the **shorter** routledge encyclopedia of **philosophy**

the **shorter** routledge encyclopedia of **philosophy**

edited by edward craig

Routledge
Taylor & Francis Group

LONDON AND NEW YORK

First published 2005
by Routledge
2 Park Square, Milton Park, Abingdon, Oxon, OX14 4RN

Simultaneously published in the USA and Canada
by Routledge
270 Madison Ave., New York, NY 10016

Routledge is an imprint of the Taylor & Francis Group

© 2005 Routledge

Introduction © Edward Craig 2005

Typeset in Bembo and Helvetica by Taylor and Francis Books

Printed and bound in Great Britain
by TJ International Ltd, Padstow, Cornwall

British Library Cataloguing in Publication Data
A catalogue record for this book is available from the British Library

Library of Congress Cataloging in Publication Data
A catalogue record for this book has been requested

ISBN 0–415–32495–5

T&F informa

Taylor & Francis Group is the Academic Division of T&F Informa plc.

Contents

Introduction

The Shorter REP has emerged out of our experience with Concise REP, the first one-volume distillation of the original ten-volume Routledge Encyclopedia of Philosophy published in 1998. Concise REP, appearing in 2000, was composed of the initial, introductory or summary sections of each of the 2,054 entries contained in the parent work, which it therefore matched everywhere for breadth, but hardly anywhere for depth. By virtue of its sheer range Concise REP fulfilled a need, but we have heard from users and reviewers who would evidently have preferred more depth – and would have been willing, we must presume, to sacrifice some breadth to get it. Thinking about this valuable feedback quickly led to a different conception of a single-volume reduction of the encyclopedia, that now embodied in The Shorter REP. By excising much of the more recondite material we have made it possible for a considerable number of entries on the more central and sought-after topics to be included in their entirety, even though in some cases that meant as much as 15,000 words or more.

The Shorter REP accordingly contains just 957 entries, but of these 119 are republished here in their full original length, and marked out by bold typeface in the headwords at the top of the page. The reader will find substantial essays on all the major figures of the Western philosophical tradition, likewise on all major topics and those we judged to be of most help to a student readership. Further, we have reprinted in full all the 'Signpost' entries, in which members of the original team of specialist subject editors surveyed in brief, usually in about 2,000 words, their specialist field. There are twenty-four of these, instantly recognisable from their light-grey background; taken together they offer the reader a highly informative outline sketch of pretty much the whole of philosophy, Latin American, African, Jewish, Arabic, Russian, Indian and East-Asian thought all included. The Shorter REP is unashamedly 'Western' in its emphasis, being designed to suit the needs of undergraduate philosophy students and the courses they are most likely to encounter. But so far as the stringencies of a single volume allow it retains the spirit of inclusivity and comprehensiveness that was such a feature of its ten-volume ancestor. Nowhere is the 'Signpost' the only entry allotted to its area – in every case there are at least two others.

The inclusion of so many complete entries has had another welcome effect, that of allowing us to do a little more justice to at least some of the encyclopedia's most eminent authors: Richard Rorty, Bernard Williams, Dagfinn Føllesdal, Tim Scanlon, Philip Kitcher, Timothy Williamson, Onora O'Neill, Gary Gutting, Anthony Appiah, Frank Jackson, Michael Friedman, Dan Garber, Malcolm Budd, Terry Irwin and the list runs on, though I have to stop, apologetically, somewhere. Entries by all these and many others appear in their original shape, unabridged.

The Shorter REP is not just a selective rearrangement of the old material. Admittedly hardly anything has been rewritten specifically for The Shorter REP, just two very short entries in fact, but it nevertheless contains a good deal that is new when compared with the original 1998 publication. Any slight suggestion of paradox is easily dispelled: since October 2000 the Routledge Encyclopedia has been available on the Internet as REP Online, in which form it has seen additions (at present towards 100 new entries) and a number (now approaching thirty) of updates and revisions, concentrating on entries near the top of our list of user-statistics. Some of the revised entries embody only minor changes, perhaps the mention of a recent book or article, others differ much more from their first versions, as for instance Wittgenstein (by Jane Heal), which as well as various smaller adjustments now has a whole new section on recent interpretative controversy about Wittgenstein's Tractatus. In one absolutely central case, of obvious prime interest to students, we have a completely rewritten replacement entry: this is David Hume, by Don Garrett. All this new material for REP Online was available to us as we made our selections for The Shorter REP, and a good deal of it is now to be found here. Some further examples of revisions now in full in The Shorter REP as well as REP Online are Plato (Malcolm Schofield), Socrates (John

Cooper), *Stoicism* and *Epicureanism* (both David Sedley), *Hobbes* (Tom Sorrell), *Justice* (Brian Barry and Matt Matravers), *Kant* (Paul Guyer), *Foucault* (Gary Gutting), *Heidegger* (Thomas Sheehan), *Quine* (Alex Orenstein), *Feminism* (Susan James), *Existentialism* (Charles Guignon), *Infinity* (Adrian Moore), and *Democracy* (Ross Harrison). In addition, as many as nineteen of the new entries, hitherto available only on the Internet in *REP Online*, are to be found here in their shorter form: *Innateness in ancient philosophy; Prolēpsis; Technē; Telos; Magic; More, Thomas; Eclecticism; Fourier, Charles; de Maistre, Joseph; Novalis; Apel, Karl-Otto; Cloning; Normativity; Globalization; Sustainability; Beccaria; Causation in the law; Justice, corrective;* and *Simulation theory.* Besides this, two new entries are printed here in full. One is *Painting, aesthetics of* (Robert Hopkins); the other is a new 'Signpost' entry: *Nineteenth-century philosophy* by Robert Stern. I hope that as General Editor I may be allowed to attach, to the second of these in particular, my personal recommendation. The nineteenth century seems to me too little studied and understood in English-speaking philosophical circles. Too few of us could give a coherent sketch of its currents and tensions, its emergence from the eighteenth century and its legacy to the twentieth. Stern can, so this new Signpost entry, together with our substantial coverage of nineteenth century philosophers, will help – if readers want it to.

In a work of this kind bibliographical information can be very costly in terms of space and has to be kept to a minimum. Nevertheless, our treatment of the bibliographies, or 'Further reading', also allows scope for revision or updating. We invited the authors of the 119 main entries (i.e. those which appear in full) to provide titles and authors of just two or three works likely to be helpful to the reader, not of course necessarily drawn from their original listing. Any especially suitable works published since the middle of 1997 – when the ten volume REP finally had to raise its drawbridge against any further text – thus had at least the chance to be considered for inclusion. The response was superb – we are delighted to be able to include over 80 revised Further reading sections.

So much for inclusion; what of the less happy matter of exclusion? Such an enterprise is bound to leave some regrets on this score in the minds of the editorial team, some disappointment amongst authors and some unfulfilled expectations amongst readers. One volume, if it is to have a readable print-size and paper thick enough not to be transparent, can be crammed so full and no fuller. Complete REP entries are on average nine times as long as their short versions, so every one had to be felt to justify its status. The thought that by printing one of the biggest entries in full we were committing space sufficient for perhaps thirty or forty short ones focussed the mind; the regrettable fact that, for example, *Schopenhauer,* and *Peirce* appear only in their shortened forms has a lot to do with that consideration. But the thinking behind such decisions often had a positive aspect as well. Entries were in competition for space not just with other topics, but also with their own shorter versions; and where this was especially well written and rich in information it on several occasions prevailed, even when the subject, in itself, might well have suggested full-length treatment. Leaving nine-tenths of an author's work out does seem a backhanded way of showing gratitude, but grateful we are, and we hope that future readers have cause to be so too.

List of entries and contributors

Below is a complete list of entries and contributors in the order in which they appear in *The Shorter Routledge Encyclopedia of Philosophy*.

A posteriori
Paul K. Moser
A priori
Paul K. Moser
Abelard, Peter
Martin M. Tweedale
Absolute, the
T.L.S. Sprigge
Absolutism
Anthony Pagden
Abstract objects
Bob Hale
Action
Jennifer Hornsby
Adorno, Theodor Wiesengrund
J.M. Bernstein
Aesthetic attitude
Malcolm Budd
Aesthetic concepts
Marcia Eaton
Aesthetics
Malcolm Budd
Aesthetics and ethics
Michael Tanner
Affirmative action
Bernard Boxill
African philosophy
K. Anthony Appiah
African philosophy, Anglophone
Kwasi Wiredu
African philosophy, Francophone
F. Abiola Irele
Agnosticism
William L. Rowe
Agrippa von Nettesheim, Henricus Cornelius
Michael H. Keefer
Akrasia
Helen Steward

Albert the Great
Alain De Libera
Alchemy
Michela Pereira
Alienation
Allen W. Wood
Alighieri, Dante
Dominik Perler
Alterity and identity, postmodern theories of
Peter Fenves
Althusser, Louis Pierre
Alex Callinicos
Ambiguity
Kent Bach
Analysis, philosophical issues in
I. Grattan-Guinness
Analytical philosophy
Thomas Baldwin
Analyticity
George Bealer
Anaphora
Nicholas Asher
Anarchism
George Crowder
Anaximander
Richard McKirahan
Anaximenes
Richard McKirahan
Ancient philosophy
David Sedley
Animal language and thought
Dale Jamieson
Animals and ethics
James Rachels
Anomalous monism
Brian P. McLaughlin
Anscombe, Gertrude Elizabeth Margaret
Michael Thompson
Anselm of Canterbury
Jasper Hopkins

A

A POSTERIORI

A prominent term in theory of knowledge since the seventeenth century, 'a posteriori' signifies a kind of knowledge or justification that depends on evidence, or warrant, from sensory experience. A posteriori truth is truth that cannot be known or justified independently of evidence from sensory experience, and a posteriori concepts are concepts that cannot be understood independently of reference to sensory experience. A posteriori knowledge contrasts with a priori knowledge, knowledge that does not require evidence from sensory experience. A posteriori knowledge is empirical, experience-based knowledge, whereas a priori knowledge is non-empirical knowledge. Standard examples of a posteriori truths are the truths of ordinary perceptual experience and the natural sciences; standard examples of a priori truths are the truths of logic and mathematics. The common understanding of the distinction between a posteriori and a priori knowledge as the distinction between empirical and non-empirical knowledge comes from Kant's *Critique of Pure Reason* (1781/1787).
See also: A PRIORI; EMPIRICISM; JUSTIFICATION, EPISTEMIC; KNOWLEDGE, CONCEPT OF

PAUL K. MOSER

A PRIORI

An important term in epistemology since the seventeenth century, 'a priori' typically connotes a kind of knowledge or justification that does not depend on evidence, or warrant, from sensory experience. Talk of a priori truth is ordinarily shorthand for talk of truth knowable or justifiable independently of evidence from sensory experience; and talk of a priori concepts is usually talk of concepts that can be understood independently of reference to sensory experience. A priori knowledge contrasts with a posteriori knowledge, knowledge requiring evidence from sensory experience. Broadly characterized, a posteriori knowledge is empirical, experience-based knowledge, and a priori knowledge is non-empirical knowledge.

Standard examples of a priori truths are the truths of mathematics, whereas standard examples of a posteriori truths are the truths of the natural sciences.
See also: A POSTERIORI; JUSTIFICATION, EPISTEMIC; KNOWLEDGE, CONCEPT OF; RATIONALISM

PAUL K. MOSER

ABDUCTION

See: DISCOVERY, LOGIC OF; INFERENCE TO THE BEST EXPLANATION; PEIRCE, CHARLES SANDERS

ABELARD, PETER (1079–1142)

Among the many scholars who promoted the revival of learning in Western Europe in the early twelfth century, Abelard stands out as a consummate logician, a formidable polemicist and a champion of the value of ancient pagan wisdom for Christian thought. Although he worked within the Aristotelian tradition, his logic deviates significantly from that of Aristotle, particularly in its emphasis on propositions and what propositions say. According to Abelard, the subject matter of logic, including universals such as genera and species, consists of linguistic expressions, not of the things these expressions talk about. However, the objective grounds for logical relationships lie in what these expressions signify, even though they cannot be said to signify any things. Abelard is, then, one of a number of medieval thinkers, often referred to in later times as 'nominalists', who argued against turning logic and semantics into some sort of science of the 'real', a kind of metaphysics. It was Abelard's view that logic was, along with grammar and rhetoric, one of the sciences of language.

In ethics, Abelard defended a view in which moral merit and moral sin depend entirely on whether one's intentions express respect for the good or contempt for it, and not at all on one's desires, whether the deed is actually carried out, or even whether the deed is in fact something that ought or ought not to be done.

Abelard did not believe that the doctrines of Christian faith could be proved by logically compelling arguments, but rational argumentation, he thought, could be used both to refute attacks on Christian doctrine and to provide arguments that would appeal to those who were attracted to high moral ideals. With arguments of this latter sort, he defended the rationalist positions that nothing occurs without a reason and that God cannot do anything other than what he does do.

See also: NOMINALISM

MARTIN M. TWEEDALE

ABORTION

See LIFE AND DEATH (§5); REPRODUCTION AND ETHICS

ABSOLUTE, THE

The expression 'the Absolute' stands for that (supposed) unconditioned reality which is either the spiritual ground of all being or the whole of things considered as a spiritual unity. This use derives especially from F.W.J. Schelling and G.W.F. Hegel, prefigured by J.G. Fichte's talk of an absolute self which lives its life through all finite persons. In English-language philosophy it is associated with the monistic idealism of such thinkers as F.H. Bradley and Josiah Royce, the first distinguishing the Absolute from God, the second identifying them.

See also: IDEALISM; KANT, I.

T.L.S. SPRIGGE

ABSOLUTISM

The term 'absolutism' describes a form of government in which the authority of the ruler is subject to no theoretical or legal constraints. In the language of Roman law – which played a central role in all theories of absolutism – the ruler was *legibus solutus*, or 'unfettered legislator'. Absolutism is generally, although not exclusively, used to describe the European monarchies, and in particular those of France, Spain, Russia and Prussia, between the middle of the sixteenth century and the end of the eighteenth. But some form of absolutism existed in nearly every European state until the late eighteenth century. There have also been recognizable forms of absolute rule in both China and Japan.

As a theory absolutism emerged in Europe, and in particular in France, in the late sixteenth and early seventeenth centuries, in response to the long Civil Wars between the Crown and the nobility known as the Wars of Religion. In the late eighteenth century, as the reform movement associated with the Enlightenment began to influence most European rulers, a form of so-called 'enlightened absolutism' (or sometimes 'enlightened despotism') emerged. In this the absolute authority of the ruler was directed not towards enhancing the power of the state, but was employed instead for advancing the welfare of the subjects.

See also: FILMER, SIR ROBERT

ANTHONY PAGDEN

ABSTRACT OBJECTS

The central philosophical question about abstract objects is: Are there any? An affirmative answer – given by Platonists or Realists – draws support from the fact that while much of our talk and thought concerns concrete (roughly, spatiotemporally extended) objects, significant parts of it appear to be about objects which lie outside space and time, and are therefore incapable of figuring in causal relationships. The suggestion that there really are such further non-spatial, atemporal and acausal objects as numbers and sets often strikes Nominalist opponents as contrary to common sense. But precisely because our apparent talk and thought of abstracta encompasses much – including virtually the whole of mathematics – that seems indispensable to our best attempts to make scientific sense of the world, it cannot be simply dismissed as confused gibberish. For this reason Nominalists have commonly adopted a programme of reductive paraphrase, aimed at eliminating all apparent reference to and quantification over abstract objects. In spite of impressively ingenious efforts, the programme appears to run into insuperable obstacles.

The simplicity of our initial question is deceptive. Understanding and progress are unlikely without further clarification of the relations between ontological questions and questions about the logical analysis of language, and of the key distinction between abstract and concrete objects. There are both affinities and, more importantly, contrasts between traditional approaches to ontological questions and more recent discussions shaped by ground-breaking work in the philosophy of language initiated by Frege. The importance of Frege's work lies principally in two insights: first, that questions about what kinds of entity there are cannot sensibly be tackled independently of the logical analysis of language; and second, that the question whether or not certain expressions should be taken to have reference cannot properly be separated from the question whether complete sentences in which those expressions occur are true or false.

See also: NOMINALISM; ONTOLOGY; REALISM AND ANTIREALISM; UNIVERSALS

BOB HALE

ACRASIA

See AKRASIA

ACTION

Philosophical study of human action owes its importance to concerns of two sorts. There are concerns addressed in metaphysics and philosophy of mind about the status of reasoning beings who make their impact in the natural causal world, and concerns addressed in ethics and legal philosophy about human freedom and responsibility. 'Action theory' springs from concerns of both sorts; but in the first instance it attempts only to provide a detailed account that may help with answering the metaphysical questions.

Action theorists usually start by asking 'How are actions distinguished from other events?'. For there to be an action, a person has to do something. But the ordinary 'do something' does not capture just the actions, since we can say (for instance) that breathing is something that everyone does, although we don't think that breathing in the ordinary way is an action. It seems that purposiveness has to be introduced – that someone's *intentionally* doing something is required.

People often do the things they intentionally do by moving bits of their bodies. This has led to the idea that 'actions are bodily movements'. The force of the idea may be appreciated by thinking about what is involved in doing one thing by doing another. A man piloting a plane might have shut down the engines by depressing a lever, for example; and there is only one action here if the depressing of the lever was (identical with) the shutting down of the engines. It is when identities of this sort are accepted that an action may be seen as an event of a person's moving their body: the pilot's depressing of the lever was (also) his moving of his arm, because he depressed the lever by moving his arm.

But how do bodies' movings – such events now as his arm's moving – relate to actions? According to one traditional empiricist account, these are *caused* by *volitions* when there are actions, and a volition and a body's moving are *alike* parts of the action. But there are many rival accounts of the causes and parts of actions and of movements. And volitional notions feature not only in a general account of the events surrounding actions, but also in accounts that aim to accommodate the *experience* that is characteristic of agency.

See also: RATIONALITY, PRACTICAL

JENNIFER HORNSBY

ADORNO, THEODOR WIESENGRUND (1903–69)

Philosopher, musicologist and social theorist, Theodor Adorno was the philosophical architect of the first generation of Critical Theory emanating from the Institute for Social Research in Frankfurt, Germany. Departing from the perspective of more orthodox Marxists, Adorno believed the twin dilemmas of modernity – injustice and nihilism – derived from the abstractive character of Enlightenment rationality. In consequence, he argued that the critique of political economy must give way to a critique of Enlightenment, instrumental reason.

Identity thinking, as Adorno termed instrumental rationality, abstracts from the sensory, linguistic and social mediations which connect knowing subjects to objects known. In so doing, it represses what is contingent, sensuous and particular in persons and nature. Adorno's method of negative dialectics was designed to rescue these elements from the claims of instrumental reason. Adorno conceded, however, that all this method could demonstrate was that an abstract concept did not exhaust its object. For a model of an alternative grammar of reason and cognition Adorno turned to the accomplishments of artistic modernism. There, where each new work tests and transforms the very idea of something being a work of art, Adorno saw a model for the kind of dynamic interdependence between mind and its objects that was required for a renewed conception of knowing and acting.

See also: ENLIGHTENMENT, CONTINENTAL

J.M. BERNSTEIN

AESTHETIC ATTITUDE

It is undeniable that there are aesthetic and non-aesthetic attitudes. But is there such a thing as *the* aesthetic attitude? What is meant by the aesthetic attitude is the particular way in which we regard something when and only when we take an aesthetic interest in it. This assumes that on all occasions of aesthetic interest the object attended to is regarded in an identical fashion, unique to such occasions; and this assumption is problematic. If an attitude's identity is determined by the features it is directed towards; if an aesthetic interest in an object is (by definition) an interest in its aesthetic qualities; and if the notion of aesthetic qualities can be explained in a uniform manner; then there is a unitary aesthetic attitude, namely an interest in an item's aesthetic qualities. But this conception of the aesthetic attitude would be unsuitable for achieving the main aim of those who have posited the aesthetic attitude. This aim is to provide a definition of the aesthetic, but the aesthetic attitude, understood as any attitude focused upon an object's aesthetic qualities, presupposes the idea of the aesthetic, and cannot be used to analyse it. So the question is whether there is a characterization of the aesthetic attitude that describes its nature without explicitly or implicitly relying on the concept of the aesthetic. There is no good reason to suppose so.

Accordingly, there is no such thing as the aesthetic attitude, if this is an attitude that is both necessary and sufficient for aesthetic interest and that can be characterized independently of the aesthetic.

See also: Aesthetic concepts

MALCOLM BUDD

AESTHETIC CONCEPTS

Aesthetic concepts are the concepts associated with the terms that pick out aesthetic properties referred to in descriptions and evaluations of experiences involving artistic and aesthetic objects and events. The questions (epistemological, psychological, logical and metaphysical) that have been raised about these properties are analogous to those raised about the concepts.

In the eighteenth century, philosophers such as Edmund Burke and David Hume attempted to explain aesthetic concepts such as beauty empirically, by connecting them with physical and psychological responses that typify individuals' experiences of different kinds of objects and events. Thus they sought a basis for an objectivity of personal reactions. Immanuel Kant insisted that aesthetic concepts are essentially subjective (rooted in personal feelings of pleasure and pain), but argued that they have a kind of objectivity on the grounds that, at the purely aesthetic level, feelings of pleasure and pain are universal responses.

In the twentieth century, philosophers have sometimes returned to a Humean analysis of aesthetic concepts via the human faculty of taste, and have extended this psychological account to try to establish an epistemological or logical uniqueness for aesthetic concepts. Many have argued that although there are no aesthetic laws (for example, 'All roses are beautiful,' or 'If a symphony has four movements and is constructed according to rules of Baroque harmony, it will be pleasing') aesthetic concepts none the less play a meaningful role in discussion and disputation. Others have argued that aesthetic concepts are not essentially distinguishable from other types of concepts.

Recently theorists have been interested in ways that aesthetic concepts are context-dependent – constructed out of social mores and practices, for example. Their theories often deny that aesthetic concepts can be universal. For example, not only is there no guarantee that the term 'harmony' will have the same meaning in different cultures: it may not be used at all.

See also: Aesthetic attitude; Art criticism; Art, definition of; Baumgarten, A.G.; Beauty; Sublime, the

MARCIA EATON

AESTHETICS

Introduction

Aesthetics owes its name to Alexander Baumgarten who derived it from the Greek *aisthanomai*, which means perception by means of the senses. As the subject is now understood, it consists of two parts: the philosophy of art, and the philosophy of the aesthetic experience and character of objects or phenomena that are not art. Non-art items include both artefacts that possess aspects susceptible of aesthetic appreciation, and phenomena that lack any traces of human design in virtue of being products of nature, not humanity. How are the two sides of the subject related: is one part of aesthetics more fundamental than the other? There are two obvious possibilities. The first is that the philosophy of art is basic, since the aesthetic appreciation of anything that is not art is the appreciation of it as if it were art. The second is that there is a unitary notion of the aesthetic that applies to both art and non-art; this notion defines the idea of aesthetic appreciation as disinterested delight in the immediately perceptible properties of an object for their own sake; and artistic appreciation is simply aesthetic appreciation of works of art. But neither of these possibilities is plausible.

The first represents the aesthetic appreciation of nature as essentially informed by ideas intrinsic to the appreciation of art, such as style, reference and the expression of psychological states. But in order for that curious feeling, the experience of the sublime – invoked, perhaps, by the immensity of the universe as disclosed by the magnitude of stars visible in the night sky (see Sublime, the) – to be aesthetic, or for you to delight in the beauty of a flower, it is unnecessary for you to imagine these natural objects as being works of art. In fact, your appreciation of them is determined by their lack of features specific to works of art, and perhaps also by their possession of features available only to aspects of nature (see Nature, aesthetic appreciation of).

The second fails to do justice to the significance for artistic appreciation of various features of works of art that are not immediately perceptible, such as a work's provenance and its position in the artist's oeuvre. A more accurate view represents the two parts of the subject as being related to each other in a looser fashion than either of these positions recognizes, each part exhibiting variety in itself, the two being united by a number of common issues or counterpart problems, but nevertheless manifesting considerable differences in virtue of the topics that are specific to them. In fact, although some issues are common to the two parts, many are specific to the philosophy of art and a few specific to the aesthetics of non-art objects. Moreover, not every object of aesthetic appreciation falls neatly on one side or the other of the art–non-art distinction, so that appreciation sometimes involves an element of both of artistic and non-artistic appreciation (see ENVIRONMENTAL AESTHETICS).

Both works of art and other objects can possess specifically aesthetic properties, such as beauty and gracefulness. If they do possess properties of this sort, they will also possess properties that are not specifically aesthetic, such as size and shape. And they will be susceptible of aesthetic and non-aesthetic appreciation, and subject to aesthetic and non-aesthetic judgments. What distinguishes an item's aesthetic from its non-aesthetic properties and what faculties are essential to detecting aesthetic properties (see AESTHETIC CONCEPTS)? What is the nature of aesthetic appreciation? It has often been thought that there is a particular attitude that is distinctive of aesthetic appreciation: you must adopt this attitude in order for the item's aesthetic properties to be manifest to you, and if you are in this attitude you are in a state of aesthetic contemplation (see AESTHETIC ATTITUDE). This supposititious attitude has often been thought of as one of disinterested contemplation focused on an item's intrinsic, non-relational, immediately perceptible properties. But perhaps this view of aesthetic interest as disinterested attention is the product of masculine bias, involving the assumption of a position of power over the observed object, a reflection of masculine privilege, an expression of the 'male gaze'. Another idea is that awareness of an object's aesthetic properties is the product of a particular species of perception, an idea which stands in opposition to the claim that this awareness is nothing but the projection of the observer's response onto the object.

An object's beauty would appear to be a relational, mind-dependent property – a property it possesses in virtue of its capacity to affect observers in a certain manner. But which observers and what manner? And can attributions of beauty, which often aspire to universal interpersonal validity, ever attain that status (see BEAUTY)? The great German philosopher Immanuel Kant presented a conception of an aesthetic judgment as a judgment that must be founded on a feeling of pleasure or displeasure; he insisted that a pure aesthetic judgment about an object is one that is unaffected by any concepts under which the object might be seen; and he tried to show that the implicit claim of such a judgment to be valid for everyone is justified. But how acceptable is his conception of an aesthetic judgment and how successful is his attempted justification of the claims of pure aesthetic judgments (see KANT, I. §12)?

1 Aesthetics of art

Those questions that are specific to the philosophy of art are of three kinds: ones that arise only within a particular art form or set of related arts (perhaps arts addressed to the same sense), ones that arise across a number of arts of heterogeneous natures, and ones that are entirely general, necessarily applying to anything falling under the mantle of art.

Here are some of the most salient facts about art. Not everything is art. Artists create works of art, which reflect the skills, knowledge and personalities of their makers, and succeed or fail in realizing their aims. Works of art can be interpreted in different ways, understood, misunderstood or baffle the mind, subjected to analysis, and praised or criticized. Although there are many kinds of value that works of art may possess, their distinctive value is their value as art. The character of a work of art endows it with a greater or lesser degree of this distinctive value.

Accordingly, the most fundamental general question about art would seem to be: what is art? Is it possible to distinguish art from non-art by means of an account that it is definitive of the nature of art, or are the arts too loosely related to one another for them to possess an essence that can be captured in a definition (see ART, DEFINITION OF)? Whatever the answer to this question may be, another entirely general issue follows hard on its heels. It concerns the ontology of art, the kind of thing a work of art is. Do some works of art fall into one ontological category (particulars) and some into another (types) or do they all fall within the same category (see ART WORKS, ONTOLOGY OF)? And a number of other important general questions quickly arise. What is a work's artistic value and which aspects of a work are relevant to or determine this value? Is the value of a work of art, considered as art, an intrinsic or an extrinsic feature of it? Is it determined solely by the work's form or by certain aspects of its content – its truth or its moral sensitivity, for example? Can judgments about a work's artistic value justifiably lay claim to universal agreement or are they merely expressions of subjective preferences? And how is a work's artistic value related to, and how important is it in comparison with, other kinds of value it may possess (see ART, VALUE OF; FORMALISM IN ART; ART AND TRUTH; ART AND MORALITY; SCHILLER, J.C.F.)? What is required to detect the critically relevant properties of artworks, over and above normal perceptual and intellectual powers, and how can judgments that attribute such properties be supported (see ART CRITICISM)? What kinds of understanding are involved in artistic appreciation, and must an acceptable interpretation of a work be compatible with any other acceptable interpretation (see ART, UNDERSTANDING OF)? In what way, if any, does the artist's intention determine the meaning or their work (see ARTIST'S INTENTION)? What is an artist's style and what is its significance in the appreciation of the artist's work?

2 Aesthetics and the arts

One question that arises only for a small set of art forms concerns the nature of depiction. It might be thought that the analysis of the nature of depiction has no special importance within the philosophy of art, for pictorial representation is just as frequent outside as inside art. But this overlooks the fact that real clarity about the ways in which pictures can acquire value as art must be founded on a sophisticated understanding of what a picture is and the psychological resources needed to grasp what it depicts. So what is it for a surface to be or contain a picture of an object or state of affairs? Must the design on the surface be such as to elicit a certain species of visual experience, and must the function of the means by which the pattern was produced, or the intention of the person who created it, be to replicate features of the visible world? Or is a picture a member of a distinctive kind of symbol system, which can be defined without making use of any specifically visual concepts (see DEPICTION)? Another question that has a limited application concerns the distinctive nature and value of a particular artistic genre, the response it encourages from us, and the insight into human life it displays and imparts. For example, whereas a comedy exploits our capacity to find something funny, a tragedy engages our capacity to be moved by the fate of other individuals, and erotic art aims to evoke a sexual reaction; and this difference in the emotional responses at the hearts of the genres goes hand in hand with the different aspects of human life they illuminate (see COMEDY; EMOTION IN RESPONSE TO ART; HUMOUR; TRAGEDY).

Questions about the individual natures and possibilities of the various arts include some that are specific to the particular art and some that apply also to other arts. On the one hand, relatively few art forms (architecture and pottery, for example) are directed to the production of works that are intended to perform non-artistic functions, or are of a kind standardly used for utilitarian purposes, and, accordingly, the issue of the relevance to its artistic value of a work's performing, or presenting the appearance of performing, its intended non-artistic function satisfactorily is confined to such arts (see ARCHITECTURE, AESTHETICS OF). Again, only in some arts does a spectator witness a performance of a work, so that issues about a performer's contribution to the interpretation of a work or about the evaluation of different performances of the same work are limited to such arts. And since only some works of art (novels, plays and films, for example) tell a story, and only some refer to fictional persons or events, questions about the means by which a story is told or how references to fictional objects should be understood have a restricted application within the arts (see NARRATIVE; FICTIONAL ENTITIES). On the other hand, most, if not all, arts allow of works within their domain being correctly perceived as being expressive of psychological states, and, accordingly, give rise to the question of what it is for a work to be expressive of such a condition (see ARTISTIC EXPRESSION). But the means available within the different arts for the expression of psychological states are various: poetry consists of words, dance exploits the human body, and instrumental music uses nothing other than sounds. And these different artistic media impose different limits on the kinds of state that can be expressed by works of art, the specificity of the states, and the significance within an art of the expressive aspects of its products (see GURNEY, E.). Furthermore, it is a general truth about the various arts, rather than one special to expression, that what can be achieved within an art is determined by the nature of the medium on which the art is based. Accordingly, an adequate philosophy of art must investigate the variety of such media and elucidate the peculiar advantages they offer and the limitations they impose (see FILM, AESTHETICS OF; HANSLICK, E.; LANGER, S.K.K.; LESSING, G.E.; MUSIC, AESTHETICS OF; OPERA, AESTHETICS OF; PAINTING, AESTHETICS OF; PHOTOGRAPHY, AESTHETICS OF; POETRY).

See also: AESTHETICS AND ETHICS; BELINSKII, V.G.; METAPHOR; RHETORIC; TOLSTOI, L.N.

References and further reading

Hegel, G. (1835) *Aesthetics: Lectures on Fine Art*, trans. T.M. Knox, Oxford: Clarendon Press, 1975. (Hegel's lectures on aesthetics, delivered in Berlin in the 1820s, are a classic introduction to the subject.)

Kant, I. (1790) *Critique of Aesthetic Judgement*, trans. W.S. Pluhar, Indianapolis, IN and Cambridge: Hackett Publishing Company, 1987.

MALCOLM BUDD

AESTHETICS AND ETHICS

The contrast between ethical and aesthetic judgments, which has provided a good deal of the subject-matter of aesthetics, stems largely from Immanuel Kant's idiosyncratic view of morality as a series of imperatives issued in accordance with the dictates of practical reason, while for him judgments of taste are based on no principles. This has led even non-Kantians to argue that aesthetic judgments are primarily concerned, as is art itself, with uniqueness, while morality has mainly to do with repeatable actions. This tends to separate art from other human activities, a separation which was encouraged by the collection of useless items by 'connoisseurs', who took over as their vocabulary of appreciation the traditional language of religious contemplation. This viewpoint has been attacked passionately by idealist aestheticians, who claim that art is a heightening of the common human activity of expressing emotions, to the point where they are experienced and rendered lucidly, as they rarely are in everyday life. Marxist aestheticians, whose roots lie in the same tradition as idealists, argue that art is inherently political, and that the realm of 'pure aesthetic experience' is chimerical. Meanwhile the analytic tradition in aesthetics has spent much effort amplifying Kant-style positions, without taking into account their historical conditioning. There is a tendency to contrast the activities of the moralist, prescribing courses of action, with that of the critic, whose only job can be to point to the unrepeatable features which constitute a work of art.

See also: ART AND MORALITY; ART, VALUE OF; ETHICS; KANT, I §12

MICHAEL TANNER

AFFIRMATIVE ACTION

The term 'affirmative action' originated in the USA under President Kennedy. Originally it was designed to ensure that employees and applicants for jobs with government contractors did not suffer discrimination. Within a year, however, 'affirmative action' was used to refer to policies aimed at compensating African-Americans for unjust racial discrimination, and at improving their opportunities to gain employment. An important implication of this shift was that affirmative action came to mean preferential treatment.

Preferential treatment was later extended to include women as well as other disadvantaged racial and ethnic groups. The arguments in favour of preferential treatment can be usefully classified as backward-looking and forward-looking. Backward-looking arguments rely on the claim that preferential treatment of women and disadvantaged racial minorities compensates these groups or the members for the discrimination and injustices they have suffered. Forward-looking arguments rely on their claim that preferential treatment of women and

disadvantaged racial minorities will help to bring about a better society.

There has been much criticism of both types of argument. The most common accusation is that preferential treatment is reverse discrimination. Other criticisms are based around who exactly should be compensated, by what means and to what extent, and at whose cost. Finally, there is the fear of the unknown consequences of such action. Arguments have been forwarded to try and solve such difficulties, but the future of preferential treatment seems to lie in a combination of the two arguments.

See also: JUSTICE

BERNARD BOXILL

AFRICAN PHILOSOPHY

Introduction

In order to indicate the range of some of the kinds of material that must be included in a discussion of philosophy in Africa, it is as well to begin by recalling some of the history of Western philosophy. It is something of an irony that Socrates, the first major philosopher in the Western tradition, is known to us entirely for oral arguments imputed to him by his student Plato. For the Western philosophical tradition is, above all else, a tradition of texts. While there are some important ancient philosophers, like Socrates, who are largely known to us through the reports of others, the tradition has developed increasingly as one which pays careful attention to written arguments. However, many of those arguments – in ethics and politics, metaphysics and epistemology, aesthetics and the whole host of other major subdivisions of the subject – concern questions about which many people in many cultures have talked and many, albeit substantially fewer, have written about outside the broad tradition of Western philosophy. The result is that while those methods of philosophy that have developed in the West through thoughtful analysis of texts are not found everywhere, we are likely to find in every human culture opinions about some of the major questions of Western philosophy. On these important questions there have been discussions in most cultures since the earliest human societies. These constitute what has sometimes been called a 'folk-philosophy'. It is hard to say much about those opinions and discussions in places where they have not been written down. However, we are able to find some evidence of the character of these views in such areas as parts of sub-Saharan Africa where writing was introduced into oral cultures over the last few centuries.

As a result, discussions of African philosophy should include both material on some oral cultures and rather more on the philosophical work that has been done in literate traditions on the African continent, including those that have developed since the introduction of Western philosophical training there.

1 Oral cultures
2 Older literate traditions
3 Recent philosophy

1 Oral cultures

Two areas of folk-philosophy have been the object of extended scholarly investigation in the late twentieth century: the philosophical psychology of people who speak the Akan languages of the west African littoral (now Ghana) and the epistemological thought of Yoruba-speaking people of western Nigeria. In both cases the folk ideas of the tradition have been addressed by contemporary speakers of the language with Western philosophical training. This is probably the most philosophically sophisticated work that has been carried out in the general field of the philosophical study of folk-philosophy in Africa. It also offers some insight into ways of thinking about both the mind and human cognition that are different from those that are most familiar within the Western tradition.

One can also learn a great deal by looking more generally at ethical and aesthetic thought, since in all parts of the continent, philosophical issues concerning evaluation were discussed and views developed before the advent of writing. Philosophical work on ethics is more developed than in aesthetics and some of the most interesting recent work in African aesthetics also focuses on Yoruba concepts which have been explored in some detail by Western philosophers. The discussion of the status of such work has largely proceeded under the rubric of the debate about ethnophilosophy, a term intended to cover philosophical work that aims to explore folk philosophies in a systematic manner. Finally, there has also been an important philosophical debate about the character of traditional religious thought in Africa.

2 Older literate traditions

Although these oral traditions represent old forms of thought, the actual traditions under discussion are not as old as the remaining African literate traditions. The earliest of these is in the writings associated with the ancient civilizations of Egypt, which substantially predate the pre-Socratic philosophers who inhabit the earliest official history of

Western philosophy. The relationship between these Egyptian traditions and the beginnings of Western philosophy have been in some dispute and there is much recent scholarship on the influence of Egypt on classical Greek thought.

Later African philosophy looks more familiar to those who have studied the conventional history of Western philosophy: the literate traditions of Ethiopia, for example, which can be seen in the context of a long (if modest) tradition of philosophical writing in the horn of Africa. The high point of such writing has been the work of the seventeenth-century philosopher, Zar'a Ya'ecob. Whose work has been compared to that of Descartes.

It is also worth observing that many of the traditions of Islamic philosophy were either the product of, or were subject to the influence of, scholars born or working in the African continent in centres of learning such as Cairo and Timbuktu (see ISLAMIC PHILOSOPHY). Similarly, the work of some of the most important philosophers among the Christian Church Fathers was the product of scholars born in Africa, like St AUGUSTINE, and some was written in the African provinces of Rome.

In considering African-born philosophers, there is Anton Wilhelm Amo, who was born in what is now Ghana and received, as the result of an extraordinary sequence of events, philosophical training during the period of German Enlightenment, before returning to the Guinea coast to die in the place he was born. Amo's considerable intellectual achievements played an important part in eighteenth- and nineteenth-century polemics relating to the 'capacity of the negro'. Unfortunately, only a portion of his work has survived.

3 Recent philosophy

Most twentieth-century work in African philosophy has been carried out by African intellectuals (often interacting with scholars outside Africa) under the influence of philosophical traditions from the European countries that colonized Africa and created her modern system of education. As the colonial systems of education were different, it is helpful to think of this work as belonging to two broadly differentiated traditions, one Francophone and the other Anglophone. While it is true that philosophers in the areas influenced by French (and Francophone Belgian) colonization developed separately from those areas under British colonial control, a comparison of their work reveals that there has been a substantial cross-flow between them (as there generally has been between philosophy in the French- and English-speaking worlds). The other important colonial power in Africa was Portugal, whose commitment to colonial education was less developed. The sole Portuguese-speaking African intellectual who made a significant philosophical contribution is Amílcar Cabral, whose leadership in the independence movement of Guinea Bissau and the Cape Verde islands was guided by philosophical training influenced by Portuguese Marxism. Cabral's influence has not been as great as that of Frantz Fanon, who was born in the French Antilles, but later became an Algerian. He was a very important figure in the development of political philosophy in Africa (and much of the Third World).

Among the most important political thinkers influenced by philosophy are Kwame Nkrumah, Kenneth Kaunda and Julius Nyerere (see AFRICAN PHILOSOPHY, ANGLOPHONE). Out of all the intellectual movements in Africa in the twentieth-century, the two most important ones of philosophical interest have been *négritude* and pan-Africanism (see AFRICAN PHILOSOPHY, FRANCOPHONE).

Philosophy in Africa has changed greatly in the decades since the Second World War and, even more, as African states have gained their independence. Given the significance of the colonial legacy in shaping modern philosophical education in Africa it is not surprising that there have been serious debates about the proper understanding of what it is for a philosophy to be African. These lively debates, prevalent in the areas of African epistemology, ethics and aesthetics, are found in both Francophone and Anglophone philosophy.

See also: MARGINALITY; POSTCOLONIALISM

References and further reading

Eze, E. (1997) *Postcolonial African Philosophy: a Critical Reader*, Cambridge, MA: Basil Blackwell. (A useful collection of important work in contemporary African philosophy.)

Masolo, D.A. (1994) *African Philosophy in Search of Identity*, Edinburgh: Edinburgh University Press. (A critical history of modern African philosophy.)

K. ANTHONY APPIAH

AFRICAN PHILOSOPHY, ANGLOPHONE

Contemporary African philosophy is in a state of flux, but the flow is not without some watersheds. The chief reason for the flux lies in the fact that Africa, in most part, is in a state of transition from a traditional condition to a modernized one. Philosophically and in other ways, the achievement of independence was the most significant landmark in this transition. Independence from European rule (which began in Libya in 1951, followed by Sudan in 1956, Ghana in 1957 and continued to be won at a rapid pace in other parts of Africa in the 1960s)

did not come without a struggle. That struggle was, of necessity, both political and cultural. Colonialism involved not only political subjection but also cultural depersonalization. Accordingly, at independence it was strongly felt that plans for political and economic reconstruction should reflect the needs not only for modernization but also for cultural regeneration. These are desiderata which, while not incompatible in principle, are difficult to harmonize in practice. The philosophical basis of the project had first to be worked out and this was attempted by the first wave of post-independence leaders. The task of devising technical philosophies cognizant of Africa's past and present and oriented to her long-term future has been in the hands of a crop of professional philosophers trained in Western-style educational institutions. Philosophical results have not been as dramatic as in the case of the political, but the process is ongoing.

The political figures that led African states to independence were not all philosophers by original inclination or training. To start with only the best known, such as Leopold Senghor of Senegal, or Kwame Nkrumah of Ghana, were trained philosophers, but others, such as Kenneth Kaunda of Zambia, brought only an educated intelligence and a good sense of their national situations to the enterprise. In all cases they were rulers enthusiastically anointed by their people to chart the new course and lead them to the promised land. An example of how practical urgency can inspire philosophical productivity can be found in the way that all these philosophers propounded blueprints for reconstruction with clearly articulated philosophical underpinnings. Circumstantial necessity, then, rather than Platonic selection made these leaders philosopher-kings. It is significant, also, to note that all the leaders mentioned (and the majority of their peers) argued for a system of socialism deriving from their understandings of African traditional thought and practice, and from their perceptions of the imperatives generated by industrialization, such as it had been. Concern with this latter aspect of the situation led to some flirtation and even outright marriage with Marxism. But, according to the leaders concerned, the outcome of this fertilization of thought had enough African input to be regarded as an African progeny. Accordingly, practically all of them proffered their theories and prescriptions under the rubric of African socialism. No such labelling is possible in the work of African philosophers, but there are some patterns of preoccupation.

See also: AFRICAN PHILOSOPHY, FRANCOPHONE

KWASI WIREDU

AFRICAN PHILOSOPHY, FRANCOPHONE

The imaginative and intellectual writings that have come out of French-speaking Africa have tended to be associated exclusively with the *négritude* movement and its global postulation of a black racial identity founded upon an original African essence. Beyond its polemical stance with regard to colonialism, the movement generated a theoretical discourse which served both as a means of self-validation for the African in particular and the black race in general. This discourse developed further as the elaboration of a new worldview derived from the African cultural inheritance of a new humanism that lays claim to universal significance.

Despite its prominence in the intellectual history of Francophone Africa and in the black world generally, *négritude* does not account for the full range of intellectual activity among the French-speaking African intelligentsia. The terms of its formulation have been challenged since its inception, leading to ongoing controversy. This challenge concerns the validity of the concept itself and its functional significance in contemporary African thought and collective life. It has involved a debate regarding the essential nature of the African, as well as the possibility of constructing a rigorous and coherent structure of ideas (with an indisputable philosophical status) derived from the belief systems and normative concepts implicit in the institutions and cultural practices subsisting from Africa's precolonial past.

The postcolonial situation has enlarged the terms of this debate in French-speaking Africa. It has come to cover a more diverse range of issues touching upon the African experience of modernity. As an extension of the 'indigenist' theme which is its point of departure, the cultural and philosophical arguments initiated by the adherents of *négritude* encompass a critical reappraisal of the Western tradition of philosophy and its historical consequences, as well as a consideration of its transforming potential in the African context. Beyond the essentialism implied by the concept of *négritude* and related theories of Africanism, the problem at the centre of French–African intellectual preoccupations relates to the modalities of African existence in the modern world.

From this perspective, the movement of ideas of the French-speaking African intelligentsia demonstrates the plurality of African discourse, as shaped by a continuing crisis of African consciousness provoked by the momentous process of transition to modernity. A convergence can be discerned between the themes and styles of philosophical discourse and inquiry in Francophone Africa and some of the significant currents of twentieth-century European philosophy and social thought engaged with the fundamental human issues raised by the impact of modern technological civilization.

Two dominant perspectives frame the evolution of contemporary thought and philosophical discourse in French-speaking Africa: the first is related to the question of identity and involves the reclamation of a cultural and spiritual heritage considered to be imperilled; the second relates to what has been called 'the dilemma of modernity' experienced as a problematic dimension of contemporary African life and consciousness.

See also: AFRICAN PHILOSOPHY, ANGLOPHONE; MARGINALITY

F. ABIOLA IRELE

AGENTS, MORAL

See MORAL AGENTS

AGNOSTICISM

In the popular sense, an agnostic is someone who neither believes nor disbelieves in God, whereas an atheist disbelieves in God. In the strict sense, however, agnosticism is the view that human reason is incapable of providing sufficient rational grounds to justify either the belief that God exists or the belief that God does not exist. In so far as one holds that our beliefs are rational only if they are sufficiently supported by human reason, the person who accepts the philosophical position of agnosticism will hold that neither the belief that God exists nor the belief that God does not exist is rational. In the modern period, agnostics have appealed largely to the philosophies of Hume and Kant as providing the justification for agnosticism as a philosophical position.

See also: ATHEISM; NATURAL THEOLOGY

WILLIAM L. ROWE

AGRIPPA VON NETTESHEIM, HENRICUS CORNELIUS (1486–1535)

Famous in the sixteenth century for writings in which he steps forward variously as magician, occultist, evangelical humanist and philosopher, Agrippa shared with other humanist writers a thoroughgoing contempt for the philosophy of the scholastics. In his more evangelical moods Agrippa could be taken for a radical exponent of the *philosophia Christi* of his older contemporary Erasmus, or mistaken for a follower of Luther, whose early writings he actively disseminated in humanist circles. However, his deepest affinities are with magically inflected philosophies: the Neoplatonism and Hermetism of Marsilio Ficino, and the syncretic Christian Kabbalah of Giovanni Pico della Mirandola, Johannes Reuchlin and Johannes Trithemius.

As well as expounding an influential magical view of language, Agrippa contributed to the sixteenth-century revival of scepticism, denounced the 'tyranny' of those who obstructed a free search for truth, criticized the subjection of women and (with a courage unusual in his time) resisted and mocked the instigators of the witch-craze. Finding in Hermetic–Kabbalistic doctrines the inner truth both of religion and of philosophy, Agrippa was also aware of parallels between these magical doctrines and the Gnostic heresies. His heterodoxy made him a target for pious slanders: within several decades of his death he became the protagonist of demonological fictions which were soon absorbed into the legend of Dr Faustus.

See also: FEMINISM §2; HERMETISM; HUMANISM, RENAISSANCE; KABBALAH; PLATONISM, RENAISSANCE §5

MICHAEL H. KEEFER

AKRASIA

The Greek word 'akrasia' is usually said to translate literally as 'lack of self-control', but it has come to be used as a general term for the phenomenon known as weakness of will, or incontinence, the disposition to act contrary to one's own considered judgment about what it is best to do. Since one variety of akrasia is the inability to act as one thinks right, akrasia is obviously important to the moral philosopher, but it is also frequently discussed in the context of philosophy of action. Akrasia is of interest to philosophers of action because although it seems clear that it does occur – that people often do act in ways which they believe to be contrary to their own best interests, moral principles or long-term goals – it also seems to follow from certain apparently plausible views about intentional action that akrasia is simply not possible. A famous version of the suggestion that genuine akrasia cannot exist is found in Socrates, as portrayed by Plato in the *Protagoras*. Socrates argues that it is impossible for a person's knowledge of what is best to be overcome by such things as the desire for pleasure – that one cannot choose a course of action which one knows full well to be less good than some alternative known to be available. Anyone who chooses to do something which is in fact worse than something they know they could have done instead, must, according to Socrates, have wrongly judged the relative values of the actions.

See also: ARISTOTLE §23; MORAL AGENTS; MORAL PSYCHOLOGY; RATIONALITY, PRACTICAL; SELF-DECEPTION, ETHICS OF; SOCRATES §6; WILL, THE

HELEN STEWARD

ALBERT THE GREAT (1200–80)

Albert the Great was the first scholastic interpreter of Aristotle's work in its entirety, as well as being a theologian and preacher. He left an encyclopedic body of work covering all areas of medieval knowledge, both in philosophy (logic, ethics, metaphysics, sciences of nature, meteorology, mineralogy, psychology, anthropology, physiology, biology, natural sciences and zoology) and in theology (biblical commentaries, systematic theology, liturgy and sermons). His philosophical work is based on both Arabic sources (including Alfarabi, Avicenna and Averroes) and Greek and Byzantine sources (such as Eustratius of Nicaea and Michael of Ephesus). Its aim was to insure that the Latin world was properly introduced to philosophy by providing a systematic exposition of Aristotelian positions.

Albert's method of exposition (paraphrase in the style of Avicenna rather than literal commentary in the style of Averroes), the relative heterogeneity of his sources and his own avowed general intention 'to list the opinions of the philosophers without asserting anything about the truth' of the opinions listed, all contribute to making his work seem eclectic or even theoretically inconsistent. This was compounded by the nature and number of spurious writings which, beginning in the fourteenth century, were traditionally attributed to him in the fields of alchemy, obstetrics, magic and necromancy, such as *The Great and the Little Albert*, *The Secrets of Women* and *The Secrets of the Egyptians*. This impression fades, however, when one examines the authentic works in the light of the history of medieval Aristotelianism and of the reception of the philosophical sources of late antiquity in the context of the thirteenth-century university.

See also: AQUINAS, T.; ARISTOTLE; IBN RUSHD; IBN SINA; LIBER DE CAUSIS; NEOPLATONISM

ALAIN DE LIBERA
Translated from the original French
by CLAUDIA EISEN MURPHY

ALBERTUS MAGNUS
See ALBERT THE GREAT

ALCHEMY

Alchemy is the quest for an agent of material perfection, produced through a creative activity (*opus*), in which humans and nature collaborate. It exists in many cultures (China, India, Islam; in the Western world since Hellenistic times) under different specifications: aiming at the production of gold and/or other perfect substances from baser ones, or of the elixir that prolongs life, or even of life itself. Because of its purpose, the alchemists' quest is always strictly linked to the religious doctrine of redemption current in each civilization where alchemy is practised.

In the Western world alchemy presented itself at its advent as a sacred art. But when, after a long detour via Byzantium and Islamic culture, it came back again to Europe in the twelfth century, adepts designated themselves philosophers. Since then alchemy has confronted natural philosophy for several centuries.

In contemporary thought the memory of alchemy was scarcely regarded, save as protochemistry or as a branch of esotericism, until interest in it was revived by C.G. Jung. Recent research is increasingly showing the complexity of alchemy and its multiple relation to Western thought.

MICHELA PEREIRA

ALCIBIADES
See PLATO

ALGAZEL
See AL-GHAZALI, ABU HAMID

ALIENATION

'Alienation' is a prominent term in twentieth-century social theory and social criticism, referring to any of various social or psychological evils which are characterized by a harmful separation, disruption or fragmentation which sunders things that properly belong together. People are alienated from one another when there is an interruption in their mutual affection or reciprocal understanding; they are alienated from political processes when they feel separated from them and powerless in relation to them. Reflection on your beliefs or values can also alienate you from them by undermining your attachment to them or your identification with them; they remain your beliefs or values *faute de mieux*, but are no longer yours in the way they should be. Alienation translates two distinct German terms: *Entfremdung* ('estrangement') and *Entäußerung* ('externalization'). Both terms originated in the philosophy of Hegel, specifically in his *Phenomenology of Spirit* (1807). Their influence, however, has come chiefly from their use by Karl Marx in his manuscripts of 1844 (first published in 1930). Marx's fundamental concern was with the alienation of wage labourers from their product, the grounds of which he sought in the alienated form of their labouring activity. In both Hegel and Marx, alienation refers fundamentally to a kind of activity in which the essence of the agent is posited as something external or alien, assuming the form of hostile domination over the agent.
See also: MARXISM, WESTERN

ALLEN W. WOOD

ALIGHIERI, DANTE (1265–1321)

Although Dante never received a systematic training in philosophy, he tackled some of the most controversial philosophical problems of his time. In his theory of science, he asked how we are to explain the fact that science is a unified, strictly ordered system of knowledge. He answered by comparing the scientific disciplines with the celestial spheres, claiming that the system of knowledge mirrors the cosmological order. In his political philosophy, he asked why all humans want to live in a peaceful society. All humans seek full use of their cognitive capacity, was his answer, and they can achieve it only if they interact socially. In his philosophy of nature, Dante asked what brings about the order of the elements, and suggested that the elements obey the laws of a universal nature in a strictly ordered cosmos. He elaborated all his answers in a scholastic framework that made use of both Aristotelian and Neoplatonic traditions.
See also: COSMOLOGY; POLITICAL PHILOSOPHY, HISTORY OF; RENAISSANCE PHILOSOPHY

DOMINIK PERLER

ALTERITY AND IDENTITY, POSTMODERN THEORIES OF

Theories of alterity and identity can be said to be 'postmodern' if they challenge at least two key features of modern philosophy: (1) the Cartesian attempt to secure the legitimacy of knowledge on the basis of a subject that immediately knows itself and (2) the Hegelian attempt to secure self-knowledge and self-recognition by showing that knowledge and recognition are mediated by the whole. Postmodern thought does not necessarily champion a wholly other, but it generally conceives of self-identity in terms of a radical alterity.
See also: POSTMODERNISM

PETER FENVES

ALTHUSSER, LOUIS PIERRE (1918–90)

Louis Althusser was the most influential philosopher to emerge in the revival of Marxist theory occasioned by the radical movements of the 1960s. His influence is, on the face of it, surprising, since Althusser's Marx is not the theorist of revolutionary self-emancipation celebrated by the early Lukács. According to Althusser, Marx, along with Freud, was responsible for a 'decentring' of the human subject. History is 'a process without a subject'. Its movement is beyond the comprehension of individual or collective subjects, and can only be grasped by a scientific 'theoretical practice' which keeps its distance from everyday experience. This austere version of Marxism nevertheless captured the imagination of many young intellectuals by calling for a 'return to Marx', with the implication that his writings had been distorted by the official communist movement. In fact, Althusser later conceded, his was an 'imaginary Marxism', a reconstruction of historical materialism reflecting the same philosophical climate that produced the post-structuralist appropriations of Nietzsche and Heidegger by Deleuze, Derrida and Foucault. Most of the philosophical difficulties in which Althusser found himself can be traced back to the impossibility of fusing Marx's and Nietzsche's thought into a new synthesis.

See also: DIALECTICAL MATERIALISM

ALEX CALLINICOS

ALTRUISM
See EGOISM AND ALTRUISM

AMBIGUITY

A word, phrase or sentence is ambiguous if it has more than one meaning. The word 'light', for example, can mean not very heavy or not very dark. Words like 'light', 'note', 'bear' and 'over' are *lexically* ambiguous. They induce ambiguity in phrases or sentences in which they occur, such as 'light suit' and 'The duchess can't bear children'. However, phrases and sentences can be ambiguous even if none of their constituents is. The phrase 'porcelain egg container' is *structurally* ambiguous, as is the sentence 'The police shot the rioters with guns'. Ambiguity can have both a lexical and a structural basis, as with sentences like 'I left her behind for you' and 'He saw her duck'.

The notion of ambiguity has philosophical applications. For example, identifying an ambiguity can aid in solving a philosophical problem. Suppose one wonders how two people can have the same idea, say of a unicorn. This can seem puzzling until one distinguishes 'idea' in the sense of a particular psychological occurrence, a mental representation, from 'idea' in the sense of an abstract, shareable concept. On the other hand, gratuitous claims of ambiguity can make for overly simple solutions. Accordingly, the question arises of how genuine ambiguities can be distinguished from spurious ones. Part of the answer consists in identifying phenomena with which ambiguity may be confused, such as vagueness, unclarity, inexplicitness and indexicality.

See also: LANGUAGE, PHILOSOPHY OF; SEMANTICS

KENT BACH

ANALECTS
See CONFUCIUS

ANALOGIES IN SCIENCE
See INDUCTIVE INFERENCE; MODELS

ANALYSIS, PHILOSOPHICAL ISSUES IN

The term 'mathematical analysis' refers to the major branch of mathematics which is concerned with the theory of functions and includes the differential and integral calculus. Analysis and the calculus began as the study of curves, calculus being concerned with tangents to and areas under curves. The focus was shifted to functions following the insight, due to Leibniz and Isaac Newton in the second half of the seventeenth century, that a curve is the graph of a function. Algebraic foundations were proposed by Lagrange in the late eighteenth century; assuming that any function always took an expansion in a power series, he defined the derivatives from the coefficients of the terms. In the 1820s his assumption was refuted by Cauchy, who had already launched a fourth approach, like Newton's based on limits, but formulated much more carefully. It was refined further by Weierstrass, by means which helped to create set theory. Analysis also encompasses the theory of limits and of the convergence and divergence of infinite series; modern versions also use point set topology. It has taken various forms over the centuries, of which the older ones are still represented in some notations and terms. Philosophical issues include the status of infinitesimals, the place of logic in the articulation of proofs, types of definition, and the (non-)relationship to analytic proof methods.

See also: CONTINUUM HYPOTHESIS

I. GRATTAN-GUINNESS

ANALYTICAL PHILOSOPHY

Philosophical analysis is a method of inquiry in which one seeks to assess complex systems of thought by 'analysing' them into simpler elements whose relationships are thereby brought into focus. This method has a long history, but became especially prominent at the start of the twentieth century and, by becoming integrated into Russell's development of logical theory, acquired a greater degree of sophistication than before. The logical positivists developed the method further during the 1930s and, in the context of their anti-metaphysical programme, held that analysis was the only legitimate philosophical inquiry. Thus for them philosophy could only be 'analytical philosophy'.

After 1945 those philosophers who wanted to expand philosophical inquiries beyond the limits prescribed by the positivists extended the understanding of analysis to include accounts of the general structures of language and thought without the earlier commitment to the identification of

13

'simple' elements of thought. Hence there developed a more relaxed conception of 'linguistic analysis' and the understanding of 'analytical philosophy' was modified in such a way that a critical concern with language and meaning was taken to be central to it, leading, indeed, to a retrospective re-evaluation of the role of Frege as a founder of analytical philosophy. At the same time, however, Quine propounded influential arguments which suggest that methods of analysis can have no deep significance because there is no determinate structure to systems of thought or language for the analytical philosopher to analyse and assess. Hence some contemporary philosophers proclaim that we have now reached 'the end of analytical philosophy'. But others, who find Quine's arguments unpersuasive, hold that analytical philosophy has virtues quite sufficient to ensure it a role as a central philosophical method for the foreseeable future.

See also: LOGICAL POSITIVISM

THOMAS BALDWIN

ANALYTICITY

In *Critique of Pure Reason* Kant introduced the term 'analytic' for judgments whose truth is guaranteed by a certain relation of 'containment' between the constituent concepts, and 'synthetic' for judgments which are not like this. Closely related terms were found in earlier writings of Locke, Hume and Leibniz. In Kant's definition, an analytic judgment is one in which 'the predicate B belongs to the subject A, as something which is (covertly) contained in this concept A' (*Critique* 1781/1787). Kant called such judgments 'explicative', contrasting them with synthetic judgments which are 'ampliative'. A paradigmatic analyticity would be: bachelors are unmarried. Kant assumed that knowledge of analytic necessities has a uniquely transparent sort of explanation. In the succeeding two centuries the terms 'analytic' and 'synthetic' have been used in a variety of closely related but not strictly equivalent ways. In the early 1950s Morton White and W.V. Quine argued that the terms were fundamentally unclear and should be eschewed. Although a number of prominent philosophers have rejected their arguments, there prevails a scepticism about 'analytic' and the idea that there is an associated category of necessary truths having privileged epistemic status.

See also: CARNAP, R.; CONCEPTS; INTENSIONAL ENTITIES; KANT, I.; LOGICAL POSITIVISM; NECESSARY TRUTH AND CONVENTION

GEORGE BEALER

ANAPHORA

Anaphora describes a dependence of the interpretation of one natural language expression on the interpretation of another natural language expression. For example, the pronoun 'her' in (1) below is anaphorically dependent for its interpretation on the interpretation of the noun phrase 'Sally' because 'her' refers to the same person 'Sally' refers to.

(1)   Sally likes her car.

As (2) below illustrates, anaphoric dependencies also occur across sentences, making anaphora a 'discourse phenomenon':

(2)   A farmer owned a donkey. He beat it.

The analysis of anaphoric dependence has been the focus of a great deal of study in linguistics and philosophy. Anaphoric dependencies are difficult to accommodate within the traditional conception of compositional semantics of Tarski and Montague precisely because the meaning of anaphoric elements is dependent on other elements of the discourse.

Many expressions can be used anaphorically. For instance, anaphoric dependencies hold between the expression 'one' and the indefinite noun phrase 'a labrador' in (3) below; between the verb phrase 'loves his mother' and a 'null' anaphor (or verbal auxiliary) in (4); between the prepositional phrase 'to Paris' and the lexical item 'there' in (5); and between a segment of text and the pronoun 'it' in (6).

(3)   Susan has a labrador. I want one too.

(4)   John loves his mother. Fred does too.

(5)   I didn't go to Paris last year. I don't go there very often.

(6)   One plaintiff was passed over for promotion. Another didn't get a pay increase for five years. A third received a lower wage than men doing the same work. But the jury didn't believe any of it.

Some philosophers and linguists have also argued that verb tenses generate anaphoric dependencies.

NICHOLAS ASHER

ANARCHISM

Anarchism is the view that a society without the state, or government, is both possible and desirable. Although there have been intimations of the anarchist outlook throughout history, anarchist ideas emerged in their modern form in the late eighteenth and early nineteenth centuries in the wake of the French and Industrial Revolutions.

All anarchists support some version of each of the following broad claims: (1) people have no general obligation to obey the commands of the state; (2) the state ought to be abolished; (3) some kind of stateless society is possible and desirable; (4) the transition from state to anarchy is a realistic prospect

Within this broad framework there is a rich variety of anarchist thought. The main political division is between the 'classical' or socialist school, which tends to reject or restrict private property, and the 'individualist' or libertarian tradition, which defends private acquisition and looks to free market exchange as a model for the desirable society. Philosophical differences follow this division to some extent, the classical school appealing principally to natural law and perfectionist ethics, and the individualists to natural rights and egoism. Another possible distinction is between the 'old' anarchism of the nineteenth century (including both the classical and individualist traditions) and the 'new' anarchist thought that has developed since the Second World War, which applies the insights of such recent ethical currents as feminism, ecology and postmodernism.

Anarchists have produced powerful arguments denying any general obligation to obey the state and pointing out the ill effects of state power. More open to question are their claims that states ought to be abolished, that social order is possible without the state and that a transition to anarchy is a realistic possibility.

GEORGE CROWDER

ANAXIMANDER (610–after 546 BC)

The Greek philosopher Anaximander of Miletus followed Thales in his philosophical and scientific interests. He wrote a book, of which one fragment survives, and is the first Presocratic philosopher about whom we have enough information to reconstruct his theories in any detail. He was principally concerned with the origin, structure and workings of the world, and attempted to account for them consistently, through a small number of principles and mechanisms. Like other thinkers of his tradition, he gave the Olympian gods no role in creating the world or controlling events. Instead, he held that the world originated from a vast, eternal, moving material of no definite nature, which he called *apeiron* ('boundless' or 'unlimited'). From this, through obscure processes including one called 'separation off', arose the world as we know it. Anaximander described the *kosmos* (world) and stated the distances of the celestial bodies from the earth. He accounted for the origin of animal life and explained how humans first emerged. He pictured the world as a battleground in which opposite natures, such as hot and cold, constantly encroach upon one another, and described this process as taking place with order and regularity.
See also: ANAXIMENES; ARCHĒ; COSMOLOGY; INFINITY; PRESOCRATIC PHILOSOPHY; THALES

RICHARD MCKIRAHAN

ANAXIMENES (6th century BC)

The Greek philosopher Anaximenes of Miletus followed Anaximander in his philosophical and scientific interests. Only a few words survive from his book, but there is enough other information to give us a picture of his most important theories. Like the other early Presocratic philosophers he was interested in the origin, structure and composition of the universe, as well as the principles on which it operates. Anaximenes held that the primary substance – both the source of everything else and the material out of which it is made – is air. When rarefied and condensed it becomes other materials, such as fire, water and earth. The primordial air is infinite in extent and without beginning or end. It is in motion and divine. Air generated the universe through its motion, and continues to govern it. The human soul is composed of air and it is likely that Anaximenes believed the entire *kosmos* (world) to be alive, with air functioning as its soul. Like other Presocratics, he proposed theories of the nature of the heavenly bodies and their motions, and of meteorological and other natural phenomena.
See also: ANAXIMANDER; ARCHĒ; COSMOLOGY; THALES

RICHARD MCKIRAHAN

ANCIENT PHILOSOPHY

Introduction

The philosophy of the Greco-Roman world from the sixth century BC to the sixth century AD laid the foundations for all subsequent Western philosophy. Its greatest figures are Socrates (fifth century BC) and Plato and Aristotle (fourth century BC). But the enormously diverse range of further important thinkers who populated the period includes the Presocratics and Sophists of the sixth and fifth centuries BC; the Stoics, Epicureans and sceptics of the Hellenistic age; and the many Aristotelian and (especially) Platonist philosophers who wrote under the Roman Empire, including the great Neoplatonist Plotinus. Ancient philosophy was principally pagan, and was finally eclipsed by Christianity in the sixth century AD, but it was so comprehensively annexed by its conqueror that it came, through Christianity, to dominate medieval and Renaissance philosophy. This eventual symbiosis between ancient philosophy and Christianity may reflect the fact that philosophical creeds in late antiquity fulfilled much the same role as religious movements, with which they shared many of their aims and practices.

Only a small fraction of ancient philosophical writings have come down to us intact. The remainder can be recovered, to a greater or lesser extent, by piecing together fragmentary evidence from sources which refer to them.

1   Main features

'Ancient' philosophy is that of classical antiquity, which not only inaugurated the entire European philosophical tradition but has exercised an unparalleled influence on its style and content. It is conventionally considered to start with THALES in the mid-sixth century BC, although the Greeks themselves frequently made Homer (c.700 BC) its true originator. Officially it is often regarded as ending in 529 AD, when the Christian emperor Justinian is believed to have banned the teaching of pagan philosophy at Athens. However, this was no abrupt termination, and the work of Platonist philosophers continued for some time in self-imposed exile (see NEOPLATONISM).

Down to and including Plato (in the first half of the fourth century BC), philosophy did not develop a significant technical terminology of its own – unlike such contemporary disciplines as mathematics and medicine. It was Plato's pupil Aristotle, and after him the Stoics (see STOICISM), who made truly decisive contributions to the philosophical vocabulary of the ancient world.

Ancient philosophy was above all a product of Greece and the Greek-speaking parts of the Mediterranean, which came to include southern Italy, Sicily, western Asia and large parts of North Africa, notably Egypt. From the first century BC, a number of Romans became actively engaged in one or other of the Greek philosophical systems, and some of them wrote their own works in Latin (see LUCRETIUS; CICERO). But Greek remained the *lingua franca* of philosophy. Although much modern philosophical terminology derives from Latinized versions of Greek technical concepts, most of these stem from the Latin vocabulary of medieval Aristotelianism, not directly from ancient Roman philosophical writers.

2   The sixth and fifth centuries BC

The first phase, occupying most of the sixth and fifth centuries BC, is generally known as PRESOCRATIC PHILOSOPHY. Its earliest practitioners (THALES; ANAXIMANDER; ANAXIMENES) came from Miletus, on the west coast of modern Turkey. The dominant concern of the Presocratic thinkers was to explain the origin and regularities of the physical world and the place of the human soul within it (see especially PYTHAGOREANISM; HERACLITUS; EMPEDOCLES; DEMOCRITUS), although the period also produced such rebels as the Eleatic philosophers (PARMENIDES; ZENO OF ELEA), whose radical monism sought to undermine the very basis of cosmology by reliance on a priori reasoning.

The label 'Presocratic' acknowledges the traditional view that SOCRATES (469–399 BC) was the first philosopher to shift the focus away from the natural world to human values. In fact, however, this shift to a large extent coincides with the concerns of his contemporaries the Sophists, who professed to teach the fundamentals of political and social success and consequently were also much concerned with moral issues (see SOPHISTS). But the persona of Socrates became, and has remained ever since, so powerful an icon for the life of moral scrutiny that it is his name that is used to mark this watershed in the history of philosophy. In the century or so following his death, many schools looked back to him as the living embodiment of philosophy and sought the principles of his life and thought in philosophical theory.

3   The fourth century BC

Socrates and the Sophists helped to make Athens the philosophical centre of the Greek world, and it was there, in the fourth century, that the two greatest philosophers of antiquity lived and taught, namely Plato and Aristotle. PLATO, Socrates' pupil, set up his school the Academy in Athens. Plato's published dialogues are literary masterpieces as well as philosophical classics, and develop, albeit unsystematically, a global philosophy which embraces ethics, politics, physics, metaphysics (see FORMS, PLATONIC), epistemology (see INNATENESS IN ANCIENT PHILOSOPHY), aesthetics and psychology.

The Academy's most eminent alumnus was ARISTOTLE, whose own school the Lyceum came for a time to rival the Academy's importance as an educational centre. Aristotle's highly technical but also often provisional and exploratory school treatises may not have been intended for publication; at all events, they did not become widely disseminated and discussed until the late first century BC. The main philosophical treatises (leaving aside his important zoological works) include seminal studies in all the areas covered by Plato, plus logic, a branch of philosophy pioneered by Aristotle. These treatises are, like Plato's, among the leading classics of Western philosophy.

Platonism and Aristotelianism were to become the dominant philosophies of the Western tradition from the second century AD at least until the end of the Renaissance, and the legacy of both remains central to Western philosophy today.

4 Hellenistic philosophy

Down to the late fourth century BC, philosophy was widely seen as a search for universal understanding, so that in the major schools its activities could comfortably include, for example, biological and historical research. In the ensuing era of Hellenistic philosophy, however, a geographical split helped to demarcate philosophy more sharply as a self-contained discipline. Alexandria, with its magnificent library and royal patronage, became the new centre of scientific, literary and historical research, while the philosophical schools at Athens concentrated on those areas which correspond more closely to philosophy as it has since come to be understood. The following features were to characterize philosophy not only in the Hellenistic age but also for the remainder of antiquity.

The three main parts of philosophy were most commonly labelled 'physics' (a primarily speculative discipline, concerned with such concepts as causation, change, god and matter, and virtually devoid of empirical research), 'logic' (which sometimes included epistemology) and 'ethics'. Ethics was agreed to be the ultimate focus of philosophy, which was thus in essence a systematized route to personal virtue (see ARETĒ) and happiness (see EUDAIMONIA). There was also a strong spiritual dimension. One's religious beliefs – that is, the way one rationalized and elaborated one's own (normally pagan) beliefs and practices concerning the divine – were themselves an integral part of both physics and ethics, never a mere adjunct of philosophy.

The dominant philosophical creeds of the Hellenistic age (officially 323–31 BC) were Stoicism (founded by ZENO OF CITIUM) and Epicureanism (founded by Epicurus) (see STOICISM; EPICUREANISM). Scepticism was also a powerful force, largely through the Academy (see CARNEADES), which in this period functioned as a critical rather than a doctrinal school, and also, starting from the last decades of the era, through Pyrrhonism

5 The imperial era

The crucial watershed belongs, however, not at the very end of the Hellenistic age (31 BC, when the Roman empire officially begins), but half a century earlier in the 80s BC. Political and military upheavals at Athens drove most of the philosophers out of the city, to cultural havens such as Alexandria and Rome. The philosophical institutions of Athens never fully recovered, so that this decentralization amounted to a permanent redrawing of the philosophical map. (The chairs of Platonism, Aristotelianism, Stoicism and Epicureanism which the philosopher-emperor Marcus Aurelius established at Athens in AD 176 were a significant gesture, but did not fully restore Athens' former philosophical preeminence.) Philosophy was no longer, for most of its adherents, a living activity within the Athenian school founded by Plato, Aristotle, Zeno or Epicurus. Instead it was a subject pursued in small study groups led by professional teachers all over the Greco-Roman world. To a large extent, it was felt that the history of philosophy had now come to an end, and that the goal now was to seek the correct interpretation of the 'ancients' by close study of their texts. One symptom of this feeling is that doxography – the systematic cataloguing of philosophical and scientific opinions – concentrated largely on the period down to about 80 BC, as did the biographical history of philosophy written c. AD 300 by DIOGENES LAERTIUS.

Another such symptom is that a huge part of the philosophical activity of late antiquity went into the composition of commentaries on classic philosophical texts. In this final phase of ancient philosophy, conveniently called 'imperial' because it more or less coincides with the era of the Roman empire, the Hellenistic creeds were gradually eclipsed by the revival of doctrinal Platonism, based on the close study of Plato's texts, out of which it developed a massively elaborate metaphysical scheme. Aristotle was usually regarded as an ally by these Platonists, and became therefore himself the focus of many commentaries (see NEOPLATONISM). Despite its formal concern with recovering the wisdom of the ancients, however, this age produced many powerfully original thinkers, of whom the greatest is PLOTINUS.

6 Schools and movements

The early Pythagoreans constituted the first philosophical group that can be called even approximately a 'school'. They acquired a reputation for secrecy, as well as for virtually religious devotion to the word of their founder PYTHAGORAS. 'He himself said it' (best known in its Latin form 'ipse *dixit*') was alleged to be their watchword. In some ways it is more accurate to consider them a sect than a school, and their beliefs and practices were certainly intimately bound up in religious teachings about the soul's purification.

It is no longer accepted, as it long was, that the Athenian philosophical schools had the status of formal religious institutions for the worship of the muses. Their legal and institutional standing is in fact quite obscure. Both the Academy and the Lyceum were so named after public groves just outside the walls of Athens, in which their public activities were held. The Stoics too got their name from the public portico, or 'stoa', in which they met, alongside the Athenian agora. Although these schools undoubtedly also conducted classes and discussions on private premises too, it was their public profile that was crucial to their identity as schools. In the last four centuries BC, prospective philosophy students flocked to Athens from all over the Greek world, and the high public visibility of the schools there was undoubtedly cultivated partly with an eye to recruitment. Only the Epicurean school kept its activities out of the public gaze, in line with Epicurus' policy of minimal civic involvement.

A school normally started as an informal grouping of philosophers with a shared set of interests and commitments, under the nominal leadership of some individual, but without a strong party line to which all members owed unquestioning allegiance. In the first generation of the Academy, for example, many of Plato's own leading colleagues dissented from his views on central issues. The same openness is discernible in the first generations of the other schools, even (if to a much lesser extent) that of the Epicureans. However, after the death of the founder the picture usually changed. His word thereafter became largely beyond challenge, and further progress was presented as the supplementation or reinterpretation of the founder's pronouncements, rather than as their replacement.

To this extent, the allegiance which in the long term bound a school together usually depended on a virtually religious reverence for the movement's foundational texts, which provided the framework within which its discussions were conducted. The resemblance to the structure of religious sects is no accident. In later antiquity, philosophical and religious movements constituted in effect a single cultural phenomenon, and competed for the same spiritual and intellectual high ground. This includes Christianity, which became a serious rival to pagan philosophy (primarily Platonism) from the third century onwards, and eventually triumphed over it. In seeking to understand such spiritual movements of late antiquity as HERMETISM, GNOSTICISM, Neo-Pythagoreanism, Cynicism and even NEO-PLATONISM itself, and their concern with such values as asceticism, self-purificaton and self-divinization, it is inappropriate to insist on a sharp division between philosophy and religion.

'Ancient philosophy' is traditionally understood as pagan and is distinguished from the Christian Patristic philosophy of late antiquity (see PATRISTIC PHILOSOPHY). But it was possible to put pagan philosophy at the service of Judaism (see PHILO OF ALEXANDRIA) or Christianity (see for example ORIGEN; AUGUSTINE; BOETHIUS; PHILOPONUS), and it was indeed largely in this latter capacity that the major systems of ancient philosophy eventually became incorporated into MEDIEVAL PHILOSOPHY and RENAISSANCE PHILOSOPHY, which they proceeded to dominate.

This extensive overlap between philosophy and religion also reflects to some extent the pervasive influence of philosophy on the entire culture of the ancient world. Rarely regarded as a detached academic discipline, philosophy frequently carried high political prestige, and its modes of discourse came to infect disciplines as diverse as medicine, rhetoric, astrology, history, grammar and law. The work of two of the greatest scientists of the ancient world, the doctor Galen and the astronomer Ptolemy, was deeply indebted to their respective philosophical backgrounds.

7 Survival

A very substantial body of works by ancient philosophical writers has survived in manuscript. These are somewhat weighted towards those philosophers – above all Plato, Aristotle and the Neoplatonists – who were of most immediate interest to the Christian culture which preserved them throughout the Middle Ages, mainly in the monasteries, where manuscripts were assiduously copied and stored. Some further ancient philosophical writings have been recovered through translations into Arabic and other languages, or on excavated scraps of papyrus. The task of reconstituting the original texts of these works has been a major preoccupation of modern scholarship.

For the vast majority of ancient philosophers, however, our knowledge of them depends on secondary reports of their words and ideas in other writers, of whom some are genuinely interested in recording the history of philosophy, but others bent on discrediting the views they attribute to them. In such cases of secondary attestation, strictly a 'fragment' is a verbatim quotation, while indirect reports are called 'testimonia'. However, this distinction is not always rigidly maintained, and indeed the sources on which we rely rarely operate with any explicit distinction between quotation and paraphrase.

It is a tribute to the philosophical genius of the ancient world that, despite the suppression and distortion which its contributions have suffered over two millennia, they remain central to any modern conspectus of what philosophy is and can be.
See also: ATOMISM, ANCIENT; ARCHĒ; LOGOS; NOUS; PNEUMA; PROLĒPSIS; PSYCHĒ; TECHNĒ; TELOS

References and further reading

Algra, K., Barnes, J., Mansfeld, J. and Schofield, M. (eds) (1998) *The Cambridge History of Hellenistic Philosophy*, Cambridge: Cambridge University Press. (Recent, reliable and comprehensive.)

Guthrie, W.K.C. (1962–81) *A History of Greek Philosophy*, Cambridge: Cambridge University Press, 6 vols. (The major work of its kind in English, but does not go beyond Aristotle.)

Sedley, D. (ed.) (2003) *The Cambridge Companion to Greek and Roman Philosophy*, Cambridge: Cambridge University Press. (Surveys all periods and most aspects, with glossary and recommendations for further reading.)

DAVID SEDLEY

ANIMAL LANGUAGE AND THOUGHT

The question of animal language and thought has been debated since ancient times. Some have held that humans are exceptional in these respects, others that humans and animals are continuous with respect to language and thought. The issue is important because our self-image as a species is at stake.

Arguments for human exceptionalism can be classified as Cartesian, Wittgensteinian and behaviourist. What these arguments have in common is the view that language and thought are closely associated, and animals do not have language. The ape language experiments of the 1960s and 1970s were especially important against this background: if apes could learn language then even the advocates of human exceptionalism would have to admit that they have thoughts. It is now generally believed that whatever linguistic abilities apes have shown have been quite rudimentary. Yet many sceptics are willing to grant that in some cases apes did develop linguistic skills to some extent, and clearly evidenced thought. Studies of other animals in captivity and various animals in the wild have provided evidence of highly sophisticated communicative behaviour. Cognitive ethology and comparative psychology have emerged as the fields that study animal thought. While there are conceptual difficulties in grounding these fields, it appears plausible that many animals have thoughts and these can be scientifically investigated.

DALE JAMIESON

ANIMALS AND ETHICS

Introduction

Does morality require that we respect the lives and interests of nonhuman animals? The traditional doctrine was that animals were made for human use, and so we may dispose of them as we please. It has been argued, however, that this is a mere 'speciesist' prejudice and that animals should be given more or less the same moral consideration as humans. If this is right, we may be morally required to be vegetarians; and it may turn out that laboratory research using animals, and many other such practices, are more problematic than, previously has been realized.

> 1 The traditional view
> 2 Challenges to the traditional view
> 3 The contemporary debate

1 The traditional view

In some Eastern systems of thought, animals are accorded great respect. The Jains of India hold that all life is sacred, drawing no sharp distinction between human and nonhuman life. They are therefore vegetarians, as are Buddhists, whose sacred writings forbid all needless killing. In the West, however, it was traditionally believed that animals were made for human use. This idea, familiar from the Old Testament book of Genesis and elaborated by a long line of Jewish and Christian thinkers, also formed part of Aristotle's worldview. Aristotle taught that 'nature does everything for a purpose', and so, just as plants exist to provide food for animals, animals exist to provide food and other 'aids in life' for humans.

This was cosmology with a moral point. AQUINAS, who emphasized that it was God himself who provided the animals for human use, made the point explicit: 'Therefore,' he said, 'it is not wrong for man to make use of them, by killing or in any other way whatever' (*Summa contra gentiles*). Are there, then, no limits on how animals may be treated? One might think we have a duty to be kind to them out of simple charity. But Aquinas insisted that this is not so. 'Charity,' he said, 'does not extend to irrational creatures.'

There was, however, one way in which animals could gain a degree of protection. They might be the incidental beneficiaries of obligations owed to humans. If someone has promised to look after your dog, she is obliged to care for it. But the obligation is owed to you, not to the dog. There might even be a general duty not to torment animals, because, as KANT put it, 'He who is cruel to animals becomes hard also in his dealings with men' (*Lectures on Ethics* 1780–1). But once again, the point was to protect the men, not the animals. (This has sometimes been called the 'indirect duty view' – that we can have duties to animals, but only indirect ones.)

This view might seem extreme in its near total disregard for nonhumans. Nevertheless, the idea that animals are essentially resources for human use was accepted by almost every important thinker in the Western tradition – including such figures as St Francis, who is popularly but wrongly believed to have advocated a more charitable stance. For this view to be defensible, however, there must be some difference between humans and other animals that would explain why humans have a privileged moral status. Traditional thought cited two such differences. For Aristotle, the difference was that humans alone are rational. Religious figures added that man alone was made in the image of God. These explanations seemed sufficient until 1859, when Darwin's *On the Origin of Species* (1859) transformed our understanding of man's relation to the rest of nature (see DARWIN, C.R.).

2 Challenges to the traditional view

Darwin demonstrated that humans are not 'set apart' from other animals, but are related to them by evolutionary descent (see EVOLUTION, THEORY OF). It is no accident that we bear such a startling resemblance to the apes. Our bones and muscles are but modified versions of the ape's bones and muscles – they are similar because we inherited them from the same ancestors. The same is true of our rational faculties. Man is not *the* rational animal, for other animals also possess a degree of rationality. How could it be otherwise, when our brains developed from a common source? Darwin went so far as to declare, 'There is no fundamental difference between man and the higher mammals in their mental faculties' (*Origin of the Species*). Such differences as do exist, he said, are matters of degree, not kind.

Today it is widely accepted that Darwin was right, at least in the main outlines of his view, and this poses an obvious ethical dilemma: if humans are similar in so many ways to other animals, and humans merit moral protection, then why should other animals not merit protection too? As Asa

Gray, Darwin's friend in America, put it, 'Human beings may be more humane when they realize that, as their dependent associates live a life in which man has a share, so they have rights which man is bound to respect' (*Natural Science and Religion* 1880). Darwin himself regarded cruelty to animals, along with slavery, as one of the two great human moral failings.

Another nineteenth-century development also cast doubt on the traditional exclusion of animals from the range of moral concern. The utilitarians, led by Jeremy Bentham and John Stuart Mill, argued that morality is fundamentally a matter of seeking to promote happiness and prevent suffering (see UTILITARIANISM). But Bentham saw no reason to limit moral concern to human suffering. In fact, in *An Introduction to the Principles of Morals and Legislation* he suggested that disregard for animals was a form of discrimination analogous to racism:

> The day may come when the rest of the animal creation may acquire the rights which never could have been withholden from them but by the hand of tyranny. The French have already discovered that the blackness of the skin is no reason why a human being should be abandoned without redress to the caprice of a tormentor. It may one day come to be recognized that the number of the legs, the villosity of the skin, or the termination of the os *sacrum* are reasons equally insufficient for abandoning a sensitive being to the same fate .... The question is not, Can they *reason*? nor, Can they *talk*? but, Can they *suffer*?
>
> (1789; original emphasis)

It must be noted, however, that for most of Western history the moral status of animals did not seem to be much of an issue, and philosophers did not write very extensively about it (Bentham's discussion, for example, is confined to a footnote). The subject began to be widely discussed among philosophers only after the publication of Peter Singer's *Animal Liberation* in 1975.

3 The contemporary debate

One of the striking things about the debate concerning animals is that it is possible to reach radical ethical conclusions by invoking only the most common moral principles. The idea that it is wrong to cause suffering, unless there is a sufficient justification, is one of the most basic moral principles, shared by virtually everyone. Yet the consistent application of this principle seems to lead straight to vegetarianism or at least to the avoidance of factory-farmed meat. The argument is disarmingly simple. In modern factory farms, animals who are raised and slaughtered for food suffer considerable pain. Since we could easily nourish ourselves without eating them, our only reason for eating them seems to be our enjoyment of how they taste. So, unless one thinks our gustatory pleasure is a sufficient justification for causing torment, the obvious conclusion is that we are wrong to produce and consume such products.

Other arguments appeal to less commonplace notions. The word 'speciesism' was coined by Richard Ryder, a British psychologist who ceased experimenting on animals after becoming convinced it was immoral, and was popularized by Singer in *Animal Liberation*. Speciesism is said to be analogous to racism. Just as racists unjustifiably give greater weight to the interests of the members of their own race, speciesists unjustifiably give greater weight to the interests of the members of their own species (see DISCRIMINATION).

Consider, for example, the very different standards we have for using humans and nonhumans in laboratory research. Why do we think it permissible to perform a painful and destructive experiment on, say, a rhesus monkey, when we would not perform the same experiment on a human? Someone might suggest that, say, humans are more intelligent than monkeys, or that their social relationships are more complex. But consider mentally retarded persons whose cognitive and social capacities are no greater than those of the animal. Would it be permissible to perform the same experiment on them? Many people think that, simply because they are human, it would not. This is speciesism laid bare: there is no difference between the human and the nonhuman in their abilities to think, feel or suffer, and yet the human's welfare counts for more.

This line of thought suggests that animals may be treated differently from humans when, and only when, there are morally relevant differences between them. It may be permissible to admit humans, but not other animals, to universities, because humans can read and other animals cannot. But in cases where there are no relevant differences, they must be treated alike. This is the sense in which humans and nonhumans can be said to be morally 'equal': the bare fact that one is human never itself counts for anything, just as the bare fact that one has one skin colour or another never itself counts for anything. So we may not treat an animal in any way in which we would not be willing to treat a human with the same intellectual and emotional capacities.

Such arguments have, of course, provoked lively opposition. Many philosophers find it difficult to believe that mere animals could have such powerful claims on us. Morality, they say, is fundamentally a human institution established to protect human rights and human interests (see MORALITY AND ETHICS). Contractarianism, which has emerged in the latter half of the twentieth century as the principal rival to utilitarianism, makes this point most clearly. According to this view, morality rests on agreements of mutual benefit. Morality arises within a community when each person agrees to 'play the social game', respecting other people's rights and interests, provided others will do so as well. This agreement makes social living possible, and everyone benefits from it. But animals are unable to participate in such agreements, so they do not come within the sphere of moral protection.

In addition to initiating a philosophical debate, Peter Singer's book is perhaps the most conspicuous example of a philosophical work triggering a social movement. The animal rights movement, with its principled opposition to such practices as factory farming, the use of animals in commercial and scientific research, and the fur trade, has become a familiar part of contemporary life. Rarely, if ever, have philosophical thinking and social activism been linked so closely.

See also: ENVIRONMENTAL ETHICS; EVOLUTION AND ETHICS; RIGHTS

References and further reading

Regan, T. (1983) *The Case for Animal Rights*, Berkeley, CA: University of California Press. (Defends the view that nonhuman animals have moral rights comparable to the rights of humans. One of the most important philosophical defences of animals.)

JAMES RACHELS

ANOMALOUS MONISM

Anomalous monism, proposed by Donald Davidson in 1970, implies that all events are of one fundamental kind, namely physical. But it does not deny that there are mental events; rather, it implies that every mental event is some physical event or other. The idea is that someone's thinking at a certain time that the earth is round, for example, might be a certain pattern of neural firing in their brain at that time, an event which is both a thinking that the earth is round (a type of mental event) and a pattern of neural firing (a type of physical event). There is just one event, that can be characterized both in mental terms and in physical terms. If mental events are physical events, they can, like all physical events, be explained and predicted (at least in principle) on the basis of laws of nature cited in physical science. However, according to anomalous monism, events cannot be so explained or predicted as described in mental terms (such as thinking, desiring, itching and so on), but only as described in physical terms. The distinctive feature of anomalous monism as a brand of physical monism is that it implies that mental events as such (that is, as described in mental terms) are anomalous – they cannot be explained or predicted on the basis of strict scientific laws.

See also: REDUCTION, PROBLEMS OF; LAWS, NATURAL; REDUCTIONISM IN THE PHILOSOPHY OF MIND

BRIAN P. MCLAUGHLIN

ANSCOMBE, GERTRUDE ELIZABETH MARGARET (1919–2001)

Elizabeth Anscombe has contributed to all principal areas of philosophy, most influentially to ethics and the philosophy of mind. She is the founder of contemporary action theory, and an important source of the revival of interest in virtue ethics. The chief influences on her thought are the work of her teacher, Ludwig Wittgenstein, much of which she has translated and of which she is an important interpreter, and the classical and medieval traditions, as found in Aristotle and Aquinas. She has also made a number of contributions to the defence of Roman Catholic religious belief.

See also: CAUSATION; FREE WILL §2; REASONS AND CAUSES

MICHAEL THOMPSON

ANSELM OF CANTERBURY (1033–1109)

Anselm of Canterbury, also known as Anselm of Aosta and Anselm of Bec or Saint Anselm, was first a student, then a monk, later prior and finally abbot of the monastery of Bec in Normandy, before being elected Archbishop of Canterbury in 1093. He remains one of the best-known and most readily engaging philosophers and theologians of medieval Europe. His literary corpus consists of eleven treatises or dialogues, the most important of which are the philosophical works *Monologion* and *Proslogion* and the magnificent theological work *Cur deus homo* (Why God Became a [God-]Man). He also left three meditations, nineteen prayers, 374 extant letters including *Epistolae de Sacramentis* (Letters on the Sacraments) and a collection of philosophical fragments, together with a compilation of his sayings (*Dicta Anselmi*) by Alexander, a monk of Canterbury, and a compilation of his reflections on virtue, *De morum qualitate per exemplorum coaptationem* (On Virtues and Vices as Illustrated by a Collage of Examples), possibly also by a monk at Canterbury.

At Bec Anselm wrote his first philosophical treatise, the *Monologion*, a title signifying a soliloquy. This work was followed by the *Proslogion*, the title meaning an address (of the soul to God). At Bec he also completed the philosophical dialogues *De grammatico* (On (an) Expert in Grammar), *De veritate* (On Truth), *De libertate arbitrii* (Freedom of Choice) and *De casu diaboli* (The Fall of the Devil). Near the end of his time at Bec, he turned his attention to themes more theological, drafting a first version of *De incarnatione Verbi* (The Incarnation of the Word) before September 1092 and completing the final revision around the beginning of 1094. During his time in office at Canterbury, which included two long exiles from England (1097–1100 and 1103–6), he wrote the *Cur deus homo*, followed by the concisely reasoned treatises *De conceptu virginali et originali peccati* (The Virgin Conception and Original Sin), *De processione Spiritus Sancti* (The Procession of the Holy Spirit) and *De concordia praescientiae et praedestinationis et gratiae dei cum libero arbitrio* (The Harmony of the Foreknowledge, the Predestination and the Grace of God with Free Choice).

Though his principal writings at Bec were more philosophical while his foremost writings as archbishop were more theological, still we must remember that Anselm himself made no express distinction between philosophy and theology, that at Bec he also wrote two meditations and sixteen prayers, and that his *Cur deus homo* and *De concordia*, in dealing with the weighty theological doctrines of atonement, predestination and grace, incorporate philosophical concepts such as *necessitas praecedens* (preceding necessity) and *necessitas sequens* (subsequent necessity).

Anselm's most famous philosophical work is certainly the *Proslogion*, while his most influential theological work is undoubtedly the *Cur deus homo*. The style of the *Proslogion* imitates that of Augustine in the *Confessiones*, where the soul invokes God as it prayerfully reflects and meditates. By contrast, the *Cur deus homo* is cast in dialogue form because, as Anselm states in I.1, 'issues which are examined by the method of question and answer are clearer, and so more acceptable, to many minds – especially to minds that are slower.' About his aims in the *Proslogion* there is no scholarly consensus. The traditional view holds that he is undertaking the twofold task of demonstrating the existence of God and demonstrating certain truths regarding God's attributes. In carrying out this task, he has recourse to a single consideration (*unum argumentum*), namely, that God is *aliquid quo nihil maius cogitari potest* (something than which nothing greater can be thought). This single consideration gives rise to a single argument form; the logical structure of the reasoning which purports to establish that *quo nihil maius* is actually existent is also the structure of the arguments which conclude that *quo nihil maius* is so existent that it cannot be thought not to exist, is alone existent *per se*, is omnipotent, merciful yet impassable, is supremely just and good, is greater than can be thought, and so on. According to this interpretation, the *Proslogion* seeks to establish most of the same conclusions that were reached in the earlier *Monologion*, but to establish them more directly, simply and tersely.

The central thrust of the *Cur deus homo* may be discerned from the title: namely, to explain why it was necessary for God, in the person of the Son, to become a man (that is, to become incarnate as a human being (*homo*)). Anselm uses the Latin word *homo* generically and not in the sense of male (*vir*). This fact is seen clearly in *Cur deus homo* II, 8: 'nil convenientius, quam ut de femina sine viro assumat [deus] illum hominem quem quaerimus' 'nothing is more fitting than that God assume from a woman without a male *that* man [human being] about whom we are inquiring'. Though the sense of *homo* varies in accordance with whether Anselm is speaking about a human being or about a human nature, there is no doubt about the meaning of the title: the Son of God assumed *a* human nature, thereby becoming *a* man; he did not assume another man (in other words, assume a human person together with a human nature) as the heretical Nestorians had taught, nor did he become man (in other words, become universal man, by assuming unindividuated human nature as such).

Anselm's detailed theory of satisfaction for sin was in large measure a putative theoretical justification of the institutionalized practices of the confessional and the penitential system as found in the medieval Christian church, which understood every sin to constitute a punishable demerit and to require both the imploring of God's forgiveness and the making of amends for having dishonoured him. Throughout the intricate and sustained reasoning of the *Cur deus homo*, Anselm seeks to show one central truth: 'because only God can make this satisfaction and only a man ought to make it, it is necessary that a God-man make it' (*Cur deus homo* II, 6).

As in the *Cur deus homo*, so also in his other treatises Anselm proceeds insofar as he deems possible, *sola ratione* (by recourse to rational considerations alone). Accordingly, he is rightly called the 'Father of Scholasticism'. He understands *ratio* in a broad sense, broad enough to encompass appeals to experience as well as to conceptual intelligibility. Although the main intellectual influence upon him was Augustine, he is less platonistic than the latter, and the influence of Aristotle's *De interpretatione* and *Categories* (from Boethius' Latin translations) is clearly discernible in his philosophical works.

See also: Free will; God, concepts of; Medieval philosophy; Omniscience

JASPER HOPKINS

ANTHROPOLOGY, PHILOSOPHY OF

Anthropology, like philosophy, is multifaceted. It studies humans' physical, social, cultural and linguistic development, as well as their material culture, from prehistoric times up to the present, in all parts of the world. Some anthropological subfields have strong ties with the physical and biological sciences; others identify more closely with the social sciences or humanities. Within cultural and social anthropology differing theoretical approaches disagree about whether anthropology can be a science. The question of how it is possible to understand cultures different from one's own, and to transmit that knowledge to others, is central to anthropology because its answer determines the nature of the discipline. Philosophy of anthropology examines the definitions of basic anthropological concepts, the objectivity of anthropological claims and the nature of anthropological confirmation and explanation. It also examines the problems in value theory that arise when anthropologists confront cultures that do not share their own society's standards.

See also: Universalism in ethics

MERRILEE H. SALMON

ANTIREALISM

See Intuitionistic logic and antirealism; Realism and antirealism; Scientific realism and antirealism

ANTI-SEMITISM

Anti-Semitism is a form of racism which sees Jews as a dangerous and despicable group in society. It has solid philosophical sources in the work of German idealism which emphasized the distinctiveness of Judaism and how it has been superseded by Christianity. Both Kant and Hegel made a sharp distinction between Judaism and what they regarded as more rational religions, and they questioned the capability of the Jewish people for playing an integral role in the state. Sartre used the notion of anti-Semitism to show how a sense of self-identity is created by the attitudes of others towards the individual and the group. That is, what makes Jews Jews is the fact that there is anti-Semitism, and there is nothing that Jews can do about anti-Semitism. Anti-Semitism is a problem for the anti-Semites themselves; anti-Semitism, by Sartre's account, is in fact an attempted solution to the difficulties of taking free and authentic decisions. Anti-Semitism has played an important role in Jews' self-definition, and in attitudes to the State of Israel and to the religion of Judaism itself.

See also: FASCISM; HOLOCAUST, THE

OLIVER LEAMAN
CLIVE NYMAN

APEL, KARL-OTTO (1922–)

The German philosopher Karl-Otto Apel is best known for his wide-ranging 'transcendental pragmatic' approach to a gamut of issues in theoretical and practical philosophy. This approach accords 'argumentative discourse' and its essential normative presuppositions a foundational role within all other philosophical inquiries for which justifiable validity claims are raised, for example epistemology, normative theories of rationality, Critical Theory and ethics. If there are such presuppositions then any interlocutor's communicative intention to waive them will clash with the construal of that debate as rationally meaningful, since it involves the interlocutor in a kind of inconsistency that Apel (like Habermas), drawing on speech-act theory, conceptualizes as a 'performative self-contradiction'. Apel (unlike Habermas) develops this concept into the doctrine of rationally definitive justification (*Letztbegründung*). Apel deserves to be better known as the originator of discourse ethics (*Diskursethik*), whose central contention (that some presuppositions of discourse have universally valid moral content) he developed in the mid-1960s.

See also: COMMUNICATIVE RATIONALITY

MATTHIAS KETTNER

APPLIED ETHICS

Introduction

Applied ethics is marked out from ethics in general by its special focus on issues of practical concern. It therefore includes medical ethics, environmental ethics, and evaluation of the social implications of scientific and technological change, as well as matters of policy in such areas as health care, business or journalism. It is also concerned with professional codes and responsibilities in such areas.

Typical of the issues discussed are abortion, euthanasia, personal relationships, the treatment of nonhuman animals, and matters of race and gender. Although sometimes treated in isolation, these issues are best discussed in the context of some more general questions which have been perennial preoccupations of philosophers, such as: How should we see the world and our place in it? What is the good life for the individual? What is the good society? In relation to these questions, applied

ethics involves discussion of fundamental ethical theory, including utilitarianism, liberal rights theory and virtue ethics.

'Applied ethics' and 'applied philosophy' are sometimes used as synonyms, but applied philosophy is in fact broader, covering also such fields as law, education and art, and theoretical issues in artificial intelligence. These areas include philosophical problems – metaphysical and epistemological – that are not strictly ethical. Applied ethics may therefore be understood as focusing more closely on ethical questions. Nevertheless, many of the issues it treats do in fact involve other aspects of philosophy; medical ethics, for example, includes such metaphysical themes as the nature of 'personhood' or the definition of death.

> 1 Definitions
> 2 Theory and practice
> 3 Method
> 4 Critics and opponents
> 5 Historical context
> 6 Professional ethics
> 7 Are there ethical experts?
> 8 Research in applied ethics
> 9 Institutions

1 Definitions

While the name 'applied ethics' is comparatively new, the idea is not. Philosophy has traditionally concerned itself with questions both of personal morality (what should I do?) and public morality (what is the good society?), but while these questions are fundamental to applied ethics, they could also be said to characterize ethics in general. Applied ethics is therefore distinguished commonly as that part of ethics that gives particular and direct attention to practical issues and controversies.

In the private sphere, ethical issues include, for example, matters relating to the family (see FAMILY, ETHICS AND THE), or to close personal relationships (see FRIENDSHIP), the care of the old or disabled, the raising of the young, particularly where matters of morality are concerned, or personal ethical problems arising for the individual in the workplace. In the public sphere, applied ethics may involve assessing policy in the light of the impact of advances in biomedical technology (see LIFE AND DEATH; TECHNOLOGY AND ETHICS), or assessing international obligations and duties to future generations in the light of environmental problems (see FUTURE GENERATIONS, OBLIGATIONS TO; POPULATION AND ETHICS). The public arena includes, too, a range of issues for the plural society, such as ethnicity or gender in relation to discrimination, cultural understanding and toleration; more widely still, it may extend to issues of interest also to political philosophy, such as terrorism and the ethics of war. In all these matters, the concern of applied ethics is not only to supply a personal ethical perspective, but also to provide guidelines for public policy.

Applied ethics includes, as well, the area of professional ethics; it examines the ethical dilemmas and challenges met with by workers in the health care field – doctors, nurses, counsellors, psychiatrists, dentists – and by a wide range of workers in other professions including lawyers, accountants, managers and administrators, people in business, police and law enforcement officers. Specific ethical issues such as confidentiality, truth-telling or conflicts of interest may arise in all or any of these areas, and most professions seek to codify their approaches and provide guidance for their members.

2 Theory and practice

Underlying all such issues are questions about justice, rights, utility, virtue and community. The practice of distinguishing between theoretical and applied ethics must, therefore, be treated with some caution. Indeed, some have regarded the term 'applied' as redundant, on the grounds that there cannot be an 'ethics' which is not applied: on the one hand, they argue, theoretical concepts such as rights and justice should not be viewed as mere abstractions; and, on the other, applied ethics should not be detached from its roots in traditional morality. But while it is important to stress this continuity, there are certain characteristic features of applied ethics which mark it out in practice from theoretical ethics. These are (a) its greater attention to context and detail and (b) its more holistic approach – its willingness to link ethical ideals to a conception of human nature and human needs (see HUMAN NATURE). Thus practitioners of applied ethics may be more willing than proponents of traditional academic moral philosophy to recognize that psychology and sociology, a knowledge of culture and history, the insights of good literature, and even an understanding of humans as biological entities, are all relevant to the determination of moral issues in personal and public life.

The demarcation line between applied and theoretical ethics which this suggests may be drawn at that point on the spectrum of ethics where ethical theory stops short of normative recommendations and confines itself to the analysis of moral concepts such as 'right', 'good', 'responsibility', 'blame' and 'virtue' and to discussion of what might be called the epistemology of ethics – such theories as ethical realism, subjectivism and relativism (see MORAL KNOWLEDGE; MORAL REALISM). This is the area sometimes described as 'meta-ethics'. Drawing the line at this point may be useful so long as it is not allowed to obscure the truth that applied and theoretical ethics are not discrete but lie on a continuum from the particular to the general, the concrete to the abstract.

The ultimate focus of applied ethics may well be entirely particular: the individual case study. And it is this that gives rise to a further characteristic feature of applied ethics: its concern with dilemmas – not necessarily in the hard logical sense of situations in which it is impossible to act rightly because each of two opposite courses of action is either judged to be mandatory or judged to be wrong; but in the looser sense of cases in which a choice between courses of action may be extremely difficult, the arguments on both sides being compelling, and the person who must act being strongly influenced in opposing directions (for example, to sanction drastic medical intervention to save a severely disabled baby which would otherwise die, or to allow nature to take its course). It should be said, though, that choosing between options which are not morally equal is not, strictly speaking, a dilemma, although it is admittedly likely to be emotionally traumatizing, while choosing between moral obligations that are indisputably of equal weight is not a *moral* problem. The question for applied ethics in such cases may well be whether or not the available options are indeed morally equal.

Because it focuses on individual dilemmas, applied ethics must confront the question of universalization, which may also be seen as a 'free rider' problem: many things are judged to be wrong as a result of asking the question, 'What if everyone did that?', even though, in a particular case, it might seem harmless and more convenient for an individual to ignore the rule, while benefiting from the fact that everyone else is following it (see UNIVERSALISM IN ETHICS). The applied ethicist, like the theoretical moral philosopher, must find a way to deal with this problem, but for the applied ethicist, the problem is bound up with the need to employ what is sometimes called moral casuistry. This ancient science is not necessarily to be despised, for while a secondary meaning of the term 'casuist' is indeed 'sophist' or 'quibbler', it was not originally a term of abuse, but simply meant accepting in a theological context people's desire to work out the 'right answer' to a difficult issue of conscience in a particular set of circumstances.

3 Method

One method of reasoning employed in applied ethics may be compared to that of a designer who starts with a blueprint, but has to adapt it to the materials to hand and to the situations in which it is required. There is some resemblance in this case to the Hegelian method of dialectical reasoning, as well as to the method of reflective equilibrium favoured by such contemporary writers as Rawls, in which intuitions in response to particular cases are measured against principles, causing them to be revised and their implications for particular cases again reappraised (see MORAL JUSTIFICATION §2). According to this view of the subject, the method of applied ethics is neither purely deductive nor purely inductive. For others, however, the deductive model is more powerful, and the question to be answered in any particular case is simply *which* (inviolable) principle it falls under. Others again would favour the inductive model, according to which, by clearly seeing what is right in particular cases, it becomes possible to formulate a general principle encompassing these and other particular judgments (see UNIVERSALISM IN ETHICS).

In general, discussion of ethical theories in applied ethics aims to pursue, in the direction of the highest degree of generality and abstraction, the question of what humans should do. In practice, discussion of theories is often confined to their implications for the resolution of particular problems, since applied ethics characteristically seeks to answer the broad question with a much greater degree of particularity.

4 Critics and opponents

In seeking answers to practical problems, applied ethics runs counter to much recent philosophy. The view that prevailed during the dominance of empiricism and positivism (the greater part of the twentieth century) is that philosophy can have nothing to say about pressing practical problems.

This view is grounded in two important philosophical arguments: (a) Hume's objection to arguments that seek to derive an 'ought' from an 'is' (see HUME, D.); and (b) Moore's argument that to identify moral characteristics with 'natural' or empirical ones is to commit a 'naturalistic fallacy' (see MOORE, G.E.; NATURALISM IN ETHICS). Both of these arguments must be resisted if applied ethics is to succeed in closing the gap between factual descriptions of situations and moral judgments, and both may partially at least be answered by insisting that some facts 'speak for themselves' – torture, child-murder, genocide, for example.

The argument that facts and values are to be kept apart is, however, less of an obstacle to philosophers outside the English-speaking world; the notion of praxis, for example, is familiar from various continental traditions, including Marxism, the Frankfurt School, and the philosophy of Habermas;

while the idea of the philosopher as *engagé* – as concerned with playing a part in the world – is an important part of French existentialist thought, made familiar in the works of Sartre. These sources have, however, produced a different kind of challenge to the notion of applied ethics as an impartial and essentially reason-based approach to ethical issues in society. Objections to the conception of universal moral norms and to foundationalist procedures in reasoning (the 'postmodernist' challenge) are associated with recent developments in Marxist theory, certain feminist approaches to ethics and epistemology, and the deconstructionist movement – schools of thought which may also adopt an analysis of power-structures in society incompatible with belief in individual freedom of action (see FEMINISM AND PSYCHOANALYSIS; DECONSTRUCTION). Supporters of these theoretical positions often make strong claims for the recognition of rights, but this is probably better seen as exploitation of the preconceptions of their opponents, rather than as recognition of universal ethical concepts and human freedom.

Other critiques of traditional ethics may, however, be more sympathetic to applied ethics. On the basis of research revealing the contextuality of many women's responses to ethical dilemmas, some feminist writers, most prominently Carol Gilligan, have argued that women in general are likely to adopt an ethic of care and responsibility to particular others rather than an abstract morality of principles, rights or justice. Such an approach may well seem better adapted to the resolution of 'hard cases' in, for example, health care or social work.

Similarly, the approach known as 'virtue ethics', with its emphasis on seeking the good in particular situations, may seem well adapted to applied ethics, even if its proponents sometimes appear to view it in opposition, regarding their own stand as more objective, and wrongly equating applied ethics with subjectivism and relativism (see VIRTUE ETHICS).

Other stereotypes to be rejected are political: applied ethics has typically been associated with vegetarianism, pacifism, feminism and environmentalism. It should be noted, however, that it also includes criticism and evaluation of these positions: defences of meat-eating or animal experiments, scepticism about feminism, and resistance to new 'ecological ethics' are to be found alongside more orthodox publications on library shelves. There is nothing wrong with variety of opinion so long as this is within a broad ethical framework, for it is of the essence of applied philosophy in general to approach individual issues in their own right and not as part of an ideological package-deal.

Applied ethics, then, is part of a whole view of the human condition and takes a broad view of ethical decision-making. Essentially, this is ethical decision-making seen as practical policy that consciously recognizes the constraints of moral norms, rights and ethical principles capable of commanding universal respect. Where this is accepted, the object of applied ethics is plain: it is to gain clearer perceptions of right and wrong, with a view to embodying these insights in manners and institutions.

5 Historical context

The inception of applied philosophy could well be said to coincide with that of the Western philosophical tradition as a whole, for the first of the early Greek philosophers, Thales (c.585 BC), is recorded as having combined his speculative philosophical interests with economic acumen and an interest in legal and political reform. Later schools of philosophy in ancient times – Pythagoreans, Epicureans, Stoics – offered their followers principles for living and even distinctive codes of practice.

For both Plato and Aristotle, ethical and political questions were posed in terms of such notions as the good for man, the ultimate good, or what is good in itself and for its own sake (see PLATO §16; ARISTOTLE §21). Their assumption was that this inquiry led both to a way of life for the individual, and to a conception of the good society. They disagreed about whether this would lead an individual necessarily to live according to the ethical insight thus gained, Aristotle, unlike Plato in his earlier writings, allowing for the intervention of weakness of will to divert the person who has recognized the good from pursuing it (see AKRASIA).

Subsequent philosophers frequently applied their ethical assumptions to particular cases, and saw this, not as a way of fractionizing moral philosophy – making it the science of the particular – but as a route to formulating guiding principles. Aquinas treated a range of practical issues including marriage and the family in *Summa theologiae*, and this tradition was developed further by Suárez and Grotius. Locke wrote on the issue of toleration, Kant on suicide and on the question of whether it is ever right to tell a lie from benevolent motives (see LOCKE, J. §7; TOLERATION; SUICIDE, ETHICS OF). Bentham put forward a complex theory of punishment, even formulating plans for a new type of prison, to be called the 'panopticon'. He also wrote on legal and political reform. Hegel's philosophy included views on the family and on punishment. J.S. Mill's writings on toleration, paternalism and feminism in *On Liberty* continue to be of interest in the present day, as the controversies involved in these areas remain subjects of disagreement and debate (see FEMINISM; PATERNALISM), and Dewey's theories of education exercised enormous practical influence on education systems in the USA and Britain (see EDUCATION, HISTORY OF PHILOSOPHY OF).

The tradition in moral philosophy unsympathetic to applied ethics is in fact of fairly recent origin. It was associated with the dominance of positivism and empiricism in the philosophy of science, and the vogue for linguistic analysis in epistemology. This is a twentieth-century phenomenon and, right up to the closing years of the nineteenth century, a more generous conception of ethics flourished. If a certain myopia on applied issues is recognized amongst philosophers in the English-speaking world, coinciding roughly with the first half of the twentieth century, various explanations may be offered for the gradual return of visual focus. For those with an interest in medical ethics, a research project in Tuskegee in the USA in which a control group with syphilis remained untreated for decades after safe treatment was known to be possible is often cited as a trigger generating widespread discussion of issues such as autonomy, beneficence and nonmaleficence, medical confidentiality, and the ethics of experiments on human subjects (see MEDICAL ETHICS). This case may have been, however, a symptom rather than a cause, for in general medicine moved during those decades from being a practice with little power to influence the natural course of disease, to being a powerful interventionist tool. Whatever the specific cause, then, from roughly this period medical ethics became an arena of critical and controversial discussion.

Again in the USA, the Vietnam War and the protests which it generated are cited as having promoted discussion of a different range of applied issues (civil disobedience, duty to conscience versus duty to society) and as having led in a fairly direct way to the setting up of the Society for Philosophy and Public Affairs and the journal *Philosophy and Public Affairs* (see CIVIL DISOBEDIENCE; CONSCIENCE).

Others, focusing on the applied philosopher's interest in animal welfare, cite the publication of the volume *Animal Liberation* (1975) by Peter Singer as ushering in a new conception of ethics as a practical and possibly even campaigning area (see ANIMALS AND ETHICS §3). Already, too, Rachel Carson's *Silent Spring* (1962) had alerted the general public to many environmental hazards and thus opened the way to an enlarged philosophical perspective in which developments in science and technology and the way in which these were applied by firms and governments to the environment were seen as matters of ethical concern. It was a decade or so later that the internal operations of businesses became matters for ethical scrutiny, prompted by scandals connected with sharp practices such as insider trading.

Finally, it must be said that philosophy itself no doubt provided a spur to the growth of applied ethics. The preoccupation of academic moral philosophy with entirely minor moral issues in a century which had witnessed two world wars and many accompanying gross violations of human rights was too remarkable to pass for long, particularly with wider access to higher education and hence to the hitherto elite and somewhat esoteric pursuit of philosophy.

This account of the rise of contemporary applied ethics raises the question of what kind of study applied ethics is exactly. Is it merely another kind of academic study, or is it committed to the promotion of change in the world? Is it conservative or radical? Reactionary or revolutionary? The answer to this last question is that it can be either. Reflection may make one seek to promote change for the better, but it may also cause one to recoil from change and seek to preserve what is best from the past. The controversial nature of most of the issues involved is itself a spur to their philosophical study, for it is probably true to say that until recently, despite differences of religious or ideological background, a common moral approach could in general be assumed, and accepted norms of moral behaviour could be taken as a starting-point for ethical reasoning. Such moral consensus cannot now be presupposed, and, while absolutist approaches are by no means inconsistent with mainstream philosophical ethics, in practice the defence of an absolute conception of morality against relativistic, subjective and utilitarian approaches is often associated with a religious perspective.

Many writers on applied ethics, however, adopt a secular utilitarian stance. These include the Australian philosopher Peter Singer, and the Oxford philosopher Jonathan Glover, who has written especially in the area of medical ethics (see UTILITARIANISM). R.M. Hare, in *Moral Thinking* (1981), puts forward a prescriptivist theory which combines utilitarianism with Kantian universalizability (see PRESCRIPTIVISM). Also influential is the ethic of care mentioned above, which is often linked to gender differences. Other views include those of the Australian philosopher John PASSMORE, who defends a liberal moral perspective, especially in relation to environmental ethics, and John RAWLS, whose notion of reflective equilibrium combines intuitionism with contract theory (see MORAL JUSTIFICATION §2). Rawls' *A Theory of Justice* (1971) inaugurated a new, more practical approach in ethics, which had implications for economics, law and political theory. Sissela Bokhas has written on the fine texture of issues in public life in *Lying: Moral Choices in Public and Private Life* (1978) and *Secrets* (1984) (see TRUTHFULNESS);

Mary Midgley, in *Beast and Man* (1978) and elsewhere, has discussed the relations between humans and other species; and Onora O'Neill has brought a Kantian ethic to bear on the issues of famine and poverty. The debate between communitarians and libertarians about the ethics of capitalism and the role of welfare can also be seen as a part of applied ethics (see COMMUNITY AND COMMUNITARIANISM; MARKET, ETHICS OF THE). The German philosopher, Jürgen HABERMAS, an influential figure both in continental Europe and the English-speaking world, has put forward a notion of consensus as the object of theory expressed in practice.

6 Professional ethics

Similar divisions may reveal themselves in professional ethics, although the idea that there should be special codes of ethics peculiar to particular professions has been current since ancient times, when the Hippocratic oath was required of those engaging in medical practice. Many modern groups, including engineers, nurses and lawyers, have adopted formal codes setting standards of ethical practice for their profession (see PROFESSIONAL ETHICS).

Ethics also plays an increasing role in the training of professionals. Often the preferred approach is through the use of case studies, sometimes fictional, sometimes using videos of actual cases. One problem with the case study approach is its possible negative effect. In stressing that there are at least two sides to many ethical problems, and in presenting ethical theories as giving conflicting outcomes, they may risk generating a facile moral or cultural relativism – the view that there are only opinions, not answers. The use of case studies and discussion based on situational ethics may also tacitly undermine principles (see SITUATION ETHICS). In contrast, some courses aim simply to increase the moral sensitivity of trainees, on the assumption that if this is successful they will go on to make good professional decisions.

7 Are there ethical experts?

Applied ethics does not involve a claim of moral expertise, but often involves collaboration with specialists in practical areas in order to arrive at policy decisions that allow ethical considerations a determining role.

There is now wide acceptance of the principle of ensuring that a philosophical or ethical viewpoint is represented in certain kinds of forums, such as public enquiries, the reports of legislative committees or commissions of inquiry, and hospital ethics committees. The USA has a President's Commission to report directly on bioethical issues to the US President, the UK has a National Bioethics Committee funded independently of government, while in France there is a French National Committee on Ethical Affairs in Public Debate. In 1985, the Council of Europe created a multi-disciplinary body with experts appointed by each member country, now called the Comité Directeur de Bioéthique (CDBI). Canada set up a Royal Commission on New Reproductive Technologies, and the European Parliament commissions advise on scientific and technological policy options. Other countries are following a similar pattern. In addition, the Council of Europe in 1990 began working on a European Convention on biomedical ethics, which would be a legally binding instrument on all countries signing it, the object being ultimately to harmonize European legislation.

Individuals are also used as consultants on public policy issues. In Europe in 1989, Jonathan Glover, in collaboration with nationals of other European countries, produced a report on fertility and the family for the European Commission, while Will Kymlicka has advised on this topic as a member of the Canadian Royal Commission and, in the USA, Arthur Caplan was a member of the President's Task Force on National Health Care Reform. In Britain, the philosopher Mary Warnock was responsible for official reports on the educational needs of children with disabilities and learning difficulties, and on new developments in reproductive medicine and embryology; Bernard Williams played a similar role in relation to pornography and censorship. The debate about euthanasia in the Netherlands has engaged philosophers, lawyers and social theorists. Less happily, a visit by Peter Singer to Germany provoked widespread protest related to the debate on euthanasia and has led to the unpopularity of bioethics in some circles, and a general and unjustified rejection of applied ethics.

Some achievements in these areas may also be recorded; examination of the ethics of clinical trials, for example, particularly in relation to AIDS, led to a total reconceptualization of what clinical trials require, and to a multi-choice system being devised which is both scientifically acceptable and also offers a more acceptable level of choice to patients and physicians.

8 Research in applied ethics

In general, those who fund research regard the gathering of facts, often called the 'generation of new knowledge', as crucial; philosophy, in contrast, appears to involve reflection on facts, while normative philosophy generates proposals for action

or policy. Applied ethics offers at its best an opportunity to combine these approaches: for facts to be made the fruitful object of analytic and morally sensitive reflection, and for philosophical inquiry to accept the discipline of the need to take account of the practical framework within which speculation is cast.

Research in applied ethics, then, ideally starts from a perceived problem and is motivated to find a solution to that problem. It is frequently inter-disciplinary. A research programme is often inspired by technological progress, for it is this that has placed ethical considerations at the heart of many areas of public debate. Typical of these are the controversies already mentioned surrounding the new technologies of reproduction – embryo research, donation of gametes, surrogate motherhood – which raise questions about the status of the human embryo and the definition of parenthood (see REPRODUCTION AND ETHICS).

Other appropriate areas where ethics impinges on practical inquiry include, for example, the ethical implications of the Human Genome Project, the ethics of confidentiality, insurance in relation to AIDS or inherited disease, the care of the elderly, homelessness, and mental illness (see GENETICS AND ETHICS; MEDICAL ETHICS). One caveat to be noted here, however, is that simply gathering data about what people think is right is sociology, not ethics, applied or otherwise.

9 Institutions

Many research centres have been created in recent decades. Their function is usually to conduct research, to produce publications and to arrange lectures, seminars and conferences on practical issues of ethical concern.

North America has the best-established institutional network. First in the field was the Hastings Center, New York (1969), then the Center for Philosophy and Public Affairs, University of Maryland and the Center for the Study of Ethics in the Professions at the Illinois Institute of Technology (1976), the Center for the Study of Values, University of Delaware (1977), and the Social Philosophy and Policy Center, Bowling Green State University, Ohio (1981). There are now many other centres in universities both in the USA and elsewhere, including, in the UK, the Centre for Philosophy and Public Affairs at the University of St Andrews, the Centre for Medical Law and Ethics at King's College London, and the Social Values Research Centre at the University of Hull. The Netherlands has Bioethics Centres in Utrecht and Maastricht and work in applied ethics in the Scandinavian countries is increasing, with a strong interest in reproductive ethics in Aarhus, Denmark and in animal welfare issues in Copenhagen. The European Business Ethics Network (EBEN) began with an initiative from Switzerland, and business ethics is also well-established in Spain and Germany. Apart from university-based units, the Society for Applied Philosophy has general interests in most areas of applied ethics and has a broad membership not confined to professional philosophers.

Australia has been a pioneer in many fields of applied ethics: Peter Singer, together with Helga Kuhse, founded the Centre for Human Bioethics (1980) at Monash University, and there are now several other applied ethics centres in Australasia; it is worth noting the particular degree of interest there in environmental ethics, where the issues of species preservation, wilderness and ecological threats such as damage to the ozone layer are of direct concern to residents.

The creation of a Chair of Environmental Ethics at Warsaw University represents the strong interest, partly political in origin, in environmental ethics in the former communist countries of Eastern Europe. Other countries where applied ethics is of growing interest are parts of Southeast Asia, including Thailand and Hong Kong, India, and several African countries.

See also: BIOETHICS; BUSINESS ETHICS; CLONING; ENVIRONMENTAL ETHICS; JOURNALISM, ETHICS OF; SEXUALITY, PHILOSOPHY OF; SUSTAINABILITY

References and further reading

La Follette, Hugh (ed.) (2003) *The Oxford Handbook of Practical Ethics*, Oxford: Oxford University Press. (A guide to ethical debate in many areas of public life, from personal matters to political, economic and environmental issues.)

La Follette, Hugh (ed.) (2004) *Ethics in Practice: an Anthology*, Oxford: Blackwell (A selection from classic and contemporary original texts in applied ethics, grouped thematically as issues of life and death, personal life, liberty and equality, and justice.)

Singer, P. (ed.) (1986) *Applied Ethics*, Oxford: Oxford University Press. (Classic articles, including Hume on suicide and Mill on the death penalty.)

BRENDA ALMOND

AQUINAS, THOMAS (1224/6–74)

Introduction

Aquinas lived an active, demanding academic and ecclesiastical life that ended while he was still in his forties. He nonetheless produced many works, varying in length from a few pages to a few volumes. Because his writings grew out of his activities as a teacher in the Dominican order and a member of the theology faculty of the University of Paris, most are concerned with what he and his contemporaries thought of as theology. However, much of academic theology in the Middle Ages consisted in a rational investigation of the most fundamental aspects of reality in general and of human nature and behaviour in particular. That vast domain obviously includes much of what is now considered to be philosophy, and is reflected in the broad subject matter of Aquinas' theological writings.

The scope and philosophical character of medieval theology as practised by Aquinas can be easily seen in his two most important works, *Summa contra gentiles* (Synopsis [of Christian Doctrine] Directed Against Unbelievers) and *Summa theologiae* (Synopsis of Theology). However, many of the hundreds of topics covered in those two large works are also investigated in more detail in the smaller works resulting from Aquinas' numerous academic disputations (something like a cross between formal debates and twentieth-century graduate seminars), which he conducted in his various academic posts. Some of those topics are taken up differently again in his commentaries on works by Aristotle and other authors. Although Aquinas is remarkably consistent in his several discussions of the same topic, it is often helpful to examine parallel passages in his writings when fully assessing his views on any issue.

Aquinas' most obvious philosophical connection is with Aristotle. Besides producing commentaries on his works, he often cites Aristotle in support of a thesis he is defending, even when commenting on scripture. There are also in Aquinas' writings many implicit Aristotelian elements, which he had thoroughly absorbed into his own thought. As a convinced Aristotelian, he often adopts Aristotle's critical attitude toward theories associated with Plato, especially the account of ordinary substantial forms as separately existing entities. However, although Aquinas, like other medieval scholars of Western Europe, had almost no access to Plato's works, he was influenced by the writings of Augustine and the pseudo-Dionysius. Through them he absorbed a good deal of Platonism as well – more than he was in a position to recognize as such.

On the other hand, Aquinas is the paradigmatic Christian philosopher-theologian, fully aware of his intellectual debt to religious doctrine. He was convinced, however, that Christian thinkers should be ready to dispute rationally on any topic, especially theological issues, not only among themselves but also with non-Christians of all sorts. Since in his view Jews accept the Old Testament and heretics the New Testament, he thought Christians could argue some issues with both groups on the basis of commonly accepted religious authority. However, because other non-Christians, 'for instance, Mohammedans and pagans – do not agree with us about the authority of any scripture on the basis of which they can be convinced . . . it is necessary to have recourse to natural reason, to which everyone is compelled to assent – although where theological issues are concerned it cannot do the whole job', since some of the data of theology are initially accessible only in Scripture (*Summa contra gentiles* I.2.11). Moreover, Aquinas differed from most of his thirteenth-century Christian colleagues in the breadth and depth of his respect for Islamic and Jewish philosopher-theologians, especially Avicenna and Maimonides. He saw them as valued co-workers in the vast project of philosophical theology, clarifying and supporting doctrine by philosophical analysis and argumentation. His own commitment to that project involved him in contributing to almost all the areas of philosophy recognized since antiquity, omitting only natural philosophy (the precursor of natural science).

A line of thought with such strong connections to powerful antecedents might have resulted in no more than a pious amalgam. However, Aquinas' philosophy avoids eclecticism because of his own innovative approach to organizing and reasoning about all the topics included under the overarching medieval conception of philosophical Christian theology, and because of his special talents for systematic synthesis and for identifying and skilfully defending, on almost every issue he considers, the most sensible available position.

1 Early years

Thomas Aquinas was born at Roccasecca, near Naples, the youngest son of a large Italian aristocratic family. As is generally true of even prominent medieval people, it is hard to determine exactly when he was born; plausible arguments have been offered for 1224, 1225 and 1226. He began his schooling in the great Benedictine abbey at Monte Cassino (1231–9), and from 1239–44 he was a student at the University of Naples. In 1244 he joined the Dominican friars, a relatively new religious order devoted to study and preaching; by doing so he antagonized his family, who seem to have been counting on his becoming abbot of Monte Cassino. When the Dominicans ordered Aquinas to go to Paris for further study, his family had him abducted en route and brought home, where he was held for almost two years. Near the end of that time his brothers hired a prostitute to try to seduce him, but Aquinas angrily chased her from his room. Having impressed his family with his high-minded determination, in 1245 Aquinas was allowed to return to the Dominicans, who again sent him to Paris, this time successfully.

At the University of Paris, Aquinas first encountered ALBERT THE GREAT, who quickly became his most influential teacher and eventually his friend and supporter. When Albert moved on to the University of Cologne in 1248, Aquinas followed him there, having declined Pope Innocent IV's extraordinary offer to appoint him abbot of Monte Cassino while allowing him to remain a Dominican.

Aquinas seems to have been unusually large, and extremely modest and quiet. When during his four years at Cologne his special gifts began to be apparent, despite his reticence and humility, Albert assigned the still-reluctant Aquinas his first active part in an academic disputation. Having failed in his efforts to shake his best student's arguments on this occasion, Albert declared, 'We call him the dumb ox, but in his teaching he will one day produce such a bellowing that it will be heard throughout the world'.

In 1252 Aquinas returned to Paris for the course of study leading to the degree of master in theology, roughly the equivalent of a twentieth-century PhD. During the first academic year he studied and lectured on the Bible; the final three years were devoted to delivering in lecture form his commentary on Peter Lombard's *Sentences*, a standard requirement for the degree at that time (see LOMBARD, P.). Produced in 1253–6, Aquinas' massive commentary (often referred to as the *Scriptum super libros Sententiarum* (Commentary on the Sentences) is the first of his four theological syntheses. It contains much valuable material, but because it is superseded in many respects by his great *Summa contra gentiles* (Synopsis [of Christian Doctrine] Directed Against Unbelievers) and *Summa theologiae* (Synopsis of Theology) the *Scriptum* has not yet been studied as much as it should be.

During that same four-year period, Aquinas produced *De ente et essentia* (On Being and Essence), a short philosophical treatise written for his fellow Dominicans at Paris. Although it owes something to Avicenna's *Metaphysics*, *De ente* is distinctively Aquinas' own, expounding many of the concepts and theses that remained fundamental to his thought throughout his career (see §9 below).

2 First Paris regency

In the spring of 1256, Aquinas was appointed regent master (professor) in theology at Paris, a position he held until the end of the academic year 1258–9. *Quaestiones disputatae de veritate* (Disputed Questions on Truth) is the first of his sets of disputed questions and the most important work he produced during those three years. It grew out of his professorship, which obliged him to conduct several formal public disputations each year. *Quaestiones disputatae de veritate* consists of twenty-nine widely ranging Questions, each devoted to some general topic such as conscience, God's knowledge, faith, goodness, free will, human emotions and truth (the first Question, from which the treatise gets its name). Each Question is divided into several Articles, and the 253 articles are the work's topically specific units: for example, q.1, a.9 is 'Is there truth in sense perception?'

The elaborate structure of each of those articles, like much of Aquinas' writing, reflects the 'scholastic method', which, like medieval disputations in the classroom, had its ultimate source in Aristotle's recommendations in his *Topics* regarding cooperative dialectical inquiry. Aquinas' philosophical discussions in that form typically begin with a yes/no question. Each article then develops as a kind of debate. It begins with arguments for the answer opposed to Aquinas' own position; these are commonly, if somewhat misleadingly, called 'objections'. Next come the arguments *sed contra* (but, on the other hand), which are in later works often reduced to a single citation of some generally accepted authority on Aquinas' side of the issue. The *sed contra* is followed by Aquinas' reasoned presentation and defence of his position. This is the master's 'determination' of the question, sometimes called the 'body' of the article (indicated by 'c' in references). An article normally concludes with Aquinas' rejoinders to each of the objections (indicated by 'ad 1', and so on, in references).

Conducting 'disputed questions' was one of the duties of a regent master in theology, but the theology faculty also provided regular opportunities for 'quodlibetal questions', occasions on which a master could, if he wished, undertake to provide replies to any and all questions proposed by members of the academic audience. These occasions were scheduled, for the master's own good, during the two penitential seasons of the church year. Aquinas seems to have accepted this challenge on at least five of the six such occasions occurring during his first regency at Paris, producing *Quaestiones quodlibetales* (Quodlibetal Questions) in which he offers his considered judgment on issues ranging from whether the soul is to be identified with its powers to whether the damned behold the saints in glory.

Aquinas' commentaries on Boethius' *De trinitate* (On the Trinity) and *De hebdomadibus* (sometimes referred to as 'How Substances are Good') are his other philosophically important writings from this period of his first regency. Although several philosophers had commented on those Boethian treatises in the twelfth century, the subsequent influx of Aristotelian works had left them almost universally disregarded by the time Aquinas wrote his commentaries (see BOETHIUS, A.M.S.). No one knows why or for whom he wrote them, but he might well have undertaken these studies for his own edification on topics that were then becoming important to his thought. The *De trinitate* commentary (*Expositio super librum Boethii De trinitate*) presents Aquinas' views on the relationship of faith and reason and on the methods and interrelations of all the recognized bodies of organized knowledge, or 'sciences'. Boethius' *De hebdomadibus* is the *locus classicus* for the medieval consideration of the relation between being and goodness. Dealing with this topic in his commentary on that treatise, Aquinas also produced his first systematic account of metaphysical participation, one of the important Platonist elements in his thought. Participation, he claims, obtains when the metaphysical composition of something includes, as one of the thing's metaphysical components, *X*, which also belongs to something else that is *X* in its own right in a way that is presupposed by the first thing's having *X*. In this way a running man participates in running, a human being participates in animal, and an effect participates in its cause (see also §9 below).

3 Naples and Orvieto: *Summa contra gentiles and biblical commentary*

Aquinas' activities between 1259 and 1265 are not well documented, but he seems definitely to have left his professorship at Paris at the end of the academic year 1258–9. He probably spent the next two years at a Dominican priory in Naples, working on the *Summa contra gentiles*, which he had begun in Paris and which he subsequently finished in Orvieto where, as lector, he was in charge of studies at the Dominican priory until 1265.

Summa contra gentiles is unlike Aquinas' three other theological syntheses in more than one respect. Stylistically, it is unlike the earlier *Scriptum* and the later *Summa theologiae* in that it does not follow the scholastic method; instead, it is written in ordinary prose divided into chapters, like his *Compendium theologiae* (Compendium of Theology) which he seems to have written immediately afterwards (1265–7). More importantly, the *Scriptum*, *Summa theologiae* and the *Compendium* are all contributions to revealed theology, which essentially includes the data of revelation among the starting points of its theorizing. In *Summa contra gentiles*, on the other hand, Aquinas postpones revealed theology to the last (fourth) book, in which he deals with the 'mysteries', the few doctrinal propositions that cannot be arrived at by natural reason alone and that have their sources in revelation only; and he takes these up with the aim of showing that even those propositions 'are not opposed to natural reason' (*Summa contra gentiles* IV.1.3348). He devotes the first three books to developing fully a natural theology, dependent on natural reason of course, but independent of revelation. As developed in Books I–III, this natural theology is able to accomplish a very large part of theology's job, from establishing the existence of God through to working out details of human morality (see also §13 below).

Discussions important for understanding Aquinas' positions in many areas of philosophy are also scattered, not always predictably, among interpretations of the text in his biblical commentaries. During Aquinas' stay in Orvieto and around the time he was writing Book III of *Summa contra gentiles*, on providence and God's relations with human beings, he also produced his *Expositio super Iob ad litteram* (Literal Commentary on Job), one of the most fully developed and philosophical of his biblical commentaries, rivalled in those respects only by his later commentary on Romans. The body of the Book of Job consists mainly of the speeches of Job and his 'comforters'. Aquinas sees those speeches as constituting a genuine debate, almost a medieval academic disputation (determined in the end by God himself), in which the thought develops subtly, advanced by arguments. His construal of the argumentation is ingenious, the more so because twentieth-century readers have tended to devalue the speeches as tedious reiterations of misconceived accusations countered by Job's slight variations on the theme of his innocence.

Aquinas' interpretation of the book's subject is also unlike the modern view, which supposes it to be the biblical presentation of the problem of evil, raised by a good God's permitting horrible suffering to be inflicted on an innocent person. Aquinas seems scarcely to recognize that Job's story raises doubts about God's goodness. As he interprets it, the book explains the nature and operations of divine providence, which he understands as compatible with permitting bad things to happen to good people. As Aquinas sees it:

> If in this life people are rewarded by God for good deeds and punished for bad, as Eliphaz [one of the comforters] was trying to establish, it apparently follows that the ultimate goal for human beings is in this life. But Job means to rebut this opinion, and he wants to show that the present life of human beings does not contain the ultimate goal, but is related to it as motion is related to rest, and a road to its destination.
>
> (*Expositio super Iob ad litteram* 7: 1–4)

The things that happen to a person in this life can be explained in terms of divine providence only by reference to the possibility of that person's achieving the ultimate goal of perfect happiness, the enjoyment of union with God in the afterlife.

In discussing Job's lament that God doesn't hear his prayers, Aquinas says that Job has that impression because God sometimes 'attends not to a person's pleas but rather to his advantage. A doctor does not attend to the pleas of the invalid who asks that the bitter medicine be taken away (supposing that the doctor doesn't take it away because he knows that it contributes to health). Instead, he attends to the patient's advantage; for by doing so he produces health, which the sick person wants most of all'. In the same way, God sometimes permits a person to suffer despite prayers for deliverance, because he knows that those sufferings are helping that person achieve what he or she wants most of all (*Expositio super Iob ad litteram* 9:16).

4 Rome: disputed questions, Dionysius and the *Compendium*

In 1265 Aquinas went from Orvieto to Rome, having been appointed to establish a Dominican *studium* (something like a twentieth-century college) and to serve as regent master there. This Roman period of his career, which lasted until 1268, was particularly productive. Some of his major works dating from 1265–8 are just what would have been expected of a regent master in theology, in particular, three sets of disputed questions, *Quaestiones disputatae de potentia* (Disputed Questions on [God's] Power), *Quaestio disputata de anima* (Disputed Question on the Soul) and *Quaestio disputata de spiritualibus creaturis* (Disputed Question on Spiritual Creatures). In the earliest of these, *De potentia*, there are eighty-three Articles grouped under ten Questions; the first six questions are on divine power, while the final four are on problems associated with combining the doctrine of Trinity with God's absolute simplicity. The much shorter *De anima* is concerned mainly with metaphysical aspects of the soul, concluding with some special problems associated with the nature and capacities of souls separated from bodies (Articles 14–21). The eleven articles of *De spiritualibus creaturis* again address many of those same concerns but also go on to some consideration of angels as another order of spiritual creatures besides human beings, whose natures are only partly spiritual.

During this same period, or perhaps while he was still at Orvieto, Aquinas wrote a commentary on the pseudo-Dionysian treatise *De divinis nominibus* (On the Divine Attributes), a deeply Neo-platonist account of Christian theology dating probably from the sixth century. Aquinas, like everyone else at the time, believed that it had been written in the apostolic period by the Dionysius who had been converted by St Paul. For that reason, and perhaps also because he had first studied the book under Albert at Cologne, it had a powerful influence on Aquinas' thought. Very early in his career, while he was writing his *Scriptum*, he thought Dionysius was an Aristotelian (*Scriptum* II, d.14, q.1, a.2), but while writing the commentary on this text he realized that its author must have been a Platonist (*Expositio super librum Dionysii de divinis nominibus*, prooemium; *Quaestiones disputatae de malo* 16.1, ad 3). His commentary, which makes clear sense of a text that is often obscure, may, like his commentaries on Boethius, have been written for his own purposes rather than growing out of a course of lectures. In any case, his study of Dionysius is one of the most important routes by which Platonism became an essential ingredient in his own thought.

The *Compendium theologiae* (Compendium of Theology), already mentioned in connection with *Summa contra gentiles*, was once thought to have been written much later and to have been left incomplete because of Aquinas' death. However, its similarity to *Summa contra gentiles* not only in style but also in content has lately led many scholars to assign it to 1265–7. Among Aquinas' four theological syntheses, the *Compendium theologiae* is unique in the brevity of its discussions and in having been organized around the 'theological virtues' of faith, hope and charity. Had it been completed, it might have provided a novel reorientation of the vast subject matter of medieval theology, but Aquinas wrote only ten short chapters of the second section, on Hope, and none at all of the third section, on Charity. He did complete the first section on Faith,

but since most of the 246 chapters in the section simply provide much briefer treatments of almost all the theological topics Aquinas had already dealt with in *Summa contra gentiles*, the *Compendium* as he left it seems important mainly as a precis of material that is developed more fully in the other work (and in *Summa theologiae*).

5 Rome: Aristotelian commentary

While some of Aquinas' prodigious output in Rome from 1265–8 is, broadly speaking, similar to work he had already done, it also includes two important innovations, one of which is the first of his twelve commentaries on works of Aristotle. At the beginning of this commentary on *De anima* (*Sententia super de anima*), his approach is still a little tentative and (for Aquinas) unusually concerned with technical details. These features of the work once led scholars to describe the commentary on the first book of *De anima* as a *reportatio* (an unedited set of notes taken at his lectures), or even to ascribe this first third of Aquinas' commentary to another author. However, Gauthier has argued persuasively that the difference between the commentary's treatments of Book I and of Books II and III of *De anima* is explained by differences between the books themselves, and that in fact none of Aquinas' commentaries on Aristotle resulted from lectures he gave on those books. Discrepancies within this work, the first of Aquinas' Aristotelian commentaries, are likely to be at least in part a consequence of the fact that he was finding his way into this new sort of enterprise, at which he quickly became very adept. In a recent volume of essays on Aristotle's *De anima*, Martha Nussbaum describes Aquinas' work as 'one of the very greatest commentaries on the work' and 'very insightful'. T.H. Irwin, a leading interpreter of Aristotle, acknowledges that at one point in the *Sententia libri Ethicorum* (Commentary on Aristotle's *Nicomachean Ethics*) Aquinas 'actually explains Aristotle's intention more clearly than Aristotle explains it himself'. Such judgments apply pretty generally to Aquinas' Aristotelian commentaries, all of which are marked by his extraordinary ability as a philosophical commentator to discern a logical structure in almost every passage he examines in every sort of text: not only Aristotle's but also those of others, from Boethius to St Paul.

Since commenting on Aristotle was a regular feature of life for a member of a medieval arts faculty but never part of the duties of an academic theologian, Aquinas' many Aristotelian commentaries were technically extra-curricular and therefore an especially impressive accomplishment for someone who was already extremely busy. Some scholars, admiring Aquinas' achievements in general but focusing on the fact that his professional career was entirely in the theology faculty, have insisted on classifying only the Aristotelian commentaries as philosophical works. Certainly these commentaries are philosophical, as purely philosophical as the Aristotelian works they elucidate. However, Aquinas wrote these commentaries not only to make good philosophical sense of Aristotle's very difficult texts but also, and more importantly, to enhance his own understanding of the topics Aristotle had dealt with. As he remarks in his commentary on *De caelo*, 'the study of philosophy has as its purpose to know not what people have thought, but rather the truth about the way things are' (*Sententia super libros de caelo et mundo* I.22.228), and he believed that the theologian's attempt to understand God and everything else in relation to God was the fundamental instance of the universal human drive to know the truth about the way things are. Moreover, his view of the best way of making intellectual progress in general looks very much like the age-old method of philosophy: 'But if any people want to write back against what I have said, I will be very gratified, because there is no better way of uncovering the truth and keeping falsity in check than by arguing with people who disagree with you' (*De perfectione spiritualis vitae* 26) (see ARISTOTLE).

6 Rome: Summa theologiae

The other important innovation from Aquinas' three-year regency in Rome is *Summa theologiae*, his greatest and most characteristic work, begun in Rome and continued through the rest of his life. *Summa theologiae*, left incomplete at his death, consists of three large Parts. The First Part (Ia) is concerned with the existence and nature of God (Questions 1–43), creation (44–9), angels (50–64), the six days of creation (65–74), human nature (75–102) and divine government (103–19). The Second Part deals with morality, and in such detail that it is itself divided into two parts. The first part of the Second Part (IaIIae) takes up human happiness (Questions 1–5), human action (6–17), the goodness and badness of human acts (18–21), passions (22–48) and the sources of human acts: intrinsic (49–89) and extrinsic (90–114). The second part of the Second Part (IIaIIae) begins with the three theological virtues and corresponding vices (Questions 1–46), goes on through the four 'cardinal virtues' and corresponding vices (47–170) and ends with special issues associated with the religious life (171–89). In the Third Part, Aquinas deals with the incarnation (Questions 1–59) and the sacraments (60–90), breaking off in the middle of his discussion of penance.

Aquinas thought of *Summa theologiae* as a new kind of textbook of theology, and its most important pedagogical innovation, as he sees it, is in its organization. He says he has noticed that students new to theology have been held back in their studies by several features of the standard teaching materials, especially 'because the things they have to know are not imparted in an order appropriate to a method of teaching': an order he proposes to introduce. It may well have been his enthusiasm for this new approach that led him to abandon work on his quite differently organized *Compendium theologiae*, and his natural preoccupation during this period with the writing of *Summa theologiae* Ia may also help to account for the fact that his other work of that time shows a special interest in the nature and operations of the human soul, the subject matter of Questions 75–89 of Ia (see §13 below).

7 Second Paris regency

In 1268 the Dominican Order again assigned Aquinas to the University of Paris, where he was regent master for a second time until, in the spring of 1272, all lectures at the university were canceled because of a dispute with the bishop of Paris. The Dominicans then ordered Aquinas to return to Italy.

Among the astounding number of works Aquinas produced in those four years is the huge Second Part of *Summa theologiae* (IaIIae and IIaIIae), nine Aristotelian commentaries, a commentary on the pseudo-Aristotelian *Liber de causis* (which, as Aquinas was the first to realize, is actually a compilation of Neoplatonic material drawn from Proclus), sixteen biblical commentaries and seven sets of disputed questions (including the set of sixteen *Quaestiones disputatae de malo* (Disputed Questions On Evil), the sixth of which provides his fullest discussion of free choice). His literary productivity during this second regency is the more amazing because he was at the same time embroiled in various controversies.

Sending Aquinas back to Paris in 1268 seems to have been, at least in part, his order's response to the worrisome movement of 'Latin Averroism' or 'radical Aristotelianism', then gaining ground among members of the arts faculty who were attracted to interpretations of Aristotle found in the commentaries of Averroes. However, only two of his many writings from these years seem to have obvious connections with the Averroist controversy. One of these, his treatise *De unitate intellectus, contra Averroistas* (On [the Theory of] the Unicity of Intellect, against the Averroists) is an explicit critique and rejection of a doctrine distinctive of the movement; the theory, as Aquinas describes it, that the aspect of the human mind 'that Aristotle calls the possible intellect ... is some sort of substance separate in its being from the body and not united to it in any way as its form; and, what is more, that this possible intellect is one for all human beings' (*De unitate intellectus*, prooemium). After briefly noting that this view's incompatibility with Christian doctrine is too obvious to warrant discussion at any length, Aquinas devotes the entire treatise to showing that 'this position is no less contrary to the principles of philosophy than it is to the teachings of the Faith', and that it is even 'entirely incompatible with the words and views' of Aristotle himself (*De unitate intellectus*, prooemium).

Besides the unicity of intellect, the other controversial theory most often associated with thirteenth-century Averroism is the beginningless-ness of the universe. In many of his works Aquinas had already considered the possibility that the world had always existed, skilfully developing and defend-ing the bold position that revelation alone provides the basis for believing that the world began to exist, that one cannot prove either that the universe must or that it could not have begun, and that a world both beginningless and created is possible (although, of course, not actual). The second of Aquinas' Parisian treatises that is plainly relevant to Averroism is *De aeternitate mundi, contra murmurantes* (On the Eternity of the World, against Grumblers), a very short, uncharacteristically indignant summary of his position. Aquinas could not complain that Aristotle had been misinterpreted regarding the eternity of the world; after initially supposing this to be the case, he had become convinced that Aristotle really did think he had proved that the world must have existed forever. Aquinas' position on this issue did not distance him enough from the Averroists in the view of their contemporary 'Augustinian' oppo-nents, most notably the Franciscans BONAVENTURE and Pecham. In fact, the 'Grumblers' against whom Aquinas directed this treatise were probably not so much the Averroists in the arts faculty as those Franciscan theologians who maintained that they had demonstrated the impossibility of a beginning-less world.

Aquinas' principled dissociation on this point from some important Franciscans must have helped to make his second Paris regency much more troubled than his first. In disputations conducted in Paris in 1266–7, the Franciscan master William of Baglione implicated Aquinas' views in the propo-sitions he attacked, claiming that things Aquinas was saying encouraged the two heretical Averroist theses denounced by Bonaventure, namely the eternity of the world and the unicity of the intellect. It has also been persuasively argued that Aquinas' *De aeternitate mundi* was directed in particular against his Francis-can colleague in theology, John Pecham. It seems, then, that Aquinas' development of a distinctly philosophical theology – which, like Albert's, was more Aristotelian than Augustinian – was dividing him from his colleagues in the Paris faculty of theology during these years. It may also have been bringing him closer to the philosophers in the arts faculty.

8 Last days

In June 1272 the Dominicans ordered Aquinas to leave Paris and go to Naples, where he was to establish another *studium* for the order and to serve as its regent master. Except for some interesting collections of sermons (originally preached in his native Italian dialect), the works dating from this period – two Aristotelian commentaries and the Third Part of *Summa theologiae* – were left unfinished. On or about 6 December 1273, while he was saying mass, something happened to Aquinas that left him weak and unable to go on writing or dictating. He himself saw the occasion as a special revelation. When Reginald of Piperno, his principal secretary and longtime friend, tried to persuade him to return to work on the Third Part of *Summa theologiae*, he said, 'Reginald, I can't'. And when Reginald persisted, Aquinas finally said, 'Everything I've written seems like straw by comparison with what I have seen and what has been revealed to me'. He believed that he had at last clearly seen what he had devoted his life to figuring out and, by comparison, all he had written seemed pale and dry. Now that he could no longer write, he told Reginald, he wanted to die. Soon afterwards he did die, on 7 March 1274 at Fossanuova, Italy, on his way to the Council of Lyons, which he had been ordered to attend.

9 Metaphysics

Every part of Aquinas' philosophy is imbued with metaphysical principles, many of which are recog-nizably Aristotelian. Consequently, concepts such as potentiality and actuality, matter and form, sub-stance, essence, accident and the four causes – all of which are fundamental in Aquinas' metaphysics – should be considered in their original Aristotelian context (see ARISTOTLE §11). He invokes such principles often, and he employs them implicitly even more often. Two of his earliest writings – *De principiis naturae* (On the Principles of Nature) and especially *De ente et essentia* (On Being and Essence) – outline much of his metaphysics, almost as if they had been designed to provide guidelines for the development of his philosophy. Perhaps the most important thesis argued in *De ente* is the one that became known as 'the real distinction', Aquinas' view that the essence of any created thing is really, not just conceptually, distinct from its existence. Metaphysically speaking, corporeal beings are composites of form and matter, but all creatures, even incorporeal ones, are composites of essence and existence. Only the first, uncreated cause, God, whose essence is existence, is absolutely simple.

Except for his commentary on Aristotle's *Metaphysics*, Aquinas devoted no mature treatise to metaphysics itself. However, since he considers metaphysics to be the science of being considered generally (*ens commune*), and since he argues that being itself is first of all God himself and that all being depends on God, his philosophy does begin with metaphysics insofar as the most systematic presentations of his thought (in *Summa contra gentiles* and *Summa theologiae*) start with the investigation of God-in-himself considered as the foundation of the nature and existence of everything (see for example, *Summa contra gentiles* III.25; *Expositio super librum Boethii de trinitate* V.4, VI.1; §14 below).

Being, Aquinas says, is intellect's most fundamental conception, 'inherently its most intelligible object and the one in which it finds the basis of all conceptions.... Consequently all of intellect's other conceptions must be arrived at by adding to being ... insofar as they express a mode of being which is not expressed by the term "being" itself' (*Quaestiones disputatae de veritate* 1.1c). There are, he claims, just two legitimate ways of making such additions. The first results in the ten Aristotelian Categories, each of which is a 'specified [or specific] mode of being' – substance, quantity, quality and the rest. The results of 'adding to being' in the second way are less familiar. Aquinas takes them to be five modes of being that are entirely general, characterizing absolutely every being. That is, being, wherever and however instantiated, exhibits these five modes, which transcend the Categories because they are necessary modes of all specified being: thing (*res*), one, something (*aliquid*), good, true. These five, together with being itself, are the 'transcendentals', predicable correctly (if sometimes a little oddly) of absolutely anything that is. 'Good' and 'true' are the philosophically interesting cases, because some beings are obviously not good and because 'true' seems applicable only to propositions.

The claim that all beings are true depends on taking 'true' in the sense of 'genuine', as in 'true friend', a sense that had been explored in detail by ANSELM OF CANTERBURY. In Anselm's view, any being is true in this sense to the extent to which it agrees with the divine idea of such a thing (and is otherwise false, but only to some extent). Absolutely every thing that is agrees to some extent with the divine idea that is an ingredient in its causal explanation. Propositions are true if they correspond

to the way things are in the world; things in the world are true if they correspond to what is in the mind, God's mind first, ours derivatively. So, Aquinas says, 'in the soul there is a cognitive and an appetitive power. The word "good", then, expresses the conformity of a being to appetite (as is said at the beginning of the *Ethics*: "The good is what all desire"). The word "true", however, expresses the conformity of a being to intellect' (*Quaestiones disputatae de veritate* 1.1c).

The central thesis of Aquinas' meta-ethics grows out of this theory of the transcendentals. The thesis is the metaphysical principle that the terms 'being' and 'good' are the same in reference, differing only in sense (*Summa theologiae* Ia.5.1). What all desire is what they take to be the good, and what is desired is at least perceived as desirable (see for example, *Summa contra gentiles* I.37; III.3). Desirability is thus an essential aspect of goodness. If a thing of a certain kind is genuinely desirable as a thing of that kind, it is desirable to the extent to which it is perfect of that kind: a complete specimen, free from relevant defect. But a thing is perfect of its kind to the extent to which it has actualized its specifying potentialities, the potentialities that differentiate its species from other species in the same genus. So, Aquinas says, a thing is desirable as a thing of its kind and hence good of that kind to the extent to which it is actualized and in being (*Summa theologiae* Ia.5.1). Generally, then, 'being' and 'goodness' have the same referent: the actualization of specifying potentialities. The actualization of a thing's specifying potentialities to at least some extent is on the one hand its existence as such a thing; it is in this sense that the thing is said to have being. However on the other hand, the actualization of a thing's specifying potentialities is, to the extent of the actualization, that thing's being whole, complete, free from defect: the state all things are naturally aimed at. It is in this sense that the thing is said to have goodness (see for example *Summa theologiae* IaIIae.1.5; 94.2; *Summa contra gentiles* III.3; *Quaestiones disputatae de veritate* 21.1–2.)

Aquinas' concept of analogy is important to his thought, though perhaps not so important as it has sometimes been made to seem. It is often presented, correctly, in terms of analogical predication. However, his concept of analogy can be explained at a more fundamental level in connection with causation. Setting aside 'accidental' causation – for example, a gardener's uncovering buried treasure – Aquinas thinks that efficient causation always involves an agent (*A*), a patient (*P*), and a form (*f*). In non-accidental efficient causation, *A* antecedently has *f*, somehow. *A*'s exercising causal power on *P* brings about *f* in *P*, somehow. Thus the efficient cause is *A*'s acting (or exercising a power it has), and the effect is

P's having *f*. The fact that *A* and *P* can have *f* in several different ways is what is brought out in 'somehow'. The paradigm – straightforward efficient causation – is the kind Aquinas calls *univocal*: cases in which first *A* and then *P* have *f* in just the same way, and in which *f* can therefore be predicated truly of each in just the same sense. The metal hotplate and the metal kettle bottom resting on it are both called hot univocally: the form heat in these two causally related objects is the same specifically and differs only numerically.

However, Aquinas also recognizes two kinds of non-univocal efficient causation. The first – *equivocal* causation – characterizes cases in which there is no obvious respect in which to say that the *f* effected in *P* is found antecedently in *A*, and yet there is a natural causal connection (as there standardly is an etymological explanation for equivocal predication). If *A* is solar power and its effect is the hardening (*f*) of some clay (*P*), then obviously the sun's power is not itself hard, as the clay is. To say what it is about solar power that hardens clay will not be as easy as explaining the heating of the kettle, and yet the hardening of the clay must, somehow, be brought about by that power. In such a case, *A* has *f* only in the sense that *A* has the power to bring about *f* in *P*.

Second, *analogical* causation occurs when, for instance, a blood sample (*P*) is correctly labelled 'anaemic', although of course the blood itself doesn't have anaemia and cannot literally be anaemic. The physiology of the sample's donor (*A*) brings about a condition (*f*) in the sample that is an unmistakeable sign of anaemia in *A*, thus justifying that (analogical) labeling of the sample. For theological purposes, Aquinas is interested not in natural analogical causation but rather in the artificial kind: the kind that involves ideas and volitions, the artisan's kind. 'In other agents [the form of what is to be brought about occurs antecedently] in keeping with *intelligible* being, as in those agents that act through intellect – the way a likeness of the house exists antecedently in the builder's mind' (*Summa theologiae* Ia.15.1c). Since the status of entirely univocal causation depends on there being a merely numerical difference between the *f* in *A* and the *f* in *P*, an intellective agent effecting its ideas is obviously not a univocal cause. But neither is this difference between the antecedent *f* and the consequent *f* so wide as to constitute equivocal causation. In fact, the kind of association between the idea and its external manifestation is closer than the kind found in natural analogical causation; and since, in Aquinas' view, 'the world was brought about not by chance but by God acting through intellect... it is necessary that there be a form in the divine mind, a form in the likeness of which the world was made'

(*Summa theologiae* Ia.15.1c). God, then, is the non-univocal, non-equivocal, intellectively analogical efficient cause of the world (see CAUSATION; GOD, CONCEPTS OF).

10 Philosophy of mind

Aquinas' philosophy of mind is part of his more general theory of soul, which naturally makes use of his metaphysics. Obviously he is not a materialist – most obviously because God, the absolutely fundamental element of his metaphysics, is in no way material. Aquinas classifies every thing other than God as either corporeal or incorporeal (spiritual); he sometimes calls purely spiritual creatures – such as angels – 'separated substances' because of their essential detachment from body of any sort. However, this exhaustive division is not perfectly exclusive because human beings, simply by virtue of the human soul, must be classified not as simply corporeal but also as spiritual in a certain respect.

Merely having a soul of some sort is not enough to give a creature a spiritual component, however. Every animate creature has a soul (*anima*) – 'soul is what we call the first principle of life in things that live among us' (*Summa theologiae* Ia.75.1c) – but neither plants nor nonhuman animals are in any respect spiritual. Aquinas holds that even the merely nutritive soul of a plant, or the nutritive + sensory soul of a beast, is like the soul of a human being in being the *form* of a body. No soul, no first principle of life, can be *matter*. On the other hand, any vegetable or animal body has the life it has only in virtue of being a body whose special organization confers on it natural potentialities: that is, in virtue of the substantial form that makes it actually be such a body. Therefore, the first principle of life in a living nonhuman body, its soul, is no bodily part of that body but is rather its form, one of the two metaphysical components of the composite of matter and form that every body is. For plants and beasts, unlike humans, the form that is the soul goes out of existence when the composite dies, and it is in that sense that the souls of plants and beasts are not spiritual.

Only the soul of a human being is analysed as nutritive + sensory + *rational*. Aquinas thinks of this soul not as three nested, cooperating forms, but as the single substantial form that gives a human being its specifically human mode of existence. (In defending this thesis of 'the unicity of substantial form', Aquinas differed from most of his contemporaries.) He often designates this entire substantial form by its distinctively human aspect of rationality. He also thinks that the human soul, unlike the souls of plants and beasts, is subsistent: that is, it continues to exist after separating from the body in death. He says, for example: 'It is necessary to say that that which is the principle of intellective activity, what we call the soul of a human being, is an incorporeal, subsistent principle' (*Summa theologiae* Ia.75.2c). The human soul, just because it is distinctively mind (the principle of intellective activity), must therefore be described not only as incorporeal but also as subsistent.

It may seem impossible for Aquinas' account to accommodate the claim that souls persist and engage in mental acts after the death of the body. If the separated soul is a form, what is it a form of? Aquinas is not a universal hylomorphist; unlike some of his contemporaries, he does not think that there is 'spiritual matter' that angels or disembodied souls have as one of their components, but rather that they are separated forms that configure no matter at all. Thus when he claims that the soul exists apart from the body, he seems to be holding the view that there can be a form with nothing of which it is the form. Moreover, Aquinas thinks that an angel or the soul separated from the body engages in mental activity. However, a form seems not to be the sort of thing that enages in acts of any sort, and so it appears that even if there were some way to explain the existence of the soul apart from the body, its acting could not be explained.

In this connection, it is helpful to examine Aquinas' broader view of form. The world is ordered metaphysically in such a way that at the top of the universal hierarchy there are forms – God and angels – that are not forms *of* anything. Near the bottom of the hierarchy are forms that configure matter but cannot exist in their own right, apart from the corporeal composites they inform. The forms of inanimate things and of animate, non-rational things are of that sort. Those forms inform matter, but when the resultant composites cease to exist, those forms also cease to exist. In the middle – 'on the borderline between corporeal and separated [that is, purely spiritual] substances' – are human souls, the metaphysical amphibians (*Quaestio disputata de anima* 1c). Like angels, human souls are subsistent, able to exist on their own; but, like the forms of inanimate things, human souls configure matter.

Seeing the soul in this light helps to explain some of what is initially puzzling in Aquinas' account. The human soul has a double character. On the one hand, unlike the forms of other material things, it is created by God as an individual entity in its own right, able to exist by itself as do purely immaterial angels. On the other hand, like the form of any corporeal thing, it exists in the composite it configures, and it comes into existence only with that composite, not before it (see SOUL, NATURE AND IMMORTALITY OF THE).

11 Theory of knowledge

Nature, Aquinas thinks, must be arranged so as to enable human beings in general to satisfy their natural desire to know (*Sententia super Metaphysicam* I.1.3–4). His view of the arrangement actually provided seems at first too tight to be true, involving some sort of formal identity between the extra-mental object (*O*) and the cognizing faculty (*F*) in its actually cognizing *O*. However, Aquinas takes that (Aristotelian) identity-claim to mean only that the form of *O* is somehow *in F* (*Summa theologiae* Ia.85.2, ad 1). *O*'s form comes to be in *F* when *F* receives *species*, either sensory or intellective, of *O*. These species may be thought of as encodings of *O*'s form. If *O* is a particular corporeal object – an iron hoop, for instance – then in *O* itself *O*'s form informs matter to produce an iron hoop of just those dimensions at just that spatio-temporal location. (In Aquinas' account of individuation, it is matter that is 'designated' or 'determinate' in this way that individuates *O*'s form: see for example *De ente et essentia* 2.) But when the appropriately encoded form is received in an external sense faculty *F* (which uses a bodily organ), then, even though it is received *materially* in *F*'s matter, it is nonetheless received differently from its reception in the matter of the hoop. The imposition of the form on the matter of the sense organ constitutes an 'intentional' or 'spiritual' reception of the form, contributing to a cognition of the hoop rather than metaphysically constituting a new, individuated matter–form composite.

Sensory species received in external senses are standardly transmitted to 'internal senses', the organs for which, Aquinas thought, must be located in the brain. Among the most important of these for purposes of cognition are 'phantasia' and 'imagination' (although Aquinas usually treats imagination as part of the power of phantasia). Phantasia and imagination produce and preserve 'phantasms', the sensory data that are necessary preconditions for intellective cognition. Imagination and phantasia are also indispensable to conscious sensory cognition. In Aquinas' view, sensible species themselves are not the objects of cognition, and what he says about phantasia suggests that having sensible species isn't sufficient for having sensory cognition. *O* itself, currently having a natural effect on the external senses, is consciously sensed because phantasia has processed *O*'s sensible species into phantasms.

The form presented in a phantasm has of course been stripped of its original, individuating matter, but a phantasm of *O* remains particularized as a phantasm in virtue of having been received in the *different* matter of phantasia's organ, while remaining recognizably the form of *O* because of the details of

O that are preserved in it. However, cognition of *O* as an iron hoop is conceptual, intellective cognition, for which phantasms are only the raw material.

In intellect itself, Aquinas distinguishes two Aristotelian 'powers'. The first is *agent intellect*, the essentially active or productive aspect of intellect, which acts on phantasms in a way that produces 'intelligible species'. These constitute the primary contents of intellect, stored in *possible intellect*, intellect's essentially receptive aspect. 'Through intellect it is natural for us to have cognition of natures. Of course, [as universals] natures do not have existence except in individuating matter. It is natural for us to have cognition of them, however, not as they are in individuating matter but as they are abstracted from it by intellect's consideration', the work of agent intellect, producing intelligible species (*Summa theologiae* Ia.12.4c). The intelligible species of *O* are unlike sensory species of it in that they are only universals, which occur as such only in possible intellect: for example, round, metallic, iron hoop. These 'universal natures' are not only received in the intellective faculty *F*, the possible intellect, but are also of course used regularly as the devices indispensable for intellective cognition of corporeal reality: 'Our intellect both abstracts intelligible species from phantasms, insofar as it considers the natures of things universally, and yet also has intellective cognition of them [the things] in the phantasms, since without attending to phantasms it cannot have intellective cognition of even those things whose [intelligible] species it abstracts' (*Summa theologiae* Ia.85.1, ad 5). It is in this way that 'in intellection we can have cognition of such [particular, corporeal, composite] things in universality, which is beyond the faculty of sense' (*Summa theologiae* Ia.12.4c).

Thus both sense and intellect have cognition of *O*, a particular corporeal thing. However, sense has cognition of *O* only in its particularity (*Sententia super Posteriora analytica* II.20.14). Further, an individual intellect that happened to have the concept 'iron hoop' would have cognition only of a universal nature that happened to be instantiated in *O*, and not also of any instantiation of that nature – unless that intellect were also attending to phantasms of *O*. It is as a result of this attending that intellect also cognizes *O* itself, but as exemplifying a universal, for example, as an iron hoop (*Summa theologiae* Ia.85.5c; *Sententia super de anima* II.12.377).

Although intellect regularly has cognition of a corporeal particular in the way described, its proper object, Aquinas says, is that particular's universal nature, or 'quiddity'. Intellect's 'first operation', then, is its cognition of a universal, its proper object (although as we have seen, agent intellect's abstracting of intelligible species is a necessary step on the way to the cognition of the quiddities of things). Aquinas sometimes calls this first operation 'understanding'. However, *scientia*, which is one of the last operations of intellect, a pinnacle of intellective cognition, also has the natures of things as its objects (see below). Universal natures, the proper objects of intellect's first operation and the objects of the culminating theoretical knowledge of nature, must then be thought of as proper objects of both the beginning and the culmination of intellective cognition. What is cognized in an unanalysed way in the first operation of the intellect – for example, *animal* – is in scientific cognition analysed into the essential parts of its nature – *sensitive animate corporeality* – which are themselves comprehended in terms of all their characters and capacities. In theory, in potentiality, the culminating cognitive state is all that could be hoped for: 'if the human intellect comprehends the substance of any thing – a rock, for example, or a triangle – *none* of the intelligible aspects of that thing exceeds the capacity of human reason' (*Summa contra gentiles* I.3.16).

Intellect's 'second operation' is the making of judgments, affirming by propositionally 'compounding' with one another concepts acquired in the first operation, or denying by 'dividing' them from one another. At every stage past initial acquisition, the cognition of quiddities will partially depend on this second operation, and on reasoning as well: 'the human intellect does not immediately, in its first apprehension, acquire a complete cognition of the thing. Instead, it first apprehends *something* about it – that is, its quiddity, which is a first and proper object of intellect; and *then* it acquires intellective cognition of the properties, accidents, and dispositions associated with the thing's essence. In doing so it has to compound one apprehended aspect with another, or divide one from another, and proceed from one composition or division to another, which is reasoning'. This is sometimes called intellect's third operation (*Summa theologiae* Ia.85.5c).

The framing of propositions and the construction of inferences involving them are necessary preconditions of the culminating intellective cognition Aquinas recognizes as *scientia*, which he discusses in greatest detail in his *Sententia super Posteriora analytica* (Commentary on Aristotle's *Posterior Analytics*). The interpretation of his account of *scientia* is controversial, but one helpful way to view it is as follows. To cognize a proposition with *scientia* is, strictly speaking, to accept it as the conclusion of a 'demonstration'. Of course, many premises in demonstrations may themselves be conclusions of other demonstrations; some, however, must be accepted not on the basis of demonstration but *per se* (*Sententia super Posteriora analytica* I.7.5–8). Such propositions, knowable *per se* (although not always *per se* knowable by us) are Aquinas' first principles. Like Aristotle, he calls them immediate propositions; that is, they cannot themselves be the conclusions of demonstrations, and their truth is evident to anyone who fully understands their terms, who not merely grasps their ordinary meaning but also comprehends the real nature of their referents. The predicate of an immediate proposition belongs to the *ratio* of the proposition's subject, and the *ratio* is the formulation of the subject's real nature (*Sententia super Posteriora analytica* I.10; 33). Thus for example, Aquinas considers 'God exists' to be self-evident, since according to the doctrine of simplicity God's nature is God's existence. 'God exists' is a good example of a proposition knowable *per se* but, as Aquinas insists in rejecting Anselm's ontological argument, not knowable *per se* by us. It is for that reason that he develops a number of *a posteriori* arguments for God's existence, among which the most famous are the 'Five Ways', found in *Summa theologiae* Ia.2.3c (see GOD, ARGUMENTS FOR THE EXISTENCE OF).

Anyone who has a developed concept of the subject's real nature is certain of the truth of such an immediate proposition, 'but there are some immediate propositions the terms of which not everyone knows. That is why although the predicate of such a proposition does belong to the ratio of its subject, the proposition need not be granted by everyone, just because its subject's [metaphysical] definition is not known to everyone' (*Sententia super Posteriora analytica* I.5.7). Because proper demonstrations are isomorphic with metaphysical reality, the facts expressed in their premises are regularly to be construed as causes of the facts in their conclusions (*Sententia super Posteriora analytica* I.2.9), although in some cases demonstrative reasoning goes the other way, from effects to causes. So, having *scientia* with respect to some proposition is the fullest possible human cognition, by which one situates the fact expressed by a conclusion in an explanatory theory that accurately maps metaphysical or physical reality.

According to Aquinas, then, what demonstration provides is not so much knowledge as it has been conceived of by foundationalists (for example, DESCARTES) as depth of understanding and explanatory insight. In general, Aquinas does not begin with self-evident principles and derive conclusions from them deductively; 'rather [he begins] with a statement to be justified (it will become the "conclusion" only in a formal restatement of the argument) and "reduce[s]" it back to its ultimate explanatory principles' (see Durbin, *St Thomas*

Aquinas 1968: 82). When Aquinas himself describes his project generally, he says that there are two different processes in which human reason engages: *discovery* (or invention) and *judgment*. When we engage in discovery, we proceed from first principles, reasoning from them to other things; in judgment we reason to first principles on the basis of a kind of analysis. In his view, it is judgment's reasoning process, not that of discovery, that leads to *scientia*, and judgment is the subject of the *Posterior Analytics*: 'Judgment goes with the certitude of *scientia*. And it is because we cannot have certain judgment about effects except by analysis leading to first principles that this part of human reasoning is called "analytics"' (*Sententia super Posteriora analytica*, prooemium).

Sceptical worries seldom intrude on Aquinas' scattered development of his systematically unified theory of knowledge, largely because it is based on a metaphysics in which the first principle of existence is an omniscient, omnipotent, perfectly good God, whose rational creatures could not have been made so as to be standardly mistaken about the rest of creation (see GOD, CONCEPTS OF; KNOWLEDGE, CONCEPT OF).

12 Will and action

Philosophy of mind is obviously relevant to epistemology in its account of the mechanisms of cognition, especially of intellect. In its account of will it is just as obviously relevant to action theory and to ethics. Aquinas' concern with moral issues is even greater than his considerable interest in epistemological issues, and his ethics is so fully developed that he integrates his systematic treatment of acts of will into it rather than including such a treatment in his philosophy of mind.

As intellect is the cognitive faculty of the distinctively human rational soul, so will is its appetitive faculty. Will's metaphysical provenance is more primitive than that of intellect; it is merely the most subtle terrestrial instantiation of an utterly universal aspect of creation. Not only every sort of soul but absolutely every form, Aquinas maintains, has some sort of inclination essentially associated with it; and so every hylomorphic thing, even if inanimate, has at least one natural inclination: 'on the basis of its form, fire, for instance, is inclined toward a higher place, and toward generating its like' (*Summa theologiae* Ia.80.1c). Inclination is the genus of appetite, and appetite is the genus of will. The human soul of course involves *natural appetites* – for example, for food – but its sensory and intellective modes of cognition bring with them *sensory appetites*, or passions – for example, for seafood – and *rational appetite*, or volition – for example, for food low in fat content.

In human beings, sensory appetite, or 'sensuality', is a cluster of inclinations (passions) to which we are subject (passive) by animal nature. Following an Aristotelian line, Aquinas thinks of sensuality as sorted into two complementary powers: the *concupiscible* – pursuit/avoidance instincts – and the *irascible* – competition/aggression/defense instincts. With the former are associated the emotions of joy and sadness, love and hate, desire and repugnance; with the latter, daring and fear, hope and despair, anger.

For philosophy of mind and for ethics, one important issue is the manner and extent of the rational faculties' control of sensuality, a control without which the harmony of the human soul is threatened and morality is impossible – especially in Aquinas' reason-centred ethics with its focus on virtues and vices. A human being who is not aberrantly behaving like a non-rational animal 'is not immediately moved in accordance with the irascible and concupiscible appetite but waits for the command of will, which is the higher appetite' (*Summa theologiae* Ia.81.3c). But the kind of control exercised by a cognitive rational faculty (standardly identified in this role as 'practical reason' rather than the broader 'intellect') is less obvious, and is particularly interesting in view of Aquinas' account of intellective cognition. The rational faculties can direct the attention of the external senses and compensate to some extent for their malfunctioning, but they cannot directly control what the external senses initially perceive on any occasion. On the other hand, sensuality and the internal senses are not directly related to mind-independent external things, and so to some extent 'they are subject to reason's command', although they too can fight against reason (*Summa theologiae* Ia.81.3, ad 3). Elaborating an Aristotelian theme (*Politics* I, 2), Aquinas observes that the soul's rule over the body is 'despotic': in a normal body, any bodily part that can be moved by an act of will will be moved immediately when and as will commands. But the rational faculties rule sensuality 'politically', because the powers and passions that are the intended subjects of this rational governance are also moved by imagination and sense, and so are no slaves to reason. 'That is why we experience the irascible or the concupiscible fighting against reason when we sense or imagine something pleasant that reason forbids, or something unpleasant that reason commands' (*Summa theologiae* Ia.81.3, ad 2).

According to Aquinas, the volition for happiness in general is an ineluctable part of human nature (see §13 below). Nonetheless, 'the movement of a creature's will is not determined in particular to seeking happiness in this, or in that' (*Quaestiones disputatae de veritate* 24.7, ad 6). This sort of freedom of will is freedom of specification or 'freedom as regards the object', freedom in the 'determining' aspect of volition. It is distinguished from freedom of exercise or 'freedom as regards the act', freedom associated with will's 'executive' capacity, for either acting or not acting to achieve something apprehended as good.

The interpretation of Aquinas' account of freedom of will is controversial. The very phrase 'freedom of will' is part of the difficulty, because it imports a concept from a later tradition. Aquinas conceives of freedom as *liberum arbitrium* (free decision or judgment), which cannot be attributed to will alone. It is a property that inheres in the system of intellect and will as a whole, that emerges from their interaction. However, it is perhaps safe to say that, since Aquinas emphatically denies that any volition caused by something extrinsic to the agent can be free, his account of freedom of will is not a version of compatibilism (see for example *Summa theologiae* IaIIae.6.4). The one apparent exception has to do with God's acting on a human will. Aquinas holds that among extrinsic forces, God alone can act directly on some other person's will without violating the will's nature, that is, without undermining its freedom (see for example *Summa theologiae* IaIIae.9.6). On this basis, some interpreters characterize Aquinas as a theological compatibilist; however, the subtle complexities of his account of God's action on human wills leads others to claim that a full appreciation of those complexities would show that Aquinas is not in any sense a compatibilist (see DETERMINISM AND INDETERMINISM; FREE WILL).

Aquinas' analysis of human action, built on his account of will and intellect, is complicated and not readily summarized. Generally speaking, he finds elaborately ordered mental components in even simple acts. For instance, in a case of raising one's hand to attract attention we are likely to suppose that the mental antecedents of the bodily movement are just the agent's combined beliefs and desires, whether or not the agent is fully conscious of them. Aquinas would of course agree that the agent need not be completely aware of the overt action's mental antecedents, but he sees them as having a complex, hierarchical structure.

On his analysis, the action begins when (I1) the agent's intellect apprehends a certain end – attracting attention – as a good to be achieved in these particular circumstances. (I1) thus gives rise to a second component: (W1) the agent's will forms a simple volition for that end. Then, (I2) the agent's intellect considers whether the end can be achieved at that time. If the result of (I2) is affirmative, then on that basis (W2) the agent's will forms an intention to achieve the end by some means or other. Next, (I3) the agent's intellect surveys the available means and settles on one or more that would be suitable to achieve the end and acceptable to the agent, and (W3) the agent's will accepts the means. If intellect has found more than one suitable and acceptable means, then (I4) intellect compares them and determines which is best in the circumstances, and (W4) will opts for that means. The process comes to its natural end when (W5) the agent's will exercises its control over the agent's arm, and the arm goes up. This ordered series looks deterministic, but as Aquinas views the interaction between intellect and will, the process could go otherwise at almost any point because will could direct intellect to reconsider, to direct attention in some other way, or even just to stop thinking about the issue (*Summa theologiae* IaIIae.6–17).

13 Ethics, law and politics

Aquinas' moral theory is developed most extensively and systematically in the Second Part of *Summa theologiae*. (Broadly speaking, the general theory is in IaIIae and the detailed consideration of particular issues is in IIaIIae.) Like almost all his predecessors, medieval and ancient, Aquinas sees ethics as having two principal topics: first, the ultimate goal of human existence, and second, how that goal is to be won, or lost. Of the 303 Questions making up *Summa theologiae*'s Second Part, 298 are concerned in one way or another with the second topic, and only the first 5 are concerned directly with the first (although in *Summa contra gentiles* III he devotes chapters 25–40 to a detailed examination of it).

Summa theologiae IaIIae.1–5, sometimes called the Treatise on Happiness, develops an argument to establish the existence and nature of a single ultimate end for all human action, or, more strictly, the kind of behaviour over which a person has 'control'. First, 'all actions that proceed from a power are caused by that power in accordance with the nature of its object. But the object of will is an end and a good', that is, an end perceived as good by the willer's intellect (*Summa theologiae* IaIIae.1.1c). From this starting point Aquinas develops an argument designed to show that a human being necessarily (though not always consciously) seeks everything it seeks for its own ultimate end, happiness.

Aquinas argues that the often unrecognized genuine ultimate end for which human beings exist (their 'object') is God, perfect goodness personified; and perfect happiness, the ultimate end with which they may exist (their 'use' of that object), is the enjoyment of the end for which they exist. That enjoyment is fully achieved only in the beatific vision, which Aquinas conceives of as an activity. Since the beatific vision involves the contemplation of the ultimate (first) cause of everything, it is, whatever else it may be, also the perfection of all knowledge and understanding (*Summa theologiae* IaIIae.1.8; 3.8).

Aquinas devotes just four questions of *Summa theologiae* IaIIae (18–21) to 'the goodness and badness of human acts in general'. Although considerations of rightness and wrongness occupy only a little more than ten per cent of the discussion in Questions 18–21, Aquinas nonetheless appears to think of rightness and wrongness as the practical, distinctively moral evaluations of actions. His emphasis on the broader notions of goodness and badness reveals the root of his moral evaluation of actions in his metaphysical identification of being and goodness (see §9 above).

What makes an action morally bad is its moving the agent not toward, but away from, the agent's ultimate goal. Such a deviation is patently irrational, and Aquinas' analysis of the moral badness of human action identifies it as fundamentally irrationality, since irrationality is an obstacle to the actualization of a human being's specifying potentialities, those that make *rational* the differentia of the human species. In this as in every other respect, Aquinas' ethics is reason-centred:

> In connection with human acts the words 'good' and 'bad' are applied on the basis of a comparison to reason, because … a human being's good is existing in accordance with reason, while what is bad for a human being is whatever is contrary to reason. For what is good for any thing is what goes together with it in keeping with its form, and what is bad for it is whatever is contrary to the order associated with its form.
>
> (*Summa theologiae* IaIIae.18.5c)

It would be a mistake, however, to suppose that Aquinas takes moral evil to consist in intellective error. Because of the very close relationship he sees between intellect and will, the irrationality of moral wrongdoing will be a function of will as well, not just of intellect. In Aquinas' view, the moral evaluation of a human action attaches primarily to the 'internal act', the volition from which the external act derives. Since 'will is inclined toward reason's good [the good presented to will by intellect] by the very nature of the power of will', bad volition stems from defective deliberation (*Summa theologiae* IaIIae.50.5, ad 3). As intellect and will continually influence each other, so bad deliberation can also be an effect of bad volition.

Moreover, practical intellect's mistakes in identifying the best available course of action may also have the passions of the sensory soul as sources.

Furthermore, 'because the good [presented by intellect] is varied in many ways, it is necessary that will be inclined through some habit toward some determinate good presented by reason so that [will's determining] activity may follow more promptly' (*Summa theologiae* IaIIae.50.5, ad 3). Habits of will are conditions necessary for our carrying out our volitions in particularly good or particularly bad ways, as regards both the 'executive' and the 'determining' aspects of volition; and the habits that play these crucial roles in Aquinas' moral theory are the virtues and the vices.

The four 'cardinal virtues' can be understood as habits of this sort. Reason's habit of good governance generally is *prudence*; reason's restraint of self-serving concupiscence is *temperance*; reason's persevering despite self-serving 'irascible' passions such as fear is *courage*; reason's governance of one's relations with others despite one's tendencies toward selfishness is *justice*. Aquinas' normative ethics is based not on rules but on virtues; it is concerned with dispositions first and only then with actions. In addition to the moral virtues in all their various manifestations, Aquinas also recognizes intellectual virtues that, like the moral virtues, can be acquired by human effort. On the other hand, the supreme theological virtues of faith, hope and charity cannot be acquired but must be directly 'infused' by God. Aquinas introduces these virtues and others in *Summa theologiae* IaIIae (49–88) and examines them in detail throughout IIaIIae (see VIRTUE ETHICS).

Passions, virtues and vices are all intrinsic principles, or sources, of human acts. However, there are extrinsic principles as well, among which is law in all its varieties. Consequently, Aquinas moves on in *Summa theologiae* IaIIae.90–108 to his Treatise on Law, a famous and original treatment of the subject. The best-known feature of the treatise is Aquinas' concept of natural law. Law in general is 'a kind of rational ordering for the common good, promulgated by the one who takes care of the community' (*Summa theologiae* IaIIae.90.4c), and 'the precepts of natural law are to practical reasoning what the first principles of demonstrations are to theoretical reasoning.... All things to be done or to be avoided pertain to the precepts of natural law, which practical reasoning apprehends naturally as being human goods' (IaIIae.94.2c). Human laws of all kinds derive, or should derive, from natural law, which might be construed as the naturally knowable rational principles underlying morality in general: 'From the precepts of natural law, as from general, indemonstrable principles, it is necessary that human reason proceed to making more particular

arrangements ... [which] are called human laws, *provided that* they pertain to the definition (*rationem*) of law already stated' (IaIIae.91.3c). As a consequence of this hierarchy of laws, Aquinas unhesitatingly rejects some kinds and some particular instances of human law, for example: 'A tyrannical law, since it is not in accord with reason, is not unconditionally a law but is, rather, a perversion of law' (IaIIae.92.1, ad 4). Even natural law rests on the more fundamental 'eternal law', which Aquinas identifies as divine providence, 'the very nature of the governance of things on the part of God as ruler of the universe' (IaIIae.91.1c) (see NATURAL LAW).

In *De regimine principum* (The Governance of Rulers), his most important political work, Aquinas begins by sounding the familiar medieval theme: monarchy is the best form of government. However, he realizes that a single ruler is easily corrupted and that monarchy therefore has a tendency to turn into tyranny. He seems not to countenance revolution against a legitimate ruler who has become tyrannical (*De regimine principium* 6), but he maintains that radical means, including tyrannicide, may be justified against a usurper. Perhaps because he came to appreciate the dangers in monarchy, he gradually works republican elements into his theory of good government. His later commentary on Aristotle's *Politics* seems to erode the dominant monarchical model further in its treatment of the notions of the commonwealth (*res publica*) and of the citizen as one who rules and is ruled in turn (see POLITICAL PHILOSOPHY, HISTORY OF).

14 Theology: natural, revealed and philosophical

Because Aquinas developed most of his thought within the formal confines of thirteenth-century theology, and because this has in turn affected his place in the history of philosophy and the assessment of his work, some attention must be paid to the ways in which much of what we recognize as philosophy was an essential component of what he thought of as theology.

Aquinas devotes the first three books of *Summa contra gentiles* to a systematic development of natural theology, which he saw as part of philosophy (*Summa theologiae* Ia.1.1, ad 2) (see NATURAL THEOLOGY). As part of philosophy, natural theology must of course be based entirely on 'principles known by the natural light of intellect' (*Summa theologiae* Ia.1.2c), principles of the sort that underlie Aristotle's metaphysics, which Aristotle himself thought of as culminating in 'theology' (see Aquinas' interpretation of that thought in the prooemium to his *Sententia super Metaphysicam*

(Commentary on Aristotle's *Metaphysics*). In fact, the way Aquinas works in *Summa contra gentiles* I–III strongly suggests that he may have thought of natural theology as a science subordinate to metaphysics, somewhat as he would have understood optics to be subordinate to geometry.

However, there is something odd about that project of his. By Aquinas' day the churchmen governing universities had overcome most of their initial misgivings about the recently recovered works of the pagan Aristotle, and had acknowledged officially that the study of Aristotelian physics and metaphysics (with their integrated minor component of natural theology) was compatible with the then universally recognized availability of revealed truths about God. Medieval Christians had come to appreciate the ancient philosophers' attempts to uncover truths about God on the basis of observation and reasoning alone as having been justified, even commendable, given their total ignorance of revelation. However, no philosopher in Aquinas' circumstances could have justifiably undertaken a new project of natural theology heuristically.

Still, no opprobrium would attach to natural theology taken up expositionally. The aim of such an enterprise would be not to develop theology from scratch but rather to show, in the spirit of Romans 1: 20, the extent to which what had been supernaturally revealed could, in theory, have been naturally discovered. Such an enterprise is what *Summa contra gentiles* I–III seems to represent.

Evidence from a chronicle written about seventy years after Aquinas began *Summa contra gentiles* once led scholars to suppose that he had written it as a manual for the use of Dominican missionaries to Muslims and Jews. If that were so, then the work's presentation of natural instead of revealed theology in its first three books would have been dictated by the practical purpose of rationally deriving the truth about God, and about God's relation to everything else, for people who would not have acknowledged the revealed texts Aquinas would otherwise have cited as the source of that truth. But nobody, and certainly not Aquinas, could have supposed that Muslims or Jews needed to be argued into perfect-being monotheism of the sort developed in those first three books, which contain nothing that he would have taken to be contrary to Judaism or Islam. If Aquinas had intended *Summa contra gentiles* as a manual for missionaries to educated Muslims, Jews or Christian heretics, he would have wasted the enormous effort represented in the 366 copiously argued chapters of Books I–III.

What Aquinas himself says about his purpose in writing *Summa contra gentiles* suggests that what he wrote had at least its formal cause not in an attempt to aid missionary activities, but instead in his

consideration of the interrelation of philosophy and Christianity. He begins by writing about the concerns of a wise person, one of those 'who give things an appropriate order and direction and govern them well' (*Summa contra gentiles* I.1.2). Obviously, such a person has to be concerned with goals and sources, and so the wisest person will be 'one whose attention is turned toward the universal goal, which is also the universal source', which Aquinas takes to be God (I.1.3). Because this natural theology is oriented as it is, 'it must be called the greatest wisdom itself, as considering the absolutely highest cause of all' (II.4.874). Therefore, the highest, most universal explanatory truth must be wisdom's concern. Anyone aspiring to wisdom will attend to metaphysics, since, Aquinas reports, Aristotle rightly identified metaphysics as 'the science of truth – not of just any truth, but of the truth that is the origin of all truth, the truth that pertains to the first principle of being for all things' (I.1.5). And, as he says in an observation that suits his own enterprise, 'sometimes divine wisdom proceeds from human philosophy's starting points' (II.4.875). However, since it is the business of one and the same science 'to pursue one of two contraries and to repel the other … the role of the wise person is to meditate on the truth, especially the truth regarding the first principle, and to discuss it with others, but also to fight against the falsity that is its contrary' (I.1.6). The truth regarding the first principle will be the truth about God, supposing natural theology can show that God exists; and so the explanatory truth associated here with metaphysics is the truth associated also with theology.

No one knows what title, if any, Aquinas himself gave to this work. In some of its medieval manuscripts, it is entitled *Liber de veritate catholicae fidei contra errores* (A Book About the Truth of the Catholic Faith, Directed Against Mistakes), a title that comes closer to accurately representing the book's aim and contents than the more pugnacious, traditional *Summa contra gentiles* (Synopsis [of Christian Doctrine] Directed Against Unbelievers). During the nineteenth century, when *Summa theologiae* (Synopsis of Theology) was instead normally referred to as *Summa theologica* (Theological Synopsis), *Summa contra gentiles* was sometimes published under the deliberately contrasting title *Summa philosophica* (Philosophical Synopsis). That contrast, although potentially misleading, has some truth in it, as may be seen in Aquinas' plan for *Summa contra gentiles* I–III: 'Since we intend to pursue by way of reason the things about God that human reason can investigate, the first consideration is of matters associated with God considered in himself [Book I]; second, of the emergence of created things from him [Book II]; third, of the ordering and directing of created things toward him as their goal [Book III]' (I.9.57).

In this pursuit by way of reason, Aquinas must and does shun 'authoritative arguments' of any sort, but he shows good sense in not restricting himself to 'demonstrative arguments' in developing natural theology. He does, of course, use demonstrative arguments when he thinks he has them, but, like almost all philosophers of any period, he recognizes philosophy's need for 'probable aguments' as well. A demonstrative argument takes as its premises propositions that explain the fact in the argument's conclusion by elucidating its causes (or, sometimes, its effects), and so it produces, or presents, scientific understanding. A probable argument – the sort that has always been most prevalent and most appropriate in philosophy – is one based on premises of any sort that are accepted widely or by experts in the relevant field, and so one group may be convinced by a probable argument that another group rejects. Of course, Aquinas has to make use of authoritative arguments in the fourth (and last) book, where he turns from natural to revealed theology, and his tolerance of them there is part of what distinguishes Book IV's argumentation from the sort that characterizes Books I–III.

In *Summa contra gentiles* IV, Aquinas engages in what has come to be called *philosophical theology*, the application of reason to revelation. Philosophical theology shares the methods of natural theology broadly conceived – in other words, analysis and argumentation of all the sorts accepted in philosophy – but it lifts natural theology's restriction on premises, accepting as assumptions revealed propositions. This includes those that are initially inaccessible to unaided reason, such as the 'mysteries' of Christian doctrine. In his many works of philosophical theology, Aquinas tests the coherence of doctrinal propositions (including the mysteries), attempts explanations of them, uncovers their logical connections with other doctrinal propositions and so on, in order to bear out his conviction that the doctrines themselves are eminently understandable and acceptable, and that the apparent incoherence of some of them is only a feature of our initial, superficial view of them.

Summa theologiae is the paradigm of philosophical theology. The very first Article of the very first Question makes it clear at once that it is not natural theology that *Summa theologiae* is a summa of, since it begins by asking whether we need any 'other teaching, besides philosophical studies'; which in Aquinas' usage means the studies that medieval beginners in theology would have just completed in the arts faculty. The question arises because philosophical studies are characterized not only as dealing with 'the things that are subject to reason', but also

as encompassing 'all beings, including God', as a consequence of which 'part of philosophy is called theology'.

Although Aquinas accepts this characterization of philosophy's subject matter as universal and as including a part that is properly called theology, he offers several arguments to support his claim that revealed theology is nonetheless not superfluous. In one of those arguments, he claims that a thing's 'capacity for being cognized in various ways brings about a difference between sciences'. By this he means that different sciences can reason to some of the same conclusions on the basis of different premises or evidence. In his example, he points out that in order to support the proposition that the earth is round a naturalist uses empirical observations, while a cosmologist might support that same conclusion on a strictly formal basis. 'And for that reason', he concludes, 'nothing prevents the same things from being treated by philosophical studies insofar as they can be cognized by the light of natural reason, and also by another science insofar as they are cognized by the light of divine revelation. That is why the theology that pertains to *sacra doctrina* [in other words, revealed theology] differs in kind from the theology that is considered a part of philosophy' (ad 2).

In this argument, Aquinas might appear willing to concede that revealed and natural theology differ only in this methodological respect, that they simply constitute two radically different ways of approaching the very same propositions about God and everything else. However, he would not actually concede this. There are propositions that belong uniquely to revealed theology's subject matter, simply because the different premises with which revealed theology begins can also lead to conclusions not available to unaided reason. And, of course, no doctrinal proposition that is initially available to human beings only in virtue of having been revealed by God can be part of natural theology's subject matter.

On the other hand, no propositions appropriate to natural theology are excluded from *Summa theologiae*'s subject matter. The propositions that belong to natural theology form a proper subset of those that belong to revealed theology:

It was necessary that human beings be instructed by divine revelation even as regards the things about God that human reason can explore. For the truth about God investigated by a few on the basis of reason [without relying on revelation] would emerge for people [only] after a long time and tainted with many mistakes. And yet all human wellbeing, which has to do with God, depends on the cognition of that truth. Therefore, it was necessary for human beings to be instructed about divine matters through divine revelation so that [the nature of human] well–being might emerge for people more conveniently and with greater certainty.

(*Summa theologiae* Ia.1.1c)

When he sums up his examination of *sacra doctrina*, or revealed theology, Aquinas says that its 'main aim . . . is to transmit a cognition of God, and not only as he is in himself, but also as he is the source of things, and their goal – especially of the rational creature' (*Summa theologiae* Ia.2, intro.). Thus the subject matter of *sacra doctrina*, the theology presented in this summa of theology, is the most basic truths about *everything*, with two provisos: first, it is about God and about things other than God as they relate to God as their source and goal; second, among things other than God it deals with, it is especially about human beings, whose study of theology should be motivated by the fact that their wellbeing depends specially on their grasp of certain theological truths. And, Aquinas insists, universal scope is just what one should expect in a rational investigation of the truth about God: 'All things are considered in *sacra doctrina* under the concept of God, either because they *are* God, or because they have an ordered relationship *to* God as to their source and goal. It follows from this that the subject of this science is really God', even though the intended explanatory scope of the science is universal (*Summa theologiae* Ia.1.7c).

In referring to *sacra doctrina* as a 'science', Aquinas means to characterize it as a systematic, reasoned presentation of an organized body of knowledge consisting of general truths about some reasonably unified subject matter. In that broadly Aristotelian sense, it is not obviously wrong to think of theology as a science (as it would be in the narrower, twentieth–century sense of 'science'). It is in that sense that the science of theology as Aquinas develops it in *Summa theologiae* would now be called philosophical theology, the enterprise of employing the techniques and devices of philosophy in clarifying, supporting and extending the propositions that are supposed to have been revealed for theology's starting points. Thus, some of the work of philosophical theology is an attempt to explain revealed propositions and systematically work out their implications.

Like natural theology, which is subordinate to metaphysics, philosophical theology is a subordinate science. However, because it begins its work on divinely revealed propositions, Aquinas identifies the 'science' to which it is subordinate as God's knowledge of himself and everything else, available to human beings directly only in the afterlife

(*Summa theologiae* Ia.1.2c). As he says earlier, 'For us, the goal of faith is to arrive at an understanding of what we believe – [which is] as if a practitioner of a subordinate science were to acquire in addition the knowledge possessed by a practitioner of the higher science. In that case the things that were only believed before would come to be known, or understood' (*Expositio super librum Boethii de trinitate* 2.2, ad 7).

Not even the doctrinal mysteries are impervious to rational investigation, although unaided reason could never have discovered them. Regarding one central mystery, for example, Aquinas says: 'It is impossible to arrive at a cognition of the Trinity of the divine persons by means of natural reason' (*Summa theologiae* Ia.32.1c). However, he says this in the twenty-second of a series of seventy-seven articles of *Summa theologiae* devoted to analysing and arguing about the details of Trinity; in other words, in the midst of subjecting this mystery to philosophical theology. As he explains in the very Article in which he rules out the possibility of rationally discovering that there are three divine persons:

There are two ways in which reason is employed regarding any matter . . . in one way to provide sufficient proof of something fundamental . . . in the other way to show that consequent effects are suited to something fundamental that has already been posited . . . . It is in the first way, then, that reason can be employed to prove that God is one, and things of that sort. But it is in the second way that reason is employed in a clarification of Trinity. For once Trinity has been posited, reasonings of that sort are suitable, although not so as to provide a sufficient proof of the Trinity of persons by those reasonings.

(*Summa theologiae* Ia.32.1c)

Aquinas is also careful to point out that it isn't mere intellectual curiosity or even a defense of the faith that is served by a rational clarification of Trinity. In his view, this application of philosophical theology – confirming faith by reason, showing that Trinity is not after all irrational, exposing the intricate connections between these and other doctrinal propositions – aids one's understanding of creation and salvation (see TRINITY).

See also: ALBERT THE GREAT; DUNS SCOTUS, J.; GOD, CONCEPTS OF; KNOWLEDGE, CONCEPT OF; MEDIEVAL PHILOSOPHY; NATURAL THEOLOGY; THOMISM

References and further reading

Aquinas, Thomas (1248–73) *Opera omnia (Complete Works)*, ed. Leonine Commission, *S. Thomae Aquinatis Doctoris Angelici. Opera Omnia. Iussu Leonis XIII, P.M. edita*, Rome: Vatican Polyglot Press, 1882–. (Many of the editions in this series are repeated in the Marietti Editions.)

Kretzmann, N. and Stump, E. (eds) (1993) *The Cambridge Companion to Aquinas*, Cambridge: Cambridge University Press. (Ten studies specifically designed to introduce all the important aspects of Aquinas' thought; includes bibliography.)

Stump, E (2003) *Aquinas*, London: Routledge.

NORMAN KRETZMANN
ELEONORE STUMP

ARABIC PHILOSOPHY

See ISLAMIC PHILOSOPHY

ARCHĒ

Archē, or 'principle', is an ancient Greek philosophical term. Building on earlier uses, Aristotle established it as a technical term with a number of related meanings, including 'originating source', 'cause', 'principle of knowledge' and 'basic entity'. Accordingly, it acquired importance in metaphysics, epistemology and philosophy of science, and also in the particular sciences. According to Aristotle's doctrine of scientific principles, all sciences and all scientific knowledge are founded on principles (*archai*) of a limited number of determinate kinds.

See also: ARISTOTLE; STOICISM

RICHARD MCKIRAHAN

ARCHITECTURE, AESTHETICS OF

The philosophy of architecture is a branch of philosophical aesthetics concerned with various issues arising from the theory and practice of building design. The oldest writings on architecture date from antiquity and link architectural principles to more general, metaphysical elements of form and order. This tradition persisted into and beyond the Renaissance, but in the eighteenth century it began to give way to new philosophies of mind and value, according to which the determining factors of aesthetic experience are the interests and attitudes of informed subjects. Thereby architecture came within the sphere of the theory of taste.

Nineteenth-century revivals of classical and Gothic styles produced renewed interest in the nature of architecture, its place within the scheme of arts and sciences, and its role in society. Following this, twentieth-century modernism offered various accounts of the rational basis of architectural form and combined these with utopian political philosophies. As it had been in antiquity and during the Renaissance, architecture was again viewed as central to and partly definitive of a culture. More recently, however, attention has returned to analytical questions such as 'What is the nature of the aesthetic experience of architecture?' and, relatedly, 'How is it possible for there to be reasoned, critical judgments about the meaning and value of buildings?'

In order to deal with such issues philosophers in different traditions have begun to develop accounts of the social aspects of architecture, recognizing that critical judgments presuppose the capacity to identify buildings as being of various types: public, domestic, formal, informal and so on. The nature of architecture is in part, therefore, a matter of social convention or more generally 'forms of life', and this limits the scope for abstract ahistorical theorizing. None the less, the resources of metaphysics, the theories of mind, action, meaning and value are all utilized in contemporary philosophy of architecture.

See also: AESTHETIC ATTITUDE; FORMALISM IN ART; HABERMAS, J.; KANT, I. §12; POSTMODERNISM

JOHN J. HALDANE

ARENDT, HANNAH (1906–75)

Hannah Arendt was one of the leading political thinkers of the twentieth century. She observed Nazi totalitarianism at close quarters and devoted much of her life to making sense of it. In her view it mobilized the atomized masses around a simple-minded ideology, and devised a form of rule in which bureaucratically minded officials performed murderous deeds with a clear conscience. For Arendt the only way to avoid totalitarianism was to establish a well-ordered political community that encouraged public participation and institutionalized political freedom. She considered politics to be one of the highest human activities because it enabled citizens to reflect on their collective life, to give meaning to their personal lives and to develop a creative and cohesive community. She was deeply worried that the economically obsessed modern age discouraged political activity, and created morally superficial people susceptible to the appeal of mindless adventurism.

B. PAREKH

ARETĒ

A pivotal term of ancient Greek ethics, *aretē* is conventionally translated as 'virtue', but is more properly 'goodness' – the quality of being a good human being. Philosophy came, largely through Plato, to recognize four cardinal *aretai*: wisdom (*phronēsis*), moderation (*sōphrosynē*), courage (*andreia*) and justice (*dikaiosynē*). Others, considered either coordinate with these or their sub-species, included piety, liberality and magnanimity. The term generated many controversies. For example, is *aretē* a state of intellect, character or both? Does it possess intrinsic or only instrumental value? Is it teachable, god-given or otherwise acquired? Is it one thing or many? If many, how are they differentiated, and can you have one without having all?

See also: ARISTOTLE §§21–3; EUDAMONIA; PLATO; SOCRATES; SOPHISTS; VIRTUE ETHICS; VIRTUES AND VICES

DAVID SEDLEY

ARISTOTLE (384–322 BC)

Introduction

Aristotle of Stagira is one of the two most important philosophers of the ancient world, and one of the four or five most important of any time or place. He was not an Athenian, but he spent most of his life as a student and teacher of philosophy in Athens. For twenty years he was a member of Plato's Academy; later he set up his own philosophical school, the Lyceum. During his lifetime he published philosophical dialogues, of which only fragments now survive. The 'Aristotelian corpus' (1,462 pages of Greek text, including some spurious works) is probably derived from the lectures that he gave in the Lyceum.

Aristotle is the founder not only of philosophy as a discipline with distinct areas or branches, but, still more generally, of the conception of intellectual inquiry as falling into distinct disciplines. He insists, for instance, that the standards of proof and evidence for deductive logic and mathematics should not be applied to the study of nature, and that neither of these disciplines should be taken as a proper model for moral and political inquiry. He distinguishes philosophical reflection on a discipline from the practice of the discipline itself. The corpus contains contributions to many different disciplines, not only to philosophy.

Some areas of inquiry in which Aristotle makes a fundamental contribution are as follows:

(1) Logic. Aristotle's *Prior Analytics* constitutes the first attempt to formulate a system of deductive formal logic, based on the theory of the 'syllogism'. The *Posterior Analytics* uses this system to formulate an account of rigorous scientific knowledge. 'Logic', as Aristotle conceives it, also includes the study of language, meaning and their relation to non-linguistic reality; hence it includes many topics

that might now be assigned to philosophy of language or philosophical logic (*Categories*, *De Interpretatione*, *Topics*).

(2) The study of nature. About a quarter of the corpus (see especially the *History of Animals*, *Parts of Animals*, and *Generation of Animals*; also *Movement of Animals*, *Progression of Animals*) consists of works concerned with biology. Some of these contain collections of detailed observations. (The *Meteorology* contains a similar collection on inanimate nature.) Others try to explain these observations in the light of the explanatory scheme that Aristotle defends in his more theoretical reflections on the study of nature. These reflections (especially in the *Physics* and in *Generation and Corruption*) develop an account of nature, form, matter, cause and change that expresses Aristotle's views about the understanding and explanation of natural organisms and their behaviour. Natural philosophy and cosmology are combined in *On the Heavens*.

(3) Metaphysics. In his reflections on the foundations and presuppositions of other disciplines, Aristotle describes a universal 'science of being *qua* being', the concern of the *Metaphysics*. Part of this universal science examines the foundations of inquiry into nature. Aristotle formulates his doctrine of substance, which he explains through the connected contrasts between form and matter, and between potentiality and actuality. One of his aims is to describe the distinctive and irreducible character of living organisms. Another aim of the universal science is to use his examination of substance to give an account of divine substance, the ultimate principle of the cosmic order.

(4) Philosophy of mind. The doctrine of form and matter is used to explain the relation of soul and body, and the different types of soul found in different types of living creatures. In Aristotle's view, the soul is the form of a living body. He examines the different aspects of this form in plants, non-rational animals and human beings, by describing nutrition, perception, thought and desire. His discussion (in *On the Soul*, and also in the *Parva Naturalia*) ranges over topics in philosophy of mind, psychology, physiology, epistemology and theory of action.

(5) Ethics and politics (*Nicomachean Ethics*, *Eudemian Ethics*, *Magna Moralia*). In Aristotle's view, the understanding of the natural and essential aims of human agents is the right basis for a grasp of principles guiding moral and political practice. These principles are expressed in his account of human wellbeing, and of the different virtues that constitute a good person and promote wellbeing. The description of a society that embodies these virtues in individual and social life is a task for the *Politics*, which also examines the virtues and vices of

actual states and societies, measuring them against the principles derived from ethical theory.

(6) Literary criticism and rhetorical theory (*Poetics*, *Rhetoric*). These works are closely connected both to Aristotle's logic and to his ethical and political theory.

1   Life

Aristotle was born in 384 BC, in the Macedonian city of Stagira, now part of northern Greece. In his lifetime the kingdom of Macedon, first under Philip and then under Philip's son Alexander ('the Great'), conquered both the Greek cities of Europe and Asia and the Persian Empire. Although Aristotle spent much of his adult life in Athens, he was not an Athenian citizen. He was closely linked to the kings of Macedon, whom many Greeks regarded as foreign invaders; hence, he was affected by the volatile relations between Macedon and the Greek cities, especially Athens.

Aristotle was the son of Nicomachus, a doctor attached to the Macedonian court. In 367 BC Aristotle came to Athens. He belonged to Plato's Academy until the death of Plato in 347; during

these years Plato wrote his important later dialogues (including the *Sophist*, *Timaeus*, *Philebus*, *Statesman*, and *Laws*), which reconsider many of the doctrines of his earlier dialogues and pursue new lines of thought. Since there was no dogmatic system of 'Platonism', Aristotle was neither a disciple of such a system nor a rebel against it. The exploratory and critical outlook of the Academy probably encouraged Aristotle's own philosophical growth.

In 347 BC Aristotle left Athens, for Assos in Asia Minor. Later he moved to Lesbos, in the eastern Aegean, and then to Macedon, where he was a tutor of Alexander. In 334 he returned to Athens and founded his own school, the Lyceum. In 323 Alexander died; in the resulting outbreak of anti-Macedonian feeling in Athens Aristotle left for Chalcis, on the island of Euboea, where he died in 322.

Aristotle married Pythias, a niece of Hermeias, the ruler of Assos. They had a daughter, also called Pythias. After the death of his wife, Aristotle formed an attachment to Herpyllis, and they had a son Nicomachus.

2   Order of Aristotle's works

By the end of Aristotle's life the Lyceum must have become a well-established school. It lasted after Aristotle's death; his successor as head of the school was his pupil Theophrastus. Many of the works in the Aristotelian corpus appear to be closely related to Aristotle's lectures in the Lyceum. The polished character of some passages suggests preparation for publication (for example, *Parts of Animals* I 5), but many passages contain incomplete sentences and compressed allusions, suggesting notes that a lecturer might expand (for example, *Metaphysics* VII 13). We cannot tell how many of his treatises Aristotle regarded as 'finished' (see §11 on the *Metaphysics* and §21 on the *Ethics*).

It may be wrong, therefore, to ask about the 'date' of a particular treatise. If Aristotle neither published nor intended to publish the treatises, a given treatise may easily contain contributions from different dates. For similar reasons, we cannot plausibly take cross-references from one work to another as evidence of the order of the works. External, biographical considerations are unhelpful, since we lack the evidence to support any detailed intellectual biography of Aristotle.

A few points, however, may suggest a partial chronology.

(1) Some of Aristotle's frequent critical discussions of Plato and other Academics may have been written (in some version) during Aristotle's years in

the Academy. The *Topics* may reflect the character of dialectical debates in the Academy.

(2) It is easier to understand the relation of the doctrine of substance in the *Categories* and *Physics* I–II to the doctrine and argument of *Metaphysics* VII if we suppose that *Metaphysics* VII is later.

(3) The Organon (see §4) does not mention matter, perhaps because (a) Aristotle had not yet thought of it, or because (b) he regarded it as irrelevant to the topics considered in the Organon. If (a) is correct, the Organon precedes the works on natural philosophy.

(4) Some of the observations used in Aristotle's biological works probably came from the eastern Aegean. Hence, Aristotle probably pursued his biological research during his years away from Athens. We might trace his biological interests to the Academy (see Plato's *Timaeus*); he may also have acquired them from his father Nicomachus, who was a doctor. Probably, then, at least some of the biological works (or versions of them) are not the latest works in the corpus.

(5) The *Magna Moralia* (if it is genuine) and the *Eudemian Ethics* probably precede the *Nicomachean Ethics* (see §21).

The order in which Aristotle's works appear in the Greek manuscripts goes back to early editors and commentators (from the first century BC to the sixth century AD); it reflects their view not about the order in which the works were written, but about the order in which they should be studied. This entry generally follows the order of the corpus, except that it discusses *On the Soul* after the *Metaphysics* (see §17), not among the works on natural philosophy (where it appears in the manuscripts).

3 Appearances

The general aim of rational inquiry, according to Aristotle, is to advance from what is 'better known to us' to what is 'better known by nature' (see *Physics* I 1; *Posterior Analytics* 71b33; *Metaphysics* 1029b3). We achieve this aim if: (1) we replace propositions that we thought we knew with propositions that we really know because they are true and we understand them; (2) we find general principles that explain and justify the more specific truths that we began from; (3) we find those aspects of reality that explain the aspects that are more familiar to us.

The things better known to us in a particular area are the relevant 'appearances' (*phainomena*). Aristotle presents them through detailed collections of empirical data, reached as a result of 'inquiry' (*historia*; for example, *Parts of Animals* 646a8). Empirical inquiry proceeds from particular observa-

tions, by means of generalizations through induction (*epagōgē*) from these particular cases, until we reach experience (*empeiria*). Experience leads us to principles that are better known by nature (*Prior Analytics* 46a17); we also rely on it to test principles we have found (*Generation of Animals* 760b28).

Philosophical inquiry also relies on 'appearances'. However, the appearances that concern it are not empirical observations, but common beliefs, assumptions widely shared by 'the many and the wise'. The critical and constructive study of these common beliefs is 'dialectic'. Aristotle's method is basically Socratic. He raises puzzles in the common beliefs, looking for an account that will do them justice as a whole. Among common beliefs Aristotle considers the views of his predecessors (for example, *Metaphysics* I; *On the Soul* I; *Politics* II), because the puzzles raised by their views help us to find better solutions than they found.

Inquiry leads us to causes and to universals. Aristotle has a realist conception of inquiry and knowledge; beliefs and theories are true in so far as they grasp the reality that we inquire into (see REALISM AND ANTIREALISM §2). Universals and causes are 'prior by nature'; they are not created by, or dependent on, any theory, but a true theory must fit them.

If we attended only to Aristotle's remarks on what is better known to us and on the process of inquiry, we might regard his position as a form of empiricism (see EMPIRICISM). But in his remarks on what is better known by nature, he insists on the reality of universals and on the importance of non-sensory forms of knowledge (see §15 on universals, §19 on thought).

4 Thought and language

One means of access to appearances, and especially to common beliefs, is the study of what words and sentences 'signify' (*sēmainein*). This is part of 'logic' (*logikē*, derived from *logos*, which may be translated 'word', 'speech', 'statement', 'argument' or 'reason': see LOGOS), which is discussed in the first section of Aristotle's works (*Categories*, *De Interpretatione*, *Prior Analytics*, *Posterior Analytics*, *Topics*). This section of the corpus came to be called the 'Organon' ('instrument'), because logic, as Aristotle conceives it, concerns statements and arguments in general, without restriction to any specific subject matter; it is therefore an instrument of philosophical inquiry in general, rather than a branch of philosophy coordinate with natural philosophy or ethics. The Organon includes some elements of philosophy of language, as well as formal logic (syllogistic; see §5) and epistemology (see §6).

According to Aristotle's account of signification (see especially *De Interpretatione* 1–4), as commonly understood, the word 'horse' signifies horse by signifying the thought of horse; in using the word, we communicate thoughts about horses. When the thoughts about horses we communicate are true, we communicate truths about the universal horse; even when our thoughts are not completely true, we may signify the same universal horse.

To understand the signification of a name 'F', we look for the corresponding definition (*logos*, *horismos*) of F. Aristotle distinguishes nominal definitions, stating the beliefs associated with the name, from real definitions, giving a true account of the universal that underlies the beliefs embodied in the nominal definition (see *Posterior Analytics* II 8–10. Aristotle himself does not use the labels 'nominal definition' and 'real definition'.).

Not every name corresponds to one nominal and one real definition. Some names correspond to no genuine universal; 'goatstag' signifies (in one way) animals that are both goats and stags, but it does not signify a genuine universal, since there is no natural kind of goatstag. Other names correspond to more than one universal, as 'chest' signifies both a container and a part of an animal. Chests are 'homonymous' (*homōnyma*) or 'multivocal' (*pollachōs legomena*; 'spoken of in many ways'); more than one definition is needed to capture the signification of the name. By contrast, since only one definition corresponds to the name 'horse', horses are 'synonymous' (*Categories* 1).

Other philosophers make serious errors, Aristotle believes, because they suppose they can give a single account of things or properties that are really multivocal. Once we see that different Fs are F in different ways, we see that different, although (in many cases) connected, accounts of what it is to be F must be given. Some philosophically important cases of multivocity are cause (Aristotle's doctrine of the four causes; see §9), being (the doctrine of the categories; see §7) and good (the criticism of Plato's belief in a Form of the Good; *Nicomachean Ethics* I 6).

5   Deduction

Part of logic, as Aristotle conceives it, is the study of good and bad arguments. In the *Topics* Aristotle treats dialectical arguments in general. In the *Prior Analytics* he examines one type of argument, a 'deduction' (*syllogismos*; literally, 'reasoning', hence the standard term 'syllogism'). This is an argument in which, if propositions *p* and *q* are assumed, something else *r*, different from *p* and *q*, follows necessarily because of the truth of *p* and *q* (*Prior Analytics* 24b18–20, paraphrased). Aristotle insists that it is not possible for the premises of a deduction to be true and the conclusion false ('follows necessarily'); that a deduction must have more

than one premise ('if *p* and *q* are assumed'); that the conclusion cannot be identical to any premise ('different from *p* and *q*'); and that no redundant premises are allowed ('because of the truth of *p* and *q*'). He takes deductions to express affirmative or negative relations between universals, taken either universally ('Animal belongs to every (no) man') or not universally ('Animal belongs (does not belong) to some man'). He takes the affirmative and negative claims to imply existence (so that 'Biped belongs to some dodo' follows from 'Biped belongs to every dodo'; the latter affirmation is not equivalent, therefore, to 'If anything is a dodo, it is biped').

These different features of an Aristotelian deduction differentiate Aristotle's account of a deduction from a more familiar account of deductively valid arguments. An argument may be valid even if it is redundant, or a premise is identical to the conclusion, or it has only one premise, or it is about particulars, or it contains neither 'some' nor 'every' nor 'belongs'; but no such argument is an Aristotelian deduction. Aristotle's theory of the different forms of deduction (often called 'the moods of the syllogism') examines the various forms of argument that necessarily preserve the truth of their premises. He begins from 'complete' (or 'perfect') deductions whose validity is evident, and classifies the different types of arguments that can be derived from (shown to be equivalent to) the complete deductions. He also explores the logical relations between propositions involving modalities ('Necessarily (possibly) animal belongs to every man' and so on). Since Aristotle accepts this relatively narrow account of a deduction, his exploration of the different forms of deduction is not a theory of valid arguments in general; the Stoics come much closer to offering such a theory (see STOICISM).

Aristotle's theory of deduction is developed for its own sake, but it also has two main philosophical applications. (1) Deduction is one type of argument appropriate to dialectic (and, with modifications, to rhetoric; see §29). Aristotle contrasts it with inductive argument (also used in dialectic), in which the conclusion does not follow necessarily from the premises, but is made plausible by them. (2) It is essential for demonstration (*apodeixis*), which Aristotle takes to be the appropriate form for exhibiting scientific knowledge.

6   Knowledge, science and demonstration

The progress from what is known to us to what is known by nature aims at *epistēmē*, the scientific knowledge whose structure is exhibited in the demonstrative pattern described in the *Posterior*

Analytics. A demonstration is a deduction in which the premises are necessarily true, prior to and better known than the conclusions, and explanatory of the conclusions derived from them. Aristotle assumes that if I know that *p*, then I can cite some justification *q*, to justify my belief that *p*, and I also know why *q* justifies *p* (*Posterior Analytics* I 2). The right sort of justification relies on things better known by nature – the general laws and principles that explain the truth of *p*. Since these are embodied in demonstrations, grasp of a demonstration of *p* expresses knowledge of *p*. Aristotle's theory of demonstration, then, is not intended to describe a procedure of scientific inquiry that begins from appearances; it is an account of the knowledge that is achieved by successful inquiry.

To show that a deduction is a demonstration, we must show that its premises are better known than the conclusion. Sometimes we can show this by demonstrating them from higher premises that are even better known. This process of justification, Aristotle claims, must be linear and finite. A circular 'justification' must eventually 'justify' a given belief by appeal to itself, and an infinite regress imposes on us a task that we can never complete. Since, therefore, neither a circle nor an infinite regress can really justify, a proper justification must ultimately appeal to primary principles of a science.

These primary principles are 'assumptions' (*hypotheseis*); we must see that they are better known and prior to other truths of a science, without being derived from any further principles. Since they are the basis of all demonstration, they cannot themselves be demonstrated; Aristotle claims that we have non-demonstrative understanding (*nous*: *Posterior Analytics* II 19) of the ultimate principles of each science (see Nous).

How are we entitled to claim understanding of an ultimate principle? Aristotle believes that the principles of a science are reached from appearances (perceptual or dialectical or both), which are the starting points known to us. He may believe that this relation of the principles to appearances justifies us in accepting them as first principles and in claiming to have understanding of them. This explanation, however, does not easily fit Aristotle's demand for linear and finite chains of justification. That demand suggests that the assumptions of a science must be self-evident (seen to be true without any inferential justification), so that his conception of knowledge expresses a foundationalist position (see Foundationalism). (On difficulties in foundationalism see Agrippa.)

Although Aristotle's aim of reaching a demonstrative science reveals some of his epistemological doctrines and assumptions, it does not evidently influence most of the structure or content of most of the surviving treatises. In his main philosophical works, the influence of dialectical methods and aims is more apparent.

7 Categories and beings

Part of the task of logic is to explain the nature of predication ('*A* is *B*', analysed by Aristotle as '*B* is predicated of *A*' or '*B* belongs to *A*', as in 'Animal belongs to every man'), which is presupposed by complex *logoi* (statements and arguments). In the *Categories* (*katēgoriai*; predications), Aristotle introduces ten 'categories' (usually called *schēmata tēs katēgorias*, 'figures (that is, types) of predication'). The categories correspond to different sorts of words (for example, count-nouns, adjectives, verbs) and to different grammatical functions (for example, subject, predicate), but they primarily classify the different non-linguistic items introduced in predications. The sentences 'Socrates is a man' and 'Socrates is a musician' are grammatically similar, but they introduce different sorts of things; the first predicates a second substance of a first substance, whereas the second predicates a non-substance of a first substance.

The first category is called *ousia* (literally, 'being'), which is translated into Latin as 'substantia', and hence usually called 'substance' (see Substance). The nine non-substance categories include quality, quantity and relative (the only ones that Aristotle refers to often; the categories are listed in *Categories* 4, *Topics* I 9). Each category contains both particulars and universals. The statement that this individual man is an animal predicates a second substance (that is, a universal in the category of substance) of a first substance (that is, a particular in the category of substance). 'White is a colour' predicates one universal quality of another.

The categories display the multivocity of beings (see §4). Whereas animals constitute an ordinary univocal genus with a single definition, beings do not constitute an ordinary genus; hence there is no single account of what it is for something to be a being. Aristotle believes Plato mistakenly pursued a single account of beings; the theory of categories is meant to avoid Platonic errors.

In marking categorial divisions, Aristotle is influenced by grammar and syntax, but also by his ontology – his classification of beings. This classification rests on his view of nature and change, which clarifies his analysis of predication.

8 Change and substance

Aristotle's *Physics* discusses nature, *physis*. The nature of *x* is a principle (or 'source'; *archē*), internal to *x*, of change and stability in *x*; hence the inquiry into nature leads to a discussion of change in natural substances (the elements, plants and animals). Aristotle proceeds dialectically, raising and solving puzzles involved in the understanding of natural change. In solving the puzzles, he introduces the different types of beings that are presupposed by a coherent account of natural change.

In *Physics* I 7–8, Aristotle analyses a simple example of change – Socrates changing from being pale to being tanned. This change involves a subject (or 'underlying thing'; *hypokeimenon*), Socrates, who loses one contrary (his pale colour) and acquires another contrary (his tan). Neither of the contraries persists, but the subject persists (otherwise there would not be a change in Socrates). This particular subject that persists through change is what the *Categories* calls a first substance. First substances differ both from second substances and from non-substances by being capable of undergoing change; they persist while receiving opposites (as Socrates is first pale and then tanned). They cannot, however, remain in existence irrespective of any properties gained or lost; Socrates' ceasing to be a man is not a change in Socrates, but the perishing of Socrates.

The properties that a first substance cannot lose without perishing constitute (approximately) the essence of that first substance (see ESSENTIALISM). These essential properties define a kind to which the first substance belongs. A kind may be a species (*eidos*), for example, man or horse, or a genus (*genos*), for example, animal. In predicating a second substance of a first substance (as in 'Socrates is a man'), we place the first substance in the kind it belongs to. If we predicate one of the contraries that the first substance can lose without perishing, we introduce an item (Socrates' pale colour, his particular height, his ignorance, his being the husband of Xanthippe) in one of the non-substance categories (quality, quantity, relative, and so on). The kinds to which these non-substantial items belong are non-substantial universals.

Aristotle also examines the coming to be and perishing of a first substance. Here again, he distinguishes a persisting subject and two contraries. If we make a statue from bronze, the lump of bronze (the subject) acquires the shape of the statue, and loses the shapelessness it had, and so changes between contraries. But although the lump remains in existence, a new subject, the statue, has come into being. In this case, the subject of the change is the matter (*hylē*), and what it acquires is the form (*eidos*, also rendered 'species').

This analysis of change suggests an argument (*Physics* II 1) to show that the genuine subject, and hence the genuine substance, is the matter, whereas the apparent substance (for example, the statue) is simply matter with a certain shape. Socrates does not become another subject if he changes shape; hence (we may argue) the lump of bronze does not become another subject simply by acquiring the shape of a statue. Similarly, then, a natural organism might be understood as a piece of matter shaped in a certain way so as to embody Socrates. Natural organic 'substances', such as Socrates and this tree, turn out to be not genuine subjects, but mere configurations of the matter that is the real substance.

Aristotle does not endorse this eliminative attitude to natural organic substances. He uses the argument to raise a puzzle about whether matter or form is substance. He discusses this puzzle in *Metaphysics* VII (see §§12–14). This discussion relies on his account of causation and explanation.

9 Causes

When we correctly answer questions such as 'Why does this event happen?' or 'Why is this object as it is?', we state the cause (or explanation; *aition*) of the event or object. Aristotle believes that causes are multivocal (see *Physics* II 3; *Metaphysics* I 3). Different accounts of a cause correspond to different answers to why-questions about (for example) a statue. (1) 'It is made of bronze' states the material cause. (2) 'It is a statue representing Pericles' states the formal cause, by stating the definition that says what the thing is. (3) 'A sculptor made it' states the 'source of change', by mentioning the source of the process that brought the statue into being; later writers call this the 'moving cause' or 'efficient cause'. (4) 'It is made to represent Pericles' states 'that for the sake of which', since it mentions the goal or end for the sake of which the statue was made; this is often called the 'final' (Latin *finis*; 'end') cause.

Each of the four causes answers a why-question. Sometimes (as in our example) a complete answer requires all four causes. Not all four, however, are always appropriate; the (universal) triangle, for example, has a formal cause, stating its definition, but no efficient cause, since it does not come into being, and no final cause, since it is not made to promote any goal or end.

Some have claimed that Aristotle's 'four causes' are not really causes at all, pointing out that he takes an *aition* to be available even in cases where the why-question (for example, 'Why do the interior angles of this figure add up to two right angles?') does not seek what we would call a cause (in Aristotle's division, an efficient cause). When explanations of changes are being sought, however, Aristotle seems to provide recognizably causal explanations. Even the *aitia* (material, formal, final) that do not initially seem to be causes turn out to play an important role in causal explanation; for this reason, the label 'four causes' gives a reasonably accurate impression of Aristotle's doctrine.

His comparison between artefacts and natural organisms clarifies his claims about formal and final causes. The definition of an artefact requires reference to the goal and the intended function. A hammer's form and essence is a capacity to hammer nails into wood. The hammer was designed to have this capacity for performing this function; and if this had not been its function, it would not have been made in the way it was, to have the properties it has. The form includes the final cause, by specifying the functions that explain why the hammer is made as it is.

Similarly, Aristotle claims, a natural organism has a formal cause specifying the function that is the final cause of the organism. The parts of an organism seem to perform functions that benefit the whole (the heart pumps blood, the senses convey useful information). Aristotle claims that organs have final causes; they exist in order to carry out the beneficial functions they actually carry out. The form of an organism is determined by the pattern of activity that contains the final causes of its different vital processes. Hence Aristotle believes that form as well as matter plays a causal role in natural organisms.

To claim that a heart is for pumping blood to benefit the organism is to claim that there is some causal connection between the benefit to the organism and the processes that constitute the heart's pumping blood. Aristotle makes this causal claim without saying why it is true. He does not say, for instance, either (1) that organisms are the products of intelligent design (as Plato and the Stoics believe), or (2) that they are the outcome of a process of evolution.

Aristotle's account of causation and explanation is expressed in the content and argument of many of his biological works (including those connected with psychology). In the *Parts of Animals* and *Generation of Animals* for instance, he examines the behaviour and structure of organisms and their parts both to find the final causes and to describe the material and efficient basis of the goal-direction that he finds in nature (*Parts of Animals* I 1). He often argues that different physiological processes in different animals have the same final cause.

Some ascribe to Aristotle an 'incompatibilist' view of the relation between final causes and the underlying material and efficient causes. Incompatibilists concede that every goal-directed process (state, event) requires some material process (as nutrition, for example, requires the various processes involved in digesting food), but they argue that the goal-directed process cannot be wholly constituted by any material process or processes; any

process wholly constituted by material processes is (according to the incompatibilist) fully explicable in material-efficient terms, and therefore has no final cause.

Probably, however, Aristotle takes a 'compatibilist' view. He seems to believe that even if every goal-directed process were wholly constituted by material processes, each of which can be explained in material-efficient terms, the final-causal explanation would still be the only adequate explanation of the process as a whole. According to this view, final causes are irreducible to material-efficient causes, because the explanations given by final causes cannot be replaced by equally good explanations referring only to these other causes. This irreducibility, however, does not require the denial of material constitution.

10 Change

Aristotle studies nature as an internal principle of change and stability; and so he examines the different types of change (or 'motion'; *kinēsis*) that are found in the natural elements and in the natural organisms composed of them. In *Physics* III 1 he defines change as 'the actuality of the potential *qua* potential'. His definition marks the importance of his views on potentiality (or 'capacity'; *dynamis*) and actuality (or 'realization'; *energeia* or *entelecheia*) (see *Metaphysics* IX 1–9).

The primary type of potentiality is a principle (*archē*) of change and stability. If x has the potentiality F for G, then (1) G is the actuality of F, and (2) x has F because G is the actuality of F. Marathon runners, for instance, have the potentiality to run 26 miles because they have been trained to run this distance; hearts have the capacity to pump blood because this is the function that explains the character of hearts. In these cases, potentialities correspond to final causes.

Potentiality and possibility do not, therefore, imply each other. (1) Not everything that is possible for x realizes a potentiality of x. Perhaps it is possible for us to speak words of Italian (because we recall them from an opera) without having a potentiality to speak Italian (if we have not learnt Italian). (2) Not everything that x is capable of is possible for x; some creatures would still have a potentiality to swim even if their environment lost all its water.

These points about potentiality help to clarify Aristotle's definition of change. The building of a house is a change because it is the actuality of what is potentially built in so far as it is potentially built. 'What is potentially built' refers to the bricks (and so on). The completed house is their complete actuality, and when it is reached, their potentiality to be built is lost. The process of building is their actuality in so far as they are potentially built. 'In so far …' picks out the incomplete actuality that is present only as long as the potentiality to be built (lost in the completed house) is still present. Aristotle's definition picks out the kind of actuality that is to be identified with change, by appealing to some prior understanding of potentiality and actuality, which in turn rests on an understanding of final causation.

In the rest of the *Physics*, Aristotle explores different properties of change in relation to place and time. He discusses infinity and continuity at length, arguing that both change and time are infinitely divisible. He tries to show that the relevant type of infinity can be defined by reference to potentiality, so as to avoid self-contradiction, paradox or metaphysical extravagance. In his view, infinite divisibility requires a series that can always be continued, but does not require the actual existence of an infinitely long series. Once again, the reference to potentiality (in 'can always…') has a crucial explanatory role.

11 Metaphysics

Some of the basic concepts of the *Categories* and *Physics* – including substance, particular, universal, form, matter, cause and potentiality – are discussed more fully in the *Metaphysics*. This is a collection of fourteen books, some of them loosely connected. Aristotle probably did not deliver a course of lectures in the order of the present treatise. Parts of book I are almost repeated in book XIII. Book V is a 'philosophical dictionary' that seems to interrupt the argument of books IV and VI. Book XI summarizes parts of book IV. Books II and XI were probably not written entirely by Aristotle.

Still, whatever their literary origins, all these books have a common subject matter, since they all contribute to the universal science that studies the common presuppositions of the other sciences. This universal science has four names. (1) 'First philosophy': it studies the 'first principles' and 'highest causes' (including the four causes of the *Physics*) presupposed by the other sciences. (2) 'The science of being': every science presupposes that it studies some sort of being, and the science of being examines and defends this presupposition. (3) 'Theology': first philosophy is not only first in so far it is most universal, but also in so far as it deals with the primary sort of being, the sort on which all other beings depend. The primary sort of being is substance, and the primary sort of substance is divine substance; hence the science of being must study divine substance. (4) 'Metaphysics' (*ta meta ta physika*; 'the things after the natural things'): it is 'after' or 'beyond' the study of nature because (a) as theology, it studies entities outside the natural order, and (b) as first philosophy, it starts from the study of nature (which is prior and better known 'to us') and goes beyond it to its foundations and presuppositions (which are prior and better known 'by nature'; see §3).

The first three of these names are used by Aristotle himself (*Metaphysics* IV 1–3, VI 1). The fourth was given to the treatise in antiquity (at an uncertain date); its use of 'after' captures Aristotle's different claims about the relation of the universal science to other sciences.

The universal science is the science of being *qua* being – that is, being in so far as it is being – just as mathematics is the science of some beings *qua* mathematical objects (see §16) and physics is the science of some beings *qua* changeable. The science of being studies the beings that are also studied by other sciences, but it isolates the relevant properties of beings by a different level of abstraction; it does not rely on the fact that they have the properties of mathematical or natural objects, but simply on the fact that they are beings studied by a science (*Metaphysics* IV 1–2).

A special science assumes that it begins with a subject that has properties. The universal science is the science of being because it studies the sort of subject that is presupposed by the other sciences; and it is primarily the science of substance because substance is the primary sort of being. Aristotle's analysis of change in *Physics* I introduces substances as subjects; the *Metaphysics* asks what sorts of subjects and substances must be recognized by special sciences.

Aristotle argues that if we are to signify a subject, it is impossible for each of its properties both to belong and not to belong to it. This principle is often called the 'Principle of Non-Contradiction' (*Metaphysics* IV 3–4). To defend the principle, Aristotle considers an opponent who is willing to assert that a single subject, man, is both a bipedal animal and not a biped animal. If the opponent really says this about a single subject, then, when he uses 'man', he must signify one and the same subject, man. If he agrees that in using 'man' he signifies a biped animal, then he cannot also deny that man is a biped animal; for if he denies this, he can no longer say what 'man' signifies, and hence cannot say what subject it is that he takes to be both a biped animal and not a biped animal. This property (which one cannot also deny of a subject) is an essential property. Hence, the attempt to reject subjects with essential properties is self-undermining.

Subjects of change must also, according to Aristotle, have objective properties (that is, properties that they have whether or not they appear to have them). An argument against Protagoras seeks to show that any attempt to reject objective properties undermines itself (*Metaphysics* IV 5). Protagoras denies that there are any objective properties, because he claims that how things appear to someone is how they are. If he is to maintain the infallibility of appearances against any possibility of correction, then, Aristotle argues, he must claim that it is possible for the same subject to change in every respect at every time (to match different appearances). This is possible, however, only if the same subject can remain in being, but change in all respects. Aristotle replies that if the same subject persists, it must keep the same essential property (the 'form'); hence it cannot change in every respect (IV 5).

12 From being to substance

In *Metaphysics* IV 2 and VII 1 Aristotle argues that, since substance is the primary type of being and other beings are in some way dependent on substances, the science of being must primarily be concerned with substance. The arguments of IV 4–5 describe some features of substances; they must be subjects with stable, objective, essential properties. Books VII–IX describe these subjects more fully, by re-examining the conception of substance that is presented in the *Categories* and *Physics* (see §§7–8).

Aristotle observes that we regard substance both as 'a this' and as 'essence' (or 'what it is'). We might assume that these two descriptions pick out two sorts of substances – a particular subject ('this') and a universal ('what it is'), corresponding to the first and second substances of the *Categories*. Aristotle, however, insists that his question 'What is substance?' will be satisfactorily answered only when we have found the one thing that best satisfies the conditions for being both a subject (a 'this') and an essence ('what it is'). Whatever best satisfies these conditions is primary substance.

The different candidates that Aristotle considers for this role are matter, form and the compound of the two. He argues against the first and third candidates, and defends the second. He regards matter and compound as types of substance, but argues that they are secondary to form because they do not meet the relevant conditions to the same degree. To show that form is primary substance, he argues that a form is both a subject and an essence of the right sort. In books VIII–IX he clarifies his answer by identifying form with the actuality for which the matter is the potentiality.

13 Why is form substance?

In claiming that form is substance, Aristotle relies on the connections between form, cause, essence

and identity. He rejects the eliminative view (§8) that the so-called 'coming-to-be' or 'perishing' of an artefact or organism is simply an alteration of the matter. According to the eliminative view, this alteration does not involve the existence or non-existence of a distinct substance, any more than Socrates' coming to be musical involves the existence of a distinct substance, musical Socrates. Aristotle replies that the production of an artefact and the generation of an organism introduce a new subject, a substance that is neither identical to nor wholly dependent on the matter that constitutes it at a time (see IDENTITY §2). Although this statue of Pericles has come into being from a particular piece of bronze, we may repair the statue by replacing damaged bits; we preserve the same statue but we cause a different bit of bronze to constitute it. Similarly, an organism remains in existence as long as it replaces its matter with new matter: it persists as long as its form persists (*Generation and Corruption* I 5).

When Aristotle speaks of the relation of form to matter, he may refer to either of two kinds of matter: (1) the proximate, organic matter (for example, the organs and limbs making up the organic body); and (2) the remote, non-organic matter (for example, blood, earth, water) of which the organic body is made. Remote matter can exist without the form of the organism, but the organism can persist without any particular piece of remote matter. Proximate matter cannot exist without the form (since it is the function of an arm or heart that makes it the limb or organ it is); the form is the actuality of which the proximate matter is the potentiality (*On the Soul* 412a10; *Metaphysics* 1038b6, 1042b10).

The role of the form in determining the persistence of an organism results from its role as the source of unity. The form, including the organism's vital functions, makes a heap of material constituents into a single organism (*Metaphysics* VII 16). A collection of flesh and bones constitutes a single living organism in so far as it has the form of a man or a horse; the vital functions of the single organism are the final cause of the movements of the different parts. The organism remains in being through changes of matter, as long as it retains its formal, functional properties. Since the structure, behaviour and persistence of the organism must be understood by reference to its form, the form is irreducible to matter (see §9); the organism, defined by its form, must be treated as a subject in its own right, not simply as a heap of matter.

These facts about organisms explain why Aristotle sees a close connection between primary substance and form. Organisms are substances primarily because of their formal properties, not because of their material composition; hence we cannot identify all the basic subjects there are unless we recognize the reality of formal properties and of subjects that are essentially formal.

14 What are substantial forms?

The conclusion that primary substance and form are closely connected, however, explains only why some substances are essentially formal; it does not explain why form itself is substance. To explain this further claim, we need to decide whether Aristotle regards a substantial form as (1) a species form (shared by all members of a given species, for example, the form of man or horse), normally taken to be a universal, or as (2) a particular form, proprietary to (for example) Socrates. (See *Metaphysics* VII 10–16, XII 5, XIII 10, *Generation of Animals* IV 3, for important evidence.)

Some points favouring the 'universal solution' are the following. (1) Aristotle often contrasts the form with the compound of form and matter, and describes particulars as compounds; hence he apparently does not regard particulars as forms. (2) Similarly, he says that a particular differs from a universal in having both form and matter; hence no particular seems to be simply a form. (3) He says the form is what is specified in a definition, but there is no definition of a particular; hence a particular apparently cannot be a form. (4) He says that substance is prior in knowledge to non-substance, but scientific knowledge of particulars is impossible; hence they apparently cannot be substances, and only a universal can be a substance.

In favour of the 'particular solution' it may be argued: (1) a substance must be a subject, whereas all universals are said of subjects; (2) a substance must be a 'this', as opposed to a 'such', and hence, apparently, some sort of particular; (3) Aristotle argues at length that no universal can be a substance.

We might be tempted to conclude that Aristotle's position is inconsistent. His conviction that substance as 'this' and substance as 'what is it' must be the same thing leads him to insist that the successful candidate for substance must satisfy the criteria for being both a this (a subject, and hence a particular) and an essence (a property, and hence a universal). If one and the same thing cannot satisfy both criteria, then no one thing can satisfy all Aristotle's conditions for being a substance.

We need not draw this conclusion, however. We can maintain that Aristotle consistently favours the universal solution, if we can show: (1) a 'this' need not be a particular; (2) some universals are subjects; (3) a species form is not the sort of universal that cannot be a substance.

We can maintain that he consistently favours the particular solution, if we can show the following.

(1) The contrast between form and matter does not imply that they are always mutually exclusive; some forms may be constituted by, or embodied in, particular bits of matter. Sometimes, indeed, Aristotle speaks as though a form is a subject that can persist and perish and can exchange its matter. (2) The sense in which particulars do not allow definition and scientific knowledge does not prevent them from also being, in an appropriate sense, prior in definition and knowledge to universals (*Metaphysics* XIII 10 may attribute the relevant priority to particular substances).

These two solutions are different ways of expressing Aristotle's belief that substances are basic. Both his metaphysics and his natural philosophy express and defend the conviction that natural organisms and their kinds are substances because they are fundamental; they are fundamental because they are irreducible to their constituent matter. It is more difficult to decide whether the individuals or their kinds are more fundamental. Perhaps, indeed, we ought not to decide; different things may be fundamental or irreducible in different ways.

15 Universals, Platonic Forms, mathematics

These disputes partly concern Aristotle's attitude to the reality of universals. One-sided concentration on some of his remarks may encourage a nominalist or conceptualist interpretation (see NOMINALISM). (1) He rejects Plato's belief (as he understands it) in separated universal Forms (see PLATO §§10, 12–16; FORMS, PLATONIC), claiming that only particulars are separable. (2) In *Metaphysics* VII 13–16 he appears to argue that no universal can be a substance. (3) He claims that the universal as object of knowledge is – in a way – identical to the knowledge of it (*On the Soul* 417b23).

Other remarks, however, suggest realism about universals. (4) He claims they are better known by nature; this status seems to belong only to things that really exist. (5) He believes that if there is knowledge, then there must be universals to be objects of it; for our knowledge is about external nature, not about the contents of our own minds.

Aristotle's position is consistent if (1)–(3) are consistent with the realist tendency of (4)–(5). The denial of separation in (1) allows the reality of universals. Similarly, (2) may simply say that no universals are primary substances (which are his main concern in *Metaphysics* VII). And (3) may simply mean (depending on how we take 'in a way') that the mind's conception of the extra-mental universal has some of the features of the universal (as a map has some of the features of the area that it maps). While Aristotle denies that universals can exist without sensible particulars to embody them, he believes they are real properties of these sensible particulars.

He offers a rather similar defence of the reality, without separability, of mathematical objects (*Physics* II 2; *Metaphysics* XIII 3). While agreeing with the Platonist view that there are truths about, for example, numbers or triangles that do not describe the sensible properties of sensible objects, he denies that these truths have to be about independently-existing mathematical objects. He claims that they are truths about certain properties of sensible objects, which we can grasp when we 'take away' (or 'abstract') the irrelevant properties (for example, the fact that this triangular object is made of bronze). Even though there are no separate objects that have simply mathematical properties, there are real mathematical properties of sensible objects.

16 Metaphysics: God

When Aristotle claims that first philosophy is also theology (see §11), he implies that the general discussion of being and substance is the basis for the special discussion of divine substance. (Hence later writers distinguish 'special metaphysics', dealing with God, from 'general metaphysics', dealing with being in general.) The different features of substance explained in *Metaphysics* VII–IX are included in the divine substance of XII. (1) Primary substance is to be identified in some way with form rather than with matter or with the compound of form and matter; divine substance is pure form without matter. (2) Primary substance is in some way numerically one, a 'this' rather than a 'such'; divine substance is completely one and indivisible. (3) Primary substance is in some way actuality rather than potentiality; divine substance is pure actuality with no potentiality. (4) Primary substance is soul rather than body (see §17); divine substance is pure intellect without sense or body.

In each case the properties of primary substance are found in a sensible substance (an animal or a plant) only in so far as they belong to an object that also has other properties; hence primary substance in sensible reality is the form and actuality of an object (a horse, for example) that also has matter and potentiality. In divine substance, however, each feature is found in separation from these other properties; that is why a divine substance lacks matter, multiplicity, parts or potentiality. Aristotle argues that a substance with these pure substantial properties must exist if any sensible substances are to exist; for the existence of potentialities that can be actualized presupposes the existence of an actuality that does not itself include any potentiality (to avoid an infinite regress).

Since this primary type of substance is divine, it is what traditional belief in the Olympian gods was about, what the Presocratics were talking about when they spoke of 'the divine', and what Plato was talking about in speaking of a supreme god. Aristotle mentions the traditional Olympian gods without committing himself to acceptance of the traditional conception of them. He rejects anthropomorphic views of the gods, but he speaks of the divine nature as a kind of mind. He believes that there is something divine about the order and workings of nature, and still more divine in the heavenly substances (*Parts of Animals* I 5). Although he continues to speak of gods in the plural, he also speaks of one divine mind as the ultimate cause of the whole universe; these remarks help to justify the later interpreters who take him to speak of the one God who is the subject of (for example) Aquinas' 'Five Ways' (*Summa theologiae* 1a q.2 a.3) (see AQUINAS, T. §11).

Aristotle's God is the ultimate cause of the physical universe, but not its creator (as Plato's demiurge is), since Aristotle believes the universe is eternal. Nor does Aristotle suggest that God has providence or foreknowledge concerned with future contingent events. But he believes that the physical universe is dependent on God. In *Physics* VIII he argues that the explanation of motion requires recognition of a first cause of motion, and in *Metaphysics* XII this first cause is identified with divine, immaterial, substance. This first mover is itself unmoved; it initiates motion only as an object of love initiates motion by attraction. It is the ultimate final cause of the various movements in the universe.

In treating the divine substance as a god, and hence as a being with a soul and an intellect, Aristotle attributes some mental life to it. But since it would be imperfect if it thought of objects outside itself (because it would not be self-sufficient), it thinks only of its own thinking. This restriction, however, is not as severe as it may seem, since Aristotle believes that the various objects of thought are in some way identical to the mind that thinks them (see §15). In so far as God thinks of his own mind, he thereby also contemplates the order of the universe as a whole; this is the order that the different movements in the universe seek to embody.

Sometimes (as in *Physics* VIII) Aristotle argues for a single first mover. In *Metaphysics* XII, however, he argues that an unmoved mover must be postulated for each of the distinct movements of the heavenly bodies. This astronomical interpretation of his theological doctrine is difficult to reconcile with his belief, reaffirmed in *Metaphysics* XII 10, that in some way the universe is unified by a single first unmoved mover.

17 Soul and body

Aristotle's treatise *On the Soul* is placed among the works on natural philosophy, but should be read with *Metaphysics* VII–IX. In Aristotle's view, disputes about soul and body are simply a special case of the more general disputes about form and matter. He rejects both the Presocratic materialist assumption that the soul is simply non-organic matter, and the Platonic dualist claim that it must be something entirely non-bodily. He argues that soul is substance because it is the form of a natural body, and that the body is the matter informed by the soul. Although the soul is a substance distinct from the non-organic body (the collection of non-organic matter belonging to a living organism; see §13), it is not immaterial (if being immaterial excludes being composed of matter), nor is it independent of some non-organic body or other.

Aristotle assumes that the soul is the primary principle of life, and hence that it distinguishes the living from the non-living. A living organism is nourished, grows and diminishes, through itself – from a causal origin within itself rather than from the action of external agents. A living organism must, therefore, be teleologically ordered, since (for Aristotle) nutrition and growth cannot be understood without appeal to final causation (see TELEOLOGY).

If life must be conceived teleologically, and the soul is the *primary* principle of life, then the soul is form rather than matter. For the primary principle is whatever explains our vital activities; since these are goal-directed activities, their explanation must refer to the goal-directed features of the subject, and so to the form rather than the matter. If the soul is what we live by primarily, it must be the final cause of the body, and so a formal, not a material, aspect of the subject. Soul must, therefore, be substance as form.

Aristotle attributes to the soul the features of substantial form (see §13). (1) It is a substance that is irreducible to a material non-organic body (remote matter); to that extent the soul is incorporeal, and not just some ordinary material stuff. (2) It is the source of unity that makes a heap of material constituents into a single organism. For a collection of flesh and bones constitutes a single living organism in so far as it is teleologically organized; the activities of the single organism are the final cause of the movements of the different parts. Since a single organism has a single final cause, it has a single soul and a single body. (3) The identity and persistence of the soul determine the identity and persistence of the creature that has it. If something has a soul in so far as it has life, then Socrates perishes if and only if his soul does. The truth of this Platonic claim (*Phaedo* 115c–e) does not imply Platonic dualism. (4) The definition of a soul must mention the proximate material subject (the organic body and its parts) whose capacities are actualized in the functions of the organism (*Metaphysics* 1036b28–30). A soul must be non-coincidentally connected to a specific sort of organic body (*On the Soul* 407b20–4).

Some of the puzzles in Aristotle's doctrine of substantial form arise in his doctrine of soul and body. If, for instance, he recognizes particular substantial forms, then he also recognizes (as the previous paragraph assumes) the individual souls of Socrates and Callias; if, however, he recognizes only one substantial form for each species, then he recognizes only one soul for human beings, another for horses, and so on.

Since the soul is the form of the living body, an account of the different 'parts' or 'capacities' (or 'faculties'; *dynameis*) of the soul does not describe the different physiological processes underlying the different activities of a living organism, but describes their formal and goal-directed aspects. Aristotle describes the capacities that distinguish the different types of souls: nutrition (characteristic of plants), perception and appearance (characteristic of animals) and rational thought (characteristic of rational animals) (see PSYCHĒ). He describes some of the physiological bases of these psychic capacities in the shorter treatises on natural philosophy, including the *Parva Naturalia*, the *Movement of Animals* and the *Progression of Animals*.

18 Perception

To define perception, Aristotle returns to his contrast between form and matter. Perception happens in so far as (1) the perceiver becomes like the object (*On the Soul* 417a18); (2) the perceiver that was potentially *F* (for example, white) becomes actually *F* when it perceives the actually *F* object (418a3); (3) the perceiver acquires the form, but not the matter, of the object (424a18–24). These descriptions express a realist view of perception and its objects; Aristotle assumes in (2) that an object is actually white, square, and so on in its own right, before we perceive it.

He is sometimes taken to imply in (1) that perception requires physical similarity; but (3) counts against this interpretation. A sense receives the form without the matter in the way in which a house without matter is in the soul of the architect before the house is built. In the latter case, nothing that looks like a house is in the builder, but features of the house correspond to features of the builder's design. Similarly, when we hear a tune, our ears do not necessarily sound like the tune, but a state of us systematically corresponds to the tune (as features of a map correspond to features of the area it maps).

A 'common sense' perceives common properties of sensible objects, such as size, shape and number, which are all perceived through the perception of motion (*On the Soul* 425a14–20). This is not a sixth sense independent of the other five, but the result of the cooperation of the five senses. Aristotle argues that we can explain our grasp of these common properties without supposing that they are objects of intellect rather than sense (contrast Plato, *Theaetetus* 184–6).

19 Appearance and thought

Appearance (or 'imagination'; *phantasia*) links perception to goal-directed movement. A lion sees or smells a deer; it takes pleasure in the prospect of eating the deer, and so wants to catch the deer. To connect perception with pleasure and desire, we need to say how the deer appears to the lion (as prey); this is what Aristotle calls the lion's appearance of the deer (*On the Soul* III 3, 7).

Aristotle denies that this appearance constitutes a belief (*doxa*). He argues that belief requires reason and inference, which non-human animals lack; in his view, they lack any grasp of a universal, and have only appearances and memory of particulars (*Nicomachean Ethics* 1147b4–5). The operations of sense, memory and experience are necessary, but not sufficient, for the grasp of a universal that is expressed in concepts and beliefs (*Posterior Analytics* II 19; *Metaphysics* I 1).

Concepts and beliefs require intellect (*nous*) actualized in 'understanding' or 'thinking' (*noein*; *On the Soul* III 4) (see NOUS). Thought differs from perception in so far as it grasps universal essences – for example, what flesh is, as opposed to flesh itself. Perception does not include grasp of the universal as such; in grasping the universal, we recognize some feature of our experience as a ground for attributing the universal to a particular that we experience.

To explain how the mind is capable of grasping universals when we interact causally with particular perceptible objects, Aristotle distinguishes two aspects of intellect – passive and 'productive' (or 'active' or 'agent') – claiming that these two aspects must combine to produce thought of universals (*On the Soul* III 5). He does not say how productive intellect contributes to our grasp of universals. Later interpreters suggest that productive intellect abstracts the aspects relevant to the universal from the other features of particulars that are combined with them in perception (Aquinas, *Summa theologiae* 1a q.79 a.3).

Aristotle takes the presence of this productive intellect to be necessary for any thinking at all. Moreover, he believes that productive intellect is capable of existing without a body. He still maintains his belief in the inseparability of soul from body; for since productive intellect is not a type of soul, its separate existence is not the separate existence of a soul.

20 Desire and voluntary action

Perception, appearance and thought are connected to goal-directed movement by means of desire. The appearance of something as desirable is the source of an animal's tendency to pursue one sort of thing rather than another. External objects, however, appear desirable to different agents in different ways. Aristotle distinguishes the appetite (*epithymia*) that animals have from the wish (rational desire; *boulēsis*) that only rational agents have; appetite is for the pleasant and wish is for the good (*On the Soul* 414b2–6, 432b5–7, *Politics* 1253a15–18).

A rational agent's wish differs from appetite in so far as it is guided by deliberation resting on one's conception of one's good. Such a conception extends beyond one's present inclinations both at a particular time and over time. Rational agents are aware of themselves as extending into past and future. Deliberation that is guided by reference to these broader aspects of one's aims and nature results in the rational choice that Aristotle calls 'decision' (*prohairesis*; *Nicomachean Ethics* III 3).

Agents who act on desire and appearance also act voluntarily (*hekousiōs*), in so far as they act on some internal principle (*archē*). While voluntary action is not confined to rational agents, their voluntary action has special significance, because it is an appropriate basis for praise and blame. Since it has an internal principle, it is in our control as rational agents, and therefore we are justly praised and blamed for it. We are held responsible for our actions in so far as they reflect our character and decisions (*Nicomachean Ethics* III 1–5).

Aristotle's defence of his belief that we are appropriately responsible agents does not confront the questions later raised by Epicurus' claim that responsibility is incompatible with the complete causal determination of our actions (see EPICUREANISM). An incompatibilist position is ascribed to Aristotle by Alexander in *On Fate*. Aristotle neither explicitly presents an incompatibilist position nor explicitly endorses a compatibilist position of the sort later defended by the Stoics.

A discussion of time, truth and necessity (the 'Sea Battle'; *De Interpretatione* 9) has suggested to some interpreters that Aristotle is an indeterminist. His opponent is a fatalist, who assumes that (1) future-tensed statements about human actions (for example, 'There will be a sea battle tomorrow') were true in the past, and infers that (2) the future is necessarily determined, independently of what we choose. Aristotle certainly rejects (2). If he accepts the validity of the fatalist's argument, and rejects (1), then he accepts indeterminism.

An alternative reply to the fatalist would be to accept (1) and to deny the validity of the argument. We might argue that the past truth of statements about my actions does not imply that my actions are determined independently of my choices. If on Friday Socrates decides to walk, and he acts on his decision on Friday, then it was true on Thursday that Socrates would walk on Friday, and also true that on Friday he would act on his decision to walk, but it was not true on Thursday that he would walk whether or not he decided to (see STOICISM). Probably Aristotle accepts this alternative reply to the fatalist, and hence does not endorse indeterminism.

21 The human good

Aristotle's account of rational agents, choice, deliberation and action is an appropriate starting point for his ethical theory. Ethics is concerned with the praiseworthy and blameworthy actions and states of character of rational agents; that is why it concerns virtues (praiseworthy states) and vices (blameworthy states) (see ARETĒ).

Aristotle's ethical theory is mostly contained in three treatises: the *Magna Moralia*, the *Eudemian Ethics* and the *Nicomachean Ethics*. The titles of the last two works may reflect a tradition that Eudemus (a member of the Lyceum) and Nicomachus (the son of Aristotle and Herpyllis) edited Aristotle's lectures. The *Magna Moralia* is widely agreed not to have been written by Aristotle; some believe, with good reason, that it contains a student's notes on an early course of lectures by Aristotle. The *Eudemian Ethics* is now widely agreed to be authentic, and generally (not universally) and reasonably taken to be earlier than the *Nicomachean Ethics*. Three books (*Nicomachean Ethics* V–VII = *Eudemian Ethics* IV–VI) are assigned by the manuscripts to both the *Eudemian Ethics* and the *Nicomachean Ethics*.

Aristotle conceives 'ethics' (*Magna Moralia* 1181a24) as a part of political science; he treats the *Nicomachean Ethics* and the *Politics* as parts of a single inquiry (*Nicomachean Ethics* X 9). Ethics seeks to discover the good for an individual and a community (*Nicomachean Ethics* I 2), and so it begins with an examination of happiness (*eudaimonia*). ('Wellbeing' and 'welfare' are alternative renderings of *eudaimonia* that may avoid some of the misleading associations carried by 'happiness'; see EUDAIMONIA.) Happiness is the right starting point for an ethical theory because, in Aristotle's view, rational agents necessarily choose and deliberate with a view to their ultimate good, which is happiness; it is the end that we want for its own sake, and for the sake of which we want other things (so that it is the ultimate non-instrumental good). If it is to be an ultimate end, happiness must be complete (or 'final'; *teleion*) and self-sufficient (*Nicomachean Ethics* I 1–5, 7).

To find a more definite account of the nature of this ultimate and complete end, Aristotle argues from the human function (*ergon*), the characteristic activity that is essential to a human being in the same way that a purely nutritive life is essential to a plant and a life guided by sense perception and desire is essential to an animal (*Nicomachean Ethics* I 7). Since a human being is essentially a rational agent, the essential activity of a human being is a life guided by practical reason. The good life for a human being must be good for a being with the essential activity of a human being; hence it must be a good life guided by practical reason, and hence it must be a life in accordance with the virtue (*aretē*) that is needed for achieving one's good. The human good, therefore, is an actualization of the soul in accordance with complete virtue in a complete life. This 'complete virtue' appears to include the various virtues described in the following books of the *Nicomachean Ethics*; this appearance, however, may be challenged by *Nicomachean Ethics* X (see §26).

22 Virtue of character

From the general conception of happiness Aristotle infers the general features of a virtue of character (*ēthikēaretē*; *Nicomachean Ethics* I 13). He agrees with Plato in recognizing both rational and non-rational desires (see PLATO §14). One's soul is in a virtuous condition in so far as the non-rational elements cooperate with reason; in this condition human beings fulfil their function well. The argument from the human function does not make it clear what states of a rational agent count as fulfilling the human function. Aristotle seeks to make this clearer, first through his general account of virtue of character, and then through his sketches of the individual virtues.

A virtue of character must be a 'mean' or 'intermediate' state, since it must achieve the appropriate cooperation between rational and non-rational desires; such a state is intermediate between complete indulgence of non-rational desires and complete suppression of them. (Aristotle is not recommending 'moderation' – for example, a moderate degree of anger or pleasure – in all circumstances.) The demand for cooperation between desires implies that virtue is more than simply control over desires; mere control is 'continence' (*enkrateia*) rather than genuine virtue.

The task of moral education, therefore, is to harmonize non-rational desires with practical reason. Virtuous people allow reasonable satisfaction to their appetites; they do not suppress all their fears; they do not disregard all their feelings of pride or shame or resentment (*Nicomachean Ethics* 1126a3–8), or their desire for other people's good opinion. Aristotle's sketches of the different virtues show how different non-rational desires can cooperate with practical reason.

23 Virtue, practical reason and incontinence

A virtuous person makes a decision (*prohairesis*) to do the virtuous action for its own sake. The correct decision requires deliberation; the virtue of intellect that ensures good deliberation is prudence (or 'wisdom', *phronēsis*; *Nicomachean Ethics* VI 4–5); hence the mean in which a virtue lies must be determined by the sort of reason by which the prudent person would determine it (1107a1–2). Virtue of character is, therefore, inseparable from prudence. Each virtue is subject to the direction of prudence because each virtue aims at what is best, as identified by prudence.

In claiming that prudence involves deliberation, Aristotle also emphasizes the importance of its grasping the relevant features of a particular situation; we need to grasp the right particulars if deliberation is to result in a correct decision about what to do here and now. The right moral choice requires experience of particular situations, since general rules cannot be applied mechanically. Aristotle describes the relevant aspect of prudence as a sort of perception or intuitive understanding of the right aspects of particular situations (*Nicomachean Ethics* VI 8, 11).

These aspects of prudence distinguish the virtuous person from 'continent' and 'incontinent' people (*Nicomachean Ethics* VII 1–10). Aristotle accepts the reality of incontinent action (*akrasia*), rejecting Socrates' view that only ignorance of what is better and worse underlies apparent incontinence (see SOCRATES §6; AKRASIA). He argues that incontinents make the right decision, but act contrary to it. Their failure to stick to their decision is the result of strong non-rational desires, not simply of cognitive error. Still, Aristotle agrees with Socrates in believing that ignorance is an important component of a correct explanation of incontinence, because no one can act contrary to a correct decision fully accepted at the very moment of incontinent action.

The error of incontinents lies in their failure to harmonize the demands of their appetites with the requirements of virtue; their strong appetites cause them to lose part of the reasoning that formed their decision. When they act, they fail to see clearly how their general principles apply to their present situation. If their failure results from an error in deliberation, it is clear why Aristotle insists that incontinent people lack prudence.

24 Choice, virtue, and pleasure

It is initially puzzling that virtuous people decide to act virtuously for its own sake as a result of deliberation. If they decide on virtuous action for its own sake, then their deliberation causes them to choose it as an end in itself, not simply as a means. Decision and deliberation, however, are not about ends but about 'the things promoting ends' (*ta pros ta telē*, often rendered 'means to ends'). Aristotle's description of the virtuous person, then, seems to attribute to decision a role that is excluded by his explicit account of decision.

This puzzle is less severe once we recognize that Aristotle regards different sorts of things as 'promoting' an end. Sometimes he means (1) that the action is external and purely instrumental to the end; in this way buying food 'promotes' eating dinner. Sometimes, however, he means (2) that the action is a part or component of the end, or that performing the action partly constitutes the achieving of the end; in this way eating the main course 'promotes' eating dinner. Deliberation about this second sort of 'promotion' shows that an action is worth choosing for its own sake, in so far as it partly constitutes our end.

This role for deliberation explains how virtuous people can decide, as a result of deliberation, on virtuous action for its own sake; they choose it as a part of happiness, not as a merely instrumental means. Prudence finds the actions that promote happiness in so far as they are parts of the happy life. Such actions are to be chosen for their own sake, as being their own end; they are not simply instrumental means to some further end. The virtuous person's decision results from deliberation about the composition of happiness; virtuous people decide on the actions that, by being non-instrumentally good, are components of happiness in their own right.

Aristotle's demand for the virtuous person to decide on the virtuous action for its own sake is connected with two further claims: (1) the virtuous person must take pleasure in virtuous action as such; (2) in doing so, the virtuous person has the pleasantest life. In these claims Aristotle relies on his views about the nature of pleasure and its role in happiness (*Nicomachean Ethics* VII 11–14, X 1–5).

He denies that pleasure is some uniform sensation to which different kinds of pleasant action are connected only causally (in the way that the reading of many boring books on different subjects might induce the same feeling of boredom). Instead he argues that the specific pleasure taken in *x* rather than *y* is internally related to doing *x* rather than *y*, and essentially depends on pursuing *x* for *x*'s own sake. Pleasure is a 'supervenient end' (1174b31–3) resulting from an activity that one pursues as an activity (*praxis* or *energeia*) rather than a mere process or production (*kinēsis* or *poiēsis*).

Aristotle insists, following Plato's *Philebus*, that the value of the pleasure depends on the value of the activity on which the pleasure supervenes (1176a3–29). The virtuous person has the pleasantest life, but the pleasantest life cannot aim exclusively at pleasure.

25 Virtue, friendship and the good of others

The virtuous person's deliberation, identifying the mean in relation to different desires and different situations, is articulated in the different virtues of character (described in *Nicomachean Ethics* III–V). The different virtues are concerned with the regulation of non-rational desires (for example, bravery, temperance, good temper), external goods (for example, magnificence, magnanimity) and social situations (for example, truthfulness, wit). Some concern the good of others to some degree (bravery, good temper, generosity).

Aristotle's Greek for virtue of character, *ēthikēaretē*, is rendered into Latin as 'virtus moralis'. The English rendering 'moral virtue' is defensible, since the virtues of character as a whole display the impartial concern for others that is often ascribed to morality. They are unified by the aim of the virtuous person, who decides on the virtuous action because it is 'fine' (*kalon*). Fine action systematically promotes the good of others; we must aim at it if we are to find the mean that is characteristic of a virtue (1122b6–7).

A second unifying element in the virtues, inseparable from concern for the fine, is their connection to justice (V 1–2). Aristotle takes justice to be multivocal (see §4), and distinguishes general justice from the specific virtue concerned with the prevention and rectification of certain specific types of injustices. General justice is the virtue of character that aims specifically at the common good of a community. Since it is not a different state of character from the other virtues, they must incorporate concern for the common good.

To explain why concern for the good of others, and for a common good, is part of the life that aims at one's own happiness, Aristotle examines friendship (*philia*; *Nicomachean Ethics* VIII–IX). All three of the main types of friendship (for pleasure, for advantage and for the good) seek the good of the other person. Only the best type – friendship for the good between virtuous people – includes *A*'s concern for *B*'s good for *B*'s own sake and because of *B*'s essential character (*Nicomachean Ethics* VIII 1–4).

In the best sort of friendship, the friend is 'another self'; *A* takes the sorts of attitudes to *B* that *A* also takes to *A*. Aristotle infers that friendship is part of a complete and self-sufficient life (IX 9–11). Friendship involves sharing the activities one counts as especially important in one's life, and especially the sharing of reasoning and thinking. Friends cooperate in deliberation, decision and action; and the thoughts and actions of each provide reasons for the future thoughts and actions of the other. The cooperative aspects of friendship more fully realize each person's own capacities as a rational agent, and so promote each person's happiness. Hence the full development of a human being requires concern for the good of others.

26 Two conceptions of happiness?

Although Aristotle emphasizes the other-regarding, social aspects of happiness, he also advocates pure intellectual activity (or 'study', *theōria*) – the contemplation of scientific and philosophical truths, apart from any attempt to apply them to practice (*Nicomachean Ethics* X 6–8). The connection between the human function and human happiness (see §21) implies that contemplation is a supremely important element in happiness. For contemplation is the highest fulfilment of our nature as rational beings; it is the sort of rational activity that we share with the gods, who are rational beings with no need to apply reason to practice. Aristotle infers that contemplation is the happiest life available to us, in so far as we have the rational intellects we share with gods (see §16).

According to one interpretation, Aristotle actually identifies contemplation with happiness: contemplation is the only non-instrumental good that is part of happiness, and the moral virtues are to be valued – from the point of view of happiness – simply as means to contemplation. If this is Aristotle's view, it is difficult to see how the virtues of character are even the best instrumental means to happiness. Even if some virtuous actions are instrumental means to contemplation, it is difficult to see how the motives demanded of the virtuous person (see §§24–5) are always useful, rather than distracting, for those who aim at contemplation.

Probably, however, Aristotle means that contemplation is the best component of happiness. If we were pure intellects with no other desires and no bodies, contemplation would be the whole of our good. Since, however, we are not in fact merely intellects (*Nicomachean Ethics* 1178b3–7), Aristotle recognizes that the good must be the good of the whole human being. Contemplation is not the complete good for a human being.

If this is Aristotle's view, then contemplation fits the conception of happiness that is upheld in the rest of the *Nicomachean Ethics* and in the other ethical works. The virtues of character, and the actions expressing them, deserve to be chosen for their own sakes as components of happiness. In the virtuous person, they regulate one's choice of other goods, and so they also regulate one's choices about contemplation. The *Politics* may be taken to develop this conception of happiness, since (in book VII) it sets contemplation in the context of a social order regulated by the moral virtues.

27 Politics: ideal states

The *Politics* pursues three connected aims: (1) it completes the discussion of happiness, by showing what kind of political community achieves the human good (mainly books I, II and VII); (2) it sets out moral and political principles that allow us to understand and to criticize the different sorts of actual states and their constitutions (mainly books III and IV); (3) it offers some proposals for improving actual states (mainly books V and VI). The order of the books probably reflects Aristotle's aim of describing an ideal state after examining the strengths and weaknesses of actual states.

An individual's desire for happiness leads eventually to the city. A human being is a 'political animal', because essential human capacities and aims are completely fulfilled only in a political community; hence (given the connection between the human function and the human good) the individual's happiness must involve the good of fellow members of a community. The relevant sort of community is a *polis* ('city' or 'state') – a self-governing community whose proper function (not completely fulfilled by every actual political community) is to aim at the common good of its citizens, who (normally) share in ruling and in being ruled. The city is the all-inclusive community, of which the other communities are parts, since it aims at advantage not merely for some present concern but for the whole of life (*Nicomachean Ethics* 1160a9–30). Since happiness is complete and self-sufficient, the city is a complete and self-sufficient community (*Politics* 1252b28), aiming at a complete and self-sufficient life that includes all the goods needed for a happy life.

The connection between human nature, human good and the political community is most easily understood from Aristotle's account of friendship. Complete friendship, which requires living together and sharing rational discourse and thought, is restricted to individuals with virtuous characters,

but this is not the only type of friendship that achieves self-realization in cooperation; a similar defence can be given for the friendship of citizens. Collective deliberation about questions of justice and benefit contributes to the virtuous person's self-realization because it extends the scope of one's practical reason and deliberation beyond one's own life and activities. Since the city is comprehensive, seeking to plan for everything that is needed for the complete good, a rational agent has good reason to want to share in its deliberations.

Since, then, Aristotle believes that political activity contributes in its own right to the human good, he argues against a 'social contract' theory that assigns a restricted instrumental function to the state (safety, or mutual protection, or the safeguarding of what justly belongs to each person; *Politics* III 9). Political life is to be valued for itself, apart from any instrumental benefit; the best city aims at the development of the moral virtues and at the political participation of all who are capable of them.

In the light of these aims, Aristotle describes the best city. It has to assume favourable external conditions (geographical and economic) to allow the development of political life. Its criteria for citizenship are restricted, since they exclude everyone (including women and manual labourers) whom Aristotle regards as incapable of developing the virtues of character. Within the class of citizens, however, Aristotle is concerned to avoid gross inequality of wealth and to ensure that everyone shares both in ruling and in being ruled. The institutions of the best state provide the political, social, economic and educational basis for the practice of the moral virtues and for contemplation.

28 Politics: imperfect states

Just as a correct conception of happiness is the basis of the ideal city, various incorrect conceptions of happiness define mistaken aims for different cities. These mistaken aims underlie the different conceptions of justice that are embodied in the constitutions of different cities. Partisans of oligarchy, for instance, take happiness to consist in wealth; they treat the city as a business partnership (*Politics* 1280a25–31). Partisans of democracy take happiness to consist simply in the satisfaction of desire; they assume that if people are equal in the one respect of being free rather than slaves, they are equal altogether, and should have an equal share in ruling (1280a24–5). Neither view is completely mistaken, since neither wealth nor freedom is irrelevant to questions of justice, but each is one-sided.

These one-sided views cause errors about the just distribution of political power or other goods. The proper basis for assigning worth in distribution will be whatever is relevant for the common good, since that is the aim of general justice. Since a correct conception of the common good requires a correct conception of happiness, a correct answer to the question about distribution must appeal to a true conception of happiness.

The criticism of existing constitutions seeks to show both how they fall short of the norms that are met by the ideal state, and how they can be improved. Aristotle wants to describe not only the ideal state, but also the best organization of each political system. In some circumstances, he believes, economic, social and demographic facts may make (for example) democracy or oligarchy difficult to avoid. Still, an imperfect constitution can be improved, by attention to the aspects of justice, and hence the aspects of happiness, that this constitution tends to ignore. Even when Aristotle may appear to be engaged in empirical political sociology, or to be offering hints for the survival of a particular regime, he is guided by the moral and political principles that he defends in the more theoretical parts of the *Politics*.

29 Rhetoric and poetics

In Aristotle's classification, rhetoric and poetics (*poiētikē*; literally 'productive') count as 'productive' rather than 'practical' disciplines; they are concerned with 'production' (*poiēsis*) – purely instrumental action aiming at some external end – rather than with 'action' (*praxis*) – action that is also an end in itself. Rhetoric is a productive discipline in so far as it aims at persuasion in public speaking, and seeks the arguments, diction, language, metaphor, appeals to emotion and so on, that are most likely to persuade different types of audiences. Hence Aristotle's treatise on rhetoric contains sections on these different topics. Dialectic and logic are useful to a student of rhetoric, even though rhetoric does not aim at the truth; for true or plausible claims tend to be persuasive. *Rhetoric* II deals with another aspect of rhetorical persuasion, by describing the different emotions; the student of rhetoric must know how to arouse emotions in an audience.

Aristotle also takes his moral and political theory to be relevant to rhetoric, for two main reasons. (1) Rhetoric is concerned with the moral and political issues discussed in public assemblies or in courts, and the orator needs to be familiar with the convictions of a given audience. (2) Even more important, the orator should be guided by correct moral and political convictions (without necessarily grasping their philosophical basis). Aristotle does not endorse the conception of oratory as a technique of persuasion that is indifferent to the moral and political aims that it serves. This conception of oratory arouses Plato's criticism in the *Gorgias* (see PLATO §7) Aristotle replies to such criticism by arguing that the orator should learn, and should be guided by, correct principles. He sets out some of these in the *Rhetoric*.

Moral and political principles are also relevant to Aristotle's treatment of literary criticism in the *Poetics*. The surviving part of this treatise deals mainly with tragedy. Some of it is similar to the *Rhetoric*, in so far as it discusses matters of technique and psychology; Aristotle describes the various sorts of plots, characters and dramatic devices that affect the audience in different ways. He is also concerned, however, about the moral aspects of tragedy; in this he may be responding to the criticisms of tragedy in book X of Plato's *Republic*. He argues that tragedy achieves its appropriate effect when it directs pity, fear, sympathy and revulsion at the appropriate sorts of people and situations; and he examines the plots and characters of various tragedies from this point of view (see KATHARSIS; MIMĒSIS).

30 Influence

Some aspects of Aristotle's philosophy have become so familiar that we do not even attribute them to him. When we say that an event was a mere 'coincidence', or that an ignorant person is 'ill-informed', or that someone's behaviour is forming good or bad 'habits', our vocabulary expresses Aristotelian assumptions, transmitted through Latin translations and interpretations.

The explicit influence of Aristotle's philosophical works and theories has been variable. In Hellenistic philosophy, he is not prominently cited or discussed; some have even doubted whether the major Stoics knew his works. From the first century BC, however, the study of Aristotle revived. This revival produced philosophers defending an Aristotelian position, often incorporating Stoic or Platonist elements, but sometimes sharpening contrasts between Aristotle and the Hellenistic schools. These Aristotelians began a long series of Greek commentaries (lasting until the sixth century AD). Many of the later commentators were Neoplatonists; some of whom tried to reconcile Aristotelian with Platonic doctrines (see NEOPLATONISM; PORPHYRY).

Between the sixth and the thirteenth centuries, most of Aristotle's works were unavailable in western Europe, although he was still studied in the Byzantine empire and the Islamic world. Two leading figures in the revival of Aristotelian studies and of Aristotelian philosophy in medieval Europe were the translator William of Moerbeke and Thomas

Aquinas. Aquinas' attempt to combine Aristotelian philosophy with orthodox Christian theology was at first rejected by ecclesiastical authority, but then came to be accepted (see AQUINAS, T.).

The 'scholastic' philosophy of Aquinas and his successors is often opposed, but often presupposed, by Descartes, Locke, Hobbes and many of their successors, who often do not distinguish it from Aristotle's own philosophy. The reader who compares their representation of the scholastic position with Aristotle's own works (or with Aquinas) will often be surprised by the sharp differences between Aristotle's (and Aquinas') own positions and the positions that are attributed to him by the seventeenth-century philosophers who reject his authority.

Modern historical study of Aristotle begins in the early nineteenth century. It has led to philosophical reassessment, and his works have once again become a source of philosophical insight and argument. Many of the themes of Aristotelian philosophy – the nature of substance, the relation of form to matter, the relation of mind to body, the nature of human action, the role of virtues and actions in morality – have reappeared as issues in philosophical debates, and Aristotle's contributions to these debates have influenced the course of philosophical discussion.

In some ways, Aristotle has suffered from his success. At different times he has been regarded as the indisputable authority in astronomy, biology, logic and ethics; hence he has represented the traditional position against which reformers have revolted. If he is regarded neither as the indisputable authority nor as a repository of antiquated and discarded doctrines, his permanent philosophical value can be more justly appreciated.

See also: ARCHĒ; BEING; CHANGE; DUALISM; FRIENDSHIP; METAPHYSICS; PNEUMA; TELEOLOGICAL ETHICS; TENSE AND TEMPORAL LOGIC; VIRTUE ETHICS; VIRTUES AND VICES

References and further reading

Ackrill, J.L. (1981) *Aristotle the Philosopher*, Oxford: Oxford University Press. (This and Barnes (1982) are the best short introductions.)

Barnes, J. (1982) *Aristotle*, Oxford: Oxford University Press. (Along with Ackril (1981), one of the best short introductions to Aristotle.)

T.H. IRWIN

ARITHMETIC, PHILOSOPHICAL ISSUES IN

The philosophy of arithmetic gains its special character from issues arising out of the status of the principle of mathematical induction. Indeed, it is just at the point where proof by induction enters that arithmetic stops being trivial. The propositions of elementary arithmetic – quantifier-free sentences such as '$7 + 5 = 12$' – can be decided mechanically: once we know the rules for calculating, it is hard to see what mathematical interest can remain. As soon as we allow sentences with one universal quantifier, however – sentences of the form '$(\forall x)\, f(x) = 0$' – we have no decision procedure either in principle or in practice, and can state some of the most profound and difficult problems in mathematics. (Goldbach's conjecture that every even number greater than 2 is the sum of two primes, formulated in 1742 and still unsolved, is of this type.)

It seems natural to regard as part of what we mean by natural numbers that they should obey the principle of induction. But this exhibits a form of circularity known as 'impredicativity': the statement of the principle involves quantification over properties of numbers, but to understand this quantification we must assume a prior grasp of the number concept, which it was our intention to define. It is nowadays a commonplace to draw a distinction between impredicative definitions, which are illegitimate, and impredicative specifications, which are not. The conclusion we should draw in this case is that the principle of induction on its own does not provide a non-circular route to an understanding of the natural number concept. We therefore need an independent argument. Four broad strategies have been attempted, which we shall consider in turn.

See also: FREGE, G.; HUSSERL, E.

MICHAEL POTTER

ARNAULD, ANTOINE (1612–94)

Antoine Arnauld, a leading theologian and Cartesian philosopher, was one of the most important and interesting figures of the seventeenth century. As the most prominent spokesperson and defender of the Jansenist community based at Port-Royal, almost all Arnauld's efforts were devoted to theological matters. But early on, with his largely constructive objections to Descartes' *Meditations* in 1641, he established a reputation as an analytically rigorous and insightful philosophical thinker. He went on to become perhaps Descartes' most faithful and vociferous defender. He found Cartesian metaphysics, particularly mind–body dualism, to be of great value for the Christian religion. In a celebrated debate with Nicolas Malebranche, Arnauld advanced something like a direct realist account of perceptual acquaintance by arguing that the representative ideas that mediate human knowledge and perception are not immaterial objects distinct from the mind's perceptions, but are just those perceptions themselves. His criticisms of Leibniz gave rise to another important debate. He also co-authored the so-called 'Port-Royal Logic', the most famous and successful logic of the early modern period. The underlying motives in all Arnauld's philosophical writings were, however, theological, and his greatest concern was to safeguard God's omnipotence and to defend what he took to be the proper Catholic view on questions of grace and divine providence

See also: DUALISM; FREEDOM, DIVINE; PERCEPTION

STEVEN NADLER

ART, ABSTRACT

The use of the term 'abstract' as a category of visual art dates from the second decade of the twentieth century, when painters and sculptors had turned away from verisimilitude and launched such modes of abstraction as Cubism, Orphism, Futurism, Rayonism and Suprematism. Two subcategories may be distinguished: first, varieties of figurative representation that strongly schematize, and second, completely nonfigurative or nonobjective modes of design (in the widest sense of that term). Both stand opposed to classic representationalism (realism, naturalism, illusionism, mimeticism) understood as the commitment to a relatively full depiction of the subject matter and construed broadly enough to cover the traditional 'high art' canon through to Post-Impressionism. Analytic and Synthetic Cubism are model cases of the first subcategory while Mondrian's neoplasticism and Pollock's classic drip works are paradigms of the second. Though the effect was revolutionary, the positive motivations for this degree of abstraction in visual art were not wholly new. What was new was the elevation of previously subordinate aims to the front rank and the pursuit of certain principal aims in isolation from the full pictorial package. Thus abstract art variously celebrates structural and colour properties of objects, scenes and patterns; effects of motion, light and atmosphere; aspects of perceptual process, whether normal or expressively loaded; and forms expressing cosmic conceptions, visionary states or utopian ambitions. With a few exceptions (for example, the Futurists) the founders of abstract art were far from lucid or forthcoming about the significance of their work, and viewers have found successive waves of abstraction initially baffling and even offensive. But abstract art now forms a secure part of the 'high art' canon, though generally its appeal is less well understood than that of the classic modes of representation. Criticisms of abstract art have also become more lucid.

The chief philosophical issues affecting abstract art concern the definition of the term and the delineation of subordinate types; the relation between abstraction and other modes of avant-garde art that superficially resemble it; the magnitude of the artistic values so far achieved by the various forms; and finally the theoretical limits of significance attainable by abstraction as compared with the limits encountered in figurative art.

See also: ADORNO, T.W.; DEPICTION; EMOTION IN RESPONSE TO ART; FORMALISM IN ART

JOHN H. BROWN

ART AND EMOTION

See EMOTION IN RESPONSE TO ART

ART AND MORALITY

A complex set of questions is raised by an examination of the relationship between art and morality. First there is a set of empirical considerations about the effect that works of art have on us – one obviously contentious case is that of pornography. Many would argue that the artistic merits of a work are independent of any attitudes or actions it may lead us to adopt or perform. This claim does not survive scrutiny, however, though there is a distinction to be drawn between artistic value and the value of art as a whole. Though there are no coercive arguments to show that we have to take into account the moral qualities of works of art, it is in practice very difficult to ignore them, especially when the point of the work is insistently moral, or when the work is conspicuously depraved.

There is a long tradition, dating back to Plato, of regarding art with suspicion for its power over our emotions, and much of Western aesthetic theorizing has been a response to Plato's challenge. The longest-lasting defence justified art in terms of a combination of pleasure and instruction, though the two never hit it off as well as was hoped. In the early nineteenth century a new, more complex account of art was offered, notably by Hegel, in the form of a historicized view in which art is one of the modes by which we come to self-awareness; the emphasis altered from truth to an independently existing reality to truthfulness to our own natures, as we explore them by creating art. Taken into the social sphere, this became a doctrine of the importance of art as an agent of political consciousness, operating in subtle ways to undermine the view of reality imposed on us by the ideologies that hold us captive.

See also: AESTHETICS AND ETHICS; ARISTOTLE; ART, UNDERSTANDING OF; ART, VALUE OF; ART WORKS, ONTOLOGY OF; COLLINGWOOD, R.G.; CROCE, B.; EMOTION IN RESPONSE TO ART; HEGEL, G.W.F. §8; JOHNSON, S.; KANT, I. §12; MORALITY AND EMOTIONS; MURDOCH, I.; POETRY; PORNOGRAPHY; SCHILLER, J.C.F.; TOLSTOY, L.N.

MICHAEL TANNER

ART AND TRUTH

Some things are true within the world of a literary work. It is true, in the world evoked by *Madame Bovary*, that Emma Roualt married Charles Bovary. Here, however, we are not concerned with truth *in* fiction but rather with what it is for a work of art to be true of, or true to, the actual world. Representational works represent states of affairs, or objects portrayed in a certain way. The concept of truth naturally gets a grip here, because we can ask whether the represented state of affairs actually exists in the world, or whether a represented object exists and really is the way it is represented to be, or whether a representation of a kind of thing offers a genuinely representative example of that kind. If so, we could call the work true, or true in the given respect.

A work will often get us to respond to what is portrayed in a way similar to what our response would have been to the real thing – we are moved to fear and pity by objects we know are merely fictions. But a work could also *portray* characters responding in certain ways to the imaginary situations it conjures, often with the implication that the response is a likely human emotional or practical response to that situation, or a response to be expected of a character of the given type, and we could reasonably call the work true if we believed the portrayed reaction was a likely one.

Arguably, if we judge a work to be in some respect true to life, we must already have known that life was like that in order to make the judgment. But, interestingly, works of art appear to be able to portray situations that we have not experienced, in which the portrayal seems to warrant our saying that the work has shown (that is, taught) us a likely or plausible unfolding of the portrayed situation, or shown us what it would have been like to experience the situation. It is also said, especially of narrative fiction, that, because of its power to show us what various alternative imaginary situations would be like, it can enlighten us about how we ought to live.

So we may consider how a work of art might be a vehicle of truths about the actual world. This gives rise to a further question – sometimes called the problem of belief – of whether the value of a work of art *as* a piece of art is related to its truth. If a work implies or suggests that something is the case, ought I to value it more highly as art if I accept what it implies as the truth? Alternatively, should I take it as an aesthetic shortcoming if I do not?

See also: ART AND MORALITY; ART, VALUE OF; FICTIONAL ENTITIES; MURDOCH, I.; NARRATIVE

PAUL TAYLOR

ART CRITICISM

To criticize a work of art is to make a judgment of its overall merit or demerit and to support that judgment by reference to features it possesses. This activity is of great antiquity; we find Aristotle, for example, relating the excellence of Sophocles' *Oedipus Rex* to the excellence of its plot construction. Criticism became a topic in philosophy because reflection on the kinds of things said by critics generated various perplexities and in some cases encouraged a general scepticism about the possibility of criticism. Two general and related problems in particular have taxed philosophers. The first is the question of whether criticism is a rational activity, that is to say, whether critics can give reasons for their judgments that would persuade potential dissenters of the rightness of those judgments. The second, a matter to which Kant and Hume made notable contributions, is the problem of the objectivity of critical judgments, it being widely believed that critical appraisals are wholly subjective or just 'a matter of taste'. Arguments that use deductive or inductive reasoning to demonstrate the possibility of proofs of critical judgments are generally agreed to have failed. Another approach redescribes the critic altogether, not as someone who uses argument to prove their judgments to an audience, but as someone who aims to help the audience perceive features of the work of art and understand their role in the work.

See also: AESTHETIC CONCEPTS; ART, UNDERSTANDING OF; ART, VALUE OF; ARTIST'S INTENTION

COLIN LYAS

ART, DEFINITION OF

Many of the earliest definitions of art were probably intended to emphasize salient or important features for an audience already familiar with the concept, rather than to analyse the essence possessed by all art works and only by them. Indeed, it has been argued that art could not be defined any more rigorously, since no immutable essence is observable in its instances. But, on the one hand, this view faces difficulties in explaining the unity of the concept – similarities between them, for example, are insufficient to distinguish works of art from other things. And, on the other, it overlooks the attractive possibility that art is to be defined in terms of a relation between the activities of artists, the products that result and the audiences that receive them.

Two types of definition have come to prominence since the 1970s: the functional and procedural. The former regards something as art only if it serves the function for which we have art, usually said to be that of providing aesthetic experience. The latter regards something as art only if it has been baptized as such through an agent's application of the appropriate procedures. In the version where the agent takes their authority from their location within an informal institution, the 'artworld', proceduralism is known as the institutional theory. These definitional strategies are opposed in practice, if not in theory, because the relevant procedures are sometimes used apart from, or to oppose, the alleged function of art; obviously these theories disagree then about whether the outcome is art.

To take account of art's historically changing character a definition might take a recursive form, holding that something is art if it stands in an appropriate relation to previous art works: it is the location of an item within accepted art-making traditions that makes it a work of art. Theories developed in the 1980s have often taken this form. They variously see the crucial relation between the piece and the corpus of accepted works as, for example, a matter of the manner in which it is intended to be regarded, or of a shared style, or of its being forged by a particular kind of narrative.

See also: AESTHETIC CONCEPTS; ARTIST'S INTENTION; COLLINGWOOD, R.G.; CROCE, B.; DEFINITION; TOLSTOY, L.N.

STEPHEN DAVIES

ART, FORMALISM IN
See FORMALISM IN ART

ART, UNDERSTANDING OF

Art engages the understanding in many ways. Thus, confronted with an allegorical painting such as Van Eyk's *The Marriage of Arnolfini*, one might want to understand the significance of the objects it depicts. Similarly, confronted with an obscure poem, such as Eliot's *The Waste Land*, one might seek to understand what it means. Sometimes, too, we claim not to understand a work of art, a piece of music, say, when we are unable to derive enjoyment from it because we cannot see how it is organized or hangs together. Sometimes what challenges the understanding goes deeper, as when we ask why some things, including such notorious productions of the avant garde as the urinal exhibited by Marcel Duchamp, are called art at all. Some have also claimed that to understand a work of art we must understand its context. Sometimes the context referred to is that of the particular problems and aims of the individual artist in a certain tradition, as when the church of St Martin-in-the-Fields is understood as a contribution by its architect to the vexing problem of combining a tower with a classical façade. Sometimes the context is social, as when some Marxists argue that works of art can best be understood as reflections of the more or less inadequate economic organizations of the societies that gave rise to them. The understanding of art becomes a philosophical problem because, first, it is sometimes thought that one of the central tasks of interpretation is to understand the meaning of a work. However, recent writers, notably Derrida, query the notion of the meaning of a work as something to be definitively deciphered, and offer the alternative view of interpretation as an unending play with the infinitely varied meanings of the text. Second, a controversial issue has been the extent to which the judgment of works of art can be divorced from an understanding of the circumstances, both individual and cultural, of their making. Thus Clive Bell argued that to appreciate a work of art we need nothing more than a knowledge of its colours, shapes and spatial arrangements. Others, ranging from Wittgenstein to Marxists, have for a variety of different reasons argued that a work of art cannot be properly understood and appreciated without some understanding of its relation to the context of its creation, a view famously characterized by Beardsley and Wimsatt as the 'genetic fallacy'.

See also: ART AND MORALITY; ART AND TRUTH; ART CRITICISM; ART, VALUE OF; ARTIST'S INTENTION

COLIN LYAS

ART, VALUE OF

Art has as many kinds of value as there are points of view from which it can be evaluated. Moreover, the benefits of art vary with the role of the participant, for there are benefits that are specific to the creation, the performance and the mere appreciation of art. But in the philosophy of art one value is basic, namely the distinctive value of a work of art, its value *as* a work of art, which can be called its 'artistic value'. This value is intrinsic to a work in that it is determined by the intrinsic, rather than the instrumental, value of an informed experience of it, an experience of it in which it is understood. Artistic value is a matter of degree, but it is not a measurable quantity, and whether one work is better than another may be an indeterminate issue. A judgment about a work's artistic value claims validity, rightly or wrongly, not merely for the person who makes the judgment but for everyone. Both David Hume and Immanuel Kant tried to show how such a claim could be well-founded, but their attempts are usually considered failures, and there is no accepted solution to the problem they addressed. Many philosophers have been concerned with the relation between artistic value and other values. The most famous attack on art, founded on its supposed relation to other values, was made by Plato, who claimed that nearly all art has undesirable social consequences and so should be excluded from a decent society. Plato overlooked many possibilities, however, and the question of art's beneficial or harmful influence is a much more complex issue than he recognized.

See also: AESTHETICS AND ETHICS; ART AND MORALITY; ART AND TRUTH; ART, UNDERSTANDING OF; KANT, I. §12

MALCOLM BUDD

ART WORKS, ONTOLOGY OF

In trying to decide what kinds of thing art works are, the most natural starting point is the hypothesis that they are physical objects. This is plausible only for certain works, such as paintings and sculptures; in such cases we say that the work is a certain marked canvas or piece of stone. Even for these apparently favourable cases, though, there is a metaphysical objection to this proposal: that works and the physical objects identified with them do not possess the same properties and so cannot be identical. There is also an aesthetic objection: that the plausibility of the thesis for painting and sculpture rests on the false view that the authentic object made by the artist possesses aesthetically relevant features which no copy could possibly exemplify. Once it is acknowledged that paintings and sculptures are, in principle, reproducible in the way that novels and musical scores are, the motivation for thinking of the authentic canvas or stone as the work itself collapses.

For literary and musical works, the standard view is that they are structures: structures of word-types in the literary case and of sound-types in the musical case. This structuralist view is opposed by contextualism, which asserts that the identity conditions for works must take into account historical features involving their origin and modes of production. Contextualists claim that works with the same structure might have different historical features and ought, therefore, to count as distinct works.

Nelson Goodman has proposed that we divide works into autographic and allographic kinds; for autographic works, such as paintings, genuineness is determined partly by history of production: for allographic works, such as novels, it is determined in some other way. Our examination of the hypothesis that certain works are physical objects and our discussion of the structuralist/contextualist controversy will indicate grounds for thinking that Goodman's distinction does not provide an acceptable categorization of works.

A wholly successful ontology of art works would tell us what things are art works and what things are not; failing that, it would give us identity conditions for them, enabling us to say under what conditions this work and that are the same work. Since the complexity of the issues to be discussed quickly ramifies, it will be appropriate after a certain point to consider only the question of identity conditions. For simplicity, this entry concentrates on works of art that exemplify written literature, scored music and the plastic and pictorial arts.

See also: ART, UNDERSTANDING OF; STRUCTURALISM; TYPE/TOKEN DISTINCTION

GREGORY CURRIE

ARTIFICIAL INTELLIGENCE

Artificial intelligence (AI) tries to make computer systems (of various kinds) do what minds can do: interpreting a photograph as depicting a face; offering medical diagnoses; using and translating language; learning to do better next time.

AI has two main aims. One is technological: to build useful tools, which can help humans in activities of various kinds, or perform the activities for them. The other is psychological: to help us understand human (and animal) minds, or even intelligence in general.

Computational psychology uses AI concepts and AI methods in formulating and testing its theories. Mental structures and processes are described in computational terms. Usually, the theories are clarified, and their predictions tested, by running them on a computer program. Whether people perform the equivalent task in the same way is another question, which psychological experiments may help to answer. AI has shown that the human mind is more complex than psychologists had previously assumed, and that introspectively 'simple' achievements – many shared with animals – are even more difficult to mimic artificially than are 'higher' functions such as logic and mathematics.

There are deep theoretical disputes within AI about how best to model intelligence. Classical (symbolic) AI programs consist of formal rules for manipulating formal symbols; these are carried out sequentially, one after the other. Connectionist systems, also called neural networks, perform many simple processes in parallel (simultaneously); most work in a way described not by lists of rules, but by differential equations. Hybrid systems combine aspects of classical and connectionist AI. More recent approaches seek to construct adaptive autonomous agents, whose behaviour is self-directed rather than imposed from outside and which adjust to environmental conditions. Situated robotics builds robots that react directly to environmental cues, instead of following complex internal plans as classical robots do. The programs, neural networks and robots of evolutionary AI are produced not by detailed human design, but by automatic evolution (variation and selection). Artificial life studies the emergence of order and adaptive behaviour in general and is closely related to AI.

Philosophical problems central to AI include the following. Can classical or connectionist AI explain conceptualization and thinking? Can meaning be explained by AI? What sorts of mental representations are there (if any)? Can computers, or non-linguistic animals, have beliefs and desires? Could AI explain consciousness? Might intelligence be better explained by less intellectualistic approaches, based on the model of skills and know-how rather than explicit representation?

MARGARET A. BODEN

ARTISTIC EXPRESSION

Many kinds of psychological state can be expressed in or by works of art. But it is the artistic expression of emotion that has figured most prominently in philosophical discussions of art. Emotion is expressed in pictorial, literary and other representational works of art by the characters who are depicted or in other ways presented in the works. We often identify the emotions of such characters in much the same way as we ordinarily identify the emotions of others, but we might also have special knowledge of a character's emotional state, through direct access to their thoughts, for instance.

A central case of the expression of emotion by works of art is the expression of emotion by a purely musical work. What is the source of the emotion expressed by a piece of music? While art engages its audience, often calling forth an emotional response, its expressiveness does not consist in this power. It is not because an art work tends to make us feel sad, for instance, that we call it sad; rather, we react as we do because sadness is present in it. And while artists usually contrive the expressiveness of their art works, sometimes expressing their own emotions in doing so, their success in the former activity does not depend on their doing the latter. Moreover, the expressiveness achieved has an immediacy and transparency, like that of genuine tears, apparently at odds with this sophisticated, controlled form of self-expression. It is because art presents emotion with simple directness that it can be a vehicle for self-expression, not vice versa. But if emotions are the experiences of sentient beings, to whom do those expressed in art belong if not to the artist or audience? Perhaps they are those of a fictional persona. We may imagine personae who undergo the emotions expressed in art, but it is not plain that we must do so to become aware of that expressive-ness, for it is arguable that art works present appearances of emotions, as do masks, willow trees and the like, rather than outward signs of occurrent feelings. Expressiveness is valuable because it helps us to understand emotions in general while contributing to the formation of an aesthetically satisfying whole.

See also: ART, VALUE OF; ARTIST'S INTENTION; COLLINGWOOD, R.G.; CROCE, B.; EMOTION IN RESPONSE TO ART; EMOTIONS, PHILOSOPHY OF; EMOTIVISM; HANSLICK, E.

STEPHEN DAVIES

ARTIST'S INTENTION

W.K. Wimsatt and Monroe C. Beardsley's famous paper 'The Intentional Fallacy' (1946) began one of the central debates in aesthetics and literary theory of the last half-century. By describing as a fallacy the belief that critics should take into account the author's intentions when interpreting or evaluating a piece of literature, they were rejecting an entrenched assumption of traditional criticism – and a natural one, since we normally take it for granted that understanding actions, including acts of speech and writing, requires a grasp of the intentions of the agent. But they were expressing an idea that has been greatly influential; it was a central claim of the 'new criticism', while the marginalization of the author is also a marked feature of structuralist and poststructuralist literary theory. Most of the debate over the artist's intentions – 'artist' here being used as a general word for writer, composer, painter, and so on – has centred on their relevance for *interpreting* art works. More particularly, the question has been whether *external* evidence about the artist's intentions – evidence not presented by the work itself – is relevant to determining the work's meaning.

See also: ART CRITICISM; ART, UNDERSTANDING OF; ARTISTIC EXPRESSION; BARTHES, R.; DERRIDA, J.; INTENTION; OTHER MINDS

PAUL TAYLOR

ASCETICISM

The term 'asceticism' is derived from the Greek word, *askēsis*, which referred originally to the sort of exercise, practice or training in which athletes engage. Asceticism may be characterized as a voluntary, sustained and systematic programme of self-discipline and self-denial in which immediate sensual gratifications are renounced in order to attain some valued spiritual or mental state. Ascetic practices are to be found in all the major religious traditions of the world, yet they have often been criticized by philosophers. Some argue that the religious doctrines that they presuppose are false or unreasonable. Others contend that they express a preference for pain that humans cannot consistently act upon.

See also: Religion and morality; Sexuality, philosophy of

PHILIP L. QUINN

ASSERTION
See Speech acts

ATHEISM

Atheism is the position that affirms the nonexistence of God. It proposes positive disbelief rather than mere suspension of belief. Since many different gods have been objects of belief, one might be an atheist with respect to one god while believing in the existence of some other god. In the religions of the West – Judaism, Christianity and Islam – the dominant idea of God is of a purely spiritual, supernatural being who is the perfectly good, all-powerful, all-knowing creator of everything other than himself. As used here, in the narrow sense of the term an atheist is anyone who disbelieves in the existence of this being, while in the broader sense an atheist is someone who denies the existence of any sort of divine reality. The justification of atheism in the narrow sense requires showing that the traditional arguments for the existence of God are inadequate as well as providing some positive reasons for thinking that there is no such being. Atheists have criticized the traditional arguments for belief and have tried to justify positive disbelief by arguing that the properties ascribed to this being are incoherent, and that the amount and severity of evils in the world make it quite likely that there is no such all-powerful, perfectly good being in control.

See also: Agnosticism; Evil, problem of; God, arguments for the existence of; God, concepts of

WILLIAM L. ROWE

ATOMISM, ANCIENT

Ancient Greek atomism, starting with Leucippus and Democritus in the fifth century BC, arose as a response to problems of the continuum raised by Eleatic philosophers. In time a distinction emerged, especially in Epicurean atomism (early third century BC), between physically indivisible particles called 'atoms' and absolutely indivisible or 'partless' magnitudes.

See also: Democritus; Epicureanism; Gassendi, P.; Leucippus; Lucretius; Matter; Stoicism; Xenocrates

DAVID SEDLEY

ATOMISM IN THE SEVENTEENTH CENTURY
See Gassendi, ierrev

AUGUSTINE (AD 354–430)

Augustine was the first of the great Christian philosophers. For well over eight centuries following his death, in fact until the ascendancy of Thomas Aquinas at the end of the thirteenth century, he was also the single most influential Christian philosopher. As a theologian and Church Father, Augustine was the person who did the most to define Christian heresy and so, by implication, to formulate Christian orthodoxy. Of the three most prominent heresies defined by Augustine – Donatism, Pelagianism and Manicheism – the latter two also have especially important philosophical implications. In rejecting Pelagianism and its thesis of human perfectibility, Augustine rejected one form of the principle, often associated with Kant, that 'ought' implies 'can', and in rejecting Manicheism, with its doctrine that good and evil are equally basic metaphysical realities, Augustine rejected one solution to the philosophical problem of evil.

The *Categories* may have been the only work of Aristotle that Augustine actually read. Plato he knew somewhat better. He seems to have been familiar with several Platonic dialogues and he clearly felt a special affinity for Plato and the Platonists, which is particularly evident in *De civitate Dei* (The City of God) and *De vera religione* (On True Religion). Although he could be said to have responded to classical Greek philosophy in consequential ways, it must be added that what he responded to had been filtered through Neoplatonism, Hellenistic scepticism and Stoicism. It was principally through the writings of Cicero that Augustine became schooled in the opinions of his philosophical predecessors, and it was through the works of the Neoplatonists that he developed his deep appreciation for Plato.

Augustine's philosophy thus draws significantly on the philosophy of late antiquity as well as on Christian revelation. Its originality lies partly in its synthesis of Greek and Christian thought, and partly in its development of a novel ego-centred approach to philosophy that anticipates modern thought, especially as exemplified in the philosophy of Descartes. In his *De trinitate* (The Trinity) and *De civitate Dei*, Augustine presents a line of thinking that foreshadows Descartes' famous *cogito, ergo sum*. Through his *Confessionum libri tredecim* (Confessions, more usually known as *Confessiones*), the first significant autobiography in Western literature, and also through his *Soliloquia* (Soliloquies), which is a dialogue between himself and Reason, Augustine introduced a first-person perspective to Western philosophy.

Early in his career, Augustine found himself attracted to philosophical scepticism. In his earliest extant work he offers his most extensive response to the main sceptical arguments of his day, including those that raise the possibility one might only be dreaming. His later responses to scepticism, though less extensive, are better focused; they concentrate on the self-knowledge he considers directly available to each knowing subject, including the knowledge that one exists. Taking the first-person perspective one can also develop, he tries to show, in his *De trinitate*, a convincing argument for mind–body dualism. But supposing, as he does, that each of us knows from our own case what a mind is raises, as Augustine is perhaps the first philosopher to realize, a problem about how one can ever know that there are minds in addition to one's own.

Augustine's account of language and meaning influenced the development of 'terminist' logic in the high middle ages. His thoughts on language acquisition in *Confessiones* provide a foil for Wittgenstein in the latter's *Philosophical Investigations*. Yet, some of Augustine's own reflections on ostensive definition in his dialogue *De magistro* (The Teacher) anticipate Wittgenstein's own views on language learning.

Augustine develops what is described as an 'active' theory of sense perception, according to which rays of vision touch objects whose consequent action on the body is 'noticed' by the mind or soul. Although his ideas on sense perception are interesting, his most influential epistemological conception is certainly his 'theory of illumination'. Instead of supposing that what we know can be abstracted from sensible particulars that instantiate such knowledge, he insists that our mind is so constituted as to see 'intelligible realities' directly by an inner illumination.

The modern concept of the will is often said to originate with Augustine. Certainly the idea of will is central to his philosophy of mind, as well as to his account of sin and the origin of evil. Strikingly, he uses psychological 'trinities', including the trinity of memory, understanding and will, to illuminate the doctrine of the Divine Trinity, where there is also a baffling unity in plurality. The theological warrant for this analogy Augustine finds in the biblical idea that God created human beings, and specifically the human mind, in his own image.

Augustine's attempts to achieve a philosophical understanding of theology and religious belief set the framework for much later medieval and early modern philosophy. On the issue of how reason should bear on religious faith, Augustine develops the idea that reason should work out an understanding of what we must first accept on faith. Yet he also displays a keen sensitivity to those issues

most likely to challenge one's religious faith. Prominent among his concerns is the philosophical problem of evil, to which he offers what has proved to be perhaps the most influential type of solution.

Particularly striking is Augustine's virtually life-long preoccupation with human freedom and how the fact that human beings are free to make their own choices can be reconciled with the Christian doctrines of God's foreknowledge, predestination and grace. Almost every important medieval philosopher in the Christian West would later contribute to the continuing effort to achieve a satisfactory reconciliation of these issues. It is significant that Leibniz, who gave the problem of freedom, foreknowledge, predestination and grace one of its most sophisticated treatments, also gave much of his philosophical attention to the equally Augustinian problem of evil.

Although Augustine did present an argument for the existence of God, it is his understanding of the divine attributes, and especially his insistence on divine 'simplicity', that is, on the idea that God is not distinct from his attributes, that has been especially influential on later thinkers. Also influential are his various attempts to understand the created world. Augustine made several important efforts, perhaps most notably in the last books of his *Confessiones* and in his *De genesi ad litteram* (The Literal Meaning of Genesis) to give a philosophically sophisticated account of the creation story in the biblical book of Genesis. His contrast between God's eternity and human temporality set the stage for later medieval and modern discussions of these issues, and his discussion of the nature of time in Book XI of his *Confessiones* is sometimes taken to epitomize philosophy.

Augustine's descriptions of mystical experience are among the most eloquent in Western literature; they belong among the classic texts of mysticism. However, Augustine's attempts to understand ritual are perhaps more remarkable for the directness with which he identifies and confronts difficult issues than for the success of his efforts to solve them. Those efforts seem to be hobbled by his version of mind–body dualism.

Augustine is a thoroughgoing intentionalist in ethics. This feature of his thought, as well as his unflinching insistence that one can do what one knows one ought not to be doing, mark him off from ethicists of the classical Greek period. Yet Augustine also preserves in his own thinking important strands of ancient Greek thought. Thus, for example, his development of the doctrine of the Christian virtues includes an echo of Plato's idea of the unity of the virtues. His insistence that 'ought' does not, in any straightforward way, imply 'can', distinguishes him, not only from his contemporary

Pelagius, whom he helped brand as a Christian heretic, but also from most modern ethicists as well.

The philosophy of history Augustine develops in *De civitate Dei* initiates a branch of philosophy that came into full flower in the nineteenth century. Also in that same work Augustine makes an influential contribution to what has come to be called 'just war theory', an applied ethical theory that has continued to develop even into the latter half of the twentieth century.

See also: Ancient philosophy; Anselm of Canterbury; Boethius, A.M.S. Evil, problem of; Illumination; Malebranche, N.; Manicheism; Neoplatonism; Omniscience; Patristic philosophy; Pelagianism; Predestination; Scepticism

GARETH B. MATTHEWS

AUSTIN, JOHN (1790–1859)

Although written in the early nineteenth century, Austin's is probably the most coherent and sustained account of the theory of legal positivism. The complex relationships between legal positivism and the concepts of morality and politics are explored by him but are often neglected or misunderstood in modern commentaries.

See also: Law, philosophy of

ROBERT N. MOLES

AUSTIN, JOHN LANGSHAW (1911–60)

J.L. Austin was a leading figure in analytic philosophy in the fifteen years following the Second World War. He developed a method of close examination of nonphilosophical language designed to illuminate the distinctions we make in ordinary life. Professional philosophers tended to obscure these important and subtle distinctions with undesirable jargon which was too far removed from everyday usage. Austin thought that a problem should therefore be tackled by an examination of the way in which its vocabulary is used in ordinary situations. Such an approach would then expose the misuses of language on which many philosophical claims were based.

In 'Other Minds' (1946), Austin attacked the simplistic division of utterances into the 'descriptive' and 'evaluative' using his notion of a performatory, or performative utterances. His notion was that certain utterances, in the appropriate circumstances, are neither descriptive nor evaluative, but count as actions. Thus to say 'I promise' is to make a promise, not to talk about one. Later, he was to develop the concepts of locutionary force (what an utterance says or refers

to), illocutionary force (what is intended by saying it) and perlocutionary force (what effects it has on others).

See also: Ordinary language philosophy, school of

J.O. URMSON

AUTHORITY

The notion of authority has two main senses: expertise and the right to rule. To have authority in matters of belief (to be 'an authority') is to have *theoretical authority*; to have authority over action (to be 'in authority') is to have *practical authority*. Both senses involve the subordination of an individual's judgment or will to that of another person in a way that is binding, independent of the particular content of what that person says or requires. If a person's authority is recognized then it is effective or *de facto* authority; if it is justified then it is *de jure* authority. The latter is the primary notion, for *de jure* authority is what *de facto* authorities claim and what they are believed to have. Authority thus differs from effective power, but also from justified power, which may involve no subordination of judgment. In many cases, however, practical authority is justified only if it is also effective.

Political authority involves a claim to the obedience of its subjects. Attempts to justify it have always been at the core of political philosophy. These include both instrumental arguments appealing to the expertise of rulers or to their capacity to promote social cooperation, and non-instrumental arguments resting on ideas such as consent or communal feeling. Whether any of these succeed in justifying the comprehensive authority that modern states claim is greatly disputed.

LESLIE GREEN

AUTONOMY, ETHICAL

The core idea of autonomy is that of sovereignty over oneself, self-governance or self-determination: an agent or political entity is autonomous if it is self-governing or self-determining. The ancient Greeks applied the term to city-states. In the modern period, the concept was extended to persons, in particular by Kant, who gave autonomy a central place in philosophical discourse. Kant argued for the autonomy of rational agents by arguing that moral principles, which authoritatively limit how we may act, originate in the exercise of reason. They are thus laws that we give to ourselves, and Kant thought that rational agents are bound only to self-given laws. Much contemporary discussion has focused on the somewhat different topic of personal autonomy, and autonomy continues to be an important value in contemporary liberalism and in ethical theory.

It is important to distinguish different senses of autonomy because of variation in how the concept is used. Self-governance or self-determination appears to require some control over the desires and values that move one to action, and some such control is provided by the capacity to subject them to rational scrutiny. Thus, autonomy is often understood as the capacity to critically assess one's basic desires and values, and to act on those that one endorses on reflection. In other contexts, autonomy is understood as a right, for example as the right to act on one's own judgment about matters affecting one's life, without interference by others. The term is also sometimes used in connection with ethics itself, to refer to the thesis that ethical claims cannot be reduced to nonethical claims.

See also: Free will; Freedom and liberty; Normativity

ANDREWS REATH

AVERROES

See Ibn Rushd, Abu'l Walid Muhammad

AVICENNA

See Ibn Sina, Abu 'Ali al-Husayn

AYER, ALFRED JULES (1910–89)

A.J. Ayer made his name as a philosopher with the publication of *Language, Truth and Logic* in 1936, a book which established him as the leading English representative of logical positivism, a doctrine put forward by a group of philosophers known as members of the Vienna Circle. The major thesis of logical positivism defended by Ayer was that all literally meaningful propositions were either analytic (true or false in virtue of the meaning of the proposition alone) or verifiable by experience. This, the verificationist theory of meaning, was used by Ayer to deny the literal significance of any metaphysical propositions, including those that affirmed or denied the existence of God. Statements about physical objects were said to be translatable into sentences about our sensory experiences (the doctrine known as phenomenalism). Ayer further claimed that the propositions of logic and mathematics were analytic truths and that there was no natural necessity, necessity being a purely logical notion. Finally the assertion of an ethical proposition, such as 'Stealing is wrong', was analysed as an expression of emotion or attitude to an action, in this case the expression of a negative attitude to the act of stealing.

During the rest of his philosophical career Ayer remained faithful to most of these theses, but came to reject his early phenomenalism in favour of a sophisticated realism about physical objects. This still gives priority to our experiences, now called percepts, but the existence of physical objects is postulated to explain the coherence and consistency of our percepts. Ayer continued to deny that there were any natural necessities, analysing causation as consisting in law-like regularities. He used this analysis to defend a compatibilist position about free action, claiming that a free action is to be contrasted with one done under constraint or compulsion. Causation involves mere regularity, and so neither constrains nor compels.

GRAHAM MACDONALD

B

BACHELARD, GASTON (1884–1962)

One indication of the originality of Bachelard's work is that he was famous for his writings both in the philosophy of science and on the poetic imagination. His work demonstrates his belief that the life of the masculine, work-day consciousness (animus), striving towards scientific objectivity through reasoning and the rectification of concepts, must be complemented by the life of a nocturnal, feminine consciousness (anima), seeking an expanded poetic subjectivity, as, in reverie, it creates the imaginary.

In common with other scientist-philosophers writing in the first half of the twentieth century, Bachelard reflected on the upheavals wrought by the introduction of relativity theory and quantum mechanics. The views at which he arrived were, however, unlike those of his contemporaries; he argued that the new science required a new, non-Cartesian epistemology, one which accommodated discontinuities (epistemological breaks) in the development of science. It was only after he had established himself as one of France's leading philosophers of science, by succeeding Abel Rey in the chair of history and philosophy of science at the Sorbonne, that Bachelard began to publish works on the poetic imagination. Here his trenchantly anti-theoretical stance was provocative. He rejected the role of literary critic and criticized literary criticism, focusing instead on reading images and on the creative imagination.

MARY TILES

BACON, FRANCIS (1561–1626)

Introduction

Along with Descartes, Bacon was the most original and most profound of the intellectual reformers of the sixteenth and seventeenth centuries. He had little respect for the work of his predecessors, which he saw as having been vitiated by a misplaced reverence for authority, and a consequent neglect of experience. Bacon's dream was one of power over nature, based on experiment, embodied in appropriate institutions and used for the amelioration of human life; this could be achieved only if the rational speculations of philosophers were united with the craft-skills employed in the practical arts.

The route to success lay in a new method, one based not on deductive logic or mathematics, but on eliminative induction. This method would draw on data extracted from extensive and elaborately constructed natural histories. Unlike the old induction by simple enumeration of the logic textbooks, it would be able to make use of negative as well as positive instances, allowing conclusions to be established with certainty, and thus enabling a firm and lasting structure of knowledge to be built.

Bacon never completed his project, and even the account of the new method in the *Novum Organum* (1620) remained unfinished. His writings nevertheless had an immense influence on later seventeenth-century thinkers, above all in stimulating the belief that natural philosophy ought to be founded on a systematic programme of experiment. Perhaps his most enduring legacy, however, has been the modern concept of technology – the union of rational theory and empirical practice – and its application to human welfare.

1 Life
2 Works
3 The division of learning
4 The new logic
5 The idols of the mind
6 Induction
7 Natural philosophy
8 Bacon's influence

1 Life

Francis Bacon was born into the political elite of Elizabethan England. His father, Nicholas, was Lord Keeper; his mother, Anne, sister-in-law to Lord Burghley, the Lord Treasurer. Much of Bacon's career and even some aspects of his philosophy can best be understood as resulting from an upbringing which made him familiar with the exercise of power, and the wealth that came with it. His perspective is always that of an insider, but of one who experienced considerable difficulty in establishing his own position as such.

In 1573 Bacon was admitted to Trinity College, Cambridge. In later recollection at least, he found little to admire in the Aristotelian philosophy to which he was introduced, and still less in the writings of such authors as Peter Ramus, who were becoming fashionable alternatives (see ARISTOTLE; RAMUS, P.). As was usual with undergraduates of his social rank, he did not take a degree. In 1576 he returned to London to train as a barrister at Gray's Inn, an institution with which he was to maintain a much more enduring connection. His father died in 1579, leaving him with only a modest inheritance. Throughout his life Bacon spent freely and lived beyond his income; quite apart from considerable personal ambition, much of his pursuit of office can be seen as an attempt to repair chronic indebtedness.

Though he was elected to successive parliaments from 1581 onwards, Bacon's career did not flourish under Queen Elizabeth, who recognized his abilities but seems to have found his personality unappealing. Burghley was more concerned to advance the career of his own son Robert, later Earl of Salisbury, and Bacon attached himself to Elizabeth's last favourite, the brilliant but insubstantial Earl of Essex. Essex's attempt in 1601 to restore his fortunes by staging an insurrection proved a complete fiasco, and made him liable to prosecution for treason. Bacon adroitly changed sides and prosecuted his former patron with a skill and vigour which provided ample confirmation both of his remarkable talents and of a fundamental coldness of character.

The accession of James I in 1603 presented the prospect – initially unfulfilled – of professional advancement. Bacon was knighted soon after the King's arrival in London, but he had to wait until 1607 before being given his first important office, that of Solicitor General. It was only after the death of Salisbury in 1612 that promotion became truly rapid: in 1613 he was appointed Attorney General, in 1617 Lord Keeper, and in 1618 Lord Chancellor. This last office brought admission to the peerage, first as Baron Verulam (1618) and then as Viscount St Albans (1621).

Bacon's fall was precipitous and catastrophic, though not entirely unpredictable. He had supplemented the income from his office by taking payments from those whose cases he heard, and though this was far from unprecedented it did make him vulnerable to attack. He was also important

enough to be a substantial sacrifice to an angry House of Commons, without being so close to James that he could not be dispensed with. At the beginning of May 1621 Bacon was deprived of office, imprisoned – albeit for only a few days – in the Tower of London, fined £40,000, barred from court and prevented from taking his place in the House of Lords.

Despite his best efforts, Bacon never returned to favour. He spent his last five years in retirement, writing incessantly – at first with the hope of regaining office, or at least influence, and then merely to leave a testament to posterity. He died on Easter Day 1626, according to John Aubrey (who had the story from Hobbes) from a cold contracted after an experiment of stuffing a chicken with snow. As has often been remarked, it was a fitting end for so fervent an advocate of experimental science.

2 Works

During the first two decades of his adult life Bacon wrote little, or at least little that survives; it was however in this period that his outlook and basic ideas were formed – certainly by the early 1590s, and probably earlier still; in 1625 he mentioned to a correspondent that forty years earlier he had advocated the reform of learning in a work (now lost) entitled *Temporis Partus Maximus* (The Greatest Birth of Time). The direction of Bacon's interests is apparent in a letter of 1592, written to Lord Burghley, in which he (rather disingenuously) disclaimed any political ambition while simultaneously indicating the scope of his intellectual projects:

> I confess that I have as vast contemplative ends, as I have moderate civil ends: for I have taken all knowledge to be my province; and if I could purge it of two sorts of rovers, whereof the one with frivolous disputations, confutations, and verbosities, the other with blind experiments and auricular traditions and impostures, hath committed so many spoils, I hope I should bring in industrious observations, grounded conclusions, and profitable inventions and discoveries; the best state of that province.
>
> (*The Works of Francis Bacon* 1857–74 VIII: 109)

These themes, developed and articulated, were to preoccupy Bacon for the remainder of his life. No echo of them was however to appear in print for several years. Apart from some political tracts, the only one of Bacon's writings to be published during Elizabeth's reign was the first edition of the *Essays* (1597); the only portion of this volume of any philosophical significance is a short tract on 'The Colours of Good and Evil', which provides early evidence of Bacon's lifelong interest in fallacies and the pathology of the intellect.

The accession of James I stimulated a new burst of literary activity, of which the most visible result was *The Advancement of Learning* (1605), dedicated to the King and evidently written in the (unfulfilled) hope of munificent royal patronage. This was not the only project to have occupied Bacon's attention during the first years of the new reign. A large number of fragmentary treatises have survived, some in English, some in Latin. Several have strange, enigmatic titles: *Temporis Partus Masculus* (The Masculine Birth of Time), *Valerius Terminus of the Interpretation of Nature with the Annotations of Hermes Stella*, *Filum Labyrinthi* (The Thread of the Labyrinth). Others are more prosaic: *Redargutio Philosophiarum* (The Refutation of Philosophies), *Cogitata et Visa de Interpretatione Naturae* (Thoughts and Conclusions on the Interpretation of Nature). The diversity of the literary form displayed by these works is as striking as their unity of message: Bacon knew at least in outline what he wanted to say, but was undecided as to the most appropriate form in which to say it.

The last of these fragments probably dates from around 1608. For the next twelve years Bacon was increasingly busy with his official duties, and much of the time that remained was spent drafting and redrafting the *Novum Organum*. He did however find time to publish a second expanded edition of the *Essays* (1612) and one new work, *De Sapientia Veterum* (On the Wisdom of the Ancients) (1609), an interpretation of ancient myths as allegories of political and physical doctrine. The same pattern of thought can be found in the unpublished *De Principiis atque Originibus* (On Principles and Origins) (*c.*1610–12?), which also shows the considerable influence of Bernardino Telesio on Bacon's physical doctrines, as do two other works written around 1612, *Descriptio Globi Intellectualis* (A Description of the Intellectual Globe) and *Thema Coeli* (Theory of the Heavens), both left unfinished and unpublished.

The first instalment of Bacon's chief work, the *Instauratio Magna*, was eventually published with appropriate magnificence in 1620, when Bacon was at the pinnacle of his success. The whole work was to contain six parts, but all that appeared at this stage were a general preface, an outline of the project as a whole (the *Distributio Operis*), an incomplete section of the second part (the *Novum Organum*), and a short *Parasceve ad Historiam Naturalem et Experimentalem* (Preparative towards a Natural and Experimental History).

In the years that followed, Bacon went some way towards filling the lacunae in his original plan. The missing first part was supplied in 1623 by *De Dignitate et Augmentis Scientarum*, a revised and greatly extended translation of *The Advancement of Learning*. Despite its evident incompleteness, nothing more was added to the *Novum Organum*; most of Bacon's efforts went into the natural histories intended to fill Part III, which he rather optimistically planned to produce at the rate of one per month. In the event only two were published before his death: on winds (*Historia Ventorum* 1622) and on life and death (*Historia Vitae et Mortis* 1623), although a work on the condensation and rarefaction of materials (*Historia Densi et Rari*) was also completed in 1623. Bacon's executors ignored this – it eventually appeared in 1658 – but did publish the *Sylva Sylvarum* (1627), a natural history in English filled with some very dubious material, which proved very popular during the remainder of the century, but which provided much material for Bacon's nineteenth-century detractors.

The final three parts of *Instauratio Magna* were never written apart from short prefaces to parts four and five. The first of these, *Ladder of the Intellect*, was to contain actual examples of the new method in operation – something closer to perfection than the mere sketches provided in the *Novum Organum*. Part V, *Forerunners, or Anticipations of the Second Philosophy*, would, by contrast, exhibit discoveries made independently of the method, by the ordinary workings of the understanding. The content of the final part, the *Second Philosophy or Active Science*, can only be conjectured; one may suspect that Bacon himself had no very precise idea of what it would contain.

Perhaps the best picture of Bacon's final vision can be found in a work of a very different kind, published in the volume containing the *Sylva Sylvarum* but of uncertain date. *The New Atlantis* is an account of an imaginary voyage to an island in the Pacific Ocean, and of the scientific institution, Salomon's House, found there. Like most utopian narratives, this is deeply revealing of its author and provides the fullest picture we have of Bacon's vision of a reformed, active science, and of the kind of institution that he saw as necessary to its flourishing. It also had a profound influence both on the millennialist, visionary Baconianism of the 1640s and on the founders and early practice of the Royal Society.

3 The division of learning

The Advancement of Learning contains two books, the first on the dignity of learning and the reasons for the discredit with which it was often regarded, the second and much longer on the classification of its various branches; in the 1623 translation this latter was expanded further, and divided into eight books.

The primary division of the branches of learning reflects the faculties of the human mind: history corresponds to memory, poetry to imagination, and philosophy to reason. Philosophy itself has three subdivisions: divine philosophy or natural theology, natural philosophy, and human philosophy, this last including the doctrine of the soul, logic, rhetoric, ethics and politics). Metaphysics is a branch of natural philosophy, concerned with formal and final causes, in contrast with physics which studies the material and the efficient. Metaphysics is a more general and more abstract discipline than physics, and rests on it, just as physics in turn rests on a foundation of natural history. The image is that of a pyramid whose vertex is the summary law of nature, known to God but perhaps beyond the bounds of human enquiry.

Rather unusually, Bacon made a distinction between metaphysics and *philosophia prima* – primitive or summary philosophy. The three main subdivisions of philosophy are not like lines meeting at a point, but like branches of a tree that join in a common stem. Arboreal metaphors of this kind may appear to suggest the Cartesian picture of science, in which the trunk of physics grows out of and is sustained by the roots of an a priori metaphysical system, but the reality is quite different. Bacon's *philosophia prima* is a mere receptacle for such miscellaneous principles as have applications in several different disciplines – for example, that the force of an agent is increased by the reaction of a contrary, a rule with applications in both physics and politics.

Bacon's most important innovation was, however, the close linking of theoretical and practical disciplines. In the Aristotelian tradition these had been kept quite separate, but now (within natural philosophy at least) each speculative discipline was to have its operative counterpart: corresponding to physics there would be mechanics; corresponding to metaphysics, natural magic. Bacon had no illusions about the pervasive fraudulence of the magical tradition, but – as in the parallel case of astrology – he sought reform, not abolition (see ALCHEMY).

This close association of theory and practice was of the utmost importance: Bacon saw the dismal record of earlier natural philosophy as stemming very largely from their divorce. The practitioners of the applied arts had made what progress they had in a purely empirical way, unaided by any method, while the philosophers – especially, although not exclusively, the schoolmen in the universities – had disdained experience and, like spiders, had spun metaphysical cobwebs out of their own insides. The only hope of progress lay in uniting the two approaches.

4 The new logic

The *Novum Organum* has had far fewer readers than either the *Essays* or *The Advancement of Learning*, partly because of its more difficult subject matter, and partly because it was written in Latin; it is, however, Bacon's most remarkable achievement, and the one which he himself regarded most highly. It cost him considerable trouble – William Rawley, his chaplain, described having seen no fewer than a dozen drafts revised year by year in the decade preceding publication. Bacon's chosen form is the aphorism: initially these are short and highly compressed, but as the work proceeds they grow longer. In the second book, clearly less thoroughly revised, Bacon's grip slackens and then loosens altogether, and the aphoristic form is abandoned except in appearance.

As its title makes plain, the *Novum Organum* was intended as an account of a new logic, designed to replace the Aristotelian syllogistic which Bacon saw as having hampered and indeed corrupted the investigation of nature. The full exposition of this is found in Book II; Book I contains a survey of the task and its difficulties.

The basic themes of the *Novum Organum* are set out in the first three aphorisms:

> Man, being the servant and interpreter of nature, can only do and understand so much … as he has observed in fact or in thought of the order of nature: beyond this he neither knows anything nor can do anything. Neither the naked hand nor the understanding left to itself can effect much. It is by instruments and helps that the work is done, which are as much wanted for the understanding as for the hand. And as the instruments of the hand either give motion or guide it, so the instruments of the mind supply either suggestions for the understanding or cautions.
>
> Human knowledge and human power meet in one, for where the cause is not known the effect cannot be produced. Nature to be commanded must be obeyed; and that which in contemplation is as the cause is in operation as the rule.
>
> (Bacon 1620: i.1–3)

Natural philosophy needs to begin with observation. Though Bacon sharply separated himself from those whom he classed as 'empirics', his objection to them lay in their lack of method and consequent recourse to unsystematic experimentation, not in their reliance on experience itself. Method is absolutely essential: unmethodical experimentation is mere groping in the dark, and is no more likely to produce results than digging for buried treasure on a purely random basis.

It is an essential feature of the new method that it can be openly described, explained and taught. The new reformed science is seen as an essentially collective activity; though undoubtedly presupposing a certain minimum of intelligence in its operatives, such an enterprise does not require, and is therefore not dependent on, the appearance of individual genius:

> But the course I propose for the discovery of sciences is such as leaves but little to the acuteness and strength of wits, but places all wits and understandings nearly on a level. For as in the drawing of a straight line or perfect circle, much depends on the steadiness and practice of the hand, if it be done by aim of hand only, but with the aid of rule or compass, little or nothing; so it is exactly with my plan.
>
> (Bacon 1620: i.61)

There is therefore nothing intuitionistic about Bacon's approach, nothing at all resembling the Cartesian reliance on clear and distinct ideas. Bacon distrusted any appeal to the supposedly self-evident at the outset of any enquiry. Validation could only be retrospective: it was the ability of a theory to endow its holders with power over nature that provided the best, and indeed the only genuinely satisfactory, evidence for its truth.

Previous attempts at discovery had failed because men had either complacently supposed the mind already to be adequately equipped for the task, or else had despaired altogether. Nature is comprehensible, but its subtlety far exceeds that of the human mind. In order for anything to be achieved, a new logic based not on the *anticipation* but on the *interpretation* of nature needs to be brought into use.

This contrast between anticipation and interpretation is central to Bacon's conception of his project. Anticipations are not hypotheses, but rather 'the voluntary collections that the mind maketh of knowledge; which is every man's reason' ([*c*.1603] *Works* III: 244). The root idea is one of superficiality: these are the notions of 'folk physics' – popular ordinary-language concepts such as arise in the ordinary conduct of life, sometimes refined and made more abstract by the labours of philosophers, but not fundamentally altered. 'There is no stronger or truer reason why the philosophy we have is barren of effects than this, that it has caught at the subtlety of common [*vulgarium*] words and notions, and has not attempted to pursue or investigate the subtlety of nature' ([*c*.1607] *Works* V: 421).

It was the all-pervasive unsoundness of the concepts used that made the old logic useless as a tool for the investigation of nature. Syllogisms incorporating confused and badly abstracted terms merely propagate error without supplying any means of correcting it; more generally, the teaching of deductive logic encourages the natural tendency of the mind to ascend hurriedly and without due examination to propositions of great generality, and then to regard these as securely established when investigating further. Bacon's method requires not the liberation but the regulation of the intellect, which '*must not . . . be supplied with wings, but rather hung with weights, to keep it from leaping and flying*' (1620: i.104).

Just as syllogisms are useless for any enquiry into nature, so too is the induction by simple enumeration described in logic textbooks. Bacon consistently regarded this with contempt – 'childish' was his favourite term of abuse. It operated on the surface of things, employing 'popular' notions, and was for that reason incapable of delivering certainty. Bacon was no fallibilist, prepared to settle for a natural philosophy of conjectures and merely provisional conclusions. Certainty was quite as important for him as it would be for Descartes, but what he was looking for was certainty of a very different kind – not immunity from sceptical doubt, but complete reliability. This could be furnished by induction, but it would have to be induction of a new and much more elaborate kind, one that could make use of negative as well as positive instances.

5   The idols of the mind

Before the new logic could be put to use, the weaknesses of the human mind which it was designed to correct or evade needed to be analysed. The central section of Book I is a counterpart to the analyses of sophistical reasoning provided in the logic textbooks. What emerged, however, was not merely a list of inductive fallacies, but rather one of the most memorable and original parts of Bacon's system.

Bacon distinguished four classes of idols. The 'Idols of the Tribe' arise from the limitations of human nature; they can be allowed for and guarded against, but not removed entirely. Bacon had in mind such weaknesses as the tendency to suppose more regularity than actually exists, to be over-influenced by the imagination, and even more by hopes and desires. A very different kind of limitation arises from the dullness of the senses. Bacon had no sympathy with radical sceptical doubts of the kind that were to preoccupy Descartes, but he was acutely aware of the weakness of the human senses, and of their complete incapacity to discern the secret workings of nature. The problem was not one to be abandoned to sceptical despair or solved by metaphysical validation. Some assistance could be gained from the use of instruments, but the real solution lay in experimental design. Hidden processes would be linked with observable consequences, and an experimental determination of the latter would reveal the nature of the former.

The 'Idols of the Cave' arise from the idiosyncrasies of individuals, either natural or implanted by education. Some minds are good at seeing distant resemblances, others at making fine distinctions; some are attracted to ancient wisdom, or what might pass for it, others only to novelty; almost everyone is influenced by those disciplines which they know well, and even more by those to which they have contributed.

The 'Idols of the Forum' (or 'Idols of the Market Place') arise from the deficiencies of human speech. Bacon had no respect for the categories of ordinary language, or the habitual thought-patterns of the uneducated; 'popular' is in his lexicon almost invariably a term of disparagement. Words devised for the ordinary purposes of life cannot provide a satisfactory vocabulary for natural philosophy, and attempts to remedy the situation by making definitions achieve nothing: words are defined by other words, which themselves share the same defects.

These three classes of idols can be guarded against and to some extent allowed for, but never extirpated entirely. The fourth class is in this respect different. This consists of the 'Idols of the Theatre' – the point of the name was that rival philosophies were like stage-plays, with different casts and different plots, but all equally fictitious. The potential variety of such systems is clearly unlimited, but Bacon distinguished three main types. The natural philosophy of Aristotle and his followers was corrupted partly by logic, and partly by a reliance on common notions – popular conceptions quite unsuited to the task in hand. The empirical school (exemplified by the alchemists, but also including William Gilbert who investigated magnetism) was misled by too narrow a line of experimental enquiry: restricted ranges of data fill the imagination and lead to one-sided accounts of the world in chemical or magnetic terms. Platonism (Bacon had in mind not so much the doctrines of Plato himself – whom he generally treats with respect – as the Platonism of his own era) (see PLATONISM, RENAISSANCE) was worst affected of all, being corrupted by theology and superstition. Bacon's own religious views are by no means easy to discern and have been very diversely interpreted, but one thing that is abundantly clear is that he was wholly opposed to the intrusion of religious doctrines, Christian or non-Christian, into natural philosophy; the result of allowing this to happen was a corruption of both, into a superstitious philosophy and a heretical religion.

6   Induction

Bacon's methodological proposals occupy Book II of the *Novum Organum*. The first stage in any investigation is the gathering together of a natural and experimental history. This might be quite broad in scope – for example, the history of heat in aphorisms 11–18 – but it could be much more narrowly focused: Bacon's own examples include histories of the rainbow, of honey and of wax. The idea of a natural history was an old one, going back through numerous Renaissance and medieval encyclopedias to Pliny, and ultimately to Aristotle's *Historia Animalium*. Bacon, however, made an innovation of crucial importance. His histories would record not only material gathered from the ordinary workings of nature, but also novel phenomena generated by human activity. In the Aristotelian tradition such artefacts would have been discounted as inappropriate material for investigation; Bacon, however, saw them not merely as legitimate subjects of enquiry, but as especially valuable: 'by the help and ministry of man a new face of bodies, another universe or theatre of things, comes into view' (*Works* IV: 253). Nature was to be put to the question – a contemporary euphemism for torture.

Histories of this kind could not be assembled quickly, and the whole project would clearly absorb a very large amount of labour and money. Bacon was acutely aware of this, but could see no alternative. The human understanding needed to be purged and cleansed, and this had to be done not by any Platonic (or Cartesian) detachment from the data of the senses, but by an immersion into the world of experience in its full individuality and variety. Bacon was a good nominalist in the English tradition: for him, individuals alone are real and our most reliable cognitions are our direct sensory awareness of them. Withdrawal to a world of abstract objects supposedly accessible to reason leads merely to illusion and the enunciation of empty generalities; for Bacon the word 'abstract' – like 'popular' – almost invariably carries negative connotations.

We have to begin, therefore, with particulars; we have also to begin with as full a range of particulars as possible. Bacon did not require all this data to be correct, though manifestly false material ought to be kept out where possible, and dubious reports marked as such. Some falsehoods were bound to creep in, but these could be dealt with; what could not be dealt with were biases which affected the whole history. Initial attempts to impose criteria of relevance had therefore to be outlawed altogether.

Most histories would contain an immense quantity of data – far too much for any individual human mind to grasp as a whole – and an ordering of this material into some kind of structure was essential. Bacon proposed the use of three tables: first a 'Table of Essence and Presence', listing all the situations in which the nature under investigation is present; then a 'Table of Deviation or Absence in Proximity', describing all those situations which are as close as possible to those in the first table but where the nature under investigation is absent; and finally a 'Table of Degrees or Comparison', a list of those situations where the nature in question varies in intensity, together with details of the circumstances accompanying that variation.

When first drawn up, the second and third tables would both, in general, be incomplete in that they would contain gaps corresponding to entries in the first. One of the chief functions of experiment was to remedy these defects: for example, given that the rays of the sun can be concentrated by a convex lens, a trial should be made to see whether such lenses can produce heat by focusing the rays of the moon, or any rays proceeding from heated stones or vessels containing boiling water.

When the tables have been drawn up it is possible to begin the inductive process itself:

> The first work therefore of true induction . . . is the rejection or exclusion of the several natures which are not found in some instance when the given nature is present, or are found in some instance where the given nature is absent, or are found to increase in some instance where the given nature decreases, or to decrease where the given nature increases.
>
> (1620: ii.16)

Only when this process of exclusion has been completed will it be possible to grasp the true essence (or form, to use Bacon's own term) of the nature in question.

This method clearly rests on several presuppositions, of which the most fundamental is a principle of limited variety. Though the world as we experience it appears unendingly varied, all this complexity arises from the combination of a finite, and indeed quite small, number of simple natures. There is an alphabet of nature, which cannot be guessed or discovered by speculation, but which will start to be revealed once the correct investigatory procedures are employed. The time needed is indeed not merely finite but quite short: once the natural histories are complete, the unearthing of all the secrets of nature will require no more than a few years.

Bacon also assumed there to be a direct one-to-one correlation between natures and the forms from which they arise. He was aware that critics might deny this and maintain (for example) that the heat of the heavenly bodies and of fire, or the red in a rose and in a rainbow, are only apparently similar, having quite different causes in reality. Bacon firmly denied this – however apparently heterogeneous, these things agree in the forms or laws which govern heat and redness; indeed even such diverse modes of death as by drowning, by hanging and by stabbing agree in the form or law which governs death.

This way of thinking reinforces a tendency already present in the alchemical tradition of considering bodies as collections of simple natures, each explicable (and therefore reproducible) in isolation. Bacon certainly did think in this way: gold is yellow, heavy, ductile, fixed (that is, unaffected chemically by fire) and so on. Whoever knows the forms of these natures can attempt to join them together in a single body, and thereby transform that body into gold. At other times, however, Bacon seems to have recognized that forms are seldom independent: 'since every body contains in itself many forms of natures united together in a concrete state, the result is that they severally crush, depress, break, and enthrall one another, and thus the individual forms are obscured' (1620: ii.24). They are not, however, hidden altogether: since expansion is part of the form of heat, all heated bodies must expand; but while the expansion of air is easily noticed, that of iron is less manifest to the senses.

The justification of the principles of limited variety and of the direct correlation of forms and natures could always be postponed; another problem, however, had to be faced at the outset. Exclusion involves the rejection of simple natures, 'and if we do not yet possess sound and true notions of simple natures, how can the process of Exclusion be made accurate?' (1620: ii.19). The old logic had proved inadequate because of this deficiency; what grounds are there for supposing that the replacement would fare any better?

Bacon was acutely aware of this problem and of the difficulty it posed for his project. His solution was to propose a series of supports of induction: the account of these occupies the last part of Book II of the *Novum Organum* and is (characteristically) lengthy, elaborate and unfinished; indeed all he managed to describe was the first of his nine kinds of support, the 'Prerogatives of Instances', of which he distinguished no fewer than twenty-seven different varieties. Bacon's account of these demonstrates, perhaps more clearly than any other passage in his writings, the distinctive strengths and weaknesses of his mind. The discussion is often shrewd and sometimes much more – the *instantia crucis* has passed into modern science, under the name of a crucial experiment – but Bacon's addiction to elaborate systems of classification and portentous schemes of nomenclature is frequently apparent, above all in the nineteen species of motion described in aphorism 48. The immensity of his intellectual distance from such contemporaries as GALILEO is nowhere more apparent than it is here.

7 Natural philosophy

Bacon's intellectual gifts were remarkable, but they were not those of a scientist. He was a lawyer, and it was here, as well as with human affairs in general, that his real area of expertise can be found. He was widely read in natural philosophy, but his approach remained that of an outsider, albeit a shrewd and exceedingly intelligent one. These limitations became particularly apparent when Bacon turned to astronomy, the most highly developed of all contemporary scientific disciplines. He rejected Copernicanism and, although he saw many of the weaknesses of the inherited astronomical tradition, unlike Kepler he had only vague and quite unhelpful ideas about how the field might be reformed.

Bacon's own physics was fundamentally non-mechanistic. Bodies contain two types of matter – tangible and spiritual – and the operation of the latter, although never explained clearly, is certainly not conceived in mechanistic terms. Bacon did, however, employ several ideas that were to be taken over by the mechanical philosophers who followed him, in particular that the observable qualities of bodies are to be explained by the constitution of their internal parts. Glass can be made white by being crushed into tiny fragments, and water white by being beaten into foam; heat is not a scholastic real quality but a kind of motion. Later Baconians such as BOYLE and Hooke were able to take over these ideas and express them in more unambiguously mechanistic terms.

8 Bacon's influence

Bacon's philosophical writings met with little appreciation in England during the 1620s and 1630s. Admirers of the older learning, from James I downwards, were for the most part uncomprehending, and the one major scientist then practising, William Harvey, was brutally dismissive. Bacon had more impact in France, where he was carefully read by Mersenne, GASSENDI and DESCARTES, but even they only responded to selected parts of the system, notably the 'Idols' and the appeal to experiment.

The political turmoil in Britain in the 1640s stimulated a new interest in Bacon's thought, both among the advocates of universal reform like Samuel Hartlib, and among such natural philosophers as Robert Boyle and Robert Hooke. Baconianism indeed became the official philosophy of the Royal Society, celebrated in Thomas Sprat's semi-official *History* (1667). The hopes thus stimulated, however, proved difficult to satisfy. NEWTON paid little attention to Bacon, and the *Principia* was an achievement utterly unlike anything projected in the *Novum Organum*. Locke's debt was rather greater, especially in *The Conduct of the Understanding*, but by the early eighteenth century interest in Baconianism had started to decline.

Following the example of Voltaire, the French encyclopedists treated Bacon with great respect as an empirical, essentially secular thinker, to be contrasted favourably with Descartes who was now seen as scientifically discredited and too deferential to the Church. In Britain Bacon was ignored by HUME, but admired by REID who helped create a widely influential methodological synthesis of Baconian and Newtonian ideas.

The Baconian revival reached its climax in the second quarter of the nineteenth century. Sir John Herschel's *Preliminary Discourse on the Study of Natural Philosophy* (1830) was a thorough attempt to recast Baconianism in a form compatible with contemporary science. John Stuart MILL and William WHEWELL, though disagreeing about almost everything, both acknowledged a deep debt to Bacon, and to the inductive method of science. The most accessible introduction to early Victorian attitudes towards Bacon is however provided by Macaulay's essay 'Lord Bacon' (1837). Though respectful towards Bacon's thought, Macaulay took a less favourable view of his character, and it was in response to his account that James Spedding undertook the labours that led to his *Life and Letters* (1857–74: vols VIII–XIV), and to the critical edition of Bacon's works produced jointly with R.L. Ellis and D.D. Heath.

In the latter part of the nineteenth century, Bacon's reputation as a methodologist began to decline. The trend continued after 1900, Bacon's reputation reaching its nadir mid-century when Karl POPPER proposed a method for science that eschewed induction altogether, and historians such as Alexandre Koyré offered accounts of the scientific revolution that made Bacon's contribution utterly marginal. Since then there has been a modest revival, but Bacon has still not recovered an assured place in the philosophical canon.

See also: CRUCIAL EXPERIMENTS; HUMANISM, RENAISSANCE; INDUCTION, EPISTEMIC ISSUES IN; INDUCTIVE INFERENCE; SCIENTIFIC METHOD; TECHNOLOGY, PHILOSOPHY OF

References and further reading

Bacon, F. (1620) *Novum Organum*; repr. ed. T. Fowler as *Bacon's Novum Organum*, Oxford: Clarendon Press, 1888; trans. P. Urbach and J. Gibson, La Salle, IL: Open Court, 1994. (Bacon's most important philosophical work, containing a detailed though still important account of his work. Fowler reproduces the original Latin text with very useful notes; Urbach and Gibson offer a good modern translation.)

Peltonen, M. (ed.) (1996) *The Cambridge Companion to Bacon*, Cambridge: Cambridge University Press. (A collection of up-to-date surveys, with a full bibliography.)

J.R. MILTON

BACON, ROGER (*c.*1214–92/4)

Associated with both the University of Paris and Oxford University, Roger Bacon was one of the first in the Latin West to lecture and comment on Aristotle's writings on subjects other than logic. After he came to know Robert Grosseteste's work in natural philosophy, he became the advocate of a curricular reform that emphasized scientific experiment and the study of languages. His views were often unpopular, and he constantly belittled all who disagreed with him.

Bacon's work in logic and semantic theory had some influence during his lifetime and immediately after his death. His work in science, however, had little impact. His renown in the history of science is due in part to his being viewed as a precursor of the Oxford Calculators, who in turn anticipated certain important developments in seventeenth-century science.

See also: GROSSETESTE, R.; OXFORD CALCULATORS

GEORGETTE SINKLER

BAKHTIN, MIKHAIL MIKHAILOVICH (1895–1975)

Bakhtin is generally regarded as the most influential twentieth-century Russian literary theorist. His writings on literature, language, ethics, authorship, carnival, time and the theory of culture have shaped thinking in criticism and the social sciences. His name is identified with the concept of dialogue, which he applied to language and numerous other aspects of culture and the psyche.

Bakhtin viewed literary genres as implicit worldviews, concrete renditions of a sense of experience. Strongly objecting to the idea that novelists simply weave narratives around received philosophical ideas, he argued that very often significant discoveries are made first by writers and are then 'transcribed', often with considerable loss, into abstract philosophy. For example, he regarded the novelists of the eighteenth century as explorers of a modern concept of historicity long before philosophers took up the topic. He argued that considerable wisdom could be achieved by probing the form, as well as the explicit content, of literary works. In literature as in life, however, much wisdom is never fully formalizable, although we may approximate some of it and gesture towards more. Such partial recuperation was, in Bakhtin's view, the principal task of literary criticism.

Bakhtin's favourite genre was the realist novel. In his view, novels contain the richest sense of language, psychology, temporality and ethics in Western thought. He revolutionized the study of novels by arguing that traditional poetics, which employed categories suitable to poetry and to drama, had been unable to appreciate just what is novelistic and especially valuable about novels. Seeking the essence of 'prosaic intelligence', he therefore formulated an alternative to poetics, which critics have called 'prosaics'. This term also designates an important part of his worldview in approaching many other topics, especially language. Bakhtin stressed the prosaic, ordinary, unsystematic, events of the world as primary. In culture, order can never be presumed, but is always a 'task', the result of work that is never completed and always upset by everyday contingent events. Better than any other form of thought, great prose, especially realistic novels, captures this prosaic sense of life.

Believing in contingency and human freedom, Bakhtin described individual people, and cultural entities generally, as 'unfinalizable'. Human beings always manifest 'surprisingness' and can never be reduced to a fully comprehensible system. Paraphrasing the implications of Dostoevskii's novels, Bakhtin located humanness in the capacity of people 'to render *untrue* any externalizing and finalizing definition of them. As long as a person is alive he lives by the fact that he is not yet finalized, that he has not uttered his ultimate word' (*Problemy poetiki Dostoevskogo* 1929; original emphasis). Ethically, the worst act is to treat people as if some 'secondhand' truth about them were exhaustible. Psychologically,

A man never coincides with himself. One cannot apply to him the formula of identity $A \equiv A$ ... the genuine life of the personality takes place at the point of non-coincidence between a man and himself ... beyond the limits of all that he is as a material being ... that can be spied upon, defined, predicted apart from its own will, 'at second hand.'

(*Problemy poetiki Dostoevskogo* 1929)

Bakhtin therefore opposed all deterministic philosophies and all cultural theories that understate the messiness of things and the openness of time. He rigorously opposed Marxism and semiotics, although, strangely enough, in the West his work has been appropriated by both schools. Stating his own thought as a paraphrase of Dostoevskii, he wrote:

> nothing conclusive has yet taken place in the world, the ultimate word of the world and about the world has not yet been spoken, the world is open and free, everything is still in the future and will always be in the future.
>
> (*Problemy poetiki Dostoevskogo* 1929)

GARY SAUL MORSON

BAKUNIN, MIKHAIL ALEKSANDROVICH (1814–76)

Bakunin was the leading proponent in the second half of the nineteenth century of a variety of anarchism rooted in a Romantic cult of primitive spontaneity, and one of the principal ideologists of Russian populism. But along with his public defence of the principle of 'absolute liberty' he attempted to set up networks of secret societies which were to direct the revolution and subsequently assume dictatorial powers. The contradiction between these two aspects of his activities has puzzled historians, many of whom have sought the answer in his personality, in which the urge to dominate was as strong as the urge to rebel.

AILEEN KELLY

BARTHES, ROLAND (1915–80)

In the field of contemporary literary studies, the French essayist and cultural critic Roland Barthes cannot be easily classified. His early work on language and culture was strongly influenced by the intellectual currents of existentialism and Marxism that were dominant in French intellectual life in the mid-twentieth century. Gradually his work turned more to semiology (a general theory of signs), which had a close association with the structuralist tradition in literary criticism. In his later work, Barthes wrote more as a post-structuralist than as a structuralist in an attempt to define the nature and authority of a text. Throughout his writings Barthes rejected the 'naturalist' view of language, which takes the sign as a representation of reality. He maintained that language is a dynamic activity that dramatically affects literary and cultural practices.
See also: DECONSTRUCTION

JAMES RISSER

BAUMGARTEN, ALEXANDER GOTTLIEB (1714–62)

The German philosopher Baumgarten is known primarily for his introduction of the word 'aesthetics' to describe the affects of art and nature, which in the course of the seventeenth century replaced the older theory of beauty. Baumgarten derived the term from the Greek *aisthanomai*, which he equated with the Latin *sentio*. He understood it to designate the outer, external or bodily sense, as opposed to the inner sense of consciousness. Thus aesthetics is the realm of the sensate, of sense perception and sensible objects. Baumgarten understood his usage to be consistent with classical sources, but he was aware also that he was extending logic and science into a new realm. Baumgarten's importance lay in adapting the rationalism of Leibniz for both the study of art and what came to be known after Kant as the aesthetic.
See also: AESTHETIC CONCEPTS; AESTHETICS; SUBLIME, THE

DABNEY TOWNSEND

BAYESIANISM

See CONFIRMATION THEORY; INDUCTIVE INFERENCE; PROBABILITY, INTERPRETATIONS OF; RAMSEY, FRANK PLUMPTON; STATISTICS

BAYLE, PIERRE (1647–1706)

Bayle was one of the most profound sceptical thinkers of all time. He was also a champion of religious toleration and an important moral philosopher. The fundamental aim of his scepticism was to curb the pretensions of reason in order to make room for faith. Human reason, he believed, suffers from two fundamental weaknesses: it has a limited capacity to motivate our actions, and it is more a negative than a positive faculty, better at uncovering the defects of various philosophical positions than at justifying any one of them. This conception of reason led Bayle to see, with an uncommon clarity, that the nature of the sceptic's arguments must be to proceed by internal demolition, showing how claims to knowledge undermine themselves in their own terms.

Bayle's moral thought is to be found essentially in his critique of attempts (such as that of Malebranche) to show how God, all-powerful and good, could have created a world in which there is evil. Such theodicies, he argued, rely on unacceptable models of moral rationality. Bayle's arguments reveal a view of moral reasoning that is of considerable interest in its own right. Like Malebranche (and contrary to Leibniz, who attacked Bayle's critique of theodicy), he believed that there are duties superior to that of bringing about the most good overall. But unlike Malebranche, Bayle saw these duties as lying not in what the rational agent owes himself but in what he owes to the inviolable individuality of others. This outlook had its psychological roots, no doubt, in Bayle's own experience as a Huguenot victim of religious persecution.

See also: SPINOZA, B. DE

CHARLES LARMORE

BEATTIE, JAMES (1735–1803)

James Beattie was famed as a moralist and poet in the late eighteenth century, and helped to popularize Scottish common-sense philosophy. At Marischal College, Aberdeen, Beattie cultivated a lecturing style which differed significantly from that of his Aberdonian predecessors. Because he believed that the form of abstract analysis characteristic of the science of the mind in his day often led students into the morass of Humean scepticism, Beattie endeavoured to inculcate sound moral and religious principles through the study of ancient and modern literature. Consequently his version of common-sense philosophy diverged from that developed by Thomas Reid. Beattie was more of a practical moralist than an anatomist of the mind, and his treatment of common-sense epistemology lacked the philosophical range and rigour of Reid's.

PAUL WOOD

BEAUTY

On the subject of beauty, theorists generally agree only on rudimentary points about the term: that it commends on aesthetic grounds, has absolute and comparative forms, and so forth. Beyond this, dispute prevails. Realists hold that judgments of beauty ascribe to their subjects either a nonrelational property inherent in things or a capacity of things to affect respondents in a way that preserves objectivity. In both cases acute problems arise in defining the property and in explaining how it can be known. Classical Platonism holds that beauty exists as an ideal supersensible Form, while eighteenth-century theorists view it as a quasi-sensory property. Kant's transcendental philosophy anchors the experience of beauty to the basic requirements of cognition, conferring on it 'subjective universality and necessity'. Sceptics complain that the alleged property is merely a reflection of aesthetic pleasure and hence lacks objective standing. Partly due to its preoccupation with weightier matters, the philosophic tradition has never developed any theory of beauty as fully and deeply as it has, say, theories in the domain of morality. Comparative neglect of the subject has been encouraged by the

generally subjectivistic and relativistic bent of the social sciences and humanities, as well as by avant-gardism in the arts. However, several recent and ambitious studies have given new impetus to theorizing about beauty.

See also: AESTHETIC ATTITUDE; AESTHETIC CONCEPTS; HUME, D. §§3, 4; KANT, I. §12; PLOTINUS

JOHN H. BROWN

BEAUVOIR, SIMONE DE (1908–86)

Simone de Beauvoir, a French novelist and philosopher belonging to the existentialist-phenomenological tradition, elaborated an anthropology and ethics inspired by Kierkegaard, Husserl, Heidegger and Sartre in *Pyrrhus et Cinéas* (1944) and *Pour une morale de l'ambiguïté* (The Ethics of Ambiguity) (1947). In her comprehensive study of the situation of women, *Le deuxième sexe* (The Second Sex) (1949), this anthropology and ethics was developed and combined with a philosophy of history inspired by Hegel and Marx. The most prominent feature of Beauvoir's philosophy is its ethical orientation, together with an analysis of the subordination of women. Her concept of woman as the Other is central to twentieth-century feminist theory.

See also: PHENOMENOLOGICAL MOVEMENT

EVA LUNDGREN-GOTHLIN

BECCARIA, CESARE BONESANA (1738–94)

Best known for writing *Dei Delitti e delle Pene* (On Crimes and Punishments), Beccaria was a leading figure of the Milanese Enlightenment who also wrote about political economy and rose to high office in the Lombard administration. His chief work combines contractarian and utilitarian arguments to offer a compromise theory of punishment. According to him, law operates as a sanction to deter harmful behaviour, and should be clear and equal for all. Punishments must be proportionate to the crime whilst preserving the liberty of individuals to pursue their interests to the benefit of themselves and society. He condemned torture and the death penalty for failing to meet these criteria.

See also: CONTRACTARIANISM; CRIME AND PUNISHMENT; ENLIGHTENMENT, CONTINENTAL; UTILITARIANISM

RICHARD BELLAMY

BEHAVIOURISM, ANALYTIC

Analytical behaviourism is the doctrine that talk about mental phenomena is really talk about behaviour, or tendencies to behave. For an analytical behaviourist, to say that Janet desires ice cream is to say that, all things being equal, she tends to seek it out. To say that Brad is now feeling jealous is to say no more than that he is now behaving in a way characteristic of jealousy, or perhaps that he would do so under appropriate provocation. Analytical behaviourism differs from methodological behaviourism in insisting that our ordinary use of mental language really is, in some sense, already about behaviour. The methodological version claims either that in doing psychology we should restrict ourselves to notions which can be defined behaviourally, or, sometimes, that our general psychological language, even if not already definable in this way, should be reformed in this general direction.

The most telling objection to this account of the mind is that it is inconsistent with the requirement that mental states are causes of behaviour. Ordinarily we might note that Brad has a tendency to display jealous behaviour with little provocation, and conjecture that this is caused by his feeling jealous (rather than, say, practising for his forthcoming part in a Jacobean tragedy). But according to analytical behaviourism his feeling jealous is merely his tendency to the behaviour, and since nothing causes itself, his jealousy cannot be the cause of the pattern of behaviour.

See also: RYLE, G.

DAVID BRADDON-MITCHELL

BEHAVIOURISM, METHODOLOGICAL AND SCIENTIFIC

Methodological behaviourism is the doctrine that the data on which a psychological science must rest are behavioural data – or, at the very least, publicly observable data – not the private data provided to introspection by the contents of an observer's consciousness. *Scientific*, or, as it was sometimes called, 'radical', behaviourism contends that scientific psychology ought to be concerned only with the formulation of laws relating observables such as stimuli and responses; not with unobservable mental processes and mechanisms such as attention, intention, memory and motivation. Methodological behaviourism is all but universally embraced by contemporary experimental psychologists, whereas scientific behaviourism is widely viewed as a doctrine in decline. Both forms of behaviourism were articulated by J.B. Watson in 1913. B.F. Skinner was the most prominent radical behaviourist.

In addition to its empiricist strictures against inferred mental mechanisms, radical behaviourism was also empiricist in its assumptions about learning, assuming that: (1) organisms have no innate principles that guide their learning; (2) learning is the result of a general-purpose process,

not of a collection of mechanisms tailored to the demands of different kinds of problems; and (3) learning is a change in the relation between responses and the stimuli that control or elicit them. Many of these ideas continue to be influential, for example, in connectionism.

C.R. GALLISTEL

BEING

Although 'being' has frequently been treated as a name for a property or special sort of entity, it is generally recognized that it is neither. Therefore, questions concerning being should not be understood as asking about the nature of some object or the character of some property. Rather, such questions raise a variety of problems concerning which sorts of entities there are, what one is saying when one says that some entity is, and the necessary conditions on thinking of an entity as something which is.

At least four distinct questions concerning being have emerged in the history of philosophy: (1) Which things are there? (2) What is it to be? (3) Is it ever appropriate to treat 'is' as a predicate, and, if not, how should it be understood? (alternatively, is existence a property?) and (4) How is it possible to intend that something is? Twentieth-century discussions of being in the analytic tradition have focused on the first and third questions. Work in the German tradition, especially that of Martin Heidegger, has emphasized the fourth.

See also: EXISTENCE; ONTOLOGY

MARK OKRENT

BELIEF

Introduction

We believe that there is coffee over there; we believe the special theory of relativity; we believe the Vice-Chancellor; and some of us believe in God. But plausibly what is fundamental is believing *that* something is the case – believing a proposition, as it is usually put. To believe a theory is to believe the propositions that make up the theory, to believe a person is to believe some proposition advanced by them; and to believe in God is to believe the proposition that God exists. Thus belief is said to be a propositional attitude or intentional state: to believe is to take the attitude of belief to some proposition. It is about what its propositional object is about (God, coffee, or whatever). We can think of the propositional object of a belief as the way the belief represents things as being – its content, as it is often called.

We state what we believe with indicative sentences in 'that'-clauses, as in 'Mary believes *that the Democrats will win the next election*'. But belief in the absence of language is possible. A dog may believe that there is food in the bowl in front of it. Accordingly philosophers have sought accounts of belief that allow a central role to sentences – it cannot be an accident that finding the right sentence is *the* way to capture what someone believes – while allowing that creatures without a language can have beliefs. One way of doing this is to construe beliefs as relations to inner sentences somehow inscribed in the brain. On this view although dogs do not have a public language, to the extent that they have beliefs they have something sentence-like in their heads.

An alternative tradition focuses on the way belief when combined with desire leads to behaviour, and analyses belief in terms of behavioural dispositions or more recently as the internal state that is, in combination with other mental states, responsible for the appropriate behavioural dispositions.

An earlier tradition associated with the British Empiricists views belief as a kind of pale imitation of perceptual experience. But recent work on belief largely takes for granted a sharp distinction between belief and the various mental images that may or may not accompany it.

1   Beliefs as sentences in mentalese: the language of thought

Fred's belief in the Devil cannot literally be a relation between Fred and the Devil. Otherwise he could not have the belief, unless the Devil existed. One response is to treat belief as a relation to sentences. To believe is to 'believe-true' a sentence: Fred believes-true 'The Devil exists'. But animals that lack a language have beliefs. My dog may believe that his master is home, or that it is time for a walk. Moreover, monolingual French speakers and monolingual English speakers may agree in what they believe, say, that it would be good if they knew more than one language, and yet they may not agree on which sentences they believe true. Finally, you might believe-true the sentence 'The Devil exists' and yet not believe that the Devil exists because you wrongly think that the word 'Devil' means 'God'. In this case what you believe is that God exists while wrongly thinking that the sentence 'The Devil exists' is a good sentence to use to express this

belief. For these reasons, and others, belief is usually thought of as a relation to a proposition. A proposition is what is expressed by a sentence; it is what is in common between sentences in French and English that mean the same; the proposition expressed is what is grasped when you understand a sentence. Monolingual speakers believe alike by believing the same propositions; dogs have beliefs by virtue of believing propositions despite not having a language to express them; someone who believes that the sentence 'The Devil exists' is true while thinking that 'Devil' means 'God' does not thereby believe that the Devil exists because they are wrong about what proposition 'The Devil exists' expresses. These remarks slide over a lively controversy concerning the ontological status of propositions. Our immediate concern will be with a popular view that gives sentences a prominent role in the account of belief, but in a way which avoids the problems just rehearsed.

According to the language of thought hypothesis (LOTH), not only do certain sentences serve to provide the propositional objects of beliefs (and thoughts in general) but, in addition, the beliefs are themselves sentence-like. A sentence may be viewed as made up of significant parts put together according to certain rules. In the same general way, according to LOTH, beliefs have parts put together in certain ways (see LANGUAGE OF THOUGHT).

How does LOTH mesh with the idea that beliefs are relations to propositions? The idea is that a belief's propositional object is determined by how it is made up from parts which have representational or semantic properties – that is, the parts stand for things, properties and relations much as the parts of a natural-language sentence do (see SEMANTICS). In English 'biscuit' represents certain things, and 'crisp' represents a certain property, and when we combine them together to form the sentence 'Biscuits are crisp' we get a sentence that makes a claim that is true or false according to whether or not the things have the property. This is how the sentence expresses the proposition that biscuits are crisp (see COMPOSITIONALITY). In the same way, there are brain structures that represent things and properties, and when these brain structures are put together in the right way we get, says LOTH, a more complex structure, a sentence in mentalese, that represents the things as having the properties – as it might be, the sentence of mentalese that says that biscuits are crisp, that expresses that proposition, and that thereby provides us with a token of the belief that biscuits are crisp.

This theory can allow that dogs have beliefs. Dogs might have a language of thought even though they do not have a public language. It can explain how monolingual speakers of different language can agree in belief – their sentences of mentalese may express the same propositions. It also provides an explanation of a number of phenomena associated with belief. First, it explains how what a person believes can be causally relevant to what else they believe and what they do. If you believe that Mary is at the party and then learn that Mary is always accompanied at parties by Tom, you will typically come to believe that Tom is at the party. What you believe combines with what you learn to produce a new belief. LOTH explains these causal transactions as transactions between the structures that are the various beliefs. Much as a computer processes information by manipulating electronically coded structures, so we arrive at new beliefs by virtue of our brains manipulating the symbols of mentalese. Similarly, what we believe contributes to explanations of what we do. My belief that there is coffee over there together with suitable desires may lead me to move over there by virtue of its being a belief that there is coffee over there. LOTH accounts for this fact in terms of the causal influence of the sentences of mentalese on the causal path to bodily movement.

Second, LOTH explains the fact that typically one who can believe that Jill loves Mary can believe that Mary loves Jill, and in general if you can believe that aRb, then you can believe that bRa (the phenomenon known as systematicity). The fact that if you can believe that aRb, then you can believe that bRa, is explained by the fact that the state that encodes the former is a re-arrangement of the parts of the state that encodes the latter. And, of course, this explanation generalizes to explain more complex cases.

Finally, LOTH can explain our ability to form quite new beliefs (the property known as productivity). Just as we can form new sentences by novel combinations of the relevant words of a public language, so the brain can form new beliefs by means of novel combinations of the relevant words of mentalese.

LOTH thus explains a lot of what needs to be explained. Nevertheless, there are two serious problems for this view as applied to belief.

2   Two problems for LOTH

First, unless the claim that mentalese exists is trivialized – no matter what neuroscience reveals about how the brain processes information, what it reveals will count as the brain containing mentalese – LOTH involves risky speculation about how our brains work. The theory gives a hostage to fortune. Some are happy to accept this. If neuroscience reveals that there is no mentalese and that we do not process information in a sentential

manner, we should say that we do not have beliefs and so embrace eliminativism about belief (see ELIMINATIVISM). This is, however, very much a minority view.

Second, LOTH leaves the intimate connection between belief and behaviour obscure. On the face of it predictions about the behaviour of highly complex organisms like ourselves should be enormously difficult. Trees bend in the wind whereas we put on jumpers, go inside houses, lean into the wind, cancel our games of tennis, or whatever. Unlike trees and simple machines, we respond to stimuli in enormously varied ways. Nevertheless we are quite good at predicting human behaviour. We all make many successful predictions of the following kind: someone who has uttered the word 'Yes' on hearing the sentence 'Would you like to come to dinner at 19.30 on the 21st?' will arrive around 19.30 on the 21st at the house of the person the sentence came from. What we do, of course, is use hypotheses about what people believe and desire and predict in terms of the rule that subjects will tend to behave in such a way that they achieve what they desire if what they believe is true. Our subject's 'Yes' tells us what they desire, and what we predict – their turning up at the named time – is behaviour that will achieve their desire for dinner.

Now we noted above how LOTH explains the way belief contributes to causing behaviour. In the same general way it explains how belief together with desire explains behaviour. For LOTH treats desires as like beliefs in being internal sentences of mentalese. The difference is that, as it is often put, the desires are stored in the 'desire' box, and the beliefs are stored in the 'belief' box. The metaphor of different locations marks the fact that beliefs and desires differ in how they relate to the world. Belief is a state that seeks to conform to how things are – the sight of coffee tends to extinguish my belief that there is no coffee near; whereas desire is a state that seeks to conform things to how it is – desire for coffee tends to bring one near coffee. The stored sentences that do the first job count as being in the belief box; the stored sentences of mentalese that do the second job count as being in the desire box. So the way belief and desire combine to produce behaviour is not a problem for the LOTH. The two 'differently located' stored sentences get together to produce the behaviour.

The problem, rather, arises from the fact that the connection between behaviour and what subjects believe and desire is most immediately one between behaviour and a rich system of belief and desire. Individual beliefs and desires grossly underdetermine behaviour. There is no behaviour that the belief that there is a mine near the tree, together with the desire to live, points to as such. It is, rather, a rich system of belief – to the effect, say, that there is a mine near the tree, that the mine is likely to be triggered by going near it, that moving one's legs in such and such a way will not bring one near the tree, that there is not a bigger mine that can only be avoided by going close to the tree, that triggering mines tends to cause death, and so on and so forth, along with the desire to live being greater than the desire to test out the trigger system of the mines – that points to behaviour. When we give little illustrations of connections between subjects' beliefs and desires and what they do, we take for granted a great deal about what they believe and desire. This is fine. It is by and large common knowledge. But the point remains that only rich systems of belief and desire have the intimate connection with behaviour. The same point could be made with the dinner invitation story. The prediction of our subject's behaviour assumed a great deal by way of belief and desire. We assumed beliefs about what the words mean, about who uttered them, about which month was intended, ..., and we assumed that there were no countervailing desires that outweighed the desire to go to dinner.

The problem for LOTH is that it takes as its starting point individual beliefs and desires. This leaves it seriously unclear what the theory has to say about the connection between a rich story about belief and desire, on the one hand, and behaviour, on the other. There is no behaviour that the individual belief that p and desire that q point to. *It is rich systems of both belief and desire that point in some reasonably determinate way to behaviour.* The challenge for LOTH is to find some kind of guarantee that the account of individual beliefs and desires it offers is such that if subjects have rich enough sets of these individual beliefs and desires, these rich enough sets of beliefs and desires will cause the reasonably determinate behaviour that tends to satisfy their desires if their beliefs are true.

3   Belief as a map by which we steer

One obvious fact about belief is the way we use sentences to state what we believe. An equally obvious fact is the connection between belief and behaviour via desire discussed above. F.P. Ramsey (1931) famously captured this idea by describing belief as a map by which we steer. The alternative to LOTH is an account of belief that sees belief as map-like.

For LOTH, individual beliefs are fundamental; while on the map view systems of belief are fundamental. Inside us is a hugely complex structure that richly represents how things around us are in an essentially holistic way. When you believe the bank is bigger than the post office, there is no individual

structure, no sentence of mentalese in your head, that represents your belief that the bank is bigger than the post office. Rather you believe that the bank is bigger than the post office by having a belief system according to which, among a great many other things, the bank is bigger than the post office. The key point can be made in terms of maps. A map of the Earth might represent the fact that the taller mountains are mostly near the deeper oceans, but there is no part of the map that says just that in the way that there may be a sentence that says just that – for instance the very sentence 'The taller mountains are mostly near the deeper oceans'. Or consider holograms. Holograms are 'laser photographs'. When light from the laser is projected through the negative, the well-known, three dimensional, coloured array is produced. The negative can be thought of as representing things as being the way the coloured array depicts them. However, no part of the negative has special responsibility for some part of the array. Each part contains information about the whole array. In consequence, what happens if you damage part of the hologram is a loss of detail, a blurring, of the three dimensional array, not a loss in any particular part of it.

Many of the phenomena explained by LOTH can equally be explained by the map theory. We noted how LOTH can explain the evolution of belief over time in terms of the causal interactions of the internal sentences with each other, and how beliefs cause behaviour in terms of how the stored sentences figure in the causal path to behaviour. But internal maps guide rockets to their targets and evolve over time. The same goes for the maps we use every day – they guide our behaviour and evolve over time. We noted that LOTH can explain the fact that those with the capacity to believe that the bookshop is bigger than the post office are also able to believe that the post office is bigger than the bookshop. But maps (and holograms) that can represent that the bookshop is bigger than the post office can equally represent that the post office is bigger than the bookshop.

It has recently been argued that there is empirical evidence that our brains represent how things are around us in something like the way an internal map or hologram might. This has led to a renewed interest in the map theory of belief (see CONNECTIONISM).

The major question for the map theory concerns whether believing is closed under entailment. On the map theory to believe that p is to have a system of belief according to which p; that is, to have a system that could not be true unless p. But if p entails q, then a system that could not be true unless p must also be a system that could not be true unless q.

This means that the map view must accept closure under entailment, the principle that if *p* entails *q*, anyone who believes *p* believes *q*. But is it not possible to believe that a triangle is equiangular without believing that it is equilateral – as many beginning geometry students know only too well? The usual reply by map theorists is to insist that one who believes that a triangle is equiangular does believe that it is equilateral; what they may lack is knowledge about the right words to capture what they believe. But this is a matter of lively debate.

See also: BEHAVIOURISM, ANALYTIC; DE RE/DE DICTO; FUNCTIONALISM; INTENTIONALITY; PROPOSITIONAL ATTITUDES

References and further reading

Quine, W.V. (1960) *Word and Object*, Cambridge, MA: MIT Press. (Detailed, sympathetic discussion of whether belief should be thought of as 'believing-true' some linguistic item. Relates the discussion to the distinction between belief *de dicto* and belief *de re* not touched on in this entry.)

Ramsey, F.P. (1931) *The Foundations of Mathematics*, London: Kegan Paul. (Classic source of the view of belief as a map by which we steer, and of treatments of degree of belief in terms of betting behaviour.)

DAVID BRADDON-MITCHELL
FRANK JACKSON

BELINSKII, VISSARION GRIGORIEVICH (1811–48)

Belinskii was considered by his followers in the nineteenth century, and by the official ideology of the Soviet period, to be not only Russia's greatest literary critic, but also a leading Russian thinker. Soviet encyclopedias label him 'critic, publicist and philosopher'. His role in Russian cultural life has been given positive as well as negative assessments, but there can be no doubt as to his huge influence. He is largely responsible for the fact that Russian literature and art, for a century and a half now, have been considered an organ of society, a mirror of the Russian nation's destiny and a vehicle of its historical progress. It is largely his merit – or fault – that in Russia, art and literature have been accorded a lofty status of leadership and authority, and also that 'art for art's sake' never became respectable there. The influence of Belinskii's philosophy of art extended through the entire political spectrum, far beyond his political legacy which was limited to the revolutionary left. The idea that art and literature are organic functions of society, nationhood and historical progress, which Belinskii took for granted, was passed on even to the Slavophile right and the liberal Westernizing centre. It remains an integral part of the doctrine of Socialist Realism.

VICTOR TERRAS

BELL'S THEOREM

Bell's theorem is concerned with the outcomes of a special type of 'correlation experiment' in quantum mechanics. It shows that under certain conditions these outcomes would be restricted by a system of inequalities (the 'Bell inequalities') that contradict the predictions of quantum mechanics. Various experimental tests confirm the quantum predictions to a high degree and hence violate the Bell inequalities. Although these tests contain loopholes due to experimental inefficiencies, they do suggest that the assumptions behind the Bell inequalities are incompatible not only with quantum theory but also with nature.

A central assumption used to derive the Bell inequalities is a species of no-action-at-a-distance, called 'locality': roughly, that the outcomes in one wing of the experiment cannot immediately be affected by measurements performed in another wing (spatially distant from the first). For this reason the Bell theorem is sometimes cited as showing that locality is incompatible with the quantum theory, and the experimental tests as demonstrating that nature is nonlocal. These claims have been contested.

See also: PROBABILITY, INTERPRETATIONS OF; QUANTUM MEASUREMENT PROBLEM

ARTHUR FINE

BENJAMIN, WALTER (1892–1940)

Walter Benjamin was one of the most influential twentieth-century philosophers of culture. His work combines formal analysis of art works with social theory to generate an approach which is historical, but is far more subtle than either materialism or conventional *Geistesgeschichte* (cultural and stylistic chronology). The ambiguous alignment of his work between Marxism and theology has made him a challenging and often controversial figure.

See also: FRANKFURT SCHOOL

JULIAN ROBERTS

BENTHAM, JEREMY (1748–1832)

Jeremy Bentham held that all human and political action could be analysed in terms of pleasure and pain, and so made comprehensible. One such analysis is how people actually do behave; according to Bentham, by seeking pleasure and avoiding pain.

Another such analysis is of how they ought to behave. For Bentham, this is that they should maximize utility, which for him is the same as producing the greatest happiness of the greatest number, which, again, is the same for him as maximizing pleasure and minimizing pain. His chief study was planning how there could be a good system of government and law; that is, how laws could be created so that people being as they actually are (seeking their own pleasure) might nevertheless do what they ought (seek the greatest pleasure of all). The instruments which government use in this task are punishment and reward, inducing action by threats and offers. For Bentham, punishment is done not for the sake of the offender, but to deter other people from doing the same kind of thing. Hence on his theory it is the apparent punishment which does all the good, the real punishment which does all the harm.

Bentham thought that the primary unit of significance was the sentence, not the word. He used this idea to produce profound analyses of the nature of law and legal terms, such as' right', 'duty' or 'property'. These are what he calls names of fictions – terms which do not directly correspond to real entities. However, this does not mean that they are meaningless. Instead, meaning can be given to them by translating sentences in which they occur into sentences in which they do not occur. Thus legal rights are understood in terms of legal duties, because sentences involving the former can be understood in terms of sentences involving the latter; these in turn can be analysed in terms of threats of punishment or, again, pleasure and pain. This gives sense to legal rights, but sense cannot be given in the same way to natural rights. For Bentham, we have no natural rights and the rights that we do have, such as property rights, are created by government, whose chief task is to protect them. Bentham also worked out how people could be protected from government itself, designing an elaborate system of constitutional law in which representative democracy was a central element.

Bentham invented the word 'international', and when he died he had an international legal and political influence. His chief influence in philosophy has been as the most important historical exponent of a pure form of utilitarianism.

See also: DEMOCRACY; HAPPINESS; LAW, PHILOSOPHY OF; MILL, J.S.; UTILITARIANISM

ROSS HARRISON

BERDIAEV, NIKOLAI ALEKSANDROVICH (1874–1948)

Nikolai Berdiaev, Russian religious idealist, was one of many non-Marxist thinkers expelled from Russia by communist authorities in 1922. Although attracted to Marxism in his youth, even then he tempered it with a Neo-Kantian ethical theory. Well before the Bolshevik Revolution, he became seriously disenchanted with Marxist philosophy (though not with the idea of socialism) and embarked on the career of elaborating a personalistic Christian philosophy that occupied him for the rest of his life.

Dubbed 'the philosopher of freedom', Berdiaev wrote prolifically on that subject and on related topics in metaphysics, philosophy of history, ethics, social philosophy and other fields (but not epistemology, which he rejected as a fruitless exercise in scepticism). Because his approach to philosophy was admittedly anthropocentric and subjective, he accepted the label 'existentialist' and acknowledged his kinship with Dostoevskii, Nietzsche and (to a lesser degree) Jaspers. Like them, he constructed no philosophical system, though he did expound views that were coherently interrelated in the main, if impressionistically and sometimes obscurely expressed. Among his more prominent ideas were his conception of freedom (for which he was indebted to the mystical philosophy of Jakob Boehme), his distinction between spirit and nature, his theory of 'objectification', his doctrine of creativity and his conception of time.

The most frequently translated of twentieth-century Russian thinkers, Berdiaev has been widely studied in the West since the 1930s, particularly in schools of religion and theology and by philosophers in the existentialist and personalist traditions. Although many Western readers considered him the voice of Russian Orthodox Christianity, his independent views drew fire from some Orthodox philosophers and theologians and also from strongly anti-Soviet Russian émigrés. His writings while an émigré were eagerly embraced in his homeland once they could be published there, beginning in the late 1980s.

See also: EXISTENTIALISM

JAMES P. SCANLAN

BERGSON, HENRI-LOUIS (1859–1941)

So far as he can be classified, Bergson would be called a 'process philosopher', emphasizing the primacy of process and change rather than of the conventional solid objects which undergo those changes. His central claim is that time, properly speaking and as we experience it (which he calls 'duration'), cannot be analysed as a set of moments, but is essentially unitary. The same applies to movement, which must be distinguished from the trajectory it covers. This distinction, he claims, solves Zeno of Elea's paradoxes of motion, and analogues of it apply elsewhere, for instance, in biology and ethics.

Bergson makes an important distinction between sensation and perception. He repudiates idealism, but claims that matter differs only in degree from our perceptions, which are always perfused by our memories. Perception free from all memory, or 'pure' perception, is an ideal limit and not really perception at all, but matter. Real perception is pragmatic: we perceive what is necessary for us to act, assisted by the brain which functions as a filter to ensure that we remember only what we need to remember. Humans differ from animals by developing intelligence rather than instinct, but our highest faculty is 'intuition', which fuses both. Bergson is not anti-intellectualist, though, for intuition (in one of its two senses) presupposes intelligence. He achieved popularity partly by developing a theory of evolution, using his *élan vital*, which seemed to allow a role for religion. In ethics he contrasted a 'closed' with a (more desirable) 'open' morality, and similarly contrasted 'static' with 'dynamic' religion, which culminates in mysticism.

See also: COMEDY; HUMOUR

A.R. LACEY

BERKELEY, GEORGE (1685–1753)

Introduction

George Berkeley, who was born in Ireland and who eventually became Bishop of Cloyne, is best known for three works that he published while still very young: *An Essay towards a New Theory of Vision* (1709), *Three Dialogues between Hylas and Philonous* (1713), and in particular for *A Treatise concerning the Principles of Human Knowledge* (1710). In the *Principles* he argues for the striking claim that there is no external, material world; that houses, trees and the like are simply collections of 'ideas'; and that it is God who produces 'ideas' or 'sensations' in our minds. *The New Theory of Vision* had gone some way towards preparing the ground for this claim (although that work has interest and value in its own right), and *the Dialogues* represent Berkeley's second attempt to defend it. Other works were to follow, including *De Motu* (1721), *Alciphron* (1732) and *Siris* (1744), but it was the three early works that established Berkeley as one of the major figures in the history of modern philosophy.

The basic thesis was certainly striking, and from the start many were tempted to dismiss it outright as so outrageous that even Berkeley himself could not have taken it seriously. In fact, however, Berkeley was very serious, and certainly a very able philosopher. Writing at a time when rapid developments in science appeared to be offering the key to understanding the true nature of the material world and its operations, but when scepticism about the very existence of the material world was also on the philosophical agenda, Berkeley believed that 'immaterialism' offered the only hope of defeating scepticism and of understanding the status of scientific explanations. Nor would he accept that his denial of 'matter' was outrageous. Indeed, he held that, if properly understood, he would be seen as defending the views of 'the vulgar' or 'the Mob' against other philosophers, including Locke, whose views posed a threat to much that we would ordinarily take to be common sense. His metaphysics cannot be understood unless we see clearly how he could put this interpretation on it; and neither will we do it justice if we simply dismiss the role he gives to God as emerging from the piety of a future bishop. Religion was under threat; Berkeley can probably be judged prescient in seeing how attractive atheism could become, given the scientific revolution of which we are the heirs; and though it could hardly be claimed that his attempts to ward off the challenge were successful, they merit respectful attention. Whether, however, we see him as the proponent of a fascinating metaphysics about which we must make up our own minds, or as representing merely one stage in the philosophical debate that takes us from Descartes to Locke and then to Hume, Kant and beyond, we must recognize Berkeley as a powerful intellect who had an important contribution to make.

1 Life

George Berkeley was born in (or near) the town of Kilkenny, Ireland, and educated at Kilkenny College and at Trinity College, Dublin, where he took the degree of B.A. in 1704, and that of M.A. in 1707, becoming a Junior Fellow in the latter year. Before long he published the books for which he is now most renowned. However, mention must first be made of two notebooks, now known as the

Philosophical Commentaries, which he filled during the years 1707–8. Since their first publication in 1871 (but more particularly since it was established that they had at some stage been bound together in the wrong order, thus giving a distorted picture of the development of Berkeley's thought) these have proved an invaluable resource for scholars seeking to understand the evolution of his thinking during this crucial period. The major fruits of that thinking were *An Essay towards a New Theory of Vision* (1709), *A Treatise concerning the Principles of Human Knowledge* (1710) – which was originally intended to be merely Part I of a three- or four-part work– and the *Three Dialogues between Hylas and Philonous* (1713), which Berkeley published after he had moved to London. In between the *Principles* and *Dialogues* he published a slighter work, *Passive Obedience* (1712), which gives the main insight into his thinking on ethics, and on the basis of which he has been described as a theological rule-utilitarian. Also dating from about this time are essays published in Richard Steele's *Guardian* during the year 1713, which evidence Berkley's disdain for the anti-religious sentiments of the 'free-thinkers'.

From this time onwards, Berkeley's life was active and interesting. He made two continental tours, the first (1713–14) as chaplain to Lord Peterborough, during which he apparently met Malebranche, and the second (1716–20) as tutor to George Ashe, son of the Bishop of Clogher. Towards the end of the second tour he wrote the Latin tract *De Motu* for submission to the Royal Academy of Sciences at Paris, which had offered a prize for an essay on the cause of motion. He published this in 1721, returned to Ireland in the same year, and was appointed Dean of Derry in 1724. Already, however, he had conceived a remarkable project that was to dominate his life for ten years. During the spring of 1722 he resolved to found a college on the island of Bermuda, and before long he set about soliciting support for and gaining a charter for St Paul's College, which would, had it come into existence, have educated a number of young Native Americans, as well as the sons of English planters.

In fact he never reached Bermuda but, newly married, he set sail for Rhode Island in 1728, where he stayed for over two years awaiting a promised government grant, and where his house is preserved as a monument to him. The grant never materialized, so there was to be no college, either in Bermuda or, as he had come to think would be preferable, on the mainland. His time in Rhode Island was not, however, wasted. While there he wrote *Alciphron: or the Minute Philosopher*, an attack on atheism and deism in dialogue form, which was published in 1732, the year after his return to London. He also became a friend of Samuel JOHNSON, later the first president of King's College, New York. Johnson's *Elementa Philosophica* (1752) is dedicated to Berkeley, and two letters from Johnson written in 1729 and 1730 (published with Berkeley's replies in volume 2 of the standard edition of Berkeley's *Works*) reveal that he was basically sympathetic to, but also an acute critic of, Berkeley's main metaphysical doctrines.

Certainly the same could not be said of Andrew Baxter, who in 1733 included as part of his *Enquiry into the Nature of the Human Soul* what was, in fact, the first extended critique of Berkeley's *Principles*. Baxter's tone was hostile throughout. Berkeley chose not to respond, though in the same year he did answer an anonymous critic of *The New Theory of Vision* – a third edition of which had been annexed to *Alciphron* – by publishing *The Theory of Vision, Vindicated and Explained*. He also published a revised edition of the *Principles* and *Dialogues* in 1734. *The Analyst* (1734), which criticizes Newton's doctrine of fluxions, also relates to his earlier work in that Berkeley refers back to his observations on mathematics in the *Principles*, and it may be that remarks Baxter had made on his treatment of the mathematicians there played at least a minor role in encouraging him to publish it. Berkeley does not name the critic who, he says, had challenged him to 'make good' what he had said in the *Principles*, but if it was Baxter he treats him dismissively as someone who 'doth not appear to think maturely enough to understand either those metaphysics which he would refute, or mathematics which he would patronize' (*The Analyst* §50).

However, Berkeley also had to think about securing his and his family's future, and his efforts to gain preferment in the church were rewarded in 1734 when he was appointed Bishop of Cloyne in Ireland. There, he thoroughly earned the reputation he has had ever since as 'the good Bishop'. The tangible legacy includes *The Querist* (1735–7), which evidences his concern for the economic wellbeing of Ireland, and *Siris* (1744), so successful at the time that it went through six editions in the year of publication but which is now regarded as little more than a curiosity. However, this was to be his last original publication of any substance. He remained in Cloyne almost to the end of his life, moving to Oxford, where one of his sons was to study, in the summer of 1752. He died there the following year.

2 Influences

The primary influence on Berkeley is unquestionably John Locke, whose *Essay concerning Human Understanding* Berkeley had studied as an undergraduate and continued to dwell on afterwards. The long introduction to Berkeley's *Principles* is for the most part a sustained attack on the view that we can frame abstract ideas, focusing on Locke's account of abstraction. Illegitimate abstraction is ultimately blamed for the supposedly untenable distinction between primary and secondary qualities, the belief in 'material substance', and the view that objects have an existence distinct from 'ideas', all of which are features of Locke's position (see LOCKE, J. §§2– 5). Yet Berkeley owed a great deal to Locke whom he likened in the notebooks to 'a Gyant' and who should be seen as his mentor as well as one of his philosophical targets. It is therefore understandable that Berkeley has most often been seen as the second of the three great British Empiricists, as successor to Locke and precursor of HUME, these three being placed in opposition to the three great Rationalist philosophers, DESCARTES, SPINOZA and LEIBNIZ. Certainly, it would be tempting to say that the importance of Locke's influence on Berkeley could hardly be overestimated, were it not for the fact that it sometimes has been.

If only as a corrective, then, it is important to stress that while it is evident that Locke was often in Berkeley's mind as he formulated his own position, and while there is no doubt that none of Berkeley's major works would have existed in their present form had Locke never published the *Essay*, Berkeley would have insisted that much more was at stake than whether Locke got things right. He targeted certain views and assumptions that were very widely held. Thus Locke is the only philosopher he actually identifies and quotes from in the attack on abstract ideas, but even there he sees himself as opposing, not simply some quirky view of Locke's, but one which, as he put it in a letter, 'Mr. Locke held in common with the Schoolmen, and I think all other philosophers' (*Works*, vol. 2: 293). These certainly included Malebranche, for example, who, Berkeley elsewhere complained, 'builds on the most abstract general ideas' (*Works*, vol. 2: 214). Again, when he says that 'Some there are who make a distinction betwixt *primary* and *secondary* qualities' (*Principles* §9), he really does mean 'some', and not just Locke; and the same could be said of his opposition to the notion of 'material substance'. In short, Berkeley often had his eye on other thinkers too, and some of these must also count as influences. As is now widely recognized, these included writers in the Cartesian tradition, most notably Malebranche but also probably Pierre Bayle.

The relationship between Berkeley and Descartes is interesting – after all, it was Descartes who had introduced a radical dualism of 'matter' and 'mind', and although Berkeley rejected matter, he adhered to a broadly Cartesian view of the mind (see DUALISM). However, MALEBRANCHE is particularly important in the story, both because Berkeley had studied his *De la recherche de la vérité* at an early stage, and because Berkeley's position struck many as remarkably close to that of Malebranche. In particular, Berkeley positively denies the existence of bodies 'without the mind', but Malebranche had already argued that it was impossible to prove their existence conclusively, thus paving the way for their dismissal. Again, Malebranche had insisted that there are no corporeal *causes,* and that, strictly speaking, God is the only cause, and Berkeley certainly holds that only spirits can act. Moreover, Malebranche held, and Berkeley at least suggested, that in perception, God's ideas are revealed to us. It is significant, then, that in his own day, despite his protestations, Berkeley was often seen as essentially a follower of Malebranche. We might note, finally, that while Malebranche had concluded that neither sense nor reason could conclusively establish the existence of bodies, he also held that faith in the Scriptures did require this belief. When in the *Principles* Berkeley considers a number of possible objections to his positive rejection of 'matter', this argument from the Scriptures is the last that he chooses to tackle. As he says, 'I do not think, that either what philosophers call *matter,* or the existence of objects without the mind, is any where mentioned in Scripture' (*Principles* §82).

There is evidence that BAYLE too was an early influence, and when, as in the preface to the *Principles*, Berkeley refers to 'those who are tainted with scepticism', arguments he found in Bayle's *Dictionnaire historique et critique* were probably towards the front of his mind. Bayle had offered arguments against regarding extension and motion as any more objective than colour or smell (which the Cartesians recognized as mere 'sensations'), and for the view that the notion of real extension (for Cartesians the essence of matter) involved contradictions. Strict reasoning, Bayle argued, would thus lead us to deny the existence of bodies, in the face of our (fortunately) ineradicable beliefs. Berkeley could welcome and adapt these arguments to the extent that he was concerned to reject bodies 'without the mind', and while, unlike Bayle, Berkeley firmly denied that they lead to scepticism or to any conflict with common sense, it is hardly surprising if many of his contemporaries took a different view. As Andrew Baxter saw it, Berkeley was committed to the conclusion that 'he has neither *country* nor *parents,* nor any *material body* (but that all these things are mere *illusions,* and have no existence but in the fancy' (*An Enquiry into the Nature of the Human Soul* 1733).

3 Berkeley's metaphysics

Berkeley is understandably best known for his (at first sight outrageous) claim that mind or spirit is the only substance, and that it is God who produces 'sensations' or 'ideas' in our minds. From the beginning, many regarded this view as sceptical at best or insane at worst, and Berkeley recognized that this might be the initial reaction. It is, then, an important feature of his position that, if rightly understood, his standpoint will be seen as common sense, and in accord with the views of the unsophisticated 'vulgar'. The purpose of the present section is to sketch in very general terms how Berkeley could see things in this way.

To begin with, we can hardly make sense of Berkeley's position unless we see him as starting from an assumption that he took both to be obviously true and to be shared by other philosophers, which was that each of us is aware only of the 'ideas', 'sensations' or 'perceptions' that are somehow or other produced in our minds. On the most common view – that taken by Descartes and Locke for example – these are produced in us by external objects, which objects we do not perceive 'immediately' because, as Locke put it (whatever precisely he meant by it), 'the Mind ... perceives nothing but its own *Ideas*' (Locke, *Essay* IV 4: §3). Berkeley's first insight, and it is one that his reading of Malebranche and Bayle must have encouraged, was that if we set things up in this way – distinguishing between the 'ideas' we perceive and the 'real' objects which lie hidden beyond them – scepticism becomes inevitable. At best we can hypothesize the existence of 'real' objects as the *most likely* causes of our ideas, but then we are vulnerable to the suggestion that there could be other causes, including, most plausibly, God. There are other difficulties too. Berkeley found it widely admitted that it is quite unclear how inert 'matter' could act on minds so as to produce ideas or perceptions in them (and Malebranche and other 'occasionalists' had denied that it in fact does) (see OCCASIONAL-ISM); moreover, Berkeley found only obscurities and incoherencies in the prevalent conceptions of 'material substance'. Yet the most fundamental insight was to follow.

This insight was that when we – ordinary men and women – talk of houses, mountains, rivers and so on, we are talking about what we experience or are aware of, not of occult objects that we are not directly aware of at all. It follows, or at least it seemed to Berkeley to follow, that if when we refer to houses, mountains and rivers we are referring to things we are aware of, and if (as other philosophers agreed) we are aware only of ideas, houses, mountains and rivers must *be* 'ideas' or appearances or, better, 'collections' of such ideas. Certainly – and this was one thing that his readers found most difficult to handle, but which Berkeley himself was most insistent on – there is no need to deny that

houses, mountains and rivers exist, but only to stress (common-sensibly) that they are the very things we perceive, which is to say that they are mind-dependent ideas. Their *esse* (being) is *percipi* (to be perceived); they exist only in the mind.

Berkeley's major philosophical works, and in particular the *Principles* and *Dialogues*, are, in the main, a sustained defence of these insights and doctrines, together with a working out of their implications. For Berkeley, the implications, including those for religion and the sciences, are as important as the basic metaphysics. Yet the fundamental case for that metaphysics is supposed to be very simple indeed. Even by the end of section six of the *Principles* (under three pages in most editions) that case has supposedly been established.

4   The New Theory of Vision

Although Berkeley's *An Essay towards a New Theory of Vision* (1709) was published just one year before the *Principles*, and Berkeley was already convinced that there was no such thing as 'matter', or bodies 'without the mind', this, his first major work, stopped short of making that claim. As he said in the *Principles*, although the earlier book had shown that 'the proper objects *of sight* neither exist without the mind, nor are the images of external things (*Principles* §44; emphasis added), it had done nothing to disabuse readers of the view that tangible objects are external. At one level, then, the work can be seen as a sort of halfway house on the route to presenting his full case for immaterialism, but it is undoubtedly also true that he was fascinated by problems concerning vision in their own right. He was clearly very well read in optical theory, he had his own highly distinctive contribution to make, and for many years that contribution was esteemed by many who had little interest in, or were possibly quite blind to, any wider implications it may have had.

Ostensibly, then, the *New Theory of Vision* is merely an attempt to 'shew the manner wherein we perceive by sight the distance, magnitude, and situation of objects', though, still in the opening section, Berkeley also announces that he will be considering 'the difference there is betwixt the ideas of sight and touch, and whether there be any idea common to both senses' (*New Theory of Vision* §1). Broadly, the issue concerning 'situation', which others had recognized, is that of how we see things the 'right' way up (so to speak) when their images are inverted on the retina; that concerning 'magnitude' is how we judge objects at a distance to be small or large (one particular problem was why the moon on the horizon looks larger than the moon in the zenith, although they are virtually the same distance from us); and that concerning 'outness' or distance is that of how we come to see things as being at various distances, given that, as Berkeley observes, it was accepted that 'distance being a line directed end-wise to the eye, it projects only one point in the fund of the eye, which point remains invariably the same, whether the distance be longer or shorter' (*New Theory of Vision* §2). Berkeley's solution is similar in each case. In the case of distance, for example, even when an object is relatively close, we do not, as others had supposed, make our judgments on the basis of what Descartes had described as a sort of 'natural geometry', and on facts such as that lines drawn from the two eyes to the object form a greater angle the closer the object is: the supposed lines and angles are only theoretical entities, and are not at any rate perceived. Rather, we *learn* to make these judgments solely on the strength of certain sensory cues including, for example, the sensations accompanying the turn of the eyes, and the increasingly confused appearance of an object as it comes closer to us. An explanation in terms of geometry is thus replaced by a psychology of vision in which, crucially, the connection between the cues and the distance discoverable by touch turns out to be purely contingent. '[I]f it had been the ordinary course of Nature that the farther off an object were placed, the more confused it should appear, it is certain the very same perception that now makes us think an object approaches would then have made us to imagine it went farther off' (*New Theory of Vision* §26).

Though often regarded as controversial, Berkeley's work on the psychology of vision was also highly influential even though, and indeed partly because, Berkeley's ultimate metaphysical commitments are not apparent, and certainly not necessarily required for an acceptance, for example, that 'a man born blind, being made to see, would at first have no idea of distance by sight'. Admittedly Berkeley's account of our judgments is in terms of 'sensations', 'appearances' and 'ideas', as all we have to go on, and we are told, for example, not only that the man just cured of blindness would take the 'objects intromitted by sight' to be 'no other than a new set of thoughts or sensations, each whereof is as near to him as the perceptions of pain or pleasure, or the most inward passions of his soul', but that he would be right to do so (*New Theory of Vision* §41). Yet nothing is said to disabuse the reader of the thought that there is, for example, a distant moon, which is not at all dependent on the mind. There is a sense, therefore, in which the *New Theory of Vision* offers us some of the fruits of idealism without explicitly announcing the immaterialism, and one of those fruits is an indication of the existence of God (see IDEALISM). By the end of the work, Berkeley has

concluded that there are no ideas common to sight and touch: the extension perceived by touch, for example, is quite distinct from, and has no likeness to, any visual idea. Here he considers a problem first raised by William Molyneux and discussed by Locke, agreeing with them that a man just cured of blindness who saw a cube and a globe for the first time would not know just by looking which was which, but seeing this answer as confirming his own view that visual ideas are merely 'signs'. These we learn to correlate with tangible ideas in much the same way as we learn a language. Berkeley takes this analogy very seriously. His conclusion in the first edition is thus that 'the proper objects of vision constitute the universal language of nature, whereby we are instructed how to regulate our actions', but by the third edition 'nature' has become 'the Author of nature', or God (*New Theory of Vision* §147).

5   The Introduction to the Principles

Berkeley prefaces *A Treatise concerning the Principles of Human Knowledge* (1710) with an important introduction which is for the most part devoted to an attack on abstract ideas, and in particular abstract general ideas. In it he quotes freely from Locke. Yet, as already stated, his target was wider, including philosophers generally and, ultimately, a variety of philosophical confusions. One needs to look outside the introduction to discover what these alleged confusions are. Sometimes this is fairly straightforward. Even in the *New Theory of Vision* the notion that there is an idea of extension common to both sight and touch is ascribed to the supposition that we can abstract it from all other visible and tangible qualities; while, in the *Principles*, the notion that the supposed 'primary' qualities exist in the outward object, although colours and the like are 'in the mind alone', is undermined by the observation that 'extension, figure, and motion, abstracted from all other qualities, are inconceivable'. Similarly, the idea of 'pure' or 'absolute' space is ruled out, it being 'a most abstract idea'. In one important case the connection is perhaps less obvious: Berkeley claims that holding that sensible objects can exist unperceived depends on illegitimate abstraction, but commentators have often found it difficult to see precisely how this is supposed to work. In yet other cases, the supposed connections have been less frequently explored in the literature, as for example when Berkeley has it that the Schoolmen were 'masters of abstraction' and, in the *Dialogues*, that Malebranche 'builds on the most abstract general ideas'. These matters can probably be sorted out. Malebranche had attacked the 'disordered abstractions' of the Schoolmen, who posited occult qualities and powers, and who supposed that matter is something distinct from its known attributes, and in particular from extension, and Berkeley had probably learned from that. Yet Malebranche himself fell foul of Berkeley's anti-abstractionism by talking of 'absolute' and 'intelligible' extension, by supposing that extension was the essence of matter, and by assuming an idea of 'being in general'. The connection between abstraction and the denial of the 'esse is percipi' principle is trickier.

Berkeley's introduction attacks the view that, although the qualities of objects are always 'blended together' in them, we can frame a separate idea of each quality; that we can form, for example, an abstract idea of colour or extension in general; and that we can frame an idea corresponding to the word 'man' or 'triangle', as distinct from the ideas of particular men or particular triangles, as Locke had suggested. This in turn requires from Berkeley an alternative account of language to Locke's, which will not require that each general term stands for an idea. This alternative account is not worked out very fully, but Berkeley does insist that 'a word becomes general by being made the sign, not of an abstract general idea but, of several particular ideas, any one of which it indifferently suggests to the mind' (Principles, Intro. §11). Moreover, suggestions towards the end of the introduction that words have other uses than to mark out ideas, including the production of appropriate emotions – 'May we not, for example, be affected with the promise of a *good thing*, though we have not an idea of what it is?' (Principles, Intro. §20) – have rightly been seen as significant, and further developments along these lines, in particular in the seventh dialogue of *Alciphron*, have even been seen as making him a precursor of WITTGENSTEIN in this area.

6   The Principles

Berkeley's basic metaphysical position is usually known as 'idealism' or, because of what it denies, as 'immaterialism', and the classic defence of this position is offered in *A Treatise Concerning the Principles of Human Knowledge*. Like all Berkeley's works, this is well structured, with just 156 short sections: sections 1–33 argue the case for his idealism, sections 34–84 anticipate and answer possible objections, and the remaining sections take 'a view of our tenets in their consequences'.

As already indicated, Berkeley takes even his opponents to accept that, whatever else there may turn out to be in the world, we perceive only ideas. This assumption emerges in the opening section of the *Principles* (which is clearly modelled on the opening sections of the first chapter of Book II of Locke's *Essay*). Here Berkeley writes, or at least

suggests, that 'the objects of human knowledge' are all 'ideas', adding that when certain ideas, for example a certain colour, smell and so on are found going together they are 'reputed as one thing'. On the face of it, this blurs Locke's distinction between 'qualities' and 'ideas', and ignores Locke's supposition of a 'substratum' for the qualities. Yet Berkeley knows what he is doing, and clearly found encouragement in Locke's own preparedness not only to use 'idea' where he means 'quality', but also to assert that we have no other ideas of particular sorts of substances 'than that which is framed by a collection of those simple *ideas* which are to be found in them'. Certainly, we are supposed to start with 'ideas', although – as Berkeley points out in the second section – there are also the minds or spirits that perceive them. However, he soon insists that there can be no substance apart from mind. Given that sensible objects are ideas, and that ideas exist only when perceived, it becomes simply absurd to suppose that these objects could have any existence apart from perception; a fact that is confirmed, in Berkeley's view, simply by attending to 'what is meant by the term *exist* when applied to sensible things'. When I say that a table 'exists', I am referring to something that I perceive, or at least that I might perceive, and certainly not applying 'exists' to some object which, because it is not an idea, is not perceived at all.

This argument, like most of Berkeley's arguments, is tricky and needs careful handling. Ostensibly, it seems to have very little to do with the word 'exists' because, as Andrew Baxter observed, neither philosophers nor ordinary people seem to mean 'is perceived' by 'exists' in sentences such as 'the table exists'. That point is a fair one, and Berkeley's actual argument does seem to depend heavily on the underlying assumption that the only perceivable objects are mind-dependent items, which must consequently be actually perceived. The stress put on the word 'exists' remains puzzling, however, and one relevant fact seems to be that Locke had held that 'existence' was a simple idea 'suggested to the Understanding, by every Object without, and every *Idea* within' (Locke, *Essay*, II 7: §7). Berkeley had convinced himself both that the idea thus described was abstract (and hence impossible), and that this idea is involved when people suppose things to exist quite independently of perception. To perceive a table as existing and to simply perceive it are one and the same experience, and the existence cannot be separated from the perception so that we can attribute an 'absolute existence' to the thing.

That is at any rate what Berkeley concludes on the basis of the first few sections. But of course he expected resistance. His tactic now becomes, therefore, to seize on supposedly unsatisfactory features of his opponents' position and, by exposing them, to further his own case. If it is suggested, for example, that our ideas are merely the *likenesses* of external qualities, the counter is that an idea (or perceived thing) can be *like* nothing but an idea (or another perceivable thing). To those who argue that the supposed 'primary' qualities exist in outward objects but that colours and the like do not, his response is twofold: first, we cannot even conceive of an object having merely extension, figure and motion, but lacking any of the qualities these other philosophers recognize as mind-dependent; second, the basic argument deployed to prove that secondary qualities are mind-dependent (that is, that the appearance varies in varying circumstances) would prove the same of any quality whatsoever. Furthermore, those who posit a material substratum as the *support* of qualities find that they can attach no clear meaning in this context even to the term 'support'. There are other arguments, including a particularly tricky and much discussed one in which he proudly claims that it is impossible to conceive that there even *might* be a mind-independent object, for to conceive it would be to frame the idea of it, which would mean that it was an object of thought or perception after all. However, Berkeley is at his rumbustious best in sections 18–20, arguing that neither sense nor reason can establish that there are external bodies, and that they cannot even be posited as an hypothesis to account for our receiving the ideas we do. Even if we suppose, arbitrarily, that there are external bodies, the materialists 'by their own confession are never the nearer knowing how our ideas are produced: since they own themselves unable to comprehend in what manner body can act upon spirit, or how it is possible it should imprint any idea in the mind' (*Principles* §19). What emerges, predictably, is that the only possible cause of our ideas is another, superior spirit, who presents our ideas to us in orderly ways which in fact *constitute* the Laws of Nature, and which Berkeley also sees as constituting the *language* of God himself.

7   The Principles (cont.)

While the first thirty-three sections of the *Principles* are in an obvious sense basic, the sections in which Berkeley deals with possible objections to his thesis are important too. Here most readers new to Berkeley are likely to find that the first objections that spring to their minds have been anticipated, while the answers Berkeley gives help to clarify his basic thesis. The objections he envisages include, for example, that, given his idealism, everything becomes illusory or unreal; that we see things at a distance from us, so they are not 'in the mind'; that, if the *esse* of sensible things is *percipi*, they will disappear when we stop perceiving them, which is absurd; and that, if objects are only ideas, or collections of ideas, there can be no causal interaction between them, so we will have to deny that fire heats and that water cools. Whether Berkeley's answers to such objections satisfy us is another matter, but the objections are at least confronted, and the answers are always interesting. On the third objection mentioned above, for example, it is eventually suggested that for an object to exist it is necessary only for some mind to perceive it, with the implication that God's perception may guarantee the continued existence of objects. The answer to the fourth objection above is that, just as we continue to say that the sun 'rises' despite scientific knowledge that it is the earth that moves, so this is another area where 'we ought to *think with the learned, and speak with the vulgar*' (*Principles* §51), recognizing that, strictly, the regularities in nature we describe as causal are ultimately down to God. In answering both these objections, Berkeley is typically quick to point out that his philosophical opponents are insecurely placed to make them. Even those who hold that there are external and material bodies are committed to the view that light and colours, or visible objects, are 'mere sensations', and thus to holding that these disappear when I shut my eyes; while, when it comes to causal relationships between objects, many other philosophers, both among the Schoolmen and modern philosophers, have held that God is the 'immediate efficient cause of all things'.

In answering the second of the above objections, Berkeley predictably refers the reader back to the *New Theory of Vision*; but his answer to the first objection is more complex. There are, he stresses, decisive differences between the 'faint, weak, and unsteady' ideas of the imagination and those imprinted on the senses by God, and though he calls both 'ideas' to emphasize that they are equally in the mind, he would not object to simply calling the latter 'things'. Nor does he deny even that there are corporeal substances, if 'substance' is taken 'in the vulgar sense, for a combination of sensible qualities'. It is, he suggests, only other *philosophers* he opposes, for they take corporeal substance to be 'the support of accidents or qualities without the mind'. We may well feel that this point glosses over the one big difference between Berkeley and the vulgar, which is that the vulgar do not recognize sensible qualities to be mind-dependent ideas, but it is one that Berkeley insists on. 'The only thing whose existence we deny, is that which philosophers call matter or corporeal substance. And in doing of this, there is no damage done to the rest of mankind, who, I dare say, will never miss it' (*Principles* §35).

8   The Principles (cont.)

The full title of the *Principles* describes it as a work 'Wherein the chief causes of error and difficulty in the Sciences, with the grounds of Scepticism, Atheism, and Irreligion, are inquired into'. While Berkeley believes idealism to be true, he is as interested in the benefits that flow from accepting it. These include establishing the existence of God and attaining a proper understanding of God's role in the world; the banishment of scepticism concerning the nature and the very existence of 'real' things, both of which result from distinguishing the 'real' from what we perceive; and the resolution of certain philosophical, scientific and mathematical perplexities. From section 85 onwards, therefore, Berkeley takes 'a view of our tenets in their consequences'.

Some of the supposed advantages are obvious once stated, and they include the resolution of three issues Berkeley mentions at the outset: 'Whether corporeal substance can think?' (a possibility mooted by Locke, which threatened belief in the natural immortality of the soul); 'Whether matter be infinitely divisible?' (a long-standing issue, with Bayle in particular having exposed the paradoxes that arise whether we suppose that it is or it is not); and 'how [matter] operates on spirit?' (a problem that had exercised the Cartesians). None of these questions arises once it has been proved that there is no 'matter'; that the soul is immaterial, or 'one simple, undivided, active being' which is therefore 'indissoluble by the force of Nature'; and that, just as we can produce ideas in our own minds when exercising our fancies, so God (the superior spirit) can produce in our minds those ideas which constitute sensible things. In addition, however, Berkeley explores at some length the implications for natural philosophy and mathematics.

These, it must be stressed, were not simply casual interests for Berkeley. His very first publication – a compilation of two titles, *Arithmetica* and *Miscellanea Mathematica*, (1707) – evidences his early proficiency in mathematics, and the philosophically more significant manuscript *Of Infinites* was written at about the same time. The latter concentrates on the 'disputes and scruples' which infect modern analytical geometry, all arising from 'the use that is made of quantitys infinitely small'. Moreover *De Motu* (1721) includes an examination of the role that such concepts as force, gravitation and attraction play in Newtonian mechanics. There would have been more on these topics in the additional parts of the *Principles* which Berkeley intended to write, as indeed there would have been on persons,

perceivers or spirits. What he does say on the latter subject in the *Principles* as we have it is thin, and it is perhaps necessary only to note that Berkeley's view is indeed broadly Cartesian, though the Berkeleian dualism is between 'indivisible, incorporeal, unextended' minds and ideas, not minds and 'matter'; that he even convinces himself that the soul always thinks; and that the stress is on Berkeley's claim that we do not know ourselves, or other spirits, by way of *idea*. This insistence underlies our earlier observation that in the opening section of the *Principles* Berkeley writes, or at least *suggests*, that all the objects of knowledge are ideas; for the truth is that, though Berkeley was prepared to give this impression at the outset (presumably so as not to raise an unnecessary complication early on), his own use of 'idea' for 'any sensible or imaginable thing', as he put it in the *Philosophical Commentaries*, rules out any 'idea' of spirit, or of the operations of the mind. Certainly, though, this is not supposed to be worrying, and Berkeley is not suggesting that the word 'mind' is insignificant. When he started penning the entries in the *Commentaries* he had indeed accepted the Lockian view that all significant words stand for ideas, but he had soon rejected that principle, partly as a result of deciding that the essentially active mind must be carefully distinguished from its passive objects or 'ideas'.

9   Three Dialogues between Hylas and Philonous

The *Principles of Human Knowledge* is the most important book in the Berkeleian corpus and, had its reception not been so disappointing to Berkeley, the *Three Dialogues between Hylas and Philonous* (1713) would probably not have been written. People were readier to ridicule than to read a treatise that denied the existence of 'matter', while those who did read it usually misunderstood it. The *Dialogues*, therefore, were written, as Berkeley says in the preface, 'to treat more clearly and fully of certain principles laid down in the First [Part of the *Principles*], and to place them in a new light', and the dialogue form proved an admirable way of allowing likely objections to be dealt with at each stage (as well as making the book still perhaps the most attractive introduction to Berkeley). The protagonists are Hylas (the name derives from the Greek word for 'matter') and Philonous (the 'lover of mind', representing Berkeley himself). At the outset Hylas assumes that the Berkeleian is the proponent of 'the most extravagant opinion that ever entered into the mind of man' (*Works*, vol. 2: 172), but, as the discussion progresses, Philonous is able to demonstrate that, although he accepts with other philosophers that 'the things immediately perceived, are ideas which exist only in the mind', his additional acceptance of the view of ordinary men and women that 'those things they immediately perceive are the real things' allies him with common sense (*Works*, vol. 2: 262).

Doctrinally there are no substantial innovations here, although Berkeley has Philonous take pains early on to convince Hylas that 'sensible qualities', or the things *immediately* perceived, are mind-dependent, making great play of how appearances vary for different perceivers, and for the same perceiver in different circumstances. Other features include a striking passage, expanded in the third edition, which contains an anticipation of, and an attempt to answer, what is normally taken to be the Humean point that material and spiritual substance are on a par, so that if one is rejected, so too should the other. It is indeed a particularly attractive feature of the work that Hylas is allowed to be a quite pugnacious opponent who really does test the idealist's position. To give just one other instance, it is likely to occur to us that, if the things we perceive are identified with 'ideas' or 'sensations', surely each idea will be dependent on the particular mind that has or perceives it, with the apparently far from common-sense consequence that 'no two can see the same thing'. Berkeley's answer may or (more likely) may not satisfy us, but there is a deeper issue underlying Hylas' challenge which Berkeley himself may not have adequately explored. This concerns the relationship between particular ideas – whether described as 'sensations' or 'appearances' – and the 'collections' of ideas which, for Berkeley, constitute publicly observable objects. There are no more than hints that Berkeley may be prepared to countenance the notion that the permanently existent table is an archetypal idea in God's mind, and that we can be said to perceive it when we perceive any of the 'fleeting... and changeable ideas' which, to some degree, correspond to it.

10 De Motu

Berkeley intended to publish additional parts of the *Principles* and apparently made some progress on the second part, telling Samuel Johnson in 1729 that 'the manuscript was lost about fourteen years ago, during my travels in Italy, and I never had leisure since to do so disagreeable a thing as writing twice on the same subject', but that was as far as he got. Remarks in the *Philosophical Commentaries* suggest that one part would have been 'our Principles of Natural Philosophy', and we can assume that it would have included the sort of material covered in a work he did publish, *De Motu* (1721). This work reiterates and develops certain points already made in the *Principles* when Berkeley was taking 'a view of

our tenets in their consequences', but although it is indeed assumed that minds are not corporeal, it would not have been apparent to the reader that Berkeley holds that the *esse* of sensible things is *percipi*. Rather, what is insisted on is that 'it is idle to adduce things which are neither evident to the senses, nor intelligible to reason' (*De Motu* §21), and that when we attribute gravity and force to bodies we are improperly positing occult qualities which take us beyond anything we can experience or conceive. 'Abstract terms (however useful they may be in argument) should be discarded in meditation, and the mind should be fixed on the particular and the concrete, that is, on the things themselves' (*De Motu* §4).

It is, therefore, idle to look to the qualities of bodies themselves in order to discover a cause of motion, for 'what we know in body is agreed not to be the principle of motion' (*De Motu* §24). Relying as we should on what we can conceive, we must look to mind for that principle, for we know from our ability to move our limbs that minds can act. On this basis we should conclude that 'all the bodies of this mundane system are moved by Almighty Mind according to certain and constant reason' (*De Motu* §32).

It is clear, then, that *De Motu* fits in with Berkeley's ultimate aim in all his philosophical writings, which is to bring out the dependence of the world upon God. Yet here, as in the case of everything he was to publish later, the elements of his metaphysics that had most perplexed the readers of the *Principles* and the *Dialogues* are either absent or in the background. Indeed, it is a feature of *De Motu* that Berkeley is anxious to present himself as representing a tradition going back to the ancient Greeks, but including the Schoolmen and the Cartesians, which recognizes the ultimate dependence of motion on God. Indeed, 'Newton everywhere frankly intimates that not only did motion originate from God, but that still the mundane system is moved by the same *actus*' (*De Motu* §32). It must be stressed, however, that it is not this supposed consensus that makes Berkeley's philosophy of science interesting, but his understanding of the proper role of the natural scientist as contrasted with that of the metaphysician. Terms such as 'gravity' and 'force', for example, have a legitimate use, in facilitating calculations on the basis of certain observable regularities in the behaviour of objects. We go wrong only if we confuse the discovery of regularities with genuine explanations of them. By contrast, absolute space and absolute motion, which were posited in Newtonian mechanics, are rejected outright, as indeed they were in the *Principles*. We should 'consider motion as something sensible, or at least imaginable', and 'be content with relative measures' (*De Motu* §66). If there were but one body in the universe, it would make no sense to suppose that it moved (see NEWTON, I.).

11 Alciphron *and* The Analyst

Berkeley published *De Motu* in 1721 and nothing of any philosophical significance for over ten years thereafter. Indeed none of his later writings matched in importance what had already appeared. Yet all were controversial, and some were taken very seriously at the time. These included *Alciphron* (1732) and *The Analyst* (1734) which represent, if in very different ways, Berkeley's commitment to defending religion against those seeking to undermine it.

Alciphron is composed of seven lively dialogues in which two Christian gentlemen, Euphranor and Crito, defend the religious and Christian standpoint against two 'free-thinkers', Alciphron and Lysicles. These are, of course, fictitious characters, but are allowed on occasion to present (or misrepresent, as many have claimed) the views of such actual, though unnamed, figures as the third Earl of Shaftesbury and Bernard MANDEVILLE. Mandeville complained bitterly that his thesis arguing private vices are public benefits had been totally distorted in *Alciphron*; others have said the same of Berkeley's treatment of Shaftesbury's ethical theory. For all that, the book remains very readable. It contains, moreover, the only account of free will published by Berkeley, and also the first explicit linking of the doctrine concerning the heterogeneity of the objects of sight and touch to a proof of the existence of God. Additionally there is a discussion in the Seventh Dialogue of particular interest in that it returns us to the topic of language.

The context is still the acceptability of religion, but at this point the objection from the free-thinker Alciphron is that the Christian religion is ultimately unacceptable, not because it can be shown to be false, but because it is straightforwardly unintelligible, involving, as it does, such meaningless notions as that of 'grace'. Here Alciphron appeals to the principle that 'words that suggest no ideas are insignificant'. Consequently this principle, which Berkeley had himself assumed in a demonstration of immaterialism nearly halfway through the *Commentaries*, now becomes his explicit target. He reiterates his objection to abstract ideas, but also stresses the role of words in directing our practices, whether in mathematics and natural science, or in the religious sphere. It has been debated whether or not what we find here marks any decided shift from the line he had taken in the introduction to the *Principles*, and it is certainly true that Berkeley had long since moved towards the position he adopts here, but the

discussion in *Alciphron* does reflect his mature consideration of the topic. It stresses the use of words as signs which, as he had put it to Samuel Johnson, 'as often terminate in the will as in the understanding, being employed rather to excite, influence, and direct action, than to produce clear and distinct ideas' (*Works*, vol. 2: 293).

By contrast with *Alciphron*, the *Analyst* is a technical work in the philosophy of mathematics, containing criticisms of Newton's calculus. The adequacy of these criticisms is still debated, but they were sufficiently acute to generate considerable controversy among the mathematicians. To this controversy Berkeley contributed two further works in 1735, *A Defence of Free-thinking in Mathematics*, and *Reasons for not replying to Mr. Walton's Full Answer*. Berkeley's theological preoccupations are again relevant in this area, for *The Analyst* was addressed to an unnamed 'infidel mathematician', who has generally been identified with Edmund Halley (of Halley's Comet fame). Halley had been reported as claiming that Christian doctrines were 'incomprehensible', and the religion an 'imposture'. Berkeley is able to take delight in answering that the objection comes ill from a mathematician. He targets what he saw as obscurities and contradictions in the calculus. Some of these result from assuming an increment of infinitesimal value which, without reaching zero, proceeds towards a limit of zero, allowing the analyst to predict the system's value at a conceptual point at which the increment becomes nothing. A consequence is that these 'ghosts of departed qualities' are both used and disregarded in one and the same proof. As already mentioned, Berkeley's interest in mathematics was of long standing, as was his opposition to infinitesimal quantities. He was able to show how these lead to absurdities in the calculus, and to argue against those who 'though they shrink at all other mysteries, make no difficulty of their own'. Moreover, he was able to do this without mentioning his own idealist view that, because *esse* is *percipi*, the smallest quantity must be what he had earlier called the *minimum sensibile*, which cannot be divided into parts.

12 Siris

Siris (1744), the last of Berkeley's writings of any substance, is also in many ways the strangest. His championship of tar-water as a useful remedy against many diseases (and as a possible panacea) is likely to strike us as foolish, though it was to some extent understandable given his apparently successful use of it in his diocese. Moreover, although it was practical experience that had led him to his belief in the virtues of tar-water, Berkeley does go deeply into the explanation of its effectiveness, relying on theories which gave prominence to the role of 'aether', or 'pure invisible fire', as the vital principle of the corporeal world. Here again we can now see that Berkeley was wrong, although he was able to appeal to authorities, both ancient and modern. Indeed, this readiness to appeal to authorities, or to seek for maximum consensus, extends to the final sections in which his chain of philosophical reflections leads him to focus on God as 'the First Mover, invisible, incorporeal, unextended, intellectual source of life and being' (*Siris* §296). Here themes familiar from the early works re-emerge – including the view that 'all phenomena are, to speak truly, appearances in the soul or mind' (*Siris* §251) and that there are, strictly, no corporeal causes. Yet these are now tied in with what appear to be alien elements. There is a tendency to disparage the senses, and Berkeley's fascination with the philosophies of the ancients extends to a degree of sympathy for the Platonic Theory of Forms. That said, Berkeley's eclectic and somewhat hesitant approach in *Siris* is such that it would be wrong to look to it for evidence of a substantially new philosophical position. Though fascinating in its way, *Siris* now seems very dated indeed.

13 Concluding remarks

Inevitably, Berkeley is famed for the metaphysics of the *Principles*, and *Dialogues*. It would be easy to multiply quotations from people who treated this metaphysics as absurd, but very wrong to suggest that all the reactions have been hostile, or that the more hostile responses have not frequently been based on misunderstandings. At the other extreme, John Stuart Mill was to refer to Plato, Locke and Kant among others when describing Berkeley as 'the one of greatest philosophic genius' (Mill 1871: 'Berkley's Life and Writings'), while A.A. Luce, the most prominent Berkeley scholar of the twentieth century, held Berkeley's views to be fundamentally correct, and to coincide with the common-sense view of the world. Even many who would be less effusive have at least seen Berkeley as playing an important role in the history of philosophy, if only as marking one important stage on the route from Locke to Hume, and then to Kant and modern idealism. Certainly, no serious commentators would judge that his views can be easily or simply dismissed, though they would often give very different accounts of what makes him important and interesting. Luce, for example, found the role God has to play in Berkeley's system attractive; Mill thought it an embarrassment. Phenomenalism, the theory of perception which Mill himself espoused, could indeed be described as 'Berkeley without God' (see MILL, J.S. §6; PHENOMENALISM).

The fact is that Berkeley was grappling with problems that are perennial in philosophy, including that of the relationship between appearance and reality, or between our experiences and what we take them to be experiences of. Their treatments of these issues have very often led philosophers to say things that would strike the 'vulgar' as strange, and if Locke's position, for example, seems initially more congenial (in that Locke never doubts the existence of a world corresponding to, but distinct from, our 'ideas', and treats scepticism in that area as absurd), Berkeley was neither the first nor the last to see him as, in effect, making knowledge of that world impossible. Berkeley did not invent the sceptical challenge that arises from insisting on a distinction between what we 'immediately' perceive and an external 'material' world; if his way of dealing with it is radical, one must recognize that 'idealism' in one form or another was to have quite a history – even now there are philosophers who are happy to use the label to describe their own philosophical positions.

Certainly Berkeley does sometimes exaggerate the extent to which he is at one with the 'vulgar', or with our ordinary views about the world. He may be quite right that he is at one with those who believe that '*those things they immediately perceive are the real things*'. Yet, as we saw in §9 above, it is only by combining this with the claim that '*the things immediately perceived, are ideas which exist only in the mind*', which he attributes to 'the philosophers', that he arrives at a theory concerning the nature of reality that is very much his own. Consequently, although he can chide his opponents for their commitment to such views as 'the Wall is not white, the fire is not hot', remarking in the *Commentaries* (entry 392) that 'We Irish men cannot attain to these truths', many of his own claims, such as that 'Strictly speaking . . . we do not see the same object that we feel; neither is it the same object perceived by the microscope, which was by the naked eye' (*Works*, vol. 2: 245), would strike the vulgar as equally odd. Berkeley's beliefs about what it is that we 'immediately' perceive may or may not be true, but clearly they are not vulgar views.

To be fair, Berkeley was not unaware that this was the position. For example, his comment that on the issue of causal relationships between objects we should '*think with the learned, and speak with the vulgar*' (*Principles* §51) suggests that the vulgar have not appreciated the truth of the matter; while claims that he opposes only other philosophers contrast with passages such as that in the *Principles* in which he actually refers to the 'mistake' of the vulgar who believe that the 'objects of perception [have] an existence independent of, and without the mind' (*Principles* §56). To be sure, in the same discussion he suggests that they cannot *really* believe this, because the supposed belief involves a contradiction, and 'Strictly speaking, to believe that which involves a contradiction, or has no meaning in it, is impossible' (*Principles* §54). The whole passage rests on the equation of the objects of perception with 'ideas', which is what *makes* the supposed belief contradictory.

The truth is, therefore, that for all his resolve in the *Commentaries* (entry 751) 'To be eternally banishing Metaphisics &c & recalling Men to Common Sense' (and what he seems to have in mind there is the arid metaphysics of the Schools), Berkeley does offer us what we would naturally describe as a metaphysics, and one that cannot be refuted simply on the ground that it might strike the average person as outrageous. His arguments must be examined on their merits, together with any underlying assumptions; attention has to be paid to the notion of 'immediate' perception which he works with; and account must be taken of possible problems generated by his metaphysical conclusions. These may include, as has often been claimed, an unrecognized tendency towards solipsism. Not that it is necessary to reject or accept his philosophy in total, for there may be insights alongside what we believe are mistakes. As with any philosopher of Berkeley's stature, doing justice to Berkeley's philosophy turns out to be a very complex, but also a rewarding exercise, which is why his philosophy still exercises the commentators today.

See also: VISION

References and further reading

Berkeley, G. (1948–57) *The Works of George Berkeley, Bishop of Cloyne*, ed. A.A. Luce and T.E. Jessop, 9 vols, Edinburgh: Thomas Nelson. (The standard edition, containing Berkeley's published and unpublished writings, both philosophical and non-philosophical. The philosophical correspondence between Berkeley and Samuel Johnson is in vol. 2.)

Berman, D. (ed.) (1989) *George Berkeley: Eighteenth-Century Responses*, New York: Garland Publishing, 2 vols. (Contains many of the early responses to various of Berkeley's works. These include some from important or influential figures such as James Beattie and Thomas Reid, the first reviews of the *Principles* and *Dialogues*, and materials not easily accessible elsewhere.)

IAN TIPTON

BERLIN, ISAIAH (1909–97)

Berlin said that he decided about 1945 to give up philosophy, in which he had worked up to that time, in favour of the history of ideas. Some of his best-known work certainly belongs to the history of ideas, but he continued in fact both to write philosophy and to pursue philosophical questions in his historical work.

His main philosophical contributions are to political philosophy and specifically to the theory of liberalism. He emphasizes a distinction between 'negative' and 'positive' concepts of liberty: the former is a Hobbesian idea of absence of constraint or obstacle, while the latter is identified with a notion of moral self-government, expressed for instance in Rousseau, which Berlin finds politically threatening. His anti-utopian approach to politics is expressed also in his view that values necessarily conflict; this irreducible 'value pluralism' may be his most original contribution to philosophy, though he advances it through example and historical illustration rather than in semantic or epistemological terms. He also expresses himself against necessitarian interpretations of history, and in favour of an anti-determinist conception of free will.

See also: ENLIGHTENMENT, CONTINENTAL; FREEDOM AND LIBERTY; HISTORICISM; INCOMMENSURABILITY; PLURALISM

BERNARD WILLIAMS

BIOETHICS

While bioethics, a part of applied ethics, is usually identified with medical ethics, in its broadest sense it is the study of the moral, social and political problems that arise out of biology and the life sciences generally and involve, either directly or indirectly, human wellbeing. Thus, environmental and animal ethics are sometimes included within it. In this regard, bioethics can be of broader concern than is either medical/biomedical ethics or the study of the moral problems that arise out of new developments in medical technology.

The interrelated issues of who or what has moral status, of what justifies a certain kind of treatment of one creature as opposed to another, and whether, if a creature has moral status, it can lose it, have proved especially important issues in this broadest sense of bioethics. The philosophical task of probing arguments for soundness appears essential to deciding these issues.

As a part of applied ethics, bioethics is exposed to the difficulty that (1) we do not agree in our moral convictions and principles about many of the cases that feature in bioethics, (2) we do not agree in the moral theories in which our moral principles find their home and by which we try to justify them, and (3) we do not agree in the test(s) of adequacy by which to resolve the disagreements at the level of moral theory. We seem left with no way of deciding between contending principles and theories.

See also: CLONING; TECHNOLOGY AND ETHICS

R.G. FREY

BIOLOGY, PHILOSOPHY OF

See EVOLUTION, THEORY OF; GENETICS; SPECIES; TAXONOMY; VITALISM

BLACKSTONE, WILLIAM (1723–80)

Blackstone produced the first systematic exposition of English law as a body of principles. His enterprise was founded upon the assumption that the detailed rules of English law embodied and enforced natural law. Blackstone's invocation of natural law has frequently been regarded as ornamental rather than substantial, but there is no good reason for taking this view. Blackstone is now remembered as much for Bentham's attacks upon him as for his own contribution.

See also: LAW, PHILOSOPHY OF

N.E. SIMMONDS

BLOCH, ERNST SIMON (1885–1977)

Bloch was one of the most innovative Marxist philosophers of the twentieth century. His metaphysical and ontological concerns, combined with a self-conscious utopianism, distanced him from much mainstream Marxist thought. He was sympathetic to the classical philosophical search for fundamental categories, but distinguished earlier static, fixed and closed systems from his own open system, in which he characterized the universe as a changing and unfinished process. Furthermore, his distinctive materialism entailed the rejection of a radical separation of the human and the natural, unlike much twentieth-century Western Marxism. His validation of utopianism was grounded in a distinctive epistemology centred on the processes whereby 'new' material emerges in consciousness. The resulting social theory was sensitive to the many and varied ways in which the utopian impulse emerges, as, for example, in its analysis of the utopian dimension in religion.

VINCENT GEOGHEGAN

BOBBIO, NORBERTO (1909–)

The foremost legal and political theorist in Italy today, Norberto Bobbio founded in the 1940s Italian analytical legal positivism, trying to merge logical positivism and Kelsen's legal positivism. As a political thinker, he defends a synthesis of liberalism and socialism, focusing in particular on the defence of human and civil rights in democratic societies.

See also: DEMOCRACY; LAW AND MORALITY; LAW, PHILOSOPHY OF; LIBERALISM

PATRIZIA BORSELLINO

BODIN, JEAN (1529/30–96)

Jean Bodin was one of the great universal scholars of the later Renaissance. Despite political distractions, he made major contributions to historiography and the philosophy of history, economic theory, public law and comparative public policy, the sociology of institutions, as well as to religious philosophy, comparative religion and natural philosophy. Among his most celebrated achievements are his theory of sovereignty, which introduced a new dimension to the study of public law, and his Neoplatonist religion, which opened new perspectives on universalism and religious toleration.

Many of these intellectual positions, moreover, were responses, at least in part, to great political issues of the time. Against doctrines of popular sovereignty and the right of resistance put forward in the course of the religious wars, Bodin sought to show that the king of France was absolute. Against the widespread corruption and laxity that weakened and undermined the monarchy, he argued for administrative reform. And against the party that pressed the king to impose religious uniformity, he cautiously supported religious toleration. In all these respects Bodin's thought helped to inform the policies of the early Bourbon dynasty esatblished by Henry IV.

See also: ABSOLUTISM; HUMANISM, RENAISSANCE; NEOPLATONISM; RENAISSANCE PHILOSOPHY; SOVEREIGNTY; TOLERATION

JULIAN H. FRANKLIN

BOEHME, JAKOB (1575–1624)

Boehme was a Lutheran mystic and pantheist. He held that God is the Abyss that is the ground of all things. The will of the Abyss to know itself generates a process that gives rise to nature, which is thus the image of God. Life is characterized by a dualistic struggle between good and evil; only by embracing Christ's love can unity be regained. Boehme was highly regarded by such diverse writers as Law, Newton, Goethe and Hegel.

See also: HEGEL, G.W.F. NEOPLATONISM; SPINOZA, B.

JEAN-LOUP SEBAN

BOETHIUS, ANICIUS MANLIUS SEVERINUS (c.480–525/6)

Boethius was a principal transmitter of classical Greek logic from Aristotle, the Stoics and the Neoplatonists to the schoolmen of the medieval Latin West. His contemporaries were largely unimpressed by his learned activities, and his writings show him to have been a lonely, rather isolated figure in a world where the old Roman aristocrats were struggling to maintain high literary culture in an Italy controlled by barbarous and bibulous Goths, whose taste in music and hairgrease Boethius found painful.

Boethius himself was born into a patrician family in Rome, but was orphaned and raised instead by Q. Aurelius Memmius Symmachus, a rich Christian heir to a distinguished pagan line; Boethius later married the latter's daughter, Rusticiana. As well as Symmachus, Boethius had a small circle of educated friends, including the Roman deacon John (who probably became Pope John I, 523–6), who shared his enthusiasm for logical problems. The Gothic king of Italy at Ravenna, Theoderic, had met high culture during his education at Constantinople and made use of experienced Roman aristocrats as administrators. He employed Boethius to design a sundial for the Burgundian king and also a water-clock, specimens of advanced technology intended to impress a barbarian; he also sent a harpist to Clovis, the Frankish king, no doubt intended to soften the latter's bellicose spirit.

By 507 Boethius had gained the title 'patrician' and received letters addressed to 'your magnitude'. Symmachus was in a position to promote his public career. He was nominated consul for the year 510, a position without political power but of high standing and requiring large disbursements of private wealth; it also carried the perquisite that the consul's name stood on all dated documents for that year. In 522 his two sons were installed as consuls, a promotion that gave their father intense pride and pleasure, and he took up seriously the political post of Master of the Offices. In this capacity, his determination to eliminate corruption earned him numerous enemies among both Goths and his fellow Roman aristocrats. His relations with the courtiers at Ravenna became disastrous.

Boethius' fall came when he rashly defended a senator who had been delated to King Theoderic for conducting treasonable correspondence with persons high in the court of the emperor at Constantinople. There is no improbability in the notion that, along with other Roman aristocrats, Boethius would have preferred to be rid of the crude Goths and to see Theoderic replaced by a ruler congenial to the emperor. His great erudition had aroused fears that he was engaged in occult practices dangerous to the Ravenna dynasty. In 524 or early 525, Boethius was imprisoned at Pavia (Ticinum). Here, while awaiting the execution already decreed against him, he composed his masterpiece, *De consolatione philosophiae* (The Consolation of Philosophy).

De consolatione philosophiae, a bitterly hostile attack on Theoderic prefacing a philosophical discussion of innocent suffering and the problem of evil, must have been smuggled out of prison, no doubt with the aid of gold coins from Rusticiana or Symmachus. In the ninth century, the work captured the imagination of Alcuin at the court of Charlemagne, became a standard textbook in schools and was set on the way to being one of the greatest books of medieval culture, especially popular among laymen.

Boethius' earlier works have been the preserve of more specialized readers, especially those concerned with the history of ancient philosophy. His stated original intention was to educate the West by translating all of Plato and Aristotle into Latin and to supply explanatory commentaries on many of their writings. That was too ambitious. He did not proceed beyond some of the logical works (Organon) of Aristotle, prefaced by a commentary on a Latin translation of Porphyry's *Isagōgē* (Introduction) made in the fourth century by Marius Victorinus, an African teaching in Rome, and then by a second commentary on a translation of the same text made by himself. This commentary underlay the medieval debates on universals. He also wrote a commentary on Aristotle's *Categories* and two commentaries on Aristotle's *De interpretatione*. In addition, Boethius adapted Nicomachus of Gerasa's *Arithmetic* for Latin readers, Nicomachus' introduction to music as a liberal art, a commentary on Cicero's *Topics*, a short treatise 'On Division', important treatises on categorical and hypothetical syllogisms and a further tract on different kinds of 'topic'.

Intricate theological debates between Rome and Constantinople convinced him that a trained logician could contribute clarification, and he composed four theological tractates on the doctrines of the Trinity and the person of Christ, concentrating on logical problems. In addition, a fifth tract became a statement of orthodox belief without much reference to logical implications. The five pieces, or *Opuscula sacra*, became hardly less influential than *De consolatione philosophiae*, especially from the twelfth century onwards. We hear of critics who thought contemporary theologians knew more about Boethius than about the Bible.

See also: GOD, CONCEPTS OF; MEDIEVAL PHILOSOPHY; NEOPLATONISM; PATRISTIC PHILOSOPHY; PLOTINUS; PORPHYRY

HENRY CHADWICK

BOHR, NIELS (1885–1962)

One of the most influential scientists of the twentieth century, the Danish physicist Niels Bohr founded atomic quantum theory and the Copenhagen interpretation of quantum physics. This radical interpretation renounced the possibility of a unified, observer-independent, deterministic description in the microdomain. Bohr's principle of complementarity – the heart of the Copenhagen philosophy – implies that quantum phenomena can only be described by pairs of partial, mutually exclusive, or 'complementary' perspectives. Though simultaneously inapplicable, both perspectives are necessary for the exhaustive description of phenomena. Bohr aspired to generalize complementarity into all fields of knowledge, maintaining that new epistemological insights are obtained by adjoining contrary, seemingly incompatible, viewpoints.

See also: Logical positivism §4; Operationalism; Quantum mechanics, interpretation of

MARA BELLER

BOLZANO, BERNARD (1781–1848)

Bernard Bolzano was a lone forerunner both of analytical philosophy and phenomenology. Born in Prague in the year when Kant's first *Critique* appeared, he became one of the most acute critics both of Kant and of German Idealism. He died in Prague in the same year in which Frege was born; Frege is philosophically closer to him than any other thinker of the nineteenth or twentieth century. Bolzano was the only outstanding proponent of utilitarianism among German-speaking philosophers, and was a creative mathematician whose name is duly remembered in the annals of this discipline. His *Wissenschaftslehre* (*Theory of Science*) of 1837 makes him the greatest logician in the period between Leibniz and Frege. The book was sadly neglected by Bolzano's contemporaries, but rediscovered by Brentano's pupils: Its ontology of propositions and ideas provided Husserl with much of his ammunition in his fight against psychologism and in support of phenomenology, and through Twardowski it also had an impact on the development of logical semantics in the Lwów-Warsaw School.

See also: Analytical philosophy

WOLFGANG KÜNNE

BONAVENTURE (*c*.1217–74)

Bonaventure (John of Fidanza) developed a synthesis of philosophy and theology in which Neoplatonic doctrines are transformed by a Christian framework. Though often remembered for his denunciations of Aristotle, Bonaventure's thought includes some Aristotelian elements. His criticisms of Aristotle were motivated chiefly by his concern that various colleagues, more impressed by Aristotle's work than they had reason to be, were philosophizing with the blindness of pagans instead of the wisdom of Christians.

To Bonaventure, the ultimate goal of human life is happiness, and happiness comes from union with God in the afterlife. If one forgets this goal when philosophizing, the higher purpose of the discipline is frustrated. Philosophical studies can indeed help in attaining happiness, but only if pursued with humility and as part of a morally upright life. In the grander scheme of things, the ascent of the heart is more important than the ascent of the mind.

Bonaventure's later works consistently emphasize that all creation emanates from, reflects and returns to its source. Because the meaning of human life can be understood only from this wider perspective, the general aim is to show an integrated whole hierarchically ordered to God. The structure and symbolism favoured by Bonaventure reflect mystical elements as well. The world, no less than a book, reveals its creator: all visible things represent a higher reality. The theologian must use symbols to reveal this deeper meaning. He must teach especially of Christ, through whom God creates everything that exists and who is the sole medium by which we can return to our creator.

Bonaventure's theory of illumination aims to account for the certitude of human knowledge. He argues that there can be no certain knowledge unless the knower is infallible and what is known cannot change. Because the human mind cannot be entirely infallible through its own power, it needs the cooperation of God, even as it needs God as the source of immutable truths. Sense experience does not suffice, for it cannot reveal that what is true could not possibly be otherwise; so, in Bonaventure's view, the human mind attains certainty about the world only when it understands it in light of the 'eternal reasons' or divine ideas. This illumination from God, while necessary for certainty, ordinarily proceeds without a person's being conscious of it.

See also: Aquinas, T.

BONNIE KENT

BOOK OF CAUSES
See Liber de causis

BOOK OF CHANGES
See Yijing

BOOLEAN ALGEBRA

Boolean algebra, or the algebra of logic, was devised by the English mathematician George Boole (1815–64) and embodies the first successful application of algebraic methods to logic.

Boole seems to have had several interpretations for his system in mind. In his earlier work he thinks of each of the basic symbols of his 'algebra' as standing for the mental operation of selecting just the objects possessing some given attribute or included in some given class; later he conceives of these symbols as standing for the attributes or classes themselves. In each of these interpretations the basic symbols are conceived as being capable of combination under certain operations: 'multiplication', corresponding to conjunction of attributes or intersection of classes; 'addition', corresponding to (exclusive) disjunction or (disjoint) union; and 'subtraction', corresponding to 'excepting' or difference. He also recognizes that the algebraic laws he proposes are satisfied if the basic symbols are interpreted as taking just the number values 0 and 1.

Boole's ideas have since undergone extensive development, and the resulting concept of Boolean algebra now plays a central role in mathematical logic, probability theory and computer design.

J.L. BELL

BOSANQUET, BERNARD (1848–1923)

One of the most prominent and prolific of the British Idealists of the late nineteenth and early twentieth centuries, Bosanquet ranged across most fields of philosophy, making his main contributions in epistemology, metaphysics, aesthetics and especially political philosophy. He was deeply influenced by Plato and by Hegel. Bosanquet and F.H. Bradley were close on many matters, and each regarded the other as a co-worker; however, Bosanquet was always more Hegelian, less rigorous in argument than Bradley and lacking his sceptical approach. Bosanquet treats knowledge and reality as a single whole, working out the implications in the concrete 'modes of experience' of philosophy, science, morality, art, religion, and social and political life. He is at his best in explaining and developing the thoughts of others, particularly of Hegel, Bradley, Rousseau and T.H. Green.

See also: ABSOLUTE, THE; HEGELIANISM; STATE, THE

PETER P. NICHOLSON

BOYLE, ROBERT (1627–91)

Boyle is often remembered for the contributions that he made to the sciences of chemistry and pneumatics. Like other natural philosophers in seventeenth-century England, however, he was a synthetic thinker who sought to advance knowledge in all areas of human concern. An early advocate of experimental methods, he argued that experimentation would not only reveal the hidden processes operative in the world but would also advance the cause of religion. Through the study of nature, experimentalists would come to understand that the intricacy of design manifest in the world must be the result of an omniscient and omnipotent creator.

Boyle's experimental investigations and theological beliefs led him to a conception of the world as a 'cosmic mechanism' comprised of a harmonious set of interrelated processes. He agreed with the leading mechanical philosophers of his day that the corpuscular hypothesis, which explains the causal powers of bodies by reference to the motions of the least parts (corpuscles) of matter, provided the best means for understanding nature. He insisted, however, that these motions and powers could not be known by reasoning alone, but would have to be discovered experimentally.

See also: ATOMISM, ANCIENT; EXPERIMENT; MATTER; SCIENTIFIC METHOD

ROSE-MARY SARGENT

BRACKETING

See PHENOMENOLOGY, EPISTEMIC ISSUES IN

BRADLEY, FRANCIS HERBERT (1846–1924)

Bradley was the most famous and philosophically the most influential of the British Idealists, who had a marked impact on British philosophy in the later nineteenth and earlier twentieth centuries. They looked for inspiration less to their British predecessors than to Kant and Hegel, though Bradley owed as much to lesser German philosophers such as R.H. Lotze, J.F. Herbart and C. Sigwart.

Bradley is most famous for his metaphysics. He argued that our ordinary conceptions of the world conceal contradictions. His radical alternative can be summarized as a combination of monism (that is, reality is one, there are no real separate things) and absolute idealism (that is, reality is idea, or consists of experience – but not the experience of any one individual, for this is forbidden by the monism). This metaphysics is said to have influenced the poetry of T.S. Eliot. But he also made notable contributions to philosophy of history, to ethics and to the philosophy of logic, especially of a critical kind. His critique of hedonism – the view that the goal of morality is the maximization of pleasure – is still one of the best available. Some of his views on logic, for instance, that the grammatical subject of a sentence may not be what the sentence is really about, became standard through their acceptance by

Bertrand Russell, an acceptance which survived Russell's repudiation of idealist logic and metaphysics around the turn of the century. Russell's and G.E. Moore's subsequent disparaging attacks on Bradley's views signalled the return to dominance in England of pluralist (that is, non-monist) doctrines in the tradition of Hume and J.S. Mill, and, perhaps even more significantly, the replacement in philosophy of Bradley's richly metaphorical literary style and of his confidence in the metaphysician's right to adjudicate on the ultimate truth with something more like plain speaking and a renewed deference to science and mathematics.

Bradley's contemporary reputation was that of the greatest English philosopher of his generation. This status did not long survive his death, and the relative dearth of serious discussion of his work until more general interest revived in the 1970s has meant that the incidental textbook references to some of his most characteristic and significant views, for example, on relations and on truth, are often based on hostile and misleading caricatures.

See also: GREEN, T.H.; HEGELIANISM; JAMES, W.; LOTZE, R.H.; MOORE, G.E.

STEWART CANDLISH

BRADWARDINE, THOMAS
See OXFORD CALCULATIORS

BRAHMAN

The Sanskrit word *brahman* (neuter) emerged in late Vedic literature and Upaniṣads (900–300 BC) as the name (never pluralized) of the divine reality pervading the universe, knowledge or experience of which is a person's supreme good. The word's earliest usage (often pluralized) is to refer to the verses of the oldest work in Sanskrit (and in any Indo-European language), the *Ṛg Veda* (*c*.1200 BC), which is a compilation of poems and hymns to Indo-European gods. The individual verses of the poems are mantras (*brahmāṇi*), whose proper enunciation in the course of ritual and sacrifice was thought to secure various aims. Thematically, the *Ṛg Veda* and other early Indian literature presents a sense of pervasive divinity. Apparently through an assimilation of the idea of the magic of mantras to the divine immanence theme the word *brahman* assumed its later meaning. In any case, Brahman – the Absolute, the supremely real – became the focus of Indian spirituality and the centre of much metaphysics for almost three thousand years, down to the present day. In the Upaniṣads, which are mystic treatises containing speculation about Brahman's nature and relation to ourselves and the world, the central positions of Vedānta schools emerge, all of which are philosophies

of Brahman. But not even in the narrow set of the earliest and most universally accepted Upaniṣads (numbering twelve or thirteen) is there expressed a consistent worldview. Important themes about Brahman may be identified, but there is no overall unity of conception, despite what later exegetes claim. The unity of the early Upaniṣads concerns the premier importance of mystical knowledge or awareness of Brahman (*brahma-vidyā*), not precisely what it is that is to be mystically known. The classical Indian philosophical schools of Vedānta systematized the thought of early Upaniṣads.

See also: PANTHEISM; VEDĀNTA

STEPHEN H. PHILLIPS

BRENTANO, FRANZ CLEMENS (1838–1917)

Brentano was a philosopher and psychologist who taught at the Universities of Würzburg and Vienna. He made significant contributions to almost every branch of philosophy, notably psychology and philosophy of mind, ontology, ethics and the philosophy of language. He also published several books on the history of philosophy, especially Aristotle, and contended that philosophy proceeds in cycles of advance and decline. He is best known for reintroducing the scholastic concept of intentionality into philosophy and proclaiming it as the characteristic mark of the mental. His teachings, especially those on what he called descriptive psychology, influenced the phenomenological movement in the twentieth century, but because of his concern for precise statement and his sensitivity to the dangers of the undisciplined use of philosophical language, his work also bears affinities to analytic philosophy. His anti-speculative conception of philosophy as a rigorous discipline was furthered by his many brilliant students. Late in life Brentano's philosophy radically changed: he advocated a sparse ontology of physical and mental things (reism), coupled with a linguistic fictionalism stating that all language purportedly referring to non-things can be replaced by language referring only to things.

See also: INTENTIONALITY

RODERICK M. CHISHOLM
PETER SIMONS

BRITISH EMPIRICISTS
See HUME, DAVID; LOCKE, JOHN

BRUNO, GIORDANO (1548–1600)

Giordano Bruno was an Italian philosopher of nature and proponent of artificial memory systems who abandoned the Dominican Order and, after a turbulent career in many parts of Europe, was burned to death as a heretic in 1600. Because of his unhappy end, his support for the Copernican heliocentric hypothesis, and his pronounced anti-Aristotelianism, Bruno has often been hailed as the proponent of a scientific worldview against supposed medieval obscurantism. In fact, he is better interpreted in terms of Neoplatonism and, to a lesser extent, Hermeticism (also called Hermetism). Several of Bruno's later works were devoted to magic; and magic may play some role in his many books on the art of memory. His best-known works are the Italian dialogues he wrote while in England. In these Bruno describes the universe as an animate and infinitely extended unity containing innumerable worlds, each like a great animal with a life of its own. His support of Copernicus in *La Cena de le ceneri* (*The Ash Wednesday Supper*) was related to his belief that a living earth must move, and he specifically rejected any appeal to mere mathematics to prove cosmological hypotheses. His view that the physical world was a union of two substances, Matter and Form, had the consequence that apparent individuals were merely collections of accidents. He identified Form with the World-Soul, but although he saw the universe as permeated by divinity, he also believed in a transcendent God, inaccessible to the human mind. Despite some obvious parallels with both Spinoza and Leibniz, Bruno seems not to have had much direct influence on seventeenth-century thinkers.

See also: Atomism, ancient; Hermetism; Neoplatonism; Nicholas of Cusa; Platonism, Renaissance; Renaissance philosophy

E.J. ASHWORTH

BUBER, MARTIN (1878–1965)

Martin Buber covered a range of fields in his writings, from Jewish folklore and fiction, to biblical scholarship and translation, to philosophical anthropology and theology. Above all, however, Buber was a philosopher, in the lay-person's sense of the term: someone who devoted his intellectual energies to contemplating the meaning of life.

Buber's passionate interest in mysticism was reflected in his early philosophical work. However, he later rejected the view that mystical union is the ultimate goal of relation, and developed a philosophy of relation. In the short but enormously influential work, *Ich und Du* (I and Thou). Buber argued that the I emerges only through encountering others, and that the very nature of the I depends on the quality of the relationship with the Other. He described two fundamentally different ways of relating to others: the common mode of 'I–It', in which people and things are experienced as objects, or, in Kantian terms, as 'means to an end'; and the 'I–Thou' mode, in which I do not 'experience' the

Other, rather, the Other and I enter into a mutually affirming relation, which is simultaneously a relation with another and a relation with God, the 'eternal Thou'.

Buber acknowledged that necessity of I–It, even in the interpersonal sphere, but lamented its predominance in modern life. Through his scholarly work in philosophy, theology and biblical exegesis, as well as his translation of Scripture and adaptations of Hasidic tales, he sought to reawaken our capacity for I–Thou relations.

See also: Hasidism; Holocaust, the

TAMRA WRIGHT

BUDDHA
See Buddhist Philosophy; Indian

BUDDHIST DOCTRINE OF MOMENTARINESS
See Momentariness, Buddhist doctrine of

BUDDHIST PHILOSOPHY, CHINESE

When Buddhism first entered China from India and Central Asia two thousand years ago, Chinese favourably disposed towards it tended to view it as a part or companion school of the native Chinese Huang–Lao Daoist tradition, a form of Daoism rooted in texts and practices attributed to Huangdi (the Yellow Emperor) and Laozi. Others, less accepting of this 'foreign' incursion from the 'barbarous' Western Countries, viewed Buddhism as an exotic and dangerous challenge to the social and ethical Chinese civil order. For several centuries, these two attitudes formed the crucible within which the Chinese understanding of Buddhism was fashioned, even as more and more missionaries arrived (predominantly from Central Asia) bringing additional texts, concepts, rituals, meditative disciplines and other practices. Buddhists and Daoists borrowed ideas, terminology, disciplines, cosmologies, institutional structures, literary genres and soteric models from each other, sometimes so profusely that today it can be difficult if not impossible at times to determine who was first to introduce a certain idea. Simultaneously, polemical and political attacks from hostile Chinese quarters forced Buddhists to respond with apologia and ultimately reshape Buddhism into something the Chinese would find not only inoffensive, but attractive.

In the fifth century AD, Buddhism began to extricate itself from its quasi-Daoist pigeonhole by clarifying definitive differences between Buddhist and Daoist thought, shedding Daoist vocabulary and literary styles while developing new distinctively Buddhist terminology and genres. Curiously, despite the fact that Mahāyāna Buddhism had few adherents in Central Asia and was outnumbered by other Buddhist schools in India as well, in China Mahāyāna became the dominant form of Buddhism, so much so that few pejoratives were as stinging to a fellow Buddhist as labelling him 'Hīnayāna' (literally 'Little Vehicle,' a polemical term for non-Mahāyānic forms of Buddhism). By the sixth century, the Chinese had been introduced to a vast array of Buddhist theories and practices representing a wide range of Indian Buddhist schools. As the Chinese struggled to master these doctrines it became evident that, despite the fact that these schools were all supposed to express the One Dharma (Buddha's Teaching), their teachings were not homogenous, and were frequently incommensurate.

By the end of the sixth century, the most pressing issue facing Chinese Buddhists was how to harmonize the disparities between the various teachings. Responses to this issue produced the Sinitic Mahāyāna schools, that is, Buddhist schools that originated in China rather than India. The four Sinitic schools are Tiantai, Huayan, Chan and Pure Land (Jingtu). Issues these schools share in common include Buddha-nature, mind, emptiness, *tathāgatagarbha*, expedient means (*upāya*), overcoming birth and death (*saṃsāra*), and enlightenment.

See also: BUDDHIST PHILOSOPHY, INDIAN; BUDDHIST PHILOSOPHY, JAPANESE; BUDDHIST PHILOSOPHY, KOREAN; CHINESE PHILOSOPHY; DAOIST PHILOSOPHY

DAN LUSTHAUS

BUDDHIST PHILOSOPHY, INDIAN

Buddhism was an important ingredient in the philosophical melange of the Indian subcontinent for over a millennium. From an inconspicuous beginning a few centuries before Christ, Buddhist scholasticism gained in strength until it reached a peak of influence and originality in the latter half of the first millennium. Beginning in the eleventh century, Buddhism gradually declined and eventually disappeared from northern India. Although different individual thinkers placed emphasis on different issues, the tendency was for most writers to offer an integrated philosophical system that incorporated ethics, epistemology and metaphysics. Most of the issues addressed by Buddhist philosophers in India stem directly from the teachings attributed to Siddhārtha Gautama, known better through his honorific title, the Buddha.

The central concern of the Buddha was the elimination of unnecessary discontent. His principal insight into this problem was that all dissatisfaction arises because people (and other forms of life as well) foster desires and aversions, which are in turn the consequence of certain misunderstandings about their identity. Discontent can be understood as frustration, or a failure to achieve what one wishes; if one's wishes are generally unrealistic and therefore unattainable, then one will naturally be generally dissatisfied. Since the Buddha saw human frustration as an effect of misunderstandings concerning human nature, it was natural for Buddhist philosophers to attend to questions concerning the true nature of a human being. Since the Buddha himself was held as the paradigm of moral excellence, it was also left to later philosophers to determine what kind of being the Buddha had been. A typical question was whether his example was one that ordinary people could hope to follow, or whether his role was in some way more than that of a teacher who showed other people how to improve themselves.

The Buddha offered criticisms of many views on human nature and virtue and duty held by the teachers of his age. Several of the views that he opposed were based, at least indirectly, on notions incorporated in the Veda, a body of liturgical literature used by the Brahmans in the performance of rituals. Later generations of Buddhists spent much energy in criticizing Brahmanical claims of the supremacy of the Veda; at the same time, Buddhists tended to place their confidence in a combination of experience and reason. The interest in arriving at correct understanding through correct methods of reasoning led to a preoccupation with questions of logic and epistemology, which tended to overshadow all other philosophical concerns during the last five centuries during which Buddhism was an important factor in Indian philosophy.

Since the Buddha saw human frustration as an effect that could be eliminated if its cause were eliminated, it was natural for Buddhist philosophers to focus their attention on a variety of questions concerning causality. How many kinds of cause are there? Can a multiplicity of effects have a single cause? Can a single thing have a multiplicity of causes? How is a potentiality triggered into an actuality? Questions concerning simplicity and complexity, or unity and plurality, figured prominently in Buddhist discussions of what kinds of things in the world are ultimately real. In a tradition that emphasized the principle that all unnecessary human pain and conflict can ultimately be traced to a failure to understand what things in the world are real, it was natural to seek criteria by which one discerns real things from fictions.

See also: BUDDHIST PHILOSOPHY, CHINESE; BUDDHIST PHILOSOPHY, JAPANESE; BUDDHIST PHILOSOPHY, KOREAN; HINDU PHILOSOPHY; JAINA PHILOSOPHY; MOMENTARINESS, BUDDHIST DOCTRINE OF

RICHARD P. HAYES

BUDDHIST PHILOSOPHY, JAPANESE

Buddhism transformed Japanese culture and in turn was transformed in Japan. Mahāyāna Buddhist thought entered Japan from the East Asian continent as part of a cultural complex that included written language, political institutions, formal iconography and Confucian literature. From its introduction in the sixth century through to the sixteenth century, Japanese Buddhism developed largely by incorporating Chinese Buddhism, accommodating indigenous beliefs and reconciling intersectarian disputes. During the isolationist Tokugawa Period (1600–1868), neo-Confucian philosophy and Dutch science challenged the virtual hegemony of Buddhist ways of thinking, but served more often as alternative and sometimes complementary models than as incompatible paradigms. Only since the reopening of Japan in 1868 has Japanese Buddhist thought seriously attempted to come to terms with early Indian Buddhism, Western thought and Christianity.

Through the centuries, Buddhism gave the Japanese people a way to make sense of life and death, to explain the world and to seek liberation from suffering. When it engaged in theorizing, it did so in pursuit of religious fulfilment rather than of knowledge for its own sake. As an extension of its practical bent, Japanese Buddhist thought often tended to collapse differences between Buddhism and other forms of Japanese religiosity, between this phenomenal world and any absolute realm, and between the means and end of enlightenment. These tendencies are not Japanese in origin, but they extended further in Japan than in other Buddhist countries and partially define the character of Japanese Buddhist philosophy.

In fact, the identity of 'Japanese Buddhist philosophy' blends with almost everything with which we would contrast it. As a development and modification of Chinese traditions, there is no one thing that is uniquely Japanese about it; as a Buddhist tradition, it is characteristically syncretistic, often assimilating Shintō and Confucian philosophy in both its doctrines and practices. Rituals, social practices, political institutions and artistic or literary expressions are as essential as philosophical ideas to Japanese Buddhism.

Disputes about ideas often arose but were seldom settled by force of logical argument. One reason for this is that language was used not predominately in the service of logic but for the direct expression and actualization of reality. Disputants appealed to the authority of Buddhist *sūtras* because these scriptures were thought to manifest a direct understanding of reality. Further, as reality was thought to be all-inclusive, the better position in the dispute would be that which was more comprehensive rather than that which was more consistent but exclusive. Politics and practical consequences did play a role in the settling of disputes, but the ideal of harmony or conformity often prevailed.

The development of Japanese Buddhist philosophy can thus be seen as the unfolding of major themes rather than a series of philosophical positions in dispute. These themes include the role of language in expressing truth; the non-dual nature of absolute and relative, universal and particular; the actualization of liberation in this world, life or body; the equality of beings; and the transcendent non-duality of good and evil.

See also: BUDDHIST PHILOSOPHY, CHINESE; BUDDHIST PHILOSOPHY, INDIAN; DŌGEN; KŪKAI; SHINTŌ

JOHN C. MARALDO

BUDDHIST PHILOSOPHY, KOREAN

Buddhism was transmitted to the Korean peninsula from China in the middle of the fourth century AD. Korea at this time was divided into three kingdoms: Kokuryô, Paekche and Silla. Both Kokuryô and Paekche accepted Buddhism as a state religion immediately after it was introduced, to Kokuryô in 372 AD and to Paekche in 384 AD. However, it was not until two centuries later that Silla accepted Buddhism as a state religion. This was because Silla was the last of the three kingdoms to become established as a centralized power under the authority of one king.

It is not coincidental that Buddhism was accepted by these three states at the very same time that a strong kingship, independent of the aristocracy, was created. These newly established kingships needed a new ideology with which to rule, separate from the age-old shamanistic tradition which had been honored among the previous loose confederations of tribes. Buddhism fulfilled this need. It became a highly valued tool which kings used shrewdly, not only to provide their societies with a political ideology but to give them a foundation from which to build a viable system of ethics and philosophical thinking. Given this historical legacy, Korean Buddhism came to possess a feature which set it apart from the other East Asian traditions: it became 'state-protection' Buddhism. Although this was not a particularly sophisticated phenomenon on a philosophical level, this feature had a lasting influence on all aspects of Buddhist thought in Korea. In general, Korean Buddhism has followed a course of development more or less parallel to that of the greater East Asian context, although with notably closer ties to China than to Japan. There is no historical evidence which indicates any direct intellectual transmission from India, Buddhism's birthplace; rather, most of the philosophical development of Buddhism in Korea occurred as Korean monks travelled to China to study and obtain Buddhist texts which had either been written in or translated into Chinese. Despite such close ties to China, however, Korean Buddhism has developed its own identity, distinct from that of its progenitor.

Compared to Indian and Central Asian Buddhism, which developed along clear historical lines, the development of Buddhism in China was largely dependent on the personalities of individual monks, and was thus affected by such factors as their region of origination and the particular texts which they emphasized. Thus, in the process of assimilating Indian Buddhism, the Chinese created and developed a number of widely varying schools of Buddhist thought. In Korea, however, such a diverse number of philosophical traditions was never established. Rather, one of the distinct features of Korean Buddhism has been its preference for incorporating many different perspectives into a single, cohesive body of thought.

See also: BUDDHIST PHILOSOPHY, CHINESE

SUNGTAEK CHO

BUNDLE THEORY OF MIND
See MIND, BUNDLE THEORY OF

BURIDAN, JOHN (*c.*1300–after 1358)
Unlike most other important philosophers of the scholastic period, John Buridan never entered the theology faculty but spent his entire career as an arts master at the University of Paris. There he distinguished himself primarily as a logician who made numerous additions and refinements to the Parisian tradition of propositional logic. These included the development of a genuinely nominalist semantics, as well as techniques for analyzing propositions containing intentional verbs and paradoxes of self-reference. Even in his writings on metaphysics and natural philosophy, logic is Buridan's preferred vehicle for his nominalistic and naturalistic vision.

Buridan's nominalism is concerned not merely with denying the existence of real universals, but with a commitment to economize on entities, of which real universals are but one superfluous type. Likewise, his representationalist epistemology accounts for the difference between universal and singular cognition by focusing on how the intellect cognizes its object, rather than by looking for some difference in the objects themselves. He differs from other nominalists of the period, however, in his

willingness to embrace realism about modes of things to explain certain kinds of physical change.

Underlying Buridan's natural philosophy is his confidence that the world is knowable by us (although not with absolute certainty). His approach to natural science is empirical in the sense that it emphasizes the evidentness of appearances, the reliability of a posteriori modes of reasoning and the application of certain naturalistic models of explanation to a wide range of phenomena. In similar fashion, he locates the will's freedom in our evident ability to defer choice in the face of alternatives whose goodness appears dubious or uncertain.

See also: NOMINALISM; UNIVERSALS; WILLIAM OF OCKHAM

JACK ZUPKO

BURKE, EDMUND (1729–97)
Edmund Burke's philosophical importance lies in two fields, aesthetics and political theory. His early work on aesthetics, the *Philosophical Enquiry into the Origin of our Ideas of the Sublime and Beautiful* (1757), explored the experiential sources of these two, as he claimed, fundamental responses, relating them respectively to terror at the fear of death and to the love of society.

Active in politics from 1759, and Member of Parliament from 1765, Burke wrote and delivered a number of famous political pamphlets and speeches, on party in politics – *Thoughts on the Causes of the Present Discontents* (1770) – on the crisis with the American colonies – *On Conciliation with America* (1775) – on financial reform and on the reform of British India – *Speech on Mr Fox's East India Bill* (1783). While clearly informed by a reflective political mind, these are, however, *pièces d'occasion*, not political philosophy, and their party political provenance has rendered them suspect to many commentators.

His most powerful and philosophically influential works were written in opposition to the ideas of the French Revolution, in particular *Reflections on the Revolution in France* (1790), which has come to be seen as a definitive articulation of anglophone political conservatism. Here Burke considered the sources and desirability of social continuity, locating these in a suspicion of abstract reason, a disposition to follow custom, and certain institutions – hereditary monarchy, inheritance of property, and social corporations such as an established Church. His *Appeal from the New to the Old Whigs* (1791) insisted on the distinction between the French and Britain's revolution of 1688; while his final works, *Letters on a Regicide Peace* (1795), urged an uncompromising crusade on behalf of European Christian civilization against its atheist, Jacobin antithesis.

See also: CONSERVATISM; CONTRACTARIANISM; REVOLUTION; RIGHTS; TRADITION AND TRADITIONALISM

IAIN HAMPSHER-MONK

BURNET, G.
See CAMBRIDGE PLATONISM

BUSINESS ETHICS

Business ethics is the application of theories of right and wrong to activity within and between commercial enterprises, and between commercial enterprises and their broader environment. It is a wide range of activity, and no brief list can be made of the issues it raises. The safety of working practices; the fairness of recruitment; the transparency of financial accounting; the promptness of payments to suppliers; the degree of permissible aggression between competitors: all come within the range of the subject. So do relations between businesses and consumers, local communities, national governments and ecosystems. Many, but not all, of these issues can be understood to bear on distinct, recognized groups with their own stakes in a business: employees, shareholders, consumers, and so on. The literature of business ethics tends to concentrate on 'stakeholders' – anyone who occupies a role within the business or who belongs to a recognized group outside the business that is affected by its activity – but not in every sort of business. Corporations are often discussed to the exclusion of medium-sized and small enterprises.

Theories of right and wrong in business ethics come from a number of sources. Academic moral philosophy has contributed utilitarianism, Kantianism and Aristotelianism, as well as egoism and social contract theory. There are also theories that originate in organized religion, in the manifestos of political activists, in the thoughts of certain tycoons with an interest in social engineering, and in the writings of management 'gurus'. Recently, business ethics has been affected by the ending of the Cold War, and the breakdown of what were once command economies. These developments have encouraged enthusiasts for the market economy to advocate moral and political ideas consistent with capitalism, and the handing over to private companies of activity in certain countries that has long been reserved for the state.

See also: APPLIED ETHICS; ECONOMICS AND ETHICS; PROFESSIONAL ETHICS

TOM SORELL

BUTLER, JOSEPH (1692–1752)

Joseph Butler the moral philosopher is in that long line of eighteenth-century thinkers who sought to answer Thomas Hobbes on human nature and moral motivation. Following the Third Earl of Shaftesbury, he rejects any purely egoistic conception of these. Instead, he analyses human nature into parts, of which he notices in detail appetites, affections and passions on the one hand and the principles of self-love, benevolence and conscience on the other. His ethics consists in the main in showing the relation of these parts to each other. They form a hierarchy, ordered in terms of their natural authority, and while such authority can be usurped, as when the particular passions overwhelm self-love and conscience, the system that they constitute, or human nature, is rightly proportioned when each part occupies its rightful place in the ordered hierarchy. Virtue consists in acting in accordance with that ordered, rightly proportioned nature.

As a philosopher of religion, Butler addresses himself critically to the eighteenth-century flowering of deism in Britain. On the whole, the deists allowed that God the Creator existed but rejected the doctrines of natural and, especially, revealed religion. Butler's central tactic against them is to argue, first, that the central theses associated with natural religion, such as a future life, are probable; and second, that the central theses associated with revealed religion, such as miracles, are as probable as those of natural religion. Much turns, therefore, on the success of Butler's case in appealing to what is present in this world as evidence for a future life.

R.G. FREY

C

CABALA
See KABBALAH

CALVIN, JOHN (1509–64)

John Calvin, French Protestant reformer and theologian, was a minister among Reformed Christians in Geneva and Strasbourg. His *Institutes of the Christian Religion* (first edition 1536) – which follows the broad outline of the Apostles' Creed and is shaped by biblical and patristic thought – is the cornerstone of Reformed theology.

Calvin's religious epistemology links self-knowledge and knowledge of God. He identifies in humans an innate awareness of God, which is supported by the general revelation of God in creation and providence. Because sin has corrupted this innate awareness, Scripture – confirmed by the Holy Spirit – is needed for genuine knowledge of God. Scripture teaches that God created the world out of nothing and sustains every part of it. Humanity, which was created good and with free will, has defaced itself and lost significant freedom due to its fall into sin. Calvin sees Christ the mediator as the fulfilment of the Old Testament offices of prophet, priest and king.

Calvin insists that God justifies sinners on the basis of grace and not works, forgiving their sins and imputing Christ's righteousness to them. Such justification, received by faith, glorifies God and relieves believers' anxiety about their status before God. On the basis of his will alone, God predestines some individuals to eternal life and others to eternal damnation.

Calvin dignifies even ordinary occupations by seeing them as service to God. He recognizes the distinction between civil government and the Church, although he says that government should protect true worship of God and Christians should obey and support their government. Calvin's thought was dominant in non-Lutheran Protestant churches until the eighteenth century and has

enjoyed a resurgence since the mid-nineteenth century.

See also: CAMBRIDGE PLATONISM; FAITH; PREDESTINATION; RENAISSANCE PHILOSOPHY; WILL, THE

RONALD J. FEENSTRA

CALVINISM
See CALVIN, JOHN

CAMBRIDGE PLATONISM

Cambridge Platonism was an intellectual movement broadly inspired by the Platonic tradition, centred in Cambridge from the 1630s to the 1680s. Its hallmark was a devotion to reason in metaphysics, religion and ethics. The Cambridge Platonists made reason rather than tradition and inspiration their ultimate criterion of knowledge. Their central aim was to reconcile the realms of reason and faith, the new natural philosophy and Christian revelation. Although loyal to the methods and naturalism of the new sciences, they opposed its mechanical model of explanation because it seemed to leave no room for spirit, God and life.

In epistemology the Cambridge Platonists were critics of empiricism and stressed the role of reason in knowledge; they also criticized conventionalism and held that there are essential or natural distinctions between things. In metaphysics they attempted to establish the existence of spirit, God and life in a manner consistent with the naturalism and method of the new sciences. And in ethics the Cambridge Platonists defended moral realism and freedom of the will against the voluntarism and determinism of Hobbes and Calvin. Cambridge Platonism was profoundly influential in the seventeenth and eighteenth centuries. It was the inspiration behind latitudinarianism and ethical rationalism, and many of its ideas were developed by Samuel

Clarke, Isaac Newton and the Third Earl of Shaftesbury.

See also: NEOPLATONISM; PLATO

FREDERICK BEISER

CAMPANELLA, GIOVANNI DOMENICO
See CAMPANELLA, TOMMASO

CAMPANELLA, TOMMASO (1568–1639)

Tommaso Campanella was a Counter-Reformation theologian, a Renaissance magus, a prophet, a poet and an astrologer, as well as a philosopher whose speculations assumed encyclopedic proportions. As a late Renaissance philosopher of nature, Campanella is notable for his early, and continuous, opposition to Aristotle. He rejected the fundamental Aristotelian principle of hylomorphism, namely the understanding of all physical substance in terms of form and matter. In its place he appropriated Telesio's understanding of reality in terms of the dialectical principles of heat and cold; and he adopted a form of empiricism found in Telesio's work that included pansensism, the doctrine that all things in nature are endowed with sense. Especially after 1602, Campanella's exposure to Renaissance Platonism also involved him in panpsychism, the view that all reality has a mental aspect. Thus his empiricism came to show a distinctly metaphysical and spiritualistic dimension that transformed his philosophy. At the same time his epistemology embraced a universal doubt and an emphasis on individual self-consciousness that are suggestive of Descartes' views.

Campanella's career as a religious dissident, radical reformer and leader of an apocalyptic movement presents a political radicalism that was oddly associated with more traditional notions of universal monarchy and the need for theocracy. The only one of his numerous writings that receives attention today, *La Città del Sole* (*The City of the Sun*) (composed 1602, but not published until 1623), has come to occupy a prominent place in the literature of utopias though Campanella himself seems to have expected some form of astronomical/apocalyptic realization.

Campanella's naturalism, especially its pansensism and panpsychism, enjoyed some currency in Germany and France during the 1620s, but in the last five years of his life it was emphatically rejected by the intellectual communities headed by Mersenne and Descartes, as well as by Galileo.

See also: GALILEI, GALILEO; PANPSYCHISM; PLATONISM, RENAISSANCE; RENAISSANCE PHILOSOPHY

JOHN M. HEADLEY

CAMPBELL, NORMAN ROBERT (1880–1949)

Campbell made important contributions to philosophy of science in the 1920s, influenced by Poincaré, Russell and his own work in physics. He produced pioneering analyses of the nature of physical theories and of measurement, but is mainly remembered for requiring a theory, for example, the kinetic theory of gases, to have an 'analogy', that is, an independent interpretation, for example, as laws of motion of a swarm of microscopic particles.

See also: MEASUREMENT, THEORY OF; MODELS; SCIENTIFIC REALISM AND ANTIREALISM

D.H. MELLOR

CAMUS, ALBERT (1913–60)

Albert Camus was awarded the Nobel Prize in 1957 for having 'illuminated the problems of the human conscience in our times'. By mythologizing the experiences of a secular age struggling with an increasingly contested religious tradition, he dramatized the human effort to 'live and create without the aid of eternal values which, temporarily perhaps, are absent or distorted in contemporary Europe' (*Le Mythe de Sisyphe* 1943). Thus the challenge posed by 'the absurd' with which he is so universally identified.

See also: EXISTENTIALISM

DAVID A. SPRINTZEN

CANTOR, GEORG (1845–1918)

Georg Cantor and set theory belong forever together. Although Dedekind had already introduced the concept of a set and naïve set theory in 1872, it was Cantor who single-handedly created transfinite set theory as a new branch of mathematics. In a series of papers written between 1874 and 1885, he developed the fundamental concepts of abstract set theory and proved the most important of its theorems. Although today set theory is accepted by the majority of scientists as an autonomous branch of mathematics, and perhaps the most fundamental, this was not always the case. Indeed, when Cantor set out to develop his conception of sets and to argue for its acceptance, he initiated an inquiry into the infinite which raised questions that have still not been completely resolved today.

See also: CANTOR'S THEOREM; INFINITY §§6–7; PARADOXES OF SET AND PROPERTY; SET THEORY

ULRICH MAJER

CANTOR'S THEOREM

Cantor's theorem states that the cardinal number ('size') of the set of subsets of any set is greater than the cardinal number of the set itself. So once the

existence of one infinite set has been proved, sets of ever increasing infinite cardinality can be generated. The philosophical interest of this result lies (1) in the foundational role it played in Cantor's work, prior to the axiomatization of set theory, (2) in the similarity between its proof and arguments which lead to the set-theoretic paradoxes, and (3) in controversy between intuitionist and classical mathematicians concerning what exactly its proof proves.
See also: CONTINUUM HYPOTHESIS

MARY TILES

CARNAP, RUDOLF (1891–1970)

Carnap was one of the most significant philosophers of the twentieth century, and made important contributions to logic, philosophy of science, semantics, modal theory and probability. Viewed as an *enfant terrible* when he achieved fame in the Vienna Circle in the 1930s, Carnap is more accurately seen as one who held together its widely varying viewpoints as a coherent movement. In the 1930s he developed a daring pragmatic conventionalism according to which many traditional philosophical disputes are viewed as the expression of different linguistic frameworks, not genuine disagreements. This distinction between a language (framework) and what can be said within it was central to Carnap's philosophy, reconciling the apparently a priori domains such as logic and mathematics with a thoroughgoing empiricism: basic logical and mathematical commitments partially constitute the choice of language. There is no uniquely correct choice among alternative logics or foundations for mathematics; it is a question of practical expedience, not truth. Thereafter, the logic and mathematics may be taken as true in virtue of that language. The remaining substantive questions, those not settled by the language alone, should be addressed only by empirical means. There is no other source of news. Beyond pure logic and mathematics, Carnap's approach recognized within the sciences commitments aptly called a priori – those not tested straightforwardly by observable evidence, but, rather, presupposed in the gathering and manipulation of evidence. This a priori, too, is relativized to a framework and thus comports well with empiricism. The appropriate attitude towards alternative frameworks would be tolerance, and the appropriate mode of philosophizing the patient task of explicating and working out in detail the consequences of adopting this or that framework. While Carnap worked at this tirelessly and remained tolerant of alternative frameworks, his tolerance was not much imitated nor were his principles well understood and adopted. By the time of his death,

philosophers were widely rejecting what they saw as logical empiricism, though often both their arguments and the views offered as improvements had been pioneered by Carnap and his associates. By his centenary, however, there emerged a new and fuller understanding of his ideas and of their importance for twentieth-century philosophy.
See also: ANALYTICAL PHILOSOPHY

RICHARD CREATH

CARNEADES (214–129 BC)

The Greek philosopher Carneades was head of the Academy from 167 to 137 BC. Born in North Africa he migrated to Athens, where he studied logic with the Stoic Diogenes of Babylon; but he was soon seduced by the Academy, to which his allegiance was thereafter lifelong. He was a celebrated figure; and in 155 BC he was sent by Athens to Rome as a political ambassador, where he astounded the youth by his rhetorical powers and outraged their elders by his arguments against justice.

Under Carneades' direction the Academy remained sceptical. But he enlarged the sceptical armoury – in particular, he deployed sorites arguments against various dogmatic positions. He also broadened the target of sceptical attack: thus he showed an especial interest in ethics, where his 'division' of possible ethical theories served later as a standard framework for thought on the subject. But his major innovation concerned the notion of 'the plausible' (*to pithanon*). Even if we cannot determine which appearances are true and which false, we are able to distinguish the plausible from the implausible – and further to distinguish among several grades of plausibility. It is disputed – and it was disputed among his immediate followers – how, if at all, Carneades' remarks on the plausible are to be reconciled with his scepticism.
See also: CICERO, M.T.; STOICISM

JONATHAN BARNES

CARROLL, LEWIS
See DODGSON, CHARLES LUTWIDGE

CARTESIANISM
See DESCARTES, RENÉ; MALEBRANCHE, NICOLAS

CĀRVĀKA
See MATERIALISM, INDIAN SCHOOL OF

CASSIRER, ERNST (1874–1945)

Cassirer is one of the major figures in the development of philosophical idealism in the first half of the twentieth century. He is known for his philosophy of culture based on his conception of 'symbolic form', for his historical studies of the problem of knowledge in the rise of modern philosophy and science and for his works on the Renaissance and the Enlightenment. Cassirer expanded Kant's critique of reason to a critique of culture by regarding the symbol as the common denominator of all forms of human thought, imagination and experience. He delineates symbolic forms of myth, religion, language, art, history and science and defines the human being as the 'symbolizing animal'. All human experience occurs through systems of symbols. Language is only one such system; the images of myth, religion and art and the mathematical structures of science are others.

Being of Jewish faith, Cassirer left Germany in 1933 with the rise of Nazism, going first to Oxford, then to university positions in Sweden and the USA. In the last period of his career he applied his philosophy of culture generally and his conception of myth specifically to a critique of political myths and to the study of irrational forces in the state.

See also: STATE, THE

DONALD PHILLIP VERENE

CAT, SCHRÖDINGER'S

See QUANTUM MEASUREMENT PROBLEM

CATEGORICAL IMPERATIVE

See KANTIAN ETHICS

CATEGORIES

Categories are hard to describe, and even harder to define. This is in part a consequence of their complicated history, and in part because category theory must grapple with vexed questions concerning the relation between linguistic or conceptual categories on the one hand, and objective reality on the other. In the mid-fourth century BC, Aristotle initiates discussion of categories as a central enterprise of philosophy. In the *Categories* he presents an 'ontological' scheme which classifies all being into ten ultimate types, but in the *Topics* introduces the categories as different kinds of predication, that is, of items such as 'goodness' or 'length of a tennis court' or 'red', which can be 'predicated of' subjects. He nowhere attempts either to justify what he includes in his list of categories or to establish its completeness, and relies throughout on the unargued conviction that language faithfully represents the most basic features of reality. In the twentieth century, a test for category membership was recommended by Ryle, that of absurdity: concepts or expressions differ in logical type when

their combination produces sentences which are palpable nonsense. Kant, working in the eighteenth century, derives his categories from a consideration of aspects of judgments, hoping in this manner to ensure that his scheme will consist exclusively of a priori concepts which might constitute an objective world. The Sinologist Graham argues that the categories familiar in the West mirror Indo-European linguistic structure, and that an experimental Chinese scheme exhibits suggestively different properties, but his relativism is highly contentious.
See also: ONTOLOGY IN INDIAN PHILOSOPHY; UNIVERSALS

ROBERT WARDY

CATHARSIS

See EMOTION IN RESPONSE TO ART; KATHARSIS; TRAGEDY

CAUSATION

Two opposed viewpoints raise complementary problems about causation. The first is from Hume: watch the child kick the ball. You see the foot touch the ball and the ball move off. But do you see the foot *cause* the ball to move? And if you do not see it, how do you know that that is what happened? Indeed if all our experience is like this, and all of our ideas come from experience, where could we get the idea of causation in the first place?

The second is from Kant. We can have no ideas at all with which to experience nature – we cannot experience the child as a child nor the motion as a motion – unless we have organized the experience into a causal order in which one thing necessarily gives rise to another. The problem for the Kantian viewpoint is to explain how, in advance of experiencing nature in various specific ways, we are able to provide such a complex organization for our experience.

For the Kantian the objectivity of causality is a presupposition of our experience of events external to ourselves. The Humean viewpoint must find something in our experience that provides sufficient ground for causal claims. Regular associations between putative causes and effects are the proposed solution. This attention to regular associations connects the Humean tradition with modern statistical techniques used in the social sciences to establish causal laws.

Modern discussions focus on three levels of causal discourse. The first is about singular causation: about individual 'causings' that occur at specific times and places, for example, 'the cat lapped up the milk'. The second is about causal laws: laws about what features reliably cause or prevent other features, as in, 'rising inflation prevents unemployment'. The third is about causal powers. These are supposed to determine what kinds of singular causings a feature can produce or what kinds of causal laws can be true of it – 'aspirins have the power to relieve headaches' for example.

Contemporary anglophone work on causality has centred on two questions. First, 'what are the relations among these levels?' The second is from reductive empiricisms of various kinds that try to bar causality from the world, or at least from any aspects of the world that we can find intelligible: 'What is the relation between causality (on any one of the levels) and those features of the world that are supposed to be less problematic?' These latter are taken by different authors to include different things. Sensible or measurable properties like 'redness' or 'electric voltage' have been attributed a legitimacy not available to causal relations like 'lapping-up' or 'pushing over': sometimes it is 'the basic properties studied by physics'. So-called 'occurrent' properties have also been privileged over dispositional properties (like water-solubility) and powers. At the middle level where laws of nature are concerned, laws about regular associations between admissible features – whether these associations are deterministic or probabilistic – have been taken as superior to laws about what kinds of effects given features produce.

See also: CAUSATION, INDIAN THEORIES OF

NANCY CARTWRIGHT

CAUSATION IN THE LAW

Causal language is pervasive in the law, especially in those areas, such as contract law, tort law and criminal law, that deal with legal responsibility for the adverse consequences of voluntary and involuntary human interactions. Yet there are widely varying theories on the nature and role of causation in the law. At one extreme, the causal minimalists claim that causation plays little or no role in attributions of legal responsibility. At the opposite extreme, the causal maximalists claim that causation is the primary or sole determinant of legal responsibility. These divergent views are rooted in different conceptions of: (1) the nature or meaning of causation, (2) the relationship between causation and attributions of legal responsibility, and (3) the basic purposes of the relevant areas of law.

Much of the disagreement and confusion stems from the ambiguous usages of causal language in the law, which follow the ambiguous usages of causal language in ordinary, non-legal discourse. In both areas, causal language is sometimes used in its primary sense to refer to the content and operation of the empirical laws of nature, but at other times it is used in a more restricted normative sense to

signify that one of the contributing conditions has been identified as being more important than the other conditions, in relation to some particular purpose. The relevant purpose in the law is the attribution of legal responsibility for some consequence. Thus, in legal discourse, causal language is ambiguously employed to grapple not only with the empirical issue of causal contribution but also with the normative issue of legal responsibility. The failure to use language that clearly identifies and distinguishes these two issues has generated considerable disagreement and confusion over each issue and the nature of the relationship between them.

Further disagreement and confusion have been generated by the difficulty of providing useful, comprehensive criteria for the resolution of each of these issues. The most widely used criterion for the empirical issue of causal contribution is the necessary-condition (*conditio sine qua non*) test. This test has been subjected to considerable criticism as being over-inclusive or under-inclusive or both, and as inviting or even requiring resort to normative policy issues to resolve what supposedly is a purely empirical issue. The deficiencies of the necessary-condition test, coupled with the difficulties encountered in trying to devise a useful alternative test that does not beg the question, have led many to conclude that there is no purely empirical concept of causation, and that there is thus no more than a minimal role for causation in the attribution of legal responsibility.

This causal-minimalist position has been especially attractive to the legal economists and the critical legal scholars, since it undermines the traditional conception of the law as an instrument of interactive justice, whereby everyone is required to avoid causing injury to the persons and property of others through interactions that fail to respect properly those others' equal dignity and autonomy. The traditional conception, with its focus on individual autonomy, rights and causation, is inconsistent with the social-welfare maximizing theories of the legal economists and the anti-liberal, deconstructionist programme of the critical legal scholars. The members of each causal-minimalist group therefore argue that the concept of causation should be: (a) jettisoned entirely and replaced by direct resort to the social policy goals which they believe do or should determine the ultimate incidence and extent of legal responsibility; (b) redefined as being reducible to those social policy goals; or (c) retained as useful rhetoric that can be manipulated to achieve or camouflage the pursuit of those social policy goals.

See also: CAUSATION; RESPONSIBILITY

RICHARD W. WRIGHT

CAUSATION, INDIAN THEORIES OF

Causation was acknowledged as one of the central problems in Indian philosophy. The classical Indian philosophers' concern with the problem basically arose from two sources: first, the cosmogonic speculations of the Vedas and the Upaniṣads, with their search for some simple unitary cause for the origin of this complex universe; and second, the Vedic concern with ritual action (*karman*) and the causal mechanisms by which such actions bring about their unseen, but purportedly cosmic, effects. Once the goal of liberation (*mokṣa*) came to be accepted as the highest value, these two strands of thought entwined to generate intense interest in the notion of causation. The systematic philosophers of the classical and medieval periods criticized and defended competing theories of causation. These theories were motivated partly by a desire to guarantee the efficacy of action and hence the possibility of attaining liberation, partly by a desire to understand the nature of the world and hence how to negotiate our way in it so as to attain liberation.

Indian philosophers extensively discussed a number of issues relating to causation, including the nature of the causal relation, the definitions of cause and effect, and classifications of kinds of causes. Typically they stressed the importance of the material cause, rather than (as in Western philosophy) the efficient cause. In India only the Cārvāka materialists denied causation or took it to be subjective. This is unsurprising given that a concern with demonstrating the possibility of liberation motivated the theories of causation, for only the Cārvākas denied this possibility. The orthodox Hindu philosophers and the heterodox Buddhists and Jainas all accepted both the possibility of liberation and the reality of causation, though they differed sharply (and polemically) about the details.

The Indian theories of causation are traditionally classified by reference to the question of whether the effect is a mode of the cause. According to this taxonomy there are two principal theories of causation. One is the identity theory (*satkāryavāda*), which holds that the effect is identical with the cause, a manifestation of what is potential in the cause. This is the Sāṅkhya-Yoga view, though that school's particular version of it is sometimes called transformation theory (*pariṇāmavāda*). Advaita Vedānta holds an appearance theory (*vivartavāda*), which is often considered a variant of the identity theory. According to the appearance theory effects are mere appearances of the underlying reality, Brahman. Since only Brahman truly exists, this theory is also sometimes called *satkāraṇavāda* (the theory that the cause is real but the effect is not).

The other principal theory of causation is the nonidentity theory (*asatkāryavāda*), which denies that the effect pre-exists in its cause and claims instead that the effect is an altogether new entity. Both adherents of Nyāya-Vaiśeṣika and the Buddhists are usually classified as nonidentity theorists, but they differ on many important details. One of these is whether the cause continues to exist after the appearance of the effect: Nyāya-Vaiśeṣika claims it does, the Buddhists mostly claim it does not.

Finally, some philosophers try to take the middle ground and claim that an effect is both identical and nonidentical with its cause. This is the position of the Jainas and of some theistic schools of Vedānta.

See also: CAUSATION

ROY W. PERRETT

CAUSATION, MENTAL

See MENTAL CAUSATION

CAVELL, STANLEY (1926–)

Born in Atlanta, Georgia, Stanley Cavell has held the Walter M. Cabot Chair in Aesthetics and the General Theory of Value at Harvard University since 1963. The range, diversity and distinctiveness of his writings are unparalleled in twentieth-century Anglo-American philosophy. As well as publishing essays on modernist painting and music, he has created a substantial body of work in film studies, literary theory and literary criticism; he has introduced new and fruitful ways of thinking about psychoanalysis and its relationship with philosophy; and his work on Heidegger and Derrida, taken together with his attempts to revitalize the tradition of Emersonian Transcendentalism, have defined new possibilities for a distinctively American contribution to philosophical culture. This complex oeuvre is unified by a set of thematic concerns – relating to scepticism and moral perfectionism – which are rooted in Cavell's commitment to the tradition of ordinary language philosophy, as represented in the work of J.L. Austin and Wittgenstein.

STEPHEN MULHALL

CAVENDISH, MARGARET LUCAS (1623–73)

The only seventeenth-century woman to publish numerous books on natural philosophy, Cavendish presented her materialism in a wide range of literary forms. She abandoned her early commitment to Epicurean atomism and, rejecting the mechanical model of natural change, embraced an organicist materialism. She also addressed the relations that hold among philosophy, gender and literary genre.

See also: ATOMISM, ANCIENT; MATERIALISM

EILEEN O'NEILL

CENSORSHIP

See FREEDOM OF SPEECH; JOURNALISM, ETHICS OF; PORNOGRAPHY

CETERIS PARIBUS LAWS

See CAUSATION; IDEALIZATIONS; LAWS, NATURAL

CHANGE

Change in general may be defined as the variation of properties (whether of things or of regions of space) over time. But this definition is incomplete in a number of respects. The reference to properties and time raises two important questions. The first concerns whether we need to specify further the kinds of properties which are involved in change. If we define change in an object as temporal variation of its properties we are faced with the problem that some properties of an object may alter without there being a consequent change in the object itself. The second question concerns the passage of time: does temporal variation constitute change only in virtue of some feature of time itself, namely the fact (or putative fact) that time passes? Some philosophers have wished to reject the notion of time's passage. Are they thereby committed to a picture of the world as unchanging?

See also: EVENTS; PROCESSES

ROBIN LE POIDEVIN

CHAOS THEORY

Chaos theory is the name given to the scientific investigation of mathematically simple systems that exhibit complex and unpredictable behaviour. Since the 1970s these systems have been used to model experimental situations ranging from the early stages of fluid turbulence to the fluctuations of brain wave activity. This complex behaviour does not arise as a result of the interaction of numerous sub-systems or from intrinsically probabilistic equations. Instead, chaotic behaviour involves the rapid growth of any inaccuracy. The slightest vagueness in specifying the initial state of such a system makes long-term predictions impossible, yielding behaviour that is effectively random. The existence of such behaviour raises questions about the extent to which predictability and determinism apply in the physical world. Chaos theory addresses the questions of how such behaviour arises and how it changes as the system is modified. Its new analytical techniques invite a reconsideration of scientific methodology.

See also: RANDOMNESS

STEPHEN H. KELLERT

CHARITY, PRINCIPLE OF

The principle of charity governs the interpretation of the beliefs and utterances of others. It urges charitable interpretation, meaning interpretation that maximizes the truth or rationality of what others think and say. Some formulations of the principle concern primarily rationality, recommending attributions of rational belief or assertion. Others concern primarily truth, recommending attributions of true belief or assertion. Versions of the principle differ in strength. The weakest urge charity as one consideration among many. The strongest hold that interpretation is impossible without the assumption of rationality or truth.

The principle has been put to various philosophical uses. Students are typically instructed to follow the principle when interpreting passages and formulating the arguments they contain. The principle also plays a role in philosophy of mind and language and in epistemology. Philosophers have argued that the principle of charity plays an essential role in characterizing the nature of belief and intentionality, with some philosophers contending that beliefs must be mostly true. A version of the principle has even served as a key premise in a widely discussed argument against epistemological scepticism.

See also: SCEPTICISM

RICHARD FELDMAN

CHINESE PHILOSOPHY

Any attempt to survey an intellectual tradition which encompasses more than four thousand years would be a daunting task even if it could be presumed that the reader shares, at least tacitly, many of the assumptions underlying that tradition. However, no such commonalities can be assumed in attempting to introduce Asian thinking to Western readers. Until the first Jesuit incursions in the late sixteenth century, China had developed in virtual independence of the Indo-European cultural experience and China and the Western world remained in almost complete ignorance of one another.

The dramatic contrast between Chinese and Western modes of philosophic thinking may be illustrated by the fact that the tendency of European philosophers to seek out the being of things, the essential reality lying behind appearances, would meet with little sympathy among Chinese thinkers, whose principal interests lie in the establishment and cultivation of harmonious relationships within their social ambiance. Contrasted with Anglo-European philosophic traditions, the thinking of the Chinese is far more concrete, this-worldly and, above all, practical.

One reason for this difference is suggested by the fact that cosmogonic and cosmological myths played such a minor role in the development of Chinese intellectual culture and that, as a consequence, Chinese eyes were focused not upon issues of cosmic order but upon more mundane questions of how to achieve communal harmony within a relatively small social nexus. The rather profound linguistic and ethnic localism of what Pliny the Elder described as a 'stay-at-home' China, reinforced by a relative freedom from intercultural contact, generated traditional radial communities in which moral, aesthetic and spiritual values could remain relatively implicit and unarticulated. By contrast, in the West these norms had to be abstracted and raised to the level of consciousness to adjudicate conflicts occasioned by the complex ethnic and linguistic interactions associated with the development of a civilization rooted almost from the beginning in the confluence of Greek, Hebrew, and Latin civilizations.

The distinctive origins and histories of Chinese and Western civilizations are manifested in a number of important ways. The priority of logical reasoning in the West is paralleled in China by the prominence of less formal uses of analogical, parabolic and literary discourse. The Chinese are largely indifferent to abstract analyses that seek to maintain an objective perspective, and are decidedly anthropocentric in their motivations for the acquisition, organization and transmission of knowledge. The disinterest in dispassionate speculations upon the nature of things, and a passionate commitment to the goal of social harmony was dominant throughout most of Chinese history. Indeed, the interest in logical speculations on the part of groups such as the sophists and the later Mohists was short-lived in classical China.

The concrete, practical orientation of the Chinese toward the aim of communal harmony conditioned their approach toward philosophical differences. Ideological conflicts were seen, not only by the politicians but by the intellectuals themselves, to threaten societal wellbeing. Harmonious interaction was finally more important to these thinkers than abstract issues of who had arrived at the 'truth'. Perhaps the most obvious illustration of the way the Chinese handled their theoretical conflicts is to be found in mutual accommodation of the three emergent traditions of Chinese culture, Confucianism, Daoism and Buddhism. Beginning in the Han dynasty (206 BC–AD 220), the diverse themes inherited from the competing 'hundred schools' of pre-imperial China were harmonized within Confucianism as it ascended to become the state ideology. From the Han synthesis until approximately the tenth century AD, strong Buddhist and religious Daoist influences continued to compete with persistent Confucian themes, while from the eleventh century to the modern period, Neoconfucianism – a Chinese neoclassicism – absorbed into itself these existing tensions and those that would emerge as China, like it or not, confronted Western civilization.

In the development of modern China, when Western influence at last seemed a permanent part of Chinese culture, the values of traditional China have remained dominant. For a brief period, intellectual activity surrounding the May Fourth movement in 1919 seemed to be leading the Chinese into directions of Western philosophic interest. Visits by Bertrand Russell and John Dewey, coupled with a large number of Chinese students seeking education in Europe, Great Britain and the USA, promised a new epoch in China's relations with the rest of the world. However, the Marxism that Mao Zedong sponsored in China was 'a Western heresy with which to confront the West'. Mao's Marxism quickly took on a typically 'Chinese' flavour, and China's isolation from Western intellectual currents continued essentially unabated.

See also: Buddhist philosophy, Chinese; Confucian philosophy, Chinese; Confucius; Daoist philosophy; Mohist philosophy

DAVID L. HALL
ROGER T. AMES

CHINESE ROOM ARGUMENT

John Searle's 'Chinese room' argument aims to refute 'strong AI' (artificial intelligence), the view that instantiating a computer program is sufficient for having contentful mental states. Imagine a program that produces conversationally appropriate Chinese responses to Chinese utterances. Suppose Searle, who understands no Chinese, sits in a room and is passed slips of paper bearing strings of shapes which, unbeknown to him, are Chinese sentences. Searle performs the formal manipulations of the program and passes back slips bearing conversationally appropriate Chinese responses. Searle seems to instantiate the program, but understands no Chinese. So, Searle concludes, strong AI is false.

See also: Artificial intelligence; Consciousness; Intentionality

ROBERT VAN GULICK

CHISHOLM, RODERICK MILTON (1916–99)

Chisholm was an important analytic philosopher of the second half of the twentieth century. His work in epistemology, metaphysics and ethics is characterized by scrupulous attention to detail, the use of a few basic, undefined or primitive terms, and extraordinary clarity. One of the first Anglo-American philosophers to make fruitful use of Brentano and Meinong, Chisholm translated many of Brentano's philosophical writings. As one of the great teachers, Chisholm is widely known for the three editions of *Theory of Knowledge*, a short book and the standard text in US graduate epistemology courses. An ontological Platonist, Chisholm defends human free will and a strict sense of personal identity.

See also: A posteriori; Commonsensism; Foundationalism; Free will; Internalism and externalism in epistemology; Knowledge and justification, coherence theory of; Perception; Scepticism

DAVID BENFIELD

CHOMSKY, NOAM (1928–)

Fish swim, birds fly, people talk. The talents displayed by fish and birds rest on specific biological structures whose intricate detail is attributable to genetic endowment. Human linguistic capacity similarly rests on dedicated mental structures many of whose specific details are an innate biological endowment of the species. One of Chomsky's central concerns has been to press this analogy and uncover its implications for theories of mind, meaning and knowledge.

This work has proceeded along two broad fronts.

First, Chomsky has fundamentally restructured grammatical research. Due to his work, the central object of study in linguistics is 'the language faculty', a postulated mental organ which is dedicated to acquiring linguistic knowledge and is involved in various aspects of language-use, including the production and understanding of utterances. The aim of linguistic theory is to describe the initial state of this faculty and how it changes with exposure to linguistic data. Chomsky characterizes the initial state of the language faculty as a set of principles and parameters. Language acquisition consists in setting these open parameter values on the basis of linguistic data available to a child. The initial state of the system is a Universal Grammar (UG): a super-recipe for concocting language-specific grammars. Grammars constitute the knowledge of particular languages that result when parametric values are fixed.

Linguistic theory, given these views, has a double mission. First, it aims to 'adequately' characterize the grammars (and hence the mental states) attained by native speakers. Theories are 'descriptively adequate' if they attain this goal. In addition,

linguistic theory aims to explain how grammatical competence is attained. Theories are 'explanatorily adequate' if they show how descriptively adequate grammars can arise on the basis of exposure to 'primary linguistic data' (PLD): the data children are exposed to and use in attaining their native grammars. Explanatory adequacy rests on an articulated theory of UG, and in particular a detailed theory of the general principles and open parameters that characterize the initial state of the language faculty (that is, the biologically endowed mental structures).

Chomsky has also pursued a second set of concerns. He has vigorously criticized many philosophical nostrums from the perspective of this revitalized approach to linguistics. Three topics he has consistently returned to are:

- Knowledge of language and its general epistemological implications
- Indeterminacy and underdetermination in linguistic theory
- Person-specific 'I-languages' versus socially constituted 'E-languages' as the proper objects of scientific study.

See also: Language, innateness of; Language, philosophy of; Nativism; Unconscious mental states

NORBERT HORNSTEIN

CHRISTIAN PHILOSOPHY, EARLY
See Patristic philosophy

CHRISTIANITY AND SCIENCE
See Religion and science

CHRISTINE DE PIZAN (1365–c.1430)

Christine de Pizan, France's 'first woman of letters', is primarily remembered as a courtly poet and a propagandist for women. Her extensive writings were influenced by the early humanists, reflecting an interest in education (particularly for women and young people) and in government. Following Aquinas, Christine defined wisdom as the highest intellectual virtue and tried to apply the concept of the just war to contemporary problems. Her works are also noteworthy for their contribution to the transmission of Italian literature to Parisian intellectual circles.

See also: Feminism §2; Humanism, Renaissance; Renaissance philosophy

CHARITY CANNON WILLARD

CHURCH'S THEOREM AND THE DECISION PROBLEM

Church's theorem, published in 1936, states that the set of valid formulas of first-order logic is not effectively decidable: there is no method or algorithm for deciding which formulas of first-order logic are valid. Church's paper exhibited an undecidable combinatorial problem $\mathcal{P}$ and showed that $\mathcal{P}$ was representable in first-order logic. If first-order logic were decidable, $\mathcal{P}$ would also be decidable. Since $\mathcal{P}$ is undecidable, first-order logic must also be undecidable.

Church's theorem is a negative solution to the decision problem (*Entscheidungsproblem*), the problem of finding a method for deciding whether a given formula of first-order logic is valid, or satisfiable, or neither. The great contribution of Church (and, independently, Turing) was not merely to prove that there is no method but also to propose a mathematical definition of the notion of 'effectively solvable problem', that is, a problem solvable by means of a method or algorithm.

See also: CHURCH'S THESIS

ROHIT PARIKH

CHURCH'S THESIS

An algorithm or mechanical procedure A is said to 'compute' a function f if, for any n in the domain of f, when given n as input, A eventually produces fn as output. A function is 'computable' if there is an algorithm that computes it. A set S is 'decidable' if there is an algorithm that decides membership in S: if, given any appropriate n as input, the algorithm would output 'yes' if $n \in S$, and 'no' if $n \notin S$. The notions of 'algorithm', 'computable' and 'decidable' are informal (or pre-formal) in that they have meaning independently of, and prior to, attempts at rigorous formulation.

Church's thesis, first proposed by Alonzo Church in a paper published in 1936, is the assertion that a function is computable if and only if it is recursive: 'We now define the notion ... of an effectively calculable function ... by identifying it with the notion of a recursive function ....' Independently, Alan Turing argued that a function is computable if and only if there is a Turing machine that computes it; and he showed that a function is Turing-computable if and only if it is recursive.

Church's thesis is widely accepted today. Since an algorithm can be 'read off' a recursive derivation, every recursive function is computable. Three types of 'evidence' have been cited for the converse. First, every algorithm that has been examined has been shown to compute a recursive function. Second, Turing, Church and others provided analyses of the moves available to a person following a mechanical procedure, arguing that everything can be simulated by a Turing machine, a recursive derivation, and so on. The third consideration is 'confluence'. Several different characterizations, developed more or less independently, have been shown to be coextensive, suggesting that all of them are on target. The list includes recursiveness, Turing computability, Herbrand–Gödel derivability, λ-definability and Markov algorithm computability.

See also: COMPUTABILITY THEORY

STEWART SHAPIRO

CICERO, MARCUS TULLIUS (106–43 BC)

Cicero, pre-eminent Roman statesman and orator of the first century BC and a prolific writer, composed the first substantial body of philosophical work in Latin. Rising from small-town obscurity to the pinnacle of Rome's staunchly conservative aristocracy, he devoted most of his life to public affairs. But he was deeply interested in philosophy throughout his life, and during two intervals of forced withdrawal from politics wrote two series of dialogues, first elaborating his political ideals and later examining central issues in epistemology, ethics and theology. Designed to establish philosophical study as an integral part of Roman culture, these works are heavily indebted to Greek philosophy, and some of the later dialogues are largely summaries of Hellenistic debates. But Cicero reworked his sources substantially, and his methodical expositions are thoughtful, judicious and, on questions of politics and morals, often creative. An adherent of the sceptical New Academy, he was opposed to dogmatism but ready to accept the most cogent arguments on topics important to him. His vigorously argued and eloquent critical discussions of perennial problems greatly enriched the intellectual and moral heritage of Rome and shaped Western traditions of liberal education, republican government and rationalism in religion and ethics. These works also afford invaluable insight into the course of philosophy during the three centuries after Aristotle.

See also: EPICUREANISM; NATURAL LAW; PLATONISM, RENAISSANCE; STOICISM

STEPHEN A. WHITE

CITIZENSHIP

Within political philosophy, citizenship refers not only to a legal status, but also to a normative ideal – the governed should be full and equal participants in the political process. As such, it is a distinctively democratic ideal. People who are governed by monarchs or military dictators are subjects, not citizens. Most philosophers therefore view citizenship theory as an extension of democratic theory. Democratic theory focuses on political institutions and procedures; citizenship theory focuses on the attributes of individual participants.

One important topic in citizenship theory concerns the need for citizens to actively participate in political life. In most countries participation in politics is not obligatory, and people are free to place private commitments ahead of political involvement. Yet if too many citizens are apathetic, democratic institutions will collapse. Another topic concerns the identity of citizens. Citizenship is intended to provide a common status and identity which helps integrate members of society. However, some theorists question whether common citizenship can accommodate the increasing social and cultural pluralism of modern societies.

See also: DEMOCRACY; REPUBLICANISM

WILL KYMLICKA

CIVIL DISOBEDIENCE

According to common definitions, civil disobedience involves a public and nonviolent breach of law that is committed in order to change a law or policy, and in order to better society. More, those classed as civilly disobedient must be willing to accept punishment. Why is the categorization of what counts as civil disobedience of practical importance? The usual assumption is that acts of civil disobedience are easier to justify morally than other illegal acts. Acts of civil disobedience, such as those committed by abolitionists, by followers of Mahatma Gandhi and Martin Luther King, Jr and by opponents of the Vietnam War, have been an important form of social protest.

The decision as to what exactly should count as civil disobedience should be guided both by an ordinary understanding of what the term conveys and by what factors are relevant for moral justification. For justification, nonviolence and publicness matter because they reduce the damage of violating the law. Tactics should be proportionate to the evil against which civil disobedience is aimed; someone who assesses the morality of a particular act of civil disobedience should distinguish an evaluation of tactics from an evaluation of objectives.

KENT GREENAWALT

CIVILIAN TRADITION
See ROMAN LAW

CLARKE, SAMUEL (1675–1729)

Regarded in his lifetime along with Locke as the leading English philosopher, Clarke was best known in his role as an advocate of a thoroughgoing natural theology and as a defender of Newtonianism, most notably in his famous correspondence with Leibniz. His natural theology was set out in his Boyle lectures of 1704 and 1705, but it left little room for revelation, and endeared him to neither side in the quarrel between deists and orthodox Anglicans. A staunch proponent of Newtonian natural philosophy, he defended it against criticisms of its notions of gravity and absolute space.

STEPHEN GAUKROGER

CLASSIFICATION
See TAXONOMY

CLONING

'Cloning' is the popular name given to Cell Nuclear Replacement (CNR) or Cell Nuclear Transfer (CNT) techniques. CNR involves a recipient cell, generally an egg (oocyte), and a donor cell. The nucleus of the donor cell is introduced into the oocyte. With appropriate stimulation the oocyte is induced to develop. In some cases, the created embryo may be implanted into a viable womb and developed to term. The first mammal to be born by CNR was Dolly the sheep (1996–2003).

It is thought that CNR may have various potential applications ranging from reproduction to treatment of some of the most serious and life-threatening diseases that afflict humankind (such as cancer, Alzheimer's, Parkinson's disease, spinal cord injuries). However, many technical problems must be addressed and resolved before CNR becomes viable for use in either therapy or reproduction. Although research on CNR is still in its early stages, CNR (cloning) attracts people's attention in a way that do few other advances in biomedical research. Public debate on cloning has unfortunately been influenced more by fiction than science. The horrendous or absurd scenarios pictured in novels and films are often mistakenly believed to be possible, or even likely, outcomes of cloning. The international community, immediately after news of the birth of Dolly, imposed restrictions that may make it difficult to refine the technique used. Against 'reproductive cloning' a prohibition is enforced virtually everywhere. 'Reproductive cloning' is considered offensive to human dignity and a threat to the well-being of the child or even to the future of humankind. Most of these objections are based on either a misunderstanding of CNR or on inconsistent philosophical arguments. Against 'therapeutic cloning' objections are also raised. The strongest are that CNR involves the creation and destruction of embryos, and this is widely believed to be unethical. Advocates of this position contend that, although CNR may save human lives, the technique still involves the taking of an innocent life and therefore is the equivalent of killing one person to save another. The debate on the moral status of the embryo is ongoing, in bioethics, philosophy and theology. However, if the arguments against the killing of the embryo for the morally important, life-saving purposes envisaged for CNR were to be accepted, then the current legal and social context of most European countries would have to be revised, and abortion and in vitro fertilization (IVF) made criminal offences. Abortion and IVF (which involves creation of extra-embryos that may be destroyed) are in fact accepted practices in most European countries. Those who believe that abortion, even in its therapeutic form, and IVF are acceptable, admit that it may be ethical to destroy an embryo either to save a life or to treat infertility. If this is accepted, it is unclear why is it unacceptable that embryos are used to treat highly serious and lethal diseases (cancer or Parkinson's disease for example).

See also: APPLIED ETHICS; BIOETHICS; GENETICS AND ETHICS; LIFE AND DEATH; MEDICAL ETHICS; REPRODUCTION AND ETHICS

References and further reading

Brink, D. (1989) *Moral Realism and the Foundations of Ethics*, Cambridge: Cambridge University Press. (An influential book-length presentation of American realism.)

Dancy, J. (1993) *Moral Reasons*, Oxford: Blackwell. (The only full-scale expression of British realism.)

Sayre-McCord, G. (ed.) (1988) *Essays on Moral Realism*, Ithaca: Cornell University Press. (A collection of influential essays by leading realists and non-cognitivists.)

JOHN HARRIS
SIMONA GIORDANO

COERCION

Coercion (also called 'duress') is one of the basic exculpating excuses both in morality and in some systems of criminal law. Unlike various kinds of direct compulsion that give a victim no choice, a coercee is left with a choice, albeit a very unappealing one. They can do what is demanded, or can refuse, opting instead for the consequences, with which they are threatened. Sometimes courts find that the coercive threat that led the defendant to act as they did was objectively resistible by any person of reasonable fortitude, especially when the defendant's conduct was gravely harmful to others or to the state.

A proposal is an offer when it projects for the recipient's consideration a prospect that is welcome in itself, and not harmful or unwelcome beyond what would happen in the normal course of events. Coercive offers, according to some writers, are those that force a specific choice from the victim while actually enhancing their freedom. Some argue, however, that genuine coercion requires the active and deliberate creation of a vulnerability, and not mere opportunistic exploitation of a vulnerability discovered fortuitously.

See also: FREEDOM AND LIBERTY; RESPONSIBLITY

JOEL FEINBERG

COHEN, HERMANN (1842–1918)

Hermann Cohen was the founder of the Marburg School of Neo-Kantianism and a major influence on twentieth-century Jewish thought. *Die Religion der Vernunft aus den Quellen des Judentums* (Religion of Reason out of the Sources of Judaism) (1919) is widely credited with the renewal of Jewish religious philosophy. Cohen's philosophy of Judaism is inextricably linked with his general philosophical position. But his system of critical idealism in logic, ethics, aesthetics and psychology did not originally include a philosophy of religion. The mainly Protestant Marburg School in fact regarded Cohen's Jewish philosophy as an insufficient solution to the philosophical problem of human existence and to that of determining the role of religion in human culture. Thinkers who favoured a new, more existentialist approach in Jewish thought, however, saw Cohen's introduction of religion into the system as a daring departure from the confines of philosophical idealism.

Cohen identified the central Jewish contribution to human culture as the development of a religion that unites historical particularity with ethical universality. At the core of this religion of reason is the interdependence of the idea of God and that of the human being. Cohen derives this theme from the Jewish canon through a philosophical analysis based on his transcendental idealism.

See also: NEO-KANTIANISM

MICHAEL ZANK

COHERENCE THEORY OF JUSTIFICATION AND KNOWLEDGE

See KNOWLEDGE AND JUSTIFICATION, COHERENCE THEORY OF

COHERENCE THEORY OF TRUTH

See TRUTH, COHERENCE THEORY OF

COLLINGWOOD, ROBIN GEORGE (1889–1943)

Collingwood was the greatest British philosopher of history of the twentieth century. His experience as a practising historian of Roman Britain led him to believe that the besetting vice of philosophy is to abstract propositions away from the context of the practical problems and questions that gave rise to them. Until we know the practical context of problems and questions to which a proposition is supposed to be an answer, we do not know what it means. In this respect his concern with the living activities of language users parallels that of the later Wittgenstein. Collingwood also believed that the interpretation of others was not a scientific exercise of fitting their behaviour into a network of generalizations, but a matter of rethinking their thoughts for oneself. His conviction that this ability, which he identified with historical thinking, was the neglected and crucial component of all human thought stamped him as original, or even a maverick, during his own lifetime. He also shared with Wittgenstein the belief that quite apart from containing propositions that can be evaluated as true or false, systems of thought depend upon 'absolute presuppositions', or a framework or scaffolding of ideas that may change with time. The business of metaphysics is to reconstruct the framework that operated at particular periods of history. Collingwood had extensive moral and political interests, and his writings on art, religion and science confirm his stature as one of the greatest polymaths of twentieth-century British philosophy.

SIMON BLACKBURN

COLOUR AND QUALIA

There are two basic philosophical problems about colour. The first concerns the nature of colour itself. That is, what sort of property is it? When I say of the shirt that I am wearing that it is red, what sort of fact about the shirt am I describing? The second problem concerns the nature of colour experience. When I look at the red shirt I have a visual experience with a certain qualitative character – a 'reddish' one. Thus colour seems in some sense to be a property of my sensory experience, as well as a property of my shirt. What sort of mental property is it?

Obviously, the two problems are intimately related. In particular, there is a great deal of controversy over the following question: if we call the first sort of property 'objective colour' and the second 'subjective colour', which of the two, objective or subjective colour, is basic? Or do they both have an independent ontological status?

Most philosophers adhere to the doctrine of physicalism, the view that all objects and events are ultimately constituted by the fundamental physical particles, properties and relations described in physical theory. The phenomena of both objective and subjective colour present problems for physicalism. With respect to objective colour, it is difficult to find any natural physical candidate with which to identify it. Our visual system responds in a similar manner to surfaces that vary along a wide range of physical parameters, even with respect to the reflection of light waves. Yet what could be more obvious than the fact that objects are coloured?

In the case of subjective colour, the principal topic of this entry, there is an even deeper puzzle. It is natural to think of the reddishness of a visual experience – its qualitative character – as an intrinsic property of the experience. Intrinsic properties are distinguished from relational properties in that an object's possession of the former does not depend on its relation to other objects, whereas its possession of the latter does. If subjective colour is intrinsic, then it would seem to be a neural property of a brain state. But what sort of neural property could explain the reddishness of an experience? Furthermore, reduction of subjective colour to a neural property would rule out even the possibility that forms of life with different physiological structures, or intelligent robots, could have experiences of the same qualitative type as our experiences of red. While some philosophers endorse this consequence, many find it quite implausible.

Neural properties seem best suited to explain how certain functions are carried out, and therefore it might seem better to identify subjective colour with the property of playing a certain functional role within the entire cognitive system realized by the brain. This allows the possibility that structures physically different from human brains could support colour experiences of the same type as our own. However, various puzzles undermine the plausibility of this claim. For instance, it seems possible that two people could agree in all their judgments of relative similarity and yet one sees green where the other sees red. If this 'inverted spectrum' case is a genuine logical possibility, as many philosophers advocate, then it appears that subjective colour must not be a matter of functional role, but rather an intrinsic property of experience.

Faced with the dilemmas posed by subjective colour for physicalist doctrine, some philosophers opt for eliminativism, the doctrine that subjective colour is not a genuine, or real, phenomenon after all. On this view the source of the puzzle is a conceptual confusion; a tendency to extend our judgments concerning objective colour, what appear to be intrinsic properties of the surfaces of physical objects, onto the properties of our mental states. Once we see that all that is happening 'inside' is a perceptual judgment concerning the properties of external objects, we will understand why we cannot locate any state or property of the brain with which to identify subjective colour.

The controversy over the nature of subjective colour is part of a wider debate about the subjective aspect of conscious experience more generally. How does the qualitative character of experience – what it is like to see, hear and smell – fit into a physicalist scientific framework? At present all of the options just presented have their adherents, and no general consensus exists.

See also: Colour, theories of; Consciousness; Qualia; Vision

JOSEPH LEVINE

COLOUR, THEORIES OF

The world as perceived by human beings is full of colour. The world as described by physical scientists is composed of colourless particles and fields. Philosophical theories of colour since the Scientific Revolution have been driven primarily by a desire to harmonize these two apparently conflicting pictures of the world. Any adequate theory of colour has to be consistent with the characteristics of colour as perceived without contradicting the deliverances of the physical sciences.

Given this conception of the aim of a theory of colour, there are three possibilities for resolving the apparent conflict between the scientific and perceptual facts. The first is to deny that physical objects have colours. Theories of this kind admit that objects appear coloured but maintain that these appearances are misleading. The conflict is resolved by removing colour from the external world. Second, it might be that colour is a relational property. For an object to possess a particular colour it must be related in the right way to a perceiver. One common version of this view analyses colour as a disposition to cause particular kinds of perceptual experience in a human being. Since the physical sciences deal only with the intrinsic properties of physical objects and their relations to other physical objects and not their relations to perceiving subjects, the possibility of conflict is removed. A third possible response is to maintain that colour really is a property of external objects and that the conflict is merely apparent. Some theories of this form maintain that colour is identical to a physical

property of objects. Others maintain that colour is a property that physical objects possess over and above all their physical properties. Philosophical discussions of colour typically take the form of either elaborating on one of these three possibilities or attempting to show more generally that one of these three types of response is to be preferred to the others.

DAVID R. HILBERT

COMEDY

In the narrowest sense, comedy is drama that makes us laugh and has a happy ending. In a wider sense it is also humorous narrative literature with a happy ending. In the widest sense, comedy includes any literary or graphic work, performance or other art intended to amuse us.

Comedy began at about the same time as tragedy, and because they represent alternative attitudes toward basic issues in life, it is useful to consider them together. Unfortunately, several traditional prejudices discriminate against comedy and in favour of tragedy. There are four standard charges against comedy: it emphasizes the animal aspects of human life, encourages disrespect for leaders and institutions, is based on malice, and endangers our morality. These charges are easily answered, for none picks out something that is both essential to comedy and inherently vicious. In fact, once we get past traditional prejudices, several of the differences between comedy and tragedy can be seen as advantages. While tragedy tends to be idealistic and elitist, for example, comedy tends to be pragmatic and egalitarian. While tragedy values honour, even above life itself, comedy puts little stock in honour and instead emphasizes survival. Tragic heroes preserve their dignity but die in the process; comic characters lose their dignity but live to tell the tale. Most generally, comedy celebrates mental flexibility and a realistic acceptance of the limitations of human life. The comic vision of life, in short, embodies a good deal of wisdom.

See also: Bergson, H.-L.; Humour; Tragedy

JOHN MORREALL

COMMON SENSE SCHOOL

The term 'Common Sense School' refers to the works of Thomas Reid and to the tradition of Scottish realist philosophy for which Reid's works were the main source. The ideas of the school were carried abroad – to France; and to the USA, where they were highly influential, particularly among leading academics critical of Calvinism. Interest in Reid and the tradition to which he gave rise was revived almost a century later by leading American philosophers and their students.

See also: BEATTIE, J.; COMMONSENSISM; MOORE, G.E.

EDWARD H. MADDEN

COMMONSENSISM

'Commonsensism' refers to one of the principal approaches to traditional theory of knowledge where one asks oneself the following Socratic questions: (1) What can I know?; (2) How can I distinguish beliefs that are reasonable for me to have from beliefs that are not reasonable for me to have? and (3) What can I do to replace unreasonable beliefs by reasonable beliefs about the same subject-matter, and to replace beliefs that are less reasonable by beliefs that are more reasonable? The mark of commonsensism is essentially a faith in oneself – a conviction that a human being, by proceeding cautiously, is capable of knowing the world in which it finds itself.

Any inquiry must set out with *some* beliefs. If you had no beliefs at all, you could not even begin to inquire. Hence any set of beliefs is better than none. Moreover, the beliefs that we *do* find ourselves with at any given time have so far survived previous inquiry and experience. And it is psychologically impossible to reject everything that you believe. 'Doubting', Peirce says, 'is not as easy as lying'. Inquiry, guided by common sense, leads us to a set of beliefs which indicates that common sense is on the whole a reliable guide to knowledge. And if inquiry were not thus guided by common sense, how would it be able to answer the three Socratic questions with which it begins?

See also: CONTEXTUALISM, EPISTEMOLOGICAL

RODERICK M. CHISHOLM

COMMUNICATION AND INTENTION

The classic attempt to understand communication in terms of the intentions of a person making an utterance was put forward by Paul Grice in 1957. Grice was concerned with actions in which a speaker means something by what they do and what is meant might just as much be false as true. He looked for the essence of such cases in actions intended to effect a change in the recipient. Grice saw successful communication as depending on the recognition by the audience of the speaker's intention. Since then there have been many attempts to refine Grice's work, and to protect it against various problems. There has also been worry that Grice's approach depends on a false priority of psychology over semantics, seeing complex psycho-

logical states as existing independently of whether the agent has linguistic means of expressing them.

See also: MEANING AND RULE-FOLLOWING

SIMON BLACKBURN

COMMUNICATIVE RATIONALITY

The concept of 'communicative rationality' is primarily associated with the work of the philosopher and social theorist Jürgen Habermas. According to Habermas, communication through language necessarily involves the raising of 'validity-claims' (distinguished as 'truth', 'rightness' and 'sincerity'), the status of which, when contested, can ultimately only be resolved through discussion. Habermas further contends that speakers of a language possess an implicit knowledge of the conditions under which such discussion would produce an objectively correct result, and these he has spelled out in terms of the features of an egalitarian 'ideal speech situation'. Communicative rationality refers to the capacity to engage in argumentation under conditions approximating to this ideal situation ('discourse', in Habermas' terminology), with the aim of achieving consensus.

Habermas relies on the concept of communicative rationality to argue that democratic forms of social organization express more than simply the preferences of a particular cultural and political tradition. In his view, we cannot even understand a speech-act without taking a stance towards the validity-claim it raises, and this stance in turn anticipates the unconstrained discussion which would resolve the status of the claim. Social and political arrangements which inhibit such discussion can therefore be criticized from a standpoint which does not depend on any specific value-commitments, since for Habermas achieving agreement (*Verständigung*) is a 'telos' or goal which is internal to human language as such. A similar philosophical programme has also been developed by Karl-Otto Apel, who lays more stress on the 'transcendental' features of the argumentation involved.

See also: HABERMAS, J.

PETER DEWS

COMMUNISM

Communism is the belief that society should be organized without private property, all productive property being held communally, publicly or in common. A communist system is one based on a community of goods. It is generally presented as a positive alternative to competition, a system that is thought to divide people; communism is expected to draw people together and to create a community. In most cases the arguments for communism advocate replacing competition with cooperation either for its own sake or to promote a goal such as equality, or to free specific groups of people to serve a higher ideal such as the state or God.

The word *communism* appears to have first been used in the above sense in France in the 1840s to refer to the ideas of thinkers such as Françoise Émile Babeuf (1760–97) and Étienne Cabet (1788–1856), both of whom advocated the collectivization of all productive property. The concept is ancient, however. Early versions of a community of goods exist in myths that describe the earliest stages of human culture; it was a major issue in ancient Athens, a key component of monasticism and became the basis for much criticism of industrial capitalism.

The word communism later became associated with the teachings of Karl MARX (§12) and his followers and came to refer to an authoritarian political system combined with a centralized economic system run by the state. This form of communism has roots in the earlier idea because the ultimate goal of communism, as seen by Marx, was a society in which goods are distributed to people on the basis of need. The older usage continues to exist in a worldwide communal movement and as a standard by which to criticize both capitalism and Marxian communism.

The idea of communism as collectively owned property first appears in the Western tradition in classical Greece. Plato's *Republic* contains a notable early defence (see PLATO §14). Prior to the invention of the word, major communist theories can be found in some parts of the Christian Bible, in medieval monasticism and in Thomas More's *Utopia* (1516). In all these cases the basis for collectively owned property is that members of society are freed from the need to devote their time to earning a living or caring for private property so that they can devote themselves to something more important such as the pursuit of knowledge, God or personal fulfilment. The assumption is that the need to provide for oneself or one's family gets in the way of matters considered more important. For example, Plato advocates abolishing the family in his *Republic* because he fears that family ties will both distract the individual from higher things and tempt people to favour one group (family members) over others (non-family members). In monastic communism, which also abolishes the family, all property is owned by the community and each individual member of the community owns nothing, not even their clothes. Everything is provided by the community for each monk or nun; they are, thereby, freed from the burden of property to devote themselves to God. In More's *Utopia* all houses and their furnishings are as near identical as

possible and, since location cannot be identical, people move from house to house in regular rotation.

Later, secularized versions of communism stressed the equitable (not necessarily equal) distribution of, or at least access to, resources, but the underlying principle is quite similar. Rather than freeing some or even all people in a society to devote themselves to a higher cause, secular communism is designed to allow everyone to pursue personal fulfilment. It may best be characterized by a slogan adopted by Marx that appears to have been first published on the title page of Cabet's *Voyage en Icarie* (1840): 'From each according to his ability, to each according to his need'. In other words, each person contributes to society to the best of their ability in the areas of work for which they are suited; in return, society provides their basic needs. The underlying assumption is that all human beings deserve to have their needs met simply because they are human beings; differential ability and talent does not make one person more deserving than another. A specific case is the assumption by most communist theorists that there should be no difference in treatment of those who contribute to society through physical labour and those who contribute through mental labour. For example, in 1888 Edward Bellamy published *Looking Backward*, a utopian novel that became an instant bestseller and produced a worldwide movement. In it, Bellamy advocated an absolutely equal income for all members of society that could then be used by each individual to meet their own felt needs. An approach adopted by many intentional communities is for the group to make collective or social decisions (either by consensus or by majority rule) about economic matters that affect the community as a whole but to provide each individual member of the community with a discretionary income to use as they wish.

Marx maintained major aspects of this approach in the stage of human development that he called 'full' or 'pure' communism or just communism. The non-alienated people of this future communism will create a world in which income will be distributed on the basis of need (see MARX, K. §4); since everyone will be a productive labourer, there will no longer be any classes; and, because there will no longer be a need for political power to enforce class dominance, the state will gradually disappear to be replaced with decentralized, non-political administrative agencies. Since everyone will work, there will be high productivity and, therefore, plenty for all. Given the changed social situation, people will begin to think differently and social distinctions between occupations and between city and country will disappear. Thus, this form of communism is, in its essentials, identical to the earliest communist tradition. At least one major twentieth-century Marxist theorist, Ernst Bloch (1885–1977) in *Das Prinzip Hoffnung* (The Principle of Hope) (1959) argued that this utopian goal should be at the centre of Marxist theory (see UTOPIANISM).

While Marxism and its version of communism predominantly took a different road, the more fundamental and historically earlier theory did not disappear. Non-Marxist forms of collective property have existed and been defended as part of the communal movement best represented by the Israeli kibbutzim and the US communal movement of the early nineteenth and mid-twentieth centuries, and by some forms of anarchism (see ANARCHISM §3). Communism as common property and as a vision of a better life for all is still a living tradition.

The arguments against communism take a number of different forms. The simplest rely on assumptions about human nature radically at variance with those of communism's proponents. The assumption is made, with little real evidence, that human beings are 'naturally' competitive and that therefore communism cannot work (see HUMAN NATURE §1). A more developed analysis argues that communism is necessarily economically inefficient and will, therefore, be unable to provide as high a standard of living as a non-communist system. Some go so far as to argue that communism is impossible to sustain over long periods of time because its inefficiency is so great that the economic system must sooner or later collapse. Of course, economic efficiency is very low in the scale of values held by most supporters of traditional communism. Proponents of communism generally take the position that economic efficiency symbolizes the competitive system that they oppose and stands in the way of the cooperative community they hope to achieve.

Today, many believe that the time of communism has passed, largely because Marxist communism has been discredited in much of the world. But communism is not, and never has been, reducible to the Marxist version. Most fundamentally, it is the economic basis for dreams of complete human fulfilment, whether it is sought in monastic orders, intentional communities or whole societies. That dream persists, and with it the ideals of communism.

See also: EQUALITY; SOCIALISM

References and further reading

Cole, G.D.H. (1953–6) *A History of Socialist Thought*, London: Macmillan, 5 vols in 7. (General history of most variants of collective ownership.)

Dawson, D. (1992) *Cities of the Gods: Communist Utopias in Greek Thought*, New York: Oxford University Press. (Early developments of communism.)

Wiles, P.J.D. (1962) *The Political Economy of Communism*, Cambridge, MA: Harvard University Press. (Includes a good discussion of 'full' or 'pure' communism.)

LYMAN TOWER SARGENT

COMMUNITARIANISM
See COMMUNITY AND COMMUNITARIANISM

COMMUNITY AND COMMUNITARIANISM

Reflections on the nature and significance of community have figured prominently in the history of Western ethics and political philosophy, both secular and religious. In ethics and political philosophy the term 'community' refers to a form of connection among individuals that is qualitatively stronger and deeper than a mere association. The concept of a community includes at least two elements: (1) individuals belonging to a community have ends that are in a robust sense *common*, not merely congruent private ends, and that are conceived of and valued as common ends by the members of the group; and (2) for the individuals involved, their awareness of themselves as belonging to the group is a significant constituent of their identity, their sense of who they are.

In the past two decades, an important and influential strand of secular ethical and political thought in the English-speaking countries has emerged under the banner of communitarianism. The term 'communitarianism' is applied to the views of a broad range of contemporary thinkers, including Alasdair MacIntyre, Charles Taylor, Michael Sandel, and sometimes Michael Walzer. It is important to note, however, that there is no common creed to which these thinkers all subscribe and that for the most part they avoid the term.

There are two closely related ways to characterize what communitarians have in common; one positive, the other negative. As a positive view, communitarianism is a perspective on ethics and political philosophy that emphasizes the psychosocial and ethical importance of belonging to communities, and which holds that the possibilities for justifying ethical judgments are determined by the fact that ethical reasoning must proceed within the context of a community's traditions and cultural understandings. As a negative view, communitarianism is a variety of anti-liberalism, one that criticizes liberal thought for failing to appreciate the importance of community.

At present the communitarian critique of liberalism is more developed than is communitarianism as a systematic ethical or political philosophy. Existing communitarian literature lacks anything comparable to Rawls' theory of justice or Feinberg's theory of the moral limits of criminal law, both of which are paradigmatic examples of systematic liberal ethical and political theory. For the most part, the positive content of the communitarians' views must be inferred from their criticisms of liberalism. Thus, to a large extent communitarianism so far is chiefly a way of thinking about ethics and political life that stands in fundamental opposition to liberalism. To some, communitarian thinking seems a healthy antidote to what they take to be excessive individualism and obsessive preoccupation with personal autonomy. To others, communitarianism represents a failure to appreciate the value – and the fragility – of liberal social institutions. The success of communitarianism as an ethical theory depends upon whether an account of ethical reasoning can be developed that emphasizes the importance of social roles and cultural values in the justification of moral judgments without lapsing into an extreme ethical relativism that makes fundamental ethical criticisms of one's own community impossible. The success of communitarianism as a political theory depends upon whether it can be demonstrated that liberal political institutions cannot provide adequate conditions for the flourishing of community or secure appropriate support for persons' identities in so far as their identities are determined by their membership in communities.

See also: Confucian Philosophy, Chinese; International relations, philosophy of; Nation and nationalism; Rawls, J.

ALLEN BUCHANAN

COMPOSITIONALITY

A language is compositional if the meaning of each of its complex expressions (for example, 'black dog') is determined entirely by the meanings of its parts ('black', 'dog') and its syntax. Principles of compositionality provide precise statements of this idea. A compositional semantics for a language is a (finite) theory which explains how semantically important properties such as truth-conditions are determined by the meanings of parts and syntax. Supposing English to have a compositional semantics helps explain how finite creatures like ourselves have the ability to understand English's infinitely many sentences. Whether human languages are in fact compositional, however, is quite controversial.

See also: Meaning and truth; Semantics

MARK RICHARD

COMPUTABILITY THEORY

The effective calculability of number-theoretic functions such as addition and multiplication has always been recognized, and for that judgment a rigorous notion of 'computable function' is not required. A sharp mathematical concept was defined only in the twentieth century, when issues including the decision problem for predicate logic required a precise delimitation of functions that can be viewed as effectively calculable. Predicate logic emerged from Frege's fundamental '*Begriffsschrift*' (1879) as an expressive formal language and was described with mathematical precision by Hilbert in lectures given during the winter of 1917–18. The logical calculus Frege had also developed allowed proofs to proceed as computations in accordance with a fixed set of rules; in principle, according to Gödel, the rules could be applied 'by someone who knew nothing about mathematics, or by a machine'.

Hilbert grasped the potential of this mechanical aspect and formulated the decision problem for predicate logic as follows: 'The *Entscheidungsproblem* [decision problem] is solved if one knows a procedure that permits the decision concerning the validity, respectively, satisfiability of a given logical expression by a finite number of operations.' Some, such as, von Neumann, believed that the inherent freedom of mathematical thought provided a sufficient reason to expect a negative solution to the problem. But how could a proof of undecidability be given? The unsolvability results of other mathematical problems had always been established relative to a determinate class of admissible operations, for example, the impossibility of doubling the cube relative to ruler and compass constructions. A negative solution to the decision problem obviously required the characterization of 'effectively calculable functions'.

For two other important issues a characterization of that informal notion was also needed, namely, the general formulation of the incompleteness theorems and the effective unsolvability of mathematical problems (for example, of Hilbert's tenth problem). The first task of computability theory was thus to answer the question 'What is a precise notion of effectively calculable function?'. Many different answers invariably characterized the same class of number-theoretic functions: the partial recursive ones. Today recursiveness or, equivalently, Turing computability is considered to be the precise mathematical counterpart to 'effective calculability'. Relative to these notions undecidability results have been established, in particular the undecidability of the decision problem for predicate logic. The notions are idealized in the sense that no time or space limitations are imposed on the calculations;

the concept of 'feasibility' is crucial in computer science when trying to capture the subclass of recursive functions whose values can actually be determined.

DANIELE MUNDICI
WILFRIED SIEG

COMPUTATIONAL THEORIES OF MIND

See MIND, COMPUTATIONAL THEORIES OF

COMPUTER SCIENCE

At first sight, computers would seem to be of minimal philosophical importance; mere symbol manipulators that do the sort of things that we can do anyway, only faster and more conveniently. Nevertheless, computers are being used to illuminate the cognitive abilities of the human and animal mind, explore the organizational principles of life, and open up new approaches to modelling nature. Furthermore, the study of computation has changed our conception of the limits and methodology of scientific knowledge.

Computers have been able to do all this for two reasons. The first is that material computing power (accuracy, storage and speed) permits the development and exploration of models of physical (and mental) systems that combine structural complexity with mathematical intransigence. Through simulation, computational power allows exploration where mathematical analysis falters. The second reason is that a computer is not merely a concrete device, but also can be studied as an abstract object whose rules of operation can be specified with mathematical precision; consequently, its strengths and limitations can be systematically investigated, exploited and appreciated. Herein lies that area of computer science of most interest to philosophers: the theory of computation and algorithms. It is here where we have learned what computers can and cannot do in principle.

See also: COMPUTABILITY THEORY

JOHN WINNIE

COMTE, ISIDORE-AUGUSTE-MARIE-FRANÇOIS-XAVIER (1798–1857)

The French philosopher and social theorist Auguste Comte is known as the originator of sociology and 'positivism', a philosophical system by which he aimed to discover and perfect the proper political arrangements of modern industrial society. He was the first thinker to advocate the use of scientific procedures in the study of economics, politics and social behaviour, and, motivated by the social and moral problems caused by the French Revolution, he held that the practice of such a science would lead inevitably to social regeneration and progress.

Comte's positivism can be characterized as an approach which rejects as illegitimate all that cannot be directly observed in the investigation and study of any subject. His system of 'positive philosophy' had two laws at its foundation: a historical or logical law, 'the law of three stages', and an epistemological law, the classification or hierarchy of the sciences. The law of three stages governs the development of human intelligence and society: in the first stage, early societies base their knowledge on theological grounds, giving ultimately divine explanations for all phenomena; later, in the metaphysical stage, forces and essences are sought as explanations, but these are equally chimerical and untestable; finally, in the positive or scientific stage, knowledge is secured solely on observations, by their correlation and sequence. Comte saw this process occurring not only in European society, but also in the lives of every individual. We seek theological solutions in childhood, metaphysical solutions in youth, and scientific explanations in adulthood.

His second, epistemological law fixed a classification or hierarchy of sciences according to their arrival at the positive stage of knowledge. In order of historical development and thus of increasing complexity, these are mathematics, astronomy, physics, chemistry, biology and sociology. (Comte rejected psychology as a science, on the grounds that its data were unobservable and therefore untestable.) Knowledge of one science rested partly on the findings of the preceding science; for Comte, students must progress through the sciences in the correct order, using the simpler and more precise methods of the preceding science to tackle the more complex issues of later ones. In his six-volume *Cours de philosophie positive* (The Positive Philosophy) (1830–42), Comte gave an encyclopedic account of these sciences, ending with an exposition of what he regarded as the most advanced: social physics or 'sociology' (a term he invented). The sociologist's job would be to discover the laws that govern human behaviour on a large scale, and the ways in which social institutions and norms operate together in a complex yet ultimately predictable system.

In his later work, Comte fleshed out his vision of the positive society, describing among other things a Religion of Humanity in which historical figures would be worshipped according to their contribution to society. Despite such extravagances, however, the broader themes of his positivism – especially the idea that long-standing social problems should be approached scientifically – proved influential both in France and, through J.S. Mill's early support, in England.

ANGÈLE KREMER-MARIETTI
Translated from the French by
MARY PICKERING

CONCEPTS

The topic of concepts lies at the intersection of semantics and philosophy of mind. A concept is supposed to be a constituent of a thought (or 'proposition') rather in the way that a word is a constituent of a sentence that typically expresses a thought. Indeed, concepts are often thought to be the *meanings* of words (and will be designated by enclosing the words for them in brackets: [city] is expressed by 'city' and by 'metropolis'). However, the two topics can diverge: non-linguistic animals may possess concepts, and standard linguistic meanings involve conventions in ways that concepts do not.

Concepts seem essential to ordinary and scientific psychological explanation, which would be undermined were it not possible for *the same concept* to occur in different thought episodes: someone could not even recall something unless the concepts they have now overlap the concepts they had earlier. If a disagreement between people is to be more than 'merely verbal', their words must express the same concepts. And if psychologists are to describe shared patterns of thought across people, they need to advert to shared concepts.

Concepts also seem essential to categorizing the world, for example, recognizing a *cow* and classifying it as a *mammal*. Concepts are also *compositional*: concepts can be combined to form a virtual infinitude of complex categories, in such a way that someone can understand a novel combination, for example, [smallest sub-atomic particle], by understanding its constituents.

Concepts, however, are not always studied as part of psychology. Some logicians and formal semanticists study the deductive relations among concepts and propositions in abstraction from any mind. Philosophers doing 'philosophical analysis' try to specify the conditions that make something the *kind* of thing it is – for example, what it is that makes an act good – an enterprise they take to consist in the analysis of concepts.

Given these diverse interests, there is considerable disagreement about what exactly a concept is. Psychologists tend to use 'concept' for *internal representations*, for example, images, stereotypes, words that may be the vehicles for thought in the mind or brain. Logicians and formal semanticists tend to use it for *sets* of real and possible objects, and

functions defined over them; and philosophers of mind have variously proposed *properties*, '*senses*', inferential *rules* or discrimination *abilities*.

A related issue is what it is for someone to *possess* a concept. The 'classical view' presumed concepts had 'definitions' known by competent users. For example, grasping [bachelor] seemed to consist in grasping the definition, [adult, unmarried male]. However, if definitions are not to go on forever, there must be *primitive* concepts that are not defined but are grasped in some other way. Empiricism claimed that these definitions were provided by sensory conditions for a concept's application. Thus, [material object] was defined in terms of certain possibilities of sensation.

The classical view suffers from the fact that few successful definitions have ever been provided. Wittgenstein suggested that concept possession need not consist in knowing a definition, but in appreciating the role of a concept in thought and practice. Moreover, he claimed, a concept need not apply to things by virtue of some closed set of features captured by a definition, but rather by virtue of 'family resemblances' among the things, a suggestion that has given rise in psychology to 'prototype' theories of concepts.

Most traditional approaches to possession conditions have been concerned with the *internal* states, especially the beliefs, of the conceptualizer. Quine raised a challenge for such an approach in his doctrine of 'confirmation holism', which stressed that a person's beliefs are fixed by what they find plausible overall. Separating out any particular beliefs as defining a concept seemed to him arbitrary and in conflict with actual practice, where concepts seem shared by people with different beliefs. This led Quine himself to be sceptical about talk of concepts generally, denying that there was *any* principled way to distinguish 'analytic' claims that express definitional claims about a concept from 'synthetic' ones that express merely common beliefs about the things to which a concept applies.

However, recent philosophers suggest that people share concepts not by virtue of any internal facts, but by virtue of facts about their external (social) environment. For example, people arguably have the concept [water] by virtue of interacting in certain ways with H_2O and deferring to experts in defining it. This work has given rise to a variety of *externalist* theories of concepts and semantics generally.

Many also think, however, that psychology could generalize about people's minds independently of the external contexts they happen to inhabit, and so have proposed 'two-factor theories', according to which there is an *internal* component to a concept that may play a role in psychological explanation, as opposed to an *external* component that determines the application of the concept to the world.

See also: CONTENT, NON-CONCEPTUAL; SEMANTICS

GEORGES REY

CONCEPTUAL ROLE SEMANTICS
See SEMANTICS, CONCEPTUAL ROLE

CONDILLAC, ETIENNE BONNOT DE (1715–80)

One of the leading figures of the French Enlightenment period, Condillac is the author of three highly influential books, published between 1746 and 1754, in which he attempted to refine and expand the empirical method of inquiry so as to make it applicable to a broader range of studies than hitherto. In the half-century following the publication of Newton's *Principia Mathematica* in 1687, intellectual life in Europe had been engaged upon a fierce debate between the partisans of Cartesian physics, who accepted Descartes' principles of metaphysical dualism and God's veracity as the hallmark of scientific truth, and those who accepted Newton's demonstration that the natural order constituted a single system under laws which could be known through painstaking observation and experiment. By the mid-eighteenth century Newton had gained the ascendancy, and it was the guiding inspiration of the French thinkers, known collectively as the *philosophes*, to appropriate the methods by which Newton had achieved his awesome results and apply them across a broader range of inquiries in the hope of attaining a similar expansion of human knowledge. Condillac was at the centre of this campaign.

Condillac's first book, *An Essay on the Origin of Human Knowledge* (1746), bears the subtitle *A Supplement to Mr. Locke's Essay on the Human Understanding*. While Condillac is usually seen as merely a disciple and popularizer of Locke offering little of any genuine originality, and while he did indeed agree with Locke that experience is the sole source of human knowledge, he attempted to improve on Locke by arguing that sensation alone – and not sensation together with reflection – provided the foundation for knowledge. His most famous book, the *Treatise on the Sensations* (1754), is based upon the thought-experiment of a statue whose senses are activated one by one, beginning with the sense of smell, with the intention of showing how all the higher cognitive faculties of the mind can be shown to derive from the notice the mind takes of the primitive inputs of the sense organs. Condillac also went beyond Locke in his carefully argued claims regarding the extent to which language affects the growth and reliability of knowledge. His *Treatise on Systems* (1749) offers a detailed critique of how language had beguiled the great seventeenth-century systems-builders like Descartes, Leibniz and Spinoza and led them into erroneous conceptions of the mind and human knowledge, the influence of which conceptions was as insidious as it was difficult to eradicate.

See also: EMPIRICISM; NEWTON, I.; RATIONALISM

PAUL F. JOHNSON

CONDITIONALS
See COUNTERFACTUAL CONDITIONALS; INDICATIVE CONDITIONALS

CONDORCET, MARIE-JEAN-ANTOINE-NICOLAS CARITAT DE (1743–94)

The Marquis de Condorcet belongs to the second generation of eighteenth-century French *philosophes*. He was by training and inclination a mathematician, and his work marks a major stage in the development of what is known today as the social sciences. He was held in high regard by contemporaries for his contributions to probability theory, and he published a number of seminal treatises on the theory and application of probabilism. He is best known today for the *Esquisse d'un tableau historique des progrès de l'esprit humain* (1795), his monumental, secularized historical analysis of the dynamics of man's progress from the primitive state of nature to modernity.

Condorcet's principal aim was to establish a science of man that would be as concise and certain in its methods and results as the natural and physical sciences. For Condorcet there could be no true basis to science without the model of mathematics, and there was no branch of human knowledge to which the mathematical approach was not relevant. He called the application of mathematics to human behaviour and organization 'social arithmetic'.

The central epistemological assumption, upon which his philosophy was based, was that the truths of observation, whether in the context of the physical or the moral and social sciences, were nothing more than probabilities, but that their varying degrees of certainty could be measured by means of the calculus of probabilities. Condorcet was thus able, through mathematical logic, to counteract the negative implications of Pyrrhonic scepticism for the notions of truth and progress, the calculus providing not only the link between the different orders of knowledge but also the way out of the Pyrrhonic trap by demonstrating man's capacity and freedom to understand and direct the march of progress in a rationally-ordered way.

In his *Esquisse* Condorcet set out to record not only the history of man's progress through nine 'epochs', from the presocial state of nature to the societies of modern Europe, but in the tenth 'epoch' of this work he also held out the promise of continuing progress in the future. He saw the gradual emancipation of human society and the achievement of human happiness as the consequence of man having been endowed by nature with the capacity to learn from experience and of the cumulative, beneficial effects of the growth of knowledge and enlightenment. Condorcet's *Esquisse* laid the basis for the positivism of the nineteenth century, and had a particularly significant impact on the work of Saint-Simon and Auguste Comte.

See also: COMTE, A.; POSITIVISM IN THE SOCIAL SCIENCES; PYRRHONISM; SAINT-SIMON, C.-H. DE R.

DAVID WILLIAMS

CONFEDERALISM

See FEDERALISM AND CONFEDERALISM

CONFIRMATION THEORY

Introduction

The result of a test of a general hypothesis can be positive, negative or neutral. The first, qualitative, task of confirmation theory is to explicate these types of test result. However, as soon as one also takes individual hypotheses into consideration, the interest shifts to the second, quantitative, task of confirmation theory: probabilistically evaluating individual and general hypotheses in the light of an increasing number of test results. This immediately suggests conceiving of the confirmation of an hypothesis as increasing its probability due to new evidence.

Rudolf Carnap initiated a research programme in quantitative confirmation theory by designing a continuum of probability systems with plausible probabilistic properties for the hypothesis that the next test result will be of a certain kind. This continuum of inductive systems has guided the search for optimum systems and for systems that take analogy into account.

Carnapian systems, however, assign zero probability to universal hypotheses. Jaakko Hintikka was the first to reconsider the confirmation of such hypotheses and using Carnap's continuum for this purpose has set the stage for a whole spectrum of inductive systems of this type.

1 Qualitative and quantitative confirmation theory

According to the hypothetico-deductive method a theory is tested by examining its implications. The result of an individual test of a general hypothesis stated in observation terms can be positive, negative or neutral. If it is neutral the test was not well devised; if it is negative, the hypothesis, and hence the theory, has been falsified. *Qualitative* confirmation theory primarily aims at further explicating the intuitive notions of neutral and positive test results. Some paradoxical features discovered by Hempel and some queer predicates defined by Goodman show that this is not an easy task.

Assuming that a black raven confirms the hypothesis 'All ravens are black' and that confirmation is not affected by logically equivalent reformulations, Hempel argued that not only a non-black non-raven but, even more counterintuitively, also a black non-raven confirms it. Goodman argued that not all predicates guarantee the 'projectibility' of a universal hypothesis from observed to non-observed cases. For example, if 'grue' means 'green, if examined before t' and 'blue, if not examined before t', a green emerald discovered before t would not only confirm 'All emeralds are green' but also 'All emeralds are grue', and hence, assuming that consequences are also confirmed, even 'All emeralds not examined before t are blue'. Whereas Goodman succeeded in formulating criteria for acceptable predicates, in terms of their relative 'entrenchment' in previously successfully projected generalizations, up to now nobody has given a generally accepted qualitative solution to Hempel's riddles (see UNDERDETERMINATION).

Below we treat *quantitative*, more specifically, probabilistic confirmation theory, which aims at explicating the idea of confirmation as increasing probability due to new evidence. Carnap introduced this perspective and pointed confirmation theory towards the search for a suitable notion of logical or inductive probability (see PROBABILITY, INTERPRETATIONS OF §5). Generally speaking, such probabilities combine indifference properties with inductive properties.

CONFIRMATION THEORY

2 The continuum of inductive systems

Mainly in his *The Continuum of Inductive Methods* (1952), Rudolf CARNAP started a fruitful research programme centring around the famous λ-continuum. The probability systems in this programme can be described in terms of individuals and observation predicates or in terms of trials and observable outcomes. The latter way of presentation will be used here. Moreover, we will presuppose an objective probability process, although the systems to be presented can be applied in other situations as well.

Consider a hidden wheel of fortune. You are told, truthfully, only that it has precisely four coloured segments, BLUE, GREEN, RED and YELLOW, without further information about the relative size of the segments. So you do not know the objective probabilities. What you subsequently learn are only the outcomes of successive trials. Given the sequence of outcomes e_n of the first n trials, your task is to assign reasonable probabilities, $p(R/e_n)$, to the hypothesis that the next trial will result in, for example, RED.

There are several ways of introducing the λ-continuum, but the basic idea behind it is that it reflects gradually learning from experience. In fact, as Zabell rediscovered, C-systems were anticipated by Johnson. According to Carnap's favourite approach $p(R/e_n)$ should depend only on n and the number of occurrences of RED thus far, n_R. More specifically, it should be a special weighted mean of the observed relative frequency n_R/n and the (reasonable) initial probability $1/4$. This turns out to leave room for a continuum of (C-)systems, the λ-continuum, $0 < \lambda < \infty$:

$$p(R/e_n) = (n_R + \lambda/4)/(n+\lambda) =$$
$$n/(n+\lambda) \cdot (n_R/n) + \lambda/(n+\lambda) \cdot (1/4)$$

Note that the weights $n/(n+\lambda)$ and $\lambda/(n+\lambda)$ add up to 1 and that the larger the value of λ the slower the first increases at the expense of the second; that is, the slower one is willing to learn from experience.

C-systems have several attractive indifference, confirmation and convergence properties. The most important are as follows:

(a) order indifference or exchangeability: the resulting prior probability, $p(e_n)$, for e_n, does not depend on the order of the results of the trials, that is, $p(R/e_n) = p(e_n^*)$ for any permutation e_n^* of e_n;

(b) instantial confirmation: if e_n is followed by RED this is favourable for RED, that is, $p(R/e_n R) > p(R/e_n)$;

(c) instantial convergence: $p(R/e_n)$ approaches n_R/n for increasing n.

However, confirmation and convergence of universal hypotheses are excluded in C-systems. The reason is that C-systems in fact assign zero prior probability to all universal generalizations, for instance to the hypothesis that all results will be RED. Of course, this is desirable in the described situation, but if you were told only that there are *at most* four coloured segments, you would like to leave room for this possibility.

3 Optimum inductive systems

Carnap proved that for certain kinds of objective probability process, such as a wheel of fortune, there is an optimal value of λ, depending on the objective probabilities, in the sense that the average mistake may be expected to be lowest for this value. Surprisingly, this optimal value is independent of n. Of course, in actual research, where we do not know the objective probabilities, this optimal value cannot be calculated. Carnap did not raise the question of a reasonable estimate of the optimal value for a specific objective process, for he saw the problem of selecting a value of λ primarily as a choice that each scientist had to make in general. However, the question of a reasonable estimate has attracted the attention of other researchers.

Festa proposed basing the estimate on 'contextual' knowledge of similar processes in nature. For example, in ecology one may know the relative frequencies of certain species in different habitats before one starts the investigation of a new habitat. For a quite general class of systems, Festa formulates a solution to the estimation problem that relates the research area of confirmation theory to that of truth approximation: the optimum solution may be expected to be the most efficient way of approaching the objective or true probabilities.

Unfortunately, wheels of fortune do not constitute a technological (let alone a biological) kind for which you can use information about previously investigated instances. But if you had knowledge of a random sample of all existing wheels of fortune, Festa's approach would work on the average for a new, randomly drawn, one.

4 Inductive analogy by similarity

Carnap struggled with the question of how to include analogy considerations into inductive probabilities. His important distinction between two kinds of analogy – by similarity and by proximity – was posthumously published. Here we will consider only the first kind.

Suppose you find GREEN more similar to BLUE than to RED. Carnap's intuition of analogy by similarity is that, for instance, the posterior probability of GREEN should be higher if, other things being equal, some occurrences of RED are replaced by occurrences of BLUE. The background intuition, not valid for artificial wheels of fortune, is that similarity in one respect (for example, colour) will go together with similarities in other respects (for example, objective probabilities). However, explicating which precise principle of analogy one wants to fulfil has turned out to be very difficult.

One interesting approach is in terms of *virtual trials*, which is a way of determining how analogy influence is to be distributed after *n* trials. In the case above, BLUE would get more analogy credits than RED from an occurrence of GREEN. The resulting systems of virtual analogy have the same confirmation and convergence properties as C–systems. Moreover, they satisfy a principle of analogy that is in general more plausible than Carnap's. Roughly, the new principle says that replacement of a previous occurrence of BLUE by GREEN makes less difference for the probability that the next trial will be BLUE than does replacement of a previous occurrence of RED by GREEN for the probability that the next trial will be RED.

Unfortunately, systems of virtual analogy are not exchangeable: the order of results makes a difference. There are, however, exchangeable systems with some kind of analogy by similarity. For example, Skyrms has sketched a Bayesian approach that uses information about possible gravitational bias of a symmetric wheel of fortune to determine the influence of analogy, and di Maio follows a suggestion of Carnap.

5 Universal generalizations

Carnap was well aware that C–systems do not leave room for non–analytic universal generalizations. In fact, all systems presented thus far have this problem. Although tolerant of other views, Carnap himself was inclined to downplay the theoretical importance of universal statements.

Hintikka took up the problem of universal statements. His basic idea was to apply Bayesian conditionalization to Carnap's C–systems with uniform λ, using a specific prior distribution on universal statements containing a parameter α. The systems belonging to the resulting α–λ–continuum have the instantial confirmation and convergence properties and also the desired property of universal confirmation; that is, that the probability of a not yet falsified universal statement increases with another instance of it. Moreover, they satisfy universal convergence: $p(H_R/e_n)$ approaches 1 for increasing *n* as long as only RED continues to occur (where H_R indicates the universal statement that

only RED will occur in the long run). For increasing parameter α, universal confirmation is smaller and universal convergence slower.

In fact, systems based on an arbitrary prior distribution and C–systems with arbitrary λ, here called H–systems, already have the general properties of instantial and universal confirmation and convergence. The subclass of H–systems based on an arbitrary prior distribution and C–systems with λ proportional to the corresponding number of possible outcomes is particularly interesting. For this subclass appears to be co–extensive with a class of systems introduced by Hintikka and by Niini-luoto, very differently from H–systems, using principles and parameters related only to finite sequences of outcomes.

There is also a plausible 'delabelled' reformulation of H–systems that can be extended to the very interesting case of an unknown denumerable number of possible outcomes. Presenting the delabelling in terms of exchangeable partitions, Zabell has studied this case by principles leading to a class of systems with three parameters.

6 Applications

The Carnap–Hintikka programme in confirmation theory, also called inductive probability theory, has applications in several directions. Systems of inductive probability were intended primarily for explicating confirmation as increasing probability. One may even define a quantitative degree of confirmation: namely, as the difference or ratio of the posterior and the initial or prior probability. There are other interesting types of application as well. Carnap and Stegmüller stressed that they can be used in decision–making, and Skyrms applies them in game theory (see DECISION AND GAME THEORY). Costantini *et al.* use them in a rational reconstruction of elementary particle statistics. Festa suggests several areas of empirical science where optimum inductive systems can be used. Finally, for universal hypotheses, Hintikka, Hilpinen and Pietarinen use systems of inductive probability to formulate rules of acceptance and Niiniluoto uses these systems to estimate degrees of verisimilitude.

See also: INDUCTION, EPISTEMIC ISSUES IN; INDUCTIVE INFERENCE; PROBABILITY, INTERPRETATIONS OF; STATISTICS

References and further reading

Hilpinen, R. (1968) *Rules of Acceptance and Inductive Logic*, Amsterdam: North Holland. (Gives a detailed analysis of Hintikka's two–dimensional continuum and corresponding rules of acceptance.)

Kuipers, T. (1978) *Studies in Inductive Probability and Rational Expectation*, Dordrecht: Reidel. (Studies the systems of Carnap, Hintikka and Niiniluoto, and their generalization, in great detail. Refers also to the related work of Carnap and Hintikka, and to the work of Hilpinen, Pietarinen and Stegmüller.)

THEO A.F. KUIPERS

CONFUCIAN ANALECTS
See CONFUCIUS

CONFUCIAN PHILOSOPHY, CHINESE

Chinese Confucian philosophy is primarily a set of ethical ideas oriented toward practice. Characteristically, it stresses the traditional boundaries of ethical responsibility and *dao*, or the ideal of the good human life as a whole. It may be characterized as an ethics of virtue in the light of its conception of *dao* and *de* (virtue). Comprising the conceptual framework of Confucian ethics are notions of basic virtues such as *ren* (benevolence), *yi* (rightness, righteousness), and *li* (rites, propriety). There are also notions of dependent virtues such as filiality, loyalty, respectfulness and integrity. Basic virtues are considered fundamental, leading or action-guiding, cardinal and the most comprehensive. In the classic Confucian sense, *ren* pertains to affectionate concern for the well-being of fellows in one's community. Notably, *ren* is often used in an extended sense by major Song and Ming Confucians as interchangeable with *dao* for the ideal of the universe as a moral community. *Yi* pertains to the sense of rightness, especially exercised in coping with changing circumstances of human life, those situations that fall outside the scope of *li*. *Li* focuses on rules of proper conduct, which have three functions: delimiting, supportive and ennobling. That is, the *li* define the boundaries of proper behaviour, provide opportunities for satisfying desires of moral agents within these boundaries, and encourage the development of noble characters which markedly embody cultural refinement and communal concerns. The *li* are the depository of insights of the Confucian tradition as a living ethical tradition. This tradition is subject to changing interpretation governed by the exercise of *quan* or the weighing of circumstances informed by the sense of rightness (*yi*).

However, the common Confucian appeal to historical events and paradigmatic individuals is criticized because of lack of understanding of the ethical uses of such a historical appeal. The pedagogical use stresses the study of the classics in terms of the standards of *ren*, *yi* and *li*. Learning, however, is not a mere acquisition of knowledge, but requires understanding and insight. Also, the companion study of paradigmatic individuals is important, not only because they point to models of emulation but also because they are, so to speak, exemplary personifications of the spirits of *ren*, *yi* and *li*. Moreover, they also function as reminders of moral learning and conduct that appeal especially to what is deemed in the real interest of the learner. The rhetorical use of the historical appeal is basically an appeal to plausible presumptions, or shared beliefs and trustworthiness. These presumptions are subject to further challenge, but they can be accepted as starting points in discourse. The elucidative use of historical appeal purports to clarify the relevance of the past for the present. Perhaps most important for argumentative discourse is the evaluative function of historical appeal. It focuses our knowledge and understanding of our present problematic situations as a basis for exerting the unexamined claims based on the past as a guidance for the present. Thus, both the elucidative and evaluative uses of historical appeal are critical and attentive to evidential grounding of ethical claims.

Because of its primary ethical orientation and its influence on traditional Chinese life and thought, Confucianism occupies a pre-eminent place in the history of Chinese philosophy. The core of Confucian thought lies in the teachings of Confucius (551–479 BC) contained in the *Analects* (*Lunyu*), along with the brilliant and divergent contributions of Mencius (372?–289 BC) and Xunzi (*fl.* 298–238 BC), as well as the *Daxue* (Great Learning) and the *Zhongyong* (Doctrine of the Mean), originally chapters in the *Liji* (Book of Rites). Significant and original developments, particularly along a quasi-metaphysical route, are to be found in the works of Zhou Dunyi (1017–73), Zhang Zai (1020–77), Cheng Hao (1032–85), Cheng Yi (1033–1107), Zhu Xi (1130–1200), Lu Xiangshan (1139–93), and Wang Yangming (1472–1529). Li Gou (1009–59), Wang Fuzhi (1619–92), and Dai Zhen (1723–77) have also made noteworthy contributions to the critical development of Confucian philosophy. In the twentieth century, the revitalization and transformation of Confucian philosophy has taken a new turn in response to Western philosophical traditions. Important advances have been made by Feng Youlan, Tang Junyi, Thomé H. Fang, and Mou Zongsan. Most of the recent works in critical reconstruction are marked by a self-conscious concern with analytic methodology and the relevance of existentialism, phenomenology, and hermeneutics. Still lacking is a comprehensive and systematic Confucian theory informed by both the history and the problems of Western philosophy.

See also: BUDDHIST PHILOSOPHY, CHINESE; CHINESE PHILOSOPHY; CONFUCIUS; DAOIST PHILOSOPHY; FAMILY, ETHICS AND THE; VIRTUE ETHICS; WANG YANGMING; XUNZI

A.S. CUA

CONFUCIUS (551–479 BC)

Confucius is arguably the most influential philosopher in human history – 'is' because, taking Chinese philosophy on its own terms, he is still very much alive. Recognized as China's first teacher both chronologically and in importance, his ideas have been the rich soil in which the Chinese cultural tradition has grown and flourished. In fact, whatever we might mean by 'Chineseness' today, some two and a half millennia after his death, is inseparable from the example of personal character that Confucius provided for posterity. Nor was his influence restricted to China; all of the Sinitic cultures – especially Korea, Japan and Vietnam – have evolved around ways of living and thinking derived from the wisdom of the Sage.

A couple of centuries before Plato founded his Academy to train statesmen for the political life of Athens, Confucius had established a school with the explicit purpose of educating the next generation for political leadership. As his curriculum, Confucius is credited with having over his lifetime edited what were to become the Chinese Classics, a collection of poetry, music, historical documents and annals that chronicled the events at the Lu court, along with an extensive commentary on the *Yijing* (Book of Changes). These classics provided a shared cultural vocabulary for his students, and became the standard curriculum for the Chinese literati in subsequent centuries.

Confucius began the practice of independent philosophers travelling from state to state in an effort to persuade political leaders that their particular teachings were a practicable formula for social and political success. In the decades that followed the death of Confucius, intellectuals of every stripe – Confucians, Legalists, Mohists, Yin–Yang theorists, Militarists – would take to the road, attracted by court academies which sprung up to host them. Within these seats of learning, the viability of their various strategies for political and social unity would be hotly debated.

D.C. LAU
ROGER T. AMES

CONNECTIONISM

Connectionism is an approach to computation that uses connectionist networks. A connectionist network is composed of information-processing units (or nodes); typically, many units process information simultaneously, giving rise to massively 'parallel distributed processing'. Units process information only locally: they respond only to their specific input lines by changing or retaining their activation values; and they causally influence the activation values of their output units by transmitting amounts of activation along connections of various weights or strengths. As a result of such local unit processing, networks themselves can behave in rule-like ways to compute functions.

The study of connectionist computation has grown rapidly since the early 1980s and now extends to every area of cognitive science. For the philosophy of psychology, the primary interest of connectionist computation is its potential role in the computational theory of cognition – the theory that cognitive processes are computational. Networks are employed in the study of perception, memory, learning and categorization; and it has been claimed that connectionism has the potential to yield an alternative to the classical view of cognition as rule-governed symbol manipulation.

Since cognitive capacities are realized in the central nervous system, perhaps the most attractive feature of the connectionist approach to cognitive modelling is the neural-like aspects of network architectures. The members of a certain family of connectionist networks, artificial neural networks, have proved to be a valuable tool for investigating information processing within the nervous system. In artificial neural networks, units are neuron-like; connections, axon-like; and the weights of connections function in ways analogous to synapses.

Another attraction is that connectionist networks, with their units sensitive to varying strengths of multiple inputs, carry out in natural ways 'multiple soft constraint satisfaction' tasks – assessing the extent to which a number of non-mandatory, weighted constraints are satisfied. Tasks of this sort occur in motor-control, early vision, memory, and in categorization and pattern recognition. Moreover, typical networks can re-programme themselves by adjusting the weights of the connections among their units, thereby engaging in a kind of 'learning'; and they can do so even on the basis of the sorts of noisy and/or incomplete data people typically encounter.

The potential role of connectionist architectures in the computational theory of cognition is, however, an open question. One possibility is that cognitive architecture is a 'mixed architecture', with classical and connectionist modules. But the most widely discussed view is that cognitive architecture is thoroughly connectionist. The leading challenge to this view is that an adequate cognitive theory must explain high-level cognitive phenomena such as the systematicity of thought (someone who can think 'The dog chases the cat' can also think 'The cat chases the dog'), its productivity (our ability to think a potential infinity of thoughts) and its inferential coherence (people can infer 'p' from 'p and q'). It has been argued that a connectionist architecture could explain such phenomena only if it implements a classical, language-like symbolic architecture. Whether this is so, however, and, indeed, even whether there *are* such phenomena to be explained, are currently subjects of intense debate.

See also: MODULARITY OF MIND

BRIAN P. MCLAUGHLIN

CONSCIOUSNESS

Philosophers have used the term 'consciousness' for four main topics: knowledge in general, intentionality, introspection (and the knowledge it specifically generates) and phenomenal experience. Here we discuss the last two uses. Something within one's mind is 'introspectively conscious' just in case one introspects it (or is poised to do so). Introspection is often thought to deliver one's primary knowledge of one's mental life. An experience or other mental entity is 'phenomenally conscious' just in case there is 'something it is like' for one to have it. The clearest examples are: perceptual experiences, such as tastings and seeings; bodily-sensational experiences, such as those of pains, tickles and itches; imaginative experiences, such as those of one's own actions or perceptions; and streams of thought, as in the experience of thinking 'in words' or 'in images'. Introspection and phenomenality seem independent, or dissociable, although this is controversial.

Phenomenally conscious experiences have been argued to be nonphysical, or at least inexplicable in the manner of other physical entities. Several such arguments allege that phenomenal experience is 'subjective'; that understanding some experiences requires undergoing them (or their components). The claim is that any objective physical science would leave an 'explanatory gap', failing to describe what it is like to have a particular experience and failing to explain why there are phenomenal experiences at all. From this, some philosophers infer 'dualism' rather than 'physicalism' about consciousness, concluding that some facts about consciousness are not wholly constituted by physical facts. This dualist conclusion threatens claims that phenomenal consciousness has causal power, and that it is knowable in others and in oneself.

In reaction, surprisingly much can be said in favour of 'eliminativism' about phenomenal consciousness; the denial of any realm of phenomenal objects and properties of experience. Most (but not all) philosophers deny that there are phenomenal objects – mental images with colour and shape, pain-objects that throb or burn, inner speech with pitch and rhythm, and so on. Instead, experiences may simply seem to involve such objects. The central disagreement concerns whether these experiences have phenomenal properties – 'qualia'; particular aspects of what experiences are like for their bearers. Some philosophers deny that there are phenomenal properties – especially if these are thought to be intrinsic, completely and immediately introspectible, ineffable, subjective or otherwise potentially difficult to explain on physicalist theories. More commonly, philosophers acknowledge qualia of experiences, either articulating less bold conceptions of qualia, or defending dualism about boldly conceived qualia.

Introspective consciousness has seemed less puzzling than phenomenal consciousness. Most thinkers agree that introspection is far from complete about the mind and far from infallible. Perhaps the most familiar account of introspection is that, in addition to 'outwardly perceiving' non-mental entities in one's environment and body, one 'inwardly perceives' one's mental entities, as when one seems to see visual images with one's 'mind's eye'. This view faces several serious objections. Rival views of introspective consciousness fall into three categories, according to whether they treat introspective access (1) as epistemically looser or less direct than inner perception, (2) as tighter or more direct, or (3) as fundamentally non-epistemic or nonrepresentational. Theories in category (1) explain introspection as always retrospective, or as typically based on self-directed theoretical inferences. Rivals from category (2) maintain that an introspectively conscious mental state reflexively represents itself, or treat introspection as involving no mechanism of access at all. Category (3) theories treat a mental state as introspectively conscious if it is distinctively available for linguistic or rational processing, even if it is not itself perceived or otherwise thought about.

See also: COLOUR AND QUALIA; DUALISM; MATERIALISM IN THE PHILOSOPHY OF MIND; PHENOMENOLOGICAL MOVEMENT; QUALIA; REDUCTIONISM IN THE PHILOSOPHY OF MIND

ERIC LORMAND

CONSENT

A concept of central importance in moral, political and legal philosophy, consent is widely recognized as justifying or legitimating acts, arrangements or expectations. In standard cases, a person's consent to another person's acts removes moral or legal objections to or liability for the performance of those acts. Thus, in medical practice the informed consent of a patient to a procedure can justify the physician's actions. In law, the maxim '*volenti non fit injuria*' (the willing person is not wronged) governs a wide range of acts and transactions, from the economic to the sexual. And in politics, it is often supposed that it is 'the consent of the governed' that justifies or makes permissible both governmental policies and the use of official coercion to compel obedience to law. Consent may be given in a variety of more and less direct forms, but its binding force always rests on the satisfaction of conditions of knowledge, intention, competence, voluntariness and acceptability of content.

See also: FREEDOM AND LIBERTY; LIBERALISM; RIGHTS

A. JOHN SIMMONS

CONSEQUENTIALISM

Introduction

Consequentialism assesses the rightness or wrongness of actions in terms of the value of their consequences. The most popular version is act-consequentialism, which states that, of all the actions open to the agent, the right one is that which produces the most good.

Act-consequentialism is at odds with ordinary moral thinking in three respects. First, it seems excessively onerous, because the requirement to make the world a better place would demand all our time and effort; second, it leaves no room for the special duties which we take ourselves to have to those close to us – family, friends and fellow citizens; and third, it might require us, on occasion, to do dreadful things in order to bring about a good result.

Consequentialists standardly try to bring their theory more into line with common thinking by amending the theory in one of two ways. Indirect act-consequentialism holds that we should not necessarily aim to do what is right. We may get closer to making the world the best possible place by behaviour which accords more with ordinary moral thought. Rule-consequentialism holds that an action is right if it is in accordance with a set of rules whose general acceptance would best promote the good. Such rules will bear a fairly close resemblance to the moral rules under which we now operate.

1 Act-consequentialism
2 Criticisms of act-consequentialism
3 Indirect act-consequentialism
4 Rule-consequentialism

1 Act-consequentialism

Although the term 'consequentialism' is a recent coinage – it appears to have first been used in its present sense by Anscombe – it refers to a type of theory which has a long history. Consequentialism builds on what may seem to be the merest truism, namely that morality is concerned with making the world a better place for all. Consequentialist considerations certainly figure importantly in issues of public policy. Penal, economic or educational programmes are standardly judged by the goodness or badness of their results.

All moral theories offer an account both of the right and of the good. They all tell us, that is, both what makes an action right or wrong, and what kinds of thing are good or valuable. It is characteristic of consequentialist theories to assess whether an action is right in terms of the amount of good it produces (see §4). Deontological ethical theories, by contrast, hold that the right is independent of the good: certain kinds of action are wrong, and others right, independently of the goodness or badness of their consequences (see DEONTOLOGICAL ETHICS; RIGHT AND GOOD).

Act-consequentialism, the simplest form of the theory, holds that the right action – the one you should do – is the one which would produce the greatest balance of good over bad consequences; that is, the one which would maximize the good. (Where two or more actions come out equal best, then it is right to do any one of them.) Which action is in fact the right one will depend on what account of the good any particular act-consequentialist theory offers.

A theory of the good is an account of those things which are intrinsically good, good in themselves, and not merely good as a means to something else which is good (see GOOD, THEORIES OF THE). A visit to the dentist is only extrinsically good, because it leads to healthy teeth and the avoidance of toothache, but it is not in itself a good thing; it is a necessary evil. By far the most popular and influential account of the good within the consequentialist camp is that offered by utilitarianism (see UTILITARIANISM). On this view, usually known as hedonism or welfarism, the good is pleasure, happiness or wellbeing (see HEDONISM; HAPPINESS). The act-utilitarian holds, therefore, that the right action is the one which maximizes happiness.

Many consequentialists reject hedonism. A pioneer in this respect was G.E. MOORE, whose theory, somewhat confusingly, used to be referred to as ideal utilitarianism, in contrast to the hedonistic variety. Among the things which have been held to be intrinsically good are knowledge, virtue, beauty, justice, and the flourishing of the environment as a whole. Many of these alternative accounts of the good are pluralist: that is, they claim that there are several different kinds of good thing which cannot all be brought under one heading. Pluralist act-consequentialism faces a difficulty. In order to determine which of the possible actions is the right one, agents must be able to rank the outcomes of each action, from the worst to the best. But if there are several distinct values which cannot be reduced to a common measure, how can one kind of value be compared with another in order to produce a definitive ranking? This is the problem of incommensurability of value.

The term 'consequentialism', though hallowed by frequent philosophical use, may be misleading since it might naturally be taken to imply that an action itself can have no intrinsic value; its value is all to be found in its consequences. Utilitarianism is indeed committed to this view – for what matters on the utilitarian account is not the nature of the act itself but the pleasure which it produces in anyone affected by it – but it is not an essential feature of consequentialism as such. Some consequentialists wish to leave room for the thought that certain kinds of action, such as lying, cheating, and killing the innocent, are intrinsically bad, while other kinds of act, such as generous, loyal, or just ones, are intrinsically good. Consequentialism can take such values into account in calculating which course of action produces the best results. In deciding whether one course of action is preferable to another, a consequentialist needs to know the total value that would be produced by taking each course of action, and that will include not only the value of the consequences but the value, if any, which attaches to the action itself.

Consequentialism is sometimes described as a teleological theory, because it conceives of a moral theory as setting a goal which we should strive to achieve (see TELEOLOGICAL ETHICS). The goal which consequentialism sets is to bring about a world containing the greatest balance of good over bad. Such a classification risks confusion, however, since a virtue ethics, such as Aristotle's, is also usually classified as teleological, yet Aristotle's theory differs from consequentialism in at least

two crucial respects. First, the good at which agents aim, on Aristotle's view (outlined in *Nicomachean Ethics*), is not the best state of the world, but the good life for humans; agents are to seek to realize distinctively human goods in their own lives. Second, Aristotle's theory, unlike consequentialism, does not define the right in terms of the good. On the contrary, a full understanding of the good life rests on a prior conception of the right, for an important part of the good life consists in acting rightly (see ARISTOTLE §§21–6; RIGHT AND GOOD; VIRTUE ETHICS).

We also need to distinguish the kind of consequentialism with which we are here concerned from ethical egoism, which is sometimes classified as a consequentialist theory (see EGOISM AND ALTRUISM). Ethical egoism, which holds that the right action is the one which would best promote the agent's own interests, is structurally similar to consequentialism in that the right action is the one which maximizes a good, in this case, the agent's own good. What distinguishes egoism from the sort of consequentialism discussed here is that the latter is an *impartial* theory, giving equal weight to each person's good (see IMPARTIALITY).

2   Criticisms of act-consequentialism

How should consequentialists set about deciding what to do? A natural answer is: by calculating, as best they may, what would produce the most good on any particular occasion when they are called upon to act. Of course, lack of time and knowledge limit what consequentialists can do by way of calculation, but they must do the best they can. So interpreted, however, act-consequentialism can be criticized for running counter to our intuitive moral convictions in a number of ways.

First, it seems excessively demanding; I shall only be acting rightly in so far as I maximize the good. Given all the bad things in the world, and the fact that few of us do much to improve them, it is clear that, in order to do what act-consequentialism requires, I would have to devote virtually all my energy and resources to making the world a better place. This would give me no time or money to pursue my own interests, or even to relax, except to refresh me ready to redouble my moral efforts on the morrow. The degree of self-sacrifice required would make the lives of the saints look self-indulgent. Ordinary morality is surely not as demanding as this; it gives us permission to pursue our own goals, provided that we are not in breach of any of our fundamental duties. Some have proposed, in order to meet this point, that the theory be modified so that an act is right if its consequences are good, or good enough, even if they are not the best. This suggestion has not been widely adopted, for it is usually held that a rational agent will always prefer the greater good to the less.

Second, act-consequentialism appears to leave no place for the duties we take ourselves to have to our family and friends (see FAMILY, ETHICS AND THE; FRIENDSHIP). Such duties are often classified as agent-relative: each of us should help *their own* family and friends, so that the persons to whom the duties are owed vary from agent to agent. Act-consequentialism, however, is an agent-neutral moral theory; the goal at which we should aim does not depend on who the agent is. I should direct my efforts towards those for whom I can do the most good; their relationship to me is irrelevant. Even if act-consequentialism places special value on the cultivation of certain relationships, such as friendship, this will still not yield a duty of friendship, as traditionally understood. If friendship is a great good, then my duty as a consequentialist is to promote friendship in general between all persons; that will not necessarily require me to give special attention to *my* friends, as distinct from helping others to give special attention to their friends.

Third, if act-consequentialism is too demanding in one respect it seems too permissive in another. For it leaves no room for the thought, central to much ordinary moral thinking, that there are certain constraints on our action, certain kinds of act, such as cheating, torturing and killing, which we ought not to contemplate, even if acting in one of these forbidden ways would maximize the good. The end, as we often say, does not justify the means. Once again, constraints seem to be agent-relative. Each of us is required not to kill or torture the innocent *ourselves* even if, by doing so, we could prevent two such tortures or killings.

3   Indirect act-consequentialism

Because it generates these counter-intuitive results, few consequentialists hold that agents should decide what to do by asking what will produce the best results. There are two theories which offer a less direct link between the overall goal of making things go as well as possible and how one should decide to act on any particular occasion. The first of these is known as indirect act-consequentialism. It retains the claim that the right action is the one with the best consequences, but denies that the virtuous agent needs be guided directly by consequentialist thoughts when deciding how to act.

Indirect act-consequentialism builds on the thought that we do not necessarily hit the target if we aim directly at it. The gunner must make allowances for wind, gravity and poorly aligned sights; the moralist may have to direct our thoughts away from the goal if we are to achieve it. Act-consequentialism, on this view, tells us what the target is, but not how to hit it. It is not itself a good guide to action for a number of reasons: the calculations are tricky and time-consuming; we may be tempted to skew the results in our favour; doing the right action may require us to go against dispositions which are both deeply rooted and generally useful. So we may actually do better, in terms of achieving the goals which consequentialism sets us, if we do not aim to do what is right, but follow a few fairly simple moral rules of the traditional type, or encourage within ourselves the development of dispositions, such as kindness and loyalty, which will normally lead us to act in beneficial ways. In adopting such rules, or developing such dispositions, we know that we will sometimes act wrongly when we could, perhaps, have acted rightly. Yet we may still get closer, in the long run, to achieving the consequentialist goal than we would have if we had attempted to aim at it directly.

Some indirect act-consequentialists go further. Since we make better decisions if we eschew consequentialist calculations, it might be best if we rejected consequentialism. It seems possible that agents might behave worse, in consequentialist terms, if they were taught the truth of consequentialism than if they were brought up to believe some other moral theory. In which case consequentialists would do well to prevent its truth being generally known. Opponents see this position as incoherent. If the adoption of consequentialism demands its suppression then in what sense can we adopt it? How could a society be said to be governed by a moral code if no-one in that society believed it?

4   Rule-consequentialism

The second alternative to direct act-consequentialism is rule-consequentialism, which offers a more substantive role for moral rules or principles. Individual acts are judged right or wrong by reference to the rules; the rules, but not the individual acts, are judged by the results of accepting them. The right action is, roughly, the one that is in conformity with a set of moral rules which, if generally accepted, would tend to produce better results than any other set of viable rules we might accept. Rule-consequentialism differs from indirect act-consequentialism in two ways. It maintains that each decision should be guided by thoughts about which action is the right one, and denies that the right action is necessarily the one with the best results. In deciding which rules to accept we should bear in mind that the rules need to be clear, reasonably simple and not too difficult to comply with, given human nature. If they meet these requirements, it is likely that such rules will not be too dissimilar to our present ones.

Rule-consequentialism might be a plausible moral theory, but should it properly be seen as a form of consequentialism? It apparently abandons a central tenet of consequentialism: the claim that our goal should be to maximize the good. The rule I should follow, on this view, is the one that *would* have better consequences, if generally accepted, than any other rule. If it is not, in fact, generally accepted, then in following it I may not get as close to maximizing the good as I would if I followed some other policy. For that reason, perhaps, act-consequentialism has remained most popular among defenders of the theory, despite its difficulties.

See also: CONSEQUENTIALISM

References and further reading

Hooker, B. (2000) *Ideal Code, Real World*. Oxford: Clarendon Press. (A clear and vigorous defence of rule-consequentialism.)

Scheffler, S. (1988) *Consequentialism and Its Critics*, Oxford: Oxford University Press. (A very useful collection of seminal articles.)

Sidgwick, H. (1874) *The Methods of Ethics*, London: Macmillan; 7th edn, 1907, esp. I (ch. 9), II (ch. 1), III (chaps 11, 13), IV (chaps 25). (The classic source of many of the strategies now discussed by consequentialists and their opponents.)

DAVID MCNAUGHTON

CONSERVATISM

Conservatism is an approach to human affairs which mistrusts both a priori reasoning and revolution, preferring to put its trust in experience and in the gradual improvement of tried and tested arrangements. As a conscious statement of position, it dates from the reaction of Burke and de Maistre to the Enlightenment and Revolutionary thought and practices in the eighteenth century. Its roots, however, go far deeper. From Plato, conservatives derive a sense of the complexity and danger of human nature, although they reject emphatically his belief in the desirability of philosophical governance. From Aristotle, conservatives derive their sense of the need for practical experience in judging both moral and political matters, and their understanding of the role of tradition in inculcating habits of virtue and wisdom in the young.

Against Plato, conservatives prefer the limited government advocated by Hobbes, because of their belief in the ignorance and corruptibility of rulers, and because of their wish to encourage the self-

reliance of subjects. They do, however, reject any conception of a social contract. In this, they follow de Maistre, who argued that creatures with the institutions and reactions necessary to form a social contract will already be in a society and hence have no need of such a thing.

While de Maistre emphasized the terror underlying political power, more characteristic of modern Anglo-Saxon conservatism is the position of Burke. For Burke, a good constitution is one adorned with 'pleasing illusions' to make 'power gentle and obedience liberal'. It is also one which dissipates power in a society through autonomous institutions independent of the state. For both these reasons the communist regimes of eastern Europe could not be defended by conservatives, even though for a time they represented a form of social order.

While conservatism is not antithetical to the free market, and while the market embodies virtues the conservative will approve of, for the conservative the market needs to be supplemented by the morality, the institutions and the authority necessary to sustain it. Human beings are by nature political, and also inevitably derive their identity from the society to which they belong. Our sense of self is established through our family relationships and also through the wider recognition and apportionment of roles we achieve in the public world beyond the family. According to Hegel, who since Aristotle has written most profoundly on the interplay of the private and the public in human life, both family and the public world of civil society need to be sustained through the authority of the state. On the other hand, the distinctions between family, civil society and the state need to be maintained against the characteristically modern tendency to treat them collectively. In his insistence both on authority and on the checks and balances needed in a good society, Hegel may be said to be the most articulate and systematic of conservative thinkers.

Conservatism has been much criticized for its tendency towards complacency and to accept the status quo even when it is unacceptable. However, in its stress on the imperfectibility of human nature and on the dangers of wholesale revolution, it may be said to be more realistic than its opponents. Conservatives can also be quite content with the claim that societies animated by conservative political structures have been more successful morally and materially than socialist or liberal societies. This claim they believe to be true, and it is a fundamental aspect of their position that the dispute between them and their opponents is, at bottom, an empirical one.

See also: HUMAN NATURE

ANTHONY O'HEAR

CONSILIENCE OF INDUCTION
See CONFIRMATION THEORY; WHEWELL, WILLIAM

CONSTANTS, LOGICAL
See LOGICAL CONSTANTS

CONSTATIVES
See PERFORMATIVES; SPEECH ACTS

CONSTITUTIONALISM

Constitutionalism comprises a set of ideas, principles and rules, all of which deal with the question of how to develop a political system which excludes as far as possible the chance of arbitrary rule. While according to one of the classic sources of constitutionalism, article sixteen of the 1789 French Declaration of the Rights of Man and of the Citizen, 'any society in which rights are not guaranteed, or in which the separation of powers is not defined, has no constitution', the scope of constitutional principles is in fact broader. In addition to these two defining principles, the following are essential: popular sovereignty; the rule of law; rules about the selection of power-holders and about their accountability to the ruled; and principles about the making, unmaking, revision, interpretation and enforcement of a constitution. Despite close affiliations, constitutionalism and democracy are not the same. Whereas democracy is an institutional device which realizes the right of the people to govern themselves, constitutionalism aims to establish institutional restraints on the power of the rulers, even if they are popularly elected and legitimized. Constitutionalism embodies the self-rationalizing and self-restraining principles of popular government.

ULRICH K. PREUß

CONSTRUCTIVISM

Originally proposed by sociologists of science, constructivism or social constructivism is a view about the nature of scientific knowledge held by many philosophers of science. Constructivists maintain that scientific knowledge is made by scientists and not determined by the world. This makes constructivists antirealists. Constructivism here should not be confused with constructivism in mathematics or logic, although there are some similarities. Constructivism is more aptly compared with Berkeley's idealism.

Most constructivist research involves empirical study of a historical or a contemporary episode in science, with the aim of learning how scientists experiment and theorize. Constructivists try not to bias their case studies with presuppositions about how scientific research is directed. Thus their approach contrasts with approaches in philosophy of science that assume scientists are guided by a particular method. From their case studies, constructivists have concluded that scientific practice is not guided by any one set of methods. Thus constructivism is relativist or antirationalist.

There are two familiar (and related) criticisms of constructivism. First, since constructivists are self-avowed relativists, some philosophers argue that constructivism fails for the same reasons that relativism fails. But many philosophers of science note that relativism can be characterized in various ways and that versions of relativism can be useful in the interpretation of science. Therefore, constructivism's relativism does not by itself render it unacceptable. Second, constructivists are accused of believing that scientists literally 'make the world', in the way some make houses or cars. This is probably not the best way to understand constructivism. Rather, constructivism requires only the weaker thesis that scientific knowledge is 'produced' primarily by scientists and only to a lesser extent determined by fixed structures in the world. This interprets constructivism as a thesis about our access to the world via scientific representations. For example, constructivists claim that the way we represent the structure of DNA is a result of many interrelated scientific practices and is not dictated by some ultimate underlying structure of reality. Constructivist research provides important tools for epistemologists specializing in the study of scientific knowledge.

STEPHEN M. DOWNES

CONTENT, NON-CONCEPTUAL

To say that a mental state has intentional content is to say that it represents features of the world. The intentional content of a belief can be characterized in terms of concepts: the content of the belief that fish swim is characterized by the concepts 'fish' and 'swimming'. The contents of beliefs are, for this reason, often described as conceptual. One way to explain this idea is to say that to have a belief, one has to possess the concepts which characterize the belief's content. However, some philosophers believe that certain mental states have non-conceptual contents: these states represent the world without the subject having to possess the concepts which characterize their contents. The main examples of these putative states are conscious perceptual experiences and the non-conscious states of cognitive information-processing systems (such as the visual system).

TIM CRANE

CONTENT: WIDE AND NARROW

A central problem in philosophy is to explain, in a way consistent with their causal efficacy, how mental states can represent states of affairs in the world. Consider, for example, that wanting water and thinking there is some in the tap can lead one to turn on the tap. The contents of these mental states pertain to things in the world (water and the tap), and yet it would seem that their causal efficacy should depend solely on their internal character-istics, not on their external relations. That is, a person could be in just those states and those states could play just the same psychological roles, even if there were no water or tap for them to refer to. However, certain arguments, based on some imaginative thought experiments, have persuaded many philosophers that thought contents do depend on external factors, both physical and social. A tempting solution to this dilemma has been to suppose that there are two kinds of content, wide and narrow. Wide content comprises the referential relations that mental states bear to things and their properties. Narrow content comprises the determi-nants of psychological role. Philosophers have debated whether both notions of content are viable and, if so, how they are connected.

See also: HOLISM: MENTAL AND SEMANTIC; METHODOLOGICAL INDIVIDUALISM; SEMANTICS

KENT BACH

CONTEXTUALISM, EPISTEMOLOGICAL

The idea that norms vary with social setting has long been recognized, but it is only in the late twentieth century that philosophers have developed precise versions of epistemological contextualism, the theory that standards of knowledge and justification vary with context. Ordinary practice seems to support this rather than the 'invariantist' view that epistemological standards are uniform.

Suppose, for example, that having seen my children a minute ago, I assert 'I know my children are in the garden'. My neighbour Harold then says, 'Good, because an escaped prisoner is seeking hostages nearby'. I may then appropriately claim, 'On second thoughts, I do not know, I should check carefully'. Standards for knowledge appear to have shifted, since they now require further investigation.

Contextualism's greatest advantage is its response to scepticism. Sceptics raise radical possibilities, such as that we might be dreaming. The contextualist grants that such doubts are legitimate in the sceptical context, but holds they are illegitimate in everyday situations. Yet contextualism can appear to be an objectionable form of relativism, and may be accused of confusing standards that we apply in practical conversational contexts with the true standards that determine whether someone has knowledge.

See also: JUSTIFICATION, EPISTEMIC; KNOWLEDGE, CONCEPT OF

BRUCE W. BROWER

CONTINUANTS

There is a common-sense distinction between terms such as 'statue' or 'chair' on the one hand, and 'concert' or 'war' on the other. A long-standing tradition in metaphysics has attached some signifi-cance to this distinction, holding that the first kind of term is used to name continuants, whereas the second kind is used to name events or processes. The difference is that continuants can be said to change, and therefore persist through change, whereas events do not. However, the distinction between continuants and events has been challenged on the grounds that no concrete object does, in fact, retain its identity through time. It has been suggested, for example, that unless we give up the notion of identity through time, we are faced with questions that we cannot answer. In addition, the notion that things persist through change is, apparently, threatened by a certain view of time. On this view there is in reality no past, present and future, but rather unchanging temporal relations between events. It has been suggested that such a view is committed to the idea that objects have temporal parts, and these by definition cannot persist through time.

See also: PROCESSES

ROBIN LE POIDEVIN

CONTINUUM HYPOTHESIS

The 'continuum hypothesis' (CH) asserts that there is no set intermediate in cardinality ('size') between the set of real numbers (the 'continuum') and the set of natural numbers. Since the continuum can be shown to have the same cardinality as the power set (that is, the set of subsets) of the natural numbers, CH is a special case of the 'generalized continuum hypothesis' (GCH), which says that for any infinite set, there is no set intermediate in cardinality between it and its power set.

Cantor first proposed CH believing it to be true, but, despite persistent efforts, failed to prove it. König proved that the cardinality of the continuum cannot be the sum of denumerably many smaller cardinals, and it has been shown that this is the only restriction the accepted axioms of set theory place on its cardinality. Gödel showed that CH was consistent with these axioms and Cohen that its negation was. Together these results prove the independence of CH from the accepted axioms.

Cantor proposed CH in the context of seeking to answer the question 'What is the identifying nature of continuity?' These independence results show that, whatever else has been gained from the introduction of transfinite set theory – including greater insight into the import of CH – it has not provided a basis for finally answering this question. This remains the case even when the axioms are supplemented in various plausible ways.

MARY TILES

CONTRACEPTION
See LIFE AND DEATH (§5); SEXUALITY, PHILOSOPHY OF

CONTRACTARIANISM
The idea that political relations originate in contract or agreement has been applied in several ways. In Plato's *Republic* Glaucon suggests that justice is but a pact among rational egoists. Thomas Hobbes developed this idea to analyse the nature of political power. Given the predominantly self-centred nature of humankind, government is necessary for society. Government's role is to stabilize social cooperation. By exercising enforcement powers, government provides each with the assurance that everyone else will abide by cooperative rules, thereby making it rational for all to cooperate. To fulfil this stabilizing role, Hobbes argued that it is rational for each individual to agree to authorize one person to exercise absolute political power. Neo-Hobbesians eschew absolutism and apply the theory of rational choice to argue that rules of justice, perhaps even all morality, can be construed in terms of a rational bargain among self-interested individuals.

John Locke, working from different premises than Hobbes, appealed to a social compact to argue for a constitutional government with limited powers. All men are born with a natural right to equal freedom, and a natural duty to God to preserve themselves and the rest of mankind. No government is just unless it could be commonly agreed to form a position of equal freedom, where agreement is subject to the moral constraints of natural law. Absolutism is unjust according to this criterion.

Rousseau developed egalitarian features of Locke's view to contend for a democratic constitution. The Social Contract embodies the General Will of society, not the unconstrained private wills of its members. The General Will wills the common good, the good of society and all of its members. Only by bringing our individual wills into accord with the General Will can we achieve civic and moral freedom.

In this century, John Rawls has recast natural rights theories of the social contract to argue for a liberal egalitarian conception of justice. From a position of equality, where each person abstracts from knowledge of their historical situations, it is rational for all to agree on principles of justice that guarantee equal basic freedoms and resources adequate for each person's independence.

T.M. Scanlon, meanwhile, has outlined a rights-based contractualist account of morality. An act is right if it accords with principles that could not be reasonably rejected by persons who are motivated by a desire to justify their actions according to principles that no one else can reasonably reject.

See also: INTERNATIONAL RELATIONS, PHILOSOPHY OF; LIBERALISM

SAMUEL FREEMAN

CONVENTION AND NATURE
See NATURE AND CONVENTION

CONVENTION AND NECESSARY TRUTH
See NECESSARY TRUTH AND CONVENTION

CONVENTIONALISM
How is it known that every number has a successor, that straight lines can intersect each other no more than once, that causes precede their events, and that the electron either went through the slit or it did not? In cases like these it is not easy to find observable evidence, and it is implausible to postulate special modes of intuitive access to the phenomena in question. Yet such theses are relied on in scientific discourse and can hardly be dismissed as meaningless metaphysical excess. In response to this problem the positivists and empiricists (notably Poincaré, Hilbert, Carnap, Reichenbach and Ayer) developed a strategy known as conventionalism. The idea was that certain statements, including fundamental principles of logic, arithmetic and geometry, are asserted as a matter of conventional stipulation, being no more than definitions of some of their constituent terms; consequently they must be true, our commitment to them cannot but be justified, and the facts in virtue of which they are true are simply the facts of our having made those particular decisions about the use of words. This doctrine was a compelling and powerful weapon in the positivist–empiricist arsenal, evolving throughout the 1920s, 1930s and 1940s. But it fell into disfavour under a barrage of serious challenges due mainly to Quine. How are 'conventions' to be identified as such? How could

they possibly provide words with meanings, or have the epistemological import that is claimed for them? How could arbitrary, contingent decisions about the use of words result in the existence of necessary facts? In the absence of satisfactory replies to these objections few philosophers these days believe that conventionalism can settle the semantic, epistemological and metaphysical questions that it was intended to answer. However, certain aspects of the view remain defensible and interesting.

See also: LOGICAL POSITIVISM; NECESSARY TRUTH AND CONVENTION

PAUL HORWICH

CONVERSATION
See PRAGMATICS

CONWAY, ANNE (*c.*1630–79)

Anne Conway (née Finch) was the most important of the few English women who engaged in philosophy in the seventeenth century. Her reputation derives from one work published after her death, *Principia philosophiae antiquissimae et recentissimae* (1690), which proposes a Neoplatonic system of metaphysics featuring a monistic concept of created substance. The work entails a critique of the dualism of both Descartes and Henry More, as well as of the materialism (as she saw it) of Hobbes and Spinoza. In her concept of the monad and her emphasis on the benevolence of God, Conway's system has some interesting affinities with that of Leibniz.

SARAH HUTTON

COPERNICUS, NICOLAUS (1473–1543)

Copernicus argued that the earth is a planet revolving around the sun, as well as rotating on its own axis. His work marked the culmination of a tradition of mathematical astronomy stretching back beyond Ptolemy, to the Greeks and Babylonians. Though it was associated with methods and assumptions that had been familiar for centuries, it was also revolutionary because of its implications for the relations between humankind and the universe at large.

See also: BRUNO, G.; COSMOLOGY; EXPLANATION; GALILEI, GALILEO; KEPLER, J.; KUHN, T.S.; RENAISSANCE PHILOSOPHY

ERNAN MCMULLIN

CORRESPONDENCE THEORY OF TRUTH
See TRUTH, CORRESPONDENCE THEORY OF

COSMOLOGICAL ARGUMENT
See GOD, ARGUMENTS FOR THE EXISTENCE OF

COSMOLOGY

The term 'cosmology' has three main uses. At its most general, it designates a worldview, for example, the Mayan cosmology. In the early eighteenth century, shortly after the term made its first appearance, Christian Wolff used it to draw a distinction between physics, the empirical study of the material world, and cosmology, the branch of metaphysics dealing with material nature in its most general aspects. This usage remained popular into the twentieth century, especially among Kantian and neo-scholastic philosophers. But recent developments in science that allow the construction of plausible universe models have, effectively, pre-empted the use of the term in order to designate the science that deals with the origins and structure of the physical universe as a whole.

Cosmology may be said to have gone through three major phases, each associated with a single major figure – Aristotle, Newton and Einstein. The ancient Greeks were the first to attempt to give a reasoned account of the cosmos. Aristotle constructed a complex interlocking set of spheres centred on an immovable central earth to account for the motions of the heavenly bodies. Newton formulated a theory of gravitational force that required space and time to be both absolute and infinite. Though the laws of nature could, in principle, be specified, nothing could be said about the origins or overall structure of the cosmos. In 1915, Einstein proposed a general theory of relativity whose field-equations could be satisfied by numerous universe-models. Hubble's discovery of the galactic red shift in 1929 led Lemaître in 1931 to choose from among these alternatives an expanding-universe model, which, though challenged in the 1950s by a rival steady-state theory, became the 'standard' view after the cosmic microwave background radiation it had predicted was observed in 1964. The 'Big Bang' theory has since been modified in one important respect by the addition of an inflationary episode in the first fraction of a second of cosmic expansion. As a 'cosmic' theory, it continues to raise issues of special interest to philosophers.

See also: ANAXIMANDER; PYTHAGOREANISM; SPACE

ERNAN MCMULLIN

COUNT TERMS
See MASS TERMS

COUNTERFACTUAL CONDITIONALS

'If bats were deaf, they would hunt during the day.' What you have just read is called a 'counterfactual' conditional; it is an 'If . . . then . . .' statement the components of which are 'counter to fact', in this case counter to the fact that bats hear well and sleep during the day. Among the analyses proposed for such statements, two have been especially prominent. According to the first, a counterfactual asserts that there is a sound argument from the antecedent ('bats are deaf') to the consequent ('bats hunt during the day'). The argument uses certain implicit background conditions and laws of nature as additional premises. A variant of this analysis says that a counterfactual is itself a condensed version of such an argument. The analysis is called 'metalinguistic' because of its reference to linguistic items such as premises and arguments. The second analysis refers instead to possible worlds. (One may think of possible worlds as ways things might have gone.) This analysis says that the example is true just in case bats hunt during the day in the closest possible world(s) where they are deaf

See also: POSSIBLE WORLDS; RELEVANCE LOGIC AND ENTAILMENT

FRANK DÖRING

COUSIN, VICTOR (1792–1867)

French philosopher, educationalist and historian, Victor Cousin is primarily associated with 'Eclecticism' and the history of philosophy, but his work also includes contributions to aesthetics, philosophy of history and political theory. He was a prolific writer and editor, and a significant figure in the development of philosophy as a professional discipline in France.

See also: HEGELIANISM; GERMAN IDEALISM

DAVID LEOPOLD

CRIME AND PUNISHMENT

Introduction

An account of how state punishment can be justified requires an account of the state, as having the authority to punish, and of crime, as that which is punished. Crime, as socially proscribed wrongdoing, may be formally censured, and may lead to the payment of compensation to those injured by it – but why should it also attract the kind of 'hard-treatment' punishment which characterizes a system of criminal law? How should we decide which kinds of wrongdoing should count as crimes?

Consequentialists justify punishment by its beneficial effects, notably in preventing crime by deterring, reforming or incapacitating potential criminals. They face the objection that the wholehearted pursuit of such goals would lead to injustice – punishment of those who do not deserve it. Even if that objection is met by imposing non-consequentialist constraints on the system, they also face the objection that a consequentialist system fails to respect criminals as responsible moral agents.

Retributivists hold that punishment must be deserved if it is to be justified, and that the guilty (and only the guilty) deserve punishment. Positive retributivists hold that the guilty should be punished as they deserve, even if this will achieve no consequential good. Negative retributivists hold that only the guilty may be punished, but that they should be punished only if their punishment will be beneficial. The main objection to retributivism is that it fails to explain why the guilty deserve punishment.

Some retributivists have argued that the guilty deserve censure, and that punishment serves to communicate that censure. But why should we use 'hard treatment' such as imprisonment or fines to communicate censure? Does the hard treatment function as a consequentialist deterrent? Or could such punishments serve to reform or educate criminals, thus bringing them to repent their crimes and restore their relationships with those they have wronged?

A theory of justified punishment must be related to our existing penal institutions. It must, in particular, have something to say about sentencing: about what kinds of punishment should be imposed, and about how sentencers should decide on the appropriate severity of punishment. A central issue concerns the role of the principle of proportionality: the demand that the severity of punishment should be proportionate to the seriousness of the crime.

But we must also ask whether our existing penal practices can be justified at all. We must face the abolitionists' argument that punishment should be abolished in favour of social practices which treat 'crimes' not as wrongdoings that must be punished, but as 'conflicts' which must be resolved by a reconciliatory rather than a punitive process.

1 Punishment, the state and the criminal law
2 Consequentialism and retributivism
3 Punishment and communication
4 Penal theory and sentencing
5 Can punishment be justified?

CRIME AND PUNISHMENT

1 Punishment, the state and the criminal law

Our focus is on punishment imposed by the state for breaches of the criminal law. Punishment can be initially defined as the deliberate infliction of something meant to be burdensome, by an authority, on an alleged offender, for an alleged offence. It needs justification because it involves doing things (depriving people of life, liberty or money) which are normally wrong. Different moral perspectives, however, generate different accounts of why punishment is morally problematic and thus of what could justify it. Is what matters the infliction of pain, for instance; or the apparent coercive infringement of rights which punishment involves?

A justification of state punishment presupposes a normative theory of the state, as having the authority to punish. Different theories of the state generate different conceptions of punishment: a liberal theory, for example, might set more modest aims for state punishment, and subject it to stricter constraints, than would a communitarian theory (see LIBERALISM; COMMUNITY AND COMMUNITARIANISM).

A justification of punishment also requires an account of crime, since it is crimes that are punished. Crime can be minimally defined as socially proscribed wrongdoing, breaching an authoritative social norm. We require an account of the proper character and scope of such norms (and of what it is to be responsible for breaching them, since crime involves a criminal who can be held responsible for it) (see RESPONSIBILITY). But not all breaches of socially (or legally) authoritative norms count as crimes which merit punishment: we must ask what kinds of response are appropriate to different kinds of wrongdoing.

Censure is one proper response to breaches of authoritative norms, and the expression of censure may be a further defining feature of punishment; this distinguishes fines, for instance, from taxes (see §3). But censure can be expressed by formal declarations, or by symbolic punishments which are painful only in virtue of their expressive meaning, whereas criminal punishments typically inflict 'hard treatment' (the loss of liberty, money or life) which is painful independently of its expressive meaning. Why should such hard treatment be an appropriate response to socially proscribed wrongdoing?

Another response to such wrongdoing is the enforced payment of compensation to those harmed by it; this is a central feature of the civil as distinct from the criminal law. But though punishment may involve the payment of compensation, it also inflicts hard treatment that is not directly compensatory

(nor do crimes always harm identifiable victims). Why should such punitive hard treatment ever be appropriate, and for what kinds of conduct? Which should count as crimes, rather than merely as civil wrongs?

Some theorists appeal to the 'harm principle' (see LAW AND MORALITY §2): only conduct which harms or endangers others should be criminal. But this provides at most a necessary, not a sufficient, condition for criminalization: not every kind of (even seriously) harmful conduct is a plausible candidate for criminalization. And, apart from the question of whether paternalistic laws, prohibiting conduct that harms only the agent, can ever be justified, we must ask what counts as 'harm'. Can we distinguish harmful from merely offensive conduct? Might we count some conduct as 'harmful' purely because of its moral character (as, for example, a breach of trust or a denial of rights) rather than because of its material effects?

Whether we talk of conduct that harms interests, or that infringes rights, or that flouts community values, we must ask which interests, rights or values should be protected by the criminal rather than the civil law. Crimes are often said to be public, rather than private or individual, wrongs: wrongs not just against some individual who may claim damages, but against the community or state. That is why while civil cases are brought (and may be dropped) by individual plaintiffs, criminal cases are brought by the state or community, even when they involve an attack on an individual victim. But can we explain crimes as public wrongs, without distorting the way in which many crimes attack individual victims? To say, for instance, that murder and rape should be crimes not because of what they do to their particular victims, but because they threaten public order, seems to deny the significance of the victim's suffering. We might suggest that even crimes against individual victims should count as 'public' wrongs in that the community should identify itself with the victim, counting the victim's wrong as 'ours'. Or we might abandon the idea of crimes as public wrongs (except for those which directly injure the collective rather than any individual, like tax evasion), and portray crimes as attacks on those central rights or interests which the state should protect. Either approach, however, leaves us with the question of which rights or interests should be thus protected, or which wrongs should thus be seen as public wrongs. Or if we say that the criminal law should protect the values which are essential to the identity or existence of the community, we must ask which those values are. (Any account of crime must also explain the distinction between *mala in se*, acts which are wrong independently of any legal rule, and *mala prohibita*, acts which are wrong only because prohibited. *Mala prohibita*, however, include many offences (notably 'regulatory' offences, such as minor traffic violations) which some think should not count as true 'crimes': they should be dealt with, not by a criminal process which censures and punishes, but by some distinct regulatory procedure.)

Instead of asking directly which kinds of conduct should be criminalized, we might ask what justifies criminal punishment, and found our principles of criminalization on our answer to that question. If the central justifying aim of punishment is deterrence, we can ask which kinds of conduct should be thus deterred; if its proper aim is 'retribution', we can ask which kinds of conduct merit such a retributive response.

2 Consequentialism and retributivism

Penal theory has long been a battleground between consequentialists and retributivists. After a period of consequentialist domination, the 1970s saw a revival in retributivist thought, as part of a wider rights–based reaction against consequentialism in social policy.

Consequentialists justify punishment by its instrumental contribution to certain goods: most obviously, the good of crime-prevention. A penal system is justified if its crime-preventive and other benefits outweigh its costs, and no alternative practice could achieve such goods more cost-effectively. Punishment prevents crime by deterring, incapacitating or reforming potential offenders: by giving them prudential disincentives to crime, by subjecting them to restraints which make it harder for them to break the law, or by so modifying their attitudes that they will obey the law willingly (see BENTHAM, J.; CONSEQUENTIALISM).

It is at most a contingent truth that such effects on potential offenders are efficiently achieved by punishing actual offenders. This generates the familiar objection to any purely consequentialist theory, that it sanctions injustice. A system of deterrent punishment must appear to punish actual offenders: but that leaves open the possibility of framing innocent scapegoats to deter others or to reassure the public. And unless actual offending is the only reliable predictor of the future crimes which reformative or incapacitative measures aim to prevent, such measures might be efficiently (but surely unjustly) inflicted on those who have not yet broken the law but are thought likely to do so. Indeed, since a person's subjection to coercive treatment by the state must depend on the predicted effects of such treatment, rather than on their past conduct, we might wonder whether consequenti-

alists can justify a system of punishment, of measures imposed for a crime, at all.

Some consequentialists do argue that we should replace punishment by other, more efficient methods of dealing with socially dangerous people. Others argue that we should accept the 'injustices' that a strictly consequentialist penal system might perpetrate (noting that we already accept, for instance, the pre-emptive detention of the mentally disordered). Most accept, however, that a justified system of punishment cannot perpetrate the kinds of gross injustice noted above.

Consequentialists might meet this objection by providing a fuller account of the goods to be achieved or protected, and of the methods by which they might practicably be achieved. Thus some argue that individual freedom is an essential good, whose protection precludes the deliberate punishment of those who have not voluntarily broken the law. Others argue that, given the fallibility of human agents, the only safe way to pursue the appropriate goods is to set strict constraints on the penal system: for instance, strictly to forbid the deliberate punishment of an innocent. Such consequentialist defences, however, depend on large empirical claims about the likely effects of penal strategies, which cannot easily be verified. Can the demands of justice to which this objection appeals really be adequately grounded in the contingencies on which this consequentialist argument depends?

Another strategy is to abandon pure consequentialism, and impose non-consequentialist side-constraints of justice on our pursuit of the consequentialist's goals: to insist, for instance, that only those who have voluntarily broken the law may be punished, since responsible agents have a right not to be subjected to such coercive measures unless they voluntarily make themselves liable to them.

One objection to even a side-constrained consequentialist theory concerns the moral standing of those who are punished or threatened with punishment: that a consequentialist system fails to respect its citizens (criminals and non-criminals) as responsible agents. A system of deterrent punishments, Hegel argued, treats all those whom it threatens with punishment like 'dogs': rather than seeking their allegiance to the law by appeal to the moral reasons which justify its demands, it coerces their obedience by threats (see HEGEL, G.W.F. §8). A consequentialist system of reform similarly treats those subjected to it as objects to be remoulded, rather than as responsible agents who must determine their own conduct.

Against such objections, some argue that a side-constrained system of deterrent punishments can respect the moral standing of those it threatens and punishes; or that 'rehabilitation' and 'reform' need not be improperly manipulative or coercive. But one stimulus to the retributivist revival in the 1970s was the claim that only retributivism respects the moral standing of criminals: their right to receive 'fair and certain punishment', rather than being 'used merely as means' to the deterrence of others, or being subjected to indefinite terms of reformative 'treatment'.

The central retributivist slogan is that (only) the guilty deserve punishment, and deserve punishments proportionate to the seriousness of their crimes. This demand for 'just deserts' may be interpreted negatively, as forbidding the punishment of the innocent (or the excessive punishment of the guilty); or positively, as requiring that the guilty be punished as they deserve. The negative reading makes guilt a necessary, but not sufficient, condition of justified punishment: it suggests a 'mixed' account, which gives punishment a consequentialist aim but subjects our pursuit of that aim to retributivist side-constraints, requiring that punishment be both deserved and consequentially beneficial. The positive reading makes guilt a necessary and sufficient condition of justified punishment: the guilty should be punished because they deserve it, whether or not their punishment achieves any consequential good (see KANT, I. §10).

The central task for any retributivist is to explain this supposed justificatory relation between guilt and punishment: what is it about crime that makes punishment an appropriate response to it? The central objection to all retributivist theories is that they fail to discharge this task: they either fail to explain this notion of penal desert, falling back on unexplained intuition or metaphysical mystery-mongering, or offer covertly consequentialist explanations.

The 'new retributivism' of the 1970s offered various accounts of the idea of penal desert. One was that criminals gained by their crimes an unfair advantage over the law-abiding, since they accepted the benefits of the law-abiding self-restraint of others, but evaded that burden of self-restraint themselves: their punishment removed that unfair advantage, thus restoring the fair balance of benefits and burdens which the law should preserve. One objection to this account is that it distorts the nature of crime: what makes rape punishable as a crime is surely the wrong done to its victim, not the unfair advantage the rapist supposedly takes over all those who obey the law.

Another trend in recent retributivist thought has rather built on the idea of punishment as an expressive or communicative practice.

3 Punishment and communication

Expressive accounts of punishment need not be retributivist: since by expressing censure we can modify wrongdoers' conduct, consequentialists can advocate expressive punishments. But the expressive or communicative aspect of punishment can explain the retributivist's slogan that the guilty deserve punishment: if they have broken a law which justifiably claimed their obedience, they deserve censure; and it is a proper task for the state, speaking on behalf of the community, to communicate that censure to them.

We should talk of communication rather than of expression here. For communication is a process which addresses (as expression need not) another as a rational agent; it captures the idea (central to recent versions of retributivism), that we must address criminals as rational and responsible agents.

But even if criminal wrongdoers should be censured, and hard-treatment punishments of the sort imposed by our penal systems can communicate that censure, we must ask why it should be communicated in this way, rather than by formal declarations or purely symbolic punishments (see §1).

Some suggest that hard treatment is necessary if the censure which wrongdoing merits is to be communicated effectively to the criminal, who might not attend to merely symbolic punishments; or that it may be necessary to 'defeat' the claim to superiority which was implicit in the wrongdoer's crime (but do all crimes make such a claim?). But why, if not for the consequentialist reason that this will make the punishment a more effective deterrent, is effective communication so crucial that we must inflict hard-treatment punishments to achieve it?

Others accept that a communicative retributivism cannot by itself justify the use of hard treatment as the communicative vehicle: it must be justified by a consequentialist concern for deterrence. This need not be the kind of 'mixed' account which portrays retributivist values merely as side-constraints on the consequentialist ends which give the penal system its positive aim. The communication of censure can itself be the central justifying aim of punishment, so that the law addresses the citizen as a responsible moral agent, appealing to the moral reasons which justify its demands and the censure that it imposes on those who flout those demands. But recognizing that, as fallible human beings, we will not always be adequately motivated by such moral reasons for obeying the law, we communicate that censure through hard treatment in order to provide an additional prudential incentive for obedience. On one version of this account, the hard treatment should provide only a modest prudential supplement which does not replace or drown the law's moral voice: the question then is whether such modest supplements will be effective. On another version, the hard treatment may be harsh enough to provide by itself an effective deterrent; but this will revive the objections noted earlier to a deterrent conception of punishment.

More ambitiously communicative accounts of punishment portray the hard treatment as a mode of moral communication which aims to reform or educate. Punishment aims to bring wrongdoers to understand and to repent their crimes, and thus to reform their future conduct. Hard treatment assists this purpose by helping to bring home to them the meaning and implications of what they have done; it can also, if it is willingly undergone, enable them to express their repentance and thus reconcile themselves with their victims and the community. Such accounts are retributivist, since punishment must be focused on the past crime as an appropriate censuring response to it, but they also give punishment a forward-looking purpose: the offender's reform or rehabilitation, the restoration of the relationships which the crime damaged, the making of symbolic (and perhaps material) reparation to the victim and the community. Such purposes, however, are not to be understood in strictly consequentialist terms, as independent ends to which punishment is a contingent means: they can be achieved only through a punitive process which aims to persuade wrongdoers that they must suffer punishment for what they have done.

We must ask, however, whether hard-treatment punishment could ever be an appropriate vehicle for such a communicative, reformative and penitential endeavour; and whether, even if it could (as it might be in, for instance, a religious community that practises penance), the state should take such a coercive interest in the moral condition of its citizens. This conception of punishment might be at home within a communitarian perspective according to which individuals can find their identity and their good only as members of a community united by shared values and mutual concerns; but it seems incompatible with a liberal insistence on the need to protect individual rights and privacy against intrusive state or community power. Liberals can argue that punishment's primary purpose should be the communication of appropriate censure, but may deny that the state should try, by such coercive means, to secure repentance and reform; in which case hard-treatment punishments could be justified only as prudential deterrents which do not seek to invade the criminal's soul.

4   Penal theory and sentencing

Philosophical discussions of punishment are typically conducted at a level of high abstraction, remote both from the actualities of penal practices and from the pressing concerns of penal practitioners. But we must try to relate them to the real penal world.

One central issue is that of sentencing. What kinds of punishment should be available to the courts (capital punishment; imprisonment; fines; community service; probation)? What makes a particular kind of punishment appropriate, either generally or for a particular crime? How should sentencers determine the severity of punishment to be imposed on particular crimes or criminals?

Discussion of the last question often focuses on the principle of proportionality: the severity of punishment should be proportionate to the seriousness of the crime. Some such principle is integral to any retributivist theory, including communicative theories: for if punishment is to communicate an appropriate degree of censure, its severity must be proportionate to the seriousness of the crime. The application of such a principle requires some way of assessing and comparing the seriousness of different crimes, and the severity of different punishments; and it is not clear either just how, or how precisely, this can be done. Furthermore, while such a principle can help to determine the relative severity of sentences, requiring that more serious crimes be punished more severely, and so on, it is not clear whether it can help to fix absolute levels of punishment.

How important is the principle of proportionality? On some views, it is paramount: the primary aim of sentencing is to do justice by assigning proportionate sentences. This means, in practice, that the available range of punishments must be limited, and that the courts should have only very limited discretion in sentencing. Others argue that the demand for proportionality must be weighed against other relevant principles, such as a principle of penal parsimony which requires courts to impose the lightest acceptable sentence, even if that is lighter than is required for strict proportionality; on this view proportionality might be seen as a limiting principle requiring that criminals be punished no more severely than is proportionate to their crimes.

There is also a tension between the demand for proportionality and any ambitious account of punishment as communication. If punishment is given an educative, reformative or penitential aim, courts should seek punishments which are materially appropriate, rather than just formally proportionate, to the crime and the criminal: punishments which will appropriately address the particular criminal. But this would require the courts to be given a more flexible and creative discretion in sentencing, to find or construct sentences appropriate to the particular case: a discretion which might undermine demands for strict and formal proportionality.

Here again we face a conflict between a liberal perspective which emphasizes the demands of formal justice, and seeks to protect the citizen against the coercive and discretionary power of the state; and a more ambitious conception of the proper role of the state and the criminal law in seeking the moral good of the citizens.

5   Can punishment be justified?

Any plausible normative theory of punishment will show our existing penal institutions to be radically imperfect. The kind and degree of suffering that they inflict cannot be plausibly portrayed as either consequentially cost-effective or retributively just, or well-suited to the aims of a communicative theory of punishment. Nor is it clear that the preconditions of justified punishment are satisfied in our own societies, especially if punishment is portrayed in retributive or communicative terms: can we truly say that most of those who are convicted by our courts have culpably flouted laws which justifiably claimed their allegiance, or that we (in whose name the law speaks) have the moral standing to censure them?

The radical imperfection of our existing penal institutions raises a serious question for any citizen. Should we accept those existing institutions (while also striving for their reform) as necessary to the prevention of yet greater disorder or injustice; or may we have to recognize that they perpetrate such serious injustice, or cause so much harm, that they cannot be justified at all?

The suggestion that, even if a practice of state punishment could in principle be justified, our existing penal institutions may lack any adequate justification, might seem frivolous: can we honestly argue that they should be abolished? But this is just what is argued by 'abolitionists', many of whom indeed argue that punishment cannot even in principle be justified: we should work not for the reform of our penal institutions, but for their abolition. Such arguments are not often considered in the philosophical literature, which tends to assume that the key issue is not whether, but how, state punishment can be justified; but they present a challenge that must be taken seriously.

Various themes run through abolitionist writings. One concerns the very concept of 'crime' as that which merits a punitive response: we should reconceptualize crimes as 'conflicts' that require

resolution rather than punishment. Relatedly, we should 'civilize' our response to crime, favouring a civil law rather than a criminal model: rather than seeking 'retributive' justice by condemning and punishing those judged to have done wrong, we should seek 'restorative' justice by striving to reconcile the conflicting parties and (where necessary) negotiating reparation for whatever harm has been done. These themes are often accompanied by an advocacy of 'informal justice': rather than allowing the state to 'steal' conflicts from the individuals and local communities to whom they properly belong, we should look for informal, participatory modes of conflict-resolution. But punishment (the deliberate infliction of suffering) is never justified: neither as retribution (which is not a proper aim), nor as deterrence (which denies the moral standing of those who are threatened and punished). And while rehabilitative facilities may be offered to those who need and seek them, they can never properly be imposed on citizens.

Against such views it may be argued that some 'conflicts' involve the commission of genuine wrongs which should be condemned; that any morally acceptable 'reconciliation' must involve the recognition and acceptance of guilt by the wrong-doer (these considerations argue in favour of a communicative conception of punishment as censure); and that a society which truly forswore the whole coercive apparatus of criminal justice would be unable to protect itself or its members against seriously destructive wrongs and social disorder. We might imagine a more perfect society in which the kinds of hard-treatment punishment currently imposed would be unjustified, because unnecessary. We may agree that we now punish too much, too harshly, that our penal institutions do not serve the ends that punishment should serve, and that too often they inflict further suffering on those who are already seriously disadvantaged by the political and economic structures from which many of us benefit. Abolitionists forcibly remind us of these points; but this is not to agree that punishment can never be justified.

See also: Justice; Law, philosophy of

References and further reading

Duff, R.A. and Garland, D. (eds) (1994) *A Reader on Punishment*, Oxford, Oxford University Press. (A collection of core readings on whether and how criminal punishment can be justified.)

Primoratz, I. (1999) *Justifying Legal Punishment*, 2nd edn, Atlantic Highlands, NJ: Humanities Press. (A useful introductory text, criticizing utilitarian and 'mixed' accounts, arguing for retributivism.)

von Hirsch, A. and Ashworth, A.J. (eds) (1998)

Principled Sentencing, 2nd ed, Oxford, Hart Publishing. (A collections of articles on the principles of sentencing, which thus also discuss different current conceptions of the proper aims of punishment.)

R.A. DUFF

CRITERIA

The concept of criteria has been interpreted as the central notion in the later Wittgenstein's account of how language functions, in contrast to the realist semantics of the *Tractatus*. According to this later account, a concept possesses a sense in so far as there are conditions that constitute non-inductive evidence for its application in a particular case. This condition on a concept's possessing a sense has been thought to enable Wittgenstein to refute both solipsism and scepticism about other minds. There are powerful objections to this conception of criteria, which have led some philosophers to look for an alternative account of the role of criteria in Wittgenstein's later philosophy.

See also: CONTEXTUALISM, EPISTEMOLOGICAL; OTHER MINDS

MARIE MCGINN

CRITICAL REALISM

Critical realism is a movement in philosophy and the human sciences starting from Roy Bhaskar's writings. It claims that causal laws state the tendencies of things grounded in their structures, not invariable conjunctions, which are rare outside experiments. Therefore, positivist accounts of science are wrong, but so is the refusal to explain the human world causally. Critical realism holds that there is more to 'what is' than 'what is known', more to powers than their use, and more to society than the individuals composing it. It rejects the widespread view that explanation is always neutral – to explain can be to criticize.

See also: EXPERIMENT; EXPLANATION IN HISTORY AND SOCIAL SCIENCE; NATURALISM IN SOCIAL SCIENCE

ANDREW COLLIER

CRITICAL THEORY

The term 'critical theory' designates the approach to the study of society developed between 1930 and 1970 by the so-called 'Frankfurt School'. Comprising a group of theorists associated with the Institute for Social Research, the School was founded in Frankfurt, Germany in 1923. The three most important philosophers belonging to it were Max Horkheimer, Theodor Wiesengrund Adorno and Herbert Marcuse.

Horkheimer, Adorno and Marcuse feared that modern Western societies were turning into closed, totalitarian systems in which all individual autonomy was eliminated. In their earliest writings from the 1930s they presented this tendency towards totalitarianism as one result of the capitalist mode of production. In later accounts they give more prominence to the role of science and technology in modern society, and to the concomitant, purely 'instrumental', conception of reason. This conception of reason denies that there can be any such thing as inherently rational ends or goals for human action and asserts that reason is concerned exclusively with the choice of effective instruments or means for attaining arbitrary ends.

'Critical theory' was to be a form of resistance to contemporary society; its basic method was to be that of 'internal' or 'immanent' criticism. Every society, it was claimed, must be seen as making a tacit claim to substantive (and not merely instrumental) rationality; that is, making the claim that it allows its members to lead a good life. This claim gives critical theory a standard for criticism which is internal to the society being criticized. Critical theory demonstrates in what ways contemporary society fails to live up to its own claims. The conception of the good life to which each society makes tacit appeal in legitimizing itself will usually not be fully propositionally explicit, so any critical theory will have to begin by extracting a tacit conception of the good life from the beliefs, cultural artefacts and forms of experience present in the society in question. One of the particular difficulties confronting a critical theory of contemporary society is the disappearance of traditional substantive conceptions of the good life that could serve as a basis for internal criticism, and their replacement with the view that modern society needs no legitimation beyond simple reference to its actual efficient functioning, to its 'instrumental' rationality. The ideology of 'instrumental rationality' thus itself becomes a major target for critical theory.

See also: FRANKFURT SCHOOL

RAYMOND GEUSS

CROCE, BENEDETTO (1866–1952)

The leading Italian philosopher of his day, Croce presented his philosophy as a humanist alternative to the consolations of religion. A Hegelian idealist, he argued that all human activity was orientated towards either the Beautiful, the True, the Useful or the Good. These ideals were the four aspects of what, following Hegel, he termed spirit or human consciousness. The first two corresponded to the theoretical dimensions of spirit, namely intuition and logic respectively, the last two to spirit's practical aspects of economic and ethical willing. He contended that the four eternal ideals were 'pure concepts' whose content derived from human thought and action. Spirit or consciousness progressively unfolded through human history as our ideas of beauty, truth, usefulness and morality were steadily reworked and developed.

Croce insisted that his idealism was a form of 'absolute historicism', since it involved the claim that all meaning and value evolved immanently through the historical process. He strenuously denied that spirit could be regarded as some form of transcendent puppet-master that existed apart from the human beings through which it expressed itself. He accused Hegel of making this mistake. He also maintained that Hegel's conception of the dialectic as a synthesis of opposites had paid insufficient attention to the need to retain the distinct moments of spirit. He argued that the Beautiful, the True, the Useful and the Good, though linked, ought never to be confused, and he criticized aestheticism and utilitarianism accordingly.

Croce developed his thesis both in philosophical works devoted to aesthetics, ethics, politics and the philosophy of history, and in detailed historical studies of Italian and European literature, culture, politics and society. Opposition to the Fascist regime led him to identify his philosophy with liberalism on the grounds that it emphasized the creativity and autonomy of the individual. In practical politics, however, he was a conservative.

See also: ARTISTIC EXPRESSION; ECONOMICS AND ETHICS; HEGELIANISM; HISTORICISM; POETRY; SOCIAL DEMOCRACY

RICHARD BELLAMY

CRUCIAL EXPERIMENTS

A 'crucial experiment' allegedly establishes the truth of one of a set of competing theories. Francis Bacon held that such experiments are frequent in the empirical sciences and are particularly important for terminating an investigation. These claims were denied by Pierre Duhem, who maintained that crucial experiments are impossible in the physical sciences because they require a complete enumeration of all possible theories to explain a phenomenon – something that cannot be achieved. Despite Duhem, scientists frequently regard certain experiments as crucial in the sense that the experimental result helps make one theory among a set of competitors very probable and the others very improbable, given what is currently known.

PETER ACHINSTEIN

CUDWORTH, RALPH (1617–88)

Ralph Cudworth was the leading philosopher of the group known as the Cambridge Platonists. In his lifetime he published only one work of philosophy, his *True Intellectual System of the Universe* (1678). This was intended as the first of a series of three volumes dealing with the general topic of liberty and necessity. Two further parts of this project were published posthumously, from the papers he left when he died: *A Treatise Concerning Eternal and Immutable Morality* (1731) and *A Treatise of Freewill* (1838).

Cudworth's so-called Cambridge Platonism is broadly Neoplatonic, but he was receptive to other currents of thought, both ancient and modern. In philosophy he was an antideterminist who strove to defend theism in rational terms, and to establish the certainty of knowledge and the existence of unchangeable moral principles in the face of the challenge of Hobbes and Spinoza. He admired and borrowed from Descartes, but also criticized aspects of Cartesianism.

Cudworth's starting point is his fundamental belief in the existence of God, conceived as a fully perfect being, infinitely powerful, wise and good. A major part of his *True Intellectual System* is taken up with the demonstration of the existence of God, largely through *consensus gentium* (universal consent) arguments and the argument from design. The intellect behind his 'intellectual system' is the divine understanding. Mind is antecedent to the world, which is intelligible by virtue of the fact that it bears the stamp of its wise creator. The human mind is capable of knowing the world since it participates in the wisdom of God, whence epistemological certainty derives. The created world is also the best possible world, although not bound by necessity. A central element of Cudworth's philosophy is his defence of the freedom of will – a meaningful system of morals would be impossible without this freedom. Natural justice and morality are founded in the goodness and justice of God rather than in an arbitrary divine will. The principles of virtue and goodness, like the elements of truth, exist independently of human beings. *A Treatise Concerning Eternal and Immutable Morality* contains the most fully worked-out epistemology of any of the Cambridge Platonists and constitutes the most important statement of innate-idea epistemology by any British philosopher of the seventeenth century.

See also: CAMBRIDGE PLATONISM; LOCKE, J.; NEOPLATONISM

SARAH HUTTON

CULTURAL RELATIVISM

See RATIONALITY AND CULTURAL RELATIVISM

CULTURE

Culture comprises those aspects of human activity which are socially rather than genetically transmitted. Each social group is characterized by its own culture, which informs the thought and activity of its members in myriad ways, perceptible and imperceptible. The notion of culture, as an explanatory concept, gained prominence at the end of the eighteenth century, as a reaction against the Enlightenment's belief in the unity of mankind and universal progress. According to J.G. Herder, each culture is different and has its own systems of meaning and value, and cannot be ranked on any universal scale. Followers of Herder, such as Nietzsche and Spengler, stressed the organic nature of culture and praised cultural particularity against what Spengler called civilization, the world city in which cultural distinctions are eroded. It is difficult, however, to see how Herder and his followers avoid an ultimately self-defeating cultural relativism; the task of those who understand the significance of human culture is to make sense of it without sealing cultures off from one another and making interplay between them impossible.

Over and above the anthropological sense of culture, there is also the sense of culture as that through which a people's highest spiritual and artistic aspirations are articulated. Culture in this sense has been seen by Matthew Arnold and others as a substitute for religion, or as a kind of secular religion. While culture in this sense can certainly inveigh against materialism, it is less clear that it can do this effectively without a basis in religion. Nor is it clear that a rigid distinction between high and low culture is desirable. It is, in fact, only the artistic modernists of the twentieth century who have articulated such a distinction in their work, to the detriment of the high and the low culture of our time.

ANTHONY O'HEAR

CUSANUS

See NICHOLAS OF CUSA

D

DANTE ALIGHIERI

See ALIGHIERI, DANTE

DAOIST PHILOSOPHY

Early Daoist philosophy has had an incalculable influence on the development of Chinese philosophy and culture. Philosophical Daoism is often called 'Lao–Zhuang' philosophy, referring directly to the two central and most influential texts, the *Daodejing* (or *Laozi*) and the *Zhuangzi*, both of which were composite, probably compiled in the fourth and third centuries BC. Beyond these two texts we might include the syncretic *Huainanzi* (*c.*140 BC) and the *Liezi*, reconstituted around the fourth century AD, as part of the traditional Daoist corpus.

Second in influence only to the Confucian school, the classical Daoist philosophers in many ways have been construed as both a critique on and a complement to the more conservative, regulatory precepts of their Confucian rivals. Daoism has frequently and unfortunately been characterized in terms of passivity, femininity, quietism and spirituality, a doctrine embraced by artists, recluses and religious mystics. Confucianism, by contrast, has been cast in the language of moral precepts, virtues, imperial edicts and regulative methods, a doctrine embodied in and administered by the state official. The injudicious application of this *yin–yang*-like concept to Daoism and Confucianism tends to impoverish our appreciation of the richness and complexity of these two traditions. Used in a heavy-handed way, it obfuscates the fundamental wholeness of both the Confucian and Daoist visions of meaningful human existence by imposing an unwarranted conservatism on classical Confucianism, and an unjustified radicalism on Daoism.

There is a common ground shared by the teachings of classical Confucianism and Daoism in the advocacy of self-cultivation. In general terms, both traditions treat life as an art rather than a science. Both express a 'this-wordly' concern for the concrete details of immediate existence rather than exercising their minds in the service of grand abstractions and ideals. Both acknowledge the uniqueness, importance and primacy of the particular person and the person's contribution to the world, while at the same time stressing the ecological interrelatedness and interdependence of this person with their context.

However, there are also important differences. For the Daoists, the Confucian penchant for reading the 'constant *dao*' myopically as the 'human *dao*' is to experience the world at a level that generates a dichotomy between the human and natural worlds. The argument against the Confucian seems to be that the Confucians do not take the ecological sensitivity far enough, defining self-cultivation in purely human terms. It is the focused concern for the overcoming of discreteness by a spiritual extension and integration in the human world that gives classical Confucianism its socio-political and practical orientation. But from the Daoist perspective, 'overcoming discreteness' is not simply the redefinition of the limits of one's concerns and responsibilities within the confines of the human sphere. The Daoists reject the notion that human experience occurs in a vacuum, and that the whole process of existence can be reduced to human values and purposes.

To the extent that Daoism is prescriptive, it is so not by articulating rules to follow or asserting the existence of some underlying moral principle, but by describing the conduct of an achieved human being – the sage (*shengren*) or the Authentic Person (*zhenren*) – as a recommended object of emulation. The model for this human ideal, in turn, is the orderly, elegant and harmonious processes of nature. Throughout the philosophical Daoist corpus, there is a 'grand' analogy established in the shared vocabulary used to describe the conduct of the achieved human being on the one hand, and the harmony achieved in the mutual accomodations of natural phenomena on the other.

The perceived order is an achievement, not a given. Because *dao* is an emergent, 'bottom-up' order rather than something imposed, the question is: what is the optimal relationship between *de* and *dao*, between a particular and its environing conditions? The Daoist response is the self-dispositioning of particulars into relationships which allow the fullest degree of self-disclosure and development. In the Daoist literature, this kind of optimally appropriate action is often described as *wuwei*, 'not acting wilfully', 'acting naturally' or 'non-assertive activity'. *Wuwei*, then, is the negation of that kind of 'making' or 'doing' which requires that a particular sacrifice its own integrity in acting on behalf of something 'other', a negation of that kind of engagement that makes something false to itself. *Wuwei* activity 'characterizes' – that is, produces the character or ethos of – an aesthetically contrived composition. There is no ideal, no closed perfectedness. Ongoing creative achievement itself provides novel possibilities for a richer creativity. *Wuwei* activity is thus fundamentally qualitative: an aesthetic category and, only derivatively, an ethical one. *Wuwei* can be evaluated on aesthetic grounds, allowing that some relationships are more productively *wuwei* than others. Some relationships are more successful than others in maximizing the creative possibilities of oneself in one's environments.

This classical Daoist aesthetic, while articulated in these early texts with inimitable flavour and imagination, was, like most philosophical anarchisms, too intangible and impractical to ever be a serious contender as a formal structure for social and political order. In the early years of the Han dynasty (206 BC–AD 220), there was an attempt in the *Huainanzi* to encourage the Daoist sense of *ethos* by tempering the lofty ideals with a functional practicality. It appropriates a syncretic political framework as a compromise for promoting a kind of practicable Daoism – an anarchism within expedient bounds. While historically the *Huainanzi* fell on deaf ears, it helped to set a pattern for the Daoist contribution to Chinese culture across the sweep of history. Over and over again, in the currency of anecdote and metaphor, identifiably Daoist sensibilities would be expressed through a range of theoretical structures and social grammars, from military strategies, to the dialectical progress of distinctively Chinese schools of Buddhism, to the constantly changing face of poetics and art. It can certainly be argued that the richest models of Confucianism, represented as the convergence of Daoism, Buddhism and Confucianism itself, were an attempt to integrate Confucian concerns with human community with the broader Daoist commitment to an ecologically sensitive humanity.

See also: CHINESE PHILOSOPHY; CONFUCIAN PHILOSOPHY, CHINESE

DAVID L. HALL
ROGER T. AMES

DARWIN, CHARLES ROBERT (1809–82)

Darwin's *On the Origin of Species* (1859) popularized the theory that all living things have evolved by natural processes from pre-existing forms. This displaced the traditional belief that species were designed by a wise and benevolent God. Darwin showed how many biological phenomena could be explained on the assumption that related species are descended from a common ancestor. Furthermore, he proposed a radical mechanism to explain how the transformations came about, namely, natural selection. This harsh and apparently purposeless mechanism was seen as a major threat to the claim that the universe has a transcendent goal.

Because Darwin openly extended his evolutionism to include the human race, it was necessary to re-examine the foundations of psychology, ethics and social theory. Moral values might be merely the rationalization of instinctive behaviour patterns. Since the process which produced these patterns was driven by struggle, it could be argued that society must inevitably reflect the harshness of nature ('social Darwinism'). Darwin's book has been seen as the trigger for a 'scientific revolution'. It took many decades for both science and Western culture to assimilate the more radical aspects of Darwin's theory. But since the mid-twentieth century Darwin's selection mechanism has become the basis for a highly successful theory of evolution, the human consequences of which are still being debated.

See also: EVOLUTION AND ETHICS

PETER J. BOWLER

DAVIDSON, DONALD (1917–2003)

Donald Davidson's views about the relationship between our conceptions of ourselves as people and as complex physical objects have had significant impact on contemporary discussions of such topics as intention, action, causal explanation and weakness of the will. His collection of essays, *Actions and Events* (1980), contains many seminal contributions in these areas. But perhaps even greater has been the influence of Davidson's philosophy of language, as reflected especially in *Inquiries into Truth and Interpretation* (1984). Among the philosophical issues connected to language on which Davidson has been influential are the nature of truth, the semantic paradoxes, first person authority, indexicals, modality, reference, quotation, metaphor, indeterminacy, convention, realism and the publicity of language.

See also: AKRASIA; ANOMALOUS MONISM; INDIRECT DISCOURSE; INTENTION; RADICAL TRANSLATION AND RADICAL INTERPRETATION

ERNIE LEPORE

161

DE BEAUVOIR, SIMONE
See BEAUVOIR, SIMONE DE

DE DICTO
See DE RE/DE DICTO

DE LA METTRIE, JULIEN OFFROY
See LA METTRIE, JULIEN OFFROY DE

DE MONTESQUIEU, CHARLES BARON
See MONTESQUIEU, CHARLES LOUIS DE SECONDAT

DE PIZAN, CHRISTINE
See CHRISTINE DE PIZAN

DE RE/DE DICTO

'*De re*' and '*de dicto*' have been used to label a host of different, albeit interrelated, distinctions. '*De dicto*' means 'of, or concerning, a dictum', that is, something having representative content, such as a sentence, statement or proposition. '*De re*' means 'of, or concerning, a thing'. For example, a *de dicto* belief is a belief that a bearer of representative content is true, while a *de re* belief is a belief concerning some thing, that it has a particular characteristic.

Consider the following example:

> John believes his next-door neighbour is a Buddhist.

This statement is ambiguous. Construed *de dicto*, it is true in the following circumstance. John has never had any contact with his next-door neighbour. Nevertheless, John believes that his next-door neighbour is bound to be a Buddhist. Construed in this *de dicto* fashion, the statement does not attribute to John a belief that is distinctively about a particular individual. In contrast, construed *de re*, it does attribute to John a belief that is about a particular individual. For example, construed *de re*, the statement is true in the following circumstance. John encounters his next-door neighbour, Fred, at a party without realizing that Fred is his next-door neighbour. On the basis of his conversation with Fred, John forms a belief about the individual who is in fact his next-door neighbour to the effect that he is a Buddhist.

See also: ESSENTIALISM; USE/MENTION DISTINCTION AND QUOTATION

ANDRÉ GALLOIS

DEATH

Reflection on death gives rise to a variety of philosophical questions. One of the deepest of these is a question about the nature of death. Typically, philosophers interpret this question as a call for an analysis or definition of the concept of death. Plato, for example, proposed to define death as the separation of soul from body. However, this definition is not acceptable to those who think that there are no souls. It is also unacceptable to anyone who thinks that plants and lower animals have no souls, but can nonetheless die. Others have defined death simply as the cessation of life. This too is problematic, since an organism that goes into suspended animation ceases to live, but may not actually die.

Death is described as 'mysterious', but neither is it clear what this means. Suppose we cannot formulate a satisfactory analysis of the concept of death: in this respect death would be mysterious, but no more so than any other concept that defies analysis. Some have said that what makes death especially mysterious and frightening is the fact that we cannot know what it will be like. Death is typically regarded as a great evil, especially if it strikes someone too soon. However, Epicurus and others argued that death cannot harm those who die, since people go out of existence when they die, and people cannot be harmed at times when they do not exist. Others have countered that the evil of death may lie in the fact that death deprives us of the goods we would have enjoyed if we had lived. On this view, death may be a great evil for a person, even if they cease to exist at the moment of death.

Philosophers have also been concerned with the question of whether people can survive death. This is open to several interpretations, depending on what we understand to be people and what we mean by 'survive'. Traditional materialists take each person to be a purely physical object – a human body. Since human bodies generally continue to exist after death, such materialists presumably must say that we generally survive death. However, such survival would be of little value to the deceased, since the surviving entity is just a lifeless corpse. Dualists take each person to have both a body and a soul. A dualist may maintain that at death the soul separates from the body, thereby continuing to enjoy (or suffer) various experiences after the body has died.

Some who believe in survival think that the eternal life of the soul after bodily death can be a good beyond comparison. But Bernard Williams has argued that eternal life would be profoundly unattractive. If we imagine ourselves perpetually stuck at a given age, we may reasonably fear that eternal life will eventually become rather boring. On the other hand, if we imagine ourselves experiencing an endless sequence of varied 'lives', each disconnected from the others, then it is questionable whether it will in fact be 'one person' who lives eternally.

Finally, there are questions about death and the meaning of life. Suppose death marks the end of all conscious experience – would our lives be then rendered meaningless? Or would the fact of impending death help us to recognize the value of our lives, and thereby give deeper meaning to life?
See also: LIFE AND DEATH; LIFE, MEANING OF; SOUL, NATURE AND IMMORTALITY OF

FRED FELDMAN

DEBORIN, A.
See MARXIST PHILOSOPHY, RUSSIAN AND SOVIET

DECISION AND GAME THEORY
Decision theory studies individual decision-making in situations in which an individual's choice neither affects nor is affected by other individuals' choices; while game theory studies decision-making in situations where individuals' choices do affect each other. Decision theory asks questions like: what does it mean to choose rationally? How should we make choices when the consequences of our actions are uncertain? Buying insurance and deciding which job to take are examples of the kind of decisions studied by this discipline. Game theory instead applies to all decisions that have a strategic component. The choices of an oligopolist, voting strategies, military tactical problems, deterrence, but also common phenomena such as threatening, promising, conflict and cooperation are its subject matter. In a strategic situation, the goal is not just to choose rationally, but to choose in such a way that a mutual solution is achieved, so that choices 'coordinate' in the right way. The formal methods developed by game theory do not require that the subject making a choice be an intentional agent: coordinated interaction between animals or computers can be successfully modelled as well.
See also: PROBABILITY, INTERPRETATIONS OF; RATIONAL CHOICE THEORY; SEMANTICS, GAME-THEORETIC

CRISTINA BICCHIERI

DECISION PROBLEM
See CHURCH'S THEOREM AND THE DECISION PROBLEM

DECONSTRUCTION
Although the term is often used interchangeably (and loosely) alongside others like 'post-structuralism' and 'postmodernism', deconstruction differs from these other movements. Unlike post-structur-

alism, its sources lie squarely within the tradition of Western philosophical debate about truth, knowledge, logic, language and representation. Where post-structuralism follows the linguist Saussure – or its own version of Saussure – in espousing a radically conventionalist (hence sceptical and relativist) approach to these issues, deconstruction pursues a more complex and critical path, examining the texts of philosophy with an eye to their various blind-spots and contradictions. Where postmodernism blithely declares an end to the typecast 'Enlightenment' or 'modernist' project of truth-seeking rational inquiry, deconstruction preserves the critical spirit of Enlightenment thought while questioning its more dogmatic or complacent habits of belief. It does so primarily through the close reading of philosophical and other texts and by drawing attention to the moments of 'aporia' (unresolved tension or conflict) that tend to be ignored by mainstream exegetes. Yet this is not to say (as its detractors often do) that deconstruction is a kind of all-licensing textualist 'freeplay' which abandons every last standard of interpretive fidelity, rigour or truth. At any rate it is a charge that finds no warrant in the writings of some – Jacques Derrida and Paul de Man chief among them.
See also: DERRIDA, J.; POST-STRUCTURALISM

CHRISTOPHER NORRIS

DEDEKIND, JULIUS WILHELM RICHARD (1831–1916)
Dedekind is known chiefly, among philosophers, for contributions to the foundations of the arithmetic of the real and the natural numbers. These made available for the first time a systematic and explicit way, starting from very general notions (which Dedekind himself regarded as belonging to logic), to ground the differential and integral calculus without appeal to geometric 'intuition'. This work also forms a pioneering contribution to set theory (further advanced in Dedekind's correspondence with Georg Cantor) and to the general notion of a 'mathematical structure'.

Dedekind's foundational work had a close connection with his advancement of substantive mathematical knowledge, particularly in the theories of algebraic numbers and algebraic functions. His achievements in these fields make him one of the greatest mathematicians of the nineteenth century.
See also: CANTOR, G.; LOGICISM

HOWARD STEIN

DEDUCTIVE CLOSURE PRINCIPLE

It seems that one can expand one's body of knowledge by making deductive inferences from propositions one knows. The 'deductive closure principle' captures this idea: if S knows that P, and S correctly deduces Q from P, then S knows that Q. A closely related principle is that knowledge is closed under known logical implication: if S knows that P and S knows that P logically implies Q, then S knows that Q. These principles, if they hold, are guaranteed by general features of the concept of knowledge. They would form part of a logic of knowledge.

An influential argument for scepticism about knowledge of the external world employs the deductive closure principle. The sceptic begins by sketching a logically possible hypothesis, or counter-possibility (for example, that one is a brain in a vat, with computer-induced sense experience) which is logically incompatible with various things one claims to know (such as that one has hands). The proposition that one has hands logically implies the falsity of the sceptical hypothesis. Supposing that one is aware of this implication, the deductive closure principle yields the consequence that if one knows that one has hands, then one knows that one is not a brain in a vat. The sceptic argues that one does not know this: if one were in a vat, then one would have just the sensory evidence one actually has. It follows that one does *not* know that one has hands. Some philosophers have sought to block this argument by denying the deductive closure principle.

See also: KNOWLEDGE, CONCEPT OF §§7–10; SCEPTICISM

ANTHONY BRUECKNER

DEEP ECOLOGY

See ECOLOGICAL PHILOSOPHY; NÆSS, ARNE

DEFINITE DESCRIPTIONS

See DESCRIPTIONS

DEFINITION

A definition is a statement, declaration or proposal establishing the meaning of an expression. In virtue of the definition, the expression being defined (the 'definiendum') is to acquire the same meaning as the expression in terms of which it is defined (the 'definiens'). For example, 'Man is a rational animal' determines the meaning of the term 'man' by making it synonymous with 'rational animal'. Classical theory maintains that a good definition captures the 'real nature' of what is defined: 'A

definition is a phrase signifying a thing's essence' (see Aristotle). Historically, philosophers have come to distinguish these 'real' definitions from 'nominal' definitions that specify the meaning of a linguistic expression rather than signify the essential nature of an object, 'making another understand by Words, what Idea, the term defined stands for' (see Locke).

A further distinction can be drawn between contextual or implicit definitions, on the one hand, and explicit definitions, on the other. Often a definition fixes meaning directly and explicitly: for example, the definition of a proper name might well take the form of an explicit identity statement ('Pegasus = the winged horse') and a definition of a predicate is usually given (or can be re-cast) in the form of an equivalence ('For every x: x is a man if and only if x is a rational animal'). But sometimes the meaning of a term is specified in context, by way of the meaning of larger expressions in which the term occurs. A paradigmatic example of this is Bertrand Russell's analysis of the meaning of the definite article.

See also: FREGE, G. §§6, 8, 9; PARADOXES OF SET AND PROPERTY

G. ALDO ANTONELLI

DEISM

In the popular sense, a deist is someone who believes that God created the world but thereafter has exercised no providential control over what goes on in it. In the proper sense, a deist is someone who affirms a divine creator but denies any divine revelation, holding that human reason alone can give us everything we need to know to live a correct moral and religious life. In this sense of 'deism' some deists held that God exercises providential control over the world and provides for a future state of rewards and punishments, while other deists denied this. However, they all agreed that human reason alone was the basis on which religious questions had to be settled, rejecting the orthodox claim to a special divine revelation of truths that go beyond human reason. Deism flourished in the seventeenth and eighteenth centuries, principally in England, France and America.

See also: MIRACLES; NATURAL THEOLOGY; RELIGION AND SCIENCE

WILLIAM L. ROWE

DELEUZE, GILLES (1925–95)

Although grounded in the history of philosophy, Gilles Deleuze's work does not begin with first principles but grasps the philosophical terrain 'in the middle'. This method overthrows subject–object relations in order to initiate a philosophy of difference and chance that is not derived from static being; a philosophy of the event, not of the signifier-signified; a form of content that consists of a complex of forces that are not separable from their form of expression; the assemblage or body without organs, not the organized ego; time, intensity and duration instead of space; in short, a world in constant motion consisting of becomings and encounters with the 'outside' that such concepts do not grasp.

This radical philosophical project is rendered most clearly in Deleuze (and his collaborator Guattari's concept of the 'rhizome'). The rhizome is a multiplicity without any unity that could fix a subject or object. Any point of the rhizome can and must be connected to any other, though in no fixed order and with no homogeneity. It can break or rupture at any point, yet old connections will start up again or new connections will be made; the rhizome's connections thus have the character of a map, not a structural or generative formation. The rhizome, then, is no model, but a 'line of flight' that opens up the route for encounters and makes philosophy into cartography.

See also: ALTERITY AND IDENTITY, POSTMODERN THEORIES OF

DOROTHEA E. OLKOWSKI

DEMARCATION PROBLEM

The problem of demarcation is to distinguish science from nonscientific disciplines that also purport to make true claims about the world. Various criteria have been proposed by philosophers of science, including that science, unlike 'non-science', (1) is empirical, (2) seeks certainty, (3) proceeds by the use of a scientific method, (4) describes the observable world, not an unobservable one, and (5) is cumulative and progressive.

Philosophers of science offer conflicting viewpoints concerning these criteria. Some reject one or more completely. For example, while many accept the idea that science is empirical, rationalists reject it, at least for fundamental principles regarding space, matter and motion. Even among empiricists differences emerge, for example between those who advocate that scientific principles must be verifiable and those who deny that this is possible, claiming that falsifiability is all that is required.

Some version of each of these five criteria – considered as goals to be achieved – may be defensible.

See also: LOGICAL POSITIVISM §5

PETER ACHINSTEIN

DEMOCRACY

Introduction

Democracy means rule by the people, as contrasted with rule by a special person or group. It is a system of decision making in which everyone who belongs to the political organism making the decision is actually or potentially involved. They all have equal power. There have been competing conceptions about what this involves. On one conception this means that everyone should participate in making the decision themselves, which should emerge from a full discussion. On another conception, it means that everyone should be able to vote between proposals or for representatives who will be entrusted with making the decision; the proposal or representative with most votes wins.

Philosophical problems connected with democracy relate both to its nature and its value. It might seem obvious that democracy has value because it promotes liberty and equality. As compared with, for example, dictatorship, everyone has equal political power and is free from control by a special individual or group. However, at least on the voting conception of democracy, it is the majority who have the control. This means that the minority may not be thought to be treated equally; and they lack liberty in the sense that they are controlled by the majority.

Another objection to democracy is that, by counting everyone's opinions as of equal value, it considers the ignorant as being as important as the knowledgeable, and so does not result in properly informed decisions. However, voting may in certain circumstances be the right way of achieving knowledge. Pooling opinions may lead to better group judgement.

These difficulties with democracy are alleviated by the model which concentrates on mutual discussion rather than people just feeding opinions into a voting mechanism. Opinions should in such circumstances be better formed; and individuals are more obviously equally respected. However, this depends upon them starting from positions of equal power and liberty; rather than being consequences of a democratic procedure, it would seem that equality and liberty are instead prerequisites which are needed in order for it to work properly.

1	What democracy is
2	The value of democracy
3	The paradox of democracy
4	Democracy and knowledge
5	The use of democracy
6	Other consequences
7	Deliberative democracy

DEMOCRACY

1 What democracy is

Democracy means rule by the people. It is a form of decision making or government whose meaning can be made more precise by contrast with rival forms, such as dictatorship, oligarchy or monarchy. In these rival forms a single person or a select group rules. With democracy this is not so. The people themselves rule and they rule themselves. The same body is both ruler and ruled.

Philosophical accounts of democracy analyse its nature and discuss its value. The two cannot be completely separated. Any account which explains the value of democracy has to provide or presuppose an account of what it is holding to be of value. Conversely, supposedly neutral analyses of the nature of democracy are influenced by values. For example, someone who thinks that democracy is a good thing is liable to analyse it in terms of other features also thought to be good.

The concept of democracy therefore may naturally be thought of as what W.B. Gallie called an essentially contested concept. Such concepts are concepts whose analysis is unresolvable because different analysts read into it their favoured values. For example, before the reunification of Germany, both East and West Germany called themselves democracies. Yet each had very different political systems, one being a Marxist single-party state, the other having economic and political competition with several parties and contested elections. A dispute about which one was really a democracy would be irresolvable.

This account and this example presuppose that democracy is desirable, so there is a competition to lay claim to the honorific title. However, for most of the time since the invention of the concept of democracy it has not been taken to be a term of honour. A kind of democracy did exist in ancient Athens. But, this was a form of government criticized by the leading Greek thinkers of the time, Plato and Aristotle. For most of the time since this early democracy ended, democracy has neither existed nor been thought to be desirable.

Much later, with the creation of the USA, we reach a system which most people today would take to be a paradigmatic example of democracy. Unsurprisingly it was defended by its founding fathers. However, what might surprise us more today is that in one of the most famous of these defences, James Madison was careful not to use 'democracy' as the name for the system he supported. He identifies things called democracies and does not support them; the description he uses instead for the fledgling USA is 'republic'.

What Madison means by a republic is 'a government in which the scheme of representation takes place', and by a democracy 'a society consisting of a small number of citizens, who assemble and administer the government in person' *The Federalist Papers* (1787–8). It might be thought that the central question here is one of size. Commentators writing just before Madison, such as ROUSSEAU (§3) and MONTESQUIEU, held that democracy was only possible in small states; and Madison can be taken to be marking the transition to the modern world, with large states rather than small ones; and a corresponding move from direct democracy to representative government. What is today standardly called democracy is very different from what was standardly so called in the ancient world.

However, size is not the only important distinction here. Individuals in very large modern political units can now be so linked together by modern technology that they can relate to each other much as if they all met together. On the other hand, political decisions by and for small groups are still made in the modern world. It can still be asked of these whether they should be made democratically; and, if so, which sort of democracy is appropriate. So, whatever the size of political unit, questions can arise about the importance of participation or discussion before decisions are made. It can be asked whether democracy should be seen primarily as a mechanism in which people vote for policies or representatives without assembly, participation or discussion. At one extreme (as with Joseph Schumpeter), we could analyse democracy as a competition for votes between professional politicians. At the other extreme, we could analyse democracy as a system in which unanimous decisions are reached after a prolonged discussion which respects the equal autonomy and participation of everyone involved. The former seems more practical, but may not uphold any (other) ideals; the latter seems impressively ideal, but may be ineffective in practice.

It has just been said that voting and representation is at least practical. However, this ignores one prominent problem. This is that the collective view which results from voting may not be related in the way we would wish to the individual views expressed in the votes. In particular this applies if there are three or more options to be arranged in order of preference and there are three or more such individual orderings (see SOCIAL CHOICE). These problems will not be discussed further here; although it should be recognized that many people think that they are an insuperable objection to democratic decision making.

2   The value of democracy

Once we have an idea of democracy, the next question is why, or whether, it is of value. The Greek historians identified the original introduction of democracy with the advance of liberty and equality. Since both liberty and equality are usually thought to be of value, this would seem to be a natural answer to the question. Democracy is of value because it produces liberty and equality. With dictatorship or other forms of special leadership, a particular person or group has more power than others. By contrast, in democracy everyone is equal. Everyone has the same (political) power. So democracy is egalitarian as compared with other forms of government or decision making.

Similarly for liberty. A democracy introduced by the overthrow of a dictator increases political liberty. People have been freed from the control of the dictator. Hence democracy promotes liberty. There are several connected terms here: liberty, freedom, autonomy. However, whichever term is used, this argument seems to work. Consider autonomy. It means, literally, self-rule. Yet this is exactly what happens in democracy, as opposed to other forms of government. The people rule themselves.

However, as always, further inspection makes matters less obvious. Suppose decisions are made by majority vote and someone is in the minority. This person is outvoted and so their wants will not be put into effect. Therefore we can question whether in this (democratic) situation, this person is really autonomous. They are being made to do something which they do not want to do. Hence they are not really autonomous. Similarly for equality. Not everyone is treated equally when majority decisions are adopted, because only the views of some people (the majority) are put into effect. The minority's views are disregarded. Hence they are not treated equally. The winner takes all, and hence winners and losers are not equally treated.

If a community is divided into two parts living in mutual antipathy, this becomes even more obvious. The majority community could, by democratic vote, bear heavily down on the minority community, restricting or removing things it holds to be of fundamental value. In such circumstances the members of the minority community could hardly be said to be at liberty; nor could it be said that they were being equally treated. Hence the phrase, used by Tocqueville in *Democracy in America* (1835) and taken over by J.S. Mill in *On Liberty* (1859), 'the tyranny of the majority'. The initial contrast between democracy and dictatorship has now been left behind. If democracy is really the dictatorship of the majority, then it is not so obvious that democracy promotes freedom and equality.

3   The paradox of democracy

If we examine democracy from the standpoint of the minority, as in the last section, this helps to focus the problem of its value. A democrat thinks that the majority view ought to be enacted. But in voting they also declare their own view about what ought to be enacted. When they are in a minority these diverge and they seem to be caught in a contradiction. There are two incompatible policies, A and not-A. Yet the minority democrat seems to think both that A ought to be enacted (because that is what the majority want) and also that not-A ought to be enacted (because that is their own view). Richard Wollheim (1962) called this the 'paradox of democracy'.

However, if democracy can be given a value, the paradox is resolvable. For what we then have is a simple (and familiar) conflict of values. The democrat's direct view of the matter indicates the value of the course of action for which they voted. But once it is defeated by the majority this rival course of action also possesses value. For it inherits the value of democracy. If, for example, democracy is taken to be an egalitarian procedure, then adopting this rival course of action has egalitarian value.

An example: four of us in a car have to decide to go either to the beach or to the town. There is only one car and we can go to only one place. We agree to decide democratically, by vote. The vote is taken. I vote for the beach, and am outvoted by three to one. The beach is of value to me. This is shown by my vote. However, I am also a democrat. After the vote, the town also has value to me. With the town three people's views are respected; with the beach only one. If I hold that people are of equal value, then I have a reason for the car to go to the town.

4   Democracy and knowledge

In his *Republic* Plato says that 'it is not in the natural course of things for the pilot to beg the crew to take his orders' (*c*.380–367 BC: 489b). The implication is that if we want as a group to go to the right place, it is not sensible to assume that everyone has an equally valid opinion. Instead we should follow the lead of those who know. Hence democracy, which treats everybody's opinions equally, is inefficient as a means of determining the right thing to do (see PLATO §14).

This argument makes several presuppositions and can be resisted by contesting them. Some people can only know more than others about something if there is indeed something to be known. That is, if there is a truth about the matter independent of people's opinions. But this is precisely what might be contested when the question is what the state should do. This being a matter of value, it might be held that no independent truth, and hence no knowledge, is available. More precisely, it might be thought that a line can be drawn between areas in which knowledge is available, and which, for example, might be handled by a professional, trained civil service; and areas for which no knowledge is obtainable, and which should be left to democratic, untrained, amateur decision. Benjamin Barber, for example, takes the area of politics to be one of action, not truth; and for him democracy takes over in the areas where metaphysics fails, creating its own epistemology.

It should be noticed, however, that an argument for the goodness of democratic decision making cannot simply be made on the basis of a complete scepticism about values. For if no truths about values are available, then no truths about the value of democracy are available either. Hence a valid argument cannot be made from this premise to a conclusion that it is true that democracy is of value.

Conversely, even if it is allowed that there are independent truths about value, it does not directly follow that democracy is an inappropriate way of discovering these truths. For it is quite possible that the truth about what in general the state should do is the kind of truth about which people have a roughly equal capacity. Furthermore, even if people do not have equal capacity, as long as it cannot be told which ones are superior, democracy may still be the appropriate method to use. The Platonic argument assumes that there is a truth about what should happen; that this truth is better known to some people than others; and that it is possible to tell independently of their views which these people are. All these assumptions could be resisted.

If people are of roughly equal capacity (or it cannot be told who is superior) then, as long as everyone is more likely than not to be right, voting and adopting the majority view is an efficient method to use. For the majority decision has a higher probability of being right than any individual decision, as CONDORCET was the first to show. In other words, if I have to make a sequence of decisions about the truth of something and I am in a group each of whose members gets the answer right more often than not, then I do much better systematically following the majority view of the group than my own initial views.

Even if some people clearly have better informed views than others, it still does not follow that democratic decision making is inefficient. For if it is obvious who the experts are, then people with an interest in discovering what is right will generally follow their views. In other words, the same answers will be arrived at as would happen if, as in Plato, the better informed were made dictators. Democracy will not be inferior in discovering of the truth, and will have other advantages.

On the other hand, if it is not obvious who the experts are, then it is indeed the case that the majority view may not follow expert opinion. But, if some people are dictators, it may also be the case that the people who are made dictators are not the ones who are better informed. The dangers of mistake in following majority opinion are matched by the dangers of mistake in making the wrong people the dictators. The Platonic argument only works if the experts can be recognized in advance, for example (as in Plato's *Republic*), because they are educated in a way which ensures that they will have expertise.

5 The use of democracy

Other justifications for democracy are possible. One standard device for justification, for many areas, is utilitarianism (see UTILITARIANISM). Something is justified if it promotes general happiness or utility. It can be asked of a form of government, just like anything else, whether it does tend to promote this. The answer, at least of the classical utilitarians such as BENTHAM and James Mill, is that democracy does.

This argument is expressed most simply in James Mill's *Essay on Government* (1820). He starts with an evaluative and a factual premise. The evaluative premise is utilitarianism. Actions are right in so far as they promote the general happiness. The factual premise is universal self-interest. People seek those things which promote their own interests. The problem is to find the form of government in which both of these premises can be true together, to find the form in which people seeking their own interest will nevertheless do those things which promote the general happiness. It is not difficult to show that representative democracy is the answer. Kings will promote the interest of kings, dictators of dictators, oligarchies of oligarchies. In all cases the interest promoted is that of the ruling group, not that of the people as a whole. However, if the people as a whole are put in charge, they will promote the interests of the people as a whole. Seeking their own interests, they will produce general happiness. Hence both premises are satisfied simultaneously.

It is perhaps unsurprising that the greatest happiness of the greatest number results if the majority (the greatest number) are put in charge. However the answer does depend upon certain presuppositions. It assumes that people act in their own interests. Even if this is what they generally intend to do (which might be disputed), it does not follow from this that they are successful. For they may not know their interests. For example, it is often held that people discount the future too severely, so they prefer less important immediate interests to more important long-term interests. If this is so, then democratic decisions will lead to too short-term results, which are not even in the interests of those voting.

A related point is that this model takes preferences as they are, without allowing them to be changed by the democratic process. Yet if people are ill informed about what is good for them, it would be better to operate on the preferences before permitting these preferences to be expressed in votes. Democracy treats all votes equally. But people may not be equally informed about their interests. So the result may be that some interests are catered for better than others. Analogously, treating votes equally means that strongly held and weakly held views are considered of equal importance. Yet if the goal is to maximize utility, it may be wrong to follow the weakly held view of a majority rather than the strongly held view of a significant minority. If the utility of getting something is supposed to be roughly proportional to the strength of the desire for it, then it could be that the total of less people multiplied by a greater utility per person is higher than the total of more people multiplied by less utility per person.

6 Other consequences

The idea of utilitarianism as a mere preference-satisfying machine, in which antecedently given preferences are satisfied, has often been criticized. One alternative is to treat the values more objectively. Democracy can then be shown to be good in terms of these independently specified consequences. Such was the approach of J.S. Mill and more recent defenders such as William Nelson. Democracy is justified as a form of education or development; it is taken to be a political system in which individuals are made to think for themselves and are therefore improved. Even if the decisions they make are not the best decisions, it is better for individuals if they try and take part in such decisions.

Another consequence which might justify democracy is the supposed promotion of dynamic economic activity; as opposed to the sluggish effects supposedly emanating from more centralized planning and control. Yet even if democracy does correlate with such beneficial economic circumstances, it is not clear that this by itself can be used as an argument for promoting democracy. Jon Elster identifies the questionable role of such arguments based on indirect effects. For it may be that these other effects only happen if people are attached to democracy for more direct reasons (such as thinking that it is a just form of government). If people were only to support democracy because they thought that it encouraged economic dynamism, then the democracy would not work, and so the economic dynamism would not follow either.

This relates to another familiar problem with starting from antecedent preferences and then taking democracy to be a sort of market mechanism in which these preferences are traded. If people only act through self-interest, trying to get their antecedently given preferences fulfilled, then it is not obvious why they should vote at all. For the advantages of voting will come to them if the others vote and their own vote seems to be merely a cost. At the national government level, it is exceedingly unlikely that any one vote will be decisive. So they would be better off not voting at all.

7 Deliberative democracy

One answer to these problems is to dispense with the idea of democracy being a mechanism for satisfying antecedently given preferences. Instead of taking these as given, democracy should instead be considered a device in which people develop and discover their proper preferences through a process of mutual deliberation. In this account of what has been called 'deliberative democracy' (also sometimes 'discursive democracy'), democracy is centrally a matter of discussion rather than of voting. Recently promoted by such thinkers as J. Cohen, A. Gutmann, or J. Dryzek, it builds on an older idea about public rationality. This is that if people have to develop their view about what is right in public discussion, they are pressed to think about what is right for the group as a whole rather than just themselves So people should participate in a form of decision making in which they share their ideas, discuss together, and, with luck, eventually reach general agreement.

The assumption here is that the arguments naturally used in public discussion are constrained by the desire to reach agreement; and that this in turn requires that people should look as if they are appealing to general principles rather than merely appealing to self-interest. The condition of publicity (that is, of what can be said publicly) imposes constraints. If people think from the general point of view rather than in terms of their own individual interest, the forms of reasoning and the antecedent judgements will be different. Discussion rather than voting therefore becomes the central feature of democracy, and it becomes important that people can meet and talk together before decisions are made.

These ideas promoting discussion and participation have several presuppositions. They presuppose that people will be better able to work out the truth (about what is good for the group) by working in groups rather than individually. This may be the case if they are all independently motivated by the same desire to discover the truth. It is less obviously the case if there are deep conflicts of interest (such as capital against labour; or country against town; or this world against the next). The supposition is that group discussion leads to more rationality; but in some circumstances group dynamics merely increase and inflame passion, so that people behave badly together in a way that they never would separately.

There are disputes about whether public deliberation is meant to replace voting completely or only to supplement it. A complete replacement is in effect a recommendation of unanimity in decision making. Although this shows full respect for every party involved, it also gives every party a veto and so can block all decision making. A more practical view is to supplement discussion with voting, enabling decisions to be made even when complete agreement cannot be reached. Votes must only be held after discussion, enabling preferences to be modified before they are expressed. There is also the question of whether all decisions should be made by this method or only some fundamental (for example, constitutional) ones. Again work might be given to both deliberation and voting, the public deliberation setting a framework inside which more particular matters might be settled by voting.

There are also problems with respect to the standing of the parties engaged in discussion and, connectedly, the formality of the operation. At the one end is a formal procedure of deliberation, operating according to antecedently adopted rules, and restricted in its membership (so that, for example, only members of a club or country may engage in decision-making discussion of what that club or country should do). At the other end, discussion may happen anywhere, at any time, with anyone who happens to be interested. Informality of operation goes with informality of result, so something nearer the formal end is required for executive decisions of legal entities such as clubs or countries. This illustrates that before discussion may take place as a means of reaching collective decisions, antecedent rules have to be established.

With this the values considered at the start of this discussion – namely, liberty and equality – reappear; only now not as the consequence of democratic activity but as its prerequisites. For if discussion is to reach the right answer, it needs to start with roughly equal power between the discussants. Otherwise discussion will be forced in the interests of the stronger. Hence the idea that democracy needs circumstances of roughly equal wealth (held by Montesquieu and Rousseau). Hence the Marxist criticism that Western liberal democracy works on the fiction of an idealized equality when the real situation is one of greatly unequal economic power. Hence John Rawls' argument that political parties should be paid for by the state to avoid the economically powerful buying votes (see RAWLS, J. §2). Hence also the objections of feminist theorists. If men and women are antecedently in a situation of different power, then the supposed equality of democracy will only result in most of the power remaining with the men.

In the more recent promoters of deliberative democracy the same considerations apply. People vary in their deliberative and rhetorical skills. Formal equal permission to speak does not entail equal ability when doing so. Thus, again, some attempt has to be made to set conditions ensuring that the discussion takes place between equal participants. Thus discussion becomes a good, but only if the forum in which the discussion takes place is subject to powerful antecedent control and regulation. Otherwise we return to the bad old world of bargaining between antecedently given preferences from which this optimistic espousal of discussion was meant to save us.

See also: CONSTITUTIONALISM; GENERAL WILL; REPRESENTATION, POLITICAL; SOCIAL DEMOCRACY

References and further reading

Cohen, J. (1989) 'Deliberation and democratic legitimacy', in A. Hamlin and P. Pettit (eds) *The Good Polity* Oxford: Blackwell, repr. J. Bohman and W. Rehg (eds) *Deliberative Democracy*, Cambridge, MA: MIT Press (1999). (Useful, clear, statement by one of the original promoters of the recent consideration of deliberative democracy; referred to in §7.)

Harrison, R. (1993) *Democracy*, London: Routledge. (Historical account and analysis of value in terms of such values as equality, knowledge and autonomy.)

Wollheim, R. (1962) 'A Paradox in the Theory of Democracy', in P. Laslett and W.G. Runciman (eds) *Philosophy, Politics and Society*, 2nd series, Oxford: Blackwell. (The article referred to in §3.)

ROSS HARRISON

DEMOCRITUS (mid 5th–4th century BC)

A co-founder with Leucippus of the theory of atomism, The Greek Philosopher Democritus developed it into a universal system, embracing physics, cosmology, epistemology, psychology and theology. He is also reported to have written on a wide range of topics, including mathematics, ethics, literary criticism and theory of language. His works are lost, except for a substantial number of quotations, mostly on ethics, whose authenticity is disputed. Our knowledge of his principal doctrines depends primarily on Aristotle's critical discussions, and secondarily on reports by historians of philosophy whose work derives from that of Aristotle and his school.

The atomists attempted to reconcile the observable data of plurality, motion and change with Parmenides' denial of the possibility of coming to be or ceasing to be. They postulated an infinite number of unchangeable primary substances, characterized by a minimum range of explanatory properties (shape, size, spatial ordering and orientation within a given arrangement). All observable bodies are aggregates of these basic substances, and what appears as generation and corruption is in fact the formation and dissolution of these aggregates. The basic substances are physically indivisible (whence the term *atomon*, literally 'uncuttable') not merely in fact but in principle: (1) because (as Democritus argued) if it were theoretically possible to divide a material thing *ad infinitum*, the division would reduce the thing to nothing; and (2) because physical division presupposes that the thing divided contains gaps. Atoms are in eternal motion in empty space, the motion caused by an infinite series of prior atomic 'collisions'. (There is reason to believe, however, although the point is disputed, that atoms cannot collide, since they must always be separated by void, however small; hence impact is only apparent, and all action is at a distance.) The void is necessary for motion, but is characterized as 'what-is-not', thus violating the Eleatic principle that what-is-not cannot be.

Democritus seems to have been the first thinker to recognize the observer-dependence of the secondary qualities. He argued from the distinction between appearance and reality to the unreliability of the senses, but it is disputed whether he embraced scepticism, or maintained that theory could make good the deficiency of the senses. He maintained a materialistic account of the mind, explaining thought and perception by the physical impact of images emitted by external objects. This theory gave rise to a naturalistic theology; he held that the gods are a special kind of images, endowed with life and intelligence, intervening in human affairs. The ethical fragments (if genuine) show that he maintained a conservative social

philosophy on the basis of a form of enlightened hedonism.

See also: ATOMISM, ANCIENT; EPICUREANISM; LEUCIPPUS; ZENO OF ELEA

C.C.W. TAYLOR

DEMONSTRATIVES AND INDEXICALS

Demonstratives and indexicals are words and phrases whose interpretations are dependent on features of the context in which they are used. For example, the reference of 'I' depends on conditions associated with its use: as you use it, it refers to you; as I use it, it refers to me. In contrast, what 'the inventor of bifocals' refers to does not depend on when or where or by whom it is used. Among indexicals are the words 'here', 'now', 'today', demonstrative pronouns such as 'this', reflexive, possessive and personal pronouns, and compound phrases employing indexicals, such as 'my mother'. C.S. Peirce introduced the term 'indexical' to suggest the idea of pointing (as in 'index finger').

The phenomenon of indexicality figures prominently in recent debates in philosophy. This is because indexicals allow us to express beliefs about our subjective 'place' in the world, beliefs which are the immediate antecedents of action; and some argue that such beliefs are irreducibly indexical. For example, my belief that I am about to be attacked by a bear is distinct from my belief that HD is about to be attacked by a bear, since my having the former belief explains why I act as I do (I flee), whereas my having the latter belief explains nothing unless the explanation continues 'and I believe that I am HD'. It seems impossible to describe the beliefs that prompt my action without the help of 'I'. Similarly, some have argued that indexical-free accounts of the self or of consciousness are necessarily incomplete, so that a purely objective physicalism is impossible. In a different vein, some have argued that our terms for natural substances, kinds and phenomena ('gold', 'water', 'light') are indexical in a way that entails that certain substantive scientific claims – for example, that water is H_2O – are, if true, necessarily true. Thus, reflection on indexicality has yielded some surprising (and controversial) philosophical conclusions.

See also: REFERENCE

HARRY DEUTSCH

DENNETT, DANIEL CLEMENT (1942–)

A student of Gilbert Ryle and a connoisseur of cognitive psychology, neuroscience and evolutionary biology, American philosopher Daniel Dennett has urged Rylean views in the philosophy of mind, especially on each title topic of his first book,

Content and Consciousness (1969). He defends a broadly instrumentalist view of propositional attitudes (such as belief and desire) and their intentional contents; like Ryle and the behaviourists, Dennett rejects the idea of beliefs and desires as causally active inner states of people. Construing them in a more purely operational or instrumental fashion, he maintains instead that belief- and desire-ascriptions are merely calculational devices.

Dennett offers a severely deflationary account of consciousness, subjectivity and the phenomenal or qualitative character of sensory states. He maintains that those topics are conceptually posterior to that of propositional-attitude content: the qualitative features of which we are directly conscious in experience are merely the intentional contents of judgments.

WILLIAM G. LYCAN

DENOTATION

See DESCRIPTIONS; PROPER NAMES; REFERENCE

DEONTIC LOGIC

Deontic logic is the investigation of the logic of normative concepts, especially obligation ('ought', 'should', 'must'), permission ('may') and prohibition ('ought not', 'forbidden'). Deontic logic differs from normative legal theory and ethics in that it does not attempt to determine which principles hold, nor what obligations exist, for any given system. Rather it seeks to develop a formal language that can adequately represent the normative expressions of natural languages, and to regiment such expressions in a logical system.

The theorems of deontic logic specify relationships both among normative concepts (for example, whatever is obligatory is permissible) and between normative and non-normative concepts (for example, whatever is obligatory is possible). Contemporary research beginning with von Wright treats deontic logic as a branch of modal logic, in so far as (as was noted already by medieval logicians) the logical relations between the obligatory, permissible and forbidden to some extent parallel those between the necessary, possible and impossible (concepts treated in 'alethic' modal logic).

MARVIN BELZER

DEONTOLOGICAL ETHICS

Deontology asserts that there are several distinct duties. Certain kinds of act are intrinsically right and other kinds intrinsically wrong. The rightness or wrongness of any particular act is thus not (or not wholly) determined by the goodness or badness of its consequences. Some ways of treating people,

such as killing the innocent, are ruled out, even if the aim is to prevent others doing worse deeds. Many deontologies leave agents considerable scope for developing their own lives in their own way; provided they breach no duty they are free to live as they see fit.

Deontology may not have the theoretical tidiness which many philosophers crave, but has some claim to represent everyday moral thought.

Deontology (the word comes from the Greek *deon* meaning 'one must') typically holds that there are several irreducibly distinct duties, such as promise-keeping and refraining from lying. Some deontologists, such as W.D. Ross (1930), maintain that one of these duties is a duty to do as much good as possible. Most deny that there is such a duty, while conceding that there is a limited duty of benevolence, a duty to do *something* for the less fortunate (see HELP AND BENEFICENCE). All agree, however, that there are occasions when it would be wrong for us to act in a way that would maximize the good, because we would be in breach of some (other) duty. In this respect they are opposed to act-consequentialism (see CONSEQUENTIALISM §§1, 2).

Most deontologies include two important classes of duties. First, there are duties which stem from the social and personal relationships in which we stand to particular people. Parents have duties to children, and children to parents; people have duties in virtue of their jobs and the associations to which they belong; debtors have a duty to repay their creditors, promisors to keep their promises and borrowers to return what has been lent to them (see FAMILY, ETHICS AND THE; FRIENDSHIP; PROFESSIONAL ETHICS; PROMISING; SOLIDARITY). Some of these social relationships are ones we enter voluntarily, but many are not. The second kind take the form of general prohibitions or constraints. We should not lie to, cheat, torture or murder *anyone*, even in the pursuit of good aims (see TRUTHFULNESS).

Deontology is often described as an agent-relative moral theory, in contrast to act-consequentialism, which is an agent-neutral theory. According to act-consequentialism the identity of the agent makes no difference to what their duty is on any particular occasion; that is determined solely by which of the courses of action open to them will produce the best consequences. In deontology, by contrast, a reference to the agent often plays an ineliminable role in the specification of the duty. This is especially clear in the case of duties which stem from social relationships. I have a duty to help *this* person. Why? Because he or she is *my* friend, or *my* child. I have a duty to pay *my* debts and to keep *my* promises.

Constraints also involve agent-relativity, though in a slightly different way. The duty not to murder does not take the form of enjoining us to minimize the number of murders. The rule tells me not to commit murder myself even if I could thereby prevent something worse being done, such as two murders being committed. Proponents of deontology think of this as moral integrity; their opponents refer to it disparagingly as 'keeping one's hands clean' (see UTILITARIANISM §5).

Many deontologists hold that our duties, though sometimes very onerous, are quite limited in scope. Provided I am in breach of no duty, I am morally at liberty to devote quite a large part of my time and effort to pursuing my own projects in whatever way I please. This latitude leaves room for acts of supererogation: heroic or saintly acts that clearly go beyond the call of duty, and deserve high praise (see SUPEREROGATION).

There is a sharp division in the deontologist camp over the status of constraints. Some, such as Fried (1978), think of them as absolute: they have no exceptions and may not be breached in any circumstances which we are likely to encounter. Others regard the fact that an act would breach a constraint as providing a weighty objection to it, but one which could be overcome if there were a sufficiently pressing duty on the other side. Conflicts between two duties which are not absolute must be settled by determining which duty is the more pressing in the circumstances.

Deontology gains much of its appeal from the fact that it seems to capture the essential outlines of our everyday moral thinking, but it is open to several objections. First, its claim that there is a plurality of distinct duties runs counter to the theoretician's search for simplicity. The deontologist will reply, of course, that a theory must do justice to the complexity of the phenomena. Second, many deontologists further defy the supposed canons of good theorizing by denying that there is any overarching explanation of why there are the duties there are; they record our conviction that there are such duties without seeking to justify them. Others, usually inspired by Kant, do attempt such an explanation based on some broader precept, such as respect for persons (see KANT, I. §§9–11; KANTIAN ETHICS). Third, those who hold that some kinds of action, such as lying, are absolutely prohibited have to provide clear and detailed criteria for determining the boundary between lying and some supposedly less nefarious activity, such as 'being economical with the truth'. Such casuistry can appear both excessively legalistic and incompatible with the spirit of morality. Fourth, deontology provides no procedure to settle conflicts of duty (though some might think that an advantage). Finally, from a consequentialist perspective, the notion of a constraint seems perverse. If what is

wrong with murder is that it is a bad thing, how can it be rational to forbid an agent to commit one murder in order to prevent two? If deontology is to answer this challenge, it must show how it can be that one's duty does not rest (wholly) on the goodness or badness of the results of acting in that way.

See also: DOUBLE EFFECT, PRINCIPLE OF

References and further reading

Fried, C. (1978) *Right and Wrong*, Cambridge, MA: Harvard University Press. (A readable and vigorous defence of an absolutist deontology.)

Nagel, T. (1986) *The View from Nowhere*. Oxford: Oxford University Press, ch. 9. (An ingenious attempt to provide a grounding for deontological intuitions.)

Ross, W.D. (1930) *The Right and the Good*. Oxford: Clarendon Press, ch 2. (The classic statement of a moderate deontology.)

DAVID MCNAUGHTON

DEPICTION

How do pictures work? How are they able to represent what they do? A picture of a goat, for example, is a flat surface covered with marks, yet it depicts a goat, chewing straw, while standing on a hillock. The puzzle of depiction is to understand how the flat marks can do this.

Language poses a similar problem. A written description of a goat will also be a collection of marks on a flat surface, which none the less represent that animal. In the case of language the solution clearly has something to do with the arbitrary way we use those marks. The word 'leg', for example, is applied to legs, but any other mark would do as well, providing we all use it in the same way. In the case of pictures, however, something different seems to be going on. There is not the same freedom in producing a picture of a goat on a hillock chewing straw – the surface must be marked in the *right* way, a way we are not free to choose. So what is the right way?

A helpful thought is that the surface must be marked so as to let us experience it in a special way. With the description, we merely need to know what the words it contains are used to stand for. With the picture, we must instead be able to *see* a goat in it. However, although this does seem right, it is difficult to make clear. After all, we do not see a goat in the same way that we see a horse in a view from a window. For one thing, there is no goat there to be seen. For another, it is not even true that looking at the picture is like looking at a goat. It is partly because of the differences that, as we look at the picture, we are always aware that it is merely a collection of marks on a flat surface. So what is this special experience, seeing a goat in the picture? This is the question that a philosophical account of depiction must try to answer.

See also: FICTIONAL ENTITIES; IMAGINATION; PAINTING, AESTHETICS OF; PERCEPTION; PHOTOGRAPHY, AESTHETICS OF

R.D. HOPKINS

DERRIDA, JACQUES (1930–2004)

Jacques Derrida was a prolific French philosopher born in Algeria. His work can be understood in terms of his argument that it is necessary to interrogate the Western philosophical tradition from the standpoint of 'deconstruction'. As an attempt to approach that which remains unthought in this tradition, deconstruction is concerned with the category of the 'wholly other'.

Derrida called into question the 'metaphysics of presence', a valuing of truth as self-identical immediacy which has been sustained by traditional attempts to demonstrate the ontological priority and superiority of speech over writing. Arguing that the distinction between speech and writing can be sustained only by way of a violent exclusion of otherness, Derrida attempted to develop a radically different conception of language, one that would begin from the irreducibility of difference to identity and that would issue in a correspondingly different conception of ethical and political responsibility.

See also: DECONSTRUCTION; POSTMODERNISM; POST-STRUCTURALISM

ANDREW CUTROFELLO

DESCARTES, RENÉ (1596–1650)

Introduction

René Descartes, often called the father of modern philosophy, attempted to break with the philosophical traditions of his day and start philosophy anew. Rejecting the Aristotelian philosophy of the schools, the authority of tradition and the authority of the senses, he built a philosophical system that included a method of inquiry, a metaphysics, a mechanistic physics and biology, and an account of human psychology intended to ground an ethics. Descartes was also important as one of the founders of the new analytic geometry, which combines geometry and algebra, and whose certainty provided a kind of model for the rest of his philosophy.

After an education in the scholastic and humanistic traditions, Descartes' earliest work was mostly in mathematics and mathematical physics, in which his most important achievements were his analytical geometry and his discovery of the law of refraction in optics. In this early period he also wrote his unfinished treatise on method, the *Rules for the Direction of the Mind*, which set out a procedure for investigating nature, based on the reduction of complex problems to simpler ones solvable by direct intuition. From these intuitively established foundations, Descartes tried to show how one could then attain the solution of the problems originally posed.

Descartes abandoned these methodological studies by 1628 or 1629, turning first to metaphysics, and soon afterwards to an orderly exposition of his physics and biology in *The World*. But this work was overtly Copernican in its cosmology, and when Galileo was condemned in 1633, Descartes withdrew *The World* from publication; it appeared only after his death.

Descartes' mature philosophy began to appear in 1637 with the publication of a single volume containing the *Geometry, Dioptrics* and *Meteors*, three essays in which he presented some of his most notable scientific results, preceded by the *Discourse on the Method*, a semi-autobiographical introduction that outlined his approach to philosophy and the full system into which the specific results fit. In the years following, he published a series of writings in which he set out his system in a more orderly way, beginning with its metaphysical foundations in the *Meditations* (1641), adding his physics in the *Principles of Philosophy* (1644), and offering a sketch of the psychology and moral philosophy in the *Passions of the Soul* (1649).

In our youth, Descartes held, we acquire many prejudices which interfere with the proper use of our reason. Consequently, later we must reject everything we believe and start anew. Hence the *Meditations* begins with a series of arguments intended to cast doubt upon everything formerly believed, and culminating in the hypothesis of an all-deceiving evil genius, a device to keep former beliefs from returning. The rebuilding of the world begins with the discovery of the self through the 'Cogito Argument' ('I am thinking, therefore I exist') – a self known only as a thinking thing, and known independently of the senses. Within this thinking self, Descartes discovers an idea of God, an idea of something so perfect that it could not have been caused in us by anything with less perfection than God Himself. From this he concluded that God must exist which, in turn, guarantees that reason can be trusted. Since we are made in such a way that we cannot help holding certain beliefs (the so-called 'clear and distinct' perceptions), God would be a deceiver, and thus imperfect, if such beliefs were wrong; any mistakes must be due to our own misuse of reason. This is Descartes' famous epistemological principle of clear and distinct perception. This central argument in Descartes' philosophy, however, is threatened with circularity – the Cartesian Circle – since the arguments that establish the trustworthiness of reason (the Cogito Argument and the argument for the existence of God) themselves seem to depend on the trustworthiness of reason.

Also central to Descartes' metaphysics was the distinction between mind and body. Since the clear and distinct ideas of mind and body are entirely separate, God can create them apart from one another. Therefore, they are distinct substances. The mind is a substance whose essence is thought alone, and hence exists entirely outside geometric categories, including place. Body is a substance whose essence is extension alone, a geometric object without even sensory qualities like colour or taste, which exist only in the perceiving mind. We know that such bodies exist as the causes of sensation: God has given us a great propensity to believe that our sensations come to us from external bodies, and no means to correct that propensity; hence, he would be a deceiver if we were mistaken. But Descartes also held that the mind and body are closely united with one another; sensation and other feelings, such as hunger and pain, arise from this union. Sensations cannot inform us about the real nature of things, but they can be reliable as sources of knowledge useful to maintaining the mind and body unity. While many of Descartes' contemporaries found it difficult to understand how mind and body can relate to one another, Descartes took it as a simple fact of experience that they do. His account of the passions is an account of how this connection leads us to feelings like wonder, love, hatred, desire, joy and sadness, from which all other passions derive. Understanding these passions helps us to control them, which was a central aim of morality for Descartes.

Descartes' account of body as extended substance led to a physics as well. Because to be extended is to be a body, there can be no empty space. Furthermore, since all body is of the same nature, all differences between bodies are to be explained in terms of the size, shape and motion of their component parts, and in terms of the laws of motion that they obey. Descartes attempted to derive these laws from the way in which God, in his constancy, conserves the world at every moment. In these mechanical terms, Descartes attempted to explain a wide variety of features of the world, from the formation of planetary systems out of an initial chaos, to magnetism, to the vital functions of animals, which he considered to be mere machines.

Descartes never finished working out his ambitious programme in full detail. Though he published the metaphysics and the general portion of his physics, the physical explanation of specific phenomena, especially biological, remained unfinished, as did his moral theory. Despite this, however, Descartes' programme had an enormous influence on the philosophy that followed, both within the substantial group that identified themselves as his followers, and outside.

1 Life
2 The programme
3 Method
4 Doubt and the quest for certainty
5 The Cogito Argument
6 God
7 The validation of reason
8 Mind and body
9 The external world and sensation
10 Philosophical psychology and morals
11 Physics and mathematics
12 Life and the foundations of biology
13 The Cartesian heritage

1 Life

René Descartes was born on 31 March 1596 in the Touraine region of France, in the town of La Haye, later renamed Descartes in his honour. In 1606 or 1607 he was sent to the Collège Royal de La Flèche, run by the Jesuit order. Here he received an education that combined elements of earlier Aristotelian scholasticism with the new humanistic emphasis on the study of language and literature. But the core of the collegiate curriculum was the study of Aristotelian logic, metaphysics, physics and ethics. Descartes left La Flèche in 1614 or 1615, and went to the University of Poitiers, where he received his *baccalauréat* and his *licence en droit* in late 1616. In Part I of the *Discours de la méthode* (*Discourse on the Method*) (1637), he discusses his education in some detail, explaining why he found it increasingly unsatisfactory. In the end, he reports, he left school, rejecting much of what he had been taught there. He chose the life of the military engineer, and set out across Europe to learn his trade, following the armies and the wars. On 10 November 1618, in the course of his travels, he met Isaac Beeckman. An enthusiastic scientific amateur since his early twenties, Beeckman introduced Descartes to some of the new currents in science, the newly revived atomist ideas, and the attempt to combine mathematics and physics (see ATOMISM,

ANCIENT). Despite the fact that they only spent a few months together, Beeckman put Descartes on the path that led to his life's work. A number of discussions between them are preserved in Beeckman's extensive notebooks (1604–34), which still survive, and include problems Beeckman set for Descartes, as well as Descartes' solutions. It was for Beeckman that Descartes wrote his first surviving work, the *Compendium musicum*, a tract on music theory, then considered a branch of what was called mixed mathematics, along with other disciplines such as mathematical astronomy and geometric optics. Exactly a year after first meeting Beeckman, this new path was confirmed for Descartes in a series of three dreams that he interpreted as a call to settle down to his work as a mathematician and philosopher.

During the 1620s, Descartes worked on a number of projects including optics and the mathematics that was eventually to become his analytic geometry. In optics, he discovered the law of refraction – the mathematical law that relates the angle of incidence of a ray of light on a refractive medium, with the angle of refraction. Though some claim that Descartes learned this law from Willebrod Snel, after whom the law is now named, it is generally thought that Descartes discovered it independently. In his mathematical programme, he showed how algebra could be used to solve geometric problems, and how geometric constructions could be used to solve algebraic problems.

Descartes' most extensive writing from this period is the *Regulae ad directionem ingenii* (*Rules for the Direction of the Mind*), a treatise on method that he worked on between 1619 or 1620 and 1628, when he abandoned it incomplete. He continued to travel extensively throughout Europe, returning to Paris in 1625, where he was to stay until spring 1629. In Paris, Descartes became closely associated with Marin Mersenne who later became a central figure in the dissemination of the new philosophy and science in Europe, the organizer of a kind of scientific academy and the centre of a circle of correspondents, as well as Descartes' intellectual patron. Through his voluminous correspondence with Mersenne, Descartes remained connected to all the intellectual currents in Europe, wherever he was to live in later years. An important event in this period took place at a gathering at the home of the Papal Nuncio in Paris in 1627 or 1628, where Descartes, responding to an alchemical lecture by one M. Chandoux, took the occasion to present his own ideas, including his 'fine rule, or natural method' and the principles on which his own philosophy was based (letter to Villebressieu, summer 1631; Descartes 1984–91 vol. 3: 32). This attracted the attention of Cardinal Bérule who, in a private meeting, urged Descartes to develop his philosophy.

In spring 1629 Descartes left Paris and moved to the Low Countries, where he set his methodological writing aside and began his philosophy in earnest. The winter of 1629–30 was largely occupied with the composition of a metaphysical treatise, which, as we shall later see, represents the foundations of his philosophy. The treatise is now lost, but Descartes told Mersenne that it had tried to 'prove the existence of God and of our souls when they are separated from the body, from which follows their immortality' (letter to Mersenne, 25 November 1630; Descartes 1984–91 vol. 3: 29). This was followed by the drafting of *Le Monde* (*The World*), Descartes' mechanist physics and physiology, a book intended for publication. In the first part, also called the *Traité de la lumière* (*Treatise on Light*), Descartes begins with a general account of the distinction between a sensation and the motion of tiny particles of different sizes and shapes that is its cause, followed by an account of the foundations of the laws of nature. After then positing an initial chaos of particles in motion (not *our* cosmos, but one made by God in some unused corner of the world), Descartes argues that by means of the laws of nature alone, this cosmos will sort itself into planetary systems, central suns around which swirl vortices of subtle matter which carry planets with them. He concludes the *Traité de la lumière* with an account of important terrestrial phenomena, including gravity, the tides and light, showing how much like our cosmos this imaginary mechanist cosmos will appear. The second part, the *Traité de l'homme* (*Treatise on Man*), begins abruptly by positing that God made a body that looks exactly like ours, but which is merely a machine. Presumably missing – or never written – is a transition between the two treatises that shows how by the laws of nature alone this human body could arise in our world. (This part of the argument is noted in Part V of the later *Discourse on the Method*.) In the text that we now have, Descartes then went on to argue that all phenomena that pertain to life (thought aside) can arise in this body in a purely mechanical way, including nutrition and digestion, the circulation of blood, the movement of the muscles and the transmission of sensory information to the brain.

By 1633 Descartes had in hand a relatively complete version of his philosophy, from method, to metaphysics, to physics and biology. But in late 1633, he heard of the condemnation of Galileo's Copernicanism in Rome, and cautiously decided not to publish his *World*, which was evidently Copernican (see GALILEO, GALILEI). Indeed, he first decided never to publish anything at all. But the despair did not last. Between 1634 and 1636, Descartes collected some of the material he had been working on, and prepared three essays for publication, the *Géométrie*, the *Météors* and the *Dioptrique*. These scientific essays were preceded by a general introduction, the *Discours de la méthode pour bien conduir sa raison et chercher la vérité dans les sciences* (*Discourse on the Method for Properly Conducting Reason and Searching for Truth in the Sciences*). The *Discourse* presents itself as autobiography, an account of the path the young author (the book was published anonymously) followed in his discoveries, including a summary of his method (Part II), of his early metaphysical speculations (Part IV) and of the programme of *The World* (Part V). In the scientific essays, Descartes presented some of his most striking results, hiding the foundational elements (such as his apparent Copernicanism and his rejection of scholastic form and matter) that would be most controversial.

While not uncontroversial, the *Discourse* and *Essays* were very successful, and induced Descartes to continue his programme for publishing his philosophy. The next work to appear was the *Meditationes* (*Meditations*) of 1641, which included an extensive selection of objections to the *Meditations* from various scholars in learned Europe, including HOBBES, GASSENDI, ARNAULD, and Mersenne himself, along with Descartes' responses, a total of seven sets in all. This was followed in 1644 by the publication of the *Principia Philosophiae* (*Principles of Philosophy*) in which, after a review of his metaphysics, Descartes gives an exposition of his physics adapted and expanded from *The World*. French translations of the *Meditations* and the *Principles* done by others, but with important variants from the original Latin (presumably introduced by Descartes himself), appeared in 1647.

By the late 1630s, Descartes' work had entered the Dutch universities, and was taught at the University of Utrecht by Henricus Reneri and, following him, by Henricus Regius. Descartes' un-Aristotelian views called down the wrath of Gisbertus Voëtius, who started a pamphlet war against Descartes and Regius that raged for some time. Descartes supported Regius, and gave him advice as to how to respond and contain the affair. Eventually, however, Descartes broke with him when Regius wrote and in 1646 published his *Fundamenta physices*, about which Descartes had severe reservations. Regius responded with a broadsheet, a kind of summary of his main theses, emphasizing their differences. Descartes, in turn, responded in 1648 with the *Notae in programma quoddam* (*Comments on a Certain Broadsheet*). There was a similar incident in Leiden, where Descartes had disciples (François du Ban, Adriaan Heereboord) as well as an influential enemy (Revius).

In the late 1640s Descartes was working on drafting and publishing more of his philosophy. Two additional parts of the *Principles* were planned, extending the work to cover elements of human biology. While notes remain in the form of an incomplete treatise on the human body (*La description du corps humain* – *Description of the Human Body*) and on the foetus (*Prima cogitationes circa generationem animalium* – *First Thoughts on the Generation of Animals*), the larger work was never finished. There are also important works concerning morals and moral psychology dating from these years. Some of this material is found in the letters to the Princess Elisabeth of Bohemia, with whom he had a long and important correspondence, starting in 1643. Descartes' account of the passions is found in the last work he published in his lifetime, the short *Passions de l'âme* – (*Passions of the Soul*), which appeared in 1649.

With the exception of a few short trips to Paris in 1644, 1647 and 1648, Descartes remained in the Low Countries until October 1649, when he was lured to Stockholm to be a member of the court of Queen Christina. There he fell ill in early 1650, and died on 11 February of that year.

2   The programme

Descartes' thought developed and changed over the years. But even so, there are a number of threads that run through it. Like most of his lettered contemporaries, Descartes was educated in a scholastic tradition that attempted to combine Christian doctrine with the philosophy of Aristotle. Indeed, at La Flèche, where he first learned philosophy, Aristotle as interpreted by Aquinas was at the centre of the curriculum. What he learned was an interconnected system of philosophy, including logic, physics, cosmology, metaphysics, morals and theology.

On his own account, Descartes rejected the Aristotelian philosophy as soon as he left school. From the notes Beeckman took on their conversations, it is probable that what dissatisfied him most in what he had been taught was natural philosophy. For an Aristotelian, the understanding of the natural world was grounded in a conception of body as composed of matter and form. Matter was that which remained constant even during the generation and corruption of bodies of different kinds, and that which all bodies of all sorts have in common; form was that which was responsible for the characteristic properties of particular sorts of bodies. For example, form was to explain why earth falls and tends to be cold, and why fire rises and tends to be hot. In contrast, though he came to reject Beeckman's rather strict atomism, Descartes seems to have been attracted to the kind of mechanistic view of the world that his mentor espoused. Descartes held from then on that the manifest properties of bodies must be explained in terms of the size, shape and motion of the tiny parts that make them up, and rejected the appeal to innate tendencies to behaviour that lay at the foundation of the Aristotelian view (see ARISTOTLE §10).

But even though he rejected much of the philosophy of the schools, there was one element that remained with him: like his teachers at La Flèche, Descartes always held that knowledge has a kind of systematic coherence. In Rule 1 of the *Rules* Descartes wrote that 'everything is so interconnected that it is far easier to learn all things together than it is to separate one from the others ... All [sciences are] connected with one another and depend upon one another'. Later, when he read Galileo's *Two New Sciences* (1638), Descartes dismissed the Italian scientist because his work lacked that kind of coherence (letter to Mersenne, 11 October 1638; Descartes 1984–91 vol. 3: 124–8). His own project was to build his own interconnected system of knowledge, a system comprising an account of knowledge, a metaphysics, a physics and other sciences. This ambition is summarized in one of his last writings, the Preface to the French edition of the *Principles*, where he wrote that 'all philosophy is like a tree, whose roots are metaphysics, whose trunk is physics, and whose branches, which grow from this trunk, are all of the other sciences, which reduce to three principle sciences, namely medicine, mechanics, and morals'. In this way, Descartes saw himself as reconstituting the Aristotelian–Christian synthesis of the scholastics, grounded not in a natural philosophy of matter and form, but in a mechanist conception of body, where everything is to be explained in terms of size, shape and motion.

Certain important features of the Cartesian programme are worth special mention. The Aristotelian–Christian synthesis is founded in a variety of kinds of authority: the authority of the senses, the authority of ancient texts and the authority of his teachers. Descartes wanted to ground his thought in himself alone, and in the reason that God gave him. Since, Descartes claimed, reason gives us genuine certainty, this means that true knowledge is certain. In Rule 3 of the *Rules* he wrote that 'concerning things proposed, one ought to seek not what others have thought, nor what we conjecture, but what we can clearly and evidently intuit or deduce with certainty; for in no other way is knowledge acquired'. The rejection of the authority of the senses, texts and teachers shaped Descartes' thought in fundamental ways. Because of it, his philosophical system began with the Cogito Argument, which establishes the self as the starting-place of knowledge. Moreover, his two most influential works, the *Discourse* and the *Meditations*, were written in the first person so as to *show* the reader how Descartes did or might have come to his own state of knowledge and certainty, rather than *telling* readers what they are to believe, and thus setting himself up as an authority in his own right. Despite his rejection of authority, however, Descartes always claimed to submit himself to the authority of the Church on doctrinal matters, separating the domain of revealed theology from that of philosophy.

Another important feature of Descartes' tree of knowledge was its hierarchical organization. Throughout his career he held firmly to the notion that the interconnected body of knowledge that he sought to build has a particular order. Knowledge, for Descartes, begins in metaphysics, and metaphysics begins with the self. From the self we arrive at God, and from God we arrive at the full knowledge of mind and body. This, in turn, grounds the knowledge of physics, in which the general truths of physics (the nature of body as extension, the denial of the vacuum, the laws of nature) ground more particular truths about the physical world. Physics, in turn, grounds the applied sciences of medicine (the science of the human body), mechanics (the science of machines) and morals (the science of the embodied mind).

3 Method

Before beginning an account of the individual parts of Descartes' tree of knowledge, it is necessary to discuss his method. Method was the focus of his earliest philosophical writing, the *Rules*, and appeared prominently in his first published writing, the *Discourse on the Method*. But what exactly that method was is somewhat obscure.

In the second part of the *Discourse*, the method is presented as having four rules: (1) 'never to accept anything as true if I did not have evident knowledge of its truth: that is, carefully to avoid precipitate conclusions and preconceptions'; (2) 'to divide each of the difficulties I examined into as many parts as possible'; (3) 'to direct my thoughts in an orderly manner, by beginning with the simplest and most easily known objects in order to ascend little by little ... to knowledge of the most complex'; and (4) 'throughout to make enumerations so complete and reviews so comprehensive, that I could be sure of leaving nothing out'. Given the general nature and apparent obviousness of these rules, it is not surprising that many of Descartes' contemporaries suspected him of hiding his *real* method from the public.

But Descartes' account of the method in the *Rules* is somewhat fuller. In Rule 5 he says: 'We shall be following this method exactly if we first reduce complicated and obscure propositions step by step to simpler ones, and then, starting with the intuition of the simplest ones of all, try to ascend through the same steps to a knowledge of all the rest'. This method is illustrated with an example in Rule 8. There Descartes considers the problem of the anaclastic line, the shape of a lens which will focus parallel lines to a single point. The first step in the solution of the problem, Descartes claims, is to see that 'the determination of this line depends on the ratio of the angles of refraction to the angles of incidence'. This, in turn, depends on 'the changes in these angles brought about by differences in the media'. But 'these changes depend on the manner in which a ray passes through the entire transparent body, and knowledge of this process presupposes also a knowledge of the nature of the action of light'. Finally, Descartes claims that this last knowledge rests on our knowledge of 'what a natural power in general is'. This last question can, presumably, be answered by intuition alone, that is, a purely rational apprehension of the truth of a proposition that has absolute certainty. Once we know what the nature of a natural power is, we can, Descartes thought, answer one by one all the other questions raised, and eventually answer the question originally posed, and determine the shape of the lens with the required properties. These successive answers are to be connected deductively (in a way outlined in the *Rules*) with the first intuition, so that successive answers follow intuitively from the first intuition.

The example of the anaclastic line suggests that Descartes' method proceeds as follows. One starts with a particular question, q_1. The reductive moment in the method then proceeds by asking what we have to know in order to answer the question originally posed. This leads us from q_1 to another question, q_2, whose answer is presupposed in order for us to be able to answer q_1; it is in this sense that q_1 is said to be reduced to q_2. This reductive process continues until we reach a question whose answer we are capable of knowing through intuition, say q_n. At that point, we begin what might be called the constructive moment of the method, and successively answer the questions we have posed for ourselves, using the answer to q_n to answer q_{n-1}, the answer to q_{n-1} to answer q_{n-2}, and so on until we arrive at q_1, the question originally posed, and answer that.

Understood in this way, the method has some very interesting properties. First, it results in knowledge that is completely certain. When we follow this method, the answer to the question originally posed is grounded in an intuition; the answers to the successive questions in the series are

to be answered by deducing propositions from propositions that have been intuitively grasped as well. Second, the method imposes a certain structure on knowledge. As we follow the series of questions that constitute the reductive step of the method, we proceed from more specific questions to more general, from the shape of a particular lens to the law of refraction, and ultimately to the nature of a natural power. The answers that are provided in the constructive stage follow the opposite path, from the metaphysically more general and more basic to the more specific.

The *Rules* was written over a long period of time, and there are numerous strata of composition evident in the work as it survives. In a passage from Rule 8 that is probably in one of the last strata of composition, Descartes raises a problem for the method itself to confront, indeed the *first* problem that it should confront: 'The most useful inquiry we can make at this stage is to ask: What is human knowledge and what is its scope? ... This is a task which everyone with the slightest love of truth ought to undertake at least once in life, since the true instruments of knowledge and the entire method are involved in the investigation of the problem'. While it is not entirely clear what Descartes had in mind here, it is not implausible to interpret him as raising the problem of the justification of intuition itself, the epistemological foundation of the method. In framing the method in the *Rules*, Descartes takes for granted that he has a faculty, intuition, by which he is capable of grasping truth in some immediate way, and what he knows by intuition is worthy of trust. But why *should* we trust intuition? This, in essence, is one of the central questions in the *Meditations*, where Descartes argues that whatever we perceive clearly and distinctly is true.

Method was a central concern of Descartes' earlier writings, in both the *Rules* and the *Discourse*. In later writings it seemed to play little explicit role in his thought, but the hierarchical structure of knowledge with which the method is closely connected – the idea that knowledge is grounded in a structure of successively more metaphysically basic truths, ultimately terminating in an intuition – remained basic to his thought. In his later work, that ultimate intuition is not the nature of a natural power, as it was in the anaclastic line example, but the intuition that establishes the existence of the knowing subject, the Cogito Argument.

4 Doubt and the quest for certainty

In the *Rules for the Direction of the Mind*, Rule 2 reads: 'We should attend only to those objects of which our minds seem capable of having certain and indubitable cognition'. While, as we shall later see, Descartes seemed to relax this demand somewhat in his later writings, the demand for certainty was prominent throughout many of his writings. Historically, this can be seen as a reaction against important sceptical currents in Renaissance thought, the so-called 'Pyrrhonist Crisis'. In the face of the rapidly expanding boundaries of the European world in the sixteenth century, from new texts to new scientific discoveries to the discoveries of new worlds, contradictions and tensions in the intellectual world abounded, making it more and more attractive to hold, with the classical sceptics, that real knowledge is simply beyond the ability of human beings to acquire (see PYRRHONISM). Against this, Descartes asserted that real, certain knowledge is possible; though his name is associated with scepticism, it is as an opponent and not an advocate.

But though certainty was central to Descartes, the path to certainty begins with doubt. In Meditation I, entitled 'What can be called into doubt', Descartes says that 'I realised that it was necessary, once in the course of my life, to demolish everything completely and start again right from the foundations if I wanted to establish anything at all in the sciences that was stable and likely to last'. Following that, he presents a series of three sceptical arguments designed to eliminate his current beliefs in preparation for replacing them with certainties. The strategy is to undermine the beliefs, not one by one but by undermining 'the basic principles' on which they rest. While at least some of these arguments can be found in versions in the *Discourse* and in other writings by Descartes, they receive their fullest exposition in the *Meditations*.

The first argument is directed at the naïve belief that everything learned via the senses is worthy of belief. Against this Descartes points out that 'from time to time I have found that the senses deceive, and it is prudent never to trust completely those who have deceived us even once'. The second, the famous dream argument, is directed against the somewhat less naïve view that the senses are at least worthy of belief when dealing with middle-sized objects in our immediate vicinity: 'A brilliant piece of reasoning! As if I were not a man who sleeps at night ... I plainly see that there are never any sure signs by means of which being awake can be distinguished from being asleep'. But even if I doubt the reliability of what the senses seem to be conveying to me right now, Descartes supposes, the dream argument still leaves open the possibility that there are some general truths, not directly dependent on my present sensations, that I can know. Descartes replies to this with his deceiving God argument.

This complex argument has two horns. Descartes first supposes 'the long-standing opinion that there is an omnipotent God who made me the kind of creature that I am'. Because God is omnipotent, he might have made me in such a way that I go wrong in even the simplest and most evident beliefs that I have – for example, that $2 + 3 = 5$, or that a square has four sides. Though God is thought to be good, the possibility that I am so deeply prone to error seems as consistent with his goodness as the fact that I go wrong even occasionally, at least at this stage of the investigation. But what if there is no God, or what if I arose by 'fate or chance or a continuous chain of events, or by some other means'? In this case, Descartes argues, the less powerful my original cause, 'the more likely it is that I am so imperfect as to be deceived all the time'.

With this, the sceptical arguments of Meditation I are complete: 'I am finally compelled to admit that there is not one of my former beliefs about which a doubt may not properly be raised'. But, Descartes notes, 'my habitual opinions keep coming back'. It is for that reason that Descartes posits his famous evil genius: 'I will suppose therefore that not God, who is supremely good and the source of truth, but rather some evil genius of the utmost power and cunning has employed all his energies in order to deceive me'. The evil genius (sometimes translated as the 'evil demon') is introduced here not as a separate argument for doubt, but as a device to help prevent the return of the former beliefs called into doubt.

These arguments have a crucial function in Descartes' project. As he notes in the introductory synopsis of the *Meditations*, these arguments 'free us from all our preconceived opinions, and provide the easiest route by which the mind may be led away from the senses'. In this way the sceptical doubt of Meditation I prepares the mind for the certainty to which Descartes aspired. But in the *Third Replies*, responding to criticisms from Hobbes, Descartes notes two other roles that the sceptical arguments play in his thought. Descartes remarks that they are introduced 'so that I could reply to them in the subsequent Meditations'. As considered below, the deceiving God argument is answered in Meditations III and IV, and the dream argument is answered in the course of his discussion of sensation in Meditation VI. (Since Descartes, quite rightly, continued to maintain that sensation is not entirely trustworthy as a guide to how things really are, the first sceptical argument is never fully answered, though in Meditation VI he carefully sets out the conditions under which we can trust the senses.) Finally, he notes that the arguments are there as a kind of standard against which he can measure the certainty of his later conclusions: 'I wanted to show the firmness of the truths which I propounded later on, in the light of the fact that they cannot be shaken by these metaphysical doubts'. In all these ways, Descartes presented himself as addressing the sceptic, and defending a kind of dogmatic philosophy.

5 The Cogito Argument

Descartes' philosophy begins in doubt. The first step towards certainty, the Archimedean point from which the whole structure will grow, is the discovery of the existence of the self. At the beginning of Meditation II, reflecting on the evil genius posited at the end of Meditation I, Descartes observes: 'Let him deceive me as much as he can, he will never bring it about that I am nothing so long as I think that I am something … I must finally conclude that this proposition, *I am, I exist*, is necessarily true whenever it is put forward by me or conceived in my mind'. In the earlier *Discourse* (Part IV) and the later *Principles of Philosophy* (Part I §7), this proposition has the more familiar form, 'I am thinking, therefore I exist,' or, 'ego cogito, ergo sum,' in its Latin formulation. Here, it is called the Cogito Argument.

There is considerable discussion about how exactly Descartes thought this argument functions. There are two strains of interpretation that derive directly from his texts. In the *Second Replies*, Descartes observes that 'when we become aware that we are thinking things, this is a primary notion which is not derived by means of any syllogism'. This suggests that the Cogito Argument is known immediately by direct intuition. In the *Principles* (Part I §10), however, Descartes notes that before knowing the Cogito, we must grasp not only the concepts of thought, existence and certainty, but also the proposition that 'it is impossible that that which thinks should not exist'. This suggests that the Cogito *is* a kind of syllogism, in which I infer my existence from the fact that I am thinking, and with the premise that whatever thinks must exist. Recent analytic philosophers have also been attracted to the Cogito, trying to understand its obvious allure through speech act theory and theories of demonstratives. These accounts, however, are distant from anything that Descartes himself conceived.

There is also some confusion about what the conclusion of the Cogito Argument is supposed to be. In the body of Meditation II, Descartes clearly establishes the existence of the self as a thinking thing or a mind. But the title of Meditation II, 'The nature of the human mind, and how it is better known than the body' suggests that Descartes believed that he had established that the nature of the human mind is thought. Further still, in parallel texts in the *Discourse* (Part IV) and the *Principles* (Part I §§7–8), Descartes suggests that the Cogito establishes the existence of a thinking substance distinct from the body, though in the text of Meditation II, this seems to be denied.

Though most closely associated with Descartes, the Cogito Argument may not be altogether original. A number of Descartes' contemporaries, both during his life and afterwards, noticed the connection between the Cogito and similar formulations in AUGUSTINE. However, what was important to Descartes about the Cogito is the foundational role it plays in his system. For Descartes, it is 'the first thing we come to know when we philosophise in an orderly way' (*Principles*: Part I §7). Common sense might think that the physical world of bodies, known through sensation, is more accessible to us than is the mind, a thinking thing whose existence is established, even though we have rejected the senses. But, as Descartes argues in Meditation II using the example of a piece of wax, despite our prejudices, bodies are not conceived through the senses or the imagination but through the same process of purely intellectual conception that gives us the conception of ourselves as thinking things. Furthermore, knowledge of the external world is less certain than knowledge of the mind, since whatever thought could lead us to a probable belief in the existence of bodies will lead us to believe in the existence of the self with certainty.

The project, then, is to build the entire world from the thinking self. It is important here that it is not just the mind that is the foundation, but *my* mind. In this way, the starting place of philosophy for Descartes was connected with the rejection of authority that is central to the Cartesian philosophy. In beginning with the Cogito, we build a philosophy detached from history and tradition.

6 God

The next stage in the system, as outlined in the *Meditations*, seeks to establish that God exists. In his writings, Descartes made use of three principal arguments. The first (at least in the order of presentation in the *Meditations*) is a causal argument. While its fullest statement is in Meditation III, it is also found in the *Discourse* (Part IV) and in the *Principles* (Part I §§17–18). The argument begins by examining the thoughts contained in the mind, distinguishing between the formal reality of an idea and its objective reality. The formal reality of any thing is just its actual existence and the degree of its perfection; the formal reality of an idea is thus its actual existence and degree of perfection as a mode of mind. The objective reality of an idea is the degree of perfection it has, considered now with respect to its content. (This conception extends naturally to the formal and objective reality of a painting, a description or any other representation.) In this connection, Descartes recognized three fundamental degrees of perfection connected with the capacity a thing has for independent existence, a hierarchy implicit in the argument of Meditation III and made explicit in the *Third Replies* (in response to Hobbes). The highest degree is that of an infinite substance (God), which depends on nothing; the next degree is that of a finite substance (an individual body or mind), which depends on God alone; the lowest is that of a mode (a property of a substance), which depends on the substance for its existence. Descartes claims that 'it is manifest by the natural light that there must be at least as much reality in the efficient and total cause as in the effect of that cause'. From that he infers that there must be as much *formal* reality in the cause of an idea as there is *objective* reality in the idea itself. This is a bridge principle that allows Descartes to infer the existence of causes from the nature of the particular ideas that are in the mind, and thus are effects of some causes or another. In Meditation III, Descartes discusses various classes of ideas, one by one, and concludes that, as a finite substance, he can conceivably be the cause of all the ideas he has in his mind except for one: the idea of God. Since the idea of God is an idea of something that has infinite perfection, the only thing that can cause that idea in my mind is a thing that formally (actually) has the perfection that my idea has objectively – that is, God himself.

Descartes used two other arguments for the existence of God in his writings. In Meditation III, following the causal argument, he offers a version of the cosmological argument for those who, still blinded by the senses, may be reluctant to accept the bridge principle that his causal argument requires. (Versions of this argument are also found in *Discourse* Part IV, and in *Principles* Part I §§20–1.) This argument begins with the author's own existence, as established in Meditation II. But, the author might ask, what could have created me? It will not do, Descartes argues, to suggest that I have been in existence always, and thus I do not need a creator, since it takes as much power to sustain me from moment to moment as it does to create me anew. I could not have created myself because then I would have been able to give myself all the perfections that I so evidently lack. Furthermore, if I could create myself, then I could also sustain myself, which I do not have the power to do; being a thinking thing, if I had such a power, I would be aware of having it. My parents cannot be my creators, properly speaking, since they have neither the ability to create a thinking thing (which is all I know myself to be at

this stage of the *Meditations*), nor to sustain it once created. Finally, I could not have been created by another creature of lesser perfection than God, since I have an idea of God, an idea I could not acquire from a lesser being. (Here one suspects that this cosmological argument really collapses into the first causal argument.) From this Descartes concludes 'that the mere fact that I exist and have within me an idea of a most perfect being ... provides a very clear proof that God indeed exists'.

These first two arguments for the existence of God play a central role in the validation of reason, as discussed below. But after reason has been validated on theological grounds, Descartes presents in Meditation V a version of the ontological argument (see GOD, ARGUMENTS FOR THE EXISTENCE OF §§2–3). After reflecting on the basis of geometric reasoning, the fact that 'everything which I clearly and distinctly perceive to belong to that thing really does belong to it', Descartes concludes that this applies to the idea of God as well. Hence he concludes that 'it is quite evident that existence can no more be separated from the essence of God than the fact that its three angles equal to two right angles can be separated from the essence of a triangle, or than the idea of a mountain can be separated from the idea of a valley'. Though apparently circular in so far as its validity seems to depend on the prior arguments for the existence of God, it is not; Descartes' point is that 'even if it turned out that not everything on which I have meditated in these past days is true, I ought still to regard the existence of God as having at least the same level of certainty as I have hitherto attributed to the truths of mathematics'. As with the other two arguments, Descartes' ontological argument is also found in the *Discourse* (Part IV) and in the *Principles* (Part I §§14–16); indeed, in the *Principles* it is the first argument he gives.

As noted above, the existence of God plays a major role in the validation of reason. But it also plays a major role in two other parts of Descartes' system. As we shall later see in connection with Descartes' physics, God is the first cause of motion, and the sustainer of motion in the world. Furthermore, because of the way he sustains motion, God constitutes the ground of the laws of motion. Finally, Descartes held that God is the creator of the so-called eternal truths. In a series of letters in 1630, Descartes enunciated the view that 'the mathematical truths which you call eternal have been laid down by God and depend on Him entirely no less than the rest of His creatures' (letter to Mersenne, 15 April 1630; Descartes 1984–91 vol. 3: 23), a view that Descartes seems to have held into his mature years. While it never again gets the prominence it had in 1630, it is clearly present both in correspondence (for example, letter to Arnauld, 29 July 1648; Descartes 1984–91 vol. 3: 358–9) and in published writings (for example, in the *Sixth Responses*).

Various commentators have proposed that Descartes was really an atheist, and that he includes the arguments for the existence of God as window dressing. While this is not impossible, the frequent appeal to God in philosophical contexts, both in private letters and in published work, suggests that it is rather unlikely.

7 The validation of reason

With the existence of God established, the next stage in Descartes' programme is the validation of reason. At the beginning of Meditation III, before proving God's existence, Descartes notes that the uncertainty that remains is due only to the fact that the meditator does not know whether or not there is a God and, if there is, if he can be a deceiver. This suggests that all one must do to restore reason and defeat the third and most general sceptical argument presented in Meditation I is to prove that there is a benevolent God. And at the end of Meditation III, after two proofs for the existence of God, Descartes concludes directly that this God 'cannot be a deceiver, since it is manifest by the natural light that all fraud and deception depend on some defect'. But this is not enough. In the course of the deceiving-God argument of Meditation I, Descartes notes that if some deception is consistent with divine benevolence, then total deception would be as well. Since it is undeniable that we do make mistakes from time to time, and are thus deceived, this raises a problem for Descartes: what, if anything, does God's benevolence and veracity guarantee?

Descartes answers this question by way of an account of error in Meditation IV. Roughly speaking, the mistakes I make are due to myself and my (improper) exercise of my free will, while the truths I come to know are because of the way God made me. More exactly, Descartes asserts that judgments depend on two faculties of the mind, 'namely, on the faculty of knowledge [or intellect] which is in me, and on the faculty of choice or freedom of the will'. A judgment is made when the will assents to an idea that is in the intellect. But the intellect is finite and limited in the sense that it does not have ideas of all possible things. On the other hand, the will is indefinite in its extent, Descartes claims: 'It is only the will or freedom of choice which I experience within me to be so great that the idea of any greater faculty is beyond my grasp'. It is in our free will that we most resemble God. In certain circumstances, Descartes held, 'a great light

in the intellect is followed by a great inclination in the will', and in this way the intellect determines the will to assent. This, he thought, is a proper use of the will in judgment. In this situation, where the intellect determines the will to assent, Descartes talks of our having a clear and distinct perception of a truth. In this case, God has made us in such a way that we cannot but assent. (Clear and distinct perceptions are very close to what he calls 'intuitions' in the *Rules*, as discussed above.) But because the will has a greater extent than the intellect, and is not restrained by it, sometimes things outside the intellect move the will to assent. This is where error enters: 'The scope of the will is wider than that of the intellect; but instead of restricting it within the same limits, I extend its use to matters which I do not understand. Since the will is indifferent in such cases, it easily turns aside from what is true and good, and this is the source of my error and sin'. In this way, I am responsible for error by extending my will beyond where it belongs. God can in no way be held accountable for my mistakes any more than he can be responsible for my sins. I cannot reproach my maker for not having given me more ideas in the intellect than I have, nor can I fault him for having made me more perfect by giving me a free will. But as a result of a limited intellect and a free will, it is possible for me both to make mistakes and to sin.

As a result of this analysis of error, Descartes is able, in Meditation IV, to assert his famous principle of clear and distinct perception, an epistemological principle to replace the principles that were rejected as a result of the sceptical arguments of Meditation I: 'If I simply refrain from making a judgement in cases where I do not perceive the truth with sufficient clarity and distinctness, then it is clear that I am behaving correctly and avoiding error. But if in such cases I either affirm or deny, then I am not using my free will correctly'. With this, reason is validated, and the deceiving-God argument answered. Yet, this does not end Descartes' engagement with the sceptical arguments of Meditation I, and in Meditation VI he also addresses the question of the reliability of the senses, presents a limited validation of sensory knowledge, and answers the dream argument.

The validation of reason, central as it is to Descartes' project in the *Meditations*, has one apparent flaw: it seems to be circular. The validation of reason in Meditation IV depends on the proof of the existence of God which, in turn, depends on the proof of the existence of the self as a thinking thing. But evidently we must assume that clear and distinct perceptions are trustworthy in order to trust the Cogito and the proofs for the existence of God that ground the validation of reason – the so-called

'Cartesian Circle'. Two of the objectors to the *Meditations* noticed this point, and elicited responses from Descartes, in the *Second* and the *Fourth Replies*. Descartes' answer is not altogether clear. In the *Second Replies* he remarks, in answer to one such objection, that 'when I said that we can know nothing for certain until we are aware that God exists, I expressly declared that I was speaking only of knowledge of those conclusions' deduced by long arguments, and not of 'first principles', such as the Cogito Argument. This suggests that Descartes would exempt immediately intuitable (self-evident) propositions from the scope of the doubt of Meditation I, and use them as tools for establishing the premises of the argument that leads to the validation of reason in Meditation IV. There are serious problems with this approach. For one, it seems arbitrary to exempt self-evident propositions from the scope of doubt. Such propositions would seem to fall quite naturally among those most obvious of things that Descartes calls into doubt there; if God could create me in such a way that I go wrong when I add two and three, he could create me in such a way that I go wrong with any other self-evident belief. Furthermore, even if those propositions that are immediately evident are outside the scope of doubt, Descartes' proofs for the existence of God, necessary premises of his validation of reason, are not self-evident. These apparent problems might be either weaknesses in Descartes' response, or reasons to doubt that we have understood Descartes correctly in his responses.

The problem of circularity and the obvious problems in Descartes' apparent answer have elicited numerous examinations of the issue in the commentary literature. It is not clear just what Descartes' own solution was, nor whether or not there is a good response to the Cartesian Circle. But whatever the answer, the problem is not a superficial oversight on Descartes' part. It is a deep philosophical problem that will arise in some form or another whenever one attempts a rational defence of reason.

8 Mind and body

One of Descartes' most celebrated positions is the distinction between the mind and the body. Descartes did not invent the position. It can be found in various forms in a number of earlier thinkers. It is a standard feature of Platonism and, in a different form, is common to most earlier Christian philosophers, who generally held that some feature of the human being – its mind or its soul – survives the death of the body (see PLATO §13). But the particular features of Descartes' way of drawing the distinction and the arguments that he used were very influential on later thinkers.

There are suggestions, particularly in the *Discourse* (Part IV) and in the *Principles* (Part I §§7–8) that the distinction between mind and body follows directly from the Cogito Argument, as discussed above. However, in the *Meditations* Descartes is quite clear that the distinction is to be established on other grounds. In Meditation VI he argues as follows: I have a clear and distinct idea of myself as a thinking non-extended thing, and a clear and distinct idea of body as an extended and non-thinking thing. Whatever I can conceive clearly and distinctly, God can so create. So, Descartes argues, the mind, a thinking thing, can exist apart from its extended body. And therefore, the mind is a substance distinct from the body, a substance whose essence is thought.

Implicit in this argument is a certain conception of what it means to be a substance, a view made explicit in the *Principles* (Part I §51), which defines a substance as 'nothing other than a thing which exists in such a way as to depend on no other thing for its existence', no other thing but God, of course. In so far as the mind can exist independently of the body, it is a substance on this definition. (God is the third kind of substance, along with mind and body, though because of his absolute independence, he is a substance in a somewhat different sense.) On Descartes' metaphysics, each substance has a principal attribute, an attribute that characterizes its nature. For mind it is thought, and for body it is extension. In addition, substances have modes, literally ways of instantiating the attributes. So, for Descartes, particular ideas, particular volitions, particular passions are modes of mind, and particular shapes, sizes and motions are modes of body.

Descartes' conception of mind and body represents significant departures from the conceptions of both notions in the late scholastic thought in which he was educated. For the late scholastics, working in the Aristotelian tradition, body is composed of matter and form. Matter is that which remains constant in change, while form is that which gives bodies the characteristic properties that they have. For Descartes, however, all body is of the same kind, a substance that contains only geometric properties, the objects of geometry made concrete. The characteristic properties of particular forms of body are explained in terms of the size, shape and motion of its insensible parts (see §11 below). For the late scholastics, the mind is connected with the account of life. On the Aristotelian view, the soul is the principle of life, that which distinguishes a living thing from a dead thing; it is also taken to be the form that pertains to the living body. The mind is the rational part of the soul, that which characterizes humans, and not usually considered a genuine substance, though by most accounts, with divine aid, it can survive the death of the body (see NOUS; PSYCHÉ). For Descartes, the majority of the vital functions are explained in terms of the physical organization of the organic body. The mind, thus, is not a principle of life but a principle of thought. It involves reason, as does the rational soul of the Aristotelians, but it also involves other varieties of thought, which pertain to other parts of the Aristotelian soul (see ARISTOTLE §17). Furthermore, it is a genuine substance, and survives the death of the body naturally and not through special divine intervention.

Mind and body are distinct because they can exist apart from one another. However, in this life, they do not. In Meditation VI Descartes observed: 'Nature also teaches me, by these sensations of pain, hunger, thirst and so on that I am not merely present in my body as a sailor is present in a ship, but that I am very closely and, as it were, intermingled with it, so that I and the body form a unit'. He sometimes went so far as to say that the human mind is the form of the human body, the only kind of form that he recognizes in nature, and that the human being – the union of a mind and a body – constitutes a genuine substance, though the context of these statements suggests that they may be made more for orthodoxy's sake than an expression of his own views (see, for example, the letter to Regius, January 1642 (Descartes 1984–91 vol. 3: 208), where he is advising Regius on the best way to answer the attacks made by the more orthodox Aristotelian Gisbertus Voëtius in connection with the controversy at Utrecht.) But be that as it may, he was clearly committed to holding that the mind and the body are united. Some of his contemporaries found it difficult to understand how two such different substances could interact and be joined. Sometimes Descartes dismissed this objection by saying that it is no more difficult than understanding how form and matter unite for the Aristotelians, something that everyone learns at school (letter to Arnauld, 29 July 1648; Descartes 1984–91 vol. 3: 358). But elsewhere, particularly in an important exchange of letters with the Princess Elisabeth of Bohemia, Descartes offered a different explanation, remarking that it is simply an empirical fact that they do unite and interact, something that we learn from everyday experience, and suggesting that just as we have innate notions that allow us to understand the notions of thinking and extended substance, we also have an innate notion that allows us to comprehend how mind and body interact, and how together they can constitute a unity (letters to Elisabeth, 21 May 1643 and 28 June 1643; Descartes 1984–91 vol. 3: 217–20, 226–9).

According to Descartes, the mind is joined to the body in one specific place: the pineal gland, a single gland in the centre of the brain, between the two lobes. This is the spot in which interaction takes place. The mind has the ability to move the pineal gland, and by doing so, to change the state of the brain in such a way as to produce voluntary motions. Similarly, the sensory organs all transmit their information to the pineal gland and, as a result of that, sensation is transmitted to the attached mind. However, because of the interconnection of the parts that make up the organic body, by virtue of being connected to the pineal gland, the mind can properly be said to be connected with the body as a whole (*Passions*: §§30–2) (see PERSONS).

9 The external world and sensation

The argument for the distinction between mind and body in Meditation VI establishes the nature of body as extension, but it does not establish the real existence of the world of bodies outside of the mind. This is the focus of the last series of arguments in the *Meditations*. The argument begins in Meditation VI with the recognition that I have 'a passive faculty of sensory perception', which would be useless unless there was also an 'active faculty, either in me or in something else' which produces the ideas of sensation. Descartes has already established in Meditation IV that the mind has only two faculties – a passive faculty of perception, and the active faculty of will. Since it is passive, perception cannot be the source of my ideas of sensation, and since sensations are involuntary, they cannot be the product of my will. So, the ideas of sense must come from somewhere else. God 'has given me a great propensity to believe that they are produced by corporeal things', and no means to correct my error if that propensity is deceptive. So, Descartes concluded, God would be a deceiver if my sensory ideas come from anything but from bodies. This argument does not prove that everything we sense about bodies is reliable, but only that 'they possess all the properties which I clearly and distinctly understand, that is, all those which, viewed in general terms, are comprised within the subject-matter of pure mathematics'. (In the *Principles* Part II §1 there is also an argument for the existence of the external world, but it is somewhat different.)

The proof of the existence of the external world tells us that, in general, bodies are the causes of our sensations and it tells us, in general, what the nature of body is. But it does not seem to tell us much about what we can (and cannot) learn about specific bodies in the world around us in specific circumstances. These questions are addressed at the end of Meditation VI in a general discussion of the reliability of sensation, the most extensive such discussion in Descartes' writings. He argues there that the senses are given to me 'simply to inform the mind of what is beneficial or harmful for the composite of which the mind is a part; and to this extent they are sufficiently clear and distinct'. That is, while they cannot tell me anything about the real nature of things – that is for the intellect or reason to determine – they can inform me about specific features of my environment that relate to maintaining the union of my mind and body. So, for example, when the senses tell us that some particular apples are red and others green, this can give us reliable information that some may be ripe (and thus nutritious) and others not, but it cannot tell us that the one is, in its nature, red, and the other really green. Similarly, when I feel a pain in my toe, this tells me that there is damage to my toe, not that there is something resembling the sensation that is actually in the toe. Even in this, the sensation may be misleading. As Descartes points out, people sometimes feel pain in limbs even after they have been amputated.

Given the nature of the extended body, and the causal process by which pains (and other sensations) are transmitted through the body to the pineal gland, where the non-extended mind is joined to the extended body, such misleading sensations are inevitable; similar sensations in the mind can be the result of very different causal processes in the body. For example, a sensation of pain-in-the-toe can be caused either by a change in the state of the toe itself, or by an appropriate stimulation of the nerve connecting the toe to the brain at any point between the two. But, Descartes claims, though sensation is fallible, 'I know that in matters regarding the well-being of the body, all my senses report the truth much more frequently than not'. Furthermore, I can use multiple senses and memory, together with the intellect, 'which has by now examined all the causes of error' in order to weigh the evidence of the senses and use it properly. And with this, Descartes is finally able to answer the dream argument of Meditation I. For my waking experience is interconnected in a way in which my dreaming experience is not; the things I see in waking life, unlike those in dreams, come to me through all my senses, and connect with my memory of other objects. I can use this inter-connectedness of waking experience, together with my intellect and my knowledge of the causes of error, to sort out veridical sensations and distinguish them from the deceptive sensory experiences of dreams. Sometimes even my waking experiences will be deceptive, of course, but we are capable of determining specific circumstances in which the senses are worthy of our trust. And so, contrary to the original doubts raised by the dreaming argument in Meditation I, there is no general reason to reject waking experience as such.

Though subordinated to reason, sensation, cast into doubt in Meditation I, re-enters as a legitimate source of knowledge about the world by the end of Meditation VI.

10 Philosophical psychology and morals

Morality was a concern of Descartes' in a variety of texts. In the third part of his *Discourse* he presents what he calls a 'provisional morality', a morality to govern our behaviour while we are in the process of revising our beliefs and coming to certainty. In the tree of philosophy in the Preface to the French edition of the *Principles*, morals is listed as one of the fruits of the tree, along with medicine and mechanics. It is also a theme in the letters he exchanged with the Princess Elisabeth of Bohemia in the mid-1640s, together with another concern – the passions, what they are and, more importantly, how to control them. These themes are intertwined again in Descartes' last major work, the *Passions of the Soul* (1649).

In one of the letters that serves as a preface to the *Passions*, Descartes announces that he will treat the passions 'only as a natural philosopher [*en physicien*], and not as a rhetorician or even as a moral philosopher'. Accordingly, the bulk of the *Passions* is taken up with detailed accounts of what the passions are, and how they arise from the connection between the human body and the human mind. As Descartes conceived them, the passions are grouped with sensation and imagination, perceptions of the mind that arise from external impulses. In this respect, Descartes differed radically from the Aristotelian scholastic philosophers who attached the passions to the appetitive faculty rather than the perceptive. But though grouped with other perceptions, the ones that concern Descartes in this treatise are a special group of perceptions, 'those whose effects we feel as being in the soul itself, and for which we do not normally know any proximate cause to which we can refer them', those 'which are caused, maintained, and strengthened by some movement of the spirits'(*Passions*: §§25, 27). (The 'spirits' in question are the animal spirits, a fluid matter that played a major role in Descartes' biology.) The principal effect of the passions is to 'move and dispose the soul to want the things for which they prepare the body. Thus the feeling of fear moves the soul to want to flee, that of courage to want to fight' and so on (*Passions*: §40). As with sensations, the passions of the soul play a role in the preservation of the mind–body union: 'The function of all the passions consists solely in this, that they dispose our soul to want the things which nature deems useful for us, and to persist in this volition; and the same agitation of the spirits which normally causes the passions also disposes the body to make movements which help us to attain these things' (*Passions*: §52).

For the schoolmen, the passions pertained to the appetitive faculty, and were principally organized around a distinction between the 'irascible' and the 'concupiscent' appetites. Descartes, however, was attempting to fashion a conception of the passions based on a very different conception of the soul, one in which there is no distinction among appetites (*Passions*: §68). His categorization of the passions was based on a list of six primitive passions, which pertain to the perceptive rather than to the appetitive faculty: wonder, desire, love and hatred, joy and sadness – 'all the others are either composed from some of these six or they are species of them' (*Passions*: §69). Much of his attention in the short book is directed at accounts of what each of these basic passions is, what it feels like and its physiological causes and effects in the body, and how all the other passions can be understood in terms of the six basic ones.

But although Descartes presents himself as examining the passions '*en physicien*', there is a moral dimension to the discussion as well. Part of the motivation for the examination of the passions is their control. While the passions, like everything given to us by God, can contribute to our wellbeing, they can also be excessive and must be controlled (*Passions*: §211). While the passions are not under our direct control, by understanding what they are and how they are caused we can learn indirect means for controlling them (*Passions*: §§45–50, 211). This, Descartes asserts, is the 'chief use of wisdom, [which] lies in its teaching us to be masters of our passions and to control them with such skill that the evils which they cause are quite bearable, and even become a source of joy' (*Passions*: §212). Important in this process is what Descartes calls *générosité*, best translated as 'nobility'. *Générosité* is the knowledge that all that belongs to us, properly speaking, is our own free will, and the resolution to use it well, 'that is, never to lack the will to undertake and carry out whatever one judges to be best' (*Passions*: §53). Understood in this way, *générosité* is both a passion (an immediate feeling) and a virtue ('a habit of the soul which disposes it to have certain thoughts') (*Passions*: §§160–1). The person who has *générosité* 'has very little esteem for everything that depends on others', and as a result, Descartes claims, is able to control their passions (*Passions*: §156).

11 Physics and mathematics

To his contemporaries, Descartes was as well known for his system of physics as he was for the metaphysical views that are now more studied. Indeed, as he indicates in the Preface to the French edition of the *Principles*, metaphysics constitutes the roots of the tree of philosophy, but the trunk is physics.

Descartes' physics was developed in two main places. The earliest is in the treatise *Le Monde* (*The World*) which he suppressed when Galileo was condemned for Copernicanism in 1633, though summarized in Part V of the *Discourse*. Later, in the early 1640s, he presented much of the material in a more carefully worked-out form, in Parts II, III and IV of the *Principles*. Like the physical thought of many of his contemporaries, his physics can be divided into two parts – a general part, which includes accounts of matter and the general laws of nature, and a specific part, which includes an account of particular phenomena.

The central doctrine at the foundations of Descartes' physics is the claim that the essence of body is extension (discussed in §8 above). This doctrine excludes substantial forms and any sort of sensory qualities from body. For the Schoolmen there are four primary qualities (wet and dry, hot and cold) which characterize the four elements. For Descartes, these qualities are sensations in the mind, and only in the mind; bodies are in their nature simply the objects of geometry made real. Descartes also rejected atoms and the void, the two central doctrines of the atomists, an ancient school of philosophy whose revival by Gassendi and others constituted a major rival among contemporary mechanists. Because there can be no extension without an extended substance, namely body, there can be no space without body, Descartes argued. His world was a plenum, and all motion must ultimately be circular, since one body must give way to another in order for there to be a place for it to enter (*Principles* II: §§2–19, 33). Against atoms, he argued that extension is by its nature is indefinitely divisible: no piece of matter in its nature is indivisible (*Principles* II: §20). Yet he agreed that, since bodies are simply matter, the apparent diversity between them must be explicable in terms of the size, shape and motion of the small parts that make them (*Principles* II: §§23, 64) (see LEIBNIZ, G.W. §4).

Accordingly, motion and its laws played a special role in Descartes' physics. The essentials of this account can be found in *The World*, but it is set out most clearly in the *Principles*. There (*Principles* II: §25), motion is defined as the translation of a body from one neighbourhood of surrounding bodies into another. Descartes is careful to distinguish motion itself from its cause(s). While, as we have seen, motion is sometimes caused by the volition of a mind, the general cause of motion in the inanimate world is God, who creates bodies and their motion, and sustains them from moment to moment. From the constancy of the way in which God sustains motion, Descartes argues, the same quantity of motion is always preserved in the world, a quantity that is measured by the size of a body multiplied by its speed (*Principles* II: §36). To this general conservation law he adds three more particular laws of nature, also based on the constancy by which God conserves his creation. According to the first law, everything retains its own state, in so far as it can. As a consequence, what is in motion remains in motion until interfered with by an external cause, a principle directly opposed to the Aristotelian view that things in motion tend to come to rest (*Principles* II: §§37–8). According to the second law, bodies tend to move in rectilinear paths, with the result that bodies in circular motion tend to move away at the tangent (*Principles* II: §39). The first and second laws together arguably constitute the first published statement of what NEWTON later called the law of inertia. Descartes' third law governs the collision between bodies, specifying when one body imposes its motion on another, and when two bodies rebound from one another without exchanging motion. The abstract law is followed by seven specific rules covering special cases (*Principles* II: §§40–52). Though the law of collision turns out to be radically inadequate, it casts considerable light on Descartes' conception of the physical world. One of the determinants of the outcome of a collision is what Descartes calls the 'force' of a body, both its force for continuing in motion, and its resistance to change in its motion (*Principles* II: §43). The role of such forces in Descartes' mechanist world has generated much discussion, since they would seem to be completely inconsistent with Descartes' view that the essence of body is extension alone.

These general accounts of matter and motion form the basis of Descartes' physical theories of particular phenomena. The *Principles* goes on to explain how the earth turns around the sun in an enormous fluid vortex and how the light that comes from the sun is nothing but the centrifugal force of the fluid in the vortex, with ingenious explanations of many other particular phenomena in terms of the size, shape and motion of their parts. Other works contain further mechanistic explanations, for example of the law governing the refraction of light (*Dioptrics* II) and the way colours arise in the rainbow (*Meteors* VIII).

Descartes' hope was that he could begin with an assumption about how God created the world, and then deduce, on the basis of the laws of motion, how the world would have to have come out (*Discourse* V, VI; *Principles* III: §46). But this procedure caused some problems. It is not easy to specify just how God might have created the world –

whether the particles that he first created were of the same size, for example, or of every possible size. Furthermore, any hypothesis of this sort would seem to be inconsistent with the account of creation in Genesis (*Principles* III: §§43–7). These difficulties aside, it seemed obvious to Descartes how to proceed. For example, from his denial of the vacuum it would seem to follow that bodies in motion would sort themselves out into circular swirls of matter, the vortices which were to explain the circulation of the planets around a central sun. Similarly, Descartes used the tendency to centrifugal motion generated by the circular motion of the vortex to explain light, which, he claimed, was the pressure of the subtle matter in the vortex. But the very complexity of the world militates against the full certainty that Descartes originally sought, particularly when dealing with the explanation of particular phenomena, such as the magnet. Indeed, by the end of the *Principles*, it can seem that he has given up the goal of certainty and come to accept the kind of probability that he initially rejected (*Principles* IV: §204–6).

Central to Descartes' physics is his rejection of final causes: 'When dealing with natural things we will, then, never derive any explanations from the purposes which God or nature may have had in view when creating them. For we should not be so arrogant as to suppose that we can share in God's plans' (*Principles* I: §28). The emphasis on efficient causes was to prove very controversial later in the century.

One especially curious feature of Descartes' physics, however, is the lack of any substantive role for mathematics. Descartes was one of the great mathematicians of his age. While it is, perhaps, anachronistic to see modern analytic geometry and so-called Cartesian coordinates in his *Geometry* (1637), there is no question but that it is a work of real depth and influence. In it he shows how one could use algebra to solve geometric problems and geometry to solve algebraic problems by showing how algebraic operations could be interpreted purely in terms of the manipulation and construction of line segments. In traditional mathematics, if a quantity was represented as a given line, then the square of that quantity was represented as a square constructed with that line as a side, and the cube of the quantity represented as a cube constructed with that line as an edge, effectively limiting the geometric representation of algebraic operations to a very few. By demonstrating how the square, cube (and so on) of a given quantity could all be represented as other lines, Descartes opened the way to a more complete unification of algebra and geometry. Also important to his mathematical work was the notion of analysis. Descartes saw himself as reviving the work of the ancient mathematician, Pappus of Alexandria, and setting out a methodology for the solution of problems, a methodology radically different from the Euclidean style of doing geometry in terms of definitions, axioms, postulates and propositions, which he regarded as a method of presentation rather than a method of discovery. According to the procedure of analysis, as Descartes understood it, one begins by labelling unknowns in a geometric problem with letters, setting out a series of equations that involve these letters, and then solving for the unknowns to the extent that this is possible.

Unlike his contemporary, Galileo, or his successors, Leibniz and Newton, Descartes never quite figured out how to apply his mathematical insights to the physical world. Indeed, it is a curious feature of his tree of knowledge that, despite the central place occupied by mathematics in his own accomplishments, it seems to have no place there.

12 Life and the foundations of biology

The last part of the Cartesian programme was his biology. First presented in the *Treatise on Man*, part of *The World* project which was abandoned in 1633 when Galileo was condemned, Descartes intended to rework some of that material and publish it – as Parts V and VI of the *Principles* under the title 'De Homine'. Although he never finished this rewriting, it is clear from the notes left behind that it was very much on his mind in years that preceded his sudden and premature death.

His hope seems to have been to show how, from matter and the laws of motion alone, life would arise spontaneously as matter came to organize itself in an appropriate way (*Discourse* V). Unfortunately he never worked out this view, suggestive of later theories of evolution, in any detail. Yet, he was quite clear that all the functions of life (with the exception of thought and reason in humans) are to be explained not in terms of the soul, the principle of life, but in terms of matter in motion. Accordingly, in the *Treatise on Man*, he accounts for a variety of phenomena, including digestion, involuntary motion, the action of the heart, and sense perception, in purely mechanical terms. (Summarized in *Discourse* Part V, with special emphasis on the circulation of the blood.)

While Descartes' biology was controversial among his contemporaries, one aspect was especially so. According to his account, there is only one kind of soul in the world, the rational soul, which humans and angels have and animals do not. Humans are organic machines, collections of matter organized so as to be able to perform vital functions, attached to rational souls. Animals, on the other hand, are just machines: their behaviour is purely mechanical and they are, strictly speaking, incapable of conscious experience of any sort (*Discourse* V).

13 The Cartesian heritage

It is difficult to overestimate the influence of Descartes. In philosophy, the Cogito Argument signalled the centrality of the self and the rejection of authority from without, the authority of both texts and teacher. For physics, Descartes represented the rejection of the scholastic physics of matter and form, and its replacement by a mechanistic physics of matter and motion. So in biology he stood for mechanism and the rejection of Aristotelian vitalism.

Descartes had many followers who took his ideas (as they understood them) as dogma, and developed them as they thought he would have wanted them to do. The most important centres of Cartesian thought were France, where he was remembered as a countryman, despite his long absence, and the Netherlands, where he had lived. In France, his thought was carried on by a circle around Claude Clerselier, who gathered and published his letters as well as other works. Louis de La Forge commented on Descartes' physiology, and wrote a Cartesian treatise on the mind, extending Descartes' ideas. Gerauld de Cordemoy, tried to blend Cartesian philosophy with atomism, to the puzzlement of most of his contemporaries. Jacques Rohault was influential in Cartesian physics well after Newton had published the work that would eventually eclipse such theories. Other followers, mainly in the Low Countries, include Henricus Regius, considered Cartesian by many despite Descartes' public rejection; Adriaan Heereboord, one of Descartes' partisans in Leiden; Johannes de Raey, one of those who attempted to reconcile Descartes with the true philosophy of Aristotle; and Johannes Clauberg, who recast Cartesianism into more scholastic garb. There were many more minor Cartesians of various nationalities. Late seventeenth-century Europe was flooded with paraphrases of and commentaries on Descartes' writings.

Other more independent thinkers were strongly influenced by Descartes without explicitly being followers. The best-known such figure is probably Nicolas MALEBRANCHE. While his thought owes much to other influences, particularly to seventeenth-century Augustinianism, in his *Recherche de la vérité* (Search after Truth) (1674–5) he follows Descartes in offering a critique of the senses, rejecting the authority of tradition, and appealing to clear and distinct perceptions. Descartes was also an important influence on the Cambridge Platonist

Henry More, who regarded Descartes' philosophy, in particular his distinction between mind and body, as support for his own attacks on materialism (see CAMBRIDGE PLATONISM). SPINOZA, too, was influenced by Descartes. His first published book was a commentary on Descartes' *Principles*, and although he later moved well outside the Cartesian camp, Descartes' doctrines helped to structure his mature thought. Spinoza's metaphysical vocabulary (substance, attribute and mode) is borrowed from Descartes, as is the centrality of the attributes of thought and extension in his metaphysics.

While many of Descartes' partisans tried to remain orthodox, there is at least one doctrine characteristic of later Cartesianism that Descartes himself probably did not hold, namely, occasionalism (see OCCASIONALISM). Malebranche and the Flemish Cartesian Arnold Geulincx are most often associated with the doctrine, but it appears in Cartesian writings long before theirs. According to occasionalism, God is the only active causal agent in the world; finite minds and bodies are not real causes, but only occasions for God to exercise his causal efficacy. Motivated by the picture of divine sustenance from moment to moment that underlies Descartes' derivation of the laws of motion, together, perhaps, with general worries about the efficacy of finite causes and specific worries about mind–body interaction, occasionalism became a standard doctrine. Though often also attributed to Descartes himself, the grounds for doing so are rather slim.

Descartes' mark can also be seen among his opponents. He was clearly a target of Hobbes' materialism and sensationalism in, for example, Part I of *Leviathan* (1651). His epistemology and treatment of God were explicitly targeted by PASCAL in the *Pensées* (1658–62, published 1670). Leibniz, too, attacked his physics, his rejection of formal logic, his conception of body and his conception of the mind, among many other things. The inadequacy of the Cartesian philosophy is a constant subtext to Locke's *Essay Concerning Human Understanding* (1689), particularly in his discussion of our knowledge of mind and his rejection of the dogmatic claim to know the essences of substances. In natural philosophy, Newton's early writings show a careful study of Descartes' writings, particularly those on motion, and book II of his *Principia* was devoted to a refutation of the vortex theory of planetary motion. Between around 1650 and the eclipse of Cartesian philosophy some time in the early eighteenth century, it was simply impossible to write philosophy without reacting in some way to Descartes.

See also: DOUBT; DUALISM; LOCKE, J.; RATIONALISM; SCEPTICISM; SUBSTANCE

References and further reading

Cottingham, J.G. (1986) *Descartes*, Oxford: Blackwell. (Good introductory study of Descartes' philosophical thought.)

Descartes, R. (1984–91) *The Philosophical Writings of Descartes*, ed. and trans. J. Cottingham, R. Stoothoff, D. Murdoch and A. Kenny, Cambridge: Cambridge University Press, 3 vols. (The now-standard English translation of Descartes' writings. It contains the entire *Rules*, *Discourse*, *Meditations* and *Passions*, as well as selections from his other writings and letters.)

Voss. S. (ed.) (1993) *Essays on the Philosophy and Science of René Descartes*, New York and Oxford: Oxford University Press. (Collection of articles that gives a good idea of recent work.)

DANIEL GARBER

DESCRIPTIONS

Introduction

'Definite descriptions' are noun phrases of the form 'the' + noun complex (for example, 'the finest Greek poet', 'the cube of five') or of the form possessive + noun complex (for example, 'Sparta's defeat of Athens'). As Russell realized, it is important to philosophy to be clear about the semantics of such expressions. In the sentence 'Aeschylus fought at Marathon', the function of the subject, 'Aeschylus', is to refer to something; it is a referential noun phrase (or 'singular term'). By contrast, in the sentence 'Every Athenian remembers Marathon', the subject noun phrase, 'every Athenian', is not referential but quantificational. Definite descriptions appear at first sight to be referential. Frege treated them referentially, but Russell held that they should be treated quantificationally in accordance with his theory of descriptions, and argued that certain philosophical puzzles were thereby solved.

1   Frege
2   Russell's theory of descriptions: informal characterization
3   Russell's theory of descriptions: formal characterization
4   Strawson's theory and criticisms of Russell
5   Ambiguity theories

1   Frege

Gottlob Frege provided the first systematic account of quantification in natural language and the first systematic theory of reference (Über Sinn und Bedeutung 1892). The class of 'singular terms' (referential noun phrases), for Frege, was delimited by a set of logical tests (for example, the licensing of existential generalization) and was recursive. It included ordinary proper names and definite descriptions. Thus '5', 'the cube of 5', 'Aeschylus' and so on were all singular terms.

If a description ⌜the F⌝ is referential, then it is natural to take its reference to be the unique entity satisfying 'F'; a sentence ⌜The F is G⌝ is true if and only if that entity is G. But what if no entity, or more than one entity, satisfies the descriptive condition, as in (1) or (2)?

(1) *The largest prime number* lies between 10^{23} and 10^{27}.

(2) *The man who landed on the moon* was American.

Such descriptions are said to be 'improper'. Frege considered it a defect of natural language that it permits the possibility of improper terms. As far as his own logical system was concerned, he thought it essential that every formula have a truth-value, and so he insisted that every singular term have a reference (or meaning): he stipulated that a specified object in the range of the quantifier(s) serve as the referent of every improper description. While this stipulation proved useful for his formal system, Frege recognized that some other account of improper descriptions in ordinary language was needed. Once he had made his distinction between the 'sense' and 'reference' of an expression, he suggested that an improper term has a sense but no reference (see FREGE, G. §3; SENSE AND REFERENCE). The main problem with this proposal is that it predicts, rather counterintuitively, that any sentence containing an improper term (in a transparent context) lacks a truth-value. For example, it predicts that (1) and (2) above lack truth-values.

2 Russell's theory of descriptions: informal characterization

Like Frege, Bertrand RUSSELL thought it important to explain how a sentence such as (1) or (2) could be meaningful. At one time he entertained the idea of a realm of non-existent entities to serve as the referents of descriptions such as 'the largest prime number' and 'the round square'; but by 1905 he thought this idea conflicted with a 'robust sense of reality' and his theory of descriptions came about, in part, as an attempt to purify his ontology (see EXISTENCE).

On Russell's account, descriptions are not singular terms at all but phrases that logical analysis

reveals to be quantificational: if ⌜the F⌝ is a definite description and ⌜ ... is G⌝ is a predicate phrase, then the proposition expressed by an utterance of ⌜The F is G⌝ is equivalent, says Russell, to the proposition expressed by an utterance of ⌜There is exactly one F, and everything that is F is G⌝. That is, ⌜The F is G⌝ is analysed as

(3) $(\exists x)((\forall y)(Fy \leftrightarrow y = x) \ \& \ Gx)$.

The proposition expressed by ⌜The F is G⌝ is 'general' ('object-independent') rather than 'singular' ('object-dependent') in the sense that there is no object for which its grammatical subject stands; upon whose existence that of the proposition expressed depends. Unlike a singular term, a definite description, even if it is in fact satisfied by a unique object, does not actually *refer* to that object. It is as wrong, on Russell's account, to inquire into the referent of ⌜the F⌝ as it is to inquire into the referent of ⌜every F⌝ or ⌜no F⌝.

On Russell's account, sentences containing improper descriptions have truth-values. For example, (1) above is false as it is not the case that there exists a largest prime number. Similarly, sentence (2) is false as it is not the case that there exists exactly one man who landed on the moon.

Russell's theory opens up the possibility of accounting for certain *de dicto/de re* ambiguities in terms of scope permutations (see DE RE/DE DICTO). For example, (4) below may be analysed as either (5) or (6), according to whether the description 'the largest prime number' is given large or small scope with respect to 'John thinks that':

(4) John thinks that the largest prime number lies between 10^{23} and 10^{27}.

(5) $(\exists x)((\forall y)(\text{largest-prime } y \leftrightarrow y = x) \ \& \ \text{John thinks that: } x \text{ lies between } 10^{23} \text{ and } 10^{27})$.

(6) John thinks that: $(\exists x)((\forall y)(\text{largest-prime } y \leftrightarrow y = x) \ \& \ x \text{ lies between } 10^{23} \text{ and } 10^{27})$.

(5) is false; but (6) may be true. Thus Russell is able to explain the intuitive ambiguity of (4) and avoid positing an ontology that includes such things as a largest prime number. Smullyan points out that Russell's theory similarly explains *de dicto/de re* ambiguities in modal contexts, for example, in 'The number of planets is necessarily odd' (see MODAL LOGIC).

Russell came to treat ordinary proper names as 'disguised' or 'truncated' descriptions. For example, the name 'Cicero' might be analysed as the description 'the greatest Roman orator', while the coreferential name 'Tully' might be analysed as the description 'the author of *De Fato*'. On the face of it, this provided Russell with accounts (not dissimilar to Frege's) of why 'Cicero was bald' and 'Tully was bald' differ in informativeness, and of why (7) and (8) need not agree in truth-value:

(7)   John believes Cicero was bald.

(8)   John believes Tully was bald.

In the light of Kripke's work on names and necessity, it is widely held that descriptive analyses of proper names cannot succeed (see KRIPKE, S.A.; PROPER NAMES). There is good reason, however, to think that at least some pronouns anaphorically linked to (referring back to), but not bound by, quantified noun phrases are understood in terms of definite descriptions (see Neale 1990).

3   Russell's theory of descriptions: formal characterization

On Russell's account, descriptions are 'incomplete' symbols; they have 'no meaning in isolation', that is, they do not stand for things. In *Principia Mathematica* (1910–13), descriptions are represented by quasi-singular terms of the form '$(\iota x)(Fx)$', which can be read as 'the unique x which is F'. Superficially, the iota-operator is a variable-binding device for forming a term from a formula. A predicate symbol 'G' may be prefixed to a description '$(\iota x)(Fx)$' to form a formula 'G $(\iota x)(Fx)$', which can be expanded in accordance with a suitable 'contextual definition'. (To define an expression ζ contextually is to provide a procedure for converting any sentence containing occurrences of ζ into an equivalent sentence that is ζ-free.)

   The analysis in (3) above does not constitute a final contextual definition of 'G $(\iota x)(Fx)$' because of the possibility of scope ambiguity where a formula containing a description is itself a constituent of a larger formula (see SCOPE). Scope ambiguity is conveniently illustrated with descriptions in the context of negation. For a genuine singular term α, there is no difference between wide and narrow scope negation: α is not-F just in case it is not the case that α is F. For a description, however, there is a formal ambiguity. Let 'Kx' represent 'x is a king of France' and 'Wx' represent 'x is wise'. Then the formula '$\neg W$ $(\iota x)(Kx)$' ('The king of France is not wise') is ambiguous between (9) and (10):

(9) $(\exists x)((\forall y)(Ky \leftrightarrow y = x)\ \&\ \neg Wx)$

(10) $\neg(\exists x)((\forall y)(Ky \leftrightarrow y = x)\ \&\ Wx)$.

These are not equivalent: only (10) can be true when there is no king of France. In *Principia Mathematica*, the scope of a description is specified by appending a copy of it within square brackets to the front of the formula that constitutes its scope.

Thus (9) and (10) are represented as (11) and (12) respectively:

(11) $[(\iota x)(Kx)]\neg\{W(\iota x)(Kx)\}$

(12) $\neg\{[(\iota x)(Kx)]W(\iota x)(Kx)\}$.

In (11) the description has what Russell calls a 'primary occurrence' by virtue of having scope over the negation; in (12) the description has a 'secondary occurrence' by virtue of lying within the scope of the negation. Where a description has smallest possible scope, it is conventional to omit the scope marker; thus (12) can be reduced to '$\neg W(\iota x)(Kx)$'.

   With the matter of scope behind us, the theory of descriptions can be stated exactly:

$$[(\iota x)(\phi x)]G(\iota x)(\phi x) =_{df} (\exists x)((\forall y)(\phi y \leftrightarrow y = x) \& Gx),$$

where φ is a formula. On Russell's account, there is no possibility of a genuine referring expression failing to refer, so no predicate letter in the language of *Principia Mathematica* stands for 'exists'. Russell introduces a symbol 'E!' ('E shriek') that may be combined with a description to create a well-formed formula. Thus

$$E!(\iota x)(\phi x) =_{df} (\exists x)(\forall y)(\phi y \leftrightarrow y = x).$$

'E!' allows a treatment of negative existentials. (According to Russell, an utterance of 'The king of France does not exist' made today would be true precisely because there is no king of France.) Successive applications will allow any well-formed formula containing a definite description to be replaced by an equivalent formula that is description-free.

   It is often objected that Russell's theory, which substitutes complex quantificational structure for 'the', is unfaithful to surface syntax. The objection is engendered by an insufficiently keen appreciation of the distinction between a theory and its formal implementation. The extent of the mismatch between 'The king is wise' and its analysis

(13) $(\exists x)((\forall y)(\text{king } y \leftrightarrow y = x) \& \text{wise } x)$

has nothing to do with descriptions *per se*. In order to characterize the logical forms of even 'some philosophers are wise' and 'every philosopher is wise' in the predicate calculus we have to use formulas containing sentence connectives, no counterparts of which occur in the surface forms of the sentences:

(14) $(\exists x)(\text{philosopher } x\ \&\ \text{wise } x)$

(15) $(\forall x)(\text{philosopher } x \rightarrow \text{wise } x)$.

And when we formalize sentences such as 'Just two philosophers are wise', we find much more complexity than there is in surface syntax:

(16) $(\exists x)(\exists y)$[philosopher x & philosopher y & wise x & wise y & $(\forall z)$((philosopher z & wise z) $\rightarrow z = x \lor z = y$)].

The supposed problem about descriptions, then, is in fact a symptom of a larger problem involving the application of first-order logic to sentences of ordinary language.

Work on 'generalized' quantification provides a solution to the larger problem (as well as treatments of quantifiers such as 'most' that cannot be handled within first-order logic; see QUANTIFIERS, GENERALIZED). Natural language quantification is normally restricted: we talk about all philosophers or most poets, not about all or most entities. A simple modification of the predicate calculus yields a language – call it 'RQ' – that captures this fact while retaining the precision of regular first-order logic. In RQ, a determiner such as 'some', 'every' or 'no' combines with a formula to create a restricted quantifier such as '[every x: philosopher x]'. And such a quantifier may combine with a formula to form a formula:

(17) [every x: philosopher x] (wise x).

The viability of such a language shows that the language of *Principia Mathematica* is not essential to the theory of descriptions. Since the word 'the' is a one-place quantificational determiner (as are 'some', 'every', 'no' and so on), RQ can treat 'the' as combining with a formula 'king x' to form a restricted quantifier '[the x: king x]'. The sentence 'The king is wise' will then be represented as

(18) [the x: king x] (wise x).

Different scope possibilities are easily captured. For instance, 'The king is not wise' is ambiguous between (19) and (20):

(19) [the x: king x] $\neg$ (wise x)

(20) $\neg$ [the x: king x](wise x).

Using a formal language in which descriptions are treated as restricted quantifiers does not mean abandoning Russell's view that descriptions are 'incomplete symbols' that 'disappear on analysis'. Rather, treating descriptions as restricted quantifiers results in an explanation of where his theory of descriptions fits into a systematic account of natural language quantification, a theory in which 'every', 'some', 'most', 'a', 'the' and so on are members of a unified syntactic and semantic category.

4 Strawson's theory and criticisms of Russell

As part of a broad critique of the idea that the semantics of formal languages can be used to analyse the meanings of statements of natural language, P.F. STRAWSON argued against Russell's theory of descriptions on the grounds that (1) it fails to recognize that referring is something done by speakers and not expressions, (2) it fails to do justice to the way speakers ordinarily use sentences containing descriptions to make statements (speakers use descriptions to refer, not to quantify) and (3) it rides roughshod over important distinctions, such as the distinction between the meaning of a sentence σ and the statement made by a particular use of σ.

Using as an example 'The present king of France is wise', Strawson argues that Russell's theory is thwarted because the same sentence can be used to say something true on one occasion and something false on another. It is certainly true that Russell paid little attention to the distinction between the linguistic meaning of a sentence type and the proposition expressed by a particular dated utterance of that sentence type; but it was the latter that actually concerned him, and Strawson could get no mileage out of Russell's inattention to the distinction. The fact that a description (or any other quantified noun phrase) may contain an indexical component ('the *present* king of France', 'every man *here*', and so on) illustrates that some descriptions are subject to both the theory of descriptions and a theory of indexicality (see DEMONSTRATIVES AND INDEXICALS). Thus contextual features play a role in fixing the proposition expressed. And this can be true also if the overt indexical element is missing, as in 'The king of France is wise'.

This appreciation of contextual factors forms the basis of the Russellian response to a second Strawsonian objection. According to this, someone who uses a description ⌜the F⌝ typically intends to refer to some object or other and say something about it; there is no question of claiming that some object uniquely satisfies F. Someone who says 'The table is covered with books', for instance, does not express a proposition that entails the existence of exactly one table. But, Strawson claimed, it is a part of the meaning of ⌜the F⌝ that such an expression is used correctly only if there is an F. If this condition is not satisfied – if the 'presupposition' that there is an F is false – a use of ⌜The F is G⌝ cannot be considered to express a proposition that is either true or false. The Russellian response to Strawson is that descriptions such as 'the table' are often understood as elliptical uses of fuller descriptions such as 'the table over there', 'the table in front of me' and so on; or else they are evaluated with respect to a restricted domain of discourse. Again the phenomenon is not confined to descriptions, but is found with quantified noun phrases more generally.

Strawson's original 1950 statement of his own theory contains an interesting ambiguity. He can be understood as claiming either that no proposition is expressed, or that a proposition which is neither true nor false is expressed, when someone uses a sentence containing an empty description. A second ambiguity comes with the notion of 'presupposition'. This can be viewed as an epistemological or pragmatic relation between a person and a statement, or as a logical relation between two statements (see PRESUPPOSITION). An epistemological or pragmatic notion of presupposition appears to have no bearing on the semantic issues Strawson wanted to address when he challenged Russell.

The Strawsonian position faces some serious obstacles. If someone were to utter (21) below right now, they would unquestionably say something false.

(21) The king of France shot my cat last night.

But on Strawson's account, the speaker will have expressed no proposition because the presupposition that there is a unique king of France is false. Descriptions occurring in the context of attitude verbs create a similar problem. For example, someone might utter a true statement using (22):

(22) Ponce de León thought the fountain of youth was in Florida,

so the presence of an empty description does not always result in a failed speech act. This is something Strawson came to concede. In order to reduce the number of incorrect predictions made by his earlier theory, he suggested that the presence of an empty description sometimes renders the proposition expressed false and at other times prevents a proposition from being expressed at all (sometimes ⌜The F is G⌝ entails the existence of a unique F, and at other times it (only) *presupposes* it).

5 Ambiguity theories

Consideration of the behaviour of descriptions in non-extensional contexts and the possibility of misdescribing an individual as the F, but successfully communicating something about that individual, has led some philosophers (for example, Donnellan 1966) to suggest that descriptions are sometimes quantificational, at other times referential. When ⌜the F⌝ is used in the Russellian way, the proposition expressed is general (object-independent); when it is used referentially the proposition expressed is singular (object-dependent). Donnellan

considers examples such as the following: (1) A detective discovers Smith's mutilated body but has no idea who killed him. Looking at the body, he exclaims, 'The murderer is insane'. (2) Jones is on trial for Smith's murder; I am convinced of his guilt; hearing Jones ranting in court, I say, 'The murderer is insane'. On Donnellan's account, in case (1) the description is being used attributively; in case (2) it is being used referentially. Cases such as (2), it is argued, cannot be treated in accordance with Russell's theory. Following Grice, however, many have argued (1) that so-called referential uses of descriptions can usually be accommodated within Russell's theory by invoking a distinction between the proposition expressed by (an utterance of) a sentence on a given occasion and the proposition the speaker primarily intends to communicate on that occasion; (2) that the phenomenon of referential usage is not specific to definite descriptions, but arises with quantified noun phrases quite generally; (3) that the referential/attributive distinction is neither exclusive nor exhaustive; and (4) that no such distinction can do the work of Russell's notion of the scope of a description. It would seem, then, that something very close to Russell's theory will probably form a component of any finally acceptable theory.

See also: REFERENCE

References and further reading

Neale, S. (1990) *Descriptions*, Cambridge, MA: MIT Press. (Discussion of various views in more detail; extensive bibliography.)

Strawson, P.F. (1972) *Subject and Predicate in Logic and Grammar*, London: Methuen. (Full statement of Strawson's views.)

STEPHEN NEALE

DESIGN, ARGUMENT FROM
See GOD, ARGUMENTS FOR THE EXISTENCE OF

DESIGNATORS
See PROPER NAMES

DESIRE

If an agent is to be moved to action, then two requirements have to be fulfilled: first, the agent must possess beliefs about the way things actually are, about the actions possible given the way things are, and about the likely effects of those actions on how things are; and, second, the agent must have or form desires to change the way things are by resorting to this or that course of action. The beliefs tell the agent about how things are and about how they can be altered; the desires attract the agent to how things are not but can be made to be.

This rough sketch of beliefs and desires is widely endorsed in contemporary philosophy; it derives in many ways from the seminal work of the eighteenth-century Scottish philosopher David Hume. The striking thing about it, from the point of view of desire, is that it characterizes desire by the job desire does in collaborating with belief and thereby generating action: it characterizes desire by function, not by the presence of any particular feeling. The account raises a host of questions. Is desire an entirely different sort of state from belief, for example, and from belief-related states like habits of inference? Does desire have to answer to the considerations of evidence and truth that are relevant to belief and inference? How does desire relate to preference and choice? And how does desire relate to the values that we ascribe to different courses of action and that influence us in what we do?

See also: ACTION; INTENTION; RATIONALITY, PRACTICAL

PHILIP PETTIT

DETERMINISM AND INDETERMINISM

Over the centuries, the doctrine of determinism has been understood, and assessed, in different ways. Since the seventeenth century, it has been commonly understood as the doctrine that every event has a cause; or as the predictability, in principle, of the entire future. To assess the truth of determinism, so understood, philosophers have often looked to physical science; they have assumed that their current best physical theory is their best guide to the truth of determinism. It seems that most have believed that classical physics, especially Newton's physics, is deterministic. And in this century, most have believed that quantum theory is indeterministic. Since quantum theory has superseded classical physics, philosophers have typically come to the tentative conclusion that determinism is false.

In fact, these impressions are badly misleading. The above formulations of determinism are unsatisfactory. Once we use a better formulation, we see that there is a large gap between the determinism of a given physical theory, and the bolder, vague idea that motivated the traditional formulations: the idea that the world in itself is deterministic. Admittedly, one can make sense of this idea by adopting a sufficiently bold metaphysics; but it cannot be made sense of just by considering determinism for physical theories.

As regards physical theories, the traditional impression is again misleading. Which theories are deterministic turns out to be a subtle and complicated matter, with many open questions. But broadly speaking, it turns out that much of classical physics, even much of Newton's physics, is indeterministic. Furthermore, the alleged indeterminism of quantum theory is very controversial: it enters, if at all, only in quantum theory's account of measurement processes, an account which remains the most controversial part of the theory.

JEREMY BUTTERFIELD

DEVLIN, LORD
See LAW AND MORALITY

DEWEY, JOHN (1859–1952)

The philosophy of John Dewey is original and comprehensive. His extensive writings contend systematically with problems in metaphysics, epistemology, logic, aesthetics, ethics, social and political philosophy, philosophy and education, and philosophical anthropology. Although his work is widely read, it is not widely understood.

Dewey had a distinctive conception of philosophy, and the key to understanding and benefiting from his work is to keep this conception in mind. A worthwhile philosophy, he urged, must be practical. Philosophic inquiry, that is, ought to take its point of departure from the aspirations and problems characteristic of the various sorts of human activity, and an effective philosophy would develop ideas responsive to those conditions. Any system of ideas that has the effect of making common experience less intelligible than we find it to be is on that account a failure. Dewey's theory of inquiry, for example, does not entertain a conception of knowledge that makes it problematic whether we can know anything at all. Inasmuch as scientists have made extraordinary advances in knowledge, it behoves the philosopher to find out exactly what scientists do, rather than to question whether they do anything of real consequence.

Moral philosophy, likewise, should not address the consternations of philosophers as such, but the characteristic urgencies and aspirations of common life; and it should attempt to identify the resources and limitations of human nature and the environment with which it interacts. Human beings might then contend effectively with the typical perplexities and promises of mortal existence. To this end, Dewey formulated an exceptionally innovative and far-reaching philosophy of morality and democracy.

The subject matter of philosophy is not philosophy, Dewey liked to say, but 'problems of men'. All too often, he found, the theories of philosophers made the primary subject matter more obscure rather than less so. The tendency of thinkers is to become bewitched by inherited philosophic

195

puzzles, when the persistence of the puzzle is a consequence of failing to consider the assumptions that created it. Dewey was gifted in discerning and discarding the philosophic premises that create needless mysteries. Rather than fret, for instance, about the question of how immaterial mental substance can possibly interact with material substance, he went to the root of the problem by challenging the notion of substance itself.

Indeed, Dewey's dissatisfaction with the so-called classic tradition in philosophy, stemming at least from Plato if not from Parmenides, led him to reconstruct the entire inheritance of the Western tradition in philosophy. The result is one of the most seminal and fruitful philosophies of the twentieth century.

JAMES GOUINLOCK

DHARMA
See DUTY AND VIRTUE, INDIAN CONCEPTIONS OF

DIALECTICAL MATERIALISM

Dialectical materialism is the official name given to Marxist-Leninist philosophy by its proponents in the Soviet Union and their affiliates elsewhere. The term, never used by either Karl Marx or Friedrich Engels, was the invention of the Russian Marxist Georgii Plekhanov, who first used it in 1891. Engels, however, favourably contrasted 'materialist dialectics' with the 'idealist dialectics' of Hegel and the German idealist tradition, and the 'dialectical' outlook of Marxism with the 'mechanistic' or 'metaphysical' standpoint of other nineteenth-century materialists.

Dialectical materialism proclaims allegiance to the methods of empirical science and opposition to all forms of scepticism which deny that science can know the nature of reality. Dialectical materialists reject religious belief generally, denying the existence of non-material or supernatural entities (such as God or an immortal human soul). Unlike other forms of materialism, however, dialectical materialists maintain that the fundamental laws governing both matter and mind are *dialectical* in the sense in which that term is used in the philosophy of G.W.F. Hegel.

Although dialectical materialism is supposed to constitute the philosophical underpinnings of Marxism, Marx's only major contribution to it was his materialist conception of history. The more fundamental philosophical views of dialectical materialism have their main source in the writings of Engels, especially *Anti-Dühring* (1878), *Dialectics of Nature* (1875–82) and *Ludwig Feuerbach and the End of Classical German Philosophy* (1886). To this last work Engels appended the eleven 'Theses on Feuerbach' written by Marx in 1845, which

contrasted the 'old' or 'contemplative' materialism with the practically oriented materialism which was to be the basis of the proletarian movement. Further developments of dialectical materialism are found in writings by V.I. Lenin and subsequent Soviet writers. Lenin's chief additions were his critique of 'empirio-criticism' (the empiricist phenomenalism of certain Russian followers of Ernst Mach, who argued that matter was to be reduced to sense data), and his conception of the 'partisanship' of all philosophical views.
See also: ENGELS, F.; MARX, K.; MATERIALISM; PLEKHANOV, G.V.

ALLEN W. WOOD

DIDEROT, DENIS (1713–84)

Chief editor of the great eighteenth-century *Encyclopédie* (1751–72), Diderot set out a philosophy of the arts and sciences which took the progress of civilization to be a measure of mankind's moral improvement. He did not regard that progress as having produced universal benefits, however, and perceived the Christian religion which had accompanied it as morally harmful to those who subscribed to it and even more dangerous to societies thus far untouched by it. Religious dogmas tended to pervert the organic development of human passions, and secular education which presumed that all minds were equally receptive to instruction threatened to thwart the natural evolution of human faculties in other ways.

Like Rousseau, Diderot subscribed to a philosophy of education which encouraged curiosity rather than promoted truth. He stressed the need for the adaptability of moral rules to the physiological characteristics of the individuals to whom they applied, pointing to a connection between human cultures and biology in a manner that would influence fresh outlooks upon the sciences of man at the end of the Age of Enlightenment.
See also: ENLIGHTENMENT, CONTINENTAL; MATERIALISM; NATURAL LAW

ROBERT WOKLER

DIGAMBARA JAINISM
See JAINA PHILOSOPHY

DILTHEY, WILHELM (1833–1911)

Wilhelm Dilthey saw his work as contributing to a 'Critique of Historical Reason' which would expand the scope of Kant's *Critique of Pure Reason* by examining the epistemological conditions of the human sciences as well as of the natural sciences. Both kinds of science take their departure from ordinary life and experience, but whereas the natural sciences seek to focus on the way things behave independently of human involvement, the human sciences take account of this very involvement. The natural sciences use external observation and measurement to construct an objective domain of nature that is abstracted from the fullness of lived experience. The human sciences (humanities and social sciences), by contrast, help to define what Dilthey calls the historical world. By making use of inner as well as outer experience, the human sciences preserve a more direct link with our original sense of life than do the natural sciences. Whereas the natural sciences seek explanations of nature, connecting the discrete representations of outer experience through hypothetical generalizations and causal laws, the human sciences aim at an understanding that articulates the fundamental structures of historical life given in lived experience. Finding lived experience to be inherently connected and meaningful, Dilthey opposed traditional atomistic and associationist psychologies and developed a descriptive psychology that has been recognized as anticipating phenomenology.

Dilthey first thought that this descriptive psychology could provide a neutral foundation for the other human sciences, but in his later hermeneutical writings he rejected the idea of a foundational discipline or method. Thus he ends by claiming that all the human sciences are interpretive and mutually dependent. Hermeneutically conceived, understanding is a process of interpreting the 'objectifications of life', the external expressions or manifestations of human thought and action. Interpersonal understanding is attained through these common objectifications and not, as is widely believed, through empathy. Moreover, to fully understand myself I must analyse the expressions of my life in the same way that I analyse the expressions of others.

Not every aspect of life can be captured within the respective limits of the natural and the human sciences. Dilthey's philosophy of life also leaves room for a kind of anthropological reflection whereby we attempt to do justice to the ultimate riddles of life and death. Such reflection receives its fullest expression in worldviews, which are overall perspectives on life encompassing the way we perceive and conceive the world, evaluate it aesthetically and respond to it in action. Dilthey discerned many typical worldviews in art and religion, but in Western philosophy he distinguished three recurrent types: the worldviews of naturalism, the idealism of freedom and objective idealism.

See also: Hegelianism; Hermeneutics; Historicism; History, philosophy of; Phenomenological movement

RUDOLF A. MAKKREEL

DIOGENES LAERTIUS (*c.* AD 300–50)

Diogenes Laertius is the author of a famous work entitled *Lives of the Philosophers* consisting of nearly one hundred accounts of individual philosophers. These contain mainly biographical information, but sometimes also include doctrinal summaries. The work is extremely valuable because it preserves much information on Greek philosophers from sources now lost.

DAVID T. RUNIA

DIOGENES OF SINOPE (412/403–324/321 BC)

Diogenes of Sinope was considered, along with Antisthenes, the founder of Cynicism. His nickname 'Cynic', literally 'doglike', reflects the highly unconventional lifestyle he lived and advocated. Radically re-evaluating mankind's relation to both nature and civilization, Diogenes redefined the individual's freedom and self-sufficiency, advocating a training (*askēsis*) for achieving both.

R. BRACHT BRANHAM

DISCOVERY, LOGIC OF

Bacon, Descartes, Newton and other makers of the Scientific Revolution claimed to have found and even used powerful logics or methods of discovery, step-by-step procedures for systematically generating new truths in mathematics and the natural sciences. Method of discovery was also the prime method of justification: generation by correct method was something akin to logical derivation and thus the strongest justification a claim could have. The 'logic' of these methods was deductive, inductive or both. By the mid-nineteenth century, logic of discovery was yielding to the more flexible and theory-tolerant method of hypothesis as the 'official' method of science. In the twentieth century, Karl Popper and most logical positivists completed the methodological reversal from generativism to consequentialism by setting their hypothetico-deductive method against logic of discovery. What is epistemologically important, they said, is not how new claims are generated but how they fare in empirical tests of their predictive consequences. They demoted discovery to the status of historical anecdote and psychological process. Since the late 1950s, however, there has been a revival of interest in methodology of discovery on two fronts – logical and historical. An earlier explosion of work in symbolic logic had led to automata theory, computers, and then artificial intelligence. Meanwhile, a maturing history of science was furnishing information on science as a process, on how historical actors and communities actually discovered or constructed their claims and practices. Now, in the 1980s and 1990s, liberal epistemologists once again admit discovery as a legitimate topic for philosophy of science. Yet attempts to both naturalize and to socialize inquiry pose new challenges to the possibility of logics of discovery. Its strong associations with 'the' method of science makes logic of discovery a target of postmodernist attack, but a more flexible construal is defensible.

See also: SCIENTIFIC METHOD

THOMAS NICKLES

DISCRIMINATION

A principle forbidding discrimination is widely used to criticize and prohibit actions and policies that disadvantage racial, ethnic and religious groups, women and homosexuals. Discriminatory actions often rely on unfavourable group stereotypes and the belief that members of certain groups are not worthy of equal treatment. A prohibition of discrimination applies to the distribution of important benefits such as education and jobs, and says that people are not to be awarded or denied such benefits on grounds of characteristics such as race, ethnicity, religion or gender. Attempts have been made to expand this principle to cover *institutional* discrimination. Discrimination is morally wrong because its premise that one group is less worthy than another is insulting to its victims, because it harms its victims by reducing their self-esteem and opportunities, and because it is unfair.

JAMES W. NICKEL

DODGSON, CHARLES LUTWIDGE (LEWIS CARROLL) (1832–98)

Dodgson, an Oxford teacher of mathematics, is best known under his pseudonym, Lewis Carroll. Although not an exceptional mathematician, his standing has risen somewhat in the light of recent research. He is also of note as a symbolic logician in the tradition of Boole and De Morgan, as a pioneer in the theory of voting, and as a gifted amateur photographer. His literary output, ranging from satirical pamphleteering, light verse and puzzle-making to an immense correspondence, is again largely amateur in nature, and would hardly have survived without the worldwide success of his three master-works, *Alice's Adventures in Wonderland* (1865), *Through the Looking-Glass* (1871) and *The Hunting of the Snark* (1876). Together with portions of his two-volume fairy-novel *Sylvie and Bruno* (1889/93) they are the only writings, ostensibly for

children, to have attracted or deserved the notice of philosophers.

PETER HEATH

DŌGEN (1200–53)

Dōgen Kigen, the founder of Japanese Sōtō Zen Buddhism, is most noted for his argument that meditation is the expression or enactment of enlightenment, not the means to attaining it. Dōgen believed that even a novice might achieve insight, however fleeting. The difficulty, however, is in expressing that insight in one's daily acts, both linguistic and non-linguistic. In developing his position, Dōgen articulated a phenomenology of incarnate consciousness and a sophisticated analysis of meaning. His theories of mind–body unity, contextualized meaning, temporality and theory–praxis influenced many prominent modern Japanese philosophers such as Watsuji Tetsurō, Tanabe Hajime and Nishitani Keiji.

See also: BUDDHIST PHILOSOPHY, JAPANESE; JAPANESE PHILOSOPHY; MEANING AND TRUTH; TRUTH, DEFLATIONARY THEORIES OF

THOMAS P. KASULIS

DOSTOEVSKII, FËDOR MIKHAILOVICH (1821–81)

Dostoevskii, regarded as one of the world's greatest novelists, is especially well known for his mastery of philosophical or ideological fiction. In his works, characters espouse intriguing ideas about theology, morality and psychology. Plots are shaped by conflicts of ideas and by the interaction of theories with the psychology of the people who espouse them. Indeed, Dostoevskii is usually considered one of the greatest psychologists in the history of Western thought, not only because of the accounts of the mind his characters and narrators elucidate in detail, but also because of the peculiar behaviour betraying the depths of their souls. Dostoevskii is particularly well known for his description of the irrational in its many modes.

Deeply engaged with the political and social problems of his day, Dostoevskii brought his understanding of individual and social psychology to bear on contemporary issues and gave them a lasting relevance. His predictions about the likely consequences of influential ideas, such as communism and the social theory of crime, have proven astonishingly accurate; he has often been regarded as something of a prophet of the twentieth century.

His reputation rests primarily on four long philosophical novels – *Prestuplenie i nakazanie* (*Crime and Punishment*) (1866), *Idiot* (*The Idiot*) (1868–9), *Besy* (*The Possessed*, also known as *The*

Devils) (1871–2) and *Brat'ia Karamazovy* (*The Brothers Karamazov*) (1879–80) – and on one novella, *Zapiski iz podpol'ia* (*Notes From Underground*) (1864). In his day, Dostoevskii was as famous for his journalistic writing as for his fiction, and a few of his articles have remained classics, including 'Mr. D–bov and the Question of Art' (1861) – a critique of utilitarian aesthetics – and 'Environment' (1873).

Dostoevskii's works have had major influence on Western and Russian philosophy. In Russia, his novels inspired numerous religious thinkers, including Sergei Bulgakov and Nikolai Berdiaev; existentialists, such as Lev Shestov; and literary and ethical theorists, most notably Mikhail Bakhtin. In the West, his influence has also been great. Here, too, his writings are repeatedly cited (along with Kierkegaard's) as founding works of existentialism. Perhaps because of a misreading, they influenced Freud and Freudianism. Directly and through the medium of Bakhtin, his ideas have played a role in the rethinking of mind and language. And his rejection of utopianism and socialism has been repeatedly cited in twentieth-century political debates and theories.

Dostoevskii's influence has been diverse and at times contradictory, in part because of the different genres in which his ideas are expressed. Not only the overall meanings of his novels but also the views of his characters, including those he meant to refute, have been attributed to him. Moreover, his essays sometimes express ideas at variance with his novels. Most recently, philosophical significance has been discovered not only in the content but also in the very form of his novels. Their odd plot structure has been shown to have implications for an understanding of authorship, responsibility and time.
See also: BAKHTIN, M.M.; BERDIAEV, N.A.; EXISTENTIALISM

GARY SAUL MORSON

DOUBLE EFFECT, PRINCIPLE OF

'Double effect' refers to the good and bad effects which may foreseeably follow from one and the same act. The principle of double effect originates in Aquinas' ethics, and is supposed to guide decision about acts with double effect where the bad effect is something that must not be intended, such as the death of an innocent person. The principle permits such acts only if the bad effect is unintended, not disproportionate to the intended good effect, and unavoidable if the good effect is to be achieved. The principle has wide relevance in the moral evaluation of acts which have foreseen double effects. Controversy arises over the identification of the agent's intention in difficult cases, and over the use of the principle to resolve issues such as abortion, euthanasia, the use of pain-relieving drugs which hasten death, self-defence, and the killing of certain sorts of non-combatants in war.
See also: INTENTION; RESPONSIBILITY

SUZANNE UNIACKE

DOUBT

Doubt is often defined as a state of indecision or hesitancy with respect to accepting or rejecting a given proposition. Thus, doubt is opposed to belief. But doubt is also contrasted with certainty. Since it seems intelligible to say that there are many things we believe without being completely certain about them, it appears that we may not have a unitary concept of doubt.

Although doubt is often associated in philosophy with scepticism, historically the relation between the two is complex. Moreover, some philosophers deny that sceptical arguments have any essential connection with inducing doubts.

Sceptical doubts, as philosophers understand them, differ from ordinary doubts in their depth and generality. We all have doubts about some things. But the philosophical sceptic wonders whether we ever have the slightest reason to believe one thing rather than another. However, the reasonableness of such doubts – and even their intelligibility – remains controversial. The various attitudes philosophers adopt with respect to the status of sceptical doubts characterize the main approaches to epistemological theory.
See also: FALLIBILISM; SCEPTICISM

MICHAEL WILLIAMS

DREAMING

We naturally think of dreams as experiences very like perceptions or imaginings, except that they occur during sleep. In prescientific thought the interpretation of dreams played a role in divining the future, and it plays a role, albeit a much more limited one, in modern psychology (although in Freudian psychoanalysis dreams have been considered to give access to some of the hidden operations of the mind). Dreaming is puzzling in many respects. We do not have ready-to-hand criteria for checking dream reports, not even our own; conscious or lucid dreams are the exception rather than the rule; and there is the puzzle of how we distinguish waking experience from a very lifelike dream. Furthermore, the nature of dreams is doubtful – some have even denied that to dream is to undergo an experience during sleep: dreams on this view are to be understood in terms of what happens when we 'recall' them.

See also: SCEPTICISM

ROBERTO CASATI

DUALISM

Introduction

Dualism is the view that mental phenomena are, in some respect, nonphysical. The best-known version is that of Descartes, and holds that the mind is a nonphysical substance. Descartes argued that, because minds have no spatial properties and physical reality is essentially extended in space, minds are wholly nonphysical. Every human being is accordingly a composite of two objects: a physical body, and a nonphysical object that is that human being's mind. On a weaker version of dualism, which contemporary thinkers find more acceptable, human beings are physical substances but have mental properties, and those properties are not physical. This view is known as property dualism, or the dual-aspect theory.

Several considerations appear to support dualism. Mental phenomena are strikingly different from all others, and the idea that they are nonphysical may explain just how they are distinctive. Moreover, physical reality conforms to laws formulated in strictly mathematical terms. But, because mental phenomena such as thinking, desiring and sensing seem intractable to being described in mathematical terms, it is tempting to conclude that these phenomena are not physical. In addition, many mental states are conscious states – states that we are aware of in a way that seems to be wholly unmediated. And many would argue that, whatever the nature of mental phenomena that are not conscious, consciousness cannot be physical.

There are also, however, reasons to resist dualism. People, and other creatures with mental endowments, presumably exist wholly within the natural order, and it is generally held that all natural phenomena are built up from basic physical constituents. Dualism, however, represents the mind as uniquely standing outside this unified physical picture. There is also a difficulty about causal relations between mind and body. Mental events often cause bodily events, as when a desire causes an action, and bodily events often cause mental events, for example in perceiving. But the causal interactions into which physical events enter are governed by laws that connect physical events. So if the mental is not physical, it would be hard to understand how mental events can interact causally with bodily events. For these reasons and others, dualism is, despite various reasons advanced in its support, a theoretically uncomfortable position.

> 1 Mental and physical
> 2 Dualism and physical science
> 3 Qualitative states
> 4 Objections to dualism
> 5 Dualism and consciousness
> 6 Dualism and the concept of mind

1 Mental and physical

Underlying dualism is the strong intuition that the ordinary functioning of people is of two fundamentally different kinds. Much of what happens to us is thoroughly physical, on a par with the properties and behaviour of things such as stones, houses and planets. But we also engage in thinking, we desire and perceive things, and we feel emotions such as joy and anger. In these ways we seem to be dramatically different from such purely physical objects as stones and planets. It is natural to want to epitomize these observations by positing the idea that all concrete reality is either mental or physical, and nothing is both. Not only do the mental and the physical exhaust everything; they are also mutually exclusive. This conclusion points to some form of dualism. Either every person consists of a nonphysical substance operating in tandem with a purely physical body, or people at least have certain states or properties that are not physical.

It is worth stressing that dualism requires the mental and the physical to be mutually exclusive. If they were not, mental substances might also be physical, and mental states such as thoughts and sensations might be not just mental, but also physical as well. Moreover, the common-sense contrast between mental and physical does not by itself imply that mental phenomena lie outside the physical realm. We often contrast a special range of phenomena with the physical, even though the phenomena under consideration are strictly speaking physical; consider the contrast in computer talk between physical and logical disk drives. Mental phenomena are unlike any others, but highly distinctive phenomena are not, just on that account, nonphysical.

Still, there are reasons to think that mental and physical are indeed disjoint categories. For one thing, it is held that if they were not disjoint we could not capture what it is that is distinctive about mind. If people were just physical substances, and their mental states just special sorts of physical states, we would not be able to explain the striking difference between people and paradigmatically physical objects such as stones and houses. Some have gone so far as to urge that what is distinctive about being mental is, at bottom, simply that it is nonphysical.

But this argument is open to challenge, since we can explain the contrast between stones and people without supposing that mental and physical are mutually exclusive categories. Consider a parallel case. When we focus on living things, it is natural to contrast biological phenomena with such physical objects as stones and stars. But that does not lead us to conclude that the biological and the physical are mutually exclusive categories, and that living things are not purely physical. Rather, living organisms are physical objects, though of a very special sort, and we need not posit anything nonphysical to characterize what is special about them (see VITALISM).

Dualism implies that things are different in the case of the mind; that is, it implies that to capture what is distinctive about mental functioning we must posit substances or properties that are not physical. If, on the other hand, we can characterize the mind without positing anything nonphysical, dualism is wrong. The hypothesis that this is possible is mind–body materialism, and it has been championed especially forcefully in a version called the identity theory of mind (see MIND, IDENTITY THEORY OF).

Can such a characterization be given? According to Descartes, it is essential to everything physical that it has spatial extension, and being spatially extended implies having parts. So we can conceive of any physical object as being divided into parts; those parts would themselves be extended, and hence physical objects. But Descartes held that the same is not true about minds. Minds, he claimed, are not mere collections of mental states, as the bundle theory maintains (see MIND, BUNDLE THEORY OF); rather, minds are essentially unified. So we cannot even conceive of a mind's being divided into parts. A satisfactory characterization of the mental, therefore, implies that minds are nonphysical (see DESCARTES, R. §8).

The bundle theory put to one side, however, there is reason to question this argument. Surgically sectioning the neural pathways that connect the two cerebral hemispheres results in striking experimental behaviour, which some researchers believe indicates the presence after surgery of two distinct conscious minds. Also, brain lesions sometimes result in dissociation of mental functions, which also suggests that a normally unified mind may come to be divided. Such results cast doubt on traditional ideas about mental unity, and the very possibility of these interpretations undermines Descartes' claim that we

cannot even conceive of a mind's being divided into parts. To sustain dualism, therefore, we would need some other reason to hold that a satisfactory characterization of mind must proceed in non-physical terms.

According to Descartes' well-known *cogito*, the statement 'I am, I exist' is true whenever I assert it or mentally conceive it, and the 'I' whose existence I thereby establish is my mind, not my body. But Descartes explicitly recognizes that these considerations do not constitute an argument for dualism. Rather, as he saw, they establish at best only a conceptual difference between mind and body, and not the 'Real Distinction' for which he argues independently by appeal to divisibility.

2 Dualism and physical science

To show that the mind is nonphysical, we need to know not only what being mental amounts to, but also what it is to be physical. Descartes relied on the alleged indivisibility of mind, and on a conception of the physical as divisible. That conception of physical reality, in turn, rested on Descartes' conviction that the essential properties of physical reality are all geometrical properties.

But there is another conception of physical reality that seems to support dualism. Scientific developments over the last four centuries present a picture in which the laws governing physical reality are invariably formulated in strict mathematical terms. As Galileo put it in *The Assayer*, the book of nature is 'written in the language of mathematics'.

This idea captures the mathematical character of the physical in terms that are more general than Descartes' claim that the essential properties of physical reality are all geometrical. So it allows for a less constrained argument for dualism, independently of particular claims about what is essential to the mind. Whatever the nature of thinking, sensing, desiring and feeling, one might well deny that there could be strictly mathematical laws that govern such states. On this conception of the physical, then, mental states would not be physical.

The argument as just formulated supports property dualism, according to which no mental states or properties are physical. But we can adjust the argument to support substance dualism as well. If mental substances exist, their behaviour would presumably not be governed by mathematically formulable laws; so such substances would not be physical. The argument is therefore more flexible than Descartes' appeal to indivisibility, which adapts less readily to the case of property dualism. This is important, since contemporary concern about dualism is almost always about dualism of properties, not substances. Partly that is because of doubts about whether the traditional notion of a substance is useful. But it is also partly because of a tendency to think of people's minds not as any kind of substance at all but rather as the totality of their mental functioning, including their dispositions and abilities to function mentally.

There are various reasons to think that mental states cannot be the subjects of mathematically formulable laws. We describe our thoughts and desires in terms of the objects they are about. The property of being about something, and its related properties, are called intentional properties (see INTENTIONALITY). Mental states can be about things that do not exist; we all sometimes think about and desire nonexistent things. So thinking and desiring are somewhat like relations one can bear to nonexistent objects. But such ostensible relations, which can hold even to nonexistent things, cannot figure in mathematical descriptions of things.

There are other sorts of mental states that aren't strictly speaking about anything; examples are bodily sensations such as pains and tickles, and perceptual states such as visual experiences. The distinguishing properties of these states are not their intentional properties, but rather certain qualitative properties – for example, the redness of a visual experience or the dull, throbbing character of a pain (see QUALIA). Again, it seems unlikely that these properties could figure in mathematically formulable laws.

These intentional and qualitative properties are, arguably, the distinguishing properties of mental states – the properties in terms of which we identify those states and distinguish them from everything else. We cannot argue that mental states are physical simply by denying that they have these properties.

But our intuitive sense that these properties resist mathematical description may not be reliable. Compare our intuitions about ordinary macroscopic objects. We ordinarily take such objects to have various common-sense properties, such as colour, taste and smell. And we conceive of these common-sense physical properties in qualitative terms that seem resistant to mathematical description. Yet we can understand these properties mathematically: for example, we can construe the colours of bodies in terms of physical reflectance (see COLOUR, THEORIES OF). Perhaps, then, we can explain the intentional and qualitative properties of mental states in ways that allow for mathematical description of those properties.

The general outline such explanations would have, moreover, is clear enough. Some have argued, for example, that a thought's being about something is a matter of its having a certain content (see PROPOSITIONAL ATTITUDES), and that we can explain content, in turn, in a scientifically satisfactory way. And there is much about qualitative mental states that succumbs to quantitative treatment, as any standard textbook on perception reveals. So a successful theory of mental properties may show how to render those properties scientifically acceptable. The intuition that mental properties resist scientific treatment may therefore reflect only the current state of theorizing, just as many common-sense physical properties seemed recalcitrant to mathematical treatment before suitable scientific advances had occurred.

3 Qualitative states

Nonetheless, many would insist that, whatever science may show, qualitative properties cannot be physical. All physical objects are composed of colourless microparticles; so it is tempting to hold that no physical objects are coloured. We do, however, describe visual sensations in colour terms, for example as red or green sensations. And if nothing physical is coloured but visual sensations are, those sensations cannot be physical. Indeed, if no physical objects are coloured, colour is arguably not a physical property.

But when we describe a physical object as red, for example, this colour is a distinct property from that which we sometimes attribute to visual sensations. Physical colour is a property of a certain kind of object, namely, physical objects. Visual sensations, however, are not objects at all; they are states of people and other sentient creatures. Since the properties objects have are distinct from those of states, the colour of visual sensations is a different property from any property physical objects might have. Denying colour of physical objects does not show, therefore, that to have colour properties visual sensations must be nonphysical.

It is sometimes argued that, unless we construe sensations as objects as opposed to states, we will not be able to distinguish among the various sensations we have at any moment. And sensations are plainly not physical objects; so if they are objects of any sort, they must be nonphysical objects. But it is likely that whatever distinctions we can draw among sensations construed as objects can be preserved if we construe them as states instead.

Since bodily and perceptual sensations are not objects of any kind, but rather states of sentient creatures, there is indeed a categorial difference between sensations and physical objects. But that categorial difference is only that between objects and their states, and so by itself is irrelevant to dualism.

4 Objections to dualism

Although the character of physics underlies one major argument for dualism, a specific principle of physics is sometimes thought to show that dualism is wrong. That principle states that in a closed physical system (that is, closed to other physical systems) the total energy remains constant. But if mental events are nonphysical, then, when mental events cause bodily events, physical motion occurs uncaused by anything physical. And this, it seems, would result in an increase of the total energy in the relevant closed physical system. Mental causation of bodily events would conflict with the principle of the conservation of energy.

No such problem arises, even if dualism is true, when bodily events cause mental events. When bodily events cause mental events, presumably they cause other physical events as well, which enables energy to be conserved. In part because this problem seems to arise only in one causal direction, some theorists have adopted a version of dualism known as epiphenomenalism, according to which mental events are nonphysical and are caused by bodily events, but are themselves causally inert (see EPIPHENOMENALISM). Epiphenomenalism thus avoids the difficulty about conservation of energy. An even more extreme variant of dualism, known as parallelism, also avoids this difficulty, by denying that any causal interaction between mental and bodily events occurs at all. To distinguish these variants from the standard view, on which causal interaction occurs in both directions, this view is sometimes called interactionism.

But the dualist need not adopt the unintuitive idea that mental events never cause bodily events. Conservation of energy dictates only that the energy in a closed physical system is constant, not also how that energy is distributed within the system. Since mental events could effect bodily changes by altering that distribution of energy, the conservation principle does not preclude minds from having bodily effects.

A second difficulty sometimes raised also has to do with the causal interaction between the physical and the nonphysical. We seem to understand well enough how physical events cause one another, but it is held that causal interaction between mind and body is simply unintelligible, and so cannot occur. We have, it is objected, no conception whatever of how nonphysical events could cause or be caused by physical events.

But we understand how things happen only relative to a theory that governs the relevant events and tells us how those phenomena fit with various others. Understanding does not require a scientific theory; we often rely on informal, common-sense folk theories. But some theory or other is needed. So physical causation seems intelligible only because we have theories that cover those cases. And because we have no theory that governs mind–body interactions, we have no way to understand how they could occur. The appearance of unintelligibility here shows not that such interactions cannot occur, but only that we have at present no useful theory that would cover them if they do occur. Moreover, even if we cannot develop such a theory, that need not be because mind–body interaction is impossible; it might instead be due only to some limitation on our ability to understand things.

A third objection pertains again to causal interaction. For nonphysical events to cause bodily events, those nonphysical events must intervene in the normal sequence of bodily causes and effects. And it is argued that this would result in a detectable time lag somewhere in that sequence of bodily events. Because there is no such lag, dualism is mistaken. But causal intervention need not result in any relevant time lag. Consider the effects of gravitational force, the propagation of which is undetectable on the time scale relevant for brain and other bodily events. All in all, standard objections to dualism seem to fare no better than the standard arguments used to establish its truth.

5 Dualism and consciousness

Descartes defined mental states as conscious states, that is as states of which we are immediately conscious. Few today would endorse this definition, since it is generally held that mental states can and do occur without being conscious (see UNCONSCIOUS MENTAL STATES). But Descartes' definition fits well with dualism, because mental states provide intuitive support for dualism only when they are conscious.

Consider Descartes' argument for dualism. He held that minds are such unqualified unities that we cannot even conceive of their being divided into parts. This claim is tempting only when we focus on conscious mental states. We represent our conscious states as all belonging to a single subject, and so as inseparable from one another. But not all mental states are conscious. So this unity of consciousness does not confer a similar unity on the mind generally.

Another example concerns bodily and perceptual sensations. Dualism strikes many as most plausible for these states, because their qualitative properties seem intuitively not to be physical. But this intuition concerns only those qualitative states which are conscious. Sensations do occur of which we are in no way conscious, for example in subliminal perception or peripheral vision. And although not conscious, these sensations belong to the same types as conscious sensations; we subliminally sense various standard colours, for example, and sounds of various types. Since we distinguish types of sensation by their qualitative properties, the non-conscious sensations that occur in subliminal perception must have the same distinguishing properties as conscious sensations have, namely qualitative properties. The only difference is that in these cases we are in no way conscious of being in states that have those properties.

But when sensations are not conscious, there is no reason to think they resist being described in terms appropriate for the physical sciences. And the same holds for mental states of whatever sort, when they are not conscious. Dualism is intuitively plausible only for conscious mental states.

Considerations raised in the previous section also help disarm this last argument. Our failure to understand how neural processes could have qualitative properties reflects only our lack of a suitable theory of how neural processes could have such properties; it does not show that they do not have those properties.

Consider a related argument. We have, it seems, no conception of how bodily states could have the qualitative properties in terms of which we characterize sensations. It seems simply unintelligible that neural occurrences, or any other physical events, could have the qualities exhibited by a conscious sensation of pain, or a conscious experience of seeing red. This has led some to argue that qualitative mental states cannot be physical. But, again, the argument has force only for conscious states. When qualitative states are not conscious, we have no intuitive problem understanding how their distinguishing properties could belong to physical states.

Consciousness is presupposed even in empirical arguments for dualism. Libet, for example, has experimentally isolated certain anomalies about the subjective timing of mental events, which he thinks suggest causal intervention by nonphysical factors. But these anomalies are detectable only when subjects report their mental states, and thus only when those states are conscious. In addition, a mental state's being conscious consists in a subject's being conscious of that state in a way that seems immediate. So anomalies about subjective timing may be due not to intervention by nonphysical causes, but to differences between when mental events occur and when subjects become conscious of them.

Evidently dualism derives no support from mental states that are not conscious. But then it is unclear why cases in which we are conscious of our mental states should make dualism more plausible.

One reason sometimes offered is the subjective differences among conscious experiences, which seem to resist treatment in physicalist terms. But these differences can very likely be explained by appeal to differences in the circumstances and perceptual apparatus of various sentient creatures. Once it is clear that nonconscious mental states lend no plausibility to dualism, it is unlikely that conscious states will either (see CONSCIOUSNESS).

6 Dualism and the concept of mind

Because dualism conflicts with the scientific consensus that at bottom everything is physical, it receives little endorsement today. But among those who reject dualism, there are some who nonetheless find compelling certain reasons for holding that mental phenomena are nonphysical. They deny, for example, that the distinguishing properties of thoughts and sensations can be construed so as to conform to the dictates of physicalist description, or they have some other reason to hold that mental phenomena are nonphysical. They combine a dualist conception of what mental states are with a rejection of dualism.

The only option for such theorists is to deny that anything mental exists. This denial, known as eliminative materialism, adopts a traditional, dualist concept of mind, but insists that this dualist conception does not apply to anything. Though certain nonmental, physical phenomena may enable us to explain and predict things we usually explain and predict by appeal to mental states, on this view nothing mental exists (see ELIMINATIVISM).

Because eliminativism relies on a dualist concept of mind, we can very likely avoid this extravagant result. As argued above, we need not construe mental states and their properties in ways that imply the dualist claim that mental phenomena are nonphysical. Accordingly, we can resist both dualism and the eliminativist alternative.

See also: MENTAL CAUSATION

References and further reading

Descartes, R. (1641) *Meditations on First Philosophy*, in *The Philosophical Writings of René Descartes*, trans. J. Cottingham, R. Stoothoff and D. Murdoch, Cambridge: Cambridge University Press, 1984, vol. 2, 1–62. (Classic statement and defence of dualism; influences all subsequent discussions.)

Lowe, E.J. *Subjects of Experience*, Cambridge and New York: Cambridge University Press (1996). Thoughtful defence of a naturalistic substance dualism.

Robinson, H. (ed.) (1993) *Objections to Physicalism*, Oxford: Oxford University Press. (Fine collection of articles defending dualism.)

DAVID M. ROSENTHAL

DUHEM, PIERRE MAURICE MARIE (1861–1916)

Duhem was a French Catholic physicist, historian of science and philosopher of science. Champion of a programme of generalized thermodynamics as a unifying framework for physical science, he was a pioneer in the history of medieval and Renaissance science, where he emphasized a continuity between medieval and early modern science. Duhem was also one of the most influential philosophers of science of his day, thanks to his opposition to mechanistic modes of explanation and his development of a holistic conception of scientific theories, according to which individual empirical propositions are not tested in isolation but only in conjunction with other theoretical claims and associated auxiliary hypotheses. Such a view of theory testing entails that there are no 'crucial experiments' deciding unambiguously for or against a given theory and that empirical evidence therefore underdetermines theory choice. Theory choice is thus partly a matter of convention. Duhem's conventionalism is similar in kind to that later advocated by Otto Neurath and by W.V. Quine.

See also: Crucial experiments; Logical positivism; Scientific method

DON HOWARD

DUHEM-QUINE THESIS

See Crucial experiments; Duhem, Pierre Maurice Marie; Quine, Willard Van Orman; Underdetermination

DUMMETT, MICHAEL ANTHONY EARDLEY (1925–)

For Michael Dummett, the core of philosophy lies in the theory of meaning. His exploration of meaning begins with the model proposed by Gottlob Frege, of whose work Dummett is a prime expositor. A central feature of that model is that the sense (content) of a sentence is given by a condition for its truth, displayed as deriving from its constituent structure. If sense so explicated is to explain linguistic practice, knowledge of these truth-conditions must be attributed to language users by identifying features of use in which it is manifested. Analysis of truth suggests we seek such manifestation in patterns of assertion. But scrutiny of those patterns shows that there is no distinction between use which manifests knowledge of classical truth-conditions, and use which manifests knowledge of a weaker kind of truth – for example, one which holds whenever we possess a potential warrant for a statement.

Such considerations motivate reconstruing sense as given by conditions for this weaker kind of truth. But rejigging Fregean semantics in line with such a conception is highly nontrivial. Mathematical intuitionism, properly construed, gives us models for doing so with mathematical language; Dummett's programme is to extend such work to everyday discourses. Since he further argues that realism consists in defending the classical semantics for a discourse, this programme amounts to probing the viability of antirealism about such things as the material world, other minds and past events.

See also: Intuitionist logic and antirealism; Knowledge, tacit; Many-valued logics, philosophical issues in; Meaning and verification

BARRY TAYLOR

DUNS SCOTUS, JOHN (c.1266–1308)

Duns Scotus was one of the most important thinkers of the entire scholastic period. Of Scottish origin, he was a member of the Franciscan order and undertook theological studies first at Oxford and later at Paris. He left behind a considerable body of work, much of which unfortunately was still undergoing revision at the time of his death. Notable among his works are questions on Aristotle's *Metaphysics*, at least three different commentaries on the *Sentences* of Peter Lombard (the required text for a degree in theology) and a lengthy set of university disputations, the quodlibetal questions. A notoriously difficult and highly original thinker, Scotus was referred to as 'the subtle doctor' because of his extremely nuanced and technical reasoning. On many important issues, Scotus developed his positions in critical reaction to the Parisian theologian Henry of Ghent, the most important thinker of the immediately preceding generation and a severe Augustinian critic of Aquinas.

Scotus made important and influential contributions in metaphysics, epistemology and ethics. In metaphysics, he was the first scholastic to hold that the concepts of being and the other transcendentals were univocal, not only in application to substance and accidents but even to God and creatures. In this, Scotus broke with the unanimous view based on Aristotle that being could not be predicated of both substance and accident, much less of, except by analogy, God and creature. Scotus argued in general that univocity was required to underwrite any natural knowledge of God from creatures or of substance from accidents. Given univocity, he concluded that the primary object of the created intellect was being, rejecting Aquinas' Aristotelian view that it was limited to the quiddity of the sense particular and Henry of Ghent's Augustinian view

205

that it was God. That is, Scotus argues that even the finite intellect of the creature is by its very nature open to knowing all being.

Scotus' proof of the existence of God is the most ambitious of the entire scholastic period. Prior efforts at demonstrating the existence of God showed little concern with connecting the eclectic body of inherited arguments. Scotus' proof stands apart as an attempt to integrate logically into a single demonstration the various lines of traditional argument, culminating in the existence of God as an actually infinite being. As a result, his demonstration is exceedingly complex, establishing within a sustained and protracted argument God as first efficient cause, as ultimate final cause and as most eminent being – the so-called triple primacy – the identity within a unique nature of these primacies, and finally the actual infinity of this primary nature. Only with this final result of infinity is Scotus prepared to claim he has fully demonstrated the existence of God. Notable features of the proof include Scotus' rejection of Aristotle's argument from *Physics* VIII (the favoured demonstration of Aquinas), the reduction of exemplar cause to a species of efficient cause, important clarifications about the causal relations at issue in arguments against infinite regress, an a priori proof constructed from the possibility of God similar to that proposed by Leibniz, and the rejection of the traditional argument that the infinity of God can be inferred from creation *ex nihilo*.

Scotus is a realist on the issue of universals and one of the main adversaries of Ockham's programme of nominalism. He endorsed Avicenna's theory of the common nature, according to which essences have an independence and priority to their existence as either universal in the mind or singular outside it. Intepreting Avicenna, Scotus argued that natures as common must have their own proper unity which is both real and less than the numerical unity of a singular; that is, natures are common prior to any act of the intellect and possess their own real, lesser unity. They are accordingly not of themselves singular, but require a principle of individuation. Rejecting the standard views that essences are individuated by either actual existence, quantity or matter, Scotus maintained that the principle of individuation is a further substantial difference added to the species. This 'individual difference' is the so-called *haecceitas* or 'thisness', a term used seldom by Scotus himself. The common nature and individual difference were said by Scotus to be really identical in the individual, but 'formally distinct'. The 'formal distinction,' developed by Scotus chiefly in connection with the Trinity and the divine attributes, is an integral part of his realism and was as such attacked by Ockham. It admits within one and the same thing a distinction between realities, formalities or entities antecedent to any act of the intellect to provide an objective foundation for our concepts. These formalities are nonetheless really identical and inseparably united within the individual.

In epistemology, Scotus is important for his demolition of Augustinian illumination, at least in the elaborate defence of it given by Henry of Ghent, and the distinction between intuitive and abstractive cognition. Scotus rejected Henry's defence as leading to nothing but scepticism, and set about giving a complete account of certitude apart from illumination. He grounded certitude in the knowledge of self-evident propositions, induction and awareness of our own states. After Scotus, illumination never made a serious recovery. Scotus' other epistemological contribution was the allocation to the intellect of a direct, existential awareness of the intelligible object. This was called intuitive cognition, in contrast to abstractive knowledge, which seized the object independently of whether it was present to the intellect in actual existence or not. This distinction, credited to Scotus by his contemporaries, was invoked in nearly every subsequent scholastic discussion of certitude.

While known primarily for his metaphysics, the importance and originality of Scotus' ethical theory has been increasingly appreciated. Scotus is a voluntarist, holding for example that not all of the natural law (the decalogue) is absolutely binding, that prudence and the moral virtues are not necessarily connected and that the will can act against a completely correct judgment of the intellect. It is Scotus' theory of will itself, however, that has attracted the most attention. He argues that the will is a power for opposites, not just in the sense that it can have opposite acts over time but in the deeper sense that, even when actually willing one thing, it retains a real, active power to will the opposite. In other words, he detaches the notion of freedom from those of time and variability, arguing that if a created will existed only for an instant its choice would still be free. In this, he has been heralded as breaking with ancient notions of modality that treated contingency principally in terms of change over time. Scotus argued that the will, as a capacity for opposites, was the only truly rational power, where the rational was opposed to purely natural agents whose action was determined. In this sense, the intellect, as a purely natural agent, was not a rational power. Finally, Scotus endowed the will with an innate inclination to the good in itself apart from any advantage it might bring to the agent. This inclination or affection for the just (*affectio iustitiae*, as it was termed by Anselm), enabled the will to escape the deterministic inclination of natures toward their own perfection and fulfilment.

See also: Being; God, arguments for the existence of; God, concepts of; William of Ockham

STEPHEN D. DUMONT

DUTY

See Kantian ethics

DUTY AND VIRTUE, INDIAN CONCEPTIONS OF

Two principal strains of ethical thought are evident in Indian religious and philosophical literature: one, central to Hinduism, emphasizes adherence to the established norms of ancient Indian culture, which are stated in the literature known as the Dharma-śāstras; another, found in texts of Buddhism, Jainism and Hinduism alike, stresses the renunciation of one's familial and social obligations for the sake of attaining enlightenment or liberation from the cycle of rebirth. The Dharmaśāstras define in elaborate detail a way of life based on a division of society into four 'orders' (varṇas) – priests, warriors, tradesmen and servants or labourers – and, for the three highest orders, four 'stages of life' (āśramas). Renunciation is valid only in the final two stages of life, after one has fulfilled one's responsibilities as a student of scripture and as a householder. The various traditions that stress liberation, on the other hand, advocate total, immediate commitment to the goal of liberation, for which the householder life presents insuperable distractions. Here, the duties of the householder are replaced by the practice of yoga and asceticism. Nevertheless, specific ethical observances are also recommended as prerequisites for the achievement of higher knowledge through yoga, in particular, nonviolence, truthfulness, not stealing, celibacy and poverty. The liberation traditions criticized the system of the Dharmaśāstras for being overly concerned with ritual and external forms of purity and condoning – indeed, prescribing – the killing of living beings in Vedic sacrifices; but it was only in the Dharmaśāstras that the notion of action solely for duty's sake was appreciated. The Hindu scripture the *Bhagavad Gītā* (Song of God) represents an effort to synthesize the two ideals of renunciation and the fulfilment of obligation. It teaches that one should integrate yoga and action in the world. Only when acting out of the state of inner peace and detachment that is the culmination of the practice of yoga can one execute one's duty without regard for the consequences of one's actions. On the other hand, without the cultivation of inner yoga, the external forms of renunciation – celibacy, mendicancy, asceticism – are without significance. It is inner yoga that is the essence of renunciation, yet yoga is quite compatible with carrying out one's obligations in the world.

JOHN A. TABER

DWORKIN, RONALD (1931–)

Ronald Dworkin's early, highly controversial, thesis that there are right answers in hard cases in law, coupled with his attack on the idea that law is simply a system of rules, gained him a prominent and distinct place in the anti-positivist strand of legal theory. He has developed and enriched his earlier insights by tying his notion of law-as-interpretation to the ideals of community and equality. Dworkin is an influential representative of liberal thought, who combines clear and analytical thinking with political involvement expressed in decisive and timely interventions in many of the important political debates of our time.

See also: Law and morality §4

EMILIOS A. CHRISTODOULIDIS

E

EARLY CHRISTIAN PHILOSOPHY

See PATRISTIC PHILOSOPHY

EAST ASIAN PHILOSOPHY

Sinitic civilization, which includes the Chinese-influenced cultures of Japan and Korea, established an early lead over the rest of the world in the development of its material culture – textiles, iron casting, paper, maritime arts, pottery, soil sciences, agricultural and water technologies, and so on. For centuries after the first sustained incursions of Europe into East Asia, there were more books printed in the classical Chinese language – the 'Latin' of East Asia – than in all of the rest of the world's languages combined. As recently as the beginning of the industrial revolution in the eighteenth century, it was China rather than Europe which, by most standards, was the arbiter of science and civilization on this planet.

If 'philosophy' – the pursuit of wisdom – is an aspiration of high cultures generally, why then was it not until the late nineteenth century, in response to a growing relationship with Western learning, that an East Asian term for 'philosophy' was coined, first by the Japanese (*tetsugaku*), and then introduced into Chinese (*zhexue*) and Korean (*ch'ŏlhak*)? If it would be absurd to suggest that East Asian cultures have no history, no sociology, no economics, then how do we explain the fact that Asian philosophy is a subject neither researched nor taught in most Anglo-European seats of higher learning?

1 Uncommon assumptions, common misconceptions

The prominent French sinologist Jacques Gernet (1985) argues that when the two civilizations of China and Europe, having developed almost entirely independently of each other, first made contact in about 1600, the seeming resistance of the Chinese to embracing Christianity and, more importantly, the philosophic edifice that undergirded it was not simply an uneasy difference in the encounter between disparate intellectual traditions. It was a far more profound difference in mental categories and modes of thought, and particularly, a fundamental difference in the conception of human agency. Much of what Christianity and Western philosophy had to say to the East Asians was, quite literally, nonsense – given their own philosophic commitments, they could not think it. In turn, the Jesuits interpreted this difference in ways of thinking quite specifically as ineptness in reasoning, logic and dialectic.

The West has fared little better in its opportunity to appreciate and to appropriate Sinitic culture. In fact, it has fared so badly that the very word 'Chinese' in the English language, found in illustrative expressions from 'Chinese revenge' and 'Chinese puzzle' to 'Chinese firedrill', came to denote 'confusion', 'incomprehensibility' or 'impenetrability', a sense of order inaccessible to the Western mind. The degree of difference between a dominant Western metaphysical sense of order and the historicist 'aesthetic' order prevalent in the radial Sinitic worldview has plagued the encounter between these antique cultures from the start. When seventeenth-century European savants such as LEIBNIZ and WOLFF were looking to corroborate their universal indices in other high cultures – the one true God, impersonal rationality, a universal language – China was idealized as a remarkable and 'curious land' requiring the utmost scrutiny. In the course of time, however, reported on by philosophers such as KANT, HEGEL, MILL and EMERSON, Western esteem for this 'curious land' plummeted from such 'Cathay' idealizations to the depths of disaffection for the inertia of what, in the context of the Europe-driven Industrial Revolution, was recast as a moribund, backward-looking and fundamentally stagnant culture.

In classical Chinese there is an expression: 'We cannot see the true face of Mount Lu because we are standing on top of it.' Although virtually all cultural traditions and historical epochs are complex and diverse, there are certain fundamental and often unannounced assumptions on which they stand that give them their specific genetic identity and continuities. These assumptions, extraordinarily important as they are for understanding the cultural narrative, are often concealed from the consciousness of the participants in the culture who are inscribed by them, and become obvious only from a perspective external to the particular tradition or epoch. Often a tradition suspends within itself competing and even conflicting elements which, although at odds with one another, still reflect a pattern of importances integral to and constitutive of its cultural identity. These underlying strands are not necessarily or even typically logically coherent or systematic, yet they do have a coherence as the defining fabric of a specific and unique culture.

Looking at and trying to understand elements of the East Asian cultural narrative from the distance of Western traditions, then, embedded as we are within our own pattern of cultural assumptions, has both advantages and disadvantages. One disadvantage is obvious and inescapable. To the extent that we are unconscious of the difference between our own fundamental assumptions and those that have shaped the emergence of East Asian philosophies, we are sure to impose upon this geographical area our own presuppositions about the nature of the world, making what is exotic familiar and what is distant near. On the other hand, a clear advantage of an external perspective is that we are able to see with greater clarity at least some aspects of 'the true face of Mount Lu': we are able to discern, however imperfectly, the common ground on which the Confucian and the Buddhist stand in debating their differences, ground which is in important measure concealed from they themselves by their unconscious assumptions.

2 One-world natural cosmology

In the dominant world view of classical East Asia, we do not begin from the dualistic 'two-world' reality/appearance distinction familiar in classical Greek metaphysics, giving rise as it does to ontological questions such as: 'What is the Being behind the beings?' Rather, we begin from the assumption that there is only the one continuous concrete world that is the source and locus of all of our experience, giving rise to cosmological and ultimately ethical questions such as: 'How do these myriad beings best hang together?' Order within the classical East Asian world view is 'immanent' and 'emergent', an indwelling regularity in things themselves. It is the always unique yet continuous graining in wood, the distinctive striations in a piece of jade, the regular cadence of the surf, the peculiar veining in each and every leaf. The power of creativity resides in the world itself. The order and regularity this world evidences is neither derived from nor imposed upon it by some independent, activating power, but inheres in the world itself. Change and continuity are equally 'real'; time itself is the persistence of this self-transformation.

The 'one' world, then, is the efficient cause of itself. Situation takes priority over agency; process and change take priority over form and stasis. The context itself is resolutely dynamic, autogenerative, self-organizing and, in a real sense, alive. This one world is constituted as a sea of qi, psychophysical energy that disposes itself in various concentrations, configurations and perturbations. There is an intelligible pattern that can be discerned and mapped from each different perspective within the world that is its dao, a 'pathway' which can, in varying degrees, be traced out to make one's place and one's context coherent. Dao is, at any given time, both what the world is and how it is, always as entertained from some particular perspective or another. In this tradition, there is no final distinction between some independent source of order, and what it orders. There is no determinative beginning or presumptive teleological end. The world and its order at any particular time is self-causing, 'so-of-itself' (ziran) (see CHINESE PHILOSOPHY; DAOIST PHILOSOPHY). Truth, beauty and goodness as standards of order are not 'givens': they are historically emergent, something done, a cultural product. Given the priority of situation over agency, there is a continuity between nature and nurture, a mutuality between context and the human being. In such a world, it is not unexpected that the Yijing (Book of Changes) is the first among the ancient classics.

3 Ars contextualis: the art of contextualizing

The 'two-world' metaphysical order inherited out of classical Greece has given the Western tradition a theoretical basis for objectivity – the possibility of standing outside and taking a wholly external view of things – a 'view from nowhere'. Objectivity is not only the basis for such universalistic claims as objective truth, impersonal reason and necessity, but further permits the decontextualization of things as 'objects' in our world. It is the basis on which we can separate objective description from subjective prescription.

By contrast, in the 'one world' of classical East Asia, instead of starting abstractly from some underlying, unifying and originating principle, one begins from one's own specific place within the world. Without objectivity, 'objects' dissolve into the flux and flow, and existence becomes a continuous, uninterrupted process. Each person is invariably experiencing the world as one perspective within the context of many. Since there is only the one world, we cannot get outside of it. From the always unique place one occupies within the cosmos of classical East Asia, one construes and interprets the order of the world around one as contrasting 'thises' and 'thats'– 'this person' and 'that person' – more or less proximate to oneself. Since each and every person or thing or event is perceived from some position or other, and hence is continuous with the position that entertains it, each thing is related to and a condition of every other.

In the human world, all relationships are continuous from ruler and subject to friend and friend, relating everyone as an extended 'family'. Similarly, all 'things', like all members of a family, are correlated and thus interdependent. Every thing is holographic in entailing all other things as conditions for its continued existence, and is what it is at the pleasure of everything else. Whatever can be predicated of one thing or one person is a function of a network of relationships, all of which combine to give it its role and to constitute its place and its definition.

There is no strict notion of identity that issues forth as some essential defining feature – a divinely endowed soul, rational capacity or natural locus of rights – that makes all human beings equal. In the absence of such equality, the various relationships which define one thing in relation to another are qualitatively hierarchical and contrastive: bigger or smaller, more noble or more base, harder or softer, stronger or weaker, more senior or more junior. Change in the quality of relationships between things always occurs on a continuum as movement between such polar oppositions.

The general and most basic language for articulating such correlations among things is metaphorical: in some particular aspect at some specific point in time, one person or thing is 'overshadowed' by another; that is, made *yin* to another's *yang*. Literally, *yin* means 'shady' and *yang* means 'sunny', defining in the most general terms those contrasting and hierarchical relationships which constitute indwelling order and regularity.

It is important to recognize the *interdependence* and correlative character of the *yin–yang* kind of polar opposites, and to distinguish this contrastive

tension from the dualistic opposition implicit in the vocabulary of the classical Greek world, where one primary member of a set such as Being transcends and stands *independent* of, and thus is more 'real' than, the world of Becoming. The implications of this difference between dualism and correlativity contrast are fundamental and pervasive.

To continue the 'person' example, generally in East Asian philosophy, a particular person is not a discrete individual defined in terms of some inherent nature, but is a centre of constitutive roles and relationships. These roles and relationships are dynamic, constantly being enacted, reinforced and ideally deepened through the multiple levels of natural, cultural and social discourse. By virtue of these specific roles and relationships, a person comes to occupy a place and posture in the context of family, community and world. The human being is not shaped by some given design which underlies natural and moral order in the cosmos, and which stands as the ultimate objective of human growth and experience. Rather, the 'purpose' of the human experience, if it can be so described, is more immediate; it is to coordinate the various ingredients which constitute one's particular world here and now, and to negotiate the most productive harmony out of them. Simply put, it is to get the most out of what you have here and now.

4 Radial harmony

A major theme in Confucianism, foundational throughout East Asia, is captured in the phrase from *Analects* 13.23, 'the exemplary person pursues harmony (*ho*), not sameness' (see CONFUCIAN PHILOSOPHY, CHINESE). This conception of 'harmony' is explained in the classical commentaries by appeal to the culinary arts. In the classical period, a common food staple throughout northern Asia was *keng*, a kind of a millet gruel in which various locally available and seasonal ingredients were brought into relationship with one another. The goal was for each ingredient – the cabbage, the radish, the bit of pork – to retain its own colour, texture and flavor, but at the same time to be enhanced by its relationship with the other ingredients. The key to this sense of harmony is that it begins from the unique conditions of a specific geographical location and the full contribution of those particular ingredients readily at hand – *this* piece of cabbage, *this* fresh, young radish, *this* tender bit of pork and so on – and relies upon artistry rather than recipe for its success.

The Confucian distinction between an inclusive harmony and an exclusive sameness has an obvious social and political application, underscoring the fertility of the kind of harmony that maximizes difference. This 'harmony' is not a given in some preassigned cosmic design, but is the quality of the combination at any one moment created by effectively correlating and contextualizing the available ingredients, whether they be foodstuffs, farmers or infantry. It is not a quest of discovery, grasping an unchanging reality behind the shadows of appearance, but a profoundly creative journey where the quality of the journey is itself the end. It is the attempt to make the most of any situation.

In summary, at the core of the classical East Asian worldview is the cultivation of radial harmony, a specifically 'centre-seeking' or 'centripetal' harmony which is productive of consensus and orthodoxy. This harmony begins from what is most concrete and immediate – that is, from the perspective of any particular human being – and draws through patterns of deference from the outside in toward its centre. Hence there is the almost pervasive emphasis on personal cultivation and refinement as the starting point for familial, social, political and cosmic order. A preoccupation in classical East Asian philosophy, then, is the cultivation of this centripetal harmony as it begins with oneself, and radiates outward.

The East Asian world view is thus dominated by this 'bottom-up' and emergent sense of order which begins from the coordination of concrete detail. It can be described fairly as an 'aestheticism', exhibiting concern for the artful way in which particular things can be correlated efficaciously to thereby constitute the *ethos* or character of concrete historical events and cultural achievements. Order, like a work of art, begins with always unique details, from 'this bit' and 'that', and emerges out of the way in which these details are juxtaposed and harmonized. As such, the order is embedded and concrete – the colouration that differentiates the various layers of earth, the symphony of the morning garden, the wind piping through the orifices of the earth, the rituals and roles that constitute a communal grammar to give community meaning. Such an achieved harmony is always particular and specific, and is resistant to notions of formula and replication.

5 Philosophical syncreticism

As one might expect in a cultural narrative which privileges interdependence and the pursuit of radial harmony, orthodoxy is neither exclusive nor systematic. Rather, traditions are porous and syncretic. In the Han dynasty, for example, Confucianism is first fortified by elements appropriated from the competing schools of pre-Qin China such as Daoism and Legalism. Later it absorbs into itself an increasingly Sinicized Buddhist tradition, evolving over time into a neo-Confucianism. At the same time, the *shuyuan* academies established by the great neo-Confucian syncretist Zhu Xi are modelled on Buddhist monastic schools. In more recent years the Western heresy, Marxism, and other elements of Western learning such as the philosophy of KANT and HEGEL, are being appropriated by China and digested to produce what today is being called the 'New Confucianism' (see MARXISM, WESTERN).

The indigenous shamanistic tradition of Korean popular religion absorbed first Buddhism and then Confucianism from China, reshaping these traditions fundamentally to suit the uniqueness of the Korean social and political conditions (see BUDDHIST PHILOSOPHY, KOREAN). Native Japanese Shintoism emerges as a distinction made necessary by the introduction of first Buddhism and then Confucianism, where each tradition assumes a complementary function within the culture (see SHINTŌ; BUDDHIST PHILOSOPHY, JAPANESE). More recently, in the work of Kyoto School thinkers such as NISHIDA, TANABE and Nishitani, German idealism is mined and alloyed with the Japanese Buddhist tradition to produce new directions.

Although Confucianism, Buddhism and Daoism – the dominant traditions of East Asia – have certainly been rivals at one level, it has been characteristic of the living philosophical traditions defining of East Asian culture to pursue mutual accommodation through an ongoing process of encounter and appropriation; hence the familiar expression *sanjiao weiyi*, 'the three teachings (Confucianism, Buddhism and Daoism) are as one'. A continuation of this process is presently underway with the ongoing East Asian appropriation of Western philosophy.

See also: ANCIENT PHILOSOPHY; CHINESE PHILOSOPHY; INDIAN AND TIBETAN PHILOSOPHY; JAPANESE PHILOSOPHY

References and further reading

Gernet, J. (1985) *China and the Christian Impact*, Cambridge: Cambridge University Press. (A reconstructed conversation between the Jesuits and Chinese intellectuals on their first encounters in the sixteenth and seventeenth centuries.)

Hall, D.L and Ames, R.T. (1997) *Thinking From the Han: Self, Truth, and Transcendence in China and the West*, Albany, NY: State University of New York Press. (An examination of several fundamental themes that distinguish the Chinese cultural narrative from the Western philosophical tradition.)

Mungello, D.E. (1985) *Curious Land: Jesuit Accommodation and the Origins of Sinology*, Honolulu, HI: University of Hawaii Press. (A discussion of the inquiry of the seventeenth-century European intellectuals into Sinitic culture.)

ROGER T. AMES

ECLECTICISM

Eclecticism in philosophy is the construction of a system of thought by combining elements of the established systems of a previous age. The term 'eclecticism' is derived from the Greek verb *eklegein/eklegesthai*: to pick out, choose, or select. Diogenes Laertius (*c.* AD 300–50) attributes an 'eclectic school' to Potamo of Alexandria (*c.* early 3rd century AD) 'who made a selection from the tenets of all the existing sects'. Many philosophers of the Greco-Roman period are known as 'eclectics', and one can find the entire period of philosophy from the second century BC to the third century AD referred to as an age of 'eclecticism'. In such cases the term is often used pejoratively to designate a discordant collection of unoriginal ideas. More recently, however, the French philosopher Victor Cousin (1792–1867) expressed an optimistic view of eclecticism while using the term in reference to his own philosophy. Cousin viewed the entire history of thought as dominated by the two competing philosophies of empiricism (or sensualism) and idealism (or rationalism). The true philosophy would eliminate conflicting elements and combine the remaining truths within a single, unified system. Cousin's eclecticism, with its strong historical orientation, was the predominant school of thought in France throughout most of the nineteenth century and was also of considerable influence in Brazil.

See also: BRAZIL, PHILOSOPHY IN; COUSIN, V.

CHRIS MCCLELLAN

ECOLOGICAL PHILOSOPHY

In the early 1970s a small number of academic philosophers in the English-speaking world began to turn their attention to questions concerning the natural environment. Environmental philosophy initially encompassed various types of inquiry, including applied ethics oriented to issues such as nuclear power and the deployment of toxic chemicals; more abstract extrapolations of traditional ethical theories, such as Kantianism and utilitarianism, into environmental contexts; and, also, a far more radical project involving the reappraisal of basic presuppositions of Western thought in the light of their implications for our relation to the natural world. The first two were basically extensions of existing areas of philosophy, and it is arguably the third project – often described as 'ecological philosophy' or 'ecophilosophy' –

which constitutes a distinctively new branch of philosophy.

Although the ecophilosophical project was explicitly normative in intent, it was quickly found to entail far-reaching investigations into the fundamental nature of the world. Indeed it was seen by many as entailing a search for an entirely new ecological paradigm – a worldview organized around a principle of interconnectedness, with transformative implications for metaphysics, epistemology, spirituality and politics, as well as ethics. Moreover, the process of elaborating a new ecological view of the world was found to uncover the contours of an already deeply embedded worldview, organized around a principle of separation or division, underlying and shaping the traditional streams of modern Western thought.

See also: ENVIRONMENTAL ETHICS; GREEN POLITICAL PHILOSOPHY; MONISM; NATURPHILOSOPHIE; PANTHEISM

FREYA MATHEWS

ECONOMICS AND ETHICS

Unlike many other sciences, economics is linked both to ethics and to the theory of rationality. Although many economists regard economics as a 'positive' science of one sort of social phenomena, economics is built around a normative theory of rationality, and has a special relevance to policy making and the criticism of social institutions. Economics complements and intersects with moral philosophy in both the concepts it has constructed and in its treatment of normative problems.

Fundamental to modern economics is its conception of human beings as rational agents, whose choices are determined by complete and transitive preferences. Although economists stress the usefulness of this notion of rationality in explaining human behaviour, rationality is clearly also a normative notion. The mathematical tools economists have developed to represent and study the implications of rational action in collective and interactive contexts are thus of immediate relevance to moral philosophers.

Also of interest to moral philosophy is the problematic attempt in welfare economics to fashion a normative theory of economic institutions and policies around the goal of helping people satisfy their subjective preferences. This project relies, controversially, on equating people's well-being with the degree of satisfaction of their subjective preferences; an individual's 'utility' on this view is no more than an index of how well their subjective preferences are satisfied. Furthermore, since most welfare economists assume that there is no meaningful way to compare degrees of preference satisfaction across people, the project also requires a scheme for weighing the effectiveness of alternative economic arrangements in satisfying preferences without weighing the comparative satisfaction levels of different individuals. Central to the project is Pareto optimality – the notion of an 'efficient' arrangement as one in which no individual can achieve higher preference satisfaction without someone else undergoing a reduction in their satisfaction level.

Economic policies and institutions can be appraised in terms of a variety of values other than efficiency. Notable both in historical and contemporary discussions are the values of liberty, justice and equality. Since a large part of economics is carried out with a view to its possible application to policy, ethics has a significant part to play in economics. By the same token, economics may be of great importance to ethics, both through its exploration of consequences and through the development of mathematical and conceptual tools.

See also: DECISION AND GAME THEORY; MARKET, ETHICS OF THE

DANIEL HAUSMAN
MICHAEL S. MCPHERSON

EDUCATION, PHILOSOPHY OF

The philosophy of education is primarily concerned with the nature, aims and means of education, and also with the character and structure of educational theory, and its own place in that structure. Educational theory is best regarded as a kind of practical theory which would ideally furnish useful guidance for every aspect and office of educational practice. Such guidance would rest in a well-grounded and elaborated account of educational aims and the moral and political dimensions of education, and also in adequate conceptions and knowledge of teaching, learning, evaluation, the structure and dynamics of educational and social systems, the roles of relevant stake-holders and the like.

Philosophers of education often approach educational issues from the vantage points of other philosophical sub-disciplines, and contribute in a variety of ways to the larger unfinished project of educational theory. These contributions may be divided into work on the nature and aims of education, on the normative dimensions of the methods and circumstances of education, and on the conceptual and methodological underpinnings of its methods and circumstances – either directly or through work on the foundations of other forms of research relied upon by education theory.

Philosophical analysis and argument have suggested certain aims as essential to education, and

various movements and branches of philosophy, from Marxism and existentialism to epistemology and ethics, have suggested aims, in every case controversially. Thus, one encounters normative theories of thought, conduct and the aims of education inspired by a broad consideration of epistemology, logic, aesthetics and ethics, as well as Marxism, feminism and a host of other '-isms'. In this mode of educational philosophizing, the objects of various branches of philosophical study are proposed as the ends of education, and the significance of pursuing those ends is elaborated with reference to those branches of study.

A second form of educational philosophy derives from substantive arguments and theories of ethics, social and political philosophy and philosophy of law, and concerns itself with the aims of education and the acceptability of various means to achieve them. It revolves around arguments concerning the moral, social and political appropriateness of educational aims, initiatives and policies, and moral evaluation of the methods, circumstances and effects of education. Recent debate has been dominated by concerns about children's rights and freedom, educational equality and justice, moral and political education, and issues of authority, control and professional ethics.

The philosophy of education has also sought to guide educational practice through examining its assumptions about the structure of specific knowledge domains and the minds of learners; about learning, development, motivation, and the communication and acquisition of knowledge and understanding. Philosophy of science and mathematics have informed the design of curriculum, pedagogy and evaluation in the teaching of science and mathematics. Philosophy of mind, language and psychology bear on the foundations of our understanding of how learning occurs, and thus how teaching may best promote it.

RANDALL R. CURREN

EDWARDS, JONATHAN (1703–58)

Jonathan Edwards' work as a whole is an elaboration of two themes – God's absolute sovereignty and the beauty of his holiness. God's sovereignty is articulated in several ways. *Freedom of the Will* (1754) defends theological determinism. God is the complete cause of everything that occurs, including human volitions. Edwards is also an occasionalist, idealist and mental phenomenalist. God is the only real cause of events. Human volitions and 'natural causes' are mere 'occasions' upon which God produces the appropriate effects. Physical objects are collections of sensible 'ideas' of colour, shape, solidity, and so on, and finite minds are collections of 'thoughts' or 'perceptions'. God's production of sensible ideas and thoughts in the order which pleases him is the only 'substance' underlying them. God is thus truly 'being in general', the 'sum of all being'.

The beauty or splendour of God's holiness is the principal theme of two late works – *End of Creation* and *True Virtue* (both published posthumously in 1765). The first argues that God's end in creation is the external manifestation of his internal splendour. That splendour primarily consists in his holiness and its most perfect external expression is the holiness of the saints, which mirrors and depends upon it. *True Virtue* defines holiness as 'true benevolence' or 'the love of being in general', and distinguishes it from such counterfeits as rational self-love, instincts like parental affection and pity, and natural conscience. Since beauty is defined as 'agreement' or 'consent' and since true benevolence consents to being in general, true benevolence alone is truly beautiful. Natural beauty and the beauty of art are merely its image. Only those with truly benevolent hearts, however, can discern this beauty.

Edwards' projected *History of Redemption* would have drawn these themes together, for it is in God's work of redemption that his sovereignty, holiness and beauty are most effectively displayed.

WILLIAM J. WAINWRIGHT

EGOISM AND ALTRUISM

Introduction

Henry Sidgwick conceived of egoism as an ethical theory parallel to utilitarianism: the utilitarian holds that one should maximize the good of all beings in the universe; the egoist holds instead that the good one is ultimately to aim at is only one's own. This form of egoism (often called 'ethical egoism') is to be distinguished from the empirical hypothesis ('psychological egoism') that human beings seek to maximize their own good. Ethical egoism can approve of behaviour that benefits others, for often the best way to promote one's good is to form cooperative relationships. But the egoist cannot approve of an altruistic justification for such cooperation: altruism requires benefiting others merely for their sake, whereas the egoist insists that one's ultimate goal must be solely one's own good.

One way to defend ethical egoism is to affirm psychological egoism and then to propose that our obligations cannot outstrip our capacities; if we cannot help seeking to maximize our own well-being, we should not hold ourselves to a less selfish standard. But this defence is widely rejected,

because psychological egoism seems too simple a conception of human behaviour. Moreover, egoism violates our sense of impartiality; there is no fact about oneself that justifies excluding others from one's ultimate end.

There is, however, a different form of egoism, which flourished in the ancient world, and is not vulnerable to this criticism. It holds that one's good consists largely or exclusively in acting virtuously, and that self-interest properly understood is therefore our best guide.

> 1 Definitions of 'egoism'
> 2 Egoism's treatment of altruism
> 3 Arguments for and against
> 4 An ancient form of egoism

1 Definitions of 'egoism'

The term 'egoism' was introduced into modern moral philosophy as a label for a type of ethical theory that is structurally parallel to utilitarianism (see UTILITARIANISM). The latter theory holds that one ought to consider everyone and produce the greatest balance of good over evil; egoism, by contrast, says that each person ought to maximize their own good. Both theories are teleological, in that they hold that the right thing to do is always to produce a certain good (see TELEOLOGICAL ETHICS). But the utilitarian claims that the good that one is to maximize is the universal good – the good of all human beings and perhaps all sentient creatures. The egoist, on the other hand, holds that the good one is ultimately to aim at is only one's own (see GOOD, THEORIES OF THE).

This way of classifying ethical theories is due to Henry SIDGWICK, who regarded the choice between utilitarianism and egoism as one of the principal problems of moral philosophy. In *The Methods of Ethics* (1874), Sidgwick frames the issue in terms that assume that the good is identical to pleasure (a doctrine called 'hedonism') (see HEDONISM). He uses 'utilitarianism' for the view that one is to maximize the amount of pleasure in the universe, and holds that the only form of egoism worth considering is hedonistic egoism. Since few philosophers now accept the identity of pleasure and the good, the terms of the debate have changed. 'Egoism' is applied to any doctrine, whatever its conception of the good, that advocates maximizing one's own good.

Often this doctrine is called 'ethical egoism', to emphasize its normative status. By contrast, the term 'psychological egoism' is applied to an empirical hypothesis about human motivation. It holds that whenever one has a choice to make, one decides in favour of the action one thinks will maximize one's own good. It is possible to agree that we are inevitably selfish in this way, but to regard this as an evil element in our nature. Conversely, it is possible to hold that although people ought to maximize their own good, they seldom try to do so. (In the remainder of this entry, 'egoism' will refer to ethical egoism, unless otherwise indicated.)

2 Egoism's treatment of altruism

A defender of egoism need not frown upon attachments to others, feelings of compassion, or beneficent acts. For it is open to the egoist to argue that these social ties are an effective means to one's own ends. For example, it is a matter of common sense that altruistic behaviour – behaviour intended to help others – is often advantageous, when it motivates others to respond in kind. What little one loses in simple acts of kindness may be more than compensated when others reciprocate.

Although egoists may argue that benefiting others is generally in one's interests, they give a controversial justification for such beneficence. It is widely agreed that one should at times benefit others for *their* sake (Aristotle, for example, in *Nicomachean Ethics*, considers this essential to the best kind of friendship). To act for the sake of others is to take their good as a sufficient reason for action. But this is exactly what egoists cannot accept. They hold that ultimately the only justification for acts of beneficence is that they maximize one's own good. Ultimately, one is not to benefit others for their sake, but for one's own. If 'altruism' is used (as it often is) to refer to behaviour that not only benefits others, but is undertaken for their sake, then egoism is opposed to altruism.

3 Arguments for and against

Philosophers have sometimes tried to refute egoism by showing that it contains a contradiction or is in some way self-undermining. The best known attempt is that of G.E. MOORE in *Principia Ethica* (1903), but he has had few followers. Instead, Sidgwick's opinion that egoism is rational is generally accepted. But even if one agrees, one may ask whether there are good reasons for choosing egoism over other alternatives. Why must it always be a mistake to sacrifice one's good for the greater good of others? If a small loss in one's wellbeing can produce great gains for others, what is wrong with accepting that loss?

The egoist might at this point take refuge in psychological egoism. Although it is possible to affirm psychological egoism and reject ethical egoism – to agree that by nature we are ultimately self-seeking, and to condemn such behaviour as

evil – few philosophers regard this as an appealing mix of theories. For what plausibility can there be in a standard of behaviour that we are incapable of achieving? The egoist may therefore respond to our question 'Why should we not sacrifice our good for the sake of others?' by urging us not to impose impossible standards upon ourselves. We do not in fact make such sacrifices, and should not blame ourselves for being the way we are.

The problem with this strategy is that psychological egoism has come under heavy attack in the modern period. HOBBES and MANDEVILLE have been widely read as psychological egoists, and were criticized by such philosophers as HUTCHESON, ROUSSEAU and HUME, who sought to show that benevolence, pity and sympathy are as natural as self-love. KANT held against psychological egoism, that the rational recognition of moral principles can by itself motivate us and overcome self-love (see KANTIAN ETHICS). Perhaps the most influential critique of psychological egoism is that of BUTLER, who argued that by its nature self-love cannot be the only component of our motivational repertoire. He also pointed out that even if we feel gratification when we satisfy our desires, it cannot be inferred that such gratification is the object of those desires. The combined force of these attacks has left psychological egoism with few philosophical defenders.

At this point, an important challenge to ethical egoism should be noticed: although my circumstances, history or qualities may differ from yours in morally significant ways, and these differences may justify me in seeking my good in preference to yours, the mere fact that I am myself and not you is not by itself a morally relevant difference between us. That my good is mine does not explain why ultimately it alone should concern me. So, if my good provides me with a reason for action, why should not your good, or the good of anyone else, also provide me with a reason – so long as there are no relevant differences between us? The ideal of impartiality seems to support the conclusion that we should have at least some concern with others (see IMPARTIALITY). In fact, egoists implicitly accept a notion of impartiality, since they say that just as my ultimate end should be my good, yours should be your good. So they must explain why they accept this minimal conception of impartiality, but nothing stronger. There is nothing morally appealing about excluding all others from one's final end; why then should one do so?

4 An ancient form of egoism

The kind of egoism we have been discussing can be called 'formal', in that it makes no claim about what in particular is good or bad for human beings. It holds instead that whatever the good is, it is one's own good that should be one's ultimate end. This is the conception one arrives at when one begins from Sidgwick's pairing of egoism with utilitarianism, then abstracts from his hedonism. A different kind of egoism, which might be called 'substantive', first proposes a concrete conception of the good, and then urges each of us to maximize our own good, so conceived. It is this form of egoism that flourished in the ancient world. Plato, Aristotle and the Stoics do not accept the formal principle that whatever the good is, we should seek only our own good, or prefer it to the good of others (see PLATO; ARISTOTLE; STOICISM). Instead, they argue for a specific conception of the good, and because the social virtues play so large a role in that conception, they regard self-love not as the enemy of virtue and the larger community but as an honourable motive, once it is developed in the proper direction (see EUDAIMONIA; VIRTUES AND VICES).

Even if psychological egoism is too simple a conception of human nature, it is undeniable that we normally have a deep concern for our own welfare. If self-love is a force that often conflicts with moral duty and inherently resists education, then human beings are necessarily deeply divided creatures. This is the Augustinian and Kantian picture. By contrast, the dominant strand of ancient ethics proposes a more optimistic conception of the human situation. It does not claim that one should seek one's own good, come what may for others; rather, by arguing that acting virtuously and acting well coincide, it seeks to undermine the common assumption that at bottom the self must come into conflict with others.

See also: MORAL MOTIVATION; MORAL SCEPTICISM

References and further reading

Plato (429–367) *Republic.* trans. Tom Griffith, (ed.) G.R.F. Ferrfari, Cambridge University Press, 2000. (Critique of the egoism in Hobbes and Sidgwick.)

Shaver, R. (1999) *Rational Egoism: A Selective and Critical History.* Cambridge University Press. (Critique of the egoism in Hobbes and Sidgwick)

Sidgwick, H. (1874) *The Methods of Ethics*, London: Macmillan; 7th edn, 1907. (Argues for the plausibility of both egoism and utilitarianism.)

RICHARD KRAUT

EINSTEIN, ALBERT (1879–1955)

Albert Einstein was a German-born Swiss and American naturalized physicist and the twentieth century's most prominent scientist. He produced the special and general theories of relativity, which overturned the classical understanding of space, time and gravitation. According to the special theory (1905), uniformly moving observers with different velocities measure the same speed for light. From this he deduced that the length of a system shrinks and its clocks slow at speeds approaching that of light. The general theory (completed 1915) proceeds from Hermann Minkowski's geometric formulation of special relativity as a four-dimensional spacetime. Einstein's theory allows, however, that the geometry of spacetime may vary from place to place. This variable geometry or curvature is associated with the presence of gravitational fields. Acting through geometrical curvature, these fields can slow clocks and bend light rays.

Einstein made many fundamental contributions to statistical mechanics and quantum theory, including the demonstration of the atomic character of matter and the proposal that light energy is organized in spatially discrete light quanta. In later life, he searched for a unified theory of gravitation and electromagnetism as an alternative to the quantum theory developed in the 1920s. He complained resolutely that this new quantum theory was not complete. Einstein's writings in philosophy of science developed a conventionalist position, stressing our freedom to construct theoretical concepts; his later writings emphasized his realist tendencies and the heuristic value of the search for mathematically simple laws.

See also POINCARÉ, H.; SPACE; SPACETIME; TIME

ARTHUR FINE
DON HOWARD
JOHN D. NORTON

ELEATIC PHILOSOPHY

See GORGIAS; PARMENIDES; PRESOCRATIC PHILOSOPHY; ZENO OF ELEA

ELIMINATIVISM

'Eliminativism' refers to the view that mental phenomena – for example, beliefs, desires, conscious states – do not exist. Although this can seem absurd on its face, in the twentieth century it has gained a wide variety of adherents, for example, scientific behaviourists, who thought that all human and animal activity could be explained in terms of the history of patterns of stimuli, responses and reinforcements; as well as some who have thought that neurophysiology alone is all that is needed.

Two immediate objections to eliminativism – for example, that it is incoherent because it claims there are no 'claims', and that it conflicts with data of which we are all immediately aware – arguably beg the question against the view. What is wanted is non-tendentious evidence for the mind. Contrary to behaviourism, this seems to be available in the intelligent behaviour of most higher animals.

See also: FOLK PSYCHOLOGY; MATERIALISM IN THE PHILOSOPHY OF MIND

GEORGES REY

EMERSON, RALPH WALDO (1803–82)

The American philosopher and poet Ralph Waldo Emerson developed a philosophy of flux or transitions in which the active human self plays a central role. At the core of his thought was a hierarchy of value or existence, and an unlimited aspiration for personal and social progress. 'Man is the dwarf of himself', he wrote in his first book *Nature* (1836). Emerson presented a dire portrait of humankind's condition: 'Men in the world of today are bugs or spawn, and are called "the mass" and "the herd"'. We are governed by moods which 'do not believe in one another', by necessities real or only imagined, but also, Emerson held, by opportunities for 'untaught sallies of the spirit' – those few real moments of life which may nevertheless alter the whole.

Emerson's lectures drew large audiences throughout America and in England, and his works were widely read in his own time. He influenced the German philosophical tradition through Nietzsche – whose *The Gay Science* carries an epigraph from 'History' – and the Anglo-American tradition via William James and John Dewey. Emerson's major works are essays, each with its own structure, but his sentences and paragraphs often stand on their own as expressions of his thought.

See also: NEOPLATONISM; PRAGMATISM

RUSSELL B. GOODMAN

EMOTION IN RESPONSE TO ART

The main philosophical questions concerning emotion in response to art are as follows. (1) What kind or type of emotions are had in response to works of art? (2) How can we intelligibly have emotions for fictional persons or situations, given that we do not believe in their existence? (This is known as 'the paradox of fiction'.) (3) Why do abstract works of art, especially musical ones, generate emotions in audiences, and what do audiences then have these emotions *towards*? (4) How can we make sense of the interest appreciators have in experiencing empathetically art that is expressive of *negative* emotions? (A particular form of this query is 'the paradox of tragedy'.) (5) Is there a special *aesthetic* emotion, raised only in the context of experience of art? (6) Is there an irresolvable tension between an emotional response to art and the demands of aesthetic appreciation? Answers to these questions depend to some extent on the conception of emotion adopted.

See also: ART, VALUE OF; EMOTIONS, PHILOSOPHY OF; FICTIONAL ENTITIES; HUMOUR; MUSIC, AESTHETICS OF; SUBLIME, THE; TRAGEDY

JERROLD LEVINSON

EMOTIONS AND MORALITY

See MORALITY AND EMOTIONS

EMOTIONS, NATURE OF

What is an emotion? This basic question was posed by William James in 1884, and it is still the focus for a number of important arguments in the philosophy of mind and ethics. It is, on the face of it, a quest for a definition, but it is also a larger quest for a way of thinking about ourselves: how should we think about emotions – as intrusive or as essential to our rationality, as dangerous or as indispensable to our humanity, as excuses for irresponsibility or, perhaps, as themselves our responsibilities? Where do emotions fit into the various categories and 'faculties' of the mind, and which of the evident aspects of emotion – the various sensory, physiological, behavioural, cognitive and social phenomena that typically correspond with an emotion – should we take to be essential? Which are mere accompaniments or consequences?

Many philosophers hold onto the traditional view that an emotion, as a distinctively mental phenomenon, has an essential 'subjective' or 'introspective' aspect, although what this means (and how accessible or articulate an emotion must be) is itself a subject of considerable dispute. Many philosophers have become sceptical about such subjectivism, however, and like their associates in the social sciences have turned the analysis of emotions to more public, observable criteria – to the behaviour that 'expresses' emotion, the physiological disturbances that 'cause' emotion, the social circumstances and use of emotion language in the ascription of emotions. Nevertheless, the seemingly self-evident truth is that, whatever else it may be, an emotion is first of all a feeling. But what, then, is a 'feeling'? What differentiates emotions from other feelings, such as pains and headaches? And how does one differentiate, identify and distinguish the enormous number of different emotions?

See also: EMOTION IN RESPONSE TO ART; EMOTIONS, PHILOSOPHY OF

ROBERT C. SOLOMON

EMOTIONS, PHILOSOPHY OF

Emotions have always played a role in philosophy, even if philosophers have usually denied them centre stage. Because philosophy has so often been described as first and foremost a discipline of reason, the emotions have often been neglected or attacked as primitive, dangerous or irrational. Socrates reprimanded his pupil Crito, advising that we should not give in to our emotions, and some of the ancient Stoic philosophers urged a life of reason free from the enslavement of the emotions, a life of *apatheia* (apathy). In Buddhism, too, much attention has been given to the emotions, which are treated as 'agitations' or *klesas*. Buddhist 'liberation', like the Stoic *apatheia*, becomes a philosophical ideal – freedom from the emotions.

Philosophers have not always downgraded the emotions, however. Aristotle defended the view that human beings are essentially rational animals, but he also stressed the importance of having the right emotions. David Hume, the eighteenth-century empiricist, insisted that 'reason is, and ought to be, the slave of the passions'. In the nineteenth century, although Hegel described the history of philosophy as the development of reason he also argued that 'nothing great is ever done without passion'. Much of the history of philosophy can be told in terms of the shifting relationship between the emotions (or 'passions') and reason, which are often at odds, at times seem to be at war, but ideally should be in harmony. Thus Plato painted a picture of the soul as a chariot with three horses, reason leading the appetites and 'the spirited part', working together. Nietzsche, at the end of the nineteenth century, suggested that 'every passion contains its own quantum of reason'.

Nietzsche's suggestion, that emotion and reason are not really opposites but complementary or commingled, has been at the heart of much of the debate about emotions since ancient times. Are emotions intelligent, or are they simply physical reactions? Are they mere 'feelings', or do they play a vital role in philosophy and in our lives?

ROBERT C. SOLOMON

EMOTIVE MEANING

Emotive meaning contrasts with descriptive meaning. Terms have descriptive meaning if they do the job of stating facts: they have emotive meaning if they do the job of expressing the speaker's emotions or attitudes, or exciting emotions or attitudes in others. Emotivism, the theory that *moral* terms have only or primarily emotive meaning, is an important position in twentieth-century ethics. The most important problem for the idea of emotive meaning is that emotive meaning may not really be a kind of meaning: the jobs of moral terms supposed to constitute emotive meaning may really be performed by speakers using moral terms, on only some of the occasions on which they use them.

There are two components in emotivist accounts of the function and meaning of moral terms. One is a matter of relations to the speaker: moral assertions serve to express the speaker's emotions or attitudes. The other is a matter of relations to the audience: moral assertions serve to commend things, or to arouse emotions or attitudes in the audience.

The most celebrated accounts of emotive meaning were developed by A.J. AYER and C.L. Stevenson. Ayer argued on general metaphysical and epistemological grounds that moral terms can only express and excite emotions. Stevenson developed a more detailed theory, relying more on distinctively ethical considerations (see EMOTIVISM). These theories are liable to make moral discussion seem irrational, and to make no distinction between moral argument and propaganda. R.M. Hare developed a theory designed to remedy these defects. He argued that sentences using paradigm moral terms like 'good', 'right' and 'ought' are really disguised imperatives. Since there is a logic of imperatives, there is room for rational moral argumentation, and moral argument can be distinguished from propaganda, even though moral assertions do not primarily state facts (see PRESCRIPTIVISM).

The most important difficulties for the idea of emotive meaning can be raised by asking whether the emotive meaning of moral terms is a matter of the speech act performed by someone using these terms, and, if so, what kind of speech act? One can distinguish between locutionary, illocutionary and perlocutionary acts (or force). Locutionary acts are simply a matter of uttering certain words with certain senses and referents. Illocutionary acts lie *in* saying things; what illocutionary act one performs in uttering a sentence is determined together by the senses and referents of the words in the sentence and the context. Perlocutionary acts are done *by* saying things. That one performs a certain perlocutionary act is not guaranteed by performing an appropriate illocutionary act: it depends on further variable features of the context. Suppose Bob utters the words 'Down with the aristocrats!' before a large crowd in a revolutionary situation. Bob performs a locutionary act just by saying words with that meaning. In this context, Bob also performs the illocutionary act of *inciting* revolution. Bob's words may also, in that context, have the perlocutionary effect of *provoking* revolution; but this is not guaranteed by the locutionary or the illocutionary force of Bob's utterance. If Bob is sufficiently unpopular, his advocating revolution may actually dampen revolutionary enthusiasm. This classification suggests that the order of explanation typically goes from the locutionary to the illocutionary and the perlocutionary: it is in virtue of the sense and reference of the words one utters and the context that one performs a certain illocutionary act, and that one performs certain perlocutionary acts. The presumption is that an account of meaning will begin with sense and reference; if it begins with illocutionary or perlocutionary acts, it may begin in the wrong place (see SPEECH ACTS).

Some early accounts of emotive meaning seem to identify the meaning of moral assertions with perlocutionary acts (for example, arousing emotions). But this seems both to be the wrong place to begin and to raise a further concern. If we think of meaning as a matter of convention, not (mere) causal variation, then causal correlations between utterances and the production of certain effects are not really meanings. Perhaps then emotive meaning is a matter of illocutionary force. Unfortunately, seeing emotive meaning as illocutionary force is also problematic; in addition to the general problem that an account of meaning apparently should not begin with the illocutionary, there is the specific problem that moral terms do not seem *always* to have the right kinds of illocutionary force. Consider the suggestion that 'good' is used to commend. While it may be true that the term 'good' as used in 'This is a good tennis racket', uttered in a sports shop has the illocutionary force of commending a tennis racket, 'good' as used in 'If you can't get a good one there, try the shop down the street' does not obviously seem to commend anything.

Moral arguments raise especially acutely a version of the same problem for the view that emotive meaning is illocutionary force. Consider the argument: 'Telling the truth is good; if telling the truth is good, getting your little brother to tell the truth is good; so getting your little brother to tell the truth is good.' This argument looks valid. But while 'telling the truth is good' in its occurrence as the first premise commends telling the truth, in its occurrence in the second premise it does not seem to commend anything. So, the suggestion is, emotivists cannot account for the validity of some moral arguments, because if meaning is understood as illocutionary force, it is not the same between different occurences of the same words in arguments. This problem is often called 'the problem of unasserted contexts' (in the second premise, 'telling the truth is good' occurs unasserted).

Fans of emotive meaning can respond to these criticisms. Hare, Blackburn and Gibbard have all offered solutions to the problem of unasserted contexts. It is certainly true that the meanings of *some* words (like 'promise') seem well explained by explaining the illocutionary act one performs in using them. Moreover, it is not an accident that, for instance, 'good' is often used to commend, while it is an accident if 'fast' is used to commend. Still, an attractive alternative to the theory that 'good' has emotive meaning is that 'good' *means* something like 'meets the relevant standards'. It is by virtue of this meaning that 'good' is often used to commend. Emotive force is then explained by meaning, not vice versa.

See also: EMOTIVISM; PRESCRIPTIVISM

References and further reading

Ayer, A.J. (1936) *Language, Truth and Logic*, New York: Dover. (Chapter 6 is Ayer's classic argument for and presentation of emotivism.)

Urmson, J.O. (1968) *The Emotive Theory of Ethics*, London: Hutchinson & Co. (Balanced consideration and development of emotive theory.)

DAVID PHILLIPS

EMOTIVISM

Emotivists held that moral judgments express and arouse emotions, not beliefs. Saying that an act is right or wrong was thus supposed to be rather like saying 'Boo!' or 'Hooray!' Emotivism explained well the apparent necessary connection between moral judgment and motivation. If people judge it wrong to lie, and their judgment expresses their hostility, then it comes as no surprise that we can infer that they are disinclined to lie. Emotivism did a bad job of explaining the important role of rational argument in moral practice, however. Indeed, since it entailed that moral judgments elude assessment in terms of truth and falsehood, it suggested that rational argument about morals might be at best inappropriate, and at worst impossible.

In the early part of the twentieth century, under the influence of logical positivism, a new view about the nature of morality emerged: emotivism (see LOGICAL POSITIVISM). Emotivists held that when people say, 'It is wrong to tell lies', they express their hostility towards lying and try to get others to share that hostility with them. Moral claims were thus supposed to be very different from claims expressing beliefs. Beliefs purport to represent the world, and so are assessable in terms of truth and falsehood. Emotions, by contrast, do not purport to represent the world, so moral claims were supposed to elude such assessment (see MORAL JUDGMENT §1). Judging acts right and wrong was thus rather like saying 'Boo!' and 'Hooray!'

Emotivism had evident appeal. It is widely agreed that there is a necessary connection of sorts between moral judgment and motivation. If someone judges telling lies to be wrong then they are motivated, to some extent, not to lie. But what people are motivated to do depends on what they approve of, or are hostile towards, not simply on what they believe (see MORAL MOTIVATION). Imagine, then, that someone's judgment that telling lies is wrong expressed a belief. In order to know whether they are inclined to lie or not we would then need to know, in addition, whether they approve of, or are hostile towards, telling lies. But we need to know no such thing. Knowing that they judge lying wrong suffices to know that they are disinclined to lie. This fits well with the idea that the judgment itself simply expresses hostility.

Emotivism also had its difficulties, however. Though emotivists admitted that rational argument about morals had an important role to play, their view entailed that this role was strictly limited. Since they agreed that less fundamental moral claims are entailed by more fundamental claims along with factual premises, and since they agreed that factual premises could be criticized rationally, they held that less fundamental moral claims must be rationally-based. Someone who judges lying wrong because they think that lies are harmful must, they thought, change their mind on pain of irrationality if shown that lying is harmless. But at the same time they insisted that fundamental moral claims – those that are not so derived, for example, the claim that it is wrong to cause harm – are immune from such rational criticism. This was the so-called 'fact/value gap' (see FACT/VALUE DISTINCTION).

It is unclear whether emotivists were consistent in allowing even this limited role for rational argument, however.

(1) If it is wrong to cause harm and lying causes harm then it is wrong to tell lies.

(2) It is wrong to cause harm.

(3) Lying causes harm.

   Therefore, it is wrong to tell lies.

This argument is valid only if 'It is wrong to cause harm' in premises (1) and (2) means the same thing. If this phrase means different things then there is an equivocation and the argument is straightforwardly invalid. Emotivism entails that someone who asserts (2) expresses hostility towards causing harm. Yet whatever 'It is wrong to cause harm' means in (1), it most certainly does not serve to express such hostility. In (1) the phrase appears in the antecedent of a conditional. Someone who asserts (1) may thus even deny that it is wrong to cause harm. They need therefore have no hostility to express towards causing harm.

Philosophers sympathetic to emotivism have tried to rescue it from this objection. There is a real question whether emotivists themselves should ever have been interested in preserving an important role for rational argument about morals, however. If the function of moral judgment is simply to express emotions and arouse like emotions in others then it follows that rational argument is at best one way, and perhaps not a very good way, of achieving these aims. We might be more effective if we distracted people from the facts and used rhetoric, humiliation and brainwashing instead. It is hard to see how emotivists could find fault with the idea that a practice in which the use of such technologies was widespread could still constitute a perfectly proper *moral* practice.

The best emotivists could say at this point was, 'Boo for persuasion and brainwashing!' Philosophers who thought this response failed to acknowledge the central and defining role played by rational argument in moral practice concluded that emotivism extracted too high a price for its explanation of the necessary connection between moral judgment and motivation. Subsequent theorists have focused on whether an alternative explanation of the necessary connection is available, one which also accommodates the idea that rational argument plays such a central and defining role. No consensus on this issue has emerged, however.

If nothing else, emotivism succeeded in making clear how difficult it is to explain the necessary connection between moral judgment and motivation, together with the idea that rational argument plays a central and defining role in moral practice, if the emotions that cause our actions are assumed to be beyond rational criticism. Much recent work about the nature of morality proceeds by calling this assumption into question.

See also: ARTISTIC EXPRESSION; AYER, A.J.; MORAL KNOWLEDGE; MORAL REALISM; MORALITY AND EMOTIONS; PRESCRIPTIVISM

References and further reading

Ayer, A.J. (1936) *Language, Truth and Logic*, London: Gollancz; 2nd edn, 1946, ch. 6. (Contains a classic statement of emotivism by a logical positivist.)

Warnock, G. (1967) *Contemporary Moral Philosophy*, London: Macmillan, ch. 3. (Contains a critical discussion of emotivism.)

MICHAEL SMITH

EMPEDOCLES (*c*.495–*c*.435 BC)

Empedocles, born in the Sicilian city of Acragas (modern Agrigento), was a major Greek philosopher of the Presocratic period. Numerous fragments survive from his two major works, poems in epic verse known later in antiquity as *On Nature* and *Purifications*.

On Nature sets out a vision of reality as a theatre of ceaseless change, whose invariable pattern consists in the repetition of the two processes of harmonization into unity followed by dissolution into plurality. The force unifying the four elements from which all else is created – earth, air, fire and water – is called Love, and Strife is the force dissolving them once again into plurality. The cycle is most apparent in the rhythms of plant and animal life, but Empedocles' main objective is to tell the history of the universe itself as an exemplification of the pattern.

The basic structure of the world is the outcome of disruption of a total blending of the elements into main masses which eventually develop into the earth, the sea, the air and the fiery heaven. Life, however, emerged not from separation but by mixture of elements, and Empedocles elaborates an account of the evolution of living forms of increasing complexity and capacity for survival, culminating in the creation of species as they are at present. There followed a detailed treatment of a whole range of biological phenomena, from reproduction to the comparative morphology of the parts of animals and the physiology of sense perception and thinking.

The idea of a cycle involving the fracture and restoration of harmony bears a clear relation to the Pythagorean belief in the cycle of reincarnations which the guilty soul must undergo before it can recover heavenly bliss. Empedocles avows his allegiance to this belief, and identifies the primal sin requiring the punishment of reincarnation as an act of bloodshed committed through 'trust in raving strife'. *Purifications* accordingly attacked the practice of animal sacrifice, and proclaimed prohibition against killing animals to be a law of nature.

Empedocles' four elements survived as the basis of physics for 2,000 years. Aristotle was fascinated by *On Nature*; his biology probably owes a good deal to its comparative morphology. Empedocles' cosmic cycle attracted the interest of the early Stoics. Lucretius found in him the model of a philosophical poet. Philosophical attacks on animal sacrifice made later in antiquity appealed to him as an authority.

See also: GORGIAS; MATTER; PARMENIDES; PRESOCRATIC PHILOSOPHY; PYTHAGORAS; PYTHAGOREANISM

MALCOLM SCHOFIELD

EMPIRICISM

In all its forms, empiricism stresses the fundamental role of experience. As a doctrine in epistemology it holds that all knowledge is ultimately based on experience. Likewise an empirical theory of meaning or of thought holds that the meaning of words or our concepts are derivative from experience. It is difficult to give an illuminating analysis of 'experience'. Let us say that it includes any mode of consciousness in which something seems to be presented to the subject, as contrasted with the mental activity of thinking about things. Experience, so understood, has a variety of modes – sensory, aesthetic, moral, religious and so on – but empiricists usually concentrate on sense experience, the modes of consciousness that result from the stimulation of the five senses.

It is obvious that not all knowledge stems directly from experience. Hence empiricism always assumes a stratified form, in which the lowest level issues directly from experience, and higher levels are based on lower levels. It has most commonly been thought by empiricists that beliefs at the lowest level simply 'read off' what is presented in experience. If a tree is visually presented to me as green I simply 'register' this appearance in forming the belief that the tree is green. Most of our beliefs – general beliefs for example – do not have this status but, according to empiricism, are supported by other beliefs in ways that eventually trace back to experience. Thus the belief that maple trees are bare in winter is supported by particular perceptual beliefs to the effect that this maple tree is bare and it is winter.

Empiricism comes in many versions. A major difference concerns the base on which each rests. A public version takes beliefs about what we perceive in the physical environment to be directly supported by experience. A phenomenalist version supposes that only beliefs about one's own sensory experience are directly supported, taking perceptual beliefs about the environment to get their support from the former sort of beliefs. The main difficulties for a global empiricism (all knowledge is based on experience) come from types of knowledge it is difficult to construe in this way, such as mathematical knowledge.

See also: A POSTERIORI; EPISTEMOLOGY, HISTORY OF; RATIONALISM

WILLIAM P. ALSTON

ENGELS, FRIEDRICH (1820–95)

Until the 1970s the most influential framework for understanding Marx's career and ideas was the one established by Engels. This framework was crucially related to his understanding of philosophy and its supposed culmination in Hegel's systematic and all-encompassing idealism.

Engels claimed that Marx had grounded Hegel's insights in a materialism that was coincident with the physical and natural sciences of his day, and that Marx had identified a dialectical method applicable to nature, history and thought. With respect to history, Marx was said to have formed a 'materialist conception', from which his analysis of capitalist society and its 'secret' of surplus value were derived. Together these intellectual features were the core of the 'scientific socialism' which, Engels argued, should form the theory, and inform the practice, of the worldwide socialist or communist movement. This was to abolish the poverty and exploitation necessarily engendered, he claimed, by modern industrial production.

Philosophically the tenets of dialectical and historical materialism have been defended and modified by orthodox communists and non-party Marxists, and expounded and criticized by political and intellectual opponents. The three laws of dialectics, and the doctrine that history is determined by material factors in the last instance, have been attacked as tautologous and indeterminate. Engels's view that scientific socialism is a defensible representation of Marx's project has also been challenged by textual scholars and historians.

See also: DIALECTICAL MATERIALSM; HEGELIANISM; MARXISM, WESTERN; MARXIST PHILOSOPHY, RUSSIAN AND SOVIET; SOCIALISM

TERRELL CARVER

ENLIGHTENMENT, CONTINENTAL

The Enlightenment is frequently portrayed as a campaign on behalf of freedom and reason as against dogmatic faith and its sectarian and barbarous consequences in the history of Western civilization. Many commentators who subscribe to this view find the Enlightenment's cosmopolitan opposition to priestly theology to be dangerously intolerant itself, too committed to uniform ideals of individual self-reliance without regard to community or diversity, or to recasting human nature in the light of science. Modern debates about the nature of the Enlightenment have their roots in eighteenth-century controversies about the arts and sciences and about ideas of progress and reason and the political consequences of promoting them. Even when they shared common objectives, eighteenth-century philosophers were seldom in agreement on substantive issues in epistemology or politics. If they were united at all, it was by virtue only of their collective scepticism in rejecting the universalist

pretensions of uncritical theology and in expressing humanitarian revulsion at crimes committed in the name of sacred truth.

See also: ENLIGHTENMENT, SCOTTISH

ROBERT WOKLER

ENLIGHTENMENT, SCOTTISH

This term refers to the intellectual movement in Scotland in roughly the second half of the eighteenth century. As a movement it included many theorists – the best known of whom are David Hume, Adam Smith and Thomas Reid – who maintained both institutional and personal links with each other. It was not narrowly philosophical, although in the Common Sense School it did develop its own distinctive body of argument. Its most characteristic feature was the development of a wide-ranging social theory that included pioneering 'sociological' works by Adam Ferguson and John Millar, socio-cultural history by Henry Home (Lord Kames) and William Robertson as well as Hume's *Essays* (1777) and Smith's classic 'economics' text *The Wealth of Nations* (1776). All these works shared a commitment to 'scientific' causal explanation and sought, from the premise of the uniformity of human nature, to establish a history of social institutions in which the notion of a mode of subsistence played a key organizing role. Typically of the Enlightenment as a whole this explanatory endeavour was not divorced from explicit evaluation. Though not uncritical of their own commercial society, the Scots were in no doubt as to the superiority of their own age compared to what had gone before.

See also: COMMONSENSISM; ENLIGHTENMENT, CONTINENTAL; MORAL SENSE THEORIES; NATURALISM IN ETHICS; NATURALISM IN SOCIAL SCIENCE

CHRISTOPHER J. BERRY

ENTAILMENT
See RELEVANCE LOGIC AND ENTAILMENT

ENTSCHEIDUNGSPROBLEM
See CHURCH'S THEOREM AND THE DECISION PROBLEM

ENVIRONMENTAL ETHICS

Theories of ethics try to answer the question, 'How ought we to live?'. An environmental ethic refers to our natural surroundings in giving the answer. It may claim that all natural things and systems are of value in their own right and worthy of moral respect. A weaker position is the biocentric one, arguing that living things merit moral consideration. An ethic which restricts the possession of moral value to human persons can still be environmental. Such a view may depict the existence of certain natural values as necessary for the flourishing of present and future generations of human beings. Moral respect for animals has been discussed since the time of the pre-Socratic philosophers, while the significance to our wellbeing of the natural environment has been pondered since the time of Kant and Rousseau. The relation of the natural to the built environment, and the importance of place, is a central feature of the philosophy of Heidegger. Under the impact of increasing species loss and land clearance, the work on environmental ethics since the 1970s has focused largely on one specific aspect of the environment – nature in the wild.

See also: ECOLOGICAL PHILOSOPHY; FUTURE GENERATIONS, OBLIGATIONS TO; SUSTAINABILITY

ANDREW BRENNAN

ENVIRONMENTALISM
See GREEN POLITICAL PHILOSOPHY

EPICUREANISM

Epicureanism is one of the three dominant philosophies of the Hellenistic age. The school was founded by Epicurus (341–271 BC). Only small samples and indirect testimonia of his writings now survive, supplemented by the poem of the Roman Epicurean Lucretius, along with a mass of further fragmentary texts and secondary evidence. Its main features are an anti-teleological physics, an empiricist epistemology and a hedonistic ethics.

Epicurean physics developed out of the fifth-century atomist system of Democritus. The only *per se* existents are bodies and space, each of them infinite in quantity. Space includes absolute void, which makes motion possible, while body is constituted out of physically indissoluble particles, 'atoms'. Atoms are themselves further measurable into sets of absolute 'minima', the ultimate units of magnitude. Atoms are in constant rapid motion, at equal speed (since in the pure void there is nothing to slow them down). Stability emerges as an overall property of compounds, which large groups of atoms form by settling into regular patterns of complex motion. Motion is governed by the three principles of weight, collisions and a minimal random movement, the 'swerve', which initiates new patterns of motion and obviates the danger of determinism. Atoms themselves have only the primary properties of shape, size and weight. All secondary properties, for example, colour, are generated out of atomic compounds; given their dependent status, they cannot be added to the list of

per se existents, but it does not follow that they are not real. Our world, like the countless other worlds, is an accidentally generated compound, of finite duration. There is no divine mind behind it. The gods are to be viewed as ideal beings, models of the Epicurean good life, and therefore blissfully detached from our affairs.

The foundation of the Epicurean theory of knowledge ('Canonic') is that 'all sensations are true' – that is, representationally (not propositionally) true. In the paradigm case of sight, thin films of atoms ('images') constantly flood off bodies, and our eyes mechanically register those which reach them, neither embroidering nor interpreting. These primary visual data (like photographs, which 'cannot lie') have unassailable evidential value. But inferences from them to the nature of external objects themselves involves judgment, and it is there that error can occur. Sensations thus serve as one of the three 'criteria of truth', along with feelings, a criterion of values and psychological data, and *prolēpseis*, naturally acquired generic conceptions. On the basis of sense evidence, we are entitled to infer the nature of microscopic or remote phenomena. Celestial phenomena, for example, cannot be regarded as divinely engineered (which would conflict with the *prolēpsis* of god as tranquil), and experience supplies plenty of models adequate to explain them naturalistically. Such grounds amount to consistency with directly observed phenomena, and are called *ouk antimarturēsis*, 'lack of counter-evidence'. Paradoxically, when several alternative explanations of the same phenomenon pass this test, all must be accepted as true. Fortunately, when it comes to the foundational tenets of physics, it is held that only one theory passes the test.

In ethics, pleasure is the one good and our innately sought goal, to which all other values are subordinated. Pain is the only bad, and there is no intermediate state. Bodily pleasure becomes more secure if we adopt a simple lifestyle which satisfies only our natural and necessary desires, with the support of like-minded friends. Bodily pain, when inevitable, can be outweighed by mental pleasure, which exceeds it because it can range over past, present and future enjoyments. The highest pleasure, whether of soul or of body, is a satisfied state, 'static pleasure'. The short-term ('kinetic') pleasures of stimulation can vary this state, but cannot make it more pleasant. In striving to accumulate such pleasures, you run the risk of becoming dependent on them and thus needlessly vulnerable to fortune. The primary aim should instead be the minimization of pain. This is achieved for the body through a simple lifestyle, and for the soul through the study of physics, which offers the most prized 'static' pleasure, 'freedom from disturbance' (*ataraxia*), by eliminating the two main sources of human anguish, the fears of god and of death. It teaches us that cosmic phenomena do not convey divine threats, and that death is mere disintegration of the soul, with hell an illusion. Being dead will be no worse than not having yet been born. Physics also teaches us how to evade determinism, which would turn moral agents into mindless fatalists: the indeterministic 'swerve' doctrine (see above), along with the logical doctrine that future-tensed propositions may be neither true nor false, leaves the will free.

Although Epicurean groups sought to opt out of public life, they respected civic justice, which they analysed not as an absolute value but as one perpetually subject to revision in the light of changing circumstances, a contract between humans to refrain from harmful activity in their own mutual interest.

See also: ATOMISM, ANCIENT; DEATH; FREE WILL; GASSENDI, P.; HEDONISM; LUCRETIUS; PERCEPTION; PROLĒPSIS; STOICISM; TELOS

DAVID SEDLEY

EPICURUS
See EPICUREANISM

EPIPHENOMENALISM

Epiphenomenalism is a theory concerning the relation between the mental and physical realms, regarded as radically different in nature. The theory holds that only physical states have causal power, and that mental states are completely dependent on them. The mental realm, for epiphenomenalists, is nothing more than a series of conscious states which signify the occurrence of states of the nervous system, but which play no causal role. For example, my feeling sleepy does not cause my yawning – rather, both the feeling and the yawning are effects of an underlying neural state.

Mental states are real, and in being conscious we are more than merely physical organisms. Nevertheless, all our experiences, thoughts and actions are determined by our physical natures. Mental states are actually as smoke from a machine seems to be, mere side effects making no difference to the course of Nature.

See also: CONSCIOUSNESS; MENTAL CAUSATION

KEITH CAMPBELL
NICHOLAS J.J. SMITH

EPISTEMIC PARADOXES
See PARADOXES, EPISTEMIC

EPISTEMIC VIRTUES
See THEORETICAL (EPISTEMIC) VIRTUES; VIRTUE EPISTEMOLOGY

EPISTEMOLOGY

Introduction

Epistemology is one of the core areas of philosophy. It is concerned with the nature, sources and limits of knowledge (see KNOWLEDGE, CONCEPT OF). There is a vast array of views about those topics, but one virtually universal presupposition is that knowledge is true belief, but not mere true belief. For example, lucky guesses or true beliefs resulting from wishful thinking are not knowledge. Thus, a central question in epistemology is: what must be added to true beliefs to convert them into knowledge?

1 The normative answers: foundationalism and coherentism
2 The naturalistic answers: causes of belief
3 Scepticism
4 Recent developments in epistemology

1 The normative answers: foundationalism and coherentism

The historically dominant tradition in epistemology answers that question by claiming that it is the quality of the reasons for our beliefs that converts true beliefs into knowledge (see EPISTEMOLOGY, HISTORY OF). When the reasons are sufficiently cogent, we have knowledge. This is the normative tradition in epistemology. An analogy with ethics is useful: just as an action is justified when ethical principles sanction its performance, a belief is justified when epistemic principles sanction accepting it (see JUSTIFICATION, EPISTEMIC; EPISTEMOLOGY AND ETHICS). The second tradition in epistemology, the naturalistic tradition, does not focus on the quality of the reasons for beliefs but, rather, requires that the conditions in which beliefs are acquired typically produce true beliefs (see INTERNALISM AND EXTERNALISM IN EPISTEMOLOGY; NATURALIZED EPISTEMOLOGY).

Within the normative tradition, two views about the proper structure of reasons have been developed: foundationalism and coherentism. By far, the most commonly held view is foundationalism. It holds that reasons rest on a foundational structure comprising 'basic' beliefs (see FOUNDATIONALISM). The foundational propositions, though justified, derive none of their justification from other propositions. (Coherentism, discussed below, denies that there are foundational propositions).

These basic beliefs can be of several types. Empiricists (such as HUME and LOCKE) hold that basic beliefs exhibit knowledge initially gained through the senses or introspection (see A POSTERIORI;

EMPIRICISM). Rationalists (such as DESCARTES, LEIBNIZ and SPINOZA) hold that at least some basic beliefs are the result of rational intuition (see A PRIORI; RATIONALISM). Since not all knowledge seems to be based on sense experience, introspection or rational intuition, some epistemologists claim that some knowledge is innate (see KNOWLEDGE, TACIT; KANT, I.; PLATO). Still others argue that some propositions are basic in virtue of conversational contextual features. That is, some propositions are taken for granted by the appropriate epistemic community (see CONTEXTUALISM, EPISTEMOLOGICAL).

Foundationalists hold that epistemic principles of inference are available which allow an epistemic agent to reason from the basic propositions to the non-basic (inferred) propositions. They suggest, for example, that if a set of basic propositions is explained by some hypothesis and additional confirming evidence for the hypothesis is discovered, then the hypothesis is justified. A notorious problem with this suggestion is that it is always possible to form more than one hypothesis that appears equally well confirmed by the total available data, and consequently no one hypothesis seems favoured over all its rivals (see INDUCTION, EPISTEMIC ISSUES IN). Some epistemologists have argued that this problem can be overcome by appealing to features of the rival hypotheses beyond their explanatory power. For example, the relative simplicity of one hypothesis might be thought to provide a basis for preferring it to its rivals (see SIMPLICITY (IN SCIENTIFIC THEORIES); THEORETICAL (EPISTEMIC) VIRTUES).

In contrast to foundationalism, coherentism claims that every belief derives some of its justification from other beliefs (see KNOWLEDGE AND JUSTIFICATION, COHERENCE THEORY OF; BOSANQUET, B.; BRADLEY, F.H.). All coherentists hold that, like the poles of a tepee, beliefs are mutually reinforcing. Some coherentists, however, assign a special justificatory role to those propositions that are more difficult to dislodge because they provide more support for the other propositions and are more supported by them. The set of these special propositions overlaps the set of basic propositions specified by foundationalism.

There are some objections aimed specifically at foundationalism and others aimed specifically at coherentism. But there is one deep difficulty with both traditional normative accounts. This problem, known as the 'Gettier problem' (after a famous three-page article by Edmund Gettier in 1963), can be stated succinctly as follows (see GETTIER PROBLEM): suppose that a false belief can be justified (see FALLIBILISM), and suppose that its justificatory status can be transferred to another proposition through deduction or other principles of inference

(see DEDUCTIVE CLOSURE PRINCIPLE). Suppose further that the inferred proposition is true. If these suppositions can be true simultaneously – and that seems to be the case – the inferred proposition would be true, justified (by either foundationalist or coherentist criteria) and believed, but it clearly is not knowledge, since it was inferred from a false proposition. It is a felicitous coincidence that the truth was obtained.

One strategy for addressing the Gettier Problem remains firmly within the normative tradition. It employs the original normative intuition that it is the quality of the reasons that distinguishes knowledge from mere true belief. This is the defeasibility theory of knowledge. There are various defeasibility accounts but, generally, all of them hold that the felicitous coincidence can be avoided if the reasons which justify the belief are such that they cannot be defeated by further truths.

2   The naturalistic answers: causes of belief

There is a second general strategy for addressing the Gettier Problem that falls outside of the normative tradition and lies squarely within the naturalistic tradition (see QUINE, W.V.). As the name suggests, the naturalistic tradition describes knowledge as a natural phenomenon occurring in a wide range of subjects. Adult humans may employ reasoning to arrive at some of their knowledge, but the naturalists are quick to point out that children and adult humans arrive at knowledge in ways that do not appear to involve any reasoning whatsoever. Roughly, when a true belief has the appropriate causal history, then the belief counts as knowledge (see KNOWLEDGE, CAUSAL THEORY OF).

Suppose that I am informed by a reliable person that the temperature outside the building is warmer now than it was two hours ago. That certainly looks like a bit of knowledge gained and there could be good reasons provided for the belief. The normativists would appeal to those good reasons to account for the acquisition of knowledge. The naturalists, however, would argue that true belief resulting from testimony from a reliable source is sufficient for knowledge (see SOCIAL EPISTEMOLOGY; TESTIMONY).

Testimony is just one reliable way of gaining knowledge. There are other ways such as sense perception, memory and reasoning. Of course, sometimes these sources are faulty (see MEMORY, EPISTEMOLOGY OF). A central task of naturalized epistemology is to characterize conditions in which reliable information is obtained. Thus, in some of its forms, naturalized epistemology can be seen as a branch of cognitive psychology, and the issues can be addressed by empirical investigation.

Now let us return to the Gettier Problem. Recall that it arose in response to the recognition that truth might be obtained through a felicitous coincidence. The naturalistic tradition ties together the belief and truth conditions of knowledge in a straightforward way by requiring that the means by which the true belief is produced or maintained should be reliable.

3 Scepticism

The contrast between normative and naturalized epistemology is apparent in the way in which each addresses one of the most crucial issues in epistemology, namely, scepticism (see SCEPTICISM). Scepticism comes in many forms. In one form, the requirements for knowledge become so stringent that knowledge becomes impossible, or virtually impossible, to obtain. For example, suppose that a belief is knowledge only if it is certain, and a belief is certain only if it is beyond all logically possible doubt. Knowledge would then become a very rare commodity (see DOUBT).

Other forms of scepticism only require good, but not logically unassailable, reasoning. We have alluded to scepticism about induction. That form of scepticism illustrates the general pattern of the sceptical problem: there appear to be intuitively clear cases of the type of knowledge questioned by the sceptic, but intuitively plausible general epistemic principles appealed to by the sceptic seem to preclude that very type of knowledge.

Another example will help to clarify the general pattern of the sceptical problem. Consider the possibility that my brain is not lodged in my skull but is located in a vat and hooked up to a very powerful computer that stimulates it to have exactly the experiences, memories and thoughts that I am now having. Call it the 'sceptical hypothesis'. That hypothetical situation is clearly incompatible with the way I think the world is. Now, it seems to be an acceptable normative epistemic principle that if I am justified in believing that the world is the way I believe it to be (with other people, tables, governments and so on), I should have some good reasons for denying the sceptical hypothesis. But, so the argument goes, I could not have such reasons; for if the sceptical hypothesis were true, everything would appear to be just as it now does. So, there appears to be a conflict between the intuition that we have such knowledge and the intuitively appealing epistemic principle. Thus, scepticism can be seen as one instance of an interesting array of epistemic paradoxes (see PARADOXES, EPISTEMIC).

Of course, epistemologists have developed various answers to scepticism. Within the normative tradition, there are several responses available. One of them is simply to deny any epistemic principle –

even if it seems initially plausible – that precludes us from having what we ordinarily think is within our ken (see COMMONSENSISM; CHISHOLM, R.M.; MOORE, G.E.; REID, T.). Another response is to examine the epistemic principles carefully in an attempt to show that, properly interpreted, they do not lead to scepticism. Of course, there is always the option of simply declaring that we do not have knowledge. Whatever choice is made, some initially plausible intuitions will be sacrificed.

Within the naturalistic tradition, there appears to be an easy way to handle the sceptical worries. Possessing knowledge is not determined by whether we have good enough reasons for our beliefs but, rather, whether the processes that produced the beliefs in question are sufficiently reliable. So, if I am a brain in a vat, I do not have knowledge; and if I am not a brain in a vat (and the world is generally the way I think it is), then I do have knowledge. Nevertheless, those within the normative tradition will argue that we are obliged to withhold full assent to propositions for which we have less than adequate reasons, regardless of the causal history of the belief.

4 Recent developments in epistemology

Some recent developments in epistemology question and/or expand on some aspects of the tradition. Virtue epistemology focuses on the characteristics of the knower rather than individual beliefs or collections of beliefs (see VIRTUE EPISTEMOLOGY). Roughly, the claim is that when a true belief is the result of the exercise of intellectual virtue, it is, *ceteris paribus*, knowledge. Thus, the virtue epistemologist can incorporate certain features of both the normative and naturalist traditions. Virtues, as opposed to vices, are good, highly prized dispositional states. The intellectual virtues, in particular, are just those deep dispositions that produce mostly true beliefs. Such an approach reintroduces some neglected areas of epistemology, for example, the connection of knowledge to wisdom and understanding.

In addition, there are emerging challenges to certain presuppositions of traditional epistemology. For example, some argue that there is no set of rules for belief acquisition that are appropriate for all peoples and all situations. Others have suggested that many of the proposed conditions of good reasoning, for example 'objectivity' or 'neutrality', are not invoked in the service of gaining truths, as traditional epistemology would hold, but rather they are employed to prolong entrenched power and (at least in some cases) distort the objects of knowledge (see FEMINIST EPISTEMOLOGY).

In spite of these fundamental challenges and the suggestions inherent in some forms of naturalized epistemology that the only interesting questions are empirically answerable, it is clear that epistemology remains a vigorous area of inquiry at the heart of philosophy.

See also: CHARITY, PRINCIPLE OF; CRITERIA; HERMENEUTICS; PHENOMENALISM; PHENOMENOLOGY, EPISTEMIC ISSUES IN; RORTY, R.M.; SOLIPSISM

References and further reading

BonJour, L. (1985) *The Structure of Empirical Knowledge*, Cambridge, MA: Harvard University Press. (Develops and defends a coherentist account of knowledge and justification)

Chisholm, R. (1966/1977/1989) *Theory of Knowledge*, Englewood Cliffs, NJ: Prentice Hall, 1st, 2nd and 3rd edns. (Successive editions contain a general introduction to many issues in epistemology and increasingly complex foundationalist accounts of knowledge.)

Luper, S. (ed.) (2004) *Essential Knowledge*, New York, NY: Pearson Longman (Contains historical and contemporary articles and book excerpts with helpful introductions to the various topics.)

PETER D. KLEIN

EPISTEMOLOGY AND ETHICS

Epistemology and ethics are both concerned with evaluations: ethics with evaluations of conduct, epistemology with evaluations of beliefs and other cognitive acts. Of considerable interest to philosophers are the ways in which the two kinds of evaluations relate to one another. Philosophers' explorations of these relations divide into two general categories: examination of potential analogies between the two fields, and attempts to identify necessary or conceptual connections between the two domains.

There is little doubt that there are at least superficial similarities between ethics and epistemology: one might say that ethics is about the appraisal of social behaviour and agents, while epistemology is about the appraisal of cognitive acts and agents. On the other hand, the widely held view that behaviour subject to moral evaluation is free and voluntary while beliefs are not, suggests one important disanalogy between the two fields.

See also: CONFUCIAN PHILOSOPHY, CHINESE; JUSTIFICATION, EPISTEMIC

RICHARD FELDMAN

EPISTEMOLOGY, HISTORY OF

Introduction

Epistemology has always been concerned with issues such as the nature, extent, sources and legitimacy of knowledge. Over the course of Western philosophy, philosophers have concentrated sometimes on one or two of these issues to the exclusion of the others; rarely has a philosopher addressed all of them. Some central questions are:

(1) What is knowledge – what is the correct analysis or definition of the concept of knowledge?
(2) What is the extent of our knowledge – about what sorts of things is knowledge actually held?
(3) What are the sources of knowledge – how is knowledge acquired?
(4) Is there any genuine knowledge?

Concern with the first question has predominated in philosophy since the mid-twentieth century, but it was also discussed at some length in antiquity. Attention to the second question seems to have begun with Plato, and it has continued with few interruptions to the present day. The third question was also important in antiquity, but has also been a central focus of epistemological discussion through the medieval and early modern periods. The fourth question raises the issue of scepticism, a topic which has generated interest and discussion from antiquity to the present day, though there were some periods in which sceptical worries were largely ignored.

Various attempts to answer these questions throughout the history of philosophy have invariably served to raise additional questions which are more narrow in focus. The principal one which will be treated below can be stated as:

(5) What is a justified belief – under which conditions is a belief justified?

There has been but occasional interest in this last question in the history of philosophy; however, it has been a crucial question for many philosophers in the twentieth century.

1   Ancient philosophy
2   Hellenistic philosophy
3   Medieval philosophy
4   Modern philosophy: Descartes
5   Modern philosophy: Spinoza and Leibniz
6   Modern philosophy: Locke and Berkeley
7   Modern philosophy: from Hume to Peirce
8   Twentieth century
9   Recent issues

1   Ancient philosophy

The extant writings of the Presocratics primarily address issues in metaphysics and cosmology; epistemological concerns appear to arise first in Plato. In the *Meno* Plato tells the story of a slave boy who has had no formal education and in particular has never studied geometry. In a conversation with Socrates, the boy is led to answer questions about a geometrical figure and his answers turn out to be correct. The boy is led to assert that when given a square with side S, so that its area is S^2, then a square of exactly $2S^2$ is formed by taking as its side the diagonal of the original square. The boy could hardly have learned this earlier, since he is uneducated. Plato takes this example to show that the boy knew the geometrical truth all along and, more generally, that the boy's soul existed earlier in a state of knowledge. Indeed, he held that the boy's soul earlier knew all truths but had since forgotten them. What the boy was really doing in his conversation with Socrates was recollecting something he had forgotten. And this Plato takes to hold for everyone: what we think of as coming to know is really recollecting.

The soul or knower may have come into existence and so it would not have always had knowledge; or it may have always been in existence but at some time acquired its stock of knowledge; or it may have always been and always had knowledge. Plato certainly rejects the first option, especially in the *Phaedo* where he argues for the indestructibility and indefinite prior existence of the soul. He also appears to reject the second option (*Meno* 86b) so that his view would be that the soul always exists and earlier had a great deal of knowledge without having acquired this knowledge at some time.

The *Meno* also contains a distinction between true belief and knowledge (97d–98b). Knowledge, Plato says, is 'tied down' or tethered in a way that true opinion is not. This view, which seems to suggest that knowledge is justified true belief, is taken up again in the *Theaetetus*, where Plato suggests that knowledge is true belief plus an account or *logos* (201d). However, several attempts to explicate the notion of an account are rejected, and the dialogue ends inconclusively. It is not clear whether Plato rejects this account of knowledge outright, or whether he is best construed as rejecting this definition given the defective notions of an account (*Theaetetus* 210a–b).

In the *Republic*, especially in Book V, Plato addresses a version of our question pertaining to the extent of knowledge. There he distinguishes between knowledge at one extreme and ignorance at the other, and he roughly identifies an intermediate state of opinion or belief. Each of these states of mind, Plato says, has an object. The object of knowledge is what is or exists; the object of ignorance is what does not exist; and the object of belief is some intermediate entity, often taken as what is becoming or the sensible physical world of objects and their qualities (*Republic* 508d–e; *Cratylus* 440a–d). What truly exists for Plato are unchanging

Forms, and it is these which he indicates as the true objects of knowledge (see FORMS, PLATONIC). Moreover, knowledge is infallible, while belief is fallible (*Republic* 477e). In thus identifying knowledge with infallibility or certainty, Plato is departing widely from the view of knowledge given in *Meno* and *Theaetetus*. And, his account of the extent of our knowledge is also severely restricted: genuine knowledge is had only of the higher realm of immutable, ideal Forms (see FALLIBILISM; PLATO §§11, 15).

Aristotle discusses a special form of knowledge, scientific knowledge, in the *Posterior Analytics*. A science, as Aristotle understands it, is to be thought of as a group of theorems each of which is proved in a demonstrative syllogism. In the first instance, a demonstrative syllogism in science S is a syllogistic argument whose premises are first principles of S. These first principles, in turn, must be true, primary, immediate, better known than and prior to the conclusion, which is further related to them as effect to cause (*Posterior Analytics* 71b 21–22). First principles are primary and immediate when they are not themselves demonstrable. Still, such principles are known; indeed, they are better known than the demonstrated conclusion, a contention which may mean either that they are more familiar than the conclusion, or perhaps more certain than the conclusion. The first principles are also said to be prior to the conclusions in an epistemic way: knowledge of the conclusion requires knowledge of the first principles, but not conversely. And the first principles must explain why it is that the demonstrated conclusion is true.

The science can be extended by taking theorems proved from first principles as premises in additional demonstrative syllogisms for further conclusions. Here, too, the premises must explain the truth of the conclusion. A science will be the sum of all such theorems, demonstrated either from first principles or from already demonstrated theorems in appropriate syllogisms. And a person who carries through all these syllogisms with relevant understanding has knowledge of all of the theorems.

The first principles, however, are also known though they are not demonstrated as theorems. On this point Aristotle gives what may be the first statement of a regress argument in favour of a kind of foundationalist position (see FOUNDATIONALISM). Some might hold that even the first principles must be demonstrated if they are to be known. This would lead to an infinite regress, as these first principles would themselves be conclusions of syllogisms whose premises were other first principles which, to be known, would have to be demonstrated. To avoid the infinite regress, one would need either to allow for circular demonstration, or to agree that the first principles are not themselves known but are mere suppositions. Aristotle rejects all these options in favour of the foundationalist view in which the first principles are known even though they are not demonstrated. For him, one has an immediate, intuitive grasp of the first principles. However, his foundationalism is to be distinguished from those discussed below, because his foundations are made up of fundamental principles of special sciences.

In *De Anima*, Aristotle discusses perception and perceptual knowledge. Among perceptible objects, he distinguishes between proper and common sensibles. Common sensibles are those objects that are perceivable by more than one sense, for example, the shape of a box which can be both seen and touched. Proper sensibles are those objects that are only perceivable by one sense, for example, colour can only be seen. With respect to these proper objects, Aristotle says that one cannot be in error, or one cannot be deceived (*De Anima* 418a 9–13; 428b 17–21). So, if a person sees a white cat, they can be deceived about whether it is a cat, but not in thinking that there is white present. The same would apply to proper objects of other senses. If we then assume, as Aristotle seems to have done, that the impossibility of being deceived about *X* is sufficient for having knowledge about *X*, then we reach the conclusion that we have certain perceptual knowledge about the proper objects of each sense. What is not clear is whether Aristotle felt that one could not be mistaken about actual qualities of physical objects, such as their colours; or rather about an object's perceived qualities. Clearly the former is much less plausible than the latter (see ARISTOTLE §6).

2 Hellenistic philosophy

The Hellenistic phase of philosophy occupies several centuries after Aristotle's death (322 BC), and is notable for its three schools of philosophy: Epicureanism, Stoicism, and Scepticism (see SCEPTICISM). The sceptical tradition, however, continued well into the second century AD.

The Epicurean school supported an even more thoroughgoing empiricism than we find in Aristotle, and is best known for its doctrine that all perceptions are true. In perception, Epicurus says, thin layers of atoms are emitted from external physical objects (*eídōla*) and reach our senses, which passively receive and register these *eídōla* exactly as they are. But this, *per se*, is not to have knowledge of the external causes of our experiences of *eídōla*. For that, we need to make well-grounded inferences to the existence and nature of the external objects. Epicurus, however, maintains that these inferences,

doubtless causal ones, can be legitimately made, and thus that there is genuine perceptual knowledge of physical objects. The fact that these inferences may fare poorly under sceptical scrutiny is not a matter to which Epicurus paid special attention, probably because he did not think that the defeat of sceptical concerns was a necessary project within epistemology (see EPICUREANISM).

The Stoic position is much less optimistic. Their central concept is that of a cognitive impression. In normal conditions a red object appears red, and one has the thought (cognitive impression) 'This is red'. Such a cognitive impression, Stoics held, cannot fail to be true. It is not, by itself, knowledge of the red object however, because the person might not assent to this impression. One has knowledge only if one assents to a cognitive impression and this assent is firm, the sort of assent that one cannot be persuaded to withhold. Ordinary people fall short of assent of this firm sort, and so really have mere opinions about objects. Only the wise man typically engages in firm assent to only cognitive impressions; so only the wise man truly has knowledge of such objects (see STOICISM).

In thus restricting knowledge, the Stoic position is actually close to a sceptical doctrine. The two schools of ancient scepticism, the Academic and the Pyrrhonian, had notable differences and each had points of development over nearly five centuries, ending with Sextus Empiricus in the late second century AD. A common feature of each school, though, is an attack on claims to knowledge. For any argument towards a conclusion which goes beyond sensory appearances, sceptics maintained that an equally strong counter-argument could be given. Other sceptical arguments point to the relativity of all perception, depending on changes in the percipient or in the observation conditions or perspectives, and conclude that we do not gain knowledge of external physical objects via perception. Also, if a criterion for knowledge-acquisition is relied upon – such as perception or causal inductive inference as in Epicurus – then this criterion could be questioned as itself being far from evidently reliable. These sceptical arguments were properly taken to lead to the suspension of belief (*epochē*), rather than to the assertion that there is no knowledge. Moreover, the Pyrrhonian sceptics noted that the ultimate goal of their arguments was a non-epistemic one, that of *ataraxía* or being undisturbed. This calm state is presumed achievable once beliefs have been suspended and one is content to carry on one's life dealing only with appearances (see PYRRHONISM; SEXTUS EMPIRICUS).

Scepticism was challenged in the early medieval period by Augustine in his *Contra Academicos*, in which he dealt critically with the arguments of

Cicero, the last of the great academic sceptics (see AUGUSTINE; CICERO, M.T.). However, scepticism was not a major concern in the Middle Ages, and did not receive special philosophical attention again until the Renaissance.

3 Medieval philosophy

Medieval philosophy is concerned primarily with issues in metaphysics, logic and natural theology, less with epistemological topics. Aquinas and Ockham, however, were two thinkers for whom epistemological questions were of great interest and importance.

Aquinas closely followed Aristotle on many points, including Aristotle's account of scientific knowledge (see §1 above). Thus, *scientia* or genuine scientific knowledge is restricted to propositions proved in demonstrative syllogisms whose premises are themselves known. And, as in Aristotle, Aquinas holds that this account of *scientia* requires as premises in some demonstrative syllogisms, first principles that are known *per se*, immediately and without inference. That there must be such first principles is shown by the fact that otherwise one is faced with either an infinite regress of items of knowledge or with circularity. The former is ruled out because nobody can achieve an infinite number of inferential steps; and circularity, wherein one knows *p* on the basis of *q* and knows *q* on the basis of *p*, is dismissed because it allows that a single proposition, *p*, can both be and not be epistemically prior to *q*. For both Aquinas and Aristotle, the premises of a demonstrative syllogism are epistemically prior to their conclusions in the sense that one cannot know the conclusion without first knowing the premises, though not vice versa.

First principles of demonstrative syllogisms, for Aquinas, are necessary truths, propositions in which there is a necessary connection between the predicate and subject concepts. To grasp or know a first principle, then, requires that one grasp this necessary connection. To achieve this, one must first possess the general concepts expressed by the subject and predicate terms. Accordingly, Aquinas gives an account of how we may acquire such concepts. To do this, one must abstract the intelligible species or forms of objects from the sense impressions received in perception of them. Ultimately, then, knowledge of the first principles depends on perception, though it is not epistemically based on perception.

William of Ockham makes an interesting break with Aquinas' conception of knowledge. Part of the break concerns the fact that Ockham allows for knowledge of contingent truths, as opposed to restricting knowledge to necessary truths. Another

difference concerns perception. Aquinas held that, in perception, one has an experience of an image or phantasm from which by some cognitive mechanism (called an agent intellect) one abstracts an intelligible species or form of the perceived object. By means of this abstracted item one knows some universal aspect of the perceived object (see AQUINAS, T. §11). Ockham disagrees with a number of these points. For him, in perception of an external physical object, there is no intermediary such as a phantasm or sensible species. Instead, the object is itself perceived directly, an experience which Ockham regards as an intuitive cognition. In this respect, Ockham's account is close to that of perceptual direct realism. But he also holds epistemic direct realism, because he argues that the direct visual awareness of the external object suffices for one to acquire immediate and certain knowledge of the existence of the object and of some of its qualities. In this regard, one is 'knowing the singular' rather than something universal; and the proposition one comes to know in perception is a contingent truth. So, in perceiving a red box, one might come to know that there is a red box before one.

Sceptical worries could intrude, even here. One might see a red box and still be mistaken in one's resulting belief. One might think, therefore, that forming the belief as a result of a red-box visual experience does not suffice for knowledge. Ockham is aware of this objection, but he has a two-part answer to it. First, he notes that the mere possibility of mistaken belief does not rule out knowledge. He also notes that aligning the concept of certainty with the impossibility of mistaken belief is itself an error. Certainty, he says, requires only the absence of actual doubt or grounds for doubt. Certainty of this weaker sort, he holds, is all that is needed for knowledge (see WILLIAM OF OCKHAM).

This is a decisive break with earlier views, both with respect to the concept of certainty and with respect to its relation to the concept of knowledge. But, with one or two notable exceptions, these ideas were not taken up by many writers until much later.

4 Modern philosophy: Descartes

It is customary to begin the story of modern philosophy with Descartes, but we need to start a little farther back with a discussion of scepticism. We have noted that ancient scepticism was hardly known during the Middle Ages. In the sixteenth century, however, the old sceptical texts of Cicero were re-published and works by Sextus Empiricus were translated into Latin and thus made available to scholars. These texts and their arguments became very important to those on both sides of disputes over the legitimacy and extent of religious knowledge, an issue given great currency by the Reformation and the Counter-Reformation. Under the direct influence of Sextus Empiricus, MONTAIGNE published his *Apology for Raimond Sebond* (1576) in which he set forth sceptical arguments and recommended suspension of belief on practically all topics. His disciple, Pierre Charron, popularized sceptical doctrines even further. This sceptical climate was well known to Descartes in the first half of the seventeenth century. Still later, Pierre Bayle's *Dictionary*, which contained a number of sceptical entries, was to have a great deal of influence on Berkeley and Hume (see BAYLE, P.).

Descartes was thoroughly aware of the sceptical writings and debates of his time, and of the development of sceptical literature since Montaigne. But Descartes himself was no sceptic; on the contrary, he set out to defeat scepticism on its own terms, that is, by finding some knowledge which is completely certain and thus immune to sceptical criticism.

To accomplish this, Descartes used the method of doubt, a method wherein a proposition is considered false provided there is even the slightest possible ground for doubting it. Whole classes of propositions would then be excluded as not known: everything which one believes on the basis of the senses is dubitable by this criterion, and so is not knowledge. The many propositions of science also qualify as dubitable, and so are not items of knowledge. Indeed, it is possible, Descartes reasons, that an evil demon systematically deceives us all, even with respect to the necessary truths of mathematics. If such a demon is even possible, then there is at least the possibility of grounds for doubt, and so virtually nothing would qualify as knowledge.

Descartes contends, however, that such an evil demon cannot deceive him in one case, namely when he thinks in any way. Even when the thinking in which he engages is a case of doubting, whenever Descartes thinks he must exist, and thus he affirms as certain 'Cogito, ergo sum' – I think, therefore I exist. This is an item about which he cannot be deceived, and it is thus for Descartes indubitable or certain, and assuredly a case of knowledge.

Descartes' epistemological project then becomes one of seeing whether any other genuine certain knowledge can be derived from this very slender base. He finds first a criterion for certainty: those thoughts or ideas which are clear and distinct are also true. In fact, he says that clarity and distinctness of a thought or idea suffices to assure him of its truth. Using this criterion together with his certain

knowledge that he exists, Descartes constructs a complex causal argument for the existence of God. The clarity and distinctness of the thoughts that God is not a deceiver and that God would not allow wholesale deception is then put to work to try to derive propositions formerly excluded as dubitable by the method. Especially important here are propositions concerning the existence of external physical objects.

Descartes' project is thus a foundationalist one of an austere sort. For him, the foundations are restricted to the propositions that he himself exists, that he has certain ideas, and that God exists. From these, utilizing the criterion of clarity and distinctness, the foundations can be augmented to include propositions about immediately experienced sensations. However, derivations of other propositions from these foundational ones have to be restricted to deductions that themselves can be seen to be clear and distinct. If the derivations were inductive, then grounds for doubting the conclusions would be possible. And even if the derivations were deductive, if one did not see that they were validly made from individually indubitable premises, once again the possibility of grounds for doubting the conclusions would arise. Only if the possibility of such grounds are eliminated can these derived conclusions count as items of knowledge.

Descartes, thus, perpetuates and even emphasizes the close conceptual connection between knowledge and the strictest sort of certainty. He also gives currency to the problem of the external world, that is, the problem of deriving propositions concerning external physical objects from foundational propositions made up mostly of propositions concerning sensations. Of course, Descartes has propositions about a non-deceiving God in his foundations, unlike later writers who grappled with this problem. So armed, Descartes claims in the sixth Meditation that he can derive the general claims that there are external physical objects and that they have at most the so-called primary qualities. But even if these claims count as items of knowledge, so that to some extent scepticism is vanquished, it does not seem that Descartes secures knowledge of individual propositions about physical objects and their qualities. For he concedes that, with respect to these, error is possible in the best of circumstances, even with God's help (see DESCARTES, R. §§3–5).

5 Modern philosophy: Spinoza and Leibniz

It is customary to classify Spinoza and Leibniz along with Descartes as rationalists. In epistemology, rationalism is the view which stresses the role of reason in the acquisition of knowledge, and correspondingly downplays the role of experience or observation. A limiting case of rationalism, then, would be a position which held that only reason is operative in knowledge acquisition. It is perhaps Spinoza who comes closest to a rationalist position of this sort (see RATIONALISM).

For Spinoza, a true idea is one which must agree with its object (*Ethics*: I, dx. 6). An adequate idea is one which, considered by itself, has an internal sign or intrinsic mark of a true idea (*Ethics*: II, def. 4). Having an adequate idea, then, suffices to recognize it as true. There is no need of a clarity-and-distinctness criterion for determining which ideas are true. In this respect, Spinoza differs sharply from Descartes.

Spinoza distinguishes three levels of knowledge. The first is that which we receive in sense perception or from what he calls 'signs', as when the sight of some printed words causes one to remember something. First-level knowledge is not strictly knowledge, however, but rather opinion or imagination. Second-level knowledge or reason (*ratio*) is knowledge of the properties of objects and of relations between properties. Third-level knowledge is intuitive science, which Spinoza says 'advances from an adequate idea of the formal essence of certain attributes of God to the adequate knowledge of the essence of things' (*Ethics*: II prop. XL, schol. 2). Third-level knowledge proceeds from one thing to another in the sense that a person who has an adequate idea of the formal essence of one of God's attributes may logically infer to adequate knowledge of the essence of things.

Knowledge is adequate when one may logically infer, merely from having an adequate idea of *x*, to some general truth about *x* (second level), or to some truth about *x*'s effects (third level). Thus, on the second level, from an adequate idea of body one may infer that all bodies are capable of motion, and thus knowledge of this proposition is adequate. And from the adequate idea of the essence of a divine attribute, one may infer to the essence or nature of objects, and thus the proposition concerning the essence of the objects is adequately known.

Spinoza certainly thinks we have adequate ideas, and so have adequate knowledge (*Ethics*: II, prop. XXXIV). And he holds that the propositions known at the second and third levels are necessarily true (*Ethics* XLI). So, it looks very much as if Spinoza is committed to the view that second- and third-level knowledge is a priori, that is, knowledge that need not rely on experience, and to this degree he would qualify as a rationalist (see SPINOZA, B. DE §§7–8).

Leibniz, the other great philosopher usually classified as a rationalist, did not develop a systematic view in epistemology. His classification as a rationalist is no doubt tied to two important strands of his thought. For simple subject-predicate propositions, fundamental for Leibniz, he proposed the predicate-in-notion principle. This is the thesis that the concept of the predicate in such a proposition is contained in the concept of the subject. It seems as though this principle implies that all subject-predicate propositions are necessarily true. For the conceptual-containment doctrine amounts to the claim that such propositions are true in virtue of their meanings or are conceptually true, and this would make them necessarily true. This has the twofold result that all truth is necessary truth, given that subject-predicate propositions are fundamental; and, that all knowledge is or can be a priori, the latter on the assumption that if a proposition is a necessary truth, then it is a priori knowable. If Leibniz held these views, his status as a rationalist is secure.

Leibniz strove to ward off these consequences, however, by an account of analysis. He held that in a necessary proposition, the concept-containment feature allows for the proposition to be analysed or reduced to an identity proposition in a finite number of steps. Contingent truths, however, cannot be so analysed, despite the concept-containment thesis. Instead, in an infinite number of steps of analysis, such propositions would converge on an identity proposition. (Sometimes Leibniz suggests that such propositions can be analysed into identity propositions by God.) So, not all truths are necessary, and thus neither is all knowledge a priori.

There is a strong rationalist side to Leibniz, however, which emerges in the second strand of his thought, namely, his defence of innate truths. In a dispute with Locke, Leibniz contended that there are numerous innate concepts and principles in pure mathematics, logic, metaphysics and ethics. These innate truths are all necessary truths, and they are all knowable a priori. The senses, Leibniz says, merely function as the occasions by and on which these truths are brought to attention (see LEIBNIZ, G.W. §§8–9).

6 Modern philosophy: Locke and Berkeley

Locke provides a strong empiricist contrast to both Spinoza and Leibniz. For Locke, the fundamental items of all cognitions are ideas, which divide into those of sensation and those of reflection. The former are acquired in perception, the latter in introspective attention to the contents and workings of one's own mind. Perception and reflection, for Locke, make up experience, and the fundamental empiricist thesis is that all ideas and all knowledge derive from experience. It follows from empiricism so construed that no ideas are innate. For Locke, the mind is a 'blank tablet' at birth, and it is only by experience that it acquires its stock of ideas.

In *An Essay concerning Human Understanding* Locke defines knowledge as the perception of the agreement or disagreement of two ideas (1689: IV, I, 1 and 5). This definition has the immediate effect of restricting all knowledge to ideas, something Locke recognizes and appears to accept (1689: IV, II, 1). It also seems to have the effect of restricting knowledge to relations between ideas. The definition and the restriction accord well with most of what Locke says about knowledge.

Intuitive knowledge is the perception of the agreement or disagreement between two ideas 'immediately by themselves, without the intervention of any other' (*Essay* (1689): IV, II, 1). Perception that white is not the same as black, for example, is immediate and requires no intermediate idea between those of white and black. Intuitive knowledge, for Locke, is the most certain: it is both irresistible and infallible.

Locke seems to desert his definition of knowledge in three important cases, however, and in two of these cases intuitive knowledge is at issue. One has, for instance, intuitive knowledge of individual ideas, as when one knows that some pain is very sharp (*Essay*: IV, II, 1). Locke also maintains that one has intuitive knowledge of oneself. In such a case, even if an idea of reflection is had, self-knowledge is not a perception of an agreement or disagreement of two ideas. Moreover, it is knowledge about the self, which is not an idea or group of ideas. In this case, Locke departs not merely from his definition, but also from his explicit claim about the extent of our knowledge.

Demonstrative knowledge, for Locke, requires that each step in the demonstration be intuitively known, and that the relation between the premises and the conclusion also be intuitively known. Meeting these constraints on demonstrative knowledge assures that it is virtually as certain as intuitive knowledge. But meeting these constraints is not easy, especially in long demonstrations where one must keep in mind inferences made earlier. In such cases, Locke indicates, one's degree of certainty with respect to the conclusion will drop and one will not have demonstrative knowledge properly speaking.

Locke's account of sensitive knowledge marks a third point at which he seems to depart from his official definition of knowledge and the restriction of knowledge to our ideas. Sensitive knowledge is knowledge of the existence of external physical objects. It is not as certain as intuitive or demonstrative knowledge, yet it is still knowledge. And Locke clearly thinks that we have such knowledge, at least in those cases when an external physical object is actually present to one's senses

(*Essay*: IV, III, 5). Locke conceives of sensitive knowledge of presently perceived physical objects as inferential knowledge. From knowledge of presently experienced ideas one infers that there is an external physical object present as the cause of those ideas. Locke is untroubled by sceptical worries over whether such inferences can be legitimately made.

The distinction between intuitive and certain knowledge of ideas, and sensitive knowledge of physical objects, with the latter knowledge inductively based on the former, is indicative of Locke's foundationalist position. It differs from that proposed by Descartes, however, in two important ways. First, the propositions making up the foundations are different. For Locke, these are confined to propositions about individually experienced ideas, or to propositions describing a perceived agreement or disagreement between ideas. Thus, Locke's commitment to empiricism dictates what the foundations shall be. Another difference comes in the inferences from the foundational propositions which Locke finds acceptable. He allows for both deductive and inductive inferences, whereas for Descartes permissible inferences may only be deductive. Locke thus marks a liberalization of the foundationalist strictures imposed by Descartes (see LOCKE, J. §§2–3).

Berkeley was critical of Locke's account of knowledge of physical objects, as was Hume (though, unlike Berkeley, Hume did not mention Locke by name). Locke notes that inductive inferences from currently experienced ideas to physical objects will succeed only when there is a conformity between the ideas and the physical object (*Essay*: IV, IV, 3). Ideas, that is, have to represent the physical objects in some way. Berkeley denies that ideas can serve this role. An idea, he says, can only be like or similar to another idea, not a physical object. Moreover, even allowing for this similarity, the needed inductive inferences depend on and so require that one establish that some ideas do adequately represent objects. To accomplish this, Berkeley argues, one must be in a position to compare the ideas and the physical object. However, as Berkeley notes, this is a position one cannot occupy given Locke's account of perception, which restricts immediate perception to ideas, and so never allows for immediate perception of physical objects. Locke's overall theory, according to Berkeley, really leads to scepticism about physical objects.

To avoid this, Locke could drop the demand that currently experienced ideas conform to or represent objects. Berkeley suggests that this manoeuvre is no help because Locke's theory still requires inductive inferences from the ideas to the physical objects. He notes that the inferences at issue would be explanatory – the supposition that there are physical objects present causally explains the ideas one experiences – but denies their cogency (*Principles of Human Knowledge* 1710). A simpler and thus better explanation of our ideas, Berkeley argues, would be the supposition that they are caused by a single powerful being such as God.

Locke's empiricist version of foundationalism is often attributed to Berkeley. However, Berkeley seems to reject such a theory in favour of a foundationalism both more expansive and more modest. It is more expansive because Berkeley allows that we have immediate and certain knowledge of physical object propositions as well as propositions about currently experienced ideas. Hence, while Berkeley accepts an empiricist version of foundationalism, the propositions he is willing to count as foundational include many more than are countenanced on Locke's theory. Berkeley's theory is more modest in regard to the concept of certainty. For him, a proposition is certain provided that one has no actual grounds for doubting it. It is not further required that mistaken belief is logically impossible. In this way, Berkeley is able to contend that physical object propositions are certain, and he can avail himself of a much more modest criterion of what is to count as a foundational proposition. On this point, Berkeley lines up with Ockham (see §3 above), and with certain twentieth-century philosophers (see §8 below).

Berkeley also aimed to refute scepticism regarding the external world. He argues that this may be achieved provided one can find a way to allow for the immediate perception of physical objects. His thought is that if we perceive physical objects immediately, then we also have immediate and certain knowledge of them. He claims that these results are all achieved by abandoning realism regarding physical objects, and embracing instead a thesis which entails that objects exist if and only if they are perceived. Thus, he defends the phenomenalist thesis that a physical object is identical to a collection of ideas (see PHENOMENALISM). Objects which are collections are immediately perceivable so long as one immediately perceives some of their constituent members. So, the phenomenalist thesis regarding objects allows Berkeley to defend the view that physical objects are immediately perceivable, and hence to argue for the claimed refutation of scepticism and a more expansive foundationalism. In these respects, Berkeley claims, he is merely defending the views of common sense (see BERKELEY, G. §§5–9).

7 Modern philosophy: from Hume to Peirce

Both Locke and Berkeley accept the theory that in every perceptual experience, one is immediately aware of at least one idea. Hume follows them in this, but he distinguishes between impressions, which are our more lively and original perceptions, and ideas, which are less lively. In seeing a red cup, one experiences a red impression (or perhaps an impression of red), while in remembering the cup one attends to an idea of the red cup. Hume's fundamental principle is that all ideas are derived from impressions, and in this regard he is a thorough-going empiricist about concepts (ideas).

He also seems to accept epistemic empiricism, at least in the sense that a proposition about an object not currently present to one's senses would count as knowledge only if that proposition were derivable from propositions about currently experienced impressions. Hume denies that physical-object propositions can be deduced from propositions about impressions. He also notes that inductive inference is not something that can be given a non-circular justification. Hence, the inductive inferences from impression propositions to physical-object propositions are not justified, and so scepticism regarding physical objects results.

Hume does note, however, that nature or our psychological make-up does not allow us actually to accept scepticism, or to refrain from making inductive inferences, especially causal ones. He may mean that the fact that we are built in such a way, psychologically, that we make inductive inferences beyond our impressions to beliefs about physical objects itself constitutes being justified in having these beliefs and making these inferences. If so, then Hume is an early externalist about justification and knowledge (see INTERNALISM AND EXTERNALISM IN EPISTEMOLOGY). Or, he may mean that we can only describe the beliefs we have and the inferences we make; questions about the justification of these inferences and whether the beliefs count as knowledge cannot be settled. In that case, Hume accepts the sceptical results noted above (see HUME, D. §2).

Two very important critics of what they regarded as Humean scepticism were REID and KANT. Reid argued that Hume's scepticism was generated by acceptance of the theory of ideas (impressions), arguing that no philosopher had ever given any good reason for accepting this theory, and that it gives a mistaken account of perception in any case. The correct account, for Reid, is a complex version of direct realism in which we gain immediate and certain knowledge of physical objects. The beliefs we gain in direct perception of objects are typically irresistible, and it is a first principle for Reid, a matter of common sense, that perception is reliable and so such beliefs are justified and constitute knowledge.

Hume's scepticism did not extend to what he called 'relations of ideas'. These included the necessary truths of mathematics, and of these Hume allowed we can have a priori knowledge

(*Enquiry Concerning Human Understanding* 1748: IV, 1). It was only with respect to some statements of matters of fact that Hume was sceptical. For Kant, relations of ideas are analytic statements, while matters of fact are synthetic (see A PRIORI; A POSTERIORI; ANALYTICITY). He felt that there was a third category, however, which Hume had missed, namely synthetic a priori propositions. These are necessary truths in which the meanings of the predicate terms are not contained in the meanings of their subject terms; hence, they are synthetic. But Kant argued that the necessary truths of geometry and arithmetic are synthetic a priori, as are some very general principles of science, and these can all be known a priori. He argues that the a priori concepts he calls categories genuinely apply to objects we experience, and that our experience actually is objective in the sense that it is of real physical objects. Kant also held that having experience of objects suffices for having knowledge of such objects, and so scepticism regarding physical objects is incorrect (see KANT, I. §§4, 6).

Hegel's *Phenomenology of Spirit* (1807) contains an extended criticism of a doctrine often thought to be common to all empiricists, namely that there is immediate knowledge of something *given* in perception (for the classical empiricists, ideas), and that this knowing is passive in the sense that it is unmediated by concepts. This criticism, of course, would apply to any variant of empiricism, including a view which holds that physical objects and not subjective ideas are perceptually given and are objects of passive, immediate knowledge. Hegel's view is that there simply is no knowledge of this sort. Rather, all knowledge is conceptually mediated. Hegel seems to have drawn the conclusion that there is nothing at all which is given, a doctrine later given great currency in the twentieth century (see HEGEL, G.W.F. §5).

Charles PEIRCE was another important critic of foundationalism, both empiricist and Cartesian. Against the former, Charles Peirce held that no empirical belief is certain – we can be mistaken in any empirical belief – and neither is it unrevisable – we can be reasonably motivated to give up any empirical belief in the light of new evidence. These two points make up part of Peirce's fallibilism (see FALLIBILISM). The Cartesian programme is criticized on the grounds that wholesale doubt is not a psychologically possible action, so that Descartes' method of securing foundations for knowledge does not succeed.

8 Twentieth century

The empiricist tradition continued into the twentieth century in sense-datum theories of the sort found in Russell, with special attention paid to knowledge of the external physical world. It was argued that, in any perceptual experience, one is immediately aware of sense-data rather than physical objects. Sense-data are taken to be phenomenal objects having qualities such as colour and shape (see SENSE-DATA). Immediate awareness of sense-data is acquaintance, itself a form of certain knowing, namely, knowing objects rather than propositions about objects. Propositional knowledge of objects is knowledge by description, and it is inferential, based upon acquaintance knowledge of sense-data.

The needed inferences were to be underwritten by analytical phenomenalism, that is, the thesis that all physical-object sentences are analysable into, and so equivalent in meaning to, sets of sense-datum sentences. Given this equivalence, it was felt, inferences from sense-datum sentences to physical-object sentences would be secured as legitimate; thus the problem of the external world was solved.

Related theories were defended by AYER and C.I. LEWIS. Ayer dropped the notion of acquaintance. Sense-data were taken as items of immediate awareness, which typically issued in incorrigible propositional knowledge. Lewis dispensed with sense-data; he expressed the foundational sentences using ordinary idioms such as 'This seems red', but he made the same demands on these as Ayer did of sense-datum sentences. They are certain, and the basis of all other empirical knowledge. As in Russell, inferences from these were supposed sanctioned by analytical phenomenalism.

Interestingly enough, G.E. MOORE also defended a sense-datum theory of perception, but did not couple it with an empiricist version of foundationalism. Rather, he defended common sense, which for him included the view that there are many particular material-object propositions which are known immediately and with certainty. For instance, Moore claimed to know, immediately and with certainty, that a certain mantelpiece was closer to his body than a specific bookcase. For Moore, knowledge of this proposition and of many other material-object propositions need not be based on more secure knowledge of sense-data. In this regard, then, Moore's view is more a version of epistemic direct realism than it is empiricist foundationalism.

The programme of empiricist foundationalism and analytical phenomenalism was widely criticized. The alleged incorrigibility or certain knowledge of sense-data was influentially attacked by J.L. AUSTIN. All empirical sentences, he argued, are corrigible because in forming a belief about an object, such as is expressed by 'This is red', one is classifying the object as among the red things and so is relying on one's wholly fallible memory of other comparably red items. Moreover, certainty or incorrigibility is not needed for knowledge. Many critics argued that certainty in the sense of lack of actual grounds for doubt was a more adequate analysis of this concept, and in this sense many physical-object sentences would count as certain. Analytical phenomenalism was also criticized, principally by Chisholm (see PHENOMENALISM). He showed that physical-object sentences do not entail sense-datum sentences, and hence are not equivalent to them.

Ayer and Lewis also were in rough agreement on the definition of the concept of knowledge. They held that propositional knowledge is justified true belief, an account shared by many others. Edmund Gettier argued that this definition was incorrect. His idea was that one could have a true justified belief which is not knowledge in a situation in which one reasons from some already justified beliefs to a new belief that, as it happens, is coincidentally true. Since it would then be a matter of coincidence that one's belief was correct, it would not count as knowledge, even though it was a justified belief because it was knowingly inferred from already justified beliefs (see GETTIER PROBLEM).

Gettier's 1963 article generated a great deal of interest. While some argued that his argument was unsatisfactory, a majority assumed that he was more or less right, and many new analyses of knowledge were proposed, including many which incorporated the justified true belief analysis as a part. What has emerged as perhaps the most promising and least prone to new counter-examples is the defeasibility analysis. The key idea is that of defeated justification: where one is justified in believing a proposition p on the basis of evidence e, one's justification is defeated when there is a true proposition q, such that the conjunction (e&q) does not justify p. The defeasibility analysis would then be that knowledge is justified, true, undefeated belief. Sophisticated versions of the defeasibility analysis have been worked out in detail by a number of authors, including Klein, Lehrer and Swain (see KNOWLEDGE, DEFEASIBILITY THEORY OF).

Closely connected to the concept of knowledge is the concept of a justified belief, and a number of important theories of epistemic justification have been developed, the principal ones being foundational theories, coherence theories and reliability theories (see JUSTIFICATION, EPISTEMIC). We have already noted Cartesian and empiricist versions of foundationalism. In recent years some philosophers have defended modest versions of foundationalism. That is, they have defended the view that a belief would be justified if and only if either it were a basic, foundational belief, or were inferrable from basic beliefs. The modesty of the theory would then

derive from the fact that basic beliefs need not be certain or incorrigible; it would suffice if the basic beliefs were to be non-inferentially justified. Beliefs are non-inferentially justified when their justification need not result from being based on or inferrable from other justified beliefs.

Many philosophers have found even modest foundationalism suspect, primarily because they have found problematic the notion of a basic, non-inferentially justified belief. Some have accordingly avoided this notion altogether, and developed coherence theories of justified belief. The core idea in all such coherence theories is that a belief is justified if and only if it is a member of a system of beliefs, and this system of beliefs is coherent. A number of different accounts of coherence have been proposed, but most favoured has been that of explanatory coherence. On such a view, some beliefs (explainees) in the coherent system are justified because they are explained by other beliefs in the system; the remaining beliefs in the system are justified in virtue of their role in explaining the explainees. A problem for these theories has been to provide a reasonable way of selecting those beliefs within the system which are to be explained (see KNOWLEDGE AND JUSTIFICATION, COHERENCE THEORY OF).

The most widely discussed reliabilist theory has been the reliable-process theory. The core idea here is that a belief is justified if and only if it is caused by, or causally sustained by, a reliable process. A process is reliable when it has a high truth-ratio; that is, when that process produces more true beliefs than false ones. Typical processes selected as reliable belief-forming or belief-sustaining ones are perception, memory, introspection, and inferring or reasoning.

A problem which has proved especially vexing for supporters of the reliable-process theory is that of generality. Any specific belief is produced (sustained) by a process token which is an instance of many different process types. The generality problem is essentially that of fixing how broadly to individuate the process types in question.

9 Recent issues

In a reliable-process theory cognizers may have no knowledge or awareness of the processes which cause or causally sustain their beliefs, or of the reliability of these processes. Most foundational and coherence theories, however, construe the notion of justification in such a way that a person's belief is justified only if they have some access to, or awareness of, whatever it is that serves to justify that belief. Theories with this access condition are generally thought of as internalist theories; those which dispense with the access requirement are externalist. Though widely discussed, no fully adequate resolution of the question of whether an access requirement should be imposed on a theory of justification has yet gained general acceptance (see INTERNALISM AND EXTERNALISM IN EPISTEMOLOGY).

Proponents of reliable-process theories have typically tried to develop a naturalistic theory (see NATURALIZED EPISTEMOLOGY). Minimally, a naturalistic epistemological theory is one in which key epistemic concepts such as knowledge and justification are analysed or explained in a form which makes use only of non-epistemic concepts. A more radical form of naturalism in epistemology, proposed by Quine, dispenses outright with the normative elements of traditional epistemology, and reconceives the subject as a part of empirical psychology (see QUINE, W.V. §2). On this view, epistemology becomes a wholly descriptive discipline, one which studies how beliefs are formed, and how they are related to what we take evidence to be. Whether a minimal or more radical form of naturalized epistemology is acceptable is an open question at present.

Issues in social epistemology have also loomed large recently, as have topics in feminist epistemology. Within the former, two important questions are whether social factors play a role in determining whether a person has knowledge or justified belief, and whether non-individuals such as groups or institutions can be said to have knowledge or justified beliefs (see SOCIAL EPISTEMOLOGY). Within feminist epistemology a leading question has been whether women acquire knowledge in ways that differ from methods of knowledge acquisition open to men. Another important issue has been whether social and cultural factors as they affect women have a bearing on what it is that women know (see FEMINIST EPISTEMOLOGY).

All these recent developments in epistemology are being vigorously pursued and explored. They have served to expand and enrich the field in ways not appreciated just a few decades ago.

See also: CHINESE PHILOSOPHY; EPISTEMOLOGY, INDIAN SCHOOLS OF; KNOWLEDGE, CONCEPT OF

References and further reading

Irwin, T. (1988) *Aristotle's First Principles*, Oxford: Clarendon. (A fine, detailed treatment of Aristotle's epistemological doctrines.)

Popkin, R. (1979) *The History of Scepticism from Erasmus to Spinoza*, Berkeley, CA: University of California Press. (A great source of information, both historical and philosophical.)

GEORGE S. PAPPAS

EPISTEMOLOGY, INDIAN SCHOOLS OF

Each classical Indian philosophical school classifies and defines itself with reference to a foundational text or figure, through elaboration of inherited positions, and by disputing the views of other schools. Moreover, the schools have literatures that define them in a most concrete sense, literatures that in some cases stretch across twenty centuries and comprise hundreds of texts. And without exception, every school takes a stance on the nature of knowledge and justification, if only, as with the Mādhyamika Buddhist, to attack the positions of others. A blend of epistemology, ontology or metaphysics, and, sometimes, religious or ethical teachings constitutes the view of most schools, and sometimes only very subtle shifts concerning a single issue differentiate one school's stance from another's.

Relabelling schools of Indian epistemology using terminology forged in Western traditions ('foundationalism', 'coherentism', and so on) risks skewing the priorities of classical disputants and distorting classical debates. Nevertheless, there are positions shared across some of the schools, as well as refinements of position that apparently because of merit received greater attention in classical discussions and appear to deserve it still. Given the broad context of world philosophy, selectivity cannot be free from bias stemming from a sense of reverberation with non-Indian traditions of thought. With these warnings in mind, we may proceed to examine three important approaches within classical Indian philosophy to questions of epistemology.

First, the late Yogācāra Buddhist philosophers, Dignāga (b. *c*.480), Dharmakīrti (*c*.600–60) and followers, present a complex first-person approach to questions about knowledge that is constrained by an anti-metaphysical theme (found in earlier Buddhist treatises), along with a phenomenalism that grows out of a vivid sense of the real possibility of *nirvāṇa* experience as the supreme good. Their thought also exhibits an academic strand that is sensitive to non-Buddhist philosophical discussions. Second, a reliabilism identifying sources of veridical awareness is the most distinctive, and most central, approach to epistemology within classical Indian philosophy as a whole. Even the Yogācāra first-person approach gets framed in terms of reliable sources (perception and inference as *pramāṇas*, 'sources of knowledge'). Philosophers of diverse allegiance make contributions to what may be called this *field* of thought (as opposed to an *approach*), since, to repeat, it is the philosophical mainstream. However, the Nyāya school (the 'Logic' school) leads in most periods. Finally, the Brahmanical school known as Mīmāṃsā ('Exegesis'), supplemented in particular by centuries of reflection under an Advaita Vedānta flag, develops what can be called an ethics of belief, namely, that we should accept what we see (for example) as real (and the propositional content of perceptual awarenesses as true), what we are told by another as true, what we infer as true, and so on, except under specific circumstances that prove a proposition false or at least draw it into question. The (Nyāya) epistemological mainstream is moved to incorporate a variation on this position; for Mīmāṃsā and Advaita, 'self-certification' (svataḥprāmāṇya), or the intrinsic veridicality of cognition, defines an alternative approach to questions about knowledge, awareness and a presumed obligation to believe.

See also: MĪMĀṂSĀ; NYĀYA-VAIŚEṢIKA; SĀṄKHYA

STEPHEN H. PHILLIPS

EPISTEMOLOGY, SOCIAL
See SOCIAL EPISTEMOLOGY

EPOCHÉ
See PHENOMENOLOGY, EPISTEMIC ISSUES IN

EQUALITY

Introduction

Equality has long been a source of political and philosophical controversy. A central question about equality is how one might link empirical or moral claims about the extent to which persons are equal to judgements about the moral acceptability or unacceptability of social inequalities, and in particular how far considerations of equality license social action to bring about greater social equality. A traditional liberal argument holds that approximate equality of human strength makes it prudent for humans to place themselves under a common political authority, thus producing a justification for equality before the law. But any generalization of this argument ignores the cases where strength is unequal and the resulting balance of power unjust. Equality of worth is a principle recognized in many philosophical traditions, but its broad acceptance leaves open many problems of interpretation. In particular, it is not clear how far the principle calls for greater equality of social conditions. Persons may derive a sense of worth from enjoying the fruits of their labour, and this will legitimately block some redistribution; certain inequalities may work to everyone's advantage; and the impartial concern of the equality principle may be at odds with the sense of ourselves as persons with specific attachments. In

this context, some have wanted to soften the interpretation of equality to mean equality of opportunity or merely that inequalities should not be cumulative, although how far these moves are justified is a matter for dispute. By contrast, challenges to the equality principle from considerations of incentives, desert or difference can more easily be met.

> 1 The idea of equality
> 2 Equality of strength
> 3 Equality of moral worth
> 4 Challenges to equality

1 The idea of equality

Nearly 2,500 years ago Aristotle remarked in *The Politics* (336–22 BC) that disputes over equality and inequality were generally behind the warfare within states. Nowadays in topics as diverse as the distribution of income and wealth, access to public services, the distribution of work and employment opportunities, the political representation of different social groups and the control of natural resources among nations, the issue of equality plays a central, but controversial, role.

The idea of equality occurs in political philosophy in three main ways. First, it has sometimes been used as a purported description of certain features of human life in society, most notably in the claim that human beings are approximately equal in strength. Second, it is used as a principle of action to the effect that persons should be treated as having equal moral worth. Third, it is used to indicate a supposedly desirable set of social conditions, for example 'one person, one vote' or a more equal distribution of income. A central issue is how far one can employ premises drawn from the first two senses of the term to evaluate social, economic and political inequalities in the third sense. In particular the question arises as to how far social inequalities are just, or at least justifiable (see JUSTICE §5).

To speak of equality without qualification is to speak elliptically. Strictly speaking, equality is a relation that holds between objects or persons in respect of some common characteristic that they share. In most respects, human beings are unequal: they exhibit differences of height, weight, intelligence, manual dexterity, earning capacity and so on. Moreover, if society or governments were to seek to equalize some goods or resources, for example income, they would render unequal some other aspect of social relations, for example hourly rates of pay when people work for different lengths of time.

The upshot of these logical points is that the idea of equality needs to be embedded within a broader theory of politics and society in order to be given a specific content. No political theory aims at equality pure and simple. It aims instead at specific types of equality thought to be morally or socially important.

2   Equality of strength

Given the diversity of human beings, can it ever be said that all human beings are equal in any respect? In *Leviathan* (1651), Hobbes suggested that, although differing in bodily and mental capacities, human beings were equal in that it would be always possible for one person to kill another, an idea picked up by Hume in the eighteenth century and H.L.A. Hart in the twentieth.

According to this tradition, such rough equality of strength makes it prudent or rational for human beings to place themselves under a common body of rules comprising a system of mutual forbearance and agreement. Thus, despite persistent differences in wealth and status in society, equality of obligation under the law flows from equality of strength in some hypothesized pre-legal situation. Political agents should therefore recognize a common system of authority not merely as wise but also as just.

This line of thought can be carried too far, however. For the equality of strength condition only holds under rather specific circumstances, and where it does not hold the weak are vulnerable. One intuitive idea of justice is that bargaining advantage should not be allowed to prevail where this would threaten certain fundamental interests of persons; political power will thus only be legitimate when it protects the vulnerable (see Justice §4).

3   Equality of moral worth

If we cannot establish a normatively adequate theory of politics solely on the notion of an approximate equality of strength, the idea of equality will have to be given an irreducible moral content. This introduces the second sense of the idea: namely, equality means that all persons are to be thought of as having the same moral worth and are entitled to equal respect and consideration in the treatment of their interests. Although associated with contemporary liberal political thought, both in its utilitarian and its Kantian variants (see Liberal-ism), this idea has also found a place in many other philosophical and religious traditions, including Jewish and Christian political thought, the Stoic tradition, and the Confucianism associated with Mencius. Currents of thought within Islam, as well as breakaway sects from Hinduism, have also advanced the idea that there is an equal moral worth of all persons. However, can any specific implications about the ordering of social relations

be derived from a principle that thinkers of such varying political and philosophical persuasions have endorsed?

One issue here concerns the terms in which we spell out the implications of greater equality. Greater social equality in principle leaves open the question of what exactly is to be equalized: should it be resources, welfare or some other aspect of human life? There are sound arguments for taking any one of these possibilities as the basis of public policy.

However the issue of measurement is resolved, the central justificatory arguments for equality claim that the principle of equal moral worth places limits on what actions a state may pursue (for example, it may not privilege the interests of some at the expense of others), and that a sense of personal worth depends upon the political, social and economic institutions in which members of society participate. Yet, it is easy to see that, although in general this claim may be true, there is no simple way in which the precise nature of these connections can be ascertained.

Suppose it is allowed that people's sense of self-worth depends upon the social institutions in which they participate, so that poverty and social deprivation will undermine a person's sense of self-worth. The extent to which this assumption will license a general equalization of social and economic resources is not obvious. Thus, some libertarians have claimed that such equalization will require practices of redistribution that in effect treat the wealthy as mere means to the attainment of some social goal, in a way that is inconsistent with the respect for persons that the principle of equal worth requires (see Libertarianism).

In this simple form the libertarian argument does not carry much conviction, since it does not show why requiring persons to fulfil putative obligations under a principle of justice is to treat them merely as means. However, it does at least indicate that there may be constraints on the way in which the practice of redistribution is accomplished and that persons should, by and large, enjoy the fruits of their own labour.

Quite apart from these libertarian objections to the equalization of property, it has also been argued that the principle of equality it should be recognized that there may be a general advantage in some forms of social inequality. Thus, Rawls has consistently argued that it would be irrational for persons seeking to advance their own interests to prefer a more equal distribution of resources to an unequal distribution of a larger stock that left the poorest persons better off than they would be under the scheme of equality. By this argument the principle of equal moral worth is seen to coexist with permissible inequalities in the allocation of resources or welfare in society.

Further complications stem from the notion of personality itself. It may be argued that the sense of ourselves as persons derives from the special attachments that we form to other persons, or particular places and institutions. Our sense of moral worth depends therefore on subjectively meaningful attachments that limit the extent to which we can take a general impartial concern in the interests of others. For example, if all people are of equal moral worth, it would seem that large-scale international redistribution is called for to realize the principle, but such a proposal could cut across the subjective attachments that persons form within the political communities of which they are members.

The distinctive feature of all three of these sorts of argument is that they do not simply counterpose the principle of equality to other principles of social organization, but seek instead to develop different aspects of that principle to cut the inference from equal moral worth to an equal allocation of rights and goods in society.

In response, one option is to weaken the implications of the principle of equality. For example, perhaps the principle of equal worth does not imply an equalization of rights and goods taken as a whole, but merely that there should be no discrimination in their allocation, so that relative advantages are not unfairly achieved. Similarly, it may be argued that the principle of equality merely requires that persons be given an equal opportunity to acquire unequal social and economic advantages. A particularly influential argument in this mode has been the claim that it is not social and economic inequality in itself that is objectionable, but the accumulation of social and economic inequalities across the different dimensions of social life. Related to this argument is the claim that it may be important to reduce or eliminate only certain social inequalities – in particular those that relate to access to health care or education – in order to be consistent with the principle of equal moral worth.

The most natural way to deal with this variety of interpretations is to allow that one can identify not one but a family of political positions, all of which claim to embody the principle of equal moral worth. The choice between these positions in part depends upon broader issues of social theory (for example, the extent to which one believes that inequalities in different dimensions can be kept separate) and in part depends upon the exercise of judgement (for example, the extent to which one judges that a sense of personal worth depends upon persons being able to retain the fruits of their labour as distinct from enjoying access to collectively shared rights and goods).

4 Challenges to equality

There have been a number of challenges to the moral claims of the equality principle. One familiar argument refers to the supposed disincentives to work that would be created by the practice of redistribution from the more productive to the less productive. From one point of view this can be regarded as a pragmatic question, with policy makers having to determine what the balance should be between greater productivity and greater equality. The Rawlsian difference principle, according to which inequalities should be allowed provided they raise the incomes of the least advantaged, can be interpreted here as one possible, but attractive, compromise on this question (see RAWLS, J. §1).

However, the issue of incentives also raises matters of principle, since one way to avoid disincentive effects would be to adopt a scheme of taxation based not on labour but on ability. Although difficult to operate, such a scheme would in principle impose a lump-sum tax (an inherited debt) upon the more able that they would have to work to pay off. Clearly, the problem of work incentives in this case leads straight back to some of the problems of combining equality with a sense of personal attachment that were identified in the previous section.

A second principle that is often set against that of equality is the principle of merit or desert. This principle does provide a direct challenge to equality, since it requires that goods be distributed in proportion to the merits of those receiving them – with the best flute players receiving the best flutes, as Aristotle put it. However, the notion of desert is not without its own problems, and it may be argued that its application only makes sense within the context of an ongoing practice, like an orchestra with its own standards of performance, and not across society as a whole.

The final challenge to the principle of equality has come from the appeal to the notion of difference. Here the argument is that equality implies a uniformity of treatment, whereas interests in society are in fact plural. Thus, instead of basing public decision making on the principle of one person, one vote, a principle of difference would require some groups to be given a special say in certain matters of public policy, for example, women being given a veto over changes to the law on abortion.

The extent to which the appeal to difference mounts a serious challenge to the principle of equality is a matter for dispute however. Requiring equal consideration of the interests of all persons is compatible with recognizing that over some questions the interests of certain groups are more deeply engaged than others, as can quite easily be seen in the protection of the rights of local communities to make decisions that affect them especially. Thus, to allow that there may be a special say for certain groups in matters of public policy may be compatible with the principle of equality, provided that the acknowledgement of the possibility is not unique to a particular group.

Despite these challenges, therefore, the principle of equality still remains as a central principle of modern political thought. But its very centrality means that continuing discussion over its exact interpretation and implications is likely for a long time to come.

References and further reading

Barry, B.M. (1989) *Theories of Justice*, London: Harvester Wheatsheaf. (An extended discussion of the implications for equality and social justice of the equality of strength argument and its weaknesses.)

Walzer, M. (1983) *Spheres of Justice*, Oxford: Martin Robertson. (A statement of the view that it is cumulative inequalities, rather than inequality itself, that is morally objectionable.)

ALBERT WEALE

ERASMUS, DESIDERIUS (*c*.1466–1536)

Although Erasmus was not a systematic philosopher, he gave a philosophical cast to many of his writings. He believed in the human capacity for self-improvement through education and in the relative preponderance of nurture over nature. Ideally, education promoted *docta pietas*, a combination of piety and learning. Erasmus' political thought is dominated by his vision of universal peace and the notions of consensus and consent, which he sees as the basis of the state. At the same time he upholds the ideal of the patriarchal prince, a godlike figure to his people, but accountable to God in turn. Erasmus' epistemology is characterized by scepticism. He advocates collating arguments on both sides of a question but suspending judgment. His scepticism does not extend to articles of faith, however. He believes in absolute knowledge through revelation and reserves calculations of probability for cases that are not settled by the authority of Scripture or the doctrinal pronouncements of the Church, the conduit of divine revelation. Erasmus' pioneering efforts as a textual critic of the Bible and his call for a reformation of the Church in its head and members brought him into conflict with conservative Catholic theologians. His support for the Reformation movement

was equivocal, however. He refused to endorse the radical methods of the reformers and engaged in a polemic with Luther over the question of free will. On the whole, Erasmus was more interested in the moral and spiritual than in the doctrinal aspects of the Reformation. He promoted inner piety over the observance of rites, and disparaged scholastic speculations in favour of the *philosophia Christi* taught in the gospel. The term 'Christian humanism' best describes Erasmus' philosophy, which successfully combined Christian thought with the classical tradition revived by Renaissance humanists.
See also: FREE WILL; HUMANISM, RENAISSANCE; LUTHER, M.; MORE, T.; RENAISSANCE PHILOSOPHY; SOVEREIGNTY; WAR AND PEACE, PHILOSOPHY OF

ERIKA RUMMEL

ERIUGENA, JOHANNES SCOTTUS (*c*.800–*c*.877)

Johannes Scottus Eriugena is the most important philosopher writing in Latin between Boethius and Anselm. A Christian Neoplatonist, he developed a unique synthesis between the Neoplatonic traditions of Pseudo-Dionysius and Augustine. Eriugena knew Greek, which was highly unusual in the West at that time, and his translations of Dionysius and other Greek authors provided access to a theological tradition hitherto unknown in the Latin West. From these sources, Eriugena produced an original cosmology with Nature as the first principle. Nature, the totality of all things that are and are not, includes both God and creation, and has four divisions: nature which creates and is not created, nature which creates and is created, nature which is created and does not create, and nature which is neither created nor creates. These divisions participate in the cosmic procession of creatures from God and in their return to God. As everything takes place within Nature, God is present in all four divisions. Eriugena influenced twelfth-century Neoplatonists but was condemned in the thirteenth century for teaching the identity of God and creation.

DERMOT MORAN

ESSENCE
See ESSENTIALISM

ESSENTIALISM

Essentialists maintain that an object's properties are not all on an equal footing: some are 'essential' to it and the rest only 'accidental'. The hard part is to explain what 'essential' means.

The essential properties of a thing are the ones it needs to possess to be the thing it is. But this can be

241

taken in several ways. Traditionally it was held that F is essential to x if and only if to be F is part of 'what x is', as elucidated in the definition of x. Since the 1950s, however, this definitional conception of essence has been losing ground to the modal conception: x is essentially F if and only if necessarily whatever is x has the property F; equivalently, x must be F to exist at all. A further approach conceives the essential properties of x as those which underlie and account for the bulk of its other properties.

Acceptance of some form of the essential/accidental distinction appears to be implicit in the very practice of metaphysics. For what interests the metaphysician is not just any old feature of a thing, but the properties that make it the thing it is. The essential/accidental distinction helps in other words to demarcate the subject matter of metaphysics. But it also constitutes a part of that subject matter. If objects have certain of their properties in a specially fundamental way, then this is a phenomenon of great metaphysical significance.

See also: ARISTOTLE §8; DEFINITION; IDENTITY OF INDISCERNIBLES; LOCKE, J. §5; NATURAL KINDS; SUBSTANCE

STEPHEN YABLO

ETERNALITY
See ETERNITY

ETERNITY

The distinctive, philosophically interesting concept of eternity arose very early in the history of philosophy as the concept of a mode of existence that was not only beginningless and endless but also essentially different from time. It was introduced into early Greek philosophy as the mode of existence required for fundamental reality (being) contrasted with ordinary appearance (becoming). But the concept was given its classic formulation by Boethius, who thought of eternity as God's mode of existence and defined God's eternality as 'the complete possession all at once of illimitable life'. As defined by Boethius the concept was important in medieval philosophy. The elements of the Boethian definition are life, illimitability (and hence duration), and absence of succession (or timelessness). Defined in this way, eternality is proper to an entity identifiable as a mind or a person (and in just that sense living) but existing beginninglessly, endlessly and timelessly.

Such a concept raises obvious difficulties. Some philosophers think the difficulties can be resolved, but others think that in the light of such difficulties the concept must be modified or simply rejected as incoherent. The most obvious difficulty has to do with the combination of atemporality and duration.

Special objections have arisen in connection with ascribing eternality to God. Some people have thought that an eternal being could not do anything at all, especially not in the temporal world. But the notion of an atemporal person's acting is not incoherent. Such acts as knowing necessary truths or willing that a world exist for a certain length of time are acts that themselves take no time and require no temporal location. An eternal God could engage in acts of cognition and of volition and could even do things that might seem to require a temporal location, such as answering a prayer.

The concept of God's eternality is relevant to several issues in philosophy of religion, including the apparent irreconcilability of divine omniscience with divine immutability and with human freedom.

See also: GOD, CONCEPTS OF

ELEONORE STUMP
NORMAN KRETZMANN

ETHICAL NATURALISM
See NATURALISM IN ETHICS

ETHICS

1 Ethics and meta-ethics
2 Ethical concepts and ethical theories
3 Applied ethics

1 Ethics and meta-ethics

What is ethics? First, the systems of value and custom instantiated in the lives of particular groups of human beings are described as the ethics of these groups. Philosophers may concern themselves with articulating these systems, but this is usually seen as the task of anthropology.

Second, the term is used to refer to one in particular of these systems, 'morality', which involves notions such as rightness and wrongness, guilt and shame, and so on. A central question here is how best to characterize this system. Is a moral system one with a certain function, such as to enable cooperation among individuals, or must it involve certain sentiments, such as those concerned with blame (see MORALITY AND ETHICS; MORAL SENTIMENTS)?

Third, 'ethics' can, within this system of morality itself, refer to actual moral principles: 'Why did you return the book?' 'It was the only ethical thing to do in the circumstances.'

Finally, ethics is that area of philosophy concerned with the study of ethics in its other senses. It is important to remember that philosophical ethics is not independent of other areas of philosophy. The answers to many ethical questions depend on answers to questions in metaphysics and other areas of human thought (see AESTHETICS AND ETHICS; METAPHYSICS). Furthermore, philosophers have been concerned to establish links between the ethical sphere of life itself and other spheres (see ART AND MORALITY; LAW AND MORALITY). Some philosophers have, for philosophical reasons, had doubts about whether philosophy provides anyway the best approach to ethics. And even those who believe philosophy has a contribution to make may suggest that ethical justification must refer outside philosophy to common sense beliefs or real-life examples (see MORAL JUSTIFICATION).

A central task of philosophical ethics is to articulate what constitutes ethics or morality. This project is that of meta-ethics. What is it that especially constitutes the moral point of view as opposed to others? Some argue that what is morally required is equivalent to what is required by reason overall, whereas others see morality as just one source of reasons (see NORMATIVITY; PRACTICAL REASON AND ETHICS). Yet others have suggested that all reasons are self-interested, and that concern for others is ultimately irrational (see EGOISM AND ALTRUISM). This has not been seen to be inimical in itself to the notion of morality, however, since a moral system can be seen to benefit its participants (see CONTRACTARIANISM; DECISION AND GAME THEORY).

The moral point of view itself is often spelled out as grounded on a conception of equal respect (see EQUALITY). But there is some debate about how impartial morality requires us to be (see IMPARTIALITY).

Another set of issues concerns what it is that gives a being moral status, either as an object of moral concern or as an actual moral agent (see MORAL AGENTS; RESPONSIBILITY). And how do our understandings of human nature impinge on our conception of morality and moral agency?

Once we have some grip on what ethics is, we can begin to ask questions about moral principles themselves. Moral principles have often been put in terms of what is required by duty, but there has been something of a reaction against this notion. Some have seen it as outdated, depending on a conception of divine law with little relevance to the modern world (see ANSCOMBE, G.E.M.; SCHOPENHAUER, A.); while others have reacted against it as a result of a masculine overemphasis on rules at the cost of empathy and care (see WOLLSTONECRAFT, M.).

These doubts are related to general concerns about the role principles should play in ethical thought. Situation ethicists suggest that circumstances can lead to the abandonment of any moral principle, particularists arguing that this is because it cannot be assumed that a reason that applies in one case will apply in others (see MORAL PARTICULARISM; SITUATION ETHICS). The casuistical tradition has employed moral principles, but on the understanding that there is no 'super-principle' to decide conflicts of principles. At the other end of the spectrum, some philosophers have sought to understand morality as itself constituted by a single principle, such as that not to lie.

Duties have been seen also as constituting only a part of morality, allowing for the possibility of heroically going beyond the call of duty (see SUPEREROGATION). This is a matter of the scope of the notion of duty within morality. There are also issues concerning the scope of moral principles more generally. Does a given moral principle apply everywhere, and at all times, or is morality somehow bounded by space or time (see MORAL RELATIVISM; UNIVERSALISM IN ETHICS)? This question is related to that concerning what is going on when someone allows morality to guide them, or asserts a moral principle (see EPISTEMOLOGY AND ETHICS; MORAL JUDGMENT; MORAL KNOWLEDGE). How is the capacity of moral judgment acquired (see MURDOCH, I.)? The view that humans possess a special moral sense or capacity for intuition, often identified with conscience, is still found among contemporary intuitionists (see CUDWORTH, R.; HUTCHESON, F.; INTUITIONISM IN ETHICS; MORAL SENSE THEORIES; MOORE, G.E.; ROSS, W.D.). Scepticism about the claims of morality, however, remains a common view (see MORAL SCEPTICISM; NIETZSCHE, F.).

In recent centuries, a dichotomy has opened up between those who believe that morality is based solely on reason, and those who suggest that some nonrational component such as desire or emotion is also involved (see HUME, D.; MORALITY AND EMOTIONS; RATIONALISM). Denial of pure rationalism need not lead to the giving up of morality. Much work in the twentieth century was devoted to the question whether moral judgments were best understood as beliefs (and so candidates for truth and falsity), or as disguised expressions of emotions or commands (see EMOTIVISM; PRESCRIPTIVISM). Can there be moral experts, or is each person entirely responsible for developing their own morality (see MORAL EXPERTISE)? These questions have been seen as closely tied to issues concerning moral motivation itself (see MORAL MOTIVATION). Moral judgments seem to motivate people, so it is tempting to think that they crucially involve a desire.

Moral principles can be understood to rest on moral values, and debate continues about how to characterize these values and about how many evaluative assumptions are required to ground ethical claims (see VALUES). Against the emotivists and others, moral realists have asserted the existence of values, some identifying moral properties with those properties postulated in a fully scientific worldview (see FACT/VALUE DISTINCTION; MORAL REALISM; NATURALISM IN ETHICS).

2 Ethical concepts and ethical theories

Some philosophical ethics is broad and general, seeking to find general principles or explanations of morality. Much, however, focuses on analysis of notions central to ethics itself. One such notion which has been the focus of much discussion in recent years is that of autonomy (see AUTONOMY, ETHICAL). The interest in self-governance sits alongside other issues concerning the self, its moral nature and its ethical relation to others (see AKRASIA; DETERMINISM AND INDETERMINISM; EVOLUTION AND ETHICS; FREE WILL; SELF-DECEPTION, ETHICS OF; WILL, THE); and the relations of these selves in a social context (see SOLIDARITY). Other topics discussed include the nature of moral ideals, and the notions of desert and moral responsibility (see IDEALS; MORAL LUCK).

The question of what makes for a human life that is good for the person living it has been at the heart of ethics since the Greek philosophers enquired into *eudaimonia* ('happiness') (see ARISTOTLE; EUDAIMONIA; HAPPINESS; LIFE, MEANING OF; PLATO; SOCRATES). Once again, a philosopher's theory of the good will almost always be closely bound up with their views on other central matters (see GOOD, THEORIES OF THE). For example, some of those who put weight on sense experience in our understanding of the world have been tempted by the view that the good consists entirely in a particular kind of experience, pleasure (see EMPIRICISM; PLEASURE). Others have claimed that there is more to life than mere pleasure, and that the good life consists in fulfilling our complex human nature. Nor have philosophers forgotten 'the bad'.

Moral philosophy, or ethics, has long been at least partly concerned with the advocacy of particular ways of living or acting. Some traditions have now declined (see ASCETICISM; MACINTYRE, A.); but there is still a large range of views on how we should live. One central modern tradition is that of consequentialism (see CONSEQUENTIALISM). On this view, as it is usually understood, we are required by morality to bring about the greatest good overall (see TELEOLOGICAL ETHICS). The nature of any particular consequentialist view, therefore, depends on its view of the good. The most influential theory has been that the only good is the welfare or happiness of individual human and other animals, which, when combined with consequentialism, is utilitarianism (see BENTHAM, J.; MILL, J.S.; UTILITARIANISM).

It is commonly said that consequentialist views are based on the good, rather than on the right (see RIGHT AND GOOD; RIGHTS). Theories based on the right may be described as deontological (see DEONTOLOGICAL ETHICS). The towering figure in the deontological tradition has been the eighteenth-century German philosopher, Immanuel Kant (see KANT, I.; KANTIAN ETHICS). Such theories will claim, for example, that we should keep a promise even if more good overall would come from breaking it, or that there are restrictions on what we can intentionally do in pursuit of the good (see DOUBLE EFFECT, PRINCIPLE OF; PROMISING).

In the second half of the twentieth century there was a reaction against some of the perceived excesses of consequentialist and deontological ethics, and a return to the ancient notion of the virtues (see ARETĒ; VIRTUE ETHICS; VIRTUES AND VICES). Work in this area has consisted partly in attacks on modern ethics, but also in further elaborations and analyses of the virtues and related concepts (see LOVE; TRUST; TRUTHFULNESS).

3 Applied ethics

Philosophical ethics has always been to some degree applied to real life. Aristotle, for example, believed that there was no point in studying ethics unless it would have some beneficial effect on the way one lived one's life. But, since the 1960s, there has been a renewed interest in detailed discussion of particular issues of contemporary practical concern (see APPLIED ETHICS).

One area in which ethics has always played an important role is medicine, in particular in issues involving life and death (see BIOETHICS; LIFE AND DEATH; MEDICAL ETHICS; SUICIDE, ETHICS OF). Recently, partly as a result of advances in science and technology, new areas of inquiry have been explored (see GENETICS AND ETHICS; REPRODUCTION AND ETHICS). In addition, certain parts of medical practice which previously lacked their own distinctive ethics have now begun to develop their own.

This development is part of a wider movement involving research into the ethical requirements on those with particular occupations. Some of this research is again related to scientific advance and its implications for public policy (see TECHNOLOGY AND ETHICS). But, again, attention has also been given to occupations not in the past subjected to much philosophical ethical analysis (see BUSINESS ETHICS; JOURNALISM, ETHICS OF; PROFESSIONAL ETHICS).

The planet, and those who live and will live on it, have in recent times become the focus of much political concern, and this has had its effect on philosophy (see ANIMALS AND ETHICS; ECOLOGICAL PHILOSOPHY; ENVIRONMENTAL ETHICS; FUTURE GENERATIONS, OBLIGATIONS TO; POPULATION AND ETHICS; SUSTAINABILITY). But just as the scope of ethical inquiry has broadened, so there has been renewed interest in the specific details of human relationships, whether personal or between society, state and individual (see ECONOMICS AND ETHICS; MARKET, ETHICS OF THE; FAMILY, ETHICS AND THE; FRIENDSHIP; PATERNALISM; POLITICAL PHILOSOPHY; PORNOGRAPHY; SEXUALITY, PHILOSOPHY OF).

See also: ARISTOTLE §§22–6; AUGUSTINE; CONFUCIAN PHILOSOPHY, CHINESE; DAOIST PHILOSOPHY; DUTY AND VIRTUE, INDIAN CONCEPTIONS OF; MENCIUS

References and further reading

Rachels, J. (1986) *The Elements of Moral Philosophy*, New York: Random House. (A helpful introduction to metaethics and ethical theory, with good use made of real-life examples. Contains suggestions for further reading.)

Singer, P. (ed.) (1991) *A Companion to Ethics*, Oxford: Blackwell. (Contains short, pithy articles on central topics in ethics, including metaethics, ethical theory and applied ethics. The articles include useful bibliographies.)

Timmons, M. (2002). *Moral Theory: An Introduction*, Lanham, MD: Rowman & Littlefield. (A clear and informed survey of various ethical theories, including divine command theory, moral relativism, natural law, utilitarianism, Kantianism, moral pluralism, virtue ethics and particularism.)

ROGER CRISP

ETHICS IN INDIAN PHILOSOPHY
See DUTY AND VIRTUE, INDIAN CONCEPTIONS OF

EUCLIDEAN GEOMETRY
See THALES

EUDAIMONIA

The literal sense of the Greek word *eudaimonia* is 'having a good guardian spirit': that is, the state of having an objectively desirable life, universally agreed by ancient philosophical theory and popular thought to be the supreme human good. This objective character distinguishes it from the modern concept of happiness: a subjectively satisfactory life. Much ancient theory concerns the question of what constitutes the good life: for example, whether virtue is sufficient for it, as Socrates and the Stoics

held, or whether external goods are also necessary, as Aristotle maintained. Immoralists such as Thrasymachus (in Plato's *Republic*) sought to discredit morality by arguing that it prevents the achievement of *eudaimonia*, while its defenders (including Plato) argued that it is necessary and/or sufficient for *eudaimonia*. The primacy of *eudaimonia* does not, however, imply either egoism (since altruism may itself be a constituent of the good life), or consequentialism (since the good life need not be specifiable independently of the moral life). The gulf between 'eudaimonistic' and 'Kantian' theories is therefore narrower than is generally thought.

C.C.W. TAYLOR

EUTHANASIA
See LIFE AND DEATH (§§3, 4)

EVENTS

Events are entities like collisions and speeches, as opposed to things like planets and people. Many are changes, for example things being first hot and then cold. All lack a thing's full identity over time: either they are instantaneous, or they have temporal parts, like a speech's words, which stop them being wholly present at an instant; whereas things, which lack temporal parts, are wholly present throughout their lives.

Events may be identified with two types of entity: facts, like the fact that David Hume dies, corresponding to truths like 'Hume dies'; or particulars which, like things, correspond to names, for example 'Hume's death'. Which one they are taken to be affects the content of many metaphysical theories: such as that all particulars are things; that times, or causes and effects, or actions, are events; or that mental events are physical.

See also: CAUSATION; MOMENTARINESS, BUDDHIST DOCTRINE OF; ONTOLOGY; REICHENBACH, H.; TIME; WHITEHEAD, A.N.

D.H. MELLOR

EVIL, PROBLEM OF

Introduction

In this context, 'evil' is given the widest possible scope to signify all of life's minuses. Within this range, philosophers and theologians distinguish 'moral evils' such as war, betrayal and cruelty from 'natural evils' such as earthquakes, floods and disease. Usually the inescapability of death is numbered among the greatest natural evils. The existence of broad-sense evils is obvious and spawns a variety of problems, most prominently the practical one of how to cope with life and the existential one of what sort of meaning human life can have.

Philosophical discussion has focused on two theoretical difficulties posed for biblical theism. First, does the existence of evils show biblical theism to be logically inconsistent? Is it logically possible for an omnipotent, omniscient and perfectly good God to create a world containing evil? One classical response to this, following Leibniz, is to argue that such a God would create the best of all possible worlds, but that such a world may contain evil as an indispensable element. Alternatively, evil may be an unavoidable consequence of the boon of free will, or it may be part of a divine plan to ensure that all souls attain perfection.

The second difficulty for biblical theism is, even if we grant logical consistency, does evil (in the form, for instance, of apparently pointless suffering) nevertheless count as evidence against the existence of the Bible's God? One frequent theistic response here is to argue that the apparent pointlessness of evil may be merely a result of our limited cognitive powers; things would appear the same to us whether or not there were a point, so it is not legitimate to argue from the evidence.

1   Problems of evil

The so-called 'logical' problem of evil rests on the contention that the following two claims of biblical theism:

(I)   God exists, and is essentially omnipotent, omniscient and perfectly good; and
(II)   evil exists,

combine with the following plausible attribute analyses:

(P1)   a perfectly good being would always eliminate evil in so far as it could;
(P2)   an omniscient being would know all about evils; and
(P3)   there are no limits to what an omnipotent being can do,

to form an inconsistent quintet, so that the conjunction of any four entails the denial of the fifth; most notably the conjunction of (P1)–(P3) with either of (I) or (II) entails that the other is false.

Such an argument can be taken aporetically, as a challenge to propose more subtle alternatives to (P1)–(P3), but it has usually (in analytical philosophy of religion since the 1950s) been advanced 'atheologically' as an argument against the existence of God (see ATHEISM; NATURAL THEOLOGY). Also important is the distinction between the abstract problem, which takes 'evil' in (II) to refer generally to some evil or other (say the pain of a single hangnail), and the concrete problem, which construes (II) as shorthand for the existence of evils in the amounts and of the kinds and with the distribution found in the actual world. While the abstract problem raises a question of conceptual interest, it is the concrete version that gives the issue its bite.

Bold responses deny (P3), maintaining variously that God cannot overcome certain natural necessities (like Plato's Demiurge), that he cannot conquer his evil twin (as in Manichean dualism), or even that he lacks the power to compel at all (see PROCESS THEISM). Some reject (P2), observing that many evils arise from free choice, while future contingents are in principle unknowable (see OMNISCIENCE). (P1) is the most obviously vulnerable because it is contrary to the common intuition that ignorance and weakness excuse, and is best replaced with:

(P4)   it is logically impossible for an omniscient, omnipotent being to have a reason compatible with perfect goodness for permitting (bringing about) evils.

Rebuttals seek to counterexemplify (P4) by identifying logically possible reasons available even to an omniscient, omnipotent God.

2   Logically necessary connections with greater goods

Since omnipotence is not bound by causally necessary connections, it is natural to look for reasons among the logically necessary connections of evils with greater goods. Because the piecemeal approach of correlating distinctive sorts of good with different kinds of evil (for example, courage with danger, forgiveness with injury) threatens to be endless, it seems advantageous to identify a single comprehensive good that logically integrates all ills. One promising strategy takes its inspiration from Leibniz and develops his 'best of all possible worlds' ('BPW') theodicy in terms of contemporary possible-worlds semantics (see LEIBNIZ, G.W. §3). If a possible world is a maximal consistent state of affairs, each of infinitely many constitutive details is essential to the possible world of which it is a part. Assuming (P5) that possible worlds as wholes have values (P6) that can be ranked relative to one another and (P7) that the value scale has a maximum (P8) occupied by one and only one world, one can interpret divine creation in terms of actualizing a possible world and reason (P9) that necessarily an essentially omniscient, omnipotent and perfectly good God would actualize the best. Given the further controversial claim that:

(P10) the BPW contains instances of evil as logically indispensable components,

it follows that the desire to create the BPW is a reason compossible with perfect goodness for God not to prevent or eliminate all instances of evil.

(P10) contradicts our *prima facie* intuition that the BPW should be homogeneously good. Defenders of BPW approaches distinguish two ways in which value-parts may be related to value-wholes. The one presupposed by the critics is simply additive: negatively and positively valued parts simply 'balance off' one another and the inclusion of any 'minuses' inevitably lowers the value total. By contrast, parts may be integrated into wholes by relations of organic unity, in such a way that the positive value of the whole may defeat the negative value of the part (for example, the way the beauty of Monet's design defeats the ugliness of some colour patches). (P10) envisages the defeat of evil within the context of the possible world as a whole.

Leibniz thought he could prove the necessity of (P10) on the basis of his a priori arguments for the necessity of (I) and (P9); he believed that (P10) followed from the fact that God had actualized this world. Yet (P10) seems to fall into that class of propositions that are logically possible if and only if logically necessary. Those who recognize no sound demonstrations of (I) are left to claim that (P10) is epistemically possible. Since the atheologian is in the same epistemic predicament with respect to (P10), this epistemic defence would be sufficient *ceteris paribus* to discharge the burden of proof imposed on the theist by the argument from evil.

This BPW approach makes several other debatable value-theory assumptions. Augustine's notion (*contra* P8) that many alternative worlds have maximum value imposes no damage. Aquinas' insistence (*contra* P7) that for every collection of creatures there is a better one would not be crippling if every possible world above a certain value-level included evil. The rejection of (P5) and (P6), however, would be fatal for BPW approaches. Some question whether our comparative evaluations of small-scale states of affairs (for example, Jones' enjoying a symphony as better than his experiencing excruciating pain) is good evidence that the values of maximal states of affairs form a hierarchy. More fundamentally, some have argued (*contra* P5) that states of affairs are not intrinsically good or bad, although they can be good or bad for certain persons or projects and can ground different moral evaluations by particular agents. Anti-consequentialists in ethics also challenge whether (P9) follows from (P5)–(P8) (see CONSEQUENTIALISM). Deontologists would let justice to individuals trump putative increases in the value of states of affairs (see DEONTOLOGICAL ETHICS). Could creating the BPW be a reason compossible with perfect goodness for permitting suffering and degradation for the relatively innocent? Even if such value-maximizing were compatible with perfect goodness, it is not obviously required. For example, divine goodness is often interpreted as grace, a disposition to show favour independently of merit.

Finally, this modified Leibnizian approach entails divine determinism, because in choosing which of infinitely many fully determinate possible worlds to actualize, God is deciding on each and every detail. Some find this theologically objectionable, either because it seems incongruous for God to hold created persons responsible to himself for actions he determined, or because it fails to put enough distance between evil and divine aims.

3 Free-will defences

The last-mentioned worries are well accommodated by the other main traditional theme – that (some or all) evil originates in the wrong or evil choices of free creatures. Free-will approaches contend that:

(A1) created free will is a very great good, whether intrinsically or as a necessary means to God's central purposes in creation;

(A2) God cannot fulfil his purposes for and with free creatures without accepting the possibility that some will misuse their freedom, thereby introducing evil into the world.

In classical developments of this defence, (A1) is supposed to be a reason compossible with perfect goodness for making free creatures, while (A2) is compatible with the claim that evil is not necessary to the perfection of the universe or any other divine purpose. Some or all evil is not something God causes or does, but something he allows, a (perhaps) known but unintended side effect of his aims. The introduction of evil into the world is explained by the doctrine of 'the Fall', according to which God made angelic and human free agents in naturally optimal condition and placed them in utopian environments. God wanted them freely to choose what is right or good, but some angels and the primordial humans Adam and Eve chose what is wrong, thereby actualizing the possibility of evil.

Contemporary attention (beginning with Plantinga) has turned away from free-will defences based on the principles of double effect and doing–allowing – the principle that agents are not as responsible for the known but unintended side effects of their actions as they are for their chosen means and ends; that they are not as responsible for what they allow as for what they do – to others that reconnect with possible-worlds semantics (see DOUBLE EFFECT, PRINCIPLE OF). Once again, God creates by actualizing a possible world, but freedom is now taken to be incompatible with determinism, with the consequence that God and free creatures collaborate in determining which possible world becomes actual. Created freedom does not so much 'distance' God from evils as limit which worlds God can create. As with BPW approaches, God evaluates possible worlds as to their global features – (P5) and (P6) are assumed true, although not necessarily (P7) and (P8) – but this time he evaluates those that are a function of created incompatibilist-free choice: for example, a very good world with the optimal balance of created moral goodness over moral evil.

In defence of (A2), both classical and possible-worlds approaches appeal first to the notion that not even God can cause someone else's incompatibilist-free choices. To the objection that God should use his foreknowledge to actualize only incompatibilist-free creatures who will never sin, free-will defenders reply that such foreknowledge is not prior in the order of explanation to God's decision to create. To the suggestion that God should use his middle knowledge of what free creatures would do in particular circumstances, some (notably Plantinga 1974) grant that such counterfactuals of freedom can be true, but argue that it is logically possible that all incompatibilist-free creatures be 'transworld depraved' – that is, that no matter which combinations of individuals and circumstances God actualized, each would go wrong at least once – and logically possible that any world containing as much moral goodness as the actual world would also include at least as much moral evil as the actual world contains. Thus, it is logically possible that God could not create a world with a better balance of moral good over moral evil – which would be a reason compossible with perfect goodness for his not doing so.

This ingenious argument is controverted both by those who agree and those who deny that counterfactuals of freedom can be true. Among the former, SUÁREZ defends middle knowledge but arguably finds transworld depravity impossible because of God's necessary resourcefulness, which he takes to have the following implication: necessarily, for any

possible person and any situation in which they can exist, there are some helps of grace that would (should God supply them) win the creature over without compromising its incompatibilist freedom. Others (notably R.M. Adams) wonder what could make such counterfactuals true about creatures considered as merely possible. Incompatibilist freedom rules out divine choices or any native features of the creative will. To appeal to a contingent condition (*habitudo*, or primitive property) independent of both is too close for comfort to the ancient doctrine of fate that falls alike on the gods and their creatures, and contradicts traditional Christian views of divine providence. To maintain that counterfactuals of freedom are true although there is nothing to make them true violates a correspondence theory of truth (see TRUTH, CORRESPONDENCE THEORY OF). Denying truth to such counterfactuals of freedom does not automatically put (A2) clear of the objection from omniscience, however, if God could know about merely possible creatures what they probably would do in any given circumstance. But the meaning and ground of such probability assessments is at least as problematic as that of the original counterfactuals.

Even if (A2) were unproblematic, it could still be asked whether (A1) necessarily constitutes a reason compossible with perfect goodness for allowing evils. Two dimensions of divine goodness may be distinguished: 'global' goodness and goodness to individual created persons. The possible-worlds approaches cite global features – 'the best of all possible worlds', 'a world a more perfect than which is impossible', 'a world exhibiting a perfect balance of retributive justice', 'a world with as favourable a balance as God can get of created moral good over moral evil' – by way of producing some generic and comprehensive reason for allowing evil. But worlds with evils in the amounts and of the kind and with the distribution found in the actual world contain horrendous evils – evils the participation in (the doing or suffering of) which gives one *prima facie* reason to doubt whether one's life could (given their inclusion in it) be a great good to one on the whole – unevenly distributed among humans and uncorrelated with variations in desert. Even if horrors thus apportioned were epistemically compatible with global perfections, these defences of divine goodness as a producer of global perfection would not so much guarantee as raise doubts about God's goodness to individual participants in horrors. Divine goodness to them would require God to defeat the disvalue of horrors not only within the context of the world as a whole, but also within the framework of the individual participant's life. Nor will precise individual retribution fit this bill where the perpetrators of horrors are concerned. 'Balancing' horror with horror only deepens the difficulty. Some Christians bite this bullet, insisting that decisive defeat of evil is promised only to the obedient, while the wicked can expect the reverse, a decisive defeat of positive meaning in their lives in the form of eternal damnation. Others insist that the doctrine of hell only makes matters worse by giving rise to a specialized version of the problem of evil (see HELL).

4 Divine goodness to creatures

Soul-making theodicies try to fill the explanatory gap regarding divine goodness to individual created persons by adding further hypotheses as to what they might get out of existence in an environment in which they are so vulnerable to sin, suffering and horrors. Some versions stipulate:

(A3) God's purpose in creation culminates in a process of spiritual development in which autonomous created persons with their own free participation are perfected, and transformed from self-centred to other-centred, God-centred, Christlike or otherwise virtuous souls; and

(A4) environmental evils are permitted because they create an environment favourable to soul-making.

(A3) is compatible both with the notion that humans are initially created with mature unobstructed agency and so are fully responsible for their choices, and with the alternative idea (retrieved from Irenaeus by Hick (1966)) that human agency began immature, so that sin was to be expected in the course of the 'growing-up' process. The idea is that life in a world with evils such as this is, or with created cooperation can be, 'good for the soul'.

Establishing (A4) is difficult thrice over because: (i) the task shatters into piecemeal cataloguing, with separate demonstrations for each sub-type of environmental evil; (ii) relevant necessary connections with the soul-making environment can be hard to show; and (iii) experience makes it *prima facie* implausible that a world with evils such as ours is a good classroom for the soul. In response to (ii), some (notably Hick 1966) ingeniously contend that 'dysteleological' evils lend an air of mystery which is itself favourable to soul-making. Others modify (A4) to acknowledge that some environmental evils are consequences of sin.

Where God's soul-making purpose succeeds, it is easy to see how the painful journey is worth the individual's while. What about where it fails? Some reply that the dignity of self-determination is enough, whatever the outcome. The credibility of this contention varies with one's estimate of the robustness of human nature as well as one's conception of the natural or punitive consequences of repeated bad choices. Pessimists argue that ante-mortem participation in horrors makes a mockery of human self-determination; *a fortiori*, so does decisive personal ruin in hell.

Others (notably Hick 1966) embrace a doctrine of universal salvation: if ante-mortem horrors remain undefeated between birth and the grave, education will continue after death, probably in a series of careers, until the soul is perfected and brought into intimacy with God. Thus, God does guarantee each created person an overall existence that is a great good to them on the whole, one in which participation in horrors is balanced by the incommensurate goodness of intimacy with God. Are such horrors likewise defeated within the context of the individual's existence? The stout of heart might say 'yes', because participation in horrors that remain undefeated within the individual's ante-mortem career contributes to the sense of mystery that makes a positive contribution to the soul-making of others. Since one is at least the agent-cause of the willy-nilly sacrifice of one's ante-mortem good, participation in horrors would constitute some sort of shift from self- to other- or God-centredness after all. Even if this putative positive dimension of participation in horrors is swamped by its negative aspect when considered within the framework of the individual's ante-mortem career, it provides a means for participation in horrors to be integrated into the overall development that gives positive meaning to the individual's life and thus which are defeated within the context of the individual's existence as a whole.

Some (notably M.M. Adams) contend, on the contrary, that divine goodness to created persons would do more to lend positive meaning to any careers in which they participate in horrors. The sacrifice involved in participation in horrors is pedagogically inept as a first lesson because it can damage the person so much as to make much further ante-mortem progress from self- to other- or God-centredness virtually impossible. This combines with the delay in gratification to another or perhaps many lives later to de-emphasize the importance of this life, leaving the impression that it would have been better skipped by those whose spiritual development was significantly set back through participation in horrors. To give this life, or any career involving participation in horrors, positive significance, some parameter of positive meaning other than contribution to soul-making must be found. Given two further assumptions – that divine metaphysical goodness is infinite, and that intimacy with God is incommensurably good for created persons – the mystical literature suggests several ways for participation in horrors to be integrated into the created person's relationship with God, ranging from divine gratitude for one's earthly career to various types of mystical identification between God and creatures in the midst of horrors. Because the identification occurs in this life and divine gratitude is for this life, they add positive significance to this life even where the creature has no ante-mortem but only postmortem recognition of these facts.

5 Methodological notes

Much contemporary discussion of BPW and free-will defences has addressed itself to the logical problem of evil because we seem epistemically in a better position to assess the compossibility of logically possible reasons with various conceptions of perfect goodness than to pronounce on what God's actual reasons are. In identifying logically possible defeaters, many of the earlier discussions confine themselves to a religion-neutral value theory, the better to answer the atheologian on their own turf. By contrast, soul-making, mystical and other explanatory theodicies draw on the resources of revelation for their speculations about God's actual reasons for the evils of this world and usually address their remarks in the first instance to the believing community. The distinction between these approaches blurs when attention is riveted on the concrete logical problem of evil – that is, on the logical compossibility of God with evils in the amounts and of the kinds and with the distribution found in the actual world. In so far as the consistency of actual religious belief is at stake, it becomes highly relevant to test the reasons supplied by revelation for logical compossibility with the existence of evils and the goodness of God. Where they pass, they can be advanced as solving the concrete logical problem of evil, whether or not their truth can be proved to the atheologian.

Once the wider resources of the religions under attack are allowed to interpret (I) and (II), it becomes clear that explanatory reasons come in two broad types: reasons why God causes or permits evils, and does not prevent or eliminate them; and explanations as to how God could be good to created persons despite their participation in evil. Reasons-why identify some great-enough good with which evils are necessarily connected, while reasons-how specify ways God could defeat evils in which the created person has participated and thus give that person a life that is a great good to them on the whole. Much philosophical discussion (Swinburne is particularly insistent on this point) presupposes that the problem cannot be solved without sufficient reasons-why. The criticized

religions arguably take a mixed approach. Assuming that what perfect goodness can permit or cause is a function of what it can defeat, they combine partial reasons-why with elaborate scenarios by which God defeats even the worst horrors.

6 The evidential problem of evil

Recently many philosophers (notably Rowe, Alston, van Inwagen and Wykstra) have concluded that the most serious version of the problem of evil concerns not the logical but the evidential relation between (I) and (II). The mere logical possibility that a student has broken all four limbs and been hospitalized for a heart attack will win them no extension of essay deadlines if the tutor can see that the student is in fact physically sound. Likewise, the evidential argument contends, many actual evils – such as the slow, painful death of a fawn severely burned in a forest fire started by lightning – appear pointless, in the sense that our composite empirical evidence constitutes strong reason to believe they have no point. But an omniscient, omnipotent being could have prevented some of them, while a perfectly good being would not allow or cause any of them it could avoid. Therefore, (II) concretely construed constitutes decisive evidence against (I).

Once again, replies could take the piecemeal approach, trying to show for each type of very intense suffering that it has a discernible point after all. It would not be necessary to complete the process to undermine the evidential argument. Success with some important cases would increase the probability that defeating goods are also present in other cases where we have not discovered any.

The favourite response (for example, by Wykstra, Alston and van Inwagen) attacks the argument at its epistemological foundations. The contention is that our composite empirical evidence could constitute strong reason to believe some actual evils pointless only if our cognitive powers would afford access to any point such evils might have were they to have one. If things would seem roughly the same to us (that is, if our evidence would be roughly the same) whether or not such evils had a point, the fact that we detect no point is not good evidence that there is no point. In particular, we are in no position to see that many instances of intense suffering are not explained by some of the reasons appealed to in traditional theodicies.

Defenders of the evidential argument (notably Rowe) grant the appeal of the underlying evidential principle, but relocate the disagreement in the richness of the theological hypothesis on which one draws. They argue that if one restricts oneself to a straightforward philosophical reading of (I), then it is likely that the situation with regard to intense suffering would be different in ways discernible by us. Expanded theism might import assumptions about the hiddenness of divine providence, mystical identification with suffering creatures, etc., but deploying these resources in the evidential debate carries a cost, because the prior probability of expanded theism is lower than that of (I).

This last point holds only if the richer theological theory is advanced as true. If instead it is used, as with the logical problem, to generate possible – this time not merely logically but epistemically possible – explanations, then no dilution in prior probabilities need be accepted. And once again, the more epistemically possible explanations there are, the greater the probability that the suffering in question is not pointless.

See also: GOD, ARGUMENTS FOR THE EXISTENCE OF; HOLOCAUST, THE

References and further reading

Hick, J. (1966) *Evil and the God of Love*, San Francisco, CA: Harper & Row, 2nd edn, 1978. (Criticizes 'Augustinian' theodicies that rely on the doctrine of the Fall, and develops a soul-making theodicy in the spirit of Irenaeus.)

Plantinga, A. (1974) *The Nature of Necessity*, Oxford: Clarendon Press, ch. 9, §10, 191–3. (Develops the possible-worlds version of the free-will defence discussed in §3 of the present entry, with considerable attention to counterfactuals of free-dom and the hypothesis of transworld depravity.)

MARILYN MCCORD ADAMS

EVOLUTION AND ETHICS

The fact that human beings are a product of biological evolution has been thought to impinge on the study of ethics in two quite different ways. First, evolutionary ideas may help account for why people have the ethical thoughts and feelings they do. Second, evolutionary ideas may help illuminate which normative ethical claims, if any, are true or right or correct. These twin tasks – explanation and justification – may each be subdivided. Evolutionary considerations may be relevant to explaining elements of morality that are culturally universal; they also may help explain why individuals or societies differ in the ethics they espouse. With respect to the question of justification, evolutionary considerations have sometimes been cited to show that ethics is an elaborate illusion – that is, to defend versions of ethical subjectivism and emotivism. However, evolutionary considerations also have been invoked to justify ethical norms. Although there is no conflict between using evolution both to explain traits that are universal and to explain traits

that vary, it is not consistent to claim both that evolution unmasks ethics *and* justifies particular ethical norms.

See also: HUMAN NATURE; SOCIOBIOLOGY; SPENCER, H.

ELLIOTT SOBER

EVOLUTION, THEORY OF

The biological theory of evolution advances the view that the variety and forms of life on earth are the result of descent with modification from the earliest forms of life. Evolutionary theory does not attempt to explain the origin of life itself, that is, how the earliest forms of life came to exist, nor does it apply to the history of changes of the non-biological parts of the universe, which are also often described as 'evolutionary'. The mechanisms of natural selection, mutation and speciation are used in evolutionary theory to explain the relations and characteristics of all life forms. Modern evolutionary theory explains a wide range of natural phenomena, including the deep resemblances among organisms, the diversity of life forms, organisms' possession of vestigial organs and the good fit or 'adaptedness' between organisms and their environment.

Often summarized as 'survival of the fittest', the *mechanism of natural selection* actually includes several distinct processes. There must be variation in traits among the members of a population; these traits must be passed on from parents to offspring; and the different traits must confer differential advantage for reproducing successfully in that environment. Because evidence for each of these processes can be gathered independently of the evolutionary claim, natural selection scenarios are robustly testable. When a trait in a population has arisen because it was directly selected in this fashion, it is called an *adaptation*.

Genetic mutation is the originating source of variation, and selection processes shape that variation into adaptive forms; random genetic drift and various levels and forms of selection dynamic developed by geneticists have been integrated into a general theory of evolutionary change that encompasses natural selection and genetic mutation as complementary processes. Detailed ecological studies are used to provide evidence for selection scenarios involving the evolution of species in the wild.

Evolutionary theory is supported by an unusually wide range of scientific evidence, gaining its support from fields as diverse as geology, embryology, molecular genetics, palaeontology, climatology and functional morphology. Because of tensions between an evolutionary view of *homo sapiens* and some religious beliefs, evolutionary theory has remained controversial in the public sphere far longer than no less well-supported scientific theories from other sciences.

See also: DARWIN, C.R.; EVOLUTION AND ETHICS

ELISABETH A. LLOYD

EXISTENCE

Philosophical problems concerning existence fall under two main headings: 'What is existence?' and 'What things exist?'. The difficulty lies in separating these questions.

The question 'What is existence?' has produced a surprising variety of answers. Some hold that existence is a property that every individual has, others that it is a characteristic that some individuals have but other (for example, imaginary) individuals lack, while proponents of the thesis that 'existence is not a predicate' hold that existence is not a property or characteristic of individuals at all.

Other philosophical issues concerning existence include: disputes about whether there are abstract objects (for example, numbers, universals) as well as concrete ones, immaterial souls as well as bodies, possible objects as well as actual ones, and so on; and questions about which entities (if any) are the fundamental constituents of reality.

See also: BEING; FREE LOGICS; ONTOLOGICAL COMMITMENT; ONTOLOGY

PENELOPE MACKIE

EXISTENTIALISM

Introduction

The term 'existentialism' is sometimes reserved for the works of Jean-Paul Sartre, who used it to refer to his own philosophy in the 1940s. But it is more often used as a general name for a number of thinkers of the nineteenth and twentieth centuries who made the concrete individual central to their thought. Existentialism in this broader sense arose as a backlash against philosophical and scientific systems that treat all particulars, including humans, as members of a genus or instances of universal laws. It claims that our own existence as unique individuals in concrete situations cannot be grasped adequately in such theories, and that systems of this sort conceal from us the highly personal task of trying to achieve self-fulfilment in our lives. Existentialists therefore start out with a detailed description of the self as an 'existing individual', understood as an agent involved in a specific social and historical world. One of their chief aims is to understand how the individual can achieve the richest and most fulfilling life in the modern world.

Existentialists hold widely differing views about human existence, but there are a number of recurring themes in their writings. First, existentialists hold that humans have no pregiven purpose or essence laid out for them by God or by nature; it is up to each one of us to decide who and what we are through our own actions. This is the point of Sartre's definition of existentialism as the view that, for humans, 'existence precedes essence'. What this means is that we first simply *exist* – find ourselves born into a world not of our own choosing – and it is then up to each of us to define our own identity or essential characteristics in the course of what we do in living out our lives. Thus, our essence (our set of defining traits) is chosen, not given.

Second, existentialists hold that people decide their own fates and are responsible for what they make of their lives. Humans have free will in the sense that, no matter what social and biological factors influence their decisions, they can reflect on those conditions, decide what they mean, and then make their own choices as to how to handle those factors in acting in the world. Because we are self-creating or self-fashioning beings in this sense, we have full responsibility for what we make of our lives.

Finally, existentialists are concerned with identifying the most authentic and fulfilling way of life possible for individuals. In their view, most of us tend to conform to the ways of living of the 'herd': we feel we are doing well if we do what 'one' does in familiar social situations. In this respect, our lives are said to be 'inauthentic', not really our own. To become authentic, according to this view, an individual must take over their own existence with clarity and intensity. Such a transformation is made possible by such profound emotional experiences as anxiety or the experience of existential guilt. When we face up to what is revealed in such experiences, existentialists claim, we will have a clearer grasp of what is at stake in life, and we will be able to become more committed and integrated individuals.

1 Historical development

Although such earlier thinkers as Augustine, Montaigne, Shakespeare and Pascal have been called existentialists, the term should be reserved for a loosely connected group of thinkers in recent times who were responding to certain views that became widespread in the nineteenth century. These views include, first, the scientific picture of reality as a meaningless, value-free collection of material objects in causal interactions, and second, the modern sense of society as an artificial construct that is inevitably in conflict with the aspirations of the individual. German Idealism had attempted to counteract the implications of these new ideas, but idealism had collapsed by the 1840s, and the result was a growing feeling that the individual is ultimately alone and unsupported in a cold and meaningless universe (see IDEALISM).

Existentialism appeared in the nineteenth century alongside romanticism, but it was different from romanticism in important respects. For one thing, where romanticism tried to evoke a sense of the individual's participation in the larger context of nature, the first great existentialist, Søren KIERKE-GAARD, held that humans are at the most basic level solitary, 'existing individuals' with no real connections to anything in this world. Instead of suggesting that we are at home in this world, Kierkegaard tried to intensify the individual's feeling of anxiety and despair in order to bring about a 'leap of faith' that would bring the person into a defining relationship to the God-man (Christ).

The next figure usually included in the pantheon of existentialists, Friedrich NIETZSCHE, began from the assumption that the development of science and critical thinking in Western history has led to the result that people have lost the ability to believe in a transcendent basis for values and belief. When Nietzsche said that 'God is dead', he meant that all the things people previously thought of as absolutes – the cosmic order, Platonic Forms, divine will, Reason, History – have been shown to be human constructions, with no ultimate authority in telling us how to live our lives. In the face of the growing 'nihilism' that results from the death of God, Nietzsche tried to formulate a vision of a healthy form of life people can achieve once they have given up all belief in absolutes (see NIHILISM).

The translation of Kierkegaard's works and the discovery of Nietzsche's writings had an immense impact on German thought after the First World War. The psychiatrist and philosopher, Karl JAS-PERS, drew on these two figures to develop what he called a 'philosophy of existence'. Martin HEIDEG-GER, influenced by Kierkegaard as well as by the movement called 'philosophy of life' (then associated with the names of Nietzsche, Wilhelm DILTHEY and Henri BERGSON), began his major work, *Being and Time* (1927), with an 'existential

analytic' aimed at describing life from the stand-point of concrete, everyday being-in-the-world (see LEBENSPHILOSOPHIE). Heidegger's thought was also influenced by Edmund Husserl's phenomenology, an approach to philosophy that emphasizes description of our experience as it is prior to reflection and theorizing.

Working independently in France, Gabriel MARCEL was building on Bergson's philosophy to develop an alternative to the dominant idealist philosophy taught in the universities. Basing his reflections on his own experience of life, Marcel claimed that a human being must be understood as an embodied existence bound up with a concrete situation. Because the body and the situation can never be completely comprehended by the intellect, Marcel sees them as part of what he calls the 'mystery'. Maurice MERLEAU-PONTY took over Marcel's notion of embodied being-in-a-situation as basic for his own existential phenomenology. Jean-Paul SARTRE also drew on Marcel's thought, but he was especially influenced by the thought of Husserl and Heidegger. It seems that the term 'existential-ism' was first used by critics of Sartre, but it came to be accepted in the 1940s by Sartre and Simone de BEAUVOIR as they replied to their critics. Merleau-Ponty and Albert CAMUS were initially associated with the movement called existentialism during its heyday after the Second World War, but both eventually rejected the term as they came to distance themselves from Sartre due to political differences.

There have been important developments out-side Germany and France. The Spanish philosopher, José ORTEGA Y GASSET, influenced by Dilthey's philosophy of life, developed a number of ideas that closely parallel those of Heidegger and other existentialist thinkers. The novels and short stories of the Russian writer, Fëdor DOSTOEVSKII, were influential not only for Russian existentialists like Nikolai BERDIAEV, but for Heidegger, Sartre and Camus as well. Existentialism has also had a profound impact on other fields. The movement of existential theology remains influential today (see EXISTENTIALIST THEOLOGY), and existential psychoanalysis (especially Ludwig Binswanger, Medard Boss and Rollo May) continues to be of interest in psychotherapy. Though existentialism is no longer a central movement in philosophy, many of its principal exponents continue to be important in current philosophical discussions.

2 The human condition

Existentialists start out from the assumption that it is no longer possible to believe that there is some transcendent justification or underlying ground for our existence. If God is dead, then we find ourselves 'abandoned', 'forlorn', 'thrown' into a world, with no pregiven direction or legitimation. Though we seek some overarching meaning and purpose for our lives, we have to face the fact that there is no 'proper function of humans' or 'plan in God's mind' that tells us the right way to be human.

This picture of our predicament leads to a particular view of human existence that is accepted by many existentialists. In contrast to traditional theories, which think of a human as a thing or object of some sort (whether a mind or a body or some combination of the two), existentialists characterize human existence as involving a deep tension or conflict between two different aspects of our being. On the one hand, we are organisms among other living beings, creatures with specific needs and drives, who operate at the level of sensation and desire in dealing with the present. At this level, we are not much different from other animals. On the other hand, there is a crucial respect in which we differ from other organisms. One way to describe this difference is to say that, because we are capable of self-awareness, we are able to reflect on our own desires and evaluate ourselves in terms of some larger vision of what our lives are adding up to. In this sense we transcend our own being as mere things. What is characteristic of our being as humans is that we *care* about the kinds of beings we are, and we therefore take a stand on our basic desires. According to the existentialists, humans are unique among entities in that they form second-order desires about their first-order desires, and they therefore have aspirations that go beyond the immediacy of their sensual lives.

Heidegger and Sartre try to capture this reflexive dimension of human existence by saying that what is unique about humans is that their own being is 'in question' or 'at issue' for them. What kind of person I am matters to me, and because I am concerned about what I am and will be, I take some concrete *stand* on my life by assuming roles and developing a specific character through my actions. But this means that my existence is characterized by a fundamental tension or clash between my immediate sensations and desires on the one hand, and my long-range aims and projects on the other. As Sartre puts it, a 'rift' or a 'gap' – a 'nothingness' – is introduced into the fullness of being in the universe by human existence. Because consciousness makes us more than what we are as creatures with immediate sensations and desires, Sartre says that human reality 'is not what it is and is what it is not'.

The conception of human existence as a tension also appears in Kierkegaard's description of the self. For Kierkegaard, humans are both finite and infinite, temporal and eternal, contingent and free. What defines our identity as selves is the concrete way we relate ourselves to this tension. In a similar way, Nietzsche holds that we are both creatures and creators, and we have to embrace both these dimensions of ourselves in order to be fully human. Heidegger and Sartre refer to the two aspects of the self as 'facticity' (our mere givenness) and 'transcendence' (our ability to surpass our givenness through our interpretations and aspirations). In their view, life is a continuous tension between these elements, a tension resolved only in death. Finally, Jaspers seems to have a similar conception of humans in mind when he points out the polarity between our being as an empirical consciousness-as-such and our desire to grasp the general and realize our freedom as *Existenz*.

If we regard the self as a tension or struggle, it is natural to think of human existence not as a thing or object of some sort, but as an unfolding event or happening – the story of how the tension is dealt with. What defines my existence, according to this view, is not some set of properties that remain the same through time, but the 'event of becoming' through which I carry out the struggle to resolve the tension that defines my condition in the world. As an ongoing happening, I *am* what I make of myself throughout the course of my life as a whole. In Ortega's words, a human 'does not have a nature, but rather a history' (see ORTEGA Y GASSET, J.). What defines my existence as an individual is the ongoing story of what I accomplish throughout my life.

To think of a human as an unfolding story suggests that human existence has a specific sort of temporal structure. We are not like rocks and cauliflowers which continue to exist through an endless sequence of 'nows'. Instead, human temporality has a kind of cumulativeness and future-directedness that is different from the enduring presence of physical things. First, our existence is directed toward the future to the extent that we are striving to realize something for our lives. Heidegger calls this element of 'futurity' our 'being-towards-death,' understood as a movement toward realizing our own being by achieving certain things throughout our active lives. Second, the past shows up for us as something retained and carried forward for the purposes of our future. Depending on our projects at any given time, our past actions show up for us as assets or as liabilities in relation to what we are doing. Finally, our present appears as a point of intersection between our future projects and our past accomplishments. Because we are time-binding beings whose lives always reach out into the future and hold on to the past, we can never achieve the kind of direct presence of self to self that Descartes thought he had found in the *Cogito* ('I think').

To say that human temporality is cumulative is to say that everything we do is contributing to creating our 'being' as a totality. In this sense, we *are* what we *do* in living out our lives: we define our own identity through the choices we make in dealing with the world. Because there is no fixed essential nature which we have in advance, our 'essence' as individuals is defined and realized through our concrete existence in the world. Whatever capacities and traits I am born with, it is up to me to take them over and make something of them in what I do. Thus, whether aware of it or not, I am creating my own identity in my actions.

3   Being-in-the-world

Existentialists are deeply suspicious of the high-level, abstract theorizing about humans found in traditional philosophy and in the sciences. In their view, the concern with subsuming all particulars under concepts and building systems tends to conceal crucial features of our lives as individuals. For this reason, existentialists generally start out from a description of ourselves as agents in everyday contexts, prior to reflection and theorizing. These descriptions reveal that it is part of our 'facticity' that we are generally caught up in the midst of things, involved with others in trying to accomplish specific goals, and affected by moods and commitments that influence our perception and thoughts. Furthermore, we are embodied beings who encounter the world only from the standpoint of a particular bodily orientation that gives us a set on things: 'I am my body' Marcel wrote, and this theme of embodiment became central to the thought of Beauvoir and Merleau-Ponty. We are also bound up with contexts of equipment in practical situations where we are trying to accomplish certain goals. Finally, as social beings, we always find ourselves embedded in a particular cultural and historical milieu that conditions our outlook and determines our basic orientation toward the world. To say that we are 'factical' beings is to say that we are always 'being-in-a-situation', where our being as selves is inseparable from a shared, meaningful life-world.

If we are always embedded in a situation, then all inquiry must start out from an 'insider's perspective' on things, that is, from a description of the world *as it appears to us* – to beings who are participants in our forms of life, with our unique sort of bodily set, feelings and modes of perception. We have no choice but to begin from where we stand in the thick of our actual lives, with our local attachments and particular cares and concerns. But this means

that there is no way to achieve the sort of global 'God's-eye view' on ourselves and our world that philosophers have sought ever since Plato. Existentialists are critical of the philosophical ideal of achieving a totally detached, disinterested, disengaged 'view from nowhere' that will provide us with completely objective knowledge. The attempt to step back from our ordinary concerns in order to achieve a totally detached and dispassionate standpoint – the stance Marcel calls 'desertion' and Merleau-Ponty calls 'high-altitude thinking' – will always give us a distorted view of the world, because it bleaches out our normal sense of the significance and worth of the things we encounter around us. In order to be able to gain an insight into the way reality presents itself to us at the most basic level, then, we need to start from a description of what Heidegger calls our 'average everydayness', our ordinary, familiar ways of being absorbed in practical affairs.

The idea that our being-in-a-situation or being-in-the-world is fundamental and inescapable gives the existentialists a way of criticizing the idea, central to philosophy since Descartes, that we are at the most basic level *minds* receiving sensory inputs and processing information. Sartre, for example, rejects the idea that the self can be thought of as a 'thinking substance' or self-encapsulated 'field of consciousness' distinct from the world. In my pre-reflective activities, Sartre says, I encounter myself not as a bundle of beliefs and desires in a mental container, but as being 'out there' *with* the things I am concerned about. When I am chasing a bus, I encounter my *self* as a 'running-toward-the-bus'. My being is found not in my head, but with the bus. Sartre thinks that this follows from Husserl's view that consciousness is always 'intentional,' always directed *towards* entities in the world (see INTENTIONALITY). If Husserl is right, according to Sartre, then the 'I' is not an object, not a 'something', but is instead sheer intentional activity directed towards things in the world. The totality of my intentional acts defines me; there is no residue of 'substantial thinghood' distinct from my acts.

The existentialist conception of our irreducible being-in-a-situation calls into question some of the dualisms that have dominated so much of Western thought. First, existentialists deny the romantic distinction between an outer self – what we *do* in the world – and an inner, 'true' self that embodies our genuine nature. If we just *are* what we *do*, as existentialists contend, then there is no basis for positing a substantive 'real me' distinct from the parts I play and the things I do. Second, the account of the primacy of being-in-the-world tends to undermine the traditional subject-object model of our epistemological situation. Existentialists suggest that the assumption that humans are, at the most basic level, subjects of experience trying to formulate beliefs about objects on the basis of their inner representations, distorts our situation. If it is true that we are initially and most basically already out there with things in the world, then there must be something wrong with traditional epistemological puzzles about how a knowing subject can 'transcend' its veil of ideas to gain knowledge of objects in the external world. Finally, the existentialist picture of our basic situation as always bound up with a practical life-world seems to raise questions about the traditional fact value distinction. Existentialists hold that we always encounter the everyday life-world as a context of equipment bound up with our aims as agents in the world. If the things we encounter are initially and most basically functional entities tied up with our purposive activities, however, then it is an illusion to think that what is given 'at first' is a collection of brute objects we subsequently invest with subjective values. In our everyday lives, fact and value are inseparable.

In general, existentialists hold that traditional dualisms arise only when we try to adopt a cool, detached, theoretical stance towards things. But since such a stance is derivative from and parasitic on a more basic way of being in which we are inseparably bound up with things in practical contexts, it cannot be regarded as providing us with a privileged insight into the way things really are.

4   Freedom and responsibility

As being-in-the-world, we are already engaged in a shared life-world that gives us a prior sense of what is possible, and we find ourselves with choices in our past that carry weight in determining how we can act in the future. This is our 'facticity', and it makes up what is just 'given' in our lives. However, existentialists regard facticity as only one aspect of human existence, for they hold that humans always have the ability to transcend their given situation by taking a stand on their own lives. As 'transcendence' we are always taking over our situations and making something of them through our choices. This ability to transcend our facticity means that we have free will. Our choices are free in the sense that (1) no outside factors determine our will, (2) in any particular case we could have acted otherwise than we did, and (3) we are therefore responsible for our choices in a way that justifies moral praise and blame (see FREE WILL). (Nietzsche is inclined to reject the third sense because of its role in imposing feelings of guilt on people, but in other respects he seems to be committed to believing in human freedom.)

The existentialist belief in human freedom is based on a phenomenological description of our everyday lives. In confronting situations where I must make a choice, I find myself facing an open range of possible courses of action where nothing compels me to choose one course of action over the others. Even in cases where I am not aware of making choices, a moment's reflection shows that I am in fact deciding my own life. Suppose that I show up for work faithfully each day, and I believe that I am compelled to do this because I need to make money to support my family. Does this mean that I am forced to do what I do? An existentialist like Sartre would say that it is self-deception to think I am *compelled* to be a conscientious worker, for I *could* always walk away from it all and join a monastery or turn to a life of crime. If I am choosing to let considerations of duty or money be deciding factors for me in this way, then this is my choice. What this suggests is that even in my habitual and seemingly 'automatic' actions I am actually *assuming* a particular identity for myself through my own free choices, and am therefore responsible for what I do.

Sartre tries to capture this idea by saying that humans are 'condemned to be free'. Because our being is 'in question' for us, we are always taking it over and giving it some concrete shape through our actions. And this means that, whether we are aware of it or not, in continuing to act in familiar ways we are constantly renewing our decisions at every moment, for we could always change our ways of living through some radical self-transformation. Moreover, since all criteria or standards for evaluating our actions are also freely chosen, in our actions we are also deciding what sorts of reasons are going to guide our actions. With no higher tribunal for evaluating reasons for acting, we are entirely responsible for what we do: we have 'no excuses behind us nor justifications before us'.

Existentialists generally hold that we are not only responsible for the direction our own lives take, but also for the way the world around us appears. This idea has its roots in Kant's view that the reality we experience is partly shaped by the constituting activity of our own minds, though existentialists differ from Kant in holding that our construction of reality depends on our own choices (see KANT, I. §5). Kierkegaard, for example, contends that one's sense of reality is determined by the 'sphere of existence' in which one lives, so that the person who lives the life of a pleasure-loving aesthete will experience a world that is quite different from that of the duty-bound follower of the ethical. Similarly, Nietzsche holds that reality is accessible to us only through some 'perspective' or other, that there is no way to get in touch with reality as it is in itself, independent of any point of view or framework of interpretation.

Sartre works out an especially strong version of this Kantian outlook by developing the theory of constitution in Husserl's phenomenology. Husserl held that the world we experience is constituted through the meaning-giving activity of consciousness. Sartre takes this account of constitution to mean that, because I shape the world around me through my meaning-giving activity, I am ultimately responsible for the way the world presents itself to me in my experience. Thus if I have had some painful experiences as a child, it is up to me to decide what these mean to me. I can use them as an excuse for going through life feeling cheated, or regard them as challenges that will make me stronger. Sartre's point is not that there are no constraints on the ways I interpret my situation, but that constraints and obstacles gain their meaning from me, and since there are indefinitely many possible meanings any situation can have, there is no way to identify any supposedly 'hard' facts that could be said to compel me to see things one way rather than another. But this means, according to Sartre, that in choosing my interpretation of myself, I simultaneously choose the world. It is our own freely chosen projects that determine how reality is to be carved up and how things are to count. Sartre even goes so far as to say that, if a war breaks out around me, then I am responsible for that war, because it is up to me to decide what the war is going to mean to me in my life.

Other existentialists have tried to formulate a more tempered conception of freedom. Kierkegaard argues that, because being human involves both necessity and possibility, the extreme sort of 'anything-goes' freedom (such as that later envisaged by Sartre) would lead to the 'despair of lack of necessity'. Both Heidegger and Merleau-Ponty work towards a notion of 'situated freedom' according to which choice is always embedded in and dependent upon the meaningful choices disclosed by a specific social and historical situation. Beauvoir tries to show how institutions and social practices can cut off the choices open to women and oppressed groups. Finally, Nietzsche calls attention to the way biological and historical factors operate 'behind our backs,' influencing our decisions without our awareness. But even when such limitations are recognized, the belief that we can rise above our situations to be 'creators' remains fundamental to existentialist thought.

5   Everyday existence, anxiety and guilt

Though existentialists agree that people are free to choose their own fates, they also hold that most people are quite unaware of their freedom. This obliviousness results not from ignorance or oversight, but from the fact that we usually try to avoid facing up to our responsibility for our lives. For the most part we are 'fleeing' from ourselves, throwing ourselves into mundane concerns and drifting into standardized public ways of acting. Existentialists are generally quite critical of everyday social existence. As they see it, there is a strong temptation to let ourselves get swallowed up by the 'public', the 'they', the 'herd' or the 'masses'. We try to do what 'one does' in familiar situations, and we assume that our lives are justified so long as we are following the norms and conventions laid out in our social context. In throwing ourselves into the kinds of busyness characteristic of contemporary society, we become more and more effective at finding means to achieving socially accepted ends, but at the same time we lose the ability to understand what is at stake in existing. Life then becomes a disjointed series of episodes with no real coherence or direction, and we end up dispersed and distracted, lacking any basis for meaningful action.

Existentialists give similar accounts of how social existence undermines our ability to realize ourselves as individuals. Kierkegaard describes the way that being a well adjusted member of 'the public' levels everything down to the lowest common denominator, with the result that nothing can really *count* or *matter* to people anymore. Similarly, Nietzsche describes the way that our being as 'herd' animals domesticates us and deadens our creativity, and Heidegger points out the 'tranquilization' and 'alienation from ourselves' that results from our absorption in the familiar social world. Sartre presents an especially harsh picture of social relations. Since, in his view, people can only see each other as objects and not as free beings, the Look of the Other always objectifies me and pressures me into thinking I am just a brute thing. As each individual struggles to affirm their being as a free 'transcendence' against the objectifying Look of others, the result is inevitable conflict: in the words of a character in one of Sartre's plays, 'Hell is the others'.

But many existentialists also see a positive side to social life. Though Heidegger criticizes the temptation to self-loss in our participation in the 'they', he also holds that all our possible ways of interpreting ourselves ultimately come from the social context in which we find ourselves. For this reason, becoming authentic is not a matter of escaping society, but of embracing our social existence in the right way. Marcel's attitude toward social existence shows how different he is from Sartre. He criticizes the 'technocratic attitude' of mass society not because it leads to conformism, but because it breeds an 'atomic individualism' that robs us of our deep sense of connection and obligation to others. And Jaspers and BUBER both emphasize the importance of 'I–Thou' relations in realizing a full and meaningful life.

Although existentialists differ in their assessment of social existence, they agree in thinking that our ordinary, day-to-day existence is shot through with concealment and self-deception. What can free us from this distorted sense of things is not rational reflection, but a profound affective experience. This emphasis on the role of emotions or moods in giving us access to the truth about ourselves is one of the most characteristic features of existentialist thought. Kierkegaard and Heidegger, for example, focus on the disclosive role of anxiety in leading us to confront the fact that we exist as finite beings who must decide the content of our own lives. Jaspers' concept of 'limit-situations' refers to situations in which our ordinary ways of handling our lives 'founder' as we encounter certain inescapable 'antinomies' of life. For Sartre, the feeling of *nausea* shows us that it is up to us to impart a meaning to things, and *anguish* reveals our 'terrible freedom' to decide our own fates. Finally, Marcel refers to the experience of *mystery* in which we encounter that which defies our ability to gain intellectual mastery through our problem-solving skills.

Some existentialists also talk about an experience of the absurd that can come over us in our rationalistic age. Sartre claims that there are no ultimate grounds that validate our choices, so that any fundamental project we adopt must be absurd in the sense that it is ultimately unjustified. Camus' conception of the absurd is perhaps the best known of all, though it is not really representative of existentialist thought. In *The Myth of Sisyphus* (1942), he describes the feeling of futility we can experience when we become aware of the repetitiveness and pointlessness of our everyday routines and rituals. For Camus, this feeling of the absurdity of existence, a feeling in which suicide begins to seem like a real possibility, is the most fundamental experience philosophy must confront.

Finally, many existentialists point to the experience of guilt as providing an insight into our own being. Existential guilt refers to something broader than the feeling we sometimes have when we have done something wrong. In its broadest significance, existential guilt refers to the fact that there is no pregiven legitimation or justification for our existence. Though we are creatures who feel the need for some 'reason for existing', we find ourselves thrown into a world where there is no higher court of appeals that could validate our lives. We are ultimately answerable only to ourselves. In a somewhat narrower sense, existential guilt can refer

to the fact that, because we are always engaged in acting in concrete situations, we are implicated in whatever happens in the world, and so we always have 'dirty hands'.

6 Authenticity

Experiences like anxiety and existential guilt are important, according to existentialists, because they reveal basic truths about our own condition as humans. Everyday life is characterized by 'inauthenticity', and in our ordinary busyness and social conformism we are refusing to take responsibility for our own lives. In throwing ourselves into socially approved activities and roles, we disown ourselves and spin a web of self-deception in trying to avoid facing up to the truth about what we are. This picture of inauthentic existence is contrasted with a vision of a way of living that does not slide into self-loss and self-deception. Such a life is (using the term found in Heidegger and Sartre) 'authentic'. Authenticity suggests the idea of being true to yourself – of owning up to who you really are. However, it is important to see that authenticity has nothing to do with the romantic ideal of getting in touch with an 'inner self' that contains one's true nature, for existentialists hold that we have no pregiven 'nature' or 'essence' distinct from what we do in the world.

If authenticity is not a matter of being true to some core of traits definitive of the 'real me', what is it? For most existentialists, becoming authentic is first of all a matter of lucidly grasping the seriousness of your own existence as an individual – the raw fact of the 'I exist' – and facing up to the task of making something of your own life. Kierkegaard, for example, holds that the only way to succeed in becoming a 'self' (understood as an 'existing individual') is by living in such a way that you have 'infinite passion' in your life. This kind of intensity is possible, he thinks, only through a total, life-defining commitment to something that gives your life an ultimate content and meaning. Nietzsche is also concerned with getting us to take hold of our own lives in a more intense and clear-sighted way. To free people from the attempt to find some overarching meaning for their lives, he proposes the idea of eternal recurrence: the idea that everything that happens in your life has happened before in exactly the same way, and will happen again and again, an endless number of times. If we accept this, Nietzsche suggests, we will be able to embrace our lives as they are, on their own terms, without regrets or dreams about how things could be different. Heidegger suggests that, in the experience of anxiety, one confronts one's own 'naked' existence as 'individualized, pure and thrown'. As we become aware of our 'being-towards-death' in this experience, we will grasp the weightiness of our own finite lives, and we will then be able to seize on our own existence with integrity, steadiness and self-constancy.

Many existentialists agree that owning up to one's own existence requires a defining commitment that gives one's life a focus and sense of direction. For Kierkegaard, a religious thinker, self-fulfilment is possible only for the 'knight of faith', the person who has a world-defining relation to a particular being which has infinite importance (the eternal being who has existed in time, the God-man). For Heidegger, authenticity requires 'resoluteness', a commitment to some specific range of possibilities opened up by one's historical 'heritage'. The fact that the ideal of commitment or engagement appears in such widely different existentialist works raises a question about the distinction, first made by Sartre, between 'religious' and 'atheist' existentialists. Kierkegaard, Marcel and Jaspers are often grouped together as religious existentialists, yet there are profound differences in their views of the nature of religious commitment. Where Kierkegaard emphasizes the importance of relating oneself to a concrete particular, Marcel and Jaspers speak of a relation to the 'mystery' or to 'transcendence' (respectively). At the same time, so-called 'atheist' existentialists like Heidegger and Sartre tend to agree with Kierkegaard's view that being 'engaged' or having a 'fundamental project' is necessary to achieving a focused, intense, coherent life. The distinction between atheist and religious existentialists becomes harder to maintain when we realize that what is important for religious thinkers is not so much the factual properties of the object of commitment as the inner condition of faith of the committed individual. Thus, Kierkegaard says that what is crucial to faith is not the 'objective truth' about what one believes, but rather the intensity of one's commitment (the 'subjective truth').

The idea that intensity and commitment are central to being authentic is shared by all types of existentialists. Another characteristic attributed to an authentic life by most existentialists is a lucid awareness of one's own responsibility for one's choices in shaping one's life. For Sartre, authenticity involves the awareness that, because we are always free to transform our lives through our decisions, if we maintain a particular identity through time, this is because we are choosing that identity at each moment. Similarly, Kierkegaard and Heidegger talk about the need to sustain our identity at each moment through a 'repetition' of our choice of who we are. In recognizing our freedom to determine our own lives, we also come to accept our responsibility for who we are.

The notion of authenticity is supposed to give us a picture of the most fulfilling life possible for us after the 'death of God'. It calls on us to assume our own identities by embracing our lives and making something of them in our own way. It presupposes lucidity, honesty, courage, intensity, openness to the realities of one's situation and a firm awareness of one's own responsibility for one's life. But it would be wrong to think of authenticity as an *ethical* ideal as this is normally interpreted. First, becoming authentic does not imply that one adopts any particular moral code or follows any particular path: an authentic individual might be a liberal or a conservative, a duty-bound citizen or a wild-eyed revolutionary. In this respect, authenticity pertains not to *what* specific kinds of things you do, but *how* you live – it is a matter of the style of your life rather than of its concrete content. Second, in formulating their different conceptions of authenticity, many existentialists describe the ideal of authenticity in terms that suggest that it can be opposed to ethics as ordinarily understood. Kierkegaard, for example, says that it is possible that the knight of faith might have to 'transcend the ethical', and Nietzsche holds that authentic individuals will live 'beyond good and evil'. Thus, authenticity seems to have more to do with what is called the 'art of self-cultivation' than it does with ethics as traditionally understood.

7 Criticisms and prospects

Existentialism has been criticized from a number of different angles. One line of criticism holds that the emphasis on individual freedom and the rejection of absolutes in existentialism tends to undermine ethics; by suggesting that everyday life is 'absurd' and by denying the existence of fixed, binding principles for evaluating our actions, existentialists promote an 'anything-goes' view of freedom that exacerbates the nihilism already present in contemporary life. Camus' novel *The Stranger* (1942), for example, has come under attack for glorifying immoral 'gratuitous acts' as a way of affirming one's own absolute freedom. In reply, supporters of existentialism have noted that the stance portrayed in the work is not at all typical of existentialist views, and that existentialism's ideal of freedom and its sense of the need for human solidarity after the 'death of God', far from undermining ethics, might provide a very good basis for a moral point of view in the modern world.

Other critics have tried to show that the basic picture of reality presupposed by existentialism necessarily leads to nihilism. Hans Jonas argues that existentialism, despite its avowed goal of overcoming Cartesianism, tends to introduce a new kind of dualism with its sharp distinction between humans (who are thought of as absolutely free centres of choice and action), and an inert, meaningless 'being' that is on hand for humans to interpret and transform as they please. Not only does this extreme opposition exclude animals from the realm of beings with intrinsic worth, its view of humans as thrown into an indifferent universe seems to give us freedom only at the cost of making nothing really worthy of choice.

This line of criticism is closely connected to the claim, formulated by various postmodern theorists, that existentialism is still trapped within the assumptions of Humanism, a view now supposed to have been discredited. Humanism in this context means the view, central to modern philosophers from Descartes to Kant, that the human subject is immediately present to itself as a centre of thought and action, and that the rest of the universe should be thought of as a collection of things on hand to be represented and manipulated by the subject. Postmodern theorists claim that a number of intellectual developments in the last two centuries have made it impossible to accept this picture of the centrality of the subject. The semiotic theories of SAUSSURE, for example, have shown how language tends to work behind our backs, controlling our capacities for thought and speech, and Freudian theory has shown how unconscious drives and desires lie behind many of our conscious thoughts and actions. Given these developments, it is claimed, we can no longer accept the idea that humans are capable of the sorts of self-transparency and self-determination that seem to be presupposed by existentialists like Sartre (see POSTMODERNISM).

In reply to this objection, one might point out that most existentialists have been very critical of the Cartesian belief in the transparency of consciousness to itself. Such themes as being-in-a-situation, 'thrownness', embodiment and mystery show the extent to which many existentialists think of humans as embedded in a wider context they can never totally master or comprehend. Moreover, the existentialist description of humans as temporal beings whose 'present' is always mediated by what is projected into the future and retained from the past undermines any Cartesian conception of the immediate presence of self to self in self-awareness. Finally, as Sonia Kruks argues, postmodern theorists seem to have run up against a wall in their attempts to 'de-centre the subject'. Having identified the pervasive background structures that influence the thoughts and actions of subjects, these theorists now find it difficult to give an account of the kind of critical thinking they see as central to the postmodern stance. In Kruks' view, existentialists have much to offer postmodern theory in formulating the conception of a 'situated subjectivity' that will fill this gap.

It is not clear what the future holds in store for existentialism understood as a philosophical movement. Many of the ideas that sounded so exciting in Paris in the 1940s now seem terribly old-fashioned. Many of the more viable themes in existentialism have been absorbed into new philosophical movements, especially into hermeneutics with its emphasis on humans as self-interpreting beings (see HERMENEUTICS). While some existentialist writers have faded from the scene, others have become more and more influential (though not always *as* existentialists). There has been an explosion of interest in Heidegger and Nietzsche recently, and the works of Kierkegaard, Sartre and Beauvoir are widely discussed.

Whether or not existentialism as such will continue to thrive, it seems that there will always be a place for the style of critique of society and the concern with the concrete realities of life that are central to existentialist thought. As a reactive movement, existentialism challenged the uncritical assumptions of mainstream philosophy as well as the complacency of everyday social existence. On a more positive note, it attempted to counteract the tendency to self-loss in contemporary life by formulating a vision of the kind of coherent, focused way of living that would provide a basis for meaningful action. These certainly seem to be valuable aims, and it is likely that existentialist writers will always have important contributions to make toward realizing them.

References and further reading

Cooper, D.E. (1990) *Existentialism: A Reconstruction*, Oxford: Blackwell, 2nd edn, 1999. (An up-to-date and thorough survey of existentialist thought. Helpful bibliography.)

Guignon, C. (ed.) (2004) *The Existentialists: Critical Essays on Kierkegaard, Nietzsche, Heidegger, and Sartre*, Lanham, MD: Rowman & Littlefield. (Scholarly essays by major Anglophone philosophers on four major representatives of the existentialist tradition.)

McBride, W.L. (ed.) (1997) *Sartre and Existentialism: Philosophy, Politics, Ethics, the Psyche, Literature, and Aesthetics*, New York: Garland, 8 vols. (Collections of classic essays in English on existentialism, with volumes on its background and development.)

CHARLES B. GUIGNON

EXPERIMENT

Experiment, as a specific category of scientific activity, did not emerge until the Scientific Revolution of the seventeenth century. Seen primarily as an arbiter in theory choice, there was little, if any, analysis of experimental techniques or the ways in which data become transformed into established facts. Philosophical analysis of experiment was typically simplistic, focusing on the role of observation alone as the foundation for experimental facts. This was challenged by Thomas Kuhn who stressed the importance of background theory and beliefs in all perception, including (its role in) scientific experiment. This interconnection between theory and experiment severely undermined the idea that experiment could stand as an independent and objective criterion for judging the merits of one theory over another.

In the 1980s new philosophical analyses of experiment began to emerge, emphasizing the ways in which experiment could be seen to have a life of its own embodying activities that could supposedly be understood without recourse to theory. Factors important in the evaluation of experimental results as well as the ways in which laboratory science differs from its theoretical counterpart became the focus for a new history and philosophy of experiment. Consequently, further debates arose regarding the relationship of experiment to theory, and whether it is possible to provide a methodological framework within which experimental practice can be evaluated.

See also: SCIENTIFIC REALISM AND ANTIREALISM

MARGARET C. MORRISON

EXPERIMENTS, CRUCIAL
See CRUCIAL EXPERIMENTS

EXPLANATION

Introduction

Philosophical reflections about explanation are common in the history of philosophy, and important proposals were made by Aristotle, Hume, Kant and Mill. But the subject came of age in the twentieth century with the provision of detailed models of scientific explanation, most notably the *covering-law* model, which takes explanations to be arguments in which a law of nature plays an essential role among the premises. In the heyday of logical empiricism, philosophers achieved a consensus on the covering-law model, but, during the 1960s and 1970s, that consensus was challenged through the recognition of four major kinds of difficulty: first, a problem about the relation between idealized arguments and the actual practice of explaining; second, the difficulty of characterizing the underlying notion of a law of nature; third, troubles in accounting for the asymmetries of explanation; and, four, recalcitrant problems in treating statistical explanations.

Appreciation of these difficulties has led to the widespread abandonment of the covering-law model, and currently there is no consensus on how to understand explanation. The main contemporary view seeks to characterize explanation in terms of causation, that is, explanations are accounts that trace the causes of the events (states, conditions) being explained. Other philosophers believe that there is no general account of explanation, and offer pragmatic theories. A third option sees explanation as consisting in the unification of the phenomena. All of these approaches have associated successes, and face particular anomalies.

Although the general character of explanation is now a subject for philosophical debate, some particular kinds of explanation seem to be relatively well understood. In particular, functional explanations in biology, which logical empiricists found puzzling, now appear to be treated quite naturally by supposing them to make tacit reference to natural selection.

1 Early history

Thinking about explanation goes back at least to Aristotle, whose discussion of four kinds of causation in the *Posterior Analytics* can properly be viewed as distinguishing modes of scientific explanation (see ARISTOTLE §9). In the modern period, the writings of Hume, Kant and Mill offer many insights on causation, laws and regularities in nature that, sometimes explicitly, sometimes implicitly, propose doctrines about the character of scientific explanation (see HUME, D. §2; KANT, I. §§4–7; MILL, J.S. §5). However questions about scientific explanation became sharply focused in the mid-twentieth century, with the emergence of an orthodoxy about scientific explanation, which, despite its later demise, stands as one of the most significant achievements of the movement known as 'logical empiricism' (see LOGICAL POSITIVISM §4). The writings of Karl Popper, R.B. Braithwaite, Ernest Nagel and especially C.G. Hempel, articulate an influential conception. Namely, scientific explanations are viewed as arguments in which a statement describing the fact (or regularity) to be explained is derived from premises, at least one of which is a law of nature. The underlying idea is that scientific explanations provide understanding by showing that the phenomena to be explained should be expected as a consequence of the general laws of nature.

2   The covering-law model

One important and much-discussed species of scientific explanation according with this general conception is *deductive-nomological* explanation (D-N explanation). In cases of this type, the argument is deductive, so that the statement describing the phenomenon to be explained (the *explanandum*) is a deductive consequence of the premises advanced in giving the explanation (the *explanans*). D-N explanations may be provided for explananda that describe particular facts or for explananda that announce general regularities. In the former case, there is a simple schema which exhibits the form of the explanation

$$C_1, C_2, \ldots, C_n$$

$$\frac{L_1, L_2, \ldots, L_m}{E}$$

where the statement E is the explanandum, describing the fact to be explained, the statements L_1, L_2, ..., L_m are laws of nature, and the statements C_1, C_2, ..., C_n describe particular facts (such as initial conditions). It is not hard to construct arguments that accord with this schema and which seem to explain their conclusions: derivations in classical Newtonian dynamics that deduce the trajectories of bodies from force laws and initial conditions supply many examples.

Not all explanatory arguments are deductive. The logical empiricist orthodoxy admitted *inductive-statistical* explanations (I-S explanations) as well as D-N explanations. In an I-S explanation, the explanandum is inferred inductively from premises at least one of which is a probabilistic law, for example a statement that assigns a value to the probability with which a particular trait is found among members of a specific class. Thus, to cite a famous example of Hempel's, we may explain why a child, Henrietta, contracted measles, by noting that she has been in contact with another child, Henry, who has measles, and that a large percentage of children who come into contact with measles' patients (say 99 per cent) subsequently come down with measles. Imitating the schema for D-N explanation, we can present this modest derivation as follows:

Henrietta has been in contact with Henry, and Henry has measles.
The frequency with which children in contact with measles' patients subsequently acquire measles is 99 per cent.

$$\frac{(0.99)}{\text{Henrietta has measles}}$$

Here, the rule indicates that the inference from premises to conclusion is inductively strong, rather than deductively valid; the figure in parentheses (0.99) reveals the strength of the inference. I-S explanations have to meet several requirements. First, the numerical strength of the inductive inference must be high (close to 1). Second, the explanans must meet a requirement of maximal specificity: there must not be known further premises which, if added to the explanans, would change the strength of the inference – as, for example, the inductive reasoning would be modified if we knew that Henrietta had received a shot for measles', and that children given such shots have a very low probability of contracting the disease.

Plainly, the explanations that scientists and others actually put forward do not look much like these stripped-down arguments. The logical empiricists claimed only that the everyday provision of explanations could be reconstructed by identifying arguments of D-N or I-S form, and that these reconstructions brought into the open what it was about the explanations that enabled them to fulfil their function. In the 1940s and 1950s, many scholars were happy to concede that the covering-law model of explanation, which assimilated explanations to arguments with laws among their premises, worked well as a reconstruction of explanations in the natural sciences – especially in physics and chemistry – but there were important debates about the application of the model to the social sciences and to explanation in everyday life. Controversy focused in particular on the activity of historical explanation. Historians construct detailed narratives that appear to explain particular events – the outbreak of the American Civil War or Henry VIII's dissolution of the monasteries. If the covering-law model is correct, then a proper reconstruction of these accounts must expose general laws. Are there indeed general laws in history? Or are the general laws that underlie historical explanation simply psychological laws that connect the motivations of historical actors with their actions (see EXPLANATION IN HISTORY AND SOCIAL SCIENCE)?

3   Four kinds of difficulty

Troubles with history aside, the covering-law model appeared remarkably successful, a rare example of a convincing solution to a philosophical problem. Yet, in the 1960s, it came under sustained attack, and, by the end of the decade, it had been almost entirely abandoned. Four separate kinds of consideration contributed to this swift reversal of fortune.

First was a complaint, articulated by Michael Scriven, that perfectly satisfactory explanations can be given, and understood, by people who are quite ignorant of the covering-laws that are essential to the supposed reconstruction. It is easy to explain to a friend why there is a mess on the floor by pointing out that your arm knocked the open ink bottle off the desk at which you were writing. Perhaps it would be possible for a knowing philosopher of science to cite the general laws that govern the behaviour of the bottle and the spilled ink, but this knowledge seems entirely irrelevant to the episode in which the chagrined mess-maker explains what has occurred. At the heart of Scriven's complaint lay the recognition that the covering-law model had failed to show how the idealized derivations that supposedly highlight how the explanatory work is done are adapted, in specific local situations, to transmit understanding from one person to another. Without a *pragmatics* of explanation, an account of how the ideal arguments that fit particular logical forms relate to what people actually do in giving explanations, it was possible to challenge the claim that the structures exposed by the logical empiricists reveal the crucial features that make the explanation successful.

A second difficulty resulted from continued inability to provide a satisfactory account of natural laws. From the earliest formulations of the covering-law model, its champions had insisted that not every generalization counts as a law. So-called *accidental* generalizations cannot discharge any explanatory function: it may be a timeless truth about the universe that all ball games played by a red-haired left-hander who forgoes lunch are won by the opposite team, but that accidental generalization sheds no light on the outcome of any particular game (see LAWS, NATURAL). Prior to Nelson Goodman's formulation of a cluster of difficulties surrounding counterfactuals, induction and laws, the problem of distinguishing laws from accidental generalizations appeared an interesting challenge to the logical empiricist project. Once the depth of Goodman's 'new riddle of induction' had become apparent, it seemed impossible to find a solution within the constraints that empiricists allowed themselves (see INDUCTION, EPISTEMIC ISSUES IN).

A third trouble emerged from the recognition that, even if the distinction between laws and accidental generalizations could be drawn, the covering-law model would still be too liberal. Introducing an example that was to become famous, Sylvain Bromberger pointed out that the model is blind to certain asymmetries in explanation. We can explain the length of the shadow cast by a flagpole by deriving a statement ascribing the pertinent numerical value from premises identifying the height of the pole and the angle of elevation of the sun, together with the law of the rectilinear propagation of light. This derivation fits the D–N schema beautifully. The trouble, however, is that we can produce a modified argument, according equally well with the D–N schema, by interchanging the premise that identifies the height of the pole with the conclusion: the height of the flagpole is deducible from the length of the shadow, the elevation of the sun and the law of rectilinear propagation of light. This new derivation does not seem explanatory, for it appears wrong to explain the heights of poles (or, more generally, the sizes of physical objects) in terms of the measurements of the shadows they cast. Scrupulous about appealing to causation, logical empiricism had tried to construct an account of explanation without invoking causal notions that would offend Humean sensibilities (hence, in part, the difficulty of characterizing natural laws). Bromberger's critique suggests that the omission of causal concepts assimilates cases that are importantly different: after all, it is tempting to characterize the difference between the two derivations by pointing out that the height of the flagpole *causes* the shadow to have the length it does, but that the length of the shadow does not cause the flagpole to have the height it does.

Perhaps the most influential difficulty, was the fourth, which focused on the failure of the account of statistical explanation. Alberto Coffa probed the conditions required of I–S explanation, revealing that they involved an essential reference to the state of knowledge, which made it impossible to develop a concept of a true inductive explanation. Coffa's critique complemented the work of Richard Jeffrey, who had earlier argued that it is possible to explain individual events that do not have high probability in the light of background conditions, and thus that the high probability requirement was also defective. At the same time, Wesley Salmon, in 'Statistical Explanation' (1970) worked out, in considerable detail, an account of statistical explanation that, like Jeffrey's, rejected the thesis that explanations are arguments. Central to Salmon's account was the idea that we explain by citing probabilistically relevant information. In the early versions of his model of statistical explanation, Salmon proposed that probabilistic explanations gain their force from the recognition that the probability that an individual has a property has been raised. Schematically, the information that a is F helps explain why a is G when the probability of something's being G is increased if that thing is F (more exactly: $P(G/F) > P(G)$). In this way, Salmon was able to respond to a difficulty noted earlier by Scriven – we may explain the fact that the mayor has paresis by noting that he previously had untreated syphilis, even though the frequency with which untreated syphilitics contract paresis is small (around 15 per cent). On Salmon's account, noting that the mayor had untreated syphilis gives an enormous boost to the probability of his having paresis, raising it from the baseline figure of close to 0 to about 15 per cent.

4 Picking up the pieces

Salmon's account of explanation was deliberately motivated by the felt need to allow for explanations in the indeterministic contexts of contemporary physics. His approach dovetailed neatly with attempts, like those of Patrick Suppes, to fashion a conception of causality that would no longer be restricted to deterministic situations (see CAUSATION; DETERMINISM AND INDETERMINISM). From 1970 to the present, one important strand in contemporary theories of explanation has taken explanation to consist in delineating the causes of events, and has tried to honour Humean concerns about the invocation of causality by providing a theory of causation that will define causal relations in statistical terms. The simplest account of probabilistic causality would propose that A is causally relevant to B just in case $P(B/A) \neq P(B)$. Unfortunately, this account is too simple. As HANS REICHENBACH pointed out in the 1950s the inequality will obtain when A and B are both effects of a common cause. Thus further conditions must be imposed to identify the statistical relations constitutive of probabilistic causation.

Since the 1970s a number of different proposals have competed to inherit the position of orthodoxy once occupied by the covering-law model. Most popular have been causal approaches to explanation, and, initially, proposals to ground explanation in a detailed conception of probabilistic causality promised to answer (or sidestep) the four principal difficulties outlined above. However, it has proved remarkably difficult to work out a satisfactory account of explanation along these lines, and a number of critiques, most notably that by Nancy Cartwright, have cast doubt on the viability of the enterprise. Faced with powerful objections, champions of causal approaches to explanation have pursued one of two options. One is to continue to honour Humean concerns about the causal relation, and to seek an analysis of causation that will not make use of metaphysical notions that empiricists consider dubious. The most thorough attempt to carry out this programme has been undertaken by Wesley Salmon, who has attempted to develop Reichenbach's account of causation in terms of the fundamental notion of mark transmission. The alternative approach is to declare victory by taking some causal notion as an unanalysed primitive,

resisting Humean scruples about how we might know how to apply this notion as misguided (perhaps the proposals of Humphreys and Cartwright should be viewed as embodying this approach).

One evident attraction of the causal programme is that it provides an immediate response to the problem posed by the asymmetries of explanation. However, not all current theories view explanation as a matter of tracing causes. In recent years, Bas van Fraassen, Peter Achinstein and Peter Railton have all made important contributions to the pragmatics of explanation, and the first two authors have defended the view that the enterprise of seeking substantive necessary conditions that apply across all contexts in which people seek and give explanations is misguided. The danger is that such pragmatic theories of explanation reduce the enterprise to triviality. For any explanation-seeking question and any proposition we choose, it seems that we can construct a context in which that proposition is licensed as an adequate (or even a perfect) explanatory answer to that question.

A third cluster of positions stays close to the covering-law model's conception of explanations as arguments, proposing that explanatory arguments are not distinguished singly but emerge from the best way of systematizing our body of knowledge. Michael Friedman and Philip Kitcher have developed (different) accounts of explanation that take arguments to be explanatory if they belong to a system of arguments that best unifies our beliefs. One virtue of this approach is its ready provision of an analysis of theoretical explanation; its principal difficulties lie in formulating appropriate criteria for unification and for addressing the asymmetries of explanation.

The present debate echoes themes from earlier chapters in the history of philosophy. Hume's scruples about causation loom behind some efforts to articulate causal theories of explanation, those who oppose Hume on causation (like Cartwright) sometimes seem to harken back to Aristotle, and the unification approach has made an explicit connection with Kant. Perhaps these affinities suggest that contemporary debates about scientific explanation turn on larger metaphysical questions that need to be confronted directly (see UNITY OF SCIENCE).

5 Functional explanation: a recent success story

Ironically, after the fragmentation of the consensus on the covering-law model of explanation, considerable progress has been made on studying a species of explanation that, despite careful studies by Hempel and Nagel, was always somewhat difficult for logical empiricist orthodoxy. Biologists often appear to explain the presence of a trait or structure by identifying its function, and it is not clear how such explanations should be assimilated to a D-N (or an I-S) schema. Thanks to pioneering work by Larry Wright, contemporary philosophers of biology are largely agreed on a central idea: functional explanations are abridged versions of explanations in terms of natural selection. The identification of the function is thus seen as picking out the kind of selection pressure that causes the trait (or structure) to become originally established (or, maybe, to be maintained). The details of this idea are worked out in different ways by different authors, but the selectionist (or etiological) account of functional explanation appears to provide a philosophically satisfactory reconstruction of parts of biological practice (see EVOLUTION, THEORY OF; FUNCTIONAL EXPLANATION).

A possible moral of the comparative success in studying functional explanation is that philosophers may be too ambitious in seeking general theories of explanation. Pragmatists like van Fraassen sometimes suggest that there are many different kinds of successful explanation, and that there may be no interesting general conditions that all must meet. Perhaps the most fundamental issue confronting the theory of explanation today is whether it is reasonable to seek a theory of explanation across all contexts and all epochs or whether the study of scientific explanation should be more local, concentrating on specific types of explanation.

References and further reading

Pitt, J. (1989) *Theories of Explanation*, New York: Oxford University Press. (A collection containing many important contemporary articles.)

Rubin, D.-H. (1994) *Explanation*, Oxford: Oxford University Press. (A collection explicitly designed to complement Pitt (1989).)

PHILIP KITCHER

EXPLANATION, FUNCTIONAL
See FUNCTIONAL EXPLANATION

EXPLANATION IN HISTORY AND SOCIAL SCIENCE

Historians and social scientists explain at least two sorts of things: (a) those individual human actions that have historical or social significance, such as Stalin's decision to hold the show trials, Diocletian's division of the Roman Empire, and the Lord Chief Justice's attempt to reform the English judicial system; and (b) historical and social events and structures ('large-scale' social phenomena), such as wars, economic depressions, social customs, the class system, the family, the state, and the crime rate. Philosophical questions arise about explanations of both kinds (a) and (b).

Concerning (b), perhaps the most pressing question is whether explanations of this sort can, ultimately, be understood as merely explanations of a large number of individual human actions, that is, as a complex set of explanations of the first kind, (a).

A causal explanation is an explanation of something in terms of its event-cause(s). Some explanations under (b) appear not to be causal explanations in this sense. There are two ways in which this appears to happen. First, we sometimes seem to explain a social structure or event by giving its function or purpose. This seems to be an explanation in terms of its effects rather than by its causes. For example, it might be claimed that the explanation for a certain social custom in a tribal society is the way in which it contributes to social stability or group solidarity. An explanation of a thing in terms of its effects cannot be a causal explanation of that thing. Second, we sometimes seem to cite social structure as the explanation of something. Whatever a social structure is, it is not itself an event, and since only (it is often said) events can be causes, such a 'structural' explanation does not seem to be a causal explanation.

A second question, then, about explanations of kind (b) is whether some of them are genuinely non-causal explanations, or whether functional and/or structural explanations of this sort can be seen as special sorts of causal explanation.

Explanations of kind (a) are a proper subset of explanations of human actions generally. Although some of the discussion of these issues began life as a distinct literature within the philosophy of history, it has now been absorbed into philosophical action theory more generally. Even so, a question that remains is just which proper subset of human actions are the ones of interest to the historical and social sciences: how can we discriminate within the class of human actions between those in which historians or social scientists have a legitimate interest and those outside their purview?
See also: FUNCTIONAL EXPLANATION

DAVID-HILLEL RUBEN

EXPRESSION, ARTISTIC
See ARTISTIC EXPRESSION

EXTERNAL WORLD SCEPTICISM
See SCEPTICISM

EXTERNALISM IN EPISTEMOLOGY
See INTERNALISM AND EXTERNALISM IN EPISTEMOLOGY

F

FACTS

The existence and nature of facts is disputed. In ordinary language we often speak of facts ('that's a fact') but it is hard to take such talk seriously since it can be paraphrased away. It is better to argue for the existence of facts on the basis of three connected theoretical roles for facts. First, facts as the referents of true sentences: 'the cat sat on the mat', if true, refers to the fact that the cat sat on the mat. Second, facts as the truth-makers of true sentences: the fact that the cat sat on the mat is what makes 'the cat sat on the mat' true. Third, facts as causal relata, related in such sentences as 'Caesar died because Brutus stabbed him'. The so-called 'slingshot' argument aims to show that these roles are misconceived.

See also: Events; Ontological commitment

ALEX OLIVER

FACT/VALUE DISTINCTION

According to proponents of the fact/value distinction, no states of affairs in the world can be said to be values, and evaluative judgments are best understood not to be pure statements of fact. The distinction was important in twentieth-century ethics, and debate continues about the metaphysical status of value, the epistemology of value, and the best characterization of value-judgments.

ROGER CRISP

FAITH

Faith became a topic of discussion in the Western philosophical tradition on account of its prominence in the New Testament, where the having or taking up of faith is often urged by writers. The New Testament itself echoes both Hellenistic concepts of faith and older biblical traditions, specifically that of Abraham in the Book of Genesis.

The subsequent attention of philosophers has been focused primarily on three topics: the nature of faith, the connection between God's goodness and human responsibility, and the relation of faith to reason. Discussions on the nature of faith, from Aquinas to Tillich, have tried to examine the subject in terms of whether it is a particular form of knowledge, virtue, trust and so on. Regarding divine goodness, the argument has primarily focused on the relationship between faith and free will, and whether lack of faith is the responsibility of the individual or of God. Concerning the relation between faith and reason, there are two quite separate issues: the relation of faith to theorizing, and the rationality of faith. Aquinas in particular argued that faith is a necessary prerequisite for reasoning and intellectual activity, while later, John Locke explored the relationship between faith, reason and rationality, and concluded that faith can be reached through reason. This latter viewpoint was later heavily criticized by Wittgenstein and his followers.

See also: Natural theology; Negative theology

NICHOLAS P. WOLTERSTORFF

FALLIBILISM

Fallibilism is a philosophical doctrine regarding natural science, most closely associated with Charles Sanders Peirce, which maintains that our scientific knowledge claims are invariably vulnerable and may turn out to be false. Scientific theories cannot be asserted as true categorically, but only as having some probability of being true. Fallibilists insist on our inability to attain the final and definitive truth regarding the theoretical concerns of natural science – in particular at the level of theoretical physics. At any rate, at this level of generality and precision each of our accepted beliefs may turn out to be false, and many of them will. Fallibilism does not insist on the falsity of our scientific claims but rather on their tentativity as inevitable estimates: it does not hold that knowledge is unavailable here, but rather that it is always provisional.

See also: Commonsensism; Epistemology and ethics; Scepticism

NICHOLAS RESCHER

FALSIFICATION

See CRUCIAL EXPERIMENTS; FALLIBILISM; POPPER, KARL RAIMUND

FAMILY, ETHICS AND THE

Do obligations to children take priority over filial and other family obligations? Do blood kin have stronger moral claims than relatives acquired through marriage? Whatever their origin, do family obligations take precedence over obligations to friends, neighbours, fellow citizens? Do family moral ties presuppose specific family feeling, love, or loyalty? Is the traditional family of a married, heterosexual couple with biological offspring morally preferable to families formed by adoptive, single, remarried or same-sex parents, or with the help of gamete donors or gestational ('maternal') surrogates? On what grounds may friends, neighbours or government agencies intrude upon 'family privacy'?

To simplify the complexity and diversity of family life, reasoned answers to such questions may stress a single dimension. A *metaphysical* approach draws on the commands of a deity or the needs of a nation. A *biological* approach appeals to physical resemblance, blood or genes. An *economic* approach focuses on family property, income, division of work and resources, and inheritance. A related *political* approach attends to power, subordination, and rights within a family, as well as to their regulation by the state. A *psychological* approach takes affection, identification, intimacy, and emotional needs as morally decisive. A *narrative* approach makes recalling and revision of family stories the basis of moral education and the definition of family ties.

Although mutually compatible, these approaches do each tend to favour particular moral theories.
See also: FRIENDSHIP; GENETICS AND ETHICS; IMPARTIALITY; LOVE; REPRODUCTION AND ETHICS; SEXUALITY, PHILOSOPHY OF

WILLIAM RUDDICK

AL-FARABI, ABU NASR (870–950)

Al-Farabi was known to the Arabs as the 'Second Master' (after Aristotle), and with good reason. It is unfortunate that his name has been overshadowed by those of later philosophers such as Ibn Sina, for al-Farabi was one of the world's great philosophers and much more original than many of his Islamic successors. A philosopher, logician and musician, he was also a major political scientist.

Al-Farabi has left us no autobiography and consequently, relatively little is known for certain about his life. His philosophical legacy, however, is large. In the arena of metaphysics he has been designated the 'Father of Islamic Neoplatonism', and while he was also saturated with Aristotelianism and certainly deploys the vocabulary of Aristotle, it is this Neoplatonic dimension which dominates much of his corpus. This is apparent in his most famous work, *al-Madina al-fadila* (The Virtuous City) which, far from being a copy or a clone of Plato's *Republic*, is imbued with the Neoplatonic concept of God. Of course, *al-Madina al-fadila* has undeniable Platonic elements but its theology, as opposed to its politics, places it outside the mainstream of pure Platonism.

In his admittedly complex theories of epistemology, al-Farabi has both an Aristotelian and Neoplatonic dimension, neither of which is totally integrated with the other. His influence was wide and extended not only to major Islamic philosophers such as Ibn Sina who came after him, and to lesser mortals such as Yahya ibn 'Adi, al-Sijistani, al-'Amiri and al-Tawhidi, but also to major thinkers of Christian medieval Europe including Thomas Aquinas.
See also: IBN SINA

IAN RICHARD NETTON

FASCISM

'Fascism' is a term referring both to a political ideology and to a concrete set of political movements and regimes. Its most prominent examples were the Italian and German regimes in the interwar period. Fascist ideology is sometimes portrayed as merely a mantle for political movements in search of power, but in reality it set forth a new vision of society, drawing on both left- and right-wing ideas. Fascists stressed the need for social cohesion and for strong leadership. They were more concerned to revitalize nations by cultural change than to propose institutional changes, but they saw themselves as offering a third way between capitalism and communism. There was no fascist philosophy as such, but fascist ideology drew inspiration from earlier philosophers, most notably Nietzsche and Sorel, and was supported by several contemporary philosophers, including Heidegger, Gentile and Schmitt.
See also: ANTI-SEMITISM; TOTALITARIANISM

ROGER EATWELL

FATALISM

'Fatalism' is sometimes used to mean the acceptance of determinism, along with a readiness to accept the consequence that there is no such thing as human freedom. The word is also often used in connection with a theological question: whether God's supposed foreknowledge means that the future is already fixed. But it is sometimes explained very differently, as the view that human choice and action have no influence on future events, which will be as they will be whatever we think or do. On the face of it this is barely coherent, and invites the assessment that fatalism is simply an expression of resigned acceptance.

See also: DETERMINISM AND INDETERMINISM; FREE WILL; MANY-VALUED LOGICS, PHILOSOPHICAL ISSUES IN; PREDESTINATION; STOICISM

EDWARD CRAIG

FECHNER, GUSTAV THEODOR (1801–87)

Fechner was a pioneer in experimental psychology and the founder of psychophysics, the speciality within psychology devoted to quantitative studies of perception. In his foundational *Elemente der Psychophysik* (*Elements of Psychophysics*) (1860), he defined the mission of the new science to be the development of an 'exact theory of the functionally dependent relations of... the physical and the psychological worlds'. It is in this work that Fechner developed the law of sensation-magnitudes (Fechner's Law): the strength of a sensation is proportional to the logarithmic value of the intensity of the stimulus. Among his contemporaries he was well known not only for basic research in the field of electricity, but also as the author of a number of satirical works under the name 'Dr Mises'.

DANIEL N. ROBINSON

FEDERALISM AND CONFEDERALISM

Federative arrangements involve two or more governments ruling over the same territory and population. They have been of interest to political philosophers because they challenge, or at least complicate, some fundamental political concepts like authority, sovereignty, democracy and citizenship. Like citizens in actual federations, philosophers do not treat the terms of federation as a merely technocratic matter: they believe that there are morally legitimate and illegitimate ways of, among other things, dividing powers between governments, determining the representation of the subunits (for example, provinces) within federal institutions and amending the constitution. Philosophers also see in federalism a means of securing a degree of self-determination for ethnic minorities who cannot realistically expect to have their own homogeneous nation-states.

See also: MULTICULTURALISM

WAYNE NORMAN

FEMINISM

Introduction

Feminism is grounded on the belief that women are oppressed or disadvantaged by comparison with men, and that their oppression is in some way illegitimate or unjustified. Under the umbrella of this general characterization there are, however, many interpretations of women and their oppression, so that it is a mistake to think of feminism as a single philosophical doctrine, or as implying an agreed political programme. Just as there are diverse images of liberation, so there are a number of feminist philosophies, yoked together not so much by their particular claims or prescriptions as by their interest in a common theme.

In the earlier phases of feminism, advocates focused largely on the reform of women's social position, arguing that they should have access to education, work or civil rights. During the latter half of the twentieth century, however, feminists have become increasingly interested in the great range of social practices (including theoretical ones) through which our understandings of femininity and masculinity are created and maintained. As a result, the scope of feminist enquiry has broadened to include, for example, jurisprudence and psychoanalysis, together with many areas of philosophy.

This type of work characteristically draws on and grapples with a set of deeply-rooted historical attempts to explain the domination of women. Aristotle's claim that they are mutilated males, like the biblical account of the sin of Eve, contributed to an authoritative tradition in which the weakness, irrationality and ineducability of women, their inconstancy, inability to control their emotions and lack of moral virtue, were all regularly assumed as grounds for controlling them and excluding them from the public realm.

1. Feminism and feminisms
2. Renaissance and early-modern forerunners
3. Claims of right
4. Sexual oppression and emancipation
5. The pervasiveness of male domination
6. Second- and third-wave feminism

1 Feminism and feminisms

Throughout the history of philosophy there have been writers who challenged sexual stereotypes of women. However their works do not form a single story. It can therefore be misleading to assimilate them too quickly to the philosophical literature and political campaigns which initiated later feminist movements, or to contemporary feminist positions. Only at the end of the eighteenth century did a stream of philosophical arguments aimed at the emancipation of women begin to gather force. Only at the end of the nineteenth century did the term *la féminisme* appear, put into circulation after the fact in France during the 1890s, and rapidly taken up in the rest of Europe and then in America. The label 'feminist' thus arose out of, and was in many ways continuous with, the sequence of nineteenth- and twentieth-century campaigns for the vote, for access to education and the professions, for the right of married women to own property and have custody of their children, for the abolition of laws about female prostitution based on the double standard, and so on. While the character and success of these movements varied from country to country (for example, women's suffrage was introduced in New Zealand in 1893, Finland in 1906 and Britain in 1928) they all drew upon, and generated, arguments about the nature and capacities of women and entertained, explicitly or implicitly, images of their liberation. Many of the most influential philosophical defences of women's emancipation dating from this period were written by people involved in political work – to name only two, John Stuart MILL, the author of *The Subjection of Women*, proposed to the British parliament in 1867 an amendment to the Reform Bill designed to give votes to women, while Emily Davies, author of *The Higher Education of Women*, was the foundress of Girton College, Cambridge, the first women's college of higher education in England.

We have no difficulty in retrospectively classifying works such as these as feminist, although this is not a description their authors would have used, because they contain analyses of women's oppression and proposals for overcoming it which mesh easily with analyses and proposals later regarded as central to the feminist cause. At the same time there are also significant divergences between feminist writers, past as well as present. Different interpretations of the disadvantages to which women are subject, allied to different conceptions of an improved distribution of power, gave rise to divergent and sometimes irreconcilable feminisms. Compare, for example, the broadly liberal view that the oppression of women consists in their lack of political equality with men and can be alleviated by giving both sexes the same political rights, with the separatist view that women's oppression lies principally in their sexual subordination to men and can only be overcome in societies that are, as far as possible, exclusively female.

Historians interested in the former are liable to focus on works such as Poulain de la Barre's *De L'Égalité des deux sexes* (1673) or MARY WOLL-

STONECRAFT's *Vindication of the Rights of Women*. By contrast, writers wishing to trace the history of the latter are more likely to pick out Mary Astell's proposal that ladies should retire from the society of men who debar them from realizing the natural desire to advance and perfect their being, or Charlotte Perkins Gilman's utopia *Herland* about an isolated society of women who are able to have children without male assistance. As these examples indicate there are many feminisms, each with a history of its own.

2 Renaissance and early-modern forerunners

Although female inferiority is the dominant note that sounds through the Western philosophical tradition, its character was never a matter of consensus. Long drawn out theological debates about whether woman is a human being, whether she is made in the image of God, whether she is a perfect creation of God or an imperfect version of man, and whether men and women are equal before God, all appeal to classical authorities, to the Bible and to the Church Fathers, and rumble on through the Middle Ages and into the Renaissance. Complementing them are a series of more secular discussions, of which one of the most consistent concentrates on women's intellectual capacities. In her *Livre de la cité des dames* (1405) CHRISTINE DE PIZAN extols the advantages of educating women, a theme subsequently taken up by Renaissance writers for whom it played a part in the so-called *Querelle des Femmes* – a series of philosophically repetitive disputes about whether fidelity in marriage should be demanded of both sexes, whether and to what extent women should be educated, and whether women were entitled to the respect and gratitude of men for the services they rendered them. On one side of these debates, women's inferiority was reasserted by appeal to example, authority and reason. On the other, their superiority was defended in a variety of genres. Some authors – for example Cornelius Agrippa – employed the rhetorical device of the paradoxical encomium, attempting to surprise and impress by ingeniously reversing conventional evaluations of men and women (see AGRIPPA VON NETTESHEIM). Others drew on a well-tried stock of cases to illustrate women's superior virtue, intelligence or judiciousness. The choice of these genres strengthens the impression that, while such champions of the female cause sometimes propose limited social reforms, they are on the whole anxious not to unsettle the status quo. Their aim is to entertain – to tease men and flatter women, and perhaps in doing so to make both reconsider their roles – rather than to foment social change.

Traces of this style endured well into the seventeenth century and are visible even in writers who in other ways broke with the terms of the *querelle*. A particularly striking change is the move away from debates about the relative inferiority or superiority of women, to works purporting to show that the sexes are equal. Marie de Gournay, who claimed that she was the first to take this view, published her *Égalité des hommes et des femmes* in 1622, and the same theme was taken up with a new determination later in the century. In France, Poulain de la Barre adopted a fresh approach when he appealed to Cartesian scientific method: a clear and distinct understanding of the issue can be arrived at, he insists, by rational demonstration. Although his *De l'Égalité des deux sexes* (1673) sometimes lapses into the older style of argument – women are more decorous and discreet than men, women's work is more valuable than that of men, and so on – Poulain is remarkable for the forthright manner with which he asserts that the relations between mind and body and the capacities of the mind are the same in both sexes, and even more for the consequences he draws from this claim. There is no reason, in his view, why women should not occupy all the public roles currently held by men. Since they are capable of equalling men in understanding all the sciences (including both civil and canon law) they could, if educated, teach in the universities, be legislators, rulers, generals of armies, judges and – most radical of all – preachers and ministers of the Church.

Poulain's willingness to contemplate such dramatic social change is more unusual than his emphasis on intellectual equality or his downplaying of the significance of the bodily differences between men and women. A number of women writing in the second half of the seventeenth century criticize men for depriving them of learning and education, and imply that women are quite capable of ruling themselves, and indeed men. For instance Anna Maria von Schurman in the Netherlands, Sor Juana Ines de la Cruz in Mexico, Jacqueline Pascal and Madame de la Maintenon in France, and Bathusa Makin in England all write in favour of the education of girls. Authors such as Margaret CAVENDISH and Mary Astell are by turns bitter and witty in their wide-ranging critical explorations of women's subjection to men.

3 Claims of right

As early as 1673, Poulain de la Barre argued that women and men possess an equal right to knowledge, conferred on them by nature. All humans pursue happiness; no one can achieve happiness without knowledge; so everyone needs knowledge.

To ensure that people are able to pursue their proper end, nature has supplied the necessary means in the form of a right. We find here the beginnings of an appeal to rights which became progressively more central until, a century or so later, it dominated debate. In the immediate wake of the French Revolution, Olymphe de Gouges presented the French Assembly with a Declaration of the Rights of Women (which it declined to ratify). Women, she argued, should have rights to employment, legal rights within the family, a right to free speech and a separate assembly in which they could represent themselves. The same theme was taken up in England by Mary WOLLSTONECRAFT, who in 1792 published *A Vindication of the Rights of Women*. Challenging Rousseau, Wollstonecraft argued that the education and emancipation of women are conditions of a truly civilized society. God has endowed all humans with reason so that they can use it to govern their passions and attain knowledge and virtue. To deprive women of the opportunity to perfect their nature and increase their capacity for happiness is to treat them as less than human and render them 'gentle, domestic brutes'. It is to trample on their rights and keep them in a state of subjection which damages both them and their male captors.

Far from being natural, Wollstonecraft explains echoing the arguments of Mary Astell, the presumed inferiority of women stems primarily from their lack of education. Cut off from learning and encouraged to care only for love and fashion, they are unable to cultivate any solid virtues, and do indeed display the flightiness and stupidity for which they are criticized. However, as well as damaging themselves, women in this condition diminish others. First, they damage men. To treat a fellow human despotically shows a lack of virtue, and just as kings are corrupted by their excessive power, so men are corrupted by the tyranny they exercise over their sisters, daughters and wives. Second, ignorant and powerless women are unfit to instil virtue into their children. 'To be a good mother – a woman must have sense and that independence of mind which few women possess who are taught to depend entirely on their husbands' (*A Vindication*).

Although Wollstonecraft's argument hinges on her claim that women are as rational as men, she has no sympathy for what she calls 'masculine women'. The aim of educating women is, in her view, to make them into virtuous wives and mothers who, by fulfilling these natural duties, will become useful members of society. Freed from male subjection, educated women would not usurp the roles of men but would freely and virtuously pursue their domestic lives to the benefit of society as a whole.

The claim that men and women are intellectual equals is here allied to the view that there are natural differences between them which fit them for distinct ways of life: rational women will see that their place is in the home.

This easy division of labour was put under increasing pressure during the nineteenth century, as feminist thinking became less concerned with women's overarching moral right to liberty and focused instead on particular legal entitlements such as the right to own property, to enter the professions, and above all to vote. Nevertheless, arguments which appeal simultaneously to the equality and difference of the sexes, and sustain the view that women excel in certain domestic virtues, remained common. The US suffragist, Elizabeth Cady Stanton, demanded the vote for women from the New York legislature during the 1850s on the grounds that 'the rights of every human being are the same and identical'. But she also argued that, if women were able to represent themselves by voting, they would make a distinctive contribution which would balance that of men.

The same wish to reconcile the demands of equality and difference is evident in John Stuart Mill's *The Subjection of Women* (1869). Mill argues that women are entitled to the same rights as men and should be able to hold public office, to work, to own property and to vote. He also argues that married women should not be required to obey their husbands and should have custody over their children. His primary ground for these conclusions is that women and men are equal, but he supplements this argument with further claims about the benefits that the freedom of women would bring. Like Wollstonecraft, he claims that the power of men over women 'perverts the whole manner of existence of the man, both as an individual and a social being', and reiterates her view that there can be no true affection between spouses who have nothing in common. It is only once women are educated that there can be the solid, enduring friendship between the sexes that heralds the moral regeneration of mankind. However, two further lines of thought appeal to assumed differences. Mill first argues that women possess a distinctive aversion to war and addiction to philanthropy, of which they would make better use if they were better informed. In addition, although women should have the right to work, Mill takes it that when they marry they make 'a choice of the management of a household, and the bringing up of a family' as the first call on their exertions. Older women who have completed this task may decide to direct their energies to public life, for instance by standing for parliament. But the first place of married women is, once again, in the home.

4   Sexual oppression and emancipation

The view that the oppression of women could be overcome once they had the same rights as men was therefore compatible with a conventional understanding of the division of male and female labour. But doubt was cast on this whole approach to emancipation by the fact that, once the vote was won, women did not on the whole use their new-found political power to press for further reform. Many suffragists were keenly disappointed, and feminists of more radical political persuasions were strengthened in their conviction that the source of women's oppression did not lie in their lack of political rights. Reforms such as the married women's property act and the right to higher education, they pointed out, benefited middle-class more than working women. More important still, the root of women's subordination lay not in their civic but in their private lives – in their roles as wives and mothers.

This latter view was partly derived from Engels' *Origins of the Family, Private Property and the State* (1884) in which he argued that women's oppression is primarily sexual. There is nothing natural about the patriarchal family. Rather, this institution came into existence at a particular point in history together with private property. To be able to hand down their property to their sons, men needed complete sexual possession of the mothers of their children, and to this end they reduced women to servitude. In capitalist society, women's subjection consists not in their lack of legal rights, but in their weak position in the labour market which in turn forces them into marriage. Women face a choice between lives of near-destitution as workers or lives of slavery as wives and mothers, or in the case of working class women, both exploitation at work and subjection in marriage. Only once capitalism is overthrown will they escape this plight and be freed from dependence.

In Russia, the predicament diagnosed by Engels was confronted by the revolutionary Alexandra Kollontai (1872–1952), who insisted in *The Social Basis of the Woman Question* (1909) that proletarian women must refuse to cooperate with the bourgeois feminist movement and attack capitalism, the source of their oppression. As Commissar of Social Welfare in the Russian Revolutionary Government of 1917, Kollontai oversaw the drafting of legal reforms designed to revolutionize the family and sexual relations between men and women and to relieve women of the 'triple load' of wage worker, housekeeper and mother. These reforms were organized around a distinction between productive and non-productive labour, and were based on the view that women should be relieved of the burden

FEMINISM

of non-productive domestic labour (cleaning, cooking, washing, caring for clothes, and many aspects of child-rearing) to engage in productive labour alongside men. In this way they would achieve economic independence. At the same time, women's work was to take account of their productive childbearing role. The work of carrying and bringing up children was no longer to be seen as the responsibility of individual families but as a task for the state, since it was in the interest of the workers' collective that children should be born and that they should grow up to be able-bodied and good revolutionaries.

In the early years of the Bolshevik government, Kollontai began to implement a series of radical though short-lived changes. Women were to have full civil rights; civil marriage and divorce laws were introduced; legitimate and illegitimate children were to have the same legal rights; and in 1920 abortion was legalized. As far as labour was concerned, women's work was to take account of childbearing. They were not to do heavy work which might damage their health or work long hours or night shifts. They were to have paid maternity leave and health care during pregnancy. Once children were out of infancy they were to be cared for in crèches, kindergartens and schools which would also provide meals and clothing.

According to Kollontai, the dictatorship of the proletariat will abolish the family and with it bourgeois sexual morality. For though the state should, in her view, concern itself with children, it does not have any more extended interest in the relations between adults. Conventional notions of romantic love must not undermine comradeship; yet Kollontai stresses that solidarity can only exist between those who are capable of love and sympathy, and envisages a society in which people are emotionally educated to feel many forms of love for different people.

In the USA, Engels' view that women's oppression is rooted in the family was used by the anarchist, Emma Goldman (1869–1940), to ground a different set of conclusions. Access to education and work, for which emancipationists had fought so hard, produced women who were 'professional automatons' and lacked 'the essence that enriches the soul'. By entering the public sphere, women had joined an impure state which prevents both women and men from developing the inner qualities that spring from sexual intimacy and constitute freedom, but is particularly distorting for women, for whom love is even more important than it is for men. The question of how to become free is therefore a question about how to foster sexual self-expression, and Goldman is adamant that this can only happen once women cease to be the sexual possessions of

their husbands. As well as eschewing the public sphere, women must reject the private institution of marriage in which, driven by economic need, they purchase financial security at the price of their independence. They must learn instead to recognize and follow what Goldman calls their instinct.

Goldman and Kollontai share with some of their liberal forebears and contemporaries the premise that an institution of marriage in which women are sexually dominated by, and economically dependent on, their husbands, makes them unfree. More radically, both claim that these evils can only be overcome by sweeping away conventional notions of marriage and family. Beyond this, however, they diverge sharply. For Kollontai, liberty consists in productive labour in which both women and men must engage if they are to be equal and equally free. In the case of women, however, productive labour can take the distinctive form of bearing children. Motherhood (women's difference), is subordinated to an overall conception of equality according to which men and women are not treated in the same way, but make the same kind of contribution by working productively. Goldman, by contrast, conceives freedom as a state of individual exploration and self-expression which needs to be pursued outside the impurity and corruption of the state and has little to do with work. Both men and women need love in order to become free, but for women, sexual intimacy plays a particularly important part in this process. While Kollontai separates reproductive sex from other erotic relations, Goldman tips the balance away from motherhood. Unconstrained love, which may or may not be the love of mothers for their children, is what enables women to fulfil themselves and become free.

5 The pervasiveness of male domination

It has become customary to distinguish a first wave of feminism, dating from the mid-nineteenth century to the 1930s, from a second wave, breaking in the 1970s. This chronology is designed to highlight the absence of specifically feminist political campaigns in the intervening period, but needs to be applied with care, since one of the most influential works of modern feminist philosophy, Simone de Beauvoir's *The Second Sex*, was published in 1949 (see BEAUVOIR, S. DE). Dissatisfied with existing accounts of women's subordination to men, Beauvoir confronted the question 'What is Woman?' by exploring the limited answers offered by historical materialism and psychoanalysis. Both these theories, she claims, beg the question. In *The Origin of the Family*, Engels asserts that the institution of private property results in the enslavement of women, but offers no means of explaining why this should have been so. Equally, Freud's account of sexual differentiation fails to say what previous evaluation of virility makes boys proud of their penises and makes girls attribute special significance to their lack of this bodily part. To explain women's oppression, in which women themselves are complicitous, it is not enough to appeal merely to economic categories or patterns of psychological development already imbued with the evaluations that constitute male power. What is needed is a theory capable of doing justice to the vast variety of practices that contribute to women's subordination.

To motivate her analysis, Beauvoir appeals to Hegel's diagnosis of the conflict underlying the relation between master and slave. There is 'in consciousness itself a fundamental hostility to every other consciousness; the subject can be posed only in being opposed – he sets himself up as the essential, as opposed to the other, the inessential, the object' (see HEGEL, G.W.F. §5). Somewhat as the master achieves subjectivity by vanquishing the opponent who becomes his slave, so man establishes himself as a free subject by dominating woman, who serves as his other. To put it in Sartrean terms, he becomes transcendent while she remains mired in immanence (see SARTRE, J.-P.). Yet this situation is puzzling. Like men, women are conscious beings capable of returning the male gaze; but they nevertheless allow themselves to be dominated. Why do they occupy this position? Why do they not try to dominate men? Although Beauvoir suggests that the comparative passivity of women originates in childbearing, she is mainly interested in analysing the multitude of social practices which conspire to keep women in the position of the other and prevent them from seeking their own transcendence. These practices, she argues, are sustained both by men, who encourage and reward female passivity, and by women, who cooperate in their own domination. The latter, however, is ultimately a form of slavery. To allow oneself to be treated as an object is to fail to realize one's being by making one's own choices, and to shirk the painful project of becoming free. How, then, are women to liberate themselves? Women, Beauvoir suggests, must avoid the roles of wives and mothers in which they are most easily objectified and discover themselves through work. Once they begin to exercise the assertiveness and courage essential to freedom, conceptions of what it is to be a woman will alter, and women and men will gradually find ways to treat one another as equals.

One of Beauvoir's most profound contributions to feminist philosophy lay in her insistence that women are dominated in all aspects of their lives. Their comparative lack of freedom does not consist merely in the absence of civic rights, or in particular institutions of motherhood and marriage, although these are contributory factors. Rather, they are kept in their inferior place by 'the whole of civilization' – by a multitude of evaluations and social practices (tellingly described in chapters on childhood, the young girl, sexual initiation and so on) which shape our understandings of male and female, masculine and feminine. As she indicates in her celebrated remark, 'One is not born, but rather becomes, a woman', Beauvoir holds that it is through social practices that bodies come to be understood and lived as male or female, and through these same practices that the differences between them are invested with evaluative significance. Becoming a woman is a cultural and historical process which is never completed. Although Beauvoir allows that there will always be differences between women and men deriving from their bodily distinctions and the effect these have on their sensuality, she suggests that there is no one thing that women intrinsically or naturally are. Correspondingly, there is no obviously discernible limit to what they may become.

6 Second- and third-wave feminism

Many of the critical and constructive themes discussed by Beauvoir were taken up again in the late 1960s and 1970s (though often without much reference to *The Second Sex*) by a generation of women who struggled, in the light of their personal experience, to revise the social and psychological theories around which academic debate revolved. On a critical plane, they enlarged Beauvoir's objections to Marxism and psychoanalysis and added criticisms of other sociological approaches such as functionalism, sometimes engendering debates which remained lively throughout the next twenty or so years. For feminists concerned with Marxism, the key issues were whether women could be satisfactorily accommodated within a theory which focused on the class structure of society, and whether women's oppression could be adequately explained in terms of their place in the relations of production and the ideologies to which these gave rise. Studies of domestic labour and of women's sexual subordination suggested that, while Marxist analyses of women in capitalist societies remained valuable, the answer to these questions was negative. Turning their attention to psychoanalysis, a number of writers launched an influential attack on Freud's construction of femininity as a passive, masochistic, narcissistic and intellectually limited condition. Their re-reading gave feminists pause, and initiated a series of fruitful reinterpretations and modifications within psychoanalytic theory (see IRIGARAY, L.; KRISTEVA, J.).

Critical interpretations of this type were also the vehicle for a number of important innovations in feminist thinking which raised fresh questions and consolidated novel approaches. Writers such as Kate Millett and Shulamith Firestone argued in the early 1970s that the forms of domination isolated by feminists are all relatively superficial in comparison with patriarchy – the sexual power that men exercise over women, primarily within the family, but also in social, economic and political institutions. In a wide range of societies, it was pointed out, men's sexuality is the source and justification of their power, the purportedly natural characteristic that gives them the right to rule women. The workings of patriarchy are evident not just in erotic relations between the sexes, but in the manifold means by which men and women are socialized as to temperament, role and status, men being taught to regard themselves as potent and active, women to perceive themselves as subordinate and sexually impure.

Patriarchy, then, relies not so much on the biological differences between men and women as on deep-seated cultural interpretations that give them value and significance. In the early 1970s this distinction came to be regarded as crucial, and writers such as Millett and Ann Oakley took over the terms 'sex' and 'gender' to mark it: sex refers to the biological traits that make a person male or female, gender to culturally variable conceptions of masculinity and femininity. Taken together, the notions of patriarchy, sex and gender provided an Anglo-American articulation of many of the themes announced by Beauvoir, and gave rise to a series of theoretical debates, some of which are still going on. Is sex really separable from gender, or is our experience and theorizing so mediated by culture that the idea of the simply biological ceases to make sense? Is patriarchy a useful analytical category, or is it either unduly general, or unduly reductionist? How, in any case, is patriarchal power related to other forms of political and economic power? And is it really as strong and pervasive as its exponents claim?

Regardless of the fate of these questions, the belief that men's domination of women may be sustained by all sorts of practices had a vast impact on the Academy, as feminists began to take a fresh look at the texts and theories they studied professionally. This approach proved exceptionally fruitful when applied to literary texts – Simone de Beauvoir had included a study of 'The Myth of Woman in Five Authors' in *The Second Sex*, and Millett's *Sexual Politics* opens with insightful readings of Henry Miller, Norman Mailer and Jean Genet. It was soon adopted by philosophers, who started to analyse the conceptions of gender embedded in the great works of the philosophical tradition. Genevieve Lloyd's *The Man of Reason* (1984) and Carole Pateman's articles on contractarian political theory are notable early examples of this kind of work, and were rapidly followed by critical scrutinies both of the various areas of philosophy and particular positions within them (see FEMINIST EPISTEMOLOGY).

While the results of this academic flowering have been extremely diverse, a number of themes stand out. First, some impressive recent work has shown how philosophical standards and doctrines that have claimed for themselves an objective and universal status reflect particular interests, values and priorities attuned to broader conceptions of masculinity. Discussions of human beings sometimes turn out upon examination to be discussions of men, and norms that are held to apply generally sometimes turn out to apply better to men than to women. In this way, philosophy has contributed to the cultural constructions of gender that play a part in legitimating and maintaining male power. Feminist philosophers have gained insight into this phenomenon by studying the history as well as the contemporary practice of their subject, paying attention not only to the substance of an author's work but also to its literary form. In an influential series of essays translated into English in 1989, Michele le Doeuff argued that an analysis of imagery and metaphor can uncover gendered presuppositions within a text. This approach has helped us to move beyond the mere identification of sexism within the works of the great philosophers, and to arrive at an enriched understanding of the resources of the past. Although it is true that traits associated with women such as imagination or emotion have often been denigrated and marginalized within the philosophical tradition, it contains ideas and arguments which can be used to advance contemporary debates.

Feminist scholarship has also revived the writings of women philosophers and examined the processes through which these came to be neglected. For example, we are acquiring a fuller appreciation of the contribution made by women during the early modern era to natural philosophy (significant figures here are Margaret Cavendish, Anne Conway, Jeanne Dumee and Aphra Behn) and the field of morals (notably in the work of Madeleine de Scudery, Damarys Masham, Mary Astell, Catherine Trotter and Gabrielle Suchon).

As feminists have opened up new philosophical questions and lines of criticism, these have been taken up by the profession at large and absorbed into the mainstream. Analyses of the political exclusion of women have been applied in multicultural contexts; moral philosophers are less inclined to think of reason and passion as opposites; and feminist arguments about the social character of power are increasingly reflected in epistemology and philosophy of language. To some extent, then, feminist philosophy is ceasing to occupy the role of the other, and is finding ways to converse on equal terms with advocates of the tradition from which it sprang. But it is also continuing to develop internally, and has recently trained its own critical techniques on its long-standing habit of making claims on behalf of 'women'. These purportedly universal pronouncements, it has been pointed out, fail to take account of the differences between women of diverse races, sexual orientations, nationalities or classes. Moreover, if gender is not a natural category there may be little to be said about women as such, and we need to become more sensitive to the many conceptions of femininity found in different societies. This anti-essentialism has profound implications for feminism, both as an academic preoccupation and as a political movement, and marks an important shift away from its own origins. Within philosophy, it has reopened debate about the nature and status of 'woman', the key term around which feminism revolves.

References and further reading

Beauvoir, S. de (1949) *The Second Sex*, trans. and ed. H.M. Parshley, Harmondsworth: Penguin, 1972. (The classic existentialist interpretation of masculinity and femininity and a path-breaking analysis of the social construction of gender.)

Millett, K. (1969) *Sexual Politics*, London: Virago, 1977. (A formative analysis of the construction of femininity in twentieth-century literature and in social theory.)

SUSAN JAMES

FEMINIST EPISTEMOLOGY

The impact of feminism on epistemology has been to move the question 'Whose knowledge are we talking about?' to a central place in epistemological inquiry. Hence feminist epistemologists are producing conceptions of knowledge that are quite specifically contextualized and situated, and of socially responsible epistemic agency. They have elaborated genealogical/interpretive methods, have advocated reconstructions of empiricism, have articulated standpoint positions and have demonstrated the potential of psychosocial and post-structural analyses to counter the hegemony of epistemological master narratives. In these reconfigured epistemologies, feminists have argued that the cognitive status and circumstances of the knower(s) are central among conditions for the possibility of

knowledge. They have demonstrated the salience, in evaluating any epistemic event, of the social arrangements of power and privilege by which it is legitimated or discredited.

Feminists are engaged at once in critical projects of demonstrating the privilege-sustaining, androcentric character of 'the epistemological project' in most of its received forms, and in transformative projects of reconstructing methodologies and justificatory procedures so as to eradicate their oppressive, exclusionary effects. They have shown that, in late-twentieth-century Western philosophy, the circumstances of mature white men continue to generate prevailing ideals and norms of 'human nature', while the ideals of reason, objectivity and value-neutrality around which most mainstream theories of knowledge are constructed, like the knowledge they legitimate, tacitly validate affluent male experiences and values. Scientific knowledge, which is still an overwhelmingly male preserve, stands as the regulative model of objective epistemic authority; and the experiences and values of non-male, non-white and otherwise differently placed knowers typically have to accommodate themselves, Procrustean-style, to an idealized scientific and implicitly masculine norm, or risk dismissal as inconsequential, aberrant, mere opinion.

In engaging with these issues, most feminists – like many other participants in 'successor epistemology' projects – retain a realist commitment to empirical evidence, while denying that facts or experiences 'speak for themselves' and maintaining that most truths are as artefactual as they are factual. Questions of cognitive authority and answerability thus figure as prominently as issues of epistemic warrant in these projects, where feminists are concentrating less on formal, universal conditions for making and justifying knowledge 'in general' than on the specificities of knowledge construction. Hence these inquiries are often interdisciplinary, producing detailed analyses of everyday knowledge-making and of scientific or social scientific inquiry; drawing out their gendered and other locational implications. In these projects feminists are showing that avowedly engaged, politically committed investigations can yield well-warranted conclusions.

See also: FEMINIST POLITICAL PHILOSOPHY

LORRAINE CODE

FEMINIST POLITICAL PHILOSOPHY

In all its forms, feminism asserts that social and political structures in society discriminate against women. Feminist political philosophy aims to show how traditional political philosophy is implicated in that discrimination and how the resources of political philosophy may nevertheless be employed in the service of women. Sometimes, feminist political philosophy extends the arguments of traditional political philosophy to indicate that women are unjustly treated and to propose ways in which that injustice might be removed. This is clearest in liberal feminism, where it is argued that since women are essentially the same as men in being rational creatures, they are entitled to the same legal and political rights as men: arguments which defend the rights of man also support the rights of women. Similarly, Marxist and socialist feminism extend the insights of Marxism and socialism in an attempt to expose and remove the oppression of women: Marxist emphasis on the exploitation of labour under capital is supplemented by Marxist feminist emphasis on the exploitation of women under patriarchy.

However, there are also forms of feminist political philosophy which are more critical of traditional political philosophy and which question the very distinctions upon which it is premised. Thus, radical feminist philosophers question the scope of the term 'political' as it is usually used by political philosophers, and argue that by excluding domestic concerns, traditional political philosophy excludes many of the things which are most important to women. The aim here is not to extend the insights of political philosophy, but rather to highlight the ways in which political philosophy itself shows a distinct gender bias.

Yet more radically, the postmodernists have been critical of philosophy's emphasis on truth and objectivity, and some feminists have extended their arguments to suggest that the very language of philosophy, and by extension of political philosophy, is 'man-made'.

Feminist political philosophy is therefore not one thing but many, and feminist political philosophers are deeply divided as to whether traditional political philosophy may be modified so as to include women's interests, or whether it is itself one of the ways in which women's politically disadvantaged position is legitimized and perpetuated.

See also: FEMINISM

SUSAN MENDUS

FEUERBACH, LUDWIG ANDREAS (1804–72)

Ludwig Feuerbach, one of the critical Young Hegelian intellectuals of the nineteenth century, has become famous for his radical critique of religious belief. In *Das Wesen des Christentums* (*Essence of Christianity*) (1841) he develops the idea that God does not exist in reality but as a human projection only, and that the Christian principles of love and solidarity should be applied directly to

fellow humans rather than being regarded as an indirect reflection of God's love. In religion, the believer 'projects his being into objectivity, and then again makes himself an object of an object, another being than himself'. Religious orientation is an illusion and is unhealthy, as it deprives and alienates the believer from true autonomy, virtue and community, 'for even love, in itself the deepest, truest emotion, becomes by means of religiousness merely ostensible, illusory, since religious love gives itself to man only for God's sake, so that it is given only in appearance to man, but in reality to God' (*Das Wesen des Christentums* 1841). In *Grundsätze der Philosophie der Zukunft* (*Principles of the Philosophy of the Future*) (1843) he extends his criticism to all forms of metaphysics and religion: 'True Dialectics is not the Monologue of the sole Thinker, rather the Dialogue between I and Thou', he writes in paragraph 62 (*Sämmtliche Werke* 1846–66 II: 345), criticizing in particular his former teacher Hegel. The philosophy of the future has to be both sensual and communal, equally based on theory and practice and among individuals. In an anonymous encyclopedia article of 1847 he defines his position: 'the principle from which Feuerbach derives everything and towards which he targets everything is "the human being on the ground and foundation of nature"', a principle which 'bases truth on sensuous experience and thus replaces previous particular and abstract philosophical and religious principles' (*Gesammelte Werke* 1964– III: 331). Feuerbach's sensualism and communalism had great influence on the young Karl Marx's development of an anthropological humanism, and on his contemporaries in providing a cultural and moral system of reference for humanism outside of religious orientation and rationalistic psychology. In the twentieth century, Feuerbach influenced existential theology (Martin Buber, Karl Barth) as well as existentialist and phenomenological thought.

See also: HEGELIANISM

HANS-MARTIN SASS

FEYERABEND, PAUL KARL (1924–94)

Feyerabend was an Austrian philosopher of science who spent most of his academic career in the USA. He was an early, persistent and influential critic of the positivist interpretation of science. Though his views have some affinities with those of Thomas Kuhn, they are in important ways more radical. Not only did Feyerabend become famous (or notorious) for advocating 'epistemological anarchism' – the position that there is no such thing as scientific method, so that in advancing scientific research 'anything goes' – he also argued that the scientific outlook is itself just one approach to dealing with the world, an approach that is not self-evidently superior in all respects to other approaches. This radicalism led to his being widely attacked as an irrationalist though perhaps he might better be seen as a sceptic in the humane and tolerant tradition of Sextus Empiricus and Montaigne.

MICHAEL WILLIAMS

FICHTE, JOHANN GOTTLIEB (1762–1814)

Fichte developed Kant's Critical philosophy into a system of his own, which he named 'Theory of Science' or *Wissenschaftslehre*. Though Fichte continued to revise this system until the end of his life, almost all of his best-known and most influential philosophical works were written in first portion of his career, when he was a professor at the University of Jena.

The task of philosophy, as understood by Fichte, is to provide a transcendental explanation of ordinary consciousness and of everyday experience, from the standpoint of which philosophy must therefore abstract. Such an explanation can start either with the concept of free subjectivity ('the I') or with that of pure objectivity (the 'thing in itself'), the former being the principle of idealism and the latter that of what Fichte called 'dogmatism' (or transcendental realism). Though neither of these first principles can be theoretically demonstrated, the principle of freedom possesses the advantage of being practically or morally certain. Moreover, according to Fichte, only transcendental idealism, which begins with the principle of subjective freedom and then proceeds to derive objectivity and limitation as conditions for the possibility of any selfhood whatsoever, can actually accomplish the task of philosophy.

One of the distinctive features of Fichte's Jena system is its thoroughgoing integration of theoretical and practical reason, that is, its demonstration that there can be no (theoretical) cognition without (practical) striving, and vice versa. Another important feature is Fichte's demonstration of the necessary finitude of all actual selfhood. The 'absolute I' with which the system seems to begin turns out to be only a practical ideal of total self-determination, an ideal toward which the finite I continuously strives but can never achieve. Also emphasized in Fichte's Jena writings is the social or intersubjective character of all selfhood: an I is an I only in relationship to other finite rational subjects. This insight provides the basis for Fichte's political philosophy or 'theory of right', which is one of the more original portions of the overall system of the *Wissenschaftslehre*, a system that also includes a foundational portion (or 'first philosophy'), a philosophy of nature, an ethics and a philosophy of religion.

See also: ENLIGHTENMENT, CONTINENTAL; IDEALISM; KANTIAN ETHICS

DANIEL BREAZEALE

FICINO, MARSILIO (1433–99)

With Giovanni Pico della Mirandola, Marsilio Ficino was the most important philosopher working under the patronage of Lorenzo de'Medici, 'Il Magnifico', in the Florence of the High Renaissance. Ficino's main contribution was as a translator of Platonic philosophy from Greek into Latin: he produced the first complete Latin version of the works of Plato (1484) and Plotinus (1492) as well as renderings of a number of minor Platonists. He supplied many of his translations with philosophical commentaries, and these came to exercise great influence on the interpretation of Platonic philosophy in the Renaissance and early modern periods. Ficino's most important philosophical work, the *Theologia platonica de immortalitate animae* (Platonic Theology, On the Immortality of the Soul) (1474), aimed to use Platonic arguments to combat the Averroists, 'impious' scholastic philosophers who denied that the immortality of the soul could be proven by reason. The most famous concept associated with his name is that of 'Platonic love'.

See also: HERMETISM; HUMANISM, RENAISSANCE; PICO DELLA MIRANDOLA, G.; PLATO; PLATONISM, RENAISSANCE; RENAISSANCE PHILOSOPHY; SOUL, NATURE AND IMMORTALITY OF THE

JAMES HANKINS

FICTIONAL ENTITIES

By 'fictional entities', philosophers principally mean those entities originating in and defined by myths, legends, fairy tales, novels, dramas and other works of fiction. In this sense unicorns, centaurs, Pegasus, the Time Machine and Sherlock Holmes are all fictional entities.

A somewhat different category of fictional entities is associated with empiricist philosophy. It includes entities apparently assumed by common discourse but which admit of no direct empirical experience. Thus Jeremy Bentham classified as 'fictitious entities' motion, relation, power and matter, as well as, notoriously, rights, obligations and duties. David Hume called substance, the self, even space and time 'fictions' and Bertrand Russell thought ordinary things, such as Piccadilly or Socrates, were fictions, on the grounds that they are 'constructed' out of simpler, more immediate objects of acquaintance.

Philosophical interest in fictional entities thus covers a surprisingly wide area of the subject, including ontology and metaphysics, epistemology, logic, philosophy of language, and aesthetics. The first question that arises is how the distinction should be drawn between fictional and nonfictional entities. As the examples from Bentham, Hume and Russell show, this is by no means a straightforward matter. The next question concerns what to do with fictional entities once they have been identified. Here the primary philosophical task has been to try to accommodate two powerful yet apparently conflicting intuitions: on the one hand, the intuition that there are no such things as fictional entities, so that any seeming reference to them must be explained away; on the other hand, the intuition that because 'things' like Sherlock Holmes and Anna Karenina are so vividly drawn, so seemingly 'real', objects of thoughts and emotions, they must after all have some kind of reality. Broadly speaking, we can discern two kinds of philosophical approach: those which incline towards the latter intuition, being in some way hospitable to fictional entities; and the less hospitable kind, which incline towards the former and seek only to show how fictional entities can be eliminated altogether in the strict regime of rational discourse.

See also: CARNAP, R.; EMOTION IN RESPONSE TO ART; EXISTENCE; ONTOLOGICAL COMMITMENT; REFERENCE; RIGHTS; SEMANTICS

PETER LAMARQUE

FILM, AESTHETICS OF

Film aesthetics has been dominated by issues of realism. Three kinds of realism attributable to film may be distinguished: (1) the realism inherent in film because of its use of the photographic method (realism of method); (2) realism as a style which approximates the normal conditions of perception (realism of style); (3) realism as the capacity of film to engender in the viewer an illusion of the reality and presentness of fictional characters and events (realism of effect). Some theorists have argued that realism of method requires us to avoid realist style, others that it requires us to adopt it. Most have agreed that realist style makes for realism of effect; they disagree about whether this is a desirable goal. It is argued here that these realisms are independent of one another, that realism of style does not entail any kind of metaphysical realism, and that realism of effect is irrelevant to understanding the normal experience of cinema. Realism of style suggests a way of making precise the claim that cinema is an art of time and of space, because this kind of realism is partially explicated in terms of the representation of time by time and of space by space. Psychological theorizing about the cinema has been strongly connected with realism of effect, and with the idea that an illusion of the film's reality is created by the identification of the viewer's position with that of the camera. Another version of illusionism has it that the experience of film-watching is significantly similar to that of dreaming. Such doctrines are undermined when we acknowledge that realism of effect is an insignificant phenomenon.

See also: DEPICTION; NARRATIVE; PAINTING, AESTHETICS OF; PHOTOGRAPHY, AESTHETICS OF; SEMIOTICS

GREGORY CURRIE

FILMER, SIR ROBERT (1588–1653)

Filmer was one of the most important political thinkers in seventeenth-century England, and the author of *Patriarcha*. Locke replied to this and other works by Filmer in the *Two Treatises of Government* – perhaps the most famous of all works of liberal political theory. Filmer argued that notions of mixed or limited government were false and pernicious, and that the powers of all legitimate rulers were derived not from the people but directly from God, to whom alone rulers were accountable. Filmer's contemporaries commonly held that the authority of a father and husband over his family stemmed not from the consent of his wife and children but from the natural and divinely appointed order of things. Filmer harnessed such ideas to the cause of royal absolutism by arguing that the state and the family were essentially the same institution.

JOHANN P. SOMMERVILLE

FINCH, ANNE
See CONWAY, ANNE

FIRST CAUSE ARGUMENT
See GOD, ARGUMENTS FOR THE EXISTENCE OF

FODOR, JERRY ALAN (1935–)

Jerry Fodor has been one of the most influential figures in the philosophy of mind, the philosophy of psychology, and 'cognitive science' through the latter part of the twentieth century. His primary concern has been to argue (vigorously) for a certain view of the nature of thought. According to this view, thinking is information processing within 'the language of thought'. The mind can be understood

as a computer, which directs action with the aid of internal representations of the world.
See also: LANGUAGE OF THOUGHT

PETER GODFREY-SMITH

FOLK PSYCHOLOGY

There is wide disagreement about the meaning of ordinary mental terms (such as 'belief', 'desire', 'pain'). Sellars suggested that our use of these terms is governed by a widely shared theory, 'folk psychology', a suggestion that has gained empirical support in psychological studies of self-attribution and in a growing literature concerning how children acquire (or, in the case of autism, fail to acquire) ordinary mental concepts. Recently, there has been a lively debate about whether people actually 'theorize' about the mind, or, instead, engage in some kind of 'simulation' of mental processes.

STEPHEN P. STICH
GEORGES REY

FORCE, ILLOCUTIONARY
See PRAGMATICS; SPEECH ACTS

FOREKNOWLEDGE
See OMNISCIENCE

FORMALISM
See HILBERT'S PROGRAMME AND FORMALISM

FORMALISM IN ART

Formalism in art is the doctrine that the artistic value of a work of art is determined solely by the work's form. The concept of artistic form is multiply ambiguous, however, and the precise meaning of formalism depends upon which sense of form it operates with. There are two main possibilities. The first understands form as the structure of a work's elements, the second as the manner in which it renders its 'content'. If form is understood as structure, formalism is still ambiguous: understood one way, it has never been denied; understood another way, it is untenable. If form is understood as manner, formalism is false.
See also: ART, VALUE OF; HANSLICK, E.; KANT, I. §12

MALCOLM BUDD

FORMALISM IN ETHICS
See UNIVERSALISM IN ETHICS

FORMS, PLATONIC

Plato thought that in addition to the changeable, extended bodies we perceive around us, there are also unchangeable, extensionless entities, not perceptible by the senses, that structure the world and our knowledge of it. He called such an entity a 'Form' (*eidos*) or 'Idea' (*idea*), or referred to it by such phrases as 'the such-and-such itself'. Thus in addition to individual beautiful people and things, there is also the Form of Beauty, or the Beautiful Itself.

It may be speculated that Plato's Presocratic predecessors gave some impetus to this theory. It is a certainty that Socrates was the major influence on it, through his search for the definitions of ethical terms. The features that a definition must have in order to satisfy Socrates' criteria of adequacy foreshadow the features that Forms have in Plato's theory.

Beginning with his *Meno*, Plato turned his attention to the presuppositions of Socrates' investigation, and the preconditions of its possibility: what has to be true about virtue, knowledge and our souls if Socratic cross-examination is to have any hope of success? He answers these questions with a set of doctrines – the existence of Forms, the soul's immortality and its knowledge of Forms through recollection – which are then developed and displayed in the great dialogues of his middle period, the *Phaedo*, *Symposium*, *Phaedrus* and *Republic*. Not all of Plato's thoughts on Forms are on display in the middle-period theory, but this is the theory of Forms that has been far and away the most influential historically, and the one that is most commonly intended when people refer to 'Plato's Forms'.

The dialogues of Plato's later period present a number of puzzles. That his views developed will be agreed by all: in the *Sophist*, *Statesman* and *Philebus* Plato is clearly pushing his metaphysical investigations in new directions. What is less clear is the degree of continuity or rupture between old and new – the *Parmenides* has sometimes been taken to signal Plato's wholesale rejection of the middle-period theory, whereas the *Timaeus* seems to confirm his endorsement of it. Further complicating matters, Aristotle reports that Plato in his last period based the Forms somehow on numbers. The reported material is obscure in itself and also hard to integrate with any of the material from Plato's dialogues.

Much of our current understanding of Plato's middle-period theory comes from a group of arguments that advert to differences between Forms and sensible objects or properties. These arguments tend to support Aristotle's report that the theory arose from a collision between Socrates' views on definition and Heraclitean views on flux. The general form of the argument claims that definitions, or knowledge, require the existence of a class of entities with certain features, and that sensibles lack those features. It concludes that there exists a class of entities distinct from the familiar sensibles, namely the Forms.

But as often in historical studies, the arguments themselves are silent or ambiguous on many of the points that critics most wish to determine: whether Plato thought Forms exist separately from particulars, whether he treated them as Aristotelian substances, whether it is possible to have knowledge of sensible objects, whether Plato came to reject the middle-period theory, and so on. For the second half of the twentieth century, the tendency was for interpreters to settle the remaining interpretative issues by ascribing to Plato their own philosophical preferences, justifying this by appeal to 'interpretative charity'.

The practice of basing interpretations of Plato's Forms solely on a handful of arguments was a mistake; the increasing tendency to broaden the evidentiary base is a salutary development. Where the interpretation of an argument has left a question unresolved, the consideration of Plato's myths and metaphors may sometimes lend strong weight to one side or the other. An example: Plato's depictions of particulars make it highly implausible that the 'imperfection' in particulars to which some arguments advert is merely the compresence of opposites.

Most of Plato's successors in the early Academy kept up the Forms. Aristotle's writing are full of references to them, and they left visible imprints on his own theory. The Hellenistic period witnessed a blanket rejection of all immaterial entities, but even here the influence of the Forms can still be discerned around the edges. The revival of Platonism at the end of the Hellenistic period saw Forms returned to philosophical respectability.

See also: ARISTOTLE; INNATENESS IN ANCIENT PHILOSOPHY; PLATO; PLOTINUS; SOCRATES; UNIVERSALS

TAD BRENNAN

FORMS, THEORY OF
See FORMS, PLATONIC

FOUCAULT, MICHEL (1926–84)

Introduction

Michel Foucault was a French philosopher and historian of thought. Although his earliest writings

developed within the frameworks of Marxism and existential phenomenology, he soon moved beyond these influences and developed his own distinctive approaches. There is no overall methodological or theoretical unity to Foucault's thought, but his writings do fall into several main groups, each characterized by distinctive problems and methods. In his early studies of psychiatry, clinical medicine and the social sciences, Foucault developed an 'archaeology of knowledge' that treated systems of thought as 'discursive formations' independent of the beliefs and intentions of individuals. Foucault's archaeology displaced the human subject from the central role it played in the humanism which had been dominant since Kant. While archaeology provided no account of transitions from one system to another, Foucault later introduced a 'genealogical' approach, which seeks to explain changes in systems of discourse by connecting them to changes in the non-discursive practices of social power structures. Like Nietzsche's, Foucault's genealogies refused all comprehensive explanatory schemes, such as those of Marx or Freud. Instead he viewed systems of thought as contingent products of many small, unrelated causes. Foucault's genealogical studies also emphasize the essential connection between knowledge and power. Bodies of knowledge are not autonomous intellectual structures that happen to be employed as Baconian instruments of power. Rather, they are essentially tied to systems of social control. Foucault first used his genealogical approach to study the relations between modern prisons and the psychological and sociological knowledge on which they are based. He next proposed a similar analysis of modern practices and 'sciences' of sexuality, but eventually decided that such a study had to begin with an understanding of ancient Greek and Roman conceptions of the ethical self. The study was published in two volumes that appeared just before his death. Foucault forbade posthumous publication of his writings, but the ban has not included the texts of his public lectures at the Collège de France, several volumes of which have already appeared, with more planned.

1 Biography
2 The history of madness
3 The archaeological method
4 Genealogy
5 Sexuality and ethics
6 Conclusion

1 Biography

Foucault was born on 15 June 1926 in Poitiers, where his father was a prominent physician. In

1946, after preparatory studies with Jean Hyppolite at the Lycée Henri IV, he entered the École Normale Supérieure. He completed advanced degrees in both philosophy and psychology, working with, among others, Maurice MERLEAU-PONTY. Dissatisfied with French culture and society, Foucault held various academic posts in Sweden, Poland and Germany from 1955 to 1960, while he also completed his thesis (on madness in the Classical Age) for the *doctorat ès lettres*, which he published in 1961. During the 1960s, Foucault held a series of positions in French universities, culminating in 1969 with his election to the Collège de France, where he was Professor of the History of Systems of Thought until he died. Throughout the 1970s and until his death, Foucault was active politically, helping to found the Groupe d'Information sur les Prisions and supporting protests on behalf of homosexuals and other marginalized groups. He also frequently lectured outside France, particularly in the USA, and in 1983 had agreed to teach annually at the University of California at Berkeley. One of the first victims of AIDS, Foucault died in Paris on 25 June 1984.

Contrary to common views of authorship as self-expression, Foucault said that he wrote to escape from himself, to become other than he was. Correspondingly, there is no methodological or theoretical unity of Foucault's thought that will support any single comprehensive interpretation. His writings instead fall into several main groups, each characterized by a distinctive problematic and method of approach. It is fruitful to follow certain themes through some or all of these groups, but the core of his effort at any point is defined by what is specific to the problems then engaging him.

2 The history of madness

Foucault's earliest publications dealt with psychology and mental illness. His initial approach, developed in a long introduction to the French translation of Ludwig Binswanger's *Traum und Existenz* (1954), was through existential phenomenology, particularly that of the early Heidegger. His 1954 book, *Maladie mentale et personnalité* (Mental Illness and Psychology), combined this approach with a Marxist analysis (which, however, Foucault soon decisively rejected). His first major work, *Folie et déraison: histoire de la folie à l'âge classique* (Madness and Civilization) (1961), tried to combine the experiential emphasis of his earlier phenomenological discussions with an essentially historical approach.

Folie et déraison is a challenge to the modern use of the terms 'mad' and 'mentally ill' as synonyms. Beginning in the early nineteenth century, doctors and other therapists rejected such traditional conceptions of madness as divine ecstasy or diabolical possession in favour of the 'enlightened' view that madness is mental illness. Standard histories of psychiatry canonize this view, telling the story of how brave and compassionate men such as Tuke and Pinel replaced superstitious cruelty with scientific treatment of the mad. Foucault's rejection of this view is based on a detailed analysis of the 'experience' of madness that prevailed in the Classical Age (roughly, 1650 to 1800). Then, he maintains, madness was regarded not as mental illness but as a fundamental choice in favour of unreason (*déraison*), where unreason is any basic rejection of the norms of rationality constituting the boundaries of bourgeois social life. Among the various forms of unreason (including sexual promiscuity and deviancy, irreligion and idleness) madness was distinguished by its embracing the animal aspect of human nature at the expense of all higher aspects. The mad were those who had stripped themselves of everything distinctive of their humanity and had chosen to live like beasts. Since, on the classical view, madness was defined by its rejection of reason, the only rational reaction to it was rejection and exclusion. (Foucault regards Descartes' dismissal of his possible madness as grounds for doubt as a paradigm of this point.) Since the Classical Age had no coherent way of giving the mad a place in society, the only alternative was to exclude them from rational society, an exclusion epitomized by the Great Confinement of 1656.

The implication of Foucault's analysis is that there was, even in the relatively recent past of our own culture, a view of madness which was radically different from our own and no less defensible. This alone, he suggests, should begin to undermine our idea that there is something inevitable about our conception of madness. Foucault drives home his point through an analysis of the development of the modern (post-French-Revolution) 'experience' of madness as mental illness. This experience restores a social locus to madness, seeing it as a deviation from norms (an illness), not a rejection of the entire framework of rationality that defines these norms. He takes particular pains to show that, in spite of its veneer of scientific objectivity, the modern view is based more on a moral disapproval of the values implicit in madness than on any objective scientific truth. Similarly, he argues that the modern treatment of the mad (in asylums) was not so much a matter of medical compassion as a concerted effort to bring the mad back beneath the yoke of bourgeois morality. Initiating a theme further developed in various literary essays during the 1960s, *Folie et déraison* continually evokes the lives and works of artists haunted by madness (Van Gogh, Roussel, Artaud, Nietzsche) as precious expressions of a truth suppressed by both classical and modern experiences of madness.

3   The archaeological method

The second major division of Foucault's work begins with his history of the origins of modern medicine, *Naissance de la clinique: une archéologie du regard médical* (The Birth of the Clinic) (1963). Its first pages suggest that it is an extension of Foucault's ethical critique of the concept of mental illness to that of physical illness. But very soon the study becomes an analysis of the linguistic and conceptual structures underlying the modern practice of medicine; or, in the phrase of its subtitle, 'an archaeology of medical perception'.

Foucault's development of his 'archaeological method' synthesized three fundamental lines of influence on his thought: the history and philosophy of science of Gaston BACHELARD and Georges Canguilhem; the modernist literature of (especially) Raymond Roussel, George Bataille and Maurice Blanchot; and the historiography of Fernand Braudel and his *Annales* School. The point of convergence of these influences was the elimination of the subject as the centre of historical and philosophical analysis. Bachelard and Canguilhem challenged what Foucault called the 'transcendental narcissism' of existential phenomenology through a philosophy of objective concepts opposed to the existentialists' philosophy of subjective experience. Bachelard worked primarily on the physical sciences and Canguilhem on the biological and medical sciences, but Foucault extended their viewpoint to the strongholds of the modern conception of subjectivity: the 'human sciences'. Modernist writing excited Foucault by its potential for, in Bataille's terminology, 'transgressing' the limits of standard knowledge and experience. As illustrated in his essay, 'What Is an Author?' (1969), Foucault was particularly impressed with the modernists' decentring of the author and their constitution of language itself as the essence of literature. Braudel and his school had obtained extremely interesting results by varying the historiographical perspective; that is, by writing history not in terms of individuals' experience but from the broader standpoint of long-term factors such as geography, climate and natural resources. Foucault's archaeology did not take over any of Braudel's specific results or methods but tried to effect a parallel change of perspective in the history of thought: a move away from the individual thinker and towards more fundamental categories and structures.

Foucault's fullest deployment of his archaeological method was in *Les Mots et les choses: une archéologie des sciences humaines* (The Order of Things) (1966), where he analysed the linguistic systems ('epistemes') characteristic of certain periods of thought. In particular, Foucault delineated the linguistic systems underlying the classical disciplines of general grammar, natural history and analysis of wealth, as well as those of the modern disciplines of philosophy, biology and economics that replaced them. He argued that there were strong structural similarities among the three classical disciplines and among the three modern disciplines, but a sharp break between classical and modern modes of thought taken as wholes. On this basis he rejected, for example, the common view that the work of nineteenth-century biologists such as Darwin was a continuous development of the work of eighteenth-century natural historians such as Lamarck. Specifically, he maintained that there is no hint of the Darwinian concept of evolution in Lamarck or any other classical thinker. He took such results as illustrative of the superiority of his archaeological approach to standard history of ideas, which focused on the specific concepts and theories of particular thinkers and not on the linguistic structures underlying them.

L'Archéologie du savoir (The Archaeology of Knowledge) (1969) systematically articulated the methodology Foucault had gradually forged in his preceding historical studies. It did this through an account of discourse, based on his notion of the statement (*l'énoncé*), which described a level of linguistic structure prior to and determining the range of objects, concepts, methodological resources and theoretical formulations available to individuals who speak and write. This account provided a theoretical elucidation of the decentring of the subject effected by Foucault's histories.

4   Genealogy

Foucault's writings during the 1970s constitute a third major division of his work. Although archaeological method is not abandoned in this period, it is subordinated to a new style of analysis that Foucault, with a bow to Nietzsche, dubs 'genealogical'. A genealogical analysis explains changes in systems of discourse by connecting them to changes in the non-discursive practices of social power structures. Foucault recognizes the standard economic, social and political causes of such changes, but he rejects the efforts of many historians to fit these causes into unitary, teleological schemata, such as the rise of the bourgeoisie or Napoleonic ambition. Rather, he sees changes in non-discursive practices as due to a vast number of minute and unconnected facts, the sorts of 'petty causes' that Nietzsche evoked in his genealogies (see GENEALOGY).

Foucault's genealogical studies emphasize the essential connection between knowledge and power. Bodies of knowledge are not autonomous intellectual structures that happen to be employed as instruments of power. Rather, precisely as bodies of knowledge, they are tied (but not reducible) to systems of social control. This essential connection of power and knowledge reflects Foucault's view that power is not merely repressive but a creative, if always dangerous, source of positive values. Although systems of knowledge may express objective truth in their own right, they are none the less always tied to current regimes of power. Conversely, regimes of power necessarily give rise to bodies of knowledge about the objects they control; but this knowledge may – in its objectivity – go beyond and even ultimately threaten the project of domination from which it arises.

Surveiller et punir: naissance de la prison (Discipline and Punish) (1975) is the best example of Foucault's genealogical approach. Here Foucault applies his conception of knowledge/power to the connection between modern disciplinary practices and modern social scientific disciplines. His primary example is the relation of the practice of imprisonment to such disciplines as criminology and social psychology. But imprisonment quickly becomes a model for the entire range of modern disciplinary practices, as employed in schools, factories, the military and so on. *Discipline and Punish* is a genealogical study in the precise sense that it shows how fundamental changes in thought (the emergence of new social scientific disciplines) were causally connected with changes in non-discursive practices (characteristically modern means of controlling the body).

Foucault's *Histoire de la sexualité* (History of Sexuality) (1976–84) was initially conceived as a straightforward extension of the genealogical approach to sexuality. His idea was that modern bodies of knowledge about sexuality (the 'sciences of sexuality', including psychoanalysis) have an intimate association with the power structures of modern society. Volume 1, published in 1976, was intended as the introduction to a series of studies on particular aspects of modern sexuality (children, women, perverts and population), outlining the basic viewpoint and methods of the project. A central contention was that the history of sexuality is distorted by our acceptance of the 'repressive hypothesis': the proposition that the primary attitude towards sex during the last three centuries was one of opposition, silencing and, as far as possible, elimination. Foucault argues that in fact this period produced a 'discursive explosion' regarding sex, beginning with the rules of the Counter-Reformation governing sacramental confession. These rules emphasized the need for penitents to examine themselves and articulate not just all their sinful sexual actions, but all the thoughts, desires and inclinations behind these actions. The distinctive modern turn is the secularization (in, for example, psychoanalysis) of this concern for knowing and expressing the truth about sex.

Foucault emphasizes the similarities in our views of sex and crime. Both are objects of allegedly scientific disciplines, which simultaneously offer knowledge and domination of their objects. In the case of sexuality, however, control is exercised not only through others' knowledge of individuals but also through individuals' knowledge of themselves. We internalize the norms laid down by the sciences of sexuality and monitor our own conformity to these norms. We are controlled not only as *objects* of disciplines but also as self-scrutinizing and self-forming *subjects*. Foucault thus sees our apparently liberating focus on our sexuality as a reinforcement of the mechanisms of social control. The self-scrutiny that overcomes psychic repression to reveal our deep sexual nature is merely a subtle means of shaping us to the norms of modern society.

5   Sexuality and ethics

Foucault planned the second volume of his history of sexuality as a study of the origins of the modern notion of the subject in the practices of Christian confession. He wrote such a study, 'Les Aveux de la chair' (The Confessions of the Flesh), but did not publish it because he decided that a proper understanding of the Christian development required a comparison with ancient conceptions of the ethical self. This led to two volumes on Greek and Roman sexuality: *L'Usage des plaisirs* (The Use of Pleasure) (1984) and *Le Souci de soi* (The Care of the Self) (1984). These two volumes mark the fourth and final period of Foucault's work, a period most striking for its emphasis on the individual self: the 'problematization' of its world and actions and the 'aesthetics of existence' whereby it makes its life a work of art. It might seem that Foucault has finally rejected the derivative and ephemeral status of the individual. But this would be doubly mistaken. On the one hand, he still sees our history as strongly structured by discursive and non-discursive practices operating at much deeper levels than that of human consciousness. On the other hand, every stage of Foucault's work was directed towards overcoming the limitations of individuals (himself and others). Previously, his effort was the negative one of dissolving the apparently necessary constraints of society and its discourses. In this final turn to what he calls 'ethics', he began to explore the positive possibilities of self-creation.

In *The Use of Pleasure* and *The Care of the Self*, Foucault compares ancient pagan and Christian ethics through studies of the test case of sexuality. He notes that the moral codes of pagans and Christians were similar, but maintains that there were fundamental differences in the ways in which individuals were subordinated to the codes (in the 'forms of subjectification'). The Greeks of the fourth and fifth centuries BC, unlike the early Christians, did not regard the domain of sexual acts (*ta aphrodisia*) as evil in its own right, but as natural and necessary. The Greeks did see sexual acts as objects of moral concern because of their animality and their great intensity. What was dangerous, however, was not sex in itself but its excesses. Therefore, the Greek mode of subjection to the code of sexual ethics was a matter of the proper use (*chresis*) of pleasures. Unlike the Christians, the Greeks allowed the full range of sexual activities (heterosexual, homosexual, in marriage, out of marriage) within proper moderation. Properly used, sex was a major part of an aesthetics of the self: the self's creation of a beautiful and enjoyable existence.

The Use of Pleasure analyses a variety of primary texts (for instance, those of Plato and Xenophon) in order to understand the classical Greek conception of an aesthetics of existence. *The Care of the Self* continues with studies (of Galen, Artemidorus and Plutarch, for example) showing how later antiquity gradually moved away from this aesthetics towards a hermeneutics of the self. The latter, fully developed only by Christianity, replaced the ideal of aesthetic self-creation with that of a deep understanding of a hidden 'real self'. Foucault regards this Christian conception as the root of our domination by the sciences of sexuality he discussed in *The History of Sexuality I*. Although insisting that there can be no question of 'going back to the Greeks', he suggests that reflection on the aesthetics of existence may help us devise liberating alternatives to the traps of modern sexuality (see SEXUALITY, PHILOSOPHY OF).

Foucault forbade posthumous publication of his writings, but the ban has not included the texts of his public lectures at the Collège de France, several volumes of which have already appeared, with more planned. The volumes published so far include important material on such topics as the hermeneutics of the subject, the concept of the abnormal, psychiatric power and the modern idea of war.

6   Conclusion

It is impossible to understand Foucault's work in the typical manner of histories of philosophy. There is

not only no system, but no sustained vision, message or project (which we find even in such mavericks as Nietzsche, Kierkegaard and Wittgenstein). For Foucault, philosophy is always just a means of overcoming some specific set of historical limits. It has no final goal, no specific truth or effect, of its own. It is merely a set of intellectual techniques, tied to a consciousness of the historical enterprise that has been known as philosophy. If philosophy ever transforms its self-conception along the lines of Foucault's practice, then he will be recognized as a great philosopher (or, more likely, as someone who played a major role in eliminating philosophy as it had been understood since Plato). Otherwise, he will in all likelihood remain a minor figure, interesting for his odd historical perspectives and his quirky social criticism.

References and further reading

Gutting, G. (2005) *Foucault: a Very Short Introduction*, Oxford: Oxford University Press. (A brief overview of Foucault's work in literary, historical, political and philosophical terms.)

Macey, D. (1993) *The Lives of Michel Foucault: a Biography*, New York: Pantheon. (The best of the several biographies of Foucault.)

McNay, L. (1994) *Foucault: a Critical Introduction*, New York: Continuum. (An excellent introductory survey of Foucault's work.)

GARY GUTTING

FOUNDATIONALISM

Some foundationalists are rationalists who rely on intuition and deduction. Others are empiricists, in a broad sense, and accept observation and induction or abduction or yet other ways to support beliefs by means of other beliefs. What they have in common is that they are all willing to hazard a positive view about what in general makes a belief epistemically justified in the way required for it to be a case of knowledge; and they all propose something of the following general form: belief b is justified if and only if either b is foundationally justified through a psychological process of direct apprehension p (such as rational intuition, observation, introspection, and so on) or else b is inferentially justified through a psychological process of reasoning r (such as deduction, induction, abduction, and so on) ultimately from beliefs all of which are acquired or sustained through p. If one rejects all forms of such foundationalism, then a question remains as to what distinguishes in general the cases where a belief is epistemically justified from the cases in which it is not. Can anything general and illuminating be said about what confers epistemic justification on a belief, and what gives a belief the epistemic status required for it to constitute knowledge (provided it is true)?

See also: EMPIRICISM; JUSTIFICATION, EPISTEMIC; KNOWLEDGE, CONCEPT OF; RATIONALISM

ERNEST SOSA

FOURIER, CHARLES (1772–1837)

Fourier was a French utopian socialist who criticized the economic and domestic structures of the modern social world for their failure to respect human nature. He discerned twelve basic human 'passions' which combined to generate 810 basic personality types. On the basis of this account of human diversity, he advocated the establishment of small voluntary communities organized to provide fulfilling work and sexual liberation. Some of the more extravagant elements of his 'social' theory (his views on cosmogony, metempsychosis and 'universal analogy') were played down by his followers.

See also: MARX, K.; SAINT-SIMON, C.-H. DE ROUVROY; UTOPIANISM

DAVID LEOPOLD

FRANKFURT SCHOOL

The origins of the circle of philosophers and social scientists now known as the Frankfurt School lie in the 1920s when a number of critics and intellectuals were attempting to adapt Marxism to the theoretical and political needs of the time. The distinguishing feature of the approach adopted by the Frankfurt School lies less in its theoretical orientation than in its explicit intention to include each of the disciplines of the social sciences in the project of a critical theory of society. The objectives of this theoretical innovation vis-à-vis all the traditional Marxist approaches were established by Max Horkheimer in various articles written in the 1920s and 1930s. His critique of neo-idealist philosophy and contemporary empiricism sought to develop a philosophy of history which would comprehend the evolution of human reason; in so doing, he drew on empirical research. Thus the Institute of Social Research, conceived as a way of realizing this plan, was founded in 1929. Its work drew on economics, psychology and cultural theory, seeking to analyse, from a historical perspective, how a rational organization of society might be achieved.

However, after the National Socialists came to power and drove the Institute into exile, historical/philosophical optimism gave way to cultural/critical pessimism. Horkheimer and Adorno now saw it as the function of a critical theory of society to try, by returning to the history of civilization, to establish the reasons for the emergence of Fascism and Stalinism. Their *Dialectic of Enlightenment*, which bears some resemblance to Heidegger, impressively testifies to this change of orientation: it asks why totalitarianism came into being and it identifies a cognitive and practical perspective on the world which, because of its concern with the technical control of objects and persons, only allows for an instrumental rationality.

But there was some opposition to this critique of reason which tended to view totalitarianism as a consequence of an inescapable cycle of instrumental reason and social control. The concept of total reification was called into question by some of the more marginal members of the Institute working under Adorno and Horkheimer. These were far more interested in asking whether, even under totalitarian conditions, they could determine the remains of a desire for communicative solidarity. The work of philosopher Walter Benjamin constitutes an analysis of the interrelation of power and the imagination; Franz Neumann and Otto Kirchheimer inquired into legal consensus culture and social control; while Erich Fromm conducted a psychoanalytic investigation of communicative needs and their potential for resistance.

After the core members of the School had returned from exile, the Institute resumed its work in Frankfurt and embarked on large-scale empirical projects. From the very beginning, however, a considerable gap existed between the empirical investigations which focused on the industrial workplace and the philosophical radicalization of negativity on which Adorno and Horkheimer worked, albeit with differing emphasis. This gap was bridged only when Habermas began to challenge the systematic bases of critical theory, causing the basic philosophical concepts and the intentions of empirical social research once again to correspond. The central idea, with which Habermas introduced a new phase in the history of the Frankfurt School, was his understanding of a form of rationality which would describe the communicative agreement between subjects rather than the instrumental control of things. The concept of communicative rationality which emerged from this idea has since formed the basis for the moral grounds and democratic application of critical theory.

See also: CRITICAL THEORY

AXEL HONNETH
Translated from the German by
BRIDGET THOMSON
Bibliographical annotations by
MICHAEL BULL

FREE LOGICS

We often need to reason about things that do not – or may not – exist. We might, for example, want to prove that there is no highest prime number by assuming its existence and deriving a contradiction. Our ordinary formal logic, however (that is, anything including standard quantification theory), automatically assumes that every singular term used has a denotation: if you can use the term 'God' – if that term is part of your language – automatically there is a denotation for it, that is, God exists. Some logicians have thought that this assumption pre-judges too many important issues, and that it is best to get rid of it. So they have constructed logics free of this assumption, called 'free logics'.

See also: EXISTENCE

ERMANNO BENCIVENGA

FREE WILL

Introduction

'Free will' is the conventional name of a topic that is best discussed without reference to the will. Its central questions are 'What is it to act (or choose) freely?', and 'What is it to be morally responsible for one's actions (or choices)?' These two questions are closely connected, for freedom of action is necessary for moral responsibility, even if it is not sufficient.

Philosophers give very different answers to these questions, hence also to two more specific questions about ourselves: (1) Are we free agents? and (2) Can we be morally responsible for what we do? Answers to (1) and (2) range from 'Yes, Yes' to 'No, No' – via 'Yes, No' and various degrees of 'Perhaps', 'Possibly', and 'In a sense'. (The fourth pair of outright answers, 'No, Yes', is rare, but appears to be accepted by some Protestants.) Prominent among the 'Yes, Yes' sayers are the *compatibilists*, who hold that free will is compatible with *determinism*. Briefly, determinism is the view that everything that happens is necessitated by what has already gone before, in such a way that nothing can happen otherwise than it does. According to compatibilists, freedom is compatible with determinism because freedom is essentially just a matter of not being constrained or hindered in certain ways when one acts or chooses. Thus normal adult human beings in normal circumstances are able to act and choose freely. No one is holding a gun to their heads. They are not drugged, or in chains, or subject to a psychological compulsion. They are therefore wholly free to choose and act even if their whole physical and psychological make-up is entirely determined by things for which they are in no way ultimately responsible – starting with their genetic inheritance and early upbringing.

Incompatibilists hold that freedom is not compatible with determinism. They point out that if determinism is true, then every one of one's actions was determined to happen as it did before one was born. They hold that one cannot be held to be truly free and finally morally responsible for one's actions in this case. They think compatibilism is a 'wretched subterfuge . . . , a petty word-jugglery', as Kant put it in his *Critique of Practical Reason* (1788). It entirely fails to satisfy our natural convictions about the nature of moral responsibility.

The incompatibilists have a good point, and may be divided into two groups. *Libertarians* answer 'Yes, Yes' to questions (1) and (2). They hold that we are indeed free and fully morally responsible agents, and that determinism must therefore be false. Their great difficulty is to explain why the falsity of determinism is any better than the truth of determinism when it comes to establishing our free agency and moral responsibility. For suppose that not every event is determined, and that some events occur randomly, or as a matter of chance. How can our claim to moral responsibility be improved by the supposition that it is partly a matter of chance or random outcome that we and our actions are as they are?

The second group of incompatibilists is less sanguine. They answer 'No, No' to questions (1) and (2). They agree with the libertarians that the truth of determinism rules out genuine moral responsibility, but argue that the falsity of determinism cannot help. Accordingly, they conclude that we are not genuinely free agents or genuinely morally responsible, whether determinism is true or false. One of their arguments can be summarized as follows. When one acts, one acts in the way one does because of the way one is. So to be truly morally responsible for one's actions, one would have to be truly responsible for the way one is: one would have to be *causa sui*, or the cause of oneself, at least in certain crucial mental respects. But nothing can be *causa sui* – nothing can be the ultimate cause of itself in any respect. So nothing can be truly morally responsible.

Suitably developed, this argument against moral responsibility seems very strong. But in many human beings, the experience of choice gives rise to a conviction of absolute responsibility that is untouched by philosophical arguments. This conviction is the deep and inexhaustible source of the free will problem: powerful arguments that seem to show that we cannot be morally responsible in the ultimate way that we suppose keep coming up against equally powerful psychological reasons why we continue to believe that we are ultimately morally responsible.

1 Compatibilism

Do we have free will? It depends what you mean by the word 'free'. More than 200 senses of the word have been distinguished; the history of the discussion of free will is rich and remarkable. David Hume called the problem of free will 'the most contentious question of metaphysics, the most contentious science' (*Enquiry Concerning Human Understanding* 1748).

According to *compatibilists*, we do have free will. They propound a sense of the word 'free' according to which free will is compatible with *determinism*, even though determinism is the view that the history of the universe is fixed in such a way that nothing can happen otherwise than it does because everything that happens is necessitated by what has already gone before (see DETERMINISM AND INDETERMINISM).

Suppose tomorrow is a national holiday. You are considering what to do. You can climb a mountain or read Lao Tse. You can mend your bicycle or go to the zoo. At this moment you are reading the *Routledge Encyclopedia of Philosophy*. You are free to go on reading or stop now. You have started on this sentence, but you don't have to... finish it.

In this situation, as so often in life, you have a number of options. Nothing forces your hand. It seems natural to say that you are *entirely* free to choose what to do. And, given that nothing hinders you, it seems natural to say that you act entirely freely when you actually do (or try to do) what you have decided to do.

Compatibilists claim that this is the right thing to say. They believe that to have free will, to be a free agent, to be free in choice and action, is simply to be free from *constraints* of certain sorts. Freedom is a matter of not being physically or psychologically forced or compelled to do what one does. Your character, personality, preferences, and general motivational set may be entirely determined by events for which you are in no way responsible (by your genetic inheritance, upbringing, subsequent experience, and so on). But you do not have to be in control of any of these things in order to have compatibilist freedom. They do not constrain or

compel you, because compatibilist freedom is just a matter of being able to choose and act in the way one prefers or thinks best *given how one is*. As its name declares, it is compatible with determinism. It is compatible with determinism even though it follows from determinism that every aspect of your character, and everything you will ever do, was already inevitable before you were born.

If determinism does not count as a constraint or compulsion, what does? Compatibilists standardly take it that freedom can be limited by such things as imprisonment, by a gun at one's head, or a threat to the life of one's children, or a psychological obsession and so on.

It is arguable, however, that compatibilist freedom is something one continues to possess undiminished so long as one can choose or act in any way at all. One continues to possess it in any situation in which one is not actually panicked, or literally compelled to do what one does, in such a way that it is not clear that one can still be said to choose or act at all (as when one presses a button, because one's finger is actually forced down on the button).

Consider pilots of hijacked aeroplanes. They usually stay calm. They *choose* to comply with the hijackers' demands. They *act* responsibly, as we naturally say. They are able to do other than they do, but they choose not to. They do what they most want to do, all things considered, in the circumstances in which they find themselves.

All circumstances limit one's options in some way. It is true that some circumstances limit one's options much more drastically than others; but it does not follow that one is not free to choose in those circumstances. Only literal compulsion, panic, or uncontrollable impulse really removes one's freedom to choose, and to (try to) do what one most wants to do given one's character or personality. Even when one's finger is being forced down on the button, one can still act freely in resisting the pressure, and in many other ways.

Most of us are free to choose throughout our waking lives, according to the compatibilist conception of freedom. We are free to choose between the options that we perceive to be open to us. (Sometimes we would rather not face options, but are unable to avoid awareness of the fact that we do face them.) One has options even when one is in chains, or falling through space. Even if one is completely paralysed, one is still free in so far as one is free to choose to think about one thing rather than another. Sartre observed that there is a sense in which we are 'condemned' to freedom, not free not to be free.

Of course one may well not be able to do everything one wants – one may want to fly unassisted, vapourize every gun in the United States by an act of thought, or house all those who sleep on the streets of Calcutta by the end of the month. But few have supposed that free will, or free agency, is a matter of being able to do everything one wants. That is one possible view of what it is to be free; but according to the compatibilists, free will is simply a matter of having genuine options and opportunities for action, and being able to choose between them according to what one wants or thinks is best.

It may be said that dogs and other animals can be free agents, according to this basic account of compatibilism. Compatibilists may reply that dogs can indeed be free agents. And yet we do not think that dogs can be free or morally responsible in the way we can be. So compatibilists need to say what the relevant difference is between dogs and ourselves.

Many suppose that it is our capacity for self-conscious thought that makes the crucial difference, because it makes it possible for us to be explicitly aware of ourselves as facing choices and engaging in processes of reasoning about what to do. This is *not* because being self-conscious can somehow liberate one from the facts of determinism: if determinism is true, one is determined to have whatever self-conscious thoughts one has, whatever their complexity. Nevertheless, many are inclined to think that a creature's explicit self-conscious awareness of itself as chooser and agent can constitute it as a free agent in a fundamental way that is unavailable to any unself-conscious agent.

Compatibilists can agree with this. They can acknowledge and incorporate the view that self-conscious awareness of oneself as facing choices can give rise to a kind of freedom that is unavailable to unself-conscious agents. They may add that human beings are sharply marked off from dogs by their capacity to act for reasons that they explicitly take to be moral reasons. In general, compatibilism has many variants. According to Harry Frankfurt's version, for example, one has free will if one wants to be moved to action by the motives that do in fact move one to action. On this view, freedom is a matter of having a personality that is harmonious in a certain way. Freedom in this sense is clearly compatible with determinism.

Compatibilism has been refined in many ways, but this gives an idea of its basis. 'What more could free agency possibly be?', compatibilists like to ask (backed by Hobbes, Locke, and Hume, among others). And this is a very powerful question.

2 Incompatibilism

Those who want to secure the conclusion that we are free agents do well to adopt a compatibilist theory of freedom, for determinism is unfalsifiable, and may be true. (Contemporary physics gives us no more reason to suppose that determinism is false than to suppose that it is true – though this is contested; for further discussion see DETERMINISM AND INDETERMINISM.) Many, however, think that the compatibilist account of things does not even touch the real problem of free will. They believe that all compatibilist theories of freedom are patently inadequate.

What is it, they say, to define freedom in such a way that it is compatible with determinism? It is to define it in such a way that a creature can be a free agent even if all its actions throughout its life are determined to happen as they do by events that have taken place before it is born: so that there is a clear sense in which it could not at any point in its life have done otherwise than it did. This, they say, is certainly not free will. More importantly, it is not a sufficient basis for true moral responsibility. One cannot possibly be truly or ultimately morally responsible for what one does if everything one does is ultimately a deterministic outcome of events that took place before one was born; or (more generally) a deterministic outcome of events for whose occurrence one is in no way ultimately responsible.

These anti-compatibilists or *incompatibilists* divide into two groups: the *libertarians* and the *no-freedom theorists* or *pessimists* about free will and moral responsibility. The libertarians think that the compatibilist account of freedom can be improved on. They hold (1) that we do have free will, (2) that free will is not compatible with determinism, and (3) that determinism is therefore false. But they face an extremely difficult task: they have to show how *indeterminism* (the falsity of determinism) can help with free will and, in particular, with moral responsibility.

The pessimists or no-freedom theorists do not think that this can be shown. They agree with the libertarians that the compatibilist account of free will is inadequate, but they do not think it can be improved on. They agree that free will is not compatible with determinism, but deny that indeterminism can help to make us (or anyone else) free. They believe that free will, of the sort that is necessary for genuine moral responsibility, is provably impossible.

The pessimists about free will grant what everyone must: that there is a clear and important compatibilist sense in which we can be free agents (we can be free, when unconstrained, to choose and to do what we want or think best, given how we are). But they insist that this compatibilist sense of freedom is not enough: it does not give us what we want, in the way of free will; nor does it give us what we believe we have. And it is not as if the compatibilists have missed something. The truth is that nothing can give us what we (think we) want, or what we ordinarily think we have. All attempts to furnish a stronger notion of free will fail. We cannot be morally responsible, in the absolute, buck-stopping way in which we often unreflectively think we are. We cannot have 'strong' free will of the kind that we would need to have, in order to be morally responsible in this way.

The fundamental motor of the free will debate is the worry about moral responsibility (see RESPON-SIBILITY). If no one had this worry, it is doubtful whether the problem of free will would be a famous philosophical problem. The rest of this discussion will therefore be organized around the question of moral responsibility.

First, though, it is worth remarking that the worry about free will does not have to be expressed as a worry about the grounds of moral responsibility. A commitment to belief in free will may be integral to feelings that are extremely important to us independently of the issue of moral responsibility: feelings of gratitude, for example, and perhaps of love. One's belief in strong free will may also be driven simply by the conviction that one is or can be *radically self-determining* in one's actions (in a way that is incompatible with determinism) and this conviction need not involve giving much – or any – thought to the issue of moral responsibility. It seems that a creature could conceive of itself as radically self-determining without having any conception of moral right or wrong at all – and so without being any sort of moral agent.

3   Pessimism

One way of setting out the no-freedom theorists' argument is as follows.

(1)   When you act, you do what you do, in the situation in which you find yourself, because of the way you are.

It seems to follow that

(2)   To be truly or ultimately morally responsible for what you *do*, you must be truly or ultimately responsible for the way you *are*, at least in certain crucial mental respects. (Obviously you don't have to be responsible for the way you are in all respects. You don't have to be responsible for your height, age, sex, and so on. But it does seem that you have to be responsible for the way you are at least in certain mental respects. After all, it is your overall mental make-up that leads you to do what you do when you act.)

But

(3)   You cannot be ultimately responsible for the way you are in any respect at all, so you cannot be ultimately morally responsible for what you do.

Why is it that you cannot be ultimately responsible for the way you are? Because

(4)   To be ultimately responsible for the way you are, you would have to have intentionally brought it about that you are the way you are, in a way that is impossible.

The impossibility is shown as follows. Suppose that

(5)   You have somehow intentionally brought it about that you are the way you now are, in certain mental respects: suppose that you have intentionally brought it about that you have a certain mental nature N, and that you have brought this about in such a way that you can now be said to be ultimately responsible for having nature N. (The limiting case of this would be the case in which you had simply endorsed your existing mental nature N from a position of power to change it.)

For this to be true

(6)   You must already have had a certain mental nature N_{-1}, in the light of which you intentionally brought it about that you now have nature N. (If you did not already have a certain mental nature, then you cannot have had any intentions or preferences, and even if you did change in some way, you cannot be held to be responsible for the way you now are.)

But then

(7)   For it to be true that you and you alone are truly responsible for how you now are, you must be truly responsible for having had the nature N_{-1} in the light of which you intentionally brought it about that you now have nature N.

So

(8)   You must have intentionally brought it about that you had that nature N_{-1}. But in that case, you must have existed already with a prior nature, N_{-2}, in the light of which you intentionally brought it about that you had the nature N_{-1}.

And so on. Here one is setting off on a potentially infinite regress. In order for one to be truly or ultimately responsible for *how one is*, in such a way that one can be truly morally responsible for *what one does*, something impossible has to be true: there has to be, and cannot be, a starting point in the series of acts of bringing it about that one has a certain nature – a starting point that constitutes an act of ultimate self-origination.

There is a more concise way of putting the point: in order to be truly morally responsible for what one does, it seems that one would have to be the ultimate cause or origin of oneself, or at least of some crucial part of one's mental nature. One would have to be *causa sui*, in the old terminology. But nothing can be truly or ultimately *causa sui* in any respect at all. Even if the property of being *causa sui* is allowed to belong (unintelligibly) to God, it cannot plausibly be supposed to be possessed by ordinary finite human beings. 'The *causa sui* is the best self-contradiction that has been conceived so far', as Nietzsche remarked in *Beyond Good and Evil*:

> it is a sort of rape and perversion of logic. But the extravagant pride of man has managed to entangle itself profoundly and frightfully with just this nonsense. The desire for 'freedom of the will' in the superlative metaphysical sense, which still holds sway, unfortunately, in the minds of the half-educated; the desire to bear the entire and ultimate responsibility for one's actions oneself, and to absolve God, the world, ancestors, chance, and society involves nothing less than to be precisely this *causa sui* and, with more than Baron Münchhausen's audacity, to pull oneself up into existence by the hair, out of the swamps of nothingness.
>
> (1886: §21)

In fact, nearly all of those who believe in strong free will do so without any conscious thought that it requires ultimate self-origination. Nevertheless, this is the only thing that could actually ground the kind of strong free will that is regularly believed in, and it does seem that one way in which the belief in strong free will manifests itself is in the very vague and (necessarily) unexamined belief that many have that they are somehow or other radically responsible for their general mental nature, or at least for certain crucial aspects of it.

The pessimists' argument may seem contrived, but essentially the same argument can be given in a more natural form as follows. (i) It is undeniable that one is the way one is, initially, as a result of heredity and early experience. (ii) It is undeniable that these are things for which one cannot be held to be in any way responsible (this might not be true if there were reincarnation, but reincarnation would just shift the problem backwards). (iii) One cannot at any later stage of one's life hope to accede to true or ultimate responsibility for the way one is by

trying to change the way one already is as a result of one's heredity and previous experience. For one may well try to change oneself, but (iv) both the particular way in which one is moved to try to change oneself, and the degree of success in one's attempt at change, will be determined by how one already is as a result of heredity and previous experience. And (v) any further changes that one can bring about only after one has brought about certain initial changes will in turn be determined, via the initial changes, by heredity and previous experience. (vi) This may not be the whole story, for it may be that some changes in the way one is are traceable to the influence of indeterministic or random factors. But (vii) it is foolish to suppose that indeterministic or random factors, for which one is *ex hypothesi* in no way responsible, can in themselves contribute to one's being truly or ultimately responsible for how one is.

The claim, then, is not that people cannot change the way they are. They can, in certain respects (which tend to be exaggerated by North Americans and underestimated, perhaps, by members of many other cultures). The claim is only that people cannot be supposed to change themselves in such a way as to be or become truly or ultimately responsible for the way they are, and hence for their actions. One can make the point by saying that the way you are is, ultimately, in every last detail, a matter of luck – good or bad.

4 Moral responsibility

Two main questions are raised by the pessimists' arguments. First, is it really true that one needs to be self-creating or *causa sui* in some way, in order to be truly or ultimately responsible for what one does, as step (2) of the pessimists' argument asserts? Addressing this question will be delayed here until §6, because a more basic question arises: What notion of responsibility is being appealed to in this argument? What exactly is this 'ultimate' responsibility that we are held to believe in, in spite of Nietzsche's scorn? And if we do believe in it, what makes us believe in it?

One dramatic way to characterize the notion of ultimate responsibility is by reference to the story of heaven and hell: 'ultimate' moral responsibility is responsibility of such a kind that, if we have it, it *makes sense* to propose that it could be just to punish some of us with torment in hell and reward others with bliss in heaven. It makes sense because what we do is absolutely up to us. The words 'makes sense' are stressed because one certainly does not have to believe in the story of heaven and hell in order to understand the notion of ultimate responsibility that it is used to illustrate. Nor does one have to believe in the story of heaven and hell in order to believe in ultimate responsibility (many atheists have believed in it). One does not have to have heard of it.

The story is useful because it illustrates the *kind* of absolute or ultimate responsibility that many have supposed – and do suppose – themselves to have. It becomes particularly vivid when one is specifically concerned with moral responsibility, and with questions of desert; but it serves equally well to illustrate the sense of radical freedom and responsibility that may be had by a self-conscious agent that has no concept of morality. And one does not have to refer to the story of heaven and hell in order to describe the sorts of everyday situation that seem to be primarily influential in giving rise to our belief in ultimate responsibility. Suppose you set off for a shop on the eve of a national holiday, intending to buy a cake with your last ten pound note. Everything is closing down. There is one cake left; it costs ten pounds. On the steps of the shop someone is shaking an Oxfam tin. You stop, and it seems completely clear to you that it is entirely up to you what you do next. That is, it seems clear to you that you are truly, radically free to choose, in such a way that you will be ultimately responsible for whatever you do choose. You can put the money in the tin, or go in and buy the cake, or just walk away. (You are not only completely free to choose. You are free not to choose.)

Standing there, you may believe that determinism is true. You may believe that in five minutes' time you will be able to look back on the situation and say, of what you will by then have done, 'It was determined that I should do that'. But even if you do believe this, it does not seem to undermine your current sense of the absoluteness of your freedom, and of your moral responsibility for your choice.

One diagnosis of this phenomenon is that one cannot really believe that determinism is true, in such situations of choice, and cannot help thinking that the falsity of determinism might make freedom possible. But the feeling of ultimate responsibility seems to remain inescapable even if one does not think this, and even if one has been convinced by the entirely general argument against ultimate responsibility given in §3. Suppose one accepts that no one can be in any way *causa sui*, and yet that one would have to be *causa sui* (in certain crucial mental respects) in order to be ultimately responsible for one's actions. This does not seem to have any impact on one's sense of one's radical freedom and responsibility, as one stands there, wondering what to do. One's radical responsibility seems to stem simply from the fact that one is fully conscious of one's situation, and knows that one can choose, and believes that one action is morally better than the other. This seems to be immediately enough to

confer full and ultimate responsibility. And yet it cannot really do so, according to the pessimists. For whatever one actually does, one will do what one does because of the way one is, and the way one is is something for which one neither is nor can be responsible, however self-consciously aware of one's situation one is.

The example of the cake may be artificial, but similar situations of choice occur regularly in human life. They are the experiential rock on which the belief in ultimate responsibility is founded. The belief often takes the form of belief in specifically moral, desert-implying responsibility. But, as noted, an agent could have a sense of ultimate responsibility without possessing any conception of morality, and there is an interesting intermediate case: an agent could have an irrepressible experience of ultimate responsibility, and believe in objective moral right and wrong, while still denying the coherence of the notion of desert.

5 Metaphysics and moral psychology

We now have the main elements of the problem of free will. It is natural to start with the compatibilist position; but this has only to be stated to trigger the objection that compatibilism cannot possibly satisfy our intuitions about moral responsibility. According to this objection, an incompatibilist notion of free will is essential in order to make sense of the idea that we are genuinely morally responsible. But this view, too, has only to be stated to trigger the pessimists' objection that indeterministic occurrences cannot possibly contribute to moral responsibility: one can hardly be supposed to be more truly morally responsible for one's choices and actions or character if indeterministic occurrences have played a part in their causation than if they have not played such a part. Indeterminism gives rise to unpredictability, not responsibility. It cannot help in any way at all.

The pessimists therefore conclude that strong free will is not possible, and that ultimate responsibility is not possible either. So no punishment or reward is ever truly just or fair, when it comes to moral matters.

This conclusion may prompt a further question: What exactly is this 'ultimate' responsibility that we are supposed to believe in? One answer refers to the story of heaven and hell, which serves to illustrate the *kind* of responsibility that is shown to be impossible by the pessimists' argument, and which many people do undoubtedly believe themselves to have, however fuzzily they think about the matter. A less colourful answer has the same import, although it needs more thought: 'ultimate' responsibility exists if and only if punishment and reward can be fair without having any pragmatic justification.

Now the argument may cycle back to compatibilism. Pointing out that 'ultimate' moral responsibility is obviously impossible, compatibilists may claim that we should rest content with the compatibilist account of things – since it is the best we can do. But this claim reactivates the incompatibilist objection, and the cycle continues.

There is an alternative strategy at this point: quit the traditional metaphysical circle for the domain of *moral psychology*. The principal positions in the traditional metaphysical debate are clear. No radically new option is likely to emerge after millennia of debate. The interesting questions that remain are primarily psychological: Why do we believe we have strong free will and ultimate responsibility of the kind that can be characterized by reference to the story of heaven and hell? What is it like to live with this belief? What are its varieties? How might it be changed by dwelling intensely on the view that ultimate responsibility is impossible?

A full answer to these questions is beyond the scope of this entry, but one fundamental cause of our belief in ultimate responsibility has been mentioned. It lies in the experience of choice that we have as self-conscious agents who are able to be fully conscious of what they are doing when they deliberate about what to do and make choices. (We choose between the Oxfam box and the cake; or we make a difficult, morally neutral choice about which of two paintings to buy.) This raises an interesting question: Is it true that any possible self-conscious creature that faces choices and is fully aware of the fact that it does so must experience itself as having strong free will, or as being radically self-determining, simply in virtue of the fact that it is a self-conscious agent (and whether or not it has a conception of moral responsibility)? It seems that we cannot live or experience our choices as determined, even if determinism is true. But perhaps this is a human peculiarity, not an inescapable feature of any possible self-conscious agent. And perhaps it is not even universal among human beings.

Other causes of the belief in strong free will have been suggested. Hume stressed our experience of serious indecision, as above. Spinoza proposed that one of the causes is simply that we are not conscious of the determined nature of our desires. Kant held that our experience of moral obligation makes belief in strong free will inevitable. P.F. Strawson argued that the fundamental fact is that we are irresistibly committed to certain natural reactions to other people, like gratitude and resentment. Various other suggestions have been made: those who think hard about free will are likely to become convinced that investigation of the complex moral psychology of the belief in freedom, and of the possible moral and psychological consequences of altering the belief, is

the most fruitful area of research that remains. New generations, however, will doubtless continue to launch themselves onto the old metaphysical roundabout.

6 Challenges to pessimism

The preceding discussion attempts to illustrate the internal dynamic of the free will debate, and to explain why the debate is likely to continue for as long as human beings can think. The basic point is this: powerful logical or metaphysical reasons for supposing that we cannot have strong free will keep coming up against equally powerful psychological reasons why we cannot help believing that we do have it. The pessimists' or no-freedom theorists' conclusions may seem irresistible during philosophical discussion, but they are likely to lose their force, and seem obviously irrelevant to life, when one stops philosophizing.

Various challenges to the pessimists' argument have been proposed, some of which appear to be supported by the experience or 'phenomenology' of choice. One challenge grants that one cannot be ultimately responsible for one's mental nature – one's character, personality, or motivational structure – but denies that it follows that one cannot be truly morally responsible for what one does (it therefore challenges step (2) of the argument set out in §3).

This challenge has at least two versions. One has already been noted: we are attracted by the idea that our capacity for fully explicit self-conscious deliberation, in a situation of choice, suffices by itself to constitute us as truly morally responsible agents in the strongest possible sense. The idea is that such full self-conscious awareness somehow renders irrelevant the fact that one neither is nor can be ultimately responsible for any aspect of one's mental nature. On this view, the mere fact of one's self-conscious presence in the situation of choice can confer true moral responsibility: it may be undeniable that one is, in the final analysis, wholly constituted as the sort of person one is by factors for which one cannot be in any way ultimately responsible; but the threat that this fact appears to pose to one's claim to true moral responsibility is simply obliterated by one's self-conscious awareness of one's situation.

The pessimists reply: This may correctly describe a strong source of *belief* in ultimate (moral) responsibility, but it is not an account of something that could *constitute* ultimate (moral) responsibility. When one acts after explicit self-conscious deliberation, one acts for certain reasons. But which reasons finally weigh with one is a matter of one's mental nature, which is something for which one cannot be in any way ultimately responsible. One can certainly be a morally responsible agent in the sense of being aware of distinctively moral considerations when one acts. But one cannot be morally responsible in such a way that one is ultimately deserving of punishment or reward for what one does.

The conviction that fully explicit self-conscious awareness of one's situation can be a sufficient foundation of strong free will is extremely powerful. The no-freedom theorists' argument seems to show that it is wrong, but it is a conviction that runs deeper than rational argument, and it survives untouched, in the everyday conduct of life, even after the validity of the no-freedom theorists' argument has been admitted.

Another version of the challenge runs as follows. The reason why one can be truly or ultimately (morally) responsible for what one does is that one's *self* – what one might call the 'agent self' – is, in some crucial sense, independent of one's general *mental nature* (one's character, personality, motivational structure, and so on). One's mental nature *inclines* one to do one thing rather than another, but it does not thereby *necessitate* one to do one thing rather than the other. (The distinction between inclining and necessitating derives from Leibniz (*Discourse on Metaphysics* 1686; *New Essays on Human Understanding* 1704–5).) As an agent-self, one incorporates a power of free decision that is independent of all the particularities of one's mental nature in such a way that one can, after all, count as truly and ultimately morally responsible in one's decisions and actions even though one is not ultimately responsible for any aspect of one's mental nature.

The pessimists reply: Even if one grants the validity of this conception of the agent-self for the sake of argument, it cannot help to establish ultimate moral responsibility. According to the conception, the agent-self decides in the light of the agent's mental nature but is not determined by the agent's mental nature. The following question immediately arises: *Why* does the agent-self decide as it does? The general answer is clear. Whatever the agent-self decides, it decides as it does because of the overall way it is; and this necessary truth returns us to where we started. For once again, it seems that the agent-self must be responsible for being the way it is, in order to be a source of true or ultimate responsibility. But this is impossible, for the reasons given in §3: nothing can be *causa sui* in the required way. Whatever the nature of the agent-self, it is ultimately a matter of luck (or, for those who believe in God, a matter of grace). It may be proposed that the agent-self decides as it does partly or wholly because of the presence of indeterministic occurrences in the decision process. But it is clear that indeterministic occurrences can never be a source of true (moral) responsibility.

Some believe that free will and moral responsibility are above all a matter of being governed in one's choices and actions by reason – or by Reason with a capital 'R'. But possession of the property of being governed by Reason cannot be a ground of radical moral responsibility as ordinarily understood. It cannot be a property that makes punishment (for example) ultimately just or fair for those who possess it, and unfair for those who do not possess it. Why not? Because to be morally responsible, on this view, is simply to possess one sort of motivational set among others. It is to value or respond naturally to rational considerations – which are often thought to include moral considerations by those who propound this view. It is to have a general motivational set that may be attractive, and that may be more socially beneficial than many others. But there is no escape from the fact that someone who does possess such a motivational set is simply lucky to possess it – if it is indeed a good thing – while someone who lacks it is unlucky.

This may be denied. It may be said that some people struggle to become more morally responsible, and make an enormous effort. Their moral responsibility is then not a matter of luck; it is their own hard-won achievement.

The pessimists' reply is immediate. Suppose you are someone who struggles to be morally responsible, and make an enormous effort. Well, that, too, is a matter of luck. You are lucky to be someone who has a character of a sort that disposes you to make that sort of effort. Someone who lacks a character of that sort is merely unlucky. Kant is a famous example of a philosopher who was attracted by the idea that to display free will is to be governed by Reason in one's actions. But he became aware of the problem just described, and insisted, in a later work (*Religion in the Limits of Reason Alone* 1793), that 'man *himself* must make or have made himself into whatever, in a moral sense, whether good or evil, he is to become. Either condition must be an effect of his free choice; for otherwise he could not be held responsible for it and could therefore be *morally* neither good nor evil'. Since he was committed to belief in ultimate moral responsibility, Kant held that such self-creation does indeed take place, and wrote accordingly of 'man's character, which he himself creates' (*Critique* 1788), and of 'knowledge [that one has] of oneself as a person who... is his own originator' (*Opus Postumum* 1993). Here he made the demand for self-creation that is natural for someone who believes in ultimate moral responsibility and who thinks through what is required for it.

In the end, luck swallows everything. This is one way of putting the point that there can be no ultimate responsibility, given the natural, strong conception of responsibility that was characterized at the beginning of §4. Relative to that conception, no punishment or reward is ever ultimately just or fair, however natural or useful or otherwise humanly appropriate it may be or seem.

The facts are clear, and they have been known for a long time. When it comes to the metaphysics of free will, André Gide's remark is apt: 'Everything has been said before, but since nobody listens we have to keep going back and beginning all over again.' It seems that the only freedom that we can have is compatibilist freedom. If – since – that is not enough for ultimate responsibility, we cannot have ultimate responsibility. The only alternative to this conclusion is to appeal to God and mystery – this in order to back up the claim that something that appears to be provably impossible is not only possible but actual.

The debate continues; some have thought that philosophy ought to move on. There is little reason to expect that it will do so, as each new generation arises bearing philosophers gripped by the conviction that they can have ultimate responsibility. Would it be a good thing if philosophy did move on, or if we became more clear-headed about the topic of free will than we are? It is hard to say.

See also: ACTION; CRIME AND PUNISHMENT; MENTAL CAUSATION; MORAL AGENTS; MORAL PSYCHOLOGY; WILL, THE

References and further reading

Cicero (43–late 50s BC) *On Fate*, trans. and commentary R.W. Sharples, Warminster: Aris & Phillips, 1991, with Latin text. (Critique, by an Academic, of Stoic and Epicurean views on determinism; sole source for the outstanding defence of incompatibilism by Carneades, the second-century BC Academic philosopher.)

Kane, R. (2002) *The Oxford Handbook of Free Will*, Oxford: Oxford University Press. (Collection of specially commissioned papers covering all main aspects of the free will problem.)

Watson, G. (2003) *Free Will*, Oxford: Oxford University Press. (Wide ranging collection of essays representing work on free will and responsibility over the last fifty years.)

GALEN STRAWSON

FREEDOM AND LIBERTY

Introduction

There are at least two basic ideas in the conceptual complex we call 'freedom'; namely, rightful self-government (autonomy), and the overall ability to do, choose or achieve things, which can be called 'optionality' and defined as the possession of open options. To be autonomous is to be free in the sense of 'self-governing' and 'independent', in a manner analogous to that in which sovereign nation states are free. Optionality is when a person has an open option in respect to some possible action, x, when nothing in the objective circumstances prevents them from doing x should they choose to do so, and nothing requires them to do x should they choose not to. One has freedom of action when one can do what one wills, but in order to have the full benefit of optionality, it must be supplemented by freedom of choice (free will), which consists in being able to will what one wants to will, free of internal psychological impediments. Autonomy and optionality can vary independently of one another. A great deal of one can coexist with very little of the other.

Perhaps the most controversial philosophical question about the analysis of freedom concerns its relation to wants or desires. Some philosophers maintain that only the actual wants that a person has at a given time are relevant to their freedom, and that a person is free to the extent that they can do what they want, even if they can do very little else. Other philosophers, urging that the function of freedom is to provide 'breathing space', insist that freedom is a function of a person's ability to satisfy possible (hypothetical) as well as actual wants. A third group consists of those who hold a 'value-oriented' theory according to which freedom is not merely the power of doing what one wants or may come to want, rather it is the capacity of doing something 'worth doing or enjoying', something that is important or significant to the person said to be free, or to others.

1 Freedom and liberty
2 Freedom as autonomy
3 Negative and positive freedom
4 Freedom as optionality

1 Freedom and liberty

These two terms are often used interchangeably, but on those occasions when they are not taken to be synonyms, the basis of the distinction between the two is usually clear. 'Freedom', when applied to persons and their actions, refers to the *ability* of a person in a given set of circumstances to act in some particular way. 'Liberty' refers to authoritative *permission* to act in some particular way. The contrast is a basis for the grammatical distinction between 'can' and 'may', between the *de facto* and the *de jure* perspectives, or between (overall) ability and permission.

The concept of a liberty is an important part of juridical systems. A set of governing rules can impose *duties* on those who are subject to their authority. But when the rules remain silent about a given type of activity, *x*, then they are said to leave the subjects *at liberty* to *x* or not to *x*, or however they see fit. To be at liberty to *x* is simply to have no duty not to *x* (see RIGHTS §2).

So conceived, freedom and liberty can vary independently. For example, when a statute is only sporadically enforced, if at all, it may leave a person's *de facto* ability to do what it prohibits virtually unimpaired. Thus a cohabiting unmarried couple in Arizona is perfectly capable of doing what the law prohibits only because the law in question is hardly ever enforced. Cohabiting couples have almost perfect *de facto* freedom to cohabit because police indifference makes the risk of detection and conviction minimal. Not only are we sometimes free (to some degree or other) to do what we are not at liberty to do; conversely, we may be at liberty to do what we are not free to do, as when circumstances other than enforced rules prevent us from doing what we are legally permitted to do.

2 Freedom as autonomy

Judgments of freedom are made not only about individual persons but also about their political communities. Many nation states at some point in their histories have had occasion to declare their independence or, what amounts to the same thing, their sovereignty or status as free states. At the same time, other countries may have lost their freedom (independence) and become mere colonies of stronger nation states. When a political state becomes unfree in this way, each citizen can think of themselves as also deprived of the same kind of freedom, or something analogous to it, for few of them remain entirely self-governed when their own country is governed from afar by masters who simply impose their directives by force. 'None of us are truly free so long as our nation is not', a local patriot might say, even while conceding that the colonial power that governs them has treated them decently, allowing them many freedoms. The question of who rightly governs them, as Sir Isaiah Berlin puts it, is logically distinct from the question of how their governors – foreign or domestic, legitimate or not – protect their liberties. The first question concerns autonomy; the second concerns optionality.

Autonomy and optionality also can vary independently. National autonomy can produce its own tyranny, as when a newly independent nation, free of its colonial repressors, refuses to govern democratically and recognizes no civil rights among its subjects. In such a case the native populace may feel as badly mistreated, if not worse, by their own government as before by the colonizers.

Autonomy or self-government can consist of sharing with one's fellow citizens political independence, or can consist of self-direction by that element of the self authorized by nature to rule (often identified with reason). To be self-governed requires that we not be governed by illegitimate outsiders and equally not by alien forces from within.

Note the close analogy to slavery. One slave owner, *A*, is very severe with his only slave, *S1*, permitting him only minimal free movement, no choice in deciding what his off-duty conduct shall be, or what he shall read, how he dresses and so on. Another slave-owner, *B*, is very easy-going. He treats his only slave, *S2*, as if he were a valued friend, and allows him to do anything short of harming others or leaving the plantation. It is clearly understood that *S2* may do all these things only because *B* permits him to, not as a matter of right. The only rights in this situation are *B*'s property rights. The rules of property ownership permit *B* to be as tough with *S2* as he wishes, but he prefers to be kind. So there is in *S2*'s situation a predominance of heteronomy (government by others) conjoined with high optionality (*de facto* freedom). It seems clear then that one can have little or no autonomy, and yet live a contented life with a high standard of living, something resembling friendship and respect, and most important – options left open for one's own choice to exercise, though not as a matter of right.

Suppose that in respect to a certain choice there are two possibilities left open for *S2*. His master can restore his autonomy and turn him loose into an unfriendly world where other human beings, even though they lack authority over him, treat him badly, effectively closing many key options that would have been left open for him by his earlier beneficent master. Should he accept this offer at the expense of much *de facto* freedom? If the question is a difficult one, it shows that it is not clear to which of the two contending values, independence or optionality, he attaches the greater importance (see AUTONOMY, ETHICAL).

3 Negative and positive freedom

Philosophical advocates of 'positive freedom' are often reacting to a tradition among English empiricists that extends from HOBBES to J.S. MILL and RUSSELL. Hobbes intended his definition to apply to the most essential of the common elements in free action and free movement generally. He defined 'free' as the absence of external impediments, to apply equally well, for example, to free-flowing (undammed) streams of water as to the purposeful conduct of human beings. Subsequent empiricists, including LOCKE (§10) and HUME (§5), also held that all freedom is essentially something negative; namely, the absence of restraint or impediment to our actions.

The family of theories to which Berlin attached the label 'positive liberty' are those that identify freedom (or liberty) with personal autonomy or self-government. One version of that theory emphasizes the internal forum that is the agent's self and the legitimate claim of the rational self to rule over the self's lesser elements. The second of the autonomy theories is less individualistic and more political. It holds that no individual can live their life autonomously except as a member of a free political community, a state that is not only independent of other states, but one that is itself organized democratically so that all citizens can share in its governance, and in that sense, at least, be self-governing.

The nineteenth-century idealist philosopher T.H. GREEN summed up these requirements in his definition of 'freedom' as a 'positive power or capacity of doing or enjoying something worth doing or enjoying, and that too, something that we do or enjoy in common with others' ('Liberal Legislation and Freedom of Contract' 1888). Green's definition also expresses a second conception of positive freedom as more than the mere absence of impediment to our desires, even more than the absence of impediment to our 'worthy' desires. In addition to the absence of constraint, genuine freedom must provide full opportunity beyond the mere non-interference of the police and other people. If a person desires above all things to own and enjoy a Mercedes, and there are no external impediments, legal or nonlegal, in the community to such ownership, then both the legal code and the neighbours leave them free to do as they desire. But if that person has no money, then that negative freedom is effectively useless. To have true freedom, say supporters of positive freedom, one must have what is required for the satisfaction of worthwhile wants, and that will usually include at least minimal wealth, physical health, talent and knowledge, including the sorts of knowledge normally imparted by formal education. The more we are able to do the things worth doing, they insist, the freer we are.

The positive freedom theorists may go on to charge that the negative theorist cannot explain why the laudatory title of freedom should ever characterize the person who is paralysed, insane, infantile, impoverished and ignorant, as generally free. It must be ironic, they claim, to say that such

an unfortunate person is well off in the manner implied by the term 'free'. Negative freedom theorists argue that to be free does not mean to be well off; one may be free but discontented, unhappy, ignorant, hungry or in pain. An individual may have freedom but find that in their circumstances it is not worth much. What this shows is that freedom is the kind of good whose worth fluctuates, or in the words of John RAWLS (§§1–2): 'the worth of liberty is not the same for everyone' (*A Theory of Justice* 1971: 204).

The pauper is *unable* to buy the Mercedes, but according to the negative freedom advocate, this is not through being *unfree* to buy one. Most writers within the negative freedom tradition deny that all inabilities are also 'unfreedoms'. The inabilities that constitute unfreedoms, they insist, are those that can be traced directly or indirectly to the deliberate actions or policies of other human beings, in particular legislators and police offers, who can intervene directly and forcefully in other persons' lives. Sometimes the relevant explanation of some other person's incapacity (for example, to earn a decent living) can be linked indirectly to various social influences. The impoverished person might be so because of a lack of technical skill, and that lack, in turn, could be a product of a poor education traceable, however obscurely, to the inequities of a national system of racial segregation, which in turn was supported as deliberate policy by an apartheid government. In that case we could say not only that they are unable to do *x*, but also that they are unfree, given the circumstances, to do so.

The gap between the positive and negative theorists can be further decreased by a theory which has a wider conception of 'restraint' and 'impediment.' Such a theory would have a place both for negative constraints like lack of money, and internal constraints like intense headaches. Such a theory could support negative freedom (that all freedom consists of the absence of impediments, whether positive, negative, internal or external), yet also encompass the important point made by positive freedom (that there is a lot more to freedom than simple non-interference from police officers and other persons, important as that is).

A large number of philosophers now reject the view that there are two irreducibly distinct concepts of freedom, one positive and the other negative. These 'single concept' theorists do not contend that one of the pair of allegedly distinct concepts is 'the only, the "truest", or the "most worthwhile"' (MacCallum, 'Negative and Positive Freedom' 1967: 312), but rather that it is a mistake to make the distinction between positive and negative concepts in the first place. According to MacCallum, there is only one concept of liberty and that is best understood as 'always one and the same triadic relation' between a person (subject or agent), an intended action (actual or possible) and what MacCallum calls a 'preventing condition' (barriers, compulsions and constraints) ('Negative and Positive Freedom': 312, 314). Freedom, in his view, is always *of* someone, *from* something, *to* do, have or be something. Disputes about the nature of freedom like that which divided adherents of positive freedom from adherents of negative freedom are, according to MacCallum, really disagreements over the proper range of one or more of the three variables in a single analytic model: what the term 'person' is to stand for, what is to count as an obstacle, or impediment, or forceful interference, and what is to count as a wanted or intended action.

4 Freedom as optionality

Among the controversies that still divide writers about freedom is the question of whether freedom (in the sense of optionality alone) should be conceived of as simply the absence of present frustration or whether it is best understood as the absence of wider opportunities to do more than one wants to do now. We can call the former concept the 'actual-want satisfaction' theory and the latter the 'hypothetical-want' or 'dispositional' theory. The former allows a person to be called free to the extent that they can satisfy their present wants, without hindrance or frustration. The dispositional concept, however, will not consider them free unless they can also do things that they do not want to do at that present moment, but could, for all they now know, come to want to do at some future time. Why, one might ask, would added dispositional freedom be of value to the person whose actual wants are always permitted their satisfaction? Why should a person miss merely hypothetical want-satisfaction when they can do everything they want without frustration? The usual answer to this question points out that the love of freedom can be a love of breathing space, or room to manoeuvre, of frequent opportunities to change one's mind. The hypothetical account of optionality, therefore, can also be called the 'breathing space' theory.

The most influential spokesmen for the 'actual-wants' concept were the ancient Stoics (see STOICISM). According to Stoic teaching, there are two ways a person can increase the degree of their want-satisfaction. One is to leave their wants as they are and work for the means to satisfy them. The second is to avoid trying to change the world – that is the path to misery – but instead to develop the techniques for changing desires so that they always accord with what happens. The Stoic does not need any breathing space. Whatever happens will please

them because their only desire is that God's will be done, and since Zeus is believed to be omnipotent, that desire cannot be frustrated.

Consider Dorothy Doe, who can choose among 1,000 things at time *t*, but is prevented from choosing, or actually doing, the one thing she wants most to do. Richard Roe, on the other hand, can only do one thing at time *t*, but it happens to be the one thing he wants most to do. Richard Roe, one should say, is not simply 'comparatively' or 'largely' unfree; rather, he is totally unfree, for to say that he can do only one thing is to say that he is forced or made to do that thing. And it is beyond controversy that one cannot be both free and compelled to do the same thing. It may be the case, however, that Richard Roe will be entirely content with the arrangement, and actually welcome the compulsion, which if so, shows again that one can sometimes find more contentment in being unfree than in being free. This at least is the message derived from the example by the hypothetical-wants theorist. The actual-wants theorist will deny that Roe is truly unfree; after all, Roe *can* do what he most wants to do.

Dorothy Doe, on the other hand, may have just lost her last chance to pursue a career as a medical researcher, or her last chance to marry the man she loves, or to find a cure for her child's disease. But she does 'enjoy' thousands more options than Richard Roe. She might seem to be freer in respect (say) to prospective marriage partners (one hundred philosophers are eager to marry her tomorrow, but she loathes them all). But her greater freedom is of no significant use. She will be unhappier but more free than Roe. This example may please the breathing space theorist more than the actual-wants theorist, but it may give still more support to the value-oriented philosopher of freedom considered next.

Is Dorothy Doe really more free simply by having more open options? Does not the superior desirability, in her judgment, of some of the options count as well as the sheer number of them? The proponent of the hypothetical-wants theory of freedom often baulks at permitting desirability into our determinations, partly because of the danger that philosophers will reduce the issue to a purely normative question to be settled by considering which definition of the word 'free' links its meaning to something that is worthy of the value we associate with the word.

The problem of counting options remains a difficulty for all the above theories. Berlin had earlier written that 'the method for counting [possibilities] can never be more than impressionistic. Possibilities of action are not discrete entities like apples, which can be exhaustively enumerated'

('Two Concepts of Liberty' 1958: 130fn1). But individuating possible actions is not the only problem for the philosopher who would apply quantitative measures to freedom's many dimensions, including comprehensiveness, fecundity, and diversity. And one does not exhaust the relevant possibilities by dividing all action into 'possible' and 'impossible.' There are also the component categories – difficult and easy, possible at great cost and possible at small cost, statistically probable and statistically improbable, multiple choices and either/or choices.

It is hard enough to deal with these problems of measurement, but they are almost equally difficult to evade, especially if we continue to speak of one individual or one society having more freedom than another. Moreover, if a philosopher maintains that both the number and the significance, importance or value of open options determines how free one is (and probably most philosophers take such a combination view), then the difficulties begin all over again when they leave off option-counting and begins option-evaluating.

See also: COERCION; FREE WILL; FREEDOM OF SPEECH; LIBERALISM

References and further reading

Miller, D. (ed.) (1991) *Liberty*, Oxford: Oxford University Press. (The most useful bibliography of philosophical analyses of freedom. Contains, among other things, influential articles by T.H. Green, Isaiah Berlin, Gerald C. MacCallum and G.A. Cohen.)

Pelczynski, Z.A. and Gray, J.N. (eds) (1984) *Conceptions of Liberty in Political Philosophy*, London: Athlone Press. (Contemporary authors discuss the differing conceptions of freedom that appear throughout the history of philosophy, from the ancient Greeks to John Rawls. A major theme is the comparison of the various views with Berlin's distinction between positive and negative freedom.)

JOEL FEINBERG

FREEDOM, DIVINE

In the theistic tradition, many thinkers have held that God is infinitely powerful, all-knowing, perfectly good and perfectly free. But since a perfectly good being would invariably follow the best course of action, what can be meant when it is said that God acts freely? Two different views of divine freedom have emerged. According to the first view, God acts freely provided nothing outside him determines him to act. So when we consider God's action of creating a world, it is clear that on the first view he acts freely since there is nothing outside him to determine him to do as he does. The difficulty with this view is that it neglects the possibility that God's own nature might require him to create one particular world rather than another or none at all. According to the second view, God is free in an action provided it was within his power not to perform that action. Unlike the first view, on this view God acts freely only if nothing beyond God's control necessitates his performing that action. The problem for this view is that since it is impossible for God, being perfectly good, not to choose to follow the best course of action, it is difficult to see how God could be free in such an action.

See also: FREE WILL; LEIBNIZ, G.W. §§3, 7; OMNIPOTENCE

WILLIAM L. ROWE

FREEDOM OF SPEECH

Freedom of speech is one of the most widely accepted principles of modern political and social life. The three arguments most commonly offered in its defence are that it is essential for the pursuit of truth, that it is a fundamental constituent of democracy, and that it is a liberty crucial to human dignity and wellbeing. Its advocates also plead the dangers of allowing governments to control what may be said or heard. Yet there is also general agreement that speech should be subject to some limits. Most contemporary controversies about free speech concern those limits; some focus upon what should count as 'speech', others upon the harms that speech may cause.

PETER JONES

FREGE, GOTTLOB (1848–1925)

Introduction

A German philosopher-mathematician, Gottlob Frege was primarily interested in understanding both the nature of mathematical truths and the means whereby they are ultimately to be justified. In general, he held that what justifies mathematical statements is reason alone; their justification proceeds without the benefit or need of either perceptual information or the deliverances of any faculty of intuition.

To give this view substance, Frege had to articulate an experience- and intuition-independent conception of reason. In 1879, with extreme clarity, rigour and technical brilliance, he first presented his conception of rational justification. In effect, it constitutes perhaps the greatest single contribution to logic ever made and it was, in any event, the most important advance since Aristotle. For the first time, a deep analysis was possible of deductive inferences involving sentences containing multiply embedded expressions of generality (such as 'Everyone loves someone'). Furthermore, he presented a logical system within which such arguments could be perspicuously represented: this was the most significant development in our understanding of axiomatic systems since Euclid.

Frege's goal was to show that most of mathematics could be reduced to logic, in the sense that the full content of all mathematical truths could be expressed using only logical notions and that the truths so expressed could be deduced from logical first principles using only logical means of inference. In this task, Frege is widely thought to have failed, but the attempted execution of his project was not in vain: for Frege did show how the axioms of arithmetic can be derived, using only logical resources, from a single principle which some have argued is, if not a logical principle, still appropriately fundamental. In addition, Frege contributed importantly to the philosophy of mathematics through his trenchant critiques of alternative conceptions of mathematics, in particular those advanced by John Stuart Mill and Immanuel Kant, and through his sustained inquiry into the nature of number and, more generally, of abstract objects.

In the course of offering an analysis of deductive argument, Frege was led to probe beneath the surface form of sentences to an underlying structure by virtue of which the cogency of inferences obtains. As a consequence of his explorations, Frege came to offer the first non-trivial and remotely plausible account of the functioning of language. Many of his specific theses about language – for instance, that understanding a linguistic expression does not consist merely of knowing which object it refers to – are acknowledged as of fundamental importance even by those who reject them.

More generally, three features of Frege's approach to philosophical problems have shaped the concerns and methods of analytic philosophy, one of the twentieth century's dominant traditions. First, Frege translates central philosophical problems into problems about language: for example, faced with the epistemological question of how we are able to have knowledge of objects which we can neither observe nor intuit, such as numbers, Frege replaces it with the question of how we are able to talk about those objects using language and, once the question is so put, avenues of exploration previously invisible come to seem plausible and even natural. Second, Frege's focus on language is governed by the principle that it is the operation of sentences that is explanatorily primary: the explanation of the functioning of all parts of speech is to be in terms of their contribution to the meanings of full sentences in which they occur. Finally, Frege insists that we not confuse such explanations with psychological accounts of the mental states of speakers: inquiry into the nature of the link between language and the world, on the one hand, and language and thought, on the other, must not concern itself with unsharable aspects of individual experience.

These three guiding ideas – lingua-centrism, the primacy of the sentence, and anti-psychologism – exercised a commanding influence on early analytic philosophers, such as Wittgenstein, Russell and Carnap. Through them, these ideas have been spread far and wide, and they have come to create and shape analytic philosophy, with whose fathering Frege, more than anyone else, must be credited.

1 Life and work

Gottlob Frege, a German philosopher and mathematician, is the father of modern logic and one of the founding figures of analytic philosophy. Trained as an algebraic geometer, he spent his professional life at the University of Jena, where, because his views about logic, mathematics and language were generally at odds with the dominant trends of the time, he laboured independently on his central philosophical project.

Frege's main work consists of his *Begriffsschrift* (*Conceptual Notation*) (1879), in which he first presents his logic; *Die Grundlagen der Arithmetik* (*The Foundations of Arithmetic*) (1884), in which he outlines the strategy he is going to employ in reducing arithmetic to logic and then goes on to provide the reduction with a philosophical rationale and justification; *Grundgesetze der Arithmetik* (*Basic Laws of Arithmetic*) (volumes 1, 1893, and 2, 1903), in which he seeks to carry out the programme in detail (a planned third volume was aborted following Bertrand Russell's communication to Frege in

1902 of his discovery of paradox in Frege's logic); and a series of philosophical essays on language, the most important of which are *Funktion und Begriff* ('Function and Concept') (1891), 'Über Sinn und Bedeutung' ('On Sense and Reference') (1892), 'Über Begriff und Gegenstand' ('On Concept and Object') (1892) and 'Der Gedanke: eine logische Untersuchung' ('Thoughts') (1918).

In general, Frege was not philosophically intrigued by what was specific to the human condition; for instance, he sought neither to probe the nature and limits of human knowledge nor to understand how humans actually reason. Yet he pursued his non-parochial philosophical interests by attending carefully to natural language and to the way it serves to express our thoughts. Frege's approach, in conjunction with his powerful tool of linguistic analysis (logic) and the collection of subtle, innovative and interwoven theses about language which he elaborated, spurred in others not only an intense interest in language as an object of inquiry but also adherence to a distinctive methodology which has come to characterize much analytic philosophy past and present.

2   Language and ontology

Frege's short book *Begriffsschrift* revolutionized the study of deductive inference. In the course of explaining how his 'conceptual notation' relates to natural language, Frege illuminates important features of language's underlying structure. He recognized that traditional grammatical categories have no logical significance and he urged the consideration instead of the categories of 'singular terms' (which he calls 'proper names') and of 'predicates' (which he calls 'concept-words'). For Frege, a singular term is a complete expression, one which contains no gaps into which another expression may be placed; for example, 'Virginia Woolf', 'the third planet from the Sun' and 'the largest prime number' are all singular terms according to Frege.

By contrast, a predicate such as '( ) was written by Virginia Woolf' is something incomplete; it is a linguistic expression which contains a gap and which becomes a sentence once this gap is filled by a singular term. (The parentheses are not part of the predicate but are intended only to indicate the location of the gap.) Thus, if we fill the gap with 'the third planet from the Sun', we get a complete sentence. This example shows that the resulting sentence may be false or perhaps even nonsense; what is important is that a complete sentence does result. Other examples of predicates are 'Leonard Woolf married ( )', '( ) orbits Jupiter' and '( ) is an even prime number greater than two'; there are infinitely many predicates in any natural language.

Frege distinguishes more finely between predicates, depending on how many gaps they contain and on the types of linguistic expressions that can fill them. The predicates we have so far considered each have just one gap and are known as 'one-place' predicates. '( ) is the mother of ( )' is an example of a 'two-place' predicate, for it contains two gaps, each to be filled by a singular term. Predicates whose gaps are to be filled by one or more singular terms, as is the case with all those mentioned so far, are said to be 'first-level'. Predicates whose gaps are to be filled by first-level predicates are said to be 'second-level', and so on. For example, when properly analysed, 'All [ ] are mammals' is seen to be a second-level predicate: its structure is really 'Everything is such that if it [ ], then it is a mammal', which makes it plainer that the gap is to be filled by a predicate of first-level. (We use square brackets to distinguish such gaps, which must be filled by first-level predicates, from those occurring in first-level predicates, which must be filled by singular terms.) And, for Frege, 'There is at least one thing which [ ]' is likewise a second-level predicate: as we shall see in a moment, this corresponds to his view that existence is not a concept that applies to objects but rather to concepts. This finer classification will not be discussed further here. Nor will the issue of how precisely to understand the incompleteness of predicates, and the corresponding completeness of singular terms, a question that continues to be debated.

The following two points, however, are not in dispute: first, Frege discerns in the categories of reality counterparts to the linguistic categories of singular term and predicate; he calls these ontological categories 'object' and 'concept', respectively. Second, Frege understands concepts on the model of functions as they are commonly encountered in mathematics.

A singular term refers to, or designates, an object. A predicate refers to, or designates, a concept. (We shall use 'designate' and 'refer' and their cognates interchangeably; in some discussions of Frege, 'denote' and 'mean' are also used.) Corresponding to the fact that a first-level predicate yields a complete sentence upon its gap being filled by a singular term, we have the fact that a first-level concept is true or false of an object – or, as Frege puts it, that an object 'falls under' or fails to fall under a concept. For this reason, Frege calls concepts 'unsaturated': unlike objects, they await completion, whereupon they yield one of the two truth-values, which Frege takes to be objects: the True and the False (see 'Function and Concept'). For example, the concept designated by '( ) is an Oxonian' yields the value the False when completed with the object designated by 'Gottlob Frege' and the value the True when completed with the object designated by 'John Locke'.

Concepts are incomplete in the way that functions in mathematics are. For example, the function designated by '2 + ( )' yields the value 8 when completed with the object 6, or, as we might more simply say, it yields that value for the argument 6. The function '2 + ( )' is not an object, but yields one upon completion by an argument. On Frege's view, concepts are a kind of function, namely those that take as their only values the True or the False.

In describing this congruence of linguistic and ontological categories, Frege is not confusing use and mention (see USE/MENTION DISTINCTION AND QUOTATION); indeed, Frege exhibited an understanding of the distinction between words and what they designate not witnessed again until well into the twentieth century. Though linguistic expressions are claimed to slot into a certain set of categories and reality into another, an intimate connection obviously exists between the two categorial schemes. Whether Frege takes the linguistic scheme or instead the ontological one as fundamental is a subject of debate and bound up with the question of whether and in what sense Frege sees philosophical reflection on language as the foundation of philosophy.

Regardless of this debate's resolution, we know that Frege takes the categories of concept and object to be fundamental ontologically, ones not amenable to further analysis. In addition, basic structural features of language raise insurmountable obstacles to expressing certain truths about these categories. This can be demonstrated by considering the obvious claim (1) seeks to articulate:

(1)   The concept designated by '( ) is a horse' is a concept.

This seems patently correct. Yet Frege recognizes in 'On Concept and Object'(1892) that we must judge (1) to be false. This is because the expression 'The concept designated by ( ) is a horse' is a singular term and hence refers to an object, not to a concept. (The expression does not contain a gap, though it does mention one.) So (1) does not succeed in expressing what we intended. To do this, we need to fill the gap in '( ) is a concept' by an expression that refers to a concept. But the straightforward way of doing this yields (2):

(2)   ( ) is a horse is a concept,

which is not even a sentence. In trying to articulate our thought, we are led either to falsity or to something that makes no claim at all. This 'awkwardness of language', as Frege calls it, has been the subject of much controversy, but it seems clear that Frege draws the lesson that there are elemental facts about language and the world that perforce escape expression.

3   Sense and reference

How do what words refer to (concepts and objects) relate to our understanding of language? In his seminal essay 'On Sense and Reference' (1892), Frege considered whether the 'sense' of an expression — what it is that we know when we understand the expression — is simply identical to what it designates (the 'reference'). Frege offers the following argument, as famous as it is simple, to show that our understanding of singular terms cannot consist just of knowing their reference:

(3)   (a)   If two singular terms t and t' have the same sense and C is any (first-level) predicate, then $C(t)$ has the same sense as $C(t')$.

(b)   'The evening star = the morning star' does not have the same sense as 'The evening star = the evening star'.

(c)   'The evening star' does not have the same sense as 'the morning star'.

[This follows from (a) and (b): let C in (a) be 'The evening star = ( )'.]

(d)   'The evening star' refers to the same object as 'the morning star'.

(e)   The reference of 'the evening star' is not identical with its sense.

[This follows from (c) and (d).]

So the sense of an expression — that which must be known in order for a speaker to understand it — cannot be identified with its reference (see SENSE AND REFERENCE). (A terminological digression: in this essay of 1892, Frege used the words '*Sinn*' and '*Bedeutung*', respectively. There is, however, no consensus on how these should be rendered in English. More importantly, there is not yet agreement about how precisely to understand these notions and how they are related to more everyday notions, such as meaning.)

Frege's justification for premise (a) relies on a 'compositionality thesis': the sense of a sentence is determined by the senses of its components (and by the way in which the sentence is constructed from them; see COMPOSITIONALITY). Premise (b) is justified by noting that an alert speaker would find the one sentence obvious, but not the other: 'The evening star = the evening star' is an uninformative statement of self-identity, whereas 'The evening star = the morning star' may impart hitherto unsuspected information. This difference in what Frege called 'cognitive value' suffices, according to him, to register distinct senses. Finally, premise (d) follows from the observation that both singular terms designate the planet Venus, an astronomical discovery that was not made for some time.

If sense is not reference, then what is it? To this, Frege provides no clear answer. He writes in 'On Sense and Reference' that the sense of an expression is 'the mode of presentation of that which is designated', but he does not offer any elaboration regarding the nature of these modes (see PROPER NAMES). Frege does, however, advance a number of other theses concerning the relation between sense and reference. In the first place, the sense of an expression determines the identity of its reference, but not vice versa. For instance, the expression 'the author of *Begriffsschrift*' designates a particular individual, Frege, and any expression with the same sense designates the same individual; yet the expression 'the author of *Die Grundlagen der Arithmetik*', which also refers to Frege, has a different sense. Likewise, though 'George Orwell' and 'Eric Blair' both designate the same person (they have the same reference), the two singular terms have distinct senses.

Second, expressions can be formed which, while possessing a sense, lack a reference. For example, 'Sherlock Holmes' is a singular term that has a sense but lacks a reference, for Holmes does not exist. This is not in conflict with saying that sense determines reference, for what this means is that if two expressions have the same sense, then they have the same reference. One might wonder, though, whether this thesis is at odds with Frege's description of sense as the way 'that which is designated' is presented: how can there be such a way when that which is designated, the reference, does not exist?

Many have found in the distinction between sense and reference relief from the philosophical distress that follows upon assuming, first, that we understand an expression by directly associating a reference with it and, second, that we understand expressions that fail to refer. Holding both of these assumptions has led philosophers to extravagant claims about the reality that is actually designated by our expressions, for instance that Holmes must exist in some fashion if we are to speak of him intelligibly (if only to deny his existence). Frege's distinction between sense and reference, and his thesis that an expression can have a sense while lacking a reference, simply dissolves the problem by rejecting the first assumption (see DESCRIPTIONS).

The argument (3) concerns singular terms, but Frege believed that other kinds of expressions have sense and reference. The distinction can also be drawn in the case of predicates:

(4) Something is a bottle of claret if and only if it is a bottle of claret.

(5) Something is a bottle of claret if and only if it is a bottle of Hume's favourite wine.

(4) does not have the same sense as (5): no one would deny the first, but the second might come as something of a gastronomic discovery. Though '( ) is a bottle of claret' and '( ) is a bottle of Hume's favourite wine' are predicates that refer to the same concept, they have different senses. (Frege identifies two concepts if an object falls under the one if and only if it falls under the other.)

What is the reference of a whole sentence? Frege answers this by observing what remains unchanged about a sentence when we substitute coreferring expressions (that is, expressions that have the same reference) in it. Assuming a compositionality thesis for reference (that the reference of a sentence is determined by the reference of its components), we then have some reason to take whatever remains unchanged to be the sentence's reference. Consider (6) and (7):

(6) George Orwell wrote *1984*.

(7) Eric Blair wrote *1984*.

What remains unchanged? Not the 'thought' expressed by each sentence: someone might believe one sentence to be true, but not the other. Rather, it is the truth-value of the sentences that is constant: (6) and (7) are either both true or both false. This leads Frege to identify the reference of a sentence with its truth-value; a sentence refers to one of the two truth-values. Frege takes the two truth-values to be objects and he observes that on his view all true (false) sentences are really singular terms that refer to the same object, the True (the False).

Because the sciences are interested in what is true, we can see why Frege holds that reference 'is thus shown at every point to be the essential thing for science' ('Ausführungen über Sinn und Bedeutung' 1892–5). Natural language permits the formation of expressions that lack reference, and so Frege judged it unsuitable as a tool of rational inquiry. For this purpose, it was inferior to his *Begriffsschrift*, a formal language he designed with the intention that no expression without reference could be constructed in it.

Frege notes that if his thesis that the reference of a sentence is its truth-value is correct, then we would predict (again on the basis of the compositionality thesis for reference) that if a subordinate sentence is replaced by a coreferential one (which will have the same truth-value), the reference of the entire containing sentence (that is, its truth-value) will remain unchanged. For instance, consider:

(8)   Ronald Reagan was elected President in 1984 and George Orwell wrote *1984*.

(9)   Ronald Reagan was elected President in 1984 and Eric Blair wrote *1984*.

(8) and (9) have the same truth-value, as predicted if the reference of a sentence is its truth-value. But now consider:

(10)   Stimpson believes that George Orwell wrote *1984*.

(11)   Stimpson believes that Eric Blair wrote *1984*.

If Stimpson does not realize that George Orwell and Eric Blair are one and the same person, (10) and (11) might have different truth-values, that is, they might differ in reference. And yet one is obtained from the other merely through substitution of what, on Frege's hypothesis, are the coreferring sentences (6) and (7).

Frege defends his hypothesis by claiming that in certain contexts expressions refer not to their ordinary reference but rather to an 'indirect' reference. And, he adds, the indirect reference of an expression is just its ordinary sense. Because 'Stimpson believes that ( ) wrote 1984' is just such a context and because 'George Orwell' has a different sense from 'Eric Blair' (and so, in this context, a different reference), the compositionality thesis for reference no longer forces us to the conclusion that (10) and (11) have the same truth-value. Frege's response inaugurated a long, fruitful and continuing debate about the nature of such linguistic contexts. (For further discussion, see INDIRECT DISCOURSE; SENSE AND REFERENCE.)

And what about the sense of a complete sentence? Given the compositionality thesis for sense, it will be preserved upon substitution of one expression in a sentence by another with identical sense. Frege says that such a substitution preserves the thought expressed by the sentence and he consequently identifies this thought with the sentence's sense. So, because 'to lie' has the same sense as 'to express something one believes to be false with the intention of deceiving', Frege would predict that the following two sentences express the same thought:

(12)   Everyone has lied.

(13)   Everyone has expressed something he believes to be false with the intention of deceiving.

And this prediction does seem to be borne out. But what precisely is the thought expressed by a sentence?

4   Thought and thinking

When one thinks the thought that lemons are sour, many different kinds of psychological events may transpire; certain memories, images or sensations may be triggered. These events, according to Frege, belong to the psychological world of the subject and, as such, are not fully shareable with others: much as one may try, one cannot experience what another does. It is a serious error, Frege says, to confuse such private events as may accompany our grasping of a thought with the thought that is grasped. One commits the sin of 'psychologism' if one does not sharply distinguish between the psychological process of thinking and the thoughts that are, as a consequence of this private activity, apprehended.

Thoughts then, in contrast to what Frege calls 'ideas', are fully shareable. When you and I grasp the sense of 'Lemons are sour', we arrive at the very same thought: there are not two different, related thoughts (as we might, for example, have two different mental images of lemons), but just the one that, through perhaps idiosyncratic and private paths, we both succeed in apprehending. And so it is in general with senses: they are not of the mental world but are objective in that different individuals can grasp them and associate them with their words. To stray from this perspective, according to Frege, is simply to abandon the view that communication is possible; that two speakers can understand a linguistic expression in the same way.

To grasp a thought is not to hold it true. For though one grasps a thought in the course of asserting it, it is no less grasped in the acts of assuming it to be true, wishing that it were true, commanding that it be made true, questioning whether it is true, and so on. These acts correspond to the different kinds of 'force' that may be attached to a thought. This is not quite Frege's position, but it is an influential one closely related to his views as given in 'On Sense and Reference'. It has been attractive to many students of language because it divides the daunting project of giving an explanation of linguistic understanding and use into two potentially more tractable components. The first task, the articulation of a 'theory of sense' or 'theory of meaning', is to explain how the sense of a sentence is determined by the senses of its parts. The second task, the articulation of a 'theory of force' (sometimes also called 'pragmatics'), is to explain, taking for granted an account of the thoughts expressed by sentences, the different speech acts into which they may enter. For example, it falls to the theory of meaning to describe the content of 'Lemurs are native to London' and to show how that thought is determined by the senses of the sentence's constituent components. It falls to the theory of force to discover what, beyond the apprehension of that thought, is involved in asking 'Are lemurs native to London?', in wishing 'Oh, would that lemurs were native to London!', and so on. Should the theory of force need to make reference to the mental states of agents, then it is not merely helpful to divide an account of linguistic understanding and use into these two components but, Frege would insist, essential if we are to keep psychology from intruding into an account of sense (see Pragmatics; Speech acts).

5 Objectivity and privacy

In the previous section, we saw that Frege insists on the objectivity of thoughts (and senses generally), intending by this that different speakers can attach the very same thoughts to their sentences. There is a second way in which Frege takes thoughts to be objective. To say that thoughts are shareable is compatible with saying that their existence and properties are dependent upon human activity. Frege's view seems to be that thoughts are also objective in that they exist independently of human activity. Thoughts are not created or shaped by the process of thinking; they exist regardless of whether we have apprehended them, regardless of whether we shall ever apprehend them. Thoughts await our grasp in somewhat the way that physical objects await our observation, though the latter are located in space and time whereas thoughts are not.

These two kinds of objectivity – shareability and independence – are taken by Frege to apply to truth as well, which he considers a property of thoughts. There are not different properties – say, 'true-for-you' and 'true-for-me' – which are private unto individuals. There is just one property, being true, which some thoughts have and others lack. Furthermore, whether a thought possesses this property is in no way dependent upon our capacity to recognize that it does. A thought's being true must be sharply distinguished from our believing it to be true or our being justified in taking it to be true. On Frege's view, the truth of a thought is not dependent upon our beliefs, not even upon our beliefs in some ideal epistemic situation. Truth is one thing, our recognition of truth something else entirely. This position regarding the independence of truth, present throughout Frege's writings, is a robust realist motif in his thought, the evaluation of which has occupied centre-stage of much contemporary philosophy of language (see Realism and antirealism §4).

Since on Frege's view a sentence is true if and only if it refers to the value the True, his realism amounts to saying that a sentence refers to what it does independently of our recognition of this fact. But a sentence refers to an object only via its sense (the thought it expresses), which is what determines its reference. And its sense is not something that it has independently of speakers (after all, an expression – like 'chat', for example – can have one sense in one language and another in another), but is associated with it through human activity. Putting all this together, we see that, according to Frege, humans associate senses with linguistic expressions – this is what their understanding of language consists of – on account of which those expressions take on references whose identity may remain forever unknown.

That such a realism should follow from the senses attached to expressions forces our attention not only to Frege's notion of sense but, relatedly, to his conception of what it is to grasp a sense and associate it with an expression. Frege's anti-psychologism with regard to sense is not extended by him to an account of the grasping of sense, for in his few remarks about the subject he appears to avow a psychological picture of the process of apprehending a thought, of judging it to be true and so on (see 'Logik' 1897). Given his view of the privacy of mental events, it might seem that for Frege one cannot always determine which thought another has associated with a sentence: not that one cannot apprehend the same thought as another (for one feature of the objectivity of thoughts, that they can be grasped by all alike, guarantees that one can); but that one cannot always ascertain that one has.

That a speaker's linguistic understanding might remain private is a view that has troubled many, especially those influenced by the work of Ludwig Wittgenstein (see Private language argument). Michael Dummett, the most influential interpreter of Frege's philosophy (see Dummett 1973), argues that, while much remains of lasting value in Frege's views on language, they should be modified in such a way that not only must senses be graspable by all, something on which Frege already insists, but the attachment of senses to expressions must be accessible as well; that is, the nature of a speaker's linguistic understanding must be a thoroughly public affair (see Private states and language). Once these modifications are made, Dummett claims, important consequences will follow about which senses can be coherently grasped: if the only intelligible senses are those the grasp of which is subject to public inspection, then we must be sceptical of any analysis of linguistic understanding in terms of senses that underwrite realism and we should instead consider seriously analyses employing senses that do not countenance the possibility of sentences being true independently of all potential human knowledge. Both Dummett's argument and his assumptions have been disputed, and the controversy continues to be a lively one. This is not an issue about which Frege explicitly said much, but it is among the many deep debates on the nature of language and thought which his work has made possible.

6   Contributions to logic

Infamous for using a notation difficult to learn to read, Frege's *Begriffsschrift* is one of the greatest logical works ever written. (Its full title in English is *Conceptual Notation: a Formula Language, Modelled Upon That of Arithmetic, for Pure Thought*.) It contains a number of major innovations, two of which are of foundational importance for contemporary logic: a satisfactory logical treatment of generality and the development of the first formal system. *Begriffsschrift* also introduces (what are essentially) truth tables, contains Frege's definition of the ancestral (§9) and sows the seeds of his philosophy of language (§§2–5).

Let us first discuss Frege's treatment of generality, that is, his logical analysis of sentences containing such words as 'everything', 'something', 'no one' and the like. The foundation for this is Frege's predicate–singular term analysis of simple sentences (§2). Sentences such as 'Tony is alive' contain a singular term, 'Tony', and a predicate, '( ) is alive'. We can extend this analysis to such sentences as 'Everything is alive' by drawing 'upon [the formula language of] arithmetic'. In arithmetic, a sentence containing a variable, 'x', is taken to be true if and only if a true sentence results no matter what x is supposed to be. For example, '$x + 2 = 2 + x$' is true if and only if, no matter what x may be, $x + 2 = 2 + x$. So, if we allow the argument of '( ) is alive' to be a variable, the resulting sentence 'x is alive' may be taken to express the generalization of 'Tony is alive'; it will be true if and only if, no matter what x may be, x is alive. Similarly, 'Everything is not alive' may be represented as 'x is not alive'. For, given the convention just explained, this will be true if and only if, no matter what x may be, x is not alive. But, as a little experimentation will show (and as can be proven), it is impossible to represent such sentences as 'Not everything is alive', so long as we use variables in this way alone. Nor can one so express 'If everything is alive, then snow is black'. One could try to represent it as 'If x is alive, then snow is black'. But this actually represents 'Everything is such that, if it is alive, then snow is black' (§11).

What is required here is some way of confining the generality expressed by the variable to a part of the sentence. In his informal discussions, Frege uses the phrase 'no matter what x may be' to do this (for example, §12). We may then represent 'Not everything is alive' as 'It is not the case that, no matter

what x may be, x is alive'; and 'If everything is alive, then snow is black' as 'If, no matter what x may be, x is alive, then snow is black'. The phrase 'no matter what x may be', and its placement in the sentence, is said to delimit the 'scope' of the variable (see SCOPE). Frege's most vital discovery is not that variables may be used to indicate generality, but that variables have scope; his most significant innovation, the development of a notation in which scope can be represented, that is, his introduction of the *quantifier*.

Frege's second fundamental contribution was his construction of the first formal system. A formal system, as Frege conceives it, has three parts: first, a highly structured 'language' in which thoughts may be expressed; second, precisely specified 'axioms', or basic truths, about the subject matter in question; and third, 'rules of inference' governing how one sentence may be inferred from others already established. Frege believed that there were a number of advantages to carrying out proofs in such formal systems, for example, that giving a proof in a formal system would better one's understanding of the proof, by revealing precisely what principles it employs. Suppose, for example, that one wants to show that a given theorem can be proven without using the axiom of choice: the obvious method would be to prove the theorem without using the axiom. But how can one be sure that the axiom has not tacitly been employed (as it was in Richard Dedekind's proof of Theorem 159 in *Was sind und was sollen die Zahlen?* in 1888)? Proving the theorem in a formal system makes this possible: the axioms which may be used are clearly specified and steps in the proof may be taken only in accordance with certain rules. (Compare the Preface of *Begriffsschrift* to *Die Grundlagen der trithmetik* §2. Formal systems are important in contemporary logic for related reasons.)

The formal system of *Begriffsschrift* does not actually live up to the standards Frege imposes upon it: not all its rules of inference are explicitly stated. However, this complaint cannot be made about the system presented in Part I of his *Grundgesetze der Arithmetik* (1893). (The first-order fragment of this system is complete; the second-order fragment is a formulation of standard, second-order logic.) The rigour of Frege's formulation was not equalled until Kurt Gödel's work in the early 1930s, almost forty years later.

It is arguable that Frege goes even further and, in *Grundgesetze*, presents a semantics for his system; that is to say, he attempts to explain, rigorously, how the formal system is to be interpreted; how its symbols are to be understood. Using these explanations, he attempts to prove that the axioms of the system, so interpreted, are true and that the rules of the system, so interpreted, preserve truth (that is, in technical parlance, to prove the system's soundness). If these controversial claims are correct, then Frege may also be credited with having anticipated, to a limited extent, the development of model theory.

7 Die Grundlagen der Arithmetik: *three fundamental principles*

In the Preface to *Begriffsschrift*, Frege announced his interest in determining whether the basic truths of arithmetic could be proven 'by means of pure logic'. Kant's answer had been negative. According to Kant, the truths of arithmetic are synthetic a priori: for example, knowledge of '7 + 5 = 12' requires appeal to intuition (see KANT, I. §§4–5). One of Frege's main goals in his *Die Grundlagen der Arithmetik* (*The Foundations of Arithmetic*) was to refute this view by giving purely logical proofs of the basic laws of arithmetic, thereby showing that arithmetical truths can be known independently of any intuition. Frege conceived the formal system of *Begriffsschrift* as an important prerequisite for this project: without it, it would be impossible to determine whether the complex proofs required do indeed depend only upon axioms of 'pure logic'.

There has been some controversy about what motivated Frege's logicism – his view that the truths of arithmetic are truths of logic (see LOGICISM). Frege says that his project is inspired by both mathematical and philosophical concerns (§§1–3). Some, notably Paul Benacerraf, have defended the view that Frege was interested in philosophical problems only in so far as they were susceptible of mathematical resolution. However that may be, Mark Wilson and Jamie Tappenden have argued that there are important connections between Frege's work on arithmetic and then recent developments in geometry to which he would have been exposed during his graduate career.

Grundlagen is important for a number of reasons. The philosophy of arithmetic developed in the book is of continuing interest. Moreover, a large number of more specific theses propounded there have had a profound influence on later philosophers, including Ludwig Wittgenstein, W.V. Quine and Michael Dummett, to name but three. More generally, *Grundlagen* is arguably the first work of analytic philosophy. At crucial points in the book, Frege makes 'the linguistic turn': that is, he recasts an ontological or epistemological question as a question about language. Unlike some 'linguistic' philosophers, his purpose is not to dissolve the philosophical problem – to unmask it as a 'pseudo-problem' – but to reformulate it so that it can be solved.

According to Frege, his work in *Grundlagen* is guided by 'three fundamental principles' he states in the Preface:

> always to separate sharply the psychological from the logical, the subjective from the objective;
> never to ask for the meaning of a word in isolation, but only in the context of a proposition;
> never to lose sight of the distinction between concept and object.
>
> (1884: x)

All of these are sufficiently important to warrant separate discussion. The first, which announces Frege's opposition to 'psychologism', has been discussed in §§4–5; the second, which is called 'the context principle', will be discussed in §8 below.

The third principle, which distinguishes the sorts of things singular terms denote – objects – from the sorts of things predicates denote – concepts – has already been discussed in §2. Of present interest is the application Frege makes of this distinction in *Grundlagen* §§45–54. Just prior to these sections, Frege has been concerned with what numbers are, his results having been almost entirely negative: numbers are neither physical objects; nor collections or properties of such; nor subjective ideas. Frege now suggests that progress may be made by asking to what, exactly, number is ascribed. The crucial observation is that different numbers seem to be assignable to the same thing: of a pack of cards, for example, one could say that it was one pack or fifty-two cards. Frege realizes that this might suggest that ascription of number is subjective; dependent upon our way of thinking about the object in question (§§25–6). But what is different in our way of regarding the pack is, specifically, the 'concept' we choose to employ: that denoted by '( ) is a pack' in the one case, or by '( ) is a card' in the other. If, with Frege, we insist that concepts, and facts about them, can be just as objective as objects and facts about them (see also 'Function and Concept' §48), there is no need to regard number as subjective. Rather, we must acknowledge that number is ascribed not to objects, nor to collections thereof, but to concepts:

> If I say 'Venus has 0 moons', there simply does not exist any moon or agglomeration of moons for anything to be asserted of; but what happens is that a property is assigned to the *concept* 'moon of Venus', namely that of including nothing under it. If I say, 'the King's carriage is drawn by four horses', then I assign the number four to the concept 'horse that draws the King's carriage'.
>
> (§46; emphasis added)

(Note that we will use '"moon of Venus"' and '( ) is a moon of Venus' to denote the same concept.) As Frege famously puts the point in §55: 'the content of a statement of number is an assertion about a concept'.

Observe here how Frege's interest in what numbers are has led him to an interest in the nature of ascriptions of number and, in particular, to an investigation of the 'logical form' of such statements. According to Frege, the most fundamental way of referring to a number is by means of an expression of the form 'the number belonging to the concept *F*'; for example, 'the number belonging to the concept "moon of the earth"' refers to the number one, for there is just one object that is a moon of the earth. This seemingly innocuous linguistic claim plays a crucial role in Frege's account of what numbers are.

8 Die Grundlagen der Arithmetik: *the context principle*

Frege denied both that numbers are physical objects and that they are objects of intuition, in Kant's sense. In *Grundlagen* §62, he therefore raises the question of how 'numbers [are] given to us, if we cannot have any ideas or intuitions of them'. This question is plainly epistemological, concerning how we can have knowledge of the objects (and so the truths) of arithmetic. What is astonishing is how Frege sets about answering it: 'Since it is only in the context of a proposition that words have any meaning, our problem becomes this: to define the sense of a proposition in which a number word occurs.' As Michael Dummett has emphasized, Frege here makes 'the linguistic turn' in a profound way: what was plainly an epistemological problem is converted into one about language. The question of how we can have knowledge about numbers becomes the question of how we refer to – that is, succeed in talking about – numbers.

Frege suggests that this question can be answered by examining whole sentences in which names of numbers occur. It is here that the second of Frege's fundamental principles, the context principle, is at work. Frege rejects any requirement that he should point out or, in some other way, display numbers for his audience. He has already asserted that this would be impossible, since numbers cannot be encountered in perception (we have no 'ideas' of them) or in intuition. Rather, Frege insists, one's ability to refer to numbers should be explained in terms of one's understanding of complete sentences in which names of numbers are employed. That is to say, Frege refuses to say what 'zero' refers to except to say what such sentences as 'Zero is the number belonging to the concept "moon of Venus"' mean. More precisely, he insists that to explain the meanings of such sentences is to say what 'zero' refers to.

Frege intends this view to be generalized: indeed, his own discussion of it does not concern numbers directly, but the analogous case of directions. So-called abstract objects pose serious philosophical problems, both ontological and epistemological. Frege's strategy for defending their existence and for defusing worries about our cognitive access to them is appealing and may well seem the only workable option. His general idea, that our capacity to refer to objects of a given kind may be explained only in terms of our understanding of sentences containing names of them, has been of continuing influence.

To return to our main thread, the immediate goal is to explain the meaning of sentences in which reference is made to numbers. Frege claims that, when we are concerned with names of *objects*, the most important such sentences are those asserting an identity. Because Frege takes numbers to be objects, he focuses upon such sentences as 'The number belonging to the concept "plate on the table" is the same as that belonging to the concept "guest at dinner"'. Frege observes that this sentence will be true if and only if there is a way of assigning plates to guests such that each guest gets exactly one plate, and each plate exactly one guest; that is, if and only if there is a one-to-one correlation between the plates and the guests. More generally, say that the concept *F* is equinumerous with the concept *G* if and only if there is a one-to-one correlation between the objects falling under *F* and those falling under *G*. Then the thought is this: the number belonging to the concept F = the number belonging to the concept G if and only if the concept *F* is equinumerous with the concept *G*. Since Frege introduces it with a quotation from Hume, this is sometimes called 'Hume's Principle' (1884: §§55–63). The principle had been known for some time, but it was only in the work of Georg Cantor that its mathematical significance was fully realized (see SET THEORY).

Of course, if Hume's Principle is to play any role in Frege's attempt to prove the axioms of arithmetic from logical principles alone, the notion of equinumerosity must be definable in purely logical terms. But Frege shows that it is, if the general theory of relations is accepted as part of logic (§§70–2).

For reasons which are not entirely clear, Frege rejects the claim that Hume's Principle suffices to explain numerical identities. His stated reason (§66; compare §56) is that it fails to decide whether Julius Caesar is the number zero! But there is little agreement about the point of this complaint or about its force. Still, Hume's Principle continues to be important to Frege, since he insists that any correct explanation of numbers must have Hume's Principle as a (relatively immediate) consequence.

He himself settles upon an explicit definition of names of numbers: the number belonging to the concept F is to be the extension of the second-level concept '[ ] is a concept equinumerous with the concept F'. (Roughly, the extension of a concept is the collection of things that fall under that concept.) Frege shows how Hume's Principle may be derived from this definition (§73). To make the definition and proof precise, however, he has to appeal to some axiom concerning extensions. Frege's idea, developed in *Grundgesetze*, was that extensions could be characterized by means of a principle analogous to Hume's Principle, namely, his Basic Law V: the extension of the concept F is the same as that of the concept G if and only if the very same objects fall under the concepts F and G (*Grundgesetze* §§3, 20). Famously and unfortunately, however, Bertrand Russell showed Frege, in 1902, that the resulting theory of extensions is inconsistent, since Russell's paradox can be derived from Basic Law V in (standard) second-order logic (see PARADOXES OF SET AND PROPERTY).

9   Frege's formal theory of arithmetic

The story of Frege's work on arithmetic might well have ended there. In *Grundlagen*, Frege does sketch proofs of axioms for arithmetic (§§70–83) and, in *Grundgesetze*, offers formal versions of them (§§78–119). But little attention was paid to these proofs for almost a century, on the ground that Frege gave his proofs in an inconsistent theory, and anything can be proven in an inconsistent theory. Frege himself decided in about 1906 that no suitable reformulation of Basic Law V was forthcoming and, his wife having died in 1904, appears to have become deeply depressed. He published nothing at all between 1908 and 1917 and only three further articles after that.

Closer attention to the structure of Frege's proofs reveals something interesting, however. As already stated, Frege requires that his explicit definition of names of numbers imply Hume's Principle, and he shows that it does (given Basic Law V). But neither the explicit definition nor Basic Law V is used essentially in the proof of any other arithmetical theorem; these other theorems are proven using only second-order logic and Hume's Principle. Thus, Frege in fact proves that axioms for arithmetic can be derived in second-order logic from Hume's Principle alone. Frege himself knew as much, but, sadly, never appreciated the philosophical and mathematical significance of this result, now known as Frege's Theorem.

The details of Frege's proof of this result are beyond the scope of this discussion. But a few points are worth mentioning. First, one cannot actually prove each of the infinitely many truths of arithmetic from logical principles, or from anything else. So any attempt to show that all truths of arithmetic follow from logical principles, or from Hume's Principle, will depend upon the identification of some finite number of basic laws, or axioms, of arithmetic from which we are confident all other arithmetical truths will follow. The most famous such axioms are those due to Dedekind (though widely known as the Peano axioms). Frege employs his own axiomatization which, while similar, is importantly different and arguably more intuitive (*Grundgesetze*: §§128–57).

Second, Frege's hardest task is to prove that there are infinitely many numbers, and his method of doing so is extremely elegant. The basic idea is as follows. Begin by noting that 0 is the number belonging to the concept 'object not the same as itself' and then that 1 is the number belonging to the concept 'identical with 0'. Further, 2 is the number belonging to the concept 'identical with 0 or 1', and so on. More generally, if n is finite, then the number of the concept 'natural number less than or equal to n' is always one more than n, which implies that every finite number has a successor and (in the presence of the other axioms) that there are infinitely many numbers (*Grundlagen*: §§82–3; *Grundgesetze*: §§114–19).

Third, Frege needs, for a variety of reasons, to define the notion of a finite, or natural, number. He also needs to prove the validity of proof by induction, since one of his (and Dedekind's) axioms is, essentially, that such proofs are legitimate. Induction is a way of proving that all natural numbers fall under a concept F; a proof by induction proceeds by showing (1) that 0 falls under F and (2) that, if a number n falls under F, $n + 1$ must also fall under F. In essence, Frege *defines* the natural numbers as those objects for which induction works. According to Frege's definition, a number is a natural number if and only if it falls under every concept F which is a concept $(1')$ under which 0 falls and $(2')$ which is 'hereditary in the number series', that is, under which $n + 1$ falls whenever n does. It then follows, immediately, that proof by induction is valid: if F is a concept satisfying (1) and (2), then, since F is then a concept satisfying $(1')$ and $(2')$, every natural number must fall under it, by definition.

It is possible to see, intuitively, that this is a good definition, that is, that what Frege calls 'the natural numbers', the things that fall under every concept satisfying $(1')$ and $(2')$, *really are* the natural numbers. Certainly, if x is a natural number, then it falls under every concept satisfying $(1')$ and $(2')$. Conversely, suppose that x falls under every concept satisfying $(1')$ and $(2')$. Well, the concept 'natural number' is such a concept: for ($1''$) 0 certainly falls under it, and ($2''$) whenever a number n falls under it, $n + 1$ also falls under it. So, since x falls under *every* concept satisfying ($1'$) and ($2'$), it must fall under this one, that is, it must be a natural number. Thus, falling under every concept satisfying ($1'$) and ($2'$) is both necessary and sufficient for being a natural number. (Objections can be made to this argument, chiefly on the grounds of its 'impredicativity'.)

This method of definition may be generalized to furnish a definition of the 'ancestral' of any given relation. Frege's definition of the ancestral, introduced in *Begriffsschrift* (and independently discovered by Dedekind), is of quite general importance in mathematics.

Frege's formal work in *Grundgesetze* does not end with his proof of the arithmetical axioms. He goes on to develop purely logical definitions both of finitude and of infinitude; he proves the so-called categoricity theorem, that any two structures which satisfy his axioms for arithmetic are isomorphic; and he proves the validity of definition by induction. (These last two results were first proven by Dedekind.) There is also some reason to believe that Frege was interested in proving results now known to depend upon the axiom of choice and that his investigations led him to discover – though not to communicate – this axiom some years before Ernst Zermelo's formulation of it in 1904. Finally, in later parts of *Grundgesetze*, Frege proves a number of preliminary results required for a logicist development of the theory of real numbers, but a projected third volume, which would have completed that part of the project, was abandoned in the wake of Russell's paradox.

10 The fate of Frege's logicism

Frege proved Frege's Theorem, that is, that axioms for arithmetic are (second-order) logical consequences of Hume's Principle. Of course, this would be of little interest but for the fact that, unlike Basic Law V, Hume's Principle is consistent. If, therefore, Hume's Principle could be argued to be a truth of logic, then the truths of arithmetic, being logical consequences of a truth of logic, would all be truths of logic and logicism would be vindicated! Work on Frege's philosophy of arithmetic has therefore tended to abstract from Frege's ill-fated explicit definition and to concern itself with the view Frege himself rejected, namely that names of numbers may be defined, or explained, by means of Hume's Principle.

No one nowadays really thinks that Hume's Principle is a truth of logic. Still, one might think that Hume's Principle is suitable as some kind of definition, or philosophical explanation, of names

of numbers. And, or so argues Crispin Wright, if the truths of arithmetic turn out to be logical consequences of an explanation, is that not almost as good as if they were truths of logic? This view is appealing precisely because Hume's Principle does seem to capture something very fundamental about (cardinal) numbers: saying that the number belonging to the concept F is the same as that belonging to G if and only if the concepts F and G are equinumerous just does seem a good way of explaining what (cardinal) numbers are. Still, there are serious worries. Saying that the extension of F is the same as the extension of G if and only if the same objects fall under F and G also *seems* to be a good way of explaining what extensions are – until one realizes this explanation is inconsistent. Hume's Principle is not inconsistent, of course, but one might wonder whether it can rightly be viewed as explanatory of what numbers are if such a kindred principle cannot rightly be viewed as explanatory of what extensions are. It is in the debate over this, the 'bad company objection' raised by George Boolos and Michael Dummett, that the fate of Frege's logicism will be decided.

See also: INTUITIONISTIC LOGIC AND ANTIREALISM; MEANING AND TRUTH

References and further reading

Dummett, M. (1973) *Frege: Philosophy of Language*, London: Duckworth, 2nd edn, 1992. (This is a long, difficult, but superb and seminal study of Frege's views on language and logic.)

Frege, G. (1884) *Die Grundlagen der Arithmetik: eine logisch-mathematische Untersuchung über den Begriff der Zahl*, Breslau: Koebner; trans. J.L. Austin, *The Foundations of Arithmetic: A Logico-Mathematical Enquiry into the Concept of Number*, Oxford: Blackwell, 2nd edn, 1980. (Includes criticism of then extant views about the nature of arithmetic, motivation for Frege's own proposal and informal proofs of the laws of arithmetic. One of Frege's most central texts.)

ALEXANDER GEORGE
RICHARD HECK

FREUD, SIGMUND (1856–1939)

Freud developed the theory and practice of psychoanalysis, one of the most influential schools of psychology and psychotherapy of the twentieth century. He established a relationship with his patients which maximized information relevant to the interpretation of their behaviour, and this enabled him to find explanations of dreams, symptoms and many other phenomena not previously related to desire. In consequence he was able radically to extend our common-sense psychology of motive.

On Freud's account everyday actions are determined by motives which are far more numerous and complex than people realize, or than common-sense understanding takes into account. The most basic and constant motives which influence our actions are unconscious, that is, difficult to acknowledge or avow. Such motives are residues of encounters with significant persons and situations from the past, often reaching back to early childhood; and they operate not to achieve realistic satisfaction, but rather to secure a form of pacification through representation. When we interpret what others say and do, we apply these patterns of satisfaction and pacification to explain their behaviour; and in so far as we succeed in understanding others in this way we support the patterns as empirical generalization. While we recognize that pacification consequent on genuine satisfaction is deeper and more lasting than that effected by representation alone, we also know that human desire outruns opportunities for satisfaction to such an extent that pacification via imagination is common. This is a view which psychoanalysis radically extends.

This understanding of the mind enabled Freud to give psychological accounts of neurosis and psychosis, and to explicate how the past gives significance to the present in normal mental functioning. Past desires, even those of infancy, are not psychologically lost; rather they are continually re-articulated through symbolism, so as to direct action towards their representational pacification throughout life. In this Freud provides both a radically holistic account of the causation of action and a naturalistic description of the generation of meaning in life. New goals acquire significance as representatives of the unremembered objects of our earliest and most visceral passions; and the depth of satisfaction we feel in present accomplishments flows from their unacknowledged pacification of unknown desires from the distant past. Thus, paradoxically, significant desires can remain forever flexible, renewable and satisfiable in their expressions, precisely because they are immutable, frustrated and unrelenting at the root.

See also: JUNG, C.G.; NIETZSCHE, F.; PSYCHOANALYSIS, METHODOLOGICAL ISSUES IN; PSYCHOANALYSIS, POST-FREUDIAN

JAMES HOPKINS

FRIENDSHIP

Philosophical interest in friendship has revived after a long eclipse. This is due largely to a renewed interest in ancient moral philosophy, in the role of emotion in morality, and in the ethical dimensions of personal relations in general. Questions about friendship are concerned with issues such as whether it is only an instrumental value (a means to other values), or also an intrinsic value – a value in its own right; whether it is a mark of psychological and moral self-sufficiency, or rather of deficiency; and how friendship-love differs from the unconditional love of *agapē*. Other issues at stake include how – if at all – friendship is related to justice; whether the particularist, partialist perspective of friendship can be reconciled with the universalist, impartialist perspective of morality; and whether friendship is morally neutral.

See also: MORALITY AND EMOTIONS; SEXUALITY, PHILOSOPHY OF; TRUST

NEERA K. BADHWAR

FROMM, ERICH
See FRANKFURT SCHOOL

FUNCTIONAL EXPLANATION

Explanations appealing to the functions of items are common in everyday discourse and in science: we say that the heart pumps blood because that is its function, and that the car fails to start because the ignition is not functioning. Moreover, we distinguish the functions things perform from other things they do: the heart makes a noise, but that is not one of its functions. Philosophical discussions in this area attempt to specify conditions under which it is appropriate to ascribe functions to items and under which it is appropriate to appeal to those functions in explanations. Difficulties arise because functions are normative: there is some sense in which items ought to perform their functions; failure to perform is a kind of error. Philosophical discussions investigate whether and how this normativity can be understood in scientifically respectable terms. This is important, because biological entities are among the most characteristically functional items. This issue gives rise to differing views as to what it is that functional explanations explain. One view is that they explain how a containing system achieves some goal or effect. Another is that functional explanations explain causally why the functional item exists.

See also: CAUSATION; TECHNOLOGY, PHILOSOPHY OF; TELEOLOGY

RICHARD N. MANNING

FUNCTIONALISM

The term 'functionalism' means different things in many different disciplines from architectural theory to zoology. In contemporary philosophy of mind, however, it is uniformly understood to stand for the view that mental states should be explained in terms of causal roles. So, to take a simple example, a functionalist in the philosophy of mind would argue that pains are states which are normally caused by bodily damage, and tend in turn to cause avoidance behaviour.

Functionalism is often introduced by an analogy between mental states and mechanical devices. Consider the notion of a carburettor, say. For something to be a carburettor it need not have any particular physical make-up. Carburettors can come in many different materials and shapes. What makes it a carburettor is simply that it plays the right causal role, namely that it mixes air with petrol in response to movements of the accelerator and choke. Similarly, argue functionalists, with the mind. The possession of mental states does not depend on the physical make-up of the brain; it depends only on its displaying the right causal structure. Since organisms with very different sorts of biological make-up, like octopuses and humans, can have states with the causal role of pain, say, it follows from functionalism that octopuses and humans can both be in pain.

There exists a number of different subspecies of functionalism. One important division depends on how the relevant causal roles are determined. 'Common-sense' functionalists take them to be fixed by common-sense psychology; 'scientific' functionalists take them to be fixed by the discoveries of scientific psychology. So, for example, common-sense functionalists will hold that emotions play the causal role that common-sense psychology ascribes to emotions, while scientific psychologists will argue that scientific psychology identifies this causal role.

Functionalism, of whatever subspecies, is open to a number of well-known criticisms. One central objection is that it cannot accommodate the conscious, qualitative aspect of mental life. Could not a machine share the causal structure of someone who was in pain, and thereby satisfy the functionalist qualification for pain, and yet have no conscious feelings?

It might seem that functionalists can respond to this difficulty by being more stringent about the requirements involved in the causal role of a given human sensation. But there is a danger that functionalism will then lose much of its appeal. The original attraction of functionalism was that its 'liberal' specification of causal roles allowed that humans could share mental states with non-humans.

This feature is likely to be lost if we switch to more 'chauvinist' specifications designed to explain why non-humans do not share our conscious life.

Another objection to functionalism is that it cannot account for mental representation. Functionalism focuses on the way mental states enter into causal structure. But it is doubtful that mental representation can be explained in purely causal terms.

Some philosophers argue that the issue of mental representation can be dealt with by adding some teleology to functionalism, that is by considering the biological purposes for which mental states have been designed, as well as their actual structure of causes and effects. However, once we do appeal to teleology in this way, it is not clear that we still need a functionalist account of representational states, for we can now simply identify such states in terms of their biological purposes, rather than their causal roles.

See also: MATERIALISM IN THE PHILOSOPHY OF MIND; REDUCTIONISM IN THE PHILOSOPHY OF MIND

DAVID PAPINEAU

FUTURE GENERATIONS, OBLIGATIONS TO

There are at least three different views concerning obligations to future generations. One is that morality does not apply here, future generations not being in any reciprocal relationship with us. Another is that, though we are not obliged to do anything for future generations, it would be praiseworthy to do so. A third view is that justice demands that we respect the interests of future generations.

Philosophers and others have discussed obligations in three main areas: the environment, and the damage inflicted upon it in pursuit of profit; savings and the accumulations of capital; and population policy.

Different theoretical approaches have been taken. According to utilitarianism, the interests of future people count equally with those of present people, and all interests are to be satisfied maximally. This may have very demanding implications. Contractarianism rests morality on the agreement of all affected parties. But whose views will be considered in the case of future generations? Perhaps the most plausible approach is communitarianism, according to which obligations can rest on a sense of community which stretches into the future.

See also: TECHNOLOGY AND ETHICS

AVNER DE-SHALIT

FUZZY LOGIC

The term 'fuzzy' refers to concepts without precise borders. Membership in a 'fuzzy' set – the set of things to which a 'fuzzy' concept (fuzzily) applies – is to be thought of as being a matter of degree. Hence, in order to specify a fuzzy set, one must specify for every item in the universe the extent to which the item is a member of the set. The engineer Lotfi Zadeh developed a theory of fuzzy sets and advocated their use in many areas of engineering and science. Zadeh and his zealous followers have attempted to develop fuzzy systems theory, fuzzy algorithms and even fuzzy arithmetic. The phrase 'fuzzy logic' has come to be applied rather imprecisely to any analysis that is not strictly binary. It does not refer to any particular formal logic, in the sense in which the term 'logic' is used by philosophers and mathematicians. ('Fuzzy logic' is sometimes used anachronistically to refer to any many-valued logic.)

CHARLES G. MORGAN

G

GADAMER, HANS-GEORG (1900–2002)

Hans-Georg Gadamer is best known for his philosophical hermeneutics. Gadamer studied with Martin Heidegger during his preparation of *Being and Time* (1927). Like Heidegger, Gadamer rejects the idea of hermeneutics as merely a method for the human and historical sciences comparable to the method of the natural sciences. Philosophical hermeneutics is instead about a process of human understanding that is inevitably circular because we come to understand the whole through the parts and the parts through the whole. Understanding in this sense is not an 'act' that can be secured methodically and verified objectively. It is an 'event' or 'experience' that we undergo. It occurs paradigmatically in our experience of works of art and literature. But it also takes place in our disciplined and scholarly study of the works of other human beings in the humanities and social sciences. In each case, understanding brings self-understanding.

Philosophical hermeneutics advocates a mediated approach to self-understanding on the model of a conversation with the texts and works of others. The concept of dialogue employed here is one of question and answer and is taken from Plato. Such understanding never becomes absolute knowledge. It is finite because we remain conditioned by our historical situation, and partial because we are interested in the truth that we come to understand. By grounding understanding in language and dialogue as opposed to subjectivity, Gadamer's philosophical hermeneutics avoids the danger of arbitrariness in interpreting the works of others.

Gadamer's most important publication is *Wahrheit und Methode* (Truth and Method) (1960). He also published four volumes of short works, *Kleine Schriften* (1967–77), containing important hermeneutical studies of Plato, Hegel, and Paul Celan among others. His many books and essays are collected into ten volumes (*Gesammelte Werke*). Gadamer was widely known as a teacher who practised the dialogue which is at the core of his philosophical hermeneutics.

KATHLEEN WRIGHT

GALILEI, GALILEO (1564–1642)

Galileo Galilei, one of the most colourful figures in the long history of the natural sciences, is remembered best today for two quite different sorts of reason. He has often been described as the 'father' of modern natural science because of his achievements in the fields of mechanics and astronomy, and for what today would be called his philosophy of science, his vision of how the practice of science should be carried on and what a completed piece of natural science should look like. While none of the elements of that philosophy was entirely new, the way in which he combined them was so effective that it did much to shape all that came after in the sciences. In the popular mind, however, as a continuing stream of biographies attest, it is his struggle with Church authority that remains the centre of attention, symbolic as it is of the often troubled, but always intriguing, relationship between science and religion.

See also: Cosmology; Explanation; Idealizations; Inductive inference; Oxford Calculators; Platonism, Renaissance; Religion and Science; Renaissance philosophy; Scientific method; Thought experiments

ERNAN MCMULLIN

GALILEO
See Galilei, Galileo

GAME-THEORETIC SEMANTICS
See Semantics, game-theoretic

GAME THEORY
See Decision and game theory; Semantics, game-theoretic

GANS, EDUARD
See Hegelianism

GASSENDI, PIERRE (1592–1655)

Pierre Gassendi, a French Catholic priest, introduced the philosophy of the ancient atomist Epicurus into the mainstream of European thought. Like many of his contemporaries in the first half of the seventeenth century, he sought to articulate a new philosophy of nature to replace the Aristotelianism that had traditionally provided foundations for natural philosophy. Before European intellectuals could accept the philosophy of Epicurus, it had to be purged of various heterodox notions. Accordingly, Gassendi modified the philosophy of his ancient model to make it conform to the demands of Christian theology.

Like Epicurus, Gassendi claimed that the physical world consists of indivisible atoms moving in void space. Unlike the ancient atomist, Gassendi argued that there exists only a finite, though very large, number of atoms, that these atoms were created by God, and that the resulting world is ruled by divine providence rather than blind chance. In contrast to Epicurus' materialism, Gassendi enriched his atomism by arguing for the existence of an immaterial, immortal soul. He also believed in the existence of angels and demons. His theology was voluntarist, emphasizing God's freedom to impose his will on the Creation.

Gassendi's empiricist theory of knowledge was an outgrowth of his response to scepticism. Accepting the sceptical critique of sensory knowledge, he denied that we can have certain knowledge of the real essences of things. Rather than falling into sceptical despair, however, he argued that we can acquire knowledge of the way things appear to us. This 'science of appearances' is based on sensory experience and can only attain probability. It can, none the less, provide knowledge useful for living in the world. Gassendi denied the existence of essences in either the Platonic or Aristotelian sense and numbered himself among the nominalists.

Adopting the hedonistic ethics of Epicurus, which sought to maximize pleasure and minimize pain, Gassendi reinterpreted the concept of pleasure in a distinctly Christian way. He believed that God endowed humans with free will and an innate desire for pleasure. Thus, by utilizing the calculus of pleasure and pain and by exercising their ability to make free choices, they participate in God's providential plans for the Creation. The greatest pleasure humans can attain is the beatific vision of God after death. Based on his hedonistic ethics, Gassendi's political philosophy was a theory of social contract, a view which influenced the writings of Hobbes and Locke.

Gassendi was an active participant in the philosophical and natural philosophical communities of his day. He corresponded with Hobbes and Descartes, and conducted experiments on various topics, wrote about astronomy, corresponded with important natural philosophers, and wrote a treatise defending Galileo's new science of motion. His philosophy was very influential, particularly on the development of British empiricism and liberalism.
See also: ATOMISM, ANCIENT; DEMOCRITUS; FREEDOM, DIVINE; WILL, THE

MARGARET J. OSLER

GEDANKENEXPERIMENTE
See THOUGHT EXPERIMENTS

GENEALOGY

'Genealogy' is an expression that has come into currency since the 1970s, a result of Michel Foucault's works *Surveiller et punir* (1975) (*Discipline and Punish*, 1977) and *The History of Sexuality* (1976, 1984). Foucault's use of the term continues Nietzsche's in his *On the Genealogy of Morals* (1887). For both philosophers, genealogy is a form of historical critique, designed to overturn our norms by revealing their origins. Whereas Nietzsche's method relies on psychological explanations, and attacks modern conceptions of equality in favour of a perfectionist ethic, Foucault's relies on microsociological explanations, and attacks modern forms of domination in favour of radical politics.

R. KEVIN HILL

GENERAL WILL

The fundamental claim for general will is that the members of a political community, as members, share a public or general interest or good which is for the benefit of them all and which should be put before private interests. When the members put the general good first, they are willing the general will of their community. The claim was given special and influential shape by Rousseau. He produced a comprehensive theory of the legitimacy of the state and of government, revolving around the general will. Some contend this solves the central problem of political philosophy – how the individual can both be obliged to obey the state's laws, and be free. If laws are made by the general will, aimed at the common good and expressed by all the citizens, the laws must be in accordance with the public interest and therefore in the interest of each, and each is obliged by the law yet free because they are its author. Rousseau's formulation has been much criticized. But others have found it essentially true and have variously adapted it.

PETER P. NICHOLSON

GENETIC MODIFICATION

Genetic modification is the heritable alteration of the genetic make-up of an organism. As a natural process this is as old as genes themselves, and has been utilized by human beings since the beginnings of agriculture. Recently, the term has come to apply specifically to newly developed DNA technologies, where the genome of an organism is modified using artificial techniques. These rely on the ability to cut DNA precisely, isolate desired fragments and insert them into a single cell of another organism. From this transformed cell a new multicellular organism can be regenerated. There is a wide range of applications of the new technology, from employing yeast to synthesize human insulin, to making crops resistant to pest and diseases. However, it has also attracted much opposition. It has been criticized for being unnatural, for posing an unassessable risk to the environment and to human health, and for providing an instrument for, the manipulation of human genetic make-up that might invite serious abuse.

MARK TESTER
EDWARD CRAIG

GENETICS

Genetics studies the problem of heredity, namely why offspring resemble their parents. The field emerged in 1900 with the rediscovery of the 1865 work of Gregor Mendel. William Bateson called the new field 'genetics' in 1905, and W. Johannsen used the term 'gene' in 1909. By analysing data about patterns of inheritance of characters, such as yellow and green peas, Mendelian geneticists infer the number and type of hypothetical genes. The major components of the theory of the gene, which proposed the model of genes as beads on a string, were in place by the 1920s. In the 1930s, the field of population genetics emerged from the synthesis of results from Mendelian genetics with Darwinian natural selection. Population geneticists study the distribution of genes in the gene pool of a population and changes caused by selection and other factors. The 1940s and 1950s saw the development of molecular genetics, which investigates problems about gene reproduction, mutation and function at the molecular level.

Philosophical issues arise: the question about the evidence for the reality of hypothetical genes, and the status of Mendel's laws, given that they are not universal generalizations. Debates have occurred about the nature of the relation between Mendelian and molecular genetics. Population genetics provides the perspective of the gene as the unit of selection in evolutionary theory. Molecular genetics

and its accompanying technologies raise ethical issues about humans' genetic information, such as the issue of privacy of information about one's genome and the morality of changing a person's genes. The nature–nurture debate involves the issue of genetic determinism, the extent to which genes control human traits and behaviour.

See also: GENETICS AND ETHICS; SPECIES

LINDLEY DARDEN

GENETICS AND ETHICS

The identification of human genes poses problems about the use of resources, and about ownership and use of genetic information, and could lead to overemphasis of the importance of genetic make-up. Genetic screening raises problems of consent, stigmatization, discrimination and public anxiety. Counselling will be required, but whether this can facilitate individual choice is unclear. It will also involve problems of confidentiality. On the other hand genetic knowledge will pave the way for genetic therapies for hereditary disease. This raises the question whether a therapy which alters an individual at the genetic level is different in kind from conventional medical treatment. Genetic alterations passed on to future generations raise problems regarding consent. Genetic intervention could also be used to make 'improvements' in human genetic potential, leading to anxieties about eugenic attempts to design the species. Transgenics, the introduction of foreign genes into a genome, raises questions about the integrity of species boundaries and the assessment of risk.

See also: APPLIED ETHICS; BIOETHICS; CLONING; GENETICS; TECHNOLOGY AND ETHICS

RUTH CHADWICK

GENTILE, GIOVANNI (1875–1944)

Best known as the self-styled philosopher of Fascism, Gentile, along with Benedetto Croce, was responsible for the ascendance of Hegelian idealism in Italy during the first half of the twentieth century. His 'actual' idealism or 'actualism' was a radical attempt to integrate our consciousness of experience with its creation in the 'pure act of thought', thereby abolishing the distinction between theory and practice. He held an extreme subjectivist version of idealism, and rejected both empirical and transcendental arguments as forms of 'realism' that posited the existence of a reality outside thought.

His thesis developed through a radicalization of Hegel's critique of Kant that drew on the work of the nineteenth-century Neapolitan Hegelian

Bertrando Spaventa. He argued that it represented both the natural conclusion of the whole tradition of Western philosophy, and had a basis in the concrete experience of each individual. He illustrated these arguments in detailed writings on the history of Italian philosophy and the philosophy of education respectively. He joined the Fascist Party in 1923 and thereafter placed his philosophy at the service of the regime. He contended that Fascism was best understood in terms of his reworking of the Hegelian idea of the ethical state, a view that occasionally proved useful for ideological purposes but which had little practical influence.

RICHARD BELLAMY

GERMAN IDEALISM

From the late eighteenth century until the middle of the nineteenth, German philosophy was dominated by the movement known as German idealism, which began as an attempt to complete Kant's revolutionary project: the derivation of the principles of knowledge and ethics from the spontaneity and autonomy of mind or spirit. However, German idealists produced systems whose relation to Kant is controversial, due to their emphasis on the absolute unity and historical development of reason.

As a movement to complete Kant's project, German idealism was punctuated by controversies about whether certain Kantian distinctions constitute *dualisms* – unbridgeable gaps between elements whose underlying unity must be demonstrated – and about how such dualisms can be overcome (see KANT, I. §3). One controversy concerned the distinction between the form of knowable objects – contributed by the mind, according to Kant – and the *matter* of sensation – contributed by mind-independent things-in-themselves. Jacobi objected that things-in-themselves lay beyond the boundaries of human knowledge, so Kant should profess 'transcendental ignorance' about the origin of sensible matter, leaving open the possibility that reality is mind-dependent. Another controversy concerned Kant's distinction between the spatio-temporal forms of sensibility and the categorial forms of understanding. Maimon argued that unless the underlying unity of this distinction were demonstrated, the applicability of categories to sensible objects could not be demonstrated against sceptics like HUME. Instead of defeating scepticism as he intended, some thought Kant had ensured its triumph by establishing unbridgeable dualisms between mind and reality, and between understanding and sensibility.

In the 1790s, some Kantians – notably REINHOLD, FICHTE and SCHELLING – sought to complete Kant's project through systematization. Troublesome dualisms would be overcome by positing distinct mental forms, as well as the distinction between mind and reality, as necessary conditions of the mind's free and unitary activity, and thus as necessary elements of a unified system. However, other Kantians – notably Buhle – accused the systematizers of undermining the distinctness of form and matter, and of attempting to generate matter from pure form. Meanwhile the systematizers, seeking to defeat scepticism, claimed metaphysical knowledge grounded in intellectual intuition of the mind's spontaneity. But Kant had explicitly denied that humans could attain such knowledge.

Professing continued allegiance to Kant despite these apparent departures, some systematizers – notably Fichte – claimed that Kant's teaching was only intelligible from a special standpoint and that, having attained that standpoint, they were expressing Kant's spirit, if not his letter. However, in his 1799 *Open Letter on Fichte's Wissenschaftslehre*, Kant publicly repudiated all attempts to discern his philosophy's spirit from a special standpoint and rejected any endeavour to bridge the gap between form and matter. But those who were repudiated did not change their ways. Finding Kant unable to complete the revolution he had started, they henceforth constructed their systems more independently of Kant's writings. The influence of pre-Kantian philosophers, notably SPINOZA, was explicitly acknowledged.

In order to overcome Kantian dualisms without ignoring his distinctions, Idealists produced a variety of developmental monisms (see FICHTE, J.G.; SCHELLING, F.W.J. VON; HEGEL, G.W.F. §4). Such systems portray a single, developing principle expressing itself in dualisms whose unstable, conflictual nature necessitates further developments. Thus reality is a developing, organic whole whose principle can be grasped and whose unity can be articulated in a philosophical system. But the dualisms encountered in everyday experience are not illusory. Rather, they are necessary stages in reality's development towards its full realization. This conception of development is often called dialectic.

Developmental monism emphasized the sociality and historicity of reason. Fichte was the first to emphasize sociality, arguing that the development of individual self-consciousness required consciousness of another mind, and deriving a theory of justice from the idea of one individual *recognizing* another as such. Hegel placed particular emphasis on historicity, portraying human history as a series of conflicts and resolutions culminating in a just society that would enable the reciprocal recognition of individuals, as well as the perfect self-recognition of reason at which philosophy had always aimed (see HEGEL, G.W.F. §8). Thus history – especially the history of philosophy – acquired unprecedented significance as the narrative of the mind's ascent to self-knowledge. And it was hoped that a philosophical account of society's historical development would correct the deficiencies of the French Revolution, which was often called the political equivalent of Kant's revolution.

Idealists disagreed about whether Kant's distinction between mind and nature was another problematic dualism. Schelling and Hegel argued that a systematic philosophy must portray nature as the mind's preconscious development. But Fichte regarded their philosophy of nature as a betrayal of Idealism that explained the mind in nonmental terms and deprived the mind of its autonomy. By 1801 the disagreement was explicit (see FICHTE, J.G.; SCHELLING, F.W.J. VON; HEGEL, G.W.F. §§3, 7).

Controversy about another putative dualism – between concept and intuition – ended the alliance between Schelling and Hegel. Without naming him, Hegel's *Phenomenology of Spirit* (1807) appeared to criticize Schelling's view that philosophy can only be understood by those innately able to intuit – to grasp non-discursively – the identity implicit in apparent dualisms. Hegel argued that the completed philosophical system must be conceptualized and rendered discursively intelligible to everyone. However, only those who transformed their accustomed ways of thinking could understand the system (see HEGEL, G.W.F. §§5, 6). So Hegel undertook to guide his readers through a series of transformations of consciousness representing the history of human thought, as well as the education of the individual. The Napoleonic wars forced Hegel from university life, but after his return in 1814, and especially after his move to Berlin in 1818, his version of idealism – with its portrayal of reason developing in both nature and culture towards conceptual articulation – became dominant.

However, Hegel died in 1831 and Schelling raised influential criticisms of Hegel when he began teaching in Berlin in 1841. In an inaugural lecture before an audience including Engels and Kierkegaard, Schelling argued that Hegel's system was an inevitably failed attempt to overcome the dualism between conceptual thought and intuited existence. Schelling's criticism was seminal for Marxism and existentialism and was more influential than his alternative proposals, which he had been developing under the influence of theosophy since 1809 (see EXISTENTIALISM; MARXISM, WESTERN; SCHELLING, F.W.J. VON; HEGELIANISM). The relationship between thought and existence remains problematic for post-idealist philosophy, and German idealism remains both an object of criticism and a source of insight.

References and further reading

Beiser, F. (2002) *German Idealism: The Struggle against Subjectivism, 1781–1801*, Cambridge, MA: Harvard University Press. (A gripping account of the development of the philosophies of Kant, Fichte, Holderlin, Novalis, Schlegel and Schelling.)

Franks, P. (2005) *All or Nothing: Systematicity, Transcendental Argument, and Skepticism in German Idealism*, Cambridge, MA: Harvard University Press. (A critical investigation of the problems to which the German idealist project of system-building is responding, and of the argumentative methods which the project calls for.)

Pinkard, T. (2002) *German Philosophy, 1760–1860: The Legacy of Idealism*, Cambridge: Cambridge University Press. (A lucid and accessible overview of German philosophy from Kant to Hegel and beyond.)

PAUL FRANKS

GESTALT PSYCHOLOGY

The term 'Gestalt' was introduced into psychology by the Austrian philosopher Christian von Ehrenfels. 'Gestalt', in colloquial German, means 'shape' or 'structure'. Ehrenfels demonstrates in his essay of 1890 that there are certain inherently structural features of experience that must be acknowledged in addition to simple tones, colours and other mental 'atoms' or 'elements' if we are to do justice to the objects towards which perception, memory and abstract thinking are directed. His essay initiated a reaction against the then still dominant atomism in psychology, a reaction that led in turn to the ideas on 'cerebral integration' of the so-called Berlin school of Gestalt psychology and thence to contemporary investigations of 'neural networks' in cognitive science. Many of the specific empirical facts discovered by the Gestaltists about the perception of movement and contour, about perceptual constancy and perceptual illusions, and about the role of 'good form' in perception and memory have been absorbed into psychology as a whole.

See also: CONNECTIONISM; PERCEPTION

BARRY SMITH

GETTIER PROBLEM

The emergence of the Gettier problem was an episode in the history of the project of trying to give necessary and sufficient conditions for knowledge. It was long supposed that knowledge could be defined as justified true belief. But in 1963 Edmund Gettier published a very short paper arguing that this was not so: there can be cases of justified true belief which are not acceptable as cases of knowledge, hence the proposed conditions are not sufficient.

Gettier described two alleged counter-examples of this kind – cases of justified true belief which are not knowledge. But first he enunciated two general principles which quickly yield a recipe for generating such counter-examples:

1   In any sense of 'justified' in which being justified in believing that p can be thought a necessary condition of knowing that p, it is possible to be justified in believing a proposition which is, in fact, false.

2   For any proposition p, if a subject S is justified in believing p, and p entails q, and S deduces q from p and accepts q as a result of this deduction, then S is justified in believing q.

If these are accepted (and neither is easy to deny), we proceed as follows. Exploiting (1), imagine circumstances in which a person is justified in believing some proposition p, which is in fact false. Now suppose this person validly to deduce from p another proposition q and to believe q as a result of this deduction. (Make sure that q is weaker than p, that is p entails it but it does not entail p.) Finally, so adjust the story that q turns out to be true (so long as q is logically weaker than p this will always be possible). Then, by (2), S's belief that q is a case of justified true belief. But surely S does not *know* that q? For so far as S is concerned the truth of q is wholly accidental: it is true not because of p – as S thought – but for some totally different reason of which S has no awareness.

Reactions have varied. Some have objected to the counter-examples themselves, others have accepted them and attempted to modify the definition of knowledge so as to avoid them. Others again have seen in them reason to rethink the whole project of defining knowledge in terms of necessary and sufficient conditions.

See also: INTERNALISM AND EXTERNALISM IN EPISTEMOLOGY

EDWARD CRAIG

AL-GHAZALI, ABU HAMID (1058–1111)

Al-Ghazali is one of the greatest Islamic jurists, theologians and mystical thinkers. He learned various branches of the traditional Islamic religious sciences in his home town of Tus, Gurgan and Nishapur in the northern part of Iran. He was also involved in Sufi practices from an early age. Being recognized by Nizam al-Mulk, the vizir of the Seljuq sultans, he was appointed head of the Nizamiyyah College at Baghdad in AH 484/AD 1091. As the intellectual head of the Islamic community, he was busy lecturing on Islamic jurisprudence at the College, and also refuting heresies and responding to questions from all segments of the community. Four years later, however, al-Ghazali fell into a serious spiritual crisis and finally left Baghdad, renouncing his career and the world. After wandering in Syria and Palestine for about two years and finishing the pilgrimage to Mecca, he returned to Tus, where he was engaged in writing, Sufi practices and teaching his disciples until his death. In the meantime he resumed teaching for a few years at the Nizamiyyah College in Nishapur.

Al-Ghazali explained in his autobiography why he renounced his brilliant career and turned to Sufism. It was, he says, due to his realization that there was no way to certain knowledge or the conviction of revelatory truth except through Sufism. (This means that the traditional form of Islamic faith was in a very critical condition at the time.) This realization is possibly related to his criticism of Islamic philosophy. In fact, his refutation of philosophy is not a mere criticism from a certain (orthodox) theological viewpoint. First of all, his attitude towards philosophy was ambivalent; it was both an object of criticism and an object of learning (for example, logic and the natural sciences). He mastered philosophy and then criticized it in order to Islamicize it. The importance of his criticism lies in his philosophical demonstration that the philosophers' metaphysical arguments cannot stand the test of reason. However, he was also forced to admit that the certainty of revelatory truth, for which he was so desperately searching, cannot be obtained by reason. It was only later that he finally attained to that truth in the ecstatic state (*fana'*) of the Sufi. Through his own religious experience, he worked to revive the faith of Islam by reconstructing the religious sciences upon the basis of Sufism, and to give a theoretical foundation to the latter under the influence of philosophy. Thus Sufism came to be generally recognized in the Islamic community. Though Islamic philosophy did not long survive al-Ghazali's criticism, he contributed greatly to the subsequent philosophization of Islamic theology and Sufism.

See also: IBN RUSHD; IBN SINA

KOJIRO NAKAMURA

GILSON, ETIENNE
See THOMISM (§3)

GIVEN, PROBLEM OF
See PHENOMENOLOGY, EPISTEMIC ISSUES IN

GLOBALIZATION

Globalization is one of the most hotly contested issues in contemporary social inquiry and public discussion. The debates mainly revolve around six points: definition, measurement, chronology, causes, consequences, and policy responses.

In regard to definition, five broad usages of 'globalization' can be distinguished: internationalization, liberalization, universalization, Westernization, and deterritorialization. Although these conceptions overlap to some extent, their emphases are substantially different.

With respect to magnitude, 'globalists' suggest that today's world is thoroughly globalized, whereas sceptics dismiss every claim of globalization as myth. Most observers agree that the incidence of globalization has been uneven, and that some countries and social circles have experienced globality more than others.

The chronology of globalization depends in good part on the definition adopted. Internationalization, liberalization, universalization and Westernization can all be traced back at least several centuries, if not millennia. On the other hand, deterritorialization has transpired on a large scale only since the third quarter of the twentieth century.

Accounts of the causal dynamics of globalization depend upon one's theoretical persuasion. However, most researchers explain globalization in some way as a product of modernity and/or capitalism. Many studies also highlight the enabling effects of certain technological developments and certain regulatory arrangements.

In terms of its consequences for social structure, some analysts treat globalization as radically transformative. Such accounts link globalization to the end of the state, the end of nationality, the end of modernity, and more. In contrast, other assessments downplay any suggestion of social change in connection with globalization. Still others conclude that globalization generates an interplay of changes and continuities in social structure.

Finally, in regard to policy, neoliberal approaches argue that globalization should be guided by market forces. In contrast, reformist strategies maintain that globalization should be deliberately steered with public policies, including in particular through suprastate laws and institutions. From a more radical position, traditionalists seek to ' de-globalize' and return to a pre-global *status quo ante*. Other radicals advocate a continuation of globalization, but in tandem with a revolutionary social transformation, for example, to a post-capitalist society.

See also: INTERNATIONAL RELATIONS, PHILOSOPHY OF; STATE, THE

JAN AART SCHOLTE

GNOSTICISM

Gnosticism comprises a loosely associated group of teachers, teachings and sects which professed to offer 'gnosis', saving knowledge or enlightenment, conveyed in various myths which sought to explain the origin of the world and of the human soul and the destiny of the latter. Everything originated from a transcendent spiritual power; but corruption set in and inferior powers emerged, resulting in the creation of the material world in which the human spirit is now imprisoned. Salvation is sought by cultivating the inner life while neglecting the body and social duties unconnected with the cult. The Gnostic movement emerged in the first and second centuries AD and was seen as a rival to orthodox Christianity, though in fact some Gnostic sects were more closely linked with Judaism or with Iranian religion. By the fourth century its influence was waning, but it persisted with sporadic revivals into the Middle Ages.

CHRISTOPHER STEAD

GOD, ARGUMENTS FOR THE EXISTENCE OF

Introduction

Arguments for the existence of God go back at least to Aristotle, who argued that there must be a first mover, itself unmoved. All the great medieval philosophers (Arabic and Jewish as well as Christian) proposed and developed theistic arguments – for example, Augustine, al-Ghazali, Anselm, Moses Maimonides, Thomas Aquinas and Duns Scotus. Most of the great modern philosophers – in particular René Descartes, Gottfried Leibniz and Immanuel Kant – have also offered theistic arguments. They remain a subject of considerable contemporary concern; the twentieth century has seen important work on all the main varieties of these arguments.

These arguments come in several varieties. Since Kant, the traditional Big Three have been the cosmological, ontological and teleological arguments. The cosmological argument goes back to Aristotle, but gets its classic statement (at least for European philosophy) in the famous 'five ways' of Aquinas, in particular his arguments for a first uncaused cause, a first unmoved mover, and a necessary being. According to the first-mover argument (which is a special case of the first-cause argument), whatever is moved (that is, caused to move) is moved by something else. It is impossible, however, that there should be an infinite series of moved and moving beings; hence there must be a first unmoved mover. Aquinas goes on to argue that a first mover would have to be both a first cause and a necessary being; he then goes on in the next parts (Ia, qq.3–11) of the *Summa theologiae* to argue that such a being must have the attributes of God.

The perennially fascinating ontological argument, in Anselm's version, goes as follows: God is by definition the being than which none greater can be conceived. Now suppose God did not exist. It is greater to exist than not to exist; so if God did not exist, a being greater than God could be conceived. Since God is by definition the being than which none greater can be conceived, that is absurd. Therefore the supposition that God does not exist implies an absurdity and must be false. This argument has had many illustrious defenders and equally illustrious attackers from Anselm's time to ours; the twentieth century has seen the development of a new (modal) version of the argument.

Aquinas' fifth way is a version of the third kind of theistic argument, the teleological argument; but it was left to modern and contemporary philosophy to propose fuller and better-developed versions of it. Its basic idea is simple: the universe and many of its parts look as if they have been designed, and the only real candidate for the post of designer of the universe is God. Many take evolutionary theory to undercut this sort of argument by showing how all of this apparent design could have been the result of blind, mechanical forces. Supporters of the argument dispute this claim and retort that the enormously delicate 'fine tuning' of the cosmological constants required for the existence of life strongly suggests design.

In addition to the traditional Big Three, there are in fact many more theistic arguments. There are arguments from the nature of morality, from the nature of propositions, numbers and sets, from intentionality, from reference, simplicity, intuition and love, from colours and flavours, miracles, play and enjoyment, from beauty, and from the meaning of life; and there is even an argument from the existence of evil.

1 Cosmological arguments

Cosmological arguments start from some obvious and general but a posteriori fact about the universe: that there are contingent beings, for example, or that things move or change. We find first steps towards such an argument in Plato (*Laws* 10); ARISTOTLE (§16) (*Metaphysics* 12; *Physics* 7, 8) gives it a fuller statement; the medieval Arabic (especially al-GHAZALI) and Jewish philosophers (especially Maimonides) gave elaborate statements of the argument; but its *locus classicus* (for Westerners, anyway) is the first three of the famous 'five ways' of Aquinas' *Summa theologiae*. Following Aquinas, DUNS SCOTUS presented a subtle and powerful version of the argument, and in modern times the most influential versions of the argument are to be found in the works of LEIBNIZ (§3) and Samuel CLARKE. (The most influential criticisms of the argument are given by HUME (§6) and KANT (§8).)

Following William Craig (1980), we may distinguish substantially three versions of the cosmological argument. First, the so-called *kalam* (Arabic, 'speculative theology') argument, developed by Arabic thinkers (for example, al-Kindi and al-Ghazali). Put most schematically, this argument goes as follows:

(1) Whatever begins to exist is caused to exist by something else.
(2) The universe began to exist.
(3) Therefore the universe was caused to exist; and the cause of its existence is God.

The second premise was supported by arguments for the conclusion that an 'actual infinite' is not possible: it is not possible, for example, that there have been infinitely many temporally non-overlapping beings each existing for at least a second; alternatively, it is not possible that an infinite number of seconds have elapsed. These arguments proceed by pointing out some of the paradoxes or peculiarities that an actual infinite involves (see INFINITY). For example, suppose there were a hotel with infinitely many rooms ('Hilbert's Hotel'). The hotel is full; a new guest arrives; despite the fact that each room is already occupied, the proprietor accommodates the guest by putting them in room 1, moving the occupant of room 1 to room 2, of room 2 to room 3, and in general the occupant of n to $n+1$. No problem! Indeed, when a large bus containing infinitely many new guests pulls up, they too can all be accommodated: for any odd-numbered room n, move its occupant into room $2n$ (moving the occupant of *that* room $n\star$ into $2n\star$, and so on), thus freeing up the infinitely many odd-numbered rooms. In fact, if it is a busy weekend and an infinite fleet of buses pulls up, each with infinitely many new guests, they too can all be easily accommodated. And the question is: is it really possible, in the broadly logical sense, that such a hotel could actually exist? The friend of the *kalam* argument thinks not, and adds that no other actual infinite is possible either. If so, then the universe has not existed for an infinite stretch of time, but had a beginning. Contemporary cosmological theory in physics has seemed to some to provide scientific, empirical support for the claim that the universe had a beginning; according to 'Big Bang' cosmology, the universe came into being something like 15 billion years ago, give or take a few billion (see COSMOLOGY).

Given that the universe has a beginning, the next step is to argue (by way of the first premise) that it must therefore have had a cause; it could not have popped into existence uncaused. And the final step is to argue that the cause of the universe would have to have certain important properties – properties of God.

The second kind of cosmological argument is the kind to be found in the first three of Aquinas' five ways. His second way, for example, goes like this:

(1) Many things in nature are caused.
(2) Nothing is a cause of itself.
(3) An infinite regress of essentially ordered efficient causes is impossible.
(4) Therefore, there is a first uncaused cause – 'to which', says Aquinas, 'everyone gives the name of God'.

There are two points of particular interest about this argument. First, Aquinas disagrees with a premise of the *kalam* argument, according to which it is impossible that there be an actual infinite. He argues that it cannot be proved that the universe had a beginning; he thinks it possible (though false) that the universe has existed for an infinite stretch of time. How then are we to understand premise (3)? Aquinas is here speaking of a certain kind of series, an 'essentially ordered' series, a series of causes in which any cause of an effect must be operating throughout the whole duration of the effect's operation. It is only such series, he says, that cannot proceed to infinity. (Aquinas gives the example of a stick moving a stone, a hand moving the stick, and so on.) So the upshot of the argument, if it is successful, is that there exists at least one thing which causes other things to exist, but is not itself caused to exist by anything else.

But could there not be many such things? And would each of them be God? This brings us to the second point of interest. Aquinas argues that there must be a first unmoved mover, a first uncaused cause, a necessary being, and the like; but his theistic argument is not finished there. In the next eight questions he argues that anything that was a first efficient cause would have to be immaterial, unchanging, eternal, simple and the possessor of all the perfections to be found in those things dependent upon it – in a word, God. It is therefore incorrect to follow the usual custom of criticizing Aquinas for hastily concluding that a first cause or unmoved mover or necessary being would have to be God.

The third sort of cosmological argument is associated especially with Leibniz and Samuel Clarke; according to this version of the argument, there must be a sufficient reason for the actuality of any contingent state of affairs. Therefore there must be a sufficient reason for the existence of any contingent being – but also, says Leibniz, for the whole series of contingent beings. This sufficient reason must be the activity of God.

2 Ontological arguments

Anselm's ontological argument has excited enormous controversy (see ANSELM OF CANTERBURY). Aquinas rejected it, Duns Scotus 'coloured' it a bit and then accepted it; DESCARTES (§6) and MALEBRANCHE endorsed it; like Duns Scotus, Leibniz thought it needed just a bit of work to be successful; Kant rejected it and delivered what many thought to be the final quietus (though others have found Kant's criticisms both intrinsically obscure and of doubtful relevance to the argument); and Schopenhauer thought it a 'charming joke'. Although in the twentieth century it was defended by (among others) Charles Hartshorne, Norman Malcolm and Alvin Plantinga, probably most contemporary philosophers reject the argument, thinking it a joke, but not particularly charming.

Anselm's version goes as follows:

Hence, even the fool is convinced that something exists in the understanding, at least, than which nothing greater can be conceived.... And assuredly that, than which nothing greater can be conceived, cannot exist in the understanding alone; for suppose it exists in the understanding alone; then it can be conceived to exist in reality; which is greater.

Therefore, if that, than which nothing greater can be conceived, exists in the understanding alone, the very being, than which nothing greater can be conceived is one, than which a greater can be conceived. But obviously this is impossible. Hence, there is no doubt that there exists a being, than which nothing greater can be conceived, and it exists both in the understanding and in reality.

(*Proslogion*, ch. 2)

This argument is a *reductio ad absurdum*: postulate the nonexistence of God, and show that this leads to an absurdity. Perhaps we can outline the argument as follows:

(1) A maximally great being (one than which nothing greater can be conceived) exists in the understanding (that is, is such that we can conceive of it).

(2) It is greater to exist in reality than to exist merely in the understanding.

(3) Therefore, if the maximally great being existed *only* in the understanding, it would be less than maximally great.

But it is impossible that the maximally great being be less than maximally great; hence this being exists in reality as well as in the understanding – that is, it exists. And clearly this maximally great being is God.

The earliest objection to this argument was proposed by Anselm's contemporary and fellow monk Gaunilo in his *On Behalf of the Fool* (Psalm 14: 'The fool has said in his heart "There is no God"'). According to Gaunilo, the argument must be defective, because we can use an argument of the very same form to demonstrate the existence of such absurdities as an island (or chocolate sundae, or hamster, for that matter) than which none greater can be conceived. (Says Gaunilo: 'I know not which I ought to regard as the greater fool: myself, supposing that I should allow this proof; or him, if he should suppose that he had established with any certainty the existence of this island.') But Anselm has a reply: the notion of a maximally great island, like that of a largest integer, does not make sense, cannot be exemplified. The reason is that the properties that make for greatness in an island – size, number of palm trees, quality of coconuts – do not have intrinsic maxima; for any island, no matter how large and no matter how many palm trees, it is possible that there be one even larger and with more palm trees. But the properties that make for greatness in a being – knowledge, power and goodness, for example – do have intrinsic maxima: omniscience, omnipotence and being perfectly good.

3 Ontological arguments (cont.)

The most celebrated criticism of the ontological argument comes from Immanuel Kant, who apparently argues in his *Critique of Pure Reason* (Transcendental Dialectic, bk II, ch. III, section 4) that if this argument were sound, the proposition 'there is a being than which none greater can be conceived' would have to be logically necessary; but there cannot be an existential proposition that is logically necessary. Sadly, his reason for making this declaration is itself maximally obscure. He adds that 'existence is not a real predicate', which is widely quoted as the principal objection to the argument. Unfortunately this dictum is of dubious relevance to

Anselm's argument and a dark saying in its own right. What might it mean to say that existence is not a real property or predicate? And if it is not, how is that relevant to the argument? Why should Anselm care whether it is or not?

Perhaps we can understand Kant as follows. The argument as stated begins with the assertion that a maximally great being exists in the understanding; the idea is that this much is obvious, whether or not this being also exists in reality (that is, actually exists). Anselm then goes on to reason about this being, arguing that a being with the properties this one has – of being maximally great – cannot exist only in the understanding, but must exist in reality as well. So the argument depends upon the assumption that there *is* a maximally great being, and now the question is: does this being actually exist? Use the term 'actualism' for the view that there are not (and could not be) things that do not exist; the things that exist are all the things there are. Note that if this is true, then existence is a very special property: it is redundant, in that it is implied by every other property; anything that has *any* property (including the property of being maximally great) also has existence. But if actualism is true, the ontological argument as formulated above cannot work. For if it is not possible that there be things that do not exist, then in saying initially that there is a maximally great being, one that at any rate exists in the understanding, we are already saying that there exists a maximally great being, thus begging the question. If no maximally great being exists, then there simply is no such thing as a maximally great being, in which case we cannot (following Anselm) suppose initially that the maximally great being does not exist in reality and then argue that this being would be greater if it did exist in reality. If actualism is true, existence is a redundant property; but then to say that there is a maximally great being that exists in the understanding is already to say that there really exists a maximally great being. So perhaps Kant's puzzling dictum should be seen as an early endorsement of actualism.

Of course Anselm might reply that the fault lies not with his argument, but with actualism; in any event, there are other versions that do not conflict with actualism. Charles Hartshorne claimed to detect two quite different versions of the argument in Anselm's work; the second version is consistent with actualism and thus sidesteps Kant's criticism. This version proceeds from the thought that a really great being would be one that would have been great even if things had been different; its greatness is stable across possible worlds, to put it in a misleading if picturesque way. So say that a being has *maximal excellence* in a given possible world W if and only if it is omnipotent, omniscient and wholly good in W; and say that a being has *maximal greatness* if it has maximal excellence in every possible world. Then the premise of the argument (thus restated) is simply:

Maximal greatness is possibly exemplified.

That is, it is possible that there be a being that has maximal greatness. But (given the widely accepted view that if a proposition is possibly necessary in the broadly logical sense, then it is necessary), it follows by ordinary modal logic that maximal greatness is not just possibly exemplified, but exemplified in fact. For maximal greatness is exemplified if and only if there is a being B such that the proposition

B is omnipotent and omniscient and wholly good (has maximal excellence)

is necessary. If maximal greatness is possibly exemplified, therefore, then some proposition of that sort is possibly necessary. By the above principle, whatever is possibly necessary is necessary; accordingly, that proposition is necessarily true and hence true.

So stated, the ontological argument breaches no laws of logic, commits no confusions and is entirely immune to Kant's criticism. The only remaining question of interest is whether its premise, that maximal greatness is possibly exemplified, is indeed true. That certainly seems to be a rational claim; but it is not one that cannot rationally be denied. A remaining problem with the argument, perhaps, is that it might be thought that the epistemic distance between premise and conclusion is insufficiently great. Once you see how the argument works, you may think that asserting or believing the premise is tantamount to asserting or believing the conclusion; the canny atheist will say that he does not believe it is possible that there be a maximally great being. But would not a similar criticism hold of any valid argument? Take any valid argument: once you see how it works, you may think that asserting or believing the premise is tantamount to asserting or believing the conclusion. The ontological argument remains as intriguing as ever.

4   Teleological arguments

Teleological arguments start from contingent premises that involve more specific features of the universe, features which in one way or another suggest that the universe has been designed by a conscious and intelligent being. These arguments have often been developed in close connection with modern science; they have been endorsed by many of the giants of modern science, including Isaac Newton. Here is a classic statement of the argument by William PALEY:

> In crossing a heath, suppose I pitched my foot against a *stone*, and were asked how the stone came to be there, I might possibly answer that for any thing I know to the contrary, it had lain there for ever: nor would it perhaps be very easy to show the absurdity of this answer. But suppose I had found a *watch* upon the ground and it should be inquired how the watch happened to be in that place, I should hardly think of the answer which I had before given, that, for any thing I know the watch might have always been there. Yet why should not this answer serve for the watch, as well as for the stone? For this reason and for no other: viz., that, when we come to inspect the watch, we perceive (what we could not discover in the stone) that its several parts are framed and put together for a purpose.
>
> (*Natural Theology* 1802)

Paley then points out that the universe and some of its parts – for example, living things and their organs – resemble a watch, in that they give the appearance of having been designed in order to accomplish certain purposes. An eye, for example, looks like an extremely subtle and sophisticated mechanism designed to enable its owner to see. But the only serious candidate for the post of designer of the universe is God.

Kant, who had little but contempt for the cosmological and ontological arguments, was much less dismissive of this one. He still rejected the argument, however, pointing out that at most it shows that it is likely that there is a designer or architect of the universe; and it is a long way from a designer to the God of the theistic religions, an almighty, omniscient, wholly good creator of the world, by whose power the universe sprang into being. Of course, a cosmic architect – a being who has designed our entire universe, with its elements ranging across many orders of magnitude from gigantic galaxies to the minutest things we know – is no mean conclusion, and it seems churlish to dismiss it with an airy wave in order to point out that there is something even stronger that the teleological argument does not show.

5   Teleological arguments (cont.)

Many people, however, have rejected the teleological argument even taken as an argument for a designer. The eighteenth-century proponents of the argument invariably mentioned the apparent teleology in the biological world; but (so say the critics) Darwin changed all that. We now know that the apparent design in the world of living things is *merely* apparent. The enormous variety of flora and fauna, those enormously elaborate and articulate mechanisms and finely detailed systems and organs such as the mammalian eye and the human brain give a powerful impression of design; but in fact they are the product of such blind mechanisms as random genetic mutation and natural selection. The idea is that there is a source of genetic variation which produces mutation in the structure and function of existing organisms. Most of these mutations are deleterious; a few are adaptive and their lucky owners will have an adaptive edge, eventually coming to predominate in a population. Given enough time, so the story goes, this process can produce all the splendid complexity and detail that characterize the contemporary living world (see EVOLUTION, THEORY OF).

Of course there is little real evidence that these processes can in fact achieve this much: naturally enough, we have not been able to follow their operation in such a way as to observe them produce, say, birds or mammals from reptiles, or even human beings from simian precursors. And even if we did observe the course of animate history (even if we had a detailed record on film), this would by no means show that blind mechanisms are in fact sufficient for this effect; for of course there would be nothing in the film record to show that those random genetic mutations were not in fact guided and orchestrated by God.

Still, the critic of the teleological argument claims not that in fact evolution has been accomplished just by these blind mechanisms, but that it could have been; if so, there is a real alternative to design. That these mechanisms really could have produced effects of this magnitude is far from clear; we have little real reason to suppose that there is a path through the space of possible animal design plans, a path leading from bacteria to human beings, and such that each new step is both adaptive and reachable from the previous step by mechanisms we understand. Still, the suggestion does perhaps damage the teleological argument by suggesting a naturalistic candidate for the post of producer of apparent design.

But organic evolution addresses only one of the areas of apparent design. There is also the origin of life; even the simplest unicellular creatures (prokaryotes such as bacteria and certain algae, for example) are enormously complex and upon close inspection look for all the world as if they have been designed; it is fair to say that no one, so far, has a decent idea as to how these creatures might have come into being just by way of the operation of the regularities of physics and chemistry. There are also the various considerations connected with the so-called 'fine

tuning' of the universe. First, there is the 'flatness' problem. The mass density of the universe is at present very close to the density corresponding to the borderline between an open universe (one that goes on expanding for ever) and a closed universe (one that expands to a certain size and then collapses). The ratio between the forces making for expansion and those making for contraction is close to one. But then shortly after the Big Bang this value would have to have been inside a very narrow band indeed. Thus Stephen Hawking, in his 'The Antisotropy of the Universe at Large Times' (1974): 'reduction of the rate of expansion by one part in 10^{12} at the time when the temperature of the Universe was 10^{10} K would have resulted in the Universe's starting to recollapse when its radius was only 1/3000 of the present value and the temperature was still 10,000 K' – much too warm for the development of life. On the other hand, if the rate of expansion had been even minutely greater, the universe would have expanded much too fast for the formation of stars and galaxies, required for the formation of the heavy elements necessary for the development of life.

Another kind of fine tuning was also necessary: of the fundamental physical constants. If any of the four fundamental forces (weak and strong nuclear forces, electromagnetic force, electron charge) had been even minutely different, the universe would not have supported life; they too must have been fine-tuned to an almost unbelievable accuracy. And the suggestion, again, is that given the infinite range of possible values for the fundamental constants, design is suggested by the fact that the actual values fall in that extremely narrow range of values that permits the development of intelligent life.

But there is a naturalistic riposte. Since the 1970s, several different sorts of 'inflationary' scenario have shown up. These postulate the formation (at very early times) of many different universes or subuniverses, with different rates of expansion, and different values for the fundamental constants. These inflationary models are motivated, in part, by a desire to avoid singularities and the accompanying appearance of design. If all possible values for the fundamental constants and the rate of expansion are actually exemplified in different subuniverses, then the fact that there is a subuniverse with the values ours displays no longer requires explanation or suggests a Designer. Many of these scenarios are wildly speculative and unencumbered by empirical evidence, but (if physically acceptable) they do tend to blunt the force of a design argument from fine tuning. (Of course, someone who already believed in God and saw no need to eliminate suggestions of design might be inclined to reject these suggestions as metaphysically extravagant.) But there are also counterarguments here; the discussion goes on. It is hard to see a verdict, at present, on the prospects of this form of the argument. The teleological argument seems to have enormous vitality; its epitaph is often read, but the argument regularly reappears in new forms. As for a final evaluation, the best perhaps comes from Kant, who said that this argument 'always deserves to be mentioned with respect. It is the oldest, the clearest and the most accordant with the common reason of mankind' (*Critique of Pure Reason*).

6 Other theistic arguments

We have examined the Big Three among theistic arguments, but there are many more. First, there are moral arguments of at least two sorts. These are arguments that the very nature of morality – the unconditioned character of the moral law – requires a divine lawgiver. You might find yourself utterly convinced that:

> Morality is objective, not dependent upon what human beings know or think or do.

You may also be convinced that:

> The objective character of morality cannot be explained in terms of any 'natural' facts about human beings (or other things), so there could not be such a thing as objective moral law unless there were a being like God who legislates it.

Then you will have a theistic argument from the nature of morality. This argument can go in either of two directions: some people think we can simply *see* that moral obligation is impossible apart from a divine will and lawgiver, while others think that the dependence of moral obligation upon the will of God is the best explanation for its objectivity and special deontological force.

A second main type of moral argument is due to Kant, who argues first that virtue deserves to be proportionally rewarded with happiness: the more virtuous you are, the more happiness you deserve. But nature by itself does not seem able to guarantee anything like this sort of coincidence. If morality is to make sense, however, it must be supposed that there is such a coincidence; practical reason, therefore, is entitled to postulate a supernatural being with enough knowledge, power and goodness to ensure that we receive the happiness we deserve as a reward for our virtue. So taken, the argument is for the rationality of making the assumption that there is a being of this sort; it is not really an

argument for the actual existence of such a being. This argument receives criticism from several sides: some hold that we do not have to assume that there is proportionality between virtue and happiness in order to carry out the moral life; others (for example, many Christians) argue that both happiness and the ability to live a moral life are gifts of grace and that if we really got what we deserve, we should all be thoroughly miserable.

There are many other theistic arguments – arguments from the nature of proper function, from the nature of propositions, numbers and sets, from intentionality, from counterfactuals, from the confluence of epistemic reliability with epistemic justification, from reference, simplicity, intuition, love, colours and flavours, miracles, play and enjoyment, morality, beauty, the meaning of life, and even from the existence of evil. There is no space even to outline all these arguments, so we will look at just three.

First, the argument from intentionality (or aboutness). Consider propositions – the things that are true or false, that are capable of being believed, and that stand in logical relations to one another. Propositions have another property: *aboutness* or *intentionality*. They represent reality or some part of it as being thus and so, and it is by virtue of this property that propositions (as opposed, for example, to sets) are true or false. Most who have thought about the matter have found it incredible that propositions should exist apart from the activity of minds. How could they just *be* there, if never thought of? Further, representing things as being thus and so – being about something or other – seems to be a property or activity of minds or perhaps thoughts. It is therefore extremely plausible to think of propositions as ontologically dependent upon mental or intellectual activity in such a way that either they just *are* thoughts, or else at any rate could not exist if not thought of. But propositions cannot be human thoughts; there are far too many of them for that. (For each real number r, for example, there is the proposition that r is distinct from the Taj Mahal.) Hence the only viable possibility is that they are divine thoughts, God's thoughts (so that when we think, we literally think God's thoughts after him).

Second, there is the argument from sets or collections. Many think of sets as displaying the following characteristics: (1) no set is a member of itself; (2) sets (unlike properties) have their extensions essentially – hence many sets are contingent beings and no set could have existed if one of its members had not; (3) sets form an iterated structure – at the first level, there are sets whose members are nonsets, at the second, sets whose members are nonsets or first level sets, ..., at the *n*th level, sets whose members are nonsets or sets of index less than *n*, . . . , and so on.

It is also natural to follow Georg Cantor, the father of modern set theory, in thinking of sets as collections – that is, as things whose existence depends upon a certain sort of intellectual activity, a collecting or 'thinking together' as Cantor put it. If sets were collections, that would explain their having the first three features. But of course there are far too many sets for them to be a product of human thinking together; there are many sets such that no human being has ever thought their members together and many such that no human being *could* think them together. That requires an infinite mind – one such as God's.

For a third example, consider the argument from appalling evil. Many philosophers offer antitheistic arguments from evil, and perhaps they have some force. But there is also a *theistic* argument from evil. The premise is that there is real and objectively horrifying evil in the world. Examples would be certain sorts of appalling evil characteristic of Nazi concentration camps: guards found pleasure in devising tortures, making mothers decide which of their children would go to the gas chamber and which be spared; small children were hanged, dying (because of their light weight) a slow and agonizing death; victims were taunted with the claim that no one would ever know of their fate and how they were treated. Of course, Nazi concentration camps have no monopoly on this sort of evil: there are also Stalin, Pol Pot and a thousand lesser villains. These states of affairs, one thinks, are objectively horrifying, in the sense that they would constitute enormous evil even if we and everyone else came perversely to approve of them.

Naturalism does not have the resources to accommodate or explain this fact about these states of affairs. From a naturalistic point of view, about all one can say is that we do indeed hate them; but this is far short of seeing them as intrinsically horrifying. How can we understand this intrinsically horrifying character? After all, as much misery and suffering can occur in a death from cancer as in a death caused by someone else's wickedness. What is the difference? The difference lies in the perpetrators and their intentions. Those who engage in this sort of evil are purposely and intentionally setting themselves to do these wicked things. But why is that objectively horrifying? A good answer (and one for which it is hard to think of an alternative) is that this evil consists in defying God, the source of all that is good and just, and the first being of the universe. What is horrifying here is not merely going contrary to God's will, but consciously choosing to invert the true scale of values, explicitly aiming at what is abhorrent to God. This is an offence and affront to God; it is defiance of God himself, and so is objectively horrifying. Appalling evil thus has a sort of cosmic significance. But of course there could be no evil of this sort if there were no such being as God.

See also: AGNOSTICISM; ATHEISM; DEISM; GOD, CONCEPTS OF; NATURAL THEOLOGY

References and further reading

Craig, W. (1980) *The Cosmological Argument from Plato to Leibniz*, London: Macmillan. (An excellent history of the cosmological argument, especially good on the versions given by the medieval Arabic and Jewish philosophers.)

Plantinga, A. (1974) *The Nature of Necessity*, Oxford: Clarendon Press. (Contains a version of the ontological argument developed in terms of the metaphysics of modality (possible worlds) that is immune to Kant's criticism (whatever precisely it was).)

Swinburne, R. (1979) *The Existence of God*, Oxford: Oxford University Press. (Contains a very full and sophisticated version of the teleological argument, developed in terms of probability.)

ALVIN PLANTINGA

GOD, CONCEPTS OF

We think of God as an ultimate reality, the source or ground of all else, perfect and deserving of worship. Such a conception is common to both Eastern and Western religions. Some trace this to human psychology or sociology: Freud regarded God as a wish-fulfilling projection of a perfect, comforting father-figure; Marxists see belief in God as arising from the capitalist structure of society. Believers, however, trace their belief to religious experience, revealed or authoritative texts, and rational reflection.

Philosophers flesh out the concept of God by drawing inferences from God's relation to the universe ('first-cause theology') and from the claim that God is a perfect being. 'Perfect-being' theology is the more fundamental method. Its history stretches from Plato and Aristotle, through the Stoics, and into the Christian tradition as early as Augustine and Boethius; it plays an important role in underwriting such ontological arguments for God's existence as those of Anselm and Descartes. It draws on four root intuitions: that to be perfect is perfectly to be, that it includes being complete, that it includes being all-inclusive, and that it includes being personal. Variously balanced, these intuitions yield our varied concepts of God.

Criticisms of perfect-being theology have focused both on the possibility that the set of candidate divine perfections may not be consistent or unique, and doubts as to whether human judgment can be adequate for forming concepts of God. Another problem with the method is that different accounts of perfection will yield different accounts of God: Ibn Sina and Ibn Rushd, for instance, appear to have held that God would be the more perfect for lacking some knowledge, while most Christian writers hold that perfection requires omniscience.

Views of God's relation to the universe vary greatly. Pantheists say that God *is* the universe. Panentheists assert that God includes the universe, or is related to it as soul to body. They ascribe to God the limitations associated with being a person – such as limited power and knowledge – but argue that being a person is nevertheless a state of perfection. Other philosophers, however, assert that God is wholly different from the universe.

Some of these think that God created the universe *ex nihilo*, that is, from no pre-existing material. Some add that God conserves the universe in being moment by moment, and is thus provident for his creatures. Still others think that God 'found' some pre-existing material and 'creates' by gradually improving this material – this view goes back to the myth of the Demiurge in Plato's *Timaeus*, and also entails that God is provident. By contrast, deists deny providence and think that once God made it, the universe ran on its own. Still others argue that God neither is nor has been involved in the world. The common thread lies in the concept of perfection: thinkers relate God to the universe in the way that their thoughts about God's perfection make most appropriate.

See also: Epicureanism; God, arguments for the existence of; Kabbalah Pantheism; Trinity

BRIAN LEFTOW

GÖDEL'S THEOREMS

Utilizing the formalization of mathematics and logic found in Whitehead and Russell's *Principia Mathematica* (1910), Hilbert and Ackermann gave precise formulations of a variety of foundational and methodological problems, among them the so-called 'completeness problem' for formal axiomatic theories – the problem of whether all truths or laws pertaining to their subjects are provable within them. Applied to a proposed system for first-order quantificational logic, the completeness problem is the problem of whether all logically valid formulas are provable in it.

In his doctoral dissertation of 1929, Gödel gave a positive solution to the completeness problem for a system of quantificational logic based on the work of Whitehead and Russell. This is the first of the three theorems that we here refer to as 'Gödel's theorems'.

The other two theorems arose from Gödel's continued investigation of the completeness problem for more comprehensive formal systems – including, especially, systems comprehensive enough to encompass all known methods of mathematical proof. Here, however, the question was not whether all logically valid formulas are provable (they are), but whether all formulas true in the intended interpretations of the systems are.

For this to be the case, the systems would have to prove either S or the denial of S for each sentence S of their languages. In his first incompleteness theorem, Gödel showed that the systems investigated were not complete in this sense. Indeed, there are even sentences of a simple arithmetic type that the systems can neither prove nor refute, provided they are consistent. So even the class of simple arithmetic truths is not formally axiomatizable.

The idea behind Gödel's proof is basically as follows. Let a given system T satisfy the following conditions: (1) it is powerful enough to prove of each sentence in its language that if it proves it, then it proves that it proves it, and (2) it is capable of proving of a certain sentence G (Gödel's self-referential sentence) that it is equivalent to 'G is not provable in T'. Under these conditions, T cannot prove G, so long as T is consistent. For suppose T proved G. By (1) it would also prove 'G is provable in T', and by (2) it would prove 'G is not provable in T'. Hence, T would be inconsistent.

Under slightly stronger conditions – specifically, (2) and (1′) every sentence of the form 'X is provable in T' that T proves is true – it can be shown that a consistent T cannot prove 'not G' either. For if 'not G' were provable in T it would follow by (2) that 'G is provable in T' would also be provable in T. But then by (1′) G would be provable. Hence, T would be inconsistent.

The proof of Gödel's second incompleteness theorem essentially involves formalizing in T a proof of a formula expressing the proposition that if T is consistent, then G. The second incompleteness theorem (that is, the claim that if T is consistent it cannot prove its own consistency) then follows from this and the first part of the proof of the first incompleteness theorem.

The two incompleteness theorems have been applied to a wide variety of concerns in philosophy. The best known of these are critical applications to Hilbert's programme and logicism in the philosophy of mathematics and to mechanism in the philosophy of mind.

See also: Church's theorem and the decision problem; Church's thesis; Computability theory; Ordinal logics; Proof theory

MICHAEL DETLEFSEN

GOETHE, JOHANN WOLFGANG VON
(1749–1832)

Goethe was a statesman, scientist, amateur artist, theatrical impresario, dramatist, novelist and Germany's supreme lyric poet; indeed he provided the Romantic generation which followed him with their conception of what a poet should be. His works, diaries and about 12,000 letters run to nearly 150 volumes. His drama *Faust* (1790–1832) is the greatest long poem in modern European literature and made the legend of Dr Faust a modern myth. He knew most of the significant figures in the philosophical movement of German idealism (though he never met Kant), but he was not himself a philosopher. His literary works certainly addressed contemporary philosophical concerns: *Iphigenie auf Tauris* (Iphigenia in Tauris) (1779–86) seems a prophetic dramatization of the ethical and religious autonomy Kant was to proclaim from 1785; in his novel *Die Wahlverwandtschaften* (The Elective Affinities) (1809) a mysterious natural or supernatural world of chemistry, magnetism or Fate, such as 'Naturphilosophie' envisaged, seems to underlie and perhaps determine a human story of spiritual adultery; in *Faust*, particularly *Part Two*, the tale of a pact or wager with the Devil seems to develop into a survey of world cultural history, which has been held to have overtones of Schelling, Hegel or even Marx. But whatever their conceptual materials, Goethe's literary works require literary rather than philosophical analysis. There are, however, certain discrete concepts prominent in his scientific work, or in the expressions of his 'wisdom' – maxims, essays, autobiographies, letters and conversations – with which Goethe's name is particularly associated and which are capable of being discussed separately. Notable among these are: Nature and metamorphosis (*Bildung*), polarity and 'intensification' (*Steigerung*), the 'primal phenomena' (*Urphänomene*), 'the daemonic' (*das Dämonische*) and renunciation (*Entsagung*).

See also: GERMAN IDEALISM; NATURPHILOSOPHIE; POETRY

NICHOLAS BOYLE

GOLDMAN, EMMA
See FEMINISM (§4)

GOOD AND RIGHT
See RIGHT AND GOOD

GOOD, THEORIES OF THE

'Good' is the most general term of positive evaluation, used to recommend or express approval in a wide range of contexts. It indicates that a thing is desirable or worthy of choice, so that normally, if you have reason to want a certain kind of thing, you also have reason to prefer a *good* thing of that kind.

A theory of the good may consist in a general account of the good, which is meant to apply to all good things; or in a definition of 'good', an account of how the term functions in the language. Theories of the good have metaphysical implications about the relations of fact and value. Many ancient and medieval philosophers believed in the ultimate identity of the real and the good. Modern philosophers reject this identification, and have held a range of positions: realists, for example, hold that the good is part of reality, while certain moral sense theorists hold that when we call something good we are projecting human interests onto reality; and emotivists hold that we use the term 'good' only to signify subjective approval.

Theorists of the good also categorize different kinds of goodness and explain how they are related. Good things are standardly classified as ends, which are valued for their own sakes, or means, valued for the sake of the ends they promote. Some philosophers also divide them into intrinsic goods, which have their value in themselves, and extrinsic goods, which get their value from their relation to something else. Various theories have been held about the relation between these two distinctions – about whether an end must be something with intrinsic value. Philosophers also distinguish subjective goods – things which are good for someone in particular – from objective goods, which are good from everyone's point of view. Views about how these kinds of goodness are related have important implications for moral philosophy.

Usually, a theory of the good is constructed in the hope of shedding light on more substantive questions, such as what makes a person, an action, or a human life good. These questions raise issues about the relation between ethical and other values. For example, we may ask whether moral virtue is a special sort of goodness, or just the ordinary sort applied to persons. Or, since actions are valued as 'right' or 'wrong', we may ask how these values are related to the action's goodness or badness. We may also pose the question of whether a life that is good in the sense of being *happy* must also be a *morally good* or virtuous life. This last question has occupied the attention of philosophers ever since Plato.

See also: HAPPINESS; PRACTICAL REASON AND ETHICS; RIGHT AND GOOD; XUNZI

CHRISTINE M. KORSGAARD

GORGIAS (late 5th Century BC)

The most important of the fifth-century BC Greek Sophists after Protagoras, Gorgias was a famous rhetorician, a major influence on the development of artistic prose and a gifted dabbler in philosophy. His display speeches, *Encomium of Helen of Troy* and *Defence of Palamedes*, are masterpieces of the art of making a weak case seem strong, and brilliant exercises in symmetrical and antithetical sentence structure. Of philosophical importance is his treatise *On Not-Being, or On the Nature of Things*, an elaborate reversal of the metaphysical argument of Parmenides, showing: (1) that nothing exists; (2) that if anything exists, it cannot be known; and (3) if anything can be known, it cannot be communicated. This nihilistic *tour de force* is probably a caricature rather than a serious statement of a philosophical position. Gorgias is a master of the persuasive use of *logos* (discourse), understood both as eloquence and as argumentative skill.

CHARLES H. KAHN

GOURNAY, MARIE DE
See FEMINISM (§2)

GREEK PHILOSOPHY
See ANCIENT PHILOSOPHY

GREEN ETHICS
See ENVIRONMENTAL ETHICS

GREEN POLITICAL PHILOSOPHY

All the major political philosophies have been born of crisis. Green political philosophy is no exception to this general rule. It has emerged from that interconnected series of crises that is often termed 'the environmental crisis'. As we enter the third millennium and the twenty-first century it seems quite clear that the level and degree of environmental degradation and destruction cannot be sustained over the longer term without dire consequences for human and other animal species, and the ecosystems on which all depend. A veritable explosion in the human population, the pollution of air and water, the over-fishing of the oceans, the destruction of tropical and temperate rain forests, the extinction of entire species, the depletion of the ozone layer, the build-up of greenhouse gases, global warming, desertification, wind and water erosion of precious topsoil, the disappearance of valuable farmland and wilderness for 'development' – these and many other interrelated phenomena provide the backdrop and justification for the 'greening' of much of modern political thinking.

The task of outlining and summarizing the state of green political philosophy is made more difficult because there is as yet no agreement among 'green' political thinkers. Indeed there is, at present, no definitive 'green political philosophy' as such. The environmental or green movement is diverse and disparate, and appears in different shades of green. These range from 'light green' conservationists to 'dark green' deep ecologists, from ecofeminists to social ecologists, from the militant ecoteurs of Earth First! to the low-keyed gradualists of the Sierra Club and the Nature Conservancy. These groups differ not only over strategy and tactics, but also over fundamental philosophy.

While there is no single, systematically articulated and agreed-upon green political philosophy, however, there are none the less recurring topics, themes, categories and concepts that are surely central to such a political philosophy. These include the idea that humans are part of nature and members of a larger and more inclusive 'biotic community' to which they have obligations or duties. This community includes both human and non-human animals, and the conditions conducive to their survival and flourishing. Such a community consists, moreover, not only of members who are alive but those who are as yet unborn. A green political philosophy values both biological and cultural diversity, and views sustainability as a standard by which to judge the justness of human actions and practices. Exactly how these themes might fit together to form some larger, systematic and coherent whole is still being worked out.

See also: ENVIRONMENTAL ETHICS

TERENCE BALL

GREEN, THOMAS HILL (1836–82)

Green was a prominent Oxford idealist philosopher, who criticized both the epistemological and ethical implications of the dominant empiricist and utilitarian theories of the time. He contended that experience could not be explained merely as the product of sensations acting on the human mind. Like Kant, Green argued that knowledge presupposes certain a priori categories, such as substance, causation, space and time, which enable us to structure our understanding of empirical reality. Physical objects and even the most simple feelings are only intelligible as relations of ideas constituted by human consciousness. However, unlike Kant, he did not draw the conclusion that things in themselves are consequently unknowable. Rather, he argued that reality itself is ultimately spiritual, the product of an eternal consciousness operating within both the world and human reason. Green adopted a similarly anti-naturalist and holistic position in ethics, in which desires are seen as orientated towards the realization of the good – both within the individual and in society at large. In politics, this led him to criticize the *laissez-faire* individualist liberalism of Herbert Spencer and, to a lesser extent, of J.S. Mill, and to advocate a more collectivist liberalism in which the state seeks to promote the positive liberty of its members.

See also: EMPIRICISM; FREEDOM AND LIBERTY; HEGELIANISM; NATURALISM IN ETHICS

RICHARD BELLAMY

GRICE, HERBERT PAUL (1913–88)

Grice was a leading member of the post-war Oxford group of analytic philosophers. His small body of published work, together with an oral tradition, has been deeply influential among both philosophers and theoretical linguists. His outline of general rules of conversation began a new era in pragmatics. Grice's analysis of speaker's meaning explicates semantic notions in terms of the psychological concepts of intention and belief. His theory of conversation is based on the nature of language as a rational, cooperative activity. His account of conversational rules gave him a tool that he applied to a wide class of philosophical problems. Although Grice is most famous for his work on language and meaning, his interests cover a full range of philosophical topics, including ethics, moral psychology and philosophical psychology.

See also: ANALYTICAL PHILOSOPHY; COMMUNICATION AND INTENTION

JUDITH BAKER

GROSSETESTE, ROBERT (c.1170–1253)

Grosseteste's thought is representative of the conflicting currents in the intellectual climate of Europe in the late twelfth and early thirteenth centuries. On the one hand, his commitment to acquiring, understanding and making accessible to his Latin contemporaries the texts and ideas of newly discovered Arabic and Greek intellectual traditions places him in the vanguard of a sweeping movement transforming European thought during his lifetime. His work in science and natural philosophy, for example, is inspired by material newly translated from Arabic sources and by the new Aristotelian natural philosophy, especially the *Physics*, *On the Heavens* and *Posterior Analytics* (Aristotle's treatise on the nature of scientific knowledge). Similarly, in his work in metaphysics, ethics and theology Grosseteste turns to ancient sources previously unknown (or incompletely known) to Western thinkers,

prominent among which are Aristotle's *Ethics* and the writings of Pseudo-Dionysius. His work as a translator of and commentator on Aristotle and Pseudo-Dionysius places Grosseteste among the pioneers in the assimilation of these important strands of the Greek intellectual heritage into the mainstream of European thought.

On the other hand, Grosseteste's views are in significant respects conservative. His greatest debt is to Augustine, and his most original ideas – such as his view that light is a fundamental constituent of all corporeal reality – are extensions of recognizably Augustinian themes. Moreover, although his work on Aristotle is groundbreaking, his approach is judicious and measured, lacking any hint of the crusader's zeal that marks the work of the later radical Aristotelians. In general his practice conforms to the traditional Neoplatonist line, viewing Aristotle as a guide to logic and natural philosophy while turning to Platonism – in Grosseteste's case, Augustinian and Pseudo-Dionysian Platonism – for the correct account of the loftier matters of metaphysics and theology.

See also: AUGUSTINE

SCOTT MACDONALD

GROTIUS, HUGO (1583–1645)

Scholar, lawyer and statesman, Grotius contributed to a number of different disciplines. His reputation as the founder both of a new international order and of a new moral science rests largely on his *De iure belli ac pacis* (The Law of War and Peace) (1625). Though the tendency today is to regard Grotius as one figure among others in the development of the concept of international law, he is increasingly regarded as one of the most original moral philosophers of the seventeenth century, in particular as having laid the foundations for the post-sceptical doctrine of natural law that flourished during the Enlightenment.

See also: LAW, PHILOSOPHY OF; PUFENDORF, S.; RIGHTS; ROMAN LAW; WAR AND PEACE, PHILOSOPHY OF

J.D. FORD

GUILT
See MORAL SENTIMENTS

GURNEY, EDMUND (1847–88)

Edmund Gurney was an English psychologist and musician. His major work, *The Power of Sound*, is a vast treatise on musical aesthetics, ranging from issues in the physiology of hearing to the question of the relation of music to morality, but is mostly devoted to central questions of form, expression and value in music. It is the most significant work of its kind in the latter half of the nineteenth century.

Commentators often couple Gurney with Hanslick as a supporter of musical formalism, but his views on the expressive dimension of music are neither as restrictive nor as doctrinaire as Hanslick's. Hanslick insisted on denying specific emotional content to music, allowing it only to convey dynamic features, which emotions, among other things, might exhibit. Gurney, on the other hand, grants that some music possesses fairly definite emotional expression, and discusses at length the grounds of such expression; he is primarily concerned to deny that musical impressiveness, or beauty, is either the same as or depends on musical expressiveness.

Gurney maintains that overall form in music is not of primary relevance to the appreciation of music. This is because the central feature of musical comprehension is the grasping of individual parts as they occur, and the grasping of connections to immediately neighbouring parts, whatever the overarching form of a piece might be. The value of a piece is directly a function of the pleasurableness of its individual parts and the cogency of sequence exhibited at the transitions between them, not a function of its global architecture.

See also: ART, UNDERSTANDING OF; ARTISTIC EXPRESSION; EMOTION IN RESPONSE TO ART; FORMALISM IN ART; MUSIC, AESTHETICS OF

JERROLD LEVINSON

H

HABERMAS, JÜRGEN (1929–)

Jürgen Habermas, German philosopher and social theorist, is perhaps best known for his wide-ranging defence of the modern public sphere and its related ideals of publicity and free public reason, but he has also made important contributions to theories of communication and informal argumentation, ethics, and the foundations and methodology of the social sciences. He studied in Göttingen, Zurich and Bonn, completing a dissertation on Schelling's philosophy in 1954. After working for a short time as Theodor Adorno's research assistant at the Institute for Social Research in Frankfurt he held professorships in Heidelberg and Frankfurt and, from 1971 to 1981, was co-director of the Max Planck Institute in Starnberg. With the publication of *Knowledge and Human Interests* (1968) he became widely recognized as the leading intellectual heir to the Frankfurt School of Critical Theory, a variant of Western Marxism that included such figures as Adorno, Max Horkheimer and Herbert Marcuse. His two-volume *The Theory of Communicative Action* (1981) is a major contribution to social theory, in which he locates the origins of the various political, economic and cultural crises confronting modern society in a one-sided process of rationalization steered more by the media of money and administrative power than by forms of collective decision-making based on consensually grounded norms and values.

See also: ADORNO, T.W.; APEL, KARL-OTTO; FRANKFURT SCHOOL; MARCUSE, H.

KENNETH BAYNES

HAECKEL, ERNST HEINRICH (1834–1919)

Haeckel was the leading German Darwinist. His evolutionary philosophy of monism differed substantially from the views of Darwin or British evolutionary philosophers such as Herbert Spencer or the dualist T.H. Huxley. Haeckel's monism asserted the unity of physical and organic nature, and included mental processes and social phenom-

ena. Its initial form was mechanistic, seeking to reduce vital processes to physicochemical laws and substances. However, his efforts to construct the history of life meant that Haeckel became preoccupied with historical processes. In its final form, his monism was pantheistic. Although Haeckel has been regarded as a forerunner of national socialism, a contextual reading of his works does not support this interpretation.

See also: EVOLUTION AND ETHICS; EVOLUTION, THEORY OF

PAUL WEINDLING

HALAKHAH

The central ideal of rabbinic Judaism is that of living by the Torah, that is, God's teachings. These teachings are mediated by a detailed normative system called *halakhah*, which might be translated as 'the Way'. The term 'rabbinic law' captures the form of *halakhic* discourse, but not its range. Appropriate sections of *halakhah* have indeed served as the law of Jewish communities for two millennia. But other sections relate to individual conscience and religious observance and are enforceable only by a 'heavenly court'.

Although grounded in Scripture, *halakhah*'s frame of reference is the 'oral Torah', a tradition of interpretation and argument culminating in the twenty volumes of the Talmud. God's authority is the foundational norm, but it is only invoked occasionally as superseding human understanding. Indeed, the rabbis disallowed divine interference in their deliberations, asserting, in keeping with Scripture, that Torah is 'not in heaven' (Bava Metzia 59b, citing Deuteronomy 30: 12).

Given the lack of binding dogma in Judaism, *halakhic* practice has often been regarded as the common denominator that unites the Jewish community. The enterprise of furnishing 'reasons of the commandments' (*ta'amei ha-mitzvot*), central to many thinkers in Judaism, accordingly reveals a great diversity of orientations. These range, in medieval Judaism, from esoteric mystical doctrines to Maimonides' rational and historical explanations; and among modern writers, from moral positivism to existentialism.

See also: LAW, PHILOSOPHY OF; MAIMONIDES, M.

NOAM J. ZOHAR

HANSLICK, EDUARD (1825–1904)

Eduard Hanslick, a music critic for the popular Viennese press, is principally known as the author of *Vom Musikalisch-Schönen* (1854). This is probably the most widely read work in the aesthetics of music for both philosophers and musicians, and remains the starting point for any discussion either of the place of emotion in music, or of the doctrine usually referred to as 'musical purism'. On the former, Hanslick maintained what he calls the negative thesis, which 'first and foremost opposes the widespread view that music is supposed to represent the feelings'; on purism, he proposed the positive thesis or antithesis, 'that the beauty of a piece of music is specifically musical, that is, is inherent in the tonal relationships without reference to an extraneous, extra-musical context'.

See also: ARTISTIC EXPRESSION; EMOTION IN RESPONSE TO ART; EMOTIONS, PHILOSOPHY OF; FORMALISM IN ART; MUSIC, AESTHETICS OF

PETER KIVY

HAPPINESS

In ordinary use, the word 'happiness' has to do with one's situation (one is fortunate) or with one's state of mind (one is glad, cheerful) or, typically, with both. These two elements appear in different proportions on different occasions. If one is concerned with a long stretch of time (as in 'a happy life'), one is likely to focus more on situation than on state of mind. If a short period of time, it is not uncommon to focus on states of mind.

By and large philosophers are more interested in long-term cases. One's life is happy if one is content that life has brought one much of what one regards as important. There is a pull in these lifetime assessments towards a person's objective situation and away from the person's subjective responses. The important notion for ethics is 'wellbeing' – that is, a notion of what makes an individual life go well. 'Happiness' is important because many philosophers have thought that happiness is the only thing that contributes to wellbeing, or because they have used 'happiness' to mean the same as 'wellbeing'.

What, then, makes a life go well? Some have thought that it was the presence of a positive feeling tone. Others have thought that it was having one's

desires fulfilled – either actual desires (as some would say) or informed desires (as others would say). It is unclear how stringent the requirement of 'informed' must be; if it is fairly stringent it can, in effect, require abandoning desire explanations and adopting instead an explanation in terms of a list of good-making features in human life.

J.P. GRIFFIN

HARMONIA
See PYTHAGOREANISM

HART, HERBERT LIONEL ADOLPHUS (1907–93)

H.L.A. Hart, Professor of Jurisprudence at Oxford University, 1952–68, is an outstanding representative of the analytical approach in jurisprudence and philosophy of law. He restated 'legal positivism' in the tradition of Jeremy Bentham and John Austin, differentiating between law's existence and its moral qualities. But he rejected the Benthamite identification of law with a sovereign's commands, advancing instead a theory of law as comprising a special, systematically organized, kind of social rules. He did this in a linguistic-analytical style, showing how attention to our way of speaking and thinking about rules can yield new insights into their nature.

See also: AUSTIN, J.; BENTHAM, J.; LAW, PHILOSOPHY OF

NEIL MACCORMICK

HASIDISM

Its name literally meaning pietism, Hasidism is a mystical renewal movement that originated in Eastern Europe in the mid-eighteenth century. It has become one of the most important spiritual and social developments of Orthodox Judaism and has exerted an influence as well on non-Jews and Jews who are not Orthodox. Early Hasidic leaders claimed their spiritual authority on the basis of heavenly revelations and mystical awakenings. But they generally differed from the more esoterically minded Kabbalists, from whom they drew their earliest following, in seeking to present the fruits of mystical inspiration to the community. Hasidic teachings fostered specific spiritual and ritual innovations, which gave outward expression to the profound nexus that the Hasidic masters saw between mundane existence and the inner, mystical meaning of God's law. According to Hasidic thinking, the divine and the human formed a single, all-encompassing unity, and it was on this basis that the Hasidic rabbis found in acts of Jewish piety means of linking divine experience with human responsiveness. Notable for its vitality and continuity in diversity, Hasidism continues its influence on religious Jewry and beyond to the present day.

See also: God, concepts of; Kabbalah

RACHEL ELIOR

HEAVEN

In Christian theology, heaven is both the dwelling place of God and the angels, and the place where all who are saved ultimately go after death and judgment to receive their eternal reward. The doctrine of the resurrection of the body requires that heaven be a place because it must contain the glorified bodies of the redeemed, but heaven is more theologically important as a state than as a place. This state is traditionally described as involving the most intimate union with God without the elimination of the individual human personality (the beatific vision); it is a state of perfect bliss beyond anything possible on earth. In high medieval theology, the happiness of heaven is understood to be so great that it is even beyond the capability of human nature to enjoy without divine aid. There are varying views on the nature of heavenly society, however, with some theologians (Augustine, Aquinas, Bonaventure) arguing that perfect happiness will be derived from the love of God alone, while others (for example, Giles of Rome) stress the joy that will be derived from the company of the elect. More recently, interest in the nature of heaven has declined, and Christian theology has tended to play down its importance.

See also: Faith; Hell; Limbo; Purgatory; Soul, nature and immortality of the

LINDA ZAGZEBSKI

HEDONISM

Hedonism is the doctrine that pleasure is the good. It was important in ancient discussions, and many positions were taken, from the view that pleasure is to be avoided to the view that immediate bodily pleasure is to be sought. More elevated views of pleasure were also taken, and have been revived in modern times. There are three varieties of hedonism. Psychological hedonists hold that we can pursue only pleasure; evaluative hedonists that pleasure is what we ought to pursue; reflective hedonists that it is what on reflection gives value to any pursuit. Arguments for psychological hedonism suggest that an agent's actions are a function of what they think will maximize their pleasure overall. Explaining altruism can lead such theories into truism. Similar arguments are used for reflective

hedonism, and the same problem arises. The difficulty for evaluative hedonism lies in deciding how we can establish certain ends as desirable. The claim that pleasure is to be maximized seems immoral to many. Hedonism also faces problems with the measurement of pleasure.

See also: Asceticism; Economics and ethics; Happiness; Moral motivation; Rational Choice Theory

JUSTIN GOSLING

HEGEL, GEORG WILHELM FRIEDRICH (1770–1831)

Introduction

Hegel was the last of the main representatives of a philosophical movement known as German Idealism, which developed towards the end of the eighteenth century primarily as a reaction against the philosophy of Kant, and whose main proponents, aside from Hegel, include Fichte and Schelling. The movement played an important role in the philosophical life of Germany until the fourth decade of the nineteenth century. Like the other German Idealists, Hegel was convinced that the philosophy of Kant did not represent the final word in philosophical matters, because it was not possible to conceive a unified theory of reality by means of Kantian principles alone. For Hegel and his two idealistic predecessors, a unified theory of reality is one which can systematically explain all forms of reality, starting from a single principle or a single subject. For Hegel, these forms of reality included not only solar systems, physical bodies and the various guises assumed by organic life, for example, plants, animals and human beings, but also psychic phenomena, social and political forms of organization as well as artistic creations and cultural achievements such as religion and philosophy. Hegel believed that one of the essential tasks of philosophy was the systematic explanation of all these various forms starting from one single principle, in other words, in the establishment of a unified theory of reality. He believed this because only a theory of this nature could permit knowledge to take the place of faith. Hegel's goal here, namely the conquest of faith, places his philosophical programme, like that of the other German Idealists, within the wider context of the philosophy of the German Enlightenment.

For Hegel, the fundamental principle which explains all reality is reason. Reason, as Hegel understands it, is not some quality which is attributed to some human subject; it is, by contrast, the sum of all reality. In accordance with this belief, Hegel claims that reason and reality are strictly identical: only reason is real and only reality is reasonable. The considerations which moved Hegel to identify reason with reality are various. On the one hand, certain motives rooted in Hegel's theological convictions play a role. According to these convictions, one must be able to give a philosophical interpretation of the whole of reality which can simultaneously act as a justification of the basic assumptions of Christianity. On the other hand, epistemological convictions also have to be identified to support Hegel's claim that reason and reality are one and the same. Among these convictions belong the assumptions (1) that knowledge of reality is only possible if reality is reasonable, because it would not otherwise be accessible to cognition, and (2) that we can only know that which is real.

According to Hegel, although reason is regarded as the sum total of reality, it must not be interpreted along the lines of Spinoza's model of substance. Reason is rather to be thought of as a process which has as its goal the recognition of reason through itself. Since reason is the whole of reality, this goal will be achieved when reason recognizes itself as total reality. It is the task of philosophy to give a coherent account of this process which leads to self-knowledge of reason. Hegel conceived this process by analogy with the model of organic development which takes place on various levels. The basic presupposition governing the conception of this process is that reason has to be interpreted in accordance with the paradigm of a living organism. Hegel thought of a living organism as an entity which represents the successful realization of a plan in which all individual characteristics of this entity are contained. He called this plan the concept of an entity, and conceived its successful realization as a developmental process, in the course of which each of the individual characteristics acquires reality. In accordance with these assumptions, Hegel distinguished the concept of reason from the process of the realization of this concept. He undertook the exposition of the concept of reason in that section of his philosophical system which he calls the *Wissenschaft der Logik* (*Science of Logic*). In this first part of his system, the various elements of the concept of reason are discussed and placed into a systematic context. He presented the process of the realization of this concept in the other two parts of his system, the *Philosophie der Natur* (*Philosophy of Nature*) and the *Philosophie des Geistes* (*Philosophy of Spirit*). Apart from their systematic function, which consists in demonstrating reason in the Hegelian sense as total reality, both parts have a specifically material function in each case. In the *Philosophy of Nature*, Hegel aims to describe comprehensively all aspects of natural phenomena as a system of increasingly complex facts. This system begins with the simple concepts of space, time and matter and ends with the theory of the animal organism. The *Philosophy of Spirit* treats of various psychological, social and cultural forms of reality. It is characterized by the assumption of the existence of something like genuine, spiritual facts, which cannot be described as subjective states of individual persons possessing consciousness, but which have an independent, objective existence. For Hegel, examples of such facts are the state, art, religion and history.

In spite of the relatively abstract metaphysical background of his philosophy, which is difficult to reconcile with common sense, Hegel's insights in his analysis of concrete facts have guaranteed him a permanent place in the history of philosophy. None the less, for contemporary readers these insights are interesting hypotheses, rather than commonly accepted truths. Of lesser importance among these insights should be counted Hegel's results in the realm of natural philosophy, which soon suffered considerable criticism from practising natural scientists. The important insights apply more specifically to the spheres of the theory of knowledge as well as the philosophy of right, and social and cultural philosophy. Hegel is thus regarded as an astute and original representative of the thesis that our conception of objectivity is largely determined by social factors which also play a significant role in constituting the subject of cognition and knowledge. His criticisms of the seventeenth- and eighteenth-century concepts of natural law and his thoughts on the genesis and significance of right in the modern world have had a demonstrable influence on the theory of right in juridical contexts. Hegel's analysis of the relationship and interplay between social and political institutions became a constituent element in very influential social theories, in particular that of Marx. The same applies to his central theses on the theory of art and the philosophy of religion and history. Hegel's thoughts on the history of philosophy made that topic a philosophical discipline in its own right. Thus Hegel was a very influential philosopher. That his philosophy has none the less remained deeply contentious is due in part to the fact that his uncompromising struggle against traditional habits of thought and his attempt to establish a conceptual perspective on reality in contrast with the philosophical tradition of the time remains characterized by a large measure of obscurity and vagueness. Unfortunately these characteristics also infect every summary of his philosophy.

HEGEL, GEORG WILHELM FRIEDRICH

1   Life and works

Hegel was born on 27 August 1770 in Stuttgart, son of a Württemberg official. In the autumn of 1788, after attending the local grammar school, he began a course of study at the Protestant Seminary in Tübingen in preparation for a career as a Protestant clergyman. Two of his fellow students and friends were F.W.J. SCHELLING and F. Hölderlin. In autumn 1793, after successfully completing this period of study, Hegel became a private tutor in Berne, Switzerland, and remained there until 1796. From January 1797 until the end of 1800 he was a private tutor in Frankfurt am Main, where he again came into contact with Hölderlin, who played an important role in the formation of Hegel's early philosophical convictions. Thanks to a legacy, Hegel was able to abandon his position as a tutor and pursue his academic ambitions. Early in 1801 he went to Jena. His student friend Schelling had become Fichte's successor and was lecturing in philosophy at the university there. With Schelling's energetic support Hegel qualified as a *Privatdozent* in the autumn of 1801 with a thesis on natural philosophy. Initially, Schelling and Hegel worked closely together, a fact which is documented by a philosophical periodical which they published jointly from 1802 (although it ceased publication following Schelling's departure from Jena in 1803). In 1805 Hegel was appointed Extraordinary Professor, but financial difficulties forced him to abandon his activities at the University of Jena in the autumn of 1806. A friend's intervention enabled him to take over as editor of a daily newspaper in Bamberg in March 1807. In November 1808 the same friend then ensured that Hegel was nominated rector and professor at a grammar school in Nuremberg. After a few years in this capacity, Hegel was able to return to university life. In 1816 he was called to the University of Heidelberg, which he left again in 1818 to take a chair at the University of Berlin, as Fichte's successor. There he revealed a considerable talent for academic teaching and succeeded in assuring a dominant position in contemporary discussions for his philosophical doctrines. Hegel died in Berlin during a cholera epidemic on 14 November 1831, at the height of his fame.

Hegel's works can be divided into three groups: (1) texts written by Hegel and published during his lifetime; (2) texts written by him, but not published during his lifetime; and (3) texts neither written by him nor published during his lifetime. Two texts from his early years in Frankfurt do not fit into this scheme. The first is the translation of a pamphlet by Cart, a Berne lawyer, on the political situation in the Canton of Vaud, which was translated and annotated by Hegel, and which he published anonymously in 1798. This is the first printed text by Hegel; the second is a fragment dating from the same period and known as the *Systemprogramm des deutschen Idealismus* (System-Programme of German Idealism). The text has survived in Hegel's handwriting, but his authorship remains controversial.

The earliest writings in the first group date from the beginning of Hegel's time in Jena. His first philosophical work is entitled *Differenz des Fichte'schen und Schelling'schen Systems der Philosophie* (The Difference between Fichte's and Schelling's System of Philosophy) (1801). This was followed later during the same year by the essay which he had to submit in order to qualify as *Privatdozent*, *De Orbitis Planetarum* (On the Orbits of the Planets). In 1802–3 Hegel published various philosophical works in the periodical which he edited with Schelling, the *Kritisches Journal der Philosophie* (Critical Journal of Philosophy). The most important among these were *Glauben und Wissen* (Faith and Knowledge), *Verhältnis des Skeptizismus zur Philosophie* (The Relationship of Scepticism to Philosophy) and *Über die wissenschaftlichen Behandlungsarten des Naturrechts* (On the Scientific Ways of Dealing with Natural Law). Immediately after his period as a university teacher in Jena and at the beginning of his period in Bamberg, Hegel published his first great philosophical work, the *Phänomenologie des Geistes* (Phenomenology of Spirit) (1807). During the eight years in which he taught at the grammar school in Nuremberg, Hegel published his three-volume *Wissenschaft der Logik* (Science of Logic) (1812, 1813, 1816). While in Heidelberg, the complete presentation of his system appeared for the first time, in his *Enzyklopädie der philosophischen Wissenschaften im Grundrisse* (Encyclopedia of the Philosophical Sciences in Outline) (1817), which was reprinted twice during his Berlin period in two completely revised editions (1827, 1830). Also during this period he published *Naturrecht und Staatswissenschaft im Grundrisse. Grundlinien der Philosophie des Rechts* (Natural Law and Politics in Outline. The Principles of the Philosophy of Right) (1821). Apart from these, Hegel published only minor writings during his lifetime. These were written partly in response to events at the time, although most articles were for the *Jahrbücher für wissenschaftliche Kritik* (Yearbooks of Scientific Criticism), which he co-edited from 1827. Among these is his final published work, *Über die englische Reform-Bill* (On the English Reform Bill) (1831).

The second group of texts includes those works which were written by Hegel but not published by him. Almost all these texts first became accessible in a more or less authentic form during the twentieth century. They can again be divided into three groups. The first group consists of the manuscripts which Hegel wrote between the end of his time as a student and the end of his time in Jena. Among the most important are the so-called *Theologische Jugendschriften* (*Early Theological Writings*), which were published in 1907 at the instigation of Wilhelm Dilthey by his pupil, H. Nohl. Today they are known as Hegel's *Frühschriften* (Early Writings). Further important texts from this period are the three *Jenaer Systementwürfe* (*Jena Drafts of a Philosophical System*), written between 1803 and 1806, partly for publication and partly as lecture notes. The second group of writings not published by Hegel consists of works produced during his period in Nuremberg. Hegel's first biographer, K. Rosenkranz, presented excerpts from these writings as the *Philosophische Propädeutik* (Philosophical Propaedeutic) (1840). In this text Hegel attempted to present his philosophical views in a form suitable for use within the framework of his grammar-school teaching courses. The third group of texts comprises manuscripts and notes which he wrote in connection with his lectures in Heidelberg and Berlin. They are partly contained in the editions in which his pupils and friends published his works after his death.

The third major group of texts covers those works which were neither written nor published by Hegel. They form almost half the texts contained in the first complete edition of Hegel's works. Among them one finds Hegel's extremely influential lectures on aesthetics, the philosophy of history, the history of philosophy and the philosophy of religion. In the form in which they have become influential, these texts are the product of students, in most cases representing the result of notes compiled during Hegel's lectures. Insufficient attention has been paid to this remarkable fact, that is, that some of Hegel's most influential texts actually have the status of second-hand sources.

The first complete edition of Hegel's work, published during the years 1832–45, proved to be influential but highly unreliable both from a historical and a critical point of view. Since the beginning of the twentieth century several attempts have been made to produce a new edition. To date, none has reached a successful conclusion. Since 1968 a new historical and critical edition of Hegel's complete works has been in preparation. By the end of 2003 eighteen volumes had been published.

2 The development of the system: the early writings

The early years of Hegel's intellectual career were characterized less by philosophical ambitions than by interests in public enlightenment and public education. In contrast to his student friends Hölderlin and Schelling, whose activities were directly based on internal philosophical discussions, Hegel aimed in his early works to find ways 'to influence men's lives' (as he wrote to Schelling). He regarded as an appropriate starting point for these attempts the analysis of the role and consequences which must be attributed to religion, especially Christianity, for the individual and for the social context of a nation. In this early approach two different interests are at work. On the one hand, Hegel aims to show how religion had developed into a power hostile to life, which produces its effect through fear and demands submission. On the other hand, however, he would like to understand the conditions under which it can prosper as a productive element in the life of the individual and society. Hegel's investigations of religion under these two aspects were strongly influenced during the early years (1793–1800) by the cultural criticism and social theories of ROUSSEAU as well as the religious philosophy of KANT (§§11, 13), and by his critical assessment of the theological positions of his academic theology teachers in Tübingen (G.C. Storr and J.F. Flatt). The most important works during this period are represented by the texts which have been preserved as fragments, and which have become known under the titles *Die Positivität der christlichen Religion* (The Positivity of the Christian Religion) (1795–6) and *Der Geist des Christentums und sein Schicksal* (The Spirit of Christianity and its Fate) (1798–9).

Hegel's religious criticism centres on the concept of 'positive religion'. For Hegel, a positive religion is one whose fundamental content and principles cannot be made comprehensible to human reason. They thus appear unnatural and supernatural, and are seen to be based on authority and to demand obedience. For Hegel, the Jewish religion represents the paradigm of a positive religion. Hegel also considers that the Christian religion has been transformed into a positive religion during the course of its history, in other words into a religion which alienates human beings from themselves and from their fellow creatures (see ALIENATION). He tries to identify cultural and social developments as an explanation for this transformation. In direct opposition to positive religion, Hegel conceives what he calls 'natural religion', which he defines as one whose doctrines correspond with human nature: one which permits or even encourages people to live not only in harmony with their own needs, inclinations and well-considered convictions, but also without being alienated from other people. Hegel's belief in the value for mankind of harmony with oneself (and others), which is strongly influenced by the Stoic ethic (which also via Rousseau had an impact on Kant's practical philosophy), is grounded in a quasi-metaphysical conception of love and life. It owes a considerable debt to the philosophical approach of Hölderlin, with whom Hegel again associated closely during his Frankfurt period. According to this conception, there is a sort of moral emotion of love, which rises above all separations and conflicts, in which persons might be involved in relation to themselves and to others. It is this emotion of love which makes people aware of their unity with others and with themselves. It cannot be adequately thematized by philosophy, which is based on reflection and (conceptual) distinction. It demonstrates vividly, however – and here metaphysics enters – the true constitution of reality, which consists of a state of unity forming the basis for all separations and conflicts and making these possible. This reality, which has to be thought of as unity, Hegel calls 'Life' (*Leben*) and also 'Being' (*Sein*). Hegel's efforts at the end of his Frankfurt period are directed towards thinking of reality in these terms in a sufficiently differentiated manner. In doing so he pursues above all the goal of conceiving of life as a process which generates as well as reconciles oppositions, a dynamic unity of generation and reconciliation. To explain this complex structure, which he conceives what he calls 'life' to be, Hegel devised in the so-called *Systemfragment von 1800* the formula 'Life is the connection of connection and non-connection'. This formula and the concept of life on which it is based already point clearly towards Hegel's later organicist metaphysics.

3 The development of the system: the Jena writings

The work of Hegel's Jena period (1801–6) can be divided into critical and systematic writings. Among the critical writings are his first philosophical publication, *The Difference between Fichte's and Schelling's Systems of Philosophy*, and most of the essays which he published during the years 1802–3 in the *Critical Journal of Philosophy*. In these essays, Hegel reveals himself as a critic of the philosophy of his age, especially of the positions of Kant, JACOBI and FICHTE whom he accuses of practising a 'reflective philosophy of subjectivity' as he calls it in the sub-title of his essay *Faith and Knowledge* (1802). For Hegel, reflective philosophy is initially an expression of an age or historical situation. Such an age is subject to the dichotomies of culture (*Bildung*), which are the products of the understanding and whose activity is regarded as divisive and isolatory. Being subject to those dichotomies, it is impossible for such an age to overcome them and

restore the harmony which the understanding has destroyed. A philosophy committed to such an age shares its fate, being also unable to remove, at least in theory, the conflicts which appear as the concrete forms of dichotomy. For even when philosophy strives to overcome these conflicts – according to Hegel, 'the only interest of reason' – and thus makes reference to a particular idea of unity or harmony, even then it remains committed to the conditions of its age and will achieve nothing except newer and even more acute conflicts. According to Hegel, we can characterize the general form underlying the various conflicts as the conflict between subjectivity and objectivity. The attempts of reflective philosophy to overcome them fail, in Hegel's view, because they are largely abstract: that is, they fail to take into account either the subjective or the objective component of the conflict, and declare it to be resolved by neglecting or abstracting from either of these components. In abstracting from subjectivity, objectivity (in Hegel's terminology) is posited as absolute, which leads to the subordination of subjectivity. This way of reconciling the conflict between subjectivity and objectivity is characteristic of all religions describable as positive by Hegel's definition. If, on the other hand, abstraction is made from objectivity, and subjectivity is thus posited as absolute, then objectivity is regarded as being dependent on subjectivity. This one-sided absolutization of subjectivity is Hegel's objection to the philosophies of Kant, Jacobi and Fichte and the reason he describes their theories as forms of a reflective philosophy of subjectivity.

During his early years in Jena, in contrast to the philosophical attitudes which he criticized, Hegel assumes along with Schelling that the described conflict between subjectivity and objectivity can only be overcome by a philosophy of identity. A philosophy of identity is characterized by the preconditions (1) that for each opposition there is a unity which must be regarded as a unity of the opposing factors, and (2) that the opposing factors are nothing more than their unity under the description or *in the form* of the opposing factors. These preconditions suggest that one should understand the overcoming of the opposition between subjectivity and objectivity as a single process which *reconstructs* the unity underlying the opposing factors and makes them possible in the first place. Following the conceptual assumptions favoured by Hegel at the time, the unity to be reconstructed in a philosophy of identity is defined as the 'subject-object', and the subject and object themselves are characterized as 'subjective subject-object' or 'objective subject-object' respectively. The process of reconstruction of the subject-object by means of the assumptions of the philosophy of identity consists of recognizing the subjective and objective subject–object in their specific one-sidedness or opposition to each other, and thus gaining an insight into the internal structure of the subject-object as the unity which underlies the two conflicting factors and makes them possible in the first place. Although Hegel did not persist in using this terminology for long, for most of his time in Jena he nevertheless remained faithful to the project of the development of a unity which he considered to be comprehensive and which consists of its internal opposing elements. The various attempts at a formal description of a process which was aimed at a unity led Hegel to various system models. All of them contained – albeit with variations of terminology and detail – a discipline initially defined by Hegel as 'logic and metaphysics' as well as a so-called 'real philosophy' (*Real-Philosophie*), in other words a 'philosophy of nature' as well as what he later called a 'philosophy of spirit'.

The systematic works of the Jena period, apart from the *Phenomenology of Spirit*, principally include the three *Jena Drafts of a Philosophical System*. Of these (in some cases) comprehensive fragments, mainly the sections dealing with the philosophy of nature and of spirit are extant. As regards the philosophy of nature, in all the Jena versions of this part of Hegel's system the description of all natural phenomena, the analysis of their processes and their interrelationships is achieved by recourse to two essential factors, which Hegel calls 'Ether' and 'Matter' (*Materie*). 'Ether' describes something like a materialized absolute, which expresses and develops itself within the realm of space and time. This entity is now introduced by Hegel in connection with the development of the determinations of nature as absolute matter or alternatively as absolute being, and the task of philosophy of nature lies in interpreting the various natural phenomena – from the solar system and the laws governing its movements to illness and death of animal organisms – as different manifestations of this absolute matter. Hegel is concerned not merely to show that any particular natural phenomenon is in its peculiar way a specific expression of absolute matter. Above all, he is concerned to prove that nature is a unity ordered in a particular manner. As a specific expression of absolute matter, each natural phenomenon represents an element in the ordered succession of natural phenomena. The position of a natural phenomenon in the order of nature is laid down by the specific way in which absolute matter is expressed in it. A consequence of this approach is that here the natural order is understood as determined by certain postulates which result from the structural conditions of the absolute matter and the methodological maxims of the complete description of these conditions. Differences between the Jena versions of Hegel's philosophy of nature mainly result from the inclusion of new facts made available by current science; but they leave his basic assumptions untouched.

Things are different in the case of the Jena writings on the second part of real philosophy – the philosophy of spirit – initially still described by Hegel as the 'philosophy of ethical life' (*Philosophie der Sittlichkeit*). They reveal many changes, all linked to modifications of his conception of spirit. Initially, he presents his philosophy of spirit as a theory of ethical life, which he then transforms into a theory of consciousness. For reasons linked to a renewed preoccupation with Fichte and certain new insights into the logical structure of self-consciousness, towards the end of his Jena period Hegel found himself obliged to present an approach which had occupied him since at least 1804–5. This approach enabled him to liberate the philosophy of spirit from its narrow systematic links to a conception of ethical life based on assumptions incompatible with his new conception of spirit. It assumes that only the formal structure of self-consciousness, which consists in its being a unity of generality and singularity, can provide the framework within which the logical-metaphysical determinations, the natural world and psychosocial phenomena unite to form a meaningful systematic context. For the philosophy of spirit this means in particular that as far as method is concerned it is better equipped for the implementation of its systematic task of being the representation of the processes of self-realization of what Hegel calls 'reason'. This insight into the formal structure of self-consciousness is the final achievement of his Jena period, and one which he never subsequently abandoned.

4 The system: metaphysical foundations

Hegel's systematic philosophy attempts to comprehend reality in all its manifestations as a self-representation of reason (*Vernunft*). His conception of what he calls 'reason' combines various specifically Hegelian connotations, both ontological and epistemological. For him, 'reason' is not merely the name for a human faculty which contributes in a specific manner to our gaining knowledge; he also uses 'reason' to describe that which is ultimately and eminently real. This is the ontological connotation. Reason is reality, and that alone is truly real which is reasonable. This programmatic credo, which has become famous from the foreword to Hegel's *Philosophy of Right*, is the basic precept determining the entire approach to his system.

At least three different convictions make up this basic precept of the ontological dignity of reason.

The first is that the everything which in one sense or another is real must be considered as the differentiation and partial realization of a primary structure which in turn forms the basis for whatever is real in whichever sense. Hegel calls this primary structure 'the absolute' or 'reason'. He shares this conviction of the necessity of assuming a primary structure he called 'reason' (interpreted ontologically) with Fichte, Schelling, Hölderlin and other members of the post-Kantian idealistic movement who used different names for it. It is this assumption which makes them all (ontological) monists. For Hegel this conviction is justified not only because it alone offers a basis for systematic philosophical considerations, following the failure of all previous philosophical attempts to conceive of a unified and complete representation of the world. It is also justified because, according to Hegel, without it one cannot make sense of the concepts of an object and of objectivity. This latter justification is part of the task of his *Phenomenology of Spirit*

This first conviction, which forms a part of Hegel's ontological conception of reason, is still too imprecise to provide a clue as to why exactly the concept 'reason' can be used to characterize the primary structure. Hegel's second important conviction, however, makes this clearer. It relates to the internal constitution of the structure which he characterizes as reason. He understands this structure to be a complex unity of thinking and being. The relevant motives for this conviction can be summarized as follows: the only philosophical approach which can organize the whole of reality into a unified and coherent picture accessible to knowledge is one which insists that everything taken to be real is only real inasmuch as it can be comprehended as the actualization of some specific structural elements of reason. This assertion of the essential reasonableness of all being, together with the first conviction of the necessity of assuming a primary structure, leads directly to the concept of this primary structure as a unity of thinking and being, understood in the very radical sense that thinking and being are one and the same, or that only thinking has being. If we now call this unity of thinking and being 'reason', and if, like Hegel, we are convinced that the requisite primary structure must be thought of as this unity of thinking and being, then reason will be declared on the one hand to represent what in the final analysis is ultimately real, and on the other that which alone is real. Since a monistic position is one in which a single entity is maintained as the ultimate and sole reality, Hegel's philosophical conception has rightly been called a 'Monism of Reason' (see MONISM).

The third conviction which enters into Hegel's basic assumption of reason as the primary structure

constituting reality and thus being ultimately and only real is that this structure constitutes reality and thus its own objectivity in a teleological process which must be understood as a process of cognition. It is this conviction which leads to the characteristically Hegelian dogma that there can be no adequate theory of reality without a dynamic or process-oriented ontology (see PROCESSES). The formula which Hegel uses to characterize this process from his early Jena works onwards shows very clearly the dominant role which he assigns to what he defines as 'reason' in the systematic approach designed to elaborate his third conviction. This process is described as 'self-knowledge of cognition' (*Selbsterkenntnis der Vernunft*). Hegel tries to integrate within this formula various aspects of his conception of reason. The first aspect is that it is necessary to take reason, understood as the primary structure, as something which is essentially dynamic. By this he means that the element of self-realization forms part of the moments which determine the primary structure. It is difficult to understand the way in which Hegel links this element of self-realization into his idea of reason as the unity of thinking and being. In order to get a rather over-simplified idea of the background for Hegel's claim, it might help to rely metaphorically on the theory of organism: just as an organism can be described as an entity whose development is linked to the concept or the structural plan of itself in such a way that the (more or less) successful realization of this concept or structural plan belongs to its being real, so we should think of Hegelian reason, understood as the ontologically relevant primary structure, as realizing in a quasi-organic developmental process the unity of thinking and being which characterizes its concept, thereby representing itself as real or as reality.

The second aspect Hegel has in mind when he speaks of 'self-cognition of reason', describing a process which must indeed be understood as that of the self-realization of reason, is that this process represents a process of *cognition* for reason. It is apparently not sufficient for Hegel to embed his idea of reason as the ontological primary structure in a conception of realization based on the paradigm of the organism. Such a grounding seems to be too unspecific for him, because it does not show how to describe a process which is typical of *all* organisms in such a way that we understand more precisely and in detail what it means for the process to be one of self-realization of *reason*. The specific way in which reason realizes itself is to be characterized first of all as a process of cognition, because only this characterization takes into account the fact that that which is being realized, namely reason, must be thought of strictly as nothing more than thinking *qua* cognition. But even this way of conceiving the realization of reason is still too imprecise, unless one includes in the concept of realization the thesis that reason is the ultimately and only real ontological primary structure. The inclusion of this thesis then leads directly to the teleologically conceived description of the process of the realization of reason as a process of self-cognition. For if only reason – by which is meant the unity of thinking and being – is real, and if an integral part of this concept of reason is the conception of its realization in the form of a process of cognition, then this process can only be directed towards the cognition of reason itself, because nothing else exists. Since this process aims to make reason aware that it alone is real, the presentation of this process, in Hegel's view, must take on the form of a system in which each manifestation of reality documents its reasonable nature. His philosophy aims to elaborate this system.

The project of exhibiting reason not only as the basis for all reality, but also as the whole of reality itself, was Hegel's sole, lifelong philosophical goal. It took him some time to be able to formulate this project explicitly. This is linked to his intellectual development (see §2 above). He also considered various approaches to the realization and development of this project (see §3 above), but he never felt any need to question the project itself.

5   *The system:* Phenomenology of Spirit

The *Phenomenology of Spirit* (1807) is Hegel's most influential work. It serves as an introduction to his philosophical system by means of a history of the experience of consciousness. The *Phenomenology of Spirit* represents only one of a number of introductory attempts he made. In the Jena writings and system drafts, a discipline which Hegel calls 'logic' assumes this function. This logic is intended to fulfil its introductory function by raising our 'normal' thinking, which is characterized by its confinement to irreconcilable oppositions, to the level of 'speculation' – Hegel's term for philosophical thinking. Speculative thought is characterized by the knowledge of the reconcilability of oppositions and of the mechanisms of their coming about. That thinking, which by its insistence on oppositions simultaneously maintains their basic irresolvability, Hegel referred to at this time as 'reflection'. He regarded the elevation of this thinking to the position of speculation as a destruction of the structures which characterize reflection, and which together constitute the finiteness of reflection. 'Finiteness' of reflection or (used by Hegel as a synonym) of the understanding (*Verstand*) is initially a way of saying that thinking whose oppositions are

irreconcilable moves within limits and must thus be regarded as finite. According to Hegel, it is now the task of logic to carry out the destruction of the finiteness of reflection or of the thinking of the understanding, thereby simultaneously leading to the standpoint of speculation or of the thinking of reason. Hegel sees the problem of a logic, which he understands as an introduction to philosophy, to be to carry out this destruction in such a way that not only the limitations of the thinking of the understanding and its preconditions are presented as mistakes and absurdities, but also that during this destructive process those structures become clear which guarantee a reasonable (that is, an intrinsic speculative) insight into the basic structures of reality.

Towards the end of his Jena period, Hegel abandoned the project of developing a logic as an introduction to his system of philosophy, and in its place presented a new discipline which he called the 'Science of the Experience of Consciousness' or 'Phenomenology of Spirit'. The declared goal of this discipline is twofold: on the one hand, it should destroy our supposedly natural picture of the world, and thus also our understanding of ourselves as the more or less consistent holders or subjects of this view, by demonstrating the contradictions which arise in our normal, complex view of the world. And second, it should thereby vindicate his ontological monism by demonstrating that our natural tendency to view the world as consisting of objects something which are both alien and different from us is not tenable. Instead we have to accept that in order to account for the real constitution of the world, and thus of objects and objectivity, we must presuppose, that we and the world represent a structural unity with the essential characteristic of being conscious of itself.

Hegel pursues this dual goal in a complex and ambitious thought-process, which attempts to combine and position within a comprehensive context a wide range of themes – historical, epistemological, psychological, meta-scientific, ideological-critical, ethical, aesthetical and religio-philosophical. This whole thought-process is based on two convictions which govern Hegel's entire construction. (1) It is possible to conceive of all epistemic attitudes of a consciousness towards a material world as relations between a subject termed 'cognition' (*Wissen*) and an object termed 'truth' (*Wahrheit*). That which is presented as cognition or truth is in each case determined by the description which the consciousness is able to furnish of its epistemic situation and its object corresponding to this situation. (2) 'Knowledge' (*Erkenntnis*) can only be taken to be that epistemic relation between cognition (subject) and truth (object) in which cognition and truth correspond with each other, which for Hegel is only the case if they are identical. A necessary, though not sufficient, condition for claiming this relationship of identity between cognition and truth is that what is regarded as cognition or as truth respectively is not formulated in a self-contradictory or inconsistent manner. For the Hegel of the *Phenomenology of Spirit*, and of the writings which were to follow, knowledge in the strict sense is thus really self-knowledge.

In characterizing the various epistemic attitudes of a consciousness to the world in the *Phenomenology of Spirit*, Hegel takes as his starting point something which he calls 'sense certainty'. He uses this term to describe an attitude which assumes that in order to know the true nature of reality we must rely on that which is sensually immediately present to us as a spatiotemporally given single object. Hegel demonstrates the untenability of this attitude by attempting to prove that in such an immediate reference to objects nothing true can be claimed of them. Moreover this immediate approach shows that any attempt to gain knowledge of what an object really is implies at the outset a different attitude towards objects. This attitude is determined by the assumption that what we are really dealing with if we refer to objects in order to know them is not the immediately given object, but the object of perception, which is characterized by Hegel as an entity defined through its qualities. According to Hegel, however, even this attitude is not tenable. Neither the perceiving consciousness, nor the object perceived, nor the relationship which is believed to exist between the two can be accepted in the manner in which they appear in this constellation: the subject, which aims to perceive the object of perception as that which it really is, can neither formulate a consistent concept of this object nor describe itself in unequivocal terms. The consciousness is thus led to a concept of an object which differentiates between what the object is in itself and what it appears to be. In order to differentiate in this manner, the consciousness must define itself as understanding, to which the inner constitution of the object in itself is disclosed as being constituted by its own laws, that is, by the laws of the understanding. Although, according to Hegel, this interpretation of the objective world through the cognizing subject also produces neither a truthful concept of the cognizing consciousness nor of the object in question, it none the less leads to the enforcement of an attitude according to which consciousness, when referring to an object, is referring to something which it is itself. The realization of this insight – that consciousness, when referring to objects, in reality relates to itself – converts consciousness into self-consciousness.

The various ways in which consciousness deals with itself and the objective manifestations corresponding with these ways as reason and spirit are comprehensively discussed by Hegel in the remainder of his *Phenomenology of Spirit*. It is in this context that he presents some of his most famous analyses, such as the account of the master–servant relationship, his critique of the Enlightenment and the French Revolution, his diagnosis of the strengths and weaknesses of the ancients' ideas of morality and ethical life and his theory of religion. The conclusion of the *Phenomenology of Spirit* forms what Hegel calls 'absolute knowledge'. Hegel characterizes this knowledge also as 'comprehending knowledge' (*begreifendes Wissen*), aiming thereby to highlight two ideas: (1) that this knowledge is only present when the subject of the knowledge knows itself to be identical *under every description* with the object of that knowledge. Comprehending knowledge therefore only occurs when the self knows itself to be 'in its otherness with itself', as Hegel puts it at the end of the *Phenomenology of Spirit*. He also aims to point out (2) that this type of identity of a subject with an object is that which constitutes the essence of that which he calls the 'Concept' (*Begriff*) of reason. The task of the *Science of Logic* is to develop this 'Concept' of reason in all its logical qualities. The goal of the *Phenomenology of Spirit*, the discipline which is to provide an introduction to logic, is achieved when it becomes evident to the consciousness that (Hegelian) truth only belongs to the (Hegelian) Concept.

But the *Phenomenology of Spirit* is not just an introduction to the system. From another point of view, Hegel describes the phenomenological process as 'self-fulfilling scepticism'. By means of this metaphor he attempts to establish a link to a subject closely connected with his critical assessment of his cultural and political environment, namely that of dichotomy (*Entzweiung*). For Hegel, the modern age is characterized by the fact that unity has disappeared from people's lives. The all-embracing unity of life can no longer be experienced, as people are no longer in a position to integrate the various aspects of their understanding of the world in a conflict-free context. So, for example, their moral convictions will force upon them a view of the world in which something like freedom and consequently something like the belief in the possibility to cause events based on free decisions occupies an irrefutable position. This view, based on moral convictions, stands in a conflicting and, finally, aporetic relationship to their scientific view of the world, which commits them to an understanding of the world in which there are no first causes or unconditioned facts, because each cause must itself be interpreted anew as an effect, whose cause can only be seen as determined by previous circumstances. In this view of the world there is apparently no place for freedom. The conflict between various aspects of the understanding of the world, cited here by way of example, is for Hegel by no means singular; instead, it runs like a leitmotif through the modern conceptualizations of all spheres of life. He initially interprets it wholly in the spirit of Rousseau as a product of culture and civilization. This conflict is what separates a human being from itself, so that it continues to be denied a coherent image of the world. As a creature living in dichotomies, the modern person is an example of what Hegel calls the 'unhappy consciousness'.

Modern consciousness now attempts to solve this conflict by making each in turn of the conflicting views into the dominant attitude of its entire interpretation of the world. In this way, however, it can only achieve a one-sided interpretation of reality, which is just as incapable of doing justice to the true nature of reality as to the need of human consciousness to integrate all aspects of reality into its understanding of the world as a coherent unity. According to Hegel, it is in this situation that the need for philosophy arises. It is philosophy's task to destroy these one-sided total interpretations of consciousness and in this destruction to lay the foundation for the true complete interpretation of reality. The *Phenomenology of Spirit* describes this process of destruction and foundation-laying. The consciousness experiences it as a process of permanent destabilization of all the convictions on which it has always based its one-sided interpretations of the world. In this sceptical approach it is forced to doubt everything and to abandon all its supposed certainties. While the phenomenological process thus concedes a philosophical value to scepticism, in Hegel's understanding it simultaneously overcomes this scepticism by claiming a truth-revealing function for it. It is also Hegel's intention that the *Phenomenology of Spirit* should in this respect be understood as a treatise on the cathartic effect of philosophical scepticism.

Two questions have often been raised in connection with Hegel's conception of the *Phenomenology of Spirit* as an introduction to his 'System of Science', especially his logic. The first is whether Hegel does not assume in advance certain central theses of the discipline to which the *Phenomenology of Spirit* is intended to provide an introduction. This question draws attention to a methodological problem which originates from Hegel's assertion that the process of consciousness described in the *Phenomenology of Spirit* is not guided by any preconditions external to this process. This assertion seems difficult to square with certain manoeuvres which Hegel makes during the course of the

Phenomenology of Spirit. The second question is of a more intrinsic nature and concerns the categorical apparatus employed by Hegel in the *Phenomenology of Spirit.* In this context, in particular his phenomenological conception of negation and identity as well as his concepts of knowledge and of cognition aroused critical interest from the very beginning.

It is difficult to determine exactly how Hegel himself later assessed the success of the *Phenomenology of Spirit* as an introduction to the point of view which is assumed at the beginning of his *Science of Logic.* On the one hand, he seems to have allotted it a certain value throughout his entire life, not only as a history of consciousness but also as an introduction. This is shown not only by the fact that he made arrangements for the publication of a second edition of the work immediately before his death, but also by later statements in the various editions of the *Science of Logic* and the *Encyclopedia of the Philosophical Sciences.* However, it is in precisely these statements that one finds Hegel expressing an increasingly critical attitude towards his project of a phenomenological introduction to the system. In this context it should also be recorded that by 1827 at the latest (that is, from the second edition of the *Encyclopedia of the Philosophical Sciences*) Hegel no longer has recourse to a version of phenomenology as 'a more detailed introduction, in order to explain and lead to the meaning and the point of view which is here allotted to logic', but for this purpose uses instead a discussion which deals with three different 'attitudes of thought to objectivity'.

6 The system: Science of Logic

The real centre of the Hegelian system is the discipline he described as 'Logic'. It contains his doctrine of the categories, to use traditional terminology (see CATEGORIES). Hegel dedicated his most comprehensive and complex work to this discipline, the *Science of Logic* (1812–16), later adding a much shorter version within the framework of the *Encyclopedia of the Philosophical Sciences.*

The starting point of the *Logic* is the insight, justified in Hegel's view by the result of the *Phenomenology of Spirit*, (1) that all true knowledge is knowledge of oneself, and (2) that the subject of this knowledge, that is to say, that which knows about itself, is reason. Because Hegel – following Schelling – only considers that to be real which can also be known, he concludes from the results of the *Phenomenology of Spirit* that only reason is real. He thinks of this reason as, internally, an extremely complex entity. Hegel now distinguishes between the 'Concept' of reason and the process of its realization. The object of the *Science of Logic* is the conceptual, that is to say, for Hegel, the logical development of this Concept. Since this Concept is the Concept of that which alone is real, Hegel can maintain that his *Science of Logic* takes the place of traditional metaphysics, which concerned itself with the elucidation of the basic ways in which we can think of reality.

Since the object whose Concept is to be logically discussed is reason, understood to be the sum of reality, the Concept of reason must include not only those aspects which account for reason's character of reality or of being, but also those aspects which do justice to the peculiar character of reason as thinking. Hegel calls both these aspects 'Determinations of the Concept' (*Begriffsbestimmungen*). Those aspects of the Concept of reason which take into account its character of being are developed by Hegel in the section 'Objective Logic' in the *Science of Logic*. He presents those aspects which are intended to do justice to its thinking character in the section called 'Subjective Logic'. He further subdivides 'Objective Logic' into 'Logic of Being' and 'Logic of Essence'.

In his 'Objective Logic', Hegel tries to show how it is possible to generate from very simple, so-called 'immediate' determinations such as 'Being', 'Nothing' and 'Becoming' other categories of quality and quantity as well as relational and modal determinations, such as 'Cause-Effect', 'Substance-Accidence' and 'Existence', 'Necessity' and the like. As in the 'Subjective Logic', the basic strategy here for the creation of categories or determinations of the Concept, assumes that (1) for every category there is an opposing one which upon closer analysis reveals itself to be its true meaning, and that (2) for every two categories opposing each other in this manner there is a third category whose meaning is determined by that which makes the opposing categories compatible. Hegel considers these two assumptions justified because only they can lead to what in his eyes is a complete and non-contingent system of categories. Hegel himself, however, did very little to make their exact sense clear, although he uses them with great skill. Immediately after his death this led to a confused and still inconclusive discussion regarding their interpretation. Many judgments concerning the worth or worthlessness of Hegel's philosophy are linked to this discussion, which has taken its place in the annals of Hegel research as a discussion concerning the meaning, significance and value of the so-called 'dialectical method'. (Hegel himself preferred 'speculative method'.)

In particular, Hegel's claims about the truth-generating function of contradiction have played a major role in the discussion of the 'dialectical method' described in the *Science of Logic*. Though highly praised by Hegel himself, his doctrine of the nature and methodological merits of contradiction has proved to be inaccessible and obscure. This may have been caused in part by Hegel's extremely concise and provocative formulations of this methodical maxim. The reader is reminded in this context not only of the succinct formulation which he chose to defend on the occasion of his Jena Habilitation – 'contradiction is the rule of truth, non-contradiction the rule of falsehood' – but also of his provocative version of the principle of contradiction, according to which 'everything is inherently contradictory'. The difficulties associated with the comprehension of the Hegelian conception of contradiction have perforce a link with his particular unconventional concept of contradiction. Two points are particularly important, in that they differentiate his concept from the classical concept of contradiction of traditional logic. (1) A contradiction between two propositions cannot be confirmed solely on the basis of their ascription to a single subject of two contradictory predicates; it is also necessary to take into account the meaning of the subject of these propositions. If the contradictory predicates cannot meaningfully be attributed to the subject, then no contradiction arises. 'Legible' and 'illegible' are predicates which will only lead to contradiction if attributed to texts, but not, for example, to bananas. For Hegel, this means among other things that the relation of contradiction is dependent on the context. (2) Hegel thinks of contradictions as analogous to positive and negative determinations, which neutralize each other but without making that whose neutralizing determinations they are into a contradictory concept which has absolutely no meaning, which therefore means nothing (the Kantian 'Nihil negativum'). Rather, the way in which positive and negative determinations neutralize each other tells us something informative about the object to which the neutralizing determinations apply. For example, possession of Euro 100 neutralizes a debt of Euro 100, without thereby making the concept of property a contradictory concept. Instead, the way in which this neutralization takes place makes clear that the concept 'property' means something which must be thought of as of a quantifiable size. For Hegel this is a consequence of 'the logical principle that what is self-contradictory does not dissolve itself into a nullity, into abstract nothingness, but essentially only into the negation of its *particular* content'. Whether these two convictions are sufficient to justify Hegel's thesis that contradictions play a 'positive' role in cognition procedures is rightly controversial.

Hegel's 'Subjective Logic', the second part of the *Science of Logic*, contains not only his so-called 'speculative' interpretation of the objects of traditional logic, that is, his own doctrine of concepts, judgments and syllogisms, but above all his theory of the 'Concept'. This theory is deeply rooted in Hegel's critique of traditional metaphysics, and is thus most easily comprehended when placed in that context. He presents this critique most tellingly in the third edition of the *Encyclopedia of the Philosophical Sciences*. His starting point here is the claim that what matters in philosophy, and what philosophy aims at, is the 'scientific recognition of truth'. This means among other things that philosophy is concerned with the recognition of 'what objects really are'. According to Hegel, the question of what objects really are has been approached in philosophy from a variety of angles, but all the different modes in which the question has been answered to date are unacceptable because they are based on false premises. Traditional metaphysics is one of the ways of approaching the question of what objects really are. Hegel characterizes this approach as 'the *unbiased* method', which is motivated by the assumption that 'through *thinking the truth becomes known*, what objects really are is brought to one's consciousness'. In contrast to other philosophical approaches that deal with the question posed, metaphysics, according to Hegel, is in principle certainly capable of contributing to the cognition of what things in truth are, because it starts from the correct assumption that 'the determinations of thought' are to be seen as 'the fundamental determinations of things'. But traditional metaphysics has not made a significant contribution to the cognition of truth, because it was only able to transform its correct initial assumption in a systematically erroneous manner.

According to Hegel, the crucial weakness of traditional metaphysics is to use the form of judgment *in an unreflective manner*, and this shows itself in various ways. First it shows in the unfounded assumption of traditional metaphysics that judgments provide a particular and direct insight into the constitution of reality or that which really exists. In Hegel's view this unfounded assumption has two consequences: the first is that it tends without reason to favour a particular ontological model of reality because it regards the subject-predicate form as the standard form of the judgment; the second consequence, in Hegel's view incomparably more problematic, consists of the unfounded tendency of traditional metaphysics to conclude from the unquestioned and assumed correspondence between the form of judgment and constitution of reality that one can express by means of judgments what objects really are. Hegel does not find problematic the assumption contained in this conviction that one can make judgments concerning objects. He believes that the problem lies rather

in the fact that one can assume *without examination* that 'the form of the judgment could be the form of truth'. In Hegel's view, however, such an examination is essential because the traditional understanding of subject and predicate does not justify the assertion that a subject-predicate judgment actually contributes something to the determination of a real object. An additional problem lies in the fact that the unconsidered use of the form of judgment has led traditional metaphysics erroneously to use a 'natural' interpretation of the concepts of subject and predicate. The consequence of this interpretation is that judgments of the subject-predicate form can lay no claim to 'truth'.

Hegel's chief criticism of traditional metaphysics therefore lies in the lack of clarity associated with its interpretation of the form of the judgment. In particular he rejects its tendency to interpret the judgment 'naturally', which for him means to encourage a subjectivist interpretation of the judgment built on the concept of representation. Such a subjectivist interpretation cannot show how to guarantee for the judgment some sort of claim to truth or recognition of what something really is. Therefore the subjectivist metaphysical interpretation of the judgment is problematic at the very outset. Moreover, it becomes downright dangerous when one considers its ontological implications, for it leads erroneously to the assumption that the objects corresponding to the subject-concepts of the judgment are to be thought of as substances to which are attributed the characteristics described by the predicate-concepts. The unreflective subjectivist interpretation implies or at least suggests what may be called a substance-ontology, according to which substances which are independent of each other are taken as the fundamental entities of reality, determined predicatively by accidental characteristics which are applicable or not applicable to them. It is this commitment to a substance-ontology which Hegel critically imputes to traditional metaphysics. From this criticism, he deduces that it is first necessary to reach an agreement as to what the object really is before one can adequately assess the function and the achievement of the judgment in the context of knowledge. To reach this agreement is the task of the Logic of the Concept.

The starting point of Hegel's theory of the Concept is the assumption which he imputes to traditional metaphysics as an insight which is in principle correct. This was the insight that only through thinking can one recognize what something really is. Since in Hegel's view thinking is concerned not with intuitions or representations, but with concepts, he identifies that which something in truth or really is with its Concept. Because of this identification, talk of the Concept acquires an ontological connotation. Hegelian Concepts must not be confused with the so-called general concepts of traditional logic. They are difficult to understand precisely and are characterized by the fact that they are (1) non-sensible – which means that they are a particular type of thought-object – and that they are (2) something objective as opposed to subjective. Regarded as these objective thoughts, these Concepts are determined in the sense that in them different relations of determinations of the Concept are to be encountered which occur as determinations of thinking or of thought (*Denkbestimmungen*). These determinations of thought can themselves be regarded as a kind of predicative characteristic. They make up the multitude of all those determinations on the basis of which the Concept of an object can be seen as completely fixed.

Now, in Hegel's view, not everything has a Concept which in one sense or another is ordinarily thought of as an object. A (Hegelian) Concept is only allotted to objects which can be thought of on the model of an organism. Hegel thus maintains that one can only regard those objects as real or as existing in truth for which there is a Concept which can be interpreted on the organic model. If, then, the 'scientific recognition of truth' consists in recognizing the Concept of something, and if a Concept is always a Concept of a organic-type object, then the question arises how one should conceive of such a Concept. For Hegel it is clear that in his concept of a Concept, he must include everything needed to describe an organism. This includes first of all what Hegel calls the subjective Concept, which one can best regard as the sum of all characteristics whose realization represents an organic-type object. For Hegel, in the case of the concept of reason, whose Concept the *Science of Logic* elaborates, these characteristics are exclusively logical data which can be presented in the form of determinations of concepts, judgments and syllogisms. Furthermore, Hegel's Concept must include the element of objectivity. 'Objectivity' here means more or less the same as reality or the state of being an object and suggests the fact that it is part of the Concept of an organism to realize itself. Since, however, Hegel holds that there is ultimately only one object which really exists, namely reason, the Concept of this object must include a characteristic which is exclusively applicable to itself. This characteristic must permit the justification of the claim that in reality there is only one Concept and therefore also only one object. Hegel calls this characteristic 'subjectivity'.

Although it is easy to see that the term 'subjectivity' describes a central element of Hegel's logical theory, it is very difficult to shed light upon

its meaning and function therein. It is relatively obvious only that Hegel attributes the characteristic of subjectivity not just to his Concept, but also to entities such as 'I', 'self-consciousness' and 'spirit'. We are therefore on safe ground if we assume that the subjectivity which is to be attributed to the Concept is precisely that which is also attributed to the I, self-consciousness or spirit and which distinguishes them from other types of organism. The ground becomes more dangerous when it is a matter of stating what subjectivity actually means. This is not merely because Hegel distinguishes between different types of subjectivity, but also because the subjectivity which is constitutive of the Concept is tied to conditions which are difficult to state with any precision. In general it seems to be correct to say that subjectivity occurs when something recognizes itself as being identical with something else. If we follow the *Science of Logic*, then this relationship of identity known as 'subjectivity' can only be established between entities which themselves can be thought of as being particular complexes of relations of similar elements or moments. Subjectivity in this sense is thus intended to describe a certain form of self-reference or self-relationship. According to Hegel, there should be only one entity to which the term 'subjectivity' can be attributed as a characteristic in the sense which has just been explained – the Hegelian 'Idea'. He says of it, 'The unity of the Idea is subjectivity'. This Idea now forms the end of the *Science of Logic*, because through it the Concept of reason has been completely explicated. He also describes this Idea as the absolute method, for it is not only the result, that is, the Concept which comprehends all his moments, but also the complete and systematically generated series of these moments.

The results of the Logic of the Concept represent the justification for Hegel's belief that, apart from a system of logic, a complete system of philosophy must include a so-called 'real philosophy', which is divided into a philosophy of nature and a philosophy of spirit. Hegel undertakes this justification within the framework of the exposition of what characterizes the fully developed (Hegelian) Concept. This exposition only becomes comprehensible if one remembers that Hegel is a supporter of the organological paradigm in metaphysics, according to which that which really is must be regarded as a particular type of organism. Hegel describes the type of organism relevant to his metaphysics as an object which has realized or objectivized its Concept in such a way that it comprehends itself as the objectivization of this Concept of itself. On the basis of this conception, Hegel now develops the following consideration: the (Hegelian) Concept is something which is to be regarded as a unity of (in some ways incompatible) determinations of the Concept. Among these determinations also belong, as Hegel believes he can show, that of objectivity. By this he means that it is a part of the nature of a Concept to become objective, to manifest itself as an object. Now, the only object which is an adequate realization of the Concept is the one to which what Hegel calls 'subjectivity' can be attributed. 'Subjectivity' is the name of a relational characteristic which is present when something *knows* itself to be identical with something else. For Hegel, it follows from these stipulations that subjectivity can only be attributed to the object which knows itself to be identical with its Concept. To produce this knowledge is therefore a demand inherent in the nature of the Concept. Since it is the sole task of the *Science of Logic* to exhibit the Concept of reason, and since this Concept contains the demand for the production of a form of knowledge which can only be acquired when (1) the Concept objectivizes itself, that is, becomes an object, and (2) this object comprehends itself as being identical with its Concept, then it is already a demand inherent in the Concept of reason that reason should be discussed (1) from under the point of view of its objectivity or as an object, and (2) under the aspect of its known identity with its Concept. The first of these topics is the subject of a philosophy of nature; the second that of a philosophy of spirit.

7   The system: philosophy of nature

Hegel's philosophy of nature is an attempt to explain how it is possible that we can recognize nature as a complex whole standing under a set of laws. He thereby takes up the question, important in particular to both Kant and Schelling, of which epistemological and ontological preconditions underlie our conviction that nature can be known. Although Hegel had thought about the problems of a philosophy of nature since his time in Frankfurt, and although he produced several versions of a philosophy of nature during his Jena period, he only published an outline of this part of his system once, quite late, in his *Encyclopedia of the Philosophical Sciences*. Hegel's philosophy of nature is of interest mainly in three respects. The first concerns the way in which he transforms his logical theory into an interpretation of natural phenomena. The second relates to the question of how far Hegel's conceptions in the field of the philosophy of nature take into account the scientific theories current at the time. Finally, the third leads to the question of what we should make of Hegel's approach to a philosophy of nature within the framework of present-day philosophy of science. Since the philosophy of

nature is that part of the Hegelian system which is traditionally regarded with the greatest suspicion and which for this reason has received the least scholarly attention, the assessment of the second and third aspects of this philosophy of nature has so far produced very few uncontroversial results.

As far as the construction of a philosophy of nature according to the requirements of the logical theory of the Concept is concerned, Hegel assumes in accordance with his organological conception of reason that we should think of nature '*in itself* as a living whole'. This living whole has to be conceived of primarily under three different determinations, which reproduce to a certain extent the central characteristics of the Concept of reason as developed by the logical process. According to the first of these determinations, nature is to be considered as a whole defined by space, time, matter and movement. This way of looking at nature makes it the object of what Hegel calls 'mechanics'. According to Hegelian mechanics, space, time, matter and movement, their characteristics and the laws of nature which describe their relationship are generated by the formal structural moments of the (Hegelian) Concept. The utilization of such a 'conceptual' procedure to gain and secure scientific results was never seen by Hegel himself as a direct alternative procedure to empirical scientific research. On the contrary, he was of the opinion that (for instance, by means of his philosophical mechanics) he only makes explicit, and secures a rational foundation for, the conceptual elements which are implicitly contained in every scientific mechanical theory that acquires its data 'from experience and then applies a mathematical treatment'.

According to Hegel, his philosophical mechanics leads to the insight that we must think of the whole of physical nature as 'qualified matter', that is, as a totality of bodies with physical characteristics. This provides the second main determination by which nature is to be comprehended. Hegel ascribes to this way of comprehending nature a discipline which he calls 'physics', including under this heading everything which can in any way be linked with the material status of a body. Accordingly, from phenomena like specific weight, through those like sound, warmth, shape, electricity and magnetism, to the chemical reactions of substances, everything is described as being a consequence of and following from the constitution of the (Hegelian) Concept. He also adds theses concerning the nature of light and a doctrine concerning the elements earth, fire, water and air. It was this part of Hegel's philosophy of nature in particular which drove Hans Scholz, among others, to the following crushing judgment: 'Hegel's philosophy of nature is an experiment which set the philosophy of nature back several centuries instead of furthering its cause, returning it to the stage it had reached at about the time of Paracelsus'. Whether this dictum has substance, however, depends very much on what conception of nature and science one favours.

The third part of Hegel's philosophy of nature consists of the so-called 'organic physics' or 'organics'. In this section the characteristic of subjectivity, familiar from his logical theory, is the determination under which nature is to be regarded. Since in the context of the philosophy of nature, Hegel interprets subjectivity as an essential characteristic of organic life, this section of his philosophy of nature is concerned with nature as a hierarchy of organisms or as an 'organic system'. He distinguishes between three forms of organic life which are exemplified in three types of organism: the general form, which is represented by the geological organism, the particular, which is realized in vegetation, and the individual, which finds its expression in animal organisms. He regards these forms as hierarchically ordered by increasing degree of complexity. In some ways Hegel thematizes relations and conditions of dependence: just as vegetable life-forms presuppose geological structures and processes, so animal organisms presuppose a fully developed plant world. Hegel links this last part of his philosophy of nature to his philosophy of spirit by means of an analysis of the phenomenon of the death of an individual natural being. Here the leading idea is that although through death all natural determinations of the individual are removed, so that we can speak of the 'death of the natural element', none the less death does not annihilate the principle of life, that which is responsible for the essential unity of animal organization and which Hegel calls the 'soul'. Since Hegel interprets the soul as a form of spirit, and since according to his conception the soul is not destroyed by death, he can now postulate the reality of spirit independently of natural determinations as the result of his philosophy of nature, and investigate this reality in its various forms within the framework of a philosophy of spirit.

The question whether Hegel's philosophy of nature integrates in a relatively informed manner the state of science during his lifetime has provoked a number of fairly controversial answers, as has the question whether his approach can still provide any promising perspectives which are relevant today. During the nineteenth century, Hegel's philosophy of nature was broadly considered scandalous by the majority of scientists, an attitude which contributed in no small measure to the discrediting of his philosophy as a whole. This assessment also meant that Hegel's philosophy of nature has never really been taken seriously again. Since 1970, however,

the situation has changed somewhat. Starting from and relying on recent investigations in the history of science regarding the development and state of the sciences during the early nineteenth century, increasing numbers of scholars are inclining towards the view that Hegel was indeed much more familiar with the science of his time and its problems than was generally believed during the nineteenth and most of the twentieth century. It seems advisable at present to refrain from passing final judgment on this matter. The same cannot, however, be said with regard to the present relevance. Here one cannot ignore the fact that Hegel's theses concerning philosophy of nature are, quite simply, meaningless for present-day scientific theory.

8 The system: philosophy of spirit

Hegel's philosophy of spirit is divided into a theory of subjective, objective and absolute spirit. The philosophy of subjective spirit contains Hegel's philosophical psychology; his philosophy of objective spirit is devoted to his theory of law and politics and his conception of world history; and his philosophy of absolute spirit presents his theory of art, religion and philosophy. Hegel presented his philosophy of subjective spirit and in particular his philosophy of absolute spirit to a wider public only in outline in a few paragraphs of the *Encyclopedia of the Philosophical Sciences*. He presented his philosophy of objective spirit not only in the *Encyclopedia*, but also in detail in a work which was already highly regarded during his lifetime, *Natural Law and Politics in Outline: The Principles of the Philosophy of Right* (1821). In this part of his system Hegel again relies on the principle developed in his logical theory that something – here the entity called 'spirit' – must experience a process of realization in order to be able to recognize its truth, or what it is.

The philosophy of subjective spirit contains an anthropology, a phenomenology of spirit and a psychology. In these sections Hegel describes and analyses all the phenomena that influence the somatic, psychophysical and mental characteristics, conditions, processes and activities of the individual. The gamut of subjects he covers runs from the natural qualities of the individual, expressed in temperament, character and physiognomy, via sensibility, feeling, awareness and desire, to self-awareness, intuition, representation, thinking and wanting. Here one finds Hegel's theory of language acquisition, of practical feeling, of the achievements and function of imagination, his defence of the life-preserving power of habit, his solution of the mind–body problem, his understanding of the origin and treatment of mental illnesses and many other subjects. In these analyses Hegel's aim is to replace the 'ordinary approach' of empirical psychology with a 'philosophical perspective' towards psychological phenomena. The dominant characteristic of this philosophical attitude, it is claimed, is that it permits an interpretation of the subject of psychic processes as the product of psychic activity and not as an object to be thought of as a substance possessing certain powers and capacities which are its characteristics.

While the philosophy of subjective spirit really only attracted attention up to the middle of the nineteenth century, Hegel's philosophy of objective spirit, in other words his theory of law and politics, received a great deal of attention during the nineteenth and especially the twentieth century. This was not only because of the theory's great importance for the Marxist and other anti–liberalistic social theories (see MARX, K.; MARXISM, WESTERN). It has also repeatedly been the object of violent controversy, especially because of its political implications. In all its versions, Hegel's political philosophy rests on three main convictions which he cherished from his early years and held for the rest of his life. The first is that every modern philosophy of law and politics must incorporate the conception of freedom which was central to the European Enlightenment, and in particular to that of Germany (see ENLIGHTENMENT, CONTINENTAL). The second is that, especially in the case of modern political philosophy, the insight that the whole takes priority over its separate parts, an insight formulated by ARISTOTLE in his *Politics*, must be maintained and brought up to date. Finally, the third conviction consists in an application of the principle which shapes Hegel's whole philosophical enterprise, namely, that political philosophy must play its part in the confirmation of the thesis that only reason is real. Hegel attempts to do justice to these three convictions within the framework of his theory of objective spirit by (1) introducing an extravagant conception of freedom, (2) identifying the whole of Aristotle with the phenomenon which he calls 'ethical life' and (3) declaring this phenomenon called 'ethical life' to be the 'reality of reason'.

Hegel fulfils his self-imposed demand for the integration of freedom by making the conception of free will the fundamental concept of his philosophy of the objective spirit; this is where his characteristic conception of freedom comes into play. According to Hegel, a will is free not because it can choose its ends from a virtually limitless number of objective alternatives; the truly free will is the will which only determines itself. For Hegel, self-determination means to refer willingly to oneself, that is, to will oneself. Thus he thinks of freedom as a case of self-reference and in this way assimilates it into his concept of cognition, which is also based on the idea of self-reference (see §5 above). This assimilation is utterly intentional on Hegel's part, because it gives him the opportunity to interpret the process of the systematic unfolding of the various determinations of the will not only as different ways of the realization of free will but also as a process of cognition (see FREEDOM AND LIBERTY; FREE WILL).

Against this background, Hegel first develops his theories of law and morality, which derive all legal relationships and the obligatory character of moral acts from the concept of free will. In his theory of law, Hegel makes his contribution to the discussion of the philosophical foundations of civil and criminal law. His basic thesis is that property, the acquisition and use of which is a presupposition for being able to act freely, is the necessary condition of law in all its different variations. In his theory of morality, Hegel discusses the moral behaviour of autonomous subjects under the aspect of the gaining of moral standpoints for the purpose of judging actions and of the conversion of moral goals into actions. According to Hegel, however, legal relationships and moral standards are *founded* in social institutions. He thinks of these institutions as forms of what he calls 'ethical life' (*Sittlichkeit*). In Hegel's language, ethical life as the basis for the possibility of law and morality is the truth of free will, that which free will really is. Since it is a characteristic of the truth of free will to be real, it follows that, for Hegel, ethical life is also the reality of free will. This reality is thus the 'presupposed whole', without reference to which the discussion of law and morality makes no sense at all. This thesis of the function of real ethical life as the basis for law and morality is intended to account for the Aristotelian maxim of the primacy of the whole in political philosophy.

For Hegel, ethical life appears in three institutional forms: family, bourgeois society and the state. The theory of the family contains his thoughts on the ethical function of marriage, his justification of monogamy, his views on family property and the laws of inheritance and his maxims for bringing up children. The theory of bourgeois society became well–known and influential, above all because of Hegel's diagnosis of the difficulties which will arise within a society based solely on economic interests and elementary needs of its individual members. This diagnosis is grounded in Hegel's analyses of a society founded solely on economic relationships. They owe much to the works on political economy by Adam Smith, J.P. Say and David Ricardo, to whom Hegel often explicitly refers. According to Hegel, a bourgeois society considered as an economic community is defined by the fact that in it people can satisfy their needs through labour. The manifold nature of these needs means that they can only be satisfied by division of labour within the society. This leads economic subjects to join together into estates (*Stände*) and corporations whose members each undertake specific tasks with regard to the socially organized satisfaction of their needs. Hegel recognizes three estates: the peasant estate, which he calls the 'substantial estate'; the tradesmen's estate, among which he includes craftsmen, manufacturers and traders; and what he calls the 'general estate', whose members fulfil judicial and policing functions. Corporations are formed mainly in the tradesmen's estate. Although this entire realm of bourgeois society organized along these lines does involve legal restrictions, and is regulated by a civil and criminal legal code, it none the less cannot remain indefinitely stable. For it is not possible to prevent the polarization of the poor majority and the rich minority which leads to overpopulation, so that eventually the entire social wealth will not suffice to satisfy even the most elementary needs of all. The consequences are colonization and the formation of the 'proletariat'. Both will tend to destroy this bourgeois society.

If one follows Hegel's arguments, bourgeois society can only avoid this fate if its members act not according to their own particular interests and needs, but recognize the state as their 'general purpose', and direct all their activities to maintaining it (see STATE, THE). Hegel thinks of the state as a constitutional monarchy with division of power. For Hegel, the constitution of a state is in no sense the product of some constitution-creating institution or the work of individual persons. It is 'absolutely essential that the constitution, although the product of past history, *should not be seen as a finished entity*'. A constitution is rather the manifestation of the spirit of a people, created during the course of history through their customs and traditions. This view permits Hegel to maintain on the one hand that each people has the constitution 'which is appropriate to it and fits it', and on the other to insist that there is not much leeway for the modification of constitutions. The constitutional form of a reasonably organized state must be a monarchy because its characteristic individuality can only be appropriately represented by a concrete individual to whom as a person the sovereign acts of the state can be attributed. Hegel also favours a hereditary monarchy, since he sees the process of determining a person as monarch by virtue of its origin as the method which is least dependent upon arbitrary decisions. Hegel's theory of the powers of the state (*Staatsgewalten*) recognizes, in addition to the princely power (*fürstliche Gewalt*) which represents the instance of ultimate decision-making within the constitutional framework, the

governmental power (*Regierungsgewalt*) and the legislative power (*gesetzgebende Gewalt*). It is the task of the governmental power, which for Hegel also includes the judicial power, to pursue the general interests of the state, ensure the maintenance of right and enforce the laws. The legislative power is responsible for the 'further determination' of the constitution and laws. It is executed by an assembly of the estates which is divided into two chambers. The first chamber consists of a certain group of powerful landowners chosen by virtue of their birth; the second chamber comprises representatives of the corporate associations of the bourgeois society, who are sent to the assembly by their various corporations. Thus in Hegel's model state, both chambers are constituted without the direct political involvement of the population. Hegel's theory of the state provoked considerable controversy, particularly during his own time, because of its resolute defence of the hereditary monarchy and its strongly anti-democratic characteristics in all questions concerning the political representation of the citizens of the state. It was this section of his political philosophy in particular which, as early as the mid-nineteenth century, gave rise to the statement that Hegel was the philosopher of the Prussian state.

Hegel forges the link to his theory of the spirit, which contains his political philosophy, by interpreting what he calls 'ethical life' as the 'spirit of a people'. This allows him to elaborate his conception of history on the one hand and on the other to introduce his theory of the absolute spirit. The philosophy of history is introduced by the idea that ethical life as the reality of free will takes on different forms for different peoples. These forms differ from each other in the degree to which the different institutions of ethical life are actually developed. Now, Hegel believes that this development has taken place during the course of a historical process which he calls 'world history' (see HISTORY, PHILOSOPHY OF). This process of world history, which he sees as 'progress in the consciousness of freedom', can be divided into four distinct epochs, which correspond to four 'empires of world history'. Hegel describes this process of world history as beginning with the 'Oriental Empire', which is followed by the 'Greek' and then by the 'Roman' empires. The process is brought to a conclusion by the 'Germanic Empire'. This empire is not to be identified with Germany alone. It includes all central European Christian nations, even Great Britain. According to Hegel, the 'Germanic peoples are given the task of accomplishing the principle of the unity of divine and human nature, of reconciling... objective truth and freedom'. Hegel now interprets this reconciliation as the conclusion of the process of the self-recognition of reason. The result of this process consists of the insight that reason *knows itself* to be the whole of reality. Thus Hegel links the theory of the objective spirit with his metaphysics of reason and can now concentrate on the various aspects of this self-knowledge of reason as a theory of absolute spirit.

Hegel's philosophy of absolute spirit contains his philosophy of art, his philosophy of religion and his theory of philosophy. Although from his very beginnings all these subjects had a fixed place in Hegel's attempts at a system, and although his philosophies of art and religion were to become very influential (the one in the history of art and the theory of aesthetics and the other in theology), none the less these sections of Hegel's philosophy are relatively little elaborated in the works published by Hegel himself. Apart from a few sketch-like hints in his first work, *Difference between the Systems of Fichte and Schelling* (see §3 above), and the two final chapters of the *Phenomenology of Spirit*, Hegel devoted only a few paragraphs to these themes at the end of the *Encyclopedia of Philosophical Sciences*. We can gather from these paragraphs that there are three different ways or modes in which reason, cognizing itself, relates to itself; these are manifested in art, religion and philosophy. They differ from each other in the way in which in each of these ways reason cognizes itself. In art, reason relates to itself *intuitively* or, as Hegel says, *cognizes itself immediately*, while in religion this cognizing relationship with itself realizes itself in the form of *representation*, which is linked with the sublation of the immediacy of knowledge. In philosophy, the self-reference of reason is accounted for in the mode of *cognition*. The theory of epistemic modes which underpins this functional analysis of art, religion and philosophy, though obviously relying on the results of the Hegelian theory of the subjective spirit, none the less contains a number of difficulties which are hard to unravel.

Against this background of different forms of cognition, Hegel first reveals his theory of art in the form of a theory of styles of art (*Kunstformen*) and of individual arts (*Kunstarten*). He recognizes three different styles of art, which he calls symbolic, classical and romantic. They differ from each other in their various means of expressing the distinguishing characteristics of the spiritual, which belong to the sensible and therefore to the intuitive manifestations which reason gives itself. These styles themselves are characterized by the ways in which a spiritual content presents itself as the meaning of a sensible object. The symbolic style of art is thus the one in which the relationship between meaning and sensible appearance is relatively contingent, since it only arises through a randomly chosen attribute. By way of example Hegel takes the lion, which

symbolizes strength. In the classical style of art the sensible appearance expresses adequately what it is intended to signify. For Hegel, the human figure serves as a paradigm for this adequate representation of the spiritual, especially in the way in which it is represented in sculpture and painting. Finally, the romantic style of art takes as its subject the representation of the 'self-conscious inwardness' of the spirit. In it, the emotional world of the subject is expressed by reference to sensible characteristics. Hegel interprets the various individual arts as realizations of styles of art in various materials. Although each individual art can present itself in each style of art, there is for each individual art an ideal style, which he calls its basic type. The first individual art which Hegel discusses is architecture. Its task is to deal with non-organic nature in an artistic manner. Its basic type is the symbolic style of art. The second individual art is sculpture, the basic type of which is the classical style. Sculpture aims to transform non-organic nature into the physical form of the human body. The remaining individual arts are painting, music and poetry, whose basic type is represented by the romantic style of art. Painting marks the beginning of the separation of the direct processing of natural materials and thus a certain intellectualization of matter, which makes it capable of representing feelings, emotions, etc. Music is the romantic style of art *par excellence*. Its material is sound, which is matter only in a figurative sense and is therefore particularly suitable for the representation of even the most fleeting affects. Finally poetry, the last of the romantic arts, has as its material only signs, which here play no part as material entities but instead are bearers of meaning. These meanings refer to the realm of imagination and other spiritual content, so that in poetry a spiritual content can be presented in a manner appropriate to its spirituality. Hegel could not resist the temptation to use his theory of individual arts and styles of art as a model for the interpretation of the history of the development of art. His historicizing of individual arts and styles of art played a significant role in making the concept of an epoch an important tool in the history of art.

In the philosophy of religion Hegel holds that only in Christianity are the conditions fulfilled which are characteristic of the representational self-cognition of reason. Philosophy of religion has as its subject not only God, but also religion itself, and for Hegel that means the way in which God is present in the religious consciousness. By this characterization he aims to distinguish philosophy of religion from the traditional *theologia naturalis*. On the basis of the two components which make up its nature, the philosophy of religion attempts in the first instance to characterize more closely the concept of God and the various kinds of religious consciousness which Hegel takes to be feeling, intuition and representation. This will be found in the first part of the philosophy of religion, which thematizes the 'concept of religion'. The second part of the philosophy of religion discusses what Hegel calls 'determinate religion'. Here, he is concerned with something resembling a phenomenology of religions, the exposition of their various forms of appearance and objectivizations. This exposition starts with so-called natural religion, which according to Hegel assumes three forms: the religion of magic, the religion of substantiality and the religion of abstract subjectivity. The specific characteristic of natural religion is that it thinks of God in direct unity with nature. Natural religion finds its historical concept in the Oriental religions. Hegel regards the 'religions of spiritual individuality' as a second stage; these assume the forms of the religion of sublimity, the religion of beauty and the religion of teleology. At this stage, God is regarded as the primary spiritual being, which is not only nature but which also rules over and determines nature. Hegel puts the Jewish, Greek and Roman religions in this category. Finally, the third stage represents the 'perfect religion', to the discussion of which he devotes the third section of his philosophy of religion. In it, God is presented as He in reality is, namely the 'infinite, absolute end in itself'. To the religious consciousness, the God of the perfect religion appears in the trinitarian form as the unity of the Father, Son and Holy Ghost. According to Hegel, this idea of religion was first realized adequately in Christianity. Hegel's philosophy of religion greatly influenced theological discussions and points of view. None the less, it was not without its critics, for whom it represented a theory which, as, for example, R. Haym claimed in the last century, contributed to the dissolution of the Godly in reason and of Piety in knowledge.

As far as philosophy is concerned, Hegel maintains that its distinguishing mode of knowledge, namely cognition, is present when something is seen to be necessary. Since reason within the sphere of the absolute spirit relates only to itself, the achievement of the cognitive reference of reason to itself lies in the fact that it understands the progress of its realization in logic, nature and spirit as a necessary process. Philosophy is the representation of this process in its necessity. This philosophical process also has its appearance in time in the form of the history of philosophy. For Hegel, the history of philosophy presents itself as a historical succession of philosophical positions in which in each case one of the essential characteristics of (Hegelian) reason is made the principle of a philosophical interpretation of the world in a one-sided and distorted way that is characteristic of its time. He sees the existence of

political freedom as a necessary precondition for a philosophical interpretation of the world. Only in societies in which free constitutions exist can philosophical thought develop. Since, he claims, the concepts of freedom and constitution only arose as the products of Greek (that is, Occidental) thought, philosophical discourse is really a specifically Western achievement. He therefore absolutely refuses to ascribe any philosophically relevant intellectual achievements to the Oriental world, the principle proponents of which are in his view China and India. All the doctrines of wisdom of the Orient can at most be accepted as codifications of religious ideas. If, for a Westerner, some of these doctrines none the less seem to express a philosophical thought, this is because they confuse the abstract generality of Oriental religious ideas with the generality which is applicable to the thoughts of reason engaged in thinking itself. Hegel divides Western philosophy into two main periods: Greek and Germanic philosophy. Up to a certain point, Greek philosophy also includes Roman, and Germanic philosophy includes not only German philosophy but that of other European peoples as well, since these peoples have 'in their totality a Germanic culture'. The difference between Greek and Germanic philosophy lies in the fact that Greek philosophy was not yet in a position to comprehend the conception of spirit in all its profundity. This only became possible through Christianity and its acceptance throughout the Germanic world. For only in this historical context was it possible for the insight to establish itself that the essence of spirit is subjectivity and hence cognition of itself. Hegel regards it as a great merit of his philosophy that it adequately explains this, and thus reconciles reason with reality in thought. In the last analysis, his message consists of a single proposition: Reason is and knows itself to be the ultimate reality. His system is brought to a conclusion in what is, in his view, a successful justification of that proposition. Even during the nineteenth century, the optimism of reason underlying Hegel's system aroused criticism, for example, from Nietzsche, Kierkegaard and the representatives of Neo-Kantianism. It seems doubtful whether, at the beginning of the twenty-first century, Hegel's indomitable faith in reason can continue to convince.

See also ABSOLUTE, THE; GERMAN IDEALISM; HEGELIANISM; NEO-KANTIANISM

References and further reading

Hegel, G.W.F. (1830) *Enzyklopädie der philosophischen Wissenschaften im Grundrisse. Dritte Ausgabe*, Heidelberg: Winter. (The last and most comprehensive version of his system.)

Stern, R. (ed.) (1993) *G.W.F. Hegel: Critical Assessments*, London: Routledge & Kegan Paul, 4 vols. (A voluminous collection of essays on Hegel.)

Taylor, C. (1975) *Hegel*, Cambridge: Cambridge University Press. (The best and most comprehensive introduction to Hegel for the English speaking reader.)

ROLF-PETER HORSTMANN
Translated from the German by
JANE MICHAEL-RUSHMER

HEGELIANISM

As an intellectual tradition, the history of Hegelianism is the history of the reception and influence of the thought of G.W.F. Hegel. This tradition is notoriously complex and many-sided, because while some Hegelians have seen themselves as merely defending and developing his ideas along what they took to be orthodox lines, others have sought to 'reform' his system, or to appropriate individual aspects and overturn others, or to offer consciously revisionary readings of his work. This makes it very hard to identify any body of doctrine common to members of this tradition, and a wide range of divergent philosophical views can be found among those who (despite this) can none the less claim to be Hegelians.

There are both 'internal' and 'external' reasons for this: on one hand, Hegel's position itself brings together many different tendencies (idealism and objectivism, historicism and absolutism, rationalism and empiricism, Christianity and humanism, classicism and modernism, a liberal view of civil society with an organicist view of the state); any balance between them is hermeneutically very unstable, enabling existing readings to be challenged and old orthodoxies to be overturned. On the other hand, the critical response to Hegel's thought and the many attempts to undermine it have meant that Hegelians have continually needed to reconstruct his ideas and even to turn Hegel against himself, while each new intellectual development, such as Marxism, pragmatism, phenomenology or existential philosophy, has brought about some reassessment of his position. This feature of the Hegelian tradition has been heightened by the fact that Hegel's work has had an impact at different times over a long period and in a wide range of countries, so that divergent intellectual, social and historical pressures have influenced its distinct appropriations. At the hermeneutic level, these appropriations have contributed greatly to keeping the philosophical understanding of Hegel alive and open-ended, so that our present-day conception of his thought cannot properly be separated from them. Moreover, because questions of Hegel interpretation have so often revolved around the main philosophical, political and religious issues of the nineteenth and twentieth centuries, Hegelianism has also had a significant impact on the development of modern Western thought in its own right.

As a result of its complex evolution, Hegelianism is best understood historically, by showing how the changing representation of Hegel's ideas have come about, shaped by the different critical concerns, sociopolitical conditions and intellectual movements that dominated his reception in different countries at different times. Initially, Hegel's influence was naturally most strongly felt in Germany as a comprehensive, integrative philosophy that seemed to do justice to all realms of experience and promised to preserve the Christian heritage in a modern and progressive form within a speculative framework. However, this position was quickly challenged, both from other philosophical standpoints (such as F.W.J. Schelling's 'positive philosophy' and F.A. Trendelenburg's neo-Aristotelian empiricism), and by the celebrated generation of younger thinkers (the so-called 'Young' or 'Left' Hegelians, such as Ludwig Feuerbach, David Strauss, Bruno Bauer, Arnold Ruge and the early Karl Marx), who insisted that to discover what made Hegel a truly significant thinker (his dialectical method, his view of alienation, his 'sublation' of Christianity), this orthodoxy must be overturned. None the less, both among these radicals and in academic circles, Hegel's influence was considerably weakened in Germany by the 1860s and 1870s, while by this time developments in Hegelian thought had begun to take place elsewhere.

Hegel's work was known outside Germany from the 1820s onwards, and Hegelian schools developed in northern Europe, Italy, France, Eastern Europe, America and (somewhat later) in Britain, each with their own distinctive line of interpretation, but all fairly uncritical in their attempts to assimilate his ideas. However, in each of these countries challenges to the Hegelian position were quick to arise, partly because the influence of Hegel's German critics soon spread abroad, and partly because of the growing impact of other philosophical positions (such as Neo-Kantianism, materialism and pragmatism). Nevertheless, Hegelianism outside Germany proved more durable in the face of these attacks, as new readings and approaches emerged to counter them, and ways were found to reinterpret Hegel's work to show that it could accommodate these other positions, once the earlier accounts of Hegel's metaphysics, political philosophy and philosophy of religion (in particular) were rejected as too crude.

This pattern has continued into the twentieth century, as many of the movements that began by defining themselves *against* Hegel (such as Neo-Kantianism, Marxism, existentialism, pragmatism, post-structuralism and even 'analytic' philosophy) have then come to find unexpected common ground, giving a new impetus and depth to Hegelianism as it began to be assimilated within and influenced by these diverse approaches. Such efforts at rapprochement began in the early part of the century with Wilhelm Dilthey's attempt to link Hegel with his own historicism, and although they were more ambivalent, this connection was reinforced in Italy by Benedetto Croce and Giovanni Gentile. The realignment continued in France in the 1930s, as Jean Wahl brought out the more existentialist themes in Hegel's thought, followed in the 1940s by Alexander Kojève's influential Marxist readings. Hegelianism has also had an impact on Western Marxism through the writings of the Hungarian Georg Lukács, and this influence has continued in the critical reinterpretations offered by members of the Frankfurt School, particularly Theodor W. Adorno, Max Horkheimer, Herbert Marcuse, Jürgen Habermas and others. More recently, most of the major schools of philosophical thought (from French post-structuralism to Anglo-American 'analytic' philosophy) have emphasized the need to take account of Hegel, and as a result Hegelian thought (both exegetical and constructive) is continually finding new directions.

See also: ABSOLUTE, THE; FRANKFURT SCHOOL; GERMAN IDEALISM; HEGEL, G.W.F.; IDEALISM; MARXISM, WESTERN

ROBERT STERN
NICHOLAS WALKER

HEIDEGGER, MARTIN (1889–1976)

Introduction

Martin Heidegger taught philosophy at Freiburg University (1915–23), Marburg University (1923–8), and again at Freiburg University (1928–45). Early in his career he came under the influence of Edmund Husserl, but he soon broke away to fashion his own phenomenological philosophy. His most famous work, *Sein und Zeit* (*Being and Time*) was published in 1927. Heidegger's energetic support for Hitler in 1933–4 earned him a suspension from teaching from 1945 to 1950. In retirement he published numerous works, including the first volumes of his *Gesamtausgabe* (*Collected Edition*). His thought has had strong influence on trends in philosophy ranging from existentialism through

hermeneutics to deconstruction, as well as on the fields of literary theory and theology.

Heidegger often makes his case in charged and dramatic language that is difficult to convey in summary form. He argues that mortality is our defining moment, that we are thrown into limited worlds of sense shaped by our being-towards-death, and that finite meaning is all the reality we get. He claims that most of us have failed to understand that radical finitude is the source of all meaning. The result of this forgetfulness is the planetary desert called nihilism, with its promise that a virtually omnipotent and ideally omniscient humanity can remake the world in its own image. Nonetheless, he holds out the hope of recovering our finite human nature, but only at the price of accepting a nothingness darker than the nihilism that now ravishes the globe. To the barely whispered admission, 'I hardly know anymore who and where I am', Heidegger answers: 'None of us knows that, as soon as we stop fooling ourselves' (*Gelassenheit* 1959).

And yet he claims to be no pessimist. He merely wants to demonstrate (1) the phenomenological principle that 'being = meaningfulness' (the two are interchangeable) and (2) the ontological principle that all the meaningfulness we encounter is grounded in the radical finitude of human being. Heidegger's main work, *Being and Time*, was such a phenomenological ontology, an investigation of human being so as to demonstrate the finitude of all forms of meaning. Only half of the book was published in 1927, but Heidegger elaborated the rest of the project in a less systematic form during the two decades that followed.

Heidegger distinguishes between things (whatever-is) and the 'world', that is, the context within which they happen to be found. A 'world' is an arena of human concerns and interests. Any such world (that of carpentry, for example, or child-rearing, or poetry) is what constitutes the meaning of the things encountered within those worlds (hammers, for example, or nappies, or words). The 'world' of a set of entities is the 'being' of those entities, that is, that which lets them *be meaningful*. Heidegger calls this distinction between world and entities the 'ontological difference'. He argues that only human beings understand this difference, and therefore only they can make sense of things and thus have language in the full sense of the term. Rewriting Aristotle's *topos eidōn*, Heidegger calls human being 'the place of meaning', the *Da of Sein: Dasein*.

Heidegger argues that Dasein is intrinsically temporal, not in the usual chronological sense of past-present-future, but in a unique existential sense. Dasein always ek-sists (stands-out) into its own possibilities (the future). Human being is therefore always in a state of becoming, and ultimately is becoming its own death ('being-unto-death'). When used of Dasein, the word temporality indicates not chronological succession but Dasein's finite becoming, delimited by mortality.

If Dasein's being is thoroughly finite, then all of human awareness is conditioned by this finitude, including all understanding of meaning or being. For Dasein, meaning is always known finitely and indeed is finite. The main thesis of *Being and Time* is that all worlds of meaning (all possibilities of *being meaningful*) are necessarily finite because Dasein, their source, is radically finite. Heidegger arrives at these conclusions by way of a phenomenological analysis of how Dasein opens up ('dis-closes') worlds of significance by living finitely ('anticipating its own death'). The disclosure of finite worlds of sense – how it comes about, what structure it has, and what it makes possible – is the central topic of Heidegger's thought.

But even as it dis-closes worlds of sense, Dasein's finitude remains relatively concealed even from ourselves. We tend to overlook the finitude that is the source of the disclosure of worlds and to focus instead on what get revealed *within* those worlds: meaningful entities. This overlooking is what Heidegger calls the 'forgottenness of being', a shorthand phrase for: the forgottenness of the disclosive *source* of all forms of being/meaning. Finitude is not a thing but a 'nothing', and as such it remains 'hidden'. Given its intrinsic hiddenness, this nothingness, even though it is the source of all meaning, is virtually bound to be overlooked. Heidegger argues that the forgetting of finitude characterizes not only everyday human existence ('fallenness') but also the entire history of metaphysics from Plato to Nietzsche.

Heidegger calls for Dasein to resolutely reappropriate its own radical finitude as the source of the disclosure of all meaningfulness. In so doing, Dasein becomes authentically itself as well as the guardian of what Heidegger calls 'the house of being', that is, the finite domain of sense.

1 Life and works

Martin Heidegger was born on 26 September 1889 in Messkirch, Southwest Germany, to Roman Catholic parents of very modest means. From 1899 to 1911 he intended to become a priest, but after two years of theological studies at Freiburg University a recurring heart condition ended those hopes. In 1911 he switched to mathematics and the natural sciences, but finally took his doctorate in philosophy (1913) with a dissertation entitled *Die Lehre vom Urteil im Psychologismus* (The Doctrine of Judgment in Psychologism) (1914). Hoping to get appointed to Freiburg's chair in Catholic philosophy, he wrote a qualifying dissertation in 1915 on a theme in medieval philosophy, *Die Kategorien- und Bedeutungslehre des Duns Scotus* (Duns Scotus' Doctrine of Categories and Meaning) (1916). However, the job went to someone else, and in the autumn of 1915 Heidegger began his teaching career at Freiburg as a lecturer.

At this time Heidegger was known as a Thomist, but his 1915 dissertation was strongly influenced by the founder of phenomenology, Edmund HUSSERL. When Husserl joined the Freiburg faculty in the spring of 1916, Heidegger came to know him personally, if not well. Their relation would blossom only after the First World War. Heidegger was drafted in 1918 and served as a weatherman on the Ardennes front in the last three months of the war. When he returned to Freiburg his philosophical career took a decisive turn. In a matter of weeks he announced his break with Catholic philosophy (9 January 1919), got himself appointed Husserl's assistant (21 January), and began lecturing on a radical new approach to philosophy (4 February).

Many influences came to bear on Heidegger's early development, including St Paul, Augustine, Meister Eckhart, Kierkegaard, Dilthey and Nietzsche. But the major influences were Husserl and Aristotle. Heidegger was Husserl's protégé in the 1920s, but he never was a faithful disciple. He preferred Husserl's early work, *Logische Untersuchungen* (Logical Investigations) (1900–1), to the exclusion of the master's later developments. Moreover, the things that Heidegger liked about *Logical Investigations* were generally consonant with the traditional scholastic philosophy he had been taught.

First, Husserl's early phenomenology considered the human 'psyche' not as a substantial thing but as an act of revealing (intentionality), one that revealed not only *what* is encountered (the entity) but also the *way in which* it is encountered (the entity's being). Second, the early Husserl held that the central issue of philosophy was not modern subjectivity but rather 'the things themselves', whatever they might happen to be, in their very appearance; and he provided a descriptive method for letting those things show themselves as they are. Third, phenomenology argued that the being of entities is known not by some after-the-fact reflection or transcendental construction but directly and immediately by way of a categorial intuition. In short, for Heidegger, phenomenology was a descriptive method for understanding the being of entities as it is disclosed in intentional acts (see PHENOMENOLOGICAL MOVEMENT).

As Heidegger took it, all this contrasted with Husserl's later commitment to pure consciousness as the presuppositionless 'thing itself' that was to be revealed by various methodological 'reductions'. Heidegger had no use either for the Neo-Kantian turn to transcendental consciousness that found expression in Husserl's *Ideen* (Ideas) (1913) or for his further turn to a form of Cartesianism. Against Husserl's later theory of an unworldly transcendental ego presuppositionlessly conferring meaning on its objects, Heidegger proposed the historical and temporal situatedness of the existential self, 'thrown' into the world, 'fallen' in among entities in their everyday meanings, and 'projecting' ahead towards death.

In the 1920s Heidegger began interpreting the treatises of ARISTOTLE as an implicit phenomenology of everyday life without the obscuring intervention of subjectivity. He took Aristotle's main topic to be 'disclosure' (*alētheia*) on three levels: entities as intrinsically self-disclosive; human *psyche* as co-disclosive of those entities; and especially the human disclosure of entities in discursive, synthetic activity (*logos*), whether that be performed in wordless actions or in articulated sentences. Going beyond Aristotle, Heidegger interpreted this discursive disclosure as grounded in a kind of movement that he named 'temporality', and he argued that this temporality was the very essence of human being.

Using this new understanding of human being, Heidegger reinterpreted how anything at all appears to human beings. He argued that humans, as intrinsically temporal, have only a temporal understanding of whatever entities they know. But humans understand an entity by knowing it in its being, that is, in terms of how it happens to be present. Therefore, as far as human being goes, all forms of being are known temporally and indeed *are* temporal. The meaning of being is time.

Heidegger developed this thesis gradually, achieving a provisional formulation in *Sein und Zeit* (Being and Time) (1927). In public he dedicated the book to Husserl 'in respect and friendship', but in private he was calling Husserl's philosophy a 'sham' (*Scheinphilosophie*). Meanwhile, in 1923 an unsuspecting Husserl helped Heidegger move from a lecturer's job at Freiburg to a professorship at Marburg University; and when Husserl retired in 1928, he arranged for Heidegger to succeed him in the chair of philosophy at

Freiburg. Once Heidegger had settled into the new job, the relationship between mentor and protégé quickly fell apart. If *Being and Time* were not enough, the three works Heidegger published in 1929 – 'Vom Wesen des Grundes' ('On the Essence of Ground'), *Kant und das Problem der Metaphysik* (Kant and the Problem of Metaphysics), and *Was ist Metaphysik?* (What is Metaphysics?) – confirmed how far apart the two philosophers had grown.

Heidegger's career entered a new phase when the Nazis came to power in Germany. On 30 January 1933 Adolf Hitler was appointed Chancellor, and within a month the German constitution and all-important civil rights were suspended. On 23 March Hitler became dictator of Germany, with absolute power to enact laws, and two weeks later, harsh anti-Semitic measures were promulgated. A conservative nationalist and staunch anti-Communist, Heidegger supported Hitler's policies with great enthusiasm for at least one year, and with quieter conviction for some ten years thereafter. He was elected rector (president) of Freiburg University on 21 April 1933 and joined the Nazi Party on May 1, with the motive, he later claimed, of preventing the politicization of the university. In his inaugural address as rector, *Die Selbstbehauptung der deutschen Universität* (The Self-Assertion of the German University) (27 May 1933), he called for a reorganization of the university along the lines of some aspects of the Nazi revolution. As rector he proved a willing spokesman for, and tool of, Nazi policy both foreign and domestic.

Heidegger resigned the rectorate on 23 April 1934 but continued to support Hitler. His remarks in the classroom indicate that he backed the German war aims, as he knew them, until at least as late as the defeat at Stalingrad in January 1943. The relation, or lack of it, between Heidegger's philosophy and his political sympathies has long been the subject of heated debate.

Heidegger published relatively little during the Nazi period. Instead, he spent those years rethinking his philosophy and setting out the parameters it would have, both in form and focus, for the rest of his life. The revision of his thought is most apparent in three texts he published much later: (1) the working notes from 1936–8 that he gathered into *Beiträge zur Philosophie. Vom Ereignis* (Contributions to Philosophy: On Ereignis), published posthumously in 1989; (2) the two volumes of his *Nietzsche*, published in 1961, which contain lecture courses and notes dating from 1936 to 1946; and (3) 'Brief über den Humanismus' ('Letter on Humanism'), written in the autumn of 1946 and published in 1947.

After the war Heidegger was suspended from teaching because of his Nazi activities in the 1930s.

In 1950, however, he was allowed to resume teaching, and thereafter he occasionally lectured at Freiburg University and elsewhere. Between 1950 and his death he published numerous works, including the first volumes of his massive *Gesamtausgabe* (Collected Edition). He died at his home in Zähringen, Freiburg, on 26 May 1976 and was buried in his home town of Messkirch. His literary remains are held at the German Literary Archives, at Marbach on the Neckar.

Heidegger, a Catholic, married Elfride Petri (1893–1992), a Lutheran, on 21 March 1917. They had two sons, both of whom served in the Wehrmacht during the Second World War and were taken prisoner on the Eastern Front. In February of 1925 Heidegger began a year-long affair with his then student, Hannah Arendt. In February of 1950 they resumed a strong but often stormy friendship that lasted until Arendt's death.

2 Temporality and authenticity

Heidegger was convinced that Western philosophy had misunderstood the nature of being in general and the nature of human being in particular. His life's work was dedicated to getting it right on both scores.

In his view, the two issues are inextricably linked. To be human is to disclose and understand the being of whatever there is. Correspondingly, the being of an entity is the meaningful presence of that entity within the field of human experience. A proper or improper understanding of human being entails a proper or improper understanding of the being of everything else. In this context 'human being' means what Heidegger designates by his technical term 'Dasein': not consciousness or subjectivity or rationality, but that distinctive kind of entity (which we ourselves always are) whose being consists in disclosing the being both of itself and of other entities. The being of this entity is called 'existence' (see §4).

Heidegger argues that the structure of human being is comprised of three co-equal moments: becoming, alreadiness and presence. (These are usually, and unfortunately, translated as: 'coming towards itself', 'is as having been' and 'making-present'.) As a unity, these three moments constitute the essence of human being, which Heidegger calls 'temporality': opening an arena of meaningful presence by anticipating one's own death. Temporality means being present by becoming what one already is.

Becoming. To be human means that one is not a static entity just 'there' among other things. Rather, being human is always a process of becoming oneself, living into possibilities, into one's future.

For Heidegger, such becoming is not optional but necessary. He expresses this claim in various co-equal formulas: (1) the essence of human being is 'existence' understood as 'ek-sistence', an ineluctable 'standing out' into concern about one's own being and into the need to become oneself; (2) the essence of human being is 'factical', always already thrust into concernful openness to itself and thus into the ineluctability of self-becoming; and (3) the essence of being human is 'to be possible' – not just able, but above all needing, to become oneself.

The ultimate possibility into which one lives is the possibility to end all possibilities: one's death. Human beings are essentially finite and necessarily mortal, and so one's becoming is an anticipation of death. Thus, to know oneself as becoming is to know oneself, at least implicitly, as mortal. Heidegger calls this mortal becoming 'being-unto-death'.

Alreadiness. Human being consists in becoming; and this becoming means becoming what one already is. Here the word 'already' means 'essentially', 'necessarily' or 'inevitably'. 'Alreadiness' (*Gewesenheit*) names one's inevitable human essence and specifically one's mortality. In becoming the finitude and mortality that one already is, one gets whatever presence one has.

Presence. Mortal becoming is the way human being (a) is meaningfully present to itself and (b) renders other entities meaningfully present to itself. To put the two together: things are present to human being in so far as human being is present to itself as mortal becoming. In both cases presence is bound up with absence.

How human being is present to itself. Since mortal becoming means becoming one's own death, human being appears as disappearing; it is present to itself as becoming absent. To capture this interplay of presence and absence, we call the essence of human being 'pres-abs-ence', that is, an incomplete presence that shades off into absence. Pres-abs-ence is a name for what classical philosophy called 'movement' in the broad sense: the momentary presence that something has on the basis of its stretch towards the absent.

Pres-abs-ence is an index of finitude. Any entity that appears as disappearing, or that has its current presence by anticipating a future state, has its being not as full self-presence but as finite pres-abs-ence. The movement towards death that defines human being is what Heidegger calls 'temporality'. The quotation marks indicate that 'temporality' does not refer to chronological succession but rather means having one's being as the movement of finite mortal becoming.

How other things are present to human being. Other entities are meaningfully present to human being in so far as human being is temporal, that is, always anticipating its own absence. Hence the meaningful presence of things is also temporal or pres-abs-ent – always partial, incomplete and entailing an absence of its own. Not only is human being temporal but the presence of things to human being is also temporal in its own right.

All of Heidegger's work argues for an intrinsic link between the temporality or pres-abs-ence that defines human being and the temporality or pres-abs-ence that characterizes the meaningful presence of things. But the meaningful presence of things is what Heidegger means by being. Therefore, Heidegger's central thesis is this: as far as human experience goes, all modes of being are temporal. The meaningful presence of things is always imperfect, incomplete, pres-abs-ential. The meaning of being is time.

Heidegger argues that this crucial state of affairs – finite human being as an awareness of the finitude of all modes of being – is overlooked and forgotten both in everyday experience and in philosophy itself. Therefore, his work discusses how one can recover this forgotten state of affairs on both of those levels.

As regards everyday life, Heidegger describes how one might recall this central but forgotten fact and make it one's own again. The act of reappropriating one's own essence – of achieving a personal and concrete grasp of oneself as finite – is called 'resolution' (in other translations, 'resoluteness' or 'resolve'). This personal conversion entails becoming clear about the intrinsic finitude of one's own being, and then choosing to accept and to be that finitude.

Awareness of one's finitude. Human being is always already the process of mortal becoming. However, one is usually so absorbed in the things one encounters ('fallenness') that one forgets the becoming that makes such encounters possible. It takes a peculiar kind of experience, more of a mood than a detached cognition, to wake one up to one's finitude. Heidegger argues that such an awakening comes about in special 'basic moods' (dread, boredom, wonder and so on) in which one experiences not things but that which is not-a-thing or 'no-thing'. Each of these basic moods reveals, in its own particular way, the absential dimension of one's pres-abs-ence.

Heidegger often uses charged metaphors to discuss this experience. For example, he describes dread as a 'call of conscience', where 'conscience' means not a moral faculty but the heretofore dormant, and now awakening, awareness of one's finite nature. What this call of conscience reveals is that one is 'guilty', not of some moral fault but of an ontological defect: the fact of being intrinsically incomplete and on the way to absence. The call

of conscience is a call to understand and accept this 'guilt'.

Choosing one's finitude. One may choose either to heed or to ignore this call of conscience. To heed and accept it means to acknowledge oneself as a mortal process of pres-abs-ence and to live accordingly. In that case, one recuperates one's essence and thus attains 'authenticity' by becoming one's proper (or 'authentic') self. To ignore or refuse the call does not mean to cease being finite and mortal but rather to live according to an improper (inauthentic or 'fallen') self-understanding. Only the proper or authentic understanding of oneself as finite admits one to the concrete, experiential understanding that all forms of being, all ways that things can be meaningfully present, are themselves finite.

Summary. The essence of human being is temporality, that is, mortal becoming or pres-abs-ence. To overlook mortal becoming is to live an inauthentic temporality and to be a fallen self. But to acknowledge and choose one's mortal becoming in the act of resolution is to live an authentic temporality and selfhood. It means achieving presence (both the presence of oneself and that of other entities) by truly becoming what one already is. This recuperation of one's own finite being can lead to the understanding that what conditions *all* modes of being is finitude: the very meaning of being is time.

3 Being-in-the-world and hermeneutics

In *Being and Time* Heidegger spells out not only the reasons why, but also the ways in which, things are meaningfully present to human being.

Being-in-the-world. In contrast to theories of human being as a self-contained theoretical ego, Heidegger understands human being as always 'outside' any supposed immanence, absorbed in social intercourse, practical tasks and its own interests. Evidence for this absorption, he argues, is that human being always finds itself caught up in a mood – that is, 'tuned in' to a given set of concerns. The field of such concerns and interests Heidegger calls the 'world'; and the engagement with those needs and purposes and the things that might fulfil them he calls 'being-in-the-world' (or equally 'care').

Heidegger's term 'world' does not mean planet earth, or the vast expanse of space and time, or the sum total of things in existence. Rather, 'world' means a dynamic set of relations, ultimately ordered to human possibilities, which lends meaning or significance to the things that one deals with – as in the phrase 'the world of the artist' or 'the world of the carpenter'. A human being lives in many such worlds, and they often overlap, but what constitutes their essence – what Heidegger calls the worldhood of all such worlds – is the significance that accrues to things by their relatedness to human interests and possibilities. Although being-in and world can be distinguished, they never occur separately. Any set of meaning-giving relations (world) comes about and remains effective only in so far as human being is engaged with the apposite possibilities (being-in). Being-in holds open and sustains the world.

In *Being and Time* Heidegger studies the world that he considers closest to human beings: the world of everyday activity. The defining moment of such a world is practical purposes ordered to human concerns – for example, the need to build a house for the sake of shelter. A group of things then gets its significance from the direct or indirect relation of those things to that goal. For example, these specific tools get their significance from their usefulness for clearing the ground, those trees get their significance from being suitable for lumber, these plants from their serviceability as thatch. A dynamic set of such relations (such as 'useful to', 'suitable as', 'needed for'), all of which refer things to a human task and ultimately to a human possibility, constitutes a 'world' and defines the current significance that certain things (for example, tools, trees and reeds) might have.

The significance of things changes according to the interplay of human interests, the relations that they generate, and the availability of material. For example, given the lack of a mallet, the significance of a stone might be its utility for pounding in a tent peg. The stone gets its current significance as a utensil from the world of the camper: the desire for shelter, the need of something to hammer with, and the availability of only a stone. (When the camper finds a mallet, the stone may well lose its former significance.)

Hermeneutical understanding. Heidegger argues that the world of practical experience is the original locus of the understanding of the being of entities. Understanding entails awareness of certain relations: for example, the awareness of this *as* that, or of this *as for* that. The 'as' articulates the significance of the thing. In using an implement, one has a practical understanding of the implement's relation to a task (X as useful for Y). This in turn evidences a practical understanding of the being of the implement: one knows the stone as *being* useful for pounding in a tent peg. In other words, prior to predicative knowledge, which is expressed in sentences of the type 'S is P', human beings already have a pre-theoretical or 'pre-ontological' understanding of the being of things (this as *being for* that).

Since the 'as' articulates how something is understood, and since the Greek verb *hermeneuein* means 'to make something understandable',

Heidegger calls the 'as' that renders things intelligible in practical understanding the 'hermeneutical as'. This 'hermeneutical as' is made possible because human being is a 'thrown project', necessarily thrust into possibilities (thrownness) and thereby holding the world open (project).

Hermeneutical understanding – that is, prepredicatively understanding the 'hermeneutical as' by being a thrown project – is the kind of cognition that most befits being-in-the-world. It is the primary way in which humans know the being of things. By contrast, the more detached and objective 'apophantic' knowledge that expresses itself in declarative sentences ('S is P') is evidence, for Heidegger, of a derivative and flattened-out understanding of being.

Summary. As long as one lives, one is engaged in mortal becoming. This becoming entails having purposes and possibilities. Living into purposes and possibilities is how one has things meaningfully present. The ability to have things meaningfully present by living into possibilities is called being-in-the-world. Being-in-the-world is structured as a thrown project: holding open the possibility of significance (project) by ineluctably living into possibilities (thrownness). This issues in a pre-predicative, hermeneutical understanding of the being of things. Thus mortal becoming *qua* being-in-the-world engenders and sustains all possible significance. In another formulation: temporality determines all the ways that things can have meaningful presence. Time is the meaning of all forms of being.

4 Dasein and disclosure

Heidegger calls human being 'Dasein', the entity whose being consists in disclosing and understanding being, whether the being of itself or that of other entities. In so far as Dasein's being is a disclosure of its *own* being, it is called 'existence' or 'ek-sistence': self-referential standing-out-unto-itself. Dasein's very being consists in being related, with understanding and concern, to itself.

But Dasein is not just related to itself. Existence occurs only as being-in-the-world; that is, the openness of human being to itself entails the openness of the world for other entities. One of Heidegger's neologisms for 'openness' is 'the there' (*das Da*), which he uses in two interrelated senses. First, human being is its own 'there': as a thrown project, existence sustains its own openness to itself. And second, in so doing, human being also makes possible the world's openness as the 'there' for other entities. Human being's self-disclosure makes possible the disclosure of other entities.

Heidegger calls human being in both these capacities 'being-the-there' – Dasein, or sometimes

Da-sein when it refers to the second capacity. In ordinary German *Dasein* means existence in the usual sense: being there in space and time as contrasted with not being at all. However, in Heidegger's usage Dasein means being disclosive of something (whether that be oneself or another entity) in its being. In a word, Dasein is disclosive. And since human being is radically finite, disclosure is radically finite.

The Greek word for disclosure is *alētheia*, a term composed of the privative prefix *a-* (un- or dis-) and the root *lēthē* (hiddenness or closure). Heidegger finds the finitude of dis-closure inscribed in the word *a-lētheia*. To disclose something is to momentarily rescue it from (*a-*) some prior unavailability (*lēthē*), and to hold it for a while in presence.

Heidegger discusses three levels of disclosure, ranging from the original to the derivative, each of which involves Dasein: (1) disclosure-as-such, (2) the disclosedness of entities in their being, and (3) disclosure in propositional statements. Heidegger's chief interest is in the first. There, disclosure/*alētheia* is the original occurrence that issues in meaningful presence (being).

Heidegger argues that levels 1 and 2 are distinct but inseparable and, taken together, make possible level 3. The word 'truth' properly applies only at the third level, where it is a property of statements that correctly represent complex states of affairs. Therefore, to the question 'What is the essence of truth?' – that is, 'What makes the truth of propositions possible at level 3?' – Heidegger answers: proximally, the disclosure of entities in their being (level 2); and ultimately, disclosure-as-such (level 1). His argument unfolds as follows.

Level 1. Disclosure-as-such is the very opening-up of the field of significance. It is the engendering and sustaining of world on the basis of Dasein's becoming-absent. In so far as it marks the birth of significance and the genesis of being, disclosure-as-such or world-disclosure is the reason why any specific entity can have meaningful presence at all.

There are three corollaries. First, the disclosure of world never happens except in Dasein's being; indeed, without Dasein, there is no openness at all. The engendering and sustaining of the dynamic relations that constitute the very possibility of significance occurs only as long as Dasein exists as mortal becoming. And conversely, wherever there is Dasein, there is world. Second, disclosure-as-such never happens apart from the disclosedness of *entities* as being this or that. In speaking of disclosure 'as such', Heidegger is naming the originating source and general structure of all possible significance that might accrue to any entity at all. The result of disclosure-as-such is the fact that referral-to-mortal-Dasein (that is, significance) is the basic state of

whatever entities happen to show up. Third, disclosure-as-such is always prior to and makes possible concrete human action in any specific world. Such concrete actions run the risk of *not* being disclosive (that is, being mistaken about the meaning of something). By contrast, world-disclosure is *always* disclosive in so far as it is the opening-up of the very possibility of significance at all.

Alētheia/disclosure-as-such – how it comes about, the structure it has, and what it makes possible – is the central topic or 'thing itself' of Heidegger's thought. He sometimes calls it the 'clearing' of being. He also calls it 'being itself' or 'being-as-such' (that is, the very *engendering* of being). Frequently, and inadequately, he calls it the 'truth' of being.

Level 2. What disclosure-as-such makes possible is the pre-predicative availability of entities in their current mode of being. This pre-predicative availability constitutes level 2, the basic, everyday disclosedness of entities as meaningfully present. This disclosedness is always finite, and that entails two things.

First, what disclosure-as-such makes possible is not simply the being of an entity but rather the being of that entity as or as not something: for instance, this stone as not a missile but as a hammer. I know the stone only in terms of one or another of its possibilities: the entity becomes present not fully and immediately but only partially and discursively. Thus the entity's being is always finite, always a matter of synthesis-and-differentiation: being-as-and-as-not. Second, disclosure-as-such lets an entity be present not in its eternal essence but only in its current meaning in a given situation; moreover, it shows that this specific entity is not the only one that might have this meaning. For example, in the present situation I understand this stone not as a paperweight or a weapon but as a hammer. I also understand it as not the best instrument for the job: a mallet would do better.

Even though it is a matter of synthesis-and-differentiation, this pre-predicative hermeneutical understanding of being requires no thematic articulation, either mental or verbal, and no theoretical knowledge. It usually evidences itself in the mere doing of something. Nevertheless, in a more developed but still pre-predicative moment, such a hermeneutical awareness might evolve into a vague sense of the entity's being-this-or-that ('whatness'), being-in-this-way-or-that ('howness'), and being-available-at-all ('thatness'). Still later, these vague notions might lose the sense of *current* meaningfulness and develop, at level 3, into the explicit metaphysical concepts of the essence, modality and existence of the entity.

The second level of disclosure may be expressed in the following thesis: within any given world, to be an entity is to be always already disclosed as something or other. This corresponds to the traditional doctrine of metaphysics concerning a trans-generic (transcendental) characteristic of anything that is: regardless of its kind or species, every entity is intrinsically disclosed in its being (*omne ens est verum*).

Heidegger argues that while it is based on and is even aware of this second level of disclosure, metaphysics has no explicit understanding of disclosure-as-such or of its source in being-in-the-world. What is more, he claims that the disclosedness of entities-in-their-being (level 2) tends to overlook and obscure the very disclosure-as-such (level 1) that originally makes it possible. He further argues that there is an intrinsic hiddenness about disclosure-as-such, which makes overlooking it virtually inevitable (see §6).

Level 3. Being-in-the-world and the resultant pre-predicative disclosedness of entities as being-thus-and-so make it possible for us to enact the predicative disclosure of entities. At this third level of disclosure we are able to represent correctly to ourselves, in synthetic judgments and declarative sentences, the way things are in the world. A correct synthetic representation of a complex state of affairs (a correct judgment) is 'true', that is, disclosive of things just as they present themselves. Such a predicative, apophantic sentence ('S is P') is able to be true only because world-disclosure has already presented an entity as significant at all and thus allowed it to be taken as thus and so. This already disclosed entity is the binding norm against which the assertion must measure itself.

At level 3, however, it is also possible to *mis*represent things in thought and language, to fail to disclose them just as they present themselves in the world. At level 1 Dasein is always and only disclosive. But with predicative disclosure at level 3 (as analogously with hermeneutical disclosure at level 2) Dasein's representing of matters in propositional statements may be either disclosive or non-disclosive, either true or false.

One of Heidegger's reasons for elaborating the levels of disclosure is to demonstrate that science, metaphysics and reason in general, all of which operate at level 3, are grounded in a more original occurrence of disclosure of which they are structurally unaware. This is what he intends by his claim 'Science does not think'. He does not mean scientists are stupid or their work uninformed, nor is he disparaging reason and its accomplishments. He means that science, by its very nature, is not focused on being-in-the-world, even though being-in-the-world is ultimately responsible for the meaningful presence of the entities against which science measures its propositions.

5   *Hiddenness,* Ereignis *and the Turn*

Hiddenness. Heidegger claims that disclosure-as-such – the very opening up of significance in Dasein's being – is intrinsically hidden and needs to remain so if entities are to be properly disclosed in their being. This intrinsic concealment of disclosure-as-such is called the 'mystery'. Since Heidegger sometimes calls disclosure-as-such 'being itself', the phrase becomes 'the mystery of being'. The ensuing claim, that the mystery of being conceals itself while revealing entities, has led to much mystification, not least among Heideggerians. Being seems to become a higher but hidden Entity that performs strange acts that only the initiated can comprehend. This misconstrual of Heidegger's intentions is not helpful.

How may we understand the intrinsic concealment of disclosure-as-such? One way is to understand the paradigm of 'movement' that informs Heidegger's discussion of revealing and concealing. Taken in the broad philosophical sense, movement is defined not as mere change of place and the like, but as the very being of entities that are undergoing the process of change. This kind of being consists in anticipating something absent, with the result that what is absent-but-anticipated determines the entity's present being. Anticipation *is* the being of such entities, and anticipation is determined from the absent-but-anticipated goal. For example, the acorn's being is its becoming an oak tree; and correspondingly the future oak tree, as the goal of the acorn's trajectory, determines the acorn's present being. Likewise, Margaret *is* a graduate student in so far as she is in movement towards her Ph.D. The still-absent degree *qua* anticipated determines her being-a-student.

The absent is, by nature, hidden. But when it is anticipated or intended, the intrinsically hidden, while still remaining absent, becomes quasi-present. It functions as the 'final cause' and *raison d'être* that determines the being of the anticipating entity. That is, even while remaining intrinsically concealed, the absent-as-anticipated 'gives being' (*Es gibt Sein*) to the anticipating entity by disclosing the entity as what it presently is. This pattern of absence-dispensing-presence holds both for the disclosure of Dasein and for the disclosure of the entities Dasein encounters.

It holds pre-eminently for Dasein. Dasein's being is movement, for Dasein exists by anticipating its own absence. Dasein's death remains intrinsically hidden, but when anticipated, the intrinsically hidden becomes quasi-present by determining Dasein's being as mortal becoming. The absent, when anticipated, dispenses Dasein's finite presence.

The same holds for other entities. The anticipated absence determines Dasein's finite being. But Dasein's being is world-disclosive: it holds open the region of meaningful presence in which other entities are disclosed as being-this-or-that. Hence, the intrinsically hidden, when anticipated, determines the presence not only of Dasein but also of the entities Dasein encounters.

Therefore, the very structure of disclosure – that is, the fact that the absent-but-anticipated determines or 'gives' finite presence – entails that its ultimate source remain intrinsically hidden even while disclosing the being of entities. This intrinsic hiddenness at the core of disclosure is what Heidegger calls the 'mystery'. Heidegger argued that the 'mystery' is the ultimate issue in philosophy, and he believed HERACLITUS had said as much in his fragment no. 123: 'Disclosure-as-such loves to hide'.

Ereignis. The paradigm of movement also explains why Heidegger calls disclosure-as-such '*Ereignis*'. In ordinary German *Ereignis* means 'event', but Heidegger uses it as a word for movement. Playing on the adjective *eigen* ('one's own'), he creates the word *Ereignung*: movement as the process of being drawn into what is one's own. For example, we might imagine that the oak tree as final cause 'pulls' the acorn into what it properly is, by drawing the acorn towards what it is meant to be. This being-pulled is the acorn's movement, its very being. Likewise, Dasein is 'claimed' by death as its final cause and 'pulled forth' by it into mortal becoming. This being-drawn into one's own absence, in such a way that world is engendered and sustained, is what Heidegger calls 'appropriation'. It is what he means by *Ereignis*.

The word '*Ereignis*', along with the image of Dasein being appropriated by the absent, emerges in Heidegger's thought only in the 1930s. However, this later language echoes what Heidegger had earlier called Dasein's thrownness, namely, the fact that Dasein is thrust into possibilities, anticipates its self-absence, and so is 'already' involved in world-disclosure. Both the earlier language of thrown anticipation *of* absence, and the later language of appropriation *by* absence, have the same phenomenon in view: Dasein's alreadiness, its constitutive mortality that makes for world-disclosure.

The paradigm of movement also helps to clarify Heidegger's claim about the concealing-and-revealing, or withdrawing-and-arriving, of being itself (that is, of disclosure-as-such). In a quite typical formulation Heidegger writes: 'Being itself withdraws itself, but as this withdrawal, being is the "pull" that claims the essence of human being as the place

of being's own arrival' (Nietzsche 1961). This sentence, which describes the structure of *Ereignis*, may be interpreted as follows:

The 'withdrawal' of disclosure-as-such

(that is, the intrinsic hiddenness of world-disclosive absence)

maintains a relation to Dasein

(which we may call either 'appropriation' or 'thrown anticipation')

that claims Dasein

(by appropriating it into mortal becoming)

so that, *in* Dasein's being,

(in so far as Dasein's being is the openness that is world)

being itself might arrive

(in the form of the relations of significance whereby entities have being-as this-or-that).

The Turn. One can notice a certain shift within Heidegger's work beginning around 1930, both in his style and in the topics he addresses. As regards style, some have claimed that his language becomes more abstruse and poetic, and his thinking less philosophical than mystical. As regards substance, he seems to introduce new topics like 'appropriation' and the 'history of being'.

The problem is to discern whether these and other shifts count as what Heidegger calls the Turn (*die Kehre*). Some argue that beginning in the 1930s Heidegger radically changed his approach and perhaps even his central topic. The early Heidegger, so the argument goes, had understood being itself (that is, disclosure-as-such) from the standpoint of Dasein, whereas the later Heidegger understands Dasein from the standpoint of being itself. But to the contrary it is clear that even the early Heidegger understood Dasein only from the standpoint of being itself.

Heidegger clarifies matters by distinguishing between (1) the Turn and (2) the 'change in thinking' that the Turn demands, both of which are to be kept distinct from (3) the various shifts in form and focus that his philosophy underwent in the 1930s. The point is that, properly speaking, the Turn is not a shift in Heidegger's thinking nor a change in his central topic. The Turn is only a further specification of *Ereignis*. There are three issues here.

First, the 'Turn' is a name for how *Ereignis* operates. *Ereignis* is the appropriation of Dasein for the sake of world-disclosure. For Heidegger, this fact stands over against all theories of the self as an autonomous subject that presuppositionlessly (that is, without a prior world-disclosure) posits its objects in meaning. In opposition to that, *Ereignis*-means that Dasein must already be appropriated into world-disclosive absence before anything can be significant at all.

Ereignis also means that Dasein's appropriation by, or throwness into, world-disclosive absence is the primary and defining moment in Dasein's projection of that disclosure. This reciprocity (*Gegenschwung*) between appropriation/throwness on the one hand and projection on the other – with the priority going to appropriation/throwness – constitutes the very structure of *Ereignis* and is what Heidegger calls the Turn. The upshot of this reciprocity is that Dasein must be already pulled into world-disclosive absence (thrown or appropriated into it) if it is to project (that is, hold open) disclosure at all. In a word, the Turn *is Ereignis*.

Second, the 'change in thinking' refers to the personal conversion that the Turn demands. To become aware of the Turn and to accept it as determining one's own being is what Heidegger had earlier called 'resolution' and what he now describes as 'a transformation in human being'. This transformation into an authentic self consists in letting one's own being be defined by the Turn.

Third, the shifts in Heidegger's work in the 1930s – and especially the development and deepening of his insights into throwness and appropriation – are just that: shifts and developments within a single, continuing project. Important as they are, they are neither the Turn itself nor the change in personal self-understanding that the Turn requires.

6 Forgetfulness, history and metaphysics

Heidegger sees a strong connection between the forgetting of disclosure-as-such, the history of the dispensations of being, and metaphysics.

Forgetting disclosure-as-such. Because disclosure-as-such is intrinsically hidden (this is what is meant by the mystery), it is usually overlooked. When the mystery is overlooked, human being is 'fallen', that is, aware of entities as being-thus-and-so, but oblivious of what it is that 'gives' being to entities. Fallenness is forgetfulness of the mystery. Another term for fallenness is 'errancy', which conveys the image of Dasein 'wandering' among entities-in-their-being without knowing what makes their presence possible. Since disclosure-as-such is sometimes called 'being itself', fallenness is also called 'the forgetfulness of being'.

However, disclosure-as-such need not be forgotten. It is possible, in resolution, to assume one's mortality and become concretely aware of disclosure-as-such in its basic state of hiddenness. Such

awareness does not undo the intrinsic hiddenness of disclosure-as-such or draw it into full presence. Rather, one accepts the concealment of being itself (this is called 'letting being be') by resolutely accepting one's appropriation by absence.

The history of the dispensations of being. Heidegger's discussions of the 'history of being' sometimes verge on the anthropomorphic, and he often uses etymologies that are difficult to carry over into English. Nevertheless, his purpose in all this is clear: to spell out the world-historical dimensions of fallenness.

As we have seen, disclosure-as-such 'gives' the being of entities while the 'giving' itself remains hidden; and this happens only in so far as Dasein is appropriated by absence. When one forgets the absence that appropriates Dasein, and thus forgets the hidden giving that brings forth the being of entities, fallenness and errancy ensue. Fallen Dasein then focuses on the given (entities-in-their-being) and overlooks the hidden giving (disclosure-as-such). None the less, the hidden giving still goes on giving, but now in a doubly hidden way: it is both intrinsically hidden *and* forgotten. When the hiddenness is forgotten, a disclosure is called a 'dispensation' (*Geschick*) of being. The word connotes a portioning-out that holds something back. A certain form of the being of entities is dispensed while the disclosing itself remains both hidden and forgotten.

In German, 'dispensation' (*Geschick*) and 'history' (*Geschichte*) have their common root in the verb *schicken*, 'to send'. Playing on those etymologies, Heidegger elaborates a 'history' of being, based on the 'sendings' or 'dispensations' of being. (The usual translations of *Geschick* as 'fate' or 'destiny' are not helpful here.) In Heidegger's view each dispensation of being defines a distinct epoch in the history of thought from ancient Greece down to today. He calls the aggregate of such dispensations and epochs the 'history of being'. Because the whole of these dispensations and epochs is correlative to fallenness, Heidegger seeks to overcome the history of being and return to an awareness of the hidden giving.

Heidegger believes the parameters of each epoch in the history of being can be glimpsed in the name that a major philosopher of the period gave to the being of entities in that age. A non-exhaustive list of such epoch-defining notions of being includes: *idea* in Plato, *energeia* in Aristotle, act in Aquinas, representedness in Descartes, objectivity in Kant, Absolute Spirit in Hegel, and will to power in Nietzsche. What characterizes each such epoch is (1) an understanding of being as some form of the presence of entities and (2) an oblivion of the absence that bestows such presence. None the less, even when forgotten the absence is never abolished, and thus traces of it remain in the various dispensations. Therefore, in studying the texts of classical philosophy Heidegger searches for and retrieves the unexpressed absence (the 'unsaid') that hides behind what the text actually expresses (the 'said').

Metaphysics. The various ways that presence or being has been dispensed, while absence has been overlooked, are called in their entirety 'metaphysics'. Heidegger argues that metaphysics as a philosophical position which began with Plato and entered its final phase with Nietzsche.

The Greek philosophers who preceded Socrates and Plato were, in Heidegger's view, pre-metaphysical in so far as they had at least a penumbral awareness of disclosure-as-such and at least named it (Heraclitus, for example, called it *logos*, *alētheia*, and *physis*). However, none of these thinkers thematically addressed disclosure-as-such or understood the correlative notions of ek-sistence and Dasein. Heidegger calls the penumbral awareness of disclosure-as-such among archaic Greek thinkers the 'first beginning'. And he hoped that a 'new beginning' would follow the end of metaphysics. If the first beginning was not yet metaphysical, the new beginning will be no longer metaphysical. Heidegger considered his own work a preparation for that new beginning.

But metaphysics persists. The history of the dispensations of being has reached its fullness in the present epoch of technology. As Heidegger uses the word, 'technology' refers not to hardware or software or the methods and materials of applied science. Rather, it names a dispensation in the history of metaphysics, in fact the final one. It names the way in which entities-in-their-being are disclosed today.

Heidegger maintains that in the epoch of technology entities are taken as a stockpile of matter that is in principle completely knowable by human reason and wholly available for human use. With this notion metaphysics arrives at its most extreme oblivion of disclosure-as-such. In our time, Heidegger says, the presence of entities has become everything, while the absence that brings about that presence has become nothing. He calls this nil-status of absence 'nihilism'.

Overcoming metaphysics. None the less, Heidegger sees a glimmer of light in the dark epoch of nihilism. In this final dispensation of metaphysics, the hidden giving does not cease to function, even when it is completely forgotten. It continues dispensing presence – paradoxically even the nihilistic presence which obscures the absence that gives it. Because the hidden giving goes on giving even when it is forgotten, we can still experience it today (in a mood not unlike dread) and retrieve it. This recovery of world-disclosive absence requires resolution or, as Heidegger now calls it, 'the entrance into *Ereignis*'. To enter *Ereignis* today is to experience a different kind of *nihil* ('nothing') from the one that defines nihilism. The absence that bestows presence is itself a kind of 'nothing' (not-a-thing). This absence is no entity, nor can it be reduced to the being of any specific entity or be present the way an entity is. That is why it is so easily overlooked. Its 'nothingness' is its intrinsic hiddenness.

To enter *Ereignis* is to become aware of and to accept the disclosive *nihil* that rescues one from nihilism. Thereupon, says Heidegger, metaphysics as the history of the dispensations of being ceases and a new beginning takes place – at least for those individuals who achieve authenticity by way of resolution. But metaphysics will continue for those who remain inauthentic, because dispensation is correlative to fallenness.

Summary. The forgetting of disclosure-as-such is metaphysics. Metaphysics knows entities-in-their-being but ignores the very giving of that being. The aggregate of the epochs of metaphysics is the history of the dispensations of being. The history of these dispensations culminates in the epoch of technology and nihilism. But world-disclosive absence can still be retrieved; and when it is retrieved, it ushers in (at least for authentic individuals) a new beginning of ek-sistence and Dasein.

7 The work of art

One of Heidegger's most challenging essays is 'The Origin of the Work of Art', originally drafted in 1935 and published in an expanded version only in 1950. There he distinguishes between the work of art as a specific entity (for example, a poem or a painting) and art itself, the latter being understood not as a collective name for, but rather as the essence and origin of, all works of art. Heidegger asks what art itself is, and he answers that art is a unique kind of disclosure.

Dasein is disclosive of the being of an entity in many ways, some of them ordinary and some of them extraordinary. An outcome common to both kinds of disclosure is that the disclosed entity is seen as what it is: it appears in its form. Examples of ordinary, everyday ways of disclosing the being of entities include showing oneself to be adept at the flute, or moulding clay into a vase, or concluding that the accused is innocent. Each of these ordinary cases of praxis, production and theory does indeed disclose some entity as being this or that, but the focus is on showing what the *entity* is rather than on showing how the entity's *being* is disclosed. On the other hand, extraordinary acts of disclosure bring to attention not only the disclosed entity but above all the event of disclosure of that entity's being. Extraordinary acts of disclosure let us see the very fact that, and the way in which, an entity has become meaningfully present in its being. In these cases not only does an entity appear in its form (as happens in any instance of disclosure), but more importantly the very disclosure of the being of the entity 'is established' (*sich einrichten*) in the entity and is seen there as such.

Heidegger lists five examples of extraordinary disclosure: the constitution of a nation-state; the nearness of god; the giving of one's life for another; the thinker's questioning as revealing that being can be questioned; and the 'installation' (*Sich-ins-Werk-Setzen*) of disclosure in a work of art. Each of these cases discloses, in its own particular way, not just an entity but the very disclosure of that entity's being. Heidegger seeks to understand the particular way in which art itself discloses disclosure by 'installing' disclosure in the work of art.

In his essay Heidegger refers mainly to two works of art: van Gogh's canvas 'Old Shoes', painted in Paris in 1886–7 and now hung in the Stedelijk Museum, Amsterdam; and the 5th century BC Doric Temple of Hera II – the so-called Temple of Poseidon – at Paestum (Lucania), Italy. Let us consider the temple at Paestum as we attempt to answer two questions: what gets disclosed in a work of art and how does it get disclosed?

(1) *What gets disclosed in a work of art?* Heidegger gives three answers. First, a work of art lets us see disclosure in the form of 'world' and 'earth'. A work of art discloses not just an entity or an ensemble of entities but the whole realm of significance whereby an ensemble of entities gets its finite meaning. The temple at Paestum not only houses (and thus discloses) the goddess Hera, but more importantly lets us see the social and historical world – rooted as it was in the natural setting of Lucania – that Hera's presence guaranteed for the Greek colonists. A work of art, Heidegger argues, reveals the very event of disclosure, which event he calls the happening of world and earth, where 'earth' refers not only to nature and natural entities but more broadly to all entities within a specific world.

Second, a work of art lets us see the radical tension that discloses a specific world of significance. Heidegger understands being-in-the-world as a 'struggle' (*Streit* or *polemos*) between a given world and its earth, between the self-expanding urge of a set of human possibilities and the rootedness of such possibilities in a specific natural environment. Here, 'struggle' is another name for the event of disclosure whereby a particular world is opened up and maintained. What a specific work of art discloses is one particular struggle that discloses one

particular world – for instance, the world of the Greek colonists at Paestum.

Third, a work of art shows us disclosure-as-such. The movement of opening up a particular world is only one instance of the general movement of *alētheia*: the 'wresting' of being-at-all from the absolute absence into which Dasein is appropriated. Thus a work of art not only shows us a particular world-disclosive struggle (the way the temple of Hera shows us the earth–world tension at Paestum) but also lets us see the 'original struggle' (*Urstreit*) of disclosure-as-such, whereby significance is wrested from the double closure of intrinsic hiddenness and fallenness.

In short, what a work of art reveals is disclosure in three forms: as world and earth; as the struggle that opens up a specific world and lets its entities be meaningful; and as the original struggle that structures all such particular disclosures.

(2) *How does a work of art disclose disclosure?* The specific way that art discloses disclosure is by 'installing' it in a given work of art. Here, 'to install' means to bring to stability; and 'to install disclosure' means to incorporate it into the physical form of a work of art. There are three corollaries:

What the installing is not. Heidegger does not claim that the work of art 'sets up' the world and 'sets forth' the earth for the first time. That is, installing the disclosure of earth and world in the work of art is not the only or even the first way that earth and world get disclosed. The sanctuary of Hera was not the first to open up the world of Paestum and disclose the fields and flocks for what they are. Tradesmen and farmers had been doing that – that is, the disclosive struggle of world and earth had been bestowing form and meaning – for at least a century before the temple was built.

What the installing is and does. Art discloses, in a new and distinctive way, a disclosure of earth and world that is already operative. Heidegger argues that the temple as disclosive (a) captures and sustains the openness of that world and its rootedness in nature, and (b) shows how, within that world, nature comes forth into the forms of entities while remaining rooted in itself. Heidegger calls these two functions, which happen only in art, the 'setting up' of world and the 'setting forth' of earth.

The work of art lets us see – directly, experientially and in all its glory – the already operative interplay of human history's rootedness in nature and nature's emergence into human history. In Heidegger's words, art 'stabilizes' (*zum Stehen bringen*) the disclosive struggle of world and earth by 'installing' it in a particular work of art, such that in and through that medium, disclosure 'shines forth' brilliantly in beauty.

The two ways art discloses disclosure, and their unity. Art itself is a specific and distinctive way in which

Dasein is disclosive: it discloses disclosure by installing disclosure in the physical form of a work of art. This installation has two moments: the creation and the preservation of the work of art.

Creation is an artist's Dasein-activity of incorporating disclosure – the world-openness that is already operative – into a material medium (stone, colour, language and so on). This incorporation of disclosure is carried out in such a way that the material medium is not subordinated to anything other than disclosure (for example, it is not subordinated to 'usefulness'). Rather, the medium becomes, for whoever experiences it, the immediate disclosure of disclosure.

Preservation is the corresponding Dasein-activity of maintaining the power of disclosure in the work of art by resolutely letting disclosure continue to be seen there. Creation and preservation are the two ways that Dasein 'projects' (holds open and sustains) the disclosure that is installed in the work of art. The unity of creation and preservation is art itself, which Heidegger calls *Dichtung* – not 'poetry' but *poiesis*, the creating-and-preserving installation of disclosure in a disclosive medium.

Disclosure is the central topic of all Heidegger's philosophy, and this fact shines brilliantly through his reflection on the origin of the work of art. Art, both as creation and as preservation, is a specific and distinctive Dasein-activity: the disclosure of disclosure in a medium that is disclosive. In the work of art, as in Heidegger's own work, it's *alētheia* all the way down.

See also: HERMENEUTICS; PHENOMENOLOGICAL MOVEMENT

References and further reading

Heidegger, Martin (1962) *Being and Time*, trans. J. Macquarrie and E. Robinson, New York: Harper & Row. (Heidegger's most famous work, which treats the structure of human being as the finite 'place' in which all meaning or 'being' appears. The unpublished second half of the work was to have shown how the finitude of human being is responsible for the finitude of all forms of meaning/being.)

Heidegger, Martin (1998) *Pathmarks* (various translators), (ed.) W. McNeill, New York: Cambridge University Press. (A collection of fourteen of Heidegger's most important and accessible essays, ranging in date from 1919 to 1961. One of the best introductions to Heidegger's work.)

Richardson, William J. (2003) *Heidegger: Through Phenomenology to Thought*, Preface by Martin Heidegger, New York: Fordham University Press. (This expanded edition of the original 1963 text is the classical presentation of Heidegger's entire oeuvre by the pre-eminent Heidegger scholar. The preface to the book is one of Heidegger's most important self-interpretations.)

THOMAS SHEEHAN

HELL

The ancient idea that the dead go to a dark subterranean place gradually evolved into the notion of divinely instituted separate postmortem destinies for the wicked and the righteous. If the former lies behind the Psalms, the latter version appears in apocalyptic works, both canonical and deutero- or non-canonical, and is presupposed by numerous passages in the New Testament. Through the patristic and medieval periods the doctrine gradually achieved ecclesiastical definition, stipulating eternal torment (both physical and spiritual) in a distinctive place for those who die in a state of mortal sin. Most reformers recognized biblical authority for this doctrine. Philosophically, the notion of postmortem survival raises many questions in the philosophy of mind about personal identity. Recent discussion, however, has concentrated on the specialized version of the problem of evil to which the doctrine gives rise.

See also: EVIL, PROBLEM OF; HEAVEN; LIMBO; PREDESTINATION; PURGATORY; SOUL, NATURE AND IMMORTALITY OF THE

MARILYN MCCORD ADAMS

HELMONT, FRANCISCUS MERCURIUS VAN (1614–98)

Although he lived in the seventeenth century, van Helmont belongs more to late Renaissance than to modern intellectual culture. He was a larger-than-life figure who, in his prime, had an international reputation as an alchemist and a physician. His metaphysical interests came increasingly to the fore, however, and he became particularly associated with Kabbalistic doctrines. A friend of Locke and Henry More, he was also closely connected with Anne Conway and Leibniz, with whom he shared many intellectual affinities. It is these connections that make his philosophy – in particular, his theodicy and his monadology – of enduring interest.

See also: ALCHEMY; CONWAY, A.; HELL; KABBALAH; LEIBNITZ, G.W.; PARACELSUS

STUART BROWN

HERACLITUS (c.540–c.480 BC)

No Greek philosopher born before Socrates was more creative and influential than Heraclitus of Ephesus. Around the beginning of the fifth century

BC, in a prose that made him proverbial for obscurity, he criticized conventional opinions about the way things are and attacked the authority of poets and others reputed to be wise. His surviving work consists of more than 100 epigrammatic sentences, complete in themselves and often comparable to the proverbs characteristic of 'wisdom' literature. Notwithstanding their sporadic presentation and transmission, Heraclitus' sentences comprise a philosophy that is clearly focused upon a determinate set of interlocking ideas.

As interpreted by the later Greek philosophical tradition, Heraclitus stands primarily for the radical thesis that 'Everything is in flux', like the constant flow of a river. Although it is likely that he took this thesis to be true, universal flux is too simple a phrase to identify his philosophy. His focus shifts continually between two perspectives – the objective and everlasting processes of nature on the one hand and ordinary human beliefs and values on the other. He challenges people to come to terms, theoretically and practically, with the fact that they are living in a world 'that no god or human has made', a world he describes as 'an ever-living fire kindling in measures and going out in measures' (fr. 30). His great truth is that 'All things are one', but this unity, far from excluding difference, opposition and change, actually depends on them, since the universe is in a continuous state of dynamic equilibrium. Day and night, up and down, living and dying, heating and cooling – such pairings of apparent opposites all conform to the everlastingly rational formula (*logos*) that unity consists of opposites; remove day, and night goes too, just as a river will lose its identity if it ceases to flow.

Heraclitus requires his audience to try to think away their purely personal concerns and view the world from this more detached perspective. By the use of telling examples he highlights the relativity of value judgments. The implication is that unless people reflect on their experience and examine themselves, they are condemned to live a dream-like existence and to remain out of touch with the formula that governs and explains the nature of things. This formula is connected (symbolically and literally) with 'ever-living fire', whose incessant 'transformations' are not only the basic operation of the universe but also essential to the cycle of life and death. Fire constitutes and symbolizes both the processes of nature in general and also the light of intelligence. As the source of life and thought, a 'fiery' soul equips people to look into themselves, to discover the formula of nature and to live accordingly.

The influence of Heraclitus' ideas on other philosophers was extensive. His reputed 'flux' doctrine, as disseminated by his follower Cratylus,

helped to shape Plato's cosmology and its changeless metaphysical foundations. The Stoics looked back to Heraclitus as the inspiration for their own conception of divine fire, identifying this with the *logos* that he specifies as the world's explanatory principle. Later still, the neo-Pyhrronist Aenesidemus invoked Heraclitus as a partial precursor of scepticism.

See also: PRESOCRATIC PHILOSOPHY

A.A. LONG

HERDER, JOHANN GOTTFRIED (1744–1803)

Herder was a central figure in the German intellectual renaissance of the late eighteenth century. His achievement spanned virtually every domain of philosophy, and his influence, especially upon Romanticism and German idealism, was immense. In social and political philosophy he played a prominent role in the development of historicism and nationalism. In metaphysics he developed the doctrine of vitalist pantheism, which later became important for Goethe, Schelling and Hegel. In the philosophy of mind he formulated an organic theory of the mind–body relationship, which was crucial for Schelling and Hegel. And in aesthetics he was among the first to defend the value of ethnic poetry and the need for the internal and historical understanding of a text.

Herder's main aim was to extend the powers of naturalistic explanation to the realm of culture, so that characteristic human activities, such as art, religion, law and language could be included within the scientific worldview. But he also wanted to avoid reductivistic forms of explanation that viewed such activities as nothing more than matter-in-motion or stimulus-response mechanisms. He insisted that explanation in the cultural sphere had to be holistic and internal as well as mechanical and external. An action had to be understood in its historical context and according to the intention of the agent and not simply as another instance of a causal regularity between events. Herder's programme, then, was to develop naturalistic yet non-reductivistic explanations for the realm of culture. He attempted to realize this programme in many spheres, especially language, history, religion and the mind.

See also: HISTORY, PHILOSOPHY OF; NATION AND NATIONALISM; VICO, G.

FREDERICK BEISER

HERMENEUTICS

Hermeneutics, the 'art of interpretation', was originally the theory and method of interpreting the Bible and other difficult texts. Wilhelm Dilthey extended it to the interpretation of all human acts and products, including history and the interpretation of a human life. Heidegger, in *Being and Time* (1927), gave an 'interpretation' of the human being, the being that itself understands and interprets. Under his influence, hermeneutics became a central theme of Continental philosophy. Hermeneutics generates several controversies. In interpreting something do we unearth the author's thoughts and intentions, imagining ourselves in his position? Or do we relate it to a wider whole that gives it meaning? The latter view gives rise to the hermeneutic circle: we cannot understand a whole (for example, a text) unless we understand its parts, or the parts unless we understand the whole. Heidegger discovered another circle: as we inevitably bring presuppositions to what we interpret, does this mean that any interpretation is arbitrary, or at least endlessly revisable?

See also: VEDĀNTA

MICHAEL INWOOD

HERMETISM

A primarily religious amalgam of Greek philosophy with Egyptian and other Near Eastern elements, Hermetism takes its name from Hermes Trismegistus, 'thrice greatest Hermes', alias the Egyptian god Thoth. Numerous texts on philosophical theology and various occult sciences, ascribed to or associated with this primeval figure, were produced in Greek by Egyptians between roughly AD 100 and 300, and are a major document of late pagan piety. Reintroduced into Western Europe during the Renaissance, they provided considerable inspiration to philosophers, scientists and magicians of the fifteenth and sixteenth centuries.

See also: ALCHEMY; BRUNO, G.; FICINO, M.; GNOSTICISM; PARACELSUS; PICO DELLA MIRANDOLA, G.; RENAISSANCE PHILOSOPHY

JOHN PROCOPÉ

HERZEN, ALEKSANDR IVANOVICH (1812–70)

Lauded by Nietzsche as 'a man of every distinctive talent' and admired by Lenin as the founder of the Russian revolutionary movement, Herzen eludes all neat categorizations. As a moral preacher he stands alongside Tolstoi and Dostoevskii (who praised him as a poet). As a philosopher, he was the principal interpreter and popularizer of Hegel's thought in Russia in the first half of the 1840s, while the rebellion against metaphysical systems in his mature work has led him to be seen as a precursor of existentialism. Through the Russian press that he

founded while an émigré he helped to shape the beginnings of a public opinion in his country and played a major role in debates on Russia's political future on the eve of the emancipation of the serfs, while laying the foundations of the Russian populist movement through his writings on Russian socialism. He is best known in the West for his memoirs, *Byloe i dumy* (*My Past and Thoughts*) (1861, 1866), which rank among the great works of Russian literature, and for *S togo berega* (*From the Other Shore*) (1850), the most brilliant and original of the works in which he expresses his rejection of all teleological conceptions of history.

AILEEN KELLY

HILBERT'S PROGRAMME AND FORMALISM

In the first, geometric stage of Hilbert's formalism, his view was that a system of axioms does not express truths particular to a given subject matter but rather expresses a network of logical relations that can (and, ideally, will) be common to other subject matters.

The formalism of Hilbert's arithmetical period extended this view by emptying even the logical terms of contentual meaning. They were treated purely as ideal elements whose purpose was to secure a simple and perspicuous logic for arithmetical reasoning – specifically, a logic preserving the classical patterns of logical inference. Hilbert believed, however, that the use of ideal elements should not lead to inconsistencies. He thus undertook to prove the consistency of ideal arithmetic with its contentual or finitary counterpart and to do so by purely finitary means.

In this, 'Hilbert's programme', Hilbert and his followers were unsuccessful. Work published by Kurt Gödel in 1931 suggested that such failure was perhaps inevitable. In his second incompleteness theorem, Gödel showed that, for any consistent formal axiomatic system T strong enough to formalize what was traditionally regarded as finitary reasoning, it is possible to define a sentence that expresses the consistency of T, and is not provable in T. From this it has generally been concluded that the consistency of even the ideal arithmetic of the natural numbers is not finitarily provable and that Hilbert's programme must therefore fail.

Despite problematic elements in this reasoning, post-Gödelian work on Hilbert's programme has generally accepted it and attempted to minimize its effects by proposing various modifications of Hilbert's programme. These have generally taken one of three forms: attempts to extend Hilbert's finitism to stronger constructivist bases capable of proving more than is provable by strictly finitary means; attempts to show that for a significant family of ideal systems there are ways of 'reducing' their consistency problems to those of theories possessing more elementary (if not altogether finitary) justifications; and attempts by the so-called 'reverse mathematics' school to show that the traditionally identified ideal theories do not need to be as strong as they are in order to serve their mathematical purposes. They can therefore be reduced to weaker theories whose consistency problems are more amenable to constructivist (indeed, finitist) treatment.

See also: ARITHMETIC, PHILOSOPHICAL ISSUES IN; INTUITIONISM; MATHEMATICS, FOUNDATIONS OF

MICHAEL DETLEFSEN

HILDEGARD OF BINGEN (1098–1179)

Hildegard of Bingen saw herself as a prophet sent by God to awaken an age in which great troubles were besieging the Church and people no longer understood Scripture. She tried to alleviate the first problem by writing letters to secular and religious leaders and preaching against those she saw as the culprits, and to this end she undertook preaching tours throughout Germany, preaching in cathedrals, monasteries and synods. Her writings, primarily interpretations of her own visions, address the second problem by trying to cast a new light on Christian revelation through illustrating it with original vivid imagery and personifications of abstract concepts. Though her works are not, for the most part, clearly philosophical, Hildegard does show philosophical insight.

See also: SOUL, NATURE AND IMMORTALITY OF

CLAUDIA EISEN MURPHY

HINDU PHILOSOPHY

Hindu philosophy is the longest surviving philosophical tradition in India. We can recognize several historical stages. The earliest, from around 700 BC, was the proto-philosophical period, when karma and liberation theories arose, and the proto-scientific ontological lists in the Upaniṣads were compiled. Next came the classical period, spanning the first millennium AD, in which there was constant philosophical exchange between different Hindu, Buddhist and Jaina schools. During this period, some schools, such as Sāṅkhya, Yoga and Vaiśeṣika, fell into oblivion and others, such as Kashmir Saivism, emerged. Finally, after the classical period only two or three schools remained active. The political and economic disturbances caused by repeated Muslim invasions hampered intellectual growth. The schools that survived were the Logic school (Nyāya),

especially New Logic (Navya-Nyāya), the grammarians and, above all, the Vedānta schools.

The central concerns of the Hindu philosophers were metaphysics, epistemological issues, philosophy of language, and moral philosophy. The different schools can be distinguished by their different approaches to reality, but all considered the Vedas (the sacred scriptures) authoritative, and all believed that there is a permanent individual self (*ātman*). They shared with their opponents (Buddhists and Jainas) a belief in the need for liberation. They used similar epistemic tools and methods of argument.

In contrast to their opponents, who were atheists, Hindu philosophers could be either theists or atheists. Actually we can observe an increased tendency towards theistic ideas near the end of the classical period, with the result that the strictly atheistic teachings, which were more philosophically rigorous and sound, fell into disuse. Hindu metaphysics saw *ātman* as part of a larger reality (Brahman).

Because these views of the world differed, they had to be proved and properly established. Accordingly, logical and epistemological tools were developed and fashioned according to the needs and beliefs of individual philosophers. Most agreed on two or three sources of knowledge: perception and inference, with verbal testimony as a possible third. In this quest for philosophical rigour, there was a need for precision of language, and there were important philosophical developments among the grammarians and the philosophers who explained the Vedas (the Mīmāṃsakas). A culmination of these linguistic efforts can be seen in the philosopher of language Bhartṛhari. One of his greatest accomplishments was the full articulation of the theory that a sentence as a whole is understood in a sudden act of comprehension.

It is customary to name six Hindu schools, of the more than a dozen that existed, thus lumping several into a single school. This is particularly the case with Vedānta. The six are listed in three pairs: Sāṅkhya–Yoga; Vedānta–Mīmāṃsā; Nyāya–Vaiśeṣika. This does not take account of the grammarians or Kashmir Saivism.

In their quest for freedom from rebirth, all the Hindu schools operated within the same framework. Their ultimate goal was liberation. How much they were truly engaged in the quest for liberation apart from their philosophical preoccupations is not always clear, yet they never doubted its real possibility.

See also: BUDDHIST PHILOSOPHY, INDIAN; JAINA PHILOSOPHY; MĪMĀṂSĀ; NYĀYA-VAIŚEṢIKA; SĀṄKHYA; VEDĀNTA

EDELTRAUD HARZER CLEAR

HISTORICISM

Historicism, defined as 'the affirmation that life and reality are history alone' by Benedetto Croce, is understood to mean various traditions of historiographical thinking which developed in the nineteenth century, predominantly in Germany. Historicism is an insistence on the historicity of all knowledge and cognition, and on the radical segregation of human from natural history. It is intended as a critique of the normative, allegedly anti-historical, epistemologies of Enlightenment thought, expressly that of Kant. The most significant theorists and historians commonly associated with historicism are Leopold von Ranke, Wilhelm Dilthey, J.G. Droysen, Friedrich Meinecke, Croce and R.G. Collingwood.

The main antecedents for the development of historicism are to be found in two key bodies of work. J.G. Herder's *Outlines of a Philosophy of the History of Man* (1784) argues against the construction of history as linear progress, stating rather that human history is composed of fundamentally incomparable national cultures or totalities. G.W.F. Hegel's *The Philosophy of History* (1826) insists on the historical situatedness of each individual consciousness as a particular moment within the total progression of all history towards a final goal. The shifting fusion of these ideas provides the foundation for both the strengths and the problems of historicism. Historicism follows both Herder, in attempting to do justice to objective history in its discontinuity and uniqueness, and Hegel, in attempting to determine general patterns of historical change. Indeed, historicism can perhaps be best termed a Hegelian philosophy of history without an all-encompassing notion of progress.

Rather than constituting a unified intellectual movement, historicism is best known for its elusiveness. Its multifarious quality can be inferred from the variety of critical positions taken up against it. Influential critiques of historicism have been written by Friedrich Nietzsche, Friedrich Rickert, Ernst Troeltsch, Walter Benjamin, Karl Löwith and Karl Popper. Critical engagement with historicism has focused on its alleged relativism, its alleged particularism, its alleged claims to totality, its alleged subjectivism and its alleged objectivism. More positive debates with historicism have significantly influenced the thought of Martin Heidegger, Edmund Husserl and Hans-Georg Gadamer.

See also: HISTORY, PHILOSOPHY OF

CHRISTOPHER THORNHILL

HISTORY, EXPLANATION IN

See EXPLANATION IN HISTORY AND SOCIAL SCIENCE

HISTORY, HOLISM AND INDIVIDUALISM IN

See HOLISM AND INDIVIDUALISM IN HISTORY AND SOCIAL SCIENCE

HISTORY, PHILOSOPHY OF

Philosophy of history is the application of philosophical conceptions and analysis to history in both senses, the study of the past and the past itself. Like most branches of philosophy its intellectual origins are cloudy, but they lie in a refinement of 'sacred' histories, especially those of Judaism and Christianity. The first major philosopher to outline a scheme of world history was Immanuel Kant in *The Idea of a Universal History from a Cosmopolitan Point of View* (1784), and German idealism also produced Hegel's *Lectures on the Philosophy of World History* (1837), a much longer and more ambitious attempt to make philosophical sense of the history of the world as a whole. According to Hegel, history is rational, the working out, in fact, of philosophical understanding itself.

The accelerating success of natural science in the nineteenth century gave rise to a powerful combination of empiricism and logical positivism which produced a philosophical climate highly unfavourable to Hegelian philosophy of history. The belief became widespread among philosophers that Hegel, and Marx after him, had developed a priori theories that ignored historical contingency in favour of historical necessity, and which were empirically unfalsifiable. Karl Popper's philosophy of science was especially influential in converting philosophy of history to a new concern with the methods of historical study rather than with the shape of the past. Two rival conceptions of historical method existed. One tried to model explanation in history on what they took to be the form of explanation in science, and argued for the existence of 'covering laws' by which historians connect the events they seek to explain. The other argued for a distinctive form of explanation in history, whose object was the meaning of human action and whose structure was narrative rather than deductive.

Neither side in this debate was able to claim a convincing victory, with the result that philosophers gradually lost interest in history and began to concern themselves more generally with the nature of human action. This interest, combined with a revival of nineteenth-century German hermeneutics, the study of texts in their social and cultural milieu, in turn revived interest among analytical philosophers in the writings of Hegel and Nietzsche. The impact of continental influences in philosophy, art criticism and social theory was considerable, and reintroduced a historical dimension that had been largely absent from twentieth-century analytical philosophy. In particular, the formation of fundamental philosophical ideas began to be studied as a historical process. The Enlightenment came to be seen as a crucial period in the development of philosophy, and of modernity more generally, and with this understanding came the belief that the contemporary Western world is postmodern. In this way, social theory and the philosophy of culture in fact returned, albeit unawares, to the 'grand narrative' tradition in philosophy of history.

See also: HERMENEUTICS; HISTORICISM

GORDON GRAHAM

HOBBES, THOMAS (1588–1679)

Introduction

Among the figures who were conscious of developing a new science in the seventeenth century, the Englishman Hobbes stands out as an innovator in ethics, politics and psychology. He was active in a number of other fields, notably geometry, ballistics and optics, and seems to have shown considerable acumen as a theorist of light. His contemporaries, especially in Continental Europe, regarded him as a major intellectual figure. Yet he did not earn a living as a scientist or a writer on politics. In 1608 he entered the service of Henry Cavendish, First Earl of Devonshire, and maintained his connections with the family for more than seventy years, working as tutor, translator, travelling companion, business agent and political counsellor. The royalist sympathies of his employers and their circle determined Hobbes' allegiances in the period preceding and during the English Civil War. Hobbes' first political treatise, *The Elements of Law* (1640), was not intended for publication but was meant as a sort of long briefing paper that royalists in parliament could use to justify actions by the king. Even *Leviathan* (1651), which is often read as if it is concerned with the perennial questions of political philosophy, betrays its origins in the disputes of the pre-Civil War period in England.

For much of his life the aristocrats who employed Hobbes brought him into contact with the intellectual life of Continental Europe. He found not just the ideas but also the spokesmen congenial. Perhaps as early as 1630 he met Marin Mersenne, then at the centre of a Parisian network of scientists, mathematicians and theologians that included Descartes as a corresponding member. It was to this group that Hobbes attached himself in 1640 when political events in England seemed to him to threaten his safety, causing him to flee to

France. He stayed for ten years and succeeded in making a name for himself, particularly as a figure who managed to bring geometrical demonstration into the field of ethics and politics. His *De cive*, a treatise that has much in common with the *Elements of Law*, had a very favourable reception in Paris in 1642.

By the time *De cive* appeared, Hobbes had taught himself enough natural philosophy and mathematics to be taken seriously as a savant in his own right. He had also conceived the plan of producing a large-scale exposition of the 'elements' of philosophy as a whole – from first philosophy, geometry and mechanics through to ethics and politics. *De cive* would be the third volume of a trilogy entitled *The Elements of Philosophy*. These books present Hobbes' considered views in metaphysics, physics and psychology against the background of a preferred scheme of science.

Metaphysics, or first philosophy, is primarily a definitional enterprise for Hobbes. It selects the terms whose significations need to be grasped if the principles of the rest of the sciences are to be taught or demonstrated. Foremost among the terms that Hobbes regards as central are 'body' and 'motion'. According to Hobbes, the whole array of natural sciences can be organized according to how each treats of motion. Geometry is the first of these sciences in the 'order of demonstration' – that is, the science whose truths are the most general and on which the truths of all the other natural sciences somehow depend. Mechanics is next in the preferred order of the sciences. It considers 'what effects one body moved worketh upon another'. Physics is the science of sense and the effects of the parts of bodies on sense. Moral philosophy or 'the science of the motions of the mind' comes next, and is informed by physics. It studies such passions as anger, hope and fear, and in doing so informs civil philosophy. Starting from the human emotional make up, civil philosophy works out what agreements between individuals will form commonwealths, and what behaviour is required within commonwealths to make them last.

The behaviour required of the public in order to maintain a commonwealth is absolute submission to a sovereign power. In practice this means abiding by whatever a sovereign declares as law, even if those laws appear to be exacting. Law-abiding behaviour is required so long as, in return, subjects can reasonably expect effective action from the sovereign to secure their safety and wellbeing. With minor variations, this is the theme of all three of Hobbes' political treatises – the *Elements of Law*, *De cive* and *Leviathan*. Government is created through a transfer of right by the many to the one or the few, in whom an unlimited power is vested. The laws of the sovereign power may seem intrusive and restrictive, but what is the alternative to compliance? Hobbes' answer is famous: a life that is solitary, poor, nasty, brutish and short. This conception of life without government is not based on the assumption that human beings are selfish and aggressive but, rather, on the idea that if each is their own judge of what is best, there is no assurance that one's safety and one's possessions will not be at the mercy of other people – a selfish few, a vainglorious minority or even members of a moderate majority who think they have to take pre-emptive action against a vainglorious or selfish few. It is the general condition of uncertainty, in conditions where people can do anything they like to pursue their wellbeing and secure their safety, that Hobbes calls 'war'.

1 Life

Hobbes was born in Westport, a parish of the town of Malmesbury in Wiltshire, England. His mother came from a yeoman family; his father was a poorly educated vicar who seems to have left his parish in disgrace, deserting his family after having come to blows with another clergyman early in Hobbes' childhood. Hobbes' uncle subsequently supported the family, and it was he who paid for Hobbes' university education. Hobbes was lucky to receive good schooling locally, and he showed an early talent for the classical languages.

In 1602 or 1603, Hobbes began study towards an arts degree at Magdalen Hall, Oxford. From his criticisms of the universities in his published writings, it is sometimes inferred that he disliked his college days, or at least that he disliked the scholasticism of Oxford at that time. (Scholasticism – the fusion of Christian with ancient Greek thought, especially the thought of Aristotle – dominated the curricula of the schools and universities of Europe in the sixteenth and early seventeenth centuries – see MEDIEVAL PHILOSOPHY.) Certainly he disliked the university curriculum in retrospect, as chapter 46 of *Leviathan* (1651) makes clear.

Hobbes completed his degree in 1608, and entered the service of William Cavendish, First Earl of Devonshire, as companion and tutor to his son. Although Hobbes was about the same age as the young Cavendish, he was put in charge of his purse as well as his education. He was the earl's representative at meetings of the Virginia Company, in which the Devonshire family had a considerable financial stake. He also accompanied the earl's son on a grand tour of the Continent in 1610, which allowed Hobbes to improve his command of French and Italian. According to some accounts, he also became acquainted then with criticisms of scholasticism current among Continental intellectuals.

It is unclear how long this grand tour lasted, but Hobbes had returned to England by 1615. At some point during these travels Hobbes seems to have met Fulgenzio Micanzio, the friend and personal assistant of the Venetian writer and politician Paolo Sarpi. He must also have met Marc Antonio de Dominis, who was involved in the translation of Bacon's writings into Italian and who also had connections with Sarpi (see BACON, F.). Hobbes' own contact with Bacon may have had its stimulus in the requests of the newly befriended Venetians for more details of the Baconian philosophy. The young Cavendish began a correspondence with Micanzio after returning to England in 1615. Hobbes translated this correspondence and through it would have been exposed to Sarpi's theory of the supremacy of temporal rulers rather than spiritual authorities. The theory went against the Papal interdict of 1606, which asserted Rome's right to overrule the decisions of local monarchs and which had encountered much criticism in England. There are apparently strong echoes of this anti-Papal line in Hobbes' own writings.

During his first twenty years of service to the Devonshires, Hobbes seems to have spent his free time immersed in classical poetry and history. His employers had a good library, and Hobbes made use of it. The first fruit of this regrounding in the classics was a translation into English of Thucydides' *History of the Peloponnesian Wars*, published in 1628. Hobbes believed that Thucydides had lessons for those who overvalued democracy and did not see the strengths of monarchy, and it may have been the Petition of Right of 1628 that led to the publication of the translation. The Petition called on Charles I not to levy taxes without the consent of Parliament, not to imprison subjects without due cause, not to billet soldiers in private homes and not to put civilians under martial law. This sort of challenge to the prerogatives of a monarch is opposed in all of Hobbes' political writings, and the opposition is foreshadowed in the translation of Thucydides.

In 1628 Hobbes chose history as the medium for a political message. Later, in writings like *Leviathan*, he thought science or philosophy was the better vehicle. In writing history it is possible for the conventions of the genre to interfere with the communication of wisdom; in writing science, he came to believe, the communication of wisdom is assured, if the audience is prepared to pay attention and able to follow a demonstration. He struggled throughout his intellectual life with the problem of combining political rhetoric with political science, and some of his best writings are experimental solutions to this problem. The translation of Thucydides is important as the first of many such experiments.

The year 1628 was a kind of turning-point in Hobbes' career. Apart from publishing the translation of Thucydides, he had to contend with the death of the second earl at the age of 43, resulting in his loss of employment with the Devonshires. Hobbes took up a new post in the house of Sir Gervase Clifton, not far from Hardwick Hall, the home of the Devonshires. Once again he was engaged as a companion on a grand tour, this one lasting from 1629 to 1631. During this journey Hobbes looked for the first time at Euclid's *Elements*, and fell in love with geometry. There is plenty of evidence in Hobbes' writings that he regarded Euclid's book as one of the supreme examples of a scientific presentation of a subject. Perhaps also during this second journey to the Continent Hobbes was present at a discussion among some well-educated gentlemen about the nature of sense-perception, in which it emerged that none of the participants could say what sense-perception was. Both episodes are significant, because they seem to mark the beginning of Hobbes' transformation from man of letters to man of science.

Perhaps the stimulus for the change was not the second grand tour alone. After his return, Hobbes went back into the service of the Devonshires and became tutor to the young third earl. At about the same time, he came into contact with a branch of his master's family who lived at Welbeck, near Hardwick Hall. The Welbeck Cavendishes were interested in science. The Earl of Newcastle is known to have sent Hobbes on an errand to London to find a book of Galileo's in the early 1630s. The earl's younger brother, Charles, had an even greater interest in science: he acted as something of a patron and distributor of scientific writings. Hobbes was one of those who looked at and gave his opinion of these writings. Charles Cavendish also had contacts among Continental scientists, including Marin Mersenne, a friar in Paris who was at the centre of a circle of scientists and philosophers that included Descartes.

Hobbes' scientific development continued when he embarked with the third earl on yet another grand tour from 1634 to 1636. During this journey he is supposed to have met Galileo in Italy, as well as Mersenne and some members of his circle in Paris in 1636. Hobbes had probably become acquainted with Mersenne five years earlier on the second tour. It is said that on the third grand tour Hobbes was much preoccupied with the nature and effects of motion, and that he started to see for the first time how many natural phenomena depended upon it.

On his return to England, Hobbes kept up with some of the scientific work being produced in Mersenne's circle. Descartes' *Discourse and Essays* were published in 1637. Hobbes was sent a copy and seems to have made a careful study of the first of the *Essays* – on optics – perhaps taking time to write something of his own on the same subject. He was not keeping abreast solely of scientific ideas. Through his association with a circle of clergy, lawyers and aristocrats at Great Tew, near Oxford, he was able to follow the continuing debates surrounding the troubles of Charles I. In 1634 the king started to raise funds for a navy by a ship-money tax levied county by county. This tax-raising met opposition, particularly in non-coastal counties. Besides the ship-money dispute, Charles I had to reckon with the consequences of trying, in 1637, to bring the Scottish Presbyterian prayer book into line with its Anglican counterpart. This provoked a National Covenant in Scotland expressing wholesale opposition to ecclesiastical innovations from England. In 1639 and 1640 the Scots raised armies to back up their opposition, and Charles was forced to recall a parliament he was used to ruling without, and which was extremely hostile to him. When Parliament acted against Stafford, a minister of the King associated with the Earl of Newcastle, Hobbes worked on arguments that could support the royalist position in parliamentary debates. The arguments were produced in a treatise, *The Elements of Law* (1640), not intended for publication but which, in fact, contains much of the doctrine of Hobbes' political philosophy. Fearing that he would be prosecuted for giving the royalists their arguments, he fled to Paris and joined the circle of philosophers and scientists around Mersenne.

Some years after 1640 Hobbes wrote that he had recently conceived a plan for expounding, in three parts, the elements of philosophy or science in general. His exposition would begin with the nature of body and the elements of what we now call physics. It would go on to discuss human nature, in particular perception and motivation, and the third part would be a discussion of moral and civic duty. Perhaps he had already drawn up this plan, and even executed some of it, by the time he reached Paris. What *is* certain, however, is that the first part of the exposition to be published was the last of the three in his outline – the part on morals and politics. Hobbes called this part of his exposition *De cive* and published a very limited edition of it in Latin in 1642.

Hobbes seems to have enjoyed good relations with most of Mersenne's circle. He was at odds with Descartes, however, whose *Meditations* he criticized in a set of 'Objections' – the anonymous 'Third Set' (see DESCARTES, R. §§4, 6). From 1641 until Mersenne's death in 1648, Hobbes applied himself to the composition of the rest of his three-part exposition of the elements of science. He produced some of the material for the first part of the exposition – on body, the part published in 1655 as *De corpore* – and took up topics that would later occupy the middle part of the exposition. In 1643 he wrote a critical commentary on *De mundo*, a treatise written by Thomas White (another English-man in Paris at that time) which was sympathetic to scholasticism. In 1646 Hobbes composed some arguments about the respects in which freedom is compatible with causal necessitation in nature, arguing once more on this occasion against scholastic positions. He suffered a serious illness in 1647 and almost died. While on his sickbed he rebuffed an attempt by Mersenne to convert him to Roman Catholicism.

In 1648 Mersenne died and the philosophical and scientific activity that had gone on around him ceased to have a focal point. Hobbes now had a place among the royalists in exile, but he was on poor terms with churchmen around the exiled Charles II in Paris and was receiving his pay rather irregularly. By the autumn of 1649 he seems to have formed the intention of going home.

Leviathan, in which Hobbes attempted to derive from his now well-worked-out political principles the right relation of Church to state, was written at the end of the 1640s, when church government in England began to run on lines of which he approved and at a time when the influence of bishops in the English royal court-in-exile in Paris was, in Hobbes' eyes, too great. In any case, the fact that the theory in the book vindicated Cromwell's policy on church government does not mean that it was a partisan work in favour of Cromwell, calculated to ease Hobbes' return to England. If that had been so, Hobbes would not have made a special presentation copy for the future Charles II. Instead, it seems that the doctrine in *Leviathan* favoured the concentration of all authority in any *de facto* sovereign power, whether republican or royal. To the Paris royalists, mostly strong Anglicans in favour of political powers for bishops, the new book was highly offensive.

By the end of 1651 Hobbes was back in London and all three statements of his political philosophy were available in some form in English. These political works were widely known before his exposition of the elements of science was complete. Even though *De cive* had been planned to complete a sequence of three treatises on these elements, it did not depend on the other treatises in order to be understood, and it has always had a readership of its own. When the other two works in the sequence appeared in the 1650s, they did not match *De cive* in quality. The treatise on which Hobbes had been working longest was the opening work of the sequence, *De corpore*, published in 1655. In it Hobbes tried to show how the mature sciences of geometry, mechanics and physics were concerned with the effects of different kinds of motion in matter. Politically motivated critics soon exposed the weaknesses in the mathematical sections of the book, and Hobbes' attempt to vindicate his work involved him in years of fruitless polemic. *De homine*, the second volume of his *Elements* and undoubtedly the least well-integrated of the three, was published in 1658. It was never widely read, and a modern English translation of it has only recently appeared.

In 1660 the monarchy was re-established in England, and on the coat-tails of Charles II there returned to political power many who regarded Hobbes as a traitor to the royalist cause. Charles himself was not hostile, however, and other influential people were also well-disposed towards him. Nevertheless, in 1666 and 1667, Parliament came close to passing a bill outlawing Christian heresy and atheism, and *Leviathan* was specifically investigated as a source of heretical and atheistic views. The danger of imprisonment and exile did not dissipate until the end of the decade. The threats to Hobbes were reflected in additions that he made to a Latin edition of his works published in Holland in 1668. He argued that punishment for heresy was illegal under English law and that his materialism was compatible with Christian faith. Two significant works from the 1660s were applications of his political philosophy. There was a history of the English Civil War, *Behemoth* (1668), and the *Dialogue between a Philosopher and a Student of the Common Laws of England*. By the time these works were composed, Hobbes was not permitted to publish, and though he busied himself with some translations of the classics and a few other minor writings of his own in the 1670s, he had come almost to the end of his working life.

In his ninetieth year, Hobbes returned to physics. His *Decameron Physiologicum* (1678) restates some of the methodology and principal results of the physical sections of *De corpore*. For the preceding three years Hobbes had divided his time between the two Devonshire houses of Chatsworth and

Hardwick Hall. In December 1679 he died of a urinary complaint. His remains are buried in a small parish church near Hardwick Hall.

2   Science and human improvement

Hobbes' writings are those of an advocate and practitioner of a new science, a system of knowledge of causes that could, as he believed, greatly benefit human life. Yet he formed his ideas during a period when human intellectual powers, including the ability to develop science, were commonly thought to be limited. According to some theories prevalent in the late sixteenth and early seventeenth centuries, the whole human race was involved in a quite general and unstoppable process of natural decay, so that all the best achievements of human beings belonged to a long-lost golden age. It was a way of understanding things that was consistent with, if not inspired by, the Biblical story of the Fall of Adam and Eve, and the loss of paradise. According to some understandings of that story, Adam's expulsion from paradise cost him not only a life of ease in harmony with God and the rest of nature, but also the gift of a natural insight into the natures of all the things he could name. Regaining the knowledge of those natures might never be possible. In France, in the late sixteenth and early seventeenth centuries, recently popularized Greek sceptical arguments against dogmatism reinforced the view that human intellectual possibilities were limited. The arguments were directed not only against the traditional learning of the schools but against the idea that any human learning – even untraditional or anti-traditional learning – could amount to a system of genuine knowledge. Hobbes' philosophy of science stands in opposition to much of this gloomy theorizing. It stands in opposition to philosophical scepticism, to the theory of the decay of nature as applied to the human intellect and, to a lesser extent, to pessimistic interpretations of the intellectual costs of the Fall.

Although Hobbes had close friends and intellectual influences among French thinkers who took sceptical arguments seriously, there is little if any solid evidence in his own writing that he studied these arguments closely or took their conclusions to heart. He seems never to have doubted the soundness or scientific status of Euclid's geometry, and he was an early enthusiast for the applied mathematics of Copernicus, Kepler and GALILEO. He was also proud of the judgment of some early readers of *De cive* that this book ushered in a demonstrative science of ethics. Hobbes called himself the inventor of civil science and thought that his politics deserved a place alongside Galileo's mechanics. The newly founded natural and moral sciences he regarded not only as great intellectual achievements, but as distinctively modern ones. Contrary to the theory of the decay of nature as applied to the human intellect, natural and civil science had not ceased with the ancients, but had only properly begun with the work of the mathematical astronomers and his own work in *De cive*. However, Hobbes also held that human beings were badly adapted by nature to do science of this kind, and that they had to work very hard to be capable of it. He thus disagrees both with the Cartesian idea that God benignly creates us with the ingredients of science latent in our minds *and* with the Aristotelian idea that knowledge of the natures of things is the unforced and inevitable by-product of repeatedly looking and seeing. To a very significant extent, according to Hobbes, our capacities for natural science are made by us rather than given to us. This position concedes something to both scepticism and the theory that life will always be difficult for Fallen Man. Although according to Hobbes sceptics are wrong to claim that we are incapable of science, they are right in insisting that we lack native scientific ability. They are also right to doubt that human beings are capable of an exalted sort of knowledge, the knowledge of what necessitates effects. For Hobbes, the scientific knowledge of which we are capable rarely rises to the level of knowledge of how effects *must* have been brought about, and it is not taken to extend to all effects. Again, although Hobbes believed that the scientific achievements of his contemporaries and himself were important, and that the then nascent sciences of nature and politics would develop further, he did not, with Descartes, suppose that we might one day complete science. Finally, while he claimed that even in their undeveloped state the sciences had delivered considerable benefits, Hobbes did not expect a more developed science to be the answer to all our problems. Like Bacon he believed that science could not entirely repair the Fall, that it could only act to relieve some of what was bad in human existence. Whatever one did, life would continue to have 'incommodities', but with the development of science life would contain fewer of them.

Science is not, then, for Hobbes, a means of regaining Eden. At best, it is our only way of cutting the costs of losing Eden. In paradise, Adam enjoyed the gift of immortality in conditions of ready abundance. Everything he could properly want was there for the taking. Punished for eating from the tree of knowledge Adam lost his immortality. He lived, as Hobbes puts it in *Leviathan*, under a death sentence ([1651] 1839 III: 438). Adam also lost the abundance of Eden. Banished to a place outside paradise, he had for the first time to work for a living, and to do so in a relatively inhospitable environment. Had they stayed in Eden, Adam and Eve would not have reproduced their kind continually or perhaps at all ([1651] 1839 III: 440). When they left they came under a necessity to multiply that worsened the life of their kind still further. Adam's descendants, the rest of humanity, inherit from him not only their mortality but also life outside Paradise. Thanks to Adam's transgression, human beings in general live in a world that demands ingenuity and hard work for survival. And thanks to human carnality, Adam's descendants have to eke out a living in the company of, and often in competition with, many others of their own kind. These facts of life do not make it easy to do well. In order to flourish in a sometimes harsh physical environment people have to know which effects they observe are beneficial and which are harmful, and they have to learn to reproduce the beneficial ones and prevent, or at least avoid, the harmful ones. In order to flourish in a heavily populated environment people have to know how to co-operate with one another. Moreover, these problems have to be coped with simultaneously.

As things naturally are, however, the problems are too great for creatures like us. For, being descended from Adam, human beings inherit the cognitive and conative capacities of someone designed to live in paradise, not the harsh world outside. If things had gone according to God's plan, Adam would not have needed to get causal knowledge of nature; he could have satisfied himself with contemplating the diversity and order in nature. Adam would not have had to make nature supply his needs. He would not have had to cope with overpopulation and the demands of co-operation. Made for a life without problems, Adam lacked the means – that is, the science – to solve problems. As Hobbes points out in *Leviathan*, there is no evidence in scripture that Adam had the vocabulary to do science (*Elements of Law* [1651] 1839 III: 19), and yet without the vocabulary to do science we should be no better off than savages or beasts (1640 pt I, ch. 5: iv; 1658 ch. 10: ii, iii). Either people reconcile themselves to living at the mercy of the elements and of one another – Hobbes thought that this was the course taken by Native Americans – or else they take the long and difficult road to a better life through science. Neither the better life nor the means to it are out of bounds to human beings, but both involve a kind of human reform. To get access to the degrees and varieties of motion that are required to understand nature, human beings need to acquire concepts more general and universal than those for everyday experience, and they need to apply principles involving these concepts in tasks of measurement

and manufacture. To solve the problems of peaceful co-operation they need to be able to recognize the consequences of everyone's trying to get what they want. This means more than knowing what moral precepts to follow. It means being able to see what overall good the moral precepts promote – something revealed by Hobbes' civil science – and adjusting one's practical reasoning to the pursuit of that good rather than something nearer and more gratifying.

Although human beings cannot live well without science, science does not come naturally to them. Science depends on the ability to impose names aptly, to join names into propositions, and to join propositions into syllogisms, but not even these prescientific linguistic skills are natural to people. People come into the world being able at most to form sensory representations of things, and to learn from experience. But experience is a far cry from science. In its raw state experience is either a disorganized stream of representations or else a coherent sequence. If it is a coherent sequence, then, according to *Leviathan*, it is 'regulated' by some design or plan, or by curiosity about an observed body's effects ([1651] 1839 III: 13). Regulated in either way, a train of experience is only regulated as past experience allows it to be. Going by its past associations of observed phenomena, the mind will focus on a means to some goal or purpose in hand, or will suggest properties it is accustomed to conjoin with other properties it is now curious about. Once there are words for the things of which the mind has conceptions – words that can be used to signify the elements of experience – the possible ways of juxtaposing the words significantly, of analysing them and drawing consequences, introduce ways of ordering the elements that are not foreshadowed in previous experience.

New ways of regulating thought become possible because, for one thing, it is not necessary for a body spoken about to be present or remembered in order for a train of thought about it to be created. The train of thought can be generated instead by exploiting logical relations or analytic truths to get from one speech or thought to another. Reasoning can thus introduce new possibilities of combining things given separately in experience; it can also introduce ways of taking apart or separating things confounded in experience. Nor are the possibilities confined to the powers of one man's reasoning. Speech enables investigation and reasoning to be carried on co-operatively, and allows one person's explanations to be tested for clarity and coherence by others. The reasonings or explanations of one person can be preserved over time and made the model for those of many other people. A method can even be extracted from the findings of the most successful or conclusive pieces of reasoning, so that conclusive reasonings and explanations – in a word, science – can deepen and spread.

Hobbes believed that science as a whole could be divided into two principal parts, one concerned with natural bodies, the other with bodies politic. Each part of science arrives by reasoning at the causes of the properties of its subject matter; and demonstrates effects, with a view to making the relevant subject matter useful and beneficial to human beings. But the two types of bodies are very different from one another, and pose different scientific problems. Natural bodies are not made by us, and so the causes of their properties have to be worked out by reasoning from the appearances they present. Since the maker of natural bodies, God, is omnipotent and able to bring about effects in more ways than can be dreamed of in our explanations, only possible causes can be assigned to the appearances they present. Bodies politic *are* made by us – they are human artefacts and so at least in principle we can be certain of the causes of *their* properties. But the philosophical challenge they present is not primarily that of knowing their causes: it is that of knowing how they should be designed so that they last. This means setting out rules by which those involved in the commonwealth – those in government on the one hand and those subject to government on the other – can conduct themselves so that civil peace is ensured. It is doubtful whether the statement of these rules is really a science of a kind of body, as is natural science, and probably the differences between natural and civil science are to be taken more seriously than the supposed analogies. Hobbes claims that civil science is not only more certain, but more widely needed, and more accessible than natural science. On the other hand, natural science is the more fundamental of the two parts of science: its explanatory concepts are more general than those of civil science and are needed if a scientific understanding of the passions and actions of agents in civil life is to be acquired from the 'first and few' elements of science as a whole.

3 The elements of philosophy: logic and metaphysics

The relative positions of the two parts of science – natural and civil – are reflected in the organization of Hobbes' trilogy on the elements of philosophy. The first volume, *De corpore*, expounds first philosophy, geometry, mechanics and physics. It is followed by *De homine*, which is half optics and half psychology; this volume in turn is supposed to prepare the ground for the exposition of the elements of ethics and politics in *De cive*.

The account of the 'elements' of science starts in *De corpore* with chapters on the ways in which philosophy depends on names, propositions and methods of reasoning. For Hobbes, logic is nothing more than the right ordering and joining of significant propositions into chains of reasoning. Propositions in turn are no more than coherent concatenations of names with significations of different extents. A name signifies an idea – whatever idea it conveys in the context of a speech to a hearer. But the idea is not what the name refers to or stands for: it refers to or stands for an object. To make a proposition, names have to be put together coherently, and coherent concatenations are concatenations of the same category of name – names of bodies with names of bodies, names of names with names of names. The 'extent' of the signification of a name has a bearing on the truth of propositions. The signification of a proper name will extend to an individual, that of a universal name – 'man', 'horse', 'tree' – to each of a plurality of individuals. In the propositions of natural science, names are universal names of bodies. Truth in the propositions of natural sciences is a matter of the inclusion of the extent of a universal subject-term within the extent of a universal predicate-term. Demonstrations are chains of syllogisms, and syllogisms are the stringing together of trios of propositions that share appropriate subjects and predicates. In a sense, then, logic is a technique for working out the consequences of relations between the significations of universal names or their extents. There are also methods belonging to logic for analysing the significations of names, and for arriving at the most general of these significations from a starting point in everyday universal names. Logical analysis of this kind is what is required to locate the terms fundamental to the various branches of science; it also has a role in making scientific questions amenable to resolution. Metaphysics or first philosophy sets out, ideally by means of definitions, the concepts necessary for conducting fruitful enquiries concerning natural bodies and for communicating the results. The relevant concepts include those of body, motion, time, place, cause and effect.

Hobbes composed no full-scale treatise on logic, and no work of his is concerned with metaphysics alone. *De corpore* contains the nearest approximation to a full first philosophy, and even here he is not entirely clear about the borderline between that 'prior' science and geometry. There is a chapter on 'syllogism', but it is not comprehensive and its relation to traditional syllogistic is never spelled out. As for the chapters on first philosophy, they are more significant for what they deny than for what they affirm. They deny that it makes sense to study 'being' in the abstract; they deny that species or genera are things; they deny that 'substance' can mean something very different from 'body'; and they deny that other predicables are more than varieties of sensory appearance caused by bodies. In short, they deny much standard Aristotelian doctrine, including the doctrine defining the subject matter of metaphysics itself – the doctrine that metaphysics studies being *qua* being. As will become clear, the chapters on first philosophy can also be understood to register disagreements between Hobbes and some of the *moderns* – Descartes and GASSENDI, among others.

Hobbes' first philosophy starts with a thought experiment. He imagines that the external world has been annihilated – all that remains is a single thinker and the traces in memory of the world he previously sensed and perceived. Hobbes claims that the disappearance of the external world would not take away conditions for thought or reasoning, even about the physical world. The annihilation of the world would not even *alter* conditions for such thought and reasoning, since the medium of thought and reasoning is never things themselves but only appearances or phantasms. Hobbes thinks that the annihilation of the external world leaves only the mind and its phantasms in existence. There is no third world of things that exist outside the mind but outside the physical world as well. So Hobbes denies that there exist without the mind abstract natures such as Descartes claims to discover in Meditation V; and, contrary to Gassendi in the *Syntagma*, he does not think that space and time are real independently of the mind. He derives the idea of space from the memory images or phantasms presenting things as if from outside the mind. He derives the idea of time from imagined motion, from succession without existence. He derives the idea of an existing thing from the imagination of an empty space suddenly getting an occupant. Existence is thus restricted to existence in space, which is in turn identified with corporeal existence. These resources allow for only a straitened conception of cause or power, and certainly not for an Aristotelian conception. There are no forms or purposes in nature; but the makings of a conception of efficient cause are available, and that is the only sense of 'cause' recognized by Hobbes' first philosophy.

Most of the concepts that Hobbes thinks are needed for natural science have now been indicated. In Part Two of *De corpore*, after defining 'time' and 'place', he thinks he is in a position to define 'body' and its most general accidents. He then deals with magnitude or real space-occupation, and the spatial relations of continuity and contiguity. Against this background he defines 'motion', and in terms of motion the ideas of length, depth and breadth. After the three spatial dimensions are explicated, he defines quantitative identity and difference for motions and bodies, and then discusses the conditions of qualitative difference between bodies over time. He goes on to consider the causes of qualitative change, concluding with a demonstration of the thesis that all change is motion, that motion is the only cause of motion, and that power (*potentia*) is nothing but motion in so far as it is a cause of motion.

Definitions dominate Hobbes' first philosophy and, officially at least, their purpose is to fix ideas necessary for the business of science proper. Hobbes thought that the mark of a prescientific branch of learning was controversy, and he traced controversy to a failure to define terms and to proceed in orderly fashion from definitions to conclusions. The task of first philosophy is to provide insurance against controversy. It does not do this by coming up with substantive truths that command assent. Instead, Hobbes describes first philosophy as a necessary *preliminary* to the demonstration of substantive truths, where demonstrator and learner are put on one another's wavelength and attach the same significations to their terms, but where their agreement is terminological rather than doctrinal. As Hobbes puts it in the *Six Lessons*, 'he that telleth you in what sense you are to take the appellations of those things which he nameth in his discourse, teacheth you but his language, that afterwards he may teach you his art. But teaching of language is not mathematic, nor logic, nor physic'.

That 'the teaching of language' underdescribes what Hobbes does in practice in stating his first philosophy, and that it suppresses entirely the revisionary character of some of his definitions when compared with Aristotelian ones (and so the controversial nature of the devices that are supposed to pre-empt controversy), should already be clear. But, up to a point, Hobbes' first philosophy is genuinely unassuming. It takes for granted no exotic powers or substances, God included, and it postulates no exotic human capacities for acquiring the concepts that are the key to natural science. The point is not just that Hobbes keeps the relevant concepts to a small number, so that he is economical in the concepts he uses and also in his assumptions about the types of real things there have to be for these concepts to be applicable. Hobbes' first philosophy is also *naturalistic*. Nothing supernatural is assumed to exist in order for natural science to be acquired; indeed, nothing besides matter in motion is postulated. What remains after the annihilation of the world in Hobbes' thought experiment is not the immaterial self of Descartes, but the corporeal body or perhaps the brain, and the motions conserved in its internal parts from past impacts of the external world on the sense-organs.

The denial of immaterialism in Hobbes' first philosophy is anticipated in his Objections to Descartes' *Meditations*. An objection that Hobbes directs at Meditation II sets the tone (see DESCARTES, R. §5). He accepts that from the fact that I am thinking it follows that I exist, but he wonders whether Descartes can properly conclude, as a corollary, that the I is a mind or an intelligence or a thinking thing. For all the *Cogito* shows, Hobbes says, the I could be corporeal. And not only does the *Cogito* leave open the possibility of the I being corporeal, he goes on, the later wax argument actually *shows* that the I is corporeal:

> We cannot conceive of jumping without a jumper, or knowing without a knower, or of thinking without a thinker.
>
> It seems to follow from this that a thinking thing is something corporeal. For it seems that the subject of any act can be understood only in terms of something corporeal or in terms of matter, as the author himself shows later [in] his example of the wax: the wax, despite the changes in its colour, hardness, shape and other acts, is still understood to be the same thing, that is, the same matter is the subject of all of these changes.
>
> (Hobbes, *The Third Set of Objections to Descartes' Meditations* 1641)

Descartes' reply concedes that acts need subjects, that it is a *thing* that is hard, changes shape and so on, and also a *thing* that thinks, but he insists that 'thing' in this sense is neutral between the corporeal and the spiritual. He insists, too, that he is non-committal about the nature of the thing that thinks in Meditation II, a claim borne out by his responding agnostically in Meditation II to the question of whether he might be a structure of limbs or a thin vapour. If Hobbes misses that, it may be because he misunderstands the rules of the method of doubt. While implementing the method of doubt, Descartes does assume rather than prove that there is no body for the thinking thing to be or for the thought to inhere in. But this is not a case of begging the question, for the belief in the existence of bodies is reinstated in Meditation VI, and with that the question of whether the subject is essentially immaterial or material.

Hobbes comes at Descartes' immaterialism from another, more revealing direction when he tries to suggest that it is not needed to underpin the distinction between imagination and conception by the mind. In his fourth objection, Hobbes equates imagination in Descartes' sense with having an idea of a thing, and conception in Descartes' sense with reasoning to the conclusion that something exists. Descartes already agrees that imagination is a partly corporeal process resulting from action on the sense organs, but his text suggests that conception by the mind is an altogether different operation. Hobbes puts forward a suggestion that allows the explanation of conception and imagination to be linked, without the postulation of immaterial things. He proposes that reasoning is the process by which labels attached to various things are concatenated into sentences according to conventions agreed by humans.

> Reasoning will depend on names, names will depend on the imagination, and imagination will depend (as I believe it does) merely on the motions of our bodily organs; and so the mind will be nothing more than motion occurring in various parts of an organic body.
>
> (*Objections* 1641)

The compatibility of this proposal with mechanistic explanation appeals to Hobbes; but Descartes raises some powerful doubts about Hobbes' idea that names alone come into reasoning. Contrary to Hobbes, Descartes takes it that reasoning is a matter of linking together the significations of names, not just the names themselves, and also that the significations of some names cannot be imaged.

As in the case of his objection concerning the subject of the thinking, which seems to overlook the constraints of the method of doubt, Hobbes' objection to Descartes on imagination and conception seems to miss the point. Descartes is not trying to explain the workings of the faculties that result in science, only to find that he has to explain them on immaterialistic principles. He is trying to show that science is possible, that real knowledge of the physical world is possible, because not all of our faculties can coherently be held to be unreliable. Conception by the mind is a case in point. It cannot be held to be unreliable, because it is autonomous and independent of unreliable sense-perception. Hobbes does not see that it is the objectivity of conception rather than the process of conception that Descartes is concerned with. And doubting the objectivity of conception himself, Hobbes does not seek to reconstruct conception as reasoning that might be guaranteed to lead to true conclusions; he wants only to reconstruct it in ways that will not multiply entities beyond those required by mechanistic explanation. The point is that a proof of the objectivity of the conceptions arrived at by science may legitimately be demanded of a metaphysics, and Hobbes' metaphysics does little if anything to meet the demand. The metaphysical economy of materialism will not impress someone who is sceptical of the existence of the external world: the undeniability of the *Cogito* might. One cost of Hobbes' naturalistic approach is that it never attempts the task of legitimizing the scientific enterprise in general, and is probably incapable of doing so.

4 Geometry, optics and physics

First philosophy is a preliminary to natural science proper, and the first of the natural sciences is geometry. Geometry is a natural science for Hobbes, because it studies the effects of moving bodies. It studies the properties of straight lines, for instance, and straight lines are the effects of the motion of a small material thing – a point. He rejects the idea that the geometrical point is an abstraction distinct from some small material mark or other. Being a body, a geometrical point is divisible and not, as Euclid had it, 'that which hath no part'. A point could no more lack quantity than a line could lack breadth and be constructed by motion. The bodies whose motions geometry studies may not have much quantity, and the quantity may not be relevant to what is being demonstrated of them, but they are bodies all the same. Though geometry is a science of bodies, it is also in a sense an a priori certain science, as physics is not, for the effects are produced by us, and we know in advance by what means they are produced. In this, Hobbes believed, geometry is like politics. In a sense, too, geometry is a very basic science – basic not in the sense that the objects it studies are higher or more real than those in nature, but in the sense that it studies bodies and motion at a very high level of generality, with much that is specific about the bodies left out of account. Hobbes thinks that geometry is also basic in another sense, for its methods of demonstration and analysis are the inspiration for the methods of the other demonstrative sciences.

Hobbes was self-taught in mathematics, and his friend and biographer, John Aubrey, says he did not encounter Euclid until he was middle-aged. Nevertheless, he was taken seriously by very able geometers in Mersenne's circle, and is even credited with inspiring a proof by Roberval of the equality of arcs of a parabola and an 'Archimedean' spiral. He is much better known, however, as a mathematical failure whose attempts at expounding geometry in *De corpore* were ridiculed by the English mathematician John Wallis. Wallis' attack was motivated by a wish to discredit the anticlerical passages in *Leviathan*, and its attack on the universities. In correspondence with Huygens, Wallis said that Hobbes 'took his courage' from mathematics, and so it 'seemed necessary for some mathematician to show him how little he understands'. Wallis' attack succeeded – it focused on Hobbes' doomed enterprise of producing a quadrature of the circle –

and was made the more effective by Hobbes' persistent refusal to concede errors.

Although the geometrical parts of *De corpore* were supposed to present some new results, Hobbes did not claim any great stature for himself in geometry. In optics, on the other hand, he regarded himself as a major figure. It was certainly a subject he turned to early in his transformation from man of letters to man of science. As early as 1636, optical questions were featuring in his correspondence with the Earl of Newcastle, and the treatment of the sensible qualities was mechanical: 'whereas I use the phrases, the light passes, or the colour passes or diffuseth itselfe, my meaning is that the motion is onely in the medium, and light and colour are but the effects of that motion in the brayne'. Perhaps more accurately, these effects were supposed to be the effects of the motion of the medium transmitted to the animal spirits in the brain.

Exactly how early Hobbes arrived at his conception of the workings of light is not entirely clear. A short treatise dated to 1630 and originally attributed to Hobbes has been claimed by some scholars to be the work of someone else in the Cavendish circle. It contains doctrines different from writings that are more certainly ascribed to Hobbes, and which probably belong to the 1640s: the *Tractatus Opticus* I and II. It also contains as 'principles' formulations that these later optical writings present as mere hypotheses. Whether the writings of the 1640s represent only a change of mind or whether they are Hobbes' first extended publications in optics, they show him adopting a mediumistic theory of the propagation of light based on the idea of continuously expanding and contracting light sources. These displace contiguous parts of an ethereal medium of uniform density and set up a chain reaction to the eye. A resistance in the eye caused by a countervailing motion from the brain produces a phantasm of a luminous object – that is, in Hobbes' terminology, light. Light is propagated instantaneously, as both luminous object and medium expand simultaneously. The account does without the postulation of an emission by luminous objects of species or replicas of themselves which subsequently inform the senses and permit perception. Instead, luminous objects illuminate by radiation: they, so to speak, send out rays or, more precisely, displace the medium along paths called 'rays'. In their passage from luminous objects to the eye, rays are supposed to describe parallelograms. Hobbes used the properties of other geometrical figures described by rays of light passing through different densities to account for refraction. Colour he regarded as light perturbed by the internal motions of rough or coarse bodies on its way to the eye. The differences between the colours on the spectrum from blue to red he accounts for as the product of refraction plus restraint or reinforcement of the lateral motion of rays of light that goes with refraction.

At no point in the process that starts with the motion of the luminous objects and ends in the production of the phantasm does Hobbes depart from a mechanical model of the causes of sense-perception. His mature theory of optics is through and through an account in terms of matter and motion. But between the *Tractatus Opticus I* and the *Tractatus Opticus II*, he seems to have revised his ideas about the organs of sensory perception. Phantasms are said to come from the heart, rather than to result from the clash of incoming motions with motions from the brain. By 1646, when Hobbes produced *A Minute or First Draught of the Optiques*, the most polished of his optical treaties, the main lines of his doctrine were settled. In addition to material on light and its propagation, refraction and reflection, there are accounts of various kinds of sensory error.

Physics, understood as the theory of the causes of appearances to sense and of the nature of the objects of sense, is in part an offshoot of optics. It is expounded at the end of *De corpore*. By an 'object' of sense Hobbes means an external body that registers in experience as being the subject of certain qualities, and that sets off the process culminating in an 'act of sense'. The object of sense is not an idea or a sense-datum or a mental image, though such a thing may be the medium in which the object of sense is registered. The greatest of the objects of sense is the world itself, as registered from some point within it. But only a few intelligible questions can be asked about the world, and these cannot be conclusively answered. One can ask whether it is of finite or infinite magnitude, whether it is full or contains empty space, and how long it has lasted. Only the second of these questions is open to a scientific answer, and even then only to a probable conclusion, while the others are for lawfully appointed churchmen to discuss. Hobbes thinks that probably there is no vacuum, that the world is full, but that some of the bodies that make it up are invisible: thus the ether and 'the small atoms disseminated through the whole space between the earth and the stars'. He adopts Copernican and Galilean hypotheses in chapter 26 of *De corpore* to explain the order, motion and relative position of the planets. He also infers explanations of, among other things, the passage of the seasons, the succession of day and night and 'the monthly simple motion of the moon'.

Hobbes goes on to consider the bodies between the earth and the stars. Foremost among these is 'the most fluid ether', which he proposes to regard as if it were first matter. He supposes that its parts only receive motion from bodies that float in them, and impart none of their own. The bodies in the ether are supposed to have some degree of cohesion or hardness and to differ from one another in shape, figure and consistency. Any more specific hypotheses about them Hobbes adopted only to explain particular phenomena. He is, however, willing to venture that many such bodies are 'unspeakably little' or minute, since God's infinite power includes a power infinitely to diminish matter. Assumptions about intersidereal bodies inform his theories of the phantasms appropriate to the different senses, not only light but also heat, sound and odour.

5 Ethics

After *physics*,' Hobbes writes in chapter 6 of *De corpore*, 'we must come to *moral philosophy*; in which we are to consider the motions of the mind, namely, *appetite, aversion, love, benevolence, hope, fear, anger, emulation, envy* &c what causes they have and of what they be causes'. The use of the term 'moral philosophy' for the doctrine of the motions of the mind is unfortunate; elsewhere Hobbes says that the precepts of his natural law doctrine add up to a moral philosophy. 'Ethics' is another label he sometimes uses, and it is preferable. The reason ethics comes after physics is that the motions of the mind 'have their causes in sense and imagination, which are the subjects of physical contemplation'. What Hobbes means is that when a body registers in a sensory representation – when, for example, a person sees something – the thing imparts motion to the innermost part of the organ of sight. One effect of the motion is to set up an outward reaction which produces visual experience. But there can be a further after-effect. As Hobbes puts it in chapter 8 of *Elements of Law*, the 'motion and agitation of the brain which we call conception' can be 'continued to the heart, and there be called passion'. The heart governs 'vital motion' in the body, that is the circulation of the blood. In general, when motion derived from an act of sense encourages vital motion, the sentient creature experiences pleasure at the sight, smell or taste of the object and is disposed to move its body so as to prolong or intensify the pleasure. If the object of the pleasure is at a distance, then the creature will typically move towards it. There is a symmetrical account of displeasure. This is an after-effect of the act of sense consisting of a hindrance of vital motion. A creature experiencing a hindrance of vital motion will try to counteract it, typically by retreating from the object of sense. Aversion consists of the small inner movements that initiate the evasive action, just as 'appetite' names the internal beginnings of approach behaviour.

381

The pursuit of pleasure and the avoidance of pain are the basic drives recognized by Hobbes' psychology, and they determine the systems of valuation of different individuals. The individual takes as good what it has learned to pursue and regards as bad what it has learned to avoid. In developing a system of valuation, a creature is not discovering an objective distinction in nature between things that are good and things that are bad. Nothing is good or bad independently of its effects on creatures, and the effects may vary from creature to creature. At most, things are good or bad *to* individuals, not good or bad 'simply and absolutely'. In the same vein, Hobbes denies that in the sphere of good and bad things there is one that is the highest and whose attainment constitutes happiness. Instead, there are many different goods for many different individuals. Becoming happy in life is not a matter of being successful in the pursuit of one favoured good, but of being continually successful in the pursuit of many.

Hobbes' account of the constraints on the pursuit of human happiness is the connecting link between his theory of the motions of the mind and his moral and political philosophy proper. To attain happiness, people need to know what goods to pursue and how to pursue them. But in the absence of a science of good and evil, pleasure is their main criterion of the good, displeasure the main criterion of bad. Both pain and pleasure, however, are unreliable guides to the good and bad. A person may find a thing pleasant on one occasion and call it 'good', only to change their mind later. Two people can react differently to the same thing, so that it produces pleasure in one and pain in the other, and is called 'good' and 'not good' simultaneously. Pleasure biases judgment in favour of the nearer and more intense good, even if the cost of pursuing this good is displeasure later, and so on. Part of the correction to these distortions is to judge the good of various things not by how they feel when they are enjoyed or shunned, but by the consequences of enjoying or shunning them. If the costs of the consequences outweigh the present benefits, then a supposed good may be merely an apparent good. Again, if someone detached from the pursuit or avoidance of a thing can judge it good or bad, then it may really be so; while if no-one else can see the attraction or repugnance, it may be illusory. Hobbes thinks only science can supply knowledge of the consequences of actions needed to counterbalance valuations derived from pain and pleasure; and he thinks science does not come naturally to people. Abiding by the value judgments of arbitrators does not come easily either, since people are attached to their valuations and unwilling to lose face by deferring to the judgments of others.

6 Politics: the state of nature

Despite the inconsistency in individual value judgments over time, and between the value judgments of different people at the same time, Hobbes thinks that there are some evils that are so large, and that interfere so markedly with everyone's pursuit of happiness, that practically no-one would knowingly pursue a course of action that resulted in them. War is such an evil, and Hobbes thinks he can show that if everyone makes themselves their own judge of what to pursue in the name of happiness, everyone will be involved in war. His argument to this conclusion is at the same time an argument for people to be guided by a judgment other than their own about what is best for them, the judgment of an existing civil power if they live in an existing commonwealth, the judgment of an as-yet-to-be designated civil power if they live outside any commonwealth.

The argument for the inevitability of war starts with assumptions about what is useful to the achievement of any goal. What is useful, no matter what good is being pursued, no matter whether the good is real or merely apparent, is power – that is, present means to future ends. 'Power' covers the physical capacities of individual agents, and also friends, riches and reputation. Not only is power in any form useful, but there can never be, according to Hobbes, too much power at the disposal of an agent in the nature of things. The reason is not that each agent naturally has an insatiable hunger for power, but that each agent is in competition with other agents for other goods, and any advantage one competitor temporarily has over another can, in principle, be overcome. The naturally strong can be toppled by a number of weak people who join forces; the man who has no enemies can be made into an object of hate with a well-judged campaign of character assassination; the wealthy can be robbed or swindled of their riches, and so on. Not only is it useful to acquire more and more power, but people cannot be blamed for doing so if all that organizes their activity in life is the pursuit of felicity.

Felicity is continual success in one's undertakings, whatever they may be. If what one undertakes is to do down one's competitors, then any means that helps to achieve it will be permissible. Or if, as is more likely, one aims at something else, doing down one's competitors can still often promote one's goal. Even the moderate man who wants only a small share of the good life can have reason to resort to foul means if he thinks he will lose everything by playing fair with rivals. And he cannot be sure he does not risk losing everything if he plays fair. In general, the goal of felicity requires one to try to get an advantage and keep it. Disabling others is a means of keeping the advantage; the outright elimination of competitors is even surer. Because these facts can be discovered by everyone, everyone who pursues felicity must bargain for severe insecurity and even worry about survival. Struggling for survival is far removed from felicity, but the pursuit of felicity, no holds barred, can quickly turn into a struggle for survival. Or to put it Hobbes' way, in the state of nature, people who pursue felicity are in a condition of war.

The argument does not depend on the idea that every human being is naturally selfish. It is true that in *De cive* Hobbes paints an unflattering picture of ordinary human behaviour, emphasizing the tendency of people to look out for themselves, to say one thing to other people's faces and another thing behind their backs, the tendency to think very well of their own opinions, but poorly of the views of others, and to fight over trivialities. This is all ordinary human behaviour, but it is not the behaviour of absolutely every human being. That it is so ordinary is enough, in Hobbes' view, to overturn the Aristotelian idea that human beings are by nature fit for society, but he is not claiming that human beings are uniform, or that their behaviour is uniformly antisocial. Hobbes recognizes a variety of temperaments in human beings, and his state of nature encompasses the vainglorious as well as the moderate. The vainglorious will seek to dispossess others because having more than anyone else is an end in itself. Moderates will go on to the attack because they want only a little and fear that the greedy will take even that. Others again will be at odds because they want something that cannot be shared. Whatever the cause, the general effect will be insecurity, and with insecurity goes many unattractive things – not only feelings of fear, but loss of society, loss of production, loss of technology, loss of art, loss of everything that enables human beings to rise above a life of bare subsistence and savagery. Life in the state of war is, in Hobbes' famous phrase, 'solitary, poor, nasty, brutish, and short'.

Is there no such thing as virtue to keep people from pursuing felicity ruthlessly? Hobbes thinks that precepts enjoining the moral virtues – what he calls 'the laws of nature' – are discoverable even in the state of nature, but people are not morally obliged to act on them if they run the risk of dying as a result: the most basic law of nature is to preserve oneself, and there is an inalienable 'right of nature' to be one's own judge of how to secure one's own preservation and wellbeing. This right may be laid down in the interest of self-preservation, but never at the cost of self-preservation. So if one has reason to think that others will take advantage of one's keeping agreements, or of showing gratitude, of not

being judge in one's own cause, of being forgiving and so on through the rest of the virtues, one is not obliged to behave in those ways. One is not obliged to act in a way which will advertise one's vulnerability to the unscrupulous. It is enough that one is willing to behave virtuously if it is not too dangerous.

7 Politics: the commonwealth

The answer to the problems of life in the state of nature is an agreement by most in it to delegate their right of nature to a person, or body of persons, empowered to secure the many against physical attack and against the severe deprivations of the state of nature. That person or body of persons is empowered by a collective submission of the wills of the many to the will of the one or few. The many agree to be guided in their behaviour by the laws of a sovereign, on the understanding that this is a more effective way of securing their safety than individual action in the state of nature. The many lend their wills to the sovereign both as potential enforcers of the law against lawbreakers and as an army of defence against foreign invasion. They lend their wills by doing only what is permitted by the sovereign's law and refraining from what the law prohibits. The law in turn expresses the sovereign's judgment regarding who should own what, who should teach what, how trade may be conducted, how wars should be waged, who should be punished and by what method of punishment, and who should be rewarded and the scale of the reward given.

The sovereign's judgment prevails because it, uniquely in the commonwealth, is still allied to a right of nature. Everyone who is subject to the sovereign thereby delegates their right of nature to the sovereign, but not in return for any forfeit or transfer of right by the sovereign himself. It is true that the commonwealth dissolves – that the obligation not to retract the right of nature lapses – if the sovereign is not able to secure the many against life-threatening incursion. But short of a reversion to the state of nature, the state in the person of the sovereign has a claim to expect the compliance of the many. The many owe it to one another to comply, because they agree between themselves to be law-abiding in return for safety if everyone else is law-abiding. They also owe it to the sovereign, at least for the time that he succeeds in making and keeping the peace, because they voluntarily and publicly submit to the sovereign, signifying to him that they will do what he decrees should be done for their safety.

Hobbes' idea that the sovereign's law can justly reach into every sector of public life had clear application to the questions being debated during the Civil War period in England. Those who complained that it was wrong for Charles I to appropriate property, to billet troops at will, to raise taxes without the consent of parliament, were given a theory that legitimized those actions. According to the theory, the limitations on a king's powers indicate that a state of nature, with its potential for open war, still prevails. Either the powers of government are separated (in which case the contention between, say, king and parliament reproduces the contention between individuals in the pre-political condition), or else the powers of government are not separated, but are limited by the rights of the subjects (in which case the right of nature has not really been transferred, and people are still liable to prefer their own judgment about what is best for them to the judgment that they have agreed to be guided by, with the same potential for slaughter).

Hobbes' theory permits the sovereign to regulate public life very stringently, but his message to sovereigns – there is no doubt that *Leviathan* in particular was intended to be read by heads of state – was not that it was *wise* to regulate public life very stringently. To begin with, there were limits to what laws could do: belief could not be commanded, so a certain tolerance of freedom of thought was inevitable. Again, people could not be expected to risk their lives in order to obey the law, as that would leave them no better off in the state than outside it. So laws that impoverished people to such an extent that they were starving, having to steal in order to live, were ill-conceived. Likewise forced military service, if it were likely to lead to death, might reasonably be seen as unacceptable according to the terms of Hobbes' social contract. Even a regime of law that secured most people from theft and common assault, but that confiscated all income above a measly minimum, could be seen as a failure by the sovereign to come up with what the many bargained for in entering the state. What the many bargain for is safety and, as Hobbes explains in chapter 30 of *Leviathan*, 'safety' signifies more than a 'bare preservation': it means a modicum of well-being over and above survival.

The arguments from prudence against over-regulation by the sovereign are also arguments against iniquitous practice by the sovereign. Hobbes distinguishes between iniquity and injustice. The sovereign does no injustice to his subjects if he decides to claim as his own all the land in a particular county or all the houses in a village: in creating the sovereign, his subjects give him the power to decree who is the owner of what. For all that, the sovereign may act iniquitously in the sense that he allows his own appetites and interests to count for more than those of anyone else, and so makes himself, for selfish reasons, the owner of more land than anyone else. There is a law of nature against iniquity, and therefore a law that decrees that the sovereign has to *try* to be equitable. But efforts are one thing; actual behaviour is another. The law of nature is not binding on the sovereign's behaviour, since he retains the right of nature and is authoritative about what to do for the best. If, in his opinion, it is for the best to behave iniquitously, then no other free agent, still less one of his subjects, can blame him for behaving accordingly. But the fact that his iniquitous acts are in this sense blameless does not mean that they are wise. If appropriating everyone's land makes people rebellious, albeit unjustly rebellious, then appropriating other people's land may have greater costs than benefits: it is subversive of the sovereign's power, which depends on the willingness of others to obey him.

Regarding the practice of religion, the relationship between Church and state is a central preoccupation of *Leviathan*. Hobbes insists there that it is for the sovereign to decide whether people can join together for purposes of worship – that is, whether a given church can lawfully exist in the commonwealth. And he appears not to have been in favour of the establishment of a plurality of churches:

> But seeing a Common-wealth is but one Person, it ought also to exhibite to God but one Worship; which then it doth, when it commandeth it to be exhibited by Private men, Publiquely. And this is Publique Worship; the property whereof, is to be *Uniforme*: For those actions that are done differently, by different men, cannot be said to be a Publique Worship. And therefore, where many sorts of Worship be allowed, proceeding from the different Religions of Private men, it cannot be said there is any Publique Worship, nor that the Commonwealth is of any Religion at all.
>
> (Hobbes [1651] 1839 III: 354)

He goes on to say that 'whereas there be an infinite number of Actions and Gestures, of an indifferent nature; such of them as the Common-wealth shall ordain to be Publiquely and Universally in use, as signes of Honour, and part of Gods Worship, are to be taken and used for such by the Subjects'. It is hard to gather from these passages even tacit approval for a pluralistic form of national religious life. On the contrary, it is strongly implied that unless all members of the commonwealth worship in the same way, it will be doubtful not merely which religion the commonwealth observes but whether it observes any. It is as if Hobbes thinks that in a babble of different religious rites there will be no clear sign of honour from the commonwealth to God. For a clear signal to be sent, the same thing must be transmitted by everyone in the commonwealth. This 'clear-signal' justification for uniformity is not as anti-tolerationist as a justification that holds that all but the appointed religious rites are idolatrous, but it lends support all the same to a highly restrictive form of public religious worship.

As chapter 12 of *Leviathan* shows, Hobbes was aware that people living together but worshipping differently could ridicule or belittle one another's ceremonies and come into conflict. This is another reason for the secular authority to regulate public worship. It is also a reason for worshippers to take religious ceremony out of the public arena altogether, and preserve their differences in private. Hobbes has no quarrel with this sort of privatization of religious practice, so long as it is thoroughgoing: driving it out of the public arena means driving it well out. To obviate regulation, worship must be not only be private (that is, practised openly by a private person) but practised by a private person in secret. As Hobbes says in chapter 31 of *Leviathan*, private worship 'when secret, is Free; but in the sight of the multitude, it is never without some restraint, either from the Laws, or the opinion of men, which is contrary to the nature of Liberty'.

Not only actions required by religious rites can be driven underground if they might disturb the peace; freedom of action in matters indifferent to religion can also be open to regulation, as chapter 31 of *Leviathan* makes clear. Arguably it is indifferent whether prayers are said in Latin or in English; arguably it is indifferent whether services are conducted by married or by celibate men; but notoriously, these are things that people look askance at or insist upon, and about which they can come to blows. For this reason, if for no other, there is a reason for the sovereign to declare what the language shall be, and who shall preside at services.

What is in the sight of the multitude and in the control of the religious is one thing; what is out of sight and uncontrollable is another: 'Internal faith is in its own nature invisible, and consequently exempted from all humane jurisdiction', Hobbes says in chapter 42 of *Leviathan*. Humane jurisdiction is not just secular jurisdiction, but also that of a body charged by a church with the inquisition of believers. Beliefs in general are not subject to the will he says in *De Politico Corpore*, a pirated edition of part two of the *Elements of Law* (1839 IV: 339). And although salvation depends on believing some things and not others, it is hard to be sure which things have to be believed beyond an uncontroversial minimum. For all of these reasons Hobbes is against the policing of religious belief, and against

preferment for any one creed. It is in connection with the policing of belief rather than religious practice that his views come close to those of Independents, who in seventeenth-century England favoured a relatively loose, relatively tolerant organization of religious life, in particular a life outside a unitary Church of England. For when he appears in *Leviathan* (chapter 47) to side with the Independents in the Primitive church it is over each person deciding whose preaching to follow, not over many different religions being openly practised ([1651] 1839 III: 695). And in countenancing a variety of religious persuasions Hobbes is not so much showing tolerance as denying the importance to civil order of what goes on below the threshold of visible action.

8 Problems with Hobbes' political theory

In order to legitimize the powers of sovereigns, Hobbes invites his readers to think of sovereigns and states as the creations of free, self-interested people. The condition of subjection to a sovereign, even if it is not entered into by an original contract, can nevertheless be freely endorsed by each subject, since there is a good argument from self-interest for the condition. The argument says that the alternative to subjection is a dangerous chaos, which is infinitely worse than an intrusive but protective civil power. This is the argument directed against people who are already subjects; is the same argument effective when directed at people who do not yet belong to a state, who are in a state of nature? The issue can be sharpened by pointing out that the process of trading the state of nature for the commonwealth involves each person giving something now for the sake of a benefit later. Each person agrees to lay down their right of nature if everyone else will do likewise for the sake of peace. Granting that the condition of peace is better for each than the condition of war, is it not even better for anyone who can get away with it, to retain their right of nature while others give away theirs? Is it not better to pretend to lay down that right and then to take advantage of those who genuinely do so? If the answer to this question is 'Yes', how can the best outcome, from the point of self-interest, be one in which everyone performs and lays down their right of nature?

The question is taken up in a famous passage in chapter 15 of *Leviathan* where Hobbes replies to the fool who pretends that there is no such thing as justice. Commentators have likened it to the question posed by 'prisoners' dilemmas' where, for example, the outcome that would be best for each of two prisoners is for the other to confess and solely take a punishment for a crime, but where it turns out to be rational for each to confess and receive a punishment less severe than the maximum. The question is how this 'lesser' outcome can be the better one. In the case of the opportunistic non-performer of covenants discussed by Hobbes, the answer is that there is more security in the performance than in the non-performance of covenants. Someone who takes advantage of another's laying down the right of nature can only do so once and expect to get away with it. And the temporary advantage they gain may in any case not counterbalance what they will lose by being opposed by all those whose trust is threatened or betrayed.

Another problem with Hobbes' theory turns on the supposed moral urgency of each person's laying down the right of nature. Hobbes thinks that the biggest threat to the stability of states is the existence of too much scope for private judgment. The more each person is entitled to think for themselves in matters of wellbeing, the worse it turns out for everyone. This implication is supported in Hobbes' theory by a supposedly scientific understanding of the diversity of the passions and the way that the passions get the better of judgment in human beings. By delegating their power of judgment to someone who is not affected by the individual passions of the people ruled over, people actually get access to a more effective (because more dispassionate) means of securing themselves than their own individual judgments. But, by the same token, they forgo any intellectual contribution to public life. They function in the state not as citizens in the full sense but as subjects only: political life for the many consists solely of submission to law. It is by their passivity rather than by the application of their powers of judgment that people promote the public good. This may have seemed persuasive in a time when the Biblical example of Adam and Eve would have been widely understood to illustrate the dangers of private judgment of good and evil, but to contemporary sensibility it verges on the paranoid. In fact, Hobbes' point is not quite that the judgments of human beings about their wellbeing can never be trusted, but rather that their *prescientific* judgments cannot be trusted. Prescientifically, people are moved by their feelings of pleasure and displeasure to call things 'good' and 'bad' – few have either the resources or the circumstances to be taught any better. But there is a better conception to be inculcated: Hobbes indicates that it consists of showing how things that are genuinely good, as opposed to pleasant, promote peace or self-preservation, while things that are genuinely bad, as opposed to unpleasant, are conducive to war and self-destruction.

Hobbes' moral and political philosophy impresses some people because it reconstructs the reasons there are for doing what morality tells us to do as reasons of self-interest. Such reasons are sometimes thought to give a more compelling answer to the question 'Why be moral?' than accounts which connect moral motivation to the recognition of transcendent Forms or to the rationally unobjectionable, or to a category of what is acceptable under conditions of ignorance of biasing considerations. Philosophers who call themselves Hobbesians in our own day sometimes cite this power of basing moral motivation on non-utopian and non-metaphysical types of reasoning as Hobbes' main contribution to moral philosophy. For these philosophers, notably David Gauthier, Hobbes anticipates a kind of scepticism about the pretensions of moral philosophy to find rationally unignorable and inescapable reasons for doing what it tells us to do. The most that moral philosophy can show us, according to this interpretation, is that many of the things that morality asks us to do are in our interest if we care about ourselves, or more about ourselves than others (see MORAL MOTIVATION).

9 The scientific status of Hobbes' ethics and politics

The main lines of Hobbes' political philosophy include the idea that the commonwealth is a solution to the ever-present threat of war in the passionate make-up of human beings, and that the commonwealth is made by delegating the right of nature to a sovereign power with unlimited power. This summarizes a theory worked out in very great detail, a theory Hobbes always regarded as ushering in the scientific treatment of morals and politics. What made the theory scientific? A number of answers get support from Hobbes' writings. The scientific status of politics is sometimes said to be owed to its derivation, in some sense, from Hobbes' natural science. Again, Hobbes' use in civil philosophy of a method applicable to natural bodies and bodies politic alike is sometimes thought to be crucial to its scientific status. These answers are consistent with some texts but sit uneasily with others. First, although Hobbes thought that there was a way of approaching the principles of morals and politics from a starting point in the workings of sense and imagination (which were treated of by physics), he consistently denied that civil science *had* to be approached by way of physics. In chapter 6 of *De corpore* he says that people entirely innocent of physics, but who enjoy introspective access to their own passionate states, are able to see in themselves evidence for the truth of the theory of human nature in the civil science. Something similar is said in the Introduction to *Leviathan*. In the same vein there is the explanation of his having been able to publish *De cive*, the third volume in his trilogy, without having first expounded the principles of parts of philosophy that were prior to politics. Hobbes said that this was possible because civil philosophy depended on principles of its own. What ties together all of these remarks is a belief in the autonomy of civil science, a belief that is not seriously called into question by his saying that the two principal parts of civil philosophy were alike in applying a certain sort of method to the investigation of bodies – bodies politic on the one hand and natural bodies on the other.

When Hobbes says that each part of philosophy deals with bodies, he makes clear that the two kinds of bodies are 'very different' from one another. And there is no evidence that 'body', when applied in the phrase 'body politic', is supposed to mean 'space-occupying thing existing without the mind'. In other words, there is no evidence that bodies politic are bodies in any more than a metaphorical sense. Finally, it is not clear that Hobbes thought that the scientific status of his politics was made more credible by an analogy between bodies politic and natural bodies. It is not as if he thought that natural bodies were well-understood scientifically, and that bodies politic might in principle be as well understood if the methods of physics were applied to them. On the contrary, Hobbes always thought that the properties of human artefacts, such as bodies politic, were much better understood than the properties of natural bodies, which had God's inscrutable will behind them.

It would be a mistake, however, to think that civil science for Hobbes was primarily an exercise in the investigation of the properties of bodies. It was an exercise in putting our judgments about what we ought to do on grounds that were far more solid than pleasure and pain. Good and bad were a matter of what conduced or interfered with self-preservation or peace, not how it felt to do or get this or that. The core of Hobbes' civil science is an attempt to recast the precepts of morality – the laws of nature – as instruments of peace, and to show how the ingredients of war are latent in any project for the pursuit of happiness. The scientific status of the doctrine of the laws of nature – the ground of its claim to be called moral philosophy – was its conforming to the pattern of a deductive system, based on two fundamental laws of nature and the rest derivative. Similarly with the deduction of the rights of sovereigns from the goal of peace. The scientific status of the argument for the inevitability of war consisted in its proceeding from principles about the passions. But these principles were by no means the property of physics or physicists; they were available in each person's introspective self-knowledge.

The deductive character of scientific demonstration was often claimed by Hobbes to interfere with its comprehensibility and its persuasiveness. But by the time of *Leviathan* Hobbes thought that he had finally managed to achieve the best of both worlds. In the third and last version of his political philosophy, persuasiveness and scientific understanding were finally married to his satisfaction. The Review and Conclusion of *Leviathan* says as much. Commentators have tried to chart Hobbes' attempts from 1640 to 1651 to balance reason and rhetoric in his political science, and it remains a controversial question whether this is managed in one way before the appearance of *Leviathan*, and managed in a different way in *Leviathan* itself.

According to a recent interpretation, due to Quentin Skinner, Hobbes constructed his civil science with a special awareness of two humanist assumptions: that there were always two sides to any question, and that arguments over what was just and unjust were never more than probable. In connection with the belief in two sides to every question, Hobbes was alive to the dangers of *paradiastole*, the rhetorical figure by which actions of an apparently vicious character are re-described as instances of a neighbouring virtue, and actions of a noble character are re-described unflatteringly. At first, in *Elements of Law* and *De cive*, Hobbes railed against humanism by arguing that 'science' in a preferred sense put certain conclusions *beyond* controversy. Questions within the scope of science would thus *not* have two sides. More, questions of justice lay squarely within the scope of science. That is, according to both *Elements of Law* and *De cive*, they could be settled by syllogistic reasoning from the definition of justice as sticking to the covenants one enters into, in particular, sticking to the covenant that one will abide by the sovereign's laws or commands. Questions about whether actions were expressions of certain other virtues could also be settled definitively, by establishing whether those actions contributed to peace or the preservation of civil order. For all virtues were means to the establishment or preservation of peace, the maintenance of the covenant establishing the commonwealth pre-eminently so. With a science of the virtues – a science deducing precepts corresponding to the virtues from an overarching requirement of seeking peace, Hobbes had a basis for showing which uses of paradiastole led to erroneous moral evaluations.

So much for the early response to paradiastole. The later response is distinguished by new background assumptions about the human capacity of reason. *Leviathan* (ch. 5) stresses that human beings are not born with the ability to reason in a way that will produce science. Nor are they likely to acquire this ability easily or recognize it in others. Again, a standard human audience cannot be counted upon to be receptive to the sort of reasoning recommended in *Elements of Law* and *De cive*. Not only does it strain attention, but when it is followed, it does not necessarily compel belief. People need to be *willing* to heed its message, and they are unwilling to do so where it goes against or *seems* to go against their interest. Eloquence or rhetoric is needed to catch the attention, keep it and neutralize the resistance of interest to its conclusions. Hobbes is not only supposed to have dropped some of his earlier strictures on rhetoric by the time he wrote *Leviathan*, but actually to have practised the techniques of Cicero and Quintillian in works composed after 1650.

Hobbes probably *did* change his mind about the uses of rhetoric, but the response to paradiastole is not as central to Hobbes' civil science as the interpretation we are considering suggests, and there is more of a separation in Hobbes between the task of a moral science and the production of conclusive-seeming moral and political conclusions for non-philosophers.

Turning first to paradiastole, let us consider the passage from chapter 15 of *Leviathan* that, according to the interpretation we are considering, is central to the understanding of the point of Hobbes' moral science:

> *Good*, and *Evill*, are names that signifie our Appetites and Aversions, which in different tempers, customes and doctrines of men, are different. And divers men differ not onely in their Judgement, on the senses of what is pleasant and unpleasant to the taste, smell, hearing, touch and sight; but also of what is conformable, or disagreeable, to Reason, in the actions of common life. Nay, the same man, in divers times, differs from himselfe; and one time praiseth, that is, calleth Good, what at another time he disperaiseth, and calleth Evill.

What is crucial here is the idea that evaluative terms in each man's mouth signify appetites or aversions – psychological dispositions to pursue or avoid things – and that these appetites and aversions can vary from person to person. Evaluative terms can accordingly also vary in sifgnification, depending on whose mouth they come from, and what that person's circumstances and history are. Although a given pattern of appetite and aversion in one person need not be idiosyncratic – people can agree in appetites and aversions if their constitutions and experiences are similar – the things that naturally determine the pattern of appetite and aversion are inconstant, and so, if evaluations are dictated by appetites and aversions, there need be no firm distinction between good and evil either, and no firm distinction between people's judgements of what they should do and what they should not do. So it is sheer luck if people do not disagree over good and evil or if they do not disagree so heatedly that they come to blows. There is incipient war, in other words, in the facts of how individual appetites and aversions are naturally formed.

Now although the re-description of vicious actions as virtuous and virtuous actions as vicious is undoubtedly one source of inconstancy and possible disagreement in valuations leading to war, it is only one among others. So the question arises why any linguistic device, let alone any so specific as paradiastolic re-description, should have central importance. Why is not any source of inconstancy in evaluations – linguistic *or* psychological *or* physical – as much a concern of Hobbes' moral science as any other? And why is not ambiguity – the fact of a term's having more than one meaning – the politically dangerous linguistic phenomenon *par excellence* rather than paradiastolic redescription? This suggestion certainly agrees with Hobbes' identification after 1650 of the chief defect of moral philosophy before his own – that it told people to do right without setting out a 'certain rule and measure of right' (*De corpore*, ch. 1, vii). It certainly agrees with his repeated denunciations of the use of each person's judgement – private judgement – as the measure of right and wrong.

See also: CONTRACTARIANISM; HUMAN NATURE; JUSTICE; MATERIALISM; MORAL MOTIVATION; SOVEREIGNTY; STATE, THE

References and further reading

Hobbes, T. (1651) *Leviathan, or the Matter, Form and Power of Commonwealth, Ecclesiastical and Civil*, in *The English Works of Thomas Hobbes*, vol. 3, ed. W. Molesworth, London: John Bohn, 1839; repr. ed. R. Tuck, Cambridge: Cambridge University Press, 1991; repr. ed. E. Curley, Chicago, IL: Hackett Publishing Company, 1994. (Hobbes' masterpiece.)

Malcolm, N. (2002) *Aspects of Hobbes*, Oxford: Clarendon Press. (Authoritative text on Hobbes's thought, selected contemporaries, and general intellectual context.)

Sorell, T. (1986) *Hobbes*, London: Routledge. (A study of Hobbes' metaphysics and politics against the background of his philosophy of science.)

TOM SORELL

HOHFELD, WESLEY NEWCOMB (1879–1918)

W.N. Hohfeld, US law professor and proponent of analytical jurisprudence, was responsible for one of the most influential analyses of the concept of a right in legal and moral philosophy. He offered to resolve all complex legal relations into a few simple and elementary ones, often confusedly referred to as 'rights'.

See also: LAW, PHILOSOPHY OF; RIGHTS

NEIL MACCORMICK

HOLISM AND INDIVIDUALISM IN HISTORY AND SOCIAL SCIENCE

Methodological individualists such as Mill, Weber, Schumpeter, Popper, Hayek and Elster argue that all social facts must be explained wholly and exhaustively in terms of the actions, beliefs and desires of individuals. On the other hand, methodological holists, such as Durkheim and Marx, tend in their explanations to bypass individual action. Within this debate, better arguments exist for the view that explanations of social phenomena without the beliefs and desires of agents are deficient. If this is so, individualists appear to have a distinct edge over their adversaries. Indeed, a consensus exists among philosophers and social scientists that holism is implausible or false and individualism, when carefully formulated, is trivially true.

Holists challenge this consensus by first arguing that caricatured formulations of holism that ignore human action must be set aside. They then ask us to re-examine the nature of human action. Action is distinguished from mere behaviour by its intentional character. This much is uncontested between individualists and holists. But against the individualist contention that intentions exist as only psychological states in the heads of individuals, the holist argues that they also lie directly embedded in irreducible social practices, and that the identification of any intention is impossible without examining the social context within which agents think and act. Holists find nothing wrong with the need to unravel the motivations of individuals, but they contend that these motivations cannot be individuated without appeal to the wider beliefs and practices of the community. For instance, the acquiescence of oppressed workers may take the form not of total submission but subtle negotiation that yields them sub-optimal benefits. Insensitivity to social context may blind us to this. Besides, it is not a matter of individual beliefs and preferences that this strategy is adopted. That decisions are taken by subtle strategies of negotiation rather than by explicit bargaining, deployment of force or use of high moral principles is a matter of social practice irreducible to the conscious action of individuals.

Two conclusions follow if the holist claim is true. First, that a reference to a social entity is inescapable even when social facts are explained in terms of individual actions, because of the necessary presence of a social ingredient in all individual intentions and actions. Second, a reference to individual actions is not even necessary when social facts are explained or understood in terms of social practices. Thus, the individualist view that explanation in social science must rely wholly and exhaustively on individual entities is hotly contested and is not as uncontroversial or trivial as it appears.

See also: INTENTION; METHODOLOGICAL INDIVIDUALISM

RAJEEV BHARGAVA

HOLISM: MENTAL AND SEMANTIC

Mental (or semantic) holism is the doctrine that the identity of a belief content (or the meaning of a sentence that expresses it) is determined by its place in the web of beliefs or sentences comprising a whole theory or group of theories. It can be contrasted with two other views: atomism and molecularism. Molecularism characterizes meaning and content in terms of relatively *small parts* of the web in a way that allows many different theories to share those parts. For example, the meaning of 'chase' might be said by a molecularist to be 'try to catch'. Atomism characterizes meaning and content in terms of *none* of the web; it says that sentences and beliefs have meaning or content independently of their relations to other sentences or beliefs.

One major motivation for holism has come from reflections on the natures of confirmation and learning. As Quine observed, claims about the world are confirmed not individually but only in conjunction with theories of which they are a part. And, typically, one cannot come to understand scientific claims without understanding a significant chunk of the theory of which they are a part. For example, in learning the Newtonian concepts of 'force', 'mass', 'kinetic energy' and 'momentum', one does not learn any definitions of these terms in terms that are understood beforehand, for there are no such definitions. Rather, these theoretical terms are all learned together in conjunction with procedures for solving problems.

The major problem with holism is that it threatens to make generalization in psychology virtually impossible. If the content of any state depends on all others, it would be extremely unlikely that any two believers would ever share a state with the same content. Moreover, holism would appear to conflict with our ordinary conception of reasoning. What sentences one accepts influences what one infers. If I accept a sentence and then later reject it, I thereby change the inferential role of that sentence, so the meaning of what I accept would not be the same as the meaning of what I later reject. But then it would be difficult to understand on this view how one could rationally – or even irrationally! – change one's mind. And agreement and translation are also problematic for much the same reason. Holists have responded (1) by proposing that we should think not in terms of 'same/different' meaning but in terms of a gradient of similarity of meaning, (2) by proposing 'two-factor' theories, or (3) by simply accepting the consequence that there is no real difference between changing meanings and changing beliefs.

NED BLOCK

HOLOCAUST, THE

The specific, tragic event of the Holocaust – the mass murder of Jews by the Nazis during the Second World War – raises profound theological and philosophical problems, particularly problems about the existence of God and the meaning of Jewish existence. Among the thinkers who have tried to wrestle with the conceptual challenge posed by the destruction of European Jewry, three who have presented original arguments that can be termed, in a relatively strict sense, philosophical are Richard L. Rubenstein, Emil Fackenheim and Arthur A. Cohen.

Rubenstein has formulated an argument that turns on the theological difficulties raised by the realities of the evil of Auschwitz and Treblinka in a world putatively created and ordered by a benign God. For him, such evil decisively refutes the traditional theological claim that a God possessed of goodness and power exists, and entails the conclusion that 'there is no [traditional] God'. In working out this conceptual position, he uses an unsatisfactory empirical theory of verification concerning religious propositions and too narrow a notion of evidence, both historical and ethical, that ultimately undermines his counterclaims and 'Death of God' affirmations.

Fackenheim seeks not to defend a religious 'explanation' of the Holocaust, but rather to provide a 'response' to it that maintains the reality of God and his continued presence in human, and particularly Jewish, history. To do so, he uses Martin Buber's understanding of dialogical revelation, asserting that revelation is an ever-present possibility, and formulates his own moral-theological demand to the effect that after the Holocaust, Jewish survival is the '614th commandment' (there are 613 commandments in classical Judaism). Fackenheim's defence of this position, however, is philosophically problematic.

Cohen provides a 'process theology' argument as an explanation of the Holocaust; that is, the Holocaust requires a revision in our understanding of God's nature and action. It forces the theological conclusion that God does not possess the traditional 'omni' predicates; God does not intervene in human affairs in the manner taught by traditional Western theology. However, Cohen's working out of a process theological position in relation to the Holocaust raises as many philosophical problems as it solves.

See also: ANTI-SEMITISM; EVIL, PROBLEM OF

STEVEN T. KATZ

HOOKER, RICHARD (1554–1600)

Hooker's *Of the Laws of Ecclesiastical Polity* (1593–1662) is the first major work of English prose in the fields of philosophy, theology and political theory. After setting out an entire worldview in terms of the single idea of law, Hooker attempted to justify – and, arguably, to transform – the religious and political institutions of his day. Hooker's work contributed to later, more narrowly political, political thought (Locke cited 'the judicious Hooker' at crucial points in his *Second Treatise of Civil Government*), but the *Laws* is chiefly significant for articulating the ideal of a society coherent in and through its religion, a body politic which succeeds in being – not merely having – a church. In Hooker's England this meant that royal authority in religion was extensive, but derived from the community and limited by law. Modern separations of politics from religion and of philosophy from edification have made him difficult to assimilate. More recent critiques of Enlightenment secularism and purely technical philosophy help make him again intelligible.

See also: AUTHORITY; BODIN, J.; LAW, PHILOSOPHY OF; LAWS, NATURAL; LOCKE, J.; NATURAL LAW; POLITICAL PHILOSOPHY, HISTORY OF; RENAISSANCE PHILOSOPHY; SOVEREIGNTY

A.S. MCGRADE

HSÜN TSU/HSÜN TZU
See XUNZI

HUMAN NATURE

Introduction

Every political philosophy takes for granted a view of human nature, and every view of human nature is controversial. Political philosophers have responded to this conundrum in a variety of ways. Some have defended particular views of human nature, while others have sought to develop political philosophies that are compatible with many different views of human nature, or, alternatively, which rest on as few controversial assumptions about human nature as possible. Some political philosophers have taken the view that human nature is an immutable given, others that it is shaped (in varying degrees) by culture and circumstance. Differences about the basic attitudes of human beings toward one another – whether selfish, altruistic or some combination – have also exercised political philosophers. Although none of these questions has been settled definitively, various advances have been made in thinking systematically about them.

Four prominent debates concern: (1) the differences between *perfectionist* views, in which human nature is seen as malleable, and *constraining* views, in which it is not; (2) the *nature/nurture* controversy, which revolves around the degree to which human nature is a consequence of biology as opposed to social influence, and the implications of this question for political philosophy; (3) the opposition between *self-referential* and *other-referential* conceptions of human nature and motivation – whether we are more affected by our own condition considered in itself, or by comparisons between our own condition and that of others; and (4) attempts to detach philosophical thought about political association from all controversial assumptions about human nature.

1	Perfectionist versus constraining views of human nature
2	The nature/nurture controversy
3	Self-referential versus other-referential conceptions of human nature
4	'Political' versus 'metaphysical' conceptions of human nature

1 Perfectionist versus constraining views of human nature

The most celebrated proponent of perfectionist views of human nature is ARISTOTLE, and his most elaborate discussion of the question appears in *The Nicomachean Ethics* (*c.*330 BC). Aristotle's view developed there is sometimes described as teleological because it was defined by reference to a fundamental contrast between untutored or brute human nature on the one hand, and human nature as it could be if we realized our essential nature or Telos on the other (see TELOS). Ethics, for Aristotle, is the science that instructs us how to get from the one to the other. When correctly employed, ethical precepts thus have the potential to transform human

beings from their rude and untutored states into the best kinds of beings they can become.

Although there is both room and need for human nature to develop and change on Aristotle's view, his is a *naturalist* one in that both the accounts of brute human nature and perfected human nature are rooted in a philosophical psychology, a theory of natural human needs and potentials. Naturalist views are generally distinguished from *anti-naturalist* accounts, in which the sources of meaning and value for human beings are externally given, whether in Platonic forms, transcendental arguments about the nature of knowledge and obligation, or some other extrinsic origin. On anti-naturalist views what is good or right is good or right regardless of actual human needs and desires, whereas for naturalists the gulf between 'is' and 'ought' is bridged via an account of human needs or psychology (see NATURALISM IN ETHICS). Naturalist perfectionism can be secular or theologically-based; indeed, much medieval Christian Aristotelianism rested on the adaptation of the story of the Garden of Eden, the Fall from Grace, and the possibility of redemption to Aristotle's ethical categories. Marxism, on the other hand, is a secular version of naturalist perfectionism. For Marx, human beings as we find them are alienated from their 'true' selves, their potential stunted by a variety of malevolent forces. But these forces are in some sense artificial impediments to human flourishing that can be understood and ultimately vanquished, opening the way for authentic human development (see ALIENATION).

Although perfectionist views can be naturalist or anti-naturalist, constraining views of human nature are invariably naturalist in character. Proponents of constraining views regard human nature as an immutable given, holding that social and political institutions must take account of it but have no effect on it. Perhaps the most extreme proponent of this view in the history of Western philosophy was Jeremy BENTHAM, who made it an axiom of his utilitarian system that nature: 'has placed mankind under the governance of two sovereign masters, *pain* and *pleasure*' (1948: 125). For Bentham, pleasure seeking and pain avoidance 'govern us in all we do, in all we say, in all we think: every effort we can make to throw off our subjection, will serve but to demonstrate and confirm it' (1948: 125). Bentham believed that the utilitarian system he advocated was uniquely scientific in that it recognized our inescapable subjection to the pleasure/pain calculus.

Although Bentham offers one of the most forthright and clear accounts of a constraining view of human nature, his is by no means the first or the only such view in the history of Western political theory. In their modern form such views are traceable at least to Hobbes' insistence, *contra* Aristotle, that human nature is rigidly fixed. For Hobbes (1651) human beings are inescapably driven by a primordial fear of death, which produces in them a 'relentless desire for power after power'. Basic human impulses can be channelled in more and less productive ways, and to some extent people can be educated to see that certain political allegiances are better than others given their basic impulses, but the impulses themselves cannot be altered (see HOBBES, T. §6).

Utilitarians since Bentham have generally regarded human nature as given and external to the operations of political and cultural institutions. Even if utilitarians have differed greatly from one another concerning the content of human nature and even how much we can reasonably aspire to know about its content, they have generally accepted Hume's dictum that 'reason is the slave of the passions'. Whereas Hume, like Bentham, thought we are all driven by the same passions in the same ways, neoclassical utilitarians of the late nineteenth and early twentieth centuries (such as Pareto) questioned this assumption, taking a view of human nature that was perhaps most decisively stated by the emotivist philosopher Charles Stevenson in his critique of Hume: that even if we are convinced that all human beings are driven by needs for gratification of some sort, there is no decisive reason to think we all have the same such needs, or even that we can intelligently compare different desires experienced by different individuals with one another. This is the standard view in modern economics and rational choice theories of politics. Preferences are thought of as exogenously determined, but the possibility of meaningful interpersonal comparisons of preferences across individuals is denied (see UTILITARIANISM; ECONOMICS AND ETHICS).

2 The nature/nurture controversy

Since time immemorial scientists and philosophers have debated the question whether human nature is biologically given or rather the result of contingencies of cultural and historical circumstance, and these debates have been thought to be pregnant with political significance. ROUSSEAU (§2), for example, was the first in a long line of political theorists who have argued that Hobbes' political system was based on a confusion of parochial traits that were the product of seventeenth-century English life with enduring features of the human condition. In Rousseau's view, Hobbes wrongly thought the impulse toward self-preservation was incompatible with a desire to preserve others: 'because of [his] having improperly included in

the savage man's care of self-preservation the need to satisfy a multitude of passions which are the product of society' (*The First and Second Discourses*). Rousseau's own account of the state of nature has been criticized on analogous grounds however. Indeed it has become a standard move in modern political argument to question every assertion about natural human traits and propensities, however qualified or historicized, by arguing that the traits in question are socially produced or 'socially constructed'. Such debates can become exceedingly heated when they become embroiled in discussions of the determinants of intelligence and such things as ethnic, racial and gender differences (see SOCIOBIOLOGY).

The nature/nurture controversy is often confused with the issue of whether or not human nature is alterable by human design. It is often said, for instance, that much or all of human nature is socially constructed rather than naturally given, and that for this reason it should not be regarded as immutable. In fact, whether a given human characteristic is a product of nature or culture may have little to do with the degree to which it is alterable by conscious human design. On the one hand, there are many features of the natural world that human beings have effectively altered and will alter more in the future; the science of genetic engineering, for example, is presumably in its infancy. On the other hand, there are many pieces of human reality that, while indisputably the product of human action, we often seem powerless to influence. Ethnic hatred may be learned, for example, yet it may be impossible to get people to unlearn it or even to stop them passing it on to the next generation.

It is sometimes thought that cultural creations can be more easily understood than natural creations because they are the products of the human will. This view was common in the seventeenth century, for example, where philosophers like Hobbes and Locke, under the strong influence of the Cartesian idea that the reflective individual has privileged access to the contents of their own mind, held that only this individual can really know 'the ghost in the machine' in Gilbert Ryle's memorable phrase. Knowing one's own motivations and understanding one's behaviour guarantees nothing, however, about one's understanding of the complexities of human interaction in the social and political arena. In any case, in a post-Freudian age the Cartesian view must be regarded as questionable. We might be confused, or wrong, or we might deceive ourselves about our motivations and purposes. For all we know Bentham might have been right when he insisted that 'it is with the anatomy of the human mind as with the anatomy and physiology of the human body: the rare case is, not that of a man's being unconversant, but of his being conversant with it' (in *Jeremy Bentham's Economic Writings* 1954, vol. III: 425). In short, the human capacity to shape human nature is a product of how well we can understand and control the causal mechanisms that lead human traits to be what they are. This is contingently related, if it is related at all, to whether a particular trait is a product of biology, culture, some combination of the two, or some third thing.

For all the attention it has received from political philosophers over the centuries, the nature/nurture controversy is a red herring in a second respect as far as politics is concerned. Since human beings are naturally conventional creatures who often achieve biological adaptation through social learning, the distinction between what is natural and what is cultural in human behaviour is not merely difficult to pin down in practice, but impossible to get at in principle. Perhaps partly for this reason, in recent years much of the discussion in Anglo–American political and moral philosophy has turned away from the nature/nurture debate towards requiring principled justifications for any differences among persons that have political consequences, regardless of their origin. John RAWLS is perhaps more responsible for this than any other single figure. In *A Theory of Justice* (1971) he makes the case that differences in talents and abilities among persons, whether natural or cultural in origin, are 'morally arbitrary'; that is, they are products of luck either in the genetic lottery or in the milieu into which one happens to be born. In either case, the differences are not chosen or produced by actions for which the relevant agents can reasonably be held responsible. By the same token, it seems unfair that benefits should accrue to persons differentially in virtue of differences in their talents and abilities, whether such differences are rooted in nature, culture or both.

Making the Rawlsian move has the effect of socializing human capacities regardless of their origins (at least as a normative matter), and although it is exceedingly difficult to find a principled basis on which to resist his reasoning, it generates problems that are in many ways as difficult as those that it resolves. A person might find it both rationally undeniable and psychologically impossible to accept that nothing they do or achieve is the autonomous result of their own efforts. Analogously, it might be argued that for both individual and species some fictions about individual responsibility for different outcomes may be required for human reproduction and wellbeing, even if we know them to be fictions. Such beliefs may be indispensable to the basic integrity of the human psyche and necessary for generating and sustaining the incentive to work on which human beings are,

after all, critically reliant. As a result, although facts about moral luck and socially produced productive capacities conspire – when confronted – to enfeeble the idea of individual responsibility for outcomes, people may none the less be powerless to abandon it (see RESPONSIBILITY). One interesting strand of modern scholarship by Ronald DWORKIN, Amartya Sen, Richard Arneson and others attempts to grapple with the issues raised by Rawls' discussion of moral arbitrariness, but it has not converged on any single or compelling conclusion.

3 Self-referential versus other-referential conceptions of human nature

A third dimension along which conceptions of human nature vary concerns the degree to which people's interests are linked to the fortunes and perceptions of others. Contrast Ronald Reagan's 1984 election slogan: 'Are you better off now than you were four years ago?' with an employee who says to his employer 'I don't care what I get paid, so long as its more than Jones down the corridor'. The Reagan slogan is based on a *self-referential* conception of human nature; it assumes that people are interested in improving their own fortunes without any necessary reference to anyone else. The latter example is *other-referential*: a person's perception of their interests is intrinsically reliant on the welfare of others. We cannot make a judgment about their welfare without reference to the welfare of others. The distinction between self- and other-referential views operates independently of whether one is a subjectivist and of the basic metric of value along which welfare is judged. For instance, Marx's measure of exploitation is radically other-referential in that it is critically reliant on the proportion of the social surplus that the workers receive as compared with employers. Thus his technical measure of the rate of exploitation may increase even if real wages are increasing and the worker's subjective sense is that his welfare is improving. Rawls, on the other hand, works with a hybrid of self- and other-referential views of human nature in that he argues that rational people will always want to improve the lot of the worst-off individual in society, relative to what it was before, even if this means that who is the worst off changes.

Whether one thinks human nature is basically self- or other-referential has substantial implications for politics and distributive justice. Utilitarians, both classical and neoclassical, tend to think of people as self-referential maximizers who want to get on as high an indifference curve as possible without reference to anyone else, although there is no necessary reason that this be so. Aristotelians like Alasdair MACINTYRE, on the other hand, are

393

necessarily committed to other-referential views. For them what people value above all is to be valued by others whom they value. 'She's a cellist's cellist' is an appellation we intuitively grasp, and to the extent that it captures something fundamental about what motivates people, models of individual maximization that ignore it will be descriptively misleading and morally unsatisfying. In this connection it is worth noting that in Hegel's (1807) *Phenomenology* the argument is made that slavery is an unstable set of social arrangements not merely because the slave can eventually be expected to resist oppression, but also because the master will find it unsatisfying; he needs recognition from someone whom he values (see HEGEL, G.W.F.).

Whether and to what extent human nature is substantially self-referential is not to be confused with whether and to what degree people are selfish. Although self-referentially motivated people may typically be indifferent – at best – to the fortunes of others; other-referential motivations may be more or less selfish. The demand to be paid 'more than Jones', 'the same as Jones' or 'less than Jones' are all other-referential in character, although they vary considerably on the dimension between selfish and altruistic motivation. Sadists and rapists exhibit what economists refer to as 'interdependent negative utilities' in that their wellbeing is intrinsically linked to the suffering of others; so too does the divorcing spouse whose utility increases if a dollar is taken out of the pocket of their spouse and burned. These are all other-referential types of motivation, no more or less than are the motivations of those who seek and experience increased happiness at another's happiness or success. In short, the self-referential/other-referential dimension refers to the structure of human psychology rather than its content. This is not to say that the structure has no implications for content. In particular, to the extent that people are other-referentially motivated, their behaviour and aspirations will tend not to be captured by rational agent models adapted from microeconomics, which rest exclusively on self-referential assumptions about human psychology. People who find arguments based on rational agent models unsatisfying descriptively or morally tend to be sceptical of the extent to which self-referential assumptions capture important dimensions of the human condition. Whether or not such scepticism is warranted is in the end an empirical question; it will not be settled by armchair reflection (see RATIONAL CHOICE THEORY).

4 'Political' versus 'metaphysical' conceptions of human nature

Given the enduring – perhaps endemic – disagreements about human nature it is perhaps unsurprising that some political philosophers have sought to develop political theories assuming as little as possible about it. One strategy that has been extensively explored since the 1960s is to try to seek political principles that are neutral between different views of human nature and conceptions of the human good. Some of Rawls' earlier formulations of his project were understood thus, and Bruce Ackerman, Charles Larmore and others subsequently attempted to formulate different neutrality arguments (see NEUTRALITY, POLITICAL). By the 1990s a fairly broad consensus had begun to emerge that neutrality arguments fail, that there is no set of political principles that can be genuinely neutral among different conceptions of human nature and the human good, and that a little digging into allegedly neutral arguments will inevitably bring their assumptions to the surface.

A subtler response to the problem is to abandon the search for neutral political standards, but retain the ambition to develop political principles that may be compatible with as many different views of the human condition as possible. Here the key idea is to try to limit what one might reasonably expect of justification in political theory, and in particular to abandon all aspirations to get at the true or right theory of human nature. This is the strategy adopted by the later Rawls, who asks: which political principles does it make most sense to agree on, given that we know we will never all agree on basic metaphysical questions about the human condition? The answer to which he is drawn is the one that tolerates as many conceptions of the human good as possible, consistent with a 'like liberty for all'. This approach explicitly abandons the agenda of coming up with right answers to questions about human nature, seeking only to tolerate as many answers as possible. It courts the possibility that it may actually lead us not to tolerate the 'true' view of human nature if, for instance, this is embedded only in a fundamentalist religion that also requires that no other views be tolerated. On a 'political not metaphysical' approach, we are not expected – as political theorists – to take any view on the question whether the fundamentalist view is correct; for all we know it might be. However, since we can never know that it is the correct view and we do know that there will always be competing views, it is never rational to accept it as governing our politics. Various difficulties confront this and other attempts to move in the 'political not metaphysical' direction, and some will find the philosophical abdication implied by this strategy impossible to live with. But in a world in which assumptions about human nature are both indispensable to politics and endemically controversial, it is difficult to see how the impulse to turn to institutional, rather than philosophical, solutions to the problems it creates can reasonably be resisted.

References and further reading

Bentham, J. (1948) *A Fragment on Government and An Introduction to the Principles of Morals and Legislation*, Oxford: Blackwell. (The *locus classicus* of Bentham's utilitarianism. Contains a programmatic statement of his assumptions about human nature, as well as applications in the fields of politics, law and economics. Easy to read despite the arcane English.)

Locke, J. (1690) *Two Treatises of Government*, ed. P. Laslett, Cambridge: Cambridge University Press, 1960. (The most elaborate statement of Locke's views on human nature and politics. Reasonably accessible.)

Rawls, J. (1971) *A Theory of Justice*. Cambridge, MA: Harvard University Press. (The most significant treatment of justice and human nature from the second half of the twentieth century. Reasonably accessible.)

IAN SHAPIRO

HUMANISM, RENAISSANCE

The early nineteenth-century German educator, F.J. Niethammer, coined the word 'humanism', meaning an education based on the Greek and Latin classics. The Renaissance (for our purposes, Europe from about 1350 to about 1650) knew no such term. The Renaissance had, instead, the Latin phrase *studia humanitatis* (literally 'the studies of humanity'), best translated as 'the humanities'. The Renaissance borrowed the phrase from classical antiquity. Cicero used it a few times, but it was the later grammarian Aulus Gellius who clearly equated the Latin word *humanitas* with Greek *paideia*, that is, with the classical Greek education of liberal learning, especially literature and rhetoric, which was believed to develop the intellectual, moral and aesthetic capacities of a child (*pais* in Greek; hence *paideia*).

Renaissance humanists understood by *studia humanitatis* a cycle of five subjects: grammar, rhetoric, poetry, history and moral philosophy, all based on the Greek and Latin classics. A humanist was an expert in the *studia humanitatis*. The dominant discipline was rhetoric. Eloquence was the highest professional accomplishment of the Renaissance humanists, and rhetorical interests coloured humanists' approach to the other parts of the *studia humanitatis*. The Renaissance humanists were the successors of the medieval rhetorical tradition and the resuscitators of the classical rhetorical tradition. Renaissance humanism was,

in the words of P.O. Kristeller, 'a characteristic phase in what may be called the rhetorical tradition in Western culture' ('The Humanist Movement' 1955).

Renaissance humanism was neither a philosophy nor an ideology. It reflected no fixed position towards religion, the state, or society. Rather it was a cultural movement centred on rhetoric, literature and history. Its leading protagonists held jobs primarily as teachers of grammar and literature. Outside academia, they served as secretaries, ambassadors and bureaucrats. Some were jurists. The Renaissance humanists reasserted the importance of the humanities against the overwhelming dominance of philosophy and science in medieval higher education. As humanism penetrated the wider culture, it was combined with other disciplinary interests and professions so that one found humanist philosophers, physicians, theologians, lawyers, mathematicians and so forth.

Ideologically humanists were a varied lot. Some were pious, some were not. Some were interested in philosophy, most were not. Some became Protestants, others remained Catholic. Some scorned the vernacular while others made important contributions to it. Humanism influenced virtually every aspect of high culture in the West during the Renaissance. Depending on the humanist under discussion, one can legitimately speak of Christian humanism, lay humanism, civic humanism, Aristotelian humanism and other combinations.

Humanism had a profound effect on philosophy. Writing outside the philosophical establishment, humanists sought to make philosophy more literary in presentation and more amenable to rhetorical concerns. No less importantly, they recovered and translated into Latin a large reservoir of Greek classical texts unknown or ignored in the Middle Ages. Platonism, Stoicism, Epicureanism and scepticism all experienced revivals. The humanists challenged medieval Aristotelianism by offering new Latin translations of Aristotle that in some respects amounted to fresh interpretations. They also significantly enriched the Aristotelian corpus by translating the *Poetics* and the late ancient Greek commentators on Aristotle.

Renaissance humanism arose out of the peculiar social and cultural circumstances of thirteenth-century Italy. It came to maturity in Italy in the fifteenth century and spread to the rest of Europe in the sixteenth. It gradually lost its vitality in the seventeenth and eighteenth centuries as its focus on Latin eloquence became out of date in a world increasingly won over to the vernacular literatures and new science. In the nineteenth century, it did not so much die as become metamorphosed. Renaissance humanism sloughed off its rhetorical impulse and became modern scholarly classicism. Today the word humanism has taken on new connotations, but the heritage of Renaissance humanism runs deep in our culture. As long as we continue to value literature and history, and the functional skills and cultural perspective attached to these disciplines, every educated person by training will be a humanist in the Renaissance sense.

See also: Erasmus, D.; Ficino, M.; Melanchthon, P.; More, T.; Pico della Mirandola, G.; Platonism, Renaissance; Renaissance philosophy

JOHN MONFASANI

HUMBOLDT, WILHELM VON (1767–1835)

Along with Schiller and Goethe, Humboldt was one of the chief representatives of Weimar classicism, a movement that aspired to revive German culture along the lines of ancient Greece. Humboldt's philosophical significance resides mainly in two areas: political theory and the philosophy of language. In political theory he was one of the founders of modern liberalism; and in the philosophy of language, he was among the first to stress the importance of language for thought, and of culture for language.

See also: Liberalism

FREDERICK BEISER

HUME, DAVID (1711–76)

Introduction

David Hume, one of the most prominent philosophers of the eighteenth century, was an empiricist, a naturalist and a sceptic. His aim, as stated in his early masterpiece, *A Treatise of Human Nature* (written and published when he was in his twenties), was to develop a 'science of man' – what would now be called a cognitive and conative psychology – that would provide a philosophical foundation for the sciences, both those that concern human life (such as 'logic, morals, criticism, and politics') and those that are merely investigated by human beings (such as 'mathematics, natural philosophy, and natural religion'). Although the Treatise itself received relatively little attention upon its publication in 1739–40, Hume's philosophical views attracted greater attention as a result of *An Enquiry concerning Human Understanding* (1748), *An Enquiry concerning the Principles of Morals* (1751), various essays and his posthumously published *Dialogues Concerning Natural Religion* (1779). He was also noted as a historian, diplomat and essayist on political and economic topics.

One aspect of Hume's empiricism was methodological, consisting in his endorsement and practice of 'the experimental method' requiring that claims in his science of man be derived from and supported by experience rather than from intellectual ratiocination independent of experience. In this, he saw himself as following in the tradition of Locke and as standing against the excesses of earlier philosophers such as Descartes. But whereas natural philosophers (that is, natural scientists) such as Newton could simply design experiments to answer questions about the behaviour of bodies in particular circumstances, the premeditation of attempts to place the mind in a particular situation could alter the mind's natural operations, he maintained, so that we must 'glean up our experiments in this science from a cautious observation of human life, and take them as they appear in the common course of the world, by men's behaviour in company, in affairs, and in their pleasures' (THN Introduction). Another aspect of his empiricism was conceptual, consisting in his doctrine – itself defended through use of the experimental method – that all ideas, and hence all concepts, must be copied from 'impressions', that is, sensory or internal experiences. He thus also followed Locke in rejecting Cartesian 'innate ideas'.

Hume's pursuit of the experimental method proved, in his conduct of it, to support his methodological empiricism as well; for he claimed to find that all beliefs concerning 'matters of fact and real existence' – as distinguished from pure 'relations of ideas' such as mathematics – depend on the relation of cause and effect, and that relations of cause and effect, in turn, can only be discovered through the observed constant conjunction of events of one type with events of another type. Yet although we (philosophers included) easily suppose that we perceive a 'necessary connexion' binding an effect to its cause in such a way that it would be a contradiction for the one not to follow the other, there is in fact no such contradiction; for a cause and its effect are always two distinct events, either of which can be conceived to occur without the other. The attribution of a 'necessary connexion' to causes and effects results from the mind's projection on to them of its own feeling of mental determination to make an inference from the occurrence of an event of the one type to an event of the other after experience of their constant conjunction. Such inferences are not themselves founded on any process of reasoning concerning the uniformity of nature, for the denial of the uniformity of nature is not contradictory, and any attempt to defend the uniformity of nature by appeal to past experience would assume what the reasoning was supposed to establish. Instead, they are based on the mental mechanism of 'custom or habit'. While he endorses – and engages in – reasoning, Hume finds that many operations of the mind, including those involved in volition and morals, owe less to reason and more to other features of the mind's operations than might have been supposed.

Hume's naturalism consisted in his determination to treat the human mind as a part of nature, equally susceptible to scientific investigation and equally subject to ordinary causal laws, without invoking either special natural properties or supernatural entities. Indeed, he emphasized the extent to which human mental operations resemble those of animals. He was a determinist concerning both physical and mental events, holding that a given set of circumstances will always produce the same outcome in accordance with uniform laws of nature. Unlike Spinoza, however, he held this doctrine only because he thought it was supported by experience as a likely extrapolation from the successes of scientific enquiry. His naturalism is evident in his treatment of morals, which he explains as deriving from the human 'moral sense' – that is, the capacity to feel a distinctive kind of approbation and disapprobation when considering features of character – that is activated primarily by natural sympathy with those who are affected by the character traits in question. Virtue and vice acquire their central role in human life primarily through their ability to inspire love and pride, hatred and humility. Hume did not ever explicitly deny the existence of a deity, and he allowed that the hypothesis of an intelligent cause for the universe has a natural persuasive force. However, he forcefully criticized arguments for the existence of God, for religious miracles, for an afterlife with rewards and punishments, and for a deity's moral goodness or moral concern. He regarded religion as being largely pernicious for both enquiry and morals.

Hume did not use the terms 'empiricist' or 'naturalist'. He did, however, call himself a sceptic. His scepticism was the consequence of his discovery, in the course of his investigations, of the many 'infirmities' of human cognitive nature, including its inability to defend by reasoning many of its own most fundamental operations. While he held that intense consideration of these infirmities can produce a state of extreme but temporary doubt and bewilderment, the scepticism that he endorsed and sought to practise was 'mitigated' in degree, consisting in a certain diffidence and lack of dogmatism in all of his judgments. In addition to this general mitigated scepticism, however, he also recommended a complete suspense of judgment concerning matters entirely beyond our experience – such as cosmological speculation concerning 'the origins of worlds'.

1 Life and writings

David Hume was born in Edinburgh on 26 April 1711, just four years after the formal union of England and Scotland that created Great Britain. The influx of Isaac Newton's natural science and John Locke's philosophy into the Scottish universities paralleled the political union (see NEWTON, I; LOCKE, J.). Both Newton and Locke were widely seen as championing an empirical approach to knowledge in which observation and experimentation were to drive, constrain and determine theory. This approach stood in broad contrast with the readiness of many Continental philosophers of the seventeenth century – such as René DESCARTES, Nicholas MALEBRANCHE, Benedict de SPINOZA, and Gottfried Wilhelm LEIBNIZ – to allow high-level theoretical commitments to structure our understanding of the world and to determine the interpretation of sensory observations. Of particular concern to eighteenth-century philosophers were questions about the contents and faculties of the mind, causal reasoning, causal necessity, free will, God, the external world, personal identity, scepticism, motivation, the foundations of morality and political obligation. Hume was to make important contributions on each of these topics.

Hume was the youngest of three children. His mother, Katherine, was the daughter of Sir David Falconer, President of the College of Justice; his father, Joseph Home, practised law and was related to the Earls of Home. (Hume altered the spelling of his surname as a young man in order to aid its proper pronunciation.) The family maintained a modest estate, Ninewells, located in Berwickshire near the English border. Joseph Hume died in 1713, and young David was raised by his mother, a steadfast Calvinist who devoted herself to her children and never remarried. (She reportedly once declared, 'Our Davie is a fine, good-natured crater [creature], but uncommon wake-minded'; the now-obscure final adjective of this famous but perhaps apocryphal remark has been interpreted variously as meaning 'stupid', 'weak-willed', and 'intellectually alert'). Hume greatly admired his mother, but he rejected all religious commitments from an early age.

Between 1723 and 1725, Hume studied at the Edinburgh Town College – now the University of Edinburgh – with his older brother John. Among his subjects of study were Greek, logic, metaphysics and Newtonian 'natural philosophy'. From 1725 until 1734, he resided at Ninewells – preparing for a legal career, although he later allowed (in his 'My Own Life') that he read more philosophy than law. An attempt at a business career in 1734 under the tutelage of a merchant in Bristol ended in disappointment after a trial of just a few months, and the 23-year-old Hume moved to rural France to live cheaply while pursuing philosophy.

After a year in Rheims, Hume settled in La Flèche, site of the Jesuit college at which Descartes had been educated. He took full advantage of the college library as he devoted himself to writing, and in 1737 he moved to London to pursue the publication of the result, which is now regarded as his most important philosophical work. The work was *A Treatise of Human Nature* (cited here as THN), described in its subtitle as 'An Attempt to introduce the experimental method of Reasoning into Moral Subjects'. By 'moral subjects' Hume meant not only ethics, but human nature and human affairs more generally; the book's aim, as he described it in the Introduction, was to provide a 'science of man' – that is, what we would now call a cognitive and conative psychology. Because much of human knowledge *concerns* human beings and all of it is *acquired by* human beings using their human cognitive faculties, Hume proposed that such a science would provide 'a foundation almost entirely new' for all of the sciences. Just as Thales' inauguration of the study of non-human nature was followed by Socrates' inauguration of the study of human nature, he wrote, so too Francis Bacon's application of the experimental method to the study of non-human nature had been followed by the application of the experimental method to the study of human nature by Locke and some other 'late philosophers of England' (see THALES; SOCRATES; BACON, F.). The unstated implication was that, just as Newton had perfected the former, Hume would endeavour to perfect the latter. Book I ('Of the Understanding') and Book II ('Of the Passions') of the Treatise were published together in 1739,

anonymously; Book III ('Of Morals') appeared, also anonymously, in the following year.

Despite his efforts to obtain a wide readership for the book – he even composed an anonymous review, *An Abstract of a Treatise of Human Nature*, explaining some of its leading points and focusing particular attention on its central account of causal inference in Book I – the book's reception was a great disappointment to him. Although it did receive a few (largely negative) reviews, he wrote later, that the *Treatise* 'fell deadborn from the press, failing to elicit even a murmur from the zealots' ('My Own Life'); and indeed, the initial printing of 1,000 copies did not sell out during Hume's lifetime. Returning to Ninewells to live with his mother and brother, he turned his hand to essay writing, and his *Essays, Moral and Political* (two volumes, 1741–2) were somewhat better received. In 1745, he was considered for a professorship (of 'moral and pneumatical philosophy') at the University of Edinburgh. Although he was friendly with many of the more liberal clergy of Edinburgh, he was denied the chair because of the perceived anti-religious tenor of the Treatise. In the course of his candidacy, he wrote a pamphlet, published as *A Letter from a Gentleman to his Friend in Edinburgh*, rebutting theistically motivated objections to the book, including the charge of denying the causal maxim that every event has a cause.

Following the disappointment at Edinburgh, Hume took a position as a tutor and caretaker to the psychologically troubled young Marquis of Annandale, a post that lasted for a year. There followed several years travelling as an aide and secretary to General St Clair (a distant relative), first on a military expedition – for which Hume's reading in law allowed him to serve in the administration of military justice as Judge Advocate – that was originally projected to be against French Canada but was ultimately directed against the coast of France (1746), and then on a series of diplomatic missions to Vienna and Turin (1747–8). In 1748 he published *An Enquiry concerning Human Understanding* (cited here as EHU), which he later described as a 'recasting' of the material of Book I of A Treatise of Human Nature in response to his judgment that the poor reception of the *Treatise* had to do 'more with the manner than with the matter' ('My Own Life') of the earlier work. He did, however, affix an 'advertisement' in 1775 to his collected Essays and Treatises on Several Subjects – which included the Enquiry but not *A Treatise of Human Nature* – asking that his philosophy not be judged on the basis of 'that juvenile work'. This request was a response to the use of substantial quotations from the Treatise made by 'that bigotted silly Fellow, Beattie' (*The Letters of David Hume*

1932, Letter 509) in Beattie's highly critical and largely uncomprehending 1770 work, *An Essay on the Nature and Immutability of Truth* (see BEATTIE, J.).

Whereas the *Treatise* had aimed at a rich and intricate 'science of man', the *Enquiry* aimed at a more streamlined 'mental geography' that omitted many elements and complexities from Book I of the earlier work in order to focus on the explanation of causal inference and its application to a selection of other topics. The often dramatic and sometimes combative tone of the *Treatise* gave way to a more urbane and conciliatory tone in the *Enquiry*. For example, in the *Treatise* the defence of the 'doctrine of necessity' against the 'doctrine of liberty' concerning the will becomes in the Enquiry, through a simple terminological modification with no change of substantive position, a 'reconciling project' between the two doctrines. But while the *Enquiry* was rhetorically more conciliatory than the *Treatise*, it was at the same time much more directly subversive, for the three applications of his theory of causal inference on which Hume chose to concentrate – concerning the freedom and necessity of the will, rewards and punishments in an afterlife, and miracles – all had obvious anti-religious implications, and he described the goal of the work in its opening section precisely as that of disentangling philosophy from the grip of 'superstition'. Indeed the section of the *Enquiry* devoted to the topic of miracles – a topic that he had cautiously excised from the manuscript of the *Treatise* – soon became the most notorious piece of writing of his career (see MIRACLES). The year 1748 also saw the publication of his *Three Essays Moral and Political*; and at the end of the year, he returned from General St Clair's service to Ninewells.

In 1751, Hume published *An Enquiry Concerning the Principles of Morals* (cited here as EPM), a 'recasting' of Book III of the *Treatise* organized around the question of what constitutes virtue or personal merit, and a work that he later described as 'of all my writings, incomparably the best'. Anxious for a return to city life, he moved to Edinburgh and set up a household with his sister, Katharine. In the following year, he published *Political Discourses* (which included essays on topics in what would now be considered economics) and was again passed over for a professorship in philosophy – this time at the University of Glasgow, where his friend Adam SMITH was vacating the Chair of Logic to take up the Chair of Moral Philosophy. Hume was obliged to accept instead the position of Librarian of the Faculty of Advocates' Library (which developed into what is now the National Library of Scotland) in Edinburgh. The primary advantage of the position lay in the ready access it provided him to the library itself, which he used to write what

ultimately proved to be a very popular six-volume *History of England*, published between 1754 and 1762. While serving as Librarian, he also published, in 1753, *Essays and Treatises on Several Subjects*, a two-volume collection of his previously published work that enjoyed many editions, and, in 1757, *Four Dissertations*, consisting of 'The Natural History of Religion', 'Of the Passions', 'Of Tragedy' and 'Of the Standard of Taste'. ('Of the Standard of Taste', devoted to the topic of aesthetic judgment, was written to replace two essays – 'Of Suicide' and 'Of Immortality', both finally published only posthumously – that Hume cautiously decided at the last moment to suppress. He had first consented to their inclusion, in turn, in order to replace a dissertation on 'the metaphisical Principles of Geometry', now lost, that a friend had already convinced him to withdraw from the volume.) After completing sufficient research for his History, he resigned the librarianship in 1757. During the last several years of his term, he had been donating his salary to the blind Scottish poet Thomas Blacklock as the result of a dispute in which the library curators had rejected, on grounds of indecency, three French books that Hume had ordered.

In 1763, Hume was invited to serve as secretary to the British ambassador in Paris, Lord Hertford, and after some hesitation, he accepted. French intellectuals admired him for his philosophical scepticism and criticism of religion, his skill as a literary stylist and his sociable character; he was quickly lionized as 'le bon David' by French salon society. Among his friends were the *philosophes* DIDEROT, d'Alembert and Baron d'Holbach. When Lord Hertford took a new post in Ireland, Hume was left in charge of the embassy until the arrival of a new ambassador. When he returned to Edinburgh in 1766, mutual friends prevailed upon him to take the controversial philosopher Jean-Jacques ROUSSEAU (who was no longer welcome in Switzerland) to Britain with him. Hume arranged on Rousseau's behalf the rental of a country house in England. Rousseau soon grew unhappy and suspicious however, and attacked Hume's motives, publicly alleging (apparently on the basis of a satirical piece written by Hume's friend Horace Walpole) that Hume was trying to ruin his reputation. Hume responded, despite his dislike of literary controversies, by writing and circulating a defence of his conduct in the case.

From 1767 to 1769, Hume held a government post as Undersecretary of State for the Northern Department – a position that, ironically enough, required him to give formal government approval to ecclesiastical appointments in Scotland. He returned to his many friends in Edinburgh in 1769. In 1775, he became aware that he was suffering from intestinal cancer and he died the following year, composing in his final weeks the brief autobiographical essay 'My Own Life' ('this funeral oration of myself', he called it) and impressing all those around him with his cheerfulness and good humour in the face of his impending demise. He left behind the completed manuscript of his *Dialogues Concerning Natural Religion* – on which he had been working for many years and which he had meant to publish only posthumously – with a request that Adam Smith see to its publication. After Smith declined the request to publish the controversial work, it was published instead by Hume's nephew. Smith did, however, write a moving remembrance of Hume, which he concluded with these words: 'Upon the whole, I have always considered him, both in his life-time, and since his death, as approaching as nearly to the idea of a perfectly wise and virtuous man, as perhaps the nature of human frailty will permit.'

2   The contents and faculties of the mind

Hume calls all of the contents of the mind *perceptions*, which he distinguishes as *impressions* and *ideas*. Ideas differ as a class from impressions not in their intrinsic content or character but rather in their lesser 'force and vivacity': in sensing or feeling, the mind has impressions, while in thinking, it has ideas. (He thus uses the term 'idea' more narrowly than do Descartes and Locke, who use the term in a way roughly equivalent to Hume's use of 'perception'.) Perceptions – both impressions and ideas – may also be distinguished as *simple* and *complex*: the former have no perceptions as parts, whereas the latter are composed of simpler perceptions. These distinctions allow the formulation of one of Hume's most fundamental principles: that all ideas are either copied from resembling impressions or composed of simpler ideas that are copied from resembling impressions. He cites as evidence for this principle (sometimes called the *Copy Principle*) the mind's possession of simple ideas corresponding to its simple impressions, the temporal priority of impressions over their corresponding ideas, and the absence of ideas of particular kinds in the minds of those who have never had the corresponding impressions (THN 1.1.1; EHU 1). This principle plays a role in many of Hume's most important arguments on a wide variety of topics, and it also gives rise to a methodological directive: where the character of an idea is unclear or uncertain, trace it to the more forceful and vivacious impression from which it is derived in order to bestow clarity on the idea. Similarly, Hume argues, if one suspects that a term is being used without a meaning – that is,

without standing for any idea – the inability to find a corresponding impression may serve to confirm the suspicion.

Within the class of impressions, Hume draws a further distinction between *impressions of sensation* and *impressions of reflection*. The former, which include impressions of colour, taste, smell, sound, heat and touch, have immediate causes that are external to the mind. The latter, which include the passions, moral sentiments, aesthetic sentiments and other internal feelings of the mind, arise as a result of other perceptions, typically ideas – for example, hatred and anger may arise from thinking of pain or harm caused by another. Within the class of ideas, he distinguishes between those that are *particular* and those that are *abstract*. For although he asserts (against Locke and with George BERKELEY) that all ideas are fully determinate in their own nature, he maintains that an idea can acquire a general signification through its association with a word or term that disposes the mind to 'revive' or 'survey' similar ideas as needed in cognitive operations (THN 1.1.7). Such an idea thereby becomes an 'abstract' idea – what we would call a concept.

Abstract ideas, for Hume, may be of kinds of *substances*, *qualities* or *modes* of things, or of *relations* between things. Relations are respects in which two or more things may be compared. While he distinguishes seven general kinds of 'philosophical relations', relations of three of these kinds can also function as 'natural relations' – by which Hume means that the holding of the relation between things can serve as a natural principle of mental association, leading the ideas of the related things to succeed one another in the mind or be combined into complex ideas (such as those of substances). These 'natural relations' are *resemblance*, *contiguity in space or time*, and cause and effect. Whereas Locke had appealed to 'the association of ideas' chiefly to explain error and insanity, Hume dramatically expands its explanatory role in normal cognitive functioning so as to make it a kind of mental analogue of the fundamental Newtonian attractive force of gravitation, but one operating on perceptions rather than on bodies.

In the course of analyzing the operations of the human mind, Hume discusses a number of cognitive faculties. In addition to *sensation* and *reflection*, which are faculties for having impressions, Hume distinguishes two faculties for having ideas. *Memory* is a faculty for having ideas that retain not only the character but also the order and a large share of the original force and vivacity of the impressions from which they are copied. The *imagination*, in contrast, does not retain this large share of the force and vivacity of the original impressions and is not constrained to preserve their order; instead, the imagination can separate and recombine ideas freely. Because it is a faculty for having ideas, the imagination is, like memory, fundamentally a representational faculty. Such additional cognitive faculties as *judgment* and *reason* are nevertheless functions of the imagination, in Hume's view, because they ultimately constitute particular *ways of* having ideas. This, in turn, is because *belief* itself, in which judgment consists and which constitutes the characteristic outcome of reasoning, is itself a lower degree of force and vivacity, or "liveliness," below that of impressions and memory.

Notably absent from Hume's account of cognitive faculties is any further representational faculty of *intellect*, of the kind proposed by such philosophers as Descartes, Malebranche, Spinoza, Leibniz – that is, a representational faculty whose representations are not derived from sensory or internal experience and which can serve as the basis for a higher kind of cognition than mere experience can provide. Hume's adoption of the Copy Principle constitutes a rejection of such a faculty, for it commits him to accounting for all human cognition exclusively in terms of representations that are images of sensory and inner impressions.

While Hume uses the term 'imagination' in a wide sense to designate 'the faculty by which we form our fainter (that is, non-memory) ideas', he also carefully distinguishes a narrower sense of the term as well, according to which it is 'the same faculty, excluding only our demonstrative and probable reasonings'. *Demonstrative reasoning*, as he characterizes it, depends only on the intrinsic content of ideas; accordingly, whatever is demonstrated has a denial that is contradictory and literally inconceivable, and the result of demonstrative reasoning is *knowledge*, in a strict and technical sense derived from Locke. All other reasoning – resulting not in knowledge, in this technical sense, but in *probability* – is *probable reasoning*, the investigation of which is a central task of Hume's philosophical project. Given this narrower sense of 'imagination' as excluding reasoning, Hume can and often does ask whether a particular feature or content of the mind derives from the senses, reason or the imagination. One of the most general theses of the *Treatise* is that the character of human thought and action is determined to a very considerable extent by features of the imagination in this narrower sense.

In contrast to the understanding are the *passions*, which determine much of human conative nature. What Hume calls the direct passions – including joy, grief, desire, aversion, hope and fear – arise immediately from 'good or evil, pleasure or pain'; the indirect passions arise also arise from pleasure and pain, but 'by the conjunction of other qualities'.

Among the most important *indirect passions* are pride, humility, love and hatred. Each of these four indirect passions has a characteristic and natural *object*, either oneself (as in the case of pride and humility) or another person (as in the case of love and hate); this object is that to which the passion directs the thought of the person undergoing it. These indirect passions arise through a process of conversion (called 'the double relation of impressions and ideas'), whereby a pleasure or pain is transformed into a resembling passion when the cause of the pleasure or pain is closely associated with the object of the passion. Voluntary action, for Hume, is the result of *the will*, or volition, which is itself just another impression of reflection, typically prompted by desire or aversion - which may, in turn, be prompted by other passions. The *moral sentiments* of approbation and disapprobation arise from reflection on traits of character – ongoing motives, dispositions and tendencies – and constitute the source of moral distinctions, much as the sentiments of *beauty* and *deformity* constitute the source of aesthetic distinctions. Indeed, Hume characterizes virtue as a kind of 'moral beauty'.

3 Causal reasoning

Seventeenth- and eighteenth-century philosophers offered many different views of the nature and extent of causal power. Descartes, for example, held that causes must contain at least as much 'perfection' as their effects and that the laws of nature can be deduced from God's immutability, while Malebranche followed the suggestion of Descartes' doctrine that God's conservation of the universe is equivalent to continuous re-creation and the implications of the proposition that causes must be connected by necessity with their effects to propose that only God has genuine causal power. Spinoza held that the laws of nature could not have been otherwise and can be discerned by the intellect, while Leibniz denied the possibility of causal interaction between substances. Locke found some but not all kinds of substantial interaction to be unintelligible, while Berkeley held that the only causal power lies in the volition of minds, either divine or finite, to produce ideas.

Of the two kinds of reasoning that he distinguishes, it is probable reasoning, Hume holds, that predominates in human life, yet he finds that it has received relatively little investigation; and it is because it has been so little investigated, he thinks, that there is so much philosophical confusion concerning the nature and extent of 'the efficacy of causes'. All probable reasoning, he argues, depends on the relation of cause and effect: whenever we infer the existence of some matter of fact that goes beyond the content of present perceptions or memories, it is always on the basis of an implicitly or explicitly supposed causal relation between what is represented by a present perception or memory and the conclusion we draw from it (THN 1.3.2; EHU 4). Yet although all probable reasoning is thus also causal reasoning, the causal relation between distinct things or events seems itself difficult to understand: causes precede their effects in time and are spatially contiguous to them (at least when they have spatial locations at all), but we also suppose that causes and effects have a 'necessary connexion' of some kind. In order to understand fully what the causal relation is, Hume holds, we must first understand the nature of the probable inferences that 'discover' it.

Contrary to those who hold that causal relations can in principle be discerned through pure thought alone, by means of the intellect, Hume argues that the attribution of causal relations always depends essentially on experience – in particular, experience that an event of one kind is regularly followed by an event of a second kind, which he calls their 'constant conjunction'. Any event may be conceived to follow any other event (that is, the imagination can form an idea of it), and prior to experience there is no basis to suppose anything about what will actually follow a given event. Although it may well seem that some causal relations – such as the communication of motion by impact central to the 'mechanistic' natural science of the seventeenth and eighteenth centuries – are so 'natural' that we could anticipate them prior to any experience of them, this is only because early and constant experience has rendered them so very familiar. A probable inference occurs when, following experience of a constant conjunction of events of one type (such as the striking of a match) with events of another type (flame), an impression or memory of a particular event of the one type leads the mind to form a belief in the existence of an event of the other type. Hume's investigation of the way in which this mental transition occurs is the occasion for his famous discussion (originally presented in the *Treatise* (1.3.6) but repeated with slight variations in the *Abstract* and the first *Enquiry* (4)) of what we now call *induction* – that is, the projection that what has held true of observed cases will also hold true of as-yet-unobserved cases.

As a 'scientist of man', Hume asks how this transition actually occurs. He argues first for a negative conclusion: that the transition is not produced – or 'determin'd', as he puts it in the *Treatise* – by reason. His argument for the negative conclusion is as follows. The transition in question spans a gap between what the mind has *experienced* –

namely, past constant conjunction between two types of events plus a present impression or memory of an event of one of the two types – and what the mind *concludes*, which is the occurrence of another event of the other type, in conformity to the previously observed regularity. This transition he calls, variously, 'making the presumption' that 'the course of nature continues always uniformly the same', 'supposing that the future will resemble the past' and 'putting trust in past experience'. If reasoning were to cause this transition, Hume argues, it would do so through an inference to a *belief* that nature is uniform, for it is only a conclusion of this kind that could span the gap and so produce the inference. Yet what kind of reasoning could this be? The reasoning could not be demonstrative, for the denial of the uniformity of nature is in every case perfectly conceivable and involves no contradiction. Nor could the reasoning be probable, for, if Hume's previous account of that species of reasoning is correct, all probable reasoning can proceed only if it *already* makes the presumption of the uniformity of nature – which is the very presumption whose causal origin is to be explained. A probable inference thus cannot be the original cause of this presumption, for the making of the presumption is a precondition for all probable inference; and, as Hume puts it in the *Treatise*, 'the same principle cannot be both the cause and effect of another'. Since all reasoning is either demonstrative or probable, and neither demonstrative nor probable reasoning can cause its key transition, probable inference is not 'determin'd by reason'.

In interpreting this conclusion, it is important to recognize that Hume is not questioning whether probable inferences constitute a *species* of reasoning – as of course they do, by his own classification. Rather, he is questioning whether the key transition in such inferences is itself mediated by a *component* piece of reasoning – in something like the way that Locke regards some demonstrative inferences as mediated by other component demonstrative inferences concerning the relations between their parts – or whether the transition is instead made by some other process. It is also important to recognize that Hume's negative conclusion is one about the *causal origin*, rather than the epistemic warrant or justification, of probable inferences. Hume's argument does, however, have important consequences for questions of justification. For if the presumption of the uniformity of nature cannot originally arise from reasoning *at all*, then it cannot be justified by the *way* in which it originally arises from reasoning. Likewise, if the claim that induction will continue to be reliable is a claim of the kind that can only be supported by reasoning that presupposes that induction will continue to be reliable, then any argument intended to justify the claim that induction will continue to be reliable must beg the question, by presupposing what it seeks to establish. Thus, the much-discussed philosophical problem of how induction *can* be justified is rightly traced to Hume's discussion of probable inference.

Although the mind does not make the presumption of the uniformity of nature by *reasoning to a belief about* that uniformity, it does indeed make the presumption in another way, Hume argues – namely, through the mechanism of 'custom or habit', which is the general tendency of the mind to 'renew' a past operation or action without any 'new reasoning or reflection'. In the case of probable inference, the mind's experience of past constant conjunctions between two types of events is renewed when the mind, upon the impression or memory of an instance of one type, proceeds immediately, without further thought or reflection, to form an idea of an instance of the other. The force and vivacity of the present impression or memory provides a measure of force and vivacity to the idea as well – and this force and vivacity, or liveliness, constitutes the *belief* that the mind reposes in the existence of the object of the idea and serves to explain its ability to affect the will. This habit-based process – which is a feature of the imagination in Hume's narrower sense – thus produces a belief in the *conclusion* of a probable inference without any *intermediate* belief or reasoning about the uniformity of nature at all. Hume's description of this process constitutes his positive answer, complementing his negative answer, to the original question of the nature of the transition.

Hume follows Lockean terminology in characterizing as 'probability' every kind or degree of assurance other than the 'knowledge' that is based entirely on perceiving relations of ideas, but he recognizes that the assurance derived from inferences from experience can be firm and unhesitating. Accordingly, he goes on to distinguish, within the range of probability in the broad Lockean sense, between *proof*, which is the high degree of belief or assurance that results from a full and exceptionless experience of the constant conjunction of two types of events, and mere *probability* in a second and narrower sense. There are three philosophically-approved species of probability (THN 1.3.11-12) in this narrower sense: the *probability of causes*, in which two types of events have been commonly experienced to be conjoined but not exceptionlessly so or only in a small number of cases; the probability of chances, in which there is uniform experience that one of a set of alternatives will definitely occur (such as the landing of a die on one of its faces), but nothing determines the mind to expect one alternative rather than another on a given occasion,

so that each alternative acquires only a limited share of assent; and *analogy*, in which belief concerns events that are somewhat similar to, but not exactly resembling, those of which one has experienced a constant conjunction. In addition to these reflectively approved species of probability, Hume also distinguishes several species of *unphilosophical probability* (THN 1.3.13) – that is, ways in which features of the imagination affect the mind's degree of belief or assurance that, upon reflection, we do not approve. In addition, he specifies a set of 'rules by which to judge of causes and effects' (THN 1.3.15), rules that result from reflection on the mind's own operations in probable reasoning and on the successes and failures of past probable inferences. He thus offers a thorough, and provocative, account of non-demonstrative reasoning as always causal and always based on inductive projection from past experience.

4 Causal necessity

On the basis of his account of causal inference, Hume offers an explanation of the 'necessary connexion' of causal relations and provides two definitions of the term 'cause' (THN 1.3.14; EHU 7). It follows from the Copy Principle that, if we have an idea of necessary connection, that idea must be copied from some impression or impressions. When the mind first observes an event of one type followed by an event of another type, however, it never perceives any necessary connection between them; it is only after repeated experience that the mind pronounces them to be necessarily connected. Yet merely repeating the experience of the conjunction of two types of events cannot introduce any new impression into the mind from the objects themselves beyond what was perceptible on the first observation. The impression of necessary connection, from which the idea of necessary connection is copied, must therefore be an internal impression resulting from the respect in which the mind itself changes as the result of experience of constant conjunction. Accordingly, the impression of necessary connection is, Hume concludes, the impression of the mind's own determination to make an inference from an impression or memory to a belief. This impression is often then projectively mislocated in or between the cause and effect themselves, in much the same way that non-spatial tastes, smells and sounds are erroneously located in bodies with which they are associated. Causal relations have a kind of necessity – an unthinkability of the opposite – that is grounded in the psychological difficulty of separating two types of events in the imagination after they have been constantly conjoined in perception and in the impossibility of believing them actually to be separated. Because of the projective illusion by which the impression of necessary connection is mislocated in the objects, however, we often conflate this causal necessity, Hume explains, with the demonstrative necessity that results from intrinsic relations among ideas. The result, he claims, is philosophical confusion, in which we suppose that we can perceive a necessary connection, amounting to a demonstration, that is intrinsic to causes and effects themselves, and then become dissatisfied when we realize that, at least in some cases, we do not perceive such a connection after all. The dissatisfaction leads to disparate theories concerning how causal powers operate and to restrictions on the range of 'genuine' causal relations. The remedy for this confusion is to realize that we never make probable inferences as the result of perceiving a necessary connection between cause and effect, but rather, that we perceive the (internal impression of) necessary connection precisely because we are disposed to make the inference. Any two types of events are capable of standing in the causal relation to one another – 'to consider the matter a *priori*, any thing may produce any thing' (THN 1.4.5.30) – and only experience can show that which are actually causally related.

Following his account of causal reasoning and causal necessity, Hume defines 'cause' in the *Treatise* both as 'an object precedent and contiguous to another, and where all objects resembling the former are placed in like relations of precedency and contiguity to those objects, that resemble the latter' and as 'an object precedent and contiguous to another, and so united with it that the idea of the one determines the mind to form the idea of the other, and the impression of the one to form a more lively idea of the other' (THN 1.3.14.31; see also EHU 7.33). It may well seem that these two definitions do not serve to pick out the same objects as causes; for objects can be constantly conjoined in fact without being observed to be so, and objects can be taken by observers of unrepresentative samples to be constantly conjoined that are not really so conjoined. In fact, however, both definitions are ambiguous, and in parallel ways. The first definition may be understood either in a subject-relative sense (concerned with what has been conjoined in the observation of a particular subject) or in an absolute sense (concerned with what is constantly conjoined at all time and places). The second definition may likewise be understood either in a subject-relative sense (concerned with what is a basis for association and inference in the mind of a particular subject) or an absolute sense (concerned with what is a basis for association and inference in an idealized human mind that has observed a representative sample of the conjunction in question and reasons in the ways that are philosophically approved). The two definitions then coincide on their subject-relative interpretations – the interpretations that Hume needs when discussing how causal relations constitute a principle of association in individual human minds, which is a matter of what a human mind will *take* to be causally related. The two definitions coincide again on their absolute interpretations – the interpretations that he needs when discussing which pairs of events are in fact causally related. Both definitions are intended to specify the class of ideas of pairs of events that are (either in a particular human mind or ideally) collected under the abstract idea of the relation of cause and effect. If cause-and-effect pairs have something else in common beyond what is captured by these two definitions, it is something inconceivable by the human mind. Interpreters differ on the question of Hume's attitude towards the prospect of such an inconceivable 'something more' – some hold that he rejects it, while some hold that he allows it, and others hold that he assumes it. In any case, however, his conception of constant conjunction as necessary and sufficient for causation is one of the most influential ideas in the history of metaphysics.

5 Free will

The question of whether the human will is free or necessitated is one of the most pressing issues raised by the scientific revolution, one that is central to morality and to the conception of the place of human beings in nature. Hume applies his account of causal reasoning and causal necessity to its solution (THN 2.3.1-2; EHU 8). He holds that his two definitions of 'cause' determine the only two possible requirements for the causal necessity of human actions: (1) constant conjunction with particular types of antecedent conditions and (2) susceptibility to association-plus-inference. Since human actions of particular kinds are constantly conjoined with particular kinds of antecedent motives, character traits and circumstances, he argues, and since these constant conjunctions clearly can and do provide a basis for inference and association on the part of observers, it follows that human actions are causally necessitated. Hume himself is a determinist, holding – on the basis of induction from the past successes of natural science in finding determining causes for events – that every event results from previous conditions in accordance with exceptionless laws of nature. However, what he calls the 'doctrine of necessity' does not require determinism, but rather only the general predictability of human action. For his primary opponents are not indeterminists, but rather defenders (such as Samuel CLARKE) of a distinction between physical causes that necessitate their effects, on the one hand, and 'moral' causes (such as human motivations) that allegedly do not necessitate their effects, on the other. Since we do not feel the impression of necessary connection when we ourselves deliberate and act, Hume argues, we suppose that our own actions are not necessitated. But this conclusion is belied by the constant conjunction of these actions with motives, traits and circumstances, and by the fact that external observers do feel the impression of necessary connection when they predict or infer our actions.

Because we mistakenly suppose that there are two kinds of causation – necessitating and non-necessitating – we also suppose that there is a kind of freedom or 'liberty' that allows constant conjunction, thus supporting association and inference, without causal necessitation. In fact, however, this is impossible; and the only kind of 'liberty' that is opposed to necessity is the *liberty of indifference* or *chance* – that is, the absence of causation and hence of predictability. As a determinist, of course, Hume denies that there is in fact any liberty of indifference at all, although he regards this as a conclusion from experience; but he also denies that anyone would *wish* their actions to be a matter of chance, for then one's actions could stand in no causal relation to one's motives, character and circumstances. The kind of liberty that we do have and want, he argues, is the *liberty of spontaneity* that consists simply in the absence of constraint – that is, the power to have one's acting or not acting determined by one's will. Indeed, both causal necessity *and* the liberty of spontaneity are required for moral responsibility, for one cannot be blamed for what is not caused by one's character, nor for what is contrary to one's will. The fact that the human will is causally determined by motives, traits and circumstances that are themselves, in turn, causally determined by other factors not ultimately subject to the will does not, in Hume's view, interfere in any way with the kind of freedom required for moral responsibility. Hume's treatment of the topic of 'liberty and necessity' is one of the best-known defences of *compatibilism* – the view that the kind of freedom required for moral responsibility is compatible with the causal determination of human deliberation and action – and constitutes an important element in his attempt to integrate the study of human nature into the natural world.

In *An Enquiry concerning Human Understanding*, Hume also considers two 'objections' to religion derived from the bearing of causal necessity and moral responsibility on the doctrine that God is the ultimate cause of the entire universe. The first objection is that this doctrine absolves human beings of responsibility for their crimes, on the grounds that what God causally necessitates must be good; the second is that the doctrine requires us to deny the moral perfection of the deity and to 'acknowledge him to be the ultimate author of guilt and moral turpitude in all his creatures' (EHU 8.33). Against the first objection, Hume argues that we may properly blame human beings for character traits that evoke sentiments of moral disapprobation regardless of their more distant causes. The second objection, however, he pronounces to be beyond the power of human philosophy to resolve – thus, in effect, leaving the objection to stand against theistic cosmology and theodicy.

6 God

In addition to his treatment of free will and divine responsibility, Hume in the first *Enquiry* also draws important consequences from his theory of causal reasoning and causal necessity for the topic of testimony for miracles (EHU 10) – a kind of testimony that, Locke had argued, could provide strong evidence to support claims of divine revelation. Hume first draws from his account of probable inference the conclusion that experience must be our only guide concerning all matters of fact, and that the 'wise' will proportion their beliefs to the experiential evidence. Thus, where there is a proof (in the sense of a widespread and exceptionless experience), the wise place a full reliance; where there is only probability (in the narrow sense distinguished from proof), they repose only a more hesitating confidence. Accordingly, where a proof comes into conflict with a mere probability, the proof ought always to prevail. Hume then applies these general principles to the specific topic of testimony. Testimony cannot possess any inherent credibility independent of its relation to experience; rather, testimony of a particular kind properly carries weight only to the extent that one has experience of the reliability (that is, conformity to the truth) of that kind of testimony. Finally, Hume applies this principle about testimony, in turn, to the special case of testimony for the occurrence of a miracle, understood as a violation of a law of nature. Since regarding a generalization as a law of nature is to regard it as having a proof (in Hume's technical sense), it follows that to suppose an event to be a miracle is, ipso facto, to allow that there is a proof against its occurring. In consequence, testimony for a miracle cannot establish the occurrence of the miracle if there is only a probability, rather than a full proof, that the testimony is reliable. Rather, testimony could establish the occurrence of a miracle only if the falsehood of that testimony would itself be an even greater miracle – and even in that case, Hume remarks, there would be 'proof against proof', requiring one to look for some greater basis for credibility in one proof than in the other (such as might be found in its 'analogy' with yet other proofs) and resulting in at most a very hesitating acceptance of whichever proof was found to be stronger. In effect, then, Hume argues that one should always accept the least miraculous explanation available for the occurrence of testimony for a miracle.

After arguing for this very high general standard for the credibility of testimony for miracles, Hume goes on to consider the quality of actually existing testimony for miracles, the psychological mechanisms that stimulate the offering and acceptance of false testimony of religious miracles, the high proportion of miracle testimony originating among 'primitive and barbarous' peoples and the counteracting effect of testimony for miracles offered in support of conflicting religions. He concludes from this survey, first, that no actual testimony for miracles has ever met the standard required, nor, indeed, has ever even amounted to a probability; and second, that no testimony could ever render a miracle credible in such a way as to serve to establish the claims of a particular religion.

Another application of Hume's account of causation and causal reasoning in the first *Enquiry* concerns 'providence and a future state' (EHU 11) and is presented in the form of a dialogue between Hume and a 'friend'. Because observed constant conjunction provides the only basis for inferences concerning the unobserved, the friend argues, we cannot infer more in an unobserved cause than we have observed to be required for an observed effect; and hence a dilemma faces those who hold that the reasonable prospect of rewards and punishments in an afterlife provides an essential motive to moral behaviour. For if the present life is not so arranged as consistently to reward the good and punish the evil, then there is insufficient experiential basis to conclude that God will be any more concerned consistently to reward the good and punish the evil in the afterlife. If, on the other hand, the present life is so arranged that the good are consistently rewarded and the evil consistently punished, then the inference to similar rewards and punishments in an afterlife may be reasonable, but the conclusion will be unnecessary to motivate moral behaviour after all – for the present life itself will offer sufficient incentives in its own right. (It might, of course, be suggested that revelation provides a different and independent source of knowledge about the nature of the afterlife; but Hume has also implicitly attacked claims to have trustworthy divine revelation by attacking the credibility of testimony

for miracles used to support claims to revelation.) Hume's final remark in the dialogue raises the question of whether, given the uniqueness of the origin of the universe and our lack of experience regarding it, anything at all can be inferred about its cause.

Dialogues Concerning Natural Religion takes up this suggestion in detail, offering an application of Hume's theory of causal reasoning to examine what is often called the 'argument from design', or 'teleological' argument, for God's existence. The character of Demea – representing philosophical theologians such as Samuel Clarke – proposes that the existence of God can be deduced from the need for a necessarily existent being to serve as the cause of the series of contingently existing beings. However, the characters of Cleanthes (a theist who accepts the view that all causal claims can be established only by experience) and Philo (a sceptic who also accepts the view that causal claims can be established only by experience) reject the notion of necessary existence – since anything can be conceived either to exist or not to exist – and agree that a good argument for the existence of God must be based on empirical evidence that the universe is the product of intelligent design. Their dispute concerns the strength of such arguments. Since we have no experience of the creation of universes, Philo argues, we are in a poor position to assess their causes, and explaining the orderliness of the universe by appealing to the activity of an orderly divine mind seems to be an unnecessary step, for the order of the divine mind itself would equally require explanation. If we must speculate, however, there are many hypotheses possible, at least some of which seem to have the advantage over that of intelligent design. Perhaps, for example, the universe arose through a process of animal generation: experience provides many examples of that process giving rise to intelligence, but no examples of intelligence giving rise to the process of animal generation. Furthermore, if we do suppose that the evidence favours the hypothesis that the cause of the universe resembles a human designer, we cannot limit ourselves to the quality of intelligence but will be obliged to treat that cause anthropomorphically – as embodied, gendered, limited and plural, just as we find the designers of complex human artefacts to be.

Yet despite these objections Philo finds himself moved and even confounded by the immediate persuasive power of Cleanthes' statement of the argument from design, despite its 'irregular' character as judged by the standards of proper causal inference. Philo reports himself to be on psychologically stronger ground when he goes on to argue that the existence, nature and distribution of evils in the world renders it improbable that an intelligent cause of the universe, if there is one, is morally good or concerned to foster human wellbeing. None the less, Philo takes a notably conciliatory tone at the end of the *Dialogues*, conceding that 'the cause or causes of the universe probably bear some remote analogy to human intelligence'. This need not be considered a complete concession to Cleanthes, however, as he has earlier allowed that 'the rotting of a turnip' also bears some remote analogy to human intelligence. While strongly criticizing the pernicious consequences for human society of religious faction and superstition, Philo suggests that the dispute between theists and sceptics is a 'verbal' one, based to a considerable degree on differences of temperament: whereas theists empha- size the admitted analogies between the universe and known products of intelligent design, sceptics emphasize the admitted disanalogies. While com- mentators continue to dispute the extent to which Philo or Cleanthes can be taken to speak for Hume, it is generally agreed that the Dialogues provide a seminal critique of the argument from design.

7 The external world

The newly mechanistic natural science of the seventeenth and eighteenth centuries sharpened the question of what and how one can know of the external world through sensation. One of Hume's aims in the *Treatise* is to investigate 'what causes induce us to believe in the existence of body' (THN 1.4.2), although he remarks at the outset of the investigation that 'it is in vain to ask, Whether there be body or not? That is a point which we must take for granted in all our reasonings'. He analyses the belief in 'bodies' (physical objects) as the belief in objects that have a 'continu'd and distinct' existence: that is, in objects that continue to exist when not perceived by the mind and that have an existence that is distinct from the mind in virtue of existing outside of it and in causal independence of it with respect to their existence and operations. The 'vulgar' – which includes even philosophers, for most of their lives – attribute a continued and distinct existence to some of what they immediately perceive, even though what they immediately perceive are in fact impressions. The opinion that these impressions have a continued and distinct existence cannot itself be an immediate product of the senses, Hume argues, for the senses themselves cannot perceive the continuation when unper- ceived, or even the distinct existence of what they perceive immediately; nor can the opinion be a proper subject of inference, since reasoning shows instead that what we immediately perceive are not continued and distinct existences, but dependent

and perishing impressions in the mind. The opinion in question must, therefore, depend on features of the imagination (in the narrow sense).

How then does the belief in bodies arise? As Hume explains it, some of our impressions (for example, those of colour, sound, taste, smell and touch) exhibit *constancy* and *coherence*. Constancy is their tendency to return despite interruptions; coherence is their tendency to occur in a certain order and to manifest elements of that order at similar times even through interruption. The coherence of impressions plays a role in the tendency to attribute continued and distinct existence to those impressions, since by means of the supposition of such existence the mind can attribute greater causal regularity to them than would otherwise be possible – and once the mind becomes accustomed to looking for causal regula- rities, it carries this tendency on even beyond what it originally finds in experience. The primary cause of the attribution of continued and distinct existence to what are in fact impressions, however, is their constancy, Hume maintains. The mind easily confuses a 'perfectly identical' – that is, invariable and uninterrupted – object with a sequence of resembling but interrupted ones, because the feeling to the mind is itself similar in the two cases. Accordingly, the mind attributes a perfect identity to some of its interrupted impressions. At times when the mind becomes aware of the interruption, it seeks to reconcile the contradiction by supposing that the very impressions themselves continue to exist uninterruptedly, distinct from the mind, during the moments when they are not perceived. The force and vivacity of the impressions provides the liveliness required for this supposition to constitute a belief.

The vulgar opinion that the very things we immediately perceive have a continued and distinct existence apart from the mind is not, Hume argues, contradictory or inconceivable; but it can, none the less, easily be shown to be false by a few simple experiments. Pressing one's eyeball, for example, doubles one's visual impressions, thereby showing that they are not causally independent of the mind for their existence or operation, and from this it can be inferred that they do not continue to exist when not perceived. Yet the opinion that there are continued and distinct existences is, Hume asserts, psychologically so irresistible that, far from giving it up, philosophers invent a new theory to reconcile their experiments with it. This is the philosophical theory of 'double existence', according to which sensory impressions are caused by a second set of objects – bodies – that resemble them qualitatively. This theory, Hume argues, has no primary recommendation to the imagination – for the imagination naturally gives rise instead to the original vulgar view that our impressions themselves are continued and distinct. Nor does the theory have any primary recommendation to reason – for causal reasoning can conclude that an object of a given kind exists only if it has been observed to be constantly conjoined with an object of another kind, yet on the philosophical theory, we directly observe only impressions, not bodies accompanying impressions. When he considers intensely the causal origin of the belief in bodies, Hume reports that he loses confidence in the belief, his earlier claim that we must take it for granted notwithstanding. However, this state of doubt is only temporary, for belief in bodies (in one form or other) immediately returns as soon as one's attention is turned away from the question.

A further problem concerning the content of the belief in bodies arises from what Hume calls 'the modern philosophy' (THN 1.4.4). It is a central contention of the modern philosophy that such qualities as extension, solidity and motion really exist in bodies, but that qualities resembling our impressions of colours, sounds, tastes, smells and tactile qualities (such as heat and cold) do not really exist in bodies. This is, for example, Locke's claim concerning what he calls 'primary' and 'secondary' qualities. Hume judges that there is, among the various arguments of the modern philosophers for this conclusion, one that is 'satisfactory'. It is found that the perception of colour, sound, taste, smell, heat and cold varies with different perspectives and different states of one's body; and hence it follows that bodies cannot have all of the qualities of colour, sound, taste, smell, heat or cold that they are perceived to have. Hence, he argues, from the principle (which is one of his 'rules by which to judge of causes and effect') that 'like effects have like causes', we may conclude that none of these qualities exist in bodies themselves. Yet the qualities of extension, solidity and motion of bodies cannot be conceived without conceiving colours or tactile qualities to fill the extension of the body in which they supposedly occur; hence, it follows that bodies cannot be determinately conceived at all in strict accordance with the modern philosophy. Since this 'satisfactory' argument is a causal one, Hume presents the outcome as a conflict between causal reasoning and 'our senses' – meaning by the latter term, more specifically, the operations of the imagination on impressions of sensation that give rise to the belief in bodies.

8 Personal identity

The second edition of Locke's *An Essay Concerning Human Understanding* (1694) offers an account of the nature of personal identity as grounded not in identity of substance but in 'sameness of consciousness' derived from memory, The account stimulated considerable discussion and controversy, and Hume, in the Treatise takes up the question of personal identity that 'has become so great a question in philosophy, especially of late years, in England' (THN 1.4.6). He rejects the proposal that we are constantly aware of a 'self' that is simple and 'perfectly identical' (that is, invariable and uninterrupted) through time. We have no idea of such a self, Hume argues, appealing to the Copy Principle, for we have no impression of it. Nor can we conceive how our particular perceptions could be related to a substantial self or mind so as to inhere in it, for the supposed concept of a substance in which qualities or perceptions inhere is a mere fiction, invented to justify the association-based tendency to think of what is really a plurality of related but changing qualities or perceptions as having something that bestows simplicity at a time and perfect identity through time on them. Instead, Hume finds, we are aware only of the sequence of perceptions themselves; as he famously puts it, 'when I enter most intimately into what I call myself, I always stumble on some particular perception or other, of heat or cold, light or shade, love or hatred, pain or pleasure. I never can catch myself at any time without a perception, and never can observe any thing but the perception' (THN 1.4.6.3). Accordingly, 'the true idea of the human mind' is that of a 'bundle' of different perceptions related by causation in such a way as to 'mutually produce, destroy, influence, and modify each other'. Because memory reproduces the intrinsic content of earlier perceptions, there is also a considerable degree of resemblance among these perceptions. These perceptions come to constitute an 'imperfect' or 'fictitious' identity, Hume explains, because their many close associative relations of causation and resemblance cause them, when surveyed in memory, to be mistaken for a perfect identity. He draws from this a corollary that has negative implications for immortality and the justice of rewards and punishments in the afterlife – namely, that 'all the nice and subtle questions concerning personal identity can never be decided' because such questions are merely 'grammatical', involving relations susceptible of insensibly diminishing degrees (THN 1.4.6.21).

In the Appendix to the *Treatise* (published with its second volume, containing Book 3), however, Hume expresses dissatisfaction with his previous account of the relations giving rise to personal identity. Because his diagnosis of the problem remains quite general, many interpretations have been offered of the precise basis of his dissatisfaction.

One possible source of dissatisfaction is that his own account of causality, as expressed in his definitions of 'cause', entails that simultaneous and spatially unlocated but qualitatively identical perceptions cannot differ in their causal relations, so that two such perceptions could not exist in two different minds if his account of the 'true idea of the human mind' were correct. In any case, he pronounces the difficulty a further ground for scepticism – that is, for entertaining 'a diffidence and modesty in all my decisions'.

9 Scepticism

As the scientific revolution of the seventeenth century brought a decline in the authority of Aristotle, it also brought renewed interest in ancient scepticism (including Pyrrhonism and the scepticism of the later Academy), and Descartes' methodological scepticism in the *Meditations* helped to make a concern with scepticism central to philosophy. Hume's strategy in the *Treatise* is to complete an investigation of human cognitive faculties, by means of those faculties, before turning to the question of whether the nature of the discoveries made undermines confidence in those faculties themselves. Thus, at the conclusion of Book I of the *Treatise* (THN 1.4.7), Hume surveys a number of considerations conducive to scepticism (to which the additional problem about personal identity from the Appendix to the *Treatise* constitutes an *ex post facto* addition). At the conclusion of the first *Enquiry*, he again surveys and assesses sceptical considerations, although the list only partially overlaps that of the *Treatise*.

Of the general sceptical considerations concerning human cognition (beyond personal susceptibilities to error) reviewed at the conclusion of the *Treatise*, the first lies in the dependence of belief on the 'seemingly trivial' quality of the imagination whereby ideas acquire force and vivacity from impressions by means of probable reasoning, memory and the senses. (It is only here, incidentally, long after his famous account of probable or inductive reasoning, that he draws any connection between it and scepticism in the *Treatise*.) The second lies in the 'contradiction' between causal reasoning and the belief in bodies, with specific qualities, discovered in connection with 'the modern philosophy'. The third consists in the illusion whereby the mind supposes that it discovers real necessary connections intrinsic to causes and effects themselves, even though such connections are in fact inconceivable.

The final sceptical consideration depends on an argument that Hume had earlier discussed in a section entitled 'Of scepticism with regard to

reason' (THN 1.4.1). Since reason is a kind of cause, he observes, of which truth is the usual but not unfailing effect, every judgment, with whatever degree of assurance it is held, may be assessed, on the basis of past experience, for the probability that one's faculties operated well – that is (presumably) did not produce too high a degree of assurance – in reaching that judgment. Yet even if one concludes with a high degree of assurance that one's faculties operated well in the initial judgment, one will find at least some low degree of probability that one's original assurance was too high; and this realization should serve to decrease somewhat the original assurance of the first judgment. Furthermore, he argues, a *third* judgment concerning the operation of one's faculties in the *second* judgment will likewise find at least some low degree of probability that one's assurance in making the second judgment – namely, the judgment that one's original assurance in the first judgment was not too high – was *itself* too high. This realization, Hume argues, should properly reduce the assurance of the second judgment – which should, in turn, again reduce further the assurance of the first judgment. Since this process may properly be reiterated indefinitely, and the amount of assurance available in any judgment is finite, the result should, in accordance with the natural operations of the 'probability of causes', be the elimination of all belief.

No such elimination of belief actually occurs, however, even when one aims to employ the probability of causes as scrupulously as possible. Hume explains this phenomenon through appeal to another 'seemingly trivial quality' of the imagination' – the unnatural ascent to higher levels of reflection strains the mind and prevents the successive reflexive reasonings from having their usual effects. When he first considers the question of reason's reflexive subversion of belief, he dismisses the question of whether he is himself a total sceptic on the grounds that such scepticism cannot be maintained with any constancy, and instead takes the argument as confirmation for his theory that belief consists in vivacity – for this best explains how the trivial quality of the imagination prevents the annihilation of belief.

Nevertheless, the conclusion that causal reasoning would, unless prevented by a seemingly trivial feature of the imagination, naturally annihilate all belief is unquestionably a disturbing one; and Hume returns to it, at the conclusion of his recital of sceptical considerations near the end of Book 1, in order to formulate what he calls a 'dangerous dilemma'. The dilemma is this: if we reject the trivial quality of the imagination that saves reason from its own reflexive self-subversion, then we must allow that all belief should be rejected; yet if we accept the trivial quality of the imagination by making it a principle to reject all 'refined and elaborate arguments', we cut off much of science (which also depends on elaborate arguments); we must, on grounds of parity, accept all other features of the imagination as well, even those that clearly lead to illusion; and we contradict ourselves, for the argument supporting the need to reject refined and elaborate arguments is itself a refined and elaborate argument. The immediate result of this dilemma, Hume reports, is a state of intense and general doubt.

This intense general doubt constitutes a 'philosophical melancholy and delirium' that cannot be removed by argument but is naturally unsustainable. It is naturally succeeded, Hume reports, by a mood of 'indolence and spleen', in which an irresistible return to belief and reasoning concerning matters of ordinary life is combined with a disposition to avoid philosophizing, which has resulted in such discomfort. He thus finds himself operating in accordance with the principle (sometimes now called the *Title Principle*): 'Where reason is lively and mixes itself with some propensity, it ought to be assented to. Where it does not, it can have no title to operate on us'. Yet the state of indolence and spleen itself proves, in turn, to be unstable. For Hume finds naturally arising within him a renewed curiosity concerning philosophical topics and an ambition to contribute to the instruction of mankind and make a name for himself by his discoveries; and his return to philosophy is confirmed by the reflection that philosophy is a safer guide to speculation than is religion. He thus finds that the Title Principle, although originating in indolence and spleen, actually supports philosophical enquiry. Indeed, it avoids the 'dangerous dilemma' and provides a principle of belief that he can normatively endorse. For it allows him to discount the 'unlively' reasoning of the indefinitely iterated probability of causes that would gradually eradicate belief while nevertheless accepting 'refined and elaborate arguments' on topics of interest to him (arguments which thereby 'mix with some propensity'). His continuing awareness of the 'infirmities' of human cognitive nature that he has discovered produce a spirit of moderate scepticism – a 'diffidence' in judgment – but he regards those infirmities themselves with diffidence and endorses assent to his faculties (as corrected by reflection), ready to continue the investigations of his science of man into the passions and morals.

At the conclusion of the first *Enquiry*, Hume distinguishes between *antecedent scepticism* and *consequent scepticism*. Antecedent scepticism, which he identifies with the methodological scepticism of Descartes, is scepticism that occurs prior to the investigation of our faculties. It recommends beginning enquiry with universal doubt, even concerning the use of one's faculties, until those faculties have been validated by reasoning from a principle that cannot possibly be fallacious. Hume rejects this kind of scepticism on the grounds that no one self-evident principle is more certain than others and that no reasoning from such a principle could take place except by means of the very faculties that are supposed to be in doubt. (He does, however, endorse a more moderate antecedent scepticism consisting simply in antecedent caution and impartiality.) Consequent scepticism, in contrast, is scepticism that arises from the results of an investigation of our faculties, and Hume's own scepticism is of this kind. The results that he cites concern *the senses*, *abstract* (that is, demonstrative) *reasoning* and *moral evidence* (that is, probable reasoning). The consideration of sensory errors and illusions, he remarks, is a 'trite' topic of scepticism, and shows only that the first appearances of the senses often stand in need of correction. A more 'profound' sceptical consideration is a feature of the belief in bodies previously explained in the *Treatise*: namely, that the original version of this belief, identifying impressions themselves as continued and distinct existences, can be shown to be false, while the theory postulating that bodies are the causes of sensory impressions cannot be supported by causal reasoning based on observed constant conjunction. A further 'profound' topic, also presented in the *Treatise*, lies in the 'contradiction' between causal reasoning and the belief in bodies that arises from 'the modern philosophy'. The consideration concerning abstract reasoning lies in mathematical demonstrations of the infinite divisibility of extension, which Hume regards as paradoxical. (He refers in a footnote to the theory of extension he had proposed in the *Treatise*, according to which finite extensions are composed of finite numbers of unextended minima, as capable of resolving this paradox.) A 'popular' objection to moral or probable reasoning lies in the vast diversity of opinions among humankind. A more 'philosophical' objection, however, lies in the recognition that we have no argument to convince us that what we have observed to be constantly conjoined in our experience will continue to be so conjoined; only a natural instinct that leads us to make this supposition. The *Enquiry* omits discussion of reasoning's reflexive annihilation of belief, and hence also of the 'dangerous dilemma' that it posed. Nor is there any mention of the Title Principle, of the stage of 'indolence and spleen' that gave rise to it, or the role of curiosity and ambition in motivating a return to philosophy. There is, however, a distinction between 'Pyrrhonian' or 'excessive' scepticism, on the one hand, and 'Academic' or 'mitigated' scepticism on the other. Intense contemplation of sceptical considerations naturally produces a 'tincture' of Pyrrhonian scepticism that is useful in moderating dogmatic self-confidence. Were Pyrrhonian doubt to remain constant, however, it would destroy human life by preventing action. Fortunately, however, the sources of belief in human nature are too powerful to allow this to occur, and the natural outcome of reflection on sceptical considerations is a more durable Academic scepticism that consists in a certain diffidence, modesty and lack of dogmatism in all one's judgments plus a determination to refrain from all 'high and distant enquiries' beyond our faculties – such as cosmological speculation concerning 'the origins of worlds' – that have no connection to 'common life'. Hume in the *Enquiry* recommends and endorses this mitigated scepticism, which he judges to be socially useful, he with a rousing call for the elimination of scholastic metaphysics and theology not based on mathematical or experimental reasoning : 'Commit it then to the flames: for it can contain nothing but sophistry and illusion'.

In order to characterize Hume's scepticism, it is useful to distinguish several different dimensions in which scepticism can vary. One of these is its *scope* – that is, the range of propositions to which it applies. Another is its *character* – that is, whether it consists in actual doubt, in a normative injunction to doubt, in a theoretical claim that a proposition lacks support through reasoning, or in a claim that a proposition lacks epistemic merit. A third is its *degree* – that is, whether it is unmitigated or mitigated. A fourth is its *basis* – that is, whether it is antecedent to enquiry or consequent to it. A fifth is its *constancy* – that is, whether it is constant or variable. In these terms, all of Hume's scepticism appears to be consequent to enquiry. He both engages in and recommends a mitigated doubt concerning all topics, as well as unmitigated doubt concerning 'high and distant' enquiries. The actual doubt in which he engages with respect to other topics is somewhat variable – potentially unmitigated in rare moments when intensely considering sceptical topics, and sometimes entirely absent in moments of special conviction. He unmitigatedly rejects the claim that the uniformity of nature and the belief in bodies *originate* with support through reasoning. But he is not committed to the view that only propositions produced or supported by reasoning have epistemic merit. On the contrary, as his endorsement of the Title Principle and his preference for 'wise' beliefs over unphilosophical probability indicate, his mitigated scepticism about the epistemic merit of beliefs generally allows him to hold that many beliefs have some degree of epistemic merit.

10 Motivation

Philosophers from PLATO to Spinoza have recommended actions motivated by reason rather than passion. Hume argues, however, that just as reason cannot produce the key transition in probable inference or the belief in an external world of bodies, so too reason alone cannot determine the will to act. His primary argument (THN 2.3.3) is as follows. All reasoning is either demonstrative or probable. Because demonstrative reasoning discovers only relations of ideas – primarily mathematical relations – and does not discover the actual existence or non-existence of things, it cannot motivate any action directly, but affects action only by facilitating the mathematical formulation and application of causal generalizations. Probable reasoning, which discovers causal relations themselves through experience, can serve to direct action by showing the means to a desired end, but cannot alone motivate it. For as long as objects do not affect one's passions (including desire and aversion), the will remains indifferent to their causal relations. Furthermore, since reason could oppose an operation of the will only by providing a contrary motivation, reason can never oppose passion in the direction of the will. Hence, Hume declares, 'reason is, and ought only to be, the slave of the passions, and can never pretend to any other office than to serve and obey them'.

In further support of this conclusion, Hume argues that passions are 'original existences' lacking any representative quality, and hence cannot be opposed to the claims to truth produced by reasoning. Reason can never oppose a passion, but only a judgment accompanying a passion. Where a passion concerns an object judged to exist but which does not really exist, or where action takes particular form due to a false belief that something stands as a causal means to a desired end, the passion itself may be called 'unreasonable', but only in an improper sense, for it is the accompanying judgment that is unreasonable. The appearance that reason and passion can struggle for the determination of the will results largely from the existence of 'calm passions' – such as the general appetite to pleasure and aversion to evil as such – that feel, in their operation, much like the calm operations of reason.

Hume is sometimes characterized as holding a limited conception of 'practical reason': namely, that passions determine one's ends, and that the only form of practical reasoning is the generation of new desires or actions from given ends and beliefs about the means to those ends. On this view, then, one acts irrationally only when one fails to pursue the means to one's ends. In fact, however, Hume rejects even this limited conception. For him, the outcome of reasoning itself is belief, not desire or action; and although reasoning can, in concert with other aspects of one's nature, contribute to the production of new desires and actions, this process of production is not itself one of reasoning. While Hume regards failing to take the acknowledged means to one's ends as folly and subject to criticism, therefore, it is only in an improper sense 'irrational'.

11 The foundations of morality

Many of Hume's predecessors – like his successor KANT and many others – held that moral distinctions are made by reason. According to Clarke, for example, morality was a matter of relations of 'fittingness' that could be discerned and demonstrated, like geometrical relations, through reason. Hume denies that moral distinctions are derived from reason alone. For this, he offers three arguments in the *Treatise* (THN 3.1.1). The first argument concerns the non-representational character of the objects of moral evaluation. Reason is a kind of discovery of truth or falsehood, which is a relation of agreement or disagreement that ideas have either to other ideas or to 'real existence and matters of fact'. Because passions, volitions and actions are non-representational, however, they are not subject to such agreement or disagreement, and hence cannot be either contrary or conformable to reason. The second argument concerns the motivational force of moral distinctions. Since morals have an immediate influence on action and affections, while reason alone has already been shown to have no such influence, Hume argues, it follows that morals cannot be derived from reason alone. The third argument involves Hume's familiar strategy of surveying the kinds of reasoning. Moral distinctions cannot be derived from demonstrative reason, he claims, since all demonstrative reasoning depends on four of the philosophical relations of ideas – resemblance, contrariety, degrees of a quality, or proportion in quantity or number. If there is some further relation that can serve as a basis for the drawing of moral distinctions by demonstration alone, it must first be discovered; and, furthermore, it must be shown both how it can be limited to the relations between the mind and external objects (as morality is) and how it can provide motivation to any being capable of demonstrative reasoning (since morality is inherently motivating). Yet moral distinctions also cannot be derived from probable reasoning, for the virtue or vice of an action does not appear merely upon reasoning concerning matters of fact about the action; rather, it becomes apparent only upon turning one's attention to one's own sentiments.

Hume's investigation of the causal basis of the key transition in probable inferences yields first a negative answer – 'not reason' – and then a positive answer: 'custom or habit'. So, too, his investigation of the origin of moral distinctions yields first a negative answer – 'not reason alone' – and a positive answer. The positive answer, in this case, is 'a moral sense'. The moral sense consists in the capacity to feel specific sentiments of moral approbation and moral disapprobation when considering a person's character 'in general' – that is, as it affects persons considered generally, independently of one's own self-interest.

In some cases, a trait may produce approbation or disapprobation immediately, but typically it does so through *sympathy* with those who are affected by it – either its possessor or others, or both. Sympathy is, like probable inference, a mechanism by which perceptions are enlivened. In sympathy, however, one infers from circumstances or behaviour the feelings and sentiments of others, and this lively idea constituting belief that another person has a given feeling or sentiment is further enlivened by the current impression of oneself, as a result of the associative relation of resemblance between one's idea of the other person and one's idea or impression of oneself. The result is that the belief itself rises to the level of an impression, so that one sympathetically feels the other person's inferred state of mind oneself. Thus, when an individual has a character trait that produces pleasure for the individual or for others affected by that individual, an observer feels sympathetic pleasure, which then causes in the observer the further pleasant sentiment of moral approbation; when an individual has a feature of character that produces pain for the individual or others affected by that individual, the observer feels sympathetic pain, which then causes the further unpleasant sentiment of moral disapprobation.

As these sentiments give rise to abstract ideas, features of character producing moral approbation come to be called 'virtues' and those producing moral disapprobation come to be called 'vices'. Actions, in turn, are considered virtuous or vicious in so far as they are manifestations of virtuous or vicious character traits. Accordingly, Hume offers two definitions of 'virtue' or 'personal merit' parallel to his two definitions of 'cause': virtue is 'every quality of the mind, which is useful or agreeable to the person himself or to others' (EPM 9.12) or 'whatever mental quality gives to a spectator the pleasing sentiment of approbation' (EPM Appendix 1.11). Actual moral sentiments may vary with the strength of one's sympathy, itself partly a function of one's distance, in various respects, from the individual evaluated and to those affected by the individual. In order to reconcile differences of sentiment among individuals and within the same individual at different times, we naturally come to 'correct' for peculiarities of perspective, much as we correct our judgments of sensory and aesthetic qualities. In the case of moral qualities, we do so by taking up imaginatively a 'general point of view' as the proper perspective from which to make moral judgments.

In claiming that moral distinctions are derived from a moral sense and not from reason alone, Hume is not denying that reasoning plays an essential role in the drawing of moral distinctions. Reasoning is required to determine the character traits of others, and reasoning is required in order to determine the likely effects of those traits on the possessor and others. Reasoning may also be required to determine what one's sentiments would be from 'the general point of view' when one is not actually occupying it. Although he is often interpreted as an expressivist non-cognitivist in ethics – that is, as holding that moral judgments express sentiments and are not strictly susceptible of truth or falsehood, his account of the 'correction' of moral sentiments through the 'general point of view' in the construction of abstract ideas of vice and virtue leaves room for a cognitivist interpretation as well, making the moral sense more closely analogous to senses for other qualities.

For Hume, as for ancient virtue ethicists, the primary object of evaluation is personal character, rather than actions, and the primary terms of moral evaluation are 'virtuous' and 'vicious', rather than 'right' and 'wrong' or 'good' and 'bad'. Because he maintains that moral distinctions depend on sentiment rather than on reason alone, Hume rejects the ideal of a morality that would have to be accepted by any rational being; and, indeed, he emphasizes that there is no reason to suppose that an intelligent deity would have the same moral sense as human beings. Morality, for Hume, is inherently motivating, to those who have a moral sense, because the moral sentiments themselves are pleasures and pains, and, as such, they also readily give rise to pride or love (which are further pleasures) and humility or hatred (which are further pains). He fully approves of morality, for the moral sense bestows approbation both on the having of a moral sense and on its own operations. At the same time, however, he treats morality as a natural phenomenon to be understood by the science of man. Indeed, he holds that by understanding the basis of morality in human nature, one is better equipped to reflectively improve one's moral evaluations (recognizing, for example, that the 'monkish virtues' such as celibacy, fasting, mortification and self-denial are not truly virtues) and to recommend morality more persuasively to others.

12 Political obligation

In his *Second Treatise of Government*, Locke grounds the political obligation to obey and sustain one's government in a social contract, a mutual promise by which individuals pool some of their natural rights in a civil society in order to better protect their property. The obligation to keep promises and to respect property, in turn, together with the basic rules that determine the acquisition of property, are features of Natural Law. While sympathetic to Locke's aim of justifying resistance to tyrannical governments that fail to protect citizens and their property, Hume offers accounts of the political obligation to obey and sustain government (which he calls *allegiance*), the obligation to respect property (which he calls *justice*), the obligation to keep promises (which he calls *fidelity*) and the relations among them, that are very different from Locke's.

Hume distinguishes *artificial virtues*, which depend on artifice and convention, from *natural virtues* (such as benevolence, cheerfulness, prudence and industry), which do not (THN 3.2). A 'convention' between two or more individuals does not demand an explicit promise; rather, it requires a presumed sense of common interest in a coordinated course of action, and an expressed and mutually understood determination to act in accordance with that coordinated course of action on the condition that others will do so as well. Rights to property and the rules that govern its acquisition are not inscribed in a pre-conventional law of nature, but rather arise as the result of a convention to protect the stability of actual possession (that is, control of goods), a convention that is originally motivated by the self-interest of all those involved. Recognition of the usefulness to the general public of the character trait of abiding by the rules of property, however, and sympathy with all those who benefit from it, causes the trait to be recognized as a virtue (THN 3.2.2). Promise making, too, arises as the result of a convention motivated by self-interest, one that allows the coordination of non-simultaneous exchanges of benefits by instituting a form of words that commits one to perform future benefits on pain of subsequent exclusion from the valuable convention in the event of non-compliance. The character trait of promise keeping, like that of obedience to the rules of property, comes to be approved as a virtue through sympathy with the broad range of those benefiting from the trait (THN 3.2.5).

The need for conventions of property and promise keeping in order to provide stable possession and mutual exchange of benefits, respectively, will lead to their invention and institution even within individual families and very small societies, Hume holds. In such circumstances, violators are, for the most part, easily detected and effectively sanctioned. Governments arise – often beginning with deference to a chieftain who has been a leader during war-time – as a convention to maintain the rules of property and promise keeping in larger societies by making it directly in the interests of some individuals to enforce those rules impartially. The convention of deferring to a chieftain for governance may indeed often originate in a promise among the members of a society. However, the obligation of citizens to allegiance is grounded, Hume argues, not in any original promise of the founders of government, nor (as Locke allowed) in a 'tacit' promise or consent on the part of current citizens, but rather on the general utility of allegiance, which gives rise to sympathetic pleasure and hence moral approbation (THN 3.2.7–8). Justice, fidelity and allegiance are all artificial virtues, each depending for its existence on a distinct convention, and the virtuousness or moral obligation of each has a similar but distinct basis in social utility. The obligation to allegiance stands on its own, and need not be derived from other obligations that themselves have a similar basis. Where a government becomes so tyrannical that it ceases to provide security and other benefits to its citizens, Hume allows, the moral obligation to obey and sustain the government naturally ceases. Although he has a lively sense – evident in his *History of England* – of the dangers of anarchy and the preferability of even quite imperfect governors to it, he is also a staunch defender of the importance to a society of free thought and expression.

13 Hume's legacy

Every philosophical generation since Hume has been obliged to understand itself in relation to his philosophy. Scottish common-sense philosophers (see COMMON SENSE SCHOOL) such as Thomas REID read it as a demonstration that Locke's 'way of ideas', according to which we can be directly aware only of the contents of our own minds, led inevitably to scepticism and must be rejected. Kant famously proclaimed that he had been 'awakened from his dogmatic slumbers' by the challenge of Hume's treatment of the concept of causation and took his own transcendental idealism to be the only way to avoid Humean scepticism. Utilitarians took inspiration from his emphasis on the essential relation of morality to what is useful

and agreeable. British Idealists such as T.H. GREEN and F.H. BRADLEY took Hume to be a prime example of the dangers of an atomistic and sensation-based account of the capacities of mind. The logical positivists of the early twentieth century saw Hume's concern to trace the content of concepts to their experiential basis as a precursor of their own methodology – which they regarded as properly purged of Hume's conflation of philosophy and psychology. To broadly empiricist and naturalistic philosophers of the present era, Hume's philosophy is a powerful example of the effort to integrate the scientific understanding of human cognitive and conative nature into the scientific understanding of nature itself, to account for the normativity of reason and morals within the structure of that understanding, and to turn that understanding on to the understanding of philosophizing itself. Now widely regarded as the greatest philosopher to write in English, perhaps no philosopher of the early modern period has proven to be of greater relevance or importance to contemporary philosophy than Hume. The best evidence of this is the number of topics – from concepts to causation, from induction to the emotions, from scepticism to free will, from theology to practical reason, from morality to politics – on which a 'Humean' approach is one of the primary live options.

See also: CAUSATION; INDUCTION, EPISTEMIC ISSUES IN; MORAL MOTIVATION; MORAL SENSE THEORIES; PERSONAL IDENTITY

References and further reading

Bailie, J. (2000) *Hume on Morality*, London: Routledge. (A good concise introduction to Hume's theory of morality and the passions.)
Noonan, H.W. (1999) *Hume on Knowledge*, London: Routledge. (A good concise introduction to Hume's epistemology.)
Stroud, B. (1977) *Hume*, London: Routledge & Kegan Paul. (Still one of the very best and philosophically most astute commentaries on Hume's philosophy.)

DON GARRETT

HUMOUR

What is meant by saying that something is humorous or funny? It is clear that humorousness must be elucidated in terms of the characteristic response to humour, namely humorous amusement, or mirth. It is plausible to define humour in this way: for something to be humorous is for it to be disposed to elicit mirth in appropriate people through their awareness or cognition of it, and not for ulterior reasons. But this invites the question, 'What is mirth?' The three leading ideas in philosophical theories of humour are those of incongruity, superiority and relief or release. Although the perception of incongruity is often involved in finding something funny, and the resolution of a perceived incongruity plays an important role in good humour, none of these, in themselves or combined with others, is capable of capturing the concept of mirth. Mirth is not identical with the pleasurable perception of an incongruity, pleasure in feeling superior, the relief of tension or release of accumulated mental energy, or any combination of these elements. A better account of mirth is that it is a certain kind of pleasurable reaction which tends to issue in laughter if the reaction is sufficiently intense. So something is funny if it in itself pleases appropriate people through being grasped, where the pleasure is of the sort that leads, though not inevitably, to laughter.

See also: BERGSON, H.-L.; COMEDY; EMOTION IN RESPONSE TO ART; TRAGEDY

JERROLD LEVINSON

HUS, JAN (*c*.1369–1415)

From his appointment as rector of the Bethlehem chapel in Prague in 1402 until his execution at the Council of Constance in 1415, Jan Hus advanced the goals of an ecclesiastical reform movement with Czech national overtones. Hus' ministerial and academic posts provided a broad platform for his leadership. He preached tenaciously against clerical abuses. At the University of Prague he taught philosophical and ecclesiological doctrines which, his opponents charged, were taken from the radical Oxford reformer, John Wyclif. Whereas Wyclif's philosophical realism (for example, the indestructibility of 'being') led him to adopt several positions condemned as heretical, Hus' polemic, in which he castigated the fiscalization and bureaucratization of the papacy, sprang more from his ideals of evangelical minority and apostolic poverty.

See also: LUTHER, M.; PREDESTINATION; WYCLIF, J.

CURTIS V. BOSTICK

HUSSERL, EDMUND (1859–1938)

Introduction

Through his creation of phenomenology, Edmund Husserl was one of the most influential philosophers of our century. He was decisive for most of contemporary continental philosophy, and he anticipated many issues and views in the recent philosophy of mind and cognitive science. However, his works were not reader-friendly, and he is more talked about than read.

Husserl was born in Moravia, received a Ph.D. in mathematics while working with Weierstraß, and then turned to philosophy under the influence of Franz Brentano. He was particularly engaged by Brentano's view on intentionality and developed it further into what was to become phenomenology. His first phenomenological work was *Logische Untersuchungen* (Logical Investigations) (1900–1). It was followed by *Ideen* (Ideas) (1913), which is the first work to give a full and systematic presentation of phenomenology. Husserl's later works, notably *Vorlesungen zur Phänomenologie des inneren Zeitbewusstseins* (On the Phenomenology of the Consciousness of Internal Time) (1928), *Formale und transzendentale Logik* (Formal and Transcendental Logic) (1929), *Kartesianische Meditationen* (Cartesian Meditations) (1931) and *Krisis der europäischen Wissenschaften und die transzendentale Phänomenologie* (Crisis of the European Sciences) (partly published in 1936), remain largely within the framework of the *Ideas.* They take up topics that Husserl only dealt with briefly or were not even mentioned in the *Ideas*, such as the status of the subject, intersubjectivity, time and the lifeworld.

Brentano had characterized intentionality as a special kind of directedness upon an object. This leads to difficulties in cases of hallucination and serious misperception, where there is no object. Also, it leaves open the question of what the directedness of consciousness consists in. Husserl therefore endeavours to give a detailed analysis of those features of consciousness that make it as if of an object. The collection of all these features Husserl calls the act's 'noema'. The noema unifies the consciousness we have at a certain time into an act that is seemingly directed towards an object. The noema is hence not the object that the act is directed towards, but is the structure that makes our consciousness be as if of such an object.

The noemata are akin to Frege's 'third world' objects, that is, the meanings of linguistic expressions. According to Husserl, 'the noema is nothing but a generalization of the notion of meaning [Bedeutung] to the field of all acts' (*Ideas* 1913). Just as distinguishing between an expression's meaning and its reference enables one to account for the meaningful use of expressions that fail to refer, so, according to Husserl, can the distinction between an act's noema and its object help us overcome Brentano's problem of acts without an object.

In an act of perception the noema we can have is restricted by what goes on at our sensory surfaces, but this constraint does not narrow our possibilities down to just one. Thus in a given situation I may perceive a man, but later come to see that it was a mannequin, with a corresponding shift of noema. Such a shift of noema is always possible, corresponding to the fact that perception is always fallible. These boundary conditions, which constrain the noemata we can have, Husserl calls 'hyle'. The hyle are not objects experienced by us, but are experiences of a kind which we typically have when our sense organs are affected, but also can have in other cases, for example under the influence of fever or drugs.

In our natural attitude we are absorbed in physical objects and events and in their general features, such as their colour and shape. These general features, which can be shared by several objects, Husserl calls essences, or 'eidos' (*Wesen*). Essences are studied in the eidetic sciences, of which mathematics is the most highly developed. We get to them by turning our attention away from the concrete individuals and focusing on what they have in common. This change of attention Husserl calls 'the eidetic reduction', since it leads us to the eidos. However, we may also more radically leave the natural attitude altogether, put the objects we were concerned with there in brackets and instead reflect on our own consciousness and its structures. This reflection Husserl calls 'the transcendental reduction', or 'epoché'. Husserl uses the label 'the phenomenological reduction' for a combination of the eidetic and the transcendental reduction. This leads us to the phenomena studied in phenomenology, that is, primarily, the noemata.

The noemata are rich objects, with an inexhaustible pattern of components. The noema of an act contains constituents corresponding to all the features, perceived and unperceived, that we attribute to the object, and moreover constituents corresponding to features that we rarely think about and are normally not aware of, features that are often due to our culture. All these latter features Husserl calls the 'horizon' of the act. The noema is influenced by our living together with other subjects where we mutually adapt to one another and come to conceive the world as a common world in which we all live, but experience from different perspectives. This adaptation, through empathy (*Einfühlung*), was extensively studied by Husserl.

Husserl emphasizes that our perspectives and anticipations are not predominantly factual: 'this world is there for me not only as a world of mere things, but also with the same immediacy as a world of values, a world of goods, a practical world' (*Ideas* 1913). Further, the anticipations are not merely beliefs – about factual properties, value properties

and functional features – but they also involve our bodily habits and skills.

The world in which we find ourselves living, with its open horizon of objects, values, and other features, Husserl calls the 'lifeworld'. It was the main theme of his last major work, *The Crisis of the European Sciences*, of which a part was published in 1936. The lifeworld plays an important role in his view on justification, which anticipates ideas of Goodman and Rawls.

1 Life
2 Intentionality
3 Noema
4 Hyle; filling; evidence
5 Intuition
6 The reductions; phenomenology
7 The past
8 Values; practical function
9 Horizon
10 Intersubjectivity
11 Existence
12 The lifeworld
13 Ultimate justification
14 Influence

1 Life

Edmund Gustav Albrecht Husserl was born of Jewish parents in Prossnitz (now Prostejov in the Czech Republic) in Moravia, in what was then Austria-Hungary on 8 April 1859. He was thus of the same age as Dewey and Bergson.

Husserl's early interests lay in the direction of mathematics and science. In 1876 he began studying mathematics and astronomy at the University of Leipzig. After three semesters he transferred to the University of Berlin in order to study with Weierstraß, Kronecker and Kummer, a trio that made Berlin a centre in the mathematical world during that period. After three years in Berlin he left for Vienna, where he received his doctorate in January 1883. He then returned to Berlin in order to become an assistant for Weierstraß. However, Weierstraß became ill, and after just one semester in Berlin Husserl entered military service for a year, spending most of it in Vienna. A growing interest in religious questions made him decide in 1884 to study philosophy with Franz BRENTANO in Vienna, who inspired him to go into philosophy full-time and exerted a decisive influence on his later phenomenology.

Husserl studied with Brentano until 1886, when Brentano advised him to go to Halle, where one of Brentano's earlier students, Carl Stumpf, was teaching philosophy and psychology. Husserl habilitated in Halle in 1887 and remained there as a *Privatdozent* until 1901, when he became Associate Professor (*außerordentlicher Professor*) in Göttingen, and in 1906 Full Professor. In 1916 he went to Freiburg, where he taught until he retired in 1928. He died in Freiburg on 27 April 1938.

Husserl's first philosophical work was his Habilitation dissertation, *On the Concept of Number*, which was printed, but not published, in 1887. This was incorporated into the first three chapters of his *Philosophy of Arithmetic*, whose first volume was published in 1891. A second volume was announced, but never came. Instead, Husserl underwent a radical philosophical reorientation. He gave up his main project in *Philosophy of Arithmetic*, which had been to base mathematics on psychology. Instead, he developed his lasting philosophical achievement, phenomenology, which was first presented in *Logische Untersuchungen* (Logical Investigations), arriving in two volumes in 1900 and 1901. In 1905–7 he introduced the idea of a transcendental reduction and gave phenomenology a turn towards transcendental idealism. This new version of phenomenology was expounded in *Ideen* (Ideas) (1913), and is the most systematic presentation of phenomenology.

Husserl's notable later works were *Vorlesungen zur Phänomenologie des inneren Zeitbewusstseins* (On the Phenomenology of the Consciousness of Internal Time) (1928), *Formale und transzendentale Logik* (Formal and Transcendental Logic) (1929), which Husserl characterized as his most mature work, and *Kartesianische Meditationen* (Cartesian Meditations) (1931). The first part of his *Krisis der europäischen Wissenschaften* (Crisis of the European Sciences) was published in 1936, but the main part of this work and about 40,000 pages of manuscripts were left after his death. These manuscripts, together with Husserl's family and his library, were rescued from Germany by the Belgian Franciscan Van Breda, who established the Husserl Archive in Louvain, where the material is now accessible to researchers. Copies of the manuscripts are kept in other Husserl archives in various parts of the world. Gradually, the most important parts of Husserl's papers and scholarly editions of his published works are being published in the series *Husserliana*. In addition, *Erfahrung und Urteil* (Experience and Judgment) was prepared by Husserl's assistant Ludwig Landgrebe in consultation with Husserl, and appeared shortly after Husserl's death in 1938. Husserl's main works are available in good English translations.

2 Intentionality

The central theme of phenomenology is intentionality. All of phenomenology can be regarded as an unfolding of the idea of intentionality (see INTENTIONALITY). Husserl's interest in intentionality was inspired by his teacher, Franz Brentano. However, there are many differences between Husserl's treatment of this notion and that of Brentano. This section deals first with these differences, then goes on to further features of Husserl's notion of intentionality reaching beyond the issues considered by Brentano.

Husserl retains the following basic idea of Brentano's: 'We understand by intentionality the peculiarity of experiences to be "consciousness of something"' (*Ideas* 1913; Husserl's emphasis). Husserl's formulation comes close to Brentano's oft-quoted passage from *Psychology from an Empirical Point of View*:

> Every mental phenomenon is characterized by what the scholastics in the Middle Ages called the intentional (and also mental) inexistence of an object, and what we could also call, although in not entirely unambiguous terms, the reference to a content, a direction upon an object.

However, there is already an important difference between Brentano and Husserl at this starting–point. While Brentano says straightforwardly that for every act there is an object towards which it is directed, Husserl focuses on the 'of'-ness of the act. There are two reasons for this difference: First, Husserl wants to get around the difficulties connected with acts that lack an object. Second, he aims to throw light on what it means for an act to be 'of' or 'about' something. Let us begin by discussing these two differences.

Acts that lack an object. Brentano's thesis may seem unproblematic in the examples Brentano considered: just as when we love there is somebody or something that we love, so there is something that we sense when we sense, something we think of when we think, and so on. However, what is the object of our consciousness when we hallucinate, or when we think of a centaur? Brentano insisted that even in such cases our mental activity, our sensing or thinking, is directed towards some object. The directedness has nothing to do with the reality of the object, he held. The object is contained in our mental activity, 'intentionally' contained in it. And Brentano defined mental phenomena as 'phenomena which contain an object intentionally'.

Not all of Brentano's students found this lucid or satisfactory, and the problem continued to disturb both them and Brentano. Brentano struggled with it for the rest of his life, and suggested, among other things, a translation theory, giving Leibniz credit for the idea: when we describe an act of hallucination, or of thinking of a centaur, we are only apparently referring to an object. The apparent reference to an object can be translated away in such a way that in the full, unabbreviated description of the act there is no reference to any problematic object. There are two weaknesses of Brentano's proposal. First, unlike Russell later, Brentano does not specify in detail how the translation is to be carried out (see RUSSELL, B.). Second, if such a translation can be carried out in the case of hallucinations and so on, then why not carry it out everywhere, even in cases of normal perception? What then happens to the doctrine of intentionality as directedness upon an object?

One of Brentano's students, Alexius MEINONG, suggested a simple way out. In his *Gegenstandstheorie* Meinong maintained that there are two kinds of objects: those that exist and those that do not exist. Hallucinations, like normal perception, are directed towards objects, but these objects do not exist. Brentano was not happy with this proposal. He objected that, like Kant, he could not make sense of existence as a property that some objects have and others lack.

Husserl's solution was, as noted, to emphasize the 'of'. Consciousness is always consciousness *of* something. Or better, consciousness is always *as if of* an object. What matters is not whether or not there is an object, but what the features are of consciousness that makes it always be 'as if of' an object. These three words, 'as if of' are the key to Husserl's notion of intentionality. To account for the directedness of consciousness by saying only that it is directed towards an object leaves us in the dark with regard to what that directedness is. This leads us to the second reason for why Husserl diverged from Brentano. Husserl wanted to throw light on just this issue: what does the directedness of consciousness consists in? He made it a theme for a new discipline: the discipline of phenomenology.

What is directedness? To get a grip on what the directedness of consciousness consists in – to understand better the word 'of', which Husserl emphasized in his definition of intentionality quoted at the beginning of §2 above – let us note that for Husserl intentionality does not simply consist in consciousness directing itself towards objects that are already there. Intentionality for Husserl means that consciousness in a certain way 'brings it about' that there are objects. Consciousness 'constitutes' objects, Husserl said, borrowing a word from the German idealists, but using it in a different sense. Above, the phrase 'brings it about' was put in quotation marks to indicate that Husserl does not mean that we create or cause the world and its objects. 'Intentionality' means merely that the various components of our consciousness are interconnected in such a way that we have an experience as of one object. To quote Husserl:

an object 'constitutes' itself – 'whether or not it is actual' – in certain concatenations of consciousness which in themselves bear a discernible unity in so far as they, by virtue of their essence, carry with themselves the consciousness of an identical X.

(*Ideas*; translation emended)

Husserl's use, here and in many other places, of the reflexive form 'an object constitutes itself', reflects his view that he did not regard the object as being produced by consciousness. Husserl considered phenomenology as the first strictly scientific version of transcendental idealism, but he also held that phenomenology transcends the traditional distinction between idealism and realism, and in 1934 he wrote in a letter to Abbé Baudin: 'No ordinary "realist" has ever been as realistic and concrete as I, the phenomenological "idealist" (a word which by the way I no longer use)'. In the preface to the first English edition of the *Ideas* (1931), Husserl stated:

Phenomenological idealism does not deny the factual [*wirklich*] existence of the real [*real*] world (and in the first instance nature) as if it deemed it an illusion. . . . Its only task and accomplishment is to clarify the sense [*Sinn*] of this world, just that sense in which we all regard it as really existing and as really valid. That the world exists . . . is quite indubitable. Another matter is to understand this indubitability which is the basis for life and science and clarify the basis for its claim.

To see more clearly what Husserl is after, consider Jastrow and Wittgenstein's duck/rabbit picture. In order to come closer to Husserl we should modify the example and consider not a picture, but a silhouette of the real animal against the sky. When we see such a silhouette against the sky, we may see a duck or a rabbit. What reaches our eyes is the same in both cases, so the difference must be something coming from us. We structure what we see, and we can do so in different ways. The impulses that reach us from the outside are insufficient to determine uniquely which object we experience; something more gets added.

3 Noema

The structure that makes up the directedness of consciousness, Husserl called the 'noema'. More accurately, the noema has two main components. First, the 'object meaning' that integrates the various constituents of our experience into experiences of the various features of *one* object, and second, the 'thetic' component that differentiates acts of different kinds, for example, the act of perceiving an object from the act of remembering it or thinking about it. The thetic component is thereby crucial for the reality-character which we ascribe to the object.

Our consciousness structures what we experience (see KANT, I.). How it structures it depends on our previous experiences, the whole setting of our present experience and a number of other factors. If we had grown up surrounded by ducks, but had never heard of rabbits, we would have been more likely to see a duck when confronted with the duck/rabbit silhouette; the idea of a rabbit would not have occurred to us.

The structuring always takes place in such a way that the many different features of the object are experienced as connected with one another, as features of one and the same object. When, for example, we see a rabbit, we do not merely see a collection of coloured patches, various shades of brown spread out over our field of vision (incidentally, even seeing coloured patches involves intentionality, since a patch is also a kind of object, but a different kind of object from a rabbit). We see a rabbit, with a determinate shape and a determinate colour, with the ability to eat, jump and so on. It has a side that is turned towards us and one that is turned away from us. We do not see the other side from where we are, but we see something which has another side.

That seeing is intentional, or object-directed, means just this, that it is as if of an object: the near side of the object we have in front of us is regarded as a side of a thing, and the thing we see has other sides and features that are co-intended, in the sense that the thing is regarded as more than just this one side. The object meaning of the noema is the comprehensive system of determinations that gives unity to this manifold of features and makes them aspects of one and the same object.

It is important at this point to note that the various sides, appearances or perspectives of the object are constituted together with the object. There are no sides and perspectives floating around before we start perceiving, which are then synthesized into objects when intentionality sets in. There are no objects of any kind, whether they be physical objects, sides of objects, appearances of objects or perspectives of objects without intentionality. And intentionality does not work in steps. We do not start by constituting six sides and then synthesize these into a die; we constitute the die and the six sides of it in one step.

We should also note that when we experience a person, we do not experience a physical object, a body, and then infer that a person is there. We experience a fully fledged person, we are encountering somebody who structures the world, experiences it from their own perspective. Our noema is a noema of a person; no inference is involved. Seeing persons is no more mysterious than seeing physical objects, and no inference is involved in either case. When we see a physical object we do not see sense-data or the like and then infer that there is a physical object there, but our noema is the noema of a physical object. Similarly, when we see an action, what we see is a fully fledged action, not a bodily movement from which we infer that there is an action.

The word 'object' must hence be taken in a very broad sense. It comprises not only physical things, but also, as we have seen, animals, and likewise persons, events, actions and processes, and sides, aspects and appearances of such entities.

Essences. Husserl distinguishes between physical objects and processes, which are temporal and normally also spatial, and essences (*Wesen*) or eidos, which are features that the object can share with other objects, such as the triangularity of a triangle or the greenness of a tree. For Husserl, an object's essence is therefore not something unique to that object, as it is for many other philosophers. Mathematics is the most highly developed study of essences.

Noema and meaning. The features of the noema that we have mentioned, in particular the role it plays in the analysis of acts without objects and the way it accounts for the object-directedness of acts, make it natural to compare the noema to the meaning of linguistic expressions. This comparison and the ensuing way of reading Husserl has been contested. However, it is well supported by textual and systematic considerations, and it is now often regarded as the standard way of interpreting Husserl. One factor contributing to this has been Husserl's own statement, in *Ideas*, that 'the noema is nothing but a generalization of the notion of meaning (*Bedeutung*) to the field of all acts'.

Noesis. The noema is an abstract structure that can in principle be the same from act to act, in the unlikely case that at two different occasions we should have the same kind of experience of the same object from the same point of view, with exactly the same anticipations, and so on. An act has a noema in virtue of comprising a kind of experience that Husserl calls a 'noesis'. The noema is the meaning given in an act, Husserl says, while the noesis is the meaning-giving aspect of the act. There is hence a close parallelism between noema and noesis. The relation between noema and noesis bears some similarity to the type/token relation in Peirce (see TYPE/TOKEN DISTINCTION). The noesis is a temporal process, in which the noema 'dwells'.

4 Hyle; filling; evidence

In acts of perception, the noema that we can have is restricted by what goes on at our sensory surfaces, but the restriction does not narrow our possibilities down to just one. Thus in a given situation I may perceive a man, but later come to see that the man was a mannequin, with a corresponding shift of noema. Such a shift of noema is always possible, corresponding to the fact that perception is always fallible. These boundary conditions, which constrain the noemata we can have, Husserl calls 'hyle'. The hyle are not objects experienced by us, but are experiences of a kind which we typically have when our sense organs are affected, but also can have in other cases, for example, under the influence of fever or drugs.

In the case of an act of perception, its noema can also be characterized as a very complex set of expectations or anticipations concerning what kind of experiences we will have when we move around the object and perceive it, using our various senses. We anticipate different further experiences when we see a duck and when we see a rabbit. In the first case we anticipate, for example, that we will feel feathers when we touch the object, while in the latter case we expect to find fur. When we get the experiences we anticipate, the corresponding component of the noema is said to be 'filled'. In all perception there will be some filling: the components of the noema that correspond to what presently 'meets the eye' are filled, and similarly for the other senses.

Such anticipation and filling is what distinguishes perception from other modes of consciousness, such as imagination or remembering. If we merely imagine things, our noema can be of anything whatsoever. In perception, however, our sensory experiences are involved; the noema has to fit in with our sensory experiences. This eliminates a number of noemata which I could have had if I were just imagining. In your present situation you can probably not have a noema corresponding to the perception of an elephant. This does not reduce the number of perceptual noemata you can have just now to one, for example, of having a book in front of you.

It is a central point in Husserl's phenomenology that I can have a variety of different perceptual noemata that are compatible with the present impingements upon my sensory surfaces. In the duck/rabbit case this was obvious, for we could go back and forth at will between having the noema of a duck and having the noema of a rabbit. In most cases, however, we are not aware of this possibility. Only when something untoward happens, when I encounter a 'recalcitrant' experience that does not fit in with the anticipations in my noema, do I start seeing a different object from the one I thought I saw earlier. My noema 'explodes', to use Husserl's phrase, and I come to have a noema quite different from the previous one, with new anticipations. This is always possible, he says. Perception always involves anticipations that go beyond what presently 'meets the eye', and there is always a risk that we may go wrong, regardless of how confident and certain we might feel.

When some components of the noema are filled, we have 'evidence'. Evidence comes in degrees, depending on how much of the noema is filled. Husserl discusses two kinds of perfect evidence: 'adequate' evidence, where every component in the noema is filled, with no unfilled anticipations, and 'apodictic' evidence, where the negation of what seems to be the case is self-contradictory. After some vacillation Husserl ended up holding that we can never attain any of these kinds of perfect evidence – we are always fallible.

5 Intuition

Husserl uses the term 'intuition' (*Anschauung*) for any act where an object is experienced as 'given', that is, as really there. Earlier philosophers have used the word 'intuition' in a variety of ways, mostly about some sort of direct, non-inferential insight. Perception has usually been classified as a kind of intuition. A key issue in medieval philosophy as well as in rationalism and empiricism was whether there are other sorts of such insight. Kant defined 'intuition' as a representation which 'relates immediately to its object and is singular' (*Critique of Pure Reason* 1781/87: A320; B376–7). Bernard BOLZANO developed this idea with great precision. For Husserl, an intuition is an act where we are constrained in how we constitute its objects, such as we typically are in perception, which is one of his two varieties of intuition. He calls the other variety 'essential insight' (*Wesensschau*). The object is here a general feature, an essence. For Husserl, as for Kant, intuition is a key kind of evidence in mathematics. This, then, is what Husserl means by the mysterious-sounding term '*Wesensschau*'. One might still claim that there is no such thing, but it is difficult to reject the notion once one agrees that the object of an act is underdetermined by what reaches our senses, and one accepts the correlated idea of intentionality.

6 The reductions; phenomenology

Husserl distinguishes between several so-called 'reductions'. First, there is the 'eidetic' reduction, which we perform each time we pass from focusing on an individual physical object to focusing on one of its essences (eidos). This kind of reduction has been carried out in mathematics since its beginning, and Husserl conceived of other eidetic sciences in addition to mathematics. Second, a reduction that is distinctive for phenomenology is a special kind of reflection. Instead of focusing on the normal objects of our acts, be they physical objects, actions, persons or general features that many objects can have in common, we reflect on the structures of our own consciousness and study the noemata, the noeses or the hyle. The noemata, the noeses and the hyle have two important features: we are normally not aware of them, and they are a *sine qua non* for the appearance of a world. Entities with these two features are called 'transcendental'. The reduction that leads to them, where the ordinary objects are bracketed, is therefore called the 'transcendental' reduction. Husserl also calls it the 'epoché', using a word that the ancient sceptics used for refraining from taking a stand. We study the features of the act that make it seem to have an object and do not ask whether or not it actually has one. Husserl got the idea of the transcendental reduction in 1905. It marks the transition from the early phenomenology of the *Logical Investigations* to the 'idealist' phenomenology of the *Ideas* and later works.

The 'phenomenological' reduction, finally, is the combination of the eidetic reduction and the transcendental reduction. That is, it is a reduction that leads us from acts directed towards physical objects via acts directed towards essences to acts directed towards the noema, noesis and hyle of acts directed towards essences. Husserl sometimes takes the two steps in the inverse order, starting with a transcendental reduction and then focusing on the essential traits of the noema, noesis and hyle. The end product is not quite the same, but the phenomenological reduction can presumably be either.

Phenomenology is the study of the transcendental elements in our experience that are uncovered through the phenomenological reduction: the noema, the noesis and the hyle. In phenomenology, all these three elements are studied, with emphasis on the noematic/noetic structures. Husserl carried out detailed analyses of temporal structures and how they are constituted, in *On the Phenomenology of the Consciousness of Internal Time*, on the structures that are basic to logic and mathematics, in *Formal and Transcendental Logic* and *Experience and Judgment*, and on intersubjectivity and the processes whereby we come to constitute a common world, in *Cartesian Meditations* and in thousands of pages of manuscripts, the most important of which have been collected by Iso Kern in *Husserliana*, vols 13–15.

For Husserl, phenomenology is a study of the subjective perspective. In science one aims for objectivity and endeavours to arrange observations and experiments in such a way as to minimize differences between different observers. Phenomenology focuses on the subjective, on the manner in which each subject structures or 'constitutes' the world differently, on the basis of different experiences and cultural background, but also on the basis of adaptation to other subjects through interaction and communication.

7 The past

We constitute not only the different properties of things, but also the relation of the thing to other objects. If, for example, I see a tree, the tree is conceived of as something which is in front of me, as perhaps situated among other trees, as seen by other people than myself, and so on. It is also conceived of as something which has a history: it was there before I saw it, it will remain after I have left, or perhaps it will eventually be cut down and transported to some other place. However, like all material things, it does not simply disappear from the world.

My consciousness of the tree is in this way also a consciousness of the world in space and time in which the tree is located. My consciousness constitutes the tree, but at the same time it constitutes the world in which the tree and I are living. If my further experience makes me give up the belief that I have a tree ahead of me because, for example, I do not find a tree-like far side or because some of my other expectations prove false, this affects not only my conception of what there is, but also my conception of what has been and what will be. Thus in this case, not just the present, but also the past and the future are reconstituted by me. To illustrate how changes in my present perception lead me to reconstitute not just the present, but also the past, Husserl uses an example of a ball which I initially take to be red all over and spherical. As it turns, I discover that it is green on the other side and has a dent:

the sense of the perception is not only changed in the momentary new stretch of perception; the noematic modification streams back in the form of a retroactive cancellation in the retentional sphere and modifies the production of sense stemming from earlier phases of the perception. The earlier apperception, which was attuned to the harmonious development of the 'red and uniformly round', is implicitly 'reinterpreted' to 'green on one side and dented'.

(*Erfahrung und Urteil* 1938)

Husserl held that time and space are constituted. In *On the Phenomenology of the Consciousness of Internal Time* and various manuscripts that have been published in Volume 10 of *Husserliana* he gives a highly interesting analysis of the way objective time is constituted.

8 Values; practical function

So far we have focused on the factual properties of things. However, things also have *value* properties, and these properties are constituted in a corresponding manner. The world within which we live is experienced as a world in which certain things and actions have a positive value, others a negative. Our norms and values, like our beliefs, are subject to change. Changes in our views on matters of fact are often accompanied by changes in our evaluations.

Husserl emphasizes that our perspectives and anticipations are not predominantly factual. We are not living a purely theoretical life. According to Husserl, we encounter the world around us primarily 'in the attitude of the natural pursuit of life', as 'living functioning subjects involved in the circle of other functioning subjects'. Husserl says this in a manuscript from 1917, but he has similar ideas about the practical both earlier and later. Thus in the *Ideas* he says: 'this world is there for me not only as a world of mere things, but also with the same immediacy as a world of values, a world of goods, a practical world'.

In later manuscripts, particularly from 1917 onwards, Husserl focused more and more on the role of the practical and the body in our constitution of the world. Just as he never held that we first perceive sense-data, or perspectives or appearances, which are then synthesized into physical objects, or that we first perceive bodies and bodily movements and then infer that there are persons and actions, so it would be a grave misunderstanding of Husserl to attribute to him the view that we first perceive objects that have merely physical properties and then assign a value or a practical function to them. Things are directly experienced by us as having the features – functional and evaluational as well as factual – that are of concern for us in our natural pursuit of life.

In our discussion of the hyle we characterized the noema of an act of perception as a very complex set of expectations or anticipations concerning what kind of experiences we will have when we move around the object and perceive it. We should note that these experiences depend not only on our sensory organs, but also on the movements of our body, on our bodily skills and our familiarity with various kinds of practical activities. In numerous passages Husserl talks about practical anticipations and the role of kinesthesis in perception and bodily activity.

9 Horizon

When we are experiencing an object, our consciousness is focused on this object, and the rest of the world and its various objects are there in the background as something we 'believe in' but are not presently paying attention to. The same holds for most of the inexhaustibly many features of the object itself. All these further features of the object, together with the world in which it is set, make up what Husserl calls the 'horizon' of that experience. The various features of the object, which are co-intended, or also-meant, but not at the focus of our attention, Husserl calls the 'inner horizon', while the realm of other objects and the world to which they all belong, he calls the 'outer horizon'.

The horizon is of crucial importance for Husserl's concept of justification, which we shall discuss later. What is particularly significant is the hidden nature of the horizon. As we noted, the horizon is that which is not attended to. Take as an example our 'expectation' that we will find a floor when we enter a room. Usually, we have not even thought about there being a floor. Typically, we cannot even recall when we first acquired the corresponding 'belief' or 'anticipation'. According to Husserl, there may never have been any occasion when we actually judged there to be a floor in some particular room. Still we have come to 'anticipate' a floor, not in the sense of consciously expecting one, but in the sense that if we entered the room and there were none, we would be astonished. In this example we would easily be able to tell what was missing, in other cases our 'anticipations' are so imperceptible that we just may feel that something has gone awry, but not be able to tell what it is.

Words like 'belief' and 'anticipate' are clearly not the proper ones here, since they have overtones of something being conscious and thought about. Both English and German seem to lack words for what we want to get at here: Husserl uses the words '*antizipieren*', '*hinausmeinen*' and '*vorzeichnen*'.

10 Intersubjectivity

Throughout his life, Husserl emphasized that the world we intend and thereby constitute is not our own private world, but an intersubjective world, common to and accessible to all of us. Thus in the *Ideas* he writes:

> I continually find at hand as something confronting me a spatiotemporal reality [*Wirklichkeit*] to which I belong like all other human beings who are to be found in it and who are related to it as I am.

Husserl's studies of intersubjectivity focus in particular on the processes by which we experience others as experiencing subjects, like ourselves, and adapt our anticipations to those that we take them to have. Thanks to this, our way of constituting the world is not solipsistic, but we constitute the world as a shared world, which we each experience from our different perspective. A notion of objectivity arises, we may come to regard ourselves as deviant, for example, as colour-blind or as cognitively biased, and we also experience ourselves as confronted with a reality to which our beliefs and anticipations have to adapt. In works that remain largely unpublished, Husserl started to develop an ethics based in part on a study of the objectifying processes whereby objective ethical principles and norms arise from our subjective likes and dislikes.

Husserl stresses the shared, intersubjective nature of the world, particularly in §29 of the *Ideas*, which he entitles 'The "Other" Ego-subjects and the Intersubjective Natural Surrounding World'. There he says:

I take their surrounding world and mine Objectively as one and the same world of which we are conscious, only in different ways [*Weise*].... For all that, we come to an understanding with our fellow human beings and together with them posit an Objective spatiotemporal reality.

In the later works one finds similar ideas, particularly in the many texts that have been collected by Iso Kern in the three volumes of the *Husserliana* devoted to intersubjectivity, but also in many other works, for example in the *Crisis*:

Thus in general the world exists not only for isolated men but for the community of men; and this is due to the fact that even what is straightforwardly perceptual is communal.

Husserl discusses in great detail empathy and the many other varieties of intersubjective adaptation that enable us to intend a common, intersubjective world. (See the three volumes on intersubjectivity referred to above.)

11 Existence

The passages quoted in §10 above express a further feature of Husserl's notion of intentionality which is rarely discussed, in spite of its importance: intentionality does not just involve directedness upon an object, but also a 'positing' of the object, corresponding to the two components of the noema discussed in §3 above. The object is experienced as real and present, as remembered, or as merely imagined, and so on. In the passages just quoted,

Husserl said, 'I continually find at hand as something confronting me a spatiotemporal reality', and 'we come to an understanding with our fellow human beings and together with them posit an Objective spatiotemporal reality'. The same point is stressed also when he discusses the lifeworld in the *Crisis*:

the lifeworld, for us who wakingly live in it, is always there, existing in advance for us, the 'ground' of all praxis, whether theoretical or extratheoretical. The world is pregiven to us, the waking, always somehow practically interested subjects, not occasionally but always and necessarily as the universal field of all actual and possible praxis, as horizon. To live is always to live-in-certainty-of-the-world.

Husserl discusses this *thetic* character of intentionality, and, correspondingly, of the noema, in many of his books and manuscripts. He was particularly concerned with what gives reality-character to the world. Like William James, whom he had read already when he made the transition to phenomenology in the mid-1890s, he stressed the importance of the body, and the inflictions upon our body, for our sense of reality. As James put it: 'Sensible vividness or pungency is then the vital factor in reality'(*The Principles of Psychology* 1890: 2, 301). Husserl could also have subscribed to James's observation that 'the *fons et origo* of all reality, whether from the absolute or the practical point of view, is thus subjective, is ourselves' (*Principles*: 2, 296–7).

This latter passage from James gets a double meaning in Husserl which expresses the core of his view of the reality of the world: the subjective (ourselves) is the *fons et origo* of all reality in two senses, a transcendental and an empirical: we constitute the world as real through our intentionality, and the reality-character we give it is derived from our being not merely transcendental subjects, but empirical subjects with a body immersed in a physical world.

12 The lifeworld

The idea of Husserl's that has become most widely known is that of the lifeworld. In particular, the word 'lifeworld' (*Lebenswelt*) itself has gained wide currency. It was used by Simmel and others before Husserl. After the Second World War it became a favourite word of many social scientists, who used it in many different senses. Several of them refer to Husserl without seeming to have studied his philosophy and therefore without knowing the many important features that the lifeworld has in his thought.

The first place Husserl uses the word 'lifeworld' in print is in his latest work, the *Crisis*, of which the first two parts were published in 1936. The rest of this unfinished work, containing the important third part, with the main discussion of the lifeworld, was not published until 1954, but it was known to some of Husserl's students and followers, including Maurice MERLEAU-PONTY, who came to the Husserl Archives in Louvain to study this part in April 1939.

Interpreters of Husserl differ widely in their views on the lifeworld. It is often thought that it constitutes a major break in Husserl's development, from the 'early' Husserl of the *Ideas* to the 'late' Husserl of the *Crisis*. Is it such a break? And second, what exactly is the lifeworld and what role does it play in phenomenology? On the former question the answer is a definite 'No'. The lifeworld is fully compatible with Husserl's earlier philosophy, and there is even a definite place for it in his phenomenology from its beginning. Husserl touches upon the lifeworld repeatedly in his earlier work and he gradually deepens and modifies his views on it, as he did with everything else in his phenomenology. Instead of regarding the lifeworld as a break with Husserl's earlier philosophy, we should view it as intimately connected with the other main themes in phenomenology. Properly to understand the lifeworld with all its nuances it is important to appreciate fully the connection between it and the rest of Husserl's philosophy.

The lifeworld arises from the distinction between the natural attitude and the transcendental or phenomenological attitude, which Husserl introduced in 1905. The first appearance of the notion for which he later introduced the term 'lifeworld' occurs shortly thereafter, in his lectures 'Fundamental Problems in Phenomenology' in 1910–11, that is, already before the *Ideas*. Husserl begins these lectures with an extended discussion of 'the natural attitude and the "natural world concept"'. Here he says:

> It could also be shown that philosophical interests of the highest dignity require a complete and comprehensive description of the so-called *natural world concept*, that of the natural attitude, on the other hand also that an accurate and profound description of this kind is not easily carried out, but on the contrary would require exceptionally difficult reflections.

Husserl here borrows the phrase 'natural world concept', which he emphasizes, from Richard Avenarius, whom he discusses later in the lecture. In a manuscript from 1915, Husserl describes this world in the following way (following Avenarius):

> All opinions, justified or unjustified, popular, superstitious, scientific, all relate to the already *pregiven world*.... All theory relates to this immediate givenness and can have a legitimate sense only when it forms thoughts which do not offend against the general sense of the immediately given. No theorizing may offend against this sense.

In the following years, Husserl repeatedly returns to this and related themes, using various labels that sometimes allude to other philosophers who had propounded similar ideas, such as Nietzsche. Quite often he uses Avenarius' phrase 'natural world'. In a manuscript from 1917, which appears to be the first place where he uses the word 'lifeworld', he introduces this new word as equivalent to the former: 'The lifeworld is the natural world – in the attitude of the natural pursuit of life are we living functioning subjects involved in the circle of other functioning subjects' (the manuscript dates from 1917, but was copied during the first half of the 1920s, and it is possible that the word 'lifeworld' appeared then).

Gradually during the 1920s and especially in the 1930s the lifeworld becomes a central theme in Husserl's writings, until his discussion culminates in the *Crisis* in 1936. One aim of this work was to provide a new and better access to phenomenology, through the notion of the lifeworld. The lifeworld is for Husserl our natural world, the world we live in and are absorbed by in our everyday activities. A main aim of phenomenology is to make us reflect on this world and make us see how it is constituted by us. Through the phenomenological reduction phenomenology will take us out of our natural attitude where we are absorbed by the world around us, into the phenomenological, transcendental attitude, where we focus on the noemata of our acts – on our structuring of reality.

Pregivenness. In the passage just quoted from Husserl's 1915 manuscript, Husserl says that the world is pregiven (*vorgegeben*). This point is also discussed in the *Ideas*, where Husserl notes that

> In my waking consciousness I find myself in this manner at all times, and without ever being able to alter the fact, in relation to the world which remains one and the same, though changing with respect to the composition of its contents. It is continually 'on hand' for me and I myself am a member of it.

and a few pages later the passage that was quoted earlier, in the section on intersubjectivity:

> I continually find at hand as something confronting me a spatiotemporal reality [*Wirklichkeit*] to which I belong like all other

human beings who are to be found in it and who are related to it as I am.

Also the passage from §37 of the *Crisis* that was quoted in the section on existence above expresses this same idea:

> The lifeworld... is always there, existing in advance for us, the 'ground' of all praxis, whether theoretical or extratheoretical. The world is pregiven to us...

Science and the lifeworld. A contested point in Husserl scholarship is the relation between the lifeworld and the sciences. Many interpreters of Husserl like to find an opposition to the sciences in the lifeworld. However, such a disdain for the sciences is out of character with Husserl's background in and continued interest in mathematics and science. It also accords poorly with the texts, which give us a different and more intriguing picture. According to Husserl, the lifeworld and the sciences are intimately connected, in three different ways:

(1) The sciences are *part* of the lifeworld. This comes out most explicitly and clearly in *Experience and Judgment*, where Husserl says:

> everything which contemporary natural science has furnished as determinations of what exists also belong to us, to the world, as this world is pregiven to the adults of our time. And even if we are not personally interested in natural science, and even if we know nothing of its results, still, what exists is pregiven to us in advance as determined in such a way that we at least grasp it as being in principle scientifically determinable.

Similar statements are also found elsewhere in Husserl's work, for example in the *Crisis*: 'Now the scientific world – [the subject matter of] systematic theory – ... like all the worlds of ends "belongs" to the lifeworld'.

(2) Scientific statements get their *meaning* by being embedded in the lifeworld. This was stressed by Husserl already in the manuscript from 1915, quoted in §12 above:

> All opinions, justified or unjustified, popular, superstitious, scientific, all relate to the already *pregiven world*.... All theory relates to this immediate givenness and can have a legitimate *sense* only when it forms thoughts which do not offend against the general sense of the immediately given. No theorizing may offend against this sense.

(emphasis added)

(3) The sciences are *justified* through the lifeworld. There is an interplay between this point and

point (1) above; the sciences are justified because they belong to the lifeworld, and at the same time they belong to the lifeworld because they are conceived of as describing the world, as claiming to be true:

> Though the peculiar accomplishment of our modern objective science may still not be understood, nothing changes the fact that it is a validity for the lifeworld, arising out of particular activities, and that it belongs itself to the concreteness of the lifeworld.

(*Crisis*)

And similarly:

> all these theoretical results have the character of validities for the lifeworld, adding themselves as such to its own composition and belonging to it even before that as a horizon of possible accomplishments for developing science. The concrete lifeworld, then, is the grounding soil [*der gründende Boden*] of the 'scientifically true' world and at the same time encompasses it in its own universal concreteness.

(*Crisis*)

13 Ultimate justification

This brings us to the final theme of this presentation of Husserl's phenomenology: the role of the lifeworld in justification. The traditional interpretation of Husserl attributes to him a 'foundationalist' position: he is alleged to hold that we can reach absolute certainty with regard to a number of matters, particularly in philosophy. However, there is considerable evidence that Husserl had a view on justification similar to that of Goodman and Rawls. An opinion is justified by being brought into 'reflective equilibrium' with the *doxa* of our lifeworld. This holds even for mathematics: 'mathematical evidence has its source of meaning and of legitimacy in the evidence of the lifeworld' (*Crisis*).

A major puzzle that many see in this idea of justification is, 'How can appeal to the subjective-relative doxa provide any kind of justification for anything? It may help to resolve disagreements, but how can it serve as justification?' Husserl answers by pointing out that there is no other way of justifying anything, and that his way is satisfactory:

> What is actually first is the 'merely subjective-relative' intuition of prescientific world-life. For us, to be sure, this 'merely' has, as an old inheritance, the disdainful colouring of the *doxa*. In prescientific life itself, of course, it has nothing of this; there it is a realm of good

verification and, based upon this, of well-verified predicative cognitions and of truths which are just as secure as is necessary for the practical projects of life that determine their sense. The disdain with which everything 'merely subjective and relative' is treated by those scientists who pursue the modern ideal of objectivity changes nothing of its own manner of being, just as it does not change the fact that the scientist himself must be satisfied with this realm whenever he has recourse, as he unavoidably must have recourse, to it.

(*Crisis*)

So far, this is a mere claim. However, Husserl elaborates his view in other parts of his work. His key observation, which is an intriguing contribution to our contemporary discussion of ultimate justification, is that the 'beliefs', 'expectations' or 'acceptances' on which we ultimately fall back are unconsidered, and in most cases have never been considered. Every claim to validity and truth rests upon this 'iceberg' of unconsidered prejudgmental acceptances discussed earlier. One would think that this would make things even worse. Not only do we fall back on something that is uncertain, but on something that we have not even thought about, and have therefore never subjected to conscious testing. Husserl argues, however, that it is just the unconsidered nature of the lifeworld that makes it the ultimate ground of justification. 'Acceptance' and 'belief' are not attitudes that we decide to have through any act of judicative decision. What we accept, and the phenomenon of acceptance itself, are integral to our lifeworld, and there is no way of starting from scratch, or 'to evade the issue here through a preoccupation with aporia and argumentation nourished by Kantor Hegel, Aristotle or Thomas' (*Crisis*). Only the lifeworld can be an ultimate court of appeal: 'Thus alone can that ultimate understanding of the world be attained, behind which, since it is ultimate, there is nothing more that can be sensefully inquired for, nothing more to understand' (*Formal and Transcendental Logic* 1929) (see PHENOMENOLOGY, EPISTEMIC ISSUES IN).

14 Influence

Husserl's phenomenology has been a major influence on philosophy in our century, primarily on the continent, but since the 1970s also in the United States, Britain and several other countries. Husserl's immediate successor in Freiburg, Martin HEIDEGGER, conceived of *Being and Time* (1927) as a phenomenological study and dedicated it to Husserl. Also Jean-Paul SARTRE received strong impulses from Husserl, particularly from Husserl's idea that our material surroundings do not uniquely determine our noema. Sartre developed this idea into a philosophy of freedom, notably in *Being and Nothingness* (1943), which has the subtitle 'A Phenomenological Essay on Ontology'. Also Emmanuel LEVINAS, Paul RICOEUR and several other French philosophers were heavily influenced by Husserl. A new generation of young French and German philosophers is now combining Husserl scholarship with work on systematic issues in epistemology, philosophy of language and philosophy of mind.

Husserl's conception of the lifeworld become important for the so-called 'new hermeneutics' (Heidegger and GADAMER; see HERMENEUTICS) and for the methodology of the humanities and the social sciences (Schütz, Luckmann), largely because it provides a framework for discussing the subjective perspective and the many features of our way of structuring the world of which we are unaware and that often reflect the culture in which we have grown up. The issues connected with intersubjectivity and Husserl's exploration of the various ways in which we adapt to one another and come to conceive the world as a common world were pursued by several of his students, notably Edith Stein, in her dissertation *On the Problem of Empathy* (1917). His ideas about the role of the body, of kinesthesis and of practical activity, recur in different versions in Heidegger's existentialism and in Merleau-Ponty's phenomenology. MERLEAU-PONTY in particular is generous in the credit he gives Husserl.

Husserl's many students and followers explored a number of other themes in Husserl and applied his ideas in a variety of fields. Thus Roman INGARDEN used them in aesthetics, Aron Gurwitsch and several others in the study of perception. Husserl's views have led to new developments in psychology and psychotherapy. They have influenced philosophers of mathematics, including Gödel, and they are beginning to have an impact on the philosophy of mind and on cognitive science.

See also: PHENOMENOLOGICAL MOVEMENT

References and further reading

Bernet, Rudolf, Kern, Iso, and Marbach, Eduard (1993) *An Introduction to Husserlian Phenomenology (Studies in Phenomenology and Existential Philosophy)*, Evanston, IL.: Northwestern University Press. (A good introduction to phenomenology by three eminent Husserl scholars.)

Smith, Barry, and Woodruff Smith, David (eds) (1995) *The Cambridge Companion to Husserl*, Cambridge: Cambridge University Press. (Essays by several prominent Husserl scholars on various aspects of Husserl's thought, followed by useful bibliographies.)

Sokolowski, R. (2000) *Introduction to Phenomenology*, Cambridge: Cambridge University Press. (A clear, lively and dependable introduction to phenomenology by one of the main contributors to the field.)

DAGFINN FØLLESDAL

HUTCHESON, FRANCIS (1694–1746)

Francis Hutcheson is best known for his contributions to moral theory, but he also contributed to the development of aesthetics. Although his philosophy owes much to John Locke's empiricist approach to ideas and knowledge, Hutcheson was sharply critical of Locke's account of two important normative ideas, those of beauty and virtue. He rejected Locke's claim that these ideas are mere constructs of the mind that neither copy nor make reference to anything objective. He also complained that Locke's account of human pleasure and pain was too narrowly focused. There are pleasures and pains other than those that arise in conjunction with ordinary sensations; there are, in fact, more than five senses. Two additional senses, the sense of beauty and the moral sense, give rise to distinctive pleasures and pains that enable us to make aesthetic and moral distinctions and evaluations.

Hutcheson's theory of the moral sense emphasizes two fundamental features of human nature. First, in contrast to Thomas Hobbes and other egoists, Hutcheson argues that human nature includes a disposition to benevolence. This characteristic enables us to be, sometimes, genuinely virtuous. It enables us to act from benevolent motives, whereas Hutcheson identifies virtue with just such motivations. Second, we are said to have a perceptual faculty, a moral sense, that enables us to perceive moral differences. When confronted with cases of benevolently motivated behaviour (virtue), we naturally respond with a feeling of approbation, a special kind of pleasure. Confronted with maliciously motivated behaviour (vice), we naturally respond with a feeling of disapprobation, a special kind of pain. In short, certain distinctive feelings of normal observers serve to distinguish between virtue and vice. Hutcheson was careful, however, not to identify virtue and vice with these feelings. The feelings are perceptions (elements in the mind of observers) that function as signs of virtue and vice (qualities of agents). Virtue is benevolence, and vice malice (or, sometimes, indifference); our moral feelings serve as signs of these characteristics.

Hutcheson's rationalist critics charged him with making morality relative to the features human nature happens at present to have. Suppose, they said, that our nature were different. Suppose we felt approbation where we now feel disapprobation. In that event, what we now call 'vice' would be called 'virtue', and what we call 'virtue' would be called 'vice'. The moral sense theory must be wrong because virtue and vice are immutable. In response, Hutcheson insisted that, as our Creator is unchanging and intrinsically good, the dispositions and faculties we have can be taken to be permanent and even necessary. Consequently, although it in one sense depends upon human nature, morality is immutable because it is permanently determined by the nature of the Deity.

Hutcheson's views were widely discussed throughout the middle decades of the eighteenth century. He knew and advised David Hume, and, while Professor of Moral Philosophy at Glasgow, taught Adam Smith. Immanuel Kant and Jeremy Bentham, among other philosophers, also responded to his work, while in colonial America his political theory was widely seen as providing grounds for rebellion against Britain.

See also: BEAUTY; EGOISM AND ALTRUISM; ENLIGHTENMENT, SCOTTISH; HUME, D.; MORAL SENSE THEORIES; SHAFTESBURY; SLAVERY; VIRTUES AND VICES

DAVID FATE NORTON

HYPATIA (*c.* AD 370–415)

The Greek philosopher Hypatia was a Neoplatonist. She was famous for her public talks on philosophy and astronomy, and her forthright attitude to sex. Although concerned with higher knowledge, she was also a political animal and had a keen sense of practical virtue. She was killed by a Christian mob, and has remained since a martyr to the cause of philosophy.

LUCAS SIORVANES

HYPPOLITE, JEAN
See HEGELIANISM

I

See Confucius

IBN MAIMON, MUSA
See Maimonides, Moses

IBN RUSHD, ABU'L WALID MUHAMMAD (1126–98)

Ibn Rushd (Averroes) is regarded by many as the most important of the Islamic philosophers. A product of twelfth-century Islamic Spain, he set out to integrate Aristotelian philosophy with Islamic thought. A common theme throughout his writings is that there is no incompatibility between religion and philosophy when both are properly understood. His contributions to philosophy took many forms, ranging from his detailed commentaries on Aristotle, his defence of philosophy against the attacks of those who condemned it as contrary to Islam and his construction of a form of Aristotelianism which cleansed it, as far as was possible at the time, of Neoplatonic influences.

His thought is genuinely creative and highly controversial, producing powerful arguments that were to puzzle his philosophical successors in the Jewish and Christian worlds. He seems to argue that there are two forms of truth, a religious form and a philosophical form, and that it does not matter if they point in different directions. He also appears to be doubtful about the possibility of personal immortality or of God's being able to know that particular events have taken place. There is much in his work also which suggests that religion is inferior to philosophy as a means of attaining knowledge, and that the understanding of religion which ordinary believers can have is very different and impoverished when compared with that available to the philosopher.

When discussing political philosophy he advocates a leading role in the state for philosophers, and is generally disparaging of the qualities of theologians as political figures. Ibn Rushd's philosophy is

seen to be based upon a complex and original philosophy of languages which expresses his critique of the accepted methods of argument in Islamic philosophy up to his time.
See also: al-Ghazali; Ibn Sina

OLIVER LEAMAN

IBN SINA, ABU 'ALI AL-HUSAYN (980–1037)

Ibn Sina (Avicenna) is one of the foremost philosophers in the Medieval Hellenistic Islamic tradition that also includes al-Farabi and Ibn Rushd. His philosophical theory is a comprehensive, detailed and rationalistic account of the nature of God and Being, in which he finds a systematic place for the corporeal world, spirit, insight, and the varieties of logical thought including dialectic, rhetoric and poetry.

Central to Ibn Sina's philosophy is his concept of reality and reasoning. Reason, in his scheme, can allow progress through various levels of understanding and can finally lead to God, the ultimate truth. He stresses the importance of gaining knowledge, and develops a theory of knowledge based on four faculties: sense perception, retention, imagination and estimation. Imagination has the principal role in intellection, as it can compare and construct images which give it access to universals. Again the ultimate object of knowledge is God, the pure intellect.

In metaphysics, Ibn Sina makes a distinction between essence and existence; essence considers only the nature of things, and should be considered apart from their mental and physical realization. This distinction applies to all things except God, whom Ibn Sina identifies as the first cause and therefore both essence and existence. He also argued that the soul is incorporeal and cannot be destroyed. The soul, in his view, is an agent with choice in this world between good and evil, which in turn leads to reward or punishment.

Reference has sometimes been made to Ibn Sina's supposed mysticism, but this would appear to be based on a misreading by Western philosophers of parts of his work. As one of the most important practitioners of philosophy, Ibn Sina exercised a strong influence over both other Islamic philosophers and medieval Europe. His work was one of the main targets of al-Ghazali's attack on Hellenistic influences in Islam. In Latin translations, his works influenced many Christian philosophers, most notably Thomas Aquinas.

SALIM KEMAL

IDEALISM

Introduction

Idealism is now usually understood in philosophy as the view that mind is the most basic reality and that the physical world exists only as an appearance to or expression of mind, or as somehow mental in its inner essence. However, a philosophy which makes the physical world dependent upon mind is usually also called idealist even if it postulates some further hidden, more basic reality behind the mental and physical scenes (for example, Kant's things-in-themselves). There is also a certain tendency to restrict the term 'idealism' to systems for which what is basic is mind of a somewhat lofty nature, so that 'spiritual values' are the ultimate shapers of reality. (An older and broader use counts as idealist any view for which the physical world is somehow unreal compared with some more ultimate, not necessarily mental, reality conceived as the source of value, for example Platonic Forms.)

The founding fathers of idealism in Western thought are Berkeley (theistic idealism), Kant (transcendental idealism) and Hegel (absolute idealism). Although the precise sense in which Hegel was an idealist is problematic, his influence on subsequent absolute or monistic idealism was enormous. In the USA and the UK idealism, especially of the absolute kind, was the dominating philosophy of the late nineteenth and early twentieth century, receiving its most forceful expression with F.H. Bradley. It declined, without dying, under the influence of G.E. Moore and Bertrand Russell, and later of the logical positivists. Not a few philosophers believe, however, that it has a future.

1   The general case for idealism

As the term will be used here, a philosopher is an idealist if and only if they believe that the physical world exists *either* (1) only as an object for mind, *or* (2) only as a content of mind, *or* (3) only as something itself somehow mental in its true character, a disjunction we shall sum up as the thesis that the physical is derivative from mind. Particular idealists may go further and say that everything whatsoever is derivative from mind except mind itself, but this would not be affirmed by, for example, KANT, who believed in things-in-themselves which may be neither mental nor mind-derivative; neither, perhaps, would it be accepted by SCHOPENHAUER, for whom Kant's things-in-themselves become an unconscious cosmic Will. Moreover, there is no one view of the status of so-called abstract objects or universals which seems required of an idealist (see ABSTRACT OBJECTS).

The mind-dependence of the physical has been argued for and developed in widely varying ways. For example, the idealist may be a monist or a pluralist about the mind(s) from which the physical is derivative. Very significant too is the contrast between idealisms which are more ontological and those which are more epistemological in their approach. The two great exemplars of each are George BERKELEY and Immanuel Kant, the founding fathers of Western idealism and sources of most subsequent arguments in its favour.

Ontological idealism affirms that a certain view of reality, in which the physical is mind-dependent, is absolutely true, and regards such elements of common sense or science as appear to conflict with this either as wrong or as only seemingly incompatible. Epistemological idealism is concerned, rather, to show that the most acceptable views of the physical world, which doubtless include the claim that it is not mind-dependent, are, indeed, only true-for-us, but that truth-for-us is the only kind of truth it makes sense to seek. (A more qualified epistemological idealism may allow that chinks of a more absolute truth may suggest themselves and be important, but hardly belong to the main body of what we should call knowledge.) Thus, for idealism of the second kind, the mind-dependence of the physical is not so much a claim as to what is true about it, as about the sort of truth which truth about it is.

2   Berkeleian ontological idealism

According to Berkeley, there are only two types of existent – spirits (or minds) and ideas. Physical objects, as we ordinarily conceive them, are collections of sensory ideas (sense impressions).

Thus an apple is simply a collection of such sensory appearances as we are immediately aware of when we say that we are perceiving it (including the sensation of eating it). As for things, or those aspects of things, which are not perceived by any finite mind, they are there: *either* in the secondary sense that they would come into our minds if we took appropriate steps (gave ourselves appropriate impressions of moving in certain ways) to have a look at them, a sniff of them or whatever; *or* they are being perceived by an infinite mind. The second alternative brings in God immediately, the first is only explicable by saying that they are ideas which God would produce in us as a result of our taking those steps. Either way, the idealist truth that physical objects are collections of ideas, taken together with the obvious fact that everything is as though they continued their existence when unobserved by finite minds, appears to Berkeley an incontestable proof of God's existence.

Two of the main reasons why Berkeley thought that the physical world must consist of ideas were:

(1) It is only if physical objects are conceived as collections of ideas which hang together in experience that we have any empirical evidence for their existence.

(2) It is generally admitted that the so-called secondary qualities of physical things only exist as ideas in our minds (see PRIMARY–SECONDARY DISTINCTION). Moreover, it could be proved by the way in which secondary qualities vary with the state of the observer, and the way in which they are inseparable from sensations of pleasure and pain. But the considerations which show that secondary qualities are mind-dependent show equally that the primary ones are too. (Presented shape varies with conditions of observation as much as colour.) Moreover, no one can conceive of primary qualities existing in the absence of secondary qualities, so that they can only exist tied up with the admittedly mind-dependent.

It is usual to say that Berkeley's line of thought works only if one already accepts doctrines which he adopted uncritically from Locke (as he understood him), namely that all we ever perceive are ideas, and that secondary qualities are mind-dependent. It is, therefore, worth emphasizing that arguments of an essentially Berkeleian sort can be presented, and have been influential, which do not depend upon this Lockean inheritance.

The core of these arguments will be: physical objects, as they present themselves to our senses, do so with qualities which we cannot suppose to exist except for a perceiving mind. Indeed, we cannot even conceive them lacking all such qualities. These qualities, with which things present themselves to the senses, include what we may call all their perspectival qualities (the thing is given with features which reflect the position from which it is seen or the way in which it is felt and so on), also hedonic and aesthetic qualities, and finally an organization of the perceptual field into foreground and background, and into certain *Gestalten*. However much you try to imagine a thing as it is in itself, apart from any observer, you will find yourself imagining it as having features which represent the rough position of an observer of it, how they feel about it, and how they organize their perceptual field. In short you can only imagine it with features which it could only have as a presence to some observer. Such reasoning continues to persuade those of a Berkeleian cast of mind that one cannot form any genuine conception of a physical world existing except as an object for an observer.

All this is likely to invite two objections. First, it may be said that you should distinguish between the representation (such as an image in your mind) and what that representation represents for you. Only certain features of the image serve a representative function. Now the fact that the image may have some of the features which an actual sense impression of it would have only if the thing were perceived in a certain way, does not mean that these features must be regarded as belonging to what is represented. To this it may be replied by the idealist that they do not deny that, by ignoring certain features of the image, you can regard only the others as playing a role in picturing the object; and that these need not include those which obviously imply presence to a subject. What they deny, in contrast, is that one can form any sort of representation which will, so-to-speak, positively depict the thing as existing without subject-implying features. And unless one can do this one has no real sense of what an unperceived thing could be like.

The second objection is that one can conceive what one cannot imagine. Surely you can *conceive* a physical thing without these subject-implying features even if you cannot *imagine* it. To this the idealist may reply that you do not really understand what you are thinking if you only think about it in words (and doubtless this is what the objector means by conceiving it). Really to bring before your mind the character of the situation you believe in requires that, using the expression broadly, you must *imagine* it, and this you cannot do except by imagining it as it would present itself to a certain observer.

Such a line of thought, though not precisely Berkeley's in detail, is Berkeleian in spirit and inspiration and it is likely to be a main plank of an ontological idealism which claims that unperceived physical reality is an impossibility. What positive view of the world can be based upon such reflections? For Berkeley it showed that there must be a God who is responsible for those ideas which (after acting in a certain way) we have no choice but to experience and who keeps the whole system of ideas available to each individual spirit in conformity with a universal system of laws determining the appearances available to each.

However, there have been philosophers who put forward a phenomenalism supposed not to imply the existence of God. According to them, one can speak meaningfully of physical things as existing unperceived. However, these only exist in a secondary sense as compared with those which are actually perceived, and their existence in this secondary sense is only the fact that they are available for perception. That is, there are definite facts for each of us (according to what we would ordinarily call our position in space) which determine what perceptions are available or compulsory for us in response to what we do or suffer (what sensations of movement we give ourselves or are given). There is no need to suppose that there is some explanation for this; it must just be accepted as a brute fact.

This phenomenalism is often not classed as idealist because its reductive account of the physical is divorced not only from theism, but from any other conception of the world as shaped by Reason or other higher forms of Mind. It is a puzzle of intellectual history that some of those most influenced by Berkeley's views of physical reality have been among the most atheistic and, in the popular sense, most 'materialist' of thinkers (for example, T.H. Huxley, A.J. AYER and, with qualifications, J.S. MILL).

3   Kantian transcendental idealism

A simple version of Kant might present him as a phenomenalist who supplemented his phenomenalism with the admission that there must be some explanation of why the sense experiences available to us are what they are, yet who regarded this explanation as unavailable to us except as the thesis that they result from unconscious operations which we (as we really are rather than as we appear to ourselves) conduct upon things-in-themselves of whose real character we can know nothing (except that it cannot be that of anything properly called physical). However, Kant's reasoning for his transcendental idealism is largely different from those deriving from, or inspired by, Berkeley (see KANT, I. §5).

For Kant there are two striking facts about our knowledge of the world which only his transcendental idealism can explain ('transcendental' means

'having to do with our cognitive powers'). First, we have a great deal of 'synthetic a priori' knowledge about it (see A PRIORI; ANALYTICITY). Thus we know that arithmetic and the axioms of Euclid apply to the physical world as a whole, that every physical or mental process occurs in conformity with universal causal laws, and that change requires a permanent substratum of matter which remains quantitatively the same. Second, neither a priori nor empirical knowledge can answer the great questions of human destiny, such as whether God exists and whether we are immortal. The only possible explanation of our synthetic a priori knowledge about the physical and, indeed, mental worlds is that it is really our knowledge of our own cognitive nature. Space and time are the forms of our perceptual intuition and the categories of causation, substance and accident and so on are the categories by which we construct the unitary world of our actual and possible experience out of unconscious stimuli which reach the hidden self from things-in-themselves (or 'noumena'), of whose character we must remain ignorant. And it is because we are ignorant of things-in-themselves that we cannot *know* the answers to the questions about God and immortality, for these concern absolute truth rather than that truth-for-us which is all that is available for knowledge. On the other hand, just because we cannot *know* the answers to these questions, we may have *faith* that they would suit our moral natures and show that, in spite of the causal determinism holding in the phenomenal world, we are responsible at some 'noumenal' level for our own adherence or otherwise to the categorical imperatives of morality.

Some of the details of Kant's theory are outmoded by the fact that science seems no longer committed to some of his supposedly synthetic a priori truths such as the axioms of Euclid and the universality of causation. However, the idea that the world as we know it owes, to an incalculable extent, its general character to our particular modes of perception and thought still has great force. In Berkeley there is no suggestion that what we know is created by our knowledge of it. The ideas which constitute the physical world are simply the ones which God has chosen to give himself and us and to organize in a certain way. Our knowledge of those we perceive is a fully accurate knowledge by direct acquaintance and the existence and character of others, as actualities or possibilities, is known by induction. In Kant, knowledge itself to a great extent creates its objects by unconscious operations upon unconscious stimuli reaching us from things-in-themselves whose real nature it leaves in darkness.

The distinction is somewhat subtle, since both the Berkeleian and Kantian, in effect, regard facts about the physical world as facts about the perceptions we may obtain through sensations of movement in certain directions. However, the Berkeleian inheritance has mainly been to insist on the way in which the physical world cannot be conceived without sensory qualities which can only occur as contents of experience, while the Kantian inheritance has mainly been to insist on the way in which our cognition of the physical world interprets it by concepts which it *brings to* experience rather than *abstracts from* it.

In fact, Kant's position is nearer to Berkeley's than he himself allowed. According to Kant his idealism is transcendental, whereas Berkeley's is empirical. What this comes to is that Berkeley's idealism professes to give the absolute truth about the physical world, as a corrective to a realism which regarded it as existing independently of mind, while Kant accepted such realism, but claimed that it was only true for us, and that, as for the absolute truth about things which underlie it, we know nothing beyond the mere fact that there must be such an absolute truth (in the moral and theistic significance of which we may have faith).

4   German absolute idealism

The great figures in German absolute idealism were J.G. FICHTE, G.W.F. HEGEL and F.W.J. VON SCHELLING (see ABSOLUTE, THE). (The character of their considerable political influence cannot be considered here.) In effect, each agreed with Kant that ordinary common sense and 'scientific' (in our usual sense, not theirs, in which it referred to their own philosophic conclusions) truth about the physical world is only truth for us. But they went beyond Kant in holding that philosophy can put this in the context of an absolute and rationally demonstrated truth about an essentially spiritual world. In fact, Kant's attempt to close the door on attempts to know the ultimate truth of things opened it to some of the most robust claims ever made to have probed the mysteries of the universe.

For Kant the physical world only exists for us, and our knowledge of it is only truth for us. However, we can recognize that there must be two hidden determinants of it, modes of cognition which take place in our own hidden depths, and the unconscious non-physical stimuli from mysterious things-in-themselves out of which they make the familiar physical world. Fichte thought the postulation of such things-in-themselves quite unnecessary. If the knowable physical world is something whose form we construct unconsciously why should not the matter be something we determine unconsciously too? Thereby we avoid the nebulous

hypothesis of things-in-themselves, and are left simply with our own indubitable existence and hidden depths thereof, of which we dimly sense the presence. Of course there is an external world or non-ego, but it exists only as something which the ego posits and does so for reasons the general character of which can be deciphered. For the ego wants to live a life of moral worth and this it can only do if it has obstacles to overcome; thus the external world it posits consists precisely in those obstacles whose over-coming is most morally valuable at its current stage of development.

But how is it that each ego shares a non-ego, as it evidently does, with other egos? Fichte has two related answers. One is that moral development is something which can only occur in a community, so that the different egos need to posit a shared non-ego giving them a common environment in which to work out their moral destiny. Second, as his thought developed, Fichte became clearer that the ego which is working out its moral destiny in each of us is really a single world-spirit living out an apparent multiplicity of lives. Fichte developed this account by way of a dialectical method which became the hallmark of German idealism (inspired by Kant for whom, however, it was rather a source of illusion than a means to truth) in which apparently opposed truths are successively reconciled in higher syntheses until absolute truth is reached. Thus was born absolute idealism, in which the reality behind both nature and finite mind is a single absolute mind or self in process of self-discovery or development. However, Fichte's brand of absolute idealism is sometimes also called 'subjective idealism', because it regards the natural world as existing only for the subjective experience of finite individuals, expressions of a single world self though they may be.

Schelling was originally a follower of Fichte, but his continually shifting versions of idealism tended to become more 'objective' or at least more positively concerned with nature for its own sake. The Absolute or universal self does not simply dream the physical world as the scene of moral endeavour but rather expresses itself in a parallel dialectic, both 'really' in the nature from which the mind arises and 'ideally' in the mind for which nature exists. The two come together eventually in philosophical understanding and, more concretely, in art.

Absolute idealism, and the dialectical method and ontology, reached its historically most important form in the philosophy of Hegel. For Hegel, the world consists in a series of terms each surpassing its (only sometimes temporal) predecessors by incorporating what was satisfactory in them, in a manner which reconciles in a higher synthesis that in which they contradicted each other. The series begins with pure concepts, leading on to actual natural and then humanly historical processes and terminates in a community in the free service of which each individual can find themselves fulfilled and in the consciousness, in the minds of philosophers, of its total nature. Thus, everything exists as path to, and as fodder for, a rich communal spiritual life, but how far this means that nothing really exists except as a component within or object for consciousness or spirit, is controversial. Therefore, it is unclear how far Hegel was an idealist in our sense (as opposed to the broader sense mentioned parenthetically above).

Hegel and Schelling had originally seen themselves as partners in developing a new philosophy, but Hegel soon surpassed his at first better known associate in fame and influence. However, Schelling had his turn again on Hegel's death, developing a new so-called positive philosophy in which he rejected the high a priori road to the nature of existence which both thinkers had taken previously. Absolute idealism must appeal partly to empirical features of the world rather than merely cite them sometimes as illustrations of what reason can independently prove must be so. This more traditionally Christian philosophy sought to give God and man a freedom effectively denied them by Hegelianism. Its somewhat bizarre ontology also seemed to many to show German idealism in its death throes.

In different ways Fichte, Schelling and Hegel each held that the world could only be understood through realizing that it is the concrete actualization of concepts whose proper home is in the mind. This binds them to Kant, but they sought to go beyond him in explaining why the relevant categories are just as they are and why there is a real unity of experience common to apparently different minds: namely that, in the end, the world is the construction of one universal Mind or Reason. Each saw himself as drawing on SPINOZA as well as Kant, but as substituting an ultimate self or subject for Spinoza's substance.

Standing quite apart from these absolute idealists is the lonely but immensely influential figure of Arthur SCHOPENHAUER. Arguably the closest metaphysically, if not in mood, to Kant, and accepting in the main his transcendental idealism, he claimed to have discovered the true nature of the realm of things-in-themselves, regarding them as aspects of a single universal Will, manifesting itself as object for a subject (which was its own self fallen into a state of wretched self-assertion), from which it can escape only by a culmination of that denial of the will to live, characteristic, as he saw it, of sainthood.

5 Anglo-American absolute idealism

As German philosophers moved away from idealism in the later part of the nineteenth century, idealism of an essentially absolute kind became the dominant mode of philosophy in the UK and the USA (where, however, there were more serious rivals to it). This was motivated partly by the search for a form of religious belief which would be less vulnerable to Lyell and Darwin than traditional Christianity had been, and by an ethical viewpoint which would be rather nobler in its conception of the possibilities of human life than Benthamite utilitarianism. Some of these philosophers (for example John and Edward Caird, and William Wallace), were doctrinal Hegelians, utilizing Hegelianism to save Christianity.

More importantly original philosophers of an idealist persuasion during this period were T.H. GREEN and F.H. BRADLEY in the UK (also the very like-minded, though more Hegelian, Bernard BOSANQUET), and Josiah ROYCE in the USA. We can only mention in passing the very distinctive idealism already advanced by J.F. Ferrier in Scotland, which draws both on Berkeley and on German idealism. These thinkers were to various extents influenced by Kant and Hegel and the other German idealists, but in the case of Bradley, at least, something of the Berkeleian tradition is, perhaps unconsciously, present.

Green was anxious above all to show that the development of human life from animal origins could not be explained purely by way of natural selection, or indeed in any naturalistic way. Rather, must it be recognized as the gradual unfolding of the life of a universal spirit aspiring to fulfilment in an eventually virtuous form of human life. For empiricism and naturalism cannot explain the connectedness of the world, and the ability of the human mind to synthesize events of different times into a unitary history. This is only possible if the world is the expression of a single universal spirit of which each of us is an actualization in which it becomes aware of itself. The general upshot is quite Hegelian, but there is little use of Hegelian dialectic.

Bradley's metaphysics derives from two main reflections: first, that nothing is genuinely conceivable except experience with its various modes and contents; second, that what we describe as distinct things in relation to each other can only be adequately conceived as abstractions from a higher unity. In the end all things must, therefore, be abstractions from one single Cosmic Experience. With his denial of time's reality and his claim that Reality is really a single cosmic *Nunc Stans* whose ingredients only seem to be passing away in time, Bradley strikes a note which is perhaps more Platonic than Hegelian. Royce's absolute idealism has a good deal in common with Bradley, but whereas for Bradley God was only a rather superior 'appearance' along with the ordinary things of daily life, for Royce the Absolute was God, being personal in a way that Bradley's Absolute was not.

6 Panpsychism

One of the main charges against idealism is that of 'cosmic impiety' (Santayana). Its tendency is to make the vast realm of nature simply a representation in a mind observing or thinking of it. This can hardly do justice either to its obstinacy (surely not primarily of our own making, whatever Fichte may have thought) or to its wonderfulness. Such reflections have led some of those who are persuaded of the basic idealist claim that unexperienced reality is impossible, to hold the panpsychist position that nature is composed of units which feel their own existence and relation to other things, just as truly, if less articulately, as we do (see PANPSYCHISM). This was the view of Royce, and Bradley thought it might be true. It was a main plank, somewhat eccentrically developed, of the German idealist Gustav FECHNER (and is perhaps adumbrated in Schelling); also of LEIBNIZ, who in this respect can be called an idealist.

Panpsychism of this sort has been most fully developed in recent times in the work of A.N. WHITEHEAD and of Charles Hartshorne. It is sometimes regarded as a synthesis of realism and idealism; realist because it gives the ultimate units of nature (whatever they are) a reality in themselves (as what they are for themselves); idealist because it denies unexperienced reality. When the inner sentient life of (the rest of) nature is thought of as unified with the subjective life of humans and animals (as it must be for a Bradley or a Royce) in one absolute consciousness, we have a form of absolute or objective idealism which quite avoids the anthropocentric character it had in the work of thinkers such as Fichte.

7 Personal idealism

Many thinkers of an idealist persuasion in the English-speaking world bridled somewhat at the downplaying of individual persons by absolute idealism, especially Bradley and to a lesser extent Royce. This led to the development, as the nineteenth century closed, of some forms of personal idealism for which reality is a community of independently real spirits (with or without a God as a *primus inter pares*) and the physical world their common object or construction. There is no great figure here, with the possible exception of J.M.E. McTAGGART who espoused a highly individual form of pluralistic idealism. Otherwise the main proponent of personal idealism was the US philosopher, G.H. Howison, although eight Oxford philosophers published a manifesto under this label in 1902 (see PERSONALISM).

Anglo-American idealism was, for a time, widely thought to have been refuted by the work of G.E. MOORE and Bertrand RUSSELL in the UK and such pragmatists as JAMES and DEWEY in the USA (though there were certainly idealist features to the thought of these two Americans), but a contrary judgement is now not uncommon. Edmund Husserl's phenomenology remains influential in some quarters, and some agree with his eventual view that it implies a form of transcendental idealism (see HUSSERL, E.). Some regard the antirealism associated with Michael DUMMETT as idealist in spirit (see REALISM AND ANTIREALISM), while some of the continuing school of Wittgensteinians regard the thought of WITTGENSTEIN as a form of social idealism. Much closer to traditional idealism, however, is the conceptual idealism of the important US philosopher Nicholas Rescher (which synthesizes idealism and pragmatism) and idealist positions (not, it must be admitted, so far very influential) advocated in the UK by John Foster and, if he may say so, by the author of this entry.

References and further reading

Kant, I. (1781) *Critique of Pure Reason*, trans. N. Kemp Smith, London: Macmillan, 1933. (The classic statement of Kant's transcendental idealism, one of the greatest and most influential works in the history of philosophy.)

Sturt, H. (ed.) (1902) *Personal Idealism: Philosophical Essays by Eight Members of the University of Oxford*, London: Macmillan. (Personal idealist manifesto against the submerging of the individual by absolute idealism. See especially the contributions of F.C.S. Schiller and Hastings Rashdall.)

T.L.S. SPRIGGE

IDEALISM, GERMAN

See GERMAN IDEALISM

IDEALIZATIONS

Scientific analyses of particular phenomena are invariably simplified or idealized. The universe does not contain only two bodies as assumed in Newton's derivation of Kepler's laws, or only one body as assumed in Schwarzschild's relativistic update; real economic agents do not act exclusively to maximize expected utilities, the surfaces of ordinary plate condensers are not infinitely extended planes, and the sine of an angle is not equal in measure to the angle itself. There are many reasons for the use of such misdescriptions. First and foremost is the need to achieve mathematical tractability. Science gets nowhere unless numbers, or numerical constraints, are produced that can form the basis of predictions and explanations. Idealizations may also be required because of the unavailability of certain data or because of the absence of necessary auxiliary theories.

The philosophical problem is to make normative sense of this common but complex scientific practice. For example, how can theories be tested given that they connect to the world only through the intermediary of idealized descriptions? In what sense can there be scientific explanations if what is to be explained must be misdescribed before theory can be brought to bear? The fact that idealizations can often be improved, with corresponding salutary effect on the accuracy of prediction or usefulness of explanation, suggests that idealizations should be understood as part of some sort of convergent process.

See also: EXPERIMENT; MODELS; THEORIES, SCIENTIFIC

RONALD LAYMON

IDEALS

Ideals are models of excellence. They can be moral or nonmoral, and either 'substantive' or 'deliberative'. Substantive ideals present models of excellence against which things in a relevant class can be assessed, such as models of the just society or the good person. Deliberative ideals present models of excellent deliberation, leading to correct or warranted ethical conclusions. Ideals figure in ethics in two opposed ways. Most centrally, ideals serve to justify ethical judgments and to guide people in how to live. Sometimes, however, ideals may conflict with moral demands, thereby testing the limits of morality.

Reliance upon ideals in the development of ethical theories seems unavoidable but raises difficult questions. How can the choice of a particular ideal be justified? How might conflicts between ideals and other values, especially moral demands, be resolved?

See also: SOLIDARITY; VIRTUE ETHICS

CONNIE S. ROSATI

IDEAS, THEORY OF
See PLATO

IDENTITY

Anything whatsoever has the relation of identity to itself, and to nothing else. Things are identical if they are one thing, not two. We can refute the claim that they are identical if we can find a property of one that is not simultaneously a property of the other. The concept of identity is fundamental to logic. Without it, counting would be impossible, for we could not distinguish in principle between counting one thing twice and counting two different things. When we have acquired the concept, it can still be difficult to make this distinction in practice. Misjudgments of identity are possible because one thing can be presented in many guises.

Identity judgments often involve assumptions about the nature of things. The identity of the present mature tree with the past sapling implies persistence through change. The non-identity of the actual child of one couple with the hypothetical child of a different couple is implied by the claim that ancestry is an essential property. Knowledge of what directions are involves knowledge that parallel lines have identical directions. Many controversies over identity concern the nature of the things in question. Others concern challenges to the orthodox conception just sketched of identity itself.

1 Exposition of a popular view
2 Alternatives

1 Exposition of a popular view

Identity is the relation that, necessarily, each thing has to itself and to nothing else. Thus Constantinople has the identity relation to Istanbul because Constantinople *is* Istanbul, the very same city. This relation is often called 'numerical' identity, to distinguish it from 'qualitative' identity, the relation of exact similarity. Although 'identical' twins might be qualitatively identical, they are not numerically identical, for there are two of them, not one. The formula '$x = y$' says that x and y are (numerically) identical.

Identity is governed by two basic logical principles, reflexivity and Leibniz's Law (see LEIBNIZ, G.W. §11). To say that the identity relation is reflexive is to say that for each thing x, $x = x$. Leibniz's Law says that if $x = y$ then whatever is true of x is also true of y; it is used in arguments such as 'Jack the Ripper was in Whitechapel last night, the Prince of Wales was not in Whitechapel last night; therefore Jack the Ripper is not the Prince of Wales'. Leibniz was not the first to formulate this law, which was known in antiquity. It is sometimes called the 'indiscernibility of identicals', not to be confused with Leibniz's principle of the 'identity of indiscernibles', a kind of converse, which says (implausibly) that qualitative identity implies numerical identity (see IDENTITY OF INDISCERNIBLES). Reflexivity and Leibniz's Law characterize identity uniquely: it is provably impossible for two non-equivalent relations to satisfy both principles. The two principles also entail that identity is symmetric (if $x = y$ then $y = x$) and transitive (if $x = y$ and $y = z$ then $x = z$).

If $a = b$, Leibniz's Law says that whatever is true of a is true of b. However, this permits the replacement of 'a' by 'b' only in contexts in which the expressions merely specify which thing is being talked about. For example, it is invalid to argue from 'Jocasta = the mother of Oedipus' and 'Oedipus knows that he married Jocasta' to 'Oedipus knows that he married the mother of Oedipus', for here 'the mother of Oedipus' does not merely specify a person; it specifies the description under which Oedipus is said to know that he married her (see PROPOSITIONAL ATTITUDES). Looking at photographs of a mature tree and a sapling, one cannot use Leibniz's Law to refute the hypothesis 'The mature tree = the sapling' on the grounds that 'The mature tree is tall' is true and 'The sapling is tall' is false. The noun phrases 'the mature tree' and 'the sapling' do not merely specify trees; they indicate the times with respect to which tallness is predicated. A correct understanding of Leibniz's Law is needed if identity through change is not to seem contradictory.

A genuine consequence of Leibniz's Law is the necessity of identity: things that are in fact identical could not have been distinct. For suppose that $x = y$. Since x could not have been distinct from itself, x could not have been distinct from y. Thus x and y cannot be contingently identical: they must be identical in all circumstances. A more complex argument concludes that they cannot be contingently distinct. They are either necessarily identical or necessarily distinct. Consequently, they are either always identical or always distinct. For example, if my headache is identical with an event in my brain, then that headache has to be that event; neither could exist without the other. Of course, a sentence such as 'Rome = the capital of Italy' is contingently true, but that is because the description 'the capital of Italy' need not have specified the city it actually specifies. The example is consistent with the necessity of identity, however, for it does not imply that one city could have been each of two.

An argument like that for the necessity of identity can be used to refute the idea that questions of identity need have no right answer. For example, it is sometimes held to be indeterminate whether a given mass of rock and ice is Everest (see VAGUENESS). However, it is determinate whether Everest is Everest. If Leibniz's Law and ordinary logic apply in this context, it follows that Everest is distinct from that mass, and the identity question has a right answer – a negative one. Thus the hypothesis of indeterminacy contradicts itself.

Statements of identity in natural languages often include a noun answering the question 'same what?', for example, 'Istanbul is the same city as Constantinople'. Since identity is uniquely characterized by its logic, the role of the noun is not to disambiguate 'same'; 'a is the same F as b' is equivalent to 'a is an F and $a = b$' (from which 'b is an F' follows by Leibniz's Law). Identity is not defined kind by kind. Rather, we use the pregiven notion of identity in defining kinds. For example, we explain the difference between rivers and collections of water molecules by saying that the same river contains different collections of water molecules at different times.

A 'criterion of identity' for a kind is a necessary and sufficient condition for members of the kind to be identical. Frege's criterion of identity for directions is that the directions of lines are identical if and only if the lines are parallel. The criterion of identity for numbers is that the number of F things is the number of G things if and only if there is a one-to-one correlation between the F things and the G things. In such cases, members of the kind can be presented in various guises: directions as the directions of various lines; numbers as the numbers of various pluralities. The criterion of identity states the condition for two guises to be guises of one member of the kind. Without a grasp of these conditions, one would not know what directions or numbers were.

A criterion of identity for a spatiotemporal kind is expected to give the condition for a member of the kind at one place and time to be identical with a member of the kind at another place and time: for example, it may have to follow a continuous trajectory between these space-time points. An account may also be required of an object's identity across hypothetical circumstances. For example, one may hold that a member of the kind could not have originated at different places and times in different possible worlds. Spatiotemporal objects can be exactly similar without being identical, for they can originate at different times or places. In contrast, purely abstract objects cannot be exactly similar without being identical.

2 Alternatives

Every aspect of the preceding view has been questioned. Although it is popular, the philosophers who accept it all may be in a minority.

That identity is a relation has been denied, both on metaphysical grounds (it cannot relate two things) and on grammatical grounds (some assimilate 'is' in 'Constantinople is Istanbul' to the 'is' of predication as in 'Constantinople is crowded'). However, the logic of '=' does single out a unique class of ordered pairs of objects to which it applies, which suffices to make identity a relation in some minimal sense.

The contrast between identity and indiscernibility has been challenged, on the grounds that indiscernibles satisfy the same descriptions and since *a* satisfies the description 'identical with *a*', so does anything indiscernible from *a*. The obvious reply is that indiscernibles merely satisfy the same *intrinsic* descriptions, but it is hard to explain what 'intrinsicness' is.

Many applications of Leibniz's Law are problematic. Some deny its applicability to contexts that treat non-actual possibilities or even non-present times, thus excluding the derivation of the necessity or permanence of identity. The intention is, for example, to permit a pot to be contingently identical with the clay of which it is made, or the clay to be temporarily identical with the pot. One question is whether the envisaged restrictions on Leibniz's Law are *ad hoc*. They would not be if so-called identity between objects in different possible worlds or at different times could not be taken at face value but was somehow reducible to relations of qualitative similarity among counterpart objects each of which was confined to a single possible world or time. Such views have been supported by appeal to the difficulty of specifying what is essential to an object, for example, to what extent a particular ship could originally have been made from different planks of wood, or how much it could change without ceasing to exist. However, the proposed reductions are both complex and hard to reconcile with ordinary assumptions about the nature of everyday objects.

Identity has also been regarded as sometimes indeterminate. Although it is usually conceded that if things are identical then it is determinate whether they are identical, in some non-standard logics it does not follow that if it is indeterminate whether they are identical then they are not identical. Such logics postulate an intermediate status that propositions can have between truth and falsity. One challenge to this view is to explain what it means for a proposition to be not true without being false.

Yet another nonstandard view is the doctrine that identity is always relative to an answer to the question 'same what?'. For example, if *a* and *b* are copies of *Middlemarch*, this view disputes the inference from '*a* is the same edition as *b*' and '*a* is a copy' to '*a* is the same copy as *b*'. The relation of being the same edition will not satisfy Leibniz's Law unrestrictedly, but the view needs to show that no other relation (for example, being the same copy) could satisfy Leibniz's Law unrestrictedly, for such a relation would be a case of non-relative identity.

Many disputes about criteria of identity for particular kinds of entity (see PERSONAL IDENTITY) concern the nature of those entities, not of identity itself. But even the concept of a criterion of identity is itself problematic. For example, can one give an adequate criterion of identity for events by saying that events are identical if and only if they have the same causes and effects? The problem is that the causes and effects of events include other events. The criterion is in some sense circular, but it is hard to state the requirement of non-circularity clearly. Even if that could be done, it is unclear why every kind of object should have a non-circular criterion of identity. There may be nothing more basic than identity to which identity could be reduced. The standard logic of identity demands no such reduction.

Perhaps identity will come to be regarded as a logical constant, no more problematic than, say, conjunction. If so, many of the issues mentioned above will remain difficult, but their difficulty will concern the nature of various kinds of object, not the relation of identity.

See also: CONTINUANTS

References and further reading

Kripke, S.A. (1980) *Naming and Necessity*, Oxford: Blackwell. (A basic work on the connection between identity and necessity.)

Noonan, H.W. (ed.) (1993) *Identity*, Aldershot: Dartmouth. (Collects many relevant articles.)

TIMOTHY WILLIAMSON

IDENTITY OF INDISCERNIBLES

The principle of the identity of indiscernibles states that objects which are alike in all respects are identical. It is sometimes called Leibniz's Law. This name is also frequently used for the converse principle, the indiscernibility of identicals, that objects which are identical are alike in all respects. Both principles together are sometimes taken to define the concept of identity. Unlike the indiscernibility of identicals, which is widely accepted as a logical truth, the identity of indiscernibles principle has frequently been doubted and rejected. The principle is susceptible of more precise formulation in a number of ways, some more dubitable than others.

PETER SIMONS

IDENTITY OF PERSONS
See PERSONAL IDENTITY

IDENTITY, POSTMODERN THEORIES OF
See ALTERITY AND IDENTITY, POSTMODERN
THEORIES OF

IDENTITY THEORY OF MIND
See MIND, IDENTITY THEORY OF

IDEOLOGY

An ideology is a set of ideas, beliefs and attitudes, consciously or unconsciously held, which reflects or shapes understandings or misconceptions of the social and political world. It serves to recommend, justify or endorse collective action aimed at preserving or changing political practices and institutions. The concept of ideology is split almost irreconcilably between two major senses. The first is pejorative, denoting particular, historically distorted (political) thought which reinforces certain relationships of domination and in respect of which ideology functions as a critical unmasking concept. The second is a non-pejorative assertion about the different families of cultural symbols and ideas human beings employ in perceiving, comprehending and evaluating social and political realities in general, often within a systemic framework. Those families perform significant mapping and integrating functions.

A major division exists within this latter category. Some analysts claim that the study of ideology can be non-evaluative in establishing scientific facts about the way political beliefs reflect the social world and propel people to specific action within it. Others hold that ideology injects specific politically value-laden meanings into conceptualizations of the social world which are inevitably indeterminate, and is consequently a means of constructing rather than reflecting that world. This also applies to interpretations undertaken by the analysts of ideology themselves.

MICHAEL FREEDEN

ILLOCUTIONARY ACT
See SPEECH ACTS

ILLOCUTIONARY FORCE
See PRAGMATICS; SPEECH ACTS

IMAGINATION

'Imagination' and 'imagine' enjoy a family of meanings, only some of which imply the use of mental imagery. If I ask you to imagine a red flower, I will likely be inviting you to form an image. But if, for example, I say that I imagine that I will go to the party after taking a nap, I am not obviously giving voice to mental imagery. A variety of questions has arisen concerning imagination in its various forms, of which the following four are central. How do internal acts of imagining come to be about particular external objects and states of affairs, actual and non-actual? How are perceptual acts similar to and different from the central cases of imagining? To what extent do routine perception and cognition use cognitive resources similar to those of creative imagination? Are there any cognitive pursuits in which imagination can play a justificatory role?

J. O'LEARY-HAWTHORNE

IMMORTALITY OF THE SOUL
See SOUL, NATURE AND IMMORTALITY OF

IMPARTIALITY

On the one hand, most of us feel that we are permitted, even required, to give special consideration to the interests of ourselves and our loved ones; on the other hand, we also recognize the appeal of a more detached perspective which demands equal consideration for the interests of all. Among writers in the utilitarian tradition, some insist that the strictly impartial perspective is the only one that is ethically tenable, while others argue that a measure of institutionalized partiality can be justified as a means to maximizing welfare. An alternative tradition, stemming from Kant, sees the demand for impartiality as deriving from the importance of fairness and equal respect for persons, but tends to leave open the degree of partiality permitted. Finally, the Aristotelian conception of ethics offers a justification of partiality based on the structure of those virtuous dispositions of character (such as those involved in friendship and self-esteem) which are required for developing our distinctively human potentialities.
See also: EQUALITY

JOHN COTTINGHAM

IMPLICATURE

A term used in philosophy, logic and linguistics (especially pragmatics) to denote the act of meaning or implying something by saying something else. A girl who says 'I have to study' in response to 'Can you go to the movies?' has *implicated* (the technical verb for making an implicature) that she cannot go. Implicatures may depend on the conversational context, as in this example, or on conventions, as when a speaker says 'He was clever but poor', thereby implying – thanks to the conventional usage of the word 'but' – that poverty is unexpected given intelligence. Implicature gained importance through the work of H.P. Grice. Grice proposed that conversational implicatures depend on a general principle of rational cooperation stating that people normally try to further the accepted purpose of the conversation by conveying what is true, informative, relevant and perspicuous. The extent and nature of the dependence, and the precise maxims involved, are matters of controversy. Other issues include whether certain implications are implicatures rather than presuppositions or parts of the senses (literal meanings) of the words used.

See also: PRAGMATICS; SEMANTICS; SPEECH ACTS

WAYNE A. DAVIS

INCOMMENSURABILITY

When one scientific theory or tradition is replaced by another in a scientific revolution, the concepts involved often change in fundamental ways. For example, among other differences, in Newtonian mechanics an object's mass is independent of its velocity, while in relativity mechanics, mass increases as the velocity approaches that of light. Earlier philosophers of science maintained that Einsteinian mechanics *reduces* to Newtonian mechanics in the limit of high velocities. However, Thomas Kuhn and Paul Feyerabend introduced a rival view. Kuhn argued that different scientific traditions are defined by their adherence to different *paradigms*, fundamental perspectives which shape or determine not only substantive beliefs about the world, but also methods, problems, standards of solution or explanation, and even what counts as an observation or fact. *Scientific revolutions* (changes of paradigm) alter all these profoundly, leading to perspectives so different that the meanings of words looking and sounding the same become utterly distinct in the pre- and post-revolutionary traditions. Thus, according to both Kuhn and Feyerabend, the concepts of mass employed in the Newtonian and Einsteinian traditions are incommensurable with one another, too radically different to be compared at all. The thesis that terms in different scientific traditions and communities are radically distinct, and the modifications that have stemmed from that thesis, became known as the thesis of incommensurability.

DUDLEY SHAPERE

INCONTINENCE
See AKRASIA

INDETERMINACY OF MEANING AND TRANSLATION
See RADICAL TRANSLATION AND RADICAL INTERPRETATION

INDETERMINISM
See DETERMINISM AND INDETERMINISM

INDEXICALITY
See DEMONSTRATIVES AND INDEXICALS

INDIAN AND TIBETAN PHILOSOPHY

Introduction

The people of South Asia have been grappling with philosophical issues, and writing down their thoughts, for at least as long as the Europeans and the Chinese. When Hellenistic philosophers accompanied Alexander the Great on his military campaigns into the Indus valley, on the western edge of what is now the Republic of India, they expressed delight and amazement upon encountering Indians who thought as they thought and lived the sort of reflective life that they recommended living.

Nearly all philosophical contributions in India were made by people writing (or speaking) commentaries on already existing texts; to be a philosopher was to interpret a text and to be part of a more or less well-defined textual tradition. It is common, therefore, when speaking of Indian philosophers, to identify them as belonging to one school or another. To belong to a school of philosophy was a matter of having an interpretation of the principal texts that defined that school. At the broadest level of generalization, Indians of the classical period were either Hindus, Buddhists or Jainas (see BUDDHIST PHILOSOPHY, INDIAN; HINDU PHILOSOPHY; JAINA PHILOSOPHY). In addition to these three schools, all of which were in some sense religious, there was a more secular school in the classical period, whose tenets were materialistic and hedonistic (see MATERIALISM, INDIAN SCHOOL OF). The end of the classical period in Indian philosophy is customarily marked by the arrival of Muslims from Turkey and Persia at the close of the first millennium. The contributions of Indian Muslims added to the richness of Indian philosophy during the medieval period (see ISLAMIC PHILOSOPHY).

Writing was introduced into Tibet not long after the arrival of Buddhism from India in the seventh century. The earliest literature of Tibet was made up

439

mostly of Buddhist texts, translated from Indian languages and from Chinese. Eventually, ideas associated with Bon, the indigenous religion of Tibet, were also written down. Tibetan philosophers followed the habit of Indians in that they made their principal contributions by writing commentaries on earlier texts. Key Buddhist philosophers from Tibet are SA SKYA PAṆḌITA (1182–1251), TSONG KHA PA BLO BZANG GRAGS PA (1357–1419), RGYAL TSHAB DAR MA RIN CHEN (1364–1432), MKHAS GRUB DGE LEGS DPAL BZANG PO (1385–1438) and MI BSKYOD RDO RJE (1507–54).

1 Hindu philosophy
2 Buddhist and Jaina philosophy
3 Pronunciation of Sanskrit words

1 Hindu philosophy

The philosophical schools associated with what we now call Hinduism all had in common respect for the authority of the Veda ('Knowledge'), scriptures accepted as a revealed body of wisdom, cosmological information and codes of societal obligations. The textual schools that systematized disciplines derived from the Veda were the Mīmāṃsā, the Nyāya, the Vaiśeṣika, the Sāṅkhya and the various Vedānta schools (see MĪMĀMSĀ; NYĀYA-VAIŚEṢIKA; SĀṄKHYA; VEDĀNTA). Concerned as all these schools were with correct interpretation of the Veda, it is natural that questions of language were of paramount importance in Indian philosophy (see LANGUAGE, INDIAN THEORIES OF; MEANING, INDIAN THEORIES OF). These involved detailed investigation into how subjects are to be defined and how texts are to be interpreted.

Closely related to questions of language were questions of knowledge in general and its sources (see EPISTEMOLOGY, INDIAN SCHOOLS OF). The two most important sources of knowledge that Indian philosophers discussed were sensation and inference, the theory of inference being important to the development of logic in India (see SENSE PERCEPTION, INDIAN VIEWS OF). Another topic about which Indian thinkers had much to say was the problem of how absences are known. Because of the importance of scriptures and religious teachers, epistemologists in India discussed the issue of the authority of texts and the question of the reliability of information conveyed through human language (see TESTIMONY IN INDIAN PHILOSOPHY). The questions associated with epistemology are in Indian philosophy often closely connected with questions of human psychology.

Most schools of Indian philosophy offered not only an epistemology but also an ontology. Many

posited a personal creator god or an impersonal godhead. Just how particular things come into being through creative agency or through impersonal natural laws was a matter of considerable debate (see CAUSATION, INDIAN THEORIES OF). Indian thinkers also debated the precise nature of matter, the ontological status of universals, and how potentials become actualities.

In addition to epistemology and metaphysics, a third area that Indian systematic philosophers nearly always commented upon were issues concerning the nature of the human being. This included thoughts on a variety of ethical questions and the rewards for living an ethical life (see DUTY AND VIRTUE, INDIAN CONCEPTIONS OF). While most thinkers dealt with individual ethics, some also gave attention to the question of collective behaviour and policy.

The Hindu tradition produced a number of important individual philosophers. Among the earliest extant philosophers from India are the political theorist Kauṭilya (fourth century BC) and the grammarian and philosopher of language Patañjali (second century BC). The legendary founder of the Nyāya school, Akṣapāda Gautama, is traditionally regarded as the author of a set of aphorisms that modern scholars believe were composed in the second or third century. These aphorisms present the basic ontological categories and epistemological principles that were followed not only by the Nyāya school but by many others as well. The philosopher of language Bhartṛhari (fifth century) developed the intriguing idea that the basic stuff of which all the universe is made is an intelligence in the form of a readiness to use language. Vātsyāyana (fifth century) and Uddyotakara (sixth century) were both commentators on Gautama. The Vedānta systematist Śaṅkara (eighth century) wrote that realizing the underlying unity of all things in the form of Brahman could set one free. The aesthetician Abhinavagupta (tenth–eleventh century) made the education of the emotions through the cultivation of aesthetic sensitivity the basis of liberation from the turmoil of life. Udayana (eleventh century) of the Nyāya school developed important arguments for the existence of God. Rāmānuja (eleventh–twelfth century) and Madhva (thirteenth century), both Vedāntins, offered systems that became serious rivals to Śaṅkara's monism. The work of the logician Gaṅgeśa (fourteenth century), who revised the classical system of logic and epistemology, became the foundation for an important new school of thought, Navya-Nyāya ('New Nyāya'). Mādhava (fourteenth century) and Vallabhācārya (fifteenth–sixteenth century) made important contributions to Vedāntin philosophy. Gadādhara (seventeenth century) continued making advances in logical theory by building on the work of Gaṅgeśa. Also important in the sixteenth century were several thinkers who commented upon the religious thinker Caitanya. Finally, there were several thinkers and movements in the nineteenth and twentieth centuries, a period during which Indian intellectuals struggled to reconcile traditional Indian ways of thinking with European and especially British influences.

2 Buddhist and Jaina philosophy

As was the case for Hindu philosophy, Buddhist and Jaina Philosophy in India tended to proceed through commentaries on already existing texts. Jainism was founded by Mahāvīra and is best known for its method of seeing every issue from every possible point of view. The principal Buddhist traditions that incorporated significant philosophical discussions were those that tried to systematize doctrines contained in various corpora of texts believed to be the words of the Buddha. An important issue for Buddhist thinkers, as for most Indian philosophers, was analysing the causes of discontent and suggesting a method for eliminating unhappiness, the cessation of suffering being a condition known as *nirvāṇa*. A doctrine of special interest to the Mādhyamika school was that everything is conditioned and therefore lacking independence. Some Buddhists developed the view that the conditioned world is so transitory that it disappears and is recreated in every moment (see MOMENTARINESS, BUDDHIST DOCTRINE OF). In the area of epistemology and philosophy of language, some Buddhists repudiated the Hindu confidence in the authority of the Veda.

The Buddhist tradition gave India a number of important philosophers, beginning with the founder of the religion, the Buddha (fifth century BC). The first important Buddhist philosopher to write in Sanskrit and the man traditionally regarded as the founder of the Mādhyamika school was Nāgārjuna (second century). A key commentator in both the Ābhidharmika schools and in the Yogācāra school was Vasubandhu (fifth century). Two key Buddhist epistemologists and logicians were Dignāga (fifth century) and Dharmakīrti (seventh century). Buddhism disappeared from northern India in the twelfth century and from southern India a few centuries later. In the twentieth century, there has been an effort to revive it, especially among the community formerly known as 'untouchables'. A remarkable leader of this community was Bhimrao Ramji Ambedkar.

3 Pronunciation of Sanskrit words

Sanskrit is an Indo-European language, closely related to Greek and Latin. In India, it is written in a variety of phonetic scripts, and in the West it is customary to write it in roman script. Many letters used to write Sanskrit are pronounced almost as they are in English; k, g, j, t, d, n, p, b, m, y, r, l, s and h can be pronounced as in English without too much distortion. The sound of the first consonant in the English word 'church' is represented by a simple 'c' in Sanskrit. In addition to these consonants there is a class of retroflex consonants, so called because the tongue is bent back so that the bottom side of the tongue touches the roof of the mouth. These sounds are represented by letters with dots under them: ṭ, ḍ, ṇ and ṣ. As in English, some consonants are heavily aspirated, so that they are pronounced with a slight puff of air. These consonants are represented by single letters in Indian scripts but by two-letter combinations in roman script; thus 'kh' is pronounced as the 'k' in English 'kill', 'th' as 't' in 'tame' (never as 'th' in 'thin' or 'there'), 'dh' as in 'mudhouse', and 'ph' as 'p' in 'pat' (never as 'ph' in 'philosophy'). The letter 'ś' is approximately like 'sh' in 'shingle'. The letter 'ṅ' is like 'ng' in 'finger' or 'nk' in 'sink', while 'ñ' is approximately like 'ny' in 'canyon'.

Vowels are pronounced approximately as in Spanish or Italian. Vowels with a macron over them (ā, ī and ū) are pronounced for twice as much time as their unmarked equivalents. The vowel 'ṛ' is pronounced with the tip of the tongue elevated towards the roof of the mouth, very much like the 'er' in the American pronunciation of 'carter'. The diphthongs 'ai' and 'au' are pronounced as 'i' in 'kite' and 'ou' in 'scout' (or almost as 'ei' and 'au' are pronounced in German) respectively. Accent tends to be on the third syllable from the end; thus the name 'Śaṅkara' sounds like 'SHANG-ka-ra', not 'shang-KA-ra'. If the second syllable from the end is long, then it is accented; 'Dignāga' is pronounced 'dig-NAA-ga'.

See also: BUDDHIST PHILOSOPHY, CHINESE

References and further reading

Mohanty, J.N. (1992) *Reason and Tradition in Indian Thought. An Essay on the Nature of Indian Philosophical Thinking*, Oxford: Clarendon Press. (A thoughtful exploration of the principal issues of Indian philosophy.)

Powers, J. (1995) *Introduction to Tibetan Buddhism*, Ithaca, NY: Snow Lion Publications. (A useful survey of the main schools of Tibetan Buddhism, as well as of the Bon tradition.)

Raju, P.T. (1985) *Structural Depths of Indian Thought*, Albany, NY: State University of New York Press. (A good survey of the different schools of Indian philosophy from ancient times to the present.)

RICHARD P. HAYES

INDICATIVE CONDITIONALS

Examples of indicative conditionals are 'If it rained, then the match was cancelled' and 'If Alex plays, Carlton will win'. The contrast is with subjunctive or counterfactual conditionals, such as 'If it had rained, then the match would have been cancelled', and categoricals, such as 'It will rain'.

Despite the ease with which we use and understand indicative conditionals, the correct account of them has proved to be very difficult. Some say that 'If it rained, the match was cancelled' is equivalent to 'Either it did not rain, or the match was cancelled'. Some say that the sentence asserts that the result of 'adding' the supposition that it rained to the actual situation is to give a situation in which the match was cancelled. Some say that to assert that if it rained then the match was cancelled is to make a commitment to inferring that the match was cancelled should one learn that it rained. This last view is often combined with the view that indicative conditionals are not, strictly speaking, true or false; rather, they are more or less assertible or acceptable.

See also: Relevance logic and entailment

FRANK JACKSON

INDIRECT DISCOURSE

Indirect discourse is a mode of speech-reporting whereby a speaker conveys the content of someone's utterance without quoting the actual words. Thus, if Pierre says, 'Paris est belle', an English speaker might truly say,

(1) Pierre said that Paris is beautiful.

In English, sentences of indirect discourse often have the form 'A said that s', where 'A' refers to a person and 's' is often called the 'content sentence' of the report.

Sentences of indirect discourse have been classed with attributions of belief (and other psychological states) in view of an apparent conflict with the 'principle of the intersubstitutability of coreferring terms', which states that the truth-value of a sentence does not alter if one term in a sentence is replaced with another referring to the same thing. If (1) is true and 'Paris' and 'the City of Light' refer to the same thing, (2) may still be false:

(2) Pierre said that the City of Light is beautiful.

GABRIEL SEGAL

INDIVIDUALISM IN HISTORY AND SOCIAL SCIENCE

See Holism and individualism in history and social science

INDUCTION, EPISTEMIC ISSUES IN

Consider the following:

(1) Emeralds have been regularly dug up and observed for centuries; while there are still emeralds yet to be observed, every one observed so far has been green.

It is easy to see why we regard (1) as evidence, if true, that:

(2) Every emerald observed up until 100 years ago was green.

(1) logically implies (2): there is no way (1) could be true without (2) being true as well. It is less easy to see why we should think that (1), if true, is any evidence at all that:

(3) All hitherto unobserved emeralds are green as well.

(1) does not logically imply (3): it is consistent with (1) that (3) be false – that the string of exclusively green emeralds is about to come to an end. None the less, we *do* regard (1) as evidence, if true, that (3). What, if anything, justifies our doing so?

To answer this question would be to take a first step towards solving what is known as the 'problem of induction'. But only a first step. There is, at least on the surface, a wide variety of arguments that share the salient features of the argument from (1) to (3): their premises do not logically imply their conclusions, yet we think that their premises, if true, constitute at least some evidence that their conclusions are true. A fully fledged solution to the problem of induction would have to tell us, for each of these arguments, what justifies our regarding its premises as evidence that its conclusion is true. Still, the question as to how this step might be taken has been the focus of intense philosophical scrutiny, and the approaches outlined in this entry have been among the most important.

See also: Confirmation theory; Inductive inference

MARK KAPLAN

INDUCTIVE INFERENCE

Introduction

According to a long tradition, an inductive inference is an inference from a premise of the form 'all observed *A* are *B*' to a conclusion of the form 'all *A* are *B*'. Such inferences are not deductively valid, that is, even if the premise is true it is possible that the conclusion is false, since unobserved *A*s may differ from observed ones. Nevertheless, it has been held that the premise can make it reasonable to believe the conclusion, even though it does not guarantee that the conclusion is true.

It is now generally allowed that there are many other patterns of inference that can also provide reasonable grounds for believing their conclusions, even though their premises do not guarantee the truth of their conclusions. In current usage, it is common to call all such inferences inductive. It has been widely thought that all knowledge of matters of fact that we have not observed must be based on inductive inferences from what we have observed. In particular, all knowledge of the future is, on this view, based on induction.

1   Paradigms of induction

The inference from 'all observed A are B' to 'all A are B', which was once taken to be the pattern for all inductive inference, is called (universal) *inductive generalization* or *enumerative induction*. A standard example is the inference from all observed ravens being black to all ravens being black. The fallibility of such inference is illustrated by the fact that, although all the swans seen by Europeans of the eighteenth century were white, black swans existed in Australia.

Some writers, such as J.S. Mill, argued that inductive generalization is the only legitimate kind of induction. However, as Mill was well aware, others have thought that there are other ways of making inferences from the observed to the unobserved. One method that has played an important role in philosophy of science is the method of hypothesis. In this method, the premises are that (i) hypothesis H implies a proposition E describing observable phenomena, and (ii) E is observed to be true; the conclusion is that H is true. In modern discussions this method is often called the hypothetico-deductive method, because E is supposed to be deduced from the hypothesis H.

The method of hypothesis is not deductively valid, since false hypotheses can have true consequences. Its defenders have argued that its premises can nevertheless make it reasonable to believe its conclusion. Descartes offered an example to support this position: if we find that a message in code makes sense when for each letter we substitute the following letter (B for A, C for B, and so on), we will be practically certain that this gives the true meaning of the message, especially if the message contains many words.

The method of hypothesis licenses conclusions that can never be reached by inductive generalization. For example, from the fact that observable phenomena are as they would be if matter consists of atoms, one may infer by the method of hypothesis that matter does consist of atoms. This conclusion could be reached by inductive generalization only if one had observed instances of matter composed of atoms, something that had not been done at the time that most scientists accepted the atomic theory of matter.

Other commonly recognized types of inductive inference are: (1) *statistical inductive generalization*, in which the premise is that x per cent of observed As have been B and the conclusion is that about x per cent of all As are B; (2) *predictive inference*, in which the premises are that x per cent of observed As have been B and that a is A, the conclusion being that a is B; (3) *direct inference*, in which the premises are that x per cent of all As are B and that a is A, the conclusion being that a is B; and (4) *inference by analogy*, in which the premises are that certain individuals have properties $F_1, \ldots, F_n$ and a also has $F_1, \ldots F_{n-1}$, the conclusion being that a also has F_n.

2   Induction in practice

It is generally allowed that the cogency of an inductive inference is greater the more observations that have been made and the more varied these observations have been. Mill also stressed that the reliability of an inductive generalization is greatly increased by finding that other similar generalizations hold up; conversely, he maintained that our knowledge of the variability of bird-colouring undermined the inductive generalization to the conclusion that all ravens are black. But the relevance of such considerations means that inductive inferences are not adequately represented by the paradigm forms listed above, since relevant information ought to be included in the premises.

Even if we added to the paradigm forms the sort of information just mentioned, they would still not adequately represent the inductive inferences that are made in everyday life and in science. For example, consider the inductive generalization to the conclusion that all ravens are black. The premise was that all observed ravens have been black. But observed by whom? If we say observed by anyone, then we cannot be sure that the premise is correct, and this ought to affect our confidence in the conclusion, though the argument does not provide for that. If we say observed by me, then the premise leaves out the very relevant information of what I know from the testimony of others. Further, even when the premise is limited to my own observation, I cannot be sure it is true; I could very well have observed a white raven and mistakenly inferred from the fact that it was white that it was not a raven. Thus my confidence in the conclusion ought to depend on how closely I have examined both what I take to be ravens and what I take to be non-black things, though this is not reflected in the premise.

Another example: suppose we have weighed an object three times and obtained measurements of 4.9, 5.0 and 5.1 grams. From these results we might infer that the true weight of the object is between 4.7 and 5.3 grams. If this is to fit one of the standard forms, it will have to be the method of hypothesis. But the hypothesis that the true weight is between 4.7 and 5.3 grams does not entail that the weighings will give the results they did. In modern presentations of the hypothetico-deductive method it is commonly said that the premises include not only the hypothesis itself but also initial conditions, such as that the object was weighed three times, and auxiliary hypotheses, such as that the balance is accurate; but even with these additional premises the evidence does not follow deductively.

Since tests of hypotheses in science typically involve measurement, the preceding example is sufficient to show that science does not have much use for a method that is truly 'hypothetico-deductive'. But if the evidence only follows from the hypothesis with some probability, then it makes a difference what that probability is, though the method of hypothesis as usually presented does not include this information in the premises. As we will see below, it also makes a difference how probable the conclusion is on competing hypotheses, another relevant consideration that is not incorporated in the premises of the method of hypothesis as standardly conceived. Finally, our background information almost always gives us at least some relevant information; for example, we usually have some approximate idea what an object should weigh, and measurements that diverge too far from this will be taken to show that the balance is faulty. If the object that was weighed at 4.9, 5.0 and 5.1 grams was a loaded truck, we will conclude that there is something seriously wrong with the measurement process. The method of hypothesis does not provide a way to incorporate such relevant information.

3   Cogency

The premises of an inductive argument may provide more or less support for the conclusion. We would like to be able to identify the factors that determine the strength of this support. Some platitudes to this effect were mentioned above, but they have several defects. In particular, despite their vagueness, they are not true in general. For example, increasing the

number of As that have been observed to be B does not always make it more probable that all A are B; thus a person who died at age 149 is a person who died before age 150, but evidence that there is such a person would *reduce* the probability that all people die before age 150. In any case, those platitudes are limited to the paradigm forms of inductive inference, which we have seen is inadequate to represent actual inductive inferences. For these reasons, many contemporary theorists have looked for a more rigorous yet flexible framework for discussing the degree to which inductive premises support their conclusions. Probability theory has often been seen as providing such a framework.

Let H be a hypothesis and E some evidence. Let $P(H)$ be the probability that H is true given the other information that we have besides E. Then the probability that we should give to H after learning E is the probability of H conditional on E, which we write as $P(H \mid E)$. A theorem of probability, called Bayes' theorem (see PROBABILITY, INTERPRETATIONS OF §5), says the following (where $\bar{H}$ means H is false):

$$P(H \mid E) = \frac{P(E \mid H)}{P(E \mid H)P(H) + P(E \mid \bar{H})P(\bar{H})}P(H)$$

We say that E confirms H if $P(H \mid E) > P(H)$. Assuming $P(H) > 0$, E confirms H just in case the fraction on the right hand side of the above equation is greater than 1. Assuming $P(H) < 1$, this condition will hold just in case $P(E \mid H) > P(E \mid \bar{H})$. Thus for evidence to confirm a hypothesis, it is not necessary that the evidence be entailed by the hypothesis, or even that the evidence be very probable given the hypothesis. Evidence that is quite improbable supposing the hypothesis to be true will confirm that hypothesis if the evidence is even less likely on the supposition that the hypothesis is false.

Another implication of the above equation is that even if evidence E does strongly confirm hypothesis H, it does not follow that the hypothesis has a high probability of being true, for its probability given other information may be quite low; that is, $P(H \mid E)/P(H)$ may be large and yet $P(H \mid E)$ small, because $P(H)$ is small. For example, when H is the hypothesis that a loaded truck weighs about 5 grams, $P(H)$ is infinitesimal.

Philosophers often refer to the method of hypothesis as 'inference to the best explanation'. This terminology has the merit of recording the fact that the inference depends not just on the relation between hypothesis and evidence but also on how other hypotheses relate to the evidence. However, it is wrong to suggest that *explanation* plays a fundamental role here; what is important in the connection between evidence and hypothesis is the probability of the evidence given the hypothesis, and this probability is not a measure of the degree to which the hypothesis explains the evidence (see EXPLANATION; INFERENCE TO THE BEST EXPLANATION). Furthermore, the terminology misleadingly suggests that the cogency of an inference is determined by the relation between the various hypotheses and the evidence, when in fact it depends also on the prior probability of the hypotheses.

4 Inference

Inductive inference has traditionally been understood as inference in the usual sense: on the basis of premises that are categorically accepted one comes to categorically accept another statement, the conclusion. For writers such as Bacon, Whewell and Mill, this conception was unproblematic. They thought that inductive inference could provide practical certainty on substantive matters of science and everyday life, and that where such certainty was lacking we should withhold assent. However, various factors, in particular the failure of such well-supported scientific theories as Newtonian mechanics, have convinced contemporary writers that substantive inductive conclusions always have some uncertainty, the best-supported scientific theories not excepted. This presents a dilemma: either we accept only those conclusions that are certain, in which case it seems we can accept very little and there will be almost no inductive inference, or else we accept conclusions that might be wrong.

Some writers on probability and induction, notably Carnap and Jeffrey, have embraced the first horn of this dilemma. They hold that induction should be conceived, not as a process by which we pass from some accepted statements to others, but rather as a process by which we assign probabilities to various hypotheses in the light of our evidence. On this view, we ought virtually never to make inductive inferences, as these have been traditionally conceived.

This rejection of inductive inference presupposes that acceptance of a hypothesis involves treating it as if it were certainly true. Some writers have argued that we can preserve the legitimacy of inductive inference by abandoning the assumption that someone who accepts a hypothesis must treat it as certainly true. A popular suggestion is that accepting a hypothesis is merely a matter of being highly confident of it, for example, of giving it a probability greater than some threshold. One

objection to this view is that the set of propositions that have high probability is not consistent. For example, in a large unbiased lottery, the probability that any particular ticket will not win is high, though we also know that some ticket will win. Thus if we accepted every proposition with high probability we would accept an inconsistent set of propositions. This is called the 'lottery paradox' (see PARADOXES, EPISTEMIC). Another objection to equating acceptance with high probability is that informativeness is a reason for accepting a hypothesis but is not a reason for giving the hypothesis high probability.

Several writers have suggested that we ought to think of acceptance as a risky decision and use decision theory to evaluate when acceptance is rational (see DECISION AND GAME THEORY). The thought is that acceptance has a certain cognitive utility, which is greater if the proposition accepted is true than if it is false; acceptance of a hypothesis is rational, at least so far as cognitive goals are concerned, if it maximizes expected cognitive utility. The cognitive utility of accepting a true hypothesis is higher the more informative the hypothesis is, and thus this account provides a place for both probability and informativeness in determining the rationality of inductive inference. Some versions of this approach take acceptance to imply certainty while others do not.

See also: CHINESE PHILOSOPHY; CONFIRMATION THEORY; CONFUCIAN PHILOSOPHY, CHINESE; INDUCTION, EPISTEMIC ISSUES IN; REICHENBACH, H.; STATISTICS

References and further reading

Fraassen, B.C. van (1989) *Laws and Symmetry*, Oxford: Clarendon Press. (Chapters 6 and 7 discuss inference to the best explanation.)

Skyrms, B. (1986) *Choice and Chance*, Belmont, CA: Wadsworth, 4th edn. (An elementary contemporary introduction to induction, probability and decision theory.)

PATRICK MAHER

INFERENCE TO THE BEST EXPLANATION

Inference to the best explanation is the procedure of choosing the hypothesis or theory that best explains the available data. The factors that make one explanation better than another may include depth, comprehensiveness, simplicity and unifying power. According to some, explanatory inference plays a central role in both everyday and scientific thinking. In ordinary life, a person might make the inference that a fuse has blown to explain why several kitchen appliances stopped working all at once. Scientists also seem to engage in inference to the best explanation; for example, astronomers concluded that another planet must exist in order to account for aberrations in the orbit of Uranus. However, despite the suggestiveness of cases like these, the extent to which we do and should rely on inference to the best explanation is highly controversial.

See also: SCEPTICISM

JONATHAN VOGEL

INFINITARY LOGICS

An infinitary logic arises from ordinary first-order logic when one or more of its finitary properties is allowed to become infinite, for example, by admitting infinitely long formulas or infinitely long or infinitely branched proof figures. The need to extend first-order logic became pressing in the late 1950s when it was realized that many of the fundamental notions of mathematics cannot be expressed in first-order logic in a way that would allow for their logical analysis. Because infinitary logics often do not suffer the same limitation, they have become an essential tool in mathematical logic.

BERND BULDT

INFINITY

Introduction

The infinite is standardly conceived as that which is endless, unlimited, immeasurable. It also has theological connotations of absoluteness and perfection. From the dawn of civilization, it has held a special fascination: people have been captivated by the boundlessness of space and time, by the mystery of numbers going on forever, by the paradoxes of endless divisibility, and by the riddles of divine perfection.

The infinite is of profound importance to mathematics. Nevertheless, the relationship between the two has been a curiously ambivalent one. It is clear that mathematics in some sense presupposes the infinite, for instance in the fact that there is no largest integer. But the idea that the infinite should itself be an object of mathematical study has time and again been subjected to ridicule. The mathematical orthodoxy has been that there can be no formal theory of the infinite. In the nineteenth century this orthodoxy was challenged, with the advent of 'transfinite arithmetic'. Many, however, have remained sceptical, believing that the infinite is inherently beyond our grasp.

Perhaps their scepticism should be trained on the infinite itself: perhaps the concept is ultimately incoherent. It is certainly riddled with paradoxes. Yet we cannot simply jettison it. This is why the paradoxes are so acute. The roots of these paradoxes lie in our own finitude: it is self-conscious awareness of that finitude which gives us our initial sense of a contrasting infinite, and, at the same time, makes us despair of knowing anything about it, or having any kind of grasp of it. This creates a tension. We feel pressure to acknowledge the infinite, and we feel pressure not to. In trying to come to terms with the infinite, we are trying to come to terms with a basic conflict in ourselves.

1 Early Greek thought
2 Aristotle
3 The rationalists and the empiricists
4 Kant
5 Post-Kantian metaphysics of the infinite
6 Modern mathematics of the infinite
7 Human finitude

1 Early Greek thought

The Greek word *peras* is usually translated as 'limit' or 'bound'. *To apeiron* denotes that which has no *peras*, the unlimited or unbounded: the infinite. *To apeiron* made its first significant appearance in early Greek thought with Anaximander of Miletus in the sixth century BC (see ANAXIMANDER). He thought of it as the boundless, imperishable, ultimate source of everything that is. He also thought of it as that to which all things must eventually return in order to atone for the injustices and disharmony which result from their transitory existence.

Anaximander was something of an exception, however. On the whole, the Greeks abhorred the infinite (as the old adage has it). More typical of that era were the Pythagoreans, a religious society founded by Pythagoras (see PYTHAGOREANISM). They believed in two basic cosmological principles, *Peras* and *Apeiron*, the former subsuming all that was good, the latter all that was bad. They held further that the whole of creation was to be understood in terms of, and indeed was ultimately constituted by, the positive integers 1, 2, 3, ...; and that this was made possible by the fact that *Peras* was continuously subjugating *Apeiron* (the integers themselves, of course, each being finite). The Pythagoreans were followed to some extent in these beliefs by Plato, who also held that it was the imposition of limits on the unlimited that accounted for all the numerically definable phenomena that surround us.

However, the Pythagoreans soon learned to their dismay that they could not simply relegate the infinite to the role of cosmic villain. This was because of Pythagoras' own discovery that the square on the hypotenuse of a right-angled triangle is equal to the sum of the squares on the other two sides. Given this theorem, the ratio of a square's diagonal to each side is $\sqrt{2} : 1$. There are some good approximations to this ratio: for example, it is a little more than 7:5 and a little less than 17:12. Indeed there are approximations of any desired degree of accuracy. Nevertheless, given the basic tenets of Pythagoreanism, it ought to be *exactly* p:q, for some pair of positive integers p and q. The problem was that they discovered a proof that it is not, which they regarded as nothing short of catastrophic. According to legend, one of them was shipwrecked at sea for revealing the discovery to their enemies. The Pythagoreans had stumbled across the 'irrational' within mathematics. They had seen the limitations of the positive integers, and had thereby been forced to acknowledge the infinite in their very midst.

At around the same time, ZENO OF ELEA was formulating various celebrated paradoxes connected with the infinite. Best known of these is the paradox of Achilles and the tortoise: Achilles, who runs much faster than the tortoise, cannot overtake it in a race if he lets it start a certain distance ahead of him. For in order to do so he must first reach the point from which the tortoise started, by which time the tortoise will have advanced a fraction of the distance initially separating them; he must then make up this new distance, by which time the tortoise will have advanced again; and so on *ad infinitum*. Such paradoxes, as well as having a profound impact on the history of thought about infinity, did much to reinforce early Greek hostility to the concept.

2 Aristotle

Aristotle's understanding of the infinite was an essentially modern one in so far as he defined it as the untraversable or never-ending. But he perceived a basic dilemma. On the one hand Zeno's paradoxes, along with a host of other considerations, show that the concept of the infinite really does resist a certain kind of application to reality. On the other hand there seems to be no prospect of doing without the concept, as the Pythagoreans had effectively realized. As well as $\sqrt{2}$, time seems to be infinite, numbers seem to go on *ad infinitum*, and space, time and matter all seem to be infinitely divisible.

Aristotle's solution to this dilemma was masterly. It has dominated all subsequent thought on the infinite, and until very recently was adopted by almost everyone who considered the topic. Aristotle distinguished between the 'actual infinite' and the 'potential infinite'. The actual infinite is that whose infinitude exists, or is given, at some point in time. The potential infinite is that whose infinitude exists, or is given, *over* time. All objections to the infinite, Aristotle insisted, are objections to the actual infinite. The potential infinite is a fundamental feature of reality. It is there to be acknowledged in any process which can never end: in the process of counting, for example; in various processes of division; or in the passage of time itself. The reason why paradoxes such as Zeno's arise is that we pay insufficient heed to this distinction. Having seen, for example, that there can be no end to the process of dividing a given racecourse, we somehow imagine that all those possible future divisions are already in effect there. We come to view the racecourse as already divided into infinitely many parts, and it is easy then for the paradoxes to take hold.

Even those later thinkers who did not share Aristotle's animosity towards the actual infinite tended to recognize the importance of his distinction. Often, though, Aristotle's reference to time was taken as a metaphor for something deeper and more abstract. This in turn usually proved to be something grammatical. Thus certain medieval thinkers distinguished between categorematic and syncategorematic uses of the word 'infinite'. Very roughly, to use the word categorematically is to say that there is something with a property that surpasses any finite measure; to use the word syncategorematically is to say that, given any finite measure, there is something with a property that surpasses it. In the former case the infinite has to be instantiated 'all at once'. In the latter case it does not.

The categorematic–syncategorematic distinction heralds another distinction, whose importance to the infinite is hard to exaggerate. This is the distinction between saying that there is something of kind X to which each thing of kind Y stands in relation R, and saying that each thing of kind Y stands in relation R to something of kind X (not necessarily the same thing each time). This is referred to below as the 'Scope Distinction' (see SCOPE).

But Aristotle himself was not thinking in these very abstract terms. He took the references to time in his own account of the actual–potential distinction quite literally, and this gave rise to his most serious difficulty. He held that time (unlike space) is infinite. He also held that time involves constant activity, as exemplified in the revolution of the heavens. When our attention is focused on the future, there is no obvious problem with this. Past revolutions, however, because they are past, seem to have an infinitude which is by now completely given to us, and hence which is actual. This difficulty, in various different guises, has been a continual aggravation for philosophers who have wanted to see the infinite in broadly Aristotelian terms.

3 The rationalists and the empiricists

For over 2,000 years Aristotle's conception of the infinite was regarded as orthodoxy. Often this conception was motivated by a kind of empiricism: the actual infinite was spurned on the grounds that we can never encounter it in experience. But does the potential infinite fare any better in this respect? Is experience of an infinitude that is given *over* time any less problematic than experience of an infinitude that is given all at once? The more extreme of the British empiricists were hostile to the infinite in all its guises. Where Aristotle had felt able to accept that space and time were infinitely divisible, BERKELEY and HUME denied even that. They thought that the concept of the infinite was one that we could, and should, do without (see EMPIRICISM).

This was partly a backlash against their rationalist predecessors. The rationalists had argued that we could form an idea of the infinite, even though we could neither experience it nor imagine it. They thought that this idea was an innate one, and that it constituted, or helped to constitute, a vital insight into reality. They did not see any difficulty in this view. As Descartes put it, the fact that we cannot grasp the infinite does not preclude our touching it with our thoughts, any more than the fact that we cannot grasp a mountain precludes our touching it (see RATIONALISM).

Descartes believed that our idea of the infinite had been implanted in our minds by God (see DESCARTES, R. §6). Indeed this was the basis of one of his proofs of God's existence. Only a truly infinite being, Descartes argued, *could* have implanted such an idea in our minds. Note here the assimilation of the infinite to the divine: this was a legacy of medieval thought which is nowadays quite commonplace. But when the assimilation was first made, at the end of antiquity – most famously, by the Neo-Platonist PLOTINUS – it marked something of a turning point in the history of thought about the infinite. Until then there had been a tendency to hear 'infinite' as a derogatory term. Henceforth, it was quite the opposite.

The empiricists, meanwhile, needed to defend their rejection of the infinite against the charge that this invalidated contemporary mathematics. They had more or less sophisticated ways of doing so, though in the case of geometry, where the problem was at its most acute, Hume took the rather cavalier step of simply denying certain crucial principles that mathematicians took for granted. (Berkeley's chief concern was with the use of infinitesimals in the recently invented calculus. In fact, his reservations were perfectly justified: a century was to pass before they were properly addressed.)

4 Kant

Kant played his characteristic role of conciliator in the debate on the infinite (see KANT §§2, 5, 8). He had an empiricist scepticism about the infinite, based on the fact that we cannot directly experience it. Nevertheless, he sided with the rationalists by insisting that there are certain formal or structural features of what we experience, which are accessible a priori and which *do* involve the infinite. Thus he thought that space and time were infinite (both in the sense of being infinitely extended and in the sense of being infinitely divisible): it is written into the form of whatever we experience that there can also be experience of how things are further out, further in, earlier or later. These, on Kant's view, were mathematical truths, a priori and unassailable.

But there is a question about how the topology of space and time *can* be a priori. Kant's celebrated reply was that space and time are not features of 'things in themselves'; they are part of an a priori framework which we contribute to our experience of things. What then of the *contents* of space and time, the physical universe as a whole? This was different. Kant did not think that what was physical was constructed a priori. Nor, on the other hand, did he think that it was ultimately real, that is to say real in a way that transcends any possible access we have to it. It had no features, on Kant's view, that exceed what we are capable of grasping through experience. So here the concept of the infinite did resist application. It still had what Kant regarded as a legitimate *regulative* use. That is, we could proceed *as if* the physical universe as a whole were infinite, thereby encouraging ourselves never to give up in our explorations. But we ultimately had no way of making sense of such infinitude. Kant was forced to take an extreme empiricist line by denying that the physical universe as a whole is infinitely big, that it has infinitely many parts and, going this time beyond Aristotle (thus bypassing the difficulty that had beset Aristotle himself), that it is infinitely old.

However, there was a dilemma. Kant was also forced to deny that the physical universe is *finite* in each of these three respects. Apart from anything else, to postulate infinite empty space or time beyond the confines of the physical universe is itself to postulate that which exceeds what we are capable of grasping through experience.

This dilemma looks acute. Kant himself presented it in the form of a pair of 'antinomies'. These antinomies consisted of the principal arguments against the physical universe's being infinite in each of the specified respects, and the principal arguments against its being finite. But he believed that the dilemma contained the seeds of its own solution. If what is physical is not ultimately real –

if there is no more to it than what we are capable of experiencing – then we are at liberty to deny that there is any such thing as the physical universe as a whole. There are only the finite physical things that are accessible to us through experience. The physical universe as a whole is neither infinite nor finite. It does not exist.

Kant's solution involved him in a direct application of the Scope Distinction (see §2 above). On the one hand he affirmed that any finite physical thing is contained within something physical (as the earth, for instance, is contained within the solar system). On the other hand he denied that there is something physical (that is, some one physical thing, the universe as a whole) within which any finite physical thing is contained. Both of these, the affirmation and the denial, were grounded in the fact that there is nothing we can identify in space and time such that we cannot identify more. This is fundamentally a fact about us: the fact that we are finite. Our identifications are always incomplete. What Kant added, in an idealist vein, was that what we cannot identify does not exist. Here, as in so many other places, we see how deeply involved with human finitude Kant's philosophy was, and how seriously he took it.

5 Post-Kantian metaphysics of the infinite

Metaphysical thought about the infinite since Kant has continued to be just as deeply involved with human finitude. Existentialists in particular have been greatly exercised by it, especially in its guise of mortality. But they have also for the most part recognized an element of the infinite within us. This too is Kantian. Kant believed that we are free rational agents, and that when our agency is properly exercised, it has an unconditioned autonomy that bears all the hallmarks of the truly infinite. For Kant, this was something which exalts us. But for many of the existentialists, still preoccupied with the fundamental fact of human finitude, it is something which is responsible for the deepest tensions within us, and thus for the absurdity of human existence (see EXISTENTIALISM §2).

Hegel agreed with Kant that the truly infinite is to be found in the free exercise of reason (see HEGEL, G.W.F. §8). But he took this further than Kant. He argued that reason is the infinite ground of everything. Everything that happens, on Hegel's view, can be understood as the activity of a kind of world-spirit, and this spirit *is* reason.

This led Hegel to a very non-Aristotelian conception of the infinite. For Hegel, the infinite was the complete, the whole, the unified. Aristotle's conception of the infinite as the never-ending was in Hegel's view quite wrong. He explained this conception as arising from our finite attempts to assimilate the truly infinite. And he described Aristotelian infinity as a 'spurious', or 'bad', infinity – a mere succession of finite elements, each bounded by the next, but never complete and never properly held together in unity. Such 'infinitude' seemed to Hegel at turns nightmarish, then bizarre, then simply tedious, but always a pale, inadequate reflection of the truly infinite.

6 Modern mathematics of the infinite

Despite Kant's influence on Hegel, and despite his own commitment to infinite reason (as well as to infinite space), Kant certainly helped to propagate the Aristotelian tradition of treating the actual infinite with hostility and suspicion. As this tradition prevailed, the actual infinite came increasingly to be understood in the more general, non-temporal sense indicated in §2 above. Eventually, exception was being taken to any categorematic use of the word 'infinite'. The most serious challenge to this tradition, at least in a mathematical context, was not mounted until the nineteenth century, by CANTOR, whose mathematical contribution to this topic is unsurpassed.

Objections to the actual infinite had tended to be of two kinds. The first kind we have already seen: objections based on the fact that we can never encounter the actual infinite in experience. Objections of the second kind were based on the paradoxes to which the actual infinite gives rise. These paradoxes fall into two groups. The first group consists of Zeno's paradoxes and their variants. By the time Cantor was writing, however, the calculus (which had then reached full maturity) had done a great deal to mitigate these. Of more concern by then were the paradoxes in the second group, which had been known since medieval times. These were paradoxes of equinumerosity. They derive from the following principle: if (and only if) it is possible to pair off all the members of one set with all those of another, then the two sets must have just as many members as each other. For example, in a non-polygamous society, there must be just as many husbands as wives. This principle looks incontestable. However, if it is applied to infinite sets, it seems to flout Euclid's notion that the whole is greater than the part. For instance, it is possible to pair off all the positive integers with those that are even: 1 with 2, 2 with 4, 3 with 6 and so on.

Cantor accepted this principle. And, consistently with that, he accepted that there are just as many even positive integers as there are positive integers altogether. Far from being worried by this, he defined precisely what is going on in such cases, and then incorporated his definitions into a coherent, systematic and rigorous theory of the actual infinite, ready to be laid before any sceptical gaze.

It might be expected that, on this understanding, all infinite sets are the same size. (If they are, that is not unduly paradoxical.) But much of the revolutionary impact of Cantor's work came in his demonstration that they are not. There are different infinite sizes. This is a consequence of what is known as Cantor's theorem: no set, and in particular no infinite set, has as many members as it has subsets. In other words, no set is as big as the set of its subsets. If it were, then it would be possible to pair off all its members with all its subsets. But this is not possible. Suppose there *were* such a pairing and consider the set of members paired off with subsets not containing them. Whichever member was paired off with *this* subset would belong to it if and only if it did not belong to it (see CANTOR'S THEOREM).

In the course of developing these ideas, Cantor laid down some of the basic principles of the set theory which underlay them; he devised precise methods for measuring how big infinite sets are; and he formulated ways of calculating with these measures. In short, he established transfinite arithmetic. No longer, it seemed, did the actual infinite have to be an object of abhorrence. But was it really so?

Cantor operated with what is often called the 'iterative' conception of a set. On this conception, a set is something whose existence is parasitic on that of its members: the members exist 'first'. Thus there are, to begin with, all those things that are not sets (planets, people, positive integers and so forth). Then there are sets of these things. Then there are sets of *these* things. And so on, without end. Each thing, and in particular each set, belongs to countless further sets. But there never comes a set to which each set belongs (another illustration of the Scope Distinction). The collection of all sets is not itself a set. It is a collection which, on Cantor's conception, is too big to be regarded as a set: its members cannot be given 'all at once'. There is something very natural about this conception. But there is also something very Aristotelian about it. Notice the temporal metaphor that sustains the conception. Sets are depicted as coming into being 'after' their members, in such a way that there are always more to come. Their collective infinitude, as opposed to the infinitude of any one of them, is potential, not actual. Moreover, it is this collective infinitude that has best claim to the title. For the properties that I listed at the outset as characterizing the standard conception of the infinite – endlessness, unlimitedness, immeasurability – more properly apply to the entire collection of sets than to any individual set. This is partly because of the

very success that Cantor enjoyed in subjecting sets themselves to careful mathematical scrutiny. Consider the set of positive integers. Exactly what Cantor showed concerning this set is that it is limited in size. (The set of sets of positive integers has more members.) Indeed, he showed that we can give a precise mathematical measure to how big it is. There is a sense, then, in which he established that the set of natural numbers is 'really' finite, and that what is 'really' infinite is something of an altogether different kind. (He was not himself averse to talking in these terms.) It may well be that, in the end, Cantor's work served to corroborate the Aristotelian orthodoxy that 'real' infinitude can never be actual.

Brouwer, meanwhile, believed that Cantor had not shown sufficient respect for the first kind of objection to the actual infinite: that we cannot encounter it in experience. All Cantor had done, in Brouwer's view, was to demonstrate certain tricks that can be played with (finite) symbols, without addressing the question of how these tricks answer to experience. The relevant experience here – the experience to which any meaningful mathematical statement must answer, according to Brouwer and other members of his intuitionistic school – is our experience of time. It is by recognizing the possibility of separating time into parts, and then indefinitely repeating that operation over time, that we arrive at our idea of the infinite. And such infinitude is again potential, not actual – in the most literal sense (see INTUITIONISM).

There was a very different critique of Cantor's ideas in the work of Wittgenstein, though it led to similar results (see WITTGENSTEIN §15). Wittgenstein believed that insufficient attention had been paid (at least by those interpreting Cantor's work, if not by Cantor himself) to what he called the 'grammar' of the infinite, that is to certain fundamental constraints on what could count as a meaningful use of the vocabulary associated with infinity. In effect, Wittgenstein argued that the word 'infinite' could not be used categorematically.

7 Human finitude

Problems about the infinite, we have seen, are grounded in our own finitude. On the one hand our finitude prevents us from being able to think of anything, including the whole of reality, as truly infinite. On the other hand it also prevents us from being able to think of anything finite – anything to that extent within our grasp – as the whole of reality. One way to reconcile these would be to deny that there is any such thing as the whole of reality and to argue that there are only bits of reality, each a part of some other. Here once again we see application of the Scope Distinction: every bit of reality is a part of something, but there is nothing of which every bit of reality is a part. Aristotle, Kant and even to an extent Cantor played out variations on this theme.

But one of the most pressing questions of philosophy still remains: in what exactly does our finitude consist? Some of the most striking features of that finitude are conditioned by our temporality. In particular, of course, there is the fact of our death. How are we to view death? Among the many subsidiary questions that this raises, there are two in particular which are superficially equivalent but between which it is important to distinguish. Putting them in the crudest possible terms (their refinement would be a large part of addressing them): (1) Is death a 'bad thing'? and (2) Would immortality be preferable to mortality?

It can easily look as if these questions must receive the same answer. True, no sooner does one begin refining them than one sees all sorts of ways in which a full, qualified response to one can differ from a full, qualified response to the other. But it is in any case important to see how, even at this crude level, there is scope for answering 'yes' and 'no' respectively. Very roughly, death is a bad thing because it closes off possibilities, but immortality would not be preferable to mortality because mortality is what gives life its most basic structure and, therewith, the possibility of meaning.

To answer 'yes' to (1) and 'no' to (2) in this way is once again to invoke the Scope Distinction. It is to affirm that at each time there is reason to carry on living for longer, while denying that there is reason to carry on living forever. Meaning, for self-conscious beings such as us, can extend further than any given limits. But it cannot extend further than them all.

If it is true that, in some sense, at some level, and with all the myriad qualifications that are called for, the answer to (1) is 'yes' and the answer to (2) is 'no', then, coherent though that is, it points to a basic conflict in us: while it would not be good never to die, it is nevertheless never good to die. That conflict is one of the tragedies of human existence. It is also a version of the original conflict which underlies all our attempts to come to terms with the infinite. In thinking about the infinite, we are thinking, at a very deep level, about ourselves.

See also: CANTOR, G.; CANTOR'S THEOREM; CONTINUUM HYPOTHESIS; DEATH

References and further reading

Maor, E. (1987) *To Infinity and Beyond: A Cultural History of the Infinite*, Stuttgart: Birkhäuser. (Entertaining examination of the role of infinity in mathematics and its cultural impact on the arts and sciences.)

Moore, A.W. (2001) *The Infinite*, London: Routledge, 2nd edn. (Introductory and partly historical study of all aspects of the infinite.)

Rucker, R. (1982) *Infinity and the Mind: The Science and Philosophy of the Infinite*, Sussex: Harvester Wheatsheaf. (Lively and fascinating account of the more mathematical aspects of the infinite. Defends a kind of mysticism.)

A.W. MOORE

INFORMATION THEORY

Information theory was established in 1948 by Claude Shannon as a statistical analysis of factors pertaining to the transmission of messages through communication channels. Among basic concepts defined within the theory are information (the amount of uncertainty removed by the occurrence of an event), entropy (the average amount of information represented by events at the source of a channel), and equivocation (the 'noise' that impedes faithful transmission of a message through a channel). Information theory has proved essential to the development of space probes, high-speed computing machinery and modern communication systems.

The information studied by Shannon is sharply distinct from information in the sense of knowledge or of propositional content. It is also distinct from most uses of the term in the popular press ('information retrieval', 'information processing', 'information highway', and so on). While Shannon's work has strongly influenced academic psychology and philosophy, its reception in these disciplines has been largely impressionistic. A major problem for contemporary philosophy is to relate the statistical conceptions of information theory to information in the semantic sense of knowledge and content.

KENNETH M. SAYRE

INGARDEN, ROMAN WITOLD (1893–1970)

Ingarden was a leading exponent of phenomenology and one of the most outstanding Polish philosophers. Representing an objectivist approach within phenomenology he stressed that phenomenology employs a variety of methods, according to the variety of objects, and aspires to achieve an original cognitive apprehension of these objects. Its aim is to reach the essence of an object by analysing the contents of appropriate ideas and to convey the results of this analysis in clear language. Ingarden applied his methods in many areas of philosophy. He developed a pluralist theory of being and an epistemology which makes it possible to practise this discipline in an undogmatic manner and to defend the value of human knowledge. In the theory of values he developed an inspiring approach to the analysis of traditionally problematic areas. He was best known for his work in aesthetics, in which he analysed the structure of various kinds of works of art, the nature of aesthetic experience, the cognition of works of art and the objective character of aesthetic values. In general, he gave phenomenology a lucid and precise shape.

In the interwar period Ingarden was the main opponent in Poland of the dominant Lwów–Warsaw School (Polish Analytic School), which had a minimalistic orientation. The main lines of his own investigations emerged largely as a result of his regular debates with Husserl, in particular those concerning Husserl's transcendental idealism. Ingarden's best-known work, *Das literarische Kunstwerk* (*The Literary Work of Art*) (1931) has its origins in this debate.

See also: PHENOMENOLOGICAL MOVEMENT

ANTONI B. STĘPIEŃ
Translated from the Polish by
PIOTR GUTOWSKI

INNATENESS

A wide range of things can be, and have been, thought to be innate: behavioural patterns, learning capacities (especially linguistic), emotional responses, concepts, beliefs and knowledge, to give some prominent examples.

The exact meaning of these claims is harder to pin down. For a philosopher committed to a doctrine like that of Plato, according to which the human soul exists before it becomes associated with a human body, the idea of being innate or inborn can be taken more or less literally – innate properties are those which the soul brings with it. But for those without any such metaphysic of pre-existence the innateness of X must be understood as a tendency to acquire or manifest X in the course of development. Innateness is then liable to appear as a matter of degree: some such tendencies (the 'most innate') may be virtually independent of the specific input (experience, diet etc.) to the organism in question, others may be activated only by any 'normal' input, others again – those that are 'acquired' (or 'least innate') – only by some quite specific course of experience.

Historically, positive claims about innateness are associated with platonism, negative ones with empiricism. Such controversies are closely related to the 'nature v. nurture' debate.

See also: INNATENESS IN ANCIENT PHILOSOPHY; LANGUAGE, INNATENESS OF; NATIVISM; RATIONALISM

EDWARD CRAIG

INNATENESS IN ANCIENT PHILOSOPHY

The idea that knowledge exists latently in the mind, independently of sense experience, is put forward in three of Plato's dialogues: the *Meno*, the *Phaedo* and the *Phaedrus*. The claim is that the human soul exists before it enters a body, and that in its pre-existent state it knows certain things, which it forgets at birth. What we call 'learning' during our mortal lives is in fact nothing but the recollection of pre-existent knowledge. In a particularly famous passage in the dialogue the *Meno*, the character Socrates sets an uneducated slave boy a geometrical puzzle. After asking a series of questions, he elicits the correct answer from the boy, which he claims existed in him all along, merely needing to be aroused by the process of recollection. Aristotle dismisses recollection quite brusquely and tries to explain human learning by appeal to sense perception. In post-Aristotelian philosophy, it unclear how far any theory of innateness was accepted. Most probably, the Stoics thought that in some sense moral concepts and beliefs arise from human nature, though they did not endorse a theory of pre-existence or recollection.

See also: CHOMSKY, N.; EMPIRICISM; EPICUREANISM; LANGUAGE, INNATENESS OF; LOCKE, J. §2; NATIVISM; PROLĒPSIS; STOICISM

DOMINIC SCOTT

INNATENESS OF LANGUAGE
See LANGUAGE, INNATENESS OF

INSTRUMENTALISM
See CONVENTIONALISM; DEWEY, JOHN; LAWS, NATURAL; SCIENTIFIC REALISM AND ANTIREALISM

INTENSIONAL ENTITIES

Intensional entities are such things as concepts, propositions and properties. What makes them 'intensional' is that they violate the principle of extensionality; the principle that equivalence implies identity. For example, the concept of being a (well-formed) creature with a kidney and the concept of being a (well-formed) creature with a heart are equivalent in so far as they apply to the same things, but they are different concepts. Likewise, although the proposition that creatures with kidneys have kidneys and the proposition that creatures with hearts have kidneys are equivalent (both are true), they are not identical. Intensional entities are contrasted with extensional entities such as sets, which do satisfy the principle of extensionality. For example, the set of creatures with kidneys and the set of creatures with hearts are equivalent in so far as they have the same members and, accordingly, are identical. By this standard criterion, each of the following philosophically important types of entity is intensional: qualities, attributes, properties, relations, conditions, states, concepts, ideas, notions, propositions and thoughts.

All (or most) of these intensional entities have been classified at one time or another as kinds of universals. Accordingly, standard traditional views about the ontological status of universals carry over to intensional entities. Nominalists hold that they do not really exist. Conceptualists accept their existence but deem it to be mind-dependent. Realists hold that they are mind-independent. *Ante rem* realists hold that they exist independently of being true of anything; *in re* realists require that they be true of something.

See also: INTENSIONAL LOGICS; NOMINALISM; SECOND-ORDER LOGIC, PHILOSOPHICAL ISSUES IN

GEORGE BEALER

INTENSIONAL LOGICS

Intensional logics are systems that distinguish an expression's intension (roughly, its sense or meaning) from its extension (reference, denotation). The purpose of bringing intensions into logic is to explain the logical behaviour of so-called intensional expressions. Intensional expressions create contexts which violate a cluster of standard principles of logic, the most notable of which is the law of substitution of identities – the law that from a = b and P(a) it follows that P(b). For example, 'obviously' is intensional because the following instance of the law of substitution is invalid (at least on one reading): Scott = the author of *Waverley*; obviously Scott = Scott; so, obviously Scott = the author of *Waverley*. By providing an analysis of meaning, intensional logics attempt to explain the logical behaviour of expressions such as 'obviously'. On the assumption that it is intensions and not extensions which matter in intensional contexts, the failure of substitution and related anomalies can be understood.

Alonzo Church pioneered intensional logic, basing it on his theory of types. However, the widespread application of intensional logic to linguistics and philosophy began with the work of Richard Montague, who crafted a number of systems designed to capture the expressive power of natural languages. One important feature of Montague's work was the application of possible worlds semantics to the analysis of intensional logic. The most difficult problems concerning intensional logic concern the treatment of propositional attitude verbs, such as 'believes', 'desires' and 'knows'. Such expressions pose difficulties for the possible worlds treatment, and have thus spawned alternative approaches.

See also: INTENSIONAL ENTITIES

JAMES W. GARSON

INTENSIONALITY

The truth or falsity of many sentences depends only on which things are being talked about. Within intensional contexts, however, truth values also depend on *how* those things are talked about, not just on which things they are. Philosophers and logicians have offered different analyses of intensional contexts and the behaviour of terms occurring within them.

The extension of a term is the thing or things it picks out: for instance, the extension of 'the Big Dipper' is the stellar constellation itself. The intension of a term can be thought of as the way in which it picks out its extension. 'The Big Dipper' and 'the Plough' have the same extension – a particular constellation – but pick it out in different ways. The two terms have different intensions. There is much debate about how we should actually understand the notion of an intension (see INTENSIONAL ENTITIES).

For many classes of sentence, the substitution of one term for another with the same extension leaves the truth value unchanged, irrespective of whether the two terms also have the same intension. This is called intersubstitution *salva veritate* (preserving truth). For instance, if it is true that the Big Dipper consists of seven stars, then it is also true that the Plough consists of seven stars. In a number of important cases, however, terms with the same extension but different intensions are not intersubstitutable *salva veritate*. Consider, for instance:

1 Tom believes that the Big Dipper consists of seven stars.
2 Tom believes that the Plough consists of seven stars.

It is quite possible that Tom mistakenly believes that 'the Plough' refers to a totally different constellation consisting of only six stars, in which case (1) could be true and (2) false. Co-extensive terms cannot be intersubstituted *salva veritate* within the scope of the verb 'believes'. Such contexts are called intensional.

Other verbs which, like 'believe', refer to propositional attitudes – verbs like 'hope', 'desire', 'fear' – also create intensional contexts. Propositional attitudes are *intentional* states (note the 't') which has led some to consider the possible connections between intenSionality and intenTionality (see INTENTIONALITY). The two must be distinguished carefully, however, not least because intensional contexts are also created by non-psychological terms, most importantly modal terms like 'necessarily' and 'possibly'. The intensionality of modal contexts leads to particular difficulties when they also involve quantification; these problems have led to controversies over the interpretation not only of modal terms but also of the quantifiers (see QUANTIFIERS, SUBSTITUTIONAL AND OBJECTUAL).

The failure of intersubstitutability *salva veritate* raises questions about the behaviour of terms in intensional contexts. Frege argues that, in intensional contexts, the term 'the Big Dipper' in (1) refers not to the Big Dipper as usual but to its own intension (or, in Frege's terminology, its sense (see INDIRECT DISCOURSE; PROPER NAMES; SENSE AND REFERENCE). Quine describes intensional contexts as *referentially opaque*, arguing that terms occurring within them do not refer at all. Davidson's *paratactic* analysis of propositional attitude statements and of indirect discourse, another intensional context, tries to preserve our intuition that terms in intensional contexts work in the same way as in any other contexts (see INDIRECT DISCOURSE).

Many philosophers think that logic should have nothing to do with intensions. But the intensionality of many natural language contexts is hard to deny, and the development of intensional logics suggests that a more tolerant attitude might well pay off (see INTENSIONAL LOGICS).

See also: CONCEPTS; REFERENCE; SEMANTICS, POSSIBLE WORLDS

References and further reading

Searle, J.R. (1983) *Intentionality*, Cambridge: Cambridge University Press. (Chapter 1 contains a useful discussion of the relationship between intensionality and intentionality.)

SIMON CHRISTMAS

INTENTION

Suppose that Kevin intends to brush up on his predicate logic, and acts on this intention, because he wants to conduct a good tutorial and he believes that some preparatory revision will help him to do so. In an example like this, we explain why Kevin intends to revise his logic, and why he (intentionally) does revise it, by appealing to the belief and desire which provide his reasons both for his intention and his corresponding intentional action.

But how does Kevin's intention to act, coming between his reasons and his action, help to explain what he does? Central questions in the theory of intention include the following: Are intentions distinct mental attitudes or are they analysable in terms of other mental attitudes – such as beliefs and desires? How is intending to do something related to judging that it is best to do it? What distinctive roles, if any, do intentions play in getting us to act? Are foreseen but undesired consequences of an intentional action intended?

See also: ACTION; BELIEF; COMMUNICATION AND INTENTION; DESIRE; PROPOSITIONAL ATTITUDES; RATIONALITY, practical

ROBERT DUNN

INTENTION, ARTIST'S
See ARTIST'S INTENTION

INTENTIONAL FALLACY
See ARTIST'S INTENTION

INTENTIONALITY

Intentionality is the mind's capacity to direct itself on things. Mental states like thoughts, beliefs, desires, hopes (and others) exhibit intentionality in the sense that they are always directed on, or at, something: if you hope, believe or desire, you must hope, believe or desire something. Hope, belief, desire and any other mental state which is directed at something, are known as intentional states. Intentionality in this sense has only a peripheral connection to the ordinary ideas of intention and intending. An intention to do something is an intentional state, since one cannot intend without intending something; but intentions are only one of many kinds of intentional mental states.

The terminology of intentionality derives from the scholastic philosophy of the Middle Ages, and was revived by Brentano in 1874. Brentano characterized intentionality in terms of the mind's direction upon an object, and emphasized that the object need not exist. He also claimed that it is the intentionality of mental phenomena that distinguishes them from physical phenomena. These ideas of Brentano's provide the background to twentieth-century discussions of intentionality, in both the phenomenological and analytic traditions. Among these discussions, we can distinguish two general projects. The first is to characterize the essential features of intentionality. For example, is intentionality a relation? If it is, what does it relate, if the object of an intentional state need not exist in order to be thought about? The second is to explain how intentionality can occur in the natural world. How can merely biological creatures exhibit intentionality? The aim of this second project is to explain intentionality in non-intentional terms.

See also: BELIEF; DESIRE; EMOTIONS, NATURE OF; IMAGINATION; INTENTION; PERCEPTION

TIM CRANE

INTERNALISM AND EXTERNALISM IN EPISTEMOLOGY

The internalism–externalism distinction is usually applied to the epistemic justification of belief. The most common form of internalism (accessibility internalism) holds that only what the subject can easily become aware of (by reflection, for example) can have a bearing on justification. We may think of externalism as simply the denial of this constraint.

The strong intuitive appeal of internalism is due to the sense that we should be able to determine whether we are justified in believing something just by carefully considering the question, without the need for any further investigation. Then there is the idea that we can successfully reply to sceptical doubts about the possibility of knowledge or justified beliefs only if we can determine the epistemic status of our beliefs without presupposing anything about which sceptical doubts could be raised – the external world for example.

The main objections to internalism are as follows. (1) It assumes an unrealistic confidence in the efficacy of armchair reflection, which is often not up to surveying our entire repertoire of beliefs and other possible grounds of belief and determining the extent to which they support a given belief. (2) If we confine ourselves to what we can ascertain on reflection, there is no guarantee that the beliefs that are thus approved as justified are likely to be true. And the truth-promoting character of justification is the main source of its value.

Externalism lifts this accessibility constraint, but in its most general sense it embodies no particular positive view. The most common way of further specifying externalism is reliabilism, the view that a belief is justified if and only if it was produced and/or sustained by a reliable process, one that would produce mostly true beliefs in the long run. This is a form of externalism because whether a particular belief-forming process is reliable is not something we can ascertain just on reflection. The main objections to externalism draw on internalist intuitions. (1) If the world were governed by an evil demon who sees to it that our beliefs are generally false, even though we have the kind of bases for them we do in fact have, then our beliefs would still be justified, even though formed unreliably. (2) If a reliable clairvoyant (one who

'sees' things at a great distance) forms beliefs on this basis without having any reason for thinking that they are reliably formed, those beliefs would not be justified, even though they pass the reliability test.

See also: JUSTIFICATION, EPISTEMIC; KNOWLEDGE, CONCEPT OF

WILLIAM P. ALSTON

INTERNATIONAL RELATIONS, PHILOSOPHY OF

The philosophy of international relations – or more precisely its *political* philosophy – embraces problems about morality in diplomacy and war, the justice of international practices and institutions bearing on economic welfare and the global environment, human rights, and the relationship between sectional loyalties such as patriotism and global moral commitments.

Not everyone believes that such a subject can exist, or rather, that it can have significant ethical content. According to political realism – a widely-held view among Anglo-American students of international relations – moral considerations have no place in decisions about foreign affairs and international behaviour. The most extreme varieties of realism deny that moral judgment can have meaning or force in international affairs; more moderate versions acknowledge the meaningfulness of such judgments but hold either that leaders have no responsibility to attend to the morality of their actions in foreign affairs (because their overriding responsibility is to advance the interests of their constituents), or that the direct pursuit of moral goals in international relations is likely to be self-defeating.

Leaving aside the more sceptical kinds of political realism, the most influential orientations to substantive international morality can be arrayed on a continuum. Distinctions are made on the basis of the degree of privilege, if any, extended to the citizens of a state to act on their own behalf at the potential expense of the liberty and wellbeing of persons elsewhere. 'The morality of states', at one extreme, holds that states have rights of autonomy analogous to those of individuals within domestic society, which secure them against external interference in their internal affairs and guarantee their ownership and control of the natural and human resources within their borders. At the other end of the continuum, one finds cosmopolitan views which deny that states enjoy any special privilege; these views hold that individuals rather than states are the ultimate subjects of morality, and that value judgments concerning international conduct should take equally seriously the wellbeing of each person potentially affected by a decision, whether compatriot or foreigner. Cosmopolitan views may acknowledge that states (and similar entities) have morally significant features, but analysis of the significance of these features must connect them with considerations of individual wellbeing. Intermediate views are possible; for example, a conception of the privileged character of the state can be combined with a conception of the international realm as weakly normative (that is, governed by principles which demand that states adhere to minimum conditions of peaceful coexistence).

The theoretical difference between the morality of states and a fully cosmopolitan morality is reflected in practical differences about the justifiability of intervention in the internal affairs of other states, the basis and content of human rights, and the extent, if any, of our obligations as individuals and as citizens of states to help redress the welfare effects of international inequalities.

See also: Globalization; State, the

CHARLES R. BEITZ

INTERPRETATION AND TRANSLATION
See Radical translation and radical interpretation

INTERPRETATION, RADICAL
See Radical translation and radical interpretation

INTUITIONISM

Ultimately, mathematical intuitionism gets its name and its epistemological parentage from a conviction of Kant: that intuition reveals basic mathematical principles as true a priori. Intuitionism's mathematical lineage is that of radical constructivism: constructive in requiring proofs of existential claims to yield provable instances of those claims; radical in seeking a wholesale reconstruction of mathematics. Although partly inspired by Kronecker and Poincaré, twentieth-century intuitionism is dominated by the 'neo-intuitionism' of the Dutch mathematician L.E.J. Brouwer. Brouwer's reworking of analysis, paradigmatic for intuitionism, broke the bounds on traditional constructivism by embracing real numbers given by free choice sequences. Brouwer's theorem – that every real-valued function on a closed, bounded interval is uniformly continuous – brings intuitionism into seeming conflict with results of conventional mathematics.

Despite Brouwer's distaste for logic, formal systems for intuitionism were devised and developments in intuitionistic mathematics began to parallel those in metamathematics. A. Heyting was the first to formalize both intuitionistic logic and arithmetic

and to interpret the logic over types of abstract proofs. Tarski, Beth and Kripke each constructed a distinctive class of models for intuitionistic logic. Gödel, in his *Dialectica* interpretation, showed how to view formal intuitionistic arithmetic as a calculus of higher-order functions. S.C. Kleene gave a 'realizability' interpretation to the same theory using codes of recursive functions. In the last decades of the twentieth century, applications of intuitionistic higher-order logic and type theory to category theory and computer science have made these systems objects of intense study. At the same time, philosophers and logicians, under the influence of M. Dummett, have sought to enlist intuitionism under the banner of general antirealist semantics for natural languages.

DAVID CHARLES MCCARTY

INTUITIONISM IN ETHICS

To intuit something is to apprehend it directly, without recourse to reasoning processes such as deduction or induction. Intuitionism in ethics proposes that we have a capacity for intuition and that some of the facts or properties that we intuit are irreducibly ethical. Traditionally, intuitionism also advances the important thesis that beliefs arising from intuition have direct justification, and therefore do not need to be justified by appeal to other beliefs or facts. So, while intuitionism in ethics is about the apprehension of ethical facts or properties, traditional intuitionism is principally a view about how beliefs, including ethical beliefs, are justified. Varieties of intuitionism differ over what is intuited (for example, rightness or goodness?); whether what is intuited is general and abstract or concrete and particular; the degree of justification offered by intuition; and the nature of the intuitive capacity. The rejection of intuitionism is usually a result of rejecting one of the views that lie behind it.

Note that 'intuition' can refer to the thing intuited as well as the process of intuiting. Also, somewhat confusingly, intuitionism is sometimes identified with pluralism, the view that there is a plurality of fundamental ethical properties or principles. This identification probably occurs because pluralists often accept the epistemological version of intuitionism.

See also: Epistemology and ethics; Moral judgment

ROBERT L. FRAZIER

INTUITIONISTIC LOGIC AND ANTIREALISM

The law of excluded middle (LEM) says that every sentence of the form $A \vee \neg A$ ('A or not A') is logically true. This law is accepted in classical logic, but not in intuitionistic logic. The reason for this difference over logical validity is a deeper difference about truth and meaning. In classical logic, the meanings of the logical connectives are explained by means of the truth tables, and these explanations justify LEM. However, the truth table explanations involve acceptance of the principle of bivalence, that is, the principle that every sentence is either true or false. The intuitionist does not accept bivalence, at least not in mathematics. The reason is the view that mathematical sentences are made true and false by proofs which mathematicians construct. On this view, bivalence can be assumed only if we have a guarantee that for each mathematical sentence, either there is a proof of the truth of the sentence, or a proof of its falsity. But we have no such guarantee. Therefore bivalence is not intuitionistically acceptable, and then neither is LEM.

A realist about mathematics thinks that if a mathematical sentence is true, then it is rendered true by the obtaining of some particular state of affairs, whether or not we can know about it, and if that state of affairs does not obtain, then the sentence is false. The realist further thinks that mathematical reality is fully determinate, in that every mathematical state of affairs determinately either obtains or does not obtain. As a result, the principle of bivalence is taken to hold for mathematical sentences. The intuitionist is usually an *antirealist* about mathematics, rejecting the idea of a fully determinate, mind-independent mathematical reality.

The intuitionist's view about the truth-conditions of mathematical sentences is not obviously incompatible with realism about mathematical states of affairs. According to Michael Dummett, however, the view about truth-conditions implies antirealism. In Dummett's view, a conflict over realism is fundamentally a conflict about what makes sentences true, and therefore about semantics, for there is no further question about, for example, the existence of a mathematical reality than as a truth ground for mathematical sentences. In this vein Dummett has proposed to take acceptance of bivalence as actually defining a realist position.

If this is right, then both the choice between classical and intuitionistic logic and questions of realism are fundamentally questions of semantics, for whether or not bivalence holds depends on the proper semantics. The question of the proper semantics, in turn, belongs to the theory of meaning. Within the theory of meaning Dummett has laid down general principles, from which he argues that meaning cannot in general consist in bivalent truth-conditions. The principles concern the need for, and the possibility of, manifesting one's

knowledge of meaning to other speakers, and the nature of such manifestations. If Dummett's argument is sound, then bivalence cannot be justified directly from semantics, and may not be justifiable at all.

See also: MEANING AND TRUTH; REALISM AND ANTIREALISM

PETER PAGIN

IRIGARAY, LUCE (1930–)

Luce Irigaray holds doctorates in both linguistics and philosophy, and has practised as a psychoanalyst for many years. Author of over twenty books, she has established a reputation as a pre-eminent theorist of sexual difference – a term she would prefer to 'feminist'. The latter carries with it the history of feminism as a struggle for equality, whereas Irigaray sees herself more as a feminist of difference, emphasizing the need to differentiate women from men over and above the need to establish parity between the sexes.

Speculum de l'autre femme (1974) (Speculum of the Other Woman) (1985), the book that earned her international recognition, fuses philosophy with psychoanalysis, and employs a lyrical 'mimesis', or mimicry, that parodies and undercuts philosophical pretensions to universality. While adopting the standpoint of universality, objectivity and uniformity, the philosophical tradition in fact reflects a partial view of the world, one which is informed by those largely responsible for writing it: men. Without the material, maternal and nurturing succour provided by women as mothers and homemakers, men would not have had the freedom to reflect, the peace to think, or the time to write the philosophy that has shaped our culture. As such, women are suppressed and unacknowledged; femininity is the unthought ground of philosophy – philosophy's other.

TINA CHANTER

ISLAMIC PHILOSOPHY

Introduction

Islamic philosophy may be defined in a number of different ways, but the perspective taken here is that it represents the style of philosophy produced within the framework of Islamic culture. This description does not suggest that it is necessarily concerned with religious issues, nor even that it is exclusively produced by Muslims.

457

ISLAMIC PHILOSOPHY

1   The early years of Islamic philosophy

Islamic philosophy is intimately connected with Greek philosophy, although this is a relationship which can be exaggerated. Theoretical questions were raised right from the beginning of Islam, questions which could to a certain extent be answered by reference to Islamic texts such as the Qur'an, the practices of the community and the traditional sayings of the Prophet and his Companions. On this initial basis a whole range of what came to be known as the Islamic sciences came to be produced, and these consisted largely of religious law, the Arabic language and forms of theology which represented differing understandings of Islam.

The early conquests of the Muslims brought them into close contact with centres of civilization heavily influenced by Christianity and Judaism, and also by Greek culture. Many rulers wished to understand and use the Greek forms of knowledge, some practical and some theoretical, and a large translation project started which saw official support for the assimilation of Greek culture. This had a powerful impact upon all areas of Islamic philosophy. Neoplatonism definitely became the prevalent school of thought, following closely the curriculum of Greek (Peripatetic) philosophy which was initially transmitted to the Islamic world. This stressed agreement between Plato and Aristotle on a range of issues, and incorporated the work of some Neoplatonic authors. A leading group of Neoplatonic thinkers were the Ikhwan al-Safa' (Brethren of Purity), who presented an eclectic philosophy designed to facilitate spiritual liberation through philosophical perfection. However, there was also a development of Aristotelianism in Islamic philosophy, especially by those thinkers who were impressed by the logical and metaphysical thought of Aristotle, and Platonism was inspired by the personality of Socrates and the apparently more spiritual nature of Plato as compared with Aristotle. There were even thinkers who seem to have been influenced by Greek scepticism, which they turned largely against religion, and Ibn ar-Rawandi and Muhammad ibn Zakariyya' al-Razi presented a thoroughgoing critique of many of the leading supernatural ideas of Islam.

Al-Kindi is often called the first philosopher of the Arabs, and he followed a broadly Neoplatonic approach. One of the earliest of the philosophers in Baghdad was in fact a Christian, Yahya Ibn 'Adi, and his pupil AL-FARABI created much of the agenda for the next four centuries of work. Al-Farabi argued that the works of Aristotle raise important issues for the understanding of the nature of the universe, in particular its origination. Aristotle suggested that the world is eternal, which seems to be in contradiction with the implication in the Qur'an that God created the world out of nothing. Al-Farabi used as his principle of creation the process of emanation, the idea that reality continually flows out of the source of perfection, so that the world was not created at a particular time. He also did an enormous amount of work on Greek logic, arguing that behind natural language lies logic, so that an understanding of the latter is a deeper and more significant achievement than a grasp of the former. This also seemed to threaten the significance of language, in particular the language – Arabic – in which God transmitted the Qur'an to the Prophet Muhammad. A large school of thinkers was strongly influenced by al-Farabi, including al-'Amiri, al-Sijistani and al-Tawhidi, and this surely played an important part in making his ideas and methodology so crucial for the following centuries of Islamic philosophy.

IBN SINA went on to develop this form of thought in a much more creative way, and he presented a view of the universe as consisting of entirely necessitated events, with the exception of God. This led to a powerful reaction from AL-GHAZALI, who in his critique of Peripatetic philosophy argued that it was both incompatible with religion, and also invalid on its own principles. He managed to point to some of the major difficulties with the developments of Neoplatonism which had taken place in Islamic philosophy, and he argued that while philosophy should be rejected, logic as a conceptual tool should be retained. This view became very influential in much of the Islamic world, and philosophy came under a cloud until the nineteenth century.

2   Philosophy in Spain and North Africa

A particularly rich blend of philosophy flourished in al-Andalus (the Islamic part of the Iberian peninsula), and in North Africa. Ibn Masarra defended a form of mysticism, and this type of thinking was important for both IBN TUFAYL and Ibn Bajja, for whom the contrast between the individual in society and the individual who primarily relates to God became very much of a theme. The argument was often that a higher level of understanding of reality can be attained by those prepared to develop their religious consciousness outside of the framework of traditional religion, a view which was supported and became part of a highly sophisticated account of the links between religion and reason as created by IBN RUSHD. He set out to defend philosophy strenuously from the attacks of al-Ghazali, and also to present a more Aristotelian account than had been managed by Ibn Sina. He argued that there are a variety of routes to God, all equally valid, and that the route which the philosopher can take is one based on the independent use of reason, while the ordinary member of society has to be satisfied with the sayings and obligations of religion. Ibn Sab'in, by contrast, argued that Aristotelian philosophy and logic were useless in trying to understand reality since those ideas fail to mirror the basic unity which is implicit in reality, a unity which stems from the unity of God, and so we require an entirely new form of thinking which is adequate to the task of representing the oneness of the world. A thinker better known perhaps for his work on history and sociology than in philosophy is Ibn Khaldun, who was none the less a significant philosophical writer; he presents an excellent summary of preceding philosophical movements within the Islamic world, albeit from a conservative (Ash'arite) point of view.

3   Mystical philosophy

Mystical philosophy in Islam represents a persistent tradition of working philosophically within the Islamic world. Some philosophers managed to combine mysticism with Peripatetic thought, while others saw mysticism as in opposition to Peripateticism. Al-Ghazali had great influence in making mysticism in its Sufi form respectable, but it is really other thinkers such as al-Suhrawardi and Ibn al-'Arabi who produced actual systematic mystical thought. They created, albeit in different ways, accounts of how to do philosophy which accord with mystical approaches to reality, and which self-consciously go in opposite directions to Peripateticism. Ibn al-'Arabi concentrated on analysing the different levels of reality and the links which exist between them, while al-Suhrawardi is the main progenitor of Illuminationist philosophy. This tries to replace Aristotelian logic and metaphysics with an alternative based on the relationship between light as the main principle of creation and knowledge, and that which is lit up – the rest of reality. This tradition has had many followers, including al-Tusi, Mulla Sadra, Mir Damad and al-Sabzawari, and has been popular in the Persian world right up to today. Shah Wali Allah extended this school of thought to the Indian subcontinent.

4   Islamic philosophy and the Islamic sciences

Islamic philosophy has always had a rather difficult relationship with the Islamic sciences, those techniques for answering theoretical questions which are closely linked with the religion of Islam, comprising law, theology, language and the study of the religious texts themselves. Many theologians such as Ibn Hazm, al-Juwayni and Fakhr al-Din al-Razi presented accounts of Islamic theology which argued for a particular theory of how to interpret religious texts. They tended to advocate a restricted approach to interpretation, rejecting the use of analogy and also the idea that philosophy is an objective system of enquiry which can be applied to anything at all. Most theologians were Ash'arites, which meant that they were opposed to the idea that ethical and religious ideas could be objectively true. What makes such ideas true, the Ash'arites argued, is that God says that they are true, and there are no other grounds for accepting them than this. This had a particularly strong influence on ethics, where there was much debate between objectivists and subjectivists, with the latter arguing that an action is just if and only if God says that it is just. Many thinkers wrote about how to reconcile the social virtues, which involve being part of a community and following the rules of religion, with the intellectual virtues, which tend to involve a more solitary lifestyle. Ibn Miskawayh and Al-Tusi developed complex accounts of the apparent conflict between these different sets of virtues.

Political philosophy in Islam looked to Greek thinkers for ways of understanding the nature of the state, yet also generally linked Platonic ideas of the state to Qur'anic notions, which is not difficult given the basically hierarchical nature of both types of account. Even thinkers attracted to Illuminationist philosophy such as al-Dawani wrote on political philosophy, arguing that the structure of the state should represent the material and spiritual aspects of the citizens. Through a strict differentiation of role in the state, and through leadership by those skilled in religious and philosophical knowledge, everyone would find an acceptable place in society and scope for spiritual perfection to an appropriate degree.

Particular problems arose in the discussions concerning the nature of the soul. According to the version of Aristotle which was generally used by the Islamic philosophers, the soul is an integral part of the person as its form, and once the individual dies the soul disappears also. This appears to contravene the notion of an afterlife which is so important a part of Islam. Even Platonic views of the soul seem to insist on its spirituality, as compared with the very physical accounts of the Islamic afterlife. Many of the philosophers tried to get around this by arguing that the religious language discussing the soul is only allegorical, and is intended to impress upon the community at large that there is a wider context within which their lives take place, which extends further than those lives themselves. They could argue in this way because of theories which presented a sophisticated view of different types of meaning that a statement may have in order to appeal to different audiences and carry out a number of different functions. Only the philosopher really has the ability to understand this range of meanings, and those who work in the Islamic sciences do not know how to deal with these issues which come outside of their area of expertise. While those skilled in dealing with the law will know how to adjudicate between different legal judgments, we need an understanding of the philosophy of law in Islam if we are to have access to what might be called the deep structure of law itself. Similarly, although the Qur'an encourages its followers to discover facts about the world, it is through the philosophy of science that we can understand the theoretical principles which lie behind that physical reality.

Many of the problems of religion versus philosophy arose in the area of aesthetics. The rules of poetry which traditionally existed in the Arabic tradition came up against the application of Aristotle's *Poetics* to that poetry. One of the interesting aspects of Islamic aesthetics is that it treated poetry as a logical form, albeit of a very low demonstrative value, along the continuum of logical forms which lie behind all our language and practices. This is explained in studies of both epistemology and logic. Logic came to play an enormous role in Islamic philosophy, and the idea that logic represents a basic set of techniques which lies behind what we think and what we do was felt to be very exciting and provocative. Many theologians who attacked philosophy were staunch defenders of logic as a tool for disputation, and Ibn Taymiyya is unusual in the strong critique which he provided of Aristotelian logic. He argued that the logic entails Aristotelian metaphysics, and so should be abandoned by anyone who wishes to avoid philosophical infection.

However, the general respect for logic provides the framework for the notion that there is a range of logical approaches which are available to different people, each of which is appropriate to different levels of society. For the theologian and the lawyer, for instance, dialectic is appropriate, since this works logically from generally accepted propositions to conclusions which are established as valid, but only within the limits set by those premises. This means that within the context of theology, for example, if we accept the truth of the Qur'an, then certain conclusions follow if we use the principles of theology; but if we do not accept the truth of the Qur'an, then the acceptability of those conclusions is dubious. Philosophers are distinguished from everyone else in that they are the only people who use entirely certain and universal premises, and so their conclusions have total universality as well as validity. When it comes to knowledge we find a similar contrast. Ordinary people can know something of what is around them and also of the spiritual nature of reality, but they are limited to the images and allegories of religion and the scope of their senses. Philosophers, by contrast, can attain much higher levels of knowledge through their application of logic and through their ability to perfect their understanding and establish contact with the principles which underlie the whole of reality.

5   Islamic philosophy in the modern world

After the death of Ibn Rushd, Islamic philosophy in the Peripatetic style went out of fashion in the Arab world, although the transmission of Islamic philosophy into Western Europe started at this time and had an important influence upon the direction which medieval and Renaissance Europe were to take. In the Persian-speaking world, Islamic philosophy has continued to follow a largely Illuminationist curriculum right up to today; but in the Arab world it fell into something of a decline, at least in its Peripatetic form, until the nineteenth century. Mystical philosophy, by contrast, continued to flourish, although no thinkers matched the creativity of Ibn al-'Arabi or Ibn Sab'in. Al-Afghani and Muhammad 'Abduh sought to find rational principles which would establish a form of thought which is both distinctively Islamic and also appropriate for life in modern scientific societies, a debate which is continuing within Islamic philosophy today. Iqbal provided a rather eclectic mixture of Islamic and European philosophy, and some thinkers reacted to the phenomenon of modernity by developing Islamic fundamentalism. This resuscitated the earlier antagonism to philosophy by arguing for a return to the original principles of Islam and rejected modernity as a Western imperialist instrusion. The impact of Western scholarship on Islamic philosophy has not always been helpful, and Orientalism has sometimes led to an overemphasis of the dependence of Islamic philosophy on Greek thought, and to a refusal to regard Islamic philosophy as real philosophy. That is, in much of the exegetical literature there has been too much concern dealing with the historical conditions under which the philosophy was produced as compared with the status of the ideas themselves. While there are still many disputes concerning the ways in which Islamic philosophy should be pursued, as is the case with all kinds of philosophy, there can be little doubt about its major achievements and continuing significance.

See also: Ancient philosophy; Jewish philosophy; Medieval philosophy; Renaissance philosophy

References and further reading

Corbin, H. (1993) *History of Islamic Philosophy*, trans. L. Sherrard, London: Kegan Paul International. (An authoritative account of most Islamic philosophy, stressing in particular the illuminationist and mystical trends.)

Leaman, Oliver (2002) *An Introduction to Classical Islamic Philosophy*, Cambridge: Cambridge University Press. (An account of some of the leading arguments and figures in the area.)

Nasr, S. and Leaman, O. (eds) (1996) *History of Islamic Philosophy*, London: Routledge. (A comprehensive account of the different schools of thought, thinkers and concepts.)

OLIVER LEAMAN

ISLAMIC PHILOSOPHY IN SPAIN

See Ibn Rushd, Abu'l Walid Muhammad

J

JAINA PHILOSOPHY

The issues in Jaina philosophy developed concurrently with those that emerged in Buddhist and Hindu philosophy. The period from the second century BC to about the tenth century AD evinces a tremendous interaction between the schools of thought and even an exchange of ideas, borne out especially in the rich commentary literature on the basic philosophical works of the respective systems. Jaina philosophy shares with Buddhism and Hinduism the aim of striving, within its own metaphysical presuppositions, for absolute liberation (*mokṣa* or *nirvāṇa*) from the factors which bind human existence. For the philosophical systems of Indian thought, ignorance (of one's own nature, of the nature of the world and of one's role in the world) is one of the chief such factors, and Jainism offers its own insights into what constitutes the knowledge that has the soteriological function of overcoming ignorance. Jainism is not exempt from the problem of distinguishing the religious and/or mystical from the 'philosophical'; the Indian tradition has no exact equivalents for these categories as they are usually employed in Western thought.

The significance ascribed to knowledge is reflected in the attention given to epistemology and logic by Jaina philosophers. The first systematic account was given by the fourth- or fifth-century philosopher Umāsvāti, who distinguished two types of knowledge: partial knowledge, which is obtained from particular standpoints, and comprehensive knowledge, which is of five kinds – sensory knowledge, scriptural knowledge, clairvoyance, telepathy and omniscience. Of these, the first two are held to be indirect (consisting in, or analogous to, inference) and the remainder are direct; Jainism is unique among Indian philosophies in characterizing sensory knowledge as indirect. The aim of the treatises on knowledge is to present what the Jainas believe would be known in the state of omniscience, as taught by Mahāvīra. Omniscience is an intrinsic condition of all souls; however, due to the influence of karma since beginningless time this essential quality of the soul is inhibited.

The Jaina interest in logic arose, as with the other schools, through a consideration of inference as a mode of knowledge. The methods and terminology of the Nyāya school were heavily drawn upon; this is evident in Siddhasena Divākara's *Nyāyāvatāra* (The Descent of Logic) (*c.* fifth century), one of the first detailed presentations of Jaina logic. The Jainas used logic to criticize other schools and defend their own. The acquaintance with other traditions that this implies is a notable aspect of classical Jainism; their interest in other schools, coupled with their belief in collecting and preserving manuscripts, makes the Jaina corpus very important for the study of classical Indian thought.

According to Jaina ontology, reality is divided into the two basic principles of sentience and non-sentience, neither of which is reducible to the other. The former is manifested in souls, of which there are an infinite number, and the latter in the five basic substances, which are matter, *dharma* and *adharma* (factors posited to explain movement and rest), space and time. Matter consists of atoms; as it becomes associated with the soul, it gets attached to it, becomes transformed into karma and thereby restricts the functions of consciousness. This pernicious process can only be reversed through ascetic practices, which ultimately lead to liberation.

Ascetic practices constitute the basis of Jaina ethics, the framework of which are the 'five great vows', according to which the ascetics vow to live. These are: nonviolence towards all forms of life, abstinence from lying, not taking what is not given, celibacy and renunciation of property. Nonviolence is strongly emphasized, since violence produces the greatest amount of karma. Hence great care has to be exercised at all times, especially because injury of life forms should be avoided also in plants, water, fire, etc. The minimization of physical activity to avoid injury is therefore an important ideal of Jaina asceticism. Inspiration for constant ethical behaviour is provided by a contemplation of the lives of the twenty-four Jinas, of whom Mahāvīra was the last. Though human, these 'conquerors of the passions' are worshipped as divine beings because of their conduct in the world and knowledge of the nature of ultimate reality.

JAYANDRA SONI

JAMES, WILLIAM (1842–1910)

The American William James was motivated to philosophize by a desire to provide a philosophical ground for moral action. Moral effort presupposes that one has free will, that the world is not already the best of all possible worlds, and, for maximum effort, according to James, the belief that there is a God who is also on the side of good.

In his famous, often misunderstood paper 'The Will to Believe', James defended one's right to believe in advance of the evidence when one's belief has momentous consequences for one's conduct and success, and a decision cannot be postponed. One such belief is the belief in objective values. Generally, a belief is objective if it meets a standard independent of the believer's own thought. In morals, objective values emerge from each person's subjective valuings, whatever their psychological source, when these valuings become the values of a community of persons who care for one another. Still, even in such a community there will be conflicting claims, and the obligations generated by these claims will need to be ranked and conflicts resolved. James' solution is to say that the more inclusive claim – the claim that can be satisfied with the lesser cost of unsatisfied claims – is to be ranked higher. This is not to be mistaken for utilitarianism: James is not a hedonist, and it is not clear what he means by the most inclusive claim.

A concern for others makes sense only if there are others who inhabit with us a common world. Pragmatism, which he co-founded with C.S. Peirce, and radical empiricism provide James' answer to those who would be sceptics concerning the existence of the common-sense world. Pragmatism is both a theory of meaning and a theory of truth. As a theory of meaning it aims at clarity; our thoughts of an object are clear when we know what effects it will have and what reactions we are to prepare. As a theory of truth, pragmatism makes clear what is meant by 'agreement' in the common formula that a belief is true if it agrees with reality. Only in the simplest cases can we verify a belief directly – for example, we can verify that the soup is too salty by tasting it – and a belief is indirectly verified if one acts on it and that action does not lead to unanticipated consequences. Contrary to a widespread misunderstanding, this does not mean that James defines truth as that which is useful; rather, he points out that it is, in fact, useful to believe what is true.

James rejects the dualism of common sense and of many philosophers, but he is neither a materialist nor an idealist, rather what he calls a 'pure experience' (for example, your seeing this page) can be taken as an event in your (mental) history or as an event in the page's (physical) history. But there is no 'substance' called 'pure experience': there are only many different pure experiences. You and I can experience the same page, because an event in your mental history and an event in mine can be taken to be events in the same physical history of the page; James may even have been tempted to say that a pure experience can be taken to belong to more than one mental history.

According to James, pragmatism mediates the so-called conflict between science and religion. James took religious experiences very seriously both from a psychologist's perspective and as evidence for the reality of the divine.

See also: EMPIRICISM; IDEALISM; PANPSYCHISM; PRAGMATISM; RELIGION AND MORALITY

References and further reading

Kierkegaard, S.A. (1843) *Enten-Eller*, trans. H.V. Hong and E.H. Hong, *Either/Or*, Princeton, NJ: Princeton University Press, 1987, 2 vols. (Presents contrasting life-views, one aesthetic and the other ethical, in the form of papers and letters attributed to two imaginary characters.)

RUTH ANNA PUTNAM

JAPANESE PHILOSOPHY

Introduction

The most distinctive characteristic of Japanese philosophy is how it has assimilated and adapted foreign philosophies to its native worldview. As an isolated island nation, Japan successfully resisted foreign invasion until 1945 and, although it borrowed ideas freely throughout its history, was able to do so without the imposition of a foreign military or colonial presence. Japanese philosophy thus bears the imprint of a variety of foreign traditions, but there is always a distinctively Japanese cultural context. In order to understand the dynamics of Japanese thought, therefore, it is necessary to examine both the influence of various foreign philosophies through Japanese history and the underlying or continuing cultural orientation that set the stage for which ideas would be assimilated and in what way.

The major philosophical traditions to influence Japan from abroad have been Confucianism, Buddhism, neo-Confucianism and Western philosophy. Daoism also had an impact, but more in the areas of alchemy, prognostication and folk medicine than in philosophy. Although these traditions often overlapped, each also had distinctive influences.

In its literary forms, Japanese philosophy began about fourteen centuries ago. Confucian thought entered Japan around the fifth century AD. Through the centuries the imprint of Confucianism has been most noticeable in the areas of social structure, government organization and ethics. Philosophically speaking, the social self in Japan has its roots mainly in Confucian ideals, blended since the sixteenth century with certain indigenous ideas of loyalty and honour developed within the Japanese *samurai* or warrior class.

The philosophical impact of Buddhism, introduced around the same time as Confucianism, has been primarily in three areas: psychology, metaphysics and aesthetics. With its emphasis on disciplined contemplation and introspective analysis, Buddhism has helped define the various Japanese senses of the inner, rather than social, self. In metaphysics, Buddhist esotericism has been most dominant; through esoteric Buddhist philosophy, the Japanese gave a rational structure to their indigenous beliefs that spirituality is immanent rather than transcendent, that mind and body (like humanity and nature) are continuous rather than separate, and that expressive power is shared by things as well as human thought or speech. This metaphysical principle of expression has combined with the introspective psychology and emphasis on discipline to form the foundation of the various aesthetic theories that have been so well developed in Japanese history.

Neo-Confucianism became most prominent in Japan in the sixteenth century. Like classical Confucianism, it contributed much to the Japanese understanding of virtue and the nature of the social self. Unlike classical Confucianism in Japan, however, neo-Confucianism also had a metaphysical and epistemological influence. Its emphasis on investigating the principle or configuration of things stimulated the Japanese study of the natural world. This reinforced a tendency initiated with the very limited introduction of Western practical sciences and medicine in the sixteenth century.

Western philosophy, along with Western science and technology, has had its major impact in Japan only since the middle of the nineteenth century. The process of modernization forced Japanese philosophers to reconsider fundamental issues in epistemology, social philosophy and philosophical anthropology. As it has assimilated Asian traditions of thought in the past – absorbing, modifying and incorporating aspects into its culture – so Japan has been consciously assimilating Western thought since the early twentieth century. The process continues today.

What in all this is distinctively Japanese? On the superficial level, it might seem that Japan has drawn eclectically from a variety of traditions without any inherent sense of intellectual direction. A more careful analysis, however, shows that Japanese thinkers have seldom adopted any foreign philosophy without simultaneously adapting it. For example, the Japanese philosophical tradition never fully accepted the emphasis on propriety or the mandate of heaven so characteristic of Chinese Confucianism. It rejected the Buddhist idea that impermanence is a reality to which one must be resigned, and instead made the appreciation of impermanence into an aesthetic. It criticized the neo-Confucian and Western philosophical tendencies toward rationalism and positivism, even while accepting many ideas from those traditions. In short, there has always been a complex selection process at work beneath the apparent absorption of foreign ideas.

Both historically and in the present, some Japanese philosophers and cultural critics have tried to identify this selection process with Shintō, but Shintō itself has also been profoundly shaped by foreign influences. The selection process has shaped Shintō as much as Shintō has shaped it. In any case, we can isolate a few axiological orientations that have seemed to persist or recur throughout the history of Japanese thought. First, there has been a tendency to emphasize immanence over transcendence in defining spirituality. Second, contextual pragmatism has generally won out over attempts to establish universal principles that apply to all situations. Third, reason has often been combined with affect as the basis of knowledge or insight. Fourth, theory is seldom formulated in isolation from a praxis used to learn the theory. Fifth, although textual authority has often been important, it has not been as singular in its focus as in many other cultures. Thus, the Japanese have not typically identified a single text such as the Bible, the *Analects*, the Qur'an or the *Bhagavad Gītā* as foundational to their culture. Although there have been exceptions to these general orientations, they do nonetheless help define the broader cultural backdrop against which the drama of Japanese philosophy has been played out through history.

1 Archaic spirituality
2 The importation of Confucianism and Buddhism
3 Metaphysical vision of ancient Japanese esoteric Buddhism

1   Archaic spirituality

The earliest accounts of Japan by Chinese visitors, archaeological remains of the prehistoric culture and the earliest recorded prayers and songs all suggest that Japan was originally an animistic culture with shamanistic qualities. The world was understood to be full of *kami*, sacred presences in the form of awe-inspiring natural objects, personal deities, ghosts and clannish guardian spirits. The ancient rituals were apparently designed for appeasing the *kami* so that humans might live in harmony with them and benefit from their powers. The early poems, recorded in such court-sponsored compilations as the *Man'yōshū*, indicate an internal relationship between humanity and nature. That is, the ancients understood humanity and nature to be parts of each other, not independently existing entities related as subject and object. The ancient myths describe the creation of Japan through the fortuitous actions of the deities. For this reason, the world is infused with *kami* or sacred presence.

According to the myths, natural objects such as rocks and streams were originally endowed with speech, a power taken from them because of their noisy bickering and querulous nature. Although natural things lost their voice, they did not necessarily lose their expressiveness. Human beings, if properly attuned to the natural world, could voice that expressiveness in thoughts, words and artefact. In ancient Japanese, the term for this expressive possibility was *kotodama*, the 'spirit' (*dama*) of 'word' (*koto*) and/or 'thing' (also *koto*).

In short, the ancient Japanese worldview understood the gods, the natural world and humanity to be an ontological continuum. It is not precise to say that rocks and trees were the dwelling place of spirits, because that would establish a bifurcation between the spiritual and material instead of a continuity. The term *kami*, therefore, applied to any object where a sacred presence was particularly manifest or concentrated: the Sun Goddess Amaterasu, Mount Fuji, a special tree or waterfall, the emperor or the vengeful spirit of a fallen warrior.

Even the sword of that warrior might be treated as *kami*. This represents one enduring idea in Japanese culture, the emphasis on spiritual immanence instead of transcendence: the sacred permeates the everyday world.

2   The importation of Confucianism and Buddhism

The Chinese writing system was introduced into Japan at about the beginning of the fifth century AD, but it was not until the eighth century that a viable adaptation was devised for rendering Japanese in written form. Therefore early Japanese thought was expressed in Chinese, and in fact many philosophical intellectuals continued to write in Chinese (or a Japanized version of Chinese) as late as the nineteenth century.

When the Chinese writing system was first introduced, the various clans had begun to form a central government under the leadership of what would become the imperial family. The government coalesced in Yamato, a large plain adjoining what is today Kyoto, Nara and Osaka. With the introduction of Chinese literacy, the Japanese elite gained access to more than a millennium of Confucian and Buddhist philosophy. These ideas were immediately put to use in organizing the state.

Confucianism gave Japan a hierarchical model for social and political order. It focused on personal interaction, explaining the responsibilities and duties relevant to the five basic dyadic relations: master–servant, parent–child, husband–wife, elder sibling–younger sibling and friend–friend. When the dyadic relationships are hierarchical, the person in the superior position is to care for the person in the lower and the person in the lower position is to be loyal to the superior. The imperial family used this system to institute a vertical bureaucracy. Although Confucianism supplied a social structure to the state, the ancient Japanese showed little interest in developing Confucian philosophy *per se*.

Buddhism, on the other hand, was initially most attractive to the Japanese for its aesthetic and thaumaturgic qualities. Buddhist artisans, often immigrants from Korea, brought new techniques of grand architecture, painting, sculpture and music. Using these elegant accoutrements in its rituals for healing, prosperity and protection of the state, Buddhism sometimes competed with the indigenous religious practices addressed to the *kami*.

From the philosophical perspective, however, the most important impact of Buddhism was its psychology. Through its meditative techniques and advanced analyses of the human predicament, Buddhism heightened the Japanese awareness of the workings of heart and mind. Buddhism teaches

465

that egoism is the primary cause of human anguish and dissatisfaction. The ego seeks permanence and control in a world of continuing flux. By controlling the desires and eliminating egoism, one can achieve peace and inner harmony. These Buddhist teachings brought a dimension of inner awareness and psychological analysis to a culture that had formerly operated only within the concepts of taboo, purification and animistic appeasement (see BUDDHIST PHILOSOPHY, JAPANESE).

At the same time, the indigenous religion began to define itself in relation to its rival, Buddhism. It took the name *kami no michi* or *shintō*, the 'way of the *kami*'. The state helped to systematize a series of myths in the eighth century, explaining the relationships among the tutelary *kami* of the various powerful clans and, presumably, the political relationships among the clans themselves. Most critically, through its familial relation with the chief *kami*, the Sun Goddess Amaterasu, the throne established itself as the blood tie between the celestial *kami* and the Japanese people (see SHINTŌ).

A major goal of philosophy in the seventh and eighth centuries, therefore, was to integrate the available ideas, both foreign and native, into a systematic worldview in the service of political stability. In this light the Seventeen Article Constitution of AD 604 is one of the first philosophical documents of ancient Japan. Attributed to Prince Shōtoku (574–622), the Constitution is really more a set of guidelines for bureaucrats than a set of laws defining political structure. In it, however, we find the early impact of Chinese thinking and its adaptation to the Japanese context of the time.

The Constitution's first article opened with a quotation from CONFUCIUS about the importance of maintaining 'harmony'. As noted already, in traditional Confucianism one achieves harmony primarily through performing actions appropriate to one's relationships in the society. Rather than discussing such Confucian principles, however, a large portion of the Constitution discussed human frailty and the need to develop a sympathetic attitude. The Constitution admonished against hypocrisy, preferential treatment, envy and egocentric motives. On the positive side, it advocated consensus and open-mindedness. In short, while the document aimed for a harmonious Confucian social order, it also drew on Buddhist psychology to explain the obstacles to harmony and to suggest an introspective understanding of personal motivations. Although the Constitution itself lacked any detailed philosophical argument, it marks an early attempt to draw on multiple philosophical traditions in a coherent manner. In effect, it advocated a Confucian social and government order supported by Buddhist practice and the insights of Buddhist

psychology. This philosophy of government remained dominant in Japan for at least a millennium.

In the Nara period (710–94), Japanese scholar-monks secured court support to accumulate and study more texts in Buddhist philosophy. They organized themselves loosely around major traditions from the mainland, and became the Six Nara Schools of Buddhism: Ritsu, Kusha, Jōjitsu, Hossō, Sanron and Kegon (see BUDDHIST PHILOSOPHY, JAPANESE). The first primarily concentrated on the study of Vinaya, the precepts and regulations for ordering monastic life. The Kusha and Jōjitsu were schools of Abhidharma Buddhism emphasizing the detailed analysis of dharmas, the basic constituents of reality or consciousness. The Hossō was primarily based in the Indian Yogācāra tradition and Sanron in the Mādhyamika. Kegon represented the tradition known in China as Huayan. Although the Six Nara Schools played an important role in both education and court politics, there is little evidence that they were philosophically creative centres. Their historical role was mainly to introduce Buddhist analysis and doctrine into Japanese culture. They provided the intellectual raw material for the later philosophical developments of the Heian period.

3 Metaphysical vision of ancient Japanese esoteric Buddhism

Although already a significant presence in the Nara period, only in the Heian period (794–1185) did Buddhism undergo a profound process of philosophical development and Japanization. Two Buddhist thinkers were particularly influential: KŪKAI (774–835; posthumous title, Kōbō Daishi) and Saichō (767–822; posthumous title, Dengyō Daishi). Of the two, Kūkai's philosophical contribution was the more comprehensive. He went to China in 804 to study esoteric Buddhism and, upon his return two years later, founded Japanese Shingon Buddhism. The analytic and systematic character of Kūkai's writings may well qualify him as the first true philosopher in Japanese history.

For Kūkai, reality is fundamentally a person. The entire cosmos is no more than the thoughts, words and deeds of the Buddha called Dainichi (literally the 'Great Sun'). Dainichi is not the creator of the universe; Dainichi is the universe. In a perpetual state of enlightened meditation, Dainichi performs the three great practices of esoteric Buddhism: the chanting of sacred syllables (*mantras*), the visualization of geometrical arrays of symbols (*mandalas*) and the performance of sacred postures or hand gestures (*mudras*). These three activities define the nature of the universe. The *mantras* are microcosmic resonances or vibrating states of matter–energy that constitute the basic elements. The *mandalas* define the essential structure, and the *mudras* constitute the patterns of change. By performing the rituals of *mantra*, *mandala* and *mudra*, a person achieves immediate insight into the nature of the cosmos. By introspection on the nature of their own thoughts, words and deeds, the Shingon Buddhist is said to achieve insight into the thoughts, words and deeds of the Buddha, Dainichi. By understanding one's own person, one understands the person that is all of reality.

Within the framework of this metaphysical system, Kūkai developed a comprehensive philosophy addressing several major philosophical issues. For example, he criticized the idea that insight or enlightenment could be purely mental or intellectual. Because the universe itself consists of thought, word and deed (or structure, resonance and patterned change), it can only be grasped by unified praxis of the whole person: mind, speech and body. To know reality is to participate in it fully, in all three of its dimensions.

Another philosophical issue of interest to Kūkai was the nature of expression. Because the cosmos is a person, reality is the expressive style of that person. Every entity is, therefore, a symbol or imprint of Dainichi's mental, somatic and verbal activity. Yet, because we contain the element of volitional consciousness, we humans can also ignore the true source of all activity, construing ourselves as independent entities. We can interpret things through the superimposition of our own imprints, covering over their (and our) more fundamental nature. This delusion is the source of human anguish and ignorance. The escape from delusion lies in recognizing and participating in the self-expressive nature of reality.

Kūkai's contemporary and major competitor, Saichō, founded Japanese Tendai Buddhism. Although Saichō's primary goal in visiting China was to bring back to Japan the teaching of the Tiantai Buddhist tradition (see BUDDHIST PHILOSOPHY, CHINESE), he also had a chance encounter with a teacher of esotericism. When he returned to Japan, therefore, his Tendai school incorporated esoteric Buddhist elements as well as exoteric Tiantai teachings. Through the exchange of Shingon and Tendai disciples in Japan, some of Kūkai's esoteric teachings also found their way into Tendai. The result was that by the end of the ninth century, the two dominant forms of Japanese Buddhism were both at least partially esoteric in nature.

We can explain the influence of the esoteric Buddhist theory of reality from both the standpoint of cultural history and the history of philosophy. Culturally, it is important that esoteric Buddhism did not either doctrinally or politically oppose the presence of the indigenous religion, Shintō. Esoteric Buddhism reinforced rather than challenged many aspects of the indigenous religious worldview: the ubiquity of the sacred, the expressiveness of nature and the nonduality of matter and spirit, for example. Furthermore, both Kūkai and Saichō correlated the various buddhas of esotericism with the various *kami* of the traditional Japanese religion. By this process, Japanese archaism was, in effect, defended by a philosophically sophisticated system of Buddhist thought imported from the mainland and adapted to the Japanese context. Buddhism and Shintō could therefore be practised alongside each other without contradiction.

This development set the metaphysical backdrop against which later Japanese thought would develop. One might say that esoteric Buddhism did for Japanese philosophy what Plato and Aristotle did for Western philosophy. It laid out a set of assumptions and a *Problematik* that had a profound influence on the thought to follow. Two assumptions were particularly influential.

First, esotericism has a distinctive view of the relation between part and whole. The whole is recursively manifest or reflected in the part. It is not that the parts constitute the whole nor that the whole is more than the sum of its parts; rather, since the part is what it is by virtue of the whole, if we truly understand the part, we find the whole imprinted in it. In Shingon's case, for example, since any individual thing is an expression of the cosmos as Dainichi, when we truly understand the part (the individual thing), we encounter the whole (Dainichi) as well.

With this orientation as a cultural presupposition, later Japanese philosophers would seldom endorse either atomistic analysis or individualism (see ATOMISM, ANCIENT; METHODOLOGICAL INDIVIDUALISM). Atomistic analysis had been introduced into Japan via the Nara Schools of Jōjitsu and Kusha. Kūkai explicitly ranked them as philosophical 'mindsets' far below Kegon and Tendai, in part because only the latter endorsed this theory of whole-as-part. Individualism, with attendant theories of social contract, entered Japan via the West only in the late nineteenth century. Since it viewed the social whole as constituted by the parts, it ran counter to this esoteric assumption. Not surprisingly, individualism has never taken hold in Japan as a basis for social, ethical or political theory.

Second, esotericism's metaphysics argued that reality is self-expressive. Human beings are, of course, part of reality. When humans speak authentically or truly, therefore, they do not refer to reality, but rather are part of its self-expression. This position undermines any philosophical tendencies toward idealism (reality as a production of mind), realism (reality as pre-existing our expressions and truth as matching our expressions with that reality) or radical nominalism (expressions refer primarily to other expressions without necessary connection to non-linguistic reality) (see IDEALISM; REALISM AND ANTIREALISM; NOMINALISM). In the Nara Schools there were variants of idealism (Hossō), realism (Kusha and Jōjitsu) and nominalism (Sanron). Again Kūkai ranked them all below Kegon and Tendai, and certainly below what he believed to be the only comprehensive mind-set, esotericism.

This presupposition about the self-expressive nature of reality underlies most Japanese aesthetic theories as well. The Heian period was the first to develop a detailed set of aesthetic terms, for example, *miyabi* (cultured, refined elegance) and *mono no aware* (the 'ah-ness of things' or the aesthetic tinge of sadness arising from an appreciation of the evanescent). In later periods, other aesthetic terms such as *yūgen* (hidden sublimity or depth), *sabi* (the 'loneliness' of an elegance allowed to age) and *wabi* (rusticity) came to the fore. These terms have rich connotations not readily translated into English. In general, though, they signify equally a quality of the object and the response of the aesthete or artist. The aesthetic is understood to be a self-expressive resonance between the object and artist. The world expresses itself through the artist as the work of art.

4 Medieval philosophical anthropology: Pure Land Buddhism

During the Heian period the highly literate and elegant culture of the Kyoto court was at its peak. The aesthetically pleasing rituals of esoteric Buddhism found a receptive audience among the aristocrats and clergy. They alone enjoyed the leisure time, education and resources to devote their lives to its study and practice. The general populace were left to their folk religions, an amalgamation of practices with roots in Buddhism, Shintō and Daoist alchemy.

By the early twelfth century, the court had become so politically effete that the provincial aristocracy began to vie for power and the newly risen *samurai* fought for control of territory. Plagues, famines and earthquakes were also unusually devastating. In short, to any sensitive observer of the times, it was easy to see the decadence of the social order, the harshness of nature and the corruption of the human spirit. There was little time for, or consolation in, metaphysical speculations. The philosophers turned their analyses to this world and their imaginations to wondering what failing in humanity had caused such suffering. By

1185 the Minamoto clan was victorious and in 1192 Yoritomo became *shōgun*, establishing his centre of government in Kamakura. Thus began the Kamakura period (1185–1333) and a new set of philosophical and religious orientations.

The Kamakura period philosophers such as Hōnen (1133–1212), Shinran (1173–1262), Yōsai or Eisai (1141–1215), DŌGEN (1200–53) and Nichiren (1222–82) responded to the decay and suffering of their times. Each developed his own interpretation of the human predicament with an accompanying solution. All had originally trained as Tendai monks, but these reformers eventually left the establishment and founded new Buddhist sects that served the masses as well as the elite echelons of Japanese society. Of the Kamakura schools of Buddhism, Pure Land and Zen have been the most influential in their theories of human being. Shinran was the founder of Shin Buddhism or the True Pure Land School; Dōgen was the founder of Sōtō Zen. Each developed most fully the philosophical foundations for his own tradition (see BUDDHIST PHILOSOPHY, JAPANESE).

These two schools differ radically in their philosophical anthropologies. As Buddhists, both Shinran and Dōgen accepted the general Buddhist analysis about the source of ignorance: egoism. Egoism defines the self as an independent agent that initiates actions and has experiences. The Buddhist view, on the other hand, maintains that 'I' is no more than a name for related actions and events, not something that lies behind them. This implies that the boundaries of the self are fuzzy rather than sharply delineated. For example, from a distance we can readily identify the general course of a river, but if we move up close enough, we cannot specify exactly where the river ends and the river bank begins. If the river were self-conscious and tried to specify for itself 'my' boundaries as opposed to 'its' boundaries, the river would lose sight of the very processes that bring it into being and help define it. Analogously, Buddhists generally maintain that egoism, by attempting to define, delineate and protect the self, ignores the self's broader context. It overlooks the self's dependence on what egoism considers to be outside and separate from it.

As a disciple of Hōnen, the founder of the Japanese Pure Land School, Shinran also accepted the specific ideas of that tradition, including the theory that humanity had entered a degenerate period in history. Left to our own devices, we are presumed to be doomed to live and relive an existence of anguish, dissatisfaction and despair. Pure Land Buddhists believe, however, that a celestial buddha called Amida has seen our situation and taken pity on us. He has vowed that if we entrust ourselves totally to his compassion and call on his name, we can be assured rebirth in his Pure Land where the conditions are conducive to Buddhist practice. In his Pure Land we can perform the necessary spiritual disciplines and then return to this world to attain enlightenment. In so doing, we can be a spiritual aid to others in this world. Such was the basic tradition of Pure Land Buddhism that Shinran accepted. Within that traditional framework, however, he developed his own distinctive philosophical analysis of human being.

Shinran believed he had found a contradiction in how most Buddhists understood practice. Specifically, they self-consciously undertook various disciplines (meditation, reading texts, chanting mantras) as a means of eliminating egoism and attaining insight into reality. The implication is that one can overcome egoism by one's own power, by 'self-power.' People believed they were 'earning merit' by their religious practices. Shinran argued that if people practise as a means of achieving merit, then the actions only feed, rather than eradicate, egoism: discipline is understood as a means by which *I* can improve *myself*. Shinran considered this emphasis on self-power to be the psychological foundation of the degenerate age in which he believed he lived. Because people misunderstood the relation between self and Buddhist practice, the teachings of Buddhism had indeed become unintelligible and the prospect for insight had disappeared.

Although Shinran did not explicitly deny the ontological reality of the Pure Land or the account of Amida's vow as historical, his philosophy focused more on the psychological and logical implications of the Pure Land position. For him the fundamental point was that people must surrender their egoistic senses of self by adopting an 'entrusting heart-and-mind' (*shinjin*). By completely abandoning the ego, people can have faith in the power of Amida's vow to help. They turn from 'self-power' to 'other-power'. Assured birth in the Pure Land, the realm devoid of egoism, the sense of a discrete or independent self will disappear. Yet, Shinran reasoned, if there is no self at that point, logically there can be no discrete 'other' either. There is just 'naturalness' and Amida in effect disappears as well. *Shinjin* continues as the entrusting that opens itself to this naturalness. In that egoless state, one can spiritually help other people. It can be said that one returns from the Pure Land to be reborn in this world. Yet, by assisting others in this world, the ego may once again be constituted as the 'I' who self-consciously helps 'others'. As soon as one begins to think that good deeds are done by virtue of one's own power, the whole process must be renewed. One must again see the delusion of the ego, again turn oneself over to Amida's power, again be reborn in the Pure Land, again allow self and Amida to

disappear, and again return to this world from the Pure Land.

In short, Shinran agreed that to eliminate ignorance one must eliminate egoism. This can be accomplished, he believed, only by the complete renunciation of the notion that one can help oneself. Only by despairing of the efficacy of self-power and by entrusting oneself to Amida's power can one become naturally what one truly is. In that egoless state one can understand reality for what it is and act freely in the world as a compassionate being. In addressing the same issue, Zen Buddhism took an almost diametrically opposed approach, however.

5 Medieval philosophical anthropology: Zen Buddhism

Like the Pure Land Buddhists, Zen Master Dōgen believed there is a fundamental flaw in the usual interpretation of Buddhist practice as the means to enlightenment. Rather than arguing that practice must be abandoned, however, he instead maintained that practice or self-discipline is an end in itself. He rejected the popular theory that his was a degenerate age in which enlightenment was no longer possible. Instead, Dōgen maintained everyone is already enlightened, but that enlightenment was not being manifested or expressed in their actions. The goal, therefore, is to authenticate what we already are.

Trained in the Zen (Chan) Buddhist tradition in China, Dōgen was sensitive to the limitations of language and mistrustful of certain types of thinking. Like other Buddhists, he understood the problem to be egoism. By hypostatizing the ego, one falls into a desire for reality to be a specific way. One seeks permanence in both self and in one's own worldview. Therefore, it is easy to project interpretations on experience, interpretations that shape the experience to meet our presuppositions, expectations and desires.

Dōgen believed that experiential immediacy is possible. In Zen meditation, one quiets the mind and merely lets phenomena appear. Dōgen called this a state of 'without-thinking' as opposed to either 'thinking' or 'not-thinking'. Thinking, for Dōgen, included any form of sustained conceptualization whether fantasy, cogitation, believing, denying, wishing, desiring or whatever. Not-thinking is the effort to blank the mind and empty it of all awareness. In without-thinking, however, there is the awareness of brute phenomena but no sustained act of bestowing meaning. There is no consciousness of a self having an experience. Furthermore, since no meaning at all is projected on the event, it is free of the distortions found in ordinary, ego-driven forms of experience. Dōgen simply called this 'the presencing of things as they are'.

Dōgen claimed this form of meditation was not a means to enlightenment. Instead, precisely because it is egoless, it is enlightenment itself. Yet, this meditation–enlightenment event is always accessible. It is, as it were, at the root of all experience, even thinking and not-thinking. In this respect we are all already enlightened but we have not authenticated that fact. Of course, to authenticate it, we must return to a state of without-thinking.

Without-thinking is, therefore, a not-yet-conceptualized immediacy. Since it is without concepts, however, it is intrinsically meaningless; but it is impossible for humans to live a life without meanings. Enlightenment must not only be authenticated in meditation. It must also be expressed in everyday life. How can this be possible?

Dōgen claimed that meaning is always contextual. He noted that the ocean has a different meaning to a fish swimming in it, a person in a boat out at sea and a deity looking down at it from the heavens. To the fish, the ocean is a translucent palace; to the person it is a great circle extending to the horizon in all directions; to the deity it is a string of jewel-like lights glittering in the sunshine. If the deity were to interpret the ocean as a circle or the person in the boat were to interpret it as a palace, however, they would not be expressing what is actually in front of them. Their interpretation would be false. Therefore, the key to truth in meaning is the appropriateness of the context.

According to Dōgen, meditative without-thinking is the 'touchstone' for determining whether the context is appropriate. Context is continually shifting and giving rise to new meanings as we live out our lives. What is 'tree branch' at one point may be 'firewood' at another and 'weapon' in a third. Dōgen referred to these points as 'occasions' of 'being-time'. For Dōgen, the problem with egoism is its resistance to accepting flux. Egoism tries to make a set of previous meanings into a fixed worldview, into *my* reality. Therefore, one projects contexts that are not actually present in the current phenomena. Through meditation, however, one can break the closed cycle of self-verifying projections. One can return to the presence of things as they are before meaning, before they are embedded in any particular context. Then, as one returns to the expressive world of everyday action, it is easier to verify the appropriateness of the contextualizing process that generates meaning (see MEANING AND VERIFICATION).

The philosophical anthropologies of Pure Land and Zen address the common problem of egoism, but their solutions to the problem are fundamentally different. In Pure Land Buddhism, recognizing the inefficacy of egoism leads to a psychodynamic of despair, entrusting and naturalness. In the Pure Land philosophy of human being, the ego is rejected in favour of a model of dependence or interdependence. It is a process of self-effacement and surrender. By contrast, Zen overcomes the negative effects of egoism not by self-effacement, but by self-analysis. One studies the dynamics of consciousness and grounds oneself in pure, but meaningless, presence. Pure Land and Zen agree that self-discipline is not a means to enlightenment. Yet, for Pure Land this entails the rejection of self-discipline; in Zen, on the other hand, it entails the acceptance of self-discipline as an end in itself.

These two philosophical anthropologies exemplify how Kamakura philosophers generally focused on the nature of praxis as part of an analysis of human existence. In the Heian period, the pressing philosophical question seems to have been the nature of the cosmos. In the Kamakura period it shifted to the nature of the self. Shinran and Dōgen produced particularly impressive analyses of human motivation and the structure of consciousness, and their models of the self remain influential in Japanese culture up to the present. It is significant, however, that their focus was primarily on the inner self instead of the social self. The social dimension was to become a major concern in the next major period in the development of Japanese philosophy.

6 Neo-Confucianism, the samurai code and Tokugawa society

Following the Kamakura period there were more periods of intermittent warfare and internal strife. A long-lasting, nationwide peace arrived only with the establishment of the Tokugawa family's regime as *shogun*s. For nearly all of the Tokugawa period (1600–1868) Japan closed itself off from most interaction with outside world. For example, Christianity, which had been introduced by missionaries in the sixteenth century, was formally proscribed. The Tokugawa *shogun*s established a highly bureaucratic government, giving them unprecedented control over Japanese society from its system of education to its business practices and religious institutions. In this context, much of philosophy turned to the interests of the state and the definition of social responsibility.

During the fifteenth and sixteenth centuries, Japan had again received a strong infusion of foreign thought. In particular, Zen Buddhist monks who had visited the mainland brought back to Japan texts of the neo-Confucian traditions established in China by Zhu Xi and WANG YANGMING. Since Japanese Buddhist philosophy taught little about social responsibility in secular contexts, the ethical dimension of these texts attracted increasing attention. Neo-Confucianism went further than traditional Confucianism by adding a metaphysical level to explain the natural world and how it could be known.

From ancient times Confucianism had played a major role in the social, bureaucratic and ethical structures of Japanese culture. In trying to organize and stabilize the government after centuries of warfare, the Tokugawa *shoguns* were naturally intrigued by this new and more comprehensive form of the social philosophy that had already served Japan in the past. Furthermore, wary of Buddhism's popularity, they probably welcomed neo-Confucianism's challenge to the near hegemony that Buddhism had established in Japanese philosophy. In any case, from early in the seventeenth century, the Tokugawa *shoguns* gave special status and support to neo-Confucianism, especially to the school called Shushigaku, the Japanese school of Zhu Xi.

With the increased peace and prosperity of the Tokugawa period, there was a new market for philosophical education, especially in the great urban centres of Kyoto, Osaka and Edo (now Tokyo). The rising merchant class wanted the social polish of an upper class education. Furthermore, because it was peacetime, many unemployed *samurai* wanted a classical education to qualify for positions in the government bureaucracy. The result was an increase in independent schools and a proliferation of teachers with different philosophical approaches.

Generally we find major philosophical development during the Tokugawa period in two areas: naturalistic metaphysics and social philosophy or ethics. The Shushigaku school introduced a theory of reality or metaphysics foreign to the Buddhist theories so entrenched in Japanese thought. In particular, it analysed reality in terms of the dynamic between 'configuration' or 'principle' (*ri*; in Chinese, *li*) and 'material energy' or 'vital force' (*ki*; in Chinese, *qi*). According to Shushigaku, *ri* gives the universe its structure and, since *ri* is also in the mind, it is the foundation of knowledge. By 'investigating the nature of things' we come to know *ri*, both in ourselves and in the things we study. *Ki*, on the other hand, was considered the basic stuff that is ordered by *ri*.

Although the notion of *ri* was known to the Japanese through Tendai and Kegon Buddhism, the neo-Confucians gave the term a distinctive emphasis. They embedded it into the broader enterprise of understanding of the natural world. During the Tokugawa period there was a practical interest in better understanding nature; in the sixteenth century traders and missionaries from Europe had introduced some Western science. With the closure

of Japan this contact was severely limited, although the occasional Dutch treatise on practical science or medicine did find its way into Japan.

For the most part, Japanese philosophers found the Shushigaku emphasis on *ri* to be overly abstract. To many, it seemed that *ri* was an unnecessary transcendent realm behind physical reality that could be known only through some mysterious half-contemplative, half-empirical study. In response, many Japanese thinkers took a more phenomenalistic approach. Kaibara Ekken (1630–1714), for example, argued for the primacy of *ki*. To him, *ki* was the basic constituent of reality and should be studied directly; *ri* was no more than the name for the patterns one could abstract from the behaviour of *ki*. Certainly from the perspectives of both medicine and the martial arts, *ki* became the more important category in Japan.

Other naturalistic philosophers such as Miura Baien (1723–89) developed intricate systems of their own for categorizing natural phenomena. Such indigenous concerns for observation and classification of the natural world may not have developed into a full-blown science in the Western sense, but the orientation did show an increasing Japanese concern for observing and understanding the natural world. This phenomenalist tendency would serve Japan well in the nineteenth century when Western science and technology were reintroduced.

In the field of social or moral philosophy, an important development was the emergence of the school of 'Ancient Learning'. Led by Yamaga Sōkō (1622–85), Itō Jinsai (1627–1705) and Ogyū Sorai (1666–1728), these philosophers rejected the metaphysical speculations of the neo-Confucianists and tried to return to the early classics of the Confucian tradition, especially the *Analects* (see CHINESE PHILOSOPHY; CONFUCIAN PHILOSOPHY, CHINESE; CONFUCIUS). They developed sophisticated philological and exegetical skills as tools for attempting to discover the original meanings of those texts. Their goal was to clarify traditional Confucian social philosophy so that it could become the basis for Japanese society. In this regard, the school of Ancient Learning put its emphasis on the nature of virtue and the development of character. Ogyū Sorai had an especially broad impact on society for his theories about education and moral training.

Some philosophers, like Yamaga Sōkō of the Ancient Learning School, mixed Confucian values with warrior values about loyalty and honour. Yamaga tried to develop a warrior mentality for service to the state that would be appropriate to peacetime. Furthermore, in their unemployment, many *samurai* entered the various Buddhist orders, especially Zen, where they found a familiar emphasis on discipline and regimentation. The combined result was an idealized code of the warrior (*bushidō*) as a way of life, even for non-*samurai* and even in times of peace.

7 Native studies: religio-aesthetic foundation of the Shintō state

The school of Ancient Learning's return to the original classics of Chinese Confucianism was mirrored in a movement to return to the early texts of Japan, the school of 'Native Studies' or 'National Studies' (*kokugaku*). Originally a literary and philological group, Native Studies scholars like Keichū (1640–1701), Kada no Azumamaro (1669–1736) and Kamo no Mabuchi (1697–1769) analysed the language and worldview of Nara and Heian poetry and prose. The school expanded beyond these literary goals, however, as it turned to questions of religion and national identity. In this development the philosophy of Motoori Norinaga (1730–1801) played a pivotal role.

The major shift in Native Studies began with Motoori's decision as a philologist to decode the antiquated writing system of the *Kojiki* (The Record of Ancient Matters). An eighth-century text, the *Kojiki* was supposedly the written version of what had formerly been an oral tradition. Mixing myth and history, it discussed the origins of the world, the formation of Japan and the succession of Japanese emperors from the beginning of time up to its present. There was a twin work in Chinese written at the same time, *Nihon shoki* (The Chronicle of Japan). Because the orthography of the *Kojiki* died out as a writing system for Japanese shortly after the Nara period, the *Nihon shoki* became the more used text, supposedly containing the same information. The *Kojiki* had in fact become virtually unintelligible even to the educated Japanese of Motoori's time. By decoding the text, therefore, Motoori hoped to bring to light the original Japanese worldview.

A devout follower of Shintō, Motoori's task assumed a profoundly religious dimension as well. He believed the *Kojiki* was a written account of what had been orally transmitted word for word from the time of creation. The *Kojiki* contained the very words of the deities who had created the world. Furthermore, since the text was written in an orthography that had soon fallen into disuse, Motoori believed the written text was uncorrupted by later interpreters, making it superior to the adulterated cosmogonies of other cultures. This firm belief sustained Motoori's lifelong devotion to the enormously complex task of decoding the text.

Based on his readings of Japanese classics, Motoori also developed a philosophy of poetic or religious expression: his theory of 'heart' (*kokoro*). As a technical term, *kokoro* designates the seat of thinking and feeling; it is the basis of sensitivity. Heart is not, however, limited to people; things and words also have heart. If poets have 'genuine heart,' they will be touched by the heart of things and the heart of words. The poetically or religiously expressive act, therefore, is an act of the heart, something shared by the things, the person and the words. Since the genuine heart is also a goal of Shintō purification, Motoori saw in this theory the basis of religious language as well. This in turn influenced his understanding of the significance of the *Kojiki*.

If the *Kojiki* represents the original words of the deities at the time of creation, to read or study the text is virtually a ritualistic re-enactment of creation. The implication for Motoori was that the ancient Japanese language of the text is not only the language of the deities, but also the most pure intimation of the heart of things. By this line of reasoning, Motoori made the *Kojiki* into the sacred scripture of Shintō. Based on his reading of the text, Motoori founded a philosophy of Shintō supposedly free of Buddhist influence. For virtually the first time, Shintō could develop a formal doctrinal system of its own (see SHINTŌ).

This line of thought readily supported a nationalist ideology. If the ancient Japanese language was the protolanguage of all languages, if that language were most purely resonant with the heart of things and if the Japanese emperor was the special link between the deities and humanity, obviously Japan would have a special place in the world. This sense of national superiority became especially strong in the next generation of Native Studies scholars such as Hirata Atsutane (1776–1843) and helped contribute to the movement to overthrow the Tokugawa shogunate and restore the emperor as the true leader of Japan. In this effort, it found an intellectual ally in the Mito School, a Shintō–Confucian synthesis, that argued for the centrality of the emperor as the 'body of the state'. The restoration of the emperor was completed in 1868, the beginning of Japan's modern era.

In summary, the introduction of neo-Confucianism from China and the establishment of a stable state under Tokugawa rule created a new fertile environment for Japanese philosophy. Ultimately, neo-Confucianism itself did not become a dominant philosophy in Japan, but its presence challenged the dominant Buddhist philosophies. In this new context Japanese philosophy grew more concerned with social ethics, the study of the natural world and cultural identity. In this period developed the idea of the warrior-turned-bureaucrat, as fiercely loyal to the organization as formerly to the lord. As there was more interest in studying and classifying the physical processes of nature, there was also a newly defined aesthetic of sensitivity and poetic expression. For the first time, Shintō became a major intellectual force in Japanese thought and there was an attendant sense of the uniqueness and superior quality of Japanese culture. All these factors became the intellectual background for the emergence of the modern era after 1868, and its related philosophies.

8   Modern Japanese philosophy and its critique of Western philosophy

The Tokugawa policy of seclusion ended with the appearance of US gunboats in 1854 and their demand that Japan open itself to international trade. To protect its sovereignty from infringement by the Western powers, Japan believed it had to become a modern industrial and military power in its own right. The government sent its brightest young intellectuals to Europe and the United States to study what was needed for modernization, such as medicine, engineering, agriculture, postal systems and education. This effort included the study of Western thought as a means to understanding Western society and the ideas behind its science and technology. Although there was some sustained interest in American pragmatism (see PRAGMATISM), most Japanese philosophers turned toward Germany for their inspiration (see GERMAN IDEALISM).

Throughout the nineteenth century, most Japanese leaders hoped Japan could superimpose Western science and technology on a society that remained true to Asian cultural values. By the first decade of the twentieth century, Japan had successfully developed the technology and military might needed to defeat both Russia and China in wars. Many Japanese intellectuals feared, however, that this was at the expense of traditional values. The ideal of detached objectivity in Western science threatened the tradition of apprenticed learning through imitation of the master. The Buddhist and Confucian theories of reality were in jeopardy of being overwhelmed by Western scientism. The new egalitarian ideals of education so helpful in developing a technological society were also part of a democratic worldview that emphasized the individual as basic unit of society and threatened the traditional Confucian virtues and social hierarchy. How to negotiate the differences between traditional Asian and modern Western values became a major concern among Japanese philosophers in the first half of the twentieth century.

The most influential development in modern Japanese philosophy was the emergence of the Kyoto School of thought. By the early twentieth century, philosophy had become an academic study in Japanese universities. An influential circle of philosophers clustered around NISHIDA KITARŌ (1870–1945), a professor at Kyoto University. This group tended to address problems about the meaning of self, the nature of knowledge, the role of spirituality and the place of both ethical and aesthetic value.

Nishida was the single most influential philosopher of the prewar period. His philosophical goal was to locate empiricism and scientific thinking within a larger system that would also give value judgements a non-subordinate place. *Zen no kenkyū* (An Inquiry into the Good), his first major work, developed the notion of 'pure experience', an idea adapted from William JAMES and perhaps developed in light of Nishida's own Zen Buddhist practice. The book's theme is that there is a thrust toward unity in all experience. Thought arises out of the disruption of the unity of immediacy and serves as a means to establishing a more comprehensive unity. In Nishida's phrase, pure experience is the 'alpha and omega of thought'.

Nishida himself subsequently decided this early effort was too 'psychologistic' and 'mystical', and developed a different philosophical system in the 1920s and 1930s that emphasized the 'logic of place (or *topos*)'. According to Nishida, every judgment is restricted by the logic of its context, which in turn derives from a broader experiential domain that it cannot explain in its own terms. An empirical judgment, for example, excludes the subject of the experience (see EMPIRICISM). Its internal logic precludes the consideration of the self. Yet, of course, there can be no empirical data without an experiencing subject; so, the logical place within which empirical judgments are made is within a broader experiential context that assumes the function of the self. If that broader context is then made the logical domain for judgments, we have idealism. In turn, according to Nishida, the experiential locus that makes idealist judgments possible cannot be spoken of logically within the domain of idealism. Nishida calls this experiential locus 'place of absolute nothingness', the ground of 'acting-intuiting'. This region cannot be expressed in any logical form, but is the basis of all logical expression. It is also the ground of value: spiritual, ethical and aesthetic.

In this way, Nishida argued that the realm of empirical judgment is necessarily grounded experientially in a realm of value that it cannot analyse from its own standpoint. Nishida's system attempted to grant Western science its logical place while showing that its experiential ground was what traditional Asian values had affirmed all along.

Religion, at least in its Asian forms, was not antagonistic to science, nor was it endangered by science. On the contrary, Nishida argued that spiritual experience is what makes science logically possible.

Nishida argued for the synthesis of Eastern values and Western values by analysing the logic of epistemology. He was joined in this logical or epistemological approach by other philosophers connected in some way with the Kyoto School such as TANABE HAJIME (1885–1962) and Nishitani Keiji (1900–90). Other Kyoto School philosophers addressed the issue from the other direction, by analysing values. Hisamatsu Shin'ichi (1889–1980), for example, analysed the religio-aesthetic worldview of Zen Buddhism, advocating it as the basis for a style of life. Miki Kiyoshi (1897–1945), on the other hand, developed a 'logic of creativity' inspired by both Buddhist and Marxist theories of praxis.

Among the modern Japanese ethicists, the most influential was Watsuji Tetsurō (1889–1960), a professor at Tokyo University and not technically a member of the Kyoto School. Watsuji explained that Western ethics takes the individual for its prime locus. Western ethics is constituted *vis-à-vis* individual needs and the focus of morality is the individual agent. In contrast, Watsuji said, Confucian ethics takes the social as its prime locus, being constituted out of the primary social relations. Watsuji maintained both traditions are faulty in seeing only one dimension of the whole. As an alternative, he developed a philosophical anthropology emphasising 'betweenness', a dialectical tension between the individual and the collective. The collective establishes norms within which one can act in a given society, whereas the individual serves as the locus of freedom. If unqualified by the opposing pole, the collective suppresses freedom and the individual rejects the objective validity of norms.

Watsuji concluded, therefore, that true ethical behaviour is possible only as a 'double negation' that rejects both poles without settling in either. In this 'betweenness' we find the dialectical tension between the social and the individual, the fundamental definition of our human being. So, the nature of ethics follows from the definition of human being, and ethics is the fundamental way of realizing our humanity. Watsuji developed these ideas first in his *Ningen no gaku to shite no rinrigaku* (Ethics as the Study of Human Being) (1934) and then more fully in his *magnum opus*, a three-volume work called simply *Rinrigaku* (Ethics) (1937–49).

9 Postwar developments

The defeat in the Second World War caused many philosophers to rethink their positions. Tanabe and Watsuji, for example, explicitly repented some of the nationalistic implications of their earlier writings. In his *Zangedō to shite no tetsugaku* (Philosophy as Metanoia) in 1946, Tanabe developed an intricate, self-critical dialectical method to check the emergence of philosophical ideologies. In conceiving this method he drew inspiration from the philosophical analysis of Shinran's thought done by one of his students, Takeuchi Yoshinori. The connection with religious philosophy has become a recurrent theme in the further development of the Kyoto school as exemplified in the works of Nishitani, Takeuchi and Ueda Shizuteru. In a spirit reminiscent of the Kamakura Buddhist thinkers, many of the postwar philosophers have turned inward to re-examine the nature of human existence, now able to be formulated in relation to the problematics of existentialism as well as Buddhism.

At the same time some Japanese philosophers have continued to specialize in the scholarly study of Western philosophy. In many Japanese universities there are departments of philosophy where much of the work is indistinguishable from what might find in a philosophy department in Europe or North America. In general, the Continental traditions of philosophy, rather than the British analytic traditions, continue to dominate.

Lastly, and especially since the 1960s, there are individuals and groups of philosophers who have explored new provocative directions, drawing their ideas from a wide variety of sources including Western science, psychoanalysis and phenomenology as well as traditional Asian thought and medicine. This phenomenon is another example of a recurrent pattern in the history of Japanese philosophy: the assimilation and adaptation of foreign ideas against the background of an ongoing tradition.

See also: BUDDHIST PHILOSOPHY, CHINESE; BUDDHIST PHILOSOPHY, JAPANESE; CONFUCIAN PHILOSOPHY, CHINESE

References and further reading

Nakamura Hajime (1969) *A History of the Development of Japanese Thought*, Tokyo: Kokusai Bunka Shinkokai (Japan Cultural Society), 2 vols, 2nd edn. (Not an integrated book but a set of seven excellent essays on different periods of Japanese philosophy. Now out-of-print, but still one of the most insightful discussions in English.)

Tsunoda, R., de Bary, W.T. and Keene, D. (eds) (1964) *Sources of Japanese Traditions*, New York: Columbia University Press, 2 vols. (Extensive collection of short excepts from philosophical texts in translation, including brief but useful introductions to each writer.)

THOMAS P. KASULIS

JASPERS, KARL (1883–1969)

Karl Jaspers is generally known as an existentialist, but he also developed interesting conceptions in other fields of philosophy: in philosophy of religion, the concepts of Transcendence, cipher and philosophical faith; in philosophy of history, the thesis of an Axial Period in history; in political philosophy, the idea of a new, reasonable politics. His existentialism deals mainly with personal moral attitudes and private aspects of individual self-realization in boundary situations and intimate interpersonal communication. His political philosophy concentrates on controversial political affairs and some of the urgent problems of his age (for example, the possibility of extinguishing all life on earth by the atom bomb, or of establishing a world-wide totalitarian regime).

KURT SALAMUN

JEN

See CONFUCIAN PHILOSOPHY, CHINESE; CONFUCIUS

JEWISH PHILOSOPHY

Introduction

Jewish philosophy is philosophical inquiry informed by the texts, traditions and experiences of the Jewish people. Its concerns range from the farthest reaches of cosmological speculation to the most intimate theatres of ethical choice and the most exigent fora of political debate. What distinguishes it as Jewish is the confidence of its practitioners that the literary catena of Jewish tradition contains insights and articulates values of lasting philosophical import. One mark of the enduring import of these ideas and values is their articulation in a variety of idioms, from the mythic and archetypal discourse of the Book of Genesis to the ethical and legislative prescriptions of the Pentateuch at large, to the admonitions of the Prophets, the juridical and allegorical midrash and dialectics of the Rabbis, and to the systematic demonstrations, flights of imagination, existential declarations and apercus of philosophers in the modern or the medieval mode.

1 The nature of Jewish philosophy

Students of Jewish philosophy, especially those who aspire to contribute a window or a wing to the edifice, must learn many languages, to read and listen to voices very different from their own. Just as the writers of the Genesis narratives or of the Pentateuch had to recast and reinvent the ancient creation myths and the ancient Babylonian laws to express the distinctively universal ethical demands and aesthetic standards of their God, and just as the Deuteronomist had to rediscover the ethical core in the original Mosaic legislation, hearing God's commands now as urgent reminders through the very human voice of Moses, so in every generation new interpreters are needed, to rediscover what is essential and living in the tradition. Such interpreters have always needed to negotiate the rapids of historical change – not just with regard to idiom but also with regard to content, refocusing and restructuring the living tradition, sculpting it philosophically with their own moieties of reason. Such thinkers have worked always with a view to the continuity of the tradition; that is, to the faithfulness of its future to its past, but also to the vitality and vivacity of what they found timeless in the tradition and therefore capable of acquiring new meanings and new spheres of application in the present.

The confidence of the practitioners of Jewish philosophy in the conceptual vitality and continually renewed moral and spiritual relevance of the tradition is typically the reflex of an existential commitment to that tradition and to the people who are its bearers. That confidence, and its repeated vindication by the richness of the tradition itself, is also a wellspring of renewal and encouragement for the commitment that energizes it – even, and especially, in times of historical crisis and external pressures, which have rarely confined themselves to purely intellectual challenges. Symptomatic of that commitment is the prominence and recurrence of the philosophy of Judaism among the concerns of Jewish philosophy. However, the two should not be confused. The philosophy of Judaism is inquiry into the nature and meaning of Jewish existence. Its questions address the sense to be given to the idea of a covenant between the universal God and the people of Israel, the meaning of that people's mission, their chosenness, their distinctive laws, customs and rituals and the relation of those norms to the more widely recognized norms of humanity, of which the Prophets of Israel were early and insistent messengers.

The philosophy of Judaism wants to understand Zionism, the Holocaust, the Jewish Diaspora and the historical vicissitudes that gave shape to Jewish

475

experience over the millennia, from the age of the biblical patriarchs to the destruction of the first and second temples in Jerusalem, to the exile of the Jewish people and the return of many, after a hundred generations, to the land they had been promised and in which they had prospered, a land which some had never left but which most, for centuries, had pictured only through the sublimating lenses of sacred history, apocalypse and philosophy. The philosophy of Judaism wants to understand the ancient Jewish liturgy, the exegetical practices and hermeneutical standards of the Jewish exegetes. Like Freud, it wants to understand Jewish humour. Like Pico della Mirandola, it wants to understand Kabbalah, Jewish mysticism, and like Buber, it wants to understand Hasidism. The concerns of the philosophy of Judaism touch every aspect of Jewish experience, just as the concerns of philosophy at large touch every aspect of experience in general. But the concerns of Jewish philosophy, like those of general philosophy, do not confine themselves to Jewish experience. They are, in fact, the same concerns as those of general philosophy, rendered distinctively Jewish by their steady recourse to the resources of the tradition, and sustained as philosophical by an insistence on critical receptivity, responsible but creative appropriation of ideas and values that withstand the scrutiny of reason and indeed grow and give fruit in its light.

2   Strengths and weaknesses

There are two weaknesses in Jewish philosophy as practised today. One is a tendency to historicism, that is, the equivocal equation of norm with facticity and facticity with norm that leads to an abdication of philosophical engagement for a detached clinical posture or an equally unwholesome surrender of judgment to the flow of events. Historicism is a natural by-product of respect for tradition, or of expectation of progress. It becomes particularly debilitating under the pressure of positivism, whether of the logical empiricist sort that dominated philosophy for much of the early twentieth century, or of the more endemic sort that thrives on the sheer givenness of any system of law and ritual or that allows itself to be overwhelmed by the press of history itself. It is not unusual, even today, when logical positivism is widely thought to be long dead, to find scholars of Jewish thought who substitute historical descriptions for philosophical investigations, often in the process begging or slighting the key philosophical questions. Nor is it unusual among those of more traditional stamp for scholars to be found who imagine that a faithful description of the contents of authentic Jewish documents constitutes doing Jewish philosophy – as

though faithfulness to the tradition were somehow a substitute for critical grappling with the issues and problems, and as though the question as to what constitutes faithfulness to the tradition, conceptually, historically, morally and spiritually, were not itself among the most crucial of those issues and problems.

The second weakness is a narrowing of the gaze, a tendency to substitute philosophy of Judaism for the wider discourse of Jewish philosophy, as though the resources of the tradition had nothing (or nothing more) to contribute to ethics, or natural theology, or metaphysics and logic, for that matter. The work of the great practitioners of Jewish philosophy has repeatedly given the lie to such narrow expectations. In every epoch of its existence, Jewish philosophy has played an active role in the philosophical conversation of humankind – which is a universal conversation precisely because and to the extent that those who take part speak every language and bring to the conversation experiences that are universal as well as those that are unique.

But if two weaknesses are to be mentioned here, at least one strength should be cited as well: Jewish philosophy, although intimately engaged throughout its history with the philosophical traditions of the West, has also been a tradition apart. The open access of most of its practitioners to the Hebrew (and Aramaic) Jewish sources has afforded a perspective that is distinctive and that can be corrective of biases found in other branchings of the tree of philosophical learning. The early access of medieval Jewish philosophers to Arabic philosophical and scientific writings, and to the Greek works preserved in Arabic, enriched and broadened their philosophical repertoire. The scholastic learning of later medieval Jewish philosophers and their collaboration with scholastic thinkers made them at once participants in and observers of the lively philosophical debates of their day. The immersion and active participation of Renaissance and Enlightenment Jewish philosophers in the movements that spawned modernity gave them a similar philosophical vantage point. All philosophers must be, to some degree, alien to their society – Socrates and Nietzsche, and for that matter even Plato, Aristotle and Descartes were, to some degree, intellectual outsiders in their own times – not so alien as to have no word or thought in common with their contemporaries, but not so well integrated as to become mere apologists, or complacent and unquestioning acquiescers in the given. Jewish philosophy has long made and continues to make a distinctive, if today underutilized, contribution to cosmopolitan philosophical discourse in this regard. It shares the problematic of Western philosophy but typically offers a distinctive slant or perspective that calls into question accepted verities and thus enhances the critical edge of philosophical work for those who study it.

3   Movements and important figures

Jewish philosophy has over the course of its history been the source of a number of different types of study based on the philosophically relevant ideas of the Hebrew Bible, Rabbinic Law (Halakhah), Rabbinic theology and Rabbinic homiletics, exegesis and hermeneutics (midrash) (see HALAKHAH; MIDRASH). The anti-Rabbinical, biblicist movement known as Karaism and the mystical tradition of the Kabbalah are examples of differing types of movements which have emerged (see KABBALAH), while Jewish voluntarism and Jewish Averroism were fields for the rivalry between intellectualist and less deterministic, more empiricist views of theology as it was played out among Jewish thinkers. More modern movements include the Jewish pietist movement founded by Israel Baal Shem Tov and known as Hasidism, the Jewish Enlightenment movement known as the Haskalah, and Zionism, the movement that led to the establishment of the modern State of Israel (see HASIDISM).

The first exponent of Jewish philosophy was PHILO OF ALEXANDRIA, a major contributor to the synthesis of Stoicism, Middle Platonism and monotheistic ideas that helped forge the tradition of scriptural philosophy in the West. Other early figures include Daud al-Muqammas and Isaac Israeli, two of the first figures of medieval Jewish philosophical theology. Al-Fayyumi Saadiah Gaon (882–942), the first systematic Jewish philosopher, was also a major biblical translator and exegete, a grammarian, lexicographer and authority on Jewish religious law and ritual. The rationalism, pluralism and intellectual honesty evident in his work made it a model of Jewish philosophy for all who came after him. Solomon ibn Gabirol (c.1020–c.1057), long known as a Hebrew poet, was discovered in the nineteenth century to have been the author as well of the famous Neoplatonic philosophical work, preserved in Latin as the *Fons Vitae*. Moses ibn Ezra (c.1055–after 1135) is notable for his poetic and philosophic conributions. Abraham ibn Ezra (c.1089–1164) is likewise noted for his hermeneutical ideas and methods; his forthright approach to the Hebrew Bible was a critical influence on the thinking of Jewish philosophers from the Middle Ages to SPINOZA and beyond. A less familiar figure is Abu 'l-Barakat al-Baghdadi (*fl. c.*1200–50), a brilliant Jewish thinker who converted to Islam late in life. He developed highly independent views about the nature of time, human consciousness, space, matter and motion. His work undercuts the notion that the medieval period was simply an age of faith and static commitment to a faith community.

A polymath of rather different spirit was Abraham bar Hayya in the eleventh century, who wrote on astronomy, mathematics, geography, optics and music as well as philosophy and who collaborated on scientific translations with the Christian scholar Plato of Tivoli, the transmitter of the Ptolemaic system to the Latin world. Bar Hayya's *Meditation of the Sad Soul* expresses the forlornness of human life in exile from the world of the divine, a forlornness tinged with the hope of future glory. Joseph ibn Tzaddik (d. 1149) similarly developed Neoplatonic ideas around the theme of the human being as a microcosm.

Bahya ibn Pakuda (early twelfth century) wrote as a pietist philosopher. He placed philosophical understanding and critical thinking at the core of the spiritual devotion called for by the sincerest form of piety. Judah Halevi (before 1075–1141), probably the greatest Hebrew poet after the Psalms, wrote a cogently argued philosophical dialogue best known as the *Kuzari*, but more formally titled, *A Defence and an Argument in behalf of the Abased Religion*. Set in the Khazar kingdom, whose king, historically, had converted to Judaism, the work mounts a trenchant critique of the intellectualism of the prevalent philosophical school and the spiritualizing and universalizing ascetic pietism that was its counterpart. Calling for a robust recovery of Jewish life and peoplehood in the Land of Israel, the work is not only a striking anticipation of Zionist ideas but a remarkable expression of the need to reintegrate the spiritual, intellectual, moral and physical dimensions of Jewish life.

Abraham ibn Daud (c.1110–80), a historian as well as a philosopher, used his historiography to argue for the providential continuity of the Jewish intellectual and religious tradition. His philosophical work laid the technical foundations that made possible the philosophical achievement of Moses MAIMONIDES (1138–1204), the greatest of the philosophers committed to the Jewish tradition. Besides his medical writings and his extensive juridical corpus, which includes the authoritative fourteen-volume code of Jewish law, the *Mishneh Torah*, Maimonides was the author of the famous *Guide to the Perplexed*. Written in Arabic and intended for an inquirer puzzled by the apparent discrepancies between traditional Judaism and Aristotelian-Neoplatonic philosophy, the *Guide* is a paradigm in the theology of transcendence, addressing questions ranging from the overt anthropomorphism of the scriptural text to the purposes of the Mosaic legislation, to the controversy over the creation or eternity of the world, the problem of evil, and the sense that can be made of the ideas of revelation, providence, divine knowledge and human perfectibility. Like Halevi's *Kuzari* and Bahya's *Duties of the Heart*, the *Guide to the Perplexed* continues to be studied to this day by Jews and non-Jews for its philosophical insights.

Abraham ben Moses Maimonides (1186–1237), the son of the great philosopher and jurist, began his scholarly life as a defender of his father's work against the many critics who feared Maimonidean rationalism. In his mature work he became the exponent of a mystical, pietist and ascetic movement, largely influenced by Sufism. Moses Nahmanides (1194–1270), exegete, theologian and a founding figure of the Kabbalistic theosophy, championed Judaism in the infamous Barcelona Disputation of 1263 and played a leading role in the Maimonidean controversy. He struggled to harmonize his conservative and reactive tendencies with his respect for reason and the unvarnished sense of the biblical text.

Ibn Kammuna (d. 1284) was a pioneer in other areas. Besides his work in the Ishraqi or Illuminationist tradition of theosophy, laid out in commentary on the Muslim philosopher IBN SINA (Avicenna), he wrote a distinctively dispassionate study of comparative religions, favouring Judaism but fairly and unpolemically presenting the Christian and Muslim alternatives.

Shem Tov ibn Falaquera (*c.*1225–*c.*1295) was a warm exponent of Maimonidean rationalism and an ardent believer in the interdependence of faith and reason. His selections in Hebrew from the lost Arabic original of Ibn Gabirol's magnum opus allowed modern scholars to identify Ibn Gabirol as the Avicebrol of the surviving Latin text, the *Fons Vitae*.

Hillel ben Samuel of Verona (*c.*1220–95), physician, translator, Talmudist and philosopher was a Maimonist who introduced numerous scholastic ideas into Hebrew philosophical discourse. Immanuel of Rome (*c.*1261–before 1336) was a prolific author of philosophical poetry and exegesis, often praising reason and intellectual love. Judah ben Moses of Rome (*c.*1292–after 1330), known as Judah Romano, was an active bridge person between the Judaeo-Arabic and the scholastic tradition of philosophical theology.

Levi ben Gershom, known as Gersonides (1288–1344), was an important astronomer and mathematician as well as a biblical exegete and philosopher. His *Wars of the Lord* grappled with the problems of creation, providence, divine knowledge, human freedom and immortality. Aiming to defend his ancestral faith, Gersonides followed courageously where the argument led, often into radical and creative departures from traditional views.

Hasdai Crescas (1340–1410), an ardent defender of Judaism against Christian conversionary pressures, was among the most creative figures of Jewish philosophy, challenging many of the givens of Aristotelianism, including the idea that the cosmos must be finite in extent. Crescas' student Joseph Albo (*c.*1360–1444) sought to organize Jewish theology into an axiomatic system, in part to render Jewish thought defensible against hostile critics.

Profiat Duran (d. *c.* 1414), also known as Efodi, used his extensive understanding of Christian culture to criticize Christianity from a Jewish perspective. Deeply influenced by Moses Maimonides and Abraham ibn Ezra and by Neoplatonic and astrological ideas, he sought to balance the practical with the intellectual aspects of the Torah. Simeon ben Tzemach Duran (1361–1444) contributed an original approach to the project of Jewish dogmatics and an implicit critical examination of that project.

The Shem Tov family included four thinkers active in fifteenth-century Spain. Their works follow the persecution of 1391 and the ensuing mass apostasy of Spanish Jews and seek to rethink the relations of philosophy to Judaism. Shem Tov, the *paterfamilias*, criticized Maimonides and endorsed Kabbalah, but his sons Joseph, a court physician and auditor of royal accounts at Castile, and Isaac, a popular teacher of Aristotelian philosophy, and Joseph's son, again named Shem Tov, wrote numerous Peripatetic commentaries. These offspring charted a more moderate course that enabled Jewish intellectuals to cultivate philosophy and the kindred arts and sciences while asserting the ultimate primacy of their revealed faith.

Isaac ben Moses Arama (*c.*1420–94), like Nahmanides, was critical of Maimonidean and Aristotelian rationalism but did not discard reason, seeing in it a crucial exegetical tool and an avenue toward understanding miracles and providence. Isaac Abravanel (1437–1508), leader of the Jews whom Ferdinand and Isabella exiled from Spain in 1492, like Arama criticized Maimonidean rationalism in the interest of traditional Judaism as he saw it, but at the same time put forward a theistic vision of history and strikingly modern views about politics and the state. His son, Judah ben Isaac Abravanel, also known as Leone Ebreo (*c.*1460–*c.*1521), wrote the *Dialoghi d'amore*. Couched in the language of courtly love, the work explores the idea that love is the animating force of the cosmos. The work stands out as a brilliant dialectical exploration of the differences and complementarities of the Platonic and Aristotelian approaches to philosophy.

Judah Messer Leon (*c.*1425–*c.*1495) was a philosopher, physician, jurist, communal leader, poet and orator. Awarded a doctorate in medicine and philosophy by the Emperor Frederick III, he could confer doctoral degrees in those subjects on the students in his *yeshivah*. He saw logic as the key to harmonizing religion and philosophy and favored scholastic logic over the Arabic logical works. His encyclopedia became a popular textbook, and his systematic elicitation of Hebrew rhetoric from the biblical text, in *The Book of the Honeycomb's Flow*, one of the first Hebrew books to be printed, was a masterpiece of cross-cultural humanistic scholarship. But Messer Leon failed to curb the spread of Kabbalah, whose underlying Platonic metaphysics he abhorred and whose appropriation by Christian Platonists he held in deep suspicion. Indeed, his own son turned toward the Kabbalah and sought to combine its teachings with the Aristotelianism favored by his father.

Yohanan ben Isaac Alemanno (1433/4–after 1503/4) brought together in his thinking Averroist, Kabbalistic, Neoplatonic and Renaissance humanist themes. He instructed PICO DELLA MIRANDOLA in Hebrew and in Kabbalah, bringing to birth what became a Christian, syncretic Kabbalism. Elijah Delmedigo (*c.*1460–93) was an Aristotelian and Averroist. He translated works into Latin for Pico della Mirandola and developed a subtle critique of the Kabbalistic ideas that in his time were rivalled and often displaced what he saw as more disciplined philosophical thinking. Abraham Cohen de Herrera (*c.*1562–*c.*1635) was a philosophically oriented Kabbalist of Spanish origin. His Spanish writings, in Latin translation, were blamed for inspiring Spinoza's views.

4   Movements and important figures (cont.)

Moses MENDELSSOHN (1729–86), a leading figure of the European Enlightenment, spread Enlightenment ideas to Hebrew literature, fought for Jewish civil rights and did pioneering conceptual work on political theory, especially with regard to religious liberty in his *Jerusalem*. Solomon Maimon (1753/4–1800) took his name in honour of Moses Maimonides. Trained as a rabbi, he pursued secular and scientific learning and became an important and original critic of the philosophy of Kant. Nachman Krochmal (1785–1840), a leader of the Jewish Enlightenment in Galicia, found anticipations of Kant, Hegel and Schelling in the ancient Jewish writings. His work shows how a thinker whose underlying assumptions differ from those of the idealist philosophers could take their views in quite a different direction from the one they chose.

Hermann COHEN (1842–1918), a major Kantian philosopher and one of the first non-baptized Jews to hold an important academic post in Germany, applied his own distinctive version of critical idealism to the understanding of Judaism as a spiritual and ethical system. Franz Rosenzweig (1886–1929), an important Hegelian thinker, went on to formulate a Jewish existential philosophy that deeply influenced many of the most prominent Jewish thinkers of the twentieth century. Martin BUBER (1878–1965), Zionist advocate of accommodation with the Palestinian Arabs and an admiring student of Hasidic traditions, added his own stamp to the Continental tradition of Jewish philosophy by developing a widely influential dialogical philosophy that privileged relationships experientially and celebrated the I–thou, a mode of relation that allows for authentic encounter.

A number of twentieth-century philosophers of Judaism have grasped at diverse threads of the Jewish experience, illustrating both the attractions of the tradition and the fragmentation produced by centuries of persecution that would culminate in the Holocaust, only to be accentuated by the centrifugal tendencies of Jewish life in post-Holocaust liberal societies. Ahad Ha'Am, the pen name of Asher Ginzberg (1856–1927), was an essayist who argued that the creation of a 'spiritual centre' of Jewish culture in Palestine would provide the sustenance needed to preserve the diaspora Jewry from the threat of assimilation. No state was needed. David Baumgardt (1890–1963) was a philosopher who sought to reconcile ethical naturalism with the ideals he found in the Jewish sources, but, unlike Hermann Cohen, Baumgardt did not explore those sources in close detail. Mordecai Kaplan (1881–1981) sought to devise a social mission and communal identity for Jews without reliance on many of the core beliefs and practices that had shaped that identity in the past. Abraham Joshua Heschel (1907–72) sought to salvage the spiritual dimensions of Jewish experience, which found expression both in ritual and in ethical and social action. Joseph Soloveitchik (1903–93) gave canonical expression to Orthodox ideals by focusing on the intellectual and ritual rigours of his archetypal figures, Halakhic man and the Lonely Man of Faith. Yeshayahu Leibowitz (1903–94), an influential Israeli thinker, struggled for the disengagement of authentic and committed religious observance from the toils of governmental officialdom. Jews are mandated, he argued, to observance, as a community. That imperative is not to be put aside. Neither can the observant pretend to ignore the State of Israel. But the State can give no mandate to religious observance, and religious faithfulness can impart none of its aura to the State. For it is essential not to place God in the service of politics. Emil Fackenheim (1916–) seeks an authentic response to the Holocaust, which he formulates in an intentionally inclusionary way, as a

'614th' commandment, not to hand Hitler a posthumous victory but to find some way, that might vary from individual to individual, of keeping alive Jewish ideas, practices and commitments.

See also: Anti-Semitism; Holocaust, the; Islamic philosophy; Medieval philosophy; Religion, philosophy of; Renaissance philosophy

References and further reading

Goodman, L. (1991) *On Justice: An Essay in Jewish Philosophy*, New Haven, CT: Yale University Press. (A theory of justice based on the biblical idea of deserts.)

Goodman, L. (1996) *God of Abraham*, Oxford: Oxford University Press. (On the connection between natural theology and the values represented in the Jewish tradition.)

Goodman, L. (1998) *Judaism, Human Rights and Human Values*, Oxford: Oxford University Press. (Detailed treatment of the author's general theory of deserts, its relationship to human rights and liberty, abortion and the legitimacy of nations.)

L.E. GOODMAN

JOHN OF ALEXANDRIA
See Philoponus

JOHN OF FIDANZA
See Bonaventure

JOHN OF ST THOMAS (1589–1644)

The seventeenth-century Portuguese Dominican, John of St Thomas or John Poinsot, was a major figure in late scholastic philosophy and theology. Educated at Coimbra and Louvain, he taught both disciplines in Spain: at Madrid, Plasencia and Alcalá. Aspiring to be a faithful disciple of Thomas Aquinas, he published a three-volume *Cursus philosophicus thomisticus* (Thomistic Philosophical Course) and before he died began the publication of a *Cursus theologicus* (Theological Course). His philosophical writing was explicitly on logic and natural philosophy. However, in both his philosophical and theological works, he treated many metaphysical, epistemological and ethical issues. His logic is divided into two parts, formal and material. Of particular interest is his semiotic doctrine which appears in the second part. In natural philosophy, he explained Aristotle with a Thomistic slant. While following Aquinas in theology, John at times developed his master's doctrine along new lines. Both in his own time and after he has had considerable authority within scholasticism, especially for Thomists. Among those whom he has influenced

in twentieth-century Thomism are Joseph Gredt, Reginald Garrigou-Lagrange, Santiago Ramirez, Jacques Maritain and Yves Simon.

See also: Aquinas, T.; Renaissance philosophy

JOHN P. DOYLE

JOHN THE GRAMMARIAN
See Philoponus

JOHNSON, SAMUEL (1696–1772)

Johnson was the first important philosopher in colonial America and author of the first philosophy textbook published there. He derived his views largely from others, combining in one system elements from diverse sources. He followed the empiricists in holding that knowledge begins with sensations but held the Augustinian view that knowledge of necessary truths comes only from the mind's illumination by divine light. With Berkeley, he denied matter's existence, viewing bodies as collections of ideas. He held that these ideas are 'faint copies' of God's archetypal ideas, which he thought of in much the same way as had Malebranche and John Norris. His ethical views, influenced by William Wollaston, take happiness to be the supreme good, stressing that human beings should seek a happiness consonant with their nature as rational, immortal and social beings.

See also: Idealism

CHARLES J. McCRACKEN

JOURNALISM, ETHICS OF

It is sometimes suggested that ethical principles, even fundamental ones like nonmaleficence and beneficence, are totally out of place in journalism, and that it should be shaped solely by market forces. This suggestion should be resisted. One reason why journalism should be ethical is that in a democracy it is expected to serve the public interest, which means that it should accept the responsibility to circulate the information and opinion without which a democracy could not operate, and to enable it to do this the freedom of the press is acknowledged.

If journalism is to serve the public interest, then a commitment to truth-telling is fundamental. Journalists should also be fair and accurate in reporting news, should publish corrections, should offer a right of reply. They should avoid discrimination, deception, harassment, betraying confidences and invasions of privacy. But ethical journalism is more than lists of requirements and prohibitions. In investigative journalism, for example, some deception or intrusion into privacy could be justified in order to uncover corruption. Ethical journalism is therefore reflective understanding of the underlying

principles of harm and benefit and the public interest, and an ability to apply them in particular cases.
See also: APPLIED ETHICS

ANDREW BELSEY

JUDAEO-ARABIC PHILOSOPHY IN SPAIN
See MAIMONIDES, MOSES

JUDAISTIC PHILOSOPHY
See JEWISH PHILOSOPHY

JUDGMENT, MORAL
See MORAL JUDGMENT

JUNG, CARL GUSTAV (1875–1961)

Jung was among the leaders in the development of depth psychology at the beginning of the twentieth century. An early follower of Sigmund Freud, he broke with the founder of psychoanalysis in 1913 and established his own school of analytical psychology.

Jung's theoretical development originated in his work on the word association test and the theory of feeling toned complexes. As he continued to explore the workings of the unconscious, he postulated the existence of instinctual patterns of cognition and behaviour which he termed 'archetypes'. Archetypal patterns are, according to Jung, common throughout the human species and constitute an inherited 'collective unconscious'.

Jung's approach to psychology was eclectic. He accepted the psychological importance of any phenomenon, even if it conflicted with current thinking in other fields. This attitude led to a deep investigation of the psychological significance of occult phenomena and alchemy, which Jung viewed as expressions of the unconscious that anticipated modern psychology. Later in life, Jung turned increasingly to considerations of the contemporary cultural expressions of psychological forces, writing extensively on what he viewed to be a deepening spiritual crisis in Western civilization.
See also: INDIAN AND TIBETAN PHILOSOPHY; PSYCHOANALYSIS, METHODOLOGICAL ISSUES IN; PSYCHOANALYSIS, POST-FREUDIAN; REDUCTIONISM IN THE PHILOSOPHY OF MIND

GEORGE B. HOGENSON

JUSTICE

Introduction

The idea of justice lies at the heart of moral and political philosophy. It is a necessary virtue of individuals in their interactions with others, and the principal virtue of social institutions, although not the only one. Just as an individual can display qualities such as integrity, charity and loyalty, so a society can also be more or less economically prosperous, artistically cultivated, and so on. Traditionally defined by the Latin tag '*suum cuique tribuere*' – to allocate to each his own – justice has always been closely connected to the ideas of desert and equality. Rewards and punishments are justly distributed if they go to those who deserve them. But in the absence of different desert claims, justice demands equal treatment.

One division of justice concerns compensation for the infliction of damage and as punishment for the commission of crimes. The other concerns the content of just principles for the distribution of benefits and (non-punitive) burdens. Conventionalists claim that what is due to each person is given by the laws, customs and shared understandings of the community of which the person is a member. Teleologists believe that an account can be given of the good for human beings and that justice is the ordering principle through which a society (or humanity) pursues that good. Justice as mutual advantage proposes that the rules of justice can be derived from the rational agreement of each agent to cooperate with others to further their own self-interest.

1 Retributive justice
2 Conventionalism
3 Teleology
4 Justice as mutual advantage
5 Egalitarian justice
6 Critics of justice

1 Retributive justice

There is general agreement that a just punishment should meet the following criteria. First, it should be imposed only on a properly convicted wrong-doer. Second, the quantum of suffering should satisfy the principle of ordinal proportionality. This means people convicted of crimes of equal seriousness should receive punishments of equal severity except where mitigating or aggravating circumstances alter the culpability of the offender. Third, the quantum of suffering should satisfy the principle of cardinal proportionality: there should be a vertical ranking of crimes and penalties by seriousness.

There is, however, disagreement over the justification for punishment, and this makes it controversial how 'seriousness', 'severity' and 'culpability' are assessed and how the scale of penalties should be fixed. Those who appeal to deterrence may regard a widespread and socially disruptive crime as serious (whatever its degree of moral wrongness), and favour a scale of penalties designed to deter criminality. Those who favour retribution, however, have traditionally regarded seriousness as a factor of moral culpability and the scale of penalties as being derived from some notion of desert (see CRIME AND PUNISHMENT).

2 Conventionalism

Turning to social, or distributive, justice, the attraction of some form of conventionalist approach is clear. Since there are institutions, conventions and systems of law that determine what is due to whom, resolving issues of justice may be thought merely to require reading off the correct answer from such sources. The earliest extant statement of a conventionalist view of justice is offered by Socrates' interlocutors, Cephalus and Polemarchus, in Book I of Plato's *Republic*. Polemarchus states that justice is giving a man his due, or what is appropriate to him, and it is clear that for Polemarchus what is appropriate to each person is dictated by the conventions prevalent in contemporary Athenian society.

A modern statement of conventionalism has been offered by Michael Walzer, who has argued that every social good (for example, health care, education or political rights) has an appropriate criterion of distribution which is internally related to how that good is understood by society. For example, in the UK (as elsewhere), health care is understood essentially to concern itself with illness and the restoration of health. This shared understanding of health care is claimed by Walzer to entail a distributive criterion: medical need. Anyone, therefore, who claims that health care in the UK (and many other societies) ought to be distributed in accordance with, say, ability to pay has either failed to grasp the nature of the good of health care or falls outside the community which is united and defined by its shared understandings. The only universal principle of distributive justice is the demand that respect be given to different shared understandings: no community ought to impose its own understanding of a given good, and its criterion for the distribution of that good, on any other community with different views. However, it is doubtful that any society is so homogeneous as to boast a single, coherent and uncontested understanding of the meaning of each of its social goods; and even if it existed, it might not determine the particular distribution. Even if both requirements are met, it still makes sense to ask if this distribution is just. For example, a society marked by gross

inequalities based on ascription at birth can surely be regarded as unjust on the basis of ideas not available to that society. It is when one asks why things are as they are that the philosophical problem of justice really begins.

3 Teleology

In the history of thought about justice, the most common justification of any given set of laws, conventions or practices has been that they are conducive to the furtherance of some good. For example, it may be held that there is a natural law which is knowable through the faculty of human reason (see NATURAL LAW). This tradition, owing its origins to the Greek Stoics, found its most lucid interpreter in CICERO and was given its definitive Christian form by AQUINAS (§13). 'True law', writes Cicero, 'is right reason in agreement with nature; it is of universal application, unchanging and everlasting' (*De republica c*.54–51 BC: III, XXII, 211). The link to human nature via human reason is important, for it then follows that human beings reach their true end, or realize their true nature, only by living in accordance with natural law. What justice is and why it is a good are, thus, answered at the same time.

A major problem for this account is its reliance on an external source. Cicero is typical in claiming in the same passage that it is God who 'is the author of this law, its promulgator, and its enforcing judge'. Natural law theory faces the difficulty of having to give an account of the existence and verifiability of the 'true and unchanging' moral order. Commonly, the natural law was conveniently said to underwrite the existing positive law: this may reflect the role of the powerful both in formulating positive law and defining natural law.

Suppose we are attracted to the notion that human institutions are to be justified by their contribution to human good, but do not believe that human reason is capable of discerning a divine plan. Then we may naturally arrive at the secular alternative embodied in utilitarianism: that the ground of justification is human wellbeing, happiness or 'utility'. When the utility of different people conflicts, the criterion for bringing their interests into relationship with one another is that aggregate utility is to be maximized (see UTILITARIANISM). However the classical utilitarians did not equate justice with utility maximization, but claimed, rather, that familiar rules of justice can be given utilitarian foundations.

Thus, David HUME (§12), in *A Treatise of Human Nature* (1739–40), described justice as an 'artificial virtue' in that individual acts of justice contribute to utility not directly (as an act of benevolence would) but indirectly *qua* adherence to an institution that is on the whole beneficial. Hume's examples were respect for property, chastity (in women), allegiance to the government and promise-keeping. For Hume, then, justice was a convention – but it made sense to ask what good was served by following it. On somewhat parallel lines, J.S. MILL (§11) argued in *Utilitarianism* (1861) that 'justice' is the name we give to those precepts whose strict observance is important for the furtherance of the utilitarian end. Thus, utilitarians argue that the arbitrary departures from social rules summoned up by anti-utilitarians as an implication of the doctrine are, in the long term, not really for the general good. Opponents of utilitarianism however have claimed that situations might still arise in which injustice (as normally understood) would be for the general good.

4   Justice as mutual advantage

If we doubt that people can be motivated by a belief in natural law or a desire to act in ways that advance the general good, we can fall back on the idea that justice is a set of constraints that is more advantageous to each individual than the unrestrained pursuit of one's ends. Versions of 'justice as mutual advantage' can be found in Thrasymachus' 'might is right' argument in Book I of Plato's *Republic* and in the fraudulent social contract identified by Rousseau in his *Discourse on Inequality* (1755: Part II) as having been perpetrated by the rich on the poor. But the *locus classicus* of this theory is undoubtedly *Leviathan* by Thomas HOBBES (§7).

If the terms of agreement are to be to the advantage of each (compared with unrestrained conflict), they must reflect the relative bargaining strengths of the cooperators. The strong and talented have little to gain (or to fear) from the weak or infirm, and the latter may even 'fall beyond the pale' of morality if the strong have no reason for taking their interests into account, as David Gauthier makes clear in a contemporary restatement of the doctrine. Intuitively, it may seem perverse to call this a theory of justice. It is true that justice as mutual advantage has much of the structure of a theory of justice in that it results in rules that constrain the pursuit of self-interest. But the content of those rules will correspond to those of ordinary ideas of justice only if a rough equality of power holds between all the parties.

Even if this objection is not regarded as decisive, the theory suffers from internal problems. These concern the determinacy of the rules and their stability. The determinacy problem arises because of the necessity for all to start from a common view of the relative bargaining strengths of the participants.

This is an immensely demanding condition, given the information about resources required and the different predictions that are liable to be made about the outcome of conflict. Even after rules have been agreed, some parties will have reason to press for changes if their bargaining power increases. Justice as mutual advantage results in rules which are no more than truces and, like truces, they are unlikely to be stable if there are changes in the balance of power between the sides (Barry 1995: 41).

Stability will also be challenged by the problem of non-compliance. Justice as mutual advantage appeals to the self-interest of each and does so by establishing rules that, if generally complied with, will further the interests of all individuals. However, this gives the agent no reason to comply with a given rule when there is greater advantage to be had by breaking it. This applies especially when the agent can free ride on the compliance of others. All that can be attempted is to increase the costs of non-compliance by increasing the sanctions if the agent is detected. To run a society using only self-interest and sanctions, however, would mean using a degree of coercion and of 'policing' hitherto unthought of in even the most totalitarian society.

5   Egalitarian justice

Egalitarian theories of justice start, like those of justice as mutual advantage, from the premise that the role of justice is to provide a framework within which people with competing ideas of the good can live together without conflict but they insist that the framework must reflect a commitment to equal treatment or equal consideration.

The accounts of the content of justice that are compatible with this covers a wide range: Robert Nozick's entitlement theory and John Rawls' theory of justice, for example, come to very different conclusions about what justice demands, even though both start with the basic idea that justice is to regulate the interactions of free and equal persons. Nozick claims that each person has a set of inviolable rights, and in this sense is treated equally. From this starting point he generates what he calls an entitlement theory of justice (see NOZICK, R.). The just pattern of distribution is that which would result from voluntary transfers, given that holdings were justly acquired in the first place (by just transfer or by an appropriation that makes no one else worse off). Nozick, then, regards the claim to an equal set of absolute rights as defining the limits of justice: any actions which interfere with those rights (such as redistribution) are unjust no matter what the pattern or outcome of the entitlement theory. Nozick does not, however, offer any account of the existence of such robust rights, and his arguments from intuition to show that any interference with individual rights is unjust are unconvincing. It is plausible that injustice may result from a large number of individual transactions each of which taken separately seems just.

John Rawls, in his classic work *A Theory of Justice* (1971), argues that justice requires the provision of equal basic liberties and fair opportunities for all, and that social and economic inequality can only be justified where it is to the benefit of the least advantaged. These two principles are derived by arguing that they would be chosen by free persons in an 'original position', the specifications of which prevent people from making unfair use of their natural and social advantages (see CONTRACTAR-IANISM; RAWLS, J. §1). Rawls then, in contrast to Nozick, believes that justice requires us to do much more for people than merely provide them with absolute property rights. Rather, the pattern of distribution is set at that which will maximally benefit the worst off, subject to the proviso that people are free to choose their own occupations, work effort, etc.

Rawls' original position has been criticized for reducing the choice of principles to an individual computation because the veil of ignorance entails that the participants are identical. Moreover, the priority of the worst off as the unique outcome depends on an extreme risk aversion on the part of the chooser. An alternative to Rawls' original position is to posit participants who are aware of their identities and motivated to seek agreement on terms that nobody could reasonably reject. Such a position has been proposed as an ethical theory by Thomas Scanlon in his *What We Owe to Each Other* (1998) and developed into a theory of justice by Brian Barry in his *Justice as Impartiality* (1995) (see CONTRACTARIANISM).

All theories of egalitarian justice face the problems of grounding the commitment to the fundamental equality of persons and giving an account of each agent's motivation to behave justly. Rawls offers two justifications for his principles. The first is that we can come to a 'reflective equilibrium' in which the principles arising from a correctly specified original position can be brought into line with our moral intuitions. The second justification is offered as a Kantian interpretation. On this account the original position provides a 'procedural interpretation' of Kant's realm of the 'kingdom of ends' (see KANT, I. §9). The original position and the choice of the principles are viewed as an attempt to replicate Kant's reduction of morality to autonomy and autonomy to rationality. Thus, by living in accordance with justice we realize our true natures as autonomous beings. This provides the motivation required.

In later papers and in his second book, *Political Liberalism* (1993), Rawls has conceded that the Kantian interpretation requires a controversial metaphysics and that it commits him to a particular view of the good life as autonomy. Instead he now emphasizes that his theory relies on nothing more than ideas 'latent in the public political culture' of modern Western democratic states. However, this raises the problem that many political cultures are inconsistent with Rawls' principles. In his subsequent *The Law of Peoples* (1999) he accepted the implication that the arguments for these principles will not be compelling for those whose political culture does not already have these ideas latent within it. This entails that some societies that violate fundamental equality can be just. It is thus incompatible with a commitment to equal treatment or equal consideration. Egalitarian theorists of justice, however, maintain that these are universally valid for all societies, and thus reject the conventionalist turn taken by Rawls' later thinking.

Meanwhile, there have been attempts to refine and extend the theory of egalitarian justice and to explore new ways of implementing its requirements. Thus, the concept of equal treatment within a society with a plurality of religious beliefs and cultural norms has come under scrutiny. Rules of apparently general application may in fact have a sharply differential impact on members of different groups. For example, uniform codes of dress and personal appearance may be incompatible with Sikh turbans, Muslim standards of female modesty or Rastafarian dreadlocks. Unless these codes can be justified as inherent necessities (perhaps hard hats on building sites), they constitute injustice in that they fail to provide equal treatment. Conversely, some egalitarian theorists have questioned some existing accommodations of religious beliefs or cultural norms on the ground that the price of equal treatment in this sense is too high. For example, permitting kosher and halal butchery enables orthodox Jews and Muslims to eat meat, but it has been argued that it inflicts unnecessary suffering and that this should be the decisive consideration.

This question can be posed in terms of responsibility: how far are members of different cultural groups responsible for adapting their behaviour to fit in with rules based on, for example, hygiene, safety or avoidance of cruelty, and how far do societies have a responsibility for ensuring that their rules do not put members of some cultures at a disadvantage in pursuing their ends? Much of post-Rawlsian egalitarian theory has been concerned with the relation between responsibility and equal treatment. Thus, a generalized form of the problem already discussed can be put as follows: have people been treated equally if they have equal resources, or is this unfair to those who do not gain as much satisfaction from an equal share of equal resources as others do, because they have 'expensive tastes'? Does equal treatment instead require that those with 'expensive tastes' should have a larger share of resources?

An important question relating responsibility to equal treatment has been raised in the following terms: when have we 'done enough' to save our fellow citizens from making choices (perhaps out of ignorance) that pose serious risks to them? For example, how far should we regard 'unhealthy lifestyles' as the responsibility of individuals, and how far are societies responsible for providing information, ensuring the availability of 'healthy' alternatives and reducing levels of stress at work or in life generally for which 'unhealthy' choices are palliatives?

One way of thinking about equal treatment and responsibility is to propose that, under conditions of equal opportunity, people are responsible for inequalities of outcome. But what conditions are required for equality of opportunity to obtain in a form that underwrites this conclusion? On a weak interpretation, it would be satisfied if jobs were filled by the best-qualified applicants, so that the selection process should not be subject to discrimination or personal connections. However, this would be compatible with extremely unequal opportunities to acquire valuable qualifications. An obvious response is to add that all schools should provide all children with an equal opportunity to attain the best educational outcomes of which they are capable provided they make enough effort to achieve them. However, this is still not enough, according to some egalitarian theorists, because home and neighbourhood environments provide different children with very unequal opportunities to take advantage of formal education. Computers, books and a quiet room for homework are obvious material advantages. But parents and peers also provide children with very unequal capacities for achievement. An intellectually stimulating environment, parental help and encouragement, and peer expectation make an enormous difference.

Early intervention, with nursery schools and kindergartens available to all children regardless of their parents' financial position, undoubtedly reduce the unequal capacities that children bring to school, but are clearly still inadequate to close the gap. Thus, the next move is to propose that educational provision should be unequal, with more intensive and better schooling being provided for those disadvantaged by environmental factors. John Roemer has proposed a way of thinking about the implications of this in his *Equality of Opportunity*

(1998). According to this, members of a society can be divided into 'types' according to some criterion associated with advantage or disadvantage (e.g., race or ethnicity, gender) and equality of opportunity would then be achieved if the members of each 'type' finished up with the same distribution of some valued good (e.g., earnings). Unequal outcomes within types would then – provided that the types were genuinely homogenous with respect to advantage or disadvantage – correspond to differences among members of the type for which they could properly be held responsible. The potentially radical implications of this are illustrated by Roemer's conjecture that, even if Americans were divided into only two types – white and black – an equal earning profile would require very many times more money to be spent on black education than on white education.

Clearly, Roemer's proposal would raise problems of deciding how types should be defined and how to assign individuals to them. Alternative methods of achieving equal opportunity that have been advocated by egalitarian theorists of justice would act directly on the distribution of income and wealth. For example, Philippe Van Parijs, in his *Real Freedom for All* (1995) has argued that we should approach as far as possible a condition in which each person has an equal opportunity to fulfil their life plan. This opportunity should extend to those whose life plans preclude paid employment. These might include people who wish to devote themselves to caring for others (whether related or not), working for voluntary associations or pursuing unprofitable artistic careers. Such people would be entitled, as would everyone, to a 'basic income' sufficient to live on. Those who preferred to make more money would, as now, be free to do so. In response to the objection that many people would not wish to underwrite another's life spent surfing off Malibu, a number of supporters of basic income have suggested that the entitlement should be conditional upon 'participation', which could take a wide variety of forms. Differences in earning potential would therefore play a much smaller role in determining the range of opportunities open to people, because those with a low capacity for turning time into money would not be forced to take low-paid, degrading or dangerous jobs.

Another important source of unequal opportunity is unequal access to capital. A capital grant at, say, the age of eighteen has been proposed by egalitarian theorists in Britain and the United States, for example by Julian Le Grand and Bruce Ackerman, as a way of reducing this kind of unequal opportunity. Ackerman also argues that it is unfair for higher education to be subsidized while those who do not go on to university receive no equivalent state benefit. A universal cash benefit which could either be used on higher education or in other ways to get started would equalize opportunities to that extent.

The egalitarian approach has then proved itself to be a fertile source of new ideas about the principles it entails and the public policy policies that might advance the realization of egalitarian justice.

6 Critics of justice

The discussion so far has proceeded on the assumption that justice is the principal virtue of institutions. The theories of justice examined here would explain this primacy in different ways: by appealing to the most important shared understandings, the most stringent demands of Nature or God, the conduciveness of justice to utility or civil peace, or the role of justice in providing a fair framework for the pursuit of different conceptions of the good. But all agree that, where justice conflicts with other values, those other values must give way.

This consensus has been challenged on the grounds that under ideal conditions justice would be unnecessary, and appeals to it would actually destroy valuable social relationships. Thus, a marriage in which the spouses were constantly arguing in terms of rights and duties would be less good than one in which mutual love created spontaneous harmony. By an extension of this sentimental line of thought, an ideal community would be one in which justice had been transcended by a spirit of what used to be called (until feminist scholars objected) fraternity. This is one strand in the thought of Marx, and it recurs in the work of some contemporary feminist and communitarian writers (see COMMUNITY AND COMMUNITARIAN-ISM; FEMINIST POLITICAL PHILOSOPHY).

The theorists of justice discussed above would not necessarily dispute such claims. Both Hume and Rawls argued that there are 'circumstances of justice' that make justice necessary. These are precisely the conditions – conflicting demands for material goods and unreconcilable aspirations – that the critics of justice believe would be transcended by a sufficiently strong community spirit. The disagreement is not analytical but turns on the view taken of the possibility and the desirability of creating a community in which justice ceased to be the first virtue. The partisans of justice can point out that the theoretical assault on 'bourgeois morality' has provided the supposed justification for the most appalling violations of rights (for example, in China, Cambodia and the former USSR), and ask if there is any reason to suppose that other social experiments driven by the same animus would be any more benign.

References and further reading

Barry, B.M. (1995) *Justice as Impartiality*, vol. 2 of *A Treatise on Social Justice*, Oxford: Clarendon Press. (Author's work. A recent statement of the case for a universal theory of justice that also contains useful discussions of justice as mutual advantage and of Rawls' theory.)

Rawls, J.B. (1971) *A Theory of Justice*, Cambridge, MA: Harvard University Press. (The only classic work of political philosophy produced in the twentieth century.)

Ryan, A. (ed.) (1993) *Justice*, Oxford: Oxford University Press. (A useful collection of key extracts on justice, including texts from Rawls and Nozick.)

BRIAN BARRY
MATT MATRAVERS

JUSTICE, CORRECTIVE

In his treatment of justice Aristotle articulated a contrast between two forms of justice, corrective and distributive. The former deals with the rectification of an injustice inflicted by one person on another, the latter with the distribution of benefits or burdens. These forms of justice have differing structures. What informs distributive justice is the notion of comparison: a greater share goes to the more meritorious under the distributive criterion. What informs corrective justice is the notion of correlativity or mutuality: an injurer has inflicted wrongful harm on a victim if and only if the victim has suffered wrongful harm through the injurer's conduct. The parties, as doer and sufferer of the same injustice, are the active and passive poles of a single wrong, which the law rectifies by holding the perpetrator liable to the victim.

In recent decades corrective justice (along with its differentiation from distributive justice) has attracted the attention of legal theorists interested in tort law as a repository of normative judgments and insights about wrongful injuries. These theorists view the notion of correlativity as crucial for understanding the relationship between the plaintiff and the defendant. An emphasis on correlativity illuminates both the arguments that properly belong within a system of liability and the connection between corrective justice as a theoretical idea and legal liability as a familiar institutional practice.
See also: JUSTICE

ERNEST J. WEINRIB

JUSTIFICATION AND KNOWLEDGE, COHERENCE THEORY OF
See KNOWLEDGE AND JUSTIFICATION, COHERENCE THEORY OF

JUSTIFICATION, EPISTEMIC

The term 'justification' belongs to a cluster of normative terms that also includes 'rational', 'reasonable' and 'warranted'. All these are commonly used in epistemology, but there is no generally agreed way of understanding them, nor is there even agreement as to whether they are synonymous. Some epistemologists employ them interchangeably; others distinguish among them. It is generally assumed, however, that belief is the target psychological state of these terms; epistemologists are concerned with what it takes for a belief to be justified, rational, reasonable or warranted. Propositions, statements, claims, hypotheses and theories are also said to be justified, but these uses are best understood as derivative; to say, for example, that a theory is justified for an individual is to say that were that individual to believe the theory (perhaps for the right reasons), the belief would be justified.

Historically, the two most important accounts of epistemic justification are foundationalism and coherentism. Foundationalists say that justification has a tiered structure; some beliefs are self-justifying, and other beliefs are justified in so far as they are supported by these basic beliefs. Coherentists deny that any beliefs are self-justifying and propose instead that beliefs are justified in so far as they belong to a system of beliefs that are mutually supportive. Most foundationalists and coherentists are internalists; they claim that the conditions that determine whether or not a belief is justified are primarily internal psychological conditions (for example, what beliefs and experiences one has). In the last quarter of the twentieth century, externalism emerged as an important alternative to internalism. Externalists argue that one cannot determine whether a belief is justified without looking at the believer's external environment. The most influential form of externalism is reliabilism.

Another challenge to traditional foundationalism and coherentism comes from probabilists, who argue that belief should not be treated as an all-or-nothing phenomenon: belief comes in degrees. Moreover, one's degrees of beliefs, construed as subjective probabilities, are justified only if they do not violate any of the axioms of the probability calculus. Another approach is proposed by those who advocate a naturalization of epistemology. They fault foundationalists, coherentists and probabilists for an overemphasis on a priori theorizing and a corresponding lack of concern with the practices and findings of science. The most radical naturalized epistemologists recommend that the traditional questions of epistemology be recast into forms that can be answered by science.

An important question to ask with respect to any approach to epistemology is, 'what implications does it have for scepticism?' Some accounts of epistemic justification preclude, while others do not preclude, one's beliefs being justified but mostly false. Another issue is the degree to which the beliefs of other people affect what an individual is justified in believing. All theories of epistemic justification must find a way of acknowledging that much of what each of us knows derives from what others have told us. However, some epistemologists insist that the bulk of the history of epistemology is overly individualistic and that social conditions enter into questions of justification in a more fundamental way than standard accounts acknowledge.

See also: EPISTEMOLOGY, HISTORY OF; INDUCTION, EPISTEMIC ISSUES IN; INTERNALISM AND EXTERNALISM IN EPISTEMOLOGY; KNOWLEDGE AND JUSTIFICATION, COHERENCE THEORY OF; KNOWLEDGE, CONCEPT OF; NATURALIZED EPISTEMOLOGY; SCEPTICISM; SOCIAL EPISTEMOLOGY; TESTIMONY

RICHARD FOLEY

JUSTIFICATION, MORAL
See MORAL JUSTIFICATION

K

KABBALAH

Kabbalah is the body of Jewish mystical writings which became important at the end of the twelfth century in Provence and has been taken up with varying degrees of enthusiasm in an attempt to explore the esoteric side of Judaism. There are two main forms of Kabbalah: one which concentrates on gaining knowledge of God through study of his name, and a theosophical tradition that approaches God through his impact on creation. On both accounts God is linked to the world through ten *Sefirot*, hypostatic numbers which mediate between the Infinite and this world and thus (among other functions) help to explain how a being who is entirely ineffable can produce so much variety as is observed in nature. God's willingness to relate to the world gives his creatures the possibility of personal knowledge of him, although this can be acquired only through difficult and strenuous spiritual exercises. The variety of works which the Kabbalists produced are a blend of philosophical and mystical ideas which attempt to explore the inner meaning of faith and represent a creative and influential stream that both draws upon and contributes to Jewish philosophy.

See also: FICINO, M.; HASIDISM; HERMETISM; PLATONISM, RENAISSANCE

OLIVER LEAMAN

KANT, IMMANUEL (1724–1804)

Introduction

Immanuel Kant was the paradigmatic philosopher of the European Enlightenment. He eradicated the last traces of the medieval worldview from modern philosophy, joined the key ideas of earlier rationalism and empiricism into a powerful model of the subjective origins of the fundamental principles of both science and morality, and laid the ground for much in the philosophy of the nineteenth and twentieth centuries. Above all, Kant was the philosopher of human autonomy, the view that by the use of our own reason in its broadest sense human beings can discover and live up to the basic principles of knowledge and action without outside assistance, above all without divine support or intervention.

Kant laid the foundations of his theory of knowledge in his monumental *Critique of Pure Reason* (1781). He described the fundamental principle of morality in the *Groundwork of the Metaphysics of Morals* (1785) and the *Critique of Practical Reason* (1788), in the conclusion of which he famously wrote:

> Two things fill the mind with ever new and increasing admiration and awe, the more often and steadily reflection is occupied with them: *the starry heaven above me and the moral law within me.* Neither of them need I seek and merely suspect as if shrouded in obscurity or rapture beyond my own horizon; I see them before me and connect them immediately with my existence.
>
> (*Collected Works* 1900: 5. 161–2)

Kant tried to show that both the laws of nature and the laws of morality are grounded in human reason itself. By these two forms of law, however, he is often thought to have defined two incommensurable realms, nature and freedom, the realm of what is and that of what ought to be, the former of which must be limited to leave adequate room for the latter. Kant certainly did devote much space and effort to distinguishing between nature and freedom. But as he also says, in the *Critique of Judgment* (1790), it is equally important 'to throw a bridge from one territory to the other'. Ultimately, Kant held that both the laws of nature and the laws of free human conduct must be compatible because they are both products of human thought imposed by us on the data of our experience by the exercise of our own powers. This was clearly stated in his last book, *The Conflict of the Faculties* (1798):

Philosophy is not some sort of science of representations, concepts, and ideas, or a science of all sciences, or anything else of this sort; rather, it is a science of the human being, of its representing, thinking, and acting – it should present the human being in all of its components, as it is and ought to be, that is, in accordance with its natural determinations as well as its relationship of morality and freedom. Ancient philosophy adopted an entirely inappropriate standpoint towards the human being in the world, for it made it into a machine in it, which as such had to be entirely dependent on the world or on external things and circumstances; it thus made the human being into an all but merely passive part of the world. Now the critique of reason has appeared and determined the human being to a thoroughly *active* place in the world. The human being itself is the original creator of all its representations and concepts and ought to be the sole author of all its actions.

(7: 69–70)

Thus, Kant derived the fundamental principles of human thought and action from human sensibility, understanding, and reason, all as sources of our autonomy; he balanced the contributions of these principles against the ineliminable inputs of external sensation and internal inclination beyond our own control; and he strove both to demarcate these principles from each other and yet to integrate them into a single system with human autonomy as both its foundation and its ultimate value and goal. These were the tasks of Kant's three great critiques. In the *Critique of Pure Reason*, the essential forms of space, time and conceptual thought arise in the nature of human sensibility and understanding and ground the indispensable principles of human experience. He then argued that reason, in the narrow sense manifest in logical inference, plays a key role in systematizing human experience, but that it is a mistake to think that reason offers metaphysical insight into the existence and nature of the human soul, an independent world, and God. In the *Critique of Practical Reason* and *Groundwork*, however, he argued that reason as the source of the ideal of systematicity is the source of the fundamental law of morality and our consciousness of our own freedom, which is the source of all value, and that we can postulate the truth of the fundamental dogmas of Christianity, our own immortality and the existence of God, as practical presuppositions of our moral conduct but not as theoretical truths of metaphysics. In the *Critique of Judgment*, Kant argued that the unanimity of taste and the systematic

organization of both individual organisms and nature as a whole could be postulated, again not as metaphysical dogmas but rather as regulative ideals of our aesthetic and scientific pursuits; he then went on to argue that it is through these ideals that we can tie together the realms of nature and freedom, because aesthetic experience offers us a palpable image of our moral freedom, and a scientific conception of the world as a system of interrelated beings makes sense only as an image of the world as the sphere of our own moral efforts. In many of his last writings, from *Religion within the Limits of Reason Alone* (1793) to his final manuscripts, the *Opus postumum*, Kant refined and radicalized his view that our religious conceptions can be understood only as analogies for the nature of human reason itself.

The Enlightenment began by attempting to bring even God before the bench of human reason – at the turn of the eighteenth century, both Shaftesbury in Great Britain and Wolff in Germany rejected voluntarism, the theory that God makes eternal truths and moral laws by fiat, and argued instead that we ourselves must know what is right and wrong before we could even recognize supposedly divine commands as divine. Kant completed their argument, concluding that the human being 'creates the elements of knowledge of the world himself, a priori, from which he, as, at the same time, an inhabitant of the world, constructs a world-vision in the idea' (*Opus postumum*, 21: 31).

1   Life and works

Immanuel Kant was born on 22 April 1724 in Königsberg, the capital of East Prussia. He was the child of poor but devout followers of Pietism, a

Lutheran revival movement stressing love and good works, simplicity of worship, and individual access to God. Kant's promise was recognized by the Pietist minister Franz Albert Schultz, and he received a free education at the Pietist gymnasium. At sixteen, Kant entered the University of Königsberg, where he studied mathematics, physics, philosophy, theology, and classical Latin literature. His leading teacher was Martin Knutzen (1713–51), who introduced him to both Wolffian philosophy and Newtonian physics, and who inspired some of Kant's own later views and philosophical independence by his advocacy of physical influx against the pre-established harmony of LEIBNIZ and Wolff. Kant left university in 1746, just as the major works of the anti-Wolffian Pietist philosopher Christian August Crusius were appearing. Kant's upbringing would have made him receptive to Crusius, and thus he left university imbued with the Enlightenment aims of Wolffian philosophy but already familiar with technical criticisms of it, especially with Crusius' critique of Wolff's attempt to derive substantive conclusions from a single and merely formal first principle such as the logical principle of non-contradiction (see WOLFF, C.).

On leaving university, Kant completed his first work, *Thoughts on the True Estimation of Living Forces* (1746, published 1749), an unsuccessful attempt to mediate between Cartesian and Leibnizian theories of physical forces. Kant then worked as a tutor, serving in households near Königsberg for the next eight years. When he returned to the university in 1755, however, he had several works ready for publication. The first of these was *Universal Natural History and Theory of the Heavens*, a much more successful scientific work than his first in which Kant argued for the nebular hypothesis, or origin of the solar system out of a nebular mass by purely mechanical means. The book was scarcely known during Kant's lifetime, however, so the French astronomer Pierre Laplace (1749–1827) developed his version of the nebular hypothesis (published 1796) independently, and the theory became known as the Kant-Laplace hypothesis only later. In 1755, Kant also published two Latin works, his MA thesis *A brief presentation of some thoughts concerning fire*, and his first philosophical work, *A new elucidation of the first principles of metaphysical cognition*, which earned him the right to offer lectures at the university as a *Privatdozent* paid directly by his students. The following year Kant published *The employment in natural philosophy of metaphysics combined with geometry, of which sample I contains the physical monadology*, which made him eligible for a salaried professorship, although he was not to receive one until 1770. In these years, Kant also published four essays on earthquakes and winds.

Kant began lecturing in the autumn of 1755, and to earn a living lectured more than twenty hours a week. His topics included logic, metaphysics, ethics, and physics, and he subsequently added physical geography, anthropology (Germany's first lectures so entitled), pedagogy, natural right and even the theory of fortifications. Except for one small essay on optimism (1759), he did not publish again until 1762, when another burst of publications began. He then published, all in German: *The False Subtlety of the Four Syllogistic Figures* (1762); *The Only Possible Argument in support of a Demonstration of the Existence of God* and *Attempt to Introduce the Concept of Negative Magnitudes into Philosophy* (1763); *Observations on the Feeling of the Beautiful and Sublime* and *Inquiry concerning the Distinctness of the Principles of Natural Theology and Morality* (1764), the latter of which was his second-place entry in a competition won by Moses MENDELSSOHN; *Dreams of a Spirit-Seer, elucidated by Dreams of Metaphysics* (1766); and *Concerning the Ultimate Ground of the Differentiation of Directions in Space* (1768). These publications earned Kant widespread recognition in Germany. During this period, Kant was deeply struck by the work of Jean-Jacques ROUSSEAU, especially by his *Social Contract* and the paean to freedom in *Émile* (both 1762). By this time Kant was also acquainted with the philosophy of David HUME, whose two *Enquiries* and other essays, but not *A Treatise of Human Nature*, were published in German as early as 1755.

Having unsuccessfully applied for several chairs at home while declining offers elsewhere, Kant was finally appointed Professor of Logic and Metaphysics in Königsberg in 1770. This event occasioned his inaugural dissertation, and last Latin work, *On the form and principles of the sensible and intelligible world*. Following correspondence about this work with Johann Heinrich Lambert, Johann Georg Sulzer, and Mendelssohn, however, Kant fell into another decade-long silence, broken only by a few progress reports to his recent student Marcus Herz and a few minor essays. Yet during this 'silent decade', Kant was preparing for his enormous body of subsequent works. Beginning in 1781, with the first edition of the *Critique of Pure Reason*, Kant released a steady torrent of books. These include: *Prolegomena to Any Future Metaphysics that shall come forth as Scientific*, an attempted popularization of the first *Critique*, in 1783; two essays, 'Idea for a Universal History from a Cosmopolitan Point of View' and 'What is Enlightenment?' in 1784; *The Groundwork of the Metaphysics of Morals* and four other essays in 1785; *The Metaphysical Foundations of Natural Science*, essays on 'The Conjectural Beginnings of Human History' and 'What Does it mean to Orient Oneself in Thinking?' and two other pieces in 1786; a substantially revised second edition of the *Critique of Pure Reason* in 1787; in 1788, the *Critique of Practical Reason* and an essay on 'The Use of Teleological Principles in Philosophy'; the *Critique of the Power of Judgment* as well as an important polemic 'On a discovery according to which any new Critique of Pure Reason is rendered dispensable by an older one' in 1790; the political essay 'On the Common Saying: "That may be right in theory but does not work in practice"' and the controversial *Religion within the Limits of Reason Alone* in 1793; *Towards Perpetual Peace* in 1795; the *Metaphysics of Morals*, comprising the 'Doctrine of Right' and the 'Doctrine of Virtue', in 1797, as well as the essay 'On a putative Right to Lie from Love of Mankind'; and his last major works in 1798, a handbook on *Anthropology from a Pragmatic Point of View* and his defence of the intellectual freedom of the philosophical faculty from religious and legal censorship in the restrictive atmosphere of Prussia after Frederick the Great, *The Conflict of the Faculties*. (With Kant's approval, some of his other lecture courses were also published, including *Logic* in 1800 and *Physical Geography* and *Pedagogy* in 1804.) Kant retired from lecturing in 1797, at the age of seventy-three, and devoted his remaining years to a work which was to be entitled 'The Transition from the Metaphysical First Principles of Natural Science to Physics', but which was far from complete when Kant ceased working on it in 1803. (Selections from his drafts were first published in 1882–4, and they were first fully published as *Opus postumum* in 1936–8.) After a lifetime of hypochondria without any serious illness, Kant gradually lost his eyesight and strength and died 12 February 1804.

2 Kant's work to 1770

In his first work, *Living Forces*, Kant tried to mediate a dispute about the measurement of forces between DESCARTES and Leibniz by employing a distinction between 'living' or intrinsic forces and 'dead' or impressed ones to argue that Leibniz's measure was correct for the former and Descartes's for the latter. This distinction could not be maintained in a uniform mechanics, and the young Kant remained ignorant of the mathematically correct solution, which had been published by D'Alembert in 1743. Nevertheless, the work already showed Kant's lifelong preoccupation with the relation between scientific laws and metaphysical foundations. It also included the observation that the three-dimensionality of physical space is a product of actually existing forces, not the only geometry that is logically possible (1900: 10, 1: 24).

Kant's works of 1755 reveal more of his originality and his enduring themes. *Universal Natural History*, deriving the present state of the planets from postulated initial conditions by reiterated applications of the laws of Newtonian mechanics, manifests not only Kant's commitment to those laws, for which he was subsequently to seek philosophical foundations, but also his commitment to thoroughly naturalistic explanations in science, in which God can be the initial source of natural laws but never intervenes within the sequence of physical causes. *New Elucidation*, while not yet a methodological break from the rationalism of Leibniz, Wolff and Alexander Gottlieb BAUMGARTEN (1714–62) (whose textbooks on metaphysics, ethics and aesthetics Kant used for decades), breaks with them on several substantive issues. Kant begins by rejecting Wolff's supposition that the principle of non-contradiction is a single yet sufficient principle of truth, arguing instead that there must be separate first principles of positive and negative truths; following Crusius, Kant was always to remain suspicious of programmes to reduce all truth to a single principle. Kant then criticized previous proofs of the Principle of Sufficient Reason, although his own proof was also a failure. More importantly, he argued that the principle of sufficient reason does not entail the theory of pre-established harmony drawn from it by the Leibnizians: the need for a sufficient reason for any change in a substance proves the necessity rather than impossibility of real interaction among a plurality of substances. Transposed into an epistemological key, this argument was to become central in the first *Critique*. The work is also noteworthy for the first suggestion of Kant's critique of Descartes's ontological argument for the existence of God (see GOD, ARGUMENTS FOR THE EXISTENCE OF), and for a first treatment of the problem of free will as well. Here Kant defended against the indeterminism of Crusius the determinism of Leibniz (see DETERMINISM AND INDETERMINISM), although he was later to criticize this as the 'freedom of a turnspit' (5: 97). Kant's later theory of free will attempts to reconcile Crusius and Leibniz.

In the *Physical Monadology* (1756), Kant tries to reconcile the infinite divisibility of space in geometry with the need for simple, indivisible substances in metaphysics – the subsequent theme of the first *Critique*'s second Antinomy (see §8). Kant does not yet appeal to a metaphysical distinction between appearance and reality, but instead argues that because bodies in space are not ultimately composed of particles but of attractive and repulsive forces (1: 484), they may be physically indivisible even when space itself is still mathematically divisible.

Kant's works of the 1760s introduce some of the methodological as well as substantive assumptions of his mature philosophy. *The Only Possible Argument* details Kant's attack upon the ontological argument, the paradigmatic rationalistic argument because of its presupposition that an existence–statement can be derived from the analysis of a concept. Kant argues that 'existence is not a predicate or a determination of a thing' (2: 72), but rather the 'absolute positing of a thing' (2: 73); that is, the existence of its subject is *presupposed* by the assertion of any proposition, not inferred from the concepts employed in it. Kant also maintains that the other rationalist argument for theism, the argument from the contingency of the world to a necessary cause of it, as well as the empiricists' favourite, the argument from design, fail to prove the existence of a necessary being with all the attributes of God. However, Kant still holds that the existence of God can be proved as a condition of the *possibility* of any reality. Finally, Kant further develops his argument that scientific explanation cannot allow divine intervention in the sequence of events, and that God must be seen only as the original ground of the laws of nature.

Negative Magnitudes announces a fundamental methodological break from rationalism. Inspired by both Crusius and Hume, Kant argues that *real opposition* (as when two velocities in opposite directions or a pleasure and a pain cancel each other out) is fundamentally different from *logical contradiction* (as between a proposition and its negation); he then applies this to causation, arguing that the *real ground* of a state does not entail its existence logically, but is connected to it in an entirely different way. This precludes any proof of the principle of sufficient reason from merely logical considerations alone (2: 202).

The *Inquiry into the Distinctness of the Principles of Natural Theology and Ethics* continues Kant's attack upon rationalism. The question for this essay was whether metaphysics could use the same method as mathematics, which Kant firmly denied: mathematics, he argues, can prove its theorems by constructing its objects from their very definitions, but metaphysics can only use analysis to tease out the definitions of its objects from given concepts, and cannot construct the objects themselves (2: 276). The claim that the method of philosophy is analysis may sound like rationalism; however, Kant insists that in both metaphysics and ethics philosophy needs *material* as well as *formal* first principles, again precluding any purely logical derivation of philosophical theses. Kant does not yet have a clear account of material first principles – he is sympathetic to Crusius's account of indemonstrable cognitions and to the suggestion of the moral sense theorists Shaftesbury and HUTCHESON that the first principles of ethics arise from *feeling*, but not

satisfied with either. Without yet naming it, Kant also introduces his distinction between hypothetical and categorical imperatives (2: 298).

Still in 1764, however, the book *Observations on the Feeling of the Beautiful and Sublime* already announces Kant's departure from moral sense theory and introduces the most fundamental theme of Kant's ethics. Virtue cannot depend merely on benevolent inclination, but only on general principles, which in turn express 'a feeling that lives in every human breast and extends itself much further than over the particular grounds of compassion and complaisance ... the *feeling of the beauty and dignity of human nature*' (2: 217). In notes in his own copy of this work, Kant went even further, and first clearly stated his enduring belief that 'freedom properly understood (moral, not metaphysical) is the supreme principle of all virtue as well as of all happiness' (20: 31).

In *Dreams of a Spirit-Seer*, Kant ridicules traditional metaphysics by comparing it to the fantasies of the Swedish theosophist Emmanuel Swedenborg; Kant argues instead that metaphysical concepts cannot be used without empirical verification, and that therefore metaphysics can at most be 'a science of the *boundaries of human reason*' (2: 368). The work also contains further thoughts on morality, suggesting that the two forces of egoism and altruism define the structure of the moral world in much the way that the forces of repulsion and attraction define that of the physical world (2: 334). But Kant does not yet argue that postulates of practical reason may be a valid alternative to the delusions of metaphysics.

Finally, the brief essay on *Directions in Space* argues that incongruent counterparts, such as right- and left-handed gloves, which have identical descriptions but cannot occupy the same space, prove that the qualities of objects are not determined by concepts alone but also by their relation to absolute space. Kant did not yet raise metaphysical questions about the nature of absolute space or epistemological questions about how we could know it, but this essay can be seen as introducing the distinction between intuitions and concepts which was to be a cornerstone of Kant's subsequent thought (see §5).

3   *The* Inaugural Dissertation *of 1770 and the problem of metaphysics*

Kant's *Inaugural Dissertation* of 1770 consolidated many of the gains he had made during the 1760s and introduced a fundamentally new theory about the metaphysics and epistemology of space and time which was to remain a constant in his subsequent thought, but also left open crucial questions about the source of our most fundamental concepts.

Although Kant hoped to proceed quickly to his projects in the philosophy of science and in moral and political theory, it was to take him all of the next decade to answer these preliminary questions.

Taking up where *Directions in Space* left off, Kant begins the dissertation with the distinction between intuitions (singular and immediate representations of objects) and concepts (general and abstract representations of them) as distinct but equally important elements in the '*two-fold genesis* of the concept [of a world] out of the nature of the mind'. The intellect (Kant does not yet divide this into understanding and reason) provides abstract concepts, under which instances are subordinated; the 'sensitive faculty of cognition' provides 'distinct intuition[s]' which represent concepts 'in the concrete' and within which different parts may be coordinated (1900: 2: 387). Kant goes on to claim that 'whatever in cognition is sensitive is dependent upon the special character of the subject', that is, the knower, so that sensation, through intuitions, represents things '*as they appear*' (*phenomena*), while the intellect, through concepts, represents things '*as they are*' (*noumena*) (2: 392). Kant then presents the 'principles of the form of the sensible world': time and space are the forms of the intuition of all objects (time is the form for all representation of objects, inner or outer, while space is the form for the representation of all outer objects) which do not arise from but are presupposed by all particular perceptions; they are singular rather than general, that is, particular times or spaces are parts of a single whole rather than instances of a general kind; and they must each be 'the subjective condition which is necessary, in virtue of the nature of the human mind, for the co-ordinating of all things in accordance with a fixed law', or a '*pure intuition*' rather than '*something objective and real*' (2: 398–400, 402–4). Only thus can we explain our knowledge of both these general claims about space and time as well as particular claims about their structure, such as the theorems of geometry (2: 404). In other words, we can explain the certainty of knowledge about space and time only by supposing that it is knowledge of the structure of our own minds, and thus of how objects appear to us, rather than knowledge about how things are in themselves. This necessarily subjective origin and significance of certainty, which Kant was later to name 'transcendental idealism', is the foundation for the active role of the human mind in knowledge of the world.

Kant has little to say about the source of intellectual concepts, but continues to believe that they give us knowledge of how things are independently of the structure of our own minds. His main claim, still Leibnizian, is that in order to conceive of things as genuinely distinct substances, yet as collectively interacting in a single world, we must conceive of them as contingent beings all depending upon a single necessary being (2: 407–8). Kant then argues that metaphysical error arises when the principles of sensitive and intellectual cognition are confused, but more particularly when 'the principles which are native to sensitive cognition transgress their limits, and affect what belongs to the intellect' (2: 411) – the opposite of what he will argue later when he claims that metaphysical illusion arises from thinking that human reason can reach beyond the limits of the senses (see §8). Finally, Kant introduces as mere 'principles of convenience' the principles of universal causation and of the conservation of substance as well as a more general 'canon' of rationality, that '*principles are not to be multiplied beyond what is absolutely necessary*' (30, 2: 418). A better account of these principles will occupy much of Kant's later work (see §7).

Early readers of Kant's dissertation objected to the merely subjective significance of space and especially time, but Kant was never to surrender this theory. What came to bother him instead was his inadequate treatment of metaphysical concepts such as 'possibility, existence, necessity, substance, cause, etc.' (2: 395). In a famous letter of 21 February 1772 to Marcus Herz (10: 129–35), Kant claimed that the 'whole secret' of metaphysics is to explain how intellectual concepts which neither literally produce their objects (as God's concepts might) nor are merely produced by them (as empirical concepts are) nevertheless necessarily apply to them. But Kant did not yet know how to answer this question.

His first progress on this issue is found in fragments from 1774–5 (Reflections 4674–84, 17: 643–73). Two key ideas are found here. First, Kant finally formulates the problem of metaphysics as that of 'synthetic' rather than 'analytic' propositions: how can we know the truth of propositions in which the predicates clearly go beyond anything contained in their subject-concepts but yet enjoy the same universality and necessity as propositions which are mere tautologies, whose predicates are contained in their subject concepts (17: 643–4, 653–5)? Second, Kant here first states that the answer to this question lies in recognizing that certain fundamental concepts, not just the intuitions of space and time, are 'conditions of the concrete representation [of objects] in the subject' (17: 644) or of the unity of '*experience* in general' (17: 658). Kant's idea is that in order to ground any determinate ordering of either subjective or objective states in temporal succession, we must use the concepts of substance, causation, and interaction, and that these must therefore be categories which originate in the understanding just as the pure forms of space and time originate in the sensibility.

4   The project of the Critique of Pure Reason

In spite of this progress in 1775, six more years passed before the *Critique of Pure Reason* finally appeared in 1781. In an unmistakeable reference to Locke's *Essay concerning Human Understanding* (see LOCKE, J.), Kant began the work with the promise to submit reason to a critique in order to obtain a 'decision about the possibility or impossibility of metaphysics in general and the determination of its sources, its scope and its boundaries' (A xii). The 'chief question' would be 'what and how much can understanding and reason know apart from all *experience*?' (A xvii). Answering this question would require discovering the fundamental principles that human understanding contributes to human experience and exposing the metaphysical illusions that arise when human reason tries to extend those principles beyond the limits of human experience.

But Kant's project was even more ambitious than that, as he was to make clear in the revised edition of the *Critique* six years later. There, in addition to more explicitly describing his strategy for explaining the certainty of the first principles of human knowledge as one of supposing that 'objects must conform to our knowledge' rather than vice versa (B xvi), Kant described his whole project in broader terms: 'I therefore had to deny *knowledge* in order to make room for *faith*' (B xxx). Kant did not mean to return to the sceptical fideism of earlier thinkers such as Pierre BAYLE, who simply substituted religious belief for theoretical ignorance. Instead, Kant argues first that the human mind supplies necessary principles of sensibility and understanding, or perception and conception; next, that if human reason tries to extend the fundamental concepts and principles of thought beyond the limits of perception for purposes of theoretical knowledge, it yields only illusion; but finally that there is another use of reason, a practical use in which it constructs universal laws and ideals of human conduct and postulates the fulfilment of the conditions necessary to make such conduct rational, including the freedom of the will, the existence of God, and the immortality of the soul. This use of reason does not challenge the limits of theoretical reason but is legitimate and necessary in its own right.

In the Introduction, Kant defines his first task as that of explaining the possibility of synthetic a priori judgments. This notion is grounded in two distinctions. First, there is a logical distinction between analytic and synthetic propositions: in analytic propositions, the predicate-concept is implicitly or explicitly contained in the subject-concept (for example, 'A bachelor is unmarried' or 'An unmarried male is male'), so the proposition conveys no new information and is true by identity alone; in synthetic propositions, the content of the predicate is clearly not contained in the subject-concept (for example, 'Bachelors are unhappy') (A 6–7/B 10–11), so the proposition conveys new information and cannot be true by identity alone. Second, there is an epistemological distinction between propositions which are a posteriori, or can be known to be true only on the basis of antecedent experience and observation, and those which are a priori, or known to be true independently of experience, or at least any particular experience (A 1–2/B 1–3). Kant maintains that anything which is known to be universally and necessarily true must be known a priori, because, following Hume, he assumes that experience only tells us how what has actually been observed is, not how everything must be (A 1–2/B 3–4). Combining these two distinctions yields four possible kinds of judgments. Two of these obviously obtain: analytic a priori judgments, in which we know a proposition to be true by analysis of its subject-concept and without observation; and synthetic a posteriori judgments, in which we know factual statements going beyond subject-concepts to be true through observation. Equally clearly, a third possibility is excluded: there are no analytic a posteriori judgments, for we need not go to experience to discover what we can know from analysis alone. What is controversial is whether there are synthetic a priori judgments, propositions that are universally and necessarily true, and thus must go beyond experience, but which cannot be reached by the mere analysis of concepts. Both rationalists and empiricists had denied such a possibility, but for Kant only it could ground an informative science of metaphysics at all.

Kant's notion of synthetic a priori judgment raises various problems. Critics have long complained that Kant provides no unequivocal criterion for deciding when a predicate is contained in a subject, and twentieth-century philosophers such as W.V. QUINE argued that there are no analytic truths because not even definitions can be held entirely immune from revision in the face of empirical facts. Lewis White Beck showed, however, that this did not affect Kant's project, for Kant himself, in a polemic with the Wolffian Johann August Eberhard, argued that analysis always presupposes synthesis, and that the adoption of any definition itself has to be justified, either by construction or observation; so even conceding that all judgments are ultimately synthetic, Kant's question remains whether any of these are synthetic a priori.

Another issue is just what synthetic a priori judgments Kant intended to justify. In the 'Prolegomena' and the 'Introduction' to the second edition of the *Critique*, Kant suggests that it is obvious that synthetic a priori judgments exist in what he calls 'pure mathematics' and 'pure physics', and that his project is to show that what explains these also explains other such propositions, in metaphysics. Elsewhere, however, Kant suggests that metaphysics must show that there are any synthetic a priori judgments, even in mathematics and physics. While much of the content of the *Critique* suggests that Kant's considered view must be the latter, he is far from clear about this.

5 Space, time and transcendental idealism

The first part of the *Critique*, the 'Transcendental Aesthetic', has two objectives: to show that we have synthetic a priori knowledge of the spatial and temporal forms of outer and inner experience, grounded in our own pure intuitions of space and time; and to argue that transcendental idealism, the theory that spatiality and temporality are only forms in which objects appear to us and not properties of objects as they are in themselves, is the necessary condition for this a priori knowledge of space and time (see SPACE; TIME).

Much of the section refines arguments from the inaugural dissertation of 1770. First, in what the second edition labels the 'Metaphysical Exposition', Kant argues that space and time are both *pure forms of intuition* and *pure intuitions*. They are pure *forms* of intuition because they must precede and structure all experience of individual outer objects and inner states; Kant tries to prove this by arguing that our conceptions of space and time cannot be derived from experience of objects, because any such experience presupposes the individuation of objects in space and/or time, and that although we can represent space or time as devoid of objects, we cannot represent any objects without representing space and/or time (A 23–4/B 38–9; A 30–1/B 46). They are pure *intuitions* because they represent single individuals rather than classes of things; Kant tries to prove this by arguing that particular spaces and times are always represented by introducing boundaries into a single, unlimited space or time, rather than the latter being composed out of the former as parts, and that space and time do not have an indefinite number of instances, like general concepts, but an infinite number of possible parts (A 24/B 39–40; A 31–2/B 47–8).

Next, in the 'Transcendental Exposition', Kant argues that we must have an a priori intuition of space because 'geometry is a science which determines the properties of space synthetically and yet a priori' (B 40). That is, the propositions of geometry describe objects in space, go beyond the mere concepts of any of the objects involved – thus geometric theorems cannot be proved without

actually constructing the figures – and yet are known a priori. (Kant offers an analogous but less plausible argument about time, where the propositions he adduces seem analytic (B 48).) Both our a priori knowledge about space and time in general and our synthetic a priori knowledge of geometrical propositions in particular can be explained only by supposing that space and time are of subjective origin, and thus knowable independently of the experience of particular objects.

Finally, Kant holds that these results prove transcendental idealism, or that space and time represent properties of things as they appear to us but not properties or relations of things as they are in themselves, let alone real entities like Newtonian absolute space; thus his position of 1768 is now revised to mean that space is epistemologically but not ontologically absolute (A 26/B 42; A 32–3/B 49–50; A 39–40/B 56–7). Kant's argument is that 'determinations' which belong to things independently of us 'cannot be intuited prior to the things to which they belong', and so could not be intuited a priori, while space and time and their properties *are* intuited a priori. Since they therefore cannot be properties of things in themselves, there is no alternative but that space and time are merely the forms in which objects appear to us.

Much in Kant's theory has been questioned by later philosophy of mathematics. Kant's claim that geometrical theorems are synthetic because they can only be proven by construction has been rendered doubtful by more complete axiomatizations of mathematics than Kant knew, and his claim that such propositions describe objects in physical space yet are known a priori has been questioned on the basis of the distinction between purely formal systems and their physical realization.

Philosophical debate, however, has centred on Kant's inference of transcendental idealism from his philosophy of mathematics. One issue is the very meaning of Kant's distinction between appearances and things in themselves. Gerold Prauss and Henry Allison have ascribed to Kant a distinction between two kinds of *concepts* of objects, one including reference to the necessary conditions for the perception of those objects and the other merely leaving them out, with no ontological consequences. Another view holds that Kant does not merely assert that the concepts of things in themselves lack reference to spatial and temporal properties, but actually denies that things in themselves are spatial and temporal, and therefore maintains that spatial and temporal properties are properties only of our own representations of things. Kant makes statements that can support each of these interpretations; but proponents of the second view, including the present author, have argued that it is entailed by both Kant's argument for and his use of his distinction, the latter especially in his theory of free will (see §8).

The debate about Kant's argument for transcendental idealism, already begun in the nineteenth century, concerns whether Kant has omitted a 'neglected alternative' in assuming that space and time must be *either* properties of things as they are in themselves or of representations, but not both, namely that we might have a priori knowledge of space and time because we have an a priori subjective representation of them while they are also objective properties of things. Some argue that there is no neglected alternative, because although the *concepts* of appearances and things in themselves are necessarily different, Kant postulates only one set of *objects*. This author has argued that the 'neglected alternative' is a genuine possibility that Kant intends to exclude by arguing from his premise that propositions about space and time are *necessarily* true: if those propositions were true *both* of our own representations and of their ontologically distinct objects, they might be necessarily true of the former but only contingently true of the latter, and thus not necessarily true throughout their domain (A 47–8/ B 65–6). In this case, however, Kant's transcendental idealism depends upon a dubious claim about necessary truth.

6 Pure concepts of the understanding

The 'Transcendental Analytic' of the *Critique* breaks new ground, arguing that the most fundamental categories of thought as well as the forms of perception are themselves human products which are necessary conditions of the possibility of experience. Like the 'Transcendental Aesthetic', its first section, the 'Analytic of Concepts', is also divided into a 'metaphysical' and a 'transcendental deduction' (B 159).

In the metaphysical deduction Kant intends to provide a principle to identify the most fundamental concepts of thought, the categories of the understanding, and then to show that our knowledge of any object always involves these categories. The key to his argument is the claim that knowledge is always expressed in a *judgment* (A 68–9/B 93–4); he then argues that there are certain characteristic forms or 'logical functions' of judgment, and that in order for our judgments to be about objects, these logical functions of judgments must also provide the basic concepts for conceiving of objects. Thus Kant first produces a table of the logical functions of judgment, based on the premise that every judgment has a *quantity*, *quality*, *relation* and *modality*, and then produces a table of categories, under the same four headings, showing how objects of such

judgments must be conceived. Thus, judgments may be universal, particular, or singular, and then their objects must be unities, pluralities, or totalities; judgments may be affirmative, negative, or infinite, and objects manifest either reality, negation, or limitation; judgments may relate a predicate to a subject (categorical judgment), or else relate one predicate-subject judgment to another as antecedent and consequent (hypothetical judgment) or as alternatives (disjunctive judgment), and objects may correspondingly manifest the relations of inherence and subsistence, causality and dependence, or community or reciprocity; finally, judgments may be problematic, assertoric, or apodeictic, thus their objects either possible or impossible, existent or non-existent, or necessary or contingent (A 70/B 95; A 80/B 106).

Kant's scheme is intuitively plausible, and he makes use of it throughout his works. But philosophers as diverse as HEGEL and Quine have questioned its coherence and necessity. What is troubling for Kant's own project, however, is that he does not show why we must use all the logical functions of judgment, hence why we must use all the categories. In particular, he does not show why we must make not only categorical but also hypothetical and disjunctive judgments. Without such a premise, Kant's arguments for causation, against Hume, and for interaction, against Leibniz, are not advanced. It is unclear whether Kant recognized this defect in the argument of the metaphysical deduction. But he addressed precisely this problem in the subsequent chapter on the 'System of all Principles of Pure Understanding', which does attempt to demonstrate the necessity of the use of each of the categories. This chapter will be discussed in the following section

Kant's aim and his strategy in the transcendental deduction remain debatable, despite his complete revision of this section in the second edition of the *Critique*. Some view the transcendental deduction as a 'regressive argument' aimed at empiricism, meant to show only that *if* we make judgments about objects then we must use a priori concepts. But if Kant already established this in the metaphysical deduction, the transcendental deduction becomes redundant. It seems more natural to see the latter as intended to fix the *scope* of our use of the categories by showing that we can have *no* experience which is immune from conceptualization under them, thus that the categories enjoy universal objective validity. Because these categories originate in the logical structure of our own thought, Kant holds, we must conceive of ourselves as the autonomous lawgivers for all of nature (A 127–8B 164).

There are many differences between the two versions of the transcendental deduction, but both employ the fundamental idea that we cannot have some form of *self*-consciousness, or 'transcendental apperception', without also having consciousness of *objects*, which in turn requires the application of the categories; then, since Kant holds that we can have no experience at all without being able to be conscious that we have it, he can argue that we can have no experience to which we cannot apply the categories. The success of this strategy is unclear. The first-edition deduction begins with a debatable analysis of the necessary conditions for knowledge of an object, which slides from the conditional necessity that we must use rules if we are to have knowledge of objects to an absolute necessity that we must have knowledge of objects, and then introduces transcendental apperception as the 'transcendental ground' of the latter necessity (A 106). In the second edition, Kant begins directly with the claim that self-consciousness of our experience is always possible, which has not met with much resistance, but then makes the inference to the necessity of knowledge of objects conceived of through the categories by equating transcendental apperception with a notion of 'objective apperception' that is equivalent to judgment about objects (B 139–40). This makes the connection between self-consciousness and the categorial judgment of objects true by definition, and undermines Kant's claim to provide a synthetic rather than analytic proof of the objective validity of the categories.

In spite of these problems, the idea that self-consciousness depends upon knowledge of objects and thus on the use of the categories to conceive of objects has remained attractive; and some of the most interesting recent work on Kant has been reconstructions of the transcendental deduction, such as those by Peter Strawson, Jonathan Bennett and Dieter Henrich. Others have concluded that Kant only establishes a convincing connection between self-consciousness and categorial thought of objects once he shows that making judgments about objects, using the categories, is a necessary condition for making judgments about the *temporal* order of our experience. This is Kant's project in the next section of the *Critique*.

7 The principles of judgment and the foundations of science

Kant proceeds from the categories to the foundations of natural science in several steps. First, he argues that the categories, which thus far have merely logical content, must be made 'homogeneous' with experience, or be recast in forms we can actually experience. Since time, as the form of both outer and inner sense, is the most general feature of our sensible experience, Kant argues that

the categories must be made homogeneous with experience by being associated with certain determinate temporal relations or 'schemata' (A 138–9/B 177–8). For example, the pure category of ground and consequence, thus far understood only abstractly as the relation of the states of objects that makes them fit to be objects of hypothetical ('if-then') judgments, is associated with the schema of rule-governed temporal succession, something closer to what we can actually experience. Focused as he is on the universality of time, Kant seems to de-emphasize spatiality unduly in the 'Schematism': for example, it would seem more natural to say that the schema of causality is the rule-governed temporal succession of states of objects within an appropriate degree of spatial contiguity.

Next, in the 'System of all Principles of Pure Understanding', Kant argues for the necessity of certain fundamental principles of all natural laws. Following the division of the categories, this chapter is divided into four parts. In the first, the 'Axioms of Intuition', Kant argues that 'All intuitions are extensive magnitudes' (B 202), and thus that all objects of experience can be represented as wholes consisting of homogeneous parts, and thus can be represented mathematically as sums of such units. In the second, the 'Anticipations of Perception', Kant proves that 'In all appearances, the real that is an object of sensation has intensive magnitude, that is, a degree' (B 207). Here he argues that sensations can be assigned a numerical measure that does not represent a sum of separable parts, but rather a position on a scale of intensity, and then infers that because our sensations manifest varying degrees of intensity we must also conceive of the qualities of objects that they represent as manifesting a reality that varies in degree. The first of these two 'mathematical' principles (A 162/B 201) does not add to results already established in the Transcendental Aesthetic, however, and the second depends upon an empirical assumption.

In the next section, the 'Analogies of Experience', dealing with the first of two kinds of 'dynamical' principles, Kant offers some of the most compelling and important arguments in the *Critique*. In the First Analogy, Kant argues that we can determine that there has been a change in the objects of our perception, not merely a change in our perceptions themselves, only by conceiving of what we perceive as successive states of enduring substances (see SUBSTANCE). Because we can never perceive the origination or cessation of substances themselves, but only changes in their states, Kant argues, the sum-total of substances in nature is permanent (B 224). In the Second Analogy, Kant argues for a further condition for making judgments about change in objects: because even when we undergo a sequence of perceptions, there is nothing in their immediate sensory content to tell us that there is an objective change, let alone what particular sequence of change there is, we can only distinguish a '*subjective sequence* of apprehension from the *objective sequence* of appearances' (A 193/B 238) by judging that a particular sequence of objective states of affairs, *a fortiori* the sequence of our perceptions of those states, has been determined in accordance with a rule that states of the second type can only follow states of the first type – precisely what we mean by a causal law. Finally, the Third Analogy argues that because we always perceive states of objects successively, we cannot immediately perceive states of two or more objects to be simultaneous, and can therefore only judge that two such states simultaneously exist in different regions of space if they are governed by laws of interaction dictating that neither state can exist without the other (A 213/B 260).

Kant's arguments have been assailed on the basis of relativity theory and quantum mechanics. But since they are epistemological arguments that our ability to make temporal judgments about the succession or simultaneity of states of affairs depends upon our judgments about substance, causation and interaction, it is not clear that they are open to objection from this quarter. If relativity tells us that the succession or simultaneity of states of affairs may depend upon the choice of inertial frame, then Kant's theory is not refuted, but merely predicts that in that case our own judgments about temporal sequence must also vary. If quantum mechanics tells us that causal laws are merely probabilistic, then Kant's theory is again not refuted but just predicts that in that case our temporal judgments cannot be entirely determinate.

In the last section of the 'Principles', Kant assigns empirical criteria to the modal concepts of possibility, actuality and necessity. The main interest of this section lies in the 'Refutation of Idealism' which Kant inserted into it in the second edition. Here Kant argues that temporal judgments about one's own states require reference to objects which endure in a way that mental representations themselves do not, and therefore that consciousness of oneself also implies consciousness of objects external to oneself (B 275–6; also B xxxix–xli). There has been controversy not only about the precise steps of the proof, but also about whether it is supposed to prove that we have knowledge of the existence of things ontologically distinct from our own representations, which seems to undercut Kant's transcendental idealism. However, the argument of 1787 was actually just the first of many drafts Kant wrote (Reflections 6311–16, 18: 606–23), and these suggest that he did mean to prove that

we know of the existence of objects ontologically distinct from ourselves and our states, although we cannot attribute to them as they are in themselves the very spatiality by means of which we represent this ontological distinctness.

Finally, in the *Metaphysical Foundations of Natural Science*, published between the two editions of the *Critique* (1786), Kant carried his a priori investigation of the laws of nature one step further by introducing not only the empirical notion of change itself but also the further empirical concept of matter as the movable in space (1900: 4: 480). With this one empirical addition, he claims, he can deduce the laws of phoronomy, the vectorial composition of motions in space; of dynamics, the attractive and repulsive forces by which space is actually filled; of mechanics, the communication of moving forces; and of phenomenology, which in Kant's sense – derived from J.H. Lambert, and very different from its later senses in Hegel or HUSSERL – means the laws for distinguishing apparent from real motions. This work is not an essay in empirical physics but rather an exploration of the conceptual framework into which the empirical results of physics must be fitted.

8 The illusions of theoretical reason

In the 'Transcendental Dialectic', Kant argues that the doctrines of traditional metaphysics are illusions arising from the attempt to use the categories of understanding to gain information about objects that are inaccessible to our forms of intuition. What makes such illusions inevitable is the tendency of human reason to seek the unconditioned, that is, to carry a chain of ideas to its assumed completion even when that lies beyond the bounds of sense. For example, understanding may tell us that wholes consist of parts, and sensibility may allow us to find a smaller part for any given whole; but only reason suggests that decomposition into parts must come to an end in something absolutely simple, something we could never perceive by sense. In its practical use, reason may produce ideas of the unconditioned, such as the idea of the universal acceptability of maxims of action, which do not tell us anything misleading about the world because they do not tell us anything about how the world is at all, only how it ought to be; but in its theoretical use reason appears to tell us things about the world that cannot be confirmed by our senses or are even incompatible with the forms of our perception.

This diagnosis of metaphysical error makes good sense of Kant's procedure in the 'Antinomy of Pure Reason', where he presents a series of conflicts between the form and limits of sensibility as structured by the understanding, on the one hand,

and the pretensions of unconditioned reason, on the other. In early sketches of the *Dialectic* (Reflections 4756–60, 1775–7, 17: 698–713) Kant's diagnoses of all the illusions of traditional metaphysics took this form. In the *Critique*, however, Kant singled out some metaphysical beliefs about the self and about God for separate treatment in the 'Paralogisms of Pure Reason' and 'Ideal of Pure Reason'. These sections offer powerful criticisms of traditional metaphysical doctrines, but require a more complex explanation of metaphysical illusion than the single idea of reason's search for the unconditioned.

In the 'Paralogisms', Kant diagnoses the doctrines of 'rational psychology' that the soul is a *substance* which is *simple* and therefore incorruptible, *numerically identical* throughout the experience of any person, and necessarily *distinct* from any external object (this is how he reformulates the Fourth Paralogism in the second edition (B 409)), as a tissue of ungrounded assertions mistaking the logical properties of the *representation* 'I' or the *concept* of the self for the properties of whatever it is in us that actually thinks (A 355/B 409). Kant's criticism of the traditional metaphysics of the soul is convincing, but does not depend on reason's postulation of the unconditioned; instead, Kant's demonstration that these doctrines arise from confusion between properties of a representation and what is represented showed that they were not inevitable illusions by destroying their credibility once and for all.

The four metaphysical disputes that Kant presents in the 'Antinomy of Pure Reason' are often read as straightforward conflicts between reason and sensibility; but Kant characterizes them as disputes engendered by pure reason itself, so a more complex reading is required. In fact, both sides in each dispute – what Kant calls the 'thesis' and 'antithesis' – reflect different forms of reason's demand for something unconditioned, and what conflicts with the limits of sensibility is the assumption that these demands give rise to a genuine dispute at all. Kant again uses the contrast between 'mathematical' and 'dynamical' to divide the four disputes into two groups, and resolves the disputes in two different ways.

In the first antinomy the dispute is between the thesis that the world has a beginning in time and a limit in space and the antithesis that it is infinite in temporal duration and spatial extension (A 426–7/B 454–5). In the second antinomy, the dispute is between the thesis that substances in the world are ultimately composed of simple parts and the antithesis that nothing simple is ever to be found in the world, thus that everything is infinitely divisible (A 434–5/B 462–3). In each case, thesis and antithesis reflect reason's search for the

unconditioned, but in two different forms: in the thesis, reason postulates an ultimate *termination* of a series, and in the antithesis, an unconditional *extension* of the series. In these 'mathematical antinomies', however, Kant argues that *neither* side is true, because reason is attempting to apply its demand for something unconditioned to space and time, which are always *indefinite* in extent because they are finite yet always extendible products of our own cognitive activity (A 504–5/B 532–3).

In the two 'dynamical antinomies' Kant's solution is different. In the third antinomy, the thesis is that 'causality in accordance with laws of nature' is not the only kind of causality, but there must also be a 'causality of freedom' underlying the whole series of natural causes and effects, while the antithesis is that everything in nature takes place in accord with deterministic laws alone (A 444–5/B 462–3). In the fourth antinomy, the thesis is that there must be a necessary being as the cause of the whole sequence of contingent beings, either as its first member or underlying it, while the antithesis is that no such being exists inside or outside the world (A 452–3/B 480–1). Again, the theses result from reason's desire for closure and the antitheses result from reason's desire for infinite extension. But now the theses do not necessarily refer solely to spatio-temporal entities, so the claims that there must be a non-natural causality of freedom and a necessary being can apply to things in themselves while the claims that there are only contingent existents linked by laws of nature apply to appearances. In this case both thesis and antithesis may be true (A 531/B 559). This result is crucial to Kant, because it means that although theoretical reason cannot prove that either freedom or God exist, neither can it disprove them, and room is left for the existence of freedom and God to gain credibility in some other way.

The last main part of the 'Dialectic' is Kant's critique of rational theology. Here Kant reiterates his earlier critique of the ontological argument as well as his claim that the arguments for the existence of God from contingency and from design – the 'cosmological' and 'physico-theological' proofs – can only get from their ideas of a first cause or architect to the idea of a *perfect* being by the supposition of the ontological argument, and thus fall along with that. But he now precedes this argument with a critique of the argument for God as the ground of all possibility that he had earlier accepted: the very idea that there is an *ens realissimum*, an individual being containing in itself the ground of 'the sum-total of all possibility' (A 573/B 602), is another of the natural but illusory ideas of reason.

Kant does not, however, conclude the first *Critique* with an entirely negative assessment of pure reason. In an appendix to the 'Transcendental Dialectic', he argues that even though reason in its theoretical use cannot yield metaphysical insight, it does supply us with indispensable 'regulative' principles, of both the maximal simplicity of natural laws and the maximal variety of natural forms, for the conduct of empirical research; and in the 'Canon of Pure Reason', he argues that practical reason supplies an ideal of the highest good, the union of virtue and happiness and ultimately the union of freedom and nature, which is indispensable for moral conduct, not as its direct object but as a necessary condition of its rationality – which in turn gives ground for the practical postulation if not theoretical proof of the existence of God. Kant expands on both of these ideas in subsequent works (see §11 and §13).

9 The value of autonomy and the foundations of ethics

In his theoretical philosophy, Kant argued that we can be certain of the principles that arise from the combination of the forms of our sensibility and understanding, as products of our own intellectual autonomy; but he also argued that any attempt to see human reason as an autonomous source of metaphysical insight valid beyond the bounds of human sensibility leads to illusion. But in his practical philosophy, Kant argues that human reason is an autonomous source of principles of conduct, immune from the blandishments of sensual inclination in both its determinations of value and its decisions to act, and indeed that human autonomy is the highest value and the limiting condition of all other values.

Traditionally, Kant has been seen as an ethical formalist, according to whom all judgments on the values of ends must be subordinated to the obligatory universality of a moral law derived from the very concept of rationality itself. This interpretation has drawn support from Kant's own characterization of his 'paradoxical' method in the *Critique of Practical Reason*, where he holds that the moral law must be derived prior to any determination of good or evil, rather than vice versa (1900: 5: 62–3). But this passage does not do justice to the larger argument of Kant's practical philosophy, which is that rationality itself is so valuable precisely because it is the means to freedom or autonomy. Kant expressed this in his classroom lectures on ethics, when he said that 'the inherent value of the world, the *summum bonum*, is freedom in accordance with a will which is not necessitated to action' (27: 1482), and even more clearly in lectures on natural right given in the autumn of 1784, the very time he was writing the *Groundwork of the Metaphysics of Morals*, where he said that 'If only rational beings can be ends in themselves, that is not because they have reason, but because they have freedom. Reason is merely a means' (27: 1321). Kant makes the same point in the *Groundwork* when he says that the incomparable dignity of human beings derives from the fact that they are 'free with regard to all laws of nature, obeying only those laws which' they make themselves (4: 435).

The strategy of the *Groundwork* is by no means obvious, and the real character of Kant's view emerges only gradually. In Section I, Kant tries to derive the fundamental principle of morality from an analysis of 'ordinary rational knowledge of morality.' The key steps in his analysis are: virtue lies in the good will of an agent rather than any natural inclination or any particular end to be achieved; good will is manifested in the performance of an action for the sake of fulfilling duty rather than for any other end; and what duty requires is the performance of an action not for the sake of its consequences but because of its conformity to law as such; thus the maxim, or subjective principle, of virtuous action can only be that 'I ought never to act except in such a way *that I can also will that my maxim should become a universal law*' (4: 402). In Section II, Kant apparently tries to reach the same conclusion from more philosophical considerations: by arguing on the one hand that a moral or practical law must be a categorical rather than hypothetical imperative, that is, one commanding unconditionally rather than depending upon the adoption of some antecedent and optional end, and on the other hand that happiness is too indeterminate an end to give rise to such an imperative, Kant concludes that a categorical imperative can contain 'only the necessity that our maxim should conform to this law', thus that 'there remains nothing to which the maxim has to conform except the universality of a law as such' (4: 421). This version of the categorical imperative is known as the Formula of Universal Law.

Kant then furnishes further formulations of the categorical imperative, especially the Formula of Humanity as an End in Itself – '*Act in such a way that you always treat humanity, whether in your own person or in the person of any other, never simply as a means, but always at the same time as an end*' (4: 429), which at the very least requires the possibility of rational consent to your action from any agent affected by it – and the formula of the kingdom of ends, the requirement that any proposed course of action be compatible with 'a whole of all ends in systematic conjunction (a whole both of rational beings as ends in themselves and also of the personal ends which each may set before himself' (4: 433). The usual interpretation is that these two formulations are supposed to follow from the Formula of Universal Law. However, several factors suggest that Kant did not mean the derivation of that formula from either common sense or 'popular moral philosophy' to be self-sufficient, and it is only with the introduction of the notion that humanity is an end in itself because of its potential for freedom, that the real 'ground of a possible categorical imperative' is discovered (4: 428). If so, then this is Kant's theory: the ultimate source of value is human freedom as an end in itself, manifested in interpersonal contexts in the possibility of freely given consent to the actions of others; conformity to the requirement of universal law is the way to ensure that this value is preserved and fostered; and the ideal outcome of the observation of such a law would be a kingdom of ends as a system of freedom, in which all agents freely pursue their freely chosen ends to the extent compatible with a like freedom for all.

10 Duties of right and duties of virtue

In the *Groundwork*, Kant's principle of morality gives rise to a fourfold classification of duties, resulting from the intersection of two divisions: between duties to oneself and to others, and between perfect and imperfect duties. Perfect duties are proscriptions of specific kinds of actions, and violating them is morally blameworthy; imperfect duties are prescriptions of general ends, and fulfilling them by means of performing appropriate particular actions is praiseworthy. The four classes of duty are thus: perfect duties to oneself, such as the prohibition of suicide; perfect duties to others, such as the prohibition of deceitful promises; imperfect duties to oneself, such as the prescription to cultivate one's talents; and imperfect duties to others, such as the prescription of benevolence (1900: 4: 422–3, 429–30). It is straightforward what a perfect duty prohibits one from doing; it requires judgment to determine when and how the general ends prescribed by imperfect duties should be realized through particular actions.

In the later *Metaphysics of Morals*, Kant works out a detailed budget of duties that is generally based on this scheme, but with one key distinction: duties of justice (*Recht*) are those of the above duties that can appropriately be enforced by means of the public, juridical use of coercion, and the remainder are duties of virtue, which are fit subjects for moral assessment but not coercion (6: 213, 219). Since freedom is Kant's chief value, coercion is permitted only where it is both necessary to preserve freedom and possible for it to do so. This means that only a small subset of our duties, namely some but not all of our perfect duties to others, are duties of justice, thus proper subjects for public legislation; the majority of our moral duties are duties of virtue which are not appropriate subjects for coercive legal enforcement.

Kant's treatment of the duties of virtue is less complicated than that of the duties of justice, and will be considered first. Kant does not explicitly characterize these as duties to preserve and promote the freedom of oneself and others, as he does in the *Groundwork*, but instead characterizes them as duties to promote one's own perfection and the happiness of others: while one can directly perfect one's own freedom, one can avoid injuring but not directly perfect the freedom of another. On close inspection, however, Kant's duties of virtue require precisely that one perfect both the internal and external conditions for the exercise of one's own freedom and at least the external conditions for the exercise of the freedom of others. Thus, ethical duties to oneself include the prohibition of injury to the physical and mental bases of one's free agency, as by suicide or drunkenness, and the prescription of efforts to improve both the physical and mental conditions for the exercise of one's freedom, as by the cultivation of talents and of one's spiritual and moral faculties themselves; and ethical duties to others include both the prohibition of injuries to the dignity of others as free agents, for example by insulting or ridiculing them ('duties of respect'), and the prescription of efforts to improve the conditions for others' exercise of their own freedom, as by beneficence and sympathy ('duties of love').

Kant's foundation of his political philosophy on the duties of justice is more complicated. From the ultimate value of freedom, Kant derives the universal principle of justice, that an action is right only if 'on its maxim the freedom of choice of each can coexist with everyone's freedom in accordance with a universal law' (6: 230). Kant then argues that coercion is justified when it can prevent a hindrance to freedom, since a hindrance to a hindrance to freedom is itself a means to freedom (6: 231). This is too simple, since coercion might only compound the injury to freedom. Kant needs to add that coercive enforcement of the law is not itself a hindrance to freedom, since the threat of juridical sanction does not deprive a would-be criminal of freedom in the way that his crime would deprive its victim of freedom: the criminal exercises the choice to risk sanction, but deprives his victim of a like freedom of choice.

Kant goes on to argue that the only proper aim of coercive juridical legislation is the prevention of injury to the person and property of others; this is 'Private Law', while 'Public Law' concerns the proper form of the state, whose function is the enforcement of private law. Kant takes the prevention of injury to persons to be an obvious requirement of duty, needing no special discussion, but the right to property receives extended discussion.

Kant recognizes three classes of property: property in things, property in contracts, and contract-like property in other persons, such as marital rights. His discussion of property in things is the most important for his political theory. The gist of Kant's account is that it would be irrational to deprive ourselves of the right to place physical objects, above all land, at our own long-term disposal, since we are rational agents who may need to use such things to realize our freely chosen ends, while the things themselves are not free agents and have no rights. But since the earth is initially undivided, specific property rights are not innate but must be acquired. Since the claim to any particular thing would limit the freedom of others who might also be able to use it, however, property rights cannot be claimed unilaterally, at least if morality's insistence upon universal acceptability is to be respected, but can only be claimed with the multilateral consent of those others, which they can reasonably give only if they too are accorded similar rights necessary for the successful exercise of their own agency (6: 255–6). For Kant, the right to property is thus not a natural right of isolated individuals, but a social creation depending upon mutual acceptability of claims. The state, finally, exists primarily to make claims to property rights both determinate and secure, and anyone claiming property rights thus has both the right and the obligation to join in a state with others (6: 256–7, 306–8). Since property exists only by mutual consent, and the state exists to secure that consent, the state necessarily has the power to permit only those distributions of property rights sufficiently equitable to gain general consent.

Both claims to property and expressions of philosophical and religious opinions, for example, are expressions of human autonomy. But while one person's property claims may directly limit the freedom of others, and are therefore subject to public regulation, his beliefs do not, and thus do not require the consent of any other. The state therefore has no right to intervene in these matters. This fundamental difference between the state's proper concern with property and its improper concern with personal belief defines Kant's liberalism. It is only implicit in the *Metaphysics of Morals*, but becomes explicit in more purely political writings.

11 Freedom of the will and the highest good

Having considered some practical implications of Kant's conception of autonomy, we now turn to its metaphysical consequences.

In Section III of the *Groundwork*, Kant attempts to prove that the categorical imperative, derived in Section II by the analysis of the concept of free and rational beings in general, actually puts *us* under an obligation by proving that *we* are indeed free and rational beings. In his terminology, he wants to show that it is not merely an analytic but a synthetic a priori proposition that our wills are constrained by this imperative. Both the interpretation and the assessment of the arguments by which he proposes to accomplish this remain controversial.

The first claim that Kant makes is that 'every being who cannot act except under the idea of freedom is just on that account really free in a practical respect, that is, all laws that are inseparably bound up with freedom are valid for it just as if its will were really declared to be free in itself and in theoretical philosophy', and that every being with a will must indeed act under the idea of freedom (1900: 4: 448) (see WILL, THE). This seems to mean that agents who conceive of themselves as choosing their own actions, whether or not they conceive of themselves as subject to determinism, do not or perhaps even cannot consider any antecedent determinants of their actions in deciding what to do, but only what now seems most rational to do; thus they must govern their actions by rational and therefore moral laws. This seems right for agents considering their own future actions, but leaves unclear how we are to assess the freedom of the actions of others or even our own past actions.

However, Kant goes on to offer what seems to be a theoretical and therefore general proof of the existence of human freedom. He argues that theoretical philosophy has shown that we must distinguish between considering ourselves as phenomena and noumena, or members of the sensible and the intelligible worlds. From the first point of view, we must consider our actions to be governed by the causality of nature, while in the second, since we cannot consider our actions there to be governed by no law at all, we must consider them to be governed by another kind of causality, namely causality in accord with laws of reason (4: 451–3). Thus while our actions appear to be determined by natural causes, in reality they not only can but in fact must accord with laws of reason, hence with the categorical imperative.

There are two problems with this argument. First, it flouts transcendental idealism by assuming positive knowledge about things in themselves. Second, as Henry SIDGWICK was to object a century later, it precludes moral responsibility for wrong-doing: if the real laws of our behaviour are necessarily rational and hence moral, any wrong-doing could only show that an agent is not rational, and therefore not responsible, at all.

Whether consciously aware of such objections or not, Kant began to alter his argument for freedom of the will in the *Critique of Practical Reason*. Here he does not argue from a theoretical proof of our freedom to the fact of our obligation under the moral law, but conversely from our consciousness of that obligation – the 'fact of reason' – to our freedom as the necessary condition of our ability and responsibility to fulfil it (5: 29–31). This argument first assumes that transcendental idealism has left open at least the theoretical possibility of freedom of the will, and then depends upon the famous principle 'ought implies can' ('Theory and Practice', 8: 287). Transcendental idealism, of course, seems problematic to many; and although the 'ought implies can' principle seems an intuitive principle of fairness, Kant does not actually argue for it. Nevertheless, since this argument assumes only that 'ought' implies '*can*', it does not imply that any agent who is obliged under the moral law necessarily *will* act in accordance with it, and thus avoids Sidgwick's problem about the very possibility of wrong-doing.

Kant depends upon this result in his next major treatment of freedom, in *Religion within the Limits of Reason Alone*, although there he seems to go too far in the other direction by assuming that evil-doing is not just possible but even necessary. Kant begins this discussion with an elegant account of wrong-doing, arguing that because no human being is simply unaware of the demand of morality – that is implied by the 'fact of reason' – acting immorally never comes from mere ignorance of the moral law, but rather from deciding to exempt oneself from this obligation. This position is compatible with the argument for freedom in the second *Critique*, although not with that of the *Groundwork*. However, Kant goes on to argue that an evil rather than virtuous choice of fundamental maxim, or 'radical evil', is not only *possible* but inevitable, to be escaped from only by a moral conversion. This doctrine hardly follows from Kant's previous argument, and seems instead to rest on an odd mixture of empirical evidence and the lingering grip of the Christian doctrine of original sin.

The reality of freedom is only the first of Kant's three 'postulates of pure practical reason'; the other two are the existence of God and the immortality of the soul. Again Kant's argument is that, as the first *Critique* showed, neither of these can be proven by theoretical metaphysics, but they can nevertheless be postulated as necessary conditions of something essential to morality. In this case, however, they are conditions not of our obligation under the categorical imperative but for the realization of the 'highest good'. This is another complex and controversial concept. Kant typically defines it as happiness in proportion to virtue, which is worthiness to be happy (5: 110), but suggests different grounds for the necessity of this conjunction. In the *Critique of Practical Reason*, Kant sometimes treats happiness and virtue as two separate ends of human beings, one our natural end and the other our moral end, which we simply seek to combine (5: 110). In other places, however, beginning with the 'Canon of Pure Reason' in the first *Critique*, he holds that since what virtue does is precisely to coordinate our mutual pursuit of ends, and happiness arises from the realization of ends, maximal happiness would inevitably follow maximal virtue under ideal circumstances (A 809/B 837). Of course, circumstances are not always ideal for morality: as far as we can see, no one achieves perfect virtue in a normal lifespan, and such virtue as is attained is hardly always rewarded with happiness. To counter this, Kant holds that we may postulate immortality, in which to perfect our virtue, and the existence of God, who can legislate a nature in which the ends of virtue are achieved.

This theory has seemed to many to be Kant's vain attempt to save his personal faith from his own scathing critique of metaphysics. Before such a claim could even be discussed, we would have to know what Kant really means by a postulate of practical reason. Kant gives several hints about this which have not been adequately explored. In the first *Critique*, he discusses the practical postulates in a section where he considers readiness to bet as a measure of belief, thus suggesting that what he actually has in mind is Pascal's wager (see PASCAL, B.): since there is no theoretical disproof of these postulates, and nothing to lose if they are false, but their value to happiness is great, it is rational to act as if they were true. In a later essay, a draft on the 'Real Progress of Metaphysics from the Time of Leibniz and Wolff' from the early 1790s (posthumously published), Kant makes an even more striking suggestion. There he says that in the assumption of the practical postulates 'the human being is authorized to grant influence on his actions to an idea which he, in accord with moral principles, has made himself, just as if he had derived it from a given object' (20: 305). Here the suggestion is that the practical postulates are nothing less than another expression of human autonomy: not theoretical beliefs at all, let alone religious dogmas, but ideas which we construct for ourselves solely to increase our own efforts at virtue. This idea, that God is in fact nothing but an idea of our own making for use within our moral practice, is a thought Kant repeatedly expressed in his very last years (see §14).

12 Taste and autonomy

Under the rubric of 'reflective judgment', defined as that use of judgment in which we seek to find unknown universals for given particulars rather than to apply given universals to particulars (5: 179–80), the *Critique of the Power of Judgment* deals with three apparently disparate subjects: systematicity in scientific concepts generally, natural and artistic beauty, and teleology or purposiveness in particular organisms and in nature as a whole (see TELEOLOGY). Even more than the idea of reflective judgment, however, what ties these subjects together is again the idea of autonomy.

In the the first *Critique*, Kant had suggested, with but few exceptions, that the search for systematicity in scientific concepts and laws – the subordination of maximally varied specific concepts and laws under maximally unified general ones – is an ideal of reason, not necessary for empirical knowledge but still intrinsically desirable. In the third *Critique*, he reassigns this search to reflective judgment, and argues that we must adopt as a transcendental but indemonstrable principle that nature is adapted to our cognitive needs (5: 185; 20: 209–10). By this reassignment Kant indicates that systematicity is a necessary condition for the acceptance of empirical laws after all, and thus a necessary condition for experience itself. Kant thereby suggests that our empirical knowledge is neither passively received nor simply guaranteed, but dependent on our active projection of the unity of nature.

Kant next turns to judgments of taste as both a further expression of human autonomy and further evidence that the adaptation of nature to our own cognitive needs is both contingent yet reasonably assumed. Judgments of taste, beginning with the simplest such as 'This flower is beautiful' and progressing to more complex ones such as 'This poem is beautiful' and 'This landscape is sublime', are connected to autonomy in two ways: while they claim universal agreement, they must always be based on individual feeling and judgment; and while they must be made free of all constraint by theoretical or moral concepts, they are ultimately symbols of moral freedom itself.

Kant begins from an analysis of the very idea of an 'aesthetic judgment'. As aesthetic, judgments of taste must both concern and be made on the basis of the most subjective of human responses, feelings of pleasure, but, as judgments, they must still claim interpersonal agreement (5: 203, 212–16). To retain their link to feelings, judgments of taste can never simply report how others respond, but must be based on one's own free response to the object itself; in this way they express individual autonomy (5: 216, 282–5). But to claim universal agreement, they must be based on cognitive capacities shared by all, yet by a condition of those faculties that is pleasurable because it is not constrained by rules (5: 187). Such a state is one of 'free play' between

imagination and understanding, in which the imagination satisfies understanding's need for unity by presenting a form that seems unitary and coherent without any concept, or, even where a concept of human use or artistic intention is inescapable, that seems to have a unity going beyond any such concept – artistic genius lies precisely in such transcendence of concepts (5: 317–18). With debatable success, Kant argues that this 'free play' must occur under the same circumstances in all human beings (5: 238–9, 290), and thus that judgments of taste can have the 'quantity' of universality and the 'modality' of necessity while retaining the 'quality' of independence from direct moral interest and 'relation' to merely subjective, cognitive interests rather than objective, practical ones.

How does aesthetic judgment so understood both express autonomy in a moral sense and also give further evidence of the contingent adaptation of nature to our own needs? Kant answers the latter question with his idea of 'intellectual interest': the very fact that beauty exists, he argues, although it cannot be derived from any scientific laws, can be taken by us as evidence that nature is receptive not only to our cognitive needs but even to our need to see a possibility for success in our moral undertakings (5: 300). Kant's answer to the first question, how taste expresses autonomy in its moral sense, is more complex but also more compelling than this.

Like other eighteenth-century authors such as Edmund BURKE, Kant draws a fundamental distinction between the beautiful and the sublime (see SUBLIME, THE). Beauty pleases us through the free play of imagination and understanding. In our response to the sublime, however – which for Kant is not paradigmatically a response to art, but to the vastness and power of nature – we enjoy not a direct harmony between imagination and understanding, which are rather frustrated by their inability to grasp such immensities, but a feeling of them which reveals the power of reason within us (5: 257). And this, although it would seem to involve theoretical reason, symbolizes the power of practical reason, and thus the foundation of our autonomy, in two ways: our power to grasp a truly universal law, such as the moral law, and our power to resist the threats of mere nature, and thus the blandishments of inclination (5: 261–2).

In this way, the sublime symbolizes the sterner side of moral autonomy. But the experience of beauty is also a symbol of morality, precisely because the freedom of the imagination that is its essence is the only experience in which any form of freedom, including the freedom of the will itself, can become palpable to us (5: 353–4). Kant thus concludes his critique of aesthetic judgment with the remarkable suggestion that it is in our enjoyment of beauty that our vocation as autonomous agents becomes not just a 'fact of reason' but a matter of experience as well.

13 Design and autonomy

Kant's critique of teleological judgment in the second half of the *Critique of Judgment* has an even more complicated agenda than his aesthetic theory. The work has roots in both eighteenth-century biology – which began the debate, lasting until the twentieth century, whether organisms could be understood on purely mechanical principles – and natural theology – that is, the great debate over the argument from design that culminated in Hume's *Dialogues concerning Natural Religion*. Yet again Kant's motive is to show that even our understanding of nature ultimately drives us to a recognition of our own autonomy.

The work is divided into three main sections: an examination of the necessary conditions for our comprehension of individual organisms; an examination of the conditions under which we can see nature as a whole as a single system; and a restatement of Kant's moral theology. First, Kant argues that an organism is a system of whole and parts manifesting both 'regressive' and 'progressive' causality: the whole is the product of the parts, but the parts in turn depend upon the whole for their own proper functioning and existence (1900: 5: 372, 376). But our conception of mechanical efficient causation includes only progressive causation, in which the state of any system depends upon the prior state of its parts (see CAUSATION). The only way we can understand the regressive causation of the whole with respect to its parts is by analogy to intelligent design, in which an antecedent *conception of the object* as a whole determines the production of the parts which in turn determine the character of the resultant whole. However, Kant insists, we have absolutely no justification for adopting a 'constitutive concept' of natural organisms as a product of actual design; we are only entitled to use an analogy between natural organisms and products of design as 'a regulative concept for reflective judgment to conduct research into objects in a remote analogy with our own causality in accordance with purposes' (5: 375). In other words, seeing organisms as products of intelligent design is a purely heuristic strategy.

However, Kant next argues that if it is natural for us to investigate organisms as if they were products of intelligent design, then it will also be natural for us to try to see nature as a whole as manifesting a purposive design (5: 380–1); and only by seeing the whole of nature as a product of intelligent design – of course, only regulatively – can we satisfy our craving to transform every particularity of nature, which must always be left contingent by our own general concepts, into something that seems necessary (5: 405–7). However, from a merely naturalistic viewpoint the ultimate purpose of nature as a system must remain indeterminate – grass might exist to feed cows, or cows exist to fertilize the grass (4: 426). Nature can be seen as a determinate system only if it can be seen as collectively serving an ultimate end that is itself an intrinsic end, that is, an end with absolute value. This can only be humanity itself (4: 427) – but not humanity merely as a part of nature, seeking happiness, which is neither a determinate end nor one particularly favoured by nature (4: 430), but only humanity as the subject of morality, able to cultivate its freedom (5: 435–6). Thus the urge to see nature as a systematic whole, an inevitable concomitant of our research into the complexities of organic life, can only be satisfied from the moral point of view in which human autonomy is the ultimate value.

Kant is still careful to remind us that this doctrine is regulative, furnishing us with a principle for our own cognitive and practical activity, not constitutive, pretending to metaphysical insight into the nature of reality independent from us. It is therefore particularly noteworthy that the last part of the critique of teleological judgment is a restatement of Kant's moral theology, the argument for belief in the existence of God as a postulate of practical reason. This restatement within a general theory of reflective judgment, the principles of which are meant above all else to guide our own activity, confirms the view that in the end the theory of practical postulates is not meant to support any form of dogma but only to serve as another expression of our own autonomy.

14 The final decade of Kant's public and private career

German intellectuals were drawn to political issues after the French revolution in 1789, and Kant was no exception. Key elements of his political philosophy were presented in essays such as 'Theory and Practice' (1793) and *Perpetual Peace* (1795) before its formal exposition in the *Metaphysics of Morals* (1797). As was argued above (§10), the foundation of Kantian liberalism is the idea that coercion is justifiable only to prevent hindrances to freedom, and thus to protect personal freedom and regulate property, every claim to which represents a potential constraint of the freedom of others unless they can reasonably agree to that claim as part of a system of property rights; but individual beliefs and conceptions of the good, whether religious or philosophical, do not directly interfere with the freedom of others and are therefore not a proper object of political regulation. Kant's development of this basic principle into a political philosophy, however, is complex and controversial.

On the one hand, Kant argued from this premise to a firm rejection of any paternalistic government, even benevolent paternalism. Government exists for the protection of the freedom individuals have to determine and pursue their own ends to the extent compatible with the like freedom of others; so a 'paternalistic government, where the subjects, as minors, cannot decide what is truly beneficial or detrimental to them, but are obliged to wait passively for the head of state to judge how they ought to be happy... would be the greatest conceivable despotism' (1900: 8: 290–1). Further, Kant held that the sovereignty of any government derives solely from the possibility of those who are governed rationally consenting to it, and thus that it is a necessary test of the legitimacy of all laws 'that they can have arisen from the united will of an entire people' (8: 297). These constraints could best be met in a republic, without a hereditary monarchy or aristocracy pitting proprietary privilege against public right. Finally, Kant argued in *Perpetual Peace*, only in a world federation of republics, where no proprietary rulers could identify the forcible extension of their domains with the aggrandizement of their personal property, could a cessation of warfare ever be expected.

On the other hand, Kant accompanied these liberal doctrines with a denial of any right to violent revolution, which has seemed surprising to many. But Kant's thought here is complex. Underlying his position as a whole is his view that in any situation in which different persons are bound to come into contact with each other we have not merely a moral right but a moral obligation to found or uphold a state. But one could easily argue that a tyranny is a state in name only, and that our moral obligation with regard to a tyranny is precisely to replace it at any cost with a legitimate state. Kant offers several reasons why this is not so. One claim is that violent revolution does not leave time for genuine reform in principles (8: 36), and another argument is that people revolt for the sake of greater happiness, which is an illegitimate reason for the overthrow of a state (8: 298). But these are empirical claims, and do not prove that people cannot revolt solely to remove illegitimate constraints to their freedom. Another argument Kant makes is that a constitution granting a legal right to rebel against the highest authority it creates would thereby not create a single highest authority after all, and would thus be self-contradictory (6: 319). This has seemed to many to be a sophism; but it may have been Kant's attempt to get his liberalism past the Prussian censorship, denying a *legal* right to rebel without ever explicitly denying a *moral* right to rebel.

Kant had been battling censorship even before the death of Frederick the Great in 1786. In 'What is Enlightenment?' (1785), he argued that while persons in an official capacity have to obey orders (in what he confusingly calls the 'private use of reason'), no official, not a professor or even a military officer, has to surrender his right to address his views to 'the entire *reading public*' (the 'public use of reason') (8: 37). But Kant's attack on the necessity of an established church in *Religion within the Limits of Reason Alone* (1793), even though legally published with the imprimatur of a non-Prussian university (Jena), outraged the conservative Frederick William II and his minister Wöllner, and Kant was threatened with punishment if he published further on religion. With an oath of loyalty to his sovereign, Kant promised to desist, but after the death of this king in 1797 he regarded himself as freed from this promise, and the next year issued his most spirited defence of intellectual freedom yet, *The Conflict of the Faculties*. Here Kant argued that while the theological faculty might have the obligation to advance certain dogmas approved by the state, it was nothing less than the official function of the philosophical faculty to subject all views to rational scrutiny; and in any case, a government genuinely concerned with its people's welfare would not want them to base their morality on fear or dogma but only on the free exercise of their own reason. The new government had no stomach for further suppression of the aged philosopher, and Kant was able to publish this defence of intellectual freedom without incident.

Privately, Kant's last years were devoted to the project of closing the gap between the metaphysical foundations of natural science and actual physics, begun about 1796. He never published the work, leaving behind only the notes later published as the *Opus postumum*. Here Kant tried to show that by using the categorial framework and the concept of force we can derive not only the most general laws of mechanics, as he had argued in 1786, but a much more detailed categorization of the forms of matter and its forces. Kant also argued that an imperceptible, self-moving ether or 'caloric' is a condition of the possibility of experience. In the latest stages of this work, however, Kant returned to the broadest themes of his philosophy, and tried to develop a final statement of transcendental idealism. Here he argued that 'The highest standpoint of transcendental philosophy is that which unites God and the world synthetically, under one principle' (21: 23) – where that principle is nothing other than human autonomy itself. God and the world are 'not substances outside my thought, but rather the thought through which we ourselves make these objects' (21: 21): the world is our experience organized by categories and laws of our own making, and God is the representation of our own capacity to give ourselves the moral law through reason. The moral law 'emerges from freedom . . . - which the subject prescribes to himself, and yet as if another and higher person had made it a rule for him. The subject feels himself necessitated through his own reason...' (22: 129). This is a fitting conclusion to Kant's philosophy of autonomy.

See also: A priori; Analyticity; Autonomy, ethical; Empiricism; Free will; Kantian ethics; Neo-Kantianism; Practical reason and ethics; Rationalism; Transcendental arguments

References and further reading

Guyer, P. (ed.) (1992) *The Cambridge Companion to Kant*, Cambridge: Cambridge University Press. (This volume contains articles on all aspects of Kant's philosophy by leading interpreters and an extensive bibliography. An entirely revised edition is currently in preparation.)

Guyer, P. and Wood, Allen W. (eds) (1992–) *The Cambridge Edition of the Works of Immanuel Kant*, Cambridge: Cambridge University Press. (Almost complete, the volumes in the Cambridge edition provide new translations of all of Kant's published works, as well as extensive translations from his lectures, correspondence and posthumous notes and fragments. The volumes also provide extensive scholarly apparatus.)

Kant, I. (1900–) *Kant's gesammelte Schriften (Kant's Collected Works)*, ed. Royal Prussian (subsequently German, then Berlin–Brandenburg) Academy of Sciences, Berlin: Georg Reimer, subsequently Walter de Gruyter, 29 vols, in 34 parts. (Divided into four parts: *Werke (Works)* (vols 1–9), *Briefe (Letters)* (vols 10–13), *Handschriftlicher Nachlaß (Handwritten remains)* (vols 14–23), and *Vorlesungen (Transcriptions of lectures by other hands)* (vols 24–9, no volume 26). The most complete collection of Kant's works.)

Kuehn, M. (2001) *Kant: A Biography*, Cambridge: Cambridge University Press. (The most recent biography of Kant, this detailed but highly readable book interprets Kant's works in the context of his time and place.)

PAUL GUYER

KANTIAN ETHICS

Introduction

Kantian ethics originates in the ethical writings of Immanuel Kant (1724–1804), which remain the most influential attempt to vindicate universal ethical principles that respect the dignity and equality of human beings without presupposing theological claims or a metaphysical conception of the good. Kant's systematic, critical philosophy centres on an account of reasoning about action, which he uses to justify principles of duty and virtue, a liberal and republican conception of justice with cosmopolitan scope, and an account of the relationship between morality and hope.

Numerous contemporary writers also advance views of ethics which they, and their critics, think of as Kantian. However, some contemporary work is remote from Kant's philosophy on fundamental matters such as human freedom and reasoning about action. It converges with Kant's ethics in claiming that we lack a substantive account of the good (so that teleological or consequentialist ethics are impossible), in taking a strong view of the equality of moral agents and the importance of universal principles of duty which spell out what it is to respect them, and in stressing an account of justice and rights with cosmopolitan scope.

Both Kant's ethics and contemporary Kantian ethics have been widely criticized for preoccupation with rules and duties, and for lack of concern with virtues, happiness or personal relationships. However, these criticisms may apply more to recent Kantian ethics than to Kant's own ethics.

> 1   Kant's ethics
> 2   Contemporary Kantian ethics
> 3   Criticisms of Kantian ethics
> 4   Back to Kant?

1   Kant's ethics

Kant's main writing on ethics and politics can be found in *Grundlegung zur Metaphysik der Sitten* (*Groundwork of the Metaphysics of Morals*) (1785), *Kritik der practischen Vernunft* (*Critique of Practical Reason*) (1788), *Die Metaphysik der Sitten* (*The Metaphysics of Morals*) (1797) and numerous sections of other works and free-standing essays. Throughout these writings he insists that we cannot derive ethical conclusions from metaphysical or theological knowledge of the good (which we lack) or from a claim that human happiness is the sole good (which we cannot establish). We lack the basis for a teleological or consequentialist account of ethical reasoning, which therefore cannot be simply a matter of means-ends reasoning towards some fixed and knowable good (see Consequentialism; Teleological ethics).

Yet if reasoning about action, that is practical reasoning, is not means-end reasoning, what can it be? Kant's alternative account proposes simply that reasons for action must be reasons for all. He insists that we can have reasons for recommending only those principles of action which could be adopted by all concerned, whatever their particular desires, social identities, roles or relationships. Correspondingly, practical reasoning must reject any principles which cannot be principles for all concerned, which Kant characterizes as *non-universalizable* principles (see UNIVERSALISM IN ETHICS).

Kant gives this rather limited modal conception of practical reasoning some grand names. He calls it the 'supreme principle of morality' and the 'categorical imperative'. He formulates this fundamental principle of ethics in various ways. The formulation most discussed in the philosophical literature runs 'act only on that maxim [principle] through which you can at the same time will that it become a universal law'. The formulation that has had and still has the greatest cultural resonance requires us to treat others with impartial respect. It runs 'treat humanity ... never simply as a means, but always at the same time as an end' ([*Grundlegung* 1785). The equivalence of these two formulations of the categorical imperative is far from obvious. One way of glimpsing why Kant thought they were equivalent is to note that if we treat others as persons rather than as things then we must not destroy or impair their abilities to act, indeed must leave it open to them to act on the same principles that we act on; hence we must act on universalizable principles. On Kant's view, one of the worst features of consequentialist ethics is that it not merely permits but requires that persons be used as mere means if this will produce good results.

Kant claims that the categorical imperative can be used to justify the underlying principles of human duties. For example, we can show by a *reductio ad absurdum* argument that promising falsely is not universalizable. Suppose that everyone were to adopt the principle of promising falsely: since there would then be much false promising, trust would be destroyed and many would find that they could not get their false promises accepted, contrary to the hypothesis of universal adoption of the principle of false promising. A maxim of promising falsely is not universalizable, so the categorical imperative requires us to reject it. Parallel arguments can be used to show that principles such as those of coercing or doing violence are not universalizable, and so that it is a duty to reject these principles.

Kant calls duties such as these *perfect* (namely, complete) duties. These are duties which can observed by each towards all others. He also provides arguments to establish the principles of certain *imperfect* (namely, incomplete) duties, such as those of helping others in need or developing one's

own talents. One way in which imperfect duties are unavoidably incomplete is that they cannot be observed towards all others: nobody can help all others, or develop all possible talents. Kant calls these imperfect duties 'duties of virtue' (see VIRTUES AND VICES §§2–3).

The derivation of principles of duty from his conception of practical reason is the core of Kant's ethics, and provides the context for his discussion of many other themes. These include: the difference between internalizing principles and merely conforming to them in outward respects ('acting out of duty' versus 'acting according to duty'); the place of happiness in a good life; the need for judgment in moving from principle to act (see MORAL JUDGMENT §2); the justification of state power; and the justification of a cosmopolitan account of justice. He also develops the connections between his distinctive conceptions of practical reason and of freedom and his equally distinctive view of religion, which he sees as a matter not of knowledge but of reasoned hope for a future in which morality can be fully realized. In some works Kant articulates reasoned hope in religious terms; in others he articulates it in political and historical terms as a hope for a better this-worldly human future.

2 Contemporary Kantian ethics

Much contemporary work on ethics is labelled Kantian, in the main because it does not derive an account of right action from one of good results, but rather sees the right as prior to the good (RIGHT AND GOOD). In contemporary Kantian work obligations and rights are the fundamental ethical notions. Such work is often called *deontological ethics* (the term derives from the Greek word for *ought*) (see DEONTOLOGICAL ETHICS). Deontological ethical theories are contrasted with teleological or consequentialist theories, which treat the good as prior to the right. Deontological theories are concerned with ethically required action, hence with principles, rules or norms, with obligations, prohibitions and permissions, and with justice and injustice, but not with virtues, good lives, moral ideals and personal relationships.

Deontological ethics has many distinct forms. Many versions endorse one or another interpretation of the Kantian demand to respect persons, and think that moral principles should be universal; few mention Kant's minimalist strategy for justifying certain universally binding principles as those we must live by if we reject non-universalizable principles. Indeed, many deontological ethical theories rely on conceptions of freedom, reason and action which are unlike Kant's, and resemble those typically used by consequentialists.

One prominent range of deontological positions seeks to justify principles of justice by showing that they would be agreed to by all concerned under certain hypothetical conditions. They draw on the thought that agreements and contracts are good reasons for action, and suggest that all ethical claims are to be justified by showing that they are based if not on actual then on hypothetical agreements or contracts. These sorts of deontological theories are often called *contractarian* or *contractualist*; they are contemporary versions of social contract theories (see CONTRACTARIANISM).

Some contractualists take a Hobbesian rather than a Kantian approach. They argue that principles of justice are those on which instrumentally rational persons, guided by their individual preferences, would agree (see HOBBES, T. §§6–7). Other contractualists take a more Kantian approach. They argue that principles of justice are those which would be accepted or agreed to by persons who are not merely instrumentally rational but can use certain reasonable procedures.

The best known exponent of Kantian contractualism is John RAWLS, whose *A Theory of Justice* (1971) identifies principles of justice as those that would be agreed by rational and self-interested beings in circumstances which ensure that their choosing will be reasonable as well as rational. He argues that principles of justice would emerge if they were chosen by all concerned in an hypothetical situation devised to ensure impartiality and hence agreement. Rawls calls this hypothetical situation 'the original position', and represents it as one in which persons are ignorant of their own social position and personal attributes, hence of their own advantage, hence cannot but be impartial.

Rawls claims that rational persons in this hypothetical situation would choose principles of justice that prescribe equal rights for all and the highest attainable level of wellbeing for the worst off. Since everything that differentiates individuals, and could thus provide a basis for disagreement, for bargaining, or for a need to seek agreement, is carefully excluded from the original position, it is not obvious why principles chosen in it should be thought of as matters of *agreement*, or why the parties to the original position should be thought of as *contracting* with one another. Nor is it clear why the fact that certain principles would be agreed to under these conditions justifies those principles to those in other situations. Why are principles which would be agreed to under conditions that do not obtain binding under conditions that actually obtain?

In *A Theory of Justice* Rawls argues that principles that would be so agreed are binding in other situations because they cohere, or form a 'reflective equilibrium' with 'our considered judgments' (see MORAL JUSTIFICATION §2). Principles are justified not merely because the instrumental reasoning of the hypothetically ignorant would select them, but because we would reasonably judge them congruent with our most carefully considered moral views. In his later *Political Liberalism* (1993) Rawls depicts these principles as the outcome not of hypothetical agreement in an original position, but as the hypothetical agreement of persons who are not only rational but reasonable, in the sense that they are willing to abide by principles given assurance that others will do so too. Principles and institutions are just if they are the focus of reasonable agreement by all concerned.

Jürgen HABERMAS has also advocated versions of Kantian ethics which stress agreement between agents. In earlier work he argued that the test of justification or legitimation is that a proposal would be agreed in a hypothetical 'ideal speech situation', in which communication was undistorted. In more recent work (1993), he has argued that legitimation of norms is achieved through processes of public discourse, to which each can contribute and in which all can agree.

3 Criticisms of Kantian ethics

Both Kant's ethics and contemporary Kantian ethics have been criticized from many quarters. The critics evidently include those who advocate one or another form of teleological or consequentialist theory, who believe that it is possible to establish an account of the good, from which a convincing account of the right, and specifically of justice, can be derived. However, they also include a variety of writers who reject consequentialist thinking, including communitarians, virtue ethicists, Wittgensteinians and feminist thinkers (see COMMUNITY AND COMMUNITARIANISM; VIRTUE ETHICS).

The most common and general criticisms are that, because it concentrates on principles or rules, Kantian ethics is doomed to be either empty and formalistic or rigidly uniform in its prescriptions (the complaints cannot both be true). The charge of empty formalism is based on the correct observation that principles underdetermine action; it is usually countered with the equally correct observation that quite indeterminate principles (such as 'Stay within the budget' or 'All religions are to be tolerated') may set significant constraints on action, so are not empty. The charge of rigidly uniform prescriptivity is based on the thought that rules prescribe, so must regiment. It is usually countered by the reminder that since rules can be indeterminate, they need not regiment: universal principles need not be uniformly prescriptive. An ethical theory that applies to principles can be more than empty and less than rigid.

Other critics, for example MacIntyre, object that since Kantian ethics focuses on obligations and rights, and in good measure on justice, it either must or does neglect other ethical categories, and in particular the virtues, good character or good lives; that 'natural and human rights... are fictions' (MacIntyre in, *After Virtue* 1981: 67); and that obligations inevitably conflict in ways that render all deontological ethics incoherent. Some critics have laid particular stress on the point that in requiring impartial respect for all, Kantian ethics wholly ignores the place of happiness, of the emotions, of personal integrity and above all of personal relationships in the good life (see MORALITY AND EMOTIONS). They have claimed that we must choose between an ethics of justice and one of care, an ethic of rules and one of relationships, an ethic of duty and one of virtue, and that the latter term of each pair is to be preferred.

4 Back to Kant?

Some of these criticisms are accurately aimed at significant features of various forms of contemporary Kantian writing in ethics; many of them are less apt as criticisms of Kant's ethics. Several recent writers have suggested that Kant's ethics is the most convincing form of Kantian ethics, and that its distinctive features are strengths rather than weaknesses. Many of these writers accept much of the critique of deontological ethics, but think that not all the criticisms apply to Kant's ethics, of which they offer detailed interpretations. Part of their effort has gone into work on Kant's conceptions of action, reason and freedom, and part into work on his ethics. They have pointed out that Kant's account of practical reason and of its vindication does not assume either that all reasoning about action is instrumentally rational pursuit of preferred ends, or that ethical vindication is located in hypothetical agreements or contracts reached by reasonable procedures. They have stressed that Kant's conception of practical reason is based on universalizability rather than impartiality or reciprocity and that he views obligations rather than rights as basic to ethics. They have insisted that impartial respect for persons and a cosmopolitan approach to justice are not morally negligible matters, and have criticized communitarians, virtue ethicists and some feminist thinkers for not taking justice seriously. They have also pointed out that Kant offers accounts of the virtues, of the role of happiness in the good life, and of judgment, and argued that his position is not damagingly individualistic and that he acknowledges the importance of institutions and of social and personal relationships in human life (see Korsgaard 1996).

See also: AUTONOMY, ETHICAL; KANT, I. §§9–11; PRACTICAL REASON AND ETHICS

References and further reading

Korsgaard, C.M. (1996) *Creating the Kingdom of Ends*, Cambridge: Cambridge University Press. (Essays on the categorical imperative and its implications.)

Williams, B. (1985) *Ethics and the Limits of Philosophy*, Cambridge, MA: Harvard University Press and London: Fontana. (Varied and thoughtful criticism of Kantian ethics.)

ONORA O'NEILL

KATHARSIS

One of the central concepts of Aristotle's *Poetics*, *katharsis* ('purgation' or 'purification'; often spelled *catharsis*) defines the goal of the tragic poet: the depiction of human vicissitudes so to provoke the spectators' feelings of pity and fear that such emotions in them are finally purged.

See also: ARISTOTLE §29; EMOTION IN RESPONSE TO ART; MIMĒSIS; POETRY; TRAGEDY

GLENN W. MOST

KELSEN, HANS (1881–1973)

Hans Kelsen was one of the foremost (positivist) legal theorists of the twentieth century. He taught in Vienna, Cologne, Geneva and Paris, and finished his life in America, teaching in Chicago, Harvard and Berkeley. He wrote widely, on legal philosophy, constitutional and international law, and political philosophy. Kelsen is best known for his *Pure Theory of Law* (*Reine Rechtslehre*) (1934). This is the basis of a theory which, with many changes, he espoused till he died.

See also: BOBBIO, N.; HART, H.L.A.; LAW, PHILOSOPHY OF; LEGAL POSITIVISM

ZENON BAŃKOWSKI

KEPLER, JOHANNES (1571–1630)

Kepler's mathematical analysis of Brahe's observations of the motions of Mars enabled him to formulate the descriptive 'laws' of planetary motion, thus giving heliocentric astronomy an empirical basis far more accurate than it had before. He insisted that astronomy had to discover the *causes* of the motions that the laws described, in this way becoming a 'physics of the sky'. In the pursuit of this goal, he formulated the notion of distance-dependent forces between sun and planet, and guessed that gravity could be explained as an attraction between heavy bodies and their home planets, analogous to magnetic action, thus pointing the way for Newton's theory of gravity.

See also: CAUSATION; COPERNICUS, N.; COSMOLOGY; EXPLANATION; GALILEI, GALILEO.; NEWTON, I.; RENAISSANCE PHILOSOPHY; SCIENTIFIC METHOD

ERNAN MCMULLIN

KIERKEGAARD, SØREN AABYE (1813–55)

Introduction

Although Kierkegaard's name has come to be chiefly associated with writings on philosophical themes, his various publications covered a wide range that included contributions to literary criticism, discourses on specifically religious topics and forays into polemical journalism. Born in Copenhagen in 1813, he led an outwardly uneventful existence there until his death in 1855. None the less much that he wrote drew upon crises and turning points in his personal life; even his theoretical works often had an autobiographical flavour.

Kierkegaard held that the philosophy of his time, largely owing to the influence of Hegelian idealism, tended to misconstrue the relation of thought to reality, wrongly assimilating the second to the first; in doing so, moreover, it reflected an age in which habits of abstract reflection and passive response had blinded people to their true concerns as self-determining agents ultimately accountable for their own characters and destinies. He sought to counter such trends, exploring different approaches to life with a view to opening his reader's eyes both to where they themselves stood and to possibilities of opting for radical change. He implied that decisions on the latter score lay beyond the scope of general rules, each being essentially a problem for the individual alone; even so, his portrayal of the religious mode of existence presented it as transcending limitations experienced in alternative forms of life. Kierkegaard, himself an impassioned believer, was at the same time crucially concerned to articulate the Christian standpoint in a fashion that salvaged it from recurrent misconceptions. Rejecting all attempts to provide objective justifications or proofs of religious claims, he endorsed a conception of faith that eschewed rational considerations and consisted instead of subjective self-

commitment maintained in the face of intellectual uncertainty or paradox. His account was set within a psychological perspective that laid stress upon freedom as an inescapable condition of action and experience. The complex implications he believed this to possess for the interpretation of pervasive human emotions and attitudes were discussed in works that later proved highly influential, particularly for the growth of twentieth-century existentialism. Here, as in other areas of his writing, Kierkegaard made a significant, though delayed, impact upon the course of subsequent thought.

1 Life
2 The limits of objectivity
3 Aestheticism and the ethical
4 The religious consciousness
5 Faith and subjectivity
6 Psychological themes and influence

1 Life

Kierkegaard was the youngest son of a prosperous and largely self-made Danish businessman. The father was a deeply religious but exacting and guilt-ridden individual who communicated his feelings of melancholy and anxiety to other members of his family; they certainly left a lasting impression on Kierkegaard's own character and development, causing him later to describe his upbringing as having been 'insane'. It was perhaps largely from a desire to please his father, towards whom he tended to exhibit an ambivalent mixture of love and fear, that at the age of seventeen he enrolled at the University of Copenhagen with the object of taking a degree in theology. Nevertheless, after passing his preliminary examinations he found himself increasingly attracted to other spheres of intellectual interest, particularly those involving developments in contemporary philosophy and literature; at the same time he cultivated a fashionably sophisticated lifestyle, following pursuits sharply at variance with the austere precepts that had been inculcated upon him at home. But in his journals, which he began during his protracted period as a student and continued to keep for the rest of his life, he is already to be found recording a growing dissatisfaction with the wayward mode of existence he had adopted, and the death of his father in 1838 appears finally to have prompted him to return to his academic studies with a view to settling down to a professional career. Thus by July 1840 he had been awarded his degree, and two months later he announced his engagement to marry Regine Olsen, the daughter of a highly placed civil servant. This, however, was not to be.

The story of Kierkegaard's abortive engagement is familiar from his journals, where he provided a detailed account of how he eventually broke off the relationship after an uneasy year during which he harboured regrets about his proposal. While his actual motives for making the final breach are left somewhat obscure, there can be no doubt as to its significance for his later thought and writings, allusions to it – often only lightly disguised – occurring in a variety of his works. In any case it certainly constituted a turning point. Henceforward he withdrew into a bachelor existence; moreover, although by now firmly committed to Christianity, he effectively abandoned any further thought of a clerical career and devoted himself instead to living as a writer on the very comfortable income he had inherited from his father's estate. The initial period of his authorship was in fact remarkably productive. He took less than a year over his master's dissertation *Om Begrebet Ironi* (*The Concept of Irony*), successfully submitting it to the university faculty in 1841, and he followed it with a series of books, all issued under pseudonyms, which were largely concerned with philosophical or psychological aspects of ethical and religious belief. The first, entitled *Enten-Eller* (*Either/Or*), came out in two substantial volumes in 1843 and was succeeded later in the same year by *Frygt og Baeven* (*Fear and Trembling*) and *Gjentagelsen* (*Repetition*); in 1844 *Philosophiske Smuler* (*Philosophical Fragments*) and *Begrebet Angest* (*The Concept of Anxiety*) appeared, and these in turn were followed by *Stadier paa Livets Vej* (*Stages on Life's Way*) in 1845 and by *Afsluttende uvidenskabelig Efterskrift* (*Concluding Unscientific Postscript*) in 1846. Two further pseudonymous works on connected themes, *Sygdommen til Døden* (*The Sickness unto Death*) and *Indøvelse i Christendom* (*Training in Christianity*), were published in 1849 and 1850 respectively.

Although it is the writings listed above that have chiefly attracted the attention of subsequent philosophers and commentators, they by no means exhaust the total of Kierkegaard's literary output during the 1840s. Apart from some critical pieces, he also produced – this time under his own name – a number of directly religious discourses in which he aimed to present the essentials of Christian teaching; thus such works as his *Opbyggelige Taler i forskjellig Aand* (Edifying Discourses in Various Spirits) of 1847 were expressly designed to communicate and illustrate the true nature of the Christian message and the demands it imposed upon the individual. In their uncompromising emphasis on the severity of these requirements, and in their manner of stigmatizing the complacency and 'double-mindedness' imputable to contemporary representatives of the faith they professed to serve, the latter books can be said to foreshadow the standpoint from which, in the culminating phase of his career, he launched a violent assault upon the established Church of Denmark. The occasion for this was the death of the Danish primate, Bishop Mynster, in 1854. Kierkegaard had increasingly come to regard Mynster as exemplifying in his own person many of the shortcomings of the Church as a whole, and he was therefore incensed by hearing the dead prelate pronounced instead to have been a 'witness to the truth'. As a result he set out in the following months to denounce the covert worldliness and hypocrisy that permeated the clerical establishment, first through articles in the public press and subsequently in a broadsheet printed at his own expense. The ferocity of his attacks, appearing after a spell when he had published relatively little, caused surprise and some consternation. The controversy they stirred up was, however, abruptly interrupted by Kierkegaard's sudden collapse in October 1855 and his death a few weeks later.

2 The limits of objectivity

In an early entry in his journals, written when he was still a student, Kierkegaard gave vent to the dissatisfaction he felt at the prospect of a life purely devoted to the dispassionate pursuit of knowledge and understanding. 'What good would it do me', he then asked himself, 'if truth stood before me, cold and naked, not caring whether I recognized her or not?' Implicit in this question was an outlook which was to receive mature articulation in much of his subsequent work, being particularly prominent in his criticisms of detached speculation of the kind attributable to those he called 'systematists and objective philosophers'. To be sure, and notwithstanding what has sometimes been supposed, he had no wish to be understood as casting aspersions on the role played by impersonal or disinterested thinking in studies comprising scholarly research or the scientific investigation of nature: such an approach was quite in order when adopted within the limits set by determinate fields of enquiry. But matters were different when philosophical attempts were made to extend it in a manner that purported to transcend all particular viewpoints and interests, this conception of the philosopher's task leading to the construction of metaphysical theories which sought to comprehend every aspect of human thought and experience within the disengaged perspective of objective contemplation. Kierkegaard considered Hegel to be the foremost contemporary representative of the latter ambition, the famous system to which it had given rise being in his opinion fundamentally misconceived.

Kierkegaard's general reaction to what he found unacceptable in the Hegelian theory is in fact crucial to an understanding of his own philosophical position. On his interpretation Hegel's philosophy ultimately rested upon a central error, one that involved the illicit identification of essence and existence, thought and reality. The German writer had endeavoured to exhibit the world, and the place of humanity within the world, in terms of an evolving sequence of logical categories that rendered its overall structure fully intelligible from the impersonal standpoint of pure reason (see HEGEL, G.W.F. §§4–8). Kierkegaard disclaimed any desire to dispute the considerable ingenuity of the Hegelian metaphysic when this was regarded simply as an 'experiment in thought'. He insisted, however, that thought was not the same as reality, nor could anything real be validly deduced from it; in particular, it was altogether mistaken to suggest that changes and developments in the sphere of actual existence were assimilable to dialectical transitions between timeless concepts – it was one thing to construct a self-contained logical or formal system, quite another to entertain the project of producing an existential one. In raising such objections, moreover, he was especially concerned to stress their relevance to Hegel's treatment of specifically human existence. The Hegelian world-picture presupposed the possibility of adopting an absolute, God-like point of view from which everything was seen as contributing to an inter-locking and rationally determined totality; as a result, human nature tended to be reduced to a philosophical abstraction, the individual to a representative of the species, and the significance of a particular person's life and actions to their role in forwarding an all-encompassing historical process that overshadowed and transcended them. At the same time, Kierkegaard suggested that the notion of an impersonal 'knowing subject' of the type postulated by thinkers of the Hegelian school was symptomatic of a corresponding inclination to forget that the speculative philosopher was himself an 'existing human being' whose status and situation imposed necessary limits upon his outlook and cognitive credentials. Far from his viewpoint on the world being from nowhere within it, such a philosopher inescapably belongs to it in his capacity as a finite empirical individual who 'sleeps, eats, blows his nose' and who has 'to face the future'.

Although Kierkegaard's attitude to Hegel is most extensively displayed in the polemical references that enliven the pages of his *Concluding Unscientific Postscript*, scattered allusions to the faults and weaknesses of 'the System' also appear in many of his other writings. The number and variety of the contexts in which they occur indicate that he regarded the current vogue of Hegelianism as having more than a purely academic significance, the popularity it enjoyed at once reflecting and helping to promote a contemporary ethos in which what he termed the 'illusions of objectivity' exercised a pervasive and corrupting influence. Thus he conceived the age to be one wherein people had lost a clear sense of their identity as individuals ultimately responsible for their own characters, outlooks and modes of living. Instead it was customary for them to take refuge in the anonymity provided by membership of collective movements or trends and to envisage themselves as being inevitably circumscribed by the social roles they occupied in a manner that absolved them from personal accountability for their pronouncements or actions. In Kierkegaard's view, they had largely forgotten what 'it means for you and me and him, each for himself, to be human beings', succumbing to a 'quantitative dialectic' in which a bemused preoccupation with large-scale historical events and a passive submission to the levelling influence of 'the crowd' took precedence over the vital constituents of human life and experience – 'the inner spirit, the ethical, freedom'.

Confronted by such tendencies, Kierkegaard considered it to be a primary part of his task as a writer to challenge habits of thought that smothered spontaneous feeling and obstructed active commitment. He held that these had had a particularly deleterious effect in the religious sphere; the widespread belief that the fundamental tenets of Christianity could be rationally interpreted and objectively justified within the framework of the Hegelian system was symptomatic of a more general disposition to treat both religion and morality alike in a blandly contemplative spirit that detached them from the contexts of inward conviction and practical engagement to which they essentially belonged. With this in mind it was necessary in the first instance to 'make people aware', bringing home to them the limitations of their present condition and awakening them to the possibility of subjective self-determination and change.

3 Aestheticism and the ethical

Kierkegaard maintained that in his early writings he had aimed to arouse and enlarge the self-understanding of his readers by eschewing abstract instruction and by employing in its place an avowedly therapeutic method he referred to as 'indirect communication'. This meant delineating particular ways of life in a fashion that enabled people to grasp concretely and from within the distinct types of outlook and motivation involved, such a procedure being a characteristically literary or 'poetic' one. Not only were alternative positions imaginatively presented as if in a novel or play; the books in which this was done were attributed to different personages in the shape of pseudonymous authors or editors. He intended thereby to avoid the kind of *ex cathedra* didacticism he associated with standard philosophical texts of his time. Instead he favoured an undogmatic approach in which competing views and attitudes were 'allowed to speak for themselves', it being left to his readers to decide where they stood in relation to these and to make up their own minds about the practical conclusions to be drawn.

Either/Or was the first of Kierkegaard's works to be published under a pseudonym and was a book he later alluded to as clearly exemplifying his use of the above method. It purports to portray two radically dissimilar modes of existence, one characterized as 'aesthetic' and the other as 'ethical'. Both are presented through the medium of allegedly edited papers or letters, the first set being ascribed to an individual referred to as 'A' and the second to an older man who is said to be by profession a judge. Aestheticism as exhibited in A's loosely related assortment of papers is seen to take on a lively variety of forms and guises; among other things, it is held to find expression in the characters of legendary figures like Don Juan and Faust, and it is also illustrated by an account in diary form of a step-by-step seduction. By contrast, the position of the ethicist is set out in two somewhat prosaic letters which are addressed by the Judge to A and which include detailed critical analyses of the younger man's motives and psychological prospects.

What did Kierkegaard understand by the categories he distinguished? From the text the aesthetic life emerges as one in which the individual is essentially concerned with exploring means to his own satisfaction and where there is a consequent absence of overall continuity in the course he follows. As has been indicated, however, the picture drawn is complex and multi-faceted. While in general outline it is suggestive of a person in pursuit of transient pleasures rather than following any long-term aim, there are passages where attention is chiefly focused on the aesthetic individual's dependence upon unpredictable vicissitudes of mood or circumstance, and others again where emphasis is laid on his need to guard against the threats posed by ennui or melancholy. Not unexpectedly, it is the problematic possibilities inherent in A's lifestyle that the Judge singles out for criticism in his comprehensive survey of the aesthetic position. Whereas the aestheticist typically allows himself to be swayed by what he conceives to be the unalterable constituents of his natural disposition, the ethically orientated individual is prone to look at himself in an altogether different light. Both his motivation and behaviour are responsive to a self-image 'in likeness to which he has to form himself', his particular aptitudes and propensities being seen as subject to the control of his will and as capable of being directed to the realization of demanding projects that reflect what he truly aspires to become. It is commitment to such projects which endows the ethical life with a coherence and self-sufficiency that its aesthetic counterpart conspicuously lacks.

Kierkegaard's treatment in *Either/Or* of the aesthetic/ethical contrast is frequently thought to echo the Kantian distinction between inclination and duty (see KANTIAN ETHICS). But although there may be discernible affinities, there are also significant differences. Thus Kant's predominantly schematic accounts of sensuous motivation are devoid of both the psychological penetration and the literary sophistication that characterize Kierkegaard's wide-ranging portrayals of the aesthetic stance. And comparable divergences are apparent in the case of the ethical. Kierkegaard's judge may be said to follow the German philosopher in highlighting the role of the will, underlining its independence of contingent circumstances and stressing its capacity to manage the sphere of natural inclination in a way that is conformable to the ethical individual's paramount concerns. Yet while he shares Kant's belief in and respect for the latter's autonomy, he differs in not presenting moral requirements in terms of the purely formal prescriptions of practical reason. The self which it is the task of each individual to choose and develop is not an 'abstract' but a 'concrete' self; it stands in 'reciprocal relations' with its actual social and cultural surroundings, things like marriage, having a job and undertaking civic and institutional responsibilities being intrinsic to personal fulfilment in the requisite sense. It is implied, moreover, that such active participation in communal affairs, involving an unconstrained and inward adherence to standards presupposed by a shared form of life, reinforces the contrast already drawn with the unreflective or wayward 'experimentalism' typified by certain manifestations of the aesthetic outlook. Thus the Judge insists upon the conceptual exclusion from the ethical of whatever savours of the arbitrary or the merely capricious. At the same time, however, he indicates that this should not be thought of as circumscribing in any fundamental fashion the subjective freedom and independence of the individual. For although moral requirements must of necessity be treated as authoritative, they are not apprehended as deriving from a source 'foreign to the personality' but are instead experienced as springing or 'breaking forth' from the latter's essential nature.

Even so, it is arguable that the internal tensions between individualistic and socially conformist strains discernible in the Judge's representation of the ethical sphere cannot always be easily or satisfactorily resolved. Kierkegaard discussed one context in which they might be said to arise in a critical form when he went on to consider a way of life that constituted an alternative to the possibilities so far portrayed. This stage of existence, transcending the other two, was the religious.

4 The religious consciousness

Central to Kierkegaard's account of religion is his treatment of the concept of faith, a treatment that throws into relief the most distinctive features of his philosophical standpoint. There are two main areas in which these manifest themselves and in which it is the crucial inadequacies of human reason, practical as well as theoretical, that are emphasized.

The first concerns limitations in the outlook of accepted morality that make themselves felt at certain levels or junctures of experience and are held to call for what is termed a 'teleological suspension of the ethical'. The implications of this *prima facie* puzzling notion are explored in *Fear and Trembling*, an intricately wrought study in which Kierkegaard's pseudonymous author – Johannes *de silentio* – treats as his central theme the biblical story of Abraham and Isaac. Johannes portrays Abraham as being ostensibly called upon to set aside ethical concerns in deference to a higher *telos* or end that altogether transcends them. Such a situation is contrasted with the predicament of what he terms the 'tragic hero', the latter being someone who is forced to make a choice between conflicting moral requirements but who in doing so still remains within the bounds of the ethical domain. Thus although the decisions taken there may be at an agonizing cost, the fact that they can none the less be seen to conform to universally recognized norms renders them rationally acceptable to others and capable of gaining their respect. This, however, is not so in the case of Abraham, who, as a solitary 'knight of faith', responds to a divine command supposedly addressed to himself alone and having a content – the killing of his own son – that must inevitably strike ordinary thought as being both outrageous and incomprehensible. No attempt is made to soften the paradoxical character of such points. On the contrary, Kierkegaard's pseudonym sets out to underline, indeed to dramatize, the disturbing nature of the demands which religious faith can impose on the life and conduct of an individual. At the same time, he takes practising churchmen severely to task for paying lip service to a phenomenon whose awesome significance they

fail to appreciate, and he also criticizes contemporary theorists of religion for construing an intrinsically transcendent category in terms drawn from social and essentially secular conceptions of ethics. This was not to suggest that from a religious point of view moral standards and principles could in general be abrogated or overruled. It did mean, on the other hand, that within that perspective they took on a radically different aspect, one where they possessed a relative rather than an absolute status and where it was the individual's own relation to God that was paramount, assuming precedence over all other considerations.

The claim that faith in the religious sense pertains to what exceeds the limits of human rationality and understanding recurs in the two subsequent writings that Kierkegaard referred to as his 'philosophical works' – *Philosophical Fragments* and *Concluding Unscientific Postscript*. Here, however, it is discussed within a wider setting and in connection with theoretical questions concerning the proper interpretation of religious assertions. Although once again ascribed to a pseudonym, albeit a different one, both books appeared under Kierkegaard's imprint as their 'editor' and in any case may be taken to have expressed views that were basically his own. Thus in each of them it is made apparent that the author totally rejects the feasibility of trying to provide religious tenets with an objective foundation. The belief that the existence and nature of God could be conclusively established from resources supplied by pure reason might have enjoyed a long philosophical career; none the less it was demonstrably unacceptable, Kierkegaard largely echoing – though in a summary form and without attribution – some of the objections that Kant had levelled against arguments traditionally advanced by theologians and metaphysicians. Nor was he any more receptive to the suggestion that religious claims of a specifically historical character, such as those relating to the doctrines of Christianity, were susceptible to justification on straightforwardly empirical grounds; it was impossible to regard them as representing ordinary historical facts of the sort to which standard appeals to inductive inference and evidence would normally be considered appropriate. As he acknowledged, Lessing and Hamann were thinkers who in different ways had already underlined the problematic issues raised by the latter. But it was perhaps Hume's contention in his first *Enquiry* that only a 'miracle in his own person', subverting all the principles of his understanding, could bring a reasonable individual to embrace the Christian religion which most strikingly foreshadowed Kierkegaard's approach to the subject. No doubt Hume himself had intended his words to be taken in a strictly ironical sense. Even so, Kierkegaard implied that it was open to believers to look at sceptical asides of the type cited in a different light. For by exposing the vanity of attempts to encompass within its grasp matters that lay beyond the scope of reason, such remarks could be said to provide salutary reminders of what was really at stake. It was not to the spheres of impersonal judgment and dispassionate assent that the religious consciousness rightfully belonged, but on the contrary to those of individual choice and inner commitment.

5 Faith and subjectivity

Kierkegaard was certainly not alone in suggesting that writers who tried to justify religious belief on cognitive grounds were more confused about its true nature than some of their sceptically minded critics and to that extent posed a greater threat to it; indeed, Kant himself had virtually implied as much when he spoke of denying knowledge to make room for faith, as opposed to seeking to give religious convictions a theoretical foundation that could only prove illusory (see KANT, I. §4). The question arose, however, of what positive account should be given of such faith, and here Kierkegaard's position set him apart from many thinkers who shared his negative attitude towards the feasibility of providing objective demonstrations. As he made amply clear, the religion that crucially concerned him was Christianity, and far from playing down the intellectual obstacles this ostensibly presented he went out of his way to stress the particular problems it raised. Both its official representatives and its academic apologists might have entertained the hope of making it rationally acceptable to a believer, but in doing so they showed themselves to be the victims of a fundamental misapprehension. From an objective point of view, neither knowledge nor even understanding was possible here, the proper path of the Christian follower lying in the direction, not of objectivity, but of its opposite. It was only by 'becoming subjective' that the import of Christianity could be grasped and meaningfully appropriated by the individual. Faith, Kierkegaard insisted, 'inheres in subjectivity'; as such it was in essence a matter of single-minded resolve and inward dedication rather than of spectatorial or contemplative detachment, of passion rather than of reflection. That was not to say, though, that it amounted to a primitive or easy option. On the contrary, faith in the sense in question could only be achieved or realized in the course of a person's life at great cost and with the utmost difficulty (see FAITH).

To understand what lay behind this claim it is important to recognize that Kierkegaard broadly distinguished between two levels or stages of development at which religious belief manifested itself. In his account of the first of these, in which he specified the criteria that any standpoint must conform to if it was to count as a religious one, he was at pains to emphasize the element of 'objective uncertainty' surrounding assertions about the transcendent, such uncertainty deriving from the absence of rational support previously alluded to. So construed, faith essentially involved personal venture or risk, preserving it being figuratively compared to 'remaining out upon the deep, over seventy thousand fathoms of water'. But to hold fast to a conviction in the face of a lack of objective justification or grounds was not the same as giving assent to something that appeared to be intrinsically contrary to reason, an 'offence' to the understanding itself. And it was in the latter terms that Kierkegaard referred to the Christian conception of the incarnation, this being an 'absolute paradox' that required the believer to 'risk his thought' in embracing its reality. Moreover, it was in the light of such a requirement that the level of faith aspired to in Christianity could be said to constitute 'the highest passion in the sphere of human subjectivity', exceeding other forms of religious belief in virtue of the unique nature of the demands it made upon an individual's mind and outlook.

According to Kierkegaard, the paradox of the incarnation lay in the notion that the eternal or timeless had entered the sphere of finite and temporal existence: this amounted to uniting contradictories in a fashion that meant a 'breach with all thinking'. Such a feature precluded treating it as if it could be vouchsafed by ordinary historical enquiry, and he set aside the scholarly pursuit of biblical research and criticism as altogether irrelevant to what was here at issue; quite apart from the specifically 'approximative' status he assigned to history as a branch of knowledge, the content of the particular 'hypothesis' under consideration defied logic in a way that contravened the principles governing any kind of accredited cognitive discipline. Furthermore, he regarded its paradoxical character as having another crucial consequence, namely, that there was no basis for the common assumption that the contemporary witnesses of what was recorded in the Gospels were in a better position to authenticate the reality of the incarnation than subsequent generations who had only the testimony of others to rely on. To suppose that in the present case the evidence of direct observation was superior to testimony was to fail to see that neither could ever function as more than an 'occasion' for belief of the sort of question. With both, a volitional leap of faith was necessary, one that involved a 'qualitative transition' from the realm of rational thought into that of the intellectually inaccessible or 'absurd'.

Kierkegaard's stress on the gap separating faith from reason, which it could need divine assistance to surmount, was reflected in the controversial account he offered of religious truth; this likewise received a subjective interpretation. Thus in a well-known passage in the *Postscript* he contrasted two distinct ways of conceiving of truth, one treating it as a matter of a belief's corresponding to what it purported to be about and the other as essentially pertaining to the particular manner or spirit in which a belief was held. And it was to the second of these conceptions that he ostensibly referred when he declared that 'subjectivity is the truth', genuineness of feeling and depth of inner conviction being the decisive criterion from a religious point of view. Admittedly he has sometimes been criticized here for a tendency to shift from construing religious truth along the above lines to doing so in terms of the objective alternative, with the questionable implication that sheer intensity of subjective acceptance was sufficient to authenticate the independent reality of what was believed. But however that may be, it is arguable that in this context – as is often the case elsewhere – his prime concerns were conceptual and phenomenological in character, rather than epistemic or justificatory. Kierkegaard's central aim was to assign Christianity to its proper sphere, freeing it from what he considered to be traditional misconceptions as well as from the falsifying metaphysical theories to which there had more recently been attempts to assimilate it. If that meant confronting what he himself called 'a crucifixion of the understanding', the only appropriate response from the standpoint in question lay in a passionate commitment to the necessarily paradoxical and mysterious content of the Christian religion, together with a complementary resolve to emulate in practice the paradigmatic life of its founder.

6 Psychological themes and influence

Kierkegaard's preoccupation with the category of subjectivity that ran like a continuous thread through his theoretical writings was integrally linked to his conception of human beings as individual and self-determining participants in the 'existential process'. The view that freedom and the possibility of change constituted fundamental conditions of human life and fulfilment was delineated in his so-called 'psychological works', *The Concept of Anxiety* and *The Sickness Unto Death*. In both books the structure of human personality is portrayed in developmental and volitional terms; individuals exist in the mode, not of being, but of becoming,

and what they become is something for which they themselves are ultimately responsible. In this connection certain pervasive attitudes and emotions can be seen to possess a special significance, Kierkegaard giving priority of place to a form of anxiety or dread (*Angst*) which differed from sentiments like fear in lacking any determinate object and in being directed instead to 'something that is nothing'. Such a state of mind might manifest itself in a variety of ways, but he made it clear that his fundamental concern was with its relation to the consciousness of freedom. Thus he referred to the particular kind of dizziness, or vertiginous ambivalence between attraction and repulsion, that was liable to afflict us when, in certain circumstances, the realization dawned that there was nothing objective that compelled us to opt for one course of action rather than another; in the last analysis what we did was up to ourselves alone, freedom being said to 'look down into its own possibility' as though into a yawning abyss or void. Kierkegaard believed that the psychological phenomenon so identified had momentous consequences, not least for its bearing on the religious alternatives of sin and salvation. On the one hand, the story of Adam represented a mythical illustration of how the awakened consciousness of freedom could arouse an anxiety whose occurrence in this case was the precursor of sin. On the other hand, however, such an emotion might also arise when there was a possibility of making a qualitative leap, not into sin and alienation from God, but towards the opposite of this, namely, faith and the promise offered by Christianity. But here Kierkegaard reiterates the point that a presentiment of the difficulties and sacrifices entailed made the latter a course which there were strong temptations to resist; it followed that people were only too prone to conceal from themselves their potentialities as free beings, such self-induced obscurity serving as a convenient screen for inaction and a failure to change. Self-deception of this sort in fact formed a component of many of the varieties of spiritual despair which Kierkegaard picked out for analysis, as well as underpinning his diagnosis of some of the broader types of malaise he detected in the social and cultural climate of his time.

In his insistence upon the ultimacy of human freedom and his correlative attention to the devices and strategies whereby people may seek to protect themselves from a recognition of some of its disturbing implications, Kierkegaard anticipated themes that were taken up, albeit much later and often in an explicitly secular setting, by a number of leading twentieth-century writers (see EXISTENTIALISM). Subjectivity and the primacy of the individual, the 'burden' of freedom, the contrast between authentic and inauthentic modes of existence – these and associated topics became familiar through the works of existentialist philosophers such as Jean-Paul SARTRE and Martin HEIDEGGER as well as figuring in the wider field of imaginative literature. Nor were those the only areas in which his ideas eventually made an impact. In the sphere of ethics his emphasis on radical choice indirectly contributed to the growth of non-cognitivist theories of value, while in religion his conception of faith had a profound influence on the development of modern Protestant theology, notwithstanding understandable reservations about some of his more extreme claims regarding its paradoxical character.

See also: HEGELIANISM; RELIGION AND SCIENCE

References and further reading

Kierkegaard, S.A. (1843) *Enten-Eller*, trans. H.V. Hong and E.H. Hong, *Either/Or*, Princeton, NJ: Princeton University Press, 1987, 2 vols. (Presents contrasting life-views, one aesthetic and the other ethical, in the form of papers and letters attributed to two imaginary characters.)

Thompson, J. (1974) *Kierkegaard*, London: Gollancz. (A penetrating critical biography.)

PATRICK GARDINER

KIRCHHEIMER, OTTO
See FRANKFURT SCHOOL

KNOWABILITY PARADOX
See PARADOXES, EPISTEMIC

KNOWLEDGE AND JUSTIFICATION, COHERENCE THEORY OF

Introduction

Coherence theories of justification represent one main alternative to *foundationalist* theories of justification. If, as has usually been thought, possessing epistemic justification is one necessary condition (along with truth and perhaps others) for a belief to constitute knowledge, then a coherence theory of justification would also provide the basis for a coherence theory of knowledge. While some proponents of coherence theories have restricted the scope of the theory to empirical justification, others have applied it to all varieties of epistemic justification. (There are also coherence theories of meaning and of truth, as well as coherence theories of ethical or moral justification.)

The initial contrast between coherence theories and foundationalist theories arises in the context of

the *epistemic regress problem*. It is obvious that the justification of some beliefs derives from their inferential relations to other, putatively justified beliefs, and that the justification of these other beliefs may depend on inferential relations to still further beliefs, and so on, so that a potential regress of epistemic justification looms, with scepticism as the threatened outcome. The foundationalist solution to this problem is that one arrives sooner or later at basic or foundational beliefs: beliefs that are epistemically justified, but whose justification does not derive from inferential relations to any further beliefs and so brings the regress to an end. The defining tenet of a coherence theory of justification is the rejection of this foundationalist solution, the coherentist insisting that any belief (of the kinds to which the theory is applied) depends for its justification on inferential relations to other beliefs and eventually to the overall system of beliefs held by the believer in question. According to the coherentist, the justification of this system of beliefs is logically prior to that of its component beliefs and derives ultimately from the *coherence* of the system, where coherence is a matter of how tightly unified or interconnected the system is by virtue of inferential connections (including explanatory connections) between its members.

Contrary to what this might seem to suggest, coherence theories do not deny that sensory observation or perception plays an important role in justification. What they do deny is that this role should be construed in a foundationalist way, insisting instead that the justification of observational beliefs ultimately derives also from considerations of coherence. Specific coherence theories may also add other requirements for justification, thereby departing from a pure coherentism, while still avoiding foundationalism.

While the idea of a coherence theory has often played the role of a dialectical foil, developed theories of this kind are relatively rare and are often in serious disagreement among themselves. In this way, coherentism is much less a unified view with standard, generally accepted features, than is foundationalism.

1 History
2 The regress problem and non-linear justification
3 The concept of coherence
4 Coherence and observation
5 The standard objections
6 The problem of access

1 History

In contrast to foundationalism, the coherence theory of justification is a relatively recent innovation in the history of philosophy. Although it is possible, albeit with some strain, to construe Spinoza and Kant as advocating versions of coherentism, the first relatively clear-cut coherentist positions are those of the late nineteenth- and early twentieth-century absolute idealists, especially F.H. BRADLEY and BERNARD BOSANQUET. Unfortunately, however, the views of these philosophers are marked by a pervasive failure to distinguish epistemological and metaphysical issues, making it hard to separate their coherence theories of justification from their distinct, though related, advocacy of coherence theories of the nature of truth. (A more recent version of essentially the same position, in which this distinction is clearly drawn, is found in the work of Brand Blanshard.)

Coherentism was also advocated in the 1930s by some of the logical positivists, mainly Otto Neurath and Carl Hempel, in response to the foundationalist views of MORITZ SCHLICK. Neurath identifies coherence with mere logical consistency; he also, while retaining something like a justificatory appeal to observation, in effect identifies observational beliefs solely by reference to their content. He thus has no apparent response to what is perhaps the most central and obvious objection to coherence theories: that there will always be indefinitely many different coherent systems between which a coherence theory will provide no basis for a reasoned choice (see below). Hempel avoids this problem to some extent by simply identifying observational beliefs as those beliefs with the right sort of content that are accepted by 'the scientists of our culture circle', but is able to offer no real rationale for such an identification. He also, like the idealists, fails to distinguish in any clear way between a coherence theory of justification and a coherentist account of the nature of truth.

More recent coherentist positions, in contrast, generally repudiate the coherence theory of truth entirely and are more explicitly and narrowly epistemological in their character and motivation. The main arguments offered in their favour almost always derive from perceived objections to foundationalism, perhaps the central one being the charge that the foundationalist can account for the status of the allegedly basic or foundational beliefs as genuinely justified (in the sense of there being some reason or basis for thinking them to be true) only by appealing to justificatory premises of some sort and so destroying the status of such beliefs as foundational (see FOUNDATIONALISM). Thus coherentists insist that there is no way to appeal for justification to anything outside of one's system of beliefs because any such supposed source of justification would have to be apprehended by the person in question in a belief or belief-like state before it could play any justificatory role, and then it

would be the belief rather than the external item that was the immediate source of justification.

As this suggests, coherentist positions are virtually always internalist rather than externalist in character, in that they insist that the basis for epistemic justification must be cognitively accessible to the believer in question; while an externalist version of coherentism is theoretically possible, it would have little philosophical point, since a foundationalist view would be vastly more straightforward if externalism were otherwise acceptable (see INTERNALISM AND EXTERNALISM IN EPISTEMOLOGY).

These recent coherentist views differ from each other in a wide variety of ways, and often seem to have little in common beyond their rejection of foundationalism and their invocation in some fashion of the idea of coherence (and indeed there is often room for doubt in a particular case about how thoroughgoing the former of these two aspects really is). Coherentism is one ingredient, though never developed in a fully systematic way, in the comprehensive and difficult philosophical system of Wilfrid SELLARS. The epistemological position of W.V. Quine is also frequently described as coherentist in character, though other features of Quine's position, especially his claim that epistemology should be naturalized (reduced to psychology), make it difficult to decide whether his view is genuinely a version of coherentism, as opposed to a qualified version of foundationalism (see NATURALIZED EPISTEMOLOGY). More overtly coherentist positions have been advocated by Gilbert Harman (influenced especially by Quine), Nicholas Rescher, Keith Lehrer, and Laurence BonJour (influenced especially by Sellars).

As the foregoing suggests, coherence theories first arise as dialectical alternatives to foundationalism, rather than as views that are claimed to be initially plausible on their own. Their defence and elaboration must confront a number of standard problems and objections, with which any such view must seemingly deal in some fashion, and it is around these that the present entry is organized.

2 The regress problem and non-linear justification

The first standard problem arises from the epistemic regress problem itself. If foundationalism is repudiated (and if a genuinely infinite regress of justification is also rejected as psychologically impossible and in any case tantamount to scepticism), then the only remaining possibility for the outcome of the initial regress of epistemic justification seems to be a circle in which the chains of justification eventually loop back upon themselves. Incautious advocates of coherentism have sometimes seemed to endorse the idea that such a result is acceptable if only the circles are 'large enough'. But the obvious objection to circular chains of justification, to which the size of the circle seems irrelevant, is that they involve circular reasoning and hence have no genuine justificatory force. This is essentially the reason that foundationalists give for rejecting the coherentist alternative and taking the regress problem to constitute a decisive argument for foundationalism.

Perhaps the most standard coherentist response to this issue, stemming originally from Bosanquet, is to reject the idea, implicit in most presentations of the regress problem, that relations of justification must involve a linear, asymmetrical order of dependence among the beliefs in question. They insist instead that justification, when properly understood, is ultimately holistic and non-linear in character, with all of the beliefs in the system standing in relations of mutual support, but none being epistemically prior to the others. In this way, it is alleged, any true circularity is avoided. Such a view amounts to making the system itself the primary unit of justification, with its component beliefs being justified only derivatively, by virtue of their membership in an appropriate sort of system. And the property of the system, in virtue of which it is justified, is of course specified as coherence.

3   The concept of coherence

But what exactly is coherence? A second obvious problem for a coherence theory is to explicate and clarify this central concept. Intuitively, coherence is a matter of how the beliefs in a system of beliefs fit together or dovetail with each other, so as to constitute one unified, organized, and tightly structured whole. And it is clear that this fitting together depends on a wide variety of logical, inferential and explanatory relations among the components of the system. But spelling out the details of this idea, particularly in a way that would allow unproblematic assessments of comparative coherence, turns out to be extremely difficult, in part at least because of its obvious dependence on more specific and still unsettled topics, such as induction, confirmation, probability and explanation.

The strongest and most demanding conception of coherence, advocated by the idealists, specifies a coherent system of beliefs as one in which each member entails and is entailed by all of the others. It seems clear, however, that this strong conception is both unrealizable by any actual system of beliefs imaginable and also of dubious cognitive value, since it would seem to make all of the beliefs but one redundant and dispensable. (These problems may be mitigated somewhat, though certainly not

eliminated, by remembering that the idealists have a quite broad conception of entailment, one in which, for example, relations of nomological necessity are regarded as a kind of entailment.)

At the opposite extreme, it seems equally mistaken to follow Schlick and some others in identifying coherence with mere logical consistency, since the beliefs of a logically consistent system might be entirely unrelated to each other, thus yielding no real degree of mutual support and no apparent reason for thinking that any of them are true. Somewhat more surprisingly, it also seems to be a mistake to make complete logical consistency even an absolutely *necessary* condition for any degree of coherence, as many coherentists have done. In light of such things as the preface paradox and general human fallibility, this would probably mean that few if any actual systems of belief are coherent to any degree at all, a result that seems unacceptably paradoxical (see PARADOXES, EPISTEMIC).

If there is a tenable conception of coherence along these general lines, it must seemingly fall somewhere between the two extremes just discussed. Coherence will be a matter of degree, with logical consistency being a highly relevant but not absolute criterion. Coherence will also require a high degree of inferential interconnectedness in the system, involving relations of necessitation, both strictly logical and otherwise, together with probabilistic connections of various kinds. An important aspect of this is what might be called probabilistic consistency, that is, the absence of relations between beliefs in the system in virtue of which some are highly unlikely to be true in relation to others. A further important ingredient of coherence that is much emphasized in recent discussions is the presence of explanatory relations among the components of the system, thus reducing the degree to which the beliefs of the system portray unexplained anomalies. (If 'inference to the best explanation' is accepted as one species of inference, then such explanatory relations can be viewed as a kind of inferential relation – see INFERENCE TO THE BEST EXPLANATION.) Indeed, some positions such as that of Harman, and perhaps also Sellars, go so far as to virtually identify coherence with the presence of such explanatory relations.

The foregoing is an approximate account of the historically standard conception of coherence. While some proponents of coherentism have employed essentially this conception, others have in effect devised more idiosyncratic conceptions of coherence, conceptions whose connection to the historical concept is often quite tenuous. In particular, Rescher in fact employs both the standard conception of coherence, for certain purposes, and also a quite different concept that involves forming maximally consistent subsets of initially conflicting 'data' or 'truth-candidates', and then choosing among these subsets in a variety of ways that involve no appeal to standard coherence. And Lehrer (1974, 1990) has offered two subtly different versions of a general view that defines coherence in relation to the believer's own subjective conception of probability or relative likelihood of truth; for a belief to cohere with the person's system of beliefs is roughly for it to be judged to be more probable or more reasonable than any relevant competitor.

The precise nature of coherence remains a largely unsolved problem. It is important to see, however, that difficulties in this area cannot yield anything like a decisive argument against coherence theories and in favour of their foundationalist rivals. This is so because the concept of coherence, or something so similar to it as to be capable of playing essentially the same role, is also an indispensable ingredient in virtually all foundationalist theories: coherence must seemingly be invoked to account for the relation between the basic or foundational beliefs and other non-foundational or 'superstructure' beliefs, in virtue of which the latter are justified in relation to the former. For this reason, giving an adequate account of coherence should not be regarded as exclusively or even primarily the responsibility of coherentists, despite the central role that the concept plays in their position.

4   Coherence and observation

As mentioned above, few if any coherentists have wished to deny the seemingly obvious fact that sensory observation or perception plays a crucial role in justification (although they have not always been fully explicit on this point). It is thus incumbent on a coherence theory to explain how such observation can be construed in a non-foundationalist way. The central idea is that a belief that is produced by the senses, rather than being arrived at inferentially, might still depend for its justification on coherence with the background system of beliefs. But it is crucial here that the justification in question should still depend also in some way on the fact that the belief was a result of perception, since justification that depended only on the coherence of the belief's propositional content with the rest of the cognitive system would make the observational status of the belief irrelevant.

One way to develop this idea is to focus on the fact that observational or perceptual beliefs are *cognitively spontaneous*; they simply strike the observer in an involuntary, coercive, non-inferential way, rather than as a product of any sort of inference or other discursive process, whether explicit or implicit. That a belief has this status, however, says nothing so far, according to the coherentist, about whether or how it is justified. Indeed, there is no reason to think that all cognitively spontaneous beliefs *are* justified, or even necessarily that most of them are, since the category would include hunches and irrational spontaneous convictions, as well as beliefs resulting from perception. But suppose that, as seems to be the case with most ordinary systems of belief, the system includes a belief to the effect that specific kinds of cognitively spontaneous beliefs (identified by their general subject matter, by their apparent mode of sensory production as reflected in the content of the belief, and by concomitant factors of various kinds) are, under specified (or perhaps 'normal') conditions, highly likely to be true. It then becomes possible to give a justifying reason for such a belief that appeals to its status as cognitively spontaneous and putatively observational, but still does so in a way that depends on the coherence with the background system of beliefs of the claim that a belief of this kind and produced in this way is true. Such a belief would be arrived at non-inferentially, but still justified by appeal to inference relations and coherence. (This view of observation is most explicit in BonJour (1985), but something like it seems implicit in Blanshard's talk of 'beliefs about the technique of acquiring beliefs', in Sellars's talk of 'language-entry transitions', in Quine's talk of the 'observational periphery' of the 'web of belief', in Rescher's idea of 'data', and in Lehrer's (1974, 1990) discussion of a person's trustworthiness in acquiring certain kinds of information).

The foregoing provides at best only the beginning of a coherentist account of observation, leaving various problems to be solved that can only be touched on here. First, the other beliefs needed to give a justifying reason for a particular observational belief must themselves be justified in some fashion, without relapsing at this point into foundationalism. These beliefs will include at least: (1) beliefs about the conditions; (2) the general belief about the reliability of the kind of cognitively spontaneous belief in question; and (3) beliefs about the occurrence of that particular belief, including the belief that it was indeed cognitively spontaneous. The justification for (1) will presumably have to include other observational beliefs, themselves justified in the same general fashion, so that any case of justified observation will normally or perhaps always involve a set of mutually supporting observations. The justification for (2) will appeal inductively to other cases of correct observation, as judged from within the system, as well as to more theoretical reasons for thinking that beliefs of the kind in question are generally produced in a reliable way. The justification for (3) will appeal to introspective beliefs, themselves constituting a species of observation, and ultimately to the believer's comprehensive grasp of their overall system of beliefs – a grasp whose status poses one of the main problems to be considered below.

Second, it is not enough for the justification of an observational belief that a reason of the foregoing sort should merely be present in a person's system of beliefs, since such an individual might completely fail to notice that this was so, and might hold the belief on some other basis or for no reason at all. Thus even though the observational belief is not arrived at by inference, the availability of the inferential justification in question, even if never explicitly rehearsed, must be the reason why the believer continues to accept the belief and to appeal to it for further purposes. A full account of coherentist observation would have to spell out exactly what this requirement amounts to and how it can be satisfied.

Third, the bare possibility of coherentist observation seems insufficient to accommodate the role that observation plays in our cognitive lives. Given the convictions that observation is not only possible but pervasive and that an appeal to observational evidence, whether direct or indirect, is essential for the justification of at least contingent beliefs about the world, an intuitively adequate coherence theory must somehow *require* and not just allow that a substantial observational element should be present in any justified system that includes such contingent beliefs. A view that insisted on such a requirement would thereby depart from a pure coherence theory, but might still avoid foundationalism if the coherentist account of observation is otherwise successful. (Such a requirement is relevant to several of the objections examined below.)

5 The standard objections

In considering objections to coherence theories, we may begin with the three that are historically most standard and familiar. The first of these is what is commonly referred to as 'the isolation problem' or 'the input objection': an account of justification that appeals entirely to coherence within a system of beliefs seems to have the consequence that the justificatory status of the beliefs in the system will not depend in any way on the relation of the system to the world that it purports to describe, or on any sort of information derived from that world. This would seem to mean in turn that the truth of the component beliefs, if they happened to be true, could only be an accident, and thus that there is no reason to think that they are true and so no epistemic justification. The coherentist account of

observation sketched above, if it can be successfully fleshed out, provides the beginning of an answer to this objection by showing how observational beliefs that are apparently generated by the world might none the less be given a coherentist justification. In this way, a coherent system that involves a putatively observational component will at least seem from the inside to have input from the world and thus not to be isolated. Whether this seeming is likely to be veridical will depend, however, on the more general issue, discussed below, of whether and why coherentist justification should be regarded as conducive to finding the truth.

The second familiar objection, already briefly alluded to earlier, is what may be called the alternative coherent systems objection: even given a relatively strong account of coherence, there will still be indefinitely many different possible systems of beliefs, each of which is as internally coherent as the others, and so all of which will be equally justified on a coherentist view – surely an absurd result. The response to this objection also depends crucially on the idea of observation. If, as suggested earlier, it will be a requirement for justification in an adequate coherence theory that there be a substantial observational component (that is, a substantial proportion of cognitively spontaneous beliefs that the system itself certifies as likely to be true and hence worthy of being accepted), then such alternative systems can no longer be freely invented and it is no longer obvious why they should be thought to exist. Only a system that is actually accepted and employed in cognitive practice can contain cognitively spontaneous beliefs and thus satisfy the requirement for observation. There is no way to guarantee that the acceptance of such beliefs will not lead quickly to incoherence in an arbitrarily devised system, even if it is initially coherent. (As this suggests, it is coherence over a period of time and not just at a moment that is ultimately the basis for justification in all coherence theories that have been seriously advocated.)

The third of the standard objections is in effect a challenge to the coherentist to give a reason for thinking that adopting beliefs on the basis of coherentist justification is likely to lead to believing the truth. Different coherentists give very different responses to this crucial question, each problematic in its own way. These can only be briefly sketched here. (1) The absolute idealists in effect solve the problem by adopting a coherence theory of truth as well, thus reducing the gap between coherentist justification and truth (though only Blanshard is very explicit about this strategy). On such a view, truth is essentially identified with long-run justification, making it relatively easy to argue that seeking justified beliefs is likely to lead eventually to finding true ones – but at the significant cost of adopting an extremely implausible conception of truth. (2) Rescher attempts to give a pragmatic argument to the effect that the practical success which results from the employment of the coherent system makes it likely that the beliefs of the system are at least approximately true (in the sense of corresponding to independent reality). Unfortunately, however, the need for justification for the claims of practical success, which must presumably also be coherentist in character, threatens the project with vicious circularity. (3) BonJour (1985) attempts to give an a priori 'metajustificatory argument', relying on a rationalist and foundationalist conception of a priori knowledge, for the conclusion that a system of beliefs that remains coherent over the relatively long run, while receiving apparent observational input, is likely to be approximately true (again in the correspondence sense of truth). The main reason offered is that only approximate truth could explain continued coherence in the face of new observations. In addition to defending the general account of a priori justification presupposed, such an approach must also claim that sceptical explanations of one's beliefs (for example their being produced by a Cartesian demon), are a priori less likely than the preferred explanation of correspondence with reality, a claim that many have found highly implausible. (4) Lehrer's approach is to construct alternative conceptions of justification that involve the hypothetical replacement of erroneous beliefs in a person's system of beliefs with their corrected alternatives, and then require that the person's initially justified beliefs remain justified after such replacements in order for such beliefs to constitute knowledge. The main difficulty here is that such an approach seems to concede that 'personal justification' – the sort of justification which exists before the hypothetical replacements – is not in itself conducive to finding the truth, even though such personal justification is the only sort that the believer is in general ever actually aware of.

6   The problem of access

In addition to the foregoing objections, there are a number of further problems with which an adequate coherence theory would have to deal. Perhaps the most urgent of these is that of whether coherentist justification is accessible to the believer in the way that it must be if an internalist position is to result. Assuming for the moment, as is the case with all the positions discussed here, that coherentist justification is taken to require coherence with the believer's entire system of beliefs, then there are three aspects to this problem: (1) whether the believer has adequate access to their system of beliefs; (2) whether the believer has an adequate grasp of the concept of coherence; and (3) whether the believer is able to apply the concept of coherence to their system of beliefs in a way that will yield a definite assessment. All these aspects pose serious problems, and (3) in particular is anything but trivial, even given satisfactory solutions to (1) and (2). But (1) is the most difficult and will accordingly be the main focus here.

A believer's access to their own system of beliefs is in fact seriously problematic in two quite different ways. First, there is the problem of the epistemological status of the result of such access if it were achieved, which we may think of as a reflective meta-belief describing the entire contents of the system. Such a meta-belief would be clearly contingent and empirical and hence one that on any coherence theory of the sort under consideration here ought to be itself justified by appeal to coherence. But since any coherentist justification that is to be accessible to the believer must appeal to such a meta-belief in order to characterize the system of beliefs with which the belief to be justified must cohere, a coherentist justification of that meta-belief itself appears to be totally and irrevocably circular (and no appeal to non-linear justification will help here, since what is being explained is how the very sort of non-linear justification advocated by the coherentist is possible).

The most explicit discussion of this issue is given by BonJour (1985), who responds by invoking what he calls 'the Doxastic Presumption'. The idea is that coherentist justification must *presume* that the believer's grasp of their overall system of beliefs is at least approximately correct (small corrections being possible by appeal to coherence). This has the consequence that the resulting justification is contingent upon the presumed correctness of this grasp, and hence that there is no possible answer on the part of a coherence theory to the specific variety of scepticism that questions whether this presumption is indeed correct. This has seemed to many to be a very drastic result, but it is unclear what the alternative might be, so long as foundationalism is eschewed.

Even if the foregoing issue were resolved in a satisfactory way, there is still the second aspect of the present problem: the quite sticky issue of whether ordinary believers ever in fact possess or could possess anything like the reflective grasp of the entire contents of their systems of beliefs that a coherence theory seems to require. On this issue, it seems likely that a coherence theory will have to concede that ordinary cases of justification are at best only an approximation, and perhaps a fairly distant one, to the ideal justification that a coherence theory portrays.

One further problem is worth a brief mention. If, as is almost always the case, a coherence theory appeals to coherence over the relatively long run, then the issue arises of how the memory beliefs upon which any access to the fact of continued coherence must seemingly rely, are themselves to be justified. Many philosophers have offered coherence theories of the justification of memory beliefs, but such a view is again threatened with vicious circularity if the only reason for thinking that coherentist justification is conductive to truth – and so that the memory beliefs in particular are true – relies on coherence over time, and so on those very memory beliefs themselves.

See also: Justification, epistemic; Knowledge, concept of; Truth, coherence theory of; Truth, correspondence theory of

References and further reading

BonJour, L. (1985) *The Structure of Empirical Knowledge*, Cambridge, MA: Harvard University Press. (The author's version of coherentism, discussed especially in §§4 and 6 previously but containing elaborations of material in other sections as well; also contains an appendix discussing the views of the positivists, the absolute idealists, Lehrer and Rescher.)

Lehrer, K. (1990) *Theory of Knowledge*, Boulder, CO: Westview Press. (A revision of Lehrer's 1974 work *Knowledge*; referred to in §§1, 3 and 4 earlier.)

LAURENCE BONJOUR

KNOWLEDGE, CONCEPT OF

Introduction

The branch of philosophy concerned with the nature and extent of human knowledge is called epistemology (from the Greek *epistēmē* meaning knowledge, and *logos* meaning theory). Knowledge seems to come in many varieties: we know people, places and things; we know how to perform tasks; we know facts. Factual knowledge has been the central focus of epistemology.

We can know a fact only if we have a true belief about it. However, since only some true beliefs are knowledge (consider, for example, a lucky guess), the central question asked by epistemologists is 'What converts mere true belief into knowledge?'. There are many, and often conflicting, answers to this question. The primary traditional answer has been that our true beliefs must be based upon sufficiently good reasons in order to be certifiable as knowledge. Foundationalists have held that the

structure of reasons is such that our reasons ultimately rest upon basic reasons that have no further reasons supporting them. Coherentists have argued that there are no foundational reasons. Rather, they argue that our beliefs are mutually supporting.

In addition to the constraints upon the overall structure of reasons, epistemologists have proposed various general principles governing reasons. For example, it seems that if my reasons are adequate to affirm some fact, those reasons should be adequate to eliminate other incompatible hypotheses. This initially plausible principle appears to lead directly to some deep puzzles and, perhaps, even to scepticism. Indeed, many of the principles that seem initially plausible lead to various unexpected and unwelcome conclusions.

Alternatives to the primary traditional answer to the central epistemic question have been developed, in part because of the supposed failures of traditional epistemology. These alternative views claim that it is something other than good reasons which distinguishes (mere) true beliefs from knowledge. Reliabilists claim that a true belief produced by a sufficiently reliable process is knowledge. Good reasoning is but one of the many ways in which beliefs can be reliably produced. The issue of whether the objections to traditional epistemology are valid or whether the proposed substitutes are better remains unresolved.

1   The varieties of knowledge

Knowledge comes in many varieties. I can know *how* to adjust a carburettor. I can know a person. I can know *that* mixing bleach and ammonia is dangerous. In the first case, I possess a skill. In the second, I am acquainted with someone. In the third, I know a fact. Epistemologists have differed on the relationships between these types of knowledge. On the one hand, it could be held that knowing a person (place or thing) should be construed as nothing more (or less) than knowing certain facts about that someone and possessing the skill of being able to distinguish that person from other objects. On the other hand, it has been held that knowing facts depends upon being acquainted with particular objects. Whether the reduction of one form of knowledge to another is ultimately successful is an area of contention among epistemologists.

Nevertheless, it is knowledge of facts, so-called *propositional knowledge*, as opposed to knowledge by acquaintance or the possession of skills, that has been the central concern of epistemologists. The central question can be put this way: which beliefs of mine are to be counted as knowledge? This question presupposes that knowledge is a species of belief, but some might think that knowledge and belief are mutually exclusive: for example, we say such things as 'I do not *believe* that; I *know* it'. But we also say such things as 'I am not *happy*; I am *ecstatic*'. A suggested paraphrase of this expression seems to capture what is meant without denying the obviously true claim that ecstasy is a form of happiness. The paraphrase is: I am not *merely* happy, I am ecstatic. The parallel is: I do not merely believe it; I know it. Thus, this type of linguistic evidence does not support the suggestion that belief and knowledge are mutually exclusive. In general, epistemologists have held that propositional knowledge is a species of belief.

2 Propositional knowledge is not mere true belief

Propositional knowledge is a species of belief; but which beliefs are knowledge? The first thing to note is that a belief must be true in order for it to count as knowledge. But that is obviously not enough. First, true beliefs can be based upon faulty reasoning. Suppose that I believe that smoking is a leading cause of fatal lung cancer because I infer it from the fact that I know two smokers who died of lung cancer. The generalization is true, but my evidence is too meagre for my belief to count as knowledge. Second, true beliefs can be based on false beliefs. Modifying an example used by Bertrand Russell, suppose that I believe truly that the last name of the President of the United States in 1996 begins with a 'C'. Also suppose this belief is based upon the false belief that the President is Winston Churchill. My true belief that the President's name begins with a 'C' is not knowledge because it is based on a false belief.

Third, even some true beliefs resulting from good reasoning based upon true beliefs are not knowledge. Suppose that I believe (truly) that my neighbours are at home. My belief is based upon good reasoning from my true belief that I see lights on and that, in the past, the lights have been on only when they were at home. But suppose further that

this time the lights were turned on by a guest and that my neighbours had just entered the house and would not have had time to turn on the lights. In this case, I fail to know that my neighbours are home. So, the central question becomes: what must be added to true belief to convert it into knowledge?

3 Warrant

The property, whatever it is, that, if added to true belief converts it into knowledge, we may refer to as 'warrant'. Knowledge, then, is true, warranted, belief. But simply to name the missing property does not bring us closer to understanding it and we must be careful not to think of 'warrant' as a sophisticated synonym for 'justified'. Let us say that a belief is *justified* just in case we are entitled to hold it on the basis of suitable reasons available to us. In the neighbour/lights case mentioned above, we have already seen that justification is not sufficient for warrant. Whether it is even necessary will be important in the discussion that follows, especially in §6.

Given the great variety of approaches to an account of warrant, is there any common, underlying starting point embraced by epistemologists? Yes: a warranted belief is one that is not held on the basis of mere cognitive luck. Plato appeals to that intuition in the *Theaetetus*; Aristotle's account of the transition from ignorance of the first principles in science to knowledge of them in the *Posterior Analytics* is designed to demonstrate that there are reliable cognitive mechanisms whose output is not the result of chance; Descartes proposes methods for acquiring beliefs that would (he thinks) necessarily lead to truth; Locke suggests that even if persons arrive at a true belief by accident, they are not thereby free from criticism.

Let us start with the assumption that a proposition is known just in case it is not an accident, from the cognitive point of view, that it is both believed and true. Hence the task becomes one of developing an account of warrant that accurately portrays what it is that makes a belief non-accidentally true from the cognitive point of view.

4 Foundationalism and coherentism

There are two main, traditional approaches to the account of justification: foundationalism and coherentism. Both are *normative* views about rules in virtue of which propositions *ought* to be accepted or *ought* to be rejected or *ought* to be suspended (see KNOWLEDGE AND JUSTIFICATION, COHERENCE THEORY OF; FOUNDATIONALISM). In order to characterize these approaches, recall how the ancient Pyrrhonian Sceptics divided the possible structures of reasons that provide a basis for accepting a belief (see EPISTEMOLOGY, HISTORY OF; PYRRHONISM). Suppose you hold a belief and offer another belief as the reason for the first – for example, suppose you believe that Ford cars are generally less expensive than BMWs. Your reason could be your belief that you were told so by a reliable person. An obvious question arises: what is your basis for believing that the person is reliable? You could answer with another reason and that reason could, itself, be supported by a further reason, and so on.

This process of providing reasons for your beliefs can have only three possible structures:

Foundationalism: The process of giving reasons could be such that not every reason is supported by another reason because there are *basic reasons* which have no need of further reasons supporting them.

Coherentism: The process of giving reasons could have no reason that is not supported by another reason, but there is not an infinite number of reasons. Thus, beliefs are mutually supporting.

Infinitism: The process of giving reasons could have no reason that is not supported by another reason, but there is an infinite number of reasons.

Foundationalism and coherentism have both been developed and defended, and there are well-known objections to each view. In contrast, the *prima facie* objections to infinitism have seemed so overwhelming that it has not been investigated carefully. Infinitism *seems* to require that a person should have an infinite number of beliefs (which *seems* on its face to be false). In addition, it *seems* to lead inevitably to the conclusion that no belief could ever be justified, since the process of justification would never come to an end.

The standard objections to foundationalism are several. First, as the Pyrrhonians would point out, there must be a distinction between what makes a belief *properly* basic and what makes it simply one for which no other reason is, in fact, given. Otherwise, the offered 'basic' reason is arbitrary. But if there is some further reason for thinking that an offered reason is not arbitrary, then there is a reason for accepting it, and the offered reason is, thereby, not basic. Hence, there can be no foundational propositions.

Second, some preferred candidates for properly basic reasons seem not to be properly basic on closer inspection. Consider perceptual judgments – the source of most of our knowledge of the external world according to many philosophers (see EMPIRICISM; A POSTERIORI). A reason for believing that

there is a tree before me is that I see a tree before me. But the latter proposition does not appear to be properly basic because one could be required to explain what it is about what is seen that leads one to believe that it is a *tree* that one sees (as opposed to an illusion). Thus, some foundationalists have retreated to sensation-beliefs (so-called sense-data propositions) as their candidates for properly basic beliefs: for example, 'I seem to see a green, brown, tallish object' (see AYER, A.J.; MOORE, G.E.). But although these propositions might seem to be properly basic, there are notorious problems with the sense-data view (see SENSE-DATA). First, the proffered basic beliefs seem to be too meagre to provide a sufficient basis for the rich scope of things we seem to know. For example, how can my knowledge that objects persist when not being perceived be traced to particular sense-data? Second, it appears that our knowledge of the way in which to characterize our sensations (private sensations accessible only to the individual having them) depends upon our knowledge of public objects (see CRITERIA; WITTGENSTEIN, L.J.J.). How could we know, for example, that we have a throbbing pain without first recognizing what it is for a public object (say, a muscle) to be throbbing?

Foundationalists have developed answers to these objections in part by liberalizing the requirements either for being properly basic or for being an acceptable pattern of inference from the foundational propositions to the non-foundational ones (see INFERENCE TO THE BEST EXPLANATION). For example, *contextualist* accounts of knowledge have been developed that hold that a proposition is properly basic just in case it is accepted by the relevant community of putative knowers. In a discussion with a friend I could offer 'I read it in the newspaper' as my reason for believing another moon of Jupiter had been discovered. I would not need further reasons for believing that I read it. In contrast, at a convention of astronomers that reason would not be accepted. Hence, contextualists claim, what counts as a basic reason is context-dependent.

There are two obvious responses to contextualism. The first is that it might be an accurate description of some aspects of our epistemic practices, but the fundamental Pyrrhonian question remains: what distinguishes a properly basic proposition from one that is merely offered and accepted by a community of putative knowers? The issue concerns what beliefs, if any, *ought* to be offered and accepted without further reasons. The question is not what beliefs *are* offered and accepted without further reason. The second response is a corollary of the first. Knowledge seems to be a highly prized state of belief (as PLATO put it). But, if the contextualists were right, I would gain knowledge by joining a community of rather epistemically gullible and permissive folk. That hardly seems right! (See CONTEXTUALISM, EPISTEMOLOGICAL.)

In sum, it remains a subject of dispute among epistemologists whether the stock of purported foundational propositions can be made sufficiently rich and abundant without including too many that clearly require evidential support, or whether the patterns of inferences can be liberalized sufficiently without allowing patterns that are not sufficiently truth-conducive.

The historical rival of foundationalism is coherentism. Coherentists deny that there are basic reasons and claim that all propositions derive their warrant, at least in part, from other propositions. The fundamental objection is this: Typically, we recognize that arguing in a circle is not an acceptable pattern of inference, so what makes it acceptable in some cases? Suppose I believe that apples contain vitamin C, at least in part because I believe that fruits contain vitamin C. I would surely be appropriately accused of circular reasoning if I believed, in part, that fruits contain vitamin C because apples do.

Coherentists would be quick to point out that they are not really suggesting that one should argue in a circle. Rather, they would point to the fact that our beliefs come in bunches with a web-like structure (see QUINE, W.V.). They are 'mutually supporting' just as the poles in a tepee are mutually supporting. A belief is warranted just in case it is a member of a set of coherent beliefs.

But whether these colourful analogies answer the basic objection is not clear. Presumably, circular reasoning is not acceptable because although it might be the case that if you believe b_1 it might be reasonable to believe b_2, and if you believe b_2 it might be reasonable to also believe b_1, their mutual support gives you no reason for believing them both. Thus, the fundamental question is this: What makes one total set of coherent beliefs, say T_1, any more acceptable than an alternative total set of coherent beliefs, say T_2?

The Pyrrhonian Sceptics would point out that coherentists either have an answer for that question or they do not. If they do, then they seem to have abandoned their central view, since there now seems to be a reason for adopting the set of beliefs, T_1, that is not one of the beliefs in T_1. Indeed, if they provide an answer, they have embraced foundationalism. If they do not have an answer, then it seems that adopting T_1 is arbitrary. Coherentists have attempted to answer this objection by giving a 'meta-justification' for thinking that certain kinds of coherent belief systems are likely to contain true members. Indeed, some have argued that coherent

beliefs are, by their very nature, likely to be true (see DAVIDSON, D.). But whether that strategy will suffice to answer the objections remains an open question in epistemology.

5   Defeasibility theories

A basic objection to the foundationalist's and coherentist's accounts of justification is that neither seems to be able to show that a true belief which satisfied their accounts would be non-accidentally true. First, as the neighbour/lights case showed, a true belief could be fully justified on their accounts, but not be knowledge. Second, as the Pyrrhonians pointed out, either the beliefs seem to rest upon arbitrary foundations or they seem to be only one of many, equally coherent sets of beliefs. The defeasibility theory was developed, in part, to address these issues. It holds, roughly, that it is not only the evidence that one possesses that makes a belief warranted; it is equally important that there is no defeating evidence that one does not possess. That is, in order for a belief to be warranted it must not only be justified (in the sense required by either the foundationalists or the coherentists) but its justification must be such that there is no truth which, if added to the reasons that justify the belief, is such that the belief would no longer be justified.

The defeasibility theory can explain why it is not a cognitive accident that the warranted belief is true. If any of the important supporting reasons (those that if removed would destroy the justification) were false, then adding the denial of those reasons (in other words, adding the truth) to one's beliefs would undermine the justification. In addition, if there is evidence that one does not possess such that it makes it an accident that the belief is true, the propositions describing that evidence would undercut the justification.

A well-known case will help to illustrate this (see GETTIER PROBLEM). Suppose that I know Tom Grabit well and I see what appears to be Tom stealing a library book: I come to believe that Tom stole a library book. And, let us suppose that Tom did indeed steal the book. Foundationalists and coherentists could deploy their accounts in order to show that the belief is justified. Nevertheless, suppose that, unknown to me, Tom has an identical twin, John, who is a kleptomaniac and was in the library on the day in question and stole a copy of the same book. Even though I arrived at a true belief as a result of good reasoning based upon true propositions, I do not know that Tom stole the book since it is accidental, from the cognitive point of view, that I arrived at the truth. I could just as easily have based my belief on having seen John stealing the book.

527

The defeasibility theorists would point out that the belief that Tom stole the book is defeated; if the true proposition describing John were added to my beliefs, I would no longer be justified in believing Tom stole the book. In general, the defeasibility theory can rule out accidentally true beliefs as warranted because those beliefs would not be able to stand up to the truth.

Nevertheless, the defeasibility theory has its problems. The primary one is that it seems to exclude too much from what we know. Returning to the Grabit Case, suppose that everything is as it was except that Tom does not have a twin but that Tom's mother sincerely avows the claims about John. Now, there is a true proposition (Tom's mother has said sincerely that Tom has an identical twin, John) that defeats the original justification. Hence the belief that Tom stole the book would be defeated. But if Tom's mother were demented and there never was a twin, it seems that I knew all along that Tom stole the book.

Defeasibility theorists have tried to answer this objection by suggesting ways to distinguish between so-called misleading defeaters (for example, Mrs Grabit sincerely avows that Tom has an identical twin, John) and genuine ones (for example, Tom has an identical twin, John), but there is no agreement among epistemologists that any of these suggestions has succeeded in correctly capturing the distinction between genuine and misleading defeaters.

6 Externalism

Partly in response to the difficulties with foundationalism and coherentism even as supplemented by the defeasibility theory, epistemologists have developed a variety of alternative accounts of warrant. They have been called 'externalistic' because their accounts of warrant focus on features of the world other than the knower's reasons for belief. Two important ones are the causal theory and the reliabilist theory.

In their purest forms, these accounts begin with the view that knowledge, and hence warrant, does not require justification. The foundationalists had already conceded that there are no reasons for properly basic beliefs. This seemed to create a problem for foundationalism only because it was assumed that all beliefs needed to be justified and the 'basic' reasons appeared to be arbitrary. But drop the requirement that beliefs need to be justified in order to be warranted, and this problem immediately disappears.

Roughly, the causal theory of warrant holds that a belief is warranted if and only if the state of affairs represented in the belief is appropriately causally related to the belief. For example, suppose I come to believe that there is a bird in a tree as a causal consequence of seeing the bird in the tree. Sometimes the causal connection is more complex; but this direct type of causal connection between the belief and what it represents will suffice for our purposes.

This theory is initially appealing because it appears to satisfy the basic requirement that a warranted belief be non-accidentally true since the state of affairs represented in the belief is a cause of my belief. However, it is easily seen to be both too weak and too strong; and there seem to be some deep problems with it as a general account of warrant. It is too weak because it would count some true beliefs as warranted that clearly are not known. Recall the Grabit case. My belief that I see Tom stealing the book is caused by Tom's stealing the book, but if he has an identical twin, I do not know that Tom stole the book. It is too strong because there seem to be many beliefs that count as knowledge which can not be appropriately *causally* related to what they represent. Suppose I know that there is no elephant smaller than a kitten: what possible *causal* connection could there be between there being no elephant smaller than a kitten and my belief? In addition, potential difficulties arise about knowledge of a priori propositions (such as 2 + 2 = 4) and counterfactuals (such as, if it were raining today, we would have called off the picnic). It looks as though there is no possible way to produce a causal connection between my belief and what is represented in the belief – at least as 'cause' is usually understood (see A PRIORI).

Nevertheless, a basic tenet of the causal theory might still be correct: Not all beliefs need to be based on reasons in order to count as knowledge. The reliabilist theory of warrant can be seen as the successor of the causal theory. Instead of requiring an appropriate causal connection between the states of affairs represented in the belief and the belief itself, a typical form of reliabilism holds that a belief is warranted just in case the process resulting in the belief produces true beliefs sufficiently often.

Thus, the non-accidental nature of the true belief receives a very straightforward analysis. The belief is non-accidentally true because the process that produces the belief produces true beliefs sufficiently often. This view has many advantages over the causal theory. My belief that elephants are larger than kittens need not be caused by that state of affairs. All that is required is that the process by which I come to believe that proposition typically (often enough) results in true beliefs. A priori or counterfactual propositions present no problem since there could be reliable processes that produce those beliefs.

Nevertheless, there are problems confronting this view. Suppose that you require that the process should produce true beliefs on 100 per cent of the occasions on which it arises. That is a very stringent condition; but it is not stringent enough! For if the belief that Tom Grabit stole a book arises only once in the history of the world – the time I saw him stealing the book – the actual process produced a true belief 100 per cent of the times it arose; but it is not knowledge. The obvious move for the reliabilist is not only to include the actual occasions when the particular belief is produced but rather to consider whether the type of process that produced this belief would produce true beliefs of this type sufficiently often. But correctly characterizing those types has not proved easy. Is the type of belief one in which Tom is involved? Or identical twins? Or libraries? That seems too narrow. Is the type of process one in which there is first a perception and then some inferences? That seems too broad. It remains an open question whether reliabilism can produce an acceptable account of the types of processes and the types of beliefs.

Finally, there is one further objection that some epistemologists have brought against reliabilism. Perhaps it is best illustrated in a case presented by Keith Lehrer in his *Theory of Knowledge* (1990) that can be summarized as follows: a certain Mr Truetemp has a thermometer-with-temperature-belief-generator implanted in his head so that within certain ranges of temperatures he has perfectly reliable temperature beliefs. When it is 50 degrees, he comes to believe that it is 50 degrees. When it is not 50 degrees, he does not come to believe that it is 50 degrees. He holds these beliefs without knowing why he does.

Such beliefs would satisfy all of the requirements suggested by the reliabilists, but many epistemologists would hold that although Mr Truetemp has true beliefs and they are not accidentally true because his thermometer-with-temperature-belief-generator is reliable, they are accidentally true *from the cognitive point of view*, as he has no reasons at all for his beliefs. Indeed, some would say that what Mr Truetemp possesses is a skill (of telling the temperature) and not propositional knowledge at all.

Here we can detect a fundamental clash of intuitions. The reliabilists would hold that Mr Truetemp does know; the traditional normativists would hold that he does not. There appears to be no way to satisfy both. But this much seems clear: There are some situations in which the steps in the process that brings about a belief include the holding of reasons. In those cases in which there is no automatic true-belief-generator (as in the Truetemp case) and in which we must rely upon our reasoning to arrive at a belief, the questions asked by the traditional normativists are crucial: what must the structure of our reasons be so as to

make a true belief acceptable? Are there foundational reasons? Can mutually supporting reasons be offered without begging the question? (Could reasons be infinite in number?) And need those reasons be such that they are not undermined by the truth, as the defeasibility theorists would hold? At least in some cases, it seems that normative standards for belief-acquisition apply and their satisfaction will determine whether a belief ought to be accepted. Thus, it appears that an evaluation of the conditions under which beliefs ought to be accepted, denied or suspended is inescapable (see INTERNALISM AND EXTERNALISM IN EPISTEMOLOGY; JUSTIFICATION, EPISTEMIC).

7 Epistemic principles

Epistemic principles describe the normative epistemic status of propositions under varying conditions. It is generally agreed that if a person, S, is justified in believing any proposition, x, then S is not at the same time justified in believing that not-x. Foundationalists and coherentists alike can, and typically do, accept this principle. Other principles are more controversial. They are intuitively plausible but they seem to provide a basis for scepticism and for some deep epistemic puzzles. Here are three of the more interesting principles.

Conjunction Principle (CON-P): If S is justified in believing that x, and S is justified in believing that y, then S is justified in believing that (x and y).

Closure Principle (CLO-P): If S is justified in believing x, and x entails y, then S is justified in believing that y.

Evidence Transfer Principle (ET-P): If there is some evidence, e, that justifies S in believing that x, and x entails y, then e justifies S in believing that y.

In each principle and with suitable grammatical modifications 'justified' could be replaced by other epistemic terms, such as 'reasonable', 'plausible', 'evident', 'certain'. Furthermore, each principle is designed to capture a basis upon which a positive normative epistemic status of a proposition can be transferred to another proposition. As a corollary, 'S is justified in believing x' is not taken to entail 'S does believe that x, justifiably'. For S may not form the belief because of a failure to see the connection between the propositions. Finally, with regard to CLO-P and ET-P, since a tautology is entailed by every proposition, the entailment must be restricted to some form of relevant entailment and/or the range of propositions must be restricted to contingent ones (see RELEVANCE LOGIC AND ENTAILMENT). Other restrictions are no doubt necessary;

but these three seemingly intuitive principles have been challenged at their core.

It is important to see some of the relationships between these principles. CLO-P does not entail CON-P since the CLO-P is about *one* proposition that S is justified in believing, not *sets* of propositions. In addition, CLO-P does not entail ET-P because CLO-P does not require that it is the *very same evidence, e,* that S has for *x* that justifies *y* for S. Thus, one can accept CLO-P without accepting either of the other principles.

8 The epistemic principles and scepticism

Scepticism – the view that we lack knowledge in those areas commonly thought to be within our ken – comes in many varieties. The most extreme view is global scepticism. It holds that we have very little, if any, knowledge. That view seems preposterous at first glance. Indeed, some epistemologists think that any theory that leads to global scepticism should, *ipso facto,* be rejected (see COMMONSENSISM; SCEPTICISM). Yet there are many arguments for global scepticism that are difficult to answer. In addition, more modest forms of scepticism about particular subject matters (for example, other minds or the future) have been developed. But since the more modest sceptics employ strategies similar to those employed by the global sceptics, I here consider only the most extreme form of scepticism – global scepticism (see OTHER MINDS).

We have already seen the basis for one such argument for global scepticism that can be gleaned from the Pyrrhonians, namely:

(1) All knowledge requires having reasons that are neither arbitrary nor question-begging nor infinitely many.

(2) The only structures for reasons are such that reasons are either arbitrary (foundationalism), question-begging (coherentism) or infinitely many (infinitism).

Therefore, there is no knowledge.

There are at least four possible responses to this argument: (1) the foundational, basic propositions are not arbitrary; (2) coherentism does not necessarily lead to question-begging arguments; (3) requiring infinitely many reasons for a belief does not entail that a belief cannot be justified; (4) not all knowledge entails having reasons. All but (3) have been systematically developed by epistemologists.

Pyrrhonism does not rely directly upon the epistemic principles discussed in the preceding section. But there are other important forms of scepticism that do. Consider this argument that can be traced to Descartes (see DESCARTES, R. §4):

(1) If I am justified in believing that there is a table before me, then I am justified in believing that I am not in one of the sceptical scenarios (evil demon worlds, for example) in which there is no table but it appears just as though there were one.

(2) I am never justified in believing that I am not in one of the sceptical scenarios in which there is no table but it appears just as though there were one.

Therefore, I am never justified in believing that there is a table before me.

Premise 1 is a clear instance of CLO-P. Since the argument is valid (if the premises are true, the conclusion must be true), there are only three plausible responses: (1) CLO-P is false; (2) the second premise is false; (3) the argument begs the question. Responses (1) and (2) are relatively easy to envisage; the third is not so obvious. Roughly, the argument goes as follows: since one of the potentially available grounds for my being justified in believing that I am not in a sceptical scenario is any proposition that entails that I am not in such a scenario, every good argument for the second premise would have to establish that I am not justified in believing that there is a table before me. But that, of course, is the very conclusion.

It is important to note that there is an apparently similar argument for scepticism employing the stronger epistemic principle, ET-P.

(1) If the evidence, *e,* that I have for believing that there is a table before me is adequate to justify that belief, then it is adequate to justify the belief that I am not in one of the sceptical scenarios.

(2) The evidence, *e,* is not adequate to justify that I am not in one of the sceptical scenarios.

Therefore, the evidence, *e,* is not adequate to justify that there is a table before me.

Of course, it is open to epistemologists to deny ET-P. Since one can deny ET-P without abandoning CLO-P (because CLO-P does not entail ET-P), that certainly seems to be a strategy worth considering. The discussion in the next section provides additional reasons for considering that strategy.

9 The epistemic principles and some paradoxes

There are many epistemic paradoxes (see PARADOXES, EPISTEMIC). I here consider two in order to show how they depend upon some of the epistemic principles considered earlier.

The Lottery Paradox: Suppose that enough tickets (say *n* tickets) have been sold in a fair lottery for you to be justified in believing that the one ticket you bought will not win. In fact, you are justified in believing about each ticket that it will not win. Thus, you are justified in believing the following individual propositions: t_1 will not win. t_2 will not win. t_3 will not win ... t_n will not win.

Now if the conjunction principle is correct, you can conjoin them, ending up with the obviously false but apparently justified proposition that no ticket will win. So, it seems that you are in the awkward position of being justified in believing each of a series of propositions individually, but not being justified in believing that they are all true. Some philosophers have thought that this seemingly awkward position is not so bad after all, since there is no outright contradiction among any of our beliefs as long as the conjunction principle is rejected. But others have thought that making it rational to hold, knowingly, a set of inconsistent beliefs is too high a price to pay.

Others have suggested that we are not actually justified in believing of any ticket that it will lose; rather what we are justified in believing is only that it is highly likely that it will lose. But the lottery can be made as large as one wants, so that any level of probability (below 1) is reached. Thus, this suggestion seems to rule out our being justified in believing any proposition with a probability of less than 1. That is a very high price to pay! There is no generally agreed-upon solution for handling the Lottery Paradox (see CONFIRMATION THEORY).

The Grue Paradox: The so-called 'Grue Paradox' was developed by Nelson Goodman and has been recast in many ways. Here is a way that emphasizes the role of ET-P:

All of the very many emeralds examined up to the present moment, t_{now}, have been green. In fact, one would think that since we have examined so many of them, we are justified in believing that (G): all emeralds are green. But consider another proposition, namely that all emeralds examined up to t_{now} are green, but otherwise they are blue. Let us use 'grue' to stand for the property of being examined and green up to t_{now} but otherwise blue. It appears that the evidence which justifies us in believing that all emeralds are green does not justify us in believing that (N): no emerald is grue.

What are we to make of this version of the paradox? First, note that it depends upon ET-P. Although (1) our inductive evidence (the many examined green emeralds) justifies (G), and although (2) (G) does entail (N), the inductive evidence does not justify

(N). In other words, this version of the paradox arises because the evidence does not transfer as the principle would require. Second, note that CLO-P is not threatened by this paradox since it is the evidence for (G) that is inadequate for (N). (The issue is not whether we are justified in believing (N) whenever we are justified in believing that (G).)

But if ET-P were not valid, then the sting of this version of the paradox can be pulled. Recall the original Grabit case. In that case, I had adequate evidence for being justified in believing that Tom stole the book, that is, the person stealing the book looked just like Tom. It seems clear that this evidence is not adequate to justify the proposition that it was not Tom's identical twin who stole the book. If it were the twin, things would appear to be just as they did appear to be. But this tends to show that we do not typically impose ET-P on our evidence.

There are other versions of the Grue Paradox that do not make explicit use of ET-P. For example, since 'all emeralds are green' and 'all emeralds are grue' are alternative hypotheses, it seems paradoxical that the very same evidence that justifies believing the first alternative also seems to support the second. But perhaps, like the version considered above, this apparent paradox rests on a mistaken intuition. Consider the Grabit Case once again. Here, the evidence which justifies the belief that Tom is the thief would also support the claim that Tom's identical twin stole the book. To generalize further, consider any hypothesis, say *h*, that is justified by some evidence that does not entail *h*. It is always possible to formulate an alternative hypothesis that is supported by that very evidence, namely (not-*h*, but it appears just as though *h* because of...). Thus, an intuitively plausible epistemic principle similar to ET-P might be invalid. That principle is: if there is some evidence, *e*, that justifies *S* in believing that *x*, and *x* is an alternative hypothesis to *y*, then *e* does not support *y*.

To sum up, if ET-P and similar epistemic principles do not accurately capture our normative epistemic practices and if the argument for scepticism that depends upon CLO-P begs the question, then the sting of Cartesian scepticism (considered in the previous section) is numbed and the Grue Paradox can be addressed. But those are big 'ifs', and the issue remains open (see INDUCTION, EPISTEMIC ISSUES IN).

10 Some challenges to traditional epistemology

A traditional question asked by epistemologists is 'what ought we to believe?' Typically, the answer is given by (1) describing the types of reasons that contribute to warranting a belief, and (2) developing a set of necessary and sufficient conditions for knowledge in which the types of reasons depicted in (1) play a prominent role. But there are many challenges to this answer.

We have already seen the challenge developed by the causal theorists and the reliabilists. Roughly, they hold that our beliefs need not be the result of proper reasoning to be counted as knowledge. Sufficiently reliable belief-acquisition methods are all that is required. Indeed, some have held that epistemology, when done correctly, is a branch of psychology because the primary issue is the study of reliable belief-acquisition methods. This programme has often been referred to as 'naturalized epistemology' and, in one form, its basic tenet is there are no a priori knowable epistemic principles (see NATURALIZED EPISTEMOLOGY; QUINE, W.V.).

Another challenge to traditional epistemology comes from 'virtue epistemology', which makes the primary object of epistemic evaluation traits of persons rather than properties of beliefs or belief-forming processes. The virtue approach has been taken farthest by Linda Zagzebski, who proposes an epistemic theory modelled on virtue ethics and argues that such a theory permits the recovering of such neglected epistemic values as understanding and wisdom (see VIRTUE EPISTEMOLOGY).

A further type of challenge is that of Edward Craig. While allowing that the debate has been shaped by real features of the concept of knowledge, he rejects the project of analysing it in necessary and sufficient conditions. Instead, he tries to 'synthesize' the concept by deriving these features from a pragmatic hypothesis about its purpose, thus explaining the debate rather than joining it.

Even more radical challenges have been developed. First, some have argued that there is no unique method of acquiring and revising beliefs that ought to be employed by all people. Second, it has been argued that the proposed conditions of good reasoning (for example, objectivity and neutrality) tacitly aim at something other than truth. They are developed to prolong entrenched power (see FEMINIST EPISTEMOLOGY). Finally, it has been argued that successful belief acquisition occurs when the future can be adequately anticipated and controlled (see PRAGMATISM).

The defenders of traditional epistemology have two basic types of reply. First, they can examine the particular arguments developed by the critics to determine whether any one of them is sound. Second, they can point out that the critics will have to defend the reasonableness of their views by at least tacitly employing the very principles of good reasoning investigated by traditional epistemologists. Of course, this would not show that the critic's position is false, but it does at least illustrate the universality of the question 'what ought we to believe?'.

See also: DAOIST PHILOSOPHY; KŪKAI; WANG YANGMING

References and further reading

BonJour, L. (1985) *The Structure of Empirical Knowledge*, Cambridge, MA: Harvard University Press. (Develops and defends a coherentist account of knowledge and justification.)

Chisholm, R. (1966/1977/1989) *Theory of Knowledge*, Englewood Cliffs, NJ: Prentice Hall, 1st, 2nd and 3rd edns. (Successive editions contain a general introduction to many issues in epistemology and increasingly complex foundationalist accounts of knowledge.)

Luper, S (ed.) (2004) *Essential Knowledge*, New York: Pearson Longman. (Contains historical and contemporary articles and book excerpts with helpful introductions to the various topics.)

PETER D. KLEIN

KNOWLEDGE, JUSTIFICATION OF
See JUSTIFICATION, EPISTEMIC

KNOWLEDGE, MORAL
See MORAL KNOWLEDGE

KNOWLEDGE, SOCIOLOGY OF
See SOCIOLOGY OF KNOWLEDGE

KNOWLEDGE, TACIT

Tacit knowledge is a form of implicit knowledge we rely on for both learning and acting. The term derives from the work of Michael Polanyi (1891–1976) whose critique of positivistic philosophy of science grew into a fully developed theory of knowledge. Polanyi believed that the 'scientific' account of knowledge as a fully explicit formalizable body of statements did not allow for an adequate account of discovery and growth. In his account of tacit knowledge, knowledge has an ineliminable subjective dimension: we know much more than we can tell. This notion of tacit knowing in science has been developed by Thomas Kuhn, has figured prominently in theoretical linguistics and has also been studied in psychology.

C.F. DELANEY

KŌBŌ DAISHI
See KŪKAI

KOLLONTAI, ALEXANDRA
See FEMINISM (§4)

KOREAN PHILOSOPHY

See BUDDHIST PHILOSOPHY, KOREAN; EAST ASIAN PHILOSOPHY

KOTARBIŃSKI, TADEUSZ (1886–1981)

Kotarbiński was one of the founders and main representatives of the Polish philosophical school known as the Lwów–Warsaw School and akin to, though independent of (and less radical than), the Vienna Circle. H was an anti-metaphysical, pro-scientific, rationalistic school of philosophy, which was very active and influential between the First and the Second World Wars.

Kotarbiński's programme for philosophy was a minimalistic and a practical one: he stressed the need to purify the field of philosophy of questions and concepts that lack factual content or logical coherence. According to him, the term 'philosophy' should be used, if at all, to denote only logic (understood as the philosophy of cognitive thought) and the philosophy of action, including moral philosophy. His numerous (more than 500) works are devoted to logic and philosophy of action in this broad sense. One of his main original ideas is the doctrine of reism or concretism, a special version of nominalism.

Kotarbiński was admired by several generations of his pupils for his unusual pedagogical gifts, his integrity and his moral courage.

See also: VIENNA CIRCLE

B. STANOSZ

KRIPKE, SAUL AARON (1940–)

Saul Kripke is one of the most important and influential philosophers of the late twentieth century. He is also one of the leading mathematical logicians, having done seminal work in areas including modal logic, intuitionistic logic and set theory. Although much of his work in logic has philosophical significance, it will not be discussed here.

Kripke's main contributions fall in the areas of metaphysics, philosophy of language, epistemology, philosophy of mind and philosophy of logic and mathematics. He is particularly well known for his views on and discussions of the following topics: the concepts of necessity, identity and 'possible worlds'; 'essentialism' – the idea that things have significant essential properties; the question of what determines the referent of an ordinary proper name and the related question of whether such names have meanings; the relations among the concepts of necessity, analyticity, and the a priori; the concept of belief and its problems; the concept of truth and its problems; and scepticism, the idea of following a

rule, and Ludwig Wittgenstein's 'private language argument'.

See also: SEMANTICS

MICHAEL JUBIEN

KRISTEVA, JULIA (1941–)

Born in Bulgaria, Kristeva entered the Parisian scene of avant-garde intellectuals in the 1960s. Her earliest work in linguistics was shaped by the post-Stalinist communism of eastern Europe, a political climate that exerts its influence on her entire corpus, even as she distanced herself from it, to embrace an increasingly psychoanalytic perspective. Dissatisfied with scientific models of language, conceived as a mere means of communicating preconceived ideas, where words simply function as isolated symbols that represent discrete concepts, Kristeva analyses language as a signifying process. As such, language is not a static and closed system of signs, but a mobile, fluid process that implicates bodily and vocal rhythms in the generation of symbolic meanings. In *La Révolution du language poétique* (1974) (*Revolution in Poetic Language*, 1984) Kristeva fuses linguistic insights with psychoanalytic inquiry as she presents two distinct yet interrelated aspects of the signifying process, the semiotic and the symbolic. The semiotic aspect of language is vocal, pre-verbal, rhythmic, kinetic and bodily. The symbolic aspect of language is social, cultural, and rule-governed. Focusing on the interplay between the semiotic and the symbolic, Kristeva is able to analyse literary and historical texts, works of art and cultural phenomena in a way that thematizes the complex relationship between materiality and representation.

TINA CHANTER

KUHN, THOMAS SAMUEL (1922–96)

The early 1960s saw substantial turmoil in the philosophy of science, then dominated by logical empiricism. Most important was the confrontation of the prevailing philosophical tradition with the history of science. Whereas the philosophy of science was mainly normatively oriented, that is it tried to delineate what good science should look like, historical studies seemed to indicate that the practice of science both past and present did not follow those prescriptions.

Thomas S. Kuhn was educated as a theoretical physicist but soon turned to the history and philosophy of science. In 1962, he published *The Structure of Scientific Revolutions* (*SSR*). This book was the single most important publication advancing the confrontation between the history and the philosophy of science; it is now a classic in science studies. *SSR* was most influential not only in the discussion within philosophy but also in various other fields, especially the social sciences. The central concepts of *SSR*, like scientific revolution, paradigm shift and incommensurability, have been in the focus of philosophical discussion for many years, and the term 'paradigm' has even become a household word (although mostly not in Kuhn's intended sense). After *SSR*, Kuhn continued to develop his theory; apart from minor modifications it is mainly the explication of *SSR*'s more intricate philosophical topics, especially of incommensurability, which is characteristic of his later work.

See also: FEYERABEND, P.K.; INCOMMENSURABILITY

PAUL HOYNINGEN-HUENE

KŪKAI (774–835)

Kūkai, also known by his posthumous honorific title Kōbō Daishi, was the founder of Japanese Shingon ('truth word' or 'mantra') Buddhism and is often considered the first comprehensive philosophical thinker in Japanese history. Building on the Buddhist esoteric tradition first developed in India and then in China, where Kūkai encountered it, he maintained that reality is a cosmic person, the Buddha Dainichi. Dainichi's cosmic thoughts, words and deeds form microcosmic configurations, resonances and patterns of change. By performing Shingon rituals, one can supposedly accord with the microcosmic constituents and know the foundational structures of reality that compose the sensory world in which we ordinarily live.

See also: BUDDHIST PHILOSOPHY, JAPANESE; JAPANESE PHILOSOPHY; KNOWLEDGE, CONCEPT OF; METAPHYSICS

THOMAS P. KASULIS

KUNDAKUNDA
See JAINA PHILOSOPHY

L

LA BARRE, POULAIN DE

See FEMINISM (§§2, 3)

LA METTRIE, JULIEN OFFROY DE (1709–51)

La Mettrie is best known as the author of the eighteenth-century materialist manifesto, *L'Homme machine* (1747). His interest in philosophical issues grew out of his preoccupation with medicine, and he developed a tradition of medical materialism within the French Enlightenment. Born in St Malo, into the family of a prosperous textile merchant, La Mettrie pursued a medical career in Paris. He also studied for two years with the renowned Hermann Boerhaave in Leiden. After a brief period of medical practice, La Mettrie devoted his efforts to his translations and commentaries on Boerhaave's medical works. He also began to publish the works that made him a pariah to both the Faculty of Medicine of Paris and to the orthodox – that is, his medical satires and his first work of materialist philosophy, *L'Histoire naturelle de l'âme* (1745). Because of the outrage provoked by these works, he was exiled to Holland in 1745. But *L'Homme machine*, the text in which he applied his materialism thoroughly and explicitly to human beings, was too radical even for the unusually tolerant Dutch, and La Mettrie was forced to seek asylum at the court of Frederick the Great where he later died. His willingness to publish ideas his contemporaries considered too dangerous led the *philosophes* to repudiate him.

See also: ENLIGHTENMENT, CONTINENTAL

KATHLEEN WELLMAN

LABRIOLA, ANTONIO (1843–1904)

Antonio Labriola was the founder of Italian theoretical Marxism. Generally situated in the Marxism of the Second International, he was more questioning than others in that movement. He profoundly influenced the development of Italian thought, constantly challenging the influential idealism of Benedetto Croce and Giovanni Gentile. His attempt to maintain a place for human creativity within a deterministic Marxist view of history influenced Antonio Gramsci and helped give Italian Eurocommunism its distinctive flexibility. His concepts of 'genetic method', 'social morphology', 'philosophy of praxis' and 'social pedagogy' are indications of this attempt.

See also: MARXISM, WESTERN

GEOFFREY HUNT

LACAN, JACQUES (1901–81)

Jacques Lacan was a French psychoanalyst and philosopher whose contribution to philosophy derives from his consistent and thoroughgoing reinterpretation of Freud's writings in the light of Heidegger and Hegel as well as structuralist linguistics and anthropology. Whereas Freud himself had disparaged philosophical speculation, claiming for himself the mantle of the natural scientist, Lacan demonstrates psychoanalysis to be a rigorous philosophical position. Specifically, Lacan suggests that the Freudian unconscious is best understood as the effect of language (what he calls 'the symbolic') upon human behaviour.

See also: FREUD, S.; PSYCHOANALYSIS, POST-FREUDIAN; STRUCTURALISM; STRUCTURALISM IN SOCIAL SCIENCE

THOMAS BROCKELMAN

LAKATOS, IMRE (1922–74)

Imre Lakatos made important contributions to the philosophy of mathematics and of science. His 'Proofs and Refutations' (1963–4) develops a novel account of mathematical discovery. It shows that counterexamples ('refutations') play an important role in mathematics as well as in science and argues that both proofs and theorems are gradually improved by searching for counterexamples and by systematic 'proof analysis'. His 'methodology of scientific research programmes' (which he presented as a 'synthesis' of the accounts of science given by

535

Popper and by Kuhn) is based on the idea that science is best analysed, not in terms of single theories, but in terms of broader units called research programmes. Such programmes issue in particular theories, but in a way again governed by clear-cut heuristic principles. Lakatos claimed that his account supplies the sharp criteria of 'progress' and 'degeneration' missing from Kuhn's account, and hence captures the 'rationality' of scientific development. Lakatos also articulated a 'meta-methodology' for appraising rival methodologies of science in terms of the 'rational reconstructions' of history they provide.

See also: EXPERIMENT; FEYERABEND, P.K.; SCIENTIFIC METHOD; THEORIES, SCIENTIFIC

JOHN WORRALL

LANGE, FRIEDRICH ALBERT (1828–75)

A German philosopher, social scientist and political activist, Lange was best known for his study of the history of materialism. He was a leading proponent of Neo-Kantianism, a critic of speculative meta-physics, and a defender of the view that philosophy should incorporate the findings of the exact sciences. As a social scientist, Lange described the emergence of a social Darwinian 'struggle for existence' in modern times due to the rapid advancement of industrialization and a growing conflict of interest among social classes.

Cognizant of the scientific trends of his time, Lange anticipated some of the central ideas of pragmatism and adopted a form of conventionalism in regard to scientific principles and concepts. Although sympathetic to materialism, Lange also saw the inevitability of an idealist element in interpretations of natural phenomena and insisted on the importance of projecting ethical, social and aesthetic ideals.

GEORGE J. STACK

LANGER, SUSANNE KATHERINA KNAUTH (1895–1985)

With roots in logic, philosophy of language and philosophy of mind, Susanne Langer sought to explicate the meaning and cognitive import of art works by developing a theory of symbolism that located works of art at the centre of a network of relations based firmly on semantic theory. Art works were non-discursive, presentational symbols that expressed an artist's 'life of feeling', by which

observers, through a process of immediate appre-hension (or intuition) came to acquire knowledge.
See also: ANTHROPOLOGY, PHILOSOPHY OF; ARTISTIC EXPRESSION; MUSIC, AESTHETICS OF

PEG BRAND

LANGUAGE, INNATENESS OF

Is there any innate knowledge? What is it to speak and understand a language? These are old questions, but it was the twentieth-century linguist, Noam Chomsky, who forged a connection between them, arguing that mastery of a language is, in part, a matter of knowing its grammar, and that much of our knowledge of grammar is inborn.

Rejecting the empiricism that had dominated Anglo-American philosophy, psychology and lin-guistics for the first half of this century, Chomsky argued that the task of learning a language is so difficult, and the linguistic evidence available to the learner so meagre, that language acquisition would be impossible unless some of the knowledge eventually attained were innate. He proposed that learners bring to their task knowledge of a 'Universal Grammar', describing structural features common to all natural languages, and that it is this knowledge that enables us to master our native tongues.

Chomsky's position is *nativist* because it proposes that the inborn knowledge facilitating learning is *domain-specific*. On an empiricist view, our innate ability to learn from experience (for example, to form associations among ideas) applies equally in any task domain. On the nativist view, by contrast, we are equipped with special-purpose learning strate-gies, each suited to its own peculiar subject-matter.

Chomsky's nativism spurred a flurry of interest as theorists leaped to explore its conceptual and empirical implications. As a consequence of his work, language acquisition is today a major focus of cognitive science research.
See also: CHOMSKY, N.; LANGUAGE, PHILOSOPHY OF; SEMANTICS

FIONA COWIE

LANGUAGE OF THOUGHT

The 'language of thought' is a formal language that is postulated to be encoded in the brains of intelligent creatures as a vehicle for their thought. It is an open question whether it resembles any 'natural' language *spoken* by anyone. Indeed, it could well be encoded in the brains of people who claim not to 'think in words', or even by intelligent creatures (for example, chimpanzees) incapable of *speaking* any language at all. Its chief function is to be a medium of *representation* over which the *computations* posited by cognitive psychologists are defined. Its language-like structure is thought to afford the best explanation of such facts about animals as the productivity, systematicity and (hyper-)intensionality of their thought, the promiscuity of their attitudes, and their ability to reason in familiar deductive, inductive and practical ways.

See also: Mind, computational theories of

GEORGES REY

LANGUAGE, PHILOSOPHY OF

Introduction

Philosophical interest in language, while ancient and enduring, has blossomed anew in the past century. There are three key historical sources of current interest, and three intellectual concerns which sustain it.

Philosophers nowadays often aspire to systematic and even mathematically rigorous accounts of language; these philosophers are in one way or another heirs to Gottlob Frege, Bertrand Russell, Ludwig Wittgenstein and the logical positivists, who strove to employ rigorous accounts of logic and of meaning in attempts to penetrate, and in some cases to dispel, traditional philosophical questions (see Logical positivism). Contemporary philosophers, too, are often attentive to the roles that philosophically interesting words (like 'know', 'true', 'good' and 'free') play in ordinary linguistic usage; these philosophers inherit from 'ordinary language philosophers', including G.E. Moore, J.L. Austin and again Wittgenstein, the strategy of finding clues to deep philosophical questions through scrutiny of the workaday usage of the words in which the philosophical questions are framed.

Philosophical interest in language is maintained by foundational and conceptual questions in linguistics, quintessentially philosophical problems about the connections between mind, language and the world, and issues about philosophical methodology. These springs sustain a rich and fascinating field of philosophy concerned with representation, communication, meaning and truth.

1 Philosophy of linguistics'
2 Meaning: language, mind and world
3 Linguistic philosophy

1 Philosophy of linguistics

Language is an impressive and fascinating human capacity, and human languages are strikingly powerful and complex systems. The science of this capacity and of these systems is linguistics. Like other sciences, and perhaps to an unusual degree, linguistics confronts difficult foundational, methodological and conceptual issues.

When studying a human language, linguists seek systematic explanations of its *syntax* (the organization of the language's properly constructed expressions, such as phrases and sentences; see Syntax), its *semantics* (the ways expressions exhibit and contribute to meaning; see Semantics), and its *pragmatics* (the practices of communication in which the expressions find use; see Pragmatics).

The study of syntax has been guided since the 1960s by the work of Noam Chomsky, who, in reaction to earlier behaviourist and structuralist movements in linguistics (see Behaviourism, analytic; Behaviourism, methodological and scientific; Structuralism in linguistics; Saussure, F. de), takes an unapologetically cognitivist approach. Human linguistic capacities, he holds, issue from a dedicated cognitive faculty whose structure is the proper topic of linguistics. Indeed, Chomsky construes at least the study of syntax and (large parts of) semantics as attempts to uncover cognitive structures. Finding impressive commonalties among all known natural languages, and noting the paucity of evidence and instruction available to children learning a language, Chomsky suggests that surprisingly many features of natural languages stem from innate characteristics of the language faculty (see Chomsky, N.; Language, innateness of).

Whereas contemporary philosophers have tended to stay at a remove from work in syntax, discussing rather than doing it, semantics is another matter entirely. Here many of the great strides have been made by philosophers, including Gottlob Frege, Bertrand Russell, Ludwig Wittgenstein, Rudolf Carnap, Richard Montague and Saul Kripke. (However, quite a number of linguists and logicians who do not call themselves philosophers also have contributed heavily to semantics.) One major strand in semantics in the past century has consisted in the development and careful application of formal, mathematical models for characterizing linguistic form and meaning (see Semantics, game-theoretic; Semantics, possible worlds; Semantics, situation).

Pragmatics, at least as much as semantics, has benefited from the contributions of philosophers. Philosophical interest in pragmatics typically has had its source in a prior interest in semantics – in a desire to understand how meaning and truth are situated in the concrete practices of linguistic communication. The later Wittgenstein, for instance, reminds us of the vast variety of uses in which linguistic expressions participate, and warns of the danger of assuming that there is something aptly called their *meanings* which we might uncover through philosophy. J.L. AUSTIN seeks in subtleties of usage clues to the meanings of philosophically interesting terms like 'intentional' and 'true'. Austin keeps a careful eye to the several different things one does all at once when one performs a 'speech act' (for instance: uttering a sound, voicing the sentence 'J'ai faim', saying that one is hungry, hinting that one's companion might share their meal, and causing them to do so). His taxonomy has provided the basis of much subsequent work (see SPEECH ACTS; PERFORMATIVES). H.P. GRICE, while critical of some of Austin's methods, shared the aim of distilling meaning from the murky waters of use. Grice portrays conversation as a rational, cooperative enterprise, and in his account a number of conceptions of meaning figure as central strategies and tools for achieving communicative purposes. Grice's main concern was philosophical methodology (see §3), but his proposals have proven extremely popular among linguists interested in pragmatics (see COMMUNICATION AND INTENTION). Recently, philosophers and linguists have become increasingly persuaded that pragmatic concerns, far from being mere addenda to semantics, are crucial to the questions of where meaning comes from, in what it consists, and how the many incompletenesses and flexibilities in linguistic meaning are overcome and exploited in fixing what speakers mean by their words on particular occasions (see PRAGMATICS; IMPLICATURE; METAPHOR).

Our focus on language should not omit a field of study with a rather broader scope, namely *semiotics*, which is the study of signs and signification in general, whether linguistic or not. In the view of the scholars in this field, the study of linguistic meaning should be situated in a more general project which encompasses gestural communication, artistic expression, animal signalling, and other varieties of information transfer (see SEMIOTICS; ANIMAL LANGUAGE AND THOUGHT).

2 Meaning: language, mind and world

Philosophy aims at intellectually responsible accounts of the most basic and general aspects of reality. Part of what it is to provide an intellectually responsible account, clearly, is for us to make sense of our own place in reality – as, among other things, beings who conceive and formulate descriptions and explanations of it.

In framing issues about our roles as describers and explainers, philosophers commonly draw a triangle in which lines connect 'Language', 'Mind' and 'World'. The three lines represent relations that

are keys to understanding our place in reality. These relations in one or another way constitute the *meaningfulness* of language.

Mind ↔ World. Between Mind and World there are a number of crucial relations studied by philosophers of mind. Among these are perception, action, the mind's bodily constitution and intentionality (the mind's ability to think *about* what is in the world) (see MIND, PHILOSOPHY OF).

Mind → Language. Using and understanding language is a heavily mental activity. Further, this activity seems to be what the real existence of meaningful language consists in. In short, mind invests *meaning* in language.

Theorists of language focus on the Mind/Language connection when they consider *understanding* to be the cornerstone concept, holding, for instance, that an account of meaning for a given language is simply an account of what constitutes the ability to understand it. Philosophy has seen a variety of accounts of wherein understanding consists. Many have been attracted to the view that understanding is a matter of associating the correct ideas or concepts with words (see, for instance, LOCKE, J.; FREGE, G.; LANGUAGE OF THOUGHT). Others have equated understanding with knowing the requirements for accurate or apt use of words and sentences (see, for instance, DAVIDSON, D.; DUMMETT, M.A.E.). Still others find the key to understanding in one's ability to discern the communicative goals of speakers and writers (see, for instance, GRICE, H.P.), or more directly in one's ability to 'pass' linguistically, without censure (see, for instance, WITTGENSTEIN, L.J.J.). Certainly, these approaches do not exclude one another.

Some philosophers focus more on production than consumption – on the speaker's side of things – analysing linguistic meaning in terms of the goals and practices of speakers, and in terms of relations among communities of speakers (see GRICE, H.P.; COMMUNICATION AND INTENTION).

Many of the philosophers who see understanding and use as the keys to linguistic meaning have held that the meaningfulness of language in some sense derives from mental content, perhaps including the contents of beliefs, thoughts and concepts. This enhances the interest of *cognitive semantics*, which is a thriving field of study (see SEMANTICS; SEMANTICS, CONCEPTUAL ROLE).

It has not gone unquestioned that mind indeed can assign meaning to language, and in fact scepticism about this has figured quite prominently in philosophical discussions of language. Wittgenstein has been read as at least flirting with scepticism that there is anything our minds *can* do that would constitute meaning one thing rather than another (see WITTGENSTEIN, L.J.J. §§10–12; MEANING AND RULE-FOLLOWING; PRIVATE STATES AND LANGUAGE). W.V. Quine, starting from the thought that meaning is whatever good translation captures, and on arguments that good translation is not squarely dictated by any real facts, concludes that meaning is highly indeterminate. Quine is not alone in the view that linguistic and mental meaning are best seen not as 'out there' to be discovered, but rather as partly constituted or constructed by our practices of interpreting and translating (see QUINE, W.V.; DAVIDSON, D.; DENNETT, D.C.; LEWIS, D.K.; RADICAL TRANSLATION AND RADICAL INTERPRETATION).

Language → Mind. If mind assigns meaning to language, so also language *enables* and *channels* mind. Acquiring and trafficking in a language brings one concepts, thoughts and habits of thought, with all sorts of consequences (see SAPIR-WHORF HYPOTHESIS). Indeed, having language is so crucial to our ability to frame the sophisticated thoughts that appear essential to language-use and understanding that many doubt whether mind is 'prior' to language in any interesting sense (see DAVIDSON, D.).

Language ↔ World. Since language is the vehicle of our descriptions and explanations of reality, philosophers are concerned about what if anything makes for a *true* or *apt* characterization of reality. Philosophers have these concerns for reasons of philosophical methodology (which we will come to in a moment), but also owing to the naturalness and plausibility of a certain picture of meaning.

According to this picture, the key to meaning is the notion of a *truth-condition*. A statement's meaning determines a condition that must be met if it is to be true. For example, my statement 'Ireland is larger than Manhattan', given what it means, is *true* just in case a certain state of affairs obtains (namely, a certain island's being larger than a certain other island). According to the truth-conditional picture of meaning, the core of what a statement *means* is its truth-condition – which helps determine the way reality is *said to be* in it – and the core of what a word means is the contribution it makes to this (perhaps, in the case of certain sorts of word, this would be what the word *refers* to) (see SEMANTICS; MEANING AND TRUTH; REFERENCE).

While the truth-conditional picture of meaning has dominated semantics, a serious challenge has been presented by philosophers, including Michael Dummett, who urge that the key to meaning is a notion of *correct use*. According to this alternative picture, the core of a sentence's meaning is the rule for its appropriate utterance. Of course, the two pictures converge if sentences are correctly used exactly when they are true. The interest of the distinction emerges only when (a 'realist' conception

of) truth is dislodged from this role, whether because of scepticism about truth itself, or because truth is seen as too remote from the crucible of social practice to be the meaning-relevant criterion for correct use (see REALISM AND ANTIREALISM; INTUITIONISTIC LOGIC AND ANTIREALISM; MEANING AND VERIFICATION; DUMMETT, M.A.E.; TRUTH, PRAGMATIC THEORY OF; TRUTH, DEFLATIONARY THEORIES OF; TRUTH, COHERENCE THEORY OF; TRUTH, CORRESPONDENCE THEORY OF). The challenge illustrates a sense in which the Mind/Language and Language/World connections can seem to place a tension on the notion of meaning (meaning is whatever we cognitively *grasp*, while the meaning of language is its bearing on the world).

3 Linguistic philosophy

Apart from language's interest as a target of science and its centrality to our self-conception as describers of reality, language plays a key methodological role in philosophy. It is this role perhaps more than anything else that has explained the continued close attention paid to language in the past century by philosophers working in such varied areas as epistemology, aesthetics, ethics, metaphysics, the philosophy of science and the philosophy of mind.

The methodological role of language in philosophy is most easily explained by example. A philosopher is interested in the nature of value; they want to know *what goodness is*. Language enters when they observe that goodness is what is attributed when we *say* of a thing that it 'is good'. So the philosopher focuses on certain statements, and seeks an understanding of what such statements *mean* and in general of how they work. They explore whether such statements are ever objectively true or false, whether their truth or aptness varies from speaker to speaker, whether a satisfying explanation of them entails that the word 'good' refers to or expresses a genuine characteristic (of actions, states of affairs, persons, and so on), and how their meaning relates to the distinctive sorts of *endorsement* that such statements commonly convey (see EMOTIVE MEANING).

The pattern exhibited in the example of value is apparent throughout philosophy. We are interested in knowledge, fiction, necessity, causation, or sensation, so we find ourselves studying statements *about* what interests us: statements attributing knowledge, describing fictions, asserting necessities, assigning causes and reporting sensations. Tools from the philosophy of language make available quite a number of views about what these statements mean and in general about how they do their expressive and communicative work; and these views inform and support philosophical positions on the real objects of philosophical interest. There have been dramatic and no doubt exaggerated claims about such techniques – for instance, that philosophy should simply *consist* in this sort of study of language. But it is if anything an understatement to say that linguistic sophistication has deepened philosophical understanding and has advanced debate in nearly all areas of philosophy.

See also: AMBIGUITY; ANALYTICITY; ANAPHORA; COMPOSITIONALITY; COUNTERFACTUAL CONDITIONALS; DECONSTRUCTION; DEMONSTRATIVES AND INDEXICALS; DESCRIPTIONS; INDICATIVE CONDITIONALS; INDIRECT DISCOURSE; LOGIC, PHILOSOPHY OF; LOGICAL POSITIVISM; MASS TERMS; MOORE, G.E.; PROPER NAMES; RUSSELL, B.; SCOPE; SEMANTICS; SEMIOTICS; SENSE AND REFERENCE; VAGUENESS

References and further reading

Lycan, William (1999) *Philosophy of Language: A Contemporary Introduction,* London: Routledge. (A clear introduction emphasizing systematic semantics and pragmatics.)

Taylor, Kenneth (1998) *Truth and Meaning: An Introduction to the Philosophy of Language,* Oxford: Blackwell. (Somewhat advanced, but assumes no prior knowledge.)

Wright, Crispin and Hale, Bob (eds) (1999) *A Companion to the Philosophy of Language,* Oxford: Blackwell. (A collection of articles describing the state of contemporary debates on central topics. For advanced readers.)

MARK CRIMMINS

LATIN AMERICA, PHILOSOPHY IN

Geographically, Latin America extends from the Mexican–US border to those regions of Antarctica to which various Latin American countries have laid claim. It includes the Spanish-speaking Caribbean. Philosophy in Latin America dates from pre-Columbian (before 1492 in Hispanic America) and precabralian times (before 1500 in Brazil).

1 Latin American philosophy up to the nineteenth century'
2 Latin American philosophy in the twentieth century

1 Latin American philosophy up to the nineteenth century

Indigenous cultures, particularly the Aztecs, Mayas, Incas and Tupi-Guarani, produced interesting and sophisticated thought systems centuries before the arrival of Europeans in America. Many cultural artefacts were lost or destroyed so that study of this period involves many challenges in deciphering the subtleties and complexities of the earliest thought in Latin America. Indigenous cosmologies were often linked to phenomena in the natural world.

Academic philosophy started up in the sixteenth century when the Catholic church began to establish schools, monasteries, convents and seminaries in Latin America. If the encounter with the New World had significant impact on the European mind, this was not initially reflected in the philosophy being taught and written in the sixteenth and seventeenth centuries, which tended to restate and reinforce medieval values. However, intriguing writings on ethics and jurisprudence grew out of the contact between Spain and Latin America. Essentially, these writings analysed the relationship between cultural differences and human rights. The Dominican friar Bartolomé de las Casas was a pivotal figure who defended the rights of native and African peoples living in the Indies in the sixteenth century.

With a few notable exceptions, the seventeenth century was largely moribund philosophically because most efforts were directed towards using academic thought to maintain the status quo, which reinforced a fundamentally medieval worldview. The main philosophical task involved justifying and protecting the Catholic faith against Protestantism and science. Scholasticism was the dominant trend. However, there were some exceptions to the dominant practices in the form of several remarkable historical and philosophical figures. Antonio Rubio's studies on logic are remarkably advanced. Juana Inés de la Cruz had a brilliant philosophical mind and is usually considered one of the earliest feminist thinkers in America.

Intellectually, the eighteenth century continued this calm traditionalism until mid-century when a generation of Jesuits tried to break with the thought of Aristotle and bring philosophy into 'modernity'. They were primarily influenced by post-Renaissance Italian and French philosophy. However, the Jesuit order was expelled from the Spanish-speaking world in 1767. This delayed the introduction of proto-modern European philosophy in Latin America. The eighteenth century has become the subject of much revisionist philosophical study, particularly in Mexico.

Academic philosophy still did not broaden in the early nineteenth century because of political turmoil both in various Latin American countries and in Europe. Universities occasionally were closed, inhibiting academic philosophical progress as universities were the locus of much philosophical activity. A more productive forum for philosophy was often the political arena in which thoughtful essays of ideas were written by non-academics on themes such as constitutional government, progress and autonomy.

Later in the nineteenth century and into the early twentieth, positivism eventually became entrenched in most Latin American countries. This movement claimed to be an objective methodology of the sciences. It was widely believed that scientific doctrines could provide the most efficient management of society through educational and political reforms. Auguste COMTE and Herbert SPENCER were the primary positivist influences in Latin America.

2 Latin American philosophy in the twentieth century

In the early twentieth century new intellectual movements began. Arising from these was a strong, thorough-going anti-positivist backlash. Ideas that positivists had promoted as 'scientific' were rejected by anti-positivists for being scientistic. Philosophers entertained idealism, vitalism, pragmatism and various political and social philosophies. Neo-Thomist thought continued to be widely studied, primarily in the Catholic universities.

A focus on regional thought in Latin America was an outgrowth of anti-positivist thought and a consequence of the arrival of Spanish philosophers who were exiled after the fall of Republican Spain. The writings of the Spaniard, José ORTEGA Y GASSET, were widely influential in shaping Latin American philosophical reflections. Philosophers addressed the question of authenticity as they explored whether Latin Americans were simply adopting European philosophies, or whether they themselves had any authentic philosophy to offer. Many concluded that Latin Americans were adapting, rather than adopting European philosophies to their own reality.

This process of critical self-examination, or 'autognosis', was twofold. First, philosophers in individual countries and regions of Latin America sought to identify what was unique or distinctive about their thought or being. Later, philosophical contributions made by Latin America as a whole were compared and contrasted with those of other regions in the world. Studying Latin American thought in comparative perspective engendered a debate of considerable longevity over whether 'Latin American philosophy' exists or whether 'philosophy in Latin America' is a more accurate denotation. Every Latin American country, including Puerto Rico, can be argued to possess unique philosophical traditions. At the same time there

exists an extensive body of argument and commentary on what kind of philosophy, if any, can claim to be 'universal'.

Since analytical philosophy presents perspectives, methods and projects which claim to have universal appeal and applicability, it is often embraced in academic circles and is most frequently entrenched institutionally in Mexico, Brazil and Argentina. Analytical philosophy in these countries, while not obviously a response to immediate regional social, political or economic circumstances, serves to include and validate its adherents in international circles by adopting a style widely practised and accepted by mainstream Anglo-American academic philosophy. Attracted to the linguistic 'rigour' of analytical philosophy, some adherents claim that it is the only way to do 'real philosophy'.

The late twentieth century reveals that it is possible to speak of both 'Latin American philosophy' and 'philosophy in Latin America'. Some areas of philosophical research imbued with regional and cosmopolitan appeal are cultural identity, feminist thought, liberation philosophy, marginality and Marxist thought in Latin America. Many of these areas are profoundly engaged with Latin American realities in historical context. Rather than blindly adopting canonical Western philosophical paradigms, writers in these traditions seek to broaden the definition of what is human by convincingly articulating and incorporating Latin American experience and values into both the crucial discourses of philosophy and the pressing themes of the modern world (see MARGINALITY).

Marxist philosophy has been and most likely will continue to be significant in Latin America, partly because of continuing problems of economic disparities. Concerns with retributive justice, human rights and issues of power and truth, as well as the belief that Marxist theory more accurately describes reality, contribute to the vitality of this thought. Despite the collapse of the Soviet Union and the passing of Maoism in China, for many the Cuban Revolution of 1959 is still idealized because it continues to threaten the US 'monster' to the north, while advancing the notion of a supportive, egalitarian and responsible community. The Peruvian José Carlos Mariátegui was an original Latin American Marxist thinker whose thought has generated interest and respect internationally.

One of the best-known and most interesting contributions of modern Latin American intellectual life is liberation philosophy. The philosophical movement originated in Argentina, although many of its practitioners reside in other Latin American countries. Philosophy of liberation should not be confused with liberation theology. Philosophy of liberation attempts to explain philosophically the theoretical underpinnings of social and political phenomena, such as dependency, and reinforces theology of liberation. These movements are responses to significant events in twentieth-century Latin America such as the Cuban Revolution (1959), the Argentine 'Dirty war' (1976–1983) and repressive regimes which began in Guatemala in 1954, in Brazil in 1964 and in Chile in 1973. Other political topics for these writers included populism, Marxism and Peronism. Philosophy of liberation differs from theology of liberation, Latin Americanist philosophy and Marxist philosophy especially in terms of its more limited accessibility. Philosophers of liberation employ a complex and specialized vocabulary which requires initiation on the part of readers. In addition, philosophy of liberation is not a unified movement: it is more appropriate to speak of philosophies of liberation. Such fragmentation in this field can be partly explained by the political orientations of thinkers whose views range from the extreme left to the extreme right. Their philosophical influences vary widely and include Francophone, German and other Latin American thinkers.

Philosophical activity in Latin America is characterized by a tremendous diversity of focus and methodologies. Latin Americans are keenly aware of philosophical developments in the rest of the world and thus entertain a variety of philosophical stances: progressive and conservative, pragmatist and idealist, materialist and spiritualist. Numerous philosophical interests and projects exist in Latin America because of a diversified and active philosophical profession, an interested public, some government support, a cultural awareness of other continents among the educated and non-educated alike and a widespread faith in education as a key to development.

AMY A. OLIVER

LAW AND MORALITY

Introduction

Within the tradition of natural law thinking which finds its roots in the philosophies of Aristotle and Aquinas, the political community has generally been understood in terms of a fundamental goal: that of fostering the ethical good of citizens. Law, on this conception, should seek to inculcate habits of good conduct, and should support a social environment which will encourage citizens to pursue worthy goals, and to lead valuable lives.

Pragmatic considerations may sometimes suggest the wisdom of restraint in the pursuit of these goals, and citizens may therefore, on appropriate occasions, be left free to indulge depraved tastes or otherwise fall short of acceptable standards. Such pragmatic arguments for the freedom to engage in vice, however, do not call into question the legitimacy of the state's concern with individual morality.

By contrast the liberal tradition has tended to place constraints of principle upon the scope and aims of the law. The most influential such attempt was J.S. Mill's advocacy of 'the harm principle': that the law may forbid only such behaviour as is liable to cause harm to persons other than the agent. Many difficulties surround this and other, more recent, attempts to formulate and defend constraining principles. For instance, should one take into account only the immediate effects of behaviour, or more remote and diffuse effects as well? Thus it is argued that immoral behaviour which in the short term 'harms nobody' may, in the long run, lead to a decline in morality in society at large and to diffuse harmful effects.

> 1 Two traditions
> 2 Mill's 'harm principle'
> 3 The Hart/Devlin debate
> 4 Dworkin on 'external preferences'

1 Two traditions

The attempt to delimit principles which confine and constrain the proper scope of legal and governmental interference is inseparable from the liberal tradition: one need only think of Locke's attempt to define such a sphere of legitimacy by reference to a body of natural rights. Yet the attempt to delineate such principles has not always focused in a clear and circumscribed way upon the particular problem of an allegedly private sphere of morality. Thus when Locke, in his *Letter Concerning Toleration* (1689), seeks to defend religious toleration, he seems to do so not by reliance on his theory of natural rights and social contract, but by means of a pragmatic argument which would have sat comfortably within the assumptions of the Thomist natural law tradition: intolerance is, for Locke, pointlessly ineffectual rather than a violation of a distinct constraining political principle (see LOCKE, J. §1). Debate began to focus clearly on the idea of constraining principles precluding the state from interference with private immorality only in consequence of essays such as Wilhelm von Humboldt's *The Sphere and Duties of Government* (published posthumously in 1852) and J.S. Mill's *On Liberty*

(1859) (see §2 below). The latter work has exerted the most fundamental influence in English-speaking countries.

Before we examine Mill's claims, however, it is worth making a couple of preliminary points. In particular, we should reflect upon the diverse motivations which may underpin rejection of the Aristotelian tradition of political thought, and may lead to the search for principles constraining the community's entitlement to enforce 'private' moral standards. It is often thought that the liberal is committed to a 'subjectivist' or noncognitivist understanding of moral judgment, and that the liberal concern for tolerance is simply a consequence of such subjectivism (see MORAL JUDGMENT §1). Such an interpretation must, however, be a mistake: for, if moral judgments are simply expressions of subjective emotion or attitude, this must apply to moral judgments about the importance of tolerance along with all other moral judgments. A better reading of liberalism would see it as flowing from the inability to reach *agreement* on moral questions, rather than from the supposedly 'subjective' character of moral judgments. This reading does not succumb to the self-subverting character of an appeal to subjectivism, but it does have its problems. In some versions, for example, it can seem to imply that the need for consensus among those who disagree is the rationale for restricting the state's role; but this seems to make the argument for tolerance dependent upon the existence of a balance of power between contending factions.

Finally, one popular line of defence claims that liberalism is reliant neither upon moral subjectivism nor upon the inconclusive nature of moral argument, but upon the value of autonomous choice: it is good that people choose their own projects and lifestyles, even when they choose degrading or unworthy options (see AUTONOMY, ETHICAL). The problem posed by this approach is that it is not wholly clear that the approach can be contrasted in any very fruitful way with the concerns of the Aristotelian tradition. After all, the Aristotelian might claim that *being freely chosen* is an essential condition of a good life, so that the state's concern to encourage good lives itself dictates a concern to protect autonomy. Viewed from this perspective, the debate with liberalism would seem to be a pragmatic argument within the parameters of the Aristotelian tradition.

Such a reconceptualization of the terrain might well be viewed as damaging by many liberals. For many of the critics of Mill and of more recent liberals have directed their fire at the very idea of abstract principles constraining legitimate interference with a realm of supposedly 'private' conduct.

They have been less concerned to oppose the concrete applications of these principles advocated by the liberals themselves. A characteristic example is James Fitzjames Stephen, who, in his book *Liberty, Equality, Fraternity*, wrote as follows:

> I object rather to Mr. Mill's theory than to his practical conclusions.... The objection which I make to most of his statements on the subject is, that in order to justify in practice what might be justified on narrow and special grounds, he lays down a theory incorrect in itself and tending to confirm views which might become practically mischievous.

2   Mill's 'harm principle'

Mill proposes what he describes as a 'very simple principle' as being 'entitled to govern absolutely the dealings of society with the individual in the way of compulsion and control'. The principle asserted that 'The only purpose for which power can rightfully be exercised over any member of a civilised community, against his will, is to prevent harm to others' (*On Liberty* 1859).

Mill's 'harm principle' has sometimes been taken to suggest an atomistic view of society such that there is an area of private conduct which does not impinge on others at all, and which falls outside the law's proper domain for that reason. As his critics were quick to point out, only the most trivial actions are devoid of effects upon others. In spite of the encouragement that Mill gives to this interpretation in some of his language, however, he explicitly conceded that 'self-regarding' actions may nevertheless affect other people. His principle is not intended to demarcate an area of conduct that is beyond the law's remit, so much as a type of reason to which the community should restrict itself: in considering whether an action should be prohibited, only *some* of the effects of an action should be taken into account. In particular, the action's effects in 'harming' others may be taken account of, while the effects upon the actor himself must be disregarded, as must the disapproval of unaffected third parties who consider the act immoral (see PATERNALISM).

In other ways, however, the suggestion that Mill adopts an unduly 'atomistic' view might seem to have some validity. For, if the harm principle is construed as prescribing a focus on fairly immediate and individuated harms, it may lead us to neglect the importance of sustaining social institutions that may be undermined in more oblique ways by the law's failure to uphold conventional moral standards.

One reply to this line of attack might be that nothing in the harm principle compels such a narrowly individuated focus: if the erosion of some social institution *is* a probable consequence of liberalization in an area of conduct, and if that erosion would be harmful, the harm principle legitimates our taking such considerations into account. The reply is problematic, however, in so far as a harm principle which invites us to take account of quite remote and diffuse effects threatens to prove empty and insubstantial in application. Mill himself is quite ready to accept that highly diffuse effects upon others can constitute 'harm' (he is, for example, critical on this ground of the unrestricted right to procreate) but the concession does represent an erosion of the integrity of the principle.

A number of other serious problems are associated with the harm principle. One question concerns the compatibility of the principle with Mill's commitment to utilitarianism (see UTILITAR-IANISM). For should not a utilitarian legislator take account of *all* of the effects of an action, before deciding upon its prohibition? If some people suffer deep unhappiness at the very thought of acts of which they disapprove being performed in private, how can this unhappiness be justifiably *ignored* from the viewpoint of utility? It has been suggested that a utilitarian legislator should disregard such unhappiness in so far as it flows from the adoption of nonutilitarian moral views. But even if this argument could be sustained, it would not go far enough: I may be upset by the thought of acts which I consider simply disgusting rather than immoral; and, in any case, the exclusion of harm to the actor himself remains unexplained by this approach.

It is likely that Mill saw the harm principle as an intermediate maxim, by which utilitarians should regulate their conduct, with the ultimate objective of advancing overall happiness in the long run. Such a view avoids inconsistency, however, only at the price of rendering the entire case dependent on largely empirical claims about the long-term effects of individual liberty. Mill's defence of the harm principle could in this way be thought to manifest an undue and ungrounded optimism. Given the aggregative conception of the common good espoused by utilitarianism, it would be remarkably fortunate if the best way of advancing the collective welfare was invariably to protect individual freedoms.

Quite apart from the compatibility or otherwise of the harm principle with Mill's utilitarianism, however, is the question of the meaning of 'harm' itself. For it has been repeatedly and justifiably pointed out that the question of what constitutes harm is an evaluative question which cannot in the end be separated from our wider ethical beliefs.

Attempts, such as that of Joel Feinberg, to analyse harm in terms of setbacks to interests simply reformulate the problem as one concerning the nature and content of our interests. Yet, without some morally neutral account of harm, Mill's principle seems to do little to exclude criminal prohibitions which are simply based upon moral disapproval of the actor's conduct. Consider, for example, the harm principle in its application to the debate about pornography. One issue concerns the suggestion that pornography fosters a social environment within which violent crimes against women are more likely: this argument appeals to an uncontroversial instance of harm, but makes the issue depend upon highly contestable empirical theses about the effects of pornography. What then if someone suggests that women are harmed *intrinsically* by pornography, in the sense that all women are harmed when some women are depicted as being objects available for sexual gratification? This suggestion employs a notion of harm which might not be universally accepted, but it challenges us to articulate criteria for what is to be regarded as harm (see PORNOGRAPHY).

A relevant suggestion has been made (in a slightly different context) by Brian Barry. He suggests (1995) that 'harm' might be defined in terms of what the great majority of people, having divergent conceptions of the good, would nevertheless agree upon as 'bad'. The suggestion builds upon the sound insight that people may have divergent ethical conceptions which nevertheless have an extensive area of overlap; but in requiring something short of complete universality and unanimity, Barry's approach seems in danger of making the scope of the harm principle itself depend upon majoritarian politics of a kind that Mill was concerned to constrain.

The above arguments may or may not be fatal to Mill's position. They do not render the harm principle wholly vacuous, because that principle serves, at a minimum, to direct our attention to an action's effects on others, rather than on the actor himself; but, if sound, the arguments dramatically reduce the value of the principle as a limitation upon the proper scope of the state's coercive power.

Even the requirement that we should have regard only to effects upon others may be a less substantial constraint than it seems, for we must remember Mill's acceptance of diffuse effects as 'harm'. Acts which are widely considered to be immoral may, in the first instance, affect only the actor himself; but, by creating a communal environment in which such acts are tolerated, they may make it harder (for example) to educate children into moral standards of conduct. When combined with the impossibility of offering a morally neutral account of the nature of 'harm', such diffuse effects seem to reduce the significance of Mill's principle to vanishing point.

3   The Hart/Devlin debate

A concern for such diffuse effects of immoral conduct lies at the bottom of an argument presented by Lord Devlin in 1959, in a British Academy Maccabean Lecture in Jurisprudence. Lord Devlin was then a judge of the Queen's Bench Division of the High Court, becoming a Lord of Appeal in 1961. His Maccabean Lecture arose out of the Wolfenden Report on Homosexual Offences and Prostitution, which had been published in 1957, and which had articulated the principle that 'private immorality' should not be the concern of the criminal law. Devlin criticized this approach, on the ground that society depends for its survival upon the existence of a shared morality, and that it was therefore in principle possible for grossly immoral conduct to threaten the survival of the society. Consequently, society has a right to enforce its shared morality as a measure of self-protection. Devlin was concerned, not with the truth or falsehood of the relevant moral views, but solely with the fact that they were widely shared and fundamental to the society's stability.

H.L.A. HART responded to Devlin's assault by pointing to the absence of empirical support for Devlin's claims that immorality could lead to social breakdown. But it has more recently been suggested (George 1993) that Devlin had in mind not a breakdown in social order so much as a loss of social cohesion, where people relate to each other purely on a basis of self-interest rather than on a basis of moral principle. If this interpretation is correct, it would make Devlin's claim both more plausible and less open to empirical refutation or confirmation.

Devlin acknowledged a debt to the Victorian judge and jurist James Fitzjames Stephen, whose book *Liberty, Equality, Fraternity* (1873) was a forceful attack upon Mill's theory. Stephen's approach was utilitarian in character, but he regarded Mill as having departed from the consistent utilitarianism of Bentham and James Mill. Hart described the works of Stephen and Devlin as revealing 'the outlook characteristic of the English judiciary'.

4   Dworkin on 'external preferences'

The 'goal-based' approach of utilitarianism is rejected by Ronald DWORKIN in favour of what he calls a 'rights-based' approach; but, in reality, there are good grounds for considering his position to be a modified form of utilitarianism, rather than a radical rejection of that approach. Dworkin takes the view that, in so far as utilitarianism possesses any genuine moral appeal, that appeal is a consequence of the extent to which it expresses our belief in a 'right to equal concern and respect'. He argues, however, that the notion of equal concern and respect receives inadequate expression within utilitarianism to the extent that the utilitarian takes account not only of 'personal preferences' (preferences for what I myself do and receive) but also of 'external preferences' (my preferences about what others do or receive). A proper concern for equality would exclude the influence of external preferences by recognizing a 'right to moral independence': the right not to suffer disadvantage simply on the ground that others consider one's conceptions of a good life to be ignoble or wrong.

Dworkin believes that rights are best understood as 'trumps' over collective goals, and that, consequently, their philosophical justification is in part relative to the goals which have been adopted. The problem with taking account of external preferences (if a utilitarian goal has been adopted) is that the external preferences 'purport to occupy the same space' as the utilitarian theory itself: utilitarianism must be neutral between pushpin and poetry, but it cannot be neutral between itself and Nazism (for example).

Dworkin insists that this argument holds even when the external preferences are not based on any general moral or political theory: they still 'invade the space claimed by neutral utilitarianism'. It is difficult to see how this argument can be sustained, however. One cannot argue, for example, that a preference 'invades the space of utilitarianism' simply because, if fully satisfied, it would necessitate a distribution not recommended by utilitarianism. Such an approach would prescribe a decision procedure which was viciously circular: for one would have to decide upon the requirements of utility before one could say whether any particular preference should be taken into account in calculating those requirements.

In any case, could it not be said that Dworkin's approach fails to show equal concern for those whose wellbeing or utility is a function of their external preferences? Suppose that my sole concern is your welfare, and my life will be a failure if your happiness is not secure. How can equality of concern dictate that my wellbeing should be disregarded?

Many will consider that the proposed 'right to moral independence' is more attractive than is the justification which Dworkin proposes for it; but then, few if any theorists have argued that people should be disadvantaged simply in consequence of a widely held disapproval of their lifestyles, so perhaps the 'right' is not very substantial after all.

See also: LIBERALISM; NATURAL LAW; PRIVACY; RULE OF LAW (RECHTSSTAAT); TOLERATION

References and further reading

Barry, B. (1995) *Justice as Impartiality*, Oxford: Oxford University Press. (An intelligent development of some recent liberal political theory.)

George, R.P. (1993) *Making Men Moral*, Oxford: Oxford University Press. (A clear and accessible discussion, which could form a good starting point for the beginner, in spite of being written from a standpoint which is quite critical of liberalism.)

N.E. SIMMONDS

LAW, PHILOSOPHY OF

Introduction

Law has been a significant topic for philosophical discussion since its beginnings. Attempts to discover the principles of cosmic order, and to discover or secure the principles of order in human communities, have been the wellsprings of inquiry into law. Such inquiry has probed the nature and being of law, and its virtues, whether those that it is considered as intrinsically possessing, or those that ought to be cultivated by lawgivers, judges or engaged citizens. A dialectic of reason and will is to be found in philosophical speculation about the underpinning principles of law. On the one side, there is the idea that the cosmos itself, and human society too, contain immanent principles of rational or reasonable order, and this order must be capable of discovery or apprehension by rational (or 'reasonable') beings. On the other side, there is the view that order, especially in society and in human conduct, is not found but made, not disclosed to reason but asserted by acts of will. Either there is a 'law of reason – and nature' or there is a 'law by command of the sovereign – or of God'. A third possible element in the discussion may then enter, that of custom as the foundation of law.

Implicit in the opposition of reason and will is the question of practical reason: does reason have a truly practical role concerning ultimate ends and nonderivative principles of action, or is it only ancillary to the pursuit of ends or fulfilment of norms set by will? Alternatively, does reason already presuppose custom and usage, and enter the lists only by way of critique of current custom and usage? In either case, what is at issue is the very existence of such a thing as 'practical reason' (see PRACTICAL REASON AND ETHICS). For law is about human practice, about societal order enforced and upheld. If there can be a law of reason, it must be that reason is a practical as well as a speculative

faculty. The radically opposed alternative sets will above reason, will oriented to the ends human beings happen to have. Norms and normative order depend then on what is willed in the way of patterns for conduct; reason plays only an ancillary part in the adjustment of means to ends.

A further fundamental set of questions concerns the linkage of the legal with the political. If law concerns good order, and if politics aims at good order in a polity, law must be a crucial part of politics; but in this case a subordinate part, for politics determines law, but not law politics. On the other hand, politics may be considered at least as much a matter of actual power-structures as a matter of speculation about their beneficial use for some postulated common good. In the latter case, we may see law as that which can in principle set limits on and control abuses of power. Politics is about power, law about the shaping and the limiting of power-structures. The issue then is how to make law a master of politics rather than its servant.

1 Law as reason'
2 Law as will
3 Law as custom
4 Laws and values
5 Law as politics

1 Law as reason

In the *Republic*, Plato depicts Thrasymachus, proponent of the thesis that justice is the will of the powerful, as being refuted comprehensively by Socrates (see PLATO §14). The refutation postulates a human capability to discern principles of right societal conduct independently of any formal enactment or legislative decision made by somebody with power. These principles in their very nature are normative, not descriptive. In Aristotle, the same general idea emerges in the form of noticing that whereas much that is observed as law is locally variable and arbitrary, there appear to be fundamental common principles across different polities. Some principles may then be legal simply 'by enactment', but others seem to be so 'by nature'. Explorations of the nature of humans as rational and political animals may then help to underpin the idea of that which is right by nature, but that exploration is more the achievement of Aristotle's successors in the Stoic tradition than of himself (see STOICISM). Roman jurists adapted some of the Stoic ideas of natural law in their expositions of the civil law, and subsequently, for medieval and early modern Europe, the existence of the Justinianic compilation of the whole body of Roman law was held by many thinkers to embody in large measure the promise of law as 'written reason' (see ROMAN LAW).

In any event, the greatest flowering of the Aristotelian idea came with its fusion into the Christian tradition in the work of Thomas Aquinas (§13), hugely influential as this has been in the developing of Catholic moral theology in the succeeding centuries. After at least a century of relative neglect among legal scholars, especially in the English-speaking world, the last quarter of the twentieth century has seen a strong revival of the Thomistic approach in the philosophy of law (see Natural law), with contemporary thinkers developing the idea of the basic goods implicit in human nature, and showing both how these can lead to the elaboration of moral principles, and then how positively enacted laws can be understood as concretizations of fundamental principles.

In the seventeenth century, other strands of essentially the same idea had led to the belief, for example, of Hugo Grotius, that basic principles of right conduct and hence of human rights are themselves ascertainable by intuition and reason (compare Pufendorf, S.). Kant's representation of the principles of practical reason is the classical restatement of this position in its most philosophically rigorous form (see Kant, I. §§9–11; Kantian ethics §1).

In a wide sense, all these approaches may be ascribed to rationalism, as contrasted with voluntarism (see Rationalism; Voluntarism). For they treat law, or its fundamental principles, as discoverable by rational and discursive means, independently of the intervention of any legislative will. They do not, of course, deny the need for legislative, or adjudicative or executive, will. Even if fundamental principles stand to reason, their detailed operationalization in actual societies requires processes of law-stating, law-applying and law-enforcement. But the issue is whether these are fundamentally answerable at the bar of reason and practical wisdom (*prudentia*), or not. To the extent that they are so answerable, we have a concept of some 'higher law', some law of reason, by which to justify, to measure and to criticize the actual practice of human legal institutions. If the rational derivation of this depends in some way on a teleological understanding of human nature and its relation to the creator and the rest of the created universe, we may reasonably enough call this a 'law of nature' or 'natural law'.

2 Law as will

But there is another possible account of higher law. It can be thought of as a law laid down by God for his creation. The divine will, not the divine reason, must be the source of law. It cannot be for created reason to presume to judge of the creator's wisdom. The omnipotence of the creator entails that the law

will be whatever the creator wills it to be, and to be law by virtue of that will, not by any independent reason and nature of things. Indeed, the nature of things will be just what the creator wills it to be, and the names of things will be matters of convention derived from human linguistic usage. Concepts are not essences that guide us to essential meanings. Nominalism and voluntarism are inevitable bedfellows (see Nominalism).

It is therefore inaccurate to suppose that the theory of natural law as a kind of higher law presupposes rationalism. There can indeed be a voluntaristic species of 'natural law', though the voluntaristic tradition will more likely speak of 'divine law' or 'God's law' than of natural law *simpliciter* (see Austin, J.). Moreover, one element in the religious upheavals associated with the Reformation was an insistence on the need for unmediated regard to the (scripturally revealed) divine law, rather than to the custom or tradition of sinful human institutions such as the Church. It is not for fallen human reason to set itself above or even beside the revealed will of God. But that revealed will must be received as a law binding above all others.

In this state of things it becomes questionable whether to accept any human law at all; and, on the voluntarist hypothesis, to see how law other than God's law can have any obligatory force at all. To the saving of human law there are only two possible moves: either it must be shown that God in fact wills our obedience to the very kings and other superiors we actually have (as in the theory of 'the divine right of kings'), or it must be the case that the binding will arises from the consent of human beings themselves, expressed through some original social contract. The divine will then enters the picture only to the extent of making obligatory the fulfilment of compacts voluntarily agreed, a point to which may be added a grimly Hobbesian acknowledgement that covenants without swords are but words, so the true binding force of the obligation of the law will derive from the effective might of the very ruler whom the social compact institutes in that office (see Hobbes, T. §§6–7). In this Hobbesian form, natural law has practically reached a vanishing point (though Locke's response envisages the state of nature as governed by reason in the form of a law of nature, grounding presocietal rights of human beings to life, liberty and estate (see Locke, J. §§9–10). The greatest legal expression of the Lockean vision of law, applied to expounding the English common law, is in the work of Sir William Blackstone. The *coup de grâce* was administered by Hume and Bentham, the latter having as his particular target Blackstone's work. They argue that the social contract is a fifth wheel on the carriage in either Hobbesian or Lockean form, since all the reasons that there are for obeying the law that we have supposedly agreed to apply with equal force even if we did not agree to it, and there is no evidence anywhere of any such agreement as a historical phenomenon (see BENTHAM, J.).

3 Law as custom

Whence then comes the law? Hume ascribes it to convention and custom primarily, coupled with reflection upon the pleasing quality (the utility) of rigorous observance of customary norms (see HUME, D. §3). Bentham and Austin restrict the role of custom or 'habit' to the issue of obedience. Whoever is habitually obeyed by the many in a numerous society is in a position to enforce their commands by effectively coercive sanctions up to and including death. Thus do they differentiate the positive law from other forms of so-called law such as scientific law, laws of honour, or personal moral codes. Law is such by command of a sovereign, the one habitually obeyed who habitually obeys no other (see SOVEREIGNTY).

Legal positivism of this stamp is an easy bedfellow with political utilitarianism, and programmes of legal reform. Codification of law is an associated ambition, justified on utilitarian grounds (see UTILITARIANISM; BECCARIA, C.B.; BENTHAM, J.). Codification is also a distinctive phenomenon of the early nineteenth century, product of the Enlightenment critique of the old customs of the *ancien régime*, though also of spadework in the exposition of civil law partly achieved under the aegis of late legal rationalism. After the Code Napoléon, promulgated in France in 1804, there followed a century of codification and legislative modernization of law in many places, and with this characteristically went approaches in legal philosophy that stress the essential emergence of law from a sovereign's will, or the will of the state as a rational association (in Hegelian vein; see HEGELIANISM). Nevertheless, this movement produced its own counter-movements, stressing the importance of the spirit of the people as the basis of law, or more prosaically locating it primarily in custom, a view particularly popular in the context of the common law.

Twentieth-century critics of classical positivism accuse its authors of confusing 'commands' with 'binding commands' (see KELSEN, H.) or of mislocating the roots of legislative authority in mere 'habit', rather than in the 'internal point of view' of those for whom the system within which authority is exercised has normative force (see HART, H.L.A.). The Kelsenian version of positivism rests it on the necessary presuppositions for a value-free science of law, and other thinkers have pursued further the question of 'legal science' (see BOBBIO, N.); the Hartian version rests it on the customs of at least the official and political classes in a state, whose practices concerning the recognition of certain criteria for the validity of legal rules define the ultimate 'living constitution' of a state, its 'rule of recognition' (see LEGAL POSITIVISM). Rival varieties of Hartian positivism have become salient in recent decades.

A notable offshoot of or development from positivistic legal study has been the development of ever-more rigorous approaches to conceptual analysis and categorization, seeking to account for the use of concepts like 'duty', 'right', 'ownership' and others in the framework of general legal norms. Hohfeld's analysis of 'fundamental legal conceptions' (see HOHFELD, W.N.) has had many followers and critics, and contemporaries in other traditions have taken a somewhat more psychologistic approach to the task. Reflection on legal concepts as institutions or 'institutional facts' has led to developing an 'institutional' theory of law that transforms what was originally a naturalistic conception into a positivistic one.

4 Laws and values

One way or another, whether in voluntaristic versions or in those that place more weight on customary or institutional aspects of law, nearly all forms of or approaches to legal positivism have insisted on the strong value-relevance of positive law. The matter of doubt has not been 'ought laws to be just?', but whether their being just is a condition of their being genuinely legal. The 'scientific' character of pure legal analysis has indeed been contrasted with the exercise of moral judgment or moral sentiment, or the engaging in ideological argumentation, that is involved in the critique of law as unjust or otherwise unsatisfactory from the viewpoint of human needs and aspirations. Some, however, have thought that critique itself can have a scientific or at least an objective basis, grounded in the fundamentals of human nature. Classical utilitarianism and nineteenth-century law reform have already been noted; they had successors in the 'jurisprudence of interests', and, albeit with certain qualifications, in the later twentieth-century 'economic analysis of law'.

The need to subject law to critique is obvious from many points of view, none more urgently than that which takes note of the burdensome impact of legal sanctions on human happiness and liberty. If laws characteristically carry punishments or awards of damages for their infraction, some theory to justify penal and compensatory institutions is called for (see CRIME AND PUNISHMENT; JUSTICE, CORRECTIVE). Whether there are any abstractly stateable limits to the legitimacy of interference with liberty through legal intervention has been another heated debate (see LAW AND MORALITY).

Nevertheless, the positivists' claim that they can combine an a-moralistic conceptual analysis of law and its institutions with a readiness for critique of actual laws on moral and political grounds, and with a last-resort readiness to disobey or defy the law when it is unjust to an extreme, has been doubted by some. Gustav Radbruch felt himself driven by his experience of the Nazi years (and also, perhaps, by the implications of the radical voluntarism of Carl Schmitt) to abandon such a claim and to insist on a conceptually necessary minimum of basic justice in anything we can recognize as 'law' at all. The interpenetration of equity with law, and the interweaving of ideas of justice, equity and law, can be taken to point to a similar moral, and idealistic approaches to legal theory give a deeper grounding for such an approach.

5 Law as politics

However one takes one's stand on will against reason, or on natural law against legal positivism, most of the theoretical approaches so far considered give some way of accounting for the independent existence of law as a distinct social phenomenon. Law's independence, at least when underpinned by an independent judiciary, has been held to promise the possibility of effective control over arbitrary state action while at the same time guaranteeing at least the justice of formal equality to citizens and the degree of predictability allegedly desired by modern rational subjects. Here we have the 'rule of law' ideal that demands government under the forms of law and law in the form of clearly identifiable rules (see RULE OF LAW (RECHTSSTAAT)). Yet the mere existence of some body of sacred or secular texts embodying rules of law is not enough for any socially realistic account of law, or for any politically persuasive vision of the rule of law (see SOCIAL THEORY AND LAW). The statute book is not self-applying or self-interpreting. To secure the rule of law it is necessary to have prospective rules published to all. But, as L.L. Fuller points out, it is necessary that they be interpreted in a reasonable and purposive way, and faithfully carried into action by the officials of the state whose rules they are. How is this to be secured?

Many schools of thought, chief among them the realists (see LEGAL REALISM) in Europe and in the USA, have stressed the widely discretionary character of legal interpretation, both in relation to the general rules of the law, and in relation to the

categorization of fact-situations as subsumable under the law for one purpose or another. On inspection, 'facts' can turn out to be as elusive as 'laws', and the study of legal processes of proof assumes a certain urgency. All in all, it is a serious and difficult question to discern what, if anything, can render decisions reasonably 'reckonable' given the broad discretion vested in those who interpret the law.

One form of response has been to find that law is reckonable not on the basis of the official rules and standard doctrine, but rather on the basis of the 'situation sense' of a judiciary with a common understanding of political and policy objectives underlying law. These insights of the 'realists' have been carried forward more boldly by contemporary feminist jurisprudence, one version of which finds social prejudice directing law through the biases of judges. Another version locates an inner masculinity in the legal rules themselves, even and especially at their most abstract; the asserted values of objectivity and impersonality ultimately come under question as presumptions of doubtful desirability.

Within more mainstream jurisprudence the developed response to realism has been to work out extended theories of the rule of law, acknowledging that law is more than positive rules but arguing for the existence of other mechanisms within law controlling the role of substantive elements in decision-making (see CAUSATION IN THE LAW). Such responses find a certain coherence within law, but by contrast the more developed critical (including critical feminist) approaches argue that there are central fractures and fault lines within the law, reflecting ultimately competing political visions of human association, often summed up as individualism versus community-values. Ronald Dworkin's argument for coherence and integrity in law evokes the idea of an interpretive community, but seems too readily to assume that for any actual legal order there can be found a single consensual interpretive project, even in principle (see DWORKIN, R.).

Taking an overall view, the project of establishing the rule of law as an independent base for the critique and control of state action is put in serious doubt, since interpretation is through-and-through political; and appeals to the rule of law can themselves be moves in a political game, expressions of ideology rather than of higher values. It may be that in the end legal philosophy is faced, today as at its beginnings, with this dilemma: either legal reasoning and moral reasoning have that kind of in-principle objectivity proposed by natural law theory in its rationalist versions, or the theatre of law is simply a theatre presenting endlessly the power-play of rival wills and visions of the good.

549

Many have sought a third way, not yet with acknowledged success.

See also: HALAKHAH

References and further reading

Harris, J.W. (1980) *Legal Philosophies*, London: Butterworth. (Straightforward and well-written introduction to issues and schools of thought in philosophy of law.)

Kelman, M. (1987) *A Guide to Critical Legal Studies*, Cambridge, MA: Harvard University Press. (Readable and sympathetic account of, and contribution to, the 'critical' approach that regards all legal activity as intrinsically political – and ideological.)

BEVERLEY BROWN
NEIL MACCORMICK

LAW, RABBINIC
See HALAKHAH

LAWS, NATURAL

It is widely supposed that science aims to identify 'natural laws'. But what are laws of nature? How, if at all, do statements of laws differ from 'mere' general truths which include generalizations true only 'accidentally'? Suppose, for example, it happens to be true that all iron spheres (past, present and future) are less than 1 km in diameter. Contrast this with the truth of 'all electrons are negatively charged'. There seems to be a clear intuitive distinction between these two truths, but is there any principled distinction between them that can be drawn and defended?

This has been the traditional focus of philosophical attention concerning laws of nature, and basically two mutually opposed philosophical accounts have been developed. According to the first account, there are real necessities in nature, over and above the regularities that they allegedly produce (whether or not these regularities are held to be observable), and law-statements are descriptions of these necessities. According to the second account, there are no necessities but only regularities (correlations, patterns), and laws are descriptions of regularities (though perhaps not of any regularity but only of the most basic or most general ones). There are significantly different variants of each account; and also positions that altogether deny the existence of general laws (or deny that science should aim to describe them).

Any one of these accounts, if it is ultimately to be coherent and defensible, has to successfully address four interrelated issues: the meaning of a law statement – the semantic issue; the fact to which a law statement refers and which makes it true – the metaphysical issue; the basis on which claims to know a law are justified – the epistemological issue; and the capacity to explain adequately the variety and roles of scientific laws – the explanatory issue.

In attempting this task, each of the available accounts faces its own distinct difficulties. For example, if there are necessities in nature, as the first account claims, how exactly do we identify them: how can we tell which of the inductively confirmed regularities are laws? On the other hand, if there are only regularities, as the second account claims, does this mean that our intuitions and scientific practices are awry and that there really is no distinction between laws and accidental generalizations?

The difficulties facing all extant accounts become even more marked when we face up squarely to the surprisingly wide variety of (putative) laws supplied by current science and to the complexity of the relations between those putative laws and regularities and causes.

See also: POSITIVISM IN THE SOCIAL SCIENCES; PRAGMATISM; SCIENTIFIC METHOD; THEORIES, SCIENTIFIC

C.A. HOOKER

LEBENSPHILOSOPHIE

In its most general sense *Lebensphilosophie* denotes a philosophy which asks after the meaning, value and purpose of life, turning away from purely theoretical knowledge towards the undistorted fullness of lived experience. In the second half of the nineteenth century and the early twentieth century the concept of 'life' assumed a central role in German philosophy. *Lebensphilosophie* typically opposes rigid abstractions with a philosophy based on feeling and intuition, and seeks to establish the priority of 'life' as an all-encompassing whole. The central claim underlying its various manifestations is that life can only be understood from within.

See also: ENLIGHTENMENT, CONTINENTAL

JASON GAIGER

LEGAL POSITIVISM

Legal positivism is the approach in the philosophy of law which treats 'positive law' – law laid down in human societies through human decisions – as a distinct phenomenon, susceptible of analysis and description independently of morality, divine law or mere natural reality. It shares with philosophical positivism the aim of dealing in facts, but these are facts about legality and legal systems. Insistence on the distinctness of positive law has been integral to the 'rule of law ideal' because of the aim of clear law applied by neutral legal officials. However, debates about positivism have been marred by a degree of conceptual confusion: positivism often appears to mean something different to its supporters and to its enemies, and many attacks are launched against straw men. Consequently, much depends on the definition of legal positivism that is used.

Attempts have been made to put some order into the discussion. Consider, for instance, H.L.A. Hart's list of meanings of legal positivism (which cumulatively count as features of positivism): (1) law as human commands; (2) absence of any necessary connection between law and morals; (3) the study of law as meaning, as distinct from sociology, history and evaluation; (4) the contention that a legal system is a closed system, sufficient in itself to justify legal decisions; (5) non-cognitivism in ethics. Norberto Bobbio's list is shorter and more orderly, but at first sight not too different: legal positivism has been conceived as: (1) a neutral, scientific approach to law; (2) a set of theories depicting the law as the product of the modern state, claiming that the law is a set of positive rules of human origin, and ultimately amounting to a set of statutes, collected in legal systems or orders; (3) an ideology of law that gives a value to positive law as such, implying that it should always be obeyed. However, in this list, unlike Hart's, the 'meanings' cannot be added together, the first and last being incompatible. The connection between the three points is as follows: for positivists the theories of Bobbio's second point (law is made up of rules produced by the state) yield a scientific and value-free approach to law; for the adversaries of legal positivism they yield only ideology, that is hidden value judgments in favour of the power of the state.

The shortest way to understand what is at issue in these abstract discussions is to proceed by contrasting legal positivism with its main critics' approach to law. It is noteworthy that on this point legal realists and natural law theorists, although starting from different and even opposite points of view, agree in concluding that legal positivism is an ideological, covertly evaluative, thesis.

See also: Bobbio, N.; Hart, H.L.A.; Law, philosophy of

MARIO JORI

LEGAL REALISM

'Legal realism' is the term commonly used to characterize various currents of twentieth-century legal thought which stand opposed to idealism. (Hence, 'realism' in this context ought to be understood not as a body of thought which opposes nominalism, but as an instance of nominalism.) In the Scandinavian countries, legal realism was modelled on Axel Hägerström's critique of idealist metaphysics, and sought ways to account for legal rights and duties without presupposing or postulating the existence of ideal objects or entities. In the USA, legal realism evolved as a critique of the idealism implicit in the vision of the common law which was promoted by C.C. Langdell, first Dean of the Harvard Law School, and in the *laissez-faire* ideology of the late nineteenth- and early twentieth-century Supreme Court. Realist jurisprudential sentiments – primarily as articulated in terms of the so-called indeterminacy critique – continue to bear an influence on late twentieth-century critical legal thought.

See also: Law, philosophy of; Nominalism; Realism and antirealism; Social theory and law

NEIL DUXBURY

LEGITIMACY

Legitimacy refers to the rightfulness of a powerholder or system of rule. The term originated in controversies over property and succession, and was used to differentiate children born of a lawful marriage from those who were 'illegitimate'. From thence the term entered political discourse via controversies over the rightful succession to the restored French throne after the Napoleonic period. However, questions about what makes government rightful have been a central issue of philosophical debate since the ancient Greeks, and in this sense the concept, if not the term, 'legitimacy' is as old as political philosophy itself. Its significance lies in the moral, as opposed to merely prudential, grounds for obedience which follow for subjects where power is rightfully acquired and exercised, and in the depth of allegiance which such political authorities can call upon in times of difficulty.

What, then, makes government legitimate? Most thinkers agree that a necessary condition is that power should be acquired and exercised according to established rules, whether these are conventionally or legally defined. However, legal validity cannot be a sufficient condition of legitimacy, since both the rules and the power exercised under them also have to be morally justifiable. Two broad criteria for moral justifiability can be distinguished: (1) political power should derive from a rightful *source* of authority; (2) it should satisfy the rightful *ends* or purposes of government. Most philosophical disputes about legitimacy take place either within or between these two broad positions; any adequate account of it must embrace both however.

DAVID BEETHAM

LEIBNIZ, GOTTFRIED WILHELM (1646–1716)

Introduction

Leibniz was one of the central figures of seventeenth-century philosophy, indeed, one of the central intellectual figures of his age. Born and educated in Germany, he travelled to Paris in 1672 and quickly entered into its lively intellectual and scientific life, acquainting himself with the most advanced ideas then in circulation. It was there that he invented the infinitesimal calculus, and laid the foundations for the philosophical and scientific programmes that were to occupy him for the rest of his life. He returned to Germany in 1676, entering the service of the House of Hanover where, except for brief absences, he remained until his death. There, along with his court duties, he had time for a wide variety of intellectual activities that eventually gained him an international reputation.

Leibniz's philosophy, particularly his metaphysics, can appear otherworldly and complex. But there are a few simple themes and basic commitments that run through his thought. At root is his philosophical optimism, the commitment that this is the best of all possible worlds, freely created by a rational God who always chooses the best for a good reason. This best of all possible worlds, Leibniz held, is 'the one which is at the same time the simplest in hypotheses and the richest in phenomena' (*Discourse on Metaphysics* §6). For this reason, the world must be governed by a variety of general principles to which Leibniz appealed in his philosophy: there must be a sufficient reason for everything in the world; there are no jumps in nature; there must be exactly the same power in the full cause as there is in the complete effect, among many others. While such principles do not deductively determine the rest of Leibniz's philosophy, they do play a major role in shaping it; they constitute a kind of lens through which he viewed the major philosophical issues of his age.

One such issue concerns the ultimate make-up of the world. Like many of his contemporaries, Leibniz adopted a mechanistic view, according to which everything in the physical world is explicable in terms of the size, shape and motion of the tiny bodies that make up the grosser bodies of

experience. But he rejected the idea that this could be the ultimate explanation for things. Behind the mechanistic world of inanimate bodies in motion, Leibniz saw a world of living things and souls – active, genuinely individual, genuinely different from one another, the true atoms of nature, the true reality – which he eventually called monads. At the deepest level, Leibniz's world was made up of an infinity of mind-like entities, each with its own perceptions that change from moment to moment according to an internal programme by way of the faculty of appetition, all in harmony with one another so that they all reflect the same world. While the world of physics is mechanistic, it is merely phenomenal, the confused appearance of a deeper reality. A consequence of this was Leibniz's famous doctrine of pre-established harmony. In contrast to Descartes, for whom mind and body interact, and in contrast to the occasionalists, for whom God is the true cause who brings about motion in the body on the occasion of a volition and a sensation in the mind on the occasion of a stimulation of the appropriate nerves in the body, for Leibniz God created the mind (a single monad) and the body (itself a collection of monads) in perfect harmony with one another so that their mental and physical states would always correspond in the appropriate way.

A second set of metaphysical issues of central concern to Leibniz involves the interlocking questions of necessity, contingency and freedom. In response to contemporaries such as Hobbes and Spinoza, Leibniz tried to find room for contingency and freedom in his world. He argued that even though God is, in a sense, constrained to choose the best, he does so freely. Consequently, the world he created, the best of all possible worlds, exists contingently, and at least some features of it are contingent, those whose contraries are not in themselves impossible. So for example, $2 + 3 = 5$, true in every possible world, is necessary, while 'Adam sins', whose contrary is not impossible, is contingent. But over and above contingency and divine freedom, Leibniz also wanted to make room for human freedom. According to Leibniz, when God created Adam as a part of this best of all possible worlds, he knew that Adam would sin; it is part of the concept of Adam that he sins, part of his internal 'programme' that he will eat the apple, and part of the internal 'programmes' of the monads that make up his body that he will actually eat the apple. But, Leibniz argued, what God builds in is that Adam *freely* chose to sin. God builds into the world the reasons that incline Adam's will without necessitating it, correctly predicting what Adam will do, and building the rest of the world around the consequences of Adam's free actions.

Important as they are, these two concerns constitute only a small portion of Leibniz's thought, even within the domain of philosophy. In psychology, he introduced a distinction between conscious and unconscious perceptions and tried to understand the way in which unconscious perceptions ('*petites perceptions*') in part determine conscious perceptions ('apperceptions'). In epistemology, he is important for his sophisticated version of the innatist hypothesis, and for appreciating the role that a mathematical theory of probability can play in understanding the world. In logic, Leibniz advanced programmes for a new formal logic more powerful than Aristotle's, and for a universal language. In ethics and political thought, he contributed to the seventeenth-century natural law tradition. In natural philosophy, he emphasized the importance of the notion of force and advanced the broadly Cartesian programme of a physics grounded in conservation laws. Outside philosophy he is well known for his work on the calculus. Though he co-discovered it with Newton, it is his notation that is still used, and his version probably had the greater influence in his day. But he was a major contributor to many other fields, including geology, natural history, linguistics and European history. Though he left no real school of followers, he deeply influenced philosophy after his death, particularly in eighteenth-century Germany.

1 Life

Gottfried Wilhelm Leibniz was born in Leipzig on 1 July 1646. He later recalled how his father, who died when he was only six years old, had instilled in him a love of learning. Leibniz started school when he was seven, but more important than his formal education in those years was his reading. He taught himself Latin at an early age in order to be able to read Livy and Calvisius, and because of that was admitted into his late father's extensive library, where he read widely. At fifteen Leibniz entered university, first the University of Leipzig (1661–6), and then the University of Altdorf (1666–7), graduating with degrees in law and in philosophy. The education he received there was conservative, a mixture of traditional Aristotelian school philosophy and Renaissance humanism. Though invited to join the faculty at Altdorf, he chose instead to enter the service of the Elector of Mainz, where he stayed until he was sent to Paris in the spring of 1672 on diplomatic business.

While he had done significant work in a number of areas before going to Paris, including law, theology, mathematics and physics, the trip was crucial to Leibniz's intellectual development. In the later part of the seventeenth century, learned Europe was in the midst of a great intellectual revolution; the older Aristotelian philosophy of the schools was being challenged by a new mechanist philosophy which rejected the form, matter and qualities of the Aristotelian world, replacing them with a world in which everything was to be explained in terms of size, shape and motion. In this new world there was a special emphasis on mathematics, which was increasingly applied to problems in physics in a way quite foreign to Aristotelian philosophy.

Though he had taken an interest in the moderns while in Germany (HOBBES was particularly influential on his early thought), it was only after he reached Paris that Leibniz was able to enter the mainstream of European intellectual life. There he came to know the important mathematician and physicist Christiaan Huygens, who introduced him to new ideas which Leibniz absorbed quickly. In those years, Leibniz laid the foundations of his calculus, his later physics and his philosophy. While there were no publications at the time, many unpublished notes survive, important for understanding the emergence of his mature thought.

Leibniz returned to Germany in December 1676, passing through Holland, where he discussed philosophy with the reclusive SPINOZA. It was then that he first entered the service of the House of Hanover. He served under Duke Johann Friedrich until his death in 1679, under Duke Ernst August from 1680 to 1698, and then, finally, under the Elector Georg Ludwig, who ascended the throne of Great Britain as King George I in 1714. Except for his travels, he remained at Hanover for the rest of his life. There Leibniz undertook a very wide variety of tasks. He served as a mining engineer (unsuccessfully supervising the draining of the silver mines in the Harz Mountains), as head librarian of a large collection of books, as a general advisor and a diplomat, and was particularly interested in finding ways for the Catholics and the Protestants to reunite. Leibniz was also given the responsibility for writing a history of the House of Hanover. While he collected and published many previously unknown historical documents and published a number of other historical writings, this project barely got off the ground. All that he seems to have completed was a geological history of the region of Lower Saxony, the *Protogaea*. While it proved to be an important work in the history of geology when it was finally published in 1749, it seems not to have pleased Leibniz's employers who had hoped for a history of somewhat more recent times.

Through the rest of his life, Leibniz continued to explore the philosophical, scientific and mathematical questions that interested him from his earliest years. The 1680s and 1690s saw some of his most important writings. In these years, he published his new infinitesimal calculus and a variety of papers outlining his new approach to physics, particularly his new science of dynamics, the science of force and its laws. The *Brevis demonstratio* of 1686 presents for the first time a refutation of Descartes' conservation law, and hints at the foundations of a more adequate physics. The details are developed in his unpublished *Dynamica* (1690), some material from which is published in the *Specimen dynamicum* in 1695, as well as in the numerous answers to attempted refutations of his argument from tenacious Cartesians. In philosophy, Leibniz published his *Meditationes de cognitione, veritate et ideis* (Meditations on Knowledge, Truth and Ideas) in 1684, and in 1686 composed the *Discours de métaphysique* (Discourse on metaphysics), eventually published in 1846; the main arguments from the latter are discussed in a series of letters with the Catholic theologian Antoine ARNAULD, letters Leibniz contemplated publishing in later years. These same themes are found, somewhat transformed, in two important publications in the 1690s, the *Système nouveau de la nature et de la communication des substances* (New system of the nature and the communication of substances) (1695) and the *De ipsa natura* (On nature itself) (1698). In the first decades of the next century, Leibniz continued to be very active. Important in these years were the *Nouveaux essais* (New essays) (1704), a close examination of Locke's *Essay Concerning Human Understanding*, abandoned at Locke's death and unpublished until 1765. But he did publish his *Théodicée* (Theodicy) (1710), a compendium of philosophical and theological ideas involving further development of themes that go far back in his thought. His final philosophical works were short summaries, intended only as brief guides to his work, the *Monadologie* (Monadology) and the *Principes de la nature et de la grâce* (Principles of nature and grace), both of which probably date from 1714.

Throughout these years Leibniz kept up a vast correspondence, including exchanges with Huygens, Johann Bernoulli, Burchardus de Volder and Bartholomaeus Des Bosses, among many others. One exchange is particularly important. Leibniz had been at war with his English counterpart, Sir Isaac Newton, for many years; their rivalry went back to at least the early 1690s, and probably to their first contact in the mid-1670s. The affair was ugly, with accusations of plagiarism regarding the calculus from both sides, and bitter disagreements over the foundations of physics. The rivalry finally resulted, in 1715–16, in a correspondence between Leibniz and Samuel CLARKE, the latter standing in for Newton himself. The exchange was published by Clarke in 1717.

When his employer Georg Ludwig went to London in 1714 to take the throne of Great Britain, Leibniz did not follow. He was out of favour for his failure to make progress on the history of the House of Hanover, as well as for his generally old-fashioned manner. Furthermore, it is likely that Georg feared that the dispute with Newton and the British intellectual establishment would cause difficulties. Whatever the reason, Leibniz remained in Hanover, where he died on 14 November 1716. Though celebrated in his life and considered a universal genius for the breadth of his interests and activities, in death he was virtually ignored, buried with little ceremony in a grave that was to remain unmarked for many years.

2 The programme

Leibniz never wrote a single work, book or article that constitutes a canonical exposition of his thought, preferring the short article or letter where he presents his thought from one or another point of view, often in response to the thought of another (DESCARTES was a favourite target), or in response to questions from a correspondent. Indeed, Leibniz's complex thought seems to resist the kind of comprehensive treatment found in works like Descartes' *Meditations* or Spinoza's *Ethics*. Furthermore, it is only to be expected that Leibniz's beliefs changed over his long career, and from one presentation of his philosophy to another.

Despite its complexity, there are some themes and characteristics that run throughout Leibniz's thought, at least in the mature period that starts after his return from Paris in the late 1670s, the period on which this entry concentrates. (While there was not a radical break from the early years to the later, there is certainly a marked development.) Basic to his thought was his philosophical optimism: this is the best of all possible worlds, freely created by a rational God, who always chooses the best for a good reason, without any arbitrariness. It is because of our limited understanding that we cannot determine a priori all the general or particular features of this world. This conception of God and his creation shaped Leibniz's philosophy: the world is ultimately both rational and in every way perfect. Furthermore, though Leibniz's philosophical intelligence ranged widely, certain problems were particularly important to him. In an untitled note from the late 1680s he wrote: 'there are two labyrinths of the human mind, one concerning the composition of the continuum, and the other concerning the nature of freedom, and they arise from the same source, infinity' (Leibniz 1989: 95). The labyrinth of the composition of the continuum concerns the ultimate make-up of the world; the labyrinth of freedom concerns how freedom and contingency are possible in the world. The solution to both involves understanding the literally infinite complexity found in the world God created. Leibniz had an opinion about virtually every philosophical and scientific issue of his day, but these two issues consistently drew his attention.

3 God: creation and theodicy

Like many of his contemporaries, Leibniz thought that the existence of God could be proved, and he was particularly attracted by the so-called Ontological Argument, invented by Anselm and revised by Descartes (see GOD, ARGUMENTS FOR THE EXISTENCE OF §§2–3). According to the Ontological Argument, as given by Descartes and paraphrased by Leibniz in *Meditations on knowledge, truth and ideas* (1684), 'whatever follows from the idea or definition of anything can be predicated of that thing. Since the most perfect being includes all perfections, among which is existence, existence follows from the idea of God . . . Therefore existence can be predicated of God'. Leibniz's contribution to the argument is the observation that, as it stands, the argument is not valid: 'from this argument we can conclude only that, if God is possible, then it follows that he exists'. For the argument to work, we must establish the self-consistency of the definition of God. But the consistency of the definition of God follows directly from the fact that God 'is without limits, without negation, and consequently without contradiction' (*Monadology* §45). In addition to this version of the ontological argument, Leibniz also used a cosmological argument for the existence of God, arguing from the existence of contingent things in the world, things whose reason lies outside of themselves, to the existence of a necessary being (*De rerum originatione*

radicali (On the ultimate origination of things) (1697); *Monadology* §45). Finally, Leibniz argued from the existence of eternal truths: 'Without [God] there would be nothing real in possibles, and not only would nothing exist, but also nothing would be possible' (*Monadology* §43).

In the opening sections of the *Discourse on Metaphysics* (1686: §6), Leibniz argued that 'God has chosen the most perfect world, that is, the one which is at the same time the simplest in hypotheses and the richest in phenomena', a formula that recurs often in his writings. While this is the main account of creation, in other texts, particularly the essay *On the ultimate origination of things*, he argued that 'there is a certain urge for existence or (so to speak) a straining toward existence in possible things or in possibility or essence itself; in a word, essence in and of itself strives for existence' *De rerum originatione radicali* 1697). Leibniz continued: 'From this it is obvious that of the infinite combinations of possibilities and possible series, the one that exists is the one through which the most essence or possibility is brought into existence'. Such an account of creation has the apparent implication that God is not necessary for it, and that creation results from a quasi-mechanistic weighing of possibilities with respect to one another. But Leibniz emphasized that God is the ground of all possibles, and that it is God who ultimately actualizes the possibles that 'win' the 'contest'. The 'striving possibles' account of creation would seem to be a metaphorical way of expressing Leibniz's usual account in terms of God's choice of the best of all possible worlds.

Leibniz's account of creation had a number of important implications. First, against Descartes and Spinoza, it entailed that there is a standard of goodness and perfection that exists independently of God; God creates the world because it is good, a world which is good not just because it is the creation of God (*Discourse* §2). Furthermore, unlike MALEBRANCHE, Leibniz held that the world could not have been created better than it is (*Discourse* §§3–4). Leibniz's doctrine of creation can also be read as a direct attack against a conception of God argued by Spinoza. Central to Spinoza's enterprise in the *Ethics* is an attack on the view that God is like us, that he has aims and goals, that he chooses things for a reason, and that he is bound by standards of goodness that exist independently of his will. This anthropomorphic view of God, Spinoza argued, is an illusion, a projection of our own nature onto nature at large (see SPINOZA, B. DE §4). Against Spinoza, Leibniz presented his own God, who deliberately chooses to create this world for a particular reason, because it is the best of all possible worlds, a reason intelligible to us. It is on this basis that Leibniz argued against both Descartes and Spinoza for the importance of final causes in nature.

Leibniz's account of creation also addressed the problem of understanding divine justice, in particular, how sin, evil and suffering are possible in a world created by God – the 'theodicy' problem, to use the word coined by Leibniz. His answer was complex, filling many pages in *Theodicy*, the only philosophical book he published in his lifetime. Briefly, his argument was that evil is a necessary and unavoidable consequence of God's having chosen to create the best of all possible worlds. However bad we might think things are in our world, they would be worse in any other.

Leibniz's account of creation was closely connected with a number of his key principles, most prominently the Principle of Sufficient Reason. As he wrote later in the *Monadology* (§53), 'since there is an infinity of possible universes in God's ideas, and since only one of them can exist, there must be a sufficient reason for God's choice, a reason which determines Him towards one thing rather than another'. The Principle of Sufficient Reason entails that the universe is in principle rational and intelligible: God must always act for a reason, and as a consequence, there must be a reason for everything. But the account of creation was also connected with a number of other principles in Leibniz's philosophy (discussed below). In this way one can say that the doctrine of creation underlies all of Leibniz's philosophy. Had we God's intellect, we would be able to derive all of the features of this world directly from its being the best of all possible worlds. As it is, our understanding of God's creation will enable us to fix certain general truths about this world, and set certain bounds on our hypotheses about the way things are.

Leibniz's interest in philosophical theology was not just the interest of a philosopher. He believed that his understanding of truths about God and nature would greatly assist the undertaking of uniting the Catholic and Protestant Churches under the umbrella of the true philosophy.

4 Metaphysics: substance, monad and the problem of the continuum

Leibniz is famous for his claim that he solved the problem of the composition of the continuum. In so far as the continuum (length, area, volume) is divisible, it would seem to be made up out of parts. But what parts could make it up? If the parts are extended (like atoms), then they too are divisible, and we require an account of their composition as well. On the other hand, if the parts are non-extended (like points), then it is difficult to see how they could make up an extended magnitude.

Leibniz's solution was this: the mathematical continuum should not be thought of as being *composed* of parts at all; while it has parts, those parts are the result of the division of the whole, and thus are posterior to it. On the other hand, Leibniz claimed, while real physical extensions have parts, there are no physical continua. Physical extended things are at root discrete multitudes whose constituents are substances ('Remarques sur les Objections de M. Foucher' (Remarks on the objections of M. Foucher) 1696; Leibniz to de Volder, 19 January 1706). This raises one of the central problems for Leibniz's philosophy: what are these substances that constitute the metaphysically ultimate constituents of the world?

While there are many paths into his views on substance, Leibniz's critique of Descartes' notion of corporeal substance is a convenient starting place. Descartes held that the essence of body is extension. What this meant is that bodies are geometrical objects made concrete, entities that have no properties that are not grounded in extension. Colour, taste, sound and so on are not themselves in bodies, but are only sensations in minds caused by our interaction with extended substances. While Leibniz as a mechanist agreed with this last claim, he rejected the Cartesian conception of body on which it is based (see DESCARTES, R. §§8, 11).

Leibniz offered a number of arguments against the Cartesian conception of bodily substance. (1) The notion of extension presupposes some quality that is extended, like whiteness in milk or resistance to new motion in every body, and so is not the kind of thing that by itself could constitute the essence of anything (Leibniz to de Volder, 30 June 1704; 'Note on Cartesian natural philosophy', 1702). (2) In so far as extended things are divisible, they are aggregates made up out of parts. But the reality of the aggregate presupposes some genuine individuals of which the aggregate is composed; no such individuals can be found in Cartesian bodies (Leibniz to Arnauld, 30 April 1687; *Monadology* §§1–3). (3) If the world is full and there are no vacua, and if the world is filled with Cartesian extended substance, then there can be no change in the world. For any supposed change would consist in one portion of body replacing another, identical in every way ('On nature itself'). (4) If body were just extension, then it would be perfectly inert, and would have to be moved by God. If so, then God's creation would be imperfect for lacking creatures which cannot themselves carry out any of God's commands. Indeed, such a world would reduce to Spinoza's world in which finite things are just modes of God ('On nature itself'). Because of arguments like these, Leibniz wanted to take the Cartesian mechanist analysis of body back one step further, and resolve even extension into something more basic still, a world of substances that are genuinely individual, genuinely active, and which contain properties that distinguish individual substances from one another.

While there are a number of important discussions of the nature of substance in Leibniz's writings, two are especially noteworthy: the one he gave in the *Discourse on Metaphysics* at the start of his mature period, and the one he gave at the very end of his life in the *Monadology*. (There is a third important conception of substance that arises in the dynamical writings, discussed below in connection with his physics.)

Leibniz begins Section 8 of the *Discourse on Metaphysics* by noting that 'it is evident that all true predication has some basis in the nature of things, and that, when a proposition is not an identity, that is, when the predicate is not explicitly contained in the subject, it must be contained in it virtually'. (This principle, which probably derived from Leibniz's logical studies a few years earlier, was closely connected with the Principle of Sufficient Reason in Leibniz's mind; the containment of the concept of the predicate in the concept of the subject constitutes the 'sufficient reason' for the truth of a proposition. This connection with his logic has caused some commentators to see Leibniz's metaphysics as fundamentally logical in its inspiration.) And so, Leibniz claims, 'the subject term must always contain the predicate term, so that one who understands perfectly the notion of the subject would also know that the predicate belongs to it'. He concludes that 'the nature of an individual substance or of a complete being is to have a notion so complete that it is sufficient to contain and to allow us to deduce from it all the predicates of the subject to which this notion is to be attributed'. Since he held that there must be something in the substance itself in virtue of which this complete notion holds of it, he also concludes that at any given time, a substance must contain marks and traces of everything that is true of it, past, present and future – though only God could see them all. (It is not clear whether this committed Leibniz to holding that all properties of a given individual are essential to that individual, making him a kind of 'superessentialist', or whether he takes the weaker position that they are merely internal to the individual, making him a 'superintrinsicalist'. Opinions differ among the commentators.)

In the *Monadology* Leibniz offers a somewhat different characterization of substance. Using the term 'monad' that he adopted to express the notion of an individual substance in the late 1690s, he expounds: 'The monad . . . is nothing but a simple substance that enters into composites – simple, that is, without parts. And there must be simple substances, since there are composites; for the composite is nothing more than a collection, or aggregate, of simples. But where there are no parts, neither extension, nor shape, nor divisibility is possible. These monads are the true atoms of nature and, in brief, the elements of things' (*Monadology* §§1–3). So understood, the Leibnizian world is grounded in non-extended simple substances, whose principal property is non-divisibility and thus, Leibniz inferred, non-extension.

From these basic characterizations of the individual or simple substance (what Leibniz called a 'monad' after the mid-1690s), he inferred a number of important properties. The individual substance or monad is a genuine unity that cannot be split, something explicit in the *Monadology* account, less so on the earlier account in the *Discourse*. Consequently, it can begin only by divine creation, and can end only with divine annihilation; it is naturally ungenerable and incorruptible. On both accounts, individual substances or monads are the sources of all their activity, and cannot be altered or changed by the direct action of others; it is in this sense that Leibniz said that 'monads have no windows through which something can enter or leave' (*Monadology* §7). In the *Discourse* he derives this from the fact that a substance contains within itself all of the grounds of all its properties; there is no need – and no room – for any external causality. In the *Monadology* it is derived directly from the fact that monads are non-extended. The apparent action of one substance on another must be analysed in terms of the relations between the internal states of the one and the internal states of the other (as discussed below). Finally, because of the relations that hold between one substance and another, Leibniz argued that each individual substance or monad reflects the entire world of which it is a part, a thesis closely connected with the hypothesis of pre-established harmony (also discussed below). Though all the individual substances reflect the same one world, they each reflect it from a different point of view, adding the perfection of variety to God's creation (*Discourse* §§9, 15; *Monadology* §§4–7). This conception of harmony can be traced back to the Paris period and, perhaps, to Leibniz's earliest writings on physics.

On Leibniz's view, substances are distinguished from one another by their momentary perceptions, and by the appetitions, the internal source of a substance's activity that lead from one perceptual state to another. In so far as a substance has such appetitions, 'the present is pregnant with the future' (*Monadology* §22). Since there can be no external influences, each monad is created by God with a kind of internal programme, as it were, which determines all of the states that it will take and the order in which it will take them. Although the Cartesian soul is an important model for the individual substance (Leibniz to de Volder, c.1699), there are significant differences. While the momentary states are called perceptions, not all such perceptions are conscious. (Conscious perceptions are said to be 'apperceptions' in Leibniz's terminology, though because nature makes no leaps in this best of all possible worlds, there must be a continuous gradation between the unconscious and the conscious.) In scholastic thought, appetition is the general faculty that leads to change in a substance, of which will (or rational appetite) is a special case in rational souls. For Leibniz, too, not all appetition is rational. For these reasons, he distinguished carefully between rational souls, like ours, and monads with lesser degrees of consciousness and rationality – what he sometimes calls 'bare monads' (*Monadology* §§8–24).

5 Metaphysics: monad, body and corporeal substance

Much of Leibniz's attention was focused on the level of the individual substance or monad, the atom of nature and the building-block of his world, that which in some sense underlies the world of bodies. But in addition to the simple substances, Leibniz often also recognized complex substances, corporeal substances, particularly in the 1680s and 1690s. Corporeal substances are understood on analogy with the human being, a soul (itself an individual substance) united with an organic body. Leibniz often used Aristotelian language to characterize the corporeal substance, calling the soul its form, and the organic body its matter (see ARISTOTLE §§8, 11). The organic body of a corporeal substance is itself made up of corporeal substances, each of which is a soul united to another, smaller organic body, in a sequence of tinier and tinier organisms that goes to infinity, a manifestation of the infinite variety in this best of all possible worlds that God created. Leibniz distinguished corporeal substances from corporeal aggregates, aggregates of animate corporeal substances whose unity is only mental, imposed by the mind, which perceives a group of substances together. While these corporeal substances are ultimately made up of non-extended individual substances, Leibniz's position (at least before 1704) seems to have been that these corporeal substances, as substances, are the genuine individuals whose reality grounds the aggregates that constitute inanimate bodies.

As discussed below, the soul of a corporeal substance is united to its body by virtue of pre-established harmony. However, by 1704, in response to criticism from René-Joseph de Tour-

nemine, Leibniz came to think that this link does not produce genuine unity, and the notion of a corporeal substance becomes problematic for him. While he continued to assert that the physical world is made up of an infinite hierarchy of organisms, after this date he was not so sure that these organisms constitute genuine substances. (Nevertheless, Leibniz always thought that every monad has a body, and cannot exist without one, even if the monad together with its body does not constitute a genuine substance. Even in death the monad has a body, just a body radically smaller than the one it had had in 'life'.) The problem of constructing complex substances from monads led Leibniz in his correspondence with Des Bosses to explore the idea of a *vinculum substantiale*, or a substantial bond. While it is not clear that he ever really endorsed this idea, he does seem to have taken the problem of corporeal substance seriously in that dialogue.

However the issue of corporeal substance is treated, body had a kind of subordinate status for Leibniz. While corporeal substances may be genuine substances, genuinely individual and genuinely active, and thus genuinely real, they are still grounded in non-extended individual substances or monads. And inanimate bodies are inevitably phenomenal, whether the appearance resulting from a multitude of organic corporeal substances, or simply the appearance presented by an infinite multitude of non-extended substances. In this way, one can see Leibniz's philosophy as an inspiration for the distinction between the noumenal and the phenomenal worlds in Kant's philosophy. But in contrast to Kant, who claimed that we cannot know the noumenal world of the thing-in-itself, Leibniz is quite confident that he knows exactly how things are in themselves: they are monads (see KANT, I. §3).

6 Metaphysics: mind, body and harmony

A basic feature of Leibniz's metaphysics was his doctrine that everything reflects the entire world in which it exists. This harmony among things derives from God at creation, who adjusts the perceptions of individual substances or monads to one another in creating a world more perfect by virtue of its variety. And so, despite the fact that individual substances cannot communicate directly with one another, and thus have no real metaphysical causal relations with one another, yet there is an extended sense in which what happens in one substance can be considered the cause of what happens in another. Leibniz wrote: 'The action of one finite substance on another consists only in the increase of the degree of expression together with the diminution of the expression of the other, insofar as God requires them to accommodate themselves to one another' (*Discourse* §15; compare *Monadology* §52). God, in creating a given substance to perform a particular action at a given time, creates all other substances in such a way as to reflect that action at that time. This is what might be called *physical* causality, as distinct from *metaphysical* causality which Leibniz denied among finite things.

While every monad or substance is related in some way to every other, there is a special relationship between the mind and the body of a living thing, such as the human being: 'Although each created monad represents the whole universe, it more distinctly represents the body which is particularly affected by it, and whose entelechy it constitutes. And just as this body expresses the whole universe through the interconnection of all matter in the plenum (that is, space without empty place), the soul also represents the whole universe by representing this body, which belongs to it in a particular way' (*Monadology* §62; compare *Discourse* §33). In this way, the mind is connected with the world by virtue of the special connection it has with the body; on Leibniz's understanding of causality, mind and body can be the 'physical' causes of changes in one another.

So Leibniz solved to his satisfaction one of the central problems in seventeenth-century metaphysics: the interaction between mind and body. Because of the special harmony between mind and body, just when my body is in the state it would be in if it were pricked by a pin, my mind is programmed to have a sensation of pain. And just when my mind is in the state of willing my arm to raise, my body is in the physical state that would result in the raising of my arm, again not because of any direct causal connection (Leibniz to Arnauld, 28 November/8 December 1686 and 30 April 1687). For that reason, Leibniz wrote: 'According to this system, bodies act as if there were no souls (though this is impossible); and souls act as if there were no bodies; and both act as if each influenced the other' (*Monadology* §81). This is what he originally called the hypothesis of concomitance, but called the hypothesis of pre-established harmony when he published it for the first time in the *New system* (1695).

The view is summarized in an analogy he often used. The mind and the body can be compared to two clocks that keep perfect agreement. One hypothesis to explain their agreement is that of natural influence, the hypothesis that there is some physical connection between the one clock and the other. This corresponds to Descartes' view of mind–body interaction, where there is real causal influence. The second hypothesis is that someone watches over the two clocks and, by tinkering with them, always keeps them in agreement. This corresponds to the occasionalism of many of Descartes' followers, in which mind–body causality is mediated by God who causes sensations in the mind on the occasion of an appropriate bodily state, and actions in the body on the occasion of the appropriate volition in the mind (see OCCASIONALISM). Finally there is the hypothesis that the clocks are so well made that they will always remain in perfect agreement with one another. This corresponds to the hypothesis of pre-established harmony, which Leibniz thought to be the most defensible (Leibniz to Basnage de Beauval 3/13 January 1696).

Leibniz offered a number of arguments directly against occasionalism. He argued, for example, that there must be genuine activity in things themselves because a world of genuinely active things is more perfect than a world of things manipulated by God; indeed, Leibniz claimed, a world of inert things is just the Spinozistic world in which God is the only substance of which other things are modes ('On nature itself'). He also argued that occasionalism posits perpetual miracles, in so far as God is called in to do that which goes beyond the power of things to do by their own nature (Leibniz to Arnauld, 30 April 1687). As noted below, the conception of the physical world that informs Leibniz's dynamics is itself a direct challenge to occasionalism. Nevertheless, Leibniz did share at least one important doctrine with occasionalism: that finite substances have no real causal relations with one another. This doctrine may strike a modern reader as eccentric, but it would have been rather less so for a seventeenth-century reader.

Leibniz often presented the hypothesis of pre-established harmony as a solution to the problem of mind–body interaction. But, at the same time, it allowed Leibniz to reconcile the mechanistic conception of the world with a conception grounded in final causes. He wrote: 'The soul follows its own laws and the body also follows its own; and they agree in virtue of the harmony pre-established between all substances. . . . Souls act according to the laws of final causes, through appetitions, ends, and means. Bodies act according to the laws of efficient causes or of motions. And these two kingdoms, that of efficient causes and that of final causes, are in harmony with each other' (*Monadology* §§78–9). In more concrete terms, behaviour (raising one's hand, for example) can be explained either in terms of a volition and the harmony God established between mind and body, or purely in terms of the laws of motion, as applied to the physical body. By pre-established harmony, these two explanations will always agree. In this way Leibniz managed to reconcile the dualism of Descartes with the stricter mechanism of Hobbes;

everything in the body can be explained in purely mechanistic terms, while, at the same time, Leibniz could also hold that human beings (and other living organisms) have souls which are the causes of much of their behaviour.

In addition to explaining the interaction between mind and body, when first introduced, Leibniz held that pre-established harmony also explains the union of mind and body, that which makes a single substance out of a mind and the collection of individual substances that constitutes its body (*Discourse* §33). In this way, pre-established harmony provided a central support for Leibniz's account of corporeal substance. Unfortunately, however, it proved inadequate to the task. In May 1703, René-Joseph de Tournemine pointed out that whatever resemblance one might suppose between two clocks, however justly their relations might be considered perfect, one can never say that the clocks are united just because the movements correspond with perfect symmetry. While it does not challenge pre-established harmony as an account of mind–body interaction, the argument is as simple as it is devastating against the somewhat different claim that pre-established harmony accounts for mind–body unity. In consequence, Leibniz came to question the place of complex corporeal substance in his philosophy, as discussed above (see MALE-BRANCHE, N.; OCCASIONALISM).

7 Metaphysics: necessity, contingency and freedom

Central to Leibniz's philosophy were a variety of problems concerning necessity, contingency and freedom, problems which arise in a variety of ways from a variety of sources. Spinoza stood behind many of Leibniz's worries. According to Spinoza, everything in the world is necessary and nothing is contingent, so that things could not be other than they are. Indeed, everything that is genuinely possible is actual and if something does not actually exist, it is because it could not. Everything follows from the divine nature, not by choice but by blind necessity. Furthermore, Spinoza argued, everything in the world is determined and what we take to be human freedom is just an illusion. We think that we are free because we are ignorant of the causes outside us that determine us to do what we do.

Other problems came from Leibniz's own views. Some came from Leibniz's principle in accordance with which 'when a proposition is not an identity, that is, when the predicate is not explicitly contained in the subject, it must be contained in it virtually' (*Discourse* §8). If every predicate true of an individual was part of its very concept, how could it fail to be necessary? A closely related

problem followed from Leibniz's claim that every individual substance contains everything that can happen to it, past, present and future, which seems to entail that everything was determined from the beginning, and there is no room for the freedom of a creature. Here the problem concerns not necessity and contingency, but determinism and human freedom. Even if it were contingent that a certain creature has a certain built-in history, given that history, there does not appear to be room for freedom.

Leibniz offered a number of approaches to this problem in his writings. His basic response to the Spinozistic attacks on contingency is the claim that God *freely* chose the best of all possible worlds. He wrote in the early 1680s in an essay entitled *De libertate* (On Freedom) 'God produces the best not by necessity but because he wills it' Leibniz [1680–2] 1989: 20). Yet, since God is perfect, it would seem that his nature necessarily determines his will to choose the best.

This led Leibniz directly to another account of contingency. In that same document, he continued by noting that 'things remain possible, even if God does not choose them'. That is, even if God *necessarily* created the best of all possible worlds (a concession Leibniz does not always make), unactualized possibles are still, in and of themselves, possible. The recognition of such unactualized possibles is what brought him back from the precipice of necessitarianism, so Leibniz wrote in another essay from the late 1680s (Leibniz 1989: 21). Elsewhere, he characterized those possibles that God chooses to create as necessary, but only *ex hypothesi*, on the hypothesis that God chose to create them. Though necessary in this limited sense, they are contingent in so far as their contraries are not self-contradictory (*Discourse* §13).

From time to time Leibniz used the kindred notion of compossibility. Two individuals are said to be compossible when they can be actualized at the same time, and are said not to be compossible when they cannot. In this way one can say that a possible world is a maximal set of compossible individuals. The notions of compossibility and incompossibility are not, however, logical notions, taken narrowly. Two individuals may fail to fit in the same possible world because they are logically in contradiction with one another (in a sense that must be specified), or because they fail to harmonize with one another.

Leibniz sometimes also suggested that it is contingent that this particular world is the best of all possible worlds. So, even if God necessarily created the best of all possible worlds, it is still contingent that he creates *this* world. These arguments address the worries that derive from Spinoza's view that God necessarily gave rise to this world (see SPINOZA, B. de §4). But, as noted previously, there are other more Leibnizian worries to address as well. If in any true proposition the concept of the predicate must be contained in the concept of the subject, how can any truth fail to be necessary? Leibniz gave one kind of answer in the *Discourse on Metaphysics* (§13) where he simply asserts that there are two kinds of conceptual containment. While all predicates are contained in the concept of the subject, some are contained necessarily, and some contingently. But in some documents, probably from the late 1680s, he attempted a different solution. He noted first that in some cases we can demonstrate that the predicate is contained in the subject in a finite number of steps. However, in other cases this cannot be done. 'In contingent truths, even though the predicate is in the subject, this can never be demonstrated, nor can a proposition ever be reduced to an equality or to an identity, but the resolution proceeds to infinity' (Leibniz 1989: 96). To demonstrate a contingent truth, one must show that a given individual with a given property is one among an infinity of individuals in a possible world that is the best among an infinity of other possible worlds, something that cannot be shown in a finite number of steps.

Beyond the question of necessity is the issue of human freedom. Take an individual substance, which contains everything that has happened, is happening and will happen to it. Even if one can establish that the sequence of 'happenings' it contains is contingent, yet by virtue of containing all these happenings, it would seem not to be free to do anything other than what it does. Contingency is thus compatible with strict determinism, which is incompatible with human freedom.

Leibniz's solution was that while God may build certain actions into a given individual, he can build them in as *free* actions: 'God sees for all time that there will be a certain Judas whose notion or idea ... contains this free and future action' (*Discourse* §30). God does make us with free will, and the ability to choose one thing over another. So, when he chooses to create a given individual with a given life-history, he will include the conditions that will lead that individual to choose one thing over another. But the actual choice is ours, and it is free, Leibniz argued. In this way, 'God inclines our soul without necessitating it' (*Discourse* §30). Furthermore, while we can choose other than the way we do, God in his omniscience can predict what we will actually choose, and build its consequences into our future programme. This divine foreknowledge does not change the character of the events themselves: 'God foresees things as they are and does not change their nature.... Thus they are assured but they are not necessary' (*Dialogue effectif*

sur la liberté de l'homme et sur l'origine du mal (An actual dialogue on human freedom and on the origin of evil) [1695] 1989: 112). Thus Leibniz had no worse problems on this score than does anyone who believes in divine omniscience.

Leibniz's doctrine did raise a knotty problem about the identity conditions for individuals, however. If all properties of a given individual are programmed in from the beginning, then though some may be contingent, and though some may be free, still, they define the individual as the particular individual that it is; were they different, then we would be dealing with another individual altogether, it would seem. From time to time Leibniz acknowledged that we might want to talk about what might have happened if Judas (*our* Judas, the Judas in *this* possible world) had not renounced Christ (Leibniz–Arnauld Correspondence, May 1686; the specific example at issue there is not Judas, as in the *Discourse*, but Adam). But often Leibniz seemed quite willing to embrace a different view: 'But someone ... will say, why is it that this man will assuredly commit this sin? The reply is easy: otherwise he would not be this man' (*Discourse* §30). In this way, given that every substance mirrors the entire world in which it finds itself, Leibniz often committed himself to the thesis that a person can belong to only *one* possible world.

8 Epistemology: ideas and sensation

Despite the fact that Leibniz is usually categorized as a continental rationalist, his main interest was not epistemological. At the same time, he did contribute to the discussions of his day on questions relating to ideas and knowledge.

In the *New Essays* (II.1.1), Leibniz defines an idea as follows: 'an idea is an immediate inner object [which] expresses the nature or qualities of things'. He emphasizes that we can think that we have an idea when we do not really have one. So, for example, there can be no idea of a fastest motion because the notion is incoherent. But, he notes, 'At first glance we might seem to have the idea of a fastest motion, for we certainly understand what we say; but yet we certainly have no idea of impossible things'. Mistaking our comprehension of the phrase 'fastest motion' for having a genuine idea can lead us into contradiction in this case. But in other cases, for example in mathematics, where we often use symbols without fixing ideas to them, we often must work symbolically because of the complexity of working directly with ideas themselves. In this sense one can have thought and even reasoning when we do not have ideas in the proper sense. This observation is connected with a distinction Leibniz drew between real and nominal definitions. A nominal definition is a definition in which one can doubt whether or not the notion defined is genuinely possible; a real definition is one in which the possibility of the notion defined has been established. One can thus say that it is only of real definitions that one can be sure that they correspond to a genuine idea (*Meditations* [1684] 1989: 25–6; *Discourse* §24).

Leibniz was a supporter of innate ideas in a number of senses. First of all, he argued that there are certain particular ideas that are innate to the mind, and do not or cannot come through the senses: 'The ideas of *being*, *possible*, and *same* are so thoroughly innate that they enter into all our thoughts and reasoning, and I regard them as essential to our minds' (*New Essays* I.3.3). He made a similar claim for other notions, such as infinity (*New Essays* II.17.3). In this connection he used his celebrated marble analogy in the preface to the *New Essays*. Ideas and truths are in the mind, he argued, just as the shape of Hercules might already be in the veins of a block of marble, making that shape more likely to emerge when the sculptor begins to hammer on it, even though considerable effort may be required to expose the shape: 'This is how ideas and truths are innate in us – as inclinations, dispositions, tendencies, or natural potentialities'.

Leibniz's metaphysics, however, committed him to a stronger position still, that *every* idea is innate, strictly speaking, since nothing can enter a mind from the outside. He wrote: 'The mind always expresses all its future thoughts and already thinks confusedly about everything it will ever think about distinctly. And nothing can be taught to us whose idea we do not already have in our mind' (*Discourse* §26). But even though all ideas are strictly innate, Leibniz could distinguish between the ideas of sensation that in a certain sense come to us from outside, and the ideas that do not and cannot do so. As with the explication of physical causality in the context of a view in which there can be no real metaphysical causality between finite things, Leibniz could say that 'we receive knowledge from the outside by way of the senses, because some external things contain or express more particularly the reasons that determine our soul to certain thoughts' (*Discourse* §27).

Sensations are distinguished from other notions not only by their causal origin (in Leibniz's somewhat extended sense), but also by the fact that they are confused, in contrast to the distinct notions one uses, say, in mathematics. A notion is distinct when one has 'marks and tests sufficient to distinguish a thing from all other similar' things; distinct notions include number, magnitude, shape and so on. A notion is confused 'when I cannot enumerate one by one marks sufficient for differ-entiating a thing from others, even though the thing does indeed have such marks and requisites into which its notion can be resolved'. In this sense 'colours, smells, tastes, and other particular objects of the senses' are confused (*Meditations* [1684] 1989: 24). Indeed, they are the confused perception of the geometrical properties of bodies that, on the mechanist programme, ground the perception of sensible qualities. 'When we perceive colours or smells, we certainly have no perception other than that of shapes and of motions, though so very numerous and so very small that our mind cannot distinctly consider each individual one in this, its present state, and thus does not notice that its perception is composed of perceptions of minute shapes and motions alone' (*Meditations* [1684] 1989: 27). Elsewhere Leibniz used the analogy of a wave to understand this phenomenon. When we hear the roar of the ocean, we are actually hearing just a large number of individual waves, lapping on the shore. But since we cannot distinguish the sounds each individual wave makes, we hear it as an undiffer-entiated roar. This is just the way the confused perception of the corpuscular microstructure of bodies results in our sensation of colour, taste and so on (*New Essays* 1704: preface). In this way Leibniz rejected the claim that the connection between a particular sensation and its mechanical cause is the result of a perfectly arbitrary divine decree; by the Principle of Sufficient Reason, there can be no such arbitrariness in the world (*New Essays* II.8.13 and following, IV.6.7). Thus, it would seem, the distinction between sensations and ideas of the intellect is not a matter of kind, but a matter of degree, degree of distinctness and confusion.

An important part of this account of sensation was Leibniz's doctrine of *petites perceptions* (minute perceptions). Like Descartes, Leibniz believed that we think all the time. However, unlike Descartes, he denied that we are always conscious of what we think. He held that 'at every moment there is in us an infinity of perceptions, unaccompanied by awareness or reflection; that is, of alterations in the soul itself, of which we are unaware because these impressions are either too minute and too numerous, or else too unvarying, so that they are not sufficiently distinctive on their own' (*New Essays* preface). Though we do not apperceive (that is, consciously perceive) each of them individually, these unconscious perceptions have their effects on us. They are what underlie and explain sensation, as suggested earlier. Furthermore, they also have their effect on the conscious choices that we make (*New Essays* II.20.6).

Finally, Leibniz also had a clear position in the debate then raging in the intellectual world over Malebranche's view that we see all things in God, that is, that ideas do not exist in finite minds, but only in the mind of God, where they are seen by finite intellects without actually being in them (see MALEBRANCHE, N.). Leibniz quite clearly rejected Malebranche's view: 'Even if we were to see everything in God, it would nevertheless be necessary that we also have our own ideas, that is, not little copies of God's, as it were, but affections or modifications of our mind corresponding to that very thing we perceived in God' (*Meditations* [1684] 1989: 27; compare *Discourse* §29).

9 Epistemology: knowledge and probability

In a famous passage of the *Monadology* (§§31–2) Leibniz writes: 'Our reasonings are based on *two great principles, that of contradiction*, in virtue of which we judge that which involves a contradiction to be false, and that which is opposed or contradictory to the false to be true, and *that of sufficient reason*, by virtue of which we consider that we can find no true or existent fact, no true assertion, without there being a sufficient reason why it is thus and not otherwise'. These two principles correspond to two different kinds of truths, 'those of *reasoning* and those of *fact*' (*Monadology* §33).

A truth of reason can be known with certainty by a finite demonstration consisting of a finite number of steps containing simple ideas, definitions, axioms and postulates; these truths are necessary and can be known a priori. Sensation can give us particular instances of these truths, but can never attain the kind of universality one finds in necessary truths. As Leibniz wrote in the preface to the *New Essays*: 'necessary truths, such as we find in pure mathematics and particularly in arithmetic and geometry, must have principles whose proof does not depend on instances nor, consequently, on the testimony of the senses, even though without the senses it would never occur to us to think of them'.

While Leibniz agreed with DESCARTES that such truths are innate, he distanced himself from Descartes' appeal to clear and distinct perception. Against those who appeal to Descartes' axiom that 'whatever I clearly and distinctly perceive about a thing is true or is assertable of the thing in question', Leibniz objected that 'this axiom is useless unless we use criteria for the clear and distinct, criteria which we have made explicit' (*Meditations* [1684] 1989: 26–7). While Leibniz agreed with Descartes that we have an innate capacity to recognize these innate truths, as a practical matter, he preferred to constrain the mind by formal rules of logic, unlike Descartes, who rejected formal logic (see §10 below).

Since in all predications, the concept of the predicate is contained in the concept of the subject,

all knowledge is in principle a priori; if we only had sufficient knowledge of the subject, we could see everything that is true of it, contained in its complete concept. But this is only possible for God. Humans, incapable of performing the analysis that will reveal the truth a priori must make appeal to the senses in order to discover truths of fact. In fact, Leibniz thought, 'we are all mere Empirics in three fourths of our actions' (*Monadology* §28).

Because of the importance of empirical knowledge, Leibniz called for a genuine logic of probability. The modern theory of probability was born in the 1650s with the correspondence between PASCAL and Fermat, and then with Christiaan Huygens' little treatise, *Tractus de ratiociniis in aleae ludo* (Treatise on reasoning in games of chance) (1657). The theory very quickly developed in the seventeenth century, as new practical applications were quickly found. But Leibniz was not satisfied that it had yet been applied to the most general question of all, the kind of reasoning we do about matters of fact on the basis of sensation when demonstration is impossible. And so, in the *New Essays* (IV.2.14) he called for a new science: 'I maintain that *the study of the degrees of probability* would be very valuable and is still lacking, and that this is a serious shortcoming in our treatises on logic. For when one cannot absolutely settle a question one could still establish the degree of likelihood on the evidence, and so one can judge rationally which side is the most plausible.... I suspect that the establishment of an *art of estimating likelihoods* would be more useful than a good proportion of our demonstrative sciences, and I have more than once contemplated it'. But even though Leibniz may have contemplated it, he himself never made a serious attempt to develop the logic of probability that he called for here. However, his call was heard by David HUME, who saw his *Treatise* as, in part, answering Leibniz's challenge.

10 Logic and language

From his youth, Leibniz dreamed of constructing a perfect, logical language, 'a certain alphabet of human thoughts that, through the combination of the letters of this alphabet and through the analysis of the words produced from them, all things can both be discovered and judged'. This programme, which Leibniz called the 'universal characteristic', gets its first expression in the very early work, *Dissertatio de arte combinatoria* (Dissertation on the art of combinations) (1666). But it is most fully developed later, from the mid–1670s into the 1680s.

Leibniz's programme had two parts. First, one must assign characteristic numbers to all concepts that show how they are built up out of simpler concepts. Leibniz tried a number of schemes for this, but one strategy was to assign simple concepts prime numbers, and then assign complex concepts the product of the characteristic numbers of its constituent simple concepts. The second part of the programme was then to find simple mechanical rules for the truth of propositions in terms of the characteristic numbers of their constituent concepts. Leibniz's fundamental rule in his Universal Characteristic was the principle discussed above in connection with his metaphysics: a predicate is true of a subject if and only if its concept is contained in the concept of the subject. If the concepts in question can be expressed numerically, then Leibniz thought that the rule can be given a mathematical form as well, and the truth of a proposition could be established by a simple arithmetical calculation. Leibniz's project in these writings was to show how this basic intuition about truth could be extended to propositions that are not in simple subject-predicate form. He also sought to extend the programme to formalize the validity of the standard inferences in Aristotelian logic. Even if he could not assign definite characteristic numbers to particular concepts, Leibniz tried to show that for certain configurations of premises and conclusions, if the premises are true (on his definition of truth), then so too must be the conclusion.

The programme was very ambitious; it if were successful, it would allow the truth or falsity of any proposition, necessary or contingent, to be determined by calculation alone. However, it soon dawned on Leibniz that the idea of finding all the conceptual dependencies necessary to express the contents of notions numerically was utopian in the extreme, particularly given the doctrine of infinite analysis of contingent truths Leibniz came to in the late 1680s. This realization still left in place the more modest programme of validating patterns of inference. But even this more modest programme turned out to be beyond Leibniz's ability to bring to completion, and after the early 1690s he seems to have given up trying to make it work, although he returned to it from time to time.

But even though this particular programme collapsed, the idea of formalism was quite basic to Leibniz's thought. Part of the reaction against the Aristotelian philosophy of the schools was an attack on formal logic. Descartes, Locke and others in the seventeenth century argued that we all have an innate ability to recognize truth, what was often called intuition, and that we should cultivate that capacity, and not waste our time learning formal rules. While Leibniz certainly agreed that we do have the innate capacity to grasp certain truths, he still thought that formalism is very important

(Leibniz to Elisabeth of Bohemia, 1678). Much of our reasoning is 'blind' or symbolic, Leibniz thought, conducted through the manipulation of symbols without having a direct hold on the ideas that underlie the symbols. For that reason we must have clear and unambiguous symbol systems, and strict rules for manipulating them (*Meditations*).

This view is evident in the papers on the Universal Characteristic. But it also underlies another project of the same period, the differential and integral calculus, one of Leibniz's greatest accomplishments, worked out by 1676 and made public from 1684. Though others before him had solved many of the particular problems his calculus could solve, problems relating to tangents, areas, volumes and so on, Leibniz invented a simple notation, still used in the calculus ('d' to represent the operation of differentiation, and '∫' to represent the operation of infinite summation (integration)), and worked out a collection of simple rules for applying these operations to equations of different kinds. In this way, Leibniz was able to produce simple algorithms for solving difficult geometrical problems 'blindly', by manipulating certain symbols in accordance with simple rules.

Another issue closely connected with Leibniz's logic is that of relations. In the *Primae veritates* (First truths) [1689] 1989: 32) Leibniz wrote: '*There are no purely extrinsic denominations* [that is, purely relational properties], denominations which have absolutely no foundation in the very thing denominated.... And consequently, whenever the denomination of a thing is changed, there must be a variation in the thing itself'. In this way, all relations must be, in some sense, grounded in the non-relational properties of things. But it is not clear that Leibniz held that relations had to be reducible to non-relational predicates of things. In one example he gives, he paraphrased 'Paris is the lover of Helen' by the following proposition: 'Paris loves, and by that very fact [*eo ipso*] Helen is loved'. While this certainly relates the relation '*A* loves *B*' to two propositions that have the form of simple subject-predicate propositions ('*A* loves' and '*B* is loved'), it should be noted that the predicates in question ('loves' and 'is loved') would seem to be implicitly relational; whether this is an accidental feature of the example Leibniz chose or a clue to Leibniz's views is a question of some dispute. Furthermore, it is important not to ignore that which connects the two propositions ('and by that very fact'), without which one cannot say that the two non-relational propositions capture the relation '*A* loves *B*'. Other texts suggest that individuals properly speaking have non-relational properties, and that the relations between things are something imposed by the mind onto the world: 'My judgement about relations is that paternity in David is one thing, sonship in Solomon another, but that the relation common to both is a merely mental thing whose basis is the modifications of the individuals' (Leibniz to Des Bosses, 21 April 1714). But in saying that the relations between individuals are 'merely mental', Leibniz does not necessarily mean to dismiss them. He wrote: 'God not only sees individual monads and the modifications of every monad whatsoever, but he also sees their relations, and in this consists the reality of relations and of truth' (letter to Des Bosses, 5 February 1712).

In addition to formal languages, Leibniz was also keenly interested in the study of natural languages. Like many of his contemporaries, he was interested in the controversies over the question of the Adamic language, the language spoken in Eden and from which all modern languages supposedly derive. This, among other motivations, led him to the empirical study of different languages and the etymology of words.

11 Natural philosophy

Leibniz is read today largely for his philosophical writings. But in his day, he was, if anything, better known for his work in mathematics and natural philosophy. Like many of his contemporaries, Leibniz was a mechanist. Indeed, he was in a sense a much stricter mechanist than the Cartesians. Because of his doctrine of pre-established harmony (see §6 above), one can always give a purely mechanistic explanation of any physical phenomenon, even in humans, unlike in the Cartesian system, where causal interaction between mind and body, direct or occasional, can disrupt the laws governing the body. However, Leibniz's version of the mechanist programme departed significantly from other main versions of the programme of his day, particularly the Cartesian version.

Leibniz rejected the Cartesian analysis of body as extended substance (see §4 above). Instead, he argued that we must go to a deeper level of analysis, behind the extension of bodies to the substances that are the ultimate constituents of reality. Below the level of inanimate extension there are tiny organisms, souls joined to organic bodies which Leibniz, in at least one period of his thought, considered genuine corporeal substances. At a deeper level still there are the non-extended simple substances or monads that ground the reality of corporeal substances. On this view, the extended bodies of the Cartesian world are phenomena, aggregates of substances that are unified by virtue of being confusedly perceived together.

Leibniz also rejected Descartes' central law of nature. For Descartes, God conserves the same quantity of motion in the world, the size times the speed of bodies taken together (see DESCARTES, R. §11). But Leibniz argued that what is conserved is not bulk times speed, but bulk times the *square* of speed, mv^2, a quantity associated with what he called *vis viva* or living force. To defend this view, he used a cluster of a posteriori arguments which assumed the Galilean law of free-fall (the distance fallen is proportional to the square of the speed acquired in free-fall) together with the Principle of the Equality of Cause and Effect, in accordance with which there is always as much ability to do work in the cause as there is in the full effect. Leibniz showed that, on these assumptions, the Cartesian conservation law entails that the ability to do work can either be gained or lost in certain circumstances, whereas on the assumption of the conservation of mv^2, this does not happen. Leibniz used this strategy in the *Brevis demonstratio* (Brief Demonstration of a Notable Error of Descartes) (1686), where he first published this result. In addition, he offered an a priori argument in which, arguing from certain abstract notions of motion, action and effect, together with an intuitive principle of the conservation of effect, he reached the same conclusion (*Discourse* §17; *Dynamics* preliminary specimen). This challenge to Descartes' conservation law elicited numerous responses from the Cartesian community in what came to be called the *vis viva* controversy.

Leibniz saw the replacement of the conservation of the quantity of motion by the conservation of mv^2 as leading us to introduce into the world of physics something over and above the purely geometrical qualities of size, shape and motion that pertain to the extended substance of the Cartesians. This something is what he called force, the new science of which he named dynamics. While force can cause motion and is sometimes manifested in motion, Leibniz carefully distinguished the two. In emphasizing the distinction between force and motion, Leibniz was rejecting not only the Cartesian tradition, but his own early physics where, following Hobbes, he identified force with motion.

Leibniz recognized a variety of different kinds of forces in nature. At the most fundamental level, he distinguished between primitive and derivative forces, and between active and passive forces. Thus, in all, there are four basic kinds of force: primitive and derivative active force, and primitive and derivative passive force. Active force is of two sorts, living force (*vis viva*), which is associated with bodies actually in motion (a ball moving with a definite velocity), and dead force, which is associated with the instantaneous push from which actual motion results, as in gravitation or elasticity. Passive force, on the other hand, is the force that arises in reaction to the active force of another body. It also has two varieties, impenetrability (the force that prevents two bodies from occupying the same place at the same time) and resistance (the force that opposes new motion). The distinction between primitive and derivative force is quite different. Primitive force, active and passive, is the metaphysical ground of activity and passivity, that in a body by virtue of which it is capable of acting (doing work) or resisting. Derivative forces, for Leibniz, were particular states of activity and passivity that exist in a body at a particular time. In this way, primitive force is not a measurable quantity, but something in body that grounds the reality of the derivative forces, which are measurable quantities.

This notion of force was linked directly to Leibniz's notion of corporeal substance: 'Primitive active force, which Aristotle calls first entelechy and one commonly calls the form of a substance, is another natural principle which, together with matter or passive force, completes a corporeal substance' ('Note on Cartesian natural philosophy' [1702] 1989: 252). At least in the 1680s and 1690s, when Leibniz recognized corporeal substances, the primitive forces seem to have been the form and matter of the corporeal substances that ground the reality of the physical world. Derivative forces would then be interpreted as the momentary states of these corporeal substances. The position is somewhat different after Leibniz began to doubt the reality of corporeal substance (see §5 above). Then, he wrote, 'I relegate derivative forces to the phenomena, but I think that it is obvious that primitive forces can be nothing but the internal strivings of simple substances, strivings by means of which they pass from perception to perception in accordance with a certain law of their nature' (Leibniz to de Volder, 1704 or 1705). In this way, the dynamics can be regarded as another perspective on the same entities discussed in Leibniz's more metaphysical writings.

Leibniz held that these forces (or better, the motion that they cause) obey rigorous mathematical laws. These laws include the conservation of living force, mv^2, virtually equivalent to the modern law of the conservation of kinetic energy, and the conservation of bulk times the velocity (a vector quantity), mv, identical to the modern law of the conservation of momentum. (Because Leibniz's conservation of mv involved the directionality of the motion, it is distinct from the Cartesian conservation of quantity of motion, which Leibniz rejected.) While he disagreed with Descartes about the specific contents of the laws, he can be seen as advancing the Cartesian programme of building a physics grounded in mathematically expressible conservation laws. But even though Leibniz's laws are expressible in mathematical terms, they – like the forces that they govern – are grounded in certain metaphysical principles that are imposed on the world by the wisdom of God: 'Although the particular phenomena of nature can be explained mathematically or mechanically... nevertheless the general principles of corporeal nature and of mechanics itself are more metaphysical than geometrical' (Discourse §18).

One such general metaphysical principle was noted in connection with the establishment of Leibniz's conservation law, the Principle of the Equality of Cause and Effect. But there were others as well. Leibniz made frequent use of the Principle of Continuity, according to which nothing happens through a leap. Leibniz used this principle to refute Descartes' laws of impact, where small changes in the initial conditions (say the comparative sizes of the bodies in question, or their motion) can result in radically different results. This principle was also used to refute atomism. If there are perfectly hard atoms, not made up of smaller separable parts, then in collision their motion would change instantaneously at the moment of impact. So, Leibniz concluded, there cannot be any such atoms in nature. Indeed, he used this argument to conclude that every body, no matter how small, is elastic. Leibniz also made appeal to the Principle of Plenitude to argue that there can be no vacuum or empty space in the world, since if God can create something consistent with his other creations, he must do so. Finally, as seen below, Leibniz used the Principle of Sufficient Reason in connection with his relativistic account of space and time.

The very fact that the world is the product of divine wisdom allowed Leibniz to appeal to final causes in his physics. This differentiates him from both Descartes and Spinoza, both of whom rejected final causes. Leibniz agreed with both that everything in nature can be explained through efficient cause alone – that is, through the laws of motion alone. But often, particularly in optics, it is much easier to solve problems by appealing to God's wisdom, and discovering the way in which a most perfect being would have created his universe (Discourse §22; Specimen of dynamics 1695: part I). However, the appeal to final cause only supplements the understanding of nature by efficient causes, and does not replace it. It is another manifestation of divine harmony that the explanations by efficient causes and by final causes always coincides: 'In general we must hold that everything in the world can be explained in two ways: through the kingdom of power, that is, through efficient causes, and through the kingdom of wisdom, that is, through final causes.... These two kingdoms everywhere interpenetrate each other... so that the greatest obtains in the kingdom of power at the same time as the best in the kingdom of wisdom' ((*Specimen of dynamics* [1695: part I] 1989: 126–7).

So far we have been discussing Leibniz's work in relation to that of other mechanists, particularly those of the Cartesian school. But it is also important to understand Leibniz's relations with another contemporary and often bitter rival, Isaac Newton.

In opposition to Newton, who held an absolutist conception of place and space, Leibniz argued that space is 'only relations or order or orders of coexistence, both for the actually existing thing and for the possible thing one can put in its place' (*Remarks on Foucher* [1696] 1989: 146). If Newton were right, Leibniz argued, and there was absolute space, then God could create a world in which what is currently east and west are exactly reversed, for example. But if so, by the Principle of Sufficient Reason, then God could have no reason to create one such world over another. Given that he did, he cannot have been faced with such a choice. Leibniz concludes that the two purported Newtonian worlds are really just one world, a world in which space is just constituted by the relations between things (Leibniz to Clarke, 3rd paper §5). Newton's absolutist account of space was supposed to ground an absolutist account of motion as well. For Newton, motion was the change of place of a body with respect to absolute space. Leibniz rejected this too, arguing that motion is a completely relativistic notion, a matter of the relation between bodies over time and that alone (*Specimen of dynamics* part I; Leibniz to Huygens, 12/22 June 1694).

Leibniz also rejected Newton's theory of universal gravitation. He read Newton as holding that gravity is an essential property of matter as such, and he was appalled. For Leibniz, all change in body had to happen through the intermediary of contact and collision; the idea of action at a distance that seemed to underlie Newton's theory of universal gravitation was an intellectual disaster, a treasonable abandonment of the new mechanical philosophy and a return to the worst abuses of the schoolmen. Leibniz, whose early mechanism seemed so radical at the time, could not adjust to the new Newtonian philosophy, soon to take over the intellectual world (see CLARKE, S.; NEWTON, I.).

While the emphasis here has been on the aspects of Leibniz's work in physics most relevant to his philosophical programme, he was much more widely interested in the natural world. He left notes on engineering problems, on chemistry, on geology and on curious observations in natural history including the report of a talking dog, and a goat with an odd hairstyle.

12 Ethics and political thought

Although Leibniz's ethical and political writings are not widely read today, they constitute an important part of his corpus, unsurprising, given Leibniz's own involvement in politics. Leibniz's ethical and political thought, squarely within the natural law tradition, was based on the notions of justice, charity and virtue (see NATURAL LAW). Leibniz wrote: 'Charity is a universal benevolence, and benevolence the habit of loving or of willing the good. Love then signifies rejoicing in the happiness of another, or, what is the same thing, converting the happiness of another into one's own' (*Codex Iuris Gentium Diplomaticus* (The diplomatic code of the law of nations) 1693: introduction). In a note on felicity (Leibniz *c.*1694–8), he connected justice, wisdom, and virtue to charity: 'Virtue is the habit of acting according to wisdom.... Wisdom is the science of felicity, [and] is what must be studied above all things.... To love is to find pleasure in the perfection of another. Justice is charity or a habit of loving conformed to wisdom. Thus when one is inclined to justice, one tries to procure good for everybody, so far as one can, reasonably, but in proportion to the needs and merits of each'.

For Leibniz, human justice is the same as God's justice, though, of course, less perfect. Leibniz wrote in the *Monita quaedam ad S. Puffendorfii principia* (Observations on the principles of Pufendorf) (1706): 'In the science of law... it is best to derive human justice, as from a spring, from the divine, to make it complete. Surely the idea of the just, no less than that of the true and the good, relates to God, and above all to God, who is the measure of all things'. Similarly, Leibniz wrote in *Méditation sur la notion commune de la justice* (Meditation on the common concept of justice) (1702–3) that 'as soon as [the concept of justice] is founded on God or on the imitation of God, it becomes universal justice, and contains all the virtues'.

In so far as charity is defined in terms of universal love and benevolence, justice is something quite distinct from power. This is true even for God. 'Justice, indeed, would not be an essential attribute of God, if He himself established justice and law by His free will'. In this sense, God is as bound by the eternal laws of justice as he is bound by truths of reason: 'Justice follows certain rules of equality and of proportion [which are] no less founded in the immutable nature of things, and in the divine ideas, than are the principles of arithmetic and of geometry' (*Observations on Pufendorf* 1706). (Here, perhaps, is the origin of the theodicy problem for Leibniz: if God is bound by the same ideal of justice that binds us, then we must show how the works of the all-perfect creator can be seen to conform to that ideal.) So, too, are we bound by a standard of justice that exists independently of our wills.

Leibniz recognized three degrees of justice. The lowest, a minimal sort of justice, is simply not to harm others. The second degree is to give each their due, what it is that is owed to them. The highest, though, is to behave with genuine beneficence toward others, and to do that which will promote their happiness; this is what Leibniz calls piety (Leibniz to Coste, 4 July 1706: appendix).

Leibniz's conception of justice as the charity of the wise also placed virtue and obligation outside of the scope of a contract. For Hobbes, for example, the notion of justice arises from a contract that we make with one another in forming a society, and the notion of justice has no applicability outside that framework. Commenting on Shaftesbury in 1712, Leibniz wrote: 'Our illustrious author refutes with reason...those who believe that there is no obligation at all in the state of nature, and outside government; for obligations by pacts having to form the right of government itself, according to the author of these principles, it is manifest that the obligation is anterior to the government which it must form' (Leibniz 1988: 196). Indeed, he noted, there are societies, among the native Americans for example, in which the sovereign thought necessary by Hobbes is altogether absent: 'entire peoples can be without magistrates and without quarrels, and...as a result men are neither taken far enough by their natural goodness nor forced by their wickedness to provide themselves with a govern-ment and to renounce their liberty'. In people sufficiently wise, then, justice and charity are sufficient to hold society together, without the need of a contract.

But Leibniz was a practical politician, as well as a theorist of politics. He generally worked for a Europe unified under the leadership of a unified church, a Christian Europe in which there are no conflicts between different Christian states. This, in part, is what was behind his plan for the reunifica-tion of the Catholics and the Protestants. It was also behind his attempt, as early as 1671, to persuade the French to attack Egypt, a non-Christian country, rather than to invade the Netherlands. In practice, however, Leibniz was an opponent of French expansionism under Louis XIV (as much as he was an admirer of French culture), and a supporter of a union of Protestant countries in Northern Europe (his *Mars Christianissimus* (1684) was a brilliant satire directed against Louis XIV's foreign policy). He was also an active participant in the successful campaign in support of the claim of the House of Hanover for the throne of England.

13 The Leibnizian tradition

It is important to remember when considering Leibniz's influence that much of what we now know of Leibniz's writings was unknown to his readers for many years after his death. The full dimensions of Leibniz's thought emerged only slowly, as new texts came to light. Indeed, there is still no complete edition of his work.

At the time of his death, and in the decade afterwards, only a small selection of Leibniz's texts was available. There were a fair number of publications in mathematics and physics, some legal writings and some documents collected in connection with his unfinished history of the house of Hanover. In philosophy, however, there were only a few essays. During his lifetime, Leibniz had published *Meditations on Knowledge, Truth, and Ideas* (1684), the *New System* (1695), *On Nature Itself* (1698) and the *Theodicy* (1710). The Leibniz–Clarke correspondence was published soon after his death, and a Latin version of the *Monadology* appeared in 1721. On the other hand, the *New Essays* did not appear until 1765, and works that we now consider central, such as the *Discourse on Metaphysics*, did not appear until 1846. Many of his philosophical writings and correspondence had to await the monumental edition of C.I. Gerhardt, which appeared between 1875 and 1890. Many texts have yet to appear.

Despite the relative paucity of his available writings, Leibniz was much read and debated in the eighteenth century. One of his early supporters was the German professor Christian WOLFF who had corresponded with Leibniz during his life. He composed numerous volumes expounding a Leib-nizian philosophy in an ordered and orderly way. Wolff's systematic philosophy made it ideal for the academy, and his ideas were widely influential. But there were opponents, particularly a group of pietist theologians at the University of Halle, but others as well, including Maupertuis, Crusius, CONDILLAC and, most famously, VOLTAIRE, who made Leibniz into the comical Dr Pangloss of his *Candide*. KANT received his philosophical education in the atmo-sphere of this debate between the Leibnizians and the anti-Leibnizians in the German intellectual world. His philosophy, both pre-critical and critical, shows the marks of his knowledge of Leibniz's writings.

See also: ATOMISM, ANCIENT; CLARKE, S.; FREEDOM, DIVINE; IDENTITY; IDENTITY OF INDISCERNIBLES; INFINITY; MALEBRANCHE, N.; MENDELSSOHN, M.; NATURAL LAW; OCCASIONALISM; SUBSTANCE; VOLTAIRE, F.-M.; WILL, THE

References and further reading

Aiton, E.J. (1985) *Leibniz: A Biography*, Bristol: Hilger. (A recent biography in English.)

Frankfurt, H. (ed.) (1972) *Leibniz: A Collection of Critical Essays*, New York: Doubleday Anchor. (Contains many classic essays, including those of Russell and Couturat.)

Leibniz, G.W. (1989) *Leibniz: Philosophical Essays*, ed. and trans. R. Ariew and D. Garber, Indianapolis, IN and Cambridge, MA: Hackett Publishing Company. (A widely available translation of a selection of Leibniz's most important philosophical texts.)

DANIEL GARBER

LESSING, GOTTHOLD EPHRAIM (1729–81)

Gotthold Ephraim Lessing occupies a central place in eighteenth-century European belles-lettres. He was a significant religious and theological thinker whose work puzzled his contemporaries and still provokes debate. He has been variously called a deist, a concealed theist, a Spinozist–pantheist, a panentheist, and an atheist. He was a significant dramatist whose major works include *Minna von Barnhelm*, known as the first modern German comedy, and *Nathan the Wise*, which places Lessing in the tradition of eighteenth-century toleration and humanism. He was an active promoter of the contemporary German theatre and an influential drama critic and theorist. He had broad classical and antiquarian interests. And he has some claims to being one of the early developers, if not a founding father, of the discipline of philosophical aesthetics.

Philosophically, Lessing belongs to the tradition of G.W. von Leibniz and Christian Wolff and was familiar with the post-Wolffian aesthetics being developed by Alexander Baumgarten and his follower Georg Friedrich Meier. Most importantly, perhaps, Lessing was acquainted with Moses Mendelssohn, to whose work his own philosophical writings bear many similarities and who read and commented on Lessing's aesthetic writings. But Lessing cannot be identified with any of these philosophical sources and influences. His work retains many rationalist presuppositions, but Lessing also consciously sought a more inductive approach. He adhered to neoclassical standards with respect to beauty and the application of rules of art, but severely qualified those standards by justifying them empirically and appealing to emotional effects rather than to ideal forms or Cartesian clarity. Lessing's aesthetics must be inferred from his work, particularly from his *Laocoon*, some of the numbers of the *Hamburg Dramaturgy*, and to a lesser extent from short works such as 'How the Ancients Represented

Death' and the letter of 26 May 1769 to Friedrich Nikolai. What emerges is a sometimes inconsistent and fragmentary aesthetic, which one might describe as a critical rationalism.

See also: POETRY; TRAGEDY

DABNEY TOWNSEND

LEUCIPPUS (5th century BC)

The early Greek philosopher Leucippus was the founder of atomism. Virtually nothing is known of his life, and his very existence was disputed in antiquity, but his role as the originator of atomism is firmly attested by Aristotle and Theophrastus, although the evidence does not allow any distinction between his doctrines and those of his more celebrated successor Democritus. He wrote a comprehensive account of the universe, the *Great World-System*. The single surviving quotation from his work asserts universal determinism.

C.C.W. TAYLOR

LEVINAS, EMMANUEL (1906–95)

In the 1930s Levinas helped to introduce the phenomenological philosophy of Husserl and Heidegger to the French. Subsequently his work attained classic status in its own right for his attempt to explore the meaning of ethics from a phenomenological starting-point. In *Totalité et infini* (1961) (*Totality and Infinity*, 1969) Levinas locates the basis of ethics in the face-to-face relation where the Other puts me in question. My obligations to the Other are not contracted by me. They not only precede any debts I incur, but also go beyond anything I could possibly satisfy. In later works, most notably *Autrement qu'être* (1974) (*Otherwise than Being*, 1981) Levinas explores further the preconditions of this account, most especially by investigating the I that was said to be put in question in the encounter with the Other. In analyses that stretch phenomenology to its limits and beyond, Levinas finds alterity within the self.

See also: ALTERITY AND IDENTITY, POSTMODERN THEORIES OF; PHENOMENOLOGY, EPISTEMIC ISSUES IN

ROBERT BERNASCONI

LEWIS, CLARENCE IRVING (1883–1964)

The American philosopher C.I. Lewis held that in all knowledge there are two elements: that which is presented to sense and the construction or interpretation which represents the creative activity of the mind. Contrary to Kant, Lewis claimed that what is fixed and unalterable is not the structure that we bring to the sensibly presented, but rather the sensibly presented itself. The categories that mind imposes do not limit experience; they determine the interpretation we place upon experience, and if too much of experience eludes our categorizations, new ones should be established. It is pragmatically necessary that we create interpretive structures which will work in getting us around in sensory experience. This important and novel doctrine, Lewis' 'pragmatic a priori', emerged through the development of ideas which took root during his study of logic. The problems of choosing among alternative logics led him to assert the need for pragmatic criteria. The way we conceptually structure or categorize experience answers to pragmatic criteria of purposes, intents and interests. Only within a context defined by a priori categorizations can empirical judgments be made. These empirical judgments proceed from apprehensions of the sensibly presented to assertions of objectivities. Moral judgments require both judgments of good and decisions of right. Judgments of value are tied to qualitative satisfactions disclosed in experience and are empirical claims. Decisions about the morally right are based on imperatives of reason.

See also: INTENTIONALITY

SANDRA B. ROSENTHAL

LEWIS, DAVID KELLOGG (1941–2001)

David Lewis made extremely important and influential contributions to many topics in metaphysics, philosophical logic, the philosophy of science, the philosophy of mind, the philosophy of language, the philosophy of probability, rational decision theory, and ethics and social philosophy. His work on counterfactuals and the philosophy of modality has been especially influential.

See also: MODAL LOGIC

PETER VAN INWAGEN

LIBER DE CAUSIS

The *Liber de causis* (Book of Causes) is a short treatise on Neoplatonist metaphysics, composed in Arabic by an unknown author probably in the ninth century in Baghdad. Through its twelfth-century Latin translation, it greatly influenced mature medieval philosophy in the West.

Drawing heavily on the Greek Neoplatonist Proclus, the *Liber de causis* represents a development of late Neoplatonism along two lines. On the one hand, the author modifies and simplifies Proclus' theory of causes to accord more closely with the three-part division of ultimate causes advanced by the founder of Neoplatonism, Plotinus. On the

other hand, the author introduces some of the metaphysical principles of Qu'ranic or biblical monotheism. The result is a metaphysically provocative reinterpretation of Neoplatonist thought which, because it seemed to accommodate Platonist philosophy to the medieval worldview, made the *Liber de causis* a natural source text for medieval philosophers.

See also: ALBERT THE GREAT; NEOPLATONISM; PLOTINUS

HANNES JARKA-SELLERS

LIBERALISM

Introduction

Liberal political philosophy explores the foundations of the principles most commonly associated with liberal politics: freedom, toleration, individual rights, constitutional democracy and the rule of law. Liberals hold that political organizations are justified by the contribution they make to the interests of individuals, interests which can be understood apart from the idea of society and politics. They reject both the view that cultures, communities and states are ends in themselves, and the view that social and political organizations should aim to transform or perfect human nature. People have purposes of their own to pursue, either economic or spiritual (or both). Since those purposes do not naturally harmonize with one another, a framework of rules may be necessary so that individuals know what they can count on for their own purposes and what they must concede to the purposes of others. The challenge for political philosophy, then, is to design a social framework that provides this security and predictability, but represents at the same time a safe and reasonable compromise among the disparate demands of individuals.

1 Liberal politics
2 Political philosophy
3 Individualism
4 The economic side of human nature
5 The social contract

1 Liberal politics

In politics, the term 'liberalism' denotes a family of positions centred around constitutional democracy, the rule of law, political and intellectual freedom, toleration in religion, morals and lifestyle, opposition to racial and sexual discrimination, and respect for the rights of the individual.

Often these positions are associated with a suspicion of state authority, with a view that the powers of government should be constrained if not minimized, and with a confidence in the ability of individuals to organize themselves on the basis of the market, the free interplay of ideas and the loose and informal associations of civil society. Liberal support for democracy is therefore sometimes qualified by fear of 'the tyranny of the majority' and by apprehensions about the extent and intrusiveness of the power that a populist state is capable of exercising.

These attitudes are not, however, characteristic of all forms of liberalism. In Britain, in the late nineteenth and early twentieth century, a group of thinkers known as the New Liberals made a case against *laissez-faire* and in favour of state intervention in social, economic and cultural life. The New Liberals, who included T.H. GREEN and L.T. Hobhouse, saw individual liberty as something to be achieved under favourable social circumstances. The poverty, squalor and ignorance in which most people lived made it impossible in their view for freedom and individuality to flourish, and the New Liberals believed that these conditions could only be ameliorated through collective action coordinated by a strong welfare-oriented interventionist state.

In the USA, since the early part of the twentieth century, the term 'liberalism' has been associated with 'progressive' economic reform, a commitment to the modest redistribution of income that takes place in a welfare state, a suspicion of business and an abiding faith in the legal regulation of economic affairs. The more *laissez-faire* version of liberalism is called 'conservatism' in the USA, and Europeans are often disconcerted to hear 'liberal' used there as label for positions that they themselves would describe as left-wing or moderately socialist.

This is not just terminological confusion. Those in the USA who call themselves 'liberals' do also hold the positions outlined at the beginning of this article, and their disagreement with 'conservative' opponents is partly a live and unresolved issue about the implications of traditional liberal premises in so far as social and economic policy is concerned. Does individual freedom require private ownership? Is poverty compatible with liberty? Can civil and political rights be equal if economic power is not? Liberalism is a family of positions, and these remain important family disputes.

2 Political philosophy

In philosophy, 'liberalism' is not just the name of a loosely organized and quarrelsome family of sub-stantive political opinions. It refers also to a heritage of abstract thought about human nature, agency, freedom, and value, and their bearing on the functions and origins of political and legal institutions.

That heritage takes its rise in early modern English political philosophy – most notably in the work of Thomas HOBBES and John LOCKE (§10). It is also the political philosophy of the European Enlightenment, represented in its most philosophically articulate form in the writings of Jean-Jacques ROUSSEAU, François-Marie Arouet VOLTAIRE, Henri-Benjamin Constant de Rebecque and, a little later, Immanuel KANT. In the nineteenth century, philosophical liberalism is represented, first, in the utilitarian theories of BENTHAM and J.S. MILL, and later in the 'Idealism' of T.H. GREEN.

Inevitably, because of our proximity, it is harder to identify canonical works of twentieth-century liberalism. There was a long period in the twentieth century in which liberal philosophers seemed to lose their taste (or their nerve) for grand theory on the scale of Hobbes or Kant, a period during which they seemed to pride themselves on the piecemeal, analytic and unsystematic character of their thought. In a Cold War context, these were regarded as healthy signs of being 'non-ideological'. That phase seems to have passed, and more confident versions of philosophical liberalism have re-emerged in the work of late-twentieth-century writers like F.A. von Hayek, Robert NOZICK, Ronald DWORKIN, Joseph Raz and, most importantly, John RAWLS (§4).

Some will quibble about one or two of the names on this list. Was Hobbes really a liberal? Was Rousseau? We should remember, however, that 'liberalism' has never been a label over which any group has exercised collective control. As a result, the term is at the mercy of its most casual users, and indeed the attempt to define 'liberalism' is undertaken most commonly not by its practitioners but by its opponents, with predictable caricatural results.

Even so, the challenge is not just to correct misrepresentations. The philosophical positions that we most plausibly identify as liberal often represent distinctive expressions of ambivalence about human nature and political life, rather than dogmatic formulae in a liberal catechism. We have seen this already in the values and principles which constitute liberalism in the political sense: liberals disagree about property, economic equality and the role of the state. At the more philosophical level, liberals disagree about the nature of value, the meaning of freedom and the connection between individual and social purposes.

What follows is an attempt to lay out some of those positions and controversies. But defining liberalism is, on the whole, a frustrating pastime. There are many ways of mapping this philosophical landscape, and there is no substitute for grappling with the disparate detail of the theories propounded by particular liberal philosophers.

3 Individualism

Let us begin with some basic ethical premises. The deepest commitment of liberal political philosophy is to *individualism*, as a fundamental proposition about value. Liberal individualism has four parts to it.

First, liberals believe that the individual person is what matters for the purposes of social and political evaluation. We may be interested in the fate of a culture, a language, a community or a nation, but for a liberal such interest is always secondary or derivative. Ultimate value has to do with how things are for ordinary men and women, considered one by one: their pains and pleasures, their preferences and aspirations, their survival, development and flourishing. Of course, people do care about each other: individualism is not the same as egoism. But individualism excludes social and collective entities from the realm of ultimate goods.

There is less agreement about the grounds for this individualization of value. John Locke, writing in the seventeenth century, based it on each person being the workmanship and property of God, which meant that we were 'made to last during His, not one anothers Pleasure' (1690). This relation to God was direct, unmediated and unconditional in the case of each individual. It therefore established a basis for our rights with respect to one another that did not presuppose validation by larger social structures.

Modern liberalism, however, is a secular tradition, and its history since Locke's time is largely a history of the attempt to establish this individualism without appealing to the idea of God. Utilitarian thinkers linked the notion of value analytically to desire or preference, and they inferred, from the fact that desiring and preferring were attributes of individuals, that the fundamentals of value must be individualistic too (see UTILITARIANISM). Those following in the tradition of Kant, on the other hand, linked value analytically to the lonely individualism of will, conscience and the sense of duty, and drew the conclusion that each person, *qua* moral agent, was entitled to be regarded as an end in themselves, not just a means to broader social ends. The Kantian view has perhaps fared better in modern political philosophy, although its underlying argument – that because moral thinking takes place at the level of individual minds and wills, individual minds and wills must also be the fundamental objects of moral concern – has yet to be rendered in a compelling form.

Second, liberals believe that there is something particularly important in the capacity of individuals to direct their actions and live their lives, each on their own terms. They believe in the importance of freedom – although what that belief amounts to is one of the controversies referred to earlier. Some define freedom in negative terms: their libertarianism amounts simply to a condemnation of force, coercion and interference in human life. Freedom, they say, is what flourishes when these constraints are taken away, and there is nothing apart from the removal of constraints that needs to be done politically in order for freedom to flourish. Positive conceptions of liberty allow the state a much greater role than this: they may see freedom or autonomy as something to be achieved, rather than taken for granted, in the life of an unrestrained individual, something that requires educated individual capacities and favourable social conditions (see FREEDOM AND LIBERTY).

Some conceptions of positive liberty go well beyond this, moving out of the liberal realm altogether. If freedom is identified with the performance of social duty, or attributed to individuals only by virtue of their participation in some social whole, then the resulting theory can hardly be described as liberal.

Also, if freedom is presented as the achievement of a happy few, something of which the ordinary mass of humanity is incapable, then again we are not dealing with a liberal conception. Although liberal freedom is sometimes a developmental concept, it is not an aristocratic or utopian one. The free direction of a human life is seen as something which ordinary people are capable of, under decent social and political circumstances. When Colonel Rainsborough exclaimed in the Putney Debates of 1647, 'Really, I think that the poorest he that is in England has a life to live as the greatest he', he gave voice to an egalitarianism that lies at the foundations of the liberal tradition.

The third aspect of liberal individualism, then, is a commitment to equality. We have to be careful how we formulate this. Liberal philosophers are not necessarily egalitarians in the economic sense. But they are committed as a matter of the basic logic of their position to a principle of underlying equality of basic worth. People are entitled to equal concern for their interests in the design and operation of their society's institutions; and they have the right to be equally respected in their desire to lead their lives on their own terms (see EQUALITY).

Feminists have sometimes questioned whether this liberal commitment to equality extends across boundaries of gender. In the writings of Locke, Rousseau and Kant it is easy to find throwaway lines that would be described today as sexist or misogynistic. No writer in the liberal canon committed himself explicitly and at length to the emancipation of women much before J.S. Mill's essay *The Subjection of Women* in 1868. Nevertheless, the legacy of liberal carelessness on this issue does not pose any major theoretical difficulties for the position that men and women are equal in their moral and political capacities and in the respect to be accorded those capacities. Indeed, the more challenging feminist critique is that liberals exaggerate (rather than deny) the similarities between men and women – that they fail to either acknowledge or accommodate crucial elements of 'difference' in moral reasoning and ethical demeanour (see FEMINIST POLITICAL PHILOSOPHY).

A fourth element of liberal individualism involves an insistence on the rights of individual reason. This involves not just freedom of thought, conscience or discussion, but a deeper demand about justification in politics: the demand that rules and institutions of social life must be justified at the tribunal of each individual's reason.

We see here an important connection between liberal thought and the philosophical legacy of the Enlightenment. The Enlightenment was characterized by a burgeoning confidence in the human ability to make sense of the world, to grasp its regularities and fundamental principles and to manipulate its powers for the benefit of mankind. That drive to understand nature is matched in Enlightenment thought by an optimism at least as strong about the possibility of understanding society and human nature. In one aspect, this optimism is the basis of modern sociology, history and economics. But it is also the source of certain normative attitudes towards social and political justification – an impatience with tradition, mystery, awe and superstition as the basis of order, and a determination to make authority answer at the tribunal of reason and convince us that it is entitled to respect. The social world, even more than the natural world, must be thought of as a world *for us* (for *each* of us) – a world whose workings are to be understood by the active enquiries of the individual mind, not by religious dogma, mindless tradition or the hysterics of communal solidarity.

4 The economic side of human nature

Liberals accord intrinsic value to people as individuals, and attach particular importance to each individual's capacity to organize a life on their own terms. What terms are these likely to be? What nature of beings are these whose individual freedom we value? And what are the uses to which their freedom is likely to be put?

Critics commonly associate liberal individualism with an egoistic and acquisitive view of human nature. They say the classic liberals all gave pride of

place, among human motivations, to the desire for power, pleasure and material possessions. Humanity, they argue, is reduced in liberal theory to nothing more than a competitive mass of market individuals – voracious consumers with unlimited appetites, hostile or indifferent to the wellbeing of others, and requiring no more of their political and legal institutions than that they secure the conditions for market activity.

The picture is not entirely a distortion. Liberal individualism does recognize that individuals' interests do not necessarily or naturally harmonize with one another. Each individual has a life of their own to lead, and there is no guarantee that one person's desires will not conflict with another's. Sometimes, as in Hobbes' theory, this is represented as an inherent hostility, a competitive diffidence and a 'mutuall will of hurting', issuing in a 'war of all against all'. Sometimes, as in John Rawls' work, it is seen simply as a postulate of mutual disinterest (rather than hostility). Mostly it is seen in Immanuel Kant's words as a matter of the 'unsociable sociability of men' – that there are things we share in common, things that drive us to society, things we can only accomplish together, as well as aspects of our nature that make us prickly, adversarial and wilfully isolated individuals.

Moreover, although – as we shall see – liberals believe that there are terms on which individuals with diverse or even opposed interests can live in peace with one another, it has never been part of their political philosophy that reason, enlightenment or socialization would put an end to this basic diversity or competitiveness. (To the extent that Rousseau suggests that the social contract might produce 'a remarkable change in man', his speculations take him outside the liberal tradition.) In the nature of things, humans will inevitably come up with diverse and opposed views of what makes life worth living, while the exigencies of our situation in the world – the moderate scarcity of material resources and our vulnerability to one another – will always furnish the raw materials for anxiety, competition and conflict (see HUMAN NATURE).

A related objection is that liberals subordinate politics to economics: they see political structures merely as instruments for securing economic peace and market interaction, and they ignore the higher calling for the state outlined, for example, in the theories of Aristotle, Hegel or Hannah Arendt.

The image is accurate, but it is not clear why it should be regarded as an objection. Certainly, liberals do not regard participation in politics as an end in itself; unlike the civic humanists, they do not think that the most important virtues and activities are those oriented towards politics and the formal exercise of power over others (see REPUBLICANISM).

It does not follow that they think of political participation as a narrow self-interested enterprise. In political science, the term 'liberalism' is commonly associated with interest group politics, but philosophical liberals are about equally divided on the question of whether voters in a democracy should orient their decisions to the common good or to their own interests (with the common good emerging as some sort of resultant from the political process). The point, however, is that even those who believe we should vote on our views about the common good still maintain that politics is, in the end, a means to promote the interests of individuals (*all* individuals), not an end in itself. They may believe in Rousseauian democracy, they may even hope that democratic participation can bring out the best in people (although many are dubious about that), but their firmest conviction is that individuals have interests and purposes of their own to pursue which have nothing intrinsically to do with politics or the state, and that the function of government is to facilitate those individual purposes not judge them or replace them with political or social ones.

To say that these purposes are individual is not necessarily to say that they are economic or materialistic in their content. It is surprising, in fact, how few liberal theorists have actually held the economically acquisitive picture of human nature. Hobbes did, certainly, and so did some of the eighteenth-century political economists. But many others in the liberal tradition see material motives as means to individual ends that may well be ethical, even spiritual in their content. John Locke, notorious in some circles as the apostle of possessive individualism, insisted that our primary mission in life is to ascertain what our creator requires of us in the way of conduct and worship: 'the observance of these things is the highest obligation that lies upon mankind, and...our utmost care, application and diligence, ought to be exercised in the search and performance of them because there is nothing in this world that is of any consideration in comparison with eternity' (*An Essay concerning Human Understanding* 1689). Modern liberals, too, tend to stress the ethical and cultural character of individual pursuits. We each have our own conception of happiness or the good life – a view about what makes a life worth living – and it is the diversity of individual ideals of this kind that political structures must accommodate.

In general, there is an intriguing ambivalence in the liberal tradition about whether this shift from economic to ethical individualism presents the social problem as more or less intractable. On the one hand, it seems to make the situation look better. Economic conflict is a zero-sum game: what you have I cannot have, or, worse still, what you have puts you in a better position to take what I have away from me; I therefore have an excellent reason of self-protection to deprive you of as many resources as I can. Ethical and spiritual individualism, by contrast, seems less intrinsically competitive: 'one man does not violate the right of another', wrote Locke, 'by his erroneous opinions...nor is his perdition any prejudice to another man's affairs' (*Essay* 1689). The appropriate social posture for religious or ethical individualists seems to be the mutual indifference of Rawls' theory rather than the competition or conflict of Hobbes.

In fact, of course, that has not been our experience. Wars of religion have been at least as deadly as wars for territory or resources. We may think of commercial life as bland or shallow, but there is a certain sense of relief in Voltaire's comment about the London Stock Exchange: 'Here Jew, Mohammedan and Christian deal with each other as though they were all of the same faith, and only apply the word infidel to people who go bankrupt'. Even Hobbes, whose *Leviathan* is the *locus classicus* for the economic war of all against all, was adamant that the problem of the struggle for resources could be solved, since people would be willing to make concessions to a strong state that could keep the peace. But sectarian religious fervour he thought of as a form of madness, and he doubted whether the partisans of rival religious ideals could ever come to terms with one another (see TOLERATION).

Critics of liberalism will no doubt persevere in their charge that the tradition flatters the materialistic side of human nature at the expense of cultural and spiritual aspirations. They will say that liberals have paid too much attention to the ways in which political and legal structures can foster market economies and too little to the contribution they can make to the quality of ethical choice. A number of liberal writers have taken this criticism seriously. Joseph Raz, for example, has argued that there is an aspiration towards value in the very concept of autonomy, so that a liberal commitment to freedom should not be thought of as incompatible with a social commitment to ethical perfectionism.

There comes a point, however, when liberal philosophers simply have to stand up and defend the channelling of political energies towards the real (but apparently soluble) problems of famine, plague and poverty, and away from moral, cultural and religious disputes, which promise little more in the way of progress than war, sectarianism and cults of ethical correctness. The preoccupation with economics is not based on scepticism about the ethical or spiritual dimensions of human life. It is based rather on a moderate sense of what politics can and cannot accomplish in a world where people disagree about God, value and the meaning of life, but largely converge in their desire to avoid hunger and disease and to better their material conditions.

5   The social contract

To the extent that liberal philosophy emphasizes diversity and conflict among individual purposes, it seems to steer us in the direction of anarchism. For what set of actually existing or realistically practicable institutions could possibly accommodate the individualism we have outlined?

In fact, liberal theorists have always held that something like the modern state, with its familiar institutions of law and representative government, *can* be made legitimate. They reject both the anarchist view that freedom is vindicated only in the absence of state authority and obligation and the utopian premise that a just society presupposes a radical change in human nature. This puts them in a rather ambivalent position in so far as existing 'liberal' societies are concerned – meaning here the constitutional democracies of North America, western Europe, Australasia and Japan. Liberalism has been a remarkably successful political ideology, inasmuch as its leading principles – freedom, toleration and equality before the law – have been accepted as part of the self-image or public relations of the world's most powerful and prosperous societies. Its proponents are uneasy, however, with the common inference that the social, economic and political reality of these societies is what liberal principles amount to in practice (just as Marxists were uneasy about the presentation of the Soviet Union and its satellites as 'actually existing socialism'). They insist, quite properly, that liberalism is a set of critical principles, not an ideology or rationalization, and that it provides a basis for condemning things like deepening poverty, secretive and oligarchical government, legal abuses and the continuing legacy of racism and sexism in modern democracies. Even so, the existence of the self-styled 'liberal' democracies is important. It helps sustain the sense that liberalism is a reformist rather than a revolutionary creed and that we already know, at least in outline, what a truly liberal society would be like. That sense of moderate reformism is not just a strategic ideological advantage. Liberalism claims to respect men and women as they are. It does not require generation after generation to undergo sacrifice for the sake of an endlessly postponed utopia. It suggests instead that political structures can be set up in now a way which represents a safe and reasonable compromise among individuals' disparate demands.

In its classical form – in the writings of Hobbes, Locke, Rousseau, and to a lesser extent Kant – the argument from liberal premises to the legitimacy of something like the modern state was presented in terms of the social contract (see CONTRACTARIANISM). The argument goes something like this.

Imagine people living outside any framework of political authority, exercising the right to direct their own lives and their own dealings with one another, in what liberal philosophers have called 'the state of nature'. Using this as a baseline, try to model the development of political institutions as a way in which individuals exercise their freedom not as a way in which their freedom is abrogated.

The social contract model represents the functions of government in terms of a set of difficulties that such people would face in a state of nature. Conceptions of these difficulties vary. There may be an internecine struggle for resources (Hobbes and Hume); there may be an appreciation of others' rights, but no reliable mechanism for enforcing them (Locke); or there may be disagreement about justice, with each person seeking to do what seems right or good in their opinion (Kant). The common element is that people in the state of nature would lack a reliable sense of what they could count on in social and economic life. What they most need is a secure set of rules, impartially administered and enforced, to provide a framework in which peaceful cooperation and long-term production is possible.

Government, then, is represented in terms of an agreement by each person with all of the others (in a given territory) to cooperate in the institution and maintenance of permanent rule-making and rule-enforcing agencies. The contract is not an agreement between the government and the individual. Instead, it presents legal and governmental institutions as structures of cooperation among individuals, and it uses that idea as a basis for deriving limits on governmental powers and restraints on particular individuals' or factions' exploitation of those powers. Tyrannical exploitation and arbitrary government are ruled out on this conception, inasmuch as they cannot be represented as any sort of improvement over the situation individuals would face if they tried to live without any political institutions at all.

Some theorists, Rousseau and Rawls for example, use the social contract idea also as a way of thinking about the content of legal rules: we can discuss what rights we have and the just distribution of resources by asking what assurances would have to be given to each individual to secure their consent to the basic structure of social arrangements. In the hands of these theorists, the social contract is a test of substantive political justification. Others see it in more procedural terms: the social contract models the construction of political and constitutional mechanisms, which will then work out substantive solutions on a basis that is relatively independent of the contract idea. Hobbes' theory is the most extreme example of this: the Hobbesian contract is simply an agreement to authorize an individual or organization (a 'sovereign') to solve the problems that generate conflict in the state of nature in any way that promises improvement. The absolute authority with which the sovereign is thus endowed has led some to deny that Hobbes is a liberal. Certainly, he is not wedded to the positions identified with liberalism at the beginning of this article. But his underlying political philosophy is liberal: his value premises are individualistic, and he is unyielding in his view that political institutions (with the powers he accords them) must be justified in relation to the interests of each individual, as well as in his optimism that such justification is possible.

Not all liberal philosophers appeal to the idea of the social contract. Many prefer to develop their theories without the mediation of this model. The arguments of J.S. Mill's 1859 essay *On Liberty*, for example – which many regard as the quintessential statement of liberal principles – are presented directly as claims that individuals are entitled to make, against their society and their government, without any historical pretence that governments were set up by individuals to validate those claims. Others use the social contract to justify some but not all of the political constraints they propose. In the theories of John Locke and Robert Nozick, the social contract argument presupposes a distribution of 'natural' property rights. For them, the function of the social contract is to support and police these rights, not reconceive or redistribute them. In other words, Locke and Nozick propose that property rights should be justified directly in moral argument, without appealing to the social contract idea. I suspect that something like this is true of all liberal theories. The social contract is an intermediate rather than a fundamental idea: one that presupposes that individuals are free, equal and rational, and that political power requires a justification which connects with the interests of each of them.

When it is understood in this way, as a method of modelling the force of certain deeper assumptions or theorems about justification, the social contract can be used as a purely hypothetical device in normative argument. As Kant and Rawls have pointed out, we need not be embarrassed by the fact that no such contract ever took place. It is still a useful test to apply to a constitution or to a set of laws. For if we conclude, even hypothetically, that our laws or our constitution would not have commanded the agreement of all those who are constrained by them, we will have discovered a significant dissonance between our political arrangements and the fundamental (pre-contract) notion of respect for each individual – a dissonance that ought to be of concern to liberal philosophers whether they are interested in the niceties of contract theory or not.

References and further reading

Manning, D. (1976) *Liberalism*, London: Dent. (A brief overview of liberal political philosophy.)
Rawls, J. (1971) *A Theory of Justice*, Oxford: Oxford University Press. (Perhaps the most famous construction of liberal theory in modern times, using the idea of a hypothetical contract to explore issues of justice and fairness.)

JEREMY WALDRON

LIBERATION PHILOSOPHY

Philosophy of liberation emerged in Argentina early in the 1970s with the explicit intention of proposing a liberating alternative to the diagnosis of structural dependence offered by the social sciences (particularly the so-called 'theory of dependence'). Some of the original intentions of liberation philosophy were to make poor and marginalized people the subjects, or authors, of philosophy and to collaborate in the process of distancing philosophy from academia and exclusively professional settings. Social conflict and pressing national needs were topics of debate at that time. All thought started with the recognition and assessment of the experience of alterity. Horacio Cerutti-Guldberg has proposed the phrase 'philosophies for liberation' as this kind of reflection deals with multiple philosophical positions and privileges the historical process over philosophy.

See also: ALTERITY AND IDENTITY, POSTMODERN THEORIES OF

HORACIO CERUTTI-GULDBERG

LIBERTARIANISM

In political philosophy 'libertarianism' is a name given to a range of views which take as their central value liberty or freedom. Although occasionally the term is applied to versions of anti-authoritarian Marxist theory (the 'libertarian left'), more commonly it is associated with a view which champions particularly pure forms of capitalism. Libertarians endorse the free market and unfettered free exchange, and oppose paternalistic or moralistic legislation (for example, laws regulating sexual behaviour or the consumption of alcohol or drugs). Liberty, on such a view, is identified with the absence of interference by the state or by others. The legitimate state exists purely to guard individual rights, protecting people and their property from force, theft and fraud. This is the 'minimal state' or 'night-watchman state' of classical liberalism. The state has no authority to engage in the redistribution of property (except to rectify the effects of theft, and so on) or, in certain versions at least, to pursue policies designed to further the common good. Such activities are viewed by the libertarian as illegitimate interferences with an individual's right to do what they wish with their own person or property.

JONATHAN WOLFF

LIBERTY

See FREEDOM AND LIBERTY

LIFE AND DEATH

Introduction

Problems concerning life and death are among the most dramatic and intractable in philosophy and they feature in all fundamental areas of philosophical inquiry, especially ethics. Most basic is the problem of what account to give of the value of life itself. This problem has had two main dimensions. One has been the controversy over what precise account to give of death; this has revolved around the issue of whether death is, as it is commonly perceived, an evil, and premature death a tragedy. The other has been the equally puzzling question of how to explain the positive value of life, and to resolve the problem that the more rich we make our account of the value of life, the more the value of life, and hence the nature of the wrong done by killing someone, seems to vary with the quality of the life of the person concerned.

A second set of problems concerns the definition of death and appropriate criteria for death. Death, as the most extreme consequence of violence, also leads one into psychological discussions of aggression and into issues of political violence, terrorism, war and capital punishment in political philosophy. Third, there has been concern with a number of practical moral issues, including abortion and euthanasia. Finally, issues have arisen concerning the relation of the value of the life of persons to other sorts of lives, those of animals, for example, or the life and survival of the ecosystem itself.

1   The value of life

It is not only the evil of death that presupposes that life has value and directs us to account for this value, but also everyday discriminations between lives of different sorts. Even the food of vegetarians involves the premature death of living things, and vegetarians usually accept priorities between different animals and between human individuals at different stages of development. If the hospital is on fire, should we attempt to rescue the patients before the hospital cat, and some patients before others? Should the terminally ill, the very old or those in persistent vegetative state be rescued before or after those with radically different life expectancy and degrees of richness and variety in their lives? Should those responsible for their own poor health (heavy smokers, for example) be preferred to the more prudent? Only an account of the value of life will tell us both why lives should be saved and whether and to what extent it is legitimate to choose between lives.

The chief recent attempts to provide a theory of the value of life have sought to identify those features of the most valuable creatures (humans) which might explain their peculiar value. Most theories combine autonomy, self-consciousness and intelligence as the relevant features (see AUTONOMY, ETHICAL). Creatures with such capacities have often been termed 'persons' (see PERSONS). Radically different accounts of how to apply such criteria of personhood have emerged. Philosophers of broadly consequentialist orientation have claimed that only creatures who actually possess the relevant characteristics count as persons (see CONSEQUENTIALISM). A major difficulty for such accounts is their counter-intuitive conclusion that creatures which most people do regard as valuable (foetuses and neonates, for example) either are valuable not in virtue of any intrinsic properties that they possess, but only in so far as they are valued by persons properly so called (their parents, perhaps), or will be valuable only in terms of future expected utility.

Others, accepting broadly the same criteria for personhood, have argued that creatures structured to possess such capacities or members of a natural kind that typically possesses such capacities are valuable whether or not particular individuals (foetuses, for instance) actually possess them. Another approach rests content with stipulating that humans are more valuable than others simply in virtue of their species membership. These 'natural kind' theorists cannot account for the discriminations people make between the moral importance of, say, foetuses, and other members of the same natural kind. If the life of a mother and her foetus are in danger and both cannot be saved, most would believe it right to prefer the mother.

Philosophers faced with the sorts of problems considered so far often produce *ad hoc*, 'common-sense' modifications to their general theories to overcome difficulties with hard cases. For example, natural kind theorists often admit of grades of natural kind membership, using terms like 'fully-fledged' humans to account for differences in attitudes to foetuses and adults.

Ronald DWORKIN, in an original account of the value of life, has argued that the sanctity of life must be understood in terms of the waste of investment in life represented by death. Dworkin distinguishes two dimensions of investment that might be wasted by death: the natural and the human. Natural investment implies that nature itself makes an investment in terms of time, trouble and natural resources when life is created and that investment increases in a linear way as the life continues. In the case of human investment, there is both the investment of the human whose life it is (in terms of self-creation both conscious and unconscious) and that of the other people who invest time, effort and resources in creating and sustaining that life. On this view the wrong of causing premature death is that of squandering this natural and human investment. A conservative view of the wrong of euthanasia and abortion, for example, prioritizes natural investment, while a more liberal view will prioritize a particular interpretation of the human contribution to a life.

This and other accounts suggesting that a life is valuable in proportion to its *richness* give importance to factors which differ across lives. On these views, lives will be more valuable the more the investment in them or the more rich and varied they are. This gives rise to the major problem that no two lives will be equally valuable and huge problems of discrimination between people are inevitable.

2 Criteria for death

Since Epicurus there has been persistent philosophical interest in the problem of accounting for the evil of death. We have already presupposed that this problem can be solved by discussing the value of life. Epicurus' problem is in a sense paradoxical. He made substantially the same point as Wittgenstein: 'death is not an event in life'. If it is not, then there is no one to whom death happens, no one for whom death is an evil. But, of course, most people fear death for the disaster it represents. Epicurus' point turns on the necessity of a harm's being experienced, yet we are all familiar with things we rationally regard as harms whether or not we experience them. I have a rational preference not to fall into a persistent vegetative state even if I will not be aware of this happening and thereafter will never be aware of anything again.

The more interesting and important problems concern the nature of the evil death represents and the importance of defining death, or rather of identifying appropriate criteria for the occurrence of death.

If, as most believe, death is an evil, and premature death a tragedy, and if we can say what makes this so, we will also be answering our first question, about what it is that makes life valuable. Here it is important to distinguish the question, 'What makes life valuable – for you?' from the question, 'In virtue of what is life the sort of thing that can be valuable?' The first question is likely to have as many answers as there are persons to whom it is put, the second question rather fewer.

If we move to the issue of criteria for death we can perhaps see why this is so. Death is as old as life, and people have seldom been at a loss as to when grief is appropriate. In other words, death is not a concept which required elucidation. Traditionally, permanent cessation of breath and/or heartbeat was accepted as a reliable indicator of death. While there may have been some uncertainty as to when cessation could be regarded as permanent, the onset of *rigor mortis* and the decomposition of the body could be relied upon to settle the matter in due course.

Problems arose when technology enabled the heartbeat and breathing of individuals to be maintained almost indefinitely. This was so even when the individuals concerned were otherwise so badly injured as to make it certain both that they would never regain consciousness, and that they would die if mechanical support were withdrawn. But are such individuals *dead*? Why is the question important? Why does it even arise?

Individuals on what is popularly known as 'life support' do not appear dead. They breathe, they are supple and perfused with blood, not cold and stiff like a corpse. In order to justify the cessation of life support (I continue with the popular term because it highlights the paradox we are discussing) with the inevitable consequence that the individual would die, it first had to be clear why it was appropriate to let this individual die; why their life had ceased to be valuable, in the sense of worth saving. Second, the technology of efficient life support narrowly preceded the development of organ transplants. If the individual on life support was to be eligible as an organ donor, their organs had to be in good condition. The condition of the organs was optimized by the maintenance of life support. Finally, pressure created by scarce resources meant that the intensive care beds necessary for life support were in demand and their occupation by one individual rather than another had to be justified.

The practical way out of the problem was to invent a new set of criteria for the occurrence of death. The idea was not to take individuals off life support and wait for them to die, but to declare them dead while still having their life systems sustained. This could be done if death of the brain were to be accepted as a necessary and sufficient condition for death of the organism as a whole. It is now generally accepted in many different societies and cultures that brain death is the criterion for death of the organism as a whole even though the rest of the organism can be kept 'alive' (breathing, blood circulating) after brain death. The major dispute has been over whether whole brain death is necessary for death to be declared to have occurred, or death of the brain stem, the conduit through which all electrical activity in the brain has to pass.

This agreement about brain death is significant, for it surely contains an acknowledgement that it is mental activity, and the things that mental activity supports, that are relevant to the value of life – that when the capacity for consciousness has departed permanently, all that matters has gone. The point of declaring individuals 'dead' was to mark the fact that all that matters about an individual had disappeared and that other things of importance could now be permitted. For example, organs could be made available for donation, intensive care beds released for other urgent cases, friends and relatives released from the often considerable burden of care and support, and grief could begin.

The acceptance of brain death marks a change in understanding of what matters about life and at the same time a reassertion of a traditional conception of respect for the sanctity of life and a correlated insistence that only death takes individuals beyond our moral concern. Brain death is such an attractive notion precisely because it permits the preservation of the concept of death as the crucial moral divide and at the same time allows us to think differently of human individuals who yet breathe. However, the artificiality of brain death as a criterion for the death of the entire organism should be borne in mind. There is an important sense in which brain death is at best a new conception of what it is to be dead and at worst an uneasy compromise between facing squarely the issue of what matters about life and harnessing the massive unreflective consensus about the significance of 'death'.

3 Persistent vegetative state

That this is so can be seen more clearly if we consider the condition of persistent vegetative state, and the landmark judgment by Britain's House of Lords in the case of Tony Bland. Bland sustained brain damage after being crushed in a crowd of spectators at a football match in 1989, at Hillsbor-

ough football stadium in Sheffield, England. The brain damage left him permanently and irrevocably unconscious, in what is now termed a 'persistent vegetative state' (PVS). PVS is not fatal; people like Bland can remain alive for thirty or more years. They are not 'brain dead'. In this they are akin to infants born with anencephaly (absence of a brain) or with their cerebral cortex destroyed.

Bland's parents, who accepted that their son had ceased to exist in any real – biographical – sense, although his body remained alive, were prevented from obtaining the solace of grief. In desperation, they asked the English courts to declare that it would be lawful for medical staff to withdraw feeding and other life-sustaining measures so that their son would die. It is not clear why there was any necessity to take the Bland case to the courts, since it was already well established that there was no obligation to sustain a baby by feeding (*Re C* [1989] 2 All ER 782 and *Re J* [1990] 3 All ER 930).

Eventually the House of Lords ruled unanimously that such a course of action would be lawful (*Airedale NHS Trust v. Bland* [1993] 1 All ER 821 H.L.). The problem was, of course, that although Tony Bland had permanently ceased to have 'a life' in any meaningful sense, he was not dead and would not die unless the courts permitted doctors to take steps to that end.

A slightly later case was concluded in the Court of Appeal in January 1994. The Master of the Rolls, Sir Thomas Bingham, held, in a bizarre judgment with which the other two lord justices of appeal concurred, that it was permissible for doctors to end the life of a patient by refusing life-prolonging treatment when the consultant and 'a number of other doctors' agreed that such a course was in the patient's best interests and 'no medical opinion contradicted it' (*Frenchay Healthcare NHS Trust v. S*, Court of Appeal, Judgment, 14 January 1994). Tony Bland's condition resembled those with brain death in that he had irrevocably lost the capacity for consciousness. The difference is that those in PVS still have electrical activity in the brain and through the brain stem. Does this difference amount to a morally relevant difference between those in PVS and those who are brain dead? Although the House of Lords was reluctant to change the definition of death, or even address that issue, it is clear from its decision that it thought Bland's life, because he had lost all capacity for consciousness, did not retain the sort of value that required it to be sustained. In the words of Lord Keith of Kinkel in his judgment in that case, 'It is, however, perhaps permissible to say that to an individual with no cognitive capacity whatever, and no prospect of ever recovering any such capacity in this world, it must be a matter of complete indifference whether he lives or dies'.

There was no question in Bland's case of competing claims on the resources required to sustain him, so that the decision to permit a course of action designed to achieve the death his parents sought was a deliberate, conscious decision to end his life. A hotly debated question is whether such a decision constitutes a form of euthanasia. Although the House of Lords strongly denied that this is what it was doing, its decision in the Bland case was thought by many to legalize, for the first time in the United Kingdom, a form (albeit very restricted) of euthanasia. That the case of Tony Bland establishes a precedent for legally sanctioned euthanasia in the United Kingdom is confirmed by the words of Lord Mustill in his judgment in that case:

> The conclusion ... depends crucially on a distinction drawn by the criminal Law between acts and omissions, and carries with it inescapably a distinction between, on the one hand what is often called 'mercy killing', where active steps are taken in a medical context to terminate the life of a suffering patient, and a situation such as the present where the proposed conduct has the aim for equally humane reasons of terminating the life of Anthony Bland by withholding from him the basic necessities of life. The acute unease which I feel about adopting this way through the legal and ethical maze is I believe due in an important part to the sensation that however much the terminologies may differ the ethical status of the two courses of action is for all relevant purposes indistinguishable.

The key features of Lord Mustill's judgment are, first, the acknowledgment that the course of action requested of, and approved by, the courts 'has the aim ... of terminating the life of Anthony Bland'; and, second, that the supposed difference between acts and omissions relied on by the common law tradition to make moral and legal distinctions, characterizes two courses of action that are ethically 'for all relevant purposes indistinguishable'. This decision made the United Kingdom the second country in Europe to have judicially recognized the necessity of bringing to an end the lives of at least some innocent individuals who have not requested death. The Netherlands legalized euthanasia under certain conditions in a High Court case decided in 1984 and later formally enshrined euthanasia in its legal system.

It is important to emphasize the proviso 'who have not requested death', for other instances of courts defending the right to die have turned on precisely this issue. The landmark United States case concerning PVS, that of Nancy Cruzan, depended crucially on whether Cruzan had expressed a wish to die prior to falling into PVS, and indeed it is often described as a case establishing the right to die (*Cruzan v. Director, Missouri Department of Health* [1990] 497 US 261).

4   The ethics of euthanasia

Arguments about the ethics of euthanasia are essentially the same as, and have been coloured by, arguments about the ethics of suicide. The wrong of suicide has, since the death of Socrates, often been seen in terms of either a violation of some idea of the sanctity of life, or the wrong of depriving a sovereign or a god of the use of a body which was theirs to dispose of. Euthanasia, as essentially assisting suicide, while of contemporary relevance as we have seen, has reawakened the centuries old debate about suicide (see SUICIDE, ETHICS OF).

Those who defend the legitimacy of euthanasia have three main approaches to defending the ethics of what they propose. First, some see euthanasia (like suicide) as a dimension of human freedom and argue that the value represented by respect for autonomy is incomplete unless it encompasses the limiting case of suicide or assisted suicide. On this view, no further justification is required. The second view is based on compassion and tends to undermine this purist approach to the ethics of euthanasia. It argues that suicide and euthanasia are legitimate ways of bringing to an end suffering which cannot be adequately controlled or ended in any other way. This approach can undermine autonomy because it lapses if there is an equally effective way of controlling the pain and suffering. The third type of defence of euthanasia is exemplified by Ronald Dworkin's account (see §1), which argues that respect for the intrinsic value of life, properly understood, sees life essentially as meaningful and valuable because of the shape given to it by the individual whose life it is, and that this shaping power must include control over life's end. Unlike the first defence of euthanasia which appeals simply to autonomy, Dworkin's approach places autonomy at the service of, and hence subordinate to, a conception of the intrinsic value of life. On this view it is not all autonomous decisions to end life that are justified, but only those which conduce to the agent's own conception of what it is that makes their life make sense.

Arguments against the legitimacy of euthanasia take two forms: they take a stand on principle or they attempt to undermine the cogency of the arguments in favour of euthanasia. The principled approach either harkens back to the idea that an individual's life is not theirs to dispose of, belonging to the sovereign or the deity or both (one via the other), or takes a stand on the sanctity of life. The more pragmatic approach tends to suggest that the freedom to end one's own life is not part of autonomy properly understood, or that there are other compassionate and effective ways of controlling pain, both physical and psychological.

It is difficult to resolve the differences over euthanasia when the issue is one of principle. Perhaps the most obvious reconciling strategy is to seek cases in which those opposed to euthanasia would concede the legitimacy of killing, and ask if related justifications might not hold good in the case of euthanasia. For example, not all opponents of euthanasia are pacifists, and even pacifists might understand extreme exceptions to the rule against killing the innocent.

One test might be how people feel about the following case. A lorry driver is trapped in the blazing cab of his vehicle following an accident. A policeman is on the scene and sees that the driver cannot be extracted before the flames get to him and he is burned alive. The policeman can let him be burned alive or can give him a quick and relatively painless end by shooting him in the head. The driver says, 'Please shoot me; do not let me be burned alive!' Those opposed to euthanasia in all circumstances must give one answer to the policeman's dilemma, those in favour will give the alternative.

There is one final sort of objection to euthanasia. It avoids the policeman's dilemma but has its own problems. Some people are not opposed to euthanasia on principle and would permit it in exceptional cases, like the policeman's dilemma. However, they regard it as constituting a 'slippery slope' which if permitted would lead to unacceptable forms of killing. They therefore object to the *legalization* of euthanasia, but can cope with isolated and exceptional instances, by forgiveness rather than by justification. The question advocates of the slippery slope objection must answer is whether it is reasonable and rational to criminalize behaviour they admit to be both moral and defensible, and whether or not the unacceptable levels of the slope can be guarded against in another way.

5   Contraception and infanticide

Contraception raises issues of life and death analogous to those we have discussed. First, there are methods of contraception which operate to effect early abortion by, for example, preventing implantation of a fertilized egg. Second, those who regard the potentiality argument as giving moral status to the foetus will, if they are consistent, see contraception as one way in which potential human beings have their potential frustrated. There is, of course, another dimension to the ethics of contraception which is not related straightforwardly to issues of life and death. That is where one sexual partner conceals from the other the nature, existence and/or reliability of the methods of contraception used or leads the other partner to believe a method of contraception is being used when it is not (see TRUTHFULNESS).

Since the advent of HIV/AIDS, a popular method of contraception has become more significant as a barrier to infection, and this has added to the moral responsibility of using one particular method of contraception. Questions are often raised as to whether someone who uses no method of contraception, or fails to use a condom, is willing to conceive and bear the responsibility of a child or is willing to run the risk of HIV infection.

It is sometimes suggested, particularly by Catholic thinkers, that contraception subverts the purpose of sex, which supposedly was designed by the deity for procreation. This is a curious argument, however, because if sexual relations are wrong except when they could conceivably result in procreation, then sex between infertile people or during pregnancy is wrong. If, on the other hand, it is practices which weaken the prospect of new people coming into existence which are to be avoided, then it looks as though it is a celibate priesthood, or the existence of nunneries, which are an affront to God's purpose.

Infanticide raises special moral problems only for those who see a morally relevant difference between the foetus and the neonate. If abortion is permissible, infanticide will surely be permissible on the same terms, unless the newborn differs in some relevant way from those foetuses the abortion of which is permissible. Attempts have been made to identify such differences in three main ways: in terms of either some capacities possessed by the newborn and not the foetus, or the newborn's supposedly greater potential for personhood, or the social relations it forms for the first time on consciously encountering other beings. All of these alleged differences are controversial, and we should note that the last, socialization, leaves unprotected any and all unloved, unwanted and unclaimed infants (see REPRODUCTION AND ETHICS).

See also: DEATH; LIFE, MEANING OF; MEDICAL ETHICS; SUICIDE, ETHICS OF

References and further reading

Kleinig, J. (1991) *Valuing Life*, Princeton, NJ: Princeton University Press. (General account of life and death issues.)

Steinbock, B. (ed.) (1980) *Killing and Letting Die,* Englewood Cliffs, NJ: Prentice Hall. (Excellent collection of essays on life and death.)

JOHN HARRIS

LIFE, MEANING OF

This is an obscure yet central topic in philosophy. Often associated with the question whether human beings are part of a larger or divine purpose, the question, 'What is the meaning of life?' seems to invite a religious answer. Much philosophical discussion, however, questions the necessity of this association. Attention to the inevitability of death has often seemed to make life's meaning problematic, but it is not obvious how immortality could make the difference between meaning and its absence. The theme of absurdity runs through much discussion of those who believe the universe to be indifferent. Though our lives have no significance, they argue, we must live as if they do. In the face of this absurdity, some advocate suicide, others defiance, others irony. One may also turn away from the issue of cosmic significance, and look for meaning elsewhere.

See also: EXISTENTIALISM; GOOD, THEORIES OF THE; NIHILISM

SUSAN WOLF

LIFE, ORIGIN OF

The appearance of maggots on meat or of intestinal tapeworms supported an ancient belief in the spontaneous generation of life. This idea was challenged in the seventeenth century but not abandoned before Pasteur's experiments. Scientists now agree that terrestrial life had a single origin, but differ in explanations. Some believe that life began with the onset of protein-based metabolism, supported by evidence of spontaneous abiotic amino acid synthesis and theoretical models of self-sustaining and evolving systems of enzymes. Others believe life began with the appearance of nucleic acid-based molecular replicators and have organized their research efforts around the vision of a primordial 'RNA world'.

See also: EVOLUTION, THEORY OF; GENETICS; UNITY OF SCIENCE

LENNY MOSS

LIMBO

According to traditional Roman Catholic teaching, limbo is the postmortem destination of those who have not been baptized, but are not guilty of sin. Lack of baptism bars such people from salvation, but

their innocence means that they do not deserve the punishment of hell. They were thought to fall into two groups: the righteous of the Old Covenant, prior to the redemption of Christ, and unbaptized children. The former were supposed to have gone to heaven after Christ's death, but the latter had to stay in limbo forever. The existence of limbo was never dogmatically defined, and it was never given as much attention as heaven, hell or even purgatory, each of which represented a fate which human beings earned in part through personal choice. Nowadays, the possibility that unbaptized babies might be consigned to hell is not widely entertained, and some thinkers hold that the requirement of baptism for salvation is open to interpretation. Consequently, the idea of limbo is not as widely discussed as it once was.

See also: EVIL, PROBLEM OF; HEAVEN; HELL; PURGATORY

LINDA ZAGZEBSKI

LINGUISTIC RELATIVITY
See SAPIR-WHORF hypothesis

LINGUISTICS, PHILOSOPHY OF
See LANGUAGE, PHILOSOPHY OF

LINGUISTICS, STRUCTURALISM IN
See STRUCTURALISM IN LINGUISTICS

LITERATURE AND PHILOSOPHY
See ALIGHIERI, DANTE; BAKHTIN, MIKHAIL MIKHAILOVICH; BARTHES, ROLAND; CAMUS, ALBERT; CAVELL, STANLEY; COMEDY; DECONSTRUCTION; DERRIDA, JACQUES; DIDEROT, DENIS; DODGSON, CHARLES LUTWIDGE (LEWIS CARROLL); DOSTOEVSKII, FËDOR MIKHAILOVICH; EMERSON, RALPH WALDO; GOETHE, JOHANN WOLFGANG VON; IRIGARAY, LUCE; JOHNSON, SAMUEL; KRISTEVA, JULIA; LESSING, GOTTHOLD EPHRAIM; MONTAIGNE, MICHEL EYQUEM DE; NARRATIVE; POETRY; RORTY, RICHARD MCKAY; ROUSSEAU, JEAN-JACQUES; SARTRE, JEAN-PAUL; SCHILLER, JOHANN CHRISTOPH FRIEDRICH; THOREAU, HENRY DAVID; TOLSTOI, COUNT LEV NIKOLAEVICH; TRAGEDY; VOLTAIRE (FRANÇOIS-MARIE AROUET)

LLULL, RAMON (1232–1316)

One of the most extraordinary figures of thirteenth-century Europe, Llull was a self-taught lay theologian and philosopher, chiefly concerned with reforming Christian society and converting unbelievers. Details of his life remain obscure, but over 200 of his writings survive. Most of these expound his personal dialectical system, the Great Universal Art of Finding Truth, an encyclopedic collation of commonplace doctrines that attempts to show how all human knowledge conforms to divine truth. Largely ignored during Llull's lifetime and denounced as heretical in the later Middle Ages, the Great Art became very popular in the Renaissance as a programme of universal knowledge.

See also: BONAVENTURE; NATURAL THEOLOGY; NICHOLAS OF CUSA

MARK D. JOHNSTON

LOCALITY
See BELL'S THEOREM

LOCKE, JOHN (1632–1704)

Introduction

John Locke was the first of the empiricist opponents of Descartes to achieve comparable authority among his European contemporaries. Together with Newton's physics, the philosophy of *An Essay concerning Human Understanding* gradually eclipsed Cartesianism, decisively redirecting European thought. Neoplatonic innatism was replaced with a modest, naturalistic conception of our cognitive capacities, making careful observation and systematic description the primary task of natural inquiry. Locke saw himself as carrying out just such a descriptive project with respect to the mind itself. Theorizing is the construction of hypotheses on the basis of analogies, not penetration to the essences of things by super-sensory means. In religion Locke took a similarly anti-dogmatic line, advocating toleration and minimal doctrinal requirements, notably in *Epistola de tolerantia* (A Letter concerning Toleration) and *The Reasonableness of Christianity*. Through his association with the Earl of Shaftesbury he became involved in government, and then in revolutionary politics against Charles II and James II. The latter involvement led to exile, and to *Two Treatises of Government*, a rejection of patriarchalism and an argument from first principles for constitutional government in the interests of the governed, and for the right of the misgoverned to rebel. Locke published his main works only after the 'Glorious Revolution' of 1688. He undertook important governmental duties for a time, and continued to write on many topics, including economics and biblical criticism, until his death. The *Essay*, *Epistola* and *Second Treatise* remain centrally canonical texts.

Locke held that all our ideas are either given in experience, or are complex ideas formed from simple ideas so given, but not that all our knowledge is based on experience. He accepted that geometry, for example, is an a priori science, but denied that the ideas which are the objects of geometrical reasoning are innate. 'Experience' includes 'reflection', that is reflexive awareness of our own mental operations, which Cartesians treated as a way of accessing innate ideas, but which Locke calls 'internal sense'. To have ideas before the mind is to be perceiving given or constructed sensory or quasi-sensory images – things as perceived by sense. In abstraction, however, we consider only aspects of what is presented: for example, a geometrical proof may consider only aspects of a drawn figure, allowing generalization to all figures similar in just those respects. Universal knowledge is thus perception of a relation between abstract ideas, but we also have immediate knowledge, in sensation, that particular external things are causing ideas in us. This awareness allows us to use the idea as a sign of its external cause: for example, the sensation of white signifies whatever feature of objects causes that sensation. Representation is thus fundamentally causal: causality bridges the gap between reality and ideas. Consequently we have sensitive knowledge of things only through their powers, knowledge of their existence without knowledge of their essence. Each way in which things act on the senses gives rise to a phenomenally simple idea signifying a quality, or power to affect us, in the object. Some simple ideas, those of the 'primary qualities', solidity, extension, figure, motion or rest, and number (the list can vary) can be supposed to resemble their causes. Others, ideas of 'secondary qualities', colour, smell, taste and so forth, do not. We also form ideas of the powers of objects to interact.

Our idea of any sort of substantial thing is therefore complex, including ideas of all the qualities and powers by which we know and define that 'substance'. Additionally, the idea includes the 'general idea of substance', or possessor of the qualities, a placemarker signifying the unknown underlying cause of their union. Locke distinguishes between the general substance, matter, and the 'particular constitution' of matter from which flow the observable properties by which we define each sort of substance – gold, horse, iron and so on. This 'real constitution' or 'real essence' is distinguishable only relatively to our definition or 'nominal essence' of the species. Locke extends this conceptualist view of classification to individuation in a famous, still influential argument that a person is individuated, not by an immaterial soul, but by unifying and continuous consciousness.

Because their real essences are unknown to us, we are capable only of probable belief about substances, not of 'science'. In mathematics, however, real essences are known, since they are abstract ideas constructible without reference to reality. So too with ideas of 'mixed modes' and 'relations', including the ideas of social actions, roles and relationships which supply the subject-matter of a priori sciences concerned with law, natural, social and positive. The three legislators are God, public opinion and government. God's authority derives from his status as creator, and natural or moral law is his benevolent will for us. Locke's political theory concerns the authority of governments, which he takes to be, at bottom, the right of all individuals to uphold natural law transferred to a central agency for the sake of its power and impartiality. Economic change, he argues, renders this transfer imperative. In a state of nature, individuals own whatever they have worked for, if they can use it and enough is left for others. But with land-enclosure (which benefits everyone by increasing productivity) and the institution of money (which makes it both possible and morally justifiable to enjoy the product of enclosure) this primitive property-right is transcended, and there is need for an authority to ordain and uphold rules of justice for the benefit of all. Any government, therefore, has a specific trust to fulfil, and should be organized so as best to safeguard this role. A ruler who rules in his own interest forfeits all rights, as a criminal at war with his subjects. Then rebellion is justified self-defence.

1 Life and main works

John Locke was born at Wrington, Somerset in England on 28 August 1632. His father was a small property owner, lawyer and minor official, who served on the side of Parliament in the civil war under the more influential Alexander Popham. Through Popham, Locke became a pupil at Westminster School, then the leading school in England. From Westminster he was elected in May 1652 to a Studentship at Christ Church, Oxford, conditionally tenable for life.

During the next fifteen years at Oxford Locke took his degrees (B.A. 1656, M.A. 1658) and fulfilled various college offices, becoming Tutor in 1661. Between 1660 and 1662 he wrote three manuscripts on issues of Church and State, individual conscience and religious authority, two now published together and known as *Two Tracts on Government*, and *An necesse sit dari in Ecclesia infallibilem Sacro Sanctae Scripturae interpretem?* (Is it necessary to have in the church an infallible interpreter of holy scripture?). Although his answer to the last question was predictably negative, in the *Tracts* he expressed a less-than-tolerant view of conscientious religious unorthodoxy, assigning to rulers the right to determine details of religious observance for the sake of public peace. While Censor of Moral Philosophy at Christ Church in 1664 he completed the Latin manuscript now known as *Essays [or Questions] on the Law of Nature*, which presaged his mature views – both his general empiricism and his conception of moral obligation as an obligation to God to obey natural law. This work also rejects wayward and dogmatic appeals to conscience, in favour of reason based on experience.

The politics of religion, at the time a large part of politics, was not Locke's only extracurricular interest. His reading-notes ('commonplace books') of this time indicate an interest in Anglican theology, and by 1658 he was reading and taking lecture notes in medicine with the assiduity appropriate to a chosen career. This interest extended to chemistry and, in the 1660s, to the new mechanical philosophy as expounded, for example, by Robert BOYLE, whom Locke had met by 1660. Locke also read the main philosophical works of Descartes, and some Gassendi, but his record focuses on their versions of corpuscularianism, bypassing metaphysical and epistemological underpinnings (see DESCARTES, R. §§11–12; GASSENDI, P.). On the evidence, natural philosophy attracted Locke more at this time than metaphysics, although the coarse empiricism of *Essays on the Law of Nature* is close to that of Gassendi. Yet Locke could hardly have remained ignorant of the battle among the new philosophers between 'gods' and 'giants' – between those, led by Descartes, in the Platonic-Augustinian metaphysical tradition and those, headed by Gassendi and HOBBES, who developed ancient empiricist and materialist theory.

In 1665 Locke's university life was interrupted by a diplomatic mission to Brandenburg as secretary to Sir Walter Vane. About this time he decided against entering the Church, but took the one way of nevertheless keeping his Studentship (without obligation to reside in Oxford) by transferring formally to medicine. In 1666 came a momentous meeting with Lord Ashley (Anthony Ashley Cooper, who became Earl of Shaftesbury in 1672), whose London household Locke subsequently joined in 1667. Here his medical and political interests alike received a more practical edge than they had previously possessed. He began collaborating closely with the pre-eminent physician, Thomas Sydenham, and in 1668 successfully supervised an operation on Lord Ashley to drain an abscess on the liver. In the years following he continued to act as medical advisor within Ashley's circle, supervising the birth of Ashley's grandson, later the philosophical Third Earl of Shaftesbury. A manuscript of this time in Locke's handwriting (but perhaps wholly or partly by Sydenham), 'De Arte Medica', is strongly sceptical of the value of hypotheses, as opposed to experience, in medicine.

During this same period, presumably influenced by his patron, Locke wrote the manuscript *Essay concerning Toleration* (1667), departing from his earlier, nervously illiberal justification of constraint and advocating toleration of any religious persuasion not constituting a positive moral or political danger − provisos excluding, respectively, atheists and Roman Catholics. In 1667 Ashley became a member of the governing 'cabal' which followed Clarendon's period as Lord Chancellor, and in 1672 became Lord Chancellor himself. Under Ashley, and for a while after Ashley's fall from office in 1673, Locke was involved in government. He began to work on economic questions, and for some years helped in the organization of the newly founded colony of Carolina. He was registrar to the commissioners of excise (perhaps a sinecure) from 1670 to 1675, secretary for presentations (in charge of ecclesiastical patronage) in 1672–3, and secretary and treasurer to the Council for Trade and Plantations (no sinecure) in 1673–4.

Nevertheless he found time for new intellectual interests. Not later than 1671 he put down for discussion by a group of friends what he later claimed (inaccurately, given *Essays on the Law of Nature*) to have been his first thoughts on the powers of the understanding. He found the topic sufficiently gripping for a more extensive treatment than such an occasion would have demanded in *Intellectus humanus cum cognitionis certitudine, et assensus firmitate* (The human intellect, the certainty of knowledge and the confirmation of belief), dated 1671, with a longer (and as strongly empiricist and imagist) redrafting in the same year entitled 'An Essay concerning the Understanding, Knowledge, Opinion and Assent' − the manuscripts now known as Drafts A and B of *An Essay concerning Human Understanding*.

In 1675 Locke moved to France, beginning at the same time to write his journal. He met physicians and philosophers, undertook a programme of reading in French philosophy and continued working on his 'Essay'. On returning to England in 1678, after the fabricated 'Popish plot', he was again caught up in politics and in attempts to exclude Charles' brother James from the succession. Charles dissolved Parliament in 1681, and Shaftesbury led a group of Whigs planning insurrection. During this period Locke probably wrote the bulk of the *Two Treatises of Government*; the first, at least, to support moves for James' exclusion, the second possibly later to advocate actual rebellion. He also wrote, with James Tyrrell, a long response (still unpublished, 1997) to Edward Stillingfleet's *Unreasonableness of Separation*, defending the position of nonconformists against Stillingfleet's criticisms. In 1682 Shaftesbury went into exile, dying soon after. When the Rye House plot to assassinate Charles and James was uncovered in 1683, Locke himself prudently moved to Holland, where he contacted other, more overtly active exiles. His connections provoked expulsion from his Christ Church Studentship in 1684, and at the time of Monmouth's rebellion he went into hiding to escape arrest. His intellectual activities continued unabated, the *Essay* being largely written by 1686. In 1685–6 he wrote *Epistola de Tolerantia* (Letter concerning Toleration), perhaps in response to the revocation of the edict of Nantes. He made friends, and discussed theological questions, with the remonstrant Philippus van Limborch and Jean Le Clerc, publishing various items in the latter's journal, *Bibliothèque universelle et historique*, including a review of Newton's *Principia* (1686) and a ninety-two page abridgement of the *Essay* (1688).

In 1688 the 'Glorious Revolution' brought the deposition of James, and Locke returned to England the following year. He declined the post of ambassador to Brandenburg, accepted an undemanding post as commissioner of appeals (annual salary, £200) and set about publishing his writings. *Epistola de Tolerantia* was published pseudonymously in Holland in May 1689, and Popple's English translation followed within months. The *Two Treatises* were revised and published anonymously, and the *Essay* followed in December (with authorship acknowledged), although both books were dated 1690. *A Second Letter concerning Toleration* (1690) and *A Third Letter for Toleration* (1692) were in response to attacks by an Anglican clergyman, Jonas Proast. *Some Considerations of the Consequences of the Lowering of Interest and Raising the Value of Money*, partly based on the manuscript of 1668, was published in 1691 (dated 1692) against Parliamentary measures of the time. In 1691, Locke accepted the invitation of an old friend, Damaris Masham and her husband to live with them, as far as his concerns permitted, at Oates in Essex. Country life seems to have ameliorated the asthma which dogged his last years. *Some Thoughts concerning Education* (1693, revised 1695), a significant work in the history of educational theory, was based on a number of letters of advice to his friend, Edward Clarke. In 1694 came the second edition of the *Essay*, with important additions including a controversial chapter on identity. In 1695 he published a new work, once more anonymously, *The Reasonableness of Christianity*. John Edwards' attacks on its liberal, minimalist interpretation of Christian faith were rebutted in two *Vindications* (1695, 1697).

Locke continued to be engaged on economic questions, and in 1695 he joined a committee to advise the Chancellor of the Exchequer on monetary policy. His recommendations, supported by further papers, were accepted. In 1696 came an important government appointment to the Council for Trade and Plantations, and for four years he fulfilled fairly onerous duties on the Board of Trade for the considerable annual salary of £1,000. At the same time he engaged in an extended controversy with Edward Stillingfleet, who found the *Essay* theologically suspect. *A Letter to the Right Reverend Edward, Lord Bishop of Worcester* was followed by two further Letters in reply to Stillingfleet's Answers. Despite its controversial style, Locke's argument is often a cogent clarification of his position. The exchange prompted significant alterations to the fourth edition of the *Essay* (1700) and long passages were included as footnotes in the posthumously published fifth edition. In June 1700 Locke resigned from the Board of Trade, a sick man, and thereafter lived mostly at Oates. Pursuing a long-standing interest in biblical criticism, he set about the work which was posthumously published as *A Paraphrase and Notes on the Epistles of St Paul*, an important contribution to hermeneutics. In 1702 he wrote the reductive *Discourse of Miracles*, and in 1704 began a *Fourth Letter on Toleration*. On 28 October 1704 he died as Damaris Masham read to him from the Book of Psalms. For the last years of his life he was generally respected as, with Newton, one of Britain's two intellectual giants, a reputation undiminished by death.

2 The structure of Locke's empiricism

Locke's mature philosophy is 'concept-empiricist', but not 'knowledge-empiricist': he held that all our concepts are drawn from experience, but not that all our knowledge is based on experience. Yet his early position, in *Essays on the Law of Nature* and the first part of *Draft A*, was 'knowledge-empiricist' in just this sense – even the axioms of geometry gain assent 'only by the testimony and assurance of our senses'

(*Draft A* I: 22–3). However, according to *Draft A*, when we find that certain relations hold without exception, we assume that they hold universally and come to employ them as 'standards' of measurement embodied in the meaning of our terms. Locke sees this as implying a choice: an axiom can *either* be interpreted as an 'instructive' but uncertain summary of experience, *or* as a quasi-definition, founded on experience but 'only verbal … and not instructive'. But later in *Draft A* he discards the notion that geometrical axioms can be interpreted empirically, taking them only in a sense in which they can be known by 'demonstration' or 'the bare shewing of things or proposing them to our senses or understandings' (*Draft A* I: 50) – that is, by intuitions with perceived or imagined instances (for example, diagrams) as their objects. At the same time he recognizes that mathematical propositions are not plausibly regarded as merely verbal. The possibility of alternative interpretations of universal propositions, *either* as certain, but verbal, *or* as instructive, but uncertain, is now restricted to propositions about substances, such as 'Man is rational'. Locke has shifted, in effect, from knowledge-empiricism towards a concept-empiricism which allows 'instructive' a priori knowledge (the last being the acknowledged ancestor of Kant's synthetic a priori – see KANT, I. §4).

Locke's intuitionism shapes his attack on the innatism characteristic of the Platonic-Augustinian-Cartesian tradition. Starting with propositions, Locke rebuts the argument from alleged universal assent, or assent by all who have come to the use of reason. But ideas are what is before the mind in thought, and propositions are ideas in relation. Locke's underlying thesis is that to take either knowledge or ideas to be innately 'imprinted on the mind' in a merely dispositional sense (and they are clearly not actual in all human beings from birth) would be contrary to any intelligible notion of being 'in the mind': 'Whatever idea was never perceived by the mind, was never in the mind' (*Essay* I.iv.20). Locke concedes dispositional knowledge and ideas, retained by the memory and capable of being revived, but he understands both intentionality and knowledge in terms of perception, and finds nonsensical the notion of perception which never has been conscious and actual. This strongly intuitionist model rules out dispositional innatism as an intelligible possibility. Rationalist intuitionism, from Locke's point of view, is simply incoherent. And since the only dispositional ideas and knowledge are what is retained in the memory, what is before the mind as the object of intuition or demonstration must be experiential or sensory.

Locke also argues that there are no general maxims of logic or mathematics to which all assent when they come to the use of reason, since many rational but illiterate people never consider such abstract principles. He does not accept that reasoning merely consonant with logical principles is equivalent to assent to them, or, for example, that distinguishing two things is tacit employment of the idea of identity. Explicit abstract principles and ideas come late and with so much difficulty that people cannot agree on ideas of impossibility, identity, duty, substance, God and the like − just the ideas most supposed innately luminous. That rational people assent to certain propositions on first proposal is beside the point, since such people will only have understood the terms of the proposition in question by abstraction from experience. Then they will assent, not because the proposition is innate, but because it is evident. To describe the bare capacity to perceive such truths as the possession of innate principles and ideas will make all universal knowledge innate, however specific or derived. Turning to practical principles and the idea of God, Locke appeals to anthropology to rebut the claim that any of these are universally recognized. The main thrust of his argument, however, is conceptual.

Locke's empiricism has another central feature. Like GASSENDI and HOBBES, he expressly accords independent authority to the particular deliverances of the senses. Descartes had argued that sensation requires interpretation employing innate, purely intellectual ideas even in order for us to conceive of its objects as independent bodies. For Descartes, moreover, natural sensory belief is defenceless in the face of sceptical argument − secure knowledge of the existence of bodies can only be achieved through a rational proof involving reflection on the role and mechanisms of sense (see DESCARTES, R. §9). This emphatic subordination of sense to reason Locke rejects just as firmly: the senses are 'the proper and sole judges' of the existence of bodies. He sees the senses as knowledge-delivering faculties in their own right, prior to any understanding of their mechanisms: 'the actual receiving of ideas from without . . . makes us know, that something doth exist at that time without us, which causes that idea in us, though perhaps we neither know nor consider how it does it' (*Essay* IX.xi.2). The sceptic's doubt about the external world is a mere pretence, not to be taken seriously: 'no body can, in earnest, be so sceptical, as to be uncertain of the existence of those things which he sees and feels'. Echoing LUCRETIUS, Locke sees the reason employed in sceptical argument itself as standing or falling with the senses: 'For we cannot act any thing, but by our faculties; nor talk of knowledge itself, but by the help of those faculties which are fitted to apprehend even what knowledge is' (*Essay* IX.xi.3). Locke does identify features of sense-experience which militate against

scepticism: for example, sensory ideas depend on physical sense-organs, and are systematically and unavoidably consequent on our situation; the deliverances of different senses cohere; there is a 'manifest difference' between ideas of sense and ideas of memory and imagination (most dramatically with respect to pain), as there is between acting in the world and imagining ourselves acting; and so on (*Essay* IX.xi.4–8). Yet all these considerations are simply 'concurrent reasons' which further, but unnecessarily confirm 'the assurance we have from our senses themselves' − 'an assurance that *deserves* the name of knowledge' (*Essay* IX.xi.3).

Locke's explanation of the certainty and extent of 'sensitive knowledge of existence' hinges on his view that in sensation we are immediately aware, not only of sensations or 'ideas', but of their being caused by things outside us. We are thus able to think of the unknown cause through its effect in us: 'whilst I write this, I have, by the paper affecting my eyes, that idea produced in my mind, which, whatever object causes, I call *white*; by which I know, that that quality or accident (i.e. whose appearance before my eyes, always causes that idea) doth really exist, and hath a being without me' (*Essay* IX.xi.2). This claim ties in with another, that ideas of simple sensory qualities are always 'true', 'real' and 'adequate': 'their truth consists in nothing else, but in such appearances, as are produced in us, and must be suitable to those powers, [God] has placed in external objects, or else they could not be produced in us' (*Essay* II.xxxii.14). Simple ideas are 'distinguishing marks' which fulfil their function well enough whatever unknown difference lies behind the sensible distinction. But this function fits them for another, as terms in the natural language of thought. The idea of white signifies, that is *indicates*, its unknown cause, and also signifies, that is *stands for*, that feature of things in thought. So the limited causal knowledge that sensation supplies allows us to have contentful thought and knowledge of the external world. The idea of power extends such pretheoretical knowledge: our idea of the melting of wax, joined to the idea of active or passive power, can be employed as a sign of whatever in the sun melts wax, or of whatever in wax causes its melting. Consequently Locke decides to treat ideas of powers as simple ideas, and knowledge of powers as observational. The senses do not give knowledge of the essence or nature of bodies, but they do give knowledge of their existence, and enable us to distinguish between them.

3 Ideas of sensation and reflection: their retention and abstraction

Locke's employment of the word 'idea' responds to a variety of antecedents. Like Descartes, he uses it

587

ambiguously both for representative states (acts, modifications) of mind and, more frequently, for the represented objects as they are represented or conceived of, the so-called 'immediate' objects of perception and thought. To have an idea before the mind is generally, for Locke, to be contemplating something under a certain conception rather than contemplating a psychological state. To 'perceive a relation between ideas' is to perceive a relation between things-as-conceived-of. But Locke's account also looks back to the Epicurean view of sensations as signs of their unknown causes in the motion of atoms or 'corpuscules' (see §2), a view which points away from the Cartesian and scholastic presumption of intrinsically representative elements in thought towards a purely causal understanding of representation, treating ideas as blank sensory effects in the mind. Locke never resolves the tension between these different conceptions of an idea, although each of them is necessary to his theory.

Locke strongly opposes the Augustinian-Cartesian view that knowledge and truth consist in the conformity of human conceptions with God's conceptions, the divine ideas or archetypes employed in creation and revealed to us in our active use of reason. For Descartes, human reason is only accidentally involved with the senses, whereas for Locke there are no purely intellectual ideas. The task traditionally assigned to intellect – universal thought – Locke assigns to 'abstraction', taken to be the mind's in some sense separating out elements of raw experience and employing them as 'standards and representatives' of a class. What this means will be considered.

Although Locke sometimes writes that all words stand for ideas, ideas are the mental correlates of terms or names: that is, words that can stand in subject or predicate place. He adheres to the traditional view that 'particles', such as prepositions, conjunctions, the copula and the negative, signify, not ideas, but 'the connection that the mind gives to ideas, or propositions, one with another' (*Essay* III.vii.1). They do not *name*, but *express* 'actions of the mind in discoursing': for example, 'but' expresses various mental operations together named 'discretive conjunction'. The mental actions or operations expressed by 'is' and 'is not' are either the 'perception of the agreement or disagreement of ideas', which is Locke's definition of (at least, general) knowledge, or the 'presumption' of such a relation, which is Locke's account of belief or judgment. As commonly in earlier logic, merely considering a proposition is not distinguished from knowing or judging it to be true.

The aim of Book II of the *Essay* is to establish that all our ideas derive from experience: that is, that the way we conceive of the world (including ourselves) is ultimately determined by the way we experience the world. 'Experience' includes not only 'sense', but reflection ('reflexion') – not reflection in today's sense but reflexive awareness of our own mental operations. Platonists, Aristotelians and Cartesians all assigned the reflexive awareness of thinking to intellect rather than to sense. For Descartes, the innateness of such ideas as *substance*, *thought* and even *God* consists in the potentiality of their becoming explicit through the mind's reflecting on itself, and Leibniz argues accordingly that, simply by admitting reflection as well as sense, Locke admits innate ideas (see LEIBNIZ, G.W. §8). Locke, however, claims that reflection, 'though it be not sense, as having nothing to do with external objects, yet it is very like it, and might properly enough be call'd internal sense' (*Essay* II.i.4). Thereafter he treats sense and reflection as theoretically equivalent (although reflexive knowledge of one's own existence is 'intuitive' rather than 'sensitive' – *Essay* IV.ix.3). This move not only extends the empiricist principle to such non-sensory notions as *willing*, *perceiving*, *contemplation* or *hope*, but also contradicts the Cartesian model of thought as transparent to itself, propounding a gap between how thinking appears to the subject and what it really is in itself – the latter being unknown. Locke also insists that reflection is second-order awareness, presupposing sense-perception as the first mental operation. And though 'ideas in the intellect are coeval with sensation' (*Essay* II.i.23), it seems that the mind must 'retain and distinguish' ideas before it can be said to 'have ideas' dispositionally, stored in the memory for employment as signifiers in thought. Ideas of reflection in particular are achieved only 'in time' – and here 'reflection' acquires some of its modern affinity with 'contemplation'. Children, Locke's accounts of both reflection and particles imply, can discern or compound ideas without having the ideas of discerning or compounding, and few of those who employ particles to *express* various mental actions ever pay them enough attention to be able to *name* them. Locke does assert that in the reception of ideas 'the understanding is merely passive', but he also allows that attention, as well as repetition, helps 'much to the fixing any ideas in the memory' (*Essay* II.x.3).

The 'retention' of ideas in the memory, therefore, is a necessary condition of discursive thought, and its description significantly echoes Hobbes' account of memory as 'decaying sense'. What decay – 'it may seem probable' – are images in the brain, and hostility to the separation of intellect from imagination pervades the *Essay*. Descartes' famous argument for such a separation – that we can accurately reason about a chiliagon although we cannot form a distinct image of it – is directly rebutted: the reasoning is made possible by our precise idea of the number of the sides (itself dependent on the technique of counting), not by a clear and distinct idea of the shape. 'Clear' ideas are, by definition, such as we receive 'in a well-ordered sensation or perception'. Locke's treatment of abstraction accords with such express sensationism. 'Abstract ideas' are particulars, universal only in 'the capacity, they are put into ... of signifying or representing many particular things' (*Essay* III.iii.11). Locke means that in abstract thought the mind relates to, and employs, sensory images in a certain way, not that it manufactures sense-transcendent objects of intellect. Abstract ideas are what we have *distinctly* before the mind in general thought, but distinctness may be achieved by 'partial consideration', not absolute separation: 'Many ideas require others as necessary to their existence or conception, which are yet very distinct ideas. Motion can neither be, nor be conceived without space' (*Essay* II.xiii.11–13). The very abstract ideas of *being* and *unity* are ideas of anything whatsoever considered as existing, or as one. Geometry gave Locke his paradigm of 'perception of the relation between ideas'. But where Cartesians saw the role of geometrical diagrams to be the stimulation of intellectual ideas, for Locke, as for Hobbes, the object of reasoning and source of 'evidence' is the diagram itself, whether actual or imagined. (Kant's 'intuition' owes something to Locke.) Given these structural features of his theory, it seems undeniable, as some have denied, that Locke's ideas are essentially sensory (or reflexive) images (see HOBBES, T. §4; KANT, I. §5).

4 Five sorts of idea

Book II of the *Essay* presents an alternative to Aristotle's doctrine of categories, the traditional typology of entities capable of being named or predicated (see ARISTOTLE §7). That Locke's classification is of *ideas* rather than of *things* stresses that the categories are purely conceptual. He identifies five broad types: simple ideas, ideas of simple modes, ideas of mixed modes, ideas of substances and ideas of relations. Simple ideas come first in the Lockean order of knowledge, as substances come first in the Aristotelian order of being. Simple ideas are necessarily given in experience, whereas complex ideas can be constructed by 'enlarging' ('repeating') or 'compounding' simple ideas. Ideas of relations result from 'comparing' ideas. 'Abstracting' is more a matter of focusing on an idea or, better, an aspect of an idea, whether given or constructed, than of creating a new one (see §3). Locke sometimes acknowledges

that the overarching compositional model is problematic in its application, but it is put into doubt even by his formal introduction of the notion of a simple idea. The ideas of the sensible qualities of a body, Locke claims, though produced by the same body, in some cases by the same sense, are evidently distinct from one another, each being 'nothing but *one uniform appearance*, or conception in the mind' (*Essay* II.ii.1). Yet to ascribe the conceptual distinctions between, for example, a thing's shape, its motion and its colour to a primitive articulation of *appearance* is to beg a crucial question.

Under the topic of simple ideas Locke expounds his famous distinction between primary and secondary qualities (*Essay* II.viii). Since the cause of a simple idea may be quite different in character from the idea itself, we should distinguish the idea in the mind from the corresponding quality (that is, the power to cause the idea) in bodies. Certain qualities, however, are necessary to our conception of bodies as such. These are the primary qualities, 'solidity, extension, figure, motion, or rest, and number', just those which figured in corpuscularian speculations. Locke's proposal (displaying the tension, described in §3 of this entry, between two conceptions of representation) is that in the perception of a primary quality the represented cause, the basis of the power in the object, is qualitatively *like* the idea caused: 'A circle and square are the same, whether in idea or existence' (*Essay* II.viii.18). Only this will allow that the action of external bodies on the senses is 'by *impulse*, the only way which we can conceive bodies operate in' (*Essay* II.viii.12) – an appeal to the seventeenth-century commonplace that mechanical explanations are peculiarly intelligible. But then ideas of 'colours, sounds, tastes, etc.', Locke's 'secondary qualities', must also be mechanically stimulated. Hence secondary qualities 'are nothing in the objects themselves, but powers to produce various sensations in us by their primary qualities, i.e. by the bulk, figure, texture, and motion of their insensible parts' (*Essay* II.viii.10). Ontologically they are in the same boat as the power of fire to cause pain or, indeed, its power to melt wax.

The idea of power itself Locke attributes to experience of regular patterns of change, giving rise first to expectations that 'like changes will for the future be made in the same things, by like agents, and by the like ways', and then to the thought that in one thing exists the possibility of being changed and in another 'the possibility of making that change' (*Essay* II.xxi.1). So we form the idea of power, active and passive: the power of fire to melt wax and the power of wax to be melted are aspects of fire and wax known and identified only through their joint effect. The idea of power is thus a place-marker for attributes which could in principle be known more directly.

The ideas or experiences of pleasure and pain are important simple ideas, since they are responsible for our ideas of good and evil, and are 'the hinges on which our passions turn' (*Essay* II.xx.3). (This hedonistic theory of motivation and value is examined in §9 of this entry.)

'Simple modes' constitute another problematic category. Locke starts with modes of extension, the subject-matter of geometry, with which he compares modes of duration. Here his thesis is that we acquire ideas of particular modes of extension (that is, determinate lengths and figures) or duration (that is, periods) in experience, and can then repeat (or divide) them so as to construct ideas of possible lengths, figures or periods not previously experienced. Roughly, 'modification' here is compounding like with like. The same model supplies Locke's account of ideas of numbers, achieved by the repetition or addition of units, aided and ordered by the linguistic technique of counting. Yet he also recognizes qualitative simple modes, effectively conceding that ideas of different 'shades of the same [experienced] colour' are constructible. Even with quantitative 'modes', where the 'repetition' model has some plausibility, it is problematic what is a simple idea. The idea of determinable *extension* is a plausible candidate, with its determinates as 'modes', but the repetition model presupposes simple units. Locke impatiently responds that the smallest sensible point 'may perhaps be the fittest to be consider'd by us as a *simple idea* of that kind' (*Essay* (5th edn) II.xv.5n.), but he was evidently more concerned to argue that ideas of novel determinate figures are *somehow* constructible from what has been given, and so to subvert a Platonic-Cartesian argument for innateness, than to insist on the adequacy of a rigid compositional model.

Another target in Locke's account of simple modes is Descartes' conceptual identification of space and matter in the thesis that the essence of matter is extension. For Locke, both the essence of matter and the nature of space are unknown. He argues that our idea of a vacuum is not contradictory, since our ordinary idea of body includes solidity as well as extension, but he declines to choose between relational and realist theories of space. Yet comparison of the *Essay* with earlier notes and drafts indicates that, having first held a Hobbesian relational view, Locke came gradually to favour a realism close to that of Newton (see DESCARTES, R. §§8, 11; NEWTON, I.).

Ideas of mixed modes arise with the combination of unlike simple ideas, as in the idea of a rainbow. But Locke's paradigms are ideas of human actions and institutions, the materials of demonstrative moral and political theory. Like ideas of geometrical figures, ideas of mixed modes can properly be formed without regard to what exists. Ethical thought is none the worse for being about a virtue or motive or political constitution which is nowhere actually instantiated. Ideas of substances are different, for they concern the real rather than the ideal: 'When we speak of *justice*, or *gratitude* ... our thoughts terminate in the abstract ideas of those virtues, and look not further; as they do, when we speak of a *horse*, or *iron*, whose specific ideas we consider not, as barely in the mind, but as in things themselves, which afford the original patterns of those ideas' (*Essay* III.v.12). Moreover, whereas ideas of substances are formed on the presumption that the complex idea represents a really or naturally united thing, the unity of mixed modes is essentially conceptual. Indeed, 'Though ... it be the mind that makes the collection, tis the name which is, as it were the knot, that ties them fast together'. Different languages slice up the field of human life and action in different ways, determined by the practices and priorities of the communities that speak them. This thesis can be extended to natural modes such as freezing, since even here it is the term tied to a striking appearance, not a natural boundary, which slices out the particular process from the general process of nature. That, Locke plausibly assumes, is not how it is with horses.

The chief thought behind Locke's somewhat confusing account of ideas of substances is that our idea of a thing or stuff is a compound of ideas of its qualities, but the thing itself is not a compound of qualities (*Essay* II.xxiii). The substance–accident structure is a feature of our ideas and language, not a structure in reality. It is a feature which marks our ignorance of the underlying nature of things, since we always conceive and talk of a substance as a *thing* possessing certain qualities, that is, as a '*substratum*, in which [the qualities] do subsist, and from which they do result, which therefore we call substance'. The mistake of dogmatic philosophers is to think that they can form *simple* conceptions of substances matching their unitary natures. Aristotelians are so misled by language that, just because, 'for quick despatch', we employ one name, 'gold' or 'swan', they think it a 'simple term' corresponding to a 'simple apprehension'. Cartesians take the simple essences of matter and spirit to be extension and thought. Yet so far are we from catching the nature of any thing in our *complex* idea of it that, if it is asked what the subject is of the qualities by which we define it (the colour and weight of gold, for example), the best answer we can give is 'the solid extended parts', that is, the mechanistic 'corpuscularian' hypothesis as advanced by Boyle. If it is asked in turn 'what it is, that solidity and extension inhere in,' we can only say, 'we know not what'. Our idea of the substance is of 'nothing, but the supposed, but unknown support of those qualities, we find existing, which we imagine cannot subsist, *sine re substante*, without something to support them'. Such an idea is 'obscure and relative'. Ideas of specific substances are 'nothing but several combinations of simple ideas, co-existing in such, though unknown, cause of their union as makes the whole subsist of itself' (*Essay* II.xxiii.6). Locke's point is that no theory, not even the corpuscular hypothesis, gives an account of the ultimate nature of things.

Finally come ideas of relations – father, son-in-law, enemy, young, blacker, lawful and so on (*Essay* II.xxv–xxviii). Like ideas of modes, ideas of relations can properly be constructed without regard to reality, in particular if they are conventional relations. Adequate ideas even of natural relations, Locke claims, are possible without adequate ideas of the things related: we can grasp the essence of fatherhood without knowing the essence of man or even the mechanisms of reproduction. His point is that the biological details are irrelevant to the rights and duties of a father – a question rationally determined in his own attack on patriarchalism in *Two Treatises*. From this point of view, relations are theoretically close to modes. Yet Locke does allow certain relations to have peculiar ontological significance. Causal, spatial and temporal relations are universal relations which pertain to all finite beings. Identity and diversity are so too: a thing is diverse from anything existing in a different place at the same time, 'how like and indistinguishable soever it may be in all other respects', and the continuity of individual substances is spatio-temporal. The last important type of relations to be picked out for special discussion is that of moral relations, or the relations of actions to some law 'whereby good or evil is drawn on us, from the will and power of the law-maker' (*Essay* II.viii.5).

5 Substances, mixed modes and the improvement of language

On Locke's account of communication (*Essay* III.i–ii), names should, by common convention or special agreement, excite in the hearer's mind just the same ideas as they are associated with in the speaker's mind. Collaborative progress in the sciences depends on 'clear and distinct' or 'determined and determinate' ideas – that is, on consistent and agreed association of ideas and words (*Essay* II.xxix; compare 'Epistle to the Reader'). Locke's discussion of language is shaped by his belief that these conditions of the transference of knowledge were in his time commonly unsatisfied, especially in two domains. First, there was no agreed classification of 'substances' (living things and chemicals) based on careful observation and experiment. Second, the ideas associated with the names of mixed modes often varied both in the usage of different people and in that of the same person at different times. Two mistakes in particular disguise these shortcomings of language. The first is the assumption that a common set of words ensures a common language in the full sense, with a shared set of meanings. So people may argue about 'honour' and 'courage' without realizing that they mean different things, or nothing at all, by the words. The second mistaken assumption is that words have meaning by standing for things directly, as if the meaning of 'salt', 'gold' or 'fish' were fixed demonstratively, by what is named. The first assumption chiefly corrupts our thought about mixed modes, the second relates 'more particularly, to substances, and their names' (*Essay* III.ii.5). Locke's radical and influential views about the latter will be considered first.

The 'idea of substance in general' employed in ideas of specific substances is the idea of something unknown underlying the attributes known by experience (see §4 of this entry). Many have objected, following Leibniz, that here Locke confusedly postulates ignorance of the subject of attributes which is not ignorance of attributes of the subject. Yet he holds that our ignorance of 'the substance of body' and 'the substance of spirit' is an ignorance of the *natures* of these things – ignorance manifested in our inability to understand the internal cohesion or (he adds in later writings) mutual attraction of bodies, or to explain what thinks in us, and how it does so. His approval of the corpuscularian hypothesis and Newton's mechanics is qualified – the best available physical theory leaves too much unexplained to be the whole truth (Newton did not disagree). The idea of substance is a place-marker for essences which are unknown, but knowable, if possibly not by human beings (see NEWTON, I.).

One feature of Locke's theory which has made difficulties for the present interpretation is the distinction he makes between substance and 'real essence'. The real essence of a thing, Locke says, may be taken for 'the very being of a thing, whereby it is what it is', the 'real internal, but generally in substances, unknown constitution of things, whereon their discoverable qualities depend' (*Essay* III.iii.15). Nevertheless, 'essence, in the ordinary use of the word, relates to sorts' (*Essay* III.vi.4). Species and genera, or sorts of things, Locke asserts, are creatures of the understanding, with membership determined by abstract ideas made on the basis of experienced resemblances, not by the presence in each of a specific form, or by a common derivation from a divine archetype. Ultimately it is a matter of arbitrary definition which observable resemblances we count as necessary for membership of this or that named sort. It is not just that specific real essences are unknown, since (Locke argues) even if we did know the real constitution of things as well as clock-makers know the works of clocks, it would still be up to us where to draw the boundaries between species, and what to include in our abstract ideas or 'nominal essences'. The real essence of a species can therefore only be 'that real constitution ... which is the foundation of all those properties, that are combined in, and are constantly found to co-exist with, the *nominal essence*' of the species (*Essay* III.vi.6). Here, the model is that of a universal matter determinately modified as a variety of particles interacting mechanically so as to constitute the material things of ordinary experience. Since at the fundamental level these observable quasi-machines differ from one another merely quantitatively, and can do so by indefinite degrees, there are no absolute boundaries among them. There are only the discernible resemblances and differences consequent on their underlying mechanical differences – 'the wheels, or springs ... within'. Even more certainly our actual classification is not based on knowledge of any such boundaries. Talk of the real essence of a species, and the distinction between its 'properties' and its 'accidents' ('properties' flowing from the essence), are therefore, contrary to Aristotelian assumptions, *de dicto* and relative to the nominal essence defining the name of that species (see ARISTOTLE §8; DE RE/DE DICTO; ESSENTIALISM).

This conception of a real essence assigns it a role closely related to that of substance. What, after all, is the 'unknown cause of the union' of any of the 'combinations of simple ideas' by which 'we represent particular sorts of substances to ourselves', if not the real essence underlying the nominal essence in question? Yet Locke sometimes distinguishes both the notion and knowledge of real essence from the notion and knowledge of substance. That is not, however, because the 'substance' is an irremediably unknown subject underlying even essence, but because it is the common stuff of a variety of species of things, 'as a tree and a pebble, being in the same sense body, and agreeing in the common nature of body, differ only in a bare modification of that common matter' (*Essay* II.xiii.18). The unknown modification is the specific 'real essence', and the equally unknown general nature of matter is the 'substance'. Locke also envisages deeper differences of kind between substances: 'God, spirits and body' are all 'substances' only because we think of each of them indeterminately as *something*, not because of a shared nature. But by the same token we distinguish spirit and body only because we cannot understand how matter could think, not because we can grasp their separate essences, as Descartes had supposed (see DESCARTES, R. §8). Indeed, since we are equally unable to understand how spirit and body might interact, or how spirits could occupy places, the issue between materialist and immaterialist accounts of minds is for Locke undecidable, and at best a matter for speculation.

Locke's corpuscularian conception of a world of machines, resembling and differing from one another by continuous degrees, is consonant with his independent epistemological conviction that names have meaning only through association with 'ideas', rather than directly with 'things as really they are'. Together they motivate his programme for improving natural classification which advocates, not the allegedly impossible Aristotelian ideal of identifying the natural hierarchy of genera and species, but general agreement on a practically useful way of gathering and ordering the things in the world, taking into account such dependable concomitances of qualities and powers as appear to careful observation and experiment. Locke saw the future of biology and chemistry – and even of mechanics – in descriptive 'natural history', justifiable as a useful, orderly record of dependable means to ends but falling short of systematic 'science'. Despite its apparent pessimism, his view has survived in biological taxonomy as a continuous tradition of scepticism as to the reality of our taxonomical divisions. In semantic theory, Locke's broad conception of how the names of substances have meaning has only recently been eclipsed by a quasi-Aristotelian view (see KRIPKE, S.A.; PUTNAM, H.).

Locke saw equal need for a programme of agreeing definitions in ethics, where his target is less the notion that moral and political terms name independent realities, than the assumption that the very existence of a word in a language ensures that it has a fixed, common meaning. 'Common use', Locke concedes, 'regulates the meaning of words pretty well for common conversation' (*Essay* III.ix.8) – for the 'civil' rather than 'philosophical' use of words. But where precision is required, as in the establishment or interpretation of a law or moral rule, reliance on ordinary usage leaves us vulnerable to the trickery of rhetoricians who prove bad qualities good by shifting the meaning of terms; or to the subtleties of interpretors, whether of civil or revealed law, who render unintelligible what started off plain. The remedy is to give the names of virtues and vices, and of social actions, roles and relations the fixed and unequivocal definitions necessary for a clear and unwavering view of right and wrong, 'the conformity or disagreement of our actions to some law'.

6 Knowledge and belief

Like Platonists and Cartesians, Locke drew a strong distinction between knowledge and belief (also called opinion, judgment, or assent), but the ground and placing of this division between two forms of propositional 'affirmation' differed from theirs fundamentally. As the distinction is expounded in Book IV of the *Essay*, universal knowledge or 'science' does not have special objects, whether a transcendent intelligible world in the mind of God or innate intellectual ideas. Its difference from general belief lies in the way in which ideas are related in the mind. In universal knowledge, the 'connection and agreement, or disagreement and repugnancy' of ideas is 'perceived', whereas in belief it is 'presumed' on the basis of 'something extraneous to the thing I believe'. To follow a proof gives knowledge of the conclusion, whereas to accept the conclusion on the authority of a mathematician constitutes only belief. Similarly in the case of 'sensitive knowledge' of particular existence, what we ourselves perceive we know to be so, but what we infer, or accept on testimony, we merely believe.

Knowledge, as well as assent, is subject to 'degrees': there are degrees, not only of probability, but of 'evidence'. The first degree of knowledge is intuitive knowledge, in which the mind 'perceives the truth, as the eye doth light, only by being directed toward it'. Intuition 'leaves no room for hesitation, doubt, or examination'. The second degree is demonstrative knowledge, where the truth is perceived by the aid of one or a chain of 'intermediate ideas'. Doubt or mistake is possible at any point in the sequence with respect to connections not currently in view. Hence, 'Men embrace often falsehoods for demonstration'. Locke's chief model for 'intermediate ideas' is geometrical: for example, the lines employed in the intermediate steps of the Euclidean proof which allow us to see that the angles of a triangle are equal to the angle on a straight line. Although his conception of intuition can seem Cartesian, the profound difference is that, for Locke, ideas which are objects of intuition are essentially a product of sense (including reflection) and imagination. As *Draft B* puts it, the angles and figures I contemplate may be 'drawn upon paper, carved in marble, or only fancied in my understanding' (*Drafts* vol. 1: 152). Consequently Locke often talks as if we can *literally* perceive a necessary relation between ideas. Another difference from Descartes, as also from Hobbes, is that he rejects the

pretensions of proposed analytical methods to uncover self-evident principles from which the phenomena can be deduced.

The third degree of knowledge is sensitive knowledge of the existence or 'co-existence' of qualities in external things. Locke's first introduction of this category seems tentative, even an afterthought, as if it is called knowledge only by courtesy. In order to fit his main definition of knowledge it has to be interpreted as the perception of the agreement of ideas of sensible qualities with the idea of existence, an analysis Locke unsurprisingly declines to develop. Yet 'sensitive knowledge of existence' does straightforwardly satisfy his other definition of knowledge: what is known in sensitive knowledge (that is, that something external is causing an idea of sense) is known directly, 'perceived' and not inferred (see §2 of this entry). Locke was writing in a context in which, despite Gassendi's Epicurean claim that sensory knowledge is the most evident of all, it was widely assumed that knowledge in the full sense comprises only knowledge of necessary first principles, demonstrated 'science', and perhaps reflexive knowledge. Locke wanted both to concede to orthodoxy that the evidence and certainty of our sensory knowledge is not as high as that of intuition and demonstration, and to insist that, nevertheless, 'sensitive knowledge of existence' does give a degree of immediate certainty and 'deserves the name of knowledge'.

Knowledge is also categorized in terms of four propositional relations (forms of 'agreement') between ideas, namely 'identity (or diversity)', 'relation', 'necessary connection or coexistence' and 'existence' (*Essay* IV.i). By 'identity' Locke intends tautologies such as 'Gold is gold' and 'Red is not blue'. Intuitive knowledge of such identities is achieved simply by discerning ideas. The category also includes such truths as 'Gold is a metal' or 'Gold is malleable', when the property predicated is included in the thinker's definition of gold. Thus 'identity' covers all and only 'trifling' or 'verbal' propositions (see §2 of this entry).

The categories, 'relation', 'necessary connection or coexistence', and 'existence', on the other hand, together include all 'instructive' propositions. The category, 'relation', in part a response to Locke's earlier difficulty over the informativeness of mathematics (see §2 of this entry), also marks his rejection of analytical methods in science. As well as geometrical axioms and theorems, 'relation' presumably includes more exciting Lockean principles: as that, if anything changes, something must have a power to make it change; that, if anything exists, something must have existed from eternity; and that a maker has rights over his artefact. Categorical propositions about natural things, however, fall either under 'existence' or under 'necessary connection or coexistence'. Our own existence is known intuitively, God's existence demonstratively (Locke employs an idiosyncratic hybrid of the cosmological and teleological proofs), and, as discussed, the existence of bodies by sense. The category 'necessary connection or coexistence' owes its disjunctive name to a rather complicated relation between particular and universal propositions. Particular *coexistences* are perceived by sense, for example, when we simply observe that yellowness, heaviness and the metallic qualities coexist in a particular subject together with malleability (that is, that this gold is malleable), without perceiving *necessary connections* between them. Locke assumes, however, with most mechanists, that necessary connections do hold between universally coexistent properties even if we cannot perceive or grasp them. Since he contends that no natural science based on the essences of substances has been achieved, he offers only very limited examples of perceived necessary connections, as 'whatever is solid is impenetrable' and 'a body struck by another will move'. (According to the short, posthumously published *Elements of Natural Philosophy*, the laws of inertia are evidently necessary, but the law of gravity is based only on experience.) In the absence of knowledge, beliefs in universal coexistences (for example, that all gold dissolves in aqua regia), when we *presume* unperceived connections, may be inductively based on sensitive knowledge of particular coexistences. That is descriptive natural 'history', not 'science'. In general, if the idea of a particular quality is deducible from the idea of a substance, that is only because the predication of that quality is an identity: that is, universal propositions about substances, if certain, are 'trifling' and, if 'instructive', are uncertain (see §2 of this entry). In contrast, instructive a priori sciences are possible just because their objects are constructed by us: our ideas of simple or mixed modes, formed without essential reference to actuality, themselves constitute the subject-matter of mathematics and ethics. In other words, these demonstrative sciences are possible, as natural science is not, just because they deal, hypothetically, with abstractions.

The degrees of assent are 'Belief, Conjecture, Guess, Doubt, Wavering, Distrust, Disbelief, etc.' (*Essay* IV.xvi). Probability is 'the measure whereby [the] several degrees [of assent] are, or ought to be regulated'. When assent is unreasonable, it constitutes 'error'. Reasonable assent is regulated according to the proposition's conformity with the thinker's own experience or the testimony of others. The proposition may concern 'matters of fact' falling within human experience, or else unobservables lying 'beyond the discovery of our

senses'. Locke identifies four broad degrees of probability with respect to 'matters of fact': (1) when the general consent of others concurs with the subject's constant experience; (2) when experience and testimony suggest that something is so for the most part; (3) when unsuspected witnesses report what experience allows might as well be so as not; and (4) when 'the reports of history and witnesses clash with the ordinary course of nature, or with one another' – a situation in which there are no 'precise rules' for assessing probability. Finally, with respect to unobservables, 'a wary reasoning from analogy' with what falls within our experience 'is the only [natural] help we have' and the only ground of probability (see DESCARTES, R. §4). Although Locke, in striking contrast to Descartes, brings probability into the centre of epistemology, 'belief' is always treated as a practical surrogate for 'knowledge', and he takes induction itself to be grounded on the assumption of underlying, unknown necessary connections: 'For what our own and other men's constant observation has found always to be after the same manner, that we with reason conclude to be the effects of steady and regular causes, though they come not within the reach of our knowledge' (*Essay* IV.xvi.6).

Another deliberate and radical difference from Descartes relates to the role of will in cognition. For Locke, knowledge is like sense perception: we may choose where and how hard to look, but we cannot then choose what we see. Belief is similar: 'Assent is no more in our power than knowledge.... And what upon full examination I find the most probable, I cannot deny my assent to' (*Essay* IV.xx.16). Yet we are morally responsible for both error and ignorance in so far as it results from our not employing our faculties as we should. In a number of chapters of the *Essay*, Locke examines the causes of error, finding them, with many writers of his time, in the same appetites, interests, passions, wayward imaginings and associations of ideas as may motivate voluntary actions. Linguistic confusion, and its deliberate exploitation (see §5 of this entry), sometimes plays a role, and sometimes, like MALEBRANCHE and others, Locke has direct recourse to physiology, explicitly merging his explanations of error with explanations of madness. In contrast to Hobbes, he places the merely habitual 'association of ideas' in the pathology of 'extravagent' thought and action: 'all which seems to be but trains of motion in the animal spirits, which...continue on in the same steps...which by often treading are worn into a smooth path, and the motion in it becomes easy and as it were natural' (*Essay* II.xxxiii.16). But culpable error arises, on Locke's official view, when we 'hinder both knowledge and assent, by stopping our enquiry, and not employing our faculties in the search of any truth' (*Essay* IV.xx.16). It is the failure to use our power to pause for 'full examination' which leaves a space for beliefs motivated by interests and passions. But this two-stage model – the first stage voluntary, the second involuntary – proves too difficult to maintain, and sometimes passions and interests are taken to act on the will *between* inquiry and judgment, by distorting our 'measures of probability' themselves. Locke's approach is more commonsensical than that of Descartes, but the psychology of motivated error is a hard nut which he also failed to crack.

7 Faith, reason and toleration

Locke's views on belief, probability and error owed much to traditional philosophy of religious belief, and to the great debate of his century about the relationship between faith and reason. He was strongly influenced by writers in the Anglican 'probabilist' tradition, who argued for toleration within the Church with respect to all but an essential core of Christian dogma. William Chillingworth had rejected as absurd the traditional conception of a moral requirement to have 'faith' in the sense of a conviction equal to that of knowledge but beyond what is rationally justified. To recognize a proposition as probable to a certain degree is to believe it just to that degree. Revelation therefore cannot be a basis for belief distinct from probability, but is something the significance of which has to be rationally assessed, capable at best of increasing the probability of certain propositions. Similarly for Locke, when revelation grounds belief that would otherwise be improbable, that is just one natural reason outweighing another: 'it still belongs to reason to judge of the truth of its being a revelation, and of the signification of the words, wherein it is delivered' (*Essay* IV.xviii.8). For if 'reason must not examine their truth by something extrinsical to the perswasions themselves; inspirations and delusions, truth and falshood will have the same measure' (*Essay* IV.xix.14).

Accordingly, like Chillingworth, MORE and others, Locke combined a purportedly reasonable acceptance of the Bible as revelation with a critical approach to its interpretation, taking into account that it was written by men in particular circumstances. An alleged revelation which conflicts with what is naturally evident loses its claim to be revelation. Certain revealed truths (such as the Resurrection) lie 'beyond the discovery of our natural faculties, and above reason', but Locke had little time for mysteries: 'to this crying up of faith, in opposition to reason, we may, I think, in good measure, ascribe those absurdities that fill almost all the religions which possess and divide mankind'

(*Essay* IV.xviii.7, 11). Locke took the existence of God and the content of moral law to be demonstrable by reason, and, according to *The Reasonableness of Christianity* and its *Vindications*, the only essentially revealed truth of the New Testament is that Christ is the Messiah, promising forgiveness of sins to those who sincerely repent and do their imperfect best to keep the law of nature. The Bible also makes that law plain to those without the leisure or capacity to reason it out – a difficult enough task for anyone, as Locke ruefully acknowledges. The meaning of scripture is thus for Locke primarily moral, and the 'truth, simplicity, and reasonableness' of Christ's teaching is itself a main reason for accepting it as revelation. Saving faith involves works, not acceptance of 'every sentence' of the New Testament under this or that preferred interpretation.

Much the same goes for immediate revelation. Even the genuinely inspired would need proofs that they really were inspired, and the errors of commonplace 'enthusiasm' are ascribed, as by More, to physiology, 'the conceits of a warmed or overweening brain'. The advocate of immediate personal revelation over reason 'does much what the same, as if he would persuade a man to put out his eyes the better to receive the remote light of an invisible star by a telescope' (*Essay* IV.xix.4). Divine illumination necessarily depends on, and is not separable from, the natural light – 'reason must be our last judge and guide in everything'. Locke echoes Chillingworth's basic principle: the lover of truth, unbiased by interest or passion, will not entertain 'any proposition with greater assurance than the proofs it is built upon will warrant'. The implication of this standard, in the actual circumstances of life, is toleration: 'For where is the man, that has incontestable evidence of the truth of all that he holds, or of the falshood of all he condemns; or can say, that he has examined, to the bottom, all his own, or other men's opinions?' (*Essay* IV.xvi.4).

Locke's *Letter on Toleration*, the mature fruit of considerably more unpublished writing directly on the issue, links his epistemology with his political thinking. Belief is not something that can be commanded or submitted to the authority of the government, whose concern is not with saving souls but the preservation of property. Necessarily each individual must judge as they see fit, and the truth needs no help, having its own efficacy. But the right to toleration is nevertheless viewed in the context of the right and duty to seek salvation and true doctrine without harm to others, harm which is at least threatened by all who deny the authority either of moral law or of the established government. Atheists therefore forfeit the right in principle, and Roman Catholics as a matter of political fact. (See SOCINIANISM.)

8 Personal identity

The main aim of the chapter of the *Essay* entitled 'Of Identity and Diversity' (II.xxvii) is to explain how immortality is compatible with materialism. In order to maintain an agnostic neutrality on the question of the immateriality of the soul, Locke had, first, to rebut the Cartesian claim that self-awareness supplies a clear and distinct idea of a simple, continuously existing substance; and, second, to show that the metaphysical issue is irrelevant to 'the great ends of morality and religion' (*Essay* IV.iii.6). He argues that, although the moral agent is indeed the continuously existing, rational, self-aware subject of consciousness, the 'person', the identity of this subject over time, is determined by the continuity of unitary consciousness itself, not the continuity of an immaterial soul. Locke can therefore accept the Resurrection and Last Judgment as tenets of his 'reasonable' Christianity, without commitment to dualism, on the supposition that the consciousness of the resurrected person is continuous, through memory, with that of the person who died. This conclusion avoids an objection to his concept of demonstrative ethics as a science of modes, that morality relates to 'man', a substance, not a mode. His response is that morality concerns, not 'man' as a biological species, but 'man' as rational, the 'moral man', indeed all rational beings. 'Person', as he puts it, is a 'forensic term'.

Locke's argument starts from the claim that questions of identity over time are always questions as to the continuous existence in space of something of a certain kind, and that difficulties may be avoided by 'having precise notions of the things to which it is attributed'. The identity of non-substances is parasitic on that of substances: 'All other things being but modes or relations ultimately terminated in substances', their identity will be determined 'by the same way' (*Essay* II.xxvii.2). Locke holds that events and processes ('actions') are not strictly identical from moment to moment, each part of what we consider one process being distinct from every other part. Substances, however, genuinely continue to exist from moment to moment. The identity of 'simple substances' – material atoms and the presumed simple 'intelligences' – is straightforward. Each excludes others of the same kind out of its place by its very existence – a principle definitive of identity. But difficulties arise with compound substances. Strictly, a body composed of many atoms is the same just as long as the same atoms compose it – yet 'an oak, growing from a plant to a great tree, and then lopped, is still the same oak'. Locke's explanation is that 'in these two cases of a mass of matter, and a living body, *identity* is not applied to the same thing' (*Essay* II.xxvii.3).

Although he does not clearly distinguish the two views, he seems to hold individuation, rather than the identity-relation, to be kind-relative. A plant or animal is not just 'a cohesion of particles anyhow united', but such an organization of parts as enables the continuation of its characteristic life, for example, as an oak. In fact the *species* of the living thing is irrelevant to Locke's theory (fortunately, given his view that the definition of 'oak' will differ from speaker to speaker). The essential claim is that life is a principle of unity and continuity distinct from simple cohesion, thus allowing a living thing and the mass of matter that momentarily composes it so to differ in kind as to be capable of occupying the same place at the same time.

Locke defines *person* as 'a thinking intelligent being, that has reason and reflection, and can consider itself as itself, the same thinking thing at different times and places' (*Essay* II.xxvii.9). His thesis is that, just as life constitutes a distinct individuative principle of unity and continuity, so does reflexive consciousness. He argues for the logical independence of the continuity of consciousness from both the continuity of substance (whether supposed material or immaterial, simple or complex) and the continuity of animal life by a series of imagined cases: for example, for someone now to possess Socrates' soul would not make him the same person as Socrates, unless he remembered Socrates' actions as his own; whereas if souls are the seat of consciousness, and the soul of a prince could migrate to the body of a cobbler, 'everyone sees he would be the same person with the prince, accountable only for the prince's actions. But who would say it was the same man?' (*Essay* II.xxvii.15). Locke viewed such cases, not necessarily as real possibilities, but as compatible with our partial understanding of things, our *ideas*: 'for such as is the idea belonging to that name [namely 'person', 'man' or 'substance'], such must be the identity'. Yet in the crucial case of the Resurrection, we are left wondering how continuous existence through time – not to speak of space – is achieved simply by a fit between present consciousness and past experience and actions. Indeed, as BERKELEY and REID argued, memory-links seem both too little and too much for the continuity of a substantial thing. Yet, despite these and other difficulties for Locke's theory, it set the agenda for subsequent discussion and versions of it still have adherents (see PERSONAL IDENTITY).

9 Ethics, motivation and free will

With Locke's conviction that a demonstrative ethics is possible went a belief that what stood in its way was the deplorable slipperiness, openly encouraged by the practice of rhetoric, of a moral language in which terms are not consistently tied to ideas (see §5 of this entry). Both were consonant with his apparently early conviction that Natural Law theory, as pursued by such as HOOKER and GROTIUS, is capable of development into a full account of our duties to God and our fellows – even though he had first seen Natural Law as empirically based (see §3 of this entry). But Natural Law theory also gave him what could not be supplied by the conception of a quasi-geometrical system of rights and duties flowing from the definitions of mixed modes and relations: the conception of an unconditional obligation to act in accordance with moral principle against what we might otherwise desire (see NATURAL LAW).

In the *Essay* the argument starts, as might be expected, with the question of how our basic concepts of value are derived from experience. Locke has no doubt about what it is in experience that makes anything matter to us. Like other empiricists of his time, he is both a psychological and an ethical hedonist. Pleasure and pain supply not only our sole motives but also our ideas of good and evil: 'That we call *good* which is *apt to cause or increase pleasure, or diminish pain in us; or else to procure, or preserve us the possession of any other good, or absence of any evil*' (*Essay* II.xx.1). The passions are 'modes' of pleasure and pain arising from, or involving, value-judgments: thus hope is 'that pleasure in the mind, which every one finds in himself, upon the thought of a probable future enjoyment of a thing, which is apt to delight him'; fear is 'an uneasiness of the mind, upon the thought of a future evil likely to befall us' (*Essay* II.xx.9–10). Desire is the 'uneasiness a man finds in himself upon the absence of any thing, whose present enjoyment carries the idea of delight with it' (*Essay* II.xx.6). This theory of motivation faces certain problems. First, how do we get from judgments of good and evil, of what conduces to pleasure and pain, to judgments of right and wrong, of what we morally ought or ought not to do? Second, having got there, if the passions, as modes of pleasure and pain, constitute our only motives, what passion could motivate us to do what is right? Third, in what, if anything, does choice and free will – moral agency – consist?

Locke's answer to the first question, already given in *Essays on the Law of Nature*, is that the concept of obligation comes with the relational concept of law: 'Morally good and evil then, is only the conformity or disagreement of our voluntary actions to some law, whereby good or evil is drawn on us, from the will and power of the lawmaker; which good and evil, pleasure or pain, ... is that we call *reward* and *punishment*' (*Essay* II.xxviii.5). Locke makes it clear that the notion of obligation presupposes the right,

as well as the power of the lawgiver to legislate and punish – in *Essays* Locke's 'power' is explicitly *potestas*, authority, rather than *potentia*, mere force. There are, he says in the *Essay*, three kinds of law: divine law, the measure of sin and moral duty; civil law, the measure of crimes and innocence; and the law of opinion or reputation, the measure of virtue and vice. God legislates by *ius creationis*, the maker's right over what is made, and divine law is binding on all rational creatures capable of pleasure and pain. God's law accords with his wisdom and benevolence, so that we can know it by reflecting on what a wise and benevolent Deity would require of us. Unsurprisingly, Locke's ethics is heavily utilitarian.

The relationship between divine law and civil law, and the standing of the civil magistrate under divine law, is the subject-matter of Locke's political theory as expounded in *Two Treatises*. The notion of a 'law of reputation', sometimes called 'the philosophical law', has a more complex role in his thought. It is Locke's explanation of popular secular morality, but it also represents his view of the possibility of non-theistic philosophical systems of ethics. Roughly, the thought is that ordinary morality, sanctioned by public approval and disapproval, exists as a means to the preservation of society, itself a condition of the happiness of individuals. As arrangements differ between societies, so do their moral concepts and what counts as virtue and vice in each, although naturally there will be overlap given their shared aim of self-preservation. Since the divine law too is concerned with the good of human beings, and with self-preservation as a duty, the law of reputation will tend to coincide with divine law. In the aborted fragment of the *Essay*, 'Of Ethick in General', Locke suggests that philosophers may have some inkling of the divine law, but they confuse it with the law of reputation. Consequently their systems reduce either (like that of Hobbes) to an advocacy of what tends to the preservation of society, or (like that of Aristotle) to the elaboration of a set of definitions of the behaviour of which a particular society approves or disapproves. Locke does not deny the social importance of the law of reputation, however, and in *Some Thoughts concerning Education* he assigns a necessary role in a child's moral education to public esteem and shame. His complaint is that an explanation of moral obligation in terms of the value of certain actions to society, and the value of society to the individual, cannot explain how we may be morally obliged to do something contrary to our own felt interest – our interest, at least, in this world. Self-interest may commonly prescribe adherence to social rules, but it may not always do so. As Locke says in the *Essays on the Law of Nature* (1664) 'a great number of virtues, and the best of them, consist only in this: that we do good to others at our own loss'.

Locke's position is, then, that in order to explain both moral obligation and moral motivation (conflated in the usual seventeenth-century notion of obligation), we need to see morality as a system of laws prescribed by a supremely rational, just and benevolent creator to whom we owe the duty of obedience as creatures, and whose power to reward and punish in the next life is capable of motivating anyone who duly considers it (see VOLUNTARISM). Like any theistic explanation of morality's binding force, this proposal is incoherent, and in its case the incoherence lies in the combination of the view that obligation is created by law with the claim that we have a natural obligation to obey the law of our creator. Locke, however, was more exercised by the problem of why consideration of the afterlife so often fails to move theists to do their duty. Indeed, he accorded the problem wider scope, since he followed Pascal in the thought that the bare possibility of there being an afterlife, given the infinite good at stake, ought in reason to motivate the Christian life (see PASCAL, B.). Locke's explanation of the human capacity to know the better and choose the worse involved a refinement of his theory of motivation which echoes his theory of error. In the first edition of the *Essay*, in the long chapter 'Of Power', he held that 'the choice of the will is everywhere determined by the greater apparent good' (*Essay* II.xxi.70). By the second, he believed that mere consideration of future benefit will not move us to action unless it gives rise to 'an *uneasiness* in the want of it' – that is, to desire. Only a present passion – and, it seems, a kind of pain – can move to present action. It may require some reflection on the situation, over and above the simple recognition of probable or possible consequences for good or ill, to bring desire up to scratch, and to 'suit the relish of our minds to the true intrinsic good or ill, that is in things'. Someone who sees the good but does not pursue it has not reflected enough: 'Morality, established upon its true foundations, cannot but determine the choice of any one that will but consider' (*Essay* II.xxi.70).

Locke's increased emphasis on the role of deliberation in his hedonistic theory of moral motivation complicates his much revised account of liberty. He adopted a self-determinist view of free will – a free action is not one that is causally undetermined, but one determined by the agent's 'own desire guided by his own judgement'. He defines 'liberty' as 'the power to act or not to act according as the mind directs' (*Essay* II.xxi.71). But another power became increasingly important to him, the power 'to stand still, open the eyes, look about, and take a view of the consequence of what

we are going to do, as much as the weight of the matter requires' (*Essay* II.xxi.67), and it is in this power, he often suggests, that the liberty of rational agents really consists. The tension is unresolved, for Locke never retracts the rhetorical question to which he himself seems to have given an answer: 'For how can we think anyone freer than to have the power to do what he will?' (*Essay* II.xxi.21) (see FREE WILL).

10 Political theory

Locke's mature political theory is set out in 'An Essay concerning the True Original, Extent, and End of Civil Government', the second of *Two Treatises of Government*, the first being a point-by-point rebuttal of Robert Filmer's biblically based patriarchalism (see FILMER, R.). Locke's primary contention is that the right to govern comes with a duty to govern in the interest of the governed. Failure by the government to recognize or observe this duty creates the right to rebel. Like the Natural Law theories of Hooker, Grotius and Pufendorf on which he draws, Locke's argument moves from first principles, in effect a fragment of his proposed demonstrative ethics; but much of its richness derives from links with his practical political concerns and interests. It presents attitudes and actions attributable to Charles II and James II as a betrayal of trust, hostile to those features of the British constitution most adapted to the essential purposes of government; but he also states principles relating to property, money, social conventions, taxation, punishment, family relations, inheritance, the rights of the poor, enclosure of land, the practice and justification of colonial settlement, and more.

Filmer had argued that both political authority and property rights exist only by divine institution – by God's giving Adam dominion over the creatures, by the subjection of Eve, and by Adam's natural paternal rights over his children. Monarchs are deemed natural inheritors of Adam's rights. A part of Locke's strategy, pursued in both Treatises, against this doctrine was to drive wedges between the possession and inheritance of property and the possession and conveyance of authority, and between paternal (or, as Locke prefers, parental) authority and political authority. For example, the right of children to inherit their parents' property stems from their natural right (not just that of the eldest child) to sustenance by their parents, a right which cannot be supposed to embrace either patriarchal authority or political power. The analogy of power and property in Filmer's argument, however, was not only in relation to inheritance, for it entailed that individual ownership is simply a grant of use by the king, making taxation – its partial withdrawal – his personal right. Locke was therefore concerned to give property a quite different role in his explanation of political society.

For Locke, government is a human invention, to which personal property is prior. In a state of nature, he argues in the Second Treatise, human beings have an obligation, in accordance with divine or natural moral law, 'to preserve the rest of mankind', their equals as creatures and servants of God, by a rational extension of their duty to preserve themselves. More specifically, 'no one ought to harm another in his life, health, liberty or possessions' (*Two Treatises* II.6). Yet, before government, 'everyone has a right to punish the transgressors of that law to such a degree, as may hinder its violation'. The 'state of nature' is not, for Locke, a merely ideal abstraction, but a historical situation in which members of simple societies have lived and still live, unless in time of war, and in which independent national governments always necessarily exist. For international relations are not governed by positive law prescribed and sanctioned by constituted authority. In this situation the victim of aggression – or indeed any onlooker, for the violation is of the natural law which maintains the welfare of all – has the right to destroy the aggressor until offered peace, reparation and security for the future. Within civil society itself this 'right of war' or self-defence exists whenever the law cannot be effectively exercised, whether in the immediate circumstances of threatened harm, or when the administration of the law is manifestly corrupt, and itself employed to commit violence and injury.

'Liberty' in the state of nature is freedom from any constraint but the moral law of nature. Under government, it is freedom from the 'arbitrary will of another man', and from any human rule but the 'standing rule... common to everyone of that society' *Two Treatises* II.22). (Locke sees slavery as continuation of war – it is just if the war is just, when it is in lieu of capital punishment, the justly enslaved, like criminals, being 'outside civil society'. Yet this hardly stands as an endorsement of contemporary colonial slavery – indeed Locke denies that the children of aggressors can be justly enslaved, or even disinherited.) 'Possessions' arise in a state of nature with the act of appropriation which is a necessary condition of the use of any of the comestibles naturally available to all: 'this law of reason makes the deer, that Indian's who hath killed it' (*Two Treatises* II.30). Such appropriation is an extension of the principle that 'every man has a property in his own person', and therefore in 'the labour of his body'. Consequently whatever someone has 'mixed his labour with' is his, provided that it is for use, and 'there is enough, and as good left in

common for others' (*Two Treatises* II.27). This principle applies also to the enclosure of land for agriculture, which vastly increases its productivity. With land, as in all else, 'labour makes the far greatest part of the value of things, we enjoy in this world' (*Two Treatises* II.42). Nevertheless, before the conventional use of money, no one would have either motive or right to produce more than they could use, give to others or exchange before it spoils. To take something from the common store and let it spoil is against natural law. Money, however, is an artifice which modifies the whole nature of property rights, since it can be stored indefinitely without spoiling. Money makes it worthwhile to exploit land fully, and supplies a just means of keeping the product. So far from wronging others, enclosure and improvement greatly increase 'the common stock of mankind', making 'a day labourer in England' better off than a king among the (Native) Americans (*Two Treatises* II.41). Significant disparity of wealth becomes both possible and morally justified, on the assumption that none will suffer absolutely (in a Board of Trade paper Locke simply assumed that everyone should have 'meat, drink, clothing and firing... out of the stock of the kingdom, whether they work or no'. But the effect is greatly to complicate the administration of the law of nature, and to render its application uncertain, as well as to encourage its breach through greed.

All this, on top of the standing need for both impartiality and sufficient force to punish malefactors, necessitates government. The chief role of such government is to determine rules to order and preserve property. Common defence is another imperative. Government with such legislative and executive powers comes into existence when people, by consent, resign their 'executive power of the law of nature... to the public' (*Two Treatises* II.89). Each individual member gives consent, but is thereafter bound to move with the majority. To the objection that no such agreement has ever taken place, Locke argues that, although 'government is everywhere antecedent to records', cases abound of new or primitive societies with elected leaders. In the first instance, this may be 'some one good and excellent man' or effective general, or indeed the father of a familial group, but experience of unrestrained monarchy encourages legislatures of 'collective bodies of men', with none above the law. In any case, consent is normally tacit, and given in the active enjoyment of the benefit of the law, whether by possession of land or 'barely travelling freely on the highway'. Such tacit consent obliges obedience to the law, although the obligation lasts only as long as the enjoyment, leaving the individual free to give up the benefit and 'incorporate himself into any other commonwealth'. Express consent, however, binds the individual to obey and assist a particular government until its dissolution (or breach of trust).

A subject's ultimate obligation is to the supreme power, which is the legislative, itself bound by the law of nature in its choice of means, 'established and promulgated laws', for the preservation of its subjects and their property. Given this role, a government has no right to tax its subjects without their consent 'either by themselves, or their representatives chosen for them'. In order to minimize the risk of the legislative acting in its own, rather than in the public interest, it is best that it be an assembly which meets from time to time, separate from the continuously acting executive. A third, 'federative' power of war, peace and alliances is less easily directed by antecedent laws than the executive power, but falls naturally into the same hands, since both depend on public force. Locke allows some qualification of the absolute separation of powers, and subordination of the executive to the legislative, in recognition of the 'prerogative' power of the English king to dissolve and convene Parliament as circumstances require, and to employ discretion in the execution of the laws (Locke notes without express approval the power to veto legislation). Yet Locke sees prerogative as justified only as falling under 'the power of doing public good without a rule' in the face of unforeseen circumstances, and as dangerously capable of abuse. Its continuous employment contrary to the public good, for example by refusing to convene the legislative or by tampering with the rules for its election, makes the king himself a rebel and destroyer of the government, at war with his own subjects, returning them to a state of nature with a right to set up a new government.

11 Influence

Perhaps no modern philosopher has had a wider influence than Locke. His immediate achievement was, with Newton, to bring to an end the dominance within Europe of Cartesian science and philosophy, unseating the broadly Neoplatonic notion that mind and world share a common, divinely imposed structure, in favour of a modest, naturalistic conception of human capacities. Careful observation and systematic description are more valuable than the construction of hypotheses purportedly achieved by super-experiential means. Locke's own 'historical' treatment of the mind as a familiar, describable but deeply mysterious part of nature had considerable influence on European thought. His theory of classification influenced later

taxonomy, and his brilliantly original theory of personal identity is still a standard text for philosophical discussion. His philosophy was one of the chief influences on Kant, but can still suggest an alternative to Neo-Kantian conceptualism. If his ethical theory appears to be the last throes of early modern natural law theory rather than a new beginning, within that structure he enunciated a classic justification of responsible, tolerant and broadly democratic political society which has remained a major resource for political theorists ever since.

See also: EMPIRICISM; RATIONALISM

References and further reading

Locke, J. (1689/90) *An Essay concerning Human Understanding*, P.H. Nidditch (ed.), Clarendon Edition, Oxford: Oxford University Press, 1975. (Originally published in December 1689 but carrying the date 1690. Locke's chief and greatest work, arguing comprehensively that what we can think and know is limited by the way we experience the world, attacking dogmatic pretensions to grasp the essences of things, and affirming that 'reason must be our last judge and guide in everything', including morals and religion.)

Lowe, E.J. (1995) *Locke on Human Understanding*, London: Routledge. (A clear philosophical introduction to the *Essay* for students, making sensible use of recent scholarship in interpreting Locke's arguments.)

Yolton, J.W. (1956) *John Locke and the Way of Ideas*, Oxford: Oxford University Press. (This short but informative book, locating Locke's thought in its English context, was a landmark for historical study of his general philosophy.)

MICHAEL AYERS

LOGIC, FUZZY
See FUZZY LOGIC

LOGIC, INTENSIONAL
See INTENSIONAL LOGICS

LOGIC, INTUITIONISTIC AND ANTIREALISM
See INTUITIONISTIC LOGIC AND ANTIREALISM

LOGIC, MANY-VALUED
See MANY-VALUED LOGICS; MANY-VALUED LOGICS, PHILOSOPHICAL ISSUES IN

LOGIC, PARACONSISTENT
See PARACONSISTENT LOGIC

LOGIC, PHILOSOPHY OF

Introduction

Philosophy of logic can be roughly characterized as those philosophical topics which have emerged either from the technical development of symbolic (mathematical) logic, or from the motivations that logicians have offered for their technical pursuits. In settling on a list of subjects to classify as philosophy of logic, therefore, there is a certain degree of arbitrariness, since the issues which emerge from the technical development of logic can equally well be assigned to such areas as semantics, philosophy of language, philosophy of mathematics, epistemology, and even ethics (see SEMANTICS; LANGUAGE, PHILOSOPHY OF; MATHEMATICS, FOUNDATIONS OF).

1 The impact of modal logic
2 Logic and language

1 The impact of modal logic

In the broad area of mathematical logic, the biggest philosophical punch is packed by modal logic, including tense logic (see MODAL LOGIC; TENSE AND TEMPORAL LOGIC). Modal logic has been important since Aristotle but has only been put on a rigorous footing in the second half of the twentieth century, by such figures as Hintikka, Kanger, Prior, and most especially Kripke (see SEMANTICS, POSSIBLE WORLDS). The most important philosophical outgrowth of this mathematical work is contained in Kripke's three lectures from January 1970 published as 'Naming and Necessity', in which Kripke draws out some ways in which possible worlds semantics is in tension with then-prevailing orthodoxies in the philosophy of language and mind. Some of Kripke's views have become new orthodoxies since (see ESSENTIALISM; PROPER NAMES; REFERENCE; for related work by David Lewis, Robert Stalnaker, David Kaplan and others that uses the possible worlds framework, see COUNTERFACTUAL CONDITIONALS; DEMONSTRATIVES AND INDEXICALS; DESCRIPTIONS).

To give some flavour of developments here, consider the familiar Fregean view that the relation of *reference* which holds between a name and its bearer is sustained by the relation of *presentation* which holds between the *sense* of the name and the bearer of the name: the name refers to such-and-such an object precisely because it expresses a sense which presents that object (see FREGE, G. §3; SENSE AND REFERENCE). When pressed for an explanation of what the senses of names are like, the natural

Fregean response is to specify them, as Frege himself did in some cases, using definite descriptions (see DESCRIPTIONS). So, for instance, the sense of the name 'Aristotle' might be 'the pupil of Plato who taught Alexander'. However, though it may well in fact have been Aristotle who taught Alexander, there are many ways things might have gone (many 'possible worlds') in which someone other than Aristotle is taught by Plato and teaches Alexander: suppose Aristotle had got the appointment but been killed in an accident before he could take it up, and had been replaced at Philip's insistence by another pupil of Plato. The description 'the pupil of Plato who taught Alexander' is therefore 'non-rigid', in Kripke's terminology. That is, it can pick out different individuals in different possible worlds, and in some worlds may pick out no one (Philip for some reason comes to distrust Platonic pedagogy and fails to conduct an equal opportunity search). But it is clear from the formal semantics for modal logic that there is conceptual 'room' for a category of expression which is 'rigid', in the sense that it picks out the same object in every possible world, or at least in every possible world where it picks out any object at all. So the formal semantics prompts the question whether names in natural language behave as if their reference is determined by a sense which presents different individuals at different worlds, or whether they behave as if they are rigid designators. With a series of brilliant examples Kripke demonstrates that names are rigid designators and therefore do not express reference-determining senses which are non-rigid (see PROPER NAMES).

The idea that a formal semantics for a kind of logic provides an account of a possible semantics for a category of natural-language expression, opening the door to debate on whether it is the right account or not, also captures some of the philosophical bearing of kinds of logic other than modal logic. Thus free logic shows how name-like expressions can function without standard existential commitment; intuitionistic logic and many-valued logic show how a language can have a compositional semantics even if its sentences are not used to make statements with verification-transcendent truth-conditions which always either obtain or fail to obtain (see COMPOSITIONALITY; INTUITIONISTIC LOGIC AND ANTIREALISM; MANY-VALUED LOGICS, PHILOSOPHICAL ISSUES IN; PRESUPPOSITION). And second-order logic offers a particular way of understanding the semantic import of a range of puzzling locutions, such as plural quantifiers (see SECOND-ORDER LOGIC, PHILOSOPHICAL ISSUES IN). In all these cases the formal semantics for the logical system prompts debates about how well the semantics carries over to natural language.

2   Logic and language

There is also a collection of long-established topics discussion of which can be much improved, in rigour at least, in the light of the development of modern logic. For example, a distinction between propositions (or statements, or sentential contexts) which are *de dicto* and propositions (and so on) which are *de re* originates in medieval philosophy. But only contemporary modal logic affords the tools for a precise characterization of this distinction, although it must be granted that the distinction remains a puzzle in *epistemic* contexts (see DE RE/DE DICTO; DESCRIPTIONS). For other topics which can be classified in this way see ESSENTIALISM, EXISTENCE, IDENTITY, INDICATIVE CONDITIONALS, QUANTIFIERS and VAGUENESS. Again, to give some of the flavour of this kind of work, consider the *de re/de dicto* contrast. There is an evident syntactic difference between 'It is necessary that parents have children' and 'Parents are such that it is necessary that they have children', but just because there is a syntactic difference, it does not follow that there is any interesting difference in meaning. But the difference can be brought out quite precisely in possible worlds semantics. To say that it is necessary that parents have children is to say that in every possible world, the people who are parents *in that world* have children in that world; and this is an obvious truth. On the other hand, to say that parents are such that it is necessary that they have children is to say that the people who are parents *in the actual world* are such that they have children in every possible world. This is clearly false, even putting aside contingency of existence of actual parents. For given anyone who is actually a parent, there is a way things could have gone – a possible world – in which that person is childless, hence not a parent (see QUANTIFIERS, SUBSTITUTIONAL AND OBJECTUAL).

When a formal semantics for a system of logic is applied to a fragment of natural language, a very precise account of the literal content of sentences in that fragment is given. But there may be aspects of the meanings of those sentences which are omitted. Philosophical views may then divide over whether the formal semantics has been shown to be wanting as an account of the semantics of the fragment, or whether instead the aspects of meaning not captured have been shown not to belong to literal content (see PRESUPPOSITION). In the case of indicative conditionals, for instance, the formal semantics that is relevant is the simplest possible kind, namely, the truth-functional account of 'if . . . then . . .'. According to this account, 'If p then q' is true if p is false or if q is true, regardless of the actual meanings of p and q. So in particular, any indicative conditional with a true consequent is true; examples would include 'If lead floats in water then lead sinks in water' and 'If the solar system has nine planets then the Conservative Party lost the British elections in 1997'. Barring an astrological justification of the latter, both these conditionals look decidedly odd. But oddness is one thing, falsity another. The idea that such conditionals are false is based on the thought that if a conditional is true, then in establishing it in the most direct manner, non-redundant use has to be made of the antecedent. Spelling this out leads to relevance logic (see RELEVANCE LOGIC AND ENTAILMENT; INDICATIVE CONDITIONALS). On the other hand, if we say the conditionals are merely odd, we are led to some theory of communication to explain the oddness (see GRICE, H.P.; IMPLICATURE).

But we should not take away the impression that the traffic is all one way, from logic to language or from pure mathematics to pure philosophy. There is a two-way street here, with the above comments on conditionals representing a common phenomenon; that of a concern in the philosophy of language giving rise to a formal development which in turn feeds back into philosophy. For example, the idea that for a conditional to be true, the most direct way of establishing it must make non-redundant use of its antecedent seems clear enough on the face of it, but familiarity with logic of conditionals literature may well lead one to reconsider. This kind of dialectical interplay should continue to be a fruitful source of philosophical research for the foreseeable future.

See also: AMBIGUITY; ANAPHORA; DUMMETT, M.A.E.; IDENTITY OF INDISCERNIBLES; INDIRECT DISCOURSE; INTENSIONAL ENTITIES; INTENSIONALITY; KRIPKE, S.A.; LOGICAL CONSTANTS; MASS TERMS; NECESSARY TRUTH AND CONVENTION; ONTOLOGICAL COMMITMENT; PRIOR, A.N.; QUANTIFIERS, GENERALIZED; QUINE, W.V.; RUSSELL, B.A.W.; SCOPE; TYPE/TOKEN DISTINCTION; USE/MENTION DISTINCTION AND QUOTATION; VAGUENESS

References and further reading

Hughes, R.I.G. (ed.) (1993) *A Philosophical Companion to First-Order Logic*, Indianapolis, IN: Hackett Publishing Company. (New and reprinted papers of varying levels of difficulty.)

Tomberlin, J.E. (ed.) (1994) *Logic and Language*, Philosophical Perspectives 8, Atascadero, CA: Ridgeview. (A collection of new papers on relevant topics.)

GRAEME FORBES

LOGIC, QUANTUM
See QUANTUM LOGIC

LOGICAL ATOMISM

The name 'logical atomism' refers to a network of theses about the parts and structure of the world and the means by which language represents the world. Wittgenstein, in his *Tractatus Logico-Philosophicus*, expounds a version of logical atomism developed by him around the time of the First World War, as does Russell in works published contemporaneously. It is no accident that their work on logical atomism shares a common surface description since it resulted from their mutual influence at Cambridge. The common theme is that the meaning of our sentences is rooted in a primitive relation between simple expressions and their simple worldly bearers, the logical atoms. In a logically perfect language, atomic sentences describe configurations of these atoms, and complex sentences are combinations of the atomic sentences. But sentences of ordinary language may have a misleading surface form which is revealed as such by analysis. The common theme masks considerable differences of doctrine. In particular, there are differences in the nature of logical atoms and in the arguments for the existence of these atoms.
See also: PLURALISM

ALEX OLIVER

LOGICAL CONSTANTS

A fundamental problem in the philosophy of logic is to characterize the concepts of 'logical consequence' and 'logical truth' in such a way as to explain what is semantically, metaphysically or epistemologically distinctive about them. One traditionally says that a sentence *p* is a logical consequence of a set *S* of sentences in a language *L* if and only if (1) the truth of the sentences of *S* in *L* guarantees the truth of *p* and (2) this guarantee is due to the 'logical form' of the sentences of *S* and the sentence *p*. A sentence is said to be logically true if its truth is guaranteed by its logical form (for example, '2 is even or 2 is not even'). There are three problems presented by this picture: to explicate the notion of logical form or structure; to explain how the logical forms of sentences give rise to the fact that the truth of certain sentences guarantees the truth of others; and to explain what such a guarantee consists in.

The logical form of a sentence may be exhibited by replacing nonlogical expressions with a schematic letter. Two sentences have the same logical form when they can be mapped onto the same schema using this procedure ('2 is even or 2 is not even' and '3 is prime or 3 is not prime' have the same logical form: '*p* or not-*p*'). If a sentence is logically true then each sentence sharing its logical form is true. Any characterization of logical consequence, then, presupposes a conception of logical form, which in turn assumes a prior demarcation of the logical constants. Such a demarcation yields an answer to the first problem above; the goal is to generate the demarcation in such a way as to enable a solution of the remaining two.

Approaches to the characterization of logical constants and logical consequence are affected by developments in mathematical logic. One way of viewing logical constanthood is as a semantic property; a property that an expression possesses by virtue of the sort of contribution it makes to determining the truth conditions of sentences containing it. Another way is proof-theoretical: appealing to aspects of cognitive or operational role as the defining characteristics of logical expressions. Broadly, proof-theoretic accounts go naturally with the conception of logic as a theory of formal deductive inference; model-theoretic accounts complement a conception of logic as an instrument for the characterization of structure.
See also: PROOF THEORY

TIMOTHY MCCARTHY

LOGICAL FORM
See LOGICAL CONSTANTS

LOGICAL POSITIVISM

Introduction

Logical positivism (logical empiricism, neo-positivism) originated in Austria and Germany in the 1920s. Inspired by late nineteenth- and early twentieth-century revolutions in logic, mathematics and mathematical physics, it aimed to create a similarly revolutionary scientific philosophy purged of the endless controversies of traditional metaphysics. Its most important representatives were members of the Vienna Circle who gathered around Moritz Schlick at the University of Vienna (including Rudolf Carnap, Herbert Feigl, Kurt Gödel, Hans Hahn, Karl Menger, Otto Neurath and Friedrich Waismann) and those of the Society for Empirical Philosophy who gathered around Hans Reichenbach at the University of Berlin (including Walter Dubislav, Kurt Grelling and Carl Hempel). Although not officially members of either group, the Austrian philosophers Ludwig Wittgenstein and Karl Popper were, at least for a time, closely associated with logical positivism.

The logical positivist movement reached its apogee in Europe in the years 1928–34, but the rise of National Socialism in 1933 marked the effective end of this phase. Thereafter, however, many of its most important representatives emigrated to the USA. Here logical positivism found a receptive audience among such pragmatically, empirically and logically minded American philosophers as Charles Morris, Ernest Nagel and W.V. Quine. Thus transplanted to the English-speaking world of 'analytic' philosophy it exerted a tremendous influence – particularly in philosophy of science and the application of logical and mathematical techniques to philosophical problems more generally. This influence began to wane around 1960, with the rise of a pragmatic form of naturalism due to Quine and a historical-sociological approach to the philosophy of science due mainly to Thomas Kuhn. Both of these later trends, however, developed in explicit reaction to the philosophy of logical positivism and thereby attest to its enduring significance.

1 Historical background
2 Relativistic physics
3 Logic and the foundations of mathematics
4 The Vienna Circle
5 Emigration, influence, aftermath

1 Historical background

Immanuel KANT, in the positivists' eyes, had made a lasting contribution to scientific philosophy – particularly in his rejection of the possibility of supersensible metaphysical knowledge and his reorientation of theoretical philosophy around the two questions 'how is pure mathematics possible?' and 'how is pure natural science possible?' In answering these questions Kant developed his famous defence of synthetic a priori knowledge – knowledge independent of sensible experience yet nonetheless substantively applicable to the empirical world. For Kant, the mathematical physics of Newton paradigmatically exemplified such synthetic a priori knowledge through its reliance on Euclidean geometry and fundamental laws of motion such as the law of inertia. Kant's theory of a priori faculties of the mind – the faculty of pure intuition or sensibility and the faculty of pure understanding – was then intended to explain the origin of synthetic a priori knowledge and thus make philosophically comprehensible the possibility of Newtonian mathematical physics.

After the intervening dominance of post-Kantian idealism, a number of German-speaking philosophers renewed the call for a scientific, epistemological and non-metaphysical form of philosophy. But these Neo-Kantian philosophers also had to face an important new challenge to the Kantian synthetic a priori: the nineteenth-century development of non-Euclidean geometry by Gauss, Bolyai, Lobachevskii, Riemann and Klein (see GEOMETRY, PHILOSOPHICAL ISSUES IN §§1, 3). Although some Neo-Kantians attempted to defend the uniqueness and apriority of Euclidean geometry nonetheless, others – especially those of the Marburg School such as Paul Natorp and Ernst Cassirer – aimed to generalize the synthetic a priori beyond its particular embodiment in classical Euclidean–Newtonian mathematical physics (see NEO-KANTIANISM). This latter tendency was similar in important respects to ideas the logical positivists were to elaborate.

But the most important nineteenth-century predecessors of logical positivism were Hermann von Helmholtz, Ernst MACH and Henri POINCARÉ. Through their efforts to comprehend the radical changes sweeping through nineteenth-century science, these three thinkers initiated a new style of scientific philosophy later taken up and systematized by the positivists. The changes in question included the rise of non-Euclidean geometry, the formulation of the conservation of energy and general thermodynamics, and the beginnings of scientific physiology and psychology. Helmholtz made fundamental contributions to all three areas. He based geometry on the postulate of 'free mobility' of rigid bodies, and, since all classical geometries of constant curvature – negative, positive or zero (Euclidean) – satisfy this postulate, he opposed the Kantian commitment to the aprioricity of geometry: whether space is Euclidean or non-Euclidean is an empirical question about the actual behaviour of rigid bodies. In physiology, Helmholtz articulated a general principle of psycho-physical correlation whereby our sensations correspond to – but are in no way pictures or images of – processes in the external physical world. These processes consist, in the end, of microscopic atoms interacting via central forces, and, on this basis, Helmholtz developed his famous interpretation of the conservation of energy.

Mach and Poincaré can be seen as reacting, in diverse ways, to Helmholtz. Mach attacked especially atomism and the idea of a psychophysical correlation between two incommensurable realms, and he advanced a programme for the unity of science based on immediately perceptible 'elements' or 'sensations'. The task of science consists solely in seeking correlations among such elements (as in phenomenological thermodynamics), and all dualistic and atomistic tendencies are to be purged as metaphysical via historico-critical analysis. This

Machian empiricism exerted a decisive influence on the logical positivists. Poincaré, on the other hand, influenced the positivists primarily through his philosophy of geometry. He agreed with Helmholtz's emphasis on the free mobility of rigid bodies but disagreed with Helmholtz's empiricism. According to Poincaré, the idea of a rigid body is an idealization that cannot be straightforwardly instantiated in the physical world. By freely choosing one of the three classical geometries as, so to speak, a definition of rigidity, we then first make it possible to carry out empirical investigations with real physical bodies. Physical geometry is thus neither synthetic a priori nor empirical: it is 'conventional' (see CONVENTIONALISM).

2 Relativistic physics

Albert Einstein's special (1905) and general (1916) theories of relativity entered this volatile intellectual situation as a revelation (see EINSTEIN, A.; RELATIVITY THEORY, PHILOSOPHICAL SIGNIFICANCE OF). And the relativistic revolution in physics directly stimulated SCHLICK, REICHENBACH and CARNAP to initiate a parallel revolution in scientific philosophy. All three thinkers agreed that relativity – especially through the general relativistic description of gravitation via a (four-dimensional) geometry of variable curvature – definitively refutes the Kantian idea that Euclidean geometry is synthetic a priori. Moreover, relativity arises from critical reflection on the empirical significance of spatiotemporal concepts in physics (in particular, the concept of simultaneity and the concept of motion) and thus demonstrates the fruitfulness of Mach's basic point of view. At the same time, however, through its use of sophisticated abstract mathematics, relativity also illustrates the limitations of Machian empiricism (according to which even mathematical concepts have an empirical origin). All three thinkers therefore attempted to formulate an intermediate position that would do justice to both Machian empiricism and the continued importance of a priori mathematical elements in physics. Poincaré's concept of convention came to play a central role.

Schlick, Reichenbach and Carnap first pursued rather different paths. Whereas Schlick emphasized from the outset that the Kantian synthetic a priori has no place at all in the new relativistic context, Reichenbach and Carnap initially attempted to salvage important aspects of Kantianism. Reichenbach began by distinguishing the idea of necessary and unrevisable truth from the idea of necessary presupposition of a given scientific conceptualization of nature. For Reichenbach, relativity refuted the former but embodied the latter. Kant was right

that the necessary presuppositions of Newtonian physics included Euclidean geometry and the laws of motion. In moving to relativistic physics, however, these are replaced by fundamentally new presuppositions. We thus end up with a relativized version of the Kantian a priori (as constituting the presuppositions of a particular theory). Carnap, by contrast, began by distinguishing metrical from topological features of physical space. The latter are indeed synthetic a priori as Kant thought (they even depend on a kind of pure intuition), but the former – as general relativity has shown – essentially involve the behaviour of empirically given bodies. We thus end up with a weakening of the Kantian a priori (from metrical to topological features).

These early attempts to salvage aspects of the synthetic a priori did not survive, however. For Schlick's view that relativity is simply incompatible with Kant eventually won the day. Although the distinction between Poincaré's conventionalism and Helmholtzian empiricism was not entirely clear (and Reichenbach, in particular, preferred to associate his later viewpoint with Helmholtz rather than Poincaré), both Reichenbach and Carnap soon came to replace the Kantian notion of the a priori with Poincaré's concept of convention. Yet this form of conventionalism (unlike Poincaré's) was forged in the crucible of a revolutionary new physics and thus demonstrated the vitality and relevance of a new philosophy.

3 Logic and the foundations of mathematics

Whereas the positivists appealed to Poincaré's concept of convention (as realized, so they thought, in relativistic physics) to give a new answer to Kant's question concerning the possibility of pure natural science, they appealed to modern developments in logic and the foundations of mathematics to give a new answer to Kant's question concerning the possibility of pure mathematics. There were in fact two distinguishable sets of developments here. The formal point of view, typified by David Hilbert's logically rigorous axiomatization of geometry, freed geometry from any reference at all to intuitively spatial forms and instead portrayed its subject matter as consisting of any things whatever that satisfy the relevant axioms (see HILBERT'S PROGRAMME AND FORMALISM). Geometry is rigorously and a priori true, not because it reflects the structure of an intuitively given space, but rather because it 'implicitly defines' its subject matter via purely logical – but otherwise entirely undetermined – formulas. Mathematical truth, on this view, is identified with logical consistency. The 'logicism' of Gottlob Frege and Bertrand RUSSELL, by contrast, aimed to construct particular mathematical disciplines (especially arithmetic) within an all-embracing system of logic. On this view mathematical disciplines (like arithmetic) indeed have a definite subject matter about which they express truths: namely, the subject matter of logic itself (propositions, classes, and so on). As thus purely logical, however, such pure mathematical disciplines express merely analytic truths and are not synthetic a priori (see LOGICISM).

Hilbert's formal point of view was pursued especially by Schlick, who in a sense made the notion of implicit definition, together with the associated distinction between undetermined form and determinate (given) content, the centrepiece of his philosophy. The logicist point of view, by contrast, was pursued especially by Carnap, who studied with Frege and then was decisively influenced by Russell. Indeed, Carnap was inspired by Russell's conception of 'logic as the essence of philosophy' to reconceive philosophy itself on the model of the logicist construction of arithmetic. He began, in *Der logische Aufbau der Welt* (1928), by developing a 'rational reconstruction' of empirical knowledge – an epistemology – within the logical framework of Russell and Whitehead's *Principia Mathematica* (1910–13). By defining or 'constituting' all concepts of empirical science within this logic from a basis of subjective 'elementary experiences', Carnap's reconstruction was to show, among other things, that the dichotomy between empirical truth and analytic/definitional truth is indeed exhaustive.

Yet the logic of *Principia Mathematica* was afflicted with serious technical difficulties: the need for special existential axioms such as the axioms of infinity and choice. Partly in response to such difficulties, Ludwig Wittgenstein asserted in his *Tractatus Logico-Philosophicus* that logic has no subject matter after all: the propositions of logic are entirely tautological or empty of content (see WITTGENSTEIN, L.J.J. §§3–7). Carnap eagerly embraced this idea, but he also attempted to adapt it to the new, post-*Principia* technical situation – which involved the articulation of the 'intuitionist' or 'constructivist' point of view by L.E.J. Brouwer and the development of meta-mathematics by Hilbert and Kurt Gödel (see INTUITIONISM; MATHEMATICS, FOUNDATIONS OF). In *Logische Syntax der Sprache* (1934) Carnap formulated his mature theory of formal languages and put forward his famous 'Principle of Tolerance' – according to which logic has no business at all looking for true or 'correct' principles. The task of logic is rather to investigate the structure of any and all formal languages – 'the boundless ocean of unlimited possibilities' – so as to map out and explore their infinitely diverse logical structures. Indeed, the construction and logical investigation of such formal languages became, for Carnap, the new task of philosophy. The concept of analyticity thereby took on an even more important role. For this concept characterizes logical as opposed to empirical investigation and thus now expresses the distinctive character of philosophy itself.

4 The Vienna Circle

Otto Neurath, Hans Hahn, and the physicist Philipp Frank initiated a discussion group in Vienna, beginning in 1907, in which they considered a combination of Machian empiricism with Poincaré's new insights into the conventional character of physical geometry. Deeply impressed by Schlick's work on relativity theory, they arranged (apparently with Einstein's help) to bring Schlick to the University of Vienna in 1922 to take over the Chair in Philosophy of the Inductive Sciences previously held by Mach. What we now know as the Vienna Circle quickly took shape. Reichenbach, who had become acquainted with Carnap through their common interest in relativity, introduced him to Schlick in 1924. In 1925 Carnap lectured to the Circle in Vienna on his new 'constitutional theory of experience' and became assistant professor under Schlick in 1926. The Circle then engaged in intensive discussions of Carnap's epistemology and Wittgenstein's *Tractatus*. Wittgenstein's view that all propositions are truth-functions of 'elementary propositions' was combined with Carnap's constitution of scientific concepts from a basis of 'elementary experiences' so as to create a new, logically rigorous form of empiricism according to which all meaningful – scientific – propositions are reducible to propositions about immediately given experience. And this was articulated as the 'official' philosophy of the Vienna Circle in the famous manifesto *Wissenschaftliche Weltauffassung* of 1929.

Neurath was the driving force in thus turning the Vienna Circle into a public philosophical movement. Trained in economics and the social sciences, Neurath was extremely active politically as a scientific neo-Marxist. In particular, he took the community of natural scientists as the model for a rationally organized human society, and, on this basis, he advocated a reorganization of both intellectual and social life from which all non-rational, 'metaphysical' elements would be definitively purged. In this sense, Neurath saw the philosophical work of the Vienna Circle as a reflection of the wider movement for a *neue Sachlichkeit* then current in Weimar culture – as typified, for example, by the Dessau Bauhaus. As in the wider culture, this movement stood in philosophy for a rejection of individualism in favour of the cooperative, piecemeal, and 'technological' approach to problems exemplified in the sciences, and it was therefore particularly hostile to what was perceived as a return to the meta-physical system-building of post-Kantian idealism by influential German philosophers such as Martin Heidegger. Carnap was especially sympathetic to Neurath's broader philosophical-political vision and clearly expresses this vision in the Preface to the *Aufbau*. Schlick, by contrast, preferred a more individualistic model of philosophy and resisted the idea of a 'movement'.

This divergence between a 'left wing' and a 'right wing' of the Circle emerged in the sphere of epistemology in a debate over 'protocol-sentences' in the years 1930–4. At issue was the status of the basic propositions or protocols in which the results of scientific observation are recorded. It had initially appeared, in Carnap's constitutional system of the *Aufbau*, that such propositions must express private, subjective sense-experience. For Neurath, however, this view was inconsistent with the publicity and intersubjectivity required by science. He therefore advocated a more naturalistic conception of proto-cols as sentences accepted by the scientific commu-nity as recording the results of observation at a given time. These sentences must thus be expressible within the public and 'physicalistic' language of unified science and hence, like all other sentences, are in principle revisable. Schlick was deeply shocked by Neurath's view – which he took to represent an abandonment of empiricism in favour of the coherence theory of truth (see TRUTH, COHERENCE, THEORY OF). Carnap attempted, in typical fashion, to mediate the dispute: at issue was simply a choice between two different languages in which to formulate or rationally reconstruct the results of unified science. Although Neurath's thoroughly intersubjective 'physicalistic' language (where, as Karl POPPER emphasized especially, every sentence is revisable) was clearly preferable on pragmatic grounds, Carnap held that this choice – like every other choice of formal language – is in the end conventional. Empiricism, in Carnap's hands, is itself framed by conventional and hence non-empirical choices (see VIENNA CIRCLE).

5 Emigration, influence, aftermath

The rise of the Nazi regime set off a wholesale migration of logical positivists to the English-speaking world. Carnap, who had become professor at Prague in 1931, moved in 1936 to the University of Chicago. Reichenbach, who had fled to Istanbul in 1933, moved in 1938 to the University of California at Los Angeles. (After Reichenbach's death in 1953 Carnap took over his position at UCLA, beginning in 1954.) Neurath, after leaving

Vienna for The Hague in 1934, fled to England in 1940 – where he worked in Oxford until his death in 1945. Friedrich Waismann fled for England as well, where he lectured at Oxford from 1939. Philip Frank emigrated to the USA (also from Prague) in 1938 and settled at Harvard in 1939. Karl Menger took up a position at Notre Dame in 1937, and Kurt Gödel became a member of the Institute for Advanced Study at Princeton in 1940. Herbert Feigl went first to the University of Iowa in 1933 and then to the University of Minnesota in 1940, where he founded the influential Minnesota Center for the Philosophy of Science in 1953. Carl Hempel joined Carnap at the University of Chicago in 1939 and, after teaching at Queens College and Yale, settled at Princeton in 1955. (Schlick was murdered by a deranged student at the University of Vienna in 1936.)

The growth of philosophy of science in the USA was decisively shaped by the work of Carnap, Reichenbach and Hempel. Reichenbach influenced especially the development of philosophy of physics through his work on geometry, relativity and the direction of time (see RELATIVITY THEORY, PHILO-SOPHICAL SIGNIFICANCE OF). Hempel published extraordinarily influential papers on the logical analysis of explanation and confirmation and thereby furthered the ideal of scientific philosophy first articulated by Carnap (see EXPLANATION; CONFIRMATION THEORY). Carnap himself contin-ued the construction of formal languages in which such concepts as testability, modality and probability could be rationally reconstructed or 'explicated' and thus contributed further to the same ideal. Indeed, Carnap's explication of concepts through the construction of formal languages influenced the English-speaking world of analytic philosophy far beyond the borders of philosophy of science. Developments in formal semantics and philosophy of language, in particular, rested on Carnap's initial work on modality (see SEMANTICS).

The Carnapian ideal of explication is based on a sharp distinction between logical and empirical investigation, analytic and synthetic truth. In his *Logical Syntax of Language* (1934) Carnap had attempted a general explication of the concept of analyticity itself – a general formal method for distinguishing, within the context of any given formal language, the analytic from the synthetic sentences of that language. After accepting Alfred Tarski's semantical conception of truth in 1935, however, Carnap abandoned the approach of *Logical Syntax* and frankly admitted that (although explica-tions for various particular languages could still be constructed) he now had no generally applicable explication of the concept of analyticity. After studying with Carnap in the early 1930s, W.V.

Quine then exploited this situation to attack the concept of analyticity as such and, on this basis, to attack the Carnapian ideal of logical explication as well (see QUINE, W.V. §§2, 4). Philosophy, for Quine, is itself a kind of empirical science – a branch of human psychology or 'naturalized epistemology' (see NATURALIZED EPISTEMOLOGY). Moreover, at the same time that Quine was articulating this new philosophical vision, Thomas KUHN published *The Structure of Scientific Revolutions* (1962) in the *International Encyclopedia of Unified Science* edited by Carnap and Charles Morris. Whereas Carnap had relegated the (conventional) choice of scientific language to the limbo of pragmatics, Kuhn concentrated on those factors – especially social factors – which, in a scientific revolution, determine precisely this kind of choice. These ideas, in harmony with Quine's more general naturalistic point of view, then led to historical and sociological approaches to the study of science and thus, in the end, to the decline of logical analyses of scientific language in the Carnapian style.

See also: ANALYSIS, PHILOSOPHICAL ISSUES IN; ANALYTICITY; EMOTIVISM; EMPIRICISM; LOGICAL ATOMISM; MEANING AND VERIFICATION; OPERATIONALISM; POSITIVISM IN THE SOCIAL SCIENCES; THEORIES, SCIENTIFIC; UNITY OF SCIENCE

References and further reading

Ayer, A. (ed.) (1959) *Logical Positivism*, New York: Free Press. (Very useful short collection. Contains, in particular, some of the most important papers from the 'protocol-sentence' debate discussed in §4.)

Frank P. (1949) *Modern Science and its Philosophy*, Cambridge, MA: Harvard University Press. (Classic discussion of the positivist movement by a participant. Contains, in particular, good discussions of the influence of Mach and Poincaré.)

MICHAEL FRIEDMAN

LOGICISM

The term 'logicism' refers to the doctrine that mathematics is a part of (deductive) logic. It is often said that Gottlob Frege and Bertrand Russell were the first proponents of such a view; this is inaccurate, in that Frege did not make such a claim for all of mathematics. On the other hand, Richard Dedekind deserves to be mentioned among those who first expressed the conviction that *arithmetic* is a branch of logic.

The logicist claim has two parts: that our knowledge of mathematical theorems is grounded fully in logical demonstrations from basic truths of logic; and that the concepts involved in such theorems, and the objects whose existence they imply, are of a purely logical nature. Thus Frege maintained that arithmetic requires no assumptions besides those of logic; that the concept of number is a concept of pure logic; and that numbers themselves are, as he put it, logical objects.

This view of mathematics would not have been possible without a profound transformation of logic that occurred in the late nineteenth century – most especially through the work of Frege. Before that time, actual mathematical reasoning could not be carried out under the recognized logical forms of argument: this circumstance lent considerable plausibility to Immanuel Kant's teaching that mathematical reasoning is not 'purely discursive', but relies upon 'constructions' grounded in intuition. The new logic, however, made it possible to represent standard mathematical reasoning in the form of purely logical derivations – as Frege, on the one hand, and Russell, in collaboration with Whitehead, on the other, undertook to show in detail.

It is now generally held that logicism has been undermined by two developments: first, the discovery that the principles assumed in Frege's major work are inconsistent, and the more or less unsatisfying character (or so it is claimed) of the systems devised to remedy this defect; second, the epoch-making discovery by Kurt Gödel that the 'logic' that would be required for derivability of *all* mathematical truths can in principle not be 'formalized'. Whether these considerations 'refute' logicism will be considered further below.

See also: ARITHMETIC, PHILOSOPHICAL ISSUES IN; HILBERT'S PROGRAMME AND FORMALISM; INTUITIONISM

HOWARD STEIN

LOGICS, FREE
See FREE LOGICS

LOGICS, INFINITARY
See INFINITARY LOGICS

LOGICS, ORDINAL
See ORDINAL LOGICS

LOGOS

The noun *logos* derives from the Greek verb *legein*, meaning 'to say' something significant. *Logos* developed a wide variety of senses, including 'description', 'theory' (sometimes as opposed to 'fact'), 'explanation', 'reason', 'reasoning power', 'principle', 'ratio' and 'prose'.

Logos emerges as a philosophical term with Heraclitus (*c.*540–*c.*480 BC), for whom it provided the link between rational discourse and the world's rational structure. It was freely used by Plato and Aristotle and especially by the Stoics, who interpreted the rational world order as immanent deity. Platonist philosophers gave pre-eminence to *nous*, the intuitive intellect expressed in *logos*. To Philo of Alexandria and subsequently to Christian theologians it meant 'the Word', a derivative divine power, at first seen as subordinate but eventually coordinated with the Father.

CHRISTOPHER STEAD

LOKAYATA

See MATERIALISM, INDIAN SCHOOL OF

LOMBARD, PETER (1095/1100–60)

Peter Lombard's philosophical views are important given the formative role his *Sententiae in IV libris distinctae* (Four Books of Sentences) played in the education of university theologians in the high Middle Ages, many of whom were also philosophers. Lombard staunchly opposes theologies, cosmologies and anthropologies of a Platonic or Neoplatonic type. While conversant with new trends in logic in his day, he is disinclined to treat theological issues as illustrations of the rules of formal logic or natural philosophy, preferring to view them from a metaphysical perspective. In his doctrine of God he deliberately eschews terminology associated with any one philosophical school. In his anthropology and sacramental theology he shows a marked preference for Aristotelianism. The hospitability of his theology to Aristotelianism and to a philosophical treatment of a range of theological questions made his *Sentences* elastic enough to accommodate the reception of Greco-Arabic thought and to serve as a pedagogical framework usable by philosophers of every persuasion during the succeeding three centuries.

See also: GOD, CONCEPTS OF; TRINITY

MARCIA L. COLISH

LOTTERY PARADOX

See PARADOXES, EPISTEMIC

LOTZE, RUDOLPH HERMANN (1817–81)

Lotze was among the pre-eminent figures in German academic philosophy between the demise of Absolute Idealism and the rise of Neo-Kantianism proper. He sought to avoid two extremes: first, that of an idealism which seeks to deduce the world from a single, general principle; and, second, that of a realism which, by divorcing reality from the mind, splits the world into two utterly separate spheres. The search for knowledge should be tempered by a recognition of the results of natural science and sobered by the awareness that reality will, by necessity, always outstrip thought. Furthermore, our mental life cannot be reduced to purely intellectual functions: feelings and evaluations, for example, are also an integral part of human existence. While there can be no a priori deduction of a metaphysical system, a teleological interpretation, which elucidates the ultimate value of man and the world, must supplement purely naturalistic explanation. The universe has the significance of an unfolding plan, where things are subject to the general laws of order, expressing spiritual import. In this way, Lotze combined a kind of respect for the findings of scientific research with his own peculiar idealistic programme.

DAVID SULLIVAN

LOVE

Love is usually understood to be a powerful emotion involving an intense attachment to an object and a high evaluation of it. On some understandings, however, love does not involve emotion at all, but only an active interest in the wellbeing of the object. On other accounts, love is essentially a relationship involving mutuality and reciprocity, rather than an emotion. Moreover, there are many varieties of love, including erotic/romantic love, friendly love, and love of humanity. Different cultures also recognize different types of love. Love has, as well, a complicated archaeology: because it has strong links with early experiences of attachment, it can exist in the personality at different levels of depth and articulateness, posing special problems for self-knowledge. It is mistake to try to give too unified an account of such a complex set of phenomena.

Love has been understood by many philosophers to be a source of great richness and energy in human life. But even those who praise its contribution have seen it as a potential threat to virtuous living. Philosophers in the Western tradition have therefore been preoccupied with proposing accounts of the reform or 'ascent' of love, in order to demonstrate that there are ways of retaining the energy and beauty of this passion while removing its bad consequences.

See also: EMOTIONS, NATURE OF; EMOTIONS, PHILOSOPHY OF; FAMILY, ETHICS AND THE; SEXUALITY, PHILOSOPHY OF

MARTHA C. NUSSBAUM

LÖWENHEIM–SKOLEM THEOREMS AND NONSTANDARD MODELS

Sometimes we specify a structure by giving a description and counting anything that satisfies the description as just another model of it. But at other times we start from a conception we try to articulate, and then our articulation may fail to pin down what we had in mind. Sets seem to have had such a fate. For millennia sets lay fallow in logic, but when cultivated by mathematics in the nineteenth century, they seemed to bear both a foundation and a theory of the infinite. The paradoxes of set theory seemed to threaten this promise. With an eye to proving freedom from paradox, versions of set theory were articulated rigorously. But around 1920, Löwenheim and Skolem proved that no such formalized set theory can come out true only in the hugely infinite world it seemed to reveal, for if it is true in such a world, it will also be true in a world of the smallest infinite size. (Versions of this remain true even if we augment the standard expressive devices used to formalize set theory.) But then, Skolem inferred, we cannot articulate sets determinately enough for them to constitute a firm foundation for mathematics.

W.D. HART

LUCRETIUS (*c.*94–*c.*55 BC)

Titus Lucretius Carus was a Roman Epicurean philosopher and poet. About his life and personality little can be said with certainty, yet his only known work, *On the Nature of Things* (*De rerum natura*), is of considerable size and one of the most brilliant achievements of Latin poetry. A didactic poem in six books, it expounds Epicurean physics. Its manifesto is to abolish the fear of gods and of death by demonstrating that the soul is mortal and the world not governed by gods but by mechanical laws.
See also: ATOMISM, ANCIENT

MICHAEL ERLER

LUKÁCS, GEORG (1885–1971)

Lukács' *Geschichte und Klassenbewusstsein* (History and Class Consciousness) (1923) is, for both its intrinsic merits and its enormous influence, the most important work of Marxist philosophy to have appeared in the twentieth century. It sought to render explicit the dependence of Marx's thought on Hegel's dialectic as a means of elucidating both the distinctive character of historical materialism as a form of theoretical inquiry and its revolutionary rejection of the modes of thinking prevailing in capitalist society. Lukács' general aim had been shared by the authors of the first philosophical reflections on Marx's project – Engels and Plekhanov,

for example, had stressed its debt to Hegel. Lukács, however, sought to draw Marx into that broad current of twentieth-century Continental thought which has drawn a sharp distinction between the methods of the physical sciences, suitable at best for analysing inanimate nature, and those of the human sciences, whose aim is to interpret human actions in the light of the thoughts which move them. Thus Lukács sees Marx as the theorist, not of the laws of the dialectic or of inevitable social transformation, but of revolutionary subjectivity, of the proletariat as 'the identical subject–object' of history. This was a version of Marxism which suited the times, in the immediate aftermath of the Russian Revolution of October 1917. As the revolutionary tides receded, Lukács found philosophical and political reasons for retreating to a more orthodox historical materialism which laid much greater stress on objective constraints and processes than his version of the early 1920s had. Yet the force of its overall argument and the quality of its individual analyses have made *History and Class Consciousness* a constant reference-point in subsequent discussions of Marxist theory.

ALEX CALLINICOS

ŁUKASIEWICZ, JAN (1878–1956)

Before 1918, Łukasiewicz's interests centred on logic (in the broad sense) and philosophy, and he worked on induction and probability. He also wrote an important historical book on the principle of contradiction in Aristotle. After 1918, Łukasiewicz concentrated almost entirely on mathematical logic and was the main organizer of the Warsaw School of Logic. The discovery of many-valued systems of logic is perhaps the most important result he achieved. He also invented an ingenious logical symbolism in which brackets (or other punctuation signs) are not necessary (bracket-free or Polish notation). Propositional calculi became a favourite topic of Łukasiewicz's logical investigations. The history of logic was another subject in which Łukasiewicz achieved important results.

JAN WOLEŃSKI

LULL, RAMON
See LLULL, RAMON

LUNYU
See CONFUCIUS

LUTHER, MARTIN (1483–1546)

Martin Luther was an Augustinian monk who found the theology and penitential practices of his times inadequate for overcoming fears about his salvation. He turned first to a theology of humility, whereby confession of one's own utter sinfulness is all that God asks, and then to a theology of justification by faith, in which human beings are seen as incapable of any turning towards God by their own efforts. Without preparation on the part of sinners, God turns to them and destroys their trust in themselves, producing within them trust in his promises made manifest in Jesus Christ. Regarding them in unity with Christ, God treats them as if they had Christ's righteousness: he 'justifies' them. Faith is produced in the sinner by the Word of God concerning Jesus Christ in the Bible, and by the work of the Holy Spirit internally showing the sinner the true subject matter of the Bible. It is not shaped by philosophy, since faith's perspective transcends and overcomes natural reason. Faith, through the working of God's Holy Spirit within the believer, naturally produces good works, but justification is not dependent upon them – they are free expressions of faith in love. Nevertheless, secular government with its laws and coercion is still necessary in this world because there are so few true Christians. Luther's theology brought him into conflict with the Church hierarchy and was instrumental in the instigation of the Reformation, in which the Protestant churches split from Rome.

See also: CALVIN, J.; ERASMUS, D.; HUS, J.; MELANCHTHON, P.; POLITICAL PHILOSOPHY, HISTORY OF; RENAISSANCE PHILOSOPHY; VOLUNTARISM

M.A. HIGTON

LYCEUM
See ARISTOTLE

LYOTARD, JEAN-FRANÇOIS (1924–98)

Jean-François Lyotard was a prominent French philosopher who is generally considered the leading theorist of postmodernism. His work constitutes an insistent critique of philosophical closure, historical totalization and political dogmatism and a re-evaluation of the nature of ethics, aesthetics and politics after the demise of totalizing metatheories.

In his early works, Lyotard confronts the limitations of dialectical philosophy and structuralist linguistics and analyses the disruptive, extradiscursive force of desire and the nonrepresentational or figurative dimensions of art and literature. In *La Condition postmoderne* (1979) (*The Postmodern Condition*, 1984), he treats narrative pragmatics and language games as the bases for a critical approach to postmodern art and politics, as well as to the problem of justice. Recent texts insist on the obligation of philosophy, politics and writing to bear witness to heterogeneity and to what is repressed or forgotten in all representations of the past. His work questions the limits of philosophy, aesthetics and political theory in terms of problems linked to the irreducible complexities of art and literature and the nonrepresentational affects of historical–political events.

See also: POSTMODERNISM

DAVID CARROLL

M

MACH, ERNST (1838–1916)

Mach was an Austrian physicist and philosopher. Though not one of the great philosophers, he was tremendously influential in the development of 'scientific philosophy' in the late nineteenth and early twentieth centuries. A vigorous opponent of 'metaphysics', he was celebrated as a progenitor of logical positivism. His work is regarded as a limiting case of pure empiricism; he stands between the empiricism of Hume and J.S. Mill, and that of the Vienna Circle.

Mach's positivist conception of science saw its aims as descriptive and predictive; explanation is downgraded. Scientific laws and theories are economical means of describing phenomena. Theories that refer to unobservable entities – including atomic theory – may impede inquiry. They should be eliminated where possible in favour of theories involving 'direct descriptions' of phenomena. Mach claimed to be a scientist, not a philosopher, but the 'Machian philosophy' was 'neutral monism'. Close to phenomenalism, it saw the world as functionally related complexes of sensations, and aspired to anti-metaphysical neutrality.

See also: RELATIVITY THEORY, PHILOSOPHICAL SIGNIFICANCE OF

ANDY HAMILTON

MACHIAVELLI, NICCOLÒ (1469–1527)

Florentine diplomat, dramatist and political thinker, Machiavelli's treatise, *Il principe* (The Prince) (1532), has earned him notoriety as a political immoralist (or at least an amoralist) and a teacher of evil. In *The Prince*, Machiavelli posits a complex relationship between ethics and politics that associates princely *virtù* with the capacity to know and act within the political world as it 'is', and with the beastly abilities to dispense violence and practise deception. Behind this argument dwells the distinctly Machiavellian insight that politics is a realm of appearances where the practice of moral or Christian virtues often results in a prince's ruin, while knowing 'how not to be good' may result in greater security and wellbeing for both prince and people. Machiavelli warns that the prince's possibilities for success in this matter are always mediated by fortune; hence the prudent prince is one who is prepared to resist fortune by adapting his procedure to the times and his nature to 'the necessity of the case'.

A less notorious but equally influential text is the *Discorsi sopra la prima deca di Tito Livio* (Discourses on the First Ten Books of Titus Livy) (1531), in which Machiavelli offers a defence of popular liberty and republican government that takes the ancient republic of Rome as its model and emphasizes the role of the people in the 'public administration' of the city. However, Machiavelli also argues that a republic is only as successful in self-governance as its citizens are infused with civic *virtù* and therefore not corrupted. Accordingly, he praises the work of political founders who craft republican laws and institutions, and religious founders who fuse God and *patria* as one in the people's hearts. The apparent tension between Machiavelli's republican sympathies in *Discourses* and his elitist proclivities in *The Prince* has helped to fuel a vast interpretive literature concerning his political attitudes, his theory of politics, and the nature and meaning of 'machiavellianism' in Western political thought.

See also: POLITICAL PHILOSOPHY, HISTORY OF; RENAISSANCE PHILOSOPHY; REPUBLICANISM

MARY G. DIETZ

MACINTYRE, ALASDAIR (1929–)

Alasdair MacIntyre has contributed to the diverse fields of social, moral and political philosophy. He is one of the leading proponents of a virtue ethical approach in moral philosophy, part of a wider attempt to recover an Aristotelian conception of both morality and politics. His return to ancient sources has been powered by a critical indictment of the modern moral predicament, which MacIntyre regards as theoretically confused and practically fragmented; only a return to a tradition which synthesizes Aristotelian and Augustinian themes will restore rationality and intelligibility to contemporary moral and political life.

See also: VIRTUE ETHICS

ALAN THOMAS

MCTAGGART, JOHN MCTAGGART ELLIS (1866–1925)

McTaggart was one of the last of the 'British Idealists', the group of British philosophers, such as B. Bosanquet and F.H. Bradley, who took their inspiration from Hegel. In his early writings from the 1890s, McTaggart gave a critical exposition of themes from Hegel's logic before advancing his own distinctive idealist positions concerning time, the mind, and reality in general. But in his writings from 1910 he developed an independent account of the structure of existence from which he then argued for the same idealist positions as before.

The thesis for which McTaggart is now most famous is that of the unreality of time; what is even more difficult to come to terms with is his thesis that the ultimate reality of the world comprises a community of selves wholly constituted by their loving perceptions of each other. This thesis is a manifestation of a mysticism that is an essential element in McTaggart's philosophy; yet this mysticism is combined with a rationalist determination, reminiscent of Spinoza, to vindicate mystical insights by the light of pure reason alone.

THOMAS BALDWIN

MAGIC

Magic is the art of influencing the workings of nature through occult powers. It can be found in most societies throughout history. It is often defined by contrast with other subjects, such as science, rationality and religion. Practitioners of magic might fashion themselves as necromancers, magi or natural philosophers; and accused practitioners were often labelled as sorcerers, heretics or witches. Concentrated, though at times incoherent, expositions of what we might call the epistemology of magic reached their height in European philosophy in late antiquity in the writings of Plotinus, Porphyry and Proclus; this interest was rekindled in the Renaissance in the writings of Agrippa, Pico, Ficino and others in what is often described as the Hermetic or Occultist tradition. Whether magic worked according to natural, demonic or divine forces was debated, and during the Renaissance demonology shifted from a theological to a natural philosophical pursuit. In the Middle Ages explaining how magic worked was a concern of theolo-gians; in the Renaissance it was a concern of natural philosophers and physicians; and in the modern period it is a concern of anthropologists and historians. Magic has always been associated with trickery and danger, and with knowledge and power.

See also: AGRIPPA VON NETTESHEIM; BRUNO, G.; CAMPANELLA, T.; FICINO, M.; HERMETISM; KABALLAH; NEOPLATONISM; PICO DELLA MIRANDOLA; PLATONISM, RENAISSANCE; POMPONAZZI, PIETRO; RENAISSANCE PHILOSOPHY

LAUREN KASSELL

MAIMON, MOSES BEN

See MAIMONIDES, MOSES

MAIMONIDES, MOSES (1138–1204)

Called the Rambam in the Hebrew sources, an acronym on his name, and known in Islamic texts as Musa ibn Maimun, Rabbi Moses ben Maimon is best known in the West as Moses Maimonides and is generally recognized as the greatest of the medieval Jewish philosophers. Maimonides lived his mature life in Egypt and earned his living as a physician. He was the author of ten medical works but gained fame in his own lifetime for his work on Jewish law (*halakhah*), chiefly the *Kitab al-Fara'id* (*Sefer ha-Mitzvot*, that is, the Book of the Commandments), cataloguing the traditional 613 commandments of the Pentateuch; *Kitab al-Siraj* (*Sefer ha-Maor, Perush ha-Mishnah*, Commentary on the Mishnah); and, above all, the *Mishneh Torah* (The Law in Review), a comprehensive and still authoritative code of rabbinic law. The clarity and definitiveness of the Mishneh Torah led to its criticism and (after Maimonides' death) even condemnation by some rabbis, who prized the ongoing dialectic of Talmudic disputation and felt suspicious of Maimonides' rationalism.

Maimonides' philosophic masterpiece, the *Dalalat al-Ha'irin* or *Guide to the Perplexed*, was written in Arabic, with a view to helping the more intellectually inquisitive readers of the Torah, who were troubled by the apparent disparity between biblical and scientific/philosophical ideas. The work frames a powerful but not supercilious rationalism that locates and accommodates many biblical postulates and profits from the instruction of the rabbinic (Talmudic) sources and from critical appropriation of the achievements of Muslim philosophers and theologians and their Greek predecessors. It defends the doctrine of the world's creation against the eternalism of Neoplatonic Aristotelians but rejects the notion that creation (or eternity) is subject to proof. Rather, Maimonides argues, creation is preferable to its alternative, and more plausible, because it preserves the idea of divine volition as an explanation for the emergence of complexity from divine simplicity, and because it marks the difference God's act made to the existence and nature of the world.

God is pure perfection and absolute simplicity. The Torah's anthropomorphisms themselves lead us to that realization, if we follow the dialectic by which prophetic language directs us to ever higher conceptions of divine transcendence. Biblical poetry and the concrete demands of the Law are accommodations to our creaturely limitations. Such accommodations are made possible by the material side of the prophet's nature, as manifested in language and imagination, which are, no less than intellect, expressions of God. For matter in general is an expression of God, apprehensible to us through what seems wilful or arbitrary in nature. It is not a positive principle or hypostasis, but it is a necessary concomitant of the act of creation itself. For without it nothing other than God would exist. Our task as humans is to discipline our material natures – not to battle or seek to destroy them but to put them to work in behalf of our self-perfection, through which our inner, intellectual affinity to God will be realized.

Maimonides' synthetic approach, accommodating to one another the insights of reason and the teachings of Scripture and tradition, was highly valued by Aquinas, who frequently cites him, and by other European philosophers such as Jean Bodin. Leibniz warmly appreciated Maimonides' thought, as his reading notes reveal. Among subsequent Jewish thinkers, Maimonides' work became the paradigm of Jewish rationalism for his admirers and detractors alike. His philosophy was at the core of the philosophic tradition that Spinoza addressed. Even today practitioners of Jewish philosophy stake out their positions in reference to Maimonides and formulate their own views as appropriations, variants or interpretations of the elements of his thought.

See also: GOD, CONCEPTS OF; HALAKHAH; MIDRASH; RELIGION, PHILOSOPHY OF

L.E. GOODMAN

MAISTRE, JOSEPH DE (1753–1821)

Count Joseph de Maistre was a major theorist of the Counter-Enlightenment, whose writings inspired generations of French Catholic royalists and stimulated thinkers diverse as Saint- Simon, Auguste Comte and Charles Maurras. He is known especially for his providential interpretation of the French Revolution, his support for a Bourbon

Restoration in France, his opposition to all contractual theories of government, his arguments in favour of papal infallibility, his philosophical speculations on violence and bloodshed, his critique of John Locke's epistemology and his attack on Francis Bacon's 'scientism'.

See also: CONSERVATISM

RICHARD A. LEBRUN

MALEBRANCHE, NICOLAS (1638–1715)

Nicolas Malebranche, a French Catholic theologian, was the most important Cartesian philosopher of the second half of the seventeenth century. His philosophical system was a grand synthesis of the thought of his two intellectual mentors: Augustine and Descartes. His most important work, *De la recherche de la vérité* (The Search After Truth), is a wide-ranging opus that covers various topics in metaphysics, epistemology, ethics, physics, the physiology of cognition, and philosophical theology. It was both admired and criticized by many of the most celebrated thinkers of the period (including Leibniz, Arnauld and Locke), and was the focus of several fierce and time-consuming public debates. Malebranche's philosophical reputation rests mainly on three doctrines. Occasionalism – of which he is the most systematic and famous exponent – is a theory of causation according to which God is the only genuine causal agent in the universe; all physical and mental events in nature are merely 'occasions' for God to exercise his necessarily efficacious power. In the doctrine known as 'vision in God', Malebranche argues that the representational ideas that function in human knowledge and perception are, in fact, the ideas in God's understanding, the eternal archetypes or essences of things. And in his theodicy, Malebranche justifies God's ways and explains the existence of evil and sin in the world by appealing to the simplicity and universality of the laws of nature and grace that God has established and is compelled to follow. In all three doctrines, Malebranche's overwhelming concern is to demonstrate the essential and active role of God in every aspect – material, cognitive and moral – of the universe.

STEVEN NADLER

MANDEVILLE, BERNARD (1670–1733)

Bernard Mandeville's *Fable of the Bees* (1714) scandalized contemporaries by arguing that the flourishing commercial society they valued depended on vices they denounced. It resulted not only from the complementary satisfaction of appetites but was also based upon pride, envy and shame, which Mandeville traced to 'self-liking'. Numerous individuals, driven by their own desires, acted independently to produce goods which required extensive, cooperative operations – an idea central to the economic concept of a market.

Mandeville initially appeared to credit 'skilful politicians' with originating morality and society. However, in defending and expounding his views, he set out 'conjectural histories' of the gradual development of many complex social activities and institutions, including language and society itself, thereby denying that they had been invented by public spirited heroes. Throughout his works, Mandeville adopted a strict criterion of virtue, repeatedly denying that he was advocating, rather than exposing, the vices he identified as inherent in human society.

M.M. GOLDSMITH

MANICHEISM

Manicheism is a defunct religion, born in Mesopotamia in the third century AD and last attested in the sixteenth century in China. Its founder, Mani (c.216–76), had some familiarity with Judaism, Christianity, Zoroastrianism and Buddhism, and aimed to supplant them all. He taught a form of dualism, influenced by earlier Gnostics: God is opposed by forces of darkness; they, not God, created human beings, who nevertheless contain particles of light which can be released by abstemious living. Two points of contrast with Catholic Christianity are particularly striking. First, in Manicheism, sinfulness is the natural state of human beings (because of their creators), and does not stem from Adam's Fall. Second, the Manichean God did not create and does not control the forces of darkness (although he will eventually triumph); hence the problem of evil does not arise in as stark a form as it does for the all-powerful Christian God.

Although Mani's own missionary journeys took him eastwards, it was in the Roman Empire to the west that the main impact of his teaching was first felt; Augustine of Hippo was an adherent for nine years. The religion was eventually suppressed in the Roman Empire, and driven east by the Arab conquest of Mesopotamia. In the West, various Christian heresies were loosely called Manichean throughout the Middle Ages.

See also: EVIL, PROBLEM OF

CHRISTOPHER KIRWAN

MANY-VALUED LOGICS

Many-valued logics may be distinguished from classical logic on purely semantic grounds. One of the simplifying assumptions on which classical logic is based is the thesis of bivalence, which states that there are only two truth-values – true and false – and every sentence must be one or the other. Many-valued logics reject the thesis of bivalence and permit more than two truth-values.

CHARLES G. MORGAN

MANY-VALUED LOGICS, PHILOSOPHICAL ISSUES IN

The first philosophically-motivated use of many-valued truth tables arose with Jan Łukasiewicz in the 1920s. What exercised Łukasiewicz was a worry that the principle of bivalence, 'every statement is either true or false', involves an undesirable commitment to fatalism. Should not statements about the future whose eventual truth or falsity depends on the actions of free agents be given some third status – 'indeterminate', say – as opposed to being (now) regarded as determinately true or determinately false? To implement this idea in the context of the language of sentential logic (with conjunction, disjunction, implication and negation), we need to show – if the usual style of treatment of such connectives in a bivalent setting is to be followed – how the status of a compound formula is determined by the status of its components.

Łukasiewicz's decision as to how the appropriate three-valued truth-functions should look is recorded in truth tables in which (determinate) truth and falsity are represented by '1' and '3' respectively, with '2' for indeterminacy. Consider the formula $A \vee B$ ('A or B'), for example, when A has the value 2 and B has the value 1. The value of $A \vee B$ is 1, reasonably enough, since if A's eventual truth or falsity depends on how people freely act, but B is determinately true already, then $A \vee B$ is already true independently of such free action. There are no constraints as to which values may be assigned to propositional variables. The law of excluded middle is invalidated in the case of indeterminacy: if p is assigned the value 2, then $p \vee \neg p$ also has the value 2. This reflects Łukasiewicz's idea that such disjunctions as 'Either I shall die in a plane crash on January 1, 2030 or I shall not die in a plane crash on January 1, 2030' should not be counted as logical truths, on pain of incurring the fatalistic commitments already alluded to.

Together with the choice of designated elements (which play the role in determining validity played by truth in the bivalent setting), Łukasiewicz's tables constitute a (logical) matrix. An alternative three-element matrix, the 1-Kleene matrix, involves putting $2 \rightarrow 2 = 2$, leaving everything else unchanged.

And a third such matrix, the 1,2-Kleene matrix, differs from this in taking as designated the set of values $\{1,2\}$ rather than $\{1\}$. The 1-Kleene matrix has been proposed for the semantics of vagueness. In the case of a sentence applying a vague predicate, such as 'young', to an individual, the idea is that if the individual is a borderline case of the predicate (not definitely young, and not definitely not young, to use our example) then the value 2 is appropriate, while 1 and 3 are reserved for definite truths and falsehoods, respectively. Łukasiewicz also explored, as a technical curiosity, n-valued tables constructed on the same model, for higher values of n, as well as certain infinitely many-valued tables. Variations on this theme have included acknowledging as many values as there are real numbers, with similar applications to vagueness and approximation in mind.

See also: INTUITIONISM; ŁUKASIEWICZ, J.; MANY-VALUED LOGICS

LLOYD HUMBERSTONE

MARCUSE, HERBERT (1898–1979)

Herbert Marcuse endured a brief moment of notoriety in the 1960s, when his best-known book, *One-Dimensional Man* (1964), was taken up by the mass media as the Bible of the student revolts which shook most Western countries in that decade. Though Marcuse's actual political influence was uneven, his public image was not wholly misleading. On the one hand, he popularized the critique of post-war capitalism that he, with the other theorists of the Frankfurt School, had helped develop: the Western liberal democracies were, they argued, 'totally administered societies' permeated by the values of consumerism, in which the manufacture and satisfaction of 'false needs' served to prevent the working class from gaining any genuine insight into their situation. On the other hand, Marcuse never fully subscribed to the highly pessimistic version of Marxism developed by the central figures of the Frankfurt School, Adorno and Horkheimer. He hoped that revolts by an underclass of 'the outcasts and the outsiders, the exploited and persecuted of other races and other colours, the unemployed and unemployable' would stimulate a broader social transformation. Underlying this affirmation of revolutionary possibilities was a conception of Being as a state of rest in which all conflicts are overcome, where rational thought and sensual gratification are no longer at war with one another, and work merges into play. Intimations of this condition – which could only be fully realized after the overthrow of capitalism (and perhaps not even then) – were, Marcuse believed, offered in art,

'the possible Form of a free society'. Imagination could thus show politics the way.

See also: FRANKFURT SCHOOL

ALEX CALLINICOS

MARGINALITY

Traditional definitions of marginal persons include those who live in two worlds, but do not feel well integrated into either, and those who live in societies which are in the process of being assimilated and incorporated into an emerging global society. The influence of Anglo-American and European cultures has brought this situation into existence. A broader, more contemporary understanding of marginality is the condition of feeling marginal in relation to various concepts of the centre. This state produces a stigmatized identity, which either aspires to inclusion or assimilation into the centre, or demands recognition of and respect for a separate but equal existence. This condition of marginality can be experienced in varying degrees by many kinds of people.

Often gender, sexual preference, age, ethnicity, geography and religion are factors which can influence perceptions of marginality. Those who perceive themselves, or who are perceived by others to be marginal are often female, dark-skinned, very young or elderly, poor, disabled, nonheterosexual, displaced, exiled, immigrant, rural, indigenous, 'foreign', outcast, persecuted, or otherwise 'different' from those who occupy positions of privilege in the centre, or the metropolis. Critics of the term 'marginality' believe it has become overused to the point of losing descriptive precision because, they argue, almost everyone has experienced some form of marginality. In philosophy, however, the phenomenon of feeling, or being, perceived as peripheral, or on the margin, has generated critical perspectives which have enlightened discourse on social integration and stratification; personal suffering and economic, political, and cultural inequality. In addition, analyses of marginality have called into question notions of the 'universal' and the 'objective' set forth by many Western philosophers.

See also: ALTERITY AND IDENTITY, POSTMODERN THEORIES OF

AMY A. OLIVER

MARKET, ETHICS OF THE

Markets are systems of exchange in which people with money or commodities to sell voluntarily trade these for other items which they prefer to have. Most economic transactions in advanced societies are of this kind, and any attempt to replace markets wholesale with a different form of economic coordination seems destined to fail. But questions about the ethics of markets are still of considerable practical concern, for two reasons at least. First, we need to make collective decisions about the proper scope of markets: are there goods and services which in principle should not be distributed and exchanged through market mechanisms – medical care, for instance? Second, markets work within a framework of property rights which sets the terms on which people can exchange with one another, and this too is subject to collective decision: for instance, should a person's labour be regarded as a commodity like any other, to be bought and sold on whatever terms the parties can agree, or does labour carry special rights that set limits to these terms? Are employees morally entitled to a share of the profits of the companies they work in, to take a concrete issue?

To guide such decisions, we need to apply general ethical principles to market transactions. First, are markets justified on grounds of efficiency, as is often claimed? What criterion of efficiency is being used when such claims are made? Second, can we regard the outcome of market exchanges as just, or, at the other extreme, should we see them as necessarily exploitative? Third, do market exchanges necessarily alienate people from one another and destroy their sense of community? These are very different questions, but an overall assessment of market ethics needs to address each of them, and perhaps others besides.

DAVID MILLER

MARX, KARL (1818–83)

Introduction

Karl Marx was the most important of all theorists of socialism. He was not a professional philosopher, although he completed a doctorate in philosophy. His life was devoted to radical political activity, journalism and theoretical studies in history and political economy.

Marx was drawn towards politics by Romantic literature, and his earliest writings embody a conception of reality as subject to turbulent change and of human beings as realizing themselves in the struggle for freedom. His identification with these elements in Hegel's thought (and his contempt for what he regarded as Hegel's apologetic attitude towards the Prussian state) brought Marx to associate himself with the Young Hegelians.

The Young Hegelians had come to believe that the implicit message of Hegel's philosophy was a radical one: that Reason could and should exist within the world, in contrast to Hegel's explicit claim that embodied Reason already did exist. Moreover, they also rejected Hegel's idea that religion and philosophy go hand in hand: that religion represents the truths of philosophy in immediate form. On the contrary, the Young Hegelians saw the central task of philosophy as the critique of religion – the struggle (as Marx himself was to put it in his doctoral dissertation) 'against the gods of heaven and of earth who do not recognize man's self-consciousness as the highest divinity'.

Marx came to be dissatisfied with the assumption that the critique of religion alone would be sufficient to produce human emancipation. He worked out the consequences of this change of view in the years 1843 to 1845, the most intellectually fertile period of his entire career. Hegel's philosophy, Marx now argued, embodied two main kinds of mistake. It incorporated, first, the illusion that reality as a whole is an expression of the Idea, the absolute rational order governing reality. Against this, Marx's position (and on this point he still agreed with the Young Hegelians) was that it is Man, not the Idea, who is the true subject. Second, he charged, Hegel believed that the political state – the organs of law and government – had priority in determining the character of a society as a whole. In fact, according to Marx, this is the reverse of the truth: political life and the ideas associated with it are themselves determined by the character of economic life.

Marx claimed that the 'species-being' of Man consists in labour, and that Man is 'alienated' to the extent that labour is performed according to a division of labour that is dictated by the market. It is only when labour recovers its collective character that men will recognize themselves as what they are – the true creators of history. At this point, the need to represent the essence of human beings in terms of their relation to an alien being – be it the Christian God or Hegelian *Geist* – will no longer exist.

In the mature writings that followed his break with the Young Hegelians, Marx presented a would-be scientific theory of history as a progress through stages. At each stage, the form taken by a society is conditioned by the society's attained level of productivity and the requirements for its increase. In pre-socialist societies this entails the division of society into antagonistic classes. Classes are differentiated by what makes them able (or unable) to appropriate for themselves the surplus produced by social labour. In general, to the extent that a class can appropriate surplus without paying for it, it is said to be an 'exploiting' class; conversely, a class that produces more than it receives is said to be 'exploited'.

Although the exploiting classes have special access to the means of violence, exploitation is not generally a matter of the use of force. In capitalism, for example, exploitation flows from the way in which the means of production are owned privately and labour is bought and sold just like any other commodity. That such arrangements are accepted without the need for coercion reflects the fact that the ruling class exercises a special influence over ideas in society. It controls the *ideology* accepted by the members of society in general.

In *Das Kapital* (Capital), the work to which he devoted the latter part of his life, Marx set out to identify the 'laws of motion' of capitalism. The capitalist system is presented there as a self-reproducing whole, governed by an underlying law, the 'law of value'. But this law and its consequences are not only not immediately apparent to the agents who participate in capitalism, indeed they are actually concealed from them. Thus capitalism is a 'deceptive object', one in which there is a discrepancy between its 'essence' and its 'appearance'.

In Marx's view, it is inevitable that capitalism should give way to socialism. As capitalism develops, he believed, the increasingly 'socialized' character of the productive process will conflict more and more with the private ownership of the means of production. Thus the transition to collective ownership will be natural and inevitable. But Marx nowhere explained how this collective ownership and social control was to be exercised. Indeed, he had remarkably little to say about the nature of this society to the struggle to which he devoted his life.

The Critique of the Gotha Programme envisaged two phases of communist society. In the first, production will be carried out on a non-exploitative basis: all who contribute to production will receive back the value of what they have contributed. But this, Marx recognized, is a form of 'equal right' that leaves the natural inequalities of human beings unchecked. It is a transitional phase, although inevitable. Beyond it there lies a society in which individuals are no longer 'slaves' to the division of labour, one in which labour has become 'not only a means of life but life's prime want'. Only then, Marx thought, 'can the narrow horizon of bourgeois right be crossed in its entirety and society inscribe on its banners: from each according to his ability, to each according to his needs!' This is the final vision of communism.

1   Life and works

Marx was born on 5 May 1818, in Trier, a small, originally Roman city on the river Moselle. Many of Marx's ancestors were rabbis, but his father, Heinrich, a lawyer of liberal political views, converted from Judaism to Christianity and Marx was baptized with the rest of his family in 1824. At school, the young Marx excelled in literary subjects (a prescient schoolteacher comments, however, that his essays were 'marred by an exaggerated striving after unusual, picturesque expression'). In 1835, he entered the University of Bonn to study law. At the end of 1836, he transferred to Berlin and became a member of the Young Hegelian *Doktorklub*, a bohemian group whose leading figure was the theologian, Bruno Bauer. The views of the *Doktorklub* became increasingly radical (to some extent, it would seem, under Marx's influence) in the late 1830s.

Marx's father died in 1838 and in the next year – perhaps not coincidentally – Marx abandoned the law in favour of a doctorate in philosophy. His thesis, *Differenz der demokritischen und epikureischen Naturphilosophie* (Difference between the Democritean and Epicurean Philosophy of Nature) was accepted by the University of Jena in 1841. Marx had hoped to use it to gain an academic position, but, after Bruno Bauer's suspension from his post at the University of Bonn, it became apparent that such hopes would have to be abandoned in the current political climate.

Marx turned instead to journalism, involving himself with the newly-founded *Rheinische Zeitung* and taking over the editorship in October 1842. However, the paper came increasingly into conflict with the Prussian government and was banned in March 1843. At this point, Marx decided to move abroad. In the summer he married Jenny von Westphalen (after an engagement of six years) and during a long honeymoon in Kreuznach worked on *Zur Kritik der Hegelschen Rechtsphilosophie* (Critique of Hegel's Philosophy of Right) and the essay 'Zur Judenfrage' ('On the Jewish Question') in which he started to formulate his disagreements with his fellow Young Hegelians. He and Jenny moved to Paris in October of that year. It was in 1844 that Marx met up again with Friedrich ENGELS (whom he had known slightly in Berlin) and the alliance was formed that was to last for the rest of Marx's life. Together Marx and Engels wrote *Die Heilige Familie* (The Holy Family) (1845), a polemic against Bruno Bauer. More important, however, was the body of writing on economics and philosophy that Marx produced at this time, generally known as the *Paris Manuscripts* (1844).

Marx was expelled from France in 1845 and moved to Brussels. In the spring of 1845, he wrote for his own clarification a series of essays on Feuerbach. These 'Theses on Feuerbach' are one of the few mature statements we have of his views on questions of epistemology and ontology. In 1845–6 Marx and Engels wrote *Die deutsche Ideologie* (The German Ideology) which, although it too remained unpublished, contains an authoritative account of their theory of history and in particular of the place of ideas in society. Marx's developing economic views were given expression in a polemic against Proudhon, *La Misère de la Philosophie* (The Poverty of Philosophy), published in 1847.

Das Kommunistische Manifest (The Communist Manifesto), written by Marx and Engels as the manifesto of the Communist League in early 1848, is the classic presentation of the revolutionary implications of Marx's views on history, politics and economics. During the revolutionary upsurge of 1848 Marx returned to Germany, but with the defeat of the revolutionary movement he was forced to leave, first for Paris, and then, in August 1849, for London, where he would live in exile for the rest of his life.

The years of exile in Britain were difficult ones for Marx (and even more so for his loyal and devoted family). He was in constant financial difficulty and had to rely heavily on Engels and other friends and relations for support. His theoretical activities were chiefly directed to the study of political economy and the analysis of the capitalist system in particular. They culminated in the publication of the first volume of *Das Kapital* (Capital) in 1867. However, *Das Kapital* is the tip of a substantial iceberg of less important publications and unpublished writings. Among the former, the Preface to *Zur Kritik der politischen Ökonomie* (A Contribution to the Critique of Political Economy) published in 1859, contains the classic statement of Marx's materialist theory of history. The second and third volumes of *Das Kapital*, left unfinished at Marx's death, were edited and published posthumously by Engels. In addition, three volumes of *Theorien über den Mehrwert* (Theories of Surplus-Value), a series of critical discussions of other political economists, written in 1862–3, were published in the early twentieth century. An extensive and more or less complete work, the *Grundrisse der Kritik der politischen Ökonomie* (known

both in English and in German as the *Grundrisse*) was written in 1857–8 but only published in 1939. The Introduction to the *Grundrisse* is the mature Marx's most extended discussion of the method of political economy. In addition, there exist numerous notebooks and preliminary drafts, many (if not, at the time of writing, all) of which have been published.

Political economy apart, Marx wrote three works on political events in France: *Die Klassenkämpfe in Frankreich* (Class Struggles in France) (1850), *Das achtzehnte Brumaire des Louis Bonaparte* (The Eighteenth Brumaire of Louis Bonaparte) (1852) and *The Civil War in France* (1871). Among his many polemical writings, the *Kritik des Gothaer Programms* (Critique of the Gotha Programme) (1875) is particularly important for the light it throws on Marx's conception of socialism and its relation to ideas of justice.

Marx was in very poor health for the last ten years of his life, which seems to have sapped his energies for large-scale theoretical work. However, his engagement with the practical details of revolutionary politics was unceasing. He died on 14 March 1883 and is buried in Highgate Cemetery, London.

2 Marx as a Young Hegelian

Marx is relevant to philosophy in three ways: (1) as a philosopher himself, (2) as a critic of philosophy, of its aspirations and self-understanding, and (3) by the philosophical implications of work that is, in Marx's own understanding of it, not philosophical at all. Broadly speaking, these three aspects correspond to the stages of Marx's own intellectual development. This and the following section are concerned with the first stage.

The Young Hegelians, with whom Marx was associated at the beginning of his career, did not set out to be critics of Hegel. That they rapidly became so has to do with the consequences they drew from certain tensions within Hegel's thought. Hegel's central claim is that both nature and society embody the rational order of *Geist* (Spirit). Nevertheless, the Young Hegelians believed, it did not follow that all societies express rationality to the fullest degree possible. This was the case in contemporary Germany. There was, in their view, a conflict between the essential rationality of *Geist* and the empirical institutions within which *Geist* had realized itself: Germany was 'behind the times' (see HEGEL, G.W.F. §§5–8; HEGELIANISM).

A second source of tension lay in Hegel's attitude towards religion. Hegel had been prepared to concede a role to religion as the expression of the content of philosophy in immediate form. The

Young Hegelians, however, argued that the relationship between the truths of philosophy and religious 'representation' was, in fact, antagonistic. In presenting reality not as the embodiment of reason but as the expression of the will of a personal god the Christian religion establishes a metaphysical dualism that is quite contrary to the secular 'this-worldliness' which (although Hegel himself might have been too cautious to spell it out fully) is the true significance of Hegel's philosophy.

This was the position endorsed by Marx at the time of his doctoral dissertation on Epicurus and Democritus. Its subject was taken from a period of Greek thought that displayed parallels with the Germany of Marx's own time. Just as the Young Hegelians faced the problem of how to continue philosophy after Hegel, so Epicurus wrote in the shadow of another great system, that of Aristotle. Epicurus is more successful than Democritus, Marx believes, in combining materialism with an account of human agency. Furthermore, Marx admires Epicurus for his explicit critique of religion, the chief task of philosophy, he asserts, in all ages.

In its destruction of the illusions of religion, the Young Hegelians believed that philosophy would provide both the necessary and the sufficient conditions for human emancipation and the achievement of a rational state. In the works that he wrote in Kreuznach in 1843 (the unpublished draft of the *Critique of Hegel's Philosophy of Right* and the essay 'On the Jewish Question') and shortly thereafter (the '*Critique of Hegel's Philosophy of Right*: Introduction') Marx called this position into question.

In the *Critique of Hegel's Philosophy of Right* Marx makes two main criticisms of Hegel. The first is that Hegel's real concern is to retrace in the political realm the outlines of his own metaphysics, rather than to develop an analysis of political institutions and structures in their own right. This gives his political philosophy an apologetic function, for it leads him to present the contradictions that he finds in reality as essentially reconciled in the supposedly higher unity of the 'Idea'. But they are not, says Marx. On the contrary, they are 'essential contradictions'.

Chief among such contradictions is that existing between the 'system of particular interest' (the family and civil society – that is, economic life) and the 'system of general interest', namely, the state. And this leads to Marx's second criticism. Hegel, Marx alleges, assumes that the state, because it is 'higher' from the point of view of Hegelian logic, can effectively reconcile the contradictions of economic life. In fact, in Marx's view, it is civil society that exists prior to the state. The state arises from the condition of civil society and is always subordinate to the form of the latter.

3   Philosophy and the critique of religion

Marx presents the implications of these criticisms for the critique of religion in the *Critique of Hegel's Philosophy of Right*: 'Introduction'. This short essay is a compressed masterpiece of vehement rhetoric, seething with antithesis and chiasmus. In Germany, Marx writes, 'the critique of religion is essentially completed'. Thus the problem is how to go beyond it. Marx's first step is to explain the significance of that critique, as he understands it.

The world of religion is a reflection of a particular form of society: 'This state, this society, produce religion, which is an inverted world-consciousness, because they are an inverted world'. That is to say, only an inverted, secular world would produce religion as its offshoot. In religious belief, Man finds himself reflected in the 'fantastic reality of heaven', whilst he can find only 'the semblance of himself, only a nonhuman being' in this world. Religion thus provides a realm in which individuals can realize themselves, at least partially, given that full and adequate self-realization is not possible in the profane world. In this way, religion preserves the social order of which it is a by-product, both by deflecting attention from its defects and by providing a partial escape from it. In Marx's famous words, 'Religion is the sigh of the oppressed creature, the heart of a heartless world and the soul of soulless conditions. It is the opium of the people'.

Thus religion and the form of life associated with it are open to criticism at three points. (1) There is, first, the impoverished and distorted world of which religion is a by-product. (2) There is the way in which the image of reality produced by religion is falsely transfigured. (3) Finally, there is the failure by human beings to recognize the fact that religion has its origins in mundane reality.

It is this last element towards which the critique of religion is directed. Critique of religion connects religion back to its unacknowledged origins in social existence. Yet this is not enough. The critique of religion, inasmuch as it is a call to people to abandon their illusions, is also, according to Marx, 'the call to abandon a condition that requires illusions'. By itself the critique of religion cannot remove the distortion and impoverishment of the world from which religion arises. This is of course Marx's real project, for which the criticism of religion has merely prepared the ground.

Once the criticism of religion has done its work, philosophy must move on 'to unmask human self-alienation in its secular forms'. The critique of religion ends, Marx says, 'in the doctrine that man is the supreme being for man; thus it ends with the categorical imperative to overthrow all conditions in which man is a debased, enslaved, neglected, contemptible being' (*Zur Kritik der Hegeleschen Rechtsphilosophie* 1843).

Much of this analysis represents common ground between Marx and his Young Hegelian former associates. Marx concedes that philosophy has both a critical role to play in exposing the illusions of religion and an affirmative one in establishing an ideal of human fulfilment. Nevertheless, Marx takes the Young Hegelians to task for thinking that philosophy alone provides a sufficient condition for human emancipation. Philosophy, he maintains, must move beyond itself: 'criticism of the speculative philosophy of right does not remain within itself, but proceeds on to tasks for whose solution there is only one means – praxis'. For this, a material force – a 'class with radical chains' – is required, namely, the proletariat.

At this stage, then, Marx is critical not so much of the content of philosophy, but of what we might call the metaphilosophical belief associated with it: that it is possible (as he puts it in relation to the Young Hegelians) 'to realize philosophy without transcending it'. A truly successful critique of religion would require the transformation of the social conditions within which religion is generated and sustained.

4   Alienated labour

In Paris, Marx threw himself into the study of political economy. His objective was to amplify his critique of Hegel and the Young Hegelians with a more far-reaching account of the nature of 'civil society'. The *Paris Manuscripts* thus provide a unique link between Marx's economic theory and his philosophical view of human nature. The concept which brings the two together is that of alienation (*Entfremdung*) (see ALIENATION). Although Marx had made little use of this term in his earlier writings, the structure of the concept is clearly anticipated in his critique of religion. The fundamental idea is that an entity or agent gives rise to a product or expression that is distinct from but at the same time essential to itself. This secondary product comes to be cut off from its origin. In consequence, the agent suffers a loss of identity in some sense. Thus, for the agent to realize itself fully, it must remove the separation that has come between itself and its own product.

In the central discussion of the *Paris Manuscripts*, Marx sets out to apply the concept of alienation to the labour process. Alienation, Marx argues, is characteristic of a situation in which (1) labour is directed towards the production of commodities (that is, goods exchangeable in the market) and (2) labour itself is such a commodity. Marx divides the alienation involved in labour into three main forms.

(1) There is, first, the separation of the worker from the product of labour. It is in the nature of the labour process that it involves 'appropriating' the external world. But when labour is alienated, the sensible, external world becomes an object to which the worker is bound, something that is hostile to them, instead of being the means to their self-realization.

(2) At the same time, the labour process itself becomes alien to the worker. Because the imperatives according to which labour takes place come to the worker 'from outside' (that is, from the market, either directly or indirectly) labour is no longer an act of self-realization. It becomes, from the worker's point of view, 'an activity directed against himself, which is independent of him and does not belong to him'.

(3) Finally, Marx says, the consequence of these two forms of alienation is to alienate man from what he calls his 'species-being' (*Gattungswesen*). The latter concept (of which Marx made frequent use in 1843–4) is adapted from Ludwig Feuerbach. Man, says Marx, is a species-being 'because he looks upon himself as the present, living species, because he looks upon himself as a *universal* and therefore free being'.

An analogy that may help to clarify this apparently circular definition can be made with the family. In a limited sense, people can be part of a family without consciously behaving accordingly (at the limit, we can think of members of a family who do not even know that they are related). But in order to be a family in a fuller sense, people must relate to one another *as* a family, and at least a part of this is that they should be aware that they *are* a family. So it is with human species-being. While the fundamental phenomenon on which the family is based is a biological relation, in human species-being it is labour. Thus, as labour is alienated in other respects, so people become alienated from their species-being. The consequence is the alienation of members of the species from one another.

Each of these three points is, one might think, somewhat questionable. Surely, in any situation in which individuals do not produce entirely for themselves, it will be inevitable that the products of labour are 'separated' from the original producer. Likewise, the labour process cannot be something that is freely chosen by individuals as long as they are objectively constrained by the nature of the material world and the resources available to them in finding efficient means to given ends. Finally, it is not at all clear what is involved in human beings 're-appropriating' their 'species-being'.

One way of making the concept of alienated labour more precise is to ask what it might be for labour to be non-alienated. Marx addresses the issue at the end of a discussion of James Mill's *Elements of Political Economy*. 'Let us suppose', Marx begins, 'that we had produced as human beings'. In that case, he claims, each of us would have 'affirmed' both ourselves and our fellows in the process of production. In the first place, I, the producer, would have affirmed myself in my production. At the same time, I would be gratifying a human need – that of my neighbour, for whom I am in this case producing. Thus, in meeting your need, I would have mediated between you and the species: 'I would be acknowledged by you as the complement of your own being, as an essential part of yourself'. In this way, production and the meeting of needs involves a mutuality of self-realization and reciprocal recognition:

> In the individual expression of my own life I would have brought about the expression of your life, and so in my individual activity I would have directly *confirmed* and *realized* my authentic nature, my *human, communal* nature.
>
> (*Paris Manuscripts*)

These ideas help to explain Marx's antagonism towards what he would call 'bourgeois' political theory. In so far as traditional political philosophy takes as its fundamental question how to reconcile competing interests, its starting point is, from Marx's point of view, unacceptably individualistic. For what entitles us to assume that the interests of individuals are bound to be antagonistic? Rather than asking how to allocate rights and duties fairly when interests conflict, the task, Marx believes, is to move humanity towards a form of life in which conflicts of interest are no longer endemic.

5   The critique of philosophy

Although the *Paris Manuscripts* show Marx's increasing engagement with political economy, they do not represent an abandonment of his concern with philosophy. The attitude that Marx takes towards philosophy, however, now becomes more critical than it had been in his earlier, Young Hegelian period. In part, this can be traced to Ludwig Feuerbach, whom Marx quotes approvingly at several points (see FEUERBACH, L.). It was Feuerbach's great achievement, Marx writes, 'to have shown that philosophy is nothing more than religion brought into thought and developed in thought, and that it is equally to be condemned as another form and mode of existence of the alienation of human nature'. Thus Marx now regards philosophy as essentially continuous with religion, not a force directed against religion, as he

had represented it at the time of his doctoral dissertation.

Marx makes a number of negative remarks regarding philosophy in general, but his more specific critical comments are directed towards Hegel. Like Feuerbach, he takes the view that Hegel has brought philosophy to a point of completion. The dynamic principle at the heart of Hegel's philosophy, according to Marx, is that of 'abstract mental labour'. Nevertheless, despite the genuinely critical elements contained within it, Hegel's philosophy is vitiated by its idealist assumptions. In the end, for Hegel, alienation is merely a matter of the separation of the products of thought from thought itself, something to be overcome by a philosophical reorientation of consciousness. To go beyond Hegel, it would be necessary to make the concept of real, concrete labour fundamental. But this, Marx suggests, leads beyond philosophy itself.

Marx pursues these ideas in the 'Theses on Feuerbach', written in the spring of 1845. Here he makes it explicit that his disagreement is not only with idealistic philosophies, such as Hegel's, but also with would-be materialist ones, Feuerbach's included. In incorporating within itself an idea of 'activity', idealism has important advantages over materialism. It is, Marx writes,

> the chief defect of all hitherto existing materialism (that of Feuerbach included)...that the thing, reality, sensuousness, is conceived only in the form of the object or of contemplation, but not as sensuous human activity, praxis, not subjectively. Hence, in contradistinction to materialism, the *active* side was developed abstractly by idealism – which, of course, does not know real sensuous activity as such.
>
> ('Theses on Feuerbach')

It should be noted that this passage is ambiguous. Is Marx envisaging a new kind of materialism (one that would not have the defects of 'hitherto existing materialism') or is it a call to leave philosophy – both materialism and idealism – behind altogether? Interpreters of Marx who take the former view have ascribed an implicit philosophical position to him (often called 'dialectical materialism'). Nevertheless, the fact remains that Marx himself never developed such a position explicitly, and the conclusion of the 'Theses on Feuerbach' appears to lead away from philosophy entirely: 'The philosophers have only *interpreted* the world in various ways; the point is to *change* it.'

The German Ideology, which Marx and Engels wrote from September 1845 to the summer of 1846, continues this line of argument. As in so many of Marx's writings, the rhetorical trope from which the criticism starts is that of an inversion of an inversion. The Young Hegelians, Marx alleges, think of themselves as engaged in a struggle with the illusions that hold the Germans in their grip. But in fact they are in the grip of an illusion themselves: the illusion that ideas are an independent, determining force in political life. Feuerbach is not excepted from this criticism. Although he purports to demystify the realm of pure ideas, he still remains, according to Marx and Engels, 'in the realm of theory'. Feuerbach, they claim, 'never arrives at really existing, active men, but stops at the abstraction "man"'.

The alternative that Marx and Engels propose is, of course, also a theory, but it is a theory, they claim, of a quite different kind. 'In direct contrast to German philosophy, which descends from heaven to earth', their purpose is to present an account which will 'ascend from earth to heaven'. Instead of translating general ideas back into equally general anthropological categories, the aim is to give a specific account of their historical origins. In so doing, it undermines the presuppositions on which the philosophical enterprise rests and philosophy, as an independent branch of knowledge, loses its medium of existence:

> The philosophers would only have to dissolve their language into the ordinary language, from which it is abstracted, to recognize it as the distorted language of the actual world, and realize that neither thoughts nor language in themselves form a realm of their own, that they are only *manifestations* of actual life.
>
> (*The German Ideology*)

6 The theory of ideology: (1) The reflection model

The German Ideology is filled with polemical assertions of the priority of material life over the world of religion, thought and speculation. But it sets out to do more than sloganize. Its aim is to develop the framework for a scientific explanation of how the material life conditions and determines thought and culture. By the time *The German Ideology* came to be written, the term 'ideology' had established itself in German as referring to systems of ideas detached from and out of proportion to empirical reality (Heinrich Heine, with whom Marx was on intimate terms in Paris, used it in that sense). In *The German Ideology* this is certainly part of the meaning of the term. But the concept also has a wider explanatory function (see IDEOLOGY).

Since the ancient world, political thinkers had been concerned with the role that 'false' or

irrational forms of consciousness play in political life. To this extent, the Young Hegelian critique of religion represented the latest manifestation of a very long tradition. However, the originality of Marx's concept of ideology lies in the way that it brings the idea of false consciousness together with a distinctively modern conception of society.

At the end of the eighteenth and the beginning of the nineteenth century, a conception of society came to the fore in Germany and France according to which societies, like organisms, have the power of maintaining and reproducing themselves through time. Marx was very much taken with this view, which he endorsed in the *Critique of Hegel's Philosophy of Right*. Chief among the conditions for a society to reproduce itself, according to Marx, are the ideas held by its members. Thus false consciousness, rather than being simply an accidental feature of human nature (albeit one with enormous political consequences) should be regarded as a phenomenon to be explained by the particular character of the society in which it is to be found.

If societies do not rest solely on coercion, then this is because those who are oppressed or exploited for some reason accept this. As Marx puts it bluntly: 'the ideas of the ruling class are in every epoch the ruling ideas'. But how does this come about? What sort of connection holds between the economic structures of a society and the ideas of its members? *The German Ideology* contains two analogies that might serve as mechanisms for the explanation of the connection between material life and ideas. The first is embodied in the following famous passage:

> If in all ideology men and their circumstances appear upside-down as in a camera obscura, this phenomenon arises just as much from their historical life-process as the inversion of objects on the retina does from their physical life-process.... We set out from real, active men, and on the basis of their real life-process we demonstrate the development of the ideological reflexes and echoes of this life-process. The phantoms formed in the human brain are also, necessarily, sublimates of their material life-process, which is empirically verifiable and bound to material premises.
>
> (*The German Ideology*)

Let us call this the 'reflection model' of ideology. The idea is that ideology relates to material life as images do to reality in a camera obscura or on the retina of the human eye: items in reality are reproduced accurately, but in reverse.

Yet brief consideration of the analogy shows that, as it stands, it is completely inadequate. It is indeed true that the images on the human retina are 'upside-down'. But does this mean that human beings do not perceive the world about them accurately? Of course not. The fact is that, as far as human perception is concerned, 'upside-down' is the right way up for images to be on our retinas. And this points the way towards the problem with Marx's analogy. By describing *all* consciousness as reversed or inverted the contrast between 'true' and 'false' loses its sense.

A further objection arises later in the quoted passage in which Marx continues the reflection analogy when he speaks of the ideological 'reflexes and echoes' of real life-processes. Ideological ideas are, he goes on to say, 'phantoms' and 'sublimates'. These metaphors carry with them an important implication: ideological thought is the effect of real processes, but it is itself insubstantial, without material reality or causal power. If this is Marx's considered view, then it is clearly disastrous for the theory of ideology. For the point of the theory of ideology was to explain how it was that certain forms of thought served to sustain particular societies. Thus these forms of thought are, by assumption, not ineffective, but have very important causal effects: helping to maintain a particular social and economic order.

Finally, it is not obvious that ideology relates to material life as mind relates to matter. Is the implication that ideology is immaterial and material life non-intellectual? This plainly contradicts Marx's basic position. Not only would it be odd for an avowed materialist to suggest that ideas are something basically insubstantial, but, even more importantly, it conflicts with the idea that economic life, so far from being unconscious or unreflective, is the central part of man's cognitive engagement with external reality.

7　The theory of ideology: (2) The interests model

There is, however, another model at work in *The German Ideology*. While the reflection model draws on the parallel between the ideological process and a traditional, realist account of perception (the immaterial mind passively mirrors a mind-independent reality) what we may call the 'interests model' develops from a more instrumentalist approach to epistemology. That Marx was (at this time, at least) attracted to such views is apparent from the 'Theses on Feuerbach'. In the second thesis he writes, 'The dispute over the reality or non-reality of thinking that is isolated from practice is a purely *scholastic* question'. From this point of view, the most significant aspect of ideas is not their relationship to a mind-independent reality, but that they are the products of practical activity, and that this practical

activity is itself guided by interests. The materialistic view of history that this leads to, Marx and Engels say, 'does not explain practice from the Idea, but explains the formation of ideas from material practice'.

The problem with the interests model does not lie in the view that ideas are the product of interests itself, which is, of course, very plausible (although it is more difficult to determine just what proportion of our ideas are products of interests in this way – surely not all of them – and to explain just how it is that interests should assert themselves in the process by which ideas are formed). The problem is that ideological ideas are not simply ideas formed in the pursuit of interests. They are, in fact, supposed to be ideas that go *against* the interests of a large number of those who hold them (and in this way further the interests of others). How do ideas of this kind come to be accepted?

Marx and Engels' answer starts from the following claim:

> The class which has the means of material production at its disposal, has control at the same time over the means of mental production, so that thereby, generally speaking, the ideas of those who lack the means of mental production are subject to it.
>
> (*The German Ideology*)

But this is not a satisfactory solution. Marx and Engels seem to view those who live under the domination of the ruling class as passive victims, taking their ideas like obedient chicks from those who control the 'means of mental production', with no critical reflection as to whether the ideas are either true or in their own rational interests. Yet why should one suppose that the ruling class is capable of promoting its interests effectively and forms its ideas in response to those interests, while the dominated classes simply accept whatever is served up to them?

Marx and Engels do, however, attempt to make their claim more plausible in their discussion of the nature of mental production. It is, they write, the most significant development in the division of labour that mental and manual labour become separated:

> Division of labour only becomes truly such from the moment when a division of material and manual labour appears.... From this moment onwards consciousness *can* really flatter itself that it is something other than consciousness of existing practice, that it *really* represents something without representing something real; from now on consciousness is in a position to emancipate itself from the

world and to proceed to the formation of 'pure' theory, theology, philosophy, ethics, etc.

(*The German Ideology*)

The separation between mental and manual labour, Marx and Engels maintain, does not really lead to the formation of autonomous ideas; the ideologists who produce ideas are still part of the ruling class whose interests their ideas represent. Nevertheless, it offers an explanation as to why such ideas should be accepted by those, the dominated classes, whose interests they oppose: they are accepted because they are apparently disinterested. The ideologist, on this view, is like a bribed referee: able to influence the outcome of a game all the more effectively for the fact that he is falsely believed to be impartial.

Are ideologists, then, engaged in deception? Do they know the partiality of their ideas but present them none the less as if they were neutral and disinterested? On the contrary. According to Marx and Engels, ideologists are sincere – and, because they sincerely believe in the independence and objective validity of their own ideas, they are able to persuade others to accept them as such all the more effectively. Herein, however, lies the problem. How are we to suppose it to be true that the ideologists should both be constrained so that they produce ideas in the interests of the ruling class of which they are, appearances to the contrary, a part, and that they (and those who accept the ideas from them) remain sincerely unaware of the nature of this connection? Why do they *think* that they are independent when in fact they are not? And, if they are not independent, how do the class interests they share with the rest of the ruling class assert themselves?

In any case, it is clear why Marx should now become so hostile to philosophy: like any supposedly 'pure' theory, philosophy represents a deceptive abstraction from the particular circumstances and material interests that it serves. This move to detach ideas that are the products of material interests from the interests that they represent is epitomized, for Marx and Engels, in Kant (the 'whitewashing spokesman' of the German bourgeoisie, as they call him). Kant, they write:

made the materially motivated determinations of the will of the French bourgeois into *pure* self-determinations of 'free will', of the will in and for itself, of the human will, and so converted it into purely ideological determinations and moral postulates.

(*The German Ideology*)

For Marx and Engels, at this stage at least, 'moral postulates' are, by their very nature, ideological.

8 Historical materialism

'Where speculation ends – in real life – there real, positive science begins', according to Marx and Engels in *The German Ideology*. The science to which they are referring is the materialist theory of history, whose classic statement is given in the Preface to *Zur Kritik der politischen Ökonomie* (A Contribution to the Critique of Political Economy) (1859).

Taken most generally, the materialist theory of history asserts that the manner in which human beings produce the necessities of life determines the form of the societies in which they live. Every society other than the most primitive produces a 'surplus' beyond what it immediately consumes. The manner in which this surplus is 'appropriated' – taken from the direct producers and redistributed – determines the class structure of the society in question. If society is divided between direct producers and those who benefit from the former's 'unpaid surplus labour' (something that is true of all societies where a surplus exists, prior to the advent of socialism) the relationship between classes is antagonistic.

At any stage, the size of the surplus is an expression of the level of development of the 'productive forces' – the resources, physical and intellectual, upon which material production draws. Every society contains both an economic 'base', composed of 'relations of production' (the relations producers have to the means of production and to one another) and a legal and political 'superstructure', corresponding to the base. The relations of production favour the development of the productive forces up to a point. Beyond this they become, Marx says, 'fetters' upon the forces of production, and a conflict arises which leads eventually to the replacement of the existing relations of production with new and superior ones.

Presented in these terms, it is clear that the materialist theory of history is intended as an exercise in social science rather than philosophy. Thus it may seem surprising that it should have attracted such enduring attention on the part of philosophers. However, scientific theories may be of concern to philosophers if their assumptions are novel, obscure or questionable, even if the intentions behind them are in no way philosophical (examples are Darwin, Freud and Newton). In the case of Marx's theory of history, it is not just the meaning of and evidence for the particular claims to be found in the theory that have been controversial. The more general issues of the form of explanation that Marx employs and the kind of entities such an explanation presupposes have been continuing matters of dispute.

Interpreters of Marx divide broadly into three groups on these questions. In the first are those for whom Marx's theory of history is intended to be scientific in the way that any other scientific theory is. With some qualifications, the majority of the earliest Marxists (for example, Engels himself, Kautsky and Plekhanov) fall into this group. On the other hand, those who believe that there is a contrast between Marx's conception of science and the natural sciences may be divided into those who see Marx's theory as a transformation of Hegel's theory of history and those for whom it is fundamentally anti-Hegelian. The most influential presentation of the former interpretation is to be found in Georg Lukács' *History and Class Consciousness* (1921), while the latter is particularly associated with the French philosopher, Louis Althusser (see ALTHUSSER, L.P.; LUKÁCS, G.; PLEKHANOV, G.V.).

In the late 1970s the first approach was revived in the English-speaking world by G.A. Cohen's seminal *Karl Marx's Theory of History: A Defence* (1978). According to Cohen, historical materialism can be presented in a way that contains nothing that should be unacceptable to anyone who accepts the legitimacy of Darwinian biology (see DARWIN, C.R.).

The two theories are, in Cohen's view, importantly parallel to one another, for both employ 'functional explanation' (see FUNCTIONAL EXPLANATION). When Marx says that the relations of production *correspond* to the forces of production, what he means, according to Cohen, is first that the relations are in some sense 'good for' the (development of the) forces and second that they obtain *because* they are good for the forces. (The same analysis, suitably adapted, applies to the correspondence between superstructure and base.) What is distinctive about Darwinian biology, however, is not just that it employs functional explanation, but that it provides a convincing account (what Cohen calls an 'elaborating explanation') of why its functional explanations are true: the process of natural selection. Does Marxism have an equivalent elaborating explanation?

All the indications are that it does not. In response to this, there have been two main lines of argument. One is that the theory should have (but lacks) such an explanation and that it is the task of a sympathetic reconstruction of Marx to provide one. On the other hand, it is also possible to argue that the search for what Jon Elster has called 'micro-foundations' is misguided. Thus the functional explanations that Marx invokes in the theory of history rest on the fact that there really are collective agents (classes, for example). On this 'collectivist' reading it is sufficient simply to appreciate the nature of collective agency to see why collective agents should feature in functional explanations: they have the power to act purposively to bring about their ends. No reductive 'elaborating explanation' is necessary.

To take this view is to align oneself with the second and third groups of Marx's interpreters and to affirm the fundamental gap between Marx's theory of history and the explanations of the natural sciences (where functional explanations are not simply left unelaborated). If so, the Marxist theory of history cannot draw on the general prestige of science for its justification.

9 Political economy

In contrast to his relatively brief and schematic statements concerning general history, Marx wrote very extensively about the economic system under which he himself lived. *Das Kapital*, which presents Marx's definitive analysis of capitalism, is a work of exceptional methodological complexity, as is already suggested by its sub-title, 'Critique of Political Economy'. The phrase is ambiguous. Is Marx's objective to criticize the bourgeois economy or bourgeois economics? In fact, Marx rejects this as a false antithesis: the subject matter of the book is both. Ten years before its publication, Marx described the work that was to become *Das Kapital* in a letter: 'The ... work in question is a *critique of the economic categories*, or, if you like, the system of bourgeois economy critically presented. It is a presentation [*Darstellung*] of the system and, simultaneously, a critique of it'.

The two aspects go together in Marx's view because economic categories are not simply the means employed by an observer to classify some inert mass of data. They are themselves a part of social reality, 'abstract forms' of the social relations of production.

Bourgeois economists, Marx alleges, characteristically fail to recognize that their categories are specific to capitalism, and so they treat the capitalist mode of production as one 'eternally fixed by nature for every state of society', Marx alleges. A 'critical presentation' of economics must counteract the false eternalization of the economy that bourgeois economics carries within itself.

As it stands, this is a criticism of the limitations in the self-understanding of bourgeois economics rather than a challenge to its empirical content. Yet empirical explanation is a central part of Marx's project. 'It is', he writes in the Preface to *Das Kapital*, 'the ultimate aim of this work to lay bare the economic law of motion of modern society.' Has bourgeois economics failed to discover this law or has it simply not put its categories in historical context? At its strongest, Marx's case is that both criticisms are true and that the former failing is a result of the latter. The 'law of value' that Marx claims to have discovered could not, he says, have been discovered by economic science 'so long as it is stuck in its bourgeois skin'.

The connection that Marx sees between the categories of economic life and the categories of economic analysis is made more complicated by the structure that he ascribes to capitalism. Marx believes that an indispensable ingredient for understanding capitalism is the contrast between its 'essence' – its underlying determinants – and its 'appearance' – the way that it immediately strikes those who live in it. Corresponding to this distinction are two kinds of bourgeois economic thought: what Marx calls 'classical economy', on the one hand, and 'vulgar economy' on the other. Classical economy (the tradition whose greatest representatives were Ricardo and Adam SMITH) aims towards the essence of capitalism: it 'nearly touches the true relation of things', although it is not able to formulate that relation explicitly. According to Marx, it is the mark of the 'vulgar economy' of his own time, by contrast, that it 'feels particularly at home in the alienated outward appearances of economic relations'. Yet this means that it is fundamentally unscientific, for 'all science would be superfluous if the outward appearance and the essence of things coincided'. A truly scientific political economy must go beyond the immediately received categories of economic life. This is what Marx believes that he himself has achieved (and he considers himself for this reason to be the heir of the tradition of classical political economy).

In a letter to Engels, written at the time of the publication of the first volume of *Das Kapital*, Marx singles out what he calls the 'twofold character of labour' as the most important point in his book. Labour, Marx claims, is both the source of value and, at the same time, under capitalism, a commodity itself. Yet this commodity (labour-power, as Marx calls it) is a commodity of a special kind. Its value is not the same as the value of the commodities produced by the labour that is exercised on behalf of its purchaser, the capitalist. This discrepancy, in Marx's view, explains the 'origin' of surplus-value – the fact that the capitalist appropriates the surplus-labour of the worker under the guise of a fair exchange. In discussing the manner in which, in capitalist society, labour is sold to capitalists as a commodity, in exchange for wages, Marx writes: 'Hence we may understand the decisive importance of the transformation of the value and price of labour-power into the form of wages, or into the value and price of labour itself. This phenomenal form, which makes the actual relation invisible, and, indeed, shows the direct opposite of that relation, forms the basis of all the juridical notions of both labourer and capitalist, of all the mystifications of the capitalist mode of production, of all its illusions as to liberty, of all the apologetic shifts of the vulgar economists'.

Thus we see Marx making three claims: (1) that we should see reality as layered, having a surface appearance governed by an underlying structure; (2) that to make such a distinction is characteristic of the scientific approach to reality in general; and (3) that the phenomenal form conceals the real relations (it 'makes the actual relation invisible and indeed shows the opposite of that relation').

However, claims (1) and (2) do not entail (3). According to claims (1) and (2) (in themselves extremely plausible) the way that we see the world is not, immediately, adequate for us to explain the way that the world is. But that does not make our immediate perception of the world false. It simply lacks a theory. Yet Marx's claim (3) is much stronger: reality presents itself in a way that deceives those who immediately perceive it. Marx's own statements to the contrary, it seems that this third claim is best understood not as a general consequence of the nature of scientific understanding but as a specific feature of capitalism. Capitalism mystifies those who live under it, Marx believes, because it is a 'deceptive object'. To penetrate its surface scientifically it is necessary to go beyond the limitations of bourgeois political economy.

10 The fetishism of commodities

The most detailed discussion that Marx provides of a case where the surface of capitalism presents itself as 'false' is to be found in 'The Fetishism of Commodities and the Secret Thereof', in *Das Kapital*. This discussion is a recognizable reworking of the central themes to be found in the treatment of alienated labour in the *Paris Manuscripts*.

In the eighteenth-century sense of the term, fetishists were those non-European peoples whose religion involved the worship of inanimate objects. Fetishism is a fallacy attributing to objects in the world some quality (power and personality) that they, in fact, lack. Marx's conception of commodity fetishism shares this structure, but differs in an important way. The fetishism of commodities is not a matter of subjective delusion or irrationality on the part of perceivers, but is somehow embedded in the reality that they face.

According to Marx, two separate facts or properties are distorted in the commodity-form. First, the 'social character' of human beings' labour appears (falsely) as 'objective characteristics of the products themselves', and second (in consequence of the first fact, as Marx asserts) the producers' own relationship to their 'collective labour' appears 'as a social relationship between objects, existing externally to the producers'.

The first issue concerns what the 'social character' that is apparently a property of the products themselves amounts to. Is it the sheer fact that the commodity *is* a commodity? This suggestion must be rejected, for the belief that the product is a commodity is in no way a false or deceptive one. Likewise, it cannot be something concealed from the producers that commodities *do* as a matter of fact exchange for one another in certain proportions: it is hard to see how anyone could live their lives within a market society without having an adequate understanding of facts of this kind (enough, at least, to be able to buy something to eat). The best interpretation of Marx's argument is that it is not such first-order facts about commodities but a second-order one that is the source of deception: it is not *that* commodities can be exchanged with one another in certain ratios but *the reason why* they exchange in the ratios that they do that is their hidden secret.

Marx's account of the illusion regarding the social character of the products of labour is complemented by the account he gives of the second element in commodity fetishism. Because commodity production takes place as a process by which the producers' activities are coordinated solely through the imperatives of a system of market exchanges, it follows, Marx says, that 'the social relations between their private acts of labour manifest themselves as what they are – that is, not as the immediate social relationships of persons in their labour but as material relationships between persons and social relationships between things'.

Implicitly, the market commensurates the labour of each individual with the labour of every other producer – individual labour has its value in relation to the way in which others perform the same labour. The socially useful character of the labour of the individual producers thus appears to them, according to Marx, 'only under those forms which are impressed upon that labour in everyday practice, in the exchange of products'.

Here again, Marx is indicating an illusion of the second rather than the first order. The individual producers are aware of the role of the market in determining the way in which they labour. In this they are quite correct. But they also believe (falsely) that it is the market that makes their labour useful (rather than recognizing it as a contingent fact about capitalist production that their socially useful labour takes on a market-determined form). Society generates such false beliefs spontaneously, Marx claims. The world of commodities 'veils rather than reveals', he says, the social character of private labour and of the relations between the individual producers.

That the true source of the value of commodities lies in the labour expended in their production is, Marx maintains, a matter of simple scientific truth.

So, too, is the fact that the social character of private labour consists in the equalization of that labour under the auspices of the market. Nevertheless, fetishism is a matter of 'objective illusion' and knowledge of these truths does not dispel such false appearance. The discovery of the law of value 'by no means dissipates the objective illusion through which the social character of labour appears to be an objective character of the products themselves' any more than 'the discovery by science of the component gases of air' altered the atmosphere that people breathed.

The analogy that Marx chooses here is not a happy one. Admittedly, it is absurd to think that a scientist's discovery about an object should change the object itself. But that is not the issue. It is not a question of whether the atmosphere itself changes after the discovery of its component gases, but whether the way in which we think about it changes. It is only if we suppose that capitalism, unlike the atmosphere, is an object of a particular kind – a deceptive object – that it is possible to claim that it will continue to encourage such false beliefs in the face of contrary knowledge.

But it is not just that the individuals who live in a society based on commodity production are deceived by it regarding the way that it works. The way that it works is itself criticized by Marx. Above all, the 'social character of labour' is made private in actuality. This is not a misperception or false belief, but a contradiction: a discrepancy between what Marx takes to be the intrinsic nature of social labour and the way that it is in fact organized. Capitalism is not just deceptive, but also defective.

11 Morality

The question whether Marx's theory has a moral or ethical dimension is one of the most controversial of all issues surrounding the interpretation of his work, and the difficulty facing interpreters is easily seen. On the one hand, Marx has a number of uncompromisingly negative things to say about morality. Moreover, after 1845 at least, he affirms that his own theory is not a utopian or ethical one but 'real, positive science'. Yet, on the other hand, much of the language that he uses to describe capitalism is plainly condemnatory (for instance, that it is antagonistic, oppressive and exploitative). Does this not represent an inconsistency on Marx's part? Is he not moralizing and rejecting morality at the same time?

This section will present a line of interpretation according to which Marx is not inconsistent. The interpretation depends on a contrast between certain doctrines typical of moral philosophy (which, it will be argued, Marx rejects) and the rejection of ethical values as such (to which, it will be argued, he is not thereby committed). However, it should be noted that this interpretation is controversial and involves considerable reconstruction of the rather sparse evidence that we have of Marx's views.

It is helpful to start, as Marx himself did, with Hegel's critique of Kant. Both Marx and Hegel share the belief that morality, as embodied in Kant's moral philosophy, is, as they put it, 'abstract' (see HEGEL, G.W.F. §8). There appear to be three interconnected elements compressed into this criticism:

(1) First, morality is alleged to be abstract in the sense that it contains principles expressed in universal form (in Kant's case, the 'categorical imperative' to 'act only according to that maxim which you can, at the same time, will to be a universal law' (see KANTIAN ETHICS)). While such principles may function as a test upon proposed actions, they do not, the argument goes, determine the content of the action to be performed. Thus, the claims of moral philosophy to the contrary, specific content is surreptitiously imported into ethics from the existing institutions or codes of behaviour of the society in question.
(2) Second, morality is abstract to the extent that it takes the form of a mere injunction: an imperative that is addressed to people's 'moral reason', telling them to act in a certain way because that is 'good in itself'. Moral action is detached thereby from other forms of human action and, as a result, moral theory has nothing to say about the conditions under which the forms of behaviour that it commends will be realized in practice.
(3) Finally, morality may be said to be abstract in that it contains an unhistorical understanding of its own status. It presents its principles as if they were the axioms of some timeless moral geometry. Yet, in fact, every system of morality is a way of seeing the world that arises in particular circumstances and responds to definite needs within those circumstances.

Although one or more of these features may be present in the forms of moral philosophy with which we are most familiar, it is not clear that they are a necessary feature of every view that one might call 'moral'. Not all ethical positions have to express themselves as systems of universal principles that we are enjoined to follow because they are good for their own sake. Admittedly, many philosophers would argue that to combine the value commitments characteristic of morality with the meta-level doctrine that such values are, in the end, expressions of interest

(Marx's version of (3) above) inevitably undermines, as Nietzsche might have put it, the value of value itself. But it is at least arguable that the two standpoints are compatible. The path from sociological determinism to moral scepticism is not as steep, slippery and remorseless as it is sometimes claimed to be.

If this is conceded, we can draw a distinction between morality in two senses: morality as a quasi-Kantian system of principles (which Marx rejects) and morality as a set of values embodying a conception of what is good for human beings (which he can consistently accept). To present things in this way, however, may seem to give insufficient weight to the vehement hostility which Marx shows towards ideas of justice and rights, in particular. On the interpretation being proposed here, Marx's animus is best understood as aimed at what he sees as the assumptions behind such values, rather than at the fact of their being values as such.

Roughly speaking, we may think of rights as things that permit individuals to act in certain ways, in given circumstances, should they wish to do so, and to be able to claim correlative duties on the part of others. A duty, correspondingly, would require individuals to act in some way, whether they wished to or not. Justice (if we do not think of it simply as a matter of rights and duties) would consist of principles on which benefits and burdens are distributed in cases where interests conflict.

What these values have in common is that they provide a framework which regulates and limits the self-seeking behaviour of individuals. They are values that assume a conflict between (to put it in Kantian terms) 'duty' and 'inclination'. Just as Marx supposes that the categories of bourgeois economics eternalize the forms of bourgeois economic life, so, he believes, discussion of rights (which he denounces in the *Critique of the Gotha Programme* as 'ideological nonsense') eternalizes a situation in which the good of each individual is independent and so can only be advanced at the expense of others. Right, moreover, can only apply a fixed and equal standard to unequal individuals, 'from outside'.

For the liberal, who is concerned to protect the individual's powers of self-direction against the intrusions of others, the attraction of the idea of rights is that it presupposes nothing about individuals' characters and personalities. For Marx, on the other hand, that is just its weakness: rights do nothing to transform human nature. Against this, it is clear that Marx, from the time of the *Paris Manuscripts*, sees social progress as characterized by a form of community in which (as he and Engels put it in the *Communist Manifesto*) 'the free development of each is the condition for the free development of all'. Marx's ethical ideal is one of solidarity in which all advance together.

Hence Marx's reluctance to use the language of justice to condemn capitalism becomes more intelligible. It is not that Marx thinks that exploitation, expropriation, oppression, slavery and misery (a few of the terms he applies to the capitalist system) are *just*. But he is reluctant to use language that would suggest that these are forms of injustice for which 'justice' (in the sense of giving 'each their due') is the final and sufficient remedy.

12 Socialism

It may seem odd, given that Marx devoted his life to the achievement of a socialist society, how brief and unspecific his accounts of it are. One explanation that is often advanced for this apparent neglect is the following. Marx believed, it is said, that thought is limited to its own time. Thus it would have been improper for him, living under capitalism, to try to anticipate the nature of the society that would replace it and to write (as he puts it in the Preface to the Second Edition of *Das Kapital*) 'recipes for the cook-shops of the future'. While this may be part of the reason for Marx's reticence, it cannot alone suffice. For, even if we grant that Marx believed that each stage of society sets a boundary which thought cannot cross (and it is by no means beyond question that he did hold this view in such a strong form) he is also committed to the view that socialism is anticipated within capitalism.

In the Preface to *Zur Kritik der politischen Ökonomie* Marx makes the general claim that new forms of society are always prefigured within the old ones that they replace. 'Mankind', he writes, 'only sets itself such tasks as it is able to solve, since closer examination will always show that the problem itself arises only when the material conditions for its solution are already present or at least in the course of formation'.

Marx describes the process by which capitalism prepares the ground for socialism at the end of the first volume of *Das Kapital*. As the productive forces developed by capitalism grow, he claims, so too does the 'mass of misery, oppression, slavery, degradation, exploitation'. A stage is reached, however, at which the monopoly of capital becomes a 'fetter' on production and 'the centralization of the means of production and the socialization of labour at last reach a point where they become incompatible with their capitalist shell'. At this point, the shell 'bursts asunder', the 'death knell' sounds for capitalism and the 'expropriators are themselves expropriated'.

The first and most obvious difference between capitalism and socialism is that common ownership leads to a quite different pattern of distribution of the products of labour. No longer will the capitalist, in virtue of his ownership of the means of production, be able to exploit the individual producer. In the *Critique of the Gotha Programme* Marx distinguishes two stages of post-capitalist society. In the first, the direct producer receives back from society (after deductions for shared costs and social expenditure) 'what he has given to it as his individual quantum of labour'.

But this, Marx points out, is a principle of distribution that merely rectifies exploitation. It does not remedy the inequalities that arise from contingent differences in natural capacities between individual producers. Later, however, society will move beyond this, Marx claims, and 'the narrow horizon of bourgeois right' will be 'crossed in its entirety'. At this point, the principle upon which society will operate will be: 'From each according to his ability, to each according to his needs!' But socialism is distinguished by more than its principle of distribution. In particular, labour will be organized quite differently from the way that it is organized under capitalism.

One of Marx's few reasonably extensive accounts of the nature of the socialist organization of production is to be found in the section on the fetishism of commodities in *Das Kapital*, as part of a comparison between capitalist and other forms of production. Marx starts with Robinson Crusoe, whose productive activity he describes as 'simple and clear'. For Robinson, Marx says, the organization of production is a purely administrative operation: the end is known, as are the resources available and the techniques by which that end could be attained. Marx then moves from 'Robinson's island, bathed in light', via feudal and patriarchal forms of production, before alighting on: 'a community of free individuals, carrying on their labour with the means of production in common, in which the labour-power of all the different individuals is consciously applied as the combined labour-power of the community'.

Here, Marx says,

> All the characteristics of Robinson's labour are . . . repeated, but with this difference, that they are social, instead of individual . . . The social relations of the individual producers to their labour and to the products of their labour remain here transparently simple, in production as well as in distribution.

> (*Das Kapital*)

The idea that labour could be 'consciously applied' in a complex modern society – resources and needs coordinated, efficient techniques adopted, innovation managed – with the same 'transparent simplicity' as an individual allocating his time to different tasks on a desert island is astonishingly implausible. And, even if it were not so, the question would still arise how that 'common and rational plan' (as Marx terms it elsewhere) would relate to the individuals whose task it was to carry it out. Would it not, from their point of view, be no less of an 'external' imperative to be followed than the dictates of the market that govern their labour under capitalism? Arguably, the idea that society under socialism would be spontaneously unified like one great, self-transparent super-individual represents an unacknowledged hangover in Marx's mature thought from Hegel's doctrine of *Geist*. However that may be, the presence of this doctrine goes a long way towards explaining why Marx had so little to say about the problems of socialist economic organization: he simply failed to see the difficulty. Few theoretical omissions, surely, have ever had more disastrous historical consequences.

See also: COMMUNISM; ECONOMICS, PHILOSOPHY OF; EXPLANATION IN HISTORY AND SOCIAL SCIENCE; HISTORY, PHILOSOPHY OF; MARXISM, WESTERN; MARXIST PHILOSOPHY, RUSSIAN AND SOVIET; POLITICAL PHILOSOPHY, HISTORY OF; REVOLUTION; SOCIALISM

References and further reading

Marx, K. (1975–) *The Pelican Marx Library*, Harmondsworth: Penguin. (Not a complete edition, but a series that contains particularly good translations of *Das Kapital*, the *Grundrisse* and the *Early Writings*, among others.)

Wood, A. (1981) *Karl Marx*, London: Routledge & Kegan Paul. (Places emphasis on the philosophical aspects of Marx's work. Contains an extended interpretation of Marx's view of morality quite different from the one advanced in this entry.)

MICHAEL ROSEN

MARXISM, WESTERN

Western Marxism is used here as an umbrella term for the various schools of Marxist thought that have flourished in Western Europe since Marx's death in 1883. It is sometimes used more narrowly to refer to those Marxist philosophers whose thinking was influenced by the Hegelian idea of dialectics and who focused their attention on the cultural as opposed to the economic aspects of capitalism. In the broader sense, Western Marxism does not denote any specific doctrine, but indicates a range of concerns that have exercised Marxist philosophers in advanced capitalist societies. These concerns primarily have been of three kinds: (1) *epistemological* – what would justify the claim that Marxist social theory and, in particular, the

materialist conception of history are true?; (2) *ethical* – does the Marxist critique of capitalism require ethical foundations, and if so, where are these to be discovered; and (3) *practical* – if the economic collapse of capitalism can no longer be regarded as inevitable, who are the agents who can be expected to carry through a socialist transformation?

In relation to the first issue, the main debate has been between those who, following Engels, adhere to 'scientific socialism' (that is, the view that Marxism is a science in the same sense as the natural sciences), and those who claim that Marxist epistemology relies on a form of dialectics quite distinct from the methods of natural science. The most prominent exponent of this second view was the Hungarian philosopher Georg Lukács, who drew upon the dialectical method of Hegel, with class consciousness replacing *Geist* (Spirit) as the vehicle of dialectical reason. Thus, for Lukács the truth of historical materialism and the goodness of communism were both established dialectically, through the class consciousness of the revolutionary proletariat. Lukács' advocacy of dialectics was later taken up and developed by the philosophers of the Frankfurt School.

In relation to the second issue, early dissenters from the orthodox Marxism of Engels like Eduard Bernstein looked outside Marxism itself, and especially to the philosophy of Kant, for the ethical principles that would justify socialism. The position changed somewhat with the rediscovery of the young Marx's *Paris Manuscripts* (1844) from which later Marxists, and in particular those associated with the Frankfurt School, were able to extract a humanistic ethics centred on the notion of alienation.

In relation to the third issue, most Western Marxists continued to look to the proletariat as the agency of revolutionary change, often distinguishing, as did Lukács, between the true consciousness of that class and the false consciousness that reflected the distorting effects of bourgeois ideology. But in the case of the Frankfurt Marxists, the critical theory that pointed the way to a liberated human future was detached from any specific agency and treated merely as critique. The most original contribution was made by the Italian Marxist Antonio Gramsci, who argued that the working class must use the power of its ideas to establish hegemony over the other classes in bourgeois society, who would then join the proletariat in overthrowing capitalism.

The disintegration of Western Marxism began in the 1960s when the French philosopher Louis Althusser attacked both the use of Hegelian dialectics by Marxists and the various forms of Marxist humanism. Althusser insisted that Marxism was a science which required no ethical foundations. His critique was informed by a conviction that human subjectivity, together with the philosophical problems generated by subject–object dualism, are illusions.

Althusserian Marxism became fashionable in English-speaking universities, but its cavalier and paradoxical style also led, by reaction, to the rise of analytic Marxism in the late 1970s. Analytic Marxists returned to interrogating Marx's texts in more conventional ways, using the methods of analytic philosophy and contemporary social science to reformulate them to withstand academic scrutiny by non–Marxists. A tendency rather than a movement, analytic Marxism perhaps marks the final stage of a process that began with Lukács, that of turning Marxism into a purely academic study remote from politics.

See also: MARXIST PHILOSOPHY, RUSSIAN AND SOVIET

JOHN TORRANCE

MARXIST PHILOSOPHY, RUSSIAN AND SOVIET

The history of Russian Marxism involves a dramatic interplay of philosophy and politics. Though Marx's ideas were taken up selectively by Russian populists in the 1870s, the first thoroughgoing Russian Marxist was G.V. Plekhanov, whose vision of philosophy became the orthodoxy among Russian communists. Inspired by Engels, Plekhanov argued that Marxist philosophy is a form of 'dialectical materialism' (Plekhanov's coinage). Following Hegel, Marxism focuses on phenomena in their interaction and development, which it explains by appeal to dialectical principles (for instance, the law of the transformation of quantity into quality). Unlike Hegel's idealism, however, Marxism explains all phenomena in material terms (for Marxists, the 'material' includes economic forces and relations). Dialectical materialism was argued to be the basis of Marx's vision of history according to which historical development is the outcome of changes in the force of production.

In 1903, Plekhanov's orthodoxy was challenged by a significant revisionist school: Russian empiriocriticism. Inspired by Mach's positivism, A.A. Bogdanov and others argued that reality is socially organized experience, a view they took to suit Marx's insistence that objects be understood in their relation to human *activity*. Empiriocriticism was associated with the Bolsheviks until 1909, when Lenin moved to condemn Bogdanov's position as a species of idealism repugnant to both Marxism and common sense. Lenin endorsed dialectical materialism, which thereafter was deemed the philosophical worldview of the Bolsheviks.

After the Revolution of 1917, Soviet philosophers were soon divided in a bitter controversy between 'mechanists' and 'dialecticians'. The former argued that philosophy must be subordinate to science. In contrast, the Hegelian 'dialecticians', led by A.M. Deborin, insisted that philosophy is needed to explain the very possibility of scientific knowledge. The debate was soon deadlocked, and in 1929 the dialecticians used their institutional might to condemn mechanism as a heresy. The following year, the dialecticians were themselves routed by a group of young activists sponsored by the Communist Party. Denouncing Deborin and his followers as 'Menshevizing idealists', they proclaimed that Marxist philosophy had now entered its 'Leninist stage' and invoked Lenin's idea of the *partiinost'* ('partyness') of philosophy to license the criticism of theories on entirely political grounds. Philosophy became a weapon in the class war.

In 1938, Marxist-Leninist philosophy was simplistically codified in the fourth chapter of the *Istoriia kommunisticheskoi partii sovetskogo soiuza (Bol'sheviki). Kraatkii kurs* (History of the Communist Party of the Soviet Union (Bolsheviks). Short Course). The chapter, apparently written by Stalin himself, was declared the height of wisdom, and Soviet philosophers dared not transcend its limited horizons. The 'new philosophical leadership' devoted itself to glorifying the Party and its General Secretary. The ideological climate grew even worse in the post-war years when A.A. Zhdanov's campaign against 'cosmopolitanism' created a wave of Russian chauvinism in which scholars sympathetic to Western thought were persecuted. The Party also meddled in the scientific, sponsoring T.D. Lysenko's bogus genetics, while encouraging criticism of quantum mechanics, relativity theory and cybernetics as inconsistent with dialectical materialism.

The Khrushchev 'thaw' brought a renaissance in Soviet Marxism, when a new generation of young philosophers began a critical re-reading of Marx's texts. Marx's so-called 'method of ascent from the abstract to the concrete' was developed, by E.V. Il'enkov and others, into an anti-empiricist epistemology. There were also important studies of consciousness and 'the ideal' by Il'enkov and M.K. Mamardashvili, the former propounding a vision of the social origins of the mind that recalls the cultural-historical psychology developed by L.S. Vygotskii in the 1930s.

However, the thaw was short-lived. The philosophical establishment, still populated by the Stalinist old guard, continued to exercise a stifling influence. Although the late 1960s and 1970s saw heartfelt debates in many areas, particularly about the biological basis of the mind and the nature of value (moral philosophy had been hitherto neglected), the energy of the early 1960s was lacking. Marxism-Leninism still dictated the terms of debate and knowledge of Western philosophers remained relatively limited.

In the mid-1980s, Gorbachev's reforms initiated significant changes. Marxism-Leninism was no longer a required subject in all institutions of higher education; indeed, the term was soon dropped altogether. Discussions of democracy and the rule of law were conducted in the journals, and writings by Western and Russian émigré philosophers were published. Influential philosophers such as I.T. Frolov, then editor of *Pravda*, called for a renewal of humanistic Marxism. The reforms, however, came too late. The numerous discussions of the fate of Marxism at this time reveal an intellectual culture in crisis. While many maintained that Marx's theories were not responsible for the failings of the USSR, others declared the bankruptcy of Marxist ideas and called for an end to the Russian Marxist tradition. Following the collapse of the Soviet Union in 1991, it seems their wish has been fulfilled.

See also: MARXISM, WESTERN

DAVID BAKHURST

MASS TERMS

Mass terms are words and phrases such as 'water', 'wood' and 'white wallpaper'. They are contrasted with count terms such as 'woman', 'word' and 'wild wildebeest'. Intuitively, mass terms refer to 'stuff'; count terms refer to 'objects'. Mass terms allow for measurement ('three kilos of wood', 'much water'); count terms allow for counting, quantifying and individuating ('three women', 'each word', 'that wildebeest over there').

Philosophical problems associated with mass terms include; (1) distinguishing mass from count terms, (2) describing the semantics of sentences employing mass terms, and (3) explicating the ontology presupposed by our use of mass versus count terms. Associated with these philosophical issues – especially the third – are the meta-philosophical issues concerning the extent to which any investigation into the linguistic practices of speakers of a language can be used as evidence for how those speakers view 'reality'.

See also: MEREOLOGY

JEFFRY PELLETIER

MASSILIANISM
See PELAGIANISM

MATERIAL IMPLICATION, PARADOXES OF
See INDICATIVE CONDITIONALS

MATERIALISM

Introduction

Materialism is a set of related theories which hold that all entities and processes are composed of – or are reducible to – matter, material forces or physical processes. All events and facts are explainable, actually or in principle, in terms of body, material objects or dynamic material changes or movements. In general, the metaphysical theory of materialism entails the denial of the reality of spiritual beings, consciousness and mental or psychic states or processes, as ontologically distinct from, or independent of, material changes or processes. Since it denies the existence of spiritual beings or forces, materialism typically is allied with atheism or agnosticism.

The forms of materialism extend from the ancient Greek atomistic materialism through eighteenth- and nineteenth-century scientifically based theories, to recent sophisticated defences of various types of materialism.

1 Materialism
2 Ancient Greek atomism
3 Modern materialism
4 Recent materialism

1 Materialism

Materialism is the general theory that the ultimate constituents of reality are material or physical bodies, elements or processes. It is a form of monism in that it holds that everything in existence is reducible to what is material or physical in nature. It is opposed to dualistic theories which claim that body and mind are distinct, and directly antithetical to a philosophical idealism that denies the existence of matter. It is hostile to abstract objects, if these are viewed as more than just a manner of speaking (see ABSTRACT OBJECTS). An implication of materialism is that the diverse qualitative experiences we have are ultimately reducible to quantitative changes in objects or in our physiological functioning. All the properties of things, including persons, are reducible to properties of matter. Although the terms referring to psychic states such as intention, belief, desire and consciousness itself have a different sense and use than terms referring to material events, a consistent materialist would deny that mentalistic terms have reference to anything other than physical events or physiological changes in our brains. The enormous advances in the sciences have contributed storehouses of empirical data that are often used to support materialism. Many philosophers have been attracted to materialism both because of its reductive simplicity and its association with scientific knowledge.

2 Ancient Greek atomism

Although LEUCIPPUS is credited with inventing the atomic theory of matter in the fifth century BC, it was DEMOCRITUS (fourth century BC) who developed a systematic theory of atomistic materialism. This theory states that matter is composed of separate and minute elements that are 'uncuttable' (*atoma*), that these elements move in empty space or the 'void'. Atoms differ only in shape and volume, and all change occurs by the transfer through direct contact of movement from atoms in motion. These elementary entities are lacking in secondary qualities and are indestructible. Democritus held that things are hot or cold, sweet or bitter, or have different colours 'by convention'. In reality, 'there are atoms and the void'.

The essentials of early atomism were retained in Epicurus' physics, with the exception that Epicurus ascribed freedom to atoms in their movement through space. Epicurean materialism is lucidly expressed in the philosophic poem by LUCRETIUS, *De rerum natura* (On the Nature of Things), in the first century BC. This popularization of Epicurean thought did much to keep alive both atomistic materialism and what is already recognizable as a naturalistic understanding of humans and world (see EPICUREANISM).

3 Modern materialism

During the first half of the seventeenth century the atomistic materialism of the Greco-Roman period was revived in a paradoxical way by Pierre GASSENDI. He appreciated the scientific interpretation of nature and the methods of science but, at the same time, preserved the Christian idea of the immortality of the soul and conceived of God as the creator of the atoms. The English philosopher Thomas HOBBES presented a systematic theory of nature and human nature that was largely, though not completely, materialistic. Apart from attributing 'drive' or *conatus* to human action and sensation, Hobbes virtually banished the concept of 'incorporeal substance'. In theory and sentiment Hobbes was a materialist thinker, although not a consistent one. The early eighteenth century saw the publication of the first of many works that defended a materialistic and mechanistic interpretation of mankind's nature on the basis of physiological theory. In *L'Homme machine* (1748) Julien de LA METTRIE, a philosophical physician, described human beings as self-moving mechanisms and sought a neurological basis for mental activity. An advance on previous attempts to develop a systematic materialism is Paul H.D. d'Holbach's 1770 *Système de la nature* (The System of Nature). Here, a consistent naturalistic materialism is expounded in that cognitive and emotive states are reduced to internal material 'modifications of the brain'. Though not calling it such, d'Holbach presents a form of physiological determinism.

With the rapid growth of the sciences, the astronomical discoveries of COPERNICUS, the theories of GALILEO, and the systematic conception of nature in the physical theory of Isaac NEWTON, naturalistic interpretations of a variety of phenomena became more and more prevalent. This scientifically founded picture of reality lent greater plausibility to the principles of materialistic theory. The astronomer and mathematician Pierre Laplace (1749–1827) produced a sophisticated astronomical theory which, he thought, illustrated that a supermind, knowing all the states and conditions of every existing entity, could predict the total state of the cosmos in the next moment. When Napoleon I was shown a copy of Laplace's work, he is supposed to have commented on the absence of any mention of God. Laplace replied, 'I have no need of that hypothesis'. Laplace's mechanistic materialism became, in the hands of many thinkers, the definitive explanatory principle of all events.

The formulation of the biological theory of evolution by means of natural selection by Charles DARWIN virtually eliminated teleological explanations of biological phenomena and thereby buttressed material and physical interpretations of organic development. With the advances in chemistry achieved by Lavoisier (1743–94) in France and John Dalton (1766–1844) in England, the reductive analysis of natural phenomena to chemical substances, elements and processes bolstered the empirical, naturalistic and materialistic interpretations of phenomena. During the nineteenth century many philosophical thinkers sought to build theories on the foundation of scientific facts, principles or laws. The historical materialism developed by Marx and Engels sought to formulate laws of social, economic and historical development, but did not defend metaphysical materialism (see DIALECTICAL MATERIALISM). The general appeal of materialism in the nineteenth century is shown by the popularity of the 1855 work by Ludwig Büchner, *Kraft und Stoff* (Force and Matter), which passed through sixteen editions. Although philosophically crude, it is an accessible compendium of popular materialism. In 1852, Jacob Moleschott had defended the reduction of force to matter, the doctrine of the conservation of matter, and a species of objective relativism in *Der Kreislauf des Lebens*

(The Cycle of Life). Following the ill-chosen analogy between the brain and thought and the digestive system in Jean Cabanis' *Rapports due physique et du moral de l'homme* (Relations of the Physical and the Mental in Man) (1802), Karl Vogt proclaimed that the brain 'secretes' thought the way the liver secretes bile. Despite such excursions into 'vulgar materialism', the nineteenth century became a period of intense debate for scientists and philosophers alike in regard to the limits of scientific knowledge and the epistemological problems of metaphysical materialism. This was fuelled by a Neo-Kantian movement which, particularly in *Geschichte des Materialismus* (History of Materialism) (1865) by F.A. LANGE, held that materialism is a useful methodological principle in science, but questionable as a reductionist metaphysics. The concepts and postulates of science are theoretical entities or conventional notions formed by the mind. Their usefulness does not, according to Lange, warrant their role as bases for materialism.

4   Recent materialism

In the twentieth century, physicalism has emerged out of positivism. Physicalism restricts meaningful statements to physical bodies or processes that are verifiable or in principle verifiable. It is an empirical hypothesis that is subject to revision and, hence, lacks the dogmatic stance of classical materialism. Herbert Feigl defended physicalism in the USA and consistently held that mental states are brain states and that mental terms have the same referent as physical terms (Feigl 1958). The twentieth century has witnessed many materialist theories of the mental, and much debate surrounding them (see BEHAVIOURISM, ANALYTIC; FUNCTIONALISM; MATERIALISM IN THE PHILOSOPHY OF MIND; MIND, IDENTITY THEORY OF).

In the field of artificial intelligence, the mind is held to be analogous to computers in so far as it functions as an information-processing entity. Daniel DENNETT has, in a qualified way, argued that information-processing machines are valid models of the mind. In addition to the scientifically informed arguments for various forms of materialism, including nonreductive materialism, the twentieth-century conception of matter as composed of electrons, protons and other subatomic particles has spawned a rich speculative literature that effectively undermines previous forms of materialism. What the late US philosopher of science, Norwood Hanson, called the 'dematerialization' of matter, raises questions concerning what 'materialism' means in terms of the theories of microphysics. Many of the arguments that sustained earlier forms of materialism (including the assumption

of causality as universal in nature) have been put in question. The confluence of contemporary theories about the structure and function of the mind and the nature of matter have introduced a complexity of detail and an array of paradoxical claims that make contemporary materialism a welter of intriguing, but conflicting and perplexing, theoretical elements.

See also: MATTER

References and further reading

Armstrong, D.M. (1968) *A Materialist Theory of the Mind*, London: Routledge & Kegan Paul. (Thorough analysis of mind and mental states in terms of central state physicalism.)

Feigl, H. (1958) 'The "Mental" and the "Physical"', in *Minnesota Studies in the Philosophy of Science*, vol. 2, Minneapolis, MN: University of Minnesota Press. (Classic statement of physicalism.)

GEORGE J. STACK

MATERIALISM, DIALECTICAL
See DIALECTICAL MATERIALISM

MATERIALISM IN THE PHILOSOPHY OF MIND

Materialism – which, for almost all purposes, is the same as physicalism – is the theory that everything that exists is material. Natural science shows that most things are intelligible in material terms, but mind presents problems in at least two ways. The first is consciousness, as found in the 'raw feel' of subjective experience. The second is the intentionality of thought, which is the property of *being about* something beyond itself; 'aboutness' seems not to be a physical relation in the ordinary sense.

There have been three ways of approaching these problems. The hardest is eliminativism, according to which there are no 'raw feels', no intentionality and, in general, no mental states: the mind and all its furniture are part of an outdated science that we now see to be false. Next is reductionism, which seeks to give an account of our experience and of intentionality in terms which are acceptable to a physical science: this means, in practice, analysing the mind in terms of its role in producing behaviour. Finally, the materialist may accept the reality and irreducibility of mind, but claim that it depends on matter in such an intimate way – more intimate than mere causal dependence – that materialism is not threatened by the irreducibility of mind. The first two approaches can be called 'hard materialism', the third 'soft materialism'.

The problem for eliminativism is that we find it difficult to credit that any belief that we think and feel is a theoretical speculation. Reductionism's main difficulty is that there seems to be more to consciousness than its contribution to behaviour: a robotic machine could behave as we do without thinking or feeling. The soft materialist has to explain supervenience in a way that makes the mind not epiphenomenal without falling into the problems of interactionism.

HOWARD ROBINSON

MATERIALISM, INDIAN SCHOOL OF

'Materialism' stands here for the Sanskrit term Lokāyata, the most common designation for the materialistic school of classical Indian philosophy. However, at the outset 'materialism' and 'Lokāyata' were not equivalent: early materialistic doctrines were not associated with Lokāyata, and early Lokāyata was neither materialistic nor even a philosophical school.

Classical Lokāyata stands apart from all other Indian philosophical traditions due to its denial of ethical and metaphysical doctrines such as karmic retribution, life after death, and liberation. Its ontology, tailored to support this challenge, allows only four material elements and their various combinations. Further support comes from Lokāyata epistemology: the validity of inference and Scriptures is denied and perception is held to be the only means of valid cognition. As offshoots, a fully fledged scepticism and a theory of limited validity of inference developed in response to criticism by other philosophers. Consistent with Lokāyata ontology and epistemology, its ethics centres on the criticism of all religious and moral ideals which presuppose invisible agents and an afterlife. Hostile sources depict its followers as promulgating unrestricted hedonism.

ELI FRANCO
KARIN PREISENDANZ

MATHEMATICS, FOUNDATIONS OF

Introduction

Conceived of philosophically, the foundations of mathematics concern various metaphysical and epistemological problems raised by mathematical practice, its results and applications. Most of these problems are of ancient vintage; two, in particular, have been of perennial concern. These are its richness of content and its necessity. Important too,

though not so prominent in the history of the subject, is the problem of application, or how to account for the fact that mathematics has given rise to such an extensive, important and varied body of applications in other disciplines.

The Greeks struggled with these questions. So, too, did various medieval and modern thinkers. The ideas of many of these continue to influence foundational thinking to the present day.

During the nineteenth and twentieth centuries, however, the most influential ideas have been those of Kant. In one way or another and to a greater or lesser extent, the main currents of foundational thinking during this period – the most active and fertile period in the entire history of the subject – are nearly all attempts to reconcile Kant's foundational ideas with various later developments in mathematics and logic.

These developments include, chiefly, the nineteenth-century discovery of non-Euclidean geometries, the vigorous development of mathematical logic, the development of rigorous axiomatizations of geometry, the arithmetization of analysis and the discovery (by Dedekind and Peano) of an axiomatization of arithmetic. The first is perhaps the most important. It led to widespread acceptance of the idea that space was not merely a Kantian 'form' of intuition, but had an independence from our intellect that made it different in kind from arithmetic. This asymmetry between geometry and arithmetic became a major premise of more than one of the main 'isms' of twentieth-century philosophy of mathematics. The intuitionists retained Kant's conception of arithmetic and took the same view of that part of geometry which could be reduced to arithmetic. The logicists maintained arithmetic to be 'analytic' but differed over their view of geometry. Hilbert's formalist view endorsed a greater part of Kant's conception.

The second development carried logic to a point well beyond where it had been in Kant's day and suggested that his views on the nature of mathematics were in part due to the relatively impoverished state of his logic. The third indicated that geometry could be completely formalized and that intuition was therefore not needed for the sake of conducting inferences within proofs. The fourth and fifth, finally, provided for the codification of a large part of classical mathematics – namely analysis and its neighbours – within a single axiomatic system – namely (second-order) arithmetic. This confirmed the views of those (for example, the intuitionists and the logicists) who believed that arithmetic had a special centrality within human thinking. It also provided a clear reductive target for such later anti-Kantian enterprises as Russell's logicism.

The major movements in the philosophy of mathematics during this period all drew strength from post-Kantian developments in mathematics and logic. Each, however, also encountered serious difficulties soon after gaining initial momentum. Frege's logicism was defeated by Russell's paradox; Russell's logicism, in turn, made use of such questionable (from a logicist standpoint) items as the axioms of infinity and reduction. Both logicism and Hilbert's formalist programme came under heavy attack from Gödel's incompleteness theorems. And finally, intuitionism suffered from its inability to produce a body of mathematics comparable in richness to classical mathematics.

Despite the failure of these non-Kantian programmes, however, movement away from Kant continued in the mid- and late twentieth century. From the 1930s on this has been driven mainly by a revival of empiricist and naturalist ideas in philosophy, prominent in the writings of both the logical empiricists and the later influential work of Quine, Putnam and Benacerraf. This continues as perhaps the major force shaping work in the philosophy of mathematics.

1 Kant's views; reactions
2 Intuitionism
3 Logicism
4 Hilbert's formalism
5 Modifications
6 Later developments

1 Kant's views; reactions

The 'Problematik' that KANT established for the epistemology of pure mathematics focused on the reconciliation of two apparently incompatible features of pure mathematics: (1) the problem of necessity, or how to explain the apparent fact that mathematical statements (for example, statements such that $1+1=2$ or that the sum of the interior angles of a Euclidean triangle is equal to two right angles) should appear to be not only true but necessarily true and independent of empirical evidence; and (2) the problem of cognitive richness, or how to account for the fact that pure mathematics should yield subjects as rich and deep in content and method, as robust in growth and as replete with surprising discoveries as the history of mathematics demonstrates.

In mathematics, Kant said, we find a 'great and established branch of knowledge' – a cognitive domain so 'wonderfully large' and with promise of such 'unlimited future extension' that it would appear to arise from sources other than those of pure unaided (human) reason (*Prolegomena*: §§6, 7).

At the same time, it carries with it a certainty or necessity that is typical of judgments of pure reason. The problem, then, is to explain these apparently conflicting characteristics. Kant's explanation was that mathematical knowledge arises from certain standing conditions or 'forms' which shape our experience of space and time – forms which, though they are part of the innate cognitive apparatus that we bring to experience, none the less shape our experience in a way that goes beyond mere logical processing.

To elaborate this hypothesis, Kant sorted judgments/propositions in two different ways: first, according to whether they required appeal to sensory experience for their justification; and, second, according to whether their predicate concepts were 'contained in' their subject concepts. A judgment or proposition was 'a priori' if it could be justified without appeal to sensory content. If not, it was 'a posteriori'. It was 'analytic' if the very act of *thinking* the subject concept contained, as a constituent part, the *thinking* of the predicate concept. If not, it was either false or 'synthetic'. In synthetic a priori judgment – the type of judgment Kant regarded as characteristic of mathematics – the predicate concept was thought not through the mere *thinking* of the subject concept, but through its 'construction in intuition'. He took a similar view of mathematical inference, believing it to involve an intuition that goes beyond the mere logical connection of premises and conclusions (*Critique of Pure Reason*: A713–19/B741–7).

Kant erected his mathematical epistemology upon these distinctions and, famously, maintained that mathematical judgment and inference is synthetic a priori in character. In this way, he intended to account for both the necessity and cognitive richness of mathematics, its necessity reflecting its a priority, its cognitive richness its syntheticity.

Kant applied this basic outlook to both arithmetic and geometry (and also to pure mechanics). He did not regard them as entirely identical, however, since he saw them as resting on different a priori intuitions. Neither did he see them as possessing precisely the same universality (*Critique*: A163–5, 170–1, 717, 734/B204–6, 212, 745, 762). None the less, he regarded their similarities as more important than their differences and therefore took them to be of essentially the same epistemic type – namely, synthetic a priori. In the end, it was this inclusion of geometry and arithmetic within the same basic epistemic type rather than his more central claim concerning the *existence* of synthetic a priori knowledge that gave rise to the sternest challenges to his views.

In the decades following the publication of the first *Critique*, the principal source of concern regarding its views was the growing evidence for and eventual discovery of non-Euclidean geometries. This led many to question whether geometry and arithmetic are of the same basic epistemic character.

The serious possibility of non-Euclidean geometries went back to the work of Lambert and others in the eighteenth century. Building on this work, some – in particular, Gauss (Letters to Olbers and Bessel) – stated their opposition to Kant's views even before the actual discovery of non-Euclidean geometries by Bolyai and Lobachevskii in the 1820s. Gauss' reasoning was essentially this: number seems to be purely a product of the intellect and, so, something of which we can have purely a priori knowledge. Space, on the other hand, seems to have a reality external to our minds that prohibits a purely a priori knowledge of it. Arithmetic and geometry are therefore not on an epistemological par with one another.

This reasoning became a potent force shaping nineteenth- and twentieth-century foundational thinking. Another such force was the dramatic development of logic and the axiomatic method in the mid- to late nineteenth century and early twentieth century. This included the introduction of algebraic methods by Boole and De Morgan, the improved treatment of relations by Peirce, Schröder and Peano, the replacement of the subject–predicate conception of propositional form with Frege's more fecund functional conception, and the advances in axiomatization and formalization brought about by the work of Frege, Pasch, Peano, Hilbert and (especially) Whitehead and Russell.

Certain developments in mathematics proper also exerted an influence. Chief among these were the arithmetization of analysis by Weierstrass, Dedekind and others, and the axiomatization of arithmetic by Peano and Dedekind. Of somewhat lesser importance, though still significant for their effects on Hilbert's thinking, were Einstein's relativistic ideas in physics.

2 Intuitionism

A variety of views concerning the asymmetry of geometry and arithmetic emerged in the late nineteenth and early twentieth centuries. That of the early intuitionists Brouwer and Weyl retained Kant's synthetic a priori conception of arithmetic.

They responded to the discovery of non-Euclidean geometries, however, by denying the a priori status of that part of geometry that could not be reduced to arithmetic by such means as Descartes' calculus of coordinates. They retained, none the less, a type of a priori intuition of time as the basis for arithmetical knowledge. They also emphasized the synthetic character of arithmetical judgment and inference, and sharply distinguished them from logical judgment and inference.

Brouwer described his intuition of time as consciousness of change *per se* – the human subject's primordial inner awareness of the 'falling apart' of a life-moment into a part that is passing away and a part that is becoming. He believed that, via a process of abstraction, one could pass from this basal intuition of time to a concept of 'bare two-oneness', and from this concept to, first, the finite ordinals, then the transfinite ordinals and, finally, the linear continuum. In this way, parts of classical arithmetic, analysis and set theory could be recaptured intuitionistically.

Brouwer thus modified Kant's intuitional basis for mathematics. He also modified his conception of knowledge of existence. Kant believed that humans could obtain knowledge of existence only through sensible intuition. Only this, he believed, had the type of involuntariness and objectivity that assures us that belief in an object is not a mere compulsion or idiosyncrasy of our subjective selves. Like the post-Kantian romantic idealists, however, Brouwer (and Weyl, too) believed as well in knowledge of existence via a kind of 'intellectual intuition' – an intuition carried by a purely internal type of mental construction.

The early intuitionists (especially Brouwer and Poincaré) remained Kantian in their conception of mathematical reasoning and took it to be essentially different in character from 'discursive' or logical reasoning. Brouwer believed logical reasoning to mark not patterns in mathematical thinking itself but only patterns in its linguistic representation. It was therefore not indicative of the inferential structure of mathematical thinking itself and had no place within genuine mathematical reasoning *per se*. This was essentially the idea expressed in Brouwer's so-called 'First Act of Intuitionism'.

Thus the early intuitionists (especially Brouwer and Weyl and, to some extent, Poincaré) discarded Kant's view of geometry, revised his conception of arithmetic and existence claims, and preserved his basic stance on the nature of mathematical reasoning and its relationship to logical reasoning. Later intuitionists (for example, Heyting and Dummett) did not keep to this plan. They rejected Brouwer's view of the divide between logical and mathematical reasoning and made a significant place for logic in their accounts of mathematical reasoning. Some of them (Dummett and his 'anti-realist' followers) even went so far as to make the question 'What is the logic of mathematical reasoning?' central to their philosophy of mathematics (see §5).

3 Logicism

The view of the logicist FREGE (and, to some extent, of Dedekind) accepted Kant's synthetic a priori conception of geometry but maintained arithmetic to be analytic. RUSSELL, another logicist, rejected Kant's views of both geometry and arithmetic (and also of pure mechanics) and maintained the analyticity of both. (See LOGICISM.)

Frege's logicism differed sharply from intuitionism. First, it differed in the place in mathematical reasoning it assigned to logic. Frege (*Die Grundlagen der Arithmetik*: preface) maintained that reasoning is essentially the same everywhere and that even an inference pattern such as that of mathematical induction, which appears to be peculiar to mathematics, is, at bottom, purely logical. Second, it differed in its conception of geometry. Like the early intuitionists, Frege regarded the discovery of non-Euclidean geometries as revealing an important asymmetry between arithmetic and geometry. Unlike them, however, he did not see this as grounds for rejecting Kant's synthetic a priori conception of geometry (*Begriffsschrift*; *Die Grundlagen*), but rather as indicating a fundamental difference between geometry and arithmetic. Frege believed the fundamental concept of arithmetic – magnitude – to be both too pervasive and too abstract to be the product of Kantian intuition (1874: 50). It figured in *every* kind of thinking and so must, he reasoned, have a basis in thought deeper than that of intuition. It must have its basis in the very core of rational thought itself; the laws of logic.

The problem was to account for the cognitive richness of arithmetic on such a view. How could the 'great tree of the science of number' (*Die Grundlagen*: §16) have its roots in bare logical or analytical 'identities'? Frege responded by offering new accounts of both the objectivity and the informativeness of arithmetic. The former he attributed to its subject matter – the so-called 'logical objects' (§§26, 27, 105). The latter he derived from a new theory of content which allowed concepts to contain (tacit) content that was not needed for their grasp. On this view, analytic judgments could have content that was not required for the mere understanding of the concepts contained in them. Consequently, they could yield more than knowledge of transparent logical identities (§§64–6, 70, 88, 91).

Unlike Kant, then, Frege maintained an important epistemic asymmetry between geometry and arithmetic – an asymmetry based upon his belief that arithmetic is more basic to human rational thought than is geometry. In addition, he departed from Kant in maintaining a realistic conception of arithmetic knowledge despite its analytic character. He saw it as being about a class of objects – so-called 'logical objects' – that are external but intimately related to the mind and therefore not the mere expression of standing traits of human cognition. The differences between arithmetical and geometric necessity were to be accounted for by separating the relationship the mind has to the objects of arithmetic from that which it has to the objects of geometry.

Russell's logicism differed from Frege's. Perhaps most importantly, Russell did not regard the existence of non-Euclidean geometries as evidence of an epistemological asymmetry between geometry and arithmetic. Rather, he saw the 'arithmetization' of geometry and other areas of mathematics as evidence of an epistemological symmetry between arithmetic and the rest of mathematics. Russell thus extended his logicism to the whole of mathematics. The basic components of his logicism were a general methodological ideal of pursuing each science to its greatest level of generality, and a conception of the greatest level of generality in mathematics as lying at that point where all its theorems are of the form '*p* implies *q*', all their constants are logical constants and all their variables of unrestricted range. Theorems of this sort, Russell maintained, would rightly be regarded as logical truths.

Russell's logicism was thus motivated by a view of mathematics which saw it as the science of the most general formal truths; a science whose indefinables are those constants of rational thought (the so-called logical constants) that have the most ubiquitous application, and whose indemonstrables are those propositions that set out the basic properties of these indefinables (Russell 1903: 8). In his opinion, such a view provided the only precise description of what philosophers have had in mind when they have described mathematics as a necessary or a priori science.

Russell thus accounted for the necessity of mathematics by pointing to its logical character. He accounted for its richness principally by invoking a new definition of syntheticity that allowed all but the most trivial logical truths and inferences to be counted as informative or synthetic. Mathematical truths would thus be logical truths, but they would not, for all that, be analytic truths. Similarly for inferences. An inference would count as synthetic so long as its conclusion was a different proposition from its premises. Cognitive richness was conceived primarily as the production of new propositions from old, and, on Russell's conception (supposing the criterion of propositional identity to be sufficiently strict), even purely logical inference could produce a bounty of new knowledge from old.

Russell was thus able to account for both the necessity and the cognitive richness of mathematics while making mathematics part of logic. What had kept previous generations of thinkers and, in particular, Kant from recognizing the possibilities of such a view was the relatively impoverished state of logic before the end of the nineteenth century. The new logic, with its robust stock of new forms, its functional conception of the proposition and the ensuing fuller axiomatization of mathematics which it made possible, changed all this forever and provided for the final refutation of Kant. Such, at any rate, was Russell's position.

4 Hilbert's formalism

Hilbert accepted the synthetic a priori character of (much of) arithmetic and geometry, but rejected Kant's account of the supposed intuitions upon which they rest (see HILBERT'S PROGRAMME AND FORMALISM). Overall, Hilbert's position was more complicated in its relationship to Kant's epistemology than were those of the intuitionists and logicists. Like Russell, he rejected Kant's specifically mathematical epistemology – in particular, his conception of the nature and origins of its a priori character. Like Russell, too, he rejected the common post-Kantian belief in the epistemological asymmetry of arithmetic and geometry. Hilbert was, however, unique among those mentioned here in endorsing the framework of Kant's general critical epistemology and making it a central feature of his mathematical epistemology. Specifically, he adopted Kant's distinction between the faculty of the understanding and the faculty of reason as the guide for his pivotal distinction between the so-called 'real' and 'ideal' portions of classical mathematics.

Hilbert took 'real' mathematics to be ultimately concerned with the shapes or forms (Gestalten) of concrete signs or figures, given in intuition and comprising a type of 'immediate experience prior to all thought' On the Infinite 1926; Foundations of Mathematics 1928. Hilbert proposed this basic intuition of shape as a replacement for Kant's two a priori intuitions of space and time. Like Kant's a priori intuitions, however, Hilbert, too regarded his finitary intuition as an 'irremissible pre-condition' of all mathematical (indeed, all scientific) judgment and the ultimate source of all genuine a priori knowledge 'Naturkennen und Logik' 1930.

The genuine judgments of real mathematics were the judgments of which our mathematical knowledge was constituted. The pseudo-judgments of ideal mathematics, on the other hand, functioned like Kant's ideas of reason. They neither described things present in the world nor constituted a foundation for our judgments concerning such things. Rather, they played a purely regulative role of guiding the efficient and orderly development of our real knowledge.

Hilbert did not, therefore, affirm the necessity of either arithmetic or geometry in any simple, straightforward way. Rather, he distinguished two types of necessity operating within both. One, pertaining to the judgments of real mathematics, consisted in the (presumed) fact that the apprehension of certain elementary spatial and combinatorial features of simple concrete objects is a precondition of all scientific thought. The other, pertaining to the ideal parts of mathematics, had a kind of psychological necessity, a necessity borne of the manner in which our minds inevitably or best regulate the development of our real knowledge.

This conception of the necessity of mathematics was different from both Kant's and those of the logicists and intuitionists. So, too, was Hilbert's view of the cognitive richness of mathematics, which he attributed both to the objective richness of the shapes and combinatorial features of concrete signs and to the richness of our imaginations in 'creating' complementary ideal objects.

In its overall structure, Hilbert's mathematical epistemology thus resembled Kant's *general* critical epistemology. This included his so-called 'consistency' requirement (that is, the requirement that ideal reasoning not prove anything contrary to that which may be established by real means), which resembled Kant's demand that the faculty of reason not produce any judgment of the understanding that could not in principle be obtained solely from the understanding (*Critique*: A328/B385).

5 Modifications

During the first four decades of the twentieth century, each of the post-Kantian programmes outlined above came under attack. Frege's logicism was challenged by Russell's paradox. Russell's logicism encountered difficulties concerning its use of certain existence axioms (namely his axioms of reducibility and infinity) which did not appear to be laws of *logic*. Both were challenged by Gödel's incompleteness theorems, as was Hilbert's formalist programme. Finally, the intuitionists were criticized both philosophically, where their idealism was called into question, and mathematically, where their ability to support a significant body of mathematics remained in doubt. Various modifications have been proposed.

Modifications of logicism. On the mathematical side, a chastened successor to logicism can perhaps be seen in the model-theoretic work of Abraham Robinson and his followers. They are interested in

·determining the mathematical content latent in purely 'logical' features of various mathematical structures or the extent to which genuinely mathematical problems concerning these structures can be solved by purely logical (that is, model-theoretic) means. They have been particularly successful in their treatment of various algebraic structures.

Philosophically, too, there have been attempts to renew logicism. It re-emerged in the 1930s and 1940s as the favoured philosophy of mathematics of the logical empiricists. They did not, however, develop a logicism of their own in the way that Dedekind, Frege and Russell did, but, rather, simply appropriated the technical work of Russell and Whitehead (modulo the usual reservations concerning the axioms of infinity and reducibility) and attempted to embed it in an overall empiricist epistemology.

This empiricist turn was a novel development in the history of logicism and represented a serious departure from both the original logicism of Leibniz (§10) and the more recent logicism of Frege (and Dedekind). It was less at odds with Russell's logicism, which saw mathematics and the empirical sciences as both making use of an essentially inductive method (the so-called 'regressive' method).

Like all empiricists, the logical empiricists struggled with the Kantian problem of how to account for the apparent necessity of mathematics while at the same time being able to explain its cognitive richness. Their strategy was to empty mathematics of all non-analytic content while, at the same time, arguing that analytic truth and inference can be substantial and non-self-evident.

Their ideas came under heavy attack by W.V. Quine, who challenged their pivotal distinction between analytic and synthetic truths. He argued that the basic unit of knowledge – the basic item of our thought that is tested against experience – is science as a whole and that this depends upon empirical evidence for its justification. Mathematics and logic are used to relate empirical evidence to the rest of science and, so, are inextricably interwoven into the whole fabric of science. They are thus part of the total body of science that is tested against experience and there is no clean way of dividing between truths of meaning (analytic truths) and truths of fact (synthetic truths).

Within a relatively brief period of time, Quine's argument became a major influence in the philosophy of mathematics and the logicism of the logical empiricists was largely abandoned. Newer conceptions of logicism have, however, continued to appear from time to time. For example, Putnam addressed the difficult (for a logicist) question of existence claims, arguing that such statements are to be seen as asserting the possible (as opposed to the actual) existence of structures. They are therefore, at bottom, logical claims, and can be established by logical (or metalogical) means. Hodes takes a somewhat different approach, arguing that arithmetic claims can be translated into a second-order logic in which the second-order variables range over functions and concepts (as opposed to objects). In this way, commitment to sets and other specifically mathematical objects can be eliminated and, this done, arithmetic can be considered a part of logic.

Field also presents a kind of logicist view – namely, that mathematical knowledge is (at least largely) logical knowledge. Mathematical knowledge is defined as that knowledge which separates a person who knows a lot of mathematics from a person who knows only a little, and it is then argued that what separates these two kinds of knowers is mainly logical knowledge; that is, knowledge of what follows from what.

Modifications of Hilbert's programme. Hilbert's programme too has its latter-day adherents. For the most part, these have adopted one of two basic stances: that of extending the methods available for proving the consistency of classical ideal mathematics; or that of diminishing the scope and strength of classical ideal mathematics so that its consistency (or the consistency of important parts of it) can more nearly be proved by the kinds of elementary means that Hilbert originally envisaged.

Some in the first group (for example, Gentzen, Ackermann and Gödel) have argued that there are types of evidence that exceed finitary evidence in strength but which have the same basic epistemic virtues as it. Others (for example, Kreisel, Feferman, Sieg) argue for a change in our conception of what a consistency proof ought to do. They maintain that its essential obligation is to realize an epistemic gain, and that finitary methods are not the only epistemically gainful methods for proving consistency.

Those in the second group – the so-called 'reverse mathematics' school of Friedman, Simpson and others – try to isolate the mathematical 'cores' of the various areas of classical mathematics and prove the consistency of these 'reduced' theories by finitary or related means. So far, significant success has been achieved along these lines. (See Hilbert's programme and formalism.)

Modifications of intuitionism. Regarding intuitionism, Heyting's work in the 1930s to formalize intuitionism and to identify its logic has led to a vigorous programme of logical and mathematical investigation. In addition to Heyting and his students, Errett Bishop and his followers have extended a constructivist approach to areas of classical mathematics to which such an approach had previously not been extended.

On the more philosophical side, the most important development is the construction by Michael Dummett and his anti-realist followers of a defence of intuitionism based upon – in their view – the best answer to the question 'What is the logic of mathematics?'. Their answer is based upon what they take to be a proper theory of meaning – a theory which, following certain ideas set out by Wittgenstein in his *Philosophical Investigations*, equates the meaning of an expression with its canonical use in the practice to which it belongs. They then identify the canonical use of an expression in mathematics with the role it plays in the central activity of proof, and from this they infer an intuitionist treatment of the logical operators.

6   Later developments

Along with the modifications of the major post-Kantian viewpoints noted above, two other developments in the second half of the twentieth century are important to note. One of these is the shift towards empiricism that was brought about by Quine's (following Duhem's) merging of mathematics and the empirical sciences into a single justificatory unit governed by a basically inductive-empirical method. On this view, mathematics may on the whole be *less* susceptible to falsification by sensory evidence than is natural science, but this is a difference of degree, not kind.

This conception of mathematics dispenses with a 'datum' of mathematical epistemology that philosophers of mathematics from Kant on down had struggled to accommodate: namely, the presumed necessity of mathematics. It puts in its place a general empiricist epistemology in which all judgments – those of mathematics and logic as well as those of the natural sciences – are seen as evidentially connected to sensory phenomena and, so, subject to empirical revision.

To accommodate the lingering conviction that mathematics is independent of empirical evidence in a way that natural science is not, Quine introduced a pragmatic distinction between them. Rational belief-revision, he said, is governed by a pragmatic concern to maximize the overall predictive and explanatory power of one's total system of beliefs. Furthermore, predictive and explanatory power are generally aided by policies of revision which minimize, both in scope and severity, the changes that are made to a previously successful belief-system in response to recalcitrant experience.

Because of this, beliefs of mathematics and logic are typically less subject to empirical revision than beliefs of natural science and common sense since revising them generally (albeit, in Quine's view, not inevitably) does more damage to a belief-system than does revising its common sense and natural scientific beliefs. The necessity of mathematics is thus accommodated in Quine's epistemology by moving mathematics closer to the centre of a 'web' of human beliefs where beliefs are less susceptible to empirical revision than are the beliefs of natural science and common sense that lie closer to the edge of the web.

In Quine's view, merging mathematics and science into a single belief-system also induces a realist conception of mathematics. Mathematical sentences must be treated as true in order to play their role in this system, and the world is to be seen as being populated by those entities that are among the values of the variables of true sentences. Mathematical entities are thus real because mathematical sentences play an integral part in our best total theory of experience.

Quine's views have been challenged on various grounds. For example, Parsons argues that treating the elementary arithmetical parts of mathematics as being on an epistemological par with the hypotheses of theoretical physics fails to capture an epistemologically important distinction between the different kinds of evidentness displayed by the two. Even highly confirmed physical hypotheses such as 'The earth moves around the sun' are more 'derivative' (that is, roughly, more theory-laden) than is an elementary arithmetic proposition such as '7+5=12'. It is therefore not plausible to regard the two claims as based on essentially the same type of evidence.

Others have challenged different aspects of Quine's position. Field and Maddy, for example, both question his merging of mathematics and natural science, though in different ways. Field argues that natural science that utilizes mathematics is a conservative extension of it and, so, has no need of its entities. The mathematical part of natural science can thus, in an important sense, be separated from the rest of it. Maddy investigates the possibility that our knowledge of at least certain mathematical objects might not be so diffuse and inextricable from the whole scheme of our natural scientific knowledge as Quine suggests. She argues that perceptual experience can be tied closely and specifically to certain mathematical objects (in particular, to certain sets) in a way that seems out of keeping with Quine's holism.

In addition to Quine, others have suggested different mergings of mathematics and natural sciences. Kitcher, for instance, presents a generally empiricist epistemology for mathematics in which history and community are important epistemological forces. Gödel, on the other hand, argued that mathematics, like the natural sciences, makes use of what is essentially inductive justification when it justifies higher-level mathematical hypotheses on the grounds of their explanatory or simplificatory effects on lower-level mathematical truths and on physics. He allowed, however, that only *some* of our mathematical knowledge arises from empirical sources and regarded as absurd the idea that all of it might do.

Another important influence on recent philosophy of mathematics is Benacerraf's 'Mathematical Truth' (1973), in which he argues that the philosophy of mathematics faces a general dilemma. It must give an account of both mathematical truth and mathematical knowledge. The former seems to demand abstract objects as the referents of singular terms in mathematical discourse. The latter, on the other hand, seems to demand that we avoid such referents. There are mathematical epistemologies (for example, various Platonist ones) that allow for a plausible account of the truth of mathematical sentences. Likewise, there are those (for example, various formalist ones) that allow for a plausible account of how we might come to *know* mathematical sentences. However, no known epistemology does both. Towards the end of the twentieth century a great deal of work has been devoted to resolving this dilemma. Field, Hellman and Chihara attempt anti-Platonist resolutions. Maddy, on the other hand, attempts a resolution at once Platonist and naturalistic. To date there is no general consensus on which approaches are the more plausible.

An earlier argument of Benacerraf's (see Benacerraf 1965) was similarly influential in shaping later work. It is the chief inspiration of the position known as 'structuralism' – the view that mathematical objects are essentially positions in structures and have no important additional internal composition or nature. Apart from the desire for a descriptively more adequate account of mathematics, the chief motivation of structuralism is epistemological. Knowledge of the characteristics of individual abstract objects would seem to require naturalistically inexplicable powers of cognition. Knowledge of at least some structures, on the other hand, would appear to be explicable as the result of applying such classically empiricist means of cognition as abstraction to observable physical complexes. Structures identified via abstraction become part of the general framework of our thinking and can be extended and generalized in a variety of ways as the search for the simplest and most effective overall conceptual scheme is pursued.

Structuralism as a general philosophy of mathematics has been criticized by Parsons, who argues that there are important mathematical objects for which structuralism is not an adequate account. These are the 'quasi-concrete' objects of mathematics – objects that are directly 'instantiated' or 'represented' by concrete objects (for example, geometric figures and symbols such as the so-called 'stroke numerals' of Hilbert's finitary arithmetic, where these are construed as types whose instances are written marks or symbols or uttered sounds). Such objects cannot be treated in a purely structuralist way because their 'representational' function cannot be reduced to the purely intrastructural relationships they bear to other objects within a given system. At the same time, however, they are among the most elementary and important mathematical entities there are.

See also: DEDEKIND, J.W.R.; PROOF THEORY

References and further reading

Benacerraf, P. (1965) 'What Numbers Could Not Be', *Philosophical Review* 74: 47–73. (Structuralist argument that arithmetic is not a science concerning particular objects – the numbers – but rather a science elaborating the structure that all arithmetical progressions share in common. Dedekind argued for such a view a century earlier.)

Heijenoort, J. van (ed.) (1967) *From Frege to Gödel: A Source Book in Mathematical Logic, 1879–1931*, Cambridge, MA: Harvard University Press. (Collection of basic papers in mathematical logic and the foundations of mathematics. Useful forewords and bibliography.)

Russell, B.A.W. (1903) *The Principles of Mathematics*, Cambridge: Cambridge University Press; 2nd edn, London: Allen & Unwin, 1937; repr. London: Routledge, 1992. (Russell's first full-length development of his logicist views.)

MICHAEL DETLEFSEN

MATTER

Viewed as arising within the framework of a more general theory of *substance*, philosophical treatments of matter have traditionally revolved around two issues: (1) The nature of matter: what are the distinguishing characteristics of matter or material substance(s) that define it and distinguish it from other substances, if any? (2) The problem of elements: do material things consist of elementary substances, or are there always further constituents? One possible view is that there is no fundamental level – that there are always further constituents, ingredients of ingredients. However, the view most often held by both philosophers and scientists has been that there are indeed fundamental *elements* out of which material things are made. Once this view is adopted, the question arises as to what they are and what properties distinguish them.

These two issues were introduced, though only gradually, in ancient Greek philosophy. A significant turn came about in the seventeenth century, in which the work of Descartes and Newton led to a picture of matter as passive, inert and dead as opposed to minds and forces, both of which were conceived as being 'active'. Many philosophical problems and doctrines have been formulated in terms of this distinction. However, later developments in science, especially in the twentieth century, have brought about such profound changes that classical concepts of matter are no longer viable. These new developments profoundly alter the statements of philosophical doctrines and problems traditionally associated with matter.

See also: SUBSTANCE; UNITY OF SCIENCE

DUDLEY SHAPERE

MAXWELL, JAMES CLERK (1831–79)

For his two achievements of unifying electricity, magnetism and light, and of inventing statistical dynamics, Maxwell stands as the founding mind of modern theoretical physics. More than any other physicist his also was a mind shaped and informed by a training in philosophy, even though, unlike Heinrich Hertz or Ernst Mach, for example, he never wrote a philosophical treatise. Therein lies the point, however. Mach's and Hertz's best discoveries seem remote from their metaphysics, Maxwell's are bound up with his. Particularly important philosophically are his interconnected uses of relation, analogy and classification. He is also responsible for introducing the word 'relativity' into physics, and for articulating the scientific problematic that led to Einstein's theory.

C.W.F. EVERITT

MEAD, GEORGE HERBERT (1863–1931)

Together with Charles Peirce, William James and John Dewey, George Herbert Mead is considered one of the classic representatives of American pragmatism. He is most famous for his ideas about the specificities of human communication and sociality and about the genesis of the 'self' in infantile development. By developing these ideas, Mead became one of the founders of social psychology and – mostly via his influence on the school of symbolic interactionism – one of the most influential figures in contemporary sociology.

Compared to that enormous influence, other parts of his philosophical work are relatively neglected.

See also: COMMUNICATION AND INTENTION; COMMUNICATIVE RATIONALITY; PRAGMATISM

HANS JOAS

MEANING
See LANGUAGE, PHILOSOPHY OF; SEMANTICS

MEANING AND RULE-FOLLOWING

Wittgenstein's discussion of rules and rule-following, and the recent responses to it, have been widely regarded as providing the deepest and most challenging issues surrounding the notions of meaning, understanding and intention – central notions in the philosophy of language and mind. The fundamental issue is what it is for words to have meaning, and for speakers to use words in accordance with their meanings. In *Philosophical Investigations* and *Remarks on the Foundations of Mathematics*, Wittgenstein explores the idea that what could give a word its meaning is a rule for its use, and that to be a competent speaker is to use words in accordance with these rules. His discussion of the nature of rules and rule-following has been highly influential, although there is no general agreement about his conclusions and final position. The view that there is no objectivity to an individual's attempt to follow a rule in isolation provides one strand of Wittgenstein's argument against the possibility of a private language.

To some commentators, Wittgenstein's discussion only leads to the sceptical conclusion that there are no rules to be followed and so no facts about what words mean. Others have seen him as showing why certain models of what it takes for an individual to follow a rule are inadequate and must be replaced by an appeal to a communal linguistic practice.

See also: PRIVATE STATES AND LANGUAGE

BARRY C. SMITH

MEANING AND TRUTH

Analytic philosophy has seen a resurgent interest in the possibility of explaining linguistic meaning in terms of truth, which many philosophers have seen as considerably more tractable than meaning. The core suggestion is that the meaning of a declarative sentence may be given by specifying certain conditions under which it is true. Thus the declarative sentence 'Venus is red' is true just in case the condition that Venus is red obtains; and this is exactly what the sentence means.

As it stands, however, this suggestion provides us with no explanation of the meanings of the words and phrases that make up sentences, since in general they are not expressions that have truth-conditions. (There are no conditions under which the word 'Venus' is true.) Furthermore, it needs to be supplemented by some method of circumscribing the truth-conditions that embody the meanings of declarative sentences, since there are many conditions under which any given sentence is true: 'Venus is red' is true not merely when Venus is red, but also, for example, when Venus is red and 7 + 5 = 12; but it does not *mean* that Venus is red and 7 + 5 = 12.

Evidently the first problem can be solved only by finding other semantic properties which indicate the meanings of words and phrases. For example, it is sometimes thought that the meaning of a name can be specified by saying what it refers to; and that of a predicate by saying what it is true of. But notice that since the meaning of a declarative sentence can be grasped by first grasping the meanings of its basic components, meaning-indicating ascriptions of semantic properties to those components must entail a meaning-indicating statement of its truth-conditions. Semantic properties such as 'referring to' and 'being true of' satisfy this requirement, at least in the context of what is sometimes called a 'truth theory' for a language.

This still leaves the problem of how to circumscribe the right meaning-indicating statement of truth-conditions for declarative sentences. Indeed we now have a further problem. For if the meanings of the components of sentences are not stated directly, but merely in terms of what they refer to or are true of (say), then we must also find a way of determining which of the many ways of specifying what they refer to, or the conditions under which they are true of something, is meaning-indicating. These problems may arguably be solved by placing an appropriate truth theory for a language in a setting that allows us to appeal to the general psychology of its speakers.

Attempts to elucidate meaning in terms of truth-conditions induce a plethora of further problems. Many are a matter of detail, concerning the kinds of properties we should associate with particular idioms and constructions or, equivalently, how we are to produce truth theories for them. As a result of Tarski's work, we have a good idea how to do this for a wide range of categories of expressions. But there are many which, superficially at least, seem to resist straightforward incorporation into such a framework. More general difficulties concern whether truth should be central at all in the analysis or elucidation of meaning; two objections are especially prominent, one adverting to antirealist

considerations, the other to the redundancy theory of truth.
See also: DAVIDSON, D.

STEPHEN G. WILLIAMS

MEANING AND VERIFICATION

The verifiability theory of meaning says that meaning is evidence. It is anticipated in, for example, Hume's empiricist doctrine of impressions and ideas, but it emerges into full notoriety in twentieth-century logical positivism. The positivists used the theory in a critique of metaphysics to show that the problems of philosophy, such as the problem of the external world and the problem of other minds, are not real problems at all but only pseudoproblems. Their publicists used the doctrine to argue that religion, ethics and fiction are meaningless, which is how verificationism became notorious among the general public.

Seminal criticism of verification from around 1950 argues that no division between sense and nonsense coincides tidily with a division between science and metaphysics, as the positivists had claimed. Quine later developed verificationism into a sort of semantic holism in which metaphysics is continuous with science. In contrast, Dummett argues from a reading of Wittgenstein's claim that meaning is use to a rejection of any sort of truth surpassing the possibility of knowledge, and thence to a defence of intuitionistic logic. But the claim that all truths can be known yields in an otherwise innocuous setting the preposterous consequence that all truths actually are known. There are ways to tinker with the setting so as to avoid this consequence, but it is best to conclude by *reductio* that some truths cannot be known and that verificationism is false. That in turn seems to show that the prospects for an empiricist theory of meaning are dim, which might well shake a complacent confidence in meaning.

W.D. HART

MEANING, EMOTIVE
See EMOTIVE MEANING

MEASUREMENT PROBLEM, QUANTUM
See QUANTUM MEASUREMENT PROBLEM

MEASUREMENT, THEORY OF

A conceptual analysis of measurement can properly begin by formulating the two fundamental problems of any measurement procedure. The first problem is that of representation, justifying the assignment of numbers to objects or phenomena. We cannot literally take a number in our hands and 'apply' it to a physical object. What we can show is that the structure of a set of phenomena under certain empirical operations and relations is the same as the structure of some set of numbers under corresponding arithmetical operations and relations. Solution of the representation problem for a theory of measurement does not completely lay bare the structure of the theory, for there is often a formal difference between the kind of assignment of numbers arising from different procedures of measurement. This is the second fundamental problem, determining the scale type of a given procedure.

Counting is an example of an absolute scale. The number of members of a given collection of objects is determined uniquely. In contrast, the measurement of mass or weight is an example of a ratio scale. An empirical procedure for measuring mass does not determine the unit of mass. The measurement of temperature is an example of an interval scale. The empirical procedure of measuring temperature by use of a thermometer determines neither a unit nor an origin. In this sort of measurement the ratio of any two intervals is independent of the unit and zero point of measurement.

Still another type of scale is one which is arbitrary except for order. Moh's hardness scale, according to which minerals are ranked in regard to hardness as determined by a scratch test, and the Beaufort wind scale, whereby the strength of a wind is classified as calm, light air, light breeze, and so on, are examples of ordinal scales.

A distinction is made between those scales of measurement which are fundamental and those which are derived. A derived scale presupposes and uses the numerical results of at least one other scale. In contrast, a fundamental scale does not depend on others.

Another common distinction is that between extensive and intensive quantities or scales. For extensive quantities like mass or distance an empirical operation of combination can be given which has the structural properties of the numerical operation of addition. Intensive quantities do not have such an operation; typical examples are temperature and cardinal utility.

A widespread complaint about this classical foundation of measurement is that it takes too little account of the analysis of variability in the quantity measured. One important source is systematic variability in the empirical properties of the object being measured. Another source lies not in the object but in the procedures of measurement being used. There are also random errors which can arise from variability in the object, the procedures or the conditions surrounding the observations.

See also: EXPERIMENT; OBSERVATION; OPERATIONALISM

PATRICK SUPPES

MEDICAL ETHICS

Medical ethics was once concerned with the professional obligations of physicians, spelled out in codes of conduct such as the ancient Hippocratic oath and elaborated by contemporary professional societies. Today this subject is a broad, loosely defined collection of issues of morality and justice in health, health care and related fields. The term 'bioethics' is often used interchangeably, though it is also used with its original broad meaning, which included issues in ecology.

The range of concerns grouped under 'medical ethics' begins with the relationship of doctor to patient, including such issues as consent to treatment, truth-telling, paternalism, confidentiality and the duty to treat. Particular moral uncertainty is engendered by contexts which demand divided allegiances of physicians, such as medical experimentation on human subjects, public health emergencies and for-profit medicine. Issues in medical ethics arise in every stage of life, from the fate of defective newborns to the withholding of life-sustaining therapies from the very old. Medical practices with patients who may not be competent to make their own medical decisions, including paediatrics and psychiatry, raise a distinctive set of ethical issues, as does medical genetics, which involves choices affecting family members, future individuals and offspring *in utero*. In recent years, medical ethics has broadened its focus beyond the individual physician or nurse to include the organization, operation and financing of the health care system as a whole, including difficult theoretical and practical uncertainties regarding the fair allocation of health care resources.

Medical ethics is at once a field of scholarship and a reform movement. The latter has campaigned in many countries on behalf of patients' rights, better care of the dying and freedom for women in reproductive decisions. As a field of scholarship, medical ethics addresses these and many other issues, but is not defined by positions taken on any of them. Though ethicists often favour an emphasis on informed consent, oppose paternalism, urge permission to end life-sustaining therapy (or choose suicide) and seek protection of human subjects of experimentation, a diversity of viewpoints finds expression in the medical ethics literature.

See also: APPLIED ETHICS; BIOETHICS; CLONING

DANIEL WIKLER

MEDIEVAL PHILOSOPHY

Medieval philosophy is the philosophy of Western Europe from about AD 400–1400, roughly the period between the fall of Rome and the Renaissance. Medieval philosophers are the historical successors of the philosophers of antiquity, but they are in fact only tenuously connected with them. Until about 1125, medieval thinkers had access to only a few texts of ancient Greek philosophy (most importantly a portion of Aristotle's logic). This limitation accounts for the special attention medieval philosophers give to logic and philosophy of language. They gained some acquaintance with other Greek philosophical forms (particularly those of later Platonism) indirectly through the writings of Latin authors such as Augustine and Boethius. These Christian thinkers left an enduring legacy of Platonistic metaphysical and theological speculation. Beginning about 1125, the influx into Western Europe of the first Latin translations of the remaining works of Aristotle transformed medieval thought dramatically. The philosophical discussions and disputes of the thirteenth and fourteenth centuries record later medieval thinkers' sustained efforts to understand the new Aristotelian material and assimilate it into a unified philosophical system.

The most significant extra-philosophical influence on medieval philosophy throughout its thousand-year history is Christianity. Christian institutions sustain medieval intellectual life, and Christianity's texts and ideas provide rich subject matter for philosophical reflection. Although most of the greatest thinkers of the period were highly trained theologians, their work addresses perennial philosophical issues and takes a genuinely philosophical approach to understanding the world. Even their discussion of specifically theological issues is typically philosophical, permeated with philosophical ideas, rigorous argument and sophisticated logical and conceptual analysis. The enterprise of philosophical theology is one of medieval philosophy's greatest achievements.

The way in which medieval philosophy develops in dialogue with the texts of ancient philosophy and the early Christian tradition (including patristic philosophy) is displayed in its two distinctive pedagogical and literary forms: the textual commentary and the disputation. In explicit commentaries on texts such as the works of Aristotle, Boethius' theological treatises and Peter Lombard's classic theological textbook, the *Sentences*, medieval thinkers wrestled anew with the traditions that had come down to them. By contrast, the disputation – the form of discourse characteristic of the university environment of the later Middle Ages – focuses not on particular texts but on specific philosophical or theological issues. It thereby allows medieval philosophers to gather together relevant passages and arguments scattered throughout the authoritative literature and to adjudicate their competing claims in a systematic way. These dialectical forms of thought and interchange encourage the development of powerful tools of interpretation, analysis and argument ideally suited to philosophical inquiry. It is the highly technical nature of these academic (or scholastic) modes of thought, however, that provoked the hostilities of the Renaissance humanists whose attacks brought the period of medieval philosophy to an end.

1 Historical and geographical boundaries

The terms 'medieval' and 'Middle Ages' derive from the Latin expression *medium aevum* (the middle age), coined by Renaissance humanists to refer to the period separating the golden age of classical Greece and Rome from what they saw as the rebirth of classical ideals in their own day. The humanists were writing from the perspective of the intellectual culture of Western Europe, and insofar as their conception of a middle age corresponds to an identifiable historical period, it corresponds to a period in the history of the Latin West. The historical boundaries of medieval intellectual culture in Western Europe are marked fairly clearly: on the one end by the disintegration of the cultural structures of Roman civilization (Alaric sacked Rome in AD 410), and on the other end by the dramatic cultural revolution perpetrated by the humanists themselves (in the late fourteenth and fifteenth centuries). There is some justification, therefore, for taking 'medieval philosophy' as designating primarily the philosophy of the Latin West from about AD 400–1400.

There were, of course, significant non-Latin philosophical developments in Europe and the Mediterranean world in this same period, in the Greek-speaking Byzantine empire, for example, and in Arabic-speaking Islamic and Jewish cultures in the Near East, northern Africa and Spain. None of these philosophical traditions, however, was radically cut off from the philosophical heritage of the ancient world in the way the Latin-speaking West was by the collapse of the Roman Empire. For that reason, those traditions are best treated separately from that of western Europe. Accordingly, they are dealt with in this article only to the extent to which they influence developments in medieval philosophy in the Latin West.

(See HUMANISM, RENAISSANCE; ISLAMIC PHILOSOPHY; JEWISH PHILOSOPHY; RENAISSANCE PHILOSOPHY.)

2 Beginnings

The general character of medieval philosophy in the West is determined to a significant extent by historical events associated with the collapse of Roman civilization. The overrunning of Western Europe by invading Goths, Huns and Vandals brought in its wake not only the military and political defeat of the Roman Empire but also the disintegration of the shared institutions and culture that had sustained philosophical activity in late antiquity. Boethius, a Roman patrician by birth and a high-ranking official in the Ostrogothic king's administration, is an eloquent witness to the general decline of intellectual vitality in his own day. He announces his intention to translate into Latin and write Latin commentaries on all the works of Plato and Aristotle, and he gives as his reason the fear that, lacking this sort of remedial aid, his own Latin-speaking and increasingly ill-trained contemporaries will soon lose access altogether to the philosophical legacy of ancient Greece. Boethius' assessment of the situation appears to have been particularly astute, for in fact in the six centuries following his death (until the mid-twelfth century), philosophers in the West depended almost entirely on Boethius himself for what little access they had to the primary texts of Greek philosophy. Moreover, since he had barely begun to carry out his plan when his execution for treason put an end to his work, Boethius' fears were substantially realized. Having translated only Aristotle's treatises on logic together with Porphyry's introduction to Aristotle's *Categories* (see ARISTOTLE; PORPHYRY) and having completed commentaries on only some of the texts he translated, Boethius left subsequent generations of medieval thinkers without direct knowledge of most of Aristotle's thought, including the natural philosophy, metaphysics and ethics, and with no texts of PLATO (though a small portion of the *Timaeus* had been translated and commented on by Calcidius in the fourth century). Medieval philosophy was therefore significantly shaped by what was lost to it. It took root in an environment devoid of the social and educational structures of antiquity, lacking the Greek language and cut off from the rich resources of a large portion of classical thought. Not surprisingly, the gradual reclamation of ancient thought over the course of the Middle Ages had a significant impact on the development of the medieval philosophical tradition.

Medieval philosophy, however, was also shaped by what was left to it and, in particular, by two pieces of the cultural legacy of late antiquity that survived the collapse of Roman civilization. The first of these is the Latin language, which remained the exclusive language of intellectual discourse in Western Europe throughout the Middle Ages and into the Renaissance and Enlightenment. Latin provided medieval thinkers with access to some important ancient resources, including CICERO, Seneca, Macrobius, Calcidius, the Latin Church Fathers (see PATRISTIC PHILOSOPHY), Augustine and Boethius. These Latin sources gave early medieval thinkers a general, if not deep, acquaintance with classical ideas. Augustine is far and away the most significant of these Latin sources. His thought, and in particular his philosophical approach to Christianity and his Christianized Neoplatonist philosophical outlook, profoundly affect every period and virtually every area of medieval philosophy (see §5).

The second significant piece of late antiquity to survive into the Middle Ages is Christianity. Christianity had grown in importance in the late Roman Empire and, with the demise of the empire's social structures, the Church remained until the twelfth century virtually the only institution capable of supporting intellectual culture. It sustained formal education in schools associated with its monasteries, churches and cathedrals, and provided for the preservation of ancient texts, both sacred and secular, in its libraries and scriptoriums. Medieval philosophers received at least some of their formal training in ecclesiastical institutions and most were themselves officially attached to the Church in some way, as monks, friars, priests or clerks. In the later Middle Ages, the study of theology was open only to men who had acquired an arts degree, and the degree of Master of Theology constituted the highest level of academic achievement. Consequently, most of the great philosophical minds of the period would have thought of themselves primarily as theologians. Moreover, in addition to providing the institutional basis for medieval philosophy, Christianity was an important stimulus to philosophical activity. Its ideas and doctrines constituted a rich source of philosophical subject matter. Medieval philosophy, therefore, took root in an intellectual world sustained by the Church and permeated with Christianity's texts and ideas (see §5).

(See AUGUSTINE; BOETHIUS, A.M.S.; LIBER DE CAUSIS; ORIGEN; PATRISTIC PHILOSOPHY; PLATONISM, MEDIEVAL; STOICISM; TERTULLIAN, Q.S.F.)

3 Historical development

The full flowering of the philosophical tradition that grows from these beginnings occurs in the period from 1100 to 1400. Two developments are particularly important for understanding the rapid growth and flourishing of intellectual culture in these centuries. The first is the influx into the West of a large and previously unknown body of philosophical material newly translated into Latin from Greek and Arabic sources. The second is the emergence and growth of the great medieval universities.

Recovery of texts. Medieval philosophers before Peter Abelard had access to only a few texts of ancient Greek philosophy: those comprising 'the old logic' (Aristotle's *Categories* and *De interpretatione* and Porphyry's *Isagōgē*) and a small part of Plato's *Timaeus*. Abelard's generation witnessed with great enthusiasm the appearance in the Latin West of the remainder of Aristotle's logical works ('the new logic': the *Prior* and *Posterior Analytics*, the *Topics* and the *Sophistical Refutations*). Over the next hundred years, most of Aristotle's natural philosophy (most importantly the *Physics* and *On the Soul*) and the *Metaphysics* and *Ethics* became available for the first time. Not all of these Aristotelian texts were greeted with the same enthusiasm, nor did medieval philosophers find them all equally congenial or accessible (even in Latin translation). However, it is impossible to overstate the impact that the full Aristotelian corpus eventually had on medieval philosophy. The new texts became the subject of increasingly sophisticated and penetrating scholarly commentary; they were incorporated into the heart of the university curriculum, and over time the ideas and doctrines medieval philosophers found in them were woven into the very fabric of medieval thought. Having never before encountered a philosophical system of such breadth and sophistication, philosophers in the thirteenth and fourteenth centuries understandably thought it appropriate to speak of Aristotle simply as 'the Philosopher'.

As medieval thinkers were rediscovering Aristotle they were also acquiring for the first time in Latin translation the works of important Jewish philosophers such as Avencebrol and MAIMONIDES, and Islamic philosophers such as Avicenna (see IBN SINA) and Averroes (see IBN RUSHD). Some of their works were commentaries on Aristotle (Averroes became known simply as 'the Commentator') whereas some (such as Avicenna's *Metaphysics* and *De anima*) were quasi-independent treatises presenting a Neoplatonized Aristotelianism. Medieval philosophers of this period turned eagerly to these texts for help in understanding the new Aristotle, and they were significantly influenced by them. Averroes's interpretation of Aristotle's *On the Soul*, for example, sparked enormous controversy about the nature of intellect, and Avicenna's metaphysical views helped shape the famous later medieval debates about universals and about the nature of the distinction between essence and existence.

Rise of the universities. As abbot of the monastery at Bec in the 1080s, Anselm of Canterbury addressed his philosophical and theological writings to his monks. By contrast, the great philosophical minds of the next generations, thinkers such as Abelard, Gilbert of Poitiers and Thierry of Chartres, would spend significant parts of their careers in the schools at Paris and Chartres and address a good deal of their work to academic audiences. The growth of these schools and others like them at centres such as Oxford, Bologna and Salerno signals a steady and rapid increase in the vitality of intellectual life in Western Europe. By the middle of the thirteenth century, the universities at Paris and Oxford were the leading centres of European philosophical activity. Virtually all the great philosophers from 1250 to 1350, including Albert the Great, Thomas Aquinas, Bonaventure, John Duns Scotus and William of Ockham, studied and taught in the schools at one or both of these centres. It is partly for this reason that early modern philosophers (who were typically not associated with universities) refer to their medieval predecessors in general as 'the schoolmen'.

The migration of philosophical activity to the universities meant not only the centralization of this activity but also its transformation into an increasingly formal and technical academic enterprise. Philosophical education was gradually expanded and standardized, philosophers themselves became highly trained academic specialists and philosophical literature came to presuppose in its audience both familiarity with the standard texts and issues of the university curriculum and facility with the technical apparatus (particularly the technical logical tools) of the discipline. These features of later medieval philosophy make it genuinely scholastic, that is, a product of the academic environment of the schools.

The philosophical disciplines narrowly construed – logic, natural philosophy, metaphysics and ethics – occupied the centre of the curriculum leading to the basic university degrees, the degrees of Bachelor and Master of Arts. Most of the great philosophers of this period, however, went beyond the arts curriculum to pursue advanced work in theology. The requirements for the degree of Master of Theology included study of the Bible, the Church Fathers and (beginning perhaps in the 1220s) Peter Lombard's *Sentences* (which was complete by 1158).

Designed specifically for pedagogical purposes, the *Sentences* is rich in quotation and paraphrase from authoritative theological sources, surveying respected opinion on issues central to the Christian understanding of the world. From about 1250, all candidates for the degree of Master of Theology were required to lecture and produce a commentary on Lombard's text. This requirement offered a formal occasion for scholars nearing their intellectual maturity to develop and present their own positions on a wide variety of philosophical and theological issues guided (often only quite loosely) by the structure of Lombard's presentation.

By virtue of its historical circumstances, medieval philosophical method had from its beginnings consisted largely in commentary on a well defined and fairly small body of authoritative texts and reflection on a canonical set of issues raised by them. Philosophers in the era of the universities took for granted a much larger and more varied intellectual inheritance, but their approach to philosophical issues remained conditioned by an established textual tradition, and they continued to articulate their philosophical views in explicit dialogue with it. Formal commentary on standard texts flourished both as a pedagogical tool and as a literary form. However, other philosophical forms, including the disputation – the most distinctive philosophical form of the thirteenth and fourteenth centuries – were essentially dialectical. In the university environment, the disputation became a technical tool ideally suited to the pressing task of gathering together, organizing and adjudicating the various claims of a complex tradition of texts and positions.

A disputation identifies a specific philosophical or theological issue for discussion and provides the structure for an informed and reasoned judgment about it. In its basic form, a disputation presents, in order: (1) a succinct statement of the issue to be addressed, typically in the form of a question admitting of a 'yes' or 'no' answer; (2) two sets of preliminary arguments, one supporting an affirmative and the other a negative answer to the question; (3) a resolution or determination of the question, in which the master sets out and defends his own position, typically by drawing relevant distinctions, explaining subtle or potentially confusing points, or elaborating the underlying theoretical basis for his answer; and (4) a set of replies specifically addressing the preliminary arguments in disagreement with the master's stated views. A disputation's two sets of preliminary arguments allow for the gathering together of the most important relevant passages and arguments scattered throughout the authoritative literature. With the arguments on both sides of the question in hand, the master is then ideally positioned to deal with both the conceptual issues

raised by the question and the hermeneutical problems presented by the historical tradition. Academic philosophers held disputations in their classrooms and at large university convocations, and they used the form for the literary expression of their ideas. Aquinas' *Summa theologiae*, the individual articles of which are pedagogically simplified disputations, is perhaps the most familiar example of its systematic use as a literary device. The prevalence of the disputational form in later medieval philosophy accounts for its being thought of as embodying 'the scholastic method'.

(On the early Middle Ages (*c.* 600–1100), see ERIUGENA, J.S.)

(On the twelfth-century philosophers, see ABELARD, P.; ANSELM OF CANTERBURY; LOMBARD, P.)

(On the thirteenth-century philosophers, see ALBERT THE GREAT; AQUINAS, T.; BACON, R.; BONAVENTURE; GROSSETESTE, R.)

(On the fourteenth-century philosophers, see ALIGHIERI, DANTE; BURIDAN, J.; DUNS SCOTUS, J.; LLULL, R.; MEISTER ECKHART; OXFORD CALCULATORS; WILLIAM OF OCKHAM; WYCLIF, J.)

(On the fifteenth-century philosophers, see HUS, J.; NICHOLAS OF CUSA.)

4 Doctrinal characteristics

At the most basic level, medieval philosophers share a common view of the world that underlies and supports the various specific developments that constitute medieval philosophy's rich detail.

Metaphysics. The common metaphysical ground of medieval philosophy holds that at the most general level reality can be divided into substances and accidents. Substances – Socrates and Browny the donkey are the stock examples – are independent existents and therefore ontologically fundamental. Corporeal substances (and perhaps also certain incorporeal substances) are constituted from matter and form (see SUBSTANCE). Matter, which in itself is utterly devoid of structure, is the substrate for form (see MATTER). Form provides a substance's structure or organization, thereby making a substance the kind of thing it is. Socrates' soul, for example, is the form that gives structure to Socrates' matter, constituting it as the living flesh and blood of a human body and making Socrates a particular human being. Accidents – Socrates' height, for example, or Browny's colour – are also a kind of form, but they take as their substrate not matter as such but a substance: Socrates or Browny. Accidents depend for their existence on substances and account for substances' ontologically derivative characteristics.

Medieval philosophers recognized matter and form, the fundamental constituents of corporeal substances, as fundamental explanatory principles. A thing's matter (or material cause) and its form (or formal cause) provide basic explanations of the thing's nature and behaviour. To these two principles they added two others, the agent (or efficient) cause and the end (or final cause). The agent cause is whatever initiates motion or change; the final cause is the goal or good toward which a particular activity, process, or change is directed.

Medieval philosophers disagreed about extensions and qualifications of this fundamental metaphysical view of the world. They debated, for example, whether incorporeal substances are like corporeal substances in being composed ultimately of matter and form, or whether they are subsistent immaterial forms. They also debated whether substances such as Socrates have just one substantial form (Socrates' rational soul) or many (one form constituting Socrates' body, another making him a living body with certain capacities for motion and cognition (an animal), and another making him a rational animal (a human being)). However, they never doubted the basic correctness of the metaphysical framework of substance and accidents, form and matter, nor are they in any doubt about whether the analytical tools which that framework provides are applicable to philosophical problems generally.

Psychology and epistemology. Medieval philosophers understood the nature of human beings in terms of the metaphysics of form and matter, identifying the human rational soul, the seat of the capacities specific to human beings, with form. All medieval philosophers, therefore, held broadly dualist positions according to which the soul and body are fundamentally distinct. But only some were also substance dualists (or dualists in the Cartesian sense), holding in addition that the soul and body are themselves substances.

Medieval philosophers devote very little attention to what modern philosophers would recognize as the central questions of epistemology (see EPISTEMOLOGY, HISTORY OF). Until very late in the period, they show little concern for sceptical worries and are not primarily interested in stating the necessary and sufficient conditions for the truth of the claim that some person knows a given proposition. For the most part they assume that we have knowledge of various sorts and focus instead on developing an account of the cognitive mechanisms by which we acquire it. They are especially interested in how we are able to acquire knowledge of universals and necessary truths – objects or truths that are immaterial, eternal and unchanging – given that the world around us is populated with

particular material objects subject to change. The answers medieval philosophers give to this question vary considerably, ranging from Platonistic accounts that appeal to our direct intellectual vision (with the aid of divine illumination) of independently existing immutable entities (such as ideas in the divine mind) to naturalistic accounts that appeal to cognitive capacities wholly contained in the human intellect itself that abstract universals from the data provided by sense perception (see UNIVERSALS).

Ethics. Medieval philosophers share a generically Greek framework of ethical theory, extended and modified to accommodate Christianity. Its main features include an objectivist theory of value, a eudaimonistic account of the human good and a focus on the virtues as central to moral evaluation (see EUDAIMONIA; ARETĒ; VIRTUES AND VICES). According to the metaphysics of goodness inherited by medieval philosophers from Greek thought, there is a necessary connection between goodness and being. Things are good to the extent to which they have being. Evil or badness is not a positive ontological feature of things but a privation or lack of being in some relevant respect. The ultimate human good or goal of human existence is happiness or beatitude, the perfection of which most medieval philosophers identified as supernatural union with God after this life. The ultimate human good is attained both through the cultivation of the moral virtues and through divine grace in the form of supernaturally infused states and dispositions such as faith, hope and charity, the so-called theological virtues.

Within this framework, medieval philosophers debated whether human beatitude is essentially an affective state (a kind of love for God) or a cognitive state (a kind of knowledge or vision of God), and whether the virtues are strictly necessary for the attainment of beatitude. They also debated whether the rightness or wrongness of some actions depends solely on God's will. Contrary to caricatures of medieval ethics, no one unequivocally endorsed a divine command theory according to which the moral rightness (or wrongness) of *all* acts consists solely in their being approved (or disapproved) by God (see VOLUNTARISM).

Logic and language. Medieval philosophers devote enormous attention – perhaps more attention than philosophers of any period in the history of philosophy apart from the twentieth century – to logic and philosophy of language. This phenomenon is explained primarily by the uniquely important role played by Aristotle's logic in the development of medieval thought. Until the early twelfth century, medieval philosophers' knowledge of Greek philosophy was restricted to a few texts of Aristotelian logic and, by default, those texts largely set the agenda for philosophical discussion. It is a passage from Porphyry's *Isagōgē*, for example, that enticed first Boethius and, following him, a long line of commentators to take up the philosophical problem of universals (see UNIVERSALS). The texts of the old logic, which remained a central part of the philosophy curriculum in the later Middle Ages, were eventually supplemented by the remaining treatises of Aristotle's logic, among which the *Topics* and the *Sophistical Refutations* in particular sparked intense interest in the forms of philosophical argument and the nature of meaning.

Natural philosophy. Medieval philosophers believed that a complete account of reality must include an account of the fundamental constituents and principles of the natural realm. Their earliest reflections on these matters were inspired primarily by two ancient accounts of the origins and nature of the universe, the biblical story of creation (in Genesis) and Plato's story of the Demiurge's fashioning of the world (in the *Timaeus*) (see PLATO). The confluence of these ancient sources produced a medieval tradition of speculative cosmological thought paradigmatically expressed in discussions of the six days of creation. This topic in particular gave medieval philosophers opportunity to reflect on the nature of the contents of the universe and the principles governing the created realm.

From the late twelfth century, medieval philosophy was profoundly affected by the new Aristotelian natural philosophy and the new scientific treatises by Islamic philosophers. Aristotle's *Physics* in particular received enormous attention, and medieval philosophers developed sophisticated tools of logical, conceptual and mathematical analysis to deal with problems raised by Aristotle's discussions of motion, change, continuity and infinity. Scientific treatises by Islamic thinkers such as Alkindi, Alpetragius, Avicenna (see IBN SINA) and Alhasen provided the material and impetus for significant developments in astronomy, medicine, mathematics and optics.

(See OXFORD CALCULATORS.)

5   Philosophical theology

Christianity is not in itself a philosophical doctrine, but it profoundly influences the medieval philosophical world-view both from within philosophy and from outside it. On the one hand, Christian texts and doctrine provided rich subject matter for philosophical reflection, and the nature and central claims of Christianity forced medieval intellectuals to work out a comprehensive account of reality and to deal explicitly with deep issues about the aims and methods of the philosophical enterprise. In

these ways, Christianity was taken up into philosophy, adding to its content and altering its structure and methods. On the other hand, Christianity imposed external constraints on medieval philosophy. At various times these constraints took institutional form in the official proscription of texts, the condemnation of philosophical positions and the censure of individuals.

Augustine laid the foundation for medieval Christian philosophical theology in two respects. First, he provided a theoretical rationale both for Christian intellectuals engaging in philosophical activity generally and for their taking Christian doctrine in particular as a subject of philosophical investigation. According to Augustine, Christian belief is not opposed to philosophy's pursuit of truth but is an invaluable supplement and aid to philosophy. With revealed truth in hand, Christian philosophers are able to salvage what is true and useful in pagan philosophy while repudiating what is false. Moreover, Augustine argued that Christianity can be strengthened and enriched by philosophy. Christian philosophers should begin by believing (on the authority of the Bible and the Church) what Christianity professes and seek (by the use of reason) to acquire understanding of what they initially believed on authority. In seeking understanding, philosophers rely on that aspect of themselves – namely, reason – in virtue of which they most resemble God; and in gaining understanding, they strengthen the basis for Christian belief. The Augustinian method of belief seeking understanding is taken for granted by the vast majority of philosophers in the Middle Ages.

Second, Augustine's writings provide a wealth of rich and compelling examples of philosophical reflection on topics ranging from the nature of evil and sin to the nature of the Trinity. Boethius stands with Augustine in this respect as an important model for later thinkers. He composed several short theological treatises that consciously attempt to bring the tools of Aristotelian logic to bear on issues associated with doctrines of the Christian creed. Inspired by the philosophical analysis and argumentation prominent in these writings, medieval philosophers enthusiastically took up, developed and extended the enterprise of philosophical theology.

With the emergence of academic structure in the new European schools and universities of the twelfth and thirteenth centuries, theology became the paramount academic discipline in a formal curriculum of higher education. However, the fact that great thinkers of the later Middle Ages typically studied philosophy as preparatory for the higher calling of theology should not be taken to imply that in becoming theologians they left philosophy behind. As a simple matter of fact, later medieval theologians continued throughout their careers to address fundamental philosophical issues in fundamentally philosophical ways. And it is clear why this should be so: those who took up the study of theology were among the most gifted and highly trained philosophical minds of their day, and they brought to theology acute philosophical sensitivities, interests and skills. Moreover, in so far as they viewed Christianity as offering the basic framework for a comprehensive account of the world, they were naturally attracted to the broadly philosophical task of building on that framework, understanding its ramifications and resolving its difficulties.

Despite the dominance of the Augustinian view of the relation between Christianity and philosophy, religiously motivated resistance to philosophy in general and to the use of philosophical methods for understanding Christianity in particular emerges in different forms throughout the Middle Ages. In the twelfth century, some influential clerics saw the flourishing study of logic at Paris as a dangerous influence on theology and used ecclesiastical means to attack Peter Abelard and Gilbert of Poitiers. In the thirteenth century the new Aristotelian natural philosophy prompted another period of sustained ecclesiastical reaction. In 1210 and 1215 ecclesiastical authorities proscribed the teaching of Aristotle's natural philosophy at Paris, and in 1277 the Bishop of Paris issued a condemnation of 219 articles covering a wide range of theological and philosophical topics. The condemnation seems largely to have been a reaction to the work of radical Averroistic interpreters of Aristotle. It is unclear how effective these actions were in suppressing the movements and doctrines they targeted.

(See NATURAL THEOLOGY.)

6   Scholarship in medieval philosophy

Contemporary study of medieval philosophy faces special obstacles. First, a large body of medieval philosophical and theological literature has survived in European libraries, but because many of these collections have not yet been fully catalogued, scholars do not yet have a complete picture of what primary source materials exist. Second, the primary sources themselves – in the form of handwritten texts and early printed editions – can typically be deciphered and read only by those with specialized paleographical skills. Only a very small portion of the known extant material has ever been published in modern editions of a sort that any reader of Latin could easily use. Third, an even smaller portion of the extant material has been translated into English (or any other modern language) or subjected to the

sort of scholarly commentary and analysis that might open it up to a wider philosophical audience. For these reasons, scholarship in medieval philosophy is still in its early stages and remains a considerable distance from attaining the sort of authoritative and comprehensive view of its field now possessed by philosophical scholars of other historical periods with respect to their fields. For the foreseeable future, its progress will depend not only on the sort of philosophical and historical analysis constitutive of all scholarship in the history of philosophy but also on the sort of textual archeology necessary for recovering medieval philosophy's primary texts.

See also: ANCIENT PHILOSOPHY; ISLAMIC PHILOSOPHY; NEOPLATONISM; RELIGION, PHILOSOPHY OF; RENAISSANCE PHILOSOPHY

References and further reading

Armstrong, A.H. (ed.) (1967) *The Cambridge History of Later Greek and Early Medieval Philosophy*, Cambridge: Cambridge University Press. (A useful survey of medieval philosophy's historical antecedents, including the philosophical movements of late antiquity, and of the main figures of the medieval period through the beginning of the twelfth century.)

Dronke, P. (ed.) (1988) *A History of Twelfth-Century Western Philosophy*, Cambridge: Cambridge University Press. (A collection of sixteen articles exploring both the background to the philosophy of the twelfth century and its innovations and major figures; contains a good bibliography and useful bio-bibliographies of twelfth-century philosophers.)

Marenbon, J. (1983) *Early Medieval Philosophy (480–1150): An Introduction*, London: Routledge, 2nd edn, 1988. (A readable and informative general introduction to the period.)

SCOTT MACDONALD

NORMAN KRETZMANN

MEINONG, ALEXIUS (1853–1920)

Meinong was an Austrian philosopher and psychologist who taught at the University of Graz. He contributed substantially to psychology, epistemology, value theory, ethics and probability theory, but is best known for his theory of objects, in which he advocates the radical view that there are objects which are wholly outside being, including impossible objects. Meinong influenced Russell and the American 'new realists'. Though widely rejected, his views have proved difficult to refute decisively and he has found sympathetic support from a number of logicians and philosophers.

PETER SIMONS

MEISTER ECKHART (*c.*1260–1327/8)

More than any other medieval thinker, Eckhart has received widely divergent interpretations. The controversies stem from the fact that his writings fall into two distinct groups, works written in the vernacular and works written in Latin. The German writings, which were intended for a wide audience, established Eckhart's long-standing fame as a mystic. Another, more academic Eckhart emerged when his Latin work was rediscovered in 1886. The study of Eckhart's thought today centres on the unity of the scholastic (Latin) and the popular (German) work.
See also: GOD, CONCEPTS OF

JAN A. AERTSEN

MELANCHTHON, PHILIPP (1497–1560)

Philipp Melanchthon was one of Luther's closest associates, helping to systematize Lutheran theology, and his *Loci communes* (Commonplaces) (1521) was one of the most influential early works of Protestant theology. He was often a moderating influence in theological debates between Catholics and Protestants. Melanchthon was also involved in controversy over the relationship between human will and God's grace in the achievement of salvation. He was responsible for the reform of Protestant German education in the sixteenth century, through the large number of textbooks which he composed, and through his revisions of the statutes of universities (notably Wittenberg) and schools. As a scholar and reformer of education, he was a staunch follower of the humanism of Agricola and Erasmus, committed to teaching the best Latin authors and the Greek language. Many of his works are textbooks (often produced in different versions), frequently based on lecture notes, summarizing or commenting on classical authors or scripture. Although more important as a summarizer and popularizer than as a source of new ideas, Melanchthon nevertheless made important contributions to the development of logic, rhetoric, ethics and psychology, as well as to aspects of Reformation theology. In logic he contributed to the growth of interest in method. In ethics he established a place for classical moral teaching alongside but subordinate to the teaching of the Bible. His favourite philosopher was Aristotle, and he tended to pour scorn on rival ancient schools of philosophy. In psychology he favoured a simplified Aristotelianism, close to medieval faculty psychology, with strong emphasis on links with

biology. He opposed scepticism wherever he encountered it.
See also: ERASMUS, D.; HUMANISM, RENAISSANCE; LUTHER, M.; RENAISSANCE PHILOSOPHY

PETER MACK

MEMORY, EPISTEMOLOGY OF

Memory appears to preserve knowledge, but there are epistemic questions about how this could be. Memory is fallible, and empirical research has identified various ways in which people systematically misremember. Even wholesale error seems possible: Russell proposed that it is logically possible for the world to have sprung into existence five minutes ago, complete with spurious ostensible memories of earlier times. In light of such possibilities, some sceptics argue that memory cannot yield knowledge.

Assuming that memory provides knowledge, there are serious epistemic issues about how it does this. For instance, does some introspectible quality of remembering provide distinctive evidence for what is remembered, or is it some other feature of memory that secures the epistemic justification needed for knowledge? How readily recollectible must a proposition be in order for it to be known while it is not being recalled? Does a full retention in memory of a previous basis for knowing something assure continuing knowledge of it? Does forgetting an original basis for knowing without replacing it imply a loss of knowledge?
See also: KNOWLEDGE, TACIT; SCEPTICISM

EARL CONEE

MENCIUS (4th century BC)

Mencius (Mengzi) was a Chinese Confucian philosopher, best known for his claim that human nature is good. He is probably the single most influential philosopher in the Chinese tradition, in that an interpretation of his thought became the basis of the civil service examinations in China in the fourteenth century and remained so for almost 600 years. The primary source for his thought is the collection of his sayings, debates and discussions known as the *Mengzi*.
See also: CONFUCIAN PHILOSOPHY, CHINESE; VIRTUES AND VICES

BRYAN W. VAN NORDEN

MENDELSSOHN, MOSES (1729–86)

A Jewish disciple of Leibniz and Wolff, Mendelssohn strove throughout his life to uphold and strengthen their rationalist metaphysics while sustaining his ancestral religion. His most important philosophic task, as he saw it, was to refine and render more persuasive the philosophical proofs for the existence of God, providence and immortality. His major divergence from Leibniz was in stressing that 'the best of all possible worlds', which God had created, was in fact more hospitable to human beings than Leibniz had supposed. Towards the end of his life, the irrationalism of Jacobi and the critical philosophy of Kant shook Mendelssohn's faith in the demonstrability of the fundamental metaphysical precepts, but not his confidence in their truth. They would have to be sustained by 'common sense', he reasoned, until future philosophers succeeded in restoring metaphysics to its former glory. While accepting Wolff's teleological understanding of human nature and natural law, Mendelssohn placed far greater value on human freedom and outlined a political philosophy that protected liberty of conscience. His philosophic defence of his own religion stressed that Judaism is not a 'revealed religion' demanding acceptance of particular dogmas but a 'revealed legislation' requiring the performance of particular actions. The object of this divine and still valid legislation, he suggested, was often to counteract forces that might otherwise subvert the natural religion entrusted to us by reason. To resolve the tension between his own political liberalism and the Bible's endorsement of religious coercion, Mendelssohn argued that contemporary Judaism, at any rate, no longer acknowledges any person's authority to compel others to perform religious acts.

See also: LEIBNIZ, G.W.; WOLFF, C.

ALLAN ARKUSH

MENG KI/MENGZI

See MENCIUS

MENTAL CAUSATION

Both folk and scientific psychology assume that mental events and properties participate in causal relations. However, considerations involving the causal completeness of physics and the apparent non-reducibility of mental phenomena to physical phenomena have challenged these assumptions. In the case of mental *events* (such as someone's thinking about Vienna), one proposal has been simply to identify not '*types*' (or classes) of mental events with *types* of physical events, but merely individual '*token*' mental events with *token* physical ones, one by one (your and my thinking about Vienna may be 'realized' by different type physical states).

The role of mental *properties* (such as 'being about Vienna') in causation is more problematic. Properties are widely thought to have three features that

seem to render them causally irrelevant: (1) they are 'multiply-realizable' (they can be realized in an indefinite variety of substances); (2) many of them seem not to supervene on neurophysiological properties (differences in mental properties do not always depend merely on differences in neurophysiological ones, but upon relations people bear to things outside their skin); and (3) many of them (for example, 'being painful') seem inherently 'subjective' in a way that no objective physical properties seem to be. All of these issues are complicated by the fact that there is no consensus concerning the nature of causal relevance for properties in general.

See also: DETERMINISM AND INDETERMINISM; DUALISM; FREE WILL

BARRY LOEWER

MENTAL ILLNESS, CONCEPT OF

The mad were once thought to be wicked or possessed, whereas now they are generally thought to be sick, or mentally ill. Usually, this is regarded as a benign decision by a more enlightened age, but some see it as a double-edged sword – one that simultaneously relieved and robbed the mad of responsibility for their actions, eventually delivering more compassionate treatment, but also disguising value-laden judgments as objective science. The issue is made more difficult by the diversity of conditions classified as psychiatric disorders, and by the extent to which their causes are still ill understood. But the difficulty is also conceptual: what, after all, is physical illness? People usually agree that it involves abnormal body functioning, but how do we decide what is normal functioning? And even supposing that we know what we mean by a sick body, is there a parallel notion of a sick mind that is more than metaphor?

See also: FOUCAULT, M. §2; MORAL AGENTS; PSYCHOANALYSIS, POST-FREUDIAN; RESPONSIBILITY

KAREN NEANDER

MENTAL STATES, UNCONSCIOUS

See UNCONSCIOUS MENTAL STATES

MENTION

See USE/MENTION DISTINCTION AND QUOTATION

MEREOLOGY

Mereology is the theory of the part–whole relation and of derived operations such as the mereological sum. (The sum of several things is the smallest thing of which they are all parts.) It was introduced by Leśniewski to avoid Russell's paradox.

Unlike the set-membership relation, the part–whole relation is transitive. This makes mereology much weaker than set theory, but gives the advantage of ontological parsimony. For example, mereology does not posit the proliferation of entities found in set theory, such as $\emptyset, \{\emptyset\}, \{\{\emptyset\}\}, \ldots$.

Mereology has occasioned controversy: over whether many things really have a mereological sum if they are either scattered or, even worse, of different categories; over the uniqueness of sums; and over Lewis' claim that the non-empty subsets of a set are literally parts of it.

See also: STRUCTURALISM

PETER FORREST

MERLEAU-PONTY, MAURICE (1908–61)

Merleau-Ponty belongs to the group of French philosophers who transformed French philosophy in the early post-war period by introducing the phenomenological methods of the German philosophers Husserl and Heidegger. His central concern was with 'the phenomenology of perception' (the title of his major book), and his originality lay in his account of the role of the bodily sense-organs in perception, which led him to develop a phenomenological treatment of the sub-personal perceptions that play a central role in bodily movements. This account of the sub-personal aspects of life enabled him to launch a famous critique of Sartre's conception of freedom, which he regarded as an illusion engendered by excessive attention to consciousness. None the less, he and Sartre cooperated for many years in French political affairs, until Merleau-Ponty became exasperated by the orthodox Marxism-Leninism of the French Communist Party in a way in which Sartre, who remained a fellow-traveller, did not. As well as several substantial political essays, Merleau-Ponty wrote widely on art, anthropology and, especially, language. He died leaving some important work incomplete.

Although his work is still esteemed within the French academic establishment, his influence in France has waned, because of a tendency there to study his German forebears almost to the exclusion of all else. But elsewhere, and most notably in the USA, Merleau-Ponty's work is widely studied, especially now that questions about the distinction between personal and sub-personal aspects of life have become so prominent.

See also: IDEALISM; MARXISM, WESTERN; PHENOMENOLOGICAL MOVEMENT

THOMAS BALDWIN

METAPHOR

A standard dictionary definition describes a metaphor as 'a figure of speech in which a word or phrase literally denoting one kind of object is used in place of another to suggest a likeness between them'. Although the theoretical adequacy of this definition may be questioned, it conveys the standard view that there is a difference between literal and nonliteral language; that figurative speech is nonliteral language; and that a metaphor is an instance of figurative speech.

The three most influential treatments of metaphor are the comparison, interaction and speech act theories. According to the first, every metaphor involves a comparison; a specific version of this view is that every metaphor is an abbreviated simile. According to the second, every metaphor involves a semantic interaction between some object or concept that is literally denoted by some word, and some concept metaphorically predicated on that word. According to the third, it is not words or sentences that are metaphorical but their use in specific situations; thus, to understand how metaphors function, one must understand how people communicate with language.

See also: COMMUNICATION AND INTENTION; DAVIDSON, D.; SPEECH ACTS

A.P. MARTINICH

METAPHYSICS

Introduction

Metaphysics is a broad area of philosophy marked out by two types of inquiry. The first aims to be the most general investigation possible into the nature of reality: are there principles applying to everything that is real, to all that is? – if we abstract from the particular nature of existing things that which distinguishes them from each other, what can we know about them merely in virtue of the fact that they exist? The second type of inquiry seeks to uncover what is ultimately real, frequently offering answers in sharp contrast to our everyday experience of the world. Understood in terms of these two questions, metaphysics is very closely related to ontology, which is usually taken to involve both 'what is existence (being)?' and 'what (fundamentally distinct) types of thing exist?' (see ONTOLOGY).

The two questions are not the same, since someone quite unworried by the possibility that the world might really be otherwise than it appears (and therefore regarding the second investigation as a completely trivial one) might still be engaged by the question of whether there were any general truths applicable to all existing things. But although different, the questions are related: one might well expect a philosopher's answer to the first to provide at least the underpinnings of their answer to the second. Aristotle proposed the first of these investigations. He called it 'first philosophy', sometimes also 'the science of being' (more-or-less what 'ontology' means); but at some point in antiquity his writings on the topic came to be known as the 'metaphysics' – from the Greek for 'after natural things', that is, what comes after the study of nature. This is as much as we know of the origin of the word (see ARISTOTLE §11 and following). It would, however, be quite wrong to think of metaphysics as a uniquely 'Western' phenomenon. Classical Indian philosophy, and especially Buddhism, is also a very rich source (see BUDDHIST PHILOSOPHY, INDIAN; HINDU PHILOSOPHY; JAINA PHILOSOPHY).

1 General metaphysics
2 Specific metaphysics

1 General metaphysics

Any attempt on either question will find itself using, and investigating, the concepts of being and existence (see BEING; EXISTENCE). It will then be natural to ask whether there are any further, more detailed classifications under which everything real falls, and a positive answer to this question brings us to a doctrine of categories (see CATEGORIES). The historical picture here is complex, however. The two main exponents of such a doctrine are Aristotle and Kant. In Aristotle's case it is unclear whether he saw it as a doctrine about things and their basic properties or about language and its basic predicates; whereas Kant quite explicitly used his categories as features of our way of thinking, and so applied them only to things as they appear to us, not as they really or ultimately are (see KANT, I.). Following on from Kant, Hegel consciously gave his categories both roles, and arranged his answer to the other metaphysical question (about the true underlying nature of reality) so as to make this possible (see HEGEL, G.W.F.).

An early, extremely influential view about reality seen in the most general light is that it consists of things and their properties – individual things, often called particulars, and properties, often called universals, that can belong to many such individuals (see PARTICULARS; UNIVERSALS). Very closely allied to this notion of an individual is the concept of substance, that in which properties 'inhere' (see SUBSTANCE). This line of thought (which incidentally had a biological version in the concepts of individual creatures and their species) gave rise to one of the most famous metaphysical controversies: whether universals are real entities or not (see SPECIES; NATURAL KINDS). In different ways, PLATO and Aristotle had each held the affirmative view; nominalism is the general term for the various versions of the negative position (see NOMINALISM).

The clash between realists and nominalists over universals can serve to illustrate a widespread feature of metaphysical debate. Whatever entities, forces and so on may be proposed, there will be a *prima facie* option between regarding them as real beings, genuine constituents of the world and, as it were, downgrading them to fictions or projections of our own ways of speaking and thinking (see OBJECTIVITY). This was, broadly speaking, how nominalists wished to treat universals; comparable debates exist concerning causality (see CAUSATION), moral value (see EMOTIVISM; MORAL REALISM; MORAL SCEPTICISM) and necessity and possibility (see NECESSARY TRUTH AND CONVENTION) – to name a few examples. Some have even proposed that the categories (see above) espoused in the Western tradition are reflections of the grammar of Indo-European languages, and have no further ontological status (see SAPIR-WHORF HYPOTHESIS).

Wittgenstein famously wrote that the world is the totality of facts, not of things, so bringing to prominence another concept of the greatest generality (see FACTS). Presumably he had it in mind that exactly the same things, differently related to each other, could form very different worlds; so that it is not things but the states of affairs or facts they enter into which determine how things are. The apparent obviousness of the formula 'if it is true that *p* then it is a fact that *p*', makes it seem that facts are in one way or another closely related to truth (see TRUTH, COHERENCE THEORY OF; TRUTH, CORRESPONDENCE THEORY OF) – although it should be said that not every philosophical view of the nature of truth is a metaphysical one, since some see it as just a linguistic device (see TRUTH, DEFLATIONARY THEORIES OF) and some as a reflection, not of how the world is, but of human needs and purposes (see TRUTH, PRAGMATIC THEORY OF; RELATIVISM).

Space and time, as well as being somewhat elusive in their own nature, are further obvious candidates for being features of everything that exists (see SPACE; TIME). But that is controversial, as the debate about the existence of abstract objects testifies (see ABSTRACT OBJECTS). We commonly speak, at least, as if we thought that numbers exist, but not as if we thought that they have any spatiotemporal properties. Kant regarded his things-in-themselves as neither spatial nor temporal; and some have urged us to think of God in the same way (see GOD, CONCEPTS OF). There are accounts of the

657

mind which allow mental states to have temporal, but deny them spatial properties (see DUALISM).

Be all this as it may, even if not literally everything, then virtually everything of which we have experience is in time. Temporality is therefore one of the phenomena that should be the subject of any investigation which aspires to maximum generality. Hence, so is change (see CHANGE). And when we consider change, and ask the other typically metaphysical question about it ('what is really going on when something changes?') we find ourselves faced with two types of answer. One type would have it that a change is an alteration in the properties of some enduring thing (see CONTINUANTS). The other would deny any such entity, holding instead that what we really have is merely a sequence of states, a sequence which shows enough internal coherence to make upon us the impression of one continuing thing (see MOMENTARINESS, BUDDHIST DOCTRINE OF). The former will tend to promote 'thing' and 'substance' to the ranks of the most basic metaphysical categories; the latter will incline towards events and processes (see EVENTS; PROCESSES). It is here that questions about identity over time become acute, particularly in the special case of those continuants (or, perhaps, processes), which are persons (see IDENTITY; PERSONS; PERSONAL IDENTITY).

Two major historical tendencies in metaphysics have been idealism and materialism, the former presenting reality as ultimately mental or spiritual, the latter regarding it as wholly material (see IDEALISM; MATERIALISM; MATERIALISM IN THE PHILOSOPHY OF MIND). In proposing a single ultimate principle both are monistic (see MONISM). They have not had the field entirely to themselves. A minor competitor has been neutral monism, which takes mind and matter to be different manifestations of something in itself neither one nor the other (see NEUTRAL MONISM). More importantly, many metaphysical systems have been dualist, taking both to be fundamental, and neither to be a form of the other (see SĀNKHYA). Both traditions are ancient. In modern times idealism received its most intensive treatment in the nineteenth century (see ABSOLUTE, THE; GERMAN IDEALISM); in the second half of the twentieth century, materialism has been in the ascendant. A doctrine is also found according to which all matter, without actually being mental in nature, has certain mental properties (see PANPSYCHISM).

2 Specific metaphysics

There is also metaphysics that arises in reference to particular subject matters, this being therefore metaphysical primarily with regard to the second question (what are things ultimately like? – or, what kinds of thing ultimately exist?) rather than the first. One of the most obvious cases, and historically the most prominent, is theology; we have already mentioned the philosophy of mind, the philosophy of mathematics and the theory of values. Less obviously, metaphysical issues also intrude on the philosophy of language and logic, as happens when it is suggested that any satisfactory theory of meaning will have to posit the existence of intensional entities, or that any meaningful language will have to mirror the structure of the world (see INTENSIONAL ENTITIES; LOGICAL ATOMISM). The political theorist or social scientist who holds that successful explanation in the social sphere must proceed from properties of societies not reducible to properties of the individuals who make them up (thereby making a society an entity that is in a sense more basic than its members) raises a metaphysical issue (see HOLISM AND INDIVIDUALISM IN HISTORY AND SOCIAL SCIENCE). Metaphysics, as demarcated by the second question, can pop up anywhere.

The relationship with metaphysics is, however, particularly close in the case of science and the philosophy of science. Aristotle seems to have understood his 'first philosophy' as continuous with what is now called his physics, and indeed it can be said that the more fundamental branches of natural science are a kind of metaphysics as it is characterized here. For they are typically concerned with the discovery of laws and entities that are completely general, in the sense that everything is composed of entities and obeys laws. The differences are primarily epistemological ones, the balance of a priori considerations and empirical detail used by scientists and philosophers in supporting their respective ontological claims. The *subject matter* of these claims can even sometimes coincide: during the 1980s the reality of possible worlds other than the actual one was maintained by a number of writers for a variety of reasons, some of them recognizably 'scientific', some recognizably 'philosophical' (see POSSIBLE WORLDS). And whereas we find everywhere in metaphysics a debate over whether claims should be given a realist or an antirealist interpretation, in the philosophy of science we find a parallel controversy over the status of the entities featuring in scientific theories (see REALISM AND ANTIREALISM; SCIENTIFIC REALISM AND ANTIREALISM).

It is true that there has been considerable reluctance to acknowledge any such continuity. A principal source of this reluctance has been logical positivism, with its division of propositions into those which are empirically verifiable and meaningful, and those which are not so verifiable and are either analytic or meaningless, followed up by its equation of science with the former and metaphysics with the latter (see LOGICAL POSITIVISM; MEANING AND VERIFICATION). When combined with the belief that analytic truths record nothing about the world, but only about linguistic convention, this yields a total rejection of all metaphysics – let alone of any continuity with science. But apart from the fact that this line of thought requires acceptance of the principle about meaninglessness, it also makes a dubious epistemological assumption: that what we call science never uses non-empirical arguments, and that what we regard as metaphysics never draws on empirical premises. Enemies of obscurantism need not commit themselves to any of this; they can recognize the continuity between science and metaphysics without robbing anyone of the vocabulary in which to be rude about the more extravagant, ill-evidenced, even barely meaningful forms which, in the view of some, metaphysics has sometimes taken.

Even the philosopher with a low opinion of the prospects for traditional metaphysics can believe that there is a general framework which we in fact use for thinking about reality, and can undertake to describe and explore it. This project, which can claim an illustrious ancestor in Kant, has in the twentieth century sometimes been called descriptive metaphysics, though what it inquires into are our most general patterns of thought, and the nature of things themselves only indirectly, if at all. Though quite compatible with a low estimate of traditional metaphysics as defined by our two primary questions, it does imply that there is a small but fairly stable core of human thought for it to investigate. Hence it collides with the view of those who deny that there is any such thing (see POSTMODERNISM).

See also: BRAHMAN; CAUSATION, INDIAN THEORIES OF; HEGELIANISM; INFINITY; MATERIALISM, INDIAN SCHOOL OF; NEO-KANTIANISM; NEOPLATONISM; PLATONISM, RENAISSANCE; PROCESS PHILOSOPHY; RELIGION, PHILOSOPHY OF

References and further reading

Kim, J. and Sosa, E. (eds) (1995) *A Companion to Metaphysics*, Oxford: Blackwell. (Encyclopedia-style volume with over 250 entries of varying length devoted to terms, theories, movements and individual philosophers. Some coverage of epistemological issues as well as metaphysics.)

EDWARD CRAIG

METHODOLOGICAL INDIVIDUALISM

Methodological individualism is the thesis that certain psychological properties are *intrinsic* properties, such as 'being made out of iron', rather than externally *relational* properties, such as 'being an aunt'. It has been challenged by influential 'anti-individualist' claims of, for example, Putnam and Burge, according to which the content of an individual's words or thoughts (beliefs, desires) is determined in part by facts about their social or physical environment. Putnam, for example, imagines a planet, 'twin earth', which is identical to the earth in 1750 (prior to modern chemistry) in all respects except that wherever earth had H_2O, twin earth had a different but superficially similar chemical, XYZ. Putnam argues that the English word 'water' in 1750 referred only to H_2O, while the twin word 'water' refers only to XYZ.

Historically, the term 'methodological individualism' has referred to the thesis that all social explanation must be ultimately expressible in terms of facts about individual human beings; not about economic classes, nations and so on. For a treatment of this subject, see EXPLANATION IN HISTORY AND SOCIAL SCIENCE.

See also: CONTENT: WIDE AND NARROW; PUTNAM, H.; SEMANTICS, CONCEPTUAL ROLE

GABRIEL SEGAL

MILESIANS
See ANAXIMANDER; ANAXIMENES; THALES

MILL, JOHN STUART (1806–73)

Introduction

John Stuart Mill, Britain's major philosopher of the nineteenth century, gave formulations of his country's empiricist and liberal traditions of comparable importance to those of John Locke. His distinctive contribution was to bring those traditions into contact with the ideas of nineteenth-century Europe. He impressively united the radicalism of Enlightenment reason with the historical insights of the nineteenth century and he infused English liberalism with high Romantic notions of culture and character.

Mill held that all knowledge is based on experience, believed that our desires, purposes and beliefs are products of psychological laws of association, and accepted Bentham's standard of the greatest total happiness of all beings capable of happiness – the principle of 'utility'. This was his Enlightenment legacy.

In epistemology Mill's empiricism was very radical. He drew a distinction between 'verbal' and 'real' propositions similar to that which Kant made between analytic and synthetic judgments. However, unlike Kant, Mill held that not only pure mathematics but logic itself contains real propositions and inferences, and unlike Kant, he denied that any synthetic, or real, proposition is a priori. The sciences of logic and mathematics, according to Mill, propound the most general laws of nature and, like all other sciences, are in the last resort grounded inductively on experience.

We take principles of logic and mathematics to be a priori because we find it inconceivable that they should not be true. Mill acknowledged the facts which underlie our conviction, facts about unthinkability or imaginative unrepresentability, and he sought to explain these facts in associationist terms. He thought that we are justified in basing logical and mathematical claims on such facts about what is thinkable – but the justification is itself a posteriori.

What then is the nature and standing of induction? Mill held that the primitive form of induction is enumerative induction, simple generalization from experience. He did not address Hume's sceptical problem about enumerative induction. Generalization from experience is our primitive inferential practice and remains our practice when we become reflectively conscious of it – in Mill's view nothing more needs to be said or can be said. Instead he traced how enumerative induction is internally strengthened by its actual success in establishing regularities, and how it eventually gives rise to more searching methods of inductive inquiry, capable of detecting regularities where enumerative induction alone would not suffice. Thus whereas Hume raised sceptical questions about induction, Mill pushed through an empiricist analysis of deduction. He recognized as primitively legitimate only the disposition to rely on memory and the disposition to generalize from experience. The whole of science, he thought, is built from these.

In particular, he did not accept that the mere fact that a hypothesis accounts for data can ever provide a reason for thinking it true (as opposed to thinking it useful). It is always possible that a body of data may be explained equally well by more than one hypothesis. This view, that enumerative induction is the only authoritative source of general truths, was also important in his metaphysics. Accepting as he did that our knowledge of supposed objects external to consciousness consists only in the conscious states they excite in us, he concluded that external objects amount only to 'permanent possibilities of sensation'. The possibilities are 'permanent' in the sense that they can be relied on to obtain if an antecedent condition is realized. Mill was the founder of modern phenomenalism.

In ethics, Mill's governing conviction was that happiness is the sole ultimate human end. As in the case of induction, he appealed to reflective agreement, in this case of desires rather than reasoning dispositions. If happiness was not 'in theory and in practice, acknowledged to be an end, nothing could ever convince any person that it was so' (*Utilitarianism* 1861). But he acknowledged that we can will to do what we do not desire to do; we can act from duty, not desire. And he distinguished between desiring a thing as 'part' of our happiness and desiring it as a means to our happiness. The virtues can become a part of our happiness, and for Mill they ideally should be so. They have a natural base in our psychology on which moral education can be built. More generally, people can reach a deeper understanding of happiness through education and experience: some forms of happiness are inherently preferred as finer by those able to experience them fully.

Thus Mill enlarged but retained Bentham's view that the happiness of all, considered impartially, is the standard of conduct. His account of how this standard relates to the fabric of everyday norms was charged with the nineteenth century's historical sense, but also maintained links with Bentham. Justice is a class of exceptionally stringent obligations on society – it is the 'claim we have on our fellow-creatures to join in making safe for us the very groundwork of our existence' (*Auguste Comte and Positivism* 1865). Because rights of justice protect this groundwork they take priority over the direct pursuit of general utility as well as over the private pursuit of personal ends.

Mill's doctrine of liberty dovetails with this account of justice. Here he appealed to rights founded on 'utility in the largest sense, grounded on the permanent interests of man as a progressive being' (*On Liberty* 1859). The principle enunciated in this essay safeguards people's freedom to pursue their own goals, so long as they do not infringe on the legitimate interests of others: save in 'backward' states of society, power should not be exercised over people for their own good. Mill defended the principle on two grounds. It enables individuals to realize their potential in their own distinctive way, and, by liberating talents, creativity and energy, it institutes the social conditions for the moral development of culture and character.

1 Life

Mill was born in London on 20 May 1806, the eldest son of a Scotsman, James MILL, and an English woman, Harriet Burrow. James educated his son himself – an education made famous by the account John Stuart gave of it in his *Autobiography* (1873). He taught John the classics, logic, political economy, jurisprudence and psychology – starting with Greek at the age of three. John was brought up in a circle of intellectual and political radicals, friends of his father, which included Jeremy BENTHAM and David Ricardo. In his twenties (not surprisingly, perhaps) he was afflicted by a deep depression from which he recovered partly through reading poetry. In those and subsequent years he also came to know some of the most interesting younger figures in English politics and culture. These included conservative critics of Benthamism, as well as radical adherents to it.

Mill followed his father into the East India Company, where he became an influential official, resigning only in 1858 when, following the Indian Mutiny, the Company was taken over by the Crown and the governance of India became the direct business of the British State. In 1851 he married Harriet Taylor, who, according to his own account, greatly influenced his social philosophy. In the 1860s he was briefly a member of Parliament, and throughout his life was involved in many radical causes. Among them was his lifelong support for women's rights – see *The Subjection of Women* (1869).

Mill made his philosophical reputation with his *System of Logic*, published in 1843. The *Principles of Political Economy* (1848) was a synthesis of classical economics which defined liberal orthodoxy for at least a quarter of a century. His two best-known works of moral philosophy, *On Liberty* and *Utilitarianism*, appeared later – in 1859 and 1861. But he had been thinking about ethics and politics all his life, and it is his moral and political philosophy which is at present most widely read.

2 Language and logic

Nevertheless, Mill's epistemology and metaphysics remain as interesting and relevant as his better-known views in ethics and politics, and it is from these aspects of his philosophy that a general survey must start. In the *System of Logic* Mill distinguishes 'verbal' and 'real' propositions, and correspondingly, 'merely apparent' and 'real' inferences. An inference is merely apparent when no move to a new assertion has been made. For this to be so, the conclusion must literally have been asserted in the premises. In such a case, there can be no epistemological

problem about justifying the apparent inference – there *is* nothing to justify. A verbal proposition can now be defined as a conditional proposition corresponding to a merely apparent inference. Propositions and inferences which are not verbal or merely apparent are real.

Mill argues that not only mathematics but logic itself contains real inferences. To demonstrate this he embarks on a semantic analysis of sentences and terms (he calls them 'propositions' and 'names'), of syllogistic logic and of the so-called 'Laws of Thought'. His analysis has imperfections and he does not unify it in a fully general account, but he supplies the foundations of such an account, and in doing so takes the empiricist epistemology of logic and mathematics to a new level.

The starting point is a distinction between the denotation and connotation of names. Names, which may be general or singular, denote things and connote attributes of things. A general name connotes attributes and denotes each object which has those attributes. Most singular names also connote attributes.

There is, however, an important class of singular names – proper names in the ordinary sense, such as 'Dartmouth' – which denote an object without connoting any property (see PROPER NAMES). Identity propositions which contain only non-connotative names, such as 'Tully is Cicero', are verbal, in Mill's view. They lack content in the sense that, according to Mill, the only information conveyed is about the names themselves: 'Tully' denotes the same object as 'Cicero' does. Mill's point is that there is no fact in the world to which 'Cicero is Tully' corresponds. But to class these propositions as verbal would require a change in the characterization of verbal propositions given above. Moreover, knowledge that Cicero is Tully is not a priori. We cannot know the proposition to be true just by reflecting on the meaning of the names – whereas Mill's overall intention is that the class of verbal propositions should be identical with the class of propositions which are innocuously a priori *because* they are empty of content. He does not comment on these difficulties.

The meaning of a declarative sentence – 'the import of a proposition' – is determined by the connotation, not the denotation, of its constituent names; the sole exception being connotationless proper names, where meaning is determined by denotation. (Again Mill does not explain how this thesis about the meaning of proper names is to be reconciled with the a posteriority of 'Cicero is Tully'.) Mill proceeds to show how the various syntactic forms identified by syllogistic theory yield conditions of truth for sentences of those forms, when the connotation of their constituent names is given.

Armed with this analysis he argues that logic contains real inferences and propositions. He assumes that to assert a conjunction, 'A and B', is simply to assert A and to assert B. He defines 'A or B' as 'If not A, then B, and if not B, then A'. 'If A then B' means, he thinks, 'The proposition B is a legitimate inference from the proposition A'. From these claims it follows that certain deductive inferences, for example, from a conjunction to one of its conjuncts, are merely apparent. But, Mill holds, the laws of contradiction and excluded middle are real – and therefore a posteriori – propositions. He takes it that 'not P' is equivalent in meaning to 'It is false that P'; if we further assume the equivalence in meaning of P and 'It is true that P', the principle of contradiction becomes, as he puts it, 'the same proposition cannot at the same time be false and true'. 'I cannot look upon this', he says, 'as a merely verbal proposition'. He makes analogous remarks about excluded middle, which turns – on these definitions – into the principle of bivalence: 'Either it is true that P or it is false that P'.

Mill adds an epistemological argument to this semantic analysis. If logic did not contain real inferences, all deductive reasoning would be a *petitio principii*, a begging of the question, and could produce no new knowledge. Yet clearly it does produce new knowledge. So logic must contain real inferences.

Unfortunately, Mill mixes up this epistemological argument with an interesting but distinct objective. He wants to show that 'all inference is from particulars to particulars', in order to demystify the role that general propositions play in thought. He argues that in principle they add nothing to the force of an argument; particular conclusions could always be derived inductively direct from particular premises. Their value is psychological. They play the role of 'memoranda' or summary records of the inductive potential of all that we have observed, and they facilitate 'trains of reasoning' (for example, as in 'This is A; All As are Bs; No Bs are Cs; so this is not C'). Psychologically they greatly increase our memory and reasoning power, but epistemologically they are dispensable.

This thesis is connected to Mill's rejection of 'intuitive' knowledge of general truths and to his inductivism (see §5 below). But there is also a deeper way in which a radical empiricist must hold that all inference is from particulars to particulars. For consider the inference from 'Everything is F' to 'a is F'. Is it a real or merely apparent inference? It is impossible to hold it real if one also wishes to argue that real inferences are a posteriori. But the only way in which Mill can treat it as verbal is to treat the premise as a conjunction: 'a is F and b is F and...'. If that approach is precluded, then all that remains is

to deny that 'Everything is F' is propositional – it must, rather, express an inferential commitment. Both approaches are very close to the surface in Mill's discussion of the syllogism, though neither emerges clearly.

3 Mathematics

The strategy which Mill applies to mathematics is broadly similar to his approach to logic. If it was merely verbal, mathematical reasoning would be a *petitio principii*, but semantic analysis shows that it contains real propositions.

Mill provides brief but insightful empiricist sketches of geometry and arithmetic. The theorems of geometry are deduced from premises which are real propositions inductively established. (Deduction is itself largely a process of real inference.) These premises, where they are not straightforwardly true of physical space, are true in the limit. Geometrical objects – points, lines, planes – are ideal or 'fictional' limits of ideally constructible material entities. Thus the real empirical assertion underlying an axiom such as 'Two straight lines cannot enclose a space' is something like 'The more closely two lines approach absolute breadthlessness and straightness, the smaller the space they enclose'.

Applying his distinction between denotation and connotation, Mill argues that arithmetical identities such as 'Two plus one equals three' are real propositions. Number terms denote 'aggregates' and connote certain attributes of aggregates. (He does not say that they denote those attributes of the aggregates, though perhaps he should have done.) 'Aggregates' are natural, not abstract, entities – 'collections' or 'agglomerations' individuated by a principle of aggregation. This theory escapes some of the influential criticisms Frege later made of it, but its viability none the less remains extremely doubtful. The respects in which aggregates have to differ from sets if they are to be credibly natural, and not abstract, entities are precisely those in which they seem to fail to produce a fully adequate ontology for arithmetic. (One can, for example, number numbers, but can there be aggregates of aggregates, or of attributes of aggregates, if aggregates are natural entities?)

However this may be, Mill's philosophical programme is clear. Arithmetic, like logic and geometry, is a natural science, concerning a category of the laws of nature – those concerning aggregation. The fundamental principles of arithmetic and geometry, as well as of logic itself, are real. Mill provides the first thoroughly empiricist analysis of meaning and of deductive reasoning itself.

He distinguishes his view from three others – 'Conceptualism', 'Nominalism' and 'Realism'.

'Conceptualism' is his name for the view which takes the objects studied by logic to be psychological states or acts. It holds that names stand for 'ideas' which make up judgments and that 'a proposition is the expression of a relation between two ideas'. It confuses logic and psychology by assimilating propositions to judgments and attributes of objects to ideas. Against this doctrine Mill insists that:

> All language recognizes a difference between doctrine or opinion, and the fact of entertaining the opinion; between assent, and what is assented to.... Logic, according to the conception here formed of it, has no concern with the nature of the act of judging or believing; the consideration of that act, as a phenomenon of the mind, belongs to another science.
>
> (*System of Logic*)

The Nominalists – Mill cites Hobbes – hold that logic and mathematics are entirely verbal. Mill takes this position much more seriously than Conceptualism and seeks to refute it in detail. His main point is that Nominalists are only able to maintain their view because they fail to distinguish between the denotation and the connotation of names, 'seeking for their meaning exclusively in what they denote' (*System of Logic*) (see NOMINALISM).

Nominalists and Conceptualists hold that logic and mathematics can be known non-empirically, while yet retaining the view that no real proposition about the world can be so known. Realists hold that logical and mathematical knowledge is knowledge of universals which exist in an abstract Platonic domain; the terms that make up sentences being signs that stand for such universals. Versions of this view were destined to stage a major revival in philosophy, and semantic analysis would be their main source, but it is the view Mill takes least seriously.

In the contemporary use of the term, Mill is himself a nominalist – he rejects abstract entities (see ABSTRACT OBJECTS). However, just as severe difficulties lie in the way of treating the ontology of arithmetic in terms of aggregates rather than sets, so there are difficulties in treating the ontology of general semantics without appealing to universals and sets, as well as to natural properties and objects. We can have no clear view of how Mill would have responded to these difficulties had they been made evident to him. But we can be fairly sure that he would have sought to maintain his nominalism.

However, his main target is the doctrine that there are real a priori propositions (see A PRIORI). What, he asks, goes on in practice when we hold a real proposition to be true a priori? We find its negation inconceivable, or that it is derived, by principles whose unsoundness we find inconceivable, from premises whose negation we find inconceivable. Mill is not offering a definition of what is meant by such terms as 'a priori', or 'self-evident'; his point is that facts about what we find inconceivable are all that lends colour to the use of these terms.

They are facts about the limits, felt by us from the inside, on what we can imagine perceiving. Mill thought he could explain these facts about unthinkability, or imaginative unrepresentability, in associationist terms, and much of his work claims to do so. This associationist psychology is unlikely nowadays to convince, but that does not affect his essential point: the step from our inability to represent to ourselves the negation of a proposition, to acceptance of its truth, calls for justification. Moreover, the justification itself must be a priori if it is to show that the proposition is known a priori.

4 'Psychologism' and naturalism

Mill is often mistakenly accused of 'psychologism' in his treatment of logic – an accusation which seems to go back to HUSSERL (and one which Frege does not make). 'Psychologism' is the view that laws of logic are psychological laws concerning our mental processes; or that 'meanings' are mental entities, and that 'judgments' assert relationships among these entities. But Mill's view, as we have seen, is that logic and mathematics are the most general empirical sciences, governing *all* phenomena. He explicitly holds that the distinction between necessary and contingent truths, understood 'metaphysically', is empty. And he dismisses the Conceptualist claim that names refer to ideas and propositions express or assert a psychological relation between them.

What explains, then, the attribution of 'psychologism' to Mill? Husserl quotes a passage from *An Examination of Sir William Hamilton's Philosophy* (1865), which has been cited many times since:

> Logic is not the theory of Thought as Thought, but of valid Thought; not of thinking, but of correct thinking. *It is not a Science distinct from, and coordinate with Psychology. So far as it is a science at all, it is a part, or branch, of Psychology; differing from it, on the one hand as the part differs from the whole, and on the other, as an Art differs from a Science. Its theoretic grounds are wholly borrowed from Psychology, and include as much of that science as is required to justify the rules of the art.*
>
> (italics show portion quoted by Husserl)

To give this a psychologistic reading is to take it out of context. Mill means that the logician must formulate rules of reasoning in a manner which will be as helpful as possible to inquirers, and must draw on the psychology of thought to do so. It is in that sense that the art of the logician borrows from the science of the psychologist. How best to promote the art of clear thinking is a psychological question. None the less,

> the laws, in the scientific sense of the term, of Thought as Thought – do not belong to Logic, but to Psychology: and it is only the *validity* of thought which Logic takes cognizance of.
>
> (Mill, *Hamilton's Philosophy*)

So it is wrong to accuse Mill of psychologism about logic. But there is a sense in which his view of our most basic forms of inductive reasoning is psychologistic, or naturalistic. For how does he respond to the Kantian claim that the very possibility of knowledge requires that there be a priori elements in our knowledge? Even if we accept his inductive account of logic and mathematics, must we not accept the principle of induction itself as a priori?

For Mill, the primitive form of reasoning – in both the epistemological and the aetiological sense – is enumerative induction, the disposition to infer that all As are B from the observation of a number of As which are all B. (Or to the conclusion that a given percentage of all As are B from the observation of that percentage of Bs among a number of As.) We spontaneously agree in reasoning that way, and in holding that way of reasoning to be sound. This method of reasoning, enumerative induction, is not a merely verbal principle. So it cannot on Mill's own account be a priori. Mill says that we learn 'the laws of our rational faculty, like those of every other natural agency', by 'seeing the agent at work'. We bring our most basic reasoning dispositions to self-consciousness by critical reflection on our actual practice. He is right to say that this reflective scrutiny of practice is, in a *certain* sense, an a posteriori process. It examines dispositions which we have before we examine them. Having examined our dispositions, we reach a reflective equilibrium in which we endorse some – and perhaps reject others. We endorse them as sound norms of reasoning. There is nothing more to be said: no further story, platonic or transcendental, to be told.

Unlike Hume, or even Reid, Mill shows no interest at all in scepticism. If one thinks that scepticism is both unanswerable and unserious this may be true philosophic wisdom. But to Mill's epistemological critics, whether they were realists or post-Kantian idealists, it seemed obvious that it was evasion, not wisdom. Naturalism could only seem to differ from scepticism by being uncritical, and in this we find the truth in the allegation that Mill's system of logic is 'psychologistic'; if it is sound criticism, it is sound criticism of all naturalistic epistemology.

5 Inductive science

Mill does not raise purely sceptical questions about simple generalization from experience; he none the less thinks it a highly fallible method. His aim is to show how reasoning methods can evolve from it which greatly reduce the fallibility of induction, even though they can never wholly eliminate it.

Humankind begins with 'spontaneous' and 'unscientific' inductions about particular unconnected natural phenomena or aspects of experience. As these generalizations accumulate and interweave, they justify the second-order inductive conclusion that *all* phenomena are subject to uniformity, and more specifically, that all have discoverable sufficient conditions. In this less vague form, the principle of general uniformity becomes, given Mill's analysis of causation, the Law of Universal Causation. It in turn provides (Mill believes) the grounding assumption for a new style of reasoning about nature – eliminative induction.

In this type of reasoning, the assumption that a type of phenomenon has uniform causes, together with a (revisable) assumption about what its possible causes are, initiates a comparative inquiry in which the actual cause is identified by elimination. Mill formulates the logic of this eliminative reasoning in his well-known 'Methods of Experimental Inquiry' (Chapter 7, Book 2 of *System of Logic*). His picture of the interplay between enumerative and eliminative reasoning, and of the way it entrenches, from within, our rational confidence in the inductive process, is elegant and penetrating.

The improved scientific induction which results from this new style of reasoning spills back onto the principle of Universal Causation on which it rests, and raises its certainty to a new level. That in turn raises our confidence in the totality of particular enumerative inductions from which the principle is derived. So the amount of confidence with which one can rely on the 'inductive process' as a whole depends on the point which has been reached in its history – though the confidence to be attached to particular inductions always remains variable.

Mill's inductivism – his view that enumerative induction is the only ultimately authoritative method of inference to new truths – was rejected by William WHEWELL, who argued that the really fundamental method in scientific inquiry was the Hypothetical Method, in which one argues to the truth of a hypothesis from the fact that it would explain observed phenomena (see INFERENCE TO THE BEST EXPLANATION). Mill had read Whewell's *History of the Inductive Sciences* (1837), and could hardly fail to be aware of the pervasiveness of hypotheses in the actual process of inquiry, or of their indispensability in supplying working assumptions – their 'heuristic' value, as Whewell called it. But what Mill could not accept was that the mere fact that a hypothesis accounted for the data in itself provided a reason for thinking it true.

Yet Whewell's appeal was to the actual practice of scientific reasoning, as observed in the history of science. An appeal of that kind was precisely what Mill, on his own principles, could not ignore. If the disposition to hypothesize is spontaneous, why should it not be recognized as a fundamental method of reasoning to truth, as enumerative induction is?

Mill's refusal to recognize it is not arbitrary. The essential point underlying it is a powerful one: it is the possibility that a body of data may be explained equally well by more than one hypothesis. Mill does not deny the increasingly deductive and mathematical organization of science – he emphasizes it. That is quite compatible with his inductivism, and indeed is central to his account of the increasing reliability of the inductive process. He further agrees that a hypothesis can sometimes be shown, by eliminative methods of inductive reasoning which he accepts, to be the only one consistent with the facts. And he allows various other cases of apparently purely hypothetical reasoning which are, in his view, genuinely inductive.

When all such cases have been taken into account, we are left with pure cases of the Hypothetical Method, in which the causes postulated are not directly observable, and not simply because they are assumed to operate – in accordance with known laws, inductively established – in regions of time or space too distant to observe. What are we to say of such hypotheses? For example of the 'undulatory' theory of light? They cannot, Mill says, be accepted as inductively established truths, not even as probable ones.

> An hypothesis of this kind is not to be received as probably true because it accounts for all the known phenomena; since this is a condition sometimes fulfilled tolerably well by two conflicting hypotheses; while there are probably many others which are equally possible, but which from want of anything analogous in our experience, our minds are unfitted to conceive.
>
> (*System of Logic*)

Such an hypothesis can suggest fruitful analogies, Mill thinks, but cannot be regarded as yielding a new truth itself. The data do not determine a unique hypothesis: it is this possibility of under-determination which stops him from accepting hypothetical reasoning as an independent method of achieving truth.

In seeing the difficulty Mill is certainly on solid ground. What he does not see, however, is how much must be torn from the fabric of our belief if inductivism is applied strictly. So it is an important question whether the difficulty can be resolved – and whether it can be resolved within a naturalistic framework which does not appeal to an underlying idealism, as Whewell did. If naturalism can endorse the hypothetical method, then among other things it can develop a more plausible empiricism about logic and mathematics than Mill's. But the ramifications of his inductivism are even wider, as becomes apparent from an examination of his general metaphysics.

6 Mind and matter

Mill sets out his metaphysical views in *An Examination of Sir William Hamilton's Philosophy*. Hamilton was the last eminent representative of the Scottish Common Sense School, and a ferocious controversialist – in Mill's eyes a pillar of the right-thinking establishment, ripe for demolition. The result is that Mill's discussion of general metaphysical issues is cast in a highly polemical form which leaves important issues shrouded in obscurity. He does however give himself space to develop his view of our knowledge of the external world.

He begins with a doctrine which he rightly takes to be generally accepted (in his time) on all sides: 'that all the attributes which we ascribe to objects, consist in their having the power of exciting one or another variety of sensation in our minds; that an object is to us nothing else than that which affects our senses in a certain manner' (*Hamilton's Philosophy*). This is 'the doctrine of the Relativity of Knowledge to the knowing mind'. It makes epistemology, in Mill's words, the 'Interpretation of Consciousness'. He proceeds to analyse what we mean when we say that objects are external to us:

> We mean, that there is concerned in our perceptions something which exists when we are not thinking of it; which existed before we had ever thought of it, and would exist if we were annihilated; and further, that there exist things which we never saw, touched or otherwise perceived, and things which have never been perceived by man. This idea of something which is distinguished from our

fleeting impressions by what, in Kantian language, is called Perdurability; something which is fixed and the same, while our impressions vary; something which exists whether we are aware of it or not, constitutes altogether our idea of external substance. Whoever can assign an origin to this complex conception, has accounted for what we mean by the belief in matter.

(*Hamilton's Philosophy*)

To assign this origin Mill postulates that

we are capable of forming the conception of Possible sensations; sensations which we are not feeling at the present moment, but which we might feel, and should feel if certain conditions were present.

(*Hamilton's Philosophy*)

These possibilities, which are conditional certainties, need a special name to distinguish them from mere vague possibilities, which experience gives no warrant for reckoning upon. Now, as soon as a distinguishing name is given, though it be only to the same thing regarded in a different aspect, one of the most familiar experiences of our mental nature teaches us, that the different name comes to be considered as the name of a different thing.

(*Hamilton's Philosophy*)

Physical objects are 'Permanent Possibilities of Sensation' (There is a change in the 'permanent' possibilities of sensation whenever there is change in the world. Mill also uses other terms, such as 'certified' or 'guaranteed'.) We often find that whenever a given cluster of certified possibilities of sensation obtains, then a certain other cluster follows. 'Hence our ideas of causation, power, activity... become connected, not with sensations, but with groups of possibilities of sensation' (*Hamilton's Philosophy*) (see PHENOMENALISM).

However, even if our notion of matter as the external cause of sensations can be explained on psychological principles, it is still possible to hold that good grounds can be given for thinking the notion to have instances. There might be a legitimate inference from the existence of the permanent possibilities and their correlations to the existence of an external cause of our sensations. It is at just this point that Mill's inductivism plays a part. The inference would be a case of hypothetical reasoning, to an explanation of experience which transcended all possible data of experience; and that is precisely what Mill rejects: 'I assume only the tendency, but not the legitimacy of the tendency, to

extend all the laws of our own experience to a sphere beyond our experience' (*Hamilton's Philosophy*).

If matter is the permanent possibility of sensation what is mind? Can it also be resolved into 'a series of feelings, with a background of possibilities of feeling'? Mill finds in this view a serious difficulty: to remember or expect a state of consciousness is not simply to believe that it has existed or will exist; it is to believe that *I myself* have experienced or will experience that state of consciousness.

If, therefore, we speak of the Mind as a series of feelings, we are obliged to complete the statement by calling it a series of feelings which is aware of itself as past and future; and we are reduced to the alternative of believing that the Mind, or Ego, is something different from any series of feelings, or possibilities of them, or of accepting the paradox, that something which *ex hypothesi* is but a series of feelings, can be aware of itself as a series.

(*Hamilton's Philosophy*)

Thus although Mill is unwilling to accept 'the common theory of Mind, as a so-called substance', the self-consciousness involved in memory and expectation drives him to 'ascribe a reality to the Ego – to my own Mind – different from that real existence as a Permanent Possibility, which is the only reality I acknowledge in Matter' (*Hamilton's Philosophy*).

This ontology, Mill thinks, is consistent with common sense realism about the world. Phenomenalism – the conception of matter as possibility of experience – allegedly leaves common sense and science untouched. In particular, mind and experience is still properly seen as a part of the natural order.

Yet if phenomenalism is right, only the experiences are real. Mill thinks we are led to that conclusion by the very standards of reasoning recognized in a naturalistic 'science of science', or 'system of logic'. If he is right, then the naturalistic vision of the world which sees minds as part of a larger causal order is self-undermining. For if we are led to the conclusion that only states of consciousness are real by *an application of naturalism's own standards*, then that conclusion has to be understood on the same level as the naturalistic affirmation that states of consciousness are themselves part of a larger causal order external to them – and therefore as inconsistent with it. Causal relations cannot exist between fictional entities which are mere markers for possibilities of sensation.

This is the fault-line in Mill's epistemology and metaphysics. Either naturalism undermines itself, or there is something wrong with Mill's inductivist analysis of our natural norms of reasoning, or with his endorsement of the doctrine of the Relativity of Knowledge, or with both. It is not obvious that Mill's most fundamental tenet – his naturalistic view of the mind – can be safeguarded by rejecting inductivism and endorsing the hypothetical method. There is still something implausible about hypothesizing the world as an explanation of pure experience. Mill himself explicitly acknowledged that memory, as well as induction, has epistemic authority. Had he analysed the significance of such an acknowledgment more thoroughly, he might have noted a parallel: on the one hand a primitive epistemic norm which warrants assertions about the past based on present memory-experiences; on the other, primitive epistemic norms which warrant assertions about the physical world based on perceptual experience. But perhaps that would have taken him too far in the direction of Reid's principles of common sense.

7 Freedom and the moral sciences

The sixth and last book of the *System of Logic* is a classical statement of methodology in the 'moral' sciences (that is, the human sciences). Its strength derives partly from the fact that Mill was a philosopher who also practised the whole range of these sciences as they then stood. He was mainly known as a political economist, but had strong interests in psychology and in the nascent science of sociology. He thought as an economist as well as a philosopher about socialism, taxation and systems of property, and he thought in sociological terms about such topics as democracy and the role of moral and intellectual elites. He also took an interest in a variety of psychological topics, including desire, pleasure and will, and the origins of conscience and justice.

The phenomena of mind and society are, in Mill's view, causal processes. If mind and society are part of the causal order, and causation is regular succession, then the general model of explanation he has proposed, according to which explanation subsumes facts under laws linking them to their causal antecedents, will apply, he thinks, to the moral sciences. It may be hard for moral science to live up to it, in view of the complexity of its data, but the model stands as an ideal. Important issues remain about the character of and relationships between the various moral sciences, and Mill treats these issues in detail. But he does not think that the very idea of a moral science raises new metaphysical or epistemological problems (see EXPLANATION IN HISTORY AND SOCIAL SCIENCE).

Psychological concepts are intentional and, correspondingly, the moral sciences are interpreta-tive. Can laws of individual behaviour be formulated, as Mill assumed, in this interpretative vocabulary? His analysis of the moral sciences takes their fundamental laws to lie in the domain of psychology. He was familiar with a different view, that of Auguste COMTE, who held that the fundamental and irreducible moral science was sociology (a term coined by Comte). There was no deeper moral science, no science of psychology; the next level below sociology was the physical science of biology. Mill rejected that view, but enthusiastically shared Comte's vision of a historical sociology. Psychology may be the irreducible theoretical basis of the moral sciences; historical sociology is to be, as far as Mill was concerned, their prime exhibit.

Associationism and a Comtean historical sociology are thus the driving ideas in Mill's logic of the moral sciences. They interlock. Associationism fortifies his belief in the mutability of human nature: different social and historical formations can build radically different patterns of association. The bridge between historical sociology and the invariant laws of associationist psychology can be provided, Mill thinks, by an innovation of his own: a science he calls 'Ethology', which will study the different forms of human character in different social formations. He intended to write a treatise on the subject; significantly, he failed.

How, on this naturalistic view of mind and society, can human beings be free? The question mattered deeply to Mill. The conclusion others drew from the doctrine of determinism, namely, that we have (in Mill's phrase) no 'power of *self-formation*', and hence are not really responsible for our character or our actions, would have destroyed his moral vision. Self-formation is the fulcrum of his ideal of life, and 'moral freedom', the ability to bring one's desires under the control of a steady rational purpose, is a condition of self-formation, of having a character in the full sense (see FREE WILL §§3–4).

Thus Mill had to show how causally conditioned natural objects can also be morally free agents. The sketch of a solution in the *System of Logic* (Book 6, ch. 2), which Mill thought the best chapter in the book, is brief but penetrating. (There is a longer discussion in *An Examination of Sir William Hamilton's Philosophy*, ch. 26.) One of its leading features is a distinction between resistible and irresistible causes; 'in common use', only causes which are 'irresistible', whose operation is 'supposed too powerful to be counteracted at all', are called necessary:

There are physical sequences which we call necessary, as death for want of food or air;

there are others which, though as much cases of causation as the former, are not said to be necessary, as death from poison, which an antidote, or the use of the stomach-pump, will sometimes avert... human actions are in this last predicament: they are never (except in some cases of mania) ruled by any one motive with such absolute sway, that there is no room for the influence of another.

(*System of Logic*)

An action caused by an irresistible motive (a 'mania') is plainly not free. This is certainly very pertinent. Yet something is added when we move from the idea of motives being resistible by other motives to the idea of moral freedom, the idea that *I* have the power to resist motives. It is the ability to recognize and respond to reasons. I act freely if I could have resisted the motive on which I in fact acted, had there been good reason to do so. A motive impairs my moral freedom if it cannot be defeated by a cogent reason for not acting on it. Mill fails to bring this connection between freedom and reason into clear view, but he relies on it in his ethical writings. He takes it that I am more or less free overall, according to the degree to which I can bring my motives under scrutiny and act on the result of that scrutiny. So I can *make* myself more free, by shaping desires or at least cultivating the strength of will to overcome them.

A person feels morally free who feels that his habits or his temptations are not his masters, but he theirs: who even in yielding to them knows that he could resist... we must feel that our wish, if not strong enough to alter our character, is strong enough to conquer our character when the two are brought into conflict in any particular case of conduct. And hence it is said with truth, that none but a person of confirmed virtue is completely free.

(*System of Logic*)

The identification of moral freedom with confirmed virtue, and (less explicitly) of confirmed virtue with steady responsiveness to reasons, is present in Mill as in Kant (see KANT, I. §11). But Mill does not address crucial questions such as what is it to grasp a reason, or how reason can be efficacious. To vindicate the coherence of his view one would have to show how to answer such questions in a way which is compatible with naturalism. The problem remains central in contemporary philosophy – certainly Mill himself never took full stock of it.

8   Happiness, desire and will

Mill's single ultimate standard of theoretical reason is enumerative induction. His single ultimate standard of practical reason is the principle of utility; its standard is the good of all. But what is the good? According to Mill, it is happiness, understood as 'pleasure, and freedom from pain' (*Utilitarianism*: ch. 5) (see HAPPINESS). His case rests on the following principle of method:

The sole evidence it is possible to produce that anything is desirable, is that people do actually desire it. If the end which the utilitarian doctrine proposes to itself were not, in theory and in practice, acknowledged to be an end, nothing could ever convince any person that it was so.

(*Utilitarianism*: ch. 5)

Mill is not claiming that the conclusion that happiness is desirable follows deductively from the premise that people in general desire it. He gives some ground for that misinterpretation when he compares the move from 'desired' to 'desirable' to those from 'seen' and 'heard' to 'visible' and 'audible'. Nevertheless, his procedure is simply an appeal to reflective practice, just as in the case of enumerative induction – where again the 'sole evidence' that enumerative induction is an ultimate norm of reasoning is that we acknowledge it as such 'in theory and in practice'.

However, a question which is appropriate by Mill's own principle of method is whether reflective practice shows that happiness is the *only* thing we desire. Do not human beings, in theory and in practice, desire things other than happiness? Mill anticipates this question and responds to it at length. He claims that when we want a particular object for its own sake and with no further end in view we desire it because we think of it as enjoyable: 'to desire anything, except in proportion as the idea of it is pleasant, is a physical and metaphysical impossibility' (*Utilitarianism*: ch. 5). But this does not mean that we desire all objects as *means* to our pleasure. The desire for an object is genuinely a desire for that *object*; it is not the desire for pleasure as such. Mill's way of marking this is to say that the object is desired as a 'part' or an 'ingredient' of happiness, not as a means to it. His rejection of psychological egoism was one of the points on which he took himself to be at odds with Bentham (see BENTHAM, J.). When a person does something because they think it will be pleasant – for example a generous person who gives a present – it does not follow that they are acting selfishly (see EGOISM AND ALTRUISM). Generous people take pleasure in the prospect of giving, not in the prospect of getting pleasure; their desire to give is not derived from the desire to get pleasure. Giving is a part of their happiness, not a means to it.

Thus Mill's case for the claim that happiness is the sole human end, put more carefully, is this: 'Whatever is desired otherwise than as a means to some end beyond itself, and ultimately to happiness, is desired as itself a part of happiness, and is not desired for itself until has become so' (*Utilitarianism*: ch. 5). Nothing here assumes Hume's view that every action must ultimately flow from an under-ived desire. That is a quite separate issue, and Mill's view of it is closer to that of Kant or Reid than to that of Hume. He insists 'positively and emphatically':

> that the will is a different thing from desire;
> that a person of confirmed virtue, or any other
> person whose purposes are fixed, carries out
> his purposes without any thought of the
> pleasure he has in contemplating them, or
> expects to derive from their fulfilment.
>
> (*Utilitarianism*: ch. 5)

This distinction between purpose and desire is central to Mill's conception of the will. When we develop purposes we can will against mere likings or aversions: 'In the case of an habitual purpose, instead of willing the thing because we desire it, we often desire it only because we will it' (*Utilitarianism*: ch. 5). Every action is caused by a motive, but not every motive is a liking or aversion:

> When the will is said to be determined by
> motives, a motive does not mean always, or
> solely, the anticipation of a pleasure or of a
> pain.... A habit of willing is commonly
> called a purpose; and among the causes of our
> volitions, and of the actions which flow from
> them, must be reckoned not only likings and
> aversions, but also purposes.
>
> (*System of Logic*)

The formation of purposes from desires is the evolution of will; it is also the development of character. Mill quotes Novalis: 'a character is a completely fashioned will' (*System of Logic*). Not that this reflects the whole of his view of character; character for him requires the cultivation of feeling as well as the cultivation of will: 'A person whose desires and impulses are his own – are the expression of his own nature, as it has been developed and modified by his own culture – is said to have a character' (*On Liberty*). Developed spontaneity of feeling is part of fully-perfected character, but certainly moral freedom is too – 'none but a person of confirmed virtue is completely free'. As noted in

§7 above, Mill does not address the crucial question of what it is for a purpose to be informed by reason. Still, the distinction between purpose and desire does allow him to recognize conscientious action, action which flows not from any inclination but solely from a habit of willing; he asserts the possibility and value of a 'confirmed will to do right' (*Utilitarianism*: ch. 5), distinct from motives of anticipated pleasure and pain. That 'virtuous will', however, is not for him an intrinsic good, as it is for Kant. It is:

> a means to good, not intrinsically a good; and
> does not contradict the doctrine that nothing
> is good to human beings but in so far as it is
> either itself pleasurable, or a means of attaining
> pleasure or averting pain.
>
> (*Utilitarianism*: ch. 5)

9 Qualities of pleasure

Happiness – pleasure and the absence of pain – is the sole final end of life. But Mill's idea of it is altogether more romantic and liberal than that of earlier utilitarians. He takes into account the fact that a variety of notions – for example, purity, elevation, depth, refinement and sublimity, and their opposites – enter into our assessments of pleasure. We do not assess pleasures along a single dimension. In his general ethical and political writing, Mill freely draws on that extensive and flexible language. He sees the need to recognize it also in utilitarian theory, but here he does so rather more mechanically by distinguishing 'quality' and 'quantity' of pleasure. From the first publication of *Utilitarianism*, at least three sorts of question have been asked about this famous distinction. The first is whether it is reconcilable with hedonism. The second is epistemological: is there a cogent way of establishing that some pleasures are superior in 'quality'? The third question, perhaps the most challenging, though less often discussed, is how the distinction fits into the framework of utilitarianism.

As to the first question: there is indeed, as Mill says, no reason in logic why more than one characteristic of pleasures should not be relevant to estimating their value – though if we call those characteristics 'quantity' and 'quality' we need to maintain a careful distinction between the quantity and quality of a pleasure on the one hand and its degree of value on the other. All that hedonism requires is that the only things that make a pleasure valuable are its characteristics as a *pleasure* (see HEDONISM).

Nevertheless, an impression lingers that Mill's discussion appeals to intuitions which are not hedonistic. For example:

Few human creatures would consent to be changed into any of the lower animals, for a promise of the fullest allowance of a beast's pleasures; no intelligent human being would consent to be a fool, no instructed person would be an ignoramus, no person of feeling and conscience would be selfish and base, even though they should be persuaded that the fool, the dunce, or the rascal is better satisfied with his lot than they are with theirs.

(*Utilitarianism*: ch. 5)

He also notes that a 'being of higher faculties requires more to make him happy, is capable probably of more acute suffering, and is certainly accessible to it at more points, than one of an inferior type' (*Utilitarianism*: ch. 5). So a being of higher faculties may be faced with a choice: on the one hand a life of acute suffering, with no access to any of the higher pleasures which its faculties make it capable of appreciating, on the other, a cure (for example, an operation) which relieves its suffering but leaves it only with the pleasures available to a fool or a dunce. Is Mill saying that in *all* such cases the life of suffering should be preferred? He does not say so explicitly and if he does adhere to hedonism he should not. For cases are surely possible in which life after the cure offers a stream of pleasures more valuable overall, taking quality as well as quantity into account, than the life of suffering in which one retains one's higher faculties but is bereft of higher pleasures.

What of the epistemological question? Mill compares assessments of the comparative quality of pleasures to assessments of their comparative quantity: both are determined by 'the feelings and judgments of the experienced' (*Utilitarianism*: ch. 5). But a judgment that the pleasure derived from film A is of a higher kind than that derived from watching film B is clearly, as Mill conceives it, an evaluative judgment. The proper comparison would have been with the evaluative judgment that pleasure as such is desirable. A higher pleasure has some feature, *qua* pleasure, that makes it more desirable overall than a lower pleasure of like quantity. And Mill could have said that with this judgment, as with basic evaluative judgments in general, the only criterion is reflective practice – self-examination and discussion. In such discussion, some people emerge as better judges than others – this is not a circularity but an inherent feature of normative judgment.

Yet now the third question becomes pressing: how are such judgments of the quality of pleasures to be registered in the utilitarian calculus? In requiring utilitarianism to take them into account Mill makes a move of political as well as ethical

significance. For what rank do we give to these pleasures in our social ordering – the rank which highly developed human natures attach to them or that which lower human natures attach to them? Mill's answer is unambiguous: it is the verdict of 'competent judges' which stands.

Suppose that beings of highly developed faculties place the pleasures of scientific discovery or artistic creation so much higher than those of material well-being that (above a certain modicum of physical comfort and security) any amount of the former, however small, is ranked by them above any amount of the latter, however large. Suppose, however, that beings of considerably less developed faculties would not share this assessment. And now suppose that the question is put to Mill, how much of the lower pleasure of the less developed being may be sacrificed to maintain the more highly developed being's higher pleasure? Mill's view is that the more highly developed being delivers the correct assessment of the relative value of the higher and lower pleasures. But, by hypothesis, it would be prepared to sacrifice any amount of the lower pleasure, down to a modicum of physical comfort and security, for the smallest amount of the higher. Must the same hold for the interpersonal case? Must it be correct for the utilitarian to sacrifice any amount of the lower pleasures of lower beings, down to a level at which they are provided with the modicum of comfort and security, in order to secure some higher pleasure for a higher being? Mill provides no answer.

10 The utility principle

Though Mill deepened the utilitarian understanding of pleasure, desire, character and will, he never adequately re-examined the principle of utility itself. When he states the utilitarian doctrine before considering what kind of proof can be given of it, he states it thus: 'Happiness is desirable, and the only thing desirable, as an end, all other things being only desirable as means to that end' (*Utilitarianism*: ch. 5). In effect, he takes his task to be that of demonstrating the truth of hedonism. All he has to say about the move from hedonism to the utility principle is that if 'each person's happiness is a good to that person' then 'the general happiness' must be 'a good to the aggregate of all persons'. In a letter in which he explains this unclear remark, he says: 'I merely meant in this particular sentence to argue that since A's happiness is a good, B's a good, C's a good, etc, the sum of all these goods must be a good' (*Later Letters*). This contains two inexplicit assumptions. The more obvious point is that an egoist may accept that Mill has shown that 'each person's happiness is a good to that person', but deny that he has shown that happiness is a good tout *court*. The egoist denies that Mill has shown that *everyone* has reason to promote the happiness of anyone. That requires a separate postulate, as Henry Sidgwick pointed out.

The second inexplicit assumption is more subtle. At the end of the last chapter of *Utilitarianism*, 'On the Connexion between Justice and Utility', Mill does explain that he takes 'perfect impartiality between persons' to be part of the very meaning of the Greatest Happiness Principle:

> That principle is a mere form of words without rational signification, unless one person's happiness, supposed equal in degree (with the proper allowance made for kind), is counted for exactly as much as another's. Those conditions being supplied, Bentham's dictum, 'everybody to count for one, nobody for more than one', might be written under the principle of utility as an explanatory commentary.
>
> (*Utilitarianism*: ch. 5)

So here Mill supplies the required postulate of impartiality. However, the concept of impartiality does not, on its own, yield utilitarianism's aggregative principle of distribution. Maximizing the *sum* of individuals' happiness, if it makes sense to talk in this way at all, is one way of being impartial: no individual's happiness is given greater weight than any other's in the procedure which determines the value of a state of affairs as a function of the happiness of individuals in that state of affairs. In this sense the procedure implements the principle, 'Everybody to count for one, nobody for more than one'; but so does maximizing the average of all individuals' unweighted happiness. Here too all individuals count for one and no more than one. In fact a wide variety of non-equivalent distributive principles is impartial in this way. The most one could get from combining a postulate of impartiality with hedonism is that ethical value is a positive impartial function of individual happiness and of nothing else. In a footnote to the paragraph Mill glosses the requirement of perfect impartiality as follows: 'equal amounts of happiness are equally desirable, whether felt by the same or by different persons'. That does yield aggregative or average utilitarianism, but it follows neither from the thesis that happiness is the only thing desirable to human beings, nor from the formal notion of impartiality (see IMPARTIALITY).

11 Morality and justice

When we turn to Mill's conception of the relationship between the utility principle and the fabric of principles which regulate everyday social life, we find him again at his most impressive. He stresses that a utilitarian standard of value cannot itself tell what practical rules, aims or ideals we should live by. In his autobiography he dates this conviction to the period of his mental crisis. He now 'gave its proper place, among the prime necessities of human well-being, to the internal culture of the individual' (*Autobiography* 1873). The prime task for human beings was to attend to that internal culture – to develop whatever was best in themselves. The indirect role in which he now cast the utility principle became a fundamental structural feature of his moral and political philosophy. For example, he accuses Auguste Comte of committing:

> the error which is often, but falsely, charged against the whole class of utilitarian moralists; he required that the test of conduct should also be the exclusive motive of it .... M. Comte is a morality-intoxicated man. Every question with him is one of morality, and no motive but that of morality is permitted.
>
> (*Auguste Comte and Positivism*)

Mill gives a succinct statement of his own doctrine at the end of the *System of Logic*. As always, he affirms 'that the promotion of happiness is the ultimate principle of Teleology'. But, he continues,

> I do not mean to suggest that the promotion of happiness should be itself the end of all actions, or even of all rules of action. It is the justification, and ought to be the controller, of all ends, but is not itself the sole end .... I fully admit that ... the cultivation of an ideal nobleness of will and conduct, should be to individual human beings an end, for which the specific pursuit either of their own happiness or of that of others (except so far as included in that idea) should, in any case of conflict, give way. But I hold that the very question, what constitutes this elevation of character, is itself to be decided by a reference to happiness as the standard.

The happiness of all is 'the test of all rules of conduct' – and not only rules of conduct but also of cultivation of feelings. How is the test applied? Here Mill learned more from Coleridge than from Bentham; that is, from historical criticism directed at the abstract social visionaries of the Enlightenment. They did not see that moral sentiments can only grow in a stable tradition and social setting. They did not grasp the conditions necessary for such a tradition and setting – education of personal impulses to a restraining discipline, shared allegiance to some enduring and unquestioned values, 'a strong and active principle of cohesion' among 'members of the same community or state'. Hence:

> They threw away the shell without preserving the kernel; and attempting to new-model society without the binding forces which hold society together, met with such success as might have been anticipated.
>
> (Coleridge)

This feeling for the historicity of social formations and genealogies of morals gives Mill's ethical vision a penetration which is absent from Bentham (and also from the excessively abstract discussions of utilitarianism in twentieth-century philosophy). On the other hand the analysis of morality, rights and justice which Mill fits into this ethical vision owes much to Bentham.

Mill examines the concept of justice in chapter 5 of *Utilitarianism*. Having observed that the idea of something which one may be constrained or compelled to do, on pain of penalty, is central to the idea of an obligation of justice, he notes that it nevertheless 'contains, as yet, nothing to distinguish that obligation from moral obligation in general':

> The idea of penal sanction, which is the essence of law, enters not only into the conception of injustice, but into that of any kind of wrong. We do not call anything wrong, unless we mean to imply that a person ought to be punished in some way or other for doing it; if not by law, by the opinion of his fellow creatures; if not by opinion, by the reproaches of his own conscience.
>
> (*Auguste Comte and Positivism*)

This is a normative, not a positive, account of morality: the morally wrong is that which *ought* to be punished, by law, social opinion or conscience. It would be a circular account if the 'ought' in question were itself a moral 'ought'. But the utility principle is the ultimate principle of 'Teleology'. Teleology is the 'Doctrine of Ends'; 'borrowing the language of the German metaphysicians', Mill also describes it as 'the principles of Practical Reason' (*System of Logic*). So the 'ought' is the 'ought' of Practical Reason – which, making appropriate use of 'laws of nature', produces the 'Art of Life'. Morality itself is only one department of this art. Moral concepts and judgments issue from the moral sentiments, the sentiments involved in guilt and blame; but are corrigible by a rational doctrine of ends. And that doctrine, in Mill's view, is the utility principle.

From this account of morality Mill moves to an account of rights and justice. A person has a moral right to a thing if there is a moral obligation on society to protect them in their possession of that thing. Obligations of justice are distinguished from moral obligations in general by the existence of corresponding rights:

> Justice implies something which it is not only right to do, and wrong not to do, but which some individual person can claim from us as his moral right.... Whenever there is a right, the case is one of justice.
>
> (*Auguste Comte and Positivism*)

Upholding rights is one of society's vital tasks. For on it depends our security – which is 'to every one's feelings the most vital of interests':

> This most indispensable of all necessaries, after physical nutriment, cannot be had, unless the machinery for providing it is kept unintermittedly in active play. Our notion, therefore, of the claim we have on our fellow-creatures to join in making safe for us the very groundwork of our existence, gathers feelings around it so much more intense than those concerned in any of the more common cases of utility, that the difference in degree (as is often the case in psychology) becomes a real difference in kind.
>
> (*Auguste Comte and Positivism*)

In this way the claim of justice comes to be felt as a claim of a higher kind than any claim of utility. Justice, Mill concludes:

> is a name for certain classes of moral rules, which concern the essentials of human well-being more nearly, and are therefore of more absolute obligation, than any other rules for the guidance of life.
>
> (*Auguste Comte and Positivism*)

Mill spells out in detail what these moral rules should be in his writings on various social questions. In *Utilitarianism*, he is concerned with the more abstract task of showing how justice-rights take priority over the direct pursuit of general utility by individuals or the state, just as they take priority over the private pursuit of personal ends. His position is thus more complex than that of philosophers in a Kantian tradition who assume, in John Rawls' phrase, that the right (or just) is prior to the good. For Mill, good is philosophically prior to right – but politically and socially right constrains the pursuit of good (see JUSTICE §3).

12 Liberty and democracy

The most celebrated part of Mill's social philosophy, his essay *On Liberty*, must be read in terms of this conception of the right and the good. Mill is not a social contract or 'natural rights' liberal. He appeals instead to 'utility in the largest sense, grounded on the permanent interests of man as a progressive being'. He has in mind the higher human nature, capable of development by self-culture, which he believes to be present in every human being. Self-culture opens access to higher forms of human happiness, but it has to be *self*-culture, first because human potentialities are diverse and best known to each human being itself, and second because only when human beings work to their own plans of life do they develop moral freedom, itself indispensable to a higher human nature.

Given the importance free self-culture thus assumes in Mill's idea of human good, and the account of rights which has just been considered, it will follow that individual liberty must be a politically fundamental right. For self-development is one of 'the essentials of human well-being'. Thus Mill is led to the famous principle enunciated in *On Liberty*:

> the only purpose for which power can be rightfully exercised over any member of a civilized community, against his will, is to prevent harm to others. His own good, either physical or moral, is not a sufficient warrant. He cannot rightfully be compelled to do or forbear because it will be better for him to do so, because it will make him happier, because, in the opinion of others, to do so would be wise, or even right.

A society which respects this principle enables individuals to realize their potential in their own way. It liberates a mature diversity of interest and feeling, and it nurtures the moral freedom of reason and will. Throwing open the gates to talent, creativity and dynamism, it produces the social conditions of moral and intellectual progress. This Millian argument remains the strongest defence of any liberalism founded on teleological ethics. It is a resource upon which teleological liberals will always be able to draw, whether or not they accept Mill's hedonistic conception of the human good or his aggregative conception of the good of all.

However, it is also connected with Mill's ambivalence about democracy. Like many other nineteenth-century thinkers, liberal as well as conservative, Mill felt a deep strain of anxiety about democratic institutions and the democratic spirit (see DEMOCRACY §2). Certainly he applauded

the end of the *ancien régime* and sympathized with the moral aims of the French Revolution – liberty, equality, fraternity – but from that revolution he also learned, as had the continental liberals, to fear an enemy on the left, as well as an authoritarian enemy on the right. In its revolutionary form the enemy on the left threatened Jacobin terror, or the disasters which attend any attempt to achieve moral ideals by restarting history at year zero. Democracy's settled form, on the other hand, could be observed in the 'democratic republic' of America: a continuous and unremitting pressure towards conforming mediocrity.

The Romantic-Hellenic ideal of human life both inspired Mill's democratic ideals and fuelled his fears about realized democracy. It was an ideal he shared with left Hegelians like Marx, who experienced less difficulty in combining it with democratic egalitarianism. Mill too had a long-term vision in which the emancipation and education of the working class could bring free self-culture to all human beings. He was able to believe, on the basis of his associationist psychology, that all human beings have an equal potential to develop their higher faculties. This warded off the possibility that utilitarianism might recommend an extremely inegalitarian pursuit of higher forms of well-being as the equilibrium state of a fully developed human society.

Thus Mill remained more of a democrat than other liberals of the nineteenth century, such as de Tocqueville or Burckhardt, but like them he saw how moral and cultural excellence and freedom of spirit could be endangered by mass democracy. Like them, his attitude to the immediate prospect of democratic politics was decidedly mixed. What he wanted was a democratic society of freely developed human beings; he did not think it a proximate or certain prospect, and he thought that bad forms of democracy could themselves pose a threat to it by drifting into 'collective despotism' – a danger to which America had already succumbed.

His advice for warding off this threat was not less democracy but more liberty:

> If the American form of democracy overtakes us first, the majority will no more relax their despotism than a single despot would. But our only chance is to come forward as Liberals, carrying out the Democratic idea, not as Conservatives, resisting it.
>
> (*Later Letters*)

This was the importance of the essay on Liberty, and particularly of the defence of liberty of thought and discussion contained therein. Nor were freedom of speech and liberty of the individual the only instruments by which Mill hoped to steer away from bad forms of democracy towards good. Some of his recommendations – plural voting, a public ballot, a franchise restricted by educational qualification – may now seem misguided or even quaint. Others, including proportional representation of minorities and, not least, his life-long advocacy of equal rights for women, make him seem ahead of his time. At any rate, in political philosophy from Plato's *Republic* to the present day, Mill's discussion of democracy has few rivals – for its open-mindedness, its historical and psychological awareness, and its underlying ethical power.

See also: Causation; Consequentialism; Empiricism; Feminism §3; Freedom and liberty; Good, theories of the; Induction, epistemic issues in; Inductive inference; Liberalism; Utilitarianism

References and further reading

Mill, J.S. (1873) *Autobiography*, in *Collected Works of John Stuart Mill*, London: Routledge, vol. 1, 1–290, 1991. (And many other editions.)

Ryan, A. (1974) *J.S. Mill*, London: Routledge & Kegan Paul. (Useful survey, not just of Mill's philosophy but of his thought as a whole.)

Skorupski, J. (ed.) (1998) *The Cambridge Companion to Mill*, Cambridge: Cambridge University Press. (Articles covering various aspects of Mill's philosophy.)

JOHN SKORUPSKI

MĪMĀṂSĀ

The school of Mīmāṃsā or Pūrva Mīmāṃsā was one of the six systems of classical Hindu philosophy. It grew out of the Indian science of exegesis and was primarily concerned with defending the way of life defined by the ancient scripture of Hinduism, the Veda. Its most important exponents, Śabarasvāmin, Prabhākara and Kumārila, lived in the sixth and seventh centuries AD. It was realist and empiricist in orientation. Its central doctrine was that the Veda is the sole means of knowledge of *dharma* or righteousness, because it is eternal. All cognition, it held, is valid unless its cause is defective. The Veda being without any fallible author, human or divine, the cognitions to which it gives rise must be true. The Veda must be authorless because there is no recollection of an author or any other evidence of its having been composed; we only observe that it has been handed down from generation to generation. Mīmāṃsā thinkers also defended various metaphysical ideas implied by the Veda – in particular, the reality of the physical world and the immortality of the soul. However, they denied the existence of God as creator of the world and author of scripture. The eternality of the Veda implies the

eternality of language in general. Words and the letters that constitute them are eternal and ubiquitous; it is only their particular manifestations, caused by articulations of the vocal organs, that are restricted to certain times and places. The meanings of words, being universals, are eternal as well. Finally, the relation between word and meaning is also eternal. Every word has an inherent capacity to indicate its meaning. Words could not be expressive of certain meanings as a result of artificial conventions.

The basic orientation of Mīmāṃsā was pragmatic and anti-mystical. It believed that happiness and salvation result just from carrying out the prescriptions of the Veda, not from the practice of yoga or insight into the One. It criticized particularly sharply other scriptural traditions (Buddhism and Jainism) that claimed to have originated from omniscient preceptors.

JOHN A. TABER

MIMĒSIS

A crucial term in the literary theories of Plato and Aristotle, *mimēsis* describes the relation between the words of a literary work and the actions and events they recount. In Plato, the term usually means 'imitation' and suggests that poetry is derived from and inferior to reality; in Aristotle, it loses this pejorative connotation and tends to mean simply 'representation' and to indicate that the world presented in a poem is much like, but not identical with, our own.

See also: Aesthetics; Aristotle §29; Katharsis; Plato §14; Tragedy

GLENN W. MOST

MIND, BUNDLE THEORY OF

This theory owes its name to Hume, who described the self or person (which he assumed to be the mind) as 'nothing but a bundle or collection of different perceptions, which succeed each other with an inconceivable rapidity, and are in a perpetual flux and movement' (*A Treatise of Human Nature* I, IV, §VI). The theory begins by denying Descartes' *Second Meditation* view that experiences belong to an immaterial soul; its distinguishing feature is its attempt to account for the unity of a single mind by employing only relations among the experiences themselves rather than their attribution to an independently persisting subject. The usual objection to the bundle theory is that no relations adequate to the task can be found. But empirical work suggests that the task itself may be illusory.

Many bundle theorists follow Hume in taking their topic to be personal identity. But the theory can be disentangled from this additional burden.

See also: CONSCIOUSNESS; DUALISM; MODULARITY OF MIND; PERSONS; STRAWSON, P.F.

STEWART CANDLISH

MIND, COMPUTATIONAL THEORIES OF

The computational theory of mind (CTM) is the theory that the mind can be understood as a computer or, roughly, as the 'software program' of the brain. It is the most influential form of 'functionalism', according to which what distinguishes a mind is not what it is made of, nor a person's behavioural dispositions, but the way in which the brain is organized. CTM underlies some of the most important research in current cognitive science, for example, theories of artificial intelligence, perception, decision making and linguistics.

CTM involves a number of important ideas. (1) Computations can be defined over syntactically specifiable symbols (that is, symbols specified by rules governing their combination) possessing semantic properties (or 'meaning'). For example, addition can be captured by rules defined over decimal numerals (symbols) that *name* the numbers. (2) Computations can be analysed into 'algorithms', or simple step-by-step procedures, each of which could be carried out by a machine. (3) Computation can be generalized to include not only arithmetic, but deductive logic and other forms of reasoning, including induction, abduction and decision making. (4) Computations capture relatively autonomous levels of ordinary psychological explanation different from neurophysiology and descriptions of behaviour.

See also: ARTIFICIAL INTELLIGENCE; CHINESE ROOM ARGUMENT; VISION

NED BLOCK
GEORGES REY

MIND, IDENTITY THEORY OF

Introduction

We know that the brain is intimately connected with mental activity. Indeed, doctors now define death in terms of the cessation of the relevant brain activity. The identity theory of mind holds that the intimate connection is identity: the mind is the brain, or, more precisely, mental states are states of the brain. The theory goes directly against a long tradition according to which mental and material belong to quite distinct ontological categories – the mental being essentially conscious, the material essentially unconscious. This tradition has been bedevilled by the problem of how essentially immaterial states could be caused by the material world, as would happen when we see a tree, and how they could cause material states, as would happen when we decide to make an omelette.

A great merit of the identity theory is that it avoids this problem: interaction between mental and material becomes simply interaction between one subset of material states, namely certain states of a sophisticated central nervous system, and other material states. The theory also brings the mind within the scope of modern science. More and more phenomena are turning out to be explicable in the physical terms of modern science: phenomena once explained in terms of spells, possession by devils, Thor's thunderbolts, and so on, are now explained in more mundane, physical terms. If the identity theory is right, the same goes for the mind. Neuroscience will in time reveal the secrets of the mind in the same general way that the theory of electricity reveals the secrets of lightning. This possibility has received enormous support from advances in computing. We now have at least the glimmerings of an idea of how a purely material or physical system could do some of the things minds can do.

Nevertheless, there are many questions to be asked of the identity theory. How could states that *seem* so different turn out to be one and the same? Would neurophysiologists actually see my thoughts and feelings if they looked at my brain? When we report on our mental states what are we reporting on – our brains?

1 Origin of the identity theory
2 Early objections
3 Qualia
4 Functionalism and the identity theory

1 Origin of the identity theory

The identity theory of mind holds that each and every mental state is identical with some state in the brain. My desire for coffee, my feeling happy, and my believing that the dog is about to bite are all states of my brain. The view is not that mental states and brain states are correlated but that they are literally one and the same. Despite its name, the identity theory of mind is strictly speaking not a view about the mind as such, but about mental phenomena. However, most protagonists of the identity theory, and most contemporary philosophers of mind if it comes to that, hold some version of the view that the mind is a construction out of its states in somewhat the way that an army is a construction out of its soldiers.

The identity theory of mind arose out of dissatisfaction with dualism, and with behaviourism as an attempt to avoid dualism. According to dualism, mental states are quite distinct from any material states, including brain states (see DUALISM). The most famous challenge to dualism is to give a satisfactory account of the causal interactions between mental states and material states, and most especially to give a satisfactory account of causation from mental states to bodily occurrences. We believe that sometimes my desire for ice cream causes my arm to move in such a way that an ice cream is in my mouth, that my pangs of hunger cause me to tighten my belt, and so on. But how do states allegedly 'outside' the material world cause material goings on like arm movements? How do they do this in such a way as to avoid violating the various conservation laws in physics? And how do they do this in such a way as not to conflict with what the physical sciences, and especially neuroscience, tell us about how bodily movements are caused?

The last question is particularly pressing. The success of the physical sciences in explaining phenomena in their own, physical, terms has been striking. We now know that lightning is not caused by Thor's actions, that epilepsy is not caused by demonic possession, and that plants do not grow because they contain a vital essence but because their cells divide (see VITALISM). It is hard to believe that bodily behaviour is unique in resisting in-principle explanation in purely physical terms. The dualist can respond to this challenge by denying the common-sense view that mental states sometimes cause bodily behaviour, a position known as epiphenomenalism. This position holds that although physical states on occasion cause mental states, mental states themselves never cause anything, being mere epiphenomena of the brain states that, along with the appropriate material surroundings, are the true causes of the behaviour we associate with mental states. Apart from flying in the face of common sense, this position makes it hard to see why the mind evolved (see EPIPHENOMENALISM).

Behaviourism treats mental states in terms of behaviour and dispositions to behaviour. Its inspiration comes from facts such as these: that those creatures we credit with mental states are precisely those manifesting sophisticated behaviour and possessing sophisticated behavioural capacities; that psychology became a serious science when psychologists started to investigate the mind via the investigation of behavioural capacities; and that there are conceptual links between mental states and behaviour – it is, for instance, part of the concept of

an intention that having an intention goes along with behaving in a way that tends to fulfil it, and it is part of the concept of intelligence that the intelligent are better problem solvers than the unintelligent (see BEHAVIOURISM, ANALYTIC).

Behaviourists delight in pointing out that it is hard to see how dualists could explain the last two points. Why should investigation of an immaterial realm be especially aided by looking at behaviour? How could the way things are in some immaterial realm be *conceptually* linked to brute behavioural facts? However, for our purposes here the crucial point is that behaviourists, like dualists, have trouble over the causation of behaviour.

The common-sense position is that mental states are causally responsible for behaviour – the itch causes the scratching – and responsible for behavioural dispositions and capacities – people's intelligence is responsible for their capacity to solve hard problems. But then mental states are not the same as behaviour and behavioural dispositions and capacities, being rather their underlying causes. And so they are, says the identity theorist. Mental states are those brain states that all the scientific evidence points to as being causally responsible for the behaviour, and behavioural dispositions and capacities, distinctive of those creatures we credit with a mental life.

2 Early objections

Here are some of the many objections that greeted the identity theory when it became well known.

It was objected that the ancients knew about mental states while knowing next to nothing about the brain. How could this be if mental states are identical with brain states? However, as identity theorists observed, science has established many identities that were unknown to the ancients. They did not know that lightning is identical with an electrical discharge, temperature in gases is mean molecular kinetic energy, and water is H_2O. The identity of mental states with brain states is, identity theorists urged, of a piece with scientific identities in general. We learned, for example, that temperature is mean molecular kinetic energy by discovering that it is mean molecular kinetic energy that is responsible for the phenomena we associate with temperature. In the same general way, identity theorists claim, we have discovered that mental states are brain states by discovering that brain states are responsible for the behavioural phenomena that we associate with mental states, and we will discover which particular brain states are which particular mental states by discovering which particular brain states are responsible for the behavioural phenomena associated with those mental states.

Identity theorists also noted that water, lightning and temperature do not present themselves to us *as* H_2O, electrical discharge and mean molecular kinetic energy, respectively; so it cannot be an objection to their theory that mental states do not present themselves *as* brain states.

Many objected that the identity theory violates Leibniz's Law that if $x = y$, then x and y share all properties (see IDENTITY), on the ground that mental states and brain states differ in their properties. An after-image is, say, yellow and in front of my face, but my brain states are not yellow, and are inside my head; again, an itch is, say, in the middle of my back, but my brain is not in the middle of my back. They also pointed out that brain states are at a certain temperature but that it is surely absurd to hold that my belief that the Earth is not flat is at a certain temperature.

Identity theorists replied by arguing that our talk about mental states is, from a logical point of view, misleading. We talk as if mental states involved relations to mental objects. We say, for example, 'I have a headache', and this apparently has the same logical structure as 'I have a car': in both cases we seem to be asserting a relation between a person, me, and an object – a headache in one case, a car in the other. However, as identity theorists noted, cars are very different from headaches: cars can exist without their owners (if I die suddenly, my car will go on existing), but headaches cannot exist independently of being experienced (if I die, any headache of mine necessarily dies with me). Headaches, and mental states in general, are necessarily someone's. In consequence, they argued, we should think of headaches in the way we think of limps: limps are not things we have when we limp. When I say that I have a limp, I am simply saying that I limp; similarly, to say that I have a headache is to say that my head aches. Attributing properties to aches and limps is really attributing properties to ach*ings* and limp*ings*. To have a bad limp is to limp badly, and to have a winning smile is to smile winningly; likewise, to have a bad headache is to have a head that aches badly. Strictly speaking, there are no mental objects, and so, in particular, no after-images to be yellow and in front of faces, and no itches to be in backs; there are experiences of having after-images and of having one's back itching. These experiences are not yellow, not in front of us or in our backs, and so the fact that brain states are not yellow, not in front of us and not in our backs is no objection to the identity theorist's claim that these experiences are identical with brain states.

The discussion of belief followed a different course. There is an important distinction between my believing something, my state of belief, and what I believe. My believing that there is a tiger before me, is, most likely, caused by seeing a tiger and is a state of mine, whereas what I believe – that there is a tiger before me, the *proposition* believed, as it is often put (see PROPOSITIONAL ATTITUDES) – is not caused by my seeing the tiger and is not a state of mine. Again, there is my belief that the Earth is not flat, thought of as a state of mine that causes me, say, to reassure a traveller that they do not have to worry about falling off the edge, and there is the proposition that the Earth is not flat, which is *what* I accept. Now, the identity theory is not a view about the objects of belief, the propositions; it restricts itself to claiming that the state of believing is a state of the brain. And, identity theorists argued, although it would be absurd to hold that the objects of belief are at a certain temperature, it is not absurd to hold that the believings are.

Finally, some philosophers objected that the behaviour associated with having a mind, and in particular, that associated with intelligence, rationality and free action, displays a flexibility and sophistication incompatible with a purely material etiology. There are complex issues here, but we can note two serious problems for this objection. First, computers have enlarged our conception of the behavioural flexibility and sophistication compatible with a purely material etiology; and, second, it is hard to see how having an *immaterial* etiology would make any difference to the conceptual issues at stake (and, of course, quantum mechanics has broken the tie between having a material etiology and being determined).

3 Qualia

There was, however, one early objection to the identity theory that proved harder to dismiss. It concerns a perennial problem in the philosophy of mind: the nature of conscious experience and the sensuous side of psychology. But first, some stage setting.

The identity theory of mind is typically seen as part of the programme of giving a purely naturalistic or physicalistic view of the mind (see MATERIALISM IN THE PHILOSOPHY OF MIND). It is not a species of dual attribute theory of mind, according to which, although mental states are brain states they are brain states with special, non-physical properties, properties quite distinct from the kinds of properties neuro-science in particular, and the physical sciences in general, might attribute to them. The problem with dual attribute theories is that the question of how, in the light of what science is teaching us about the physical nature of the causation of behaviour, these non-physical properties could be causally relevant to behaviour seems just as pressing as the question, raised earlier, of how non-physical states could be causally relevant to behaviour. In consequence, most identity theorists see their theory as a purely naturalistic account of the mind: the denial of 'spooky' properties or attributes is as much part of the theory as the denial of 'spooky' entities or states.

The perennial objection is that the identity theory, when seen, as it should be, as part of a purely naturalistic view of the mind, leaves out the nature of conscious mental experience, the phenomenal side of psychology. We distinguish those mental states that are not associated with a characteristic 'feel' from those that are. Paradigmatic examples are belief, on the non-sensuous side, and bodily sensations and sensory perceptions, on the sensuous side. My belief that the world is round does not have a characteristic conscious feel available to introspective awareness; my itch and my sensing of a red sunset do. But, runs the objection, no amount of neurophysiological information about our brains tells us what it is like to itch, see a sunset, or smell a rose. Protagonists of this objection often use the term 'qualia' ('quale' is the singular) for the special properties that they insist that the identity theory leaves out of account. Typically, they hold that these qualia are epiphenomenal features. They avoid the implausibility of denying that pains and sensings of red *per se* are causally inefficacious but acknowledge that they have to allow that the *distinctive feel* of pains and sensings of red is causally irrelevant (see QUALIA).

4 Functionalism and the identity theory

When identity theorists first discussed the qualia objection they urged that when we itch, smell a rose, and quite generally when we are in a mental state, we are not introspectively aware of the intrinsic nature of the mental state. For they granted, as we noted earlier, that mental states do not present themselves to us as states of the brain. The identity theorists held that what happens when we introspect is that we are aware of highly relational properties of our mental states, properties like being like what goes on in me when a pin is stuck in me (in the case of pain), being like what goes on in me when I see blood and geranium petals (in the case of sensing red), and being of a kind apt for the production of scratching behaviour (in the case of itches). In bringing relational properties into the picture, the early identity theorists can be seen as precursors of functionalist theories of mind. For functionalism is a theory according to which what makes something the mental state it is is a highly relational feature of it, that feature known as its functional role.

According to functionalism, we can think of mental states as causal intermediaries between inputs and mental states as causal intermediaries between inputs from the environment, outputs in the form of behavioural responses, and other mental states. Pain, for instance, is an internal state that is typically caused by bodily damage, and typically causes the desire that it itself cease along with behavioural responses that tend to minimize the damage. The perception that there is coffee in front of me is an internal state typically caused by coffee in front of me, which in turn causes belief that there is coffee in front of me, and this belief, when combined with desire for coffee, typically causes movement towards the coffee. Mental states are, that is, specified in terms of their place in a huge network of interlocking states (of which we have just described a tiny fragment) (see FUNCTIONALISM). Our concern here is with the implications of this general approach for the identity theory.

Functionalism can be, and often is, regarded as entirely consonant with the identity theory, being indeed a good way of arguing for it; or functionalism can be, and often is, regarded as a major objection to the identity theory. It all depends on the kind of identity theory.

If mental states are defined by their place in a network, then the question of what some given mental state *is* comes down to the question of what state occupies the relevant place in the network. An analogy: money can be defined in terms of a characteristic functional role, a role we are all only too familiar with through our knowledge of what you can do if you have money, and cannot do if you do not have money. In consequence, the question of what money is is the question of what plays, or occupies, the money-functional role, be it paper notes, coins, cowrie shells, or whatever. But, identity theorists observe, by far the most plausible candidates for what play the functional roles associated with mental states are various states of the brain. Thus, functionalism gives us a simple argument for the identity theory of the following structure: pain = what plays the pain-role; what plays the pain-role = a state of the brain (say, C-fibres firing); therefore, pain = C-fibres firing. And likewise for all the mental states. Identity theorists who see the identity theory as a natural offshoot of functionalism, often refer to the identity theory as 'central state materialism'.

Approaching the identity theory through functionalism commits identity theorists to an anti-essentialist theory of mind. For the brain state that occupies the pain-role and so is, according to them, pain, might not have done so, and so might not have been pain. And the same goes for all mental states. Early expositions of the identity theory made this point by insisting that the identity of pain with, say, C-fibres firing was a *contingent* identity, and drew an analogy in this regard with the scientific identities we mentioned before. However, at least some of these identities are arguably necessarily true. It is arguable that water is necessarily H_2O. Certainly, we had to discover the identity of water and H_2O by empirical investigation, which makes it an a posteriori matter, but what we discovered was an essential feature of water. However, the identity theory must hold that the identities it posits are contingent. They are like the identity of the President of the United States in 1997 with Bill Clinton, which is contingent because that which occupies the role definitive of being President in 1997 is a contingent matter. (Dole was swimming against an economic tide, not a logical one.)

Although functionalism is a good way of arguing for the identity theory, it is a major objection to one kind of identity theory. We noted that identity theorists appeal to scientific identities in explaining and introducing their theory. These identities concern kinds or *types*. When scientists tell us that lightning is an electrical discharge, they are not merely telling us that the instance or *token* of lightning we saw last night is an instance or token of an electrical discharge; they are telling us, in addition, about what kind of happening lightning in general is. Again, the claim that temperature is mean molecular kinetic energy is a claim about kinds or types; it tells us what the property of temperature (in gases, anyway) is – namely, mean molecular kinetic energy. This suggests that we should think of the (mind-brain) identity theory as a type-type identity theory. Moreover, the theorists' favourite illustration – 'Pain = C-fibres firing' – is a type-type identity statement.

The problem is that different types of state might occupy the pain-role in different creatures. Perhaps it is C-fibres firing in humans but D-fibres firing in dolphins. But dolphins with their D-fibres firing would then be just as much in pain as we are when our C-fibres are firing. It is the role occupied, not the occupier, that matters for being in pain according to functionalism. And the point is independently plausible. We feel sorry for dolphins that exhibit all the signs of pain despite not knowing in any detail how intrinsically alike our and their brains are. But the identity theorist cannot allow both that pain = C-fibres firing, and that pain = D-fibres firing. That would, by the transitivity of identity, lead to the false contention that C-fibres firing = D-fibres firing.

Two responses are possible. Identity theorists can retreat to a token-token identity theory. Each and every token or instance of mental state M is some token brain state, but mental types are not brain types, being instead functional types. Alternatively, they can allow that the identities between mental types and brain types may need to be restricted.

Think again of the example of money. Although different types of things are money in different societies, we can make true identity claims about the types of things that are money in the different societies. For instance, money in our society = notes and coins produced by the mint, whereas money in early Polynesian society = cowrie shells (or whatever). Similarly, although temperature in gases = mean molecular kinetic energy, in substances of which the molecules do not move freely it is something else. In the same way, if indeed it is C-fibres in us but D-fibres in dolphins that play the pain-role, then identity theorists must restrict themselves to 'Pain in humans = C-fibres firing' and 'Pain in dolphins = D-fibres firing'. The question of what humans in pain and dolphins in pain have in common would remain, of course, for they would not *ex hypothesi* share the same kind of brain state. And the identity theorists' answer must be that what they would have in common would be that each has a state inside them playing the pain-role, although not the same state.

See also: REDUCTIONISM IN THE PHILOSOPHY OF MIND

References and further reading

Armstrong, D.M. (1991) *The Mind–Body Problem: An Opinionated Introduction*, Oxford: Westview Press. (Very clearly written text book by one of the most important defenders of the identity theory.)

Chalmers, David J. (ed.) (2002) *Philosophy of Mind: Classical and Contemporary Readings*, Oxford: Oxford University Press. (Large collection of important articles covering the philosophy of mind. Includes some important recent material.)

Rosenthal, D.M. (ed.) (1991) *The Nature of Mind*, London: Oxford University Press. (Large collection of important articles and extracts from books covering the philosophy of mind in general. Not as up to date as the Chalmers collection but contains an excellent bibliography.)

FRANK JACKSON

MIND, MATERIALISM IN THE PHILOSOPHY OF
See MATERIALISM IN THE PHILOSOPHY OF MIND

MIND, MODULARITY OF
See MODULARITY OF MIND

MIND, PHILOSOPHY OF

Introduction

'Philosophy of mind', and 'philosophy of psychology' are two terms for the same general area of philosophical inquiry: the nature of mental phenomena and their connection with behaviour and, in more recent discussions, the brain.

Much work in this area reflects a revolution in psychology that began mid-century. Before then, largely in reaction to traditional claims about the mind being non-physical (see DUALISM; DESCARTES), many thought that a scientific psychology should avoid talk of 'private' mental states. Investigation of such states had seemed to be based on unreliable introspection, not subject to independent checking (see PRIVATE LANGUAGE ARGUMENT), and to invite dubious ideas of telepathy. Consequently, psychologists like B.F. Skinner and J.B. Watson, and philosophers like W.V. QUINE and Gilbert RYLE argued that scientific psychology should confine itself to studying publicly observable relations between stimuli and responses.

However, in the late 1950s, several developments began to change all this: (1) The experiments behaviourists themselves ran on animals tended to refute behaviouristic hypotheses, suggesting that the behaviour of even rats had to be understood in terms of mental states. (2) The linguist Noam CHOMSKY drew attention to the surprising complexity of the natural languages that children effortlessly learn, and proposed ways of explaining this complexity in terms of largely unconscious mental phenomena. (3) The revolutionary work of ALAN TURING (see TURING MACHINES) led to the development of the modern digital computer. This seemed to offer the prospect of creating ARTIFICIAL INTELLIGENCE, and also of providing empirically testable models of intelligent processes in both humans and animals. (4) Philosophers came to appreciate the virtues of realism, as opposed to instrumentalism, about theoretical entities in general.

1 Functionalism and the computational theory of mind

These developments led to the emergence in the 1970s of the loose federation of disciplines called 'cognitive science', which brought together research from, for example, psychology, linguistics, computer science, neuroscience and a number of sub-areas of philosophy, such as logic, the philosophy of language, and action theory. In philosophy of mind, these developments led to FUNCTIONALISM,

according to which mental states are to be characterized in terms of relations they bear among themselves and to inputs and outputs, for example, mediating perception and action in the way that belief and desire characteristically seem to do. The traditional problem of OTHER MINDS then became an exercise in inferring from behaviour to the nature of internal causal intermediaries.

This focus on functional organization brought with it the possibility of multiple realizations: if all that is essential to mental states are the roles they play in a system, then, in principle, mental states, and so minds, could be composed of (or 'realized' by) different substances: some minds might be carbon-based like ours, some might be computer 'brains' in robots of the future, and some might be silicon-based, as in some science-fiction stories about 'Martians'. These differences might also cause the minds to be organized in different ways at different levels, an idea that has encouraged the co-existence of the many different disciplines of cognitive science, each studying the mind at often different levels of explanation.

Functionalism has played an important role in debates over the metaphysics of mind. Some see it as a way of avoiding DUALISM and arguing for a version of materialism known as the identity theory of mind (see MIND, IDENTITY THEORY OF). They argue that if mental states play distinctive functional roles, to identify mental states we simply need to find the states that play those roles, which are, almost certainly, various states of the brain. Here we must distinguish identifying mental state tokens with brain state tokens, from identifying mental types with brain types (see TYPE/TOKEN DISTINCTION). Many argue that multiple realizability shows it would be a mistake to identify any particular kind or type of mental phenomenon with a specific type of physical phenomenon (for example, depression with the depletion of norepinephrine in a certain area of the brain). For if depression is a multiply realized functional state, then it will not be identical with any particular type of physical phenomenon: different instances, or tokens, of depression might be identical with tokens of ever different types of physical phenomena (norepinephrine deletion in humans, too little silicon activation in a Martian). Indeed, a functionalist could allow (although few take this seriously) that there might be ghosts who realize the right functional organization in some special dualistic substance. However, some identity theorists insist that at least some mental state types – they often focus on states like pain and the taste of pineapple, states with QUALIA (see also the discussion later) – ought to be identified with particular brain state types, in somewhat the way that lightning is identified with electrical discharge, or water with H_2O. They typically think of these identifications as necessary a posteriori.

An important example of a functionalist theory, one that has come to dominate much research in cognitive science, is the computational theory of mind (see MIND, COMPUTATIONAL THEORIES OF), according to which mental states are either identified with, or closely linked to, the computational states of a computer. There have been three main versions of this theory, corresponding to three main proposals about the mind's Cognitive architecture. According to the 'classical' theory, particularly associated with Jerry FODOR, the computations take place over representations that possess the kind of logical, syntactic structure captured in standard logical form: representations in a so-called LANGUAGE OF THOUGHT, encoded in our brains. A second proposal, sometimes inspired by F.P. RAMSEY's view that beliefs are maps by which we steer (see BELIEF), emphasizes the possible role in reasoning of maps and mental imagery. A third, recently much-discussed proposal is CONNECTIONISM, which denies that there are any structured representations at all: the mind/brain consists rather of a vast network of nodes whose different and variable excitation levels explain intelligent learning. This approach has aroused interest especially among those wary of positing much 'hidden' mental structure not evident in ordinary behaviour (see Ludwig WITTGENSTEIN §3 and Daniel DENNETT).

The areas that lend themselves most naturally to a computational theory are those associated with logic, common sense and practical reasoning, and natural language syntax (see RATIONALITY, PRACTICAL; SYNTAX); and research on these topics in psychology and ARTIFICIAL INTELLIGENCE has become deeply intertwined with philosophy (see SEMANTICS; LANGUAGE, PHILOSOPHY OF).

A particularly fruitful application of computational theories has been to VISION. Early work in GESTALT PSYCHOLOGY uncovered a number of striking perceptual illusions that demonstrated ways in which the mind structures perceptual experience, and the pioneering work of the psychologist, David Marr, suggested that we might capture these structuring effects computationally. The idea that perception was highly cognitive, along with the functionalist picture that specifies a mental state by its place in a network, led many to holistic conceptions of mind and meaning, according to which parts of a person's thought and experience cannot be understood apart from the person's entire cognitive system (see HOLISM: MENTAL AND SEMANTIC; SEMANTICS, CONCEPTUAL ROLE).

However, this view has been challenged recently by work of Jerry FODOR. He has argued that perceptual systems are 'modules', whose processing is 'informationally encapsulated' and hence isolatable from the effects of the states of the central cognitive system (see MODULARITY OF MIND). He has also proposed accounts of meaning that treat it as a local (or 'atomistic') property to be understood in terms of certain kinds of causal dependence between states of the brain and the world. Others have argued further that perception, although contentful, is also importantly non-conceptual, as when one sees a square shape as a diamond but is unable to say wherein the essential difference between a square and a diamond shape consists (see CONTENT, NON-CONCEPTUAL; PERCEPTION).

2 Mind and meaning

As these last issues indicate, any theory of the mind must face the hard topic of meaning (see SEMANTICS). In the philosophies of mind and psychology, the issue is not primarily the meanings of expressions in natural language, but of how a state of the mind or brain can have meaning or content: what is it to believe, for example, that snow is white or hope that you will win. These latter states are examples of propositional attitudes: attitudes towards propositions such as that snow is white, or that you will win, that form the 'content' of the state of belief or hope. They raise the general issue of intentionality, or how a mental state can be about things (for example, snow) and properties (for example, white), and, particularly, 'about' things that do not exist or will not happen, as when someone believes in Santa Claus or hopes in vain for victory.

There have been three main proposals about mental content. A state might possess a specific content: (1) by virtue of the role it plays in reasoning (see SEMANTICS: CONCEPTUAL ROLE); (2) by virtue of certain causal and lawful relations the state bears to phenomena in the world (see FUNCTIONALISM); or (3) by virtue of the function it plays in the evolution and biology of the organism (see FUNCTIONAL EXPLANATION). Related to these proposals are traditional philosophical interests in CONCEPTS, although this latter topic raises complicating metaphysical concerns with UNIVERSALS, and epistemological concerns with A PRIORI knowledge.

Special problems are raised by indexical content, or the content of thoughts involving concepts expressed by, for example, 'I myself', 'here', 'now', 'this', and 'that' (see DEMONSTRATIVES AND INDEXICALS; PROPOSITIONAL ATTITUDES). Does the thought that it is hot here, had in Maryland, have the same content as the thought that it is hot here, had in Canberra? The conditions under which such thoughts are true obviously depends upon the external context – for example, the time and place – of the thinking.

This dependence on external context is thought by many to be a pervasive feature of content. Drawing on recent work on reference (see REFERENCE; PROPER NAMES), Hilary PUTNAM and Tyler Burge have argued that what people think, believe and so on depends not only on how they are, but also upon features of their physical and social environment. This raises the important question of whether an organism's psychology can be understood in isolation from the external world it inhabits. Defenders of methodological individualism insist that it can be (see METHODOLOGICAL INDIVIDUALISM); Putnam, Burge and their supporters that it can't. Some theorists respond to the debate by distinguishing between wide and narrow content: narrow content is what 'from the skin in' identical individuals would share across different environments, whereas wide content might vary from one environment to the next (see CONTENT: WIDE AND NARROW). These theorists then give distinctive roles to the two notions in theoretical psychology, although this is a matter of great controversy.

3 Alternatives to functionalism

Not everyone endorses functional and computational theories of mind. Some, influenced by RYLE and the later WITTGENSTEIN, think that such concern with literally inner processes of the brain betrays a fundamental misunderstanding of mental talk, which, they argue, rests largely on outward CRITERIA. Others think that computational processes lack the means of capturing the basic properties of CONSCIOUSNESS and INTENTIONALITY that are essential to most mental phenomena. JOHN SEARLE, in particular, regards his CHINESE ROOM ARGUMENT as a devastating objection to computational approaches. He thinks that mental phenomena should be understood not functionally, but directly in biological or physical terms.

The hardest challenge for functionalism is posed by QUALIA – the properties that distinguish pain, the look of red, the taste of pineapple, and so on, on the one hand, from mental states like belief and understanding on the other. (See also SENSE-DATA; PERCEPTION). Some argue that unnecessary problems are produced in this area by an excessive reification of inner experience, and recommend instead an adverbial theory of mental states. However, some problems persist, and can be made vivid by considering the possibility of 'inverted qualia'. It seems that two people might have colour experiences that are the complements of one another (red for green, yellow for blue, etc.), even though their behaviour and functional organization are identical. This issue is explored in COLOUR AND QUALIA and leads inevitably to the hard problems of CONSCIOUSNESS: What is it? What things have it? How do we tell? What causal role, if any, does it play the world?

There is also an issue for functionalists over MENTAL CAUSATION. A principal reason why DUALISM has few adherents today is the problem of explaining how non-physical or non-natural phenomena can causally affect a physical world. And although some dualists retreat to EPIPHENOMENALISM, the view that mental phenomena are caused by but do not themselves cause any physical phenomena, this is widely seen as implausible. However, functionalists also have a problem. Even though they can and do insist that functional states are realized physically, arguably the functional states *per se* do no causing; what does the causing would seem to be the underlying physical properties of the physical realization. So, although functionalists avoid giving causal roles to the 'non-natural', it seems they must allow that mental properties *per se* do no causing.

Although the view that the mind is a natural phenomenon is now widely accepted (principally because of the causal problem for dualism), what this implies is highly contentious. Some hold that it simply means that mental phenomena supervene on physical nature in the sense that there can be no mental difference without a physical difference. Donald DAVIDSON thinks this can be true without there being any strict laws connecting the physical and the mental (see ANOMALOUS MONISM). Others insist that a naturalist about the mind must reduce the mental to the physical in somewhat the way thermodynamics has been reduced to statistical mechanics, so delivering neat lawful biconditionals linking the mental and the physical (see REDUCTIONISM IN THE PHILOSOPHY OF MIND).

Much in this discussion turns on the status of FOLK PSYCHOLOGY, the theory of mind allegedly implicit in ordinary (folk) thought and talk about the mind. On one view, mental states are simply the states that fill the roles of this implicit theory, and the reduction consists in finding which internal physical states fill the roles and are, thereby, to be identified with the relevant mental states. However, defenders of ELIMINATIVISM, noting that any theory – especially a folk one – can turn out false, argue that we should take seriously the possibility that the mental states postulated by folk psychology do not exist, much as it turned out that there are no witches or phlogiston.

4 Issues in empirical psychology

Empirical psychology has figured in philosophy not only because its foundations have been discussed in the above ways, but also because some of its specific findings have been relevant to traditional philosophical claims. Thus, experiments on split brains have undermined traditional conceptions of personal identity (see also MIND, BUNDLE THEORY OF), and research on the reliability of people's self-attribution of psychological states has cast doubts on introspection as a source of specially privileged knowledge about the mind. The work of FREUD on psychopathology (see PSYCHOANALYSIS, POST-FREUDIAN; PSYCHOANALYSIS, METHODOLOGICAL ISSUES IN) and of CHOMSKY in linguistics, suggests that the states of most explanatory interest are not introspectively accessible (see KNOWLEDGE, TACIT; UNCONSCIOUS MENTAL STATES). Chomsky's ideas also seem to revive RATIONALISM's postulation of innate knowledge that was long thought to have been discredited by EMPIRICISM. And they have stimulated research beyond knowledge of grammar, into infant cognition generally (some of which treats the Molyneux problem of whether newly sighted people would be able to recognize shapes that they had previously only touched). Other questions about the basic categories in which people understand the world have benefited from work on how these categories are understood and evolve in childhood (see PIAGET, J.; MOLYNEUX PROBLEM). A particularly important issue for the philosophy of mind concerns the origin of our mental concepts, a topic of lively current research that affects our understanding of folk psychology.

5   Philosophy of action

Whether or not it is ultimately vindicated by empirical research, folk psychology is a rich fund of distinctions that are important in human life. The examination of them has tended to focus on issues in the explanation of ACTION, and, in a related vein, on psychological issues relevant to ethics (see MORAL PSYCHOLOGY).

The traditional view of action, most famously advocated by David HUME, is that an action needs both a desire and a belief. The desire provides the goal, and the belief the means of putatively achieving it (see also REASONS AND CAUSES; DESIRE; BELIEF). But what then is the role, if any, of INTENTION? Are intentions nothing more than some complex of belief and desire? And how, if at all, do we find a place in the Humean picture for the will? Is it something that can somehow act independently of beliefs and desires, or is it some kind of manifestation of them, some kind of 'all things considered' judgment that takes a person from dithering to action? (See WILL, THE.) Notoriously difficult questions in this regard concern whether there actually is anything as

FREE WILL, and how it is possible for a person to act against their better judgement, as they seem to do in cases of AKRASIA, or 'weakness of will'.

Beliefs and desires seem intimately connected with many other mental states. Belief about the past is of the essence of memory. Perception delivers belief about how things are around one, and dreaming seems to be the having of experiences during sleep akin to (rather fragmented) perceptions in the way they tend to make you believe that certain things are happening. Even emotions and bodily sensations seem to have belief and desire components (see EMOTIONS, NATURE OF): anger involves both a belief that one has been wronged and a desire to do something about it, and pain involves the belief that something is amiss and the desire that it stop. Much contemporary philosophy of mind and action is concerned with teasing out the relationship between beliefs and desires and various other mental states, although approaches in cognitive science often focus upon more computationally active states, such as: noticing, deciding, and 'on line' processes of reasoning.

See also: IMAGINATION; JUNG, C.G.; MATERIALISM IN THE PHILOSOPHY OF MIND; NEUTRAL MONISM; NOUS; PLEASURE

References and further reading

Braddon-Mitchell, D. and Jackson, F. (1997) *Philosophy of Mind and Cognition*, Oxford: Blackwell. (Discusses most of the live positions in the philosophy of mind; sympathetic to analytical functionalism.)

Guttenplan, S . (ed.) (1994) *A Companion to the Philosophy of Mind*, Oxford: Blackwell. (Collection of substantial essays by some the best-known figures in the philosophy of mind field.)

Rey, G. (1997) *Contemporary Philosophy of Mind*, Oxford: Blackwell. (Discusses most of the live positions in the philosophy of mind; sympathetic to the representational theory of mind.)

FRANK JACKSON
GEORGES REY

MINDS, OTHER
See OTHER MINDS

MIRACLES

Introduction

Does God at times miraculously intervene in earthly affairs? That is, do some events occur because God has entered our space-time continuum and directly modified or circumvented the relevant natural laws? Few philosophers today deny that this is possible. But many question whether we could ever justifiably maintain that such intervention has taken place.

According to some philosophers, it is not even necessary to grant that the types of events believers label miracles – for instance, healings or resurrections – actually occur as reported. Since the evidence supporting the occurrence of such events is the personal testimony of a few, possibly biased, individuals, while the basis for doubt is the massive amount of objective research upon which the relevant laws are based, it is always justifiable, according to this view, to conclude that such reports are erroneous. Others contend, however, that the presence of some forms of evidence – for instance, independent confirmation from reputable sources – could make it most reasonable in some cases to acknowledge that even the most unexpected of events had actually occurred.

Some philosophers also deny that we could ever justifiably conclude that an event could not have been produced by natural causes alone. Since we will never be in a position to identify all that nature can produce, they declare, it will always be most reasonable for the scientist facing a currently unexplainable counterinstance to a natural law to continue to look for a natural explanation. Many believers, however, are quite willing to grant that nature could in principle produce any event, since what they wish to maintain is only that nature does not do so in the case of miraculous interventions.

Finally, while many philosophers acknowledge that belief in direct divine intervention may at times be justifiable for those who already believe that God exists, some also argue that no single event or series of events could ever compel all thoughtful individuals to acknowledge the existence of a perfectly good supernatural causal agent, given all we experience – for instance, the tremendous amount of horrific evil in our world. Many believers, though, are also willing to grant this point.

1 Definition

The term 'miracle' is sometimes used in ordinary discussions to refer to the occurrence of any unexpected event – from the sudden discovery of a lost possession to the unanticipated passing of an exam. Within philosophical circles, however, 'miracle' is almost always discussed in its more restricted sense: as a designation for an unusual event that is the result of direct divine circumvention or modification of the natural order.

Philosophers, as well as religious believers, differ on the exact nature of the conceptual relationship between miraculous divine interventions and the natural order. For those who understand miracles to be violations of natural laws, a miracle is not simply an event that nature *did* not alone produce. It is an event that nature *could* not have produced on its own – an event that will always be incompatible with the relevant natural laws (see LAWS, NATURAL). For example, as proponents of the violation model understand it, to maintain that someone has miraculously been healed, it is not sufficient to maintain simply that God was directly involved. It is also necessary to maintain that the state of affairs in question could not have occurred naturally (that no totally natural explanation could be forthcoming).

Other philosophers, and many believers, however, deny that a miraculous divine intervention must be defined as an event for which no plausible natural explanation is, or could be, available. It is sufficient, they believe, to maintain that God was directly involved. For example, to maintain that someone's cancer has miraculously entered remission, it is not necessary to hold that nature alone could not have brought it about (to maintain that it could not have happened naturally). It is sufficient to maintain that nature alone did not do so in this case.

2 The possibility of miracles

Some philosophers have claimed that the concept of a miracle, if defined as a violation of a natural law, is incoherent. Natural laws, they point out, are really only generalized descriptions of what does in fact happen. That is, these laws summarize for us the actual course of events. Accordingly, to claim that an occurrence is a violation of a natural law is to claim that the event in question is a suspension of the actual course of events and this is, of course, impossible. Events may well occur, they acknowledge, that seem at present to be incompatible with how we believe things normally happen. But a true counterinstance to what we now believe to be a natural law only shows the law to be inadequate. Since natural laws, by definition, only summarize what actually occurs, we must always be willing in principle to expand our laws to accommodate any occurrence, no matter how unusual. We can never have both the exception and the rule.

Others, however, take this line of reasoning to be based on a confusion. To maintain that a natural law accurately describes the natural order, they point out, is to say only that it correctly identifies that which will occur under a specific set of natural conditions. But to maintain that an event is a miraculous counterinstance to a natural law is not to maintain that some event has occurred under the exact set of natural conditions covered by this law and nothing more. To say that water has miraculously turned into wine, for example, is not to say that water has turned into wine only under the exact set of natural conditions under which the relevant laws tell us this will not occur. It is to maintain that an additional non-natural causal factor, namely direct divine activity, was also present in this case. Accordingly, these philosophers contend, unless it is assumed that supernatural activity is impossible, it cannot be assumed that a miraculous counterinstance to a natural law – a counterinstance produced in part by divine circumvention or modification of the natural order – is conceptually impossible. That is, unless it is assumed that supernatural intervention is impossible, we can have both the exception and the rule.

Of course, many individuals do in fact deny the existence of any type of supernatural being. And even some who affirm the existence of such a being – for example, process theists (see PROCESS THEISM) – deny that this being can unilaterally intervene in earthly affairs in the sense necessary to produce miraculous events. However, few philosophers today maintain that the existence of a supernatural being, or the ability of such a being (if it exists) to intervene, can be demonstrated to be impossible. That is, while most philosophers agree that the existence of a supernatural being who intervenes in earthly affairs can justifiably be denied, most also agree that it is possible to maintain justifiably that such a being does exist. Consequently, few deny that miracles, even if defined as violations of natural laws, could occur. Since the time of David HUME (§6), however, philosophers have continued to debate vigorously a number of questions related to our ability to *identify* miraculous events.

3   The credibility of personal testimony

One such question is whether we need even acknowledge that alleged counterinstances to well-confirmed natural laws actually occur. Most philosophers agree that reports of repeatable counterinstances – counterinstances that can in principle be produced by anyone under a specified set of natural conditions – cannot justifiably be dismissed. But there are a number of philosophers who believe that if the events in question are nonrepeatable – if they cannot be reproduced under

specifiable natural conditions – the situation is quite different. It is clearly possible, they acknowledge, that nonrepeatable counterinstances to well-confirmed natural laws have occurred (or will occur). They acknowledge, for instance, that nonrepeatable counterinstances to our current laws describing the properties of water or human tissue may have occurred (or might occur). However, the evidence supporting the adequacy of laws of this type, they point out, is very strong. These laws not only can be, but are, tested and reconfirmed daily by people with no vested interest in the outcome.

On the other hand, they are quick to add, reports of presently nonrepeatable counterinstances to such laws – a claim, for instance, that water has turned into wine or that someone has been raised from the dead – will be supported at best only by the personal testimony of a few people who may well have a vested interest in the outcome. Consequently, as long as alleged counterinstances remain nonrepeatable, we can never possess better reasons for believing that the events in question have actually occurred as reported than for believing that they have not. And therefore, following the Humean maxim that the wise person proportions belief to the evidence, these philosophers conclude that it is always justifiable to deny the accuracy of such reports.

However, there are those (for instance, Swinburne) who believe that this conclusion is much too strong. They acknowledge that reports of seemingly nonrepeatable counterinstances to well-established laws must be approached with appropriate scepticism, since deception or misperception is always possible. But from their perspective it is unreasonable to assume that the evidence supporting even the most highly confirmed laws would *always* furnish a sufficient basis for dismissing reports of counterinstances to them.

First and foremost, they argue that to make this assumption fails to take into account the *prima facie* reliability of our visual belief-forming faculties. We all rely on these faculties daily and, in general, they serve us quite well. In fact, the general reliability of such faculties must be presupposed by those formulating our natural laws. Thus, in cases where we had no reason to doubt the reliability of these belief-forming faculties – for instance, if we were to observe a seeming counterinstance ourselves or if it were directly observed by a friend whose character and objectivity were beyond question – it is not clear, they maintain, that it would always be justifiable to decide in favour of the natural laws in question, even if they were very well established.

Moreover, these philosophers add, we might in some cases have compelling physical traces to consider. In the case of an alleged healing that runs counter to well-established laws, for instance, we might have more than personal testimony. We might have objective data – photographs or videotapes or X-rays or medical records – that would stand as strong evidence for the occurrence of the event in question, evidence so convincing that it would be unreasonable to reject it. Thus they conclude that decisions concerning the accuracy of reports of alleged counterinstances – even if the events in question are nonrepeatable – must be made on a case-by-case basis.

4 Miracles as events unexplainable by natural causes

Even if some occurrences can justifiably be labelled counterinstances to our current laws, could we ever be in a position to maintain justifiably that any such event is permanently unexplainable scientifically? That is, could we ever be in a position to maintain that an acknowledged counterinstance is a state of affairs that nature could never produce on its own?

In addressing this question, it is important to clarify a potential ambiguity that has been glossed over so far in this entry. By definition, no specific state of affairs produced even in part by direct supernatural activity (by direct circumvention or modification of the natural cause/effect patterns) could ever be given a totally natural explanation. Accordingly, if we were ever in a position to maintain justifiably that some event was actually a direct act of God, we would automatically be in a position to maintain justifiably that this specific occurrence was, itself, permanently unexplainable scientifically.

As currently understood by most philosophers, however, the primary purpose of natural science is not to determine what nature has in fact produced. The main objective of science, rather, is to determine what nature is capable of producing – what can occur under solely natural conditions. For instance, the primary purpose of natural science is not to determine whether natural factors alone actually did cause any specific person's cancer to enter remission. The primary purpose of science is to determine whether natural factors alone could have done so.

Hence, when philosophers ask whether we could ever be in a position to maintain justifiably that an event is permanently unexplainable scientifically, they are not asking whether we could ever be in a position to maintain justifiably that a specific state of affairs *was* not produced by nature alone. They are asking, rather, whether we could ever be in a position to maintain justifiably that a specific event *could* not have been produced by nature alone.

In considering this question, it should first be noted that no philosopher believes that we as

human beings are in a position to state with absolute certainty what nature could or could not produce on its own. All acknowledge that the scientific enterprise is continually discovering new, often startling and unexpected, information about the causal relationships that obtain in our universe. And all freely admit that the annals of science record numerous instances in which supposed counterinstances to natural laws were later demonstrated to be consistent with such laws or revisions of them.

However, as some philosophers (such as Swinburne) see it, some of our natural laws are so highly confirmed that any modification we might suggest to accommodate counterinstances would be clumsy and so *ad hoc* that it would upset the whole structure of science. For example, from their perspective, to attempt to modify our current laws relating to the properties of water to allow for the possibility that water could turn into wine naturally, or to attempt to modify our current laws relating to the properties of nonliving human tissue to allow for the possibility that a dead body could be resuscitated naturally, would make these laws of little practical value. Consequently, if we were in a position to maintain justifiably that a counterinstance to a law of this type had actually occurred, we would be required, for the sake of the scientific enterprise, to maintain that this event was permanently unexplainable by natural causes – that this event could never have been produced by nature on its own.

Critics consider this line of reasoning to contain a false dilemma. If faced with an acknowledged counterinstance to a natural law, even one that was very highly confirmed, we would not, they contend, be required at that moment either to modify the law to accommodate the occurrence or to affirm the adequacy of the law and declare the event permanently unexplainable by natural causes. Rather, since only naturally repeatable counterinstances falsify natural laws, the appropriate initial response to the occurrence of any seeming counterinstance to any law, no matter how highly confirmed, would be to acknowledge both the law and the counterinstance while further research was undertaken.

Moreover, these critics argue that such research could never make it most reasonable to conclude that something beyond the ability of nature to produce had actually occurred. If it were discovered that the seeming counterinstance was naturally repeatable – if it were found that the event in question could be produced with regularity under some set of purely natural conditions – a revision of the relevant laws would indeed be necessary. But then this event would no longer be naturally unexplainable. On the other hand, if natural repeatability could not be achieved, the appropriate response, they contend, would still not be to maintain that this occurrence was permanently unexplainable. Since nonrepeatable counterinstances do not present us with competing hypotheses to the relevant law(s), the appropriate response, rather, would be to label the counterinstance an anomaly while continuing to accept the functional adequacy of the law(s) in question.

Even if this line of reasoning is correct, however, nothing of significance follows for those who maintain only that a miracle is an event that would not have occurred at the exact time and in the exact manner it did if God had not somehow directly circumvented or modified the natural order in the specific case in question. Only those who believe that a miracle must be a violation of a natural law – who believe that a miracle must be an event that nature could not have produced – are affected.

5   Miracles as acts of God

Regardless of the perceived relationship between miracles and nature, however, questions concerning our ability (or inability) to identify events as direct acts of God remain important. For many philosophers, the most significant question of this sort continues to be whether there are imaginable conditions under which all rational individuals would be forced to acknowledge that God has directly intervened. And although most philosophers believe the answer to be no, some (for example, Larmer) believe an affirmative response is required. They acknowledge that with respect to many states of affairs which believers do in fact maintain have been brought about by God – for example, many alleged cases of divine healings – it is possible for a rational person to grant that the event has occurred as reported and yet justifiably deny that it was the result of direct divine intervention. But let us assume that someone who has been dead for twenty-four hours is raised from the dead when divine intervention is requested. Or let us assume that the missing fingers of a leper instantaneously reappear following a prayer for healing. In such cases, they argue, there would be very strong evidence supporting supernatural causation and no evidence supporting purely natural causation. In fact, the evidence would be so strong that to continue to hold out indefinitely for a totally natural explanation in such contexts would be unjustified in that this would simply demonstrate an unreasonable a priori naturalistic bias.

In response, critics do not deny that there might be conceivable cases which, if considered in isolation, would appear to make divine intervention a very plausible causal hypothesis. However, to acknowledge that God exists and has beneficially intervened in some specific case(s), they point out, is also to acknowledge that God's existence is compatible with all we experience – for example, that it is compatible with the tremendous amount of horrific human pain and suffering that appears to fall disproportionately on the innocent and disadvantaged. And even if it is possible to claim justifiably that God's existence is compatible with all we experience, it cannot be argued successfully that everyone must agree. Disbelief in God also remains a justifiable response (see EVIL, PROBLEM OF §6). Consequently, these critics conclude, the belief that there exists a solely natural cause for any specific occurrence always remains a justifiable option, regardless of the extent to which it may appear that divine intervention was involved.

For many philosophers, though, the crucial question is not whether there are imaginable conditions under which all rational individuals would be compelled to acknowledge divine intervention but rather whether there are conditions under which those who already believe in God would be justified in doing so. Even if it is true that the occurrence of no single event (or set of events) can justifiably compel belief in divine intervention, it is also true (so some philosophers contend) that the occurrence of no event (or set of events) – for instance, no amount of evil – can rule out justified belief in God's existence as a supernatural causal agent in our world. And given this fact, it is argued, as long as believers themselves possess good theistic reasons for assuming that God has directly intervened in a given case – for instance, because the occurrence appears clearly to fit an accepted pattern of divine action – they are justified in making this assumption.

It must be added, however, that even if this is correct, an important inverse relationship between miracles and evil remains. For instance, to respond to evil by claiming that God cannot both grant humans significant freedom and yet beneficially intervene on a consistent basis is, at the same time, to cite a reason why miracles should not be expected with frequency. And to respond to evil by claiming that 'God's ways are above our ways' places the believer in a less secure position to say when and where miraculous intervention has occurred.

See also: DEISM; OCCASIONALISM; RELIGION AND SCIENCE; REVELATION

References and further reading

Johnson, David (1999) *Hume, Holism, and Miracles,* Ithaca, NY: Cornell University Press. (An interesting challenge to the Humean case against the rational credibility of reports of miracles.)

Larmer, R.A.H. (ed.) (1996) *Questions of Miracle*, Kingston, Ont.: McGill-Queen's University Press. (Helpful discussions of both the relationship between miracles and laws of nature and the question of miracles as evidence for God's existence.)

Swinburne, Richard (ed.) (1989) *Miracles*, New York: Macmillan Publishing Company. (A balanced set of essays addressing what would count as evidence for miracles and whether it really matters whether they occur.)

DAVID BASINGER

MO TI/MO TZU

See MOHIST PHILOSOPHY; MOZI

MODAL LOGIC

Modal logic, narrowly conceived, is the study of principles of reasoning involving necessity and possibility. More broadly, it encompasses a number of structurally similar inferential systems. In this sense, deontic logic (which concerns obligation, permission and related notions) and epistemic logic (which concerns knowledge and related notions) are branches of modal logic. Still more broadly, modal logic is the study of the class of all possible formal systems of this nature.

It is customary to take the language of modal logic to be that obtained by adding one-place operators '$\Box$' for necessity and '$\Diamond$' for possibility to the language of classical propositional or predicate logic. Necessity and possibility are interdefinable in the presence of negation:

$$\Box A \leftrightarrow \neg\Diamond\neg A \text{ and}$$
$$\Diamond A \leftrightarrow \neg\Box\neg A$$

hold. A modal logic is a set of formulas of this language that contains these biconditionals and meets three additional conditions: it contains all instances of theorems of classical logic; it is closed under *modus ponens* (that is, if it contains A and $A \rightarrow B$ it also contains B); and it is closed under substitution (that is, if it contains A then it contains any substitution instance of A; any result of uniformly substituting formulas for sentence letters in A). To obtain a logic that adequately characterizes metaphysical necessity and possibility requires certain additional axiom and rule schemas:

$$K \quad \Box(A \rightarrow B) \rightarrow (\Box A \rightarrow \Box B)$$
$$T \quad \Box A \rightarrow A$$
$$5 \quad \Diamond A \rightarrow \Box\Diamond A$$

Necessitation $A/\Box A$.

By adding these and one of the $\Box$–$\Diamond$ biconditionals to a standard axiomatization of classical propositional logic one obtains an axiomatization of the most important modal logic, S5, so named because it is the logic generated by the fifth of the systems in Lewis and Langford's *Symbolic Logic* (1932). S5 can be characterized more directly by possible-worlds models. Each such model specifies a set of possible worlds and assigns truth-values to atomic sentences relative to these worlds. Truth-values of classical compounds at a world w depend in the usual way on truth-values of their components. $\Box A$ is true at w if A is true at all worlds of the model; $\Diamond A$, if A is true at some world of the model. S5 comprises the formulas true at all worlds in all such models. Many modal logics weaker than S5 can be characterized by models which specify, besides a set of possible worlds, a relation of 'accessibility' or relative possibility on this set. $\Box A$ is true at a world w if A is true at all worlds accessible from w, that is, at all worlds that would be possible if w were actual. Of the schemas listed above, only K is true in all these models, but each of the others is true when accessibility meets an appropriate constraint.

The addition of modal operators to predicate logic poses additional conceptual and mathematical difficulties. On one conception a model for quantified modal logic specifies, besides a set of worlds, the set D_w of individuals that exist in w, for each world w. For example, $\exists x \Box A$ is true at w if there is some element of D_w that satisfies A in every possible world. If A is satisfied only by existent individuals in any given world $\exists x \Box A$ thus implies that there are necessary individuals; individuals that exist in every accessible possible world. If A is satisfied by non-existents there can be models and assignments that satisfy A, but not $\exists x A$. Consequently, on this conception modal predicate logic is not an extension of its classical counterpart.

The modern development of modal logic has been criticized on several grounds, and some philosophers have expressed scepticism about the intelligibility of the notion of necessity that it is supposed to describe.

STEVEN T. KUHN

MODELS

Of the many kinds of things that serve as 'models', all function fundamentally as representations of what we wish to understand or to be or to do. Model aeroplanes and other scale models share selected structural properties with their originals, while differing in other properties, such as construction materials and size. Analogue models, which resemble their originals in some aspect of structure or internal relations, are important in the sciences, because they can facilitate inferences about complicated or obscure natural systems. A collection of billiard balls in random motion is an analogue model of an ideal gas; the interactions and motions of the billiard balls are taken to represent – to be analogous to – the interactions and motions of molecules in the gas.

In mathematical logic, a model is a structure – an arrangement of objects – which represents a theory expressed as a set of sentences. The various terms of the sentences of the theory are mapped onto objects and their relations in the structure; a model is a structure that makes all of the sentences in the theory true. This specialized notion of model has been adopted by philosophers of science; on a 'structuralist' or 'semantic' conception, scientific theories are understood as structures which are used to represent real systems in nature. Philosophical debates have arisen regarding the precise extent of the resemblances between scientific models and the natural systems they represent.

See also: Scientific method; Scientific realism and antirealism; Theories, scientific

ELISABETH A. LLOYD

MODI
See Mozi

MODULARITY OF MIND

A common view in recent philosophy of science is that there is no principled distinction between theoretical and observational claims, since perception itself is thoroughly contaminated by the beliefs and expectations of the observer. However, recent psychological and neurological evidence casts doubt on this latter claim and suggests, instead, that perceptual processing is to a significant extent 'cognitively impenetrable': it takes place in informationally encapsulated 'modules' that cannot be rationally influenced by beliefs or other 'central' cognitive states, or even other portions of the perceptual system.

See also: Perception; Vision

ZENON W. PYLYSHYN

MOHIST PHILOSOPHY

Mohist philosophy describes the broad-ranging philosophical tradition initiated by Mo Ti or Mozi (Master Mo) in the fifth century BC. Mozi was probably of quite humble origins, perhaps a member of the craft or artisan class. Early in life, he may have studied with followers of Confucius.

However, he went on to become the first serious critic of Confucianism.

Mozi's philosophy was part of an organized utopian movement whose members engaged in direct social action. He was a charismatic leader who inspired his followers to dedicate themselves to his unique view of social justice. This required them to lead austere and demanding lives, as he called upon them to participate in such activities as the military defence of states unjustly attacked.

Mozi is arguably the first true philosopher of China. He was the first to develop systematic analyses and criticisms of his opponents and present carefully argued positions of his own. This led him and his later followers to develop an interest in and study of the forms and methods of philosophical argumentation, which contributed significantly to the development of early Chinese philosophy.

Mozi saw ideological differences and the factionalism they spawned as the primary source of human suffering, and he hotly criticized the familially-based ethical and political system of Confucius for its inherent partiality. In its place he advocated three basic goods: the wealth, order and the population of the state. Against the Confucians, he argued for *jian'ai* (impartial care). *Jian'ai* is often translated as 'universal love', but this is misleading. Mozi saw the central ethical problem as an excess of partiality, not a lack of compassion; he was interested not in cultivating emotions or attitudes, but in shaping behaviour. He showed remarkably little interest in moral psychology and embraced an extremely thin picture of human nature, which led him away from the widely observed Chinese concern with self-cultivation. His general lack of appreciation for psychological goods and the need to control desires and shape dispositions and attitudes also led him to reject the characteristic Confucian concern with culture and ritual.

Mozi believed human beings possess an extremely plastic and malleable nature, and he advocated a strong form of voluntarism. For several different reasons, he believed that people could be induced to take up almost any form of behaviour. First, he shared a common early Chinese belief in a psychological tendency to respond in kind to the treatment one receives. He further believed that, in order to win the favour of their rulers, many people are inclined to act as their rulers desire. Those who do not respond to either of these influences can be motivated and controlled by a system of strict rewards and punishments, enforced by the state and guaranteed by the support of Heaven, ghosts and spirits. Most important of all, Mozi believed that rational arguments provide extremely strong if not compelling motivation to act: presented with a superior argument, thinking people act accordingly.

The social and political movements of the later Mohists lasted until the beginning of the Han Dynasty (206 BC). They continued Mozi's early interests and developed sophisticated systems of logical analysis, mathematics, optics, physics, defensive warfare technology and strategy and a formal ethic based upon calculations of benefit and harm. All the philosophical concerns of the later Mohists can be found in the early strata of the *Mozi*, and seem to reflect the teachings of the tradition's founder.

See also: CHINESE PHILOSOPHY; CONFUCIAN PHILOSOPHY, CHINESE; DAOIST PHILOSOPHY; MOZI

PHILIP J. IVANHOE

MOLINA, LUIS DE (1535–1600)

A leading figure in sixteenth-century Iberian scholasticism, Molina was one of the most controversial thinkers in the history of Catholic thought. In keeping with the strongly libertarian account of human free choice that marked the early Jesuit theologians, Molina held that God's causal influence on free human acts does not by its intrinsic nature uniquely determine what those acts will be or whether they will be good or evil. Because of this, Molina asserted against his Dominican rivals that God's comprehensive providential plan for the created world and infallible foreknowledge of future contingents do not derive just from the combination of his antecedent 'natural' knowledge of metaphysically necessary truths and his 'free' knowledge of the causal influence – both natural (general concurrence) and supernatural (grace) – by which he wills to cooperate with free human acts. Rather, in addition to God's natural knowledge, Molina posited a distinct kind of antecedent divine knowledge, dubbed 'middle knowledge', by which God knows pre-volitionally, that is, prior to any free decree of his own will regarding contingent beings, how any possible rational creature would in fact freely choose to act in any possible circumstances in which it had the power to act freely. And on this basis Molina proceeded to forge his controversial reconciliation of free choice with the Catholic doctrines of grace, divine foreknowledge, providence and predestination.

In addition to his work in dogmatic theology, Molina was also an accomplished moral and political philosopher who wrote extensive and empirically well-informed tracts on political authority, slavery, war and economics.

See also: FREEDOM, DIVINE; GASSENDI, P.; GOD, CONCEPTS OF; OMNISCIENCE; PREDESTINATION; RENAISSANCE PHILSOPHY; SUÁREZ, F.

ALFRED J. FREDDOSO

MOLYNEUX PROBLEM

The origin of what is known as the Molyneux problem lies in the following question posed by William Molyneux to John Locke: if a man born blind, and able to distinguish by touch between a cube and a globe, were made to see, could he now tell by sight which was the cube and which the globe, before he touched them? The problem raises fundamental issues in epistemology and the philosophy of mind, and was widely discussed after Locke included it in the second edition of his *Essay concerning Human Understanding*.

MENNO LIEVERS

MOMENTARINESS, BUDDHIST DOCTRINE OF

The object of the Buddhist doctrine of momentariness is not the nature of time, but existence within time. Rather than atomizing time into moments, it atomizes phenomena temporally by dissecting them into a succession of discrete momentary entities. Its fundamental proposition is that everything passes out of existence as soon as it has originated and in this sense is momentary. As an entity vanishes, it gives rise to a new entity of almost the same nature which originates immediately afterwards. Thus, there is an uninterrupted flow of causally connected momentary entities of nearly the same nature, the so-called continuum (*santāna*). These entities succeed each other so fast that the process cannot be discerned by ordinary perception. Because earlier and later entities within one continuum are almost exactly alike, we come to conceive of something as a temporally extended entity even though the fact that it is in truth nothing but a series of causally connected momentary entities. According to this doctrine, the world (including the sentient beings inhabiting it) is at every moment distinct from the world in the previous or next moment. It is, however, linked to the past and future by the law of causality in so far as a phenomenon usually engenders a phenomenon of its kind when it perishes, so that the world originating in the next moment reflects the world in the preceding moment.

At the root of Buddhism lies the (never questioned) conviction that everything that has originated is bound to perish and is therefore, with the exception of factors conducive to enlightenment, ultimately a source of frustration. There is no surviving textual material that documents how this law of impermanence came to be radicalized in terms of momentariness. It seems that by the fourth century the doctrine of momentariness had already assumed its final form. Characteristically, the debate became more and more dominated by epistemological questions, while the metaphysical aspect faded into the background.

See also: BUDDHIST PHILOSOPHY, INDIAN

ALEXANDER VON ROSPATT

MONISM

'Monism' is a very broad term, applicable to any doctrine which maintains either that there is ultimately only one thing, or only one kind of thing; it has also been used of the view that there is only one set of true beliefs. In these senses it is opposed to the equally broad term 'pluralism'. But it is also often contrasted with 'dualism', since so much philosophical debate has focused on the question whether there are two different kinds of thing, mind and matter, or only one.

See also: PLURALISM

EDWARD CRAIG

MONTAIGNE, MICHEL EYQUEM DE (1533–92)

Montaigne was a sixteenth-century French philosopher and essayist, who became known as the French Socrates. During the religious wars between the Catholics and the Protestants in France, he was a friend and adviser to leaders of both sides, including the Protestant leader Henri de Navarre, who converted to Catholicism and became King Henri IV. Montaigne counselled general toleration for all believers, a view promulgated by the new king in the Edict of Nantes (1598). His main literary work was in the form of *essais* (a word originally meaning 'attempts'), or discussions of various subjects. In these he developed various themes from the sceptical and Stoic literature of antiquity, and in his unique digressive way presented the first full statement in modern times of Pyrrhonian scepticism and cultural relativism. In particular, he presented and modernized the ancient sceptical arguments about the unreliability of information gained by the senses or by reason, about the inability of human beings to find a satisfactory criterion of knowledge, and about the relativity of moral opinions. His advocacy of complete scepticism and relativism was coupled with an appeal to accept religion on the basis of faith alone. His writings became extremely popular, and the English translation by John Florio, first published in 1603, was probably known to Shakespeare and Francis Bacon. Montaigne, whose essays provided the basic vocabulary for modern philosophy written in vernacular languages, was one of the most influential thinkers of the Renaissance,

and his works are regarded as classics of literature and philosophy.

See also: FAITH; HUMANISM, RENAISSANCE; POLITICAL PHILOSOPHY, HISTORY OF; PYRRHONISM; RENAISSANCE PHILOSOPHY; SEXTUS EMPIRICUS

RICHARD H. POPKIN

MONTESQUIEU, CHARLES LOUIS DE SECONDAT (1689–1755)

Montesquieu, one of the greatest figures of the Enlightenment, was famous in his own century both in France and in foreign lands, from Russia to the American colonies. Later generations of French *philosophes* took for granted his concern to reform the criminal laws, to replace the Inquisition with a reign of tolerance, and to repudiate the vicious conquests of the Spaniards in the Americas. They also accepted his finding that Protestant, commercial, and constitutionalist England and Holland represented all the best possibilities of Europe; whereas Catholic, economically backward, and politically absolutist Portugal and Spain represented the worst of the Western world and constituted a warning to the French.

Although the findings and specific reforms proposed by Montesquieu were repeated by many another figure of the French Enlightenment, his work in certain respects remained unique in the circles of the most advanced thinkers. In his efforts to think systematically about politics and to do so by employing the comparative method, he stands virtually alone in his age. Other thinkers sharing his commitments resorted to the universalizing language of natural rights when they ventured into the realm of political philosophy. Or, like Voltaire, they tied their thoughts about politics to a succession of specific issues, each essay bearing so indelibly the imprint of specific time and place that there was no room for theory in their writings. Finally, as is true of Diderot or D'Alembert, many of the *philosophes* were slow to recognize what Montesquieu knew from the outset, that if Enlightenment does not extend to politics it is futile.

Steeped in Montaigne's scepticism, Montesquieu found that in the absence of absolutes there were good reasons to appreciate the 'more than/less than' and 'better than/worse than' judgments of comparative analysis. In his notebooks he commented that the flaw of most philosophers had been to ignore that the terms beautiful, good, noble, grand, and perfect are 'relative to the beings who use them'. Only one absolute existed for Montesquieu and that was the evil of despotism, which must be avoided at all costs.

Montesquieu wrote three great works, each teaching lessons about despotism and freedom, *The Persian Letters* (1721), the *Considerations of the Grandeur of the Romans and the Cause of Their Decline* (1734), and *The Spirit of the Laws* (1748).
See also: HISTORY, PHILOSOPHY OF

MARK HULLIUNG

MOORE, GEORGE EDWARD (1873–1958)

G.E. Moore was one of the most influential British philosophers of the twentieth century. His early writings are renowned for his rejection of idealist metaphysics and his insistence upon the irreducibility of ethical values, and his later work is equally famous for his defence of common sense and his conception of philosophical analysis. He spent most of his career in Cambridge, where he was a friend and colleague of Russell, Ramsey and Wittgenstein.

The best-known thesis of Moore's early treatise on ethics, *Principia Ethica* (1903), is that there is a fallacy – the 'naturalistic fallacy' – in almost all previous ethical theories. The fallacy is supposed to arise from any attempt to provide a definition of ethical values. The validity of Moore's arguments is much disputed, but many philosophers still hold that Moore was right to reject the possibility of a reductive definition of ethical values. The book is also renowned for Moore's affirmation of the pre-eminence of the values of Art and Love.

Moore's later writings concern the nature of the external world and the extent of our knowledge of it. In opposition to idealist doubts about its reality and sceptical doubts concerning our knowledge of it, Moore defends 'common sense' by emphasizing the depth of our commitment to our familiar beliefs and criticizing the arguments of those who question them. But although he insists upon the truth of our familiar beliefs, he is remarkably open-minded concerning their 'analysis', which is intended to clarify the facts in which their truth consists.
See also: ANALYTICAL PHILOSOPHY

THOMAS BALDWIN

MORAL AGENTS

Moral agents are those agents expected to meet the demands of morality. Not all agents are moral agents. Young children and animals, being capable of performing actions, may be agents in the way that stones, plants and cars are not. But though they are agents they are not automatically considered moral agents. For a moral agent must also be capable of conforming to at least some of the demands of morality.

This requirement can be interpreted in different ways. On the weakest interpretation it will suffice if the agent has the capacity to conform to some of the external requirements of morality. So if certain agents can obey moral laws such as 'Murder is wrong' or 'Stealing is wrong', then they are moral agents, even if they respond only to prudential reasons such as fear of punishment and even if they are incapable of acting for the sake of moral considerations. According to the strong version, the Kantian version, it is also essential that the agents should have the capacity to rise above their feelings and passions and act for the sake of the moral law. There is also a position in between which claims that it will suffice if the agent can perform the relevant act out of altruistic impulses. Other suggested conditions of moral agency are that agents should have: an enduring self with free will and an inner life; understanding of the relevant facts as well as moral understanding; and moral sentiments, such as capacity for remorse and concern for others.

Philosophers often disagree about which of these and other conditions are vital; the term moral agency is used with different degrees of stringency depending upon what one regards as its qualifying conditions. The Kantian sense is the most stringent. Since there are different senses of moral agency, answers to questions like 'Are collectives moral agents?' depend upon which sense is being used. From the Kantian standpoint, agents such as psychopaths, rational egoists, collectives and robots are at best only quasi-moral, for they do not fulfil some of the essential conditions of moral agency.
See also: ACTION; KANTIAN ETHICS; MORAL JUSTIFICATION; MORAL MOTIVATION

VINIT HAKSAR

MORAL JUDGMENT

Introduction

The term 'moral judgment' can refer to four distinguishable things. First, the activity of thinking about whether a given object of moral assessment (be it an action, person, institution or state of affairs) has a particular moral attribute, either general (such as rightness or badness) or specific (insensitivity, integrity). Second, the state that can result from this activity: the state of judging that the object has the attribute. Third, the content of that state: what is judged by us, rather than our judging it. And fourth, the term can be read as commendatory, referring to a moral virtue that we might also call 'moral discernment' or 'moral wisdom'. There are three principal questions regarding moral judgment. The first asks what kind of state the state of moral judgment is, and in particular whether this state is to be characterized, either wholly or in part, as a state of belief. The second is concerned with the activity of moral judgment, investigating especially the role within this activity that is played by the application of rules. The third examines the conditions under which a person is justified in making a moral judgment with a given content.

> 1 Cognitivism versus noncognitivism
> 2 Moral rules and deliberation
> 3 Moral rules and justification
> 4 The virtue of moral judgment and moral epistemology

1 Cognitivism versus noncognitivism

When I think that something has a certain moral attribute (that an action is wrong, say), the state I am in seems to have features both of cognitive (belief-based) and noncognitive states. First, my moral attributions aspire to objective truth – to being true independently of my attitude towards them. For my moral attitudes can take the form 'This action is wrong, and would have been wrong even if I had approved of it', committing me to moral facts of the matter that I can be right or wrong about (see MORAL REALISM). And a state that aims to be true to independently obtaining facts must be thought of as a belief, it seems (see BELIEF). However, attributing a moral or any other evaluative feature to something seems to go beyond being in a merely cognitive state: it seems to involve orienting myself towards or away from the object of the attribution. In particular, it is often maintained that there is a certain sort of 'internal connection' between the state of moral judgment and the judge's motivation: it is part of the concept of judging something to be wrong that if I judge that it is wrong to perform this action in these circumstances, then (provided I am not weak-willed, and other things equal) I am motivated to avoid it in these circumstances (see MORAL MOTIVATION §§1–2).

Thus cognitivism about the state of moral judgment – the view that it consists essentially in a belief – seems to be supported by its objectivity-presupposing character, while noncognitivism (the denial of cognitivism) seems to be supported by the internal connection to motivation. The problem is not simply resolved by characterizing moral judgment as a compound state, comprising both a belief and a noncognitive companion state. For this would seem to require as an isolable component a pure belief that the action is wrong, and the possibility of such a belief is precisely what is at issue.

Beyond this, four main options present themselves. Each side of the dispute can either deny the claim being adduced in support of the other, or accept the claim while denying the relationship of support. Thus, first, a cognitivist might deny the internal connection, insisting that to the (unsurprisingly widespread) extent that moral judges tend to care about morality, this is only contingently true. A second, less plausible view is a noncognitivism that simply denies that moral judgments presuppose objectivity. Perhaps, as emotivism suggests, objectivity-presupposing moral judgments ought to be rejected and replaced with something else (see EMOTIVISM); it seems hard to deny that moral judgment as it actually exists does have this objectivity-presupposing character. This leaves two possibilities, each of which attempts to allow for both the objectivity-presupposing nature of moral judgment and its internal connection to motivation. According to the cognitivist internalism of John McDowell (1979), moral judgments are indeed beliefs, but beliefs of a special kind, in being internally connected to the believer's motivational states. And according to the noncognitivist objectivism of Simon Blackburn (1984), the objectivity-presupposing character of moral judgments can be explained without construing them as beliefs. The central thought here is that the attitude expressed by 'This action is wrong, and would have been wrong even if I had approved of it' can be explained as a noncognitive attitude that ranges across counterfactual as well as actual possibilities – as an attitude of approval of the action not only in the world as it is, but in the world as it would have been if I had happened to approve of the action but the world were otherwise unchanged.

It remains unclear, however, whether noncognitivism can supply a satisfactory treatment of the full range of semantic features of moral judgment-contents, and in particular, of unendorsed occurrences of moral terms, such as the first occurrence of 'wrong' in 'If blasphemy is very seriously wrong, then it is wrong to associate with blasphemers'. If not, we should be cognitivists about our actual states of moral judgment. Whether sense can be made of the objective moral facts seemingly presupposed by moral judgment is a further question – the question of moral realism (see MORAL REALISM).

2 Moral rules and deliberation

What is the role of rule-application in good deliberation about the moral attributes of things?

A widespread view is this: good moral thinking identifies correct moral principles under which the moral judge then subsumes particular instances to produce a moral verdict about them (see UNIVERSALISM IN ETHICS).

On this view, though, not much actual moral deliberation can qualify as good. Few moral judges are equipped with an exhaustive set of exceptionless moral principles by reference to which all their moral judgments are made. Most of the time, when we deliberate about whether a case instantiates a moral concept, we are engaged in an activity of moral discernment or judgment that is not simply a matter of applying a fully determinative, independently articulable rule to the case. Moreover, there seem to be good reasons not to conceive of moral deliberation as consisting ideally in the application of an exhaustive set of exceptionless moral rules. This view confronts a dilemma. Either our set of principles would be small and readily comprehensible – perhaps consisting of a single member, as in direct utilitarianism (see UTILITARIANISM) – but would need to be framed in such general terms as to make their application to even the simplest cases a difficult matter to determine; or they would be framed in terms specific enough to make the assessment of their application to particular circumstances straightforward, but would thereby need to be so numerous and highly qualified as to be unusable.

This does not yet show that good deliberation cannot consist solely in the application of rules, however. On R.M. Hare's consequentialist view, the response to this problem should be to equip ourselves with a set of familiar moral rules of thumb (for instance, 'Promise-breaking is wrong, other things being equal'), together with a meta-rule that in cases where these rules conflict we should apply a fundamental principle of direct consequentialism (see CONSEQUENTIALISM). Alternatively, Barbara Herman's Kantian theory (1985) tells us to equip ourselves with an equally familiar set of rules of moral salience – rules identifying certain features of the maxims on which actions are performed as those showing that the actions bear the burden of moral justification – together with a meta-rule that, when an action has a morally salient feature, its permissibility is to be judged in terms of the fundamental categorical imperative principle (see KANTIAN ETHICS).

3   Moral rules and justification

The views just described allow that it is proper for much of our deliberation to proceed by appealing to merely *prima facie* rules – rules specifying defeasible reasons (reasons capable of being outweighed) for making a moral attribution – but they supplement them with more fundamental, fully determinative rules governing judgment in cases where the *prima facie* rules conflict. But why should we seek rules of the fully determinative kind? The natural answer is this: good moral deliberation issues in judgments that are justified; if an all-things-considered judgment I make, in a case where my *prima facie* rules conflict, is to be justified, it cannot be arbitrary; and a judgment of mine can only be non-arbitrary if it instantiates a fully determinative rule.

When it is said that judgments are only justified by the existence of rules, two things might be intended:

(a) What makes it right to apply this concept to this object is a rule for doing so.
(b) What warrants me in judging that this concept applies to this object is a rule for doing so.

Claim (a), we might say, concerns the 'constitutive justification' of a judgment-content, whereas (b) concerns the epistemic justification of a state of judging (see JUSTIFICATION, EPISTEMIC).

Claim (a) pictures constitutive justification as consisting in the subsuming of instances under rules. This picture has been attacked, on the ground that it betrays a fallacy about rule-following (see WITTGENSTEIN, L.J.J. §10; MEANING AND RULE-FOLLOWING). Our ability to discern whether a given case falls under a rule cannot consist in our grasp of an independent meta-rule, on pain of regress. This applies to the rule 'Identify instances falling under concept *c*' as much as to any other. Proceeding correctly in the application of a concept cannot require sensitivity to an independently articulable rule which one's practice of applying the concept follows. If so, then this leaves open the possibility that there are no such further rules that justify our practice of moral concept-application. The onus is on a proponent of such rules to produce compelling examples that do square with our practice; the criticism is that they have failed to do so.

According to opponents of (a), then, there is no obstacle to the claim of 'moral pluralists' that the only defensible moral rules are *prima facie* ones. A further claim is that there are not even rules of this limited kind. This is held by moral 'particularists', who claim that there are no properties that always count as reasons for the same moral attribution. Often, the fact that an action of mine will harm someone is a reason for the wrongness of the action; but sometimes (for instance, if I am rightly administering a just punishment), it will count morally as a reason for its rightness. If so, we need to exercise a form of moral judgment that goes beyond the application of rules not only in order to determine how moral reasons relate to each other, but to determine when a consideration counts as a moral reason (see VIRTUE ETHICS §6)

4 The virtue of moral judgment and moral epistemology

If claim (a), with its subsumptive picture of constitutive moral justification, ought to be rejected, then so should (b), concerning epistemic justification. If there need be no independently articulable rule for a correct moral attribution, then there need be no such rule for my being warranted in judging that the attribution is correct. This still leaves it open to claim a relation of mutual epistemic support between my judgments concerning *prima facie* moral principles and my judgments concerning the existence of moral reasons on particular occasions, given a coherence conception of epistemic justification (see KNOWLEDGE AND JUSTIFICATION, COHERENCE THEORY OF). However, concerning the justification of my judging that, all things considered, a particular object has a given moral attribute, it seems that we must say simply that this is justified provided it is the attribution that would be made by a person with the virtue of moral judgment or discernment.

How can one ever be warranted in believing this? If the correctness of a moral judgment depends on its endorsement by an agent with a virtue the conditions for the possession of which are not independently specifiable, then it seems that any claims to epistemic justification will amount to dubious claims of self-evidence (see INTUITIONISM IN ETHICS). To progress beyond this, we should need to be able to cite the convergence in judgment of those whom we have independent reason to identify as good moral judges.

See also: EPISTEMOLOGY AND ETHICS; MORAL JUSTIFICATION; MORAL KNOWLEDGE; OBJECTIVITY

References and further reading

Blackburn, Simon (1984) 'Evaluations, Projections, and Quasi-Realism', ch. 6 of *Spreading the Word*, Oxford: Clarendon, 181–223. (A prominent defence of non-cognitivism against the objection that it cannot accommodate the objectivity-presupposing character of moral judgment.)

Herman, Barbara (1993) *The Practice of Moral Judgment*, Cambridge, MA: Harvard University Press. (A Kantian account of the role of rules in moral judgment.)

McDowell, John (1979) 'Virtue and Reason', *The Monist* 63: 331–350. (A defence of cognitivism and the need for the virtue of moral judgment for the possession of moral knowledge.)

GARRETT CULLITY

Introduction

Questions of justification arise in moral philosophy in at least three ways. The first concerns the way in which particular moral claims, such as claims about right and wrong, can be shown to be correct. Virtually every moral theory offers its own account of moral justification in this sense, and these accounts naturally differ from each other. A second question is about the justification of morality as a whole – about how to answer the question, 'Why be moral?' Philosophers have disagreed about this, and about whether an answer is even possible. Finally, some philosophers have claimed that justification of our actions to others is a central aim of moral thinking. They maintain that this aim provides answers to the other two questions of justification by explaining the reasons we have to be moral and the particular form that justification takes within moral argument.

1 Three questions of justification
2 Justification within morality
3 Justification of morality
4 Justification as an aim of morality

1 Three questions of justification

Questions of justification arise in moral philosophy in at least three different ways. First, it is generally taken as a central task of moral philosophy to clarify the structure of first-order moral thinking. A theory should, for example, explain 'what makes acts right'(see MORALITY AND ETHICS). Is the status of an action as morally right or wrong determined by its actual or expected consequences, by its conformity to certain rules or standards, or in some other way (see CONSEQUENTIALISM; DEONTOLOGICAL ETHICS)? Any theory that answers these questions provides us with an account of moral justification, that is to say, of justification *within* morality.

A second task of moral philosophy is to explain why we should care about morality and give its requirements priority over other considerations. This can be seen as a matter of providing a justification of morality.

Third, some philosophers have argued that it is a central aim of morality (or of some part of it, such as principles of justice) to provide a basis for justifying our actions or our institutions to one another, and that this aim provides a basis for understanding the importance of morality and for determining its content. According to these writers, justification is an aim of morality.

2   Justification within morality

Every moral theory offers its own account of moral justification. There is, however, a more general methodological question that transcends particular accounts of 'what makes acts right', namely the question of how the claim of any such account to be the correct account of moral justification can itself be justified.

One answer to this general methodological question has been formulated by RAWLS as the method of 'reflective equilibrium'. According to this method, one begins by identifying one's 'considered moral judgments', those judgments in which one has the highest degree of initial confidence. These may be judgments of any degree of abstraction: judgments about the rightness or wrongness of particular actions, about the correctness of general moral principles, or about the moral relevance of various considerations. One then tries to find the set of principles (the account of the particular area of morality in question) that best fits with these judgments. This fit will almost certainly be imperfect, so one then proceeds to consider whether and how to modify the principles one has formulated to yield a better fit with one's considered judgments, and whether and how to modify these judgments in the light of the principles at which one has arrived. This process of revision leads to a new set of principles, and hence to a new stage of adjustments of principles and judgments. The process continues until 'equilibrium' between principles and judgments is reached; the principles one has formulated at that stage are to be taken as justified as an account of the area of morality in question.

This account of how moral principles are to be justified has been attacked, chiefly on the ground that it gives too much authority to the considered judgments with which the process begins. This is sometimes put in the form of a charge that it is circular to base an argument for a particular form of moral justification on some of the very beliefs that are to be justified. It is also objected that two people, using this same method, might arrive at quite different principles, because they began with a high degree of confidence in different sets of judgments. In reply, it can be said that the charge of circularity is misplaced, since the aim of the process is not to supply a needed justification for every moral belief we have, but rather to come up with the best general account of the subject matter. How else could we arrive at justified conclusions about a subject except by relying, at the outset, on

those beliefs about that subject that seem to us most likely to be true? Moreover, in the search for reflective equilibrium no particular judgment is assumed, irrevocably, to be correct. Any reasons we might have for mistrusting particular beliefs are taken account of in the process as described, either as possible reasons for denying them the status of considered judgments to begin with or as reasons for abandoning them later when their incompatibility with the best account of our other beliefs comes to light.

3   Justification of morality

Turning now to the question of justifying morality itself, circularity looms when the bases of a proposed justification seem themselves to be moral in character. One cannot answer the question 'Why care about right and wrong?' by saying that it would be morally deficient not to. There is a dilemma here, however, since a justification for morality that appeals ultimately to values that are clearly not moral (such as those of self-interest) does not seem to give the right kind of explanation of morality's importance. It does not seem that virtuous people care about what is morally right because doing so is conducive to their self-interest.

Prichard concluded from this dilemma that moral philosophy, or at least that part of it that seeks to provide a justification of morality, 'rests on a mistake'. A less pessimistic conclusion would be that an adequate justification, or explanation, of the authority of moral requirements must appeal ultimately to considerations which are evidently relevant to morality yet have a significance which is not wholly dependent on it. The appeal of utilitarianism for some people, and the conviction of others that morality must have a basis in religion, can be explained in part by the fact that the ideas of the greatest happiness of the greatest number and of divine will appear, to members of these groups, to be the only plausible solutions to this problem. That is to say, these reasons have seemed to represent values both relevant to morality and able to supply it with the proper authority, but not (so it is claimed) dependent on it. One question is whether there are other kinds of reasons that have this status.

The task of finding such reasons is made more difficult by morality's claim to unconditional authority, and to priority over all other values. A justification for such authority seems to require starting points that are peculiarly inescapable, and it may seem that reasons grounded in what is merely one value among others could not meet this test. Accordingly, many have attempted to justify morality by showing that it is entailed, or presupposed, by something to which everyone is committed. So, for example, KANT argued that we must take ourselves to be bound by morality in so far as we regard ourselves as rational agents, and HABERMAS has maintained that moral requirements are entailed by the idea of communication with others.

4 Justification as an aim of morality

Moral and political theories that may be broadly classed as 'contractualist' emphasize justification as an aim of morality (see CONTRACTARIANISM). They argue, for example, that our thinking about right and wrong is guided by the idea of what could be justified to others on the grounds they could not reasonably reject, or that principles of justice are to be defended on the ground of their suitability to serve as public standards for the assessment of claims against the basic institutions of a society.

These ideas are related to questions of justification of the two kinds already discussed. First, it can be claimed that the aim of justifiability to others determines the content of justification within morality. Rawls, for example, concludes that principles of justice and the basic institutions of a society must be justifiable on a basis that is independent of controversial worldviews and conceptions of the good life. Second, it can be argued that the value of being able to justify one's actions to others has the right combination of connection with morality and independence of it to serve as an explanation of the significance that morality has for us. These claims are, however, controversial. Against them it can be maintained that the idea of justifiability to others lacks sufficient importance to account for the authority of morality and that some deeper standard of right and wrong must be presupposed as a standard of justifiability.

See also: FALLIBILISM; MORAL JUDGMENT; MORAL MOTIVATION §§4–7; MORAL SCEPTICISM

References and further reading

Brink, D. (1989) *Moral Realism and the Foundations of Ethics*, Cambridge: Cambridge University Press. (Critical discussion of issues concerning moral justification, defending a method like that of reflective equilibrium; see esp. ch. 5.)

T.M. SCANLON

MORAL KNOWLEDGE

One possesses moral knowledge when, but only when, one's moral opinions are true and held justifiably. Whether anyone actually has moral knowledge is open to serious doubt, both because moral opinions are so hard to justify and because there is reason to think moral opinions are expressions not of belief (which might be evaluated as true or false) but of taste or preference. A successful defence of the view that people do have moral knowledge requires assuaging these doubts. Attempts in this direction standardly emphasize the respects in which our moral opinions, and the evidence we have for them, are analogous to the opinions and evidence we have concerning non-moral matters, such as logic, mathematics, science, psychology and history. In the process they attempt to show that we do have good reason to think some of our moral opinions are true.

See also: EMOTIVISM; JUSTIFICATION, EPISTEMIC; KNOWLEDGE, CONCEPT OF; MORAL JUDGMENT; PRESCRIPTIVISM

GEOFFREY SAYRE-MCCORD

MORAL LUCK

The term 'moral luck' was introduced by Bernard Williams in 1976 to convey the idea that moral status is, to a large extent, a matter of luck. For example, that Bob grows up to be vicious and Tom to be virtuous depends very much on their different family conditions and educational background. Following Williams, Thomas Nagel widened the scope of moral luck. The position taken by both stands in stark contrast to the widely-held view, influenced by Kant, that one is morally accountable only for what is under one's control, so that moral accountability is not a matter of luck. This idea is so deeply entrenched in our modern concept of morality that rejecting it would call for a rethinking and reformulation of the most basic notions of morality. Some have argued that the paradox of moral luck provides a strong reason to abandon traditional moral theories, and lends support to virtue ethics.

DANIEL STATMAN

MORAL MOTIVATION

Introduction

Questions about the possibility and nature of moral motivation occupy a central place in the history of ethics. Philosophers disagree, however, about the role that motivational investigations should play within the larger subject of ethical theory. These disagreements surface in the dispute about whether moral thought is necessarily motivating – 'internalists' affirming that it is, 'externalists' denying this.

The disagreement between externalists and internalists reflects a basic difference in how the subject matter of ethics is conceived: externalism goes with the view that ethics is primarily about the truth of theories, construed as sets of propositions, while internalists see morality as a set of principles meant to guide the practical deliberations of individual agents. Internalists interpret questions of objectivity in ethics as questions of practical reason, about the authority of moral principles to regulate our activities. Here controversy has centred on whether the authority of practical principles for a given agent must be grounded in that agent's antecedent desires, or whether, instead, practical reason can give rise to new motivations.

There are also important questions about the content of moral motivations. A moral theory should help us to make sense of the fact that people are often moved to do the right thing, by identifying a basic motive to moral behaviour that is both widespread and intelligible, as a serious source of reasons. Philosophers have accounted for moral motivation in terms of self-interest, sympathy, and a higher-order concern to act in accordance with moral principles. But each of these approaches faces difficult challenges. Can egoistic accounts capture the distinctive character of moral motivation? Can impartial sympathy be integrated within a realistic system of human ends? Can we make sense of responsiveness to moral principle, as a natural human incentive?

1   Internalism and externalism

Internalism states that moral considerations are necessarily motivating for those who grasp them. The most common version of this position is the claim that sincere acceptance of a moral judgment implies that the person who accepts it has some motive – not necessarily overriding – for compliance with the judgment. Externalists deny this, insisting that one might sincerely accept a moral judgment without any corresponding motivation. On this view, psychological questions about human motivation are completely distinct from issues about the truth of moral judgments or the nature and constitution of moral facts (see MORAL JUDGMENT §1; MORAL REALISM §1).

The categories 'internalism' and 'externalism' were introduced only in the middle of the twentieth

century. It is often unclear how exactly these categories are to be understood, inviting confusion about their precise extension. (Which moral judgments are supposed to be motivationally effective? How are we to understand the notion of a motive that is present, but not necessarily overriding?) So it is often hard to classify moral philosophers as internalists or externalists as such.

Nevertheless, David Hume is presumably giving voice to an internalist point of view when he makes central to his theory the idea that 'morals excite passions, and produce or prevent actions' (*A Treatise of Human Nature* 1739/40). In characteristic internalist fashion, Hume interprets this idea as placing the important constraint on an account of moral distinctions that it must explain how grasping moral distinctions could immediately give rise to passions and actions, in the way it seems to do. By contrast, the hermetic distinction drawn by John Stuart Mill in *Utilitarianism* (1861), between the proof of the principle of utility and the sanctions for compliance with it, suggests an externalist position. On this position, it would be possible to accept a moral principle without having any tendency to act in accordance with it; the question of the truth of a moral principle is thus taken to be completely distinct from the psychological issue of whether and how the principle can be rendered effective in people's motivations (see HUME, D. §10; MILL, J.S. §§7–8).

2   Implications

The issue of moral motivation is a crux in discussions about the nature and status of moral judgments and moral values. Noncognitivists, who hold that moral judgments express emotions or preferences rather than report genuine truths, often start out by affirming that moral judgment is directly motivating, a version of internalism (see MORAL JUDGMENT §1; EMOTIVISM). Underlying the position that only noncognitivism can explain this fact is the assumption that the cognitive states through which we grasp judgments capable of genuine truth are motivationally inert.

In a more metaphysical vein, irrealists or error theorists, who deny the reality of moral values in the world, similarly argue from internalist assumptions. Real moral values would have to have the distinctive property of affecting the will directly. But, it is argued, items with this property would be mysterious – utterly unlike the other kinds of things with which we are familiar in the world – and so we should be reluctant to include them in the inventory of reality (see MORAL REALISM).

Philosophers who wish to resist these conclusions may either accept internalism, and try to show that cognitivist or realist views can account for the motivational effects of ethical reflection, or reject internalism (see MORAL REALISM). Those who pursue the second option need not deny that people are often motivated to do what they judge to be morally right or good. Like Mill, however, they insist that motivations of this kind are not necessarily built into moral reflection; rather it is the task of moral education to supply them.

The interest of this dispute lies in its connection with fundamentally divergent ways of thinking about moral objectivity and the subject matter of ethics. Externalism goes naturally with the view that moral philosophy is essentially about moral theories, construed as sets of propositions setting out what it is morally right or good to do. On this conception, questions of objectivity in ethics turn primarily on the truth of the propositions that make up competing moral theories. But whether a given proposition is true or false seems independent of the psychological question of whether and how people may be moved to act in accordance with it. Taking this approach seriously, we may be led to the conclusion that the true moral theory should be esoteric, so that the theory itself provides good reasons for discouraging people from accepting it, a conclusion countenanced by SIDGWICK and other utilitarians.

Internalist approaches, by contrast, conceive of moral philosophy as dealing with common principles for public moral discourse and practical deliberation. On this view, the issue of objectivity in ethics is conceived primarily as an issue of practical reason, about the title of moral principles to regulate our activities. Moral reflection is accordingly thought of as a form of practical deliberation, yielding verdicts about what is to be done, and questions about the truth of moral propositions assume a subsidiary role. If we conceive of the subject in this way, then some form of internalism will seem inevitable, since it is the distinguishing mark of practical deliberation that it affects the will directly. Furthermore, it will hardly make sense to suppose that the criteria of right defined by the correct moral theory should be esoteric, since the kind of objectivity aimed at primarily in ethical theory is precisely an objectivity within practical reason (see PRACTICAL REASON AND ETHICS).

3 Reason and desire

Within the internalist camp, there are striking disagreements about the degree to which the motivational consequences of practical reason effectively constrain our philosophical options. On one side are the Humeans, who hold that practical

reasoning must always be grounded in the non-cognitive psychological states of individual agents – what Bernard WILLIAMS calls their 'subjective motivational sets'. Combined with internalism, this view has the consequence that moral principles are hostage to antecedent, empirical facts about the motivational sets of the agents to whom the principles apply. This conclusion in turn exerts some pressure in the direction of relativism, since motives to comply with moral principles may, as a matter of empirical fact, fail to show up in the subjective sets of all agents (see MORAL RELATIVISM).

On the other side, Kantians deny that empirical facts about people's subjective motivational sets place substantive restrictions on the content or normative force of moral principles. They point out that any theory of practical reason must allow for the phenomenon of motivational irrationality (see AKRASIA). Thus I may fail to take steps that I know to be necessary if I am to attain some end that I hold dear. The principle that I ought to pursue those means that are necessary for realizing my ends does not entail that I will necessarily be motivated accordingly, but only that I will be motivated accordingly in so far as I am rational. This has been pointed out by Christine Korsgaard. If she is right, then it cannot be inferred from the fact that a given agent lacks an empirical motive for compliance with a candidate principle that the principle is not binding on the agent, since it is possible that the agent is irrational. To decide whether that is the case, however, we will need to determine – in a way that is not circumscribed by antecedent facts about people's motives – the content of principles of practical reason.

A central question in this dispute concerns the role of desires in the explanation of motivation. Humean resistance to the idea of practical principles that are not grounded in people's subjective sets stems from the idea that motivation is essentially a noncognitive orientation to the world. Kantians – most notably including Thomas NAGEL (1970) – have granted that motivation always involves a state of desire, but suggested that reasoning in accordance with practical principles may give rise to new desires, so that the validity of such principles for a given agent need not be constrained by the items already contained in that agent's subjective motivational set.

4 Explanation and justification

However this dispute is resolved, it cannot be denied that the disposition to respond to moral principles is reliably awakened and strengthened in the normal course of human psychological development. Furthermore, moral reasons often weigh heavily with people in their practical deliberations, leading them to take remarkable steps to avoid doing what would be wrong. It seems a reasonable constraint on moral theories that they should help us to make sense of these facts. A theory on which it appeared utterly mysterious that people naturally respond to moral considerations and take them seriously in their deliberations would be to that extent implausible.

What is needed is an account of the content of our moral incentives. Moral theories typically identify some common pattern of motivation, such as sympathy or self-interest, and try to show how motivations of that type might lead people to comply with principles of right, as the theory characterizes them. In practice, human motives are heterogeneous, complex and fluid; why should we suppose that there is any general account to be had of our responsiveness to moral considerations? This supposition is linked to two controversial normative assumptions. First, there is the assumption that moral considerations hang together in such a way that a uniform account can be provided of what makes actions morally wrong (in terms, for instance, of the effects of the actions on general utility, or the failure of universalizability). Philosophers who accept this assumption naturally expect to find a complementary general pattern of moral motivation, while those who deny it – some virtue theorists, perhaps – will be more sceptical.

Second, it is commonly assumed that modern morality aspires to a kind of objectivity within practical reason, providing public principles that make claims on virtually all agents. Here controversy centres not so much on whether morality represents itself as authoritative in this way, as on its title to such authority. How this controversy is resolved will depend in part on whether we can identify incentives to moral behaviour that are both widespread in human nature and intelligible as serious sources of reasons, for the availability of such common motivational structures would seem a necessary condition for the objective authority of morality.

It would not, however, be sufficient. If Nietzsche and Freud are right, for instance, then there are common motivational structures at the root of moral responsiveness, involving internal mechanisms for enforcing compliance with moral norms that draw on the redirection of aggressive impulses back against the self (see NIETZSCHE, F. §§8–9; FREUD, S.). These accounts suggest a ready explanation of the urgency with which moral demands are invested in the deliberations of many agents; indeed, they have the further advantage of being able to explain the characteristic pathologies of the moral life, such as moralistic forms of extreme self-denial. But the explanations provided by these accounts seem to undermine rather than to vindicate the authority of morality, suggesting that the common patterns of moral motivation are essentially harmful for the individuals subject to them.

This shows that the authority of morality will depend not just on the availability of a common incentive to moral behaviour, but on the content of the common incentive that is identified. An account of moral motivation congenial to morality's normative ambitions would, at a minimum, identify a motive to moral behaviour that can be cultivated without necessarily causing dire psychological harm to the individual who has the motive. Beyond this, an effective moral motive should be capable of being integrated within an agent's overall system of ends, so as to produce a stable and self-reinforcing personality.

5 Egoism and self-interest

Very few philosophers accept egoism, construed as the psychological thesis that our motives are uniformly self-interested. This bald thesis flies in the face of the many occasions on which people act without any apparent concern for their own interests, however broadly conceived. Even when our motives are self-interested, the specification of our interests would seem to presuppose some core of nonegoistic concerns, a point well made by Joseph Butler (see BUTLER, J.; EGOISM AND ALTRUISM §3).

Still, self-interest is an undeniably widespread and powerful pattern of motivation, and this makes it an obvious candidate in terms of which to reconstruct moral concern. Thus, suppose that compliance with moral principles could be shown to conduce to the long-term interest of each individual. We would then have a ready explanation to hand of the ease with which moral incentives emerge in the course of psychological development, and of the urgency with which moral considerations present themselves in practical deliberation: these phenomena would reflect the natural concern of humans for their own wellbeing, and the equally natural use of practical reason in the service of this concern. This explanation would in turn support rather than undermine the authority of morality. Those who make morality regulative of their activities would thereby achieve integration and stability of personality in an exemplary degree, since morality, far from being inimical to our other interests, would represent the condition for their effective pursuit.

This broadly Hobbesian strategy for understanding morality rests on the idea that each of us benefits enormously from the availability of certain public goods – such as peace, security, and trustworthiness – that can be secured only through general compliance with moral norms (see HOBBES, T. §5). Discussions of the strategy have become highly sophisticated, drawing on advances in the theory of rational choice (see RATIONAL CHOICE THEORY). But the increasing sophistication of its formulation cannot compensate for the inadequacy of the strategy as an account of moral motivation. The strategy might show that something like moral norms make claims on all of us. But to the extent that our incentive to comply with these norms is self-interest, the norms themselves seem to lose their distinctively moral character, for it is part of our understanding of moral requirements that they are to be followed even when it is inexpedient for us to do so. The problem is made vivid by the figure of the prospective 'free rider', who asks why they should comply with social norms when sufficiently many other people follow them to secure the public goods of cooperation. However this question may be answered, the very fact that it needs to be asked shows that the prospective free rider is not an ordinary moral agent at all.

6 Altruism and sympathy

A genuinely moral agent – as opposed to an egoist – is altruistic, in the sense of having some immediate concern for the interests of others. Furthermore, the capacity for sympathetic identification seems natural to human beings; it is the rare person who is not directly moved by exposure to human suffering, and this tendency to sympathetic response can be nurtured through moral education. For these reasons, many have followed Hume and Schopenhauer in taking sympathy to be the paradigmatic moral motivation (see HUME, D. §10; SCHOPENHAUER, A.; MORAL SENTIMENTS).

If sympathy is to play this role, however, then it will need to be corrected and refined. Actual sympathy is notoriously partial and erratic, directed (for instance) at those individuals with whom one has some personal connection, whereas morality seems to demand impartiality of response. Thus, whether morality requires that I help a given person should not depend just on whether I happen to know them, but also (for instance) on the comparative urgency of the claims of others. The standard way to deal with this problem is to subject the mechanism of sympathetic identification to the discipline of impartial reflection. One is to adopt the perspective of an informed spectator, abstracting from one's knowledge of one's own position in the world, and treating each person's welfare as equally important; the morally right action is what sympathy, refined by this procedure of reflection, would then

lead one to approve of. Though liable to many different interpretations, this general approach to moral motivation has been associated traditionally with utilitarianism (see IMPARTIALITY; UTILITARIANISM).

The utilitarian approach yields an impersonal conception of ethical impartiality, on which moral requirements take an agent-neutral rather than agent-relative form. Consider the familiar moral prohibition on murder. This is ordinarily understood as an agent-relative requirement, proscribing my killing another person even if by doing so I could prevent a number of other murders. But a prohibition of this kind would not survive utilitarian impartial reflection. Once we abstract from our knowledge of our local position in the world, it is no longer possible to sustain a proprietary concern for the character of our own actions. When sympathy is subjected to a filter of impersonal reflection, it can only endorse requirements that are agent-neutral in form, and hence capable of being accepted and acted on by any other agent as well (an injunction to prevent murder, say, instead of the conventional agent-relative prohibition on killing people oneself). In this way, the impersonal interpretation of impartiality defines a standpoint that is available to be occupied by any moral agent.

Questions arise, however, about the authority and motivational effectiveness of the claims made from this point of view. To take the latter first, it is supposed to be an advantage of the utilitarian approach that it accounts for moral motivation in terms of the familiar operations of sympathy. But there is a vast difference between the immediate, impulsive sympathy that develops naturally in human beings and the impersonal concern to maximize the good. The utilitarian claims that sympathy is transformed into a responsiveness to agent-neutral reasons as a result of moral reflection, but one may wonder whether sympathy, thus transformed, remains a natural pattern of motivation.

As for authority, the question is whether impersonal sympathy can be integrated into a person's system of ends. It gives us a standing first-order aim – the maximization of the good – which is set over against our other first-order aims, and likely to conflict fundamentally with them (given the demands that the maximization of the good notoriously imposes on individuals). The result is that we must either radically curtail the pursuit of our ordinary interests for the sake of morality, or resign ourselves to living in a way that is not morally justifiable. Utilitarians reply that morality is a hard thing, and that we should not expect to be able to accommodate its demands within the contours of ordinary bourgeois life. But the difficulty of integrating impersonal sympathy within a normal system of human ends is likely to raise a doubt about the authority of a morality construed in these terms: by what right does it demand this degree of sacrifice of us?

7 Principle-dependent motives

Kantian approaches typically trace moral concern to a higher-order motive, such as the concern to act only in ways that are permitted by moral principles (see KANTIAN ETHICS). Motives of this type will sometimes give an agent first-order ends, namely when moral principles require a certain course of action (keeping a promise, say). But when moral principles do not impose requirements in this way it will be open to agents to pursue their first-order ends while at the same time completely satisfying their higher-order moral concern. Morality regulates our first-order pursuits, but because the moral motive does not automatically supply a standing first-order end it is not inevitably in conflict with those pursuits, and so the possibility of integrating moral concern within a realistic system of human ends is left open.

Whether this possibility is realized will depend on the content of moral principles. If those principles instructed us always to maximize the good, then they would in effect determine a standing first-order end. In that case the higher-order concern to act in ways that are permitted by moral principles might be as difficult to integrate with our other ends as impersonal sympathy would be. But Kantians reject such maximizing interpretations of morality, taking moral requirements to derive from reflection on the universalizability of our aims, and contending that these universality procedures yield specific agent-relative obligations that function as limiting conditions on our activities.

The idea that morality supplies a higher-order motive invites the charge that it is self-indulgent, reflecting a fastidious concern for one's own virtue rather than a direct responsiveness to the needs of others. Further, the involvement of moral principles in Kantian moral motivation seems to deny moral worth to spontaneous and heartfelt actions, and threatens to erect an alienating screen of reflection between moral agents and their projects. A more fundamental question is whether the motive of duty can be rendered intelligible, as a natural human incentive. Why should the concern to act in ways that are universalizable emerge so readily in moral development, and present itself to us as a serious source of reasons?

To this, Kant replies that the motive of duty is constitutively rational, and that acting on it enables us to realize the supreme good of autonomy (see KANT, I. §9). Somewhat less ambitiously, T.M.

Scanlon observes that people commonly want to be able to justify their conduct to others on grounds that could not reasonably be rejected, arguing that moral principles tell us what we have to do to satisfy this familiar desire. Either of these strategies might derive support from the readiness with which people respond to 'golden rule' arguments, in which we invite them to consider what it would be like to change positions with those who would be affected by their actions. This phenomenon suggests that the concern to act in ways that are universalizable may be a powerful and *sui generis* pattern of human motivation.

See also: MORAL JUSTIFICATION §3

References and further reading

Nagel, T. (1970) *The Possibility of Altruism*, Princeton, NJ: Princeton University Press, 1978. (Challenging and suggestive argument that practical reason can give rise to new motivations, and that altruism is based in reflection from an impersonal point of view.)

Scanlon, T.M. (1998) *What We Owe to Each Other*, Cambridge, MA: Harvard University Press. (Defence of a contractualist account of morality, which includes important discussions of the relation between reasons and desires, the influence of normative reasons on the will, and the distinctive focus and force of moral motivation.)

Scheffler, S. (1992) *Human Morality*, New York: Oxford University Press. (Subtle and wide-ranging discussion of naturalistic approaches to moral motivation and their implications for the content and authority of moral demands; contains extensive bibliographic references.)

R. JAY WALLACE

MORAL PARTICULARISM

Moral particularism is a broad set of views which play down the role of general moral principles in moral philosophy and practice. Particularists stress the role of examples in moral education and of moral sensitivity or judgment in moral decision-making, as well as criticizing moral theories which advocate or rest upon general principles. It has not yet been demonstrated that particularism constitutes an importantly controversial position in moral philosophy.

See also: AESTHETICS AND ETHICS

ROGER CRISP

MORAL PHILOSOPHY

See ETHICS

Introduction

Moral psychology as a discipline is centrally concerned with psychological issues that arise in connection with the moral evaluation of actions. It deals with the psychological presuppositions of valid morality, that is, with assumptions it seems necessary for us to make in order for there to be such a thing as objective or binding moral requirements: for example, if we lack free will or are all incapable of unselfishness, then it is not clear how morality can really apply to human beings. Moral psychology also deals with what one might call the psychological accompaniments of actual right, or wrong, action, for example, with questions about the nature and possibility of moral weakness or self-deception, and with questions about the kinds of motives that ought to motivate moral agents. Moreover, in the approach to ethics known as 'virtue ethics' questions about right and wrong action merge with questions about the motives, dispositions, and abilities of moral agents, and moral psychology plays a more central role than it does in other forms of ethical theory.

> 1 Psychology and the possibility of morality
> 2 Psychology and moral judgment

1 Psychology and the possibility of morality

We can divide the main traditional concerns of moral psychology as a distinctive philosophical discipline into questions about the psychological assumptions necessary to the validity of morality, or moral rules, in general, and questions about the psychological concomitants or underpinnings of particular actions evaluated either as good/right or as bad/wrong. The question of whether human beings have free will or freedom of choice (see FREE WILL) naturally falls within the first of these areas. If human beings lack free will, then, it has over the millennia typically (though not universally) been assumed, they cannot be held responsible for their actions and cannot be bound by moral obligations any more than are animals or small children. Thus those who have systematically elaborated one or another view of moral right and wrong have usually thought it necessary to defend, or at least explicitly assume, the existence of human free will, or freedom of choice.

In the first instance this standardly involves saying something about free agency in relation to universal causal/nomic determinism. If the world is universally governed by causal or physical laws, then it is unclear how anyone could possibly have behaved otherwise than they in fact did, and so have been responsible for what they did. So defenders of (objective) morality typically feel called upon either to argue that human beings are in important ways not subject to iron-clad causal determination, or else to show that causal determinism does not in fact deprive us of free will (see DETERMINISM AND INDETERMINISM).

Another metaphysical or quasi-metaphysical issue that looms large in moral psychology concerns the human capacity for morality. Most moral codes and moral philosophies require, for example, that people occasionally put aside self-interest in the name of honour, fairness, decency, compassion, loyalty or the general good. But if one believes in psychological egoism, one will hold that people lack the capacity for these forms of self-sacrifice, and it then becomes problematic whether human beings really have the obligations that various non-egoistic moral views/theories claim that they do (see EGOISM AND ALTRUISM).

But even if one rejects both psychological and ethical egoism, there are moral-psychological issues about how much morality can fairly be demanded of people. These issues arise especially in connection with utilitarianism (see UTILITARIANISM) and Kantianism (see KANTIAN ETHICS). Utilitarianism is usually stated in a 'maximizing' form that treats it as a necessary and sufficient condition of right action that one do the best/most one circumstantially can to advance the happiness of humankind (or sentient beings). But such a doctrine seems to entail that if one is in a position to relieve the suffering, hunger or disease of others, one is morally obliged to do so, even if that means giving up one's own life plans and most of what one really cares about in life. The traditional utilitarian moral standard is thus very demanding, and some philosophers have questioned whether morality can properly, or, one might say, fairly, require so much of people. In particular, it may be wondered whether most people have the capacity to live up to such a stringent morality as is presented by maximizing utilitarianism.

Certain doctrines of Kantian ethics can likewise be seen as going against the grain of human nature or capacities, not by demanding too much of a sacrifice of self-interest, but by laying down rather stringent or narrow psychological conditions for the moral admirability of actions. According to Kant, if one helps someone in need or in trouble out of fellow-feeling or friendship, one's act lacks all moral worth, because it was not performed out of a sense of duty and respect for the moral law. And many ethical thinkers have either implicitly or explicitly held such a view of moral virtue to be too narrow and out of keeping with realistic human psychology, and have argued that certain primary, immediate or natural motives such as compassion or friendly feeling not only have moral worth, but can often even more praiseworthy than a cool appeal to duty or to something as abstract as the moral law. But Kantians question the durability and reliability of mere feeling or emotion, and there remains considerable debate in this area.

2 Psychology and moral judgment

Another topic that has recently occupied moral psychologists and ethicists is the relevance of so-called 'moral emotions' to moral judgments. Some philosophers have considered the validity of one or another moral theory to depend, in part, on whether people tend to feel guilty for violating its dictates. But others have held that there are situations where guilt is inevitable, but that that fact constitutes no sort of evidence of wrongdoing. Indeed, it is sometimes argued that the question of whether guilt for some action is *appropriate* or *justified* is separate from the issue of whether that action was actually wrong (Greenspan 1988). (Is it, for example, appropriate to feel guilty about injuries one caused in a traffic accident that was someone else's fault entirely?) Other philosophers, however, seek to connect the moral emotions with morality by arguing that the seeming *ineradicability* of our emotions of anger and resentment provides some sort of underpinning for human judgments about justice and injustice, praiseworthiness and blameworthiness (see MORALITY AND EMOTIONS; MORAL SENTIMENTS).

In addition, moral psychologists concern themselves with various forms of situational moral failure, such as self-deception and weakness of will (see AKRASIA). The very existence of these phenomena is often questioned on grounds of their paradoxical character. If one is motivated to deceive oneself about some difficult matter (for example, the needs of one's children), how can one possibly succeed unless one knows what it is one has to deceive oneself about – in which case, in what way is one actually deceived? Similarly, if moral weakness, or weakness of will more generally, means allowing anger or passion to lead one to act against one's better judgment, is it not natural to reconfigure our understanding of what is happening so as to suppose that the reasons for anger or passion warp one's sense of what really is best (for one) – in which case, in what way has one actually acted against one's (however momentary) better judgment?

Both weakness of will and self-deception are, therefore, inherently problematic, and moral psychology has sought ways of either making sense of these moral phenomena or showing them definitively to be incoherent and consequently impossible (see, for example, Pears 1984). Either 'solution' has bearing on the moral assessment of actions (and desires). If self-deception is possible, what sort of blame attaches to it when it leads to bad consequences (for example, neglect of children)? Should it be counted as a deliberate, intentional act; or it is more like negligence, or heedlessness? But if self-deception is not possible, then what masquerades as such may be more like intentional wrongdoing, and perhaps even more blameworthy, than it initially appears (see SELF-DECEPTION, ETHICS OF). Then too, if weakness of will is not possible, many cases we are inclined (at most) partially to excuse on grounds of weakness may be cases in which the agent is actually compelled, psychologically, to act wrongly – or else perhaps momentarily ignorant of the difference between right and wrong. Such conclusions are bound to affect the character and/or severity of the blame or punishment directed at those who initially seemed to be acting weakly.

Another set of issues in moral psychology arises within the tradition of moral theory known as virtue ethics, which treats issues of moral psychology as essential to our understanding of right and wrong action (see VIRTUE ETHICS). Thus, rather than basing morality on moral rules or on the production of 'good consequences', Aristotelian virtue ethics denies the possibility of universal moral rules and thinks of the virtuous individual as someone who intuitively perceives what is right or noble in various situations and, fairly effortlessly, acts accordingly. To that extent, the Aristotelian tradition in virtue ethics approaches the idea of moral rightness in some measure indirectly, by focusing on the character, habits and abilities of the virtuous individual who tracks rightness in thought and actions.

In addition, there is a more radical tradition of virtue ethics in which the moral evaluation of actions and moral rules is directly derived from characterizations of good and bad motivation and how these may be expressed or realized in someone's actions. Perhaps the best-known historical example of such an approach can be found in Plato's *Republic* (Book IV), where it is said that good actions are those that enhance or support the health and harmony of the soul (see PLATO §14).

A more recent and 'purer' example (because it does not mention anything like the Form of the Good) can be found in James Martineau's *Types of Ethical Theory*. Martineau ranks all human motives on an absolute scale – for example, compassion is placed above ambition, the latter above sexual desire, and the latter, in turn, above vindictiveness – and claims that right action is action that comes from the higher or highest motive operating in any given situation of moral choice. This then allows moral rules of thumb to be derived from generalizations about which motives are likely to operate in various morally familiar situations.

These varying virtue-ethical approaches put moral psychology at the very centre of ethics. However, for the foreseeable future, the chief role of moral psychology will probably be as a discipline ancillary to, rather than as the main focus of, moral theory.

References and further reading

Greenspan, P. (1988) *Emotions and Reasons: An Inquiry into Emotional Justification*, New York: Routledge. (A full-scale examination of the rational status of emotions.)

Pears, D. (1984) *Motivated Irrationality*, Oxford: Oxford University Press. (An extended analysis of weakness of will and other forms of irrationality.)

MICHAEL SLOTE

MORAL REALISM

Introduction

Moral realism is the view that there are facts of the matter about which actions are right and which wrong, and about which things are good and which are bad. But behind this bald statement lies a wealth of complexity. If one is a full-blown moral realist, one probably accepts the following three claims.

First, moral facts are somehow special and different from other sorts of fact. Realists differ, however, about whether the sort of specialness required is compatible with taking some natural facts to be moral facts. Take, for instance, the natural fact that if we do this action, we will have given someone the help they need. Could this be a moral fact – the same fact as the fact that we ought to do the action? Or must we think of such a natural fact as the natural 'ground' for the (quite different) moral fact that we should do it, that is, as the fact in the world that makes it true that we should act this way?

Second, realists hold that moral facts are independent of any beliefs or thoughts we might have about them. What is right is not determined by what I or anybody else thinks is right. It is not even determined by what we all think is right, even if we could be got to agree. We cannot make actions right by agreeing that they are, any more than we can make bombs safe by agreeing that they are.

Third, it is possible for us to make mistakes about what is right and what is wrong. No matter how carefully and honestly we think about what to do, there is still no guarantee that we will come up with the right answer. So what people conscientiously decide they should do may not be the same as what they should do.

1 Realism, objectivism, cognitivism

These three terms are hard to keep separate, but it is worth the effort. Cognitivism is the claim that moral attitudes are cognitive states rather than noncognitive ones. The distinction between cognitive and noncognitive states is not clear; the best way of drawing it is by appeal to the distinction between two 'directions of fit'. Beliefs, which are the paradigm examples of a cognitive state, have one direction of fit; desires, which are the paradigm examples of a noncognitive state, have the other. A belief, that is, has to fit the world; the world is given, as it were, and it is the belief's job to fit that world, to get it right. A desire is not like that; the desire's job, if anything, is to get the world to fit it, to make things be the way it wants them to be. Crucially, a desire is not at fault if things are not as it wants them to be; a belief is at fault if things are not as it takes them to be. The question whether moral attitudes are cognitive states or noncognitive ones is the question whether they have the direction of fit of a belief, or that of a desire. They could, of course, be complex states with a mixture of both; but noncognitivism is the view that moral attitudes have either wholly or partly the direction of fit of a desire. This is normally expressed more briefly as the view that moral attitudes either are, or at least contain, desires; to think an action right is a sort of 'pro-attitude', and pro-attitudes are wantings (see BELIEF; DESIRE; MORAL JUDGMENT §1).

Realists, believing that there are distinct moral facts, are likely to be cognitivists, since the appropriate attitude to a fact is belief rather than desire. It is for this reason that the opposition to realism is normally called 'noncognitivism'. Realists, holding there to be moral facts, maintain for that reason that moral attitudes are beliefs; noncognitivists, holding that moral attitudes either are or include desires, claim for that reason that there are no facts to be the objects of those attitudes.

Objectivism is harder to distinguish from realism, since the two are very closely linked. Objectivity is something to do with independence from us. Realism, as characterized above, combines three theses: a distinctness thesis, a metaphysical thesis and an epistemological thesis. The metaphysical thesis is the claim that moral facts are objective. If moral facts are independent in some way, what exactly is it that they are independent of? To say 'independent of us' is little help at best, and straightforwardly wrong at worst. Moral facts concern agents and actions, which are human matters, and so they are not completely independent of us; if we were different, different actions would be wrong. The phrasing used above, 'independent of any beliefs and thoughts we might have about them', attempts to be more precise, at the cost of excluding too much. Is the limitation involved in 'about them' justified? If not, what other limitation would be better? This matter is very difficult to resolve (see OBJECTIVITY).

Realism, on this showing, is a complex of claims. The distinctness claim carves out a distinctive subject matter for ethics. The independence claim tells us something about the sort of fact that ethics is concerned with. The epistemological claim tells us that we have a less than perfectly secure grip on those facts. Moral realists have, however, generally been willing to say that we are capable of moral knowledge, even if we do not achieve it very often. They would all agree that are we capable of justified moral beliefs (if they are cognitivists).

Readers should be aware that the characterization of moral realism is a matter of hot debate. In particular, as well as the sort of account offered here, there is a form of realism that, taking its start from the claim that there are facts of the matter in ethics, and so moral truths, holds that there must therefore be 'truth-makers' – things that make the truths true. In the moral case, what makes moral truths true must be the possession of moral properties by suitable agents and actions. Realism, so understood, is the commitment to moral properties and relations as no less 'real' than other properties. It is possible, however, to combine these two strands of realist thinking without strain.

2 Arguments for realism, and an outline of its history

Corresponding to the three elements of realism, there are three things commonly urged by realists in favour of their position. In different ways, they all suggest that we should take seriously the way things initially appear to us. Realists try to hold that things are as they appear, despite noncognitivist arguments that they cannot possibly be. This is sometimes called 'the appeal to phenomenology'.

First, realists claim that moral thought appears to have its own subject matter, distinct from science and all natural inquiry. Second, they argue that moral judgment appears to be an attempt to determine a matter of fact that is independent of any beliefs we might have about it; the fact is one thing, and what we think about it another. Third, realists hold that moral judgment presents itself to the judger as risky and fallible. When facing a difficult choice, especially, we have a sense of thin ice; we know that, with the best will in the world, the view we come to may be wrong. Only the second two of these three claims may properly be termed 'phenomenological'.

Most moral theorists have been realists, from Plato and Aristotle through Price and Hutcheson to Sidgwick and Mill, and then, in the twentieth century, to Moore and the intuitionist tradition (see INTUITIONISM IN ETHICS). It is the opposition to realism that needs to be documented. Here the patron saint of noncognitivism is Hume, whose work flowered, though altered in many respects, in the noncognitivist tradition of Stevenson, Ayer and Hare (see EMOTIVISM). Leading contemporary noncognitivists are Blackburn and Gibbard.

Advances in the philosophy of language, philosophy of mind and philosophy of science in the 1960s and 1970s persuaded many that the noncognitivist arguments against realism, which had dominated the intellectual scene since 1930, were less powerful than they had appeared. Two quite distinct forms of moral realism emerged, American and British. (This means only that most proponents of the first form are American, and most proponents of the second are British.) In the next two sections, the differences between these two positions will be charted in three areas: metaphysics, epistemology and theory of motivation.

3 American moral realism

Metaphysics. American moral realists are naturalists: they suppose that moral facts are either natural facts or configurations of natural facts (see NATURALISM IN ETHICS). As suggested in the initial summary, it is possible that the fact that if I do this I will have helped someone and harmed nobody else is the fact that I ought to do this action. Perhaps, however, the moral fact is more complex than this natural fact (and than any other single natural fact), without this meaning that it is not some combination of natural facts. If so, those natural facts will have to be combined in the right sort of way – in the sort of way that they are here – if they are together to make the moral fact that I ought to do this action. Then the moral fact will be identical with this configuration of natural facts.

This form of naturalism in ethics is often, though not always, accompanied by some form of consequentialism. A certain sort of natural fact is a moral fact because there is a relation between that fact and certain consequences (see CONSEQUENTIALISM). Naturalism in ethics is now a live option again because of a growing sense that G.E. Moore's 'open question' argument is flawed (see MOORE, G.E.).

Epistemology. American moral realists, seeing moral facts as natural facts, suppose that they are knowable in whatever ways natural facts can be known, including science. To identify those facts as moral facts, we will need to combine the best scientific theory with the best moral theory.

Theory of motivation. How is it possible to reconcile the claim that moral facts are natural facts with the widespread sense that moral facts have an intrinsic authority – that they make demands on us to which we should respond, whatever our personal choices and preferences? This 'intrinsic authority' is hard to understand in any detail. Perhaps the best attempt is Kant's distinction between categorical and hypothetical imperatives (see KANT §1; KANTIAN ETHICS). Moral imperatives such as, 'Help those less fortunate than you', are categorical, in the sense that one cannot escape their relevance to oneself by saying, 'I just don't care very much about that sort of thing'. By contrast, a hypothetical imperative such as, 'Use fresh eggs to make an omelette', has no grip on those who just do not care about how their omelettes taste.

However we understand it, the idea of the authority of moral facts does not sit easily with ethical naturalism. Natural facts, however configured, do not seem able to have any such authority over the will (see MORAL MOTIVATION §§1–2). American realists generally respond to this by doubting the claim that any fact could have that sort of authority. The world, whether in its moral or its more obviously natural clothes, is one whose grip on us depends on our bringing to it a sort of moral concern (which will have been the product either of evolution or of education). If we lack that concern, we will be unmotivated by moral distinctions, even though we will be still perfectly capable of discovering which actions are right and which are wrong. To know the right is one thing, and to bend one's will to it another. Moral judgment is cognitive; it is the discovery of facts. But facts are motivationally inert; whether one is motivated by them depends not so much on them as on what one cares about. So moral imperatives are hypothetical, despite appearances.

In these thoughts, American realists adopt what is sometimes called a 'Humean' theory of motivation. Neither belief nor desire alone can lead to action;

only a combination of the two can do that. (For an action we need two mental states, one with each direction of fit.) Moral facts are the objects of belief. No such belief can motivate alone; for there to be an action, the agent must have some desire or preference as well as the belief. Moral facts cannot motivate in their own right, thus; their ability to make a difference to how we act depends upon the independent contribution of a desire. This being so, they cannot have such a thing as an intrinsic authority over us; for whether they can make a difference to how we act depends on something over which they have no control (see PRACTICAL REASON AND ETHICS §2).

4 British moral realism

The British variety of moral realism denies everything that the American variety claims.

Metaphysics. British moral realism is non-naturalist: moral facts are not natural facts, nor are they are natural configurations of natural facts. They may be non-natural configurations of natural facts, but that is another matter. Natural facts are relevant to moral ones, of course, since they are the reasons why actions are right or wrong. It follows from this that any two situations that are naturally indistinguishable must be morally indistinguishable (see SUPERVENIENCE). But this sort of supervenience is a far cry from any identity between the natural and the moral.

In terms of the characterization of moral realism given earlier, the British thus attribute far greater distinctness to moral facts, considering them to be metaphysically distinct from natural ones. The Americans have a harder task in showing what is distinctive about the moral, though not an impossible one. They can say, for instance, that moral facts are distinguished by their subject matter, or by the sort of configuration of natural facts that they are.

Epistemology. If moral facts are not natural facts, the normal methods of finding out how things are will not suffice for the discovery of the moral. Admittedly, British realists have been prone to talk of seeing that an action is right. But it appears that they mean by this neither that rightness is visible, nor that there is a moral sense in addition to the normal five senses. Talk of seeing that the action is right is intended to echo Aristotle's remark that right and wrong are not matters of rules so much as of the nature of the case before us, and that to discern what is right we have to concentrate on the details of the present situation (see VIRTUE ETHICS §6). They deny, therefore, that moral judgment is a matter of subsumption, of bringing the present case under some moral rule. Moral judgment is the application of concepts, but those concepts are not rules. Indeed, it is characteristic of British realists to be sceptical about the very possibility of moral rules or principles. For them, moral judgment is a matter of recognizing the reasons for action as they present themselves in the present case, and responding to them as such (see UNIVERSALISM IN ETHICS). This sort of recognition is not perceptual, but it is cognitive and practical at once – for what one is recognizing is a reason for action, that is, a normative state of the world.

Theory of motivation. American realists are 'externalists' about moral judgment. They hold that the ability of a moral judgment to motivate, that is, to make a difference to how one acts, is dependent on the presence of a quite different mental state, namely some sort of desire. British moral realists are generally 'internalists', holding that a moral judgment motivates in its own right, and does not get its ability to affect action from a desire that is present at the same time (see MORAL MOTIVATION §1). To make this out, they have to reject the standard Humean picture of motivation, though they do not agree among themselves about quite how to do this. Wiggins and McDowell hold that action does require a combination of belief and desire, but that in the moral case it is belief that leads and desire that follows. Dancy suggests that it is belief alone that motivates, since mere recognition of relevant reasons should be enough for action; he sees desire as a state of being motivated (by the reasons), not as what motivates. Either way, the suggestion that there are genuinely normative and non-natural facts is combined with the claim that recognition of these facts motivates in its own right, in a way that is not dependent on the presence of an independent desire.

This raises problems. The first is that Humeanism is more or less received wisdom; so the British are fighting an uphill battle in rejecting it. The second is that it is very hard to make sense of the idea of a state of the world, or fact, that stands in some intrinsic relation to the will. It is normal to think that facts are motivationally inert; to recognize them is one thing, and to bend the will to them another. The British hold that the response to the fact, which we call recognition, is itself motivational. The preferred way of doing this is by appeal to the 'dispositional conception of value'. This conception is inspired by a supposedly similar dispositional conception of colour: a red object is one that is disposed to cause in us a characteristic sort of experience (see COLOUR, THEORIES OF). Similarly, a valuable object is conceived as one which is disposed to elicit a certain response from us, an inclination of the will. As such, it is not totally independent of us, since it consists (at least partly) in a certain relation to us; and this means that it is not

fully objective, if objectivity is to be understood in terms of independence from us. But it is still objective in a weak sense, since value can still be conceived as there for us to recognize and there whether we recognize it or not.

There are two difficulties with this appeal to dispositions. The first is that the analogy with colours is hotly disputed. The second is that, in order to keep values in the world, their objectivity has had to be diminished. For some, this weaker conception of objectivity is hardly to be distinguished from subjectivity.

5 Realism and minimalism

In this entry, realism has been seen as a combination of three distinct theses. But there is an alternative account of what realism is that sees it as nothing more than a claim about truth. The realist, on this account, holds that moral statements are capable of truth, and indeed that some are true. If we say this, we can still distinguish between realism and objectivism in ethics. Realism is the claim that moral judgments are sometimes true; objectivism is the claim that the sort of truth they have is objective truth.

We can distinguish two sorts of opposition to this form of realism. The first accepts that moral statements are capable of truth, but holds that all are false (see MORAL SCEPTICISM); the second holds that truth is not the appropriate form of success for a moral judgment, and that we would do better to think of them as sincere or insincere, or as more or less well connected with other judgments, or as ones that we ourselves would agree with. One should not try to combine these two sorts of opposition.

Crispin Wright has suggested that, if this is what is at issue between realism and noncognitivism, the matter will be quickly resolved in favour of realism. In his view, the mere fact that moral discourse is assertive, and that moral utterances are governed by norms of warranted assertibility, is enough to establish that we make no mistake in calling some true and others false. The question should not be, then, whether moral judgments are capable of truth, since everyone really admits that they are. Instead, the debate about realism should focus on other questions. According to Wright, among these questions are:

(1) Is it a priori that differences of moral opinion can only be explained in terms of divergent input, unsuitable conditions or malfunction (such as prejudice and dogma)?
(2) Do the supposed moral facts serve to explain anything at all? Suppose that they explain (some of) our moral beliefs. Do they explain anything else in a way that is not mediated by our beliefs?

That is to say, do moral facts directly explain anything about how the world goes?

Wright suggests that we only get a 'full-blooded' moral realism if our answer to these questions is 'yes'. There will, therefore, be degrees of realism, and in a way the question is not whether we should be realists, but what sort of realists we should be. How far should our realism go?

6   Arguments against realism

Since realism comes in different forms, arguments against it are more likely to attack some particular form than to attack realism as such. The main difficulties for the American and the British realist schools have already been mentioned. In both cases they were metaphysical. The Americans have difficulty in keeping moral facts both natural and moral. The British have difficulty in explaining how the world can be other than 'motivationally inert'.

The two general challenges to realism that are most often mentioned are those made by John Mackie and Gilbert Harman. Harman asks what, if anything, is explained by moral facts that cannot be equally well explained by moral beliefs. If moral belief alone is enough for all such explanations, why suppose that the facts exist in addition to the beliefs? The facts appear to be explanatorily redundant. We might suggest that at least the facts explain the beliefs, but Harman replies that the beliefs can be equally well explained in other ways, for example, by appeal to upbringing and education. This leaves the facts explaining nothing; they are mere metaphysical danglers, hanging in the air and not related to anything else at all. We are better off without such things. (This is different from Wright's view above, because Wright allows that moral facts could explain moral beliefs; he only asks whether they could explain anything else 'directly'.)

Mackie (1977) suggests that values, if they existed, would be very peculiar things, unlike anything else in the universe; so queer are they that, if they existed, we would need a special faculty of moral perception or intuition to perceive them. Their queerness lies in the idea that an objective value would necessarily be pursued by anyone who recognized it, because such values have 'to-be-pursuedness' built into them. Even if such things are possible, which nobody influenced by Hume would allow, something of that sort is of a different order from anything else with which we are acquainted.

Mackie also asks about the supposed relation between moral facts and natural facts. We ordinarily say, for instance, that an action was wrong because it was cruel. But 'just what *in the world* is signified by this "because"?' (1977: 41; original emphasis). Not only is there the wrongness and the cruelty, but also a totally mysterious 'consequential link' between the two.

These arguments of Mackie's are answered in different ways by the different varieties of realism. The Americans deny the possibility of 'to-be-pursuedness'; the British admit it, but try to explain it by appeal to the dispositional theory of value. As for the mysterious 'consequential link', both sides would, in their different ways, try to say that the wrongness is somehow 'constituted' by the cruelty.

See also: MORAL JUSTIFICATION; MORAL KNOWLEDGE; MORAL RELATIVISM; REALISM AND ANTIREALISM

References and further reading

Mackie, J. (1977) *Ethics: Inventing Right and Wrong*, Harmondsworth: Penguin, ch. 1. (A very influential introductory text, which starts by attempting to undermine realism.)

JONATHAN DANCY

MORAL RELATIVISM

Introduction

Often the subject of heated debate, moral relativism is a cluster of doctrines concerning diversity of moral judgment across time, societies and individuals. Descriptive relativism is the doctrine that extensive diversity exists and that it concerns values and principles central to moralities. Meta-ethical relativism is the doctrine that there is no single true or most justified morality. Normative relativism is the doctrine that it is morally wrong to pass judgment on or to interfere with the moral practices of others who have adopted moralities different from one's own. Much debate about relativism revolves around the questions of whether descriptive relativism accurately portrays moral diversity and whether actual diversity supports meta-ethical and normative relativism. Some critics also fear that relativism can slide into nihilism.

1 Descriptive relativism
2 Meta-ethical relativism
3 Normative relativism
4 Relativism and moral confidence

1   Descriptive relativism

From the beginnings of the Western tradition philosophers have debated the nature and implications of moral diversity. Differences in customs and values the Greeks encountered through trade, travel and war motivated the argument attributed to the sophist Protagoras in Plato's *Theaetetus*: that human custom determines what is fine and ugly, just and unjust (see PROTAGORAS). Anthropologists in the twentieth century have emphasized the fundamental differences between the moralities of small-scale traditional societies and the modern West. For example, many traditional societies are focused on community-centred values that require the promotion and sustenance of a common life of relationships, in contrast to both the deontological morality of individual rights and the morality of utilitarianism that are the most prominent within modern Western moral philosophy. Within this philosophy itself moral diversity is represented by the debates between utilitarians and deontologists, and more recently criticism of both camps by defenders of virtue theory and communitarianism (see DEON-TOLOGICAL ETHICS; UTILITARIANISM; VIRTUE ETHICS; COMMUNITY AND COMMUNITARIANISM). Such differences have motivated the doctrine of *descriptive relativism*: that there exists extensive diversity of moral judgment across time, societies and individuals, and that it concerns central moral values and principles.

Critics of descriptive relativism argue that it fails to account for important moral similarities across cultures such as prohibitions against killing innocents and provisions for educating and socializing the young. A relativist response given by Michael Walzer is to argue that shared norms must be described in an extremely general way and that once one examines the concrete forms they take in different societies, one sees significant variety, for example, in which persons count as 'innocent'. The descriptive relativist might go so far as to assert that no significant similarities exist, but an alternative position is that broad similarities exist that are compatible with significant differences among the moralities human beings have held.

Critics of descriptive relativism also argue that many moral beliefs presuppose religious and metaphysical beliefs, and that these beliefs, rather than any difference in fundamental values, give rise to much moral diversity (see RELIGION AND MORALITY). Also, differences in moral belief across different societies may not arise from differences in fundamental values but from the need to implement the same values in different ways given the varying conditions obtaining in these societies. One relativist reply is that while such explanations apply to some moral disagreements, they cannot apply to many others, such as disagreements over the rightness of eating animals or the moral status of the foetus or the rightness of sacrificing an innocent person for the sake of a hundred more.

2 Meta-ethical relativism

The most heated debate about relativism revolves around the question of whether descriptive relativism supports *meta-ethical relativism*: that there is no single true or most justified morality. There is no direct path from descriptive to meta-ethical relativism; the most plausible argument for meta-ethical relativism is that it is part of a larger theory of morality that best explains actual moral diversity.

Critics of meta-ethical relativism point out that moral disagreement is consistent with the possibility that some moral judgments are truer or more justified than others, just as disagreement among scientists does not imply that truth is relative in science. Some relativists are unimpressed by the analogy with science, holding that disagreements about the structure of the world can be sufficiently radical to undermine the assumption that there is an absolute truth to be found. This defence of meta-ethical relativism amounts to founding it upon a comprehensive *epistemological relativism* that expresses scepticism about the meaningfulness of talking about truth defined independently of the theories and justificatory practices of particular communities of discourse.

An alternative relativist response is to take a nonrelativist stance towards science and to drive a wedge between scientific and moral discourse. Defenders of such a *morality-specific meta-ethical relativism* argue that scientific disagreements can be explained in ways that are consistent with there being a nonrelative truth about the structure of the physical world while moral disagreements cannot be treated analogously. For example, much scientific disagreement may be traced to insufficient or ambiguous evidence or distortions of judgment stemming from personal interests. Relativists have argued that such explanations will not work for moral disagreements such as the ones mentioned above concerning the eating of animals, abortion, and the sacrifice of an innocent to save more lives.

In offering alternative explanations of moral disagreement, morality-specific relativists tend to adopt a 'naturalistic' approach to morality in the sense that they privilege a scientific view of the world and fit their conceptions of morality and moral disagreement within that view. They deny that moral values and principles constitute an irreducible part of the fabric of the world and argue that morality is best explained on the theory that it arises at least in part from custom and convention. On Wong's view (1984), for example, a good part of morality arises out of the need to structure and regulate social cooperation and to resolve conflicts of interest. Meta-ethical relativism is true because there is no single valid way to structure social cooperation.

Morality-specific relativism divides into *cognitive* and *non-cognitive* versions (see MORAL JUDGMENT §1). On C.L. Stevenson's emotivist view, for example, moral discourse merely expresses emotion and influences the attitudes and conduct of others (see EMOTIVISM). Cognitive relativists, such as Mackie, Harman, Foot and Wong, interpret moral judgments as expressing belief, on the grounds that moral judgments are often argued or judged true or false on the basis of reasons. Within cognitive relativism, there are those who believe that there is no single true morality because more than one morality is true, and those who believe that there is no single true morality because all are false. J.L. Mackie (1977) represents the latter camp, on the ground that while morality actually arises out of custom and convention, the meanings of moral terms presuppose a mistaken reference to *sui generis* properties that provide everyone with a reason for acting according to morality. Other cognitive relativists see no need to construe moral terms as containing a reference to nonexistent properties and instead tie their cognitive content to certain standards and rules.

According to such a standards relativism, moral language is used to judge and to prescribe in accordance with a set of standards and rules. Different sets of standards and rules get encoded into the meaning of ethical terms such as 'good', 'right' and 'ought' over time, and into individuals, groups, or societies in such a way that two apparently conflicting moral beliefs can both be true. Though under a relativist analysis the beliefs express no conflicting claims about what is true, they do conflict as prescriptions as to what is to be done or as to what kinds of things are to be pursued. The disagreement is purely pragmatic in nature, though parties to the disagreement may not be aware of this if they erroneously assume they share the relevant standards.

Another crucial question for the standards relativist concerns *whose* standards and rules apply when someone makes a moral judgment. Suppose that Jones makes a moral judgment about what Smith ought to do, but that the standards Jones applies to guide his own conduct are not the same as the standards Smith uses to guide hers. One possibility is that Jones uses Smith's standards to judge what she ought to do. Another possibility offered by Harman in some of his writing about relativism is that one must judge others by standards one shares with them. His theory is that morality consists of implicit agreements for the structuring of social cooperation. Moral judgments implying that the subjects have a reason to do what is prescribed make sense only as prescriptions based on what the

speakers and subjects (and the intended audience of the judgments) have agreed to do. Other standards relativists observe that people use their own standards in judging the conduct of others, whether or not they believe these others share their standards.

There are *radical* and *moderate* versions of meta-ethical relativism. Radical relativists hold that any morality is as true or as justified as any other. Moderate relativists, such as Foot (1978) and Wong (1984), deny that there is any single true morality but also hold that some moralities are truer or more justified than others. On Wong's view, for instance, certain determinate features of human nature and similarities in the circumstances and requirements of social cooperation combine to produce universal constraints on what an adequate morality must be like. It may be argued, for example, that a common feature of adequate moralities is the specification of duties to care and educate the young, a necessity given the prolonged state of dependency of human offspring and the fact that they require a good deal of teaching to play their roles in social cooperation. It may also be a common feature of adequate moralities to require of the young reciprocal duties to honour and respect those who bring them up, and this may arise partly from the role that such reciprocity plays in ensuring that those who are charged with caring for the young have sufficient motivation to do so. Such common features are compatible with the recognition that adequate moralities could vary significantly in their conceptions of what values that cooperation should most realize. Some moralities could place the most emphasis on community-centred values that require the promotion and sustenance of a common life of relationships, others could emphasize individual rights, and still others could emphasize the promotion of utility.

3 Normative relativism

Does meta-ethical relativism have substantive implications for action? *Normative relativism* – the doctrine that it is morally wrong to pass judgment on or to interfere with the moral practices of others who have adopted moralities different from one's own – is often defended by anthropologists, perhaps in reaction to those Western conceptions of the inferiority of other cultures that played a role in colonialism. It also has application to disagreements within a society such as that concerning the morality of abortion, where the positions of the disputing parties seem ultimately to be based on fundamentally different conceptions of personhood.

As in the case of descriptive and meta-ethical relativism, however, there is no direct path from metaphysical to normative relativism. One could hold consistently that there is no single true morality while judging and interfering with others on the basis of one's own morality. Wong has proposed a version of normative relativism consistent with the point that nothing normative follows straightforwardly from meta-ethical relativism. Meta-ethical relativism needs to be supplemented with a liberal contractualist ethic to imply an ethic of nonintervention. A liberal contractualist ethic requires that moral principles be justifiable to the individuals governed by these principles. If no single morality is most justified for everyone, *liberal normative relativism* may require one not to interfere with those who have a different morality, though the requirement of noninterference may not be absolute when it comes into conflict with other moral requirements such as prohibitions against torture or the killing of innocents (see LIBERALISM).

4 Relativism and moral confidence

A reason why relativism has been feared is the thought that it could easily slide into moral nihilism. Could one continue living according to one's moral values, which sometimes require significant personal sacrifice, if one can no longer believe that they are truer or more justified than other values that require incompatible actions? One relativist response is that one may reasonably question the importance of certain features of one's morality upon adopting a view of their conventional origin. Consider that duties to give aid to others are commonly regarded as less stringent than duties not to harm them. Gilbert Harman has proposed that this difference results from the superior bargaining position of those with greater material means in the implicit agreement giving rise to morality. Those with lesser material means may reasonably question this feature of morality, if they are persuaded of Harman's explanation. Notice, however, that it is not merely the supposition that this feature arose from convention that may undermine one's confidence in it. With regard to other features of one's morality, one may adopt a relativist view of them and continue to prize them simply because they are as good as any other and because they help to constitute a way of life that is one's own.

Admittedly, people who condemn torture and unremitting cruelty as an offence against the moral fabric of the world may possess a certitude not available to relativists and may find it easier to make the personal sacrifices morality requires. Moral certitude has its own liabilities, however, and has itself contributed to the unremitting cruelty that human beings have inflicted upon each other.

See also: MORALITY AND ETHICS; RELATIVISM; SOCIAL RELATIVISM

References and further reading

Foot, P. (1978) *Moral Relativism (The Lindley Lectures)*, Lawrence, KS: University of Kansas Press. (Defends a form of moderate relativism.)

Mackie, J.L. (1977) *Ethics: Inventing Right and Wrong*, Harmondsworth: Penguin. (Defends a sceptical form of relativism under which moral judgments lack the objectivity they purport to have. Hence no standard moral judgments are true.)

Wong, D. (1984) *Moral Relativity*, Berkeley, CA: University of California Press. (A defence of moderate relativism based on a naturalistic approach. Some chapters presuppose a contemporary philosophy of language that some may regard as technical.)

DAVID B. WONG

MORAL SCEPTICISM

Scepticism in general is the view that we can have little or no knowledge; thus moral scepticism is the view that we can have little or no moral knowledge. Some moral sceptics argue that we cannot have moral knowledge because we cannot get the evidence necessary to justify any moral judgments. More radical moral sceptics argue that we cannot have moral knowledge because in morality there are no truths to be known. These radical sceptics argue either that moral judgments are all false because they erroneously presuppose the real existence of 'objective values', or that moral judgments aim to express feelings or influence behaviour instead of stating truths. Critics of moral scepticism, in turn, argue that in at least some cases moral judgments aim to state truths, some of these judgments are in fact true, and we have enough evidence to say that we know these moral truths.

See also: MORAL JUSTIFICATION

MARK T. NELSON

MORAL SENSE THEORIES

In *Leviathan* (1651), Thomas Hobbes argued that since good and evil are naturally relative to each individual's private appetites, and man's nature is predominantly selfish, then morality must be grounded in human conventions. His views provoked strong reactions among British moral philosophers in the seventeenth and eighteenth centuries. Moral sense theories comprise one set of responses. A moral sense theory gives a central role to the affections and sentiments in moral perception, in the appraisal of conduct and character, and in deliberation and motivation. Shaftesbury and Francis Hutcheson argued that we have a unique faculty of moral perception, the moral sense. David Hume and Adam Smith held that we cultivate a moral sensibility when we appropriately regulate our sympathy by an experience-informed reason and reflection.

See also: CAMBRIDGE PLATONISM; MORAL MOTIVATION

JACQUELINE TAYLOR

MORAL SENTIMENTS

Moral sentiments are those feelings or emotions central to moral agency. Aristotle treated sentiments as nonrational conditions, capable of being moulded into virtues through habituation. The moral sense theorists of the Enlightenment took sentiments to provide the psychological basis for our common moral life. Kantian approaches deny the primacy of sentiments in moral personality, and treat moral sentiments as conditioned by our rational grasp of moral principles.

A central issue is whether moral sentiments incorporate moral beliefs. Accounts which affirm a connection with moral beliefs point to the complex intentionality (object-directedness) of such states as resentment or indignation. Against this, some observe that moral emotions may be felt inappropriately.

Of special interest are the sentiments of guilt and shame. These seem to reflect different orientations towards moral norms, and questions arise about the degree to which these different orientations are culturally local, and whether either orientation is superior to the other.

See also: CONSCIENCE; MORAL JUDGMENT; MORAL KNOWLEDGE; MORAL MOTIVATION

R. JAY WALLACE

MORALITY AND ART

See ART AND MORALITY

MORALITY AND EMOTIONS

Emotions such as anger, fear, grief, envy, compassion, love and jealousy have a close connection to morality. Philosophers have generally agreed that they can pose problems for morality in a variety of ways: by impeding judgment, by making attention uneven and partial, by making the person unstable and excessively needy, by suggesting immoral projects and goals.

The place of emotions in moral theories depends on whether they are conceived of merely as impulses without thought or intentional content, or as having some sort of cognitive content. Plato argued that emotions form a part of the soul separate from thought and evaluation, and moved, in the course of his writings, from a sceptical view of their contribution to morality to a more positive appraisal. Aristotle connected emotions closely with judgment and belief, and held that they can be cultivated through moral education to be important components of a virtuous character. The Stoics identified emotions with judgments ascribing a very high value to uncontrolled external things and persons, arguing that all such judgments are false and should be removed. Their cognitive analysis of emotion stands independent of this radical normative thesis, and has been adopted by many philosophers who do not accept it.

Modern theories of emotion can be seen as a series of responses and counter-responses to the Stoic challenge. Descartes, Spinoza, Kant and Nietzsche all accepted many of the Stoics' normative arguments in favour of diminishing the role played by emotions in morality; they differed, however, in the accounts of emotion they proposed. Focusing on compassion or sympathy, Hutcheson, Hume, Rousseau, Adam Smith and Schopenhauer all defended the role of some emotions in morality, returning to a normative position closer to Aristotle's (though not always with a similarly cognitive analysis).

Contemporary views of emotion have been preoccupied with the criticism of reductive accounts that derive from behaviourist psychology. By now, it is once again generally acknowledged that emotions are intelligent parts of the personality that can inform and illuminate as well as motivate. Philosophers' views have been enriched by advances in cognitive psychology, psychoanalysis and anthropology. Feminist accounts of emotion differ sharply, some insisting that we should validate emotions as important parts of moral character, others that emotions shaped by unjust conditions are unreliable guides.

See also: EMOTIVISM; FAMILY, ETHICS AND THE; NORMATIVITY

MARTHA C. NUSSBAUM

MORALITY AND ETHICS

Morality is a distinct sphere within the domain of normative thinking about action and feeling (see NORMATIVITY); the whole domain, however, is the subject of ethics.

How should the moral sphere be characterized? The three most influential suggestions are that morality should be characterized by its *function*, by the *supremacy* of the moral, or by the distinctive moral *sentiments*. It is plausible that moral codes have a social function, such as that of maintaining beneficial cooperation; but it does not seem an a priori truth. In contrast, it may be true a priori that moral obligations are supreme – accepting an obligation as moral is accepting that it should be carried out whatever else may be said against doing so. But even if this is a priori, it does not provide a criterion for demarcating the moral. A better characterization takes an obligation to be moral if and only if certain sentiments, those invoked in blame, are justified towards an agent who fails to comply with it.

This provides a criterion for demarcating the moral, but only if the sentiments can be identified. The sentiment at the core of blame is sometimes held to be a species of anger – indignation, for example. However it seems that one may feel the sentiment involved in guilt or blame without feeling indignation. A view deriving from Hegel's conception of wrongdoing may be more accurate. Whereas indignation disposes to aggressive restorative action, the sentiment of blame itself disposes to withdrawal of recognition, expulsion from the community. Punishment can then be seen, with Hegel, as a route whereby recognition is restored.

Criticisms of morality are broadly of two kinds, though they often overlap: that moral valuation rests on incoherent presuppositions, and that morality is a dysfunctional system. The leading source of the first kind of criticism (and one source of the second) is Nietzsche; in contemporary philosophy related ideas are developed by Bernard Williams. One of Williams' criticisms centres on something which does indeed seem to be presupposed by moral valuation, at any rate in modern moral thought: that moral obligations exist independently of one's desires and projects yet of themselves give one a reason to act. Other doubts about the coherence of the moral focus on a conception which, again, may be distinctively modern – being associated particularly with some forms of Protestant Christianity and with Kant; the conception takes it that all are equally autonomous and that the only true worth is moral worth. Criticisms of this conception occur (in different ways) in Nietzsche's treatment of modern morality and in Hegel's treatment of what he calls *Moralität*.

The idea that morality is dysfunctional, that blame and guilt deny life or impose pain without securing compensating gains, has considerable influence in contemporary culture (as does the idea that they are compromised by the interests of those who can shape them). Such criticism must come from a conception of ethical value, and assume that there is an alternative to morality. Unless one believes in the possibility of a communal life unmediated by any disciplinary forces at all, the assumption being made must be that there could be

a discipline which was better, ethically speaking, than the discipline of guilt and blame.

See also: MORAL AGENTS; MORAL JUDGMENT; MORAL REALISM; UNIVERSALISM IN ETHICS

JOHN SKORUPSKI

MORALITY AND LAW
See LAW AND MORALITY

MORALITY AND RELIGION
See RELIGION AND MORALITY

MORE, THOMAS (1477–1535)

Thomas More was a classical, biblical and patristic scholar, an author in many genres, a lawyer who became Lord Chancellor, a humanist 'born for friendship' according to Erasmus, a widowed husband who remarried and could not decide which wife he loved more, a father who established a 'school' with the best of tutors in his home so that his daughters could have the same formal education (denied to women) as his son, and a martyr who refused to recognize Henry VIII as head of the church in England and was therefore beheaded by the king he had vindicated against Martin Luther. With his *Utopia* he coined a word and inspired subsequent writers to imagine both ideal and non-ideal societies.
See also: ERASMUS; HUMANISM, RENAISSANCE

CLARE M. MURPHY

MOSES BEN MAIMON
See MAIMONIDES, MOSES

MOSES MAIMONIDES
See MAIMONIDES, MOSES

MOTIVATION, MORAL
See MORAL MOTIVATION

MOTOORI NORINAGA (1730–1801)

Motoori Norinaga was a pivotal figure in Japan's 'Native Studies' or 'National Learning' (*kokugaku*) movement. An accomplished philologist, he helped decipher the idiosyncratic eighth-century orthography of the Japanese chronicle of history and myth, the *Kojiki* (Records of Ancient Matters). This was part of his broader scholarly project of defining the nature of the ancient Japanese sensitivity or 'heart-and-mind' (*kokoro*). In so doing, he articulated an influential religious philosophy of Shintō and an axiology of traditional Japanese values, which he considered as primarily emotivist and aesthetic.
See also: JAPANESE PHILOSOPHY; SHINTŌ

THOMAS P. KASULIS

MOZI (5th century BC)

Mozi was the first philosopher to question the ideas of Confucius. Scholarly debate centres around the issue of whether Mozi was a 'weak' or a 'strong' utilitarian, an 'act' or 'rule utilitarian', and whether he was a 'language utilitarian' or rather placed the religious authority of a personalized Heaven at the centre of his system. He is noteworthy for being the first thinker to develop a tripartite methodology for verifying claims to knowledge and for attacking the Confucian emphasis on ritual and the centrality of the family as the basis for social and political action.

See also: Chinese philosophy; Confucian philosophy, Chinese; Mohist philosophy

ROBIN D.S. YATES

MULTICULTURALISM

Multicultural political philosophy explores ways of accommodating cultural diversity fairly. Public policies often have different consequences for members of different cultural groups. For example, given the importance of language to culture, and the role of the modern state in so many aspects of life, the choice of official languages will affect different people very differently. Similar issues arise concerning the cultural content of education and the criminal law, and the choice of public holidays. To avoid policies that create unfair burdens, multicultural theory turns to abstract inquiries about such things as the relation between culture and individual wellbeing, or the relation between a person's culture and the appropriate standards for judging them. Multiculturalism raises related questions for democratic theory also. Culture may be important to deciding on appropriate units of democratic rule and to the design of special mechanisms for representing minorities within such units. Each of these questions is made more difficult in the context of cultures that reject the demands of liberty or equality. The challenge for philosophers is to develop a principled way of thinking about these issues.

See also: Citizenship; Culture

ARTHUR RIPSTEIN

MURDOCH, IRIS (1919–99)

Iris Murdoch was an Oxford moral philosopher and a prolific novelist. Her philosophy was marked by a strong sense of the moral significance of our inner lives: the quality of our seeing, feeling and imagining is significant, both in itself and as a background for our active lives. Moral effort, Murdoch believed, consists mainly in the struggle against our natural egoism. She thought ethics should discuss the techniques of this struggle and took a particular interest in the role art might play in such a context. Insisting on the irreducible plurality of the moral 'field of force', Murdoch did not develop a moral theory; yet she also believed that moral experience is haunted by a sense of unity. Her thought revolved around this tension. Inspired by Plato, she referred to this unity as 'Good' and understood it as a distant perfect reality present in imperfect human lives as a baffling but magnetic force. The phenomena and problems that had Murdoch's philosophical interest were also explored in her fiction, despite her insistence that she was not a philosophical novelist.

See also: Art and morality; Egoism and altruism; Ethics; Fact/value distinction; Free will; Good, theories of the; Moral realism; Moral sense theories; Morality and emotions; Plato; Religion and morality; Rights; Utilitarianism; Virtue ethics; Virtues and vices; Weil, Simone

THOMAS NORGAARD

MUSIC, AESTHETICS OF

The aesthetics of music comprises philosophical reflection on the origin, nature, power, purpose, creation, performance, reception, meaning and value of music. Some of its problems are general problems of aesthetics posed in a musical context; for example, what is the ontological status of the work of art in music, or what are the grounds of value judgments in music? Other problems are more or less peculiar to music, lacking a clear parallel in other arts; for example, what is the nature of the motion perceived in music, or how can the marriage of music and words best be understood?

Attempts to define the concept of music generally begin with the fact that music involves sound, but also posit such things as cultural tradition, the fulfilment of a composer's aims or the expression of emotions as essential features of music. Perhaps any plausible concept, though, has to involve the making of sounds by people for aesthetic appreciation, broadly conceived. In deciding what is meant by a musical work, further considerations come into play, such as might lead to the identification of it with a sound structure as defined by a given composer in a particular musico-historical context.

In what sense can a piece of music be said to have meaning? Some hold it has meaning only internally – in its structure as an arrangement of melodies, harmonies, rhythms and timbres, for instance – while others have claimed that its meaning lies in the communication of things not

715

essentially musical – such as emotions, attitudes or the deeper nature of the world. The most popular of these beliefs is that music expresses emotion. This is not to say, however, that the emotion expressed in a work is necessarily experienced by those involved in its composition or performance: composers can create peaceful or furious music without themselves being in those states, and the same goes for the performance of such music by performers. Also, the emotions evoked in listeners seem of a different nature from those directly experienced: negative emotions expressed in music do not preclude the audience's appreciation, and in fact commonly facilitate it. Ultimately, a work's expressiveness should be seen as something directly related to the experience of listening to that work. Music is often said to have value primarily in so far as it is beautiful, its beauty being whatever affords pleasure to the listener. But the quality of a work's expressiveness, its depth, richness and subtlety, for example, also seems to form an important part of any value judgment we make about the work.

See also: ART WORKS, ONTOLOGY OF; ARTISTIC EXPRESSION; EMOTION IN RESPONSE TO ART; GURNEY, E.; HANSLICK, E.; LANGER, S.K.K.; OPERA, AESTHETICS OF

JERROLD LEVINSON

MYSTICISM, JEWISH
See KABBALAH

N

NÆSS, ARNE (1912–)

As professor of philosophy in Oslo between 1939 and 1970, Arne Næss contributed to a strengthening of the position of philosophy in Norwegian academic life. During the German occupation (1940–5) he played an active part in the resistance movement. In the 1940s and 1950s he was the inspiration for and centre of a group of students of philosophy and social science, the 'Oslo School', whose members became influential in the later development of these fields. His philosophical thinking passed through an early 'scientistic' period of radical empiricism to 'possibilist' and pluralist views, and an undogmatic scepticism. After resigning his professorship in 1970, he became the protagonist of a version of ecological philosophy, 'deep ecology'. He has always been an admirer of Spinoza and has also sought inspiration in Spinozism for his ecological philosophy.

See also: ECOLOGICAL PHILOSOPHY

INGEMUND GULLVÅG

NAGEL, ERNEST (1901–85)

Ernest Nagel was arguably the pre-eminent American philosopher of science from the mid-1930s to the 1960s. He taught at Columbia University for virtually his entire career. Although he shared with Bertrand Russell and with members of the Vienna Circle a respect for and sensitivity to developments in mathematics and the natural sciences, he endorsed a strand in the thought of Charles S. Peirce and John Dewey that Nagel himself called 'contextual naturalism'. Among the main features of contextual naturalism is its distrust of reductionist claims that are not the outcomes of scientific inquiries.

Nagel's contextual naturalism infused his influential, detailed and informed essays on probability, explanation in the natural and social sciences, measurement, history of mathematics, and the philosophy of law. It is reflected, for example, in his trenchant critiques of Russell's reconstruction of the external world and Russell's epistemology as well as cognate views endorsed at one time or another by members of the Vienna Circle.

See also: LOGICAL POSITIVISM

ISAAC LEVI

NAGEL, THOMAS (1937–)

The comprehensiveness of Thomas Nagel's approach to philosophy sets him apart among late-twentieth-century analytic philosophers. Nagel develops a compelling analysis of the fundamental philosophical problems, showing how they result from our capacity to take up increasingly objective viewpoints that detach us from our individual subjective viewpoints as well as from the viewpoints of our community, nation and species. Our essentially dual nature, which allows us to occupy objective as well as subjective viewpoints, poses unsolvable problems for us because subjective and objective viewpoints reveal conflicting facts and values. Our ability to undertake increasingly detached viewpoints from which objective facts come into view indicates that we are contained in a world that transcends our minds; similarly, our ability to examine our values and reasons from a detached or impartial objective viewpoint implies that moral values are real in the sense that they transcend our personal motives and inclinations. Yet Nagel also holds that our capacity for objective thought is limited by the fact that we cannot detach ourselves completely from our own natures in our attempts either to know our world or to act morally. Subjective facts are equally a part of reality and our moral outlook is essentially the outlook of individual agents with personal and communal ties. Consequently, Nagel argues against any form of reductionism which holds that only objective facts and values are real or which attempts to explain subjective facts and values in terms of objective ones.

See also: REDUCTION, PROBLEMS OF

SONIA SEDIVY

NAMES
See PROPER NAMES

NARRATIVE

Narrative, in its broadest sense, is the means by which a story is told, whether fictional or not, and regardless of medium. Novels, plays, films, historical texts, diaries and newspaper articles focus, in their different ways, on particular events and their temporal and causal relations; they are all narratives in the above sense. Accounts of mathematical, physical, economic or legal principles are not. A narrower sense of narrative requires the presence of a narrator mediating between audience and action, and contrasts with imitative discourse wherein the action is presented directly, as in drama. The boundary between narration narrowly construed and imitation is disputed, some writers arguing that apparently imitative forms are covertly narrated.

Attempts have been made to characterize fictional narratives in linguistic terms; another view is that fictions are things which have certain (intended or actual) effects on the audience. Theorists of narrative have mostly concentrated on narratives of the fictional kind and have developed a complex taxonomy of the various narrative devices. Recently, pressure has been placed on the distinction between historical and fictional narrative by those who believe that history is nothing distinct from the various and conflicting narrative versions we have. It has also been argued that value accrues to an agent's life and acts when those acts conform to a conception of that life as exemplifying narrative.

See also: BARTHES, R.; HISTORY, PHILOSOPHY OF; NIETZSCHE, F.

GREGORY CURRIE

NATION AND NATIONALISM

No one observing political events in the world today could deny the continuing potency of nationalism. Many of the most intractable conflicts arise when one national community tries to break away from another, or when two such communities lay claim to the same piece of territory. Yet to outsiders the basis for such conflicts often seems mysterious. People are prepared to fight and die for their nation, yet what exactly is this 'nation' that commands such loyalty? Why should it matter so much that a person is governed by leaders drawn from one community rather than from another?

Philosophers are often inclined to dismiss nationalism as having no rational basis, but as resting merely on tribal instincts and brute emotions. Such a response overlooks the different forms

that nationalism has taken: in particular, the contrast between authoritarian nationalism, which allows national cultures to be imposed by force and which may justify acts of aggression against neighbouring peoples, and liberal nationalism, which upholds the rights of individuals to form political communities with those with whom they feel identified and to protect their common culture. We need to examine carefully the arguments that have been advanced by nationalist thinkers in order to decide which form of nationalism, if any, is rationally defensible.

See also: GLOBALIZATION; JUSTICE, INTERNATIONAL; STATE, THE

DAVID MILLER

NATIVISM

Traditional empiricism claims that the mind is initially equipped only with the capacity for experience and the mechanisms that make it possible for us to learn from experience. Nativists have argued that this is not enough, and that our innate endowment must be far richer, including information, ideas, beliefs, perhaps even knowledge.

Empiricism held the advantage until recently, partly because of a misidentification of nativism with rationalism. Rationalists such as Descartes and Leibniz thought nativism would explain how a priori knowledge of necessary truths is possible. However, the fact that something is innate does not establish that it is true, let alone that it is necessary or a priori.

More recently, nativism has been reanimated by Chomsky's claims that children must have innate language-specific information that mediates acquisition of their native tongue. He argues that, given standard empiricist learning procedures, the linguistic data available to a child underdetermines the grammar on which they converge at a very young age, with relatively little effort or instruction.

The successes in linguistics have led to fruitful research on nativism in other domains of human knowledge: for example, arithmetic, the nature of physical objects, features of persons, and possession of concepts generally.

JERRY SAMET

NATORP, PAUL
See NEO-KANTIANISM

NATURAL DEDUCTION, TABLEAU AND SEQUENT SYSTEMS

Different presentations of the principles of logic reflect different approaches to the subject itself. The three kinds of system discussed here treat as fundamental not logical truth, but consequence, the relation holding between the premises and conclusion of a valid argument. They are, however, inspired by different conceptions of this relation. Natural deduction rules are intended to formalize the way in which mathematicians actually reason in their proofs. Tableau systems reflect the semantic conception of consequence; their rules may be interpreted as the systematic search for a counter-example to an argument. Finally, sequent calculi were developed for the sake of their metamathematical properties.

All three systems employ rules rather than axioms. Each logical constant is governed by a pair of rules which do not involve the other constants and are, in some sense, inverse. Take the implication operator '→', for example. In natural deduction, there is an introduction rule for '→' which gives a sufficient condition for inferring an implication, and an elimination rule which gives the strongest conclusion that can be inferred from a premise having the form of an implication. Tableau systems contain a rule which gives a sufficient condition for an implication to be true, and another which gives a sufficient condition for it to be false. A sequent is an array $\Gamma \vdash \Delta$, where Γ and Δ are lists (or sets) of formulas. Sequent calculi have rules for introducing implication on the left of the '⊢' symbol and on the right.

The construction of derivations or tableaus in these systems is often more concise and intuitive than in an axiomatic one, and versions of all three have found their way into introductory logic texts. Furthermore, every natural deduction or sequent derivation can be made more direct by transforming it into a 'normal form'. In the case of the sequent calculus, this result is known as the cut-elimination theorem. It has been applied extensively in metamathematics, most famously to obtain consistency proofs. The semantic inspiration for the rules of tableau construction suggests a very perspicuous proof of classical completeness, one which can also be adapted to the sequent calculus. The introduction and elimination rules of natural deduction are intuitionistically valid and have suggested an alternative semantics based on a conception of meaning as use. The idea is that the meaning of each logical constant is exhausted by its inferential behaviour and can therefore be characterized by its introduction and elimination rules.

Although the discussion below focuses on intuitionistic and classical first-order logic, various other logics have also been formulated as sequent, natural deduction and even tableau systems: modal logics, for example, relevance logic, infinitary and higher-order logics. There is a gain in understanding the role of the logical constants which comes from formulating introduction and elimina-

tion (or left and right) rules for them. Some authors have even suggested that one must be able to do so for an operator to count as logical.

A.M. UNGAR

NATURAL KINDS

Objects belonging to a natural kind form a group of objects which have some theoretically important property in common. For example, rabbits form a natural kind, all samples of gold form another, and so on. Natural kinds are contrasted with arbitrary groups of objects such as the contents of dustbins, or collections of jewels. The latter have no theoretically important property in common: they have no unifying feature. Natural kinds provide a system for classifying objects. Scientists can then use this system to predict and explain the behaviour of those objects. For these reasons, the topic of natural kinds is of special interest to metaphysics and to the philosophy of science.
See also: MASS TERMS; REFERENCE

CHRIS DALY

NATURAL LAW

When made within the discourse of ethics, political theory, or legal theory or philosophy of law, the claim that there is a natural law is an offer to explain and defend certain claims often made, in different terms, in the discourse of moral argument, politics or law. In pre-theoretical moral discourse, certain choices, actions or dispositions may be asserted to be 'inhuman', 'unnaturally cruel', 'perverse' or 'morally unreasonable'. In pre-theoretical political discourse, certain proposals, policies or conduct may be described as violations of 'human rights'. In international law and jurisprudence, certain actions may be described as 'crimes against humanity' and citizens may claim immunity from legal liability or obligations by appealing to a 'higher law'. A natural law theory offers to explain why claims of this sort can be rationally warranted and true. It offers to do so by locating such claims in the context of a general theory of good and evil in human life so far as human life is shaped by deliberation and choice. Such a general theory can also be called a general theory of right and wrong in human choices and actions. It will contain both (1) normative propositions identifying types of choice, action or disposition as right or wrong, permissible, obligatory and so on, and (2) non-normative propositions about the objectivity and epistemological warrant of the normative propositions.
See also: GROTIUS, H.; LAW, PHILOSOPHY OF; LEGAL POSITIVISM

JOHN FINNIS

NATURAL LAWS
See LAWS, NATURAL

NATURAL THEOLOGY

Natural theology aims at establishing truths or acquiring knowledge about God (or divine matters generally) using only our natural cognitive resources. The phrase 'our natural cognitive resources' identifies both the methods and data for natural theology: it relies on standard techniques of reasoning and facts or truths in principle available to all human beings just in virtue of their possessing reason and sense perception. As traditionally conceived, natural theology begins by establishing the existence of God, and then proceeds by establishing truths about God's nature (for example, that God is eternal, immutable and omniscient) and about God's relation to the world.

A precise characterization of natural theology depends on further specification of its methods and data. One strict conception of natural theology – the traditional conception sometimes associated with Thomas Aquinas – allows only certain kinds of deductive argument, the starting points of which are propositions that are either self-evident or evident to sense perception. A broader conception might allow not just deductive but also inductive inference and admit as starting points propositions that fall short of being wholly evident.

Natural theology contrasts with investigations into divine matters that rely at least in part on data not naturally available to us as human beings. This sort of enterprise might be characterized as *revelation-based* theology, in so far as the supernatural element on which it relies is something supernaturally revealed to us by God. Revelation-based theology can make use of what is ascertainable by us only because of special divine aid. Dogmatic and biblical theology would be enterprises of this sort.

Critics of natural theology fall generally into three groups. The first group, the majority, argue that some or all of the particular arguments of natural theology are, as a matter of fact, unsuccessful. Critics in the second group argue that, in principle, natural theology cannot succeed, either because of essential limitations on human knowledge that make it impossible for us to attain knowledge of God or because religious language is such as to make an investigation into its truth inappropriate. The third group of critics holds that natural theology is in some way irrelevant or inimical to true religion. They argue in various ways that the objectifying, abstract and impersonal methods of natural theology cannot capture what is

fundamentally important about the divine and our relation to it.

See also: AGNOSTICISM; ATHEISM; GOD, ARGUMENTS FOR THE EXISTENCE OF; GOD, CONCEPTS OF; MENDELSSOHN, M.; REVELATION

SCOTT MACDONALD

NATURALISM IN ETHICS

Ethical naturalism is the project of fitting an account of ethics into a naturalistic worldview. It includes nihilistic theories, which see no place for real values and no successful role for ethical thought in a purely natural world. The term 'naturalism' is often used more narrowly, however, to refer to cognitivist naturalism, which holds that ethical facts are simply natural facts and that ethical thought succeeds in discovering them.

G.E. Moore, attacked cognitivist naturalism as mistaken in principle, for committing what he called the 'naturalistic fallacy'. He thought a simple test showed that ethical facts could not be natural facts (the 'fallacy' lay in believing they could be), and he took it to follow that ethical knowledge would have to rest on nonsensory intuition. Later writers have added other arguments for the same conclusions. Moore himself was in no sense a naturalist, since he thought that ethics could be given a 'non-natural' basis. Many who elaborated his criticisms of cognitivist naturalism, however, have done so on behalf of generic ethical naturalism, and so have defended either ethical nihilism or else some more modest constructive position, usually a version of noncognitivism. Noncognitivists concede to nihilists that nature contains no real values, but deny that it was ever the function of ethical thought to discover such things. They thus leave ethical thought room for success at some other task, such as providing the agent with direction for action.

Defenders of cognitivist naturalism deny that there is a 'naturalistic fallacy' or that ethical knowledge need rest on intuition; and they have accused Moore and his successors of relying on dubious assumptions in metaphysics, epistemology, the philosophy of language and the philosophy of mind. Thus many difficult philosophical issues have been implicated in the debate.

See also: MORAL JUDGMENT; MORAL KNOWLEDGE

NICHOLAS L. STURGEON

NATURALISM IN SOCIAL SCIENCE

Naturalism is a term used in several ways. The more specific meanings of 'naturalism' in the philosophy of social sciences rest on the great popular authority acquired by modern scientific methods and forms of explanation in the wake of the seventeenth-century scientific revolution. For many of the thinkers of the European Enlightenment and their nineteenth-century followers the success of science in uncovering the laws governing the natural world was used as an argument for the extension of its methods into the study of morality, society, government and human mental life. Not only would this bring the benefit of consensus in these contested areas, but also it would provide a sound basis for ameliorative social reform. Among the most influential advocates of naturalism, in this sense, was the early nineteenth-century French philosopher Auguste Comte.

The authority of the new mechanical science, even as an account of non-human nature, continued to be resisted by romantic philosophers. However, the more limited task of resisting the scientific 'invasion' of human self-understanding was taken up by the Neo-Kantian philosophers of the latter part of the nineteenth century, in Germany. Followers and associates of this tradition (such as Windelband, Rickert, Dilthey and others) insist that there is a radical gulf between scientific knowledge of nature, and the forms of understanding which are possible in the sphere of humanly created meanings and cultures. This view is argued for in several different ways. Sometimes a contrast is made between the regularities captured in laws of nature, on the one hand, and social rules, on the other. Sometimes human consciousness and self-understanding is opposed to the non-conscious 'behaviour' of nonhuman beings and objects, so that studying society is more like reading a book or having a conversation than it is like studying a chemical reaction.

TED BENTON

NATURALISTIC FALLACY

See MOORE, GEORGE EDWARD; NATURALISM IN ETHICS

NATURALIZED EPISTEMOLOGY

The term 'naturalized epistemology' was coined by W.V. Quine to refer to an approach to epistemology which he introduced in his 1969 essay 'Epistemology Naturalized'. Many of the moves that are distinctive of naturalized epistemology were made by David Hume, but Quine's essay fixes the sense of the term as it is used today.

Naturalized epistemology has critical as well as constructive thrusts. In a critical spirit, 'naturalists' (theorists who identify with the label 'naturalized epistemology') abandon several assumptions that are part of the tradition. They reject Descartes' vision of

epistemology as the attempt to convert our beliefs into an edifice resting on a foundation about which we have complete certainty. Descartes is wrong to equate knowledge with certainty, and wrong to think that knowledge is available through a priori theorizing, through reasoning which makes no use of experience. Nor should epistemology continue as David Hume's attempt to rest knowledge on an introspective study of the mind's contents. Moreover, the global sceptic's claim that there is no way to justify all our views at once, should either be conceded or ignored.

On the constructive side, naturalists suggest that in investigating knowledge we rely on the apparatus, techniques and assumptions of natural science. Accordingly, naturalized epistemology will be a scientific (and hence neither indefeasible nor a priori) explanation of how it is that some beliefs come to be knowledge. Issues of scepticism will be addressed only when they come up in the course of a scientific investigation.

Quine's seminal essay lays out the core of naturalized epistemology, but subsequent naturalists disagree on the appropriate responses to several issues, among them the following: First, may theories be tested on the basis of (independently plausible) theory-neutral observation, or are observations simply more theory? Second, after being naturalized, does epistemology survive as an autonomous discipline? Quine argues that epistemology should become a subfield of natural science, presumably a part of psychology, so that there is no separate field left specifically to philosophers. But can all our questions about knowledge be answered by natural scientists? Third, the claim that epistemology explains how knowledge comes to be suggests that epistemology will merely describe the origins of beliefs we take to be known; but what is the relationship between such descriptive issues and normative issues such as that of how we ought to arrive at our views? Fourth, to what extent is the new approach to epistemology susceptible to sceptical concerns such as those that so plagued traditional epistemologists, and how effective a response can be made to those concerns?
See also: KNOWLEDGE, CONCEPT OF; SOCIAL EPISTEMOLOGY

STEVEN LUPER

NATURE, AESTHETIC APPRECIATION OF

In the Western world, aesthetic appreciation of nature and its philosophical investigation came to fruition in the eighteenth century. During that time, aestheticians made nature the ideal object of aesthetic experience and analysed that experience in terms of disinterestedness, thereby laying the groundwork for understanding the appreciation of nature in terms of the sublime and the picturesque. This philosophical tradition reached its zenith with Kant, while popular aesthetic appreciation of nature continued primarily in terms of the picturesque.

In the late twentieth century, renewed interest in the aesthetics of nature has produced various positions designed to avoid assimilating appreciation of nature with traditional models for aesthetic appreciation of art. Three are especially noteworthy. The first holds that the appreciation of nature is not in fact aesthetic; the second rejects the traditional analysis of aesthetic experience as disinterested, arguing instead that the aesthetic appreciation of nature involves engagement with nature; the third attempts to maintain the traditional analysis, while distinguishing aesthetic appreciation of nature by dependence on scientific knowledge.

These positions have a number of ramifications. In freeing aesthetic appreciation of nature from artistic models, they pave the way for a general environmental aesthetics comparable to other areas of philosophy, such as environmental ethics. Moreover, the significance given to scientific knowledge in the third position both explains the aesthetic appreciation associated with environmentalism and provides aesthetic appreciation of nature with a degree of objectivity that may make aesthetic considerations more effectual in environmental assessment.

See also: AESTHETIC ATTITUDE; ENVIRONMENTAL AESTHETICS; HEGEL, G.W.F. §8; KANT, I. §12; NATURPHILOSOPHIE; SUBLIME, THE

ALLEN CARLSON

NATURE AND CONVENTION

The nature–convention distinction opposes instinctual or 'spontaneous' modes of comportment (those which follow from 'human nature') to those which are socially instituted or culturally prescribed. Its philosophic interest resides in its use to justify or contest specific forms of human behaviour and social organization. Since the 'conventional' is opposed to the 'natural' as that which is in principle transformable, the adherents of a particular order in human affairs have standardly sought to prove its 'naturality', while its critics have sought to expose its merely 'conventional' status. Relatedly, 'conventions' may be associated with what is distinctive to 'human', as opposed to 'bestial' nature, or denounced for their role in repressing our more 'natural' impulses.

See also: CONVENTIONALISM; CULTURE; NATURALISM IN SOCIAL SCIENCE

KATE SOPER

NATURE, PHILOSOPHY OF
See NATURPHILOSOPHIE

NATURPHILOSOPHIE

Naturphilosophie refers to the philosophy of nature prevalent especially in German philosophy, science and literary movements from around 1790 to about 1830. It pleaded for an organic and dynamic worldview as an alternative to the atomist and mechanist outlook of modern science. Against the Cartesian dualism of matter and mind which had given way to the mechanist materialism of the French Encyclopedists, Spinoza's dual aspect theory of mind and matter as two modes of a single substance was favoured. The sources of this heterogeneous movement lie in the philosophy of German idealism as well as in late classicism and Romanticism. The leading figure, Schelling, assimilated and stimulated the major trends and ideas through his work.

After the death of Hegel (1831) and of Goethe (1832), *Naturphilosophie* quickly disappeared from the mainstream. Yet it survived in various different forms, especially as an undercurrent of German culture and science, until the twentieth century.

See also: GERMAN IDEALISM

MICHAEL HEIDELBERGER

NAVYA-NYĀYA
See NYĀYA-VAIŚEṢIKA

NECESSARY TRUTH AND CONVENTION

Necessary truths have always seemed problematic, particularly to empiricists and other naturalistically-minded philosophers. Our knowledge here is a priori – grounded in appeals to what we can imagine or conceive (or can prove on that basis) – which seems hard to reconcile with such truths being factual, short of appealing to some peculiar faculty of a priori intuition. And what mysterious extra feature do necessary truths possess which makes their falsity impossible? Conventionalism about necessity claims that necessary truths obtain by virtue of rules of language, such as that 'vixen' means the same as 'female fox'. Because such rules govern our descriptions of all cases – including counterfactual or imagined ones – they generate necessary truths ('All vixens are foxes'), and our a priori knowledge is just knowledge of word meaning. Opponents of conventionalism argue that conventions cannot ground necessary truths, particularly in logic, and have also challenged the notion of analyticity (truth by virtue of meaning). More recent claims that some necessary truths are a posteriori have also fuelled opposition to conventionalism.

See also: CONVENTIONALISM; ESSENTIALISM

ALAN SIDELLE

NEGATIVE THEOLOGY

The term 'negative theology' refers to theologies which regard negative statements as primary in expressing our knowledge of God, contrasted with 'positive theologies' giving primary emphasis to positive statements. The distinction was developed within Muslim, Jewish and Christian theism. If the negative way (*via negativa*) is taken to its limits, two questions arise: first, whether one may speak of God equally well in impersonal as in personal terms (blurring the distinction between theism and, say, the philosophical Hinduism of Śaṅkara); and second, whether it leads ultimately to rejecting any ultimate being or subject at all (blurring the distinction between theism and, say, the atheism of Mahāyāna Buddhism). However, within their original theistic context, positive and negative statements about God are interdependent, the second indispensably qualifying the first, the negative statements taken alone useless.

Negative qualifications on positive statements attributing so-called 'perfections' to God – for example, existence, life, goodness, knowledge, love or active power ('strength') – are obviously necessary if God is unimaginable. If his presence is always of his whole being and life all at once, in each place in space and time, he must be non-spatial and non-temporal in being and nature, and clearly he must be unimaginable. However, his supposed 'simplicity' and 'infinity' imply that he is much more radically outside the reach of understanding or 'comprehension', imposing the negative way at a deeper level than mere unimaginability. This unimaginability and incomprehensibility are key to theistic accounts of prayer and the mystical life.

See also: PATRISTIC PHILOSOPHY

DAVID BRAINE

NÉGRITUDE

See AFRICAN PHILOSOPHY, ANGLOPHONE; AFRICAN PHILOSOPHY, FRANCOPHONE

NEO-KANTIANISM

In contrast to earlier research, which chose to distinguish up to seven schools of thought within the field of Neo-Kantianism, more recent scholarship takes two basic movements as its starting point: the Marburg School and the Southwest German School, which are based respectively on systematically oriented works on Kant published during the 1870s and 1880s by Hermann Cohen and Wilhelm Windelband.

Cohen held that Kant's concern in all three Critiques was to reveal those a priori moments which above all give rise to the domains of scientific experience, morality and aesthetics. Windelband on the other hand held that Kant's achievement lay in the attempt to create a critical science of norms which, instead of giving a genetic explanation of the norms of logic, morality and aesthetics, aimed instead to elucidate their validity. In both approaches, an initial phase during which Kant's doctrines were appropriated subsequently developed into the production of systems. Thus Cohen published a 'System of Philosophy' during the early years of the twentieth century, which consisted of the *Logik der reinen Erkenntnis* (Logic of Pure Knowledge) (1902), the *Ethik des reinen Willens* (Ethics of Pure Will) (1904) and the *Ästhetik des reinen Gefühls* (Aesthetics of Pure Feeling) (1912) and which radicalized the operative approach of his work on Kant. Later, Cohen conceived a *Religion der Vernunft aus den Quellen des Judentums* (*Religion of Reason from the Sources of Judaism*) (1919). Windelband, on the other hand, who made a name for himself primarily in the sphere of the history of philosophy, understood philosophy to be essentially concerned with value, anchored in transcendental consciousness. He emphatically linked the classical division of philosophy into logic, ethics and aesthetics to the values of Truth, Goodness and Beauty and also tried to situate the philosophy of religion in this context.

Apart from Cohen, the Marburg School is represented by Paul Natorp and Ernst Cassirer, whose early works followed Cohen's philosophical views (compare Natorp's interpretation of the Platonic doctrine of ideas and Cassirer's history of the problem of knowledge), but whose later works modified his approach. Nevertheless, their extensions and developments can also be explained within the framework of the original Marburg doctrines. The ontological turn which Natorp undertook in his later years can be seen as a radicalization of Cohen's principle of origin, which Natorp believed could not be expressed in terms of pure intellectual positing, and the operative moment introduced by Cohen lives on as a theory of creative formation in Cassirer's theory of symbolic forms.

In addition to Windelband, the Southwest German school of Neo-Kantianism is represented by Heinrich Rickert, Emil Lask, Jonas Cohn and Bruno Bauch. Windelband instigated the systematic approach of the Southwest School, but it was left to Rickert to develop it fully. Unlike Windelband, who traced the difference between history and science back to the difference between the idiographic and the nomothetic methods, Rickert distinguished between the individualizing concepts of history and the generalizing concepts of science. During his middle period he turned his attention to the problem of articulating a system of values. In his later works, Rickert also turned towards ontology, a development which should not necessarily be interpreted as a break with the constitutional theories of his early years. In concrete terms, building on his earlier theories concerning the constitutive role of concepts in experience, Rickert henceforth distinguishes not only the realm of scientific and cultural objects and the sphere of values, but also the further ontological domains of the world of the free subject and the metaphysical world, which is the object of faith and which can only be comprehended by thinking in symbols.

Lask's theoretical philosophy was characterized by a turn to objectivism. In contrast to the classical Neo-Kantian conception of knowledge, according to which everything given is determined by the forms of cognition, Lask sees matter as that element which determines meaning. Accordingly, at the centre of his theory of knowledge is not the subject's activity in constituting the object, but the subject's openness to the object. In the final stage of his philosophy, however, he once more attributed to the subject an autonomous role in the actualization of knowledge. Cohn contributed to Southwest German Neo-Kantianism not only his *Allgemeine Ästhetik* (General Theory of Aesthetics) (1901), but also works on the philosophy of culture and education as well as on the systematic articulation of values and the problem of reality. During the 1920s Cohn moved towards dialectics. In contrast to Hegel, however, he understood this to mean critical dialectics inasmuch as it does not aim to sublate or overcome opposition, but merely sets itself the unending task of attempting to resolve irreconcilable contradictions.

Finally, Bauch can be regarded as the most essentially synthetic thinker of the Southwest German Neo-Kantian school. He tried to demonstrate the inseparable connectedness of individual problems which had generally been treated separately. Apart from his great Kantian monographs, these ideas are also put forward in his systematic works on the questions of theoretical and practical philosophy, such as his study *Wahrheit, Wert und Wirklichkeit* (Truth, Value and Reality) (1923) and his *Grundzüge der Ethik* (Fundamentals of Ethics) (1935).

Despite the one-sidedness of its reception of Kant's doctrines, Neo-Kantianism was important for the momentum it gave to research into Kantian philosophy during the twentieth century. Its systematic achievement lies in its development of the normative concept of validity and its programmatic outline for a philosophy of culture.

See also: COHEN, H.; NISHIDA KITARŌ

HANS-LUDWIG OLLIG
Translated from the German
by JANE MICHAEL and NICHOLAS WALKER

NEOPLATONISM

Neoplatonism was the final flowering of ancient Greek thought, from the third to the sixth or seventh century AD. Building on eight centuries of unbroken philosophical debate, it addressed questions such as: What is the true self? What is consciousness and how does it relate to reality? Can intuition be reconciled with reason? What are the first causes of reality? How did the universe come into being? How can an efficient cause retain its identity and yet be distributed among its effects? Why does the soul become embodied? What is the good life?

There were several flavours of Neoplatonism, reflecting the concerns and backgrounds of its practitioners, who ranged from Plotinus and his circle of freelance thinkers to the heads of the university schools of the Roman Empire, Proclus, Ammonius and Damascius. In the later, more analysed form, we see a rich scheme of multi-layered metaphysics, epistemology and ethics, but also literary theory, mathematics, physics and other subjects, all integrated in one curriculum. Neoplatonism was not just a philosophy but the higher education system of its age.

The Neoplatonism that came to dominate the ancient world from the fourth century was an inseparable mixture of inspired thought and scholastic order. To this may be traced some of its internal conceptual conflicts: for example, the free individual soul versus the ranks of being, personal experience versus demonstrative knowledge. To this may also be traced its appeal to polar audiences: mystics and mathematizing scientists, romantics and rationalists.

To the Neoplatonist, knowledge consists of degrees of completion. Take the example of tutor and student. Both study the same things, but the tutor has a wider and more intimate knowledge. The tutor opens the student's mind to the breadth and intricacies of the study-matter, and corrects the student's deliberations. So it is with the Neoplatonic levels of knowledge. Every level has access to the entire spectrum of what there is to know, but each with its appropriate adverbial modifier. At the 'lower' level an individual comprehends things 'particularly' and is concerned with the 'images' or presentations of mind and sense-impressions of the qualities of physical things. At the 'higher' level, an individual apprehends things 'wholly', as universal statements (often called 'laws' and 'canons'). The concern is with propositions about what is true or false, self-grounded and logically necessary. Thus the higher level corrects and supplies the 'criterion' for the lower level.

Knowledge, however, is not an end in itself, but a means to salvation. Increasing awareness puts us in touch with the levels of reality of which we ourselves are part. The ultimate reality is none other than the fundamental unity out of which all came into being: God. In this union we recover our true good.

As the summation of ancient Greek philosophy, Neoplatonism was transmitted to Byzantium, Islam and western Europe. It was the prime intellectual force behind the protagonists of the Italian Renaissance, and its influence was felt until the nineteenth century.

See also: HYPATIA; KABBALAH; RENAISSANCE PHILOSOPHY

LUCAS SIORVANES

NEUMANN, FRANZ
See FRANKFURT SCHOOL

NEUTRAL MONISM

Neutral monism is a theory of the relation of mind and matter. It holds that both are complex constructions out of more primitive elements that are 'neutral' in the sense that they are neither mental nor material. Mind and matter, therefore, do not differ in the intrinsic nature of their constituents but in the manner in which the constituents are organized. The theory is monist only in claiming that all the basic elements of the world are of the same fundamental type (in contrast to mind–body dualism); it is, however, pluralist in that it admits a plurality of such elements (in contrast to metaphysical monism).

See also: BEHAVIOURISM, ANALYTIC; FUNCTIONALISM; MIND, IDENTITY THEORY OF; MONISM

NICHOLAS GRIFFIN

NEUTRALITY, POLITICAL

The principle of political neutrality, which requires the state to remain neutral on disputed questions about the good, is an extension of traditional liberal principles of toleration and religious disestablishment. However, since neutrality is itself a contested concept, the principle remains indeterminate: is it,

for example, a requirement of neutral reasons for legislation (or neutral legislative intentions) or is it a more exacting requirement of equal impact in so far as legislative consequences are concerned? The answer must surely reflect the deeper values that are used to justify the neutrality principle. This raises further problems, however. If the principle is based upon certain value commitments – such as the importance of equality or individual autonomy – then it cannot require us to be neutral about all values. It requires some sort of distinction between principles of right (of which neutrality is one) and conceptions of the good (among which neutrality is required). Critics believe that liberal principles of right are symptomatic of a deeper liberal bias in favour of individuality as a way of life. Perhaps liberals should embrace this point, and accept that the neutrality they advocate is quite superficial compared to the depth of their own value commitments.

See also: LIBERALISM

JEREMY WALDRON

NEWTON, ISAAC (1642–1727)

Newton is best known for having invented the calculus and formulated the theory of universal gravity – the latter in his *Principia*, the single most important work in the transformation of natural philosophy into modern physical science. Yet he also made major discoveries in optics, and put no less effort into alchemy and theology than into mathematics and physics.

Throughout his career, Newton maintained a sharp distinction between conjectural hypotheses and experimentally established results. This distinction was central to his claim that the method by which conclusions about forces were inferred from phenomena in the *Principia* made it 'possible to argue more securely concerning the physical species, physical causes, and physical proportions of these forces'. The law of universal gravity that he argued for in this way nevertheless provoked strong opposition, especially from such leading figures on the Continent as Huygens and Leibniz: they protested that Newton was invoking an occult power of action-at-a-distance insofar as he was offering no contact mechanism by means of which forces of gravity could act. This opposition led him to a tighter, more emphatic presentation of his methodology in the second edition of the *Principia*, published twenty-six years after the first. The opposition to the theory of gravity faded during the fifty to seventy-five years after his death as it fulfilled its promise on such issues as the non-spherical shape of the earth, the precession of the

equinoxes, comet trajectories (including the return of 'Halley's Comet' in 1758), the vagaries of lunar motion and other deviations from Keplerian motion. During this period the point mass mechanics of the *Principia* was extended to rigid bodies and fluids by such figures as Euler, forming what we know as 'Newtonian' mechanics.
See also: Cosmology; Relativity theory, philosophical significance of; Space; Theories, scientific

WILLIAM L. HARPER
GEORGE E. SMITH

NICHOLAS OF CUSA (1401–64)

Also called Nicolaus Cusanus, this German cardinal takes his distinguishing name from the city of his birth, Kues (or Cusa, in Latin), on the Moselle river between Koblenz and Trier. Nicholas was influenced by Albert the Great, Thomas Aquinas, Bonaventure, Ramon Llull, Ricoldo of Montecroce, Master Eckhart, Jean Gerson and Heimericus de Campo, as well as by more distant figures such as Plato, Aristotle, Proclus, Pseudo-Dionysius and John Scottus Eriugena. His eclectic system of thought pointed in the direction of a transition between the Middle Ages and the Renaissance. In his own day as in ours, Nicholas was most widely known for his early work *De docta ignorantia* (On Learned Ignorance). In it, he gives expression to his view that the human mind needs to discover its necessary ignorance of what the Divine Being is like, an ignorance that results from the infinite ontological and cognitive disproportion between Infinity itself (that is, God) and the finite human or angelic knower. Correlated with the doctrine of *docta ignorantia* is that of *coincidentia oppositorum in deo*, the coincidence of opposites in God. All things coincide in God in the sense that God, as undifferentiated being, is beyond all opposition, beyond all determination as *this* rather than *that*.

Nicholas is also known for his rudimentary cosmological speculation, his prefiguring of certain metaphysical and epistemological themes found later in Leibniz, Kant and Hegel, his ecclesiological teachings regarding the controversy over papal versus conciliar authority, his advocacy of a religious ecumenism of sorts, his interest in purely mathematical topics and his influence on the theologian Paul Tillich in the twentieth century. A striking tribute to Nicholas' memory still stands today: the hospice for elderly, indigent men that he caused to be erected at Kues between 1452 and 1458 and that he both endowed financially and invested with his personal library. This small but splendid library, unravaged by the intervening wars and consisting of

726

some three hundred volumes, includes manuscripts written in Nicholas' own hand.
See also: Bruno, G.; Cosmology; Negative theology; Ontology; Platonism, Renaissance; Renaissance philosophy

JASPER HOPKINS

NICOLE, PIERRE
See Arnauld, Antoine

NIETZSCHE, FRIEDRICH (1844–1900)

Introduction

Appointed professor of classical philology at the University of Basel when he was just 24 years old, Nietzsche was expected to secure his reputation as a brilliant young scholar with his first book, *Die Geburt der Tragödie* (*The Birth of Tragedy*) (1872). But that book did not look much like a work of classical scholarship. Bereft of footnotes and highly critical of Socrates and modern scholarship, it spoke in rhapsodic tones of ancient orgiastic Dionysian festivals and the rebirth of Dionysian tragedy in the modern world. Classical scholars, whose craft and temperament it had scorned, greeted the book with scathing criticism and hostility; even Nietzsche eventually recognized it as badly written and confused. Yet it remains one of the three most important philosophical treatments of tragedy (along with those of Aristotle and Hegel) and is the soil out of which Nietzsche's later philosophy grew. By 1889, when he suffered a mental and physical collapse that brought his productive life to an end, Nietzsche had produced a series of thirteen books which have left a deep imprint on most areas of Western intellectual and cultural life, establishing him as one of Germany's greatest prose stylists and one of its most important, if controversial, philosophers.

Nietzsche appears to attack almost everything that has been considered sacred: not only Socrates and scholarship, but also God, truth, morality, equality, democracy and most other modern values. He gives a large role to the will to power and he proposes to replace the values he attacks with new values and a new ideal of the human person (the *Übermensch* meaning 'overhuman' or 'superhuman'). Although Nazi theoreticians attempted to associate these ideas with their own cause, responsible interpreters agree that Nietzsche despised and unambiguously rejected both German nationalism and anti-Semitism. Little else in his thought is so unambiguous, at least in part because he rarely writes in a straightforward, argumentative style, and because his thought changed radically over the course of his productive life. The latter is especially true of his early criticism of Socrates, science and truth.

Nietzsche's philosophizing began from a deep sense of dissatisfaction with modern Western culture, which he found superficial and empty in comparison with that of the ancient Greeks. Locating the source of the problem in the fact that modern culture gives priority to science (understood broadly as including all forms of scholarship and theory), whereas Presocratic Greece had given priority to art and myth, he rested his hopes for modern culture on a return to the Greek valuation of art, calling for a recognition of art as 'the highest task and the truly metaphysical activity of this life'.

He soon turned his back on this early critique of science. In the works of his middle period he rejects metaphysical truth but celebrates the valuing of science and empirical truth over myth as a sign of high culture. Although he had earlier considered it destructive of culture, he now committed his own philosophy to a thoroughgoing naturalistic understanding of human beings. He continued to believe that naturalism undermines commitment to values because it destroys myths and illusions, but he now hoped that knowledge would purify human desire and allow human beings to live without preferring or evaluating. In the works of his final period, Nietzsche rejects this aspiration as nihilistic.

In his final period, he combined a commitment to science with a commitment to values by recognizing that naturalism does not undermine all values, but only those endorsed by the major ideal of value we have had so far, the ascetic ideal. This ideal takes the highest human life to be one of self-denial, denial of the natural self, thereby treating natural or earthly existence as devoid of intrinsic value. Nietzsche saw this life-devaluing ideal at work in most Western (and Eastern) religion and philosophy. Values always come into existence in support of some form of life, but they gain the support of ascetic religions and philosophies only if they are given a life-devaluing interpretation. Ascetic priests interpret acts as wrong or 'sinful' because the acts are selfish or 'animal' – because they affirm natural instincts – and ascetic philosophers interpret whatever they value – truth, knowledge, philosophy, virtue – in non-natural terms because they share the assumption that anything truly valuable must have a source outside the world of nature, the world accessible to empirical investigation. Only because Nietzsche still accepted this assumption of the ascetic ideal did naturalism seem to undermine all values.

According to his later thought, the ascetic ideal itself undermines values. First it deprives nature of value by placing the source of value outside nature. Then, by promoting the value of truth above all else, it leads to a denial that there is anything besides nature. Among the casualties of this process are morality and belief in God, as Nietzsche indicated by proclaiming that 'God is dead' and that morality will gradually perish. Morality is not the only possible form of ethical life, however, but a particular form that has been brought about by the ascetic ideal. That ideal has little life left in it, according to Nietzsche, as does the form of ethical life it brought about. Morality now has little power to inspire human beings to virtue or anything else. There is no longer anything to play the essential role played by the ascetic ideal: to inspire human beings to take on the task of becoming more than they are, thereby inducing them to internalize their will to power against themselves. Modern culture therefore has insufficient defences against eruptions of barbarism, which Nietzsche predicted as a large part of the history of the twentieth and twenty-first centuries.

But Nietzsche now saw that there was no way to go back to earlier values. His hope rested instead with 'new philosophers' who have lived and thought the values of the ascetic ideal through to their end and thereby recognized the need for new values. His own writings are meant to exhibit a new ideal, often by exemplifying old virtues that are given a new, life-affirming interpretation.

1 Life

Nietzsche was born in Rocken, a small village in the Prussian province of Saxony, on 15 October 1844. His father, a Lutheran minister, became seriously ill in 1848 and died in July 1849 of what was diagnosed as 'softening of the brain'. His brother died the following year, and Nietzsche's mother moved with her son and daughter to Naumberg, a town of 15,000 people, where they lived with his father's mother and her two sisters. In

1858, Nietzsche was offered free admission to Pforta, the most famous school in Germany. After graduating in 1864 with a thesis in Latin on the Greek poet Theogonis, he registered at the University of Bonn as a theology student. The following year he transferred to Leipzig where he registered as a philology student and worked under the classical philologist Friedrich Ritschl. The events of his Leipzig years which had the most profound and lasting influence on his later work were his discoveries of Schopenhauer's *Die Welt als Wille und Vorstellung* (*The World as Will and Representation*) and F.A. Lange's *Geschichte des Materialismus* (*History of Materialism*), and the beginning of a personal relationship with Richard Wagner (see SCHOPENHAUER, A.; LANGE, F.A.). Nietzsche became Ritschl's star pupil, and on Ritschl's recommendation he was appointed to the Chair of Classical Philology at Basel in 1869 at the age of twenty-four. Leipzig proceeded to confer the doctorate without requiring a dissertation.

Basel's proximity to the Wagner residence at Tribschen allowed Nietzsche to develop a close relationship with Richard and Cosima Wagner. Sharing with the composer a deep love of Schopenhauer and a hope for the revitalization of European culture, he initially idealized Wagner and his music. His first book, *Die Geburt der Tragödie* (*The Birth of Tragedy*) (1872), used Schopenhauer's philosophy to interpret Greek tragedy and to suggest that Wagner's opera constituted its rebirth and thereby the salvation of modern culture. Torn between philology and philosophy since shortly after his discovery of Schopenhauer, Nietzsche devoted much of his teaching to the texts of ancient Greek and Roman philosophy and hoped that his first book would establish his credentials as a philosopher. Instead, its unorthodox mixture of philosophy and philology merely served to damage his reputation as a philologist.

In 1879, he resigned his chair at Basel because of health problems that had plagued him for years. In the meantime, he had become progressively estranged from Wagner, a process that culminated in the 1878 publication of the first volume of *Menschliches, Allzumenschliches* (*Human, All Too Human*), a positivist manifesto that praised science rather than art as indicative of high culture. The ten productive years left to him after his retirement were marked by terrible health problems and a near absence of human companionship. Living alone in Italian and Swiss boarding houses, he wrote ten books, each of which has at least some claim to being a masterpiece. His last seven books mark a high point of German prose style.

In January 1889, Nietzsche collapsed in Turin. He wrote a few lucid and beautiful (although insane) letters during the next few days, and after that nothing of which we can make any sense. Following a brief institutionalization, he lived with his mother and then his sister until his death in Weimar on 25 August 1900.

2 Writings and development

During the sixteen years between his first book and his last productive year, Nietzsche's thinking underwent remarkable development, usually with little notification to his readers. The traditional grouping of his writings into three major periods is followed here, although there is significant development within each period. In addition to *The Birth of Tragedy* his early work consists of four essays of cultural criticism – on David Strauss, history, Schopenhauer, and Wagner – published separately but linked together as *Unzeitgemäße Betrachtungen* (*Unfashionable Observations*) (1873–6), plus a number of largely finished essays and fragments that belong to the *Nachlaß* of the period. The most important of the essays are 'Über Wahrheit und Lüge im außermoralischen Sinne' ('On Truth and Lies in a Nonmoral Sense'), 'Homer's Wettkampf' ('Homer's Contest'), and 'Die Philosophie im tragischen Zeitalter der Griechen' ('Philosophy in the Tragic Age of the Greeks').

These early writings sound a note of great dissatisfaction with European (Enlightenment) culture, of which Socrates is taken as the earliest representative and continuing inspiration. At the base of Socratic culture Nietzsche finds the belief that life's highest goal is the theoretical grasp of truth at which science and philosophy aim. Theory's claim to provide truth has been undermined, he thinks, by the doctrine of Kant and Schopenhauer that discursive thought gives access not to things-in-themselves but only to 'appearance' (see KANT, I. §5; SCHOPENHAUER, A.). Nietzsche's suggestion for saving European culture is that art should replace theory as the most valued, the 'truly metaphysical', human activity. At first, his main argument for elevating art is that it is more truthful than theory. But he also suggests a very different argument: that theory is destructive of culture unless it is guided and limited by the needs of life which art serves. In his essay on history, the second argument has largely replaced the first. He argues that when practised as autonomous theory, devoted solely to truth, history destroys the limited and mythical horizons required by life and action. And if we emphasize for another generation the naturalistic understanding of human beings at which Socratic culture has now arrived (for example, the denial of a cardinal distinction between humans and other animals), we will only further our culture's disintegration into chaotic systems of individual and group egoism. Nietzsche suggests that history can be harnessed to serve the needs of life, for instance when it is written to emphasize great lives and other aspects that encourage individuals to set lofty and noble goals for themselves. Such history is as much art as it is theory or science.

Nietzsche turns decisively away from such criticism of pure theory in the writings of his middle period, *Human, All Too Human* (1878–80) and *Morgenröte* (*Daybreak*) (1881). He here celebrates as a sign of high culture an appreciation of the little truths won by rigorous method, and presents his own philosophy as a form of natural science that serves only truth. He also commits himself to the truth of the naturalism he earlier considered so dangerous: there is no cardinal distinction between humans and other animals; everything about human beings, including their values, can be explained as a development from characteristics found among other animals. At the beginning of this period Nietzsche struggles with how naturalism can be compatible with a commitment to values, for he sees it as exposing and thereby undermining the illusions that are needed in order to find value in life. In *Human*, his hope is that knowledge will gradually purify 'the old motives of violent desire' until one can live 'as in *nature*', without preferring or evaluating, but 'gazing contentedly, as though at a spectacle' (*Human* §34). Nietzsche later has Zarathustra mock this spectator conception of knowledge and life as 'immaculate perception' (*Zarathustra* II: §15).

Nietzsche's final period begins with *Die Fröhliche Wissenschaft* (*The Gay Science*) (1882), which replaces the spectator conception with one in which the 'knower' belongs to the dance of existence and is one of its 'masters of ceremony' (*The Gay Science* §54). This formulation expresses his new confidence that naturalism, which he often calls 'knowledge', is compatible with commitment to values. In this period, Nietzsche once again celebrates art, criticizes Socrates and denies the autonomy of theory, suggesting to some that he has reverted to the viewpoint of his early period. Evidence is provided throughout this entry for an alternative interpretation: the later Nietzsche does not deny that theory can provide truth, and he remains as committed to the pursuit of truth as he was in his middle period. The difference is that he now recognizes in even the apparently autonomous theory of his middle period a commitment to an ideal that is external to and served by theory, namely, the ascetic ideal. Nietzsche returns to the suggestion of his first book, that theory is not autonomous; however, he now objects not to theory, but only to the ideal that theory has served (see §§6 and 7 of this entry). The

works of Nietzsche's final period are largely devoted to uncovering, criticizing and offering an alternative to that ideal.

Gay Science was followed by *Also Sprach Zarathustra* (*Thus Spoke Zarathustra*) (1883–5), a fictional tale used as a vehicle for Nietzsche's most puzzling and infamous doctrines, including the overhuman (*Übermensch*), will to power and eternal recurrence. He considered this to be the deepest work in the German language and suggested that chairs of philosophy might one day be devoted to its interpretation. Our surest guides to it at present are the other books of his final period, especially the two that followed it: *Jenseits von Gut und Böse* (*Beyond Good and Evil*) (1886) and *Zur Genealogie der Moral* (*On the Genealogy of Morality*) (1887). These masterpieces show Nietzsche at the height of his powers as a thinker, an organizer and an artist of ideas. Yet some prefer his last five books. At the beginning of 1888, Nietzsche published *Der Fall Wagner* (*The Case of Wagner*) and then composed four short books before the year was out: *Die Götzen-Dämmerung* (*The Twilight of the Idols*), an obvious play on Wagner's *Götterdämmerung* (*Twilight of the Gods*), puts the finishing touches to his accounts of knowledge and philosophy and offers his final critique of Socrates; *Der Antichrist* (*The Antichrist*), a critique of Pauline Christianity, offers a relatively sympathetic portrait of Jesus; and *Ecce Homo*, Nietzsche's own portrait of his life and work under such chapter headings as 'Why I write such good books'. It is easy to hear signs of his impending insanity in the shrill tone and self-promotion that sometimes takes over in these books (although not in the very funny and brilliantly anti-Socratic chapter headings of *Ecce Homo*), and perhaps also in the fall-off in organizational and artistic power from the masterpieces of the previous two years. *Nietzsche Contra Wagner*, which he dated Christmas 1888, leaves a different impression. Nietzsche's shortest and perhaps most beautiful book, it is a compilation of passages from earlier works, with a few small improvements, as if aiming at perfection. He collapsed nine days later.

3 The Nachlaß

Nietzsche left behind a large body of unpublished material, his *Nachlaß*, which technically should include *The Antichrist* and *Ecce Homo*, published by his sister in 1895 and 1908 respectively. However, Nietzsche had made arrangements for their publication and prepared a printer's copy of each. For purposes of understanding his philosophy, these are therefore accorded the same status as his earlier works and are not usually considered to be part of his *Nachlaß*. This entry gives a very secondary role to the remainder of Nietzsche's *Nachlaß*, which includes the relatively polished essays written in the early 1870s (mentioned in §2 of this entry). These essays are informative about Nietzsche's early views, and are sometimes also thought to provide a clearer statement of his later views of truth and language than do the works he published. The interpretation of Nietzsche's development offered here supports a very different view: that Nietzsche chose not to publish these essays because he soon progressed beyond them to quite opposed views.

Another issue that divides interpreters concerns the weight to give to the notes of Nietzsche's later years. Many treat them as material he would have published if he had remained productive for longer. But since he might instead have rejected and disposed of much of this material, others advise great caution in its use. Further, we often cannot determine the use Nietzsche had in mind for particular notes even when he wrote them. Nietzsche *composed* his books to lead prepared readers to certain views. The rich context and clues for reading supplied by his books, when they are attended to, provide a check on interpretive licence and a basis for getting at Nietzsche's own thinking that has no parallel in the case of the *Nachlaß* material. This applies to the entire contents of *Der Wille zur Macht* (*The Will to Power*), which some have regarded as Nietzsche's magnum opus. Although he did announce it as 'in preparation', there is evidence that he dropped his plans to publish a work of this title; the book we have is actually a compilation of notes from the years 1883–8 selected from his notebooks and arranged in their present form by his sister and editors appointed by her. Such notes may sometimes help in understanding what Nietzsche actually did publish. But it is difficult to justify giving them priority when they suggest views that differ from and are even contrary to those suggested by a careful reading of Nietzsche's books (see §§11–12 of this entry).

4 Truth and metaphysics

In the writings of his early and middle periods, Nietzsche often appears to deny that any of our theories and beliefs are really true. By the end of his final period, he denies only metaphysical truth. The rejection of metaphysics forms the cornerstone of his later philosophy.

What Nietzsche rejects as metaphysics is first and foremost a belief in a second world, a metaphysical or true world. *Human, All Too Human* offers a genealogy of this belief. Receiving their first idea of a second world from dreams, human beings originally share with 'everything organic' a belief in the existence of permanent things (substance) and

free will. When reflection dawns and they fail to find evidence of these in the world accessible to empirical methods, they conclude that these methods are faulty, and that the real world is accessible only to non-empirical methods. They thus take the empirical world to be a mere appearance or distortion of a second world, which is thereby constituted as the true one. Metaphysics is purported knowledge of this non-empirical world. *The Birth of Tragedy* affirms metaphysics in this sense – 'an artists' metaphysics' he later called it – in the suggestion that perception and science confine us to mere appearance, whereas truth is accessible in the special kind of preconceptual experience characteristic of Dionysian art.

Human, All Too Human sets out to undermine metaphysics by showing that knowledge of a non-empirical world is cognitively superfluous. Nietzsche's Enlightenment predecessors had already established the adequacy of empirical methods to explain what goes on in the nonhuman world. However, belief in a metaphysical world persisted because that world is assumed to be necessary to account for the things of the highest value in the human world. Nietzsche sought to explain the origin of this assumption and to undermine it. The assumption was made, he claims, because thinkers were unable to see how things could originate from their opposites: disinterested contemplation from lust, living for others from egoism, rationality from irrationality. They could deny this origination only by positing for 'the more highly valued thing a miraculous source in the very kernel and being of the "thing-in-itself"'. Nietzsche offers a naturalistic account of higher things, which presents them as sublimations of despised things and therefore as 'human, all too human'. Once it is clear that we can explain their origin without positing a metaphysical world, he expects the interest in such a world to die out. We cannot deny the bare possibility of its existence, however, because 'we view all things through the human head and cannot cut this head off; yet the question remains what of the world would still be there if we had cut it off' (*Human* §§1, 9).

Nietzsche later goes a step further and denies the very existence of a metaphysical world. His history of the 'true' world in *Twilight of the Idols* offers a six-stage sketch of how the metaphysical world came to be recognized as a 'fable'. Stage Four corresponds to the position of *Human*: the 'true' world is cognitively superfluous. In Stage Five, its existence is denied. Stage Six adds that without a true world, there is no merely apparent world either: the empirical world originally picked out as 'merely apparent' is the only world there is. Nietzsche thus makes clear that he has moved beyond the assumption that there *might* be a metaphysical world to a positing of the empirical world as the only one. He dismisses the whole idea of a second world as unintelligible. The books after *Beyond Good and Evil* proceed on this assumption: they no longer claim that the empirical world is a mere appearance or, what amounts to the same thing, that empirical truths are illusions or falsifications.

5 Knowledge

The position on knowledge to which Nietzsche is led by his rejection of metaphysics is a combination of empiricism, antipositivism and perspectivism. Claiming in his later works that 'all evidence of truth comes only from the senses', and that we have science 'only to the extent that we have decided to *accept* the testimony of the senses – to the extent to which we sharpen them further, arm them, and think them through', he considers the rest of purported knowledge 'miscarriage and not yet science', or formal science, like pure logic and mathematics (*Beyond Good and Evil* §134; *Twilight* III §3). The latter, he now insists, departing from his earlier stand that they falsify reality, make no claim about reality at all. Nietzsche's empiricism amounts to a rejection of any wholesale disparaging of sense experience, an insistence that the only bases for criticizing or correcting particular deliverances of the senses are other sense experiences or theories based on them.

Nietzsche's antipositivism involves a rejection of two aspects associated with some other versions of empiricism. First, he rejects foundationalism. Anticipating many later critics of positivism, he denies that there is any experience that is unmediated by concepts, interpretation or theory. Sense experience, our only evidence of truth, is always already interpreted, and knowledge is therefore interpretation, as opposed to the apprehension of unmediated facts. Nietzsche also avoids the problem of needing an a priori theory to establish his empiricism, which he bases instead on his genealogy of the belief in a metaphysical world (a genealogy that is itself empirical in that it accepts the testimony of the senses) and a diagnosis and working-through of the intellectual confusions that have locked previous philosophers into that belief. Clearing away these confusions (especially pictures of knowledge that set the world's true nature over against its appearances) removes all intellectual basis for considering sense experience in principle problematic, and all intellectual motivation for pursuing a priori knowledge. Philosophers may, however, still have non-intellectual motives for this pursuit (see §6 of this entry). The upshot of Nietzsche's antipositivism is that what counts as knowledge is always

revisable in the light of new or improved experience. This reinforces his empiricism, and in no way devalues empirical theories or denies that they can give us truth.

Nietzsche's perspectivism is often thought to imply that empirical knowledge offers us 'only a perspective' and not truth. But is perspectivism itself only a perspective? If not, it is false; if so, it is not clear why we should accept perspectivism rather than some other perspective. And Nietzsche himself puts forward as truths not only perspectivism, but also many other claims.

We can avoid saddling Nietzsche with these problems by recognizing that, at least in its mature and most important formulation (at *Geneology* III §12), perspectivism is a claim about knowledge; it is not a claim about truth, and it does not entail that truth is relative to perspective. Further, 'perspectives' are constituted by affects, not beliefs. The point is *not* that knowledge is always from the viewpoint of a particular set of beliefs and that there are always alternative sets that would ground equally good views of an object (see RELATIVISM). Such a view inevitably saddles perspectivism with relativism and problems of self-reference. Nietzsche's explicit point in describing knowledge as perspectival is to guard against conceiving of knowledge as 'disinterested contemplation'.

His early essay 'Truth and Lie' did use the impossibility of disinterested knowledge to devalue empirical knowledge, arguing that the latter was only a perspective and an illusion. But the point of the *Genealogy*'s claim that there is 'only a perspective knowing' is quite the reverse: to guard against using the idea of 'pure' knowing to devalue the kind of knowledge we have. The metaphor of perspective sets up disinterested knowing as the equivalent of the recognizably absurd notion of seeing something from nowhere. If the conception of knowledge ruled out by perspectivism really is absurd, however – and Nietzsche insists that it is – then it excludes only a kind of knowledge of which we can make no sense and which we could not really want. This explains why so many find perspectivism obvious and even self-evident; but so interpreted, it does nothing to devalue empirical knowledge.

Why does Nietzsche deny the possibility of disinterested knowledge? That surely does not follow from the impossibility of seeing something from nowhere. His early basis for this denial was Schopenhauer's doctrine that the intellect originates as servant to the will, but he accepted the same doctrine in later works on the basis of a thoroughgoing Darwinian naturalism. Human cognitive capacities exist because of the evolutionary advantage they confer on the species, and no such advantage is to be found in attending to any and all features of reality. The intellect must be directed to certain features – initially at least, those most relevant to human survival and reproduction. Affect – emotion, feeling, passion, value orientations – turns the mind in a particular direction, focusing its attention on certain features of reality and pushing it to register them as important; knowledge is only acquired when the intellect is so pushed and focused. Nietzsche's perspectivism is a metaphorical formulation of this naturalistic understanding of knowledge.

Because knowledge is always acquired from the viewpoint of particular interests and values, there are therefore always other affective sets that would focus attention on different aspects of reality. Nietzsche's use of the metaphor of perspective thus implies that knowledge is limited in the sense that there are always other things to know, but not that perspectives block our access to truth. Affects are our access, the basis of all access to truth. If its perspectival character raises any problems for knowledge, it is only because being locked into a particular perspective can make one unable to appreciate features of reality that are apparent from other perspectives. Nietzsche's solution is simple: the more affects we know how to bring to bear on a matter, the more complete our knowledge of it will be.

This does not mean that true knowledge requires assuming as many perspectives as possible. Knowledge does not require complete knowledge, and complete knowledge is not Nietzsche's epistemological ideal. In fact, he suggests that the greatest scholars tend to serve knowledge by immersing themselves deeply and thoroughly in some particular perspective, so much so that they damage themselves as human beings. The situation is different for philosophers because their ultimate responsibility is not knowledge, but values. To undertake the task to which Nietzsche assigns them, they need practice in shifting perspectives. This explains much that is distinctive about his way of writing philosophy: why it involves so much affect and seems so given to extremes of expression. He uses different affective stances – assuming them for a while – in order to show us features of reality that are visible from them. More importantly, by moving from one perspective to another, he attempts to show philosophers the kind of 'objectivity' that is required for their task: objectivity understood not as disinterested contemplation, but as a matter of not being *locked into* any particular valuational perspective, as an ability to move from one affective set to another.

6 Philosophy and the ascetic ideal

According to Nietzsche, philosophy has been understood as an a priori discipline, a deliverance

of pure reason. Given his empiricism, what role can he allow philosophy? In *Human, All Too Human* he claims to practise 'historical philosophy' and denies that it can be separated from natural science, suggesting that he counts empirical theories as philosophy if they illuminate topics of traditional philosophical concern. Attention to the more conceptual aspects of such theories might especially count as continuing the philosopher's traditional role (§§8–9 of this entry provide an example).

Further, Nietzsche's thinking on topics of traditional philosophical concern (§§4–5 of this entry) is philosophical in a more traditional sense, to the extent that it deals with conceptual as opposed to empirical matters. Such 'pure' philosophy is a matter of battling the images and pictures that beguile the mind and lead philosophers into thinking that there are purely philosophical questions to be answered concerning knowledge, truth and reality. Philosophy in this sense functions as therapy, and to the extent that Nietzsche practises it, he counts as a forerunner of Wittgenstein (see WITTGENSTEIN, L.J.J. §§9–12).

Like Wittgenstein, Nietzsche gives language a major role in generating the problems and confusions of previous philosophy. He sometimes seems to criticize language itself for falsifying reality, holding the subject–predicate structure of Indo-European languages responsible for philosophers' propensity to think that reality itself must consist of ultimate subjects that could never be part of the experienced world: God and the ego, or indivisible atoms of matter. But he would probably say of language what he ultimately says of the senses: only what we make of their testimony introduces error. Language misleads us into traditional philosophy only if we erroneously assume that linguistic structure offers us a blueprint of reality that can be used to challenge the adequacy of empirical theories. This is similar to Wittgenstein's diagnosis that philosophical problems arise when language is taken away from the everyday tasks for which it is suited and expected to play a different game. Nietzsche's philosopher forces language to play the 'game' of affording insight into a non-empirical world.

Unlike Wittgenstein, however, Nietzsche fights the confusions of traditional philosophy to free us not *from* the need to do philosophy, but *for* what he considers the true task of genuine philosophy. And this task is not a matter of offering empirical theories. In his later work, Nietzsche insists that philosophers should not be confused with scholars or scientists, that scholarship and science are only means in the hands of the philosopher. Gradually it has become clear to him, he says, that philosophers' values are the 'real germ' from which their systems grow. While pretending to be concerned only to discover truth, philosophers have actually been wily advocates for prejudices (values) they call 'truths'. They interpret the world in terms of their own values, and then claim that their interpretation, which they present as objective knowledge, gives everyone reason to accept these values – as the Stoics justified their ideal of self-governance on the grounds that nature itself obeys laws, an interpretation they arrived at by projecting their ideal of self-governance onto nature (*Beyond Good and Evil* §§1–9).

Because Nietzsche believes that interpretations of the world in terms of values provide something that is as important as truth, he wants the philosophy of the future to preserve this function of traditional philosophy. He does not, however, wish to preserve two aspects of the way in which previous philosophers have gone about this task: the lack of courage evident in their failure to recognize that they were reading values into the world rather than discovering truth, and the particular values they read into the world.

These values, he claims, have been expressions of the ascetic ideal, the ideal that takes the highest human life to be one of self-denial, denial of the natural self. Behind this ideal, which he finds in most major religions, Nietzsche locates the assumption that natural or earthly existence (the only kind he thinks we have) is devoid of intrinsic value, that it has value only as a means to something else that is actually its negation (such as heaven or nirvana). He claims that this life-devaluing ideal infects all the values supported by most religions (although *The Antichrist* retracts this in the case of Buddhism). Having come into existence in support of some form of life, values gain the support of the ascetic priest only if they are given a life-devaluing interpretation. Acts are interpreted as wrong or 'sinful', for instance, on the grounds that they are selfish or animal, that they affirm natural instincts. Traditional ('metaphysical') philosophers are successors to the ascetic priest because they interpret what they value – truth, knowledge, philosophy, virtue – in non-natural terms. In the background of their interpretations Nietzsche spies the assumption of the ascetic ideal: that whatever is truly valuable must have a source outside the world of nature, the world accessible to empirical investigation. What ultimately explains the assumption that philosophy must be a priori, and therefore concerned with a metaphysical world, is philosophers' assumption that nothing as valuable as philosophy or truth could be intimately connected to the senses or to the merely natural existence of human beings.

The philosophy of Nietzsche's early and middle periods can itself be diagnosed as an expression of the ascetic ideal. We can understand his devaluation of human knowledge in 'Truth and Lie' (his claim that human truths are 'illusions') as a response to the recognition that knowledge is rooted in the world of nature and thereby lacks the 'purity' demanded by the ascetic ideal. And we can surmise that he considered Darwinian naturalism dangerous because he saw that it deprives human life of value – if one accepts the ascetic ideal (see DARWIN, C.R.). Indeed, when he embraced the truth of naturalism in *Human* (to the extent of accepting philosophy itself as an empirical discipline), he drew the conclusion that follows from the combination of naturalism and the ascetic ideal: that human life is without value. From the viewpoint of Nietzsche's later philosophy, it is hardly surprising that his early philosophy turns out to be another expression of the ascetic ideal. According to his *Genealogy*, the ascetic ideal is the only ideal of any widespread cultural importance human beings have had so far; it has dominated the interpretation and valuation of human life for millennia. To have escaped the ascetic ideal without having to work through its influence on him would have been impossible.

On the other hand, Nietzsche was also fighting the ascetic ideal. Naturalism works against the supernatural interpretation of human life that has been promoted by the ascetic ideal, and as modern science increasingly shows how much of the world can be understood in naturalistic terms, the influence of the ascetic ideal wanes. Or, rather, it goes underground. Nietzsche denies that science and the naturalism it promotes are themselves opposed to the ascetic ideal. The commitment to science is actually the latest and most noble form of the ascetic ideal, based as it is on the Platonic/Christian belief that God is truth, that truth is divine. This amounts to the assumption that truth is more important than anything else (for instance, life, happiness, love, power) an assumption Nietzsche traces to the ascetic ideal's devaluation of our natural impulses. Thus the development of science and naturalism has been promoted by inculcating the discipline of the scientific spirit – the willingness to give up what one would like to believe for the sake of what there is reason to believe – as the heir to the Christian conscience cultivated through confession. This has thereby worked against the exterior of the ascetic ideal, against the satisfaction it has provided – in particular, the sense that this life, and especially its suffering, has a meaning, that it shall be redeemed by another life. But to work against such satisfaction is not to oppose the ascetic ideal; it is simply to require more self-denial.

Nietzsche believes that we need a new ideal, a real alternative to the ascetic ideal. If philosophers are to remain true to the calling of philosophy and not squander their inheritance, they must create new values and not continue merely to codify and structure the value legislations of ascetic priests. To create new values, however, it will be necessary for philosophers to overcome the ascetic faith that truth is more important than anything else, for truth is not sufficient support for any ideal. Although they must therefore overcome the ascetic ideal to create a new one, undertaking this task responsibly requires the training in truthfulness promoted by the ascetic ideal. The overcoming of the ascetic ideal that Nietzsche promotes is thus a self-overcoming.

7 The 'death of God' and nihilism

Nietzsche is perhaps best known for having proclaimed the death of God. He does in fact mention that God is dead, but his fullest and most forceful statement to this effect actually belongs to one of his fictional characters, the madman of *Gay Science*. Nietzsche's madman declares not only that God is dead and that churches are now 'tombs and sepulchres of God', but also that we are all God's 'murderers'. Although the madman may accept these statements as literally true, they clearly function as metaphors for Nietzsche. The 'death of God' is a metaphor for a cultural event that he believes has already taken place but which, like the death of a distant star, is not yet visible to normal sight: belief in God has become unbelievable, the Christian idea of God is no longer a living force in Western culture.

Nietzsche views all gods as human creations, reflections of what human beings value. However, pagan gods were constructed from the qualities human beings saw and valued in themselves, whereas the Christian God was given qualities that were the opposite of what humans perceived in themselves, the opposite of our inescapable animal instincts. Our natural being could then be reinterpreted as 'guilt before God' and taken to indicate our unworthiness. Constructed to devalue our natural being, the Christian God is a projection of value from the viewpoint of the ascetic ideal (see §6 of this entry). That this God is dead amounts to a prediction that Christian theism, along with the ascetic ideal that forms its basis, is nearing its end as a major cultural force and that its demise will be brought about by forces that are already and irreversibly at work.

One such force, to which Nietzsche himself contributed, is the development of atheism in the West, a development that stems from Christian morality itself and the will to truth it promotes. The will to truth, a commitment to truth 'at any price', is the latest expression of the ascetic ideal, but it also undermines the whole Christian worldview (heaven, hell, free will, immortality) of which 'God' is the symbol. Inspired by the will to truth, philosophy since Descartes has progressively undermined the arguments that supported Christian doctrines, and science has given us reason to believe that we can explain all the explicable features of empirical reality without appealing to God or any other transcendent reality. Theism has thus become cognitively superfluous. In this situation we can justify atheism without demonstrating the falsity of theism, Nietzsche claims, if we also have a convincing account of how theism could have arisen and acquired its importance without being true. Even if there is no cognitive basis for belief in God, however, might not one still accept something on the order of William James' will to believe? (see JAMES, W.). Nietzsche nowhere treats this option as irrational, but he does deny that it is now a serious option for those who have taken most strictly and seriously Christianity's ascetic morality. It may not be irrational, but it is psychologically impossible, Nietzsche thinks, to accept theism if the commitment to truthfulness has become fully ingrained, if hardness against oneself in matters of belief has become a matter of conscience. Atheism is 'the awe-inspiring *catastrophe* of a two-thousand year discipline in truth that finally forbids itself the *lie involved in belief in God*' (*Genealogy* III §27).

Although atheism, especially among the most spiritual and intellectual human beings, undoubtedly weakens Christianity, depriving it of both creative energy and prestige, it does not bring about the death of God by itself. The modern world, as KIERKEGAARD had seen already, contains many other factors that weaken the influence of Christianity and its ideal; among these Nietzsche includes the development of money-making and industriousness as ends in themselves, democracy, and the greater availability to more people of the fruits of materialistic pursuits. Zarathustra's statement that 'when gods die, they always die several kinds of death' suggests that just as the ascetic ideal has been accepted by different kinds of people for different reasons, the death of God and the ascetic ideal is also brought about by a multiplicity of causes that operate differently on different kinds of people. What matters, says Zarathustra, is that 'he is gone' (*Zarathustra* IV §6).

According to Nietzsche, the loss of belief in God will initiate a 'monstrous logic of terror' as we experience the collapse of all that was 'built upon this faith, propped up by it, grown into it; for example, the whole of our European morality' (*Gay Science* §343). In notes made late in his career (published in *The Will to Power*), Nietzsche calls this collapse of values 'nihilism', the 'radical repudiation of value, meaning, and desirability'. He predicts '*the advent of nihilism*' as 'the history of the next two centuries', and calls himself 'the first perfect nihilist of Europe'. However, he adds that he has 'lived through the whole of nihilism, to the end, leaving it behind' (*Will to Power* Preface). Nihilism is therefore not his own doctrine, but one he diagnoses in others (including his own earlier self). He *does not* believe that nothing is of value (or that 'everything is permitted') if God does not exist, but that this form of judgment is the necessary outcome of the ascetic ideal. Having come to believe that the things of the highest value – knowledge, truth, virtue, philosophy, art – must have a source in a reality that transcends the natural world, we necessarily experience these things as devoid of value once the ascetic ideal itself leads to the death of God, to the denial that any transcendent reality exists.

8 Morality

Nietzsche's criticism of morality is perhaps the most important and difficult aspect of his later philosophy. Calling himself an 'immoralist' – one who opposes all morality – he repeatedly insists that morality 'negates life'. He turned against it, he claims, inspired by an 'instinct that aligned itself with life' (*Birth of Tragedy* Preface). Whatever Nietzsche might mean by suggesting that morality is 'against life', his point is *not* that morality is 'unnatural' because it restricts the satisfaction of natural impulses. He finds what is natural and 'inestimable' in any morality in the hatred it teaches of simply following one's impulses, of any 'all-too-great freedom': it teaches 'obedience over a long period of time and in a single direction' (*Beyond Good and Evil* §188). Nietzsche analyses the directive to 'follow nature' as commanding something that is either impossible (if it means 'be like the nonhuman part of nature') or inevitable (if it means 'be as you are and must be').

His objection to morality sometimes seems to be not that it is 'against life', but that it promotes and celebrates a kind of person in which he finds nothing to esteem: a 'herd animal' who has little idea of greatness and seeks above all else security, absence of fear, absence of suffering. To complicate matters still further, he sometimes uses 'morality' to refer to what he approves of, for instance, 'noble morality' and 'higher moralities'.

The last of these interpretive problems can be resolved by recognizing that Nietzsche uses 'morality' in both a wider and a narrower sense. Every ethical code or system for evaluating conduct is 'a morality' in the wider, but not in the narrower sense. A system that determines the value of conduct solely in terms of 'the retroactive force of success or failure', for instance, is an instance of 'morality' in the wider sense, but Nietzsche counts it as 'pre-moral' in the narrower sense (*Beyond Good and Evil* §32). And it is the narrower sense Nietzsche is using when he commits himself to 'the overcoming of morality' and claims that it 'negates life'. His immoralism does not oppose all forms of ethical life. Although he opposes morality in the narrower sense, Nietzsche accepts another ethical system in terms of which he considers himself 'bound' or 'pledged'. Indeed, he claims that, contrary to appearances, 'we immoralists' are human beings 'of duty', having 'been spun into a severe yarn and shirt of duties [which we] *cannot* get out of' (*Beyond Good and Evil* §226).

Why didn't Nietzsche just say that he opposed *some* moralities and call his own ethical system his 'morality'? He undoubtedly thought that would be more misleading than his use of the term in a dual sense because it would trivialize the radical nature of his position. He called himself an 'immoralist' as a 'provocation' that would indicate what distinguishes him from 'the whole rest of humanity' (*Ecce Homo* IV §7). And it could so function, he thought, even though he actually opposes morality only in the narrower sense, precisely because this is the sense 'morality' has had until now. That word has been monopolized, he thinks, for a particular kind of ethical system on which all our currently available choices for an ethics are mere variations.

Genealogy provides a genealogy of morality in the narrower sense (the sense 'morality' will have hereafter in this entry) and a complex and sophisticated analysis of that concept of morality. Although there is no agreed-upon definition, we all have a feeling for what 'morality' in this sense means. But both the feeling and the 'meaning' are actually products of a complicated historical development that synthesized meanings of diverse origins into a unity, one that is difficult to dissolve or analyse and impossible to define. If conceptual analysis were a matter of formulating necessary and sufficient conditions for the use of a term, we might analyse the concept of morality by specifying the characteristics that are both necessary and sufficient to qualify a code of conduct as 'a morality'. But this approach has never delivered great clarification, and Nietzsche's understanding of concepts explains why: our concepts need clarification precisely because they are products of a complicated historical development. Different strands have been tied together into such a tight unity that they seem inseparable and are no longer visible as strands. To analyse or clarify such a concept is to disentangle these strands so that we can see what is actually involved in the concept. History can play a role in analysing a concept because at earlier stages the 'meanings' that constitute it are not as tightly woven together and we can still perceive their shifts and rearrangements. Looking at the history of the corresponding phenomenon can therefore make it easier for us to pick out the various strands that make up the concept and better able to recognize other possible ways of tying them together. Nietzsche's genealogy of morality aims to show that there are distinct aspects of morality, each with a separate pre-moral source, which makes the synthesis we call 'morality' something that can be undone, so that its strands might be rewoven into a different form of ethical life.

The three essays of *Genealogy* separate out for examination three main strands of morality: the good (in the sense of virtue), the right (or duty), and a general understanding of value. Each essay focuses on the development of one strand without paying much attention to the other two, even though any developed form of ethical life will actually involve all three aspects in some form and interconnection. The overall account of morality constitutes a 'genealogy' precisely because it traces the *moral* version of each strand back to pre-moral sources – thus to *ancestors of morality*. Its upshot is that what we call 'morality' emerged from these pre-moral ancestors when the right and the good become tied together under the interpretation of value provided by the ascetic ideal. This explains why Nietzsche claims that morality 'negates life': morality is an ascetic interpretation of ethical life.

The first essay in *Genealogy* finds the central pre-moral ancestor of morality's idea of goodness among politically superior classes in the ancient world whose members called themselves 'the good' and used 'good' and 'virtue' as their marks of distinction, the qualities that distinguished them from commoners or slaves. 'Good' and 'virtuous' were the same as 'noble' in the sense of 'belonging to the ruling class'; their contrasting term was 'low-born' or 'bad' (the German, *schlecht*, originally meant 'simple' or 'common').

As Nietzsche uses 'bad' (he does not claim to reflect contemporary usage), it involves no connotation of blame, whether applied to the poor person or the liar. 'Bad' certainly expresses a value judgment: that the person so described is inferior. The nobles regard themselves as superior and look down on the bad (sometimes with contempt, sometimes with pity). But they do not blame them for being inferior, or think that the inferior ought to be good (much less that inferiority deserves punishment or goodness a reward). Such judgments make sense only if one is judging inferiority in moral terms – that is, if 'bad' has become 'morally bad' or 'evil'.

To explain the origin of the good/evil (the specifically moral) mode of valuation, Nietzsche

postulates a 'slave revolt in morality', a revaluation inspired by *ressentiment* (grudge-laden resentment) against the nobles. Nietzsche does not claim that the nobles' actions were considered wrong because they were resented. He is dealing only with ideas of goodness or virtue in this essay; he seeks to explain how goodness became connected to praise and blame, reward and punishment. His postulated 'slave revolt' was led not by slaves but by priests, the 'great haters' in human history precisely because their spirituality is incompatible with the direct discharge of resentment and revenge. They hated the nobles not because they were oppressed by them but because the nobles considered themselves superior and had been victorious over them in gaining the respect and admiration of the people. Because this hatred could not be expressed directly, it grew to monstrous proportions until it finally found an outlet in revaluing the nobles and their qualities as inferior. As a result, certain qualities – useful to those in a slavish or dependent position – were called 'good', not because anyone found them particularly admirable, but from a desire to 'bring down' people with the opposite qualities. Simply 'looking down' at the nobles and their qualities would not have done the trick, especially since the majority envied and admired them. Only through the transformation of bad into evil, of inferiority into something for which one could be blamed, could the revaluation succeed. Pent-up *ressentiment* could then be vented in acts of blaming and moral condemnation, which Nietzsche sees as acts of 'imaginary revenge' that 'bring down' hated opponents 'in effigy' and elevate those who do the blaming, at least in their own imagination. Blaming, for Nietzsche, evidently involves the judgment that the person blamed is deserving of punishment, in this case for their inferiority. Therefore, once 'bad' is transformed into 'evil', God and his judgment along with heaven and hell can be used to support the revaluation by winning over to it those who would not feel sufficiently elevated by mere moral condemnation of the nobles. Nietzsche suggests that this is how the issue of free will became connected to morality. Blaming or holding people responsible for their actions does not raise the issue; it is raised by holding them responsible for what they are. And that is precisely what was required for the revaluation of noble values.

9 Morality (cont.)

Priests did not invent the idea of 'evil' on the spot, however. The notion of blame required for the revaluation emerged in a quite different sphere, that of right conduct or duty, the development of which

Nietzsche sketches in the second essay of *Genealogy*. The pre-moral ancestor to which this essay traces moral versions of right and wrong, duty or obligation, is the ethics of custom (*Sittlichkeit der Sitte*), an early system of community practices that gained the status of rules through the threat of punishment. These rules were perceived as imperatives, but not as moral imperatives: violation was punished, but not considered to be a matter of conscience or thought to incur guilt.

Nietzsche finds an ancestor of guilt in the realm of trade, in the creditor–debtor relation. Guilt arises, Nietzsche claims, when the idea of debt is put to the uses of the 'bad conscience', the sense of oneself as unworthy, which develops when the external expression of aggressive impulses becomes restricted to such an extent that they can be expressed only by being turned back against the self. This internalization does not take place automatically, however; human beings must learn techniques that promote it, and Nietzsche views priests as the great teachers in this field. One such technique exploits the idea that a debt is owed to ancestors (who eventually come to be perceived as gods) for the benefits they continue to bestow and for violations of community laws which represent their will. Priests use this idea to teach the people that they must make difficult sacrifices to the gods – for example, to sacrifice one's first-born – and that certain instances of apparent bad luck and suffering constitute the extraction of payment for violations of divine law, hence are deserved punishments.

So conceived, the debts are still mere debts, material rather than moral 'owings'. The moralization of debt (and thereby of duty) removes the idea that it can simply be paid off and connects it to one's worth or goodness. This moralization takes place by means of the third strand of morality analysed in *Genealogy*, the understanding of value, which in the case of morality is guided by the ascetic ideal. We enter what Nietzsche calls the 'moral epoch' only when the divine being to whom the debt is owed is considered the highest being and is conceived in non-naturalistic or ascetic terms, as a purely spiritual being and thus as a repudiation of the value of natural human existence (see §§6–7 of this entry). What must now be sacrificed to the divine is 'one's own strongest instincts, one's "nature"' (*Beyond Good and Evil* §55). The affirmation of these instincts is conceived as rebellion against God, and the normal sufferings of human life as punishments for this rebellion. The debt is now owed precisely for what one is and continues to be, for being part of the natural world. This debt can no longer be considered material, a mere debt, for while it is owed and payment must be made, it can never be paid off. And the punishment one deserves is now

completely bound up with one's (lack of) goodness or virtue, which is interpreted in ascetic terms as self-denial, the denial of one's natural impulses, or at least as selflessness.

The priest now has the notion of 'evil' required for the revaluation of the noble values: the moralized notion of virtue as self-denial provides the standard against which the nobles could be judged inferior, whereas the moralized notion of debt provides the basis for blaming the nobles for that inferiority. Both notions (of virtue and duty) were moralized by being tied together under the understanding of value provided by the ascetic ideal. Morality connects duty and virtue in such a way that blameable violations of duty are taken to show lack of virtue and lack of virtue is blameable (luck has nothing to do with it). Because he sees this connection as having been brought about by means of the ascetic ideal, Nietzsche regards that ideal as a major element of morality.

His own ideal is a very different one. Named after the Greek god Dionysus, Nietzsche's ideal celebrates the affirmation of life even in the face of its greatest difficulties, and thus gives rise to a doctrine and valuation of life that is fundamentally opposed to the one he finds behind morality. Committed to finding the sources of value in life, he rejects all non-naturalistic interpretations of ethical life, those that make reference to a transcendent or metaphysical world. It therefore seems likely that what he opposes in morality is not the idea of virtue, or standards of right and wrong, but the moralization of virtue and duty brought about by the ascetic ideal. Morality 'negates life' because it is an ascetic interpretation of ethical life. By interpreting virtue and duty in non-natural terms, it reveals the assumption of the ascetic ideal: that things of the highest value must have their source 'elsewhere' than in the natural world. This is why Nietzsche says that what 'horrifies' him in morality is 'the lack of nature, the utterly gruesome fact that *antinature* itself received the highest honours as morality and was fixed over humanity as law and categorical imperative' (*Ecce Homo* IV §7).

But how is this connected to Nietzsche's complaints against 'herd morality'? 'Herd' is his deliberately insulting term for those who congregate together in questions of value and perceive as dangerous anyone with a will to stand alone in such matters. He calls the morality of contemporary Europe 'herd animal morality' because of the almost complete agreement 'in all major moral judgments'. Danger, suffering, and distress are to be minimized, the 'modest, submissive, conforming mentality' is honoured, and one is disturbed by 'every severity, even in justice'. Good-naturedness and benevolence are valued, whereas the 'highest and strongest drives, if they break out passionately and drive the individual far above the average and the flats of the herd conscience', are slandered and considered evil (*Beyond Good and Evil* §§201–2).

This morality does not seem to involve the ascetic ideal. In fact, it is more likely to be packaged as utilitarianism, which offers a naturalistic, and therefore presumably unascetic, interpretation of duty and virtue in terms of happiness (see UTILITARIANISM). We might, in fact, formulate Nietzsche's main objection to herd morality as a complaint that there is nothing in it to play the role of the ascetic ideal: to hold out an ideal of the human person that encourages individuals to take up the task of self-transformation, self-creation, and to funnel into it the aggressive impulses, will to power and resentment that would otherwise be expressed externally. Although it horrifies him, Nietzsche recognizes the greatness of the ascetic ideal. It is the only ideal of widespread cultural importance human beings have had so far, and it achieved its tremendous power, even though it is the 'harmful ideal *par excellence*', because it was necessary, because there was nothing else to play its role. 'Above all, a counterideal was lacking – until Zarathustra' (*Ecce Homo* III GM).

The problem is that the ascetic ideal is now largely dead (as part of the 'death of God'). Nietzsche thinks we need something to replace it: a great ideal that will inspire the striving, internalization, virtue, self-creation that the ascetic ideal inspired. 'Herd animal morality' is what we are left with in the absence of any such ideal. It is what morality degenerates into once the ascetic ideal largely withdraws from the synthesis it brought about. The virtuous human being no longer is anything that can stir our imagination or move us. For Nietzsche, this is the 'great danger' to which morality has led: the sight of human beings makes us weary.

10 The overhuman (Übermensch)

Nietzsche's apparent alternative to 'herd-animal morality' is his most notorious idea, the *Übermensch*. (There is no really suitable English translation for this term: 'overhuman' has been chosen instead of 'superman' or 'overman' because it seems best able to bring out the idea of a being who overcomes in itself what has defined us as human.) The idea actually belongs to the protagonist of *Thus Spoke Zarathustra*, Nietzsche's work of philosophical fiction, and it can never be assumed that Zarathustra's ideas are the same as those of Nietzsche. As the story opens, Zarathustra is returning from ten years of solitude in the wilderness, bringing human beings a gift: his teaching that humanity is not an end or

goal, but only a stage and bridge to a higher type of being, the overhuman. He teaches that now that God is dead, it is time for humanity to establish this higher type as the goal and meaning of human life, a goal that can be reached only if human beings overcome what they now are, if they overcome the merely human.

The idea of becoming a higher kind of being by overcoming one's humanity can seem frightening. For some, it calls up images of Nazi stormtroopers seeking out 'inferior' human beings to annihilate. However, *Zarathustra* suggests that Nietzsche has something very different in mind. 'Zarathustra' is another name for Zoroaster, the founder of Zoroastrianism (see ZOROASTRIANISM). Nietzsche claims that the historical Zarathustra 'created the most calamitous error, morality', because his doctrine first projected ethical distinctions into the metaphysical realm (as a cosmic fight between good and evil forces). Nietzsche bases his character on Zarathustra because the creator of the error 'must also be the first to recognize it' (*Ecce Homo* IV §3).

Zarathustra is thus the story of a religious leader, the inventor of one of the world's oldest religions, who comes to recognize the 'error' of traditional (moralized) religions. Far from turning against every aspect of traditional religion, however, Zarathustra commits himself to its central task: urging human beings to raise their sights above their usual immersion in materialistic pursuits to recognize the outlines of a higher form of being that calls them to go beyond themselves, to become something more than they are. Zarathustra's overhuman can thus be seen as a successor to the images of 'higher humanity' offered by traditional religions. His teaching is not intended to encourage human beings to throw off the constraints and shackles of morality (something Nietzsche sees as well underway without his help). Its point is, rather, to combat the forces of barbarism by encouraging us to take on a more demanding ethical task than modern morality requires: that of becoming what Nietzsche had earlier called a 'true human being'. When he used that phrase, however, Nietzsche believed it applied only to 'those no-longer animals, the philosophers, artists, and saints'. Animal (purely natural) existence was a senseless cycle of becoming and desire, and only those who escape it by extinguishing egoistic desire counted as truly human. The saint in particular counted as 'that ultimate and supreme becoming human', in which 'life no longer appears senseless but appears, rather, in its metaphysical meaningfulness' (*Unfashionable Observations* III §5). From the viewpoint of his later philosophy, early Nietzsche's conception of true humanity is an obvious expression of the ascetic ideal; it devalues natural existence relative to something that is its opposite. Once one recognizes this opposite as unattainable (as Nietzsche did in *Human*), the conception can be seen for what it really is: a devaluation and condemnation of human life.

Nietzsche never abandoned his early belief that the modern world is threatened by forces of both conformism and barbarism and that our great need is therefore for educators who will inspire human self-overcoming by the force of a lofty ideal. But since he rejects the ascetic ideal, he must abandon his earlier image of a true human being. At the end of *Genealogy*'s second essay, Nietzsche suggests that what the overhuman overcomes is not the 'natural' inclinations against which the ascetic ideal has been directed, those that make apparent our connection to other animals, but rather the 'unnatural' inclinations, the aspirations to a form of existence that transcends nature and animality. In other words, the overhuman must overcome all the impulses that led human beings to accept the ascetic ideal, an ideal that has so far defined what counts as 'human'. As we will see in §2, however, Zarathustra's call for the overcoming of the human is still too bound up with the old ideal.

11 The will to power

Zarathustra teaches that life itself is will to power, and this is often thought to be Nietzsche's central teaching as well. However, will to power first appears in Nietzsche's work in *Daybreak* (1881), and there it is one human drive among others, the striving for competence or mastery. It is usefully thought of as a second-order drive or will: a need or desire for the effectiveness of one's first-order will. In *Daybreak*, Nietzsche finds this drive at work in large areas of human life: in asceticism, revenge, the lust for money, the striving for distinction, cruelty, blaming others, blaming oneself. He explains the drive's apparent omnipresence in human life by saying not that life is will to power (or that power is the only thing humans want), but that power has a special relation to human happiness. He calls love of power a 'demon' because human beings remain unhappy and low-spirited if it is not satisfied even if all their material needs are satisfied, whereas power can make them as happy as human beings can be, even if everything else is taken away (*Daybreak* §262). In *Genealogy* (1887) he expresses a similar idea in more positive terms when he calls the will to power 'the most life-affirming drive', that is, the one whose satisfaction contributes most to finding life worth living (*Genealogy* III §18).

Zarathustra claims that this 'will to be master' is found in all that lives, and that this explains why life is 'struggle and becoming', always overcoming itself, always opposing what it has created and loved: 'Verily, where there is perishing and a falling of leaves, behold, there life sacrifices itself – for power' (*Zarathustra* II §12). But this seems a clearly anthropomorphic conception of life, the projection of the human will to power onto nonhuman nature. Nietzsche rejects anthropomorphic conceptions of nature, insists that will is to be found only in beings with intellects, and complains that Schopenhauer's idea of will 'has been turned into a metaphor when it is asserted that all things in nature possess will' (*Human* II §5).

Yet Nietzsche does say that life, and even reality itself, is will to power. The idea seems to be that reality consists of fields of force or dynamic quanta, each of which is essentially a drive to expand and thus to increase its power relative to all other such quanta. However, almost all the passages to this effect are found in Nietzsche's notebooks. He actually argues that reality is will to power in only one passage he chose to publish, and this passage gives us good reason to doubt that Nietzsche actually accepted the argument. He neither says nor implies that he accepts its conclusion, and he argues against its premises in earlier passages of the same book (*Beyond Good and Evil* §36).

Why would Nietzsche construct a rather elaborate argument from premises he clearly rejects? Perhaps it was to illustrate the view of philosophy presented earlier in the same book. Philosophers' ultimate aim, he claims, is not to obtain knowledge or truth, but to interpret the world in terms of their own values (see §6 of this entry) – to 'create [in thought] a world before which [they] can kneel' (*Zarathustra* II §12). Yet they present their interpretations as true, and argue for them on the basis of amazingly 'little': 'any old popular superstition from time immemorial', a play on words, a seduction by grammar, or 'an audacious generalization of very narrow, very personal, very human, all too human facts' (*Beyond Good and Evil* Preface). This seems an apt diagnosis of Nietzsche's own argument, since he elsewhere identifies its first premise as 'Schopenhauer's superstition' and the exaggeration of a popular prejudice, and its second and third premises as part of the 'primeval mythology' Schopenhauer 'enthroned' (*Beyond Good and Evil* §§16–19; *Gay Science* §127). Furthermore, the effect of the argument is an 'audacious generalization' to the whole universe of the will to power, which Nietzsche originally understands as one human drive among others. In generalizing this drive, Nietzsche can be seen as generalizing and glorifying what he values, just as he claims philosophers have always done and must do. For Nietzsche's own answer to 'what is good?' is 'everything that heightens the feeling of power in human beings, the will to power, power itself' (*Antichrist* §2).

739

Why does Nietzsche value the will to power? He certainly came to recognize it as responsible for the violence and cruelty of human life and as the prime ingredient in what he had earlier called the 'cauldron full of witches' brew' that threatens the modern world with 'horrible apparitions' (*Unfashionable Observations* III §4). But he also saw it as 'the most life-affirming drive' and as responsible for the great human accomplishments – political institutions, religion, art, morality and philosophy. His basic psychological claim is that human beings are subjected to intense experiences of powerlessness and that such experience leads to depression unless some means is found for restoring a feeling of power. What we call 'barbarism' is largely a set of direct and crude strategies for restoring the feeling of power by demonstrating the power to hurt others. What we call 'culture' is a set of institutions and strategies for achieving the same feeling in a sublimated or less direct fashion. The most important strategies have all involved directing the will to power back against the self. Such internalization is responsible for all the ethical achievements of human life, all the ways in which human beings have changed and perfected their original nature by taking on a new and improved nature. But the internalization of the will to power has been promoted by the ascetic ideal's condemnation of our original nature, especially of the will to power. This is what Zarathustra attempts to overcome with his overhuman teaching, which directs the will to power back against the self to overcome the inclinations that led to the old ideal. He therefore does not condemn the will to power, but celebrates it.

12 Eternal recurrence

Nietzsche identifies himself above all else as the teacher of eternal recurrence, which is often interpreted as a cosmological theory to the effect that the exact history of the cosmos endlessly repeats itself. Although he did sketch arguments for such a theory in his notebooks, he actually does not argue for or commit himself to a recurrence cosmology in any work he published. And, although he presents eternal recurrence as the 'basic conception' of *Zarathustra*, he does not commit its protagonist to a cosmology. He identifies this 'basic conception' not as a cosmology, but as 'the highest formula for affirmation that is at all attainable' (*Ecce Homo* III §1).

As first articulated in *Gay Science*, eternal recurrence is a heuristic device used to formulate Nietzsche's Dionysian ideal (see §9 of this entry). How well disposed we are to life is to be measured by how we would react upon being told by a demon (in a manner designed to induce uncritical acceptance) that we will have to live again and again the

exact course of life we are now living. Would we experience despair or joy, curse the demon or greet him as a god? Nietzsche's ideal is the *affirmation of eternal recurrence*, to be a person who would respond to the demon with joy. This is *not* equivalent to having no regrets, since it has no implication concerning how to respond if given the choice of variations on history. Nietzsche's ideal is to love life enough to be joyfully willing to have the whole process repeated eternally, including all the parts that one did not love and even fought against. Eternal recurrence gives him a formula for what it is to value the process of life as an end and not merely as a means.

Nietzsche's special self-identification with eternal recurrence can be explained in terms of his view regarding the importance of the ascetic ideal and his explanation of its power: 'a *counterideal* was lacking – until Zarathustra'. There are only two plausible candidates for the counterideal Zarathustra offers: the overhuman and the affirmation of eternal recurrence. The overhuman is one who overcomes the ascetic ideal. But, as Zarathustra first preaches it, the overhuman ideal can be seen as another variation on the ascetic ideal. Like the ascetic priest, Zarathustra treats our lives as valuable only as a means to a form of life that is actually their negation. Like the ascetic priest, he turns his will to power against human life and takes revenge against it (for the powerlessness it induces) by excluding it from what he recognizes as intrinsically valuable. The ideal of affirming eternal recurrence, in contrast, values the whole process of living, and thereby overcomes the ascetic ideal's devaluation of human life, even while pushing us to go beyond its present form. It provides us with the image of a higher form of human life, but does not take revenge against the latter by refusing to call its higher form 'human'. It therefore appears to be Zarathustra's true alternative to the ascetic ideal.

It may seem, however, that happy pre-moral barbarians should be able to affirm eternal recurrence. How then can it provide an image of a higher form of human life towards which to strive, one that could inspire internalization, virtue and self-creation comparable to that inspired by the ascetic ideal? One relevant factor is Nietzsche's hope for new philosophers who will create new values. Perhaps he did not expect his counterideal to provide the full content of new values, just as the ascetic ideal did not provide the full content of the old values. The ascetic priests did not create their values from scratch. They took over virtues, duties, forms of life that were already there and gave them a new interpretation, one that denied the value of natural human existence. Nietzsche seems to hope that new philosophers will do something comparable – that they will provide a new life-affirming interpretation of virtues, duties and forms of life that are already there. Eternal recurrence would function as the form of new values, a test that they must pass to count as non-ascetic or life-affirming. The test for teachers of new values would be: can you endorse and teach these values while affirming eternal recurrence?

If this suggestion is correct, Nietzsche's relation to the modern world is not quite as revolutionary as it sometimes appears. The role of his new philosophers is not to overturn everything, but to take what is in pieces due to the dissolution of the old interpretation of value and to provide a new interpretation. This kind of philosophizing is not just for the future, but is found in Nietzsche's own writings. He praises old virtues – justice and generosity, for instance – but gives us a new interpretation of them, a different way of seeing them as valuable. Generosity is valuable not because it is selfless, but because it exhibits the soul's richness and power. And justice is perhaps the greatest virtue not because it is disinterested or obeys a higher law, but because it is the rarest and highest mastery that is possible on earth. And Nietzsche does not merely talk about these matters. His writings show us a new kind of person and a new kind of philosopher in the virtues he exhibits in them, not least of all in the interpretations he gives of his virtues. Truthfulness or honesty, justice, generosity are all exhibited in his writings, but are given life-affirming interpretations that bring to our attention the role of the will to power in them.

This is not to say that Nietzsche's new values are simply repackaged old ones. Nietzsche's ideal leads him to value qualities that he claims have never before been considered part of greatness, such as malice, exuberance and laughter. But even in their new interpretations of old values, the aim of Nietzsche's new philosophers is to push culture in new directions, for instance, towards giving explicit expression at the higher levels of culture to what the old ideal excluded from the highest forms of life. This is what Nietzsche exhibits, for instance, in the positive and negative emotion, the exuberance and malice, the aggression and eros, that permeates his writings. At this level, his philosophy is art, but it is an art that completes and is no longer used to devalue knowledge, which can now be recognized as its sometimes contentious partner in Nietzsche's soul and writings.

See also: GENEALOGY

References and further reading

Nietzsche, F. (1888) *Der Antichrist*, 1895; trans. W. Kaufmann as *The Antichrist*, in *The Portable Nietzsche*, New York: Viking, 1954. (Nietzsche's version of 'Why I am not a Christian'. Distinguishes original Christianity from the Pauline version and gives a relatively sympathetic portrait of the former and of the one who lived it. Fairly straightforward and accessible.)

Schacht, R. (1983) *Nietzsche*, London: Routledge & Kegan Paul. (Careful and detailed survey of all the main themes of Nietzsche's philosophy. Here Nietzsche has a basically naturalistic orientation, but nevertheless accepts the will to power as the basic principle of life.)

MAUDEMARIE CLARK

NIHILISM

As its name implies (from Latin *nihil*, 'nothing'), philosophical nihilism is a philosophy of negation, rejection, or denial of some or all aspects of thought or life. Moral nihilism, for example, rejects any possibility of justifying or criticizing moral judgments, on grounds such as that morality is a cloak for egoistic self-seeking, and therefore is a sham; that only descriptive claims can be rationally adjudicated and that moral (prescriptive) claims cannot be logically derived from descriptive ones; or that moral principles are nothing more than expressions of the subjective choices, preferences or feelings of the people who endorse them.

Similarly, epistemological nihilism denies the possibility of justifying or criticizing claims to knowledge, because it assumes that a foundation of infallible, universal truths would be required for such assessments, and no such thing is available; because it views all claims to knowledge as entirely relative to historical epochs, cultural contexts or the vagaries of individual thought and experience, and therefore as ultimately arbitrary and incommensurable; because it sees all attempts at justification or criticism as useless, given centuries of unresolved disagreement about disputed basic beliefs even among the most intelligent thinkers; or because it notes that numerous widely accepted, unquestioned beliefs of the past are dismissed out of hand today and expects a similar fate in the future for many, if not all, of the most confident present beliefs.

Political nihilism calls for the complete destruction of existing political institutions, along with their supporting outlooks and social structures, but has no positive message of what should be put in their place. Cosmic nihilism regards nature as either wholly unintelligible and starkly indifferent to basic human concerns, or as knowable only in the sense of being amenable to scientific description and explanation. In either case, the cosmos is seen as giving no support to distinctively human aims or values, and it may even be regarded as actively hostile to human beings. Existential nihilism negates the meaning of human life, judging it to be irremediably pointless, futile and absurd.

See also: ANARCHISM; LIFE, MEANING OF; MORAL SCEPTICISM; SCEPTICISM

DONALD A. CROSBY

NINETEENTH-CENTURY PHILOSOPHY

Introduction

In the first part of the nineteenth century, the reigning philosophical outlook was idealist in one form or another, as the attempt was made to complete the intellectual revolution which Kant had begun, but which he was seen as having compromised in a variety of ways. Culminating in the dominance of Hegel and Hegelianism in the 1830s, this idealist position was criticised in the second half of the century from a number of perspectives, including Neo-Kantianism (which sought a return to an idealism closer to Kant's own), materialism (which rejected idealism altogether) and positivism (which sought to revive elements of empiricism that Kant had put in doubt). Nonetheless, idealism never fully lost its influence, and there are interesting and important cross-currents between all these positions throughout the nineteenth century. From our present viewpoint many of these debates can be seen to foreshadow contemporary controversies, such as those between naturalism and transcendentalism, and between various forms of idealism and realism, as well as wider issues concerning the nature of philosophy and the relation between science and religion.

1 From the eighteenth to the nineteenth century
2 Nineteenth-century idealism
3 The turn against idealism: materialism, positivism, empiricism, naturalism
4 The re-emergence of idealism
5 The legacy of nineteenth-century philosophy

1 From the eighteenth to the nineteenth century

In his *Autobiography* (written in the 1850s and 1860s), J.S. MILL famously identified 'the reaction of the nineteenth century against the eighteenth' as a central feature of intellectual life in this period. The 'reaction' he is referring to is the way in which many early nineteenth-century thinkers saw the Enlightenment conception of reason, naturalism and liberalism as leading to scepticism, materialism and anarchy; if rationalism, science and freedom were to be defended, they argued, it could only be achieved against the background of some kind of idealism, which required thinking about religion, nature, and the social and historical world in a new way. To their critics, however, this claim by the idealists who sought to question the outlook of the eighteenth century was no more than a cover for a return to the kind of reactionary metaphysical thinking that the Enlightenment had swept away; these critics therefore sought to defend empiricism, the authority of science, and naturalism against these charges, and so began a counter-reaction on behalf of the ideals of the eighteenth century. Mill characterizes the struggle this engendered in a memorable image: 'The fight between the nineteenth century and the eighteenth always reminded me of the battle about the shield, one side of which was white and the other black. I marvelled at the blind rage with which the combatants rushed against one another' (in *Autobiography*). (See ENLIGHTENMENT, CONTINENTAL)

The origins of this struggle can be found in the eighteenth century itself, and can be traced back to KANT, who thus remains a key figure in the nineteenth century. While at one level Kant was deeply committed to the ideas of the eighteenth-century Enlightenment – freedom, reason, Newtonian science, religious toleration – it appeared to him that the epistemology and metaphysics of the Enlightenment – empiricism, realism, materialism – led to the undermining of these ideals, as freedom was threatened by causal determinism, reason and science were threatened by scepticism, and religion by dogmatic materialism and militant atheism. Kant therefore sought to retain the Enlightenment ideals, but to overturn the epistemology and metaphysics that seemed to undermine them. His solution was what he called 'transcendental idealism', where the strategy was to argue that scepticism, determinism and atheism can be avoided once the empirical world is treated as an appearance: scepticism is thus avoided, because we can now be sure that this world will conform to our concepts; determinism is thus avoided, because causality only operates in the sphere of appearances and not in relation to things in themselves, where the self is located; and atheism can be avoided, because we can still postulate the existence of God and immortality and so leave room for faith. However, in preserving the ideals of the Enlightenment in this way, Kant was consciously overturning its epistemology and metaphysics: he argued that experience no longer gives us access to a mind-independent reality that is purely material and causally determined; rather, what we experience this way is only the world as it appears to us. Nonetheless, he tried to sweeten the pill by pointing out that the empiricists and materialists themselves had accepted that this was true of many aspects of the world that common-sense takes to be straightforwardly real, such as colour and taste; all he was doing was applying the same idea at a higher level, to matter in time and space itself. Once this step was taken, he argued, it could be seen that pushed to their limit, empiricism and materialism themselves lead to transcendental idealism, and that it is therefore the natural next stage of Enlightenment thinking.

For those who came after Kant in the nineteenth century – such as the German idealists FICHTE, SCHELLING and HEGEL; the young Romantics Hölderlin, NOVALIS and SCHLEGEL; and the Protestant theologian Schleiermacher – the general project was the same, and the diagnosis was shared; but the Kantian solution was rejected. That is, for this generation of thinkers it was clear that despite its high ideals, the Enlightenment outlook of the British empiricists and the French encyclopedists was threatened by collapse into scepticism, materialism and nihilism. Likewise, they shared with Kant a sense that the fault lay with the metaphysics and epistemology of the eighteenth-century thinkers. However, they felt that as it stood, Kant's appeal to transcendental idealism as an alternative was inadequate, in part because in itself was too much indebted to the eighteenth-century outlook it had sought to transcend, with its atomistic view of experience, its scepticism about the world as it is in itself and its commitment to Newtonian mechanics as a scientific paradigm. (This dissatisfaction with Kant was influenced in part by the somewhat earlier critique of his work offered by Jacobi, Hamann and HERDER, amongst others.) In different ways, therefore, these post-Kantians sought other solutions to the crisis in eighteenth-century thought that Kant had been responding to, as it was agreed that Kant's radically dualistic picture of appearances and 'the thing-in-itself' could not avoid collapsing into scepticism, determinism and atheism. (Although ignored at the time, the only major thinker in this period who was still trying to work largely within the Kantian framework was SCHOPENHAUER, while outside Germany Kant continued to find followers, for example ROSMINI-SERBATI in Italy.)

2   Nineteenth-century idealism

While the post-Kantian German idealists and Romantics had a shared sense of the difficulties to be overcome, and of the way in which Kant himself had failed to resolve these difficulties, they differed amongst themselves over what alternative solution to propose, and the struggle between them was at times intense (see GERMAN IDEALISM). In terms of historical influence, however, there is no doubt that Hegel emerged as the thinker with the greatest impact in the 1820s and 1830s, both within his native Germany and through much of the rest of Europe and, later, America (see BAKUNIN, M.A.; BELINSKII, V.G.; COUSIN, V.; HEGELIANISM), although Schelling also had a following outside Germany during this period, as did KRAUSE in Spain and Argentina.

However, if it appeared to some that Hegel had brought the great cycle of Western thought to a satisfactory close, and that there would be no going further or back, this sense was quickly lost, partly because difficulties and tensions emerged as Hegel's thought was increasingly questioned, and partly because from the 1840s onwards there was an increasing revival of the eighteenth-century outlook that idealism had seemed to have eclipsed. Thus, on the one hand, Hegel's grand synthesis faced critique and reform at the hands of a series of younger radical thinkers such as FEUERBACH, Hess, Ruge, Bauer, Cieszkowski, HERZEN, MARX, Heine and KIERKEGAARD, some of whom were inspired in part by Schelling's attack on Hegel after the latter's death (see SCHELLING), and by other critics such as TRENDELENBURG; on the other hand, it appeared that the idealist critique of eighteenth-century thought as leading to determinism, immoralism, atheism and scepticism was misguided – or, if it were right, just had to be accepted and lived with, as the harsh but inescapable truth concerning the world and our place within it. Deprived of its underlying motivation, post-Kantian idealism now appeared as reactionary, simply trying to obscure the fundamental truths that the eighteenth century empiricists and materialists had uncovered: namely, that we are natural creatures living in a godless universe governed by scientific laws, to which experience gives us adequate but limited access. The most profound thinkers of the second half of the nineteenth century – such as Marx, Mill and NIETZSCHE – can be seen as struggling to come to terms with and find something progressive in this conclusion, without requiring any return to idealism.

3   The turn against idealism: materialism, positivism, empiricism, naturalism

After the authority of Hegelian idealism was questioned from the 1840s onwards, the remainder of the century is marked by a battle between those who sought to go back to the eighteenth century and re-think the doctrines of LOCKE, HUME, BENTHAM or the French materialists, and those who believed that this was a retrograde step, which could only lead to the same mistakes and with them a threat to freedom, reason, morality and religion.

Perhaps the most obvious sense in which the second half of the nineteenth century saw a return to the eighteenth was in the way that the major movements of the period – materialism, positivism, empiricism – went back to a conception of science and of science's relation to philosophy that belonged to the seventeenth and eighteenth centuries, when the scientific revolution had decisively shaped philosophical thinking. It would be wrong to characterize the German idealism of the first half of the nineteenth century as crudely 'anti-scientific'; nonetheless, it did see itself as opposed to the scientific paradigms of the seventeenth and eighteenth centuries, particularly Newtonianism. In the early nineteenth century, the new approach of NATURPHILOSOPHIE, espoused primarily by Schelling, GOETHE and Hegel, in fact became the favoured scientific outlook with some researchers, and bore real fruit in the work of Lorenz Oken, Hans Christian Ørsted, and Johann Wilhelm Ritter, amongst others; but in the second half of the nineteenth century, this idealist *Naturphilosophie* was viewed as mere metaphysical speculation, divorced from true science, which was once again seen as requiring a commitment to the mechanistic paradigms of explanation which the *Naturphilosophen* had sought to question. Thus, in relation to the natural sciences in the second half of the nineteenth century, philosophy can be seen as returning to positions it had adopted previously, when under the influence of the scientific revolution in the seventeenth and eighteenth centuries.

In the eighteenth century, one way in which that influence was most directly felt was in the conception philosophers came to have of the ultimate nature of reality, as physicalistic, mechanistic and deterministic. This view was adopted by the radical *philosophes* of the Enlightenment, particularly Julien de LA METTRIE and Paul d'Holbach, who were uncompromising in their scientific materialism. While aiming to overcome the Cartesian dualism of mind and matter, they also (and much more broadly) saw the material world in essentially mechanistic terms. They also used the authority and methods of science to challenge all metaphysical speculation and apriorism, and instead defended a thoroughgoing empiricism. Likewise, materialism in the nineteenth century came to adopt a similar view, taking this to be the lesson of contemporary science, which they saw as continuous with seventeenth- and eighteenth-century physicalism. The thinking of La Mettrie and d'Holbach thus has

its nineteenth-century counterpart in the work of Carl Vogt, Jacob Moleschott, Ludwig BÜCHNER and Heinrich Czolbe in Germany; John Tyndall in Britain; and Nikolai Chernyshevskii in Russia (see also NIHILISM). The impact of DARWIN and Darwinism also played a vital role in underlining the authority of this broadly materialist and naturalistic outlook, and extending it to the understanding of the processes of history (see MATERIALISM §3).

While materialism represents perhaps the most direct influence of science on philosophy, a less direct influence can be found in the revival of empiricism and the related position of positivism, where philosophers looked to science and scientific methods to understand how knowledge of the world is acquired, what form that knowledge takes and how far it can extend. As in the seventeenth and eighteenth centuries, this view rested on a sense that scientific inquiry was hugely successful, and so must form a model for all our cognitive endeavours. This model was inductivist: using observations and generalizations based on observations, science is able to uncover the law-governed causal relations between natural phenomena. According to this view, we are thereby able to reach an adequate understanding of the world, in the sense of an understanding that is perfectly satisfactory to science, without engaging in metaphysical speculation or attempting to transcend the boundaries of experience; no further kind of knowledge is possible for us, or even desirable, insofar as empirical science provides us with a fully adequate understanding of the world around us. As Mill makes clear, in adopting this sort of position, the empiricists and positivists of the nineteenth century saw themselves as returning to the earlier empiricist tradition of the seventeenth and eighteenth centuries:

[T]he truth, on this much-debated question (concerning the sources of our knowledge) lies with the school of Locke and of Bentham. The nature and laws of Things in themselves, or of the hidden causes of the phenomena which are the objects of experience, appear to us radically inaccessible to the human faculties. We see no ground for believing that anything can be the object of our knowledge except our experience, and what can be inferred from our experience by the analogies of experience itself; nor that there is any idea, feeling, or power in the human mind, which, in order to account for it, requires that its origin should be inferred to any other source.

(*Coleridge* 1840)

We have here a characteristic mix of empiricist and positivist themes, built around a renewed faith in the methods and results of science as these were conceived of in the seventeenth and eighteenth centuries, together with a sharp awareness of the limits of scientific inquiry from a metaphysical perspective: metaphysical questions concerning the 'hidden causes of the phenomena' must be left unanswered, but in a way that leaves the adequacy of our investigations untouched. The sharp distinction between metaphysics and science that emerged in the seventeenth and eighteenth centuries can be seen to mark the positivism and empiricism of the second half of the nineteenth century, where in both periods the distinction was used to prioritize science over metaphysics, whereas in the early part of the century, the order of priority had been the opposite. (See BRENTANO, F.C.; COMTE, A.; MACH. E.; POSITIVISM IN THE SOCIAL SCIENCES.)

A third respect in which science came to influence philosophy from the 1840s onwards, in a manner that paralleled the influence it possessed in the seventeenth and eighteenth centuries, was the way in which respect for science (particularly physiology and psychology) led to a naturalistic view of the mind, as operating in accordance with processes and laws occurring in the natural causal order, with no place for any Kantian 'transcendental subject' outside this order. This has implications both for philosophy of mind and for epistemology, where the issue is to show how various mental capacities and forms of knowledge (such as innateness, a priori knowledge, intentionality or the normativity of thought) are compatible with this naturalistic picture, or (if they are not) how they can be explained away. This programme can be seen at its clearest and most thoroughgoing in Mill, and also in the work of Hermann von Helmholtz, Herbert SPENCER and William JAMES.

Thus the emergence of these three strands of thought – metaphysical materialism, empiricism and positivism, and naturalism – can be set against the dominant idealism of the first half of the century, and each can be seen as a revival of positions from the seventeenth and eighteenth centuries, shaped by a return to views of science and its relation to philosophy that first emerged in this early modern period. Nonetheless, there are important tensions between these strands that marked nineteenth-century debate, as had been the case when these positions first emerged. One tension was between metaphysical materialism on the one hand, and positivism on the other: for, from a positivist perspective, it appeared that materialism could not be justified, as it involved claims about the ultimate nature of reality that could not be supported on the basis of normal scientific inquiry, so transcending the epistemological limits that the positivists set themselves. Likewise, positivism encouraged an

instrumentalist or conventionalist conception of scientific theories that threatened to lead to a kind of anti-realist constructivism concerning the natural world, which was also at odds with materialistic realism (see CONVENTIONALISM; DUHEM, P.M.M.; MACH, E.; POINCARÉ, J.H.). Another tension was between positivism and empiricism, where (as COMTE argued) positivism could make greater concessions to the rationalist and Kantian traditions than could an empiricist such as Mill, by accepting that scientific inquiry in fact involved observation shaped by some sort of prior theorizing. A further tension can be seen in the relation between empiricism and naturalism, for example in the way that Mill's empiricism led to phenomenalism, which holds that minds and experiences are all that exist; but this position seems to be at odds with his commitment to naturalism, which normally involves taking the human mind to be part of the natural world realistically conceived. Finally, while Comte sought to give the scientific understanding of society and historical development its own special status, the fact that this understanding was modelled on paradigms from the natural sciences inevitably threatened to make this form of social theory reductionistic (see POSITIVISM IN THE SOCIAL SCIENCES).

4 The re-emergence of idealism

As well as these internal tensions, the three strands of materialism, positivism and naturalism were also faced by counter-currents from idealism and the idealist tradition, which in different ways questioned the conception of science that these positions had taken up. So first, for example, the materialism of Büchner, Vogt and Moleschott was questioned by ENGELS, who was more sympathetic to the critique of mechanism offered by the *Naturphilosophen*, while opposing what he saw as their idealism. Engels argued that precisely because it was based around an early modern scientific paradigm, metaphysical materialism was outdated, with contemporary scientific developments such as electromagnetic field theory suggesting a less mechanistic and atomistic metaphysical picture (see also DIALECTI-CAL MATERIALISM). It was also argued by various Hegelians (such as Johann Bernard Stallo, an influence on EMERSON) that Hegel's conception of the dialectic and his emphasis on time and change made his position compatible with evolutionary theory, which in turn suggested less mechanistic ways of understanding the processes involved, as more than chance variation and natural selection. Similarly, in France Ravaisson adopted a more Romantic conception of nature based on the irreducibility of the higher mental faculties to material processes, while the British psychologist James Ward was equally critical of mechanism. Moreover, while the Neo-Kantians were opposed to what they saw as the anti-scientific speculative metaphysics of Hegelian idealism, they nonetheless questioned how far human cognition could be reduced to natural processes, arguing that Kant's transcendental approach to epistemology is needed to provide a proper foundation for science (see COHEN, H.; NEO-KANTIANISM; RENOUVIER, C.B.).

Second, where positivism was committed to a unified conception of the scientific method, on the grounds that the human and the natural were continuous domains, those working in the Kantian tradition saw the need to reassert a fundamental division between the natural and the human sciences, and so questioned the assumption on which positivism was based. The most significant figure here is Wilhelm DILTHEY, who in the 1880s and beyond argued that human cultures required investigation not through classification and causal explanations, but from within, through lived experience, which was conceived of in historical terms, in contrast to the ahistorical paradigms of the natural sciences. Thus, according to Dilthey, while the positivists were right to hold that the natural sciences look for general laws, the *Geisteswissenschaften* have the different goal of seeking the meaning of particular human situations, thereby acquiring hermeneutic understanding rather than predictive control. (See also NATURALISM IN SOCIAL SCIENCE; NEO-KANTIANISM.)

Third, Mill's empiricist assumption that the scientific method was purely inductivist was challenged as a misrepresentation and oversimplification of actual scientific method by William WHEWELL, who offered a more Kantian picture, according to which ideas are prescribed to, and not derived from, sensations. He also claimed that positivism took its empiricist claims about the limits of inquiry too far, arguing that we must speculate about causes if we are to posit laws. Likewise, PEIRCE combined a commitment to the methods of science with a recognition of their metaphysical underpinnings, in a manner that led him to take the *Naturphilosophie* of Schelling and Hegel quite seriously, together with their anti-nominalist idealism.

Finally, as regards naturalism, some of the various schools of Neo-Kantianism in Germany stood against both the empiricist rejection of the a priori, and psychologism about the a priori, which seemed to subsume logic and epistemology under psychology. This non-naturalism was to have a decisive influence on twentieth-century philosophy through the anti-psychologism of FREGE. Opposition to naturalism can also be found in Royce's idealistic alternative (see ROYCE, J.) to James' naturalistic

pragmatism and in the work of the British idealists, where T.H. GREEN in particular played Kant to Mill's Hume, accusing Mill and other empiricists of naivety in the face of Kant's recognition of Hume's lesson that naturalism leads to scepticism. Britain, along with other European countries, thus ended the nineteenth century with a revival of positions that had been dominant at the start of the century, but which had apparently been eclipsed by the 'return to the eighteenth century' that took place from the 1840s onwards. (See BERDIAEV, N.A.; BERGSON, H.-L.; BOSANQUET, B.; BRADLEY, F.H.; CROCE, B.; GENTILE, G.; McTAGGART, J.M.E.)

Given the polarity that developed from the middle of the century onwards between idealism on the one hand, and various strands of materialism, positivism and naturalism on the other, it is not surprising that some thinkers sought ways of compromising between them. One route was to take up a kind of Kantian modesty, whereby positivism and naturalism are adopted with respect to the material world, but where this is said to place limits on our scientific knowledge, beyond which traditional metaphysical possibilities are left open and unresolvable by us. This allowed for a dualistic compromise between science and religion, of the sort favoured by Spencer, Thomas Huxley (who coined the term 'agnosticism'), William Hamilton, Leslie Stephens, Rudolph Virchow and Emil Du Bois-Raymond (who in a speech to the Berlin Academy of Science in 1880 famously delivered the verdict of 'Ignorabimus!' – 'we will never know!' – on the question of the origin of sensation and consciousness, amongst other 'world riddles'). To some, this humility appeared the highest wisdom; to others (such as Ernest HAECKEL) it appeared incoherent, obscure and in bad faith. Another strategy was to attempt to integrate idealism with these apparently competing positions: this led to the eclecticism of COUSIN (see ECLECTICISM), and also the similarly syncretic approaches of Taine, Renan, Cournot, Boutroux, LANGE and LOTZE, while many of the American pragmatists attempted to combine elements of idealism and naturalism, as in Dewey's attempt to reconcile Hegelianism and Darwinism in his early papers (an attempt he later abandoned, as he lost faith in the value of Hegel's idealism) (see DEWEY, J.).

However, even to some enthusiastic proponents of the revival of eighteenth-century paradigms in science and philosophy, it was still recognized that aspects of the social, ethical and religious picture offered by the idealists and Romantics were of value and should be retained. It was in these areas that Mill, for example, was keen to stress the true contribution of Coleridge and Carlyle and the school of German philosophy they represented, as a counterbalance to the ahistoricism and abstract rationalising of the *philosophes*, the early utilitarians and the political radicals. Thus Mill, like many commentators since, sought to preserve the social and historical insights of the idealist tradition, but to divorce them from what he saw as their wrong-headed epistemological and metaphysical underpinnings.

5 The legacy of nineteenth-century philosophy

It can be seen therefore that the 'fight between the nineteenth century and the eighteenth' runs like a thread though the philosophical debates in the period we have been discussing (and where European ideas spread, a similar trajectory can be found in other countries: see LATIN AMERICA, PHILOSOPHY IN). Moreover, in an important sense, this fight continues even now, as Kantians and idealists question the positions of materialists, empiricists and positivists, in the light of scientific developments and disputes about the methodologies of science. While aspects of the nineteenth-century debate may perhaps be less strongly felt – such as the religious implications of these issues – the issues remain as central and pivotal to large areas of philosophy as previously, insofar as they concern not only our conception of the nature of reality, knowledge and the mind, but also of ethics, human freedom, society, historical understanding and politics. Many intellectual movements of the twentieth century – such as EXISTENTIALISM, phenomenology (see PHENOMENOLOGICAL MOVEMENT), CRITICAL THEORY and HERMENEUTICS – have underlying them this tension between 'naturalism' and various forms of 'anti-naturalism'. To understand our own preoccupations properly, we must understand the nineteenth-century debates that first reflected this tension.

References and further reading

Gardiner, P.L. (ed.) (1969) *Nineteenth-Century Philosophy*, New York: The Free Press and London: Collier-Macmillan. (A useful collection of primary texts, with a helpful introduction.)

Mandelbaum, M. (1971) *History, Man, and Reason: A Study of Nineteenth Century Thought*, Baltimore and London: John Hopkins University Press. (A classic study.)

Solomon, R. and Higgins, K. (eds) (1993) *Routledge History of Philosophy, vol VI: The Age of German Idealism*, London and New York: Routledge. (Clear and accessible articles focused on the major figures of German idealism and their successors.)

ROBERT STERN

NISHIDA KITARŌ (1870–1945)

Considered Japan's first original modern philosopher, Nishida not only transmitted Western philosophical problems to his contemporaries but also used Buddhist philosophy and his own methods to subvert the basis of traditional dichotomies and propose novel integrations. His developmental philosophy began with the notion of unitary or pure experience before the split between subject and object. It developed to challenge other traditional opposites such as intuition and reflection, fact and value, art and morality, individual and universal, and relative and absolute. In its organic development, Nishida's philosophy reacted to critiques that it neglected the social dimension with political essays that sometimes aligned it with Japanese imperialism. It culminated in the 'logic of place', a form of thinking that would do justice to the contradictory world of human actions.

See also: JAPANESE PHILOSOPHY; POLITICAL PHILOSOPHY, HISTORY OF

JOHN C. MARALDO

NOMINALISM

'Nominalism' refers to a reductionist approach to problems about the existence and nature of abstract entities; it thus stands opposed to Platonism and realism. Whereas the Platonist defends an ontological framework in which things like properties, kinds, relations, propositions, sets and states of affairs are taken to be primitive and irreducible, the nominalist denies the existence of abstract entities and typically seeks to show that discourse about abstract entities is analysable in terms of discourse about familiar concrete particulars.

In different periods, different issues have provided the focus for the debate between nominalists and Platonists. In the Middle Ages, the problem of universals was pivotal. Nominalists like Abelard and Ockham insisted that everything that exists is a particular. They argued that talk of universals is talk about certain linguistic expressions – those with generality of application – and they attempted to provide an account of the semantics of general terms rich enough to accommodate the view that universals are to be identified with them.

The classical empiricists followed medieval nominalists in being particularists, and they sought to identify the kinds of mental representations associated with general terms. Locke argued that these representations have a special content. He called them abstract ideas and claimed that they are formed by removing from ideas of particulars those features peculiar to the particulars in question. Berkeley and Hume, however, attacked Locke's doctrine of abstraction and insisted that the ideas corresponding to general terms are ideas whose content is fully determinate and particular, but which the mind uses as proxies for other particular ideas of the same sort.

A wider range of issues has dominated recent ontological discussion, and concern over the existence and status of things like sets, propositions, events and states of affairs has come to be every bit as significant as concern over universals. Furthermore, the nature of the debate has changed. While there are philosophers who endorse a nominalist approach to all abstract entities, a more typical brand of nominalism is that which recognizes the existence of sets and attempts to reduce talk about other kinds of abstract entities to talk about set-theoretical structures whose ultimate constituents are concrete particulars.

See also: ABSTRACT OBJECTS; INTENSIONAL ENTITIES

MICHAEL J. LOUX

NON-CONCEPTUAL CONTENT
See CONTENT, NON–CONCEPTUAL

NON-MONOTONIC LOGIC

A relation of inference is 'monotonic' if the addition of premises does not undermine previously reached conclusions; otherwise the relation is non-monotonic. Deductive inference, at least according to the canons of classical logic, is monotonic: if a conclusion is reached on the basis of a certain set of premises, then that conclusion still holds if more premises are added.

By contrast, everyday reasoning is mostly non-monotonic because it involves risk: we jump to conclusions from deductively insufficient premises. We know when it is worthwhile or even necessary (for example, in medical diagnosis) to take the risk. Yet we are also aware that such inference is 'defeasible' – that new information may undermine old conclusions. Various kinds of defeasible but remarkably successful inference have traditionally captured the attention of philosophers (theories of induction, Peirce's theory of abduction, inference to the best explanation, and so on). More recently logicians have begun to approach the phenomenon from a formal point of view. The result is a large body of theories at the interface of philosophy, logic and artificial intelligence.

ANDRÉ FUHRMANN

NONSTANDARD MODELS
See LÖWENHEIM–SKOLEM THEOREMS AND NONSTANDARD MODELS

NORMATIVITY

Something is said by philosophers to have 'normativity' when it entails that some action, attitude or mental state of some other kind is justified, an action one ought to do or a state one ought to be in. The philosophical area most distinctively concerned with normativity, almost by definition, is ethics. Arguably, every ethical concept or category involves normativity of some kind. One area of lively debate within ethics concerns the precise kind of normativity that is possessed by different ethical concepts: moral wrongness, virtue, wellbeing and so on. For example, if an action is wrong, does that entail that there is reason not to do it or just that there is reason to take a certain attitude (blame) towards those who do act in that way?

A second way in which ethics is concerned with normativity is in investigating how an ethical proposition's normative claim might be vindicated and considering whether it actually is vindicated. For example, if an action is morally wrong only if there is reason not to do it, can we then satisfactorily establish that any actions actually are wrong?

Yet a third kind of engagement with normativity concerns the very sources of normativity itself. An attempt to vindicate or debunk the implicit normativity of some specific ethical claim will ultimately face the question of what could support claims to normativity in general. Here we find a fertile debate between Humeans, who seek to ground practical normativity in instrumental rationality, and Kantians, who argue that practical reason necessarily includes formal constraints that extend beyond means/end coherence.

Philosophical discussion of normativity is by no means restricted to ethics, however. Epistemology has an irreducibly normative aspect, in so far as it is concerned with norms for belief. And the idea that meaning is implicitly normative has sparked some of the most exciting discussions in recent philosophy of language.

See also: AESTHETICS; ARISTOTLE; AUTONOMY, ETHICAL; BELIEF; DAVIDSON, D.; ETHICS; EUDAIMONIA; HUME, D.; JUSTIFICATION, EPISTEMIC; KANT, I.; KANTIAN ETHICS; LANGUAGE, PHILOSOPHY OF; MEANING AND RULE-FOLLOWING; MIND, PHILOSOPHY OF; MORAL JUSTIFICATION; MORAL REALISM; NATURALISM IN ETHICS; PRACTICAL REASON AND ETHICS; RATIONAL CHOICE THEORY; TELOS; UTILITARIANISM; VIRTUE ETHICS; VIRTUES AND VICES; WELFARE

STEPHEN DARWALL

NOUS

Commonly translated as 'mind' or 'intellect', the Greek word *nous* is a key term in the philosophies of

ÅYA-VAIŚEṢIKA

Plato, Aristotle and Plotinus. What gives *nous* its special significance there is not primarily its dictionary meaning – other nouns in Greek can also signify the mind – but the value attributed to its activity and to the metaphysical status of things that are 'noetic' (intelligible and incorporeal) as distinct from being perceptible and corporeal. In Plato's later dialogues, and more systematically in Aristotle and Plotinus, *nous* is not only the highest activity of the human soul but also the divine and transcendent principle of cosmic order.

See also: NEOPLATONISM; PSYCHĒ

A.A. LONG

NOVALIS (GEORG PHILIPP FRIEDRICH VON HARDENBERG) (1772–1801)

Novalis (the name is a pseudonym adopted for his published writings) was, together with Friedrich Schlegel and Friedrich Schleiermacher, the leading philosophical thinker of 'early German Romanticism'. Until recently Novalis was regarded primarily as a poet and as the author of the novel *Heinrich von Ofterdingen*, who wrote some philosophical work in conjunction with his writings on natural science and on the political matters of his day. In the wake of the renewed philosophical interest in the philosophy of J.G. Fichte and other German idealist thinkers, there has been a reassessment of the writings of both Schlegel and Novalis. It is now apparent that, far from being, as most commentators present them, defenders of Fichte's 'subjective idealism', Novalis and Schlegel arrived at significant criticisms of Fichte's idealism and initiated an anti-foundationalist tendency in modern philosophy which still has significant resonances today.

See also: FICHTE, J.G.

ANDREW BOWIE

NOVUM ORGANUM

See ARISTOTLE

NOZICK, ROBERT (1938–2002)

Although Robert Nozick published on an enormous range of topics, he is best known as a political philosopher, and especially for his powerful and entertaining statement of libertarianism. In *Anarchy, State, and Utopia* (1974), Nozick presents an image of a fully voluntary society, in which people cooperate only on terms which violate no one's rights.

Nozick's other major contributions to philosophy include an analysis of knowledge, and an accompanying response to scepticism, an account of personal identity and contributions to decision theory and the theory of rationality.

See also: KNOWLEDGE, CONCEPT OF; OBJECTIVITY; PERSONAL IDENTITY; RATIONAL CHOICE THEORY; SCEPTICISM

JONATHAN WOLFF
SIMON BLACKBURN

NYĀYA

See NYĀYA-VAIŚEṢIKA

NYĀYA-VAIŚEṢIKA

The Nyāya school of philosophy developed out of the ancient Indian tradition of debate; its name, often translated as 'logic', relates to its original and primary concern with the method (*nyāya*) of proof. The fully fledged classical school presents its interests in a list of sixteen categories of debate, of which the first two are central: the means of valid cognition (perception, inference, analogy and verbal testimony) and the soteriologically relevant objects of valid cognition (self, body, senses, sense objects, cognition, and so on). The latter reflect an early philosophy of nature added to an original eristic-dialectic tradition. On the whole, classical Nyāya adopts, affirms and further develops, next to its epistemology and logic, the ontology of Vaiśeṣika. The soteriological relevance of the school is grounded in the claim that adequate knowledge of the sixteen categories, aided by contemplation, yogic exercises and philosophical debate, leads to release from rebirth. Vaiśeṣika, on the other hand, is a philosophy of nature most concerned with the comprehensive enumeration and identification of all distinct and irreducible world constituents, aiming to provide a real basis for all cognitive and linguistic acts. This endeavour for distinction (*viśeṣa*) may well account for the school's name. Into the atomistic and mechanistic worldview of Vaiśeṣika a soteriology and orthodox ethics are fitted, but not without tensions; still later the notion of a supreme god, whose function is at first mainly regulative but later expanded to the creation of the world, is introduced. In the classical period the Vaiśeṣika philosophy of nature, including the highly developed doctrine of causality, is cast into a rigorous system of six, later seven, categories (substance, quality, motion, universal, particularity, inherence, nonexistence). Nyāya epistemology increasingly influences that of Vaiśeṣika.

The interaction and mutual influences between Nyāya and Vaiśeṣika finally led to the formation of what may be styled a syncretistic school, called

749

Nyāya-Vaiśeṣika in modern scholarly publications. This step, facilitated by the common religious affiliation to Śaivism, occurs with Udayana (eleventh century), who commented on texts of both schools. Subsequently, numerous syncretistic manuals attained high popularity. Udayana also inaugurated the period of Navya-Nyāya, 'New Logic', which developed and refined sophisticated methods of philosophical analysis.

See also: HINDU PHILOSOPHY

ELI FRANCO
KARIN PREISENDANZ

O

Introduction

Objectivity is one of the central concepts of metaphysics. Philosophers distinguish between objectivity and agreement: 'Ice-cream tastes nice' is not objective merely because there is widespread agreement that it is true. But if objectivity is not mere agreement, what is it? We often think that some sorts of claim are less objective than others, so that a different metaphysical account is required of each. For example, ethical claims are often held to be less objective than claims about the shapes of middle-sized physical objects: 'Murder is wrong' is held to be less objective than 'The table is square'. Philosophers disagree about how to capture intuitive differences in objectivity. Those known as non-cognitivists say that ethical claims are not, strictly speaking, even apt to be true or false; they do not record facts but, rather, express some desire or inclination on the part of the speaker. Others, dubbed subjectivists, say that ethical statements are in some sense about human desires or inclinations. Unlike the non-cognitivist, the subjectivist views ethical claims as truth-apt, but as being true in virtue of facts about human desires or inclinations. Some philosophers, referred to as anti-realists, disagree with both non-cognitivism and subjectivism, and attempt to find different ways of denying objectivity. Quietists, on the other hand, think that there are no interesting ways of distinguishing discourses in point of objective status.

1 Non-cognitivism and subjectivism
2 Anti-realist views of objectivity
3 Objectivity of meaning and quietism

1   Non-cognitivism and subjectivism

Intuitively, an ethical claim such as 'It is right to help those in distress' is less objective than a claim such as 'The table is square'. What does this intuition amount to? Non-cognitivists, such as Ayer, Blackburn and Gibbard, focus on the semantic function of the two claims. 'The table is square' has the function of asserting that a fact obtains in the world. If that fact obtains – if the table is square – then the claim is true; if not, it is false. Thus 'The table is square' is apt to be true or false: it is truth-apt. On the other hand, the non-cognitivist views 'It is right to help those in distress' as having a different semantic function: despite appearances, its function does not consist in asserting that a fact obtains in the world. It is not truth-apt; rather, it expresses an inclination, desire, or some other non-cognitive attitude of the speaker, in the same way that 'Hurrah!' or 'Boo!' merely expresses a favourable or unfavourable attitude. This is why some versions of non-cognitivism are called 'expressivism'. Ethical claims are less objective than claims like 'The table is square' since the latter are genuine truth-apt assertions, whereas the former are not. Non-cognitivists have viewed ethical claims as not objective in this sense for various reasons: because of widespread disagreement over moral matters, because moral facts seem 'queer' or 'odd', and because of the normative character of moral discourse.

There are problems with this way of capturing differences in objective status. Consider the inference:

1 If lying is wrong, then getting little brother to lie is wrong.
2 Lying is wrong.
3 Getting little brother to lie is wrong.

According to non-cognitivism, 'Lying is wrong' and 'Getting little brother to lie is wrong' are not truth-apt. But the inference is intuitively *valid*. And to say that an inference is valid is to say that the truth of the premises guarantees the truth of the conclusion. How can non-cognitivism explain the validity of the inference, given that it denies that (2) and (3) are even apt to be true? Relatedly, the non-cognitivist has a difficulty with (1). What sense can be made of a conditional whose antecedent and consequent are not truth-apt? Non-cognitivism has had difficulty in finding satisfactory answers to these questions.

Subjectivists take a different tack. They admit that 'It is right to help those in distress' is truth-apt, that its sincere utterance makes a genuine assertion. They thus avoid the sort of difficulty outlined above. But if an ethical claim genuinely asserts that a fact obtains, what sort of fact is it? According to the subjectivist, it is simply a fact about the person making the claim: when I say 'It is right to help those in distress' I am asserting that I desire to help them. Ethical claims are truth-apt, but the facts they assert to exist are facts about us, our desires, inclinations or subjective states. When I say 'It is right to help those in distress' I literally *mean* 'I desire to help those in distress'. This contrasts with claims like 'The table is square' which, though truth-apt, are not analysable in terms of facts about human subjectivity. In this sense, 'The table is square' is the more objective.

Subjectivism has difficulty in accounting for moral disagreement. If Jones says 'It is right to help those in distress' and Smith says 'It is wrong to help those in distress', they are disagreeing with each other, indeed contradicting one another. But if Jones means 'I (Jones) desire to help the unfortunate', whereas Smith means 'I (Smith) do not desire to help the unfortunate', there is no contradiction. So in what sense do they disagree?

Subjectivism may try to deal with this by focusing on a wider range of desires than those possessed by the individual who utters the statement. 'It is right to help those in distress' literally means 'Most people desire to help the unfortunate', so that its content is spelled out in terms of intersubjective agreement in desires. But this also faces problems. If it were true, it would be a contradiction to say that helping the unfortunate is right even though most people do not desire to do it. But it is not a contradiction, so even this wider subjectivist analysis must be flawed.

2 Anti-realist views of objectivity

Suppose we admit that two types of claim are truth-apt and yet do not have an anthropocentric subject matter. Do we have to view them as equally objective? Anti-realists, such as Wright and Dummett, think not. They try to show how differences in objectivity can be captured, without adopting either non-cognitivism or subjectivism. How can we distinguish between 'It is right to help those in distress' and 'The table is square' if we allow that both are truth-apt, and that neither is susceptible to a subjectivist analysis? One way would be to develop an analogue of the distinction between primary and secondary qualities, the *locus classicus* for which is Locke's *An Essay Concerning Human Understanding* (1689/90) (see PRIMARY–SECONDARY

DISTINCTION). The standard example of a secondary quality is colour, while shape is usually held to be primary. What is involved in the claim that redness, for example, is a secondary quality? The idea is that there is a close relationship between facts about certain of our subjective states and statements like 'The mailbox is red'. In order to explain this relationship, we need to explain the notion of a best judgment. A judgment that an object is red is best when it is made in conditions that are optimally good for appraising whether or not the mailbox is red. These conditions could be specified very roughly as those that obtain out of doors, in the shade, at lunch time on a lightly overcast summer afternoon. To say that redness is a secondary quality is to say that our best judgments concerning the redness of objects determine the extension of the concept red. The extension of a concept is the class of things to which that concept can correctly be applied. So our best judgments about whether objects are red *determine* which class of objects the concept red can properly be applied to. In contrast, a primary quality like squareness is one whose extension is determined independently of facts about best judgments concerning squareness. Best judgments in this case merely detect an independently determined extension.

This way of saying how 'The mailbox is red' is less objective than 'The table is square' is different from the subjectivist analysis. To say that redness is secondary is not to say that 'The mailbox is red' literally means that 'If conditions were best, we would judge that the mailbox is red'. The claim is the weaker one, that our best judgments determine whether the mailbox falls in the extension of red. The proposal that redness is a secondary quality can therefore avoid the problems associated with subjectivism. And since it does not deny that 'The mailbox is red' is truth-apt, it avoids the problems associated with non-cognitivism. One way, then, to claim that ethical claims are less objective than claims like 'The table is square' is to argue that ethical qualities such as right, wrong, good and bad are secondary rather than primary.

According to the anti-realist, there can be more than one way of saying that one type of claim is less objective than another. Even if we cannot show that ethical qualities are secondary, there might be other ways of contrasting ethical claims with different claims. One way concerns what Wright calls 'objectivity of truth'. This notion of objectivity features prominently in Dummett's discussions of realism. To say that a class of statements exhibits objectivity of truth is to say that '[they] may be fully intelligible to us even though resolving their truth-values may defeat our cognitive powers (even when idealized)' (Wright in *Realism, Meaning and Truth*,

1986: 5). Their truth might be 'evidence-transcendent': they are determinately either true or false, even if we are in principle incapable of citing evidence for or against them. Take Goldbach's Conjecture (that every even number greater than two is the sum of two primes), or some claim about past happenings in some far distant galaxy. We understand these claims, but we are in principle incapable of resolving their truth-values. This gives us one way of claiming that mathematical or cosmological claims are more objective than claims about morals or comedy. There is little temptation to think that claims about the moral status of an action, or about the comic quality of a joke, may in principle transcend our best cognitive efforts. There are no difficulties akin to those affecting non-cognitivism and subjectivism: there is no denial of truth-aptitude, nor an assignment of an anthropocentric subject matter.

3   Objectivity of meaning and quietism

The main danger for the anti-realist story about objectivity comes from Wittgenstein's rule-following considerations (RFC). According to Wright, the RFC endanger the objectivity of meaning. This is the view that 'the meaning of a statement is a real constraint, to which we are bound ... by contract, and to which verdicts about its truth-value may objectively conform, quite independently of our considered opinion on the matter' (Wright in *Realism, Meaning and Truth*, 1986: 5). The meaning of a statement imposes requirements on what counts as correct use of the statement, which determine what uses are correct and incorrect independently of any opinions we may subsequently form. The problem is that if the RFC destroy the idea that meanings are objective in this sense, they thereby threaten the various ways in which anti-realists attempt to draw comparisons concerning objectivity. For example, Wright believes that objectivity of truth implies objectivity of meaning. If the RFC force us to reject objectivity of meaning, they also force us to reject objectivity of truth. And if no discourses possess objectivity of truth, appealing to failure of objectivity of truth will be useless for drawing comparisons between discourses. Likewise, since the truth of any statement is a function of its meaning together with facts about the world, rejection of objectivity of meaning may entail that all qualities are secondary. The possibility of appealing to the primary–secondary distinction in order to draw a contrast will be endangered. In short, the RFC seem to threaten us with quietism about objectivity: the view that no principled, metaphysically interesting contrasts concerning objectivity can be drawn.

Anti-realists try to find ways of avoiding quietism, while retaining their interpretation of the RFC (Wright 1992: Ch. 6). Note that some philosophers, such as McDowell, think that there is a different way in which quietism about objectivity can open up. McDowell does not view the RFC as threatening the objectivity of meaning. So the relevance of the primary–secondary distinction and evidence-transcendent truth is not threatened in the direct manner envisaged in the previous paragraph. The distinctions the anti-realist wishes to draw can still be drawn: instead, what the RFC threaten is the idea that there is any interesting metaphysical *point* to be made by appealing to the distinctions in the first place. For example, it might be argued that the thought that the anti-realist primary–secondary distinction is of metaphysical relevance depends upon a conception of detecting or tracking facts that the RFC display to be untenable.

See also: PROJECTIVISM; REALISM AND ANTIREALISM

References and further reading

Leiter, B. (ed.) (1997) *Objectivity in Law and Morals*, Cambridge: Cambridge University Press. (Collection of articles on the nature and role of objectivity in law and morality.)

Rosen, G. (1994) 'Objectivity and Modern Idealism: What is the Question?', in M. Michael and J. O'Leary-Hawthorne (eds) *Philosophy in Mind: The Place of Philosophy in the Study of Mind*, (Dordrecht: Kluwer Academic Publishers). (State-of-the-art survey, together with a powerful argument for quietism).

Wright, C. (1992) *Truth and Objectivity*, Cambridge, MA: Harvard University Press. (Further development of anti-realism. Chapter 6 contains a useful discussion of quietism.)

ALEXANDER MILLER

OBJECTUAL INTERPRETATION OF QUANTIFIERS

See QUANTIFIERS, SUBSTITUTIONAL AND OBJECTUAL

OBLIGATION, POLITICAL

The problem of political obligation has been one of the central concerns of political philosophy throughout the history of the subject. Political obligations are the moral obligations of citizens to support and comply with the requirements of their political authorities; and the problem of political obligation is that of understanding why (or if) citizens in various kinds of states are bound by such obligations. Most theorists conservatively assume that typical citizens in reasonably just states are in fact bound by these obligations. They take the problem to be that of advancing an account of the ground(s) or justification(s) of political obligation that is consistent with affirming widespread obligations. Other theorists, however, anarchists prominent among them, do not accept the conservative assumption, leaving open the possibility that the best theory of political obligation may entail that few, if any, citizens in actual states have political obligations.

Much of the modern debate about political obligation consists of attempts either to defend or to move beyond the alleged defects of voluntarist theories. Voluntarists maintain that only our own voluntary acts (such as freely consenting to the authority of our governments) can bind us to obedience. Because actual political societies appear not to be voluntary associations, however, voluntarism seems unable to satisfy conservative theoretical ambitions. Some individualists turn as a result to nonvoluntarist theories of political obligation, attempting to ground obligations in the receipt by citizens of the benefits governments supply or in the moral quality of their political institutions. Others reject individualism altogether, defending communitarian theories that base our political obligations in our social and political roles or identities. Individualist anarchists reject instead the conservative ambitions of such theories, embracing a voluntarism which entails that most citizens simply have no political obligations.

See also: CIVIL DISOBEDIENCE

A. JOHN SIMMONS

OBSERVATION

Observation is of undeniable importance in the empirical sciences. As the source of information from the world itself, observation has the role of both motivating and testing theories. Playing this role requires more than just opening our eyes and letting nature act upon us. It requires a careful attention to the information conveyed from the world so that an observation is meaningful. Scientific observation, in other words, is more than a physical act of sensation; it must be an epistemic act as well, with sufficient meaning and credibility to contribute to knowledge. A report of an observation, therefore, must be more than a 'Yes, I see'. It must describe just what is seen, 'I see that _____'.

This obligation to make observation relevant to theory suggests that there is an essential influence of background theories on the observations themselves. The theories we believe or wish to test tell us which observations to make. And describing the results of observations, that is, bringing out their informational content, will always be done in the language of the conceptual and theoretical system already in place. For these reasons, observation is said to be indelibly theory-laden. And the influence of background beliefs is even greater in cases of indirect observation where machines, like microscopes and particle detectors, are used to produce images of the objects of observation. Here, the reliability of the machines, and hence the credibility of the observation, must be based on a theoretical understanding of the interactions that are the links in the chain of information.

The influence of theory on observation is often seen as a threat to the objectivity of the process of testing and verification of theories, and hence of science in general. If theories are allowed to, indeed required to, select their own evidence and then to give meaning and credibility to the observations, the testing process seems to be unavoidably circular and self-serving. Observation that is theory-laden would guarantee success. But a look at the history of science shows that it does not. There are plenty of cases of observations that are used to disconfirm theories or at least undermine the theorist's confidence. Perhaps there is a kind of observation that is not influenced by scientific theory and can serve as a common, objective source of information to put theories to a rigorous and meaningful test. Or perhaps all scientific observation does bear the influence of background scientific theories, but not necessarily of the theory the observation is being used to test. This independence between the theories that support an observation and the theory for which the observation serves as evidence can break the circle in the process of testing and perhaps restore objectivity.

See also: EXPERIMENT; INFORMATION THEORY; MEASUREMENT, THEORY OF; THEORIES, SCIENTIFIC

PETER KOSSO

OCCASIONALISM

Occasionalism is often thought of primarily as a rather desperate solution to the problem of mind–body interaction. Mind and body, it maintains, do not in fact causally affect each other at all; rather, it is God who causes bodily movements to occur 'on the occasion of' appropriate mental states (for example, volitions), and who causes mental states, such as sensations, on the occasion of the corresponding bodily states (for example, sensory stimulation).

This characterization, while correct in so far as it goes, is seriously incomplete. Occasionalists have seen the lack of real causal influence between mind and body as merely a special case of the more general truth that no two created beings ever causally affect each other. The one and only 'true cause' is God, with created beings serving as the occasions for his causal and creative activity, but never as causes in their own right. (The one possible exception to this is that created agents may themselves bring about their own acts of will; this is necessary if they are to be in any sense free agents.) Occasionalism has always been held primarily for religious reasons, in order to give God the honour due to him as the Lord and ruler of the universe. It has never, however, been a majority view among philosophical theists.

See also: EDWARDS, J.; MIRACLES; RELIGION AND SCIENCE

WILLIAM HASKER

OCKHAM, WILLIAM OF

See WILLIAM OF OCKHAM

OMNIPOTENCE

Traditional theism understands God to be the greatest being possible. According to the traditional conception, God possesses certain great-making properties or perfections, including necessary existence, omniscience, perfect goodness, and omnipotence. Philosophical reflection upon the notion of omnipotence raises many puzzles and apparent paradoxes. Could an omnipotent agent create a stone so massive that that agent could not move it? It might seem that however this question is answered, it turns out that, paradoxically, an omnipotent agent is not truly all-powerful. Could such an agent have the power to create or overturn necessary truths of logic and mathematics? Could an agent of this kind bring about or alter the past? Is the notion of an omnipotent agent other than God an intelligible one? Could two omnipotent agents exist at the same time? If there are states of affairs which an omnipotent agent is powerless to bring about, then how is the notion of omnipotence to be intelligibly defined? Yet if the notion of omnipotence is unintelligible, then traditional theism must be false. Another obstacle to traditional theism arises if it is impossible for God to be both perfectly good, and omnipotent. If an omnipotent God is powerless to do evil, then how can God be omnipotent?

See also: FREEDOM, DIVINE; GOD, CONCEPTS OF; PROCESS THEISM

JOSHUA HOFFMAN
GARY ROSENKRANTZ

OMNIPRESENCE

Western Scripture and religious experience find God present everywhere. Western thinkers make sense of this as their concepts of God dictate. Pantheists hold that God's being everywhere is every bit of matter's being a part or an aspect of God. Panentheists say that as God is the soul of the universe, God's being everywhere is his enlivening the whole universe as souls enliven bodies. But most theists reject these views, as most think that if God is perfect, he cannot be, be made of, or be embodied in, a flawed and material universe. Most theists think God intrinsically spaceless, that is, able to exist even if no space exists. Still, theists argue that God's knowledge of and power over creation make him present within it without occupying space or being embodied in matter. Some add that God is present in space not just by power and knowledge but in his very being. These try to explain a spaceless God's presence in space by likening it to the presence of a universal attribute like hardness. Hardness is not spread over hard surfaces, occupying them by having parts of itself in parts of them. Each part of a hard surface is hard. So all of hardness is in each part of a hard surface. So too, theists say, God is not spread out over space, filling parts of it with parts of himself. Rather, all of God is wholly present at each point in space and in each spatial thing.

See also: OCCASIONALISM

BRIAN LEFTOW

OMNISCIENCE

The concept of omniscience has received great attention in the history of Western philosophy, principally because of its connections with the Western religious tradition, which views God as perfect in all respects, including as a knower. Omniscience has often been understood as knowledge of all true propositions, and though several objections to any simple propositional account of omniscience have been offered, many philosophers continue to endorse such an analysis. Advocates of divine omniscience have discussed many problems connected with both the extent of omniscience and the relation between this property and other alleged divine attributes. Three such issues are: Can an omniscient being properly be viewed as immutable? Would an omniscient being have knowledge of the future, and is such knowledge consistent with our future actions' being genuinely free? And should omniscience be thought of as including middle knowledge? That is, would an omniscient being know (but have no control over) what other free beings would in fact freely do if placed in various different situations?

See also: GOD, CONCEPTS OF

THOMAS P. FLINT

ONTOLOGICAL ARGUMENT

See GOD, ARGUMENTS FOR THE EXISTENCE OF

ONTOLOGICAL COMMITMENT

A person may believe in the existence of God, or numbers or ghosts. Such beliefs may be asserted, perhaps in a theory. Assertions of the existence of specific entities or kinds of entities are the intuitive source of the notion of ontological commitment, for it is natural to think of a person who makes such an assertion as being 'committed' to an 'ontology' that includes such entities. So ontological commitment appears to be a *relation* that holds between persons or existence assertions (including theories), on the one hand, and specific entities or kinds of entities (or ontologies), on the other.

Ontological commitment is thus a very rich notion – one in which logical, metaphysical, linguistic and epistemic elements are intermingled. The main philosophical problem concerning commitment is whether there is a precise *criterion* for detecting commitments in accordance with intuition. It once seemed extremely important to find a criterion, for it promised to serve as a vital tool in the comparative assessment of theories. Many different criteria have been proposed and a variety of problems have beset these efforts.

Many important philosophical topics are closely connected with ontological commitment. These include: the nature of theories and their interpretation; interpretations of quantification; the nature of kinds; the question of the existence of merely possible entities; extensionality and intensionality; the general question of the nature of modality; and the significance of Occam's razor.

See also: ONTOLOGY; QUINE, W.V.

MICHAEL JUBIEN

ONTOLOGY

The word 'ontology' is used to refer to philosophical investigation of existence, or being. Such investigation may be directed towards the concept of being, asking what 'being' means, or what it is for something to exist; it may also (or instead) be concerned with the questions 'What exists?', or 'What general sorts of thing are there?' It is common to speak of a philosopher's ontology, meaning the kinds of thing they take to exist, or the ontology of a theory, meaning the things that would have to exist for that theory to be true.

1 Existence and being
2 What is there?
3 Ontological commitment

1 Existence and being

Since so many central debates of philosophy concern what types of things exist, scrutiny of the arguments used in them was bound to lead to investigation of the concept of existence and its logic. The most famous case of this kind is the Ontological Argument for the existence of God, and one of the most famous moves in the ensuing debate is Kant's claim that existence is not a property or predicate of existing things: 'cats exist' clearly tells us something, but it does not tell us of things which, in addition to being furry, feline and fleet of foot, have the further property of existence (see GOD, ARGUMENTS FOR THE EXISTENCE OF §§2–3; EXISTENCE).

This point, with which modern logic agrees, may teach us to formulate 'cats exist' as 'there are things which are cats' – in which it doesn't even look as if existence is functioning as a predicate. But many will think that this does not take us very far. It does not tell us how to describe the difference between a world in which cats exist and one in which they do not – other than by repeating the formula 'there are cats'; it will not advance our understanding of what it is for something to exist. Nor will it touch the somewhat dizzying question 'why does anything exist, rather than nothing?'.

Some philosophers, however, have taken an interest in existence or 'being' (as it tends to appear in their works or in the English translations), not because it appears as part of so many philosophical claims but because they take it for the central concept of philosophy. The most prominent examples are, in antiquity, PARMENIDES, and in the twentieth century, Martin HEIDEGGER.

2 What is there?

In its characteristically philosophical form, this is not a question of detail (for example, are there mammoths?) but about the most general *kinds* of thing: are there universals, or only particulars? – is there mind or spirit, or is there only matter? – is there anything that exists without being in space and time? Thus the debate on the first of these questions between Platonists and nominalists, or on the second between idealists and materialists, might in each case be described as a difference of opinion about the correct ontology. So might the conflict over whether values are objective aspects of reality, or rather 'in the eye of the beholder', a matter of how we react to things rather than the things themselves (see EMOTIVISM; PROJECTIVISM).

The questions 'What kinds of thing *ultimately* exist?' or '... *really* exist?' or '... exist *in themselves*?' are even more characteristically philosophical forms of the general ontological question.

To understand what usually lies behind these additional terms one needs a grasp of (1) the concept of a *reduction* and (2) the distinction between appearances and things-in-themselves.

Reduction. Berkeley famously claimed that material objects were just collections of 'ideas' (see BERKELEY, G. §3). He did not mean that there were no chairs or tables, but that such things did not have a material, non-mental component; what really existed was all mental. There are spirits and their ideas, and we speak of chairs and so on when the latter occur in familiar, stable groupings. In modern terminology, he was claiming that material objects can be *reduced to* ideas. There are other common examples. In political discourse we often speak of what a particular state has done – but without having to suppose that there are such things as states distinct from the individual people who compose them. A once-popular thesis about the nature of mind was that there is nothing but bodies and their behaviour, and that words apparently naming mental states and happenings are just convenient ways of indicating types of behaviour (see BEHAVIOURISM, ANALYTIC; REDUCTIONISM IN THE PHILOSOPHY OF MIND).

Things-in-themselves. We may distinguish between the way a thing appears, which will depend partly on the faculties and situation of whoever is perceiving it, and the way it is, independently of how anyone perceives it. The latter is the thing-in-itself. The terminology was made instantly famous by Kant, who argued that space and time (and therefore everything in space or time) were merely the way in which a non-spatiotemporal reality, things-in-themselves, appeared to humans (see KANT, I. §5).

3 Ontological commitment

The notion of ontological commitment has come to prominence in the second half of the twentieth century, mainly through the work of QUINE (§5). On Quine's view the right guide to what exists is science, so that our best guide to what exists is our best current scientific theory: what exists is what acceptance of that theory commits us to.

But what is that? How do we determine what existents the acceptance of a given theory commits us to? Quine proposes a criterion, often summarized in the famous slogan 'to be is to be the value of a variable'. We are to see what types of thing are quantified over when the theory is stated in canonical form with predicate calculus as the underlying logic; the theory's ontological commitment is precisely to things of those types. This line of thought has given rise to much discussion (see ONTOLOGICAL COMMITMENT).

See also: ABSTRACT OBJECTS; BEING; IDEALISM; REALISM AND ANTIREALISM; UNIVERSALS

References and further reading

Kant, I. (1781/1787) *Critique of Pure Reason*, trans. N. Kemp Smith, London: Macmillan, 1929. (For the famous passage about existence not being a predicate, A598/B626–A601/B629; for the distinction between appearances and things-in-themselves a good example is A45/B62–A46/B63.)

Quine, W.V. (1948) 'On What There is', in *From a Logical Point of View*, Cambridge, MA: Harvard University Press, 1953. (Classic paper on existence and ontological commitment. First published in the *Review of Metaphysics*.)

EDWARD CRAIG

OPACITY

See INDIRECT DISCOURSE; INTENSIONAL LOGICS; SEMANTICS, POSSIBLE WORLDS

OPERA, AESTHETICS OF

Opera, which may be defined as a dramatic action set in large part to music, is an inherently unstable art form, more so than any other. It has been characteristic of its practitioners and critics to call it periodically to order, in idioms which vary but carry much the same message: the music exists to further the drama. This has often been taken to be a matter of settling the priority of two elements: music and text. But in fact three are involved: music, text and plot (or action).

Opera began very abruptly in northern Italy at the end of the sixteenth century, partly as the result of discussions about its possibility. To begin with, familiar Greek myths were employed, set in the vernacular, with simple accompaniments so that every word could be heard. This led to pre-eminence for the singers and for spectacle. After each wave of excess – vocal prowess, dance interludes, stilted plots and texts, then once again, in the nineteenth century, empty display, and later gargantuan orchestras – there was a movement of revolt. Philosophers rarely took part in these aesthetic disputes, most of them being uninterested in music, and possibly more relevantly, being uninterested in any subject which can only be studied in historical terms. But it is fruitless to think about opera apart from its manifestations; every great operatic composer makes his own treaty between the potentially warring elements, Wagner being the most passionate propagandist for his own conception. In the twentieth century the aesthetics of opera have become pluralistic, as has, to an unprecedented degree, the form itself. The perpetual danger is that opera should degenerate into entertainment, and it is always the same message that recalls it to its original function – one which most spectators and listeners are happy to ignore: opera is a form of drama.

See also: MUSIC, AESTHETICS OF

MICHAEL TANNER

OPERATIONALISM

'Operationalism', coined by the physicist Percy W. Bridgman, has come to designate a loosely connected body of similar but conflicting views about how scientific theories or concepts are connected to reality or observation via various measurement and other procedures. Examples of an operation would be the procedure of laying a standard yardstick along the edge of a surface to measure length or using psychometric tests to measure sexual orientation. In the 1920s through to the 1950s different versions of operationalism were produced by, amongst others: Bridgman, who was concerned with the ontology of basic units in physics; behaviourists such as E.C. Tolman and S.S. Stevens, who were concerned with the measurement of intervening variables or hypothetical constructs not accessible to direct observation, as well as B.F. Skinner, who sought to eliminate such nonobservables; and positivistic philosophers of science who were analysing the meaning of terms in scientific language. Conflation of their different operationalist philosophies has led to a great deal of nonsense about operational definition, methodology of observation and experiment, and the meaning of scientific concepts. Operationalist doctrines were most influential in the social sciences, and today the primary legacy is the practice of operationally defining abstract social science concepts as measurable variables.

See also: BEHAVIOURISM, ANALYTIC; LOGICAL POSITIVISM; SCIENTIFIC METHOD

FREDERICK SUPPE

ORDINAL LOGICS

By an ordinal logic is meant any uniform effective means of associating a logic (that is, an effectively generated formal system) with each effective ordinal representation. This notion was first introduced and studied by Alan Turing in 1939 as a means to overcome the incompleteness of sufficiently strong consistent formal systems, established by Kurt Gödel in 1931.

The first ordinal logic to consider, in view of Gödel's results, would be that obtained by iterating into the constructive transfinite the process of adjoining to each system the formal statement expressing its consistency. For that ordinal logic,

Turing obtained a completeness result for the class of true statements of the form that all natural numbers have a given effectively decidable property. However, he also showed that any ordinal logic (such as this) which is strictly increasing with increasing ordinal representation cannot have the property of invariance: in general, different representations of the same ordinal will have different sets of theorems attached to them. This makes the choice of representation a crucial one, and without a clear rationale as to how that is to be made, the notion of ordinal logic becomes problematic for its intended use.

Research on ordinal logics lapsed until the late 1950s, when it was taken up again for more systematic development. Besides leading to improvements of Turing's results in various respects (both positive and negative), the newer research turned to restrictions of ordinal logics by an autonomy (or 'boot-strap') condition which limits the choice of ordinal representations admitted, by requiring their recognition as such in advance.

See also: TURING, A.M.

SOLOMON FEFERMAN

ORDINARY LANGUAGE PHILOSOPHY, SCHOOL OF

The label 'ordinary language philosophy' was more often used by the enemies than by the alleged practitioners of what it was intended to designate. It was supposed to identify a certain kind of philosophy that flourished, mainly in Britain and therein mainly in Oxford, for twenty years or so, roughly after 1945. Its enemies found it convenient to group the objects of their hostility under a single name, while the practitioners thus aimed at were more conscious of divergences among themselves, and of the actual paucity of shared philosophical doctrine; they might have admitted to being a 'group' perhaps, but scarcely a 'school'. The sharp hostility which this group aroused was of two quite different sorts. On the one hand, among certain (usually older) philosophers and more commonly among the serious-minded public, it was labelled as philistine, subversive, parochial and even deliberately trivial; on the other hand, some philosophers (for instance, Russell, Popper and Ayer), while ready enough to concede the importance in philosophy of language, saw a concern with ordinary language in particular as a silly aberration, or even as a perversion and betrayal of modern work in the subject.

How, then, did 'ordinary language' come in? It was partly a matter of style. Those taken to belong to the school were consciously hostile to the lofty, loose rhetoric of old-fashioned idealism; and to the 'deep' paradoxes and mystery-mongering of their continental contemporaries; but also to any kind of academic jargon and neologism, to technical terms and aspirations to 'scientific' professionalism. They preferred to use, not necessarily without wit or elegance, ordinary language. (Here G.E. Moore was an important predecessor.) Besides style, however, there were also relevant doctrines, though less generally shared. Wittgenstein, perhaps the most revered philosopher of the period, went so far as to suggest that philosophical problems in general actually consisted in, or arose from, distortions and misunderstandings of ordinary language, a 'clear view' of which would accomplish their dissolution; many agreed that there was some truth in this, though probably not the whole truth. Then it was widely held that ordinary language was inevitably fundamental to all our intellectual endeavours– it must be what one starts from, supplying the familiar background and terms in which technical sophistications have to be introduced and understood; it was therefore not to be neglected or carelessly handled. Again it was urged, notably by J.L. Austin, that our inherited everyday language is, at least in many areas, a long-evolved, complex and subtle instrument, careful scrutiny of which could be expected to provide at least a helpful beginning in the pursuit of philosophical clarity. It was probably this modest claim– overstated and even caricatured by its detractors – which was most frequently supposed to be the credo of ordinary language philosophers. It was important that Russell – like, indeed, Wittgenstein when composing his *Tractatus Logico-Philosophicus* (1922) – firmly believed, on the contrary, that ordinary language was the mere primitive, confused and confusing surface beneath which theorists were to seek the proper forms of both language and logic.

GEOFFREY WARNOCK

ORGANON
See Aristotle

ORIGEN (*c*.185–*c*.254)

An ascetic Christian, prodigious scholar and dedicated teacher, Origen devoted his life to exploring God's revelation. Much of his work takes the form of commentaries on Scripture. He argued that Scripture has three levels: the literal, the moral and the spiritual. The literal level veils the others, and we need God's help to find the divine mysteries behind the veil. His commentaries directly or indirectly influenced the practice of exegesis throughout the patristic period and the Middle Ages.

Origen used his spiritual exegesis, as well as arguments, concepts and models drawn from philosophy, to tackle the theological problems of his day: the compatibility of providence and freedom, the relation of the Father, Son and Holy Spirit to each other and to rational creatures, the problem of evil, and the origin and destiny of the soul. He is famous – or infamous – for arguing that the souls of angels, demons and human beings enjoyed a previous heavenly existence, but that they sinned and fell. God created the world to punish and remedy their faults.

See also: Patristic philosophy; Revelation; Trinity

JEFFREY HAUSE

ORIGINAL SIN
See Sin

ORTEGA Y GASSET, JOSÉ (1883–1955)

The Spanish philosopher Ortega borrowed themes from early twentieth-century German philosophy and applied them with new breadth and urgency to his own context. Calling his philosophy 'vital reason' or 'ratiovitalism', he employed it initially to deal with the problem of Spanish decadence and later with European cultural issues, such as abstract art and the mass revolt against moral and intellectual excellence. Vital reason is more a method for coping with concrete historical problems than a system of universal principles. But the more disciplined the method became, the deeper Ortega delved into Western history to solve the theoretical and practical dilemmas facing the twentieth century.

NELSON R. ORRINGER

OTHER MINDS

Introduction

It has traditionally been thought that the problem of other minds is epistemological: how is it that we know other people have thoughts, experiences and emotions? After all, we have no direct knowledge that this is so. We observe their behaviour and their bodies, not their thoughts, experiences and emotions. The task is seen as being to uncover the justification for our belief in other minds. It has also been thought that there is a conceptual problem: how can we manage to have any conception of mental states other than our own? It is noteworthy that there is as yet no standard view on either of these problems. One answer to the traditional (epistemological) problem has been the analogical inference to other minds, appealing to the many similarities existing between ourselves and others. This answer, though it is no longer in general favour among philosophers, still has its defenders. Probably the favoured solution is to view other minds as logically on a par with the unobservable, theoretical entities of science. That other people have experiences, like us, is seen as the best explanation of their behaviour.

1   What generates the two problems of other minds?

The epistemological problem arises from two facts. We lack direct knowledge of the mental states of other people. We have such knowledge of at least some of our own mental states. Put the two claims together and we have the traditional problem of other minds. The relevant asymmetry, between our own case and that of others, turns on the question of direct knowledge, not observation. Being able to observe the mental states of others would not enable us to avoid the problem. What would be needed would be the ability to observe those mental states as the mental states of others. They would have to come labelled. The situation would only then be symmetrical. We would have the direct knowledge we lack.

The same asymmetry generates the conceptual problem. How can we have the concept of other people's experiences given that we have direct knowledge only of our own experiences, labelled as our own? Once again, the problem is not that we cannot observe the pains of others. What would be needed would be observing such pains as, indeed, the pains of others.

There has been comparatively little discussion of the conceptual problem, and no more will be said here about the conceptual problem of other minds, other than to note that solving it would not, other than controversially at best, remove the epistemological problem. That problem will be hereinafter the one under discussion.

2   Who has the epistemological problem?

The heroic way of avoiding the problem of other minds is to deny that the claimed asymmetry,

between ourselves and others, holds. Some have done so by insisting that we have direct knowledge of the mental states of others, though this has generally been seen as implausible. However, there seems to be an important strand of thinking within feminist theory that would endorse this rejection of our asymmetry. Similarly, Continental European philosophy has commonly taken the view that other people are needed for us to acquire our own sense of ourselves as persons (see ALTERITY AND IDENTITY, POSTMODERN THEORIES OF). So our sense of others goes before our sense of self. That would seem to demand some capacity to know about others before one knows about oneself. The asymmetry would, presumably, be reversed, and the problem of other minds give way to the problem of our own minds.

Given that the asymmetry is accepted, and thus the traditional understanding of the problem of other minds, it has been almost a commonplace to believe that only a traditional dualist view of the mind produces a difficult problem of other minds (see DUALISM). Though generally theories of mind accept the asymmetry, not all are thought to have a difficult problem. Behaviourism (see BEHAVIOURISM, ANALYTIC) is a theory of mind that either is thought to have no problem at all, or, if it does, nevertheless has no difficulty in solving the problem. There is no special problem about knowing about the behaviour and behavioural dispositions of another.

Functionalism is another theory of mind that is thought not to have a difficult problem. Mental states are viewed as internal states of the organism, regulating its responses to its surroundings. The various mental states are differentiated by their various roles, and they have no other features relevant to their being the mental states they are (see FUNCTIONALISM). It is then claimed to be straightforward, faced with the behaviour of others, to infer that such internal states exist, in the appropriate relations to the behaviour. Eliminative materialists have been seen as not having any problem. If there are no minds, then there are no other minds, therefore there is no problem of other minds (see ELIMINATIVISM).

However, it has been argued that all theories of mind leave the other minds problem intact, and difficult. Theories of mind are, indeed, theories of mind, all minds, one's own and others. Given that they are to be true of all minds, including other minds, they cannot, it has been argued, be used to show that there are, indeed, other minds. It is unacceptable to argue that, say, functionalism is true, and then use this to solve the other minds problem, since it cannot be known to be true, to hold of minds in general, unless it holds of other minds.

OTHER MINDS

How could that be known without the other minds problem having been, somehow, solved?

In conjunction with this line of argument, it has been pointed out that a theory of mind, embracing all minds, needs to embrace its propounder's mind as well as other minds. So a crucial part of the evidence (generally implicit) for a theory of mind will be that the theory fits the propounder's experience. That is the only way direct evidence in its favour can be obtained. So the propounder's experience is crucial. It has been argued that there is no escaping dependence on that experience and, as we shall see, any such dependence has been seen to be a fatal weakness, whenever it exists, in any would-be justification for belief in other minds.

3   The analogical inference to other minds

The traditional solution to the problem of other minds has been the analogical inference to other minds. Other people behave like me in similar circumstances and have the same physico-chemical composition. When I burn myself it hurts and I cry out and wince. When other people are burned they cry out and wince. I can thus infer that they are in pain too. More generally, others are very like me. I know I have beliefs, experiences and emotions. So I am entitled, given how like me they are, to infer that other people also have beliefs, experiences and emotions.

This traditional analogical inference to other minds is now generally incorporated in a hypothetic inference (scientific inference, inference to the best explanation) to other minds. That there are alternative hypotheses about others which have to be ruled out requires that the argument take the form of a hypothetic inference (see INFERENCE TO THE BEST EXPLANATION). But the appeal to one's own case, and to similarities, remains crucial in this analogical/hypothetic inference.

That, indeed, one's own case is crucial, gives rise to the classical, continuing objection to the analogical inference to other minds, that it is a generalization from one case. Such generalizations are almost invariably unsound. Though there have been attempts to put the analogical inference to other minds in a form that avoids this objection, it is generally accepted that such attempts have not succeeded.

However, its supporters argue that, even so, the analogical/hypothetic inference remains a sound inference, despite its dependence on one case. More than one case is needed where what is at issue is the question of a causal link between events. Where it can be known from one case that there is such a causal link, that one case will then be enough. It is claimed that the relevant causal link, involving

mental states, can be known to hold from one's own case. Though it has traditionally been insisted that the relevant causal link is between mental states and behaviour, it has been urged that the relevant causal link needs to be between brain states and mental states if the analogical/hypothetic inference is to be defensible.

The other classical objection to the analogical inference to other minds has been that its conclusion was impossible to check, not just in fact, but in principle. This feature no longer seems to be seen as having any epistemological relevance.

4   Other minds as theoretical entities

This is probably, among Anglo-American philosophers, the favoured solution to the problem of other minds. The justification is in the form of a hypothetic inference. That others have mental states is hypothesized to account for how they behave. However, one proceeds purely from the outside. No evidence gathered from one's own case is used to support this hypothesis. The one case objection thought widely to be fatal to the analogical inference is, crucially, avoided, so it is widely believed.

It is generally considered that treating other minds in this way, as theoretical entities, will succeed if one has a functionalist (or some such) view of the mind. The two seem made for each other. However, the argument in §1, that no theory of mind has an advantage over any other in supporting belief in other minds, would, if successful, apply to this particular attempt to avoid dependence on one's own case.

It has been argued, conversely, that unless one enlists the help of a functionalist (or some such) theory of the mind, treating other minds as theoretical entities will not succeed. A traditional view of mental states, allowing that they have intrinsic content – in particular, phenomenal properties, such as the hurtfulness of pain (see QUALIA) – cannot be supported by this method. Treating the mental states of others as theoretical entities, it is argued, will not provide those states with the needed intrinsic properties. That content can only be filled in by an appeal to one's own case.

5   Criteria and other minds

Treating other minds as theoretical entities, though an alternative to the analogical inference, takes the form of a hypothetic inference. Criterialists, by contrast, have sought to avoid the one case problem by eschewing any form of inference. They have insisted that the link between behaviour and mental states is neither entailment (as in behaviourism) nor

761

an inductive inference. The link is claimed to be conceptual and such links are characterized as criterial. Behaviour is a criterion for the presence of mental states. It has been claimed by some that such a non-inferential connection is required if we are to have any concept of the experiences of others.

An example of such a claimed non-inferential link would be the claim that itching is conceptually linked to scratching, not merely contingently correlated. Our concept of itching is that it disposes one to scratch. It is further claimed that scratching is, thereby, evidence of itching, given that itching disposes one to scratch.

That there are such conceptual links has been widely argued and widely denied. That, if there are, they would provide a sufficient basis for belief in the mental states of other people has been, if anything, even more vigorously contested. The thrust of the attack on the use of criteria to support belief in other minds seems to be that such conceptual links fail to bridge the gap between observed behaviour and the unobserved inner states to which they are conceptually linked. If there is no entailment directly from the one to the other, and there is no appeal to some form of inductive inference, it is argued that we are left with the gap. The gap cannot be crossed by *fiat*, as it were.

One way of understanding what has been called the attitudinal approach to other minds, is to see it as going beyond other uses of criteria in insisting that our conception of other human figures is that they are souls, that they have experiences. That is how we perceive them. It is as immediate as that, preceding any belief. This criterial view seems, however, to inherit the criterial gap. However we conceive of reality, our conceptions might be mistaken. There are attitudes to things and people which, though more immediate and deeper than inferential belief, are, nevertheless, mistaken (racist and sexist attitudes might be given as instances).

6 Private language and other minds

It has been widely accepted that language is a public phenomenon. Some have insisted that it is essentially public. One way of understanding this claim is classically associated with Wittgenstein. A language that is necessarily private, that is, such that only one person can understand it, is (logically) impossible (see PRIVATE LANGUAGE ARGUMENT).

The connection with the problem of other minds has been controversial. However, it seems clear that the connection exists in the reason given for the impossibility of such a private language. That reason bears directly on the analogical inference to other minds.

A necessarily private language is claimed to be impossible because a language has to be, in principle, subject to checking by someone other than an individual user of the language. Generally, a user of the analogical inference to other minds is in breach of this principle. They have insisted that each of us knows what psychological terms mean (at any rate, some of them) from our own case and only from our own case. Their usage would not then be, in principle, one that could be checked for consistency. Functionalists, by contrast, make no such claim, and it should be noted that the connection from private language to other minds depends on the use of terms whose meaning would be private in the relevant sense. The connection is not directly to any particular argument to other minds.

The argument that a check is needed (in principle, so Robinson Crusoe is not in trouble) has generally been that, in its absence, no distinction can be made between its seeming to the language user that their usage is consistent, and its being so. They have only their impression to go on. The issue has been vigorously contested.

That a private language is impossible has not generally been used explicitly as an argument for other minds. Nor could it be. After all, it is only in principle that a language is to be checkable by other people. An important, though indirect role, however, could be seen as its supporting the criterialist insistence on the need for a conceptual connection between inner states and publicly observable states (see CRITERIA).

References and further reading

Buford, T.O. (ed.) (1970) *Essays on Other Minds*, Chicago, IL: University of Illinois Press. (A useful, varied collection, including some classical items, particularly two by N. Malcolm expounding Wittgenstein.)

ALEC HYSLOP

OXFORD CALCULATORS

'Oxford Calculators' is a modern label for a group of thinkers at Oxford in the mid-fourteenth century, whose approach to problems was noticed in the immediately succeeding centuries because of their tendency to solve by 'calculations' all sorts of problems previously addressed by other methods. If for example the question was, what must a monk do to obey the precept of his abbot to pray night and day, a 'calculator' might immediately rephrase the question to ask whether there is a minimum time spent in prayer that would be sufficient to fulfil the abbot's precept, or a maximum time spent that would be insufficient to fulfil the precept. Or, if grace was supposed to be both what enables a Christian to act meritoriously and a reward for having so acted, then a calculator might ask whether the degree of grace correlated with a meritorious act occurs at the moment of the meritorious act, before the act when the decision to act is being made, or after the act when the reward of increased grace is given. If a body was hot at one end but cold at the other, then a calculator might ask not whether it is to be labelled hot or cold, but *how* hot it is as a whole. Finally, if it was asked whether a heavy body acts as a whole or as the sum of its parts, then a calculator might take the case of a long thin rod falling through a tunnel pierced through the centre of the earth and attempt to calculate how the rod's velocity would decrease as parts of the rod passed the centre of the cosmos, if it acted as the sum of its parts.

Of these four questions, the last two were asked by Richard Swineshead, a mid-fourteenth century fellow of Merton College, Oxford, whose *Liber calculationum* (Book of Calculations) led to his being given the name 'Calculator'. By association with Richard Swineshead, other Oxford masters including Thomas Bradwardine, Richard Kilvington, William Heytesbury, Roger Swineshead and John Dumbleton have been labelled the 'Oxford Calculators'. Their work contains a distinctive combination of logical and quantitative techniques, which results from the fact that it was often utilized in disputations on sophismata (*de sophismatibus*). This same group of thinkers, with emphasis on their mathematical rather than logical work, has been called the 'Merton School', because many but not all of the Calculators were associated with Merton College, Oxford. Besides calculatory works, the same authors wrote works in which calculatory techniques are not so prominent, including commentaries on Aristotle, mathematical compendia and commentaries on Peter Lombard's *Sentences*.

EDITH DUDLEY SYLLA

P

PAINE, THOMAS (1737–1809)

Thomas Paine, born in Norfolk, England, spent his early years as an undistinguished artisan and, later, an excise officer. In 1774 he emigrated to America and settled in Philadelphia where he became a journalist and essayist. His *Common Sense* (1776) and sixteen essays on *The Crisis* (1776–83) were stunning examples of political propaganda and theorizing. In the late 1780s, in Europe, Paine wrote *The Rights of Man* (1791–2) and attacked the English political system. During the French Revolution he was a Girondin in the French Convention and wrote *The Age of Reason* (1794, 1796), savagely criticizing Christianity. He died in New York in 1809, an important figure in the sweep of the revolutionary politics in America, England, and France at the end of the eighteenth century.

BRUCE KUKLICK

PAINTING, AESTHETICS OF

Introduction

Why care about painting as an art? Does it offer to engage our aesthetic interest in ways that other art forms do not, or does it merely reproduce the aesthetic satisfactions they provide? Most paintings involve both marks on a surface, and something represented by those marks. Some attempts to say what is distinctive about painting concentrate on the former feature, understanding the art as an exploration of the two-dimensional picture plane. Others concentrate on the representational aspect, seeking to find something special about the things painting can represent, or the way in which it achieves this. The most promising approach acknowledges both aspects, and does so as essential elements in the *experience* we have of painting. If successful, this allows us to see painting as offering aesthetic values found elsewhere, but in a distinctive form. It also helps us to say something about a set of

paintings we are otherwise in danger of ignoring – abstract works.

1   The question

What is there to value, aesthetically, in painting? At first glance, there are many things. Painting can, for instance, present us with beauty, express emotion or illuminate an abstract idea by embodying it in the representation of something concrete. These virtues are found in many other arts. This may seem to render it rather arbitrary to ask about the aesthetics of painting in particular. However, the inquiry makes perfect sense provided there is something distinctive in what painting has to offer. It may be that painting offers a unique combination of values, each of which can be found elsewhere; or it may be that some of what painting offers is found nowhere else. Each possibility provides an approach to our topic.

History provides instances of both approaches, sometimes within the work of a single author (see, for instance, Ruskin 1843–60). But either approach faces a further issue, that of just how circumscribed the realm of painting is taken to be. For example, the eighteenth-century theorist LESSING sought to describe values found in both pictorial art and sculpture, using these to draw aesthetic distinctions between the pair (which he called 'painting') and literature, above all poetry. Others, such as the American art critic Clement Greenberg, have hoped to distinguish the pictorial from the sculptural, in aesthetic terms. Even the pictorial itself presents difficulties: is it to include only painting proper, or some or all of the many other ways in which art pictures can be made – fresco, drawing, etching and photography?

'Painting' is here taken to cover all the pictorial arts, bar photography. This approach presents special problems for aesthetics. We will ask whether there are things to value in these arts that are not found in other art forms. Why do we pursue this approach? One reason is the poverty of accounts of art in general, a poverty in part inherited from accounts of general artistic values. Another is that s/he who does not look, does not find. Since philosophical aesthetics stands in a two-way relationship with criticism, each able, at their best, to learn from the other, and since something parallel is true of criticism and ordinary aesthetic engagement, the worry is that if we do not look for what is special about painting from the viewpoint of philosophical aesthetics, an engagement with painting as it is actually practised might be impoverished both critically and on a day-to-day basis.

Not discussed here are two themes which have a certain topicality. One is the speculation that painting is dead, that it has run its course as an art form. The other is the radical overhaul in recent years of the self-conception of art history, as an academic discipline. The latter involves either a theme too large to tackle here – the idea that the aesthetic is itself an outmoded concept; or a theme that is irrelevant – the idea that art history should be concerned, at least in part, with non-aesthetic matters. The former does not undermine, but presupposes, our question. For if painting is dead, it is because it has explored to the full whatever aesthetic potential it has.

2 Some basic observations

It is unlikely that we could define 'painting', construed either narrowly or as broadly as is here required, except in terms that themselves import aesthetic considerations. So our inquiry cannot have a definition as a neutral starting point. However, there are some simple features common to all, or at least very many, of the items that concern us. Our topic is surfaces that have been marked by human hand, with the intention of stimulating the eye. The vast majority of these surfaces represent something. Matisse's *The Dance*, for instance, shows a group of circling dancers, holding hands and lost to the music. When surfaces are marked so as to represent in this way, they have two aspects. One, the *configurational* aspect, is a matter of what marks lie where. The other, *representational*, aspect is a matter of what the marks stand for, or represent.

This type of representation is found in many pictures which are not our concern, either because they involve methods of picture production we have

here set aside (photography) or because they do not aspire to aesthetic interest (consider the illustrations in a car repair manual). There is a good deal of argument over how to characterize this representation (see DEPICTION). One approach will, however, be of particular relevance (see below). It sees pictorial representation as involving a special experience on the part of the viewers of the picture. In this experience, the precise nature of which is also controversial, we see the marks which make up the picture as organized in a special way, around the thought of whatever is represented: we see things in the marks, as for instance, the dancers in Matisse's canvas.

3 Answers stressing configuration

Although many paintings represent, it is at least not obvious that all do. One very natural way to understand abstract pictorial art is precisely as art that foregoes representation. So understood, abstract paintings will have a configurational aspect, since they are marked surfaces, but not a representational one. Anyone determined to stress the distinctiveness of painting as an art form, but also determined to give a central place to abstraction, is thus under pressure to concentrate on the configurational aspect of pictures. The clearest expression of these tendencies is in the work of Clement Greenberg.

Greenberg thought that painting had often succumbed to 'the confusion of the arts', importing values which properly belong in literature. The true purpose of painting is the exploration of the 'flatness' of the marked surface. What it uniquely offers is the opportunity to draw attention to the two-dimensional pattern of marks on the canvas, emphasizing their status as such, and exploring the opportunities for stimulation, commentary and surprise which such emphasis affords. Painting can do this while representing, but that representation is essentially irrelevant to its pursuit of this, its proper task. Greenberg saw the history of art in terms of the prominence or recession of this central preoccupation, citing Ingres' portraiture, for instance, as work which, while representational, stresses the picture plane. But it is only with abstraction that this tendency reaches its purest, and most elevated, form. For, while Greenberg allows that even most abstract paintings are not completely 'flat', they are the paintings where there is least to distract from the investigation of flatness. Abstract pictorial art is thus not just properly part of painting, but the purest embodiment of its ideals.

Greenberg's writing provides a crude but powerful formulation of themes of more general import. One is his emphasis on painting as a tradition, as a historically extended activity working through a common problematic. Later exponents of the art draw on and react to the achievements and failures of their predecessors, and their work cannot be understood properly except as part of that ongoing, practically embodied, discussion. Another is Greenberg's stress on features of form, rather than content, as central to proper appreciation. The notion of form is very elastic, and in consequence 'formalism' names not one position but many (see FORMALISM IN ART). Not all of these positions exclude representation from the realm of the aesthetically significant. However, Greenberg is not alone in rejecting the relevance of representation; even if, in concentrating exclusively on painting, his claims apply far more narrowly than some formalist views.

Nonetheless, in the end Greenberg's position is unsatisfactory. A great part of the history of painting has been concerned with extending its powers of representation, or at least realistic representation. Indeed, it is possible to see these efforts as the fulcrum around which the history of Western pictorial art turns. Greenberg is forced to construe these efforts either as the pursuit of something other than painting altogether, or as misdirected fire which, somehow, nonetheless hits the real target, that of emphasis on the picture plane. He thus marginalizes what has some claim to be central, and which looks distorting. If there are other, better, ways to deal with abstraction, and less one-sided ways to identify distinctive pictorial values, they merit our attention.

4   Pure content

Positions geometrically opposed to that of Greenberg insist that the value of painting is entirely a matter of representation. Such views are the inheritors of the Aristotelian tradition that sees art as essentially *mimēsis*, or imitation (see MIMĒSIS). (ARISTOTLE distinguished these notions but the tradition following him did not.) If we reduce imitation to the bare power to represent something else, the tradition holds little promise. For even the crudest images or simplest combinations of words represent. Mere representing is thus neither special to pictorial art, nor in itself of aesthetic interest. However, perhaps we can progress further if we identify something distinctive about the representational content of pictures, something which might be developed by pictorial art.

At this point emerges a theme which has great prominence in the literature on painting, both philosophical and art historical. If there is something special about pictorial content, it lies in some kind of tie to vision. It is not just that pictures must be seen to be understood – that much is true of written language. It is that pictures represent things we see, and represent them in something like the way in which vision itself does. Something like this underlies the commonplace, developed by Ruskin into a principle of criticism, that pictorial art can sharpen our visual engagement with the world around us. Thus it is perhaps to painting that we owe the discovery that shadows can be coloured or our sense of the varieties of appearance which can be presented by clouds, trees or mountainsides (Ruskin 1843–60). And it is a closely related suggestion that painting might take visual experience as its explicit subject matter, capturing, for instance, the way that visual detail is distributed across the field of vision in response to shifts in focus and attention. But perhaps the most systematic development of ideas in this vein lies in Lessing's *Laocoon* (1766) (see LESSING, G.E.).

Lessing's attempt to separate painting from poetry begins with a feature they have in common: the aim of both is what he calls 'illusion'. The name may be misleading – Lessing's position is that each art aims to stimulate vivid sensory imaginings. The difference between the two arts stems from the signs each uses to represent. Since those of painting are simultaneously existing and spatially organized, they can 'express only objects whose wholes or parts coexist'. Poetry, in contrast, exploits signs which follow one another, and can thus 'express' only items made up of consecutive parts, that is, actions.

An important corollary is that painting can capture the aesthetic merit things have by virtue of the interrelations of their co-existing parts, i.e. 'material beauty'. Poetry is unable to imitate this, since our psychological limitations prevent us forming decent sensory images of the simultaneous on the basis of exposure to the successive. It is thus restricted to imitating the *effects* of material beauty, or beauty in movement, which Lessing calls 'charm'. Painting's task is to imitate material beauty. Lessing at least comes close to a stronger claim: that a painting's beauty – for him its main aesthetic merit – reduces to that of the thing represented.

There is much to question here. It is certainly false that a painting is only as beautiful as its represented object. There is more to a work, and to our awareness of it, than its representational aspect. We are aware of configurational properties too, and this alone makes it likely that the beauty of the whole comes apart from that of the represented object. Examples are easy to find. Bellini's *Doge Leonardo Loredan* is a work of an exquisite and delicate beauty; the represented Doge, while undeniably an impressive figure, does not have these qualities. Perhaps more damagingly, Lessing's prizing of beauty above all other painterly values seems, if only in the light of developments in art since his day, severely constricting.

These problems can be eased, if not entirely solved, without sacrificing the spirit of Lessing's view. We can explicitly deny that a painting is only as beautiful as its object, without thereby losing one of Lessing's key insights – that represented beauty can at least contribute to the beauty of the representation. And the narrow focus on beauty can be expanded to include other aesthetic qualities accessible to vision. Once we cease directly to link the aesthetic character of the work to that of its object, these need not even be positive qualities, as encountered face to face. We can allow that painting can succeed by virtue of capturing the repulsive and visually disturbing, as well as the erotic, the visually intoxicating and the sublime.

5 Painting and experience

The last section focused on construals of the Aristotelian formula, namely that art is mimēsis, which make do with a thin notion of imitation. A rather different set of views opens up if we draw on another of our basic observations outlined above. Perhaps the way pictures imitate is unique, essentially a matter of how they are experienced. This idea receives particularly clear expression in a view which there are some grounds for attributing to Lessing. As noted, we cannot put much weight on his talk of 'illusion' per se. However, he not only identifies illusion with vivid sensory imagining, he also seems to hold that imagining differs from sense perception only in terms of vivacity. If so, the most vivid acts of imagination will be indistinguishable, in terms of phenomenology, from acts of perception. *Illusionism* is the view that our experience of pictures is phenomenally identical with our experience of what they represent. The idea that this is painting's special gift, or at least its proper aim, has a very long history. Moreover, it links painting to vision in the strongest possible way. Can it also form the basis for a distinctive painterly aesthetic?

It cannot. The problem is not that many pictures do not generate illusion, in this sense. That is true, but shows the view to be false only as an account of pictorial representation, not as stating an ideal at which pictorial art should aim. Nor is the problem that this ideal has never been recognized by painting, or never attained. There are genuinely illusionistic moments in some pictorial art in the Western tradition. In the foreground of Caravaggio's *The Lute Player* (Metropolitan Museum, New York) lies a flute so realistic that one really does seem to be looking at polished wood glinting in the light. The problem is rather that too much great pictorial art does not even aspire to these effects. Consider the achievements of the twentieth century, the great Japanese woodcuts or medieval icon painting.

Nonetheless, illusionism does raise two problems of more general significance. First, if a painting's worth lies in its generating an experience as of its object, what does the picture have to offer that is not already on offer from the object itself? Of course, the latter may not be to hand, or may not even exist. But if the value of painting reduces to that of a convenient visual substitute, it is hard to understand the place it has held in Western culture. We might hope to circumvent this difficulty by saying that painting's value lies not in the nature of the experience it affords, but in the achievement involved in engendering that experience. It is nothing for a flute to present the appearance of one, but a considerable achievement for paint on canvas to do so.

However this, while appealing, runs into the second difficulty. It is very tempting to think that aesthetic value is peculiarly bound to experience. The most compelling form of this thought is that, if I experience two objects in exactly the same way, they cannot differ in value for me. Illusionism, as an aesthetic doctrine, precisely advocates such matching of experiences, of the painting and its object, as an ideal for pictorial art. But then painting and object cannot differ in value after all. Of course, illusionism can allow that the achieving of illusion may be manifest in experience of the painting, but only to the extent that the achievement is partial; the painting, by revealing its own presence, fails to present the appearance of the object. Thus we are forced into the paradox that, the greater the achievement, the less it is present. Art does not so much conceal, as annihilate, itself.

Both these problems hold more widely. The principle behind the second is at the heart of the problem of forgery, of how an original can be of differing aesthetic value from a perfect copy. And the difficulty of differentiating aesthetically between a painting and its object threatens many views which attempt to understand the value of painting in terms of its relations to vision. However, illusionism raises these difficulties in a particularly acute form. To make progress with them, we need a less extreme position.

6 Seeing-in and related phenomena

Illusionism is an accurate account of our experience of only a few pictures. Can an account which fits all pictorial representation fare better as the basis for an aesthetic of painting? Such an account would have to begin by recognizing the fact illusionism overlooks, namely that we are aware of both the representational and configurational aspects of pictures. As noted above (see §2), we experience the latter as organized around the thought of the former.

Schematic as this is, it already provides some help. By acknowledging the role of the configuration, we distance our experience of the picture from that of the represented object. We are thus able to explain at least how it is possible for the two to differ aesthetically. More than this, by stressing that we are aware of both aspects of the painting, we make room for the idea that it has a beauty which amounts neither to that of what is represented, nor to that of the marks considered merely as such, but to the way the one emerges from the other. This does indeed seem to be the case for many paintings – consider Bellini's *Doge Leonardo Loredan* again. This beauty is both important to painting and distinctively pictorial. For, while other art forms too can exhibit a beauty constituted by how what they represent emerges from the means by which it is so, only painting achieves this in the special experience by which pictorial content is grasped.

However, one lesson we took from discussing Lessing is that there must be more to pictorial art than beauty. When a painting is not beautiful, or when its beauty is only a part, perhaps a small part, of its aesthetic interest, what else is involved? We cannot here appeal, in the style of Aristotle, to the imitation itself, not even if we understand that as essentially involving our two-sided experience, seeing-in. For *every* picture sustains that experience, even those of no value. Moreover, we have no account of why that experience should, in itself, be of aesthetic significance. What, then, can we say?

We need to adopt a new strategy. Rather than searching for values found only in painting, or resorting to values found in exactly the same form elsewhere, we should try to understand painting as embodying more general values in a distinctive way. That distinctiveness is to stem from the way those values present themselves in pictorial experience. Seeing-in is thus not merely the means by which we grasp the representational content of a picture: it is also the conduit along which all pictorial value passes, and which gives the values thus accessed a distinctively pictorial shape. Seeing-in is not, now we have definitively rejected illusionism, face-to-face visual experience differently caused. But it is importantly related to ordinary vision. And it is so in such a way that what is aesthetically available in seeing-in is significantly linked to what is available in face-to-face visual contact with the world.

Thus, suppose that seeing things in the flesh not only presents us with certain individuals and their properties, but can also, on occasion, embody an affective response to those things. The skyscraper looks not merely grey and towering, but threatening, hostile. Perhaps seeing-in can similarly incorporate the affective, as when a De Chirico does not merely show strange buildings and alleys with long shadows, but captures a certain affective response to them, of poignant melancholy. If so, seeing-in offers not just a distinctively pictorial way to represent things, but the chance to represent them along with an affective response they merit. The response need not be one we would standardly have to such objects, and might even be one which, in real contact, no such object would ever elicit from us. Painting, then, seems to offer us the chance to explore how another might see the world and feel about it. It promises to initiate us into another sensibility.

This is something literature can do also, of course. What is distinctive about painting is that it does this in a specially visual form. It exploits the intermingling of percept and affect in everyday experience; and the way in which seeing-in is able to preserve such structural features of ordinary vision within what is, phenomenally, a quite different experience. It thereby allows the artist to speak to us by means, not of words and the images they can convey, but manipulated complexes of seeing and feeling.

This is, at most, only the start of an answer to our question. To flesh out our argument we would need to understand more about seeing-in, and in particular how it is able to deploy the resources of seeing face-to-face. We would need to understand those resources themselves far better, for instance, describing properly the role in ordinary vision of feeling. We would then need to spell out the significance provided by the possibility, in painting, of the artist's *controlling* our response, and the hold thus created for the notion of communication. We would need to explain how such control manifested itself in our experience. And we would need to expand our sense of the phenomena this structure allows for – is the above unique, or the model for a whole range of distinctively visual forms of more general artistic values which painting can offer? Having done all this, we would need to fit the values thus described into a plausible account of the tradition of painting, in something like Greenberg's sense of an historically extended, practically embodied, discussion between practitioners of the art (see §3).

We cannot do these things here. Although he does not frame them this way, the most serious attempt to tackle these questions is to be found in the work of Richard Wollheim (1987). The interested reader is directed there. Instead we may end by returning to just one of many matters outstanding – the question of abstract art. The above programme for constructing a pictorial aesthetic may seem already, even in this inchoate state, to ignore abstraction. For if pictorial values are distinctive through their involvement with seeing-in, and seeing-in is the experience by which pictorial content is grasped, what are we to say of those pictures which, *prima facie*, have no such content? Wollheim has an answer. We do see things in abstract paintings. It is just that those things are highly schematic – not flutes, doges and dancers, but, for example, triangles intersecting with rectangles, simple shapes arranged in various planes. Perhaps this is not true of all abstract painting, but it is true of by far the greater part of it. Even Greenberg himself seems to concede as much. For it is hard to know what else to make of his acknowledgement that most abstract painting is not completely 'flat'. This tactic allows us at least to hope to treat most abstract painting as exploring the very same, perhaps multiple, values as the rest of the tradition. And if some pictures remain thereby excluded – Wollheim cites early Mondrian and Barnett Newman at his most distinctive – then perhaps that is a price that the aesthetic, once properly developed, can afford to pay.

See also: DEPICTION; FORMALISM IN ART; LESSING, G.E.; MIMESIS; PERCEPTION

References and further reading

Lessing, Gotthold Ephraim (1766) *Laocoon*, trans. E.A. McCormick, Indianapolis: Bobbs Merrill. (A seminal piece, from the errors of which much can be learned.)

Ruskin, John (1843–60) *Modern Painters*, 5 vols, repr. 1906, London: J.M. Dent & Co (A magisterial, insightful and idiosyncratic exploration, both critical and theoretical, of painting, with special reference to the work of Turner.)

Wollheim, Richard (1987) *Painting As An Art*, London, Thames & Hudson. (As well as providing the archetype for all accounts of pictorial experience which acknowledge both aspects of pictures, this is the most extensive, sophisticated and accomplished attempt to answer our question.)

ROBERT HOPKINS

PAKṢILASVĀMIN
See VĀTSYĀYANA

PALEY, WILLIAM (1743–1805)

William Paley, theologian and moral philosopher, expressed and codified the views and arguments of orthodox Christianity and the conservative moral and political thought of eighteenth-century England. Paley says that his works form a unified system based on natural religion. Like others during this period, Paley thought that reason alone, unaided by revelation, would establish many Christian theses.

He is confident that a scientific understanding of nature will support the claim that God is the author of nature. Paley belongs to the anti-deist tradition that holds that revelation supplements natural religion. The most important revelation is God's assurance of an afterlife in which the virtuous are rewarded and the vicious are punished. Natural and revealed religion, in turn, provide the foundation for morality. God's will determines what is right and his power to reward and punish us in the afterlife provide the moral sanctions. On the whole, Paley is concerned with sustaining Christian faith, and ensuring that people know what their duties are and do them.

See also: UTILITARIANISM

CHARLOTTE R. BROWN

PANENTHEISM
See GOD, CONCEPTS OF

PANPSYCHISM

Panpsychism is the thesis that physical nature is composed of individuals each of which is to some degree sentient. It is somewhat akin to hylozoism, but in place of the thesis of the pervasiveness of life in nature substitutes the pervasiveness of sentience, experience or, in a broad sense, consciousness. There are two distinct grounds on which panpsychism has been based. Some see it as the best explanation of the emergence of consciousness in the universe to say that it is, in fact, universally present, and that the high-level consciousness of humans and animals is the product of special patterns of that low-level consciousness or feeling which is universally present. The other ground on which panpsychism is argued for is that ordinary knowledge of the physical world is only of its structure and sensory effects on us, and that the most likely inner content which fills out this structure and produces these experiences is a system of patterns of sentient experience of a low level.

T.L.S. SPRIGGE

PANTHEISM

Pantheism contrasts with monotheism (there is one God), polytheism (there are many gods), deism (God created the world in such a way that it is capable of existing and operating on its own, which God then allows it to do) and panentheism (in God there is a primordial and unchanging nature, and a consequent nature that changes and develops). Etymologically, pantheism is the view that Deity and Cosmos are identical. Theologically, it embraces divine immanence while rejecting divine transcendence. If atheism is the denial that anything is divine, pantheism is not atheism; if atheism is the claim that there is no Creator, Providence, transcendent Deity, or personal God, pantheism is atheistic.

Spinoza, perhaps the paradigm figure for pantheism, was described by some as 'a God-intoxicated man' and by others as an atheist. On his account, only *God or Nature* exists, a single, necessarily existing substance whose modes and qualities exhaust reality. Conceivable equally properly as physical or as mental, God or Nature is no proper object of worship, creates nothing, grants freedom to none, hears no prayer, and does not act in history. Personal immortality, on Spinoza's view, not only does not occur, but is logically impossible. It is one thing to value nature so highly that one calls it a divinity, another to believe in God in any monotheistic sense.

This much said, it must be admitted that 'pantheism' is not easy to define precisely. As conceived here, pantheism need not be a variety of materialism, and if it is materialistic it includes a high view of the worth of matter. Yet 'pantheism' has served as a term of abuse, and as another term for 'atheism' and 'materialism' and 'deism', terms bearing quite different senses.
See also: GOD, CONCEPTS OF

KEITH E. YANDELL

PARACELSUS (PHILIPPUS AUREOLUS THEOPHRASTUS BOMBASTUS VON HOHENHEIM) (1493–1541)

Paracelsus (pseudonym of Theophrastus Bombastus von Hohenheim) was an itinerant Swiss surgeon and physician who formulated a new philosophy of medicine based on a combination of chemistry, Neoplatonism and the occult, all within a Christian framework. His works, usually in German rather than Latin, were mostly published after his death. His importance for medical practice lay in his insistence on observation and experiment, and his use of chemical methods for preparing drugs. He rejected Galen's explanation of disease as an imbalance of humours, along with the traditional doctrine of the four elements. He saw the human being as a microcosm that reflected the structure and elements of the macrocosm, thus presenting a unified view of human beings and a universe in which everything was interconnected and full of vital powers. Paracelsian chemical medicine was very popular in the late sixteenth and seventeenth centuries, largely due to its presentation as part of a general theory.
See also: ALCHEMY; HERMETISM; HUMANISM, RENAISSANCE; RELIGION AND SCIENCE; RENAISSANCE PHILOSOPHY

E.J. ASHWORTH

PARACONSISTENT LOGIC

A logic is paraconsistent if it does not validate the principle that from a pair of contradictory sentences, A and ~A, everything follows, as most orthodox logics do. If a theory has a paraconsistent underlying logic, it may be inconsistent without being trivial (that is, entailing everything). Sustained work in formal paraconsistent logics started in the early 1960s. A major motivating thought was that there are important, naturally occurring, inconsistent but non-trivial theories. Some logicians have gone further and claimed that some of these theories may be true. By the mid-1970s, details of the semantics and proof-theories of many paraconsistent logics were well understood. More recent research has focused on the applications of these logics and on their philosophical underpinnings and implications.

GRAHAM PRIEST

PARADIGMS
See KUHN, THOMAS SAMUEL (§4)

PARADOXES, EPISTEMIC

The four primary epistemic paradoxes are the lottery, preface, knowability, and surprise examination paradoxes. The lottery paradox begins by imagining a fair lottery with a thousand tickets in it. Each ticket is so unlikely to win that we are justified in believing that it will lose. So we can infer that no ticket will win. Yet we know that some ticket will win. In the preface paradox, authors are justified in believing everything in their books. Some preface their book by claiming that, given human frailty, they are sure that errors remain. But then they justifiably believe both that everything in the book is true, and that something in it is false.

The knowability paradox results from accepting that some truths are not known, and that any truth is knowable. Since the first claim is a truth, it must be knowable. From these claims it follows that it is possible that there is some particular truth that is known to be true and known not to be true.

The final paradox concerns an announcement of a surprise test next week. A Friday test, since it can be predicted on Thursday evening, will not be a surprise yet, if the test cannot be on Friday, it cannot be on Thursday either. For if it has not been given by Wednesday night, and it cannot be a surprise on Friday, it will not be a surprise on Thursday. Similar reasoning rules out all other days of the week as well; hence, no surprise test can occur next week. On Wednesday, the teacher gives a test, and the students are taken completely by surprise.
See also: SCEPTICISM

JONATHAN L. KVANVIG

PARADOXES OF SET AND PROPERTY

Emerging around 1900, the paradoxes of set and property have greatly influenced logic and generated a vast literature. A distinction due to Ramsey in 1926 separates them into two categories: the logical paradoxes and the semantic paradoxes. The logical paradoxes use notions such as set or cardinal number, while the semantic paradoxes employ semantic concepts such as truth or definability. Both often involve self-reference.

The best-known logical paradox is Russell's paradox concerning the set S of all sets x such that x is not a member of x. Russell's paradox asks: is S a member of itself? A moment's reflection shows that S is a member of itself if and only if S is not a member of itself – a contradiction.

Russell found this paradox by analysing the paradox of the largest cardinal. The set U of all sets has the largest cardinal number, since every set is a subset of U. But there is a cardinal number greater than that of any given set M, namely the cardinal of the power set, or set of all subsets, of M. Thus the cardinal of the power set of U is greater than that of U, a contradiction. (The paradox of the largest ordinal, is similar in structure.)

Among the semantic paradoxes, the best known is the liar paradox, found by the ancient Greeks. A man says that he is lying. Is what he says true or false? Again, either conclusion leads to its opposite. Although this paradox was debated in medieval Europe, its modern interest stems from Russell, who placed it in the context of a whole series of paradoxes, including his own.

GREGORY H. MOORE

PARETO PRINCIPLE

A social state is said to be Pareto-efficient when there is no feasible alternative to it in which at least one individual is better off while no individual is worse off. The Pareto principle tells us to move from Pareto-inefficient to Pareto-efficient states. Suppose a large basket of fruit is shared among a group in some way or another – one apple, two peaches, a dozen cherries each, for instance. If the fruit can be exchanged so that at least some people get more enjoyment from what they have, and no one gets less, the Pareto principle instructs us to do so; indeed, it instructs us to carry on exchanging until no more improvements of this kind are possible.

DAVID MILLER

PARMENIDES (early to mid 5th century BC)

Parmenides of Elea, a revolutionary and enigmatic Greek philosophical poet, was the earliest defender of Eleatic metaphysics. He argued for the essential homogeneity and changelessness of being, rejecting as spurious the world's apparent variation over space and time. His one poem, whose first half largely survives, opens with the allegory of an intellectual journey by which Parmenides has succeeded in standing back from the empirical world. He learns, from the mouth of an unnamed goddess, a dramatically new perspective on being. The goddess's disquisition, which fills the remainder of the poem, is divided into two parts; the Way of Truth and the Way of Seeming.

The Way of Truth is the earliest known passage of sustained argument in Western philosophy. First a purportedly exhaustive choice is offered between two 'paths' – that of being, and that of not-being. Next the not-being path is closed off: the predicate expression ' . . . is not' could never be supplied with a subject, since only that-which-is can be spoken of and thought of. Nor, on pain of self-contradiction, can a third path be entertained, one which would conflate being with not-being – despite the fact that just such a path is implicit in the ordinary human acceptance of an empirical world bearing a variety of shifting predicates. All references, open or covert, to not-being must be outlawed. Only ' . . . is' (or perhaps ' . . . is . . .') can be coherently said of anything.

The next move is to seek the characteristics of that-which-is. The total exclusion of not-being leaves us with something radically unlike the empirical world. It must lack generation, destruction, change, distinct parts, movement and an asymmetric shape, all of which would require some not-being to occur. That-which-is must, in short, be a changeless and undifferentiated sphere.

In the second part of the poem the goddess offers a cosmology – a physical explanation of the very world which the first half of the poem has banished as incoherent. This is based on a pair of ultimate principles or elements, the one light and fiery, the other heavy and dark. It is presented as conveying the 'opinions of mortals'. It is deceitful, but the goddess nevertheless recommends learning it, 'so that no opinion of mortals may outstrip you'.

The motive for the radical split between the two halves of the poem has been much debated in modern times. In antiquity the Way of Truth was taken by some as a challenge to the notion of change, which physics must answer, by others as the statement of a profound metaphysical truth, while the Way of Seeming was widely treated as in some sense Parmenides' own bona fide physical system.

See also: BEING; PRESOCRATIC PHILOSOPHY

DAVID SEDLEY

PASCAL, BLAISE (1623–62)

Blaise Pascal was a mathematical prodigy who numbered among his early achievements an essay on conic sections and the invention of a calculating machine. In his early twenties he engaged in the vigorous European debate about the vacuum, undertaking, or causing to be undertaken, a series of experiments which helped to refute the traditional view that nature abhors a vacuum and setting out clearly the methodology of the new science. In 1646 he came under the influence of Jansenism; this he seems to have rejected for a short time in the early 1650s, but he then underwent a profound spiritual experience which transformed his life and drew him into close association with leading Jansenists, with whom he collaborated in producing the polemical *Lettres provinciales* (1656–7). At the same time he planned to write an apology for the Christian religion, but ill-health so affected his final years that this only survives in the fragmentary form of the *Pensées* (1670). He made significant contributions to mathematics, especially in the fields of geometry, number theory and probability theory, and he also helped to describe the *'esprit géométrique'* which characterized the new science of the 1650s. He argued that geometry was superior to logic in that it could provide not only demonstrative procedures but also axioms from which to work; and he set down appropriate rules of argument. His religious writings were published shortly after his death; many attempts have been made to reconstruct the apology which they encapsulate. It seems most likely that this would have fallen into two parts, the first setting out the wretchedness of humans without God, the second demonstrating the truth of Christianity and the felicity of the religious life. Humans are portrayed in Augustinian terms as corrupt, vapid creatures, prey to their passions and the delusions of imagination; but they are also shown to possess greatness through their reason and self-awareness, which can bring them to recognize that Christianity alone has represented their predicament accurately, and that they should turn to religion, even if initially they lack the instinctive faith which is the hallmark of the saved. In the 'wager' fragment, Pascal employs his mathematical insights to revivify an old apologetic argument (that it is wiser to bet on God existing rather than on his not existing) and to link it to an existential imperative (that we all are obliged to choose between these alternatives). The adroit interplay between scepticism, rationalism and faith of the first part is succeeded by a second part which argues the veracity of Christianity from Biblical interpretation, prophecies and miracles. Pascal concedes that this cannot carry absolute conviction; but he insists that the rejection of such arguments is caused not by man's rational powers but by his corrupt passions. Pascal's *Pensées* are written for the most part in terse aphoristic form; he aspired to a style that was so accessible that the reader would believe he was experiencing as his own the thoughts that he read. Although Pascal said at the end of his life that he considered his mathematical pursuits a quite separate enterprise from his religious writings, a common epistemology can be found in both, together with a scientific outlook which Pascal saw as superior to the philosophical alternatives of his day.

See also: DECISION AND GAME THEORY

IAN MACLEAN

PASSMORE, JOHN ARTHUR (1914–)

John Passmore was born in New South Wales and studied at the University of Sydney. He taught there before moving to Otago in New Zealand and then to the Australian National University. He is perhaps best known for *A Hundred Years of Philosophy* which has been widely recognized as a major feat of philosophical scholarship. He has contributed widely to topics in the history of philosophy, philosophy of education, philosophy of science and philosophy of the environment. He is one of the pioneers of what has come to be called applied philosophy.

FRANK JACKSON

PATERNALISM

Restriction of people's liberty of action is paternalistic when it is imposed for the good of those whose liberty is restricted and against their will. The argument in favour of paternalism is that, if one can prevent people from harming themselves, there is no reason not to do so. Versions of the ethical creed of liberalism tend to oppose paternalism. One argument is that as a practical matter the policy of permitting paternalism tends to do more harm than good in the long run, or at least less good than a strict refusal to countenance paternalism would achieve. Another argument appeals to a right of autonomy which paternalism is held to violate whether or not its consequences on the whole are undesirable. Paternalist advocacy can be 'hard' or 'soft'; soft paternalism is the doctrine that paternalism can only be justifiable when the individual action that is being restricted was not chosen in a substantially voluntary way.

See also: CONFUCIAN PHILOSOPHY, CHINESE; CONSENT; FREEDOM AND LIBERTY; LIBERALISM

RICHARD ARNESON

PATRISTIC PHILOSOPHY

Early Christian writers used terminology and ideas drawn from Graeco-Roman philosophical literature in their theological writings, and some early Christians also engaged in more formal philosophical reflection. The term 'patristic philosophy' covers all of these activities by the 'fathers' (*patres*) of the Church. The literature of nascent Christianity thus contains many concepts drawn from Graeco-Roman philosophy, and this early use of classical ideas by prominent Christians provided an authoritative sanction for subsequent philosophical discussion and elaboration.

Early Christians were drawn to philosophy for many reasons. Philosophy held a pre-eminent place in the culture of the late Hellenistic and Roman world. Its schools provided training in logical rigour, systematic accounts of the cosmos and directions on how to lead a good and happy life. While philosophical movements of the period, such as Neoplatonism or Stoicism, varied widely in their doctrines, most presented accounts of reality that included some representation of the divine. These rationally articulated accounts established the theological and ethical discourse of Graeco-Roman culture. As such, philosophy had a natural appeal to Hellenistic Jewish and early Christian thinkers. It provided a ready language in which to refine ideas about the God of the ancient Hebrew scriptures, and to elaborate the trinitarian God of Christianity. It also helped to bring conceptual coherence to the ideas found in the scriptures of both religions. Finally, it provided the common intellectual discourse that those communities required in order to present their central tenets to the majority culture of the Roman empire.

To a considerable extent, the notion of 'philosophy' suggested to the ancients a way of life as much as an intellectual discipline. This too drew Christians to the teachings of the philosophers. While there were doctrines and prescriptions of behaviour specific to the major schools, philosophers in general tended to advocate an ethically reflective and usually rather ascetic life, one which conjoined intellectual with moral discipline. This ethical austerity was prized by early Christians as an allied phenomenon within Graeco-Roman culture to which they could appeal in debates about the character of their new movement. The tacit validation that philosophy offered to the Christian movement was thus multifaceted, and, while it was sometimes thought to be associated with unacceptable aspects of pagan religious culture, philosophy provided some educated Christians with a subtle social warrant for their new life and beliefs.

It should be noted that ancient Christianity was itself a complex movement. Like Graeco-Roman philosophy, Christianity included a broad spectrum of beliefs and practices. Thus those early Christians who developed their beliefs with reference to philosophy endorsed a wide range of metaphysical and ethical doctrines, ranging from materialism to extreme transcendentalism, from asceticism to spiritual libertinism. Yet, while diversity is evident, it is also true that the Christian movement came to develop a rough set of central beliefs and some early forms of community organization associated with those beliefs. This incipient 'orthodoxy' came to value some sorts of philosophy, especially Platonism, which seemed best suited to its theological agenda. This tacit alliance with Platonism was fraught with ambiguity and uncertainty, and it was never a reciprocal relationship. Nonetheless, in the second and third centuries a type of Christian philosophical theology emerged which owed much to the Platonic school and became increasingly dominant among orthodox Christian authors. It was this trajectory that defined the character of patristic philosophy.

Early Christian thought had its origins in Hellenistic Judaism, and its initial character was defined by the dominant patterns of that tradition. This early phase extended through the first half of the second century AD, as Christianity began to define its distinctive themes associated with the nature and historical mission of Jesus Christ. Throughout the second century, Christianity became increasingly a movement made up of gentile converts; some of these new members had educations that had included philosophy and a few were even trained as philosophers. Thus Christian thought began to show increased contact with the Graeco-Roman philosophical schools, a trend no doubt reinforced by the critical need for Christians – as a proscribed religious minority – to defend their theology, ritual practices and ethics in the face of cultural and legal hostility.

This so-called 'age of the apologists' lasted throughout the second and third centuries, until Christianity began to enjoy toleration early in the fourth century. However, it would be a mistake to consider Christian philosophical thought in that period as primarily directed towards the surrounding pagan society. In many respects philosophy, as the intellectual discourse of Graeco-Roman culture, offered gentile Christians a means to clarify, articulate and assimilate the tenets of their new faith. This process of intellectual appropriation appears to have been of considerable personal importance to many Graeco-Roman converts. Christian philosophical theology helped them to recover ideas familiar from their school training and to find unfamiliar concepts defended with the rigour much prized within Graeco-Roman culture.

After Christianity became a licit religion in the fourth century, philosophical activity among

Christians expanded. The task of theological self-articulation became increasingly significant as Christianity grew in the fourth and fifth centuries towards majority status within the Empire, with imperial support. In this later period the range and sophistication of Christian thought increased significantly, due in part to the influence of pagan Neoplatonism, a movement that included a number of the finest philosophers active since the classical period of Plato and Aristotle. Later patristic philosophy had a defining influence upon medieval Christian thought through such figures as Augustine and Dionysius the pseudo-Areopagite, establishing both the conceptual foundations and the authoritative warrant for the scholasticism of the Latin West and Greek East.

See also: AUGUSTINE; BOETHIUS, A.M.S.; GNOSTICISM; MANICHEISM; NEOPLATONISM; ORIGEN; PELAGIANISM; TERTULLIAN, Q.S.F.

JOHN PETER KENNEY

PEACE

See WAR AND PEACE, PHILOSOPHY OF

PEIRCE, CHARLES SANDERS (1839–1914)

Peirce was an American philosopher, probably best known as the founder of pragmatism and for his influence upon later pragmatists such as William James and John Dewey. Personal and professional difficulties interfered with his attempts to publish a statement of his overall philosophical position, but, as the texts have become more accessible, it has become clear that he was a much more wide-ranging and important thinker than his popular reputation suggests.

He claimed that his pragmatism was the philosophical outlook of an experimentalist, of someone with experience of laboratory work. His account of science was vigorously anti-Cartesian: Descartes was criticized for requiring an unreal 'pretend' doubt, and for adopting an individualist approach to knowledge which was at odds with scientific practice. 'Inquiry' is a cooperative activity, whereby fallible investigators progress towards the truth, replacing real doubts by settled beliefs which may subsequently be revised. In 'The Fixation of Belief' (1877), he compared different methods for carrying out inquiries, arguing that only the 'method of science' can be self-consciously adopted. This method makes the 'realist' assumption that there are real objects, existing independently of us, whose nature will be discovered if we investigate them for long enough and well enough.

Peirce's 'pragmatist principle' was a rule for clarifying concepts and hypotheses that guide scientific investigations. In the spirit of laboratory practice, we can completely clarify the content of a hypothesis by listing the experiential consequences we would expect our actions to have if it were true: if an object is fragile, and we were to drop it, we would probably see it break. If this is correct, propositions of a priori metaphysics are meaningless. Peirce applied his principle to explain truth in terms of the eventual agreement of responsible inquirers: a proposition is true if it would be accepted eventually by anyone who inquired into it. His detailed investigations of inductive reasoning and statistical inference attempted to explain how this convergence of opinion was achieved.

Taken together with his important contributions to formal logic and the foundations of mathematics, this verificationism encouraged early readers to interpret Peirce's work as an anticipation of twentieth-century logical positivism. The interpretation is supported by the fact that he tried to ground his logic in a systematic account of meaning and reference. Much of his most original work concerned semiotic, the general theory of signs, which provided a novel framework for understanding of language, thought and all other kinds of representation. Peirce hoped to show that his views about science, truth and pragmatism were all consequences of his semiotic. Doubts about the positivistic reading emerge, however, when we note his insistence that pragmatism could be plausible only to someone who accepted a distinctive form of metaphysical realism. And his later attempts to defend his views of science and meaning bring to the surface views which would be unacceptable to an anti-metaphysical empiricist.

From the beginning, Peirce was a systematic philosopher whose work on logic was an attempt to correct and develop Kant's philosophical vision. When his views were set out in systematic order, positions came to the surface which, he held, were required by his work on logic. These include the theory of categories which had long provided the foundations for his work on signs: all elements of reality, thought and experience can be classified into simple monadic phenomena, dyadic relations and triadic relations. Peirce called these Firstness, Secondness and Thirdness. He also spoke of them as quality, reaction and mediation, and he insisted that the error of various forms of empiricism and nominalism was the denial that mediation (or Thirdness) was an irreducible element of our experience. Peirce's 'synechism' insisted on the importance for philosophy and science of hypotheses involving continuity, which he identified as 'ultimate mediation'. This emphasis upon continuities in thought and nature was supposed to ground his realism. Furthermore, his epistemological work came to focus increasingly upon the requirements for rational self-control, for our ability to control our inquiries in accordance with norms whose validity we can acknowledge. This required a theory of norms which would explain our attachment to the search for truth and fill out the details of that concept. After 1900, Peirce began to develop such an account, claiming that logic must be grounded in ethics and aesthetics.

Although pragmatism eliminated a priori speculation about the nature of reality, it need not rule out metaphysics that uses the scientific method. From the 1880s, Peirce looked for a system of scientific metaphysics that would fill important gaps in his defence of the method of science. This led to the development of an evolutionary cosmology, an account of how the world of existent objects and scientific laws evolved out of a chaos of possibilities through an evolutionary process. His 'tychism' insisted that chance was an ineliminable component of reality, but he argued that the universe was becoming more governed by laws or habits through time. Rejecting both physicalism and dualism, he defended what he called a form of 'Objective Idealism': matter was said to be a form of 'effete mind'.

See also: DOUBT; EMPIRICISM; HEGELIANISM; INDUCTION, EPISTEMIC ISSUES IN; PRAGMATISM; SCEPTICISM; SCIENTIFIC REALISM AND ANTIREALISM; SEMIOTICS; TRUTH, PRAGMATIC THEORY OF

CHRISTOPHER HOOKWAY

PELAGIANISM

Pelagius, a Christian layman, was active around AD 400. The thesis chiefly associated with his name is that (i) human beings have it in their own power to avoid sin and achieve righteousness. Critics objected that this derogates from human dependence on the grace of God. Pelagius did not deny that the power to avoid sin is itself a gift of God, an *enabling* grace; but he was understood to deny the need for *cooperative* grace, divine aid in using the power rightly, or at least to assert that (ii) such aid is a reward for human effort, and so not an act of grace. Later thinkers who held that God's aid, though not a reward, goes only to those who do make an effort, were accused of believing that (iii) there is no need of *prevenient* grace in causing the effort in the first place. So Pelagianism is a tendency to magnify human powers: its defenders saw it as a (frightening) challenge to humans, its detractors as an insult to God. It was hard without Pelagianism to find a place for free will, or with it for original sin.

See also: PREDESTINATION; SIN

CHRISTOPHER KIRWAN

PELAGIUS
See PELAGIANISM

PERCEPTION

Introduction

Sense perception is the use of our senses to acquire information about the world around us and to become acquainted with objects, events, and their features. Traditionally, there are taken to be five senses: sight, touch, hearing, smell and taste.

Philosophical debate about perception is ancient. Much debate focuses on the contrast between appearance and reality. We can misperceive objects and be misled about their nature, as well as perceive them to be the way that they are: you could misperceive the shape of the page before you, for example. Also, on occasion, it may seem to us as if we are perceiving, when we do not perceive at all, but only suffer hallucinations.

Illusions and hallucinations present problems for a theory of knowledge: if our senses can mislead us, how are we to know that things are as they appear, unless we already know that our senses are presenting things as they are? But the concern in the study of perception is primarily to explain how we can both perceive and misperceive how things are in the world around us. Some philosophers have answered this by supposing that our perception of material objects is mediated by an awareness of mind-dependent entities or qualities: typically called sense-data, ideas or impressions. These intermediaries allegedly act as surrogates or representatives for external objects: when they represent aright, we perceive; when they mislead, we misperceive.

An alternative is to suppose that perceiving is analogous to belief or judgment: just as judgment or belief can be true or false, so states of being may be correct or incorrect. This approach seeks to avoid intermediary objects between the perceiver and the external objects of perception while still taking proper account of the possibility of illusion and hallucination. Both responses contrast with that of philosophers who deny that illusions and hallucinations have anything to tell us about the nature of perceiving proper, and hold to a form of naïve, or direct, realism.

The account of perception one favours has a bearing on one's views of other aspects of the mind and world: the nature and existence of secondary qualities, such as colours and tastes; the possibility of giving an account of the mind as part of a purely physical, natural world; how one should answer scepticism concerning our knowledge of the external world.

1 Perception, objects, appearance and illusion

We perceive objects, features of objects, and events: I can see a lilac bush, notice the texture of a piece of velvet, hear an explosion. We can also perceive facts, that things are a certain way: I may see that there are three empty coffee cups in my office, or smell that the milk has gone off. When we perceive things, they appear a certain way to us and we come to acquire knowledge concerning them, but one can also perceive facts without perceiving any object in particular: scanning the horizon you might see that there is nothing at all in your vicinity; you have perceived that something is the case, but there is no object that you have seen.

Objects can vary in their appearance: how something looks to you depends on the point of view from which you see it; how things appear to you depends on the conditions under which you perceive, for example whether the lighting is good; and they depend on your powers of perception, for example, how much you can smell or taste may depend on whether you have a cold. The same object may appear differently to different observers. Furthermore, you may not only perceive different aspects of an object from others, you may misperceive it, or suffer an illusion concerning it.

One misperceives something where one does perceive it, but it appears differently to one from how it really is. Misperceptions occur in different ways: one might mistake a clump of grass for a rabbit; in odd lighting the walls of a room may look peach, even when they are really off-white; one may be subject to illusions due to disease. Other examples of illusion happen in normal conditions of perception to all perceivers. Here is one example, common in psychology text books, called the Ponzo illusion:

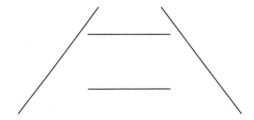

The two horizontal lines are in fact the same length, even though the top one looks longer. Psychologists and neuroscientists are adept at causing other illusions as well: in one alarming example, subjects are made to feel as if their noses are growing back into their heads.

It is also possible to bring about hallucinations. These are cases in which it seems to subjects as if they are really seeing or feeling something, when in fact they are seeing nothing at all. They are most commonly caused by psychological disturbance, but it is also possible to bring them about through appropriate stimulation of the brain: apparent sightings of lights, called phosphenes, arise from stimulation of the visual cortex.

Philosophers tend to draw the same conclusion from all these of kinds of example: it is possible for things to seem a certain way to you, even if they are not that way. Just as one cannot determine from the object of perception how things appear to a perceiver, so one cannot determine from how things appear to a perceiver what the object of perception is, or even whether there is such an object. This implies that an account of perception involves two distinct tasks: on the one hand, it needs to explain what perceptual experience is, the state of mind when things sensorily appear a certain way to one; on the other, it needs to explain what it is for such an experience to be a genuine perception of some object, as opposed to a mere illusion or hallucination.

Under what conditions is a perceptual experience the perception of a given object? One might think that how things appear must match the object in some respect, but there seems to be no particular respect in which I must perceive correctly in order to perceive an object: one can misperceive the colour, shape, location, taste, smell or texture of things. Even if how things appear to me matches perfectly the scene before me, I do not necessarily perceive the scene: if a scientist has induced a visual hallucination in me as of an orange, merely placing an orange in front of my blindfolded eyes will not thereby make me see it. In response to such examples of veridical hallucination, some philosophers have suggested that one can perceive an object only if it causes one's perception of it. This condition is not sufficient by itself to distinguish veridical hallucinations from perceptions: the orange before my blindfolded eyes may be resting on the switch of the machine inducing the hallucination. Various attempts have been made to refine the causal condition in order to give a complete account of the difference between hallucination and perception, but none as yet seems entirely satisfactory in explaining our ability to discern a difference between the two.

The basic task for any theory of perceptual experience is to explain the following. In perceiving, things appear to you a certain way. For example, when you see a red patch on the wall in front of you, it can look to you as if there is a red patch there. In such a case, where you perceive things to be the way that they are, a case of veridical perception, a description of what your experience is like – that is, of how things appear to you – is also a true description of what you can see. In this case, it seems as if a description of your experience is also a description of the things in the world which you can perceive. However, you could have an experience just the same for you even if you were having an illusion, and not seeing something red, or a hallucination and not seeing anything at all. In either case, you would be inclined to give the same description of your experience as in the veridical case, but in neither would the description be true of what was before you in the world, since no red patch would be there. So, how can it be correct to describe your experience in terms of objects in the world, when the description can be true when applied to your experience, but false when applied to the world? This is the question which lies behind the so-called argument from illusion, and different theories of perception answer it in different ways.

2 Sense-datum theories of perception

Some philosophers claim that we are not aware, or anyway not immediately aware, of objects in the world around us, but only of things which depend on the mind for their existence and nature. Suppose that there is no red patch on the wall before me, but that a neuroscientist has so affected my brain that it looks to me as if there is a red patch before me. One might think that it could only appear to me as if some red thing was before me, if there actually was something red of which I was aware. Since the neuroscientist can give me the hallucination just by affecting my brain in the right way, it seems as if bringing about the experience was sufficient for there to be such a red patch for me to be aware of. At least in the case of hallucination, I would be aware of an entity which depended for its existence on my awareness of it; philosophers have used the term sense-datum, for such entities (see SENSE-DATA).

The hallucination could be just the same for me as the experience I would have were I actually looking at a physical red patch on the wall. And the neuroscientist could be bringing this about by stimulating my visual cortex in just the way it would be stimulated if I was looking at the wall. So, it may seem plausible to suppose that my hallucination is of the same sort as the experience I would have were I genuinely perceiving. If the hallucinatory

experience is of a kind which involves being aware of a sense-datum, then even in the case of veridical perception I will be aware of such a mind-dependent entity. Hence we arrive at the sense-datum theory of experience: that we are aware of mind-dependent entities in all perceptual experience.

One criticism of this line of thought is that it involves a form of fallacious reasoning. If I believe that there are fifteen elephants in the next room, it does not follow that there are fifteen elephants in the next room which I believe to be there – after all, my belief may be false – so it would be a mistake to accept the latter claim on the basis of the former. Critics suggest that in the above claim, when one moves from the uncontroversial claim that it looks to me as if there is a red patch before me, to the conclusion that there is a red patch which looks to be before me, just such a mistake in reasoning has been made. However defenders of sense-datum theories of perception would agree that the claim does not follow simply as a matter of logic. Rather, they claim that we can only offer an adequate explanation of what experience is like, if we accept that the latter claim is true when the former is.

How good an explanation of what experience is like does this offer? The theory is committed to claiming that when things appear a certain way to you, then some sense-datum actually is that way. Suppose it seems to you as if there is a rabbit in the field before one; is one then aware of some mind-dependent bunny? In order to resist this conclusion, the sense-datum theorist needs to restrict the range of qualities which can strictly be apparent to us; namely to only those which sense-data might plausibly be thought to have. In the case of vision, this has traditionally been restricted to colour, shape and size (there is some dispute over whether visual data are located in a two-dimensional or a three-dimensional visual space). Hence, it could not strictly look (in the relevant sense) as if a rabbit was before one, only as if something rabbit-shaped were there.

If appearances are to be accounted for solely in terms of mind-dependent entities, what connection holds between experience and the objects of perception, such as the rabbit? Representative theories of perception typically hold that material objects are the indirect or mediate objects of perception in virtue of reliably causing our experiences of sense-data. I can perceive the rabbit in front of me, because the visual experience of something rabbit-shaped is caused by the rabbit. One traditional objection to representative theories of perception is that they lead to scepticism concerning the external world (see SCEPTICISM). In response, some philosophers adopt an alternative view of the connection between objects of perception and experience, taking physical objects to be no more than constructions out of mind-dependent entities or experiences (see PHENOMENALISM; IDEALISM §2). Few philosophers find this position acceptable. Must a sense-datum theorist choose between scepticism and idealism? One may deny that representative theories of perception introduce any special sceptical problems. Whether this is so or not depends on whether sense-data should be thought of as cutting us off from the external world, as a veil of perception, rather than providing us with our only access to the world.

Are the metaphysical implications of the sense-datum theory acceptable? It requires us to accept that in addition to such familiar things as rocks and chairs, and discoveries such as black holes and neutrinos, there are mind-dependent objects which come into and go out of existence as each person has an experience. Philosophers have complained that such entities must be inherently mysterious and that we can discern no readily agreed method of determining when one has the same or a different sense-datum. Furthermore, their existence would rule out explaining how the mind comes to be part of a purely physical, natural world (see MATERIALISM IN THE PHILOSOPHY OF MIND).

Some philosophers have thought that these worries would be lessened if we eliminated inner objects of awareness, and appealed instead simply to ways in which one senses. According to this view, when one senses a red patch, one should not suppose that there has to be some object, a patch which one senses, but rather that one senses redly or in a red manner. One might compare this to singing a lullaby: we need not suppose that there is some thing which the singer sings, rather that they have sung in a certain, quieting manner. Where the sense-datum theory posits inner objects and qualities in order to explain the character of perceptual experience, this adverbial theory of experience appeals just to the manners or qualities of experiencing, sometimes called qualia, subjective qualities or sensational properties of experience.

Critics of the adverbial theories have pointed out that we make a distinction between on the one hand sensing a red square and green triangle, and on the other sensing a green square and a red triangle. It is difficult to explain this difference without appealing to the idea that an object is both square and red in the one case, and square and green in the other. There seems to be no sense in which a state of mind, or a sensing, could literally be square or round.

There is a further objection to be made from how we describe our experiences which applies to both adverbial and sense-datum theories. Various philosophers have denied that introspection of one's visual experience reveals the mind-independent objects which one perceives, and the features which one perceives them to have. Our experience of the world is diaphanous or transparent: introspection of it takes one through to the objects and features in the world, much as in staring at a pane of glass head on, one's attention is taken through to what lies beyond it.

The objection has two aspects to it. On the one hand, there is a negative claim that no introspective evidence can be found for the existence of mind dependent objects or qualities. Since such things are introduced as just that of which one is aware, one might expect that if there are such things, they should just be obvious through introspection. It is not evident that this negative claim is correct: opponents have claimed that evidence for them is provided by the example of after-images; or in the way that a nearer object can fill up more of one's field of view than a more distant object, even though both look the same size; or in our awareness of the fact that we are seeing the shape of an object rather than feeling it. Whether such examples really do demonstrate the existence of subjective qualities is a matter of further dispute, but the other element of the transparency objection can be made without having to settle that matter. It points out a positive element of the character of experience, as revealed through introspection, namely that mind-independent objects of perception are there in your experience. An account of experience which appeals solely to sense-data and qualia would not predict that these mind-independent elements should be part of our experience.

One reply to this is to deny that perceptual experiences really do have this diaphanous character. So, it has been suggested that we describe an experience as of a cube merely in order to indicate the typical cause of such experiences. But this suggestion is implausible. We do sometimes pick out experiences indirectly by reference to their typical cause, as when we call a certain distinctive pain a nettle sting. In this case it does not seem as if the term nettle should be applied directly to a description of what the pain is like. But one may claim that visual experience is not like that, the description of experience as of something red, or square or hard involves applying those terms directly to what one senses.

The objection is more pressing against adverbial theories than sense-datum theories. We describe our visual and tactual experiences in terms of shape properties. As noted above, a sense-datum theorist will dispute whether we also have to describe our experiences in terms of other qualities which could only be the properties of material objects. However, even if the objection is not decisive, it has been influential as a motivation for an alternative account of perceptual experience.

3 Intentional theories of perception

If it can seem to me that there is a red patch on the wall in front of me, when nothing physical is there, and the patch in question seems to be a part of the objective world external to me, then perhaps it can seem to me as if something is so, without anything actually having to be that way. We are all familiar with the fact that one may think that something is the case, when it is not so, as when one believes England will win the World Cup at cricket, and one may think about something, even if it does not really exist, as when small children hope that Santa Claus will visit their house that night. An intentional theory of perception claims that the case of perceptual experience is parallel to these examples: perceptual experience is intentional, and allows for incorrectness in its content, and non-existence of its objects in just the way that beliefs and judgments may do so (see INTENTIONALITY).

When it appears to one as if there is a red patch before one, one's experience represents the world as containing such a patch. If there is no patch there, how one's experience represents the world to be is incorrect, and one's experience is illusory. If the object of one's experience is non-existent, like Santa Claus, then one's experience is a hallucination and not the perception of anything. For the intentional approach, experience is ascribed a representational content which may be correct or incorrect; the experience is veridical, or illusory depending on the correctness of this content. What the experience is like for the subject, as revealed through reflection on it, is to be explained by that representational content. It is important to note that the intentional theory does not introduce the representational content of experience as an object of awareness, in the way that a sense-datum theory introduces sense-data as objects of awareness. Rather, the intentional theory claims that, in the case of perceiving, the objects of awareness are the mind-independent objects that one perceives, and which one's experience represents to be present. In the case of hallucination, there are no objects of awareness, but the character of experience is just the same as that in the case of perception: in both cases it is to be explained by the representational content that the experience has. So the intentional theory offers an account not of the objects of awareness, but rather the mode in which we can be aware of objects in the world.

How like belief could experience be? One view is that we can identify experience with the acquiring of beliefs, or with dispositions to acquire belief. A problem for this suggestion is that one can disbelieve one's senses. Those familiar with the Ponzo illusion do not believe that the top line is

longer, but it still looks longer. A belief theory of experience may respond to this example by claiming that you are still disposed to believe that the top line is longer, it is just that other beliefs you have prevent you forming that belief. But this response is not really satisfactory: when you look at the illusion, you then have an experience which could have led to the belief in question; no mere disposition to acquire a belief can be identified with an occurrent state of mind which interacts with one's other mental states.

This suggests that experiencing is not believing, but one might still claim that both states have the same representational content. That claim has also been denied. For the conditions needed for thinking something may be different from the conditions for having certain kinds of experience: it seems conceivable that we can have the same experiences as infant humans or as other animals, but they cannot share the same thoughts as us; our beliefs are expressible linguistically, and rest on sophisticated conceptual abilities which neither infants nor other animals need have. One may also claim that the character of experience is too rich to be encompassed by any one set of categories, or set of concepts that one can bring to bear on it. For these, and related reasons, some philosophers have claimed that the content of experience is different from that of thought or belief in not being purely conceptual: experience has a non-conceptual content as well (see CONTENT, NON-CONCEPTUAL).

Is this sufficient to explain the character of experience, and the differences between experiencing things to be a certain way and merely believing or thinking them to be that way? Many philosophers have thought not. They have insisted that there must be some form of non-representational quality to experience in addition to any representational content it may have (see QUALIA). The issue here returns us to the first part of the transparency objection to sense-datum theories: it is an open question whether there are evidently subjective, or qualitative aspects of experience other than how the world is presented to us. If one accepts that there are, then there is more agreement than one might initially have supposed between traditional sense-datum theories, which supplement awareness of sense-data with interpretation, and alternatively intentional theories, which supplement representational content with subjective qualities.

4 Naïve realism and disjunctive theories of appearance

Sense-datum theories of perception appeal to illusions and hallucinations in arguing for the existence of inner objects of perception, and intentional theories of perception appeal to illusions to justify the view that experience is representational. But there is a strand of philosophical criticism which denies that one can draw any conclusion about perception from cases of illusion and hallucination. One motive for such criticism is an endorsement of a certain kind of naïve, or direct, realism concerning perception.

Defenders of sense-datum theories claim that the best account of experience commits one to thinking that one can sense a quality only if there actually is an instance of that quality which one senses – the argument from illusion then leads them to suppose that such qualities must be mind-dependent; defenders of intentional theories claim that the best account of experience commits one to thinking that experience is directed at, or of, mind-independent objects – the example of illusion leads them to claim that one's experience merely represents these things. A naïve realist might endorse both the initial claim of the sense-datum theorist and that of the intentional theorist, while trying to resist their conclusions: on this view, when one perceives, one is aware of some mind-independent objects and their features, and such objects and features must actually be there for one to have such an experience. This cannot be true of cases where there is no appropriate physical object of perception, as in hallucination, so the naïve realist must claim that the account applies only to cases of perception. Hence they must deny that the state of mind one is in when one perceives something is of a sort which could have occurred even were one having an illusion or hallucination. They must claim that when it appears to one as if there is a red patch there, then either there is a red patch which is apparent to one, or it is merely as if there were such a red patch apparent to one: nothing more need be in common between the situations, such as an inner object of which one is aware, or a representational content. The view, which we can call a disjunctive theory of appearances, claims that perceptual experience does not form a common kind of state across perception, illusion and hallucination.

The view has been thought objectionable for a number of reasons. First, as all sides agree, for any perception one has, one could have a matching illusion or hallucination which one could not distinguish from the perception. According to the disjunctive view, there is a genuine difference here, but how can there be a difference in the conscious state of mind which the subject is unable to detect? The disjunctive view is committed to claiming that we can be misled about the kind of conscious state we are in; indeed one might sum up the view as claiming that illusions and hallucinations mislead

one not only about objects in the world, but about themselves as well.

Second, the same brain activity as can bring about perceptions can bring about hallucinations. Furthermore, any physical outcome a case of perceiving can produce, for example kicking a ball, could equally well be caused by a matching hallucination. So the disjunctive view must claim that there is a real difference between experience which is a perceiving and one which is a hallucination even though there is no causal difference between them. But many philosophers claim that there can only be a real difference between things where they differ in their causal powers. It remains a matter of dispute whether the consequences of the view are unacceptable or the objections without answer – a similar set of arguments attends debates about the nature of content and thought (see CONTENT: WIDE AND NARROW).

See also: EMPIRICISM; VISION

References and further reading

Cornman, J. (1975) *Perception, Common Sense and Science*, New Haven, CT: Yale University Press. (A very comprehensive presentation of the debate and its implications for metaphysics and theory of knowledge.)

Yolton, J. (1984) *Perceptual Acquaintance from Descartes to Reid*, Minneapolis, MN: Minnesota University Press. (A discussion of the history of philosophy of perception which questions the popular attribution of representative theories of perception to various early modern philosophers, including Descartes and Locke.)

M.G.F. MARTIN

PERCEPTION, INDIAN VIEWS OF
See SENSE PERCEPTION, INDIAN VIEWS OF

PERFORMATIVES

There are certain things one can do just by saying what one is doing. This is possible if one uses a verb that names the very sort of act one is performing. Thus one can thank someone by saying 'Thank you', fire someone by saying 'You're fired' and apologize by saying 'I apologize'. These are examples of 'explicit performative utterances', statements in form but not in fact. Or so thought their discoverer, J.L. Austin, who contrasted them with 'constatives'. Their distinctive self-referential character might suggest that their force requires special explanation, but it is arguable that performativity can be explained by the general theory of speech acts.

See also: AUSTIN, J.L.; SEARLE, J.; SPEECH ACTS

KENT BACH

PERLOCUTIONARY ACT

See PRAGMATICS; SPEECH ACTS

PERSIAN PHILOSOPHY

See AL-GHAZALI, ABU HAMID

PERSONAL IDENTITY

Introduction

What is it to be the same person today as one was in the past, or will be in the future? How are we to describe cases in which (as we might put it) one person becomes two? What, if anything, do the answers to such questions show about the rationality of the importance we attach to personal identity? Is identity really the justifier of the special concern which we have for ourselves in the future? These are the concerns discussed here.

In order to answer the question about the persistence-conditions of persons we must indulge in some thought experiments. Only thus can we tease apart the strands that compose our concept of personal identity, and thereby come to appreciate the relative importance of each strand. There are plausible arguments against attempts to see the relation of personal identity as constitutively determined by the physical relations of same body, or same brain. I can survive with a new body, and a new brain. But it does not follow; nor is it true, that a person's identity over time can be analysed exclusively in terms of psychological relations (relations of memory, belief, character, and so on). To the contrary, the most plausible view appears to be a mixed view, according to which personal identity has to be understood in terms of both physical and psychological relations. This is the view which can be extracted from our core (that is, minimally controversial) set of common-sense beliefs about personal identity.

The possibility of the fission of persons – the possibility that, for example, a person's brain hemispheres might be divided and transplanted into two new bodies – shows that the mixed view has to incorporate a non-branching or uniqueness clause in its analysis. The concept of personal identity, contrary to what we might first be inclined to believe, is an extrinsic concept (that is, whether a given person exists can depend upon the existence of another, causally unrelated, person).

Some philosophers have recently tried to forge an important connection between theories of personal identity and value theory (ethics and rationality). The possibility of such a connection had not previously been investigated in any detail. It has been argued that, on the correct theory of personal identity, it is not identity that matters but the preservation of psychological relations such as memory and character. These relations can hold between one earlier person and two or more later persons. They can also hold to varying degrees (for example, I can acquire a more or less different character over a period of years). This view of what matters has implications for certain theories of punishment. A now reformed criminal may deserve less or no punishment for the crimes of their earlier criminal self. Discussions of personal identity have also provided a new perspective on the debate between utilitarianism and its critics.

1	Criteria of personal identity
2	Physical criteria
3	Psychological and mixed criteria
4–5	Fission of persons
6	Value theory

1 Criteria of personal identity

What is it to be a person? What is it for a person at one time to be identical to some person at a later time? Although the two questions are obviously related, my concern in this entry will be with the second question. (For more on the first question, see PERSONS; MIND, BUNDLE THEORY OF.) However, I assume this much about what it is to be a person: a person is a rational and self-conscious being, with a (more or less) unified mental life. There are indeed cases (multiple personality, split-brain patients, and so on) in which the apparent lack of mental unity casts doubt on whether a single person occupies a given body. But such cases are exceptional. A normal person is a mentally unified individual. The central question of personal identity is the question of what distinguishes the sorts of changes we mentally unified individuals can survive from the sorts of changes which constitute our death.

On one very familiar view (associated with Plato, Descartes and the Christian tradition) a person can survive bodily death. Bodily death is not the sort of change which constitutes personal death. On this view, a person is an immaterial (that is, non-spatial) soul, only contingently attached to a physical body (see SOUL, NATURE AND IMMORTALITY OF THE). This view has few philosophical adherents today. It is fraught with metaphysical and epistemological difficulties. (For example: how can an immaterial soul interact with the material world? How can I know that you have a soul?) In what follows I simply assume, without further argument, that our continued existence is not the continued existence of an immaterial soul.

I do not have to deny that in some possible worlds, there are persons who are immaterial souls; but ours is not such a world. And our concern here is with the conditions for the identity over time of actual (human) persons. Once we have given up the immaterialist view of ourselves, we can say the following. A person is a psychophysical entity, which is essentially physically embodied. That is, a person (a typical adult human, for example) consists of a biological organism (a human body), with a control centre (the brain) that supports their mental life. Persons are essentially mental, and essentially physically embodied. But this is not the end of puzzles about personal identity; it is just the beginning.

When we judge that a friend before us now is identical to the friend we saw yesterday, we typically make this judgment of personal identity under optimal conditions. In such a case, our friend today is physically continuous with our friend yesterday (they possess the very same brain and body). And our friend today is also psychologically continuous with our friend yesterday (they possess the very same beliefs, character, desires, memories, and so on, with only very slight changes). In this case, our identity judgment is true in virtue of the obtaining of both physical and psychological continuities. The puzzle of personal identity is: which continuity (if any) is the more important or central to our concept of personal identity? Evidently, reflection on the paradigm case just described will not help us to answer that question. We need to consider thought experiments where the continuities come apart.

There are three broad accounts or criteria of personal identity over time: the physical criterion, the psychological criterion, and the mixed criterion. These criteria do not purport just to offer quite general ways of telling or of finding out who is who. They also purport to specify what the identity of persons over time consists in: what it is to be the same person over time. According to the physical criterion, the identity of a person over time consists in the obtaining of some relation of physical continuity (typically either bodily continuity or brain continuity). On this view, to be the same person is to be the same living biological object (whether body or brain).

According to the psychological criterion, the identity of a person over time consists in the obtaining of relations of psychological continuity (overlapping memory chains, or memory together with the retention of other psychological features such as well-entrenched beliefs, character, basic desires, and so on). The psychological criterion splits into a narrow version and a wide version. According to the narrow version, the cause of the psychological continuity must be normal (that is, the continued existence of one's brain) if it is to preserve personal identity; according to the wide version, any cause will suffice (normal or abnormal). Sub-versions of the wide and narrow versions differ over the question of whether any one psychological relation is privileged with respect to identity preservation. (For example, Locke, in his *An Essay Concerning Human Understanding*, thought that memory was such a privileged relation.)

Each of the physical and psychological criteria divides into many different versions. The distinctive claim of the mixed criterion is that no version of either the physical or psychological criterion is correct. The best account of a person's identity over time will make reference to both physical and psychological continuities.

I now want to examine in more detail different versions of the physical and psychological criteria. My conclusion will be that all familiar versions of these criteria are open to objection, and that we should accept the mixed criterion. The mixed criterion best captures our core (that is, minimally controversial) beliefs about personal identity.

We can begin with the physical criterion. As noted, this criterion divides into two criteria: the bodily criterion and the brain criterion.

2 Physical criteria

Physical criteria: the bodily criterion. According to the bodily criterion, person A at time t_1 is identical to person B at t_2 if and only if A and B have the same body (that is, they are bodily continuous). Note that A and B can truly be said to have the same body, even though the body at the later time has no matter in common with the body at the earlier time (see CONTINUANTS). In such a case, however, the replacement of matter must be gradual, and the new matter must be functionally absorbed into the living body. This is how it is in the life of a normal human being.

The bodily criterion accords with most of our ordinary judgments of personal identity. However, there appear to be logically possible cases in which the deliverances of the bodily criterion conflict with our considered judgments. The particular case I have in mind is that of brain transplantation. Such transplants are, of course, technologically impossible at present; but that is hardly relevant. The speculations of philosophers are not confined to what is technologically possible.

Sydney Shoemaker was the first to introduce such cases into the philosophical literature. In his work *Self-Knowledge and Self-Identity* he wrote:

> It is now possible to transplant certain organs... it is at least conceivable ... that a human body could continue to function normally if its brain were replaced by one taken from another human body.... Two men, a Mr. Brown and a Mr. Robinson, had been operated on for brain tumors, and brain extractions had been performed on both of them. At the end of the operations, however, the assistant inadvertently put Brown's brain in Robinson's head, and Robinson's brain in Brown's head. One of these men immediately dies, but the other, the one with Robinson's head and Brown's brain, eventually regains consciousness. Let us call the latter 'Brownson'.... When asked his name he automatically replies 'Brown'. He recognizes Brown's wife and family ..., and is able to describe in detail events in Brown's life... of Robinson's life he evidences no knowledge at all.

We can suppose, in addition, that Brown and Robinson are physically very similar, and that their bodies are equally suited for the realization of particular dispositions or abilities (for example, playing the piano, or hang-gliding).

The description of this case which commands almost universal assent is that Brown is the same person as Brownson. Virtually no one thinks that the correct description is: Robinson acquires a new brain. Receiving a new skull and a new body seems to be just a limiting case of receiving a new heart, new lungs, new legs, and so on. If Brown is the same person as Brownson, and yet Brownson's body is not the same body as Brown's body, then it follows that the bodily criterion is false.

Physical criteria: the brain criterion. In the light of this example, it would be natural for a defender of the physical criterion to move to the brain criterion: A at t_1 is the same person as B at t_2 if and only if A and B possess the same brain. But is this a plausible criterion of personal identity? I think not. The following scenario is conceivable. Imagine that robotics and brain science have advanced to such a stage that it is possible to construct a silicon brain which supports the very same kind of mental life as that supported by a flesh-and-blood human brain. Imagine also that parts of a human brain (say, a cancerous part) can be replaced by silicon chips which subserve the very same mental functions as the damaged brain tissue.

Suppose that the whole of my brain gradually becomes cancerous. As soon as the surgeons detect a cancerous part, they replace it with silicon chips.

My mental life continues as before – the same beliefs, memories, character, and so on, are preserved. Eventually, the surgeons replace all my biological brain with a silicon brain. Since my mental life, and physical appearance and abilities, are unaffected by this replacement, we have no hesitation in judging that I have survived the operation. The procedure preserves personal identity. But is this judgment of personal identity consistent with the brain criterion? The answer to this question depends on whether my (later) silicon brain is deemed to be identical to my (earlier) human brain.

It is plausible to suppose that, if an object (such as a heart, brain or liver) is biological, then that very object is essentially biological. That is, for example, my flesh-and-blood brain could not have been anything but a biological entity. This essentialist thesis is consistent with the view that the function of any given biological object (a human heart, for example) could, in principle, be carried out by a non-biological object (a mechanical pump, say). Hence, I am happy to concede that my later silicon brain is indeed a brain; but it is not remotely plausible to think that it is the same brain as my earlier human brain. Rather, the effect of all the tissue removals and bionic insertions in my skull is to destroy one brain and replace it with another.

Our brain example shows that the sort of matter or stuff with which we replace an object's removed parts can affect the overall identity of that object, even if continuity of form or function is preserved. My (earlier) human brain is not identical to my (later) silicon brain. Yet I survived the operation. Hence, the brain criterion is false.

However, there is a deeper worry about the tenability of the brain criterion. Why did we move to the brain criterion, in response to counter-examples to the bodily criterion? Was it because the human brain is a three-pound pinkish-grey spongy organ that occupies human skulls? No, we moved to the brain criterion because of what the human brain does, namely, supports directly our mental life. It is surely because of its mind-supporting function that we are inclined to single out the brain as the seat of personal identity. Consequently, we should not see our identity over time as tied necessarily to the continued existence of the human brain we presently have. What matters most is that our stream of mental life continues to be supported by some physical object, not that it continues to be supported by the very same biological organ.

Since the mid-1990s there has been a vigorous debate, sparked by Eric Olson's book *The Human Animal* (1997), over a version of the Physical Criterion called 'Animalism'. According to Animalism, each of us is identical to a particular animal (in our case, of the kind *human being*). Hence our conditions of identity are just those of human beings. Animalism, like all versions of the Physical Criterion, is vulnerable to the objections raised in §3. However, Olson nicely brings out the following difficulty for any denier of Animalism: if I and the animal I share my matter with (call him 'A') are not identical, then how do we block the absurd conclusion that there are two thinkers/subjects of experience in my shoes? I and A are atom-for-atom identical: why should I have the status of a person while A is denied that status? Olson thinks no good answer can be given to these questions; hence the only way to avoid the absurd conclusion is to embrace Animalism. It is fair to say that responding to Olson's reasoning is one of the most pressing issues in the current discussion of personal identity.

3 Psychological and mixed criteria

The bionic brain example appears to undermine not just the brain criterion, but also the narrow version of the psychological criterion – I survive with a bionic brain, yet the cause of my psychological continuity is abnormal. Hence, it might be thought, the combined effect of these conclusions is to push us towards the wide version of the psychological criterion. Indeed, there are other thought-experiments which might be thought to establish the wide version of the psychological criterion.

Bernard Williams describes a device which can wipe a brain clean while recording all the information stored in the brain. This machine can then reprogramme that information into another brain. The machine can thus preserve psychological continuity in the absence of any physical continuity. And Derek Parfit has made use of the Star Trek fantasy of teletransportation. Here a physical and psychological blueprint is made of a person, who is then painlessly destroyed. The blueprint is transmitted to another location where, out of different matter, an exact physical and psychological replica of the original person is made.

Some philosophers have claimed that, in both these examples, the original person is identical to the later person, and so concluded that physical continuity is not necessary for personal identity over time. Other philosophers have taken the opposite view, and concluded that physical continuity is necessary for personal identity over time. But these are judgments in which theory is being allowed to dictate intuitions. In truth, there simply is no general agreement about whether the original is the same person as the replica, in cases in which there is psychological continuity but no physical continuity.

Further, there appears to be a decisive objection to the wide version of the psychological criterion –

the criterion which holds that personal identity over time consists in psychological continuity, however that continuity is caused. (A defender of the wide version would agree with my verdicts about the counterexamples to the body and brain criteria, and would also regard the normal operation of the brain-state transfer device and the teletransporter as identity-preserving.) Imagine that I step into the teletransporter booth. My psychophysical blueprint is constructed, and sent to another location, where a replica is created. Unfortunately, the machine malfunctions and fails to destroy me. I step out of the booth, intrinsically no different from when I went in. In this case, we have no hesitation in judging that I continue to exist in the same body, and therefore that the replica is not me. But both me-later and my replica stand to me-earlier in the relation of psychological continuity. If the cause of that continuity is deemed to be irrelevant to personal identity, as in the wide version of the psychological criterion, then it ought to be the case that both later candidates have an equal claim to be me. Yet, as we have seen, we strongly believe that I am identical to the later person who is physically and psychologically continuous with me. Consequently, the wide version of the psychological criterion cannot be correct.

I conclude that the best account of personal identity over time is provided by the mixed criterion. We have seen that neither continuity of body nor brain (nor, by extension, the continuity of any other human organ) is a necessary condition for personal identity over time. But we should not conclude from this that psychological continuity, whatever its cause, is sufficient for personal identity over time. As just noted, that thesis does not accord with our intuitions. The most consistent and plausible view that can be recovered from our core set of common-sense judgments appears to be the following: psychological continuity is necessary for personal identity over time; a sufficient condition of personal identity over time is not psychological continuity with any cause, but psychological continuity with a cause that is either normal or continuous with the normal cause (this is why I continue to exist with a bionic brain). One might well ask: why do we have only this concept of personal identity and not some other (such as the wide version of the psychological criterion)? Here, as with other conceptual analyses, there may be no non-trivial answer to this question.

Our discussion thus far has made a certain simplification. The counterexample to the wide version of the psychological criterion exploited the fact that relations of psychological continuity are not logically one-one. In that example, one of the streams of psychological continuity did not have a normal cause. However, it is logically possible for a person at one time to be psychologically continuous with two or more later persons, even when both streams of psychological continuity have their normal cause (that is, the continued existence of the brain hemispheres). But the relation of identity is logically one-one: I cannot be identical to two distinct people. It seems, therefore, that the sufficient condition for personal identity endorsed in the previous paragraph will have to be modified, unless either such branching is impossible or the possibility of branching can be redescribed so that it does not conflict with our sufficient condition. The problem raised by the possibility of branching continuities is known as the problem of fission.

4   Fission of persons

As we have seen, much work in personal identity has made use of various thought experiments or imaginary scenarios. The method of thought experiments in personal identity has recently been subject to criticism. It has been claimed that we should not take our intuitions about thought experiments as guides to philosophical truth, since such intuitions may be prejudiced and unreliable. These criticisms are, I think, misplaced. For one thing, such criticisms ignore the frequent and legitimate use of thought experiments in virtually all traditional areas of philosophy (for example, in theories of knowledge and in ethics). Why is their use in discussions of personal identity singled out for criticism? Second, and more important, thought experiments can be useful in understanding the structure of a concept and the relative importance of its different strands, provided that there is general agreement about the best description of the thought-experiment. There is such general agreement about the counterexamples to the body and brain criteria. Some philosophers have tried to gain mileage from thought experiments in the absence of such general agreement – for example, the case of teletransportation discussed above. But it would be unwarranted to infer from the existence of such abuses that thought experiments can never perform any useful function in discussions of personal identity (see THOUGHT EXPERIMENTS).

One thought experiment which has been much discussed in recent years, and which does not fall into the teletransporter category of thought experiments, is that of the fission or division of persons. This thought experiment is interesting because it shows us something about the nature or metaphysics of personal identity, about what it is to be the same person over time.

Fission is a situation in which one thing splits into two (or more) things. Fission does occur in nature (amoebae, for example). Fission of persons, of course, does not occur – but it might. We can devise a thought experiment to flesh out this possibility. Consider a person, Arnold. Like us, Arnold has a mental life that is crucially dependent upon the normal functioning of his brain. Arnold also has a property which most of us do not have, but might have done: each of his brain hemispheres support the very same mental functions. If one of Arnold's hemispheres developed a tumour, that hemisphere could simply be removed and Arnold's mental life would be unaffected.

Suppose that Arnold's body develops cancer. The surgeons cannot save his body, but they can remove Arnold's brain and transplant both hemispheres into two brainless bodies, cloned from Arnold's body many years ago. Arnold agrees to this and the operation is successfully carried out. The fission of Arnold has taken place. We now have two people – call them Lefty and Righty – both of whom are psychologically continuous with Arnold (same character, beliefs, apparent memories of a common past, and so on). They are also physically similar to Arnold, and each contain a hemisphere from Arnold's brain. There is both physical and psychological continuity linking Arnold with Lefty and with Righty. Suppose also that Lefty and Righty are in different rooms in the hospital, and exercise no causal influence on each other. How should this case be described – who is who? A number of responses have been suggested, which we shall examine in turn.

(1) *'The case is not really possible, so we can say nothing about it and learn nothing from it.'* This view is implausible. Hemisphere transplants may be technologically impossible; but they are surely not logically impossible. Indeed, hemisphere transplants, like other organ transplants, appear to be nomologically possible (that is, consistent with the laws of nature). If so, such transplants are also logically possible. Response (1) is not a serious contender.

(2) *'Arnold has survived the operation, and is one or the other of Lefty or Righty.'* Immediately after fission, Lefty and Righty are physically and psychologically indistinguishable. Both stand in the same psychological and physical relations to Arnold. They both believe that they are Arnold. According to response (2), one is right and the other wrong.

Response (2) is implausible for two reasons. First, since Lefty and Righty are symmetrically related to Arnold in respect of physical and psychological continuities, the claim that, for example, Arnold is Lefty, can only be sustained on something like the Cartesian view of persons. If we think of the person as an immaterial ego that typically underlies streams of psychological life, we can suppose that Arnold's ego pops into the left-hand stream of consciousness, leaving the right-hand stream ego-less or with a new ego. As noted at the beginning of §1, this view of persons is bizarre. The postulation of such an ego is idle, and conflicts with both science and common sense.

Second, the metaphysical absurdity of the Cartesian view has an epistemic counterpart. According to response (2), when Arnold divides, he survives in one of the two streams. So either Arnold is Lefty or Arnold is Righty. But how can we know which? From the third-person point of view, we have no reason to make one identification rather than the other. Nor is appeal to the first-person perspective of any help: both Lefty and Righty take themselves to be Arnold. Nothing in either stream of consciousness will reveal to its bearer that it is Arnold. So if, for example, Arnold is Lefty, this truth will be absolutely unknowable. There may be no incoherence in the idea of unknowable truths, but we should be suspicious of any theory of personal identity which implies that truths about who is who can be, in principle, unknowable. For these reasons, we should reject response (2).

(3) 'Arnold survives fission as both Lefty and Righty.' There are three ways in which we can understand this response. According to the first way, Lefty and Righty are sub-personal components of a single person, Arnold. According to the second way, Arnold is identical to both Lefty and Righty (hence, Lefty is Righty). According to the third way, Lefty and Righty together compose Arnold (so that two persons are parts of one larger person, just as Scotland and England are parts of one larger country).

These views are hard to believe. It seems plain common sense that Lefty and Righty are both persons (not sub-personal entities), and that they are numerically distinct. Lefty and Righty both satisfy the normal physical and psychological criteria for personhood. They qualify as persons. And they are two. They may be exactly alike immediately after fission, but exact similarity does not imply numer-ical identity. (Two red billiard balls may be exactly similar, yet numerically distinct.) Further, they will soon begin to differ, mentally and physically, so that it would be intolerable to regard them as anything but distinct persons.

According to the remaining version of response (3), Arnold exists after fission composed of Lefty and Righty, now regarded as persons in their own right. This is sheer madness. The postulation of Arnold's existence in this circumstance (in addition to that of Lefty and Righty) does no work whatsoever. It is completely idle. Second, can we really make any sense of the idea that one person might be composed of two separate persons? That

one person might be composed of two bodies and two minds? To be a single person is to possess a unified mental life. (This is why we are sometimes reluctant to regard a split-brain patient as constitut-ing a single person.) Yet, supposedly, after fission Arnold is permanently composed of two uncon-nected spheres of consciousness. How could they possibly constitute a single person? If Lefty believes that Clinton will win the next election, and Righty believes that he will not, does Arnold believe that Clinton will both win and lose the next election? Such problems multiply. It seems that all ways of understanding response (3) skew our concept of a person to such an extent that they cannot be taken seriously.

5 Fission of persons (cont.)

(4) 'The case of Arnold's fission has been misdescribed. Lefty and Righty exist prior to fission, but only become spatially separate after fission.' This theory also has different versions. Some philosophers think that only Lefty and Righty occupy the pre-fission body, and that the name Arnold is ambiguous. Others think that three people (Arnold, Lefty and Righty) occupy the pre-fission body, but that only Lefty and Righty survive fission. The differences between these versions of the theory will not concern us.

This theory is very strange. It involves a tremendous distortion of our concept of a person to suppose that more than one person occupies the pre-fission body. Surely to one body and a unified mind there corresponds only one person? However, the strangeness of response (4) may depend on one's general metaphysics. In particular, the degree of strangeness may depend on whether we accept a three- or four-dimensional view of continuants such as persons.

On the three-dimensional view of persons, persons are wholly present at all times at which they exist (much as a universal, such as redness, is said to be wholly present in each of its instantia-tions). On this view, persons are extended only in space, not in time, and have no temporal parts. On the four-dimensional view of persons, persons are four-dimensional entities spread out in space and time. Persons have temporal parts as well as spatial parts. Hence, at any given time, say 1993, only a part of me is in existence, just as only a part of me exists in the spatial region demarcated by my left foot. (See the entry on TIME for more on the contrast between three- and four-dimensional views.)

On the three-dimensional view of persons, response (4) is not just strange but barely intelligible. Consider a time just prior to fission. On this view, two wholly present persons (entities of the same kind) occupy exactly the same space at the same time. This ought to be as hard to understand as the claim that there are two instantiations of redness in some uniformly coloured red billiard ball. On the four-dimensional view, however, Lefty and Righty are distinct persons who, prior to fission, share a common temporal part. It ought to be no more remarkable for two persons to share a common temporal part than for two persons (Siamese twins) to share a common spatial part.

Suppose, for present purposes, that we accept the four-dimensional view. Response (4) is still counter-intuitive. It is implausible to hold that two persons (Lefty and Righty) share a common temporal segment in the absence of any psychological disunity. We should be loath to give up the principle that to each psychologically unified temporal segment there corresponds just one person. Second, there is the problem of how we are to account for the coherence and unity of the I-thoughts associated with the locus of reflective mental life that occupies the pre-fission body. How can there be such unity if two persons occupy that body? These objections to response (4) may not be decisive, but they do show that the multiple occupancy view is problematic, and we should avoid it if we can.

(5) *'What's the problem? When Arnold divides into Lefty and Righty, Arnold ceases to exist (one thing cannot be two). Lefty and Righty then come into existence, and are numerically distinct, though initially very similar, persons.'* This is the response I favour. When Arnold divides, there are two equally good candidates for identity with him. Since they are equally good, and since one thing cannot be two things, Arnold is identical to neither. And since there is no one else with whom we could plausibly identify Arnold, Arnold no longer exists. This response respects the logic of identity, and does not violate our concept of a person by supposing that one (post-fission) person is composed of two persons or that more than one person occupies the pre-fission body. This is a victory for common sense!

Indeed it is so. But it is important to realize that, in embracing response (5), we are committing ourselves to a quite particular conception of the identity over time of persons. On this view, Arnold is not Lefty. Why is this true? The reason given is not: because Arnold and Lefty do not have the same body, or because Arnold and Lefty do not have the same (whole) brain. (These would anyway be bad reasons – see §1.) The reason is that one thing cannot be two. Arnold is not Lefty because Righty also exists. Whether Arnold continues to exist depends upon whether he has one continuer or two. Since Lefty and Righty are causally isolated from each other, this implies that the identity over

time of a person can be determined by extrinsic factors. Theories that allow for such extrinsicness are sometimes called best-candidate theories of personal identity. According to these theories, B at t_2 is the same person as A at t_1 if and only if there is no better or equally good candidate at t_2 for identity with A at t_1. If there are two equally good candidates, neither is A.

Are such theories, and hence response (5), acceptable? Some philosophers have thought not, but for bad reasons. It has been thought that best-candidate theories violate the widely accepted thesis that identity sentences are, if true, necessarily true and, if false, necessarily false. Is not the upshot of response (5) precisely that Arnold is not Lefty, but that had Righty not existed (had the surgeon accidently dropped the right hemisphere, for example), Arnold would have been Lefty? Here we have to be careful. The widely accepted thesis is that identity sentences containing only rigid singular terms (that is, terms which do not shift their reference across possible worlds) are, if true, necessarily true and, if false, necessarily false. We can read the term Lefty as rigid or as non-rigid. If it is non-rigid (perhaps abbreviating the definite description 'the person who happens to occupy the left-hand branch'), then it is true that, had Righty not existed, Arnold would have been Lefty. But this result is consistent with the necessity of identity and distinctness. If Lefty is rigid, then the best-candidate theorist, if he is to respect the necessity of identity, must deny that Arnold would have been Lefty if Righty had not existed. If Righty had not existed, Arnold would then have occupied the left-hand branch, but that person (namely, Arnold) is not Lefty. Lefty doesn't exist in the nearest world in which Righty does not exist, though an exact duplicate of Lefty – twin Lefty – exists there.

Best-candidate theories do not violate the necessity of identity. However, they do have consequences that might be thought objectionable. Consider again the world in which Arnold divides into Lefty and Righty. According to the best-candidate theory, Lefty can truly say, 'Thank goodness Righty exists, otherwise I wouldn't have existed'. Given that Lefty and Righty exert no causal influence on each other, such dependency is apt to seem mysterious.

These consequences are not objectionable. They simply illustrate the fact that properties like being occupied by Lefty (where Lefty is understood to be rigid) are extrinsic properties of bodies. That is, whether the left-hand body has the property of being occupied by Lefty, rather than by Twin Lefty, is fixed by an extrinsic factor (namely, the existence or non-existence of Righty). But this is not counter-intuitive. The property being occupied by Lefty is not a causal property of a body. In contrast with properties of shape and weight, and so on, this identity-involving property does not contribute to the causal powers of any body in which it inheres. (The causal powers of the left-hand body are unaffected by whether Lefty or Twin Lefty is the occupant.) It is typical of a non-causal property that its possession by an object may depend upon what happens to other objects which exercise no causal influence on it. For example, the property of being a widow is not a causal property and, unsurprisingly, whether a woman is a widow may depend upon what happens to someone who, at the relevant time, exercises no causal influence on her. Response (5) teaches us that identity-involving properties (like being occupied by Lefty) are also extrinsic. This is not a counter-example, merely a consequence.

The best-candidate theory provides the most satisfying response to the case of fission. It also reveals something important about our concept of personal identity: its structure is that of an extrinsic concept. This result may be surprising, but it is not objectionable. If we combine this result with the central claim of the last section, we arrive at the following modified sufficient condition for personal identity over time: A at t_1 is identical to B at t_2 if A stands to B in the relation of psychological continuity with a cause that is either normal or continuous with the normal cause, and there is no better or equally good candidate at t_2 for identity with A at t_1.

6   Value theory

In this final section, I investigate the implications (if any) of the metaphysics of personal identity for value theory. A contemporary philosopher, Derek Parfit, is the most well-known advocate of such implications: he argues that the most plausible metaphysics of persons yields radical conclusions for ethics and rationality (value theory).

It has, of course, long been acknowledged that there is a link between theories of persons and value theory. For example, a religious person's belief that we are immaterial souls will obviously bear on their view of the morality of abortion and euthanasia. However, in this case, the value of persons is not called into question; what is in question is simply the extension of the concept person. The intent of Parfit's project is far more subversive: it is to undermine the significance we currently attach to personal identity and distinctness. Whether or not it is ultimately successful, it is important to recognize the form or shape of this project.

The central feature of Parfit's value theory is the thesis that personal identity is not, in itself, an important relation. It is various psychological relations which matter, relations which are concomitants of personal identity in the normal case (but not, for example, in the case of fission). According to this theory, it would be irrational of me strongly to prefer my own continued existence to death by fission.

I will be concerned with arguments for the thesis that personal identity is not what matters. This thesis has two strands. One strand is that personal identity over time is unimportant; the other strand is that personal identity at a time is unimportant. (These are the diachronic and synchronic strands, respectively.) The thesis that the identity of a person over time is unimportant has been taken to undermine the self-interest theory of rationality, and has implications for the tenability of transtemporal moral notions such as compensation, responsibility and personal commitment. The thesis that the identity and distinctness of persons at a time is unimportant has been thought to lend support to utilitarianism.

The thesis that personal identity over time is unimportant implies that pure self-interested concern is irrational. That is, it is irrational for me to be especially concerned about the fate of some future person just because that person is me. It follows that the self-interest theory of rationality is false. According to this theory, which has dominated so much thinking about rationality (see RATIONALITY, PRACTICAL), there is only one future person that it is supremely rational for me to benefit: the future person identical to me. Since the self-interest theory places immense weight on a relation which has no rational significance, this theory cannot be correct.

Further, if we do not believe that personal identity over time is important, this may change our attitude to punishment, compensation and commitment. Consider a case where there are only weak psychological connections between different stages of the same life. (For example, a one-time criminal may now be completely reformed, with a new and more respectable set of desires and beliefs.) On the present view, the grounds are thereby diminished for holding the later self responsible for the crimes of the earlier self, or for compensating the later self for burdens imposed on the earlier self, or for regarding earlier commitments as binding on the later self. The truth that the earlier person is the later person is too superficial or unimportant to support the opposite view.

The thesis that the identity and distinctness of persons at a time is unimportant has been taken to imply that the fact of the 'separateness of persons' is not 'deep', and that less weight should be assigned to distributive principles. The synchronic thesis thus supports (in part) the utilitarian doctrine that no weight should be assigned to distributive principles: we should simply aim to maximize the net sum of benefits over burdens, whatever their distribution (see UTILITARIANISM).

These are radical claims. They are all underwritten by the thesis that personal identity is not what matters. What are the arguments for this thesis? I shall discuss one argument for the diachronic thesis (the argument from fission), and one argument for the synchronic thesis (the argument from reductionism).

Recall our earlier discussion of fission. I argued that the most plausible description of fission is that the pre-fission person is numerically distinct from the post-fission offshoots. This constitutes the first premise of the argument from fission (which I will present in the first person): (1) I am not identical to either of my fission products. The second premise is this: (2) fission is not as bad as ordinary death. This premise is taken to imply a third: (3) my relation to my offshoots contains what matters. The first and third premises jointly imply that personal identity is not what matters.

This is an interesting argument, which has had many adherents in recent years. But there is a problem with it. The problem concerns the move from the second to the third premise. The second premise is certainly true: the prospect of fission is not as bad as that of ordinary death. What grounds this premise, and what exhausts its true content, is simply that presented with a choice between those two options, virtually everyone would choose fission. Such a choice is both explicable and reasonable: after fission, unlike after ordinary death, there will be people who can complete many of my projects, look after my family, and so on. However, if the third premise is grounded in the second, the claim that my relation to my offshoots contains what matters merely reflects the innocuous truth that fission is preferable to ordinary death. This robs the argument of any radical import. Its conclusion does nothing to undermine the rationality of self-interest, or the rationality of strongly preferring continued existence to both fission and ordinary death. (This argument is not improved if it is merely asserted that fission is just as good as ordinary death. What is the argument for this claim?)

What of the argument from reductionism? Reductionism is the view that a description of reality which refers to bodies and experiences, but omits reference to persons, can be complete. It would leave nothing out (see PERSONS §3). The argument from reductionism attempts to show that, if reductionism is true, the fact of the separateness of persons (the fact that you and I are distinct persons, for example) is not deep or significant, and hence less weight should be assigned to distributive principles.

The argument can be presented as follows. Suppose that reductionism is true: reality can be completely described without reference to persons. If such a complete and impersonal description is possible, how can the boundaries between persons be important? Failing an answer to this question, the argument from reductionism concludes that the boundaries between persons are not morally significant.

The validity of this argument turns on the truth of the general principle that if reality can be completely described without referring to Fs, then the boundaries between Fs cannot be of any importance. Both the interpretation and plausibility of this principle are unclear. A more definite worry is that reasons may be presented for dissatisfaction with the argument's premise, reductionism about persons. (In particular: can our mental life really be completely described in impersonal or identity-neutral terms?) Unless those objections can be met, we should reject the argument from reductionism.

The central arguments for the thesis that identity is not what matters are both open to dispute. The failure of these arguments emphasizes how difficult it is to undermine the importance I attach to the fact that such-and-such a person tomorrow is me, and to the fact that you are not me. Unless other arguments are forthcoming, we can continue reasonably to believe that personal identity is important, and to endorse the traditional views in ethics and rationality which that belief supports.

See also: ALTERITY AND IDENTITY, POSTMODERN THEORIES OF; CONSCIOUSNESS

References and further reading

Olson, E. (1997) *The Human Animal*, Oxford: Oxford University Press. (Personal identity conceived in terms of life-sustaining processes rather than any kind of psychological continuity.)

Unger, P. (1992) *Persons, Consciousness and Value*, New York: Oxford University Press. (Thorough and imaginative contemporary discussion. Defence of the physical criterion of personal identity.)

BRIAN GARRETT

PERSONALISM

Personalism is the thesis that only persons (self-conscious agents) and their states and characteristics exist, and that reality consists of a society of interacting persons. Typically, a personalist will hold that finite persons depend for their existence and continuance on God, who is the Supreme Person, having intelligence and volition. Personalists are usually idealists in metaphysics and construct their theories of knowledge by inference from the data of self-awareness. They tend to be nonutilitarian in ethics and to place ultimate value in the person as a free, self-conscious, moral agent, rather than in either mental states or in apersonal states of affairs. Typically, holding that a good God will not allow what has intrinsic value to lose existence, they believe in personal survival of death.

The term 'personalism', even as a term for philosophical systems, has myriad uses. There is said to be, for example, atheistic personalism (as in the case of McTaggart, famous for embracing both atheism and the immortality of the soul), absolute idealistic personalism (Hegel, Royce, Calkins), and theistic personalism (Bowne, Brightman, Bertocci). Leibniz and Berkeley are seen as early personalists; both were theists and idealists. Kant, while not strictly a personalist, was influential in personalism's history. In particular, B.P. Bowne (1847–1910) borrowed freely from Kant, while refusing to accept a Kantian transcendentalism in which our basic concepts or categories apply in a knowledge-giving way only to appearances and not to reality. R.H. Lotze made personality and value central to his worldview, and was a European precursor of American personalism.
See also: IDEALISM

KEITH E. YANDELL

PERSONS

We are all persons. But what are persons? This question is central to philosophy and virtually every major philosopher has offered an answer to it. For two thousand years many philosophers in the Western tradition believed that we were immaterial souls or Egos, only contingently attached to our bodies. The most well-known advocates of this view were Plato and Descartes. Few philosophers accept this view now, largely because it is thought to face a number of intractable metaphysical and epistemological problems (for example: how can an immaterial soul or mind interact with the material world? How can I know that you have a soul?). The recoil from Cartesianism has been in three different directions. One direction (the animalist) emphasizes the fact that persons are human beings, evolved animals of a certain sort. A second direction (the reductionist) is represented by David Hume: the self or person is not a Cartesian entity, it is a 'bundle of perceptions'. Finally, there is a theory of persons influenced by the views of John Locke, according to which persons are neither essentially animals nor reducible to their bodies or experiences.
See also: MIND, BUNDLE THEORY OF; REDUCTIONISM IN THE PHILOSOPHY OF MIND

BRIAN GARRETT

PHENOMENALISM

On its most common interpretation, phenomenalism maintains that statements asserting the existence of physical objects are equivalent in meaning to statements describing sensations. More specifically, the phenomenalist claims that to say that a physical object exists is to say that someone would have certain sequences of sensations were they to have certain others. For example, to say that there is something round and red behind me might be to say, in part, that if I were to have the visual, tactile and kinaesthetic (movement) sensations of turning my head I would seem to see something round and red. If I were to have the sensations of seeming to reach out and touch that thing, those sensations would be followed by the familiar tactile sensations associated with touching something round.

Rather than talk about the meanings of statements, phenomenalists might hold that the fact that something red and round exists is no more than the fact that a subject would have certain sequences of sensations following certain others. The phenomenalist's primary motivation is a desire to avoid scepticism with respect to the physical world. Because many philosophers tied the meaningfulness of statements to their being potentially verifiable, some phenomenalists further argued that it is only by reducing claims about the physical world to claims about possible sensations that we can preserve the very intelligibility of talk about the physical world.

There are very few contemporary philosophers who embrace phenomenalism. Many reject the foundationalist epistemological framework which makes it so difficult to avoid scepticism without phenomenalism. But the historical rejection of the view had more to do with the difficulty of carrying out the promised programme of translation.
See also: EMPIRICISM; IDEALISM

RICHARD FUMERTON

PHENOMENOLOGICAL MOVEMENT

The phenomenological movement is a century-old international movement in philosophy that has penetrated most of the cultural disciplines, especially psychiatry and sociology. It began in Germany with the early work of Edmund Husserl, and spread to the rest of Europe, the Americas and Asia. In contrast with a school, a movement does not have a body of doctrine to which all participants agree; rather, there is a broad approach that tends to be shared. The phenomenological approach has at least four components.

First, phenomenologists tend to oppose naturalism. Naturalism includes behaviourism in psychology and positivism in social sciences and philosophy, and is a worldview based on the methods of the natural sciences. In contrast, phenomenologists tend to focus on the socio-historical or cultural lifeworld and to oppose all kinds of reductionism. Second, they tend to oppose speculative thinking and preoccupation with language, urging instead knowledge based on 'intuiting' or the 'seeing' of the matters themselves that thought is about. Third, they urge a technique of reflecting on processes within conscious life (or human existence) that emphasizes how such processes are directed at (or 'intentive to') objects and, correlatively, upon these objects as they present themselves or, in other words, as they are intended to. And fourth, phenomenologists tend to use analysis or explication as well as the seeing of the matters reflected upon to produce descriptions or interpretations both in particular and in universal or 'eidetic' terms. In addition, phenomenologists also tend to debate the feasibility of Husserl's procedure of transcendental *epoché* or 'bracketing' and the project of transcendental first philosophy it serves, most phenomenology not being transcendental.

Beyond these widely shared components of method, phenomenologists tend to belong to one or another of four intercommunicating and sometimes overlapping tendencies. These tendencies are 'realistic phenomenology', which emphasizes the seeing and describing of universal essences; 'constitutive phenomenology', which emphasizes accounting for objects in terms of the consciousness of them; 'existential phenomenology', which emphasizes aspects of human existence within the world; and 'hermeneutical phenomenology', which emphasizes the role of interpretation in all spheres of life. All tendencies go back to the early work of Husserl, but the existential and hermeneutical tendencies are also deeply influenced by the early work of Martin Heidegger. Other leading figures are Nicolai Hartmann, Roman Ingarden, Adolf Reinach and Max Scheler in realistic phenomenology, Dorion Cairns, Aron Gurwitsch and Alfred Schutz in constitutive phenomenology, Hannah Arendt, Jean-Paul Sartre, Maurice Merleau-Ponty, and Simone de Beauvoir in existential phenomenology, and Hans-Georg Gadamer and Paul Ricoeur in hermeneutical phenomenology.

LESTER EMBREE

PHENOMENOLOGY, EPISTEMIC ISSUES IN

Phenomenology is not a unified doctrine. Its main proponents – Husserl, Heidegger, Sartre and Merleau-Ponty – interpret it differently. However, it is possible to present a broad characterization of what they share. Phenomenology is a method of philosophical investigation which results in a radical ontological revision of Cartesian Dualism. It has implications for epistemology: the claim is that, when the foundations of empirical knowledge in perception and action are properly characterized, traditional forms of scepticism and standard attempts to justify knowledge are undermined.

Phenomenological method purports to be descriptive and presuppositionless. First one adopts a reflective attitude towards one's experience of the world by putting aside assumptions about the world's existence and character. Second, one seeks to describe particular, concrete phenomena. Phenomena are not *contents* of the mind; they all involve an experiencing subject and an experienced object. Phenomenological description aims to make explicit essential features implicit in the 'lived-world' – the world as we act in it prior to any theorizing about it. The phenomenological method reveals that practical knowledge is prior to propositional knowledge – knowing *that* arises from knowing *how*.

The key thesis of phenomenology, drawn from Brentano, is that consciousness is intentional, that is, directed onto objects. Phenomenologists interpret this to mean that subjects and objects are essentially interrelated, a fact which any adequate account of subjects and objects must preserve. Phenomenological accounts of subjects emphasize action and the body; accounts of objects emphasize the significance they have for us.

The aim to be presuppositionless involves scrutinizing scientific and philosophical theories (Galileo, Locke and Kant are especially challenged). Phenomenology launches a radical critique of modern philosophy as overinfluenced by the findings of the natural sciences. In particular, epistemology has adopted from science its characterization of the basic data of experience.

The influence of phenomenology on the analytic tradition has been negligible. The influence on the Continental tradition has been greater. The phenomenological critique of modern science and philosophy has influenced postmodern thought which interprets the modernist worldview as having the status of master narrative rather than truth. Postmodern thought also criticizes the positive phenomenological claim that there are essential features of the lived-world.

See also: BRENTANO, F.C.; CONSCIOUSNESS; KNOWLEDGE, TACIT

JANE HOWARTH

PHILO JUDAEUS
See PHILO OF ALEXANDRIA

PHILO OF ALEXANDRIA (c.15 BC–c.AD 50)

Philo of Alexandria is the leading representative of Hellenistic-Jewish thought. Despite an unwavering loyalty to the religious and cultural traditions of his Jewish community, he was also strongly attracted to Greek philosophy, in which he received a thorough training. His copious writings – in Greek – are primarily exegetical, expounding the books of Moses. This reflects his apologetic strategy of presenting the Jewish lawgiver Moses as the sage and philosopher *par excellence*, recipient of divine inspiration, but not at the expense of his human rational faculties. In his commentaries Philo makes extensive use of the allegorical method earlier developed by the Stoics. Of contemporary philosophical movements, Philo is most strongly attracted to Platonism. His method is basically eclectic, but with a clear rationale focused on the figure of Moses.

Philo's thought is strongly theocentric. God is conceived in terms of being. God's essence is unreachable for human knowledge (negative theology), but his existence should be patent to all (natural theology). Knowledge of God is attained through his powers and, above all, through his *Logos* ('Word' or 'Reason'), by means of which he stands in relation to what comes after him. In his doctrine of creation Philo leans heavily on Platonist conceptions drawn from reflection on Plato's *Timaeus*. The conception of a creation *ex nihilo* ('from nothing') is not yet consciously worked out. Philo's doctrine of human nature favours the two anthropological texts in Genesis 1–2, interpreting creation 'according to the image' in relation to the human intellect. With regard to ethics, both Stoic concepts and peculiarly Jewish themes emerge in Philo's beliefs. Ethical ideals are prominent in the allegorical interpretation of the biblical patriarchs.

Philo's influence was almost totally confined to the Christian tradition, which preserved his writings. He was unknown to medieval Jewish thinkers such as Maimonides.

DAVID T. RUNIA

PHILOPONUS (c.490–c.570 BC)

John Philoponus, also known as John the Grammarian or John of Alexandria, was a Christian philosopher, scientist and theologian. Philoponus' life and work are closely connected to the city of Alexandria and its famous Neoplatonic school. In the sixth century, this traditional centre of pagan Greek learning became increasingly insular, located as it was at the heart of an almost entirely Christian community. The intense philosophical incompatibilities between pagan and Christian beliefs come to the surface in Philoponus' work.

His œuvre comprised at least forty items on such diverse subjects such as grammar, logic, mathematics, physics, psychology, cosmology, astronomy, theology and church politics; even medical treatises have been attributed to him. A substantial body of his work has come down to us, but some treatises are known only indirectly through quotations or translations. Philoponus' fame rests predominantly on the fact that he initiated the liberation of natural philosophy from the straitjacket of Aristotelianism, though his non-polemical commentaries on Aristotle as well as his theological treatises deserve to be appreciated in their own right.

Philoponus' intellectual career began as a pupil of the Neoplatonic philosopher Ammonius, son of Hermeas, who had been taught by Proclus and was head of the school at Alexandria. Some of his commentaries profess to be based on Ammonius' lectures, but others give more room to Philoponus' own ideas. Eventually, he transformed the usual format of apologetic commentary into open criticism of fundamental Aristotelian-Neoplatonic doctrines, most prominently the tenet of the eternity of the world. This renegade approach to philosophical tradition, as well as the conclusions of his arguments, antagonized Philoponus' pagan colleagues; they may have compelled him to abandon his philosophical career. Philoponus devoted the second half of his life to influencing the theological debates of his time; the orthodox clergy condemned him posthumously as a heretic, because of his Aristotelian interpretation of the trinitarian dogma, which led him to enunciate three separate godheads (tritheism).

The style of Philoponus' writing is often circuitous and rarely entertaining. However, he combines an almost pedantic rigour of argument and exposition with a remarkable freedom of spirit, which allows him to cast off the fetters of authority, be they philosophical or theological. Although his mode of thinking betrays a strong Aristotelian influence, it also displays a certain doctrinal affinity to Plato, stripped of the ballast of Neoplatonic interpretation. His works were translated into Arabic, Latin and Syriac, and he influenced later thinkers such as Bonaventure, Gersonides, Buridan, Oresme and Galileo.

CHRISTIAN WILDBERG

PHILOSOPHY OF LIFE
See Lebensphilosophie

PHOTOGRAPHY, AESTHETICS OF

Claims that photography is aesthetically different from and, in many versions of the argument, inferior to the arts of painting and drawing have taken various forms: that photography is a mechanical process and therefore not an artistic medium; that it is severely limited in its capacity to express the thoughts and emotions of the artist; that its inability to register more than an instantaneous 'slice' of events restricts its representational capacity; that it is not a representational medium at all. Some of these arguments are thoroughly mistaken, while others have an interesting core of truth that will emerge only after some clarification. Central to this clarification is an account of the precise sense in which photography is mechanical, and an explication of our intuition that a photograph puts us 'in touch with' its subject in a way that a painting or drawing cannot. Both these ideas need to be separated from the mistaken view that it is the nature of photography to provide images that are superlatively faithful to the objects they represent.

See also: FILM, AESTHETICS OF; PAINTING, AESTHETICS OF; SEMIOTICS

GREGORY CURRIE

PHYSICALISM

See MATERIALISM IN THE PHILOSOPHY OF MIND

PHYSICS, PHILOSOPHY OF

See BELL'S THEOREM; BOHR, NIELS; BOYLE, ROBERT; EINSTEIN, ALBERT; EXPERIMENT; GALILEI, GALILEO; MACH, ERNST; MATTER; MAXWELL, JAMES CLERK; MEASUREMENT, THEORY OF; NEWTON, ISAAC; OXFORD CALCULATORS; QUANTUM MEASUREMENT PROBLEM; QUANTUM MECHANICS, INTERPRETATION OF; REDUCTION, PROBLEMS OF; RELATIVITY THEORY, PHILOSOPHICAL SIGNIFICANCE OF; UNITY OF SCIENCE

PIAGET, JEAN (1896–1980)

The Swiss psychologist Jean Piaget was the founder of the field we now call cognitive development. His own term for the discipline was 'genetic epistemology', reflecting his deep philosophical concerns. Among Piaget's most enduring contributions were his remarkably robust and surprising observations of children. Time after time, in a strikingly wide variety of domains, and at every age from birth to adolescence, he discovered that children understood the world in very different ways from adults.

But Piaget was really only interested in children because he thought they exemplified basic epistemological processes. By studying children we could discover how biological organisms acquire knowledge of the world around them. The principles of genetic epistemology could then be applied to other

creatures, from molluscs to physicists. Piaget's other enduring legacy is the idea that apparently foundational kinds of knowledge were neither given innately nor directly derived from experience. Rather, knowledge was constructed as a result of the complex interplay between organisms and their environment. Piaget saw this view as an alternative to both classical rationalism and empiricism.

ALISON GOPNIK

PICO DELLA MIRANDOLA, GIOVANNI (1463–94)

Giovanni Pico della Mirandola, today the best known of Renaissance philosophers, was a child prodigy and gentleman scholar who studied humanities, Aristotelianism and Platonism with the greatest teachers of his day. He claimed to have mastered, by the age of 24, all known theological systems, Christian and non-Christian, from Moses to his own time. He was the first important Christian student of the Jewish mystical theology known as Kabbalah. The purpose of Pico's philosophical and theological studies was to produce a grand synthesis of religious wisdom which would both deepen understanding of Christian truth and also serve as an apologetic weapon against non-Christians. This was the project outlined in Pico's most famous work, *De dignitate hominis* (*On the Dignity of Man*) (1486), and further illuminated by his *Conclusiones* (1486) and *Apologia* (1487). As part of this larger project, Pico planned to write a concord of Plato and Aristotle, of which only a fragment, the treatise *De ente et uno* (*On Being and the One*) (1491), was ever finished. Although he proposed to found a new theological school based on an esoteric reading of all theologies past and present, he did not believe that these theologies were the same in substance, differing only in expression. He insisted on the differences between Platonism and Christianity, while holding that every major theological tradition did contain some elements of truth.

In addition to other, non-philosophical works, Pico wrote the *Commento* (1486), a commentary on a Neoplatonic poem that in effect constituted a critique of Marsilio Ficino's most famous work, the dialogue *De amore* (*On Love*) (1469). He criticized Ficino as too literary and defended the use of precise technical language in philosophy. Pico used Neoplatonic metaphysics to rediscover the 'secret mysteries' of pagan theology (though he sometimes criticized the reliability of the Neoplatonists as guides to Plato's thought) and offered a fresh interpretation of the metaphysics of love based on his own reading of Platonic sources, seeing human erotic love as a psychological process distinct from cosmic love.

See also: FICINO, M.; HERMETISM; KABBALAH; PLATONISM, RENAISSANCE; PLOTINUS; RENAISSANCE PHILOSOPHY

JAMES HANKINS

PLATO (427–347 BC)

Introduction

Plato was an Athenian Greek of aristocratic family, active as a philosopher in the first half of the fourth century BC. He was a devoted follower of Socrates, as his writings make abundantly plain. Nearly all are philosophical dialogues – often works of dazzling literary sophistication – in which Socrates takes centre stage. Socrates is usually a charismatic figure who outshines a whole succession of lesser interlocutors, from sophists, politicians and generals to docile teenagers. The most powerfully realistic fictions among the dialogues, such as *Protagoras* and *Symposium*, recreate a lost world of exuberant intellectual self-confidence in an Athens not yet torn apart by civil strife or reduced by defeat in the Peloponnesian War.

Some of Plato's earliest writings were evidently composed in an attempt to defend Socrates and his philosophical mission against the misunderstanding and prejudice which – in the view of his friends – had brought about his prosecution and death. Most notable of these are *Apology*, which purports to reproduce the speeches Socrates gave at his trial, and *Gorgias*, a long and impassioned debate over the choice between a philosophical and a political life. Several early dialogues pit Socrates against practitioners of rival disciplines, whether rhetoric (as in *Gorgias*) or sophistic education (*Protagoras*) or expertise in religion (*Euthyphro*), and were clearly designed as invitations to philosophy as well as warnings against the pretensions of the alternatives. Apologetic and protreptic concerns are seldom entirely absent from any Platonic dialogue in which Socrates is protagonist, but in others among the early works the emphasis falls more heavily upon his ethical philosophy in its own right. For example, *Laches* (on courage) and *Charmides* (on moderation) explore these topics in characteristic Socratic style, relying mostly on his method of elenchus (refutation), although Plato seems by no means committed to a Socratic intellectualist analysis of the virtues as forms of knowledge. That analysis is in fact examined in these dialogues (as also, for example, in *Hippias Minor*).

In dialogues of Plato's middle period like *Meno*, *Symposium* and *Phaedo* a rather different Socrates is presented. He gives voice to positive positions on a much wider range of topics: not just ethics, but metaphysics and epistemology and psychology too. And he is portrayed as recommending a new and constructive instrument of inquiry borrowed from mathematics, the method of hypothesis. While there are continuities between Plato's early and middle period versions of Socrates, it is clear that an evolution has occurred. Plato is no longer a Socratic, not even a critical and original Socratic: he has turned Socrates into a Platonist.

The two major theories that make up Platonism are the theory of Forms and the doctrine of the immortality of the soul. The notion of a Form is articulated with the aid of conceptual resources drawn from Eleatic philosophy. The ultimate object of a philosopher's search for knowledge is a kind of being that is quite unlike the familiar objects of the phenomenal world: something eternal and changeless, eminently and exclusively whatever – beautiful or just or equal – it is, not qualified in time or place or relation or respect. An account of the Form of Beautiful will explain what it is for something to be beautiful, and indeed other things are caused to be beautiful by their participation in the Beautiful. The middle period dialogues never put forward any proof of the existence of Forms. The theory is usually presented as a basic assumption to which the interlocutors agree to subscribe. Plato seems to treat it as a very general high-level hypothesis which provides the framework within which other questions can be explored, including the immortality of the soul. According to *Phaedo*, such a hypothesis will only stand if its consequences are consistent with other relevant truths; according to the *Republic* its validity must ultimately be assured by its coherence with the unhypothetical first principle constituted by specification of the Good.

The Pythagorean doctrine of the immortality of the soul, by contrast, is something for which Plato presents explicit proofs whenever he introduces it into discussion. It presupposes the dualist idea that soul and body are intrinsically distinct substances, which coexist during our life but separate again at death. Its first appearance is in *Meno*, where it is invoked in explanation of how we acquire a priori knowledge of mathematical truths. Socrates is represented as insisting that nobody imparts such truths to us as information: we work them out for ourselves, by recollecting them from within, where they must have lain untapped as latent memory throughout our lives. But innate forgotten knowledge presupposes a time before the soul entered the body, when it was in full conscious possession of truth. *Phaedo* holds out the promise that the souls of philosophers who devote their lives to the pursuit of wisdom will upon death be wholly freed from the constraints and contaminations of the body, and achieve pure knowledge of the Forms once again.

Republic, Plato's greatest work, also belongs to this major constructive period of his philosophizing. It gives the epistemology and metaphysics of Forms a key role in political philosophy. The ideally just city (or some approximation to it), and the communist institutions which control the life of its elite governing class, could only become a practical possibility if philosophers were to acquire political power or rulers to engage sincerely and adequately in philosophy. This is because a philosopher-ruler whose emotions have been properly trained and disciplined by Plato's reforming educational programme, and whose mind has been prepared for abstract thought about Forms by rigorous and comprehensive study of mathematics, is the only person with the knowledge and virtue necessary for producing harmony in society. Understanding of Forms, and above all of the Good, keystone of the system of Forms, is thus the essential prerequisite of political order.

It remains disputed how far Plato's vision of a good society ruled by philosopher-statesmen (of both sexes) was ever really conceived as a blueprint for practical implementation. Much of his writing suggests a deep pessimism about the prospects for human happiness. The most potent image in *Republic* is the analogy of the cave, which depicts ordinary humanity as so shackled by illusions several times removed from the illumination of truth that only radical moral and intellectual conversion could redeem us. And its theory of the human psyche is no less dark: the opposing desires of reason, emotion and appetite render it all too liable to the internal conflict which constitutes moral disease.

While *Republic* is for modern readers the central text in Plato's *œuvre*, throughout much of antiquity and the medieval period *Timaeus* was the dialogue by which he was best known. In this late work Plato offers an account of the creation of an ordered universe by a divine craftsman, who invests preexisting matter with every form of life and intelligence by the application of harmonious mathematical ratios. This is claimed to be only a 'likely story', the best explanation we can infer for phenomena which have none of the unchangeable permanence of the Forms. None the less *Timaeus* is the only work among post-*Republic* dialogues, apart from a highly-charged myth in *Phaedrus*, in which Plato was again to communicate the comprehensive vision expressed in the Platonism of the middle period dialogues.

Many of these dialogues are however remarkable contributions to philosophy, and none more so than

the self-critical *Parmenides*. Here the mature Parmenides is represented as mounting a powerful set of challenges to the logical coherence of the theory of Forms. He urges not abandonment of the theory, but much harder work in the practice of dialectical argument if the challenges are to be met. Other pioneering explorations were in epistemology (*Theaetetus*) and philosophical logic (*Sophist*). Theaetetus mounts a powerful attack on Protagoras' relativist theory of truth, before grappling with puzzles about false belief and problems with the perennially attractive idea that knowledge is a complex built out of unknowable simples. *Sophist* engages with the Parmenidean paradox that what is not cannot be spoken or thought about. It forges fundamental distinctions between identity and predication and between subject and predicate in its attempt to rescue meaningful discourse from the absurdities of the paradox.

In his sixties Plato made two visits to the court of Dionysius II in Sicily, apparently with some hopes of exercising a beneficial influence on the young despot. Both attempts were abysmal failures. But they did not deter Plato from writing extensively on politics in his last years. *Statesman* explores the practical knowledge the expert statesman must command. It was followed by the longest, even if not the liveliest, work he ever wrote, the twelve books of *Laws*, perhaps still unfinished at his death.

1 Life

Evidence about Plato's life is *prima facie* plentiful. As well as several ancient biographies, notably that contained in book III of Diogenes Laertius' *Lives of the Philosophers*, we possess a collection of thirteen letters which purport to have been written by Plato.

Unfortunately the biographies present what has been aptly characterized as 'a medley of anecdotes, reverential, malicious, or frivolous, but always piquant'. As for the letters, no scholar thinks them all authentic, and some judge that none are.

From the biographies it is safe enough to accept some salient points. Plato was born of an aristocratic Athenian family. He was brother to Glaucon and Adimantus, Socrates' main interlocutors in the *Republic*; his relatives included Critias and Charmides, members of the bloody junta which seized power in Athens at the end of the Peloponnesian War. He became one of the followers of Socrates, after whose execution he withdrew with others among them to the neighbouring city of Megara. His travels included a visit to the court of Dionysius in Sicily. On returning from Sicily to Athens he began teaching in a gymnasium outside the city, called the Academy.

The *Seventh Letter*, longest and most interesting of the collection of letters, gives a good deal of probably trustworthy information, whether or not it was written by Plato himself. It begins with an account of his growing disenchantment with Athenian politics in early adulthood and of his decision against a political career. This is prefatory to a sketch of the visit to Dionysius in Syracuse, which is followed by an elaborate self-justifying explanation of why and how, despite his decision, Plato later became entangled in political intrigue in Sicily, once the young Dionysius II had succeeded to his father's throne. There were two separate visits to the younger Dionysius: one (*c.*366 BC) is represented as undertaken at the behest of Dion, nephew of Dionysius I, in the hope of converting him into a philosopher-ruler; the other (*c.*360 BC) was according to the author an attempt to mediate between Dionysius and Dion, now in exile and out of favour. Both ventures were humiliating failures.

Of more interest for the history of philosophy is Plato's activity in the ACADEMY. We should not conceive, as scholars once did, that he established a formal philosophical school, with its own property and institutional structures. Although he acquired a house and garden in the vicinity, where communal meals were probably taken, much of his philosophical teaching and conversation may well have been conducted in the public space of the gymnasium itself. Some sense of the Academy's distinctive style may be gleaned from evidence of the contemporaneous writings of the philosophical associates he attracted, notably his nephew Speusippus, Xenocrates, ARISTOTLE and the mathematician EUDOXUS. Discussion of Plato's metaphysical ideas figured prominently in these; but orthodoxy was not expected, to judge from their philosophical disagreements with him and with each other.

Aristotle's early *Topics* suggests that an important role was played by formal disputation about philosophical theses.

From the educational programme of the *Republic* one might have guessed that Plato would have attached importance to the teaching of mathematics as a preparation for philosophy, but we have better evidence for his encouraging research in it. While he was not an original mathematician himself, good sources tell us that he formulated problems for others to solve: for example, what uniform motions will account for the apparent behaviour of the planets. Otherwise there is little reliable information on what was taught in the Academy: not much can be inferred from the burlesque of comic playwrights. Since almost certainly no fees were charged, most of those who came to listen to Plato (from all over the Greek world) must have been aristocrats. Some are known to have entered politics or to have advised princes, particularly on constitutional reform. But the Academy had no political mission of its own. Indeed the rhetorician Isocrates, head of a rival school and admittedly not an unbiased witness, dismissed the abstract disciplines favoured by the Academy for their uselessness in the real world.

2 Writings

Thrasyllus, astrologer to the emperor Tiberius, is the unlikely source of the arrangement of Platonic writings adopted in the manuscript tradition which preserves them. For his edition of Plato he grouped them into tetralogies, reminiscent of the trilogies produced in Athenian tragic theatre. These were organized according to an architectonic scheme constructed on principles that are now only partially apparent, but certainly had nothing to do with chronology of composition. His arrangement began with a quartet 'designed to show what the life of the philosopher is like' (Diogenes Laertius, III 57): *Euthyphro*, or 'On Piety', classified as a 'peirastic' or elenctic dialogue (see SOCRATES §§3–4), which is a species of one of his two main genres, the dialogue of inquiry; *Apology*, *Crito* and *Phaedo* are all regarded as specimens of exposition, his other main genre, or more specifically as specimens of ethics. These four works are all concerned in one way or another with the trial and death of Socrates.

There followed a group consisting of *Cratylus*, or 'On the Correctness of Names', *Theaetetus*, or 'On Knowledge', *Sophist* and *Politicus* (often Anglicized as *Statesman*). Plato himself indicates that the last three of this set are to be read together. They contain some of his most mature and challenging work in epistemology, metaphysics and philosophical methodology. In this they resemble *Parmenides*, with its famous critique of the theory of Forms, the first of the next tetralogy, which was completed by three major dialogues all reckoned 'ethical' by Thrasyllus: *Philebus*, an examination of pleasure, *Symposium* and *Phaedrus*, both brilliant literary divertissements which explore the nature of love.

A much slighter quartet came next: two dialogues entitled *Alcibiades*, plus *Hipparchus* and *Rivals*. None of these, with the disputed exception of the first *Alcibiades*, is thought by modern scholarship to be authentic Plato. They were followed by *Theages*, a short piece now generally reckoned spurious, *Charmides*, *Laches* and *Lysis*. These latter three works are generally regarded by modern scholars as Socratic dialogues: that is, designed to exhibit the distinctive method and ethical preoccupations of the historical Socrates, at least as Plato understood him, not to develop Plato's own philosophy. Thrasyllus would agree with the latter point, since he made them dialogues of inquiry: *Laches* and *Lysis* 'maieutic', in which the character 'Socrates' attempts as intellectual midwife to assist his interlocutors to articulate and work out their own ideas on courage and friendship respectively; *Charmides* elenctic, with the interlocutors Charmides and Critias and their attempts to say what moderation is put to the test of cross-examination, something Thrasyllus interestingly distinguished from philosophical midwifery.

The next group consisted of *Euthydemus*, *Protagoras*, *Gorgias*, *Meno*, important works in which modern scholarship finds analysis and further elaboration by Plato of the Socratic conception of virtue. The first three present a Socrates in argumentative conflict with sophists of different sorts (see SOPHISTS), so it is understandable that under the general heading 'competitive' Thrasyllus characterized *Euthydemus* and *Gorgias* as dialogues of refutation, and *Protagoras* as a dialogue of display – presumably because Protagoras and Socrates are each portrayed as intent on showing off their debating skills. *Meno*, on the other hand, is labelled an elenctic work. It was followed by the seventh tetralogy: *Hippias Major* and *Hippias Minor*, two very different dialogues (of refutation, according to Thrasyllus), both featuring the sophist of that name; *Ion*, a curious piece on poetic performance; and *Menexenus*, a still more curious parody of a funeral oration, put in the mouth of Pericles' mistress Aspasia.

For the last two tetralogies Thrasyllus reserved some of Plato's major writings. The eighth contained the very brief (and conceivably spurious) *Clitophon*, in which a minor character from the *Republic* plays variations on themes in the *Republic*, the second dialogue in the group, and generally regarded nowadays as Plato's greatest work. This quartet was completed by *Timaeus* and its unfinished sequel *Critias*, no doubt because these dialogues represent themselves as pursuing further the discussions of the *Republic*. The pre-Copernican mathematical cosmology of *Timaeus* no longer attracts readers as it did throughout antiquity, and particularly in the Middle Ages, when the dialogue was for a period the only part of Plato's œuvre known to the Latin West. Finally, the ninth tetralogy began with the short *Minos*, a spurious dialogue taking up issues in the massive *Laws*, Plato's longest and probably latest work, which was put next in the group. Then followed *Epinomis*, an appendix to *Laws* already attributed to one of Plato's pupils in antiquity (Philip of Opous, according to a report in Diogenes Laertius, III 37). Last were placed the *Letters*, briefly discussed above.

3 Authenticity and chronology

Thrasyllus rejected from the canon a variety of minor pieces, some of which still survive through the manuscript tradition. Modern judgment concurs with the ancient verdict against them. It also questions or rejects some he thought genuinely Platonic. But we can be fairly sure that we still possess everything Plato wrote for publication.

Attempting to determine the authenticity or inauthenticity of ancient writings is a hazardous business. Egregious historical errors or anachronisms suffice to condemn a work, but except perhaps for the *Eighth Letter*, this criterion gets no purchase on the Platonic corpus. Stylistic analysis of various kinds can show a piece of writing to be untypical of an author's œuvre, without thereby demonstrating its inauthenticity: *Parmenides* is a notable example of this. Most of Plato's major dialogues are in fact attested as his by Aristotle. The difficult cases are short pieces such as *Theages* and *Clitophon*, and, most interestingly, three more extended works: the *Seventh Letter*, *Alcibiades I* and *Hippias Major*. Opinion remains divided on them. Some scholars detect crude or sometimes brilliant pastiche of Plato's style; a parasitic relationship with undoubtedly genuine dialogues; a philosophical crassness or a misunderstanding of Platonic positions which betrays the forger's hand. Yet why should Plato not for some particular purpose recapitulate or elaborate things he has said elsewhere? And perhaps he did sometimes write more coarsely or didactically or long-windedly than usual. Such assessments are inevitably matters of judgment, on which intelligent and informed readers will legitimately differ.

Prospects for an absolute chronology of Plato's writings are dim. There are no more than two or three references to datable contemporaneous events in the entire corpus (leaving aside the *Letters*).

Relative chronology is another matter. Some dialogues refer back to others. A number of instances have been mentioned already, but we can add a clear reminiscence of *Meno* in *Phaedo* (72e–73b), and of *Parmenides* in both *Theaetetus* (183e–184a) and *Sophist* (217c). According to one ancient tradition *Laws* was unfinished at Plato's death, and Aristotle informs us that it was written after *Republic* (*Politics* 1264b24–7), to which it appears to allude (see, for example, *Laws* 739a–e). Attempts have sometimes been made to find evidence, whether internal or external, for the existence of early versions of works we possess in different form. One example is the suggestion that Aristophanes' comedy *Ecclesiazousae* or *Assembly of Women* (388 BC) was parodying an early version of book V of *Republic*. But while the idea that Plato may have revised some of his writings is plausible, concrete instances in which such revision is plainly the best explanation of the phenomena are hard to find. Even if they were not, it is unlikely that the consequences for relative chronology would be clear.

For over a century hopes for a general relative chronology of Plato's writings have been pinned on the practice of stylistic analysis. This was pioneered by Lewis Campbell in his edition of *Sophist* and *Politicus*, published in 1867. His great achievement was to isolate a group of dialogues which have in common a number of features (added to by subsequent investigators) that set them apart from all the rest. *Timaeus, Critias, Sophist, Politicus, Philebus* and *Laws* turn out to share among other things a common technical vocabulary; a preference for certain particles, conjunctions, adverbs and other qualifiers over alternatives favoured in other dialogues; distinctive prose rhythms; and the deliberate attempt to avoid the combination of a vowel at the end of one word followed by another vowel at the beginning of the next. Since there are good independent reasons for taking *Laws* to be Plato's last work, Campbell's sextet is very likely the product of his latest phase of philosophical activity. Application of the same stylistic tests to the Platonic corpus as a whole, notably by Constantin Ritter, established *Republic, Theaetetus* and *Phaedrus* as dialogues which show significantly more of the features most strongly represented in the late sextet than any others. There is general agreement that they must be among the works whose composition immediately precedes that of the *Laws* group, always allowing that *Republic* must have taken several years to finish, and that parts of it may have been written earlier and subsequently revised. *Parmenides* is ordinarily included with these three, although mostly on non-stylistic grounds.

Since Campbell's time there have been repeated attempts by stylometrists to divide the remaining dialogues into groups, and to establish sequences within groups. The heyday of this activity was in the late nineteenth and early twentieth centuries. Since the 1950s there has been a revival in stylistic study, with the use of increasingly sophisticated statistical techniques and the resources of the computer and the database. Secure results have proved elusive. Most scholars would be happy to date *Phaedo, Symposium* and *Cratylus* to a middle period of Plato's literary and philosophical work which may be regarded as achieving its culmination in *Republic*. But while this dating is sometimes supported by appeal to stylistic evidence, that evidence is in truth indecisive: the hypothesis of a middle period group of dialogues really rests on their philosophical affinities with *Republic* and their general literary character. The same can be said *mutatis mutandis* of attempts to identify a group assigned to Plato's early period.

The cohesiveness of Campbell's late group has not gone unchallenged. For example, in 1953 G.E.L. Owen mounted what for a while seemed to some a successful attack on his dating of *Timaeus* and *Critias*, on the ground that these dialogues belong philosophically in Plato's middle period. Broadly speaking, however, stylistic studies have helped to establish an agreed chronological framework within which most debates about philosophical interpretation now take place. This is not to say however that there is unanimity about the way Plato's thought developed; and some scholars refuse to assign any importance to the notion of development for understanding his philosophical project or projects in the dialogues.

4 The Platonic dialogue

Who invented the philosophical dialogue, and what literary models might have inspired the invention, are not matters on which we have solid information. We do know that several of Socrates' followers composed what Aristotle calls *Sōkratikoi logoi*, discourses portraying Socrates in fictitious conversations. The only examples which survive intact besides Plato's are by XENOPHON, probably not one of the earliest practitioners of the genre.

One major reason for the production of this literature was the desire to defend Socrates against the charges of irreligion and corrupting young people made at his trial and subsequently in Athenian pamphleteering, as well as the implicit charge of guilt by association with a succession of oligarchic politicians. Thus his devotion to the unstable and treacherous Alcibiades was variously portrayed in, for example, the first of the *Alcibiades* dialogues ascribed to Plato and the now fragmentary *Alcibiades* of Aeschines of Sphettos, but both emphasized the gulf between Alcibiades' self-conceit and resistance to education and Socrates' disinterested concern for his moral wellbeing. The same general purpose informed the publication of versions of Socrates' speech (his 'apology') before the court by Plato, Xenophon and perhaps others. Writing designed to clear Socrates' name was doubtless a particular feature of the decade or so following 399 BC, although it clearly went on long after that, as in Xenophon's *Memorabilia*. After starting in a rather different vein *Gorgias* turns into Plato's longest and angriest dialogue of this kind. Socrates is made to present himself as the only true politician in Athens, since he is the one person who can give a truly rational account of his conduct towards others and accordingly command the requisite political skill, which is to make the citizens good. But he foresees no chance of acquittal by a court of jurors seeking only gratification from their leaders.

Placing Socrates in opposition to Alcibiades is a way of defending him. Arranging a confrontation between a sophist (Protagoras or Hippias) or a rhetorician (Gorgias) or a religious expert (Euthyphro) or a Homeric recitalist (Ion) and Socrates is a way of exposing their intellectual pretensions, and in most cases their moral shallowness, while celebrating his wit, irony and penetration and permitting his distinctive ethical positions and ethical method to unfold before the reader's eyes. The elenchus (see SOCRATES §§3–4) is by no means the only mode of argument Socrates is represented as using in these fictional encounters. Plato particularly enjoys allowing him to exploit the various rhetorical forms favoured by his interlocutors. But it is easy to see why the dialogue must have seemed to Plato the ideal instrument not only for commemorating like Xenophon Socrates' style of conversation, but more importantly for exhibiting the logical structure and dynamic of the elenchus, and its power in Socrates' hands to demolish the characteristic intellectual postures of those against whom it is deployed.

In these dialogues of confrontation Socrates seldom succeeds in humbling his interlocutors into a frank recognition that they do not know what they thought they knew: the official purpose – simultaneously intellectual and moral – of the elenchus. It would not have been convincing to have him begin to convert historical figures with well-known intellectual positions. The main thing registered by their fictional counterparts is a sense of being manipulated into self-contradiction. In any case, the constructive response to the extraordinary figure of Socrates which Plato really wants to elicit is that of the reader. We have to suppose that, as conversion to philosophy was for Plato scarcely

distinguishable from his response to Socrates (devotion to the man, surrender to the spell of his charisma, strenuous intellectual engagement with his thought and the questions he was constantly pursuing), so he conceived that the point of writing philosophy must be to make Socrates charismatic for his readers – to move us to similar devotion and enterprise. In short, the dialogues constitute simultaneously an invitation to philosophy and a critique of its intellectual rivals.

Whatever Plato's other accomplishments or failures as a writer and thinker, one project in which he unquestionably succeeds is in creating a Socrates who gets under the reader's skin (see SOCRATES §7). Plato has a genius for portrayal of character: the 'arrogant self-effacement' of Socrates' persona; the irony at once sincere and insincere; the intellectual slipperiness in service of moral paradox; the nobility of the martyr who loses everything but saves his own soul, and of the hero who stands firm on the battlefield or in face of threats by the authorities; relentless rationality and almost impregnable self-control somehow cohabiting with susceptibility to beautiful young men and their erotic charm. Also important is the ingenious variety of perspectives from which we see Socrates talking and interacting with others. Sometimes he is made to speak to us direct (for example, *Apology, Gorgias*). Sometimes Plato invites us to share complicity in a knowing narrative Socrates tells of his own performance (as in *Charmides* and *Protagoras*). Sometimes someone else is represented as recalling an unforgettably emotional occasion when Socrates dominated a whole roomful of people, as in the most powerfully dramatic dialogues of all, *Phaedo* and *Symposium*. Here we have the illusion that Socrates somehow remains himself even though the ideas advanced in them must go beyond anything that the historical Socrates (or at any rate the agnostic Socrates of *Apology*) would have claimed about the soul and its immortality or about the good and the beautiful.

5 The problem of writing

It might seem strange that an original philosopher of Plato's power and stature should be content, outside the *Letters* if some of them are by him, never to talk directly to the reader, but only through the medium of narrative or dramatic fiction, even granted the pleasure he plainly takes in exhibiting his mastery of that medium. This will become less mysterious if we reflect further on Socrates and Socratic questioning. At any rate by the time of the *Meno*, Plato was wanting to suggest that the elenchus presupposes that understanding is not something one person can transmit in any straightforward way to another, but something which has to be worked out for oneself and recovered from within by recollection. The suggestion is made by means of an example from mathematics, where it is transparently true that seeing the answer to a problem is something that nobody else can do for us, even if Socrates' questions can prompt us to it. The moral we are to draw is that in pressing his interlocutors on what they say they believe, Socrates is merely an intellectual midwife assisting them to articulate for themselves a more coherent and deeply considered set of views, which will ideally constitute the truth.

The Platonic dialogue can be interpreted as an attempt to create a relationship between author and reader analogous to that between Socrates and his interlocutors. Given that that relationship is to be construed in the way indicated in *Meno*, the point of a dialogue will be like that of the elenchus: not to teach readers the truth (it is strictly speaking unteachable), but to provoke and guide them into working at discovering it for themselves. Most of the dialogues of Campbell's late sextet are admittedly more didactic than one would expect on this view of the dialogue, and it is significant that except in *Philebus* Socrates is no longer the main speaker. Yet even here use of the dialogue form can be taken as symbolizing that responsibility for an active philosophical engagement with what Plato has written rests with the reader, as the difficulty and in some cases the methodological preoccupations of most of these works confirms.

In a much discussed passage at the end of *Phaedrus* (275–8), Socrates is made to speak of the limitations of the written word. It can answer no questions, it cannot choose its readers, it gets misunderstood with no means of correcting misunderstanding. Its one worthwhile function is to remind those who know of what they know. By contrast with this dead discourse live speech can defend itself, and will be uttered or not as appropriate to the potential audience. The only serious use of words is achieved when speech, not writing, is employed by dialecticians to sow seeds of knowledge in the soul of the learner. If they commit their thoughts to writing they do so as play (*paidia*). The *Seventh Letter* (341–2) makes related remarks about the writing of philosophy; and at various points in, for example, *Republic*, *Timaeus* and *Laws*, the discussions in which the interlocutors are engaged are described as play, not to be taken seriously.

Interpreters have often taken these written remarks about writing with the utmost seriousness. In particular the Tübingen school of Platonic scholarship has connected them with references, especially in Aristotle, to unwritten doctrines of Plato. They have proposed that the fundamental principles of his philosophy are not worked out in the dialogues at all, but were reserved for oral discussions in the Academy, and have to be reconstructed by us from evidence about the unwritten doctrines. But this evidence is suspect where voluble and elusive when apparently more reliable. There are two star exhibits. First, according to the fourth-century BC music theorist Aristoxenus, Aristotle used to tell of how when Plato lectured on the good he surprised and disappointed his listeners by talking mostly about mathematics (*Harmonics* II, 30.16–31.3). Second, at one point in the *Physics* (209b13–6) Aristotle refers to Plato's 'so-called unwritten teachings'; and the Aristotelian commentators report that Aristotle and other members of the Academy elsewhere wrote more about them. Plato's key idea was taken to be the postulation of the One and the great and the small, or 'indefinite dyad', as principles of all things, including Forms. In his *Metaphysics* (I.6) Aristotle seems to imply that in this theory the Forms were construed in some sense as numbers. It remains obscure and a subject of inconclusive scholarly debate how far the theory was worked out, and what weight we should attach to it in comparison to the metaphysical explorations of the dialogues of Plato's middle and late periods (see for example Guthrie 1975, 1978).

The general issue of how far we can ascribe to Plato things said by interlocutors (principally Socrates) in his dialogues is something which exercises many readers. The position taken here will be that no single or simple view of the matter is tenable: sometimes, for example, Plato uses the dialogue form to work through a problem which is vexing him; sometimes to recommend a set of ideas to us; sometimes to play teasingly with ideas or positions or methodologies without implying much in the way of commitment; and frequently to suggest to us ways we should or should not ourselves try to philosophize. As for the Tübingen school, we may agree with them that when it introduces the Form of the Good the *Republic* itself indicates that readers are being offered only conjectures and images, not the thorough dialectical discussion necessary for proper understanding. But the notions of seriousness and play are less straightforward than they allow. Playing with ideas – that is, trying them out and developing them to see what might work and what will not – is the way new insights in philosophy and science are often discovered. When we meet it in Plato's dialogues it usually seems fun without being frivolous. Nor should we forget that the Platonic dialogue represents itself as a spoken conversation. It seems hard to resist the thought that we are thereby invited to treat his dialogues not as writing so much as an attempt to transcend the limitations of writing. Perhaps the idea is that they can achieve the success of living speech if treated not as texts to be interpreted (despite Plato's irresistible urge to produce texts devised precisely to elicit attempts at interpretation), but as stimuli to questions we must put principally to ourselves, or as seeds which may one day grow into philosophy in our souls.

6 Early works

There is widespread scholarly agreement that the following are among Plato's earliest writings: *Apology, Crito, Ion, Hippias Minor, Laches* and *Charmides. Apology*, as we have noted, best fits into the context of the decade following Socrates' death, and so does *Crito*, which explores the question why he did not try to escape from the condemned cell; the others are all short treatments of questions to do with virtue and knowledge, or in the case of *Ion*, with expertise (*technē*), and all are relatively simple in literary structure. The brief *Euthyphro* and the much longer *Protagoras* and *Gorgias* (with which *Menexenus* is often associated) are usually seen as having many affinities with these, and so are put at least fairly early, although here anticipations of the style or content of the mature middle-period dialogues have also been detected. The connections in thought between *Lysis, Euthydemus* and *Hippias Major* and middle-period Plato may be argued to be stronger still, even though there remain clear similarities with the dialogues generally accepted as early. We do not know whether Plato wrote or published anything before Socrates' death; *Menexenus* cannot be earlier than 386 BC, *Ion* might be datable to around 394–391 BC, but otherwise we can only guess.

All those listed above fall under the commonly used description 'Socratic dialogues', because they are seen as preoccupied with the thought of the historical Socrates as Plato understood him, in contrast with writings of the middle period, where 'Socrates' often seems to become a vehicle for exploring a more wide-ranging set of ideas (see SOCRATES §2). In the Socratic dialogues discussion is confined almost exclusively to ethical questions, or problems about the scope and credentials of expertise: metaphysics and epistemology and speculation about the nature and powers of the soul are for the most part notable by their absence. Use of the elenchus is prominent in them as it is not, for example, in *Republic* (apart from book I, sometimes regarded as an early work subsequently reused as a preface to the main body of the dialogue). The hypothesis that philosophizing in this style was the hallmark of the historical Socrates is broadly consistent with what we are given to understand about him by Xenophon, Aristotle and Plato's *Apology* – which is usually thought to be particularly authoritative evidence, whether or not it is a faithful representation of what Socrates really said at his trial.

How historical the historical Socrates of the hypothesis actually is we shall never know. The conjecture that many of the Socratic dialogues are early works is likewise only a guess, which gets no secure support from stylometric evidence. None the less the story of Plato's literary and philosophical development to which it points makes such excellent sense that it has effectively driven all rival theories from the field. The placing of individual dialogues within that story remains a matter for controversy; and doubts persist over how far interpretation of Plato is illuminated or obstructed by acceptance of any developmental pattern. With these provisos, the account which follows assumes the existence of a group of early Socratic dialogues in the sense explained.

The convenience of the description 'Socratic dialogues' should not generate the expectation of a single literary or philosophical enterprise in these writings. It conceals considerable variety, for example as between works devoted to articulating and defending the philosophical life and works which problematize Socratic thought as much as they exhibit its attractions. This distinction is not an exhaustive one, but provides useful categories for thinking about some of the key productions of Plato's early period.

7 Apologetic writings

Moral, or indeed existential, choice, to use an anachronistic expression, is the insistent focus of *Apology*. God has appointed Socrates, as he represents it to his judges, to live the philosophical life, putting himself and others under constant examination. The consistency of his commitment to this mission requires him now to face death rather than abandon his practice of philosophy, as he supposes for the sake of argument the court might require him to do. For confronted with the choice between disobeying God (that is, giving up philosophy) and disobeying human dictate (that is, refusing to do so), he can only take the latter option. What governs his choice is justice:

> It is a mistake to think that a man worth anything at all should make petty calculations about the risk of living or dying. There is only one thing for him to consider when he acts: whether he is doing right or wrong, whether he is doing what a good man or a bad man would do.
>
> (*Apology* 28b)

Whether death is or is not a bad thing Socrates says he does not know. He does know that behaving wrongly and disobeying one's moral superior – whether divine or human – is bad and shameful. The demands of justice, as his conscience (or 'divine sign') interpreted them, had earlier led him to choose the life of a private citizen, conversing only with individuals, rather than the political life: for justice and survival in politics are incompatible. When he did carry out the public obligations of a citizen and temporarily held office, justice again compelled him to choose the dangerous and unpopular course of resisting a proposal that was politically expedient but contrary to the law. As for those with whom he talked philosophy, they too faced a choice: whether to make their main concern possessions and the body, or virtue and the soul; that is, what belongs to oneself, or oneself. And now the judges too must choose and determine what is just as their oath requires of them.

Crito and *Gorgias* continue the theme in different ways. *Crito* has often been found difficult to reconcile with *Apology* when it argues on various grounds (paternalistic and quasi-contractual) that citizens must always obey the law, unless they can persuade it that it is in the wrong. Hence, since the law requires that Socrates submit to the punishment prescribed by the court, he must accept the sentence of death pronounced on him. The higher authority of divine command stressed in *Apology* seems to have been forgotten. Once again, however, the whole argument turns on appeal to justice and to the choices it dictates: we must heed the truth about it, not what popular opinion says; we must decide whether or not we believe the radical Socratic proposition that retaliation against injury or injustice is never right (see SOCRATES §4). *Gorgias*, one of the longest of all the dialogues, ranges over a wide territory, but at its heart is the presentation of a choice. Socrates addresses Callicles, in whose rhetoric Nietzsche saw an anticipation of his ideal of the superman:

> You see that the subject of our arguments – and on what subject should a person of even small intelligence be more serious? – is this: what kind of life should we live? The life which you are now urging upon me, behaving as a *man* should: speaking in the assembly and practising rhetoric and engaging in politics in your present style? Or the life of philosophy?
> (*Gorgias* 5th century BC)

The dialogue devotes enormous energy to arguing that only philosophy, not rhetoric, can equip us with a true expertise which will give us real power, that is power to achieve what we want: the real not the apparent good. Only philosophy can articulate a rational and reliable conception of happiness – which turns out to depend on justice.

8 Laches *and* Charmides

Contrast the works outlined in §7 with *Laches* and *Charmides*, which were very likely conceived as a pair, the one an inquiry into courage, the other into *sōphrosynē* or moderation. Both engage in fairly elaborate scene setting quite absent from *Crito* and *Gorgias*. In both there is concern with the relation between theory and practice, which is worked out more emphatically in *Laches*, more elusively in *Charmides*. For example, in *Laches* Socrates is portrayed both as master of argument about courage, and as an exemplar of the virtue in action – literally by reference to his conduct in the retreat from Delium early in the Peloponnesian War, metaphorically by his persistence in dialectic, to which his observations on the need for perseverance in inquiry draw attention.

A particularly interesting feature of these dialogues is their play with duality. Socrates confronts a *pair* of main interlocutors who clearly fulfil complementary roles. We hear first the views of the more sympathetic members of the two pairs: the general Laches, whom Socrates identifies as his partner in argument, and the young aristocrat Charmides, to whom he is attracted. Each displays behavioural traits associated with the virtue under discussion, and each initially offers a definition in behavioural terms, later revised in favour of a dispositional analysis: courage is construed as a sort of endurance of soul, *sōphrosynē* as modesty. After these accounts are subjected to elenchus and refuted, the other members of the pairs propose intellectualist definitions: according to Nicias (also a general), courage is knowledge of what inspires fear or confidence, while Critias identifies *sōphrosynē* with self-knowledge.

Broad hints are given that the real author of these latter definitions is Socrates himself; and in *Protagoras* he is made to press Protagoras into accepting the same definition of courage. There are also hints that, as understood by their proponents here, this intellectualism is no more than sophistic cleverness, and that neither possesses the virtue he claims to understand. Both are refuted by further Socratic elenchus, and in each case the argument points to the difficulty of achieving an intellectualist account which is not effectively a definition of virtue in general as the simple knowledge of good and bad. *Laches* explicitly raises the methodological issue of whether one should try to investigate the parts of virtue in order to understand the whole or vice versa (here there are clear connections with the main argument of *Protagoras*).

Aristotle was in no doubt that Socrates 'thought all the virtues were forms of knowledge' (*Eudemian Ethics* 1216b6); and many moves in the early dialogues depend on the assumption that if you know what is good you will *be* good (see SOCRATES §5). But *Laches* and *Charmides* present this Socratic belief as problematical. Not only is there the problem of specifying a unique content for the knowledge with which any particular virtue is to be identified. There is also the difficulty that any purely intellectual specification of what a virtue is makes no reference to the dispositions Charmides and Laches mention and (like Socrates) exemplify. In raising this difficulty Plato is already adumbrating the need for a more complex moral psychology than Socrates', if only to do justice to how Socrates *lived*. If the viewpoints of Laches and Nicias are combined we are not far from the account of courage in *Republic*, as the virtue of the spirited part of the soul, which 'preserves through pains and pleasures the injunctions of reason concerning what is and is not fearful' (442b).

9 Other dialogues of inquiry

In *Protagoras* it is Socrates himself who works out and defends the theory that knowledge is sufficient for virtuous action and that different virtues are different forms of that knowledge (see ARETĒ). He does not here play the role of critic of the theory, nor are there other interlocutors who might suggest alternative perceptions: indeed Protagoras, as partner not adversary in the key argument, is represented as accepting the key premise that (as he puts it) 'wisdom and knowledge are the most powerful forces governing human affairs' (352c–d). It would be a mistake to think that Plato found one and the same view problematic when he wrote *Laches* and *Charmides* but unproblematic when he wrote *Protagoras*, and to construct a chronological hypothesis to cope with the contradiction. *Protagoras* is simply a different sort of dialogue: it displays Socratic dialectic at work from a stance of some detachment, without raising questions about it. *Protagoras* is an entirely different kind of work from *Gorgias*, too: the one all urbane sparring, the latter a deadly serious confrontation between philosophy and political ambition. *Gorgias* unquestionably attacks hedonism, *Protagoras* argues for it, to obtain a suitable premise for defending the intellectualist paradox that nobody does wrong willingly, but leaves Socrates' own commitment to the premise at best ambiguous (see SOCRATES §6). Incommensurabilities of this kind make it unwise to attempt a relative chronology of the two dialogues on the basis of apparent incompatibilities in the positions of their two Socrates.

Space does not permit discussion of *Ion*, a debate about poetry (is it craft or inspiration?), or of *Hippias Minor*, in which Socrates is made to tease us with the paradox – derived from his equation of virtue and knowledge – that someone who *did* do wrong knowingly and intentionally would be better than someone who did it unintentionally through ignorance. Interpretation of *Euthyphro* remains irredeemably controversial. Its logical ingenuity is admired, and the dialogue is celebrated for its invention of one of the great philosophical questions about religion: either we should do right because god tells us to do so, which robs us of moral autonomy, or because it is right god tells us to do it, which makes the will of god morally redundant.

Something more needs to be said about *Lysis* and *Euthydemus* (which share a key minor character in Ctesippus, and are heavy with the same highly charged erotic atmosphere) and *Hippias Major*. They all present Socrates engaging in extended question and answer sessions, although only in *Hippias* is this an elenchus with real bite: in the other dialogues his principal interlocutors are boys with no considered positions of their own inviting refutation. All end in total failure to achieve positive results. All make great formal play with dualities of various kinds. Unusually ingenious literary devices characterize the three works, ranging from the introduction of an *alter ego* for Socrates in *Hippias* to disruption of the argument of the main dialogue by its 'framing' dialogue in *Euthydemus*, at a point where the discussion is clearly either anticipating or recalling the central books of *Republic*. All seem to be principally preoccupied with dialectical method (admittedly a concern in every dialogue). Thus *Hippias* is a study in definitional procedure, applied to the case of the fine or beautiful, *Lysis* a study in thesis and antithesis paralleled in Plato's *œuvre* only by *Parmenides*, and *Euthydemus* an exhibition of the contrast between 'eristic', that is, purely combative sophistical argument, demonstrated by the brothers Euthydemus and Dionysodorus, and no less playful philosophical questioning that similarly but differently ties itself in knots. It is the sole member of the trio which could be said with much conviction to engage – once more quizzically – with the thought of the historical Socrates about knowledge and virtue. But its introduction of ideas from *Republic* makes it hard to rank among the early writings of Plato. Similarly, in *Lysis* and *Hippias Major* there are echoes or pre-echoes of the theory of Forms and some of the causal questions associated with it. We may conclude that these ingenious philosophical exercises – 'gymnastic' pieces, to use the vocabulary of *Parmenides* – might well belong to Plato's middle period.

10 The introduction of Platonism

Needless to say, no explicit Platonic directive survives that encourages us to read *Meno, Symposium* and *Phaedo* together. But there are compelling reasons for believing that Plato conceived them as a group in which *Meno* and *Symposium* prepare the way for *Phaedo*. In brief, in *Meno* Plato introduces his readers to the non-Socratic theory of the immortality of the soul and a new hypothetical method of inquiry, while *Symposium* presents for the first time the non-Socratic idea of a Platonic Form, in the context of a notion of philosophy as desire for wisdom. It is only in *Phaedo* that all these new ideas are welded together into a single complex theory incorporating epistemology, psychology, metaphysics and methodology, and constituting the distinctive philosophical position known to the world as Platonism.

Meno and *Symposium* share two features which indicate Plato's intention that they should be seen as a pair, performing the same kind of introductory functions, despite enormous differences for example in dialogue form, scale and literary complexity. First, both are heavily and specifically foreshadowed in *Protagoras*, which should accordingly be reckoned one of the latest of Plato's early writings. At the end of *Protagoras* (361c) Socrates is made to say that he would like to follow up the inconclusive conversation of the dialogue with another attempt to define what virtue is, and to consider again whether or not it can be taught. This is exactly the task undertaken in *Meno*. Similarly, not only are all the *dramatis personae* of *Symposium* except Aristophanes already assembled in *Protagoras*, but at one point Socrates is represented as offering the company some marginally relevant advice on how to conduct a drinking party – which corresponds exactly to what happens at the party in *Symposium* (347c–348a).

Second, both *Meno* and *Symposium* are exceedingly careful not to make Socrates himself a committed proponent either of the immortality of the soul or of the theory of Forms. These doctrines are ascribed respectively to 'priests and priestesses' (*Meno*) and to one priestess, Diotima, in particular (*Symposium*); in *Meno* Socrates says he will not vouch for the truth of the doctrine of immortality, in *Symposium* he records Diotima's doubts as to whether he is capable of initiation into the mysteries (a metaphor also used of mathematics in *Meno*) which culminate in a vision of the Form of the Beautiful. In *Symposium* these warning signs are reinforced by the extraordinary form of the dialogue: the sequence of conversations and speeches it purports to record are nested inside a Chinese box of framing conversations, represented as occurring some years later and with participants who confess to inexact memory of what they heard.

Phaedo for its part presupposes *Meno* and *Symposium*. At 72e–73b *Meno*'s argument for the immortality of the soul is explicitly recalled, while

the Form of Beauty is regularly mentioned at the head of the lists of the 'much talked about' Forms which *Phaedo* introduces from time to time (for example, 75c, 77a, 100b). It is as though Plato relies upon our memory of the much fuller characterization of what it is to be a Form supplied in *Symposium*. Unlike *Meno* and *Symposium*, *Phaedo* represents Socrates himself as committed to Platonist positions, but takes advantage of the dramatic context – a discussion with friends as he waits for the hemlock to take effect – and makes him claim prophetic knowledge for himself like a dying swan (84e–85b). The suggestion is presumably that Platonism is a natural development of Socrates' philosophy even if it goes far beyond ideas about knowledge and virtue and the imperatives of the philosophical life to which he is restricted in the early dialogues.

11 Meno

Meno is a dialogue of the simplest form and structure. It consists of a conversation between Socrates and Meno, a young Thessalian nobleman under the spell of the rhetorician Gorgias, interrupted only by a passage in which Socrates quizzes Meno's slave, and then later by a brief intervention in the proceedings on the part of Anytus, Meno's host and one of Socrates' accusers at his trial. The dialogue divides into three sections: an unsuccessful attempt to define what virtue is, which makes the formal requirements of a good definition its chief focus; a demonstration in the face of Meno's doubts that successful inquiry is none the less possible in principle; and an investigation into the secondary question of whether virtue can be taught, pursued initially by use of a method of hypothesis borrowed from mathematics. Although the ethical subject matter of the discussion is thoroughly Socratic, the character and extent of its preoccupation with methodology and (in the second section) epistemology and psychology are not. Nor is *Meno*'s use of mathematical procedures to cast light on philosophical method; this is not confined to the third section. Definitions of the mathematical notion of shape are used in the first section to illustrate for example the principle that a definition should be couched in terms that the interlocutor agrees are already known. And the demonstration of an elenchus with a positive outcome which occupies the second is achieved with a geometrical example.

It looks as though Plato has come to see in the analogy with mathematics hope for more constructive results in philosophy than the Socratic elenchus generally achieved in earlier dialogues. This is a moral which the second and third sections of *Meno* make particularly inviting to draw. In the second

Socrates is represented as setting Meno's untutored slave boy a geometrical problem (to determine the length of the side of a square twice the size of a given square) and scrutinizing his answers by the usual elenctic method. The boy begins by thinking he has the answer. After a couple of mistaken attempts at it he is persuaded of his ignorance. So far so Socratic. But then with the help of a further construction he works out the right answer, and so achieves true opinion, which it is suggested could be converted into knowledge if he were to go through the exercise often. The tacit implication is that if elenchus can reach a successful outcome in mathematics, it ought to be capable of it in ethics too.

None the less, and perhaps significantly, Socrates does not press or indeed even articulate that point; direct engagement with the original problem of what virtue is is in fact abandoned at this juncture, and the discussion turns to the issue of its teachability, and to the method of hypothesis. Here the idea is that instead of investigating the truth of proposition p directly 'you hit upon another proposition h ('the hypothesis'), such that p is true if and only if h is true, and then investigate the truth of h, undertaking to determine what would follow (quite apart from p) if h were true and, alternatively, if it were false' (as formulated by Vlastos). After illustrating this procedure with an exceedingly obscure geometrical example, Socrates makes a lucid application of it to the ethical problem before them, and offers the Socratic thesis that virtue is knowledge as the hypothesis from which the teachability of virtue can be derived. The subsequent examination of this hypothesis comes to conclusions commentators have found frustratingly ambiguous. But the survival and development of the hypothetical method in *Phaedo* and *Republic* are enough to show Plato's conviction of its philosophical potential.

The slave boy episode is originally introduced by Socrates as a proof of something much more than the possibility of successful inquiry. The suggestion is that the best explanation of that possibility is provided by the doctrine of the immortality of the soul, a Pythagorean belief which makes the first of its many appearances in Plato's dialogues in *Meno* (see PSYCHĒ; PYTHAGORAS; PYTHAGOREANISM). More specifically, the idea as Socrates presents it is that the soul pre-exists the body, in a condition involving conscious possession of knowledge. On entry into the body it forgets what it knows, although it retains it as latent memory. Discovery of the sort of a priori knowledge characteristic of mathematics and (as Plato supposes) ethics is a matter of recollecting latent memory. This is just what happens to the slave boy: Socrates does not

impart knowledge to him; he works it out for himself by recovering it from within. Once again, although the Socrates of *Meno* does not in the end subscribe to belief in learning as recollection of innate knowledge, it is embraced without equivocation in *Phaedo*, as also in the later *Phaedrus*. But *what* exactly is recollected? *Phaedo* will say: knowledge of Forms. *Meno* by contrast offers no clues. The introduction of the theory of Forms is reserved for *Symposium*.

12 Symposium

Symposium has the widest appeal of all Plato's writings. No work of ancient Greek prose fiction can match its compulsive readability. Plato moves through a rich variety of registers, from knockabout comedy and literary parody to passages of disturbing fantasy or visionary elevation, culminating in a multiply paradoxical declaration of love for Socrates put in the mouth of a drunken Alcibiades. Love (*erōs*) is the theme of the succession of *encōmia* or eulogies delivered at the drinking party (*symposion*) hosted by the playwright Agathon: not sublimated 'Platonic' love between the sexes, but the homoerotic passion of a mature man for a younger or indeed a teenager. This continues until Aristophanes (one of the guests) and Socrates broaden and transform the discussion. Socrates' speech, which is a sort of anti-eulogy, develops a general theory of desire and its relation to beauty, and it is in this context that the idea of an eternal and changeless Form makes its first unequivocal appearance in Plato's *œuvre*. Thus Plato first declares himself a metaphysician not in a work devoted to philosophical argument, but in a highly rhetorical piece of writing, albeit one in which fashionable models of rhetoric are subverted.

Love and beauty are first connected in some of the earlier *encōmia*, and notably in Agathon's claim that among the gods 'Love is the happiest of them all, for he is the most beautiful and best' (195a). This thesis is subjected to elenchus by Socrates in the one argumentative section of the dialogue. Agathon is obliged to accept that love and desire are necessarily love and desire *for something*, namely, something they are in need of. Following his concession Socrates argues that beauty is not what love possesses but precisely the thing it is in need of. This argument constitutes the key move in the philosophy of the dialogue, which Plato elaborates in various ways through the medium of Diotima, the probably fictitious priestess from whom Socrates is made to claim he learned the art of love in which he has earlier (177d) claimed expertise. First she tells a myth representing Love as the offspring of poverty and resource, and so – according to her interpretation – occupying the dissatisfied inter-mediate position between ignorance and wisdom which characterizes philosophy: hence presumably the explanation of Socrates' claim to be an expert in love, since the pursuit of wisdom turns out to be the truest expression of love. Then she spells out the theoretical basis for this intellectualist construction of what love is. The theory has rightly been said to combine 'a psychology that is strictly or loosely Socratic with a metaphysics that is wholly Platonic' (see Price, *Mental Conflict* 1995).

This psychology holds that a person who desires something wants not so much the beautiful as the good, or more precisely happiness conceived as permanent possession of the good. Love is a particular species of desire, which occurs when perception of beauty makes us want to reproduce. (Socrates is made to express bafflement at this point: presumably an authorial device for indicating that Diotima's line of thought is now moving beyond anything Plato considered strictly Socratic.) Dio-tima goes on to explain that reproduction is the way mortal animals pursue immortality, interpreted in its turn in terms of the longing for permanent possession of good with which she has just identified desire. Other animals and many humans are content with physical reproduction, but humans are capable of *mental* creation when inspired by a beautiful body, and still more by a beautiful soul or personality. This is how the activities of poets and legislators and the virtuous are to be understood.

Perhaps Plato thought these ideas, although no longer Socratic, provided a convincing explanation of the drive which powered Socrates' philosophical activity in general, and made him spend so much time with beautiful young men in particular. However that may be, in what follows he has Diotima speak of greater mysteries which 'I do not know whether you [that is, Socrates] would be able to approach'. These are the subject of a lyrical account of how a true lover moves step by step from preoccupation with the beauty of a single beloved, to appreciating that there is one and the same beauty in all bodies and so loving them all, and then to seeing and loving beauty in souls or personalities and all manner of mental creations, until he 'turns to the great sea of beauty, and gazing upon this gives birth to many gloriously beautiful ideas and theories, in unstinting love of wisdom [that is, philosophy]' (210d). The final moment of illumina-tion arrives when the philosopher-lover grasps the Beautiful itself, an experience described as the fulfilment of all earlier exertions. Unlike other manifestations of beauty the Form of the Beautiful is something eternal, whose beauty is not qualified in place or time or relation or respect. It is just the one sort of thing it is, all on its own, whereas other things that are subject to change and decay are beautiful by participation in the Form. Only someone who has looked upon it will be capable of giving birth not to images of virtue (presumably the ideas and theories mentioned a little earlier), but to virtue itself, and so achieving immortality so far as any human can.

It is striking that the doctrine of the immortality of the soul forms no part of Diotima's argument. If we assume the scholarly consensus that *Symposium* postdates *Meno*, this poses something of a puzzle. One solution might be to suppose that, although *Meno* presents the doctrine, Plato is himself not yet wholly convinced of its truth, and so gives it no role in his account of the desire for immortality in *Symposium*. This solution might claim support from the fact that *Phaedo* takes upon itself the task of arguing the case for the immortality of the soul much more strenuously than in *Meno*, and in particular offers a much more careful and elaborate version of the argument from recollection. Addi-tionally or alternatively, we may note that when Plato presents the doctrine of the immortality of the soul in the dialogues, he always treats it as some-thing requiring explicit proof, unlike the theory of Forms, which generally figures as a hypothesis recommending itself by its explanatory power or its ability to meet the requirements of Plato's episte-mology. Since Diotima's discourse is not con-structed as argument but as the explication of an idea, it is not the sort of context which would readily accommodate the kind of demonstration Plato apparently thought imperative for discussion of the immortality of the soul.

13 Phaedo

The departure point for *Phaedo*'s consideration of the fate of the soul after death is very close to that idea of love as desire for wisdom which Diotima offers at the start of her speech in *Symposium*. For Socrates starts with the pursuit of wisdom, which he claims is really a preparation for death. This is because it consists of an attempt to escape the restrictions of the body so far as is possible, and to purify the soul from preoccupation with the senses and physical desires so that it can think about truth, and in particular about the Forms, which are accessible not to sense perception but only to thought. Pure knowledge of anything would actually require complete freedom from the body. So given that death is the separation of soul from body, the wisdom philosophers desire will be attainable in full only when they are dead. Hence for a philosopher death is no evil to be feared, but something for which the whole of life has been a training. The unbearably powerful death scene at the end of the dialogue presents Socrates as someone whose serenity and cheerfulness at the end bear witness to the truth of this valuation.

Symposium implied that a long process of intellectual and emotional reorientation was required if someone was to achieve a grasp of the Form of Beauty. *Phaedo* has sometimes been thought to take a different view: interpreters may read its argument about recollecting Forms as concerned with the general activity of concept formation in which we all engage early in life. In fact the passage restricts recollection of Forms to philosophers, and suggests that the knowledge they recover is not the basic ability to deploy concepts (which Plato seems in this period to think a function of sense experience), but hard-won philosophical understanding of what it is to be beautiful or good or just. The interlocutors voice the fear that once Socrates is dead there will be nobody left in possession of that knowledge; and the claim that pure knowledge of Forms is possible only after death coheres with the *Symposium* account very well, implying as it does that the path to philosophical enlightenment is not just long but a journey which cannot be completed in this life.

The proposal that the soul continues to exist apart from the body after death is immediately challenged by Socrates' interlocutors. Much of the rest of *Phaedo* is taken up with a sequence of arguments defending that proposal and the further contention that the soul is immortal, pre-existing the body and surviving its demise for ever. The longest and most ambitious of these arguments is the last of the set. It consists in an application of the method of hypothesis, which is explained again in a more elaborate version than that presented in *Meno*. The hypothesis chosen is the theory of Forms, or rather the idea that Forms function as explanations or causes of phenomena: beautiful things are beautiful by virtue of the Beautiful, large things large by virtue of the Large, and so on. Socrates is made to represent his reliance on this apparently uninformative or 'safe and simple' notion of causation as a position he has arrived at only after earlier intellectual disappointments: first with the inadequacies of Presocratic material causes, then with the failure of Anaxagoras' promise of a teleological explanation of why things are as they are (see ANAXAGORAS).

He soon goes on to argue however that the hypothesis can be used to generate a more sophisticated model of causation. Instead of proposing merely that (for example) hot things are hot by virtue of the Hot, we may legitimately venture the more specific explanation: 'Hot things are hot by virtue of fire', provided that it is true that wherever fire exists, it always heats things in its vicinity, being

itself hot and never cold. After elaborating this point Socrates is ready to apply the model to the case of life and soul. By parity of reasoning, we may assert that living things are alive not just in virtue of life, but in virtue of soul, given that wherever soul exists it makes things it occupies alive, being itself alive and never dead. From this assertion there appears to follow the conclusion whose derivation is the object of the exercise: if soul is always alive and never dead, it must be immortal (that is, incapable of death) and so imperishable.

Phaedo, like *Republic*, ends with a sombre myth of last judgment and reincarnation, designed primarily to drive home the moral implications of Plato's distinctive version of soul–body dualism. It reminds us of the Pythagorean origins of the doctrine of the immortality of the soul. Yet the Platonism of *Phaedo* owes a great deal also to the metaphysics of PARMENIDES. Both here and in *Symposium* the characterization of Forms as simple eternal beings, accessible only to thought, not the senses, and the contrast both dialogues make with the changing and contradictory world of phenomena, are couched in terms borrowed from Parmenides and the Eleatic tradition which he inaugurated. Platonism can accordingly be seen as the product of an attempt to understand a fundamentally Socratic conception of philosophy and the philosophical life in the light of reflection on these two powerful Presocratic traditions of thought, using the new methodological resources made available by geometry.

14 Republic

Republic is misleadingly titled. The Greek name of the dialogue is *Politeia*, which is the standard word for constitution or ordering of the political structure: 'political order' would give a better sense of what Plato has in mind. There is a further and deeper complication. Once you start reading the dialogue you find that it is primarily an inquiry into justice, conceived as a virtue or moral excellence of individual persons. The philosophical task it undertakes is the project of showing that justice so conceived is in the best interests of the just person, even if it brings nothing ordinarily recognizable as happiness or success, or indeed (as with the sentence of death passed on Socrates) quite the opposite. Thus *Republic* carries forward the thinking about justice begun in early dialogues such as *Apology*, *Crito* and *Gorgias*. Why, then, the title's suggestion that it is a work of political rather than moral philosophy?

One way of answering this question is to attend to the formal structure of *Republic*. After book I, an inconclusive Socratic dialogue which none the less introduces, particularly in the conversation with

Thrasymachus, many of the themes pursued in the rest of the work, the interlocutors agree to take an indirect approach to the problem of individual justice: they will consider the nature of justice and injustice in the *polis*, that is the (city-)state, in the hope that it will provide an illuminating analogy. Books II–IV spell out the class structure required in a 'good city'. It is suggested that in such a state political justice consists in the social harmony achieved when each class (economic, military, governing) performs its own and only its own function. This model is then applied to the individual soul (see PSYCHĒ). Justice and happiness for an individual are secured when each of the parts of the soul (appetite, emotion, reason) performs the role it should in mutual harmony. In working out the idea of psychic harmony, Plato formulates a conception of the complexity of psychological motivation, and of the structure of mental conflict, which leaves the simplicities of Socratic intellectualism far behind, and one which has reminded interpreters of Freudian theory, particularly in books VIII–IX. Here he examines different forms of *un*just political order (notably oligarchy, democracy and tyranny) and corresponding conditions of order, or rather increasing *dis*order, in the soul.

Political theory therefore plays a large part in the argument of the dialogue, even though the ultimate focus is the moral health of the soul, as is confirmed by the conclusion of book IX. Socrates suggests that it may not matter whether we can actually establish a truly just political order, provided we use the idea of it as a paradigm for founding a just city within our own selves.

This account of *Republic* omits the central books V–VII. These explore the notion of political order much further than is necessary for the purposes of inquiry into individual justice. This is where Plato develops the notion of a communistic governing class, involving the recruitment of talented women as well as men, the abolition of the family, and institution of a centrally controlled eugenic breeding programme. And it is where, in order to meet the problem of how the idea of the just city he has been elaborating might ever be put into practice, he has Socrates introduce philosopher-rulers:

> Unless either philosophers rule in our cities or those whom we now call rulers and potentates engage genuinely and adequately in philosophy, and political power and philosophy coincide, there is no end, my dear Glaucon, to troubles for our cities, nor I think for the human race.
>
> (*Republic* 473c–d)

What Plato perhaps has most in mind when he makes Socrates speak of 'troubles' is as well as civil war the corruption he sees in all existing societies. As he acknowledges, this makes the emergence of an upright philosopher-ruler an improbability – and incidentally leaves highly questionable the prospects of anyone but a Socrates developing moral order within the soul when society without is infected with moral disorder.

Here we touch on another broadly political preoccupation of *Republic*, worked out at various places in the dialogue. It offers among other things a radical critique of Greek cultural norms. This is highlighted in the censorship of Homer proposed in books II and III, and in the onslaught on the poets, particularly the dramatists, in book X, and in their expulsion from the ideal city. But these are only the more memorable episodes in a systematic attack on Greek beliefs about gods, heroes and the departed, on the ethical assumptions underlying music, dance and gymnastics (see MIMĒSIS), and again erotic courtship, and on medical and judicial practice. *Republic* substitutes its own austere state educational programme, initially focused on the training of the emotions, but subsequently (in books VI and VII) on mathematics and philosophy. Plato sees no hope for society or the human race without a wholesale reorientation, fostered by an absolute political authority, of all the ideals on which we set our hearts and minds.

Republic itself is written in such a way as to require the reader to be continually broadening perspectives on the huge range of concerns it embraces, from the banalities of its opening conversation between Socrates and the aged Cephalus to its Platonist explication of the very notion of philosophy in the epistemology and metaphysics of books V–VII. At the apex of the whole work Plato sets his presentation of the Form of the Good, as the ultimate goal of the understanding that philosophy pursues by use of the hypothetical method. The dialogue offers a symbol of its own progress in the potent symbol of the cave. We are like prisoners chained underground, who can see only shadows of images flickering on the wall. What we need is release from our mental shackles, and a conversion which will enable us gradually to clamber out into the world above and the sunlight. For then, by a sequence of painful reorientations, we may be able to grasp the Good and understand how it explains all that there is.

15 Critical dialogues

Parmenides is that rare phenomenon in philosophy: a self-critique. Plato here makes his own theory of Forms the subject of a penetrating scrutiny which today continues to command admiration for its ingenuity and insight. *Theaetetus* (datable to soon after 369 BC) also reverts to Plato's critical manner. It applies an enriched variant of the Socratic elenchus to a sequence of attempts to define knowledge. The confidence of *Phaedo* and *Republic* that Platonist philosophers are in possession of knowledge and can articulate what it consists in is nowhere in evidence, except in a rhetorical digression from the main argument. Methodological preoccupations are dominant in both works. *Parmenides* suggests that to defend the Forms against its critique, one would need to be much more practised in argument than is their proponent in this dialogue (a young Socrates fictively encountering a 65 year-old Parmenides and a middle-aged Zeno). And it sets out a specimen of the sort of exercise required, running to many pages of purely abstract reasoning modelled partly on the paradoxes of ZENO OF ELEA, partly on Parmenides' deductions in the Way of Truth (see PARMENIDES). *Theaetetus* likewise presents itself, initially more or less explicitly, later implicitly, as a model of how to go about testing a theory without sophistry and with due sympathy. While the conclusions achieved by this 'midwifery' – as Socrates here calls it – are as devastatingly negative as in the early dialogues, we learn much more philosophy along the way. Many readers find *Theaetetus* the most consistently rewarding of all the dialogues.

A sketch of the principal concerns of the two dialogues will bring out their radical character. *Parmenides* raises two main questions about Forms. First, are there Forms corresponding to every kind of predicate? Not just *one* and *large*, or *beautiful* and *just*, familiar from the middle period dialogues, but *man* and *fire*, or even *hair* and *dirt*? Socrates is represented as unclear about the issue. Second, the idea that other things we call for example 'large' or 'just' are related to the Form in question by participation is examined in a succession of arguments which seek to show that, however Forms or the participation relation are construed, logical absurdities of one kind or another result. The most intriguing of these has been known since Aristotle as the Third Man: if large things are large in virtue of something distinct from them, namely the Form of Large, then the Large itself and the other large things will be large in virtue of *another* Form of Large – and so on *ad infinitum*.

Theaetetus devotes much of its space to considering the proposal that knowledge is nothing but sense perception, or rather to developing and examining two theories with which that proposal is taken to be equivalent: the view of Protagoras that truth is relative, since 'man is the measure of all things', and that of Heraclitus that everything is in flux, here considered primarily in application to the nature of sense perception. The dialogue is home to

some of Plato's most memorable arguments and analogies. For example, Protagoreanism is attacked by the brilliant (although perhaps flawed) self-refutation argument: if man is the measure of *all* things, then the doctrine of the relativity of truth is itself true only in so far as it is believed to be true; but since people in general believe it to be false, it must be false. The next section of *Theaetetus* worries about the coherence of the concept of false belief. Here the soul is compared to a wax tablet, with false belief construed as a mismatch between current perceptions and those inscribed on the tablet, or again to an aviary, where false belief is an unsuccessful attempt to catch the right bird (that is, piece of knowledge). In the final section the interlocutors explore the suggestion that knowledge must involve the sort of complexity that can be expressed in a *logos* or statement. Socrates' 'dream' that such knowledge must be built out of unknowable simples fascinated WITTGENSTEIN (§5), who saw in it an anticipation of the theory of his *Tractatus*.

Are we to infer that in opening or reopening questions of this kind Plato indicates that he is himself in a real quandary about knowledge and the Forms? Or is his main target philosophical complacency in his readers, as needing to be reminded that no position is worth much if it cannot be defended in strenuous argument? Certainly in the other two dialogues grouped here with *Parmenides* and *Theaetetus* the theory of Forms is again in evidence, presented as a view the author is commending to the reader's intellectual sympathies. *Cratylus* is a work whose closest philosophical connections are with *Theaetetus*, although its relative date among the dialogues is disputed. It is a pioneering debate between rival theories of what makes a word for a thing the right word for it: convention or, as Cratylus holds, a natural appropriateness – sound somehow mirroring essence. Underlying Cratylus' position is an obscurely motivated commitment to the truth of Heracliteanism. For present purposes what is of interest is the final page of the dialogue, which takes the theory of Forms as premise for an argument showing that the idea of an absolutely universal Heraclitean flux is unsustainable. As for *Phaedrus*, it contains one of the most elevated passages of prose about the Forms that Plato ever wrote.

The context is an exemplary rhetorical exercise in which *Symposium*'s treatment of the philosophical lover's attraction to beauty is reworked in the light of *Republic*'s tripartition of the soul. Subsequently Plato has Socrates dismiss the speech as 'play', useful only for the methodological morals about rhetorical procedure we happen to be able to derive from it – together with a preceding denunciation of love by

Socrates, capping one by his interlocutor Phaedrus – if we are dialecticians. This comment has led some readers to conjecture that Phaedrus accordingly marks Plato's formal leave-taking of the theory of Forms: in retrospect he sees it more as rhetoric than as philosophy or dialectic, which will henceforward confine itself to something apparently less inspiring – the patient, thorough, comprehensive study of similarities and differences. Yet Phaedrus is pre-eminently a dialogue written not to disclose its author's mind, but to make demands on that of the sophisticated reader. Perhaps Socrates' great speech on the philosophical lover is 'play' not absolutely, but only relative to the controlling and unifying preoccupation of the dialogue, which is to work through a fresh examination of rhetoric, going beyond Gorgias in explaining how it can be a genuine form of expertise, based on knowledge of truth and variously geared to the various psycho-logical types to which oratory addresses itself. We might speculate that Plato writes the speech as he does precisely because he thinks or hopes many of his readers will be of a type persuadable to the philosophical life by its vision of the soul's desire for the Beautiful.

16 Later dialogues

The theory of Forms also figures prominently in Timaeus. Timaeus is Plato's one venture into physical theory, and appropriately has in the Italian Greek Timaeus someone other than Socrates as main speaker. It is presented as an introduction to the story of Atlantis, allegedly an island power defeated by the prehistoric Athenians, and mentioned only by Plato among the classical Greek authors. The conflict between Atlantis and Athens was to be the subject of Critias, conceived as a dialogue that would demonstrate the political philosophy of Republic in practice. But Critias was never com-pleted, so Timaeus stands as an independent work.

The argument of Timaeus is based on the premise that the universe is not eternal but created – although debate has raged from antiquity onwards whether this means created in time, or timelessly dependent on a first cause. From the order and beauty of the universe Plato infers a good creator or craftsman (dēmiourgos), working on pre-existing materials (with their own random but necessary motions) from an eternal blueprint encoding life and intelligence: namely, the Form of Animal. The greater part of Timaeus consists in an account of how first the universe (conceived of as a living creature), then humans, are designed from the blueprint for the best. Much use is made of mathematical models, for example for the move-ments of the heavenly bodies and the atomistic

construction of the four elements from triangular surfaces. The account is presented as inevitably only a 'likely story', incapable of the irrefutable truth of metaphysics.

There is no more austere or profound work of metaphysics in Plato's œuvre than Sophist. Like many of the post-Republic dialogues it is 'professional' philosophy, probably written primarily for Plato's students and associates in the Academy. The style of Sophist and the remaining works to be discussed is syntactically tortuous and overloaded with abstrac-tion and periphrasis; they are altogether lacking in literary graces or dramatic properties which might commend them to a wider readership. Sophist's main speaker is a stranger from Elea, symbolizing the Parmenidean provenance of the problem at the heart of the long central section of the dialogue: how is it possible to speak of what is not (see PARMENIDES)? This puzzle is applied for example both to the unreality of images and to falsehood, understood as what is not the case. The solution Plato offers required some revolutionary moves in philosophical logic, such as the explicit differentia-tion of identity from predication, and the idea that subject and predicate play different roles in the syntax of the sentence. These innovations and their bearing on analysis of the verb 'to be' have made Sophist the subject of some of the most challenging writing on Plato in the twentieth century.

The companion dialogue Politicus or Statesman addresses more squarely than Republic did the practical as distinct from the theoretical knowledge of the ideal statesman. Its contribution to this topic consists of three major claims. First is the rejection of the sovereignty of law. Plato has nothing against law as a convenient but imprecise rule of thumb in the hands of an expert statesman, provided it does not prevent him using his expertise. Making law sovereign, on the other hand, would be like preferring strict adherence to a handbook of navigation or a medical textbook to the judgment of the expert seafarer or doctor. If you have no such expert available, a constitution based on adherence to law is better than lawlessness, but that is not saying much. What law cannot do that expert rulers can and must is judge the kairos: discern the right and the wrong 'moment' to undertake a great enterprise of state. This proposition follows from the second of Plato's key claims, which is represented as one true of all practical arts: real expertise consists not of measuring larger and smaller, but in determining the norm between excess and defect – a notion which we ordinarily think more Aristotelian than Platonic (see ARIS-TOTLE §22), although it recurs in a different guise in Philebus. Finally, Plato thinks we shall only get our thinking straight on this as on any matter if we find the right – usually homely – model. *Statesman* makes the statesman a sort of weaver. There are two strands to the analogy. First, like weaving statesmanship calls upon many subordinate skills. Its job is not to be doing things itself, but to control all the subordinate functions of government, and by its concern for the laws and every other aspect of the city weave all these strands together. Second, the opposing temperaments of the citizens are what most need weaving together if civil strife is to be avoided, and (as in *Republic*) expert rulers will use education and eugenics to that end.

Statesman shares themes with both *Philebus* and *Laws*. *Philebus* is the one late dialogue in which Socrates is principal speaker, as befits its ethical topic: the question whether pleasure or understanding is the good, or at least the more important ingredient in the good life. After so much insistence in middle-period dialogues on the Form as a unity distinct from the plurality of the phenomena, it comes as a shock to find Socrates stressing at the outset that there is no merit in reiterating that pleasure or understanding is a unity. The skill resides in being able to determine what and how many forms of understanding and pleasure there are. What *Philebus* goes on to offer next is a model for thinking about how any complex structure is produced, whether a piece of music or the universe itself. It requires an intelligent cause creating a mixture by imposing limit and proportion on something indeterminate. This requirement already indicates the main lines of the answer to our problem, at any rate, if it is accepted that pleasure is intrinsically indeterminate. Clearly intelligence and understanding will be shaping forces in the good life, but pleasures are only admissible if suitably controlled. At the adjudication at the end of the dialogue, this is just the result we get. The majority of the many forms of pleasure defined and examined in the course of the dialogue are rejected. They do not satisfy the criteria of measure and proportion which are the marks of the good.

17 Laws

The vast *Laws* is in its way the most extraordinary of all Plato's later writings, not for its inspiration (which flags) but for its evidence of tireless fascination with things political. Its relation to *Republic* and *Statesman* has been much debated. What is clear is that Plato is legislating – through the last eight of its twelve long books – for a second best to the ideal state and ideal statesman of *Republic*, with greater zeal than *Statesman* might have led one to expect. Is this because he has lost faith in those ideals, which still seemed alive in *Statesman* at least as ideals? That view is in danger of overlooking

Republic's own indication that it would be wrong to expect in practice anything but an approximation of the ideal.

And an approximation is precisely what the *Laws* presents. Communistic institutions are abandoned, but land holdings are to be equalized to guard against the division between rich and poor which *Republic* saw as the most severe threat to social harmony, and land is to be used as though it were the common property of the whole city. The family is reinstated, but women are not therefore regarded as confined to domestic concerns – they are still to be regarded as half of the city's whole human resource. Educational provisions are given even greater prominence than in *Republic*. They deal explicitly with what *Republic* left largely undiscussed: the irrationality of human nature and the prospects for bringing it under rational control.

If the ideal city of *Republic* is a community shaped and governed by philosophy, *Laws* founds the second-best state on religion. The very first word of the whole work is 'God', and in one way or another religion not philosophy dominates the discussion. The interlocutors are pious elderly men, two of them from the cultural backwaters of Sparta and Crete and without any prior experience of philosophy at all. Together with a more philosophically sophisticated Athenian Stranger they are engaged on a journey to the shrine of Zeus on Mount Ida in Crete, making this the only Platonic dialogue set outside Athens. The city whose constitution and laws they are represented as establishing is to be a theocracy; and the first thing its original settlers are to understand is the need for all their conduct to be governed by consideration of divine justice. In a famous anti-Protagorean phrase they are instructed that 'God is the measure of all things'.

It is already clear by this stage (Book IV) that what Plato has in mind here is not undiluted traditional religion. The theological vocabulary employed is mainly the language of Orphic and Pythagorean rationalized religion; and by theocracy Plato indicates that he means the rule of reason as embodied in law. Moreover, when the Athenian Stranger turns next to consider the principles of legislation, he introduces a novel idea which perhaps constitutes the most interesting proposal in the dialogue. It is the notion of a 'prelude' to a law, which is the attempt the legislator should make to *persuade* citizens, albeit not always by rational means, of the necessity of the prescriptions of the law itself. Here is a theme which relates interestingly to conceptions of reason, necessity and persuasion found in several other dialogues, notably *Republic* and *Timaeus*. In due course the Athenian Stranger will give a reasoned justification of the religious assumptions which underpin his whole approach to legislation. In Book X, presented as an extended 'prelude' to laws against impiety, Plato imagines an atheist challenge to the whole religious framework of his enterprise, and in response develops an unequivocally philosophical argument for a natural theology which posits soul as divine first cause of motion and change in the universe.

Plato seems to have wanted two things above all of the discourse he developed in the *Laws*: first, that it should reflect and embody a sense of a transcendent moral framework for political and social existence; second, that it should be capable of being persuasive –because *inter alia* generally intelligible – to a population at large, not to just an intellectual elite. As he judged the matter, it was religious discourse, reformed and redirected as necessary, which could most palpably meet these two requirements.

18 Plato's influence

Plato's influence pervades much of subsequent Western literature and thought. Aristotle was among those who came to listen to him in the 'school' he founded in the Academy; and a great deal of Aristotle's work is conceived in explicit or implicit response to Plato. Other philosophical traditions flourished after Aristotle's time in the last centuries BC, and the Academy of the period read Plato through sceptical spectacles. But from the first century AD onwards Platonism in various forms, often syncretistic, became the dominant philosophy of the Roman Empire (see PLATONISM, EARLY AND MIDDLE), especially with the rise of Neoplatonism in late antiquity (see NEOPLATONISM). Some of the Fathers of the early Greek Church articulated their theologies in Platonist terms; and through Augustine in particular Plato shaped, for example, the Western Church's conception of time and eternity (see PATRISTIC PHILOSOPHY). A Neoplatonist version of him prevailed among the Arabs.

With the translation of Plato into Latin in the high Middle Ages and the revival of Greek studies in the Renaissance, Platonism (again in a Neoplatonic guise) once more gripped the minds of learned thinkers in the West, for example at the Medici court in fifteenth-century Florence. But none of the great philosophers of the modern era has been a Platonist, even if Plato was an important presence in the thought of a Leibniz or a Hegel or a Russell. Probably he has never been studied more intensively than in the late twentieth and early twenty-first centuries. Thanks to the availability of cheap translations in every major language and to his position as the first great philosopher in the Western canon, he figures in most introductory

courses offered every year to tens of thousands of students throughout the developed world.

See also: FORMS, PLATONIC; INNATENESS IN ANCIENT PHILOSOPHY; NEOPLATONISM; PLATONISM, RENAISSANCE; TECHNÊ

References and further reading

Fine, G. (1999) *Plato 1, Plato 2*, Oxford: Oxford University Press. (Two volumes of important articles on the main aspects of Plato's thought, all first published in the last thirty years of the twentieth century; they include extensive selected bibliographies.)

Grube, G. (1980) *Plato's Thought*, London: Athlone Press. (Accessible introductory account of Plato's thought, with new introduction and bibliography by D. Zeyl.)

Guthrie, W.K.C. (1975, 1978) *A History of Greek Philosophy, vol. 4, Plato, The Man and his Dialogues: Earlier Period, vol. 5, The Later Plato and the Academy*, Cambridge: Cambridge University Press. (The Plato volumes of the most detailed and comprehensive English-language account of Greek philosophy; indispensable for bibliography and general orientation; volume 5 includes an assessment of the Tübingen school's interpretation of Plato.)

MALCOLM SCHOFIELD

PLATONISM, RENAISSANCE

Though it never successfully challenged the dominance of Aristotelian school philosophy, the revival of Plato and Platonism was an important phenomenon in the philosophical life of the Renaissance and contributed much to the new, more pluralistic philosophical climate of the fifteenth and sixteenth centuries. Medieval philosophers had had access only to a few works by Plato himself, and, while the indirect influence of the Platonic tradition was pervasive, few if any Western medieval philosophers identified themselves as Platonists. In the Renaissance, by contrast, Western thinkers had access to the complete corpus of Plato's works as well as to the works of Plotinus and many late ancient Platonists; there was also a small but influential group of thinkers who identified themselves as Christian Platonists. In the fifteenth century, the most important of these were to be found in the circles of Cardinal Bessarion (1403–72) in Rome and of Marsilio Ficino (1433–99) in Florence. Platonic themes were also central to the philosophies of Nicholas of Cusa (1401–64) and Giovanni Pico della Mirandola (1463–94), the two most powerful and original thinkers of the Quattrocento. While the dominant interpretation of the Platonic dialogues throughout the Renaissance remained Neoplatonic, there was also a minority tradition that revived the sceptical interpretation of the dialogues that had been characteristic of the early Hellenistic Academy.

In the sixteenth century Platonism became a kind of 'countercultural' phenomenon, and Plato came to be an important authority for scientists and cosmologists who wished to challenge the Aristotelian mainstream: men like Copernicus, Giordano Bruno, Francesco Patrizi and Galileo. Nevertheless, the Platonic dialogues were rarely taught in the humanistic schools of fifteenth-century Italy. Plato was established as an important school author in the sixteenth century, first at the University of Paris and later in German universities. In Italy chairs of Platonic philosophy began to be established for the first time in the 1570s. Although the hegemony of Aristotelianism was in the end broken by the new philosophy of the seventeenth century, Plato's authority did much to loosen the grip of Aristotle on the teaching of natural philosophy in the universities of late Renaissance Europe.

See also: HUMANISM, RENAISSANCE; FICINO, M.; FORMS, PLATONIC; PICO DELLA MIRANDOLA, G.; PLATO

JAMES HANKINS

PLEASURE

From Plato and beyond, pleasure has been thought to be a basic, and sometimes the only basic, reason for doing anything. Since there are many forms that pleasure can take and many individual views of what pleasure consists in, much attention has been given to how pleasures may be distinguished, what their motivational and moral significance might be, and whether there may not be some objective determination of them, whether some may be good or bad, or some better as pleasures than others.

But first there is the question of what pleasure is. It has been variously thought to be a state of mind like distress only of the opposite polarity; merely the absence or cessation of or freedom from pain; a kind of quiescence like contentment; or the experiencing of bodily sensations which, unlike sensations of pain, one does not want to stop. We also identify and class together particular sources of pleasure and call them pleasures of the table, company, sex, conversation, solitude, competition, contemplation or athletic pleasures. In this sense there may be some pleasures which we do not enjoy. But most generally pleasure is what we feel and take when we do enjoy something. This raises the questions of what is encompassed by 'something', what it is to enjoy anything, and the extent to which theories of

pleasure can accommodate both our passivity and activity in pleasure. The most influential theories have been those of Plato, Aristotle and empiricists such as Hume and Bentham.

GRAEME MARSHALL

PLEKHANOV, GEORGII VALENTINOVICH (1857–1918)

Known as 'the Father of Russian Marxism', Plekhanov was the chief popularizer and interpreter of Marxism in Russia in the 1880s. His interest in the philosophical aspects of Marxism made him influential outside as well as inside Russia. He was a prolific writer, and dealt with several aspects of Marxist thought.

Plekhanov was an important figure in the Russian revolutionary movement. He was a founder member of the Russian Social Democratic Party, and a leading figure in its Menshevik wing after it split into Bolsheviks and Mensheviks in 1903. As a politician, Plekhanov was constantly involved in polemics with political and ideological opponents. Most of his theoretical works are to some degree polemical, and it was the conflicts among Russian revolutionary groups that shaped Plekhanov's interpretation of Marx's thought.

A basic feature of this interpretation was that Russia's historical development was like that of Western European countries, and would pass through a capitalist phase before progressing to socialism. Accordingly, Plekhanov gave prominence to those of Marx's writings which could be presented in a deterministic way. Plekhanov insisted that Marxism was a materialist doctrine (as opposed to an idealist one) and as such recognized the primacy of matter in all spheres of existence.

Plekhanov was in many ways an innovator, being the writer who first coined the term 'dialectical materialism', and who drew attention to the Hegelian origins of Marx's system. His writings were quickly translated into several European languages. His interpretation of Marxism was much admired by Lenin, and was to form the basis of the official ideology of the Soviet Union. The conception of Marxism that Plekhanov propounded continues to exercise a profound influence on conceptions of Marxism throughout the world.

JAMES D. WHITE

PLOTINUS (AD 204/5–70)

Plotinus was the founder of Neoplatonism, the dominant philosophical movement of the Graeco-Roman world in late antiquity, and the most significant thinker of the movement. He is sometimes described as the last great pagan philosopher. His writings, the so-called *Enneads*, are preserved as whole. While an earnest follower of Plato, he reveals other philosophical influences as well, in particular those of Aristotle and Stoicism. Plotinus developed a metaphysics of intelligible causes of the sensible world and the human soul. The ultimate cause of everything is 'the One' or 'the Good'. It is absolutely simple and cannot be grasped by thought or given any positive determination. The One has as its external act the universal mind or 'Intellect'. The Intellect's thoughts are the Platonic Forms, the eternal and unchanging paradigms of which sensible things are imperfect images. This thinking of the forms is Intellect's internal activity. Its external act is a level of cosmic soul, which produces the sensible realm and gives life to the embodied organisms in it. Soul is thus the lowest intelligible cause that is immediately in contact with the sensible realm. Plotinus, however, insists that the soul retains its intelligible character such as nonspatiality and unchangeability through its dealings with the sensible. Thus he is an ardent soul–body dualist. Human beings stand on the border between the realms: through their bodily life they belong to the sensible, but the human soul has its roots in the intelligible realm. Plotinus sees philosophy as the vehicle of the soul's return to its intelligible roots. While standing firmly in the tradition of Greek rationalism and being a philosopher of unusual abilities himself, Plotinus shares some of the spirit of the religious salvation movements characteristic of his epoch.

See also: FORMS, PLATONIC; NEOPLATONISM

EYJÓLFUR KJALAR EMILSSON

PLURALISM

'Pluralism' is a broad term, applicable to any doctrine which maintains that there are ultimately many things, or many kinds of thing; in both these senses it is opposed to 'monism'. Its commonest use in late twentieth-century philosophy is to describe views which recognize many sets of equally correct beliefs or evaluative standards; and in this sense it is akin to 'relativism'. Societies are sometimes called 'pluralistic', meaning that they incorporate a variety of ways of life, moral standards and religions; one who sees this not as undesirable confusion but a proper state of things, espouses pluralism.

See also: CITIZENSHIP; MONISM; MULTICULTURALISM; POSTMODERNISM; PRAGMATISM; RELATIVISM; TOLERATION

EDWARD CRAIG

PNEUMA

Pneuma, 'spirit', derives from the Greek verb *pneo*, which indicates blowing or breathing. Since breathing is necessary for life and consciousness, *pneuma* came to denote not only wind and breath but various vital functions, including sensation and thought, and was understood by some philosophers as a cosmological principle. It became especially important in Stoicism, which explained the world in terms of matter and the rational structure exhibited in all its forms; this is established by rhythmical variations in the *tonos* or 'tension' of the *pneuma*.

In Hebrew tradition, where Greek was used, *pneuma* stood for life, consciousness, and for invisible conscious agents, angels or demons. In Christian thought it denotes divine inspiration, in particular the Holy Spirit acknowledged as a divine Person. At *John* 4: 24 it is used, unusually, to describe God himself.

CHRISTOPHER STEAD

POETRY

Though poetry today seems a relatively marginal topic in philosophy, it was crucial for philosophy's own initial self-definition. In ancient Greece, poetry was revered as the authoritative expression of sacred myth and traditional wisdom. With Socrates and Plato, philosophy began by distinguishing itself from poetry as a new, superior form of knowledge which could provide better guidance for life and even superior pleasure. Just as the sophists were attacked for relativism and deception, so were poets stridently criticized for irrationality and falsehood. For Plato, not only did poetry stem from and appeal to the emotional, unreasoning aspects of human nature; it was also far removed from truth, being only an imitation of our world of appearances which itself was but an imitation of the real world of ideas or forms. He therefore insisted that poets be banished from his ideal state because they threatened its proper governance by reason and philosophy.

Subsequent philosophy of poetry has been devoted to overcoming Plato's condemnatory theory, while tending to confirm philosophy's superiority. This task, begun by Aristotle, was for a long time pursued primarily under Plato's general model of poetry (and indeed all art) as imitation or *mimesis*. The main strategy here was to argue that what poetry imitates or represents is more than mere superficial appearance, but rather general essences or the ideas themselves. For such theories, poetry's relation to truth is crucial. Other theories were later developed that preferred to define and justify poetry in terms of formal properties or expression, or its distinctively beneficial effects on its audience. These strategies became increasingly influential from the time of Romanticism, but can be traced back to more ancient sources.

The vast majority of theories follow Plato in treating poetry as a distinct domain, separate from and subordinate to philosophy. But since Romanticism, some have argued for the essential unity of these two enterprises. Great philosophy is here seen as the poetic creation of new ways of thinking and new forms of language, and the role of poetry as uniting and gathering things together so that the truth and presence of being shines forth.

See also: ARISTOTLE §29; ARTISTIC EXPRESSION; HEGEL, G.W.F. §8; LESSING, G.E.

RICHARD M. SHUSTERMAN

POINCARÉ, JULES HENRI (1854–1912)

Although primarily a mathematician, Henri Poincaré wrote and lectured extensively on astronomy, theoretical physics, philosophy of science and philosophy of mathematics at the turn of the century. In philosophy, Poincaré is famous for the conventionalist thesis that we may choose either Euclidean or non-Euclidean geometry in physics, claiming that space is neither Euclidean nor non-Euclidean and that geometry is neither true nor false. However, Poincaré's conventionalism was not global, as some have claimed. Poincaré held that only geometry and perhaps a few principles of mechanics are conventional, and argued that science does discover truth, despite a conventional element.

Poincaré followed new developments in mathematics and physics closely and was involved in discussion of the foundations of mathematics and in the development of the theory of relativity. He was an important transitional figure in both of these areas, sometimes seeming ahead of his time and sometimes seeming very traditional. Perhaps because of the breadth of his views or because of the way in which philosophers focused on issues or small pieces of his work rather than on accurate history, interpretations of Poincaré vary greatly. Frequently cited by the logical positivists as a precursor, and widely discussed in the philosophy of science and the philosophy of mathematics, Poincaré's writings have had a strong impact on English-language philosophy.

See also: CONVENTIONALISM

DAVID J. STUMP

POINSOT, JOHN
See JOHN OF ST THOMAS

POLANYI, MICHAEL (1891–1976)

Michael Polanyi was almost unique among philosophers in not only fully acknowledging but in arguing from the tacit dimensions of our knowledge which concern the many things which we know but cannot state nor even identify. He argued that our knowledge is a tacit, personal integration of subsidiary clues into a focal whole, and he elaborated this structure of knowing into a corresponding ontology and cosmology of a world of comprehensive entities and actions which are integrations of lower levels into higher ones. Polanyi used these accounts of knowing and being to argue against the 'critical' demands for impersonal, wholly objective and fully explicit knowledge, against reductionist attempts to explain higher levels in terms of lower ones, and to defend the freedom of scientific research and a free society generally.

R.T. ALLEN

POLITICAL PHILOSOPHY

Introduction

Political philosophy can be defined as philosophical reflection on how best to arrange our collective life – our political institutions and our social practices, such as our economic system and our pattern of family life. (Sometimes a distinction is made between *political* and *social* philosophy, but I shall use 'political philosophy' in a broad sense to include both.) Political philosophers seek to establish basic principles that will, for instance, justify a particular form of state, show that individuals have certain inalienable rights, or tell us how a society's material resources should be shared among its members. This usually involves analysing and interpreting ideas like freedom, justice, authority and democracy and then applying them in a critical way to the social and political institutions that currently exist. Some political philosophers have tried primarily to justify the prevailing arrangements of their society; others have painted pictures of an ideal state or an ideal social world that is very different from anything we have so far experienced (see UTOPIANISM).

Political philosophy has been practised for as long as human beings have regarded their collective arrangements not as immutable and part of the natural order but as potentially open to change, and therefore as standing in need of philosophical justification. It can be found in many different cultures, and has taken a wide variety of forms. There are two reasons for this diversity. First, the methods and approaches used by political philosophers reflect the general philosophical tendencies of their epoch. Developments in epistemology and ethics, for instance, alter the assumptions on which political philosophy can proceed. But second, the political philosopher's agenda is largely set by the pressing political issues of the day. In medieval Europe, for instance, the proper relationship between Church and State became a central issue in political philosophy; in the early modern period the main argument was between defenders of absolutism and those who sought to justify a limited, constitutional state. In the nineteenth century, the social question – the question of how an industrial society should organize its economy and its welfare system – came to the fore. When we study the history of political philosophy, therefore, we find that alongside some perennial questions – how can one person ever justifiably claim the authority to govern another person, for instance – there are some big changes: in the issues addressed, in the language used to address them, and in the underlying premises on which the political philosopher rests his or her argument. (For the development of the Western tradition of political philosophy, see POLITICAL PHILOSOPHY, HISTORY OF.)

One question that immediately arises is whether the principles that political philosophers establish are to be regarded as having universal validity, or whether they should be seen as expressing the assumptions and the values of a particular political community. This question about the scope and status of political philosophy has been fiercely debated in recent years. It is closely connected to a question about human nature (see HUMAN NATURE). In order to justify a set of collective arrangements, a political philosophy must say something about the nature of human beings, about their needs, their capacities, about whether they are mainly selfish or mainly altruistic, and so forth. But can we discover common traits in human beings everywhere, or are people's characters predominantly shaped by the particular culture they belong to?

If we examine the main works of political philosophy in past centuries, they can be divided roughly into two categories. On the one hand there are those produced by philosophers elaborating general philosophical systems, whose political philosophy flows out of and forms an integral part of those systems. Leading philosophers who have made substantial contributions to political thought include PLATO, ARISTOTLE, AUGUSTINE, AQUINAS, HOBBES, LOCKE, HUME, HEGEL and J.S. MILL. On the other hand there are social and political thinkers whose contribution to philosophy as a whole has had little lasting significance, but who have made influential contributions to

political philosophy specifically. In this category we may include CICERO, Marsilius of Padua, MACHIAVELLI, GROTIUS, ROUSSEAU, BENTHAM, FICHTE and MARX. Two important figures whose work reflects non-Western influences are Ibn Khaldhun and Kauṭilya. Among the most important twentieth-century political thinkers are ARENDT, BERLIN, DEWEY, FOUCAULT, Gandhi, Gramsci, HABERMAS, Hayek, Oakeshott, RAWLS, SARTRE and TAYLOR.

> 1 Political institutions and ideologies
> 2 Contemporary political philosophy

1 Political institutions and ideologies

What are the issues that, historically and today, have most exercised political philosophers? To begin with, there is a set of questions about how political institutions should be arranged. Today we would think of this as an inquiry into the best form of state, though we should note that the state itself is a particular kind of political arrangement of relatively recent origin – for most of their history human beings have not been governed by states (see STATE, THE). Since all states claim AUTHORITY over their subjects, two fundamental issues are the very meaning of authority, and the criteria by which we can judge forms of political rule legitimate (see LEGITIMACY; CONTRACTARIANISM; TRADITION AND TRADITIONALISM). Connected to this is the issue of whether individual subjects have a moral obligation to obey the laws of their state (see OBLIGATION, POLITICAL), and of the circumstances under which politically-inspired disobedience is justifiable (see CIVIL DISOBEDIENCE; REVOLUTION). Next there is a series of questions about the form that the state should take: whether authority should be absolute or constitutionally limited (see ABSOLUTISM; CONSTITUTIONALISM); whether its structure should be unitary or federal (see FEDERALISM AND CONFEDERALISM); whether it should be democratically controlled, and if so by what means (see DEMOCRACY; REPRESENTATION, POLITICAL). Finally there is the question of whether any general limits can be set to the authority of the state – whether there are areas of individual freedom or privacy that the state must never invade on any pretext (see FREEDOM OF SPEECH; COERCION; PROPERTY; SLAVERY), and whether there are subjects such as religious doctrine on which the state must adopt a strictly neutral posture (see NEUTRALITY, POLITICAL; TOLERATION).

Beyond the question of how the state itself should be constituted lies the question of the general principles that should guide its decisions.

What values should inform economic and social policy for instance? Part of the political philosopher's task is to examine ideas that are often appealed to in political argument but whose meaning remains obscure, so that they can be used by politicians from rival camps to justify radically contrasting policies. Political philosophers try to give a clear and coherent account of notions such as EQUALITY, FREEDOM AND LIBERTY, JUSTICE, Needs and interests, Public interest, RIGHTS and WELFARE. And they also try to determine whether these ideas are consistent with, or conflict with, one another – whether, for instance, equality and liberty are competing values, or whether a society might be both free and equal at once.

Further questions arise about the principles that should guide one state in its dealings with other states. May states legitimately pursue what they regard as their national interests, or are they bound to recognize ethical obligations towards one another? More widely, should we be seeking a cosmopolitan alternative under which principles of justice would be applied at global level? (See INTERNATIONAL RELATIONS, PHILOSOPHY OF; GLOBALIZATION.) When, if ever, are states justified in going to war with each other? (See WAR AND PEACE, PHILOSOPHY OF.)

Over about the last two centuries, political debate has most often been conducted within the general frameworks supplied by rival ideologies. We can think of an ideology as a set of beliefs about the social and political world which simultaneously makes sense of what is going on, and guides our practical responses to it (see IDEOLOGY). Ideologies are often rather loosely structured, so that two people who are both conservatives, say, may reach quite different conclusions about some concrete issue of policy. Nevertheless they seem to be indispensable as simplifying devices for thinking about a political world of ever-increasing complexity.

No political philosopher can break free entirely from the grip of ideology, but political philosophy must involve a more critical scrutiny of the intellectual links that hold ideologies together, and a bringing to light of the unstated assumptions that underpin them. The most influential of these ideologies have been LIBERALISM, CONSERVATISM, SOCIALISM, nationalism (see NATION AND NATIONALISM) and Marxism (see MARXISM, WESTERN; MARXIST PHILOSOPHY, RUSSIAN AND SOVIET). Other ideologies are of lesser political significance, either because they have drawn fewer adherents or because they have been influential over a shorter period of time (see ANARCHISM, COMMUNISM, FASCISM, LIBERTARIANISM, REPUBLICANISM, SOCIAL DEMOCRACY and TOTALITARIANISM).

2 Contemporary political philosophy

The last quarter of the twentieth century has seen a powerful revival of political philosophy, which in Western societies at least has mostly been conducted within a broadly liberal framework. Other ideologies have been outflanked: Marxism has gone into a rapid decline, and conservatism and socialism have survived only by taking on board large portions of liberalism. Some have claimed that the main rival to liberalism is now communitarianism (see COMMUNITY AND COMMUNITARIANISM); however on closer inspection the so-called liberal – communitarian debate can be seen to be less a debate about liberalism itself than about the precise status and form that a liberal political philosophy should take – whether, for example, it should claim universal validity, or should present itself simply as an interpretation of the political culture of the Western liberal democracies. The vitality of political philosophy is not to be explained by the emergence of a new ideological revival to liberalism, but by the fact that a new set of political issues has arisen whose resolution will stretch the intellectual resources of liberalism to the limit.

What are these issues? The first is the issue of social justice, which in one form or another has dominated political philosophy for much of the century. Most of the many liberal theories of justice on offer have had a broadly egalitarian flavour, demanding at least the partial offsetting of the economic and social inequalities thrown up by an unfettered market economy (see MARKET, ETHICS OF THE; JUSTICE; RAWLS, J.; DWORKIN, R.; though for dissenting views see NOZICK, R.). These theories rested on the assumption that social and economic policy could be pursued largely within the borders of a self-contained political community, sheltered from the world market. This assumption has become increasingly questionable, and it presents liberals with the following dilemma: if the pursuit of social justice is integral to liberalism, how can this be now be reconciled with individual freedoms to move, communicate, work and trade across state boundaries?

The second issue is posed by feminism, and especially the feminist challenge to the conventional liberal distinction between public and private spheres (see FEMINIST POLITICAL PHILOSOPHY). In many respects feminism and liberalism are natural allies, but when feminists argue for fundamental changes in the way men and women conduct their personal relationships, or advocate affirmative action policies for employment that seem to contravene firmly-entrenched liberal principles of desert and merit, they pose major challenges to liberal political philosophy.

Third, there is a set of issues arising from what we might call the new politics of cultural identity.

Many groups in contemporary societies now demand that political institutions should be altered to reflect and express their distinctive cultures; these include, on the one hand, nationalist groups asserting that political boundaries should be redrawn to give them a greater measure of self-determination, and on the other cultural minorities whose complaint is that public institutions fail to show equal respect for those attributes that distinguish them from the majority (for instance their language or religion) (see NATION AND NATIONALISM; MULTICULTURALISM; POSTCOLONIALISM). These demands once again collide with long-established liberal beliefs that the state should be culturally neutral, that citizens should receive equal treatment under the law, and that rights belong to individuals, not groups (see CITIZENSHIP; AFFIRMATIVE ACTION; DISCRIMINATION). It remains to be seen whether liberalism is sufficiently flexible to incorporate such demands.

Finally, liberalism is challenged by the environmental movement, whose adherents claim that liberal political principles cannot successfully address urgent environmental concerns, and more fundamentally that the liberal image of the self-sufficient, self-directing individual is at odds with the ecological picture of humanity's subordinate place in the system of nature as a whole (see GREEN POLITICAL PHILOSOPHY; ENVIRONMENTAL ETHICS; SUSTAINABILITY). Liberalism, it is said, is too firmly wedded to the market economy and to consumption as the means of achieving personal wellbeing to be able to embrace the radical policies needed to avoid environmental disaster.

None of these problems is capable of easy solution, and we can say with some confidence that political philosophy will continue to flourish even in a world in which the sharp ideological divisions of the mid-twentieth century no longer exist. We may also expect a renewal of non-Western traditions of political philosophy as free intellectual inquiry revives in those countries where for half a century or more it has been suppressed by the state. Political questions that have concerned philosophers for two millennia or more will be tackled using new languages and new techniques, while the ever-accelerating pace of technological and social change will generate new problems whose solutions we can barely begin to anticipate.

See also: ALIENATION; ANTI-SEMITISM; CONSENT; CRITICAL THEORY; CULTURE; ECONOMICS AND ETHICS; EVOLUTION AND ETHICS; FAMILY, ETHICS AND THE; HISTORICISM; LAW, PHILOSOPHY OF; PARETO PRINCIPLE; PATERNALISM; POPULATION AND ETHICS; VIOLENCE; WORK, PHILOSOPHY OF; SOVEREIGNTY

References and further reading

Kymlicka, W. (1990) *Contemporary Political Philosophy*, Oxford: Oxford University Press, 2nd edn. (Each chapter covers a major school of contemporary political thought.)

Miller, David (2003) *Political Philosophy: A Very Short Introduction*, Oxford: Oxford University Press. (An accessible introduction for those coming to political philosophy for the first time.)

Swift, Adam (2001) *Political Philosophy: A Beginner's Guide for Students and Politicians*, Cambridge: Polity Press. (A selective discussion of some of the most important concepts in contemporary political philosophy.)

DAVID MILLER

POLITICAL PHILOSOPHY, AFRICAN
See AFRICAN PHILOSOPHY, ANGLOPHONE

POLITICAL PHILOSOPHY, HISTORY OF

The history of political philosophy attempts to yield a connected account of past speculation on the character of human association at its most inclusive level. 'History' or 'philosophy' may be stressed depending on whether the organizing principle is the temporal sequence or conceptual framework of political thought. Anglophone work has increasingly been organized around distinctive political 'languages' defined by specific vocabularies, syntaxes and problems, for example, classical republicanism, Roman law, natural law, utilitarianism. Chronologically it has been usual to observe divisions between ancient, medieval, Renaissance, early modern and modern periods of study.

Ancient Greece is the source of the earliest political reflection, with a continuous history in the West. Here reflection on the nature and proper organization of political community stimulated inquiry into the difference between nature and convention, the public and the domestic realm, the distinctive character of political rule, the relationship between political life and philosophy, the identity of justice, and the taxonomy of state-forms – as well as a more sociological investigation of the stability and decline of political regimes.

Greek political vocabulary was adapted to existing Roman republican practice (by Polybius and Cicero for example), which soon gave way to an imperial constitution stressing peace, order and unity. Rome thus generated two contrasting political ideals – that of the virtuous active republican citizen, and that of the unified empire governed by Roman law. Together with questions about the causes of its own rise and decline, Rome thus provided political values and historical material for subsequent philosophical and historical reflection.

Christianity undermined the pagan autonomy of politics in the name of a higher, transcendent ideal. However, it adapted much of Greek rationalism and the political vocabulary of classical culture in elaborating a creed and an institutional form. In turn it lent legitimacy to imperial and royal officeholders of Rome and barbarian successor-kingdoms.

Medieval political philosophy was characteristically preoccupied with the relationship between pope and king, church and *regnum*, but philosophy as a discipline was subordinated to theology. This was challenged by the rediscovery of Aristotle's self-sufficiently secular political ideal, a challenge met for a while by Aquinas' synthesis. However, the autonomy of secular politics was continually reasserted by a sequence of writers – Bartolus of Sassoferrato, Marsilius of Padua, Bruni and Machiavelli – who revived and reformulated classical republicanism using both Roman law and new Renaissance techniques and insights.

The Reformation, although initially politically quiescent, gave rise to new conflicts between secular and sacred rule. In particular, radical claims about the responsibility of all believers for their own salvation fed through in various ways into more individualistic political philosophies. In early modern Europe, using the strikingly new (and originally Catholic) vocabulary of natural right, Hugo Grotius aspired to provide a common secular basis for a shared political morality, on the basis of individual rights derived from a universal right of self-preservation. This was widely explored by seventeenth- and eighteenth-century thinkers, notably Hobbes and Locke, and culminated politically in the American and French Revolutions. In the aftermath of the French Revolution, language of natural rights was rejected both by conservative thinkers, such as Burke, and by a new, utilitarian radicalism largely forged by Bentham.

Attempts to grasp the political character of economic transformations and Empire in early modern Europe resulted in a growing engagement with the essentially historical character of politics, the dynamic of which republican discourse was particularly well suited to exploring. Avoiding the loss of liberty which the acquisition of Empire had seemed to entail in Rome involved rethinking possible patterns of politico-economic development, providing a new definition of liberty which stressed personal and economic over political freedom, and proposing that impersonal institutional devices could replace virtuous motives in guaranteeing political liberty and stability. Such possibilities were explored by Montesquieu and Constant in France, Hume and Smith in Britain and 'Publius' (Madison,

Hamilton and Jay) in America. They were rejected outright by Rousseau, for whom only the active citizen could guarantee rights, civic or civil.

The French Revolution was not only an event in which political philosophy played an important if hotly contested role; it also, like the rise and fall of Rome, provided a central topic for subsequent political reflection. The character of modernity, the nature of revolution, the relationship of political ideas to political action, the strength or weakness of rationalism as an informing principle, the viability and desirability of the Revolutionary ideals of liberty, equality and fraternity, all became topics of philosophical speculation by post-Revolutionary thinkers such as Constant, Cabet, de Tocqueville, Burke, de Maistre, Saint-Simon, Owen and Coleridge, as well as a later generation including Comte, Carlyle and Marx.

In contrast to his predecessors' use of Lockean psychology and the conditioning effects of experience and association to understand the processes of socio-economic change, Kant's postulation of the transcendent self initiated a new vocabulary of idealism. This culminated in Hegel's attempt to show how philosophical and historical (including political) change could be understood as the development and realization of a trans-historical consciousness or *Geist*, seeking to overcome internal tensions through a process of projection and transcendence.

The notion that human self-understanding and practices are to be understood historically greatly influenced subsequent political thinking, being central to the ideas of Marx, Nietzsche and Freud (as well as shaping many of J.S. Mill's modifications of classical utilitarianism). All three of the former owed insights to Hegel's claims about the crucial and emblematic character of the master–slave struggle. However, while for Hegel and Marx the slave's insights represent the transition to a higher form of consciousness – mediated in Marx's case by a class revolution – for Nietzsche (despairingly) and Freud (resignedly) repression was a constitutive and self-perpetuating feature of modern politics.

While nineteenth-century political thought was preoccupied with the historical conditioning of political sensibilities, Freud's discovery of the unconscious was accompanied by the emergence of a mass, irrationalist politics, characteristic of the twentieth century, and more suited to sociological than philosophical analysis. Nevertheless rationalist political theory, deriving from utilitarianism, and frequently drawing on (and contributing to) economic thought, remains the dominant accent in contemporary political philosophy.

See also: WILLIAM OF OCKHAM

IAIN HAMPSHER-MONK

POMPONAZZI, PIETRO (1462–1525)

Pietro Pomponazzi was the leading Aristotelian philosopher in the first quarter of the sixteenth century. His treatise *De immortalitate animae* (*On the Immortality of the Soul*) (1516) argues that although faith teaches immortality, natural reason and Aristotelian principles cannot prove it. In *De incantationibus* (On Incantations) (first published in 1556), Pomponazzi attempts to demonstrate on rational grounds that all reported miraculous suspensions or reversals of natural laws can be explained by forces within nature itself. Separating faith and reason once again, Pomponazzi proclaims his belief in all canonical miracles of the Church. These arguments cast doubt on morality, for without an afterlife, humanity is deprived of rewards for virtue and punishment for evil; and nature itself appears to be governed by impersonal forces unconcerned with human affairs. However, morality is restored to the universe by the human powers of rational reflection which lead to the pursuit of virtue. Yet in *De fato* (On Fate) (first published in 1567), Pomponazzi challenges the very basis of his own ethical doctrine by arguing that all activity of insentient and sentient beings is directed to preordained ends by environmental factors. Unable to justify human freedom on rational grounds, he then seeks to re-establish it using arguments derived from Christian natural theology, thus reversing his usual separation of faith and reason.

See also: Ficino, M.; Free will; Mersenne, M.; Miracles; Renaissance philosophy; Soul, nature and immortality of

MARTIN L. PINE

POPPER, KARL RAIMUND (1902–94)

Introduction

Popper belongs to a generation of Central European émigré scholars that profoundly influenced thought in the English-speaking countries during the twentieth century. His greatest contributions are in philosophy of science and in political and social philosophy. Popper's 'falsificationism' reverses the usual view that accumulated experience leads to scientific hypotheses; rather, freely conjectured hypotheses precede, and are tested against, experience. The hypotheses that survive the testing process constitute current scientific knowledge. His general epistemology, 'critical rationalism', commends the Socratic method of posing questions and critically discussing the answers offered to them.

He considers knowledge in the traditional sense of certainty, or in the modern sense of justified true belief, to be unobtainable.

After the *Anschluss*, Popper was stimulated by the problem of why democracies had succumbed to totalitarianism and applied his critical rationalism to political philosophy. Since we have no infallible ways of getting or maintaining good government, Plato's question 'Who should rule?' is misdirected. To advocate the rule of the best, the wise or the just invites tyranny disguised under those principles. By contrast, a prudently constructed open society constructs institutions to ensure that any regime can be ousted without violence, no matter what higher ends it proclaims itself to be seeking. Couched in the form of extended critiques of Plato and Platonism as well as of Marx and Marxism, Popper's political philosophy has had considerable influence in post-war Europe, East and West.

1 Life and works
2 Theory of science
3 Later ideas
4 Democracy, society and individualism

1 Life and works

Born in Vienna in 1902, the youngest child of a barrister, Karl Raimund Popper was educated at the University of Vienna, where he studied mathematics, music, psychology, physics and philosophy. He taught in secondary school between 1930 and 1936. Apprehension about Nazism persuaded him to emigrate in 1937, to become lecturer in philosophy at Canterbury University College, Christchurch, New Zealand. In January 1946 he became Reader in Logic and Scientific Method at the London School of Economics, was promoted to professor in 1949, and retired from full-time teaching in 1969. Among many honours, he was knighted in 1965, elected Fellow of the Royal Society in 1976, and made a Companion of Honour in 1982.

After a specialized start in the philosophy of science, Popper revealed himself as a philosopher of wide reach, making contributions across the spectrum from Presocratic studies to modern logic, from politics to probability, and from the mind–body problem to the interpretation of quantum theory. With all of his books in print, and translated into many languages, Popper's is one of the most discussed philosophies of the century. Yet, he insisted, his ideas are systematically misunderstood and misrepresented; this led him to devote uncommon energy to issues of interpretation and commentary on his own work.

Popper published three major works between 1935 and 1945. The first, *Logik der Forschung* (1935), his theory of science, appeared in English as *The Logic of Scientific Discovery* only in 1959. The second, *The Poverty of Historicism* (1957), first appeared in 1944–5 and extended his theory of science to history and society, severely criticizing the notion of historical laws. The third, *The Open Society and Its Enemies* (1945), is a two-volume treatise on the philosophy of history, politics and society.

Popper's other principal works consist of two collections of major papers, *Conjectures and Refutations* (1962), and *Objective Knowledge* (1972); a Library of Living Philosophers volume (1974) containing an intellectual autobiography and a set of replies to his critics, the former appearing separately as *Unended Quest* (1976); a collaboration with Sir John Eccles on a study of the mind–body problem, *The Self and Its Brain* (1977); *Die Beiden Grundprobleme der Erkenntnistheorie* (The Two Basic Problems of the Theory of Knowledge) (1979), the extant fragment of the book he was writing before *Logik der Forschung* superseded it; and the long-delayed *Postscript to the Logic of Scientific Discovery* (1982–3), much of which dates from the period 1955–7. Most of these books have seen multiple editions, involving sometimes minor and sometimes major changes. Throughout his career Popper also produced many original papers on diverse topics, and lectured all over the world. His manuscripts and correspondence fill some 450 archive cartons at the Hoover Institution, Stanford University.

2 Theory of science

Two problems structure Popper's theory of science: he calls them 'the problem of induction' and 'the problem of demarcation'. The problem of induction can be formulated as: what relation holds between theoretical knowledge and experience? The problem of demarcation can be formulated as: what distinguishes science from metaphysics as well as from logic and mathematics?

The received answers to these problems are: we get knowledge from experience by means of induction, that is, by inferring universal theories from accumulations of particular facts; and the inductive method demarcates science from metaphysics as well as from logic and mathematics. However, HUME showed that inductive inferences are invalid, hence the *problem* of induction: either we get knowledge from experience by invalid means (irrationalism) or we do not get any at all (scepticism); and induction collapses as a demarcation criterion (see DEMARCATION PROBLEM; INDUCTION, EPISTEMIC ISSUES IN).

In Part I of *The Logic of Scientific Discovery*, Popper's solutions to these two problems are set out

and shown to converge: knowledge results when we accept statements describing experience that contradict and hence refute our hypotheses; thus a deductive rather than an inductive relation holds between theoretical knowledge and experience. Experience teaches us by correcting our errors. Only hypotheses *falsifiable* by experience should count as scientific. There is no need for the inductive leap that Hume thought illogical but unavoidable; and the Hobson's choice between irrationalism or scepticism is avoided. To the question, 'Where do hypotheses come from, if not inductively from experience?', Popper answers, like Francis Bacon, that they come from our propensity to guess (see BACON, F. §6); in any case they cannot come from observation alone because there is no observation without hypotheses. Hypotheses are both logically and psychologically prior to observation. We are theorizing all the time in order to navigate in the world, and our encounters with negative evidence are the bumps that deliver information about the shape of reality.

The Logic of Scientific Discovery is dialectical in style, dealing with the traditional alternatives and the objections to each idea as it goes along. It is remarkable how frequently critics rediscover objections set out and answered in the book. The commonest objection is that, just as no amount of experience will conclusively verify a statement, so no amount of experience will conclusively falsify it. To answer this objection Popper points to a logical asymmetry. A universal statement cannot be derived from or verified by singular statements, no matter how many are marshalled. It can, however, be contradicted by one singular statement. The logic of falsification is the issue; conclusiveness is a red herring. Another argument, to the effect that the force of falsifying evidence can always be evaded by *ad hoc* definition or simple refusal to countenance it, Popper finds insuperable. The way to proceed, he concludes, is to entrench falsifiability in a methodology.

For Popper, a methodology is a policy decision governing action and embodied in norms or 'methodological rules'. Our decisions concern which course of action will best foster our aims. Thus falsificationism is made into a supreme rule to the effect that the 'rules of scientific procedure must be designed in such a way that they do not protect any statement in science against falsification' (*The Logic of Research* 1935). The rule for causality is typical of the small number offered: 'we are not to abandon the search for universal laws and for a coherent theoretical system, nor ever to give up our attempts to explain causally any kind of event we can describe' (*The Logic of Research*). A broad epistemological ambition is revealed when Popper generalizes: 'It might indeed be said that the majority of problems of theoretical philosophy, and the most interesting ones, can be reinterpreted . . . as problems of method' (*The Logic of Research*) (see SCIENTIFIC METHOD §2).

Throughout *The Logic of Scientific Discovery*, Popper defines his position by debate and contrast with logical positivist positions regarding meaning, and with two traditional views regarding science, inductivism and the conventionalism of POINCARÉ and DUHEM (see CONVENTIONALISM; LOGICAL POSITIVISM §4). It is notable that, like the logical positivists, Popper expresses unbounded respect for science. Unlike them, he grants a constructive (historical) role to metaphysics in science, seen as directly descended from the earliest Greek speculations about the nature of the world. The demarcation between science and metaphysics is thus a matter for decision, not a discovery about the nature of things. Popper's attacks on central logical positivist contentions contributed to the demise of that movement.

Popper respects conventionalism as self-contained, defensible and most likely consistent. His objection is that it risks treating obsolete or floundering science as incontrovertible truth. Yet Popper is a conventionalist in one respect: methodology. As opposed to the 'methodological naturalism' of the logical positivists, who treat the demarcation between science and metaphysics as a difference existing in the nature of things, or rather, in the nature of language, Popper is a 'methodological conventionalist', proposing rules that embody choices or decisions – which are in turn governed by aims. His demarcation should be judged, Popper maintains, by whether it proves fruitful in furthering the aims of discovering new ideas and new problems.

Part II of *The Logic of Scientific Discovery* consists of chapters on theories, falsifiability, the empirical basis, testability, simplicity, probability, quantum theory and corroboration. Each is an expansion, development and defence of the ideas briefly stated in Part I and parries a particular cluster of critical objections. The chapters on probability and corroboration, for example, deal at length with the objections that the pervasive probability statements of modern science are not falsifiable, and that they measure the strength of our inductive evidence. The chapters endeavour to show how probability statements can be falsified in relevant ways, and how they are better interpreted as statements of frequencies rather than as measures of inductive support.

3 Later ideas

The English translation of *The Logic of Scientific Discovery* is palimpsestic: while translating it Popper

intercalated comments, glosses, developments and corrections in new footnotes and appendices, as well as drafting a supplementary work, the three-volume *Postscript* of 1982–3. Opinion differs over whether all this is fully consistent. A case in point is 'The Aim of Science' section of the *Postscript*, published already in 1957, which argues that science aims at satisfactory explanations. It centres around a historical example (Galileo, Kepler, Newton), showing how each theory superseded and explained its predecessor. Satisfactory explanation, in addition to being testable, must fulfil other conditions, making it a rather stronger aim than falsifiability, one that may or may not be the same as the aim of science articulated at the end of *The Logic of Scientific Discovery*, of discovering 'new, deeper and more general problems'.

Certainly Popper acknowledges some changes of view. Since metaphysical dispute surrounded the concept of truth, he carefully avoided using it in *The Logic of Scientific Discovery*, making do with logical relations (implication, tautology, contradiction). Later, convinced by Tarski's work, he made free use of the concept of truth and of getting nearer to the truth (verisimilitude). Again, his criticisms of conventionalism in *The Logic of Scientific Discovery* were methodological. In later years they were also openly metaphysical, as Popper espoused a robust realism and indeterminism.

Throughout *The Logic of Scientific Discovery* there are Darwinian metaphors – the struggle for survival among theoretical systems, natural selection, fitness to survive – although, in the last pages of the book, the view that science is an instrument of biological adaptation is rejected. This Darwinian leitmotif became a controversial issue in Popper's later work: did evolutionary biology yield to the same methodological analysis as physics? Were the central ideas of DARWIN or of the modern synthesis falsifiable? To complicate matters, Popper changed his mind on this central question, viewing Darwinism as a historical hypothesis in *Objective Knowledge*, and as an unfalsifiable near tautology in *Unended Quest*. In contrast to his earlier view, Popper also began to advocate an evolutionary epistemology, that is, an attempt to explain the very existence of a truth-seeking science within the framework of natural selection, in effect to give a biological twist to Kant's problem, 'How is knowledge possible?' His second Herbert Spencer Lecture (1975) treats both endosomatic and exosomatic adaptations as forms of knowledge. Biological considerations also weigh heavily in Popper's part of *The Self and Its Brain*. Pitting himself against the reductionist materialism of most contemporary mind–body specialists, Popper there marshalled mainly indirect arguments for an interactive pluralism.

Reflections on biology seem to have been behind a bold new metaphysical initiative of 1967–8, especially the provocatively entitled 'Epistemology Without a Knowing Subject' (*Objective Knowledge* 1972: ch. 3). Distinguishing the world of physical things from the world of mental things, Popper argued that objective knowledge is located in neither, but in 'World 3' – the world of humanly created objective contents of thought. Such intellectual products have an objective existence: theories, problems, problem–situations, theoretical situations and critical arguments have properties and logical interrelations that lack physical or mental analogues. Stored knowledge exists even if no living person retrieves it. Critics of World 3 find some of its consequences counterintuitive: for example, it contains not only all truths, but also all falsehoods, which thus have an equally objective 'existence'.

In the late 1940s Popper published a particularly forceful and elegant system of natural deduction that is of considerable interest, both intrinsically and because in it he views deductive logic as the *organon* of criticism. He reports that while he has repaired some defects in it, he never brought it to completion. His technical attentions became focused on the theory of probability, to which he had already contributed in *The Logic of Scientific Discovery*. The result was a highly abstract axiomatic system that made no explicit assumptions about any logical relations among the elements on which probability is defined, and thereby established that probability is a genuine generalization of deducibility. The system is open to many new interpretations of probability statements. A particularly important one, superseding the frequency interpretation of *The Logic of Scientific Discovery*, views probabilities as measures of the 'propensities' of states of the world to develop one way rather than another. In the *Postscript* (1982) and *A World of Propensities*, this view was developed into a striking new metaphysics (see PROBABILITY, INTERPRETATIONS OF §4).

4 Democracy, society and individualism

In *Unended Quest*, Popper recounts how, as a politically conscious adolescent, he flirted with communism. He was quickly disillusioned when he judged communist actions irresponsible in leading to the deaths of some demonstrators. (Individual autonomy, responsibility, Socratic fallibilism and the obligation to reduce suffering are the keynotes of his scattered remarks about ethics.) In the 1920s he began a critique of Marx and Marxism, first tried out in a talk of 1935, 'The Poverty of Historicism'. 'Historicism' is Popper's name for the idea that there are inexorable laws of historical development: the demand that if natural science can predict eclipses then social science ought to be able to predict political revolutions. In a highly systematic way, Popper set out to show how both those who think the social sciences are not at all like the natural sciences (the 'anti-naturalists'), and those who think the social sciences very like the natural sciences (the 'naturalists'), share the aim of predicting history. Both recommend the methodology of historicism, which he sees as impoverished and inclined to treat societies as wholes responding to the pressures of inchoate social forces (see HISTORICISM).

Instead, Popper recommends 'methodological individualism': rules to the effect that the behaviour and actions of collectives should be explained by the behaviour of human individuals acting appropriately to the logic of their social situation as best they can and as best they see it. Not only was the alternative unfruitful, he argued, but the best social explanations of Plato and Marx were individualist. What look like holistic phenomena are to be explained as the 'unintended consequences' of such individual actions reverberating through the social set-up (see HOLISM AND INDIVIDUALISM IN HISTORY AND SOCIAL SCIENCE).

According to methodological individualism, social theories are tested not by historical predictions, which are little more than prophecies, Popper argues, but by attempts to invent institutions that correct social faults by social engineering. Man-made social institutions are hypotheses in action, he says. If we are to refute these hypotheses we need to avoid complicating matters with large-scale experiments, or too many at once, otherwise assessment will be impossible. For we must also reckon with the interference factor of 'the Oedipus effect', that is, the way in which a prediction about the future becomes an altering factor in the situation as human beings are aware of it, thus 'interfering' with the outcome.

The Open Society and Its Enemies was a 'truly unintended consequence' of an attempt to expand aspects of *The Poverty of Historicism* to satisfy puzzled friends. When it grew too large, Popper made it a separate work. On publication in 1945 it elevated him from academic obscurity to academic fame. He became a controversial and well-known public intellectual.

Described modestly as a 'critical introduction to the philosophy of politics and of history', *The Open Society* had become, in the seven years of its gestation, a major treatise on the intellectual and social ills of the time, offering an explanation of how totalitarianism had gained intellectual respectability and how purging post-war society of it would involve rethinking politics, education and social morality. Its title refers to two ideal-types used throughout. A closed society is one which takes a magical or tabooistic attitude to tradition and custom, which does not differentiate between nature and convention. An open society marks that difference and confronts its members with personal decisions and the opportunity to reflect rationally on them. Heraclitus, Aristotle and Hegel are briefly discussed, but the book's two intellectual anti-heroes are PLATO in volume 1 and MARX in volume 2.

The volume entitled 'The Spell of Plato' answers two questions: first, why Plato espoused totalitarian ideas and second, why students of Plato have whitewashed that fact and beautified him. The answer to the first question, a deeply sympathetic piece of writing, sketches a portrait of the young Plato contemplating with dismay the closed world of tribal Athens giving way to a more liberal and open society, with loss of social privilege and chaos arriving hand in hand. Popper insists on the brilliance of Plato's sociological analysis of the causes of change and of his proposals to arrest it and staunch the deterioration it brings. In answer to the second, Popper courts controversy by suggesting that Plato's intellectual followers, flattered by the role offered them, engaged in a long-running *trahison des clercs* by presenting as liberal and enlightened the doctrine of the philosopher-king.

To expose the commitment of Plato and Platonists to totalitarianism, Popper had to clarify our ideals of a liberal and democratic social order and show how Plato indulges in persuasive definitions, while attempting to show that his totalitarian *Republic* is 'just'. (Popper also mounts a general attack on the idea that philosophy should seek out the essence of universal words such as justice, democracy and tyranny. He argues that natural science uses the methodology of nominalism, not of essentialism, and social science and philosophy would do well to follow suit.) Mindful of Plato's distaste for majority rule, as rule of the mob or rule of the worst, Popper carefully discusses tyranny, and concludes that the problem is not the question of what is popular, for certain kinds of tyrants are very popular and could easily be elected. So an open and liberal society is not to be identified with a popularly elected government. No more is it a matter of what is just, good or best, for none of these offers insurance against tyranny in their name. In line with his theory of science, and of knowledge generally, he proposes a *via negativa*. The issue is not what regime we want, but what to do about ones we do not want. The problem with tyranny is that the citizens have no peaceful way in which to rid themselves of it, should they want to. Popper

proposes a now famous and generally endorsed criterion for democracy as that political system which permits the citizens to rid themselves of an unwanted government without the need to resort to violence. He exposes Plato's question, 'Who should rule?' and all similar discussions of sovereignty as subject to paradoxes because the question permits an inconsistency to develop between the statement designating the ruler (for example, the best or wisest should rule) and what the ruler commands (for example, the best or wisest may then tell us: obey the majority, or the powerful). Popper noticed that the question carries the authoritarian implication that whoever is so named is *entitled* to rule. He replaces them with the practical question 'How can we rid ourselves of bad governments without violence?', with its implication that rulers are on permanent parole. Popper's is a fundamentally pessimistic view that all governments are to one extent or the other incompetent and potentially criminal in their misbehaviour, and that only a political system which allows them to govern at the sufferance of citizens who can withdraw their support readily is one with more or less effective checks against abuse. Even so, the fallibility of our institutional hypotheses enjoin upon us an eternal vigilance.

The second volume, 'The High Tide of Prophecy, Hegel and Marx', argues that the prophetic tendency in Heraclitus and Plato produced in Hegel a damaging incoherence and charlatanry, and in Marx a project for the scientific study of society that, despite noble emancipating aims, foundered, especially among the followers, on the confusion of prediction with unscientific historical prophecy and hence on a fundamental misconstruction of scientific method. The chapters on Marx are among the most penetrating commentaries ever written on him, and are both sympathetic in their appreciation and unremitting in their criticism. Although Popper clearly regards Plato as the deeper thinker, he argues that Marx has much to teach us about how moral and emancipatory impulses can go awry. Marxists and the radical experimenters of the Soviet Union are judged harshly, as are all forms of nationalism.

Appearing in 1945 just after the end of the war, a war that had forged an alliance with the Soviet Union, the book antagonized many powerful intellectual interest groups. Platonists were taken aback to be accused of being apologists for totalitarian tendencies in Plato (even though Popper was not the first to point these out) and Marxists were equally affronted. The aftermath was strange. Although Popper was at first widely read and indignantly denounced, it later became bad form among Marxists and classicists to mention him by name. Yet, to an extraordinary extent, in the following decades his work set the agenda for apologetic Platonists, Hegelians and Marxists. In many cases a book or article makes most sense when seen as covertly engaged in trying to confute some point Popper made in *The Open Society.*

As a teacher of philosophy, Popper displayed ambivalence: philosophical problems emerge from science, so the best preparation was an education in a first-order subject, preferably scientific. In the classroom, he had the charisma of one possessed by intellectual problems, thinking about them all the time. In lecture or seminar he could be intellectually fierce and confrontational, in personal encounter sweet and encouraging. He regularly displayed an astonishingly quick intuitive grasp of the logic of any position presented to him, even from the most meagre of clues, and an eagerness to strengthen and elaborate on it before setting about criticizing it. He thus exemplified the values he advocated: intellectual seriousness, personal responsibility and disinterestedness, that is, doing justice to ideas regardless of their temporary embodiment. The failure of much critical commentary to meet these standards lies behind his complaint of misrepresentation. But there are also other reasons. If Popper is correct, not only is much in the traditional way of doing philosophy misdirected, but even the questions are wrongly put. Any attempt to map Popper's ideas into traditionally oriented discussions risks misrepresentation. The frequent practice of reconstructing Popper's philosophy timelessly, plucking materials from works published as far apart as fifty years, flies in the face of his emphasis on the structuring role of problems and problem–situations in all intellectual activity, particularly inquiry. To do justice to the originality and creativity of his work, scholarship needs in the first instance to respect its intellectual context of production.

See also: Carnap, R.; Discovery, logic of; Explanation in history and social science; Fallibilism; Inductive inference; Liberalism; Meaning and verification; Natural deduction, tableau and sequent systems; Scientific realism and antirealism; Vienna Circle

References and further reading

Hacohen, Malachi (2000). *Karl Popper: The Formative Years, 1902–1945,* Cambridge: Cambridge University Press. (An intellectual biography that situates Popper in the milieux of Central European thinking, and which also offers critical assessments of his ventures into different philosophical questions.)

Miller, David (ed.) (1985) *Popper Selections,* Princeton, NJ: Princeton University Press. (Miller offers

an authoritative introduction to Popper's thought and an astutely chosen anthology of selections.)

Stokes, Geoffrey (1998) *Popper: Philosophy, Politics, and Scientific Method.* Cambridge: Polity Press. (One of the better attempts at an overall critical study of Popper's thought.)

IAN C. JARVIE

POPULATION AND ETHICS

Ethical concern with population policies and with the issue of optimal population size is, generally speaking, a modern phenomenon. Although the first divine injunction of the Bible is 'be fertile and multiply', systematic theoretical interest in the normative aspects of demography has become associated largely with recent developments which have provided humanity with unprecedented control over population size, mainly through medical and economic means. Once the determination of the number of people in the world is no longer a natural given fact, but rather a matter of individual or social choice, it becomes subject to moral evaluation.

However, the extension of traditional ethical principles to issues of population policies is bedevilled by paradoxes. The principle of utility, the ideal of self-perfection, the idea of a contract as a basis for political legitimacy and social justice, the notion of natural or human rights, and the principle of respect for persons – all these presuppose the existence of human beings whose interests, welfare, rights and dignity are to be protected and promoted. But population policies deal with the creation of people and the decision concerning their number. They relate to the creation of the very conditions for the application of ethical principles. And it need not be just their number – advances in genetics and reproductive technology may soon bring what sort of people they are to be to some extent under human control.

See also: Contractarianism; Environmental ethics; Future generations, obligations to; Genetics and ethics; Kantian ethics; Utilitarianism

DAVID HEYD

POPULISM, RUSSIAN
See Herzen, Aleksandr Ivanovich

PORNOGRAPHY

There are three main questions about pornography. (1) How is pornography to be defined? Some definitions include the contention that it is morally wrong, while others define it neutrally in terms of its content and function. (2) Why is it wrong? Some accounts see the moral wrong of pornography in its tendency to corrupt individuals or to have detrimental effects on the morality of society; other accounts declare pornography to be objectionable only in so far as it causes physical harm to those involved in its production, or offence to unwilling observers. (3) Should pornography be restricted by law? Controversy here centres around whether the law should be used to discourage immorality, and whether the importance of free speech and individual autonomy are such as to rule out legislating against pornography. Here, the pornography debate raises very general questions about law and about autonomy in liberal societies.

See also: LIBERALISM; SEXUALITY, PHILOSOPHY OF

SUSAN MENDUS

PORPHYRY (c.233–309 AD)

The late ancient philosopher Porphyry was one of the founders of Neoplatonism. He edited the teachings of Plotinus into the form in which they are now known, clarified them with insights of his own and established them in the thought of his time. But, in reaction to Plotinus, he also advanced the cause of Aristotle's philosophical logic. Indeed, Porphyry is responsible for the resurgence of interest in Aristotle, which continued to the Middle Ages and beyond. Because of Porphyry, later Greek philosophy recovered both its Platonic and its Aristotelian roots, and Neoplatonism aimed to combine inspired thought with academic precision.

He was a scholar of great learning, with interests ranging from literary criticism and history to religion. An example is his defence of vegetarianism, which anticipated the modern debate on ecological preservation. Humans and animals belong to the same family. Seeking to preserve life is a matter of extending philanthropy and respect to all living species, which are our natural siblings. Ideally we ought to display 'harmlessness' even towards plants, except that our bodies, being composite and mortal, need to consume something else for food. Thus we should be ever conscious of the destructive effect that our eating habits and consumerism have on the creation of which we are part, and should try to keep to a simple lifestyle.

Porphyry's attention to logic, metaphysics and all other topics was driven by his firm belief that reason exercised by pure mind leads to the true essence of things, the One God. Intellectual activity detaches the soul from passions and confusions, and concentrates its activity on the real things. Porphyry attacked Christianity and Gnosticism because he thought they appealed to the irrational. Mysteries and rituals are fitted for those who are unable to practise inward contemplation. Salvation comes to those leading the life of the philosopher-priest.

See also: NEOPLATONISM

LUCAS SIORVANES

POSITIVISM

See COMTE, ISIDORE-AUGUSTE-MARIE-FRANÇOIS-XAVIER; LEGAL POSITIVISM; LOGICAL POSITIVISM; POSITIVISM IN THE SOCIAL SCIENCES

POSITIVISM IN THE SOCIAL SCIENCES

Positivism originated from separate movements in nineteenth-century social science and early twentieth-century philosophy. Key positivist ideas were that philosophy should be scientific, that metaphysical speculations are meaningless, that there is a universal and a priori scientific method, that a main function of philosophy is to analyse that method, that this basic scientific method is the same in both the natural and social sciences, that the various sciences should be reducible to physics, and that the theoretical parts of good science must be translatable into statements about observations. In the social sciences and the philosophy of the social sciences, positivism has supported the emphasis on quantitative data and precisely formulated theories, the doctrines of behaviourism, operationalism and methodological individualism, the doubts among philosophers that meaning and interpretation can be scientifically adequate, and an approach to the philosophy of social science that focuses on conceptual analysis rather than on the actual practice of social research. Influential criticisms have denied that scientific method is a priori or universal, that theories can or must be translatable into observational terms, and that reduction to physics is the way to unify the sciences. These criticisms have undercut the motivations for behaviourism and methodological individualism in the social sciences. They have also led many to conclude, somewhat implausibly, that any standards of good social science are merely matters of rhetorical persuasion and social convention.

HAROLD KINCAID

POSSIBLE WORLDS

The concept of possible worlds arises most naturally in the study of possibility and necessity. It is relatively uncontroversial that grass might have been red, or (to put the point another way) that there is a possible world in which grass is red. Though we do not normally take such talk of possible worlds literally, doing so has a surprisingly large number of benefits. Possible worlds enable us to analyse and help us understand a wide range of problematic and difficult concepts. Modality and modal logic, counterfactuals, propositions and properties are just some of the concepts illuminated by possible worlds.

Yet, for all this, possible worlds may raise more problems than they solve. What kinds of things are possible worlds? Are they merely our creations or do they exist independently of us? Are they concrete objects, like the actual world, containing flesh and blood people living in alternative realities, or are they abstract objects, like numbers, unlocated in space and time and with no causal powers? Indeed, since possible worlds are not the kind of thing we can ever visit, how could we even know that such things exist? These are but some of the difficult questions which must be faced by anyone who wishes to use possible worlds.

See also: ABSTRACT OBJECTS; INTENSIONAL ENTITIES; INTENSIONAL LOGICS; MODAL LOGIC

JOSEPH MELIA

POSTCOLONIALISM

The term 'postcolonialism' is sometimes spelled with a hyphen – post-colonial – and sometimes without. There is no strict general practice, but the hyphenated version is often used to refer to the condition of life after the end of colonialism while the non-hyphenated version denotes the theory that attempts to make sense of this condition. The term is regularly used to denote both colonialism and imperialism even though these refer to different historical realities.

Like postmodernism and poststructuralism, postcolonialism designates a critical practice that is highly eclectic and difficult to define. It involves a studied engagement with the experience of colonialism and its past and present effects at the levels of material culture and of representation. Postcolonialism often involves the discussion of experiences such as those of slavery, migration, suppression and resistance, difference, race, gender, place and analysis of the responses to the discourses of imperial Europe, such as history, philosophy, anthropology and linguistics. Since conditions under imperialism and colonialism proper are as much the subject of postcolonialism as those coming after the historical end of colonialism, postcolonialism allows for a wide range of applications and a constant interplay between the sense of an historical transition, a cultural location and an epochal condition. Postcolonialism is seen to pertain as much to conditions of existence in former colonies as to conditions in diaspora. Both

are frequently linked to the continuing power and authority of the West in the global political, economic and symbolic spheres and the ways in which resistance to, appropriation of and negotiation with the West's order are prosecuted. However the term is construed, there is as much focus on the discourse and ideology of colonialism as on the material effects of colonial subjugation. Because it has its source in past and continuing oppression, postcolonialism furthermore has affinities with multicultural, feminist, and gay and lesbian studies.

ATO QUAYSON

POSTMODERNISM

The term 'postmodernism' appears in a range of contexts, from academic essays to clothing advertisements in the *New York Times*. Its meaning differs with context to such an extent that it seems to function like Lévi-Strauss' 'floating signifier': not so much to express a value as to hold open a space for that which exceeds expression. This broad capacity of the term 'postmodernism' testifies to the scope of the cultural changes it attempts to compass.

Across a wide range of cultural activity there has been a sustained and multivalent challenge to various founding assumptions of Western European culture since at least the fifteenth century and in some cases since the fifth century BC: assumptions about structure and identity, about transcendence and particularity, about the nature of time and space. From physics to philosophy, from politics to art, the description of the world has changed in ways that upset some basic beliefs of modernity. For example, phenomenology seeks to collapse the dualistic distinction between subject and object; relativity physics shifts descriptive emphasis from reality to measurement; the arts move away from realism; and consensus politics confronts totalitarianism and genocide. These and related cultural events belong to seismic changes in the way we register the world and communicate with each other.

To grasp what is at stake in postmodernism it is necessary to think historically and broadly, in the kind of complex terms that inevitably involve multidisciplinary effort. This multilingual impetus, this bringing together of methods and ideas long segregated both in academic disciplines and in practical life, particularly characterizes postmodernism and largely accounts for such resistance as it generates.

Although diverse and eclectic, postmodernism can be recognized by two key assumptions. First, the assumption that there is no common denominator – in 'nature' or 'truth' or 'God' or 'the future' – that guarantees either the One-ness of the world or the possibility of neutral or objective thought. Second, the assumption that all human systems operate like language, being self-reflexive rather than referential systems – systems of differential function which are powerful but finite, and which construct and maintain meaning and value.

See also: FOUCAULT, M.; PHENOMENOLOGY, EPISTEMIC ISSUES

ELIZABETH DEEDS ERMARTH

POST-STRUCTURALISM

Introduction

Post-structuralism is a late-twentieth-century development in philosophy and literary theory, particularly associated with the work of Jacques Derrida and his followers. It originated as a reaction against structuralism, which first emerged in Ferdinand de Saussure's work on linguistics. By the 1950s structuralism had been adapted in anthropology (Lévi-Strauss), psychoanalysis (Lacan) and literary theory (Barthes), and there were hopes that it could provide the framework for rigorous accounts in all areas of the human sciences.

Although structuralism was never formulated as a philosophical theory in its own right, its implicit theoretical basis was a kind of Cartesianism, but without the emphasis on subjectivity. It aimed, like Descartes, at a logically rigorous system of knowledge based on sharp explicit definitions of fundamental concepts. The difference was that, for structuralism, the system itself was absolute, with no grounding in subjectivity. Post-structuralist critiques of structuralism typically challenge the assumption that systems are self-sufficient structures and question the possibility of the precise definitions on which systems of knowledge must be based.

Derrida carries out his critique of structuralist systems by the technique of deconstruction. This is the process of showing, through close textual and conceptual analysis, how definitions of fundamental concepts (for example, presence versus absence, true versus false) are undermined by the very effort to formulate and employ them. Derrida's approach has particularly influenced literary theory and criticism in the USA. In addition, Richard Rorty, developing themes from pragmatism and recent analytic philosophy, has put forward a distinctively American version of post-structuralism.

1 Structuralism

In his lectures on linguistics, Ferdinand de SAUSSURE proposed a view of language (*langue*) as a formal structure, defined by differences between systemic elements. According to Saussure, this structure is simultaneously present in and unites the two domains of thought and words. A given linguistic term (a sign) is the union of an idea or concept (the 'signified') and a physical word (the 'signifier'). A language is a complete system of such signs, which exists not as a separate substance but merely as the differentiating form that defines the specific structure of both signifiers (physical words) and signifieds (ideas). Saussure's view rejects the common-sense picture of the set of signifiers and the set of signifieds as independent givens, with the signifieds having meaning in their own right and the signifiers obtaining meaning entirely through their association with corresponding signifieds. Saussure denies this independence and instead maintains that signifiers and signifieds alike have meaning only in virtue of the formal structure (itself defined by differences between elements) that they share (see STRUCTURALISM IN LINGUISTICS).

Saussure's structuralist approach was very successful within linguistics, where it was applied and extended by, among others, Jakobson and Troubetzkoy. By the 1950s the approach had been adapted in anthropology (Lévi-Strauss), psychoanalysis (Lacan) and literary theory (Barthes); and there were hopes that it could provide the framework for rigorous accounts in all areas of the human sciences. Three distinguishing features of this framework were: (1) a rejection of all idealist views of concepts and meanings as derived from the activity of consciousness; (2) an understanding of concepts and meanings as, instead, grounded in the structural relations among the elements of abstract systems; (3) an explication of such structural relations solely in terms of bipolar differences (for example, real/unreal, temporal/nontemporal, present/absent, male/female).

2 Post-structuralism: terminology

Post-structuralism is obviously closely tied to structuralism, but commentators have characterized the relationship in a variety of mutually inconsistent ways. Some writers make no distinction between structuralism and post-structuralism, applying the single term 'structuralist' to the entire range of thinkers from Saussure through to Derrida. More commonly, post-structuralism is distinguished as a separate development, but there is disagreement as to whether it is primarily a reaction against structuralism or an extension of it (as the term *Neostrukturalismus*, commonly used by Manfred Frank and other German commentators, suggests). Apart from matters of definition, there is even disagreement as to whether major figures such as Barthes, Lacan and Foucault are structuralists or post-structuralists.

Michel Foucault's book, *Les Mots et les choses* (translated under the title *The Order of Things*) is an instructive example. In one sense it is quintessentially structuralist. The book first uncovers the fundamental epistemic systems (which Foucault calls 'epistemes') that underlie and delimit the subjective thought of particular eras. It then goes on to show how the apparent ultimacy of subjectivity is itself just the product of one contingent episteme, that of modernity, which is even now disappearing (the famous 'death of man'). Nevertheless, Foucault's essentially historical viewpoint in the work demonstrates the limitation of structuralism: its inability to give any account of the transitions from one system of thought to another. Foucault seems to have seen from the beginning that structuralism cannot be historical, a fact that explains his constant insistence that he was not a structuralist, in spite of his obvious deployment of structuralist methods and concepts. So, although *Les Mots et les choses* is a structuralist book, it at the same time makes clear the limits of structuralism and prepares the way for Foucault's later work on power and ethics which is distinctly post-structuralist (see FOUCAULT, M.).

Despite these ambiguities and disagreements, the concept of post-structuralism is useful, if not essential, for understanding philosophy in France during the latter part of the twentieth century. One fruitful approach is to think of post-structuralism as a philosophical reaction to the structuralism that was such a powerful force during the 1960s in linguistics, psychology and the social sciences. It was neither a simple rejection or extension of structuralism but a series of philosophical reflections on the structuralist programme and achievement.

3   Two major post-structuralist theses

Although structuralism was never formulated as a philosophical theory in its own right, its implicit theoretical basis was, as noted above, a kind of Cartesianism without the subject. (Hence, the association of structuralism with the notion of the 'death of the subject'.) Post-structuralist critiques of structuralism are typically based on two fundamental theses: (1) that no system can be autonomous (self-sufficient) in the way that structuralism requires; and (2) that the defining dichotomies on which structuralist systems are based express distinctions that do not hold up under careful scrutiny.

The first thesis is not understood so as to support the traditional idealist view that systematic structures are dependent on the constitutive activities of subjects. Post-structuralists retain structuralism's elimination of the subject from any role as a foundation of reality or of our knowledge of it. But, in opposition to structuralism, they also reject any logical foundation for a system of thought (in, for example, its internal coherence). For post-structuralists, there is no foundation of any sort that can guarantee the validity or stability of any system of thought.

The second thesis is the key to post-structuralism's denial of the internal coherence of systems. The logical structure of a system requires that the applications of its concepts be unambiguously defined. (In the formalism of elementary number theory, for example, there must be no question as to whether a given number is odd or even.) As a result, the possibility of a systematic structure depends on the possibility of drawing sharp distinctions between complementary concepts such as odd/even, charged/uncharged, living/non-living, male/female and so on. Post-structuralist philosophers have been particularly concerned with the fundamental dichotomies (or oppositions) underlying structuralist theories in the human sciences. Saussure's linguistics, for example, is based on the distinction of the signifier from the signified; Lévi-Strauss's anthropology of myths employs oppositions such as raw/cooked, sun/moon and so on. In each case, post-structuralists have argued that the dichotomy has no absolute status because the alternatives it offers are neither exclusive nor exhaustive.

4   Derrida's critique of logocentrism

This sort of critique was extended to philosophy, particularly by Jacques DERRIDA, who finds Western philosophical thought pervaded by a network of oppositions – appearance/reality, false/true, opinion/knowledge, to cite just a few examples – that constitute what he calls the system of 'logocentrism'. This term derives from Derrida's conviction that at the root of Western philosophical thought is a fundamental distinction between speech (*logos*) and writing. Speech is privileged as the expression of what is immediate and present, the source, accordingly, of what is real, true and certain. Writing, on the other hand, is derogated as an inferior imitation of speech, the residue of speech that is no longer present and, therefore, the locus of appearance, deceptions and uncertainty. Plato's devaluation of writing in comparison with living dialogue is the most famous and influential example of this distinction. But Derrida finds the distinction pervading Western philosophy and regards it as not just a preference for one form of communication over another but the basis for the entire set of hierarchical oppositions that characterize philosophical thought. Speech offers presence, truth, reality, whereas writing, a derivative presentation employed in the absence of living speech, inevitably misleads us into accepting illusions.

Derrida's critiques of the speech/writing opposition – and of all the hierarchical oppositions that attend it – proceed by what he calls the method of 'deconstruction' (see DECONSTRUCTION). This is the process of showing, through close textual and conceptual analysis, how such oppositions are contradicted by the very effort to formulate and employ them. Consider, for example, the opposition between presence and absence, which plays a fundamental role in Husserl's phenomenology (and many other philosophical contexts). Husserl requires a sharp distinction between what is immediately present to consciousness (and therefore entirely certain) and what is outside of consciousness (and therefore uncertain). But once Husserl undertakes a close analysis of the immediately present, he discovers that it is not instantaneous but includes its own temporal extension. The 'present', as a concrete experiential unit, involves both memory of the just-immediately-past (retention, in Husserl's terminology) and anticipation of the immediate future (protention). Thus, the past and the future, both paradigms of what is absent (not present), turn out to be integral parts of the present. Husserl's own account of the presence/absence opposition overturns it.

Deconstruction maintains that there is no stability in any of thought's fundamental oppositions. Their allegedly exclusive alternatives turn out to be inextricably connected; their implicit hierarchies perpetually reversible. As a result, there is an ineliminable gap between the intelligibility of a rational system and the reality it is trying to capture. Derrida expresses this gap through a variety of terms. He frequently speaks of *différance* (a deliberately misspelled homophone of the French *différence*) to emphasize, first, the difference between systematic structures and the objects (for example, experiences, events, texts) they try to make intelligible, and, second, the way in which efforts to make absolute distinctions are always deferred (another

sense of the French *différer*) by the involvement of one polar opposite in the other. This latter phenomenon Derrida also discusses in terms of the 'trace' of its opposite always lingering at the heart of any polar term. He also employs the term 'dissemination' to refer to the way that objects of analysis slip through the conceptual net spread by any given system of intelligibility we devise for it.

5 Post-structuralism and literary theory

Thus far the discussion has focused on Derrida's deconstruction of the meaningful structures philosophers purport to find in reality and to express in their philosophical texts. But Derrida's approach is also readily applicable to literary texts (and the 'worlds' they create). This is because – like philosophical systems – poems, novels and other literary texts are typically thought to embody complete and coherent systems of meaning, which it is the task of literary criticism to extract. Although Derrida himself has dealt primarily with philosophical texts, his approach has been widely adopted by analysts of literature. (Of course, as should be expected, Derrida and his followers reject any sharp distinction between the philosophical and the literary.)

Traditional literary analysis has understood the meaning of a text as the expression of its author's mind; that is, as thoughts the author intended to convey in writing the text. The first stage of deconstructive criticism is the structuralist one of detaching meaning from authorial intention, locating it instead in the text itself as a linguistic structure. Roland Barthes, for example, showed how to analyse a text by Balzac entirely in terms of the formal codes it embodies, with no reference to what Balzac supposedly 'meant'. This structuralist move effects a 'death of the author' parallel to the anti-Cartesian 'death of the subject'. But the post-structuralists take the future step of denying a fixed meaning to even the autonomous text itself. It is not that a text lacks all meaning but that, on the contrary, it is the source of an endless proliferation of conflicting meanings. As deconstructionists delight in showing, any proposed privileged meaning of a text can be undermined by careful attention to the role in it of apparently marginal features. (For example, an orthodox Christian reading of Milton's *Paradise Lost* is deconstructed by a close study of certain details in its treatment of Satan.) There is no doubt, of course, that texts are often produced by authors trying to express what they think or feel. But what they write always goes beyond any authorial intention and in ways that can never be reduced to a coherent system of meaning.

The deconstructionist's point can also be understood as an undermining of the distinction between primary text and commentary. On the traditional view, a commentary is an effort to formulate as accurately as possible the content (meaning) of the text. To the extent that it is successful, a commentary expresses nothing more and nothing less than this meaning. But for deconstructionists the meaning in question does not exist, and the commentary must be understood as nothing more than a free elaboration of themes suggested, but not required, by the text. Unable to be a secondary reflection, the commentary becomes as much an independent creation as the text itself.

6 Rorty's post-structuralist pragmatism

Richard Rorty's work is far removed, in both antecedents and style, from that of continental post-structuralists (see RORTY, R.M.). His critique of Cartesianism, derived more from Dewey than from Heidegger, is aimed at twentieth-century analytic philosophy rather than the structuralist human sciences; and his urbanely lucid prose contrasts sharply with the wilfully playful convolutions of Derrida and his followers. None the less, Rorty's analyses lead him to a critique of traditional philosophy very similar to that of the post-structuralists.

The focal point of Rorty's critique is the project (called foundationalism) of providing a philosophical grounding for all knowledge. Modern foundationalism originates with Descartes, but Rorty sees it as also the *leitmotif* of Descartes' successors, through Hume and Kant down to the logical positivists. Like Derrida, Rorty attacks traditional systematic thought by calling into question some of its key distinctions. Unlike Derrida, however, he does not carry out his attacks through close readings of classic texts but by deploying the results of recent analytic philosophy. He uses, for example, Quine's critique of the distinction between analytic and synthetic statements to argue that there are no foundational truths about the meaning of concepts. He appeals to Wilfrid Sellars' undermining of the distinction between theory and observation to reject empirical foundations of knowledge in interpretation-free sense data. He employs Donald Davidson's questioning of the distinction between the formal structure and the material content of a conceptual framework to reject Kantian attempts to ground knowledge in principles that define the framework of all possible thought.

In Rorty's view the upshot of these various critiques is to cut off every source of an ultimate philosophical foundation for our knowledge. Accordingly, he maintains, philosophy must give up its traditional claim to be the final court of appeal in disputes about truth. We have no alternative but to accept as true what we (the community of knowers) agree on. There is no appeal beyond the results of the 'conversation of mankind' so far as it has advanced to date. For us, there is no (upper-case) Truth justified by privileged insights and methods. There is only the mundane (lower-case) truth: what our interlocutors let us get away with saying.

It might seem that this rejection of foundationalism is a rejection of the entire tradition of Western philosophy since Plato. Rorty, however, distinguishes two styles of philosophy. First, there is *systematic philosophy*, the mainline of the Western tradition since Plato, which is defined by the foundationalist goal of ultimate justification. But, on the other hand, there is another enterprise, always marginal to the tradition, that Rorty calls *edifying philosophy*. Whereas systematic philosophers undertake elaborate and purportedly eternal constructions (which are always demolished by the next generation), edifying philosophers are content to shoot ironic barbs at the systematic thought of their day, exploding its pretensions and stimulating intriguing lines of counter-thought. The tradition of edifying thought can be traced back at least to the ancient Cynics and has been more recently represented by Kierkegaard, Nietzsche and the later Wittgenstein. Derrida's deconstructions are, on Rorty's view, a prime contemporary example of edifying philosophy.

Edifying philosophers, however, are philosophers only because they react against systematic philosophy. They do not differ from other sorts of cultural critics (novelists, literary theorists, social scientists) because of any distinctively philosophical method or viewpoint. If, in the wake of thinkers such as Derrida and Rorty, systematic philosophy is abandoned, philosophy will be too. The triumph of post-structuralism would, for better or worse, be the end of philosophy as we have known it.

See also: DERRIDA, J.; FOUCAULT, M.; POSTMODERNISM; RORTY, R.M.; STRUCTURALISM; STRUCTURALISM IN LINGUISTICS

References and further reading

Dews, P. (1987) *Logics of Disintegration: Poststructuralist Thought and the Claims of Critical Theory*, London: Verso. (Analytic and critical essays on Derrida, Lacan, Foucault and Lyotard.)

Gutting, G. (2001) *French Philosophy in the Twentieth Century, Part III, Structuralism and Beyond*, Cambridge: Cambridge University Press. (Part III covers structuralist and post-structuralist thinkers.)

Howells, C. (1999) *Derrida: Deconstruction from Phenomenology to Ethics*, Cambridge: Polity Press. (A comprehensive, clearly written survey of Derrida's work.)

GARY GUTTING

PRACTICAL ETHICS

See Animals and ethics; Applied ethics; Bioethics; Business ethics; Civil disobedience; Environmental ethics; Family, ethics and the; Genetics and ethics; Journalism, ethics of; Life and death; Market, ethics of the; Medical ethics; Population and ethics; Pornography; Professional ethics; Reproduction and ethics

PRACTICAL RATIONALITY

See Rationality, practical

PRACTICAL REASON AND ETHICS

Introduction

Practical reason is reasoning which is used to guide action, and is contrasted with theoretical reason, which is used to guide thinking. Sometimes 'practical reason' refers to any way of working out what to do; more usually it refers to proper or authoritative, hence *reasoned*, ways of working out what to do.

On many accounts practical reasoning is solely instrumental: it identifies ways of reaching certain results or ends, but has nothing to say about which ends should be pursued or which types of action are good or bad, obligatory or forbidden. Instrumental reasoning is important not only for ethics and politics, but for all activities, for example, in working out how to travel to a given destination.

Other accounts of practical reason insist that it is more than instrumental reasoning: it is concerned not only with working out how to achieve given ends, but with identifying the ethically important ends of human activity, or the ethically important norms or principles for human lives, and provides the basis for all ethical judgment.

No account of objective ethical values can be established without showing how we can come to know them, that is, without showing that some form of *ethical cognitivism* is true. However, ethical cognitivism is not easy to establish. Either we must show that some sort of intuition or perception provides direct access to a realm of values; or we must show that practical reasoning provides less direct methods by which objective ethical claims can be established. So anybody who thinks that

there are directly objective values, but doubts whether we can intuit them directly, must view a plausible account of practical reason as fundamental to philosophical ethics.

1   Introduction

Most ethical positions or theories rely on one or more conceptions of practical reason, yet many fail to explicate, let alone to vindicate, the particular conceptions on which they rely. The only positions or theories which offer no account of practical reason are those which construe ethical claims either as noncognitive or as based directly on particular cognitions such as perceptions or intuitions that do not need to be linked to any reasoning process (see Analytic ethics; Emotivism; Intuitionism in ethics; Moral realism).

One pervasive disagreement among the proponents of various accounts of practical reason is between those who think that practical reasons should both justify and motivate action and those who think that they should justify, but need not motivate. The claim that reasons both justify and motivate is often labelled *internalism*, the thought being that anything that motivates (whether a desire, or a certain sort of belief, or some other internal state) must be internal to the agent who is motivated. The claim that reasons must justify but need not motivate is correspondingly termed *externalism* (see Moral motivation §§1–2). Broadly speaking, internalists think that externalists fail to show how reason can be practical, since they do not adequately address the question of motivation, and externalists think that internalists lose sight of the fact that practical reason must be reasoned, since they build an account of the contingencies of motivation into their account of reason. There are many versions both of internalism and of externalism.

Accounts of practical reasoning can be grouped under two very general headings. Many accounts of practical reason are *end-oriented* (also known as *teleological* or *consequentialist*): they seek to show how reason can select action (also attitudes and policies) that will contribute to certain ends or results (see CONSEQUENTIALISM; TELEOLOGICAL ETHICS). Many proponents of end-oriented practical reasoning think that practical reason can do no more. Since no objective account of the proper ends of human life can be found, we must settle for *subjective* accounts of human ends. We must agree with Hume that reason 'is, and ought only to be the slave of the passions' (*A Treatise of Human Nature* 1739–40) (see RATIONALITY, PRACTICAL). However, there are other accounts of end-oriented practical reasoning which insist that reason can also identify certain *objective* ends, and so has the dual task of identifying the proper ends of action and guiding action towards those ends.

Yet other conceptions of practical reason do not view it as focused solely on ends and means to those ends. *Act-oriented* accounts of practical reason take it that action (also attitudes and policies) are guided by norms or principles, and that it is the task of practical reason to identify appropriate, reasoned norms and principles. Some norms and principles formulate very general ends, others point to quite specific acts: the Jesuit maxim 'For the greater glory of God' defines the end of an entire life; the homely advice 'Do not eat oysters unless there is a letter "r" in the name of the month' offers limited and specific advice. Although some norms and principles define ends, norm- and principle-guided reasoning cannot be assimilated to end-oriented reasoning, which sees all practical reasoning as bearing on a means-ends complex. Act-oriented reasoning sees it as bearing on practical propositions (norms, rules, principles) and as guiding action without reference either to supposed objective ends or to the subjective ends of any agents.

Many accounts of act-oriented reasoning see it as norm-based: they take it that the fundamental ethical orientations (norms, categories, commitments, beliefs, senses of identity: hereafter *norms*) accepted in a society or tradition, or in an individual's life, provide the fundamental premises for practical reasoning. On such accounts, practical reasoning is internal to societies: it appeals to the norms that constitute the bedrock of certain lives or ways of life, so cannot coherently be brought into question by those who live these lives.

Other critical accounts of act-oriented ethical reasoning object that uncritical appeal to accepted norms cannot provide acceptable premises for practical reasoning; arguing from accepted norms is quite arbitrary, hence quite unreasoned. Any conclusions reached in this way will be relative to the assumed norms, so can support no more than one or another version of ethical relativism (see MORAL RELATIVISM). Exponents of critical accounts of practical reason think that adequate act-oriented reasoning must offer reasons which do not presuppose any specific norms (or traditions, or identities), but rather must be public in the sense that they are relevant to an unrestricted audience, or, as Kant put it vividly in an early version of this thought, that they must 'address... the world at large' (*An Answer to the Question: 'What is Enlightenment?'* 1784). The possibility of vindicating any critical, universal conception of act-oriented practical reason is questioned by proponents of other conceptions.

The search for a convincing account of practical reason raises issues fundamental not only to ethics and politics, but to a wide range of philosophical problems. They include the problem of seeing whether, and if so how, any account of practical reason can be vindicated without begging questions, the connection between practical and theoretical reason and the problem of showing how and how far various conceptions of practical reason can guide action, attitudes or policies.

2 End-oriented reasoning: reason is instrumental

Scepticism about the idea that reason has any objective ends of its own was put succinctly by Hume, who scoffed that ''tis not contrary to reason to prefer the destruction of the whole world to the scratching of my finger' (*A Treatise of Human Nature* 1739–40), insisted that ''tis in vain to pretend, that morality is discover'd only by a deduction of reason' and concluded that *ought* cannot be derived from *is*. If morality has no ends that are discovered by reason, then practical reason's only task is to show how the pursuit of the passions – of subjective ends – is to be organized effectively and efficiently. The central task of practical reason is the instrumental one of deploying our knowledge of causal relations to guide action: practical reason is simply an application of and derivative from aspects of theoretical reason; it needs no separate justification.

There is, however, a great deal to be said about the detailed operations of instrumental reasoning. In particular, if some metric can be found for the ends which are to be sought (for example, if there is a metric for the satisfaction of desires or preferences), and if the probabilities of achieving various ends can be quantified, then instrumental reasoning can be used to show which available actions maximize the satisfaction of preferences, and hence how given ends can be pursued efficiently. If this metric permits the desires or preferences of different persons to be measured using a common unit, practical reasoning may be able to guide social as well as individual decision-making and policy. Utilitarian ethical theory, game theory and a wide range of economic and social calculi have discussed numerous versions of subjective, end-oriented practical reasoning which are held to be appropriate for various contexts (see RATIONALITY, PRACTICAL; RATIONAL CHOICE THEORY; UTILITARIANISM.)

Merely instrumental accounts of practical reason have been criticized at least since Kant. The critics do not doubt that instrumental reasoning is a necessary aspect of practical reasoning, but they insist that it cannot be sufficient. All that it provides is an account of the use of empirical, and in particular causal, knowledge in pursuit of intrinsically arbitrary ends. Instrumental reasoners may show that it is necessary to break eggs if one wants to make an omelette, but they have nothing but preferences to cite as reasons for making or not making omelettes: all their conclusions are conditional on subjective ends. Instrumental reasoning in pursuit of individual preferences can support efficient egoism, or strategic thinking or certain limited and distinctively modern conceptions of prudence: but this is all it can do (see MORAL MOTIVATION §§4–6).

Contemporary work on instrumental reasoning has addressed this criticism up to a point by insisting that practical reasoning requires not only that choices of action be instrumentally sound, but that they be based on well-ordered (for example, connected and transitive) preference-orderings. However, since these coherence conditions can be met by many different sets of preferences, the requirement of well-orderedness provides little further reasoned guidance. It does not add enough to an account of instrumental rationality to satisfy those who think that an account of practical reason should provide a more complete guide to reasoned choice, or to rebut the charge that instrumental reasoning gets no further than showing how intrinsically arbitrary (unreasoned) ends are to be pursued by rational means.

Some advocates of subjective end-oriented practical reasoning have held that desires and preferences, although subjective, provide an approximation to an objective account of the good. Some utilitarians, for example, have held that happiness is the sole good, that it is achieved by satisfying desires, and that therefore the optimal satisfaction of desires leading to maximal happiness produces the greatest good; they then claim that instrumental reasoning provides a sufficient account of practical reasoning for ethical as well as for egoistical, strategic and merely prudential purposes. Critics have countered that happiness is not the sole good, and moreover that it is not all of a sort, and cannot be aggregated, so that instrumental reasoning alone will not be enough to guide ethical choice. Others have objected that some sorts of happiness, such as

happiness in the satisfaction of evil desires, or happiness produced by violating others' rights, does not contribute to the good at all, and conclude that the instrumentally rational pursuit of happiness cannot be what ethics demands.

3 End-oriented reasoning: reason identifies objective ends

All of these difficulties would be resolved if reason could also identify objective ends. Instrumental reasoning is only one aspect of an older and more ambitious conception of end-oriented practical reasoning, which claims that reason both identifies the proper ends of action – the good – and can be used to steer action towards those ends. Such a position can be attributed to PLATO, on whose account reason not merely can know its proper object, the [Form of the] Good, but strives for the Good. Far from being inert, reason is intrinsically active, and has its own desires and its own end. In this picture there is no gap between theoretical reason, which guides right cognition, and practical reason, which guides right action. Human knowledge and desire have a common focus on the Good; *nous* and *eros* are aspects of one capacity, and the remaining practical problem is to align human life as that capacity directs.

The metaphysical and epistemological claims needed to support this more traditional vision of practical reason are hugely ambitious. Yet despite the difficulty of justifying objective conceptions of end-oriented practical reason, it has been widely accepted in varied forms. Aristotle, for example, took issue with Plato's unitary conception of the Good, and insisted that there are many goods, but held that they include the Good for man, which constitutes the proper end for human action (see ARISTOTLE §§20–1; EUDAIMONIA). He offers a complex account of supplementary patterns of practical reasoning which can be used to identify action that contributes to the good for man. These include the *doctrine of the mean*, which purportedly offers a nonmechanistic way of selecting 'intermediate' action, so avoiding unacceptable extremes, and the so-called *practical syllogism*, by which conclusions about action (or possibly actions themselves) are inferred from general principles and claims about particular situations. Many later Neoplatonist and Christian thinkers also combine the ideas that the Good can be known by reason and that it is the proper end of human life. Plato's teleological view of reason has been widely if tacitly shared by countless other writers who neither share his metaphysical position nor provide any alternative, but who speak of certain ends as 'reasonable' without much by way of explanation, and often with far less by way of defence than Plato offers.

Of course, knowing what the Good is – what the true ends of human life are – is never enough to guide action. The effective pursuit of these ends also requires the use of reason to calculate which of various available acts contributes to those ends most effectively, as well as to identify any actions, attitudes or policies that are components of those ends. However, by itself this calculating, predominantly instrumental, side of end-oriented practical reason, as discussed in §2, cannot guide action without assuming subjective ends.

4 Act-oriented reasoning: reason appeals to norms

Other accounts of practical reason hold that it must guide action without reference either to subjective ends (because its conclusions would then be conditional on something wholly arbitrary) or to objective ends (because there is none). An adequate account of practical reason must bear more directly on action, and more specifically on the practical propositions (norms, rules, principles) which agents follow or embody in their lives. Just as theoretical reasoning prescribes ways of moving between elements that have syntactic and semantic structure, so too must practical reasoning. The central problem in using any act-oriented conception of practical reason for ethical purposes is to show *why* some but not other norms or principles, and so some but not other types of action and ends, attitudes and policies, are either good or ethically required.

Many forms of act-oriented practical reasoning maintain that the basis for distinguishing certain types of action from others can be found in the categories, beliefs and norms that form the constitutive elements of a society or of a sense of identity. These constitutive norms cannot be brought into question by anyone for whom they constitute the horizons of life and thought, so can provide basic premises for reasoning about what is good or bad, required or forbidden.

Once some fundamental norms have been identified, practical reasoning can be extended both by instrumental reasoning and by analysing the logical connections and implications between different norms (for example, between requirements, prohibitions and permissions) and the structure of systems of norms. At its most formal this sort of analysis draws on deontic logic; less formal conceptual investigations of types and systems of rules have also been undertaken, particularly by philosophers of law (see DEONTIC LOGIC). However, since act-oriented practical

reasoning does not provide any metric for ends it cannot use the maximizing patterns of practical reasoning which some subjective forms of end-oriented reasoning favour.

Norm-based practical reasoning is uncontroversially part and parcel of daily life, but philosophical argument that it is the basis for all ethical reasoning is highly controversial. Arguments that all ethical reasoning appeals to norms can be found in the work of Hegel, in historicist, communitarian and relativist writing, and (in more individualistic forms) in work by Wittgensteinians and by Bernard Williams.

Hegel's view that there is no gap between *is* and *ought* expresses not the implausible thought that whatever is accepted is acceptable, that (contrary to Hume) *ought* can be generally be derived from *is*, but the more profound view that all thinking and action must grow not out of abstract theories and principles but out of the deep structures of our actual situations (Hegel's term is *Sittlichkeit*, often translated as *ethical life*) (see HEGEL, G.W.F. §8). The deep facts of our histories and lives are ones that we cannot 'go behind' and bring into question; rather they form the inescapable framework of our action, and so constitute legitimate, indeed unavoidable, starting points for all practical, including ethical, reasoning.

Similar positions can be found in Wittgenstein and in certain Wittgensteinians. In Wittgenstein's assertion that 'there must be agreement... in judgments' (*Philosophical Investigations* 1953: para. 242) and in the widespread view that certain issues are 'not a matter for decision', we see further versions of the thought that certain categories and norms form inescapable frameworks for life and thought, and that those who live within them lack any external vantage point from which to question or undermine them. More individualistic versions of the same approach can be found in Bernard Williams' contention that certain identity-constituting personal projects and commitments are part of the framework which reasoning must assume, so cannot query (see WILLIAMS, B.A.O.)

Practical reasoning which appeals to constitutive norms, coupled with ordinary patterns of instrumental reasoning, has powerful means of guiding action at its disposal. Critics fear, however, that this power is bought too dearly. One alleged cost is that norm-based practical reasoning is supposedly conservative: it will always already have presupposed established (usually establishment) categories, norms, identities and commitments, and provides no vantage point from which they can be criticized. This criticism is rebutted by many proponents of norm-based reasoning who, like Hegel, point out that any constitutive norm, sense of identity or the like will be but part of a wider set of beliefs and norms, whose elements can be used to challenge, revise and renew one another. Once norms and identities are seen in developmental, historical context there is no reason to suppose that practical reasoning that starts from those of a given place and time must be intrinsically conservative.

Perhaps a more worrying criticism of norm-based practical reasoning is that even if it is not intrinsically conservative, it is nevertheless unavoidably designed for those who have internalized a certain outlook and its categories and norms: it is insiders' reasoning. For outsiders, treating insiders' shared categories and norms, and the established practices and identities they support, as bedrock for practical reasoning lacks all justification, because it adopts arbitrary premises. Like instrumental reasoning, norm-based reasoning can at best reach conditional conclusions. Its advocates can only retort that there is no external vantage available from which these starting points can be rebutted or called into question.

5 Act-oriented reasoning: reason appeals to 'the world at large'

If act-oriented reasoning is to escape the confines and the criticisms which it incurs by treating socially specific categories and norms as the bedrock for ethical reasoning, then it must find some way of 'going behind' and criticizing these assumptions.

The classic version of a critical conception of act-oriented practical reasoning was developed by Immanuel Kant, who held that reasoning should address 'the world at large' (that is, all reasoners) rather than the limited groups who share specific but intrinsically arbitrary norms and practices (Kant, *An Answer to the Question* and *What is Orientation in Thinking?*; O'Neil 1989 part I). If practical reasoning is to meet this standard, its first requirement must be the rejection of any principles which cannot be adopted by all, regardless of their social background, their accepted categories and norms, their established practices, their senses of identity or their desires (see UNIVERSALISM IN ETHICS). Kant summarized this requirement in the words: 'Act only on that maxim through which you can at the same time will that it should be a universal law' (*Grundlegung zur Metaphysik der Sitten* 1785). He claims that this principle of practical reason provides the supreme principle of morality, and should be called the 'categorical imperative' because it is the only way of reasoning practically which does not introduce arbitrary assumptions, and so the only one that can reach unconditional, namely categorical, conclusions. The component norms of social traditions and senses of identity may be scrutinized using

the categorical imperative; if they cannot be willed as universal laws they must be rejected as unreasoned.

Kant's attempt to vindicate this critical account of practical reasoning is based on the thought that anything which deserves to be called reasoning must be something that can be given or received, exchanged or followed, among the widest 'public', that is universally, and correspondingly that anything which invokes the norms and beliefs of limited groups, let alone the favoured projects of individual lives, calls for rather than provides reasons. The authority of reason is simply the requirement of living by fundamental principles that are fit for universal use (in other words, that are *lawlike*). Since we know no intrinsic sources of authoritative standards – we have no account of the objectively good – the only meagre authority with which we are left is the injunction to reject principles which cannot be principles for all.

Once this fundamental use of practical reason has been used to identify certain core ethical principles or rules, critical practical reasoning can be extended by some of the moves used by instrumental and norm-based practical reasoning. Kant insists that instrumental reasoning is indispensable (although he cannot reinstate the metric assumptions or maximizing calculi advocated by those who hinge reasoning on subjective ends). He speaks of instrumental reasoning as guided by the principle of the 'hypothetical imperative', since by itself it can only licence conditional conclusions. His full account of practical reasoning also relies on the transitions between different modalities of required action (for example, between claims about obligations, permissions and prohibitions) that are used in norm-based reasoning.

There are many passages in which Kant indicates that the principles of theoretical and practical reason are fundamentally the same (such as in *Grundlegung*). However in his case this appears to be the result neither of the derivation of practical from theoretical reason (as in instrumental reasoning) nor of the fusion of theory and practice (as in Platonism) but because his vindication of reason unites practical and theoretical reason (see O'Neill 1989 part II).

Kant's vindication of practical reason is controversial, and its adequacy as a guide to action is even more so. Since Hegel criticized Kant, many commentators have concluded that this stripped-down conception of practical reason is simply not enough to guide action, or alternatively that it will guide it in the 'wrong' direction. Some object that virtually any principle can be universally adopted and that this account of practical reason is not robust enough to guide action; others object (with little plausibility) that the universality requirement makes rigidly uniform demands and leaves no room for the differentiation of action which human life requires.

These classic (and incompatible) objections are respectively said to target empty 'formalism' and insensitive 'rigourism' (see O'Neill 1989 part II).

Kantian conceptions of practical reason have recently been taken up in two bodies of literature. Some writers have returned to Kant to look for more plausible interpretations of the procedures by which his conception of practical reason can guide action (see O'Neill 1989 part II) and to explicate his distinctive vindication of practical reason (see O'Neill 1989 part I). Others have offered a range of contemporary interpretations of the idea that the fundamental feature of practical reason is its capacity to be public (see Rawls 1993).

6   Other aspects of practical reason

Few, if any, accounts of practical reason claim to offer a total guide for action (the exception may be certain utilitarian versions of subjective end-oriented reasoning, which supposedly reduce everything to calculation). Most insist that good practical reasoning must be linked with careful empirical reasoning, and that it will also need judgment to determine the specific way in which an end should be pursued or a norm or principle instantiated (see MORAL JUDGMENT). There is general acceptance of the point (emphasized by both Kant and Wittgenstein) that rules cannot provide instructions for their own application, and must be supplemented by judgment. Real life appeals to instrumental reasoning, to socially specific norms and to abstract principles, are all inevitably indeterminate and must be augmented with judgment.

Reasoning practically is always a task rather than an automatic process, and there are therefore many ways in which it can fail. Some are cognitive failures (due, for example, to mistaken views about causal links or risks); others are closely linked to questions about motivation. Some central types of failure in practical reasoning have been the subject of extensive study (see AKRASIA).

See also: GOOD, THEORIES OF THE

References and further reading

O'Neill, O. (1989) *Constructions of Reason: Explorations of Kant's Practical Philosophy*, Cambridge: Cambridge University Press. (Papers on Kant's vindication of reason and on patterns of ethical reasoning that start from the categorical imperative.)

Rawls, J. (1993) *Political Liberalism*, New York: Columbia University Press. (Reformulation of his earlier political philosophy basing it on a conception of public reason.)

ONORA O'NEILL

PRAGMATIC THEORIES OF TRUTH
See TRUTH, PRAGMATIC THEORY OF

PRAGMATICS

Analytic philosophers have made lasting contributions to the scientific study of language. Semantics (the study of meaning) and pragmatics (the study of language in use) are two important areas of linguistic research which owe their shape to the groundwork done by philosophers.

Although the two disciplines are now conceived of as complementary, the philosophical movements out of which they grew were very much in competition. In the middle of the twentieth century, there were two opposing 'camps' within the analytic philosophy of language. The first – 'ideal language philosophy', as it was then called – was that of the pioneers, Frege, Russell and the logical positivists. They were, first and foremost, logicians studying formal languages and, through these formal languages, 'language' in general. Work in this tradition (especially that of Frege, Russell, Carnap, Tarski and later Montague) gave rise to contemporary *formal semantics*, a very active discipline developed jointly by logicians, philosophers and grammarians. The other camp was that of so-called 'ordinary language philosophers', who thought important features of natural language were not revealed, but hidden, by the logical approach initiated by Frege and Russell. They advocated a more descriptive approach, and emphasized the 'pragmatic' nature of natural language as opposed to, for example, the 'language' of *Principia Mathematica*. Their own work (especially that of Austin, Strawson, Grice and the later Wittgenstein) gave rise to contemporary pragmatics, a discipline which (like formal semantics) has developed successfully within linguistics in the past thirty years.

From the general conception put forward by ordinary language philosophers, four areas or topics of research emerged, which jointly constitute the core of pragmatics: speech acts; indexicality and context-sensitivity; non-truth-conditional aspects of meaning; and contextual implications. Looking at these topics from the point of view of ordinary language philosophy, pragmatics is seen as an *alternative* to the truth-conditional approach to meaning associated with ideal language philosophy (and successfully pursued within formal semantics). Looking at them from a contemporary point of view, pragmatics merely *supplements* that approach.

See also: STRAWSON, P.F.; WITTGENSTEIN, L.J.J.

FRANÇOIS RECANATI

PRAGMATISM

Introduction

Pragmatism is a philosophical tradition founded by three American philosophers: Charles Sanders Peirce, William James and John Dewey. Starting from Alexander Bain's definition of belief as a rule or habit of action, Peirce argued that the function of inquiry is not to represent reality, but rather to enable us to act more effectively. He was critical of the 'copy theory' of knowledge which had dominated philosophy since the time of Descartes, and especially of the idea of immediate, intuitive self-knowledge. He was also a prophet of the linguistic turn, one of the first philosophers to say that the ability to use signs is essential to thought.

Peirce's use of Bain was extended by James, whose *The Principles of Psychology* (1890) broke with the associationism of Locke and Hume. James went on, in *Pragmatism* (1907) to scandalize philosophers by saying that '"The true" . . . is only the expedient in our way of thinking'. James and Dewey both wanted to reconcile philosophy with Darwin by making human beings' pursuit of the true and the good continuous with the activities of the lower animals – cultural evolution with biological evolution. Dewey criticized the Cartesian notion of the self as a substance which existed prior to language and acculturation, and substituted an account of the self as a product of social practices (an account developed further by George Herbert Mead).

Dewey, whose primary interests were in cultural, educational and political reform rather than in specifically philosophical problems (problems which he thought usually needed to be dissolved rather than solved), developed the implications of pragmatism for ethics and social philosophy. His ideas were central to American intellectual life throughout the first half of the twentieth century.

All three of the founding pragmatists combined a naturalistic, Darwinian view of human beings with a deep distrust of the problems which philosophy had inherited from Descartes, Hume and Kant. They hoped to save philosophy from metaphysical idealism, but also to save moral and religious ideals from empiricist or positivist scepticism. Their naturalism has been combined with an anti-foundationalist, holist account of meaning by Willard van Orman Quine, Hilary Putnam and Donald Davidson – philosophers of language who are often seen as belonging to the pragmatist tradition. That tradition also has affinities with the work of Thomas Kuhn and the later work of Ludwig Wittgenstein.

1 Classical pragmatism
2 Pragmatism after the linguistic turn
3 Pragmatism as anti-representationalism
4 Pragmatism and humanity's self-image

1 Classical pragmatism

Charles Sanders PEIRCE, William JAMES and John DEWEY – often referred to as the three 'classical pragmatists' – had very different philosophical concerns. Except for their shared opposition to the correspondence theory of truth, and to 'copy theories' of knowledge, their doctrines do not overlap extensively (see TRUTH, PRAGMATIC THEORY OF). Although each knew and respected the other two, they did not think of themselves as belonging to an organized, disciplined philosophical movement. Peirce thought of himself as a disciple of Kant, improving on Kant's doctrine of categories and his conception of logic. A practising mathematician and laboratory scientist, he was more interested in these areas of culture than were James or Dewey. James took neither Kant nor Hegel very seriously, but was far more interested in religion than either Peirce or Dewey. Dewey, deeply influenced by Hegel, was fiercely anti-Kantian. Education and politics, rather than science or religion, were at the centre of his thought.

Peirce was a brilliant, cryptic and prolific polymath, whose writings are very difficult to piece together into a coherent system. He is now best known as a pioneer in the theory of signs, and for work in logic and semantics contemporaneous with, and partially paralleling, that of Frege. Peirce's account of inquiry as a matter of practical problem-solving was complemented by his criticisms of the Cartesian (and empiricist) idea of 'immediate knowledge', and of the project of building knowledge on self-evident foundations (of either a rationalist or empiricist kind).

Peirce protested against James' appropriation of his ideas, for complex reasons to do with his obscure and idiosyncratic doctrine of 'Scotistic realism' – the reality of universals, considered as potentialities or dispositions. Peirce was more sympathetic to metaphysical idealism than James, and found James' version of pragmatism simplistic and reductionist. James himself, however, thought of pragmatism as a way of avoiding reductionism of all kinds, and as a counsel of tolerance. Particularly in his famous essay 'The Will to Believe' (1896), he attempted to reconcile science and religion by viewing both as instruments useful for distinct, non-conflicting purposes.

Although he viewed many metaphysical and theological disputes as, at best, exhibitions of the diversity of human temperament, James hoped to construct an alternative to the anti-religious, science-worshipping positivism of his day. He approvingly cited Giovanni Papini's description of pragmatism as 'like a corridor in a hotel. Innumerable chambers open out of it. In one you may find a man writing an atheistic volume; in the next someone on his knees praying for faith; in a third a chemist investigating a body's properties ... they all own the corridor, and all must pass through it'. His point was that attention to the implications of beliefs for practice offered the only way to communicate across divisions between temperaments, academic disciplines and philosophical schools.

Dewey, in his early period, tried to bring Hegel together with evangelical Christianity. Although references to Christianity almost disappear from his writings around 1900, in a 1903 essay on Emerson he still looked forward to the development of 'a philosophy which religion has no call to chide, and which knows its friendship with science and with art'. The anti-positivist strain in classical pragmatism was at least as strong as its anti-metaphysical strain, and so James and Dewey found themselves attacked simultaneously from the empiricist left and from the idealist right – by Bertrand RUSSELL as well as by F.H. BRADLEY. Both critics thought of the pragmatists as fuzzy and jejune thinkers. This sort of criticism was repeated later in the century by the disciples of CARNAP, most of whom dismissed the classical pragmatists as lacking in precision and argumentative rigour.

James wrote a few remarkable essays on ethics – notably 'The Moral Philosopher and the Moral Life' (1891), in which, echoing Mill's *Utilitarianism*, he says that every desire and need has a *prima facie* right to be fulfilled, and that only some competing desire or need can provide a reason to leave it unsatisfied. But neither James nor Peirce attempted any systematic discussion of moral or political philosophy. Dewey, however, wrote extensively in this area throughout his life – from *Outlines of a Critical Theory of Ethics* (1891) to *Human Nature and Conduct* (1922) and *Theory of Valuation* (1939).

Dewey urged that we make no sharp distinction between moral deliberation and proposals for change in sociopolitical institutions, or in education (the last being a topic on which he wrote extensively, in books which had considerable impact on educational practice in many countries). He saw changes in individual attitudes, in public policies and in strategies of acculturation as three interlinked aspects of the gradual development of freer and more democratic communities, and of the better sort of human being who would develop within such communities. All of Dewey's books are permeated by the typically nineteenth-century conviction that human history is the story of expanding human freedom and by the hope of substituting a less professionalized, more politically oriented conception of the philosopher's task for the Platonic conception of the philosopher as 'spectator of time and eternity'.

In *Reconstruction in Philosophy* (1920) he wrote that 'under disguise of dealing with ultimate reality, philosophy has been occupied with the precious values embedded in social traditions. ... has sprung from a clash of social ends and from a conflict of inherited institutions with incompatible contemporary tendencies'. For him, the task of future philosophy was not to achieve new solutions to traditional problems, but to clarify 'men's ideas as to the social and moral strifes of their own day'. This conception of philosophy, which developed out of Hegel's and resembled Marx's (see HEGEL, G.W.F.; MARX, K.), isolated Dewey (particularly after the rise of analytic philosophy) from colleagues who thought of their discipline as the study of narrower and more precise questions – questions that had remained substantially unchanged throughout human history.

2 Pragmatism after the linguistic turn

Peirce was one of the first philosophers to emphasize the importance of signs. 'The word or the sign which man uses *is* the man himself,' he wrote, ' ... my language is the sum total of myself; for the man is the thought'. But, with the exception of C.I. LEWIS and Charles Morris, philosophers did not take Peirce's work on signs very seriously. Indeed, for decades Peirce remained largely unread: he had never published a philosophical book, and most of his articles were collected and republished only in the 1930s.

By that time philosophy in the English-speaking world was already in the process of being transformed by admirers of Frege, notably Carnap and Russell. These philosophers accomplished what Gustav Bergmann was to baptize 'the linguistic turn' in philosophy. They thought that it would be more fruitful, more likely to yield clear and convincing results, if philosophers were to discuss the structure of language rather than, as Locke and Kant had, the structure of the mind or of experience. The early analytic philosophers, however, accompanied this turn with a revival of the traditional empiricist idea that sense-perception provides foundations for empirical knowledge – an idea which, at the beginning of the century, the idealists and the classical pragmatists had united in rejecting. These philosophers also insisted on a strict distinction between conceptual questions (the analogue of Kant's 'transcendental' questions), now reinterpreted as questions about the meaning of linguistic expressions, and empirical questions of fact.

It was not until that distinction was questioned by Willard van Orman Quine in his groundbreaking 'Two Dogmas of Empiricism' (1951) that pragmatism was able once again to obtain a hearing (see QUINE, W.V. §8). James and Dewey had been viewed during the heyday of logical positivism as having prefigured the logical positivist's verifiability criterion of empirical meaningfulness, but as unfortunately lacking the powerful analytic tools which the new logic had made available. However, Quine's suggestion that empirical observation of linguistic behaviour could not detect a difference between necessary, analytic truths and contingent, synthetic, yet unquestioned truths helped revive the pragmatists' combination of holism, anti-foundationalism and naturalism.

That suggestion was reinforced by other publications which were roughly simultaneous with Quine's. In *Philosophical Investigations* (1953), Ludwig Wittgenstein mocked the idea that logic is both 'something sublime' and the essence of philosophy, an idea which the younger Wittgenstein had shared with Russell (see WITTGENSTEIN, L.J.J. §8). That book also reinvigorated the pragmatists' claim that most philosophical problems should be dissolved rather than solved. Wilfrid Sellars' 'Empiricism and the Philosophy of Mind' (1953) renewed both Peirce's assault on the idea of 'immediate experience' and his claim that the intentionality of the mental is derived from the intentionality of the linguistic, rather than conversely (see SELLARS, W.S.). In America, this article had the same devastating effect on the notion of 'sense-datum', and thus on the empiricist roots of logical positivism, that J.L. Austin's work was simultaneously having in Britain (see AUSTIN, J.L.). The work of Sellars and Austin conspired to deprive empiricism of the prestige which it had traditionally enjoyed in the Anglophone philosophical world.

Somewhat later, Thomas Kuhn's *The Structure of Scientific Revolutions* (1962) broke the grip of the positivist notion that natural science, because it offered paradigmatically rational methods and procedures, should be imitated by the rest of culture (see KUHN, T.S.). The effect of these various anti-empiricist and anti-positivist writings was to make many post-positivistic analytic philosophers sympathetic to Dewey's suspicions of the Cartesian-Kantian problematic of modern philosophy. Hilary PUTNAM, the best-known contemporary philosopher to identify himself as a pragmatist, has written appreciatively about all three classical pragmatists, praising their refusal to distinguish 'the world as it is

in itself' from the world as it appears in the light of human needs and interests.

On Putnam's account in his *The Many Faces of Realism* (1987), 'the heart of pragmatism ... was the insistence on the agent point of view. If we find that we must take a certain point of view, use a certain 'conceptual system', when we are engaged in practical activity ... then we must not simultaneously advance the claim that it is not really the way things are in themselves'. Putnam holds that our moral judgments are no more and no less 'objective' than our scientific theories, and no more and no less rationally adopted. He agrees with Dewey that the positivists' attempt to separate 'fact' from 'value' is as hopeless as their pre-Quinean attempt to separate 'fact' from 'language'.

Putnam has also come to the defence of the most notorious and controversial of the classical pragmatists' doctrines: the so-called 'pragmatist theory of truth'. Peirce said 'the opinion which is fated to be ultimately agreed to by all who investigate is what we mean by the truth, and the object represented in this opinion is the real'. Putnam has revived this idea, arguing that even if we cannot follow Peirce in *defining* 'true' as 'idealized rational assertibility', the latter notion is, as a regulative ideal, inseparable from an understanding of the concept of truth. He has criticized the correspondence theory of truth by arguing that any such correspondence of a belief to reality can only be to reality under a particular description, and that no such description is ontologically or epistemologically privileged. Putnam follows Nelson Goodman in saying that 'there is no one Way the World Is'.

3 Pragmatism as anti-representationalism

Putnam is chary, however, of endorsing James' claim that '"The true" ... is only the expedient in the way of our thinking, as "the right" is only the expedient in our way of behaving'. That formulation was attacked by James' contemporaries as at worst an invitation to self-deception, and at best a confusion of truth with justifiability. Dewey tried to avoid the controversy by ceasing to use the word 'truth', and speaking instead of 'warranted assertibility'. But this did not shield him from charges of confusion and inconsistency. Russell, reviewing Dewey, said that 'there is a profound instinct in me which is repelled by [Dewey's] instrumentalism: the instinct of contemplation, and of escape from one's own personality'. He and many other critics complained that pragmatism is unable to take account of the eternity and absoluteness of truth – of the fact that a sentence that contains no demonstratives is, if true, true in utter independence of changes in human needs or purposes. Putnam's treatment of truth is designed to avoid the appearance of relativism, and to escape such strictures as Russell's.

Despite its paradoxical air and its apparent relativism, however, James' claim does bring out pragmatism's strongest point: its refusal to countenance a discontinuity between human abilities and those of other animals. Pragmatists are committed to taking Darwin seriously. They grant that human beings are unique in the animal kingdom in having language, but they urge that language be understood as a tool rather than as a picture. A species' gradual development of language is as readily explicable in Darwinian terms as its gradual development of spears or pots, but it is harder to explain how a species could have acquired the ability to *represent* the universe – especially the universe as it really is (as opposed to how it is usefully described, relative to the particular needs of that species).

In a weak sense of 'represent', of course, an earthworm or a thermostat can be said to contain 'representations of the environment', since there are internal arrangements in both which are responsible for the reactions of each to certain stimuli. But it makes little sense to ask whether those representations are *accurate*. Philosophers who take epistemological scepticism seriously (as pragmatists do not) have employed a stronger sense of 'representation', one in which it does make sense to ask whether the way in which it best suits human purposes to describe the universe is an accurate representation of the universe as it is in itself (see SCEPTICISM).

The idea that knowledge is accurate representation and the idea that reality has an intrinsic nature are inseparable, and pragmatists reject both. In rejecting these ideas pragmatists are rejecting the problematic of realism and antirealism – the question of whether there is or is not a 'matter of fact' about, for example, mathematics or ethics, whether beliefs in these areas are attempts to correspond to reality. Whatever may be said about truth, pragmatists insist, we cannot make sense of the notion of 'correspondence', nor of that of 'accurate representation of the way things are in themselves' (see TRUTH, CORRESPONDENCE THEORY OF).

Donald DAVIDSON is the philosopher of language whose work is most reminiscent of the classical pragmatists' attempts to be faithful to Darwin. Davidson has said that 'Beliefs are true or false, but they represent nothing. It is good to be rid of representations, and with them the correspondence theory of truth, for it is thinking that there are representations that engenders thoughts of relativism' ('The Myth of the Subjective' 1989). He has argued that we need to get rid of what he calls 'the third dogma of empiricism', the distinction between the mind or language as organizing

scheme, and something else (for example, the sensible manifold, the world) as organized content – the Kantian version of the dualism of subject and object (see 'On the Very Idea of a Conceptual Scheme' 1974). In 'A Nice Derangement of Epitaphs' (1986), an attempt to radicalize and extend Quine's naturalistic approach to the study of linguistic behaviour, he has suggested that we 'erase the boundary between knowing a language and knowing our way about in the world generally', and that 'there is no such thing as a language, not if a language is anything like what many philosophers and linguists have supposed'.

Davidson does not wish to be called a pragmatist, however, since he equates pragmatism with unfeasible attempts to reduce truth to some form of assertibility, thereby making it an epistemic concept, rather than a merely semantic one. Unlike Peirce and Putnam, Davidson thinks that we should treat 'true' as a primitive term, and should neither attempt to revitalize the correspondence theory of truth nor replace it with a better theory of truth. Davidson's strategy is summed up in his recommendation that we not say 'that truth is correspondence, coherence, warranted assertibility, ideally justified assertibility, what is accepted in the conversation of the right people, what science will end up maintaining, what explains the convergence on single theories in science, or the success of our ordinary beliefs' ('The Structure and Content of Truth' 1990). We should, he says in the same article, not offer an analysis of the meaning of 'true', but rather confine ourselves to describing 'the ultimate source of both objectivity and communication', namely, 'the triangle that, by relating speaker, interpreter and the world determines the contents of thought and speech'. The trouble with the correspondence theory, on Davidson's view, is that it cuts out the 'interpreter' side of the triangle, and treats truth as relation of 'matching' between speaker and world.

If one follows Davidson's advice, one can give up the pragmatist theory of truth without giving up the Darwinian naturalism which that theory was a paradoxical-sounding attempt to articulate. Such naturalism, however, entails an abandonment of much of the problematic of contemporary philosophy. If truth is never the name of a relation ('corresponding', 'representing', 'getting right', 'fitting') which holds between sentences and non-sentences, there is no point in asking whether this relation holds for some true sentences (for example, perceptual reports or scientific theories) and not for others (for example, sentences about numbers or values). On this latter point, Putnam and Davidson are in agreement (see TRUTH, CORRESPONDENCE THEORY OF).

841

Michael DUMMETT has suggested, plausibly, that the problematic of realism and antirealism is at the heart of the Western philosophical tradition (see REALISM AND ANTIREALISM). If he is right, and if Davidson is right in thinking that we should now abandon that problematic, then James' and Dewey's suggestions about how to end the traditional and seemingly sterile quarrels between materialists and idealists, positivists and metaphysicians, theists and atheists, science-worshippers and poetry-worshippers, look more promising. The heart of both men's pragmatism was not any particular doctrine about the nature of truth, of knowledge, or of value, but rather the hope that philosophy could renew itself by moving out from under traditional dualisms (subject–object, mind–world, theory–practice, morality–prudence) which recent science and recent social changes had, they believed, rendered obsolete.

The classical pragmatists saw themselves as responding to Darwin in the same way as the great philosophers of the seventeenth and eighteenth centuries had responded to Galileo and Newton. Philosophers such as Descartes, Locke and Kant attempted to accommodate old, precious, moral and spiritual aspirations to new scientific developments. James and Dewey thought that these attempts had been made obsolete by Darwin's new account of the origin of our species, and that fresh attempts were needed. If one reads Quine's and Davidson's naturalization of semantics as a continuation of philosophy's attempt to come to terms with Darwin, one can also read these two philosophers as continuing the larger enterprise which James and Dewey inaugurated.

4 Pragmatism and humanity's self-image

By stepping back from its relation to traditional empiricism on the one hand and to the linguistic turn on the other, one can put pragmatism in a larger context. Much twentieth-century philosophy has been devoted to a criticism of the view, shared by Plato and Aristotle, that a capacity to know things as they really are is central to being human. Philosophers influenced by Nietzsche – notably Heidegger, SARTRE and DERRIDA – have argued against the idea that cognition is the distinctively human capacity. Heidegger's treatment of inquiry as a species of coping, in his discussion of *Vorhandenheit* in *Being and Time* (1927), has much in common with Dewey's and Kuhn's attempts to see scientific progress as problem-solving – as the overcoming of obstacles to the satisfaction of human needs, rather than as convergence towards a special, specifically cognitive, relation to reality. Both Dewey and HEIDEGGER saw the Greek quest for certainty as

debilitating. Neither granted the traditional assumption that, in addition to all the other needs human beings have, there is a need to know the truth.

Heidegger's criticism of what he called 'onto-theology' – Western philosophy viewed as a series of attempts to find solace and support in the non-temporal – has much in common with Dewey's criticism of what he called 'intellectualism'. Both of these men saw the tradition which begins with Plato as a self-deceptive attempt to give the eternal priority over the temporal. So did BERGSON and WHITEHEAD, the founders of the tradition known as 'process philosophy', a tradition to which James (especially in his *Essays in Radical Empiricism*) made important contributions (see PROCESS PHILO-SOPHY). This downgrading of the eternal is characteristic of a great deal of twentieth-century philosophy. It is found in James' criticisms of Bradley, in Putnam's criticism of Bernard Williams' claim that we can use an 'absolute conception of the world' as a regulative ideal of inquiry, in Heidegger's criticism of Husserl, and in Derrida's criticism of Heidegger.

Downgrading eternity means downgrading both the idea of truth as eternal and the assumption that knowledge of eternal truth is the distinctively human activity. From a Davidsonian, as from a Deweyan, point of view, the only point of the doctrine that truth is eternal is to contrast truth with justification (which is obviously neither eternal nor absolute, because it is relative to the composition of the audience to which justification is offered, and thus to historical circumstance). But that contrast can be formulated without treating 'truth' as the name of a goal to be reached, or as an object to be admired. Davidson's treatment of truth forbids us to think of inquiry as subject to a norm of acquiring true beliefs, in addition to the norm of providing adequate justification. There is no way to seek for truth apart from seeking for justification. Justification gets better as the community to which justification is offered becomes more sophisticated and complex, more aware of possible sources of evidence and more capable of dreaming up imaginative new hypotheses and proposals. So pragmatists place the capacity to create complex and imaginative communities at the centre of their image of humanity, superseding the ability to know. Dewey and Putnam agree that the aim of inquiry is what Putnam calls 'human flourishing' – the kind of human life which is possible in free, democratic, tolerant, egalitarian societies. These are the societies in which the arts and the sciences proliferate and progress, and within which idiosyncrasy is tolerated.

The obvious difference between James, Dewey and Putnam on the one hand and Nietzsche, Heidegger and Foucault on the other – between the two most prominent sections of the twentieth-century revolt against the Greek self-image of humanity – is that these three Europeans do not share the Americans' enthusiasm for, and optimism about, liberal-democratic society. Nietzsche's, and the early Heidegger's, insistence on the resolute authenticity of the lonely individual, and their exaltation of will as opposed to intellect, are equally foreign to Dewey and to Putnam (though they have some echoes in certain passages of James). Rather than replace intellect by will, in the manner of SCHOPENHAUER, pragmatists tend to replace knowledge by love, in the manner of Kierkegaard's contrast between Socrates and Christ (see KIERKE-GAARD, S.A.).

For Dewey, the pragmatist who speculated most daringly, and developed the greatest historical self-consciousness, the glory of human beings is their ability to become citizens of a liberal-democratic society, of a community which constantly strives to see beyond its own limits – both with an eye to the inclusion of presently excluded or marginalized human beings and with respect to innovative intellectual and artistic initiatives. This is the capacity which most clearly sets us apart from other animals. It presupposes, of course, the capacity to use language, but for Dewey the point of having language, and therefore thought, was not to penetrate through the appearances to the true nature of reality, but rather to permit the social construction of new realities. For him, language was not a medium of representation, but a way of coordinating human activities so as to enlarge the range of human possibilities. These processes of coordination and enlargement, which make up cultural evolution, do not have a destined terminus called the Good or the True, any more than biological evolution has a destined terminus called The Ideal Life-Form. Dewey's imagery is always of proliferating novelty, rather than of convergence.

The naturalist strain in pragmatism, the attempt to come to terms with Darwin, is thus from a Deweyan point of view important mainly as a further strategy for shifting philosophers' attention from the problems of metaphysics and epistemology to the needs of democratic politics. Dewey once said that he agreed with Plato that politics was 'the science of the whole', a remark which summarized the following train of reasoning. Finding out what there is is a matter of finding out what descriptions of things will best fulfil our needs. Finding out what needs we should fulfil is a task for communal reflection about what human beings might become. Such cooperative inquiry into the possibilities of self-transcendence is best accomplished within a democratic society. So philosophers should stop asking about the nature of reality or of knowledge,

and instead try to strengthen and improve the institutions of such societies by clarifying 'men's ideas as to the social and moral strifes of their own day'.

See also: DARWIN, C.R.; DOUBT; EMPIRICISM; LOGICAL POSITIVISM; SCIENTIFIC REALISM AND ANTIREALISM

References and further reading
Murphy, J.P. (1990) *Pragmatism: From Peirce to Davidson*, Boulder, CO: Westview Press. (An introductory textbook. Murphy sees Quine and Davidson as continuing the pragmatist tradition. Contains a substantial bibliography.)
Scheffler, I. (1974) *Four Pragmatists: A Critical Introduction to Peirce, James, Mead and Dewey*, London: Routledge & Kegan Paul. (Combines sympathetic presentation with detailed criticism.)

RICHARD RORTY

PRAGUE SCHOOL
See STRUCTURALISM IN LINGUISTICS

PREDESTINATION

Predestination appears to be a religious or theological version of universal determinism, a version in which the final determining factor is the will or action of God. It is most often associated with the theological tradition of Calvinism, although some theologians outside the Calvinist tradition, or prior to it (for example, Augustine and Thomas Aquinas), profess similar doctrines. The idea of predestination also plays a role in some religions other than Christianity, perhaps most notably in Islam.

Sometimes the idea of predestination is formulated in a comparatively restricted way, being applied only to the manner in which the divine grace of salvation is said to be extended to some human beings and not to others. John Calvin, for example, writes:

> We call predestination God's eternal decree, by which he compacted with himself what he willed to become of each man. For all are not created in equal condition; rather, eternal life is foreordained for some, eternal damnation for others. Therefore, as any man has been created to one or the other of these ends, we speak of him as predestined to life or to death.
> (*Institutes*, bk 3, ch. 21, sec. 5)

At other times, however, the idea is applied more generally to the whole course of events in the world; whatever happens in the world is determined by the will of God. Philosophically, the most interesting aspects of the doctrine are not essentially linked with salvation. For instance, if God is the first cause of all that happens, how can people be said to have free will? One answer may be that people are free in so far as they act in accordance with their own motives and desires, even if these are determined by God. Another problem is that the doctrine seems to make God ultimately responsible for sin. A possible response here is to distinguish between actively causing something and passively allowing it to happen, and to say that God merely allows people to sin; it is then human agents who actively choose to sin and God is therefore not responsible.

See also: ETERNITY; OMNISCIENCE

GEORGE I. MAVRODES

PREDICATE CALCULUS

The predicate calculus is the dominant system of modern logic, having displaced the traditional Aristotelian syllogistic logic that had been the previous paradigm. Like Aristotle's, it is a logic of quantifiers – words like 'every', 'some' and 'no' that are used to express that a predicate applies universally or with some other distinctive kind of generality, for example 'everyone is mortal', 'someone is mortal', 'no one is mortal'. The weakness of syllogistic logic was its inability to represent the structure of complex predicates. Thus it could not cope with argument patterns like 'everything Fs and Gs, so everything Fs'. Nor could it cope with relations, because a logic of relations must be able to analyse cases where a quantifier is applied to a predicate that already contains one, as in 'someone loves everyone'. Remedying the weakness required two major innovations.

One was a logic of connectives – words like 'and', 'or' and 'if' that form complex sentences out of simpler ones. It is often studied as a distinct system: the propositional calculus. A proposition here is a true-or-false sentence and the guiding principle of propositional calculus is truth-functionality, meaning that the truth-value (truth or falsity) of a compound proposition is uniquely determined by the truth-values of its components. Its principal connectives are negation, conjunction, disjunction and a 'material' (that is, truth-functional) conditional. Truth-functionality makes it possible to compute the truth-values of propositions of arbitrary complexity in terms of their basic propositional constituents, and so develop the logic of tautology and tautological consequence (logical truth and consequence in virtue of the connectives).

The other invention was the quantifier-variable notation. Variables are letters used to indicate things in an unspecific way; thus 'x is mortal' is read as predicating of an unspecified thing x what 'Socrates is mortal' predicates of Socrates. The connectives can now be used to form complex predicates as well as propositions, for example 'x is human and x is mortal'; while different variables can be used in different places to express relational predicates, for example 'x loves y'. The quantifier goes in front of the predicate it governs, with the relevant variable repeated beside it to indicate which positions are being generalized. These radical departures from the idiom of quantification in natural languages are needed to solve the further problem of ambiguity of scope. Compare, for example, the ambiguity of 'someone loves everyone' with the unambiguous alternative renderings 'there is an x such that for every y, x loves y' and 'for every y, there is an x such that x loves y'.

The result is a pattern of formal language based on a non-logical vocabulary of names of things and primitive predicates expressing properties and relations of things. The logical constants are the truth-functional connectives and the universal and existential quantifiers, plus a stock of variables construed as ranging over things. This is 'the' predicate calculus. A common option is to add the identity sign as a further logical constant, producing the predicate calculus with identity. The first modern logic of quantification, Frege' in 1879, was designed to express generalizations not only about individual things but also about properties of individuals. It would nowadays be classified as a second-order logic, to distinguish it from the first-order logic described above. Second-order logic is much richer in expressive power than first-order logic, but at a price: first-order logic can be axiomatized, second-order logic cannot.

TIMOTHY SMILEY

PREFACE PARADOX
See PARADOXES, EPISTEMIC

PRESCRIPTIVISM

Prescriptivism is a theory about moral statements. It claims that such statements contain an element of meaning which serves to prescribe or direct actions. The history of prescriptivism includes Socrates, Aristotle, Hume, Kant and Mill, and it has been influential also in recent times.

Moral statements also contain a factual or descriptive element. The descriptive element of morality differs between persons and cultures, but the prescriptive element remains constant.

Prescriptivism can allow for moral disagreement, and explain moral weakness. It can also explain better than other theories the rationality and objectivity of moral thinking.

R.M. HARE

PRESOCRATIC PHILOSOPHY

The Presocratics were the first Western philosophers. The most celebrated are Thales, Anaximander, Pythagoras, Heraclitus, Parmenides, Zeno of Elea, Empedocles, Anaxagoras and Democritus. Active in Greece throughout the sixth and fifth centuries BC, they concentrated on cosmogony and cosmology – the tasks of explaining the world's origin and order, without recourse to mythology.

Socrates (469–399 BC) is perceived as marking a watershed in philosophy – a shift of focus from the origin and nature of the universe to human values. 'Presocratic' philosophy thus represents the era intellectually antecedent to Socrates, even though its exponents included contemporaries of his (some his juniors). Those thinkers contemporary with Socrates who shared his concentration on human values it is better not to call Presocratic (see SOPHISTS). No complete Presocratic text survives. We have only later writers' quotations ('fragments'), summaries, criticisms, and so on, from which to glimpse the originals.

A mythological construction of the world was already integral to the earliest poetry familiar to the Greeks (c.700 BC). Philosophers' rationalizations of this picture concentrated initially on such questions as what the world's primeval stuff is, why the earth remains stable and, more generally, what made the world orderly. In time *kosmos* ('ordering'), came to mean 'world'. To explain cosmic order, biological, mechanical and even political models were developed. However, Presocratic philosophy was interested equally in the human soul and its destiny (see PSYCHÉ), and never altogether ignored human values. Another dominant issue was the possibility of human knowledge.

The main movements and phases were as follows. The three sixth-century BC Milesian philosophers, starting with Thales, were monists: each posited a single primeval stuff – for example, water, air. These came to function not just as the world's originative stuff but also perhaps as its enduring substrate (see ARCHÉ; THALES; ANAXIMANDER; ANAXIMENES; MONISM).

Pythagoreanism, although a secretive movement with cultic leanings, was highly influential throughout this era. Beyond a concern with the soul and survival, it promoted a mathematicizing approach to cosmology (see PYTHAGORAS; PYTHAGOREANISM).

Heraclitus (c.540–480 BC) kept the formal focus on the cosmos and the soul, but his approach was largely governed by metaphysical concerns, especially the paradoxical interdependence of opposites (see HERACLITUS). Metaphysics and logic took centre stage soon after in the Eleatic movement, initiated by PARMENIDES and continued by ZENO OF ELEA and Melissus. Eleaticism was a radical critique of ordinary notions of being, defending instead a strict monism which outlawed all phenomenal distinctions and changes as illusory (see also GORGIAS).

The later fifth-century BC cosmologists sought to deflect this Eleatic critique. Most were pluralists, positing more than one underlying element. Their contributions culminated in the atomic system of DEMOCRITUS, which reduced all reality to atoms and void, conceding much to Eleaticism (see ATOMISM, ANCIENT; EMPEDOCLES; LEUCIPPUS)

Presocratic philosophy is often seen as materialistic. However, no philosopher before Leucippus and Democritus reduced life and intelligence to something inanimate. Previous Presocratics considered these ineliminably present in things – either as already intrinsic to the primordial stuff(s) or, in Anaxagoras' system, by virtue of an irreducible dualism of mind and matter.

See also: ANCIENT PHILOSOPHY; SOCRATES

References and further reading

Barnes, J. (1979) *The Presocratic Philosophers*, London: Routledge & Kegan Paul. (The most philosophically satisfying work on the Presocratics.)

Kirk, G.S., Raven, J.E. and Schofield, M. (1983) *The Presocratic Philosophers*, Cambridge: Cambridge University Press, 2nd edn (An invaluable survey of Presocratic philosophy, including texts and translations.)

Long, A.A. (2000) (ed.) *The Cambridge Companion to Greek and Roman Philosophy*, Cambridge: Cambridge University Press. (Up-to-date and accessible survey, with very full bibliography.)

DAVID SEDLEY

PRESUPPOSITION

There are various senses in which one statement may be said to 'presuppose' another, senses which are in permanent danger of being confused. Prominent among them are Strawsonian presupposition, a relation which obtains between statements when the falsity of one deprives the other of truth-value (for example, 'There was such a person as Kepler' is a Strawsonian presupposition of 'Kepler died in misery'); semantic presupposition, which obtains between a statement and a particular use of a sentence type, when the falsity of the statement

845

means that that use will not after all constitute the making of a statement (for example, 'The name "Kepler" has a bearer' is a semantic presupposition of 'Kepler died in misery'); and pragmatic presupposition, a broader notion exemplified by the legitimate presumption that accepting or denying the statement 'Fred knows that the earth moves' means accepting 'The earth moves'.

See also: DESCRIPTIONS; IMPLICATURE; PRAGMATICS

IAN RUMFITT

PRIMARY–SECONDARY DISTINCTION

The terminology of 'primary and secondary qualities' is taken from the writings of John Locke. It has come to express a position on the nature of sensory qualities – those which we attribute to physical objects as a result of the sensuous character of sensations they produce when they are perceived correctly by us. Since our senses can be differentiated from each other by the type of sensations they produce, sensory qualities are what Aristotle called 'proper sensibles' – those perceptible by one sense only. Colours, sounds, scents and tastes are always regarded as proper to their respective senses. What are the proper sensibles of touch, and whether there is similarly a single family of them, is a matter of controversy; but temperature at least is standardly regarded as proper to this sense. It is such sensory qualities that are candidates for being given the status of secondary qualities.

To regard sensory qualities as secondary is to hold that an object's possession of one is simply a matter of its being disposed to occasion a certain type of sensation when perceived; the object in itself possesses no sensuous character. Primary qualities, by contrast, are those which characterize the fundamental nature of the physical world as it is in itself. They are always taken to include geometrical attributes, and often some space-occupying feature; Locke's candidate for this latter was solidity. Although the terminology dates from the seventeenth century, this general doctrine goes back to the Greek atomists.

See also: QUALIA

A.D. SMITH

PRINCIPLE OF CHARITY
See CHARITY, PRINCIPLE OF

PRIOR, ARTHUR NORMAN (1914–69)

Prior is most often thought of as the creator of tense logic. (Tense logic examines operators such as 'It will be the case that' in the way that modal logic examines 'It must be the case that'.) But his first

book was on ethics, and his views on metaphysical topics such as determinism, thinking, intentionality, change, events, the nature of time, existence, identity and truth are of central importance to philosophy. Using methods akin to Russell's in his Theory of Descriptions, Prior showed that times, events, facts, propositions and possible worlds were logical constructions. For example, we get rid of events by recognizing among other things that to say that the event of Caesar's crossing the Rubicon took place later than the event of Caesar's invading Britain is to say that it has been the case that both Caesar is crossing the Rubicon and it has been the case that Caesar is invading Britain. The title of the posthumous work, *Worlds, Times and Selves* (1977), indicates the breadth and depth of his thought. He is also fun to read. Prior died at the age of fifty-four, at the height of his powers.

C.J.F. WILLIAMS

PRIVACY

The distinction between private and public is both central to much legal and political thought and subject to serious challenge on philosophical, practical and political grounds by critics of the status quo. Privacy – the state of being withdrawn from the world, free from public attention, interference or intrusion – is a cherished social value that is being offered ever more protection. Increasingly, laws require people to respect the privacy of others: privacy is recognized as a fundamental right in international documents and national constitutions, and recent customs and social norms forbid intrusions that were once accepted. The concept of privacy is also widely abused: it has been used to justify private racial discrimination and state neglect of domestic violence, as well as social abdication of general economic welfare through *laissez-faire* policies and the so-called privatization of social services. Critique of the public–private distinction is an important part of many critical theories, especially feminism and critical legal theory. These critics object that the public–private distinction is exaggerated, manipulable or incoherent.

FRANCES OLSEN

PRIVATE AND PUBLIC
See PRIVACY

PRIVATE LANGUAGE ARGUMENT

Ludwig Wittgenstein argued against the possibility of a private language in his 1953 book *Philosophical Investigations*, where the notion is outlined at §243: 'The words of this language are to refer to what can be known only to the speaker; to his immediate, private, sensations. So another cannot understand the language.' The idea attacked is thus of a language in principle incomprehensible to more than one person because the things which define its vocabulary are necessarily inaccessible to others; cases such as personal codes where the lack of common understanding could be remedied are hence irrelevant.

Wittgenstein's attack, now known as the private language argument (although just one of many considerations he deploys on the topic), is important because the possibility of a private language is arguably an unformulated presupposition of standard theory of knowledge, metaphysics and philosophy of mind from Descartes to much of the cognitive science of the late twentieth century.

The essence of the argument is simple. It is that a language in principle unintelligible to anyone but its user would necessarily be unintelligible to the user also, because no meanings could be established for its signs. But, because of the difficulty of Wittgenstein's text and the tendency of philosophers to read into it their own concerns and assumptions, there has been extensive and fundamental disagreement over the details, significance and even intended conclusion of the argument. Some, thinking it obvious that sensations are private, have supposed that the argument is meant to show that we cannot talk about them; some that it commits Wittgenstein to behaviourism; some that the argument, self-defeatingly, condemns public discourse as well; some that its conclusion is that language is necessarily social in a strong sense, that is, not merely potentially but actually. Much of the secondary (especially the older) literature is devoted to disputes over these matters.

An account of the argument by the influential American philosopher Saul Kripke has spurred a semi-autonomous discussion of it. But Kripke's version involves significant departures from the original and relies on unargued assumptions of a kind Wittgenstein rejected in his own treatment of the topic.

See also: Consciousness; Criteria; Kripke, S.A.; Wittgenstein, L.J.J.

STEWART CANDLISH

PRIVATE STATES AND LANGUAGE

Something is 'private' if it can be known to one person only. Many have held that perceptions and bodily sensations are in this sense private, being knowable only by the person who experiences them. (You may know, it is often said, that we both call the same things 'green'; but whether they really look the same to me as they do to you, you have no

means of telling.) Regarding the relation between private states and language two main questions have arisen:

(1) Could there be a 'private language', that is, a language in which a person communicates to themselves, or records for their own use, information about their own private states – this language being in principle incomprehensible to others, who do not know the nature of the events it is used to record? This question is primarily associated with Ludwig Wittgenstein.

(2) Can the nature of our private states affect the meaning of expressions in the public language, that is, the language we use for communicating with each other? Or must everything that affects the meaning of expressions in the public language be something which is itself public, and knowable in principle by anyone? Michael Dummett has argued that we must accept the second of these alternatives, and that this has far-reaching consequences in logic and metaphysics.

See also: Intuitionistic logic and antirealism; Private language argument

EDWARD CRAIG

PROBABILITY, INTERPRETATIONS OF

Introduction

The term 'probability' and its cognates occur frequently in both everyday and philosophical discourse. Unlike many other concepts, it is unprofitable to view 'probability' as having a unique meaning. Instead, there exist a number of distinct, albeit related, concepts, of which we here mention five: the classical or equiprobable view, the relative frequency view, the subjectivist or personalist view, the propensity view, and the logical probability view. None of these captures all of our legitimate uses of the term 'probability', which range from the clearly subjective, as in our assessment of the likelihood of one football team beating another, through the inferential, as when one set of sentences lends a degree of inductive support to another sentence, to the obviously objective, as in the physical chance of a radioactive atom decaying in the next minute. It is often said that what all these interpretations have in common is that they are all described by the same simple mathematical theory – 'the theory of probability' to be found in most elementary probability textbooks – and it has traditionally been the task of any interpretation to conform to that theory. But this saying does not hold up under closer examination, and it is better to consider each approach as dealing with a separate subject matter, the structure of which determines the structure of the appropriate calculus.

1   The project

The task of interpreting probability might be approached in three distinct ways. The first way is to see the project as one of providing an explicit definition of the term 'probability' or, more usually, of the predicate 'has a probability of value p'. The second is to provide operational content to this predicate; in other words, to provide a set of procedures by means of which various probability values can be measured or attributed. This second task may result only in the provision of sufficient conditions for attributing the predicate, and conversely a solution to the first task may be accomplished without the definition providing us with a way to measure probability values. At one time, when verificationism held sway, a failure to provide measurement criteria was considered fatal to a definition (see LOGICAL POSITIVISM §4; OPERATIONALISM), but we should keep separate these two tasks. The third approach is to provide an implicit definition of the predicate 'has a probability of value p' by means of an axiomatized theory of probability, followed by an interpretation or model for that theory. That is, because the concept of probability is often considered to be mysterious and inaccessible to observation in a way that the concept of, say, blue, is not, the best and perhaps the only way of providing content to the concept is by constructing a detailed theory of probability and providing a model within which the theory is true. This third project consists in putting structural constraints on possible interpretations of a probability function, and it will not ordinarily result in an explicit definition. It will also not usually assign specific values to outcomes, except for certain extremal values, such as the certain or the impossible event.

2   The formal theory

The structure of elementary probability theory is often motivated by an appeal to familiar facts about relative frequencies. Suppose that a chance process, such as rolling a die, has N possible outcomes which form an outcome space $\Omega = \{1, 2, 3, 4, 5, 6\}$. By taking subsets of Ω, such as $\{2, 4, 6\}$, we have an event consisting in the die coming up even. Then take all possible subsets of Ω and this will form an algebra A of subsets of Ω, for example, a set of subsets of Ω closed under complementation ('negation') and union ('disjunction'). Let us say that an event E in A occurs if the elementary outcome, such as '2', is in E. Then we can define a probability function P over A by letting $P(E) =$ the number of times E occurs/the total number of repetitions of the chance process. This immediately gives us that

(1) $P(\Omega) = 1$

(2) $P(E) \geq 0$

(3)   If two events E and F are mutually exclusive, then $P(E \cup F) = P(E) + P(F)$.

For mathematical convenience, this elementary theory is usually extended by requiring countable additivity, wherein (3) is replaced by

(3') $P(\cup_{i=1}^{\infty} E_i) = \sum_{i=1}^{\infty} P(E_i)$ when the E_i are all mutually disjoint.

(The structure of A then needs to be more complex in ways that are inessential here.)

An important definition to add is that of conditional probability, $P(A \mid B)$, the probability of A given B, defined as $P(A \mid B) = P(A \cap B)/P(B)$. Two elements of A are *independent* if and only if $P(A \mid B) = P(A)$ or, equivalently, if $P(A \cap B)P(A) \times P(B)$.

This abstract calculus is now no longer tied to the particular interpretation with which we began, and the algebra can be one of propositions rather than events, an ontology preferable for logical or subjective interpretations. Different accounts of probability can now be compared to this axiomatic theory.

3   Relative frequency theories

Here the ontology is one of event types, and the probability is explicitly defined either as the actual finite relative frequency as in §2 above, or as the limit value of the relative frequency when the total number of repetitions goes to infinity. This gives the value of the probability as an empirical property of the sequence or reference class of outcomes which generates the frequency, rather than absolutely. A naïve finite frequency interpretation is clearly unsatisfactory. Suppose a die is rolled a finite number of times N. Then no outcome, say a '6', can have a probability value more fine-grained than on a scale 0, $1/N$, $2/N$, ..., 1. Thus, after two throws, a '6' could only have a probability of 0, 0.5, or 1. This problem could be circumvented by requiring sufficiently many repetitions, where 'sufficiently many' would be a function of the number of possible outcomes and degree of precision required. A more standard remedy for this problem is to move to a limiting relative frequency interpretation, wherein the probability value is simply defined as the limit of m/N as $N \rightarrow \infty$, where m is the number of successes. This solves our first, definitional, task, but it produces a difficulty for the measurement project, for there is no guarantee that the value of the relative frequency after, say, 1,000 repetitions, will be the same as, or close to, the limiting value, because an unusual run of outcomes could occur initially. What one can do is appeal to the strong law of large numbers for binary valued outcomes, which asserts that if the repetitions of the experiment are independent and identically distributed (that is, the probability does not vary from repetition to repetition) then

for every $\varepsilon > 0$, with probability one $|m/N - p| > \varepsilon$ only finitely often.

This provides assurance that in the long run, the probability that the limiting frequency will differ from the 'true' value of p is zero, but at the cost of introducing a second order probability which in turn needs to be interpreted. As an additional requirement, Richard von Mises correctly insisted that limiting frequency values can only be drawn from random sequences of data. Thus, if our die gave us the sequence of outcomes 1, 2, 3, 4, 5, 6, 1, 2, 3, 4, 5, 6, ..., the limiting frequency of a '2' would be 1/6, but quite clearly on every $(6N + 2)$nd throw ($N = 0, 1, 2, ...$) the probability of '2' would be 1, and would be 0 on any other throw. This highlights what is known as the problem of single-case probabilities – how do we transfer a probability value from a class to a single outcome? A standard answer is that the appropriate frequency for an outcome type is one drawn from a random sequence. Attempts to solve this single-case problem have led to complex and fascinating theories of randomness and statistical relevance, each of which is of philosophical interest in its own right.

4 Propensity theories

We have seen above that relative frequencies are defined relative to a class of outcomes. If we focus on the fact that outcomes can be produced by a fixed set of generating conditions, then it is reasonable to attribute probabilities to a system in a physical context, especially when the system producing the outcomes is irreducibly indetermi-

nistic. This gives us a chance disposition or *propensity* to produce a given outcome. For example, the probability of decay within the next minute is a physical property of a radioactive atom, just as is its atomic weight. This view, which seems to have originated with C.S. Peirce, and was resurrected by KARL POPPER (§3), has been criticized as excessively metaphysical. This is an unfair criticism, for the propensity value can be measured empirically for a system with a fixed propensity by employing the strong law of large numbers, mentioned above, together with statistical estimation techniques, thus satisfying the operational criterion. Being a thoroughly ontological interpretation, propensity accounts do not provide an explicit reductionist definition of probability, for propensities are basic, often primitive, properties of the world. However, no satisfactory solution has yet been given for the third project of providing a propensity calculus. Nor, despite a number of efforts by Popper and others, has a satisfactory argument been provided that quantum probabilities are obviously propensities in any detailed sense (see CAUSATION; QUANTUM MECHANICS, INTERPRETATION OF; STATISTICS).

5 Subjective probabilities

In contrast to the objective interpretations just described, probability has always had a close relation with degrees of rational belief. Within this tradition, one can measure such degrees of belief operationally by means of betting behaviour. Here the elements to which the probabilities attribute values are propositions or sentences rather than events. By means of an ingenious operational process, known as the Dutch book method, within which the probability value is defined in terms of the lowest odds at which the gambler will accept a bet, one can show that plausible constraints on rational behaviour are satisfied if and only if axioms (1)–(3) and the definition of conditional probability of §2 hold. The subjective probability assignments are then said to be coherent. Thus we have satisfied the second and third criteria cited earlier, although it should be noted that different individuals can assign widely different values to a contingent proposition and both be coherent. De Finetti, however, held that (3′) was not true for subjective probabilities because placing an infinite number of bets makes no sense for human agents. The Dutch book method will give us what are called prior probabilities but, except for extremal values, these are not arrived at by an a priori process. Rather, they are the expression of an unarticulated amalgamation of background knowledge. Although there is some controversy over how best to revise beliefs in the light of empirical evidence, the traditional way to do this is via conditionalization, using Bayes' theorem. If H_j is a hypothesis (say that the die is fair), E is empirical evidence (say data from throws) and P_0 is our prior subjective probability assignment, then

$$P_1(H_j) = P_0(H_j \mid E)$$
$$= P_0(E \mid H_j)P_0(H_j) / \sum_i P_0(E \mid H_i)P_0(H_i)$$

where $\{H_i\}$ is the set of hypotheses under consideration and P_1 is the new, posterior, probability assignment. Provided that the members of $\{H_i\}$ are distinct hypotheses (only one can be true at any time) and that $\sum_i P_0(H_i) = 1$ (the possibility that no member of $\{H_i\}$ is true is not entertained), $\sum_i P_0(E \mid H_i)P_0(H_i) = P_0(E)$, which gives $P_1(H_j) = P_0(H_j \mid E)P_0(H_j)/P_0(E)$.

The above gives us a normative theory of how agents should distribute their degrees of belief, but there has always been a divergence between this normative Bayesianism and individuals' actual degrees of belief. Investigations by psychologists and economists have revealed systematic differences from Bayesian prescriptions, even by agents well versed in probabilistic reasoning.

6 Classical interpretations of probability

This approach allocates probability values by dividing the outcomes into equipossible cases, and then using a principle of indifference to give each equipossible case an equal probability. Thus, if one considers, on the basis of symmetry, that each side of a die is just as likely to come up as any other side, then the classical theory attributes a value of 1:6 to each such outcome. This is not, contrary to many claims, always an a priori attribution, because it generally depends upon some specific empirical knowledge about symmetries of the system. The classical approach is unsatisfactory for a variety of reasons. First, it is limited to situations in which equipossible cases are available. Second, there are straightforward paradoxes associated with this approach, which allow different probability values to be attached to the same event. The simplest is one introduced by Bertrand. Suppose you have wine and water mixed, in a ratio somewhere between one part of water to one of wine, and two parts water to one of wine. Using an indifference principle on the ratio water:wine, we have that the probability of the ratio lying between 1 and 1.5 is 1:2. Now consider the ratio wine:water. This can lie between 1:2 and 1, and the water:wine ratio of 1:5 is a wine:water ratio of 2:3. The indifference principle then says that the probability of this ratio lying between 1 and 2:3 has a probability of 2:3. This is contradictory.

7 Logical interpretations and other approaches

The logical approach takes propositions as the objects to which probabilities are ascribed, and interprets a conditional probability as a logical relation giving a degree of inductive support from the conditioning sentence to the conditioned. Thus, $P(H \mid E)$ is the degree of inductive support that the evidence statement E gives to the hypothesis H. To measure $P(H \mid E)$, CARNAP considered state descriptions. In the simplest case, one lists all the individuals $a_1 \dots a_n$ in a world and all the predicates $F_1 \dots F_r$. Then a state description is an attribution of F_i or $\sim F_i$ to each individual a_j for all i and j, that is, a maximally consistent description of some possible world. If we now attribute, in an a priori way, a measure m on state descriptions (and this can be done in a number of ways), then the conditional logical probability is just $m(H \& E)/m(E)$. The principal drawback to using state descriptions is that learning from experience is impossible, simply because all predicates are logically independent and hence observing an instance of the property it represents gives no information about instances of any other. For this reason, Carnap switched to structure descriptions, within which individuals are indistinguishable. Interestingly, the differences between Maxwell–Boltzmann statistics, Bose–Einstein, and Fermi–Dirac statistics in physics are representable as differences that depend upon which states are physically possible. Because it is an empirical fact which particles satisfy which statistics, this sheds considerable doubt upon the whole enterprise of making a priori probability attributions.

There are now well-entrenched theories of comparative probability within which numerical values are not assigned, but one outcome is simply considered to be at least as probable as another. Alternatively, rather than assigning specific values to a proposition, intervals of probability can be assigned to mirror our uncertainty about the correct value via upper and lower probabilities. The connections between subjective probability and objective chance are now also the subject of much interest.

See also: CARNAP, R.; CONFIRMATION THEORY; DECISION AND GAME THEORY; INDUCTIVE INFERENCE; RATIONAL CHOICE THEORY; REICHENBACH, H.

References and further reading

Feller, W. (1968) *An Introduction to Probability Theory and Its Applications*, New York: John Wiley & Sons. (Still the best introduction to the mathematical theory of probability. Volume 1 treats discrete outcome spaces; volume 2 (2nd edn; 1971) deals with continuous outcome spaces.)

Gillies, D. (2000) *Philosophical Theories of Probability*, London: Routledge. (A comprehensive, readable, and balanced evaluation of the principal interpretations.)

Kahneman, D., Slovic, P. and Tversky, A. (eds) (1982) *Judgement under Uncertainty: Heuristics and Biases*, Cambridge: Cambridge University Press. (A collection of papers by psychologists describing how individuals reason probabilistically.)

PAUL HUMPHREYS

PROBLEM OF EVIL

See EVIL, PROBLEM OF

PROCESS PHILOSOPHY

In the broad sense, the term 'process philosophy' refers to all worldviews holding that process or becoming is more fundamental than unchanging being. For example, an anthology titled *Philosophers of Process* (1965) includes selections from Samuel Alexander, Henri Bergson, John Dewey, William James, Lloyd Morgan, Charles Peirce and Alfred North Whitehead, with an introduction by Charles HARTSHORNE. Some lists include Hegel and Heraclitus. The term has widely come to refer in particular, however, to the movement inaugurated by Whitehead and extended by Hartshorne. Here, process philosophy is treated in this narrower sense.

Philosophy's central task, process philosophers hold, is to develop a metaphysical cosmology that is self-consistent and adequate to all experienced facts. To be adequate, it cannot be based solely on the natural sciences, but must give equal weight to aesthetic, ethical and religious intuitions. Philosophy's chief importance, in fact, derives from its integration of science and religion into a rational scheme of thought. This integration is impossible, however, unless exaggerations on both sides are overcome. On the side of science, the main exaggerations involve 'scientific materialism' and the 'sensationalist' doctrine of perception. On the side of religion, the chief exaggeration has been the idea of divine omnipotence. Process philosophy replaces these ideas with a 'panexperientialist' ontology, a doctrine of perception in which nonsensory 'prehension' is fundamental, and a doctrine of divine power as persuasive rather than coercive.

See also: PROCESS THEISM; PROCESSES

DAVID RAY GRIFFIN

PROCESS THEISM

Process theism is a twentieth-century school of theological thought that offers a nonclassical understanding of the relationship between God and the world. Classical Christian theists maintain that God created the world out of nothing and that God not only can, but does, unilaterally intervene in earthly affairs. Process theists, in contrast, maintain that God and the basic material out of which the rest of reality is composed are coeternal. Moreover, process theists believe that all actual entities always possess some degree of self-determination. God, it is held, does present to every actual entity at every moment the best available course of action. And each entity does feel some compulsion to act in accordance with this divine lure. But process theists deny that God possesses the capacity to control unilaterally the activity of any entity. Thus, what occurs in relation to every aspect of reality involving a multiplicity of entities – for example, what happens in relation to every earthly state of affairs – is always a cooperative effort.

This understanding of the God–world relationship has significant theological implications. For instance, while classical Christians must attempt to explain why God does not unilaterally intervene more frequently to prevent horrific evils, process theists face no such challenge since the God of process thought cannot unilaterally control any earthly state of affairs. On the other hand, while most classical Christians maintain that God at times unilaterally intervenes in our world primarily because divine assistance has been requested, process theists naturally deny that God can be petitioned efficaciously in this sense since they believe that God is already influencing all aspects of reality to the greatest possible extent. Moreover, while most Christian theists believe that God will at some point in time unilaterally bring our current form of existence to an end, process theists maintain that the same co-creative process now in place will continue indefinitely.

Not everyone finds the process characterization of the God–world relationship convincing or appealing. But few deny that process theism has become a significant force in modern American theology.

See also: NATURAL THEOLOGY; PROCESS PHILOSOPHY

DAVID BASINGER

PROCESSES

A process is a course of change with a direction and internal order, where one stage leads on to the next. Processes can be physical (such as atomic decay), biological (such as the growth of living things), artificial (such as building a house) and social (such

as carrying out a criminal investigation). Much of what is said about processes can be said about sequences of events. The concept of event, however, suggests a separate occurrence, whereas that of a process suggests something which is ongoing. There are matters, such as development in organisms, where to see what is happening as part of a process has an advantage over thinking of it as an event. Causes are generally spoken of as events, but the more dynamic concept of causal processes may get nearer to expressing the transition between cause and effect. Moreover, to explain something as a stage in a process can take account not only of what has happened in the past, but of what might happen in the future. This may (but need not) involve purpose; with organisms it involves development through functionally interrelated activities. In some social processes there can be a practical, moral significance in seeing a situation as a stage in a process, since this can encourage us to look to a further stage where something constructive might be brought out of what could otherwise be seen as simply an untoward event or an unhappy situation.
See also: CAUSATION; CHANGE; EVENTS; PROCESS PHILOSOPHY; PROCESS THEISM

DOROTHY EMMET

PROFESSIONAL ETHICS

Professional ethics is concerned with the values appropriate to certain kinds of occupational activity, such as medicine and law, which have been defined traditionally in terms of a body of knowledge and an ideal of service to the community; and in which individual professionals have a high degree of autonomy in their practice. The class of occupations aiming to achieve recognition as professions has increased to include, for example, nursing, while at the same time social and political developments have led to criticism of and challenge to the concepts of professions and professionalism. Problems in professional ethics include both regulation of the professional–client relationship and the role and status of professions in society. A central question for ethics is whether there are values or virtues specific to particular professions or whether the standards of ordinary morality are applicable.
See also: APPLIED ETHICS; BUSINESS ETHICS; JOURNALISM, ETHICS OF; MEDICAL ETHICS; TECHNOLOGY AND ETHICS

RUTH CHADWICK

PROJECTIVISM

'Projectivism' is used of philosophies that agree with Hume that 'the mind has a great propensity to spread itself on the world', that what is in fact an aspect of our own experience or of our own mental organization is treated as a feature of the objective order of things. Such philosophies distinguish between nature as it really is, and nature as we experience it as being. The way we experience it as being is thought of as partly a reflection or projection of our own natures. The projectivist might take as a motto the saying that beauty lies in the eye of the beholder, and seeks to develop the idea and explore its implications.

The theme is a constant in the arguments of the Greek sceptics, and becomes almost orthodox in the modern era. In Hume it is not only beauty that lies in the eye (or mind) of the beholder, but also virtue, and causation. In Kant the entire spatio-temporal order is not read from nature, but read into it as a reflection of the organization of our minds. In the twentieth century it has been especially non-cognitive and expressivist theories of ethics that have adopted the metaphor, it being fairly easy to see how we might externalize or project various sentiments and attitudes onto their objects. But causation, probability, necessity, the stances we take towards each other as persons, even the temporal order of events and the simplicity of scientific theory have also been candidates for projective treatment.
See also: RELATIVISM

SIMON BLACKBURN

PROLĒPSIS

In post-Aristotelian Greek philosophy, the term *prolēpsis* (plural *prolēpseis*) was used, first by Epicurus and then by the Stoics, to refer to basic general concepts. These concepts were held to be preconditions of rational thought and language. For the most part, the Epicureans and Stoics thought that *prolēpseis* were formed by experience.
See also: CONCEPTS; EPICUREANISM; INNATENESS IN ANCIENT PHILOSOPHY; NATIVISM; STOICISM

DOMINIC SCOTT

PROMISING

Promising is often seen as a social practice with specific rules, determining when a promise has been made and requiring that duly made promises be kept. Accordingly, many philosophers have sought to explain the obligation to keep a promise by appealing to a duty to abide by such rules, whether because of the social benefits of the practice or because fairness requires one to abide by it. Others see breaking a promise as a direct wrong to the person whose expectations are disappointed.

See also: TRUST; TRUTHFULNESS

T.M. SCANLON

PRONOUNS
See ANAPHORA

PROOF THEORY

Proof theory is a branch of mathematical logic founded by David Hilbert around 1920 to pursue Hilbert's programme. The problems addressed by the programme had already been formulated, in some sense, at the turn of the century, for example, in Hilbert's famous address to the First International Congress of Mathematicians in Paris. They were closely connected to the set-theoretic foundations for analysis investigated by Cantor and Dedekind – in particular, to difficulties with the unrestricted notion of system or set; they were also related to the philosophical conflict with Kronecker on the very nature of mathematics. At that time, the central issue for Hilbert was the 'consistency of sets' in Cantor's sense. Hilbert suggested that the existence of consistent sets, for example, the set of real numbers, could be secured by proving the consistency of a suitable, characterizing axiom system, but indicated only vaguely how to give such proofs model-theoretically. Four years later, Hilbert departed radically from these indications and proposed a novel way of attacking the consistency problem for theories. This approach required, first of all, a strict formalization of mathematics together with logic; then, the syntactic configurations of the joint formalism would be considered as mathematical objects; finally, mathematical arguments would be used to show that contradictory formulas cannot be derived by the logical rules.

This two-pronged approach of developing substantial parts of mathematics in formal theories (set theory, second-order arithmetic, finite type theory and still others) and of proving their consistency (or the consistency of significant sub-theories) was sharpened in lectures beginning in 1917 and then pursued systematically in the 1920s by Hilbert and a group of collaborators including Paul Bernays, Wilhelm Ackermann and John von Neumann. In particular, the formalizability of analysis in a second-order theory was verified by Hilbert in those very early lectures. So it was possible to focus on the second prong, namely to establish the consistency of 'arithmetic' (second-order number theory and set theory) by elementary mathematical, 'finitist' means. This part of the task proved to be much more recalcitrant than expected, and only limited results were obtained. That the limitation was inevitable was explained in 1931 by Gödel's theorems; indeed, they refuted the attempt to establish consistency on a finitist basis – as soon as it was realized that finitist considerations could be carried out in a small fragment of first-order arithmetic. This led to the formulation of a general reductive programme.

Gentzen and Gödel made the first contributions to this programme by establishing the consistency of classical first-order arithmetic – Peano arithmetic – relative to intuitionistic arithmetic – Heyting arithmetic. In 1936 Gentzen proved the consistency of Peano arithmetic relative to a quantifier-free theory of arithmetic that included transfinite recursion up to the first epsilon number, ε_0; in his 1941 Yale lectures, Gödel proved the consistency of the same theory relative to a theory of computable functionals of finite type. These two fundamental theorems turned out to be most important for subsequent proof-theoretic work. Currently it is known how to analyse, in Gentzen's style, strong subsystems of second-order arithmetic and set theory. The first prong of proof-theoretic investigations, the actual formal development of parts of mathematics, has also been pursued – with a surprising result: the bulk of classical analysis can be developed in theories that are conservative over (fragments of) first-order arithmetic.

See also: HILBERT'S PROGRAMME AND FORMALISM

WILFRIED SIEG

PROPER NAMES

Introduction

The Roman general Julius Caesar was assassinated on 14 March 44 BC by conspirators led by Brutus and Cassius. It is a remarkable fact that, in so informing or reminding the reader, the proper names 'Julius Caesar', 'Brutus' and 'Cassius' are used to refer to three people each of whom has been dead for about two thousand years. Our eyes could not be used to see any of them, nor our voices to talk to them, yet we can refer to them with our words.

The central philosophical issue about proper names is how this sort of thing is possible: what exactly is the mechanism by which the user of a name succeeds in referring with the name to its bearer? As the example indicates, whatever the mechanism is, it must be something that can relate the use of a name to its bearer even after the bearer has ceased to exist.

PROPER NAMES

In modern philosophy of language there are two main views about the nature of the mechanism. On one account, which originated with Frege, a use of a name expresses a conception or way of thinking of an object, and the name refers to whatever object fits, or best fits, that conception or way of thinking. Thus with 'Cassius', for example, I may associate the conception 'the conspirator whom Caesar suspected because of his size' (recalling a famous speech in Shakespeare's *Julius Caesar*). Conception theories are usually called 'sense' theories, after Frege's term '*Sinn*'. The other account is the 'historical chain' theory, due to Kripke and Geach. In Geach's words, 'for the use of a word as a proper name there must in the first instance be someone acquainted with the object named.... But...the use of a given name for a given object...can be handed on from one generation to another...Plato knew Socrates, and Aristotle knew Plato, and Theophrastus knew Aristotle, and so on in apostolic succession down to our own times. That is why we can legitimately use "Socrates" as a name the way we do' (1969–70: 288–9).

> 1 Sense theories: introduction
> 2 Sense theories: do names express senses?
> 3 Sense theories: do senses determine reference?
> 4 Historical chains
> 5 Direct reference and Frege's puzzle

1 Sense theories: introduction

The idea that names express reference-determining conceptions or 'senses' originated with Frege. But Frege was led to it not by wondering about the mechanism of reference, but rather about the difference in 'cognitive value' between two true identity statements of the respective forms $a = a$ and $a = b$ (for example, 'Clark Kent is Clark Kent' and 'Clark Kent is Superman'). Statements of the former sort, he says, are a priori, while the latter 'often contain very valuable extensions of our knowledge and cannot always be established a priori' ('Über Sinn und Bedeutung' 1892). Frege takes this to show that the propositions expressed by $a = a$ and $a = b$ cannot be the same even when a and b are names of the same person. Yet if the names do corefer, there is no difference in the references of the constituents of $a = a$ and $a = b$; moreover, these two sentences are assembled in the same way. So either they cannot express different propositions, or else – and this is the inference Frege drew – what determines the proposition a sentence S expresses cannot just have to do with the structure of S and

the *references* of its constituent words and phrases (see FREGE, G. §§3–4; SENSE AND REFERENCE).

Frege's proposal was that in addition to possessing a reference, any meaningful expression has a sense, the sense being a 'way of thinking' of the reference. The proposition a sentence expresses is determined by the senses of the words in it, not their references. Thus 'Clark Kent is Clark Kent' and 'Clark Kent is Superman' express different propositions because 'Clark Kent' and 'Superman' express different senses, senses which happen to be ways of thinking of the same reference. Taking the Superman fiction to be fact, the sense of 'Clark Kent' might be 'the mild-mannered reporter on *The Daily Planet* who has a crush on Lois Lane' while the sense of 'Superman' might be 'the blue-suited extraterrestrial who flies'. Here we specify different conceptions of the same individual in two definite descriptions (expressions of the form 'the so-and-so' – see DESCRIPTIONS). The proposition that Superman is Clark Kent therefore has the content that the blue-suited extraterrestrial who flies is the mild-mannered reporter on *The Daily Planet* who has a crush on Lois Lane, which may indeed be, in Frege's phrase, an extension of our knowledge.

It was Frege's view that in an ideal language each name would have a fixed sense and reference for everyone; in an ordinary natural language, there are names that fail to refer, and users may fail to agree on the sense of a name for a specific individual, which Frege thought of as deficiencies of natural language. In a modification of Frege's views, Searle allowed that a name may be associated with a whole range of descriptions, different users using different ranges; the bearer of the name need not satisfy all the conditions mentioned in the descriptions, only 'a sufficient number', an intentionally vague condition.

Sense theories along such lines as these have been called 'famous deeds' sense theories. Famous deeds sense theories appear to have been conclusively refuted by Kripke (1972). Kripke objects to such sense theories both as they respond to Frege's own puzzle about the difference between $a = a$ and $a = b$, and as they address our initial question about the mechanism of reference. Let us consider these two issues in turn.

2 Sense theories: do names express senses?

According to Kripke, the propositions one expresses using names do not involve senses or ways of thinking expressed by the names, otherwise some such propositions would be both metaphysically necessary and a priori, which they are clearly not. For example, suppose the sense of 'Aristotle' is 'the

854

pupil of Plato who tutored Alexander'. Then the sentence

(1)   Aristotle was a pupil of Plato

would express the proposition with the content

(2)   The pupil of Plato who tutored Alexander was a pupil of Plato.

But (2) is, in a certain sense, necessary, while (1) is not. There is no way things could have gone in which (a) a unique pupil of Plato who tutored Alexander exists and (b) that person was not a pupil of Plato. On the other hand, there are many ways things could have gone in which (a′) Aristotle exists but (b′) Aristotle was not a pupil of Plato (for example, he died young). In other words, granted that there is such a person as Aristotle, he may be a pupil of Plato or he may not be. But granted that there is such a person as the pupil of Plato who tutored Alexander, it follows that he is a pupil of Plato.

This example brings out Kripke's famous distinction between 'rigid' and 'non-rigid' designators. In thinking about or describing other ways things could have gone (other possible worlds) we use a proper name such as 'Aristotle' consistently to denote the same person; this makes proper names rigid designators. But we use definite descriptions such as 'the pupil of Plato who tutored Alexander' differently. With respect to the actual world, this description picks out Aristotle; with respect to a possible world where someone else is the one and only pupil of Plato who tutored Alexander, the description picks out that other person, not Aristotle; and with respect to a possible world where either Plato or Alexander does not exist, the description fails to pick out anyone, even if Aristotle does exist. Hence such descriptions are non-rigid designators. Certain descriptions, such as 'the positive square root of 9', are as rigid as proper names, but this is on account of their subject matter, not their semantic role. It is because the typical famous deeds description is non-rigid that the contrast between pairs such as (1) and (2) vis-à-vis necessity and contingency arises (see REFERENCE).

Just as (1) and (2) differ in modal status, they differ epistemically: bracketing the question of existence, (2) is, in a limited sense, knowable a priori, while (1) is not. That is, granted that there was such a person as Aristotle, it is a further, empirical question whether he was a pupil of Plato (there may be a controversy among historians about this). But granted that there was such a person as the pupil of Plato who tutored Alexander, it is not a further question, a fortiori not an empirical one, whether he was a pupil of Plato.

The same objections arise to Searle's modified version of the sense theory. For example, no matter what range of descriptions we associate with a name, they will generate statements that are a priori in the manner of (2). If being φ logically implies being φ', then

(3)   The thing which is F-and-G or G-and-H is F' or G' or H'

is essentially the same as (2), just more complicated. But if the predicates F, G and H encapsulate famous deeds, the corresponding

(4) NN is F' or G' or H',

where 'NN' is the name with which 'the thing which is F or G or H' is associated, will be no more a priori than (1).

3   Sense theories: do senses determine reference?

Kripke demonstrates another flaw in famous deeds sense theories, namely, that they do not provide an adequate answer to the question about the mechanism of reference. This is because (1) the likely candidate for the sense of a name may pick out an object which is not in fact the name's bearer, or may fail to pick out anything, and (2) we can succeed in referring with a name even when we do not have a 'famous deeds' description associated with it.

Kripke illustrates (1) with two examples. If any description is associated with the name 'Gödel' it is 'the discoverer of the incompleteness of arithmetic'. Does this mean that 'Gödel' refers to that person? What if the theorem was actually proved by Schmidt, who died in strange circumstances, and Gödel got hold of Schmidt's work and represented it as his own? The very fact that we can understand this 'what if' shows that the reference of 'Gödel' is not fixed as whoever discovered the incompleteness of arithmetic. And though this example is fictional, there are similar actual cases: Peano's Axioms are not due to Peano; and Einstein was not the inventor of the atomic bomb. For a case where there are descriptions that do not pick out any object although the relevant name still refers, Kripke gives the example of the prophet Jonah, who really existed (according to the scholarly consensus), but whose career as described in the Bible is essentially fictitious. Again, the mere intelligibility of the claim 'Jonah was a historical person but everything uniquely identifying that the Bible says about him is fictitious' is enough to show that the reference of 'Jonah' is not fixed as the Hebrew prophet who was swallowed by a whale, or by any other condition, no matter how complicated or disjunctive, derived from the Book of Jonah.

As for (2), successful reference without associated (definite) descriptions, Kripke points out that most people can use the names 'Richard Feynman' and 'Murray Gell-Mann' to refer to those two people, but that, at best, all the typical person knows about either is that he is a famous physicist who won a Nobel Prize (this was before Feynman achieved popular fame for his role in the *Challenger* disaster inquiry). So we have difference in reference with no difference in associated descriptions; therefore associated descriptions are not at the heart of how proper name reference works.

Perhaps these examples only establish such a conclusion for descriptions that encapsulate famous deeds. Kripke considers some other approaches and concludes that they violate an important non-circularity condition: that candidate descriptions must not themselves embed the notion of reference in a way that cannot eventually be eliminated. For example, we might suggest that the reference of 'Socrates' is fixed as 'the man called "Socrates"'. Since 'called' just means 'referred to as', we do not explain how reference to Socrates is possible in this way: what we want to know is how Socrates *gets to be* the man referred to as 'Socrates'. So this goes nowhere as a proposal about the mechanism of reference, and Kripke plausibly argues that the same would be true for more complicated versions of the idea, for example, that 'Gödel' refers to the person to whom the proof of the incompleteness of arithmetic is commonly attributed. So these attempts at a non-famous-deeds description theory fail. However, in view of Kripke's critique of the famous deeds approach, it seems that if any sense theory is to work, it will have to be a non-famous-deeds account of some sort.

4   Historical chains

The main competing account of the mechanism of reference is the Geach–Kripke historical chain account, in which competence to refer with the name is transmitted across generations in the style adverted to in the quotation from Geach above. The historical chain account is sometimes called the 'causal' chain account, since it is held that the links in the chain are forged by transactions of a causal sort. In Kripke's own version, which he says is a 'picture' rather than a theory, a name is introduced into a community by some 'initial baptism' of an object with the name, and then the name is passed on from link to link, it being required at each step that the receiver of the name 'intend...to use it with the same reference as the [person] from whom he heard it'.

If we regard being told about, or otherwise hearing about, an object, as a way of becoming 'acquainted' with it, then the Geach–Kripke account instantiates an approach championed by Bertrand RUSSELL, who made acquaintance with an object necessary for referring to it. However, Russell's notion of acquaintance was rather idiosyncratic: apart from my own sense-data, my self, universals and perhaps the present moment, I lack acquaintance with things, according to Russell. Since the ordinary names I use, ostensibly for other people and things, are not names of sense-data, Russell claimed that in a 'logical' sense, ordinary names are not 'proper' names. Rather, he suggested, they are definite descriptions in disguise. For this reason, Kripke sometimes calls the view he opposes the 'Frege–Russell theory of names'. The point to bear in mind is that Frege and Russell had different accounts of how reference works (so there is no 'Frege–Russell theory of reference'), but because on Russell's account ordinary names do not really refer, the two philosophers end up saying similar-sounding things about such names.

Returning to Kripke's account of the mechanism of reference in terms of informational exchanges in which the intention to preserve reference is present, the obvious question is whether it is any improvement on circular description theories. After all, the notion of reference enters explicitly into Kripke's necessary condition for successful passing on of the name, and it also enters at the start of the chain, where some kind of demonstrative reference to the object being baptized is standardly made. To put the same question another way, if this account is explanatory, would there be anything wrong with a description theory which attributed to a name '*NN*' and a user of the name *U* the sense 'the object at the start of the chain of reference-preserving links by which I came into mastery of this name', in which 'I' refers to *U*?

One problem with this version of a description theory is that no ordinary speaker of a natural language associates any such description with a proper name, since the description embodies a philosophical theory, and it is difficult to see how one could justify claiming that the association is 'implicit'. Here there is a contrast with Kripke's proposal, which only requires speakers to have the intention to preserve the reference of the new name they have just learned, and it is surely plausible that speakers do have such an intention. Still, there is some sense in which the fundamental nature of the mechanism of reference is left unexplained. For instance, what exactly is it about an actual baptismal service, or about parents announcing their choice of name, that causes a new 'common currency' name to be added to the language? Or is the request for further explanation here a demand for a 'reductive' account of reference in terms of non-semantic notions (see REFERENCE), something perhaps impossible?

The causal chain picture is not without other difficulties, as Kripke mentions. For instance, straightforward application of the picture could lead to the conclusion that 'Santa Claus' is the name of a certain central European king, which seems wrong. Evans proposed a different causal account on which the 'causal source' of the information associated with the name determines whom it refers to, though in a possibly complex way. Evans observes that the reference of a name in a linguistic community can change over time if it was originally a name for x that was mistakenly but consistently misapplied to y:y would ultimately become the bearer of the name, being the dominant causal source of the information associated with it (unless, as Evans notes, younger members of the community defer in their use of the name towards those for whom it was once a name for x). Evans subsequently elaborated upon this account.

5 Direct reference and Frege's puzzle

A striking feature of the Geach–Kripke picture is that it leaves no role for sense to play as that which determines reference. The only candidate for the 'meaning' of a name is therefore the name's reference itself. A theory which claims that the meaning of a name is just its reference, pure and simple, is often called a 'direct reference' theory, 'direct' signifying that reference is not mediated via sense. Such theories trace their origins through Russell back to Mill; more recently, the idea is prominent in the writings of Marcus on reference, and has subsequently been developed and defended in a sustained form by Salmon and Soames.

The main problem which direct reference theories face is the puzzle about the difference between $a = a$ and $a = b$. The general 'failure of substitutivity' puzzle is the puzzle of how it is possible for the meanings of two sentences to differ if the sentences have the same structure and their corresponding parts have the same meaning. For example,

(5) It is self-evident to any rational thinker that if Superman exists, then Superman = Superman

seems true and 'Superman' and 'Clark Kent' have the same reference. Therefore, according to direct reference theory, (5) should have the same meaning as

(6) It is self-evident to any rational thinker that if Superman exists, then Superman = Clark Kent.

But at first sight, (6) does not even have the same truth-value as (5), never mind the same meaning.

Failure of substitutivity is handled straightforwardly on a sense theory of names which allows that coreferential names can have different senses. The claim would be that (not merely the reference but) the sense of 'Superman' enters into the truth-condition of (5), while in (6) the sense of 'Clark Kent' is also involved. There are various mechanisms which might be invoked here, Frege's own being the simplest: in (5) and (6), according to Frege, the proper names refer to their *senses*, rather than to the person they normally refer to (see SENSE AND REFERENCE §5). But the trouble with any explanation of substitutivity failure for proper names that invokes senses is that sense theories of proper names have been so thoroughly battered by Kripke.

Direct reference theory seems to have less to work with to explain the semantic difference between (5) and (6). On perhaps the best known version of the theory, that of Salmon, it is simply denied that there is a semantic difference between (5) and (6). The appearance that substitution changes truth-value in cases such as (5) and (6) is explained as being due to pragmatic effects (see PRAGMATICS). Apparently, the only alternative for a direct reference theorist is to identify some assumption in the argument that substitution of coreferring names ought not to change meaning and deny that assumption. This strategy produces a possible target. We suggested that what makes substitutivity failure puzzling is that sentences with the same structure whose corresponding parts have the same meaning should themselves have the same meaning. But this presupposes that the meaning of the entire sentence is wholly determined by the meaning of its parts and their manner of composition (see COMPOSITIONALITY). However, the notion of structure alluded to in the phrase 'manner of composition' is one which is sensitive only to syntactic categories of expression, not to the identity of expressions. There is another, more 'logical' notion of structure, on which use of a different word, even one with the same meaning, can disrupt structure. In this logical sense, the structure of 'if Superman exists, then Superman = Superman' is 'if Et then tt', while 'if Superman exists, then Superman = Clark Kent' has the different structure 'if Et then $t = t\star$'. If we hold that substitution is acceptable only when it does not change logical structure, then from (5) we can infer merely

(7) It is self-evident to any rational thinker that if Clark Kent exists, then Clark Kent = Clark Kent

which is presumably true if (5) is. Of course, this does not help with cases of substitutivity failure in which there is only one occurrence of the name being substituted ('Lois believes that Superman is an extraterrestrial'), but some direct reference theorists have tried to develop a more general notion of structure for these cases.

It is the handling of substitutivity puzzles that is the deciding issue between sense theories and direct reference theories of proper names. Sense theorists need to find a viable account of the senses of names and direct reference theorists need to find a persuasive account either of why substitutivity fails in cases such as (5), or else of why it gives such a convincing appearance of doing so.

See also: DE RE/DE DICTO; KRIPKE, S.A.

References and further reading

Geach, P.T. (1969–70) 'The Perils of Pauline', *Review of Metaphysics* 23: 287–300; repr. in *Logic Matters*, Berkeley, CA: University of California Press, 1972, 153–65. (States the historical chain view and discusses the use of names in intentional contexts.)

Kripke, S.A. (1972) 'Naming and Necessity', in D. Davidson and G. Harman (eds) *Semantics of Natural Language*, Dordrecht: Reidel, 252–355. (One of the most influential and widely discussed works in post-war philosophy.)

GRAEME FORBES

PROPERTIES

See ABSTRACT OBJECTS; NATURAL KINDS; UNIVERSALS

PROPERTY

Introduction

Most of the great philosophers have expressed views on property, its justification and limits, and especially on the justification of having private property; generally, one must understand these views against the background of the economic and social conditions of their times. Notable theories include first possession (roughly, 'whoever gets their hands on it justifiably owns it'), labour ('whoever made it deserves to own it'), utility and/ or efficiency ('allowing people to own things is the most effective way of running society') and personality ('owning property is necessary for personal development').

Few thinkers now defend the first possession theory but all the other three have their contemporary supporters. Some philosophers combine two or more theories into multi-principled or 'pluralist'

justifications of property ownership. Many express concern about wide gaps between rich and poor and argue for constraints on inequalities in property holdings.

> 1 Concept of property
> 2 History of theorizing about property
> 3 Systematic justifications of private property
> 4 Constraints on the distribution of property

1 Concept of property

The concept of property is understood in two main ways. First, it applies to material things such as tools, houses and land. Second, it applies to bundles of 'rights'. Most lawyers and philosophers stress the second understanding over the first. The first is too narrow to accommodate intangibles such as copyrights, patents and trademarks. Moreover, for purposes of legal and philosophical analysis the second understanding is more useful.

Here the word 'rights' covers many normative modalities (see RIGHTS §2). Following Hohfeld and Honoré, the package of rights called 'property' includes: claim rights to possess, use and receive income; powers to transfer, waive and exclude; a disability (a no-power) of others to force a sale; liberty rights to consume or destroy; and immunity from expropriation by the government. It is probably a vain enterprise to try to specify necessary and sufficient conditions for all and only those 'rights' that pertain to property rather than, say, to contract or tort. Yet it is a worthy undertaking to try to identify those 'rights' that seem most central to property or those rules that create such 'rights'.

The second understanding of property finds favour for many reasons. It applies to widely different cultures. It is useful in both legal and philosophical analysis. It can accommodate both 'will' and 'interest' theories of rights. It can capture both full ownership and limited property rights (such as easements), and both tangible and intangible property. It permits distinguishing among different sorts of property depending on the identity of the rightholder. Thus, a single person or a corporation has *private* property, a tribe has *communal* property and a government has *public* or *state* property.

This explanation of the concept of property is neutral with respect to which kinds of things can be the subject of property rights. Few would defend slavery, which is the most extreme form of property in the bodies or persons of others. More disputed are whether people can have property rights in the whole of their own bodies, in bodily parts for use in transplantation, in information, in cultural practices, in welfare payments or other forms of government largesse, or in seabed resources or objects in outer space.

The approach of Guido Calabresi and Douglas Melamed to the notion of property, which philosopher-economists and lawyer-economists often use, is not conceptually distinct from that of Hohfeld and Honoré. For Calabresi and Melamed the basic idea is an 'entitlement'. An entitlement is, roughly, an interest that the law does or should protect. Decisions must be made as to which entitlements to protect and how to protect them. As to the latter decision, the law may use what Calabresi and Melamed call 'property rules', 'liability rules' and 'rules of inalienability'. These technical terms can be restated in Hohfeld's vocabulary. If a person's entitlement is protected by a property rule, then others have a disability (a no-power) with regard to obtaining the entitlement except at a price agreed to by its holder. If a person's entitlement is protected by a liability rule, then others have a disability with regard to obtaining or reducing the value of the entitlement unless they compensate its holder by an officially determined amount. If a person's entitlement is protected by a rule of inalienability, its holder has no power to transfer the entitlement to others. The real value of Calabresi and Melamed's approach rests in the light that it sheds on the integration of property and tort, on its application to pollution control, on its sensitivity to distributional as well as efficiency considerations, and on the choice between civil and criminal sanctions for violations of property rights.

2   History of theorizing about property

Many of the great philosophers have offered views on property. Plato actually expresses two different views (see PLATO §§14, 17). In the *Republic* he portrays an ideal society in which the rulers and auxiliaries have political power but almost no private property. Ordinary citizens possess private property, with limits on unequal distribution, but have almost no political power. In contrast, the *Laws* depicts a practical, second-best society. It favours individual private possession with underlying communal ownership. Regulations maintain a roughly equal distribution of property.

ARISTOTLE advocates private rather than communal ownership on grounds that relate to the smooth functioning of a society and its economy. His *Politics* fails, however, to show how property should, or can, be 'in a certain sense common, but, as a general rule, private'.

Locke, at least in the *Second Treatise*, offers a labour theory of property (see LOCKE, J. §10). The interpretation of his theory is disputed. It is unclear

how much the theory rests on 'mixing' one's labour with unowned things, or on barring the idle from taking the benefit of the labourer's pains, and the extent to which the needs of others and restrictions on spoilage limit the acquisition of property by labour. It is also disputed whether Locke's theory is proto-capitalist or stems from some conception of natural law.

Hume and Bentham are the first important utilitarian theorists of property. For Hume, utility in the sense of common interest explains how private property arises (see HUME, D. §§4–5). It also justifies the general institution of private property and specific rules of property law. BENTHAM understands utility as the balance of pleasure over pain, and views property in terms of expectations. The security of expectations, rather than equality in distribution, is for Bentham the weightier consideration in favour of private property. Nevertheless, Bentham is sharply critical of the English law of property of his day.

Kant and Hegel are also linked, although less closely and in more complicated ways than Hume and Bentham. For Kant, as for Locke, a form of private property can exist in the state of nature (see KANT, I. §10). But Kant has a social contract theory under which only society can give individual possession full normative significance as private property. Hegel regards Kantian private property as excessively individualistic and belonging to the domain of 'abstract right' (see HEGEL, G.W.F. §8). A more sophisticated form of property exists in 'civil society' – roughly, the social correlate of *laissez-faire* capitalism. Only in the 'state' does private property emerge fully transformed; private property, unequally distributed, still exists, but is subject to heavier state regulation in the organic interest of all citizens.

MARX dismisses Hegel's dialectical defence of private property as so much claptrap. Marx believes that capitalist production, not unequal distribution, is the more serious problem, because 'capitalism' distorts human relationships. In particular, private property under capitalism involves 'alienation' – that is, a separation of persons from nature, the products of their labour, other human beings and even themselves (see ALIENATION). *Pace* Marx, it is unclear that all forms of private property must involve alienation, or that alienation will be absent from the mature communist society that he envisages.

3   Systematic justifications of private property

First possession and entitlement. Attempts to justify the acquisition of property by being the first person to possess it have won few converts. The general difficulty is to show why first possession should support full ownership rather than limited rights of use. Specific difficulties include articulating which acts of possession count, explaining how long they must continue, and identifying the item or area possessed. Suppose that someone claims title to an acre of farmland by standing in one place for an hour. Why should that person not have to farm rather than merely stand, to remain there for a year rather than just an hour, and to perform appropriate acts over the entire acre rather than only on an area two feet square? To many these difficulties have no ready solution. Still, those sympathetic to the rights of aboriginal peoples sometimes invoke first possession.

A related account is the libertarian entitlement theory of Robert NOZICK. Nozick's position is hazy on which acts are appropriate acts of acquisition under his principle of justice in acquisition. The literature contains sharp attacks on his position. Among them are objections as to how any individual can, by unilateral action, impose moral duties on others to refrain from using certain resources, worries about inequalities of property holdings, and scepticism that anyone living today has morally valid property rights by transfer from some original acquirer. Nozick has not responded to these attacks. Other libertarian theories are either grounded in economics or based on strong conceptions of freedom and individual rights (see LIBERTARIANISM).

Labour. More promising are efforts to recast the labour theory in terms of the desert of the labourer. Lawrence Becker and Stephen Munzer offer somewhat different accounts of a labour–desert principle.

Becker (1977) holds that if a worker adds value to the lives of others in some morally permissible way and without being required to do so, that person deserves a fitting benefit. Property rights may be the most fitting benefit, and which benefit is 'most fitting' depends on purposes. However, Becker's theory leaves it unclear which purposes (for example, an attempt to gain property rights?) and whose purposes (the labourer's or those of other individuals?) are relevant. Also, he does not show why purpose should be the sole test of fittingness. Nevertheless, Becker rightly insists that losses inflicted by the labourer's work require some reduction in property rights or some offsetting compensation or taxation.

Munzer argues that if workers use their bodies to produce something or provide a service, then they have a *prima facie* claim to deserve property rights in the product or in wages. This claim is qualified by scarcity, by the needs and rights of others, and by some post-acquisition changes in situation. Restrictions on transfer may also apply. Moreover, since work is a social activity, a wage policy is in order that makes wages commensurate so far as possible with desert. The heavy qualifications that surround this version of the labour theory support moderate egalitarianism rather than the wide disparities in income and wealth that libertarian theories allow. Critics of Munzer's labour–desert principle have objected that its intellectual underpinnings are not sufficiently clear and that in both theory and practice no precise correlations exist between desert claims and property rights.

Utility and efficiency. Contemporary justifications of this sort owe a distant obligation to Hume and Bentham. These justifications often stress 'efficiency', which does not allow interpersonal comparison of individual preference satisfaction, over 'utility', which does allow them. Because of the invocation of efficiency, the most sophisticated advocates are frequently economists or academic lawyers influenced by economics rather than philosophers.

Utility and efficiency can, given some plausible assumptions about individuals' preferences, justify some public property as well as some rights of private property. They tend (again given certain assumptions about preferences) to justify moderate egalitarianism rather than highly unequal distributions of private property. However, more detailed information is needed to show how utility and efficiency can justify particular rules of property law or radical changes in existing property institutions. Perhaps the most influential theoretical result of applying efficiency to the law of nuisance bears the sobriquet 'Coase's Theorem'. It holds that, under perfect competition and perfect information and with costless transactions, an efficient allocation of resources will result no matter what the decision of the courts concerning liability for damage.

Personality. Contrary to some reports, the personality theory of property did not die with Hegel and the British neo-Hegelians. The basic idea is that people need at least some private property in order to develop healthy character structures. The account of 'property for personhood' by Margaret Radin is probably the best-known and most fully developed contemporary theory of this sort. She applies her theory to many practical legal problems, but some readers find the foundations of her account no clearer than those of Hegel. Her books also suggest that some things are so personal that they ought not to be property or 'commodities' at all.

Pluralist theories. The variety of possible justifications of property has suggested to some writers that the most plausible account of property is 'pluralist' – that is, contains two or more irreducible principles. Becker and Munzer explicitly embrace pluralist accounts. Other writers do so implicitly. Some critics dismiss such pluralism as eclectic. Other critics contend that if it is impossible to show that the principles never conflict, it is necessary to establish that conflict between principles is logically consistent and otherwise free from objection. Further, it may be harder to apply a pluralist theory rather than a unitary theory to practical problems. Still, those who favour a unitary theory − a theory with a single principle or at least a single supreme principle − must show how it can accommodate the complexity of considered moral judgments concerning property. For anyone who shares Proudhon's worry that property is theft, justification remains the key problem in the theory of property (see PROUDHON, P.-J.).

4   Constraints on the distribution of property

Justice and equality. The liberal tradition in political theory, stemming particularly from Mill, often tries to limit inequalities of property holdings (see MILL, J.S. §§11–12). The limitation can take the form of a side constraint or, in a pluralist theory, of a separate principle of justice and equality. Few philosophers argue for strictly equal holdings. More modest is the 'difference principle' of John RAWLS (§§1–2). Applied to property, this principle would hold that differences in holdings are justifiable only if they are to the greatest benefit of the least advantaged. A related view might concentrate on both the floor and the ceiling: everyone should be ensured a minimum amount of property, and remaining inequalities, if any, should not undermine a fully human life for anyone in society.

Absence of exploitation. The radical tradition in political theory, traceable especially to Marx, stresses the need to eliminate exploitation and other differences in power that derive from unequal property holdings. Roughly, persons are exploited if others secure a benefit by using them as a tool or resource so as to cause them serious harm. Exploitation theory often concentrates as much on problems of economic production as it does on the real or imagined evils of unequal distributions of property. The 'Critical Legal Studies movement', in some of its forms, objects to exploitation and differences in power as they relate to property. More rigorous accounts of exploitation come from the work of John E. Roemer.

References and further reading

Becker, L.C. (1977) *Property Rights: Philosophic Foundations*, London, Henley and Boston, MA: Routledge & Kegan Paul. (Admirably concise introduction.)

Ryan, A. (1984) *Property and Political Theory*, Oxford: Blackwell (Elegantly written historical survey.)

STEPHEN R. MUNZER

PROPOSITIONAL ATTITUDES

Examples of propositional attitudes include the belief that snow is white, the hope that Mt Rosea is twelve miles high, the desire that there should be snow at Christmas, the intention to go to the snow tomorrow, and the fear that one shall be killed in an avalanche. As these examples show, we can distinguish the kind of attitude − belief, desire, intention, fear and so on − from the content of the attitude − that snow is white, that there will be snow at Christmas, to go to the snow, and so forth. The term 'propositional attitudes' comes from Bertrand Russell and derives from the fact that we can think of the content of an attitude as the proposition the attitude is towards. It can be typically captured by a sentence prefixed by 'that', though sometimes at the cost of a certain linguistic awkwardness: it is more natural, for example, to talk of the intention to go to the snow rather than the intention that one go to the snow. The most frequently discussed kinds of propositional attitudes are belief, desire and intention, but there are countless others: hopes, fears, wishes, regrets, and so on.

Some sentences which contain the verbs of propositional attitude − believes, desires, intends, and so on − do not make ascriptions of propositional attitudes. For example: 'Wendy believes me', 'John fears this dog' and 'He intends no harm'. However, while these sentences are not, as they stand, ascriptions of propositional attitudes, it is arguable − though not all philosophers agree − that they can always be analysed as propositional attitude ascriptions. So, for example, Wendy believes me just in case there is some p such that Wendy believes that p because I tell her that p; John fears this dog just in case there is some X such that John fears that this dog will do X and so on.

Discussions of propositional attitudes typically focus on belief and desire, and, sometimes, intention, because of the central roles these attitudes play in the explanation of rational behaviour. For example: Mary's visit to the supermarket is explained by her desire to purchase some groceries, and her belief that she can purchase groceries at the supermarket; Bill's flicking the switch is explained by his desire to illuminate the room, and his belief that he can illuminate the room by flicking the switch; and so on. It is plausible − though not uncontroversial − to hold that rational behaviour can always be explained as the outcome of a suitable belief together with a suitable desire.

Some philosophers (examples are Grice and Schiffer) have used the propositional attitudes to explain facts about meaning. They hold that the meanings of sentences somehow derive from the contents of relevantly related beliefs and intentions. Roughly, what I mean by a sentence S is captured by the content of, say, the belief that I express by saying S.

One fundamental question which divides philosophers turns on the ontological status of the propositional attitudes and of their contents. It is clear that we make heavy use of propositional attitude ascriptions in explaining and interpreting the actions of ourselves and others. But should we think that in producing such ascriptions, we attempt to speak the truth – that is, should we think that propositional attitude ascriptions are truth-apt – or should we see some other purpose, such as dramatic projection, in this usage? Or, even more radically, should we think that there is nothing but error and confusion – exposed by modern science and neurophysiology – in propositional attitude talk?

See also: ACTION; COMMUNICATION AND INTENTION; DESIRE; FOLK PSYCHOLOGY; INTENTION

GRAHAM OPPY

PROPOSITIONAL CALCULUS
See PREDICATE CALCULUS

PROUDHON, PIERRE-JOSEPH (1809–65)

Pierre-Joseph Proudhon was a French social theorist, political activist and journalist. Claiming to be the first person to adopt the label 'anarchist', he developed a vision of a cooperative society conducting its affairs by just exchanges and without political authority. In his lifetime he exercised considerable influence over both militants and theorists of the European left, and he is remembered today as one of the greatest exponents of libertarian socialism. His last writings, though still strongly libertarian, advocated a federal state with minimal functions.

See also: ANARCHISM; FREEDOM AND LIBERTY; PROPERTY; SOCIALISM

RICHARD VERNON

PSYCHĒ

Conventionally translated 'soul', *psychē* is the standard word in classical Greek for the centre of an animal's, and especially a human being's, 'life'. In its earliest usage (in Homer) *psychē* is a breath-like material persisting after death as a mere ghost. Its precise reference to the locus of thought and emotion only began under the influence of philo-

sophy. From the beginning of the fourth century BC it became normal to pair and contrast *psychē* with 'body' (*soma*). The term generated sophisticated discussions. Leading questions include: Is *psychē* immortal? Is it corporeal or incorporeal? What are its parts or functions?

See also: ANAXIMENES; DEMOCRITUS; NEOPLATONISM; SOUL, NATURE AND IMMORTALITY OF THE; THALES

A.A. LONG

PSYCHOANALYSIS, METHODOLOGICAL ISSUES IN

Philosophers have subjected psychoanalysis to an unusual degree of methodological scrutiny for several interconnected reasons. Even a cursory look at the Freudian corpus reveals a slender base of evidence: eleven 'case histories', including those published jointly with Breuer. On the other hand, the theoretical claims have broad scope: all psychopathology can be traced to repressed sexuality. Further, Freud and his followers have disdained the most widely accepted means of establishing theories – experimental confirmation – while allowing themselves to appeal to such apparently dubious sources of support as dream interpretation, literature and everyday life. Together, these factors conjure a picture of a 'science' with a large gap between theory and evidence that has not and cannot be filled by solid data.

The central methodological question about psychoanalysis is whether there is now or ever has been any evidence supporting its truth. Popper rejected psychoanalysis as a science on the grounds that there could be no possible evidence against it which could test its truth. More recently, Grünbaum has objected that there are serious logical difficulties with appealing to cures as evidence of truth. Grünbaum and others have attacked both the theory of dreams and the use of dream interpretation as evidence. Sulloway and Kitcher have argued that several tenets of psychoanalysis were supported by their nineteenth-century scientific context, particularly certain aspects of Darwinian biology, but that those crucial supports have been eroded by later scientific developments. Eysenck and Wilson have examined experimental results that have been offered in support of various claims of psychoanalysis and rejected them as inadequate to establish any specifically psychoanalytic claims. By contrast, Glymour (and others) have explained how even single case histories could provide evidence in favour of psychoanalysis. Other philosophers have argued that psychoanalysis is continuous with 'common-sense' psychology and is supported by the continual reaffirmation of the essential correctness of common-sense psychological prediction and explanation.

See also: FREUD, S.; PSYCHOANALYSIS, POST-FREUDIAN; UNCONSCIOUS MENTAL STATES

PATRICIA KITCHER

PSYCHOANALYSIS, POST-FREUDIAN

The basic concepts of psychoanalysis are due to Sigmund Freud. After establishing psychoanalysis Freud worked in Vienna until he and other analysts fled the Nazi occupation. Post-Freudian psychoanalysis has evolved in distinct ways in different countries, often in response to influential analysts who settled there.

Freud's patients were mainly adults who suffered from neurotic rather than psychotic disturbances. He found their psychological difficulties to be rooted in conflict between love and hate, caused by very disparate, often fantastic, images deriving from the same parental figure. These images provided the basic representations of the self and others, formed by processes of projection (representing the other via images from the self) and introjection (representing the self via images from the other). The internalized image of a parent could be used to represent the self as related to some version of the other, as in the formation of the punitive super-ego, or as like the other, as in the identification with the parent of the same sex through which the Oedipus complex was dissolved.

Later analysts, including Anna Freud and Melanie Klein, observed that the uninhibited play of children could be seen to express fantasies involving such images, often with striking clarity. This made it possible to analyse children, and to see that their representations of the self were regularly coordinated with fantastic representations of others, with both organized into systematically interacting systems of good and bad. Emotional disturbance was marked by a fantasy world in which the self and idealized good figures engaged in conflict with hateful bad objects, unmitigated by any sense that all derived from the same self and parental figures.

Such observations made it possible to confirm, revise and extend Freud's theories. Klein saw that symptoms, character and personality could be understood in terms of relations to internalized fantasy-figures, laid down in early childhood; and this extended to psychotic disturbances, such as schizophrenia and manic-depressive illness, which turned on the particular nature of the figures involved. This gave rise to the British object-relations approach to psychoanalysis. It also influ-

enced the development of ego-psychology and self-psychology by Hartmann, Kohut and others in the United States, and Lacan's attempt to relate psychoanalysis to language, in France.

See also: FREUD, S.; PSYCHOANALYSIS, METHODOLOGICAL ISSUES IN

JAMES HOPKINS

PSYCHOLOGY, PHILOSOPHY OF
See MIND, PHILOSOPHY OF

PUFENDORF, SAMUEL (1632–94)

Pufendorf was the first university professor of the law of nature and nations. His *De iure naturae et gentium* (On the Law of Nature and Nations) (1672) and *De officio hominis et civis iuxta legem naturalem* (On the Duty of Man and Citizen according to Natural Law) (1673) greatly influenced the handling of that subject in the eighteenth century. As a result Pufendorf has been recognized as an important figure in the development of the conception of international law as a body of norms commonly agreed to have universal validity by sovereign states. He regarded himself as an exponent of a new moral science founded by Hugo Grotius which transformed the natural law tradition by starting from identifiable traits of human nature rather than ideas about what human beings ought to be.

See also: DESCARTES, R.; HOBBES, T.; HOHFELD, W.N.; LAW, PHILOSOPHY OF

J.D. FORD

PUNISHMENT
See CRIME AND PUNISHMENT

PURGATORY

According to Roman Catholic teaching, purgatory is the place or state of purification after death in which those who die in a state of grace (and hence are assured of being saved) make expiation for unforgiven venial sins or endure temporal punishment for mortal and venial sins already forgiven. The concept evolved to resolve the theological confusion about the state of souls between personal death and the general resurrection and Last Judgment, to explain what happens to those persons who repent before death but do not live long enough to do penance for their sins, and to make intelligible the widespread practice of praying for the souls of the departed. The doctrine developed in conjunction with a 'high' Eucharistic theology, according to which all the faithful departed take part in the liturgy of the Church. The idea of purgatory is therefore intimately connected with Christian ideas of sin, judgment, retributive punishment, the communion of saints and the idea that salvation occurs in history. It was rejected by the Reformers and, in the second half of the twentieth century, interest from Catholic theologians waned. Nevertheless, some modern Protestant thinkers have defended the concept as an intermediate phase in salvation.

See also: HELL; LIMBO

LINDA ZAGZEBSKI

PURPOSE IN NATURE
See TELEOLOGY

PURVA MĪMĀṂSĀ
See MĪMĀṂSĀ

PUTNAM, HILARY (1926–)

Putnam's work spans a broad spectrum of philosophical interests, yet nonetheless reflects thematic unity in its concern over the question of realism. A critic of logical positivism, Putnam opposed verificationism and conventionalism, arguing for a realist understanding of scientific theories. He rejected the traditional conception of meaning according to which speakers' mental states determine meaning and consequently, reference, and put forward a conception of meaning on which external reality, for example, what one talks about, contributes essentially to meaning. Further, citing what he called the division of linguistic labour, Putnam saw the conferring of meaning as a social rather than an individual enterprise. In response to the relativistic challenge that the incommensurability of different theories precludes any possibility of intertheoretical dialogue, Putnam invoked a causal theory of reference construing reference as relatively insensitive to theoretical variation, so that the continuity and rationality of science and communication are upheld. The Copenhagen interpretation of quantum mechanics posed yet another difficulty for realism. Putnam saw quantum logic as an alternative which was compatible with realism, and argued that logic, like geometry, can be revised on the basis of empirical considerations. In the philosophy of mind, Putnam proposed functionalism, the view that mental states are characterized by function rather than material constitution. Putnam also made a substantial contribution to mathematics through his work on the insolvability of Hilbert's tenth problem.

In 1976, Putnam launched an attack on the coherence of the view he termed 'metaphysical realism'. Arguing that relativism and scepticism are disguised forms of metaphysical realism, and likewise incoherent, he suggested an alternative, referred to as 'internal realism'. Clarification of this position and its viability as a third way between realism and relativism is the focus of Putnam's later writings, and of much of the criticism they have incurred.

See also: REFERENCE

YEMIMA BEN-MENAHEM

PYRRHONISM

Pyrrhonism was the name given by the Greeks to one particular brand of scepticism, that identified (albeit tenuously) with Pyrrho of Elis, who was said (by his disciple Timon of Phlius) to have declared that everything was indeterminable and accordingly to have suspended judgment about the reality of things – in particular whether they were really good or bad. After Timon's death Pyrrhonism lapsed, until revived by Aenesidemus. Aenesidemus held that it was inadmissible either to affirm or to deny that anything was really the case, and in particular to hold, with the Academic sceptics, that certain things really were inapprehensible. Instead, the Sceptic (the capital letter denotes the Pyrrhonists, who adopted the term, literally 'inquirer', as one of the designations for their school) should only allow that things were no more the case than not, or only so under certain circumstances and not under others. Aenesidemean Scepticism took the form of emphasizing the disagreement among both lay people and theoreticians as to the nature of things, and the fact that things appear differently under different circumstances (the various ways of doing this were systematized into the Ten Modes of Scepticism); the result was meant to be suspension of judgment about such matters, which would in turn lead to tranquillity of mind. Thus 'Scepticism' denotes a particular philosophical position, not simply, as in modern usage, that of any philosopher inclined towards doubt. Later Pyrrhonists, notably Agrippa, refined the Sceptical method and concentrated on undermining the dogmatic (that is, anti-Sceptical) notion of the criterion – there is no principled way to settle such disputes without resorting to mere assertion, infinite regress or circularity. We owe to Sextus Empiricus our most complete account of Pyrrhonian argument and the clearest exposition of the Pyrrhonian attitude. Faced with endemic dispute, Sceptics reserve judgment; but this does not render life impossible for them, since they will still react to the way things appear to be, although without believing in any strong sense that things really are as they seem. Furthermore, when Pyrrhonians describe their affective states, they do so undogmatically – and the Sceptical slogans ('I determine nothing', 'nothing is apprehended', and so on) are to be understood in a similar way, as merely reporting a state of mind and not expressing a commitment. Thus the slogans apply to themselves, and like cathartic drugs are themselves purged along with the noxious humour of dogmatism.

R.J. HANKINSON

PYTHAGORAS (*c.*570–*c.*497 BC)

Pythagoras of Samos was an early Greek sage and religious innovator. He taught the kinship of all life and the immortality and transmigration of the soul. Pythagoras founded a religious community of men and women in southern Italy that was also of considerable political influence. His followers, who became known as Pythagoreans, went beyond these essentially religious beliefs of the master to develop philosophical, mathematical, astronomical, and musical theories with which they tended to credit Pythagoras himself. The tradition established by Pythagoras weaves through much of Greek philosophy, leaving its mark particularly on the thought of Empedocles, Plato, and later Platonists.

See also: PRESOCRATIC PHILOSOPHY

HERMANN S. SCHIBLI

PYTHAGOREANISM

Pythagoreanism refers to a Greek religious–philosophical movement that originated with Pythagoras in the sixth century BC. Although Pythagoreanism in its historical development embraced a wide range of interests in politics, mysticism, music, mathematics and astronomy, the common denominator remained a general adherence among Pythagoreans to the name of the founder and his religious beliefs. Pythagoras taught the immortality and transmigration of the soul (reincarnation) and recommended a way of life that through ascetic practices, dietary rules and ethical conduct promised to purify the soul and bring it into harmony with the surrounding universe. Thereby the soul would become godlike since Pythagoras believed that the cosmos, in view of its orderly and harmonious workings and structure, was divine. Pythagoreanism thus has from its beginnings a cosmological context that saw further evolution along mathematical lines in the succeeding centuries. Pythagorean philosophers, drawing on musical theories that may go back to Pythagoras, expressed the harmony of the universe in terms of numerical relations and possibly even claimed that things are numbers. Notwithstanding a certain confusion in Pythagorean number philosophy between abstract and concrete, Pythagoreanism represents a valid attempt, outstanding in early Greek philosophy, to explain the world by formal, structural principles. Overall, the combination of religious, philosophical and mathematical speculations that characterizes Pythagoreanism exercised a significant influence on Greek thinkers, notably on Plato and his immediate successors as well as those Platonic philosophers known as Neo-Pythagoreans and Neoplatonists.

See also: PRESOCRATIC PHILOSOPHY

HERMANN S. SCHIBLI

Q

QUALIA

The terms 'quale' and 'qualia' (plural) are most commonly understood to mean the qualitative, phenomenal or 'felt' properties of our mental states, such as the throbbing pain of my current headache, or the peculiar blue of the afterimage I am experiencing now. Though it seems undeniable that at least some of our mental states have qualia, their existence raises a number of philosophical problems.

The first problem regards their nature or constitution. Many theorists have noted great differences between our intuitive conceptions of qualia and those of typical physical properties such as mass or length, and have asked whether qualia could nonetheless be identical with physical properties. Another problem regards our knowledge of qualia, in particular, whether our beliefs about them can be taken to be infallible, or at least to have some kind of special authority.

See also: COLOUR AND QUALIA; CONSCIOUSNESS; SENSE-DATA

JANET LEVIN

QUANTIFIERS

The quantifiers 'some' and 'every' were the object of the very first logical theory, Aristotelian syllogistic. An example of a syllogism is 'Every Spartan is Greek, every Greek is European, therefore every Spartan is European'. In such inferences, no quantifier is governed by another one. Contrast this with 'Everybody loves somebody'. Modern logic is often taken to have begun when Frege systematized for the first time the logic of quantifiers, including such dependent ones. In general, much of what has passed as logic over the centuries is in effect the study of quantifiers. This is especially clear with the area of logic variously known as quantification theory, lower predicate calculus or elementary logic. Some philosophers have even sought to limit the scope of logic to such a study of quantifiers. Yet the nature of quantifiers is

a delicate matter which is captured incompletely by the logic initiated by Frege and Russell.
See also: LOGICAL CONSTANTS

JAAKKO HINTIKKA
GABRIEL SANDU

QUANTIFIERS, GENERALIZED

Generalized quantifiers are logical tools with a wide range of uses. As the term indicates, they generalize the ordinary universal and existential quantifiers from first-order logic, '$\forall x$' and '$\exists x$', which apply to a formula $A(x)$, binding its free occurrences of x. $\forall x A(x)$ says that $A(x)$ holds for all objects in the universe and $\exists x A(x)$ says that $A(x)$ holds for some objects in the universe, that is, in each case, that a certain condition on $A(x)$ is satisfied. It is natural then to consider other conditions, such as 'for at least five', 'at most ten', 'infinitely many' and 'most'. So a quantifier Q stands for a condition on $A(x)$, or, more precisely, for a property of the set denoted by that formula, such as the property of being non-empty, being infinite, or containing more than half of the elements of the universe. The addition of such quantifiers to a logical language may increase its expressive power.

A further generalization allows Q to apply to more than one formula, so that, for example, $Qx(A(x),B(x))$ states that a relation holds between the sets denoted by $A(x)$ and $B(x)$, say, the relation of having the same number of elements, or of having a non-empty intersection. One also considers quantifiers binding more than one variable in a formula. $Qxy,zu(R(x,y),S(z,u))$ could express, for example, that the relation (denoted by) $R(x,y)$ contains twice as many pairs as $S(z,u)$, or that $R(x,y)$ and $S(z,u)$ are isomorphic graphs.

In general, then, a quantifier (the attribute 'generalized' is often dropped) is syntactically a variable-binding operator, which stands semantically for a relation between relations (on individuals), that is, a second-order relation. Quantifiers are studied in mathematical logic, and have also been applied in other areas, notably in the semantics of natural languages.

DAG WESTERSTÅHL

QUANTIFIERS, SUBSTITUTIONAL AND OBJECTUAL

Understood substitutionally, 'Something is F' is true provided one of its substitution instances (a sentence of the form 'a is F') is true. This contrasts with the objectual understanding, on which it is true provided 'is F' is true of some object in the domain of the quantifier. Substitutional quantifications have quite different truth-conditions from objectual ones. For instance, 'Something is a mythological animal' is true if understood substitutionally, since the substitution instance 'Pegasus is a mythological animal' is true. But understood objectually, the sentence is not true, since there are no mythological creatures to make up a domain for the quantifier.

Since substitutional quantifiers do not need domains over which they range, it is easy to introduce substitutional quantifiers which bind predicate or sentential variables, even variables within quotation marks. One reason for interest in substitutional quantification is the hope that it may provide a way to understand discourse which appears to be about numbers, properties, propositions and other 'troublesome' sorts of entities as being free of exceptional ontological commitments. Whether natural language quantification is sometimes plausibly construed as substitutional is not, however, clear.

See also: ONTOLOGICAL COMMITMENT

QUANTUM LOGIC

The topic of quantum logic was introduced by Birkhoff and von Neumann in 1936, who described the formal properties of a certain algebraic system associated with quantum theory. To avoid begging questions, it is convenient to use the term 'logic' broadly enough to cover any algebraic system with formal characteristics similar to the standard sentential calculus. In that sense it is uncontroversial that there is a logic of experimental questions (for example, 'Is the particle in region R?' or 'Do the particles have opposite spins?') associated with any physical system. Having introduced this logic for quantum theory, we may ask how it differs from the standard sentential calculus, the logic for the experimental questions in classical mechanics. The most notable difference is that the distributive laws fail, being replaced by a weaker law known as orthomodularity.

All this can be discussed without deciding whether quantum logic is a genuine logic, in the sense of a system of deduction. Putnam argued that quantum logic was indeed a genuine logic, because taking it as such solved various problems, notably that of reconciling the wave-like character of a beam of, say, electrons, as it passes through two slits, with the thesis that the electrons in the beam go through one or other of the two slits. If Putnam's argument succeeds this would be a remarkable case of the empirical defeat of logical intuitions. Subsequent discussion, however, seems to have undermined his claim.

PETER FORREST

QUANTUM MEASUREMENT PROBLEM

In classical mechanics a measurement process can be represented, in principle, as an interaction between two systems, a measuring instrument M and a measured system S, during which the classical states of M and S evolve dynamically, according to the equations of motion of the theory, in such a way that the 'pointer' or indicator quantity of M becomes correlated with the measured quantity of S. If a similar representation is attempted in quantum mechanics, it can be shown that, for certain initial quantum states of M and S, the interaction will result in a quantum state for the combined system in which neither the pointer quantity of M nor the measured quantity of S has a determinate value. On the orthodox interpretation of the theory, propositions assigning ranges of values to these quantities are neither true nor false. Since we require that the pointer readings of M are determinate after a measurement, and presumably also the values of the correlated S-quantities measured by M, it appears that the orthodox interpretation cannot accommodate the dynamical representation of measurement processes. The problem of how to do so is the quantum measurement problem.

See also: QUANTUM MECHANICS, INTERPRETATION OF

JEFFREY BUB

QUANTUM MECHANICS, INTERPRETATION OF

Quantum mechanics developed in the early part of the twentieth century in response to the discovery that energy is quantized, that is, comes in discrete units. At the microscopic level this leads to odd phenomena: light displays particle-like characteristics and particles such as electrons produce wave-like interference patterns. At the level of ordinary objects such effects are usually not evident, but this generalization is subject to striking exceptions and puzzling ambiguities.

The fundamental quantum mechanical puzzle is 'superposition of states'. Quantum states can be added together in a manner that recalls the superposition of waves, but the effects of quantum superposition show up only probabilistically in the statistics of many measurements. The details suggest that the world is indefinite in odd ways; for example, that things may not always have well-defined positions or momenta or energies. However, if we accept this conclusion, we have difficulty making sense of such straightforward facts as that measurements have definite results.

Interpretations of quantum mechanics are, in one way or another, attempts to understand the superposition of quantum states. The range of interpretations stretches from the metaphysically daring to the seemingly innocuous. But, so far, no single interpretation has commanded anything like universal agreement.

ALLEN STAIRS

QUINE, WILLARD VAN ORMAN (1908–2000)

Introduction

Quine is the foremost representative of naturalism in the second half of the twentieth century. His naturalism consists of an insistence upon a close connection or alliance between philosophical views and those of the natural sciences. Philosophy so construed is an activity within nature wherein nature examines itself. This contrasts with views which distinguish philosophy from science and place philosophy in a special transcendent position for gaining special knowledge. The methods of science are empirical; so Quine, who operates within a scientific perspective, is an empiricist, but with a difference. Traditional empiricism, as in Locke, Berkeley, Hume and some twentieth-century forms, takes impressions, ideas or sense-data as the basic units of thought. Quine's empiricism, by contrast, takes account of the theoretical as well as the observational facets of science. The unit of empirical significance is not simple impressions (ideas) or even isolated individual observation sentences, but systems of beliefs. The broad theoretical constraints for choice between theories, such as explanatory power, parsimony, precision and so on, are foremost in this empiricism. He is a fallibilist, since he holds that each individual belief in a system is in principle revisable. Quine proposes a new conception of observation sentences, a naturalized account of our knowledge of the external world, including a rejection of a priori knowledge, and he extends the same empiricist and fallibilist account to our knowledge of logic and mathematics.

Quine confines logic to first-order logic and clearly demarcates it from set theory and mathematics. These are all empirical subjects when empiricism is understood in its Quinian form. They are internal to our system of beliefs that make up the natural sciences. The language of first-order logic serves as a canonical notation in which to express our ontological commitments. The slogan 'To be is to be the value of a variable' (*From a Logical Point of View* 1953) encapsulates this project. Deciding which ontology to accept is also carried out within the naturalistic constraints of empirical science – our ontological commitments should be to those objects to which the best scientific theories commit us. On this basis Quine's own commitments are to physical objects and sets. Quine is a physicalist and a Platonist, since the best sciences require physical objects and the mathematics involved in the sciences requires abstract objects, namely, sets.

The theory of reference (which includes notions such as reference, truth and logical truth) is sharply demarcated from the theory of meaning (which includes notions such as meaning, synonymy, the analytic–synthetic distinction and necessity). Quine is the leading critic of notions from the theory of meaning, arguing that attempts to make the distinction between merely linguistic (analytic) truths and more substantive (synthetic) truths has failed. They do not meet the standards of precision which scientific and philosophical theories adhere to and which are adhered to in the theory of reference. He explores the limits of an empirical theory of language and offers a thesis of the indeterminacy of translation as further criticism of the theory of meaning.

1 Life

Willard Van Orman Quine was born on 25 June 1908 and died at the age of 92 on 25 December 2000. He was an undergraduate at Oberlin College and a graduate student at Harvard, where he studied with A.N. Whitehead, C.I. Lewis and Sheffer. In his dissertation 'The Logic of Sequences: A Generalization of *Principia Mathematica*' there already appears a prominent theme of Quine's philosophy – a concern with matters of ontology.

In 1931, Quine had what he has described as his 'most dazzling exposure to greatness', when Bertrand RUSSELL came to lecture at Harvard. Russell is one of the most influential figures on Quine's thought. Both share a preoccupation with questions concerning what there is. For example, Quine adopted and improved upon Russell's view of how we express ontological claims. More significantly, as the dissertation already reveals, Russell's influence was that of a rival whose theories spur Quine on to the creation of more acceptable alternatives. Wherever possible, Quine tries to get on with the fewest and most precise assumptions which will suffice to do the job at hand. Whereas *Principia Mathematica* is constructed on the basis of an ontology that comprises propositional functions, which are properties of a sort, Quine's revision tries to accomplish the same goals with concrete physical objects and sets or classes. In addition, some of Quine's most famous systems of logic and set theory are designed to achieve the same effects as *Principia Mathematica*, while avoiding Russell's theory of types (see THEORY OF TYPES).

A travelling fellowship to Europe in 1932 exposed Quine to the latest developments in logic and in philosophy. In Vienna he attended meetings of the Vienna Circle, and described the following weeks spent in Prague and Warsaw as 'the intellectually most rewarding months I have known' (see VIENNA CIRCLE). In Prague, Quine met Rudolf CARNAP, one of the most careful expositors of prominent themes of analytic philosophy and especially those of the logical empiricists, such as the verifiability criterion for the empirical meaningfulness of sentences, the linguistic (analytic) character of a priori knowledge, as in mathematics and logic, and the triviality or meaninglessness of ontology as a species of metaphysics. Quine subjected each of these themes to severe criticism, resulting in some of the most important philosophical debates of the century. In Warsaw, he attended the lectures of Lesniewski, Łukasiewicz and Tarski and in the next few years was to adopt Tarski's and Gödel's 'classic' formulation of logic in formulating his most famous works. Quine was quite sympathetic to the extensionalist and the nominalist side of the Warsaw school.

At Harvard in the period prior to the Second World War, Quine worked out some of his most distinctive positions: his conception of ontological commitment (best known from his 1948 essay 'On What There Is'); his two most distinctive systems of logic and set theory 'New Foundations for Mathematical Logic' (1937) and *Mathematical Logic* (1940); and his criticisms of the position that a priori knowledge as it purportedly exists in logic and mathematics is merely linguistic. These criticisms began to appear in 1934, when Quine lectured on Carnap's work. Some of this material can be found in 'Truth by Convention' (1936) and his most famous paper, 'Two Dogmas of Empiricism' (1951).

Quine served as a naval officer in the Second World War, and afterwards continued his work on the above topics (see *From a Logical Point of View* (1953)). Much of his most original work since then has been the formulation of a new holistic variety of empiricism and the exploration of its consequences: 'The point of holism, stressed by Pierre Duhem . . . , is that the observable consequence by which we test a scientific hypothesis is ordinarily not a consequence of the hypothesis taken by itself; it is a consequence only of a whole cluster of sentences . . . *Quiddities* (1987: 141). Beginning with 'Two Dogmas', and eventually in *Word and Object* (1960), Quine employed this new holistic empiricism to criticize the concepts of meaning, synonymy and analyticity. In *Word and Object* he presented a thesis of the indeterminacy of translation as a further criticism of these notions. Later, in *Ontological Relativity* (1969), *The Roots of Reference* (1974), *Pursuit of Truth* (1992) and *From Stimulus to Science* (1995) he took a similar critical stance on concepts from the theory of reference. In essays dating from this period Quine's naturalism also comes to the fore. Though the theme of the continuity of philosophy and science is found in earlier works, he explores it more explicitly in 'Epistemology Naturalized' (1969), *Theories and Things* (1981), *Pursuit of Truth* and *From Stimulus to Science*.

2 Epistemology naturalized – nature know thyself

The problem of our knowledge of the external world is traditionally stated as one of how a self with private mental states can come to have knowledge of the external world. Quine's restatement is strikingly more naturalistic:

> I am a physical object sitting in a physical world. Some of the forces of this physical world impinge on my surface. Light rays strike

my retinas; molecules bombard my eardrums and fingertips. I strike back, emanating concentric air waves. These waves take the form of a torrent of discourse about tables, people, molecules, light rays, retinas, air waves, prime numbers, infinite classes, joy and sorrow, good and evil.

(*The Ways of Paradox and Other Essays* 1966)

In its traditional statement the problem lies in how, starting with 'experience' in the form of immediately given impressions or sense-data, we justify our claims to know objects such as tables, chairs or molecules. This vantage point was that of a first philosophy, intended as providing a foundation of certainty for the sciences by standing outside of them and legitimizing their accomplishments. Quine rejects this formulation. His naturalized epistemology rephrases the problem as one of how we learn to talk about or refer to objects (ordinary as well as scientific). What are the conditions that lead to reference? How is scientific discourse possible?

The traditional accounts of the linkage between 'experience' and our knowledge vary from mentalistic conceptions, like that of Hume, in which all our ideas are copies of sense impressions, to more neutral linguistic formulations, in which cognitive claims are to be translated into observation sentences. On Quine's holistic account, one cannot deal with the empirical content of sentences, much less of terms – the linguistic correlates of ideas – one by one, either via definition, translation or some other sort of linkage. To study the relation of knowledge and science to observation sentences is to trace the psychological and linguistic development of the knower, that is, the potential user of scientific language. Observation sentences serve as both the starting point in human language learning as well as the empirical grounds for science. The problem of knowledge now is how, starting with observation sentences, we can proceed to talk of tables, chairs, molecules, neutrinos, sets and numbers. One of the reasons for doing epistemology by studying the roots of reference is simply the failure of the traditional empiricists' programme mentioned above. Another is that it enables one to dispense with mentalistic notions such as 'experience' or 'observation'. One relies instead on two components which are already part of a naturalist's ontology: the physical happening at the nerve endings, the neural input or stimulus; and the linguistic entity, the observation sentence. These two serve as naturalistic surrogates for 'experience' and 'observation'. On Quine's empiricist and behaviourist account, observation sentences are those that can be learned independently of other

language acquisition. They are the sentences that can be learned purely by ostension and as such are causally most proximate to the stimulus. This account is not vulnerable to attacks on the notion of observation as dependent on the theories one holds, since observation sentences are precisely those which are learnable without any background information. Another point of difference with empiricists concerns the alleged certainty or incorrigibility of observation. Though Quine's observation sentences are assented to with a minimum of background information and are thus included among those sentences less likely to be revised, they are not in principle immune from revision.

Unlike traditional epistemology, then, Quine's epistemology is naturalistic: we cannot stand apart from our place as part of nature and make philosophical judgments (see NATURALIZED EPISTEMOLOGY). This is part of the theme that philosophy is continuous with science, science being the part of nature most suitable for knowing itself.

> The naturalistic philosopher begins his reasoning within the inherited world theory as a going concern. He tentatively believes all of it, but believes also that some unidentified portions are wrong. He tries to improve, clarify and understand the system from within.
>
> (*Theories and Things* 1981)

There is no cognitive standpoint outside of nature: philosophy, and in particular, epistemology, is no exception. We cannot stand apart from our scientific worldview and make philosophical judgments. As an example consider the problem of induction. It is frequently stated as scepticism about knowing whether the future will resemble the past. If this scepticism is stated as requiring a justification of induction in the sense that we provide a deductive or an inductive argument for the future (in relevant respects) resembling the past, then we should refuse to accede to that request. It is well known that such arguments are either question-begging or require a standpoint beyond our natural cognitive abilities which there is little reason for thinking we can attain to. 'The Humean predicament is the human predicament' (*Ontological Relativity and Other Essays* 1969). Since justification in the above sense is out of the question, what should and what can we do? Quine dealt with this problem by adopting the stance of a scientist examining scientific practice. The psychogenesis of reference consists of hypotheses as to how we get to talk about objects. This involves hypothesizing an innate ability to spot similarities. Induction in its most primitive forms is of a piece with recognizing similarities. We have a built-in mechanism to expect similarities. However, it does not guarantee that we will find them.

> Perceptual similarity is the basis of all expectations, all learning, all habit formation. ... This is primitive induction.
>
> Since learning hinges thus on perceptual similarity, perceptual similarity cannot itself have been learned – not all of it. Some of it is innate.
>
> The survival value of primitive induction is anticipation of something edible, or of some creature by which one might be eaten. Thus it is that natural selection has endowed us with standards of perceptual similarity that mesh pretty well with natural trends. The future is as may be, but we persist hopefully.
>
> (*From Stimulus to Science* 1995)

Such is Quine's treatment of Hume's problem of why we believe that similar causes have similar effects. He deals with the problem in the setting of evolutionary psychology where Hume dealt with it in terms of the associationist psychology of his times. Quine, like Hume, is not attempting to justify induction in the sense of providing an argument for something like the uniformity of nature. Parallel to Hume, Quine offers an empirical account – a theory within empiricism of why we believe the future will resemble the past. Both hold that the source of this belief is 'subjective', i.e. found in the human subject. They differ in that Hume holds that the subject acquires this belief as a result of 'experience' and association whereas Quine says its source is a gene-determined disposition to spot similarities, which Quine supplements with an account from evolutionary psychology.

3 Dethroning the a priori

A purported stumbling block for empiricism is a priori knowledge in logic and mathematics and in such purportedly conceptual truths as 'All bachelors are unmarried' and 'Nothing is larger than itself'. Such subject matter appears to defy justification in terms of observation. J.S. Mill's empiricist programme foundered on this point, and the various forms of rationalism are unacceptable to an empiricist. A proposed solution, the dominant one favoured by analytic philosophers, involved the analytic–synthetic distinction: all a priori knowledge was said to be analytic, in the sense that the truth of sentences claimed to be known independent of experience was reducible to matters of language, for example, linguistic convention, definitions, and truth in virtue of the meaning of the expressions involved.

Quine's critique is that of an empiricist reforming empiricism, supplanting reductionist-atomistic empiricism with Duhemian holism. Experimental testing is a juncture where observation ('experience') enters as a factor in deciding whether to accept or reject a claim. An oversimplified model of how observation counts in testing is that given a hypothesis and a statement of initial conditions, we deduce by logic and/or mathematics some observation sentence as an observable consequence. If the expected observation occurs, we take this as evidence for the hypothesis. If it does not, we take this as evidence that the hypothesis is false. Such a model makes use of the dogma of reductionism by assuming that individual sense experiences-observation sentences function unequivocally for or against isolated sentences-hypotheses. Pierre DUHEM showed that this model is flawed and Quine extends Duhem's point into a holistic one that embodies a critique of reductionism and the a priori.

Duhem had pointed out that where the observation fails to occur, one has leeway in dealing with the situation. All serious testing involves background assumptions, implicit in the hypothesis or in the statement of the initial conditions. A test situation underdetermines which factor should be revised and there is no way of knowing in advance where the revision should be made. Quine's insight was to take cognizance of all the assumptions that can be questioned in a test situation. The underdetermination of theory by observation does not stop with revising background assumptions relative to the hypothesis and the initial conditions. Both the purportedly disconfirming observation made and the principles involved in deriving the observable consequence can also be revised. In test situations whole systems of beliefs go into the hopper and we have leeway as to how we make the consistency-preserving revisions. We can edit the observation. We can even question the logic and or mathematics used in deriving the observable conclusion. No sentence is in principle immune from being revised. In this spirit, all knowledge is empirical; there is no a priori knowledge. The quest for certainty is replaced by fallibilism, the associated foundationalist programmes are abandoned, as is the verifiability theory of the logical empiricists. Instead, the broad constraints on what to do in a test situation are the natural scientist's criteria for preferring one hypothesis, theory or system of beliefs over another. These criteria include explanatory power, simplicity or parsimony, conservatism, modesty and precision. Conservatism cautions, other things being equal, that we should accept that hypothesis-theory which clashes least with our other beliefs. This 'maxim of minimal mutilation' comes into play in explaining why logic, while in principle revisable (for example, some suggest adopting a three-valued logic), is the least likely item to be revised. Doing so would have far-reaching consequences for our other beliefs. Modesty says that all other things being equal we should hypothesize as little as is necessary for the job at hand. Precision mandates standards on introducing and explaining philosophical or scientific concepts. It requires that philosophical explications be couched in acceptable terms, the extensional or empirical notions of logic, set theory and the sciences. For example, abstract objects should not be posited without a precise account of what they are, that is to say, 'no entity without identity' (see A PRIORI; ANALYTICITY; FALLIBILISM).

4 Logic as first-order logic

Quine distinguishes the theory of reference from the theory of meaning. He is sceptical of notions associated with the theory of meaning, such as those of meaning, intension, synonymy, analyticity and necessity. By contrast, he relies on and makes contributions to the theory of reference, for example, to the understanding of logical truth, truth, reference and ontological commitment.

For Quine, the notion of logical truth falls squarely in the theory of reference. His most characteristic definition of logical truth is that a sentence is a logical truth if it is true and if it remains true when one uniformly replaces its nonlogical parts. The logical parts are the logical constants, signs for negation, disjunction, quantification and identity. 'Brutus killed Caesar or it is not the case that Brutus killed Caesar' is such a logical truth. In Quine's terminology the logical constants 'or' and 'it is not the case that' occur essentially, while the nonlogical part 'Brutus killed Caesar' can be uniformly varied and the resulting sentence will still be true. In other words a logical truth cannot be changed into a falsehood by varying the nonlogical expressions, whereas an ordinary truth can be.

The same concept of logical truth is found in BOLZANO and Ajdukiewicz. One of its virtues lies in its being parsimonious, that is, in what it does not say. Logical truth and related notions are often explained in modal terms. That is, logical truths are said to be distinguished by being 'necessary' or 'true in all possible worlds', and a valid argument is defined as one in which, if the premises are true, the conclusion 'must be true'. These accounts make logic presuppose modal notions. Quine's definition leaves logic autonomous in this respect. Indeed Quine is a critic of modal logic, challenging various attempts to explain the notion of necessity. Logical truth, as defined by Quine, is a precisely explained

species of truth, fitting squarely inside the theory of reference. Quine relies on the concept of truth, which he construes along the lines of Tarski's theory (see TARSKI).

If logical truths are those in which only logical constants occur essentially, then the scope of logic is in part determined by what we take to be a logical constant. Quine lists as the logical constants the truth-functional connectives 'not', 'and', 'or', 'if... then', 'if and only if'; the quantifiers 'all' and 'some'; and the identity predicate '$a = b$'. The language of logic so construed is that of sentences formed out of truth-functional connectives, quantifiers, identity, schematic predicate letters and individual variables. Quantificational logic of this sort is also known as first-order logic. For Quine, logic *is* first-order logic with identity. Ruled out as logic on this construal are modal logic, because 'necessity' is not taken as a logical constant. Also excluded is higher-order logic, which has quantifiers for predicate positions (it is 'set theory in sheep's clothing' (*Philosophy of Logic* 1986)). On other grounds other proposals such as intuitionist logic are also ineligible. Set theory, and with it mathematics, are not logic (see LOGICAL CONSTANTS).

Quine falls in the camp of the logicist programme in holding that mathematics is reducible to set theory. Set theory is the theory of the 'is a member of' predicate and is stated in the language of first-order logic. Given the theory of membership and logic as first-order logic plus identity, Quine introduces mathematical notions as definitional abbreviations: for example, a number is defined as a special set, addition as a special function on these sets and so on. He argues that logic does not include set theory because membership should not be considered a logical constant for the following reasons. (1) There is a general consensus about elementary logic, which, given paradoxes such as Russell's, is lacking in the case of set theory. Alternative set theories have the status of so many tentative hypotheses. This lends credence to Quine's view that mathematics based on set theory is not very different from other sciences. (2) The incompleteness of set theory contrasts sharply with the completeness of elementary logic. (3) The ontology of set theory is not as topic-neutral as that of logic. The second item in the membership relation is restricted to sets. Logic is the most general of subjects, since the variables of logic are not restricted to any one category of objects (see LOGICISM §1).

5 Canonical notation and ontological commitment

Ever since Frege and Russell, existential quantification has been the prevalent way in which existence assertions have been understood. The idea is that existence sentences in natural language can be paraphrased in the language of logic and 'existence' explicated by the existential quantifier of predicate logic. 'Existence is what existential quantification expresses' (*Ontological Relativity*). The functions that the predicate 'exists' performs in English can be accomplished by the '∃x' quantifier. Quine's version of this theme is incorporated into his account of ontological commitment. The language of first-order predicate logic in which our ontological commitments are made is his 'canonical notation'.

> Taking the canonical notation thus austerely... we have just these basic constructions: predication, quantification... and the truth functions... What thus confronts us as a scheme for systems of the world is that structure so well understood by present-day logicians, the logic of quantification or calculus of predicates.
>
> Not that the idioms thus renounced are supposed to be unneeded in the market place or in the laboratory... The doctrine is only that such a canonical idiom can be abstracted and then adhered to in the statement of one's scientific theory. The doctrine is that all traits or reality worthy of the name can be set down in an idiom of this austere form if in any idiom.
>
> It is in spirit a philosophical doctrine of categories, ... philosophical in its breadth however continuous with science in its motivation.
>
> ('Carnap on Logical Truth' 1960)

A key reason for regarding this language as canonical is that in it one's use of the existential quantifier is explicit. To discover the existence assumptions or ontological commitments of a theory, we first state it in the language of truth-functional connectives and quantification, and then look at the existential quantifications we have made. The logic of '∃x' is the logic of existence, and a notation that makes '∃x' explicit accordingly makes our existence assumptions or ontological commitments explicit.

One of Quine's most famous remarks, 'to be is to be the value of a variable' (*From a Logical Point of View* [1953] 1988), sums up this criterion of ontological commitment. The slogan also incorporates one of Quine's elaborations on Russell's theory of definite descriptions. Russell held that in most sentences ordinary names are disguised definite descriptions, which on his theory are analysed as existential generalizations. Thus 'Socrates is human' becomes 'The one husband of Xanthippe is human' which in turn becomes the existential generalization

'There is one and only one husband of Xanthippe and he is human'. Quine's elaboration dispenses with names entirely. Wherever a name occurs in the original sentence, we can get by in the canonical notation with variables, predicates and the logical constants. If we do not have a definite description on hand to put in place of the name, we can form a predicate, such as 'Socratizes', then encapsulate the coined predicate in a definite description and define away the descriptions via Russell's theory. So names disappear and are not part of the canonical notation. Dispensing with names not only has the virtue of a more parsimonious notation: it also specifies that variables are the vehicles of reference and as such the grounds of ontological commitment. Being the value of a variable is what 'being' is all about (see ONTOLOGICAL COMMITMENT).

6 Competing ontologies

Some important philosophical differences concern competing ontologies. Physicalists, for instance, have as their basic objects physical objects, while phenomenalists have sense-data. A twentieth-century version of the problem of universals involves a dispute over the relative merits of: (1) a nominalistic ontology according to which only concrete individuals exist; and (2) realist ontologies, such as those of Platonists, which involve the existence of abstract objects. The issue of nominalism versus Platonism arises for Quine in connection with the mathematics required for science and the question whether it requires hypothesizing abstract objects such as sets. Another area of ontological controversy is whether Platonist assumptions should include only extensional objects such as sets or intensional ones such as properties or propositions (see ABSTRACT OBJECTS; NOMINALISM).

While we look to the existential generalizations of a theory stated in canonical notation to see what its ontological commitments are, this does not answer the question of which ontological commitments we should have. As a naturalist and scientific realist, Quine regards this as a matter of epistemology. It is the question of which theory we ought to accept. Deciding on a theory (scientific or philosophical) and its attendant ontology is once again done within a scientific perspective. Appeal is made to the same theoretical concerns mentioned earlier, that is, explanatory power, parsimony, conservatism, precision and so on. Quine's own ontological commitments are the result of just such considerations. He is a physicalist, no longer taking seriously the phenomenalist programme; partly on grounds connected with the dogma of reductionism and partly on the grounds that sense-data are not needed in a naturalized epistemology (the functions performed by sense-data are accomplished by nerve hits and observation sentences which are already part of our physicalist ontology). But he is a Platonist (a reluctant one) because of the mathematics that is required by our best scientific theories. In canonical notation, this mathematics requires quantifying over at least as many extensional abstract objects, namely sets, as there are real numbers. In an early essay co-authored with Nelson Goodman, 'Steps Towards A Constructive Nominalism' (1947), the possibilities of taking a nominalist stance were surveyed. But unlike Goodman, Quine reluctantly concluded that the nominalist programme failed. He has considered later attempts at nominalism such as by an appeal to substitutional quantification. The success of these attempts depends on whether impredicative notions are required by the mathematics embedded in the natural sciences. Others such as Field try to make the case for nominalism by abiding by some and abandoning other of Quine's constraints.

However, Quine has consistently argued against theories which require abstract objects of an intensional sort. An intensional notion might provisionally be characterized as one requiring for its explanation notions which do not conform to certain basic assumptions of first-order logic and standard set theories. Intensional contexts are not truth-functional, or do not allow the substitutability of coextensive singular terms or predicates. Modal notions are a case in point. 'Necessarily P' is not a truth-functional operation; we cannot replace singular terms or predicates in P, or the whole sentence P, with coextensive expressions and be guaranteed that if the original sentence is true then the subsequent one will also be true. In non-intensional contexts, that is, extensional contexts, such replacements are truth-preserving. Intensional objects are those that require intensional notions to account for them, such as properties or propositions. Extensional objects are those that do not require intensional notions to account for them, such as sets or sentences. So sets are identical if they have the same members, for example, the set of humans is the same as the set of featherless bipeds. Properties, on the other hand, are identical only if they necessarily belong to the same objects. So the properties of being human and being a rational animal are identical, but differ from the property of being a featherless biped.

Given Quine's views on the precision of notions from first-order logic and set theory, it is not surprising that he is critical of intensional notions which are not based on standard assumptions of first-order logic and set theory. His arguments against hypothesizing intensional objects are numerous and can be sketchily listed as cases where their

explanatory power is questioned, where parsimony is invoked and where precise accounts of the identity conditions of such items is lacking ('no entity without identity'). Sometimes he argues that extensional ersatz constructions can achieve the same purpose for which the intensional objects were introduced: for instance, eternal sentences rather than propositions, sets rather than properties, ordered pairs rather than relations (construed intensionally), non-modal notions rather than modal ones, and so on (see INTENSIONAL ENTITIES).

7 Indeterminacy of reference and global structuralism

Quine's views on ontology undergo refinements in his later writings. Most important is the recognition that empiricism does not uniquely determine which objects are required as the values of our variables. There is an indeterminacy of reference which is in keeping with empiricist strictures on deciding which ontology to accept.

The thesis of ontological relativity, also known as the inscrutability or indeterminacy of reference, is in accord with Quine's naturalistic empiricism. It has been generalized into a view which he refers to as global structuralism. Since it is only at the observation sentences construed holophrastically as indissoluble wholes that the system is externally constrained, there are different but equally plausible ways of meeting these observational constraints and these can involve diverse ontologies, such as an ontology of rabbits or of rabbit parts. It is the structural part of the system that must be saved in order to meet the observational constraints. But this can be accomplished with quite different objects being the values of the variables. Quine endorses this global structuralist perspective by generalizing from his own cases and by noting a less global structuralist argument from the philosophy of mathematics. Quite different objects can be taken as the values of the variables for arithmetic, for example, numbers can be taken as Frege–Russell sets or as von Neumann sets without changing the truths of arithmetic. For Quine the question of whether we are really committed to rabbits as opposed to sums of rabbit parts, or to a given number as the set of all sets equinumerous to a given set (as on the Frege–Russell account) or to some different set (as on von Neumann's view) is without sense. It is without sense in that there is no natural-empirical way of raising this question. Global structuralism is a consequence of the denial of a first philosophy – a point of view in nature that transcends all natural points of view.

Quine's best-known cases which serve as evidence for his global structuralism are his rabbits case and his proxy functions, especially that of cosmic complements. Intertwined with his discussion in *Word and Object* of a linguist translating a native speaker's utterance of 'Gavagai', Quine points out that construing that expression as a referring expression leaves no empirical way of deciding whether it is used to refer to rabbits, rabbit parts, or rabbit stages and so on. As a later example he asks us to consider how sentences about concrete objects can be reinterpreted in terms of different ontologies assigned as values of the variables so that there is no empirical way of saying which is the correct one. Indeed the message of structuralism is that it is an error to speak as though there were a uniquely correct referent. The sentence 'This rabbit is furry' is true and is usually interpreted as being about individual rabbits and individual furry things. However, if we reinterpret the referring portions in terms of mereological cosmic complements the sentence remains true and there is no empirical way if we do this uniformly to say which is the correct ontology. Thus assign to 'This rabbit' the entire cosmos less this rabbit (imagine a complete jigsaw puzzle with a rabbit piece removed; the cosmic complement would be the puzzle without the rabbit piece). Assign to the predicate 'is furry' each of the cosmic complements of individual furry things. The sentence 'This rabbit is furry' is true under such an interpretation because the cosmos less this rabbit is a member of the set of cosmic complements of individual furry things (that is, that set includes the cosmic complement of that individual rabbit). One can extend this treatment of singular sentences to the remaining referential sentences.

8 The theory of meaning: its myths and dogmas

Quine's reaction in the 1930s to Carnap's work was a sceptical critique of the prevalent view among analytic philosophers that logic and mathematics are justified in some distinctively linguistic way, that is, that they are based on merely analytic-linguistic truths – truths by convention. The scepticism then and later questions proposed accounts of the distinction. Linguistic truth or truth by convention, as opposed to non-conventionally based empirical truths, appears in the end to be a purported distinction without a real difference. Of special importance is the failure to satisfy the requirement of precision in explaining the distinction. In 'Truth By Convention' (1936) and 'Carnap on Logical Truth' (1960), Quine takes up different attempts to characterize such truths and finds that for the most part they are either too broad – not distinctive of logic or mathematics – or require non-linguistically based truth. There are as many of these character-

izations as there are different senses of 'convention'. Quine considers truth by convention as based on the following: the arbitrary factor in axiomatization; formalization–disinterpretation; the arbitrary element in hypothesizing; and definition. But neither logic nor mathematics is distinguished by being axiomatized, or formalized-disinterpreted. The same can be done for other disciplines, such as physics and biology. The somewhat arbitrary choice of which sentences to take as axioms, so long as we can prove the right sentences, is also not distinctive of them. If truth by convention is taken as the somewhat arbitrary element in framing hypotheses, then this too is not distinctive of logic or mathematics. Nor are the formulas involved distinguished by being true by definition. Thus, if 'p →p' is defined in terms of '−p ∨ p', then the truth of the defined formula depends on the truth of the defining formula, and that formula's truth is not a matter of definition or convention. For Quine, logic and mathematics can be precisely characterized in terms from the theory of reference. Logic is described in terms of truth, the logical constants and interchange of the extralogical elements; mathematics can be characterized in terms of set theory. But neither of these subjects is distinct in having a different epistemological basis which results in their being in some interesting sense 'analytic' or mere 'linguistic truths'.

The 'Two Dogmas' of Quine's 1951 essay were the dogma of reduction (see §3 earlier) and the dogma of the analytic/synthetic distinction. In discussing the dogma of analyticity, Quine questions, as he did in 'Truth by Convention', whether the distinction can be well made. Here he rejects five ways of explaining analyticity. These involve appeals to: (1) meanings, (2) definition, (3) interchangeability, (4) semantic rules and (5) the verifiability theory of meaning.

(1) 'Bachelors are unmarried men' might be regarded as analytic, where that notion is explained as truth in virtue of the meanings of its words. One suggestion is that the meaning of 'unmarried man' is included in the meaning of 'bachelor'. Another approach would hypothesize the existence of meanings to explain synonymy and then use synonymy in turn to show how the above sentence is a synonymous instance of a logical truth. The success of the above explanations requires assuming that there are such things as precisely characterizable meanings. Quine is sceptical of this assumption. He rejects three accounts of meanings: (a) referential theories – meanings as referents; (b) mentalism – meanings as ideas; and (c) intensionalism – meanings as intensional entities. Meaning (or sense), as Frege taught, must be distinguished from reference.

The notion of meaning that is to explain synonymy and analyticity cannot simply be reference, because coreferential terms need not be synonymous and so will not distinguish analytic sentences from true non-analytic ones. Truth in virtue of meaning where meaning is simply reference is too broad as all truths would then be analytic. As to meanings as ideas, Quine brings to bear empiricist and behaviourist qualms. The account of meanings as abstract intensional entities is found in Frege, Carnap and Church. Quine maintains that such intensional objects are neither required as posits by our theories of language, nor are they precisely accounted for. The attempt to explain intensional notions is either circular or unhelpful. There is a circle of intensional notions, meaning, synonymy, analyticity, necessity, and we can define one in terms of another. Quine's criticism is that if we do not break out of this intensional circle, then the account has failed to clarify the matter. For example, if the meaning of a predicate 'is human' is the property of being human, how would one go about identifying whether 'being a rational animal' or 'being a featherless biped' stood for the same property or had the same meaning? One answer is that the sentence 'humans are rational animals' is analytic, while the sentence 'humans are featherless bipeds' is not. But this relies on the notion of 'analytic' – which we haven't yet defined. Another approach at giving an identity condition uses modal notions and says that the first sentence is a necessary truth while the second is not. This, however, raises the problem of giving a precise account of modal notions. Explaining modal claims in terms of analyticity, for example, 'Necessarily humans are rational' as explained by '"Humans are rational" is analytic', will not do – since we have not defined 'analytic'. Quine's challenge is that one break out of this intensional circle and explain notions from the theory of meaning in more acceptable terms.

(2) He next rejects accounts of analyticity in terms of logical truth and synonymy. On this account a sentence is analytic if it is a synonymous instance of a logical truth, that is, 'All bachelors are unmarried men' is analytic in that it is derivable from the first-order logical truth 'All bachelors are bachelors' by putting a synonym 'unmarried man' for the second occurrence of 'bachelor'. One account attempts to explain synonymy in terms of definition. However, the various forms of definition either presuppose synonymy or stipulate it; none explain it. Quine is sceptical of definitions or philosophical analysis when thought of as capturing or analysing some concept or meaning. Instead philosophical explication is thought of in terms of the theory of reference and scientific hypothesizing and thus again embodying the naturalistic theme of the continuity of science and philosophy. One does not capture 'the meaning' of an expression; one explicates or proposes a theory of the referential features one is interested in preserving.

(3) Another attempt to define synonymy asserts that two expressions are synonymous if they are interchangeable. But it is not enough to say expressions are synonymous when the interchange of the one with the other within extensional contexts does not change the truth value of the sentences involved. This has the unacceptable consequence that merely coextensive terms would be synonyms. To do better one has to require interchangeability within intensional contexts. However, this raises the problem of breaking out of the circle of intensional notions.

(4) The fourth approach is another of Carnap's. It consists in constructing an artificial language and then defining 'analytic' for it. While it is possible to construct a language and specify that relative to it logic, mathematics and such truths as 'All bachelors are unmarried men' and 'Nothing is larger than itself' are analytic, this language-relative specification of analyticity does not clarify matters. It does not help to be told that in one language, language 1 (artificial or otherwise), we have a list of sentences that are analytic 1, and that in another language, language 2, we have the list analytic 2 and so on. What we want of an explication of analyticity is an account of what analytic 1, analytic 2 and so on have in common. The appeal to artificial languages fails to provide this characterization. Moreover, the problem is precisely why 'All bachelors are unmarried' is on the list and 'No bachelors are six-legged' is not. To be told that a sentence is analytic because it is on a list (even the list of an artificial language) provides no real distinction.

(5) The last attempt to define analyticity that Quine considers appeals to the verification theory of meaning. According to this theory, 'the meaning of a statement is the method of empirically confirming or infirming it'; 'statements are synonymous if and only if they are alike in point of method of empirical confirmation or infirmation' ([1953] 1988). Though sympathetic towards the empiricist thrust of this theory Quine does not think it survives the holistic criticism of the dogma of reductionism.

Quine's critique of the theory of meaning has amounted to a challenge to provide precise accounts of its notions. What counts as precise could take the form of reducing intensional notions to extensional ones. His criticisms of modal concepts has spurred a generation of responses in what is known as possible world semantics, which in one of its variations can be seen as trying to provide a reduction of intensional modal notions via extensional metalinguistic truth conditions for modal statements. The success of this reduction is still challenged by Quinians. More in keeping with Quine's challenge to explicate the theory of meaning is Davidson's work on letting a Tarskian theory of truth serve as surrogate for a theory of meaning. Another way in which scepticism about the theory of meaning might be overcome would be by an empirical and behaviouristically constrained account of such notions. Carnap took up this challenge and sketched a programme for empirically identifying meanings by testing translation hypotheses, for example, a linguist's hypotheses for translating the terms 'Pferd' from German to English as 'horse'. Quine's response was the topic of radical translation and his thesis of the indeterminacy of translation.

9 Indeterminacy of translation

How much of language is susceptible to empirical analysis? Like Carnap, Quine takes the case of linguists hypothesizing about translations as the subject matter for empirical inquiry. Both take as their data the intersubjectively available public phenomena of native speakers responding to appropriate stimuli. Quine introduces the concept of the stimulus meaning of a sentence for a person as the class of stimulations which would prompt them to assent to it. But Quine deals with the stimulus meaning of whole sentences, such as 'This is a horse', construed as holophrastic fused expressions, such as 'Here-is-a-horse', and not terms, such as 'horse'. Quine's linguist offers a hypothesis equating two such fused sentences (one is the native's and the other the linguist's) and checks it against a native speaker's assenting or dissenting to the native sentence in the presence of some nonverbal stimulus. One reason for adopting such holophrastic sentences is that we are dealing with the entering wedge in learning a language. In the crucial radical translation case Quine's field linguist is in a somewhat similar position to an infant who is learning a language without having any prior linguistic skills. That is, we are initially concerned with the public conditions in learning those parts of a language (one-word sentences) that do not involve knowledge of other parts of the language, especially those parts that are remote from the stimulus conditions. These sentences that serve as the entering wedge are Quine's observation sentences, and they also serve as an observational base for testing scientific theories. Carnap considered translation for languages such as German and English, which are known to have much in common. For Quine, the critical case is that of radical translation, that is, translations between languages that have little or nothing in

common. Think of a linguist among some radically foreign tribe. The linguist observes a certain correlation between a native utterance of 'Gavagai' and the presence of rabbits and proceeds to frame a hypothesis which equates 'Gavagai' and the one-word sentence 'Rabbit', short for 'Here's-a-rabbit'. The linguist could, on learning how to recognize the native's assent and dissent, question the native by uttering 'Gavagai' when a rabbit appears and seeing whether the native assents. Carnap would presumably want this to count as evidence that the terms in a sentence 'gavagai' and 'rabbit' have the same meaning. But does the evidence really go that far? All that we have as data is the native's expression and the rabbit stimulation. Quine claims that on these grounds one could equally well translate the holophrastic sentence 'Gavagai' as 'Here's-a-rabbit', 'Here's-a-rabbit-stage' or 'Here's-a-temporal-part-of-a-rabbit' or something else. For wherever there are rabbit stimulations there are also rabbit-stage stimulations, etc. On what basis then would one decide between these different translations? In the case of culturally similar languages one assumes a stock of more theoretical guides to translations and thus one can ask the German whether all horses are Pferde and all Pferde are horses. Such theoretical guides (Quine refers to them as 'analytical hypotheses') appear among the remoter parts of language that cannot be what the infant or field linguist has access to at the initial stage of learning a language. In the case of radical translation, the linguist is not in a position to pose more theoretical questions about the remoter portions of a language. At this point hypotheses less directly connected to the data – to the stimulus conditions – may be introduced by the linguist. These analytical hypotheses can be framed so as to do justice to quite different incompatible translations. Thus radical translation provides evidence for the conjecture of the indeterminacy of translation (see RADICAL TRANSLATION AND RADICAL INTERPRETATION).

To illustrate this matter for the Gavagai case we must note that in order to ask the question 'Is this rabbit the same as that?' the linguist must have decided how to translate articles, pronouns, identity predicates and so on. To translate these sentences is to go far beyond the data provided by the stimuli and involves selecting from different sets of analytical hypotheses, that is, different possible manuals of translation. On one set of these we translate the question as 'Is this the same rabbit as that?', while on another as 'Is this rabbit stage of the same series as that?' Each of these translations is equally good, yet they are mutually incompatible. Since neither of these has any immediate connection with the Gavagai stimulation there is no way of deciding between them.

This indeterminacy provides further grounds for discrediting the notion of meaning. Philosophers have talked as if meanings are related to expressions in somewhat the same way as paintings in a museum are related to their labels. Quine dubs this 'the myth of the museum'. According to this view, two expressions are synonymous when they are related to a unique meaning, like two labels for the same painting. In the case of translation, one English expression is a translation of another in a different language when the two bear a relation to one and the same interlinguistic object which is their meaning. Quine is attempting to dislodge this model for thinking about language and to put in its place a more empirically based conception. According to the museum model, an expression has its meaning, pure and simple, and two synonymous expressions relate uniquely to one meaning which, as interlinguistic, is independent of the languages in which it is expressed. What Quine has shown is that it makes no sense to speak of language-independent meanings. Translation from one language to another is relative to a set of analytical hypotheses. There is no independent meaning of 'Gavagai' which the linguist can link to 'Here's-a-rabbit' and not 'Here's-a-rabbit-stage'. The three sentences are stimulus synonymous. The public data does not yield the result that it is only the first two which are supposed to be synonymous in the full-blooded/museum model sense of expressing one and the same unique proposition. The linguist is at best in a position of saying that 'Gavagai' and 'Here's-a-rabbit' are synonymous relative to the assumption of certain analytical hypotheses. We have to study language in terms of linguistic behaviour in the face of publicly accessible stimulus conditions; in turn this behaviour must be interpreted in relation to more theoretical background assumptions. With the exception of observation sentences, we have at best relative notions of meaning (synonymy and analyticity), and these will not do the job philosophers have frequently assigned to them according to the myth of the museum. If one cannot empirically uniquely determine the full blooded meaning/proposition that is posited in the theory of meaning for sentences so close to stimulus conditions then the prospects are even worse for the rest of language which is remote from these conditions, sentences like: 'Frank's uncle is overweight', 'Heredity is a matter of genes' or '2 + 2 = 4'.

Quine and the later WITTGENSTEIN are two of the most rigorous thinkers who anchor language in public conditions. For Wittgenstein this leads to the denial of private languages and Kripke's puzzle about acquiring determinate rules. (see KRIPKE, S.A.). For Quine the public learning of language yields in the theory of reference the thesis of the indeterminacy/inscrutability of reference and in the theory of meaning the conjecture of the indeterminacy of meaning. Quine insists on behaviourism as the required method for studying language learning. He argues that we learn language by observing verbal behaviour and having our verbal behaviour reinforced by others. But there are naturalistic accounts of language learning which are scientifically respectable and not behaviourist (see CHOMSKY, N.). Yet although Quine insists on behaviourism as the method for studying and acquiring languages, he is not a behaviourist in psychology or the philosophy of mind. On the mind–body problem he endorses Davidson's anomalous monism – the view that our ways of speaking of the mental, for example, of perceptions and beliefs, cannot be stated in terms of the natural laws which govern the underlying physiological states, even though our mental states just are such states. Quine construes the matter so that mental ascriptions have a role in everyday life and the social sciences that cannot be precisely specified in purely physiological or physicalist terms.

See also: ANALYTICAL PHILOSOPHY; BEHAVIOURISM, METHODOLOGICAL AND SCIENTIFIC

References and further reading

Orenstein, A. (2002) *W.V. Quine*, Chesham, Bucks: Acumen Press and Princeton: Princeton University Press. (An exposition of Quine's thought, its place in twentieth-century philosophy, and some challenges to it.)

Quine, W.V. (1964) *Word and Object*, New York: Boston, MA: MIT Press. (A major source for Quine's views on meaning, translation, reference, modality and propositional attitudes.)

Quine, W.V. [1953] (1988) *From a Logical Point of View*, Cambridge, MA: Harvard University Press. (A collection of some of his most famous essays, including 'New Foundations for Mathematical Logic', 'On What There Is' and 'Two Dogmas of Empiricism'.)

ALEX ORENSTEIN

QUOTATION
See USE/MENTION DISTINCTION AND QUOTATION

R

RABBINIC LAW

See HALAKHAH

RADICAL TRANSLATION AND RADICAL INTERPRETATION

Radical translation is the setting of a thought experiment conceived by W.V. Quine in the late 1950s. In that setting a linguist undertakes to translate into English some hitherto unknown language – one which is neither historically nor culturally linked to any known language. It is further supposed that the linguist has no access to bilinguals versed in the two languages, English and (what Quine called) 'Jungle'. Thus, the only empirical data the linguist has to go on in constructing a 'Jungle-to-English' translation manual are instances of the native speakers' behaviour in publicly recognizable circumstances. Reflecting upon the fragmentary nature of these data, Quine draws the following conclusions.

(1) It is very likely that the theoretical sentences of 'Jungle' can be translated as wholes into English in incompatible yet equally acceptable ways. In other words, translation of theoretical sentences is indeterminate. On the assumption that a sentence and its translation share the same meaning, the import of indeterminacy of translation is indeterminacy of meaning: the meanings of theoretical sentences of natural languages are not fixed by empirical data. The fact is, the radical translator is bound to impose about as much meaning as they discover. This result (together with the dictum 'no entity without identity') undermines the idea that propositions are meanings of sentences.

(2) Neither the question of which 'Jungle' expressions are to count as terms nor the question of what object(s), if any, a 'Jungle' term refers to can be answered by appealing merely to the empirical data. In short, the empirical data do not fix reference.

The idea of *radical interpretation* was developed by Donald Davidson in the 1960s and 1970s as a modification and extension of Quine's idea of radical translation. Quine is concerned with the extent to which empirical data determine the meanings of sentences of a natural language. In the setting of radical interpretation, Davidson is concerned with a different question, the question of what a person could know that would enable them to interpret another's language. For example, what could one know that would enable the interpretation of the German sentence 'Es regnet' as meaning that it is raining? The knowledge required for interpretation differs from the knowledge required for translation, for one could know that 'Es regnet' is translated as 'Il pleut' without knowing the meaning (the interpretation) of either sentence. Beginning with the knowledge that the native speaker holds certain sentences true when in certain publicly recognizable circumstances, Davidson's radical interpreter strives to understand the meanings of those sentences. Davidson argues that this scenario reveals that interpretation centres on one's having knowledge comparable to an empirically verified, finitely based, recursive specification of the truth-conditions for an infinity of sentences – a Tarski-like truth theory. Thus, Quine's radical translation and Davidson's radical interpretation should not be regarded as competitors, for although the methodologies employed in the two contexts are similar, the two contexts are designed to answer different questions. Moreover, interpretation is broader than translation; sentences that cannot be translated can still be interpreted.

See also: DAVIDSON, D.; HERMENEUTICS; MEANING AND TRUTH; QUINE, W.V.; REFERENCE

ROGER F. GIBSON

RAMBAM

See MAIMONIDES, MOSES

RAMÉE, PIERRE DE LA

See RAMUS, PETRUS

RAMIFIED TYPE THEORY
See THEORY OF TYPES

RAMSEY, FRANK PLUMPTON (1903–30)

Before Ramsey died at the age of 26 he did an extraordinary amount of pioneering work, in economics and mathematics as well as in logic and philosophy. His major contributions to the latter are as follows. (1) He produced the definitive version of Bertrand Russell's attempted reduction of mathematics to logic. (2) He produced the first quantitative theory of how we make decisions, for example about going to the station to catch a train. His theory shows how such decisions depend on the strengths of our beliefs (that the train will run) and desires (to catch it), and uses this dependence to define general measures of belief and desire. This theory also underpins his claim that what makes induction reasonable is its being a reliable way of forming true beliefs, and it underpins his equation of knowledge generally with reliably formed true beliefs. (3) He used the equivalence between believing a proposition and believing that it is true to define truth in terms of beliefs. These in turn he proposed to define by how they affect our actions and whether those actions fulfil our desires. (4) He produced two theories of laws of nature. On the first of these, laws are the generalizations that would be axioms and theorems in the simplest true theory of everything. On the second, they are generalizations that lack exceptions and would if known be used to support predictions ('I'll starve if I don't eat') and hence decisions ('I'll eat'). (5) He showed how established, for example optical, phenomena can be explained by theories using previously unknown terms, like 'photon', which they introduce. (6) He showed why no grammatical distinction between subjects like 'Socrates' and predicates like 'is wise' entails any intrinsic difference between particulars and universals.

See also: BELIEF; FREGE, G.; MIND, IDENTITY THEORY OF; UNIVERSALS

D.H. MELLOR

RAMUS, PETRUS (1515–72)

Petrus Ramus, for many years a professor of philosophy and eloquence at the University of Paris, wrote textbooks and controversial works in grammar, logic, rhetoric, mathematics, physics and philosophy. He was also a university reformer. His followers were prolific with commentaries, Ramist analyses of classical texts and handbooks of their own. His logical works and those of his school exercised a large influence between 1550 and 1650.

His formation was humanist, in that he attacked scholasticism and encouraged the study (and logical analysis) of classical texts, as Agricola, Sturm and Melanchthon had done. But he was far more independent-minded than them, a stern critic of the textbooks of Aristotle and Cicero, as well as an admirer of their style and intellect. His most important innovation was the method, a theory of organization which he used to simplify his textbooks. He emphasized the need for learning to be comprehensible and useful, with a particular stress on the practical aspect of mathematics. His critics would say he oversimplified. He was also a student of Gaulish pseudo-antiquities and an important proponent of the French language. His *Dialectique* (1555) was the first book on dialectic in French.

See also: PLATONISM, RENAISSANCE; RENAISSANCE PHILOSOPHY; RHETORIC

PETER MACK

RANDOMNESS

The fundamental intuition underlying randomness is the absence of order or pattern. To cash out this intuition philosophers and scientists employ five approaches to randomness.

(1) Randomness as the output of a chance process. Thus an event is *random* if it is the output of a chance process. Moreover, a sequence of events constitutes a *random sample* if all events in the sequence derive from a single chance process and no event in the sequence is influenced by the others.

(2) Randomness as mimicking chance. Statisticians frequently wish to obtain a random sample (in the sense of (1)) according to some specified probability distribution. Unfortunately, a chance process corresponding to this probability distribution may be hard to come by. In this case a statistician may employ a computer simulation to mimic the desired chance process (for example, a random number generator). Randomness *qua* mimicking chance is also known as *pseudo-randomness*.

(3) Randomness via mixing. Consider the following situation: particles are concentrated in some corner of a fluid; forces act on the fluid so that eventually the particles become thoroughly mixed throughout the fluid, reaching an equilibrium state. Here randomness is identified with the equilibrium state reached via mixing.

(4) Randomness as a measure of computational complexity. Computers are ideally suited for generating bit strings. The length of the shortest program that generates a given bit string, as well as the minimum time it takes for a program to generate the string, both assign measures of

complexity to the strings. The higher the complexity, the more random the string.

(5) Randomness as pattern-breaking. Given a specified collection of patterns, an object is random if it breaks all the patterns in the collection. If, on the other hand, it fits at least one of the patterns in the collection, then it fails to be random.

WILLIAM A. DEMBSKI

RATIONAL CHOICE THEORY

Rational choice theory is the descendant of earlier philosophical political economy. Its core is the effort to explain and sometimes to justify collective results of individuals acting from their own individual motivations – usually their own self interest, but sometimes far more general concerns that can be included under the rubric of preferences. The resolute application of the assumption of self-interest to social actions and institutions began with Hobbes and Machiavelli, who are sometimes therefore seen as the figures who divide modern from early political philosophy. Machiavelli commended the assumption of self-interest to the prince; Hobbes applied it to everyone. Their view of human motivation went on to remake economics through the work of Mandeville and Adam Smith. And it was plausibly a major factor in the decline of virtue theory, which had previously dominated ethics for many centuries.

Game theory was invented almost whole by the mathematician von Neumann and the economist Morgenstern during the Second World War. Their theory was less a theory that made predictions or gave explanations than a framework for viewing complex social interactions. It caught on with mathematicians and defence analysts almost immediately, with social psychologists much later, and with economists and philosophers later still. But it has now become almost necessary to state some problems game theoretically in order to keep them clear and to relate them to other analyses. The game-theory framework represents ranges of payoffs that players can get from their simultaneous or sequential moves in games in which they interact. Moves are essentially choices of strategies, and outcomes are the intersections of strategy choices. If you and I are in a game, both of us typically depend on our own and on the other's choices of strategies for our payoffs.

The most striking advance in economics in the twentieth century is arguably the move from cardinal to ordinal value theory. The change had great advantages for resolving certain classes of problems but it also made many tasks more difficult. For example, the central task of aggregation from individual to collective preferences or utility could be done – at least in principle – as a matter of mere arithmetic in the cardinal system. In that system, Benthamite utilitarianism was the natural theory for welfare economics. In the ordinal system, however, there was no obvious way to aggregate from individual to collective preferences. We could do what Pareto said was all that could be done: we could optimize by making those (Pareto) improvements that made at least one person better off but no one worse off. But we could not maximize. In his impossibility theorem, Arrow showed that, under reasonable conditions, there is no general method for converting individual to collective orderings.

After game theory and the Arrow impossibility theorem, the next major contribution to rational choice theory was the economic theory of democracy of Downs. Downs assumed that everyone involved in the democratic election system is primarily self-interested. Candidates are interested in their own election; citizens are interested in getting policies adopted that benefit themselves. From this relatively simple assumption, however, he deduced two striking results that ran counter to standard views of democracy. In a two-party system, parties would rationally locate themselves at the centre of the voter distribution; and citizens typically have no interest in voting or in learning enough to vote in their interests even if they do vote.

The problem of the rational voter can be generalized. Suppose that I am a member of a group of many people who share an interest in having some good provided but that no one of us values its provision enough to justify paying for it all on our own. Suppose further that, if every one of us pays a proportionate share of the cost, we all benefit more than we pay. Unfortunately, however, my benefit from my contribution alone might be less than the value of my contribution. Hence, if our contributions are strictly voluntary, I may prefer not to contribute a share and merely to enjoy whatever follows from the contributions of others. I am then a free-rider. If we all rationally attempt to be free-riders, our group fails and none of us benefits.

A potentially disturbing implication of the game-theoretic understanding of rationality in interactive choice contexts, of the Arrow impossibility theorem, of the economic theory of democracy and of the logic of collective action is that much of philosophical democratic theory, which is usually normative, is irrelevant to our possibilities. The things these theories often tell us we should be doing cannot be done.

See also: Decision and game theory; Social choice

RUSSELL HARDIN

RATIONALISM

Rationalism is the view that reason, as opposed to, say, sense experience, divine revelation or reliance on institutional authority, plays a dominant role in our attempt to gain knowledge. Different forms of rationalism are distinguished by different conceptions of reason and its role as a source of knowledge, by different descriptions of the alternatives to which reason is opposed, by different accounts of the nature of knowledge, and by different choices of the subject matter, for example, ethics, physics, mathematics, metaphysics, relative to which reason is viewed as the major source of knowledge. The common application of the term 'rationalist' can say very little about what two philosophers have in common.

Suppose we mean by reason our intellectual abilities in general, including sense experience. To employ reason is to use our individual intellectual abilities to seek evidence for and against potential beliefs. To fail to employ reason is to form beliefs on the basis of such non-rational processes as blind faith, guessing or unthinking obedience to institutional authority. Suppose too that we conceive of knowledge as true, warranted belief, where warrant requires that a belief be beyond a reasonable doubt though not beyond the slightest doubt. Here, then, is a version of rationalism: reason is the major source of knowledge in the rational sciences. This is a weak version of rationalism which simply asserts that our individual intellectual abilities, as opposed to blind faith and so on, are the major source of knowledge in the natural sciences. It is clearly not very controversial and is widely accepted.

Suppose, however, we take reason to be a distinct faculty of knowledge distinguished from sense experience in particular. To employ reason is to grasp self-evident truths or to deduce additional conclusions from them. Suppose we conceive of knowledge as true, warranted belief, where warrant now requires that a belief be beyond even the slightest doubt. Let us also extend our attention to metaphysics and issues such as the existence of God, human free will and immortality. Here is a much stronger version of rationalism which asserts that the intellectual grasp of self-evident truths and the deduction of ones that are not self-evident is the major source of true beliefs warranted beyond even the slightest doubt in the natural sciences and metaphysics. Clearly it is highly controversial and not very widely accepted.

The term 'rationalism' has been used to cover a range of views. Scholars of the Enlightenment generally have in mind something like the first example – a general confidence in the powers of the human intellect, in opposition to faith and blind acceptance of institutional authority, as a source of knowledge – when they refer to the rationalist spirit of the period and the work of such philosophers as Voltaire. Most frequently, the term 'rationalism' is used to refer to views, like the second one above, which introduce reason as a distinct faculty of knowledge in contrast to sense experience. Rationalism is then opposed to empiricism, the view that sense experience provides the primary basis for knowledge.

See also: EMPIRICISM; ENLIGHTENMENT, CONTINENTAL

PETER J. MARKIE

RATIONALITY AND CULTURAL RELATIVISM

Under what conditions may we judge the practices or beliefs of another culture to be rationally deficient? Is it possible that cultures can differ so radically as to embody different and even incommensurable modes of reasoning? Are norms of rationality culturally relative, or are there culture-independent norms of rationality that can be used to judge the beliefs and practices of all human cultures?

In order to be in a position to make judgments about the rationality of another culture, we must first understand it. Understanding a very different culture itself raises philosophical difficulties. How do we acquire the initial translation of the language of the culture? Can we use our categories to understand the social practices of another culture, for instance, our categories of science, magic and religion? Or would the mapping of our categories on to the practices of culturally distant societies yield a distorted picture of how they construct social practices and institutions?

A lively debate has revolved around these questions. Part of the debate involves clarifying the difficult concepts of rationality and relativism. What sort of judgments of rationality are appropriate? Judgments about how agents' reasons relate to their actions? Judgments about how well agents' actions and social practices conform to the norms of their culture? Or judgments about the norms of rationality of cultures as such? Can relativism be given a coherent formulation that preserves the apparent disagreements for which it is meant to account?

Can there be incommensurable cultures, such that one culture could not understand the other? According to Donald Davidson's theory of interpretation, radical translation requires the use of a principle of charity that in effect rules out the possibility of incommensurable cultures. If this result is accepted, then a strong form of cultural relativism concerning norms of rationality is also ruled out.

Davidson's theory, some argue, does not eliminate the possibility of attributing irrational beliefs and practices to agents in other cultures, and thus still leaves some room for debate about how to understand and evaluate such beliefs and practices. Three positions frame the debate. The intellectualist position holds that judgments of rationality are in order across cultures. The symbolist and functionalist positions, here taken together, try to avoid such judgments by attributing functions or symbolic meanings to cultural practices that are generally not understood as such by the agents. The fideist position, wary of too easily being ethnocentric, assumes a more relativist stance with regard to cross-cultural judgments of rationality.

See also: MORAL RELATIVISM; RELATIVISM; SOCIAL RELATIVISM

LAWRENCE H. SIMON

RATIONALITY, PRACTICAL

Whereas theoretical reason is that form of reason that is authoritative over belief, practical reason is that form of reason that applies, in some way, to action: by either directing it, motivating it, planning it, evaluating it or predicting it. Accounts of practical reason include theories of how we should determine means to the ends we have; how we should define the ends themselves; how we should act given that we have a multiplicity of ends; how requirements of consistency should govern our actions; and how moral considerations should be incorporated in our deliberations about how to act.

Economics has provided, in recent times, what many regard as the most compelling portrait of practical reason, called 'expected utility theory' (hereafter 'EU theory'). On this theory, rational action is that action which yields the highest expected utility, which is calculated by measuring the utility – or the 'goodness' or 'badness' – of the possible outcomes of the action, multiplying the utility of each outcome by the probability that it will occur, and, finally, adding together the results for all the possible outcomes of each action. The action that has the highest expected utility is the rational action. Other technical representations of practical reason have been explored in the branch of social science called 'game theory', which studies 'strategic' situations in which the action that is rational for any agent depends in part on what other agents do.

A theory of practical reason can have one or more of several different goals. If it sets out how human beings *actually* reason, it functions as a

descriptive theory of reasoning. If it sets out a conception of how our reasoning *ought* to proceed, it functions as a *normative* theory of reasoning. Theories of reason can also be about actions themselves: if a theory presents a conception of the way our actions should be intelligible or consistent or useful (regardless of the quality of the deliberation that preceded it), it functions as a (normative) theory of behavioural rationale. If it merely presents an account of consistent action that allows us to predict the behaviour of an agent whose previous actions fit this account of consistency, it functions as a descriptive theory.

One might say that whereas theoretical reason is supposed to pursue truth, practical reason is supposed to pursue some sort of good or value in human action. Theories that take rational action to be that which achieves, furthers or maximizes (what is regarded as) good, are *consequentialist* or *teleological* theories. Theories that believe rational action must sometimes be understood as action that has an intrinsic value or 'rightness' regardless of how much good it will accomplish or manifest, are non-consequentialist or non-teleological conceptions of reason. If the theory defines reason as that which serves ends defined by something other than itself, it is an *instrumental* conception. If it allows reason to have a non-instrumental role, itself capable of establishing at least some of our ends of action, it is setting out a non-instrumental conception. Theories of practical reason that recognize the existence of a special moral reasoning procedure tend to represent that procedure as non-instrumental.

Philosophers have disagreed about whether practical reason gives us a way of reasoning prior to choice that can actually motivate us to behave in the way that it directs. Many believe it lacks motivational power, so that it can only give us authoritative directives that must be motivated by something else (for example, by our desires). Finally, the study of practical reason also considers the variety of ways in which one can fall short of being rational; and issues about the nature and possibility of irrational 'weakness of will' have been central to this discussion.

See also: ECONOMICS AND ETHICS; RATIONALITY AND CULTURAL RELATIVISM

JEAN HAMPTON

RAWLS, JOHN (1921–2002)

Introduction

Rawls' main work, *A Theory of Justice*, presents a liberal, egalitarian, moral conception – 'justice as fairness' – designed to explicate and justify the institutions of a constitutional democracy. The two principles of justice outlined in this text affirm the priority of equal basic liberties over other political concerns, and require fair opportunities for all citizens, directing that inequalities in wealth and social positions maximally benefit the least advantaged. Rawls develops the idea of an impartial social contract to justify these principles: free persons, equally situated and ignorant of their historical circumstances, would rationally agree to them in order to secure their equal status and independence, and to pursue freely their conceptions of the good.

In *Political Liberalism*, his other major text, Rawls revises his original argument for justice as fairness to make it more compatible with the pluralism of liberalism. He argues that, assuming that different philosophical, religious and ethical views are inevitable in liberal society, the most reasonable basis for social unity is a public conception of justice based in shared moral ideas, including citizens' common comception of themselves as free and equal moral persons. The stability of this public conception of justice is provided by an overlapping consensus; all the reasonable comprehensible philosophical, religious and ethical views can endorse it, each for their own specific reasons.

1 Justice as fairness
2 Democratic institutions
3 Stability
4 Political liberalism

1 Justice as fairness

Rawls' overriding aim is 'to provide the most appropriate moral basis for a democratic society' (1971: viii). Despite its many strengths, he sees the dominant utilitarian tradition as providing deficient foundations for democracy. Rawls begins with a normative conception of persons, whom he describes as free, equal, rational and endowed with a moral capacity for a sense of justice. Because of differences in knowledge and situations, free persons inevitably will develop different conceptions of the good. To pursue their good, they make conflicting claims on scarce resources. Principles of justice regulate the division of benefits and burdens resulting from social cooperation. Rawls contends that the appropriate way to decide principles for a democratic society is by conjecturing what principles free persons would agree to among themselves to regulate basic social institutions (the political constitution, property, markets and the family). But to ensure this agreement is fair, they

must abstract knowledge of their own situations – of their talents and social positions and their conceptions of the good. Since these principles will be used to assess the justice of existing institutions and the reasonableness of existing desires and claims, Rawls further envisages that contracting parties abstract not just awareness of their own, but everyone's historical circumstances, desires and conceptions of the good. They are to be placed behind a thick 'veil of ignorance'. What such free individuals do know are general social, economic, psychological, and physical theories of all kinds. They also know there are certain all-purpose means that are essential to achieving their good, whatever it might be. These 'primary social goods' are rights and liberties, powers and opportunities, income and wealth, and the basis of self-respect.

The effect of these restrictions on knowledge is to render Rawls' parties strictly equal. This enables Rawls to carry to the limit the intuitive idea of the democratic social contract tradition: that justice is what could, or would, be agreed to among free persons from a position of equality (see CONTRACTARIANISM). Rawls sees his strong equality condition, along with other moral conditions on agreement (that principles be universal, general, publicly known, final, and so on), as reasonable restrictions on arguments for principles of justice for the basic structure of society. These conditions define the 'original position', the perspective from which rational agents are to unanimously agree. Parties to the original position are presented with a list of all known feasible conceptions of justice and consider them in pairwise comparisons. The parties are rational, in that all utilize effective means to secure their ends, and are motivated by their interests, and so are moved to acquire an adequate share of the primary social goods needed to pursue their interests. The parties are also assumed to be rationally prudent (with zero time-preference), mutually disinterested (of limited altruism) and without envy.

Given these conditions, Rawls argues that the parties would unanimously agree to justice as fairness over the classical and average principles of utility, perfectionist and intuitionistic conceptions, and rational egoism. Its main principles state: (1) each person has an equal right to a fully adequate scheme of equal basic liberties, compatible with a similar scheme of liberties for all; and (2) social and economic inequalities must be attached to offices and positions open to all under conditions of fair equality of opportunity and must be to the greatest benefit of the least advantaged members of society (the 'difference principle'). The basic liberties of the first principle are liberty of conscience, freedom of thought, equal political rights, freedom of association, freedoms specified to maintain the liberty and integrity of the person (including rights to personal property), and the rights and liberties covered by the rule of law. These liberties are basic in that they have priority over the difference principle; their equality cannot be infringed, even if inequalities would increase the opportunities or wealth of those least advantaged. Moreover, the rights implied by both principles have priority over all other social values: they cannot be infringed or traded for the sake of efficiency, others' likes and dislikes or perfectionist values of culture.

Rawls' argument for these principles is that, given complete ignorance of everyone's position, it would be irrational to jeopardize one's good to gain whatever marginal advantages might be promised by other alternatives. For included in one's conception of the good are the religious and philosophical convictions and ethical ways of life that give one's existence meaning. It is fundamentally irrational, Rawls contends, to gamble with these given complete ignorance of risks and probabilities. In his later work, Rawls contends that parties in the original position are also moved by 'higher-order interests' to develop and exercise the 'moral powers' that enable them to engage in social cooperation – the capacity to form, revise and rationally pursue a conception of the good, and the capacity to understand, apply and act from a sense of justice. Parties agree on the two principles underlying justice as fairness since they provide each with primary goods adequate to realize these powers; other alternatives jeopardize these conditions.

One objection to Rawls' theory is that the parties' 'maximin' strategy of choice is too conservative. Harsanyi, in 'Morality and the Theory of Rational Behaviour' (1982), contends that Rawls' parties should assume an equal probability of being any member in society. Given sympathetic identification with each person's interests, they should choose (as if they were following) the principle of average utility (see UTILITARIANISM). But Harsanyi's ideal chooser, although ignorant of their own identity, still has full knowledge of everyone's desires and situations; Harsanyi views such knowledge as necessary for sympathetic identification. But Rawls' parties are without knowledge of anyone's desires and circumstances, and thus are rendered incapable of sympathetic identification, as well as making interpersonal comparisons of utility. Rawls also finds that, especially under conditions of radical uncertainty, gambling freedom to practise one's conscientious convictions against added resources betrays a failure to understand what it is to have a conception of the good. For these and other reasons Rawls contends that it is difficult to see how the

argument for average utility can arise from his original position. More important, assuming publicity of basic principles, a utilitarian society will not command the willing allegiance of everyone (especially those made worse off), and so will not evince stability (see §3). That basic political principles be publicly known is required by democratic freedom; otherwise citizens are under illusions about the bases of their social relations and are manipulated by forces placed beyond their control. With Rawls' liberal egalitarian principles, nothing is, nor need be, hidden from public view in order to maintain social stability.

2 Democratic institutions

For Rawls the role of democratic legislation is not to register citizens' unconstrained preferences and let majority preferences rule, but to advance the interests of all citizens, so that each has the status of equal citizen, is suitably independent and can freely pursue a good consistent with justice. The two principles of justice as fairness designate a common good that provides the end of democratic legislation. Ideally it should not be individual or group interests voting, but citizens and legislators, whose judgments are based on laws that best realize the common good of justice, as defined by the two principles. These principles imply a liberal constitution that specifies basic liberties immune from majority infringement. The first principle also requires maintaining the fair value of each citizen's political rights, thereby establishing a limit on inequalities in wealth allowable by the difference principle. The second principle, the 'difference principle', preserves the 'fair value' of the remaining basic liberties. It suggests a criterion for deciding the basic minimum of resources each citizen needs to fairly and effectively exercise the basic liberties: property and economic institutions are to be so designed that those least advantaged have resources exceeding what the worst off would acquire under any alternative economic scheme (consistent with the first principle). This implies (depending on historical conditions) either a property-owning democracy (with widespread private ownership of the means of production) or liberal socialism. In either case, Rawls assumes markets are needed for efficient *allocation* of factors of production; but use of markets for *distribution* of output is constrained by the difference principle. Whatever effect redistributions from the market have on allocative efficiency is not a problem for Rawls, since justice has priority over efficiency. The end of justice is not to maximize productive output whatever the distributive effects, any more than it is to maximize aggregate utility (see JUSTICE §5).

3 Stability

The argument from the original position aims to show that justice as fairness best coheres with our considered judgments of justice (in 'reflective equilibrium'). But why should we care about justice enough to allow its requirements to outweigh our other aims? Stability addresses this issue of motivation. A conception of justice is 'stable' whenever departures from it call into play forces within a just system that tend to restore the arrangement. Unstable conceptions are utopian, not realistic possibilities. HOBBES argued that stability required a nearly absolute sovereign. This is incompatible with Rawls' democratic aim. To argue that justice as fairness is stable, Rawls appeals to principles of moral psychology to show how citizens in a 'well-ordered society' can acquire a settled disposition to act on and from the principles of justice. He then argues that justice as fairness is compatible with human nature, and is even 'congruent' with citizens' good in a society well ordered by justice as fairness.

A person's good is the plan of life they would rationally choose based on their considered interests from an informed position of 'deliberative rationality'. Rawls' congruence argument contends that it is rational, part of a person's good, to be just and reasonable for their own sake in a well-ordered society. Assuming citizens there have a sense of justice, it is instrumentally rational for them to cultivate this capacity by doing justice, in order to achieve the benefits of social cooperation. On the Kantian interpretation of justice as fairness, the capacity for justice is among the powers that define our nature as rational agents; by developing and exercising this power for its own sake, citizens realize their nature and achieve moral autonomy. The Aristotelian principle is a psychological law which implies that it is rational to want to develop the higher capacities implicit in one's nature. Since the circumstances of a well-ordered society describe optimal conditions for exercising one's sense of justice, it is rational to want to cultivate the virtue of justice for its own sake and achieve moral autonomy. Justice and moral autonomy are then intrinsic and supreme goods in a well-ordered society, so the Right and the Good are 'congruent'. If so, it is not rational to depart from justice, and a well-ordered society manifests inherent stability.

HEGEL argued that Rousseau's social contract, like Hobbes', was individualistic and incompatible with the values of community. Contemporary communitarians re-state Hegel's criticism, contending that Rawls' original position presupposes abstract individualism, with a metaphysical conception of persons as essentially devoid of the final ends and commitments that constitute their identity (see COMMUNITY AND COMMUNITARIANISM). In *Political Liberalism* ([1993] 1996) Rawls contends that this is mistaken. In *A Theory of Justice* he presupposes, not a metaphysical conception of persons, but a practical account of the conditions of political agency, as grounded in the moral powers. Given congruence, maintaining justice and just institutions is the shared good that underwrites the values of community (or 'social union') among free and equal moral persons.

Rawls' Kantian congruence argument addresses the classical aim of showing how justice can be compatible with the human good. It is one of Rawls' most original contributions to moral philosophy. It also bears implications that led Rawls subsequently to revise his view.

4 Political liberalism

The problem with congruence is that it conflicts with the 'reasonable pluralism' of liberal societies, which should tolerate a wide range of religious, philosophical and moral views. The 'burdens of judgment' imply certain limitations on judgment, so that under free institutions we cannot expect agreement upon a comprehensive metaphysical, religious, or moral doctrine or conception of the good. But congruence implies that widespread acceptance of the intrinsic good of moral autonomy is a condition of liberal stability. By hypothesis, most conceptions of the good in a well-ordered society can endorse Rawls' principles of justice. The problem is, some may not accept the intrinsic goodness of moral autonomy. Teleological views, such as liberal Thomism or a reasonable utilitarianism, will gain adherents in a well-ordered society, and for these views justice and autonomy are at best but instrumental to the one rational and intrinsic good (the Vision of God, and aggregate or average utility, respectively). The incompatibility of congruence with reasonable pluralism then undermines Rawls' original argument for stability.

In *Political Liberalism* Rawls reformulates the justification of justice as fairness as a 'freestanding' political conception. He aims to provide a public justification for justice as fairness acceptable to all citizens of a well-ordered democracy. This requires an argument that is not grounded in Kant's or some other comprehensive ethical doctrine, but rather in certain fundamental intuitive ideas implicit in democratic culture. Rawls argues that the features of the original position can be construed as a 'procedural representation' of the idea of social cooperation among free and equal citizens implicit in a democracy. The principles of justice can then be represented as 'constructed' from a 'model conception' of democratic citizens as free, equal and possessed of the two moral powers that enable them to participate in social cooperation. These principles are politically justified since they are presented, not as true, but as most reasonable; they fit best with the considered political convictions of justice shared by democratic citizens, at all levels of generality, in wide reflective equilibrium (see LIBERALISM §5).

To complete this freestanding political justification, however, Rawls needs an alternative stability argument, one that, unlike congruence, does not rely upon premises peculiar to Kant's moral philosophy. The idea of 'overlapping consensus' says that the conception of justice that is politically justified as reasonable on grounds of individuals' shared conception of themselves as democratic citizens, will also be judged most reasonable or true on independent grounds, specific to each of the reasonable comprehensive doctrines gaining adherents in a well-ordered society. For its own particular reasons, each comprehensive view (for example, Kantians, utilitarians, pluralists, and religions accepting a doctrine of free faith) can endorse justice as fairness as true or reasonable. Justice as fairness then has one public, but many non-public, justifications in a well-ordered society. Assuming an overlapping consensus of reasonable comprehensive views exists there, justice as fairness evinces willing compliance, and hence stability.

See also: EQUALITY; FREEDOM AND LIBERTY; RIGHTS

References and further reading

Freeman, Samuel (ed.) (2003) *The Cambridge Companion to Rawls*, Cambridge: Cambridge University Press. (Critical commentary by several major political philosophers on Rawls's works.)

Rawls, J. (1971) *A Theory of Justice*, Cambridge, MA: Harvard University Press. (Rawls's major work.)

Rawls, J. [1993] (1996), *Political Liberalism*, New York: Columbia University Press (A major restatement of Rawls' position, taking pluralism into account)

SAMUEL FREEMAN

REALISM

See MORAL REALISM; REALISM AND ANTIREALISM; SCIENTIFIC REALISM AND ANTIREALISM

REALISM AND ANTIREALISM

Introduction

The basic idea of realism is that the kinds of thing which exist, and what they are like, are independent of us and the way in which we find out about them; antirealism denies this. Most people find it natural to be realists with respect to physical facts: how many planets there are in the solar system does not depend on how many we think there are, or would like there to be, or how we investigate them; likewise, whether electrons exist or not depends on the facts, not on which theory we favour. However, it seems natural to be antirealist about humour: something's being funny is very much a matter of whether we find it funny, and the idea that something might really be funny even though nobody ever felt any inclination to laugh at it seems barely comprehensible. The saying that 'beauty is in the eye of the beholder' is a popular expression of antirealism in aesthetics. An obviously controversial example is that of moral values; some maintain that they are real (or 'objective'), others that they have no existence apart from human feelings and attitudes.

This traditional form of the distinction between realism and its opposite underwent changes during the 1970s and 1980s, largely due to Michael Dummett's proposal that realism and antirealism (the latter term being his own coinage) were more productively understood in terms of two opposed theories of meaning. Thus, a realist is one who would have us understand the meanings of sentences in terms of their truth-conditions (the situations that must obtain if they are to be true); an antirealist holds that those meanings are to be understood by reference to assertability-conditions (the circumstances under which we would be justified in asserting them).

1 Facets of the debate
2 Ontological realism/antirealism
3 Epistemological versions
4 Logical and semantic versions

1 Facets of the debate

Realism became a prominent topic in medieval times, when it was opposed to nominalism in the debate concerning whether universals were independent properties of things or if classification was just a matter of how people spoke or thought (see NOMINALISM). The impetus for the debate in modern times comes from Kant's doctrine that the familiar world is 'empirically real' but 'transcendentally ideal', that is to say a product of our ways of experiencing things, not a collection of things as they are 'in themselves' or independently of us. Kant's 'empirical realism', confusingly, is thus a form of antirealism (see KANT, I. §5).

Closely related is 'internal realism', as represented by Hilary PUTNAM, according to which something may be real from the standpoint marked out by a particular theoretical framework, while the attempt to ask whether it is real *tout court* without reference to any such framework is dismissed as nonsensical. This reaffirms the thesis propounded by Rudolf CARNAP, that there are 'internal' and 'external' questions about existence or reality. An internal question is asked by someone who has adopted a language of a certain structure and asks the question on that basis. Only philosophers attempt to ask external questions (are there really – independently of the way we speak – physical objects?). But this is either nonsense or a misleading way of asking whether our linguistic framework is well suited to our practical purposes. 'Internal realism', it should be noted, is certainly not a form of realism, since it admits only language- or theory-relative assertions of existence.

By the mid-1980s, largely as a result of the work of Putnam and DUMMETT, it had become common to formulate the distinction between realism and antirealism in a variety of what are *prima facie* quite different ways. A realist, it was said, thinks of truth in terms of correspondence with fact, whereas an antirealist defines truth 'in epistemic terms', for instance as 'what a well-conducted investigation under ideal circumstances would lead us to believe'. A realist holds that there are, or could be, 'recognition-transcendent facts', whereas an anti-realist denies this. Also present was the idea that an antirealist believes that there can be a 'reductive analysis' (see §2 below) of whatever subject matter their antirealism relates to, whereas a realist holds such analysis to be impossible. Seemingly still further from the origins of the distinction, it was said to be characteristic of realism to accept, and of antirealism to deny, the general validity of the law of excluded middle. Yet another version located the basic difference in the respective theories of meaning: a realist gave the meaning of a sentence by specifying its truth-conditions, an antirealist by specifying the conditions under which it could properly be asserted.

To come to terms with this debate, the reader therefore needs an awareness of the interrelations of the many definitions of the realism–antirealism distinction, and of the inexactness of fit between some of them and others.

2   Ontological realism/antirealism

The primary form of the definition deals directly in terms of what really exists. A realist about Xs, for example, maintains that Xs (or facts or states of affairs involving them) exist independently of how anyone thinks or feels about them; whereas an antirealist holds that they are so dependent. We are not speaking here of causal (in)dependence: the fact that there would be no houses if people had not had certain thoughts should not force us into antirealism about houses. So the point of the definition is better brought out by saying that *what it is for an X to exist* does not involve any such factors (whatever their causal role in the production of Xs may be). Nor does the definition entail an antirealist stance towards the mental. Realism about mental states is a *prima facie* plausible option, holding that our mental states are what they are whatever we think they are, or whatever we would come to think they were if we investigated.

Where philosophers have argued for realism about some particular subject matter (for example, universals, ethical value, the entities of scientific theory), one particular argument is repeatedly found. For the subject matter in question, it is claimed, we find that everyone's opinion is the same, or tends to become the same if they investigate, or that (in science) theory seems to 'converge', later theories appearing to account for the partial success of their predecessors. Why should this be, unless it is the effect of a reality independent of us, our opinions and our theorizing? (See UNI-VERSALS; SCIENTIFIC REALISM AND ANTIREALISM.)

In consequence, there are two broad antirealist strategies, both common. One is to argue that the supposed conformity of opinion, actual or potential, does not exist – so we hear of the diversity of ethical or aesthetic judgements, for instance, or the extent to which judgements of colour depend on viewing conditions and the state of the observer. The other is to accept the conformity, but explain it as arising from a uniformity of *our* nature rather than the independent nature of things. Thus it is argued that moral 'objectivity' is really 'inter-subjectivity' – that is, a result of shared human psychological responses rather than of independent moral properties in the world – or that the similarity between different languages' schemes of classification is a product of shared basic human interests, not something forced on us by 'real' universals.

In modern times nobody has made a more radical use of this method of explaining conformity of judgement in terms of intersubjectivity than Kant. He argued that even the experience of our environment as extended in space and time was a human reaction to things that were in themselves not of a spatiotemporal nature, and to which other beings might just as legitimately react altogether differently. In the face of this it may be felt that the argument from conformity is better used to establish a very abstract realism, namely that there must be *something* independent of us, rather than that any specific property or type of thing must be so.

Two other objections have been used against certain forms of realism. One is that the realist provides no account of how the supposed real things or properties can actually have an effect on our experience. What sense do we have, it is asked, that is affected by the ethical properties of the moral realist, or by the real properties of necessity and possibility that the modal realist posits? The common realist practice of speaking of 'intuition' in these contexts is rejected as providing only a word, not an answer. The second type of objection (christened the 'argument from queerness' by John Mackie, who used it in the moral context) claims that the things or properties in which the realist believes would need to be too strange to be credible (see MORAL REALISM).

A closely related definition of the realism–antirealism distinction focuses not on the independence of things but on the truth of judgements about them: realism takes truth to be correspondence with fact and our knowledge of truth to be a separate matter, whereas antirealism defines truth 'in epistemic terms', that is to say as what human beings would believe after the best possible application of their cognitive faculties. This is much more a change of perspective than of substance. It is natural to think that if some object exists independently of us, then judging truly must consist in getting our judgement to match the way the object is; while if the object is determined by (perhaps a projection of) our cognitive and/or affective faculties, judging truly can only mean judging as those very faculties lead us to judge.

Harder to assess is the position of *reductive analysis* in the debate. A reductive analysis exists where what makes statements about one kind of thing, *A*, true or false are the facts about another kind *B*. (*A*s are then said to be reducible to *B*s.) Classically, phenomenalism claims that statements about physical objects are thus reducible to statements about sensory experiences; behaviourism holds that propositions about mental states are reducible to ones about dispositions to physical behaviour. Does accepting such a reduction mean accepting antirealism about the *A*s, while rejecting reduction of *A*-statements means accepting realism? Some philosophers speak in this way, and there is a clear point to doing so: if a reduction is possible, then a complete statement of everything there 'really is' would not need to mention *A*s – it could speak of *B*s instead. Besides, reductive analyses have usually been offered in opposition to a different conception of what *A*s are, and in relation to *that* (rejected) conception of an *A* the reducer is certainly saying that there are no *A*s. But it is not thereby said that

*A*s and facts about them are dependent upon us – only that they are really certain sorts of fact about *B*s; our attitude to their independence is therefore a question of whatever we think about the latter (see REDUCTION, PROBLEMS OF).

3 Epistemological versions

It is common to hear realism characterized in terms of the limits of knowledge as the belief that there are, or could be, 'recognition-transcendent facts' (meaning thereby facts which lie beyond *our* cognitive powers – there is no intention to saddle the realist with the view that there may be facts which simply could not be recognized at all). Antirealism then becomes the view that no such facts are possible.

The motivation for this epistemic version of the realism–antirealism divide is not hard to see. If the way something is is independent of the way we are, what could rule out the possibility that there should be facts about it beyond our powers of knowledge? Conversely, if its whole nature is due to the way we 'construct' it through our style of experience and investigation, how could there be anything about it that our cognitive faculties cannot recover? Although understandable, this is quick and imprecise. Consider someone who holds that the nature of the physical world is utterly independent of what human beings may believe it to be, but also has such anthropocentric theological inclinations as to hold that God must have given us cognitive powers equal, in principle, to discovering every fact about it. If we call this philosopher an antirealist on these grounds, we have surely changed the original subject, not just drawn it from another perspective.

This brings out the significance of formulating the epistemic criterion in terms of mere possibility (there *could be* recognition-transcendent facts) rather than actuality, thus allowing the philosopher who thinks, for whatever reason, that our cognitive powers are in fact a match for reality, still to be a realist by virtue of accepting that our powers might have been more limited without reality being any different.

It is one thing to suggest that there may be facts beyond our powers of recognition, quite another to hold that this is true of certain specific facts; the former is just modesty about our cognitive capacities, the latter a positive scepticism. So to imply an intrinsic connection between realism and scepticism, as some do, is very different from identifying realism with a belief in the possibility of recognition-transcendent facts.

Again, there is a plausible line of thought linking realism closely to scepticism. If a certain type of fact is as it is quite independently of us, then our knowledge of it must depend on an intermediary, namely the effect that it has upon us. But then we encounter the sceptical argument of which Descartes' fiction of a malicious demon represents the classic formulation: how are we ever to know that this intermediary effect is produced by the sort of thing we think it is produced by, and not rather by something completely different? Hence, starting with realism, we arrive at scepticism.

However, it seems undesirable to use scepticism (and the absence of it) to characterize the realism–antirealism distinction. The classic argument from realism (as independence of the subject) to scepticism may be a formidable one, but it nevertheless involves substantial assumptions which can be challenged; to adopt terminology which makes it sound as if its conclusion were true by definition invites confusion. Besides, scepticism is not itself a precise notion, and there may be forms of it which apply even under certain antirealist conceptions. For instance, one who thinks that truth is to be understood as the opinion that would be reached under ideal conditions may still be a sceptic, because they remain sceptical of our ability to recognize ideal conditions or know how closely we have approximated to them.

4 Logical and semantic versions

It is often said that realism and antirealism can be distinguished by their attitude towards the law of excluded middle (the logical principle that, given two propositions one of which is the negation of the other, one of them must be true): the realist accepts it, the antirealist does not. Again, we can understand this if we think back to the original characterization of the distinction in terms of what is independently there and what we 'construct', what is the case 'in itself' and what is so because of our ways of experiencing (see INTUITIONISTIC LOGIC AND ANTIREALISM).

For explanatory purposes we may consider the world of literary fiction. Most people will be happy enough with the idea that, in so far as anything can be said to be true of the world of Macbeth, just those things are true which Shakespeare wrote into it. But in that case neither 'Lady Macbeth had two children' nor its negation 'Lady Macbeth did not have two children' is true, since Shakespeare's text (we may suppose) does not touch on that question; the law of excluded middle fails in this 'constructed' world.

Passing now to a genuinely disputed case, there are those who think that whether a mathematical statement is true is one thing, whether it can be proved quite another; and there are those who think that truth in mathematics can only mean provability.

For the latter the law of excluded middle is unsafe. From the fact that not-p cannot be proved, it does not follow that p can be proved; perhaps neither is provable and hence, on this view of mathematical truth, perhaps neither is true. And anyone who equates truth, in whatever sphere, with verifiability-in-principle by us will be liable to the parallel conclusion: only for those propositions p where failure to refute p is ipso facto to verify p may we rely on the law of excluded middle. Where verifying p and verifying not-p are distinct procedures, excluded middle fails. (It is because they are characteristically distinct when the proposition in question makes some claim about an infinite totality that we hear so much about infinite totalities and the rejection of excluded middle.) This explains why some writers (in particular Dummett) often say that the difference between realist and antirealist lies in the difference between their conceptions of truth.

It can also be seen why it should have become common to express the realism–antirealism opposition as an opposition between theories of meaning, and why philosophers should be found speaking of realist and antirealist semantics. Any theory which ties meaning to verification, which equates the understanding of a sentence with a knowledge of those conditions that would verify it or would justify us in asserting it, promotes the view that we have no other idea of what it is for it to be true than for these conditions to be satisfied. Hence the realism–antirealism debate often exhibits neo-verificationist features; sometimes (especially by Dummett) antirealism is presented as the outcome of Wittgensteinian ideas about meaning, sometimes (especially by Putnam) of the alleged impossibility of explaining how our language could ever come to refer to the mind-independent items that realism posits (see MEANING AND VERIFICATION).

References and further reading

Dummett, M.A.E. (1963) 'Realism', in *Truth and Other Enigmas*, London: Duckworth, 145–65. (Seminal – and fairly difficult – paper, shifting the debate from the perspectives of §2 above to those of §4.)

James, W. (1907) 'Pragmatism's Conception of Truth', Lecture VI of *Pragmatism in Pragmatism and the Meaning of Truth*, Cambridge, MA, and London: Harvard University Press, 1978. (Popular, polemical presentation of the doctrine that 'truth is *made*'.)

Putnam, H. (1981) 'Two Philosophical Perspectives', in *Reason, Truth and History*, Cambridge: Cambridge University Press. (Putnam links the traditional form of the debate to the question of the rival accounts of truth and problems about linguistic reference. For the most part not difficult reading; full understanding of some points calls for acquaintance with the two preceding chapters.)

EDWARD CRAIG

REALISM AND ANTIREALISM, SCIENTIFIC
See SCIENTIFIC REALISM AND ANTIREALISM

REALISM, MORAL
See MORAL REALISM

REASONS AND CAUSES

Imagine being told that someone is doing something for a reason. Perhaps they are reading a spy novel, and we are told that their reason for doing so is that they desire to read something exciting and believe that spy novels are indeed exciting. We then have an explanation of the agent's action in terms of the person's reasons. Those who believe that reasons are causes think that such explanations have two important features. First, they enable us to make sense of what happens. Reading a spy novel is the rational thing for an agent to do if they have that particular desire and belief. Second, such explanations tell us about the causal origins of what happens. They tell us that the desires and beliefs that allow us to make sense of actions cause those actions as well.

The idea that reasons are causes has evident appeal. We ordinarily suppose that our reasons make a difference to what we do. In the case just described, for example, we ordinarily suppose that had the agent had appropriately different desires and beliefs then they would have acted differently: had the person desired to read something romantic instead of exciting, or had the person believed that spy novels are not exciting, a spy novel would not have been chosen. But if what they desire and believe makes a difference to what they do then the desires and beliefs that are those reasons must, it seems, be the cause of the person's actions.

Despite its evident appeal, however, the view that reasons are causes is not without its difficulties. These all arise because of the manifest differences between explanations in terms of reasons and causal explanations.
See also: ACTION; AKRASIA; INTENTION; MENTAL CAUSATION

MICHAEL SMITH

RECHTSSTAAT
See RULE OF LAW

REDUCTION, PROBLEMS OF

Reduction is a procedure whereby a given domain of items (for example, objects, properties, concepts, laws, facts, theories, languages, and so on) is shown to be either absorbable into, or dispensable in favour of, another domain. When this happens, the one domain is said to be 'reduced' to the other. For example, it has been claimed that numbers can be reduced to sets (and hence number theory to set theory), that chemical properties like solubility in water or valence have been reduced to properties of molecules and atoms, and that laws of optics are reducible to principles of electromagnetic theory. When one speaks of 'reductionism', one has in mind a specific claim to the effect that a particular domain (for example, the mental) is reducible to another (for example, the biological, the computational). The expression is sometimes used to refer to a global thesis to the effect that all the special sciences, for example chemistry, biology, psychology, are reducible ultimately to fundamental physics. Such a view is also known as the doctrine of the 'unity of science'.
See also: LAWS, NATURAL; LOGICAL POSITIVISM; REDUCTIONISM IN THE PHILOSOPHY OF MIND; SIMPLICITY (IN SCIENTIFIC THEORIES); SUPERVENIENCE

JAEGWON KIM

REDUCTIONISM IN THE PHILOSOPHY OF MIND

Reductionism in the philosophy of mind is one of the options available to those who think that humans and the human mind are part of the natural physical world. Reductionists seek to integrate the mind and mental phenomena – fear, pain, anger and the like – with the natural world by showing them to be natural phenomena. Their inspirations are the famous reductions of science: of the heat of gases to molecular motion, of lightning to electric discharge, of the gene to the DNA molecule and the like. Reductionists hope to show a similar relationship between mental kinds and neurophysiological kinds.
See also: REDUCTION, PROBLEMS OF

KIM STERELNY

REFERENCE

It is usual to think that referential relations hold between language and thoughts on one hand, and the world on the other. The most striking example of such a relation is the naming relation, which holds between the name 'Socrates' and the famous philosopher Socrates. Indeed, some philosophers in effect restrict the vague word 'reference' to the naming relation, or something similar. Others use 'reference' broadly (as it is used in this entry) to cover a range of semantically significant relations that hold between various sorts of terms and the world: between 'philosopher' and all philosophers, for example. Other words used for one or other of these relations include 'designation', 'denotation', 'signification', 'application' and 'satisfaction'.

Philosophers often are interested in reference because they take it to be the core of meaning. Thus, the fact that 'Socrates' refers to that famous philosopher is the core of the name's meaning and hence of its contribution to the meaning of any sentence – for example, 'Socrates is wise' – that contains the name. The name's referent contributes to the sentence's meaning by contributing to its truth-condition: 'Socrates is wise' is true if and only if the object referred to by 'Socrates' is wise.

The first question that arises about the reference of a term is: what does the term refer to? Sometimes the answer seems obvious – for example, 'Socrates' refers to the famous philosopher – although even the obvious answer has been denied on occasions. On other occasions, the answer is not obvious. Does 'wise' refer to the property wisdom, the set of wise things, or each and every wise thing? Clearly, answers to this should be influenced by one's ontology, or general view of what exists. Thus, a nominalist who thinks that properties do not really exist, and that talk of them is a mere manner of speaking, would not take 'wise' to refer to the property wisdom.

The central question about reference is: in virtue of what does a term have its reference? Answering this requires a theory that explains the term's relation to its referent. There has been a great surge of interest in theories of reference in this century.

What used to be the most popular theory about the reference of proper names arose from the views of Gottlob Frege and Bertrand Russell and became known as 'the description theory'. According to this theory, the meaning of a name is given by a definite description – an expression of the form 'the F – that competent speakers associate with the name; thus, the meaning of 'Aristotle' might be given by 'the last great philosopher of antiquity'. So the answer to our central question would be that a name refers to a certain object because that object is picked out by the name's associated description.

Around 1970, several criticisms were made of the description theory by Saul Kripke and Keith Donnellan; in particular, they argued that a competent speaker usually does not have sufficient knowledge of the referent to associate a reference-determining description. Under their influence, many adopted 'the historical–causal theory' of names. According to this theory, a name refers to

its bearer in virtue of standing in an appropriate causal relation to the bearer.

Description theories are popular also for words other than names. Similar responses were made to many of these theories in the 1970s. Thus, Kripke and Hilary Putnam rejected description theories of natural-kind terms like 'gold' and proposed historical–causal replacements.

Many other words (for example, adjectives, adverbs and verbs) seem to be referential. However we need not assume that all other words are. It seems preferable to see some words as syncategorematic, contributing structural elements rather than referents to the truth-conditions and meanings of sentences. Perhaps this is the right way to view words like 'not' and the quantifiers (like 'all', 'most' and 'few').

The referential roles of anaphoric (cross-referential) terms are intricate. These terms depend for their reference on other expressions in their verbal context. Sometimes they are what Peter Geach calls 'pronouns of laziness', going proxy for other expressions in the context; at other times they function like bound variables in logic. Geach's argument that every anaphoric term can be treated in one of these two ways was challenged by Gareth Evans.

Finally, there has been an interest in 'naturalizing' reference, explaining it in scientifically acceptable terms. Attempted explanations have appealed to one or more of three causal relations between words and the world: historical, reliable and teleological.

See also: SEMANTICS

MICHAEL DEVITT

REFERENTIAL/ATTRIBUTIVE
See DESCRIPTIONS; REFERENCE

REICHENBACH, HANS (1891–1953)

Philosophy of science flourished in the twentieth century, partly as a result of extraordinary progress in the sciences themselves, but mainly because of the efforts of philosophers who were scientifically knowledgeable and who remained abreast of new scientific achievements. Hans Reichenbach was a pioneer in this philosophical development; he studied physics and mathematics in several of the great German scientific centres and later spent a number of years as a colleague of Einstein in Berlin. Early in his career he followed Kant, but later reacted against his philosophy, arguing that it was inconsistent with twentieth-century physics.

Reichenbach was not only a philosopher of science, but also a scientific philosopher. He insisted that philosophy should adhere to the same standards of precision and rigour as the natural sciences. He unconditionally rejected speculative metaphysics and theology because their claims could not be substantiated either a priori, on the basis of logic and mathematics, or a posteriori, on the basis of sense-experience. In this respect he agreed with the logical positivists of the Vienna Circle, but because of other profound disagreements he was never actually a positivist. He was, instead, the leading member of the group of logical empiricists centred in Berlin.

Although his writings span many subjects Reichenbach is best known for his work in two main areas: induction and probability, and the philosophy of space and time. In the former he developed a theory of probability and induction that contained his answer to Hume's problem of the justification of induction. Because of his view that all our knowledge of the world is probabilistic, this work had fundamental epistemological significance. In philosophy of physics he offered epoch-making contributions to the foundations of the theory of relativity, undermining space and time as Kantian synthetic a priori categories.

See also: SCIENTIFIC METHOD

WESLEY C. SALMON

REID, THOMAS (1710–96)

Thomas Reid, born at Strachan, Aberdeen, was the founder of the Scottish school of Common Sense philosophy. Educated at Marishal College, Aberdeen, he taught at King's College, Aberdeen until appointed professor of moral philosophy at Glasgow. He was the co-founder of the Aberdeen Philosophical Society or 'Wise Club', which counted among its members George Campbell, John Stewart, Alexander Gerard and James Beattie. His most noteworthy early work, *An Inquiry into the Human Mind: Or the Principles of Common Sense* attracted the attention of David Hume and secured him his professorship. Other important works are *Essays on the Intellectual Powers of Man* (1785) and *Essays on the Active Powers of the Human Mind* (1788).

Reid is not the first philosopher to appeal to common sense; Berkeley and Butler are notable British predecessors in this respect, in the discussions of perception and of free will respectively. It fell to Reid, however, to collect and systematize the deliverances of common sense – the first principles, upon the acceptance of which all justification depends – and to provide adequate criteria for that status. Reid insists we rightly rely on our admittedly fallible faculties of judgment, including the five senses, as well as memory, reason, the moral

sense and taste, without need of justification. After all, we have no other resources for making judgments to call upon in justification of this reliance. We cannot dispense with our belief that we are continually existing and sometimes fully responsible agents, influenced by motives rather than overwhelmed by passions or appetites. In Reid's view major sceptical errors in philosophy arise from downgrading the five senses to mere inlets for mental images – ideas – of external objects, and from downgrading other faculties to mere capacities for having such images or for experiencing feelings. This variety of scepticism ultimately reduces everything to a swirl of mental images and feelings. However we no more conceive such images than perceive or remember them; and our discourse, even in the case of fiction, is not about them either. Names signify individuals or fictional characters rather than images of them; when I envisage a centaur it is an animal I envisage rather than the image of an animal. In particular the information our five senses provide in a direct or non-inferential manner is, certainly in the case of touch, about bodies in space.

Reid thus seems to be committed to the position that our individual perceptual judgments are first principles in spite of his admission that our perceptual faculties are fallible. Moreover, moral and aesthetic judgments cannot be mere expressions of feeling if they are to serve their purposes; a moral assessor is not a 'feeler'. Reid is therefore sure that there are first principles of morals, a view that scarcely fits the extent and degree of actual moral disagreement.

Reid offers alternative direct accounts of perception, conception, memory and moral and aesthetic judgment. He stoutly defends our status as continuing responsible agents, claiming that the only genuine causality is agency and that although natural regularities are held to be causes they cannot be full-blooded causes. Continuing persons are not reducible to material entities subject to laws of nature (pace Priestley); nor does the proper study of responsible agents belong within natural philosophy. Morals may be adequately systematized on a human rights basis according to which private property is not sacrosanct, once moral judgment is recognised to be based on first principles of morals. Judgments of beauty likewise rest on a body of first principles, even though Reid readily allows that there are no properties that all beautiful objects must have in common.

See also: COMMON SENSE SCHOOL; COMMONSENSISM; ENLIGHTENMENT, SCOTTISH; MORAL SENSE THEORIES; PRIMARY–SECONDARY DISTINCTION

ROGER GALLIE

REINHOLD, KARL LEONHARD (1757–1823)

A catalyst in the rise of post-Kantian idealism, Reinhold popularized Kant's critical philosophy by systematizing it in the form of a theory of consciousness. Reinhold shifted from one position to another, however, each time declaring his latest philosophical creed as ultimate. For this he was ridiculed by his more famous contemporaries, including Fichte, Schelling and Hegel, and his historical reputation suffered accordingly. Recent re-evaluations, however, suggest that there was considerable coherence to his philosophical wanderings.

A sometime priest who converted to Protestantism, active freemason and popular teacher, Reinhold advocated political intervention in the promotion of enlightened practices. He steadfastly defended the French Revolution.

See also: ENLIGHTENMENT, CONTINENTAL; GERMAN IDEALISM

GEORGE DI GIOVANNI

RELATIVISM

Someone who holds that nothing is simply good, but only good *for someone* or from a certain point of view, holds a relativist view of goodness. Protagoras, with his dictum that 'man is the measure of all things', is often taken to be an early relativist. Quite common are relativism about aesthetic value, about truth in particular areas such as religious truth, and (arising from anthropological theory) about rationality. There are also a number of ways of answering the question 'relative to what?' Thus something might be said to be relative to the attitudes or faculties of each individual, or to a cultural group, or to a species. Relativism therefore has many varieties; some are very plausible, others verge on incoherence.

See also: ANTHROPOLOGY, PHILOSOPHY OF; MORAL RELATIVISM; PLURALISM; RATIONALITY AND CULTURAL RELATIVISM; SOCIAL RELATIVISM

EDWARD CRAIG

RELATIVISM, MORAL
See MORAL RELATIVISM

RELATIVITY THEORY, PHILOSOPHICAL SIGNIFICANCE OF

There are two parts to Albert Einstein's relativity theory, the special theory published in 1905 and the general theory published in its final mathematical form in 1915. The special theory is a direct development of the Galilean relativity principle in classical Newtonian mechanics. This principle affirms that Newton's laws of motion hold not just when the motion is described relative to a reference frame

at rest in absolute space, but also relative to any reference frame in uniform translational motion relative to absolute space. The class of frames relative to which Newton's law of motion are valid are referred to as inertial frames. It follows that no mechanical experiment can tell us which frame is at absolute rest, only the *relative* motion of inertial frames is observable. The Galilean relativity principle does not hold for accelerated motion, and also it does not hold for electromagnetic phenomena, in particular the propagation of light waves as governed by Maxwell's equations. Einstein's special theory of relativity reformulated the mathematical transformations for space and time coordinates between inertial reference frames, replacing the Galilean transformations by the so-called Lorentz transformations (they had previously been discovered in an essentially different way by H.A. Lorentz in 1904) in such a way that electromagnetism satisfied the relativity principle. But the classical laws of mechanics no longer did so. Einstein next reformulated the laws of mechanics so as to make them conform to his new relativity principle. With Galilean relativity, spatial intervals, the simultaneity of events and temporal durations did not depend on the inertial frame, although, of course, velocities were frame-dependent. In Einstein's relativity the first three now become frame-dependent, or 'relativized' as we may express it, while for the fourth, namely velocity, there exists a unique velocity, that of the propagation of light *in vacuo*, whose magnitude c is invariant, that is, the same for all inertial frames. It can be argued that c also represents the maximum speed with which any causal process can be propagated. Moreover in Einstein's new mechanics inertial mass m becomes a relative notion and is associated via the equation $m = E/c^2$ with any form of energy E. Reciprocally inertial mass can be understood as equivalent to a corresponding energy mc^2.

In the general theory Einstein ostensibly sought to extend the relativity principle to accelerated motions of the reference frame by employing an equivalence principle which claimed that it was impossible to distinguish observationally between the presence of a gravitational field and the acceleration of a reference frame. Einstein here elevated into a fundamental principle the known but apparently accidental numerical equality of the inertial and the gravitational mass of a body (which accounts for the fact that bodies move with the same acceleration in a gravitational field, independent of their inertial mass). By extending the discussion to gravitational fields which could be locally, but not globally, transformed away by a change of reference frame, Einstein was led to a new theory of gravitation, modifying Newton's theory of gravitation, which could explain a number of observed phenomena for which the Newtonian theory was inadequate. This involved a law (Einstein's field equations) relating the distribution of matter in spacetime to geometrical features of spacetime associated with its curvature, considered as a four-dimensional manifold. The path of an (uncharged spinless) particle moving freely in the curved space-time was a geodesic (the generalized analogue in a curved manifold of a straight line in a flat manifold).

Einstein's theories have important repercussions for philosophical views on the nature of space and time, and their relation to issues of causality and cosmology, which are still the subject of debate.

See also: COSMOLOGY

MICHAEL REDHEAD

RELEVANCE LOGIC AND ENTAILMENT

'Relevance logic' came into being in the late 1950s, inspired by Wilhelm Ackermann, who rejected certain formulas of the form A→B on the grounds that 'the truth of A has nothing to do with the question whether there is a logical connection between B and A'.

The central idea of relevance logic is to give an account of logical consequence, or entailment, for which a connection of relevance between premises and conclusion is a necessary condition. In both classical and intuitionistic logic, this condition is missing, as is highlighted by the validity in those logics of the 'spread law', A→B; a contradiction 'spreads' to every proposition, and simple inconsistency is equivalent to absolute inconsistency. In relevance logic the spread law fails, and the simple inconsistency of a theory (that a set of formulas entails a contradiction) is distinguished from absolute inconsistency (or triviality: that a set of formulas entails every proposition). The programme of relevance logic is to characterize a logic, or a range of logics, satisfying the relevance condition, and to study theories based on such logics, such as relevant arithmetic and relevant set theory.

See also: MODAL LOGIC

STEPHEN READ

RELEVANT ALTERNATIVES

See SCEPTICISM

RELIGION AND MORALITY

The relationship between religion and morality has been of special and long-standing concern to philosophers. Not only is there much overlap between the two areas, but how to understand their proper relationship is a question that has stimulated much debate. Of special interest in philosophical discussions has been the question of divine authority and the moral life. If there is a God, how are we to understand the moral status of his commands? Are there moral standards that even God must acknowledge? Or does God's commanding something *make* it morally binding? Secular thinkers have insisted that these questions pose a serious dilemma for any religiously based ethic: either the moral standards are independent of God's will, with the result that God's authority is not supreme, or God's will is arbitrary, which means that what appears to be a morality is really a worship of brute power. Many religious ethicists have refused to acknowledge the dilemma, arguing for an understanding of divine moral directives as expressions of the complexities and excellences of God's abiding attributes.

The impact of religion on moral selfhood has also been much disputed. Secularists of various stripes have insisted that religion is not conducive to moral maturity. Religious thinkers have responded by exploring the ways in which one's notion of moral maturity is shaped by one's larger worldview. If we believe that there is a God who has provided us with important moral information, then this will influence the ways we understand what is to count as a 'mature' and 'rational' approach to moral decision making.

Religious ethicists have had a special interest in the ways in which worldviews shape our understandings of moral questions. This interest has been necessitated by the fact of diversity within religious communities. Different moral traditions coexist in Christianity, for example, corresponding to the rich diversity of theological perspectives and the plurality of cultural settings in which Christian beliefs have taken shape. This complexity has provided some resources for dealing with the 'postmodern' fascination with moral relativism and moral scepticism.

The relationship between religion and morality is also important for questions of practical moral decision. Religious ethical systems have often been developed with an eye to their 'preachability', which means that religious ethicists have a long record of attempting to relate theory to practice in moral discussion. The ability of a moral system to provide practical guidance is especially important during times of extensive moral confusion.

See also: HALAKHAH

RICHARD J. MOUW

RELIGION AND SCIENCE

Philosophical discussion of the relation between modern science and religion has tended to focus on Christianity, because of its dominance in the West. The relations between science and Christianity have been too complex to be described by the 'warfare' model popularized by A.D. White and J.W. Draper.

An adequate account of the past two centuries requires a distinction between conservative and liberal positions. Conservative Christians tend to see theology and science as partially intersecting bodies of knowledge. God is revealed in 'two books': the Bible and nature. Ideally, science and theology ought to present a single, consistent account of reality; but in fact there have been instances where the results of science have (apparently) contradicted Scripture, in particular with regard to the age of the universe and the origin of the human species.

Liberals tend to see science and religion as complementary but non-interacting, as having concerns so different as to make conflict impossible. This approach can be traced to Immanuel Kant, who distinguished sharply between pure reason (science) and practical reason (morality). More recent versions contrast science, which deals with the what and how of the natural world, and religion, which deals with meaning, or contrast science and religion as employing distinct languages. However, since the 1960s a growing number of scholars with liberal theological leanings have taken an interest in science and have denied that the two disciplines can be isolated from one another. Topics within science that offer fruitful points for dialogue with theology include Big-Bang cosmology and its possible implications for the doctrine of creation, the 'fine-tuning' of the cosmological constants and the possible implications of this for design arguments, and evolution and genetics, with their implications for a new understanding of the human individual.

Perhaps of greater import are the indirect relations between science and theology. Newtonian physics fostered an understanding of the natural world as strictly determined by natural laws; this in turn had serious consequences for understanding divine action and human freedom. Twentieth-century developments such as quantum physics and chaos theory call for a revised view of causation. Advances in the philosophy of science in the second half of the twentieth century provide a much more sophisticated account of knowledge than was available earlier, and this has important implications for methods of argument in theology.

See also: PERSONALISM; WITTGENSTEIN, L.J..

NANCEY MURPHY

RELIGION, PHILOSOPHY OF

Introduction

Philosophy of religion is philosophical reflection on religion. It is as old as philosophy itself and has been a standard part of Western philosophy in every period (see RELIGION, HISTORY OF PHILOSOPHY OF). In the last half of the twentieth century, there has been a great growth of interest in it, and the range of topics philosophers of religion have considered has also expanded considerably.

Philosophy of religion is sometimes divided into philosophy of religion proper and philosophical theology. This distinction reflects the unease of an earlier period in analytic philosophy, during which philosophers felt that reflection on religion was philosophically respectable only if it confined itself to mere theism and abstracted from all particular religions; anything else was taken to be theology, not philosophy. But most philosophers now feel free to examine philosophically any aspect of religion, including doctrines or practices peculiar to individual religions. Not only are these doctrines and practices generally philosophically interesting in their own right, but often they also raise questions that are helpful for issues in other areas of philosophy. Reflection on the Christian notion of sanctification, for example, sheds light on certain contemporary debates over the nature of freedom of the will.

> 1 Philosophy and belief in God
> 2 Philosophy and religious doctrines and practices

1 Philosophy and belief in God

As an examination of mere theism, the core of beliefs common to Western monotheisms, philosophy of religion raises and considers a number of questions. What would anything have to be like to count as God? Is it even possible for human beings to know God's attributes (see GOD, CONCEPTS OF; NEGATIVE THEOLOGY)? And if so, what are they? Traditionally, God has been taken to be a necessary being, who is characterized by omniscience, omnipotence, perfect goodness, immutability and eternity (see OMNISCIENCE; OMNIPOTENCE), who has freely created the world (see FREEDOM, DIVINE), and who is somehow specially related to morality (see RELIGION AND MORALITY).

This conception of God takes God to be unique, unlike anything else in the world. Consequently, the question arises whether our language is capable of representing God. Some thinkers, such as Moses MAIMONIDES, have argued that it is not and that terms applied to God and creatures are equivocal. Others have argued that our language can be made to apply to God, either because some terms can be used univocally of God and creatures, or because some terms used of creatures can be applied to God in an analogical sense.

Not everyone accepts the traditional characterization of God, of course. Pantheists, for example, reject the distinction between God and creation (see PANTHEISM). Certain philosophers have objected to the traditional conception on the grounds that it leaves certain philosophical problems, such as the problem of evil, insoluble (see PROCESS THEISM). And many feminists reject it as patriarchal.

Given the traditional conception of God, can we know by reason that such a God exists? There are certain arguments that have been proposed to demonstrate the existence of God so understood (see GOD, ARGUMENTS FOR THE EXISTENCE OF; NATURAL THEOLOGY). The ontological argument tries to show that a perfect being must exist (see ANSELM OF CANTERBURY). The cosmological argument argues that the existence of the world demonstrates the existence of a transcendent cause of the world. And the teleological argument argues from design in nature to the existence of a designer. Some philosophers have maintained that the widespread phenomenon of religious experience also constitutes an argument for the existence of a supernatural object of such experience. Most contemporary philosophers regard these arguments as unsuccessful (see ATHEISM; AGNOSTICISM).

But what exactly is the relation between reason and religious belief? Do we need arguments? Or is faith without argument rational? What is faith? Is it opposed to reason? Some philosophers have argued that any belief not based on evidence is defective or even culpable. This position is not much in favour any more. On the other hand, some contemporary philosophers have suggested that evidence of any sort is unnecessary for religious belief. This position is also controversial (see FAITH; RELIGION AND EPISTEMOLOGY).

Some philosophers have supposed that these questions are obviated by the problem of evil (see EVIL, PROBLEM OF), which constitutes an argument against God's existence. In their view, God and evil cannot coexist, or at any rate the existence of evil in this world is evidence which disconfirms the existence of God. In response to this challenge to religious belief, some philosophers have held that religious belief can be defended only by a theodicy, an attempt to give a morally sufficient reason for God's allowing evil to exist. Others have thought that religious belief can be defended without a theodicy, by showing the weaknesses in the versions of the argument from evil against God's existence. Finally, some thinkers have argued that only a practical and political approach is the right response to evil in the world.

Those who use the existence of evil to argue against the existence of God assume that God, if he existed, could and should intervene in the natural order of the world. Not everyone accepts this view

(see DEISM). But supposing it is right, how should we understand God's intervention? Does he providentially intervene to guide the world to certain ends? Would an act of divine intervention count as a miracle? What is a miracle, and is it ever rational to believe that a miracle has occurred (see MIRACLES)? Some people have supposed that a belief that miracles occur is incompatible with or undermined by a recognition of the success of science. Many people also think that certain widely accepted scientific views cast doubt on particular religious beliefs (see RELIGION AND SCIENCE).

2 Philosophy and religious doctrines and practices

In addition to the issues raised by the traditional conception of God, there are others raised by doctrines common to the Western monotheisms. These include the view that the existence of a human being does not end with the death of the body but continues in an afterlife (see SOUL, NATURE AND IMMORTALITY OF THE). Although there is wide variation in beliefs about the nature of the afterlife, typically the afterlife is taken to include heaven and hell. For some groups of Christians, it also includes limbo and purgatory. All of these doctrines raise an array of philosophical questions (see HEAVEN; HELL; LIMBO; PURGATORY).

There is equally great variation in views on what it takes for a human being to be accepted into heaven. Christians generally suppose that faith is a necessary, if not a sufficient, requirement. But they also suppose that faith is efficacious in this way because of the suffering and death of Jesus Christ (see TRINITY). Christians take sin to be an obstacle to union with God and life in heaven, and they suppose that Christ's atonement is the solution to this problem (see SIN). Because of Christ's atonement, divine forgiveness and mercy are available to human beings who are willing to accept it. Most Christians have supposed that this willingness is itself a gift of God, but some have supposed that human beings unassisted by grace are able to will or even to do what is good (see PELAGIANISM). How to interpret these doctrines, or whether they can even be given a consistent interpretation, has been the subject of philosophical discussion.

The religious life is characterized not only by religious belief and experience but by many other things as well. For many believers, ritual and prayer structure religious life. Christians also suppose that sacraments are important, although Protestants and Catholics differ on the nature and number of the sacraments. For Christians, the heart of the religious life, made possible by the atonement and the believer's acceptance of grace, consists in the theological virtues – faith, hope, and charity.

897

Many religious believers suppose they know that these and other things are essential to the religious life because God has revealed them (see REVELATION). This revelation includes or is incorporated in a book, the Qur'an for Muslims, the Hebrew Bible for Jews, and the Old and New Testaments for Christians. How the texts in this book are to be understood and the way in which religious texts are to be interpreted raise a host of philosophical issues.

Certain thinkers who are not themselves philosophers are none the less important for the philosophy of religion. These include, for example, John CALVIN and Martin LUTHER, whose views on such issues as justification and atonement significantly influenced the understanding of these notions, and Jacques Maritain and Pierre Teilhard de Chardin, whose influence on contemporary philosophical theology has been significant.

See also: AQUINAS, T.; AUGUSTINE; BOEHME, J.; BRAHMAN; BUDDHIST PHILOSOPHY, CHINESE; BUDDHIST PHILOSOPHY, INDIAN; BUDDHIST PHILOSOPHY, JAPANESE; BUDDHIST PHILOSOPHY, KOREAN; EAST ASIAN PHILOSOPHY; EDWARDS, J.; GNOSTICISM; INDIAN AND TIBETAN PHILOSOPHY; ISLAMIC PHILOSOPHY; JAINA PHILOSOPHY; JEWISH PHILOSOPHY; MANICHEISM; OCCASIONALISM; OMNIPRESENCE; PERSONALISM; PREDESTINATION; SHINTŌ; VOLUNTARISM; ZOROASTRIANISM

References and further reading

Murray, M. and Stump, E. (eds) (1999) *Philosophy of Religion: The Big Questions*, Oxford: Blackwell. (A broad and inclusive anthology of readings in philosophy of religion.)
Quinn, P. and Taliaferro, C. (1997) *A Companion to Philosophy of Religion*, Oxford: Blackwell. (A helpful and comprehensive reference work for philosophy of religion.)

ELEONORE STUMP

REN
See CONFUCIAN PHILOSOPHY, CHINESE; CONFUCIUS

RENAISSANCE HUMANISM
See HUMANISM, RENAISSANCE

RENAISSANCE PHILOSOPHY

Introduction

The term 'Renaissance' means rebirth, and was originally used to designate a rebirth of the arts and literature that began in mid-fourteenth century Italy

(see HUMANISM, RENAISSANCE). Here the term is simply used to refer to the period from 1400 to 1600, but there are ways in which Renaissance philosophy can be seen as a rebirth, for it encompasses the rediscovery of Plato and Neoplatonism (see PLATONISM, RENAISSANCE), the revival of such ancient systems as Stoicism and scepticism (see STOICISM), and a renewed interest in magic and the occult. Continuity with the Middle Ages is equally important. Despite the attacks of humanists and Platonists, Aristotelianism predominated throughout the Renaissance, and many philosophers continued to work within the scholastic tradition.

> 1 Historical and social factors
> 2 Humanism and the recovery of ancient texts
> 3 Scholasticism and Aristotle
> 4 Philosophical themes

1 Historical and social factors

Three historical events were of particular importance. First is the Turkish advance, culminating in the capture of Constantinople in 1453. This advance produced a migration of Greek scholars (like George of Trebizond) and Greek texts into the Latin-speaking West (see HUMANISM, RENAISSANCE; PLATONISM, RENAISSANCE). It also led to a search for new trade routes. The European discovery of the Americas and the first voyages to China and Japan widened intellectual horizons through an awareness of new languages, religions and cultures. New issues of colonialism, slavery and the rights of non-Christian peoples had an impact on legal and political philosophy (see VITORIA, F. DE; SUÁREZ, F.). The study of mathematics and science (especially astronomy) was also affected by developments in navigation, trade and banking, by new technology such as the telescope and other instruments (see KEPLER, J.; GALILEI, GALILEO), as well as by the recovery of Greek mathematics and the favourable attitude of Plato towards mathematical studies.

Second is the development of printing in the mid-fifteenth century. This allowed for the publication of scholarly text editions, for the expansion of learning beyond the universities, and for the increased use of vernacular languages for written material (see HUMANISM, RENAISSANCE §4). These changes particularly affected women, who were most often literate only in the vernacular. CHRISTINE DE PIZAN, PARACELSUS, RAMUS, MONTAIGNE, BRUNO and Charron are among those who used vernacular languages in at least some of their works.

Third is the Protestant reformation in the first part of the sixteenth century (see LUTHER, M.; CALVIN, J.). Protestant insistence on Bible reading in the vernacular strengthened both the use of the vernacular and the spread of literacy (see MELANCHTHON, P.). The Catholic Counter-Reformation also affected education, particularly through the work of the Jesuit Order (founded 1540), which set up educational institutions throughout Europe, including the Collegio Romano in Rome (founded 1553) and the secondary school at La Flèche, where DESCARTES was educated. Political philosophy took new directions (see HOOKER, R., for example) and theological studies changed. As the Protestants abandoned the *Sentences* of Peter LOMBARD and emphasized the church fathers, so the Catholics replaced the *Sentences* with the *Summa theologiae* of Thomas AQUINAS. In turn, these changes affected the undergraduate curriculum, which (for other reasons as well) became less technically demanding, especially in relation to logic studies. Personal liberties, too, were affected. Both Catholics and Protestants censored undesirable views, and the first Roman Catholic Index of Prohibited Books was drawn up in 1559. BRUNO was burnt for heresy, CAMPANELLA was imprisoned and the philosophical atheism of VANINI led to his execution. Calls for tolerance by such men as MONTAIGNE and LIPSIUS were not always favourably received. The books of all these men, and others such as ERASMUS, MACHIAVELLI and Rabelais, were placed on the Index or required to be revised. At the same time, Calvinist Geneva prohibited the printing of Thomas AQUINAS and Rabelais.

Social factors also affected philosophy which, as an academic discipline, was tied to the universities. These continued to accept only male students, and to teach in Latin, the universal language of learning and of the Roman Catholic Church, but more students came from higher social classes than during the Middle Ages. They expected a curriculum with less emphasis on technical logic and natural science and more on rhetoric, modern languages, history and other practical disciplines. Such curricular changes owed much to humanism, as did the spread of new secondary schools (see HUMANISM, RENAISSANCE; MONTAIGNE, M. DE).

The Renaissance was also notable for the spread of learning outside the university. Some men largely relied on the patronage of nobles, princes and popes (among them Valla, FICINO, PICO DELLA MIRANDOLA and ERASMUS), some were medical practitioners (including PARACELSUS and Cardano), some had private resources (like MONTAIGNE). Nor was it only men that were involved: CHRISTINE DE PIZAN, for example, was a court poet (see FEMINISM §2).

Jewish thinkers, too, were active outside the university (see JEWISH PHILOSOPHY §3). Yohanan ben Isaac see Alemanno and Judah ben Isaac Abravanel (known as Leone Ebreo) are particularly important figures of the Italian Renaissance.

2 Humanism and the recovery of ancient texts

Humanism was primarily a cultural and educational programme (see HUMANISM, RENAISSANCE; ERASMUS, D.; MORE, T.). Humanists were very much concerned with classical scholarship, especially the study of Greek, and with the imitation of classical models. Despite their frequent criticisms of scholastic jargon and techniques, they were not direct rivals of scholastic philosophers, except in so far as changes to the university curriculum brought about by the influence of humanist ideals diluted or squeezed out scholastic subjects. It was humanism that led to the rediscovery of classical texts, and their dissemination in printed form, in Greek and in Latin translation. Plato is the most notable example, but he was rediscovered with the Neoplatonists, and was often read through Neoplatonic eyes (see FICINO, M.; PLATONISM, RENAISSANCE). The so-called ancient wisdom of Hermeticism (also known as HERMETISM) was also recaptured within a Neoplatonic framework (see FICINO, M.), and, along with the Kabbalah (see KABBALAH), led to a revived interest in magic and the occult (see ALCHEMY; AGRIPPA VON NETTESHEIM, H.C.; BRUNO, G.; PARACELSUS). These streams also fed into the new vitalistic philosophy of nature (in such thinkers as PARACELSUS, BRUNO, CAMPANELLA, Cardano and Telesio). Other ancient schools of thought that were revived include Epicureanism, scepticism (see AGRIPPA VON NETTESHEIM, H.C.; ERASMUS, D.; SANCHES, F.; MONTAIGNE, M. DE) and Stoicism.

Some humanists wrote important works on education, including the education of women (see ERASMUS, D.). The Lutheran Aristotelian MELANCHTHON was also an educational reformer; and the Jesuits drew up the *Ratio Studiorum* (Plan of Studies) which prescribed texts for all Jesuit institutions. Humanism also affected Bible studies (see ERASMUS, D.; LUTHER, M.; HUMANISM, RENAISSANCE) and Aristotelianism itself.

3 Scholasticism and Aristotle

Scholastic philosophy was the philosophy of the schools, the philosophy which was taught in institutions of higher learning, whether the secular universities or the institutions of religious orders. The association of late scholastic philosophy with institutions of higher learning carried with it a certain method of presentation, one which is both highly organized and argumentative, with a clear account of views for and against a given thesis. It also carried with it a focus on Aristotle, for it was Aristotle who provided most of the basic textbooks in the sixteenth- and even the seventeenth-century university. Nor was the study of Aristotle necessarily carried on in a rigidly traditional manner, for many different Aristotelianisms were developed. Moreover, particularly within the Jesuit order, there was a strong inclination to include new developments in mathematics and astronomy within the framework of Aristotelian natural philosophy.

Aristotelians include Paul of Venice, George of Trebizond, Vernia, Nifo, POMPONAZZI, MEL-ANCHTHON, Zabarella and the Thomists (see below). Anti-Aristotelians include Petrarch, Blasius of Parma, Valla, RAMUS, SANCHES, Telesio, Patrizi da Cherso and CAMPANELLA. Some philosophers sought to reconcile Platonism and Aristotelianism (see PICO DELLA MIRANDOLA, G.; PLATONISM, RENAISSANCE).

A very important characteristic of late scholastic philosophy is its use of medieval terminology, along with its continued, explicit, concern both with problems stemming from medieval philosophy and with medieval philosophers themselves. There are fashions here as elsewhere. Albertism (the philosophy of ALBERT THE GREAT) was important in the fifteenth century; nominalism more or less disappeared after a final flowering in the early sixteenth century. Scotism declined significantly, but was still present in the seventeenth century. Thomism underwent a strong revival especially through the work of the Dominicans (Capreolus, Cajetan, Silvestri, VITORIA, Soto, Báñez and John of St Thomas) and the Jesuits (Fonseca, Toletus, SUÁREZ and Rubio: see THOMISM).

4 Philosophical themes

It is difficult to map the interests of Renaissance philosophers on to the interests of contemporary philosophers, especially as the main form of writing remained the commentary, whether on Aristotle or Aquinas. SUÁREZ is the first well-known author to write a major systematic work of metaphysics that is not a commentary, though earlier authors (such as Nifo and POMPONAZZI) had written shorter works on particular themes. Nonetheless, certain general themes can be isolated:

4.1 Logic and language. Logic was basic to the curriculum of all educational institutions, and many Renaissance philosophers wrote on logic. Individual humanists who worked in this field include Valla (§4), Agricola, Vives; MELANCHTHON and RAMUS;

individual scholastics include Soto, Toletus and Fonseca. Theories of logic and language were often closely related to metaphysics and philosophy of mind, as well as to science.

4.2 Metaphysics and philosophy of mind. Among the themes that overlapped with theories of logic and language were: (i) mental language (see LANGUAGE OF THOUGHT); (ii) analogy; (iii) objective and formal concepts (see SUÁREZ, F.); (iv) beings of reason (see JOHN OF ST THOMAS). A specifically Thomistic theme in metaphysics was the relation between essence and existence (see AQUINAS, T. §9; SUÁREZ, F.). Other metaphysical issues include: (i) universals (see SUÁREZ, F.); (ii) individuation (see SUÁREZ, F.); and (iii) the Great Chain of Being (see FICINO, M.; POMPONAZZI, P.; BRUNO, G.). Issues in the philosophy of mind included the existence of an agent sense and of intelligible species).

4.3 Immortality. The biggest single issue was the nature of the intellectual soul, whether it was immortal, and if so, whether its immortality could be proved (see FICINO, M.; POMPONAZZI, P.; SUÁREZ, F.; JOHN OF ST THOMAS; SOUL, NATURE AND IMMORTALITY OF THE).

4.4 Free will. Free will was a topic closely connected with the religious issues of grace, predestination and God's foreknowledge (see POMPONAZZI, P.; LUTHER, M.; ERASMUS, D.; CALVIN, J.; MOLINA, L. DE).

4.5 Science and philosophy of nature. The discussion of scientific method also overlaps with logic. Themes include: (i) traditional Aristotelian discussions about the object of natural philosophy (see JOHN OF ST THOMAS); (ii) anti-Aristotelian materialism; (iii) the new philosophies of nature which saw the universe as full of life (see PARACELSUS; BRUNO, G.; CAMPANELLA, T.) or as explicable in terms of light-metaphysics; (iv) tentative approaches to empiricism (see RAMUS, P.; SANCHES, F.). Finally, there are the thinkers who set science on a new path by using a combination of mathematical description and experiment (such as COPERNICUS, KEPLER and GALILEO).

4.6 Moral and political philosophy. Humanists were deeply concerned with moral and political philosophy (see HUMANISM, RENAISSANCE; ERASMUS, D.), as were Protestant reformers (see MELANCHTHON, P.; CALVIN, J.). Although the central focus remained on Aristotle, Epicurean moral philosophy was taken up by Valla and Stoic moral philosophy was also influential. Major political thinkers included MACHIAVELLI, VITORIA and BODIN. Many discussions of forms of government, the status of law, and the notion of a just war grew out of the Aristotelian–Thomistic tradition – prominent contributors to this tradition include CHRISTINE DE

PIZAN, VITORIA, Soto, Toletus, SUÁREZ, MOLINA and HOOKER. Other significant types of Renaissance political philosophy include: (i) conciliarism (see NICHOLAS OF CUSA); (ii) utopianism (see UTOPIANISM; MORE, T.; CAMPANELLA, T.); (iii) neostoicism. (See also POLITICAL PHILOSOPHY, HISTORY OF; NATURAL LAW.)

4.7 The human being. Themes related to the human being that were prominent in the Renaissance include: (i) the distinction between microcosm and macrocosm (NICHOLAS OF CUSA; PICO DELLA MIRANDOLA, G.; PARACELSUS; CAMPANELLA, T.); (ii) love (FICINO, M.; PICO DELLA MIRANDOLA, G.); (iii) the ability to shape one's own nature (PICO DELLA MIRANDOLA, G.; POMPONAZZI, P.).

References and further reading

Grendler, P.F. (ed.) (1999) *Encyclopedia of the Renaissance*, New York: Scribner's in association with the Renaissance Society of America, 6 vols. (An invaluable resource for all aspects of the Renaissance, including philosophy and science.)

Kraye, J. (ed.) (1997) *The Cambridge Translations of Renaissance Philosophical Texts. Vol. I. Moral Philosophy. Vol. II. Political Philosophy*, Cambridge: Cambridge University Press. (Forty new translations of works on moral and political philosophy with introductions and bibliographies. To be used as a companion to *The Cambridge History of Renaissance Philosophy*.)

Schmitt, C.B., Skinner, Q., Kessler, E. (eds) (1988) *The Cambridge History of Renaissance Philosophy*, Cambridge: Cambridge University Press. (A monumental work, arranged thematically.)

E.J. ASHWORTH

RENOUVIER, CHARLES BERNARD (1815–1903)

Charles Renouvier is the main representative of French Neo-Kantianism in the nineteenth century. Following Kant, he delimited the conditions for the legitimate exercise of the faculty of knowledge, and denounced the illusions of past metaphysics. Wishing to go further than Kant in this direction, he criticized the notions of substance and of actual infinity. According to him, relation is the basis of all our representations, reality is finite, and certainty rests on liberty. In ethics, he took into consideration, beyond the ideal of duty, the existence of the desires and interests to which history testifies.

See also: NEO-KANTIANISM; PERSONALISM

LAURENT FEDI
Translated from the French
by ROBERT STERN

RENUNCIATION IN INDIAN PHILOSOPHY
See DUTY AND VIRTUE, INDIAN CONCEPTIONS OF

REPRESENTATION IN ART
See DEPICTION

REPRESENTATION, POLITICAL

Political representation – the designation of a small group of politically active citizens to serve as representatives of the political community as a whole – is a central feature of contemporary states, especially of those that claim to be democratic. But what does it mean to say that one person or one group of people represents a larger group? Representatives are sometimes understood as agents of those they represent, sometimes symbolizing them, sometimes typifying their distinctive qualities or attitudes. Although political representation has something in common with each of these, it has its own special character. The missing idea here may be that the group represented *authorizes* the representative to make decisions on its behalf. This still leaves open one crucial question, however: how far should political representatives remain answerable to those they represent, and how far should they have the freedom to act on their own judgment?

ANDREW REEVE

REPRODUCTION AND ETHICS

Introduction

The first reproductive issue debated extensively by philosophers was abortion. Debates about its morality were, and still are, dominated by the issue of the moral status of the foetus, on which a wide variety of views has been defended. The most 'conservative' view is usually associated with very restrictive abortion policies, inconsistent with 'a woman's right to choose' (though the connection has been challenged by Judith Jarvis Thomson). However, all but the most conservative find it hard to ground prevailing moral intuitions concerning the newer issue of using human embryos for research purposes. Embryos, and even gametes, also assume importance in the context of methods for overcoming infertility (artificial insemination by donor (AID), egg and embryo donation involving in vitro fertilization (IVF), surrogacy) where issues about rights and ownership may arise. Considerations of 'the welfare of the child', often used to settle surrogacy disputes, also bear on questions of what should, or may, be done to avoid bringing a child with a genetic abnormality into the world. Current philosophical literature on reproductive issues is largely limited to a vocabulary of rights and little attention is paid to the social and familial contexts in which reproductive decisions are usually made

1   The status of the foetus

A wide range of views on the moral status of the foetus, and whether it is the sort of thing that may, or may not, be killed has been defended. (1) According to the 'conservative' position, the foetus has, from the moment of conception, the same moral status as an adult human being. (2) At the other, 'liberal', extreme, the foetus is claimed to be nothing but a collection of cells, part of the pregnant woman's body, like her appendix, until the moment of birth. Oddly enough, these diametrically opposed views share two assumptions; both assume that the moral status of the foetus remains unchanged from conception to birth and both assume that the foetus is, morally speaking, like something else – an adult or an appendix. Three other views reject at least one of these assumptions. (3) A 'moderate' view claims that the moral status changes at some determinate 'cut-off point' such as motility or viability. (4) According to the 'gradualist' view, the moral status changes gradually, increasing as the foetus develops. (5) According to the 'potentiality' view, the foetus has a unique moral status, being quite unlike anything else, that of a potential human being, from the moment of conception. Minor variations on these views exist, beyond the scope of the discussion presented here; however, a well-known sixth must be mentioned. (6) According to Michael Tooley and his followers, whatever the foetus is, it is not a person, that is, it does not have a right to life; and the same is true of infants (see RIGHTS).

Each of these views has been not only defended, but contested. None has an argument to establish what the moral status of the foetus is that its opponents regard as conclusive and each has difficulties concerning its *prima facie* consequences, which may be seized upon by opponents as unacceptable. So, for example, the potentiality view's 'difficulty' is that it hardly counts as yielding

any consequences at all. The conservative view appears to yield the consequence that if you can save only a baby or a two-day-old embryo in vitro from certain death, you are faced with just the same moral dilemma as when you can save only one of two babies in cradles. Tooley's view, notoriously, licenses infanticide, and so on. The difficulties become even more acute when we come to consider the treatment of foetuses not *in utero*.

2   Embryonic and foetal research

The debate about the status of the foetus assumed prominence in the days when abortion came to be seen as an issue of women's rights, and this was well before we had acquired the technique of fertilizing extracted ova in vitro, or discovered that foetal brain tissue might help adult human beings suffering from Parkinson's disease, or started on the 'genome project' (see GENETICS AND ETHICS). The gradualist or moderate positions were, perhaps, gaining ground, as the views that underpinned the legislation governing abortion in many Western countries – wherein increasingly 'serious' reasons for abortion are required as the pregnancy develops but abortion 'on demand' is allowed in the first trimester – until the new questions about the treatment of first-trimester-age foetuses (or embryos) hit the headlines and people started manifesting qualms. In fact, research on quite well-developed – even viable – foetuses had been going on, but few people knew about it, and, in many countries, there was no legislation that covered it. Now there is, but the substantial restrictions laid down seem to fit badly with the policies which are fairly 'liberal' about first trimester abortions. If the moral status of a ten-week-old foetus is so minimal that abortion 'on demand' is morally permissible, why do we insist on laws restricting the use of even two- or three-day-old embryos for research? In particular, why is it always assumed (as it is) that embryos may only be used as a last resort (when, that is, no other animals can be used to further the research), a restriction that those concerned about our exploitation of other animals rightly point out calls for some justification (see ANIMALS AND ETHICS).

In fact, the debates about these issues tend to dodge questions about morality and centre instead around legislation where considerations of the general consequences of allowing or forbidding certain practices become obviously relevant. Hence *prima facie* inconsistent positions which combine liberal abortion legislation with very restrictive legislation on the use of embryos and foetuses may be defended on the grounds that, as things are at the moment, liberal abortion legislation is a necessary evil, the only available way of avoiding desperate women resorting to backstreet abortionists or suffering the emotional and economic hardship of having babies they did not want and could not afford. However, this is hardly a defence that conservatives about the moral status of the foetus can employ; nor does it tend to recommend itself to those who defend 'a woman's right to choose'.

3   The right over one's own body

The prevailing emphasis on the status of the foetus has an odd effect; one could, if ignorant of the facts of human reproduction, read hundreds of articles written on abortion and be left wondering what they were. Those who maintain that, at least in the early stages, the foetus is just a growth in the woman's body, fail to mention the fact that it is a growth like no other, namely a growth that, uniquely, results from the cells of two human beings, and is a growth that will usually become a baby, someone's child, if allowed to develop. Those who hold the 'conservative' or 'potential' view emphasize the fact that a fertilized ovum naturally develops into a baby; some mention the fact that an ovum is fertilized by a male cell and that this usually happens as a result of sexual intercourse, but remarkably few mention the fact that the nine-month development into a baby standardly – and arduously – takes place in a woman's body. If one did not know better, one might reasonably infer that parthenogenesis was common and that many of the results of sexual intercourse were raised in incubators as in Aldous Huxley's *Brave New World*.

Conservatives about not only the status of the foetus, but also abortion, do not deny that we all have some sort of right over our own bodies; they merely claim that it is restricted, or outweighed, by the foetus' right to life. This initially plausible move has been challenged, however, in a deservedly famous article by Judith Jarvis Thomson, which, despite its age, still stands almost alone in its attempt to take account of what is special about abortion, namely that it is the termination of a (human) pregnancy. A human pregnancy, regardless of one's views about the status of the foetus, is a condition of a human body, and usually results from sexual intercourse, voluntary or involuntary, in the hope, or not, of conceiving. Thomson daringly allows the conservatives their premise about the moral status of the foetus and argues that, even if this is granted, the impermissibility of abortion does not follow in many cases. Her argument depends on the claim that the right to life does not, as such, include the right to the use of another person's body to survive. If you can survive only by being connected to my circulatory system for nine months, then my right to decide what happens to my body allows me not

only to refuse and let you die, but, moreover, to disconnect us and thereby kill you if I have not granted you the right to use my body but have been kidnapped and connected up to you while unconscious.

The wild unlikelihood of the latter scenario reflects Thomson's heroic attempt to describe something that is not a pregnancy but is like at least unintended pregnancies in the (assumed) relevant respects, namely that one person (the foetus, granting the conservative view) needs the use of another person's body to survive, while the second person has not done anything that can be construed as giving them the right to use it. The strained nature of Thomson's analogies has attracted much criticism, but few of her critics have paused to reflect that any analogies to pregnancy are bound to be strained because there simply is not any other condition of the human body remotely like it.

Her article manages to take cognizance of remarkably many of the unique features of pregnancy but still leaves several out. When we turn from the issue of abortion to those of surrogacy, artificial insemination by donor (AID) and in vitro fertilization (IVF), the fact that a fertilized ovum has resulted from the cells of two human beings, a man and a woman, and the fact that it would become a baby, someone's child, if enabled and allowed to develop *in utero*, assume unavoidable prominence. Moreover, questions about what is involved in 'the right to decide what happens to my body' and, more generally, what counts as 'mine', become increasingly problematic.

4   Rights and ownership

AID, IVF and surrogacy, as moral and political issues, revolve around those people who very much want to have a child; hence the question of whether the foetus has the moral status of something that may be killed tends to fade into the background, and passionate feelings about parenthood, families and 'my (our) child' come to the foreground. Those who espouse the conservative view on the status of the foetus do indeed object to the current practice of IVF on the ground that it tends to involve producing 'spare' embryos, which must either be allowed to die or be frozen and stored; but the various methods of alleviating infertility involve many further problems.

Feminists have found themselves divided over what to say about surrogacy, inclined, on the one hand, to defend the view that a woman's right to decide what happens to her body surely extends to deciding whether or not to act as a surrogate mother but inclined, on the other, to liken surrogacy to female prostitution, regarding both as practices in which the woman's body is *used* in an exploitative and degrading manner, even if she has, in some sense, freely consented.

Anyone who is, for whatever reason, inclined to defend at least some forms of surrogacy, has to consider what should be done when the agreement between the parties concerned breaks down – when, say, the surrogate mother changes her mind, and wants to keep the child, or the commissioning couple change theirs and do not want to take it. Some aim to settle these unhappy questions by arguing that surrogacy is a form of 'pre-natal adoption', whereby the commissioning couple acquire parental rights (and duties) to the embryo as soon as fertilization takes place; the surrogate mother cannot abort it, nor claim it, nor can the commissioning couple refuse to take it without this counting as their immorally abandoning it. Others aim to settle them by considering who owned the sperm and ovum involved initially, who can be said to have 'donated' or given up their rights to these gametes and who has retained them, whether the surrogate mother acquires a right to the baby by (in a new sense of the phrase) 'mixing her labour with it', and hence who 'owns' the baby, as though gametes, foetuses and children were like any other possessions. But, like the two most extreme positions on the moral status of the foetus, each of these approaches takes cognizance of only some of the facts relevant to human reproduction, ignoring those emphasized by the other side and leaving some out entirely.

5 Welfare considerations

What about, in particular, 'the welfare of the child', the consideration which, in practice, has pre-eminently been appealed to in resolving disputes when surrogacy agreements have broken down? This undoubtedly goes beyond the debates about the various adults' rights but it is not, thereby, a consideration independent of the facts that are appealed to in those debates. For, it may be said, it is in the best interests of any child not only to be wanted and loved by two adults, but also for its mother's love to spring from the natural bond that exists between the child and the mother who carries it and gives birth to it and, even further, for it to have the opportunity to know, and, we hope, love, its genetic parents. But these considerations resolve a surrogacy-agreement breakdown adequately (if that) only in the particular case in which the surrogate child is the genetic offspring of the surrogate mother and her partner and they decide mutually they want to keep the child. Otherwise, the decision has to be over the circumstances in which the child will be least disadvantaged.

That surrogacy and, indeed, AID, and egg and embryo donation are all methods of overcoming infertility that, arguably, lead to the production of a disadvantaged child probably forms the strongest basis for those who are morally opposed to them all. Common claims that they are all unnatural, or introduce a third party into what should be 'the exclusive relationship between wife and husband', thus undermining the family, tend to fall foul of the obvious counter that few things are more 'natural', or more affirmative of the value of family life, than a couple's desire to have a child. But no-one thinks that this natural, proper, and in some cases, quite consuming, desire can, morally, be satisfied by any means. You cannot steal a child in order to have one, and, it may be said, you cannot set about bringing a disadvantaged child into the world in order to have one either.

The extent to which different methods of overcoming infertility produce, or would produce, a disadvantaged child is usually thought to vary. As I write, many people in Britain have said that it would be a terrible thing for a child to know that its 'mother' was an aborted foetus and, on those grounds, supported legislation designed to forbid any future use of the ova already present in female foetuses. It is important to remember in cases such as these that the very existence of the child whose welfare would be at stake depends on the decision taken. The choice here, for example, is not between existence with a foetus as mother and existence without, but between existence with a foetus as mother and nonexistence. However, egg donation by mature women, embryo donation and AID, when uncomplicated by surrogacy, often pass unquestioned – though the recent discovery that an unscrupulous doctor at an infertility clinic in America was the genetic father of hundreds of children, having used his own sperm to fertilize all his patients, gave some people pause for thought.

Considerations of what sort of life a child produced in certain circumstances will have may also form the basis of adverse moral judgments of people's selfishness and irresponsibility. Many condemned a fifty-nine-year-old woman who chose to have a child by IVF (though the same judgment is rarely passed on even older men who father children), and some insist that people carrying certain genes should get themselves sterilized and resign themselves to childlessness or adoption. It is sometimes even said that it is selfish and irresponsible of pregnant women to reject screening for genetic abnormality or to reject abortion when it is identified; but whether this is so surely depends on their reasons for the rejections. If they think, for instance, that the genetic abnormality does not prevent one's life being a good one (perhaps because they or their partner have it themselves), or if they think that abortion, at least in their circumstances, is wrong, then they have a good reason for not trying to 'maximize happiness' on this occasion (see UTILITARIANISM).

6 Morality, legislation and rights

At this point we return to the abortion debate, but now under a new aspect and in a way that brings questions about infanticide more clearly to the fore. The most fundamental objection to the conservative position on the status of the foetus is that it puts abortion, at any stage, on a par with infanticide, and, in the usual context of the abortion debate, infanticide equals murder; on the conservative view, abortion in the case of rape is not one whit more justifiable than murdering a child conceived through rape, and arguably less justifiable or excusable (given the innocence of the child) than the woman murdering the rapist. But in the context of euthanasia, killing an infant, or allowing it to die, without its consent, may well not be counted as murder, even on a conservative view; not because, quite generally, infants fail to be 'persons' with a right to life, who can thereby be killed for any old reason (as Tooley suggests), but because, when a human being is by virtue of extreme youth (or perhaps extreme impairment) incapable of autonomy, 'paternalistic' considerations of their welfare form, quite properly, the determining factor (see LIFE AND DEATH).

So even on the conservative view on the status of the foetus, abortion in the form of 'foetal euthanasia' may be justified, as infant euthanasia may be; and on any view that ranks the foetus as somehow not quite the same as a born baby, the possibilities of justification increase. But a new twist has been added; 'euthanasia' has its motivation built in, since it is done for the sake of the one who dies. Morally speaking, there is all the difference in the world between seeking an abortion because one wants a 'designer baby', and seeking it because one thinks it is wrong to bring a disadvantaged child into the world, just as there is a difference between my instructing the doctors to take my mother off life support for her sake, and my doing it to save myself the medical bills. But, given that people can and will lie about their motives, there is no way in which legislation can effectively permit the well-motivated cases but prohibit the callous ones.

Much of the literature devoted to reproductive ethics in fact vacillates between discussing morality and legislation, frequently leaving it unclear which is at issue. This is, no doubt, in part the result of the current tendency to talk almost exclusively in terms of rights, for we tend to think of (moral) rights as

things that should be protected by good legislation. But we too readily forget that, particularly within families, it may be morally quite wrong for me to exercise a right that I certainly have, and, more generally, that there is much opportunity within families for acting morally well or ill where questions of rights, and even duties, do not arise. Most reproductive decisions are made by couples who love each other, who discuss what 'their' decision will be; the discussion is often extended to other members of the family who will say 'we' decided; most of the couples want to be good parents, and morally good people. This is, indeed, how things should mostly be, but none of it can be brought about by legislation, and all of it is almost universally ignored in the current literature (see FAMILY, ETHICS AND THE).

See also: APPLIED ETHICS; BIOETHICS; CLONING

References and further reading

Alpern, K.D. (1992) *The Ethics of Reproductive Technology*, Oxford: Oxford University Press. (A wide range of readings, not exclusively modern, with useful case studies.)

Feinberg, J. (1984) *The Problem of Abortion*, Belmont, CA: Wadsworth, 2nd edn. (Still the most comprehensive collection of articles on the topic, including ones by Judith Jarvis Thomson and Michael Tooley, with a helpful introduction.)

ROSALIND HURSTHOUSE

REPUBLICANISM

Significant divisions exist in all societies and communities of any size. The expression of these divisions in politics takes many forms, one of them republican. The hallmark of republican politics is the subordination of different interests to the common weal, or what is in the interest of all citizens. To ensure this outcome, government in a republic can never be the exclusive preserve of one interest or social order; it must always be controlled jointly by representatives of all major groups in a society. The degree of control exercised by representatives of different social elements may not be equal, and different styles of government are compatible with republican objectives. However, all republican governments involve power-sharing in some way. Even in a democratic republic political majorities must share power with minorities for the common good to be realized.

Maintaining an appropriate balance of political power is the chief problem of republicans. One or another faction may obtain control of government and use it to further its own interests, instead of the common weal. To prevent this republicans have developed a variety of strategies. Some rely on constitutional 'checks and balances' to cure the mischief of factionalism. Others seek to minimize factionalization itself by regulating the causes of faction – for example, the distribution of land and other forms of property. Still others promote civic religions in order to bind diverse people together. All these methods accept the inevitability of conflicting interests, and see the need to accommodate them politically. Hence, civic life is at the heart of republicanism.

RUSSELL L. HANSON

RESPONSIBILITY

To be responsible for something is to be answerable for it. We have *prospective* responsibilities, things it is up to us to attend to: these may attach to particular roles (the responsibilities of, for instance, parents or doctors), or be responsibilities we have as moral agents, or as human beings. We have *retrospective* responsibilities, for what we have done or failed to do, for the effects of our actions or omissions. Such responsibilities are often (but not always) moral or legal responsibilities.

The scope of our retrospective moral responsibilities is controversial. We are responsible for the intended results of our actions, but how far we are responsible for their foreseen effects, or for harms that we do not prevent when we could, depends on how we should define our prospective responsibilities, that is, on how far we should regard such foreseen effects, or such preventable harms, as our business. To say that I am responsible for some foreseen effect, or for a harm which I did not prevent, is to say that I should have attended to that effect or to that harm in deciding how to act; our retrospective responsibilities are partly determined by our prospective responsibilities.

I am responsible for something only if it is within my control. It is sometimes argued that I am therefore not responsible for that whose occurrence is a matter of luck; but it is not clear that we can or should try to make responsibility wholly independent of matters of luck.

We have responsibilities not merely as individuals, but also as members of organizations (organizations themselves have responsibilities in so far as they can be seen as agents). This raises the question of how far we are responsible for the actions of groups or organizations to which we belong.

See also: ACTION; CONFUCIAN PHILOSOPHY, CHINESE

R.A. DUFF

REVELATION

All major theistic religions have claimed that God has revealed himself in some way, both by showing something of himself in events and also by providing some true, important and otherwise unknowable propositions. Event-revelation may include both general revelation (God revealing himself in very general events, observable by all, such as the existence of the universe and its conformity to natural laws), and special revelation (God revealing himself in certain particular historical events). The events are a revelation in the sense that God has brought them about and they show something of his character. Thus Judaism teaches that God manifested his nature and his love for Israel when he brought his people out of Egypt and led them to the promised land through the agency of Moses. Christianity traditionally affirms that God has revealed himself in a much fuller sense in Jesus Christ – because Jesus did not merely show us something of the character of God but was God himself. God reveals propositions by some chosen prophet or society telling us truths orally or in writing which we would not have adequate grounds for believing unless they had been announced to us by persons who showed some mark of God-given authority. Thus Islam teaches that God inspired Muhammad to write the Qur'an in the seventh century AD, and that its success (its proclamation throughout a large part of the civilized world), content and style (deep thoughts expressed in a beautiful way, not to be expected of an uneducated person) show its divine origin.

See also: NATURAL THEOLOGY

RICHARD SWINBURNE

REVOLUTION

There have been revolutions in politics, science, philosophy and most other spheres of human life. Here we discuss revolution mainly through concepts pertaining especially to the political realm. Attempts to define political revolution have been controversial; as a consequence there is dispute about whether specific occurrences were revolutions, rebellions, *coups d'état* or reformations.

If we define revolution as the illegal introduction of a radically new situation and order for the sake of obtaining or increasing individual or communal freedom, we may list those characteristics most often ascribed to it. These characteristics distinguish it from its earlier use where revolution referred to the return of an original state of affairs, as in astronomy; they also allow its distinction from related concepts such as reformation. At least at a superficial level this definition can do justice to early modern (seventeenth and eighteenth) as well as late modern (nineteenth and twentieth century) revolutions. Through these periods there has, however, been sufficient change in concepts closely related to revolution to require the definition's openness to nuances for it to apply to both periods. It is unclear whether even such a nuanced definition can apply in postmodern thought.

PETER A. SCHOULS

RHETORIC

Rhetoric is the power to persuade, especially about political or public affairs. Sometimes philosophy has defined itself in opposition to rhetoric – Plato invented the term 'rhetoric' so that philosophy could define itself by contrast, and distinctions like that between persuasion and knowledge have been popular ever since. Sometimes philosophy has used rhetorical techniques or materials to advance its own projects. Some of its techniques, especially topics of invention, the classification of issues, and tropes or figures of speech, are occasionally employed by philosophers. The philosophical question is whether these techniques have any interest beyond efficacy. What is the relation between techniques effective in persuading others and methods for making up one's own mind? Is there any connection between the most persuasive case and the best decision? Is there a relation between the judgments of appropriateness and decorum exercised by the rhetorician, and the judgments of appropriateness exercised by the person of practical wisdom? Do judgments about probability, ambiguity and uncertainty, and judgments under constraints of time or the need for decision, aspire to the ideal of perfect rationality, to which they are doomed to fall short, or do these kinds of judgment have an integrity of their own? Apart from supplying useful techniques, an art of persuasion also raises philosophic questions concerning the relation between rhetoric and logic, rhetoric and ethics, and rhetoric and poetics.
See also: ARISTOTLE §29; CICERO, M.T.; MELANCHTHON, P.; RAMUS, P.

EUGENE GARVER

RICKERT, H.
See NEO-KANTIANISM

RICOEUR, PAUL (1913–)

Paul Ricoeur is one of the leading French philosophers of the second half of the twentieth century. Along with the German philosopher Hans-Georg Gadamer, Ricoeur is one of the main contemporary exponents of philosophical hermeneutics: that is, of a philosophical orientation which places particular emphasis on the nature and role of interpretation. While his early work was strongly influenced by Husserl's phenomenology, he became increasingly concerned with problems of interpretation and developed – partly through detailed inquiries into psychoanalysis and structuralism – a distinctive hermeneutical theory. In his later writings Ricoeur explores the nature of metaphor and narrative, which are viewed as ways of creating new meaning in language.
See also: HERMENEUTICS

JOHN B. THOMPSON

RIGHT AND GOOD

'Right' and 'good' are the two basic terms of moral evaluation. In general, something is 'right' if it is morally obligatory, whereas it is morally 'good' if it is worth having or doing and enhances the life of those who possess it.

Acts are often held to be morally right or wrong in respect of the action performed, but morally good or bad in virtue of their motive: it is right to help a person in distress, but good to do so from a sense of duty or sympathy, since no one can supposedly be obliged to do something (such as acting with a certain motive) which cannot be done at will.

Henry Sidgwick distinguished between two basic conceptions of morality. The 'attractive' conception, favoured by the ancient Greeks, views the good as fundamental, and grounds the claims of morality in the self-perfection to which we naturally aspire. The 'imperative' conception, preferred in the modern era, views the right as fundamental, and holds that we are subject to certain obligations whatever our wants or desires.
See also: CONFUCIAN PHILOSOPHY, CHINESE; GOOD, THEORIES OF THE

CHARLES LARMORE

RIGHTS

Introduction

There is widespread consensus that rights are ways of acting or of being treated that are beneficial to the rightholder. Controversy begins, however, when one attempts to specify the notion of rights further.

(1) It is sometimes said, perhaps too casually, that all rights carry with them correlated obligations –

things that other persons are supposed to do or refrain from doing when some given person is said to have a right to something. The question is: how is it best to state this relationship between rights and correlated obligations?

(2) Most people think that rights are, in some sense, justified. But there is considerable controversy as to what, precisely, is the proper focus of justification. Some say that rights are practices (certain ways of acting or of being treated) that are established, typically socially established. Thus, the issue for them is whether the fact of social recognition and enforcement is justified (or could be). Others say that rights themselves are claims; hence a right is a justified claim or principle of some sort (whether the practice identified in that claim exists or not). This dispute, between rights as justified practices and rights as justified claims, needs to be explored and, if possible, resolved.

Other topics need addressing beyond the question of the initial characterization of rights. One of them is the question of the function of rights: What good are they anyway? What can one do with rights? Another is the question of how best to justify particular kinds of rights, such as human rights and basic constitutional rights. Is there a substantive theory of critical morality that can do the job? Many people are concerned, especially, with whether utilitarianism (one of the dominant ethical theories in the West today) is up to this task. Finally, mention should be made of one other issue much talked about of late: what kinds of beings can have rights, and under what conditions of possession and dispossession?

1 Initial characterization and some points of consensus

Rights are an important issue in contemporary social and political philosophy. For it is widely held that rights, by providing a significant protection of important interests of individuals against the state and against other persons (even a majority), give a person something to stand on. One may not want to go so far as to say that rights are 'trumps' (as some have), but it is none the less clear that rights are valuable things. So it seems natural to ask: 'what, then, is a right?'

Rights are socially established ways of acting or ways of being treated (or, alternatively, such ways as ought to be so established). More specifically, a right so understood is a right *to* something that is (1) fairly determinate and that (2) can be similarly distributed on an individual basis to each and all of those who are said to be rightholders. A right is always regarded as (3) a beneficial way of acting or of being treated both for the rightholder and, more generally, for society. Thus, (4) it is or should be something socially accepted – recognized and protected in given societies. Such acceptance would be (5) deemed reasonable, even by outsiders, in that it made explanatory sense. For the way of acting or of being treated in question could be exhibited, plausibly, as a means to or as a part of accomplishing some interest or perceived benefit or other good (or desirable) thing. Accordingly, (6) directives could be issued to others, to those who are not rightholders. And (7) further initiatives could be taken as a feature of any such successful claim to rights status.

This initial characterization constitutes common ground in the arguments people make about rights. Indeed, several of its features are not particularly controversial at all. Thus, there would today be widespread consensus on the idea that rights are ways of acting or ways of being treated that are (1) appropriately determinate, (2) equitably distributable on an individual basis and (3) beneficial. Even the central characterization, concerning social acceptability in (4), is not unduly contestable as stated; but dispute would break out as soon as we tried to determine what to emphasize – whether rights are *socially established* or merely *ought* to be. Finally, the idea (6) that rights always involve some sort of normative direction of the behaviour of others might also appear to be universally agreed upon; but there are problems with alleging consensus on this particular point.

2 Normative direction

The view in question in (6) is often put by saying that rights correlate with duties – meaning thereby that a right always implies or has attached some distinctive and closely related duty of others. But serious difficulties arise for the thesis in this precise form.

The most interesting arguments against such correlations derive from Wesley Hohfeld's highly influential classification of rights (see HOHFELD, W.N.). On his view a legal right could be constituted by any one of four elements: a claim; a liberty; a power; or an immunity. And each type of right has a unique second-party correlative. Thus, for a legal *claim right* to some thing the correlative element is a legal duty of some second party. Analogously, a person's *immunity right* from some thing is necessarily correlated with a lack of power – with a legal disability – on the part of others to do that thing (for example, the constitutional inability of the US Congress to 'abridge' free political speech). Hohfeld's point is simply that a legal duty and a no-power (a legal *in*ability) are significantly different. Accordingly, the existence of immunity rights tells against the view that the correlative of every right is always going to be a closely related second-party duty.

Thus, the thesis that rights logically correlate with specific duties is not sound. A weaker but more defensible view is that any genuine right must involve some normative direction of the behaviour of persons other than the holder. Even this weaker thesis, however, seems to run up against the authority of HOBBES (in his account of rights in the state of nature) and of Hohfeld. We can see this most clearly by looking at the Hohfeldian liberty right.

Here the legal *liberty right* to do some thing – which consists in the absence of any duty on the agent's part to refrain from doing that thing – is matched with other people's lack of a claim that such a thing not be done by the agent. The point is, this is the *only* directive incumbent on the conduct of second parties in the case of a liberty. They can make no claim on the duties of a liberty-rightholder (to refrain); beyond that their own action is relatively unencumbered.

A liberty right, so conceived, is indeed an odd one. For it fails to capture the common-sense notion that when one has a liberty right to do a thing someone else is directed not to interfere with that doing. The problem is that literally *no* normative direction at all is involved for second parties (in Hobbes' case) and no *significant* normative direction against interference is involved (in Hohfeld's).

If the common-sense notion of a liberty right is correct, there ought always to be some sort of strong mandate for non-interference, either explicitly stated in our formulation of a given liberty or present at least in the context in which that liberty normally occurs. Thus, to take the latter case, certain standing duties of second parties (such as the duty not to assault or batter others or to trespass on their property), even though these are relatively independent of a given liberty (for example, the liberty to paint one's barn a shocking purple), would none the less afford the exercise of that liberty a considerable degree of protection. Without some such fairly robust mandates against interference (either closely connected to the liberty in question or permanently and independently in place on the 'perimeter' of its usual exercise), we would

probably be inclined to call that liberty, not a right, but a *mere* liberty or a privilege.

The upshot, then, is that we should state our main contention so as to emphasize *significant* normative direction (on the conduct of second parties). This is the focal point of what appears to be an emerging consensus on the matter at issue.

3 Accreditation

No real consensus has emerged, however, on the point we now turn to: whether rights, in order to be rights, require social recognition (and beyond that, social maintenance). In considering this issue one school of thought – embracing both classical natural rights theorists and contemporary advocates of human rights – has tended to emphasize that individuals can have rights independently of organized society, of social institutions, and hence of social recognition and maintenance in any form. The rather common characterization that rights are essentially claims can be taken as a way of emphasizing that rights hold irrespective of whether they have been acknowledged, either in the society or, more specifically, by that person against whom the claim is made.

Against the view that rights are essentially claims are ranged a number of philosophers. BENTHAM comes most readily to mind, and his polemic on this very point against natural rights as 'nonsense' still adds relish to philosophical discussions. T.H. GREEN, in his insistence that rights require social recognition and that without it they are something less than rights, would be another. And, oddly enough, Lenin would be a third.

The problem we are examining arises, in part, because the procedure for deciding whether something is a right is not wholly settled. We find that the vocabulary of rights, in particular, of human rights, may actually be used at any of several steps: that of mere claim, that of entitlement (where only the claim-to element is really settled), that of fully validated claim (where we have the idea both of a justified claim *to* something and of a justified claim *against* someone for it) and, finally, that of satisfied or enforced claim (where the appropriate measures required to support or to fulfil the claim have been given effective embodiment as well). The presence of these possible stages has introduced a degree of ambiguity into assertions that a right exists.

Accordingly, we find a significant variety of contemporary opinion as to the point at which such assertions can most plausibly be thought to take hold. While some have said simply that rights are *claims*, others say they are *entitlements*, and yet others (most notably, Feinberg 1973) say they are *valid claims*. Ranged against them have been those (such as Sumner 1987) who emphasize that rights, even human rights, are basically established ways of acting or being treated. And, last of all, some have treated rights as legitimate expectations and, hence, have landed more or less in the middle (see RAWLS, J.).

The main backdrop to the view that rights are (valid) claims is, I think, the common opinion (emphasized by Dworkin, Raz, MacCormick and Held among others) that to have a right is to have a justification for acting in a certain way, or a justification for being treated in a certain way (see DWORKIN, R.). Now, suppose that a candidate for rights status had all the rights-making features (mentioned in §1) but one. Although accredited (in the sense of justified), it was not established; it lacked the *social* recognition which it ought to have.

Why should the lack of such recognition deprive it of rights status? For, clearly, if we modelled the rights-making features on what was justified (what was accredited in *that* sense), the thing was already a right even before it was recognized, even before it became a practice. And when it was recognized it would be recognized as a *right* (as something that was fully justified) and would not simply *become* a right in being recognized.

The opposing view, that rights are socially recognized practices, rests on three main contentions. The first of these is the contention that the notions of authoritative recognition (if not explicit, then at least implicit, as evidenced by conduct) and of governmental promotion and maintenance (usually on a wide variety of occasions) are themselves part of the standard notion of a *legal* right, that is, when we are concerned with rights that are more than merely nominal ones.

Thus, on the social recognition view, the fatal flaw in the theory of rights as valid claims (in any of its formulations) is the suggestion that practices of governmental recognition and enforcement in law can be dispensed with in the case of legal rights. Indeed, this is the very point at which both Dworkin and Raz, who might otherwise be taken to be supporters of some form of the valid claims thesis, desert that thesis for one that emphasizes the necessity of institutionally establishing ways of acting/being treated, if these are to count as *legal* rights.

The second point put forward by the social recognition view is that it is desirable to have, if possible, a single, unequivocal sense of 'rights': one that is capable of capturing both legal rights and human (and other moral) rights under a single generic heading. Now, if the argument just sketched is to be credited, then the view of rights as valid claims does not provide an adequate generalized notion of rights, one that can comfortably include both legal and human rights. For we have already

seen that legal rights cannot be satisfactorily accounted for under the heading of valid claims.

This brings us to the third point urged by the social recognition view. Here the argument is that *all* moral rights can, indeed must, be construed as involving established practices of recognition and maintenance. Since human rights (as a special case of moral rights) are thought to be addressed to governments in particular, we must regard practices of governmental recognition and promotion as being the form for such recognition and maintenance to take for these rights. Here we have, in brief compass, then, the social recognition view that opposes the contention that rights are essentially justified or valid claims.

4 Functions of rights

Rights have many functions. Two in particular are emphasized in the contemporary literature: the conferring of liberty or autonomy (on rightholders) and the protection of their interests, especially their basic interests.

Rights in the seventeenth and eighteenth centuries were largely discussed as if they were simply liberties and, hence, ways of acting on the part of the rightholder. Indeed, this tendency is deeply rooted in the tradition of rights discourse. It is hard to say when 'a right' was first spoken of in a way continuous with current usage, but many careful expositors locate that first recognizable use with WILLIAM OF OCKHAM, when he talked of a right (*ius* or *jus*) as a power or capacity (*potestas*) to act in accordance with 'right reason' or, in the special case of a legal right (*ius fori*), with an agreement. Such a usage was well established by the seventeenth century (with Hobbes and, some would say, with Locke) and has been widespread ever since.

It constitutes, none the less, a drastic oversimplification – even if the rights referred to are, as they often are, the classic rights of the eighteenth-century declarations. For these rights include important rights to ways of being treated and such rights are *not* things the rightholder does or can do. Even so, the oversimplification continues to prevail in philosophical literature (for example, Rawls 1993). Thus, Rawls' 'equal basic liberties' (enshrined in his first principle of justice) include both liberties of action and ways of being treated, typically ways of not being injured by the actions of others (see FREEDOM AND LIBERTY §3).

It is clearly possible to have both important functions (the conferring of liberty on rightholders and the protection of their interests) as functions of rights, often of a single right. Thus it seems arbitrary, where both functions are normally served by almost all rights, to single out just one of these functions (typically the function of conferring autonomy) and to give it *definitional* weight (see Sumner 1987).

In fact, in line with the contemporary understanding of rights (as expressed, for example, in the UN's *Universal Declaration of Human Rights* of 1948), it might be best to stress three main functions of rights. Thus, the central content of some rights will be a way of acting (for example, a liberty of conduct of some sort). But at the core of other rights will be a way of being treated: a non-injury of some sort or, alternatively, the provision of a service.

Corresponding to each main heading or class of rights (as determined by these central cores), there is an appropriate or characteristic normative response enjoined for the conduct of others. But the essential character of this normative direction of the conduct of second parties shifts from main case to main case. Allowing or even encouraging a piece of conduct is what these parties are normatively directed to do in the case of a liberty; prohibiting their doing of an injury to the rightholder or requiring of them a service, again to the rightholder, is the incumbent directive in the other two cases.

5 Critical justification

Rights are eminently plausible candidates for justification, an idea that I tried to capture with the notion that rights are *accredited* ways of acting or of being treated. This section will consider some of the main full-blown theories offered to justify rights. One proviso is that the most important rights are universal rights – in particular, human rights and constitutional rights, which are fundamental or basic civil rights of all persons (or all citizens) within a given politically organized society. My account is limited to theories that attempt to justify such universal rights.

All civil rights are important rights and all reflect a high level of social commitment. But not all can be justified as representing individuated and practicable and universal moral claims which serve as proper conclusions to sound arguments from objective principles of critical morality (or at least from principles widely regarded as reasonable).

Some can be, however. Indeed, in the social recognition view (described in §3), human rights would be, simply, constitutional rights that embodied precisely such morally valid claims. These claims, then, when on their own, could be described (relatively noncontroversially and giving due weight to both the opposing views canvassed in §3) as human rights *norms*.

We can ask: what might be involved, then, in the justification of human rights – or human rights

norms – and of those constitutional rights susceptible of the same sort of justification? One thing seems clear: the norms which constitute or back up human rights are moral norms. Thus human rights can exist only if substantive moral norms in some sense exist (or, at least, can be objectively described and argued for). Now, it is possible for moral, and hence human, rights to exist even if moral norms are conventional or are relative to culture. But if human rights – or human rights norms – are to serve their role as international standards of political criticism then such a conventional morality would have to include some norms that are accepted worldwide. More important, if such norms are to have weight and bearing for future human beings in societies not yet existing (and this much would seem to be involved if we are to call these norms *universal* in any significant sense), then these norms cannot be merely conventional.

Thus, in classifying human rights as moral rights one may wish to distinguish between actual and critical moralities. What seems especially crucial to human rights, then, is the belief that there are objectively correct, or objectively reasonable, critical moral principles. Often, human rights – or human rights norms – are traced back to such foundational ideas as human dignity or moral personality or moral agency or moral community. But the exploration of such possibilities has failed to gain widespread support, perhaps because such notions as moral agency do not themselves seem sufficiently distinct from the very norms or rights they are being called upon to justify. Or perhaps because such notions seem, in the end, to stand in need of a more basic sort of justification themselves. Thus, we might do well to consider other grounding principles, principles that could be regarded as rock bottom and, arguably, as objectively reasonable.

One appropriate way to narrow the field among these is to consider first those substantive theories of critical justification that have grown up in proximity to serious talk about human and constitutional rights. Three important contemporary theories fit this description: utilitarianism (in particular, the theory developed by J.S. MILL (§10) and advocated recently under the name of 'indirect' utilitarianism), the theory of John Rawls, and rational-choice ethical theory, especially that of David Gauthier (see CONTRACTARIANISM). I will confine the discussion to one example.

Rawls' theory (like Dworkin's) emphasizes the standing priority of basic liberties and other constitutional rights over such things as the common good or perfectionist values (for example, the value of holiness, as religiously conceived, or the values of Nietzschean elitism). In his 1993 book

Political Liberation Rawls sketches a complex theory of justification comprising two main parts. He starts with what he calls a 'freestanding' justification of the political conception of justice, drawing here on certain fundamental ideas which he finds 'implicit' in the contemporary democratic tradition. Next he claims that this political conception will also be endorsed and supported as the focus of an 'overlapping consensus' among the proponents of various comprehensive religious and moral doctrines that exist in the Western world today. Historic utilitarianism is prominently mentioned as one of these doctrines.

But it is doubtful that the utilitarian principle of general happiness could support the assignment of basic rights – constitutionally guaranteed benefits – to individuals if such rights prevented the utilitarian politician from allowing policies favourable to corporate or aggregate interests to override or supersede constitutional rights when those interests could be seen to conduce to greater benefit. In that sense, then, philosophical utilitarianism is incompatible with the notion of basic rights developed by Rawls, Dworkin and others. For utilitarianism cannot possibly accept a critical justification of a scheme of basic institutions in which constitutional civil rights have a standing priority over policies favouring corporate goods or aggregate welfare.

Much hinges, it would seem, then, on how discussion of the critical justification of rights is set up and conducted. And if questions regarding the distribution of rights are best taken up *after* successful or at least plausible attempts at justification, then such issues as what kinds of beings can have rights are seen to hang in the balance as well.

Currently, we find highly agitated discussions about whether foetuses have rights or whether animals can have them or about limits to the right to life (in cases of mercy killing, for example, or in requests for assisted suicide). But a serious attempt to give answers to questions such as these, questions of distribution and of scope and of defeasibility, cannot be clearly addressed until they can be considered in the light of adequate accounts of the function of rights and with one or more substantive theories of critical justification in hand (see ANIMALS AND ETHICS; REPRODUCTION AND ETHICS).

References and further reading

Feinberg, Joel (1973) *Social Philosophy*, Foundations of Philosophy Series. Englewood Cliffs, NJ: Prentice-Hall. (Referred to in §3. Feinberg is probably the leading US writer on the concept of rights; his argument that rights are valid claims has been especially influential. This book is intended for introductory reading by students in political studies. Chs 4–6 are relevant to rights.)

Rawls, John (1993) *Political Liberalism*, New York: Columbia University Press, 2nd edn (expanded), 1996. (Although Rawls here attempts a more conversational style, this book is ultimately no easier than his 1971 book, *Theory of Justice*. Here Rawls attempts to rework his theory of justice as a *political* theory. Also contains, unrevised, his important 1982 essay, 'The Basic Liberties and Their Priority'. Rawls's theory of critical justification is described and criticized in §5.)

Sumner, L. Wayne (1987) *The Moral Foundation of Rights*, Oxford: Oxford University Press. (This well-written book also represents one of the most important attempts to provide a critical justification of rights on a utilitarian basis.)

REX MARTIN

RISK ASSESSMENT

Probabilistic or quantitative risk assessment (QRA) aims to identify, estimate and evaluate a variety of threats to human health and safety. These threats arise primarily from particular technologies (such as commercial nuclear fission) or from environmental impacts (such as deforestation). Defined in terms of the probability that some consequence will occur, 'risk' typically is expressed as the average annual probability of fatality that a particular activity imposes on one individual. For example, because of normal lifetime exposure to dichloromethane (DCM), a multipurpose solvent, the average member of the public has an annual probability of dying from cancer of 0.0000041 or (4.1×10^{-6}). Or, for every million persons exposed to DCM throughout their lifetimes, on average the chemical will cause four cancer deaths each year.

Although risks may be *individual* (such as those from consuming saturated fats) or *societal* (such as those from liquified natural gas facilities), government typically regulates only societal risks. By definition, they are largely involuntarily imposed, whereas individual risks affect only the persons voluntarily choosing them. Most QRAs address societal risks, either because a government seeks a scientific basis for particular risk regulations, because some industry wishes to determine possible liability for its processes or products, or because actual or potential victims want to protect themselves or to allocate risks by means other than market mechanisms.

Philosophical contributions to QRA are of three main types: assessments of particular risks, criticisms of existing assessments, and clarifications of important QRA concepts, methods or theories. Such contributions usually focus on either epistemology (including philosophy of science) or ethics. Epistemological analyses address, for example, the adequacy and appropriateness of some scientific, probabilistic or policy techniques used in QRA; the status of a specific causal hypothesis about risk; or the rationality of alternative decision rules for evaluating risks. Ethical analyses investigate, for instance, the equity of the risk distributions presupposed in a specific QRA or by general QRA methodology; the degree to which a particular method of risk evaluation accounts for crucial social values, such as free informed consent and due process; and the extent to which a given QRA technique, such as discounting the future, begs important ethical questions such as rights of future generations.

See also: CONFIRMATION THEORY; ENVIRONMENTAL ETHICS; OBSERVATION; SCIENTIFIC METHOD

KRISTIN SHRADER-FRECHETTE

ROMAN LAW

Law was Rome's greatest gift to the intellect of modern Europe. Even today the Roman law library, and the achievements of the jurists who built it up, live on in the law of the Continental jurisdictions and of other countries farther afield. It is true that over the past two centuries codification has largely interrupted the long tradition of direct recourse to the Roman materials, but the concepts applied in civilian jurisdictions and the categories of legal thought which they use are still in large measure those of the Roman jurists. In England, perhaps for no better reason than that from the late thirteenth century the judges of the King's Bench and Common Pleas happened to come from a background which cut them off from the clerical education which had given their predecessors access to the Roman library, there was no reception of Roman law. Post-Norman England thus became the second Western society to set about building up a mature law library from scratch. The common law (being the law common to the whole realm of England) and the civil law (being the *ius civile*, the law pertaining to the *civis*, the citizen, initially of course the Roman citizen) thus became the two principal families within the Western legal tradition. It is wrong, however, to suppose that the development of the common law was constantly isolated. There have on the contrary been important points of contact at almost all periods. One result is that the categories of English legal thought are not in fact dissimilar to those of the jurisdictions of continental Europe. The study of Roman law has contributed immeasurably to the idea of a rational

normative order, an idea fundamental to legal philosophy as indeed to all practical philosophy.
See also: LAW, PHILOSOPHY OF

P.B.H. BIRKS

ROMAN STOICISM
See STOICISM

RORTY, RICHARD MCKAY (1931–)

Richard Rorty is a leading US philosopher and public intellectual, and the best-known contemporary advocate of pragmatism. Trained in both analytic and traditional philosophy, he has followed Dewey in attacking the views of knowledge, mind, language and culture that have made both approaches attractive, drawing on arguments and views of the history of philosophy from sources ranging from Heidegger and Derrida to Quine and Wilfrid Sellars. He takes pragmatism to have moved beyond Dewey by learning from analytical philosophy to make 'the linguistic turn', and from Thomas Kuhn that there is no such thing as 'scientific method'. Language and thought are tools for coping, not representations mirroring reality. Rorty's characteristic philosophical positions are what might be called 'anti-isms', positions defined primarily by what they deny. In epistemology he endorses anti-foundationalism, in philosophy of language anti-representationalism, in metaphysics anti-essentialism and anti- both realism *and* antirealism, in meta-ethics ironism. He extols pragmatism as the philosophy that can best clear the road for new ways of thinking which can be used to diminish suffering and to help us find out what we want and how to get it. In the public arena, he is a leading exponent of liberalism and critic of both left and right.
See also: LIBERALISM; PRAGMATISM

MICHAEL DAVID ROHR

ROSENKRANZ, KARL
See HEGELIANISM

ROSMINI-SERBATI, ANTONIO (1797–1855)

In the reactionary, anti-Enlightenment, spiritualistic climate of Italy and Europe in the first decades of the nineteenth century, the Italian philosopher Rosmini set out to elaborate a Christian, Catholic system of philosophy which drew elements from Platonic, Augustinian and Thomist thought, while also taking account of recent philosophical developments, especially Kantian ones, as well as of the new liberal political trends in the culture of the time. His aim was to restore the principle of objectivity in the field of gnoseology, as well as in ethics, law and political thought.

GUIDO VERUCCI
Translated from the Italian
by VIRGINIA COX

ROSS, WILLIAM DAVID (1877–1971)

W.D. Ross was a British ancient and moral philosopher. In terms of his moral thinking, he was a pluralist, who held that there are several distinct moral considerations which bear on the rightness of an action. Among the things we need to take into account are promises we have made, the need to avoid harming others, gratitude to benefactors, and the amount of good our action will produce. That these considerations are morally relevant is something we can know, but which action is the right one is a matter of fallible judgment, because that will depend upon how these considerations are to be weighed against each other in the particular case. Ross' contributions to the study of ancient philosophy mainly concerned Aristotle. He is now best known, however, for his moral philosophy.

See also: INTUITIONISM IN ETHICS

DAVID MCNAUGHTON

ROUSSEAU, JEAN-JACQUES (1712–78)

Introduction

Rousseau was born in Geneva, the second son of Isaac Rousseau, watchmaker. His mother died a few days after his birth. From this obscure beginning he rose to become one of the best-known intellectual figures of the eighteenth-century French Enlightenment, taking his place alongside Diderot, Voltaire and others as one of the emblematic figures of this period, for all that he came to differ violently in view from them. He died in 1778 and in 1794 his body was transferred to the Panthéon in Paris.

Rousseau always maintained that he regretted taking up a career of letters. His first love was music and he composed a number of operas in the 1740s with some success. The turning point in his life occurred in July 1749. He was on his way to see his then friend Diderot who was imprisoned at Vincennes. He read in the newspaper a prize essay question, asking whether advances in the sciences and arts had improved morals. So overcome was he by the flood of ideas that this question aroused in

him, he had to break his journey. The rest of his life's work was, he claimed, determined for him at that moment. Rousseau's primary claim to fame depends on his ideas about morals, politics and society. Perhaps his best-known remark is 'Man is born free; and everywhere he is in chains'; this reveals his preoccupation with issues of freedom in the state.

In answer to the prize essay question Rousseau argued that men and morals were corrupted and debilitated by advances in higher learning. The goal of prestigious distinction is substituted for that of doing useful work for the good of all. This theme, of people seeking invidious ascendancy by doing others down – the effect of exacerbated *amour-propre* – pervades Rousseau's social theorizing generally. His essay, *Discourse on the Sciences and Arts* (1750), won the prize; related concerns shape the more profound *Discourse on the Origin of Inequality* of 1755. In his most famous work of political theory, *The Social Contract* (1762), Rousseau presents an alternative approach to how we might achieve a just and legitimate civil order. All members of society should take an equal place as members of the sovereign authority and societal laws should come from the general will by which a people gives rules to itself. Only under such a system, Rousseau argues, will humankind live on equal terms bound by fraternal ties, enjoying as much freedom and rights of self-determination as is possible in a stable community. Speaking up in this way for the equal political standing of all, regardless of birth or wealth, Rousseau points the way towards the dissolution of the *ancien régime* and the emergence of more democratically based polities. Precisely what influence his ideas had on the French Revolution is impossible to determine, although his name was often invoked.

Rousseau also wrote extensively on education. In his *Émile* (subtitled *On Education*, 1762) he tries to show how a child could be brought up free of the aggressive desire to dominate others. Instead that child can be caused to want to cooperate with others on a footing of mutual respect. He hopes by this to show that his social proposals are not an unrealizable dream. In this work there are also criticisms of religious dogma and church practices which brought severe condemnation onto Rousseau. He had to flee Paris in 1762 to avoid imprisonment. This, and other related experiences, plunged him into a protracted period of mental distress in which he feared he was the object of the plotting of others. These others came to include David Hume, with whom Rousseau had hoped to find refuge in England in 1766.

Still troubled in mind, Rousseau returned to France the next year, and during the last decade of his life he wrote several works of self-explanation and self-justification. The greatest of these is his autobiography, *Confessions* (written between 1764 and 1775, published posthumously), but there are other more prolix writings. After an accident in 1776, the worst of Rousseau's mental disturbance seems to have cleared and his last substantive work, an album of miscellaneous reflections on his life, ideas and experiences (*Reveries of the Solitary Walker*, written 1776–8), has a clarity and balance which had been absent for so long.

1 Life and writings
2 Works leading up to *The Social Contract*
3 *The Social Contract*
4 *Émile* (or *On Education*)
5 Controversial works
6 *La Nouvelle Héloïse* and other literary works
7 Autobiography and other personal works

1 Life and writings

Brought up by his father for the first ten years of his life after the death of his mother, Rousseau traced his love of republican Rome to the reading of Plutarch that he and his father used to do. This love, along with the idolization of his native Geneva, provided the inspiration for many of his political ideas. After being involved in a fight, Rousseau's father fled Geneva in 1722 and Rousseau was sent to live with his cousin not far from Geneva for a couple of years. This period in his youth is exquisitely evoked by Rousseau in Book One of *Confessions* (1764–75). When he returned to Geneva his more lowly social station became apparent and he was indentured to an engraver, Abel Ducommun, a brutal and ill-educated man.

Restless and dissatisfied, Rousseau was more than glad to take advantage of the mischance of being locked out of the city on a Sunday in 1728. He walked away from that life, seeking the help of a Catholic priest who sent him to see Françoise-Louise de la Tour, Baronne de Warens, who was in receipt of money to secure more Catholic converts. She sent him, in turn, to Turin for instruction and Rousseau was admitted to the Church in April 1728. It is doubtful that Rousseau had any deep spiritual involvement in this process; he was more anxious to retain others' interest in him. He had a number of shortlived jobs in Turin. In one of these, he lied about stealing a ribbon and put the blame on a servant girl. This wicked deed preyed on his mind for the rest of his life.

The next year, he made his way back to Madame de Warens. He learned the rudiments of music and his passion for music was a dominant force in his life

at this time. By the autumn of 1731 he had moved in permanently with Madame de Warens. They lived a life of innocent delight for some years, she calling him *petit* and he calling her *maman*. He became her lover in 1733, although he appears never to have enjoyed this almost incestuous relationship. He read avidly during this time, laying a foundation for many of his later writings.

This idyll did not endure, however. Rousseau was displaced in Madame de Warens's affections in 1738. Considerably aggrieved, he took up the post of tutor to the two sons of Jean Bonnot de Mably in Lyons in 1740. Not an adept teacher, he gave up the post after a year, determined to make his way in the larger world of Paris where he moved in 1742 (two short essays on education date from this time).

Once there, he presented a paper on musical notation to the Academy of Sciences; this was published in 1743 as *Dissertation on Modern Music*. In that year, Rousseau went to Venice as secretary to the French Ambassador. They quarrelled and Rousseau returned to Paris to resume his musical compositions. About this time he set up home with his mistress, Thérèse Levasseur, who was to be his lifelong companion. He had a number of children by her, whom he abandoned to his later shame. Rousseau had also begun to keep the company of the rising Parisian intelligensia. DIDEROT was a personal friend and it was while on the way to visit him during one of his periodic bouts of imprisonment that Rousseau had the experience that fixed the course of the rest of his life. The Academy at Dijon had advertised a prize essay question asking whether the advancements in the sciences and arts had improved morals. Rousseau saw this and was so overwhelmed by a flood of insights evoked by it that (he said) he spent the rest of his life trying to put into words what he had seen in one hour. Rousseau, answering the question with a firm 'No', won the prize and his essay was published in 1750 under the title *Discourse on the Sciences and Arts*. He was poised to begin a new career as social critic, moralist and philosopher, but his last triumphs as a composer and musical theoretician also occur about this time. His opera *Le Devin du Village* was performed before the King at Fontainebleau in 1752 and his *Letter on French Music* (1753) created an enormous stir as part of a large-scale argument over the relative merits of the French and Italian styles.

Rousseau was soon to turn his back on Parisian society. He wrote a further, very original, essay on social questions, *Discourse on the Origin of Inequality* (1755) but then withdrew to the countryside the better to meditate and write about his new concerns, attracting the scorn of many of his erstwhile friends. Around this time he returned to the Protestant faith of his childhood, and reclaimed his citizenship of Geneva. The *Discourse on the Origin of Inequality* has a passionate dedication to Geneva.

During the next six years, Rousseau wrote the bulk of his greatest work: his masterpiece of educational theory, *Émile* (1762); of political theory, *The Social Contract* (1762); but also a best-selling novel, *La Nouvelle Héloïse* (1761) and a host of smaller pieces: the *Letter to M. d'Alembert on the Theatre* (1758); the *Letter to Voltaire on Providence* (1756), the *Moral Letters* (1757–8), written to Sophie d'Houdetot with whom Rousseau was then desperately in love.

Catastrophe befell Rousseau in 1762 after the publication of *Émile*. A section of it, the so-called *Creed of a Savoyard Vicar*, was judged unacceptable by the religious authorities and out of fear of being imprisoned Rousseau fled Paris in June 1762. Unsettled years followed, mostly spent in different parts of Switzerland. Rousseau wrote extensively in defence of himself and his work during this time, including his *Letter to Christophe de Beaumont, Archbishop of Paris* (1763) written in reply to the condemnation of the *Creed of a Savoyard Vicar*; and his *Lettres Écrites de la Montagne* (Letters Written from the Mountain) (1764), a response to criticism of him made by Geneva's attorney-general. From January 1766 Rousseau spent just over a year in England at the invitation and in the company of David HUME. Rousseau, almost always a touchy and suspicious person, was at that time in the grip of a severe paranoiac breakdown and he became convinced Hume was plotting to humiliate him. An account of this sorry episode was given by Hume (*A Concise Account*, 1766). Exhausted and ill, Rousseau returned to France in early 1767 and sought refuge well away from the public gaze near Grenoble where he married Thérèse.

The tide of public opinion was slowly turning, and in 1770 he returned to Paris very much a celebrated figure and object of curiosity, even though he was banned from writing and speaking on controversial matters. Despite his grave mental distress, Rousseau had, from around 1764, been working on his great autobiography, *Confessions*. He completed part one by 1770. He gave some private readings of parts of the text; these also were banned. Other personal works occupied the bulk of the last decade of his life. There is an extensive essay in self-justification and defence, *Rousseau Judge of Jean-Jacques: Dialogues* (1772–6). Its completion was marked by another episode of desperate mental anguish as Rousseau attempted to place the manuscript on the altar at Nôtre Dame. Later in 1776, returning home from a walk, Rousseau was knocked down by a dog. This accident seems, miraculously, to have cleared his mind and his last

work, *Reveries of the Solitary Walker* (1776–8), has a simplicity and clarity of manner missing from the writings of the preceding years.

Not all his work was in self-vindication however. He wrote at length on the political problems of Poland (*Considerations on the Government of Poland*) (1769–70), prepared a *Dictionary of Music* (1767) and botanized extensively, also writing some short works on the topic (*Elementary Letters on Botany* and *Dictionary of Botanical Terms*, uncompleted). He died at Ermenonville in June 1778, outlived by Thérèse for twenty-two years.

It is useful to give more information about Rousseau's life than is usual for most philosophers or political theorists, since so much of his work arises from events in his life or is directly about himself. This is, however, not so true of his principal works of social and political theory, just because they are works more purely of theory. They provide the most solid basis for Rousseau's reputation, and an account of these follows.

2 Works leading up to The Social Contract

From 1750 onwards, Rousseau developed increasingly deeper and more sophisticated ideas about the origin and nature of the condition of man in society and about what could and should be done to ameliorate that condition. His discussion of these themes in his first serious work, *Discourse on the Sciences and Arts*, is fairly shallow. He argues that increasing scientific knowledge and refinement of arts and letters does not at all produce an improvement of morals either in individuals or in society at large. On the contrary, such sophistication is the offshoot of luxury and idleness and it has developed principally to feed people's vanity and desire for ostentatious and aggressive self-display. All these features work against the moral virtues of loyalty to one's country, courage in its defence and dedication to useful callings. Rousseau allows for the fact that there are a few people of genius who genuinely enrich humanity by their ideas. But the majority of us are not improved, but harmed, by exposure to the 'higher learning'.

This essay attracted considerable notice and a number of replies, to which Rousseau responded with care. But he did not continue immediately with his works of social criticism. His musical interests intervened, although with some of these his social and moral ideas became entwined. In his *Letter on French Music* (1753), Rousseau criticizes French music as monotonous, thin and without colour because the spoken language (in which all music is rooted) is thus also. This is because, as Rousseau explains in his *Essay on the Origin of Languages* (1755–60, but never completed), the

French language has been shaped by the imperatives of calling for help and controlling other people, which require harshness and clarity above all else. In warmer southern climes it is the sweet accents of love and passion which colour the language hence the supremacy of Italian opera. Thus social and political demands shape even the nature of music, according to Rousseau. Effective government also requires sharp, impressive utterance, he maintains, and it is to the origin and function of government that Rousseau turns in his so-called second *Discourse*, the *Discourse on the Origin and Foundations of Inequality*, to give it its full title. This is a very substantial essay and one of Rousseau's most important works.

In *Discourse on the Origin and Foundations of Inequality* Rousseau gives an account of the 'fall' of natural humankind, its degeneration and corruption as it joins together with others to make up tribes, societies and eventually states. Natural man (the 'noble savage') left alone in his natural environment is self-sufficient, largely absorbed in present feeling without foresight or recollection, solitary, peaceable and, in fact, most often asleep. (Rousseau may well have had the orang-utan in view here.) Inclement circumstances, increase in numbers (arising from hasty couplings in the forest devoid of all the artificial trappings of romantic love), force people to live together. Sexual jealousy, the desire for domination, vindictive resentments grow up as men come to demand esteem and deference. *Amour-propre*, an anxious concern for tribute to be paid to one's status, replaces *amour de soi*, a simple healthy concern for one's own natural wellbeing. Men begin to compete for precedence and life is tainted by aggression and spite. Those who have acquired dominance then conspire together to consolidate their position. They argue that everyone needs a more peaceable and stable society, which can only be achieved through the apparatus of government, law, punishments. Thus it is that they consolidate the *status quo*, but without right or justice and acting only to perpetuate unfair privilege and the oppression of the weak.

This extraordinarily subversive essay seems to have attracted no official censure; that came later in connection with other works. Rousseau's other significant essay on political themes from this period is the so-called *Discourse on Political Economy*(1755, first published separately 1758), which began life as an entry for Diderot and D'Alembert's *Encyclopaedia* (1751–72). A very eloquently written piece, it shows clear signs of being a preliminary study for *The Social Contract*. Much play is made with the idea of the sovereignty of all the people over themselves, expressing their legislative intent through the general will. Emphasis is laid on the need to cultivate patriotic republican loyalties in citizens if a just society of equals united by common care and respect is ever to arise and to survive. The essay ends with a discussion of taxation and fiscal issues, but the principal force of the argument lies in the discussion of the source of legitimate law in 'the people'. It is this same issue which Rousseau places at the centre of his now most famous work, *The Social Contract*.

3 The Social Contract

This work is generally regarded as an essential entry in the canon of classic works in political theory and as Rousseau's masterpiece. Many people read nothing else of his. This is a pity, for many of the themes in it are rendered unnecessarily hard to understand by being taken in isolation. Also, the work is in some ways poorly constructed and uses idea drawn from different times in Rousseau's development. As he says in a prefatory note to the work, it is the only residue remaining of a project begun many years before. However, we must take the work as we find it. Its present reputation would perhaps have surprised contemporary readers. *Émile* was considered a more seditious work; and *La Nouvelle Héloïse* regarded as the most perfect exhibition of Rousseau's genius. Certainly Hume regarded Rousseau's own good opinion of *The Social Contract* as quite absurd.

The Social Contract is divided into four parts. Roughly speaking, Book One concerns the proper basis for the foundation of a legitimate political order; Book Two the origin and functions of the sovereign body within that order; Book Three considers the role of government, which Rousseau treats as a subsidiary body in the state deriving its powers from the sovereign; and Book Four considers more issues regarding a just society, treating of the Roman republic at some length and of the functions of civil religion. It is important always to remember that the book is subtitled: *The Principles of Political Right*. Rousseau's paramount concerns are normative, with the nature and basis of legitimacy, justice and right and not simply with *de facto* political structures. A useful brief summary of the principal themes of the work is given in Book Five of *Émile*, as part of Émile's political education.

Rousseau argues that it is our lack of individual self-sufficiency that requires us to associate together in society. But, when we do so, we do not want to have to accept a condition of enslavement as the price of our survival. Freedom is an essential human need and the mark of humanity; mere survival without that does not constitute a human life. Rousseau holds that freedom and association can only be combined if all the persons of the association make up the sovereign body for that association, that is, the final authoritative body which declares the law by which the people wish to bind themselves. This law is a declaration of the 'general will'.

The notion of the general will is wholly central to Rousseau's theory of political legitimacy (see GENERAL WILL). It is, however, an unfortunately obscure and controversial notion. Some commentators see it as no more than the dictatorship of the proletariat or the tyranny of the urban poor (such as may perhaps be seen in the French Revolution). Such was not Rousseau's meaning. This is clear from the *Discourse on Political Economy* where Rousseau emphasizes that the general will exists to protect individuals against the mass, not to require them to be sacrificed to it. He is, of course, sharply aware that men have selfish and sectional interests which will lead them to try to oppress others. It is for this reason that loyalty to the good of all alike must be a supreme (although not exclusive) commitment by everyone, not only if a truly general will is to be heeded, but also if it is to be formulated successfully in the first place.

This theme is taken up in Book Two. Here Rousseau appeals to the charisma of a quasi-divine legislator to inspire people to put the good of their whole community above their own narrow selfish interest and thereby gain a greater good for themselves. In the course of this Book, Rousseau alludes to Corsica as having a people who have the sentiments and capacities to establish just laws and a good state (Book Two, ch. 10). His passing remark that 'I have the feeling that some day that little island will astonish Europe' has caused some fancifully to suppose that he foresaw the emergence of Napoléon.

Book Three of *The Social Contract* concerns the role of government. Rousseau knows that governors often rule in their own interest, not in the interests of their community. For this reason he argues that governmental functions must be thoroughly subordinate to the sovereign judgment of the people and that it is essential to adjust the form and powers of government to suit the different circumstances (size, dispersion and so on) of different states. It still surprises some readers that Rousseau has no particular enthusiasm for democratic government. Of course, the constitution and functions of the sovereign body are a different matter.

Book Four has something of a disjointed character. Rousseau discusses the Roman republic at considerable length, principally to hold it up as a model from which, in his opinion, there has been a terrible falling away. But he also discusses civil religion, arguing that divine sanctions should be joined to civil laws the better to procure obedience

to them and people's loyalty to the common good of all in their nation.

Rousseau made wholly central to his vision of political right the union of free and equal men devising for themselves the laws under which they shall then proceed to live their lives as citizens one with another of their own state. In doing so he depicted a form of political community which exerts a very great appeal and influence on the modern imagination. We are still learning to live with the consequences of that appeal.

Rousseau's political concerns were not confined to theory alone. On two occasions he was approached for help with the political affairs and constitutional problems of countries. In 1764 he wrote an unfinished fragment, *Project for a Constitution for Corsica*, in response to a plea for help and guidance from the Corsican rebels. Then again, in 1769–70, Rousseau wrote extensively on the constitutional and legislative problems facing Poland (*Considerations on the Government of Poland*) in response to a request from persons opposed to Russian domination. This work (not properly published in Rousseau's lifetime) is a substantial essay which throws a lot of light on how Rousseau envisaged his theoretical notions working out in historically specific situations. He reveals many shrewd and hard-headed practical insights.

4 Émile (*or* On Education)

There is some evidence that Rousseau regarded *Émile* as his most mature and well-achieved work. In his self-evaluating *Rousseau Judge of Jean-Jacques: Dialogues* (1772–6) he specifies it as the book in which someone who is truly concerned to understand him will find his ideas most deeply and comprehensively expressed. Posterity has, perhaps unfortunately, not generally endorsed this evaluation.

Precisely when he began work on *Émile* is unclear, but it must have been around 1759 when Rousseau was at the peak of his creative powers. Its immediate occasion seems to have been a request from certain of his distinguished women friends to give them his advice about the upbringing of their children; and indeed, the subtitle of the book is *On Education*. However, within this framework Rousseau gives us his deepest ideas about the origins of human evil and wickedness and about the prospects for a whole and happy life.

Émile is structured as the narrative of the upbringing of a young man (Émile himself) who is to be spared the pain and loss of human corruption but made whole and entire by following the teachings of 'nature'. The work also includes in Book Four a long more-or-less self-contained essay on the basis and nature of religious belief, called the *Creed of a Savoyard Vicar*. Rousseau puts his religious ideas into the mouth of a fictitious priest, although one modelled on priests he had previously known. It was this section which attracted the condemnation of the Catholic authorities and led to the burning of the book in June 1762. Rousseau then fled Paris, condemned to almost ten years of distress and displacement. He wrote at some length in defence of these religious ideas, in his *Letter to Christophe de Beaumont, Archbishop of Paris* of 1763 (see §5).

Rousseau held that most men and women in contemporary society were corrupted and their lives deformed because of the nature and basis of their social relationships and of the civil order (see §2). That man is good by nature, but is perverted by society, is perhaps the dominant theme of *Émile*. Thus, if a person is to live a whole and rewarding life they must first be protected from such damaging influences and then be given the personal resources and emotional and moral dispositions to enable them to develop in a creative, harmonious and happy way once they do enter society. The principal discussions in *Émile* are devoted to studying the deepest causes of health or sickness in human development, both those internal to the individual and those coming from external influences, at each stage in the growth and maturation of a person from infancy to adulthood.

In early life it is the tendency to imperious rage and the petulant demand for others' immediate compliance to one's wishes that must be checked. Children must certainly not be tormented, but neither must they be indulged since that gives rise to both misplaced expectations and to even less capacity to cope with setbacks. Children need to be treated in a steady, predictable and methodical way, as if not in contact with other humans at all at first. Thus they learn to manage in a practical and efficacious way with concrete issues and not to engage in a battle of wills and in contention for dominance.

This motif of living according to nature – that is, according to the actualities of our powers and real circumstances – continues as Émile matures. As and when he needs to find a place for himself in society he will not try to control all that is around him and be aggrieved if he cannot as if he were a despot. Rather, he will seek to establish relations grounded in friendship, mutual respect and cooperation proper to finite and needy beings. Our capacity to feel compassion for each other and our acceptance of compassion with gratitude forms, in Rousseau's view, the fundamental basis for human union and the true explanation of the Golden Rule. Real moral demands are not imposed on us from outside,

nor are they precepts discovered by reason. Rather, they express the requirements by which a bond of creative respect can be sustained between equals. This same issue of maintaining self-possession and mutual respect shapes Rousseau's treatment of marriage and sexual relations in Book Five. Such intimate union holds out the greatest hopes of human happiness, but can also lead to enslavement to the whims of the beloved. Feminist critics have found Rousseau's depiction of the character and role of Émile's intended, Sophie, objectionable, in that she appears to be stereotyped as largely passive and destined for traditional domestic occupations.

In the controversial material on religious belief Rousseau argues that we know God not by reason, but through simple feelings and convictions much deeper and more permanent than any theorems of reason. Such feelings teach us that the world is animated by a loving and powerful intelligence, who is God. Rousseau spends some time denouncing religious factionalism and intolerance which he sees as wholly incompatible with Christ's message of love and forgiveness. There can be no serious doubt that these are Rousseau's own thoughts. The rhetorical distance provided by the figure of the vicar is very slight.

In his deep and subtle psychological insights into the damage aggression does, not just simply to the victims of aggression, but in a complex and concealed way to the aggressors themselves, Rousseau shows the greatness of his mind in *Émile*.

5 Controversial works

Rousseau did not take the condemnation of the *Creed of a Savoyard Vicar* lightly. Almost as soon as he had settled again after his flight from Paris, he wrote a lengthy reply to the criticism of his work made by Christophe de Beaumont, Archbishop of Paris. Written in the form of a letter, Rousseau defends the fundamental tenets of his work. He has always held, he says, that man is naturally good, but corrupted by society. It is therefore a mystery why his work should only now be singled out for condemnation. He then mounts a point-by-point reply to the Archbishop's criticisms, arguing that the religion of the priests and the dogmas of the Church must never be confused with the true gospel of charity and love taught by Christ. This *Letter to Christophe de Beaumont, Archbishop of Paris* was published in 1763. It ends on a note of self-aggrandizement. So far from being reviled, Rousseau says, statues of himself should be erected throughout Europe.

Just a year later, Rousseau published his extensive *Lettres Écrites de la Montagne* (Letters Written from the Mountain). In 1763, the Genevan attorney-general, Jean-Robert Tronchin, had written in defence of the authorities in their condemnation of Rousseau's works in his *Letters Written from the Country* (hence Rousseau's oppositional title). Rousseau again replies at length, arguing that the Geneval political system had become very corrupt, but also defending once more the basic principles of his thought.

These two works date from the period just after the condemnation of Rousseau's most famous works. But prior to that he had also been engaged in some controversial exchanges. In 1758 he wrote the *Letter to M. d'Alembert on the Theatre* in which he argues that to establish a theatre in Geneva would corrupt the honest morals and civil integrity of that city-state. This was in opposition to d'Alembert's argument, presented in an article on Geneva for the *Encyclopaedia*, that a theatre would improve the cultural life of that city. However, such sophistication is not a benefit, in Rousseau's opinion; it goes along with deceit and the abandonment of morally commendable activities. Rousseau writes with great verve in this essay, harking back to some of his themes in his first discourse, *Discourse on the Sciences and Arts*.

A similar clash between urbane civilization and (what Rousseau liked to see as his own) plainness and simplicity of heart occurs in the exchange with VOLTAIRE on the providence of God (written in 1756; Voltaire may also have been an influence on d'Alembert). Voltaire, in his poem on the Lisbon earthquake, had written scornfully of Leibnizian optimism that all is for the best in the best of all possible worlds. Rousseau retorts that one must rest one's certainty of God's providence in feeling, not on the subtleties of philosophical reasoning. More personally, he says that it is surprising to find the wealthy and successful Voltaire complaining against God when he, Rousseau, who lives in poverty and obscurity, sees only the blessings of existence. This *Letter to Voltaire on Providence* also makes some very sharp points against religious intolerance, prefiguring the ideas of the *Creed of a Savoyard Vicar*. Rousseau's controversial writings are among his most eloquent, even though they do not generally add much to our appreciation of his overall intellectual achievement.

6 La Nouvelle Héloïse *and other literary works*

Outside the narrow circle of the intelligensia and his aristocratic patrons, Rousseau was probably best known during his lifetime for his novel of illicit passion, reconciliation and self-transcendence, *Julie, ou La Nouvelle Héloïse*. At a time when works in different genres were not so sharply compartmentalized, David Hume for one saw in this novel the most perfect expression of Rousseau's genius and could not understand why Rousseau seemed to value *The Social Contract* more.

Rousseau professed himself surprised and dismayed to be writing the work. In 1756 he had turned his back on the hot-house world of fashionable Parisian society, wishing to dedicate the rest of his life to working for the good of humankind. However, as he took solitary walks in the forest of Montmorency, be became absorbed in an imaginary world of passion and illicit love. In a fever of erotic ecstasy he wrote the first of the letters between Julie, her tutor-lover Saint-Preux and her friend and cousin Claire. Saint-Preux confesses his love for Julie; a love which she tries to fend off through intimate conversations instructing him to be virtuous and pure. Of course, this does not work and she finally gives herself over to him in a passion. But her father has other plans for her. She is betrothed to the Baron de Wolmar; Saint-Preux leaves and not until much later does he return to become tutor once more, but now to Julie's two young sons. Wolmar (who has come to know of their earlier intimacy), leaves Julie and Saint-Preux alone on his model estate at Clarens. Saint-Preux confesses that he had never ceased to love Julie, but the novel ends tragically with the death of Julie, who has contracted pneumonia after having saved one of her children from drowning.

As Rousseau wrote this work nature seemed to imitate art. Sophie d'Houdetot, the sister-in-law of Madame d'Épinay whose house Rousseau was then living in, visited him and Rousseau fell in love with her. He saw in her the incarnation of his imaginary Julie. The relationship did not endure. Rousseau became morbidly suspicious that his middle-aged love was being mocked behind his back by his erstwhile friends.

La Nouvelle Héloïse was published in 1761 and was a bestseller. It is seldom read these days, except to be mined for ideas which might illuminate Rousseau's social and political philosophy. Wolmar's model estate is sometimes argued to be Rousseau's own vision of an ideal community, with rigid paternalistic control and substantial manipulation of the inhabitants by the all-seeing, all-knowing Wolmar. It is scarcely clear that this was Rousseau's intention. The fact that Julie dies, despite living at Clarens, may be taken to imply that it provides no adequate human habitation.

The rest of Rousseau's literary output is slight. It includes a number of mostly short poems, dating from the early 1740s, some plays (also mostly early), one of which, *Narcissus* (Self-Lover), received performance in 1752 and for which Rousseau wrote a substantial preface explaining how his theatrical writing could be squared with his then political and social polemic against civilized letters.

7 Autobiography and other personal works

The last ten or so years of Rousseau's life were primarily given over to the writing of works of autobiography and other substantial essays of self-explanation and justification. These were presaged in his four *Letters to Malesherbes* written in 1762, just before the catastrophe of the banning of *Émile* and *The Social Contract*. Malesherbes, although official censor and likely to be suspicious of Rousseau's subversive ideas, in fact took a highly intelligent and sympathetic interest in his work. Rousseau became fearful that the printing of *Émile* was being held up by Jesuit plotting. Through Madame de Luxembourg, Malesherbes was contacted and able to put Rousseau's mind to rest. Rousseau expressed his gratitude by writing to Malesherbes four semi-confessional letters, setting out the principal events of his life and trying to make his motives and character plain to Malesherbes. Rousseau writes that he is not a misanthrope; he seeks the country only because he can live there more freely and fully as himself. He wants, in fact, nothing more than to serve humankind, but he can best do this by keeping himself apart and not getting embroiled in quarrels and back-stabbing.

Around this time Rousseau began to assemble materials towards writing an autobiography. He worked on and off at this until 1767, by which time part one of what we now know as *Confessions* was completed. This still extraordinary work of self-disclosure and candour is one of the most remarkable books ever written. It includes some beautiful writing about childhood and about his travels, but also revelations of a most intimate and shameful kind. Part one covers the period up to 1741–2, when Rousseau left Madame de Warens to make his way in Paris. Part two (1769–70) is less successful. Rousseau's morbid fears sometimes surface here as he describes the events of the years 1742–65, including his foolish passion for Sophie d'Houdetot, the writing and publication of *Émile*, and so on. The book breaks off in 1765, just as Rousseau is about to leave for England in the company of Hume, there (he believed) further to be ensnared. As the revelation of the quality of being of another human soul, *Confessions* is almost without equal.

Another lengthy work of self-explanation is *Rousseau Judge of Jean-Jacques: Dialogues* (published, like *Confessions*, posthumously). This is in three parts, cast in the form of dialogues between 'Rousseau' and 'a Frenchman', who together try to delve beneath the surface to find out the true nature of 'Jean-Jacques', the real Rousseau. The

innumerable lies put about regarding Jean-Jacques are considered and exposed in the first part; in the second, a visit is paid to him and his true character is revealed; in the third part, a careful reading of his works is made and their true meaning explained. Although sometimes obsessively detailed and very repetitive, this work has considerable interest for the light it throws on Rousseau's own estimate of his achievement. The overall tone is, it is thought, marred by lengthy self-justification.

Rousseau's last work of self-accounting is *Reveries of the Solitary Walker* (left unfinished at his death). Cast in the form of 'Walks', it comprises a series of reflections, ideas and meditations which supposedly occurred to Rousseau as he went on his perambulations in and around Paris. Rousseau returns to special moments in his life – his love for Mme de Warens; the episode of the stolen ribbon; his 'illumination' on the way to see Diderot. But he also reflects for one last time on some of his major intellectual preoccupations – on the depth of *amour-propre*; on the sources of malice; and on the nature of happiness. There is a clear steadiness of vision which pervades this work which contrasts markedly with the often distressed and distressing writing of the preceding five years.

After his death, Rousseau's grave on the Île des Peupliers at Ermenonville became a place of pilgrimage for Parisians and Rousseau was embraced as one of the great sons of France. His influence remains very great, not only because of his political writings which have become part of the permanent canon of works in political theory, but also because of his more imponderable effect on sensibility and attitudes. His love of nature and stress on the value of the simple life, as well as his far-reaching explorations of his own character and feelings, make him a central figure in the development of romanticism. The emphasis in his educational writings on discouraging the coercion of the child into tasks which are apparently pointless undoubtedly influenced the work of Montessori and A.S. Neill. Even Rousseau's musical writings and compositions, seldom studied these days, made a marked impact on the history of opera in particular. His place as one of the major figures of Western civilization is secure, even though he can still attract violent differences of opinion.

See also: CONTRACTARIANISM; ENLIGHTENMENT, CONTINENTAL; POLITICAL PHILOSOPHY, HISTORY OF; SOCIETY, CONCEPT OF

References and further reading

Cole, G.D.H. (ed. and trans.) (1973) *The Social Contract and Discourses*, London: Dent. (Revised and augmented by J.H. Brumfitt and J.C. Hall.

Contains principal writings on political theory; an excellent selection in English.)

Dent, N.J.H. (1988) *Rousseau*, Oxford: Blackwell. (Covers most of the psychological and political works.)

Grimsley, R. (ed.) (1970) *Rousseau: Religious Writings*, Oxford: Clarendon Press. (Selected works in French.)

NICHOLAS DENT

ROYCE, JOSIAH (1855–1916)

Josiah Royce rose from a humble background in the California of the Gold Rush period to become Professor of the History of Philosophy at Harvard University and one of the most influential American philosophers of the so-called 'period of classical American philosophy' from the late nineteenth to the early twentieth century. He was also (along with F.H. Bradley) one of the two most important English-speaking philosophers of the period who defended philosophical idealism: the doctrine that in some sense or other all things either are minds or else are the contents of minds. Royce remained loyal to his own idealist commitments throughout his life, despite the fact that his friend and Harvard colleague William James was extremely hostile to idealism, and that his intellectual environment was increasingly dominated by the 'pragmatism' of which James was an outspoken champion. In later years, however, under the influence of another pragmatist, Charles S. Peirce, Royce gave the themes of his idealist thought a naturalistic social foundation rather than the abstract metaphysical foundation of his earliest writings. Royce's entire corpus is perhaps best seen as representing a bridge from the German world of Neo-Kantianism and various varieties of philosophical idealism to the American world of pragmatism and of philosophical naturalism.

See also: ABSOLUTE, THE; HEGELIANISM; PRAGMATISM

ROBERT W. BURCH

RULE OF LAW (RECHTSSTAAT)

The 'rule of law' most simply expresses the idea that everyone is subject to the law, and should therefore obey it. Governments in particular are to obey law – to govern under, or in accordance with, law. The rule of law thus requires constitutional government, and constitutes a shield against tyranny or arbitrary rule: political rulers and their agents (police and so on) must exercise power under legal constraints, respecting accepted constitutional limits. The British and US conceptions of this ideal find a parallel in the Germanic concept of the *Rechtsstaat*, or 'state-under-law', where the state as an organized entity is conceived to be limited by laws and by fundamental principles of legality, rather than being a purely political organization that can dispense with law in the interests of policy. Such concepts play an essential part in the political philosophy of liberalism; yet, characteristically, their more detailed exposition and indeed their nature and meaning are contested and controversial.

In a wider sense, the rule of law articulates values of procedural fairness or due process which affect the *form* of legal rules and govern the manner of their application. Those values both enhance the utility of legal regulation and also acknowledge underlying ideas of human dignity and autonomy. In a further sense, the rule of law refers to the faithful application of those rules and principles which constitute the law of a particular legal system. It expresses the idea that legal obligation should always be determined in particular cases by analysis of existing law – as opposed to *ad hoc* legislation by judges – even where disagreement may exist about the true meaning or content of the law.

The connection between the rule of law and justice is complex. The rule of law cannot itself guarantee justice, but it forms an essential precondition. In so far as it imposes formal constraints on the laws enacted or enforced, which ensure that they are capable of being obeyed and that they are fairly administered, the rule of law assumes a conception of moral personality – of how individuals should be treated, as responsible human beings, capable of a sense of justice – which links the idea with the values of freedom and autonomy, and the ideal of equality.

See also: LAW, PHILOSOPHY OF; SOCIAL THEORY AND LAW

T.R.S. ALLAN

RULES AND LANGUAGE
See MEANING AND RULE-FOLLOWING

RUSSELL, BERTRAND ARTHUR WILLIAM (1872–1970)

Bertrand Russell divided his efforts between philosophy and political advocacy on behalf of a variety of radical causes. He did his most important philosophical work in logic and the philosophy of mathematics between 1900 and 1913, though later he also did important work in epistemology, metaphysics and the philosophy of mind, and continued to contribute to philosophy until the late 1950s. He wrote relatively little on ethics. His political work went on until his death in 1970.

In the philosophy of mathematics Russell's position was logicism, the view that all of mathematics can be derived from logical premises, which he attempted to establish in detail by actual derivations, creating in the process what is essentially now the standard formulation of classical logic. Early in this work he discovered the self-referential paradoxes which posed the main difficulty for logicism and which he eventually overcame by the ramified theory of types.

Logic was central to Russell's philosophy from 1900 onwards, and much of his fertility and importance as a philosopher came from his application of the new logic to old problems. Among his most important logical innovations were the modern theory of relations and the theory of descriptions. The latter enabled him to re-parse sentences containing the phrase 'the so-and-so' into a form in which the phrase did not appear. The importance of this theory for subsequent philosophy was that it enabled one to recast sentences which apparently committed one to the existence of the so-and-so into sentences in which no such commitment was suggested. This laid the basis for a new method in metaphysics (widely pursued by Russell and others in the first half of the century) in which theories about items of a given kind are reformulated so as to avoid reference to items of that kind.

Logicism itself offers just such a treatment of mathematics and in his later work Russell used the method repeatedly, though the reformulations he suggested were rarely so explicit as the ones he had offered in mathematics. In 1914 he proposed a solution to the problem of the external world by constructing matter out of sensibilia. After 1918 he proposed to construct both mind and matter out of events. After 1940 he treated all particulars as bundles of qualities. In each case his motivation was to avoid postulating anything that could be constructed, thereby eliminating ontological commitments which had no independent evidential support. Outside mathematics, his starting-point was the empirically given and he attempted to make his constructions depend as little as possible upon items not given in experience. He was not, however, a strict empiricist, since he did not think that empirical evidence alone would be sufficient for the constructions and he was always prepared to supplement it in order to obtain them. He wanted to construct, not those items which were empirically warranted, but those which were required by the relevant scientific theories, for he regarded science as the best available, though by no means an infallible, source of truth. The task, in each case, was therefore to reveal the least amount of apparatus that would have to be assumed in addition to the empirical data in order for the constructions required by science to be possible. This methodology, which he pursued throughout his career, gives an underlying unity to what, more superficially, appears as a series of abrupt changes of position.

See also ANALYTICAL PHILOSOPHY; IDEALISM §§5, 7; LOGICISM; MONISM; MOORE, G.E.

NICHOLAS GRIFFIN

RUSSIAN PHILOSOPHY

Introduction

Russian thought is best approached without fixed preconceptions about the nature and proper boundaries of philosophy. Conditions of extreme political oppression and economic backwardness are not conducive to the flowering of philosophy as a purely theoretical discipline; academic philosophy was hence a latecomer on the Russian scene, and those (such as the Neo-Kantians of the end of the nineteenth century) who devoted themselves to questions of ontology and epistemology were widely condemned for their failure to address the country's pressing social problems. Since Peter the Great's project of Westernization, Russian philosophy has been primarily the creation of writers and critics who derived their ideals and values from European sources and focused on ethics, social theory and the philosophy of history, in the belief that (as Marx put it in the first 'Thesis on Feuerbach') philosophers had hitherto merely interpreted the world: the task was now to change it. This passionate social commitment generated much doctrinaire fanaticism, but it also inspired the iconoclastic tendency made philosophically respectable by Nietzsche: the revaluation of values from an ironic outsider's perspective. The principal contribution of Russian thinkers to world culture has so far consisted not in systems, but in experiments in the theory and practice of human emancipation. Some of these led to the Russian Revolution, while others furnished remarkably accurate predictions of the nature of utopia in power. Like Dostoevskii's character Shigalëv who, starting from the ideal of absolute freedom, arrived by a strict logical progression at the necessity of absolute despotism, Russian philosophers have specialized in thinking through (and sometimes acting out) the practical implications of the most seductive visions of liberty that Europe has produced over the last 200 years.

1 The development of Russian philosophy

What Berdiaev called the 'Russian Idea' – the eschatological quest that is the most distinctive feature of Russian philosophy – can be explained in terms of Russian history. The Mongol yoke from the twelfth to the fourteenth century cut Russia off from Byzantium (from which it had received Christianity) and from Europe: it had no part in the ferment of the Renaissance. Its rise as a unified state under the Moscow Tsardom followed closely on the fall of the Orthodox Byzantine Empire, and the emerging sense of Russian national identity incorporated a messianic element in the form of the monk Philotheus' theory of Moscow as the 'Third Rome', successor to Rome and Constantinople as guardian of Christ's truth in its purity. 'There will not be a fourth', ran the prophecy: the Russian Empire would last until the end of the world. Russian thought remained dominated by the Greek patristic tradition until the eighteenth century, when the Kievan thinker Skovoroda (sometimes described as Russia's first philosopher) developed a religious vision based on a synthesis of ancient and patristic thought. He had no following however; by the mid-century Russia's intellectual centre was St Petersburg, where Catherine the Great, building on the achievements of her predecessor Peter, sought to promote a Western secular culture among the educated elite with the aid of French Enlightenment ideas. But representatives of the 'Russian Enlightenment' were severely punished when they dared to cite the *philosophes'* concepts of rationality and justice in criticism of the political status quo. The persecution of advanced ideas (which served to strengthen the nascent intelligentsia's self-image as the cultural and moral leaders of their society) reached its height under Nicolas I (1825–55), when philosophy departments were closed in the universities and thought went underground. Western ideas were the subject of intense debate in small informal circles of students, writers and critics, the most famous of which in Moscow and St Petersburg furnished the philosophical education of such intellectual leaders as the future socialists Herzen and Bakunin, the novelist and liberal Ivan Turgenev, the literary critic Belinskii (from whose 'social criticism' Soviet Socialist Realism claimed descent), and the future Slavophile religious philosophers Kireevskii and Khomiakov. As a critic has noted: 'In the West there is theology and there is philosophy; Russian thought, however, is a third concept'; one which (in the tsarist intellectual underground as in its Soviet successor) embraced novelists, poets, critics, religious and political thinkers – all bound together by their commitment to the goals of freedom and justice.

In the 1830s these beleaguered individuals encountered German idealism: an event of decisive significance for the future development of Russian thought. The teleological structures of idealist thought provided Russian intellectuals with a redemptive interpretation of their conflicts and struggles as a necessary stage in the dialectical movement of history towards a transcendent state of harmony. Idealism (notably in its Hegelian forms) left its mark on the vocabulary of subsequent Russian philosophy, but its principal legacy was the belief, shared by the vast majority of Russian thinkers, that an 'integral worldview', a coherent and unified vision of the historical process and its goal, was the essential framework both for personal moral development and social theorizing. The question of history's goal became a matter for intense debate among the intelligentsia with the publication in 1836 of Chaadaev's 'Philosophical Letter', which posed Russia's relationship to the West as a central philosophical problem, maintaining that Russia's historical separation from the culture of Western Christianity precluded its participation in the movement of history towards the establishment of a universal Christian society. Chaadaev's version of the march of progress was much indebted to French Catholic conservatism, while the nationalist riposte to his ideas drew heavily on the Romantics' critique of the Age of Reason and Schelling's organic conception of nationhood: the Slavophiles held that Western culture was in a state of terminal moral and social decline, suffering from an excess of rationalism, which had led to social atomization and the fragmentation of the individual psyche. These divisions could be healed only by religious faith in its purest form, Russian Orthodoxy, whose spirit of organic 'togetherness', uncontaminated by Western rationalism, they presented as a model for Russian society and a beacon for mankind. They thereby laid the foundations of a distinctively Russian tradition of cultural and religious messianism which includes Dostoevskii's political writings, the Pan-Slavist and Eurasian movements (see DOSTOEVSKII, F.M.), and the apocalyptic vision of Berdiaev, whose philosophy was highly popular among the Soviet underground.

Secular and Westernist thinkers tended to be scarcely less messianic in their response to Chaadaev's pessimism. The first philosophers of Russian liberalism interpreted their country's past and future development in the light of Hegel's doctrine of the necessary movement of all human societies towards the incarnation of Reason in the modern constitutional state, while the Russian radical tradition was shaped successively by the eschatological visions of the French utopian socialists, the Young Hegelians and Karl Marx. Herzen defined the distinctive characteristic of Russian radical thought as the 'implacable spirit of negation' with which, unrestrained by the European's deference to the past, it applied itself to the task of freeing mankind from the transcendent authorities invented by religion and philosophy; and the radical populist tradition that he founded argued that the 'privilege of backwardness', by permitting Russia to learn both from the achievements and the mistakes of the West, had placed it in the vanguard of mankind's movement towards liberty.

Russian religious philosophers tended to see themselves as prophets, pointing the way to the regeneration of human societies through the spiritual transformation of individuals. Vladimir SOLOV'ËV (regarded by many Russians as their greatest philosopher) believed that his country's mission was to bring into being the Kingdom of God on Earth in the form of a liberal theocracy, which would integrate knowledge and social practice and unite the human race under the spiritual rule of the Pope and the secular rule of the Russian tsar. His metaphysics of 'All-Unity' was a dominant force in the revival of religious and idealist philosophy in Russia in the early twentieth century, inspiring an entire generation of thinkers who sought to reinterpret Christian dogma in ways that emphasized the links of spiritual culture and religious faith with institutional and social reform, and progress in all other aspects of human endeavour. Among them were leading Russian émigré philosophers after 1917, such as Semën Frank, Bulgakov (who sought to create a new culture in which Orthodox Christianity would infuse every area of Russian life), BERDIAEV (who was strongly influenced by the messianic motifs in Solov'ëv), and Hessen, who offered a Neo-Kantian and Westernist interpretation of the notion of 'All-Unity'. A number of émigré philosophers (notably Il'in and Vysheslavtsev) interpreted Bolshevism as the expression of a spiritual crisis in modern industrialized cultures. Many blamed the Russian Revolution on infection from a culturally bankrupt West which (echoing the Slavophiles, Dostoevskii and Leont'ev) they presented as corrupted by rationalism, positivism, atheism and self-centred individualism (although few have gone as far as the fiercely polemical LOSEV who, up until his death in the Soviet Union in 1988, maintained that electric light expressed the spiritual emptiness of 'Americanism and machine-production'). Most maintained a historiosophical optimism throughout the catastrophes of the first half of the twentieth century, which Berdiaev saw as a precondition for messianic regeneration, while Hessen believed that religious and cultural values would emerge triumphant from the carnage in a dialectical *Aufhebung*.

2   Major themes in Russian philosophy

The main impetus of Russian philosophy has always been towards the future, as its representatives strained to discern the features of the 'new man' (the term favoured by the left from the 1860s, with the addition of the adjective 'Soviet' after 1917), or the 'integral personality', as Slavophiles and neo-idealists preferred to describe the individual who would one day be free from the cognitive and moral defects that had hitherto prevented mankind from realizing its potential. The nature of these flaws and the specifications of the regenerated human being were the subject of bitter disputes between rival movements. Even on the left, models of the 'new man' varied widely, from the narrow rationalist who was the ideal of the 'nihilists' of the 1860s and subsequently of Lenin and Plekhanov, to Bakunin's eternal rebel, who would embody the spontaneous spirit of freedom in defiance of all established authorities and orders. At the end of the nineteenth century, in the cultural ferment produced by new movements in philosophy and the arts emanating from the West, radical thinkers began *en masse* to renounce their predominantly rationalist models of the individual and society. Nietzsche's Superman had a pervasive influence on the ensuing 'revaluation of values', undertaken with the aim of formulating moral and social ideals that would embrace the many-sidedness of human creativity. Some radical philosophers (such as Berdiaev and Frank), in the process of moving from Marxism to neo-idealism, sought to reconcile Nietzsche's aesthetic immoralism with Christian ethics, while the 'Empiriocriticist' group of Bolsheviks attempted to inject Russian Marxist philosophy with an element of heroic voluntarism by synthesizing it with Nietzschean self-affirmation and the pragmatism of Ernst Mach. Nietzschean influences combined with the mechanistic scientism of Soviet Marxism in the Soviet model of the 'new man' (whose qualities Lysenko's genetics suggested could be inherited by successive generations). In the post-Stalin 'thaw' some Soviet philosophers, including Il'enkov and Mamardashvili, began a critical rereading of Marx's texts from an anthropocentric standpoint which emphasized the unpredictable and limitless potential of human consciousness (see MARXIST PHILOSOPHY, RUSSIAN AND SOVIET).

This open-ended view of progress (officially encouraged in the Gorbachev period) is uncommon in Russian philosophy, where epistemological scepticism is more often to be encountered in uneasy combinations with eschatological faith. Like other rootless groups, Russian intellectuals were drawn to compensating certainties that seemed capable of resisting their corrosive critique. The radical humanism of much Russian thought placed it at the forefront of the developing critical insistence on the context-dependent nature of truth; but many thinkers who attacked the claims of systems and dogmas to encompass and explain the experience and creative needs of living individuals in specific historical contexts, nevertheless retained a belief in a final, ideal state of being in which the fragmentation of knowledge would be overcome and all human purposes would coincide: a condition for whose principles some looked to science, others to religious revelation. The nihilists, who rejected metaphysics and all that could not be proven by rational and empirical methods, fervently believed that progress would inevitably lead to the restoration of a natural state of harmony between the individual and society. The empiriocriticist movement within Russian Marxism opposed the idolatry of formulas with the claim that experience and practice were the sole criteria of truth, but the group's leading philosopher, BOGDANOV, looked forward to a metascience that would unify the fragmented world of knowledge by reducing 'all the discontinuities of our experience to a principle of continuity', predicting that under communism, when all would share the same modes of organizing experience, the phenomenon of individuals with separate mental worlds would cease to exist. Solov'ëv's pervasive influence on subsequent Russian religious idealism owed much to the charms of his vision of 'integral knowledge' and 'integral life' in an 'integral society'. Religious and socialist motifs were combined in some visions of an earthly paradise, such as Bulgakov's 'Christian Socialism', or Gorkii's and Lunacharskii's creed of 'God-building', which called for worship of the collective humanity of the socialist future. In the revolutionary ferment of the first two decades of the twentieth century many religious and radical philosophers, together with Symbolist writers and poets, envisaged the leap to the harmonious future in apocalyptic terms: the novelist and critic Merezhkovskii prophesied the coming of a 'New Christianity' which would unite Christian faith with pagan self-affirmation in a morality beyond good and evil. In the aftermath of 1917 some thinkers (notably Berdiaev and members of the Eurasian movement) found consolation in apocalyptic fantasies of a new light from the East shining on the ruins of European culture.

Herzen memorably ascribed such doctrinaire utopianism to the Russian tendency to march 'in fearless ranks to the very limit and beyond it, in step with the dialectic, but out of step with the truth'. The most original and subversive Russian thinker, he was the first of a significant minority who directed the iconoclastic thrust of Russian philo-

sophy against all forms, without exception, of messianic faith. Contending that there was no basis in experience for the belief in a purposeful universe on which the great optimistic systems of the nineteenth century were built, he urged his contemporaries to adapt their categories to the flow of life, to accept (and even welcome) the dominant role of contingency in human existence, on the grounds that individual freedom and responsibility were possible only in an unprogrammed world. Herzen's critique of the claims of metaphysical systems to predict or regulate the course of history was echoed by the 'subjective sociology' developed by Mikhailovskii and Lavrov in opposition to the deterministic scientism of the dominant Russian radical tradition. TOLSTOI pointed to the chanciness of life and history in order to demonstrate the inadequacy of all attempts to formulate general rules for human societies; Dostoevskii confronted the systematizers with the lived experience of human freedom as the ability to be unpredictable; in their symposium of 1909 (frequently cited in the West as a pioneering analysis of the psychology of political utopianism) the neo-idealists of the *Signposts* movement explored the ways in which obsession with an ideal future impoverishes and distorts perception of the historical present.

Under the Soviet system a few representatives of this anti-utopian tradition ingeniously evaded the pressure on philosophers (backed up by the doctrine of the 'partyness' of truth) to endorse the official myths of utopia in power. The history of the novel form was the vehicle for Bakhtin's reflections on the 'unfinalizability' of human existence (see BAKHTIN, M.M.); similar insights were expressed by the cultural-historical school of psychology established by Vygotskii, who drew on Marx to counter the mechanistic determinism of Soviet Marxist philosophy with a view of consciousness as a cultural artefact capable of self-transcendence and self-renewal. In the 1960s Soviet psychologists and philosophers such as Il'enkov helped to revive an interest in ethics with their emphasis on the individual as the centre of moral agency, while in its historical studies of culture as a system of semiotic signs, the Moscow-Tartu school brought a richly documented and undoctrinaire approach to important moral and political topics.

The insights of some of these individuals and movements into the attractions and delusions of utopian thought are lent added conviction by their own often spectacularly unsuccessful efforts to overcome what Nietzsche called 'the craving for metaphysical comfort'. Tolstoi was torn all his life beween his pluralist vision and his need for dogmatic moral certainties, while Dostoevskii in his last years preached an astonishingly crude variety of religio-political messianism. The humanism of some later religious philosophers (including the *Signposts* authors Berdiaev and Bulgakov) is hard to reconcile with their eschatological impatience.

References and further reading

Edie, J.M., Scanlan, J.P. and Zeldin, M.B. (eds) (1966) *Russian Philosophy*, Chigaco, IL: Quadrangle Books, 3 vols. (A selection of texts, well annotated and introduced, from the beginnings of Russian philosophy until the Soviet period.)

Masaryk, T.G. (1955) *The Spirit of Russia. Studies in History, Literature and Philosophy*, trans. E. and C. Paul, with additional chapters and bibliographies by J. Slavik, London: Allen & Unwin, 3 vols. (First published in German in 1913, and still an excellent introduction to Russian philosophy.)

Walicki, A. (1980) *Russian Thought From the Enlightenment to Marxism*, Oxford: Clarendon Press. (Covers the main movements in Russian thought from the eighteenth to the early twentieth century.)

AILEEN KELLY

RYLE, GILBERT (1900–76)

Alongside Wittgenstein and Austin, Ryle was one of the dominant figures in that middle period of twentieth-century English language philosophy which became known as 'Linguistic Analysis'. His views in philosophy of mind led to his being described as a 'logical behaviourist' and his major work in that area, *The Concept of Mind* (1949), both by reason of its style and content, has become one of the modern classics of philosophy. In it Ryle attacked what he calls 'Cartesian dualism' or the myth of 'the Ghost in the Machine', arguing that philosophical troubles over the nature of mind and its relation with the body arose from a 'category mistake' which led erroneously to treating statements about mental phenomena in the same way as those about physical phenomena. For Ryle, to do something was not to perform two separate actions – one mental, one physical – but to behave in a certain way.

Much of Ryle's work had a similar theme: philosophical confusion arose through the assimilation or misapplication of categorically different terms, and could only be cleared up by a careful analysis of the logic and use of language. He later became preoccupied with the nature of reflective thinking, since this stood as an example of an activity which seemed to evade the behaviouristic analysis that he recommended. Ryle was also a considerable Plato scholar, though his work in this area has been less influential.

WILLIAM LYONS

S

SAINT-SIMON, CLAUDE-HENRI DE ROUVROY, COMTE DE (1760–1825)

An influential French social theorist, Saint-Simon propounded a philosophy of history and an account of the future organization of industrial society. He predicted a 'golden age', where harmony between individual capacities and social structures, reflected in a reordering of 'temporal' and 'spiritual' power, would overcome disorder and banish idleness. He has been variously portrayed as a utopian socialist, the founder of sociology and a prescient madman.

See also: HISTORY, PHILOSOPHY OF; POSITIVISM IN THE SOCIAL SCIENCES; SOCIALISM; UTOPIANISM

DAVID LEOPOLD

SĀṂKHYA
See SĀṄKHYA

SANCHES, FRANCISCO (1551–1623)

Francisco Sanches was a sceptical philosopher and a professor of medicine at the University of Toulouse in southern France in the late sixteenth and early seventeenth century. He was born in Spain to a family of Jewish ancestry that had been forcibly converted to Catholicism, but he was brought up in France. Though he was a distant cousin of the sceptic Michel de Montaigne, he independently advanced what was perhaps the strongest sceptical critique of Aristotelianism and Platonism. In addition he developed a scepticism about mathematical knowledge claims. At the same time, he offered the first form of constructive scepticism, a way of solving intellectual problems without antecedently overcoming the sceptical challenge to traditional kinds of knowledge. He thus presented science as a way of dealing with experience, rather than as a way of gaining knowledge, and in this his views anticipate some twentieth-century philosophies. Sanches was also an important empirical medical practitioner, who presented the newest medical findings in his courses at Toulouse. His sceptical-critical views were influential in the first half of the seventeenth century, and were still being studied in Leibniz's time.

See also: MONTAIGNE, M. DE; RENAISSANCE PHILOSOPHY; SCEPTICISM; SCIENTIFIC METHOD

RICHARD H. POPKIN

SĀṄKHYA

Considered one of the oldest classical Hindu schools by Indian tradition, Sāṅkhya is most famous in Indian philosophy for its atheism, its dualist model of *puruṣa* (passive, individual consciousness) and *prakṛti* (non-conscious, cognitive-sentient body) and its theory that effects pre-exist in their cause. In its classical formulation the *puruṣa-prakṛti* model is analysed into twenty-five components (*tattva*) intended to encompass entire metaphysical, cognitive, psychological, ethical and physical worlds in terms of their embodiment as individual constituents and the creative and interpretive projection of those worlds as experience by and for individuals. Both the world and the individual, in other words, are considered a phenomenological refraction and projection of the underlying and constitutive components of the conscious body.

Falsely identifying with the cognitive and sensory components of *prakṛti* (which according to orthodox Sāṅkhya performs cognitive and sentient operations, but is bereft of consciousness; *puruṣa* alone is conscious), Sāṅkhyans believe themselves to be the agents of their actions, rather than recognizing that actions are processes lacking any selfhood. Sāṅkhyans claim that liberation from the suffering of repeated rebirths can only be achieved through a profound understanding of the distinction between *puruṣa* and *prakṛti*. The latter is not abandoned after liberation, but continues to operate, observed with detachment by *puruṣa*. However, according to some versions of Sāṅkhya, *prakṛti* eventually becomes dormant. *Puruṣa* and *prakṛti* both are considered to be eternal and to have no beginning. Since liberation is achieved through knowledge, Sāṅkhya stresses the importance and efficacy of knowledge over ritual and other religious endeavours.

Sāṅkhya is cognate to *saṅkhyā*, meaning 'to count' or 'enumerate'. Thus Sāṅkhya seeks to enumerate the basic facts of reality so that people will understand them and find liberation. Basic Sāṅkhyan models and terms appear in some Upaniṣads and underlie important portions of the epic *Mahābhārata*, especially the *Bhagavad Gītā* and *Mokṣadharma*. No distinct Sāṅkhyan text prior to Īśvarakṛṣṇa's *Sāṅkhyakārikā* (*c*.350–*c*.450) is extant. It enumerates and explains the twenty-five components and a subsidiary list of sixty topics (*ṣaṣṭitantra*), which are then subdivided into further enumerative lists. Most of the subsequent Sāṅkhyan literature consists of commentaries and expositions of the *Sāṃkhyakārikā* and its ideas, which continued to be refined without major alterations well into the eighteenth century. Sāṅkhyan models strongly influenced numerous other Indian schools, including Yoga, Vedānta, Kashmir Shaivism and Buddhism.

See also: DUALISM

DAN LUSTHAUS

SANTAYANA, GEORGE (1863–1952)

George Santayana was a philosopher, essayist, novelist and poet. Born in Spain, he moved to America as a child and attended Harvard, studying under William James and Josiah Royce. The philosophical world first took note of Santayana for his work in aesthetics. *The Sense of Beauty* (1896), his attempt to give a naturalistic account of the beautiful, remains influential. He wrote exquisitely crafted essays on literature and religion, viewing both as articulating important symbolic truths about the human condition. His mature philosophical system is a classical edifice constructed out of positions adopted from Plato and Aristotle, which he modified in light of the naturalistic insights of his beloved Lucretius and Spinoza and steeped in pessimism reminiscent of Schopenhauer. Although in close touch with the philosophical developments of his day, he always viewed human life and its problems in a calming cosmic perspective.

JOHN LACHS

SAPIR, EDWARD

See SAPIR-WHORF HYPOTHESIS

SAPIR-WHORF HYPOTHESIS

The Sapir-Whorf hypothesis is a widely used label for the linguistic relativity hypothesis, that is, the proposal that the particular language we speak shapes the way we think about the world. The label derives from the names of American anthropological linguists Edward Sapir and Benjamin Lee Whorf, who persuasively argued for this idea during the 1930s and 1940s – although they never actually characterized their ideas as a 'hypothesis'. In contrast to earlier European scholarship concerned with linguistic relativity, their approach was distinguished by first-hand experience with native American languages and rejection of claims for the superiority of European languages.

See also: AUSTIN, J.L.; CASSIRER, E.; CONDILLAC, E.B. DE; DETERMINISM AND INDETERMINISM; DIDEROT, D.; LANGUAGE, PHILOSOPHY OF; PUTNAM, H.; QUINE, W.V.; RADICAL TRANSLATION AND RADICAL INTERPRETATION; RELATIVISM; SEARLE, J.; WITTGENSTEIN, L.J.J.

JOHN A. LUCY

SARTRE, JEAN-PAUL (1905–80)

Introduction

Sartre was a philosopher of paradox: an existentialist who attempted a reconciliation with Marxism, a theorist of freedom who explored the notion of predestination. From the mid-1930s to the late 1940s, Sartre was in his 'classical' period. He explored the history of theories of imagination leading up to that of Husserl, and developed his own phenomenological account of imagination as the key to the freedom of consciousness. He analysed human emotions, arguing that emotion is a freely chosen mode of relationship to the outside world. In his major philosophical work, *L'Être et le Néant* (*Being and Nothingness*) (1943), Sartre distinguished between consciousness and all other beings: consciousness is always at least tacitly conscious of itself, hence it is essentially 'for itself' (*pour-soi*) – free, mobile and spontaneous. Everything else, lacking this self-consciousness, is just what it is 'in-itself' (*en-soi*); it is 'solid' and lacks freedom. Consciousness is always engaged in the world of which it is conscious, and in relationships with other consciousnesses. These relationships are conflictual: they involve a battle to maintain the position of subject and to make the other into an object. This battle is inescapable.

Although Sartre was indeed a philosopher of freedom, his conception of freedom is often misunderstood. Already in *Being and Nothingness* human freedom operates against a background of facticity and situation. My facticity is all the facts about myself which cannot be changed – my age, sex, class of origin, race and so on; my situation may be modified, but it still constitutes the starting point for change and roots consciousness firmly in the world. Freedom is not idealized by Sartre; it is always within a given set of circumstances, after a particular past, and against the expectations of both myself and others that I make my free choices. My personal history conditions the range of my options.

From the 1950s onwards Sartre became increasingly politicized and was drawn to attempt a reconciliation between existentialism and Marxism. This was the aim of the *Critique de la raison dialectique* (*Critique of Dialectical Reason*) (1960) which recognized more fully than before the effect of historical and material conditions on individual and collective choice. An attempt to explore this interplay in action underlies both his biography of Flaubert and his own autobiography.

1   Background

Sartre's prestige as a philosopher was at its peak, in France at least, in the late 1940s, in the aftermath of the Second World War, when a philosophy of freedom and self-determination fitted the mood of a country recently liberated from the Occupation. It was at its nadir in the late 1960s and 1970s when structuralism had discredited, temporarily, both humanism and existentialism, and proclaimed 'man' to be no more than a locus of forces traversed and indeed produced by social and linguistic structures (see STRUCTURALISM). The British analytic tradition has never had much time for the literary and dramatic aspects of existentialism and phenomenology, though some recent critics, such as Phyllis Morris and Gregory McCulloch, have attempted to take Sartre seriously as a philosopher and to assess his contribution in terms more accessible to analytically trained minds.

The emotive responses tend in their different ways to distort Sartre's arguments and to focus, for example, on one of the poles of the many paradoxes which his philosophy implies. For Sartre is indeed a philosopher of paradox – deliberately facing his readers with logically 'impossible' or self-contradictory statements in order to force them to think beyond the confines of the binary oppositions to which common sense and analytic reason have accustomed them. For example, 'Man is what he is not and is not what he is' (1943: 97) provocatively compels the reader who perseveres to confront the

difficult issues of the relationship between essence, existence and negation. 'Man is what he is not', that is to say, man is a being without an essential nature, a being who operates through negation, who cannot be identified with his past, or indeed his present self, and so 'who is not what he is'.

The Paris of the 1940s overestimated Sartre's faith in human freedom and lauded him for it; 1960s Paris made the same mistake and discarded him along with all other relics of mid-century humanism. Neither period read Sartre carefully enough to recognize the constraints and limits within which freedom was, from the outset, deemed to operate.

2   Early philosophy

Sartre's first published philosophical works were *L'Imagination* (1936), a history of theories of imagination up to the theory of Edmund HUSSERL, and 'La Transcendance de l'ego' (*The Transcendence of the Ego*) (1936). *The Transcendence of the Ego* shows hostility to any kind of essentialism of the self. In it Sartre argues (against Husserl) that the ego is not transcendental but transcendent, that is, it is not an inner core of being, a source of my actions, emotions and character, but rather a construct, a product of my self-image and my image in the eyes of others, of my past behaviour and feelings. Sartre maintains that consciousness is not essentially first-person but is impersonal, or at most pre-personal, and that it is characterized by intentionality, that is to say it is always directed at something other than itself. In this context Sartre positions himself in relation to the Kantian 'unity of apperception', arguing that although the 'I think' must be able to accompany all my representations, it does not always do so, at least explicitly. I may turn my attention at any moment away from what I am doing and direct it towards myself as agent, but this reflexivity is not a permanent, thetic feature of consciousness. Later, in *L'Être et le Néant* (*Being and Nothingness*) (1943), Sartre claims that it is precisely this very reflexivity – the self-consciousness of consciousness – that personalizes consciousness and constitutes the human subject, but in *The Transcendence of the Ego* such a notion is absent and he is more concerned to argue against the identification of consciousness with selfhood than to explore the ways in which consciousness relates to the notion of subject.

In his *Esquisse d'une théorie des émotions* (*Sketch for a Theory of Emotions*) (1939) Sartre turns his attention to another area of human experience in order to show that this, in its turn, cannot be described in essentialist terms. Emotions, in Sartre's account, are chosen rather than caused: emotion involves a 'magical' attempt to transform reality by changing what can be changed (my own feelings) rather than what is less easily malleable, that is, the outside world. In the face of extreme danger I may faint from fear: the danger has not disappeared but I am no longer conscious of it. Sartre here takes a radical position which he maintained but modified in later years, as his recognition of the degree to which we are formed by external conditions gradually increased. He is careful to distinguish between various areas related to emotion – passion, feeling and so on. Emotion is not sustainable continuously through time, but is subject to fluctuations of intensity, and may at times be replaced by alternative feelings. In this sense too Sartre rejects essentialism: like Proust he believes in the 'intermittances of the heart': love, for example, is not a continuous emotional state, but an amalgam of affection, desire, passion, as well as, perhaps, jealousy, resentment and even occasionally hatred. Love is not the permanent compelling state we may like to imagine: it is the product of a decision and a commitment (see EMOTIONS, NATURE OF; EMOTIONS, PHILOSOPHY OF).

These two works form the grounding for Sartre's early theory of human freedom along with a second work on the imagination. In *L'Imaginaire, psychologie phénoménologique de l'imagination* (*The Psychology of the Imagination*) (1940) Sartre picks up the threads of Husserl's theory of imagination and develops it further by showing how phenomenological psychology works in practice. Unlike traditional empirical psychology it is not based in a positivist methodology in which evidence depends on an accumulation of examples. The phenomenological method operates through a particular type of introspection or intuition in which the phenomenologist examines a single example, or a series of examples, of the phenomenon to be analysed (here imagination) and deduces from the example the general principles and features of the phenomenon. In this way Sartre describes what he calls the 'poverty' of the image – the fact, that is, that I can never find in it any more than I have already put there. If, say, I do not know the number of columns in the Parthenon, I can count them if I look at the temple in reality; if I merely imagine the temple the number of pillars will depend not on the real building but merely on my own implicit estimate. I cannot learn anything from imagination as I can from perception. But the reverse of this 'poverty' of the imagination is its *freedom* – in imagination I am not constrained as I am in perception by the material world around me. Indeed, imagination is not merely image formation – in Sartre's account it is itself constitutive of the freedom of consciousness. Without imagination we would be 'stuck in the real', unable to escape from the present moment of time and our immediate surroundings. It is imagination that allows us to step back from our material environment and take up an (imaginary) distance from it, in Sartre's terms to 'totalize' it, to see it as a 'world' with order and pattern. In *Being and Nothingness* Sartre will also maintain that the imagination is the source of the purpose and finality we see in the world, but *The Psychology of the Imagination* concentrates rather on the different functions of imagination and image formation in the narrower sense (see IMAGINATION).

3 Being and Nothingness

Being and Nothingness sets out the main philosophical tenets of the 'classical' Sartre. Being is subdivided, as it were, into two major regions – being for-itself (*l'être pour-soi*) or consciousness, and being-in-itself (*l'être en-soi*) which is everything other than consciousness, including the material world, the past, the body as organism and so on. To being-in-itself Sartre devotes no more than six of his 660 pages; there is little to be said about it other than it is, it is what it is, and it is 'in itself'. Only through the 'for-itself' of consciousness does the 'in-itself' become a world to speak of. Indeed, Sartre argues, we cannot know anything about being as it is, only about being as it appears to us. It is through consciousness that the world is endowed with temporality, spatiality and other qualities such as usefulness. This is where the imagination in its broadest sense may be seen as primary: 'imagination is the whole of consciousness as it realizes its freedom' ('L'Imaginaire, psychologie phénoménologique de l'imagination' 1940: 236). Imagination makes a world of the 'in-itself', it totalizes and 'nihilates' it. Nihilation (*néantir*) is a term that is specific to Sartre, and means not annihilation but rather the special type of negation that consciousness operates when it 'intends' an object: it differentiates the object from its surroundings and knows itself *not* to be that object. But consciousness is not alone in the world it has created from the brute 'in-itself', indeed it has not created the world individually, but rather as part of an intersubjective community. And other people, or their consciousnesses, are not an afterthought for Sartre. Like HEIDEGGER he sees man as always already engaged in relationships with others; unlike Heidegger he sees these not in terms of *Mitsein* (Being-with), but in terms of conflict in a manner reminiscent of the account given by HEGEL of the relationship between masters and slaves. The other is in permanent competition with me. I wish to be a subject and make of the other an object, while he or she attempts to make me an object in my turn. In Sartre's account, this battle is the key to all human relationships, and not merely those which might appear conflictual, but also those of sexual desire and even love. Consciousness is engaged in a permanent struggle to maintain its freedom in the face of onslaughts from all sides.

These aspects of Sartre's early philosophy are probably the best known. Less familiar but no less significant are his accounts of the limits within which human freedom operates. The battle of consciousnesses is not disembodied, and my own body constitutes not only the condition of possibility but also one of the major constraints on my freedom. Consciousness and imagination are free, but they are free against a background of facticity and situation. Facticity in particular is rarely given due weight by exegetes of Sartre's philosophy. My facticity is all the facts about myself which cannot be changed – my age, sex, height, class of origin, race, nationality, for example. (Later Sartre comes to include in facticity more psychological elements of genetic or environmental origin.) One's situation may be modified, but it still constitutes the starting point for any change, and roots consciousness firmly in the world about it. All this means that the Sartrean philosophy of freedom is less idealized than it might at first appear. I am not free to change a whole multiplicity of aspects of my condition, and those I am free to change may not prove easy. As I live I create a self which does not bind me but which certainly makes some courses of action easier and more attractive than others. My own self-image and the image others hold of me also condition the range of possibilities open to me. I make a character for myself over the years, and though it is always open to me to act 'out of character' – after all it is a self I have constituted, not an essence I was born with – such a decision is not usually easy. Sartre describes this self-constitution in terms not so much of character as of 'project', each person having a fundamental project of being, which is not necessarily the result of a conscious decision, and possibly elaborated gradually over time. This project forms the core of a whole nexus of choices and behavioural decisions which form the totality that constitutes my self. My actions form a meaningful whole, each act relates to others before and since, and so the decision to make significant changes always comes up against resistance from already existent patterns and structures. Discussing, for example, an episode when a man gives up on a long hike declaring he is 'too tired' to continue, Sartre discusses the abandonment of the walk in terms of a project which does not put persistence in the face of setbacks at much of a premium. He 'could have acted differently, of course,' Sartre comments, 'but at what cost?' (1943: 531). Our personal history does not eradicate our freedom, but in practice it is often easier to deny our freedom than to employ it. We hide behind the selves we have constructed, fearing change and convincing ourselves that our choices are limited. Freedom is threatening to us, it opens up a range of possibilities which we find daunting, and we flee from it in what Sartre calls 'bad faith'. Ideally we would like the positive aspect of liberty – free choice, a lack of constraints – together with the security and comfort of a fixed character or nature. The two are incompatible, and our desire to combine them is termed by Sartre a 'useless passion' (see SELF-DECEPTION, ETHICS OF).

In 1943, then, Sartre already sets freedom firmly against a background of constraint – constraints which arise from the features of the material world, from other people whose projects may not coincide with mine, from bodily existence, from facticity and from fear of freedom itself. Freedom is always within and starting from situation, and it is on the determinants and conditioning power of situation that Sartre increasingly focuses in his later writings.

4 Literary works

The 1940s were the period of Sartre's most prolific literary production. From *La Nausée* (*Nausea*) (1938) which explores the relationship of contingency and necessity in life and art through the experiences of Roquentin, Sartre moves on in the war years to a contemporary trilogy *Les Chemins de la liberté* (The Roads to Freedom) (1945–9). The trilogy (or unfinished quadrology?) portrays the lives of a varied group of Parisian intellectuals at the outbreak of war, and in particular the ways in which they hide their freedom from themselves while convincing themselves that it is their ultimate goal. Mathieu, a university academic, is the main focus for such ambivalence as he tries to find money for an abortion for his long-term mistress Marcelle.

Sartre also wrote several very successful plays in this period – *Les Mouches* (*The Flies*) (1943), a wartime allegory of resistance to German occupation, which uses the Orestean myth to explore the power of human liberty in the face of oppression. *Huis Clos* (*In Camera*) (1944) shows the deadly consequences of conflictual human relations and self-deception in a hell comprising three characters doomed to remain together for ever in a Second Empire drawing room. *Les Mains Sales* (*Dirty Hands*, or *Crime Passionel*) (1948) debates the issues of realism and idealism, means and ends, truth, lies and political commitment in Illyria, an imaginary communist country in Eastern Europe. This finely balanced and complex play received an unexpectedly positive response from the bourgeois press who interpreted it, against Sartre's intentions, as predominantly anti-communist. In consequence Sartre felt obliged to ban its production for about ten years.

5 Later philosophy

The increasing politicization of Sartre's postwar writing meant that he left both literature and philosophy to one side in the 1950s as he became increasingly engaged as a writer, lecturer and public figure in concrete political issues and endeavours. His next major philosophical work, the *Critique de la raison dialectique* (*Critique of Dialectical Reason*), did not appear until 1960 and is clearly marked by his increasing intellectual engagement with MARX. The *Critique* is an attempt to do the impossible: to reconcile existentialism and Marxism; to revivify Marxism, which Sartre believed was becoming sclerotic, by reawakening its awareness of individual and collective subjectivity; and to bring existentialism into closer contact with the material conditions of historical existence. Sartre examines social and political issues such as group action, historical change, revolution and behaviour in the face of material scarcity of resources. He modifies his radical position on the extent of human freedom by recognizing more fully than before the effect of historical and material conditions on individual and collective choice. He takes as his own the famous slogan of Engels: 'Men make history on the basis of what history has made them'. We are not pawns or cogs in a machine, nor do we simply participate in processes of internalization and externalization: we are free agents, but agents who are profoundly and inescapably situated in specific social and material conditions. Indeed Sartre later uses the (Jansenist) term 'predestination' to explain how his views differ from positivist theories of human determinism. Material conditions set up the environment in which we operate. They do not causally determine our behaviour, but they do prescribe the (limited) range of options open to us. A white bourgeois male in a prosperous suburb has a vastly wider range of choices on which to exercise his freedom than an elderly black women living in the poverty of an inner city ghetto. Both are free in the ontological sense, but their possibilities for making use of that freedom are not comparable. And in 1960 Sartre is as concerned with the restrictions imposed on freedom by the material world as with human liberty itself.

It is this preoccupation with the absolute and yet circumscribed nature of human freedom that underpins Sartre's two last major works: his autobiography, *Les Mots* (*Words*) (1963), a brief and finely wrought literary masterpiece, and *L'Idiot de la famille* (*The Idiot of the Family*) (1971–2), a 3,000-page biography of Flaubert which draws on a vast range of different disciplines. 'What can one know of a man, today?' was the question Sartre set out to answer in his account of Flaubert, and in it he synthesizes not only existentialism, phenomenology and Marxist theory and method, but also psycho-analysis, sociology, history of literature, aesthetics and anthropology. What did Flaubert make of what was made of him? Educated in a family embodying the historical conflicts of its age, second son of a doctor and expected to become a lawyer, the young Gustave Flaubert constructed a very different career for himself. Resistant to adult pressures to perform, he learned to read late (hence the *Idiot* of the title), lived in his elder brother's shadow and opted out of law school through a hysterico-epileptic crisis ('intentional' but not 'deliberate', in Sartre's terms) which made him an invalid – the 'hermit of Croisset' – and thus permitted him to live in the family home and become a writer. Sartre's account of his own choice of the same career is more succinct and more ironic: the Sartre and Schweitzer (maternal grandfather) families are not spared in the biting and witty descriptions of the 'family comedy' which made of young Jean-Paul a precocious charlatan, writing to please adults, writing for future fame – a superman author – and finally writing as a professional. The gap between choice and destiny is shown to be very small, but it has not closed. Even when analysing with cruel perspicacity his own formation, Sartre maintains the framework he set up thirty years earlier: freedom within situation, even when the situation may leave little room for manoeuvre. Subjectivity is now defined as the *décalage* or difference between the processes of internalization and externalization; liberty may be no more than the 'play' in the mechanism, but the permanent dialectic between the poles of freedom and conditioning remains untotalized.

See also: BEAUVOIR, S. DE; CAMUS, A.; EXISTENTIALISM; MERLEAU-PONTY, M.; PHENOMENOLOGICAL MOVEMENT

References and further reading

Cohen-Solal, A. (1987) *Sartre: A Life*, New York: Pantheon, and London: Heinemann. (Much the best biography of Sartre so far; well-informed and not uncritical.)

Howells, Christina (ed.) (1992) *The Cambridge Companion to Sartre*, Cambridge: Cambridge University Press. (An interesting and varied collection of philosophical essays by some of the foremost interpreters of Sartre in the US and Europe.)

Sartre, J.-P. (1943) *L'Être et le Néant. Essai d'ontologie phénoménologique*, Paris: Gallimard; trans. H.E. Barnes, *Being and Nothingness: An Essay of Phenomenological Ontology*, New York: Philosophical Library, 1956; repr. London: Methuen, 1957. (Sartre's major philosophical work: a study of the relationship between consciousness and the world, and between consciousness and other consciousnesses.)

CHRISTINA HOWELLS

SAUSSURE, FERDINAND DE (1857–1913)

Though he made a major contribution to the comparative and historical studies which dominated nineteenth-century linguistics, Saussure is best known today for the development of a radically different conception of language and of the methodology of linguistics which became central to twentieth-century structural linguistics. According to this conception a language is a system of signs which are radically arbitrary, so that their significations are determined only by the historically constituted systems of conventions to which they belong – such a system Saussure called '*la langue*'. It follows, therefore, that a linguistic study is first and foremost one of *la langue*, that is, of the conventional relations obtaining at a given time between signs belonging to the same system, rather than one of the development of linguistic forms over time, as the comparativists had maintained.

See also: SEMIOTICS; STRUCTURALISM IN SOCIAL SCIENCE

DAVID HOLDCROFT

SCEPTICISM

Introduction

Simply put, scepticism is the view that we fail to know anything. More generally, the term 'scepticism' refers to a family of views, each of which denies that some term of positive epistemic appraisal applies to our beliefs. Thus, sceptical doctrines might hold that none of our beliefs is certain, that none of our beliefs is justified, that none of our beliefs is reasonable, that none of our beliefs is more reasonable than its denial, and so on. Sceptical doctrines can also vary with respect to the kind of belief they target. Scepticism can be restricted to beliefs produced in certain ways: for example, scepticism concerning beliefs based on memory, on inductive reasoning or even on any reasoning whatsoever. And sceptical views can be restricted to

beliefs about certain subjects: for example, scepticism concerning beliefs about the external world, beliefs about other minds, beliefs about value and so on. Solipsism – the view that all that exists is the self and its states – can be seen as a form of scepticism based on the claim that there are no convincing arguments for the existence of anything beyond the self.

The philosophical problem of scepticism derives from what appear to be very strong arguments for sceptical conclusions. Since most philosophers are unwilling to accept those conclusions, there is a problem concerning how to respond to the arguments. For example, one kind of sceptical argument attempts to show that we have no knowledge of the world around us. The argument hinges on the claim that we are not in a position to rule out the possibility that we are brains-in-a-vat being artificially stimulated to have just the sensory experience we are actually having. We have no basis for ruling out this possibility since if it were actual, our experience would not change in any way. The sceptic then claims that if we cannot rule out the possibility that we are brains-in-a-vat, then we cannot know anything about the world around us.

Responses to this argument often fall into one of two categories. Some philosophers argue that we can rule out the possibility that we are brains-in-a-vat. Others argue that we do not need to be able to rule out this possibility in order to have knowledge of the world around us.

1 The philosophical problem of scepticism
2 Responses to scepticism
3 Relevant alternatives fallibilism
4 *Modus ponens* fallibilism
5 The role of intuitions

1 The philosophical problem of scepticism

Most contemporary discussions of scepticism have focused on scepticism concerning the external world. We can use this type of scepticism to illustrate the broader philosophical problem, as many of the arguments we consider can be applied *mutatis mutandis* to other types of scepticism.

One type of scepticism denies that we know anything about the external world. The view is not simply that, for example, by gathering more evidence we could come to know. Rather, it is that we are unable to attain knowledge. On the plausible assumption that knowledge entails justified belief, scepticism concerning knowledge follows from scepticism concerning justified belief – the view that justified belief about the external world is unattainable.

Scepticism is of philosophical interest because there appear to be very strong arguments that support it. This presents us with the problem of how to respond to these arguments. One way would be to accept their conclusion. Of course, very few philosophers are willing to do this. There are very few actual sceptics. So the problem of scepticism is how to refute or in some way neutralize or deflate the force of these arguments.

In the history of philosophy, some sceptical arguments have been based on the unreliability or relativity of our senses (see PYRRHONISM), or upon the inability of reason to produce non-question begging arguments for our beliefs (see HUME, D.). Nearly all sceptical arguments exploit sceptical hypotheses or alternatives. Sceptical alternatives suppose that the world is very different from what we would normally believe on the basis of our sensory evidence. This entails that our sensory evidence is radically misleading. More precisely, suppose we claim to know a proposition q on the basis of evidence e. Let (proposition) h be an *alternative* to q just in case h is incompatible with q (q and h cannot both be true). Then h is a *sceptical alternative* to q provided h is an alternative to q compatible with e. An alternative of this kind has sceptical force precisely because it is compatible with the evidence we claim gives us knowledge of q. For example, ordinarily, I would claim to know on the basis of my visual evidence that I am currently looking at my computer monitor. One sceptical alternative, introduced by Descartes, is that the world of familiar objects does not exist and that I am being deceived into thinking it does by a powerful demon. The demon causes me to have just the sensory experiences I would have if the world of familiar objects existed (see DESCARTES, R. §4). According to a modern version of this alternative, I am a brain-in-a-vat being artificially stimulated to have all the experiences I would have if I had a body and interacted, in the normal way, with the world of familiar objects. These alternatives are incompatible with what I claim to know about the familiar world around me since according to those alternatives, that world does not exist. Moreover, since these alternatives entail that it appears to me as if that world exists, they are compatible with my evidence.

Sceptical alternatives provide the basis for very powerful sceptical arguments. Exactly how they do this is a matter of some controversy. The quickest route to scepticism is through what I will call the entailment principle:

S knows q on the basis of (evidence) e only if e entails q.

Since a sceptical alternative is, by definition, a proposition incompatible with q but compatible with e, it follows from the mere existence of sceptical alternatives of the kind we have been considering that we do not know those empirical propositions we ordinarily claim to know. But, this argument is only as good as the entailment principle. Should we accept this principle? In effect, the principle says I can know p only if my evidence precludes the possibility of error. Though many philosophers concede that this principle has considerable intuitive force, most have thought, in the end, that it should be rejected. This position is sometimes called fallibilism (see COMMONSENSISM; FALLIBILISM). Of course, few philosophers believe that scepticism should be avoided at all costs. But when given a choice between scepticism and fallibilism, most philosophers opt for fallibilism (at the expense of the entailment principle).

Does fallibilism beg the question against scepticism? After all, precisely what the sceptic claims is that the existence of alternatives consistent with our evidence undermines our claims to know. Fallibilists merely respond that the alternatives the sceptic has invoked do not undermine our knowledge claims: that is, we can know even when there are such alternatives. Since this is the point at issue, fallibilists seem to need an argument in support of this crucial claim.

Here, fallibilists can appeal to our strong intuition that in many cases we do know things, despite the existence of sceptical alternatives. And it is not clear that the sceptic can undermine those intuitions except by appealing to the entailment principle – which is itself undermined by those very intuitions. Thus neither side of the debate may be able to defend its position without begging the question.

Unfortunately scepticism is not so easily dispatched. The sceptic can turn the appeal to our ordinary intuitions against fallibilism. For some of those intuitions can provide the basis for a new sceptical argument. This argument begins by claiming, quite plausibly, that whatever else we may say about the significance of sceptical alternatives, we cannot claim, plausibly, to know they are false. For example, we cannot claim, plausibly, to know that we are not brains-in-a-vat being artificially stimulated to have exactly the same experience we would have as normal human beings. None of our evidence counts against this hypothesis since if it were true, we would have precisely that evidence.

But how, exactly, does this permit the sceptic to conclude we do not know the propositions we ordinarily claim to know? At this point, the sceptic appeals to a very intuitive principle that is weaker than the entailment principle. This principle says that the set of known (by S) propositions is closed under known (by S) entailment:

If S knows q, and S knows that q entails not-h, then S knows not-h.

While one could quibble with some details about this principle, it (or something very much like it) seems compelling (see DEDUCTIVE CLOSURE PRINCIPLE). From this principle and the claim that we fail to know sceptical alternatives are false, it follows that we fail to know the propositions we ordinarily claim to know (since we know those propositions entail the falsity of sceptical alternatives).

2 Responses to scepticism

This argument presents problems for fallibilism, as I have characterized it, since the argument at no point presupposes the entailment principle. The sceptical argument we are now considering merely exploits the fallibilist position that permits the existence of alternatives to known propositions.

Fallibilist responses come in two forms, each of which corresponds to the denial of one of the two premises of the sceptical argument. One response denies the closure principle. For example, Dretske has argued that the fact that we do not know the falsity of sceptical alternatives shows that the closure principle is false, since we do know the truth of many empirical propositions that (we know) entail the falsity of sceptical alternatives. According to this view, certain alternatives are not relevant to whether one knows a proposition: one does not have to know such an alternative to q is false in order to know q. So, for example, one can know that one sees a zebra without knowing that the alternative – that one sees a cleverly disguised mule – is false, because that alternative is not relevant. This version of fallibilism is sometimes called the 'relevant alternatives' view.

The other fallibilist response to the sceptical argument agrees with the sceptic that the closure principal is true. But, against the sceptic, these fallibilists deny the claim that we fail to know the falsity of sceptical alternatives. One version of this fallibilist response uses the closure principle along with the claim that we do have knowledge, to reject the claim that we do not know that sceptical alternatives are false. They argue from the premise that we know some ordinary proposition q and the premise that if we know q then we know any proposition that we know is entailed by q (the closure principle), to the conclusion that we know that we are not seeing a cleverly disguised mule. We can call this view 'modus ponens fallibilism'.

3 Relevant alternatives fallibilism

As we have noted, the sceptic attempts to undermine our claims to know by calling attention to sceptical alternatives. The relevant alternatives response to this sceptical manoeuvre is to deny that these alternatives are relevant. An alternative, h, to q, is relevant just in case we need to know h is false in order to know q. So if h is not a relevant alternative, we can still know q even if we fail to know h is false. This view entails that the deductive closure principle is false.

There are two ways to argue for this view. The direct way is to cite alleged counterexamples to the deductive closure principle. Some philosophers have done this by appealing both to our intuition that we know many propositions about the external world and to our intuition that we fail to know the falsity of sceptical alternatives. So my strong intuition that I know I am looking at my computer monitor and my strong intuition that I fail to know I am not a brain-in-a-vat constitute the basis for such a counterexample.

A more indirect way to argue for this view is to construct a theory of knowledge that has as a consequence the failure of the closure principle, as in Nozick. The basic idea of these kinds of theories is that knowing requires the truth of certain subjunctive conditionals. On one (simplified) version, my knowing q requires that:

(S)   If q were false, I would not believe q.

This requirement for knowledge precludes my knowing I am not a brain-in-a-vat. For I would still believe I am not a brain-in-a-vat, even if I were a brain-in-a-vat. But, this requirement allows me to know I see a computer monitor. For it seems plausible to claim that I would not believe I see the computer monitor if I were not seeing it.

A significant difficulty for the direct way of arguing for the relevant alternatives view – the appeal to counterexamples to the closure principle – is that the intuitions that support the counter-examples seem no more compelling than the intuitions in favour of the closure principle. Many think that the closure principle expresses a funda-mental truth about our concept of knowledge. So much so that if a certain theory of knowledge entails the falsity of the closure principle, some philosophers are inclined to take the fact as a *reductio ad absurdum* of that theory.

But this presents problems for the indirect way of arguing for the relevant alternatives view: some philosophers reject theories that endorse condition (S), for the very reason that it entails the falsity of the closure principle. Moreover, there are other difficulties for theories that endorse conditions like

(*S*). One problem for these theories is that they seem to preclude our knowing much of what we take ourselves to know inductively. Consider an example where you leave a glass containing some ice cubes outside on an extremely hot day. Several hours later, while you are still inside escaping the heat, you remember the glass you left outside. You infer that the ice must have melted by now. Here we have an ordinary case of knowledge by inductive inference. According to the theories we are now considering, my knowing that the ice cubes have melted requires the truth of this subjunctive conditional:

(*S′*) If the ice cubes had not melted, I would not believe that they had.

But (*S′*) looks false. It seems plausible to claim that had the ice cubes not melted, it might have been for some reason (for example, someone putting them in a styrofoam cooler) that would still leave me believing they had melted. Thus, it looks as if theories which endorse this condition are too strong. If this is correct, then the anti-sceptical results afforded by condition (*S*) come at the cost of scepticism about certain kinds of inductive knowledge.

We should note, however, that there is some controversy over the evaluation of subjunctive conditionals like (*S′*). But I think it is fair to say that standard semantics for subjunctive conditionals would render (*S′*) as false (see DEDUCTIVE CLOSURE PRINCIPLE).

4 Modus ponens *fallibilism*

Modus ponens fallibilists accept, along with the sceptic, the deductive closure principle. But they attempt to turn that principle against the sceptic. Like relevant alternatives fallibilists, they take as a starting point the strongly intuitive claim that we do know many things about the world. They then note that, given the closure principle, it follows that we know the falsity of sceptical alternatives. For example, I now know that I am looking at my computer monitor. I also know that my looking at a computer monitor precludes my being a brain-in-a-vat. It follows by the closure principle that I know I am not a brain-in-a-vat.

Is this piece of reasoning legitimate? One might challenge those who reason in this way to explain how we know sceptical alternatives are false. How, for example, do I know I am not a brain-in-a-vat? After all, the sceptical problem arises because we seem to lack any reason for believing sceptical alternatives are false. These alternatives are constructed so as to make it impossible for our evidence

to count against them. Presumably, our recognition of this explains, at least in part, our intuition that we fail to know that sceptical alternatives are false.

One way for the *modus ponens* fallibilist to try to meet this challenge is to claim that I can know:

not-*h*: I am not a brain-in-a-vat

by inferring it from:

q: I am looking at my computer monitor

According to this way of proceeding, even though none of my evidence for *q* counts in favour of not-*h*, it does not follow that I have no reason to believe not-*h*. For *q* itself can be that reason. Since I know *q* (on the basis of my visual evidence) and I know that *q* entails not-*h*, I can infer not-*h* from *q* and thereby come to know not-*h*.

Is this reasoning legitimate? Let's compare it with another case. Suppose I park my car in front of the market and go inside. Although I am not currently looking out the window I can still know:

p: My car is parked in front of the store

Can I then come to know:

r: My car has not been towed away

simply by inferring it from *p*? Notice that *p* entails *r*. It seems, none the less, that I would already need to have sufficient evidence to know *r* before I could infer *p*. And if my initial evidence is insufficient for me to know *r*, I cannot infer *p* and so I cannot infer *r* from *p*.

The *modus ponens* fallibilist reasoning concerning sceptical alternatives looks suspicious because it seems like the reasoning in the parked car case. Intuitively, I need to have reason to believe not-*h* before I can infer (and thereby come to know) *q*. Thus I cannot first infer *q* and then go on to infer (and thereby come to know) non-*h*.

Another version of fallibilism argues for the claim that we know sceptical alternatives are false by appealing to principles of inductive inference. One version of this view argues that the hypothesis that the familiar world of objects exists is the best explanation of our sensory evidence (and so a better explanation than sceptical alternatives). This licenses an inference from our sensory evidence to the familiar-world hypothesis (see INFERENCE TO THE BEST EXPLANATION). We can thereby come to know that this familiar world exists. And since we know that the familiar-world hypothesis rules out the sceptical alternatives, it follows by the closure principle that we know that sceptical alternatives are false.

The burden for this view is to say why the familiar-world hypothesis is a better explanation of our sensory evidence than any sceptical alternative. This is not easy to do since sceptical alternatives are designed to explain our sensory evidence. Proponents of the view that sceptical alternatives provide inferior explanations often appeal to pragmatic considerations like simplicity and conservatism. But there are several problems with this approach. Even if we could establish that the familiar-world hypothesis is, for example, simpler than any sceptical alternative, why should we think that this supports the claim that the hypothesis is true? Unless this crucial link can be made, it is not clear how this response to the sceptic can succeed (see THEORETICAL (EPISTEMIC) VIRTUES).

Moreover, often arguments that the familiar-world hypothesis is the best explanation of our sensory data are quite sophisticated and complex. This raises the worry that only those who are philosophically sophisticated enough to follow such an argument can have knowledge of the external world.

5 The role of intuitions

Many fallibilist responses to the sceptic take as their starting point our ordinary intuitions about knowledge or our everyday pattern of knowledge attributions. But how exactly can our everyday pattern of knowledge attributions have force against sceptical arguments, since the sceptic is calling into question precisely these attributions?

The reason our ordinary intuitions about knowledge have force against the sceptic is that these intuitions persist even in the face of sceptical arguments. When we confront a sceptical argument, even though we may not be able to say where the argument goes wrong, we are reluctant to withdraw our everyday knowledge attributions. This is the basis of G.E. Moore's famous response to sceptical arguments. Moore claimed to be more sure that he knew some things, for example, that he has a hand, than he is that the sceptical argument is sound. So even though he could not say where the sceptical argument goes wrong, he thought it more rational to suppose that there is a mistake in the sceptical argument than to suppose that the conclusion of the argument – we fail to know anything – is true (see MOORE, G.E.; COMMONSENSISM).

The sceptic could try to dismiss the significance of our reluctance to withdraw our everyday knowledge attributions as nothing more than the persistence of old habits. This persistence of our habitual ways of thinking about knowledge even after we have been confronted with sceptical arguments was noticed by Descartes and by Hume.

But in response, we can note that, often, we find our everyday pattern of knowledge attributions compelling even while we are in the midst of sincere philosophical reflection. The fact is that when we think about sceptical arguments, we often find ourselves pulled in two directions. We feel the pull of the sceptical argument and yet we remain reluctant to give up our claims to know. This phenomenon cannot be dismissed as nothing more than an unreflective habit. So the fallibilist can maintain that our everyday knowledge attributions reflect deep-seated intuitions about our concept of knowledge. Since our intuitions are a kind of data that any theory of knowledge must explain, they present a formidable challenge to the sceptical position.

Nevertheless, there is something unsatisfying about rejecting scepticism just because it conflicts with our intuitions about knowledge. For, again, it is hard to deny the force of the sceptical argument. And just as our intuitions about our everyday knowledge attributions present a problem for scepticism, so our sceptical intuitions present a challenge to our everyday knowledge attributions. If scepticism is a strongly counterintuitive view, then why do sceptical arguments have any grip on us at all? Why do we not immediately respond to sceptical arguments by objecting, for example, that sceptical hypotheses are too remote and fanciful to undermine our knowledge claims? (Either we can know that sceptical alternatives are false or we need not know they are false in order to know things about the external world.) Sometimes we are inclined to do just that. But the sceptical problem arises precisely because we cannot always sustain that attitude. Sometimes, when we consider sceptical arguments, we begin to worry that sceptical alternatives really do threaten our knowledge claims.

What we are confronting here is a paradox – a set of inconsistent propositions, each of which has considerable independent plausibility:

(1) We know some ordinary empirical propositions.
(2) We do not know that sceptical alternatives are false.
(3) If S knows q, and S knows that q entails not-h, then S knows not-h.

One of these propositions must be false (on the assumption that we know q entails not-h). Yet each of them is very difficult to deny. This is what explains our vacillation over scepticism. The arguments for scepticism and for fallibilism attempt to exploit the intuitions favourable to them. The sceptic appeals to (2) and (3), and concludes that (1) is false. Relevant alternatives fallibilism appeals to

(1) and (2), and concludes that (3) is false. *Modus ponens* fallibilism appeals to (1) and (3), and concludes that (2) is false. Because each member of the set has independent plausibility, it seems arbitrary and unsatisfying to appeal to any two members of this triad as an argument against the third. Such a strategy does not provide what any successful resolution of a paradox should provide, namely an explanation of how the paradox arises in the first place. Any satisfying resolution of the paradox that defends our claims to know against the sceptic must explain the appeal of sceptical arguments. For it is that very appeal that gives rise to the paradox.

This is where Moore's response to the sceptic goes wrong. Many philosophers think that Moore begged the question against scepticism. In a way he did, but no more so than the sceptic begs the question against him. Still, there is something quite unsatisfying, philosophically, about Moore's treatment of the sceptical argument. But the problem with it is not that it begs the question against the sceptic. Rather the problem is that it fails to explain the dialectic force of sceptical arguments. Though it is possible that the apparent cogency of sceptical arguments is explained by some very subtle error in our reasoning, the simplicity of these arguments suggests that their appeal reveals something deep and important about our concept of knowledge. That is why we can learn much about the nature of knowledge by grappling with the problem of scepticism.

See also: INDUCTION, EPISTEMIC ISSUES IN; INTERNALISM AND EXTERNALISM IN EPISTEMOLOGY; JUSTIFICATION, EPISTEMIC; KNOWLEDGE, CONCEPT OF; PHENOMENOLOGY, EPISTEMIC ISSUES IN; SOLIPSISM

References and further reading

Cornman, J. (1980) *Scepticism, Justification, and Explanation,* Dordrecht: Reidel. (Defends inference to the best explanation response – see §4.)

Unger, P. (1975) *Ignorance,* New York: Oxford University Press. (Influential defence of scepticism.)

STEWART COHEN

SCEPTICISM, MORAL

See MORAL SCEPTICISM

SCHELER, MAX FERDINAND (1874–1928)

Max Scheler, usually called a phenomenologist, was probably the best-known German philosopher of the 1920s. Always an eclectic thinker, he was a pupil of the neo-idealist Rudolph Eucken, but was also strongly influenced by the life-philosophies of Dilthey and Bergson. While teaching at Jena he regularly met Husserl, the founder of the phenomenological movement, and his mature writings have a strongly phenomenological, as well as a Catholic, stamp. Later he turned towards metaphysics and the philosophical problems raised by modern science.

Scheler's interests were very wide. He tried to do justice to all aspects of experience – ethical, religious, personal, social, scientific, historical – without doing away with the specific nature of each. Above all, he took the emotional foundations of thought seriously. Many of his insights are striking and profound, and sometimes his arguments are very telling, but his power to organize his material consistently and to attend conscientiously to the business of justification is poorly developed.

Scheler is best known for his anti-Kantian ethics, based on an a priori emotional grasp of a hierarchy of objective values, which precedes all choice of goods and purposes. He himself describes his ethics as 'personalist', and makes personal values supreme, sharply distinguishing the 'person' from the 'ego', and linking this with his analysis of different types of social interaction. In epistemology he defends a pragmatist approach to science and perception; thus philosophy, as the intuition of essences, requires a preparatory ascetic discipline. His philosophy of religion is an attempt to marry the Augustinian approach through love with the Thomist approach through reason. In his later work, to which his important work on sympathy provides the transition, he defends a dualist philosophical anthropology and metaphysics, interpreting the latter in activist terms as a resolution of the tensions between spiritual love and vital impulse.

FRANCIS DUNLOP

SCHELLING, FRIEDRICH WILHELM JOSEPH VON (1775–1854)

Like the other German idealists, Schelling began his philosophical career by acknowledging the fundamental importance of Kant's grounding of knowledge in the synthesizing activity of the subject, while questioning his establishment of a dualism between appearances and things in themselves. The other main influences on Schelling's early work are Leibniz, Spinoza, J.G. Fichte and F.H. Jacobi. While adopting both Spinoza's conception of an absolute ground, of which the finite world is the consequent, and Fichte's emphasis on the role of the I in the constitution of the world, Schelling seeks both to overcome the fatalism entailed by Spinoza's monism, and to avoid the sense in Fichte that nature only exists in order to be subordinated to the I. After adopting a position close to that of Fichte between 1794 and 1796, Schelling tried in his various versions of *Naturphilosophie* from 1797 onwards to find new ways of explicating the identity between thinking and the processes of nature, claiming that in this philosophy 'Nature is to be invisible mind, mind invisible nature'. In his *System des transcendentalen Idealismus* (System of Transcendental Idealism) (1800) he advanced the idea that art, as the 'organ of philosophy', shows the identity of what he terms 'conscious' productivity (mind) and 'unconscious' productivity (nature) because it reveals more than can be understood via the conscious intentions that lead to its production. Schelling's 'identity philosophy', which is another version of his *Naturphilosophie*, begins in 1801, and is summarized in the assertion that 'Existence is the link of a being as One, with itself as a multiplicity'. Material nature and the mind that knows it are different aspects of the same 'Absolute' or 'absolute identity' in which they are both grounded. In 1804 Schelling becomes concerned with the transition between the Absolute and the manifest world in which necessity and freedom are in conflict. If freedom is not to become inexplicable, he maintains, Spinoza's assumption of a logically necessary transition from God to the world cannot be accepted. *Philosophische Untersuchungen über das Wesen der menschlichen Freiheit und die damit zusammenhängenden Gegenstände* (Of Human Freedom) (1809) tries to explain how God could create a world involving evil, suggesting that nature relates to God somewhat as the later Freud's 'id' relates to the developed autonomous 'ego' which transcends the drives which motivate it.

The philosophy of *Die Weltalter* (The Ages of the World), on which Schelling worked during the 1810s and 1820s, interprets the intelligible world, including ourselves, as the result of an ongoing conflict between expansive and contractive forces. He becomes convinced that philosophy cannot finally give a reason for the existence of the manifest world that is the product of this conflict. This leads to his opposition, beginning in the 1820s, to Hegel's philosophical system, and to an increasing concern with theology. Hegel's system claims to be without presuppositions, and thus to be self-grounding. While Schelling accepts that the relations of dependence between differing aspects of knowledge can be articulated in a dynamic system, he thinks that this only provides a 'negative' philosophy, in which the fact of being is to be enclosed within thought. What he terms 'positive' philosophy tries to come to terms with the facticity of 'being which is absolutely independent of all thinking' (2 (3): 164). Schelling endeavours in his *Philosophie der*

Mythologie (Philosophy of Mythology) and *Philosophie der Offenbarung* (Philosophy of Revelation) of the 1830s and 1840s to establish a complete philosophical system by beginning with 'that which just exists ... in order to see if I can get from it to the divinity' (2 (3): 158), which leads to a historical account of mythology and Judeo-Christian revelation. This system does not, however, overcome the problem of the 'alterity' of being, its irreducibility to a philosophical system, which his critique of Hegel reveals. The direct and indirect influence of this critique on Kierkegaard, Nietzsche, Heidegger, Rosenzweig, Levinas, Derrida and others is evident, and Schelling must be considered as the key transitional figure between Hegel and approaches to 'post-metaphysical' thinking.

See also: GERMAN IDEALISM

ANDREW BOWIE

SCHILLER, JOHANN CHRISTOPH FRIEDRICH (1759–1805)

Schiller was an artist first – a major poet and the leading dramatist of eighteenth-century Germany – and an aesthetician second. At the height of his involvement in aesthetics, he calls the philosopher 'a caricature' beside 'the poet, the only true human being'. But reflection had deep roots in his nature, to the point where he felt it inhibited his creativity, yet would also have to be the means to restore it. He eventually came to terms with this paradox by devising a typology of 'naïve' and 'reflective' artists that explained his problem – and incidentally the evolution of modern European literature (*On Naïve and Reflective Poetry*) (1796). Schiller was also driven by a passionate belief in the humanizing and social function of art. His early speech *The Effect of Theatre on the People* (1784; later title *The Stage considered as a Moral Institution*) celebrated the one meeting-place where our full humanity could be restored. In the mature essays of the 1790s, an immensely more complex argument cannot hide the ultimate simplicity of his faith in art, even and especially in the midst of historical crisis: his culminating statement on beauty, *On the Aesthetic Education of Man* (1795), is at the same time a considered response to events in France, where a 'rational' Revolution had turned into a Reign of Terror. Schiller proposes an education for humane balance as the only sufficiently radical answer to the violent excesses of impulse, and argues that art is its only possible agent. Schiller's ideas are imaginative, generous and intuitively appealing as an account of what art is and might do. With the authority of his poetic standing and the high eloquence of his prose, they are powerful cultural criticism. Arguably they could have been more effective still and less vulnerable if he had not tried to make them something else by giving them a systematic quasi-Kantian form, as a result of which philosophical commentators have often patronized him while the Common Reader has been scared off.

See also: AESTHETICS AND ETHICS; BURKE, E.; CASSIRER, E.; GOETHE, J.W. VON; SUBLIME, THE

T.J. REED

SCHLEGEL, FRIEDRICH VON (1772–1829)

Schlegel was the major aesthetician of the Romantic movement in Germany during its first formative period (1797–1802). In these years he developed his influential concepts of Romantic poetry and irony, created an original approach to literary criticism and edited the journal of the early Romantic circle, *Athenäum*. Along with F. von Hardenberg (Novalis), F.W.J. Schelling and F.D.E. Schleiermacher, he was also a guiding spirit in the development of a Romantic metaphysics, ethics and politics. His metaphysics attempted to synthesize Fichte's idealism and Spinoza's naturalism. His ethics preached radical individualism and love against the abstract formalism of Kant's ethics. In his early politics Schlegel was very radical, defending the right of revolution and democracy against Kant. In his later years, however, he became much more conservative. His final works are a defence of his neo-Catholic mysticism.

FREDERICK BEISER

SCHLEIERMACHER, FRIEDRICH DANIEL ERNST (1768–1834)

Friedrich Daniel Ernst Schleiermacher was the most notable German-speaking protestant theologian of the nineteenth century. He gave significant impetus to the re-orientation of theology after the Age of Enlightenment (see his speeches *Über die Religion* (*On Religion*) (1799), and also *Kurze Darstellung des theologischen Studiums* (*Brief Outline of Theology as a Field of Study*) (1811)) and he enjoyed a wide audience in Berlin both as preacher and professor of theology and philosophy. Throughout his life he was a fervent advocate of the union between the Lutheran and the Reformed Church established in the so-called Old Prussian Union, and his compendium *Der christliche Glaube* (*The Christian Faith*) (1821, 1822) is held to be the first dogmatics transcending the denominational boundaries between the Reformation Churches. His translation of Plato attained the status of a classic. In his university lectures and academic speeches on philosophy he made a profound and lasting impression

on his audience, both in his historical and systematic thought. He also had an important hand in the reform of the German universities. In theology and philosophy he strove to find an independent and intermediate position between the Enlightenment, German idealism and Romanticism.

See also: HERMENEUTICS

GÜNTER MECKENSTOCK
Translated from the German
by J.G. FINLAYSON

SCHLICK, FRIEDRICH ALBERT MORITZ (1882–1936)

Moritz Schlick is usually remembered as the leader of the Vienna Circle, a group that flourished from the late 1920s to the mid-1930s, and made an important contribution to the philosophical movement known as 'logical empiricism'. Yet many of Schlick's most original contributions to philosophy antedated the hey-day of the Circle, providing the foundations for much of its subsequent development. He started his academic career as a physicist, and his early contributions to philosophy include an influential conventionalist interpretation of general relativity and a new account of the definitions of the basic terms of theoretical science. In the debates that flourished within the Vienna Circle he is famous for his commitment to the Principle of Verifiability and his defence of a correspondence theory of truth. In addition, his works during the final years of the Vienna Circle represent some of the most sober reflections on the problems that vexed the early logical empiricists. Although few of the views identified with logical empiricism currently find favour among philosophers, their approach to philosophy, especially their identification of its central perplexities, still wields enormous influence among contemporary thinkers. Since Schlick contributed significantly to the form logical empiricism assumed during its period of dominance, there can be little doubt that his thought continues to inspire much philosophical thinking today.

See also: LOGICAL POSTIVISM; MEANING AND VERIFICATION

THOMAS OBERDAN

SCHOPENHAUER, ARTHUR (1788–1860)

Schopenhauer, one of the great prose-writers among German philosophers, worked outside the mainstream of academic philosophy. He wrote chiefly in the first half of the nineteenth century, publishing *Die Welt als Wille und Vorstellung* (*The World as Will and Representation*), Volume 1 in 1818 and Volume 2 in 1844, but his ideas became widely

941

known only in the half-century from 1850 onwards. The impact of Schopenhauer's philosophy may be seen in the work of many artists of this period, most prominently Wagner, and in some of the themes of psychoanalysis. The philosopher most influenced by him was Nietzsche, who originally accepted but later opposed many of his ideas.

Schopenhauer considered himself a follower of Kant, and this influence shows in Schopenhauer's defence of idealism and in many of his central concepts. However, he also departs radically from Kant. His dominant idea is that of the will: he claims that the whole world is will, a striving and mostly unconscious force with a multiplicity of manifestations. Schopenhauer advances this as a metaphysical account of the world as it is in itself, but believes it is also supported by empirical evidence. Humans, as part of the world, are fundamentally willing beings, their behaviour shaped by an unchosen will to life which manifests itself in all organisms. His account of the interplay between the will and the intellect has been seen as a prototype for later theories of the unconscious.

Schopenhauer is a pessimist: he believes that our nature as willing beings inevitably leads to suffering, and that a life containing suffering is worse than nonexistence. These doctrines, conveyed in a literary style which is often profound and moving, are among his most influential. Equally important are his views on 'salvation' from the human predicament, which he finds in the denial of the will, or the will's turning against itself. Although his philosophy is atheist, Schopenhauer looks to several of the world religions for examples of asceticism and self-renunciation. His thought was partially influenced by Hinduism at an early stage, and he later found Buddhism sympathetic.

Aesthetic experience assumes great importance in Schopenhauer's work. He suggests that it is a kind of will-less perception in which one suspends one's attachments to objects in the world, attaining release from the torment of willing (desire and suffering), and understanding the nature of things more objectively. The artistic genius is the person abnormally gifted with the capacity for objective, will-free perception, who enables similar experiences in others. Here Schopenhauer adopts the Platonic notion of Ideas, which he conceives as eternally existing aspects of reality: the genius discerns these Ideas, and aesthetic experience in general may bring us to comprehend them. Music is given a special treatment: it directly manifests the nature of the will that underlies the whole world.

In ethics Schopenhauer makes thorough criticisms of Kant's theory. He bases his own ethical views on the notion of compassion or sympathy, which he considers a relatively rare quality, since

human beings, as organic, willing beings, are egoistic by nature. Nevertheless, compassion, whose worldview minimizes the distinctness of what are considered separate individuals, is the only true moral impulse for Schopenhauer.

See also: ART, VALUE OF; SEXUALITY, PHILOSOPHY OF

CHRISTOPHER JANAWAY

SCHRÖDINGER'S CAT
See QUANTUM MEASUREMENT PROBLEM

SCIENCE AND RELIGION
See RELIGION AND SCIENCE

SCIENCE, PHILOSOPHY OF

Introduction and historical background

Science grew out of philosophy; and, even after recognizable, if flexible, interdisciplinary boundaries developed, the most fruitful philosophical investigations have often been made in close connection with science and scientific advance. The major modern innovators – Bacon, Descartes, Leibniz and Locke among them – were all centrally influenced by, and in some cases significantly contributed to, the science of their day. Kant's fundamental epistemological problem was generated by the success of science: we have obtained certain knowledge, both in mathematics and – principally due to Newton – in science, how was this possible? Unsurprisingly, many thinkers who are principally regarded as great scientists, had exciting and insightful views on the aims of science and the methods of obtaining scientific knowledge. One can only wonder why the epistemological views of Galileo and of Newton, for example, are not taught along with those of Bacon and Locke, say, in courses on the history of modern philosophy. Certainly it can be argued very convincingly that the former two had at least as much insight into the aims and methods of science, and into how scientific knowledge is gained and accredited, as the latter two (see GALILEI, G.; NEWTON, I.; also see BOYLE, R.; COPERNICUS, N.; KEPLER, J.).

In the nineteenth century, MAXWELL, Hertz and Helmholz all had interesting views about explanation and the foundations of science, while POINCARÉ, who was undoubtedly one of the greatest mathematicians and mathematical physicists, was arguably also one of the greatest philosophers of science – developing important and influential views about, amongst other things, the nature of theories and hypotheses, explanation, and the role of probability theory both within science and as an account of scientific reasoning (also see DUHEM, P.M.M.).

The period from the 1920s to the 1950s is sometimes seen as involving a movement towards more formal issues to the exclusion of detailed concern with the scientific process itself (see LOGICAL POSITIVISM). While this has been over-exaggerated – CARNAP, Hempel, POPPER and especially REICHENBACH for example all show sophisticated awareness of a range of issues from contemporary science (also see OPERATIONALISM) – there is no doubt that general attention in philosophy of science has been redirected back to the details of science, and in particular of its *historical* development, by 'post-positivist' philosophers such as Hanson, FEYERABEND, KUHN, LAKATOS and others.

Current philosophy of science has developed this great tradition, addressing many of the now standard philosophical issues – about knowledge, the nature of reality, determinism and indeterminism and so on – but by paying very close attention to science both as an exemplar of knowledge and as a source of (likely) information about the world. This means that there is inevitably much overlap with other areas of philosophy – notably epistemology (the theory of scientific knowledge is of course a central concern of philosophy of science) and metaphysics (which philosophers of science often shun as an attempted a priori discipline but welcome when it is approached as an investigation of what current scientific theories and practices seem to be telling us about the likely structure of the universe). Indeed one way of usefully dividing up the subject would see scientific epistemology and what might be called scientific metaphysics as two of the main branches of the subject (these two together in turn forming what might be called general philosophy of science), with the third branch consisting of more detailed, specific investigations into foundational issues concerned with particular scientific fields or particular scientific theories (especial, though by no means exclusive, attention having been paid of late to foundational and interpretative issues in quantum theory and the Darwinian theory of evolution). Again not surprisingly, important contributions have been made in this third sub-field by scientists themselves who have reflected carefully and challengingly on their own work and its foundations (see BOHR, N.; DARWIN, C.R.; EINSTEIN, A.), as well as by those who are more usually considered philosophers.

1   Contemporary philosophy of science: the theory of scientific knowledge

Scientists propose theories and assess those theories in the light of observational and experimental evidence; what distinguishes science is the careful and systematic way in which its claims are based on evidence (see SCIENTIFIC METHOD). These simple claims, which I suppose would win fairly universal agreement, hide any number of complex issues.

First, concerning theories: how exactly are these best represented? Is Newton's theory of gravitation, or the neo-Darwinian theory of evolution, or the general theory of relativity, best represented – as logical empiricists such as Carnap supposed – as sets of (at least potentially) formally axiomatized sentences, linked to their observational bases by some sort of correspondence rules? Or are they best represented, as various recent 'semantic theorists' have argued, as sets of models (see MODELS; THEORIES, SCIENTIFIC)? Is this simply a representational matter or does the difference between the two sorts of approach matter scientifically and philosophically? This issue ties in with the increasingly recognized role of idealizations in science and the role of models as intermediates between fundamental theory and empirical laws (see CAMPBELL, N.R.; IDEALIZATIONS). It also relates to an important issue about how best to think of the state of a scientific field at a given time: is a scientist best thought of as accepting (in some sense or other) a single theory or set of such theories or rather as accepting some sort of more general and hierarchically organized set of assumptions and techniques in the manner of Kuhnian paradigms or Lakatosian research programmes? It seems likely that arriving at the correct account of scientific development and in particular of theory-change in science will depend on identifying the 'right' account of theories.

Next concerning the *evidence*: it has long been recognized that many of the statements that scientists are happy to regard as 'observation sentences' in fact presuppose a certain amount of theory, and that *all* observation sentences, short perhaps of purely subjective reports of current introspection, depend on some sort of minimal theory (even 'the needle points to around 5 on the scale' presupposes that the needle and the scale exist independently of the observer and that the observer's perception of them is not systematically deluded by a Cartesian demon). Does this mean that there is no real epistemic distinction between observational and theoretical claims? Does it mean that there is no secure basis or foundation for science in the form of observational and experimental results (see OBSERVATION)? If so, what becomes of the whole empiricist idea of basing scientific theories on the evidence? It can be argued that those who have drawn dire consequences from these considerations have confused fallibility with (serious) corrigibility: that there are observation statements, such as reports of meter readings and the like, of a sufficiently low level as to be, once independently and intersubjectively verified, not seriously corrigible despite being trivially strictly fallible (see MEASUREMENT, THEORY OF). Aside from this issue, experiment was for a long time regarded as raising barely any independent, philosophical or methodological concern – experiments being thought of as very largely simply means for testing theories (see EXPERIMENT). More recently, there has been better appreciation of the extent to which experimental science has a life of its own, independent of fundamental theory, and of the extent to which philosophical issues concerning testing, realism, underdetermination and so on can be illuminated by studying experiments.

Suppose that we have characterized scientific theories and drawn a line between theoretical and observational statements, what exactly is involved in 'basing' theoretical claims 'systematically and carefully' on the evidence? This question has of course been perhaps *the* central question of general philosophy of science in this century. We have known at least since David HUME that the answer cannot be that the correct theories are *deducible* from observation results. Indeed not only do our theories universally generalize the (inevitably finite) data as Hume pointed out, they also generally 'transcend' the data by explaining that data in terms of underlying, but non-observable, theoretical entities. This means that there must always in principle be (indefinitely) many theories that clash with one another at the theoretical level but yet entail all the same observational results (see UNDERDETERMINATION). What extra factors then are involved over and beyond simply having the right observational consequences? What roles do such factors as simplicity (see SIMPLICITY (IN SCIENTIFIC THEORIES)) and explanatory power (see EXPLANATION), play in accrediting theories on the basis of evidence? Moreover what status do these factors have – are they purely pragmatic (the sorts of features *we* like theories to have) or are they truth-indicating, and if so why? Some have argued that the whole process can be codified in probabilistic terms – the theories that we see as accredited by the evidence being the ones that are at any rate *more probable* in the light of that evidence than any of their rivals (see CONFIRMATION THEORY; INDUCTIVE INFERENCE).

Finally, suppose we have characterized the correct scientific way of reasoning to theories from evidence, what exactly does this tell us about

the theories that have been thus 'accredited' by the evidence? And what does it tell us about the entities – such as electrons, quarks, and the rest – apparently postulated by such theories? Is it reasonable to believe that these accredited theories are *true* descriptions of an underlying reality, that their theoretical terms refer to real, though unobservable, entities? (Or at least to believe that they are *probably* true? or *approximately* true? Or perhaps probably approximately true?) More strongly still, is any one of these beliefs the *uniquely* rational one? Or is it instead more, or at least equally, reasonable – at least equally explanatory of the way that science operates – to hold that these 'accredited' theories are no more than empirically adequate, even that they are simply instruments for prediction, the theoretical 'entities' they involve being no more than convenient fictions (see CONVENTIONALISM; INCOMMENSURABILITY; PUTNAM, H.; SCIENTIFIC REALISM AND ANTIREALISM)? One major problem faced by realists is to develop a plausible response to once accepted theories that are now rejected either by arguing that they were in some sense immature – not 'fully scientific' – or that, despite having been rejected, they nonetheless somehow live on as 'limiting cases' of current theories (see ALCHEMY; VITALISM).

Clearly an antirealist view of theories would be indicated *if* it could convincingly be argued that the accreditation of theories in science is not simply a function of evidential and other truth-related factors or even of epistemic pragmatic factors, but *also* of broader cultural and social matters. Although such arguments are heard increasingly often, many remain unconvinced – seeing those arguments as based *either* on confusion of discovery with validational issues *or* on fairly naïve views of evidential support (see CONSTRUCTIVISM; DISCOVERY, LOGIC OF).

2 Contemporary philosophy of science: 'scientific metaphysics'

Suppose that we take a vaguely realist view of current science; what does it tell us about the general structure of reality? Does a sensible interpretation of science require the postulation, for example, of natural kinds (see NATURAL KINDS) or universals? Does it require the postulation of a notion of physical necessity to distinguish natural laws from 'mere' regularities (see LAWS, NATURAL)? What is the nature of probability (see PROBABILITY, INTERPRETATIONS OF) – is a probabilistic claim invariably an expression of (partial) ignorance or are there real, irreducible 'objective chances' in the world? What exactly is involved in the claim that a particular theory (or a particular system described by such a theory) is deterministic (see DETERMIN-ISM AND INDETERMINISM), and what would it mean for the world as a whole to be deterministic? Does even 'deterministic' science eschew the notion of *cause* (as Russell argued)? Does this notion come into its own in more 'mundane' contexts, involving what might be called 'causal factors' and probabilistic causation? What exactly is the relationship between causal claims – such as 'smoking causes heart disease' – and statistical data (see CAUSATION)? How should spacetime be interpreted (see SPACETIME): as substantive or as 'merely' relational? Does current science plus whatever ideas of causality are associated with it unambiguously rule out the possibility of time travel (see TIME TRAVEL), or does this remain at least logically possible given current science?

Finally, and most generally, what is science (or, perhaps more significantly, the *direction* of scientific development) telling us about the overall structure of the universe – that it is one simple system governed at the fundamental level by one unified set of general laws, or rather that it is a 'patchwork' of interconnected but separate, mutually irreducible principles (see UNITY OF SCIENCE; REDUCTION, PROBLEMS OF)? Although it is of course true – despite some exaggerated claims on behalf of 'theories of everything' – that science is very far from reducing everything to a common fundamental basis, and although it is of course true that, even in cases where reduction is generally agreed to have been achieved, such as that of chemistry to physics, the reduction is *ontological* (that is, chemistry has been shown to need no essential, non-physical primitive notions) rather than *epistemological* (no one would dream of trying actually to *derive* a full description of any chemical reaction from the principles of quantum mechanics), some would nonetheless still argue that the overall *tendency* of science is in the reductionist direction.

These are examples of the more or less general, and impressively varied, 'metaphysical' issues informed by science that have attracted recent philosophical attention.

3 Contemporary philosophy of science: foundational issues from current science

Many of the most interesting issues in current philosophy of science are closely tied to foundational or methodological concerns about current scientific theory. One fertile source of such concerns is quantum theory. How much of a revolutionary change in our general metaphysical view of the world does it require? Is the theory irreducibly indeterministic or do 'hidden variable' interpretations of some sort remain possible despite

the negative results? What does quantum mechanics tell us about the notion of cause? Does quantum mechanics imply a drastic breakdown of 'locality', telling us that the properties of even vastly spatially separated systems are fundamentally interconnected – so that we can no longer think of, for example 'two' spatially separated electrons as separate, independent 'particles'? More directly, is there, in view of the 'measurement problem' a coherent interpretation of quantum mechanics at all? (It has been argued that when the theory is interpreted universally so that *all* systems, including 'macroscopic' ones, such as measuring apparatuses, are assigned a quantum state then the two fundamental principles of quantum theory – the Schrödinger equation and the projection postulate – come into direct contradiction (see BELL'S THEOREM; QUANTUM MEASUREMENT PROBLEM; QUANTUM MECHANICS, INTERPRETATION OF; see also RANDOMNESS; STATISTICS).)

Although perhaps attracting relatively less attention than quantum theory, the other two great theories that form the triumvirate at the heart of contemporary physics – relativity (both special and general) and thermodynamics – pose similarly fascinating problems. In the case of relativity theory, philosophers have raised both ontological issues (for example, concerning the nature of spacetime) and epistemological issues (concerning for example the real role played in Einstein's development of the theory by Machian empiricism, the role of allegedly crucial experiments such as that of Michelson and Morley (see CRUCIAL EXPERIMENTS), and the evidential impact on the general theory of the Eddington star-shift experiment). There are also important issues about the consistency of relativity and quantum theory – issues that in turn feed into the more general questions concerning the unity of science and realism (see RELATIVITY THEORY, PHILOSOPHICAL SIGNIFICANCE OF).

Thermodynamics raises issues about, amongst other things, probability and the testing of probabilistic theories, about determinism and indeterminism, and about the direction of time (see THERMODYNAMICS; DETERMINISM AND INDETERMINISM; DUHEM, P.M.M.; TIME). Other current areas of physics, too, raise significant foundational issues (see CHAOS THEORY; COSMOLOGY).

For a long time, philosophy of science meant in effect philosophy of *physics*. A welcome broadening-out has occurred recently – especially in the direction of philosophy of biology. The central concern here has been with foundational issues in the Darwinian theory of evolution (or more accurately the neo-Darwinian synthesis of natural selection and genetics). Questions have been raised about the testability and, more generally, the empirical credentials of that theory, about the scope of the theory (in particular what it can tell us about humans and human societies), about the appropriate 'unit of selection' (individual, gene, group), about what exactly are genes and what exactly are species, and about whether evolutionary biology involves distinctive – perhaps even in *some* sense 'teleological' – modes of explanation (see DARWIN, C.R.; EVOLUTION, THEORY OF; FUNCTIONAL EXPLANATION; GENETICS; LIFE, ORIGIN OF; SOCIOBIOLOGY; SPECIES; TAXONOMY). More recently philosophy of biology has started to widen its own scope by considering issues outside of evolutionary theory, where, however, issues of reductionism and of the possibility of distinctive modes of explanation still loom large.

See also: ATOMISM, ANCIENT; COLOUR, THEORIES OF; COMPUTER SCIENCE; DECISION AND GAME THEORY; DEMARCATION PROBLEM; DEMOCRITUS; FACTS; INFORMATION THEORY; JUNG, C.G.; MATTER; MEAD, G.H.; RELIGION AND SCIENCE; RISK ASSESSMENT; SPACE; TECHNOLOGY, PHILOSOPHY OF; THOUGHT EXPERIMENTS

References and further reading

Kitcher, P. (1993) *The Advancement of Science: Science without Legend, Objectivity without Illusions*, New York and Oxford: Oxford University Press. (Thorough and illuminating account of the general issues surrounding theory-change in science; also useful as an introduction to the methodological issues raised by Darwinian theory.)

Papineau, D. (ed.) (1996) *The Philosophy of Science*, Oxford Readings in Philosophy, Oxford: Oxford University Press. (Recent collection of articles, especially on the realism/antirealism issue, but also on issues of empirical support.)

Salmon, M.H. *et al.* (1992) *Introduction to the Philosophy of Science*, Englewood Cliffs, NJ: Prentice Hall. (A text written by members of the internationally celebrated History and Philosophy of Science Department at the University of Pittsburgh and covering general philosophy of science, as well as philosophy of physics, of biology, and of the behavioural and social sciences.)

JOHN WORRALL

SCIENTIFIC METHOD

Introduction

Procedures for attaining scientific knowledge are known as scientific methods. These methods include formulating theories and testing them against observation or experiment. Ancient and medieval thinkers called any systematic body of knowledge a 'science', and their methods were aimed at knowledge in general. According to the most common model for scientific knowledge, formulated by Aristotle, induction yields universal propositions from which all knowledge in a field can be deduced. This model was refined by medieval and early modern thinkers, and further developed in the nineteenth century by Whewell and Mill.

As Kuhn observed, idealized accounts of scientific method must be distinguished from descriptions of what scientists actually do. The methods of careful observation and experiment have been in use from antiquity, but became more widespread after the seventeenth century. Developments in instrument making, in mathematics and statistics, in terminology, and in communication technology have altered the methods and the results of science.

1 'Method' and 'science'
2 Ideas of method from the Greeks to Thomas Kuhn
3 Scientific method in scientific practice

1 'Method' and 'science'

'Method' comes from the Greek *meta* (after) plus *hodos* (path or way). A method is a way to achieve an end; a scientific method is a way to achieve the ends of science. What those ends are depends on what science is or is taken to be. The word 'science' now means primarily natural science, examples of which are physics, astronomy, biology, chemistry, geology and psychology, and it applies secondarily to social sciences such as economics and sociology. Discussions of method focus on the cognitive aims of science, which may include knowledge, understanding, explanation, or predictive success, with respect to all or part of nature or to some domain of natural or social phenomena. Abstractly described, scientific method is the means for attaining these aims, especially by forming models, theories, or other cognitive structures and testing them through observation and experiment (see EXPERIMENT; MODELS; OBSERVATION; THEORIES, SCIENTIFIC). Investigations of scientific method may describe the methods actually employed by scientists, or they may formulate proposals about the procedures that should be followed to achieve scientific knowledge.

The main features traditionally ascribed to 'the scientific method' – including clear statement of a problem, careful confrontation of theory with fact, open-mindedness, and (potential) public availability or replicability of evidence – are common to many cognitive endeavours, including much work in the humanities. Although there is no single method that distinguishes science from other intellectual practices, the following features are characteristic of the natural and social sciences: the use of quantitative data and of theories formulated mathematically; the use of artificially created experimental situations; and an interest in universal generalizations or laws (see DEMARCATION PROBLEM; LAWS, NATURAL; UNITY OF SCIENCE). (But note that biological taxonomies are not intrinsically quantitative, and that neither astronomy nor economics is based primarily on experiment.) In both the natural and social sciences, the formation of models or theories may involve skills in mathematical computation and derivation, in evaluating consistency, in imagining new theoretical possibilities, in assessing the structure of a taxonomy, or in relating one area of investigation to other areas. The means for testing theories or generating new empirical knowledge vary widely, and include systematic observation, unsystematic observation, checks against background theories or knowledge, and various experimental procedures, including sophisticated statistical techniques, the construction of special instruments or apparatus and the use of specially bred laboratory animals.

2 Ideas of method from the Greeks to Thomas Kuhn

Because 'science' originally meant any systematic body of knowledge, ranging from mathematics to theology, the method of science was the method for obtaining, or perhaps merely for presenting and teaching, knowledge in general. Methods varied in relation to beliefs about what there is to be known.

The writings of Plato and Aristotle embody contrasting conceptions of both the objects of knowledge and the method for knowing them. In *Republic* VI, Plato divided the objects of knowledge into two realms: the visible and the intelligible (see PLATO §14). He considered the former to include the objects of the senses, about which only opinion but not genuine knowledge is possible, and the latter to include geometry and astronomy, in which investigators assume the existence of their objects (such as geometrical objects) and reason from them as from hypotheses. In the highest reaches of the intelligible realm, reason attempts to reach 'the first principle of all that exists', from which it then 'comes down to a conclusion . . . proceeding by means of Forms and through Forms to its conclusions which are Forms', without any reference to the visible world. Plato conceived the sensible world as a dim reflection of the intelligible Forms, and he held that the Forms themselves are best known through direct intellectual contemplation, independent of

sensory experience. The notion of an intelligible world behind the sensible world, and especially of a world described by mathematics, has played an important role in physical science since Plato's time.

ARISTOTLE rejected Plato's intelligible realm because it removed the objects of mathematical sciences such as astronomy from the sensible world, where he believed the forms of things are to be found. He carried out extensive observations (including dissections) in biology and developed a preliminary taxonomic scheme. Aristotle's principal discussion of method is the *Posterior Analytics*, a founding work in the philosophy of science. He accepted the Platonic distinction between a direction of cognition that is going 'to the forms' and the direction of cognition (as in syllogistic demonstration) that proceeds 'from the forms', but he conceived these processes as starting from sensible objects and arriving at knowledge of the common natures or essences of things as existing in those objects. Such knowledge (for instance, of the essence of a specific kind of mineral, or kind of living thing) yields a set of core propositions in each science, from which other knowledge is to be deductively derived.

Medieval philosophers, including Roger BACON, John DUNS SCOTUS and WILLIAM OF OCKHAM, commented extensively on Aristotle's methodological writings, which were later discussed at the University of Padua together with those of Galen. A central topic was the distinction between analysis and synthesis, or, as it was sometimes called, between resolution and composition. In the analytic phase of inquiry, one resolves the object of investigation into its basic constituents or least elements so as to determine its first principles. In the synthetic phase, one explains a subject matter from its first principles, or presents a body of knowledge by deriving it from such principles. In a common example, the analytic phase would include the search for the axioms, postulates and definitions of geometry; the synthetic phase the demonstration of theorems from those axioms and postulates. Bacon suggested that the first principles achieved in the analytic or inductive phase can be tested by deducing and checking new consequences (a feature of 'hypothetico-deductive' tests of theories). Scotus outlined a method of agreement, in which a possible cause for an effect is found by listing the circumstances that co-occur with the effect and looking for one that is present every time. Ockham suggested a method of difference, in which a circumstance that is present when the effect is present and absent when it is absent is considered as a possible cause for the effect.

The seventeenth century, a time of fundamental change in physics and astronomy, saw continuing attention to method within the inductive–deductive framework established by Aristotle. Francis BACON outlined inductive procedures in detail, calling for extensive collections of data (named 'histories') which are to be culled systematically for general principles or laws. Galileo urged that mathematical descriptions be fitted to natural phenomena through observation and experiment (see GALILEI, G.). Descartes wrote in *Discourse on the Method* (1637) that the derivation of an effect from a cause may serve as an explanation of the effect, and also as an empirical 'proof' of the posited cause (see DESCARTES, R. §6). Newton, in *Mathematical Principles of Natural Philosophy* (1729), laid down several 'hypotheses' or 'rules' for reasoning in natural philosophy. He advised investigators to avoid multiplying causes in relation to effects, to generalize from properties found in bodies that have been observed to all bodies in the universe, and to accept inductively supported propositions as 'accurately or very nearly true' until new observations improve upon their accuracy or limit their scope (see NEWTON, I.).

During the nineteenth century, the 'philosophy of science' or the 'logic of science' became, in the writings of William WHEWELL, John Stuart MILL and others, a main staple of philosophy. Whewell's *Philosophy of the Inductive Sciences* (1840) analyses scientific knowledge of 'external' nature (excluding the mind itself). Whewell held that scientific knowledge is based upon sensations and ideas, the former being the 'objective' element (caused by objects), the latter a 'subjective' element (provided by the knowing subject). Consciously entertained facts and theories correspond to sensations and ideas, but not completely, because all facts implicitly include ideas (and so, possibly, theory). Whewell divided the methods of science into methods of observation, of obtaining clear ideas, and of induction. The methods of observation include quantitative observation (as in chemistry or astronomy) and the perception of similarities (as in natural history); observation includes both the collection and classification of facts. Clear ideas result from intellectual education (including both the mathematical sciences and natural history), and from discussion, including (sometimes metaphysical) discussions of definitions, such as whether uniform force acting in free fall should be defined relative to space or to time. Science proceeds by 'induction', including the use of quantitative techniques to smooth out the irregularities of observation (that is, the 'method of curves' by which a curve is fitted to data points, the 'method of means' and the 'method of least squares') and the formation and empirical testing of tentative hypotheses. Laws of phenomena are usually formed first, but theories of true causes

are desired, such as (Whewell explained) have been found in physical astronomy, physical optics, and geology, and might be found with respect to heat, magnetism, electricity, chemical compounds and living organisms.

In *A System of Logic* (1843), Mill analysed the methods of science even more fully than had Whewell, now including psychology and the social sciences (also known as the 'mental' and 'moral' sciences). In his analysis of experimental method, Mill included the methods of agreement and difference already mentioned, and added the method of residues, which directs the investigator to look for the (as yet unknown) causes of those effects that remain after all other effects have been assigned to known causes, and the method of concomitant variations, according to which those phenomena that vary regularly in quantitative degree with one another are assumed to be causally related. Like Whewell, Mill emphasized the role of new or pre-existing concepts and names in scientific observation, and the role that classification plays in induction. He proposed that psychology and the social sciences should adopt the explanatory structures of the natural sciences, a proposal frequently criticized since his time, notably by the Neo-Kantians Wilhelm DILTHEY, Heinrich Rickert and Ernst CASSIRER, who discussed methods pertaining to the 'social' or 'human' sciences, and who included the humanities as a form of 'science' (in German, *Wissenschaft*) (see NEO-KANTIANISM; POSITIVISM IN THE SOCIAL SCIENCES).

Philosophers in the first half of the twentieth century, especially the Vienna Circle and Karl POPPER, sought to analyse science and to reconstruct scientific reasoning using the new symbolic logic or the new theory of probability (see VIENNA CIRCLE). They continued the investigation of theory confirmation, focusing on recent theories in physics (see CONFIRMATION THEORY). Rudolph CARNAP attempted unsuccessfully to develop a quantitative theory of inductive support. Carl Hempel, who favoured a hypothetico–deductive account of scientific confirmation (involving the testing of theories by their deductive consequences), revealed certain paradoxes that result when the relation between scientific generalizations and confirming instances are expressed in predicate logic and certain (plausible) assumptions are made. Popper concluded that the defining feature of the empirical methods of science is that statements are always subjected to falsification by new data.

In the second half of the twentieth century philosophical analyses of scientific method broadened to again include sciences such as biology and geology, and paid greater attention to the history of science. N.R. Hanson recalled the often implicit role of theory in observation, questioning the notion of a theory-neutral observation language (see OBSERVATION). Thomas S. KUHN emphasized the social nature of scientific communities and the common training that produces a shared vocabulary and set of experimental procedures. Kuhn and Paul FEYERABEND stressed the need to distinguish the idealized accounts of scientific method given by some scientists and philosophers from the actual methodological practices of scientists. In studying the latter, historical and sociological investigation supplements the participatory acquaintance with scientific research possessed by scientists themselves and by some philosophers.

3   Scientific method in scientific practice

The methods of careful observation and description (including quantitative description) and of controlled experiment arose in antiquity and were practised by Greek, Hellenistic and Islamic investigators. Examples include Aristotle's biological observations, the many Greek and Arabic (and earlier Babylonian) tables of astronomical data, Ptolemy and Alhazen's careful studies of binocular vision and distance perception, and Galen's use of the ligature and other experimental techniques in physiology.

From antiquity, instruments aided the precision of observation in astronomy and optics. In the early seventeenth century Johannes KEPLER used Tycho Brahe's precise astronomical data (obtained with improved instruments) to establish the elliptical orbits of the planets and to determine the relations among the sizes and periods of those orbits. In 1609 Galileo used the newly invented telescope to observe previously unseen heavenly bodies (including the moons of Jupiter). Later in the century the microscope opened new fields of observation. The nineteenth and twentieth centuries have seen the development of refined and often complex instrumentation in all branches of natural science, including biology, chemistry and psychology, ranging from improved balances to the electron microscope and the space telescope. Photography has been used to record data in nearly every field. The computer permits collection and manipulation of larger bodies of data than was previously practical. In psychology, the computer allows generation of precisely controlled stimuli and the recording of data with highly accurate temporal measurement.

The development of mathematics, including probability and statistics, has yielded new forms of theory statement and new descriptions of observational or experimental data. Mathematical sciences from antiquity to the seventeenth century used

geometry almost exclusively. The development of algebraic geometry and of the calculus permitted new statements of Newtonian mechanics in the eighteenth century, and opened up new possibilities (theoretical as well as experimental) for describing and investigating functional relations among quantities. In the nineteenth and twentieth centuries, new mathematics has been demanded by or has facilitated mathematical physics. Thus, the discovery of non-Euclidean geometries opened up hitherto unforeseen theoretical possibilities in physical cosmology. The development of probability and statistics permitted the formulation of statistical laws, as in mathematical genetics, quantum physics and sociology (see PROBABILITY, INTERPRETATIONS OF; STATISTICS; STATISTICS AND SOCIAL SCIENCE). Inferential statistics is widely used in the analysis of quantitative data in psychology and other sciences.

Clear and precise terminology is an important feature of scientific methodology. Astronomy, optics (as the science of vision), natural history and medicine developed technical vocabularies in antiquity. Newton profoundly altered the terminology of physics, which continues to change as theories change. Carl von Linnaeus invented important taxonomies in botany and zoology; after Darwin's theory of natural selection gained acceptance, evolutionary history influenced biological taxonomy (see EVOLUTION, THEORY OF; TAXONOMY). Molecular biology has produced another new terminology. In psychology, long-standing mentalistic terminology was purged by twentieth-century behaviourists (see BEHAVIOURISM, METHODOLOGICAL AND SCIENTIFIC), and has since been reintroduced, partly under the influence of the computer metaphor for mental processes (see MIND, COMPUTATIONAL THEORIES OF). Likewise, economics, anthropology and sociology use refined technical vocabularies.

A sense of the various instruments and techniques of data collection and analysis now used can be gleaned from the materials, methods and results sections of scientific journals. Journals and other means of communication are themselves of methodological significance. The available methods for presenting observational data were radically altered by the development of printing (for both text and images), and again through computer-generated images and electronic communication. The mass production of standardized illustrations and printed data permits worldwide dissemination, utilization and hence testing of scientific findings.

The structure of scientific research groups and their interaction with scientific institutions, including the processes for deciding whether to fund research or to publish results, are also part of the method of science (broadly conceived). The methodological effectiveness of science can be evaluated at various scales, including the individual experiment, the individual investigator, the laboratory group, or the institutional structures by which collective instruments such as particle accelerators are administered. One might further examine the normative consequences of having relative homogeneity of methodological and theoretical belief across an active science, as opposed to the hedged bet of methodological and theoretical diversity. The student of scientific methods may investigate any aspect of the linguistic, conceptual, psychological, instrumental, social and institutional features of the sciences that affects their cognitive products.

See also: CRUCIAL EXPERIMENTS; DISCOVERY, LOGIC OF; EXPLANATION; INDUCTIVE INFERENCE; OBJECTIVITY

References and further reading

Hanson, N.R. (1958) *Patterns of Discovery*, Cambridge: Cambridge University Press. (Important study of fundamental concepts in science, with reference to actual historical cases.)

Kitcher, P. (1993) *The Advancement of Science: Science without Legend, Objectivity without Illusions*, New York and Oxford: Oxford University Press. (Advanced work in philosophy of science, relevant to method.)

Losee, J. (2001) *Historical Introduction to the Philosophy of Science*, Oxford: Oxford University Press, 4th edn. (An introduction, with references, to many topics in the philosophy of science.)

GARY HATFIELD

SCIENTIFIC REALISM AND ANTIREALISM

Introduction

Traditionally, scientific realism asserts that the objects of scientific knowledge exist independently of the minds or acts of scientists and that scientific theories are true of that objective (mind-independent) world. The reference to knowledge points to the dual character of scientific realism. On the one hand it is a metaphysical (specifically, an ontological) doctrine, claiming the independent existence of certain entities. On the other hand it is an epistemological doctrine asserting that we can know what individuals exist and that we can find out the truth of the theories or laws that govern them.

Opposed to scientific realism (hereafter just 'realism') are a variety of antirealisms, including

phenomenalism and empiricism. Recently two others, instrumentalism and constructivism, have posed special challenges to realism. Instrumentalism regards the objects of knowledge pragmatically, as tools for various human purposes, and so takes reliability (or empirical adequacy) rather than truth as scientifically central. A version of this, fictionalism, contests the existence of many of the objects favoured by the realist and regards them as merely expedient means to useful ends. Constructivism maintains that scientific knowledge is socially constituted, that 'facts' are made by us. Thus it challenges the objectivity of knowledge, as the realist understands objectivity, and the independent existence that realism is after. Conventionalism, holding that the truths of science ultimately rest on man-made conventions, is allied to constructivism.

Realism and antirealism propose competing interpretations of science as a whole. They even differ over what requires explanation, with realism demanding that more be explained and antirealism less.

> 1 Arguing for realism
> 2 Piecemeal realisms
> 3 Alternatives to realism
> 4 The constructivist challenge

1 Arguing for realism

Late nineteenth- and early twentieth-century debates over the reality of molecules and atoms polarized the scientific community on the realism question. Antirealists like MACH, DUHEM and POINCARÉ – representing (roughly) phenomenalist, instrumentalist and conventionalist positions – at first carried the day with a sceptical attitude towards the truth of scientific theories and the reality of the 'theoretical entities' employed by those theories (see PHENOMENALISM; CONVENTIONALISM). Led by the successes of statistical mechanics (see THERMODYNAMICS) and relativity (see RELATIVITY THEORY, PHILOSOPHICAL SIGNIFICANCE OF), however, Planck and EINSTEIN helped turn the tide towards realism. That movement was checked by two developments. In physics the quantum theory of 1925–6 quickly ran into difficulties over the possibility of a realist interpretation (see QUANTUM MECHANICS, INTERPRETATION OF) and the community settled on the instrumentalist programme promoted by BOHR and Heisenberg. This was a formative lesson for logical empiricism whose respect for developments in physics and whose positivistic orientation led it to brand the realism question as metaphysical, a pseudo-question. Thus for a while empiricist and instrumentalist trends in science and philosophy eclipsed scientific realism.

The situation changed again in the 1960s, by which time science and its technological applications had become a ubiquitous and dominant feature of Western culture. In this setting philosophers like Smart and PUTNAM proposed what came to be known as the 'miracles' argument for scientific realism. They argued that unless the theoretical entities employed by scientific theories actually existed and the theories themselves were at least approximately true of the world at large, the evident success of science (in terms of its applications and predictions) would surely be a miracle. It is easy to see, at least with hindsight, that the most one could conclude from scientific success, however impressive, is that science is on the right track. That could mean, as the argument concludes, on the track to truth or it could just mean on the track to empirical success, perhaps with deeply flawed representations of reality. The 'miracles' argument is inconclusive. Nevertheless, during the next two decades it was compelling for many philosophers. Indeed, during this period realism became so identified with science that questioning realism was quickly put down as anti-science.

Realist orthodoxy found support in Popper's attack on instrumentalism, which he criticized as unable to account for his own falsificationist methodology (see POPPER, K.R.). Broadening this line, Boyd developed an explanationist version of the 'miracles' argument that focused on the methods of science and tried as well to give proper due to the human-centred (constructivist and conventionalist) aspects of science emphasized by KUHN and FEYERABEND. Boyd asks why methods crafted by us and reflecting our interests and limitations lead to instrumentally successful science. Contrasting realism with empiricism and constructivism, he finds that realism offers the best (indeed, the only) explanation. That is because, he argues, if we begin with truths or near-truths the methods we have crafted for science produce even more of the same. Since it is only realism that demands the truth of our scientific theories, then realism wins as giving the best explanation for the instrumental success of science. Hence, like a scientific hypothesis, realism is most likely to be true and we should believe in it.

The explanationist argument is carefully framed so that we ask only about the instrumental success of science; that is, success at the observational level. To take science as successful (for example, truth-producing) at the theoretical level would beg the question against empiricism and instrumentalism. Once this is recognized, however, we can see a significant gap in the reasoning. The argument is driven by a picture of science as generating new

truths from old truths, but the explanatory issue raised is only about truths at the level of observation, not about truths in general. Antirealists might well reject this as an illegitimate request for explanation. If they accept it, there is an obvious empiricist or instrumentalist response: namely, that our scientific methods are made by us to winnow out instrumentally reliable information. If we begin with fairly reliable statements, the methods we have crafted for science will produce even more. Thus the explanation for scientific success at the instrumental level need not involve the literal truth of our scientific principles or theories, just their instrumental reliability. This move nicely converts the argument for realism as the best explanation of scientific success into an argument for instrumentalism.

There is a second problem with the explanationist tactic, perhaps even more serious. The conclusion in support of realism depends on an inference to the best explanation (see INFERENCE TO THE BEST EXPLANATION). That principle, to regard as true that which explains best, is a principle that antirealisms (especially instrumentalism and empiricism) deny. Van Fraassen, for example, regards being the best explanation as a virtue, but one separate from truth. (He reminds us that the best may well be the best of a bad lot.) Although not required, there could perhaps be an instrumentalist principle of inference to the best explanation. It would not infer to the truth of the explanation but to its instrumental reliability (or empirical adequacy) – precisely the strategy pursued above where we infer instrumentalism from the instrumental success of science. Thus the explanationist argument uses a specifically realist principle of inference to the best explanation and, in so doing, begs the question of truth versus reliability, one of the central questions at issue between realism and antirealism.

2 Piecemeal realisms

Inference to the best explanation promised the most cogent version of the 'miracles' argument. Its inadequacy hastened a retreat from realism's original undertaking as a global interpretation of science. Retreat was fostered by two other antirealist developments. One was the pessimistic meta-induction to the instability of current science, a conclusion based on the repeated overthrow of scientific theories historically and the consequent dramatic alterations in ontology. The other was a sharpening of the underdetermination thesis associated with Poincaré and Duhem, suggesting that there may be empirically equivalent theories between which no evidence can decide (see UNDERDETERMINATION). Both developments tended to undermine claims for the reality of the objects of scientific investigation and the truth of scientific theories.

Pursuing a salvage operation, several philosophers suggested that realism could confine itself to being a doctrine about the independent existence of theoretical entities ('entity realism') without commitment to the truth of the theories employing them. Hacking proposed an 'experimental argument' for this entity realism; roughly, that if you can deploy entities experimentally to discover new features of nature (for example, use an electron gun to learn about quarks), then the entities must be real whether or not the covering theories are true (see EXPERIMENT). Cartwright suggested that the strategy of inference to the best explanation be confined to an inference to the causes of phenomena, since causes are unquestionably real. To the antirealist, however, these related strategies seem far from compelling. For one thing, it is not clear that one can so neatly disengage theoretical entities from their covering theories. Moreover, in both cases, we can see that the basis on which one is asked to draw a realist conclusion need support no more than a conclusion about utility or reliability. In Hacking's case one need conclude only that electrons are a useful theoretical construct (perhaps a useful fiction?) and in Cartwright's that certain causal hypotheses are reliable in certain domains.

Faced with these difficulties realism has fragmented even further. Sometimes it takes an historicist turn, countering the pessimistic meta-induction by endorsing as real only those fruitful entities that survive scientific revolutions. Sometimes realism becomes highly selective in other ways; for example, looking only at what seems essential in specific cases of explanatory or predictive success, or at entities that stand out as supported by only the very best scientific evidence. Although each of these principles locates matters of scientific significance, it is not clear that such criteria overcome the general strategies that have undone global realist arguments. In particular they do not seem to discriminate effectively between what is real and what is merely useful (and so between realism and instrumentalism).

3 Alternatives to realism

Several alternatives to realism have developed during the course of these debates. Principal among them are Putnam's 'internal realism' (see PUTNAM, H.), van Fraassen's 'constructive empiricism' and what Fine calls 'the natural ontological attitude', or NOA. In a chameleon-like move, Putnam switched from being realism's champion to its critic. Rejecting what he called 'metaphysical

realism' (associated with a 'God's eye view'), Putnam proposed a perspectival position in which truth is relative to language (or conceptual scheme). He could then allow scientific claims to be true in their proper domain but deny that they tell the whole story, or even that there is a whole story to tell. His picture was that there could be other truths – different stories about the world – each of which it may be proper to believe. Van Fraassen's constructive empiricism eschews belief in favour of what he calls commitment. He takes the distinguishing features of realism as twofold: realism seeks truth as a goal, and when a realist accepts a theory it is accepted as true. Constructive empiricism, by contrast, takes empirical adequacy (not truth) as the goal of science, and when it accepts a theory it accepts it as empirically adequate. This involves commitment to working within the framework of the theory but not to believing in its literal truth. Unlike these others, Fine's NOA is not a general interpretive scheme but simply an attitude that one can take to science. The attitude is minimal, deflationary and expressly local. It is critically positive, looking carefully at particular scientific claims and procedures, and cautions us not to attach any general interpretive agenda to science. Thus NOA rejects positing goals for science as a whole, as realists and constructive empiricists do. NOA accepts 'truth' as a semantic primitive, but rejects any general theories or interpretations of scientific truth, including the perspectivalism built into internal realism and the external-world correspondence built into realism itself. NOA is perhaps better classified as a nonrealism than as an antirealism.

It is interesting to contrast how these positions respond to good science. Realism accepts good science as true of an observer-independent world; internal realism accepts it as true relative to our scheme of things; constructive empiricism accepts it only as empirically adequate. NOA simply accepts it. This brings out two significant features of the recent debates. One is that they are more about the reach of evidence (what kind of acceptance is warranted) than about the metaphysical character of the objects of belief. The contrast also shows that major contenders, whether realist or not, share a basically positive attitude towards science. This has not always been acknowledged and a contrary suspicion still attaches to constructivism, which is frequently regarded as anti-science.

4 The constructivist challenge

Contemporary developments in the history and sociology of science have revived constructivist approaches (see CONSTRUCTIVISM). Sharing with instrumentalism and other forms of pragmatism an emphasis on science as an activity, constructivism borrows the Marxist vocabulary of the 'production' of ideas to place science among the manufacturing institutions. Specifically, what science makes is knowledge, which includes concepts and theories, along with things and even facts. Constructivism also emphasizes that science is open-ended. It highlights the role of unforced judgment in scientific practice, challenging the picture of a strict scientific method and of decision-making forced by rationality at every turn. The upshot is to see science as a form of human engagement like others; just people doing their own thing as best they can. Many regard this placement of science as a displacement, demoting science from its privileged position as the paradigm of rational and objective inquiry.

The emphasis on human constructions may challenge the mind-independence that is the hallmark of realist metaphysics. The respective roles of the social order and of nature in shaping these constructions, however, differ among constructivists, making for strong idealism at one pole (see IDEALISM) and pragmatic realism at the other. Despite these differences, constructivism challenges the unique position that realism marks out for itself with respect to ongoing science. If we look beyond the relatively sophisticated arguments for realism rehearsed above, perhaps realism's major hold on our attention is its claim to offer the only viable setting for understanding scientific practice. We are told that unless we take scientists to be engaged in finding out about a world not of their own making we cannot begin to understand how science works. The major constructivist challenge is right here. The heart of constructivism consists in richly detailed studies of science in action. These studies set out to understand how science actually proceeds while bracketing the truth-claims of the area of science under investigation. Instead, constructivists typically employ little more than everyday psychology and an everyday pragmatism with respect to the common objects of experience. To the extent to which these studies succeed they paint a picture of science quite different from realism's, a constructivist picture that may undermine not only the arguments but also the intuitions on which scientific realism rests.

See also: DEWEY, J.; EMPIRICISM; PRAGMATISM; REALISM AND ANTIREALISM; THEORIES, SCIENTIFIC

References and further reading

Papineau, D. (ed.) (1996) *The Philosophy of Science*, Oxford: Oxford University Press. (Essays by leading figures touching on many of the themes related to §2 and §3.)

ARTHUR FINE

SCIENTIFIC THEORIES
See THEORIES, SCIENTIFIC

SCOPE

Scope is a notion used by logicians and linguists in describing artificial and natural languages. It is best introduced in terms of the languages of formal logic. Consider a particular occurrence of an operator in a sentence – say, that of → in eqn (1), or that of the universal quantifier ∀ in eqn (2).

(1) $\quad A \rightarrow (B \ \& \ C)$

(2) $\quad \forall x(Bxy \rightarrow \exists y Axy)$

Speaking intuitively, the scope of the operator is that part of the sentence which it governs. The scope of → in (1) is the whole sentence; this renders the whole sentence a conditional. The scope of &, on the other hand, is just $(B \ \& \ C)$. In (2), the scope of the quantifier ∀ is the whole sentence, which allows it to bind every occurrence of x. The scope of ∃ is only $\exists y Axy$. Since Bxy is outside its scope, the y in Bxy is left unbound.

See also: ANAPHORA; DESCRIPTIONS; QUANTIFIERS, SUBSTITUTIONAL AND OBJECTUAL

MARK RICHARD

SCOTUS, JOHN DUNS
See DUNS SCOTUS, JOHN

SEARLE, JOHN (1932–)

John Searle was a pupil of J.L. Austin at Oxford in the 1950s. He is the Mills Professor of Mind and Language at the University of California, Berkeley, where he has taught philosophy since 1959. According to Searle, the primary objects of analysis in the philosophy of language are not expressions but the production of expressions, speech acts, in accordance with rules. Learning a language involves (often unconsciously) internalizing rules that govern the performance of speech acts in that language. Speech-act theory aims to discover these rules and is itself a part of action theory, which concerns intentional states directed at or about something. It follows that speech-act theory is part of a more comprehensive theory of intentionality.

See also: ANALYTICAL PHILOSOPHY; INTENTIONALITY; ORDINARY LANGUAGE PHILOSOPHY, SCHOOL OF; SPEECH ACTS

ERNIE LEPORE

SECOND-ORDER LOGIC, PHILOSOPHICAL ISSUES IN

Typically, a formal language has variables that range over a collection of objects, or domain of discourse. A language is 'second-order' if it has, in addition, variables that range over sets, functions, properties or relations on the domain of discourse. A language is third-order if it has variables ranging over sets of sets, or functions on relations, and so on. A language is higher-order if it is at least second-order.

Second-order languages enjoy a greater expressive power than first-order languages. For example, a set S of sentences is said to be categorical if any two models satisfying S are isomorphic, that is, have the same structure. There are second-order, categorical characterizations of important mathematical structures, including the natural numbers, the real numbers and Euclidean space. It is a consequence of the Löwenheim–Skolem theorems that there is no first-order categorical characterization of any infinite structure. There are also a number of central mathematical notions, such as finitude, countability, minimal closure and well-foundedness, which can be characterized with formulas of second-order languages, but cannot be characterized in first-order languages.

Some philosophers argue that second-order logic is not logic. Properties and relations are too obscure for rigorous foundational study, while sets and functions are in the purview of mathematics, not logic; logic should not have an ontology of its own. Other writers disqualify second-order logic because its consequence relation is not effective – there is no recursively enumerable, sound and complete deductive system for second-order logic.

The deeper issues underlying the dispute concern the goals and purposes of logical theory. If a logic is to be a calculus, an effective canon of inference, then second-order logic is beyond the pale. If, on the other hand, one aims to codify a standard to which correct reasoning must adhere, and to characterize the descriptive and communicative abilities of informal mathematical practice, then perhaps there is room for second-order logic.
See also: THEORY OF TYPES

STEWART SHAPIRO

SELF-DECEPTION, ETHICS OF

Self-deception is complicated and perplexing because it concerns all major aspects of human nature, including consciousness, rationality, motivation, freedom, happiness, and value commitments. In a wide sense, 'self-deception' refers to intentional activities and motivated processes of avoiding unpleasant truths or topics and the resulting mental

states of ignorance, false belief, unwarranted attitudes, and inappropriate emotions. Deceiving oneself, like deceiving other people, raises a host of questions about immorality. These include whether self-deception is always immoral or only when it conceals and supports wrongdoing; whether self-deception about wrongdoing and character faults compounds or mitigates guilt for causing harm; how important the value of authenticity is, and whether it can be sacrificed in an attempt to cope with reality; what the relation is between self-deception and responsibility; and whether groups can be self-deceived. Ultimately, the moral status of any instance of self-deception depends on the particular facts of the case.

MIKE W. MARTIN

SELLARS, WILFRID STALKER (1912–89)

Wilfrid Sellars was among the most systematic and innovative of post-war American philosophers. His critical destruction of the 'Myth of the Given' established him as a leading voice in the Anglo-American critique of 'the Cartesian concept of mind' and in the corresponding shift of attention from the categories of thought to public language. His own positive views were naturalistic, combining a robust scientific realism with a thoroughgoing nominalism which rejected both traditional abstract entities and ontologically primitive meanings. In their place, Sellars elucidated linguistic meaning and the content of thought in terms of a sophisticated theory of conceptual roles, instantiated in the linguistic conduct of speakers and transmitted by modes of cultural inheritance. He combined this theory with a form of 'verbal behaviourism' to produce the first version of functionalism in the contemporary philosophy of mind. Besides his profoundly original philosophical contributions, his long career as a distinguished teacher and influential editor earned him justified acclaim as one of the definitive figures of the post-war period.
See also: CATEGORIES; CONCEPTS; FOUNDATIONALISM; INTENTIONALITY; NOMINALISM; ONTOLOGY

JAY F. ROSENBERG

SEMANTIC VIEW OF THEORIES
See MODELS; THEORIES, SCIENTIFIC

SEMANTICS

Semantics is the systematic study of meaning. Current work in this field builds on the work of logicians and linguists as well as of philosophers. Philosophers are interested in foundational issues in semantics because these speak to the nature of meaning, as it embeds in our thinking and in our relations to each other and to the world. Of special interest are questions about how a semantic theory should respect the connections of meaning to truth and to understanding. In addition, numerous semantic problems concerning particular linguistic constructions bear philosophical interest, sometimes because the problems are important to resolving foundational semantical issues, sometimes because philosophical problems of independent interest are expressed using the constructions, and sometimes because clarity about the semantic function of the constructions enables clarity in the development of philosophical theories and analyses.

See also: AMBIGUITY; ANALYTICITY; EMOTIVE MEANING; INTUITIONISTIC LOGIC AND ANTIREALISM; LOGICAL CONSTANTS; MASS TERMS; ONTOLOGICAL COMMITMENT; SEMIOTICS; STRUCTURALISM IN LINGUISTICS

MARK CRIMMINS

SEMANTICS, CONCEPTUAL ROLE

According to conceptual role semantics (CRS), the meaning of a representation is the role of that representation in the cognitive life of the agent, for example, in perception, thought and decision-making. It is an extension of the well-known 'use' theory of meaning, according to which the meaning of a word is its use in communication and, more generally, in social interaction. CRS supplements external use by including the role of a symbol *inside* a computer or a brain. The uses appealed to are not just actual, but also counterfactual: not only what effects a thought *does* have, but what effects it *would* have had if stimuli or other states had differed. Of course, so defined, the functional role of a thought includes all sorts of causes and effects that are non-semantic, for example, perhaps happy thoughts can bolster one's immunity, promoting good health. Conceptual roles are functional roles minus such non-semantic causes and effects.

The view has arisen separately in philosophy (where it is sometimes called 'inferential' or 'functional' role semantics) and in cognitive science (where it is sometimes called 'procedural semantics').

See also: CONCEPTS

NED BLOCK

SEMANTICS, GAME-THEORETIC

Game-theoretic semantics (GTS) uses concepts from game theory to study how the truth and falsity of the sentences of a language depend upon the truth and falsity of the language's atomic sentences (or upon its sub-sentential expressions). Unlike the Tarskian method (which uses recursion clauses to determine satisfaction conditions for nonatomic sentences in terms of the satisfaction conditions of their component sentences, then defines truth in terms of satisfaction), GTS associates with each sentence its own semantic game played on sentences of the language. This game defines truth in terms of the existence of a winning strategy for one of the players involved. The structure of the game is determined by the sentence's structure, and thus the semantic properties of the sentence in question can be studied by attending to the properties of its game.

See also: DECISION AND GAME THEORY; SEMANTICS

MICHAEL HAND

SEMANTICS, POSSIBLE WORLDS

Possible worlds semantics (PWS) is a family of ideas and methods that have been used to analyse concepts of philosophical interest. PWS was originally focused on the important concepts of necessity and possibility. Consider:

(a) Necessarily, 2 + 2 = 4.
(b) Necessarily, Socrates had a snub nose.

Intuitively, (a) is true but (b) is false. There is simply no way that 2 and 2 can add up to anything but 4, so (a) is true. But although Socrates did in fact have a snub nose, it was not necessary that he did; he might have had a nose of some other shape. So (b) is false.

Sentences (a) and (b) exhibit a characteristic known as *intensionality*: sentences with the same truth-value are constituent parts of otherwise similar sentences, which nevertheless have different truth-values. *Extensional semantics* assumed that sentences stand for their truth-values, and that what a sentence stands for is a function of what its constituent parts stand for and how they are arranged. Given these assumptions, it is not easy to explain the difference in truth-value between (a) and (b), and hence not easy to give an account of necessity.

PWS takes a sentence to stand for a function from worlds to truth-values. For each world, the function yields the truth-value the sentence would have if that world were actual. Thus '2 + 2 = 4' stands for a function that yields the truth-value 'true' for every world, while 'Socrates had a snub nose' stands for a different function that yields 'true' for some worlds and 'false' for others, depending on what Socrates' nose is like in the world. Since these two sentences stand for different things, sentences that have them as constituents, such as (a) and (b), can also stand for different things.

This basic idea, borrowed from Leibniz and brought into modern logic by Carnap, Kripke and others, has proven extremely fertile. It has been applied to a number of intensional phenomena in addition to necessity and possibility, including conditionals, tense and temporal adverbs, obligation and reports of informational and cognitive content. PWS spurred the development of philosophical logic and led to new applications of logic in computer science and artificial intelligence. It revolutionized the study of the semantics of natural languages. PWS has inspired analyses of many concepts of philosophical importance, and the concept of a possible world has been at the heart of important philosophical systems.

See also: INTENSIONAL ENTITIES; POSSIBLE WORLDS

JOHN R. PERRY

SEMANTICS, SITUATION

Situation semantics attempts to provide systematic and philosophically coherent accounts of the meanings of various constructions that philosophers and linguists find important. It is based on the old idea that sentences stand for facts or something like them. As such, it provides an alternative to extensional semantics, which takes sentences to stand for truth-values, and to possible worlds semantics, which takes them to stand for sets of possible worlds.

Situations are limited parts or aspects of reality, while states of affairs (or infons) are complexes of properties and objects of the sort suitable to constitute a fact. Consider the issue of whether Jackie, a dog, broke her leg at a certain time T. There are two states of affairs or possibilities: that she did or she did not. The situation at T, in the place where Jackie was then, determines which of these states of affairs (infons) is *factual* (or *is the case* or *is supported*). *Situation theory*, the formal theory that underlies situation semantics, focuses on the nature of the *supports* relation.

Situation semantics sees *meaning* as a relation among *types of situations*. The meaning of 'I am sitting next to David', for example, is a relation between types of situations in which someone A utters this sentence referring with the name 'David' to a certain person B, and those in which A is sitting next to B. This relational theory of meaning makes situation semantics well suited to treat indexicality, tense and other similar phenomena. It has also inspired relational accounts of information and action.

JOHN R. PERRY

SEMIOTICS

As the study of signification, semiotics takes as its central task that of describing how one thing can mean another. Alternatively, since this philosophical problem is also a psychological one, its job could be said to be that of describing how one thing can bring something else to mind, how on seeing 'x' someone can be induced to think about 'y' even though 'y' is absent.

A person in whose head 'y' has been brought to mind may be responding to an 'x' someone else has transmitted with the intention of its signifying 'y'; or, mistakenly, responding to an 'x' someone has transmitted in the guileless expectation of its signifying some 'z'; or, often, responding to an 'x' that comes to his notice without anybody's apparent intention at all. Words, for example, generally signify because someone intends them to, and ideally (though not always) they signify what is intended; whereas clouds signify – a coming storm, a whale – because we so interpret them, not because they shaped themselves to convey some meaning.

Obviously the study of signification forms an integral part of the study of thinking, since no object can itself enter the brain, barring fatal mischance, and so it must be represented by some mental (that is, neural) 'x' that signifies it.

Signifiers are equally essential for creatures far lower than humans, as when a chemical signal 'x' emitted by some bacterium signifies to one of its colleagues some 'y' such as 'There's a dearth of food hereabouts'.

There are a number of ways in which an 'x' can signify some 'y', but for humans these are chiefly: by physical association; by physical resemblance; and/or by arbitrary convention.

When we take some 'x' as signifying some 'y' we are often guessing; our guess is subject to checking by interpretative (re)appraisal.

See also: LANGUAGE, PHILOSOPHY OF

W.C. WATT

SENGHOR, LEOPOLD

See AFRICAN PHILOSOPHY, ANGLOPHONE; AFRICAN PHILOSOPHY, FRANCOPHONE

SENSE AND FORCE

See PRAGMATICS

SENSE AND REFERENCE

The 'reference' of an expression is the entity the expression designates or applies to. The 'sense' of an expression is the way in which the expression presents that reference. For example, the ancients used 'the morning star' and 'the evening star' to designate what turned out to be the same heavenly body, the planet Venus. These two expressions have the same reference, but they clearly differ in that each presents that reference in a different way. So, although coreferential, each expression is associated with a different 'sense'. The distinction between sense and reference helps explain the cognitive puzzle posed by identity statements. 'The morning star is the evening star' and 'The morning star is the morning star' are both true, yet the sentences differ in cognitive significance, since the former may be informative, whereas the latter definitely is not. That difference in cognitive significance cannot be explained just by appeal to the references of the terms, for those are the same. It can, however, be naturally accounted for by appeal to a difference in sense. The terms 'the morning star' and 'the evening star' used in the first sentence, having different senses, present the referent in different ways, whereas no such difference occurs in the second sentence.

The distinction between sense and reference applies to all well-formed expressions of a language. It is part of a general theory of meaning that postulates an intermediate level of sense between linguistic terms and the entities the terms stand for. Senses give significance to expressions, which in and of themselves are just noises or marks on a surface, and connect them to the world. It is because linguistic terms have a sense that they can be used to express judgments, to transmit information and to talk about reality.

See also: INTENSIONAL ENTITIES

GENOVEVA MARTÍ

SENSE PERCEPTION, INDIAN VIEWS OF

Sense perception is considered in classical Indian thought in the context of epistemological issues – in particular, perception as a source of knowledge – and of psychological and metaphysical issues, for example, the relations of sense experiences to objects, to language and to the perceiving self or subject. The Sanskrit word used most commonly in philosophical investigations of sense perception is *pratyakṣa*, a compound of *prati*, 'before', and *akṣa*, 'eye' or any 'organ of sense'; thus it should be understood as 'being before the eyes' or 'experientially evident' as an adjective, and 'immediate experience' or 'sense experience' as a noun. The meaning 'sense perception' is normal within philosophical inquiries. But just how many sense modalities there are is not to be taken for granted. In addition to the five types of sense experience commonly identified, 'mental' perception (as of pleasures, pains and desires), apperception (awareness of awareness) and extraordinary or yogic perception are sometimes counted as *pratyakṣa*.

Views about the psychology of perception or, more broadly, about perception considered as part of the world are developed in religious and soteriological literature (literature about enlightenment and lib-

eration) predating classical philosophical discussions. In Upaniṣadic, Buddhist and Jaina texts over two millennia old, perception is painted in broad strokes within spiritual theories of self and world that promote ideas of the supreme value of a mystical experience. Sense perception is usually devalued comparatively. Later, the psychology of perception becomes very advanced and is treated in some quarters independently of soteriological teachings.

Classical Indian philosophy proper is marked by tight argumentation and self-conscious concern with evidence. The justificational value of perception is recognized from the outset, in so far as any justifiers, or knowledge sources, are admitted at all. Nāgārjuna and others challenge the epistemological projects of Nyāya and other positive approaches to knowledge, prompting deep probing of perception's epistemic role. Views about veridicality, fallibility and meaningful doubt become greatly elaborated.

What do we perceive? Throughout classical thought, sharp disagreements occur over the perceptibility of universals, relations, absences or negative facts (such as Devadatta's not being at home), parts versus wholes, and the self or awareness itself. Issues about perceptual media (such as light and ether, *ākāśa*, the purported medium of sound), about occult or spiritual perceptibles and about the very existence of objects independently of consciousness are hotly debated. A Buddhist phenomenalism is polemically matched by a Mīmāṃsā and Nyāya realism on a range of concerns.

Probably through the influence of mysticism, verbalization of experience, however simple and direct, becomes suspect in comparison with experience itself; this suspicion is evident in concerns over the value of each in presenting reality, as well as in other, sometimes rather indefinite, ways. The judgment is prevalent that what prevents a person from living in an enlightened or liberated state is thinking – verbalizing experience, calculating, planning, and so on – instead of having pure experience, perceptual and otherwise, and thus living with a 'silent mind'. This attitude emerges in treatments of sense experience, reinforcing what is perhaps a natural tendency among philosophers to find the relations of experience and language problematic. Even in the root text of Nyāya, where the influence of yoga and mysticism is not so strong, perception is said to be a cognition that is nonverbal, *avyapadeśya*, although there is considerable dispute about precisely what this means. The relations between various modes of experience and the language used with respect to them remains an ongoing concern of the very latest and most complex classical Indian philosophy.

See also: MĪMĀṂSĀ; PERCEPTION

STEPHEN H. PHILLIPS

SENSE-DATA

A philosophical theory of perception must accommodate this obvious fact: when someone perceives, or seems to perceive something, how things appear may differ from how they are. A circular coin tilted will look elliptical. A stick partially immersed in water will look bent. Noting that appearance and reality do not always coincide, some philosophers have given the following account of the contrast between the two. Suppose someone seems to see a book with a red cover. Whether or not there is any book to be seen, the individual seeming to see the red book will be aware of something red. What they are aware of is called a sense-datum. According to a sense-datum theory, any perceptual experience involves awareness of a sense-datum whether or not it is an experience of a physical object.

Some philosophers link a sense-datum theory with certain views about knowledge. According to foundationalists all knowledge of the external world must rest on a foundation of beliefs that are beyond doubt. We can always be mistaken about what physical objects are like. On the other hand, we cannot be mistaken about what sense-data are like. So, all knowledge about the external world rests on beliefs about sense-data. In this way a sense-datum theory is supposed to do double duty in contributing towards an account of perception, and an account of knowledge based on perception.

See also: FOUNDATIONALISM

ANDRÉ GALLOIS

SEQUENTS/SEQUENT CALCULI

See NATURAL DEDUCTION, TABLEAU AND SEQUENT SYSTEMS

SET THEORETIC PARADOXES

See PARADOXES OF SET AND PROPERTY

SET THEORY

In the late nineteenth century, Georg Cantor created mathematical theories, first of sets or aggregates of real numbers (or linear points), and later of sets or aggregates of arbitrary elements. The relationship of element a to set A is written $a \in A$; it is to be distinguished from the relationship of subset B to set A, which holds if every element of B is also an element of A, and which is written $B \subseteq A$. Cantor is most famous for his theory of transfinite cardinals, or numbers of elements in infinite sets. A subset of an infinite set may have the same number of elements as the set itself, and Cantor proved that the sets of natural and rational numbers have the same number of elements, which he called $\aleph_0$; also that the sets of

real and complex numbers have the same number of elements, which he called **c**. Cantor proved $\aleph_0$ to be less than **c**. He conjectured that no set has a number of elements strictly between these two.

In the early twentieth century, in response to criticism of set theory, Ernst Zermelo undertook its axiomatization; and, with amendments by Abraham Fraenkel, his have been the accepted axioms ever since. These axioms help distinguish the notion of a set, which is too basic to admit of informative definition, from other notions of a one made up of many that have been considered in logic and philosophy. Properties having exactly the same particulars as instances need not be identical, whereas sets having exactly the same elements are identical by the axiom of extensionality. Hence for any condition Φ there is at most one set $\{x|\Phi(x)\}$ whose elements are all and only those x such that $\Phi(x)$ holds, and $\{x|\Phi(x)\} = \{x|\Psi(x)\}$ if and only if conditions Φ and Ψ hold of exactly the same x. It cannot consistently be assumed that $\{x|\Phi(x)\}$ exists for every condition Φ. Inversely, the existence of a set is not assumed to depend on the possibility of defining it by some condition Φ as $\{x|\Phi(x)\}$.

One set x_0 may be an element of another set x_1 which is an element of x_2 and so on, $x_0 \in x_1 \in x_2 \in \ldots$, but the reverse situation, $\ldots \in y_2 \in y_1 \in y_0$, may not occur, by the axiom of foundation. It follows that no set is an element of itself and that there can be no universal set $y = \{x|x = x\}$. Whereas a part of a part of a whole is a part of that whole, an element of an element of a set need not be an element of that set.

Modern mathematics has been greatly influenced by set theory, and philosophies rejecting the latter must therefore reject much of the former. Many set-theoretic notations and terminologies are encountered even outside mathematics, as in parts of philosophy:

pair	$\{a,b\}$	$\{x|x = a \text{ or } x = b\}$
singleton	$\{a\}$	$\{x|x = a\}$
empty set	$\emptyset$	$\{x|x \neq x\}$
union	$\cup X$	$\{a|a \in A \text{ for some } A \in X\}$
binary union	$A \cup B$	$\{a|a \in A \text{ or } a \in B\}$
intersection	$\cap X$	$\{a|a \in A \text{ for all } A \in X\}$
binary intersection	$A \cap B$	$\{a|a \in A \text{ and } a \in B\}$
difference	$A - B$	$\{a|a \in A \text{ and not } a \in B\}$
complement	$A - B$	
power set	$\wp(A)$	$\{B|B \subseteq A\}$

(In contexts where only subsets of A are being considered, $A-B$ may be written $-B$ and called the complement of B.)

While the accepted axioms suffice as a basis for the development not only of set theory itself, but of modern mathematics generally, they leave some questions about transfinite cardinals unanswered. The status of such questions remains a topic of logical research and philosophical controversy.

See also: CANTOR'S THEOREM

JOHN P. BURGESS

SEXTUS EMPIRICUS (*fl. c.* AD 200)

Sextus Empiricus is our major surviving source for Greek scepticism. Three works of his survive: a general sceptical handbook (*Outlines of Pyrrhonism*), a partly lost longer treatment of the same material, and a series of self-contained essays questioning the utility of the individual liberal arts.

R.J. HANKINSON

SEXUALITY, PHILOSOPHY OF

The philosophy of sexuality, like the philosophy of science, art or law, is the study of the concepts and propositions surrounding its central protagonist, in this case 'sex'. Its practitioners focus on conceptual, metaphysical and normative questions.

Conceptual philosophy of sex analyses the notions of sexual desire, sexual activity and sexual pleasure. What makes a feeling a sexual sensation? Manipulation of and feelings in the genitals are not necessary, since other body parts yield sexual pleasure. What makes an act sexual? A touch on the arm might be a friendly pat, an assault, or sex; physical properties alone do not distinguish them. What is the conceptual link between sexual pleasure and sexual activity? Neither the intention to produce sexual pleasure nor the actual experience of pleasure seems necessary for an act to be sexual. Other conceptual questions have to do not with what makes an act sexual, but with what makes it the type of sexual act it is. How should 'rape' be defined? What the conceptual differences are, if any, between obtaining sex through physical force and obtaining it by offering money is an interesting and important issue.

Metaphysical philosophy of sex discusses ontological and epistemological matters: the place of sexuality in human nature; the relationships among sexuality, emotion and cognition; the meaning of sexuality for the person, the species, the cosmos. What is sex all about, anyway? That sexual desire is a hormone-driven instinct implanted by a god or nature acting in the service of the species, and that it has a profound spiritual dimension, are two – not necessarily incompatible – views. Perhaps the significance of sexuality is little different from that of eating, breathing and defecating; maybe, or in addition, sexuality is partially constitutive of moral personality.

Normative philosophy of sex explores the perennial questions of sexual ethics. In what circumstances is it morally permissible to engage in sexual activity or experience sexual pleasure? With whom? For what purpose? With which body parts? For how long? The historically central answers come from Thomist natural law, Kantian deontology, and utilitarianism. Normative philosophy of sex also addresses legal, social and political issues. Should society steer people in the direction of heterosexuality, marriage, family? May the law regulate sexual conduct by prohibiting prostitution or homosexuality? Normative philosophy of sex includes nonethical value questions as well. What is good sex? What is its contribution to the good life?

The breadth of the philosophy of sex is shown by the variety of topics it investigates: abortion, contraception, acquaintance rape, pornography, sexual harassment, and objectification, to name a few. The philosophy of sex begins with a picture of a privileged pattern of relationship, in which two adult heterosexuals love each other, are faithful to each other within a formal marriage, and look forward to procreation and family. Philosophy of sex, as the Socratic scrutiny of our sexual practices, beliefs and concepts, challenges this privileged pattern by exploring the virtues, and not only the vices, of adultery, prostitution, homosexuality, group sex, bestiality, masturbation, sadomasochism, incest, paedophilia and casual sex with anonymous strangers. Doing so provides the same illumination about sex that is provided when the philosophies of science, art and law probe the privileged pictures of their own domains.

See also: FAMILY, ETHICS AND THE; FRIENDSHIP; KANTIAN ETHICS; LOVE; MORALITY AND EMOTIONS; REPRODUCTION AND ETHICS

ALAN SOBLE

SHAME
See MORAL SENTIMENTS

SHINTŌ

Shintō means the 'way of the *kami* (gods)' and is a term that evolved about the late sixth or early seventh century – as Japan entered an extended period of cultural borrowing from China and Korea – to distinguish the amalgam of native religious beliefs from Buddhism, a continental import. Shintō embraces the most ancient and basic social and religious values of Japan. It is exclusively Japanese, showing no impulse to spread beyond Japan. The exportation of Shintō would in any case be exceedingly difficult since its mythology is so closely bound to the creation of Japan and the Japanese people, and since many of its deities are believed to make their homes in the mountains, rivers, trees, rocks and other natural features of the Japanese islands.

Shintō comprises both great and little traditions. The great tradition, established in the mythology that was incorporated into Japan's two oldest extant writings, *Kojiki* (Record of Ancient Matters) and *Nihon Shoki* (Chronicle of Japan), both dating from the early eighth century, is centred on the imperial institution. According to the mythology the emperorship was ordained by the sun goddess, Amaterasu, who sent her grandson from heaven to earth (Japan) to found a dynasty 'to rule eternally'. The present emperor is the 125th in a line of sovereigns officially regarded, until Japan's defeat in the Second World War, as descended directly from Amaterasu.

Shintō's little tradition is a mixture of polytheistic beliefs about *kami*, manifested in nature worship (animism), ancestor worship, agricultural cults, fertility rites, shamanism and more. Lacking a true scriptural basis, Shintō derives from the faith of the people, and from earliest times has had its roots firmly planted in particularistic, localistic practices. Thus it has always been strongest in its association with such entities as families, villages and locales (for example, mountains thought to be the homes of certain *kami* or, indeed, to be the *kami* themselves).

See also: BUDDHIST PHILOSOPHY, JAPANESE; JAPANESE PHILOSOPHY; RELIGION, PHILOSOPHY OF

PAUL VARLEY

SIDGWICK, HENRY (1838–1900)

Henry Sidgwick was a Cambridge philosopher, psychic researcher and educational reformer, whose works in practical philosophy, especially *The Methods of Ethics* (1874), brought classical utilitarianism to its peak of theoretical sophistication and drew out the deep conflicts within that tradition, perhaps within the age of British imperialism itself. Sidgwick was profoundly influenced by J.S. Mill, but his version of utilitarianism – the view that those social or individual actions are right that maximize aggregate happiness – also revived certain Benthamite doctrines, though with more cogent accounts of ultimate good as pleasure, of total versus average utility, and of the analytical or deductive method. Yet Sidgwick was a cognitivist in ethics who sought both to ground utilitarianism on fundamental intuitions and to encompass within it the principles of common-sense ethics (truthfulness, fidelity, justice, etc.); his highly eclectic practical

philosophy assimilated much of the rationalism, social conservatism and historical method of rival views, reflecting such influences as Butler, Clarke, Aristotle, Bagehot, Green, Whewell and Kant. Ultimately, Sidgwick's careful academic inquiries failed to demonstrate that one ought always to promote the happiness of all rather than one's own happiness, and this dualism of practical reason, along with his doubt about the viability of religion, led him to view his results as largely destructive and potentially deleterious in their influence.

See also: COMMON SENSE SCHOOL; COMMONSENSISM; ETHICS; MILL, J.S. §§8–12; MORAL SCEPTICISM; MORALITY AND ETHICS; TELEOLOGICAL ETHICS; UNIVERSALISM IN ETHICS

BART SCHULTZ

SIMMEL, GEORG (1858–1918)

Georg Simmel was a prolific German philosopher and sociologist, who was one of the principal founders of sociology in Germany. His philosophy and social theory had a major impact in the early decades of the twentieth century, both among professional philosophers and sociologists and within the cultural and artistic spheres. This is true of his foundation for sociology, his philosophy of art and culture, his philosophy of life and his philosophy of money. His thought ranged from substantive issues within the philosophical tradition to a concern with the everyday world and its objects.

DAVID FRISBY

SIMPLE TYPE THEORY
See THEORY OF TYPES

SIMPLICITY (IN SCIENTIFIC THEORIES)

In evaluating which of several competing hypotheses is most plausible, scientists often use simplicity as a guide. This raises three questions: What makes one hypothesis simpler than another? Why should a difference in simplicity make a difference in what we believe? And how much weight should simplicity receive, compared with other considerations, in judging a hypothesis' plausibility? These may be termed the descriptive, the normative, and the weighting problems, respectively. The aesthetic and pragmatic appeal of more simple theories is transparent; the puzzle is how simplicity can be a guide to truth.

See also: CONFIRMATION THEORY; INDUCTIVE INFERENCE; INFERENCE TO THE BEST EXPLANATION;

SCIENTIFIC REALISM AND ANTIREALISM; STATISTICS; THEORETICAL (EPISTEMIC) VIRTUES

ELLIOTT SOBER

SIMULATION THEORY

Mental simulation is the simulation, replication or re-enactment, usually in imagination, of the thinking, decision-making, emotional responses or other aspects of the mental life of another person. According to simulation theory, mental simulation in imagination plays a key role in our everyday psychological understanding of other people. The same mental resources that are used in our own thinking, decision-making or emotional responses are redeployed in imagination to provide an understanding of the thoughts, decisions or emotions of another.

Simulation theory stands opposed to the 'theory theory' of folk psychology. According to the theory theory, everyday psychological understanding depends on deployment of an empirical theory or body of information about psychological matters, such as how people normally think, make decisions or respond emotionally. Simulation theory does not altogether deny that third-personal psychological knowledge is implicated in our folk psychological practice, prediction, interpretation and explanation. But it maintains that, over a range of cases, the first-personal methodology of mental simulation allows us to avoid the need for detailed antecedent knowledge about how psychological processes typically operate.

See also: FOLK PSYCHOLOGY

MARTIN DAVIES
TONY STONE

SIMULTANEITY

See CONVENTIONALISM; RELATIVITY THEORY, PHILOSOPHICAL SIGNIFICANCE OF; TIME; TIME TRAVEL

SIN

The most archaic conception of human fault may be the notion of defilement or pollution, that is, a stain or blemish which somehow infects a person from without. All the major religious traditions offer accounts of human faults and prescriptions for dealing with them. However, it is only when fault is conceived within the context of a relationship to a personal deity that it makes sense to speak of it as an offence against the divine will. The concept of sin is the concept of a human fault that offends a good God and brings with it human guilt. Its natural home is in the major theistic religions of Judaism, Christianity and Islam.

These religious traditions share the idea that actual or personal sins are individual actions contrary to the will of God. In the Hebrew Bible, sin is understood within the context of the covenantal relation between Yahweh and his chosen people. To be in covenant with Yahweh is to exist in holiness, and so sin is a deviation from the norms of holiness. In the Christian New Testament, Jesus teaches that human wrongdoing offends the one whom he calls Father. The Qur'an portrays sin as opposition to Allah rooted in human pride.

According to Christian tradition, there is a distinction to be drawn between actual sin and original sin. The scriptural warrant for the doctrine of original sin is found in the Epistles of Paul, and the interpretation of Paul worked out by Augustine in the course of his controversy with the Pelagians has been enormously influential in Western Christianity. On the Augustinian view, which was developed by Anselm and other medieval thinkers with considerable philosophical sophistication, the Fall of Adam and Eve had catastrophic consequences for their descendants. All the progeny of the first humans, except for Jesus and his mother, inherit from them guilt for their first sin, and so all but two humans are born bearing a burden of guilt. The Augustinian doctrine of original sin is morally problematic just because it attributes innate guilt to humans. It was criticized by John Locke and Immanuel Kant.

See also: HELL; PURGATORY

PHILIP L. QUINN

SINGULAR TERMS

See REFERENCE

SINN UND BEDEUTUNG

See SENSE AND REFERENCE

SITUATION ETHICS

'Situation ethics' accords morally decisive weight to particular circumstances in judging whether an action is right or wrong. Thus we should examine critically all traditional rules prohibiting kinds of actions. Proponents of these views have exerted their greatest influence in Europe and North America in the twentieth century, although such influence had waned by 1980. The views received extensive scrutiny in Christian communities. Three quite different warrants were offered for privileging discrete situations. First, we should remain dispositionally open to God's immediate command in a particular time and place (theological contextualism).

Second, we should take the actual consequences of particular actions as morally decisive (empirical situationism). Third, we should be ready to perform actions that compromise moral ideals when doing so improves matters in ways a given situation, with its distinctive constraints, makes viable (mournful realism).

See also: INTUITIONISM IN ETHICS; MORAL JUDGMENT; MORAL REALISM; MORAL SENSE THEORIES

GENE OUTKA

SITUATIONAL SEMANTICS
See SEMANTICS, SITUATION

SLAVERY

The moral, economic and political value of slavery has been hotly disputed by philosophers since ancient times. It was defended as an institution by Plato and Aristotle, but became increasingly subject to attack in the modern period, until its general abolition in the Western world in the nineteenth century.

In the twentieth century our belief that slavery is fundamentally unjust has become a benchmark against which moral and political philosophies may be tested. Both utilitarians and contractarian philosophers have argued against slavery in general and the enforceability of slavery contracts more specifically, although for very different moral reasons. Others have argued that only by viewing slavery from the standpoint of the slave can its moral significance be understood.

STEPHEN L. ESQUITH
NICHOLAS D. SMITH

SMITH, ADAM (1723–90)

Despite his reputation as the founder of political economy, Adam Smith was a philosopher who constructed a general system of morals in which political economy was but one part. The philosophical foundation of his system was a Humean theory of imagination that encompassed a distinctive idea of sympathy. Smith saw sympathy as our ability to understand the situation of the other person, a form of knowledge that constitutes the basis for all assessment of the behaviour of others. Our spontaneous tendency to observe others is inevitably turned upon ourselves, and this is Smith's key to understanding the moral identity of the individual through social interaction. On this basis he suggested a theory of moral judgment and moral virtue in which justice was the key to jurisprudence. Smith developed an original theory of rights as the

core of 'negative' justice, and a theory of government as, primarily, the upholder of justice. But he maintained the political significance of 'positive' virtues in a public, non-governmental sphere. Within this framework he saw a market economy developing as an expression of humanity's prudent self-interest. Such self-interest was a basic feature of human nature and therefore at work in any form of society; but commercial society was special because it made the pursuit of self-interest compatible with individual liberty; in the market the poor are not personally dependent upon the rich. At the same time, he recognized dangers in commercial society that needed careful institutional and political management. Smith's basic philosophy is contained in *The Theory of Moral Sentiments* (1759), but a major part concerning law and government was never completed to Smith's satisfaction and he burnt the manuscript before he died. Consequently the connection to the *Wealth of Nations* (1776) can only be partially reconstructed from two sets of students' notes (1762–3 and 1763–4) from his *Lectures on Jurisprudence* at Glasgow. These writings are complemented by a volume of essays and student notes from lectures on rhetoric and belles-lettres.

Although a philosopher of public life and in some measure a public figure, Adam Smith adhered to the Enlightenment ideal of privacy to a degree rarely achieved by his contemporaries. He left no autobiographical accounts and, given his national and international fame, the surviving correspondence is meagre. The numerous eyewitness reports of him mostly relate particular episodes and individual traits of character. Just as there are only a few portraits of the man's appearance, there are no extensive accounts of the personality, except Dugald Stewart's 'Life of Adam Smith' (1793), written after Smith's death and designed to fit Stewart's eclectic supplementation of common sense philosophy. While Smith was a fairly sociable man, his friendships were few and close only with men who respected his desire for privacy. David Hume was pre-eminent among them.

See also: ECONOMICS AND ETHICS; JUSTICE; MARKET, ETHICS OF THE; MORAL SENSE THEORIES; PROPERTY; WORK, PHILOSOPHY OF

KNUD HAAKONSSEN

SMITH, JOHN
See CAMBRIDGE PLATONISM

SOCIAL CHOICE

Social choice theory is the branch of economics concerned with the relationships between individual values, preferences and rights and collective decision making and evaluation. Social choice theory therefore provides connections between the formal analysis of rational choice, the debate on political process, and ethics. A central theme in social choice theory has been the aggregation of individual preferences into either a social decision rule or a social evaluation rule. The most famous result in social choice theory – Arrow's impossibility theorem – is that such aggregation is impossible if individual preferences are conceived as ordinal in nature, and if the aggregation procedure is to satisfy certain apparently reasonable conditions. This result implies that neither a voting system nor a system of moral evaluation can be found that satisfies all of the required conditions. Further impossibility theorems arise from attempts to model the role of individual rights.

Much of social choice theory is concerned with interpreting, extending and questioning these impossibility theorems in a variety of contexts. This discussion has generated an extensive interchange at the margins of economics and ethics on topics such as the commensurability of values and the relationship between morality and rationality.

See also: ECONOMICS AND ETHICS; RATIONAL CHOICE THEORY; RIGHTS; UTILITARIANISM; WELFARE

ALAN HAMLIN

SOCIAL CONSTRUCTIVISM
See CONSTRUCTIVISM

SOCIAL CONTRACT
See CONTRACTARIANISM

SOCIAL DEMOCRACY

The idea of social democracy is now used to describe a society the economy of which is predominantly capitalist, but where the state acts to regulate the economy in the general interest, provides welfare services outside of it and attempts to alter the distribution of income and wealth in the name of social justice. Originally 'social democracy' was more or less equivalent to 'socialism'. But since the mid-twentieth century, those who think of themselves as social democrats have come to believe that the old opposition between capitalism and socialism is outmoded; many of the values upheld by earlier socialists can be promoted by reforming capitalism rather than abolishing it.

Although it bases itself on values like democracy and social justice, social democracy cannot really be described as a political philosophy: there is no systematic statement or great text that can be pointed to as a definitive account of social democratic ideals. In practical politics, however, social democratic ideas have been very influential, guiding the policies of most Western states in the post-war world.

See also: DEMOCRACY; JUSTICE

DAVID MILLER

SOCIAL EPISTEMOLOGY

Social epistemology is the conceptual and normative study of the relevance to knowledge of social relations, interests and institutions. It is thus to be distinguished from the sociology of knowledge, which is an empirical study of the contingent social conditions or causes of what is commonly taken to be knowledge. Social epistemology revolves around the question of whether knowledge is to be understood individualistically or socially.

Epistemology has traditionally ascribed a secondary status to beliefs indebted to social relations – to testimony, expert authority, consensus, common sense and received wisdom. Such beliefs could attain the status of knowledge, if at all, only by being based on first-hand knowledge – that is, knowledge justified by the experience or reason of the individual knower.

Since the work of the common sense Scottish philosopher Thomas Reid in the mid-eighteenth century, epistemologists have from time to time taken seriously the idea that beliefs indebted to social relations have a primary and not merely secondary epistemic status. The bulk of work in social epistemology has, however, been done since Thomas Kuhn depicted scientific revolutions as involving social changes in science. Work on the subject since 1980 has been inspired by the 'strong programme' in the sociology of science, by feminist epistemology and by the naturalistic epistemology of W.V. Quine. These influences have inspired epistemologists to rethink the role of social relations – especially testimony – in knowledge. The subject that has emerged may be divided into three branches: the place of social factors in the knowledge possessed by individuals; the organization of individuals' cognitive labour; and the nature of collective knowledge, including common sense, consensus and common, group, communal and impersonal knowledge.

See also: FEMINIST EPISTEMOLOGY; NATURALIZED EPISTEMOLOGY

FREDERICK F. SCHMITT

SOCIAL RELATIVISM

People in different societies have very different beliefs and systems of belief. To understand such diversity is a prime task of the student of society. The task is especially pressing when alien beliefs seem obviously mistaken, unreasonable or otherwise peculiar. A popular response is social relativism. Perhaps beliefs which seem mistaken, unreasonable or peculiar viewed from our perspective, are by no means mistaken, unreasonable or peculiar viewed from the perspective of the society in which they occur. Different things are not just thought true (reasonable, natural) in different societies – rather, they are true (reasonable, natural) in different societies. Relativism recognizes diversity and deals with it even-handedly.

Relativism has absurd results. Consider the view that what is true in society A need not be true in society B. So if society A believes in witches while society B does not, there are witches in A but not in B. Relativism regarding truth drives us to different 'worlds', one with witches in it and another without. This seems absurd: people who live in different societies do not in any literal sense live in different worlds. The challenge is to do justice to social diversity without falling into absurdities such as this.

See also: MORAL RELATIVISM; RATIONALITY AND CULTURAL RELATIVISM; RELATIVISM

ALAN MUSGRAVE

SOCIAL SCIENCE, CONTEMPORARY PHILOSOPHY OF

Some philosophers think that the study of social phenomena must apply methods from natural science. Researchers should discover causal regularities (whenever C operates, E occurs) and fit them into systematic theories. Some philosophers hold that social phenomena call for an entirely different approach, in which researchers seek to interpret fully the meaning of people's actions, including their efforts to communicate and cooperate. On this view, the nearest that researchers will come to regularities will be to discover rules (whenever the situation is S, everyone must do A). The nearest that they will get to systematic theories will be systematic expositions of rules, like the rules of a kinship system.

Besides the naturalistic school and the interpretive school, the philosophy of social science harbours a critical school. This finds researches endorsed by the other two schools shot through with bias. It inclines to agree with the interpretive school in resisting naturalistic methods. However, its charges against naturalistic researches extend to interpretations. For interpretations may give untroubled pictures of societies in deep trouble, or picture the trouble in ways that serve the interests of the people who profit from it, for example, by leaving current rules about taking workers on and laying them off unquestioned. Here the critical school may itself use naturalistic methods. If it contends that ignoring ways of reassigning authority over employment increases the chances of private enterprises' retaining their present authority, the critical school is talking about a causal connection. There is no rule that says anyone must increase the chances.

Yet the researches sponsored by the three schools are complementary to the degree that researches into regularities and into rules are complementary. Settled social rules have counterparts in causal regularities, which may be expressed in similar terms, although the evidence for regularities need not include intended conformity. Some regularities are not counterparts of rules, but involve rules notwithstanding. If the proportion of marriages in Arizona ending in divorce is regularly one-third, that is not (as it happens) because one-third of Arizonans who marry must divorce. Yet marriage and divorce are actions that fall under rules.

The three schools do more than endorse studies of rules or regularities. The critical school denies that any study of social phenomena can be value-free, in particular on the point of emancipating people from the oppressions of current society. Either researchers work with the critical school to expose oppression; or they work for the oppressors. The interpretive school brings forward subjective features of human actions and experiences that overflow the study of rules. These features, too, may be reported or ascribed correctly or incorrectly; however, the truth about them may be best expressed in narrative texts more or less elaborate.

Postmodernism has generalized these themes in a sceptical direction. Every text can be read in multiple, often conflicting, ways, so there are always multiple, often conflicting, interpretations of whatever happens. Every interpretation serves a quest for power, whether or not it neatly favours or disfavours an oppressive social class. Such contentions undermine assumptions that the three schools make about seeking truth regarding social phenomena. They do even more to undermine any assumption that the truths found will hold universally.

The assumption about universality, however, is a legacy of the positivist view of natural science. Positivism has given way to the model-theoretic or semantic view that science proceeds by constructing models to compare with real systems. A model – in social science, a model of regularities or one of rules – that fits any real system for a time is a scientific achievement empirically vindicated. Renouncing demands for universality, the philosophy of social science can make a firm stand on issues raised by postmodernism. It can accept from postmodernists the point that scientific success happens in local contexts and only for a time; but resist any further-reaching scepticism.

See also: EXPLANATION IN HISTORY AND SOCIAL SCIENCE; HOLISM AND INDIVIDUALISM IN HISTORY AND SOCIAL SCIENCE; NATURALISM IN SOCIAL SCIENCE; STRUCTURALISM IN SOCIAL SCIENCE

DAVID BRAYBROOKE

SOCIAL SCIENCE, METHODOLOGY OF

Each of the sciences, the physical, biological, social and behavioural, have emerged from philosophy in a process that began in the time of Euclid and Plato. These sciences have left a legacy to philosophy of problems that they have been unable to deal with, either as nascent or as mature disciplines. Some of these problems are common to all sciences, some restricted to one of the four general divisions mentioned above, and some of these philosophical problems bear on only one or another of the special sciences.

If the natural sciences have been of concern to philosophers longer than the social sciences, this is simply because the former are older disciplines. It is only in the last century that the social sciences have emerged as distinct subjects in their currently recognizable state. Some of the problems in the philosophy of social science are older than these disciplines, in part because these problems have their origins in nineteenth-century philosophy of history. Of course the full flowering of the philosophy of science dates from the emergence of the logical positivists in the 1920s. Although the logical positivists' philosophy of science has often been accused of being satisfied with a one-sided diet of physics, in fact their interest in the social sciences was at least as great as their interest in physical science. Indeed, as the pre-eminent arena for the application of prescriptions drawn from the study of physics, social science always held a place of special importance for philosophers of science.

Even those who reject the role of prescription from the philosophy of physics cannot deny the relevance of epistemology and metaphysics for the social sciences. Scientific change may be the result of many factors, only some of them cognitive. However, scientific advance is driven by the interaction of data and theory. Data controls the theories we adopt and the direction in which we refine them. Theory directs and constrains both the sort of experiments that are done to collect data and the apparatus with which they are undertaken: research design is driven by theory, and so is

methodological prescription. But what drives research design in disciplines that are only in their infancy, or in which for some other reason, there is a theoretical vacuum? In the absence of theory how does the scientist decide on what the discipline is trying to explain, what its standards of explanatory adequacy are, and what counts as the data that will help decide between theories? In such cases there are only two things scientists have to go on: successful theories and methods in other disciplines which are thought to be relevant to the nascent discipline, and the epistemology and metaphysics which underwrites the relevance of these theories and methods. This makes philosophy of special importance to the social sciences. The role of philosophy in guiding research in a theoretical vacuum makes the most fundamental question of the philosophy of science whether the social sciences can, do, or should employ to a greater or lesser degree the same methods as those of the natural sciences? Note that this question presupposes that we have already accurately identified the methods of natural science. If we have not yet done so, the question becomes largely academic. For many philosophers of social science the question of what the methods of natural science are was long answered by the logical positivist philosophy of physical science. And the increasing adoption of such methods by empirical, mathematical, and experimental social scientists raised a second central question for philosophers: why had these methods so apparently successful in natural science been apparently far less successful when self-consciously adapted to the research agendas of the several social sciences?

One traditional answer begins with the assumption that human behaviour or action and its consequences are simply not amenable to scientific study, because they are the results of free will, or less radically, because the significant kinds or categories into which social events must be classed are unique in a way that makes non-trivial general theories about them impossible. These answers immediately raise some of the most difficult problems of metaphysics and epistemology: the nature of the mind, the thesis of determinism, and the analysis of causation. Even less radical explanations for the differences between social and natural sciences raise these fundamental questions of philosophy.

Once the consensus on the adequacy of a positivist philosophy of natural science gave way in the late 1960s, these central questions of the philosophy of social science became far more difficult ones to answer. Not only was the benchmark of what counts as science lost, but the measure of progress became so obscure that it was no longer uncontroversial to claim that the social sciences' rate of progress was any different from that of natural science.

ALEX ROSENBERG

SOCIAL SCIENCES, PHILOSOPHY OF

Introduction

Although some of the topics and issues treated in the philosophy of social science are as old as philosophy itself (for example, the contrast between nature and convention and the idea of rationality are dealt with by Aristotle), the explicit emergence of a subdiscipline of philosophy with this name is a very recent phenomenon, which in turn may itself have stimulated greater philosophical activity in the area. Clearly, this emergence is tied to the development and growth of the social sciences themselves.

1 Historical approach
2 Problems
3 Contemporary movements
4 Specific social sciences

1 Historical approach

There are, perhaps, four distinct ways in which to gain an understanding of the subdiscipline. These ways are, of course, complementary. First, just as with most other areas of philosophy, one might approach the philosophy of the social sciences historically, by studying major schools or philosophers of an earlier period. There is much to recommend this approach. There are a number of classical texts (by Weber and Durkheim, for example) of which any interested student of the philosophy of the social sciences should be aware, much as there is in epistemology or ethics. This provides an interesting contrast with the philosophy of the natural sciences; far less could be said in favour of gaining an understanding of the latter in this way.

Compared with other areas of philosophy, the history of the philosophy of the social sciences is somewhat truncated, since it can only begin properly with the earliest attempts at social science, in the late eighteenth and early nineteenth centuries, first in the Scottish Enlightenment and subsequently in Germany. Prior to this period, there had been speculation about the nature of society, some of it quite rich and rewarding (Hobbes and Vico provide two examples of this), but it is only in the period of the Scottish Enlightenment and after that writers begin to reflect the first systematic attempts to study and understand society.

There is no clear line of demarcation between philosophers of social science and of society on the one hand and social theorists on the other, especially in this early period. Conventionally, to select only a few examples, G.W.F. Hegel, Wilhelm DILTHEY, F.H. BRADLEY and T.H. GREEN are considered to be examples of the former, and Adam SMITH, Karl MARX, Émile Durkheim, and Max WEBER, examples of the latter, but the line is sometimes somewhat arbitrary.

2 Problems

A second way in which to gain an understanding of the philosophy of social science is through the study of the issues and problems that these writers, and their contemporary counterparts, address (see SOCIAL SCIENCE, METHODOLOGY OF). Many of these problems arise in ordinary as well as in more scientific discussions of and thought about the social realm. It is not only social scientists who think about the social world; all of us do, a great deal of the time. Even in those cases in which the social scientist introduces neologisms, for example, 'demand curves' or 'anomie', they seem closely connected to, and sometimes only a refinement of, concepts already grasped by the lay person.

This nonscientific reflection arises quite apart from any specialized scientific work. It is, to a certain extent, misleading to think of the field as only the philosophy of the social *sciences*. Since so much of the motivation for critical discussion of the problems in this area comes from philosophical reflection on these quite ordinary modes of thought and understanding, the field should perhaps be called 'the philosophy of *society*', to reflect this nonscientific, as well as the scientific, interest in those problems.

Most of the things that social science is about, social structures (like families or society itself), norms and rules of behaviour, conventions, specific sorts of human action, and so on, are items that find a place in the discourse of the ordinary lay person who has as good a grasp of common talk about social class and purchase, voting and banking, as does the social scientist. This raises, in a direct way, metaphysical questions about the nature of these things. Are these social structures anything more than just individuals and their interrelations? Many philosophers, in the grip of the ideal of the unity of science, have held out the prospect that social science can be derived from, and is therefore reducible to, psychology (the latter eventually being reducible to chemistry and physics). For such thinkers, the world is ultimately a simple place, with only many different ways in which to speak about it. Other thinkers have been struck by the reality and integrity of the social world, and how it seems to impress itself on the individual willy-nilly (see SOCIETY, CONCEPT OF; HOLISM AND INDIVI-DUALISM IN HISTORY AND SOCIAL SCIENCE).

What is an action, and how does it differ from the mere movement of one's body? It seems hard to say in what this difference consists in a way that remains plausible and true to what action is like. Whatever an action is, what makes some actions *social* actions? One might think that an action is social in virtue of its causal consequences on others. Another line of thought holds that an action is social in virtue of its intrinsic character, quite apart from the question of its effects. Much of the philosophical discussion of action arose in the philosophy of history, over the explanation of historically impor-tant action, but has now been absorbed into a separate area of philosophy, the theory of action (see HISTORY, PHILOSOPHY OF; ACTION; SOCIAL ACTION).

The alleged contrast between nature and con-vention occurs to those who think about human-kind and its development, whether they be scientists and philosophers or not. Anyone who has travelled widely and noticed the social differences between peoples and cultures may have wondered whether all social practice was rational in its own terms, wherever found and no matter how apparently peculiar by our home-grown standards. Or perhaps, on the other hand, there are some universal standards of rationality, in the light of which evaluation of social practices and criticism of some of them can be mounted (see NATURE AND CONVENTION; RATIONALITY AND CULTURAL RELATIVISM; SOCIAL RELATIVISM).

The relationship between scientific theory and ordinary modes of thought is, of course, interactive, since many of the concepts or issues that have become part of ordinary lore have their roots in earlier scientific theory (our modern, and by most accounts, confused, concept of race might be an example of this).

Another set of problems arise in thinking through the nature of the social scientific enterprise itself. What standards must full explanation in social science meet? Causal explanation is a mode of explanation in natural science that is, relatively speaking, well understood. Explanations of a ritual or practice in society do not appear to be causal explanations, nor do explanations of human action. The first are often functional explanations (for example, a certain ritual exists because it produces such-and-such) and this appears to be an explana-tion of something by its effects rather than by its

causes. Explanations of human action are intentional explanations, whereby an action is explained by the goal or end at which it is directed. This also appears not to be causal. But perhaps appearances are deceptive, and these can be recast as causal explanations after all (see EXPLANATION IN HIS-TORY AND SOCIAL SCIENCE).

Natural scientists believe that their work is ethically neutral. To be sure, their work can be put to good and bad uses, but this presumably reflects on the users rather than on the content of the science itself. The relationship between social science and the values of the social scientist seems far more immediate and direct than this, and this alleged contrast has been the subject for continuing discussion and debate.

Is social science like natural science in important ways? In the developed natural sciences, there are controlled experiments and predictions. Neither seem available to the social scientist. Natural scientists attempt to formulate the laws that govern the phenomena they study. Is this a reasonable goal for the social scientist? Certainly, there are not many candidate laws for the social sciences one can think of. Does the social scientist use statistical evidence in the same way as the natural scientist? (See STATISTICS AND SOCIAL SCIENCE.) Finally, in natural science, we distinguish between theory and observation in a relatively sharp way, and we believe that a rational person should accept that theory which is best confirmed by observations. It is not clear that we can make the same distinction in the social sciences, nor that theory is supported by observation in just the same way. Our observations of the social world seem even more coloured by the theory we employ than is the case in the natural sciences.

3 Contemporary movements

A third way in which to approach the subject is through the study of either contemporary move-ments and schools of philosophy, or specific philosophers, who bring a specific slant to the subdiscipline. Controversy marks the natural as well as the social sciences, but observers have noted that there seems to be even less consensus, even less of an agreed paradigm at any particular time, in the latter than in the former.

Critical reflection on society, or on social science, or both, is very different in France and Germany from the way it is in the English-speaking world. The problems are the same, but the traditions and the manner in which the discussions proceed are markedly distinctive. The hope is that each tradition may learn something from the other (see SOCIAL SCIENCE, CONTEMPORARY PHILOSOPHY OF; CRITICAL

REALISM; MacIntyre, A.; Naturalism in social science; Positivism in the social sciences; Sociology of knowledge; Structuralism in social science).

4   Specific social sciences

Fourth and finally, one might approach the philosophy of the social sciences by studying the philosophical problems that arise specifically within each of the social sciences. Some, although not all, of the social sciences have thrown up philosophical industries of their own. Economics is the most salient example. In many ways, it is the most developed of all the social sciences, and this may be the reason why some of the best-defined controversies in the philosophy of social science arise from within it. Questions about the philosophical foundations of economics touch on the philosophically central issues of rationality, choice and the nature of wants or desires and their connection with action (see Economics, philosophy of; Social choice; Rational choice theory). But other social sciences have also given rise to specific problems, including history, psychology, sociology and anthropology (see Anthropology, philosophy of).

References and further reading

Martin, M. and McIntyre, L. (eds) (1994) *Readings in the Philosophy of Social Science*, Cambridge, MA: MIT Press. (A useful collection of recent and contemporary articles, grouped around some of the main issues in the philosophy of social science.)

Root, M. (1993) *Philosophy of Social Science*, Oxford: Blackwell. (Argues that some of the most prominent research programmes in the social sciences flout the ideal of moral and political philosophy.)

Ruben, D.-H. (1998) 'The Philosophy of Social Sciences', in A. Grayling (ed.) *Philosophy 2: Further Through the Subject*, Oxford: Oxford University Press, vol. 2. (A discussion of the main problems in the philosophy of social science, intended for the philosophy student. Assumes some prior knowledge of philosophy.)

DAVID-HILLEL RUBEN

SOCIAL THEORY AND LAW

Social theory embodies the claim that philosophical analyses, reflections on specific historical experience and systematic empirical observations of social conditions may be combined to construct theoretical explanations of the nature of society – that is,

of patterned human social association in general and of the conditions that make this association possible and define its typical character. Social theory, in this sense, can be defined broadly as theory seeking to explain systematically the structure and organization of society and the general conditions of social order or stability and of social change. Since law as a system of ideas can also be thought of as purporting to specify, reflect and systematize fundamental normative structures of society, it has appeared as both a focus of interest for social theory and, in some sense, a source of competition with social theory in explaining the character of social existence.

The relation of legal thought to social theory is, thus, in important respects, a confrontation between competing general modes of understanding social relationships and the conditions of social order. In one sense, this confrontation is as old as philosophy itself. But as an element in modern philosophical consciousness it represents a gradual working-out in Western thought, over the past two centuries, of the implications of various 'scientific' modes of interpreting social experience, all in one way or another the legacy of Enlightenment ideas.

From the late eighteenth century and throughout the nineteenth century, criteria of 'scientific' rationality were carried into the interpretation of social phenomena through the development of social theory. These criteria also significantly influenced the development of modern legal thought. The classic social theory of the late nineteenth and early twentieth centuries, which established an enduring vocabulary of concepts for the interpretation of social phenomena, treated law as an object of social inquiry within its scope. It sought scientific understanding of the nature of legal phenomena in terms of broad systems of explanation of the general nature of social relationships, structures and institutions.

In the late twentieth century the relationship between social theory and law has been marked by fundamental changes both in the outlook of social theory and in forms of contemporary regulation. On the one hand, social theory has been subjected to wide-ranging challenges to its modern scientific pretensions. It has had to respond to scepticism about claims that social life can usefully be analysed in terms of historical laws, or authoritatively interpreted and explained in terms of founding theoretical principles. On the other hand, the inexorable expansion of Western law's regulatory scope and detail appears, sociologically, as largely uncontrollable by moral systems and relatively unguided by philosophical principles. Hence, in some postmodern interpretations, contemporary law is presented as a system of knowledge and interpretation of social life of great importance, yet one that has ultimately evaded the Enlightenment ambition systematically to impose reason and principle – codified by theory – on agencies of political and social power.

See also: LAW, PHILOSOPHY OF

ROGER COTTERRELL

SOCIALISM

While socialist ideas may retrospectively be identified in many earlier forms of protest and rebellion against economic injustice and political oppression, socialism both as a relatively coherent theoretical doctrine and as an organized political movement had its origins in early nineteenth-century Europe, especially in Britain, France and Germany. It was, above all, a critical response to early industrial capitalism, to an unregulated market economy in which the means of production were privately owned and propertyless workers were forced to sell their labour power to capitalists for often meagre wages. The evils of this system seemed manifest to its socialist critics. Not only was the relationship between workers and capitalists inherently exploitative, and the commodification of labour an affront to human dignity, but it generated widespread poverty and recurrent unemployment, massive and unjust inequalities of wealth and economic power, degrading and soul-destroying work, and an increasingly atomized and individualistic society.

Socialists were not alone in criticizing some of these features of industrial capitalism and its accompanying ideology of economic liberalism. In particular, antipathy towards individualism was also a characteristic of conservative thought. But whereas conservatives found their inspiration in the hierarchically structured organic communities of the past, and were deeply hostile to the political radicalism of the French Revolution, socialists looked forward to new forms of community consistent with the ideals of liberty, equality and fraternity. For them, the evils of capitalism could be overcome only by replacing private with public or common ownership of the means of production, abolishing wage labour and creating a classless society where production geared to capitalist profits gave way to socially organized production for the satisfaction of human needs. In such a society, the human potential for a genuinely 'social' mode of existence would be realized, with mutual concern for others' wellbeing rather than unbridled pursuit of self-interest, with cooperation for common ends rather than competition for individual ones, and with generosity and sharing rather than greed and acquisitiveness – a truly human community.

For most nineteenth-century socialist theorists, the historic task of creating such a society was assigned to the organized industrial working class; most notably by Marx, the pre-eminent figure in the history of socialism. It was Marx who (along with Engels) provided the socialist movement not only with a theoretically sophisticated economic analysis of capitalism and a biting critique of its social consequences, but also, through his scientific, materialist theory of historical development, with the confident belief that the inherent contradictions and class antagonisms of capitalism would eventually give birth to a socialist society.

In marked contrast to such earlier optimism, contemporary socialists are faced with the continued resilience of capitalist societies and the collapse of at least nominally socialist regimes in the USSR and elsewhere, regimes in which state ownership and centralized planning have been accompanied by political repression and economic failure. For those who reject the idea that a suitably regulated form of welfare capitalism is the most that can be hoped for, the task is to construct some alternative model of a socialist economy which is preferable to this yet which avoids the evils of centralized state socialism.

See also: BAKUNIN, M.A.; ENGELS, F.; MARKET, ETHICS OF THE; MARX, K.; MARXISM, WESTERN; MARXIST PHILOSOPHY, RUSSIAN AND SOVIET; POLITICAL PHILOSOPHY, HISTORY OF; PROUDHON, P.-J.

RUSSELL KEAT
JOHN O'NEILL

SOCIETY, CONCEPT OF

The term 'society' is broader than 'human society'. Many other species are described as possessing a social way of life. Yet mere gregariousness, of the kind found in a herd of cattle or a shoal of fish, is not enough to constitute a society. For the biologist, the marks of the social are cooperation (extending beyond cooperation between parents in raising young) and some form of order or division of labour. In assessing the merits of attempts to provide a more precise definition of society, we can ask whether the definition succeeds in capturing our intuitive understanding of the term, and also whether it succeeds in identifying those features of society which are most fundamental from an explanatory point of view – whether it captures the Lockean 'real essence' of society.

One influential approach seeks to capture the idea of society by characterizing social action, or interaction, in terms of the particular kinds of awareness it involves. Another approach focuses on social order, seeing it as a form of order that arises spontaneously when rational and mutually aware individuals succeed in solving coordination problems. Yet another approach focuses on the role played by communication in achieving collective agreement on the way the world is to be classified and understood, as a precondition of coordination and cooperation.

See also: ANTHROPOLOGY, PHILOSOPHY OF; CONFUCIAN PHILOSOPHY, CHINESE

ANGUS ROSS

SOCINIANISM

Socinianism was both the name for a sixteenth- and seventeenth-century theological movement which was a forerunner of modern unitarianism, and, much less precisely, a polemic term of abuse suggesting positions in common with that 'heretical' movement. Socinianism was explicitly undogmatic but centred on disbelief in the Trinity, original sin, the satisfaction, and the natural immortality of the soul. Some Socinians were materialists. Socinians focused on moralism and Christ's prophetic role; the elevation of reason in interpreting Scripture against creeds, traditions and church authority; and support for religious toleration. The term was used polemically against many theorists, including Hugo Grotius, William Chillingworth, the Latitudinarians, and John Locke, who emphasized free will, moralism, the role and capacity of reason, and that Christianity included only a very few fundamental doctrines necessary for salvation.

See also: DEISM; NATURAL LAW

JOHN MARSHALL

SOCIOBIOLOGY

Following Darwin, biologists and social scientists have periodically been drawn to the theory of natural selection as the source of explanatory insights about human behaviour and social institutions. The combination of Mendelian genetics and Darwinian theory, which did so much to substantiate the theory of evolution in the life sciences, however, has made recurrent adoption of a biological approach to the social sciences controversial. Excesses and errors in social Darwinism, eugenics and mental testing have repeatedly exposed evolutionary approaches in the human sciences to criticism.

Sociobiology is the version of Darwinism in social and behavioural science that became prominent in the last quarter of the twentieth century. Philosophical problems of sociobiology include challenges to the explanatory relevance of Darwinian theory for human behaviour and social institutions, controversies about whether natural selection operates at levels of organization above or below the individual, questions about the meaning of the nature–nurture distinction, and disputes about Darwinism's implications for moral philosophy.

See also: HUMAN NATURE; METHODOLOGICAL INDIVIDUALISM; REDUCTION, PROBLEMS OF; SPECIES; UNITY OF SCIENCE

ALEX ROSENBERG

SOCIOLOGY OF KNOWLEDGE

Sociologists of knowledge contribute to the enterprise of generating a naturalistic account of knowledge by describing and explaining the observed characteristics of shared cultures. They assume that knowledge can be treated as an object of empirical investigation (rather than mere celebration or condemnation). Because science is understandably taken as our best example of knowledge, the sociology of scientific knowledge plays a pivotal role in the field. It is argued that our natural reasoning capacities, and our sense experience, are necessary but not sufficient conditions for scientific knowledge. Sociologists looking for the causes of its content and style focus on the contribution of conventions and institutions.

See also: CONSTRUCTIVISM; FEMINIST EPISTEMOLOGY; FOUCAULT, M.; NATURALISM IN SOCIAL SCIENCE

DAVID BLOOR

SOCRATES (469–399 BC)

Introduction

Socrates, an Athenian Greek of the second half of the fifth century BC, wrote no philosophical works but was uniquely influential in the later history of philosophy. His philosophical interests were restricted to ethics and the conduct of life, topics which thereafter became central to philosophy. He discussed these in public places in Athens, sometimes with other prominent intellectuals or political leaders, sometimes with young men, who gathered round him in large numbers, and other admirers. Among these young men was Plato. Socrates' philosophical ideas and – equally important for his philosophical influence – his personality and methods as a 'teacher' were handed on to posterity in the 'dialogues' that several of his friends wrote after his death and which depicted such discussions. Only those of Xenophon (*Memorabilia*, *Apology*, *Symposium*) and the early dialogues of Plato survive (for example *Euthyphro*, *Apology*, *Crito*). Later Platonic dialogues such as *Phaedo*, *Symposium* and *Republic* do not present the historical Socrates' ideas; the 'Socrates' appearing in them is a spokesman for Plato's own ideas.

Socrates' discussions took the form of face-to-face interrogations of another person. Most often they concerned the nature of some moral virtue, such as courage or justice. Socrates asked what the respondent thought these qualities of mind and character amounted to, what their value was, how they were acquired. He would then test their ideas for logical consistency with other highly plausible general views about morality and goodness that the respondent also agreed to accept, once Socrates presented them. He succeeded in showing, to his satisfaction and that of the respondent and any bystanders, that the respondent's ideas were not consistent. By this practice of 'elenchus' or refutation he was able to prove that politicians and others who claimed to have 'wisdom' about human affairs in fact lacked it, and to draw attention to at least apparent errors in their thinking. He wanted to encourage them and others to think harder and to improve their ideas about the virtues and about how to conduct a good human life. He never argued directly for ideas of his own, but always questioned those of others. None the less, one can infer, from the questions he asks and his attitudes to the answers he receives, something about his own views.

Socrates was convinced that our souls – where virtues and vices are found – are vastly more important for our lives than our bodies or external circumstances. The quality of our souls determines the character of our lives, for better or for worse, much more than whether we are healthy or sick, or rich or poor. If we are to live well and happily, as he assumed we all want to do more than we want anything else, we must place the highest priority on the care of our souls. That means we must above all want to acquire the virtues, since they perfect our souls and enable them to direct our lives for the better. If only we could know what each of the virtues is we could then make an effort to obtain them. As to the nature of the virtues, Socrates seems to have held quite strict and, from the popular point of view, paradoxical views. Each virtue consists entirely in knowledge, of how it is best to act in some area of life, and why: additional 'emotional' aspects, such as the disciplining of our feelings and desires, he dismissed as of no importance. Weakness of will is not psychologically possible: if you act wrongly or badly, that is due to your ignorance of how you ought to act and why. He thought each of the apparently separate virtues amounts to the same single body of knowledge: the comprehensive knowledge of what is and is not good for a

human being. Thus his quest was to acquire this single wisdom: all the particular virtues would follow automatically.

At the age of 70 Socrates was charged before an Athenian popular court with 'impiety' – with not believing in the Olympian gods and corrupting young men through his constant questioning of everything. He was found guilty and condemned to death. Plato's *Apology*, where Socrates gives a passionate defence of his life and philosophy, is one of the classics of Western literature. For different groups of later Greek philosophers he was the model both of a sceptical inquirer who never claims to know the truth, and of a 'sage' who knows the whole truth about human life and the human good. Among modern philosophers, the interpretations of his innermost meaning given by Montaigne, Hegel, Kierkegaard, and Nietzsche are especially notable.

1 Life and sources

Socrates, an Athenian citizen proud of his devotion to Athens, lived his adult life there engaging in open philosophical discussion and debate on fundamental questions of ethics, politics, religion and education. Going against the grain of the traditional education, he insisted that personal investigation and reasoned argument, rather than ancestral custom, or appeal to the authority of Homer, Hesiod and other respected poets, was the only proper basis for answering these questions. His emphasis on argument and logic and his opposition to unquestioning acceptance of tradition allied him with such Sophists of a generation earlier as Protagoras, GORGIAS and Prodicus, none of whom was an Athenian, but all of whom spent time lecturing and teaching at Athens (see SOPHISTS). Unlike these Sophists Socrates did not formally offer himself or accept pay as a teacher. But many upper-class young Athenian men gathered round him to hear and engage in his discussions, and he had an inspirational and educational effect upon them, heightening their powers of critical thought and encouraging them to take seriously their individual responsibility to think through and decide how to conduct their lives. Many of his contemporaries perceived this education as morally and socially destructive – it certainly involved subverting accepted beliefs – and he was tried in 399 BC before an Athenian popular court and condemned to death on a charge of 'impiety': that he did not believe in the Olympian gods, but in new ones instead, and corrupted the young. Scholars sometimes mention specifically political motives of revenge, based on guilt by association: a number of prominent Athenians who were with Socrates as young men or were close friends did turn against the Athenian democracy and collaborated with the Spartans in their victory over Athens in the Peloponnesian war. But an amnesty passed by the restored democracy in 403 BC prohibited prosecution for political offences before that date. The rhetorician Polycrates included Socrates' responsibility for these political crimes in his *Accusation of Socrates* (see Xenophon, *Memorabilia* I 2.12), a rhetorical exercise written at least five years after Socrates' death. But there is no evidence that, in contravention of the amnesty, Socrates' actual accusers covertly attacked him, or his jurors condemned him, on that ground. The defences PLATO and Xenophon constructed for Socrates, each in his respective *Apology*, imply that it was his own questioning mind and what was perceived as the bad moral influence he had on his young men that led to his trial and condemnation.

Socrates left no philosophical works, and apparently wrote none. His philosophy and personality were made known to later generations through the dialogues that several of his associates wrote with him as principal speaker. Only fragments survive of those by Aeschines of Sphettus and Antisthenes, both Athenians, and Phaedo of Elis (after whom Plato's dialogue *Phaedo* is named). Our own knowledge of Socrates depends primarily on the dialogues of Plato and the Socratic works of the military leader and historian Xenophon. Plato was a young associate of Socrates' during perhaps the last ten years of his life, and Xenophon knew him during that same period, though he was absent from Athens at the time of Socrates' death and for several years before and many years after.

We also have secondary evidence from the comic playwright Aristophanes and from Aristotle. Aristotle, although born fifteen years after Socrates' death, had access through Plato and others to first-hand information about the man and his philosophy. Aristophanes knew Socrates personally; his *Clouds* (first produced *c.*423 BC) pillories the 'new' education offered by Sophists and philosophers by showing Socrates at work in a 'thinkery', propounding outlandish physical theories and teaching young men how to argue cleverly in defence of their improper behaviour. It is significant that in 423, when Socrates was about 45 years old, he could plausibly be taken as a leading representative in Athens of the 'new' education. But one cannot expect a comic play making fun of a whole intellectual movement to contain an authentic account of Socrates' specific philosophical commitments.

However, the literary genre to which Plato's and Xenophon's Socratic works belong (along with the other, lost dialogues) also permits the author much latitude; in his *Poetics* Aristotle counts such works as fictions of a certain kind, alongside epic poems and tragedies. They are by no means records of actual discussions (despite the fact that Xenophon explicitly so represents his). Each author was free to develop his own ideas behind the mask of Socrates, at least within the limits of what his personal experience had led him to believe was Socrates' basic philosophical and moral outlook. Especially in view of the many inconsistencies between Plato's and Xenophon's portraits (see §7 later), it is a difficult question for historical-philosophical interpretation whether the philosophical and moral views the character Socrates puts forward in any of these dialogues can legitimately be attributed to the historical philosopher. The problem of interpretation is made more difficult by the fact that Socrates appears in many of Plato's dialogues – ones belonging to his middle and later periods (see PLATO §§10–16) – discussing and expounding views that we have good reason to believe resulted from Plato's own philosophical investigations into questions of metaphysics and epistemology, questions that were not entered into at all by the historical Socrates. To resolve this problem – what scholars call the 'Socratic problem' – most now agree in preferring Plato to Xenophon as a witness. Xenophon is not thought to have been philosopher enough to have understood Socrates well or to have captured the depth of his views and his personality. As for Plato, most scholars accept only the philosophical interests and procedures, and the moral and philosophical views, of the Socrates of the early dialogues, and, more guardedly, the Socrates of 'transitional' ones such as *Meno* and *Gorgias*, as legitimate representations of the historical personage. These dialogues are the ones that predate the emergence of the metaphysical and epistemological inquiries just referred to. However, even Plato's early dialogues are philosophical works written to further Plato's own philosophical interests. That could produce distortions, also; and Xenophon's relative philosophical innocence could make his portrait in some respects more reliable. Moreover, it is possible, even probable, that in his efforts to help his young men improve themselves Socrates spoke differently to the philosophically more promising ones among them – including Plato – from the way he spoke to others, for example Xenophon. Both portraits could be true, but partial and needing to be combined (see §7). The account of Socrates' philosophy given below follows Plato, with caution, while giving independent weight also to Xenophon and to Aristotle.

2 Life and sources (cont.)

Xenophon's *Apology* of Socrates, *Symposium* and *Memorabilia* (or *Memoirs*) may well reflect knowledge of Plato's own *Apology* and some of his early and middle period dialogues, as well as lost dialogues of Antisthenes and others. Xenophon composed the *Memorabilia* over many years, beginning only some ten years after Socrates' death, avowedly in order to defend Socrates' reputation as a good man, a true Athenian gentleman, and a good influence upon his young men. The same intention motivated his *Apology* and *Symposium*. Anything these works contain about Socrates' philosophical opinions and procedures is ancillary to that apologetic purpose. Plato's *Apology*, of course, is similarly apologetic, but it and his other early dialogues are carefully constructed discussions, strongly focused upon questions of philosophical substance. Plato evidently thought Socrates' philosophical ideas and methods were central to his life and to his mission. Xenophon's and Plato's testimony agree that Socrates' discussions consistently concerned the *aretai*, the recognized 'virtues' or excellences of character (see ARETÊ), such as justice, piety, self-control or moderation (*sōphrosynē*), courage and wisdom; what these individual characteristics consist in and require of a person, what their value is, and how they are acquired, whether by teaching or in some other way. In his *Apology* and elsewhere Plato has Socrates insist that these discussions were always inquiries, efforts made to engage his fellow-discussants in coming jointly to an adequate understanding of the matters inquired into. He does not himself know, and therefore cannot teach anyone else – whether by means of these discussions or in some other way – either how to be virtuous or what virtue in general or any particular virtue is. Furthermore, given his general characterization of virtue (see §§4–5), Plato's Socrates makes a point of suggesting the impossibility in principle of teaching virtue at all, by contrast with the Sophists who declared they could teach it. Virtue was not a matter of information about living or rote techniques of some sort to be handed on from teacher to pupil, but required an open-ended personal understanding that individuals could only come to for themselves. Xenophon, too, reports that Socrates denied he was a teacher of *aretē*, but he pays no attention to such issues of philosophical principle. He does not hesitate to show Socrates speaking of himself as a teacher (see *Apology* 26, *Memorabilia* I 6.13–14), and describes

him as accepting young men from their fathers as his pupils (but not for a fee), and teaching them the virtues by displaying his own virtues to them for emulation, as well as through conversation and precepts. Perhaps Socrates did not insist on holding to strict philosophical principles in dealing with people on whom their point would have been lost.

In his *Apology* Plato's Socrates traces his practice of spending his days discussing and inquiring about virtue to an oracle delivered at the shrine of Apollo at Delphi. Xenophon also mentions this oracle in his *Apology*. A friend of Socrates', Chaerephon, had asked the god whether anyone was wiser than Socrates; the priestess answered that no one was. Because he was sure he was not wise at all – only the gods, he suspected, could actually *know* how a human life ought to be led – Socrates cross-examined others at Athens with reputations for that kind of wisdom. He wanted to show that there were people wiser than he and thus discover the true meaning of the oracle – Apollo was known to speak in riddles requiring interpretation to reach their deeper meaning. In the event, it turned out that the people he examined were not wise, since they could not even give a self-consistent set of answers to his questions: obviously, true knowledge requires at least that one think and speak consistently on the subjects one professes to know. So he concluded that the priestess's reply had meant that of all those with reputations for wisdom only he came close to deserving it; he wisely did not profess to know these things that only gods can know, and that was wisdom enough for a human being. Because only he knew that he did *not* know, only he was ready earnestly to inquire into virtue and the other ingredients of the human good, in an effort to learn. He understood therefore that Apollo's true intention in the oracle had been to encourage him to continue his inquiries, to help others to realize that it is beyond human powers actually to *know* how to live – that is the prerogative of the gods – and to do his best to understand as far as a human being can how one ought to live. The life of philosophy, as led by him, was therefore something he was effectively ordered by Apollo to undertake.

We must remember that Socrates was on trial on a charge of 'impiety'. In tracing his philosophical vocation back to Apollo's oracle, and linking it to a humble recognition of human weakness and divine perfection, he was constructing a powerful rebuttal of the charges brought against him. But it cannot be literally true – if that is what he intended to say – that Socrates began his inquiries about virtue only after hearing of the oracle. Chaerephon's question to Apollo shows Socrates had established a reputation in Athens for wisdom before that. That reputation cannot have rested on philosophical inquiries of another sort. In Plato's *Phaedo* Socrates says he had been interested as a young man in philosophical speculations about the structure and causes of the natural world, but he plainly did not take those interests very far; and in any event, his reputation was not for that kind of wisdom, but wisdom about how to lead a human life. In fact we do not hear of the duty to Apollo in Xenophon, or in other dialogues of Plato, where we might expect to find it if from the beginning Socrates thought Apollo had commanded his life of philosophizing. However, we need not think Socrates was false to the essential spirit of philosophy as he practised it if in looking back on his life under threat of condemnation for impiety he chose, inaccurately, to see it as initially imposed on him by Apollo's oracle.

Despite its impressiveness, Socrates' speech failed to convince his jury of 501 male fellow citizens, and he died in the state prison by drinking hemlock as required by law. His speech evidently offended the majority of the jurors by its disdain for the charges and the proceedings; Xenophon explains his lofty behaviour, which he thinks would otherwise have been lunatic – and damaging to his reputation – by reporting that he had told friends in advance that as a 70-year-old still in possession of his health and faculties it was time for him to die anyhow, before senility set in. Furthermore, his 'divine sign' – the 'voice' he sometimes heard warning him for his own good against a contemplated course of action – had prevented him from spending time crafting a defence speech. (This voice seems to have been the basis for the charge of introducing 'new' gods.) So he would do nothing to soften his manner in order to win his freedom. Even if this story is true, Plato could be right that Socrates put on a spirited, deeply serious defence of his life and beliefs – one that he thought should have convinced the jurors of his innocence, if only they had judged him intelligently and fairly.

3 Socratic elenchus, or refutation

In cross-examining those with reputations for wisdom about human affairs and showing their lack of it, Socrates employed a special method of dialectical argument that he himself had perfected, the method of 'elenchus' – Greek for 'putting to the test' or 'refutation'. He gives an example at his trial when he cross-examines Meletus, one of his accusers (Plato, *Apology* 24d–27e). The respondent states a thesis, as something he *knows* to be true because he is wise about the matter in question. Socrates then asks questions, eliciting clarifications, qualifications and extensions of the thesis, and seeking further opinions of the respondent on

related matters. He then argues, and the respondent sees no way not to grant, that the original thesis is logically inconsistent with something affirmed in these further responses. For Socrates, it follows at once that the respondent did not know what he was talking about in stating his original thesis: true knowledge would prevent one from such self-contradiction. So the respondent suffers a personal set-back; *he* is refuted – revealed as incompetent. Meletus, for example, does not have consistent ideas about the gods or what would show someone not to believe in them, and he does not have consistent ideas about who corrupts the young, and how; so he does not know what he is talking about, and no one should take *his* word for it that Socrates disbelieves in the gods or has corrupted his young men. In many of his early dialogues Plato shows Socrates using this method to examine the opinions of persons who claim to be wise in some matter: the religious expert Euthyphro on piety (*Euthyphro*), the generals Laches and Nicias on courage (*Laches*), the Sophist Protagoras on the distinctions among the virtues and whether virtue can be taught (*Protagoras*), the rhapsodist Ion on what is involved in knowing poetry (*Ion*), the budding politician Alcibiades on justice and other political values (*Alcibiades*), the Sophist Hippias on which was the better man, Odysseus or Achilles (*Lesser Hippias*), and on the nature of moral and aesthetic beauty (*Greater Hippias*). They are all refuted – shown to have mutually inconsistent ideas on the subject discussed (see PLATO §§4, 6, 8–9).

But Socrates is not content merely to demonstrate his interlocutor's lack of wisdom or knowledge. That might humiliate him into inquiring further or seeking by some other means the knowledge he has been shown to lack, instead of remaining puffed up with self-conceit. That would be a good thing. But Socrates often also indicates clearly that his cross-examination justifies him and the interlocutor in rejecting as false the interlocutor's original thesis. Logically, that is obviously wrong: if the interlocutor contradicts himself, at least one of the things he has said must be false (indeed, all of them could be), but the fact alone of self-contradiction does not show where the falsehood resides. For example, when Socrates leads Euthyphro to accept ideas that contradict his own definition of the pious as whatever pleases all the gods, Socrates concludes that that definition has been shown to be false (*Euthyphro* 10d–11a), and asks Euthyphro to come up with another one. He does not usually consider that perhaps on further thought the additional ideas would seem faulty and so merit rejection instead – thus leaving room to retain the definition.

Socrates uses his elenctic method also in discussion with persons who are not puffed up with false pride, and are quite willing to admit their ignorance and to reason out the truth about these important matters. Examples are his discussions with his long-time friend Crito on whether he should escape prison and set aside the court's death sentence (Plato, *Crito*), and with the young men Charmides, on self-control (*Charmides*), and Lysis and Menexenus, on the nature of friendship (*Lysis*). Socrates examines Crito's proposal that he escape on the basis of principles that he presents to him for his approval, and he, together with Crito (however half-heartedly), rejects it when it fails to be consistent with them. And he examines the young men's successive ideas about these virtues, rejecting some of them and refining others, by relying on their own acceptance of further ideas that he puts to them. Again, he is confident that the inconsistencies brought to light in their ideas indicate the inadequacy of their successive proposals as to the nature of the moral virtue in question.

In many of his discussions, both with young men and the allegedly wise, Socrates seeks to know what some morally valuable property is – for example, piety, courage, self-control or friendship (see §4). Rejecting the idea that one could learn this simply from attending to examples, he insisted on an articulated 'definition' of the item in question – some *single* account that would capture all at once the presumed common feature that would entitle anything to count as a legitimate instance. Such a definition, providing the essence of the thing defined, would give us a 'model' or 'paradigm' to use in judging whether or not some proposed action or person possesses the moral value so defined (*Euthyphro* 6d–e). Aristotle says (in *Metaphysics* I, 6) that Socrates was the first to interest himself in such 'universal definitions', and traces to his interest in them Plato's first impetus towards a theory of Forms, or 'separated' universals (see PLATO §10).

In none of his discussions in Plato's early works does Socrates profess to think an adequate final result has actually been established – about the nature of friendship, or self-control, or piety, or any of the other matters he inquires about. Indeed, on the contrary, these works regularly end with professions of profound ignorance about the matter under investigation. Knowledge is never attained, and further questions always remain to be considered. But Socrates does plainly think that progress towards reaching final understanding has taken place (even if only a god, and no human being, could ever actually attain it). Not only has one discovered some things that are definitely wrong to say; one has also achieved some positive insights that are worth holding onto in seeking further systematic understanding. Given that

Socrates' method of discussion is elenctic throughout, what does he think justifies this optimism?

On balance, our evidence suggests that Socrates had worked out no elaborate theory to support him here. The ideas he was stimulated to propound in an elenctic examination which went against some initial thesis seemed to him, and usually also to the others present, so plausible, and so supportable by further considerations, that he and they felt content to reject the initial thesis. Until someone came up with arguments to neutralize their force, it seemed the thesis was doomed, as contrary to reason itself. Occasionally Socrates expresses himself in just those terms: however unpalatable the option might seem, it remains open to someone to challenge the grounds on which his conclusions rest (see *Euthyphro* 15c, *Gorgias* 461d–462a, 509a, *Crito* 54d). But until they do, he is satisfied to treat his and his interlocutor's agreement as a firm basis for thought and action. Later, when Plato himself became interested in questions of philosophical methodology in his *Meno*, this came to seem a philosophically unsatisfactory position; Plato's demand for justification for one's beliefs independent of what seemed on reflection most plausible led him to epistemological and metaphysical inquiries that went well beyond the self-imposed restriction of Socratic philosophy to ethical thought in the broadest sense. But Socrates did not raise these questions. In this respect more bound by traditional views than Plato, he had great implicit confidence in his and his interlocutors' capacity, after disciplined dialectical examination of the issues, to reach firm ground for constructing positive ideas about the virtues and about how best to lead a human life – even if these ideas never received the sort of final validation that a god, understanding fully the truth about human life, could give them.

4 Elenchus and moral progress

The topics Socrates discussed were always ethical, and never included questions of physical theory or metaphysics or other branches of philosophical study. Moreover, he always conducted his discussions not as theoretical inquiries but as profoundly personal moral tests. Questioner and interlocutor were equally putting their ways of life to what Socrates thought was the most important test of all – their capacity to stand up to scrutiny in rational argument about how one ought to live. In speaking about human life, he wanted his respondents to indicate what they truly believed, and as questioner he was prepared to do the same, at least at crucial junctures. Those beliefs were assumed to express not theoretical ideas, but the very ones on which they themselves were conducting their lives. In losing an argument with Socrates you did not merely show yourself logically or argumentatively deficient, but also put into question the very basis on which you were living. Your way of life might ultimately prove defensible, but if you cannot now defend it successfully, you are not leading it *with* any such justification. In that case, according to Socrates' views, your way of life is morally deficient. Thus if Menexenus, Lysis and Socrates profess to value friendship among the most important things in life and profess to be one another's friends, but cannot satisfactorily explain under pressure of elenctic investigation what a friend is, that casts serious doubt on the quality of any 'friendship' they might form (Plato, *Lysis* 212a, 223b). Moral consistency and personal integrity, and not mere delight in argument and logical thought, should therefore lead you to repeated elenctic examination of your views, in an effort to render them coherent and at the same time defensible on all sides through appeal to plausible arguments. Or, if some of your views have been shown false, by conflicting with extremely plausible general principles, it behoves you to drop them – and so to cease living in a way that depends upon accepting them. In this way, philosophical inquiry via the elenchus is fundamentally a personal moral quest. It is a quest not just to understand adequately the basis on which one is actually living, and the personal and moral commitments that this contains. It is also a quest to change the way one lives as the results of argument show one ought to, so that, at the logical limit of inquiry, one's way of life would be completely vindicated. Accordingly, Socrates in Plato's dialogues regularly insists on the individual and personal character of his discussions. He wants to hear the views of the one person with whom he is speaking. He dismisses as of no interest what outsiders or most people may think – provided that is not what his discussant is personally convinced is true. The views of 'the many' may well not rest on thought or argument at all. Socrates insists that his discussant shoulder the responsibility to explain and defend rationally the views he holds, and follow the argument – reason – wherever it may lead.

We learn a good deal about Socrates' own principles from both Plato and Xenophon. Those were ones that had stood up well over a lifetime of frequent elenctic discussions and had, as he thought, a wealth of plausible arguments in their favour. Foremost is his conviction that the virtues – self-control, courage, justice, piety, wisdom and related qualities of mind and soul – are essential if anyone is to lead a good and happy life. They are good in themselves for a human being, and they guarantee a happy life, *eudaimonia* – something that he thought all human beings always wanted, and wanted more

than anything else. The virtues belong to the soul – they are the condition of a soul that has been properly cared for and brought to its best state. The soul is vastly more important for happiness than are health and strength of the body or social and political power, wealth and other external circumstances of life; the goods of the soul, and preeminently the virtues, are worth far more than any quantity of bodily or external goods. Socrates seems to have thought these other goods *are* truly good, but they only *do* people good, and thereby contribute to their happiness, under the condition that they are chosen and used in accordance with virtues indwelling in their souls (see Plato, *Apology* 30b, *Euthydemus* 280d–282d, *Meno* 87d–89a).

More specific principles followed. Doing injustice is worse for oneself than being subjected to it (*Gorgias* 469c–522e): by acting unjustly you make your soul worse, and that affects for the worse the whole of your life, whereas one who treats you unjustly at most harms your body or your possessions but leaves your soul unaffected. On the same ground Socrates firmly rejected the deeply entrenched Greek precept to aid one's friends and harm one's enemies, and the accompanying principle of retaliation, which he equated with returning wrongs for wrongs done to oneself and one's friends (*Crito* 49a–d). Socrates' daily life gave witness to his principles. He was poor, shabbily dressed and unshod, and made do with whatever ordinary food came his way: such things matter little. Wealth, finery and delicacies for the palate are not worth panting after and exerting oneself to enjoy. However, Socrates was fully capable of relishing both refined and plain enjoyments as occasion warranted (see §7).

5 The unity of virtue

The Greeks recognized a series of specially prized qualities of mind and character as *aretai* or virtues. Each was regarded as a distinct, separate quality: justice was one thing, concerned with treating other people fairly, courage quite another, showing itself in vigorous, correct behaviour in circumstances that normally cause people to be afraid; and self-control or moderation, piety and wisdom were yet others. Each of these ensured that its possessor would act in some specific ways, regularly and reliably over their lifetime, having the justified conviction that those are ways one *ought* to act – *agathon* (good) and *kalon* (fine, noble, admirable or beautiful) ways of acting. But each type of virtuous person acts rightly and well not only in regularly recurring, but also in unusual and unheralded, circumstances; the virtue involves always getting something right about how to live a good human life. Socrates thought these virtues were essential if one was to live happily (see §4). But what exactly were they? What was it about someone that made them just, or courageous, or wise? If you did not know that, you would not know what to do in order to acquire those qualities. Furthermore, supposing you did possess a virtue, you would have to be able to explain and defend by argument the consequent ways in which you lived – otherwise your conviction that those are ways one *ought* to act would be shallow and unjustified. And in order to do that you would have to know what state of mind the virtue was, since that is essential to them (see Plato, *Charmides* 158e–159a). Consequently, in his discussions Socrates constantly asked for 'definitions' of various virtues: what is courage (*Laches*), what is self-control or moderation (*Charmides*), what is friendship (*Lysis*) and what is piety (*Euthyphro*). As this context shows, he was asking not for a 'dictionary definition', an account of the accepted linguistic understanding of a term, but for an ethically defensible account of an actual condition of mind or character to which the word in common use would be correctly applied. In later terminology, he was seeking a 'real' rather than a 'nominal' definition (see DEFINITION; PLATO §§6–9).

Socrates objected to definitions that make a virtue some external aspect of a virtuous action (such as the manner in which it is done – for example its 'quiet' or measured quality in the case of moderation; *Charmides* 160b–d), or simply the doing of specific types of action, described in terms of their external circumstances (such as, for courage, standing one's ground in battle; *Laches* 190e–191d). He also objected to more psychological definitions that located a virtue in some non-rational and non-cognitive aspect of the soul (for example, in the case of courage, the soul's endurance or strength of resistance; *Laches* 192d–193e). For his own part, he regularly shows himself ready to accept only definitions that identify a virtue with some sort of knowledge or wisdom about what is valuable for a human being. That 'intellectualist' expectation about the nature of virtue, although never worked out to his satisfaction in any Platonic dialogue, is central to Socrates' philosophy.

Given that in his discussions he is always the questioner, probing the opinions of his respondent and not arguing for views of his own, we never find Socrates stating clearly what led him to this intellectualism. Probably, however, it was considerations drawn from the generally agreed premise that each virtue is a condition motivating certain voluntary actions, chosen because they are good and fine or noble. He took it that what lies behind and produces any voluntary action is the idea under which it is done, the conception of the action in the agent's mind that makes it seem the thing to do just then. If so, each virtue must be some state of the mind, the possessor of which constantly has certain distinctive general ideas about how one ought to behave. Furthermore, since virtues get this *right*, these are true ideas. And since a virtuous person acts well and correctly in a *perfectly reliable* way, they must be seated so deeply in the mind as to be ineradicable and unwaveringly present. The only state of mind that meets these conditions is knowledge: to know a subject is not just to be thoroughly convinced, but to have a deep, fully articulated understanding, being ready with explanations to fend off objections and apparent difficulties and to extend old principles into new situations, and being prepared to show with the full weight of reason precisely why each thing falling under it is and must be so. Each virtue, then, must be knowledge about how one ought to behave in some area of life, and why – a knowledge so deep and rationally secure that those who have it can be counted upon never to change their minds, never to be argued out of or otherwise persuaded away from, or to waver in, their conviction about how to act.

In Plato's *Protagoras* Socrates goes beyond this, and identifies himself with the position, rejected by Protagoras in their discussion, that the apparently separate virtues of justice, piety, self-control, courage and wisdom are somehow one and the same thing – some single knowledge (361a–b). Xenophon too confirms that Socrates held this view (*Memorabilia* III 9.5). Protagoras defends the position that each of the virtues is not only a distinct thing from each of the others, but so different in kind that a person could possess one of them without possessing the others (329d–e). In opposing him, Socrates sometimes speaks plainly of two allegedly distinct virtues being 'one' (333b). Given this unity of the virtues, it would follow that a person could not possess one without having them all. And in speaking of justice and piety in particular, Socrates seems to go further, to imply that every action produced by virtue is equally an instance of *all* the standardly recognized virtues: pious as well as just, wise and self-controlled and courageous also. Among his early dialogues, however, Plato's own philosophical interests show themselves particularly heavily in the *Protagoras*, so it is doubtful how far the details of his arguments are to be attributed to the historical Socrates. The issues raised by Socrates in the *Protagoras* were, none the less, vigorously pursued by subsequent 'Socratic' philosophers (as Plutarch's report in *On Moral Virtue* 2 demonstrates). And the positions apparently adopted by Plato's Socrates were taken up and ingeniously defended by the Stoic philosopher Chrysippus (see STOICISM). As usual, because of his questioner's role, it is difficult to work out Socrates' grounds for holding to the unity of virtue; and it is difficult to tell whether, and if so how, he allowed that despite this unity there were some real differences between, say, justice and self-control, or courage and piety. Apparently he thought the same body of knowledge – knowledge of the whole of what is and is not good for human beings, and why it is so or not – must at least underlie the allegedly separate virtues. If you did not have that vast, comprehensive knowledge you could not be in the state of mind which is justice or in that which is courage, and so on; and if you did have it you would necessarily be in those states of mind. It seems doubtful whether Socrates himself progressed beyond that point. Efforts to do that were made by Chrysippus and the other philosophers referred to above. And despite denying that all virtues consist in knowledge, Plato in the *Republic* and Aristotle in *Nicomachean Ethics* VI follow Socrates to the extent of holding, in different ways, that you need to have all the virtues in order to have any one.

6 Weakness of will denied

In Plato's *Protagoras* Socrates also denies the possibility of weakness of will – being 'mastered' by some desire so as to act voluntarily in a way one knows is wrong or bad (see also Xenophon, *Memorabilia* III 9.4, IV 5.6.) All voluntary wrong-doing or bad action is due to ignorance of how one ought to act and why, and to nothing else. This would be easy to understand if Socrates were using 'knowing' quite strictly, to refer to the elevated and demanding sort of knowledge described in §6 (sometimes called 'Socratic knowledge'). Someone could know an action was wrong or bad, with full 'Socratic knowledge', only if they were not just thoroughly convinced, but had a deep, fully articulated understanding, being ready with explanations to fend off objections and apparent difficulties, and prepared to show precisely *why* it was so. That would mean that these ideas were seated so deeply in the mind as to be ineradicable and unwaveringly present. Accordingly, a person with 'Socratic knowledge' could not come to hold even momentarily that the action in question would be the thing to do, and so they could never do it voluntarily.

However, Plato's Socrates goes further. He explains his denial of weak-willed action by saying that a person cannot voluntarily do actions which, in doing them, they even *believe* to be a wrong or bad thing to do (*Protagoras* 358c–e). He gives a much-discussed, elaborate argument to establish this stronger conclusion, starting from assumptions identifying that which is pleasant with that which is good (352a–357e). These assumptions, however,

he attributes only to ordinary people, the ones who say they believe in the possibility of weak-willed action; he makes it clear to the careful reader, if not to Protagoras, that his own view is simply that pleasure is a good thing, not 'the' good (351c–e; see 354b–d). Although some scholars have thought otherwise, Socrates himself does not adopt a hedonist analysis of the good in the *Protagoras* or elsewhere either in Plato or Xenophon; indeed, he speaks elsewhere against hedonist views (see HEDONISM). The fundamental principle underlying his argument – a principle he thinks ordinary people will accept – is that voluntary action is always 'subjectively' rational, in the sense that an agent who acts to achieve some particular sort of value always acts with the idea that what they are doing achieves *more* of that value than alternatives then thought by them to be available would achieve. If someone performs an overall bad action because of some (lesser) good they think they will get from it, they cannot do it while *believing* it is bad overall. That would mean they thought they could have got *more* good by refraining, and their action would violate the principle just stated. Instead, at the time they acted (despite what they may have thought before or after acting), they believed (wrongly and ignorantly) that the action would be good overall for them to do. Thus ignorance, and only ignorance, is responsible for voluntary error. Weakness of will – knowingly pursuing the worse outcome – is psychologically impossible: 'No one does wrong willingly'.

The details of this argument may not represent explicit commitments of the historical Socrates. None the less, his denial of weakness of will, understood as presented in Plato's *Protagoras*, was the centre of a protracted debate in later times. First Plato himself, in *Republic* IV, then Aristotle in *Nicomachean Ethics* VII, argued against Socrates' conclusion, on the ground that he had overlooked the fact that human beings have other sources of motivation that can produce voluntary actions, besides their ideas about what is good or bad, or right or wrong to do. 'Appetites' and 'spirited desires' exist also, which can lead a person to act in fulfilment of them without having to adopt the idea, in their beliefs about what is best to do, that so acting would be a good thing (see PLATO §14; ARISTOTLE §20, 22–3). The Stoics, however, and especially Chrysippus, argued vigorously and ingeniously in defence of Socrates' analysis and against the Platonic-Aristotelian assumption of alternative sources of motivation that produce voluntary action on their own (see STOICISM). In fact, during Hellenistic times it was the Socratic, 'unitary' psychology of action that carried the day; the Platonic-Aristotelian alternative, dominant in the 'common sense' and the philosophy of modern times, was a minority view. The issues Socrates raised about weakness of will continue to be debated today.

7 Socrates' personality

Socrates drew to himself many of the brightest and most prominent people in Athens, securing their fascinated attention and their passionate friendship and support. His effectiveness as a philosopher, and the Socratic 'legend' itself, depended as much on the strength and interest of his personality as on the power of his mind. Plato's and Xenophon's portraits of Socrates as a person differ significantly, however. Plato's Socrates is aloof and often speaks ironically, although also with unusual and deeply held moral convictions; paradoxically, the depth and clarity of his convictions, maintained alongside the firm disclaimer to know what was true, could seem all the stronger testimony to their truth, and made them felt the more strongly as a rebuke to the superficiality of one's own way of living. In Xenophon, Socrates is also sometimes ironical and playful, especially in the *Symposium*, but his conversation is usually direct, even didactic, and often chummy in tone; his attitudes are for the most part conventional though earnest; and there is nothing to unsettle anyone or make them suspect hidden depths. It is much easier to believe that the Socrates of Plato's dialogues could have had such profound effects on the lives of the brightest of his contemporaries than did the character in Xenophon. That is one reason given for trusting Plato's more than Xenophon's portrait of the historical personage. But perhaps Socrates used the more kindly and genial manner and conventional approach depicted by Xenophon to draw out the best in some of his young men and his friends – ones who would have been put off by the Platonic subtleties. The historical Socrates may have been a more complex person than even Plato presents.

Plato and Xenophon both represent Socrates as strongly attracted to good-looking young men in the 'bloom' of their middle to late teens, just the period when they were also coming of age morally and intellectually. In both he speaks of himself as unusually 'erotic' by temperament and constantly 'in love'. But he explains his 'erotic' attachments in terms of his desire to converse with bright and serious young men, to question them about virtue and how best to live a human life, and to draw out what was best in their minds and characters. In Xenophon he describes his love as love for their souls, not their bodies, and he vigorously condemns sexual relations with any young man: using him that way disgraces him and harms him by encouraging a

loose attitude as regards physical pleasures (*Symposium* 8). The overheated sexuality of Plato's own accounts (*Symposium* and *Phaedrus*) of *erōs*, sexual love, for a young man's beauty as motivating an adult male to pursue philosophical truth into an eternal realm of Forms (see PLATO §12) is to be distinguished sharply from Socrates' ideas, as we can gather them from Xenophon and from Plato's own early dialogues.

Xenophon emphasizes Socrates' freedom from the strong appetites for food, drink, sex and physical comfort that dominate other people; his *enkrateia* or self-mastery is the first of the virtues that Xenophon claims for him (*Memorabilia* I 2.1). He was notorious for going barefoot even in winter and dressing always in a simple cloak. Socrates' self-mastery was at the centre of Antisthenes' portrayal, and is reflected also in several incidents reported in Plato, such as his serene dismissal of the young Alcibiades' efforts to seduce him sexually (Plato, *Symposium* 217b–219e), or, perhaps when engrossed in a philosophical problem, his standing in the open (during a break in the action while on military service) from morning to night, totally indifferent to everything around him (*Symposium* 220c–d). This 'ascetic' Socrates, especially as presented by Antisthenes – rejecting conventional comforts and conventional behaviour – became an inspiration for the 'Cynics' of later centuries.

8 Socrates in the history of philosophy

Looking back on the early history of philosophy, later philosophers traced to Socrates a major turn in its development. As Cicero puts it: 'Socrates was the first to call philosophy down from the heavens ... and compel it to ask questions about life and morality' (*Tusculan Disputations* V 10–11). Previously it had been concerned with the origins and nature of the physical world and the explanation of celestial and other natural phenomena. Modern scholarship follows the ancients' lead in referring standardly to philosophers before Socrates collectively as 'Presocratics' (see PRESOCRATIC PHILOSOPHY). This includes DEMOCRITUS, in fact a slightly younger contemporary of Socrates; Cicero's verdict needs adjustment, in that Democritus, independently of Socrates, also investigated questions about ethics and morality. With the sole exception of Epicureanism, which developed separately out of Democritean origins, all the major movements of Greek philosophy after Socrates had roots in his teaching and example. This obviously applies to Plato, whose philosophical development began with a thorough reworking and assimilation of Socratic moral inquiry, and through him to Aristotle and his fellow members of Plato's

Academy, Speusippus and Xenocrates and others, as well as to later Platonists. Among Socrates' inner circle were also Aristippus of Cyrene, who is traditionally thought to have founded the hedonist Cyrenaic school, and Antisthenes, an older rival of Plato's and major teacher in Athens of philosophical dialectic. Both of these figure in Xenophon's *Memorabilia* (Antisthenes also in his *Symposium*), where they are vividly characterized in conversation with Socrates. Another Socratic, Euclides, founded the Megarian school. These 'Socratic schools' developed different themes already prominent in Socrates' own investigations, and competed in the claim to be his true philosophical heirs.

In the third to first centuries BC, both the Stoics and their rivals the Academic sceptics claimed to be carrying forward the Socratic tradition. In both cases this was based upon a reading of Plato's dialogues and perhaps other eye-witness reconstructions of Socrates' philosophy. The Academic Arcesilaus interpreted the Platonic Socrates as a sceptical inquirer, avidly searching but never satisfied that the truth on any disputed question had been finally uncovered. He could point to much about Plato's Socrates in support: his modest but firm denial that he possessed any knowledge, and his constant practice of inquiring into the truth by examining others' opinions on the basis of ideas which they themselves accepted, without formally committing himself to these ideas even when he was the one to first suggest them. Arcesilaus, however, applied his sceptical Socratic dialectic to more than the questions of ethics and human life about which Socrates himself had argued, making it cover the whole range of philosophical topics being investigated in his day. The Stoics read the dialogues (especially the *Euthydemus* and *Protagoras*) quite differently. They found Socrates espousing a complete doctrine of ethics and the psychology of human action. He posed his questions on the basis of this doctrine, leaving the respondent (and the reader) to recover for themselves the philosophical considerations underlying it. They thus emphasized the conceptions of virtue as knowledge, of virtue as unified in wisdom, and of voluntary action as motivated always by an agent's beliefs about what is best to do, that emerged through Socrates' examination of Protagoras (see §§6–7). They thought these constituted a positive, Socratic moral philosophy, and in their own moral theory they set out to revive and strengthen it with systematic arguments and with added metaphysical and physical speculations of their own. Later Stoics regularly referred to Socrates as a genuine wise man or 'sage', perhaps the only one who ever lived. He had brought to final, systematic perfection his knowledge, along Stoic lines, of what is good and bad for human beings, and what is not, and therefore possessed all the virtues and no vices, and lived unwaveringly the best, happy life, free from emotion and all other errors about human life. It is a tribute to the complexity and enigmatic character of Socrates that he could stand simultaneously as a paragon both of sceptical, non-committal inquiry and life led on that uncommitted basis, and of dogmatic knowledge of the final truth about all things human.

The figure of Socrates has continued to fascinate and to inspire ever-new interpretations of his innermost meaning. For MONTAIGNE, he proved that human beings can convincingly and attractively order their own lives from their own resources of mind, without direction from God or religion or tradition. In the nineteenth century KIERKEGAARD and NIETZSCHE offered extensive interpretations of him, both heavily dependent upon Hegel's absolute-idealist analysis. HEGEL interpreted Socrates as a quintessentially negative thinker, aiming at making people vacillate in their superficial moral beliefs and endorse none of them wholeheartedly, thus hinting that the truth, although universal and objective, lies deep within the freedom of their own subjectivity. For Kierkegaard he represents, on the contrary, the possibility of living wholeheartedly by occupying an unarticulated position somehow beyond the negative rejection but expressed through it: 'infinite absolute negativity'. In *Die Geburt der Tragödie* (*The Birth of Tragedy*) Nietzsche treats Socrates principally as having poisoned the 'tragic' attitude that made possible the great achievements of classical culture, by insisting that life should be grounded in rational understanding and justified by 'knowledge'; but his fascinated regard for Socrates led him to return to him repeatedly in his writings. Socrates was paradigmatically a philosopher whose thought, however taken up with logic and abstract argument, is inseparable from the search for self-understanding and from a deeply felt attachment to the concerns of human life. His power to fascinate and inspire is surely not exhausted.

See also: PLATO

References and further reading

Grote, G. (1875) *Plato and the Other Companions of Socrates*, London: Murray, 3 vols. (Judicious, perceptive older account of Socrates in Plato's works and of the other Socratics; still a valuable work.)

Reeve, C.D.C. (1989) *Socrates in the* Apology, Indianapolis, IN: Hackett. (Commentary on Plato's *Apology* in the light of Socrates' general philosophy; accessible to the general reader.)

JOHN M. COOPER

SOLIDARITY

Solidarity exists among a group of people when they are committed to abiding by the outcome of some process of collective decision-making, or to promoting the wellbeing of other members of the group, perhaps at significant cost to themselves. Many regard solidarity as an important political ideal on the grounds that it is related to community and fraternity, and conducive to social cohesion and stability. Some individualists, however, believe that it is incompatible with autonomy on the grounds that full autonomy requires one always to take the final decision oneself about what one should do.

See also: FAMILY, ETHICS AND THE; FRIENDSHIP

ANDREW MASON

SOLIPSISM

'Solipsism' (from the Latin *solus ipse* – oneself alone) is the doctrine that only oneself exists. This formulation covers two doctrines, each of which has been called solipsism, namely (1) that one is the only self, the only centre of consciousness, and, more radically, (2) that nothing at all exists apart from one's own mind and mental states. These are not always distinguished from corresponding epistemic forms: for all we know, (1) or (2) might be true.

A more recent coinage is 'methodological solipsism', which has a quite different meaning: that the content of an individual's thoughts is fully determined by facts about them, and is independent of facts about their environment.

EDWARD CRAIG

SOLOV'ËV, VLADIMIR SERGEEVICH (1853–1900)

It has been widely acknowledged that Vladimir Solov'ëv is the greatest Russian philosopher of the nineteenth century; his significance for Russian philosophy is often compared to the significance of Aleksandr Pushkin for Russian poetry. His first works marked the beginning of the revolt against positivism in Russian thought, followed by a revival of metaphysical idealism and culminating in the so-called Religious-Philosophical Renaissance of the early twentieth century.

Unlike the Russian idealists of the Romantic epoch, Solov'ëv was a professional, systematic philosopher. He created the first all-round philosophical system in Russia and thus inaugurated the transition to the construction of systems in Russian philosophical thought. At the same time he remained faithful to the Russian intellectual tradition of reluctance to engage in purely theoretical problems; his ideal of 'integrality' postulated that theoretical philosophy be organically linked to religion and social practice. He saw himself not as an academic philosopher, but rather as a prophet, discovering the way to universal regeneration.

One of the main themes of Solov'ëv's philosophy of history was Russia's mission in universal history. Owing to this he was interested in the ideas of the Slavophiles and, in the first period of his intellectual evolution, established close relations with the Slavophile and Pan-Slavic circle of Ivan Aksakov. He was close also to Dostoevskii, on whom he made a very deep impression. At the beginning of the 1880s he began to dissociate himself from the epigones of Slavophilism; his final break with them came in 1883, when he became a contributor to the liberal and Westernizing *Vestnik Evropy* (European Messenger). The main reason for this was the pro-Catholic tendency of his thought, which led him to believe that Russia had to acknowledge the primacy of the Pope. In his view, this was a necessary condition of fulfilling Russia's universal mission, defined as the unification of the Christian Churches and the establishment of a theocratic Kingdom of God on earth.

In the early 1890s Solov'ëv abandoned this utopian vision and concentrated on working out an autonomous ethic and a liberal philosophy of law. This reflected his optimistic faith in liberal progress and his confidence that even the secularization of ethics was essentially a part of the divine–human process of salvation. In the last year of his life, however, historiosophical optimism gave way to a pessimistic apocalypticism, as expressed in his philosophical dialogue *Tri razgovora* (Three Conversations) (1900), and especially the 'Tale of the Antichrist' appended to it.

ANDRZEJ WALICKI

SOPHISTS

The Sophists were itinerant educators, the first professors of higher learning, who appeared in Greece in the middle and later fifth century BC. The earliest seems to have been Protagoras, who was personally associated with the statesman Pericles. The next most eminent was Gorgias, an influential author and prose stylist. The Sophists succeeded in earning very large sums for their instruction. They lectured on many subjects, including the new natural philosophy, but their most important teaching was in rhetoric, the art of influencing political assemblies and law courts by persuasive speech. In conservative circles their great influence was regarded with hostility, as corrupting the young.

CHARLES H. KAHN

SOREL, GEORGES (1847–1922)

The French social theorist Georges Sorel is best known for his controversial work *Réflexions sur la violence* (*Reflections on Violence*), first published in 1908. He here argued that the world could be saved from 'barbarism' through acts of proletarian violence, most notably the general strike. This, he believed, would not only establish an ethic of the producers but would also serve to secure the economic foundations of socialism. Moreover the inspiration for these heroic deeds would be derived from a series of 'myths' that encapsulated the highest aspirations of the working class. More broadly Sorel should be seen as an innovator in Marxist theory and the methodology of the social sciences.

See also: REVOLUTION; SOCIALISM

JEREMY JENNINGS

SORITES ARGUMENTS
See VAGUENESS

SOUL, NATURE AND IMMORTALITY OF THE

For the Greeks, the soul is what gives life to the body. Plato thought of it as a thing separate from the body. A human living on earth consists of two parts, soul and body. The soul is the essential part of the human – what makes me me. It is the part to which the mental life of humans pertains – it is the soul which thinks and feels and chooses. Soul and body interact. Bodily states often cause soul states, and soul states often cause bodily states. This view is known as substance dualism. It normally includes the view that the soul is simple, that it does not have parts. If an object has parts, then one of those parts can have properties which another part does not. But for any experience that I have, an auditory or visual sensation or thought, it happens to the whole me. Plato also held that at death, soul and body are separated; the body decays while the soul departs to live another life. Aristotle, by contrast, thought of the soul simply as a 'form', that is, as a way of behaving and thinking; a human having a soul is merely the human behaving (by moving parts of the body) and thinking in certain characteristic human ways. And just as there cannot be a dance without people dancing, so there cannot be ways of behaving without embodied humans to behave in those ways. Hence, for Aristotle, the soul does not exist without the body.

Christian theology, believing in life after death, found it natural to take over Plato's conception of the soul. But in the thirteenth century, St Thomas Aquinas sought to develop an Aristotelian conception modified to accommodate Christian doctrine. The soul, Aquinas taught, was indeed a form, but a special kind of form, one which could temporarily exist without the body to which it was naturally fitted. It has always been difficult to articulate this view in a coherent way which makes it distinct from Plato's. Descartes restated Plato's view. In more modern times, the view that humans have souls has always been understood as the view that humans have an essential part, separable from the body, as depicted by Plato and Aquinas. The pure Aristotelian view has more normally been expressed as the view that humans do not have souls; humans consist of matter alone, though it may be organized in a very complicated way and have properties that inanimate things do not have. In other words, Aristotelianism is a kind of materialism.

If, however, one thinks of the soul as a thing separable from the body, it could still cease to exist at death, when the body ceases to function. Plato had a number of arguments designed to show that the soul is naturally immortal; in virtue of its own nature, because of what it is, it will continue to exist forever. Later philosophers have developed some of these arguments and produced others. Even if these arguments do not show it (and most philosophers think that they do not), the soul may still be naturally immortal; or it may be immortal because God or some other force keeps it in being forever, either by itself or joined to a new body. If there is an omnipotent God, he could keep it in existence forever; and he might have revealed to us that he is going to do so.

See also: MENDELSSOHN, M.; PSYCHĒ

RICHARD SWINBURNE

SOUTH AMERICA, PHILOSOPHY IN
See LATIN AMERICA, PHILOSOPHY IN

SOVEREIGNTY

In legal and political philosophy sovereignty is the attribute by which a person or institution exercises ultimate authority over every other person or institution in its domain. Traditionally, the existence of a final arbiter or legislator is said to be essential if people are to live together in peace and security. The example brought most readily to mind by the word 'sovereign' is the individual monarch, and the theory of sovereignty was at one time closely linked with the defence of monarchy. But leading theorists of sovereignty, like Jean Bodin and Thomas Hobbes, recognize that authority can be exercised by sovereign bodies of people; and later writers, like Rousseau and Austin, locate sovereignty in the people, to whom the officials of more democratic institutions are ultimately accountable.

Traditionally, too, it is deduced from the nature of the state or law that the sovereign's authority must be absolute, not limited by conditions; perpetual, not merely delegated for a time; and indivisible, not distributed between different persons or institutions. It is further deduced that the sovereign must be independent from external domination as well as internally supreme. All these inferences have been subjected to criticism, not least because they can be difficult to reconcile with the actual practice of states and legal systems.

See also: ABSOLUTISM; AUTHORITY; CONSTITUTIONALISM; GENERAL WILL; GLOBALIZATION; LAW, PHILOSOPHY OF; RULE OF LAW (RECHTSSTAAT); SHINTŌ; STATE, THE

J.D. FORD

SPACE

In some of its uses, the word 'space' designates an empty or potentially empty expanse among things, for example, when a driver finds a space in a crowded parking lot, or when a typesetter increases the space between words on a page. In other uses, 'space' is meant to stand for a boundless extension which supposedly contains everything, or every thing of a certain sort. The former sense is well-grounded in ordinary experience and can be traced back to the etymology of the word (from the Latin word *spatium*, meaning 'race-track', or generally 'distance', 'interval', 'terrain'). The latter sense originated in scholarly circles – possibly as late as the fourteenth century – by a bold extrapolation of the former; it does not refer to anything that can be exhibited in sense-perception; and yet, through the influence of Newtonian science on Euro-American common sense, it has become so entrenched in ordinary usage that it is normally viewed as the primary meaning of 'space', from which all others are derived.

According to Cornford, the 'invention of space' as a boundless, all-encompassing container happened in the fifth century BC. However, it is more likely to have occurred in the late Middle Ages. At any rate, the idea was rampant in Cambridge in the 1660s, when Newton made it a fundamental ingredient in his framework for the description of the phenomena of motion. In a posthumous paper, Newton stressed that space evades the traditional classification of entities into substances and attributes, and has 'its own manner of existence'. Until the publication of this paper in 1962, philosophers took Newtonian space for a substance, and most of them thought this to be utterly absurd. In view of the role of all-encompassing space in Newtonian physics, Kant opted for regarding it as a precondi-

tion of human knowledge, contributed once and for all by the human mind. Newton had written that the points of space owe their individual identity to the relational system in which they are set. Nineteenth-century mathematicians vastly extended this concept of space by conceiving many such relational systems. They thus made it possible for relativity theory to substitute four-dimensional spacetime for Newtonian space and time, and for current string theory to countenance a ten-dimensional physical space. These developments confirm the productivity, but not the fixity, of the knowing mind.

ROBERTO TORRETTI

SPACETIME

Spacetime is the four-dimensional manifold proposed by current physics as the arena for Nature's show. Although Newtonian physics can very well be reformulated in a spacetime setting, the idea of spacetime was not developed until the twentieth century, in connection with Einstein's theories of special and general relativity. Due to the success of special relativity in microphysics and of general relativity in astronomy and cosmology, every advanced physical theory is now a spacetime theory. *Spacetime* is undoubtedly an artificial concept, which our hominid ancestors did not possess, but the same is true of Newtonian *space* and *time*.

ROBERTO TORRETTI

SPEAKER'S INTENTION

See COMMUNICATION AND INTENTION

SPECIES

The diversity of life is not seamless but comes in relatively discrete packages, species. Is that packaging real, or an artefact of our limited temporal perspective on the history of life? If all living forms are descended from one or a few ancestors, there may be no real distinction between living and ancestral forms, or between closely related living animals.

Received wisdom holds that species are the 'units of evolution', for it is they that evolve. They are the *upshot* of evolutionary processes, but, if species and not just their component organisms compete with one another, they are also important *agents* in the evolutionary process. If so, species are real units in nature, not arbitrary segmentations of seamless variation.

The 'species problem' has been approached from two angles. One focus has been on specific taxa of the tree of life. What would settle whether some arbitrarily chosen organism is a member of *homo sapiens* or *canis familiaris*? This is sometimes known as the 'species taxon' problem. An alternate way of approaching diversity has been to ask what all species have in common. What do all the populations we think of as species share? This is the 'species category' problem.

One idea is to group organisms into species by appealing to the overall similarity. This 'phenetic' conception is in retreat. Most contemporary species definitions are relational, the animals that compose *pan troglodytes* are a species, not because they are all very similar (they are very like the pygmy chimps as well) but because of their relations amongst themselves and with their ancestors. The most famous relational definition is the 'biological species concept', according to which conspecific organisms are organisms that can interbreed, however different they look.

Relational species definitions aim to define a category of theoretical and explanatory interest to evolutionary and ecological theory. Given that there are many explanatory interests, one problem in evaluating these accounts is to determine whether they are genuinely rivals.

See also: Evolution, theory of; Taxonomy

KIM STERELNY

SPEECH ACTS

Making a statement may be the paradigmatic use of language, but there are all sorts of other things we can do with words. We can make requests, ask questions, give orders, make promises, give thanks, offer apologies and so on. Moreover, almost any speech act is really the performance of several acts at once, distinguished by different aspects of the speaker's intention; there is the act of saying something, what one does in saying it, such as requesting or promising, and how one is trying to affect one's audience.

The theory of speech acts is partly taxonomic and partly explanatory. It must systematically classify types of speech acts and the ways in which they can succeed or fail. It must reckon with the fact that the relationship between the words being used and the force of their utterance is often oblique. For example, the sentence 'This is a pig sty' might be used nonliterally to state that a certain room is messy, and further to demand indirectly that it be tidied up. Even when this sentence is used literally and directly, say to describe a certain area of a farmyard, the content of its utterance is not fully determined by its linguistic meaning – in particular, the meaning of the word 'this' does not determine which area is being referred to. A major task for the theory of speech acts is to account for how speakers can succeed in what they do despite the various ways in which linguistic meaning underdetermines use.

In general, speech acts are acts of communication. To communicate is to express a certain attitude, and the type of speech act being performed corresponds to the type of attitude being expressed. For example, a statement expresses a belief, a request expresses a desire, and an apology expresses a regret. As an act of communication, a speech act succeeds if the audience identifies, in accordance with the speaker's intention, the attitude being expressed.

Some speech acts, however, are not primarily acts of communication and have the function not of communicating but of affecting institutional states of affairs. They can do so in either of two ways. Some officially judge something to be the case, and others actually make something the case. Those of the first kind include judges' rulings, referees' decisions and assessors' appraisals, and the latter include sentencing, bequeathing and appointing. Acts of both kinds can be performed only in certain ways under certain circumstances by those in certain institutional or social positions.

See also: Grice, H.P.; Language, philosophy of; Pragmatics; Semantics

KENT BACH

SPEECH, FREEDOM OF
See Freedom of speech

SPENCER, HERBERT (1820–1903)

Herbert Spencer is chiefly remembered for his classical liberalism and his evolutionary theory. His fame was considerable during the mid- to late-nineteenth century, especially in the USA, which he visited in 1882 to be lionized by New York society as the prophetic philosopher of capitalism. In Britain, however, Spencer's reputation suffered two fatal blows towards the end of his life. First, collectivist legislation was introduced to protect citizens from the ravages of the Industrial Revolution, and Spencer's spirited defence of economic *laissez-faire* became discredited. Second, his evolutionary theory, which was based largely on the Lamarckian principle of the inheritance of organic modifications produced by use and disuse, was superseded by Darwin's theory of natural selection. Nearly a century after his death, however, there is renewed interest in his ideas, partly because the world has become more sympathetic to market philosophies, and partly because the application of evolutionary principles to human society has become fashionable once more.

See also: DARWIN, C.R.; EVOLUTION, THEORY OF; FREEDOM AND LIBERTY; HOLISM AND INDIVIDUALISM IN HISTORY AND SOCIAL SCIENCE; RELIGION AND SCIENCE

TIM S. GRAY

SPINOZA, BENEDICT DE (1632–77)

Introduction

A Dutch philosopher of Jewish origin, Spinoza was born Baruch de Spinoza in Amsterdam. Initially given a traditional Talmudic education, he was encouraged by some of his teachers to study secular subjects as well, including Latin and modern philosophy. Perhaps as a result of this study, he abandoned Jewish practices and beliefs and, after receiving stern warnings, he was excommunicated from the synagogue in 1656. Alone and without means of support, he Latinized his name and took up the trade of lens grinder with the intention of devoting his life to philosophy. He remained in Amsterdam until 1660, lived for the next decade in nearby villages, and in The Hague from 1670 until his death from consumption in 1677. During these years he worked continuously on his philosophy and discussed it with a small circle of friends and correspondents. His masterpiece, *Ethica Ordine Geometrico Demonstrata* (*Ethics Demonstrated in a Geometrical Manner*), was completed in 1675; but because of its radical doctrines, it was only published after his death.

The full scope of Spinoza's *Ethics* is not indicated by its title. It begins with a highly abstract account of the nature of substance, which is identified with God, and culminates in an analysis of human beings, their nature and place in the universe, and the conditions of their true happiness. Written in a geometrical form modelled after Euclid, each of its five parts contains a set of definitions, axioms and propositions which are followed by their demonstrations and frequently by explanatory scholia.

The defining feature of Spinoza's thought is its uncompromising rationalism. Like other philosophers of the time, Spinoza is a rationalist in at least three distinct senses: metaphysical, epistemological and ethical. That is to say, he maintains that the universe embodies a necessary rational order; that, in principle, this order is knowable by the human mind; and that the true good for human beings consists in the knowledge of this order and a life governed by this knowledge. What is distinctive of Spinoza's brand of rationalism, however, is that it allows no place for an inscrutable creator-God distinct from his creation, who acts according to hidden purposes. Instead, Spinoza boldly identifies God with nature, albeit with nature regarded as this necessary rational order rather than as the sum-total of particular things.

In its identification of God with nature, Spinoza's philosophy is also thoroughly naturalistic and deterministic. Since nature (as infinite and eternal) is all-inclusive and all-powerful, it follows that nothing can be or even be conceived apart from it: this means that everything, including human actions and emotions, must be explicable in terms of nature's universal and necessary laws. Moreover, given this identification, it also follows that knowledge of the order of nature specified through these laws is equivalent to the knowledge of God. Thus, in sharp opposition to the entire Judaeo-Christian tradition, Spinoza claims that the human mind is capable of adequate knowledge of God.

The attainment of such knowledge is, however, dependent on the use of the correct method. In agreement with Descartes and Thomas Hobbes (the two modern philosophers who exerted the greatest influence on his thought) and thoroughly in the spirit of the scientific revolution, Spinoza held that the key to this method lies in mathematics. This conviction is obviously reflected in the geometrical form of the *Ethics*; but it actually runs much deeper, determining what for Spinoza counts as genuine knowledge as opposed to spurious belief. More precisely, it means that an adequate understanding of anything consists in seeing it as the logical consequence of its cause, just as the properties of a geometrical figure are understood by seeing them as the logical consequence of its definition. This, in turn, leads directly to the complete rejection of final causes, that is, the idea that things in nature (or nature as a whole) serve or have an end, and that understanding them involves understanding their end. Not only did Spinoza reject final causes as unscientific, a view which he shared with most proponents of the new science, he also regarded it as the source of superstition and a major obstacle to the attainment of genuine knowledge.

The same spirit underlies Spinoza's practical philosophy, which is marked by his clinical, dispassionate analysis of human nature and behaviour. In contrast to traditional moralists (both religious and secular), he rejects any appeal to a set of absolute values that are independent of human desire. Since the basic desire of every being is self-preservation, virtue is identified with the capacity to preserve one's being, the good with what is truly useful in this regard and the bad with what is truly harmful. In the case of human beings, however, what is truly useful is knowledge; so virtue consists essentially in knowledge. This is because knowledge is both the major weapon against the passions (which are the chief sources of human misery) and, in so far as it is directed to God or the necessary order of nature, the source of the highest satisfaction.

Apart from the *Ethics*, Spinoza is best known for his contributions to the development of an historical approach to the Bible and to liberal political theory. The former is contained in the *Tractatus Theologico-politicus* (*Theological-Political Treatise*), which he published anonymously in 1670 as a plea for religious toleration and freedom of thought. The latter is contained both in that work and in the unfinished *Tractatus Politicus* (*Political Treatise*) of 1677, in which Spinoza attempts to extend his scientific approach to questions in political philosophy.

1 The geometrical method

Although Spinoza uses the geometrical method in the *Ethica Ordine Geometrico Demonstrata* (*Ethics Demonstrated in a Geometrical Manner*) (1677), he does not attempt to justify or even explain it. This has led many readers to view its argument as an intricate and fascinating chain of reasoning from arbitrary premises, which, as such, never touches reality. Nevertheless, Spinoza was very much aware of this problem and dealt with it both in an important early and unfinished work on method, *Tractatus de Intellectus Emendatione* (*Treatise on the Emendation of the Intellect*) (1677) and in some of his correspondence.

At the heart of the problem is the nature of the definitions (and to a lesser extent the axioms) on the basis of which Spinoza attempts to demonstrate the propositions of the *Ethics*. In a 1663 letter to a young friend, Simon De Vries, who queried him about this very problem, Spinoza offers his version of the traditional distinction between nominal and real definitions. The former kind stipulates what is meant by a word or thought in a concept. Such a definition can be conceivable or inconceivable, clear or obscure; but, as arbitrarily invented, it cannot, strictly speaking, be either true or false. By contrast, the real definition, which supposedly 'explains a thing as it exists outside of the understanding', defines a thing rather than a term (*The Correspondence of Spinoza*: letter 9: 106–7). Consequently, it can be either true or false.

Since the definitions of the *Ethics* are typically introduced by expressions such as 'by ... I mean that', or 'a thing is called', it would seem that they are of the nominal type, which gives rise to the charge of arbitrariness. It is clear from their use, however, that Spinoza regards them as real definitions. Like the definitions of geometrical figures in Euclid, they are intended to express not merely the names used, but the objects named.

The question, then, is how can one know that one has arrived at a true definition. Spinoza's answer reveals the depth of his commitment to the geometrical way of thinking, especially to the method of analytic geometry developed by DESCARTES. He appeals to the example of the mathematician, who knows that one has a real definition of a figure when one is able to construct it. The definition of a figure is thus a rule for its construction, what is usually called a 'genetic definition'. Spinoza develops this point in *On the Emendation of the Intellect* (1677) by contrasting the nominal definition of a circle as 'a figure in which the lines drawn from the centre to the circumference are equal' with the genetic definition as 'the figure that is described by any line of which one end is fixed and the other movable'. The point is that the latter definition, but not the former, tells us how such a figure can be constructed and from this rule of construction we can deduce all its essential properties.

Spinoza's claim, then, is that the principles that apply to mathematical objects and perhaps other abstract entities also apply to reality as such. Thus, we have a real definition, an adequate, true or clear and distinct idea of a thing (all of these terms being more or less interchangeable) in so far as we know its 'proximate cause' and can see how its properties necessarily follow from this cause.

But if knowledge of a thing reduces to knowledge of its proximate cause, then either we find ourselves involved in an infinite regress, which would lead to a hopeless scepticism, or the chain of reasoning must be grounded in a single first principle. Furthermore, this first principle must have a unique status: if it is to provide the ultimate ground in terms of which everything else is to be explained, it must somehow be self-grounded or have the reason for its existence in itself. In the scholastic terminology which Spinoza adopts, it must be *causa sui* (self-caused). Thus, Spinoza's rationalist method leads necessarily to the concept of God, which he defines as 'a being absolutely infinite, i.e., a substance consisting of an infinity of attributes, of which each one expresses an eternal and infinite essence' (*Ethics*: I, def. 6).

Given this concept, together with other essential concepts such as substance, attribute and mode (which are treated in the definitions of part one), the argument of the *Ethics* proceeds in a deductive manner. Its goal is to enable us to understand reality as a whole in light of this concept in just the same way that the mathematician can understand all the essential properties of a geometrical figure in terms of its concept or genetic definition. At least this is the project of part one of the *Ethics* (On God). The remainder of the work is devoted to the demonstration of the most important consequences of this result in so far as they concern the human condition.

2 Substance-monism

The first fourteen propositions of the *Ethics* contain an argument intended to show that 'Except God, no substance can be or be conceived' (*Ethics*: I, prop. 14). Since it follows from an analysis of the concept of substance that whatever is not itself substance must be a modification thereof, Spinoza concludes in the next proposition that 'Whatever is, is in God, and nothing can be or be conceived without God'. Together they express Spinoza's substance-monism, which can be defined as the complex thesis that there is only one substance in the universe; that this substance is to be identified with God; and that all things, as modes of this one substance are, in some sense 'in God'.

The argument for this thesis is based largely on the analysis of the concept of substance, defined as 'what is in itself and is conceived through itself, i.e., that whose concept does not require the concept of another thing, from which it must be formed' (*Ethics*: I, def. 3). This definition is quite close to Descartes who likewise made a capacity for independent existence the criterion of substance; but the two philosophers drew diametrically opposed conclusions from their similar definitions. Although Descartes held that God is substance in a pre-eminent sense, he also maintained that there are two kinds of created substance – thinking things or minds, and extended things, both of which depend for their existence on God but not on each other. For Spinoza, by contrast, there is only the one substance – God – and thought and extension are among its attributes.

Spinoza argues indirectly for his monism by criticizing the two major alternatives that a substance-based metaphysics can provide: that there is a plurality of substances of the same nature or attribute and that there is a plurality of substances with different natures or attributes. Since Descartes

is committed to both forms of pluralism, both parts of the argument cut against his views. In considering Spinoza's position, however, it should be kept in mind that his target is not merely Descartes, but an entire philosophical and theological tradition which conceived of the universe as composed of a number of finite substances created by God (see MEDIEVAL PHILOSOPHY). In spite of his radical critique of scholastic ways of thinking and his appeal to mathematics as the ideal of knowledge, Descartes remained in many ways a part of that tradition.

The argument against the first form of pluralism turns on the claim that 'In nature there cannot be two or more substances of the same nature or kind' (*Ethics*: I, prop. 5). This is at once one of the most important and controversial propositions in the *Ethics*. It is important because of its pivotal role in the overall argument for monism, controversial because of the demonstration offered in its support which is based on a consideration of the grounds on which two or more substances might be distinguished. This could be done either on the basis of their attributes, if they are substances of different types (for example, Descartes' thinking and extended substances), or on the basis of their modifications, if they are distinct substances of the same kind (for example, particular minds or bodies). The claim is that neither procedure can distinguish two or more substances of the same kind; and since these are the only possible ways of distinguishing substances, it follows that such substances could not be distinguished from one another.

The unsuitability of the first alternative seems obvious and would be recognized as such by Descartes. Since a substance-type for Descartes is defined in terms of its attribute, it follows that two or more substances of the same kind could not be distinguished on the basis of their attributes. As obvious as this seems, however, it was criticized by Leibniz on the grounds that two substances might have some attributes in common and others that were distinct. For example, substance A might have attributes x and y, and substance B attributes y and z. Although a Cartesian would reject this analysis on the grounds that a substance cannot have more than one attribute, Spinoza (for whom God is a substance with infinite attributes) could hardly accept this Cartesian principle. Moreover, we shall see that it is essential to the overall argument for monism to eliminate the possibility suggested by Leibniz (see LEIBNIZ, G.W. §§4–7).

Various strategies for dealing with this problem have been suggested in the literature, perhaps the most plausible of which turns on the principle that if two or more substances were to share a single attribute, they would have to share all, and would, therefore, be numerically identical. Although

Spinoza never argues explicitly in this way, it seems a reasonable inference from his conception of attribute as 'what the intellect perceives of a substance as constituting its essence' (*Ethics*: I, def. 4). This entails that attribute *y* of substance *A* is identical to attribute *y* of substance *B* just in case they express the same nature or essence – that is, are descriptions of the same kind of thing. But if they are things of the same kind, then any attribute *A* has will be possessed by *B* as well.

Against the second alternative Spinoza argues that, since by definition substance is prior to its modifications, if we consider substance as it is in itself then we cannot distinguish one substance from another. Although the claim is surely correct, the suggestion that we set the modifications aside seems to beg the question against Descartes. After all, two Cartesian thinking substances share the same nature or attribute and are distinguished precisely by their different modifications (thoughts).

Spinoza's reasoning at this point is unclear, but one could respond that, on the hypothesis under consideration, the substances must be assumed to be indistinguishable prior to the assignment of modifications. Moreover, it follows from this that the assignment of modifications could not serve to distinguish otherwise indistinguishable substances unless it is already assumed that they are numerically distinct. In other words, while we can distinguish two Cartesian substances by means of their modifications, we can only do so by presupposing that the distinct modifications belong to numerically distinct substances. But it is just this assumption to which the Cartesian is not entitled.

3   Substance-monism (cont.)

This, however, is only the first step in the argument for monism. It is also necessary to rule out the possibility of a plurality of substances of different kinds. Essential to this project is the demonstration that substance is infinite not merely 'in its own kind', that is, unlimited by anything of the same kind, but 'absolutely infinite', that is, all-inclusive or possessing all reality, which, for Spinoza, means infinite attributes. For example, Descartes' extended substance is infinite in the first sense because it is not limited or determined by anything outside itself (for example, empty space); but it is not infinite in the second and decisive sense because it does not constitute all reality. Moreover, this is precisely why the first sense of infinity is not sufficient to preclude a plurality of substances.

The basis of the argument for the absolute infinity of substance is the claim that 'The more reality or being each thing has the more attributes belong to it' (*Ethics*: I, prop. 9). This is a direct challenge to the Cartesian conception of substance as defined in terms of a single attribute, resting on the dual assumption that some things can possess more reality than others and that this superior degree of reality is manifested in a greater number of attributes. Unfortunately, in defence of this claim Spinoza merely refers to the definition of attribute as 'what the intellect perceives of a substance as constituting its essence' (*Ethics*: I, def. 4). Nevertheless, it does seem possible to understand Spinoza's point if we interpret attributes as something like distinct descriptions under which substance or reality can be taken. Consider, for example, a simple human action such as raising an arm. Although it may be possible to give a complete neurophysiological account of such an action in terms of impulses sent to the brain, the contraction of muscles and the like, one could still argue that no such account, no matter how detailed, is adequate to understanding it as an action. This requires reference to psychological factors such as the beliefs and intentions of an agent, which in Spinoza's metaphysics belong to the attribute of thought. Thus, we might say both that there is 'more reality' to an action than is given in a purely neurophysiological account and that this 'greater reality' can be understood as the possession of a greater number of attributes.

It follows from this that a being possessing all reality – that is, God, or the *ens realissimum* (most real being) of the tradition – may be described as possessing infinite attributes. It also follows that the Cartesian must either accept the possibility of a substance with infinite attributes or deny the possibility of God. And since the orthodox Cartesian could hardly do the latter, the former must be admitted.

Even granting this, however, at least two problems remain. One is how to understand the infinity of attributes. This might mean either that substance possesses infinitely many attributes, of which the human mind knows only two (thought and extension), or that it possesses all possible attributes, which is compatible with there being only two. Although scholars are divided on the point and there are indications from Spinoza's correspondence that he held the former view, it is important to realize that the argument for monism requires only the latter. This argument turns on the claim that God is a substance that possesses all the attributes there are and, therefore, that there are none left for any other conceivable substance. Combining this with the proposition that two substances cannot share an attribute, it follows that there can be no substance apart from God.

The second problem is that the argument up to this point is completely hypothetical. It shows that *if* we assume the existence of God, defined as a substance possessing infinite attributes, then it follows that no substance apart from God is possible; but it has not yet established the existence of substance so conceived. Spinoza had, however, laid the foundation for this claim in *Ethics* (I, prop. 7) with the demonstration that existence pertains to the nature of substance; so it remains merely to apply this result to God. This is the task of proposition eleven, which contains Spinoza's arguments for the existence of God. Spinoza offers three separate proofs, the major one being his version of the ontological argument, which was first developed by Anselm and later reformulated by Descartes (see ANSELM; DESCARTES, R. §6). Like his predecessors, Spinoza attempts to derive God's existence from the mere concept; but unlike them he makes no reference to God's perfection. Instead he appeals merely to the definition of God as a substance, from which it follows (by proposition seven) that God necessarily exists.

The nerve of the overall argument is, therefore, the proposition that existence pertains to the nature of substance or, equivalently, that its essence necessarily involves existence. Moreover, Spinoza's argument for this claim reveals the extent of his rationalism. From the premise that substance cannot be produced by anything external to itself (since such a cause would have to be another substance of the same nature, which has already been ruled out), he concludes that it must be the cause of itself, which is just to say that existence necessarily follows from its essence. Underlying this reasoning is what, at least since Leibniz, is usually termed the principle of sufficient reason, that is, the principle that everything must have a ground, reason or cause (these terms often being used interchangeably) why it is so and not otherwise. Although followers of Leibniz such as Christian WOLFF attempted to demonstrate this principle, Spinoza, like most rationalists before Kant (including Leibniz), seems to have regarded it as self-evident.

This characterization of substance as self-caused or self-sufficient being anticipates its identification with God. Quite apart from the question of its validity, however, perhaps the most interesting feature of Spinoza's argument for the necessary existence of his God-substance is that it is at the same time an argument for the non-existence of God the creator. Nevertheless, it should not be inferred from this that the result is purely negative or that Spinoza is concerned to deny the existence of God in every sense. On the contrary, his real concern in the opening propositions of the *Ethics* is to show that necessary existence and, therefore, the property of being a self-contained, self-explicated reality is to be predicated of the order of nature as a whole rather than of some distinct and inscrutable ground of this order. And this also expresses the deepest meaning of his monism.

4 God and the world

Spinoza's monism does not, however, mean the end of all dualities. In fact, the identification of God with nature leads immediately to the distinction between two aspects of nature, which he terms *natura naturans* (active or generating nature), and *natura naturata* (passive or generated nature). The former refers to God as conceived through himself, that is, substance with infinite attributes, and the latter to the modal system conceived through these attributes (which includes, but is not identical to, the totality of particular things). Consequently, the task is to explain the connection between these two aspects of nature, a task which is the Spinozistic analogue to the traditional problem of explaining the relationship between God and creation.

Like the theologians, whose procedure he adopts even while subverting their claims, Spinoza divides his analysis into two parts: a consideration of the divine causality as it is in itself (or as *natura naturans*) and a consideration of it as expressed in the modal system (or as *natura naturata*). Given what we have already seen, the former holds few surprises. The basic claim is that 'From the necessity of the divine nature there must follow infinitely many things in infinitely many ways, (i.e., everything which can fall under an infinite intellect)' (*Ethics*: I, prop. 16). Spinoza here characterizes both the nature and extent of the divine causality or power. By locating this power in the 'necessity of the divine nature' rather than creative will and by identifying its extent with 'everything which can fall under an infinite intellect', that is, everything conceivable, Spinoza might seem to be denying freedom to God. Certainly he is denying anything like freedom of choice. To object on these grounds, however, is to ignore the conception of freedom which Spinoza does affirm and to appeal to the very anthropomorphic conception of the deity against which his whole analysis is directed. To be free for Spinoza is not to be undetermined but to be self-determined (*Ethics*: I, def. 7); and God, precisely because he acts from the necessity of his own nature, is completely self-determined and, therefore, completely free.

The question of the relationship between God, so construed, and the 'infinitely many things' or modes that supposedly follow from God in 'infinitely many ways', which is perhaps the central question in Spinoza's metaphysics, is greatly complicated by the fact that Spinoza distinguishes between two radically distinct types of modes. As modifications of the one substance, both types are dependent on and in a sense 'follow from' God, but they do so in quite different ways.

First, there are those modes that either follow directly from an attribute of substance or follow from one that does directly follow. These are termed respectively 'immediate' and 'mediate eternal and infinite modes'. They are eternal and infinite because they follow (logically) from an attribute of substance, but they are not eternal and infinite in the same manner as substance and its attributes. Although Spinoza tells us very little about these modes in the *Ethics*, we know from his correspondence and the *Short Treatise on God, Man, and his Well-Being* (c.1660–5) which contains the earliest statement of his system, that he regarded 'motion' or 'motion and rest', and 'intellect' or 'infinite intellect', as immediate eternal and infinite modes in the attributes of extension and thought respectively. As an example of a mediate eternal and infinite mode, he mentions only the 'face of the whole universe' (*facies totius universi*) which pertains to extension.

Given the highly schematic and fragmentary nature of the surviving accounts of these eternal and infinite modes, any interpretation is hazardous. Nevertheless, both their systematic function as mediators between God or substance and the particular things in nature (finite modes), and the names chosen for the modes of extension, suggest that the latter are best construed as the fundamental laws of physics. In fact, Spinoza's characterization of motion and rest as an eternal and infinite mode may be seen as his attempt to overcome a basic difficulty in Cartesian physics. Having identified matter with extension, Descartes could not account for either motion or the division of matter into distinct bodies without appealing to divine intervention. On Spinoza's view, however, this is not necessary, since extended substance has its principle within itself. Otherwise expressed, matter is inherently dynamical, a property which cannot be explained in terms of Descartes' purely geometrical physics.

The 'face of the whole universe', which is identified with corporeal nature as a whole, may be understood in a similar fashion. By claiming that this is a mediate eternal and infinite mode of extension following directly from motion and rest, Spinoza is implying that the proportion of motion and rest in corporeal nature as a whole remains constant, even though it may be in continual flux in any given region. Moreover, this is equivalent to affirming the principle of the conservation of motion, which is a basic principle of Cartesian physics.

Viewing Spinoza's account in the light of seventeenth-century physics also helps to understand his doctrine of finite modes, or the series of

particular things, which is usually regarded as one of the more problematic aspects of his metaphysics. The problem is how to conceive the relationship between the series of these modes and God. If one assumes that, like the mediate eternal and infinite modes, they follow mediately from the attributes of God, then they too become eternal and infinite; but this is absurd, since it is of the essence of such modes to be transitory. If, however, one denies that they follow from God at all, then the dependence of all things on God, and with it Spinoza's monism, is negated. Accordingly, it must be explained how, in spite of their finitude, particular things and occurrences depend on God and participate in the divine necessity.

Spinoza's solution to this dilemma consists in claiming that the series of finite modes constitutes an infinite causal chain, wherein each finite mode is both cause and effect of others, *ad infinitum*, while the entire series (viewed as a totality) is dependent on the attributes of God and the eternal and infinite modes. Expressed in scientific terms, this means that every occurrence in nature is to be understood in terms of two intersecting lines of explanation. On the one hand, there is a set of general laws which for Spinoza are logically necessary (since they follow from the divine attributes); on the other hand, there must be a set of antecedent conditions. Both are required to explain a given phenomenon, say a clap of thunder. Clearly, no such explanation is possible without appealing to the relevant physical laws; but of themselves these laws are not sufficient to explain anything. It is also necessary to refer to the relevant antecedent conditions: in this case the state of the atmosphere. But, given these laws and the atmospheric state at t_1, it is possible to deduce the occurrence of thunder at t_2. And this means that nature is to be conceived as a thoroughly deterministic system.

Spinoza concludes from this that 'In nature there is nothing contingent, but all things have been determined from the necessity of the divine nature to exist and to produce an effect in a certain way' (*Ethics*: I, prop. 29). But because of this denial of contingency, he is sometimes accused of conflating determinism with the stronger thesis (usually termed 'necessitarianism') according to which the entire order of nature, that is, the infinite series of finite modes, could not have been different. The point is that determinism entails merely that, given the laws of nature and the set of appropriate antecedent conditions, any particular occurrence is necessary; but this leaves room for contingency, since it leaves open the possibility of a different set of antecedent conditions.

In response, one might distinguish between a consideration of finite modes, or a subset thereof, taken individually and a consideration of the series of such modes as a whole. The former fails to eliminate contingency, since any particular mode or subset of modes, viewed in abstraction from the whole, can easily be thought (or imagined) to be different. But the same cannot be said of the series taken as a whole. Since this series (considered as a totality) depends on God, it could not be different without God being different (which is impossible). The problem here is with the idea that the set of modes as a whole requires an explanation or grounding distinct from that of its constituent elements. Such a move is usually dismissed as a 'category mistake' (treating a collection as if it were a higher-order individual). But if it is a mistake, it is one to which Spinoza is prone in virtue of his rationalism; for nothing could be less Spinozistic than the idea that while particular events may be intelligible, the order of nature as a whole is not. And since for Spinoza making something intelligible involves demonstrating its necessity, this commits him to necessitarianism.

5   The human mind

Just as the target of part one of the *Ethics* is the dualism of God and created nature, so that of part two is the dualism of mind and body. Rather than holding with Descartes that the mind and the body are two distinct substances that somehow come together to constitute a human being, Spinoza maintains that they constitute a single individual expressed in the attributes of thought and extension. Since the fundamental modifications of thought are ideas (other modifications, such as desires and volitions, presuppose an idea of their object), while those of extension are bodies, this means that the human mind is an idea of a rather complex sort and that together with its correlate or object in extension (the body), it constitutes a single thing or individual. The great attractiveness of this view, particularly when contrasted with both Descartes' dualism and Hobbes' reductive materialism, is that it allows for the conception of persons as unified beings with correlative and irreducible mental and physical aspects (see HOBBES, T.). Unfortunately, this attractiveness is diminished considerably by its inherent obscurity. How can the mind be identified with an idea (even a very complex one)? And how can such an idea constitute a single thing with its object?

The place to begin a consideration of these questions is with Spinoza's elusive conception of an idea, which he defines as 'a conception of the mind that the mind forms because it is a thinking being' (*Ethics*: II, def. 3). As he makes clear in his explication of this definition through the distinction

between conception and perception, the emphasis falls on the activity of thought. To say that the mind has the idea of x is to say that it is engaged in the activity of conceiving x, not merely passively perceiving its mental image. Indeed, in one sense of the term, an idea for Spinoza just is the act of thinking. Moreover, this helps to remove at least some of the mystery in the identification of the mind with an idea. On the Spinozistic view, this means that the mind is identified with its characteristic activity, thinking; that its unity is the unity of this activity.

As acts of thinking, ideas may be identified with beliefs or 'believings'; but this reflects only one dimension of Spinoza's conception of an idea. For beliefs have propositional content and this, too, is an essential aspect of every idea. In short, ideas have both psychological and logical (or epistemological) properties. Moreover, although Spinoza is often charged with conflating these, he was well aware of the difference and of the importance of keeping them apart. This is evident from his appeal to the scholastic distinction, also invoked by Descartes, between the 'formal' and the 'objective reality' of ideas. The former refers to the psychological side of ideas as acts of thinking or mental events, the latter to their logical side or propositional content. Construed in the former way, ideas have causes which, in view of the self-contained nature of each attribute, are always other ideas. Construed in the latter way, they have rational grounds which likewise are always other ideas.

Spinoza differs from Descartes, however, in his understanding of the objective reality of ideas. For Descartes, talk about the objective reality of an idea as it exists in someone's mind refers to that idea *qua* intentional object to which a 'real' (extra-mental) object may or may not correspond. For Spinoza, by contrast, the idea viewed objectively just is its object (a corresponding mode of extension) as it exists in thought. This is a direct consequence of Spinoza's mind–body monism and we shall see that it has important implications for his epistemology.

6   The human mind (cont.)

Our immediate concern, however, is with the implications of this conception of ideas for Spinoza's account of the mind–body relationship. Unquestionably, the key feature in this account is the principle that 'The order and connection of ideas is the same as the order and connection of things' (*Ethics*: II, prop. 7). Taken by itself, this might be viewed as the assertion of a parallelism or isomorphism between the two orders, thereby leaving open the possibility that the elements contained in these orders might be ontologically distinct, as, for example, in Leibniz's pre-established harmony (see LEIBNIZ, G.W. §§4–7). In the scholium attached to this proposition, however, Spinoza indicates that he takes it to entail something more. Thus, he explains that just as thinking and extended substance are 'one and the same substance, comprehended now under this attribute and now under that. So also a mode of extension and the idea of that mode are one and the same thing, but expressed in two ways' (*Ethics*: II, prop. 7). In other words, rather than there being two series, one of extended things and the other of ideas, there is only a single series of finite modes, which may be regarded from two points of view, or taken under two descriptions. This also defines the sense in which Spinoza affirms an identity between mind and body. In claiming that mind and body constitute the same thing, he is not asserting that ultimately there is only one set of properties (which would make him a reductionist like Hobbes); rather, he is denying that the two sets of properties or, better, the two descriptions, can be assigned to two ontologically distinct things (as they are for Descartes).

Although the proposition makes a completely general claim about the relationship between the attributes of thought and extension, and their respective modifications, it also provides the metaphysical foundation for Spinoza's descent from the attribute of thought to its most interesting finite modification – the human mind. The descent is somewhat circuitous, however, since in subsequent propositions Spinoza stops to dwell on some topics that do not seem directly germane, such as the status of ideas of non-existent things; but the main line of the argument is clear enough. As a finite mode of thought, the essence of the mind must be constituted by an idea. Since the mind itself is something actual (an actual power of thinking), it must be the idea of an actually existing thing. And since this actually existing thing can only be a corresponding modification of extension, that is, a body, Spinoza concludes that 'The object of the idea constituting the human mind is the body, or a certain mode of extension which actually exists, and nothing else' (*Ethics*: II, prop. 13).

Even if one accepts Spinoza's premises and the chain of reasoning leading to the conclusion, this 'deduction' of the human mind as the idea of the body raises at least two major questions. One is how to reconcile the identification of the body as the unique object of the mind with the capacity of the mind to know and, therefore, presumably, to have ideas of things quite distinct from the body with which it is identified. This will be discussed in the next section in connection with Spinoza's

epistemology. The other question concerns how this enables us to understand what is distinctive about the human mind. As Spinoza himself remarks in the scholium to proposition thirteen, this result is perfectly general, applying no more to human beings than to other individuals. And, by way of accentuating the point, he adds that these other individuals are 'all animate [*animata*], albeit in different degrees'. Now, given the principles of Spinoza's metaphysics, it certainly follows that there must be 'in God' an idea corresponding to every mode of extension in the same way as an idea of a human body corresponds to that body. Thus, the claim that the human mind is the idea of the body may serve to determine its ontological status, but it does not enable us to understand its specific nature and activity. But unless Spinoza's deduction of the mind can accomplish this result, it cannot be judged a success, even on his own terms. Moreover, by suggesting that all individuals in nature are to some extent *animata*, he introduces a fresh element of paradox into his discussion. Indeed, this is particularly so if we take Spinoza to be claiming that something like a soul, or a rudimentary mind, must be attributed to all individuals.

Since the Latin '*animatus*' is cognate with the English 'animate', the sense of paradox can be lessened somewhat if we take the claim to be merely that all individuals are alive. Although this itself might seem bizarre, it becomes more plausible when one considers Spinoza's conception of life which, in the appendix to his early work *Descartes's 'Principles of Philosophy'*, he defines as 'the force through which things persevere in their being'. Since, as we shall see, Spinoza's conatus doctrine consists in the claim that each thing, in so far as it can, strives to preserve its being, it follows that every thing is in this sense 'alive'. And from this it is perhaps not too large a step to the conclusion that every thing has a 'soul' in the sense of an animating principle. But, of course, it does not follow from this that everything has a mental life that is even remotely analogous to that enjoyed by the human mind.

This makes it incumbent on Spinoza to account for the different degrees of animation and to explain thereby the superiority of the human mind to the 'minds' of other things in the order of nature. And he proceeds to do so by focusing on the nature of body. In essence, Spinoza's view is that 'mindedness' is a function of organic complexity; so the greater the capacity of a body (that is, brain and central nervous system) to interact with its environment, the greater the capacity of the mind to comprehend it. Thus, in a kind of speculative biophysics, Spinoza attempts to demonstrate that the human body is, indeed, a highly complex individual, which stands in a complex and reciprocal relationship with its environment. Although this account is extremely cryptic, it is also highly suggestive and points in the direction of an analysis of the phenomenon of life that goes far beyond the crude mechanism of the Cartesians (for whom the body is merely a machine). Perhaps more to the point, it also provides a theoretical basis for locating conscious awareness and rational insight on a continuum of mental powers, all of which are strictly correlated with physical capacities, rather than viewing them with Descartes as unique properties of a distinct mental substance.

7   Theory of knowledge

Although Spinoza does not assign to epistemological questions the priority given them by Descartes and the British empiricists, he certainly does not neglect them. In fact, his analysis of human knowledge, which follows directly upon his account of the mind, may be viewed as an attempt to show how the human mind, so conceived, is capable of the kind of knowledge presupposed by the geometrical method of the *Ethics*. In Spinoza's own terms, this means that what must be shown is nothing less than that the human mind is capable of adequate knowledge of the eternal and infinite essence of God.

Since adequate knowledge rests on adequate ideas, Spinoza must demonstrate that the human mind possesses such ideas. He defines an adequate idea as one which 'considered in itself, without relation to an object, has all the properties or intrinsic denominations of a true idea' (*Ethics*: II, def. 4). The term 'intrinsic' functions to rule out the extrinsic feature of a true idea: namely, agreement with its object. Thus, Spinoza's view is that truth and adequacy are reciprocal concepts: all adequate ideas are true (agree with their object) and all true ideas are adequate. Moreover, this enables him to dismiss the radical doubt regarding even our most evident conceptions envisaged by Descartes, which is supposedly overcome only by the manifestly circular appeal to God as the guarantor of truth. Since adequacy is an intrinsic feature of all true ideas, it serves as the criterion of truth. Consequently, someone who has a true idea immediately recognizes it as such and there is no longer room for Cartesian doubt. As Spinoza puts it with uncharacteristic elegance: 'As the light makes both itself and the darkness plain, so truth is the standard both of itself and of the false' (*Ethics*: II, prop. 43, scholium).

The intrinsic property through which truth manifests itself is explanatory completeness. An idea of x is adequate and, therefore, true just in case it suffices for the determination of all of the essential properties of x. For example, the mathematician's idea of a triangle is adequate because all of the mathematically relevant properties of the figure can be deduced from it. Conversely, the conception of a triangle by someone ignorant of mathematics is inadequate because it is incapable of yielding any such consequences.

It does not follow from this, however, that inadequate ideas are simply false. On the contrary, since every idea agrees with its object, every idea must in some sense be true. Specifically, 'All ideas, insofar as they are related to God, are true' (*Ethics*: II, prop. 32). Error or falsity arises because not every idea possessed by the human intellect is related by that intellect to God, that is, viewed as a determinate member of the total system of ideas. In other words, error or falsity is a function of incomplete comprehension, of partial truth being taken as complete. Spinoza illustrates the point by an example also used by Descartes: the imaginative, non-scientific idea of the sun as a disk in the sky located a few hundred feet above the earth. This idea is 'true' in so far as it is taken as an accurate representation of how the sun appears to us under certain conditions; but since it is not understood in this way by someone ignorant of optics and astronomy, such a person's idea is false in the sense of being inadequate or incomplete. It is not, however, 'materially false' in the Cartesian sense that there is nothing in the realm of extension corresponding to it.

Correlative with the distinction between inadequate and adequate ideas is a contrast between two mutually exclusive ways in which ideas can be connected in the mind: either according to the 'common order of nature' or the 'order of the intellect'. The former refers to the order in which the human mind receives its ideas in sense perception or through imaginative association. Since these correspond exactly to the order in which the body is affected by the objects of these ideas, it reflects the condition of the body in its interaction with its environment rather than the true nature of an independent reality. And from this Spinoza concludes that all such ideas are inadequate. In fact, he argues that, in so far as its ideas reflect this order or, equivalently, are based on sense perception or imagination, the mind is incapable of adequate knowledge of either external objects in nature, its own body or even of itself. Spinoza also contends, however, that adequate knowledge of all three is possible in so far as the mind conceives things according to the order of the intellect, that is, the true order of logical and causal dependence, which, once again, is precisely why the correct method is so essential.

8 Theory of knowledge (cont.)

The central problem of Spinozistic epistemology is thus to explain how conception according to the order of the intellect is possible for the human mind. This is a problem because the possibility of such conception seems to be ruled out by the ontological status of the mind as the idea of the body. For how could a mind, so conceived, have any ideas that do not reflect the condition of its body? The gist of Spinoza's answer is that there are certain ideas that the human mind possesses completely and hence can conceive adequately because, unlike ideas derived from sense perception or imagination, they do not 'involve', or logically depend on, ideas of particular modifications of the body.

Spinoza's doctrine is particularly obscure at this point; but it is perhaps best approached by comparing it to the doctrine of innate ideas, which was appealed to by Descartes and later Leibniz to deal with a similar problem. Like Spinoza, they held that sensory experience cannot account for the possibility of knowledge of necessary and universal truth. Instead, they claimed that the source of such knowledge must lie in the mind and reflect its very structure. This was not understood in a naïve psychological sense, however, as if an infant were born with knowledge of the basic principles of mathematics. Rather, innate ideas were viewed more as dispositions that pertain essentially to the human mind, but of which individuals are not necessarily conscious.

Although Spinoza's account of the mind as the idea of the body precludes the distinction drawn by Descartes between innate and adventitious ideas (that is, those that come from the mind and those that come from sensory experience), it does allow for an analogous distinction, which leads to much the same result. This is the distinction between ideas that are correlated with specific features of particular bodies and those whose correlates are common to all bodies or a large proportion thereof. The latter fall into two classes, corresponding to two levels of generality, which Spinoza terms respectively 'common notions' and 'adequate ideas of the common properties of things'. Their distinctive feature is that they do not arise in connection with an encounter with any particular kind of thing; and this enables Spinoza to claim that the mind possesses them in their totality and comprehends them adequately. Unfortunately, he does not provide examples of either class of these adequate ideas; but it seems reasonable to assume that the common notions include the axioms of geometry and first principles of physics (which are common to all bodies). Correlatively, since the adequate ideas of common properties of things correspond to properties that are common and peculiar to the human body and to other bodies by which it is affected (*Ethics*: II, prop. 39), it is likely that Spinoza was here referring to the basic principles of biology (or perhaps physiology). In any event, the crucial point is that the commonality of these ideas enables the human mind to grasp them completely, which is what is required for adequate knowledge.

The epistemological teaching of the *Ethics* culminates in the distinction between three kinds of knowledge (*Ethics*: II, prop. 40, scholium 2). The first is an experientially determined knowledge, which can be based either on the perception of particular things or on signs, which for Spinoza includes both sensory and memory images. The second is knowledge through reason, which is based on common notions and ideas of the common properties of things. Since the former mode of knowledge involves inadequate ideas and the latter adequate ones, this is just the contrast one would expect. At this point, however, Spinoza unexpectedly introduces a third kind of knowledge, termed 'intuitive knowledge' (*scientia intuitiva*), which supposedly 'proceeds from an adequate idea of the formal essence of certain attributes of God to the adequate knowledge of the essence of things'. He also attempts to clarify the difference between all three by comparing their respective treatments of the problem of finding a fourth proportional. Someone with the first kind of knowledge proceeds by rule of thumb, multiplying the second by the third and dividing the product by the first, thereby arriving at the correct answer without really understanding the principle at work. Someone with the second kind understands the principle and is, therefore, able to derive the result from the common property of proportionals as established by Euclid. Someone who possesses the third kind of knowledge, however, immediately grasps the result, without applying a rule or relying on a process of ratiocination.

Although both reason and intuition are sources of adequate knowledge, Spinoza recognizes two senses in which intuition is superior. First, whereas the province of reason concerns general truths based on common notions and consequently is abstract and general, that of intuition concerns the individual case and consequently is concrete and particular. This difference is not directly germane to Spinoza's epistemology, but it plays a significant role in his practical philosophy. Second, and of more immediate relevance, knowledge from general principles alone remains ultimately ungrounded. Accordingly, as in Spinoza's example, while the conclusion is inferred correctly from the principle, the status of the principle itself remains in question.

Within the framework of Spinoza's metaphysics, this question can be resolved only by grounding the principle in the nature of God, which is supposedly what is accomplished by intuitive knowledge.

But grounding our knowledge of things in the eternal and infinite essence of God obviously presupposes a knowledge of that essence; and even for a rationalist such as Descartes, this far transcends the capacity of the human intellect. This is not the case for Spinoza, however, given his unique conception of God. Since 'it is of the nature of reason to regard things as necessary, not as contingent' (*Ethics*: II, prop. 44), and since to conceive things in this way is to conceive them in relation to God, Spinoza in effect concludes that in so far as the mind has an adequate idea of anything at all, it must have an adequate idea of God. Moreover, since it presumably has been established that the human mind knows some things (has some adequate ideas), it follows that the mind has an adequate idea of God. Although initially this seems paradoxical in the extreme, it becomes much less so if one keeps in mind the nature of Spinoza's God.

9 The emotions

Nowhere is Spinoza's unique combination of rationalism and naturalism more evident than in his doctrine of the emotions, the topic of the third part of the *Ethics*. Appealing to the conception of the mind as the idea of the body, he defines the emotions or affects (*affectiones*) as 'affections of the body by which the body's power of acting is increased or diminished, aided or restrained, and at the same time, the ideas of these affections' (*Ethics*: III, def. 3). Emotions are, therefore, directly related to the body's capacity for action or level of vitality and have both a physiological and a psychological side. Moreover, given mind–body identity, these are seen as distinct expressions of the same thing. Thus, a conscious desire for some object and a corresponding bodily appetite are the same state considered under the attributes of thought and extension respectively.

Among other things, Spinoza's conception of mind precludes the assumption of a distinct power of will through which the mind can exert control over the bodily appetites. Strictly speaking, there is nothing pertaining to the mind but ideas, that is, acts of thinking; but these ideas have a conative or volitional and affective as well as a cognitive dimension. In other words, to have an idea of *x* is to have not only a belief or propositional attitude with respect to *x*, but also some sort of evaluative attitude (pro or con). Moreover, this enables Spinoza to avoid concluding from his denial of will that the mind is powerless, condemned to being

the passive observer of the bodily appetites. The mind, for Spinoza, is active in so far as it is the 'adequate', that is sufficient, cause of its states; and it is such in so far as it possesses adequate ideas, that is, in so far as its desires and hence its 'decisions', are grounded in rational considerations – for example, when it desires a particular food because of the knowledge (adequate idea) that it is nutritious. Conversely, it is passive when its desires reflect inadequate ideas connected with sense perception and imagination.

But regardless of whether it is active or passive, the mind's evaluative attitude is always an expression of its conatus, which is identified with the endeavour of each thing to persist in its own being. This endeavour pertains to the nature of every finite mode; but in human beings, who are conscious of this endeavour, it becomes the desire for self-preservation. Spinoza thus agrees with Hobbes in regarding this desire as the basic motivating force in human behaviour. But rather than inferring this from observation, he deduces it from the ontological status of human beings as finite modes. This allows him to affirm not merely that this desire is, as a matter of fact, basic to human beings, but that it constitutes their very essence. Accordingly, one can no more help striving to preserve one's being than a stone can help falling when it is dropped.

Perhaps under the influence of Hobbes, Spinoza also identifies this endeavour to preserve one's being with a striving for greater perfection, understood as an increased power of action. Just as Hobbes insisted that individuals continually desire to increase their power because there can never be any assurance that it is sufficient for self-preservation, so Spinoza maintains that the endeavour of an organism to preserve its existence is identical to its effort to increase its power of acting or level of vitality. This is because anything that lessens an organism's power, lessens its ability to preserve its being, while anything that increases this power enhances that ability.

The so-called primary emotions (pleasure, pain and desire) are correlated with the transition from one state of perfection or level of vitality to another. Thus, pleasure or joy (*laetitia*) is defined as the emotion whereby the mind passes to a greater state of perfection, and pain or sorrow (*tristitia*) is that by which it passes to a lesser state. Both reflect changes brought about in the organism through interaction with its environment. Although particular desires are directly related to pleasures, desire is none the less a distinct primary emotion because a desire for a particular object viewed as a source of pleasure is distinct from that pleasure.

The great bulk of part three of the *Ethics* is devoted to showing how the other emotions can be derived from the primary ones by means of combination and association with other ideas. Central to this project is the thesis that pleasure, pain and desire relate to present objects, which cause the affections of the body to which these emotions (as ideas) correspond. Accordingly, the derivative emotions are all species or combinations of pleasure, pain or desire, which are directed in various ways either to objects that do not presently affect the body or to those that are not themselves directly the cause of these affections. For example, love and hatred are defined respectively as pleasure and pain accompanied by the idea of an external cause. Similarly, hope and fear are understood as pleasures and pains that arise under conditions of uncertainty, when the image of some past or future thing is connected with an outcome that is in doubt. This analysis is extended with considerable subtlety, showing, among other things, how ambivalence is possible; and how, through various forms of association, the mind can come to feel love, hatred, hope or fear towards things with regard to which it has no direct desire or aversion. The key point, however, is that, like everything else in nature, these emotions do not arise capriciously, but in accordance with universal and necessary laws.

But these laws concern the mind only in so far as it is passive, that is, in so far as its ideas are inadequate and it is, therefore, only the partial or inadequate cause of its affections. Accordingly, at the end of his lengthy account of the passive emotions or passions, Spinoza turns briefly to the active emotions, which are connected with adequate ideas. Of the three primary emotions, only desire and pleasure have active forms, because only they can be grounded in adequate ideas. Active desire has already been described; it is simply rational desire. Active pleasure is a concomitant of all adequate cognition; for when the mind cognizes anything adequately it is necessarily aware of this and, therefore, of its own power or activity. And it is the awareness of its activity, not the nature of the object known, that is the source of pleasure. Finally, since pain or sorrow reflects a diminution of the mind's power of activity (adequate ideas), Spinoza concludes that it can never be the result of this activity, but must always result from the mind's inadequate knowledge and determination by external forces.

10 Moral theory

Spinoza's moral theory is based on his analysis of the emotions and is formulated with the same clinical detachment as the remainder of the *Ethics*. In sharp contrast to Judaeo-Christian moralists and their secular counterparts, he proposes neither a set of obligations nor a list of actions, the performance of which make one morally 'good', and their omission or neglect morally 'evil': all such moral systems and concepts are based on inadequate ideas, particularly the ideas of free will and final causes. Instead, he is concerned to determine the means through which and the extent to which human beings, as finite modes, are capable of attaining freedom, understood as the capacity to act rather than to be governed by the passions. Morality in the traditional sense is, therefore, replaced by a kind of therapy, which is one reason why Spinoza is frequently compared with FREUD. The concept of virtue is retained; but it is given its original meaning as power, which is itself understood in light of the conatus doctrine as the power to preserve one's being. In the same spirit, the good is identified with what is truly useful in this regard and the bad with what is truly harmful.

In spite of his amoralism, Spinoza does not equate virtue with the ability to survive or the good with what is in one's self-interest, narrowly conceived. What matters is not mere living, but living well; and this means being active – that is, being, to the fullest extent possible, the adequate cause of one's condition. And since being an adequate cause is a function of adequate ideas, virtue is directly correlated with knowledge. Knowledge, however, has a dual role in the Spinozistic scheme. It is the major weapon in the struggle against the passions, since it is through understanding our passions and their causes that we are able to gain some measure of control over them. But it is also itself constitutive of the good life, since our freedom is manifested essentially in the exercise of reason.

Nevertheless, Spinoza was under no illusions about the extent of the power of reason. Human virtue or perfection is merely relative and its attainment a rare and difficult feat. Thus, the first eighteen propositions of part four of the *Ethics*, which is significantly entitled 'On Human Bondage, or the Powers of the Affects', are concerned with the limits of the power of reason in its conflict with the passions. The basic point is that, as finite modes, the force through which human beings endeavour to preserve their being is infinitely surpassed by other forces in nature and, therefore, to some extent at least, they will always be subject to the passions. Moreover, knowledge itself has no motivating power simply *qua* knowledge, but only in so far as it is also an affect. Now knowledge is, indeed, an affect for Spinoza, since all ideas have an affective component, that is, possess a certain motivational force. But, as he attempts to demonstrate by means of an elaborate psychodynamics, the affective component of even an adequate idea is strictly limited and can easily be overcome by other (inadequate) ideas, which is why rational desires, based on a knowledge of what is truly beneficial, all too frequently give way to irrational urges.

After his analysis of human weakness, Spinoza turns to the question of what reason, limited as its power may be, prescribes. The basic answer, of course, is knowledge and, given Spinoza's metaphysics and epistemology, this ultimately means knowledge of God. Thus, he concludes that 'Knowledge of God is the mind's greatest good; its greatest virtue is to know God' (*Ethics*: IV, prop. 28). At this point, however, the discussion takes a surprising turn, one which indicates both the complexity of, and the inherent tensions in, Spinoza's thought. For while this austere intellectualism suggests the picture of the isolated, asocial thinker, devoted exclusively to the life of the mind, what is affirmed instead is the essentially social character of human existence. For Spinoza, as for Aristotle, human beings are social animals; and the life lived under the guidance of reason is, at least to some extent, a social life (see ARISTOTLE §22). This is not because human beings are intrinsically altruistic, but rather because, as relatively limited and weak finite modes, they are ineluctably interdependent. Thus, Spinoza argues that those who live under the guidance of reason desire nothing for themselves that they do not also desire for others (*Ethics*: IV, prop. 37). This reflects his undoubtedly idealized portrait of those devoted to the life of the mind. In so far as this devotion is pure (which it can never be completely), such individuals will not come into conflict because the good which they all seek, knowledge, can be held in common. In fact, not only will genuine seekers after truth not compete, they will cooperate; for in helping others acquire knowledge and the control of the passions that goes with it, one is also helping oneself. Moreover, although only the few capable (to some extent) of living under the guidance of reason may be able to grasp adequately and, therefore, internalize this truth, the need for cooperation applies to all; for all are members of the same human community of interdependent beings.

11 Moral theory (cont.)

Spinoza's account of the specific virtues reflect his general principles. These virtues are identified with certain affects or emotional states and their value is regarded as a function of their capacity to promote an individual's conatus. For this purpose the affects are divided into three classes: those that are intrinsically good and can never become excessive (the virtues); those that are intrinsically bad; and a large group that are good in moderation but bad if they become excessive. In identifying the virtues with affects that can never become excessive, Spinoza differs from Aristotle for whom virtues are regarded as means between two extremes.

Paramount in the group of virtuous affects is pleasure or joy. Since it reflects in the attribute of thought an increase in the body's power of activity, it can never be harmful. This gives Spinoza's thought a strongly anti-ascetic tone which stands in sharp contrast to the Calvinistic austerity of many of his countryman. Nevertheless, it is crucial to distinguish between genuine pleasure, which reflects the wellbeing of the organism as a whole, and titillation (*titillatio*) or localized pleasure, which merely reflects that of a part. Although the latter can be good, it can also be quite harmful. Other affects in this mixed category include cheerfulness and self-esteem. In the latter case, the crucial factor is whether or not the affect is grounded in reason. Pride, or self-esteem, without any rational basis is obviously harmful and is to be avoided at all costs. But, in so far as self-approval arises from an adequate idea of one's power, it is the highest thing we can hope for, since it is simply the consciousness of one's virtue. Perhaps even more than his anti-asceticism, this indicates how much closer Spinoza is to the classical ideal of the virtuous life than he is to traditional religious morality.

In addition to pain, Spinoza assigns first place among the intrinsically harmful affects to hate. Closely associated with hate, and rejected in similarly unqualified terms, are affects such as envy, derision, contempt, anger and revenge. These might be termed the social vices, since they serve to alienate human beings from one another. It is also noteworthy that Spinoza here locates many of the traditional religious virtues: hope, fear, humility, repentance and pity. Since they all reflect ignorance and lack of power, they cannot be regarded as beneficial, or assigned any place in the life of reason. Nevertheless, in a concession to human frailty, Spinoza does acknowledge that because human beings rarely live in this manner, these affects have a certain pragmatic value as checks on our more aggressive tendencies.

The affects that can be either good or bad include – besides titillation – desire and love. If directed towards an object that stimulates or gratifies a part of the organism or one of its appetites at the expense of the whole, they can become excessive and hence harmful. And this is precisely what occurs in pathological states such as avarice, ambition, gluttony and, above all, lust. In spite of his generally anti-ascetic attitude, Spinoza tended to regard sexual desire as an unmitigated evil. In sharp contrast to it stands the one kind of love that can never become excessive: the love of God.

12 The love of God and human blessedness

Although it does not enter into the account of virtue, the love of God plays a central role in the final part of the *Ethics*. The situation is complicated, however, by the fact that this part deals with two distinct topics, which may be characterized as mental health and blessedness; and the love of God is crucial to both. The question of health is the subject of the first twenty propositions, which are concerned with reason's unremitting struggle with the passions. Here Spinoza functions explicitly as therapist, providing his alternative not only to the religious tradition, but also to the training of the will advocated by the Stoics and Descartes (see STOICISM). Since what is crucial is that, as far as possible, one be moved by pleasurable thoughts (rather than reactive, negative affects), Spinoza's account amounts to an essay on the power of positive thinking. Moreover, since the ultimate positive thought is the love of God, this love serves as the chief remedy against the passions.

In spite of the religious language in which it is expressed, this claim is readily understandable in Spinozistic terms. Since by 'love' is meant simply pleasure accompanied by the idea of its cause, any pleasure accompanied by God as its cause counts as the love of God. But all adequate cognition is both inherently pleasurable, since it expresses the activity of the mind, and involves the idea of God as cause, since it consists in an idea of the object as following from God (the third kind of knowledge). Thus, the adequate knowledge of anything involves the love of God as its affective dimension. Moreover, since, in principle at least, it is possible to acquire an adequate idea of any modification of substance, it follows that this love can be occasioned by virtually anything. Consequently, it is its potential ubiquity, together with its superior affective force as expression of pure activity, that qualifies this love-knowledge of God as the supreme remedy against the passions.

In the second half of part five, the love of God is now explicitly characterized as 'intellectual' and paradoxically identified with the love with which God loves himself. And if this were not puzzling enough, Spinoza introduces the new discussion by proclaiming: 'With this I have completed everything which concerns this present life ... so it is now time to pass to those things which pertain to the mind's duration without relation to the body' (*Ethics*: V, prop. 20, scholium). This sets the agenda for the final propositions, the basic concern of which is to show that 'The human mind cannot be absolutely destroyed with the body, but something of it remains which is eternal' (*Ethics*: V, prop. 23). It is within this context that Spinoza refers to the intellectual love of God.

Because of their apparent incompatibility with the central teachings of the *Ethics*, these final propositions remain a source of perplexity. Nevertheless, it does seem possible to make sense of Spinoza's thought here, if we see it in the context of a shift of focus from the concern with reason (including the love of God) in its struggle with the passions, to a concern with the life of reason as the highest condition of which human beings are capable and, therefore, as constitutive of human blessedness. So construed, the abrupt change of tone is simply Spinoza's way of marking that shift rather than an indication of a lapse into a mysticism that is totally at variance with the spirit of his philosophy. Such a reading leads to an essentially epistemological rather than a metaphysical reading of the doctrine of the eternity of the mind. According to this reading, the human mind is 'eternal' to the extent to which it is capable of grasping eternal truth and ultimately of understanding itself by the third kind of knowledge, which, in turn, leads to the intellectual love of God. To be sure, this is not the eternal life promised by religion; but it is a state of blessedness or perfection in the sense that it involves the full realization of our capacities. Moreover, it is precisely the mode of life to which the *Ethics* as a whole points the way.

Such a reading is also supported by the final proposition in which Spinoza returns to the theme of virtue and links it with both health and blessedness. As he there puts it, 'Blessedness is not the reward of virtue, but virtue itself; nor do we enjoy it because we restrain our lusts; on the contrary, because we enjoy it, we are able to constrain them' (*Ethics*: V, prop. 41). There is not a trace of mysticism here, but merely the familiar Spinozistic emphasis on the connection between blessedness and knowledge on the one hand, and knowledge and power on the other. Accordingly, the point is that we do not acquire this knowledge by first controlling our lusts, but that we have the power to control them (virtue) only to the extent to which we already possess adequate knowledge. And it is in this knowledge, also characterized as peace of mind, that blessedness consists.

13 Politics

Spinoza's concern with political theory has its philosophical roots in his conception of human beings as social animals, which entails the necessity of living in a state under a system of laws; but it was also triggered by the political situation in his own time. In the Netherlands, the monarchist party was intent on overthrowing the republican form of government, and their allies, the Reformed clergy, desired to establish a state church. In spite of his commitment to a life of philosophical contemplation, Spinoza was keenly aware of this situation and the dangers it posed to freedom of thought and expression, which he regarded as essential. His philosophical response to this threat, as well as the statement of his own views about the nature and function of the state, are to be found in the *Tractatus Theologico-politicus* (*Theological-Political Treatise*) and the *Tractatus Politicus* (*Political Treatise*). The former is a polemical work, intended, at least in part, as a response to the Reformed clergy, while the latter is a dispassionate essay in political science. But despite this difference in tone and some disagreement on substantive matters, both works argue for freedom as the supreme political value and both investigate the conditions under which it can be realized and preserved.

Spinoza's political thought is best approached by way of a comparison with Hobbes. Both thinkers view human beings as thoroughly determined parts of nature and as driven by the desire for self-preservation; both are amoralists in the sense that they hold that everyone has a 'natural right' to do whatever is deemed necessary for self-preservation; as a direct consequence of this view of natural right, both view the state of nature (the pre-political condition) as one of unavoidable conflict and insecurity; and, finally, both maintain that peace and security can be attained only if everyone surrenders all of their natural right to a sovereign power (which takes the form of a social contract). But whereas Hobbes concludes from his account the necessity of an absolute sovereign power, preferably in the form of a monarchy, Spinoza infers from substantially the same premises that the true end of the state is freedom, and, at least in the *Theological-Political Treatise*, that democracy is 'the most natural form of state'.

To some extent, these differences can be understood in terms of the different social and political conditions under which the two thinkers lived. There are also important philosophical differences, however, one of which is their respective conceptions of human reason. For Hobbes, reason has a merely instrumental value as a means to the attainment of ends dictated by desire. We have seen, however, that for Spinoza the goal is to transform desire through reason, which naturally leads him to focus on the conditions under which the life of reason can best be lived. Moreover, Spinoza seems to have arrived at his conclusions through a kind of internal critique of Hobbes. As he informed a correspondent in 1674:

> With regard to politics, the difference between Hobbes and me ... consists in this, that I ever preserve the natural right intact so

that the supreme power in a state has no more right over a subject than is proportionate to the power by which it is superior to the subject. This is what always takes place in the state of nature.

> (*The Correspondence of Spinoza* 1966 letter 50: 269)

By suggesting that Hobbes did not keep natural right intact, Spinoza is implying that he did not consistently equate right with power. This is indeed true; but it does not explain how the identification of might with right enables Spinoza to arrive at his conclusions. The gist of the answer, as suggested by this passage, is that the identification applies also to sovereign power. In other words, rather than gaining absolute right over its subjects through the social contract, as Hobbes maintained, the sovereign's right is limited by its power; and since this power is inevitably limited, so too are the things that a sovereign may 'legitimately' demand of its subjects.

Among the things that a sovereign cannot require are acts so contrary to human nature that no threat or promise could lead a person to perform them. These include things such as forcing people to testify against themselves or to make no effort to avoid death. But Spinoza does not stop at such obvious cases. He also emphasizes the limitation of legislative power with respect to private morality; and he finds an argument for freedom of thought in the fact that a government is powerless to prevent it. More importantly, he points out that there are some things which a government can do by brute force, but in doing so inevitably undermines its own authority. And since a government cannot do these things with impunity, it does not have the 'right' to do them at all. Thus, he argues on entirely pragmatic grounds for the limitation of governmental power through the power of public opinion.

Spinoza's main concern as political theorist, however, is not to determine what the state cannot do, but rather what it should do in order to realize the end for which it was established. Moreover, while verbally agreeing with Hobbes in construing this end as peace and security, Spinoza understands these in a much broader sense. Accordingly, peace is not merely an absence of war or the threat thereof, but a positive condition in which people can exercise their virtue. Thus, the goal of the state is to create this condition, which is also the social condition necessary for the life of reason as depicted in the *Ethics*.

But the life of reason is only for the few, and political arrangements must concern the many. Moreover, since it is the many who determine the public opinion to which the government must pay heed if it is to rule effectively, it follows that there can be valid laws, approved at least tacitly by a majority, which are none the less inimical to true virtue. Spinoza was keenly aware of this problem; but his way of dealing with it indicates the tension between his democratic tendencies and his elitism that runs throughout his theory. Thus on the one hand he insists on the right of free expression, including the right to protest against laws deemed unjust, while on the other hand he emphasizes the necessity of total obedience to the existing law, no matter how contrary to reason it may be. The reason for this conservative turn, which is also reflected in the complete rejection of revolution as a political remedy, lies in his profound sense of the irrationality of the multitude. Given this irrationality, which poses a constant threat to the power of reason, Spinoza concludes with Hobbes that even under a tyrannical regime, obedience to the established authority is the lesser evil.

14 Scripture

Spinoza's revolutionary treatment of the Bible in the *Theological-Political Treatise* must also be understood within the framework of his political thought. In line with his concern to secure the freedom to philosophize, he launches a systematic attack on the authority of Scripture: its claim to be the revealed word of God. But rather than offering an external philosophical critique in the manner of the *Ethics*, he attempts, in a somewhat paradoxical fashion, to show from Scripture itself that it makes no such claim to authority. This strategy, in turn, rests on a new method of Biblical exegesis, one based on the Cartesian principle that nothing should be attributed to the text that is not clearly and distinctly perceived to be contained in it. In light of this principle, he rejects both the Calvinist doctrine that a supernatural faculty is required for interpreting the Bible and the older Jewish rationalism of Maimonides, which held that if the literal reading of a passage conflicts with reason, it must be interpreted in some metaphorical sense (see MAIMONIDES, M.). Both of these approaches he regards as not only useless for interpreting the Bible, but as dangerous politically, since they lead to the establishment of spiritual authorities.

Applying his method, Spinoza argues that neither prophecy nor miracles, the twin pillars of biblical authority, are able to support the orthodox claims. The prophets are shown to differ from other individuals in their superior imaginations, not in their intellects. Similarly, biblical miracles are treated as natural occurrences, which only appeared mysterious to the biblical authors because of their limited understandings and, as such, have no

probative value. More generally, the Bible is viewed as a document which reflects the limited understandings of a crude people rather than the dictates of an omniscient deity. And by analysing Scripture in this way, Spinoza laid the foundation for the subsequent historical study of the Bible ('higher criticism'), which endeavours to interpret it by the same methods applicable to any other ancient text.

Spinoza's critique of the Bible is, however, largely directed against its speculative content and claim to be a source of theoretical truth. Thus, he affirms that in moral matters the Bible has a consistent and true teaching, which reduces essentially to the requirement to love one's neighbour. Moreover, precisely because it appeals to the imagination rather than the intellect, it has the great virtue of presenting morality in a form which the multitude can grasp. Such a view of religion as morality for the masses is hardly original to Spinoza. It had already been expressed in the twelfth century by Averroes (see IBN RUSHD), and it found expression in many subsequent politically minded thinkers, including MACHIAVELLI. But, if not original to Spinoza, it is still an integral part of his political thought, since it enables him to 'save' religion while also protecting the autonomy of philosophy. And the latter is, of course, necessary for the life of reason as depicted in the *Ethics*.

See also: ARETÉ; EUDAIMONIA; GOD, CONCEPTS OF; MONISM; SUBSTANCE; WILL, THE

References and further reading

Donagan, A. (1989) *Spinoza*, Chicago, IL: University of Chicago Press. (Good, scholarly introduction to Spinoza's thought.)

Spinoza, B. de (1677) *Ethica Ordine Geometrico Demonstrata* (Ethics Demonstrated in a Geometrical Manner), in *The Collected Works of Spinoza*, vol. 1, ed. and trans. E. Curley, Princeton, NJ: Princeton University Press, 1985. (Spinoza's major systematic work.)

HENRY E. ALLISON

STATE, THE

States are inescapable, powerful and fundamentally important in the modern world. They spend a substantial portion of their members' wealth; they tax, confiscate or compulsorily purchase private property; conscript; impose punishments, including capital punishment; defend their members from aggression and protect their rights; and provide educational, health and other essential social services.

States are also central to modern political philosophy, and figure in its main topics. For instance, the various theories of social justice concern which principle or principles of justice should be followed by states. Again, discussions of the rights of individuals, or of groups, presuppose states to make the preferred rights effective. The answers to traditional questions, such as whether one is morally obliged to obey the laws of a state, or whether freedom is reduced by the state or made possible by it, must depend in part on what a state is taken to be.

The principal features of the modern state are basically agreed upon (population, territory, effective and legitimate government, independence). But there are underlying assumptions needing notice, and many questions about the state, especially concerning its proper activities, are controversial and disputed. Moreover, the value of the state can be challenged, and its future doubted, especially in the light of increasing economic and political globalization and moral cosmopolitanism.

PETER P. NICHOLSON

STATEMENTS
See SPEECH ACTS

STATISTICS

The discipline of statistics encompasses an extremely broad and heterogeneous set of problems and techniques. These include problems of statistical inference, which have to do with inferring from a body of sample data (for example, the observed results of tossing a coin or of drawing a number of balls at random from an urn containing balls of different colours) to some feature of the underlying distribution from which the sample is drawn (for example, the probability of heads when the coin is tossed, or the relative proportion of red balls in the urn).

There are two conflicting approaches to the foundations of statistical inference. The classical tradition derives from ideas of Ronald Fisher, Jerzy Neyman and Egon Pearson and embodies the standard treatments of hypothesis testing, confidence intervals and estimation found in many statistics textbooks. Classicists adopt a relative-frequency conception of probability and, except in special circumstances, eschew the assignment of probabilities to hypotheses, seeking instead a rationale for statistical inference in facts about the error characteristics of testing procedures. By contrast, the Bayesian tradition, so-called because of the central role it assigns to Bayes' theorem, adopts a subjective or degree-of-belief conception

of probability and represents the upshot of a statistical inference as a claim about how probable a statistical hypothesis is in the light of the evidence.
See also: INDUCTION, EPISTEMIC ISSUES IN; INDUCTIVE INFERENCE; STATISTICS AND SOCIAL SCIENCE

JAMES WOODWARD

STATISTICS AND SOCIAL SCIENCE

There are a number of distinct uses for statistics in the social sciences. One use is simply to provide a summary description of complicated features in a population.

A second use of statistics is to predict (some) features of a unit or group in a population, given other features of the unit or group. For example, a company may charge lower health insurance rates for people who do not smoke, because smokers have a lower risk of lung cancer. Some companies could also charge lower health insurance rates for people who do not have a heavy cough, because the probability of having lung cancer is lower for such people. Predictions can be made by developing a probabilistic model of the joint distribution of incidence of smoking, lung cancer, and incidence of heavy coughs in the population.

A third use of statistics is to help predict the probable effects of adopting different policies. For example, the government may consider a number of alternative policies for reducing the rate of lung cancer. One policy would ban smoking. Another policy would make everyone who coughs take cough medicine. Both smoking and coughing are predictors of lung cancer. But because smoking is a cause of lung cancer, while coughing is an effect of lung cancer, the first policy seems as if it might achieve the desired effect, while the second does not. In order to answer policy questions we need to know not only how the variables are distributed in the actual population, but also how they are causally related. A causal model specifies the causal relations between features in a population, as well as specifying a probability distribution of the features. Statistical information together with causal information can be used to predict the effects of adopting a certain policy.

A fourth use of statistics is in helping decide which policies should be adopted in order to achieve specific goals. Such decisions are based not only on the probable effects of each policy, but also on assigning different utilities to each possible outcome. This use of statistics is a branch of decision theory.
See also: STATISTICS

PETER SPIRTES

STATUS AND ETHICS
See MORAL RELATIVISM

STEWART, DUGALD (1753–1828)

Dugald Stewart was, after Thomas Reid, the most influential figure of the Common Sense School; he was a major influence on Victor Cousin and Théodore Jouffroy in France and on most academic philosophers in the United States. Along with Reid and Cousin, Stewart made the Scottish tradition the dominant philosophy in America for half a century. His *Elements of the Philosophy of the Human Mind* and *Philosophy of the Active and Moral Powers of Man* were his most important works and went through a number of printings. The abridged edition of his *Active and Moral Powers* was reprinted ten times from 1849 to 1868.

Stewart followed Reid in claiming that any philosophy which contravenes the principles of common sense must be false, and the problem is to discover and eliminate the premise which yields such results. He added the requirement that philosophical propositions must not change the *meanings* of concepts in ordinary life, and he also added a new dimension to Reid's agency theory. More than any other writer he emphasized correctly the epistemic similarities between Reid and Immanuel Kant, but he followed Reid in avoiding Kant's distinction between phenomena and noumena.

Stewart disagreed with Reid in avoiding the phrase 'principles of common sense' as misleading, rejected his mentor's realistic interpretation of universals and provided his own nominalistic alternative. He also modified to some extent, though quite cautiously, Reid's rigid inductivism and made some concessions to a realistic interpretation of scientific hypotheses. Stewart was equipped to discuss issues in the philosophy of science since he was well versed in mathematics and physics, having been professor of mathematics at Edinburgh for ten years before being named professor of moral philosophy. Stewart was arguably the first and finest philosopher of science in the Scottish tradition.

See also: COMMON SENSE SCHOOL; COMMONSENSISM; THEORIES, SCIENTIFIC

EDWARD H. MADDEN

STILLINGFLEET, E.
See CAMBRIDGE PLATONISM; LOCKE, JOHN

STIRNER, MAX (1806–56)

Max Stirner is the author of *Der Einzige und sein Eigentum* (*The Ego and Its Own*), first published in Germany in 1844 and best known for its idiosyncrasies of argument and idiom. Stirner condemns modernity as entrenched in religious modes of thought and envisages a positive egoistic future in which individuals are liberated from the tyranny of those ideas and social arrangements which restrict autonomy. *The Ego and Its Own* was an impulse to the decline of the Hegelian left as a coherent intellectual movement, and played an important role in the genesis of Marxism; Stirner has also been variously portrayed as a precursor of Nietzsche, an individualist anarchist and a forerunner of existentialism.

See also: ANARCHISM; EGOISM AND ALTRUISM

DAVID LEOPOLD

STOICISM

Stoicism is the Greek philosophical system founded by Zeno of Citium *c*.300 BC and developed by him and his successors into the most influential philosophy of the Hellenistic age. It views the world as permeated by rationality and divinely planned as the best possible organization of matter. Moral goodness and happiness are achieved, if at all, by replicating that perfect rationality in oneself, and by finding out and enacting one's own assigned role in the cosmic scheme of things.

The leading figures in classical, or early, Stoicism are the school's first three heads: Zeno of Citium, Cleanthes and Chrysippus. It is above all the brilliant and indefatigable Chrysippus who can be credited with building Stoicism up into a truly comprehensive system. 'Early Stoicism', discussed here, is in effect largely identical with his philosophy.

No formal philosophical writings of the early Stoics survives intact. We are mainly dependent on isolated quotations and secondary reports, many of them hostile. Nevertheless, the system has been reconstructed in great detail, and, despite gaps and uncertainties, it does live up to its own self-description as a unified whole. It is divided into three main parts: physics, logic and ethics.

The world is an ideally good organism, whose own rational soul governs it for the best. Any impression of imperfection arises from misleadingly viewing its parts (including ourselves) in isolation, as if one were to consider the interests of the foot in isolation from the needs of the whole body. The entire sequence of cosmic events is pre-ordained in every detail. Being the best possible sequence, it is repeated identically from one world phase to the next, with each phase ending in a conflagration followed by cosmic renewal. The causal nexus of 'fate' does not, however, pre-empt our individual responsibility for our actions. These remain 'in our power', because we, rather than external circumstances, are their principal causes, and in some appropriate sense it is 'possible' for us to do otherwise, even though it is predetermined that we will not.

At the lowest level of physical analysis, the world and its contents consist of two coextensive principles: passive 'matter' and active 'god'. At the lowest observable level, however, these are already constituted into the four elements earth, water, air and fire. Air and fire form an active and pervasive life force called *pneuma* or 'breath', which constitutes the qualities of all bodies and, in an especially rarefied form, serves as the souls of living things.

'Being' is a property of bodies alone, but most things are analysed as bodies – even moral qualities, sounds, seasons and so forth – since only bodies can causally interact. For example, justice is the soul in a certain condition, the soul itself being *pneuma* and hence a body. A scheme of four ontological categories is used to aid this kind of analysis. In addition, four incorporeals are acknowledged: place, void, time and the *lekton* (roughly, the expressed content of a sentence or predicate). Universals are sidelined as fictional thought constructs, albeit rather useful ones.

The world is a physical continuum, infinitely divisible and unpunctuated by any void, although surrounded by an infinite void. Its perfect rationality, and hence the existence of an immanent god, are defended by various versions of the Argument from Design, with apparent imperfections explained away, for example, as blessings in disguise or unavoidable concomitants of the best possible structure.

'Logic' includes not only dialectic, which is the science of argument and hence logic in its modern sense, but also theory of knowledge, as well as primarily linguistic disciplines like rhetoric and grammar. Stoic inferential logic takes as its basic units not individual terms, as in Aristotelian logic, but whole propositions. Simple propositions are classified into types, and organized into complex propositions (for example, conditionals) and complete arguments. All arguments conform to, or are reducible to, five basic 'indemonstrable' argument formats. The study of logical puzzles is another central area of Stoic research.

The Stoics doggedly defended, against attacks from the sceptical Academy, the conviction that cognitive certainty is achieved through ordinary sensory encounters, provided an entirely clear impression (*phantasia*) is attained. This, the 'cognitive impression' (*phantasia kataleptikē*), is one of such a nature that the information it conveys could not be false. These self-certifying impressions, along with the natural 'preconceptions' (*prolēpseis*) which constitute human reason, are criteria of truth, on which fully scientific knowledge (*epistēmē*) – possessed only by the wise – can eventually be built.

Stoic ethics starts from *oikeiōsis*, our natural 'appropriation' first of ourselves and later of those around us, which makes other-concern integral to human nature. Certain conventionally prized items, like honour and health, are commended by nature and should be sought, but not for their own sake. They are instrumentally preferable, because learning to choose rationally between them is a step towards the eventual goal of 'living in agreement with nature'. It is the coherence of one's choices, not the attainment of their objects, that matters. The patterns of action which promote such a life were systematically codified as *kathēkonta*, 'proper functions'.

Virtue and vice are intellectual states. Vice is founded on 'passions': these are at root false value judgments, in which we lose rational control by overvaluing things which are in fact indifferent. Virtue, a set of sciences governing moral choice, is the one thing of intrinsic worth and therefore genuinely 'good'. The wise are not only the sole possessors of virtue and happiness, but also, paradoxically, of the things people conventionally value – beauty, freedom, power, and so on. However geographically scattered, the wise form a true community or 'city', governed by natural law.

The school's later phases are the 'middle Stoicism' of Panaetius and Posidonius (second to first century BC) and the 'Roman' period (first to second century AD) represented for us by the predominantly ethical writings of Seneca, Epictetus and Marcus Aurelius.

See also: PROLĒPSIS

DAVID SEDLEY

STRAWSON, PETER FREDERICK (1919–)

Strawson taught at the University of Oxford from 1947, becoming Waynflete Professor of Metaphysical Philosophy in 1968, and retiring in 1987. A sequence of influential books and articles established him as one of the leading philosophers in Oxford during that period. He had a crucial role in the transition there from the dominance of Austin and linguistic philosophy in the 1950s to the more liberal and metaphysical approaches in the 1960s and later. The principal topics about which he has written are the philosophy of language, metaphysics, epistemology and the history of philosophy.

Strawson became famous with 'On Referring' (1950), in which he criticized Russell for misconstruing our ordinary use of definite descriptions. Strawson endorses the slogan 'ordinary language has no exact logic', a viewpoint which is explored in *Introduction to Logical Theory* (1952). He argues that the utility of formal logic in its application to ordinary speech does not imply that the meaning of ordinary language is captured by the semantics of standard formal systems.

In *Individuals* (1959), Strawson's most discussed work, his task is descriptive metaphysics. He attempts to describe the referentially basic subject matter of our thought. They are relatively enduring, perceptible and re-identifiable bodies. The other element in the basic framework is what Strawson calls persons, enduring entities with both material and psychological features. In *The Bounds of Sense* (1966), Strawson continued the development of his metaphysical and epistemological ideas, by combining a critical study of Kant's *Critique of Pure Reason*, with the defence of some transcendental claims similar to Kant's. To think of oneself as an enduring subject of experience requires that one recognize objects which are independent of oneself. So the major epistemological problem in the empiricist tradition, of building up to the external world from private experiences, cannot arise.

Skepticism and Naturalism; Some Varieties (1985) studies the conflicts between fundamental opinions which are natural to us, such as that we know things, and philosophical viewpoints claiming that these opinions are mistaken. Strawson argues that scepticism about these natural views can and should be resisted. Throughout his career, Strawson has tried to describe the basic content of our thoughts and experiences, to counter scepticism about or revisions of such thoughts, to illuminate them by making analytical connections between their basic elements, as well as investigating language, our vehicle for expressing these thoughts. He has linked his explorations to the insights of philosophers of the past, while engaging in critical debate with the period's other leading philosophers, such as Austin, Quine, Davidson and Dummett.

PAUL F. SNOWDON

STRUCTURALISM

The term 'structuralism' can be applied to any analysis that emphasizes structures and relations, but it usually designates a twentieth-century European (especially French) school of thought that applies the methods of structural linguistics to the study of social and cultural phenomena. Starting from the insight that social and cultural phenomena are not physical objects and events but objects and events with meaning, and that their signification must

therefore be a focus of analysis, structuralists reject causal analysis and any attempt to explain social and cultural phenomena one-by-one. Rather, they focus on the internal structure of cultural objects and, more importantly, the underlying structures that make them possible. To investigate neckties, for instance, structuralism would attempt to reconstruct (1) the internal structure of neckties (the oppositions – wide/narrow, loud/subdued – that enable different sorts of neckties to bear different meanings for members of a culture) and (2) the underlying 'vestimentary' structures or system of a given culture (how do neckties relate to other items of clothing and the wearing of neckties to other socially-coded actions).

Ferdinand de Saussure, the founder of structural linguistics, insists that to study language, analysts must describe a linguistic system, which consists of structures, not substance. The physical sound of a word or sign is irrelevant to its linguistic function: what counts are the relations, the contrasts, that differentiate signs. Thus in Morse code a beginner's dot may be longer than an expert's dash: the structural relation, the distinction, between dot and dash is what matters.

For structuralism, the crucial point is that the object of analysis is not the corpus of utterances linguists might collect, that which Saussure identifies as *parole* (speech), but the underlying system (*la langue*), a set of formal elements defined in relation to each other and which can be variously combined to form sentences. Arguing that the analysis of systems of relation is the appropriate way to study human phenomena, that our world consists not of things but of relations, structuralists often claim to provide a new paradigm for the human sciences. In France, structuralism displaced existentialism in the 1960s as a public philosophical movement. Philosophically, proponents of structuralism have been concerned to distinguish it from phenomenology.

See also: STRUCTURALISM IN LINGUISTICS; STRUCTURALISM IN SOCIAL SCIENCE

JONATHAN CULLER

STRUCTURALISM IN LINGUISTICS

The term structural linguistics can be used to refer to two movements which developed independently of each other. The first is European and can be characterized as post-Saussurean, since Saussure is generally regarded as its inspiration. The central claim of this movement is that terms of a language of all kinds (sounds, words, meanings) present themselves in Saussure's phrase 'as a system', and can only be identified by describing their relations to other terms of the same language; one cannot first identify the terms of a language and then ask which system they belong to. Moreover, because a language is a system of signs, one cannot identify expression-elements (sounds, words) independently of the content-elements (meanings), so that a study of language cannot be divorced from one of meaning. The second movement is an American one, which developed from the work of Leonard Bloomfield and dominated American linguistics in the 1940s and 1950s. It attached great importance to methodological rigour and, influenced by behaviourist psychology, was hostile to mentalism (any theory which posits an independent category of mental events and processes). As a result, unlike the first movement, it excluded the study of meaning from that of grammar, and tried to develop a methodology to describe any corpus in terms of the distribution of its expression-elements relative to each other. Whereas the first movement provided a model for structuralist thought in general, and had a significant impact on such thinkers as Barthes, Lacan and Lévi-Strauss, the second made a major contribution to the development of formal models of language, however inadequate they may seem now in the light of Chomsky's criticisms.

See also: STRUCTURALISM; SYNTAX

DAVID HOLDCROFT

STRUCTURALISM IN SOCIAL SCIENCE

Any school of thought in the social sciences that stresses the priority of order over action is 'structural'. In the twentieth century, however, 'structuralism' has been used to denote a European, largely French language, school of thought that applied methods and conceptions of order developed in structural linguistics to a wide variety of cultural and social phenomena. Structuralism aspired to be a scientific approach to language and social phenomena that, in conceiving of them as governed by autonomous law-governed structures, minimized consideration of social-historical context and individual as well as collective action. Structural linguistics was developed in the early part of the twentieth century primarily by the Swiss linguist, Ferdinand de Saussure. After the Second World War, it fostered roughly three phases of structural approaches to social phenomena. Under the lead of above all the French anthropologist Claude Lévi-Strauss, classical structuralism applied structural linguistic conceptions of structure with relatively little transformation to such social phenomena as kinship structures, myths, cooking practices, religion and ideology. At the same time, the French

psychoanalyst Jacques Lacan appropriated Saussure's conceptual apparatus to retheorize the Freudian unconscious. In the 1960s, a second phase of structural thought, neo-structuralism, extended structural linguistic notions of order to a fuller spectrum of social phenomena, including knowledge, politics and society as a whole. Many of Saussure's trademark conceptions were abandoned, however, during this phase. Since the 1970s, a third phase of structuralism has advanced general theories of social life that centre on how structures govern action. In so refocusing structural theory, however, the new structuralists have broken with the conception of structure that heretofore reigned in structural thought.

THEODORE R. SCHATZKI

SUÁREZ, FRANCISCO (1548–1617)

Francisco Suárez was the main channel through which medieval philosophy flowed into the modern world. He was educated first in law and, after his entry into the Jesuits, in philosophy and theology. He wrote on all three subjects. His philosophical writing was principally in the areas of metaphysics, psychology and philosophy of law, but in both his philosophical and theological works he treated many related epistemological, cosmological and ethical issues. While his basic outlook is that of a very independent Thomist, his metaphysics follows along a line earlier drawn by Avicenna (980–1037) and Duns Scotus (1266–1308) to treat as its subject 'being in so far as it is real being'. By the addition of the word 'real' to Aristotle's formula, Suárez emphasized Aristotle's division of being into categorial being and 'being as true', as well as Aristotle's exclusion of the latter from the object of metaphysics. Divided into a general part dealing with the concept of being as such, its properties and causes, and a second part which considers particular beings (God and creatures) in addition to the categories of being, Suárez's metaphysics ends with a notable treatment of mind-dependent beings, or 'beings of reason'. These last encompass negations, privations and relations of reason, but Suárez's treatment centres on those negations which are 'impossible' or self-contradictory. Inasmuch as such beings of reason cannot exist outside the mind, they are excluded from the object of metaphysics and relegated to the status of 'being as true'. In philosophy of law he was a proponent of natural law and of a theory of government in which power comes from God through the people. He was important for the early development of modern international law and the doctrine of just war. While his brand of Thomism was opposed in his own time and after by some scholastics, especially Dominicans, he had great authority among his fellow Jesuits, as well as other Catholic and Protestant authors. Outside scholasticism, he has influenced a variety of modern thinkers.

See also: ABSOLUTISM; AQUINAS, T.; INTERNATIONAL RELATIONS, PHILOSOPHY OF; MOLINA, L. DE; NATURAL LAW; RENAISSANCE PHILOSOPHY; WAR AND PEACE, PHILOSOPHY OF

JOHN P. DOYLE

SUBJECT

See PERSONS

SUBJECTIVISM/SUBJECTIVITY

See OBJECTIVITY

SUBJUNCTIVE CONDITIONALS

See COUNTERFACTUAL CONDITIONALS

SUBLIME, THE

The origin of the term 'the sublime' is found in ancient philosophy, where, for example, Longinus linked it with a lofty and elevated use of literary language. In the eighteenth century, the term came into much broader use, when it was applied not only to literature but also to the experience of nature, whereafter it became one of the most hotly debated subjects in the cultural discourse of that age.

The theories of Addison, Burke and Kant are especially significant. Addison developed and extended the Longinian view of the sublime as a mode of elevated self-transcendence, while Burke extended John Dennis' insight concerning sublimity's connection with terror and a sense of self-preservation. While Addison and Burke encompassed both art and nature in their approaches, Kant confined the experience of the sublime to our encounters with nature. In his theory, the sublime is defined as a pleasure in the way that nature's capacity to overwhelm our powers of perception and imagination is contained by and serves to vivify our powers of rational comprehension. It is a distinctive aesthetic experience.

In the 1980s and 1990s Kant's and (to a much lesser extent) Burke's theories of the sublime became the objects of a massive revival of interest, in the immediate context of a more general discussion of postmodern society. Kant's theory, for example, has been used by J.-F. Lyotard and others to explain the sensibility – orientated towards the enjoyment of complexity, rapid change and a

breakdown of categories – that seems to characterize that society.

See also: BURKE, E.; KANT, I. §12; LYOTARD, J.-F.; NATURE, AESTHETIC APPRECIATION OF; SCHILLER, J.C.F.

PAUL CROWTHER

SUBSTANCE

For Aristotle, 'substances' are the things which exist in their own right, both the logically ultimate subjects of predication and the ultimate objects of scientific inquiry. They are the unified material objects, as well as the natural stuffs, identifiable in sense-experience, each taken to be a member of a natural species with its 'form' and functional essence. Entities in other categories – qualities, actions, relations and so forth – are treated as dependent on, if not just abstracted aspects of, these independent realities.

With the rise of mechanistic physics in the seventeenth century, the Aristotelian multiplicity of substances was reduced to universal matter mechanically differentiated. This move sharpened the issue of the relation of mind to the physical world. The consequent variety of ways in which the notion of substance was manipulated by materialists, dualists, immaterialists and anti-dogmatists encouraged later scepticism about the distinction between independent realities and human abstractions, and so idealism.

Twentieth-century conceptualism, like some earlier versions of idealism, rejects the distinction altogether, commonly ascribing the logical priority of material things in natural language to the utility of a folk physics, as if they were the theoretical entities of everyday life. As such, their identity and existence are determined only through applications of a theory outdated by modern science. Yet this 'top-down', holistic philosophy of language is belied by the detailed insights of traditional logic, which point clearly to a 'bottom-up' account of classification and identity, that is an account which recognizes the possibility of perceptually picking out material objects prior to knowledge of their kind or nature, and of subsequently classifying them. The idea that material things are theoretical entities, and that their individuation is accordingly kind-dependent, is a hangover from an atomistic approach to perception which calls on theory to tie sensory information together. A more accurate understanding of sensation as the already integrated presentation of bodies in spatial relations to one another and to the perceiver is consonant with the possibility denied by the idealist– namely, that, with respect to its primitive referents, language and thought are shaped around reality itself, the independent objects given in active sense-experience. That the coherence or discrete unity of material objects has a physical explanation does not mean that physics explains it away.

See also: BEING; CONTINUANTS; IDENTITY; MATTER; ONTOLOGY; PHENOMENOLOGICAL MOVEMENT; REALISM AND ANTIREALISM; SCIENTIFIC REALISM AND ANTIREALISM; THEORIES, SCIENTIFIC

MICHAEL AYERS

SUBSTITUTIONAL INTERPRETATION OF QUANTIFIERS

See QUANTIFIERS, SUBSTITUTIONAL AND OBJECTUAL

SUFISM

See AL-GHAZALI, ABU HAMID

SUICIDE, ETHICS OF

Suicide has been condemned as necessarily immoral by most Western religions and also by many philosophers. It is argued that suicide defies the will of God, that it is socially harmful and that it is opposed to 'nature'. According to Kant, those who commit suicide 'degrade' humanity by treating themselves as things rather than as persons; furthermore, since they are the subject of moral acts, they 'root out' morality by removing themselves from the scene.

In opposition to this tradition the Stoics and the philosophers of the Enlightenment maintained that there is nothing necessarily immoral about suicide. It is sometimes unwise, causing needless suffering, but it is frequently entirely rational and occasionally even heroic. Judging by the reforms in laws against suicide and the reactions to the suicides of prominent persons in recent decades, it appears that the Enlightenment position is becoming very generally accepted.

See also: BIOETHICS; DEATH; LIFE AND DEATH; MEDICAL ETHICS

PAUL EDWARDS

SUPEREROGATION

Supererogatory actions are usually characterized as 'actions above and beyond the call of duty'. Historically, Catholic thinkers defended the doctrine of supererogation by distinguishing what God commands from what he merely prefers, while Reformation thinkers claimed that all actions willed by God are obligatory. In contemporary philosophy, it is often argued that if morality is to permit us to pursue our own personal interests, it must recognize that many self-sacrificing altruistic acts are supererogatory rather than obligatory. The need for some category of the supererogatory is particularly urgent if moral obligations are thought of as rationally overriding. There are three main contemporary approaches to defining the supererogatory. The first locates the obligatory/supererogatory distinction within positive social morality, holding that the former are actions we are blameworthy for failing to perform, while the latter are actions we may refrain from performing without blame. The second holds that obligatory actions are supported by morally conclusive reasons, while supererogatory actions are not. On this approach the personal sacrifice sometimes involved in acting altruistically counts against it from the moral point of view, making some altruistic actions supererogatory rather than obligatory. The third approach appeals to virtue and vice, holding that obligatory actions are those failures to perform which reveal some defect in the agent's character, while supererogatory actions are those that may be omitted without vice.

GREGORY VELAZCO Y TRIANOSKY

SUPERVENIENCE

Supervenience is used of the relationship between two kinds of properties that things may have. It refers to the way in which one kind of property may only be present in virtue of the presence of some other kind: a thing can only possess a property of the first, supervening kind because it has properties of the underlying kind, but once the underlying kind is fixed, then the properties of the first kind are fixed as well. The supervening features exist only because of the underlying, or 'subjacent' properties, and these are sufficient to determine how the supervening features come out. For example, a person can only be good in virtue of being kind, or generous, or possessing some other personal qualities, and an animal can only be alive in virtue of possessing some kind of advanced physical organization. Equally, a painting can only represent a subject in virtue of the geometrical arrangement of light-reflecting surfaces, and its representational powers supervene on this arrangement. A melody supervenes on a sequence of notes, and the dispositions and powers of a thing may supervene on its physical constitution.

Although the word supervenience first appears in twentieth-century philosophy, the concept had previously appeared in discussion of the 'emergence' of life from underlying physical complexity. The central philosophical problem lies in understanding the relationship between the two levels. We do not want the relationship to be entirely mysterious, as if it is just a metaphysical accident that properties of the upper level arise when things are suitably organized at the lower level. On the other hand, if the relationship becomes too close so that, for instance, it is a logical truth that once the lower-level properties are in place the upper-level ones emerge, the idea that there are two genuinely distinct levels becomes problematic: perhaps the upper-level properties are really nothing but lower-level ones differently described.

If this problem is dealt with, there may still remain difficulties in thinking about the upper-level properties. For example, can they be said to cause things, or explain things, or must these notions be reserved for the lower-level properties? Supposing that only lower-level properties really do any work leads to epiphenomenalism – the idea that the upper-level properties really play no role in determining the course of events. This seems to clash with common-sense belief in the causal powers of various properties that undoubtedly supervene on others, and also leads to a difficult search for some conception of the final, basic or lowest level of fact on which all else supervenes.

See also: CAUSATION

SIMON BLACKBURN

SURPRISE EXAMINATION PARADOX
See PARADOXES, EPISTEMIC

SUSTAINABILITY

Sustainability is a property of any activity, practice, process or institution that has the capacity to be continued in more or less the same way indefinitely. The concept has risen to prominence in recent years in response to the realization that continued social and economic development may not be sustainable in view of the unprecedented environmental changes that it brings about. Development is said to be sustainable, in the words of the 'Brundtland Report', when it 'meets the needs of the present without compromising the ability of future generations to meet their own needs'. This prescription is widely perceived to capture and to integrate a number of existing social and political objectives (justice, the alleviation of poverty and the protection of the environment), and following the United Nations Conference on Environment and Development held in Rio de Janeiro in 1992 it is now the declared objective of local and national governments worldwide, as well as of a large number of business and non-government organizations. Given its purported practical relevance, a great deal of intellectual effort has been concentrated upon developing a viable conception of sustainability for policy purposes. Economic and ecological models of the concept have been developed, and criticized. Recent attention has focused more on the political and institutional dimensions of the problem.

See also: ECONOMICS AND ETHICS; GREEN POLITICAL PHILOSOPHY; POPULATION AND ETHICS; TECHNOLOGY AND ETHICS

ALAN HOLLAND

ŚVETĀMBARA JAINISM
See JAINA PHILOSOPHY

SWINESHEAD, RICHARD
See OXFORD CALCULATORS

SYNTAX

Syntax (more loosely, 'grammar') is the study of the properties of expressions that distinguish them as members of different linguistic categories, and 'well-formedness', that is, the ways in which expressions belonging to these categories may be combined to form larger units. Typical syntactic categories include noun, verb and sentence. Syntactic properties have played an important role not only in the study of 'natural' languages (such as English or Urdu) but also in the study of logic and computation. For example, in symbolic logic, classes of well-formed formulas are specified without mentioning what formulas (or their parts) mean, or whether they are true or false; similarly, the operations of a computer can be fruitfully specified using only syntactic properties, a fact that has a bearing on the viability of computational theories of mind.

The study of the syntax of natural language has taken on significance for philosophy in the twentieth century, partly because of the suspicion, voiced by Russell, Wittgenstein and the logical positivists, that philosophical problems often turned on misunderstandings of syntax (or the closely related notion of 'logical form'). Moreover, an idea that has been fruitfully developed since the pioneering work of Frege is that a proper understanding of syntax offers an important basis for any understanding of semantics, since the meaning of a complex expression is compositional, that is, built up from the meanings of its parts as determined by syntax.

In the mid-twentieth century, philosophical interest in the systematic study of the syntax of natural language was heightened by Noam Chomsky's work on the nature of syntactic rules and on the innateness of mental structures specific to the acquisition (or growth) of grammatical knowledge.

This work formalized traditional work on grammatical categories within an approach to the theory of computability, and also revived proposals of traditional philosophical rationalists that many twentieth-century empiricists had regarded as bankrupt. Chomskian theories of grammar have become the focus of most contemporary work on syntax.

See also: ANALYTICAL PHILOSOPHY; CHOMSKY, N.; LANGUAGE OF THOUGHT; MIND, COMPUTATIONAL THEORIES OF; SCOPE

STEPHEN NEALE

T

TABLEAU SYSTEMS

See NATURAL DEDUCTION, TABLEAU AND SEQUENT SYSTEMS

TACIT KNOWLEDGE

See KNOWLEDGE, TACIT; POLANYI, MICHAEL

TANABE HAJIME (1885–1962)

Tanabe Hajime was a central figure of the so-called Kyoto School, and is generally acknowledged to be one of the most important philosophers of modern Japan. He held Kant in high esteem, and used a Neo-Kantian critical methodology in his early studies in epistemology. In the 1920s he was chiefly influenced by Nishida Kitarō's original cosmological system. He adapted Nishida's idea of 'absolute nothingness' to political situations and, in so doing, contributed much to establishing the foundations of what became the most influential philosophical school in Japan up until the end of the Second World War.

See also: JAPANESE PHILOSOPHY

HIMI KIYOSHI

TAOIST PHILOSOPHY

See DAOIST PHILOSOPHY

TARSKI, ALFRED (1901–83)

Alfred Tarski was a Polish mathematician and logician. He worked in metamathematics and semantics, set theory, algebra and the foundations of geometry. Some of his logical works, in particular his definition of truth, were also significant contributions to philosophy. He was a successful teacher and a master of writing simply and with great clarity about complicated matters.

ROMAN MURAWSKI

TAXONOMY

The fundamental elements of any classification are its theoretical commitments, basic units and the criteria for ordering these basic units into a classification. Two fundamentally different sorts of classification are those that reflect structural organization and those that are systematically related to historical development.

In biological classification, evolution supplies the theoretical orientation. The goal is to make the basic units of classification (taxonomic species) identical to the basic units of biological evolution (evolutionary species). The principle of order is supplied by phylogeny. Species splitting successively through time produce a phylogenetic tree. The primary goal of taxonomy since Darwin has been to reflect these successive splittings in a hierarchical classification made up of species, genera, families, and so on.

The major point of contention in taxonomy is epistemological. A recurrent complaint against classifications that attempt to reflect phylogeny is that phylogeny cannot be 'known' with certainty sufficient to warrant using it as the object of classification. Instead, small but persistent groups of taxonomists have insisted that classifications be more 'operational'. Instead of attempting to reflect something as difficult to infer as phylogeny, advocates of this position contend that systematists should stick more closely to observational reality.

See also: THEORIES, SCIENTIFIC

DAVID L. HULL

TAYLOR, CHARLES (1931–)

Among the most influential of late twentieth-century philosophers, Taylor has written on human agency, identity and the self; language; the limits of epistemology; interpretation and explanation in social science; ethics; and democratic politics. His work is distinctive because of his innovative treatments of long-standing philosophical problems, especially those deriving from applications of

Enlightenment epistemology to theories of language, the self and political action, and his unusually thorough integration of 'analytic' and 'Continental' philosophical concerns and approaches.

Taylor's work is shaped by the view that adequate understanding of philosophical arguments requires an appreciation of their origins, changing contexts and transformed meanings. Thus it often takes the form of historical reconstructions that seek to identify the paths by which particular theories and languages of understanding or evaluation have been developed. This reflects both Taylor's sustained engagement with Hegel's philosophy and his resistance to epistemological dichotomies such as 'truth' and 'falsehood' in favour of a notion of 'epistemic gain' influenced by H.G. Gadamer.

CRAIG CALHOUN

TECHNĒ

Technē (plural *technai*) is the ancient Greek term for an art or craft; examples include carpentry, sculpting and medicine. Philosophical interest in the *technai* stems from their use as a model and metaphor for all aspects of practical rationality, including its perfection in philosophy (the 'art of living'). From Socrates onwards, the notion of *technē* is employed for thinking about the connections between reason, ends and action. *Technai* are held to possess epistemological virtues (such as coherence and explanatory power) and practical virtues (their delivering of detailed instructions for action) against which other bodies of belief or practical systems can be studied and judged.

TAD BRENNAN

TECHNOLOGY AND ETHICS

Only within the modern period have philosophers made a direct and sustained study of ethics and technology. Their work follows two philosophical traditions, each marked by distinct styles: the Continental or phenomenological tradition, and the Anglo-American or analytical tradition.

Hans Jonas articulated one of the basic premises of Continental approaches when he argued for technology as a special subject of ethics: because technology has fundamentally transformed the human condition, generating problems of global magnitude extending into the indefinite future, it calls for a new approach to ethics. Jonas' basic premise is expressed variously in the works of Karl Marx, Max Scheler, José Ortega y Gasset, Martin Heidegger and others.

Work within the Anglo-American tradition tends not to deal with technology as a whole but to be organized around particular technologies, such as computing, engineering, and medical and biological sciences. It draws on concepts and principles of traditional ethical theory at least as a starting point for analyses. Although each of the technologies has a unique set of problems, certain themes, such as responsibility, risk, equity and autonomy, are common to almost all.

Social scientists have also raised important issues for the field of ethics and technology. Their work has yielded two dominant schools of thought: technological determinism and social constructivism.

CARL MITCHAM
HELEN NISSENBAUM

TECHNOLOGY, PHILOSOPHY OF

The philosophy of technology deals with the nature of technology and its effects on human life and society. The increasing influence of modern technology on human existence has triggered a growing interest in a philosophical analysis of technology. Nevertheless, the philosophy of technology as a coherent field of research does not yet exist. The subject covers studies from almost every branch of thinking in philosophy and deals with a great variety of topics because of a lack of consensus about the primary meaning of the term 'technology', which may, among others, refer to a collection of artefacts, a form of human action, a form of knowledge or a social process.

Among the most fundamental issues are two demarcation problems directly related to the definition of technology. The first concerns the distinction between technological (artificial) and natural objects. It involves the relation between man, nature and culture. The second pertains to the distinction between science and technology as types of knowledge. The science–technology relationship has become of central importance because of the widespread assumption that the distinguishing feature of modern technology, as compared to traditional forms of technology, is that it is science-based. Another much discussed issue is the autonomy of technology. It deals with the question of whether technology follows its own inevitable course of development, irrespective of its social, political, economic and cultural context.

See also: FUNCTIONAL EXPLANATION; RISK ASSESSMENT

PETER KROES

TELEOLOGICAL ARGUMENT

See GOD, ARGUMENTS FOR THE EXISTENCE OF

TELEOLOGICAL ETHICS

The Greek *telos* means final purpose; a teleological ethical theory explains and justifies ethical values by reference to some final purpose or good. Two different types of ethical theory have been called teleological, however. Ancient Greek theories are 'teleological' because they identify virtue with the perfection of human nature. Modern utilitarianism is 'teleological' because it defines right conduct as that which promotes the best consequences.

See also: INTUITIONISM IN ETHICS; KANTIAN ETHICS; STOICISM; UTILITARIANISM

CHRISTINE M. KORSGAARD

TELEOLOGICAL SEMANTICS

See SEMANTICS, TELEOLOGICAL

TELEOLOGY

Introduction

Teleology is the study of purposes, goals, ends and functions. Intrinsic or immanent teleology is concerned with cases of aiming or striving towards goals; extrinsic teleology covers cases where an object, event or characteristic serves a function for something.

Teleological explanations attempt to explain X by saying that X exists or occurs for the sake of Y. Since the question 'For what purpose . . . ?' may be construed either intrinsically or extrinsically, such explanations split into two broad types: those that cite goals of an agent, and those that cite functions.

The history of Western philosophy and science has been characterized by major debates about the logic, legitimacy and proper domains of these types of explanation. They still raise problems in contemporary biology and psychology. The modern debates have progressed considerably from the earlier ones, although continuities do exist.

1 Goals
2 Functions

1 Goals

Aristotle's views about the domain of striving that is present in nature were challenged during the Renaissance. Aristotle held that goals were 'final causes', that inanimate things seek natural places or states which are proper to their kind, and that growth and development in living things is directed towards the attainment of maturity.

The term 'final cause' misled some commentators, who assumed that a final cause is an efficient cause that comes after its effect. This could not have been Aristotle's view. Aristotle believed that trees grow leaves in order to protect their fruit (*Physics:* 199a, 26–9), but he recognized that the fruit is not always successfully protected. If birds eat the fruit, and hence the final cause fails to come about, this fact in no way undermines the teleological explanation. If he had meant that fruit-protection was an efficient cause working backwards in time, the failure to come about would undercut the efficient causal explanation. A final cause, for Aristotle, is a 'that for the sake of which' (see ARISTOTLE §9).

Still, there were other objections to his explaining the movements of inorganic bodies by ascribing goals to them. Francis BACON, GALILEO and NEWTON eschewed such explanations on the grounds that they were entirely speculative and otiose. First, the alleged striving could not be identified independently of the changes that actually occurred to the body, nor could its goal be identified – the hypothesis was untestable. Second, the hypothesis was unnecessary, at least in the fields of mechanics and dynamics, since a complete explanation could be provided in terms of antecedent causes and the laws of motion. As Bacon put it, 'Inquiry into final causes is sterile, and, like a virgin consecrated to God, produces nothing' (*De Augmentis Scientiarum* 1623).

Modern science does not sanction the ascription of goals or strivings to inanimate objects, except possibly to such artefacts as guided missiles, autonomous robots, and mechanical searching devices, which were first designed in the 1940s. But here the goal-talk is perhaps only 'as if' (Woodfield 1976: ch. 11).

In the life sciences, however, it is accepted that human beings and animals *do* strive after goals. The conviction that we are intentional agents is central to our self-image and to society. Moreover, animal and human goals can be identified in advance of the behaviour that they explain. The hypothesis that an animal is striving for food, for example, can be tested experimentally. So it is not true that goal-explanations are *in principle* vacuous.

Whether plants strive is, perhaps, unclear. Although we speak as if they did ('The flower turned in order to face the sun' and so on), such locutions may be merely a hangover from an Aristotelian tradition. They survive because we find them picturesque or convenient. In late-twentieth-century biology, vitalistic teleological theories of growth and development are not thought to be respectable, even though such processes cannot quite be explained in wholly physico-chemical terms (see VITALISM).

Are goal-explanations restricted, then, to the domain of intentional behaviour performed by intelligent organisms? The central case is surely that of the animate agent, conscious of what it wants, sensitive to information about its environment and able to represent alternative plans to itself. If goals always involve desires, beliefs and other mental states, then intrinsic teleological explanations are a species of mentalistic explanation. The main problem that arises next is to provide a satisfactory account of intentionality (see INTENTIONALITY).

Several philosophers in the twentieth century have tried to make room for a distinctive form of goal-explanation which is not necessarily mentalistic (see, for example, Wright 1976). Such theories may be viewed as broadly Aristotelian in the sense that they locate striving in activity which exhibits a distinctive pattern or causal structure.

2 Functions

Aristotle maintained that if an item X is a part of a system S in which X performs a characteristic activity that benefits S, then X exists and acts for the sake of S. S might be a living organism or something bigger, such as a bee-colony, an ecosystem or even the world as a whole. The fact that X serves a function for S is supposed to explain why X is present in S. Aristotle's doctrine was naturalistic in the sense that it did not postulate a supernatural designer, but it was not wholly naturalistic, since it employed the notion of *benefiting*. The main problem with extrinsic teleological explanations in biology is to see precisely how they work.

Even supposing that it is a 'fact' that X does good to a bigger system S, that fact alone is insufficient to account for X's existence. Some additional premise or principle seems to be required. For example, if nature had been designed and created by a benevolent and omnipotent God, the existence of X in S would be explicable in terms of God's wishes, beliefs and creative acts. This form of functional explanation has a familiar logic: we use such explanations when giving the reasoning that leads human beings to design and produce useful artefacts. By supplementing the explanation in this way, we present extrinsic teleology as being derivative upon the intrinsic teleology of the designer (see GOD, ARGUMENTS FOR THE EXISTENCE OF §4). This solution is unsatisfactory, however, since neither biologists nor laypeople feel that the validity of 'natural function' explanations is dependent upon any theological assumptions. Either the explanations have some other form, then, or they are not genuine explanations at all.

In 1859, Darwin's theory of evolution by natural selection showed how harmonious systems could have arisen naturally, without the need for a designer. Darwin's theory explains the existence of X in S as the outcome of a gradual process. Ancestors of S who possessed parts similar to X survived and reproduced more successfully than their relatives who lacked parts similar to X, and these ancestors reproduced true to form (their offspring had organs like X, including S who has X).

Darwin made the designer-hypothesis redundant. Was his theory anti-teleological? Darwin took it as a datum that biological parts and characteristics which have survived the selection process are normally useful for their owners; his theory asserted that they persisted *because* they were useful. This looks like a vindication of Aristotelian extrinsic teleology. Upon further reflection, however, it hardly amounts to a ringing endorsement since Darwin's theory can be stated without employing the term 'function' or any teleological language at all (see DARWIN, C.R.; EVOLUTION, THEORY OF).

Contemporary philosophers separate into two camps on the question of the logic of functional explanations in biology. The 'naturalistic revisionists' *redefine* the concept of function in terms of the causal-historical Darwinian selection hypothesis. They keep the old teleological language but sanitize it (Wright 1976). The other camp consists of 'semantic conservationists' who maintain that natural functionality cannot be *defined* in terms of Darwin's theory (Woodfield 1976). On the latter view, talk of natural functions is committed to assumptions about benefit and harmony and goodness that are extraneous to science and probably perspective-dependent. This view implies that functional explanations are still potentially problematic.

It is possible to maintain that functional explanations of undesigned phenomena have some scientific merit even if they are not wholly objective. Kant argues that the attribution of natural functions to organs is heuristic: it helps to systematize our knowledge of organisms and generates further 'How?' questions. Kant's sophisticated defence does not license the unbridled attribution of good consequences to everything in nature – a tendency ridiculed earlier by Voltaire (see KANT, I. §13).

In the 1980s, naturalistic revisionists, notably Millikan, began to exploit the Darwinian account of functionality as a tool for solving the problem of intentionality. The key insight is that desires, intentions and other mental states with intentional contents can themselves be seen as biologically adaptive states or as the products of mechanisms that are adaptive. The hope is to provide a naturalistic reduction of intentionality. This ambitious research-programme would make extrinsic teleology more fundamental than intrinsic teleology.

After more than two millennia of debates since Aristotle, teleology continues to provoke lively controversy among analytic philosophers.

See also: FUNCTIONAL EXPLANATION

References and further reading

Woodfield, A. (1976) *Teleology*, Cambridge: Cambridge University Press. (Monograph defending a unified analysis of teleological language.)

Wright, L. (1976) *Teleological Explanations*, Berkeley, CA: University of California Press. (Monograph arguing that such explanations are a special kind of causal explanation.)

ANDREW WOODFIELD

TELOS

Telos is the ancient Greek term for an end, fulfilment, completion, goal or aim; it is the source of the modern word 'teleology'. In Greek philosophy the term plays two important and interrelated roles, in ethics and in natural science; both are connected to the most common definitional account of the *telos*, according to which a *telos* is that for the sake of which something is done or occurs.

In ethical theory, each human action is taken to be directed towards some *telos* (i.e. end), and practical deliberation involves specifying the concrete steps needed to attain that *telos*. An agent's life as a whole can also be understood as aimed at the attainment of the agent's overall *telos*, here in the sense of their final end or *summum bonum* ('highest good'), generally identified in antiquity as *eudaimonia* (happiness). Rival ancient ethical theories are distinguished primarily by their rival specifications of the end; the Epicurean *telos* is pleasure, the Stoic *telos* is life according to nature, and so on.

In the natural science of Aristotle, the *telos* of a member of a species is the complete and perfect state of that entity in which it can reproduce itself (so, insects reach their *telos* when they become adults). The *telos* of an organ or capacity is the function it plays in the organism as a whole, or what it is for the sake of; the *telos* of the eye is seeing. Carrying on the tradition of Anaxagoras and Plato, Aristotle centres his scientific methodology around the claim that there are ends in nature, i.e. that some natural phenomena occur for the sake of something; Galen and the Stoics enthusiastically second this; Epicurus rejects it.

See also: FUNCTIONAL EXPLANATION; TELEOLOGY

TAD BRENNAN

TEMPORAL LOGIC
See TENSE AND TEMPORAL LOGIC

TENSE AND TEMPORAL LOGIC

A special kind of logic is needed to represent the valid kinds of arguments involving tensed sentences. The first significant presentation of a tense logic appeared in Prior's work of 1957. Sentential tense logic, in its simplest form, adds to classical sentential logic two tense operators, *P* and *F*. The basic idea is to analyse past and future tenses in terms of prefixes 'It was true that' and 'It will be true that', attached to present-tensed sentences. (Present-tensed sentences do not need present tense operators, since 'It is true that Jane is walking' is equivalent to 'Jane is walking'.) Translating the symbols into English is merely a preliminary to a semantics for tense logic; we may translate '*P*' as 'it was true that' but we still have the question of the meaning of 'it was true that'. There are at least two versions of the tensed theory of time – the minimalist version and the maximalist version – that can be used for the interpretation of the tense logic symbols.

The minimalist version implies that there are no past or future particulars, and thus no things or events that have properties of pastness or futurity. What exists are the things, with their properties and relations, that can be mentioned in certain present-tensed sentences. If 'Jane is walking' is true, then there is a thing, Jane, which possesses the property of walking. 'Socrates was discoursing', even if true, does not contain a name that refers to a past thing, Socrates, since there are no past things. The ontological commitments of past and future tensed sentences are merely to propositions, which are sentence-like abstract objects that are the meanings or senses of sentences. 'Socrates was discoursing' merely commits us to the proposition expressed by the sentence 'It was true that Socrates is discoursing'.

The maximalist tensed theory of time, by contrast, implies that there are past, present and future things and events; that past items possess the property of pastness, present items possess the property of presentness, and future items possess the property of being future. 'Socrates was discoursing' involves a reference to a past thing, Socrates, and implies that the event of Socrates discoursing has the property of being past.

See also: CONTINUANTS; DEMONSTRATIVES AND INDEXICALS; INTENSIONAL LOGICS; MODAL LOGIC; TIME

QUENTIN SMITH

TERMS, LOGICAL
See LOGICAL CONSTANTS

TERTULLIAN, QUINTUS SEPTIMUS FLORENS (*c.* AD 160–*c.* AD 220)

Tertullian was the first Christian theological author to write in Latin, and is responsible for initiating the Latin vocabulary of Christian theology, including such important terms as *persona* (person) and *substantia* (substance). His early works, including the *Apologeticum*, refute pagan misconceptions about Christianity and argue on philosophical and juridical grounds for religious freedom. His later theological treatises, such as *De anima* (On the Soul) and *Adversus Marcionem* (Against Marcion), reflect Tertullian's adherence, in about AD 205–6, to Montanism, a Christian sect which emphasized asceticism, apocalypticism and prophecy. These lengthy works represent an effort to oppose those forms of Christianity that sought to ally themselves with Platonism, such as Gnosticism. After these defences of apocalyptic Christianity, Tertullian fades from historical view around AD 220, leaving a legacy of charismatic truculence.

See also: Gnosticism; God, concepts of; Neoplatonism; Patristic philosophy; Stoicism; Trinity

JOHN PETER KENNEY

TESTIMONY

Philosophical treatment of the problems posed by the concept of knowledge has been curiously blind to the role played by testimony in the accumulation and validation of knowledge or, for that matter, justified belief. This is all the more surprising, given that an enormous amount of what any individual can plausibly claim to know, whether in everyday affairs or in theoretical pursuits, is dependent in various ways upon what others have to say. The idea that someone can only really attain knowledge if they get it entirely by the use of their own resources provides a seductive ideal of autonomous knowledge that may help explain the way epistemologists have averted their gaze from the topic of testimony. But, unless they are prepared to limit the scope of knowledge dramatically, theorists who support this individualist ideal of autonomy need to explain how our wide-ranging reliance upon what we are told is consistent with it. Characteristically, those who consider the matter acknowledge the reliance, but seek to show that the individual cognizer can 'justify' dependence upon testimony by sole resort to the individual's resources of observation, memory and inference. Testimony is thus viewed as a second-order source of knowledge. But this reductionist project is subject to major difficulties, as can be seen in David Hume's version. It has problems with the way the proposed justification is struc-

tured, with its assumptions about language and with the way the individual's epistemic resources are already enmeshed with testimony. The success or failure of the reductionist project has significant implications for other areas of inquiry.

See also: Social epistemology; Testimony in Indian philosophy

C.A.J. COADY

TESTIMONY IN INDIAN PHILOSOPHY

A prominent topic in Indian epistemology is *śābdapramāṇa*, knowledge derived from linguistic utterance or testimony. The classical material is extensive and varied, initially concerned with providing grounds for accepting the wisdom of *śruti* or 'the heard word', that is, the canonical scriptures. The Buddhists, however, saw no need for *śābdajñāna* (information gained through words) as an independent source of knowledge, because any utterance (including the Buddha's) that has not been tested in one's own experience cannot be relied upon; and in any case, the operation of such knowledge can be accounted for in terms of inference and perception.

The Nyāya, following the Mīmāṃsā, developed sophisticated analyses and a spirited defence of the viability and autonomy of testimony. The problem is recast thus: is *śābdapramāṇa* linguistic knowledge *eo ipso*, or does verbal understanding amount to knowledge only when certain specifiable conditions, in addition to the generating conditions, are satisfied? The more usual answer is that where the speaker is reliable and sincere, and there is no evidence to the contrary, the generating semantic and phenomenological conditions suffice to deliver valid knowledge. If doubt arises, then other resources can be utilized for checking the truth or falsity of the understanding, or the reliability of the author (or nonpersonal source), and for overcoming the defects.

PURUSHOTTAMA BILIMORIA

THALES (*fl. c.*585 BC)

Known as the first Greek philosopher, Thales initiated a way of understanding the world that was based on reason and nature rather than tradition and mythology. He held that water is in some sense the basic material, that all things are full of gods and (purportedly) that all things possess soul. He predicted an eclipse of the sun and was considered the founder of Greek astronomy and mathematics.

RICHARD MCKIRAHAN

THEORETICAL ENTITIES

See OBSERVATION; SCIENTIFIC REALISM AND
ANTIREALISM; THEORIES, SCIENTIFIC

THEORETICAL (EPISTEMIC) VIRTUES

When two competing theories or hypotheses
explain or accommodate just the same data (and
both are unrefuted), which should be preferred?
According to a classical, purely formal confirmation
theory, neither – each is confirmed to the same
degree, and so the two hypotheses are precisely
equal in epistemic status, warrant or credibility. Yet
in real life, one of the two may be preferred very
strongly, for any of a number of pragmatic reasons: it
may be simpler, more readily testable, more fruitful
or less at odds with what we already believe. The
philosophical question is whether such pragmatic
virtues are of no specifically epistemic, truth-
conducing value, or are instead genuine reasons
for accepting a theory as more likely to be true than
is a competitor that lacks them.

See also: JUSTIFICATION, EPISTEMIC; SCEPTICISM

WILLIAM G. LYCAN

THEORIES, SCIENTIFIC

The term 'theory' is used variously in science to
refer to an unproven hunch, a scientific field (as in
'electromagnetic theory'), and a conceptual device
for systematically characterizing the state-transition
behaviour of systems. Philosophers of science have
tended to view the latter as the most fundamental,
and most analyses of theories focus on it.

The Einsteinian revolution involved the rejection
of the chemical ether on experimental grounds. It
thus prompted philosophers and scientists to
examine closely the nature of scientific theories
and their connections to observation. Many sought
normative analyses that precluded the introduction
of 'fictitious' theoretical entities such as the ether.
Such analyses amounted to criteria for demarcating
scientific or cognitively significant claims from
unscientific or metaphysical claims.

Logical positivism sought to develop an ideal
language for science that would guarantee cognitive
significance. The language was symbolic logic with
the nonlogical vocabulary bifurcated into observational and theoretical subvocabularies. Observation
terms directly designated observable entities and
attributes, and the truth of statements using them
was unproblematic. To prevent postulation of
fictitious unobservable entities, theoretical terms
were allowed only in the context of a theory which
guaranteed the cognitive significance of theoretical
assertions. Theories were required to contain
correspondence rules that interpret theoretical

terms by coordinating them in some way with
observational conditions.

In the 1960s this 'received view' was attacked on
grounds that the observational–theoretical distinction
was untenable; that the correspondence rules were a
heterogeneous confusion of meaning relationships,
experimental design, measurement and causal relationships; that the notion of partial interpretation associated
with more liberal requirements on correspondence
rules was incoherent; that theories are not axiomatic
systems; that symbolic logic is an inappropriate
formalism; and that theories are not linguistic entities.

Alternative analyses of theories were suggested –
construing theories as answers to scientific problems
or as paradigms or conceptual frameworks. Gradually
analyses that construe theories as extra-linguistic set-
theoretic structures came to dominate post-positivistic
thought. The *semantic conception* identifies theories
with abstract theory structures like configurated state
spaces that stand in mapping relations to phenomena
and are the referents of linguistic theory formulations. Depending on the sort of mapping relationship
required for theoretical adequacy, realist, quasi-
realist or antirealist versions are obtained. Correspondence rules are avoided and some versions
eschew observational–nonobservational distinctions
altogether. Development of the semantic conception
has tended to focus on the mediation of theories
and phenomena via observation or experiment, the
relations between models and theories, confirmation of theories, their ontological commitments,
and semantic relations between theories, phenomena and linguistic formulations. The *structuralist*
approach also analyses theories set-theoretically as
comprised of a theory structure and a set of intended
applications, but is neopositivistic in spirit and in its
reliance on a relativized theoretical–nontheoretical
term distinction. It has been used to explore
theoreticity, the dynamics of theories as they undergo
development, and incommensurability notions.

One's analysis of theories tends to influence
strongly the position one takes on issues such as such
as observation, confirmation and testing, and
realism versus instrumentalism versus antirealism.

See also: EXPERIMENT; IDEALIZATIONS; LOGICAL
POSITIVISM; MODELS; OBSERVATION;
OPERATIONALISM; RELATIVITY THEORY,
PHILOSOPHICAL SIGNIFICANCE OF; SCIENTIFIC
REALISM AND ANTIREALISM

FREDERICK SUPPE

THEORY OF TYPES

The theory of types was first described by Bertrand
Russell in 1908. He was seeking a logical theory
that could serve as a framework for mathematics,

and, in particular, a theory that would avoid the so-called 'vicious-circle' antinomies, such as his own paradox of the property of those properties that are not properties of themselves – or, similarly, of the class of those classes that are not members of themselves. Such paradoxes can be thought of as resulting when logical distinctions are not made between different types of entities, and, in particular, between different types of properties and relations that might be predicated of entities, such as the distinction between concrete objects and their properties, and the properties of those properties, and so on. In 'ramified' type theory, the hierarchy of properties and relations is, as it were, two-dimensional, where properties and relations are distinguished first by their order, and then by their level within each order. In 'simple' type theory properties and relations are distinguished only by their orders.

See also: INTENSIONAL LOGIC

NINO B. COCCHIARELLA

THERMODYNAMICS

Thermodynamics began as the science that elucidated the law-like order present in the behaviour of heat and in its transformations to and from mechanical work. It became of interest to philosophers of science when the nature of heat was discovered to be that of the hidden energy of motion of the microscopic constituents of matter.

Attempts at accounting for the phenomenological laws of heat that make up thermodynamics on the basis of the so-called kinetic theory of heat gave rise to the first fundamental introduction into physics of probabilistic concepts and of probabilistic explanation. This led to so-called statistical mechanics.

Some of the issues of thermodynamics with importance to philosophers are: the meaning of the probabilistic claims made in statistical mechanics; the nature of the probabilistic explanations it proffers for the observed macroscopic phenomena; the structure of the alleged reduction of thermodynamic theory to the theory of the dynamics of the underlying microscopic constituents of matter; the place of cosmological posits in explaining the behaviour of local systems; and the alleged reducibility of our very notion of the asymmetry of time to thermodynamic asymmetries of systems in time.

See also: DUHEM, P.M.M.; MAXWELL, J.C.

LAWRENCE SKLAR

THOMISM

Deriving from Thomas Aquinas in the thirteenth century, Thomism is a body of philosophical and theological ideas that seeks to articulate the intellectual content of Catholic Christianity. In its nineteenth and twentieth-century revivals Thomism has often characterized itself as the 'perennial philosophy'. This description has several aspects: first, the suggestion that there is a set of central and enduring philosophical questions about reality, knowledge and value; second, that Thomism offers an ever-relevant set of answers to these; and third, that these answers constitute an integrated philosophical system.

In its general orientation Thomism is indeed preoccupied with an ancient philosophical agenda and does claim to offer a comprehensive, non-sceptical and realist response based on a synthesis of Greek thought – in particular that of Aristotle – and Judaeo-Christian religious doctrines. However, in their concern to emphasize the continuity of their tradition, Thomists have sometimes overlooked the extent to which it is reinterpretative of its earlier phases. The period from the original writings of Thomas Aquinas to late twentieth-century neo-scholastic and 'analytical' Thomism covers eight centuries and a stretch of intellectual history more varied in its composition than any other comparable period.

Not only have some self-proclaimed Thomists held positions with which Aquinas would probably have taken issue, some have advanced claims that he would not have been able to understand. Examples of the first are found in Neo-Kantian treatments of epistemology and ethics favoured by some twentieth-century Thomists. Examples of the second include attempts to reconcile Aquinas' philosophy of nature with modern physics, and his informal Aristotelian logic with quantified predicate calculus and possible world semantics.

The term 'Thomism' is sometimes used narrowly to refer to the thought of Aquinas, and to its interpretation and elaboration by sixteenth- and seventeenth-century commentators such as Cajetan, Sylvester of Ferrara, Domingo Bañez and John of St Thomas. At other times it is employed in connection with any view that takes its central ideas from Aquinas but which may depart from other of his doctrines, or which combines his ideas with those of other philosophers and philosophies. Prominent examples of Thomists in this wider sense include Francisco Suárez (1548–1617) who also drew on the epistemology and metaphysics of another great medieval thinker Duns Scotus; and, more recently, Joseph Marechal (1878–1944), whose 'Transcendental Thomism' accepted as its starting point the Kantian assumption that experience is of phenomena and not of reality as it is in itself. An example drawn from the ranks of contemporary analytical philosophers is Peter Geach who draws in equal measure from Aquinas, Frege and Wittgenstein.

In the twentieth century there have been two major proponents of the philosophy of Aquinas, namely Jacques Maritain and Etienne Gilson, both of whom contributed significantly to the development of Neo-Thomism in North America. Interestingly, both men were French, neither had been trained in a Thomistic tradition and both were drawn into philosophy by attending lectures by Henri Bergson at the Collège de France in Paris. The Neo-Thomism they inspired declined following the Second Vatican Council (1962–5) as Catholics looked to other philosophical movements, including existentialism and phenomenology, or away from philosophy altogether. Today Thomists tend to be close followers and interpreters of the writings of Aquinas, but there is also a growing interest among mainstream English-language philosophers in some of his central ideas. While not a movement, this approach has been described as 'analytical' Thomism.

See also: RELIGION, PHILOSOPHY OF

JOHN J. HALDANE

THOREAU, HENRY DAVID (1817–62)

Thoreau was one of the founders of the new literature that emerged within the fledgling culture of the United States in the middle decades of the nineteenth century. He inherited an education in the classics and in the transcendentalism of his older friend and teacher Ralph Waldo Emerson. Thoreau forged a means of writing which was dedicated to recording particular events in all their transience but capable of rendering graphic the permanent laws of nature and conscience. His incorporation of both confidence and self-questioning into the texture of his writing forms the ground of his standpoint as an observer of human lives and other natural histories.

Thoreau's relation to philosophy goes beyond his inheritance from Plato, Kant, Emerson and Eastern thought. Above all, his quest for philosophy is evident in the ways his writing seeks its own foundations. It is in the act of writing that Thoreau locates the perspectives within which to give an account of the humanness of a life. His project is to report sincerely and unselfconsciously a life of passion and simplicity, using himself as a representative of basic human needs and projects. Influenced by Plato's *Republic*, Thoreau gives an account of some basic human needs, such as food, shelter and society. But also, like Plato, he shows that the particular institutions by which human needs are met are very far from being necessary. Tracing the relationship between need and necessity is one of the primary goals of Thoreau's work.

TIMOTHY GOULD

THOUGHT EXPERIMENTS

Thought experiments are strange: they have the power to present surprising results and can profoundly change the way we view the world, all without requiring us to examine the world in the way that ordinary scientific experiments do. Philosophers who view all hypothetical reasoning as a form of thought experimentation regard the method as being as old as philosophy itself. Others maintain that truly informative thought experiments are found only in mathematics and the natural sciences. These emerged in the seventeenth century when the new experimental science of Bacon, Boyle, Galileo, Newton and others forced a distinction between the passive observation of Aristotelian mental narratives and the active interventions of real-world experiment. The new science gave rise to a philosophical puzzle: how can mere thought be so informative about the world? Rationalists argue that thought experiments are exercises in which thought apprehends laws of nature and mathematical truths directly. Empiricists argue that thought experiments are not exercises of 'mere thought' because they actually rely upon hidden empirical information – otherwise they would not count as experiments at all. More recently it has been argued that thought experiments are not mysterious because they are constructed arguments that are embedded in the world so as to combine logical and conceptual analysis with relevant features of the world.

See also: EMPIRICISM; EXPERIMENT; RATIONALISM; SCIENTIFIC METHOD

DAVID C. GOODING

THOUGHT, LANGUAGE OF
See LANGUAGE OF THOUGHT

TILLOTSON, J.
See CAMBRIDGE PLATONISM

TIME

Introduction

Time is the single most pervasive component of our experience and the most fundamental concept in our physical theories. For these reasons time has received intensive attention from philosophy. Reflection on our ordinary-tensed language of time has led many to posit a relation of metaphysical importance between time and existence. Closely connected with such intuitions are claims to the effect that time is unlike space, and in deep and important ways.

The development of physical theories from Newtonian dynamics through relativistic theories, statistical mechanics, and quantum mechanics has had a profound effect on philosophical views about time. Relativity threatens the notion of a universal, global present, and with it the alleged connections of time to existence. The connection between temporal order and causal order in relativity theories, and between the asymmetry of time and entropic asymmetry in statistical mechanics, suggest various 'reductive' accounts of temporal phenomena.

Finally, the radical differences between time as it appears in our physical theory and time as it appears in our immediate experience, show important and difficult problems concerning the relation of the time of 'theory' to the time of 'our immediate awareness'.

1   Time and existence
2   Relationism and its problems
3   Time in relativistic theories
4   Time and causation
5   Time in experience and time in nature

1   Time and existence

There is much philosophical debate about the degree to which the temporality of the world is like or unlike its spatiality. All agree that space and time differ in their dimensionality, and all agree, even in a relativistic context, that the temporality of the world is not a spatial dimension. Spatial and temporal aspects of the world are, for example, differentially interconnected with causal features.

One aspect that distinguishes time from space is the intuitive asymmetry of the former, unmatched by any related feature of the latter. While there is debate about what this asymmetry consists in, and how it is connected to other features of the world such as entropic asymmetry, there is not much question that it is uniquely characteristic of the temporal structure of the world (see THERMODYNAMICS).

But that distinction alone is often thought insufficient to capture the special nature of time. Expressions such as the 'flux' or 'flow' of time are often invoked metaphorically to capture what is intended, as in Bergson's treatment of temporality (see BERGSON, H.-L.). McTaggart distinguished between those aspects of time that could be characterized using timeless temporal relations (such as one event being after another), called by him the B-series, and those aspects of time that were expressed in tensed discourse, called by him

the A-series. It was McTaggart's contention that only the A-series captured the essence of temporality, but that since this essence was self-contradictory, time was 'unreal' (see McTAGGART, J.M.E.).

The core of such claims lies, perhaps, in the intuition expressed by St Augustine that while being elsewhere than here hardly reduced the reality of an object, that which was not presently existing had no genuine existence at all (see AUGUSTINE). Other versions of this line take it that only past and present have 'determinate reality', the future, not yet having come into being, having no genuine determinate reality at all.

An important response to such ideas argues that there is no ultimate distinction in 'reality' between the present as contrasted with the past and future or between the present and past as contrasted with the future. This approach admits that past and future do not 'exist', of course, if 'exist' is being used in its tensed form, but finds in that only an interesting feature of natural language (having tensed-verb forms but no parallel structure for spatial location) and not anything of metaphysical importance.

McTaggart's claim that tensed expressions cannot be translated into tenseless ones, since the former have truth-values that vary with time and the latter do not, is admitted, but the proponents of the view that nothing metaphysical is represented by tense take it that this shows only that tensed discourse has an ineliminable 'token reflexive' or 'indexical' nature. To say 'x occurred' is to say 'x occurred before now'. 'Now' is a term whose reference varies with its use, since it refers to any moment of time at which it is uttered. Only this implicit indexicality, it is claimed, distinguishes tensed from untensed discourse, not some ability of the former but not the latter to capture the essential metaphysical nature of time.

Those who reject this line offer several ways of trying to express what they think is missing in its account. Tense logics and models of splitting worlds (with the past as unique and the future as still offering manifold possibilities) are one approach. Others note the analogy with modal logic where the actual world is (in most accounts) metaphysically distinguished in its reality from the other possible worlds, much as the present is, allegedly, distinguished in its reality from other temporal moments of past and future (see TENSE AND TEMPORAL LOGIC). The analogy goes only so far, however, since each moment of time is, when it is the present, the moment of reality. Formulating a fully fledged metaphysical perspectivalism that would capture the essence of the metaphysical claims of those who think time is specially connected with existence has proven a difficult task.

2 Relationism and its problems

Just as in philosophical explorations of space, the idea that time can be considered as nothing but a structured family of relations of material events is an important one (see SPACE). The doctrine is, perhaps, already implicit in Aristotle's description of time as 'the measure of motion' and becomes explicit in Leibniz's fully fledged relationism for space and time (see LEIBNIZ, G.W. §11).

One question that immediately arises in a relationist perspective is whether there could be passage of time without change (see CHANGE). One response to this is to introduce modality into the discourse. Just as empty space can be thought of as given by unactualized possibilities of spatial relations, so one might think of time intervals without actual change as given by possible but not actual changes. Important insights are contained in the notion of limits to situations themselves relationally acceptable (such as the limit of a sequence of ever-larger regions of the universe that abide without change).

NEWTON introduces novel elements into the philosophical discussion in his insistence on 'absolute time' to accompany space as a reference frame for absolute inertial motions. Many relationists like to think of the time interval as being arbitrarily specified by any periodic process. Newton emphasizes the distinction between the ideal process and any actual one. More importantly his theory, with its notion of distinguished, absolutely uniform motions, presupposes that uniformity of time interval is fixed by physical processes other than arbitrarily chosen periodic processes. Without an absolute notion of equality of time interval the absolute notion of uniformity of motion is incoherent.

Within contemporary relativistic theories the issue of the adequacy of a relationist account of time becomes absorbed into the more general issues concerning the opposition between relationistically and substantivally interpreted spacetime theories (see RELATIVITY THEORY, PHILOSOPHICAL SIGNIFICANCE OF).

3 Time in relativistic theories

The introduction of the novel conceptualization of space and time forced upon us by the theories of special and general relativity once again illustrates the crucial interdependence of philosophical and physicist thought in this area.

In the special theory of relativity, the notion of simultaneity for events spatially separated from one another, and with it the time interval between any two separated non-simultaneous events, becomes relative to a chosen inertial reference frame (see RELATIVITY THEORY, PHILOSOPHICAL SIGNIFICANCE OF). There is no longer a global 'now' that selects one and the same set of events for all observers, no matter what their state of motion relative to one another. Such a relativization of the notion of time is not to be confused with the relationist conception of time described above. With the advent of special relativity one has the beginning of the radical divergence between our intuitive notions of time and those posited by physical theories.

It is often claimed that within the relativistic picture the doctrines that connect existence with temporality (as discussed above) are no longer viable. If what is present and what is past can vary from observer to observer, then how can one maintain that past and future (or, alternatively, future alone) have no genuine reality? A frequent claim is that relativity forces upon us the view of the timelessness of existence contrasted with the 'essentially tensed nature of existence' theories.

As is so often the case, however, such an inference from physics to philosophy is premature. One could, for example, relativize one's notion of existence, thus claiming that past and future are unreal, but that events unreal for one observer can be real for another observer itself real to the first. Alternatively, one could utilize only invariant spacetime features in the account. In one version of this approach the past remains real at a spacetime point-event, in the sense of the past light-cone at the point-event constituting the real (see RELATIVITY THEORY, PHILOSOPHICAL SIGNIFICANCE OF). In another version reality is collapsed even more radically than in the Augustinian view, so that what is real at a place–time is only that unextended point place–time and its features.

General relativity, with its dynamic spacetime, makes matters even more peculiar. Models of the world in this theory exist with closed timelike curves. In such a world an event can be (globally) in its own past and future (see TIME TRAVEL). Such possibilities led Kurt Gödel to assert that time was 'ideal' and that the 't' parameter of physics did not stand for time at all.

4 Time and causation

Various claims have been made to the effect that time 'is defined by' or 'reduces to' some other feature of the world. Causal theories date back to Leibniz, who pointed out that simultaneity for events could be characterized by their not being causally connectable. The breakdown of this association in the special theory of relativity is often taken as the key factor in claims to the effect that distant simultaneity is a matter of convention.

The issue of the extent to which temporal notions are, or are not, causally definable in relativistic theories is a complex one. In the special theory there is a relation framed in terms of causal connectability that is coextensive with simultaneity. In general relativity causal definitions of temporal metric and topological notions utilizing causal connectability alone fail in general. But one can characterize topological spatiotemporal notions in terms of the continuity of causal (timelike) paths. This suggests a reduction of the spatiotemporal notions not to causal notions *per se*, but to the epistemically accessible topological features of the spacetime, those directly available to an observer (see RELATIVITY THEORY, PHILOSOPHICAL SIGNIFICANCE OF).

Both the physical connections of spatial and temporal (and spatiotemporal) features to causal features of the world, and the philosophical understanding of what these might tell us about 'what time is' in the world, remain controversial issues (see CAUSATION).

5 Time in experience and time in nature

Temporality enters our conceptual framework both as a descriptive component of our immediate experience and as a component of our theoretical description of the physical world. But how are these aspects of time related to one another? This would be a problem for philosophy even if we took the time of nature to have the features we think of time having prescientifically. Once we have been told by science that time in nature is radically unlike anything we encounter in our immediate experience, as we seem to be told in relativistic theories and as we are likely to be even more radically informed when a fully quantum mechanical account of spacetime is forthcoming, the problem of relating experienced time to the time of theory becomes even more pressing.

One tradition starts from the time of our immediate experience and suggests that the time of nature is in some way or another a construct dependent on the time of conscious awareness. A seminal version of this approach is the treatment of time in Kant (*Critique of Pure Reason* 1781/1787). Time is, along with space, one of the structuring principles of all experience, called by Kant a pure intuition. As such it is a feature of the phenomenal world and not of 'things-in-themselves'. Both outer experience of physical objects and inner experience of psychological states are framed in the format of the temporal intuitive structure. Behind the temporal psychological self is the transcendental self,

that which unifies all our experience with its implicit 'I think'. Non-temporal, the transcendental self is the ground of the temporal structuring of physical and psychological experience (see KANT, I. §§5–7).

The idealist tradition is continued in Husserl's phenomenological account of the ground and nature of our experience of time. Here emphasis is placed on what the necessary features of such experience must be like in order that we experience things as past, present and future, and have the sense that we do of time as passage. In Heidegger's pragmatist-phenomenology, time as it functions in human activity is the ground of time altogether (see HEIDEGGER, M. §§1–2). One begins with time as it appears in our experienced world of the fixed past, the present of action and the future of projected intentions. The time of nature and science, the time of the 'present-at-hand', is only derivative from the primordial time of experience as decision and action. In these (external, transcendental) idealist accounts of time, the time of past, present and future is taken as central.

Contrasted with such approaches is that of the physicalist-naturalist, to whom the time of the physical world is basic and the time of human experience supervenient at best. In these accounts it is the timeless temporal relations of the B-series that are usually taken as fundamental. Time in experience is usually thought of in something in the vein of a secondary quality.

But even such naturalistic accounts have their problematic aspects. Any proposal to make time as experienced a mere secondary quality (such as that of Gödel noted above), and that takes the 't' of physics to be a parameter disconnected from time as we immediately encounter it, leaves little ground for understanding how physical theories can receive a realistic (as opposed to instrumentalistic) interpretation, or for theoretical realism in general (see SCIENTIFIC REALISM AND ANTIREALISM).

See also: CONTINUANTS

References and further reading

Davies, P. (1974) *The Physics of Time Asymmetry*, Berkeley, CA: University of California Press (Direction of time and physical theory.)

Le Poidevin, R. and MacBeath, M. (eds) (1993) *The Philosophy of Time*, Oxford: Oxford University Press. (Collection of important philosophical articles on time.)

Sklar, L. (1993) *Physics and Chance*, Cambridge: Cambridge University Press. (Discussion of entropic theory of time order in ch. 10.)

LAWRENCE SKLAR

1021

TIME TRAVEL

The prospect of a machine in which one could be transported through time is no longer mere fantasy, having become in this century the subject of serious scientific and philosophical debate. From Einstein's special theory of relativity we have learned that a form of time travel into the future may be accomplished by moving quickly, and therefore ageing slowly (exploiting the time dilation effect). And in 1949 Kurt Gödel announced his discovery of (general relativistic) spacetimes whose global curvature allows voyages into the past as well. Since then the study of time travel has had three main strands. First, there has been research by theoretical physicists into the character and plausibility of structures, beyond those found by Gödel, that could engender closed timelike lines and closed causal chains. These phenomena include rotating universes, black holes, traversable wormholes and infinite cosmic strings. Second, there has been concern with the semantic issue of whether the terms 'cause', 'time' and 'travel' are applicable, strictly speaking, to such bizarre models, given how different they are from the contexts in which those terms are normally employed. However, one may be sceptical about the significance of this issue, since the questions of primary interest – focused on the nature and reality of the Gödel-style models – seem independent of whether their description requires a shift in the meanings of those words. And, third, there has been considerable discussion within both physics and philosophy of various alleged paradoxes of time travel, and of their power to preclude the spacetime models in which time travel could occur.
See also: RELATIVITY THEORY, PHILOSOPHICAL SIGNIFICANCE OF; SPACETIME; TIME

PAUL HORWICH

TOKEN

See TYPE/TOKEN DISTINCTION

TOLERATION

Toleration emerged as an important idea in the seventeenth century, receiving its fullest defence in John Locke's *A Letter Concerning Toleration* (1689). Initially developed in the context of attempts to restore peace in a Europe convulsed by religious conflicts, in the nineteenth and twentieth centuries it came to be extended to the accommodation of disputes about racial, sexual and social differences. Toleration is widely thought to be an essential element of a free society, especially one marked by moral and cultural pluralism, and it figures particularly prominently in the political theory of liberalism.

The paradigm example of toleration is the deliberate decision to refrain from prohibiting,

hindering or otherwise coercively interfering with conduct of which one disapproves, although one has the power to do so. The principal components of the concept of toleration are: a tolerating subject and a tolerated subject (either may be an individual, group, organization or institution); an action, belief or practice which is the object of toleration; a negative attitude (dislike or moral disapproval) on the part of tolerator toward the object of toleration; and a significant degree of restraint in acting against it.

Philosophical arguments have mostly concerned: the range of toleration (what things should or should not be tolerated?); the degree of restraint required by toleration (what forms of opposition are consistent with toleration?); and, most importantly, the justification of toleration (why should some things be tolerated?).
See also: FREEDOM OF SPEECH; LIBERALISM; MULTICULTURALISM

JOHN HORTON

TOLSTOI, COUNT LEV NIKOLAEVICH (1828–1910)

Tolstoi expressed philosophical ideas in his novels *Voina i mir* (*War and Peace*) (1865–9) and *Anna Karenina* (1875–7), which are often regarded as the summit of realism, as well as in shorter fictional works, such as *Smert' Ivana Il'icha* (The Death of Ivan Il'ich) (1886), often praised as the finest novella in European literature. In addition, he wrote numerous essays and tracts on religious, moral, social, educational and aesthetic topics, most notably 'Chto takoe iskusstvo?' ('What Is Art?') (1898), *Tsarstvo Bozhie vnutri vas* (*The Kingdom of God Is Within You*) (1893) and his autobiographical meditation 'Ispoved' (A Confession) (1884).

Tolstoi apparently used his essays, letters and diaries to explore ideas by stating them in their most extreme form, while his fiction developed them with much greater subtlety. Critics have discerned a sharp break in his work: an earlier period, in which he produced the two great novels, is dominated by deep scepticism; and a later period following the existential trauma and subsequent conversion experience described in 'Ispoved'. Tolstoi stressed the radical contingency of events, valued practical over theoretical reasoning, and satirized any and all overarching systems. After 1880, he assumed the role of a prophet, claiming to have found the true meaning of Christianity. He 'edited' the Gospels by keeping only those passages containing the essence of Christ's teaching and dismissed the rest as so many layers of falsification imposed by ecclesiastics. Tolstoi preached pacifism, anarchism, vegetarianism, passive resistance to evil (a doctrine that influenced Gandhi), a radical asceticism that would have banned sex even within marriage, and a theory of art that rejected most classic authors, including the plays of Shakespeare and Tolstoi's own earlier novels.

See also: WAR AND PEACE, PHILOSOPHY OF

GARY SAUL MORSON

TOTALITARIANISM

A term adopted in the 1920s by the Italian philosopher Giovanni Gentile to describe the ideal fascist state, 'totalitarianism' quickly acquired negative connotations as it was applied to the regimes of Hitler in Germany and Stalin in the USSR. Within political science it has generally been used to refer to a distinctively modern form of dictatorship based not only on terror but also on mass support mobilized behind an ideology prescribing radical social change. Controversially, the specific content of the ideology is considered less significant than the regime's determination to form the minds of the population through control of all communications.

Totalitarianism has attracted the attention of philosophers as well as political scientists because a number of classic philosophical systems have been suspected of harbouring totalitarian aspirations, and also because the model of total power exercised through discourse has been used by critical theorists to mount an attack on modernity in general.

MARGARET CANOVAN

TRADITION AND TRADITIONALISM

Tradition is that body of practice and belief which is socially transmitted from the past. It is regarded as having authority in the present simply because it comes from the past, and encapsulates the wisdom and experience of the past. For some, the very idea of tradition is anathema. It is characteristic of modernity to reject the authority of the past in favour of the present deployment of reason, unencumbered by tradition or prejudice. While prior to the seventeenth century tradition was largely unquestioned as a source of insight, and in need of no defence, since the Enlightenment the notion of tradition has been defended by traditionalists such as Burke and, more recently, Hayek. Upon inspection, however, traditionalism, if not indefensibly irrational, turns out to be a demonstration of the overlooked rationality contained within traditions. Traditions often turn out upon inspection to be not so much irrational as subtle and flexible deployments of reason in particular spheres.

See also: CONSERVATISM

ANTHONY O'HEAR

TRAGEDY

Tragedy is primarily a type of drama, though non-dramatic poetry ('lyric tragedy') and some novels (for example, *Moby Dick*) have laid claim to the description. As a genre, it began in ancient Greece and forms a part of the Western European tradition. Historically, it has carried prestige for playwrights and actors because it dealt with persons, generally men, of 'high' or noble birth, who, by virtue of their stature, represented the most profound sufferings and conflicts of humanity, both morally and metaphysically. The history of the genre is part of the history of how art and culture reflect views about class and gender.

Tragic theory has concentrated primarily on how to define the genre. A persistent feature is the tragic hero, who begins by occupying a position of power or nobility, but comes to a catastrophic end through some action of his own. According to the Aristotelian tradition, the audience is supposed to experience pity and fear in response to the sufferings of the tragic hero, and perhaps pleasure from its cathartic effects. Hegel initiated a paradigm shift in tragic theory in proposing that tragic plots essentially involve conflicts of duty rather than suffering.

Greek tragedy and Shakespearean tragedy provide two different exemplars of the genre. The tradition inspired by Greek tragedy emphasized a rigidly defined genre of dramatic poetry; French neoclassic tragedy is part of this tradition. Shakespearean tragedy, on the other hand, is written partly in prose, and includes comic elements and characters who are not nobly born. Lessing and Ibsen also resisted restraints imposed on the genre in terms of its representation of social class and gender in favour of drama that was more realistic and relevant to a bourgeois audience. Twentieth-century criticism has questioned the viability of the genre for modern times.

See also: COMEDY; EMOTION IN RESPONSE TO ART; HEGEL, G.W.F. §8; KATHARSIS; LESSING, G.E.; MIMĒSIS; NIETZSCHE, F.; POETRY

SUSAN L. FEAGIN

TRANSCENDENTAL ARGUMENTS

Introduction

Transcendental arguments seek to answer scepticism by showing that the things doubted by a sceptic are in fact preconditions for the scepticism to make sense. Hence the scepticism is either meaningless or false. A transcendental argument works by finding the preconditions of meaningful thought or judgment. For example, scepticism about other minds suggests that only the thinker themselves might have sensations. A transcendental argument which answered this scepticism would show that a precondition for thinking oneself to have sensations is that others do so as well. Expressing the scepticism involves thinking oneself to have sensations; and the argument shows that if this thought is expressible, then it is also false.

Arguments with such powerful consequences have, unsurprisingly, been much criticized. One criticism is that it is not possible to discover the necessary conditions of judgment. Another is that transcendental arguments can only show us how we have to think, whereas defeating scepticism involves showing instead how things really are.

1 Nature of argument
2 Problems
3 Further criticisms

1 Nature of argument

The name 'transcendental argument' originally comes from Kant, who called the most difficult part of his most difficult work a 'transcendental deduction' (see KANT, I. §6). In the twentieth century, the name has been applied by both proponents and critics to a loosely similar set of arguments, sometimes directly inspired by Kant, sometimes not. The central figure in re-launching such arguments was P.F. STRAWSON in his work on metaphysics, *Individuals* (1959), and his reconstruction of Kant, *The Bounds of Sense* (1966). Subsequently the work of Davidson, Putnam and Searle on the relations between language and the world has been called 'transcendental argument' both by themselves and by others; indeed Richard Rorty calls Davidson's argument a 'transcendental argument to end all transcendental arguments'.

One example of a transcendental argument is Strawson's attack on scepticism about other minds. He maintains that the ability to attribute mental states to others is a precondition for attributing mental states to oneself. Therefore, if the scepticism is stated in its standard form of wondering whether anyone apart from the thinker has thoughts or feelings, it is also answerable. For the argument shows that a precondition for any such wondering is that we also attribute such states to others. Hence, if scepticism makes sense at all, it is mistaken; the sceptic is reduced to either error or silence.

This particular example is a kind of private language argument (see PRIVATE LANGUAGE ARGU-MENT). Wittgenstein has retrospectively been seen as having made these kinds of arguments, as more

obviously and recently has Donald DAVIDSON. The closest analogy to them in Kant is not the *Transcendental Deduction* but, rather, the *Refutation of Idealism*, where Kant argued that knowledge of outer states is a precondition for knowledge of inner states, and hence claimed that 'the game played by idealism has been turned against itself' (*Critique of Pure Reason* 1781/1787: B276). As in Strawson, the way that the sceptical position (here idealism) enters the game means that it can be defeated.

This briefly sketched family of arguments illustrates several things about modern transcendental arguments. They are arguments about the preconditions of thought or judgment. They start with a supposition about our thoughts, such as that we have thoughts of some particular kind. A necessary condition for having such thoughts is then derived, followed by a necessary condition for this necessary condition, and so on. Assuming that the first assumption is correct, all its necessary conditions will then have been found also to apply.

2 Problems

As an answer to scepticism, a transcendental argument is only as strong as its initial assumption. In the example in §1 above, the assumption is that we think ourselves to have mental states. However, a sceptic could try to meet this by claiming that we might be mistaken about the content of our thoughts. Similarly Putnam's transcendental argument that we would not even be able to think that we were seeing an apple unless this kind of state was typically caused by real apples (and hence that external–world scepticism must be false) could be met by doubting whether I correctly identify my thoughts as being of the apple variety.

If, however, the initial assumption is not about the contents of thoughts but is just that there is thought (or language), then the sceptical move can be met. For this is something which no one, and hence no sceptic, can properly think that they doubt. Hence the most robust transcendental arguments concern themselves merely with the preconditions of there being thought or language at all. Examples are (again) the Private Language Argument, or Davidson's argument that there is only one conceptual scheme. The next possible point of weakness after the initial assumption is the discovery of its necessary conditions. Obviously this must not have a purely observational basis. The argument that people could not think without brains – we think, hence we have brains, hence the external world exists – would not be an effective answer to scepticism. So the arguments have to be (at least relatively) a priori.

Some people have therefore held that transcendental arguments may only draw out the purely conceptual, or analytic, consequences of their initial assumptions. This gives them better security against scepticism but makes their chances of reaching interesting conclusions rather slim. Others have held, rather more ambitiously, that the connections do not need to be narrowly analytic: transcendental arguments show the necessary conditions for having thoughts. Therefore, if the having of one kind of thought is a necessary condition for having another kind of thought, this will be good enough, even if the contents of the thoughts themselves are not analytically connected.

3 Further criticisms

In transcendental arguments, necessary conditions are often demonstrated by discovering the unique conditions which enable some kind of thought to be had. Yet it has been claimed, most prominently by Stefan Körner (1969), that the uniqueness of a conceptual structure cannot be established. Uniqueness, he says, could only be demonstrated by the elimination of all possible rivals. Yet although we may eliminate all rivals that occur to us, there may always be a possibility that we might have overlooked or might not be able to envisage. Other people have similarly claimed that, at best, we can only describe how we currently think, or the limits of currently imaginable alternatives. However, neither of these can show how we must think; they cannot demonstrate the necessary conditions of thought.

Another criticism is that, even if it can be shown what we must think, this will not defeat scepticism. Defeating scepticism demands a demonstration that we are justified in thinking that our beliefs show how things actually are. However, showing that we must think something does not show that the thought is correct – a necessary illusion is still an illusion. The force of this criticism depends on the kinds of necessary conditions derived in transcendental arguments. If some matter of fact is shown to be a necessary condition for having thoughts, then it does not apply. However, in modern arguments, the necessary conditions derived for having one kind of thought are frequently other kinds of thought. For example in the Strawson argument discussed above in §1, it is belief in other people's pains that is the required presupposition. It can be objected that this is insufficient to answer scepticism (in this case about other minds) since the crucial point is not whether we have to believe that others have pains, but, rather, whether this belief is correct.

A version of this objection is the one which Stroud mounts against Strawson and others in his highly influential paper of 1968 about transcendental arguments. This is his claim that transcendental arguments need a version of the Verification Principle in order to work (see MEANING AND VERIFICATION). However, Stroud continues, if we are entitled to presuppose the Verification Principle, then transcendental arguments are not needed, since the Verification Principle by itself will do the anti-sceptical work. The principle shows that it makes no sense to suppose that our best-verified beliefs might not be true. Analogously, it can show that it makes no sense to suppose that beliefs that we must have are not true. However it is the verificationist assumption which is doing the deadly anti-sceptical work, not the transcendental argument which gets us from belief to necessary belief. Therefore the route through necessary belief is superfluous; transcendental arguments are either redundant or invalid.

Alternatively, the transition from what we (have to) believe to how things actually are can be made by shrinking the distance between them. A supposition of idealism would do this; so that in the end we do not distinguish between the structure of thought and an independent, real world waiting to be described. In Kant, some kind of idealism was required in order to make the transcendental arguments work, and it has been suggested by Bernard Williams (1973) and others that this also applies to modern users of transcendental arguments. However, some modern users would not take this to be a criticism (see IDEALISM; REALISM AND ANTIREALISM).

See also: SCEPTICISM

References and further reading

Körner, S. (1969) *Fundamental Questions in Philosophy*, Harmondsworth: Allen Lane, The Penguin Press. (Chapter 12 contains the objection mentioned in §2; moderately difficult work.)

Stroud, B. (1968) 'Transcendental Arguments', *Journal of Philosophy* 65 (9): 241–56. (Mentioned in §3; frequently cited article which is not particularly difficult.)

Williams, B. (1973) *Problems of the Self*, Cambridge: Cambridge University Press. (The argument referred to in §3 is contained in paper number 8; a fairly difficult work.)

ROSS HARRISON

TRANSLATION, RADICAL

See RADICAL TRANSLATION AND RADICAL INTERPRETATION

TRINITY

The doctrine of the Holy Trinity is a central and essential element of Christian theology. The part of the doctrine that is of special concern in here may be stated in these words: the Father, the Son and the Holy Spirit are each God; they are distinct from one another; and yet (in the words of the Athanasian Creed), 'they are not three Gods, but there is one God'. This is not to be explained by saying that 'the Father', 'the Son' and 'the Holy Spirit' are three names that are applied to the one God in various circumstances; nor is it to be explained by saying that the Father, the Son, and the Holy Spirit are parts or aspects of God (like the leaves of a shamrock or the faces of a cube). In the words of St Augustine:

> Thus there are the Father, the Son, and the Holy Spirit, and each is God and at the same time all are one God; and each of them is a full substance, and at the same time all are one substance. The Father is neither the Son nor the Holy Spirit; the Son is neither the Father nor the Holy Spirit; the Holy Spirit is neither the Father nor the Son. But the Father is the Father uniquely; the Son is the Son uniquely; and the Holy Spirit is the Holy Spirit uniquely.
>
> (*De doctrina christiana* I, 5, 5)

The doctrine of the Trinity seems on the face of it to be logically incoherent. It seems to imply that identity is not transitive – for the Father is identical with God, the Son is identical with God, and the Father is not identical with the Son. There have been two recent attempts by philosophers to defend the logical coherency of the doctrine. Richard Swinburne has suggested that the Father, the Son and the Holy Spirit be thought of as numerically distinct Gods, and he has argued that, properly understood, this suggestion is consistent with historical orthodoxy. Peter Geach and various others have suggested that a coherent statement of the doctrine is possible on the assumption that identity is 'always relative to a sortal term'. Swinburne's formulation of the doctrine of the Trinity is certainly free from logical incoherency, but it is debatable whether it is consistent with historical orthodoxy. As to 'relative identity' formulations of the doctrine, not all philosophers would agree that the idea that identity is always relative to a sortal term is even intelligible.

See also: IDENTITY; SUBSTANCE

PETER VAN INWAGEN

TRUST

Most people writing on trust accept the following claims: trust involves risk; trusters do not constantly monitor those they trust; trust enhances the effectiveness of agency; and trust and distrust are self-confirming. Three further claims are widely accepted: trust and distrust are contraries but not contradictories; trust cannot be willed; and trust has noninstrumental value. Accounts of trust divide into three families: risk-assessment accounts, which are indifferent to the reasons why one trusts; will-based accounts, which stress the importance of the motives of those who are trusted; and affective attitude accounts, which claim that trust is a feeling as well as a judgment and a disposition to act. One of the central questions concerns when trust is justified, and, in particular, whether justified trusting can outstrip evidence for the belief that the person trusted is trustworthy. If trust can leap ahead of evidence of trustworthiness, then trust poses a problem for evidentialism, or the view that one should never believe anything without sufficient evidence. Further central questions include whether trusting is a virtue and trustworthiness morally required, while a final set of questions concerns the role of trust in politics and the connection between interpersonal trust and trust in institutions.

See also: PROFESSIONAL ETHICS; PROMISING; SOLIDARITY; TRUTHFULNESS

KAREN JONES

TRUTH AND MEANING
See MEANING AND TRUTH

TRUTH BY CONVENTION
See CONVENTIONALISM; NECESSARY TRUTH AND CONVENTION

TRUTH CONDITIONS
See MEANING AND TRUTH

TRUTH, COHERENCE THEORY OF

The term 'coherence' in the phrase 'coherence theory of truth' has never been very precisely defined. The most we can say by way of a general definition is that a set of two or more beliefs are said to cohere if they 'fit' together or 'agree' with one another. Typically, then, a coherence theory of truth would claim that the beliefs of a given individual are true to the extent that the set of all their beliefs is coherent. Such theories, thus, make truth a matter of a truth bearer's relations to other truth bearers rather than its relations to reality. This latter implication is the chief hindrance to plausibility faced by coherence theories, and most coherence theorists try to escape the problem by denying that there is any extra-mental reality.

See also: MEANING AND TRUTH; TRUTH, DEFLATIONARY THEORIES OF; TRUTH, PRAGMATIC THEORY OF

RICHARD L. KIRKHAM

TRUTH, CORRESPONDENCE THEORY OF

The two oldest theories of truth in Western philosophy, those of Plato and Aristotle, are both correspondence theories. And if the non-philosopher can be said to subscribe to a theory of truth, it would most likely be to a correspondence theory; so called because such theories are often summed up with the slogans 'truth is correspondence with the facts' or 'truth is agreement with reality'. Aristotle puts it thus: 'to say that [either] that which is is *not* or that which is not *is*, is a falsehood; and to say that that which is is and that which is not is not, is true'. In epistemology, such theories offer an analysis of that at which, supposedly, investigation aims: truth. But correspondence theories are also now thought to play important roles in philosophical semantics and in the physicalist programme, which is the task of reducing all non-physical concepts to the concepts of logic, mathematics, and physics.

See also: MEANING AND TRUTH; REALISM AND ANTIREALISM; TRUTH, COHERENCE THEORY OF; TRUTH, DEFLATIONARY THEORIES OF; TRUTH, PRAGMATIC THEORY OF

RICHARD L. KIRKHAM

TRUTH, DEFLATIONARY THEORIES OF

So-called deflationary theories of truth, of which the best known are the redundancy, performative and prosentential theories, are really theories of truth *ascriptions*. This is because they are not theories of what truth *is*; rather, they are theories of what we are saying when we make utterances like '"Routledge editors are fine folks" is true'. The surface grammar of such utterances suggests that we use them to predicate a property, truth, of sentences or propositions; but the several deflationary theories all deny this. Indeed, they all endorse the deflationary thesis that there is no such property as truth and thus there is no need for, or sense to, a theory of truth distinct from a theory of truth ascriptions. Thus, for deflationists, the classical theories of truth, such as correspondence, coherence and pragmatic, are not wrong. They are something worse: they are wrong-

headed from the start, for they are attempting to analyse something which simply *is not there*.

See also: JUSTIFICATION, EPISTEMIC; MEANING AND TRUTH; TRUTH, COHERENCE THEORY OF; TRUTH, CORRESPONDENCE THEORY OF; TRUTH, PRAGMATIC THEORY OF

RICHARD L. KIRKHAM

TRUTH, PRAGMATIC THEORY OF

Two distinctly different kinds of theories parade under the banner of the 'pragmatic theory of truth'. First, there is the consensus theory of C.S. Peirce, according to which a true proposition is one which would be endorsed unanimously by all persons who had had sufficient relevant experiences to judge it. Second, there is the instrumentalist theory associated with William James, John Dewey, and F.C.S. Schiller, according to which a proposition counts as true if and only if behaviour based on a belief in the proposition leads, in the long run and all things considered, to beneficial results for the believers. (Peirce renamed his theory 'pragmaticism' when his original term 'pragmatism' was appropriated by the instrumentalists.) Unless they are married to some form of ontological anti-realism, which they usually are, both theories imply that the facts of the matter are not relevant to the truth-value of the proposition.

See also: MEANING AND TRUTH; PRAGMATISM; REALISM AND ANTIREALISM; TRUTH, COHERENCE THEORY OF; TRUTH, CORRESPONDENCE THEORY OF; TRUTH, DEFLATIONARY THEORIES OF

RICHARD L. KIRKHAM

TRUTH-CONDITIONAL SEMANTICS
See MEANING AND TRUTH

TRUTHFULNESS

Humans are the only species capable of speech and thus of lies. Choices regarding truthfulness and deceit are woven into all that they say and do. From childhood on, everyone knows the experience of being deceived and of deceiving others, of doubting someone's word and of being thought a liar. Throughout life, no moral choice is more common than that of whether to speak truthfully, equivocate, or lie – whether to flatter, get out of trouble, retaliate, or gain some advantage.

All societies, as well as all major moral, religious and legal traditions have condemned forms of deceit such as bearing false witness; but many have also held that deceit can be excusable or even mandated under certain circumstances, as, for instance, to deflect enemies in war or criminals bent on doing violence to innocent victims. Opinions diverge about such cases, however, as well as about many common choices about truthfulness and deceit. How open should spouses be to one another about adultery, for example, or physicians to dying patients? These are quandaries familiar since antiquity. Others, such as those involving the backdating of computerized documents, false claims on résumés in applying for work, or misrepresenting one's HIV-positive status to sexual partners, present themselves in new garb.

Hard choices involving truthfulness and lying inevitably raise certain underlying questions. How should truthfulness be defined? Is lying ever morally justified, and if so under what conditions? How should one deal with borderline cases between truthfulness and clear-cut falsehood, and between more and less egregious forms of deceit? And how do attitudes towards truthfulness relate to personal integrity and character? The rich philosophical debate of these issues has focused on issues of definition, justification, and line-drawing, and on their relevance to practical moral choice.

See also: SELF-DECEPTION, ETHICS OF; TRUST; VIRTUES AND VICES

SISSELA BOK

TULLY
See CICERO

TURING, ALAN MATHISON (1912–54)

Alan Turing was a mathematical logician who made fundamental contributions to the theory of computation. He developed the concept of an abstract computing device (a 'Turing machine') which precisely characterizes the concept of computation, and provided the basis for the practical development of electronic digital computers beginning in the 1940s. He demonstrated both the scope and limitations of computation, proving that some mathematical functions are not computable in principle by such machines.

Turing believed that human behaviour might be understood in terms of computation, and his views inspired contemporary computational theories of mind. He proposed a comparative test for machine intelligence, the 'Turing test', in which a human interrogator tries to distinguish a computer from a human by interacting with them only over a teletypewriter. Although the validity of the Turing test is controversial, the test and modifications of it remain influential measures for evaluating artificial intelligence.

JAMES H. MOOR

TURING MACHINES

Turing machines are abstract computing devices, named after Alan Mathison Turing. A Turing machine operates on a potentially infinite tape uniformly divided into squares, and is capable of entering only a finite number of distinct internal configurations. Each square may contain a symbol from a finite alphabet. The machine can scan one square at a time and perform, depending on the content of the scanned square and its own internal configuration, one of the following operations: print or erase a symbol on the scanned square or move on to scan either one of the immediately adjacent squares. These elementary operations are possibly accompanied by a change of internal configuration. Turing argued that the class of functions calculable by means of an algorithmic procedure (a mechanical, stepwise, deterministic procedure) is to be identified with the class of functions computable by Turing machines. The epistemological significance of Turing machines and related mathematical results hinges upon this identification, which later became known as Turing's thesis; an equivalent claim, Church's thesis, had been advanced independently by Alonzo Church. Most crucially, mathematical results stating that certain functions cannot be computed by any Turing machine are interpreted, by Turing's thesis, as establishing absolute limitations of computing agents.

GUGLIELMO TAMBURRINI

TYPES, THEORY OF
See THEORY OF TYPES

TYPE/TOKEN DISTINCTION

The type/token distinction is related to that between universals and particulars. C.S. Peirce introduced the terms 'type' and 'token', and illustrated the distinction by pointing to two senses of 'word': in one, there is only one word 'the' in the English language; in the other, there are numerous words 'the' on the physical page you are now looking at. The latter are spatiotemporal objects composed of ink; they are said to be word tokens of the former, which is said to be the word type and is abstract. Phonemes, letters and sentences also come in types and tokens.

See also: ABSTRACT OBJECTS; UNIVERSALS

LINDA WETZEL

U

UNCONSCIOUS MENTAL STATES

Unconscious phenomena are those mental phenomena which their possessor cannot introspect, not only at the moment at which the phenomenon occurs, but even when prompted ('Do you think/ want/ . . . ?'). There are abundant allusions to many kinds of unconscious phenomena from classical times to Freud. Most notably, Plato in his *Meno* defended a doctrine of *anamnesis* according to which a priori knowledge of, for example, geometry is 'recollected' from a previous life. But the notion of a rich, unconscious mental life really takes hold in nineteenth-century writers such as Herder, Hegel, Helmholtz and Schopenhauer. It is partly out of this latter tradition that Freud's famous postulations of unconscious, 'repressed' desires and memories emerged.

Partly in reaction to the excesses of introspection and partly because of the rise of computational models of mental processes, twentieth-century psychology has often been tempted by Lashley's view that 'no activity of mind is ever conscious'. A wide range of recent experiments do suggest that people can be unaware of a multitude of sensory cognitive factors (for example, pupillary dilation, cognitive dissonance, subliminal cues to problem-solving) that demonstrably affect their behaviour. And Weiskrantz has documented cases of 'blindsight' in which patients with damage to their visual cortex can be shown to be sensitive to visual material they sincerely claim they cannot see.

The most controversial cases of unconscious phenomena are those which the agent could not possibly introspect, even in principle. Chomsky ascribes unconscious knowledge of quite abstract principles of grammar to adults and even newborn children that only a linguist could infer.

Many philosophers have found these claims about the unconscious unconvincing, even incoherent. However, they need to show how the evidence cited above could be otherwise explained, and why appeals to the unconscious have seemed so perfectly intelligible throughout history.
See also: CONSCIOUSNESS; PSYCHOANALYSIS, METHODOLOGICAL ISSUES IN

GEORGES REY

UNDERDETERMINATION

The term underdetermination refers to a broad family of arguments about the relations between theory and evidence. All share the conclusion that evidence is more or less impotent to guide choice between rival theories or hypotheses. In one or other of its guises, underdetermination has probably been the most potent and most pervasive idea driving twentieth-century forms of scepticism and epistemological relativism. It figures prominently in the writing of diverse influential philosophers. It is a complex family of doctrines, each with a different argumentative structure. Most, however, suppose that only the logical consequences of an hypothesis are relevant to its empirical support. This supposition can be challenged.
See also: CONFIRMATION THEORY; CRUCIAL EXPERIMENTS; INDUCTIVE INFERENCE; SCIENTIFIC METHOD

LARRY LAUDAN

UNITY OF SCIENCE

How should our scientific knowledge be organized? Is scientific knowledge unified and, if so, does it mirror a unity of the world as a whole? Or is it merely a matter of simplicity and economy of thought? Either way, what sort of unity is it? If the world can be decomposed into elementary constituents, must our knowledge be in some way reducible to, or even replaced by, the concepts and theories describing such constituents? Can economics be reduced to microphysics, as Einstein claimed? Can sociology be derived from molecular genetics? Might the sciences be unified in the sense of all following the same method, whether or not they are all ultimately reducible to physics? Considerations of the unity problem begin at least with Greek cosmology and the question of the one and the many. In the late twentieth century the increasing tendency is to argue for the disunity of science and to deny reducibility to physics.

JORDI CAT

UNIVERSALISM IN ETHICS

The claim that ethical standards or principles are universal is an ancient commonplace of many ethical traditions and of contemporary political life, particularly in appeals to universal human rights. Yet it remains controversial. There are many sources of controversy. Universalism in ethics may be identified with claims about the form, scope or content of ethical principles, or with the very idea that ethical judgment appeals to principles, rather than to particular cases. Or it may be identified with various claims to identify a single fundamental universal principle, from which all other ethical principles and judgments derive. These disagreements can be clarified, and perhaps in part resolved, by distinguishing a number of different conceptions of universalism in ethics.

See also: CRITICAL THEORY; INTUITIONISM IN ETHICS

ONORA O'NEILL

UNIVERSALS

Introduction

In metaphysics, the term 'universals' is applied to things of two sorts: properties (such as redness or roundness), and relations (such as kinship relations like sisterhood, or the causal relation, or spatial and temporal relations). Universals are to be understood by contrast with particulars. Few universals, if any, are truly 'universal' in the sense that they are shared by all individuals – a universal is characteristically the sort of thing which some individuals may have in common, and others may lack.

Universals have been conceived to be things which enable us intellectually to grasp a permanent, underlying order behind the changing flux of experience. Some of the gods of ancient mythologies correspond roughly to various important underlying universals – social relations for instance, as for example if Hera is said to be the goddess of Marriage and Ares (or Mars) is said to be the god of War. Many traditions, East and West, have dealt

with the underlying problem which generates theories of universals; nevertheless the term 'universals' is closely tied to the Western tradition, and the agenda has been set largely by the work of Plato and Aristotle.

The term often used in connection with Plato is not 'universals' but 'Forms' (or 'Ideas', used in the sense of ideals rather than of thoughts), the term 'universals' echoing Aristotle more than Plato. Other terms cognate with universals include not only properties and relations, but also qualities, attributes, characteristics, essences and accidents (in the sense of qualities which a thing has not of necessity but only by accident), species and genus, and natural kinds.

Various arguments have been advanced to establish the existence of universals, the most memorable of which is the 'one over many' argument. There are also various arguments against the existence of universals. There are, for instance, various vicious regress arguments which derive from Aristotle's so-called 'third man argument' against Plato. Another family of arguments trades on what is called Ockham's razor: it is argued that we can say anything we need to say, and explain everything we need to explain, without appeal to universals; and if we can, and if we are rational, then we should. Those who believe in universals are called Realists, those who do not are called Nominalists.

1 Sources in ancient mathematics and biology
2 Samenesses and differences
3 Arguments for and against
4 Nominalism and Realism
5 Frege exhumes universals

1 Sources in ancient mathematics and biology

Plato looked to mathematics as a model to find ideal 'Forms' which can be grasped by the intellect and which we find to be imperfectly reflected in the world of the senses. Moral and political ideals too, Plato thought, are reflected only very imperfectly in the world of appearances. Aristotle's conception of universals was tailored to fit not mathematics but biology. Individual animals and plants fall into natural kinds, or species, such as pigs or cabbages. Various different species, in turn, fall under a genus.

Universals impose a taxonomy on the plurality of different individuals in the world. Regularities in the world can then be understood by appeal to the universals, or species, under which individuals fall, explaining why pigs never give birth to kittens, for instance, and in general why each living thing generates others of its kind.

Plato conceived of universals as transcendent beings, *ante rem* in Latin ('before things'): the existence of universals does not depend on the existence of individuals which instantiated them. This is a natural thought if your model of universals lies in mathematics: geometrical truths about circles, for instance, do not depend on the existence of any individuals which really are perfectly circular. Aristotle, in contrast, held a theory of universals as immanent beings, *in rebus* ('in things'): there can be no universals unless there are individuals in which those universals are instantiated. This is a natural thought if your model of universals lies in biology: a species cannot exist, for instance, if there are no animals of that species. Thus, one of the key distinctions between Plato's transcendent and Aristotle's immanent realism is that the Platonist allows, and Aristotle does not allow, the existence of uninstantiated universals (see ARISTOTLE §15; PLATO).

2 Samenesses and differences

When a property is shared by two individuals, there is something which is in or is had by both. But it is in a quite distinctive sense that one universal can be 'in' two distinct individuals. An individual person may be 'in' two places at once if, for instance, their hand is in the cookie jar and their foot is in the bath. But a universal is 'in' distinct individuals in a way which does not mean that there is one part of the universal in one thing and a distinct part of it in another. Thus, a universal is said to be the sort of thing which can be wholly present in distinct individuals at the same time: a person cannot be wholly present in two places at once, but justice can.

Some draw a distinction between certain special properties and relations which qualify for the label 'universals', and other properties and relations which do not. It is suggested that, whenever something is true of an individual (whenever a description can truly be predicated of an individual), then there is always a 'property' which that individual may be said to have. On this view, a 'property' is just a shadow of a predicate, whereas a genuine universal is something more. A genuine universal has to be something which is literally identical in each of its instances. Alternatively, the sorts of 'properties' which are just shadows of predicates are sometimes construed as set-theoretical constructions of various sorts, as for instance if we say that the 'property' of redness is the set of actual red things, or of actual and possible red things. In this spirit it is now standard practice in mathematics to use the term 'relations' to refer just

to any set of ordered pairs. Set-theoretical constructions are not, however, universals – or at least they are not to be confused with the universals which are the subject matter of traditional debates.

3 Arguments for and against

Various arguments have been advanced to establish the existence of universals, the most memorable of which is the 'one over many' argument. Although it is memorable, there is little consensus on just how this argument works. Very roughly, it begins with an appeal to the manifest fact of recurrence, the fact that, as it says in the biblical text of *Ecclesiastes* (1: 9), 'What has been is what will be, and what has been done is what will be done; and there is nothing new under the sun'. There are many things, and yet they are all in some sense just the very same things over and over again. From this manifest fact of recurrence, the argument purports to derive the conclusion that there are universals as well as particulars.

There are also various arguments against the existence of universals. One family of such arguments derives from Aristotle's so-called 'third man argument' and is designed to demonstrate that Plato's theory of Forms entails an unacceptable infinite regress. Roughly, Plato's problem is that he needs some relation to hold between the Form of Man and individual men before this Form can help to explain what it is that individual men have in common. So the theory would seem to call into being another Form, a third man, which is what the Form of Man has in common with individual men. This leads to an infinite regress, hence Plato's theory of Forms is unacceptable. Of course, Aristotle had only intended to demonstrate the non-existence of Plato's Forms, not of universals in general; but enemies of universals frequently advance related infinite-regress arguments against the existence of universals of any kind. Whatever you call the instantiation relation between particulars and universals, if you think of it as another universal then you are off on a regress, and this seems to count against any theory of universals.

Another argument against the existence of universals trades on what is called 'Ockham's razor' – the principle that you should not postulate more entities when everything you want to explain can be explained using fewer (see WILLIAM OF OCKHAM). It is sometimes argued that everything you can explain with universals can be explained just as well without them. Things which superficially seem to refer to universals can, it is maintained, generally be rephrased in ways which make no apparent reference to universals – reference to universals can be paraphrased away. If we can do without universals, then obviously we should; when you supplement this Ockhamist argument with allusions to the interminable and unresolvable internecine conflicts among Realists over numerous details, you have an even stronger case against the existence of universals.

4   Nominalism and Realism

During the Middle Ages in Europe, universals played a focal role in the intellectual economy: many issues revolved around what became known as the problem of universals. Famously, a commentary by BOETHIUS on Porphyry's *Isagoge*, which in turn was intended as an introduction to Aristotle's Categories, set very crisply but vividly and tantalizingly what came to be taken as a compulsory question in the medieval pursuit of learning: whether genera and species are substances or are set in the mind alone; whether they are corporeal or incorporeal substances; and whether they are separate from the things perceived by the senses or set in them (Boethius *c*.510; Spade 1994). The initial problem for many was not one of deciding whether there are any universals, but of choosing between Plato and Aristotle and then fine-tuning further details.

Later in the Middle Ages, however, a growing number of philosophers and theologians became more and more impressed by arguments against the existence of universals. They began to adopt the position called 'Nominalism' which was opposed to all the various forms of Platonic or Aristotelian Realism. According to Nominalists like ABELARD and Ockham, the only thing which distinct individuals share is a common name, a label which we choose to apply to each of those individuals and not to others.

Nominalistic claims were echoed by many of the champions of the modern sciences as they emerged at the end of the Middle Ages. It was standardly said to be granted on all hands that all existing things are merely particular. Being assumed as granted on all hands, it was not up for debate, and so the problem of universals, explicitly so described, settled into the shadowy background of scientific and philosophical discussion. For example, an archaeologist of ideas might argue that, in Kant, the problem of universals is really alive and working very hard in the background, playing a role in discussions on almost every topic that arises. Nonetheless the problem of universals, under that name or any clear equivalent, is not featured on Kant's explicit agenda. Kant speaks of intuitions and concepts in ways which have some relation to the old problem of particulars and universals, but more has shifted than just the labels. Hence the problem of universals has received

little attention across a great span of philosophical history, right through to twentieth-century philosophy in France and Germany (see NOMINALISM; REALISM AND ANTIREALISM).

5   Frege exhumes universals

In the twentieth century, the problem of universals has re-emerged under its familiar name, accompanied by more or less the same guiding illustrations used by Plato and Aristotle. This rebirth has occurred in the tradition of analytic philosophy, notably in the work of FREGE, RUSSELL, WITTGENSTEIN, QUINE and Armstrong.

A new twist to the theory of universals can be traced to groundbreaking work by Frege on the nature of natural numbers in his *Die Grundlagen der Arithmetik* (The Foundations of Arithmetic) (1884). As for Plato, so too for Frege, Russell and others in recent times, advances in mathematics have been the source of a philosophical focus on the problem of universals. Frege's analysis of natural numbers $(1, 2, 3, \ldots)$ proceeded in three very different stages (see FREGE, G. §9).

In the first stage of his analysis of numbers, Frege introduced the idea that numbering individuals essentially involves not the attribution of properties to individuals but, rather, the attribution of properties to properties. To illustrate: when asked 'How many are on the table?', Frege notes that there will be many different possible answers, as for instance (1) 'Two packs of playing cards' or (2) '104 playing cards'. The metaphysical truth-makers identified by Frege for these two sample answers are (1) that the property of being a pack of playing cards on the table is a property which has the property of having two instances, and (2) that the property of being a playing card on the table is a property which has the property of having one hundred and four instances. In general, natural numbers number individuals only via the intermediary of contributing to second-order properties, or properties of properties, namely properties of the form 'having *n* instances'. Like Kant, Frege speaks of concepts (*Begriffe*) rather than of 'universals'. Yet Frege's concepts are definitely not private mental episodes, but are thoroughly mind-independent, more like Plato's Forms than Aristotelian universals.

In the second stage of his analysis of numbers, Frege gives a very new twist to the theory of universals. He argues that the nature of universals, or concepts, is such as to make it impossible in principle ever to refer to a universal by any name or description. Thus for instance, in saying 'Socrates is wise', the universal which is instantiated by Socrates is something which is expressed by the whole arrangement of symbols into which the name

'Socrates' is embedded to yield the sentence 'Socrates is wise'. Suppose you were to try to name this universal by the name 'wisdom'. Then, compare 'Socrates is wise' with the concatenation of names – 'Socrates wisdom'. The mere name 'wisdom' clearly leaves out something which was present in the attribution of wisdom to Socrates. Hence a universal cannot be referred to by a name.

Thus, a property can only be expressed by a predicate, never by a name or by any logical device which refers to individuals. Indeed, if we wish to attribute existence to universals, we cannot do so by the use of the same sort of device (the first-order quantifier) as that used to attribute existence to individuals. Thus, for instance, from 'Socrates is wise' we may infer 'There exists something which is wise', and 'There exists something which is Socrates':

$$(\exists x)(\text{wise}(x)), \text{ and}$$
$$(\exists x)(x = \text{Socrates}).$$

Yet we may not infer that 'There exists something which Socrates possesses', or that 'There exists something which is wisdom':

$$(\exists x)(\text{has}(\text{Socrates}, x)), \text{ or}$$
$$(\exists x)(x = \text{wisdom}).$$

Frege does, however, allow us to attribute existence to universals, using logical devices called higher-order quantifiers, which he introduced in his *Begriffsschrift* (1879). That is, we can infer from 'Socrates is wise' to 'There is somehow such that: Socrates is that-how':

$$(\text{E}f)(f(\text{Socrates})).$$

But although there is somehow that Socrates is, this does not entail that there is anything which is the somehow that Socrates is: universals (concepts) can only have second-order existence, not first-order existence.

For Frege, numbering things essentially involved attribution of properties to properties. So the sorts of things being attributed are not the sorts of things which can be named. Yet, Frege argued, numbers can be named – numbers are abstract individuals, he says, objects not concepts. Hence the third stage of Frege's analysis of numbers consists in the attempt to find individuals – objects – which could be identified with the numbers. It was this stage of the analysis which resulted in the emergence of modern set theory. For every property, Frege argued, there is a corresponding individual: the extension of that universal, the set of all the things (or all the actual and possible things) which

instantiate that universal. Thus, for instance, corresponding to the property of being a property which has two instances, there will be a set of sets which have two members. Modern mathematics has selected different candidates for identification with the natural numbers, but it has followed Frege hook, line and sinker with respect to the broad strategy of identifying numbers, and functions and relations, with sets.

Frege's legacy has significantly changed the agenda for any theory of universals which, like Plato's, aspires to do justice to mathematics. It leaves three courses open for exploration. One course is that charted by Quine, of allowing the existence of sets but not of any other nameable things which might be called universals, nor of any of Frege's higher-order, unnameable universals. Another course is that of allowing the existence of nameable things other than sets: this is a course charted, for example, by Armstrong (1978). A third course allows also the irreducible significance of higher-order quantification.

See also: ABSTRACT OBJECTS

References and further reading

Armstrong, D.M. (1978) *Universals and Scientific Realism*, London: Cambridge University Press, 2 vols. (A groundbreaking resuscitation of a broadly Aristotelian realism about universals as extra 'objects' in Frege's sense.)

Spade, P.V. (trans. and ed.) (1994) *Five Texts on the Medieval Problem of Universals*, Indianapolis, IN: Hackett. (Great works from the heyday of the problem of universals, including those mentioned at the beginning of §4; requires no formal logic, but both historically and conceptually difficult.)

JOHN C. BIGELOW

USE/MENTION DISTINCTION AND QUOTATION

Speakers 'use' the expressions they utter and 'mention' the individuals they talk about. Connected with the roles of used expressions and mentioned individuals is a way of uniting them and a characteristic mistake involving them. Usually the expression used in an utterance will not be the same as the individual mentioned, but the two can be made to converge. The means is quotation. Quotation is a special usage in which an expression is used to mention itself. A failure to distinguish between the roles of used expressions and mentioned individuals can lead to mistakes. Such mistakes are called use/mention confusions. In themselves use/mention confusions are a minor linguistic *faux pas*, but under unfavourable conditions, they have the potential to cause greater problems.

See also: DE RE/DE DICTO

COREY WASHINGTON

UTILITARIANISM

Introduction

Utilitarianism is a theory about rightness, according to which the only good thing is welfare (wellbeing or 'utility'). Welfare should, in some way, be maximized, and agents are to be neutral between their own welfare, and that of other people and of other sentient beings.

The roots of utilitarianism lie in ancient thought. Traditionally, welfare has been seen as the greatest balance of pleasure over pain, a view discussed in Plato. The notion of impartiality also has its roots in Plato, as well as in Stoicism and Christianity. In the modern period, utilitarianism grew out of the Enlightenment, its two major proponents being Jeremy Bentham and John Stuart Mill.

Hedonists, believing that pleasure is the good, have long been criticized for sensualism, a charge Mill attempted to answer with a distinction between higher and lower pleasures. He contended that welfare consists in the experiencing of pleasurable mental states, suggesting, in contrast to Bentham, that the quality, not simply the amount, of a pleasure is what matters. Others have doubted this conception, and developed desire accounts, according to which welfare lies in the satisfaction of desire. Ideal theorists suggest that certain things are just good or bad for people, independently of pleasure and desire.

Utilitarianism has usually focused on actions. The most common form is act-utilitarianism, according to which what makes an action right is its maximizing total or average utility. Some, however, have argued that constantly attempting to put utilitarianism into practice could be self-defeating, in that utility would not be maximized by so doing. Many utilitarians have therefore advocated non-utilitarian decision procedures, often based on common-sense morality. Some have felt the appeal of common sense moral principles in themselves, and sought to reconcile utilitarianism with them. According to rule-utilitarianism, the right action is that which is consistent with those rules which would maximize utility if all accepted them.

There have been many arguments for utilitarianism, the most common being an appeal to reflective belief or 'intuition'. One of the most interesting is

Henry Sidgwick's argument, which is ultimately intuitionist, and results from sustained reflection on common sense morality. The most famous argument is Mill's 'proof'. In recent times, R.M. Hare has offered a logical argument for utilitarianism.

The main problems for utilitarianism emerge out of its conflict with common sense morality, in particular justice, and its impartial conception of practical reasoning.

1   Introduction and history

Defining utilitarianism is difficult, partly because of its many variations and complexities, but also because the utilitarian tradition has always seen itself as a broad church. But before offering a history, we must supply a working definition. First, utilitarianism is, usually, a version of *welfarism*, the view that the only good is welfare (see WELFARE). Second, it assumes that we can compare welfare across different people's lives (see ECONOMICS AND ETHICS). Third, it is a version of consequentialism (see CONSEQUENTIALISM). Consequentialists advocate the impartial maximization of certain values, which might include, say, equality. Utilitarianism is welfarist consequentialism, in its classical form, for instance, requiring that any action produce the greatest happiness (see HAPPINESS).

The concern with welfare, its measurement and its maximization is found early, in Plato's *Protagoras*. In the process of attempting to prove that all virtues are one, Socrates advocates hedonism, the welfarist view that only pleasurable states of mind are valuable, and that they are valuable solely because of their pleasurableness (see PLATO §9; SOCRATES; HEDONISM).

The debate in the *Protagoras* is just one example of the many discussions of welfare in ancient ethics (see EUDAIMONIA). Some have seen Greek ethics as primarily egoistic, addressing the question of what each individual should do to further their own welfare (see EGOISM AND ALTRUISM §4). Utilitarianism, however, is impartial.

The Stoics, who followed Plato and Aristotle, began to develop a notion of impartiality according to which self-concern extended rationally to others, and eventually to the whole world (see STOICISM). This doctrine, allied to Christian conceptions of self-sacrifice, and conceptions of rationality with roots in Plato which emphasize the objective supra-individual point of view, could plausibly be said to be the source of utilitarian impartiality (see IMPARTIALITY).

In the modern period, the history of utilitarianism takes up again during the Enlightenment. The idea of impartial maximization is found in the work of the eighteenth-century Scottish philosopher Francis HUTCHESON. The work of his contemporary, David Hume, also stressed the importance to ethics of the notion of 'utility' (see HUME, D. §4). A little later, the so-called 'theological utilitarians', Joseph Priestley and William PALEY, argued that God requires us to promote the greatest happiness. Meanwhile, in France, Claude Helvétius advocated utilitarianism as a political theory, according to which the task of governments is to produce happiness for the people. He influenced one of the most extreme of all utilitarians, William Godwin.

It was Jeremy BENTHAM, however, who did most to systematize utilitarianism. Bentham's disciple, J.S. MILL, was the next great utilitarian, and he was followed by Henry SIDGWICK. G.E. MOORE distanced himself from Mill's hedonism, and offered an influential 'ideal' account of the good. One of the most important recent versions of utilitarianism is that of R.M. Hare.

2 Conceptions of utility

Before you can maximize utility, you need to know what utility is. It is essential to note that the plausibility of utilitarianism as a theory of right action does not depend on any particular conception of welfare. An account of the good for a person is different from an account of right action (see RIGHT AND GOOD).

Utilitarians have held many different views of utility. The 'classical' utilitarians – primarily Bentham and Mill – were hedonists. There are many objections to hedonism. What about masochists, for example, who seem to find pain desirable? Well, perhaps pain can be pleasurable. But is there really something common – pleasure – to all the experiences that go to make up a happy life? And would it be rational to plug oneself into a machine that gave one vast numbers of pleasurable sensations? Here there may be a move towards the more eclectic view of Sidgwick, that utility consists in desirable consciousness of any kind. Some philosophers, however, such as Nietzsche, have suggested that a life of mere enjoyment is inauthentic.

Hedonists have been criticized for sensualism. For millennia J.S. Mill sought to answer the charge, suggesting that hedonists do not have to accept that all pleasurable experiences – drinking lemonade and reading Wordsworth – are on a par, to be valued only according to the *amount* of pleasure they contain. Bentham and others had suggested that the value of a pleasure depends mainly on its intensity and its duration, but Mill insisted that the *quality* of a pleasure – its nature – also influences its pleasurableness, and hence its value. But why must the effect on value of the nature of an experience be filtered through pleasurableness? Why cannot its nature by itself add value?

Perhaps the most serious objection to any theory that welfare consists in mental states is the so-called 'experience machine'. This machine is better than the pleasure machine, and can give you the most desirable experiences you can imagine. Would it be best for you to be wired up to it throughout your life? Note that this is not the question whether it would be *right* to arrange for yourself to be wired up, leaving all your obligations in the real world unfulfilled. Even a utilitarian can argue that that would be immoral.

Some people think it makes sense to plug in, others that it would be a kind of death. If you are one of the latter, then you might consider moving to a desire theory of utility, according to which what makes life good for you is your desires being maximally fulfilled. On the experience machine, many of your desires will remain unfulfilled. You want not just the experience of, say, bringing about world peace, but actually to bring it about. Desire theories have come to dominate contemporary thought because of economists' liking for the notion of 'revealed preferences' (see RATIONALITY, PRACTICAL). Pleasures and pains are hard to get at or measure, whereas people's preferences can be stated, and inferred objectively from their behaviour.

A simple desire theory fails immediately. I desire the glass of liquid, thinking it to be whisky. In fact it is poison, so satisfying my desire will not make me better off. What desire theorists should say here is that it is the satisfaction of intrinsic desires which counts for wellbeing. My intrinsic desire is for pleasure, the desire for the drink being merely derived.

The usual strategy adopted by desire theorists is to build constraints into the theory in response to such counterexamples: what makes me better off is not the fulfilment of my desires, but of my informed desires.

But why do desire theorists so respond to such counterexamples? It is probably because they already have a view of utility which guides them in the construction of their theories. This means that desire theories are themselves idle, which is to be expected once we realize that the fulfilment of a desire is in itself neither good nor bad for a person. What matters is whether what the person desires, and gets, is good or bad.

For reasons such as this, there is now a return to ancient *ideal* theories of utility, according to which certain things are good or bad for beings, independently in at least some cases of whether they are desired or whether they give rise to pleasurable experiences. Another interesting ancient view which has recently been revived is that certain non-hedonistic goods are valuable, but only when they are combined with pleasure or desire-fulfilment (see Plato, *Philebus* 21a–22b). The non-hedonistic goods suggested include knowledge and friendship. Questions to ask of the ideal theorist include the following. What will go on your list of goods? How do you decide? How are the various items to be balanced?

3 Types of utilitarianism

Theories of right and wrong have to be about something, that is, have to have a focus. Usually, at least in recent centuries, they have focused on actions, attempting to answer the questions, 'Which actions are right?', and 'What makes those actions right?' The ancients also asked these questions, but were concerned to focus on lives, characters, dispositions and virtues. Nearly all forms of utilitarianism have focused on actions, but in recent decades there has been some interest in utilitarianism as applied to motives, virtues and lives as a whole.

Utilitarianism is a form of consequentialism. But it is important to note that, since utilitarians can attach intrinsic moral importance to acts (especially, of course, to the act of maximizing itself), there are problems in attempting to capture the nature of utilitarianism using the act/consequence distinction. A recent alternative has been to employ the 'agent-neutral'/'agent-relative' distinction. Agent-neutral theories give every agent the same aim (for example, that utility be maximized), whereas agent-relative theories give agents different aims (say, that *your* children be looked after). Logically, however, there is nothing to prevent a utilitarian from insisting that *your* aim should be that *you* maximize utility. Though this theory would be practically equivalent to an agent-neutral theory, its possibility suggests there may be problems with attempting to use the agent-neutral/agent-relative distinction to capture the essence of utilitarianism.

What clearly distinguishes utilitarianism from other moral theories is what it requires and why, so we should now turn to that. The commonest, and most straightforward, version of utilitarianism is *act-utilitarianism*, according to which the criterion of an action's rightness is that it maximize utility.

Act-utilitarians might offer two accounts of rightness. The objectively right action would be that which actually does maximize utility, while the subjectively right action would be that which maximizes expected utility. Agents would usually be blamed for not doing what was subjectively right.

Another distinction is between *total* and *average* forms. According to the total view, the right act is the one that produces the largest overall total of utility. The average view says that the right action is that which maximizes the average level of utility in a population. These theories are inconsistent only in cases in which the size of a population is under consideration. The most common such case occurs when one is thinking of having a child. Here, the average view has the absurd conclusion that I should not have a child, even if its life will be wonderful and there will be no detrimental effects from its existence, if its welfare will be lower than the existing average.

But the total view also runs into problems, most famously with Derek Parfit's 'repugnant conclusion', which commits the total view to the notion that if a population of people with lives barely worth living is large enough it is preferable to a smaller population with very good lives. One way out of this problem is to adopt a *person-affecting* version of utilitarianism, which restricts itself in scope to existing people. But there are problems with this view. Recently, certain writers have suggested that one way to avoid the 'repugnant conclusion' would be to argue that there are *discontinuities* in value, such that once welfare drops below a certain level the loss cannot be compensated for by quantity. There is a link here with Mill's view of the relation of higher pleasures to lower.

Imagine being an act-utilitarian, brought up in an entirely act-utilitarian society. You will have to spend much time calculating the utility values of the various actions open to you. You are quite likely to make mistakes, and, being human, to cook the books in your own favour.

For these reasons, most act-utilitarians have argued that we should not attempt to put act-utilitarianism into practice wholesale, but stick by a lot of common sense morality. It will save a lot of valuable time, is based on long experience, and will keep us on the straight and narrow. Act-utilitarians who recommend sole and constant application of their theory as well as those who recommend that we never consult the theory and use common sense morality can both be called *single-level* theorists, since moral thinking will be carried on only at one level. Most utilitarians have adopted a *two-level* theory, according to which we consult utilitarianism only sometimes – in particular when the principles of ordinary morality conflict with one another.

The main problem with two-level views is their psychology. If I really accept utilitarianism, how can

I abide by a common sense morality I know to be a fiction? And if I really do take that common sense morality seriously, how can I just forget it when I am supposed to think as a utilitarian? The two-level response here must be that this is indeed a messy compromise, but one made to deal with a messy reality.

Act-utilitarianism is an extremely demanding theory, since it requires you to be entirely impartial between your own interests, the interests of those you love, and the interests of all. The usual example offered is famine relief. By giving up all your time, money and energy to famine relief, you will save many lives and prevent much suffering. Utilitarians often claim at this point that there are limits to human capabilities, and utilitarianism requires us only to do what we can. But the sense of 'can' here is quite obscure, since in any ordinary sense I can give up my job and spend my life campaigning for Oxfam.

The demandingness objection seems particularly serious when taken in the context of widespread non-compliance with the demands of act-utilitarian morality. Most people do little or nothing for the developing world, and this is why the moral demands on me are so great. An argument such as this has been used to advocate *rule-utilitarianism*, according to which the right action is that which is in accord with that set of rules which, if generally or universally accepted, would maximize utility. (The version of the theory which speaks of the rules that are *obeyed* is likely to collapse into act-utilitarianism.)

Unlike act-utilitarianism, which is a *direct* theory in that the rightness and wrongness of acts depends directly on whether they fit with the maximizing principle, rule-utilitarianism is an *indirect* theory, since rightness and wrongness depend on rules, the justification for which itself rests on the utilitarian principle.

The demandingness of act-utilitarianism has not been the main reason for adopting rule-utilitarianism. Rather, the latter theory has been thought to provide support for common sense moral principles, such as those speaking against killing or lying, which appear plausible in their own right.

Rule-utilitarianism has not received as much attention as act-utilitarianism, partly because it detaches itself from the attractiveness of maximization. According to rule-utilitarianism there may be times when the right action is to bring about less than the best possible world (such as when others are not complying). But if maximization is reasonable at the level of rules, why does it not apply straightforwardly to acts?

4 Arguments for utilitarianism

The most famous argument for utilitarianism is John Stuart Mill's 'proof'. This has three stages:

(1) Happiness is desirable.
(2) The general happiness is desirable.
(3) Nothing other than happiness is desirable.

Each stage has been subjected to much criticism, especially the first. Mill was an empiricist, who believed that matters of fact could be decided by appeal to the senses (see EMPIRICISM). In his proof, he attempted to ground evaluative claims on an analogous appeal to desires, making unfortunate rhetorical use of 'visible' and 'desirable'. The first stage suggests to the reader that if they consult their own desires, they will see that they find happiness desirable.

The second stage is little more than assertion, since Mill did not see the vastness of the difference between egoistic and universalistic hedonism (utilitarianism). In an important footnote (1861: ch. 5, para. 36), we see the assumption that lies behind the proof: the more happiness one can promote by a certain action, the stronger the reason to perform it. Egoists will deny this, but it does put the ball back in their court.

The final stage again rests on introspection, the claim being that we desire, ultimately, only pleasurable states. Thus even a desire for virtue can be seen as a desire for happiness, since what we desire is the pleasure of acting virtuously or contemplating our virtue. One suspects that introspection by Mill's opponents would have had different results.

Perhaps the most common form of utilitarianism, as of any other moral theory, is, in a weak sense, intuitionist. To many, utilitarianism has just seemed, taken by itself, reasonable – so reasonable, indeed, that any attempt to prove it would probably rest on premises less secure than the conclusion. This view was expressed most powerfully by Henry Sidgwick. Sidgwick supported his argument with a painstaking analysis of common sense morality. Sidgwick also believed that egoism was supported by intuition, so that practical reason was ultimately divided (see EGOISM AND ALTRUISM §§1, 3).

In the twentieth century, R.M. Hare wished to avoid appeal to moral intuition, which he saw as irrational. According to Hare, if we are going to answer a moral question such as, 'What ought I to do?', we should first understand the logic of the words we are using. In the case of 'ought', we shall find that it has two properties: prescriptivity (it is action-guiding) and universalizability (I should be ready to assent to any moral judgment I make when it is applied to situations similar to the present one in their universal properties) (see PRESCRIPTIVISM). Hare argues that putting yourself in another's position properly – 'universalizing' – involves taking on board their preferences. Once this has been done, the only rational strategy is to maximize overall preference-satisfaction, which is equivalent to utilitarianism.

Hare's moral theory is one of the most sophisticated since Kant's, and he does indeed claim to incorporate elements of Kantianism into his theory (see KANTIAN ETHICS). Objectors have claimed, however, that, rather like Kant himself, Hare introduces 'intuitions' (that is, beliefs about morality or rationality) through the back door. For example, the logic of the word 'ought' may be said not to involve a commitment to the rationality of maximization even in one's own case.

5   Problems for utilitarianism

There are many technical problems with the various forms of utilitarianism. How are pleasure and pain to be measured? Which desires are to count? Is knowledge a good in itself? Should we take into account actual or probable effects on happiness? How do we characterize the possible world which is to guide us in our selection of rules? These are problems for the theorists themselves, and there has been a great deal said in attempts to resolve them.

More foundational, however, is a set of problems for any kind of utilitarian theory, emerging out of utilitarianism's peculiarly strict conception of impartiality. A famous utilitarian tag, from Bentham, is, 'Everybody to count for one, nobody for more than one'. This, however, as Mill implies (1861: ch. 5, para. 36), is slightly misleading. In a sense, according to utilitarianism, no one matters; all that matters is the level of utility. What are counted equally are not persons but pleasures or utilities.

This conception of impartiality has made it easy for opponents of utilitarianism to dream up examples in which utilitarianism seems to require something appalling. A famous such example requires a utilitarian sheriff to hang an innocent man, so as to prevent a riot and bring about the greatest overall happiness possible in the circumstances (see CRIME AND PUNISHMENT §2).

Utilitarians can here respond that, in practice, they believe that people should abide by common sense morality, that people should accept practical principles of rights for utilitarian reasons (see §2). But this misses the serious point in many of these objections: that it matters not just how much utility there is, but how it is shared around. Imagine, for example, a case in which you can give a bundle of resources either to someone who is well-off and rich through no fault of their own, or to someone who is poor through no fault of their own. If the utility of giving the bundle to the rich person is only slightly higher than that of giving it to the poor

person, utilitarianism dictates giving it to the rich person. But many (including some consequentialists) would argue that it is reasonable to give some priority to the worse-off.

These are problems at the level of the social distribution of utility. But difficulties arise also because of the fact that human agents each have their own lives to live, and engage in their practical reasoning from their own personal point of view rather than from the imaginary point of view of an 'impartial spectator'. These problems have been stated influentially in recent years by Bernard WILLIAMS, who puts them under the heading of what he calls 'integrity'.

In a famous example, Williams asks us to imagine the case of Jim, who is travelling in a South American jungle. He comes across a military firing squad, about to shoot twenty Indians from a nearby village where some insurrection has occurred. The captain in charge offers Jim a guest's privilege. Either Jim can choose to shoot one of the Indians himself, and the others will go free, or all twenty will be shot by the firing squad.

Williams' point here is not that utilitarianism gives the wrong answer; indeed he himself thinks that Jim should shoot. Rather, it is that utilitarianism reaches its answer too quickly, and cannot account for many of the thoughts we know that we should have ourselves in Jim's situation, such as, 'It is I who will be the killer'. Practical reasoning is not concerned only with arranging things so that the greatest utility is produced. Rather it matters to each agent what role they will be playing in the situation, and where the goods and bads occur. This point emerges even more starkly if we imagine a variation on the story about Jim, in which the captain asks Jim to commit suicide so as to set an example of courage and nobility to the local populace, on the condition that if he does so the twenty Indians will go free. The utility calculations are as clear, perhaps clearer, than in the original story. But it is only reasonable that Jim in this story should think it relevant that it is he who is going to die. To any individual, it matters not only how much happiness there is in the world, but who gets it.

See also: ANIMALS AND ETHICS; DEONTOLOGICAL ETHICS; GOOD, THEORIES OF THE; TELEOLOGICAL ETHICS

References and further reading

Mill, J.S. (1861) *Utilitarianism*, ed. R. Crisp, Oxford: Clarendon Press, 1998. (One of the most important and widely studied works in moral philosophy. Contains the argument that pleasures can be seen as higher and lower.)

Scarre, G. (1996) *Utilitarianism*, London: Routledge. (Useful introduction, including history. Contains bibliography.)

Shaw, W.H. (1999). *Contemporary Ethics: Taking Account of Utilitarianism*, Malden, MA: Blackwell. (A nicely balanced and well-written introduction to ethics, from a utilitarian point of view. Contains extensive bibliography.)

ROGER CRISP
TIM CHAPPELL

UTOPIANISM

Utopianism is the general label for a number of different ways of dreaming or thinking about, describing or attempting to create a better society. Utopianism is derived from the word 'utopia', coined by Thomas MORE. In his book *Utopia* (1516) More described a society significantly better than England as it existed at the time, and the word *utopia* (good place) has come to mean a description of a fictional place, usually a society, that is better than the society in which the author lives and which functions as a criticism of the author's society. In some cases it is intended as a direction to be followed in social reform, or even, in a few instances, as a possible goal to be achieved.

The concept of utopianism clearly reflects its origins. In *Utopia* More presented a fictional debate over the nature of his creation. Was it fictional or real? Was the obvious satire aimed primarily at contemporary England or was it also aimed at the society described in the book? More important for

later developments, was it naïvely unrealistic or did it present a social vision that, whether achievable or not, could serve as a goal to be aimed at? Most of what we now call utopianism derives from the last question. In the nineteenth century Robert Owen in England and Charles Fourier, Henri Saint-Simon and Étienne Cabet in France, collectively known as the utopian socialists, popularized the possibility of creating a better future through the establishment of small, experimental communities. Karl Marx, Friedrich Engels and others argued that such an approach was incapable of solving the problems of industrial society and the label 'utopian' came to mean unrealistic and naïve. Later theorists, both opposed to and supportive of utopianism, debated the desirability of depicting a better society as a way of achieving significant social change. In particular, Christian religious thinkers have been deeply divided over utopianism. Is the act of envisaging a better life on earth heretical, or is it a normal part of Christian thinking?

Since the collapse of communism in Eastern Europe and the former Soviet Union, a number of theorists have argued that utopianism has come to an end. It has not; utopias are still being written and intentional communities founded, in the hope that a better life is possible.

See also: FOURIER, C.; MORE, THOMAS; SAINT-SIMON, COMTE DE

LYMAN TOWER SARGENT

UTTERER'S INTENTION
See COMMUNICATION AND INTENTION

V

VAGUENESS

It seems obvious that there are vague ways of speaking and vague ways of thinking – saying that the weather is hot, for example. Common sense also has it that there is vagueness in the external world (although this is not the usual view in philosophy). Intuitively, clouds, for example, do not have sharp spatiotemporal boundaries. But the thesis that vagueness is real has spawned a number of deeply perplexing paradoxes and problems. There is no general agreement among philosophers about how to understand vagueness.

See also: Many-valued logics, philosophical issues in

MICHAEL TYE

VAIHINGER, HANS (1852–1933)

Hans Vaihinger was a German philosopher and historian of philosophy. Much of his work was a response to Kant's philosophy, and he contributed to the revival of interest in Kant at the end of the nineteenth century both through his published commentaries and by founding a journal and society for the discussion of Kant's thought. He developed his own philosophy, the philosophy of 'as-if', which was derived from the Kantian notion of 'heuristic fictions'.

CHRISTOPHER ADAIR-TOTEFF

VAIŚEṢIKA
See Nyāya-Vaiśeṣika

VALUES AND FACTS
See Fact/value distinction

VAN HELMONT, FRANCISCUS MERCURIUS
See Helmont, Franciscus Mercurius van

VEDĀNTA

Indian philosophical speculation burgeoned in texts called Upaniṣads (from 800 BC), where views about a true Self (*ātman*) in relation to Brahman, the supreme reality, the Absolute or God, are propounded and explored. Early Upaniṣads were appended to an even older sacred literature, the Veda ('Knowledge'), and became literally Vedānta, 'the Veda's last portion'. Classical systems of philosophy inspired by Upaniṣadic ideas also came to be known as Vedānta, as well as more recent spiritual thinking. Classical Vedānta is one of the great systems of Indian philosophy, extending almost two thousand years with hundreds of authors and several important subschools. In the modern period, Vedānta in the folk sense of spiritual thought deriving from Upaniṣads is a major cultural phenomenon.

Understood broadly, Vedānta may even be said to be the philosophy of Hinduism, although in the classical period there are other schools (notably Mīmāṃsā) that purport to articulate right views and conduct for what may be called a Hindu community (the terms 'Hindu' and 'Hinduism' gained currency only after the Muslim invasion of the South Asian subcontinent, beginning rather late in classical times). Swami Vivekananda (1863–1902), the great popularizer of Hindu ideas in the West, spoke of Vedānta as an umbrella philosophy of a Divine revealed diversely in the world's religious traditions. Such inclusivism is an important theme in some classical Vedānta, but there are also virulent disputes about how Brahman should be conceived, in particular Brahman's relation to the individual.

In the twentieth century, philosophers such as Sarvepalli Radhakrishnan, K.C. Bhattacharyya and T.M.P. Mahadevan have articulated idealist worldviews largely inspired by classical and pre-classical Vedānta. The mystic philosopher Sri Aurobindo propounds a theism and evolutionary theory he calls Vedānta, and many others, including political leaders such as Gandhi and spiritual figures as well as academics, have developed or defended Vedāntic views.

See also: BRAHMAN; HINDU PHILOSOPHY

STEPHEN H. PHILLIPS

VERIFICATION PRINCIPLE

See LOGICAL POSITIVISM; MEANING AND VERIFICATION

VERIFICATION THEORY OF MEANING

See MEANING AND VERIFICATION

VIA NEGATIVA

See NEGATIVE THEOLOGY

VICES

See VIRTUES AND VICES

VICO, GIAMBATTISTA (1668–1744)

Vico lived in a period in which the successes of the natural sciences were frequently attributed to the Cartesian method of a priori demonstration. His own first interest, however, was in the cultivation of the humanist values of wisdom and prudence, to which this method was irrelevant. Initially, therefore, he sought a methodology for these values in the techniques of persuasion and argument used in political and legal oratory. But he soon came to believe that the Cartesian method was too limited to explain even the advances in the natural sciences and he developed an alternative constructivist theory of knowledge by which to establish the degree of certainty of the different sciences. Wisdom and prudence, however, came low on this scale.

Through certain historical studies in law, he became convinced that, although there were no eternal and universal standards underlying law at all times and places, the law appropriate to any specific historical age was dependent upon an underlying developmental pattern of social consciousness and institutions common to all nations except the Jews after the Fall. His *New Science* (1725, 1730 and 1744) was a highly original attempt to establish this pattern, originating in a primeval mythic consciousness and concluding in a fully rational, but ultimately corrupt, consciousness. He believed that knowledge of the pattern would enable us to interpret a wide range of historical evidence to provide continuous and coherent accounts of the histories of all actual gentile nations. The primacy of consciousness in the pattern led him to claim that there must be a necessary sequence of ideas upon which institutions rested, which would provide the key to the historical interpretation of meaning in all

the different gentile languages. He supported this conception by extensive comparative anthropological, linguistic and historical enquiries, resulting most famously in his interpretation of the Homeric poems. He also advanced a more developed account of his earlier theory of knowledge, in which the work of philosopher and historian were mutually necessary, to show how this conception of 'scientific history' was to be achieved.

Vico believed that the knowledge that wisdom and prudence vary in different historical ages in accordance with an underlying pattern could provide us with a higher insight into those of our own age and enable us to avoid a collapse into barbarism which, in an overrational age in which religious belief must decline, was more or less inevitable. Unfortunately, the metaphysical status of his pattern rendered this impossible. Much of his thought was expressed in a context of theological assumptions which conflict with important aspects of his work. This has given rise to continuous controversy over his personal and theoretical commitment to these assumptions. Despite this, however, his conceptions of the historical development of societies, of the relation between ideas and institutions, of social anthropology, comparative linguistics and of the philosophical and methodological aspects of historical enquiry in general, remain profoundly fruitful.

See also: HISTORY, PHILOSOPHY OF

LEON POMPA

VIENNA CIRCLE

The Vienna Circle was a group of about three dozen thinkers drawn from the natural and social sciences, logic and mathematics who met regularly in Vienna between the wars to discuss philosophy. The work of this group constitutes one of the most important and most influential philosophical achievements of the twentieth century, especially in the development of analytic philosophy and philosophy of science.

The Vienna Circle made its first public appearance in 1929 with the publication of its manifesto, *The Scientific Conception of the World: The Vienna Circle*. At the centre of this modernist movement was the so-called 'Schlick Circle', a discussion group organized in 1924 by the physics professor Moritz Schlick. Friedrich Waismann, Herbert Feigl, Rudolf Carnap, Hans Hahn, Philipp Frank, Otto Neurath, Viktor Kraft, Karl Menger, Kurt Gödel and Edgar Zilsel belonged to this inner circle. Their meetings in the Boltzmanngasse were also attended by Olga Taussky-Todd, Olga Hahn-Neurath, Felix Kaufmann, Rose Rand, Gustav Bergmann and Richard von Mises, and on some occasions by visitors from abroad such as Hans Reichenbach, Alfred Ayer, Ernest Nagel, Willard Van Orman Quine and Alfred Tarski. This discussion circle was pluralistic and committed to the ideals of the Enlightenment. It was unified by the aim of making philosophy scientific with the help of modern logic on the basis of scientific and everyday experience. At the periphery of the Schlick Circle, and in a more or less strong osmotic contact with it, there were loose discussion groups around Ludwig Wittgenstein, Heinrich Gomperz, Richard von Mises and Karl Popper. In addition the mathematician Karl Menger established in the years 1926–36 an international mathematical colloquium, which was attended by Kurt Gödel, John von Neumann and Alfred Tarski among others.

Thus the years 1924–36 saw the development of an interdisciplinary movement whose purpose was to transform philosophy. Its public profile was provided by the Ernst Mach Society through which members of the Vienna Circle sought to popularize their ideas in the context of programmes for national education in Vienna. The general programme of the movement was reflected in its publications, such as the journal *Erkenntnis* ('Knowledge', later called The Journal for Unified Science), and the *International Encyclopedia of Unified Science*. Given this story of intellectual success, the fate of the Vienna Circle was tragic. The Ernst Mach Society was suspended in 1934 for political reasons, Moritz Schlick was murdered in 1936, and around this time many members of the Vienna Circle left Austria for racial and political reasons; thus soon after Schlick's death the Circle disintegrated. As a result of the emigration of so many of its members, however, the characteristic ideas of the Vienna Circle became more and more widely known, especially in Scandinavia, Britain and North America where they contributed to the emergence of modern philosophy of science. In Germany and Austria, however, the philosophical and mathematical scene was characterized by a prolongation of the break that was caused by the emigration of the members of the Vienna Circle.

See also: ANALYTICAL PHILOSOPHY; ENLIGHTENMENT, CONTINENTAL; LOGICAL POSITIVISM; MEANING AND VERIFICATION

FRIEDRICH STADLER
Translated from the German
by C. PILLER

VIOLENCE

Violence is a central concept for much discussion of moral and political life, but lots of debate employing the concept is confused by the lack of clarity about its meaning and about the moral status it should have in our development of public policy. Wide understandings of the term – for instance, structural violence – not only include too much under the name of violence, but also place an excessively negative moral loading onto the concept. This is also a problem for some other definitions of violence, such as legitimist definitions, which treat violence as essentially the illegitimate use of force. It is better to confront directly the important and disturbing claim that violence is sometimes morally permissible than to settle it by definitional fiat.

See also: CIVIL DISOBEDIENCE

C.A.J. COADY

VIRTUE EPISTEMOLOGY

'Virtue epistemology' is the name of a class of theories that analyse fundamental epistemic concepts such as justification or knowledge in terms of properties of persons rather than properties of beliefs. Some of these theories make the basic concept constitutive of justification or knowledge that of a reliable belief-forming process, or a reliable belief-forming faculty or, alternatively, a properly functioning faculty. Others make the fundamental concept that of an epistemic or intellectual virtue in the sense of virtue used in ethics. In all these theories, epistemic evaluation rests on some virtuous quality of the person that enables them to act in a cognitively effective and commendable way, although not all use the term 'virtue'. The early, simple forms of process reliabilism are best treated as precursors to virtue epistemology since the latter arose out of the former and has added requirements for knowledge intended to capture the idea of epistemic behaviour that is subjectively responsible as well as objectively reliable.

Proponents of virtue epistemology claim a number of advantages. It is said to bypass disputes between foundationalists and coherentists on proper cognitive structure, to avoid sceptical worries, to avoid the impasse between internalism and externalism, and to broaden the range of epistemological inquiry in a way that permits the recovering of such neglected epistemic values as understanding and wisdom.

See also: CONFUCIAN PHILOSOPHY, CHINESE; JUSTIFICATION, EPISTEMIC

LINDA ZAGZEBSKI

VIRTUE ETHICS

Introduction

Virtue ethics has its origin in the ancient world, particularly in the writings of Plato and Aristotle. It has been revived following an article by G.E.M. Anscombe critical of modern ethics and advocating a return to the virtues.

Some have argued that virtue ethics constitutes a third option in moral theory additional to utilitarianism and Kantianism. Utilitarians and Kantians have responded vigorously, plausibly claiming that their views already incorporate many of the theses allegedly peculiar to virtue ethics.

Virtue *theory*, the study of notions, such as character, related to the virtues, has led to the recultivation of barren areas. These include: What is the good life, and what part does virtue play in it? How stringent are the demands of morality? Are moral reasons independent of agents' particular concerns? Is moral rationality universal? Is morality to be captured in a set of rules, or is the sensitivity of a virtuous person central in ethics?

From virtue ethics, and the virtue theory of which it is a part, have emerged answers to these questions at once rooted in ancient views and yet distinctively modern.

1   Aristotle and ancient virtue ethics

Modern virtue ethicists often claim ARISTOTLE as an ancestor. Aristotle, however, was himself working through an agenda laid down by PLATO and SOCRATES. Socrates asked the question at the heart of Greek ethics: 'How should one live?' All three of these philosophers believed that the answer to this question is 'Virtuously' (see VIRTUES AND VICES §§1–3).

The ancient philosophical task was to show how living virtuously would be best for the virtuous person. Plato's *Republic* attempts to answer Thrasymachus' challenge that rational people will aim to get the most pleasure, honour and power for themselves. His argument is that justice, broadly construed, is to be identified with a rational ordering of one's soul. Once one sees that one identifies oneself with one's reason, one will realize that being just is in fact best for oneself. Thrasymachus, of course, might respond that he identifies himself with his desires.

Aristotle continued the same project, aiming to show that human *eudaimonia*, happiness, consists in the exercise (not the mere possession of) the virtues

(see EUDAIMONIA; HAPPINESS). The linchpin of his case is his 'function' argument that human nature is perfected through virtue, a standard objection to which is that it confuses the notions of a good man and the good for man. Ultimately, Aristotle's method is similar to Plato's. Much of *Nicomachean Ethics* is taken up with portraits of the virtuous man intended to attract one to a life such as his.

For Aristotle, all of the 'practical' virtues will be possessed by the truly virtuous person, the man of 'practical wisdom' (Aristotle's central 'intellectual' virtue). Socrates believed that virtue was a *unity*, that it consisted in knowledge alone. Aristotle's position is one of *reciprocity*: the possession of one virtue implies the possession of all. At this point he joined Socrates and Plato in their opposition to Greek 'common sense'. This opposition to common sense is not something that characterizes modern virtue ethics.

2   Modern virtue theory

Virtue theory is that general area of philosophical inquiry concerned with or related to the virtues. It includes *virtue ethics*, a theory about how we should act or live. This distinction is a rough one, but it is important to grasp that much of modern virtue theory is by writers not themselves advocating virtue ethics.

Virtue theory has undergone a resurgence since G.E.M. Anscombe's article 'Modern Moral Philosophy' (1958) (see ANSCOMBE, G.E.M.). Anscombe believed that it was a mistake to seek a foundation for a morality grounded in legalistic notions such as 'obligation' or 'duty' in the context of general disbelief in the existence of a divine lawgiver as the source of such obligation. She recommended that philosophy of psychology should take the place of moral philosophy, until adequate accounts of such central notions as action and intention were available. Then, she suggested, philosophers might return to moral philosophy through an ethics of virtue.

What is virtue ethics? It is tempting to characterize it as a theory advocating acting virtuously, but this is insufficiently precise. Virtue ethics is usually seen as an alternative to utilitarianism or consequentialism in general (see CONSEQUENTIALISM; UTILITARIANISM). To put it roughly, utilitarianism says that we should maximize human welfare or utility. A utilitarian, however, may advocate acting virtuously for reasons of utility. Ethical theories are best understood in terms not of what acts they require, but of the reasons offered for acting in whatever way is in fact required.

Which properties of actions, then, according to virtue ethics, constitute our reason for doing them?

The properties of kindness, courage and so on. It is worth noting that there is a difference between acting virtuously and doing a virtuous action. One's doing a virtuous action may be seen as doing the action a virtuous person would do in those circumstances, though one may not oneself be a virtuous person. Virtue ethics, then, concerns itself not only with isolated actions but with the character of the agent. There are reasons for doing certain things (such as kind things), and also for being a certain type of person (a kind person).

This account of virtue ethics enables us to distinguish it from its other main opponent, deontology or Kantianism (see DEONTOLOGICAL ETHICS; KANT, I. §§9–10; KANTIAN ETHICS). A Kantian, for example, might claim that my reason for telling the truth is that to do so would be in accordance with the categorical imperative. That is a property of the action of telling the truth quite different from its being honest.

3 The good of the agent and the demandingness of morality

A pure form of virtue ethics will suggest that virtuous properties – 'thick' properties as opposed to thin properties such as 'rightness' and 'goodness' – of actions constitute our only reasons for performing them. Aristotle came close to this position, but it is perhaps more plausible to interpret him as claiming that the rationality of virtue lies in its promotion of the agent's *eudaimonia*. Aristotle's view is nevertheless radical. Since my *eudaimonia* consists only in the exercise of the virtues, I have no reason to live a non-virtuous life.

More common than pure forms of virtue ethics are pluralistic views according to which there are other reason-constituting properties, some perhaps of the kind advocated by utilitarians and Kantians. The open-mindedness of virtue ethics contrasts sharply at this point with what Bernard WILLIAMS has identified as the peculiar narrowness of focus in modern ethics. Considerations other than the moral are relevant to the question of how one should live. Modern virtue ethicists can thus adopt a position on the demandingness of morality between the extremes of Aristotle and their modern opponents. For they need claim neither that self-interest is constituted entirely by being moral nor that morality completely overrides self-interest.

Much of virtue theory has been concerned to develop Williams' criticism of utilitarianism and Kantianism that, through their impersonality and impartiality, the two violate the *integrity* of moral agents. Philippa Foot has developed these critical arguments in a direction favourable to virtue ethics. According to both the principle of utility and the Kantian categorical imperative, moral reasons, being universal, are independent of the desires of agents. Foot, impressed by the rationality of fulfilling one's own desires, has argued that moral reasons do depend on the desires of the agent, so that a person who acts consistently ungenerously may be described as ungenerous, but not necessarily as having any reason to act generously, unless they have a desire which would thereby be fulfilled. Foot is here expressing a doubt similar to Anscombe's about the possibility of ungrounded 'ought' judgments.

4 Agency and motivation

Imagine that you are thanking a friend for visiting you in hospital. She replies, 'Oh, it was nothing. It was obvious that morality required me to come.' This case, taken from an influential 1976 article by Michael Stocker, and related to the discussion in the previous section concerning the demandingness of morality and the pervasiveness of the moral point of view, serves to illustrate an ideal of agency which lies implicit in much modern ethical theory (see MORAL MOTIVATION; MORAL REALISM). The unattractiveness of this ideal can be avoided by utilitarians, who may argue that thinking in the way your friend did about morality is likely to be self-defeating in utilitarian terms. Even the utilitarians, however, can be charged with missing the point. What is wrong with your friend is not that moral thinking like hers fails to maximize utility. Nevertheless, the case constitutes a far more serious problem for Kantians, given Kant's insistence on the explicit testing of courses of action using the categorical imperative, and his view that the moral worth of an action lies entirely in its being done out of a sense of duty.

Modern virtue ethicists such as Lawrence Blum have endeavoured to replace this conception of moral agency with a virtue-centred ideal allowing agents to be moved directly by emotional concern for others. This ideal can once again be seen as emerging from Anscombe's attack on the notion of duty. A morality of duty is said to pay insufficient attention to the inner life: the dutiful agent is not doing, or feeling, enough (this criticism is an interesting counterpoint to the accusation that Kantianism is excessively demanding). The charge, then, is not only that modern moral theory fails to provide plausible justifying reasons for action, but that the motivational structure of what is clearly moral agency is quite different from what the theories lead us to expect. Moral agency consists at least partly in acting and feeling in ways prompted by bonds of partiality, requiring no further backing from impersonal ethical theory (see FRIENDSHIP).

5 Universality and tradition

We have already seen how some virtue theorists link moral reasons to motivation. This is one route to a narrowing of the scope of moral reasons. Without any motivation to do so, there is no reason, say, to maximize utility or respect the moral law. Another route is followed by writers such as Alasdair MacIntyre who ground moral rationality in traditions.

MacIntyre's critique of modern ethical theory, outlined in *After Virtue* (1981), is the most stringent in virtue theory. He claims that present moral discussion is literal nonsense: we unreflectively use a mix of concepts left over from moribund traditions; since these traditions are incommensurable, arguments using concepts from rival traditions are irresoluble and interminable. MacIntyre does not, however, follow through the implications of this critique into a Nietzschean moral scepticism, advocating instead a return to Aristotelian virtue ethics (see NIETZSCHE, F.). The question of how he accomplishes this is an example of a puzzle about virtue theory present since Anscombe's original article: after the sustained critique of modern ethical theory by virtue theorists, is the remaining conceptual apparatus sufficiently strong to support an alternative prescriptive ethics?

The relationship between modern virtue ethicists and Aristotle is complex. Most virtue ethicists, including Foot and MacIntyre, combine an Aristotelian emphasis on the virtues with a modern scepticism about the possibility of an objective theory of the good for an individual. Likewise, MacIntyre's stress on the importance of context is quite Aristotelian, but the relativism to which this leads him would be anathema to Aristotle (see MORAL RELATIVISM). MacIntyre claims that goods are internal to practices, and not assessable from some external point of view, while Aristotle believed that teleological reflection on universal human nature enabled one to identify those practices which are good *haplōs*, 'simply good'.

The relativism of modern virtue ethics has emerged also in political theory in the debate between communitarians, such as MacIntyre, and liberals (see COMMUNITY AND COMMUNITARIANISM; LIBERALISM). Along with a predilection for virtue-centred over rule-centred ethics go preferences for the local and particular to the universal, the specific to the general, the embedded to the abstracted, the communal to the individual, the inexplicit to the explicit, the traditional to the revised, the partial to the impartial. In MacIntyre's work, the notion of goods internal to diachronic practices and grounded in traditions is tied to a criticism of a free-floating liberal self, choosing goods from some Archimedean standpoint. MacIntyre's narrative conception of a self opens another door for the readmittance of the notion of character into moral philosophy.

The most serious problem for relativism has yet to be resolved in modern virtue ethics. What are we to say of practices and ways of life constituting internally coherent traditions, yet containing undeniably evil components?

6 Practical reason

One reason for the fading of the notion of character in ethical theory is that utilitarianism and Kantianism have commonly been developed as ethics of rules to resolve dilemmas. An argument against a rule-based ethics is found in Aristotle's discussion of the legal virtue of *epieikeia*, 'equity'. Rules will always run out in hard cases, and some sensitivity is required on the part of the judge to fill the gap between the law and the world. Likewise, for Aristotle, the virtuous man possesses *phronēsis*, 'practical wisdom', a sensitivity to the morally salient features of particular situations which goes beyond an ability to apply explicit rules.

This view has been revived in virtue ethics, by among others Iris MURDOCH and John McDowell, in his 1979 article, 'Virtue and Reason'. McDowell argues that we cannot postulate a world as seen by both the virtuous and the unvirtuous, and then explain the moral agency of the virtuous through their possessing some special desire. Since moral rules run out, any object of desire could not be made explicit. McDowell uses Wittgenstein to support his claim that rational action does not have to be rule-governed (see WITTGENSTEIN, L.J.J. §§10–12). This has clear implications for moral education: it should consist in enabling the person to see sensitively, not (or at least not only) in inculcating rigid and absolute principles. This is one of the strands in the feminist critique of modern ethical theory, itself closely tied to virtue theory. Writers such as Carol Gilligan argue that the moral sensibility of women is less rule-governed than that of men, and this has influenced the 'ethics of care' of, for example, Nel Noddings.

The emphasis in virtue ethics on non-rational factors in moral motivation sits well with the notion of moral sensitivity. And this latter notion provides another standpoint from which one might criticize the basing of morality on the categorical imperative. As we have seen, Foot claims that immorality is not necessarily irrational, since moral reasons depend on the agent's desires. Writers such as McDowell who depict practical reason as perceptual can also deny that immorality is irrational. The unvirtuous lack not any capacity of the theoretical or calculative intellect, but moral sensitivity. Unlike Foot, however, McDowell would argue that this is in fact a failure to perceive genuine reasons for action independent of the agent's motivations.

Again, in McDowell, we see the pastiche, characteristic of virtue ethics, of ancient and modern: rationality is made to depend on social practice, and yet, as Socrates thought, virtue turns out to be a kind of knowledge.

See also: IMPARTIALITY; LIFE, MEANING OF; MENCIUS; MORAL JUDGMENT

References and further reading

Crisp, R. and Slote, M. (1997) *Virtue Ethics*, Oxford: Oxford University Press. (A collection of well-known papers on the virtues, with introductory essay. Includes bibliography on various topics.)

Darwall, S. (ed.) (2003) *Virtue Ethics*, Malden, MA: Blackwell. (A useful collection of excerpts from classical texts alongside significant modern articles.)

MacIntyre, A. (1981) *After Virtue*, London: Duckworth. (Influential critique of modern ethics, and advocacy of Thomistic virtue ethics.)

ROGER CRISP

VIRTUE, INDIAN CONCEPTIONS OF

See DUTY AND VIRTUE, INDIAN CONCEPTIONS OF

VIRTUES AND VICES

Introduction

The concept of a virtue can make an important contribution to a philosophical account of ethics, but virtue theory should not be seen as running parallel to other 'ethical theories' in trying to provide a guide to action.

Modern accounts of the virtues typically start from Aristotle, but they need to modify his view substantially, with respect to the grounding of the virtues in human nature; the question of what virtues there are; their unity; and their psychological identity as dispositions of the agent. In particular, one must acknowledge the historical variability of what have been counted as virtues.

Aristotle saw vices as failings, but modern opinion must recognize more radical forms of viciousness or evil. It may also need to accept that the good is more intimately connected with its enemies than traditional views have allowed. Virtue theory helps in the discussion of such questions by

offering greater resources of psychological realism than other approaches.

1 Virtues and theory

Ethical theories are standardly presented as falling into three basic types, centring respectively on *consequences*, *rights* and *virtues* (see CONSEQUENTIALISM; DEONTOLOGICAL ETHICS; RIGHTS; VIRTUE ETHICS). One way of understanding this division into three is in terms of what each theory sees, at the most basic level, as bearing ethical value. For the first type of theory, it is *good states of affairs*; for the second, it is *right action*; while virtue theory puts most emphasis on the idea of a *good person*, someone who could be described also as an ethically admirable person. The last is an important emphasis, and the notion of a virtue is important in ethics; but its importance cannot be caught in this way, as the focus of a theory which is supposedly parallel to these other types of theory. Consequentialist and rights theories aim to systematize our principles or rules of action in ways that will, supposedly, help us to see what to do or to recommend in particular cases. A theory of the virtues cannot claim to do this: the theory itself says that what one needs in order to do and recommend the right things are virtues, not a theory about virtues. Moreover, the thoughts of a virtuous person do not consist entirely, or even mainly, of thoughts about virtues or about paradigms of virtuous people. Indeed, they will sometimes be thoughts about rights or good consequences, and this makes it clear that thoughts about the good person cannot displace these other ethical concepts, since a good person will have to use some such concepts. 'Virtue theory' cannot be on the same level as the other types of theory.

An emphasis on virtues is important to moral philosophy for other reasons. Although it need not exclude cognitivism, it shifts attention from morality as a system of propositions or truths to its psychological (and hence, eventually, social) embodiment in individual dispositions of action, thought and emotional reaction. It draws attention to the variety of reasons for action and judgment that may play a part in ethical life, beyond the theorists' favourites, duty and utility (see MORAL MOTIVATION §§1–3; MORALITY AND EMOTIONS). Such reasons will not typically embody virtue concepts themselves, or, still less, involve reflection on the agent's own virtues. But virtue theory can help to explain how considerations such as 'she needs it', for instance, or 'he relied on what you said', can function as an agent's reasons. An approach through the virtues also leaves room for the important idea that ethically correct action may be only partly codifiable and may involve an essential appeal to judgment (see MORAL JUDGMENT §4; UNIVERSALISM IN ETHICS).

2 Beyond Aristotle: ground; content

The first systematic investigation of the virtues was made by Plato, in such works as *Gorgias* and the *Republic*, and it was extremely significant, for instance in setting the problem of the unity of the virtues (see §3). Plato also posed in a particularly challenging form questions about the value of virtues to their possessor. The classical account of the virtues, however, to which all modern treatments refer, is that of Aristotle (*Nicomachean Ethics*) (see ARISTOTLE §22–5). Just because of the power and the influence of this account, it is easy to underestimate the extent to which a modern theory needs to distance itself from Aristotle. A modern account is likely to agree with Aristotle that virtues are dispositions of character, acquired by ethical training, displayed not just in action but in patterns of emotional reaction. It will agree, too, that virtues are not rigid habits, but are flexible under the application of practical reason. But there are at least four matters on which it is likely to disagree with Aristotle, which may be labelled *ground*; *content*; *unity*; and *reality*.

Ground. Aristotle held that the virtues (for which the word in his language means only 'excellences' – see ARETĒ) had a teleological ground, in the sense that they represented the fullest development of a certain kind of natural creature, a nondefective male human being. No one now is going to agree with Aristotle that there are creatures who are biologically human beings but who are excluded from this full development by their nature as women or as 'natural slaves'. Having abandoned his views about women and slaves, modern thinkers face the harder question of how far they agree with Aristotle about the natural basis of the virtues. This in turn raises the question of how strongly one should feel about Aristotle's own teleological view. On one interpretation, he had a comprehensive functional conception of the contents of the universe, with each kind of creature fitting into a discoverable overall pattern. On such a conception, substantial parts of the theory of the virtues will be discoverable by top-down systematic inquiry which will tell us what sorts of creatures human beings are, and hence what their best life will be (see TELEOLOGICAL

ETHICS). Other interpreters give a more moderate account of Aristotle's enterprise, according to which his intentions will be honoured by a hermeneutical inquiry into what we, now, regard as the most basic and valuable aspects of human beings.

Content. What is undeniably lacking from Aristotle's thought, as from that of other ancient thinkers, is an historical dimension. Some modern virtue theorists share this weakness. Aristotle's account is in several respects different from any account of the virtues one would give now, with respect both to what it puts in and what it leaves out. He gives a particularly important place to a quality called *megalopsuchia*, 'greatness of soul', which has a lot to do with a grand social manner and which bears even less relation to a contemporary ethic than its name, in itself, might suggest. A modern person, asked for the principal virtues, might well mention kindness and fairness. Fairness bears a relation to an important Aristotelian virtue, justice, but the latter is defined to an important extent in political and civic terms, and gives a fairly restricted account of fairness as a personal characteristic. Kindness is not an Aristotelian virtue at all. Moreover, there is no account of an important modern virtue, truthfulness; what Aristotle calls the virtue of truth is (surprisingly, as it seems to us) concerned exclusively with boasting and modesty.

There has been obvious historical variation in what is seen as the content of the virtues. Aquinas, who notably developed Aristotle's account, of course modified it to accommodate Christianity, holding in particular that besides the moral virtues, there were 'theological' virtues, which have God as their immediate object. The pagans were not in a position to display these, but so far as the moral virtues were concerned, they could be truly virtuous in the light of natural reason. However, there was still something imperfect about their virtue even at this level since, Aquinas held, the whole of ethical life is properly grounded in the virtue called charity, which has a divine origin.

For Hume, on the other hand, Aristotle's account and other pagan sources served to support an ethics of the virtues that was precisely designed to discredit and exclude Christianity (see HUME, D. §4). The historical variation, both in philosophical formulations and in cultural realizations of the virtues, raises wider issues of how theories of the virtues are to be understood. The conceptions of human nature and human circumstances that underlie such theories are open to wide reinterpretation in the face of changing values, and the Aristotelian presupposition that an understanding of human nature could yield a determinate account of the virtues – even if that idea is interpreted relatively unambitiously – looks unrealistic. There are of course constants in the psychology and circumstances of human beings that make certain virtues, in some version or other, ubiquitous: in every society people need (something like) courage, (something like) self-control with regard to anger and sexual desire, and some version of prudence. These platitudes, which are stressed by those who look to a substantive universal virtue theory, severely underdetermine the content of such a theory. This is shown by the very simple consideration that the constant features of human life are indeed constant, but the virtues that have been recognized at different times and by different cultures vary considerably.

3 Beyond Aristotle (cont.): unity; reality

Unity. Aristotle inherited from Plato, and ultimately from Socrates, an interest in the unity of the virtues (see SOCRATES §5). Socrates seems to have held that there was basically only one virtue, which he called wisdom or knowledge. The conventional distinctions between the various virtues – justice, self-control, courage and the rest – were taken to mark only different fields of application of this power. Aristotle did think that there were separate virtues, but nevertheless his view came almost to the same thing as Socrates', since he thought that one could not have one virtue without having them all. One could not properly possess any one virtue unless one had the intellectual virtue which is called in Aristotle's language *phronēsis* (often translated as 'practical wisdom', but better rendered as 'judgment' or 'good sense'); but, Aristotle held, if one had this quality, then one had all the virtues.

It is not hard to see the general idea underlying this position. Generosity is linked to justice – someone who gives only what justice demands is not being generous. Similar points can be made about the interrelations of some other virtues. However, it is important to the theory of the virtues that they provide psychological explanations as well as normative descriptions, and from a realistic psychological point of view it is hard to deny (as many ancient Greeks other than Socrates and Aristotle agreed) that someone can have some virtues while lacking others. In particular, the so-called 'executive virtues' of courage and self-control can be present without other virtues; indeed, they themselves can surely be deployed in the interests of wicked projects. The refusal to acknowledge this may simply represent an ethical reluctance to give moral accolades to bad people.

The fact that the virtues can, to some degree, be separated from one another itself helps to give point to virtue theory. Some modern ethical theories do imply that there is basically only one moral disposition. Utilitarianism, at least in its direct form, places everything on impartial benevolence (see UTILITARIANISM; IMPARTIALITY); and though Kant himself did have a theory of the virtues, Kantianism insists on the primacy of a sense of duty (see KANT, I. §§9–11; KANTIAN ETHICS). An advantage of virtue theory is that it allows for a more complex and realistic account of ethical motivation.

Relatedly, it can acknowledge psychological connections between the ethical and other aspects of character, accepting that people's temperaments have something to do with how they conduct themselves ethically. For the same reason, virtue theory is implicitly opposed to sharp boundaries between the 'moral' and the 'nonmoral', and is likely to acknowledge that there is a spectrum of desirable characteristics, and that no firm or helpful line can be drawn around those that are specifically of moral significance. Aristotle did not even try to draw such a line: his own terminology distinguishes only between excellences of character and intellectual excellences, and one of the latter, *phronēsis*, is itself necessary to the excellences of character. Hume, who, unlike Aristotle, was surrounded by moralists who wanted to draw such a line, goes out of his way to mock the attempt to draw it, and his deliberately offensive treatment of the subject is still very instructive.

Reality. Aristotle conceived of the virtues as objective dispositional characteristics of people which they possess in at least as robust a sense as that in which a magnet possesses the power to attract metals, though people, unlike magnets, have of course acquired the dispositions – in the way appropriate to such things – by habituation. Modern scepticism, however, to some extent supported by social and cognitive psychology, questions whether we can take such a naïve view of what it is for someone to have a virtue. There are at least two different sources of doubt. One is the extent to which people's reactions depend on situation: it is claimed that they will act in ways that express a given virtue only within a rather narrow range of recognized contexts, and if the usual expectations are suspended or even, in some cases, slightly shifted, may not act in the approved style.

The other doubt concerns ascription. When we understand people's behaviour in terms of virtues and vices, or indeed other concepts of character, we are selecting in a highly interpretative way from their behaviour as we experience it, and the way in which we do this (as, indeed, we understand many other things) is in terms of stereotypes, scripts, or standard images, which may range from crude 'characters' to sophisticated and more individuated outlines constructed with the help of types drawn, often, from fiction. The available range of such images forms part of the shifting history of the virtues. At different times there have been pattern books of virtue and vice, and one of the first was the *Characters* written by Theophrastus, a pupil of Aristotle.

Even assuming such ideas to be correct, it is not clear exactly to what extent they have a negative impact on virtue theory. Everyone knows that virtues do not express themselves under all circumstances, and also that agents may be very rigid in their ability to understand how a situation is to be seen in terms of virtues. Again, with regard to ascription, it is very important that if it is true that we construct our interpretations of another person's character in terms of a stock of images, it is equally true that the other person does so as well. The point is not so much that there is a gap between the interpreter and the person interpreted, but rather that all of us, as interpreters of ourselves and of others, use shared materials that have a history. There are lessons in such ideas for ethics generally and for virtue theory, but they need not be entirely sceptical. The points about the situational character of the virtues and about their ascription serve to remind us that an agent's virtues depend in many different ways on their relations to society: not simply in being acquired from society and reinforced or weakened by social forces, but also in the ways in which they are constructed from socially shared materials.

4   Vices, failings and evil

Aristotle named a variety of vices, each of which was basically constituted by the absence of the restraining or shaping influence of virtue, together with the operation of some natural self-centred motive. Thus cowardice was the disposition, in the absence of courage, to give in to fear; self-indulgence and irascibility the dispositions to give in to bodily pleasure and to anger. In this range of what may be called 'failings', actions that are expressions of vices do have distinctive motives, but those are not in themselves distinctively bad motives: it is rather that natural motives are expressed in ways in which they would not be expressed by a virtuous person. There are other failings in which the agent's motivation is distinctively deplorable, because it is constituted by the exaggeration, parody or perversion of a virtue: an ostentatious disposition to distribute gifts or favours, in place of generosity, or, to take a modern example, sentimentality in place of kindness. Aristotle notices some failings of this type, but, in line with his 'doctrine of the mean', he oversimplifies

their psychology under an unexamined category of 'excess'.

A peculiar case, in Aristotle's treatment, is justice. At the level of actions, at least, it might be thought that there were no distinctive motives to injustice; a person can act unjustly from a variety of motives, and indeed Aristotle mentions the possibility that a coward might treat others unjustly, by 'getting an unfair share of safety'. If this is generalized, an unjust person might be understood not as one with some characteristic motive, but rather as one who is simply insensitive to considerations of justice. However, Aristotle does introduce a distinctive motive for injustice – 'greed', or the desire to have more than others. An unjust person, then – as opposed to someone who has some other vice as a result of which he acts unjustly – is, for Aristotle, a particular greedy type, one who might roughly be recognized in modern terms as 'a crook'.

Aristotle also notices another kind of failing or deficiency, a lack of perception or feeling for others, but this is typically registered by him only as an extreme characteristic, lying off the scale of the ethical, in the form of a brutality or beastliness which virtually falls out of the category of the human. The fact that he does not have anything to say about the more domesticated forms of such a failing, very familiar to us, is a corollary to his not recognizing a virtue of kindness.

It follows from Aristotle's holistic and teleological conception of virtue as the fulfilment of the highest human capacities that vices should basically be failings, instances of a lack or an absence. This hardly leaves room for a notion of the *vicious*: the nearest that Aristotle gets to such an idea is the figure of an obsessional and unscrupulous hedonist. We possess, only too obviously, notions of viciousness deeper and more threatening than this. They point to a concept conspicuously lacking from Aristotle (though to a lesser extent, perhaps, lacking from Plato) – the concept of evil.

This leads decisively beyond the conception of vices as failings, even very serious failings. Among evil or vicious motivations, a basic type is cruelty, the desire to cause suffering, a disposition which, as Nietzsche pointed out, contrasts markedly with brutality: it has to share, rather than lack, the sensitivity to others' suffering that is displayed by kindness. In the most typical modes of cruelty, agents derive their pleasure from the sense of themselves bringing about the pain or frustration of others, and their cruel behaviour is directly an attempted expression of power. Rather different from this, though close to it, is maliciousness, as it might be called; this comprises a motivation in the style of envy, where the desire is merely that other people's happiness should not exist. Persons in this state of mind may be pleased if others come to grief, even though they do not bring it about themselves. Alberich, in Wagner's *Götterdämmerung*, says, 'Hagen, mein Sohn! hasse die Frohen!' – 'hate the happy'; such a hatred can have many expressions, only some of which involve the specifically active pleasures of cruelty.

Sometimes, cruelty may not only share, as it must, the perceptions that kindness uses, but model itself negatively on kindness, calculating what a kind person might want to do, in order to parody or subvert it. It then takes on the character of perversity. This style of reversal can be applied to virtues other than kindness. There is counter-justice, the disposition to frustrate the ends of justice, not simply in one's own interests, or to hurt or frustrate a particular person whom one hates or envies, but to take pleasure in the frustration of justice as such and the disappointments inflicted on those of good will. At the limit, this can constitute an almost selfless aesthetic of horribleness, one of the less obvious forms that may be taken by the satisfactions of Milton's Satan, with his resolve that evil should be his good.

5 Links between virtue and vice

Unlike the failings recognized by Aristotle, these evil motivations are more than mere negations. It is important, however, that this need not be taken as a metaphysical claim: one need not be committed to a Manichean view (or even the very various compromises with such a view that have been negotiated by orthodox Christianity), to the effect that human nature or the world itself contains some perversely destructive principle. One might, for instance, hold, as some optimistic programmes of psychotherapy do, that vicious and cruel motivations are, indeed, perversions, produced by a failure of love or other deficiency in the individual's upbringing. This is an encouraging position, inasmuch as it holds out the hope of a world free of such motivations, but it does not think that such motivations, while they exist, are to be understood simply in terms of the lack of a shaping or restraining influence. It would accept that vicious motivations were specially and inventively active.

Other psychological and social views are less hopeful. It is not simply that they see no ground for utopian hopes that the world could ever be freed from vicious motivations. Some of them detect deeper ways in which virtue, and more generally the good, depend on their opposites. At the most superficial level, there are contemporary versions of the point made in Mandeville's *Fable of the Bees* (1714) (see MANDEVILLE, B.): many benefits, including ethical benefits, have come from the development of commercial society, but there is no known way of replacing greed as a means of sustaining such a society. At another level, there is no doubt that valuable human achievements, for instance in the arts and sciences, have come about only because of a certain indifference to values of justice and benevolence, both at an institutional level and in the lives of those who have brought about these achievements. (Here, as so often, moralists have to face the question whether or not they are relieved that the values which they think should prevail have not always done so.)

At the deepest level, however, it is not a question simply whether nonethical values may often require the neglect or denial of morality, but whether morality itself does not require it. One of the metaphysicians' illusions, Nietzsche said in 1886, is 'the belief in opposing values'. In fact, he believed that moral values always turn out to implicate their opposites – historically (in terms of how new moral values come to exist), socially (in terms of how they sustain themselves), and psychologically (in terms of how they are learned and how they derive their energy).

Even if we accept the force of the Nietzschean suspicions, this need not damage, but rather encourages, the project of thinking about morality in ways that give an important place to virtues and vices. A theory of virtues, handled in a truthful way, offers better hope of being psychologically realistic than other prominent pictures of the ethical life do. If, further, it extends its realism to the motivations of immorality as well, and does not treat them as mere negations of the moral dispositions, it will better understand morality itself. It will be more successful in this than other theories of morality, which usually pass over in silence the forces that oppose it, or register them simply as objects of moral disapproval, or treat them as the products of a (typically unexplained) cognitive failure.

See also: HUMAN NATURE; JUSTICE; MENCIUS; MORAL JUDGMENT §4; NIETZSCHE, F.; TRUTHFULNESS

References and further reading

French, P.A., Uehling, T.E. and Wettstein, H.K. (eds) (1988) *Ethical Theory: Character and Virtue*, Midwest Studies in Philosophy, vol. 13, Notre Dame, IN: University of Notre Dame Press. (A useful collection of papers on contemporary virtue theory.)

Sherman, N. (1989) *The Fabric of Character: Aristotle's Theory of Virtue*, Oxford: Clarendon Press. (A useful philosophical and interpretative discussion.)

BERNARD WILLIAMS

VISION

Vision is the most studied sense. It is our richest source of information about the external world, providing us with knowledge of the shape, size, distance, colour and luminosity of objects around us. Vision is fast, automatic and achieved without conscious effort; however, the apparent ease with which we see is deceptive. Since Kepler characterized the formation of the retinal image in the early seventeenth century, vision theorists have known that objects do not look the way they appear on the retina. The retinal image is two-dimensional, yet we see three dimensions; the size and shape of the image that an object casts on the retina varies with the distance and perspective of the observer, yet we experience objects as having constant size and shape. The primary task of a theory of vision is to explain how useful information about the external world is recovered from the changing retinal image.

Theories of vision fall roughly into two classes. *Indirect* theories characterize the processes underlying visual perception in psychological terms, as, for example, inference from prior data or construction of complex percepts from basic sensory components. *Direct* theories tend to stress the richness of the information available in the retinal image, but, more importantly, they deny that visual processes can be given any correct psychological or mental characterization. Direct theorists, while not denying that the processing underlying vision may be very complex, claim that the complexity is to be explicated merely by reference to non-psychological, neural processes implemented in the brain.

The most influential recent work in vision treats it as an information-processing task, hence as indirect. Computational models characterize visual processing as the production and decoding of a series of increasingly useful internal representations of the distal scene. These operations are described in computational accounts by precise algorithms. Computer implementations of possible strategies employed by the visual system contribute to our understanding of the problems inherent in complex visual tasks such as edge detection or shape recognition, and make possible the rigorous testing of proposed solutions.

See also: Colour and qualia; Consciousness; Molyneux problem; Perception

FRANCES EGAN

VITALISM

Vitalists hold that living organisms are fundamentally different from non-living entities because they contain some non-physical element or are governed by different principles than are inanimate things. In its simplest form, vitalism holds that living entities contain some fluid, or a distinctive 'spirit'. In more sophisticated forms, the vital spirit becomes a substance infusing bodies and giving life to them; or vitalism becomes the view that there is a distinctive organization among living things. Vitalist positions can be traced back to antiquity. Aristotle's explanations of biological phenomena are sometimes thought of as vitalistic, though this is problematic. In the third century BC, the Greek anatomist Galen held that vital spirits are necessary for life. Vitalism is best understood, however, in the context of the emergence of modern science during the sixteenth and seventeenth centuries. Mechanistic explanations of natural phenomena were extended to biological systems by Descartes and his successors. Descartes maintained that animals, and the human body, are 'automata', mechanical devices differing from artificial devices only in their degree of complexity. Vitalism developed as a contrast to this mechanistic view. Over the next three centuries, numerous figures opposed the extension of Cartesian mechanism to biology, arguing that matter could not explain movement, perception, development or life. Vitalism has fallen out of favour, though it had advocates even into the twentieth century. The most notable is Hans Driesch (1867–1941), an eminent embryologist, who explained the life of an organism in terms of the presence of an *entelechy*, a substantial entity controlling organic processes. Likewise, the French philosopher Henri Bergson (1874–1948) posited an *élan vital* to overcome the resistance of inert matter in the formation of living bodies.

See also: Aristotle; Bergson, H.-L.; Life, origin of

WILLIAM BECHTEL
ROBERT C. RICHARDSON

VITORIA, FRANCISCO DE (*c.*1486–1546)

Francisco de Vitoria, who spent most of his working life as Prime Professor of Theology at Salamanca, Spain, was one of the most influential political theorists in sixteenth-century Catholic Europe. By profession he was a theologian, but like all theologians of the period he regarded theology as the 'mother of sciences', whose domain covered everything governed by divine or natural, rather than human, law; everything, that is, which belonged to what we would describe as jurisprudence. Vitoria's writings covered a wide variety of topics, from the possibility of magic to the acceptability of suicide. But it is on those which deal with the most contentious juridical issues of the period – the nature of civil power and of kingship, the power of the papacy and, above all, the legitimacy of the Spanish conquest of America – that his fame chiefly rests.

See also: INTERNATIONAL RELATIONS, PHILOSOPHY OF; POLITICAL PHILOSOPHY, HISTORY OF; RENAISSANCE PHILOSOPHY; WAR AND PEACE, PHILOSOPHY OF

ANTHONY PAGDEN

VOLTAIRE (FRANÇOIS-MARIE AROUET) (1694–1778)

Voltaire remains the most celebrated representative of the reformers and free-thinkers whose writings define the movement of ideas in eighteenth-century France known as the Enlightenment. He was not, however, a systematic philosopher with an original, coherently argued worldview, but a *philosophe* who translated, interpreted and vulgarized the work of other philosophers. His own writings on philosophical matters were deeply influenced by English empiricism and deism. His thought is marked by a pragmatic rationalism that led him, even in his early years, to view the world of speculative theorizing with a scepticism that was often expressed most effectively in his short stories. As a young man, Voltaire was particularly interested in Locke and Newton, and it was largely through his publications in the 1730s and 1740s that knowledge of Lockean epistemology and Newtonian cosmology entered France and eventually ensured the eclipse of Cartesianism.

After his stay in England Voltaire became interested in philosophical optimism, and his thinking reflected closely Newton's view of a divinely ordered human condition, to which Alexander Pope gave powerful poetic expression in his *Essay on Man* (1733–4). This was reinforced for the young Voltaire by Leibnizian optimism, which offered the view that the material world, being necessarily the perfect creation of an omnipotent and beneficent God, was the 'best of all possible worlds', that is to say the form of creation chosen by God as being that in which the optimum amount of good could be enjoyed at the cost of the least amount of evil.

Voltaire's later dissatisfaction with optimistic theory brought with it a similar loss of faith in the notion of a meaningful order of nature, and his earlier acceptance of the reality of human freedom of decision-taking and action was replaced after 1748 with a growing conviction that such freedom was illusory. The 1750s witness Voltaire's final abandonment of optimism and providentialism in favour of a more deterministically orientated position in which a much bleaker view of human life and destiny predominates. Pessimistic fatalism was a temporary phase in his thinking, however, and was replaced in turn by a melioristic view in which he asserted the possibilities of limited human action in the face of a hostile and godless condition.

See also: EMPIRICISM; ENLIGHTENMENT, CONTINENTAL; RATIONALISM; WILL, THE

DAVID WILLIAMS

VOLUNTARISM

Voluntarism is a theory of action. It traces our actions less to our intellects and natural inclinations than to simple will or free choice. Applied to thinking about God's actions, voluntarism led late medieval philosophers to see the world's causal and moral orders as finally rooted in God's sheer free choice, and to take God's commands as the source of moral obligation. Medieval voluntarism helped pave the way for empiricism, Cartesian doubt about the senses, legal positivism and Reformation theology.

See also: FREEDOM, DIVINE; OCCASIONALISM

BRIAN LEFTOW

VON HUMBOLDT, WILHELM
See HUMBOLDT, WILHELM VON

VON WRIGHT, GEORG HENRIK (1916–2003)

G.H. von Wright was one of the most influential analytic philosophers of the twentieth century. Born in Helsinki, Finland, von Wright did his early work on logic, probability and induction under the influence of logical empiricism. In 1948–51 he served as Ludwig Wittgenstein's successor at Cambridge, but returned to his homeland and later became a member of the Academy of Finland. He did pioneering work on the new applications of logic: modal logic, deontic logic, the logic of norms and action, preference logic, tense logic, causality and determinism. In the 1970s his ideas about the explanation and understanding of human action helped to establish new links between the analytic tradition and Continental hermeneutics. Von Wright's later works, which are eloquent books and essays written originally in his two native languages (Swedish and Finnish), deal with issues of humanism and human welfare, history and the future, technology and ecology.

See also: ACTION; DEONTIC LOGIC; INDUCTION, EPISTEMIC ISSUES IN; MODAL LOGIC

ILKKA NIINILUOTO

W

WAHL, JEAN
See HEGELIANISM

WANG YANGMING (1472–1529)

Wang Yangming was an influential Confucian thinker in sixteenth-century China who, like other Confucian thinkers, emphasized social and political responsibilities and regarded cultivation of the self as the basis for fulfilling such responsibilities. While sometimes drawing on ideas and metaphors from Daoism and Chan Buddhism, he criticized these schools for their neglect of family ties and social relations. And, in opposition to a version of Confucianism which emphasized learning, he advocated directly attending to the mind in the process of self-cultivation.

See also: CONFUCIAN PHILOSOPHY, CHINESE

SHUN KWONG-LOI

WAR AND PEACE, PHILOSOPHY OF

The war/peace dichotomy is a recurrent one in human thought and the range of experience it interprets is vast. Images of war and peace permeate religion, literature and art. Wars, battles, pacts and covenants appear as outcomes and antecedents in historical narratives. Recurrent patterns of warlike and pacific behaviour invite scientific explanations in terms of underlying biological, psychological or economic processes. War and peace are also often matters of practical concern, predicaments or opportunities that call for individual or collective action. While philosophers have explored all these ways of looking at war and peace, they have paid most attention to the practical aspects of the subject, making it part of moral and political philosophy.

Practical concern with war and peace can go in either of two main directions, one focusing on war and the other on peace. Those who doubt that war can be abolished naturally worry about how it can be regulated. So long as war is possible, there will be principles for waging it. Whether such principles should limit war-making to ends like self-defence or leave the choice to the discretion of political and military leaders is a matter of continuing dispute. Nor is there agreement regarding restrictions on the conduct of war, some holding that belligerents need only avoid disproportionate damage, others that it is morally wrong to harm innocents (for example, noncombatants). In situations of emergency both limits may give way, and moralists have debated whether this relaxation of standards is defensible. Disputes over the principles governing war raise difficult questions about action, intention and the character of morality itself.

If we think that wars can be prevented, it becomes important to focus on the conditions of permanent peace. Some who do this conclude that peace depends on the conversion of individuals to an ethic of nonviolence, others that it requires strengthening the rule of law. According to a powerful version of the latter argument, the absence of law creates a condition in which persons and communities are at liberty to invade one another: a condition that, in Hobbes's classic metaphor, is a 'state of nature' which is also a perpetual state of war. While treaties of peace may terminate particular wars, only political institutions that establish the rule of law within and between communities can provide security and guarantee peace.

See also: INTERNATIONAL RELATIONS, PHILOSOPHY OF

TERRY NARDIN

WEAKNESS OF WILL
See AKRASIA

WEBER, MAX (1864–1920)

Max Weber, German economist, historian, sociologist, methodologist and political thinker, is of philosophical significance for his attempted reconciliation of historical relativism with the possibility of a causal social science; his notion of a *verstehende* (understanding) sociology; his formulation, use and epistemic account of the concept of 'ideal types'; his views on the rational irreconcilability of ultimate value choices, and particularly his formulation of the implications for ethical political action of the conflict between ethics of conviction and ethics of responsibility; and his sociological account of the causes and uniqueness of the Western rationalization of life.

These topics are closely related: Weber argued that the explanatory interests of the historian and social scientist vary historically and that the objects of their interest were constituted in terms of cultural points of view, and that consequently their categories are ultimately rooted in evaluations, and hence are subjective. But he also argued that social science cannot dispense with causality, and that once the categories were chosen, judgments of causality were objective. The explanatory interests of the sociologist, as he defined sociology, were in understanding intentional action causally, but in terms of categories that were culturally significant, such as 'rational action'. Much of his influence flowed from his formulation of the cultural situation of the day, especially the idea that the fate of the time was to recognize that evaluations were inescapably subjective and that the world had no inherent 'meaning'. The existential implications of this novel situation for politics and learning were strikingly formulated by him: science could not tell us how to live; politics was as a choice between warring gods. Weber's scholarly work and his politics served as a model for Karl JASPERS, and a subject of criticism and analysis for other philosophers, such as Karl Löwith, Max Scheler, and the FRANKFURT SCHOOL.

STEPHEN P. TURNER
REGIS A. FACTOR

WEIL, SIMONE (1909–43)

Simone Weil's life and work represent an unusual mixture of political activism, religious mysticism and intense speculative work on a wide range of topics, including epistemology, ethics and social theory. Much of her most important writing survives in fragmentary form, in notebooks published after her untimely death. Though Jewish by family, her attitude to Judaism was largely hostile; and despite a deep commitment in the later part of her life to Christian ideas and symbols, she consistently refused to be baptized. Her religious views are eclectic in many ways, drawing on Plato and on Hindu sources. In everything she wrote, she was preoccupied with the dehumanizing effects of economic unfreedom and the servile labour required by industrial capitalism, but this is only

one instance, for her, of the experience of 'necessity' or 'gravity' that dominates material transactions. The essence of moral and spiritual action is the complete renunciation of any privileged position for an ego outside the world of 'necessity'. Such renunciation is the only escape from necessity, in fact: what she calls 'decreation' becomes our supremely creative act, since only in the ego's absence is love, or an apprehension of non-self-oriented goods, possible. Marx, Kant and the gospels are all in evidence here.

ROWAN WILLIAMS

WELFARE

Notions of welfare occur widely in political philosophy and political argument. For example, utilitarianism is a social ethic that may be interpreted as giving a pre-eminent place to the idea that the welfare of society should be the overriding goal of public policy. Discussion of the ethics of redistribution focuses upon the institutions and practices of the so-called welfare state. Even those not convinced that we can validly speak of animal rights will often accept that considerations of animal welfare should play a part in legislation and morals. Moreover, the concept of welfare is clearly related to, and indeed overlaps with, concepts like 'needs' or 'interests', which are also central to public decision-making and action.

Welfare can be thought of in three ways. First, there is a subjective sense, in which to say that something contributes to a person's welfare is to say that it makes for the satisfaction of a preference. However, people can adapt their preferences to their circumstances, and happy slaves might be better off changing their preferences than having them satisfied. This thought leads on to the second sense of welfare as doing well according to some objective measure, like the possession of property. However, this conception can ignore subjective differences between people and fail to account for their capacity to take advantage of their objective circumstances. Hence, a third conception of welfare would make the capacity to take advantage of one's possessions an essential element of welfare. A satisfactory overall conception will have to bring these ideas together.

See also: HAPPINESS

ALBERT WEALE

WESENSSCHAU (PERCEPTION OF ESSENCE)

See PHENOMENOLOGY, EPISTEMIC ISSUES IN

WHEWELL, WILLIAM (1794–1886)

William Whewell's two seminal works, *History of the Inductive Science, from the Earliest to the Present Time* (1837) and *The Philosophy of the Inductive Sciences, Founded upon their History* (1840), began a new era in the philosophy of science. Equally critical of the British 'sensationalist' school, which founded all knowledge on experience, and the German idealists, who based science on a priori ideas, Whewell undertook to survey the history of all known sciences in search of a better explanation of scientific discovery. His conclusions were as bold as his undertaking. All real knowledge, he argued, is 'antithetical', requiring mutually irreducible, ever-present, and yet inseparable empirical and conceptual components. Scientific progress is achieved not by induction, or reading-out theories from previously collected data, but by the imaginative 'superinduction' of novel hypotheses upon known but seemingly unrelated facts. He thus broke radically with traditional inductivism – and for nearly a century was all but ignored. In *Philosophy* the antithetical structure of scientific theories and the hypothetico-deductive account of scientific discovery form the basis for novel analyses of scientific and mathematical truth and scientific methodology, critiques of rival philosophies of science, and an account of the emergence and refinement of scientific ideas.

See also: CONVENTIONALISM; DISCOVERY, LOGIC OF; SCIENTIFIC METHOD

MENACHEM FISCH

WHICHCOTE, B.

See CAMBRIDGE PLATONISM

WHITEHEAD, ALFRED NORTH (1861–1947)

Whitehead made fundamental contributions to modern logic and created one of the most controversial metaphysical systems of the twentieth century. He drew out what he took to be the revolutionary consequences for philosophy of the new discoveries in mathematics, logic and physics, developing these consequences first in logic and then in the philosophy of science and speculative metaphysics. His work constantly returns to the question: What is the place of the constructions of mathematics, science and philosophy in the nature of things?

Whitehead collaborated with Bertrand Russell on *Principia Mathematica* (1910–13), which argues that all pure mathematics is derivable from a small number of logical principles. He went on in his philosophy of science to describe nature in terms of overlapping series of events and to argue that

scientific explanations are constructed on that basis. He finally expanded and redefined his work by developing a new kind of speculative metaphysics. Stated chiefly in *Process and Reality* (1929), his metaphysics is both an extended reflection on the character of philosophical inquiry and an account of the nature of all things as a self-constructing 'process'. On this view, reality is incomplete, a matter of the becoming of 'occasions' which are centres of activity in a multiplicity of serial processes whereby the antecedent occasions are taken up in the activities of successor occasions.

JAMES BRADLEY

WHORF, BENJAMIN LEE

See SAPIR-WHORF HYPOTHESIS

WIENER KREIS

See VIENNA CIRCLE

WILL, FREEDOM OF THE

See FREE WILL

WILL, THE

As traditionally conceived, the will is the faculty of choice or decision, by which we determine which actions we shall perform. As a faculty of decision, the will is naturally seen as the point at which we exercise our freedom of action – our control of how we act. It is within our control or up to us which actions we perform only because we have a capacity to decide which actions we shall perform, and it is up to us which such decisions we take. We exercise our freedom of action through freely taken decisions about how we shall act.

From late antiquity onwards, many philosophers took this traditional conception of the will very seriously, and developed it as part of a general theory of specifically human action. Human action, on this theory, is importantly different from animal action. Not only do humans have a freedom of or control over their action which animals lack; but this freedom supposedly arises because humans can act on the basis of reason, while animal action is driven by appetite and instinct. Both this freedom and rationality involve humans possessing what animals are supposed to lack: a will or rational appetite – a genuine decision-making capacity.

From the sixteenth century on, this conception of the will and its role in human action met with increasing scepticism. There was no longer a consensus that human action involved mental capacities radically unlike those found in animals. And the idea that free actions are explained by free decisions of the will came to be seen as viciously regressive: if our freedom of action has to come from a prior freedom of will, why shouldn't that freedom of will have to come from some yet further, will-generating form of freedom – and so on ad infinitum?

Yet it is very natural to believe that we do have a decision-making capacity, and that it is up to us how we exercise that capacity – that it is indeed up to us which actions we decide to perform. The will-scepticism of early modern Europe, which persists in much modern Anglophone philosophy of action, may then have involved abandoning a model of human action and human rationality that is deeply part of common sense. We need to understand this model far better before we can conclude that its abandonment by so many philosophers really was warranted.

See also: ACTION; FREE WILL; INTENTION; PRACTICAL REASON AND ETHICS; VIRTUE ETHICS

THOMAS PINK

WILLIAM OF OCKHAM (c.1287–1347)

William of Ockham is a major figure in late medieval thought. Many of his ideas were actively – sometimes passionately – discussed in universities all across Europe from the 1320s up to the sixteenth century and even later. Against the background of the extraordinarily creative English intellectual milieu of the early fourteenth century, in which new varieties of logical, mathematical and physical speculation were being explored, Ockham stands out as the main initiator of late scholastic nominalism, a current of thought further exemplified – with important variants – by a host of authors after him, from Adam Wodeham, John Buridan and Albert of Saxony to the school of John Mair far into the sixteenth century.

As a Franciscan friar, Ockham taught theology and Aristotelian logic and physics from approximately 1317 to 1324, probably in Oxford and London. He managed to develop in this short period an original and impressive theological and philosophical system. However, his academic career was interrupted by a summons to the Papal Court at Avignon for theological scrutiny of his teachings. Once there, he became involved in the raging quarrel between Pope John XXII and the Minister General of the Franciscan Order, Michael of Cesena, over the poverty of the church. Ockham was eventually excommunicated in 1328. Having fled to Munich, where he put himself under the protection of the Emperor Ludwig of Bavaria, he fiercely continued the antipapal struggle, devoting the rest of his life to the writing of polemical and politically-oriented treatises.

Because he never was officially awarded the title of Doctor in Theology, Ockham has been traditionally known as the *venerabilis inceptor*, the 'venerable beginner', a nickname which at the same time draws attention to the seminal character of his thought. As a tribute to the rigour and strength of his arguments, he has also been called the 'Invincible Doctor'.

The core of his thought lies in his qualified approach to the old problem of universals, inherited by the Christian world from the Greeks through Porphyry and Boethius. Ockham's stand is that only individuals exist, generality being but a matter of signification. This is what we call his nominalism. In the mature version of his theory, species and genera are identified with certain mental qualities called concepts or intentions of the mind. Ontologically, these are individuals too, like everything else: each individual mind has its own individual concepts. Their peculiarity, for Ockham, lies in their representative function: a general concept *naturally signifies* many different individuals. The concept 'horse', for instance, naturally signifies all singular horses and the concept 'white' all singular white things. They are not arbitrary or illusory for all that: specific and generic concepts, Ockham thought, are the results of purely natural processes safely grounded in the intuitive acquaintance of individual minds with real singular objects; and these concepts do cut the world at its joints. The upshot of Ockham's doctrine of universals is that it purports to validate science as objective knowledge of necessary connections, without postulating mysterious universal entities 'out there'.

Thought, in this approach, is treated as a mental language. Not only is it composed of signs, but these mental signs, natural as they are, are also said to combine with each other into propositions, true or false, just as extra-mental linguistic signs do; and in so doing, to follow rules of construction very similar to those of spoken languages. Ockham thus endowed mental discourse with grammatical categories. However, his main innovation in this respect is that he also adapted and transposed to the fine-grained analysis of mental language a relatively new theoretical apparatus that had been emerging in Europe since the twelfth century: the theory of the 'properties of terms' – the most important part of the *logica modernorum*, the 'logic of the moderns' – which was originally intended for the semantical analysis of spoken languages. Ockham in effect (along with some of his contemporaries, such as Walter Burley) promoted this new brand of semantical analysis to the rank of philosophical method *par excellence*. In a wide variety of philosophical and theological discussions, he made sustained use of the technical notions of 'signification', 'connotation' and, above all, 'supposition' (or reference) and all their cognates. His distinctive contribution to physics, for example, consists mainly in semantical analyses of problematic terms such as 'void', 'space' or 'time', in order to show how, in the end, they refer to nothing but singular substances and qualities.

Ockham's rejection of universals also had a theological aspect: universals, if they existed, would unduly limit God's omnipotence. On the other hand, he was convinced that pure philosophical reasoning suffices anyway for decisively refuting realism regarding universals, since all its variants turn out to be ultimately self-contradictory, as he endeavoured to show by detailed criticism.

On the whole, Ockham traced a sharper dividing line than most Christian scholastics before him between theological speculation based on revealed premises and natural sciences in the Aristotelian sense, that is those based on empirical evidence and self-evident principles. He wanted to maintain this clear-cut distinction in principle through all theoretical and practical knowledge, including ethics and political reasoning. In this last field, in particular, to which Ockham devoted thousands of pages in the last decades of his life, he strenuously defended the independence of secular power from ecclesiastical power, stressing whenever he could the autonomy of right reason in human affairs.

See also: BURIDAN, J.; DUNS SCOTUS, J.; EMPIRICISM; NOMINALISM; UNIVERSALS

CLAUDE PANACCIO

WILLIAMS, BERNARD ARTHUR OWEN (1929–2003)

Bernard Williams wrote on the philosophy of mind, especially personal identity, and political philosophy; but the larger and later part of his published work is on ethics. He is hostile to utilitarianism, and also attacks a view of morality associated in particular with Kant: people may only be properly blamed for what they do voluntarily, and what we should do is the same for all of us, and discoverable by reason. By contrast Williams holds that luck has an important role in our evaluation of ourselves and others; in the proper attribution of responsibility the voluntary is less central than the Kantian picture implies. Williams thinks shame a more important moral emotion than blame. Instead of there being an independent set of consistent moral truths, discoverable by reason, how we should live depends on the emotions and desires that we happen to have. These vary between people, and are typically plural and conflicting. Hence for Williams ethical judgment could not describe independent or real

values – by contrast with the way in which he thinks that scientific judgment may describe a real independent world.

ROSS HARRISON

WINDELBAND, WILHELM
See NEO-KANTIANISM

WITTGENSTEIN, LUDWIG JOSEF JOHANN (1889–1951)

Introduction

Ludwig Wittgenstein was born in Vienna on 26 April 1889 and died in Cambridge on 29 April 1951. He spent his childhood and youth in Austria and Germany, studied with Russell in Cambridge from 1911 to 1914 and worked again in Cambridge (with some interruptions) from 1929 to 1947.

His first book, the *Tractatus Logico-Philosophicus*, was published in German in 1921 and in English translation in 1922. It presents a logical atomist picture of reality and language. The world consists of a vast number of independent facts, each of which is in turn composed of some combination of simple objects. Each object has a distinctive logical shape which fits it to combine only with certain other objects. These objects are named by the basic elements of language. Each name has the same logical shape, and so the same pattern of possibilities of combination, as the object it names. An elementary sentence is a combination of names and if it is true it will be a picture of the isomorphic fact formed by the combination of the named objects. Ordinary sentences, however, are misleading in their surface form and need to be analysed before we can see the real complexity implicit in them.

Other important ideas in the *Tractatus* are that these deep truths about the nature of reality and representation cannot properly be *said* but can only be *shown*. Indeed Wittgenstein claimed that pointing to this distinction was central to his book. And he embraced the paradoxical conclusion that most of the *Tractatus* itself is, strictly, nonsense. He also held that other important things can also be shown but not said, for example, about there being a certain truth in solipsism and about the nature of value. The book is brief and written in a simple and elegant way. It has inspired writers and musicians as well as being a significant influence on logical positivism.

After the *Tractatus* Wittgenstein abandoned philosophy until 1929, and when he returned to it he came to think that parts of his earlier thought had been radically mistaken. His later ideas are worked out most fully in the *Philosophical Investigations*, published in 1953.

One central change is from presenting language as a fixed and timeless framework to presenting it as an aspect of vulnerable and changeable human life. Wittgenstein came to think that the idea that words name simple objects was incoherent, and instead introduced the idea of 'language games'. We teach language to children by training them in practices in which words and actions are interwoven. To understand a word is to know how to use it in the course of the projects of everyday life. We find our ways of classifying things and interacting with them so natural that it may seem to us that they are necessary and that in adopting them we are recognizing the one and only possible conceptual scheme. But if we reflect we discover that we can at least begin to describe alternatives which might be appropriate if certain very general facts about the world were different or if we had different interests.

A further aspect of the change in Wittgenstein's views is the abandonment of sympathy with solipsism. On the later view there are many selves, aware of and co-operating with each other in their shared world. Wittgenstein explores extensively the nature of our psychological concepts in order to undermine that picture of 'inner' and 'outer' which makes it so difficult for us to get a satisfactory solution to the so-called 'mind–body problem'.

Although there are striking contrasts between the earlier and later views, and Wittgenstein is rightly famous for having developed two markedly different philosophical outlooks, there are also continuities. One of them is Wittgenstein's belief that traditional philosophical puzzles often arise from deeply gripping but misleading pictures of the workings of language. Another is his conviction that philosophical insight is not to be gained by constructing quasi-scientific theories of puzzling phenomena. Rather it is to be achieved, if at all, by seeking to be intellectually honest and so to neutralize the sources of confusion.

1 Life

Wittgenstein was the eighth and last child of a wealthy Austrian industrialist. From 1903–8 he was educated on the assumption that he would be an engineer and in 1908 he came to Manchester to study aeronautics. He continued with this for three years, but at the same time developed his interest in philosophy. He was particularly engaged with logic and the foundations of mathematics, in connection with which he read FREGE (§§6–10) and RUSSELL. In October 1911 he gave up engineering and, on Frege's advice, came to Cambridge to study with Russell. In the 1914–18 war he served in the Austro-Hungarian army and during this time completed the *Tractatus Logico-Philosophicus* (1922).

For a time Wittgenstein thought that the *Tractatus* said everything which could be said in philosophy, and so he turned to other things. From 1920 to 1926 he was a schoolteacher in Austria, though this was not a success, since he was severe and demanded too much of his pupils. In 1926–8 he helped to design a house for his sister. In 1927 he resumed philosophical discussion with some members of the Vienna Circle, and in 1929 he returned to Cambridge, lecturing there from 1930 to 1936. From 1936 to 1938 he visited Norway and Ireland, returning to Cambridge in 1938 and being appointed professor there in 1939. He held the chair until 1947, although from 1941 to 1944 he was given leave of absence to work first at Guy's Hospital, London, then at the Royal Victoria Infirmary, Newcastle. After resigning his chair in 1947 he lived in various places, Ireland chief among them, and also visited America.

Wittgenstein impressed those who met him with the power both of his intellect and personality. He had an intense concern for truth and integrity which exerted great attraction, but which also made him difficult to deal with since he was liable to accuse others of superficiality or dishonesty. He greatly disliked what he perceived as the artificiality and pretentiousness of academic life. His later ideas became known in the 1930s and 1940s through the circulation of copies of *The Blue and Brown Books* (1958) and reports of his lectures. They acquired considerable influence with some who found them inspiring, but others thought them irritatingly obscure.

2 Works and method of writing

Throughout his life Wittgenstein wrote down his thoughts in notebooks, returning to the same topics many times, trying to get the most direct and compelling formulation of the ideas. He then made selections and arrangements from these remarks, followed by yet further selection, reworking and rearrangement. The *Tractatus* was the only book published during his lifetime. In 1930 he assembled what we now know as the *Philosophical Remarks*, a work still having much of the outlook of the *Tractatus* and also showing considerable sympathies with verificationism, and in 1932–4 he wrote the *Philosophical Grammar*, in which some central themes of the later philosophy are foreshadowed. But he was not satisfied with either of these, and from 1936 onwards worked on various versions of what we now know as the *Philosophical Investigations* (1953), which he hoped would provide a definitive presentation of his thought. The earlier half of the volume is the part of his work with which he was most nearly satisfied, but he was never fully content with any of it, and in 1949 he abandoned the project of completing it.

The other books we have under his name are all early or intermediate versions of material, left in his papers and edited and published after his death. The *Notebooks* are preliminary versions of ideas which later became the *Tractatus*. The *Blue and Brown Books* were prepared so as to help his students in 1932 and 1933. *Remarks on the Foundations of Mathematics* (1956) contains ideas he worked on from 1937 to 1944 and which he intended at that time to form the second part of the *Investigations* (rather than the psychological topics we now have). From 1944 onwards he worked mainly on philosophical psychology: *Zettel* (1967), *Remarks on the Philosophy of Psychology I and II* (1980) and *Last Writings on Philosophical Psychology I and II* (1982) are from these years. From 1950 to 1951 we also have *On Certainty* (1969) and *Remarks on Colour* (1977). Another source for his views is his conversations and lectures as recorded by friends and pupils.

3 The picture theory of meaning

The *Tractatus* consists of nearly eighty printed pages of numbered remarks. The numbers do not run consecutively but are designed to indicate the relative importance and role of the remarks. There are seven major sentences and each of them (except 7) has subordinate and clarificatory remarks following it, labelled '2.2', '5.4' and so on, down as far as such numbers as '4.0312'.

The topics that preoccupied Wittgenstein when he arrived in Cambridge included the nature of logical truth and Russell's Theory of Types (see THEORY OF TYPES). On both of these matters Russell held that we need an account of very general features of the world and of the kinds of things in it. But Wittgenstein soon came to think that the route to insight was through the contemplation of the nature and presuppositions of individual meaningful sentences such as 'Socrates is wise' and that this contemplation showed Russell's approach to be misguided.

The central fact about such individual sentences is that each says one thing – that Socrates is wise, for example – but is essentially such that it may be either true or false. A false sentence is both out of touch with the world, inasmuch as it is false, but also in touch with the world, inasmuch as it succeeds in specifying a way that things might be. Wittgenstein holds that all this is possible only because the sentence is complex and has components which represent elements of reality, which exist whether the sentence is true or false and are (potentially) constituents of states of affairs. So, in rough illustration, 'Socrates' represents Socrates and 'is wise' represents wisdom. The truth or falsity of the sentence then depends on whether these elements are or are not assembled into a fact.

Not all sequences of sentence components are acceptable. A mere list of names (for example, 'Socrates Plato') does not hang together as a sentence. And although it looks as if we may apply a predicate to itself (as in 'is in English is in English' or 'is wise is wise'), it seems important to disallow such sequences as truth-evaluable sentences, on pain of falling into Russell's paradox. Russell's account of these matters is that elements of reality come divided into different types – individuals, properties and so on – and that a sentence is to be allowed as meaningful, and so truth-evaluable, only if the elements picked out by the components are of suitably related types.

Wittgenstein maintains, against this, that we do not need rules to bar sentences which would lead to paradox, because when we properly understand the nature of our language we see that we cannot formulate the supposed sentences in the first place. We think we can only because we have misidentified that component in 'Socrates is wise' the presence of which in the sentence attributes wisdom to Socrates. This component is not the phrase 'is wise' but the property which the word 'Socrates' has when the words 'is wise' are written to the right of it. To see why this is plausible, consider the fact that there could be a language in which properties are attributed to people by writing their names in different colours. For example, we could claim that Socrates is wise by writing 'Socrates' in red letters. In such a language we could never formulate any analogue to 'is wise is wise' because we could not take the redness of 'Socrates' and make it red. And although in English we have given a linguistic role to 'Plato' (as representing Plato), we have not given any role to the property of a name which it acquires when we write 'Plato' to the right of it. That is why a mere list of names does not hang together to make a statement.

Wittgenstein generalizes this idea to claim that the formal properties of any element of the world, that is, the properties which fix its potential for combining into facts with other elements, must be mirrored in the formal properties of the linguistic component which represents it. So the kind of item which says something, and which we often wrongly think to be a complex object, is really a fact. In a sentence certain linguistic components are put together experimentally in a structure which mirrors the formal structure of some possible state of affairs (see THEORY OF TYPES).

4   Negation and tautology

This account does away with the need for a theory of types and Wittgenstein holds that the ideas invoked by Russell to explain the nature of logical truth are similarly unnecessary. Russell's view was that logical truths, such as that all sentences of the form 'p or not p' are true, should be explained by pointing to relations holding between some very abstract kind of logical items – negation, disjunction and the like.

Wittgenstein maintains that the negation sign is not a component of a sentence and so does not represent any element of a possible fact (in the quasi-technical sense of 'component', 'element' and 'represent' introduced above). Rather it is the visible mark of an operation one can perform on a meaningful sentence to produce another sentence. The role of the second sentence is to deny that things are as they would need to be to make the first sentence true.

To see the force of this, we must look again at the account of truth given above. What makes a negative sentence true is not the presence of some 'not-ness' in a fact but rather the absence of that (the combination of elements) which would have made the unnegated sentence true. Similar accounts are to be given of the other so-called logical constants. Thus 'or' does not stand for a possible element in a fact but is a sign by which one can correctly link two sentences if the components of either are so combined as to yield a truth.

Logical tautologies thus do not reveal the nature of special logical objects. Such sentences as 'It is raining or it is not raining' do not say anything. But their possibility is a corollary of the existence of a language adequate to say the kind of thing which can be said. So contemplating them can draw our attention to the logical structure of the world (see LOGICAL CONSTANTS).

5   Simples

The ideas outlined in the last two sections are already present in the sets of notes which Wittgenstein wrote in late 1913 and 1914. But the *Tractatus* in its complete form incorporated several further important ideas. One of these, perhaps adopted from Frege, is the view that sense must be determinate, that is, that every meaningful sentence must be either true or false in every possible state of affairs. But Wittgenstein differs from Frege in thinking that ordinary language, although misleading in surface form, is in order, and so already fulfils this condition of determinacy.

Determinacy entails that there must be what Wittgenstein calls 'objects', that is, utterly simple, eternal and unalterable elements, out of which all facts are composed. Moreover the links between our language system and reality must be set in place at this basic level. Suppose that language-world links were set up so as to connect a basic linguistic component with some element of reality which was not basic. The existence of this element would be contingent and would depend upon some simpler elements being suitably combined in a fact. A sentence containing this imagined basic component is clearly not true in a world where the simpler elements are not suitably combined. But it is equally unhappy to say that it is false, because the component itself does not specify what the simpler elements are or that they must be combined, and so it is no part of its meaning that their failure to be combined is relevant to its falsehood. To insist on the undefinability of this imagined basic element of language is to insist that it has meaning only through its connection with the item it represents. So in a world lacking that item it has no meaning, and sentences containing it are neither true nor false. But this, given the assumption of determinacy of sense, is a *reductio ad absurdum* of the idea that meaning can be conferred in this imagined way.

We may have an apparently basic sentence component which is linked to a contingently existing item (for example 'Socrates' as a name of Socrates). But this is only possible because a definition of that component can be given in our language system. The link between Socrates and his name is thus not a basic point of attachment between language and the world (contrary to the impression given in our earlier rough-and-ready example). It is a consequence of these ideas that there must be a complete analysis of every sentence of our language which reveals it to be a truth-functional combination of elementary propositions, the components of which are simple signs representing objects.

But what are these simple objects? Wittgenstein, like Russell but unlike Frege, does not allow for any contrast between sense and reference within the meaning possessed by names of simples. This puts one demand on simples: they cannot be items with distinguishable aspects, that is, items which can be conceived of in several logically distinct ways. If they were, then there would also be the possibility of one name for a simple as conceived one way and another non-synonymous name for it as conceived another way – contrary to the denial of the sense-reference distinction. So a simple is the kind of thing which, if apprehended in such a way that it can be named, is apprehended exactly as it is in its entirety.

In so far as Wittgenstein drops any hints, it is that simples are phenomenally presented items, such as points in the sensory field and the properties they have, for example, shades of experienced colour. But he cannot give this answer officially because to do so would clash with another of the themes brought to prominence in the later development of the *Tractatus*. This is the claim that all necessity is logical necessity, and hence would be revealed as tautological in a complete analysis (see §7). A corollary of this is that all atomic facts are independent of each other and no elementary proposition can entail or be the contrary of any other. Such things as colours cannot then be 'objects' because attribution of different colours to one thing, as in 'a is red' and 'a is green', produces sentences which are contraries.

The topics so far discussed are treated primarily in the remarks following the main sentences numbered 2, 3 and 4. The remarks following 5 and 6 deal mainly with implications of this atomist conception for certain issues in logic (generality and identity for example) and for the nature of science, mathematics and statements of probability. On the last mentioned subject, Wittgenstein's brief remarks are one important source for the approach later developed by Rudolf Carnap (see CARNAP, R.; LOGICAL ATOMISM).

6 Thought, self and value

Wittgenstein writes, 'There is no such thing as the subject that thinks or entertains ideas' (5.631). His grounds for this are similar to those of Hume, namely that a unified, conscious self cannot be an element in any encountered fact. Hence no such item can be among those objects represented in thought. So reports of the form 'A believes that p', which seem to mention such a subject, are really of the form '"p" says that p'. They report the existence of a sentential complex, the components of which are correlated with the elements of the potential fact that p. There are then no selves in the contingent, encountered world but, at best, bundles of sentence-like items.

But Wittgenstein does not discard the notion of subject completely. The notion he rejects is that of the subject 'as conceived in psychology'. But the notion of the 'metaphysical' subject he thinks important. On this latter he says, 'What the solipsist means is quite correct; only it cannot be said but makes itself manifest' (5.62), and 'The subject does not belong to the world: rather, it is a limit of the world' (5.632).

One reading of this sees it as holding that I cannot prise apart the world and my experience of it. My own experience is directly available to me and any claim I make about the world must at the same time articulate that experience. Others' experiences, by contrast, are available to me only through noises or movements in my world. Another interpretation stresses the idea that a representation is always from a point of view which is not represented in it. A third view connects these remarks with the idea of projection. Wittgenstein speaks of using a propositional sign as a projection of a possible situation by thinking out its sense. So a subject might be the origin of the lines of projection which link representing items with what they represent and whose existence is thus presupposed by their meaningfulness. 'The world is *my* world: this is manifest in the fact that the limits of *language* (of that language which alone I understand) mean the limit of *my* world' (5.62). So perhaps Wittgenstein's idea is that the existence of a unique self (me) at the limit of the world is shown by the existence of representations which are meaningful to me.

Wittgenstein also offers, in the closing pages of the *Tractatus*, a number of gnomic remarks about value, death and the mystical, among them that no value exists in the world, that ethics cannot be put into words, that the will as a subject of ethical attributes cannot alter facts but only the limits of the world, that at death the world does not alter but comes to an end, that feeling the world as a limited whole is the mystical and that the solution of the problem of life is seen in the vanishing of the problem. These claims are to some extent intelligibly grounded in ideas concerning the self and what can be said. But they also represent a leap of development beyond those, a leap which comes in part from Wittgenstein's experiences in the First World War and the religious convictions to which his always intense and serious outlook then led him.

7 Saying and showing

Wittgenstein says that by reading the *Tractatus* one may come to grasp certain things about the nature of meaning, reality and value, among them the kinds of things outlined above. But he also claims that these things cannot be *said* but only *shown*, and that the attempt to say them ends up producing nonsense (6.54). Most of the *Tractatus* itself is thus nonsense. This claim is highly paradoxical and may seem to be unnecessary and grandiose mysticism, especially when viewed as part of the same package as the difficult remarks about the will and solipsism. But this is unfair. In many of its applications, the claim is well motivated, given the picture theory of meaning (see §3).

Most of the linguistic manoeuvres which Wittgenstein condemns as nonsensical are attempts to say things which are both necessary but also substantive – that is, not mere tautologies. Thus they include moves to assign elements of reality or language to their logical types ('Socrates is a particular'), related attempts to describe the logical forms of sentences or facts and also efforts to list the simples. (Claims about what is valuable could also have this status of seeming to be both substantial and necessary.) But if the picture theory of meaning holds in complete generality there cannot be such stable necessary truths. To say, for example, that object b is F we require that there be a linguistic representative of b ('b') and one of F-ness (the property of having 'F' to the right) which can be combined or not, just as b and F-ness can be combined or not. There must be complexity and there must therefore be the possibility of dissociation as well as association. But if b and F-ness necessarily go together (for example, Socrates must be a particular) then b cannot be dissociated from F-ness and it is a confusion to imagine that its being F is a fact with a composite structure. Hence it is also a confusion to imagine that it is something of the kind which can be said, on the account of saying which is offered by the picture theory.

8 Variant interpretations of the Tractatus

The above account summarizes what the *Tractatus* seems to say. Wittgenstein's overall intention in writing it is disputed. One traditional 'metaphysical' reading takes him to present a strongly realist outlook. There is a world of simple objects with a determinate structure independent of thought and this structure constrains and explains the nature of meaningful representation. We cannot say what this structure is, or describe the relation between reality and language. But the *Tractatus* aims to show us these things.

A second 'therapeutic' reading sees Wittgenstein as seeking to undermine the temptation to make such metaphysical claims. '"Is wise" is wise' is plain nonsense, like 'Frabble is wise', because we have given no meaning to 'is wise' as a referring expression. No further explanation of its nonsensicality is needed or could be given. The attempt to find one, by appeal to some further fact about the nature of what predicates represent merely leads us to formulate more nonsensical verbiage. We may explore the form of our language from the inside but we cannot explain that form by appeal to something external to it. Reflection on the articulation of reality must at the same time be reflection on the articulation of representation since the idea of reality can only be the idea of what makes representations true. 'What is not representable by meaningful representations' can only mean 'what is represented by nonsense'. But nonsense represents nothing.

Defenders of this second interpretation believe that Wittgenstein's intention in writing the *Tractatus* was to release us from the temptation to fruitless philosophical theorizing. Some of them also believe that Wittgenstein intends the completion of the therapy to be relinquishing the show–say distinction itself as nonsensical, and hence relinquishing also the idea of there being any insights to be gained by reading the book. In favour of this so-called 'resolute' interpretation are the facts that some therapeutic intentions are plainly embodied in the work and that Wittgenstein's project looks inconsistent without the final move. He strives to make apparent to us what he takes to be the requirements for any speech to be meaningful, namely that it be capable of picturing contingent states of affairs. Can it be that he then, in all seriousness, suggests that there are linguistic moves by which things are shown (moves which are therefore meaningful in some sense) which do not meet the requirements?

Against the resolute reading one may note that the removal of a muddle which hinders fruitful thought may also present itself as an increase in self-understanding or a coming to know better how to think. The process of reflection which dissolves the muddle and the better view it results in may both have natural verbal expressions. Wittgenstein's *Tractatus* view of language, as solely a system for picturing contingent states of affairs, does not allow for the meaningfulness of such utterances. But his later view recognises a greater variety of kinds of meaningful speech, including (for example) utterances which have the form of indicative statements but whose role is that of acknowledgements of rules of language. We may thus think of Wittgenstein in the *Tractatus* as either irresolute and inconsistent but in practice already recognizing the variety of human discourse, or as resolute and consistent but closing his eyes to that variety.

The *Tractatus*, whether read in a metaphysical or a therapeutic way, shows Wittgenstein gripped by the conviction that there is just one set of possible concepts. The basic constituents of thought and of reality are, he takes it, fixed once and for all, independent of any contingencies of the interests and circumstances of human beings. And sentences have an analysis which if spelt out would make clear to us something we are not now (explicitly) aware of, namely the nature of the fundamental objects which compose states of affairs and which are represented by the simple signs of any meaningful language. These commitments – to analysis, objects and simplicity – themselves embody substantial philosophical claims and they provide central targets for Wittgenstein's later reconsiderations.

9 Transition

At the time of writing the *Tractatus* Wittgenstein took a lofty tone about simple objects; he had proved that they existed and it was of no importance that we cannot say what they are. But in the first years of his return to philosophy in 1927–31 one thing which occupied his attention was the detailed workings of various parts of our language, notably those involved in talking of shape, length and colour and other observable properties of items around us. His aim in considering them was to fill in that earlier gap by giving an account of the fundamental features of both language and the world.

He soon became convinced that the idea of independent elementary propositions was indefensible. For example, the incompatibility of 'a is red' and 'a is green' cannot be explained (contrary to what he had urged in the *Tractatus*) by analysing the two propositions and showing that one contains some elementary proposition which contradicts an elementary proposition in the analysis of the other. Rather the whole collection of colour judgments come as one set, as the marks along the edge of a ruler come as a set. To measure an object we hold a ruler with its marks against the object, that is, in effect we hold up a whole set of possible judgments of length, and we read off which is correct; to see that one judgment is correct is to see at the same time that all the others are incorrect. Something similar holds for colour and for many other concepts, except that in these cases the 'ruler' is not physically present. The differences between concepts have to do with the logical shapes of their 'rulers' and with the different methods by which they are compared to reality.

Other topics which occupied Wittgenstein at this time were those of psychological phenomena

and the use of the word 'I'. And he also worked extensively on the nature of mathematics. Ideas in common with those of the logical positivists are apparent in some of the writings of this time. Indeed the slogan known as the verification principle – 'the meaning of a proposition is its method of verification' – may have originated with Wittgenstein. But he found it impossible to accept this as a clear statement which could provide one of the starting points for elaborating a philosophical system. He was aware of further puzzles and was temperamentally incapable of putting them on one side for the purpose of building an intellectual construct which might be based on misapprehension and which failed to address questions which still perplexed him (see Logical positivism §§3–4; Vienna Circle).

10 Dismantling the Tractatus picture

Paragraphs 1–242 of the *Philosophical Investigations* (roughly the first third of the book) are generally agreed to provide the most focused presentation of some of the central ideas of Wittgenstein's later outlook, in the context of which his views on philosophy of mind, mathematics and epistemology can helpfully be seen. We may divide the paragraphs into three groups: §§1–88 raise a variety of interrelated difficulties for the outlook of the *Tractatus*, §§89–142 discuss the nature of logic, philosophy and truth, and §§143–242 contain the so-called rule-following considerations.

The first group has two main targets: first, the idea that most words have meaning in virtue of naming something and, second, the idea that meaning requires determinacy and so exactness. Against the former Wittgenstein points out that different words function in different ways. To understand 'five', for example, a person needs to be able to count and behave appropriately on the result of a counting; to understand a colour term might, by contrast, involve knowing how to compare the specimen to be judged with a sheet of samples. To teach language one must train a person to produce and respond to words in the context of everyday activities such as fetching things, measuring, building, buying and selling. We can throw light on meaning by reflecting on simple 'language games', involving such integration of speech and action. To say that every word names something is like saying that every tool in the tool box modifies something. We can describe things this way if we insist: 'The saw modifies the shape of the board; the ruler modifies our knowledge of a thing's length'. But such assimilation may lead us to overlook important variety rather than representing a useful insight. To get someone to understand a word it is not enough to bring them face-to-face with the supposed referent while repeating the word. In order to profit from the confrontation, the learner must know what kind of word is being taught (for a number, shape, colour, and so on). And this in turn involves already being at home with the everyday activities into which remarks using the word are woven. 'For a *large* class of cases – though not for all – in which we employ the word meaning it can be defined thus: the meaning of a word is its use in the language' (Wittgenstein 1953: §43).

On the second topic Wittgenstein remarks that drawing a contrast between 'simple' and 'complex' depends upon context and interest. Items which might be seen as complex in one context could be taken as simple in another and vice versa. So these notions and the related notion of exactness are context-relative. A word does not become unusable and hence meaningless because its use is not everywhere bounded by rules. That we can imagine circumstances in which a given description would seem inappropriately vague or in which we would not know whether to say that it was true or false is no criticism of its current use and hence no argument that it does not have meaning. Thus the idea that every meaningful sentence must have some underlying analysis in terms of simples is mistaken.

Each sort of word is at home in its own language game. But there are not always clear-cut relations of subordination or dependence between different language games. There are many predicates (for example, 'intention', 'thought', 'statement', 'number', 'game') which clearly do not name simples, because they have interesting richness and apply to complex items. But it is not the case that such predicates must have an analysis in terms of 'simpler' predicates. Search for such an analysis may reveal instead a 'family resemblance'. Persons who recognizably belong to the same family may have various resemblances, of build, features, colour of eyes, gait, temperament and so on, which 'form a complicated network of similarities, overlapping and criss-crossing' (1953: §66), without one set of such resemblances being necessary and sufficient for having the appearance of a member of that family.

On the basis of this survey of the actual workings of language, Wittgenstein then concludes that the *Tractatus* picture of a detailed crystalline structure present in both world and language is an illusion.

But perhaps the considerations outlined require only minor tinkering with the *Tractatus* picture? We might say: 'Certainly linguistic representations of states of affairs are put to various uses, in commands, jokes, stories etc., as well as in straight reports; also what degree of exactness we need is fixed by context; hence we should accept that for many

practical purposes vague remarks are adequate. But none of this shows that we must discard the *Tractatus* picture of a fully determinate world, structured by simples; nor does it show that the idea of constructing a complete and exhaustive description of it need be abandoned. All it shows is that our everyday language mirrors the world less accurately than an imaginable ideal scientific language.' That such a reading is inadequate is shown by considering the remarks on rule-following found in paragraphs 143–242.

11 Rule-following

By 'rule' Wittgenstein does not mean an abstract standard according to which some act may be judged right or wrong. Rather he means a concrete item, such as a noise, mark or gesture, which is presented to a person and by attending to which they direct their behaviour, the link between rule and response being learned and conventional. An enormous number of human activities can be seen as instances of rule-following. They include imitating the gestures and noises which others make, copying shapes, converting marks into noises as in reading music, chanting the number sounds in sequence, and so on. More generally, both non-verbal behaviour in response to verbal instruction (fetching a book when told to do so) and also producing linguistic reports (where the world itself is the guide and the utterance is the response) may be described as rule-following. Rule-following is thus at the heart of linguistic competence. If we further accept that coming to use a rich and expressive language is an indispensable part of coming to grasp complex concepts and to make reflective judgments, then rule-following is also at the heart of our lives as thinking creatures.

It is generally agreed that Wittgenstein has telling negative points to make about one attractive but misleading picture of rule-following. On this picture, to understand a rule, for example, to grasp what is meant by 'Add two', it is necessary and sufficient to have a certain sort of item, an image, feeling or formula, occur in the mind when the instruction is heard. For example, having a mental image of two blocks appearing at the end of a line of blocks is the sort of thing which might be imagined to constitute understanding 'Add two'. This image is supposed to do two things. First, it helps bring about that the person goes on to produce a particular response, for example saying 'Eight' if the previously given number was six; second, it sets a standard by which that response can be judged correct or incorrect.

But the picture will not do. A person might have such an image while responding to 'Add two' as if it meant 'Multiply by two'. Moreover their behaviour (the regular patterns of action, what seems to be regarded as a mistake, and so on) could show that for them, 'Add two' actually means 'Multiply by two'. So images guarantee neither subsequent behaviour nor the appropriateness of a particular standard of assessment.

What this case makes us see is that an image, feeling or formula is merely another rule-like object (that is, a potential vehicle of meaning) rather than the meaning itself. An item is not automatically a self-interpreting sign, that is, one which fixes and enforces a certain reading of itself, simply in virtue of existing in the mind rather than in the outer public world. So images and the like are not sufficient for understanding; but neither are they necessary, since in many cases they do not occur. Typically when someone responds to everyday and familiar language they just act unhesitatingly and spontaneously, without consulting any inner item.

To teach someone to follow a rule, for example to understand 'Add two', we put them through a finite amount of training, primarily by working through examples of adding two. These examples may appear to be another resource for pinning down meaning. But being only finite in number, they are bound to have more than one feature in common. Thus they do not themselves determine a unique interpretation for the sign we associate with them. A learner might exhibit a future bizarre divergence from what is expected, for instance by saying that adding two to 1,000 yields 1,004. And if this occurred it would suggest that they had all along been struck by some feature other than the one intended.

The central point here is that, for there to be meaning, the rule-followers must have fixed on one rather than another of the various similarities between the teaching examples and have associated it with the rule, that is, with the mark or sign to which they respond. 'The use of the word rule and the use of the word same are interwoven' (1953: §224). But neither the examples nor the rule itself determine which similarity this is; and imagined inner surrogates, in which we would like to see the relevant resemblance encapsulated, turn out to be equally inefficacious.

These reflections do not just undermine one picture of the psychology of understanding. They are also relevant to the picture presented by the *Tractatus*. If there were a fixed structure for world and language as envisaged in the *Tractatus*, then there would exist items, namely the simple objects, which would fix the one and only absolute standard of similarity. If there is a simple which is a common element in two separate facts then there is a basic real resemblance between those facts; if not, not.

Every other real resemblance which can be meaningfully labelled, for example by the predicates of everyday language or science, must be founded in simples. A putative linguistic expression which is not tied to some definite combination of simples is, on the *Tractatus* view, an expression without meaning which is merely randomly applied. Further, as we saw earlier, a simple is the kind of thing which, when apprehended, must be apprehended as it is. So representing a simple, whether by a direct cognition of it or by having in mind something which encapsulates its nature, is to be aware of a self-interpreting item, something which dictates what is to count as 'the same'. But this sort of confrontation is what the rule-following considerations suggest to be unintelligible.

Thus the discussions of §§143–242 can be seen as interweaving with and reinforcing those of §§1–88. The whole undermines not only the idea of closeness of fit between a *Tractatus* world and everyday language, but the underlying conception of that world itself, namely as already determinately articulated into facts by simples which we can apprehend (see MEANING AND RULE-FOLLOWING).

12 The later picture of meaning

The *Tractatus* offers us a world articulated, independently of our detailed human concerns, into value-free facts which are the subject matter of the natural sciences together with a mind confronting that world and attempting to mirror it in its thoughts. It also tells us that there is (in some sense) only one subject and that it is an item at the limit of the world which cannot act responsibly in the world.

However attractive the first element here, everyone would agree that there is something seriously wrong with the solipsism of the second. So one essential move in amendment is to reintegrate the psychological and the metaphysical subjects of the *Tractatus*, by making the self responsibly active, bringing it in from the limit and locating it firmly in the world, together with other selves. We may do this while leaving in place the idea of the world as the totality of value-free facts. Then the existence of the self which is now located in the world must be some subset of such facts. This yields an extremely powerful and attractive overall picture, namely the picture of reductive naturalism. But it also generates many philosophical puzzles, those to do, for example, with giving naturalistic accounts of consciousness, free will, rationality and so on.

This overall picture cannot be Wittgenstein's, however, if §11 is right in its reading of the rule-following considerations. The idea of an independently articulated world is not acceptable to him.

We cannot understand our concepts by pointing to simples which reveal themselves as the ultimate constituents in any world and so make evident to us the necessity and defensibility of our way of thinking. To understand meaning we must look at use, at how our actions and concepts are inter-woven. The fact that makes a sentence true is grasped through seeing when the sentence is correctly used, and that in turn is grasped only by seeing the full shape of the language games in which it is used. For a concept to be truly applicable to the world, and so for its corresponding property to have instances, is not for it to pick out some simple which is among the timelessly given building-blocks of all worlds. Rather it is for the life of which use of that concept is a part to be liveable in this world. Wittgenstein thus moves from a form of the correspondence theory of truth in the *Tractatus* to a redundancy theory in the *Investigations* (see TRUTH, CORRESPONDENCE THEORY OF; TRUTH, DEFLATIONARY THEORIES OF).

The self need not, on this view, be an assemblage of value-free facts. Neither need we conceive it as a unique metaphysical limit to the world. It is rather a living, human locus of abilities, a person who can be trained to follow rules, to use and respond to language, in the way that normal humans can. And since concepts are aspects of our way of life rather than items built into the one conceptual scheme and underpinned by simple objects, understanding what it is to have a particular concept involves 'assembling reminders' about how it works for us and how our various activities and ways of talking build together into our way of life.

If it is correct to conceive of understanding as an ability, then the exercise of this ability in everyday situations will often be just some confident, spontaneous action or utterance, which the subject will not be able to justify by pointing to something, other than the situation or words responded to, which guided them.

> 'How am I able to obey a rule?' – if this is not a question about causes, then it is about the justification for my following the rule in the way I do. If I have exhausted the justification I have reached bedrock and my spade is turned. Then I am inclined to say: 'This is simply what I do'.
>
> (1953: §217)

But this need not worry us. 'To use a word without justification does not mean to use it without right' (1953: §289). The fact is that we do find such confident and unhesitating responses in ourselves. Also we (usually) agree with others; and where we do not we (usually) agree on how to settle the dispute. So we have no reason to doubt that in general we do indeed mean what we take ourselves to mean.

Indeed we can put things more strongly than this. It is not just that it is sensible, practically speaking, for me to make a leap of faith and decide to carry on as if I and others mean what it seems we mean. We have no more choice about this than we do about taking 'Eight' to be the right response to 'Add two to six'. The language game of ascribing meanings to the remarks of ourselves and others is as central and indispensable to a recognizably human life as anything in our linguistic repertoire. More-over the rich and complex social world in which we find ourselves sustains our practice of so doing. So we and our meanings are just as much part of the world as the stars, rocks and trees around us. And since we are no longer committed to the idea of one totality of facts, those of value-free natural science, this recognition does not now produce cramps or pressures to reductive manoeuvres (see PRIVATE STATES AND LANGUAGE).

13 Alternative readings

The account of §§10–12 presents Wittgenstein as inviting us to abandon the idea of our meanings and judgments being securely moored to something given to us and for which we have no responsibility. We see that there is no guarantee of any unique conceptual scheme to be revealed by analysis, or of a world articulated once and for all in terms of its categories. We are instead to become aware of our involvement in and responsibility for our own judgments and the way of life of which they are part. We are also to acknowledge that we cannot prove the unique correctness of our way of life and its associated concepts. (The arguments of the *Investigations* against the position of the *Tractatus* thus have much in common with themes explored by other late-nineteenth-century and twentieth-century thinkers, such as Nietzsche, William JAMES, Heidegger, Quine and DERRIDA (see NIETZSCHE, F.; HEIDEGGER, M. §§2–4; QUINE, W.V. §5).) But, the reading given in §12 implicitly suggests, this need not lead us to scepticism about the notions of meaning, fact, objectivity or truth.

This interpretation, although not idiosyncratic, is by no means generally accepted. There are a large number of differing construals of Wittgenstein's overall intention, many of which have in common that they present the consequences of abandoning the *Tractatus* view as more radical and/or more deflationary than is suggested in §12.

One interpretation stresses a contrast between the *Tractatus* and the later writings which is different from any highlighted earlier. It takes the rule-following considerations to show that we cannot make sense of a grasp of meaning which fixes truth conditions independent of our ability to verify that they obtain. The later Wittgenstein is thought to insist (as against his earlier self) that all meaning be explicated by appeal to assertibility conditions rather than such possibly verification-transcendent truth conditions, and he is recruited onto the antirealist side of the debate in the dispute between realism and antirealism.

Another much discussed view is presented by Saul KRIPKE. If there were facts about meaning, he argues, they would have to be constituted by something about past behaviour or present occurrences in the mind. So §§143–242 can be read as showing that there are no facts about meaning. Our practice of labelling remarks 'correct' or 'incorrect' and ascribing 'meanings' to them has a role in our social life. But such linguistic moves do not have truth conditions. Instead they have only appropriateness conditions. We are licensed to make them when others in our community keep in step with us in certain ways in their patterns of utterance.

Yet a third interpretation takes it that Wittgenstein espouses relativism. One response to the idea that there are no simples is to take it that the world is a featureless mush or unknowable something. Any apparent structure in it is then imposed by us. Hence the familiar physical and social world we experience is a creation of ours. But there are several possible but incompatible ways of imposing structure, one of which we are physiologically and/or socially caused to adopt. So no judgment can claim to be 'true' in a non-relative sense; at best it can be 'true for us'.

An important issue in assessing this third view is what status Wittgenstein intended for the sketched alternative ways of responding to language teaching. Certainly they need enough feasibility to dislodge the conviction that there is one and only one possible way of dividing up the world. On the other hand it is not clear that he takes us to be entitled to assert that there are conceptual schemes which are both incompatible with ours and also fully possible.

Many other readings are also possible, detecting in his writings elements of pragmatism, behaviourism and even deconstructionism (see BEHAVIOURISM, ANALYTIC; DECONSTRUCTION; PRAGMATISM §2; REALISM AND ANTIREALISM §4; RELATIVISM).

A general question is whether Wittgenstein should be read as a philosophical theorist or as a therapist offering to relieve us of the impulse to construct philosophical theories. To take him to be offering anti-realist, sceptical or relativist views is to see him as a theorist. Those who read him as a theorist in his later work are also likely to favour a metaphysical reading of the *Tractatus*, seeing it too as expressing a philosophical theory, for example

some version of realism. Other commentators (representing a mainstream view) see him as shifting from a theoretical stance in the *Tractatus* to a therapeutic one in the later work. Yet a third group favours a therapeutic reading of his intentions throughout and believes that the ideas offered in the *Tractatus* are much more similar to those of the later work than is often supposed.

This entry assumes that the second approach is right, at least in that the *Tractatus* embodies commitments which are, in effect, theoretical and which Wittgenstein later recognized and criticized as such. But it allows also that the third group may well be correct in thinking that Wittgenstein's overt intentions always had a therapeutic aspect. (It may also be that the distinction between theory and therapy is less clear-cut than previously assumed.)

14 Philosophy of mind

The *Tractatus* picture of the relation of language to its subject matter is especially attractive in the case of some psychological notions. A sensation such as pain is easily conceived as a phenomenon which impresses its nature and identity conditions on one who has it, independent of external circumstances or bodily behaviour. The private language argument (§§243–71) examines this idea in the light of the earlier discussion of meaning. One aim is to show that our actual use of terms for sensations does not and could not conform to the pattern suggested.

The rule-following considerations suggest that no standard for what is to count as 'the same' can be fixed merely by uttering a word to oneself while being vividly aware of what one experiences. For one kind of item rather than another to come into focus out of the indefinite variety potentially presented in an experience, that experience must be embedded in one kind of life rather than another. Relatedly, for a word to have meaning there must be some extended practice in which its use has a point. This is as true of sensation words as of any others. We teach and use them in a complex setting of physical circumstances and expressive bodily behaviour. This setting, says Wittgenstein, is not externally and contingently linked to sensation but is an integral part of the sort of life in which the general category 'sensation' makes sense and in which particular sensations can be individuated.

Wittgenstein considers many other topics in philosophical psychology, among them intention, expectation, calculating in the head, belief, dreaming and aspect perception. A constant theme is the need to counter the attraction of the model of name and object, which (together with such things as the special authority which each person has to pronounce on their own psychological states) leads us to conceive of the 'inner' as a special mysterious realm, distinct from the 'outer' or physical. He offers such general remarks as 'An inner process stands in need of outward criteria' (1953: §580). He also returns repeatedly to the idea that authoritative first-person psychological claims should be seen as expressions or avowals of those states which we are inclined to insist that they describe. These sorts of moves have led to the idea that he denies the existence of the 'inner' and is really a behaviourist.

Wittgenstein was aware of the risk of this reading:

'But you will surely admit that there is a difference between pain-behaviour accompanied by pain and pain-behaviour without any pain?' – Admit it? What greater difference could there be? – 'And yet you again and again reach the conclusion that the sensation itself is a *nothing*.' Not at all. It is not a *something*, but not a *nothing* either!

(1953: §304)

Thoughts and experiences are, on his view, necessarily linked to expressive behaviour. 'Only of a living human being and what resembles (behaves like) a living human being can one say: it has sensations; it sees; is blind; hears; is deaf; is conscious or unconscious' (1953: §281). But this does not mean either that any reduction of the mental to the behavioural is possible or that the psychological is not real. To see Wittgenstein's view sympathetically it is important to keep in mind the upshot of §§1–242. There is no a priori guarantee of some privileged set of classifications (for instance, those of natural science) in terms of which all others must be explained. To understand any phenomenon we must get a clear view of the language games in which terms for it are used; and the logical shapes of these may be very different from those which are initially suggested by the pictures which grip us (see PRIVATE LANGUAGE ARGUMENT).

15 Philosophy of mathematics

Platonism in mathematics involves two claims, that there is a realm of necessary facts independent of human thought and that these facts may outrun our ability to get access to them by proofs. Platonism is attractive because it accounts for several striking features of mathematical experience: first that proofs are compelling and yet may have conclusions which are surprising, and second that we seem to be able to understand some mathematical propositions without having any guarantee that proofs of them exist.

Wittgenstein never accepted Platonism because he always took the view that making substantive

statements is one thing, while articulating the rules for making them is another. So-called necessary truths clearly do present rules of language, inasmuch as accepting them commits one to allowing and disallowing certain linguistic moves. Wittgenstein holds that it is therefore a muddle to think that such formulations describe some particularly hard and immovable states of affairs. Thus in the *Tractatus* mathematical propositions are treated together with tautologies as sets of signs which say nothing, but show the logic of the world.

Nevertheless the *Tractatus* view has some kind of affinity with at least the first claim in Platonism, inasmuch as the rules of our language, on which mathematics rest, are rules of the only logically possible language. But when Wittgenstein comes to see linguistic rules as features internal to our (possibly varying) practices, the resulting picture is unwelcoming even to this. We cannot now assume there to be such a thing as 'the logic of the world', whether to be shown or said. Instead, in *Remarks on the Foundations of Mathematics*, he explores ideas of the following kinds.

At a given time we have linguistic practices directed by certain rules. Someone may now produce a proof of a formula which if accepted would be a new rule – for example, '14 + 3 = 17'. It is natural to think that to accept this is to unpack what we were already committed to by our understanding of '17', '+', and so on. But the rule-following considerations unsettle this assumption because they undermine the idea of an intellectual confrontation with an abstract item which forces awareness of its nature upon us and they also bring to our attention the element of spontaneity in any new application of a given term. Rather to accept the proof and its outcome is to change our practices of applying signs like '17', because it is to adopt a new criterion for judging that seventeen things are present, namely that there are two groups of fourteen and three. Hence to accept the proof is to alter our concepts. What makes mathematics possible is that we nearly all agree in our reaction to proofs, and in finding them compelling. But to seek to explain this by pointing to Platonic structures is to fall back into incoherent mythology.

The present author's own view is that it is persistent uneasiness with the first claim in Platonism which primarily motivates Wittgenstein's reflections on mathematics. But those who see him as an antirealist will put more stress on hostility to the second claim (the idea of verification transcendence) and certainly some of Wittgenstein's remarks (for example, his suspicion of the application of the law of excluded middle to mathematical propositions) have affinities with ideas in intuitionistic logic. A third reading will bring out the conventionalist-sounding elements, on which we choose what linguistic rules to adopt on pragmatic grounds.

In addition to reflections on the nature and use of elementary arithmetical claims, Wittgenstein also applies his ideas to some more complex constructs in mathematical logic, such as the Frege–Russell project of deriving mathematics from logic, Cantor's diagonal argument to the non-denumerability of the real numbers, consistency proofs and Gödel's theorem. His general line here is not that there is anything wrong with the mathematics but that the results have been misconstrued, because they have been interpreted against a mistaken background Platonism. Some mathematical logicians claim that Wittgenstein has not understood properly what he is discussing. His views on consistency and Gödel in particular have aroused annoyance (see INTUITIONISM).

16 Ethics, aesthetics and philosophy of religion

In the *Tractatus* Wittgenstein consigns ethics to the realm of the unsayable, and he takes the same line in his 'Lecture on Ethics' (1929). Here he says that ethics (which he links to aesthetics and religion) arises from a tendency in the human mind to try to express in words something – roughly the existence and nature of absolute value – which seems to manifest itself to us in certain experiences. (He gives as an instance the experience of finding the existence of the world miraculous.) It is essential to this impulse that it seeks to go beyond the world and significant language; so it is bound to issue in utterances which are nonsensical. Nevertheless, he says, he has the greatest respect for this impulse and would not for his life ridicule it.

This position resembles the emotivism associated with logical positivism in distinguishing ethical utterances sharply from those of science (that is, those which are capable of rational assessment, and can be true or false). But it also differs from it in being, in spirit, an ethical realism, albeit of a mystical kind.

In his later writing Wittgenstein rethought his views on meaning, mathematics and the mind but did not return to any sustained discussion of ethics or aesthetics (although there are scattered remarks, particularly on the aesthetics of music, in *Culture and Value* (1980)). One interpretation of the later outlook, however, provides a hospitable setting for an ethical realism of a less mysterious kind, one which allows for the statement and rational discussion of truth-evaluable ethical claims. Philosophers of meta-ethics taking themselves to be

working within a Wittgensteinian outlook have urged that our inclination to insist on a dichotomy between fact and value, or between cognition and feeling, should be resisted, as the outcome of the grip on us of some misapplied picture. Moreover Wittgenstein's emphasis on attention to the actual workings of language could encourage a distinctive approach to first order ethical questions. But he himself never developed this position, nor does he engage with issues in political philosophy.

The later outlook enjoins us to study each distinctive area of language as far as possible without preconceptions. If we do this for religious language, Wittgenstein holds, we shall see that religion is not a kind of science and hence is not open to criticism on the grounds that, as science, it is unconvincing (see, for example, 'Remarks on Frazer's *Golden Bough*' (1931)). Some take it that this implies that no religious utterance can be properly subject to any criticism other than that coming from inside the same religious community or tradition.

17 Epistemology

One familiar traditional philosophical problem is that of scepticism, that is, whether we can rightly claim to know such things as that physical objects exist independent of our perception, that the world was not created five minutes ago and so forth.

Wittgenstein's most extended discussion of these issues is in *On Certainty* (1969). He starts from the kinds of examples invoked by G.E. MOORE in his attempt to combat scepticism, such as 'Here is a hand' and 'The Earth has existed for a long time before my birth'. Moore is wrong, Wittgenstein thinks, in taking it that we are plainly entitled to assert that we know these things. But Moore is right in thinking that the claims form an interesting class. It is impossible to conduct life and thought without taking some things entirely for granted, and the propositions Moore identifies are the articulated forms of things which play this role for us. They help to define our world picture and underpin the procedures by which other claims (ones that are in fact doubted and tested) can be assessed. But they cannot themselves be assessed because there is nothing relatively more certain by which we can get leverage on them. Someone who seems to doubt them is thought mad and, from a first-person point of view, when I imagine doubting such things I contemplate a situation in which I would no longer know how to reason about anything. There are close links between these themes and the idea that the workability of any language game presupposes certain very general facts of nature.

The relevance of this for the traditional question of scepticism is that it is, in its form, misconceived.

The central use of 'know' is in connection with propositions where testing is possible. Hence one who uses it in connection with the propositions which help define our worldview (as is in fact done only in philosophy and not in ordinary life) has extended the word to a situation where procedures do not exist for assessing either the first-order claim or the claim to knowledge of it. This is not to say that the word 'know' is unintelligibly and wrongly used in the philosophical debate. We can sympathize with the sceptical impulse, which springs from awareness of the fact that our language games are not based on grounds which compel us to adopt them or guarantee their continued success. But we can also sympathize with the anti-sceptical position which insists that acceptance of these central propositions underpins our being able to do any thinking at all, so that claims to doubt them are empty (see SCEPTICISM).

18 Wittgenstein's conception of philosophy

In two central respects Wittgenstein stands squarely within the main historical tradition of philosophy, first in the nature of the issues which excited and intrigued him intellectually – meaning, the self, consciousness, necessity – and second (going back to the roots of the tradition) in his being a 'lover of wisdom', that is, one who is seriously concerned about having a right stance to the world both intellectually and practically and who is committed to the use of the intellect (among other things) in helping to achieve this.

But he differs from many philosophers in his conviction that a great number of traditional philosophical problems are the result of some deep kind of muddle, and in his belief that the answers given and the way they are debated hinder rather than help us in achieving wisdom. This conviction gripped him from very early on and philosophical thought therefore presented itself to him as a tormentingly difficult struggle to be honest and to free himself from misleading preconceptions.

So the word 'philosophy' has, in all his writings, two uses. On one it describes a body of confused utterances and arguments, arising largely from misunderstanding of the workings of language, and on the other it describes an activity of helping people to get free of the muddles. Another important continuity is his insistence that there cannot be philosophical theories and that the helpful activity of philosophy ought only to consist of making uncontentious statements, of describing and assembling reminders. In the context of the picture theory of meaning, this is comprehensible (see §7). But it is less clear that it is required by the later view.

In part Wittgenstein is here stressing that we cannot have the kind of explanation of our concepts which the *Tractatus* picture seemed to promise. Our form of life cannot be grounded but only described and lived. In part he is questioning the impulse to look for quasi-scientific theories of the nature of philosophically puzzling phenomena. But these two interrelated points do not obviously add up to a complete embargo on anything which could be called 'philosophical theory'. It is in the spirit of the later philosophy to point out that there are many different kinds of things which can be called 'theories'. Everyone engaged in reflection on the topics Wittgenstein considers (including Wittgenstein himself) finds it natural to articulate in words the states they arrive at and to engage with these words and those of others in the mode of further comment and assessment.

We become aware here, and at many other places, of the open-ended and unfinished nature of Wittgenstein's reflections. His writings have aroused great devotion because of the honesty and depth which many find in them. But it is important not to treat them with superstitious reverence. Rather they should be read in the spirit in which he intended, namely as an invitation to explore with as much integrity as possible one's own perplexities and what would resolve them.

See also: CRITERIA; FREGE, G.; KRIPKE, S.A.; LOGICAL ATOMISM; MEANING AND RULE-FOLLOWING; MOORE, G.E.; ORDINARY LANGUAGE PHILOSOPHY, SCHOOL OF; PRIVATE LANGUAGE ARGUMENT; VIENNA CIRCLE

References and further reading

Monk, R. (1990) *Ludwig Wittgenstein*, London: Jonathan Cape. (A full and illuminating biography.)

Wittgenstein, L.J.J. (1922) *Tractatus Logico-Philosophicus*, trans. C.K. Ogden and F.P. Ramsey, London: Routledge; trans. D.F. Pears and B.F. McGuinness, London: Routledge, 1961. (The major work of Wittgenstein's early period and the only book published during his lifetime. The first English translation was revised and approved by Wittgenstein himself, though the later version is now standard. The German version was published in 1921 in *Annalen der Naturphilosophie*.)

Wittgenstein, L.J.J. (1953) *Philosophical Investigations*, ed. G.E.M. Anscombe and R. Rhees, trans. G.E.M. Anscombe, Oxford: Blackwell. (The most polished and worked over of all Wittgenstein's later works and the one with which he was most nearly satisfied. It contains presentations of his later ideas on meaning and philosophical psychology, including discussions of concepts such as 'language game', 'form of life' and 'family resemblance'.)

JANE HEAL

WOLFF, CHRISTIAN (1679–1754)

Christian Wolff was a rationalistic school philosopher in the German Enlightenment. During the period between the death of Leibniz (1716) and the publication of Kant's critical writings (1780s), Wolff was perhaps the most influential philosopher in Germany.

There are many reasons for this, including Wolff's voluminous writings in both German and Latin in nearly every field of philosophy known to his time, their unvarying employment of a strict rationalistic method to establish their conclusions, the attention directed to Wolff and his views as a result of bitter controversies with some theological colleagues, his banishment from Prussia by King Frederick Wilhelm I in 1723 and triumphant return from Hesse–Cassel in 1740 after Frederick the Great assumed the throne, and his active teaching at the Universities of Halle and Marburg for nearly fifty years. Through his work as a university professor, his prolific writings, and the rigour and comprehensiveness of his philosophy, Wolff influenced a very large group of followers, educators and other writers. Even after his influence had begun to wane, Kant still referred to 'the celebrated Wolff' and spoke of 'the strict method of the celebrated Wolff, the greatest of all dogmatic philosophers'.

Wolff thought of philosophy as that discipline which provides reasons to explain why things exist or occur and why they are even possible. Thus, he included within philosophy a much broader range of subjects than might now be recognized as 'philosophical'. Indeed, for Wolff all human knowledge consists of only three disciplines: history, mathematics and philosophy.

The reasons provided by Wolff's philosophy were to be established through unfailing adherence to a strict demonstrative method. Like Descartes, Wolff first discovered this method in mathematics, but he concluded that both mathematical and philosophical methods had their ultimate origins in a 'natural logic' prescribed to the human mind by God. In fact, the heart of Wolff's philosophical method is a deductive logic making use of syllogistic arguments.

For Wolff, the immediate objective of philosophical method is to achieve certitude by establishing an order of truths within each discipline and a system within human knowledge as a whole. The ultimate goal is to establish a reliable foundation for the conduct of human affairs and the enlargement of knowledge.

Wolff applied his philosophical method unfailingly in each of the three principal parts of philosophy: metaphysics – knowledge of those things which are possible through being in general, the world in general, human souls, and God; physics – knowledge of those things which are possible through bodies; and practical philosophy – knowledge of those things which are concerned with human actions. Wolff's philosophical system also includes logic, an art of discovery (to guide the investigation of hidden truth and the production of new insights), some experiential disciplines (for example, empirical psychology) and several bodies of philosophical knowledge that were not well developed in Wolff's time concerning law, medicine, and both the practical and liberal arts.

See also: Enlightenment, Continental; Rationalism

CHARLES A. CORR

WOLLSTONECRAFT, MARY (1759–97)

Wollstonecraft used the rationalist and egalitarian ideas of late eighteenth-century radical liberalism to attack the subjugation of women and to display its roots in the social construction of gender. Her political philosophy draws on Rousseau's philosophical anthropology, rational religion, and an original moral psychology which integrates reason and feeling in the production of virtue. Relations between men and women are corrupted by artificial gender distinctions, just as political relations are corrupted by artificial distinctions of rank, wealth and power. Conventional, artificial morality distinguishes between male and female virtue; true virtue is gender-neutral, consists in the imitation of God, and depends on the unimpeded development of natural faculties common to both sexes, including both reason and passion. Political justice and private virtue are interdependent: neither can advance without an advance in the other.

See also: Feminism; Morality and emotions

SUSAN KHIN ZAW

WORK, PHILOSOPHY OF

Unlike play, work is activity that has to involve significant expenditure of effort and be directed toward some goal beyond enjoyment. The term 'work' is also used to signify an individual's occupation, the means whereby they gain their livelihood. In modern market economies individuals contract to work for other individuals on specified terms. Beyond noting this formal freedom to choose how one shall work, critics of market economies have maintained that one's occupation should be a realm of substantive freedom, in which work is freely chosen self-expression. Against this unalienated labour norm, others have held that the freedom of self-expression is one good among others that work can provide, such as lucrative pay, friendly social contact and the satisfaction of the self-support norm, and that none of these various work-related goods necessarily should have priority over others. Some philosophers place responsibility on society for providing opportunities for good work for all members of society; others hold that the responsibility for the quality of one's occupational life appropriately falls on each individual alone. Finally, some theorists of work emphasize that performance of hard work renders one deserving of property ownership (John Locke) or enhances one's spiritual development (Mahatma Gandhi).

RICHARD ARNESON

WRIGHT, GEORG HENRIK VON
See von Wright, Georg Henrik

WU FORMS
See Confucian philosophy, Chinese

WUNDT, WILHELM (1832–1920)
The German philosopher, psychologist and physician Wilhelm Wundt founded the world's first psychological laboratory in Leipzig in 1879 – at a time when psychology was still generally regarded as a theoretical and institutional part of philosophy. This event typified his life's work and its reception in many respects. On the one hand Wundt tried to develop psychology as an independent science by defining its subject matter and methodology; on the other, he wanted to integrate psychology into the context of philosophy, cultural theory and history. With both attempts he acquired world fame and at the same time became a most controversial figure. Systematizing his approach, Wundt worked on a great amount of material in very different disciplines. He has been called the last philosophical 'polyhistor' in the tradition of Leibniz and Hegel, as well as the first modern scientist in psychology.
See also: Dualism

JENS BROCKMEIER

WYCLIF, JOHN (*c.*1330–84)
John Wyclif was a logician, theologian and religious reformer. A Yorkshireman educated at Oxford, he first came to prominence as a logician; he developed some technical notions of the Oxford Calculators, but reacted against their logic of terms to embrace with fervour the idea of the real existence of universal ideas. He expounded his view as a theologian, rejecting the notion of the annihilation of substance (including the eucharistic elements) and treating time as merely contingent. The proper understanding of universals became his touchstone of moral progress; treating scripture as a universal idea, he measured the value of human institutions, including the Church and its temporal property, by their conformity with its absolute truth. These views, though temporarily favoured by King Edward III, were condemned by Pope Gregory XI in 1377 and by the English ecclesiastical hierarchy in 1382, forcing him into retirement but leaving him to inspire a clandestine group of scholarly reformers, the Lollards.
See also: Trinity; Universals

JEREMY CATTO

X

XUN KUANG
See XUNZI

XUN QING
See XUNZI

XUNZI (*fl.* 298–238 BC)

Xunzi is one of the most brilliant Confucian thinkers of ancient China. His works display wide-ranging interest in such topics as the relation between morality and human nature, the ideal of the good human life, the nature of ethical discourse and argumentation, and the ethical uses of history, moral education and personal cultivation. Because of the comprehensive and systematic character of his philosophical concerns, Xunzi is sometimes compared to Aristotle. Noteworthy is his emphasis on *li*, or rules of proper conduct, and the holistic character of *dao*, the Confucian ideal of the good human life. He criticized other philosophers not because of their mistakes, but because of their preoccupation with one aspect of *dao* to the exclusion of others.

See also: CONFUCIAN PHILOSOPHY, CHINESE; ETHICS

A.S. CUA

Y

YI

See CONFUCIAN PHILOSOPHY, CHINESE; CONFUCIUS

YIN–YANG

Yin and *yang* always describe the relationships that obtain among unique particulars. Originally these terms designated the shady side and the sunny side of a hill, and gradually came to suggest the way in which one thing 'overshadows' another in some particular aspect of their relationship. Any comparison between two or more unique particulars on any given topic is necessarily hierarchical: one side is *yang* and the other is *yin*. The nature of the opposition captured in this pairing expresses the mutuality, interdependence, hierarchical relationship, diversity and creative efficacy of the dynamic relationships that are immanent in and give value to the world. The full range of difference in the world is deemed explicable through this pairing.

Yin and *yang* are elements of a correlative pairing which are pragmatically useful in sorting out 'this' and 'that', and are not, as often claimed, dualistic principles of light and dark, male and female, action and passivity where light and dark both exclude each other and logically entail each other and, in their complementarity, constitute a totality. Rather, *yin* and *yang* are first and foremost a vocabulary of qualitative contrasts which have application to specific situations and enable us to make specific distinctions.

To bring this observation to bear on our understanding of *yin* and *yang*, we must start with the relationship that obtains between any two particular things or events. For example, in a given relationship, 'this' older woman might by virtue of her wisdom be regarded as *yang* in contrast to 'that' younger woman who is *yin*. However, if we were to focus on their fecundity or physical strength, the correlation would likely be the opposite. Important here is the primacy of the particular and the fluidity of the relationship. Although things in this world – that is, particular things – are resolutely hierarchical, no one thing

excels in all respects, making this same hierarchy the basis for their complementarity.

In the classical Chinese world, things of the same 'kind' are not defined in terms of their essences as natural kinds but by virtue of their affinity or 'kinship' resemblances that associate them, their 'family resemblances'. Important here is the primacy of particular difference and the absence of any assumed sameness or strict identity. Things are deemed to have resemblances based upon analogous roles or functions. Thus one thing, by virtue of its relationships, evokes many. The suggestiveness of each phenomenon in calling up other similar phenomena is comparable to the multivalence of poetic images. Describing a particular phenomenon does not require the discovery of some underlying determinative and originative principle – a basis for making 'many' one – but a mapping out and an unravelling of the phenomenon's multiple correlations and of the relationships and conditions that make up its context. *Yin* and *yang* define the tension between multiple perspectives on phenomena, and they enable us to interpret and bring coherence to our circumstances by allowing us to discern the patterns in relationships within particular contexts. They provide a vocabulary for sorting out the relationships that obtain among things as they come together and constitute themselves in unique compositions.

Thus, *yin* and *yang* as correlatives are not universal principles that define some essential feature of phenomena, but are explanatory categories that register a creative tension in specific differences and thus make the immediate concrete things of the world intelligible. It is only through a process of generalization that feminine and male gender traits are construed as predominantly *yin* and *yang* respectively, and vocabulary such as vaginal orifice (*yinmen*) and virility (*yangdao*) emerges to essentialize the *yin* and *yang* contrast.

The *yin–yang* vocabulary is functional. In order to evaluate the propensity of a situation and manipulate it in advance, we must make distinctions. This is where the vocabulary of *yin* and *yang* comes into play. We begin from the assumed uniqueness of each situation and the uniqueness of the components that constitute it. The *yin–yang* contrast provides a line, enabling us to divide a continuous situation into distinct yet interdependent particulars. *Yin* is a becoming-*yang*; *yang* is a becoming-*yin*. We must come to know the particular conditions that govern a situation so that we can manipulate them to advantage. This requires that one translate the situation into the *yin–yang* vocabulary of complementary opposites: strong–weak, fast–slow, many–few, regular–irregular and so on. *Yin–yang* is a vocabulary that enables us to discriminate among the many factors which together constitute the force of circumstances, and that allows us to control this force through the strategic adjustments. Once we have arrived at an understanding of the circumstances, we must identify those critical factors which will enable us to turn the configuration of an unfolding situation into an opportunity.

References and further reading

Graham, A.C. (1989) *Disputers of the Tao: Philosophical Argument in Ancient China*, LaSalle, IL: Open Court. (A survey of ancient Chinese thought.)

Hall, D.L. and Ames, R.T. (1995) *Anticipating China: Thinking Through the Narratives of Chinese and Western Culture*, Albany, NY: State University of New York Press. (A comparative study of the uncommon assumptions that ground the Chinese and Western philosophical traditions.)

ROGER T. AMES

Z

ZEN

See BUDDHIST PHILOSOPHY, JAPANESE; BUDDHIST PHILOSOPHY, CHINESE

ZENO OF CITIUM (334–262 BC)

Zeno of Citium, a Greek philosopher from Cyprus, founded the Stoic school in Athens c.300 BC. His background and training lay in various branches of the Socratic tradition, including the Platonic Academy, but especially Cynicism. His controversial *Republic* was a utopian treatise, founded on the abolition of most civic norms and institutions. He laid the main foundations of Stoic doctrine in all areas except perhaps logic.

DAVID SEDLEY

ZENO OF ELEA (*fl. c.*450 BC)

The Greek philosopher Zeno of Elea was celebrated for his paradoxes. Aristotle called him the 'founder of dialectic'. He wrote in order to defend the Eleatic metaphysics of his fellow citizen and friend Parmenides, according to whom reality is single, changeless and homogeneous. Zeno's strength was the production of intriguing arguments which seem to show that apparently straightforward features of the world – most notably plurality and motion – are riddled with contradiction. At the very least he succeeded in establishing that hard thought is required to make sense of plurality and motion. His paradoxes stimulated the atomists, Aristotle and numerous philosophers since to reflect on unity, infinity, continuity and the structure of space and time. Although Zeno wrote a book full of arguments, very few of his actual words have survived. Secondary reports (some from Plato and Aristotle) probably preserve accurately the essence of Zeno's arguments. Even so, we know only a fraction of the total.

According to Plato the arguments in Zeno's book were of this form: if there are many things, then the same things are both F and not-F; since the same things cannot be both F and not-F, there cannot be many things. Two instances of this form have been preserved: if there were many things, then the same things would be both limited and unlimited; and the same things would be both large (that is, of infinite size) and small (that is, of no size). Quite how the components of these arguments work is not clear. Things are limited (in number), Zeno says, because they are just so many, rather than more or less, while they are unlimited (in number) because any two of them must have a third between them, which separates them and makes them two. Things are of infinite size because anything that exists must have some size: yet anything that has size is divisible into parts which themselves have some size, so that each and every thing will contain an infinite number of extended parts. On the other hand, each thing has no size: for if there are to be many things there have to be some things which are single, unitary things, and these will have no size since anything with size would be a collection of parts.

Zeno's arguments concerning motion have a different form. Aristotle reports four arguments. According to the Dichotomy, motion is impossible because in order to cover any distance it is necessary first to cover half the distance, then half the remainder, and so on without limit. The Achilles is a variant of this: the speedy Achilles will never overtake a tortoise once he has allowed it a head start because Achilles has an endless series of tasks to perform, and each time Achilles sets off to catch up with the tortoise it will turn out that, by the time Achilles arrives at where the tortoise was when he set off, the tortoise has moved on slightly. Another argument, the Arrow, purports to show that an arrow apparently in motion is in fact stationary at each instant of its 'flight', since at each instant it occupies a region of space equal in size to itself. The Moving Rows describes three rows (or streams) of equal-sized bodies, one stationary and the other two moving at equal speeds in opposite directions. If each body is one metre long, then the time taken for a body to cover two metres equals the time taken for it to cover four metres (since a moving body will pass two stationary bodies while passing four bodies moving in the opposite direction), and that might be thought impossible.

Zeno's arguments must be resolvable, since the world obviously does contain a plurality of things in motion. There is little agreement, however, on how they should be resolved. Some points can be identified which may have misled Zeno. It is not true, for example, that the sum of an infinite collection of parts, each of which has size, must itself be of an infinite size (it will be false if the parts are of proportionally decreasing size); and something in motion will pass stationary bodies and moving bodies at different velocities. In many other cases, however, there is no general agreement as to the fallacy, if any exists, of Zeno's argument.

STEPHEN MAKIN

ZI MOZI
See Mozi

ZOROASTRIANISM

Zarathushtra, better known to the Classical and modern world in the Greek form of his name 'Zoroaster', revealed his vision of truth, wisdom and justice in the verse texts known as the *Gāthās* (*c*.1200–1000 BC) and is revered by Zoroastrians as their holy prophet. The religion is correctly described as *mazdāyasna*, 'the worship of Ahura ('Lord') Mazdā, creator of the world and source of all goodness. Since the Avestan word *mazdā* means 'wise, wisdom', Zoroastrians see their prophet as the original *philosophos*, 'lover of wisdom'. Zarathushtra's message is primarily ethical and rationalistic. Zoroastrianism teaches a life based on (1) the avoidance of evil, through rigorous discrimination between good and evil, and (2) the service of wisdom through the cherishing of seven ideals. These latter are personified as seven immortal, beneficent spirits: Ahura Mazdā himself, conceived as the creative 'holy' spirit; Sublime Truth; Virtuous Power; Good Purpose/Mind; Beneficent Piety; Wholeness/Health; and, finally, Immortality. Evil originates neither from God nor from his creatures, but from a wholly other source, personified as Angra Mainyu, the 'Hostile Spirit', whose existence is ritually and doctrinally rejected as being pretended and parasitic. Real existence is solely the domain of Ahura Mazdā and his creation; Angra Mainyu and his demons are actually states of negativity, denial or, as the religion puts it, 'the Lie'. Thus the charge that the religion is ontologically dualistic is no more true than it is of other systems which conceive of good and evil as being in fundamental opposition. Equally, the allegation that its theology is ditheistic or polytheistic is a misunderstanding of the Zoroastrian theological and ritual tradition. The influence which this religion has exerted on classical philosophy and the thought and practice of Judaism, Christianity and Islam is being reappraised by scholars in modern times.

See also: NEOPLATONISM; RELIGION, PHILOSOPHY OF

ALAN WILLIAMS